John Milton

COMPLETE POEMS
and
MAJOR PROSE

Edited by
MERRITT Y. HUGHES

Notes and *Introductions* by the *Editor*

THE ODYSSEY PRESS

A Division of Bobbs-Merrill Educational Publishing
Indianapolis

The Bobbs-Merrill Company, Inc.
4300 West 62nd Street
Indianapolis, Indiana 46268

First Edition
Twentieth Printing—1980

Library of Congress Catalog Card Number 57-4209
ISBN 0-672-63178-4

For

Jane and David, Elspeth and John

Preface

The only justification of the present attempt to pack all Milton's poems and much of his prose into a single volume is the practical need of undergraduate as well as graduate students who are increasingly tasting, swallowing, or chewing and digesting large Miltonic rations in courses ranging from a quarter to an academic year in length. The object of this book is to make Milton and what is known about his work as easily accessible as space will permit. On that principle three decisions have been made, two of which are compromises about the wisdom of which there may be a variety of opinions.

The first decision has been to arrange each of the main divisions of the book—poetry and prose—chronologically. This plan, with which Sir Herbert Grierson experimented in his edition of Milton's poems in 1925, is the best substitute for the impossible royal road to an understanding of the development of the poet, the pamphleteer, and the amateur theologian. Though assignments of reading may seldom be made mainly for biographical reasons, and though explicators may rarely resort to dates, it is usually helpful to have a given document unobtrusively charted in time. Whenever possible, the exact or approximate dates of Milton's works are given, and in doubtful cases the way is pointed to discussions of the problem by J. M. French in his *Life Records of John Milton* (Vols. I to IV, Rutgers University Press, 1949–1956) or by J. H. Hanford, W. R. Parker, A. S. P. Woodhouse, or others in the journals.

The second decision—one which has meant a compromise—has been to combine modernization of Milton's spelling and punctuation with preservation of his most conspicuous seventeenth century typographical peculiarities. In the major poems it has been decided to preserve his distinction between the unemphatic and the emphatic forms of the pronouns *he, she, me, we,* and *thir* vs. *hee, shee, mee, wee,* and *their.* I shall not try to defend a doubtful decision which has been ably defended by Miss Helen Darbishire in her edition of *Milton's Poetical Works* (Oxford, at the Clarendon Press, 1953–1955), nor shall I disguise the fact that I sympathize with some of her critics' objections to her practice. But there is no doubt that the distinction in the spelling of the pronouns was frequently important for Milton and his early readers, though it is by no means certain that the two editions of *Paradise Lost* which he saw through the press constantly represented his judgment rather than the taste or caprice of his printers. The present text has been compared with the edition of 1674 in the Folger Shakespeare Library in Washington, D.C. The result is not a scholar's text, but it is a not untrustworthy one for many scholarly purposes. The preservation of Milton's capitalization is justified by the fact that it was clearly important to him and his public. Miss Darbishire is unquestionably right in believing that he capitalized the word *spirit* when it meant an angelic or divine being, but otherwise wrote it with a small *s.* So sure is she of such distinctions in his capitalizations of words like *spirit, man, world,* etc., that she has ventured to alter their treatment in the early editions, in a number of cases, even more boldly than I have done. In the three major poems my modernization of the spelling is largely complete except for the pronouns and the *-t* endings (instead of *-ed*) in the past participles and past tense of many weak verbs. In the other poems and the prose, the early editions of which lack the orthographical authority of the second edition of *Paradise Lost,* the modernization has been more drastic. The distinction between the pronouns is disregarded, names of persons and places are not italicized as they are in the major poems, and the capitalization follows modern practice.

The third decision—also a compromise—relates to notes and introductions. The latter have been supplied at some length for *Paradise Lost, Paradise Regained, Samson Agonistes, Comus, Lycidas,* and a few other poems, but—aside from bibliographical headnotes—not for the prose.   The object has been to synthesize the criticism and scholarship of the past half-century with as much reference to major books and articles as the scale of the volume permits.   There is a bibliography of modern books about *Paradise Lost,* and there are lists of books and articles dealing with *Paradise Regained* and *Samson.*   No attempt has been made to write introductions to the prose works of a kind which would place them in the intellectual history of their time—as the introductions to Don Wolfe's edition of *Milton's Prose Works* (Vol. I, Yale University Press, 1953) do—or to place them in the spiritual development of their author—as Arthur Barker does in *Milton and the Puritan Dilemma* (University of Toronto Press, 1942); but the notes on prose and poetry alike seek to help the reader to make the links which Milton expected his first readers to make between his pages and the events and books of their own time, or with the traditions of the past, biblical and classical.   When the importance of modern studies of specific passages has seemed to require references to them, I have mentioned them in the notes.   Their scale throughout the volume is the same, except that no annotation is provided for the selections from *The Christian Doctrine.*   In them I have preserved the text of Bishop Sumner's translation intact (including the biblical citations), but I have dropped his notes.   The substance of many of them can be found in the notes to *Paradise Lost* which link it with *The Christian Doctrine,* and in Maurice Kelley's *This Great Argument* the parallels between the two works can be found fully tabulated.

The notes seem to me to be a service which is due from an editor working for intelligent amateur readers.   In rendering it I have tried to remember that all annotation should be concise and clear enough for a reader to see at a glance whether it is—for him—a red herring or a momentarily helpful road sign or a window on the sea.   A glance at the patristic background of the "darkness visible" of Milton's hell may enrich the esthetic pleasure of a reader who, without it, might regard the oxymoron as evidence of the weakness of Milton's visual imagination, or of his mind.   A few words about the meaning of his account of poetry as "more simple, sensuous, and passionate" than prose, in *Of Education,* may exorcise hobgoblins which seem to some readers to have plagued his esthetic and his pedagogy.

For whatever may be valuable in this book I am indebted to the many scholars who have helped me with suggestions: particularly to William Haller, who discussed my problems almost daily with me in the Folger Library.   Douglas Bush and his colleagues in the Department of English and on the staff of the libraries at Harvard have done much to forward my work during three months in Cambridge.   I owe much to Louis B. Wright and the staff of the Folger Library for doing everything within their power to secure modern works of reference for me and to make their great collection of seventeenth century books conveniently accessible.   My greatest debt is to my tri-une co-worker, audience, and critic, whose constant help in Washington and Cambridge has alone made it possible to finish this book.

MERRITT Y. HUGHES

University of Wisconsin
Madison

Contents

Poems

THE MINOR POEMS

ix

PARADISE LOST

Prose

Appendix

1608, Dec. 9.   Birth in Bread Street, Cheapside, London.

1620 (?).   Admission to St. Paul's School in London.

1625, Feb. 12.   Admission to Christ's College, Cambridge.

1632, July 3.   Admission to degree of M. A.

1632–1635.   Residence at Hammersmith in Middlesex.

1634, Sept. 29.   First performance of *Comus*.

1635–1638.   Residence at Horton in Buckinghamshire.

1637. *Lycidas* written.   Published in 1638.

1638, May, to July, 1639.   Italian journey.

1639 or early 1640.   Residence and teaching in London begun.

1640 (?).   Design for a tragedy to be called "Paradise Lost."

1641, May.   *Of Reformation in England* published.

June or July.   *Of Prelatical Episcopacy* published.

Sept. *Animadversions upon the Remonstrant's Defence against SMECTYMNUUS* published.

1642, Jan. or Feb.   The Reason of Church-Government Urg'd *against Prelaty* published.

April.   *An Apology against a Pamphlet* . . . published.

June (?).   Marriage to Mary Powell.

Aug. (?).   Return of Mary Powell Milton to her home in Buckinghamshire.

1643, Aug. 1.   *The Doctrine and Discipline of Divorce* published.

1644, June 5.   *Of Education* published.

Aug. 6.   *The Judgement of Martin Bucer concerning Divorce* published.

Nov. 23.   *Areopagitica* published.

1645, March 4.   *Tetrachordon* and *Colasterion* published.

Summer (?).   Return of Mary Powell Milton.

October.   Beginning of Milton's residence with Mary in Barbican, Cripplegate.

1646. Jan. 2.   *Poems of Mr. John Milton* published.

July 29.   Birth of Milton's daughter Anne.

1648, Oct. 25.   Birth of daughter Mary.

1649, Feb. 13.   *The Tenure of Kings and Magistrates* published.

March 3.   Appointment by the Council of State as its Secretary for Foreign Tongues.

Oct. 5.   *Eikonoklastes* published.

1650, June 14.   Assignment by the Council to a lodging in Whitehall.

1651, Feb. 24.   *Defensio pro populo Anglicano* published.

March 16.   Birth of son John.

1652, Feb. (?).   Milton's blindness almost total.   Removal to a residence in Petty-France, Westminster.

May 2.   Birth of daughter Deborah.

May 5 (?).   Death of Mary Powell Milton.

June 16.   Death of son John.

1654, May 30.   *Defensio secunda pro populo Anglicano* published.

1655, Aug. 8.   *Pro Se Defensio* published.

1656, Nov. 12.   Marriage to Katherine Woodcock.

1658, Feb. 3.   Death of Katherine Woodcock Milton.

1659, Feb.   *A Treatise of Civil Power in Ecclesiastical Causes* published.

Aug. *Considerations touching the Likeliest Means to Remove Hirelings out of the Church* published.

1660, Feb. *The Ready and Easy Way to Establish a Free Commonwealth* published.

May. Milton retires to a house in Bartholomew Close.

June 16. Parliament resolves upon Milton's arrest.

Dec. 15. Parliament resolves upon Milton's release from the custody of its Serjeant at Arms.

1661–1663. Residence in Jewin Street.

1663, Feb. 24. Marriage to Elizabeth Minshul.

Removal from Jewin Street to Bunhill Fields.

1665, June (?)–1666, Feb. (?). Retreat from the plague to Chalfont St. Giles in Buckinghamshire.

1667, Aug. 20. *Paradise Lost, A Poem in Ten Books* published.

1670. *The History of Britain* published.

1671. *Paradise Regain'd* and *Samson Agonistes* published.

1673, Spring. *Of True Religion, Heresy, Schism, and Toleration* published.

1674. *Paradise Lost, A Poem in Twelve Books* published.

Nov. 8. Death.

Nov. 12. Burial in St. Giles, Cripplegate.

ABBREVIATIONS OF TITLES OF MILTON'S WORKS

NOTE: Not all Milton's titles are included. Those which are not included are cited in full in the notes.

Animadversions – *Animadversions upon the Remonstrant's Defense against Smectymnuus*
Apology – *An Apology against a Pamphlet Called "A Modest Confutation of the Animadversions upon the Remonstrant's Defense against Smectymnuus"*
Arc – *Arcades*
Areop – *Areopagitica*
Britain – *The History of Britain*
Bucer – *The Judgment of Martin Bucer concerning Divorce*
Carrier I etc. – *Upon the University Carrier* I etc.
CB – *Commonplace Book*
CD – *De doctrina Christiana* (*The Christian Doctrine*)
CG – *The Reason of Church Government Urged against Prelaty*
Circumcision – *On the Circumcision*
Civil Power – *A Treatise of Civil Power*
Colas – *Colasterion*
Damon – *Epitaphium Damonis* (*Damon's Epitaph*)
DDD – *The Doctrine and Discipline of Divorce*
Def 1 – *Johannis Miltoni, Angli, pro populo Anglicano defensio contra Claudii Salmasii defensionem regiam* (*The Defense of the English People . . . against Salmasius*)
Def 2 – *Johannis Miltoni, Angli, pro populo Anglicano defensio secunda . . .* (*The Second Defense of the English People*)
Def se – *Defensio pro se* (*A Defense of Himself*)
Educ – *Of Education*
Eikon – *Eikonoklastes*
El I etc. – *Elegy I* etc.
Ely – *In obitum praesulis Eliensis* (*On the Death of the Bishop of Ely*)
Forcers – *On the New Forcers of Conscience under the Long Parliament*
Hirelings – *Considerations Touching the Likeliest Means to Remove Hirelings out of the Church*
Idea – *De idea Platonica* (*On the Platonic Idea*)
IlPen – *Il Penseroso*
Infant – *On the Death of a Fair Infant Dying of a Cough*
L'All – *L'Allegro*
Leon 1 etc. – *Ad Leonoram Romae canentem* (*To Leonora Singing in Rome* 1 etc.)
Logic – *Artis logicae plenior institutio ad Petri Rami methodum concinnata* (*A Fuller Treatment of the Art of Logic, Adjusted to the Method of Peter Ramus*)
Lyc – *Lycidas*
Manso – *Mansus* (*Manso*)
May – *Song. On May Morning*
Muscovia – *A Brief History of Muscovia*
Music – *At a Solemn Music*
Nat – *On the Morning of Christ's Nativity*
Naturam – *Naturam non pati senium* (*That Nature is Not Subject to Old Age*)
Pas – *The Passion*
Patrem – *Ad patrem* (*To His Father*)
Peace – *Observations on Ormond's Articles of the Peace with the Irish Rebels*)

PL – Paradise Lost
Plot – In proditionem bombardicam (*On the Gunpowder Plot*)
PR – Paradise Regained
Prol I etc. – *Prolusiones oratoriae* (*Academic Exercises* I etc.)
Ps i etc. – Psalm i etc. Milton's translations of individual Psalms are cited in the usual way.
QNov – In quintum Novembris (*On the Fifth of November*)
Ref – Of Reformation Touching Church Discipline in England
Rous – Ad Johannem Rousium, Oxoniensis Academiae Bibliothecarium (*To John Rouse, Librarian of Oxford University*)
SA – Samson Agonistes
Salsillo – Ad Salsillum, Poetam Romanum, aegrotantem (*To Salzilli, a Roman Poet, When He Was Ill*)
Shak – On Shakespeare
Sonn I etc. – *Sonnet* I etc.
Tetr – Tetrachordon
TKM – The Tenure of Kings and Magistrates
TR – Of True Religion, Heresy, Schism, and Toleration
Vac – At a Vacation Exercise
Way – A Ready and Easy Way to Establish a Free Commonwealth
Winchester – An Epitaph on the Marchioness of Winchester

References to Milton's prose works, insofar as they are not contained in this volume, are to *The Works of John Milton*, Columbia University Press, 1931–1942. The abbreviation is C.E.

ABBREVIATIONS OF TITLES OF LITERARY AND CRITICAL WORKS CITED IN THE NOTES

NOTE: Works of one-book authors such as Natale Conti's *Mythology* (*Mythologiae libri decem*, Frankfurt, 1696), Diodorus Siculus' *Library of History*, Pausanius' *Description of Greece*, Persius' *Satires*, Pliny's *Natural History*, and Propertius' *Elegies* are cited simply by the authors' names, followed by the appropriate reference.

Advancement – Francis Bacon, *The Advancement of Learning*
Aen. – Virgil, *Aeneid*
Anatomy – Robert Burton, *The Anatomy of Melancholy* (Everyman Ed.)
Angels – Robert H. West, *Milton and the Angels* (1955)
Antiquities – Josephus, *Antiquities of the Jews*
Argument – Maurice Kelley, *This Great Argument* (1941)
Background – Sister Mary Corcoran, *Milton's Paradise with Reference to the Hexaemeral Background* (1945)
Britannia – William Camden, *A Chorographical Description of Britain* (1607)
Chariot – G. Wilson Knight, *Chariot of Wrath*
Commentary – John S. Diekhoff, *Milton's "Paradise Lost," A Commentary on the Argument* (1946)
Conflicts – Joseph R. Tanner, *Constitutional Conflicts of the Seventeenth Century* (1928)
Counterpoint – James Whaler, *Counterpoint and Symbol*
Critics – A. J. A. Waldock, *"Paradise Lost" and Its Critics* (1947)

Cycle – Watson Kirkconnell, *The Celestial Cycle: The Theme of "Paradise Lost" in World Literature* (1952)

Dictionaries – DeWitt T. Starnes and Ernest W. Talbert, *Classical Myth and Legend in Renaissance Dictionaries* (1955)

Dilemma – Arthur Barker, *Milton and the Puritan Dilemma* (1942)

Diodatis – Donald Dorian, *The English Diodatis* (1950)

D.N.B. – *Dictionary of National Biography*

Documents – Samuel R. Gardiner, *The Constitutional Documents of the Puritan Revolution* (1889)

Dogma – Malcolm M. Ross, *Poetry and Dogma* (1954)

Ec. – Virgil, *Eclogues*

E.H.W.C. – *Essays in Honor of Walter Clyde Curry* (1954)

Englishman – James Holly Hanford, *John Milton: Englishman*

Ep. – Horace, *Epodes*

Expositor – Arnold Williams, *The Common Expositor* (1948)

F.Q. – Edmund Spenser, *The Faerie Queene*

Génie – Canon Camille Looten, *J. Milton: quelques espects de son génie* (1938)

Georg. – Virgil, *Georgics*

Haller – William Haller, *Tracts on Liberty in the Puritan Revolution*, 3 Vols.

Handbook – James Holly Hanford, *A Milton Handbook*, 4th Ed. (1946)

Heresy – George N. Conklin, *Biblical Criticism and Heresy in Milton* (1949)

Hexaemeral Lit. – Frank H. Robbins, *The Hexaemeral Literature: A Study of the Greek and Latin Commentaries on Genesis* (1912)

Hierarchie – Thomas Heywood, *The Hierarchie of the Blessed Angels*

Humanism – Douglas Bush, *The Renaissance and English Humanism* (1939)

I.E.M.V. – F.T. Prince, *The Italian Element in Milton's Verse* (1954)

Ikon – Robert Adams, *Ikon: John Milton and the Modern Critics* (1955)

Il. – Homer, *Iliad*

Inf. – Dante, *Inferno*

J.D. – Torquato Tasso, *Jerusalem Delivered (La Gerusalemme Liberata)*

Knowledge – J. Howard Schultz, *Milton and Forbidden Knowledge* (1955)

LRJM – J. M. French (Ed.) *Life Records of John Milton.*

Laws – Plato, *Laws*

Met. – Ovid, *Metamorphoses*

Milieu – George W. Whiting, *Milton's Literary Milieu* (1939)

M.P.L.C. – John Arthos, *On a Mask Presented at Ludlow Castle* (1954)

M.R.R. – Harris Fletcher, *Milton's Rabbinical Readings* (1930)

M.&S. – Kester Svendsen, *Milton and Science* (1956)

M.S. – E.M.W. Tillyard, *The Miltonic Setting* (1938)

Od. – Homer, *Odyssey*

Odes – Horace, *Odes (Carmina)*

O.E.D. – *Oxford English Dictionary*

O.F. – Ludovico Ariosto, *Orlando Furioso*

Oracle – G. Wilson Knight, *The Burning Oracle* (1939)

Our Time – Douglas Bush, *"Paradise Lost" in Our Time* (1945)

Ovid – Davis P. Harding, *Milton and the Renaissance Ovid* (1946)

Par. – Dante, *Paradiso*

Pastoral – William Empson, *Some Versions of Pastoral* (n.d.)

Poetic – Ruth Wallerstein, *Studies in Seventeenth Century Poetic* (1950)

Polity – Richard Hooker, *Of the Laws of Ecclesiastical Polity* (Everyman Ed.)

P.&M. – Irene Samuel, *Plato and Milton*

Preface – C. S. Lewis, *A Preface to "Paradise Lost"* (1942)
Prom. – Aeschylus, *Prometheus*
Purg. – Dante, *Purgatorio*
Read – *Studies for William A. Read,* ed. by Nathaniel M. Caffee (1940)
Reader – B. Rajan, *"Paradise Lost" and the Seventeenth Century Reader* (1947)
Relation – George Sandys, *A Relation of a Journey*
Rep. – Plato, *Republic*
Royalism – Malcolm M. Ross, *Milton's Royalism: A Study of the Conflict of Symbol and Idea in the Poems* (1943)
Sat. – Juvenal, *Satires*
S.C.S.H.G. – *Seventeenth Century Studies Presented to Sir Herbert Grierson* (1938)
Semitic – Harris F. Fletcher, *Milton's Semitic Studies and Some Manifestations of Them in His Poetry* (1926)
Serpents – Edward Topsell, *A Historie of Serpents*
S.M. – E. M. W. Tillyard, *Studies in Milton* (1951)
Stuarts – Godfrey Davies, *The Early Stuarts, 1603–1660* (1937)
Style – Arnold Stein, *Answerable Style* (1953)
Summa Theol. – St. Thomas Aquinas, *Summa Theologica*
T.G.C.T. – Arnold Williams, ed., *A Tribute to George Coffin Taylor* (1952)
Theog. – Hesiod, *Theogony*
Thinker – Denis Saurat, *Milton: Man and Thinker* (1925)
Tim. – Plato, *Timaeus*
Tradition – Elizabeth M. Pope, *"Paradise Regained": The Tradition and the Poem* (1947)
Vanity – Joseph Glanvill, *The Vanity of Dogmatizing*
Verse – W. B. C. Watkins, *An Anatomy of Milton's Verse* (1955)
Vision – Don Cameron Allen, *The Harmonious Vision* (1954)
V.&M. – Sir Maurice Bowra, *From Virgil to Milton*
Wars – Josephus, *The Wars of the Jews*

ABBREVIATIONS OF TITLES OF PERIODICALS CITED IN THE NOTES

AR – *American Review*
CJ – *Cambridge Journal*
ColE – *College English*
CR – *Classical Review*
EA – *Etudes Anglaises*
ELH – *ELH: A Journal of English Literary History*
EM – *English Miscellany*
ESEA – *Essays and Studies by Members of the English Association*
Exp. – *Explicator*
HSCP – *Harvard Studies in Classical Philology*
HLQ – *Huntington Library Quarterly*
HTR – *Harvard Theological Review.*
JEGP – *Journal of English and Germanic Philology*
JHI – *Journal of the History of Ideas*
JWCI – *Journal of the Warburg and Courtauld Institute*
KR – *Kenyon Review*
MLN – *Modern Language Notes*
MLQ – *Modern Language Quarterly*
MLR – *Modern Language Review*

MP – Modern Philology
N&Q – Notes and Queries
PBA – Proceedings of the British Academy
PMLA – Publications of the Modern Language Association of America
PQ – The Philological Quarterly
QQ – Queen's Quarterly
RES – Review of English Studies
RHPR – Revue d'Histoire et de Philosophie religieuses
RR – Romanic Review
RSUL – Research Studies of the University of Louisiana
RSUW – Research Studies of the University of Washington
SAB – Shakespeare Association Bulletin
SAMLA – SAMLA Studies in Milton, by Members of the South Atlantic Modern Language Association
SCN – Seventeenth Century News
SP – Studies in Philology
Spec – Speculum
SR – Sewanee Review
TLS – The London Times Literary Supplement
TRSL – Transactions of the Royal Society of Literature
UTQ – University of Toronto Quarterly
UTSE – University of Texas Studies in English

Complete Poems
and
Major Prose

POEMS

OF
Mr. *John Milton*,

BOTH

ENGLISH and LATIN,
Compos'd at several times.

Printed by his true Copies.

The SONGS were set in Musick by
Mr. HENRY LAWES Gentleman of
the KINGS Chappel, and one
of His MAIESTIES
Private Musick.

——*Baccare frontem*
Cingite, ne vati noceat mala lingua futuro,
Virgil, Eclog. 7

Printed and publish'd according to
ORDER.

Jan: 2 LONDON,
Printed by *Ruth Raworth* for *Humphrey Moseley;*
and are to be sold at the signe of the Princes
Arms in S. *Pauls* Church-yard. 1645.

The Minor Poems

A PARAPHRASE ON *PSALM CXIV*

Milton's interest in the Psalms began when he paraphrased Psalm CXIV in English, and later in Greek. His first attempts, like his translations of 1648 and 1653, were influenced by the simple rhythms and rhymes of the Sternhold and Hopkins version (c1547), which was widely used in congregational singing. His treatment of the original Hebrew was no freer than that of other translators. It does not justify him in calling Egypt the *"Pharian fields"* (in CXIV, 3), after the island of Pharos at the mouth of the Nile; but, for doing so he had the immediate example of George Buchanan in his Latin paraphrase of the Psalms, and, in general, he had the example of Ovid and many classical poets for his learnedly allusive geographical names both here and in *PL*. His extravagant language in passages like that on the crossing of the Red Sea (the *"Erythraean* main" of CXXXVI, 46) reflects the bombast of Sylvester's translation of Du Bartas' account of it in the *Divine Weeks* (Ed. of 1608, pp. 476–7);

> . . . on each side is flanked all along
> With walls of crystal, beautiful and strong, . . .
> Two Walls of Glass, built with a word alone.

His quaintly "huge-bellied Mountains" that "skip like rams" are less quaint than the "hillocks" of Sir Philip Sidney's translation of the Psalm CXIV, which

> . . . capreold soe, as wanton by the dammes
> We capreoll see the lusty lambs.

This and the following *Psalm* were done by the Author at fifteen years old.

> When the blest seed of *Terah's* faithful Son,
> After long toil their liberty had won,
> And past from *Pharian* fields to *Canaan* Land,
> Led by the strength of the Almighty's hand,
> *Jehovah's* wonders were in *Israel* shown,　　　　　　　5
> His praise and glory was in *Israel* known.
> That saw the troubl'd Sea, and shivering fled,
> And sought to hide his froth-becurled head
> Low in the earth; *Jordan's* clear streams recoil,
> As a faint host that hath receiv'd the foil.　　　　　　10
> The high, huge-bellied Mountains skip like Rams
> Amongst their Ewes, the little Hills like Lambs.
> Why fled the Ocean? And why skipt the Mountains?
> Why turned *Jordan* toward his Crystal Fountains?
> Shake earth, and at the presence be aghast　　　　　　15
> Of him that ever was, and aye shall last,
> That glassy floods from rugged rocks can crush,
> And make soft rills from fiery flint-stones gush.　　　(1624)

---

1. Milton changed the reading of the original—which calls the Israelites the "house of Jacob"—for the sake of the allusion to Abraham. Though his father *Terah* was an idolater, "by faith Abraham, when he was called to go out into a place which he should after receive for an inheritance, obeyed" (Heb. xi, 8). Cf. *PL* XII, 151–52.

10. *foil:* defeat (in battle).

3

PSALM CXXXVI

Let us with a gladsome mind
Praise the Lord, for he is kind,
   For his mercies aye endure,
   Ever faithful, ever sure.

Let us blaze his Name abroad,   5
For of gods he is the God;
   For, &c.

O let us his praises tell,
That doth the wrathful tyrants quell.   10
   For, &c.

That with his miracles doth make
Amazed Heav'n and Earth to shake.
   For, &c.   15

That by his wisdom did create
The painted Heav'ns so full of state.
   For, &c.   20

That did the solid Earth ordain
To rise above the wat'ry plain.
   For, &c.

That by his all-commanding might,   25
Did fill the new-made world with light.
   For, &c.

And caus'd the Golden-tressed Sun,
All the day long his course to run.   30
   For, &c.

The horned Moon to shine by night,
Amongst her spangled sisters bright.
   For, &c.   35

He with his thunder-clasping hand,
Smote the first-born of *Egypt* Land.
   For, &c.   40

And in despite of *Pharaoh* fell,
He brought from thence his *Israel*.
   For, &c.

The ruddy waves he cleft in twain,   45
Of the *Erythraean* main.
   For, &c.

The floods stood still like Walls of Glass,
While the Hebrew Bands did pass.   50
   For, &c.

But full soon they did devour
The Tawny King with all his power.
   For, &c.   55

His chosen people he did bless
In the wasteful Wilderness.
   For, &c.   60

29. *Golden-tressed* may be a reminiscence of *auricomum solem* in Buchanan's version of this Psalm, or it may have been written with a characteristically Miltonic side-glance at the use of that epithet for Apollo in the Greek paeans.

In bloody battle he brought down
Kings of prowess and renown.
　　For, &c.
He foil'd bold *Seon* and his host,　　　　　　　　　　　　　65
That rul'd the *Amorrean* coast.
　　For, &c.
And large-limb'd *Og* he did subdue,
With all his over-hardy crew.　　　　　　　　　　　　　　　70
　　For, &c.
And to his servant *Israel*,
He gave their Land therein to dwell.
　　For, &c.　　　　　　　　　　　　　　　　　　　　　　　75
He hath with a piteous eye
Beheld us in our misery.
　　For &c.　　　　　　　　　　　　　　　　　　　　　　　80
And freed us from the slavery
Of the invading enemy.
　　For, &c.
All living creatures he doth feed,　　　　　　　　　　　　　85
And with full hand supplies their need.
　　For, &c.
Let us therefore warble forth
His mighty Majesty and worth.　　　　　　　　　　　　　　90
　　For, &c.
That his mansion hath on high
Above the reach of mortal eye.
　　For his mercies aye endure,　　　　　　　　　　　　　　95
　　Ever faithful, ever sure.　　　　　　　　　　(1624)

65–69. In *PL* I, 406–11, there is an allusion in like vein to the defeat of the Amorite king, Seon or Sihon; and Og reappears among the giants of old in *SA,* 1080.

Milton's Latin poems have been well edited by Walter MacKellar (New Haven, 1930) and will be edited by Douglas Bush in *A Variorum Commentary on the Poems of John Milton* to be published as a supplement to the Columbia Edition of Milton's *Works*. The dating of the poems here rests mainly on A. S. P. Woodhouse's "Notes on Milton's Early Development" in *UTQ* XIII (1943), 66–101, and W. R. Parker's study in *A Tribute to George Coffin Taylor* (Chapel Hill, 1952), pp. 113–31. More light is shed on the psychological interest of the poems and their relations to Milton's epic plans and to his style in *PL* by J. H. Hanford in *Studies in Shakespeare, Milton, and Donne* (New York, 1925); by E. K. Rand in *SP* XIX (1922), 109–35; and by E. M. W. Tillyard in *The Miltonic Setting* (London, 1947), pp. 168–204, and *Milton* (2nd ed. London, 1949). In *MP* XXXVII (1940), 351–6, F. R. B. Godolphin has traced Milton's greater fondness for Propertius and Ovid than for Tibullus as models for love poetry and familiar letters in elegiac meter, but there is no adequate study of his place in the tradition of Renaissance Latin poetry that includes Dante, Petrarch, Mantuan, Pontano, Sannazaro and Buchanan.

CARMINA ELEGIACA (ELEGIAC VERSES)

In his Commonplace Book, from which these verses come, Milton gave them no title except *Carmina Elegiaca* (*Elegiac Verses*).

Surge, age, surge, leves, iam convenit, excute somnos,
  Lux oritur; tepidi fulcra relinque tori.
Iam canit excubitor gallus, praenuncius ales
  Solis, et invigilans ad sua quemque vocat.
Flammiger Eois Titan caput exerit undis,   5
  Et spargit nitidum laeta per arva iubar.
Daulias argutum modulatur ab ilice carmen
  Edit et excultos mitis alauda modos.
Iam rosa fragrantes spirat silvestris odores;
  Iam redolent violae luxuriatque seges.   10
Ecce novo campos Zephyritis gramine vestit
  Fertilis, et vitreo rore madescit humus.
Segnes invenias molli vix talia lecto,
  Cum premat imbellis lumina fessa sopor.
Illic languentes abrumpunt somnia somnos,   15
  Et turbant animum tristia multa tuum.
Illic tabifici generantur semina morbi.
  Qui pote torpentem posse valere virum?
Surge, age, surge, leves, iam convenit, excute somnos,
  Lux oritur; tepidi fulcra relinque tori. (1625) 20

5. *Titan* is the sun (or sun god) whom Ovid describes (*Met.* I, 10) as infusing life into the earth.

7. Daulis, in Phocis, was the scene of Ovid's story (*Met.* VI, 668–74) of Procne's wrongs by her husband Tereus and of his pursuit of her and her sister Philomela, which ended in his transformation into a hoopoe and theirs into a swallow and a nightingale respectively.

Arise, haste, arise! Now that the time is right, shake off gentle slumbers. The light is springing up; leave the posts of your languid couch. Now sings the sentinel cock, the harbinger bird of the sun, alert to call every man to his task. Flaming Titan[5] lifts his head above the eastern waves and scatters his shining radiance over the happy fields. The Daulian[7] modulates her thrilling song from the oak-tree and the gentle lark pours out her skilful notes. Now the wild rose is breathing its fragrant perfumes; now the scent of violets is sweet and the corn is flourishing. Look, the bounteous daughter of Zephyr is clothing the fields with new verdure and the turf is moist with dew like beads of glass. Lazy one, you will hardly find such delights in your soft bed, when relaxing slumber weighs on your tired eyes. There dreams break in upon your dull sleep and many griefs disturb your spirit. There the seeds of a consuming illness are bred. What strength can a sluggard enjoy?

Arise, haste, arise! Now that the time is right, shake off gentle slumbers. The light is springing up; leave the posts of your languid couch.

To the following eight verses, in lesser Aesclepiad meter, Milton gave no heading.

Ignavus satrapam dedecet inclytum
Somnus qui populo multifido praeest.
Dum Dauni veteris filius armiger
Stratus purpureo procubuit toro.
Audax Eurialus, Nisus et impiger   5
Invasere cati nocte sub horrida
Torpentes Rutilos castraque Volscia:
Hinc caedes oritur clamor et absonus. . . . (1625)

3. The son of *Daunus* is Turnus, the leader of the *Rutilians, Volscians,* and other Italian tribes with which Aeneas had to contend for the mastery of Italy, and whose camp Virgil describes (*Aen.* IX, 176–449) as being successfully raided by Aeneas' followers, *Nisus* and *Eurialus.*

Slothful sleep is disgraceful to a famous governor who presides over the hosts of a people. While the warrior son of old Daunus[3] lay prone on his purple couch, bold Euryalus and keen Nisus cunningly attacked the sleeping Rutilians and the Volscian camp in the dreadful night. Hence slaughter arose and a hideous outcry. . . .

APOLOGUS DE RUSTICO ET HERO (FABLE OF PEASANT AND LANDLORD)

Like the verses from the Commonplace Book, this poem is probably an early school exercise of the kind which D. L. Clark describes in *Milton at St. Paul's School* (New York,

1948), p. 233.   It is a fable of Aesop which—as Walter MacKellar notes—was assigned for imitation by schoolboys in William Bullokar's *Aesop's Fables in True Orthography* (London, 1585); but—as H. F. Fletcher has shown in *JEGP* LV (1956), 230-3—its model was a metrical version of the fable in the fourth book of Mantuan's *Sylvarum* (Paris, 1513). The fact that Milton's version was not published until 1673 suggested to Masson that it might have been written or revived during Milton's active political career, and that it may hide a political "sting."

Rusticus ex Malo sapidissima poma quotannis
  Legit, et urbano lecta dedit Domino:
Hic, incredibili fructus dulcedine Captus,
  Malum ipsam in proprias transtulit areolas.
Hactenus illa ferax, sed longo debilis aevo,   5
  Mota solo assueto, protinus aret iners.
Quod tandem ut patuit Domino, spe lusus inani,
  Damnavit celeres in sua damna manus;
Atque ait, 'Heu quanto satius fuit illa Coloni,
  Parva licet, grato dona tulisse animo!   10
Possem Ego avaritiam frenare, gulamque voracem:
  Nunc periere mihi et foetus et ipsa parens.'

                (1625)

A peasant gathered most savory fruit year after year from his apple-tree and gave the choice specimens to his city-dwelling landlord. The latter, pleased with the unbelievable sweetness of the fruit, transferred the tree itself to his own gardens. The tree, though it had long been fruitful, was enfeebled by old age and, when it was moved out of its accustomed soil, it forthwith withered past all bearing. When it was clear at last to the master that he had been tricked by a vain hope, he cursed the hands that were so swift to their own undoing:

"Alas!" he cried, "how much more satisfactory it was to receive my tenant's offerings with a grateful heart, small though they were! If only I might bridle my cupidity and my voracious gullet! Now both the fruit and the parent tree are lost to me."

ELEGIA PRIMA (ELEGY I)

AD CAROLUM DIODATUM (TO CHARLES DIODATI)[1]

Tandem, care, tuae mihi pervenere tabellae,
  Pertulit et voces nuntia charta tuas,
Pertulit occidua Devae Cestrensis ab ora
  Vergivium prono qua petit amne salum.
Multum, crede, iuvat terras aluisse remotas
  Pectus amans nostri, tamque fidele caput,
Quodque mihi lepidum tellus longinqua sodalem
  Debet, at unde brevi reddere iussa velit.
Me tenet urbs reflua quam Thamesis alluit unda,
  Meque nec invitum patria dulcis habet.   10

At last, dear friend, your letter has come to me and its news-laden pages have brought me your words —brought them from the western bank of the Dee beside Chester,[3] where with precipitate current it seeks the Irish Sea. There is great delight, believe me, in the fact that remote regions have bred a heart that is loving and a head so devoted to me, that I have a claim for a charming comrade upon a distant land, which is willing soon to return him to me at my bidding.

[1] Milton was rusticated (suspended) after a quarrel with his tutor in the Lent term of his second year at Cambridge, in 1626. His friend Diodati was a student at Oxford, but was visiting in Chester. Their friendship is the subject of a chapter in D. C. Dorian's *The English Diodatis*

(New Brunswick, 1950), but its best records are *El 1* and *El VI* and *Damon.*
3. The associations of the river Dee for Milton in *Lyc*, 55 are illuminated by his references to it here and in *Vac*, 98.

Iam nec arundiferum mihi cura revisere Camum,
　　Nec dudum vetiti me laris angit amor.
Nuda nec arva placent, umbrasque negantia molles,
　　Quam male Phoebicolis convenit ille locus!
Nec duri libet usque minas perferre magistri　　15
　　Caeteraque ingenio non subeunda meo.
Si sit hoc exilium patrios adiisse penates,
　　Et vacuum curis otia grata sequi,
Non ego vel profugi nomen, sortemve recuso,
　　Laetus et exilii conditione fruor.　　20
O utinam vates nunquam graviora tulisset
　　Ille Tomitano flebilis exul agro;
Non tunc Ionio quicquam cessisset Homero
　　Neve foret victo laus tibi prima, Maro.
Tempora nam licet hic placidis dare libera Musis,　　25
　　Et totum rapiunt me mea vita libri.
Excipit hinc fessum sinuosi pompa theatri,
　　Et vocat ad plausus garrula scena suos.
Seu catus auditur senior, seu prodigus haeres,
　　Seu procus, aut posita casside miles adest,　　30
Sive decennali foecundus lite patronus
　　Detonat inculto barbara verba foro,
Saepe vafer gnato succurrit servus amanti,
　　Et nasum rigidi fallit ubique Patris;
Saepe novos illic virgo mirata calores　　35
　　Quid sit amor nescit, dum quoque nescit, amat.
Sive cruentatum furiosa Tragoedia sceptrum
　　Quassat, et effusis crinibus ora rotat,
Et dolet, et specto, iuvat et spectasse dolendo,
　　Interdum et lacrymis dulcis amaror inest:　　40
Seu puer infelix indelibata reliquit

21–22. The bard is Ovid, who was irrevocably banished to the city of Tomis on the northwest shore of the Black Sea by Augustus in 8 A.D.
23. For Homer's traditional Ionian origin see *Manso*, 22, n.
24. *Maro*, Virgil's family name, was as familiar in Milton's time as the name *Virgilius*, by which we know him best.
27. The language suggests the "curving theater" of Ovid's *Art of Love* I, 89, or the "sinuous awnings" of the splendid Roman theaters in Propertius I, iv, 15. The characters and plots that Milton seems to have in mind resemble those of Roman comedy rather than any to be found in contemporary English drama except academic plays imitating Plautus and Terence. One such play, George Ruggle's *Ignoramus* (c1615), added a pettifogging lawyer to the stock characters that Milton mentions.
37–46. Milton's personification is like the "violent Tragedy" of Ovid's *Amores* III, i, 11–13, "moving with mighty strides, her brow gloomy under her locks, and her robe thrown down to let her brandish a royal scepter in her left hand." But the characters suggest plays like the *Agamemnon*, *The Libation Bearers*, and the *Eumenides* of Aeschylus, which tell the tragic stories of the descendants of *Pelops*, or plays like Sophocles' *Oedipus* trilogy, in all of which *Creon* has a part. Cf. *IlPen*, 99.

I am in the city which the Thames washes with its tidal waters and I am willingly detained in my dear native place. At present I feel no concern about returning to the sedgy Cam and I am troubled by no nostalgia for my forbidden quarters there. The bare fields, so niggardly of pleasant shade, have no charm for me. How wretchedly suited that place is to the worshippers of Phoebus! It is disgusting to be constantly subjected to the threats of a rough tutor and to other indignities which my spirit cannot endure. But if this be exile, to have returned to the paternal home and to be carefree to enjoy a delightful leisure, then I have no objection to the name or to the lot of a fugitive and I am glad to take advantage of my banishment. Ah! Would that the bard who was a pitiful exile in the land of Tomis[22] had never had to bear anything worse! Then he would have yielded nothing to Ionian Homer[23] and you, O Maro,[24] would have been conquered and stripped of your prime honors.

Here my hours are free to be dedicated to the quiet Muses; and my books, which are my life, quite carry me away. When I am tired, the magnificence of the arched theater[27] diverts me and the chattering actors invite me to applaud them. Sometimes the speaker is a shrewd old man, sometimes he is the wastrel heir, and sometimes the wooer. Or the soldier lays aside his helmet and appears, or the barrister who has fattened on a ten-year suit volleys his barbarous verbiage at an illiterate court-room. Often a wily slave comes to the rescue of a love-struck son and seems ubiquitous as he dupes the stiff-necked father under his very nose. And often the virgin, who is surprised by the strange fire within her and has no idea what love is, falls in love without knowing what she does.

Or Tragedy, with streaming hair and rolling eyes, tosses her blood-stained scepter in her frenzy.[37] The sight is painful, but still I watch and find pleasure in watching and suffering, and sometimes there is a sweet pain even in tears: at times when an unhappy youth must leave his joys untasted and is torn away

Gaudia, et abrupto flendus amore cadit,
Seu ferus e tenebris iterat Styga criminis ultor,
 Conscia funereo pectora torre movens;
Seu maeret Pelopeia domus, seu nobilis Ili,   45
 Aut luit incestos aula Creontis avos.
Sed neque sub tecto semper nec in urbe latemus,
 Irrita nec nobis tempora veris eunt.
Nos quoque lucus habet vicina consitus ulmo
 Atque suburbani nobilis umbra loci.   50
Saepius hic blandas spirantia sidera flammas
 Virgineos videas praeteriisse choros.
Ah quoties dignae stupui miracula formae
 Quae possit senium vel reparare Iovis;
Ah quoties vidi superantia lumina gemmas,   55
 Atque faces quotquot volvit uterque polus;
Collaque bis vivi Pelopis quae brachia vincant,
 Quaeque fluit puro nectare tincta via,
Et decus eximium frontis, tremulosque capillos,
 Aurea quae fallax retia tendit Amor;   60
Pellacesque genas, ad quas hyacinthina sordet
 Purpura, et ipse tui floris, Adoni, rubor!
Cedite laudatae toties Heroïdes olim,
 Et quaecunque vagum cepit amica Iovem.
Cedite Achaemeniae turrita fronte puellae,   65
 Et quot Susa colunt, Memnoniamque Ninon,
Vos etiam Danaae fasces submittite Nymphae,
 Et vos Iliacae, Romuleaeque nurus,
Nec Pompeianas Tarpeia Musa columnas
 Iactet, et Ausoniis plena theatra stolis.   70
Gloria Virginibus debetur prima Britannis,
 Extera, sat tibi sit, foemina, posse sequi.
Tuque urbs Dardaniis Londinum structa colonis
 Turrigerum late conspicienda caput,
Tu nimium felix intra tua moenia claudis   75
 Quicquid formosi pendulus orbis habet.

from his love to perish lamentably; or when the stern avenger of crime returns from the shades across the Styx and his fatal torch perturbs hearts that are conscious of guilt; or when the house of Pelops or of noble Ilus is stricken with grief; or the palace of Creon expiates the incest of its sires.[46] But I am not always hiding indoors nor even in the city, and the spring does not pass without some profit to me. I also am a visitor in the grove where the elms stand close together and in the magnificent shade of a place just beyond the city's confines. Here, like stars that breathe out soft flames, you may see groups of maidens go dancing past. Ah, how many times have I been struck dumb by the miraculous grace of a form which might make decrepit Jove young again! Ah, how many times have I seen eyes which outshine jewels and all the stars that wheel about either pole, necks which excel the arms of Pelops the twice-living[57] and the Way that flows tinctured with pure nectar, and a brow of surpassing loveliness, and waving tresses which were golden nets flung by Cupid, the deceiver! How often have I seen seductive cheeks beside which the purple of the hyacinth and even the blush of your flower, Adonis, turn pale.[62] Give way, ye Heroïdes[63] so much praised in olden times, and every mistress who made inconstant Jove her captive.[64] Give way, you Achaemenian[65] damsels with the turrets on your brows, and you, whose home is Susa or Memnonian Nineveh,[66] and you Greek maidens also, and you women of Troy and of Rome, make your submission. Let not the Tarpeian Muse boast of Pompey's colonnade[69] or of the theaters crowded with Italian robes. The prime honor is due to the virgins of Britain; be content, foreign woman, to follow after. And you, London, the city built by Trojan colonists and now widely conspicuous with towered head,[74] yours is the excessive happiness of bounding within your walls whatever beauty the pendant world[76] possesses. The ministrant

57. Ovid tells the story (*Met.* VI, 407–11) of *Pelops'* dismemberment by his own father, and of the search for his scattered limbs by the gods, who failed to find one of his shoulders and had to substitute an ivory shoulder before they restored him to life.
62. According to Ovid's story (*Met.* X, 735–9), Venus caused the anemone to grow from the blood of the dying Adonis. Cf. *Comus*, 999.
63–64. Milton was thinking of Ovid's imaginary letters by famous women (the *Heroides*) and his many stories of the love-affairs of Jove in the *Metamorphoses*.
65–66. *Achaemenes* was the founder of the Persian dynasty whose capital, *Susa*, was supposed to have been founded by Tithonus, father of *Memnon*. In *PL* X, 308, Susa is rightly called "Memnonian." No known legend connects Tithonus with *Nineveh*.
69. *Pompey's colonnade* was in the Campus Martius below the *Tarpeian* Rock, near which Ovid lived on the Capitoline Hill.
74. Cf. the "Tower'd Cities" of *L'All*, 117. Both phrases recall Virgil's "tower-bearing cities" (*Aen.* X, 253).

76. Ovid's picture of the newly-created world "supported by its own weight" (*Met.* I, 12–13) was later to inspire Milton's "pendulous round earth"

Non tibi tot caelo scintillant astra sereno
  Endymioneae turba ministra deae,
Quot tibi conspicuae formaque auroque puellae
  Per medias radiant turba videnda vias.   80
Creditur huc geminis venisse invecta columbis
  Alma pharetrigero milite cincta Venus,
Huic Cnidon, et riguas Simoentis flumine valles,
  Huic Paphon, et roseam posthabitura Cypron.
Ast ego, dum pueri sinit indulgentia caeci,   85
  Moenia quam subito linquere fausta paro;
Et vitare procul malefidae infamia Circes
  Atria, divini Molyos usus ope.
Stat quoque iuncosas Cami remeare paludes,
  Atque iterum raucae raucae murmur adire Scholae.   90
Interea fidi parvum cape munus amici,
  Paucaque in alternos verba coacta modos.   (1626)

hosts of Endymion's[78] goddess, the stars that shine down upon you in the calm sky, are fewer than the radiant host in your streets—maidens whose forms and golden ornaments dazzle the eye. Venus, the giver of life (it is believed) has come hither, drawn by her twin doves and escorted by her quiver-bearing soldiery, and she will prefer this city to Cnidus[81] and to the valleys that are watered by the river Simois,[84] and to Paphos and rosy Cyprus.

But for my part—while the blind boy's indulgence permits it—I am preparing the speediest possible departure from this city of delights—preparing, with the help of divine moly,[87] to secure the safety of distance from the infamous halls of the deceiver, Circe.[88] It is decided also that I am to go back to the reedy fens of the Cam and return again to the hum of the noisy school. Meanwhile, accept this small tribute of a loyal friend and these few words that have been forced into alternating measures.[92]

(PL IV, 1000) and "Pendant world" (PL II, 1052).

78. *Endymion*, says the Gloss to Spenser's *Shepheardes Calendar* (July 63), was feigned by the poets "To have bene so beloved by Phoebe, sc. the moone, that he was by her kept a sleepe in a cave by the space of xx yeares, for to enjoye his companye."

81-84. In the background is Lucretius' cosmic Venus, whose haunts, as Spenser recalled (*F.Q.* III, vi, 39, 4–8), were as various as "*Paphos*, or Cythaeron Hill, Or . . . *Gnidus*." Paris awarded the apple of strife that caused the Trojan war to Venus on the bank of the river *Simois*, which rises on Mt. Ida.

87-88. Cf. the allegorical part played by the herb moly in *Comus*, 636.

92. The alternating measures are the alternating hexameters and pentameters of the elegiac couplet.

THE FIFTH ODE OF HORACE, LIB. I

Quis multa gracilis te puer in Rosa, Rend'red almost word for word without Rhyme according to the Latin Measure, as near as the Language will permit.

What slender Youth bedew'd with liquid odors
Courts thee on Roses in some pleasant Cave,
    Pyrrha? for whom bind'st thou
    In wreaths thy golden Hair,
Plain in thy neatness? O how oft shall he   5
On Faith and changed Gods complain: and Seas
    Rough with black winds and storms
    Unwonted shall admire:
Who now enjoys thee credulous, all Gold;
Who always vacant, always amiable   10
    Hopes thee; of flattering gales
    Unmindful. Hapless they
To whom thou untried seem'st fair. Me in my vow'd
Picture the sacred wall declares t' have hung
    My dank and dropping weeds   15
    To the stern God of Sea.   (1626?)

AD PYRRHAM. ODE V

Horatius ex Pyrrhae illecebris tanquam e naufragio enataverat, cuius amore irretitos, affirmat esse miseros. [Milton subjoined the Latin text to his translation.]

Quis multa gracilis te puer in rosa
Perfusus liquidis urget odoribus,
    Grato, *Pyrrha,* sub antro?
    Cui flavam religas comam,
Simplex munditie? Heu quoties
    fidem
Mutatosque deos flebit, et aspera
    Nigris aequora ventis
    Emirabitur insolens,
Qui nunc te fruitur credulus aurea:
Qui semper vacuam, semper amabi-
    lem
    Sperat, nescius aurae
    Fallacis. Miseri, quibus
Intentata nites. Me tabula sacer
Votiva paries indicat uvida
    Suspendisse potenti
    Vestimenta maris Deo.

IN OBITUM PROCANCELLARII MEDICI (ON THE DEATH OF THE VICE-CHANCELLOR, A PHYSICIAN)

Anno Aetatis 16 [*17*]   *At Age 16* [*17*]

Parere fati discite legibus,
Manusque Parcae iam date supplices,
  Qui pendulum telluris orbem
    Iapeti colitis nepotes.
Vos si relicto mors vaga Taenaro
Semel vocarit flebilis, heu morae
  Tentantur incassum dolique;
    Per tenebras Stygis ire certum est.
Si destinatam pellere dextera
Mortem valeret, non ferus Hercules
  Nessi venenatus cruore
    Aemathia iacuisset Oeta.
Nec fraude turpi Palladis invidae
Vidisset occisum Ilion Hectora, aut
  Quem larva Pelidis peremit
    Ense Locro, Iove lacrymante.
Si triste fatum verba Hecateia
Fugare possint, Telegoni parens
  Vixisset infamis, potentique
    Aegiali soror usa virga.
Numenque trinum fallere si queant
Artes medentum, ignotaque gramina,
  Non gnarus herbarum Machaon
    Eurypyli cecidisset hasta.
Laesisset et nec te, Philyreie,
Sagitta echidnae perlita sanguine,
  Nec tela te fulmenque avitum
    Caese puer genitricis alvo.
Tuque O alumno major Apolline,
Gentis togatae cui regimen datum,
  Frondosa quem nunc Cirrha luget,

Learn obedience to the laws of destiny and lift suppliant hands to the Goddess of Fate, you descendants of Iapetus[4] who inhabit the pendulous orb of the earth. If Death, [5] the grievous rover from Tartarus, once summons you, alas! it is vain to try delays and tricks. The journey through the shadows of the Styx is inevitable. If the human arm had [10] power to repel fated death, the poisonous blood of Nessus[10] would not have laid the untamable Hercules low on Thessalian Oeta;[12] nor would Troy have seen Hector slain by the shameful deceit of vengeful [15] Athene,[13] nor Sarpedon killed—though Jove shed tears—by the Locrian disguised in Achilles' armor.[16] If the spells of Hecate could banish sad fate, Circe[18] would have lived [20] on in her infamy and Medea would have survived to use her potent wand.[20] If the arts of the physicians and mysterious herbs had power to deceive the triple deity, Machaon,[23] with his knowledge of medicinal [25] plants, would not have succumbed to the wound of Eurypylus'[24] spear; nor would the arrow smeared with serpent's blood have stricken you, O son of Philyra;[25] nor would you [30] have been smitten with the bolts and thunder of your grandsire, O boy cut from your mother's womb.[26] And you[29]—who are greater than your pupil, Apollo, to whom the government of our gowned society was given, and whom leafy Cirrha[31]

1–4. Again, as in *El 1*, 76, we have Ovid's newborn and self-poised world, and with it a reference to his account of the creation of man by Prometheus, the son of *Iapetus* (*Met.* I, 82–83).

10–12. Cf. *Hercules'* vengeance on *Nessus* in *PL* II, 542, n.

13–16. Sarpedon's death at the hands of Patroclus the *Locrian* (*Il.* XVI, 477–91) was a link in the chain of events that led to *Hector's* overthrow by *Achilles* with the help of *Athene* (*Il.* XXII, 275–99).

18–20. *Telegonus'* mother was Circe (Cf. *Comus,* 50). In Trogus' *History* XLII, iii, 1, *Aegialeus* is named as the brother of the enchantress Medea.

23–24. Homer mentions *Machaon* and *Eurypylus* as Greek leaders (*Il.* II, 732–6; XI, 541) and makes Machaon their healer. His death at Eurypylus' hands is described by Quintus of Smyrna in *The Fall of Troy* VI, 391–428.

25–26. Though the centaur Chiron, the son of

the nymph *Philyra*, was immortal and was the tutor of the god of healing, Aesculapius, whom his father Apollo cut from the womb of his mother Coronis, he had to beg his death from the Fates as a cure for his wounds by Hercules' poisoned arrows (*Met.* II, 596–654). Aesculapius was killed by Jupiter, as Milton goes on to say that the Vice-Chancellor was by Persephone, because his medical skill saved too many lives.

29. Dr. John Gostlin, who had been Regius Professor of Medicine and Vice-Chancellor at Cambridge since 1623, died Oct. 21, 1626.

31. Milton speaks as if the god of medicine, *Apollo* himself, had been Dr. Gostlin's pupil—as if Cambridge were more famous than Apollo's city of *Cirrha,* near his oracle at Delphi.

Et mediis Helicon in undis,
Iam praefuisses Palladio gregi
Laetus, superstes, nec sine gloria,
  Nec puppe lustrasses Charontis   35
  Horribiles barathri recessus.
At fila rupit Persephone tua
Irata, cum te viderit artibus
  Succoque pollenti tot atris
  Faucibus eripuisse mortis.   40
Colende praeses, membra precor tua
Molli quiescant cespite, et ex tuo
  Crescant rosae, calthaeque busto,
  Purpureoque hyacinthus ore.
Sit mite de te iudicium Aeaci,   45
Subrideatque Aetnaea Proserpina,
  Interque felices perennis
  Elysio spatiere campo.   (1626)

37. The queen of hell, *Persephone*, is called
Sicilian because she was kidnapped from Enna in
Sicily by Pluto (Cf. *PL* IV, 269).

mourns and Helicon in the midst of its streams—you would be the happy and glorious leader of the flock of Athena instead of traversing the frightful depths of hell in Charon's boat. But Persephone broke the thread of your life,[37] angered because she saw you snatching so many victims from the black jaws of death by your arts and powerful potions.

Reverend Chancellor, may your limbs find rest in the soft turf, I pray, and from your grave may roses and marigolds and the purple-lipped hyacinth spring. May the judgement of Aeacus upon you be gentle, and may Sicilian Proserpina [46] smile! May you walk forever among the blessed in Elysium!

46. *Proserpina*, Latin equivalent of Persephone.

ELEGIA SECUNDA (ELEGY II)

Anno Aetatis 17 (At Age 17)

IN OBITUM PRAECONIS ACADEMICI CANTABRIGIENSIS (ON THE DEATH OF THE BEADLE OF CAMBRIDGE UNIVERSITY)

Te, qui conspicuus baculo fulgente solebas
  Palladium toties ore ciere gregem,
Ultima praeconum praeconem te quoque saeva
  Mors rapit, officio nec favet ipsa suo.
Candidiora licet fuerint tibi tempora plumis   5
  Sub quibus accipimus delituisse Iovem,
O dignus tamen Haemonio iuvenescere succo,
  Dignus in Aesonios vivere posse dies,
Dignus quem Stygiis medica revocaret ab undis
  Arte Coronides, saepe rogante dea.   10
Tu si iussus eras acies accire togatas,
  Et celer a Phoebo nuntius ire tuo,

1–5. Richard Ridding, for whom this elegy was written, had been senior beadle or official crier of the University for thirty years when he died in 1626. As marshall of all its academic processions he had been familiar to all the students—"the host of Pallas Athene" as Milton calls them with perhaps mock solemnity.

5–6. Milton was thinking of the story that Jove "turnd into a snowy swan / To win faire Leda to his lovely trade" (*F.Q.* III, xi, 32, 1–2).

7. Ovid tells the story (*Met.* VII, 263–93) of Medea's rejuvenation of old *Aeson* by dissecting him and reuniting his limbs after boiling them in a brew of "Haemonian roots." Haemonia (Thrace) was traditionally a land of magic. Cf. *Manso*, 75 and *Comus*, 38.

9–10. *Coronides*, Aesculapius, the god of heal-

You, who were so often conspicuous with your glittering mace[1] when your voice assembled the Palladian host—beadle though you were—you have become the prey of the last of beadles, Death, who shows no favor even to her own profession. Though your brows were whiter than the plumes in which we are told that Jove was disguised,[5] you were none the less worthy to have your youth restored by the drugs of Haemonia[7] and to be endued with the power to live to an Aesonian old age. You deserved that, at the repeated prayer of the goddess, Coronides[9] should use his healing art to recall you from the Stygian waves.[10] If you were bidden by your Apollo[12] to go—a swift messenger—and convene the files of gownsmen, you were like wing-

ing, was a son of Coronis, the story of whose unfaithful love for his father Apollo Ovid tells (*Met.* II, 542–6 and 596–611). Spenser retold the story (*F.Q.* I, v, 37–44) of his restoration of Hippolytus to life at the prayer of Diana.

12. The beadle's *Phoebus Apollo* was the Vice-Chancellor.

Talis in Iliaca stabat Cyllenius aula
  Alipes, aetherea missus ab arce Patris.
Talis et Eurybates ante ora furentis Achillei   15
  Rettulit Atridae iussa severa ducis.
Magna sepulchrorum regina, satelles Averni
  Saeva nimis Musis, Palladi saeva nimis,
Quin illos rapias qui pondus inutile terrae?
  Turba quidem est telis ista petenda tuis.   20
Vestibus hunc igitur pullis, Academia, luge,
  Et madeant lacrimis nigra feretra tuis.
Fundat et ipsa modos querebunda Elegeia tristes,
  Personet et totis naenia moesta scholis.   (1626)

13. *Cyllenius* (i. e. Mercury, who was born on Mt. Cyllene in Arcadia), was the beadle or messenger of the gods. Cf. *Arc*, 98.
15. *Eurybates* was one of the heralds of Agamemnon, the son of *Atrides* (*Il.* I, 320–33).
17. Because Lake *Avernus*, near Naples, was traditionally an entrance to hell its name came to mean hell itself.
22. In these tears and the "tears of perfect moan" of *Winchester*, 55 and the "melodious tear" of *Lyc*, 14, there may be a reference to an old practice of fastening mourning verses to the biers of the dead.

footed Cyllenius[13] when he was dispatched from the heavenly citadel of his father and stood in the palace at Ilium. You were like Eurybates[15] when he delivered the stern orders of his chief, Atrides, in the presence of the angry Achilles.

Great queen of sepulchers, accomplice of Avernus[17]—too terrible to the Muses and too terrible to Pallas—why do you not make your prey of those who are useless burdens of the earth? That is the rabble which ought to be made the target of your darts.

Therefore grieve for this man, O Academe, in robes of black, and make his dark hearse wet with your tears.[22] Let wailing Elegy herself pour out her sad dirge and fill all the schools with its sound.

IN PRODITIONEM BOMBARDICAM (ON THE GUNPOWDER PLOT)

Cum simul in regem nuper satrapasque Britannos
  Ausus es infandum, perfide Fauxe, nefas,
Fallor? an et mitis voluisti ex parte videri,
  Et pensare mala cum pietate scelus?
Scilicet hos alti missurus ad atria caeli,   5
  Sulphureo curru flammivolisque rotis:
Qualiter ille, feris caput inviolabile Parcis,
  Liquit Iordanios turbine raptus agros.

7. Elijah, whose escape from death by translation to heaven from the banks of the river Jordan is described in II Kings ii, 7. The *Parcae* are the Fates. Cf. *Manso*, 19.

Perfidious Fawkes, when you attempted your recent unspeakable outrage against the King and the English nobles—do I misjudge, or did you wish to seem merciful in one way and to atone for your crime with a kind of wicked piety? You were going, obviously, to send them to the courts of high heaven in a sulphurous chariot with wheels of whirling fire—as he whose head proved inviolable by the fell Parcae[7] was rapt away in a whirlwind, leaving the banks of the Jordan behind him.

IN EANDEM (ON THE SAME)

Siccine tentasti caelo donasse Iäcobum
  Quae septemgemino Bellua monte lates?
Ni meliora tuum poterit dare munera numen,
  Parce, precor, donis insidiosa tuis.
Ille quidem sine te consortia serus adivit   5
  Astra, nec inferni pulveris usus ope.
Sic potius foedos in caelum pelle cucullos,

1. James I died on March 5, 1625.
2. The *beast* is the monster described by St. John as rising "out of the sea, having seven heads and ten horns . . . and upon his heads the name of blasphemy" (Rev. xiii, 1).
7. Cf. the Paradise of Fools in *PL* II, 476–97.

Was this the kind of attempt that you made to bestow heaven upon James, you beast[2] in ambush on the Seven Hills? Unless your divinity has better gifts in its power, O weaver of plots, I implore you to spare your largess. Without your help, it is true, and without the aid of your infernal gunpowder, the King has gone at a ripe old age to be with his kindred, the stars.

Blow your detestable cowls, rather, up to the skies,[7] and all the idol

Et quot habet brutos Roma profana Deos;
Namque hac aut alia nisi quemque adiuveris arte,
Crede mihi, caeli vix bene scandet iter.   10

gods that profane Rome contains; for, unless you help them in this way or in some other, believe me, not one of them will climb very prosperously on the path to heaven.

IN EANDEM (ON THE SAME)

Purgatorem animae derisit Iäcobus ignem,
Et sine quo superum non adeunda domus.
Frenduit hoc trina monstrum Latiale corona
Movit et horrificum cornua dena minax.
Et "Nec inultus," ait, "temnes mea sacra, Britanne;   5
Supplicium spreta religione dabis.
Et, si stelligeras unquam penetraveris arces,
Non nisi per flammas triste patebit iter."
O quam funesto cecinisti proxima vero,
Verbaque ponderibus vix caritura suis!   10
Nam prope Tartareo sublime rotatus ab igni
Ibat ad aethereas, umbra perusta, plagas.

James made a jest of the purgatorial fire without which there is no way for the soul to reach the heavenly mansions. At that the Latin monster with its triple crown gnashed its teeth and wagged its ten horns with menace horrid:

"Englishman," it cried, "you shall not despise my sanctities with impunity; you shall pay a forfeit for the insult to religion. And if ever you attain the starry citadels, the only way open to you will be the sad one through fire."

How close your vaticinations came to the grim truth and how little your utterances lacked of fulfilment! For he did—almost—go to the celestial shores, a cindery ghost, whirled aloft by Tartarean fire.

IN EANDEM (ON THE SAME)

Quem modo Roma suis devoverat impia diris,
Et Styge damnarat, Taenarioque sinu,
Hunc, vice mutata, iam tollere gestit ad astra,
Et cupit ad superos evehere usque Deos.

1. The reference is to the formal interdict under which James I lay because of his assumption of the headship of the English church.
2. Cf. *El V*, 66, n.

Him whom impious Rome had consigned to her curses[1] and condemned to the Styx and the Taenarian gulf,[2] him—quite contrarily—she sets about to lift to the stars and wishes to hoist among the celestial gods.

IN INVENTOREM BOMBARDAE (ON THE INVENTOR OF GUNPOWDER)

Iapetionidem laudavit caeca vetustas,
Qui tulit aetheream solis ab axe facem;
At mihi major erit, qui lurida creditur arma,
Et trifidum fulmen surripuisse Iovi.   (1626?)

1. Cf. the reference to Prometheus as *Iapetus'* son in *On the Death of the Vice-Chancellor*, 4, and to his theft of fire from heaven in *Patrem*, 20.

The ancients in their blindness paid honor to the son of Iapetus,[1] who brought down the celestial fire from the chariot of the sun; but in my eyes he will be a greater man who is credited with having stolen his flaming weapons and three-forked thunderbolt from Jove.

IN QUINTUM NOVEMBRIS (ON THE FIFTH OF NOVEMBER)

Anno Aetatis 17 (At Age 17)

November 5, 1605, might have been fatal to James I if Guy Fawkes had not been detected under the Parliament House as he was preparing to explode a charge of 32cwt. of gunpowder at the opening of the session. Fawkes and eight other conspirators were tried and executed. By act of Parliament "an annual and constant memorial of that day" was to be observed so that—as Thomas Fuller said in *The Church-History of Britain* X, 17—it might "be solemnly transmitted to all posterity, . . . how bad man can be to destroy, and how good God hath been to deliver." In the universities the day was celebrated with epic poems like Milton's and the longer and even more bitterly anti-papal *Locustae* and *Apolyonists* of Phineas Fletcher (1627). In such poems an inevitable feature was the formal conspiracy of the devils in hell as the beginning of the plot against the English king. Milton was familiar with many demonic councils in classical literature and in *PL* he was destined to create a very different kind of infernal council from the bitterly propagandic one that he described here, perhaps mainly under the influence of a similar council in Bernardino Ochino's *A Tragedy or Dialogue of the unjust and usurped Primacy of the Bishop of Rome* (1549).

Iam pius extrema veniens Iacobus ab arcto
Teucrigenas populos, lateque patentia regna
Albionum tenuit, iamque inviolabile foedus
Sceptra Caledoniis coniunxerat Anglica Scotis:
Pacificusque novo felix divesque sedebat   5
In solio, occultique doli securus et hostis:
Cum ferus ignifluo regnans Acheronte tyrannus,
Eumenidum pater, aethereo vagus exul Olympo,
Forte per immensum terrarum erraverat orbem,
Dinumerans sceleris socios, vernasque fideles,   10
Participes regni post funera moesta futuros;
Hic tempestates medio ciet aere diras,
Illic unanimes odium struit inter amicos,
Armat et invictas in mutua viscera gentes;
Regnaque olivifera vertit florentia pace,   15
Et quoscunque videt purae virtutis amantes,
Hos cupit adiicere imperio, fraudumque magister
Tentat inaccessum sceleri corrumpere pectus,
Insidiasque locat tacitas, cassesque latentes
Tendit, ut incautos rapiat, ceu Caspia Tigris   20

2. Milton makes poetic use of Geoffrey of Monmouth's story of the settlement of England by the followers of Erutus, a grandson of Aeneas—a story retold by Spenser in *F.Q.* II, x, 9 and iii, 9, 46–51.

7. *Acheron*, like the other infernal river *Phlegethon* in l. 74 below, stands for hell itself. Cf. *Comus*, 604 and *PL* II, 578.

8. In this allusion to Virgil's treatment of Pluto as the father of the *Eumenides*, the avengers of crime, there may be a suggestion of a Christian tradition that made Satan the father of Sin and Death in *PL* II, 747–89.

20. Cf. the note on the Caucasus and the *Caspian* in *PR* III, 318.

Now the devout James, coming from the remote north, assumed the lordship of the Troy-born race[2] and of the wide-spreading realms of the English, and now an inviolable league had united the English and the Scottish scepters. The establisher of peace was seated on his new throne, fortunate and affluent, with no suspicion of a secret conspiracy or of a foe, when the cruel tyrant who governs the fiery streams of Acheron,[7] the father of the Eumenides,[8] the wandering outcast from the celestial Olympus, chanced to range through the vast circle of the earth, counting the companions of his wickedness, his faithful slaves, who are destined after their miserable deaths to take their share in his kingdom.

Here he stirs up wild tempests in mid air; there he instigates hatred among loyal friends. He arms unconquerable nations for a death-struggle together and overturns kingdoms which are flourishing under the olive of peace. Whatever lovers of pure virtue he can find, he seeks to add to his empire and—master of guile that he is—he tries to corrupt even the heart that is locked against sin. He lays silent plots and stretches unseen nets to capture the unwary, like the Caspian[20] tigress pursuing her trem-

Insequitur trepidam deserta per avia praedam
Nocte sub illuni, et somno nictantibus astris.
Talibus infestat populos Summanus et urbes
Cinctus caeruleae fumanti turbine flammae.
Iamque fluentisonis albentia rupibus arva   25
Apparent, et terra Deo dilecta marino,
Cui nomen dederat quondam Neptunia proles
Amphitryoniaden qui non dubitavit atrocem
Aequore tranato furiali poscere bello,
Ante expugnatae crudelia saecula Troiae.   30
  At simul hanc opibusque et festa pace beatam
Aspicit, et pingues donis Cerealibus agros,
Quodque magis doluit, venerantem numina veri
Sancta Dei populum, tandem suspiria rupit
Tartareos ignes et luridum olentia sulphur.   35
Qualia Trinacria trux ab Iove clausus in Aetna
Efflat tabifico monstrosus ab ore Typhoeus.
Ignescunt oculi, stridetque adamantinus ordo
Dentis, ut armorum fragor, ictaque cuspide cuspis,
Atque "Pererrato solum hoc lacrymabile mundo   40
Inveni," dixit, "gens haec mihi sola rebellis,
Contemtrixque iugi, nostraque potentior arte.
Illa tamen, mea si quicquam tentamina possunt,
Non feret hoc impune diu, non ibit inulta."
Hactenus; et piceis liquido natat aere pennis;   45
Qua volat, adversi praecursant agmine venti,
Densantur nubes, et crebra tonitrua fulgent.
  Iamque pruinosas velox superaverat alpes,
Et tenet Ausoniae fines; a parte sinistra
Nimbifer Apenninus erat, priscique Sabini,   50
Dextra veneficiis infamis Hetruria, nec non
Te furtiva, Tibris, Thetidi videt oscula dantem;
Hinc Mavortigenae consistit in arce Quirini.
Reddiderant dubiam iam sera crepuscula lucem,
Cum circumgreditur totam Tricoronifer urbem,   55
Panificosque Deos portat, scapulisque virorum

23. In Charles Stephanus' *Dictionary* Milton
knew that his audience could find Pliny (II, 51)
and Ovid (*Fasti* VI) cited as authorities for identifying Pluto with a forgotten god of midnight
storms, *Summanus*.

28. "Albion, a giant son of *Neptune,* who called
the island after his own name," Milton recalled
in *Britain* (Book I; *C.E.* X, 4) was supposed to
have "ruled it forty-four years. Till, passing over
into Gaul, in aid of his brother Lestrygon, against
whom Hercules was hasting out of Spain, he was
there slain in fight."

32. Cf. the allusion to *Ceres,* the goddess of
grain, in *PL* IV, 980.

36. Behind this comparison of Satan with *Typhoeus* is Ovid's account (*Met.* V, 346–58) of him
as requiring the whole weight of the island of
Sicily to hold him down, and of the eruptions
of Mt. Aetna as due to his struggles. Cf. *PL* I,
199.

52. The sea-nymph Thetis stands for the sea,
which is "kissed" by the god of the Tiber because
its waters fall gently into the Mediterranean.

bling prey through trackless deserts
at night in the moonless darkness
when the stars are drowsily glimmering. With horrors like his does
Summanus,[23] girdled with a smoking tornado of lightning flame, beset
peoples and cities. And now he sees
the white fields and wave-beaten
cliffs of the favorite land of the sea-
god, the land to which Neptune's
son long ago gave his name,[28] he
who was bold enough to cross the
sea and challenge Hercules to a dire
combat before the dreadful times of
the conquest of Troy.

As soon as he catches sight of this
land in its enjoyment of the blessings of wealth and festal peace, with
its fields rich in the gifts of Ceres[32]
and—what irked him worse—a people worshipping the sacred deity of
the true God, he broke into sighs
that were redolent of lurid sulphur
and the fires of Tartarus. Such
sighs the horrid and monstrous
Typhoeus, whom Jove imprisoned
under Sicilian Aetna,[36] emits from
his consuming mouth. His eyes
flash and his adamantine array of
teeth grinds like the clash of arms
and the blow of spear against spear.
"After wandering throughout the
whole world," says he, "I find this
my only grief, this nation alone rebellious against me, contemptuous
of my yoke and stronger than my
art. Yet if my efforts avail at all,
they shall not go on so with impunity, they shall not continue unpunished." That much he said and
oared away on pitch-black wings
through the liquid air. Wherever
he flies warring winds run before
him; clouds mass up and thunderbolts flash incessantly.

Now his speed had carried him
beyond the frosty Alps and he
reaches the borders of Italy. To his
left was the cloud-wrapped Apennine chain, the home of the ancient
Sabines; to his right, Etruria, infamous for its magic potions; and
not far away he sees the furtive
kisses which you are giving to the
sea, O Tiber.[52] Thence he came to
rest on the citadel of Quirinus, the
son of Mars. The dusk of evening
had already made the light uncertain, when the wearer of the Triple
Crown, borne on men's shoulders, makes a circuit of the whole

Evehitur, praeeunt submisso poplite reges,
Et mendicantum series longissima fratrum;
Cereaque in manibus gestant funalia caeci,
Cimmeriis nati in tenebris, vitamque trahentes.   60
Templa dein multis subeunt lucentia taedis
(Vesper erat sacer iste Petro) fremitusque canentum
Saepe tholos implet vacuos, et inane locorum.
Qualiter exululat Bromius, Bromiique caterva,
Orgia cantantes in Echionio Aracyntho,   65
Dum tremit attonitus vitreis Asopus in undis,
Et procul ipse cava responsat rupe Cithaeron.
    His igitur tandem solenni more peractis,
Nox senis amplexus Erebi taciturna reliquit,
Praecipitesque impellit equos stimulante flagello,   70
Captum oculis Typhlonta, Melanchaetemque ferocem,
Atque Acherontaeo prognatam patre Siopen
Torpidam, et hirsutis horrentem Phrica capillis.
    Interea regum domitor, Phlegetontius haeres,
Ingreditur thalamos (neque enim secretus adulter   75
Producit steriles molli sine pellice noctes);
At vix compositos somnus claudebat ocellos,
Cum niger umbrarum dominus, rectorque silentum,
Praedatorque hominum falsa sub imagine tectus
Astitit. Assumptis micuerunt tempora canis;   80
Barba sinus promissa tegit; cineracea longo
Syrmate verrit humum vestis; pendetque cucullus
Vertice de raso; et ne quicquam desit ad artes,
Cannabeo lumbos constrinxit fune salaces,
Tarda fenestratis figens vestigia calceis.   85
Talis, uti fama est, vasta Franciscus eremo
Tetra vagabatur solus per lustra ferarum,
Silvestrique tulit genti pia verba salutis
Impius, atque lupos domuit, Libycosque leones.
    Subdolus at tali Serpens velatus amictu   90
Solvit in has fallax ora execrantia voces;
    "Dormis, nate? Etiamne tuos sopor opprimit artus?

60. Cf. *Cimmerian* in *L'All*, 10.
62. St. Peter's feast is on June 28.
65–67. *Aracynthus* and *Cithaeron* are mountains
in Boeotia, where Ovid says (*Met.* III, 702) that
the rites of Bacchus were first celebrated. *Echion*
was one of the heroes who sprang from the dragon's teeth sown by Cadmus, whose son Pentheus
was slain by the followers of *Bacchus* in Euripides'
Bacchanals.
69. Cf. *eldest Night* in *PL* II, 894. Milton
imagined her as Virgil describes her, "black Night,
riding through the sky in her chariot" (*Aen.* V,
721). "Her twyfold Teme," of which Spenser
said (*F.Q.* I, v, 28) two were "blacke as pitch,
And two were brown." had no traditional names.
Milton's epithets are translations of the names
that he invented for them.
80–85. Thomas Warton compared Satan's disguise here with that in which he approaches Christ
in *PR* I, 314–20, and compared the passage with
analogous ones in Buchanan's *Franciscannus* and
Somnium. Francis is St. Francis of Assisi.
92. The line parodies Mercury's greeting of
Aeneas (*Aen.* IV, 564).

city, carrying with him his gods
made of bread. Kings went before
him with bended knee and the vast
procession of mendicant brothers.
They carried wax candles in their
hands—those men who are born and
lead their lives in Cimmerian darkness.[60] Then they enter the temples
that gleam with many a torch (it
was the eve sacred to St. Peter[62])
and the cry of the chanters often fills
the hollow domes and void spaces.
Such are the shrieks of Bacchus and
the followers of Bacchus when they
chant their orgies on Theban Aracynthus,[65] while astonished Asopus
shudders under his glassy waves and
in the distance Cithaeron[67] itself
gives back the sound from its hollow cliff.
    When at last these rites had been
performed with solemn pomp,
Night[69] silently left the embraces
of old Erebus to drive her swift
coursers with the goading whip;
blind Typhlos, cross-grained Melan-
chaetes, torpid Siope born of an infernal sire, and Phrix with his
shaggy, rough hair.
    Meanwhile the tamer of kings,
and heir of hell enters his chamber
(for the secret adulterer passes no
barren nights without a gentle concubine); but sleep was hardly quiet-
ing and closing his eyes when the
dark lord of shadows, the ruler of
the speechless dead, who preys upon
men, stood beside him, covered with
a false shape. His temples shone
under the disguise of grey hairs;[80]
a long beard covered his breast;
his ash-colored robe trailed with a
long train on the ground; a hood
dangled from his shaven crown;
and—to make his wiles complete—
his lustful loins are bound with a
hempen rope and his slow feet are
thrust into laced sandals.[85] In such
a guise, the story goes, Francis used
to wander in the expanse of the
desert, alone among the hideous
haunts of wild beasts; and, though
he was impious himself, he bore the
pious word of salvation to the wood-
land folk, and tamed the wolves and
the Libyan lions.
    Dressed in such a garb the De-
ceiver, the Serpent, lyingly shaped
his execrable lips to these words:
    "Do you sleep, my son?[92] Does
slumber weigh down your limbs?

Immemor O fidei, pecorumque oblite tuorum!
Dum cathedram, venerande, tuam diademaque triplex
Ridet Hyperboreo gens barbara nata sub axe,   95
Dumque pharetrati spernunt tua iura Britanni.
Surge, age, surge piger, Latius quem Caesar adorat,
Cui reserata patet convexi ianua caeli,
Turgentes animos, et fastus frange procaces,
Sacrilegique sciant, tua quid maledictio possit,   100
Et quid Apostolicae possit custodia clavis;
Et memor Hesperiae disiectam ulciscere classem,
Mersaque Iberorum lato vexilla profundo,
Sanctorumque cruci tot corpora fixa probrosae,
Thermodoontea nuper regnante puella.   105
At tu si tenero mavis torpescere lecto
Crescentesque negas hosti contundere vires,
Tyrrhenum implebit numeroso milite Pontum,
Signaque Aventino ponet fulgentia colle:
Relliquias veterum franget, flammisque cremabit,   110
Sacraque calcabit pedibus tua colla profanis,
Cuius gaudebant soleis dare basia reges.
Nec tamen hunc bellis et aperto Marte lacesses;
Irritus ille labor; tu callidus utere fraude,
Quaelibet haereticis disponere retia fas est;   115
Iamque ad consilium extremis rex magnus ab oris
Patricios vocat, et procerum de stirpe creatos,
Grandaevosque patres trabea, canisque verendos;
Hos tu membratim poteris conspergere in auras,
Atque dare in cineres, nitrati pulveris igne   120
Aedibus iniecto, qua convenere, sub imis.
Protinus ipse igitur quoscunque habet Anglia fidos
Propositi, factique mone: quisquamne tuorum
Audebit summi non iussa facessere Papae?
Perculsosque metu subito, casumque stupentes,   125
Invadat vel Gallus atrox, vel saevus Iberus.
Saecula sic illic tandem Mariana redibunt,
Tuque in belligeros iterum dominaberis Anglos.

O, heedless of the faith and neglectful of your flocks! While a savage nation born under the northern sky mocks your throne and your triple crown and while the archer-English[96] insult your rights, O venerable one. Up and act![97] Up from this indolence, you whom the Roman Emperor venerates and for whom the locked gate of the vault of heaven lies open; break their insolent spirit and upstart pride, and let the sacrilegious know the force of your malediction and the power of your control of the Apostolic key. Remember to avenge the scattered Spanish Armada, the Iberian standards swallowed by the sea's depths, and the bodies of so many saints shamefully hung on gallows[104] during the recent reign of the Amazonian virgin. If you prefer to lie languid in your soft bed and refuse to crush the growing strength of the foe, he will soon fill the Tyrrhene Sea with a numerous host and plant his glittering standards on the Aventine hill.[109] He will destroy and burn with fire what remains of the ancients and with profane feet he will trample upon your neck—you, whose shoes kings were once glad to kiss. Yet you must not attack him with open war. To do so would be lost labor. Rather be shrewd enough to use treachery. It is lawful to spread nets of any kind for heretics. Just now the great king is summoning the patricians from distant places to council, summoning men sprung from distinguished stock and the venerable old fathers, gowned and grey-haired. You have it in your power to scatter their dismembered bodies through the air, to burn them to cinders, by exploding nitrous powder under the halls where they will assemble. Immediately therefore give notice to whatever faithful there are in England of the deed proposed. Will any of your people dare neglect the commands of the sovereign Pope? Then let the fierce Gaul or savage Spaniard attack them instantly, while they are panic-stricken and stupefied by the catastrophe. So at last the Marian[127] epoch will return to that land and you will rule again over the warlike English. And—so that you may

96. Since the victories of Crecy and Poitiers English archery had been famous.

97. A parody of the divine call to Aeneas: "Up and act" (*Aen.* III, 169).

104. In Elizabeth's main persecution of 1577–83 Philip Hughes lists 183 victims "claimed by the Catholic Church as martyrs for religion." *The Reformation in England* (London, 1954), Vol. III, 349.

109. The *Aventine* is the southernmost of Rome's seven hills.

127. There is a pun in *Mariana,* for the word occurs in Florus' *Epitome* (III, xii, 11 and IV, ii, 2), where it refers to Marius' brutal troops in the civil war with Sulla.

Et nequid timeas, divos divasque secundas
Accipe, quotque tuis celebrantur numina fastis."   130
    Dixit et adscitos ponens malefidus amictus
Fugit ad infandam, regnum illaetabile, Lethen.
    Iam rosea Eoas pandens Tithonia portas
Vestit inauratas redeunti lumine terras;
Maestaque adhuc nigri deplorans funera nati   135
Irrigat ambrosiis montana cacumina guttis;
Cum somnos pepulit stellatae ianitor aulae,
Nocturnos visus et somnia grata revolvens.
    Est locus aeterna septus caligine noctis
Vasta ruinosi quondam fundamina tecti,   140
Nunc torvi spelunca Phoni, Prodotaeque bilinguis
Effera quos uno peperit Discordia partu.
Hic inter caementa iacent praeruptaque saxa,
Ossa inhumata virum, et traiecta cadavera ferro;
Hic Dolus intortis semper sedet ater ocellis,   145
Iurgiaque, et stimulis armata Calumnia fauces,
Et Furor, atque viae moriendi mille videntur,
Et Timor, exanguisque locum circumvolat Horror,
Perpetuoque leves per muta silentia Manes
Exululant, tellus et sanguine conscia stagnat.   150
Ipsi etiam pavidi latitant penetralibus antri
Et Phonos, et Prodotes, nulloque sequente per antrum,
Antrum horrens, scopulosum, atrum feralibus umbris,
Diffugiunt sontes, et retro lumina vortunt;
Hos pugiles Romae per saecula longa fideles   155
Evocat antistes Babylonius, atque ita fatur:
    "Finibus occiduis circumfusum incolit aequor
Gens exosa mihi, prudens natura negavit
Indignam penitus nostro coniungere mundo.
Illuc, sic iubeo, celeri contendite gressu,   160
Tartareoque leves difflentur pulvere in auras
Et rex et pariter satrapae, scelerata propago,
Et quotquot fidei caluere cupidine verae
Consilii socios adhibete, operisque ministros."

132. Again one of the infernal rivers, *Lethe*,
represents hell. Cf. ll. 7 and 74 above, and *PL*
II, 583.
133. The transition recalls Homer's: "Now
Dawn rose from her bed, from the side of lordly
Tithonus, to bear light to the immortals and to
mortal men" (*Od.* V, 1–3). Her son is Memnon,
who was slain by Achilles (*Od.* XI, 521). Cf.
PL V, 1–2, and VI, 12–15, and *IlPen*, 18.
141. Cf. the personified children of Chaos in
Milton's *Pro!* I, and *PL* II, 959–67.
149. Ovid's "mute silences of night" (*Met.* VII,
184) left its trace again on *IlPen*, 55.
150. So Ovid speaks (*Met.* II, 438) of the "conscious forest" which knew of Jove's love-thefts.
Cf. the "conscious Night" of *PL* VI, 521.
156. Cf. the reference to Rome as Babylon in
Sonn XVIII.

fear nothing—accept the fact that
the gods and goddesses are favorable, as many deities as are honored
in your feast days."
    So the deceiver spoke and, doffing
his disguise, fled to Lethe,[132] the
unspeakable and joyless kingdom.
    Now rosy Dawn,[133] throwing
open the eastern gates, dresses the
gilded world with returning light,
and grieving for the sad death of
her swarthy son she sprinkles the
mountain-tops with ambrosial tears.
Then the keeper of the starry vault
banished slumber, turning over his
nocturnal visions and delightful
dreams.
    There is a place wrapped eternally
in the darkness of night, once the
vast foundation of a structure now
ruinous which has become the den
of brutal Murder and double-
tongued Treason, twins whom savage Discord bore. Here amid
rubble and shattered rock lie the
unburied bones of men and corpses
pierced by steel; here forever sits
dark Guile with eyes distorted, and
Contentions and Calumny with her
fang-armed jaws, and Fury and a
thousand ways of dying and Fear
are seen.[141] Pale Horror wings
about the place and unsubstantial
ghosts shriek perpetually through
the mute silences.[149] The conscious
earth[150] rots with blood. Murder
and Treason themselves shudder in
the inmost depths of the cavern and,
though no one pursues them,
through the cave—a horrid cave
with outcropping rocks and dark
with deathly shadows—the guilty
pair flee away with many a backward glance. The Babylonian high
priest[156] summons these defenders
of Rome which have been faithful
to her for centuries, and thus he
speaks:
    "A race that is odious to me lives
on the western verge of the world
amid the surrounding ocean. Prudent Nature has cut that unworthy
people off from our continent.
Thither, for so I command, you are
to go with all speed; you are to
bring all who are fired with love for
the true faith into the plot and make
them the tools of its execution. Let
the king and his nobles together,
the whole wicked race, be blown
into thin air by Tartarean powder."

Finierat, rigidi cupide paruere gemelli.   165
   Interea longo flectens curvamine caelos
Despicit aetherea dominus qui fulgurat arce,
Vanaque perversae ridet conamina turbae,
Atque sui causam populi volet ipse tueri.
   Esse ferunt spatium, qua distat ab Aside terra   170
Fertilis Europe, et spectat Mareotidas undas;
Hic turris posita est Titanidos ardua Famae
Aerea, lata, sonans, rutilis vicinior astris
Quam superimpositum vel Athos vel Pelion Ossae.
Mille fores aditusque patent, totidemque fenestrae,
Amplaque per tenues translucent atria muros;   176
Excitat hic varios plebs agglomerata susurros;
Qualiter instrepitant circum mulctralia bombis
Agmina muscarum, aut texto per ovilia iunco,
Dum Canis aestivum caeli petit ardua culmen.   180
Ipsa quidem summa sedet ultrix matris in arce,
Auribus innumeris cinctum caput eminet olli,
Queis sonitum exiguum trahit, atque levissima captat
Murmura, ab extremis patuli confinibus orbis.
Nec tot, Aristoride servator inique iuvencae   185
Isidos, immite volvebas lumina vultu,
Lumina non unquam tacito nutantia somno,
Lumina subiectas late spectantia terras.
Istis illa solet loca luce carentia saepe
Perlustrare, etiam radianti impervia soli.   190
Millenisque loquax auditaque visaque linguis
Cuilibet effundit temeraria, veraque mendax
Nunc minuit, modo confictis sermonibus auget.
   Sed tamen a nostro meruisti carmine laudes
Fama, bonum quo non aliud veracius ullum,   195
Nobis digna cani, nec te memorasse pigebit
Carmine tam longo. Servati scilicet Angli
Officiis, vaga diva, tuis tibi reddimus aequa.
Te Deus aeternos motu qui temperat ignes,

168. Cf. the repeated echoes in *PL* II, 731; V,
737; and VIII, 78, of Psalm ii, 4: "He that sitteth
in the heavens shall laugh."
   172. Fame, said Virgil (*Aen.* IV, 178–80), was
the youngest of the Titans. Her description here
is drawn partly from Virgil but mainly from Ovid
(*Met.* XII, 39–63).
   174. So Homer describes the Titans as throwing
the Thessalian mountains Pelion and Ossa one on
top of the other in their assault on the gods of
Olympus (*Od.* XI, 312–15).
   185. Ovid calls the hundred-eyed Argus the son
of *Arestor* (*Met.* I, 624) when he describes Argus'
commission by Juno to watch Io after Jove had
transformed her into a heifer in a vain attempt
to hide their secret love. Conti (VIII, xviii) identifies Io with the Egyptian goddess Isis.

He ended and the cruel twins were
eager in their obedience.
   Meanwhile the Lord, who turns
the heavens in their wide revolution
and hurls the lightning from his
skyey citadel, laughs[168] at the vain
undertakings of the degenerate
mob and is willing to take upon
himself the defence of his people's
cause.
   There is a place situated, men say,
with its aspect toward Lake Mare-
otis, in the gulf between fertile
Europe and Asia. Here is the lofty
tower of Titanean Fame[172]—a
brazen structure, broad, noise-
haunted, and closer to the glowing
stars than Athos or Pelion, piled
upon Ossa.[174] A thousand doors
and entrances and no fewer windows are open wide and the courts
within shine through the unsubstantial walls. Here a crush of
people start various whispers. So
swarms of flies buzz and hum
about the milk-pails or in the
wattled sheepfolds, when in summer
the Dog Star climbs aloft to the
summit of the skies. Fame herself,
the avenger of her mother, sits atop
of her citadel and raises her head,
which is girt about with innumerable ears, so as to catch the faintest
sound and seize the lightest murmur from the uttermost ends of the
wide world. You, O Argus, spite-
ful guardian of the heifer, Io, had
not so many eyes in your cruel
face, eyes never winking in silent
sleep, eyes gazing abroad over the
lands below.[185] With them it is
Fame's habit to pry into dark places
where the sun's rays never penetrate.
With a thousand tongues the blab
recklessly pours out what she has
heard and seen to any auditor, and
lyingly she pares down the truth or
enlarges it with fabrications.
   Nevertheless, O Fame, you deserved the praise of our song, for
one good deed than which there
was never any more genuine. You
deserve that I should sing about
you and I shall never regret this
commemoration of you at such
length in my song. Because we
English plainly owe our safety to
your good offices, O vagrant goddess, we render you a just return.
God, who controls the eternal fires
in their motion, hurled his thunder-

Fulmine praemisso alloquitur, terraque tremente: 200
"Fama, siles? an te latet impia Papistarum
Coniurata cohors in meque meosque Britannos,
Et nova sceptrigero caedes meditata Iacobo?"
Nec plura, illa statim sensit mandata Tonantis,
Et satis ante fugax stridentes induit alas,   205
Induit et variis exilia corpora plumis;
Dextra tubam gestat Temesaeo ex aere sonoram.
Nec mora, iam pennis cedentes remigat auras,
Atque parum est cursu celeres praevertere nubes;
Iam ventos, iam solis equos, post terga reliquit.   210
Et primo Angliacas solito de more per urbes
Ambiguas voces, incertaque murmura spargit,
Mox arguta dolos, et detestabile vulgat
Proditionis opus, nec non facta horrida dictu,
Authoresque addit sceleris, nec garrula caecis   215
Insidiis loca structa silet. Stupuere relatis,
Et pariter iuvenes, pariter tremuere puellae,
Effoetique senes pariter, tantaeque ruinae
Sensus ad aetatem subito penetraverat omnem.
Attamen interea populi miserescit ab alto   220
Aethereus Pater, et crudelibus obstitit ausis
Papicolum. Capti poenas raptantur ad acres;
At pia thura Deo et grati solvuntur honores;
Compita laeta focis genialibus omnia fumant;   224
Turba choros iuvenilis agit: Quintoque Novembris
Nulla dies toto occurrit celebratior anno. (1626)

bolt and, while the earth still trembled, he said to you:
"Fame, are you silent? Or have you no inkling of the impious band of Papists conspiring against me and my English, nor of the novel kind of murder designed against scepter-bearing James?"

He said no more, but she instantly responded to the Thunderer's command and—swift though she was before—she assumes strident wings and covers her slender body with parti-colored feathers, and in her right hand she takes a trumpet of Temesan brass.[207] She makes no delay, but on her wings goes oaring through the yielding air. Not content to outstrip the swift clouds in her flight, she passes now the winds and now the horses of the sun. First, in her usual way, she scatters ambiguous rumors and uncertain whispers through the English cities. Presently, grown clear-voiced, she publishes the plots and the detestable work of treason—not merely the deeds which are abominable to utter, but also the authors of the crime; nor does her garrulity make a secret of the places prepared for the treacherous attempt. Men are aghast at what is reported. Youths and maidens and weak old men alike tremble, and folk of all ages are reached by the sense of so great ruin impending. But meanwhile the heavenly Father takes pity on his people from on high and thwarts the outrages which the Papists have dared. They are seized and dragged to painful punishments. Pious incense and grateful honors are paid to God. The joyous streets are all lurid with genial bonfires. In throngs youth goes dancing. Throughout the whole year there shall be no day more celebrated than the fifth of November.

207. Homer mentions the Calabrian city of *Tamesa* as famous for its copper mines (*Od.* I, 184).

ELEGIA TERTIA (ELEGY III)

Anno Aetatis 17 (At Age 17)

In Obitum Praesulis Wintoniensis (On the Death of the Bishop of Winchester)

The poem reflects the sincere public grief at the death of Lancelot Andrewes on September 25, 1626. He had been Master of Pembroke College, Cambridge (1589–1605) and later successively Bishop of Chichester, Ely, and Winchester.

Moestus eram, et tacitus nullo comitante, sedebam.
  Haerebantque animo tristia plura meo,
Protinus en subiit funestae cladis imago
  Fecit in Angliaco quam Libitina solo;   4
Dum procerum ingressa est splendentes marmore turres
  Dira sepulchrali mors metuenda face;
Pulsavitque auro gravidos et iaspide muros,
  Nec metuit satrapum sternere falce greges.
Tunc memini clarique ducis, fratrisque verendi
  Intempestivis ossa cremata rogis;   10
Et memini Heroum quos vidit ad aethera raptos,
  Flevit et amissos Belgia tota duces.
At te praecipue luxi, dignissime praesul,
  Wintoniaeque olim gloria magna tuae;
Delicui fletu, et tristi sic ore querebar: 15
"Mors fera, Tartareo diva secunda Iovi,
Nonne satis quod silva tuas persentiat iras,
  Et quod in herbosos ius tibi detur agros,
Quodque afflata tuo marcescant lilia tabo,
  Et crocus, et pulchrae Cypridi sacra rosa,   20
Nec sinis ut semper fluvio contermina quercus
  Miretur lapsus praetereuntis aquae?
Et tibi succumbit liquido quae plurima caelo
  Evehitur pennis, quamlibet augur, avis,
Et quae mille nigris errant animalia sylvis,   25
  Et quod alunt mutum Proteos antra pecus.
Invida, tanta tibi cum sit concessa potestas,
  Quid iuvat humana tingere caede manus?
Nobileque in pectus certas acuisse sagittas,
  Semideamque animam sede fugasse sua?"   30
Talia dum lacrymans alto sub pectore volvo,
  Roscidus occiduis Hesperus exit aquis,
Et Tartessiaco submerserat aequore currum
  Phoebus, ab eöo littore mensus iter.
Nec mora, membra cavo posui refovenda cubili,   35

I was grief-stricken, and without any companion I was sitting in silence. Many sorrows were besetting my spirit, when, lo, suddenly there arose a vision of the baneful destruction which Libitina[4] wrought upon English soil when dire death —terrible with his sepulchral torch —entered the bright, marble palaces of the patricians, attacked the walls that are weighted with jasper and gold, and presumed to mow down hosts of princes with his scythe. Then I remembered that glorious duke and his brother,[9] whose bones were burned on untimely pyres; and I remembered the Heroes whom Belgia saw rapt into the skies—the lost leaders whom the whole nation mourned. But my greatest grief was for you, most worthy Bishop, and in time past the noble ornament of your Winchester. I melted in tears and complained in this sad language:

"O fell Death, goddess second to Tartarean Jove,[16] are you not satisfied that the forest suffers your fury, that power is given to you over the herb-bearing fields and that the lilies, the crocuses and the rose, that is sacred to the beautiful Cypris,[20] wither when touched by your poisonous breath? And you do not permit the oak on the riverbank to watch the flow of the ebbing water forever. And all the countless birds that are borne through the liquid sky on their pinions—in spite of their gift of prophecy— succumb to you, and so do the myriad wild creatures that stray in the dark forests and the dumb herd[26] which the caves of Proteus nourish. Envious one, when such vast power has been granted you, what pleasure is there in staining your hands with human slaughter, in sharpening your unerring darts against a noble breast, and driving a spirit that is half-divine from its habitation?"

While I was weeping and entertaining such meditations in my heart, the dewy Hesperus[32] rose out of the western sea and Phoebus— after measuring his course from the Orient—had sunk his chariot in the Spanish ocean. Not delaying, I sought rest for my limbs in the depths of my bed, and night and

---

4. *Libitina,* an ancient Italian goddess of corpses, symbolizes the plague that raged severely in 1625–6 in London.

9. The lost leaders may be Count Ernest of Mansfield, who was killed on November 29, 1626, and Duke Christian of Brunswick-Wolfenbüttel, who died on June 6, 1626. Both were strong supporters of James I's son-in-law, the Elector Palatine, Frederick V, in the Thirty Years War.

16. *Tartarean Jove* is the ruler of Hades, the brother of Jove, Pluto. Cf. *nether Jove* in *Comus,* 20.

20. Cf. Venus' title of the Cyprian in *El VII,* 48.

26. Cf. *Proteus' herd,* the seals, in *Damon,* 99.

32. The evening star *Hesperus* is dew-bearing as it is in Ovid's *Fasti* II, 314—as Milton makes the moon in *Damon,* 140.

Condiderant oculos noxque soporque meos;
Cum mihi visus eram lato spatiarier agro,
  Heu! nequit ingenium visa referre meum.
Illic punicea radiabant omnia luce,
  Ut matutino cum iuga sole rubent.   40
Ac veluti cum pandit opes Thaumantia proles,
  Vestitu nituit multicolore solum;
Non dea tam variis ornavit floribus hortos
  Alcinoi Zephyro Chloris amata levi.
Flumina vernantes lambunt argentea campos,   45
  Ditior Hesperio flavet arena Tago.
Serpit odoriferas per opes levis aura Favoni,
  Aura sub innumeris humida nata rosis.
Talis in extremis terrae Gangetidis oris
  Luciferi regis fingitur esse domus.   50
Ipse racemiferis dum densas vitibus umbras
  Et pellucentes miror ubique locos,
Ecce mihi subito praesul Wintonius astat,
  Sidereum nitido fulsit in ore iubar;
Vestis ad auratos defluxit candida talos,   55
  Infula divinum cinxerat alba caput.
Dumque senex tali incedit venerandus amictu,
  Intremuit laeto florea terra sono.
Agmina gemmatis plaudunt caelestia pennis,
  Pura triumphali personat aethra tuba.   60
Quisque novum amplexu comitem cantuque salutat,
  Hosque aliquis placido misit ab ore sonos:
"Nate, veni, et patrii felix cape gaudia regni;
  Semper ab hinc duro, nate, labore vaca."
Dixit, et aligerae tetigerunt nablia turmae; 65
  At mihi cum tenebris aurea pulsa quies,
Flebam turbatos Cephaleia pellice somnos.
  Talia contingant somnia saepe mihi.   (1626)

41. The child of *Thaumas* is Iris, goddess of
the rainbow.
44. *Chloris* the goddess of flowers, Ovid says
(*Fasti* V, 195–398), was wooed by the West Wind
Zephyr. Cf. the comparison of Paradise with Alcinous' gardens in *PL* V, 340–1 and IX, 441.
46. The *Tagus*, which flows into the Atlantic
at Lisbon, as Ovid testified (*Met.* II, 251), was
famous for its golden sand.
47. *Favonius* is the Latin equivalent for *Zephyr*,
which Homer describes (*Od.* IV, 567) as blowing
in the Elysian Fields. Cf. *PL* IV, 329 and *Sonn*
XX, 6.
50. *Lucifer* is the sun as Ovid describes him
in his palace (*Met.* II, 1–18), which he locates
east of India (*Met.* I, 778–9).
59. The line recalls the applause of the happy
spirits in Virgil's Elysium (*Aen.* VI, 644), which
mingle at once with the blessing on "the dead
which die in the Lord" (Rev. xiv, 13) and the
"voice of the harpers harping with their harps"
(Rev. xiv, 2) which St. John heard in heaven.
68. The final line boldly adapts Ovid's prayer

sleep had fast closed my eyes, when
I seemed to be walking in a broad
field—but, alas! my faculties cannot
report what I saw. There all things
were radiant with rosy light, like
mountain-crests flushing in the
morning sunshine. The earth was
brilliant in a garb of many colors,
as it is when the child of Thaumas[41] scatters her wealth abroad.
Chloris,[44] the goddess beloved by
delicate Zephyr, did not deck the
gardens of Alcinous with such various flowers. Silver rivers washed
the green fields and their sands
gleamed with greater wealth than
Hesperian Tagus.[46] Through the
perfumed opulence stole the light
breath of Favonius[47]—the dewy
breath that is born beneath myriad
roses. Such a place, on the most
distant shores of the land of the
Ganges, do men imagine the home
of the monarch, Lucifer,[50] to be.
While I was looking with admiration at the shining landscape all
around and at the shady retreats
under the clustering vines, lo, suddenly Winchester's bishop stood before me and a starry light shone in
his glorious face. A robe of shining
white fell flowing down to his
golden sandals and a white fillet en-
circled his divine head. And while
the reverend old man, arrayed in
this way, walked forward, the
flowery earth was vibrant with
joyous sound. The heavenly host
applauded[59] with their jewelled
wings and the clear air of heaven
rang with the triumphal trumpet.
Everyone saluted his new companion with an embrace and a song,
and one of them uttered these words
from his serene lips:
  "Come, my son, and joyously
enter into the delights of your
father's kingdom; and rest here
from your labors forever."
  He spoke, and the winged hosts
touched their harps. But my
golden rest was banished with the
night and I wept for the slumber
that was disturbed by the Dawn.
May dreams like these often befall
me![68]

(*Amores* I, v, 26) for the return of a golden day
spent with his Corinna.

IN OBITUM PRAESULIS ELIENSIS (ON THE DEATH OF THE BISHOP OF ELY)

Anno Aetatis 17 (At Age 17)

Nicholas Felton, Bishop of Ely at his death on October 6, 1626, was a Cambridge alumnus and a former Master of Pembroke College.

Adhuc madentes rore squalebant genae,
  Et sicca nondum lumina
Adhuc liquentis imbre turgebant salis,
  Quem nuper effudi pius,
Dum moesta caro iusta persolvi rogo   5
  Wintoniensis praesulis;
Cum centilinguis Fama (proh! semper mali
  Cladisque vera nuntia)
Spargit per urbes divitis Britanniae,
  Populosque Neptuno satos,   10
Cessisse morti, et ferreis sororibus,
  Te, generis humani decus,
Qui rex sacrorum illa fuisti in insula
  Quae nomen Anguillae tenet.
Tunc inquietum pectus ira protinus   15
  Ebulliebat fervida,
Tumulis potentem saepe devovens deam:
  Nec vota Naso in Ibida
Concepit alto diriora pectore,
  Graiusque vates parcius   20
Turpem Lycambis execratus est dolum,
  Sponsamque Neobolen suam.
At ecce! diras ipse dum fundo graves,
  Et imprecor neci necem,
Audisse tales videor attonitus sonos   25
  Leni, sub aura, flamine:
"Caecos furores pone, pone vitream
  Bilemque et irritas minas.
Quid temere violas non nocenda numina,
  Subitoque ad iras percita?   30
Non est, ut arbitraris elusus miser,
  Mors atra Noctis filia,
Erebove patre creta, sive Erinnye,
  Vastove nata sub Chao:
Ast illa, caelo missa stellato, Dei   35
  Messes ubique colligit;
Animasque mole carnea reconditas
  In lucem et auras evocat,
Ut cum fugaces excitant Horae diem,

My cheeks were still drenched and stained with tears and my eyes, not yet dry, were still swollen with the rain of salt water which but now my reverent affection poured out as I paid my debt of sorrow to the bier of Winchester's beloved bishop, when hundred-tongued Fame—alas! always the true messenger of evil and disaster—spreads through the cities of affluent Britain and the people who are descended from Neptune[10] the news that you —the ornament of mankind, who were the prince of the saints in the island called Ely[13]—had yielded to death and the implacable sisters.[11] Suddenly then my disquieted breast surged with hot anger and frequent imprecations upon the goddess who is powerful in the grave. Ovid, in the depths of his heart, conceived no worse curses against Ibis,[18] and the Greek poet was more restrained in his abuse of the shameful deceit of Lycambes and Neobule,[22] his betrothed. But behold, while I am pouring out these grievous curses and calling down death upon death[24]—astonished—I seem to hear these sounds in the gently moving air:

"Leave your blind anger, leave your madness and furious curses. Why do you offer rash violence to deities which cannot be harmed and are swift to anger? Contrary to your notion, O deluded wretch, Death is not the dark daughter of Night, nor of Erebus nor of Erynis;[33] nor was she born in the gulf of Chaos. But she is sent from the starry sky to reap God's harvest everywhere. As the flying Hours,[39] the daughters of Justice

10. Cf. *QNov*, 28–30.
11. The *sisters* are the Fates: Clotho, Lachesis, and Atropos.
13. Literally, *Ely* means "Eel-island."
18. Ovid's *Ibis* (*The Crane*) satirizes an enemy.
22. Archilochus of Paros is traditionally said to have written his satires against *Lycambes*, the father of his fiancée *Neobule*, for refusing to permit their marriage.

24. The play on *death* recalls Hosea xiii, 14: "O death, I will be thy plagues; O grave, I will be thy destruction." The Vulgate reads: *ero mors tua, o mors.*
33. Cf. *Night* in *QNov*, 69, and *Chaos* in *PL* II, 891–910.
39. Cf. the *Hours* in *Sonn* I, 4 and *Comus,* 986.

Themidos Iovisque filiae;
Et sempiterni ducit ad vultus patris;
  At iusta raptat impios
Sub regna furvi luctuosa Tartari,
  Sedesque subterraneas.
Hanc ut vocantem laetus audivi, cito
  Foedum reliqui carcerem,
Volatilesque faustus inter milites
  Ad astra sublimis feror,
Vates ut olim raptus ad caelum senex,
  Auriga currus ignei.
Non me Boötis terruere lucidi
  Sarraca tarda frigore, aut
Formidolosi Scorpionis brachia,
  Non ensis, Orion, tuus.
Praetervolavi fulgidi solis globum,
  Longeque sub pedibus deam
Vidi triformem, dum coercebat suos
  Fraenis dracones aureis.
Erraticorum siderum per ordines,
  Per lacteas vehor plagas,
Velocitatem saepe miratus novam,
  Donec nitentes ad fores
Ventum est Olympi, et regiam Crystallinam, et
  Stratum smaragdis Atrium.
Sed hic tacebo, nam quis effari queat
  Oriundus humano patre
Amoenitates illius loci? Mihi
  Sat est in aeternum frui."   (1627)

40 and Jove, arouse the day, so she summons into the light and air the spirits which are buried under the weight of flesh, and she leads them into the presence of the eternal Father; but because she is just she 45 sweeps the wicked away to the realms of grief in dark Tartarus, to the infernal abodes. I was glad when I heard her calling and eagerly I left my sordid prison. Among 50 the winged warriors I was carried aloft, clear to the stars, like the venerable prophet of old, charioteer of a fiery chariot, who was caught up to heaven.[49] I was not terrified either by the wain of bright 55 Boötes,[51] slow-moving with the cold, nor by the claws of the frightful Scorpion, nor by your sword, O Orion. I flew beyond the globe of the glittering sun and far below 60 my feet I saw the triform goddess[57] controlling her dragons with reins of gold. Through the ranks of the planets and the Milky Way I was borne, wondering often at my strange speed, until I reached the 65 shining portals of Olympus, the palace of crystal and the beryl-paved courts. But here I fall silent, for who that is begotten of a mortal father can tell the delights of that place? For me it is enough to enjoy them forever."

49. Cf. Elijah's translation in *PR* II, 16–17.
51. *Boötes,* the "ox-driver," (the constellation of the bright star Arcturus) drives his traditionally "lagging team" (Ovid, *Met.* II, 176) around the north pole.
57. The *triform goddess* is Ovid's "triple deity" (*Met.* VII, 94) Luna, the moon, whose names of Hecate, Diana, and Proserpina are discussed with

many quotations from the poets by Conti (III, xvii). Davis P. Harding explains (*Ovid*, p. 50) how her team of horses came to be the dragons that draw her in "the silent sliding of the night" in Sandys' translation of Ovid.

ELEGIA QUARTA (ELEGY IV)

Anno Aetatis 18 (At Age 18)

AD THOMAM IUNIUM, PRAECEPTOREM SUUM, APUD MERCATORES ANGLICOS HAMBURGAE AGENTES PASTORIS MUNERE FUNGENTEM (TO THOMAS YOUNG, HIS TUTOR, PERFORMING THE DUTIES OF A PASTOR AMONG THE ENGLISH MERCHANTS RESIDENT IN HAMBURG)

Thomas Young (1588–1665) was a Scot who came to London early enough to be Milton's tutor at St. Paul's School between 1618 and 1620. By 1620 Young was in Hamburg, but in 1628 he was established in the church in Stowmarket, Suffolk, which he held until his death. In 1641 he was one of the five antiepiscopal pamphleteers the successive initials of whose names composed the signature to the tract that Milton defended in his *Animadversions upon the Remonstrant's Defence against Smectymnuus.* D. L. Clark discusses Milton's friendship with Young in *John Milton at St. Paul's School* (New York, 1948). The extensive reflection of Ovid's *Amores* and *Tristia* in this elegy is studied by D. P. Harding in

Milton and the Renaissance Ovid (Urbana, 1946) and by Mary C. Brill in her Cornell thesis, "Milton and Ovid" (1935, unpublished).

Curre per immensum subito, mea littera, pontum;
I, pete Teutonicos laeve per aequor agros;
Segnes rumpe moras, et nil, precor, obstet eunti,
Et festinantis nil remoretur iter.
Ipse ego Sicanio fraenantem carcere ventos   5
Aeolon, et virides sollicitabo Deos,
Caeruleamque suis comitatam Dorida Nymphis,
Ut tibi dent placidam per sua regna viam.
At tu, si poteris, celeres tibi sume iugales,
Vecta quibus Colchis fugit ab ore viri;   10
Aut queis Triptolemus Scythicas devenit in oras,
Gratus Eleusina missus ab urbe puer.
Atque, ubi Germanas flavere videbis arenas,
Ditis ad Hamburgae moenia flecte gradum,
Dicitur occiso quae ducere nomen ab Hama,   15
Cimbrica quem fertur clava dedisse neci.
Vivit ibi antiquae clarus pietatis honore
Praesul Christicolas pascere doctus oves;
Ille quidem est animae plusquam pars altera nostrae,
Dimidio vitae vivere cogor ego.   20
Hei mihi, quot pelagi, quot montes interiecti,
Me faciunt alia parte carere mei!
Carior ille mihi quam tu, doctissime Graium,
Cliniadi, pronepos qui Telamonis erat;
Quamque Stagirites generoso magnus alumno,   25
Quem peperit Lybico Chaonis alma Iovi.
Qualis Amyntorides, qualis Philyrëius Heros
Myrmidonum regi, talis et ille mihi.

Swiftly, my letter, dart across the boundless ocean; go, and over the smooth sea seek Teutonic lands. Shake off slothful delays and let nothing, I implore, stand in the way of your dispatch or interfere with the speed of your journey. I myself will offer prayers to the glaucous deities and to Aeolus, who bridles the winds in his Sicanian cave,[5] and to cerulian Doris, escorted by her nymphs,[7] to give you a quiet journey through their kingdoms. Obtain for yourself, if you can, the swift team by which the Colchian[10] was borne away in her flight from the face of her husband, or that by which the boy, Triptolemus,[11] reached the bounds of Scythia, when he was sent, a welcome messenger, from the Eleusinian city. But when you see the sands of Germany shining yellow, turn your steps toward the walls of opulent Hamburg, which is said to derive its name from Hama, who, they say, was slain by a Danish club.[15] There a pastor lives, who is illustrious for his honor of the primitive faith and well instructed how to feed the sheep that love Christ. Truly, that man is more than the other half of my soul[20] and without him I am compelled to live a life which is but the half of itself. Alas for me—how many seas and mountains lying between us make me miss that other half of myself! Dearer is that man to me than you were, O wisest of the Greeks, to Cliniades,[24] who traced his ancestry back to Telamon—dearer than was the great Stagirite[25] to his magnanimous pupil, whom the bountiful daughter of Chaonia bore to Libyan Jove.[26] What the son of Amyntor[27] and what Philyra's heroic son were to the Myrmidons' king, such is this man to me. Under his guidance I first visited the

5. The line closely parallels Ovid's picture of the god *Aeolus* bridling the winds (*Met.* XIV, 224), and the *glaucous deities* are Ovid's *virides . . . Deos* (*Tristia* I, ii, 59).

7. The nymphs are the daughters of *Doris:*
All goodly damsels, deckt with long greene haire,
Whom of their sire *Nereides* men call,
All which the Ocean's daughter to him bare
That gray eyde *Doris:* all which fifty are.
            (*F.Q.* IV, xi, 48, 2–5)

10. The *Colchian* is Medea, whose flight in a dragon-drawn chariot after her murder of her children in the palace of her husband Jason, was familiar to Milton in Euripides' *Medea* and Ovid's tragic retelling of the tale (*Heroides* VI, 129–38).

11. Ovid (*Met.* V, 643–50) tells how Ceres sent *Triptolemus* in her chariot from *Eleusis* in Attica to sow the world with wheat as far as *Scythia.* Later Ovid wished for Triptolemus' chariot to carry him back from Thrace to Rome (*Tristia* III, viii, 1–4).

15. Tradition names *Hamburg* after *Hama,* a Saxon champion who is supposed, said Warton, to have been killed on its site by the Dane, Starchater.

20. Wishing Virgil a prosperous voyage, Horace (*Odes* I, iii, 8) called him *animae dimidium meae*—"the half of my soul."

24. *Cliniades* is Alcibiades, who, in Plato's *Alcibiades* (120d) boasts of his descent from Eurysaces, the grandson of *Telamon.*

25. The *Stagirite* is Aristotle, who was the tutor and life-long friend of Alexander the Great.

26. *Chaonia* is Epirus, where Alexander's mother Olympias was born. For his divine father see *Pl* IX, 508, n.

27. Phoenix, son of *Amyntor,* was one of Achilles' tutors; the other was Chiron, son of *Philyra.* Cf. *Manso.* 60.

Primus ego Aonios illo praeeunte recessus
    Lustrabam, et bifidi sacra vireta iugi,   30
Pieriosque hausi latices, Clioque favente,
    Castalio sparsi laeta ter ora mero.
Flammeus at signum ter viderat arietis Aethon,
    Induxitque auro lanea terga novo,
Bisque novo terram sparsisti, Chlori, senilem   35
    Gramine, bisque tuas abstulit Auster opes;
Necdum eius licuit mihi lumina pascere vultu,
    Aut linguae dulces aure bibisse sonos.
Vade igitur, cursuque Eurum praeverte sonorum;
    Quam sit opus monitis res docet, ipsa vides.   40
Invenies dulci cum coniuge forte sedentem,
    Mulcentem gremio pignora cara suo;
Forsitan aut veterum praelarga volumina patrum
    Versantem, aut veri biblia sacra Dei,
Caelestive animas saturantem rore tenellas,   45
    Grande salutiferae religionis opus.
Utque solet, multam sit dicere cura salutem,
    Dicere quam decuit, si modo adesset, herum.
Haec quoque paulum oculos in humum defixa mo-
    destos,
    Verba verecundo sis memor ore loqui: 50
"Haec tibi, si teneris vacat inter praelia Musis,
    Mittit ab Angliaco littore fida manus.
Accipe sinceram, quamvis sit sera, salutem;
    Fiat et hoc ipso gratior illa tibi.
Sera quidem, sed vera fuit, quam casta recepit   55
    Icaris a lento Penelopeia viro.
Ast ego quid volui manifestum tollere crimen,
    Ipse quod ex omni parte levare nequit?
Arguitur tardus merito, noxamque fatetur,
    Et pudet officium deseruisse suum.   60
Tu modo da veniam fasso, veniamque roganti;
    Crimina diminui, quae patuere, solent.

30. The twin peaks of Mt. Parnassus, the haunt
of the Muses, were in *Aonia;* the *Castalian spring*
at its foot was sacred to them. Cf. *PL I,* 15.
    31. Hesiod (*Theog.,* 52–79) represents the Muses
(of whom *Clio,* the Muse of History, stands first)
as being born to Zeus by Mnemosyne (Memory) on
Mt. Pierus in Macedonia.
    33. Ovid (*Met.* II, 153) makes *Aethon* one of
the sun's four horses. Since the sun has entered
the zodiacal sign of the Ram three times since
Young's departure, he must have left England in
the winter of 1624-5.
    35. Cf. *Chloris* in *El III,* 44.
    36. *Auster:* the south wind.
    39. *Eurus:* the east wind. Cf. *PL* X, 705.
    43. So Ovid speeds a letter to his Perilla on its
way to find her with her dear mother or among her
books (*Tristia* III, vii, 1-4).
    51. In 1626 the Protestant allies under Christian
IV of Denmark were defeated by the Imperialists
under Tilly at Lütter-am-Bandenberge in Brunswick,
and Hamburg was in danger.
    56. So in the *Odyssey* (XXIII, 1-208) *Penelope*

Aonian retreats and the sacred
lawns of the twin-peaked mountain.[30] I drank the Pierian[31] waters
and by the favor of Clio I thrice
wet my blessed lips with Castalian
wine. Three times has fiery Aethon[33] looked upon the sign of the
Ram and gilded his woolly back
afresh with gold; and twice,
Chloris,[35] have you sown the old
earth with new herbage, and twice,
Auster,[36] you have swept her riches
away; and not yet have my eyes
been allowed to feast on his face
or my ears to drink in the sweet
sounds of his tongue.

Be off, then, and speed on your
way faster than shrieking Eurus.[39]
How necessary is my urging the
situation itself suggests and you
yourself perceive. Perhaps you will
find him sitting with his sweet
wife, fondling the dear pledges of
their love on his lap, or perhaps
turning over the mighty volumes of
the old Fathers[43] or the Holy Scriptures of the true God, or watering
tender souls with the dew of heaven
—which is the grand affair of healing religion. As the custom is, be
careful to give him generous greeting and to speak as it would become your master to do, if only he
were present; and remember to fix
your eyes for a little while modestly
upon the ground and to speak these
words with reverent lips:

"These verses—if there is leisure
for the delicate Muses in the midst
of the fighting[51]—a devoted hand
sends to you from English shores.
Even though it be late, accept this
sincere greeting and may it be the
more welcome to you on that very
account. Late, indeed, but loyal
was the greeting which the daughter
of Icarius, Penelope,[56] received from
her long-delaying husband. But
why should I wish to deny a manifest fault, which the delinquent
himself is utterly unable to mitigate? He is justly accused of being
dilatory and confesses the crime and
is ashamed of his neglect of his
duty. Only grant me forgiveness,
because I confess my fault and ask
for absolution; for offences acknowledged are half wiped out. No wild

is slowly convinced that Ulysses has indeed returned
to her from Troy.

Non ferus in pavidos rictus diducit hiantes,
  Vulnifico pronos nec rapit ungue leo.
Saepe sarissiferi crudelia pectora Thracis   65
  Supplicis ad moestas deliceuere preces;
Extensaeque manus avertunt fulminis ictus,
  Placat et iratos hostia parva Deos.
Iamque diu scripsisse tibi fuit impetus illi,
  Neve moras ultra ducere passus Amor;   70
Nam vaga Fama refert—heu nuntia vera malorum!
  In tibi finitimis bella tumere locis,
Teque tuamque urbem truculento milite cingi,
  Et iam Saxonicos arma parasse duces.
Te circum late campos populatur Enyo,   75
  Et sata carne virum iam cruor arva rigat.
Germanisque suum concessit Thracia Martem;
  Illuc Odrysios Mars pater egit equos.
Perpetuoque comans iam deflorescit oliva,
  Fugit et aerisonam Diva perosa tubam,   80
Fugit, io! terris, et iam non ultima virgo
  Creditur ad superas iusta volasse domos.
Te tamen interea belli circumsonat horror,
  Vivis et ignoto solus inopsque solo;
Et, tibi quam patrii non exhibuere penates,   85
  Sede peregrina quaeris egenus opem.
Patria, dura parens, et saxis saevior albis
  Spumea quae pulsat littoris unda tui,
Siccine te decet innocuos exponere foetus,
  Siccine in externam ferrea cogis humum,   90
Et sinis ut terris quaerant alimenta remotis
  Quos tibi prospiciens miserat ipse Deus,
Et qui laeta ferunt de caelo nuntia, quique
  Quae via post cineres ducat ad astra, docent?
Digna quidem Stygiis quae vivas clausa tenebris, 95
  Aeternaque animae digna perire fame!
Haud aliter vates terrae Thesbitidis olim
  Pressit inassueto devia tesqua pede,
Desertasque Arabum salebras, dum regis Achabi

64. The experience of the sleeping Oliver with
the lion in *As You Like It* IV, iii, 119–20, proves
that it is
    The royal disposition of that beast
    To prey on nothing that doth seem as dead.
74. The Elector of Saxony, John George I, was
lukewarm in opposition to the Imperialists, but six
of the sons of Duke John of Saxe-Weimar were their
active opponents. Hamburg wished to be neutral.
75. In Homer (*Il.* V, 333) *Enyo* is goddess of
war and "devastator of cities."
77. Homer (*Od.* VIII, 361) makes Thrace, which
was anciently called *Odrysia,* the home of Ares or
Mars.
81. Cf. Milton's question in *Prol* IV of "that
Ovidian story; whether . . . Astraea was the last
of the goddesses to leave the earth." Cf. *Nat,* 141–
4.
  97. Cf. Elijah in *PR* I, 353, and II, 19 and 277.

beast opens its maw upon victims
that tremble nor does the lion do
violence with his rending paw to
those who are prostrate.[64] The
cruel hearts of Thracian spearmen
have often melted at a suppliant's
sad appeals. Outstretched hands
avert the stroke of the thunder-bolt
and even a small sacrifice pacifies
the gods when they are angry.

  "He has long felt the impulse
to write to you and now Love
would not endure any further delay,
for vagrant Rumor—alas, the vera-
cious reporter of disasters—says that
in regions bordering upon you wars
are ready to burst out, that you and
your city are beset by insolent troops,
and that the Saxon leaders[74] have
already prepared their munitions of
war. All around you Enyo[75] is
laying waste the fields and blood
is watering the ground which has
been sown with human flesh.
Thrace has given up Mars to the
Germans[77] and father Mars has
driven his Odrysian horses into
their territories. The ever-flourish-
ing olive-tree is withering and the
goddess who hates the brazen blare
of the trumpet has fled—look, fled
from the earth[81]—and it is believed
that the just virgin was not the
last to fly for refuge to the heavenly
mansions. Nevertheless, you live
resourceless and alone on that
strange soil, where the horror of
war echoes all around you; and on
alien soil you seek in your poverty
for the livelihood which your native
country withholds. O Fatherland,
hard parent, more cruel than the
white cliffs that are battered by the
frothing waves of your coast, does
it become you thus to expose your
innocent offspring; do you drive
them away thus with iron implac-
ability to foreign soil and do you
allow men to seek their subsistence
in strange lands whom God himself
in his providence has sent to you—
men who bring glad tidings from
heaven and teach the way which
leads beyond the grave to the stars?
Indeed, you deserve to live shut up
in Stygian darkness and to perish
by undying hunger of the soul. In
just this way the Tishbite[97] prophet
long ago walked the byways of the
desert with unaccustomed steps and
trod the rough sands of Arabia

Effugit atque tuas, Sidoni dira, manus.   100
Talis et horrisono laceratus membra flagello,
  Paulus ab Aemathia pellitur urbe Cilix;
Piscosaeque ipsum Gergessae civis Iesum
  Finibus ingratus iussit abire suis.
At tu sume animos, nec spes cadat anxia curis,   105
  Nec tua concutiat decolor ossa metus.
Sis etenim quamvis fulgentibus obsitus armis,
  Intententque tibi millia tela necem,
At nullis vel inerme latus violabitur armis,
  Deque tuo cuspis nulla cruore bibet.   110
Namque eris ipse Dei radiante sub aegide tutus;
  Ille tibi custos, et pugil ille tibi;
Ille Sionaeae qui tot sub moenibus arcis
  Assyrios fudit nocte silente viros;
Inque fugam vertit quos in Samaritidas oras   115
  Misit ab antiquis prisca Damascus agris;
Terruit et densas pavido cum rege cohortes,
  Aere dum vacuo buccina clara sonat,
Cornea pulvereum dum verberat ungula campum,
  Currus arenosam dum quatit actus humum,   120
Auditurque hinnitus equorum ad bella ruentum,
  Et strepitus ferri, murmuraque alta virum.
Et tu (quod superest miseris) sperare memento,
  Et tua magnanimo pectore vince mala.
Nec dubites quandoque frui melioribus annis,   125
  Atque iterum patrios posse videre lares."   (1627)

when he fled from the hands of King Ahab and from your hands also, O vindictive Sidonian woman.[100] In this way Cilician Paul was driven out of the Emathian city with his flesh bleeding from the hissing scourge;[102] and the ungrateful citizenry of fishy Gergessa[103] bade Jesus himself to depart from their coasts.

"But take heart and do not let your anxious hope yield to your embarrassments nor pale fear strike palsy to your bones. Even though you are beset by flashing arms and though a thousand shafts threaten you with death, your unarmed breast shall not be violated by any weapon and no spear shall drink of your blood.[109] For you shall be secure under the radiant aegis of God.[111] He will be your guardian and he will be your champion—He, who wiped out so many Assyrian soldiers[112] in a silent night under the walls of Zion, who turned to flight the men whom ancient Damascus sent from her venerable fields into the coasts of Samaria,[115] and smote their massed cohorts and their trembling king with terror when the loud trumpet sounded in the empty air, and the horny hoof beat the dusty plain,[119] and the hard-driven chariot shook the sandy earth, and the neigh of horses plunging into battle was heard, and the din of steel weapons and the deep roar of the voices of men.

"And for your part—because hope is the right of the unhappy—remember to hope, and let your magnanimous heart triumph over your misfortunes. Do not doubt that some time you will enjoy better years and be able once more to see your native land."

100. The *Sidonian woman* is Jezebel, "the daughter of Ethbaal, king of the Zidonians" (I Kings xvi, 31), Ahab's queen, who threatened Elijah's life (II Kings xix, 2) and drove him into the desert.

102. When St. *Paul*, often called Saul of Tarsus (in *Cilicia*), visited Philippi in Macedonia (otherwise called *Emathia*), he was publicly scourged (Acts xvi, 22–3). Cf. *Sonn* VIII, 10, and *PR* III, 290.

103. When at *Gergessa* on the Sea of Galilee Jesus healed a man possessed of a legion of devils and allowed them to destroy a herd of swine, the Gergesenes "besought him that he would depart from their coasts" (Matt. viii, 34).

109. Cf. Ps. xci, 4–5: "His truth shall be my shield and buckler. Thou shalt not be afraid for the terror by night, nor for the arrow that flieth by day."

111. Both Jove and Minerva had shields of superlative powers, one of which was that of routing any attacker (*Il.* V, 738).

112. When Sennacherib attacked Jerusalem, "the angel of the Lord . . . smote in the camp of the Assyrians an hundred and fourscore and five thousand" (II Kings xix, 35).

115. When Ben Hadad of Damascus attacked Samaria "the Lord . . . made the host of the Syrians

to hear a noise of horses, even the noise of a great host. . . . Wherefore they arose and fled in the twilight" (II Kings vii, 6).

119. The line imitates Virgil's onomatopoetic verse:

Quadrupedante putrem sonitu quatit ungula campum.

(*Aen.* VIII, 596)

AT A VACATION EXERCISE IN THE COLLEGE,
PART LATIN, PART ENGLISH

The Latin *speeches ended, the* English *thus began*

Anno Aetatis 19

The first of the Latin speeches was an oration which has been lost. The second was Milton's *Prolusion* VI, and the third part of the entertainment was the present poem. Milton took advantage of an invitation to be the "Father" of a group of students in this traditional gay ceremony at the beginning of the long vacation in July, 1628. After avenging himself on the men who were responsible for his nickname of "the Lady" in the *Prolusion,* he now goes on to play with the scholastic logic that was a part of education at Cambridge, and his thesis is to be: "That occasional indulgence in sportive activities is not inconsistent with academic studies." He appears as the Aristotelian principle of *Ens,* or Absolute Being, and his ten "sons" impersonate the Aristotelian categories of the accidents of Substance: Quantity, Quality, Relation, Place, Time, Posture, Possession or Having, Action, and Passion.

Hail native Language, that by sinews weak
Didst move my first endeavoring tongue to speak,
And mad'st imperfect words with childish trips,
Half unpronounc't, slide through my infant lips,
Driving dumb silence from the portal door,   5
Where he had mutely sat two years before:
Here I salute thee and thy pardon ask,
That now I use thee in my latter task:
Small loss it is that thence can come unto thee,
I know my tongue but little Grace can do thee: 10
Thou needst not be ambitious to be first,
Believe me, I have thither packt the worst:
And, if it happen as I did forecast,
The daintiest dishes shall be serv'd up last.
I pray thee then deny me not thy aid   15
For this same small neglect that I have made:
But haste thee straight to do me once a Pleasure,
And from thy wardrope bring thy chiefest treasure;
Not those new fangled toys, and trimming slight
Which takes our late fantastics with delight,   20
But cull those richest Robes, and gay'st attire
Which deepest Spirits, and choicest Wits desire:
I have some naked thoughts that rove about
And loudly knock to have their passage out;
And weary of their place do only stay   25
Till thou hast deck't them in thy best array;
That so they may without suspect or fears
Fly swiftly to this fair Assembly's ears;
Yet I had rather, if I were to choose,
Thy service in some graver subject use,   30
Such as may make thee search thy coffers round,

18. Cf. *wardrope* (a frequent 17th century form) for "wardrobe" in *Lyc,* 47.

20. Milton is not thinking of the metaphysical poets but of the "metaphysical fume" of some of his fellow students whom he accused in *An Apology for Smectymnuus* (C.E. III, 347) of not knowing how "to write or speak in a pure style," or to "distinguish . . . the various kinds of style in Latin barbarous, and oft not without solecisms."

22. *Spirits* is usually treated as a monosyllable in Milton's verse. Cf. *Pl.* I, 139 and 146.

Before thou clothe my fancy in fit sound:
Such where the deep transported mind may soar
Above the wheeling poles, and at Heav'n's door
Look in, and see each blissful Deity   35
How he before the thunderous throne doth lie,
Listening to what unshorn *Apollo* sings
To th' touch of golden wires, while *Hebe* brings
Immortal Nectar to her Kingly Sire:
Then passing through the Spheres of watchful fire,   40
And misty Regions of wide air next under,
And hills of Snow and lofts of piled Thunder,
May tell at length how green-ey'd *Neptune* raves,
In Heav'n's defiance mustering all his waves;
Then sing of secret things that came to pass   45
When Beldam Nature in her cradle was;
And last of Kings and Queens and *Heroes* old,
Such as the wise *Demodocus* once told
In solemn Songs at King *Alcinous'* Feast,
While sad *Ulysses'* soul and all the rest   50
Are held with his melodious harmory
In willing chains and sweet captivity.
But fie, my wand'ring Muse, how thou dost stray!
Expectance calls thee now another way,
Thou know'st it must be now thy only bent   55
To keep in compass of thy Predicament:
Then quick about thy purpos'd business come,
That to the next I may resign my Room.

Then Ens *is represented as Father of the Predicaments his ten Sons, whereof the Eldest stood for* Substance *with his Canons, which* Ens *thus speaking, explains.*

Good luck befriend thee Son; for at thy birth
The Fairy Ladies danc't upon the hearth;   60
Thy drowsy Nurse hath sworn she did them spy
Come tripping to the Room where thou didst lie;
And sweetly singing round about thy Bed
Strew all their blessings on thy sleeping Head.
She heard them give thee this, that thou should'st still   65
From eyes of mortals walk invisible;
Yet there is something that doth force my fear,
For once it was my dismal hap to hear
A *Sibyl* old, bow-bent with crooked age,
That far events full wisely could presage,   70
And in time's long and dark Prospective Glass

33. Imitating a Latin usage, Milton used *deep* to mean "high."

37. *Apollo's* classical epithet *unshorn* goes back to Homer (*Il.* XX, 39).

38. *Hebe,* goddess of youth, serves the gods with the *nectar* that confers immortality. Cf. *L'All,* 29 and *Lyc,* 175.

40. The planets are *watchful fires* because Plato said that, "by the design of God . . . the planets came into existence for determining and watching over the numbers of time" (*Tim.,* 38c).

48. Milton thought of Homer's story of Ulysses' tears as he listened to the bard *Demodocus* at the table of *Alcinous* (*Od.* VIII, 521).

56. In scholastic logic the *predicaments* corresponded to Aristotle's categories.

66. Because scholastic logic described Substance as unknowable except through its "accidents," Milton pretends that a fairy godmother gave it the gift of invisibility in its cradle.

69. *Sibyl* here is simply an old woman like Othello's

> sibyl, that had number'd in the world
> The sun to course two hundred compasses,
> (*Othello* III, iv, 69–70)

71. *Prospective Glass:* a magic glass for looking into the *future.*

Foresaw what future days should bring to pass!
  "Your son," said she, "(nor can you it prevent)
Shall subject be to many an Accident.
O'er all his Brethren he shall Reign as King,   75
Yet every one shall make him underling,
And those that cannot live from him asunder
Ungratefully shall strive to keep him under;
In worth and excellence he shall outgo them,
Yet being above them, he shall be below them;   80
From others he shall stand in need of nothing,
Yet on his Brothers shall depend for Clothing.
To find a Foe it shall not be his hap,
And peace shall lull him in her flow'ry lap;
Yet shall he live in strife, and at his door   85
Devouring war shall never cease to roar:
Yea it shall be his natural property
To harbour those that are at enmity."
What power, what force, what mighty spell, if not
Your learned hands, can loose this Gordian knot?   90

The next Quantity *and* Quality, *spake in Prose, then* Relation *was call'd by his Name.*

Rivers, arise; whether thou be the Son
Of utmost *Tweed,* or *Ouse,* or gulfy *Dun,*
Or *Trent,* who like some earth-born Giant spreads
His thirty Arms along the indented Meads,
Or sullen *Mole* that runneth underneath,   95
Or *Severn* swift, guilty of maiden's death,
Or Rocky *Avon,* or of Sedgy *Lee,*
Or Coaly *Tyne,* or ancient hallowed *Dee,*
Or *Humber* loud that keeps the *Scythian's* Name,
Or *Medway* smooth, or Royal Tow'red *Thame.*   100
        The rest was Prose.   (July, 1628)

74. There is a play on the literal meaning of *substance*—that which "stands beneath" or "underlies" other things.

88. Some of the predicaments, such as action and passion, are mutually exclusive.

90. The knot which the Phrygian king Gordius tied as a magical protection to his realm, could be loosened by no one until Alexander the Great cut it with his sword.

92. The passage looks back to Drayton's catalogues of English rivers in *Polyolbion* and to Spenser's marriage of the Thames and the Medway (*F.Q.* IV, xi, 24–39).

96. The maiden is Sabrina. Cf. *Comus*, 826.

98. The *Dee,* says Spenser (*F.Q.* IV, xi, 39), "Britons long ygone Did call divine." Changes in its course and flow were supposed to foretell the national future. Cf. *Lyc,* 55, n. and *El I,* 3.

NATURAM NON PATI SENIUM (THAT NATURE IS NOT SUBJECT TO OLD AGE)

This exercise may be the set of verses that Milton described in a letter to his former teacher Alexander Gill (July 2, 1628) as having been written for a candidate for the M.A. to read as a conclusion to his public defence of his thesis. Its background in the history of thought is traced by E. L. Tuveson in *Millennium and Utopia: A Study in the Background of the Idea of Progress* (Berkeley, 1949), pp. 22–74, and by Victor Harris in *All Coherence Gone* (Evanston, 1949), pp. 1–161. The subject and side were probably arbitrarily assigned and not of Milton's own choice. Because his arguments harmonize with those of George Hakewell in his great controversial *An Apologie or Declaration of the Power and Providence of God* (London, 1627), E. M. W. Tillyard seems right in regarding his cosmic "optimism" as mainly due to his faith in the current hope of the Puritans for the fulfilment of their religious and political hopes, perhaps by the fulfilment of prophecy in the beginning of Christ's reign on earth. His attitude toward the complex problems of physical, moral, and political decay is studied by Z. S. Fink in *The Classical Republicans* (Evanston, 1945), pp. 91–122, and by J. A. Bryant, Jr. in *SAMLA*, pp. 1–19.

Heu quam perpetuis erroribus acta fatiscit
Avia mens hominum, tenebrisque immersa profundis
Oedipodioniam volvit sub pectore noctem!
Quae vesana suis metiri facta deorum
Audet, et incisas leges adamante perenni   5
Assimilare suis, nulloque solubile saeclo
Consilium fati perituris alligat horis.
  Ergone marcescet sulcantibus obsita rugis
Naturae facies, et rerum publica mater
Omniparum contracta uterum sterilescet ab aevo?   10
Et se fassa senem male certis passibus ibit
Sidereum tremebunda caput? Num tetra vetustas
Annorumque aeterna fames, squalorque situsque,
Sidera vexabunt?   An et insatiabile Tempus
Esuriet Caelum, rapietque in viscera patrem?   15
Heu, potuitne suas imprudens Iupiter arces
Hoc contra munisse nefas, et Temporis isto
Exemisse malo, gyrosque dedisse perennes?
Ergo erit ut quandoque, sono dilapsa tremendo,
Convexi tabulata ruant, atque obvius ictu   20
Stridat uterque polus, superaque ut Olympius aula
Decidat, horribilisque retecta Gorgone Pallas;
Qualis in Aegaeam proles Iunonia Lemnon
Deturbata sacro cecidit de limine caeli.
Tu quoque, Phoebe, tui casus imitabere nati   25
Praecipiti curru, subitaque ferere ruina
Pronus, et extincta fumabit lampade Nereus
Et dabit attonito feralia sibila ponto.
Tunc etiam aerei divulsis sedibus Haemi
Dissultabit apex, imoque allisa barathro   30
Terrebunt Stygium deiecta Ceraunia Ditem,

Alas! how persistent are the errors by which the wandering mind of man is pursued and overwearied, and how profound is the darkness of the Oedipean night in his breast![3] His insane mind dare make its own acts the measure of those of the gods[4] and compare its own laws to those that are written upon eternal adamant; and it binds the eternally immutable plan of fate to the perishing hours.[7]

Shall the face of Nature, then, be overspread with wrinkles and shall the common mother[9] contract her all-generating womb and become sterile? Shall she confess herself old and move with uncertain steps, her starry head a-trembling? Shall the stars be vexed by foul old age and the undying hunger of the years, and by squalor and mold? Shall insatiable Time devour the heavens and gorge the vitals of his own father? Alas! could not Jupiter, the improvident, fortify his citadels against this outrage and make them immune from the harm of time? Could he not endue them with perpetual revolutions? Some day, then, it will come to pass that the vaulted floor of heaven, collapsing with a mighty uproar, will fall and both poles will rattle with the impact, while Olympian Jove drops down from his celestial hall, and with him Pallas Athene, spreading horror from her exposed Gorgon shield.[22] So the child of Juno[23] fell upon Aegean Lemnos, where he was tossed down from the sacred threshold of heaven. And you also, Phoebus Apollo,[25] shall share the fate of your son in your precipitate chariot and be swept down in sudden ruin; and at the quenching of your light Nereus[27] shall send up jets of steam and dreadful hisses from his astonished waters. Then the rending of the foundations of lofty Haemus[29] shall shatter its summit and the Ceraunian Mountains,[31]

3. The hero's deliberate blinding of himself in Sophocles' *Oedipus the King* symbolizes wilful human blindness of soul.

4–7. The lines adapt Isa. lv, 8: "For my thoughts are not your thoughts, neither are your ways my ways, saith the Lord."

9. Hesiod describes Earth as the mother of Heaven, the mountains, Time, Hyperion, and many of the elder gods (*Theog.*, 117–52). Cf. *PL* V, 338.

22. Ovid (*Met.* IV, 773–803) describes the Gorgon Medusa, whose dreadful eyes and snaky locks turned all beholders to stone, but the story that Athene wore the Gorgon's head on her shield goes back to Homer (*Il.* V, 741).

23. The *child of Juno* is Hephaestus (in Latin Vulcan or Mulciber). Cf. *El VII*, 81 and *PL I*, 740.

25. Cf. the allusion to Apollo's son Phaeton in *El V*, 92.

27. *Nereus*, oldest of Ocean's children (*Theog.*, 233), stands for the sea.

29. *Haemus*: a steep mountain range in Thrace.

31. The *Ceraunian Mountains* are in what was

ancient Epirus. Cf. Hesiod's account (*Theog.*, 617–735) of the piling up of the mountains by the assailants of the gods on Mt. Olympus.

In superos quibus usus erat, fraternaque bella.
   At Pater omnipotens, fundatis fortius astris,
Consuluit rerum summae, certoque peregit
Pondere fatorum lances, atque ordine summo   35
Singula perpetuum iussit servare tenorem.
Volvitur hinc lapsu mundi rota prima diurno,
Raptat et ambitos socia vertigine caelos.
Tardior haud solito Saturnus, et acer ut olim
Fulmineum rutilat cristata casside Mavors.   40
Floridus aeternum Phoebus iuvenile coruscat,
Nec fovet effoetas loca per declivia terras
Devexo temone Deus; sed semper amica
Luce potens eadem currit per signa rotarum.
Surgit odoratis pariter formosus ab Indis   45
Aethereum pecus albenti qui cogit Olympo,
Mane vocans, et serus agens in pascua caeli,
Temporis et gemino dispertit regna colore.
Fulget, obitque vices alterno Delia cornu,
Caeruleumque ignem paribus complectitur ulnis.   50
Nec variant elementa fidem, solitoque fragore
Lurida perculsas iaculantur fulmina rupes.
Nec per inane furit leviori murmure Corus,
Stringit et armiferos aequali horrore Gelonos
Trux Aquilo, spiratque hiemem, nimbosque volu-
    tat.   55
Utque solet, Siculi diverberat ima Pelori
Rex maris, et rauca circumstrepit aequora concha
Oceani Tubicen, nec vasta mole minorem
Aegaeona ferunt dorso Balearica cete.
Sed neque, Terra, tibi saecli vigor ille vetusti   60
Priscus abest; servatque suum Narcissus odorem;
Et puer ille suum tenet et puer ille decorem,
Phoebe, tuusque, et Cypri tuus, nec ditior olim
Terra datum sceleri celavit montibus aurum   64
Conscia, vel sub aquis gemmas. Sic denique in aevum

which Stygian Dis once used against the gods in fratricidal conflicts, shall be cast down to terrify him in the lowest depth of the abyss.

But by founding the stars more strongly the omnipotent Father has taken thought for the universe. He has fixed the scales of fate with sure balance and commanded every individual thing in the cosmos to hold to its course forever. Therefore the Prime Wheel[37] of the universe turns in daily rotation and transmits its movement to its enclosed spheres. Saturn is no slower than his wont and Mars, as fierce as he was of old, darts lightning from his crested helmet. Phoebus shines with the ruddy beauty of eternal youth. He does not drive his team down descending slopes to warm exhausted lands, but, strong in his friendly light, he pursues his course forever through the same signs of the Zodiac. Equally beautiful, the planet[45] which drives in the heavenly flock through the sky at dawn and at evening drives them out into the pastures of heaven, rises out of the perfumed Indies and divides the kingdoms of time with its two-fold radiance. Delia[49] still shines and wanes with alternating horns and holds her heavenly effulgence in undiminished arms. The elements do not vary from their faith and with their accustomed uproar the lightning-bolts strike and shatter the rocks. Corus[53] goes raging with no gentler voice through the void and the ferocious Aquilo[55] torments the armed Scythians with undiminished chill as he breathes out winter and sweeps the clouds along. In his accustomed style the sea king smites the foundations of Sicilian Pelorus[56] and the trumpeter[58] of the ocean still blows his hoarse conch throughout the seas. The Balearic whales[59] bear upon their backs an Aegaeon of no less vast bulk. Nor has the pristine vigor of your earliest time forsaken you, O Earth. Narcissus[61] still preserves his fragrance. Your beloved youth, O Phoebus,[62] and yours, O Cypris,[63] still keep their beauty; nor did the earth in times past conceal beneath the mountains a greater wealth of the gold which her bad conscience knows is to be the root of evil, nor hide more gems beneath the seas.[65]

37. The *Prime Wheel* is that *high first-moving sphere* of *Infant*, 39.
45. Cf. Venus as the morning star, Lucifer, in *Nat*, 74.
49. Diana, goddess of the moon, is called *Delia* from her birthplace on the island of Delos.
53. *Corus*: the northwest wind.
55. *Aquilo*: northeast wind. Cf. map, p. 432.
56. Cf. *thund'ring Aetna* on the Sicilian promontory of *Pelorus* in *PL* I, 232–3. The *sea king* is Neptune.
58. Cf. the sea-god Triton blowing his conch in *Comus*, 18–23.
59. Hesiod's hundred-armed giant *Aegaeon* (*Theog.*, 147) is described by Ovid (*Met*. II, 9–10) as clasping the vast backs of whales in his arms.
61. The flower is personified in allusion to Ovid's story of its origin in the metamorphosis of the youth *Narcissus* (*Met*. III, 509–10).
62. Cf. the reference to Apollo's accidental slaying of Hyacinth in *Lyc*, 106, and the reference to Venus' love for Adonis in *Comus*, 999. From his blood Ovid says (*Met*. X, 735–9) Venus created the anemone.
63–65. Cf. *Comus, 732–6* and *PL* I, 686–9, n.

Ibit cunctarum series iustissima rerum,
Donec flamma orbem populabitur ultima, late
Circumplexa polos, et vasti culmina caeli;
Ingentique rogo flagrabit machina mundi.

(June, 1628)

Thus, in a word, the righteous sequence of all things shall go on perpetually, until the final fire shall destroy the world, enveloping the poles and summits of vast heaven, while the fabric of the universe consumes in a mighty funeral pyre.[67]

67. Milton thought of the prophecy of the coming of Christ in II Peter iii, 10, "the day of the Lord," when "the elements shall melt with fervent heat; the earth also and the works that are therein shall be burned up." Cf. *PL* XI, 900.

ON THE DEATH OF A FAIR INFANT DYING OF A COUGH

Anno Aetatis 17

The *flower* of line 1 seems to have been Anne, daughter of Milton's sister Anne, who married Edward Phillips on November 27, 1623. The child was born on January 12, 1625, and in *TLS* for December 17, 1938, p. 802, W. R. Parker shows that she was almost certainly the Anne Philips who was buried in the church of St. Martin-in-the-Fields, London, on January 22, 1628. J. M. French (*Life Records* I, 102), after reviewing the evidence, agrees with Parker that the poem was written in 1628. It was first published in the volume of 1673.

There has been much discussion of this poem for its "metaphysical" conceits, the first of which prompts J. W. Saunders to say (*ELH*, XXII. 274) that such imagery is no more characteristic of Donne than it is of the religious poetry of the Renaissance generally: "the religious poem of the Renaissance was essentially a love song." The stanza of this poem is that of the induction to *Nativity*, and the two poems both indulge in several conceits— facts which encourage the suspicion that they were written less than three years from each other. — *maybe 1-year apart?*

I

O fairest flower no sooner blown but blasted,
Soft silken Primrose fading timelessly,
Summer's chief honor if thou hadst outlasted
Bleak winter's force that made thy blossom dry;
For he being amorous on that lovely dye
   That did thy cheek envermeil, thought to kiss   *— Kiss that kills*   5
But kill'd alas, and then bewail'd his fatal bliss.

II

For since grim Aquilo his charioteer
By boist'rous rape th' Athenian damsel got,   *— asks Classical world for consolation*
He thought it toucht his Deity full near,
If likewise he some fair one wedded not,   10
Thereby to wipe away th' infamous blot,
   Of long-uncoupled bed, and childless eld,
Which 'mongst the wanton gods a foul reproach was held.

III

So mounting up in icy-pearled car,   15
Through middle empire of the freezing air
He wander'd long, till thee he spy'd from far,

8. *Aquilo*, the northeast wind, Ovid says (*Met.* VI, 682–713) wooed the *Athenian* princess Orithyia and snatched her away over the mountains in storm and darkness. Cf. *Salsillus*, 11.
16. Cf. *mid air* in *PL* II, 718, n.

There ended was his quest, there ceast his care.   *Classical world still cold.*
Down he descended from his Snow-soft chair,
   But all unwares with his cold-kind embrace   20
Unhous'd thy Virgin Soul from her fair biding place.

IV

Yet art thou not inglorious in thy fate;
For so *Apollo*, with unweeting hand   *using classical conceits.*
Whilom did slay his dearly-loved mate,
Young *Hyacinth* born on *Eurotas'* strand,   25
Young *Hyacinth* the pride of *Spartan* land,
   But then transform'd him to a purple flower;·   *some color, but no luck*
Alack, that so to change thee winter had no power.

recurrent image of Milton's

V

Yet can I not persuade me thou art dead
Or that thy corse corrupts in earth's dark womb,   30
Or that thy beauties lie in wormy bed,
Hid from the world in a low delved tomb;
Could Heav'n for pity thee so strictly doom?
   Oh no! for something in thy face did shine   *assurance of soul*
Above mortality that show'd thou wast divine.   35

VI

Resolve me then oh Soul most surely blest
(If so it be that thou these plaints dost hear)
Tell me bright Spirit where'er thou hoverest
Whether above that high first-moving Sphere
Or in the Elysian fields (if such there were).   40
   Oh say me true if thou wert mortal wight
And why from us so quickly thou didst take thy flight.

VII

Wert thou some Star which from the ruin'd roof   *classical world again.*
Of shak't Olympus by mischance didst fall;
Which careful *Jove* in nature's true behoof   45
Took up, and in fit place did reinstall?
Or did of late earth's Sons besiege the wall
   Of sheeny Heav'n, and thou some goddess fled
Amongst us here below to hide thy nectar'd head?

VIII

Or wert thou that just Maid who once before   50
Forsook the hated earth, O tell me sooth,
And cam'st again to visit us once more?
Or wert thou [Mercy] that sweet smiling Youth?
Or that crown'd Matron, sage white-robed Truth?

25. *Cf*. the allusion to the myth of *Hyacinth* in
Lyc, 106, n.
   31. Cf. Peter in Acts ii, 27, quoting Ps. xvi, 10:
"Thou wilt not leave my soul in hell; neither wilt
thou suffer thy Holy One to see corruption."
   39. The *first-moving Sphere* is the *primum mobile* or *first mov'd* of *PL* III, 483. Cf. the *nine enfolded Spheres* of *Arc*, 63, and the interest in the
abodes of souls in *IlPen*, 88–92.
   40. In *PR* II, 358–60, Milton speaks of another
pagan paradise, the Gardens of the Hesperides, as
fabulous, like the *Elysian fields* here.

45. *true behoof*: true interest. Cf. *PL* II, 982.
   47. *earth's Sons*: the earth-born giants who, Ovid
says (*Met*. I, 151–62), assailed heaven in the iron
age when the goddess of justice, *Astraea* (the *just
Maid* of l. 50), forsook mankind because of their
wickedness. Cf. *PL* IV, 998.
   53. *Mercy* is the conjecture of most editors to
complete this defective line. Cf. *Nat*, 141–4.
   54. Cf. *Truth* triumphing in *PL* III, 338; Truth
"as impossible to be soiled as a sunbeam" in *DDD*;
and Truth "a perfect shape most glorious to look on"
in *Areop*.

Or any other of that heav'nly brood   55
Let down in cloudy throne to do the world some good?

IX

Or wert thou of the golden-winged host, —
Who having clad thyself in human weed,
To earth from thy prefixed seat didst post,
And after short abode fly back with speed,   60
As if to show what creatures Heav'n doth breed,
   Thereby to set the hearts of men on fire
To scorn the sordid world, and unto Heav'n aspire?

X

But oh! why didst thou not stay here below
To bless us with thy heav'n-lov'd innocence,   65
To slake his wrath whom sin hath made our foe
To turn Swift-rushing black perdition hence,
Or drive away the slaughtering pestilence,
   To stand 'twixt us and our deserved smart?
But thou canst best perform that office where thou art.   70

XI

Then thou the mother of so sweet a child
Her false imagin'd loss cease to lament,
And wisely learn to curb thy sorrows wild;
Think what a present thou to God hast sent,
And render him with patience what he lent;   75
   This if thou do, he will an offspring give
That till the world's last end shall make thy name to live.   (1628)

68. Plague was claiming many victims in London.

76. The line echoes Isaiah's promise (lvi, 5) to the childless:

"Even unto them will I give . . . a name better than sons or daughters: I will give them an everlasting name that will not be cut off."

ELEGIA QUINTA (ELEGY V)

Anno Aetatis 20 (At Age 20)

IN ADVENTUM VERIS (ON THE COMING OF SPRING)

In *The Youth of Milton* (p. 116) J. H. Hanford has compared this poem with Buchanan's *Majae Calendae (The First of May)*, and Mario Praz (in *Seventeenth Century Studies in Honor of Sir Herbert Grierson*, p. 200) regards ll. 115–130 as "the best commentary on Poussin's 'Bacchanalian Dance' "! The spirit (if not the style) of *Elegies V* and *VII* reflects the treatment of their theme by works as diverse as Botticelli's "Springtime" and Ben Jonson's mask *The Vision of Delight*.

In se perpetuo Tempus revolubile gyro
   Iam revocat Zephyros, vere tepente, novos.
Induiturque brevem Tellus reparata iuventam,
   Iamque soluta gelu dulce virescit humus.
Fallor? an et nobis redeunt in carmina vires,   5
   Ingeniumque mihi munere veris adest?

3. *Tellus:* Earth, "the mother of fruits," as Ovid calls her in *Fasti* I, 671.

Now, in the growing warmth of the spring, Time—as it turns in its perpetual cycle—is calling back the Zephyrs afresh. Earth,[3] with her strength renewed, is donning her brief youth and the frost-free soil is putting forth its sweet greenness. Am I deluded? Or are my powers of song returning? And is my inspiration with me again by grace of

Munere veris adest, iterumque vigescit ab illo
(Quis putet?) atque aliquod iam sibi poscit opus.
Castalis ante oculos, bifidumque cacumen oberrat,
Et mihi Pyrenen somnia nocte ferunt.   10
Concitaque arcano fervent mihi pectora motu,
Et furor, et sonitus me sacer intus agit.
Delius ipse venit—video Peneide lauro
Implicatos crines—Delius ipse venit.
Iam mihi mens liquidi raptatur in ardua caeli,   15
Perque vagas nubes corpore liber eo.
Perque umbras, perque antra feror, penetralia vatum;
Et mihi fana patent interiora Deum.
Intuiturque animus toto quid agatur Olympo,
Nec fugiunt oculos Tartara caeca meos.   20
Quid tam grande sonat distento spiritus ore?
Quid parit haec rabies, quid sacer iste furor?
Ver mihi, quod dedit ingenium, cantabitur illo;
Profuerint isto reddita dona modo.
Iam, Philomela, tuos foliis adoperta novellis   25
Instituis modulos, dum silet omne nemus.
Urbe ego, tu silva, simul incipiamus utrique,
Et simul adventum veris uterque canat.
Veris, io! rediere vices; celebremus honores
Veris, et hoc subeat Musa perennis opus.   30
Iam sol, Aethiopas fugiens Tithoniaque arva,
Flectit ad Arctoas aurea lora plagas.
Est breve noctis iter, brevis est mora noctis opacae,
Horrida cum tenebris exulat illa suis.
Iamque Lycaonius plaustrum caeleste Boötes   35
Non longa sequitur fessus ut ante via,
Nunc etiam solitas circum Iovis atria toto
Excubias agitant sidera rara polo.
Nam dolus et caedes, et vis cum nocte recessit,
Neve Giganteum Dii timuere scelus.   40

9. Cf. *Castaly* in *El IV*, 30.
10. Near the fountain of *Pirene*, at Corinth, Pindar says (*Olympians* XIII, 64–8) that the poets' steed Pegasus was tamed by Bellerophon. Cf. *Rous*, 36.
13. *Apollo* wears a crown of *laurel*, the tree into which his beloved *Daphne* was transformed (*Met.* I, 548–52).
19. *Olympus:* the home of the gods, either on Mt. Olympus in Thessaly or in heaven.
25. Cf. the nightingale, *Philomel*, in *IlPen*, 56.
31. Cf. the *Ethiop Line* (for the equator) in *PL* IV, 282. The *fields of Tithonus:* the east. Cf. l. 49 below.
35. Cf. *Boötes* in *Ely*, 51. Because he is identified with the constellation of the Little Bear he is *Lycaonian* (northern).
40. Cf. the heaven-storming giants in *Infant*, 48.

the spring? By the spring's grace it is with me and—who would guess such a thing?—it is already clamoring for some employment. Castaly[9] and the riven peak float before my eyes and by night I am beside Pirene[10] in my dreams. My breast is aflame with the excitement of its mysterious impulse and I am driven on by the madness and the divine sounds within me. Apollo himself is approaching—I see the locks that are braided with Daphne's laurel[13] —Apollo himself comes. Already my mind is being borne up into the sheer liquid heights of the sky and, quit of the body, I go through the wandering clouds. I am carried through shadows and grottoes, the secret haunts of the poets; and the innermost shrines of the gods are open to me. My spirit surveys all that is done on Olympus[19] and the unseen infernal world is not impervious to my eyes. What mighty song is my soul pouring from its full throat? What is to be the offspring of this madness and this sacred ecstasy? The spring shall be the song of the inspiration that it has given to me, and so she may profit by her gift's return.

Already, Philomela,[25] you are beginning your trills in your covert among the budding leaves, while all the woods guard their silence. I in the city and you in the forest, let us both begin together and let us both together sing the advent of the spring. Ho, for the change of spring is returning. Let us celebrate the honors of the spring and let the Muse take up the task that she perennially assumes. Now the sun, in full flight from the Ethiopians[31] and the fields of Tithonus,[31] is turning his golden reins toward northern lands. Brief is the journey and brief the tarrying of gloomy night; the frightful night is an exile with its shadows. Lycaonian Boötes[35] no longer plods wearily— as of yore—over a long course after the heavenly wain; now even the stars are but few as they keep their accustomed watch about the courts of Jove throughout the whole sky, for fraud, murder and violence vanish with the night and the gods have no fear of outrage by the giants.[40] Some shepherd, perhaps,

Forte aliquis scopuli recubans in vertice pastor,
   Roscida cum primo sole rubescit humus,
"Hac," ait, "hac certe caruisti nocte puella,
   Phoebe, tua, celeres quae retineret equos."
Laeta suas repetit silvas, pharetramque resumit   45
   Cynthia, Luciferas ut videt alta rotas,
Et tenues ponens radios gaudere videtur
   Officium fieri tam breve fratris ope.
"Desere," Phoebus ait, "thalamos, Aurora, seniles;
   Quid iuvat effoeto procubuisse toro?   50
Te manet Aeolides viridi venator in herba:
   Surge; tuos ignes altus Hymettus habet."
Flava verecundo dea crimen in ore fatetur,
   Et matutinos ocius urget equos.
Exuit invisam Tellus rediviva senectam,   55
   Et cupit amplexus, Phoebe, subire tuos.
Et cupit, et digna est; quid enim formosius illa,
   Pandit ut omniferos luxuriosa sinus,
Atque Arabum spirat messes, et ab ore venusto
   Mitia cum Paphiis fundit amoma rosis?   60
Ecce, coronatur sacro frons ardua luco,
   Cingit ut Idaeam pinea turris Opim;
Et vario madidos intexit flore capillos,
   Floribus et visa est posse placere suis,
Floribus effusos ut erat redimita capillos,   65
   Taenario placuit diva Sicana Deo.
Aspice, Phoebe, tibi faciles hortantur amores,
   Mellitasque movent flamina verna preces.
Cinnamea Zephyrus leve plaudit odorifer ala,
   Blanditiasque tibi ferre videntur aves.   70
Nec sine dote tuos temeraria quaerit amores
   Terra, nec optatos poscit egena toros:
Alma salutiferum medicos tibi gramen in usus
   Praebet, et hinc titulos adiuvat ipsa tuos.
Quod si te pretium, si te fulgentia tangunt   75
   Munera (muneribus saepe coemptus Amor)
Illa tibi ostentat quascunque sub aequore vasto,

44. Cf. *Phoebus* as the sun-god in *El III*, 34.

46. *Cynthia*, the moon, is personified as the huntress Diana. Cf. *IlPen*, 59.

49. The bed shared by *Aurora* with Tithonus is *impotent* because he had the gift of immortality but not of youth. Cf. *QNov*, 133. Aurora's love for Cephalus figures in *El III*, 67. *Aeolides*: Cephalus, who, Ovid says (*Met*. VII, 700-15), was violently stolen from his wife Procris by Aurora.

60. *Paphian roses* suggest Venus' temple at Paphos in Cyprus.

62. Ovid makes the fertility goddess *Ops* the wife of Saturn (*Met*. IX, 498).

66. The *Taenarian* god is Pluto, who kidnapped Proserpina as she was gathering flowers in *Sicania* (Sicily). Cf. *PL* IV, 269.

74. In the background are invocations to Apollo the healer—like that in the first chorus of Aeschylus' *Agamemnon*.

as he lies on the top of a crag, says, while the dewy earth reddens under the first rays of the sun: "Last night, surely, O Phoebus,[44] last night you were unprovided with a fair bed-fellow who would delay your swift coursers."

Delighted, Cynthia[46] returns to her forests and resumes her quiver, when from on high she sees the wheels of Lucifer; and, laying aside her delicate rays, she seems to be happy that by her brother's help her own task is cut short.

"Leave the couch of an old man, O Aurora,"[49] is the cry of Phoebus; "what pleasure is there in the bed of impotence? On the green lawns the hunter, Aeolides, is waiting for you. Up! the heights of Hymettus are in possession of your fires."

With blushing face the bright goddess acknowledges her guilt and urges the horses of the dawn to greater speed. The reviving earth throws off her hated old age and craves thy embraces, O Phoebus. She craves them and she is worthy of them; for what is lovelier than she as she voluptuously bares her fertile breast and breathes the perfume of Arabian harvests and pours sweet spices and the scent of Paphian[60] roses from her lovely lips? Behold, her towering brow is girdled with a sacred grove as Idaean Ops[62] is turreted with pines. She twines her dewy hair with various bloom and with her flowers seems powerful to charm, as the Sicanian goddess with the flowers plaited in her flowing hair was charming to the Taenarian god.[66] Look Phoebus, facile loves are calling to you and the winds of spring carry honied appeals. Perfume-bearing Zephyr gently fans his cinnamon-scented wings and the birds seem to carry their blandishments to you. The earth is not so bold as to beg for your love without offering a dowry in return and she makes no pauper's appeal for the nuptials that she desires. In her bounty she provides you with health-giving herbs for healing and so she adds to your titles of honor.[74] If a bribe and if glittering gifts have power over you—and love is often bought with gifts—she spreads before you all the wealth in the

Et superiniectis montibus, abdit opes.
Ah, quoties cum tu clivoso fessus Olympo
    In vespertinas praecipitaris aquas,   80
"Cur te," inquit, "cursu languentem, Phoebe, diurno
    Hesperiis recipit caerula mater aquis?
Quid tibi cum Tethy? quid cum Tartesside lympha?
    Dia quid immundo perluis ora salo?
Frigora, Phoebe, mea melius captabis in umbra,   85
    Huc ades, ardentes imbue rore comas.
Mollior egelida veniet tibi somnus in herba,
    Huc ades, et gremio lumina pone meo.
Quaque iaces circum mulcebit lene susurrans
    Aura per humentes corpora fusa rosas.   90
Nec me, (crede mihi) terrent Semeleia fata,
    Nec Phaetonteo fumidus axis equo.
Cum tu, Phoebe, tuo sapientius uteris igni,
    Huc ades, et gremio lumina pone meo."
Sic Tellus lasciva suos suspirat amores;   95
    Matris in exemplum caetera turba ruunt.
Nunc etenim toto currit vagus orbe Cupido,
    Languentesque fovet solis ab igne faces.
Insonuere novis lethalia cornua nervis,
    Triste micant ferro tela corusca novo.   100
Iamque vel invictam tentat superasse Dianam,
    Quaeque sedet sacro Vesta pudica foco.
Ipsa senescentem reparat Venus annua formam,
    Atque iterum tepido creditur orta mari.   104
Marmoreas iuvenes clamant Hymenaee per urbes;
    Litus io Hymen, et cava saxa sonant.
Cultior ille venit, tunicaque decentior apta;
    Puniceum redolet vestis odora crocum.
Egrediturque frequens ad amoeni gaudia veris
    Virgineos auro cincta puella sinus.   110
Votum est cuique suum; votum est tamen omnibus
    unum,

83. Cf. *Tethys* in *Comus*, 870, n.
91. *Semele*, who bore Bacchus to Jove, was induced by Juno to ask him to come to her in his
divine glory, but "her mortal body could not bear
that celestial violence and she was consumed by her
marriage gift" (*Met.* III, 308–9).
92. Ovid tells the story (*Met.* II, 19–328) of
Apollo's unwilling consent that his son *Phaeton*
should drive the chariot of the sun for a day,
and of the wild drive that threatened heaven and
earth with destruction until Jove struck Phaeton
dead with a thunderbolt. Cf. *Patrem*, 38 and 97–
100.
101. The grant of eternal chastity by Zeus to
Artemis (*Diana*) is mentioned as early as Callimachus' *Hymn to Artemis*, 5.
102. For *Vesta* see *IlPen*, 23–24, n.
104. Venus' birth from the sea was the subject of
famous paintings by Apelles and Botticelli.
105. The lines echo the chorus in Catullus' epithalamium for Malius Torquatus (LXI). *Hymen*
was god of marriage. Cf. *PL* XI, 591 and *L'All*,
125–6.

vast ocean and under the mass of the mountains. Ah, how often, when, wearied from the steep of heaven, you would plunge into the western sea, she cries:

"Why, O Phoebus, should the blue mother receive you into the Hes-perian waves when you are fainting from your daily course? What have you to do with Tethys?[83] What have you to do with Tartessian streams? Why do you bathe your divine face in the unclean salt water? You will find coolness much better, Phoebus, in my shadow. Come hither and steep your glowing locks in dew. A gentler sleep will be yours in the cool grass. Come hither and lay your glories in my lap. Where you lie a gently murmuring breeze will soothe our bodies on their couch of humid roses. I have no fear, be-lieve me, of a fate like that of Semele,[91] nor of the axle that smoked when Phaeton was the driver of the horses.[92] When you shall have put your fire to wiser use, come hither and lay your glories in my lap."

Thus the wanton earth breathes out her passion, and her thronging children follow hard after her ex-ample. Now wandering Cupid runs at large throughout the whole world and kindles his dying torch in the flame of the sun. The lethal horns of his bow are resonant with new strings, and his gleaming shafts, tipped with new steel, are ominously glittering. And now he attempts the conquest of even the unconquerable Diana[101] and of the chaste Vesta,[102] whose seat is the sacred hearth. Venus herself is making her annual renewal of her aging form and appears to have sprung afresh out of the warm sea.[104] Through marble cities the youths are chanting Hymenaee;[105] the shores and the caverns echo with the cry, Io, Hymen. And Hymen appears in festal attire, properly robed in a becoming tunic, and his fragrant vestment diffuses the per-fume of the purple crocus. Many a damsel with her virgin breast girdled with gold goes forth to the pleasures of the lovely spring. Each one has her own prayer and the prayer of each is the same—that

Ut sibi quem cupiat det, Cytherea virum.
Nunc quoque septena modulatur arundine pastor,
　Et sua quae iungat carmina Phyllis habet.
Navita nocturno placat sua sidera cantu,　　　　115
　Delphinasque leves ad vada summa vocat.
Iupiter ipse alto cum coniuge ludit Olympo,
　Convocat et famulos ad sua festa Deos.
Nunc etiam Satyri, cum sera crepuscula surgunt,
　Pervolitant celeri florea rura choro,　　　　120
Sylvanusque sua Cyparissi fronde revinctus,
　Semicaperque Deus, semideusque caper.
Quaeque sub arboribus Dryades latuere vetustis
　Per iuga, per solos expatiantur agros.
Per sata luxuriat fruticetaque Maenalius Pan,　125
　Vix Cybele mater, vix sibi tuta Ceres;
Atque aliquam cupidus praedatur Oreada Faunus,
　Consulit in trepidos dum sibi Nympha pedes,
Iamque latet, latitansque cupit male tecta videri,
　Et fugit, et fugiens pervelit ipsa capi.　　　　130
Dii quoque non dubitant caelo praeponere silvas,
　Et sua quisque sibi numina lucus habet.
Et sua quisque diu sibi numina lucus habeto,
　Nec vos arborea, dii, precor, ite domo.
Te referant miseris te, Iupiter, aurea terris　　135
　Saecla! quid ad nimbos aspera tela redis?
Tu saltem lente rapidos age, Phoebe, iugales
　Qua potes, et sensim tempora veris eant;
Brumaque productas tarde ferat hispida noctes,
　Ingruat et nostro serior umbra polo!　(1629)　140

Cytherea will give her the man of her desire.

Now also the shepherd is making music on his pipe of reeds and Phyllis[114] has her songs which she adds to his. With his chant by night the sailor wins the favor of his stars and calls up the fleet dolphins to the surface of the waves.[116] On the heights of Olympus Jove himself sports with his spouse and invites even the gods that serve in his household to his feast. And now, as the late shadows thicken, even the satyrs go darting through the flowery fields in swift bands, and Sylvanus[121] also, crowned with cypress leaves, the god who is half goat and the goat who is half god.[121] The Dryads who have been in hiding under the ancient trees are ranging over the mountains and through the lonely fields. Maenalian Pan takes his wanton pleasure in the sown fields and the copses. There[126] mother Cybele is hardly safe from him and Ceres herself is hardly safe. The lustful Faunus[127] seeks to make some Oread his victim. The nymph takes to her trembling heels for safety. And now she hides but as she does so her hope is to be seen in her poor covert. She darts away, but, though she runs, she hopes to be overtaken. The gods do not hesitate to prefer our woods to their heaven and every grove possesses its own deities.

And long may every grove possess its deities! And my prayer to you, O gods, is not to desert your forest home. Let the Age of Gold restore you, Jupiter, to a wretched world. Why go back to live with your thunderbolts in the clouds? At least, O Phoebus, drive your swift coursers as moderately as you can and let the spring-tide pass slowly. Let the foul winter be long in bringing back its endless nights and let the shadows be later than their wont in attacking our pole.

114. Cf. *Phyllis* in *L'All*, 86.
116. For the fancy about the *dolphins* see *Patrem*, 60.
121. Cf. *Sylvanus* in *Comus*, 268. Milton seems to confuse Sylvanus with the satyrs, as he did in *PR* II, 191. The description fits the half-goat, half-god Pan, whom Sannazaro described in exactly these words in his *Elegies*, and to whom the *Maenalian* mountains in Arcadia were sacred.
126. Cf. the reverend goddesses *Cybele* and *Ceres* in *Arc*, 21 and *El IV*, 11, *Patrem*, 48, and *PL* IV, 271.
127. Cf. *Faunus* in *PL* IV, 708.

SONG: ON MAY MORNING

Now the bright morning Star, Day's harbinger,
　Comes dancing from the East, and leads with her

1. Perhaps Milton thought of the identification of the *morning Star*, Lucifer, with Venus, for whom the induction to Lucretius' *De rerum natura* describes the earth as bringing forth its flowers. But

The Flow'ry *May,* who from her green lap throws
The yellow Cowslip, and the pale Primrose.
Hail bounteous *May* that dost inspire   5
Mirth and youth and warm desire!
Woods and Groves are of thy dressing,
Hill and Dale doth boast thy blessing.
Thus we salute thee with our early Song,
And welcome thee, and wish thee long.   (1629–30)   10

his inspiration is the beauty of the English meadows   The freckled cowslip, burnet, and green clover.
which bring   *(Henry V* V, ii, 47–8)
         sweetly forth

ON THE MORNING OF CHRIST'S NATIVITY

Composed 1629

The theme of this *Ode*—the triumph of the infant Christ over the gods of paganism—was dear to Christian humanists, Protestant and Catholic alike.   Its most mysterious aspect, the silencing of the oracles (to which stanza XIX refers), attracted the Greek Lecturer at Cambridge in Milton's time there, Joseph Mead, who discussed Plutarch's explanation of it in his essay *On the Cessation of the Oracles.*   Challenging Plutarch's theories about "those false lights of the Heathen," Mead said (in his *Discourses on Divers Texts of Scripture* I, XXXV) that they failed simply because they had to "vanish when the Sun of righteousness, Christ *Jesus,* arose into the world."   Milton's full development of the theme in stanzas XVI to XXV anticipates his review of the pagan deities in *PL* I, 392–540.   The paradox of the Son or Word of God incarnating himself in a speechless infant to silence the oracles and rout the pagan deities was later to inspire a passage in the *Socrate chrétien* of Jean-Louis-Guez Balzac in France.

The paradoxes in the *Ode* have been condemned as "metaphysical," and in its "dissonances" Wylie Sypher finds reason—in *Four Stages of Renaissance Style* (New York, 1955), p. 106—for classifying it as "mannerist" poetry.   But the dissonances hardly amount to the lack of "poetic continuity" of which M. M. Ross accuses the *Ode* in *Poetry and Dogma* (New Brunswick, 1954), p. 191.   The charge of discontinuity really roots into the theological objection that "the Person of Christ" is subordinated to "a series of separate symbolizations of the might and goodness of God."   But the orthodoxy of Milton's view of Christ in the *Ode* is established by J. H. Hanford in *The Youth of Milton* and assumed by Brooks and Hardy in their analysis in *Poems of Mr. John Milton* (New York, 1951), pp. 95–104. The essential unity of the *Ode* is traced by Arthur Barker in *UTQ,* X (1941), 167–81, in the pattern which merges the images of silence in stanzas I to VIII into the "enrapturing harmony of the angelic choir" in IX to XV and then moves on to a challenge of that harmony by the pagan gods who are finally controlled by the "dreaded Infant's hand." The last stanza takes us back to the silent Christmas eve and the pastoral note of the opening stanzas, which E. K. Rand compared with Virgil's beautiful "Messianic Eclogue" in *SP,* XIX (1922), 127–9.

The best of the many illustrated editions is *On the Morning of Christ's Nativity.*   With illustrations by William Blake and a Note by Geoffrey Keynes.   Cambridge, 1923.

Some poems by comparison with which Milton's *Ode* may profit: Robert Southwell, *The Burning Babe;* Henry Vaughan, *Christ's Nativity;* Thomas Traherne, *On Christmas Day;* Robert Herrick, *An Ode on the Birth of Our Saviour;* Richard Crashaw, *In the Holy Nativity of Our Lord God.*

I

This is the Month, and this the happy morn
Wherein the Son of Heav'n's eternal King,
Of wedded Maid, and Virgin Mother born,
Our great redemption from above did bring;
For so the holy sages once did sing,   5
    That he our deadly forfeit should release,
And with his Father work us a perpetual peace.

II

That glorious Form, that Light unsufferable,
And that far-beaming blaze of Majesty,
Wherewith he wont at Heav'n's high Council-Table,   10
To sit the midst of Trinal Unity,
He laid aside; and here with us to be,
    Forsook the Courts of everlasting Day,
And chose with us a darksome House of mortal Clay.

III

Say Heav'nly Muse, shall not thy sacred vein   15
Afford a present to the Infant God?
Hast thou no verse, no hymn, or solemn strain,
To welcome him to this his new abode,
Now while the Heav'n by the Sun's team untrod,
    Hath took no print of the approaching light,   20
And all the spangled host keep watch in squadrons bright?

IV

See how from far upon the Eastern road
The Star-led Wizards haste with odors sweet:
O run, prevent them with thy humble ode,
And lay it lowly at his blessed feet: 25
Have thou the honor first, thy Lord to greet,
    And join thy voice unto the Angel Choir,
From out his secret Altar toucht with hallow'd fire.

THE HYMN

I

It was the Winter wild,
While the Heav'n-born child,   30
    All meanly wrapt in the rude manger lies;
Nature in awe to him
Had dofft her gaudy trim,
    With her great Master so to sympathize:

5. *the holy sages:* the prophets who sang "the times of great Messiah" (*PL* XII, 243–4).

10. So Phineas Fletcher developed Genesis i, 26 into the idea of "That Trine-one with himself in council" deliberating on man's creation in *The Purple Island* I, xliv, 3.

21. Nehemiah's saying that "the host of heaven worshippeth thee" (i. e. God—Neh. ix, 6) was a challenge to the worship of "the host of heaven" by Israel's idolatrous neighbors. Nehemiah's worshipping stars fit into the pattern of the Platonic music of the spheres in ll. 125–32, and of the following overthrow of the pagan gods by "the dreaded Infant." Cf. *Arc*, 63.

23. *Wizards:* the "wise men from the east" (Matt. ii, 1) who brought gifts to the infant Christ. Spenser called them

    those Aegyptian wizards old,
Which in star-read were wont have best insight.
                                (*F.Q.* V, Prologue VIII, 1–2)

28. Cf. the coal from the altar which a seraph laid on the prophet's lips (Isa. vi, 6).

It was no season then for her   35
To wanton with the Sun, her lusty Paramour.

II

Only with speeches fair   — metaphysical and
She woos the gentle Air   neoplatonism
   To hide her guilty front with innocent Snow,
And on her naked shame,   Form incorruptible,   40
Pollute with sinful blame,   matter isn't.
   The Saintly Veil of Maiden white to throw,
Confounded, that her Maker's eyes   Opposite of
Should look so near upon her foul deformities.   Romantics

III

But he her fears to cease,
Sent down the meek-ey'd Peace; Peace-deliberate Baroque image 45
   She crown'd with Olive green, came softly sliding
Down through the turning sphere,
   His ready Harbinger,
   With Turtle wing the amorous clouds dividing, — soft sounding
And waving wide her myrtle wand,   Set up next   50
She strikes a universal Peace through Sea and Land.   stanzas

IV

No War, or Battle's sound
Was heard the World around:
   The idle spear and shield were high up hung;   55
The hooked Chariot stood
Unstain'd with hostile blood,
   The Trumpet spake not to the armed throng,
And Kings sat still with awful eye,
As if they surely knew their sovran Lord was by.   60

V

But peaceful was the night
Wherein the Prince of light
   His reign of peace upon the earth began:
The Winds, with wonder whist,
Smoothly the waters kiss't,   65
   Whispering new joys to the mild Ocean,
Who now hath quite forgot to rave,
While Birds of Calm sit brooding on the charmed wave.

36. Cf. the earth as the sun's beloved in *El V*, 55–56.

41. *pollute:* polluted.

42. Cf. Rev. iii, 18: ". . . buy white raiment . . . that the shame of the nakedness do not appear."

46. Milton's personified *Peace* owes something to masques like Jonson's *Entertainments at the Coronation of James I*, in which *Peace* was the "principal person," and something to allegorical prints like that of Theodore Galle.

48. The *sphere* is "the visible Diurnal Sphere" (*PL* VII, 22), the starry globe of the heavens turning daily about the earth.

50. *Turtle wing:* the wings of the turtle dove. *amorous:* fond (of Peace).

53. Popularly it was believed—as Lyly said (*Euphues*, Ed. Arber, p. 456)—that "Christ would not be borne, untill there were peace throughout the whole worlde." The Roman world was at peace for seven years before the traditional date of Christ's birth.

56. War-chariots often had hooks or blades projecting from the hubs of the wheels.

59. *awful:* full of awe, reverent.

64. *whist:* hushed. Cf. "The wild waves whist" in *The Tempest* I, ii, 379.

68. The *Birds of Calm* are the halcyons, which Ovid describes (*Met.* XI, 745–6) as sitting on their floating nests in the quiet spring weather.

VI

The Stars with deep amaze   — *perfect Zodiac*
Stand fixt in steadfast gaze,   70
  Bending one way their precious influence,
And will not take their flight,
For all the morning light,
  Or *Lucifer* that often warn'd them thence;
But in their glimmering Orbs did glow,   75
Until their Lord himself bespake, and bid them go.

VII

And though the shady gloom
Had given day her room,
  The Sun himself withheld his wonted speed,
And hid his head for shame,   80
As his inferior flame,
  The new-enlight'n'd world no more should need;
He saw a greater Sun appear
Than his bright Throne, or burning Axletree could bear.

VIII

The Shepherds on the Lawn,   85
Or ere the point of dawn,
  Sat simply chatting in a rustic row;
Full little thought they then,
That the mighty *Pan*°
  Was kindly come to live with them below;   90
Perhaps their loves, or else their sheep,
Was all that did their silly thoughts so busy keep.

IX

When such music sweet
Their hearts and ears did greet,   — *Music of the*
  As never was by mortal finger struck,   *Spheres*   95
Divinely-warbled voice   *everything in perfect*
Answering the stringed noise,   *harmony.*
  As all their souls in blissful rapture took:
The Air such pleasure loath to lose,
With thousand echoes still prolongs each heav'nly close.   100

69. *amaze:* amazement. Cf. *PR* II, 38 and *SA*, 1645.

71. In *PL* IV, 668–72 Milton explains the stars' *influence.*

74. *Lucifer* may mean the morning star, Venus, or the sun itself, as it does in *El III*, 50 and *El V*, 46.

75. Cf. the planets understood as turning in their respective *orbs* in *PL* I, 287; III, 668; VIII, 30; and the fixed stars "fixed in their orb that flies" (*PL* V, 176). Cf. l. 21 above.

80. So St. John describes Christ as "the light of men" (i, 4) and Malachi (iv, 2) sees a vision of "the Sun of righteousness" rising "with healing in his wings."

84. The *Axletree* is a metonymy for the sun's chariot. Cf. *Comus*, 96.

89. *Pan,* Virgil's "guardian of flocks" (*Georg.* I, 17), who is clothed with mystery and power in the Orphic *Hymn to Pan*, was associated with Christ as the Good Shepherd in Renaissance poetry. Christ, says the Glosse to Maye in Spenser's *Shepheardes Calendar*, "calleth himselfe the greate and good shepherd. The name is most rightly . . . applyed to him for Pan signifieth all, or omnipotent, which is onely the Lord Jesus."

90. In *Images and Themes*, p. 90, R. Tuve reads *kindly* as meaning both "according to nature" and "gently."

100. *close* cadence.

X

Nature that heard such sound
Beneath the hollow round
    Of *Cynthia's* seat, the Airy region thrilling,
Now was almost won
To think her part was done,   105
    And that her reign had here its last fulfilling;
She knew such harmony alone
Could hold all Heav'n and Earth in happier union.

XI

At last surrounds their sight
A Globe of circular light,   110
    That with long beams the shame-fac't night array'd,
The helmed Cherubim
And sworded Seraphim
    Are seen in glittering ranks with wings display'd,
Harping in loud and solemn choir,   115
With unexpressive notes to Heav'n's new-born Heir.

XII

Such Music (as 'tis said)
Before was never made,   *Notice compression of time*
    But when of old the sons of morning sung,
While the Creator Great   120
His constellations set,
    And the well-balanc't world on hinges hung,
And cast the dark foundations deep,
And bid the welt'ring waves their oozy channel keep.

XIII

Ring out ye Crystal spheres,   125
Once bless our human ears,
    (If ye have power to touch our senses so)
And let your silver chime
Move in melodious time;
    And let the Bass of Heav'n's deep Organ blow,   130
And with your ninefold harmony
Make up full consort to th'Angelic symphony.

XIV

For if such holy Song
Enwrap our fancy long,
    Time will run back, and fetch the age of gold,   135

102. *the hollow round:* the orb or sphere of the moon. Cf. l. 75 above, l. 130 below, and *Comus*, 131.

103. This half-technical use of *region* is illustrated in *PL* II, 718, n., *Infant*, 16, and *Vac*, 41.

110. Cf. the *Globe of fiery Seraphim* in *PL* II, 512.

116. *unexpressive:* inexpressible. Cf. *Lyc*, 176.

117. So Job is asked (xxxviii, 6–7): "Whereupon are the foundations thereof fastened? or who laid the corner-stone thereof, When the morning stars sang together, and all the sons of God shouted for joy." Cf. *Music*, 6–16 and *PL* XI, 55–56.

122. Again in *PL* VII, 242, Milton remembered Job xxvi, 7: "He . . . hangeth the earth upon

nothing."

125–135. Memories of the promised golden age of Virgil's *Eclogue IV* and of Plato's cyclical "Great Year" (*Timaeus*, 39) mingle with the Pythagorean tradition that the music of the spheres would be audible to sinless men. Cf. *Arc*, 63, n.

133–136. Perhaps Milton thought of Hesiod's Golden Age, when men were so good that Zeus changed them into immortal spirits (*Works and Days*, 111–26). *Vanity* stands for all "the sins to which the creature was made subject" (Rom. viii, 20), and from which Milton says that the angels' song might redeem human nature so that men could hear "the heavenly tune" (*Arc*, 72–3).

And speckl'd vanity
Will sicken soon and die,
    And leprous sin will melt from earth.y mold,
And Hell itself will pass away,
And leave her dolorous mansions to the peering day.   140

- Aerial view of bombed city? - Allusion

XV

Yea, Truth and Justice then
Will down return to men,
    Th'enamel'd *Arras* of the Rainbow wearing,
And Mercy set between,
Thron'd in Celestial sheen,   145
    With radiant feet the tissued clouds down steering,
And Heav'n as at some festival,
Will open wide the Gates of her high Palace Hall.

Personifying concepts Very Baroque

XVI

But wisest Fate says no,
This must not yet be so,   150
    The Babe lies yet in smiling Infancy,
That on the bitter cross
Must redeem our loss;   *} - future act.*
    So both himself and us to glorify:
Yet first to those ychain'd in sleep,   155
The wakeful trump of doom must thunder through the deep,

XVII

With such a horrid clang
As on mount *Sinai* rang
    While the red fire, and smold'ring clouds outbrake:
The aged Earth aghast   160
With terror of that blast,
    Shall from the surface to the center shake,
When at the world's last session,
The dreadful Judge in middle Air shall spread his throne.

XVIII

And then at last our bliss   165
Full and perfect is,
    But now begins; for from this happy day
Th'old Dragon under ground,
In straiter limits bound,
    Not half so far casts his usurped sway,   170

141. Cf. Ps. lxxxv, 10–11: "Mercy and Truth are met together; righteousness and peace have kissed each other. Truth shall spring out of the earth. . . ."   Or perhaps Milton was mainly influenced by allegorical figures of the four daughters of God in the morality plays, or by similar figures in contemporary masks and paintings.

143–144. In 1673 Milton changes these lines to read:

    Orb'd in a Rainbow; and like glories wearing
    Mercy will sit between.

155. ychain'd, like yclep'd in *L'All*, 12, keeps the Old English prefix *ge-*, reduced to *y-*. Milton added it here, as he did mistakenly to a present parti-

ciple in *Snak*, 4, because—as the Glosse to Spenser's April explains—"Y is a poetical addition." *sleep* is death, 'that sleep in the dust of the earth" from which Daniel (xii, 2) prophesied that men "shall awake."

157. The stanza rests on the account of the "thunders and lightnings and the voice of the trumpet exceeding loud" on Mt. Sinai when the Ten Commandments were given to Moses (Ex. xix, 16) and Christ's prophecy of the Last Judgment, when "they shall see the Son of man coming in the clouds of heaven with power and great glory" (Matt. xxiv, 30).

158. Cf. the dragon of Rev. xii, 9 in *PL* IV, 3.

And wroth to see his Kingdom fail,   *— cf. Faerie Queen*
Swinges the scaly Horror of his folded tail.

XIX

The Oracles are dumb,
No voice or hideous hum
    Runs through the arched roof in words deceiving.   175
Apollo from his shrine
Can no more divine,
    With hollow shriek the steep of *Delphos* leaving.
No nightly trance, or breathed spell,
Inspires the pale-ey'd Priest from the prophetic cell.   180

XX

account of Rachel

The lonely mountains o'er,   *— Jeremiah weeping for her*
And the resounding shore,   *children*
    A voice of weeping heard, and loud lament;
From haunted spring and dale
Edg'd with poplar pale,   *— Gentle exit here*   185
    The parting Genius is with sighing sent;
With flow'r-inwov'n tresses torn
The Nymphs in twilight shade of tangled thickets mourn.

XXI

In consecrated Earth,
And on the holy Hearth,   190
    The *Lars* and *Lemures* moan with midnight plaint;
In Urns and Altars round,   *— vestiges of old household*
A drear and dying sound   *gods*
    Affrights the *Flamens* at their service quaint;   *kitchen witches*
And the chill Marble seems to sweat,   195
While each peculiar power forgoes his wonted seat.

XXII

Peor and *Baalim*
Forsake their Temples dim,
    With that twice-batter'd god of *Palestine,*
And mooned *Ashtaroth,*   200
Heav'n's Queen and Mother both,
    Now sits not girt with Tapers' holy shine,
The Libyc *Hammon* shrinks his horn,
In vain the *Tyrian* Maids their wounded *Thammuz* mourn.

174–220. Many details of the flight of the pagan gods seemed to A. S. Cook to come from the *Apotheosis* of Prudentius or the *Parthenicae* (III, i) of Mantuan.

178. *Delphos:* Delphi, Apollo's most famous oracle, which lay on the precipitous upper slopes of Mt. Parnassus.

186. *Genius:* local god. Cf. *Lyc,* 184 and *Arc,* 44–60.

191. *Lars:* tutelary gods of cities or houses. *Lemures:* spirits of the dead, who were revered in ancient Rome.

194. *Flamens:* priests serving any particular Roman diety.

195. So Virgil speaks of the sweating of the god's statues (in *Georg.* I, 480) as a portent of evil to come.

197. Cf. *Baal Peor* in *PL* I, 412, n.

199. The *twice-batter'd god* is Dagon, whose image in Ashdod was twice miraculously broken, so that "only the stump of Dagon was left to him" (I Sam. v, 4). Cf. *PL* I, 457–66 and *SA,* 13.

200. *Ashtoroth* appears under the name *Astarte* in *PL* I, 438.

204. *Thammuz,* whom the Greeks knew as Adonis, was worshipped in an annual ceremony of mourning for him as a symbol of the beauty of summer slain by the boar, winter. Cf. *PL* I, 446–57.

XXIII

And sullen *Moloch,* fled,   205
Hath left in shadows dread
  His burning Idol all of blackest hue;
In vain with Cymbals' ring
They call the grisly king,
  In dismal dance about the furnace blue;   210
The brutish gods of *Nile* as fast,
Isis and *Orus,* and the Dog *Anubis* haste.

— notice Masculinity of lines and baroqueness.

XXIV

Nor is *Osiris* seen   *—last god to depart*
In *Memphian* Grove or Green,
  Trampling the unshow'r'd Grass with lowings loud: 215
Nor can he be at rest
Within his sacred chest,
  Naught but profoundest Hell can be his shroud:
In vain with Timbrel'd Anthems dark
The sable-stoled Sorcerers bear his worshipt Ark.   220

intentionally hard? fitting end for this god?

XXV

He feels from Judah's Land
The dreaded Infant's hand,
  The rays of *Bethlehem* blind his dusky eyn;
Nor all the gods beside,
Longer dare abide,   *— quieter force.*   225
  Nor *Typhon* huge ending in snaky twine:
Our Babe, to show his Godhead true,
Can in his swaddling bands control the damned crew.   *— Hercules image*

XXVI

So when the Sun in bed,   *— conceited nature image*
Curtain'd with cloudy red,   230
  Pillows his chin upon an Orient wave,
The flocking shadows pale
Troop to th'infernal jail;
  Each fetter'd Ghost slips to his several grave,
And the yellow-skirted *Fays*   235
Fly after the Night-steeds, leaving their Moon-lov'd maze.

205. The decree against any man's making "his son or his daughter to pass through the fire to *Moloch*" (II Kings xxiii, 10) suggests the worship of the "Idoll of brasse hauing the head of a Calfe, the rest of a kingly figure, with armes extended to receive the miserable sacrifice," which George Sandys described in his *Travels* (1637, p. 186), with particular stress on the din of cymbals that was used to drown the cries of the suffering infants. Cf. *PL* I, 392.
  211. Cf. the *brutish gods* of Fanatic Egypt in *PL* I, 480–2.
  212–213. *Isis,* sister and wife of *Osiris* and mother of the hawk-headed *Orus,* was represented with the disc of the sun and the horns of a cow on her head. *Anubis* was usually represented with a jackal's head.
  215. *unshow'r'd* refers to the rainless Egyptian climate.
  219. So Herodotus (II, 63) describes Osiris' priests bearing his "image, placed in a small wooden temple, gilded all over," from one of his temples

to another amid the sound of timbrels or tambourines.
  223. *eyn* was already obsolescent as a plural of *eye.*
  226. *Typhon* is either the Egyptian evil deity who slays Osiris in the myth which Milton told in *Areop,* p. 742, or he is Hesiod's primeval serpent which figures in *PL* I, 199.
  229. Cf. this fancy with Marvell's *Upon Appleton House,* 661–4:
    The sun himself of her aware,
    Seems to descend with greater care,
    And, lest she see him go to bed,
    In blushing clouds conceals his head.
  231. *Orient:* oriental, eastern. Cf. *PL* II, 399 and IV, 644.
  234. So in *A Midsummer Night's Dream* III, ii, 380–2 Puck warns of Aurora's harbinger,
    At whose approach ghosts, wandering here and there,
    Troop home to churchyards . . .

XXVII

But see! the Virgin blest,
Hath laid her Babe to rest.
  Time is our tedious Song should here have ending;
Heav'n's youngest-teemed Star   240
Hath fixt her polisht Car,
  Her sleeping Lord with Handmaid Lamp attending:
And all about the Courtly Stable,
  Bright-harness'd Angels sit in order serviceable. ⟶ Milton's word (Dec., 1629)

240. *Heav'n's youngest-teemed* (newest-born)
Star has guided the three Wise Men from the east
and has now come to rest "over where the young
child was" (Matt. ii, 9).

243. The stable is *Courtly* because it houses Christ
the king.
244. *Bright-harness'd*: clad in bright armor.

ELEGIA SEXTA (ELEGY VI)

Ad Carolum Diodatum, Ruri Commorantem (To Charles Diodati When He Was Visiting in the Country)

(Qui cum idibus Decemb. scripsisset, et sua carmina excusari postulasset si solito minus essent bona, quod inter lautitias quibus erat ab amicis exceptus, haud satis felicem operam Musis dare se posse affirmabat, hunc habuit responsum.) (Who, when he wrote on the thirteenth of December, begging that his verses might be excused if they were not so good as usual, pled that, in the magnificence of his reception by his friends, he was not able to cultivate the Muses very prosperously. He had this answer:)

E. M. W. Tillyard's treatment of this poem as a serious self-dedication to poetry in *Setting*, pp. 177–9, is qualified but not discredited by W. R. Parker's view of it in *MLN*, LV (1940), 215–8, as a rhetorical debate like *Prol* I. In *SP*, XIX (1922), 111, E. K. Rand suggests that Milton was "a young Ovid" when he wrote the first thirty-five lines of *El VI*, and that he developed the traditional Renaissance theory of the austerity of character becoming an epic poet in ll. 55–90 in a playful rather than serious spirit.

Mitto tibi sanam non pleno ventre salutem,
  Qua tu distento forte carere potes.
At tua quid nostram prolectat Musa camenam,
  Nec sinit optatas posse sequi tenebras?
Carmine scire velis quam te redamemque colamque;
  Crede mihi vix hoc carmine scire queas,   6
Nam neque noster amor modulis includitur arctis,
  Nec venit ad claudos integer ipse pedes.
Quam bene solennes epulas, hilaremque Decembrim
  Festaque caelifugam quae coluere Deum,   10
Deliciasque refers, hiberni gaudia ruris,
  Haustaque per lepidos Gallica musta focos.
Quid quereris refugam vino dapibusque poesin?
  Carmen amat Bacchum, Carmina Bacchus amat.

On an empty stomach I send you a wish for the good health of which you, with a full one, may perhaps feel the lack. But why does your Muse provoke mine, instead of permitting her to seek the obscurity that she craves? You would like to be informed by a song how I return your love and how fond I am of you. Believe me, you can hardly learn it from this song, for my love is not confined by narrow meters and it is too sound to use the lame feet of elegy.[8]

How well you report the splendid feasts and the hilarious December—the festivals which do honor to the heaven-forsaking[10] God—the sports and pleasures of winter in the country and the French vintages quaffed beside merry fires. But why do you complain that poetry is a fugitive from wine and feasting? Song loves Bacchus[14] and Bacchus loves

8. *The lame feet of elegy* are the alternate hexameters and pentameters, which Ovid himself had playfully described in that way (*Tristia* III, i, 2).
10. The *heaven-forsaking God* is Christ coming to earth.
14. *Bacchus* is the Muses' friend because, as Conti says (V, xiii, p. 506), "the heat of wine awakens genius."

Nec puduit Phoebum virides gestasse corymbos,   15
  Atque hederam lauro praeposuisse suae.
Saepius Aoniis clamavit collibus Euoe
  Mista Thyoneo turba novena choro.
Naso Corallaeis mala carmina misit ab agris;
  Non illic epulae, non sata vitis erat.   20
Quid nisi vina, rosasque racemiferumque Lyaeum
  Cantavit brevibus Teia Musa modis?
Pindaricosque inflat numeros Teumesius Euan,
  Et redolet sumptum pagina quaeque merum;
Dum gravis everso currus crepat axe supinus,   25
  Et volat Eleo pulvere fuscus eques.
Quadrimoque madens Lyricen Romanus Iaccho
  Dulce canit Glyceran, flavicomamque Chloen.
Iam quoque lauta tibi generoso mensa paratu
  Mentis alit vires ingeniumque fovet.   30
Massica foecundam despumant pocula venam,
  Fundis et ex ipso condita metra cado.
Addimus his artes, fusumque per intima Phoebum
  Corda; favent uni Bacchus, Apollo, Ceres.
Scilicet haud mirum tam dulcia carmina per te   35
  Numine composito tres peperisse Deos.
Nunc quoque Thressa tibi caelato barbitos auro
  Insonat arguta molliter icta manu;
Auditurque chelys suspensa tapetia circum,
  Virgineos tremula quae regat arte pedes.   40
Illa tuas saltem teneant spectacula Musas,
  Et revocent quantum crapula pellit iners.
Crede mihi, dum psallit ebur, comitataque plectrum
  Implet odoratos festa chorea tholos,
Percipies tacitum per pectora serpere Phoebum,   45
  Quale repentinus permeat ossa calor;
Perque puellares oculos digitumque sonantem
  Irruet in totos lapsa Thalia sinus.
Namque Elegia levis multorum cura deorum est,
  Et vocat ad numeros quemlibet illa suos;   50

16. Cf. Apollo's *laurel* in *El V*, 13.
17. Cf. the *Aonian Hills* and the Muses in *El IV*, 30.
18. Bacchus is called *Thyoneus* because his mother Semele was also called Thyone. His other name of *Lyaeus* means "the releaser" (of genius and high spirits).
19. Cf. the allusion in *El I*, 22 to Ovid's banishment to Pontus, where he complained in the *Epistles from Pontus* IV, viii, 80–83 that the barbarous inhabitants, the Coralli, had no vineyards and no wine.
22. The *Teian Poet* is Anacreon, whose drinking songs are in short verses.
23. *Teumesian Euan* is still another name for Bacchus, who is now the inspirer of Pindar's odes celebrating the victories of the charioteers in the Olympic Games at Elis.
28. *Glycera* and blond *Chloe* both appear in Horace's *Odes*.
37. The lyre is *Thracian* because it belonged to Orpheus, the *Thracian* bard of *PL* VII, 34. Cf. *Lyc*, 63.
48. *Thalia*, the Muse of Comedy, inspired sports

songs. Phoebus was not ashamed to wear the green garland of ivy and to prefer its leaves to his own laurel.[16] On the Aonian hills[17] the chorus of the Nine has often mingled with the rout of Thyoneus[18] and raised the cry, *Euoe*. Ovid sent bad verses from the Corallian[19] fields because there were no banquets in that land and the vine had not been planted. O what but wine and roses and Lyaeus wreathed with clusters did the Teian Poet sing in his short measures?[22] Teaumesian Euan inspires the Pindaric Odes[23] and their every page is redolent of the consumed wine; as he paints the crash of the heavy chariot overturned by a shattered axle, and the rush of the horseman, all blackened with the Elean dust. In his potations of four-year-old wine the Roman lyrist sang of Glycera and of golden-haired Chloe.[28] In your case also the sumptuous board with its generous provision gives strength to your mind and fire to your genius. Your Campanian cups foam with creative impulse and you decant the store of your verses out of the wine-jar itself. To all this we add the arts and Apollo's presence in your secret heart. In your single self the favor of Bacchus, Apollo, and Ceres is united. No wonder, then, if the three gods by their combined potency should have brought forth such sweet songs through you!

Now also for you the Thracian lyre,[37] inlaid with gold and gently touched by a skilled hand, is sounding; and in tapestried halls you have the music of the harp that rules the dancing feet of maidens by its rhythmic art. At least, let these scenes hold the attention of your Muse and recall whatever power dull dissipation drives away. Believe me, when the ivory key is played and the festive throng dances through the perfumed halls to the sound of the lute, you will feel the silent approach of Phoebus in your breast like a sudden heat that permeates to the marrow; and through a maiden's eyes and music-making fingers Thalia[48] will glide into full possession of your breast.

For many of the gods patronize the gay elegy and she calls whom

Liber adest elegis, Eratoque, Ceresque, Venusque,
　Et cum purpurea matre tenellus Amor.
Talibus inde licent convivia larga poetis,
　Saepius et veteri commaduisse mero.
At qui bella refert, et adulto sub Iove caelum,　　　55
　Heroasque pios, semideosque duces,
Et nunc sancta canit superum consulta deorum,
　Nunc latrata fero regna profunda cane,
Ille quidem parce Samii pro more magistri
　Vivat, et innocuos praebeat herba cibos.　　　60
Stet prope fagineo pellucida lympha catillo,
　Sobriaque e puro pocula fonte bibat.
Additur huic scelerisque vacans et casta iuventus,
　Et rigidi mores, et sine labe manus.
Qualis veste nitens sacra, et lustralibus undis,　　　65
　Surgis ad infensos augur iture Deos.
Hoc ritu vixisse ferunt post rapta sagacem
　Lumina Tiresian, Ogygiumque Linon,
Et lare devoto profugum Calchanta, senemque
　Orpheon edomitis sola per antra feris.　　　70
Sic dapis exiguus, sic rivi potor Homerus
　Dulichium vexit per freta longa virum
Et per monstrificam Perseiae Phoebados aulam,
　Et vada foemineis insidiosa sonis,
Perque tuas, rex ime, domos, ubi sanguine nigro　　　75
　Dicitur umbrarum detinuisse greges.
Diis etenim sacer est vates, divumque sacerdos,
　Spirat et occultum pectus et ora Iovem.
At tu si quid agam scitabere (si modo saltem
　Esse putas tanti noscere siquid agam)　　　80
Paciferum canimus caelesti semine regem,
　Faustaque sacratis saecula pacta libris;
Vagitumque Dei, et stabulantem paupere tecto
　Qui suprema suo cum patre regna colit;

---

she will to her measures. Liber and Erato, Ceres and Venus are at hand to help her, and beside his rosy mother is the stripling Cupid. For such poets, then, grand banquets are allowable and frequent potations of old wine. But he whose theme is wars and heaven under Jupiter in his prime, and pious heroes and chieftains half-divine, and he who sings now of the sacred counsels of the gods on high, and now of the infernal realms where the fierce dog[58] howls, let him live sparingly, like the Samian teacher;[59] and let herbs furnish his innocent diet. Let the purest water stand beside him in a bowl of beech and let him drink sober draughts from the pure spring. Beyond this, his youth must be innocent of crime and chaste, his conduct irreproachable and his hands stainless. His character should be like yours, O Priest, when, glorious with sacred vestments and lustral water, you arise to go into the presence of the angry deities.

By this rule it is said that the wise Tiresias[68] lived after the loss of his eyes, and Ogygian Linus, and Calchas[69] when he was a fugitive from his doomed home, and Orpheus in his old age, when he tamed the wild beasts among the lonely caves. So Homer, the spare eater and the water-drinker,[71] carried Ulysses through vast stretches of ocean, through the monster-making palace of the daughter of Phoebus and Perseis, through the seas made treacherous by the songs of the Sirens, and through your mansions, O infernal King, where he is said to have constrained the hosts of shades by means of a libation of dark blood. For truly, the bard is sacred to the gods and is their priest.[77] His hidden heart and his lips alike breathe out Jove.

But if you will know what I am doing (if only you think it of any importance to know whether I am doing anything)—I am singing the heaven-descended King, the bringer of peace, and the blessed times promised in the sacred books—the infant cries of our God and his stabling under a mean roof who, with his Father, governs the realms above. I am singing the starry

---

of all kinds. *Erato* is the Muse of erotic and lyric poetry.

58. The *dog* is Cerberus, the three-headed guardian of Hades.

59. Pythagoras, the *Samian teacher*, in Ovid's account (*Met.* XV, 60–142) of his teaching, stressed the "impiety" of eating meat. Cf. *Music,* 14 and 19, nn.

68. Cf. *Tiresias* in PL III, 36 and *Idea,* 25. *Linus* was a legendary Theban bard.

69. *Calchas* was the soothsayer of the Greeks in the Trojan War.

71. Milton perhaps remembered Boccaccio's account in the *Genealogy of the Gods* XIV, xix, of the blind Homer living something like the life of a Christian hermit on the mountains and composing the story of Ulysses—the ideal hero because he resisted the charms of Circe and the Sirens and passed unscathed through the realm of the dead.

77. So Ovid asserts the poet's divine inspiration because he sings of divine things (*Fasti* VI, 5–7).

Stelliparumque polum, modulantesque aethere turmas,
  Et subito elisos ad sua fana Deos.   36
Dona quidem dedimus Christi natalibus illa;
  Illa sub auroram lux mihi prima tulit.
Te quoque pressa manent patriis meditata cicutis;
  Tu mihi, cui recitem, iudicis instar eris.   90

(Dec., 1629)

sky and the hosts that sang high in air, and the gods that were suddenly destroyed in their own shrines.

These are my gifts for the birthday of Christ—gifts which the first light of its dawn brought to me. For you these simple strains that have been meditated on my native pipes[90] are waiting; and you, when I recite them to you, shall be my judge.

90. The *strains . . . on my native pipes* (i. e. written in English) are the *Nativity Ode,* which we know was written at Christmas time, 1629.

SONNET I

O Nightingale

The opening recalls several sonnets by Giovanni della Casa, Giacomo Cenci, and Cardinal Bembo. In tone it resembles the following Italian group as much as it does *Elegies V* and *VII,* and its date was probably very close to that of the Italian sonnets.

O Nightingale, that on yon bloomy Spray
  Warbl'st at eve, when all the Woods are still,
  Thou with fresh hope the Lover's heart dost fill,
While the jolly hours lead on propitious *May*
Thy liquid notes that close the eye of Day,   5
  First heard before the shallow Cuckoo's bill,
  Portend success in love; O, if *Jove's* will
Have linkt that amorous power to thy soft lay,
Now timely sing, ere the rude Bird of Hate
  Foretell my hopeless doom in some Grove nigh: 10
  As thou from year to year hast sung too late
For my relief; yet hadst no reason why.
  Whether the Muse, or Love call thee his mate,
  Both them I serve, and of their train am I.   (1630)

2. Cf. *El V,* 25–6.
4. Portrayals of the personified *hours* go back in classical poetry as far as the Orphic Hymn which Conti quotes (V, 13, p. 418) with Hesiod's account of them as born of Zeus and the goddess of Justice, Themis (*Theog.,* 901).
6. In Sir Thomas Clanvowe's *The Cuckoo and the Nightingale* (which Milton found in Speght's edi-

tion of Chaucer) a poet dreams of hearing love's champion the nightingale debate with its enemy the cuckoo, and he recalls

how lovers had a tokeninge,
And among hem it was a comune tale,
That it were good to here the nightingale
Rather than the lewd cukkow singe.

SONNET II

Donna leggiadra! (Beautiful Lady)

The resemblance of this and the following sonnets to *Elegies V* and *VII* is the best justification for their dating here. The closing lines of *Sonn* VI seem like an echo of *Elegy VII,* 89–90, though as a whole it has been compared with sonnets by Petrarch and Tasso. The significance of Milton's mastery of the technique of the Italian sonneteers as a factor in his style in all his later poetry is traced by F. T. Prince in *The Italian Elements in Milton's Verse* (Oxford, 1954). The romantic legend of the composition of the Italian sonnets during the Italian journey was finally disproved by J. M. Smart in his edition of *The Sonnets of John Milton* (Glasgow, 1921).

Donna leggiadra, il cui bel nome onora
  L'erbosa val di Reno, e il nobil varco,
  Ben è colui d' ogni valore scarco
  Qual tuo spirto gentil non innamora,
Che dolcemente mostrasi di fuora,   5
  De' suoi atti soavi giamai parco,
  E i don', che son d' Amor saette ed arco,
  Là onde l' alta tua virtù s' infiora.
Quando tu vaga parli, o lieta canti
  Che mover possa duro alpestre legno,   10
  Guardi ciascun agli occhi, ed agli orecchi
L'entrata, chi di te si trova indegno;
  Grazia sola di sù gli vaglia, innanti
  Che'l disio amoroso al cuor s' invecchi.   (1630)

Gentle and beautiful lady,[1] whose fair name honors the verdant valley of Reno and the glorious ford, surely he is a man void of all worth who is not inspired with love by your gracious spirit. Sweetly it expresses itself in the bounty of fair looks and the gifts which are the arrows and the bow of Love,[7] there where your high virtue wears its garland.

When you speak in your beauty and sing in your happiness, so that the tough trees on the mountains might respond, let every man who finds himself unworthy of you ward well the approaches to the eye and ear. Grace from above alone can avail him to prevent the desire of a lover from becoming fixed immovably in his heart.

1. The lady's name is Aemilia, for that is the name of the Italian province through which flow both the Reno and the Rubicon, whose ford Caesar made famous by the crossing that led to his dictatorship in Rome. She may have been a relative of Charles Diodati or a friend of his family in London.
7. Countless Renaissance sonnets were developed from the "Platonism" which identified a woman's glances with the weapons of Cupid, whose darts—as Spenser declared in *Amoretti* VIII, 6—may serve "to base affections wound."

SONNET III

Qual in colle aspro (As on a Rugged Mountain)

Qual in colle aspro, al' imbrunir di sera,
  L' avezza giovinetta pastorella
  Va bagnando l' erbetta strana e bella,
  Che mal si spande a disusata spera,
Fuor di sua natia alma primavera,   5
  Così Amor meco insù la lingua snella
  Desta il fior nuovo di strania favella,
  Mentre io di te, vezzosamente altera,
Canto, dal mio buon popol non inteso,
  E'l bel Tamigi cangio col bel Arno.   10
  Amor lo volse, ed io a l' altrui peso
Seppi ch' Amor cosa mai volse indarno.
  Deh! foss' il mio cuor lento e'l duro seno
  A chi pianta dal ciel sì buon terreno.   (1630)

As, on a rugged mountain when twilight is darkening, the young shepherd girl, familiar with the spot, waters a strange and lovely little plant which spreads its leaves feebly in the alien clime, remote from its fostering, native springtime; so on my prompt tongue Love calls forth the novel flower of a foreign speech, when I sing of you, graciously proud lady, and change the fair Thames for the fair Arno[10]—not understood by my own good countrymen. Love willed it, and at the cost of others I know that Love never willed anything in vain.

Ah, that my dull heart and hard breast might be as good a soil for Him who plants from heaven.

10. To change the *Thames* for the *Arno* is to exchange English for Tuscan, the pure Italian spoken in Florence in Tuscany, on the Arno.

CANZONE

Ridonsi donne e giovani amorosi,
M' accostandosi attorno, e, "Perchè scrivi,
Perchè tu scrivi in lingua ignota e strana

Amorous young men and maidens press about me, jesting: "Why write —why do you write in a language

Verseggiando d'amor, e come t'osi?
Dinne, se la tua speme sia mai vana,   5
E de' pensieri lo miglior t' arrivi."
Così mi van burlando; "Altri rivi,
Altri lidi t' aspettan, ed altre onde,
Nelle cui verdi sponde
Spuntati ad or ad or a la tua chioma   10
L'immortal guiderdon d'eterne frondi.
Perchè alle spalle tue soverchia soma?"
    Canzon, dirotti, e tu per me rispondi:
Dice mia Donna, e'l suo dir è il mio cuore,
"Questa è lingua di cui si vanta Amore."   (1630)   15

unknown and strange, versifying of
love, and how do you dare? Speak,
if your hope is ever to prove not
vain and if the best of your desires
is to come to pass."
    And thus they make sport of me;
"Other rivers, other shores and
other waters are waiting for you, on
whose green banks now, even now,
an immortal guerdon of undying
leaves is putting forth its shoots to
crown your locks. Why the superfluous burden on your shoulders?"
    Canzone,[13] I will tell you, and
you shall answer for me. My lady,
whose words are my very heart,
says, "This is the language of which
Love makes his boast."

13. A *canzone* ended with an envoy called the *commiato,* in which the poet often addressed his poem as Milton does here, and as Spenser did in the last stanza of his *Epithalamion.* Spenser's stanza is an elaboration of the Italian *canzone,* whose strict rhyme scheme is only approximated here by Milton.

SONNET IV

DIODATI, E TE'L DIRÒ (DIODATI, and I will say it to you)

Diodati, e te 'l dirò con maraviglia,
    Quel ritroso io, ch' Amor spreggiar soléa
    E de' suoi lacci spesso mi ridéa
    Già caddi, ov' uom dabben talor s' impiglia.
Nè treccie d' oro nè guancia vermiglia   5
    M' abbaglian sì, ma sotto nuova idea
    Pellegrina bellezza che 'l cuor bea,
    Portamenti alti onesti, e nelle ciglia
Quel sereno fulgor d' amabil nero,
    Parole adorne di lingua più d' una,   10
    E 'l cantar che di mezzo l' emisfero
Traviar ben può la faticosa Luna;
    E degli occhi suoi avventa si gran fuoco
    Che l' incerar gli orecchi mi fia poco.   (1630)

Diodati—and I will say it to you
with amazement—that obstinate I,
who used to pour contempt upon
Love and often mocked his snares,
have fallen where a good man sometimes entangles himself. No tresses
of gold nor vermeil cheeks have
dazzled me so, but an alien beauty
under a new pattern,[6] which rejoices
my heart—a manner nobly decorous,
and in her eyes that quiet radiance
of lovely black, speech that is
adorned with more than one language, and a gift of song which
might draw the laboring moon[12]
from its course in mid-sky. And
so potent a fire flashes from her
eyes that it would be of little avail
to me to seal up my ears.[14]

6–7. The lines seem to retract the praise of Eng-lishwomen as the loveliest in the world of *El I,* 71–72. The following description may owe some-thing to Petrarch's sonnet CCXIII.
12. So again *PL* II, 665 uses Virgil's figure (*Georg.* II, 478) of the *laboring moon.* Virgil also described the moon as lured from her course by the songs of enchantresses (*Ec.* VIII, 69).

14. A glance at Homer's story of Ulysses' escape from the Sirens by stopping the ears of his men with wax against their song. Cf. *Comus,* 253–9.

SONNET V

PER CERTO I BEI VOSTR' OCCHI (IN TRUTH, YOUR FAIR EYES)

Per certo i bei vostr' occhi, Donna mia,
    Esser non può che non sian lo mio sole,
    Si mi percuoton forte, come ei suole
    Per l' arene di Libia chi s' invia,

1–4. Cf. the turn of this time-worn Petrarchan image in *El VII,* 56–57.

In truth, your fair eyes, my lady,
cannot but be my sun,[1] for they
beat upon me as powerfully as the
sun beats upon one who pursues
his way through the sands of Libia.
Meanwhile an ardent vapor, such as

Mentre un caldo vapor (nè senti' pria)   5
  Da quel lato si spinge ove mi duole,
  Che forse amanti nelle lor parole
  Chiaman sospir; io non so che si sia:
Parte rinchiusa, e turbida si cela
  Scossomi il petto, e poi n' uscendo poco,   10
  Quivi d' attorno o s' agghiaccia, o s' ingiela;
Ma quanto a gli occhi giunge a trovar loco
  Tutte le notti a me suol far piovose
  Finchè mia Alba rivien colma di rose.   (1630)

6. The painful side is the side of the heart.

I never felt before, presses up from that side[6] where my pain lies. Perhaps lovers in their language call it a sigh; I do not know what it may be. A turbulent part hidden in the confinement of my breast makes it heave and, a little escaping, it then turns frosty and congeals. But the part of it which comes to find a place in my eyes makes all my nights rainy, until my Dawn returns, surcharged with roses.

SONNET VI

Giovane piano, e semplicetto amante (Young, Gentle, and Candid Lover)

Giovane piano, e semplicetto amante,
  Poichè fuggir me stesso in dubbio sono,
  Madonna, a voi del mio cuor l' umil dono
  Farò divoto; io certo a prove tante
L' ebbi fedele, intrepido, costante,   5
  Di pensieri leggiadro, accorto, e buono.
  Quando rugge il gran mondo, e scocca il tuono,
  S' arma di se, e d' intero diamante,
Tanto del forse, e d' invidia sicuro,
  Di timori, e speranze al popol use,   10
  Quanto d' ingegno, e d' alto valor vago,
E di cetra sonora, e delle Muse:
  Sol troverete in tal parte men duro
  Ove Amor mise l' insanabil ago.   (1630)

Young, gentle and candid lover that I am, because I am doubtful, my lady, how[2] to fly from myself, I shall make the humble gift of my heart in devotion to you. In countless ordeals I have proved it faithful, courageous and constant, and in its thoughts gracious, courteous and good.[5] When the world is in an uproar and the thunder crashes, it arms itself from within itself with perfect adamant[7]—as secure against fortune, envy, and the fears and hopes of ordinary men as it is keen in its desire for the mind's gifts, high courage, and the sounding lyre, and the Muses. Only at a single point will you find it less unyielding—the point where Love's dart has pierced incurably.

2. It is hard to tell whether the poet is doubtful *how* or *whether* to flee from himself. The former idea was a Petrarchan convention, but the latter harmonizes better with the Stoic ideal which colors Milton's self-portrait.

5. Stoic doctrine was that, "It is a true marke of vulgar basenesse, for a man to expect neither good nor harme from himselfe, but all from externall euents. Contrariwise, the true note of a Philosopher, is to repose all his expectation, vpon himselfe

alone" (Healey's tr. of *Epictetus his Manuell*, ed. of 1616, p. 91).

7-9. Cf. Horace's just man invulnerable against the worst that Fate can do (*Odes* III, iii). As a whole, the tone of these sonnets corresponds with the autobiographical passage in the selection from *Apology* which is found below on p. 694.

DE IDEA PLATONICA QUEMADMODUM ARISTOTELES INTELLEXIT (ON THE PLATONIC IDEA AS UNDERSTOOD BY ARISTOTLE)

This is a college exercise—dating somewhere between 1628 and 1630, and resembling the second Prolusion in its ironical treatment of Aristotle, "the envious and perpetual calumniator of Pythagoras and Plato." In form, the poem is dramatic—a series of questions supposed to be drawn from Aristotle's *Metaphysics* by a disciple who naïvely admires its criticism of Plato's theory of an archetypal man made in a divine image.

Dicite, sacrorum praesides nemorum deae,
Tuque O noveni perbeata numinis

Reveal, you goddesses[1] who preside over the sacred groves, and you

1. The *goddesses* are the Muses, called daughters of Zeus and Memory by Hesiod (*Theog.* 53-4).

Memoria mater, quaeque in immenso procul
Antro recumbis otiosa Aeternitas,
Monumenta servans, et ratas leges Iovis,
Caelique fastos atque ephemeridas Deum,
Quis ille primus cuius ex imagine
Natura solers finxit humanum genus,
Aeternus, incorruptus, aequaevus polo,
Unusque et universus, exemplar Dei?
Haud ille, Palladis gemellus innubae,
Interna proles insidet menti Iovis.
Sed quamlibet natura sit communior,
Tamen seorsus extat ad morem unius,
Et, mira, certo stringitur spatio loci.
Seu sempiternus ille siderum comes
Caeli pererrat ordines decemplicis,
Citimumve terris incolit Lunae globum.
Sive inter animas corpus adituras sedens
Obliviosas torpet ad Lethes aquas;
Sive in remota forte terrarum plaga
Incedit ingens hominis archetypus gigas,
Et diis tremendus erigit celsum caput,
Atlante maior portitore siderum.
Non, cui profundum caecitas lumen dedit,
Dircaeus augur vidit hunc alto sinu;
Non hunc silenti nocte Pleiones nepos
Vatum sagaci praepes ostendit choro;
Non hunc sacerdos novit Assyrius, licet
Longos vetusti commemoret atavos Nini,
Priscumque Belon, inclytumque Osiridem.
Non ille trino gloriosus nomine
Ter magnus Hermes (ut sit arcani sciens)
Talem reliquit Isidis cultoribus.
At tu perenne ruris Academi decus

too, O happy mother of the ninefold deity, and you, Eternity, far
5 away where you lie at ease in some
vast cave,[4] guarding the records and
the immutable decrees of Jove and
the calendars of heaven and the
day-books of the gods, reveal who
was that first being—eternal, in-
10 corruptible, unique yet universal,
coeval with the heavens and made
in the image of God—in whose likeness skilful Nature has molded the
human race. Certainly he does not
15 lurk, a twin of the virgin Athene,
unborn in the brain of Jove.[11] But,
though all men have a share in his
nature, yet—strange as it may be—
he exists by himself as an individual
apart and is limited by his own
20 definite bounds in space. Or is he
a comrade of the eternal stars who
goes wandering through the ten-fold
spheres of heaven or inhabits the
neighbor of this world, the moon?
25 Or perhaps he sits torpidly beside
the stream of Lethe among the
spirits waiting to re-enter the
body.[20] Or perhaps the human
archetype is a huge giant, a tremendous figure in some remote
30 region of the earth who lifts his
head higher than the star-bearer,
Atlas,[24] to terrify the gods. Even
in the depths of the soul of the
Dircean[26] seer, to whom blindness
brought a profound illumination, no
35 vision of him appeared. Never in
the silent night was any revelation
of him made to the wise company of
the prophets by the swift grandchild[27] of Pleione. This being was
unknown to the Assyrian priest,[29]
though he was familiar with the
long line of the progenitors of old
Ninus and with primeval Belus[31]
and with renowned Osiris. Not
even thrice-great Hermes,[33] glorious
for his triple name, in spite of all
his esoteric knowledge, left any such
tradition to the worshippers of
Isis.[34]

But you, the eternal glory of the
Academy[35] that was set among the

4. Milton is thinking here of Boccaccio's description of *Eternity* in the *Genealogy of the Gods* I, ii,
as a man of vast age, coeval with Demogorgon and
Chaos, and living in a remote cave where the gods
themselves can never come. Boccaccio's source was
Claudian *On Stilicho's Consulship*, 424–40.

11. The myth of the birth of *Athene*, adult and
armed, from the brain of Zeus, is interpreted by
Conti (IV, v, p. 308) as an allegory of the mind
as the seat of memory and wisdom.

20. In a Pythagorean passage Virgil has Anchises
explain the doctrine of metempsychosis to Aeneas—
how after death all spirits drink the oblivion-giving
waters of Lethe and suffer various purifications before rebirth (*Aen.* VI, 713–51).

24. The giant *Atlas*, whom Hesiod describes
(*Theog.*, 507–20) as supporting the heavens, was
vaguely identified with Mt. Atlas in Morocco. Cf.
PL IV, 985–9.

26. Milton's most interesting allusion to the *Dircean seer Tiresias* is in *PL* III, 36.

27. The *grandchild of Pleione* is Hermes, whose
mother Maia was one of the Pleiades and the daughter of the sea-nymph Pleione.

29. The *priest* may be one of the sages to whom
Herodotus refers (I, 1) as authorizing his account
(I, 7) of the Assyrian king Ninus, the husband of
Semiramis.

31. The Assyrian Bel is identified with the Baal of
Nat, 197 and *PL* I, 422.

33. Cf. *Hermes* in *Il Pen,* 88, n.

34. Cf. *Isis* in *Nat,* 212, n.

35. The *glory of the Academy*—Plato, whose ex-
clusions of the poets from his ideal state (*Rep.* III,
395–8 and X, 595–607) Sir Philip Sidney refused
to take seriously because, "in the body of his work,
though the inside and strength were philosophy,

(Haec monstra si tu primus induxti scholis)
Iam iam poetas, urbis exules tuae,
Revocabis, ipse fabulator maximus,
Aut institutor ipse migrabis foras.   (1630)

the skinne as it were, and beautie depended most
of Poetrie" (*Elizabethan Critical Essays*, ed. Gregory Smith, I, 152).

fields—if you were the first who brought these absurdities into the schools—must surely now call home again those exiles from your city, the poets, for you are the supreme fabler yourself. Either that, or, even though you are the founder, you shall go into exile yourself.

ELEGIA SEPTIMA (ELEGY VII)

ANNO AETATIS UNDEVIGESIMO (AT AGE 19)

Though most authorities date this poem in 1628, when Milton was nineteen, the date assumed here is 1630—partly because (as Parker suggests in *A Tribute to George Coffin Taylor,* p. 119) *undevigesimo* may be a printer's mistake for *uno & vigesimo,* but mainly because its position after *El VI* in the editions of 1645 and 1673 indicates that Milton probably regarded it as last in order of composition.   The "retractation" that immediately follows it and is separated from the end of *El VII* only by a thin rule in those editions, may imply early composition, but it may also mean that all the elegies were written in a vein that Milton felt himself to be outgrowing under the influence of "the divine volumes of Plato." Cf. p. 694, col. 1, below.   *El VII* is a half-serious game with the traditional Ovidian theme of the poet conquered by Cupid.

Nondum blanda tuas leges, Amathusia, noram,
  Et Paphio vacuum pectus ab igne fuit.
Saepe cupidineas, puerilia tela, sagittas,
  Atque tuum sprevi maxime, numen, Amor.
"Tu puer imbelles," dixi, "transfige columbas,   5
  Conveniunt tenero mollia bella duci.
Aut de passeribus tumidos age, parve, triumphos;
  Haec sunt militiae digna trophaea tuae.
In genus humanum quid inania dirigis arma?
  Non valet in fortes ista pharetra viros."   10
Non tulit hoc Cyprius—neque enim Deus ullus ad iras
  Promptior—et duplici iam ferus igne calet.
Ver erat, et summae radians per culmina villae
  Attulerat primam lux tibi, Maie, diem:
At mihi adhuc refugam quaerebant lumina noctem,
  Nec matutinum sustinuere iubar.   16
Astat Amor lecto, pictis Amor impiger alis;
  Prodidit astantem mota pharetra Deum;
Prodidit et facies, et dulce minantis ocelli,
  Et quicquid puero dignum et Amore fuit.   20

O charming Amathusia,[1] I did not yet know your laws and my breast was free from Paphian fire. Often I poured scorn on the arrows of Cupid as childish weapons, and upon thy divinity particularly, O Love.

"Boy," I said, "go shoot the unwarlike doves; gentle combats suit a tender champion; or else, little one, go keep your boasted triumphs over the sparrows. Why do you aim your contemptible weapons at mankind?   Against strong men that quiver of yours has no power."

Cupid would not bear the insult—for no deity is swifter to anger—and the vengeful boy burned with double heat.

It was spring, and the light pouring over the roof-tops of the town had brought your first day, O May. But my eyes still craved the retreating night and could not endure the radiance of dawn.   Then Love stood beside my bed,[18] Love the indefatigable with his painted wings. The swaying quiver betrayed the god as he stood; his features and his sweetly menacing eyes betrayed him and so did all else beseeming the boy who is Love.   So the Phrygian youth appeared when he mixed the flowing cups for amorous

1. Venus' most famous temples were at Amathus and Paphos in Cyprus.
18. So, in the *Cheat of Cupid,* which develops an Ovidian fancy that goes back to Anacreon, Herrick dreamed of Cupid standing beside his bed:
    I saw he had a bow,
      And wings too, which did shiver;
    And looking down below,
      I spied he had a quiver.

Talis in aeterno iuvenis Sigeius Olympo
  Miscet amatori pocula plena Iovi;
Aut, qui formosas pellexit ad oscula nymphas,
  Thiodamantaeus Naiade raptus Hylas.
Addideratque iras, sed et has decuisse putares;   25
  Addideratque truces, nec sine felle minas.
Et "Miser exemplo sapuisses tutius," inquit;
  "Nunc mea quid possit dextera testis eris.
Inter et expertos vires numerabere nostras,
  Et faciam vero per tua damna fidem.   30
Ipse ego, si nescis, strato Pythone superbum
  Edomui Phoebum, cessit et ille mihi;
Et, quoties meminit Peneidos, ipse fatetur
  Certius et gravius tela nocere mea.
Me nequit adductum curvare peritius arcum,   35
  Qui post terga solet vincere, Parthus eques.
Cydoniusque mihi cedit venator, et ille
  Inscius uxori qui necis author erat.
Est etiam nobis ingens quoque victus Orion,
  Herculeaeque manus, Herculeusque comes.   40
Iupiter ipse licet sua fulmina torqueat in me,
  Haerebunt lateri spicula nostra Iovis.
Caetera quae dubitas melius mea tela docebunt,
  Et tua non leviter corda petenda mihi.
Nec te, stulte, tuae poterunt defendere Musae,   45
  Nec tibi Phoebaeus porriget anguis opem."
Dixit, et, aurato quatiens mucrone sagittam,
  Evolat in tepidos Cypridos ille sinus.
At mihi risuro tonuit ferus ore minaci,
  Et mihi de puero non metus ullus erat.   50
Et modo qua nostri spatiantur in urbe Quirites,
  Et modo villarum proxima rura placent.

Jove on everlasting Olympus;[21] and
so Hylas, the son of Theomadas,
who lured the lovely nymphs to his
kisses and was carried off by a
Naiad.[24] He was wrathful, but you
would have thought his wrath becoming to him; and he poured out
cruel threats, full of gall.

  "Wretch," he said, "you might
more safely have learned wisdom
from the experience of others; but
now you yourself shall be a witness
to the power of my right hand.
You shall be counted among those
who have felt my strength and by
your agony, truly, I shall establish
the truth. You may not be aware
that it was I—I my very self—
who tamed Phoebus in all his pride
after he had slain the Python,[31] and
that he yielded to me. As often as
he remembers Daphne, he confesses
that my arrows harm more certainly and more gravely than his
own. The Parthian horseman,[36]
who makes victory out of retreat,
cannot draw the taut bow more
skilfully than I. The Cydonian
hunter[37] yields to me and he
who was the unwitting author of
his own wife's death.[38] Gigantic
Orion[39] was a victim of mine and
so were strong-handed Hercules and
the companion of Hercules.[40] And
though Jove himself hurls his thunderbolts at me, my darts shall first
pierce the side of Jove.[41] Whatever
other doubts you have shall be resolved by my shafts and by your
own heart, at which I must aim no
gentle stroke. Fool! Neither will
your Muses be able to protect you
nor will the serpent of Apollo[46]
afford you any help."

  Thus he spoke, and, shaking the
arrow with the point of gold, he
flew away to the warm breast of
Cypris. But I was inclined to laugh
at the threats that the angry fellow
thundered at me and I had not the
least fear of the boy.

  Sometimes parts of the town
where our citizens walk abroad and

21. The "Phrygian Ganymede" for whose love
Jove took an eagle's form to steal him away—Ovid
says (Met. X, 155–61)—is still pouring nectar for
his captor in heaven.
    24. Cf. Hylas in PR II, 353, n.
    31. After shooting the monster Pytho, Apollo
boasted that he was a better archer than Cupid,
who—says Ovid (Met. I, 38–9)—then wounded him
with a dart that inspired love for Daphne, and
Daphne with a dart inspiring hate for him.
    36. The Parthian mounted archers were famous
for defeating Crassus' legions in 53 B.C.
    37. Virgil mentions the Cretan port of Cydon as
breeding archers as good as the Parthians (Aen. XII,
859).
    38. Ovid's story (Met. VII, 791–862) of the hun-
ter Cephalus' accidental slaying of his wife Procris
was famous.
    39. Conti (VIII, xii, pp. 881–6) involves Aurora,
Aerope, and Diana herself with the giant hunter
Orion, from whose pursuit the Pleiades were saved
only when Jove raised them to heaven.
    40. Conti lists over sixty marriages and amorous
involvements of Hercules (VII, i; pp. 681 and 697–
8). The companion may be Jason, who divorced
Medea to marry Creusa, for they went together on
the expedition to Argos.

41. In Alciati's Emblemata (Padua, 1661; No.
108) Cupid is pictured catching the lightning above
a translation of a Greek epigram declaring his power
to break Jove's thunderbolts. Alciati lists many of
Jove's amorous adventures.
    46. Apollo's serpent was the emblem of the heal-
ing art that he bequeathed to his son Aesculapius.
(Cf. Met. XV, 626–744.)

Turba frequens, facieque simillima turba dearum,
   Splendida per medias itque reditque vias.
Auctaque luce dies gemino fulgore coruscat.   55
   Fallor? an et radios hinc quoque Phoebus habet?
Haec ego non fugi spectacula grata severus,
   Impetus et quo me fert iuvenilis agor.
Lumina luminibus male providus obvia misi,
   Neve oculos potui continuisse meos.   60
Unam forte aliis supereminuisse notabam;
   Principium nostri lux erat illa mali.
Sic Venus optaret mortalibus ipsa videri,
   Sic regina Deum conspicienda fuit.
Hanc memor obiecit nobis malus ille Cupido,   65
   Solus et hos nobis texuit ante dolos.
Nec procul ipse vafer latuit, multaeque sagittae,
   Et facis a tergo grande pependit onus.
Nec mora; nunc ciliis haesit, nunc virginis ori,
   Insilit hinc labiis, insidet inde genis;   70
Et quascunque agilis partes iaculator oberrat,
   Hei mihi! mille locis pectus inerme ferit.
Protinus insoliti subierunt corda furores;
   Uror amans intus, flammaque totus eram.
Interea misero quae iam mihi sola placebat   75
   Ablata est, oculis non reditura meis.
Ast ego progredior tacite querebundus, et excors,
   Et dubius volui saepe referre pedem.
Findor; et haec remanet, sequitur pars altera votum,
   Raptaque tam subito gaudia flere iuvat.   80
Sic dolet amissum proles Iunonia caelum,
   Inter Lemniacos praecipitata focos.
Talis et abreptum solem respexit ad Orcum
   Vectus ab attonitis Amphiaraus equis.
Quid faciam infelix, et luctu victus? Amores   85
   Nec licet inceptos ponere, neve sequi.
O utinam spectare semel mihi detur amatos
   Vultus, et coram tristia verba loqui!

sometimes the suburban fields offer me their pleasures. Groups of radiant girls with divinely lovely faces come and go along the walks. When they add their glory, the day shines with double splendor. Am I deceived, or is it from them also that Phoebus has his rays? I did not turn puritanically away from the pleasant sights, but was carried where the impulse of youth led me. Heedlessly I sent my glances to encounter theirs and lost all control of my eyes. Then, by chance, I caught sight of one who was supreme above all the rest; her radiance was the beginning of my disaster. In such a guise Venus herself might choose to appear to mortals. Glorious to look upon, like her, must the queen of the gods have been.[64] She was thrown in my way by the grudge-harboring rascal, Cupid; he alone has woven these snares in my path. Not far away the rogue was hiding with his store of arrows and his mighty torch burdening his back. Without delay he fixed himself now on the maiden's eyelids, now on her mouth; then sped away between her lips or perched on her cheek; and wherever the agile dart-thrower strayed—alas for me—he struck my defenseless breast in a thousand places. In an instant unfamiliar passions assailed my heart. Inwardly I was consumed by love and was all on fire.

While I suffered, she who alone could give me happiness was borne away, never to return to my eyes again. Distressed and dispirited, I went on my way, often questioning whether I should not turn my steps backward. I am rent asunder; one part of me stays here, but the other follows after my desire. There was pleasure in weeping for delights so suddenly snatched away. Such was the grief of Hephaestus[81] for his lost heaven when he was hurled down among the hearths of Lemnos; such was the grief of Amphiaraus[84] when he looked his last upon the sun as he was swept away to Hades by his thunder-driven horses. Unhappy and grief-stricken as I was, what should I do? I can neither dismiss nor pursue my incipient love. O, would that it

---

64. The *queen of the gods:* Hera (Juno). Cf. *Arc,* 23.

81. Cf. *Hephaestus* (Vulcan or Mulciber) in *Naturam,* 23 and *PL* I, 740–5.

84. Like Dante (*Inf.* XX, 29–36), Milton was struck by Statius' references (*Thebaid* VII, 818–23 and VIII, 8–12) to the punishment of death by lightning that Jove inflicted on *Amphiaraus* for joining the expedition against Thebes though, as a prophet, he knew that it was impious.

Forsitan et duro non est adamante creata,
  Forte nec ad nostras surdeat illa preces.   90
Crede mihi, nullus sic infeliciter arsit;
  Ponar in exemplo primus et unus ego.
Parce, precor, teneri cum sis Deus ales amoris;
  Pugnent officio nec tua facta tuo.
Iam tuus O certe est mihi formidabilis arcus,   95
  Nate dea, iaculis nec minus igne potens;
Et tua fumabunt nostris altaria donis,
  Solus et in superis tu mihi summus eris.
Deme meos tandem, verum nec deme, furores;
  Nescio cur, miser est suaviter omnis amans.   100
Tu modo da facilis, posthaec mea siqua futura est,
  Cuspis amaturos figat ut una duos.

101. The prayer echoes an epigram of Rufinus in the *Palatine Anthology* V, 97. For the *monuments to my wantonness* see the headnote.

might be given me once to look into those beloved features and to tell her the story of my pain face to face. Perhaps she is not made of hard adamant; perhaps she would not be deaf to my prayers. Believe me! No one ever suffered such misery in the fire of love. I may be rated the first and unique example. Spare me, I pray, since you are the winged god of tender love. Do not let your deeds conflict with your duty. Now, O child of the goddess, with your darts no less powerful than fire, your bow is beyond all doubt dreadful to me. Your altars shall smoke with my sacrifices, and, as far as I am concerned, you shall be sole and supreme among the gods. Take away madness, then! But rather, do not take it away. I cannot tell why, but every lover's misery is sweet. Only be gracious enough to grant, if any maiden is ever to be mine, that a single dart shall transfix the destined lovers.[101]

Haec ego mente olim laeva, studioque supino,
  Nequitiae posui vana trophaea meae.
Scilicet abreptum sic me malus impulit error,
  Indocilisque aetas prava magistra fuit;
Donec Socraticos umbrosa Academia rivos   5
  Praebuit, admissum dedocuitque iugum.
Protinus, extinctis ex illo tempore flammis,
  Cincta rigent multo pectora nostra gelu;
Unde suis frigus metuit puer ipse Sagittis,
  Et Diomedeam vim timet ipsa Venus.   (1630)   10

These are the monuments to my wantonness that with a perverse spirit and a trifling purpose I once erected. Obviously, mischievous error led me astray and my undisciplined youth was a vicious teacher until the shady Academy offered its Socratic streams and taught me how to escape from the yoke to which I had submitted. From that hour those flames were extinct and thenceforward my breast has been rigid under a thick case of ice, of which the boy himself fears the frost for his arrows, and Venus herself is afraid of my Diomedean strength.

THE PASSION

This failure to capture an inspiration equal to that of the *Nativity Ode* seems to have been written at Easter in 1630.

I

    Erewhile of Music and Ethereal mirth,
    Wherewith the stage of Air and Earth did ring,
    And joyous news of heav'nly Infant's birth,
    My muse with Angels did divide to sing

1. *Ethereal:* heavenly. Cf. the ethereal people of PL X, 27.

4. *divide.* share in a song of two or more parts.

But headlong joy is ever on the wing,   5
  In Wintry solstice like the short'n'd light
Soon swallow'd up in dark and long outliving night.

II

For now to sorrow must I tune my song,
And set my Harp to notes of saddest woe,
Which on our dearest Lord did seize ere long,   10
Dangers, and snares, and wrongs, and worse than so,
Which he for us did freely undergo:
  Most perfect *Hero,* tried in heaviest plight
Of labors huge and hard, too hard for human wight.

III

He sovereign Priest, stooping his regal head   15
That dropt with odorous oil down his fair eyes,
Poor fleshly Tabernacle entered,
His starry front low-rooft beneath the skies;
O what a Mask was there, what a disguise!
  Yet more; the stroke of death he must abide,   20
Then lies him meekly down fast by his Brethren's side.

IV

These latter scenes confine my roving verse,
To this Horizon is my *Phoebus* bound;
His Godlike acts and his temptations fierce,
And former sufferings other-where are found;   25
Loud o'er the rest *Cremona's* Trump doth sound;
  Me softer airs befit, and softer strings
Of Lute, or Viol still, more apt for mournful things.

V

Befriend me Night, best Patroness of grief,
Over the Pole thy thickest mantle throw,   30
And work my flatter'd fancy to belief,
That Heav'n and Earth are color'd with my woe;
My sorrows are too dark for day to know:
  The leaves should all be black whereon I write,
And letters where my tears have washt, a wannish white.   35

VI

See, see the Chariot and those rushing wheels
That whirl'd the Prophet up at *Chebar* flood;
My spirit some transporting *Cherub* feels,
To bear me where the Towers of *Salem* stood,
Once glorious Towers, now sunk in guiltless blood;   40

13. Christ's sufferings—greater than the labors of Hercules—make him more heroic than any hero of mythology. Cf. paragraph 22, page 479 below.

14. *wight:* creature, being.

15. Christ sets aside his divinity "to be made like unto his brethren, that he might be a merciful and faithful High Priest . . ." (Heb. ii, 17). At his consecration the High Priest was anointed with oil.

22. In 1673 Milton changed *latter* to *latest.*

23. As patron of poetry, Phoebus Apollo is mentioned as the Muse has been mentioned in l. 4.

26. *Cremona's Trump:* the *Christias* or epic on the life of Christ by Marco Girolamo Vida of Cremona.

28. *still:* gentle. Cf. *IlPen,* 127.

30. Cf. the classical use of *Pole* for the sky in *PL* IV, 724 and *Comus,* 99.

37. Ezekiel's vision of the creatures which appeared "as it were a wheel in the middle of a wheel" (Ezek. i, 16) was "by the river of Chebar" (Ezek. i, 1), a name which may have meant the Euphrates and certainly stood for some Babylonian stream.

39. *Salem:* Jerusalem, which represents the seat of sacred poetry.

There doth my soul in holy vision sit,
In pensive trance, and anguish, and ecstatic fit.

VII

Mine eye hath found that sad Sepulchral rock
That was the Casket of Heav'n's richest store,
And here though grief my feeble hands up-lock,   45
Yet on the soft'ned Quarry would I score
My plaining verse as lively as before;
  For sure so well instructed are my tears,
  That they would fitly fall in order'd Characters.

VIII

Or should I thence hurried on viewless wing,   50
Take up a weeping on the Mountains wild,
The gentle neighborhood of grove and spring
Would soon unbosom all thir Echoes mild,
And I (for grief is easily beguil'd)
  Might think th'infection of my sorrows loud   55
  Had got a race of mourners on some pregnant cloud.

*This Subject the Author finding to be above the years he had, when he
wrote it, and nothing satisfied with what was begun, left it unfinisht.*
(March, 1630)

43. The *rock* is the new tomb where Joseph of
Arimethea laid the body of Jesus.
  50. *viewless:* invisible. Cf. *Comus,* 92.
  51. The extravagance is an echo of Jeremiah ix,

10: "For the mountains will I take up a weeping
and a wailing, and for the habitations of the wilderness a lamentation."

ON SHAKESPEARE, 1630

In the Second Folio of Shakespeare's plays (1632) these lines appeared under the title *An
Epitaph on the Admirable Dramatic Poet W. Shakespear.* Milton's questionable date,
1630, suggests that the poem was written some time before its publication, possibly with the
expectation that the Stratford monument instead of the Droeshout portrait would be represented as the frontispiece of the Folio.

What needs my *Shakespeare* for his honor'd Bones
The labor of an age in piled Stones,
Or that his hallow'd relics should be hid
Under a Star-ypointing *Pyramid?*
Dear son of memory, great heir of Fame,   5
What need'st thou such weak witness of thy name?
Thou in our wonder and astonishment
Hast built thyself a livelong Monument.
For whilst to th'shame of slow-endeavoring art,
Thy easy numbers flow, and that each heart   10
Hath from the leaves of thy unvalu'd Book

4. Cf. the *y-* prefix in *Nat,* 155 and *L'All,* 12.
  5. As the *son of memory* Shakespeare is a brother
of the Muses, whom Hesiod describes as the daughters of Zeus by Mnymosyne (Memory) (*Theog.,*
53–9).
  8. The thought has countless parallels stretching
from Horace's boast (*Odes* II, xx) that his poetry
would be his world-wide tomb to an epitaph on
Sir Edward Stanley which has been attributed by

Sir Edmund Chambers to Shakespeare himself:
Not monumentall stones preserves our Fame;
Nor sky-aspiring Piramides our name;
The memory of him for whom this standes
Shall outlive marble and defacers hands
  When al to times consumption shall be given,
  Standly for whom this stands shall stand in
    Heaven.
  11. *unvalu'd:* invaluable, precious.

Those Delphic lines with deep impression took,
Then thou our fancy of itself bereaving,
Dost make us Marble with too much conceiving;
And so Sepulcher'd in such pomp dost lie,   15
That Kings for such a Tomb would wish to die.   (1630)

12. *Delphic* means "inspired by the god of Del-   14. *Dost make us Marble:* cf. *IlPen*, 42, n.
phi, Apollo," and therefore genuinely poetical.   — *says nothing*

ON THE UNIVERSITY CARRIER

Who sicken'd in the time of his vacancy, being forbid to go to *London*, by reason of the Plague

Thomas Hobson drove a weekly coach between Cambridge and London from 1564 until shortly before his death on January 1, 1631.   Milton's witty poems on his death were two among many by various students, a score of which are collected by G. B. Evans in *MLQ*, IV (1943), 281–90; and IX (1948), 10 and 184.   Cf. Willa Evans on "Hobson in Comic Song" in *PQ*, XXVI (1947), 321–7.   W. R. Parker argues for Milton's authorship of a third Hobson poem in *MLR*, XXXI (1936), 395–402.

Here lies old *Hobson,* Death hath broke his girt,
And here, alas, hath laid him in the dirt,
Or else the ways being foul, twenty to one,
He's here stuck in a slough, and overthrown.
'Twas such a shifter, that if truth were known,   5
Death was half glad when he had got him down;
For he had any time this ten years full,
Dodg'd with him, betwixt *Cambridge* and the Bull.
And surely, Death could never have prevail'd,
Had not his weekly course of carriage fail'd;   10
But lately finding him so long at home,
And thinking now his journey's end was come,
And that he had ta'en up his latest Inn,
In the kind office of a Chamberlain
Show'd him his room where he must lodge that night,   15
Pull'd off his Boots, and took away the light:
If any ask for him, it shall be said,
    "*Hobson* has supt, and 's newly gone to bed."   (1631)

5. *shifter:* dodger, evader.   14. *Chamberlain:* a man-servant about an inn.
13. Taken a room in the last inn that he will
ever visit.

ANOTHER ON THE SAME

Here lieth one who did most truly prove
That he could never die while he could move,
So hung his destiny never to rot
While he might still jog on and keep his trot,
Made of sphere-metal, never to decay   5
Until his revolution was at stay.

5. *sphere-metal:* the *Ethereal Mold* of which God   heavenly substance is indestructible (*De Coelo* I,
frames the celestial bodies (*PL* VII, 353–6). The   iii).
thought rests on the Aristotelian doctrine that the

Time numbers motion, yet (without a crime
'Gainst old truth) motion number'd out his time;
And like an Engine mov'd with wheel and weight,
His principles being ceast, he ended straight.   10
Rest that gives all men life, gave him his death,
And too much breathing put him out of breath;
Nor were it contradiction to affirm
Too long vacation hast'ned on his term.
Merely to drive the time away he sick'n'd,   15
Fainted, and died, nor would with Ale be quick'n'd;
    "Nay," quoth he, on his swooning bed outstretch'd,
    "If I may not carry, sure I'll ne'er be fetch'd,
But vow, though the cross Doctors all stood hearers,
For one Carrier put down to make six bearers."   20
Ease was his chief disease, and to judge right,
He died for heaviness that his Cart went light.
His leisure told him that his time was come,
And lack of load made his life burdensome,
That even to his last breath (there be that say't)   25
As he were prest to death, he cry'd, "more weight";
But had his doings lasted as they were,
He had been an immortal Carrier.
Obedient to the Moon he spent his date
In course reciprocal, and had his fate   30
Linkt to the mutual flowing of the Seas,
Yet (strange to think) his wain was his increase:
His Letters are deliver'd all and gone,
Only remains this superscription.   (1631)

7. According to Platonic doctrine (*Tim.*, 37–38, 47) motion measures time. So Aristotle affirmed (*De Coelo* I, ix), and it became an axiom of the schools. "*Time* is made by *Motion*, all confesse," says John Davies of Hereford in *Mirum in Modum* (London, 1602; G4r).

10. *principles* signified either the power moving a machine or the faculties of the human body.

14. The play is on the vacations and college terms.

22. *heaviness*: "the dumpish heavinesse, that proceedeth of Melancholy" as Barnabe Googe (quoted by *O.E.D.*) calls it.

26. The victims of the punishment by pressing to death often asked for more weight to hasten the inevitable.

32. *wain*: wagon, puns with "wane"—diminishing (as of the moon).

AN EPITAPH ON THE MARCHIONESS OF WINCHESTER

As lines 55–60 imply, this poem was one of several "flowers" which Cambridge students sent to strew the laureate hearse of Jane Paulet, who died on April 15, 1631. The poem was published by Milton in 1645, but an early MS version contains a substantial variant passage which is published by Miss Darbishire (II, 312). The simplicity of the verse shows the influence of Ben Jonson. Its intimate resemblances to the varying trochaic and iambic rhythms of *L'All* and *IlPen* are studied by E. S. Sprott in *Milton's Art of Prosody* (Oxford, 1953), pp. 16–20, and by Ants Oras in *N&Q*, CXCVIII (1953), 332–3. Interesting proof of Milton's budding interest in Dante is spotted by J. H. Hanford in lines 61–70 in the thought of the two mothers who died in childbed, Rachel and the Marchioness, as together in the third rank of the Celestial Rose, where Dante placed the former with Beatrice in the *Paradiso* (XXXII, 7–10).

This rich Marble doth inter
The honor'd Wife of *Winchester*,
A Viscount's daughter, an Earl's heir,

Besides what her virtues fair
Added to her noble birth,
More than she could own from Earth.   5
Summers three times eight save one
She had told; alas too soon,
After so short time of breath,
To house with darkness, and with death.   10
Yet had the number of her days
Been as complete as was her praise,
Nature and fate had had no strife
In giving limit to her life.
Her high birth, and her graces sweet,   15
Quickly found a lover meet;
The Virgin choir for her request
The God that sits at marriage feast;
He at their invoking came
But with a scarce-well-lighted flame;   20
And in his Garland as he stood,
Ye might discern a Cypress bud.
Once had the early Matrons run
To greet her of a lovely son,
And now with second hope she goes,   25
And calls *Lucina* to her throes;
But whether by mischance or blame
Atropos for *Lucina* came,
And with remorseless cruelty,
Spoil'd at once both fruit and tree: 30
The hapless Babe before his birth
Had burial, yet not laid in earth,
And the languisht Mother's Womb
Was not long a living Tomb.
So have I seen some tender slip   35
Sav'd with care from Winter's nip,
The pride of her carnation train,
Pluck't up by some unheedy swain,
Who only thought to crop the flow'r
New shot up from vernal show'r;   40
But the fair blossom hangs the head
Sideways as on a dying bed,
And those Pearls of dew she wears,
Prove to be presaging tears
Which the sad morn had let fall   45
On her hast'ning funeral.
Gentle Lady, may thy grave
Peace and quiet ever have:
After this thy travail sore
Sweet rest seize thee evermore,   50
That to give the world increase,

18. *The God:* Hymen. Perhaps in a mask at the lady's wedding he had appeared in his saffron robe as Ovid describes him (*Met.* X, 1) at the marriage of Orpheus and Eurydice, where he failed to bring a lucky omen and his torch sputtered out in spite of his best efforts to keep it ablaze. Cf. *L'All*, 125.

24. The son was Charles, afterward first Duke of Bolton.

26. *Lucina:* the Roman goddess of childbirth.

28. *Atropos*, the "inflexible," was the Fate who cut the thread of human lives. Cf. *Arc*, 63–69 and *Lyc*, 75–76.

46. *funeral:* death.

50. *seize:* possess.

Short'ned hast thy own life's lease;
Here, besides the sorrowing
That thy noble House doth bring,
Here be tears of perfect moan   55
Wept for thee in *Helicon,*
And some Flowers and some Bays
For thy Hearse to strew the ways,
Sent thee from the banks of *Came,*
Devoted to thy virtuous name;   60
Whilst thou, bright Saint, high sitt'st in glory,
Next her much like to thee in story,
That fair *Syrian* Shepherdess,
Who after years of barrenness
The highly favor'd *Joseph* bore   65
To him that serv'd for her before,
And at her next birth, much like thee,
Through pangs fled to felicity,
Far within the bosom bright
Of blazing Majesty and Light;   70
There with thee, new welcome Saint,
Like fortunes may her soul acquaint,
With thee there clad in radiant sheen,
No Marchioness, but now a Queen.   (1631)

56. *Helicon* is the Boeotian mountain "where the Muses haunt" (*PL* III, 27).
59. *Came:* the river Cam, standing for Cambridge. Cf. *Lyc,* 103.

63. The *Syrian Shepherdess* is Rachel, who kept her father's sheep (Gen. xxix, 9) and died in giving birth to Benjamin (Gen. xxxv, 18). Cf. the headnote.

L'ALLEGRO AND IL PENSEROSO

The companion poems still resist criticism's best efforts to appraise their wealth. It is the pride of Kester Svendsen's study of their complementary sound imagery (*Exp.,* VIII, 1950, No. 49) merely to have opened a new vein in the mine. The same can be said of Brooks' and Hardy's treatment of light or "half-light in both poems as a sort of symbol of the aesthetic distance which the cheerful man, no less than the pensive man, constantly maintains" (*Poems,* p. 139). The octosyllabic couplets keep their simplicity even after Ants Oras has shown, in *N&Q,* CXCVIII (1953), 332–3, how symmetrically their metrical parallelism extends to their diminishingly trochaic lines. Structural analysis will never exhaust the correspondences between l'Allegro's idealized day in the country and night in the balls and theaters of "tower'd cities" as they are contrasted with Il Penseroso's night of meditative walking in the woods, followed by browsing among beloved books in a "high lonely Tower," and then by a day in "the studious Cloister's pale." R. M. Lumiansky's verbal analysis, in *MLN,* LV (1940), 591–4, ended the delusion that the language of the companion poems is Latinate or anything other than simple Anglo-Saxon English, but left their evocative power unexplained. Their final secret escapes all the criticism which J. B. Leishman surveys in *Essays and Studies,* n. s. IV (1951), 1–36.

Both the poems have long roots. They draw nourishment from verse like the *Abstract of Melancholy* prefixed to Burton's *Anatomy of Melancholy:*

Methinks I hear, methinks I see,
Sweet musick, wondrous melody,
Towns, Palaces, and Cities fine;
Here now, then there; the world is mine.
Rare beauties, gallant ladies shine.

In a comparison of l'Allegro's entertainments with Burton's theory of pleasure as a cure for the dangerous melancholy which ends in insanity, W. J. Grace has shown in *SP*, LII (1955), 579–83 that Milton understood what we may call the psychiatry of his time as well as he did the contemplative ideal of cultivation of the sciences that lead both to the mastery of nature and to the vision of God.   The backgrounds of that intellectual melancholy are traced by Lawrence Babb (*SP*, XXXVII, 1940, 257–73) and Erwin Panofsky (*Albrecht Dürer*, Princeton, 1948, I, 156–71).   But the roots of the poems extend as far as the drama and probably as far as the song of the Passionate Mad Man in John Fletcher's *Nice Valour*:

> Hence all you vain delights,
>   As short as are the nights,
>   Wherein you spend your folly.
> There's nought in this life sweet,
>   If men were wise to see't,
>   But only melancholy,
>   O, sweetest melancholy.

L'Allegro and *Il Penseroso* seem to have been written late in Milton's years at Cambridge, before he went to Horton.   Perhaps, as E. M. W. Tillyard suggests (*M.S.*, pp. 4–21), their exorcisms of Melancholy and Mirth are parodies of mythological descriptions like that in *In quintum Novembris*, 139–56.   If they were parodies of hackneyed themes in undergraduate courses in mythology, they were none the less intended to strike exactly the right introductory note for the sympathetically contrasted moods of the two poems.   Their balanced themes surely owe something to the exercises of students on stock themes like the respective merits of Day and Night, or of Learning and Ignorance, as we find them illustrated by Milton's own *Prolusions* I and VII.

Blake's illustrations of the companion poems are splendidly reproduced in the Nonesuch edition of *Milton's English Poems*, in the Limited Editions Club volume of 1954, and in Adrian Van Sinderin's *Blake, the Mystic Genius* (Syracuse, 1949).   Bernard Meinsky's illustrations in *L'Allegro and Il Penseroso* (London, 1947) excel Blake's in emphasis on the erotic potential in *L'Allegro*, but do not try to compete with him in interpretation of the "Platonic" element in *Il Penseroso*, which D. C. Allen has shown (*Vision*, pp. 12–23) to be the dominant theme of the second poem.

L'ALLEGRO

> Hence loathed Melancholy
>   Of *Cerberus* and blackest midnight born,
> In *Stygian* Cave forlorn
> 'Mongst horrid shapes, and shrieks, and sights unholy,
>   Find out some uncouth cell,   5
>   Where brooding darkness spreads his jealous wings,
>   And the night-Raven sings;
>   There under *Ebon* shades, and low-brow'd Rocks,
>   As ragged as thy Locks,
>   In dark *Cimmerian* desert ever dwell.   10
> But come thou Goddess fair and free,
>   In Heav'n yclep'd *Euphrosyne*,

[margin annotation:] = slow, not allegro but Adante

5. *uncouth*: unknown, strange and dreadful.

10. So Ovid describes (*Met.* XI, 592–6) the cave of the slumber-god Morpheus in the cloudy land of the Cimmerians on a far ocean shore.   "Darker than Cimmeria" was proverbial.

12. *yclep'd*: called. Cf. *Nat*, 155, n. above. Milton first follows the tradition that makes *Venus*

and *Bacchus* the parents of *Euphrosyne* (Mirth) and her *sister Graces* Aglaia and Thalia; then he invents his own myth about *Zephyr* and *Aurora*, as Ben Jonson invented a myth of Zephyr's courtship of Spring, mother of the flowers, in his mask of *Chloridia*.

And by men, heart-easing Mirth,

3/4 time

Whom lovely *Venus* at a birth
With two sister Graces more   15
To Ivy-crowned *Bacchus* bore;
Or whether (as some Sager sing)
The frolic Wind that breathes the Spring,
Zephyr with *Aurora* playing,
As he met her once a-Maying,   20
There on Beds of Violets blue,
And fresh-blown Roses washt in dew,
Fill'd her with thee a daughter fair,
So buxom, blithe, and debonair.
Haste thee nymph, and bring with thee   25
Jest and youthful Jollity,
Quips and Cranks, and wanton Wiles,
Nods, and Becks, and Wreathed Smiles,
Such as hang on *Hebe's* cheek,
And love to live in dimple sleek;   30
Sport that wrinkled Care derides,
And Laughter holding both his sides.
Come, and trip it as ye go
On the light fantastic toe,
And in thy right hand lead with thee,   35
The Mountain Nymph, sweet Liberty;

Mirth combined with Liberty

And if I give thee honor due,
Mirth, admit me of thy crew
To live with her, and live with thee,
In unreproved pleasures free;   40
To hear the Lark begin his flight,
And singing startle the dull night,
From his watch-tow'r in the skies,
Till the dappled dawn doth rise;
Then to come in spite of sorrow,   45
And at my window bid good-morrow,
Through the Sweet-Briar, or the Vine,
Or the twisted Eglantine;
While the Cock with lively din,
Scatters the rear of darkness thin,   50
And to the stack, or the Barn door,
Stoutly struts his Dames before;
Oft list'ning how the Hounds and horn
Cheerly rouse the slumb'ring morn,
From the side of some Hoar Hill,   55
Through the high wood echoing shrill;
Some time walking not unseen
By Hedgerow Elms, on Hillocks green,

18. *breathes:* exhales. Cf. the North Wind *breathing* winter in *Naturam*, 55.

24. *buxom:* compliant and friendly. *debonair:* graceful, gentle.

27. *Quips and Cranks:* smart jests and witticisms.

29. Cf. *Hebe*, the Goddess of Youth, pouring Jove's nectar in *Vac*, 38.

40. *unreprov'd:* unreprovable. Cf. *uninchanted* in *Comus*, 395.

55. The *O.E.D.* defines *Hoar* as here meaning "grey from absence of foliage," but cf. Shakespeare's mention of the willow

That shows his hoar leaves in the glassy stream
(*Hamlet* IV, vii, 168)

The season in *L'All* ranges from spring to harvest; perhaps early or late enough for a hoarfrost to be meant.

57. *not unseen:* not trying to keep out of sight. Contrast *IlPen*, 65.

Right against the Eastern gate,
Where the great Sun begins his state,   60
Rob'd in flames, and Amber light,
The clouds in thousand Liveries dight;
While the Plowman near at hand,
Whistles o'er the Furrow'd Land,
And the Milkmaid singeth blithe,   65
And the Mower whets his scythe,
And every Shepherd tells his tale
Under the Hawthorn in the dale.
Straight mine eye hath caught new pleasures
Whilst the Landscape round it measures,   70
Russet Lawns and Fallows Gray,
Where the nibbling flocks do stray;
Mountains on whose barren breast
The laboring clouds do often rest;
Meadows trim with Daisies pied,   75
Shallow Brooks, and Rivers wide.
Towers and Battlements it sees
Bosom'd high in tufted Trees,
Where perhaps some beauty lies,
The Cynosure of neighboring eyes.   80
Hard by, a Cottage chimney smokes,
From betwixt two aged Oaks,
Where *Corydon* and *Thyrsis* met,
Are at their savory dinner set
Of Herbs, and other Country Messes,   85
Which the neat-handed *Phillis* dresses;
And then in haste her Bow'r she leaves,
With *Thestylis* to bind the Sheaves;
Or if the earlier season lead
To the tann'd Haycock in the Mead.   90
Sometimes with secure delight
The upland Hamlets will invite,
When the merry Bells ring round,
And the jocund rebecs sound
To many a youth, and many a maid,   95
Dancing in the Checker'd shade;
And young and old come forth to play
On a Sunshine Holiday,
Till the livelong daylight fail;
Then to the Spicy Nut-brown Ale,   100
With stories told of many a feat,
How *Faery Mab* the junkets eat;
She was pincht and pull'd, she said,

60. *state:* stately march (like a king's in a car of state). Cf. *PL* II, 1 and VI, 12–15.

62. *Liveries:* gorgeous costumes. Cf. *Comus,* 455. *dight:* clad.

67. The *O.E.D.* interprets *tells his tale* as "tells his story" (i.e., of love), but the interpretation "counts his tale" or tally of sheep is tempting beside Dryden's line:
Once she takes the tale of all the lambs.
    (Translations of Virgil's *Pastorals* III, 51)

75. *pied:* variegated, spotted. Cf. Shakespeare's song:

When daisies pied and violets blue . . .
Do paint the meadows with delight.
    (*Love's Labors Lost* V, ii, 882–5)

80. Cf. *Cynosure* in *Comus,* 342, n.

83. Beginning with Theocritus' *Idyls,* the rustic names come from countless classical and Renaissance pastoral poems.

87. *Bow'r* probably keeps its early meaning of "cottage."

91. *secure:* free from care. Cf. *PL* IV, 791 and VI, 672.

94. *rebecs:* primitive fiddles with three strings.

And he, by Friar's Lantern led,
Tells how the drudging *Goblin* sweat   105
To earn his Cream-bowl duly set,
When in one night, ere glimpse of morn,
His shadowy Flail hath thresh'd the Corn
That ten day-laborers could not end;
Then lies him down the Lubber Fiend,   110
And, stretch'd out all the Chimney's length,
Basks at the fire his hairy strength;
And Crop-full out of doors he flings,
Ere the first Cock his Matin rings.
Thus done the Tales, to bed they creep,   115
By whispering Winds soon lull'd asleep.
Tow'red Cities please us then,
And the busy hum of men,
Where throngs of Knights and Barons bold,
In weeds of Peace high triumphs hold,   — no warring, must have   120
With store of Ladies, whose bright eyes   peace.
Rain influence, and judge the prize
Of Wit, or Arms, while both contend
To win her Grace, whom all commend.
There let *Hymen* oft appear   ↓ why does marriage   125
In Saffron robe, with Taper clear,   come into the city.
And pomp, and feast, and revelry,
With mask, and antique Pageantry—
Such sights as youthful Poets dream
On Summer eves by haunted stream.   130
Then to the well-trod stage anon,
If *Jonson's* learned Sock be on,
Or sweetest *Shakespeare,* fancy's child,
Warble his native Wood-notes wild.
And ever against eating Cares,   135
Lap me in soft *Lydian* Airs,
Married to immortal verse,
Such as the meeting soul may pierce
In notes, with many a winding bout
Of linked sweetness long drawn out,   140
With wanton heed, and giddy cunning,
The melting voice through mazes running;
Untwisting all the chains that tie
The hidden soul of harmony;

104. *Friar's Lantern:* the will-o'-the-wisp.

105–110. So in *A Midsummer Night's Dream* II, i, 16–41 Puck answers to the name of *Lob of spirits* and *Hobgoblin* and is a willing household drudge for
    Those that Hobgoblin call you and sweet Puck.

111. *Chimney* keeps its primitive meaning of "fireplace."

120. *triumphs:* festivals. Cf. Bacon's essay *Of Masques and Triumphs.*

122. The ladies' eyes are metaphorical stars shedding *"influence"* like the real stars in *Nat,* 71. Cf. *Sonn* VI, 7–8.

125. So the god of marriage appears in Jonson's *Masque of Hymen* "in a saffron-coloured robe, . . . in his right hand a torch of pine-tree." Cf. *Winchester,* 18.

132. Comedy resembles the figure on the title page of Jonson's *Workes* (1616), which fits Cesare Ripa's traditional picture in his *Iconographia* of "a lady of mature age and noble aspect, with a flute and wearing socks" (i.e., slippers, in contrast to Tragedy's buskins in *IlPen,* 102).

133. *fancy:* the spontaneously creative gift which Milton attributed to Shakespeare in supreme degree (in *Shak,* 13).

134–144. Ignoring the traditional prejudice against Lydian music as morally enervating— in contrast with both the chaste Dorian and the spiritually stimulating Ionian modes—Milton remembered Cassiodorus' account of Lydian music as relaxing and delightful, "being invented against excessive cares and worries." The point is made by James Hutton in *EM* 2 (1951), 46.

That *Orpheus'* self may heave his head   145
From golden slumber on a bed
Of heapt *Elysian* flow'rs, and hear
Such strains as would have won the ear
Of *Pluto,* to have quite set free
His half-regain'd *Eurydice.*   150
These delights if thou canst give,
Mirth, with thee I mean to live.   (1631?)

145. On their wedding day *Orpheus* lost his wife *Eurydice,* but when he followed her to Hades, his music won the consent of Proserpina, Pluto's queen, that he should take back his wife. But the consent—Ovid says (*Met.* X, 50–63)—was given on the impossible condition that he should not once look back at her as he led her up into the sunlight.

IL PENSEROSO

Hence vain deluding joys,
    The brood of folly without father bred,
How little you bested,
    Or fill the fixed mind with all your toys;
Dwell in some idle brain,   5
    And fancies fond with gaudy shapes possess,
As thick and numberless
    As the gay motes that people the Sunbeams,
Or likest hovering dreams,
    The fickle Pensioners of *Morpheus'* train.   10
But hail thou Goddess, sage and holy,
Hail divinest Melancholy,
Whose Saintly visage is too bright
To hit the Sense of human sight;
And therefore to our weaker view,   15
O'erlaid with black, staid Wisdom's hue.
Black, but such as in esteem,
Prince *Memnon's* sister might beseem,
Or that Starr'd *Ethiop* Queen that strove
To set her beauty's praise above   20
The Sea Nymphs, and their powers offended.
Yet thou art higher far descended;
Thee bright-hair'd *Vesta* long of yore,
To solitary *Saturn* bore;
His daughter she (in *Saturn's* reign,   25

10. For *Morpheus* see *L'All,* 10, n.

16. Albrecht Dürer's engraving *Melencolia I* (Z. S. Fink suggests in *PQ,* XIX (1940), 310) may have contributed to Milton's picture of a dark goddess of melancholy. Burton said (*Anatomy* I, iii, 1, 3; Vol. I, 397) that men in whose horoscope Saturn predominated were "very austere, sullen, churlish, and black of colour. . . ."

18. Homer's handsome Ethiopian *Prince Memnon* (*Od.* XI, 521) had, according to Dictys, a sister named Hemera.

19. The *Starr'd Ethiop Queen* is Cassiopeia, who, according to Hyginus' *Astronomica* II, x, was transformed into the familiar constellation for boasting that her daughter Andromeda (not herself) was more beautiful than the Nereids.

23. Most classical writers made *Vesta* a virgin daughter of Saturn, but in making her the mother of Melancholy (i.e. of the contemplative temperament) Milton may have remembered that for the mythographer Conti (VIII, xix; p. 910) the important thing about her was her enthronement in the heavens in an Orphic Hymn and in Plato's *Phaedrus,* 247-b.

25. Milton thought of the Golden Age when *Saturn* reigned on Mt. Ida in Crete, where Jove was born to him and later overthrew him (Cf. *PL* I, 510–22). Saturn's share in Vesta's fanciful parentage is due in part to Neoplatonic conceptions of him as "the collective angelic mind" and in part to the astrological theory that all melancholic persons were born under

            ill-disposed skyes,
When oblique *Saturne* sate in the house of agonyes.
                                    (*F.Q.* II, ix, 52, 8–9)

Such mixture was not held a stain).
Oft in glimmering Bow'rs and glades
He met her, and in secret shades
Of woody *Ida's* inmost grove,
While yet there was no fear of *Jove*.   30
Come pensive Nun, devout and pure,
Sober, steadfast, and demure,
All in a robe of darkest grain,
Flowing with majestic train,
And sable stole of *Cypress* Lawn,   35
Over thy decent shoulders drawn.
Come, but keep thy wonted state,
With ev'n step, and musing gait,
And looks commercing with the skies,   — *ignores earth, wisdom with god.*
Thy rapt soul sitting in thine eyes: 40
There held in holy passion still,
Forget thyself to Marble, till
With a sad Leaden downward cast,
Thou fix them on the earth as fast.
And join with thee calm Peace and Quiet,   45
Spare Fast, that oft with gods doth diet,
And hears the Muses in a ring
Aye round about *Jove's* Altar sing.
And add to these retired Leisure,
That in trim Gardens takes his pleasure; — *cf. Montaigne* 50
But first, and chiefest, with thee bring
Him that yon soars on golden wing,
Guiding the fiery-wheeled throne,
The Cherub Contemplation;
And the mute Silence hist along,   55
'Less *Philomel* will deign a Song,
In her sweetest, saddest plight,
Smoothing the rugged brow of night,
While *Cynthia* checks her Dragon yoke,
Gently o'er th' accustom'd Oak;   60
Sweet Bird that shunn'st the noise of folly,
Most musical, most melancholy!
Thee Chantress oft the Woods among,
I woo to hear thy Even-Song;
And missing thee, I walk unseen   65
On the dry smooth-shaven Green,
To behold the wand'ring Moon,
Riding near her highest noon,
Like one that had been led astray
Through the Heav'n's wide pathless way;   70
And oft, as if her head she bow'd,
Stooping through a fleecy cloud.
Oft on a Plat of rising ground,

33. *grain*: color.

35. *Cypress Lawn*: cf. "Cyprus black as e'er was crow" (*Winter's Tale* IV, iv, 219).

42. Mr. Garrod compares Thomas Tomkins' *Albumazor* (I, iv, 3–4): "*Wonder* for me, admire and be *astonished*, Marvel thyself to Marble." Cf. *Shak*, 13.

43. *sad*: serious. Cf. *Comus*, 189.

52. Ezekiel (i, 4–6) inspired this imagery as it did that of the "Cherubic shapes" which convoy the "Chariot of Paternal deity" in *PL* VI, 750–3.

56. *Philomel*: the "lover of song," the Greek name of the nightingale.

59. *Cynthia*: the goddess of the moon. See *Ely*, 57.

I hear the far-off *Curfew* sound,   ~ alone
Over some wide-water'd shore,   75
Swinging slow with sullen roar;
Or if the Air will not permit,
Some still removed place will fit,
Where glowing Embers through the room
Teach light to counterfeit a gloom,   80
Far from all resort of mirth,
Save the Cricket on the hearth,
Or the Bellman's drowsy charm,
To bless the doors from nightly harm:
Or let my Lamp at midnight hour,   85
Be seen in some high lonely Tow'r,
Where I may oft outwatch the *Bear,*
With thrice great *Hermes,* or unsphere
The spirit of *Plato* to unfold
What Worlds, or what vast Regions hold   90
The immortal mind that hath forsook
Her mansion in this fleshly nook:
And of those *Dæmons* that are found
In fire, air, flood, or underground,
Whose power hath a true consent   95
With Planet, or with Element.
Sometime let Gorgeous Tragedy   ~ not theatric, but literate
In Scepter'd Pall come sweeping by,
Presenting *Thebes,* or *Pelops'* line,
Or the tale of *Troy* divine,   100
Or what (though rare) of later age,
Ennobled hath the Buskin'd stage.
But, O sad Virgin, that thy power
Might raise *Musaeus* from his bower,
Or bid the soul of *Orpheus* sing   105
Such notes as, warbled to the string,
Drew Iron tears down *Pluto's* cheek,
And made Hell grant what Love did seek.
Or call up him that left half told

83. The cry of the *Bellman* (night-watchman) calling the hours is like a chant (*charm,* which originally meant "song").

86. The *Tow'r,* as Allen notes (*Vision,* p. 18), is Plato's "acropolis of the soul" (*Rep.* 560b) and the "watchtower" where Isaiah said (xxi, 8), "I am set in my ward whole nights." There Milton contemplates the constellation of the Great *Bear,* which never sets, and which the *thrice-great Hermes* taught was a symbol of perfection.

87. To *outwatch the Bear* is to work through the night; the Great Bear circles the North Pole without ever setting.

88. *Hermes Trismegistus* was identified with both Egyptian Thoth and the Greek Hermes and was supposed to have been the author of numerous esoteric writings which were actually written in Alexandria in the third and fourth centuries A.D. Milton probably knew them in the translation of the Florentine Platonist Marsilio Ficino (Paris, 1494). He was *thrice great,* said Raleigh (*History* II, vi, 6), "because he spake of the Trinitie, affirming that there is one God in Trinitie," but in the Dedication to the *Advancement* Bacon made his triplicity consist in "the power and fortune of a king, the knowledge and illumination of a priest, and the learning and universality of a philosopher."

89. For *Plato* see *Comus,* 10–11, n.

93. In Burton's "Digression of Spirits" (*Anatomy* I, ii, 1, 2; Vol. I, 190) evil spirits are classified as "fiery, aerial, terrestrial, watery, and subterranean devils besides those fairies, satyrs, nymphs, &c." The doctrine is traced by E. C. Baldwin (*MLN,* XXXIII [1918], 184) to the Hermetic *Definitions of Asclepius to King Amon* xiii, though Burton attributes it to Psellus.

97. *Tragedy* suggests dramas like Aeschylus' *Seven against Thebes,* plays about Pelops' descendants Agamemnon, Orestes, Iphigenia, and Electra, and Trojan plays like Euripides' *Trojan Dames, Andromache,* and *Hecuba.*

104. Perhaps Milton remembered Virgil's picture of the mythical bard *Musaeus* standing "foremost of all the heroes and poets" in Elysium (*Aen.* VI, 656–8).

105. Cf. *Orpheus* in *L'All,* 145, n.

The story of *Cambuscan* bold,　　　　　　　　110
Of *Camball,* and of *Algarsife,*
And who had *Canace* to wife,
That own'd the virtuous Ring and Glass,
And of the wondrous Horse of Brass,
On which the *Tartar* King did ride;　　　　　115
And if aught else great Bards beside
In sage and solemn tunes have sung,
Of Tourneys and of Trophies hung,
Of Forests, and enchantments drear,
Where more is meant than meets the ear.　*literary*　120
　　　　　　　　　　　　　　　　　criticism?
Thus night oft see me in thy pale career,
Till civil-suited Morn appear,
Not trickt and frounc't as she was wont
With the Attic Boy to hunt,
But kerchieft in a comely Cloud,　　　　　125
While rocking Winds are Piping loud,
Or usher'd with a shower still,
When the gust hath blown his fill,
Ending on the rustling Leaves,
With minute-drops from off the Eaves.　　　130
And when the Sun begins to fling
His flaring beams, me Goddess bring
To arched walks of twilight groves,
And shadows brown that *Sylvan* loves
Of Pine or monumental Oak,　　　　　　135
Where the rude Axe with heaved stroke
Was never heard the Nymphs to daunt,
Or fright them from their hallow'd haunt.
There in close covert by some Brook,
Where no profaner eye may look,　　　　　140
Hide me from Day's garish eye,
While the Bee with Honied thigh,
That at her flow'ry work doth sing,
And the Waters murmuring
With such consort as they keep,　　　　　145
Entice the dewy-feather'd Sleep;
And let some strange mysterious dream
Wave at his Wings in Airy stream,
Of lively portraiture display'd,
Softly on my eyelids laid.　　　　　　　150
And as I wake, sweet music breathe　*associated with*
　　　　　　　　　　　　　religion and study
Above, about, or underneath,
Sent by some spirit to mortals good,

110–115. In *The Squire's Tale* Chaucer left *half told* the story of the "Tartre Cambyuskan" and his children Algarsyf, Camball, and Canacee, whose guest offered him a *Horse of Brass* and gave her a ring which possessed its wearer with symbolic powers which have been identified by Allen (*Vision,* p. 13) with those to which Milton aspires in the closing lines of the poem.

122. *civil-suited:* soberly dressed.

123. Cf. the story of Aurora's love for Cephalus in *El* V, 49–51, n.

128. *his:* its. The modern form for the neuter had not yet become established.

130. *minute-drops:* drops falling at intervals of a minute.

134. *brown:* dark. Cf. *PR* II, 293, n. The wood-god *Sylvanus* has the forest setting that he has in *Aen.* VIII, 597–9.

145. *consort:* harmony.

147. Cf. Jonson's image in Night's speech in *The Vision of Delight:*

Break, Phant'sie, from thy cave of cloud,
　　And spread thy purple wings;
Now all thy figures are allowed,
　　And various shapes of things;
Create of airy forms a stream, . . ."

Or th'unseen Genius of the Wood.
But let my due feet never fail   155
To walk the studious Cloister's palc,
And love the high embowed Roof,
With antic Pillars massy proof,
And storied Windows richly dight,
Casting a dim religious light.   160
There let the pealing Organ blow
To the full voic'd Choir below,
In Service high and Anthems clear,
As may with sweetness, through mine ear,
Dissolve me into ecstasies,   165
And bring all Heav'n before mine eyes.
And may at last my weary age
Find out the peaceful hermitage,
The Hairy Gown and Mossy Cell, — *like Thomas More*
Where I may sit and rightly spell   170
Of every Star that Heav'n doth shew,
And every Herb that sips the dew;
Till old experience do attain
To something like Prophetic strain.
These pleasures *Melancholy* give,   175
And I with thee will choose to live.   (1631?)

156. *pale:* enclosure. The word repeats the meaning of *Cloister*.

158. *antic:* quaint, fantastic.

159. *storied Windows:* stained-glass windows representing Bible stories.

170. *spell:* consider, speculate.

171. Scientific prose and poetry alike were full of the belief about "the beautiful stars," for every one of which Raleigh declared (*History* I, xi) that, "in the treasury of His wisdom, who is infinite, there [could not] be wanting, even for every star, a peculiar virtue and operation, as every herb, plant, fruit, and flower adorning the face of the earth hath the like."

SONNET VII

How Soon Hath Time

   Although Milton's twenty-third birthday fell on December 9, 1631, his practice in dating his poems and his retirement to Hammersmith after taking his degree at Cambridge in July, 1632, suggests a time early in that year as the date of this sonnet. A few months after writing it he enclosed a copy of it in a letter to a friend who, he said, had accused him of "too much love of learning" and of dreaming away his "years in the arms of a studious retirement." R. M. Smith suggests (*MLN,* LX (1945), 394–8) that Spenser is one of the "more timely-happy spirits" of line 8, and that the sonnet has more than accidental resemblances to Spenser's defense of himself against a similar accusation in a Latin verse-letter to Gabriel Harvey. In *Astrophel and Stella* XXIII Sidney writes a somewhat similar defense of himself.

How soon hath Time, the subtle thief of youth,
   Stol'n on his wing my three and twentieth year!
   My hasting days fly on with full career,
   But my late spring no bud or blossom show'th.
Perhaps my semblance might deceive the truth,   5
   That I to manhood am arriv'd so near,
   And inward ripeness doth much less appear,
   That some more timely-happy spirits endu'th.

Yet be it less or more, or soon or slow.
   It shall be still in strictest measure ev'n   10
     To that same lot, however mean or high,
Toward which Time leads me, and the will of Heav'n;
   All is, if I have grace to use it so,
     As ever in my great task-Master's eye.   (1632)

10. *still:* always, forever.

10–12. The lines are compared by Lewis Campbell (*CR*, Oct. 1894) with Pindar, *Nemean Odes* IV, 43: "Whatever merit King Fate has given me, I shall know that time in its course will accomplish what is destined."

13. Instead of regarding *All* as the antecedent of *it*, Kester Svendsen prefers (*Exp.* VII (1949), 53) to have it refer to *ripeness* in l. 7.

14. Donald Dorian interprets *ever* as meaning *eternity* and interprets the line to mean, "All time is, if I have grace to use it so, as eternity in God's sight." Cf. A. S. P. Woodhouse on the punctuation in *UTQ*, XIII (1943), 96.

ARCADES

Part of an Entertainment presented to the Countess Dowager of *Derby* at *Harefield*, by some Noble persons of her Family, who appear on the Scene in pastoral habit, moving toward the seat of State, with this Song.

1. Song

Look Nymphs, and Shepherds look,
What sudden blaze of majesty
Is that which we from hence descry,
Too divine to be mistook:
   This, this is she   5
To whom our vows and wishes bend,
Here our solemn search hath end.

Fame that her high worth to raise,
Seem'd erst so lavish and profuse,
We may justly now accuse   10
Of detraction from her praise,
   Less than half we find exprest,
   Envy bid conceal the rest.

Mark what radiant state she spreads,
In circle round her shining throne,   15
Shooting her beams like silver threads.
This, this is she alone,
   Sitting like a Goddess bright,
   In the center of her light.

Might she the wise *Latona* be,   20
Or the tow'red *Cybele*,

1. The *Nymphs and Shepherds*—the Arcades— are natives of *Arcady* (l. 28) or Arcadia, the Greek state in the Peloponnesus within which lay the rivers *Alpheus* (l. 30) and *Ladon* (l. 97) and the mountains *Cyllene* (l. 98), *Erymanth* (l. 100), and *Maenalus* (l. 102). Ovid laid the story of Pan's unsuccessful courtship of the nymph *Syrinx* (l. 106; cf. *Met.* I, 689) there and began that idealization of Arcadia which produced the *Arcadias* of Sannazaro and Sir Philip Sidney in the Renaissance.

5. *she:* Alice Spencer, whose loss of her husband, the Earl of Derby, was lamented by Spenser in *Colin Clout's Come Home Again* in 1595. In 1600 she married Sir Thomas Egerton and became the stepmother of Sir John Egerton, who (now Earl of Bridgewater) gave the entertainment in her honor for which *Arcades* was written.

7. The searchers are the Earl's children and other members of his household, among them probably his little daughter Alice Egerton, the Lady of *Comus*.

8. Cf. *Fame* in *QNov*, 173–202.

20. With her children around her, the Countess is like *Latona*, the mother of Apollo and Diana.

21. *Cybele* appears in the *Aeneid* (X, 252–3) wearing a turreted crown because she first taught men to build fortified cities, and again (VI, 789) as the mother of a hundred gods.

Mother of a hundred gods;
Juno dares not give her odds;
  Who had thought this clime had held
  A deity so unparallel'd?   25

As they come forward, the Genius of the Wood appears, and turning toward them, speaks.

Genius. Stay gentle Swains, for though in this disguise,
I see bright honor sparkle through your eyes.
Of famous *Arcady* ye are, and sprung
Of that renowned flood, so often sung,
Divine *Alpheus,* who by secret sluice,   30
Stole under Seas to meet his *Arethuse;*
And ye the breathing Roses of the Wood,
Fair silver-buskin'd Nymphs as great and good,
I know this quest of yours and free intent
Was all in honor and devotion meant   35
To the great Mistress of yon princely shrine,
Whom with low reverence I adore as mine,
And with all helpful service will comply
To further this night's glad solemnity;
And lead ye where ye may more near behold   40
What shallow-searching *Fame* hath left untold;
Which I full oft amidst these shades alone
Have sat to wonder at, and gaze upon:
For know by lot from *Jove* I am the pow'r
Of this fair Wood, and live in Oak'n bow'r,   45
To nurse the Saplings tall, and curl the grove
With Ringlets quaint, and wanton windings wove.
And all my Plants I save from nightly ill,
Of noisome winds, and blasting vapors chill;
And from the Boughs brush off the evil dew,   50
And heal the harms of thwarting thunder blue,
Or what the cross dire-looking Planet smites,
Or hurtful Worm with canker'd venom bites.
When Ev'ning gray doth rise, I fetch my round
Over the mount, and all this hallow'd ground,   55
And early ere the odorous breath of morn
Awakes the slumb'ring leaves, or tassell'd horn
Shakes the high thicket, haste I all about,
Number my ranks, and visit every sprout
With puissant words and murmurs made to bless; 60
But else in deep of night, when drowsiness
Hath lockt up mortal sense, then listen I

---

23. Even the queen of the gods, *Juno,* dares not compete on equal terms with the Countess.

26. *Genius.* Roman religion attached a genius or protecting deity to every wood and locality. Cf. *IlPen,* 154 and *Lyc,* 183.

31. Ovid (*Met.* V, 574–641) has *Arethusa* tell the story of her pursuit by the god of the river *Alpheus,* of her transformation into a stream by Diana, and of her escape in that form under the Adriatic Sea to Sicily, only to be overtaken there by the pursuing waters of the Alpheus. Cf. *Lyc,* 85 and 132.

39. *solemnity:* festival. Cf. *Comus,* 142.

47. *quaint:* cunningly made, ingenious. *wove:* woven.

51. Cf. "the cross blue lightning" of *Julius Caesar* I, ii, 51.

52. The *Planet* is Saturn, whose oblique rays fall like a dart in *Damon,* 79–80.

53. Cf. Titania's dispatch of her fairies "to kill cankers (i. e. cankerworms) in the musk-rose buds" (*Midsummer Night's Dream* II, ii, 3).

59. The Genius counts the ranks of his trees. Cf. *PL* IV, 140.

60. *puissant words:* magically powerful words. *murmurs:* charms. Cf. *Comus,* 526.

To the celestial *Sirens'* harmony,
That sit upon the nine infolded Spheres
And sing to those that hold the vital shears   65
And turn the Adamantine spindle round,
On which the fate of gods and men is wound.
Such sweet compulsion doth in music lie,
To lull the daughters of *Necessity,*
And keep unsteady Nature to her law,   70
And the low world in measur'd motion draw
After the heavenly tune, which none can hear
Of human mold with gross unpurged ear;
And yet such music worthiest were to blaze
The peerless height of her immortal praise,   75
Whose luster leads us, and for her most fit,
If my inferior hand or voice could hit
Inimitable sounds; yet as we go,
Whate'er the skill of lesser gods can show,
I will assay, her worth to celebrate,   80
And so attend ye toward her glittering state;
Where ye may all that are of noble stem
Approach, and kiss her sacred vesture's hem.

2. Song

O'er the smooth enamell'd green
Where no print of step hath been,   85
    Follow me as I sing,
    And touch the warbled string.
Under the shady roof
Of branching Elm Star-proof,
    Follow me;   90
I will bring you where she sits
Clad in splendor as befits
    Her deity.
Such a rural Queen
All *Arcadia* hath not seen.   95

3. Song

Nymphs and Shepherds dance no more
    By sandy *Ladon's* Lillied banks.

63. Plato describes the *Sirens* as sitting on the eight celestial spheres, each "uttering her voice in one monotone, but all of them, being eight, composed one harmony." The spheres turn on "the distaff of Necessity, by which all the revolutions of the universe are maintained, whose spindle and point are both of adamant." And "at equal distances" are the Fates, Lachesis, Clotho, and Atropos, the daughters of Necessity, sitting enthroned" (*Rep.,* 616–7). Atropos traditionally held the shears to cut "the thin-spun life." Milton was probably thinking of a tradition which assigned Urania to the sphere of the fixed stars and seven other Muses to respective planets as their "sirens"—as James Hutton recalls in *EM* 2 (1951), 25. In the Pythagorean doctrine behind Plato's passage the music of the spheres was said to be audible only to men of pure heart, as Milton's *Prol* II explains. He regards it as harmonizing with the songs of the angels in heaven, which are no less inaudible to the "gross unpurged ear" of men. Cf. *Nat,* 125–32; *Music,* 6–16; *Comus,* 1020–1; *Patrem,* 33–34; and Shakespeare's *Merchant of Venice* V, i, 60–87.

74. *blaze:* proclaim.

80. *assay:* try.

82. *stem:* line, family.

84. Perhaps, as in *Lyc,* 139, *enamell'd* indicates that the grass was sprinkled with flowers. Cf. *PL* IV, 149.

89. Though Latin and English poetry have many parallels for the description of elms as *star-proof,* C. G. Osgood is probably right in suggesting, in *JEGP,* IV (1905), 372, that Milton had in mind an avenue of thick elms under which Queen Elizabeth like the Countess of Derby, had been welcomed by maskers, when she visited Harefield in 1602.

97. *Ladon:* an Arcadian river. Cf. l. 1 above, n.

On old *Lycæus* or *Cyllene* hoar,
  Trip no more in twilight ranks,
Though *Erymanth* your loss deplore,   100
  A better soil shall give ye thanks.
From the stony *Mænalus,*
Bring your Flocks, and live with us.
Here ye shall have greater grace,
To serve the Lady of this place.   105
  Though *Syrinx* your *Pan's* mistress were,
  Yet *Syrinx* well might wait on her.
    Such a rural Queen
    All *Arcadia* hath not seen.   (1632)

98. *Lycæus* is mentioned by Theocritus (I, 123) as a haunt of Pan. Like *Erymanth,* it is an Arcadian mountain. Virgil associates Pan with mounts *Lycæus* and *Mænalus* (*Georg.* I, 16–17).

ON TIME

Fly envious *Time,* till thou run out thy race,
Call on the lazy leaden-stepping hours,
Whose speed is but the heavy Plummet's pace;
And glut thyself with what thy womb devours,
Which is no more than what is false and vain,   5
And merely mortal dross;
So little is our loss,
So little is thy gain.
For when as each thing bad thou hast entomb'd,
And, last of all, thy greedy self consum'd,   10
Then long Eternity shall greet our bliss
With an individual kiss;
And Joy shall overtake us as a flood,
When everything that is sincerely good
And perfectly divine,   15
With Truth, and Peace, and Love, shall ever shine
About the supreme Throne
Of him, t'whose happy-making sight alone,
When once our heav'nly-guided soul shall climb,
Then all this Earthy grossness quit,   20
Attir'd with Stars, we shall for ever sit,
  Triumphing over Death, and Chance, and thee
  O Time.   (1633)

3. The allusion to the *Plummet* or weight moving the works of a clock was appropriate in a poem which, as a manuscript sub-title indicates, was intended "to be set on a clock-case."

12. *individual:* undividable, like the *individual Soul* of the united angels in *PL* V, 610. Hence, everlasting.

18. The *happy-making sight* is the Beatific Vision to which Dante devoted the last canto of the *Paradiso.* In *PL* III, 61–2 the angels from God's "sight receiv'd Beatitude past utterance."

UPON THE CIRCUMCISION

Ye flaming Powers, and winged Warriors bright,
  That erst with Music and triumphant song

1. The *Powers* were usually placed sixth among the nine traditional orders of angels, but in referring to the *Powers . . . that in Heav'n sat on Thrones* in *PL* I, 360 and elsewhere Milton did not think of their hierarchical position.

2. *erst:* formerly; i. e. at Christ's birth.

First heard by happy watchful Shepherds' ear,
So sweetly sung your Joy the Clouds along
Through the soft silence of the lis:'ning night,   5
Now mourn; and, if sad share with us to bear
Your fiery essence can distill no tear,
Burn in your sighs, and borrow
Seas wept from our deep sorrow:
He, who with all Heav'n's heraldry whilere   10
Enter'd the world, now bleeds to g:ve us ease;
Alas, how soon our sin
   Sore doth begin
     His Infancy to seize!
O more exceeding love or law more just?   15
Just law indeed, but more exceeding love!
For we by rightful doom remediless
Were lost in death, till he that dwelt above
High-thron'd in secret bliss, for us frail dust
Emptied his glory, ev'n to nakedness;   20
And that great Cov'nant which we still transgress
Entirely satisfi'd,
And the full wrath beside
Of vengeful Justice bore for our excess,
And seals obedience first with wounding smart   25
This day; but Oh! ere long
   Huge pangs and strong
     Will pierce more near his heart.   (1632-3?)

15. Cf. the antithesis of *law* with *love* in the prophecy of Christ's satisfaction of *high Justice* in *PL* XII, 401-404.
17. *doom:* judgment. Cf. *PL* X, 769.
20. So St. Paul described Christ, "Who, being in the form of God, . . . took upon him the form of a servant, and was made in the likeness of men" (Phil. ii, 6-7).
21. The *Cov'nant* is the Law of Moses. *still:* constantly. Cf. *Sonn* VII, 10.

AT A SOLEMN MUSIC

Blest pair of *Sirens,* pledges of Heav'n's joy,
Sphere-born harmonious Sisters, Voice and Verse,
Wed your divine sounds, and mixt power employ
Dead things with inbreath'd sense able to pierce,
And to our high-rais'd fantasy present   5
That undisturbed Song of pure concent,
Aye sung before the sapphire-color'd throne
To him that sits thereon,
With Saintly shout and solemn Jubilee,
Where the bright Seraphim in burning row   10
Their loud uplifted Angel-trumpets blow,
And the Cherubic host in thousand choirs

1. The two "sphere-born" sirens are distinguished by James Hutton—in *EM* 2 (1951), 48-49—from the seven "celestial sirens" of *Arc,* 63. The "sphere-born sirens" represent the earthly music of which Proclus spoke in the *Platonica Theologia* VII, 36, as the "ultimate image" of heaven's music, and as capable of reconciling men through their imagination with the divine.
5. *fantasy:* imagination.
6. *concent:* harmony.
7-16. Over the heads of the seraphs in Ezekiel's vision "was the likeness of a throne, as the appearance of a sapphire stone; and upon the likeness of the throne was the likeness as the appearance of a man above upon it" (Ezek. i, 26). The vision of Ezekiel fuses with St. John's vision of the *just Spirits* of the redeemed with "palms in their hands," singing a "new song before the throne" of God (Rev. xiv, 3-4). Cf. the angels singing before the throne of God in *PL* VII, 597-8, and in *Nat,* 117-120.

Touch their immortal Harps of golden wires,
With those just Spirits that wear victorious Palms,
Hymns devout and holy Psalms   15
Singing everlastingly;
That we on Earth with undiscording voice
May rightly answer that melodious noise;
As once we did, till disproportion'd sin
Jarr'd against nature's chime, and with harsh din   20
Broke the fair music that all creatures made
To their great Lord, whose love their motion sway'd
In perfect Diapason, whilst they stood
In first obedience and their state of good.
O may we soon again renew that Song,   25
And keep in tune with Heav'n, till God ere long
To his celestial consort us unite,
To live with him, and sing in endless morn of light.   (1633)

19. Cf. *Sin, that first distemper'd all things* in *PL* XI, 55–56.

23. *Diapason* means both "the concord of the octave" and "spiritual harmony." The *O.E.D.* compares Burton's *Anatomy*: "A true correspondence, perfect amity, a diapason of vows and wishes" among friends.

27. Cf. George Herbert in *The Temple, Employment vi:*

Lord place me in thy consort; give one strain
        To my poore reed.

Milton's audience was familiar with the principle that the universe from sand-grain to sun and from grass-blade to seraph, is "one mighty, sweet-toned instrument . . . acted and guided by one Spirit" (as John Everard put it in *Some Gospel Treasures Opened,* 1653). Cf. *Nat,* 125, n.

AD PATREM (TO HIS FATHER)

This poem has been speculatively dated as early as the Sonnet "How soon hath Time, the subtle thief of Youth" and as late as Milton's preparations for publishing his poems in 1645. In and between its lines the main facts and forces in Milton's early development can be read: his passionate devotion to the study of the classical languages, Hebrew, and—later—French and Italian; his encouragement by his father, though perhaps with some hesitation, in preferring poetry to law, which—as J. M. French's *Milton in Chancery* shows—played a great part in his father's life, and was to be the profession of his brother, Christopher; his pleasure in music and in his father's fame as an amateur composer; and his faith in his own destiny as an epic poet.

Nunc mea Pierios cupiam per pectora fontes
Irriguas torquere vias, totumque per ora
Volvere laxatum gemino de vertice rivum;
Ut, tenues oblita sonos, audacibus alis
Surgat in officium venerandi Musa parentis.   5
Hoc utcunque tibi gratum, pater optime, carmen
Exiguum meditatur opus, nec novimus ipsi
Aptius a nobis quae possint munera donis
Respondere tuis, quamvis nec maxima possint
Respondere tuis, nedum ut par gratia donis   10
Esse queat, vacuis quae redditur arida verbis.
Sed tamen haec nostros ostendit pagina census,

Now I wish that the Pierian[1] fountains would send their waters flooding through my breast and make my lips the channel for the whole stream that pours from the twin peaks, so that my Muse—her trivial songs forgotten—might rise on bold wings to do honor to my revered father. The song that she is meditating is a poor attempt, dearest father, and not at all certain to please you. Yet I do not know what gifts of mine could more aptly repay yours—though my greatest gifts could never repay yours, for they cannot be equalled by any barren gratitude of futile words. On this page, however, you have an account of my means, and whatever

1. Like the Castalian spring in *El IV,* 30, the *Pierian fountains* on Mt. Pierus in Thessaly were haunts of the Muses.

Et quod habemus opum charta numeravimus ista,
Quae mihi sunt nullae, nisi quas dedit aurea Clio
Quas mihi semoto somni peperere sub antro,   15
Et nemoris laureta sacri, Parnassides umbrae.
  Nec tu vatis opus divinum despice carmen,
Quo nihil aethereos ortus, et semina caeli,
Nil magis humanam commendat origine mentem,
Sancta Prometheae retinens vestigia flammae.   20
Carmen amant superi, tremebundaque Tartara carmen
Ima ciere valet, divosque ligare profundos,
Et triplici duros Manes adamante coercet.
Carmine sepositi retegunt arcana futuri
Phoebades, et tremulae pallentes ora Sibyllae;   25
Carmina sacrificus sollennes pangit ad aras,
Aurea seu sternit motantem cornua taurum,
Seu cum fata sagax fumantibus abdita fibris
Consulit, et tepidis Parcam scrutatur in extis.
Nos etiam, patrium tunc cum repetemus Olympum,
Aeternaeque morae stabunt immobilis aevi,   30
Ibimus auratis per caeli templa coronis,
Dulcia suaviloquo sociantes carmina plectro,
Astra quibus geminique poli convexa sonabunt.
Spiritus et rapidos qui circinat igneus orbes   35
Nunc quoque sidereis intercinit ipse choreis
Immortale melos et inenarrabile carmen;
Torrida dum rutilus compescit sibila serpens,
Demissoque ferox gladio mansuescit Orion,
Stellarum nec sentit onus Maurusius Atlas.   40
Carmina regales epulas ornare solebant,
Cum nondum luxus, vastaeque immensa vorago
Nota gulae, et modico spumabat coena Lyaeo.
Tum de more sedens festa ad convivia vates,
Aesculea intonsos redimitus ab arbore crines,   45
Heroumque actus imitandaque gesta canebat,
Et chaos, et positi late fundamina mundi,

14. *Clio,* the Muse of history, might be called
upon to help the epic Muse, *Calliope,* as she is twice
in *The Faerie Queene* (III, iii, 4, 6 and VII, vi, 37,
9) when the theme becomes historical.

20. Prometheus' theft of heaven's fire for men
was interpreted by Conti (IV, vi, p. 329) as meaning that he first gave them "cognizance of philosophy and divine things."

25. *Apollo's priestesses* who gave oracles at
Delphi trembled under the god's inspiration as
Virgil said that the *Sibyl* trembled as she prophesied
to Aeneas (*Aen.* VI, 46–49).

30–33. The lines glance at St. John's account of
the heavenly elders who are crowned with gold
(Rev. iv, 4) and of the "voice of the harpers harping with their harps" (Rev. xiv, 22). Cf. the very
Christian description of Olympus in *Ely,* 63–65.

38. So Ovid describes Phaeton riding the sun's
chariot and being threatened by the *Serpent,* the
constellation lying between the two bears (*Met.*
II, 173–5).

39. Cf. *Orion* in *Ely,* 54.
40. Cf. *Atlas* in *Idea,* 24.
43. Cf. *Lyaeus* in *El VI,* 21.

wealth I possess I have reckoned
up on this paper, for I have nothing
except what golden Clio[14] has given
and what has been the fruit of
dreams in a remote cavern and of
the laurel groves of the sacred wood
and of the shadows of Parnassus.

You should not despise the poet's
task, divine song, which preserves
some spark of Promethean fire[20]
and is the unrivalled glory of the
heaven-born human mind and an
evidence of our ethereal origin and
celestial descent. The gods on high
love song and song has power to
move the frightful depths of Tartarus and to bind the gods below
and control the implacable shades
with triple adamant. By song
Apollo's priestesses[25] and the trembling Sibyl, with blanched features,
lay bare the mysteries of the far-
away future. Songs are composed
by the sacrificing priest at the altar,
both when he smites the bull that
tosses its gilded horns and when
his acute eye consults the secrets of
destiny in the steaming flesh and
reads fate in the warm entrails.
When we return to our native
Olympus and the everlasting ages
of immutable eternity are established, we shall walk, crowned with
gold,[30] through the temples of the
skies and with the harp's soft accompaniment we shall sing sweet
songs to which the stars shall echo
and the vault of heaven from pole
to pole.[33] Even now the fiery spirit
who flies through the swift spheres
is singing his immortal melody and
unutterable song in harmony with
the starry choruses. Meanwhile the
shining Serpent restrains his burning hisses,[38] fierce Orion[39] grows
gentle and drops his sword, and
Mauretanian Atlas[40] no longer feels
the load of the stars.

Songs were the usual ornaments
of royal tables in the times before
luxury and the bottomless appetite
of gluttony were known, when
Lyaeus[43] sparkled at the banquet in
temperate cups. Then the custom
was that the bard should sit at the
festal banquet, wearing a garland of
oak leaves on his unshorn locks,
and should sing of the deeds and
emulable achievements of heroes,
and of chaos and of the broad
foundations on which the earth

Reptantesque Deos, et alentes numina glandes,
Et nondum Aetnaeo quaesitum fulmen ab antro.
Denique quid vocis modulamen inane iuvabit   50
Verborum sensusque vacans, numerique loquacis?
Silvestres decet iste choros, non Orphea, cantus,
Qui tenuit fluvios, et quercubus addidit aures,
Carmine, non cithara, simulacraque functa canendo
Compulit in lacrymas; habet has a carmine laudes.   55
    Nec tu perge, precor, sacras contemnere Musas,
Nec vanas inopesque puta, quarum ipse peritus
Munere mille sonos numeros componis ad aptos,
Millibus et vocem modulis variare canoram
Doctus, Arionii merito sis nominis haeres.   60
Nunc tibi quid mirum si me genuisse poetam
Contigerit, caro si tam prope sanguine iuncti
Cognatas artes studiumque affine sequamur?
Ipse volens Phoebus se dispertire duobus,
Altera dona mihi, dedit altera dona parenti,   65
Dividuumque Deum genitorque puerque tenemus.
    Tu tamen ut simules teneras odisse Camenas,
Non odisse reor. Neque enim, pater, ire iubebas
Qua via lata patet, qua pronior area lucri,
Certaque condendi fulget spes aurea nummi;   70
Nec rapis ad leges, male custoditaque gentis
Iura, nec insulsis damnas clamoribus aures.
Sed magis excultam cupiens ditescere mentem,
Me procul urbano strepitu, secessibus altis
Abductum, Aoniae iucunda per otia ripae,   75
Phoebaeo lateri comitem sinis ire beatum.
    Officium cari taceo commune parentis;
Me poscunt maiora. Tuo, pater optime, sumptu

rests, of the deities who once went creeping about in search of their acorn-food,[48] and of the thunderbolt not yet sought out of the depths of Aetna.[49] And now, to sum it all up, what pleasure is there in the inane modulation of the voice without words and meaning and rhythmic eloquence? Such music is good enough for the forest choirs, but not for Orpheus,[52] who by his song —not by his cithara—restrained rivers and gave ears to the oaks, and by his singing stirred the ghosts of the dead to tears. That fame he owes to his song.

Do not persist, I beg of you, in your contempt for the sacred Muses, and do not think them futile and worthless whose gift has taught you to harmonize a thousand sounds to fit numbers, and given you skill to vary the voice of the singer with countless modulations, so that you are deservedly the heir of Arion's[60] name. Now, since it is my lot to have been born a poet, why does it seem strange to you that we, who are so closely united by blood, should pursue sister arts and kindred interests? Phoebus himself,[64] wishing to part himself between us two, gave some gifts to me and others to my father; and, father and son, we share the possession of the divided god.

You may pretend to hate the delicate Muses, but I do not believe in your hatred. For you would not bid me go where the broad way lies wide open, where the field of lucre is easier and the golden hope of amassing money is glittering and sure; neither do you force me into the law and the evil administration of the national statutes. You do not condemn my ears to noisy impertinence. But rather, because you wish to enrich the mind which you have carefully cultivated, you lead me far away from the uproar of cities into these high retreats of delightful leisure beside the Aonian[75] stream, and you permit me to walk there by Phoebus' side, his blessed companion.

I will not mention a father's usual generosities, for greater things have a claim on me. It was at your expense, dear father, after I had got the mastery of the language of

48. The *deities* seem to be the Titans before they learned agriculture from Ceres, as Apollonius of Rhodes says that they did (*Argonautica* IV, 982).
49. Virgil describes the forging of Jove's *thunderbolts* by the Cyclops under Mt. *Aetna* (*Georg.* IV, 170–3).
52. Cf. *Orpheus* in *L'All*, 145 and *IlPen*, 105.
60. Herodotus (I, 23–24) describes the rescue of the poet *Arion* from the sea by dolphins whom he charmed with his lyre.
64. Cf. the references to *Phoebus* Apollo as god of music and poetry in *Vac*, 37, *Comus*, 478, *Shak*, 12, and *Manso*, 2.
75. Again the *Aonian* fountain on Mt. Helicon symbolizes the Muses and Apollo. Cf. *El IV*, 29; *VI*, 17, and *PL* I, 15.

Cum mihi Romuleae patuit facundia linguae,
Et Latii veneres, et quae Iovis ora decebant   80
Grandia magniloquis elata vocabula Graiis,
Addere suasisti quos iactat Gallia flores,
Et quam degeneri novus Italus ore loquelam
Fundit, Barbaricos testatus voce tumultus
Quaeque Palaestinus loquitur mysteria vates.   85
Denique quicquid habet caelum, subiectaque caelo
Terra parens, terraeque et caelo interfluus aer,
Quicquid et unda tegit, pontique agitabile marmor,
Per te nosse licet, per te, si nosse libebit.
Dimotaque venit spectanda scientia nube,   90
Nudaque conspicuos inclinat ad oscula vultus,
Ni fugisse velim, ni sit libasse molestum.
   I nunc, confer opes, quisquis malesanus avitas
Austriaci gazas Peruanaque regna praeoptas.
Quae potuit maiora pater tribuisse, vel ipse   95
Iupiter, excepto, donasset ut omnia, caelo?
Non potiora dedit, quamvis et tuta fuissent,
Publica qui iuveni commisit lumina nato,
Atque Hyperionios currus, et fraena diei,
Et circum undantem radiata luce tiaram.   100
Ergo ego iam doctae pars quamlibet ima catervae
Victricis hederas inter laurosque sedebo,
Iamque nec obscurus populo miscebor inerti,
Vitabuntque oculos vestigia nostra profanos.
Este procul, vigiles curae, procul este, querelae,   105
Invidiaeque acies transverso tortilis hirquo,
Saeva nec anguiferos extende, Calumnia, rictus;
In me triste nihil, foedissima turba, potestis,
Nec vestri sum iuris ego; securaque tutus
Pectora vipereo gradiar sublimis ab ictu.   110
   At tibi, care pater, postquam non aequa merenti
Posse referre datur, nec dona rependere factis,
Sit memorasse satis, repetitaque munera grato

79. Tradition made *Romulus* the progenitor of
the Romans,
   "Great *Romulus* the Grandsyre of them all,"
as Spenser called him (*F.Q.* I, v, 49, 5).
85. The prophetic *Palestinian* mysteries stand for
the Old Testament.
98. The *common light* is one of Ovid's titles for
the sun god *Hyperion* when Phaeton begs the
privilege of driving the sun's chariot (*Met.* II, 35).
102. The confidence of fame echoes similar boasts
of Horace (*Odes* I, i, 29–34 and III, xxx, 1) and
echoes a mood of assurance in Milton which corresponds with W. R. Parker's dating of *Ad Patrem*
shortly after the success of *Comus*.
106. The odd syntax of the allusion to the
"evil eye" of envy (as MacKellar notes) stems from
Virgil's reference to the superstition (*Ec.* III, 8).

Romulus[79] and the graces of Latin,
and acquired the lofty speech of
the magniloquent Greeks, which is
fit for the lips of Jove himself, that
you persuaded me to add the flowers
which France boasts and the eloquence which the modern Italian
pours from his degenerate mouth—
testifying by his accent to the barbarian wars—and the mysteries
uttered by the Palestinian prophet.[85]
And finally, all that heaven contains
and earth, our mother, beneath the
sky, and the air that flows between
earth and heaven, and whatever the
waters and the trembling surface of
the sea cover, your kindness gives
me the means to know, if I care for
the knowledge that your kindness
offers. From the opening cloud
science appears and, naked, she
bends her face to my kisses, unless
I should wish to run away or unless
I should find her enjoyment irksome.
   Go now, gather riches, whoever
you are whose morbid preference is
for the ancient treasures of Austria
and the lucre of Peru. What
greater gift could come from a
father, or from Jove himself if he
had given everything, with the
single exception of heaven? He
who gave to his young son the common light,[98] the chariot of Hyperion
and the reins of day and the aureole
radiating a flood of glory (even
assuming that those gifts were
harmless) bestowed no grander
gifts. Therefore, however humble
my present place in the company of
learned men, I shall sit with the ivy
and laurel of a victor.[102] I shall
no longer mingle unknown with
the dull rabble and my walk shall
be far from the sight of profane
eyes. Begone, sleepless cares and
complaints, and the twisted glance
of envy with goatish leer.[106] Malevolent Calumny, open not your
dragon gorge. You have no power
to harm me, O detestable band; and
I am not under your jurisdiction.
I shall walk with heart secure, lifted
high above your viper stroke.
   But to you, dear father, since no
requital equal to your desert and
no deeds equal to your gifts are
within my power, let it suffice that
with a grateful mind I remember
and tell over your constant kind-

Percensere animo, fidaeque reponere menti.
Et vos, O nostri, iuvenilia carmina, lusus,   115
Si modo perpetuos sperare audebitis annos,
Et domini superesse rogo, lucemque tueri,
Nec spisso rapient oblivia nigra sub Orco,
Forsitan has laudes, decantatumque parentis
Nomen, ad exemplum, sero servabitis aevo.   120

(1637)

nesses, and lay them up in a loyal heart.

And you, my juvenile verses and amusements, if only you dare hope for immortality and a life and a glimpse of the light beyond your master's funeral pyre, and if dark oblivion does not sweep you down into the throngs of Hades, perhaps you will preserve this eulogy and the name of the father whom my song honors as an example to remote ages.

A MASK

PRESENTED AT LUDLOW CASTLE
1634:
ON MICHELMAS NIGHT, BEFORE THE RIGHT HONORABLE JOHN, EARL OF BRIDGEWATER, VISCOUNT BRACKLEY, LORD PRESIDENT OF WALES, AND ONE OF HIS MAJESTY'S MOST HONORABLE PRIVY COUNCIL.

Eheu quid volui misero mihi! floribus austrum Perditus . . . Virgil, *Eclogue* II, 58–59.

(The title-page of the first (1637) edition of the then anonymous mask which we know as *Comus* read as above, and the volume carried the following dedication by Henry Lawes.)

To the Right Honorable John, Lord Viscount Brackley, Son and heir-apparent to the Earl of *Bridgewater, &c.*

MY LORD,
    This Poem, *which received its first occasion of Birth from your Self, and others of your Noble Family, and much honor from your own Person in the performance, now returns again to make a final Dedication of itself to you. Although not openly acknowledged by the Author, yet it is a legitimate offspring, so lovely, and so much desired, that the often Copying of it hath tired my Pen to give my several friends satisfaction, and brought me to a necessity of producing it to the public view; and now to offer it up in all rightful devotion to those fair Hopes, and rare Endowments of your much-promising Youth, which give a full assurance, to all that know you, of a future excellence. Live sweet Lord to be the honor of your Name, and receive this as your own, from the hands of him who hath by many favors been long obliged to your most honored Parents, and as in this representation your attendant* Thyrsis, *so now in all real expression*
Your faithful, and most
humble Servant
H. LAWES.

1. Our nearest approach to the mask which was actually presented at Ludlow Castle in 1634 is through the manuscript still in the hands of the Egerton family and known as the Bridgewater MS. Before the mask was printed—anonymously in 1637 by Henry Lawes, who had written the music for its songs and acted the part of the Attendant Spirit at Ludlow, and again in 1645 by Milton himself—he had worked it over in the Trinity MS into a form approaching that of the somewhat divergent printed texts. When he reprinted it in 1673 he made no important changes and kept the original caption of *A Mask presented at Ludlow Castle.* It seems to have been given the un-Miltonic title of *Comus* first by Dr. John Dalton when he printed it as *Comus, A Mask, Now Adapted to the Stage,* in 1738.

2. Today habit makes *Comus* seem the inevitable title, though if Milton had given the Lady a name, either mythological or allegorical, it might seem more appropriate.   But to him the title *Comus* might have seemed no more appropriate for his mask than would *Satan* for his epics.   It was no accident that he discarded the title which had been used by Hendrik van der Putten (Puteanus) for his neo-Latin play of *Comus*, which R. H. Singleton has shown—in *PMLA*, LXVIII (1943), 948–55—was widely known in French and Flemish versions and was popular enough in England to be acted at Oxford in 1634.   It was from Puteanus that Milton learned to give life to the shadowy classical genius of revelry whom Philostratus described as an allegorical figure, gracefully drunk, standing with an inverted torch in his hand.   As the captain of a rout like his "Monsters, headed like sundry sorts of wild Beasts" in Milton's mask, Puteanus made him the garrulous prophet of the life of revelry.   But in the Flemish play there is nothing like the speech of Milton's Comus pleading that the Lady's chastity blasphemes Nature as she pours "her bounties forth, . . . Covering the earth with odors, fruits, and flocks."

3. That wonderful speech of Comus has been studied from many angles: from that of the long stream of the tradition of gathering "the rose of love while yet 'tis prime" by Fredella Bruser in *SP*, XLIV (1947), 625–44; from the point of view of the seductions in Marlowe's *Hero and Leander* and Shakespeare's *Venus and Adonis* by Hermann Schaus in *UTSE* (1945–6), 129–41; by contrast with the perverted "Platonism" of court plays like D'Avenant's *The Fair Favourite* by G. F. Sensabaugh in *SP*, XLI (1944), 238–49; and as a dominant psychological theme in Milton's work by J. H. Hanford in *SP*, XV (1918), 176–94, and J. Blondel in *RHPR*, XXXVIII–XXXIX (1949), 43–48.   It is possible—as does G. W. Knight (*Oracle*, pp. 66–67)—to see in Comus' appeal to Nature's fecundity as sanctioning unchastity the high point in all Milton's poetry because there he was "dramatizing a conflict in his own mind."   But Comus' appeal to the Lady to "be wise and taste" is no more private a struggle in Milton's mind than is Satan's seduction of Eve.   What Dyson calls Comus' "sensuous, suasive, insidious style" had traditionally been pitted against the neo-Platonic ideal of chastity (in the wide sense of the word) as long ago as Porphyry's *On Abstinence* I, 16–17.   Indeed, as Martin Litz suggests in his unpublished thesis, *The Tong and the Heart*, the essence of the drama in *Comus* is the contrast between the tempter's play with syllogisms on the mundane level of fallen mankind and the clarity of the Lady's statement of her vision of Platonic universals.

4. In spite of its length, Milton thought of his poem as comparable with court masks like Jonson's *Pleasure Reconciled to Virtue*.   Its conventions of "a world of perfection, with persons representing ideals and types and powers" seem to John Arthos to make it a true mask in essence if not in form.   Analysis of its revisions in the Trinity MS by C. S. Lewis in *RES*, VIII (1932), 170–6, and by John Diekhoff in *PMLA*, LV (1940), 748–72, shows Milton subordinating its language to those conventions and to a corresponding harmony of tone.   Its songs, its dance measure in Comus' octosyllabic address to his rout (ll. 93–144), and its poetry everywhere take us into the realm of "masks and antique pageantry" which l'Allegro associated with Jonson.   And the next line goes on, significantly, to mention "sweetest Shakespeare," the Shakespeare of *Romeo and Juliet* and *The Tempest*, whose mask-like imagery and language have been traced in *Comus* by Ethel Seaton in *ESEA*, XXXI (1945), 68–80.

5. Shakespeare is only one among many questionably dramatic influences in *Comus*. One of the most obvious has been thought to be George Peele's *Old Wives Tale*, with its romantic plot of the delivery of a maiden from an enchanter, not by her two brothers, who have long been searching for her, but by "a Lady who is neither maid, nor wife, nor widow." Clear proof of the influence is lacking, and the elements in Milton's plot which have been traced to Peele are plausibly traced by Gretchen L. Finney—in *SP*, XXXVII (1940), 493—

to *The Chain of Adonis* (*La Catena d'Adone*) of Ottavio Tronsarelli and Domenico Maz-zocchi and to their source in *L'Adone* of Giambattista Marino. *The Chain of Adonis* is a good example of an operatic development of the court mask in Italy, the *dramma per musica*. Such drama tried to assimilate Greek elements like the prologue-soliloquy and the swift exchange of alternate speeches of single lines in dialogue (stichomythia), which in *Comus* are usually traced to plays like Euripides' *Bacchae* and *Iphigeneia in Tauris*. Miss Finney makes a strong case, but it must be judged in comparison with Mario Praz's confi-dent claim for Tasso's *Aminta* as Milton's model (in *S.C.S.H.G.*, pp. 202-03), which sug-gests wider Italian influences on Milton than she has recognized. The *Aminta* is a pas-toral drama with resemblances to *Comus* so much greater than those of the English play to which it is often compared, John Fletcher's *Faithful Shepherdess*, that Sir Walter Greg's classification of *Comus* in that literary type—in *Pastoral Poetry and Pastoral Drama* (Lon-don, 1906), p. 396—seems true, insofar as it is true, mainly in the light of the *Aminta*.

6. The technical reasons for denying the name of a mask to *Comus* have been fully stated by Enid Welsford in *The Court Masque* (Cambridge, 1927, pp. 314-23) and in Eugene Haun's "Inquiry into the Genre of *Comus*" (*E.H.W.C.*, pp. 221-40). If it is to be treated as a pastoral drama, it must be judged by dramatic standards far too strict for it. Dr. Johnson, who wrote a prologue for one of its eighteenth century performances, de-plored its lack of dramatic unity, and that weakness has been severely stressed by D. C. Allen in *Vision* (pp. 29-40), to the point of denying it any unity whatsoever. If it is to be judged by dramatic rules, there is no reply to Allen's charge except to ridicule it, as Robert Adams does in IKON (p. 31), for demanding an organic unity hardly to be found even in Greek tragedy. But if, with Arthos, we think of *Comus* as an entertainment whose cen-tral human character is moved by a "passion which makes it possible to identify reason with the image of an individual"; if, with B. A. Wright (in *TLS*, 27 Oct., 1945, p. 511), we think of the entire poem as interpreting "virtue in the genuine platonic sense, identifying it with the rule of reason and with knowledge"; the question of dramatic unity is less urgent. The lady avoids too easy condemnation on psychological grounds. Not many readers now see the Lady as a mere projection of Milton's own "cold' stoicism" and inexperienced faith in "the magic power of chastity," which Denis Saurat attributed to him in 1929, in *Milton: Man and Thinker* (p. 9). Yet in 1939 Paul Phelps-Morand still regarded Milton's faith in "magical chastity" as reducing "the drama almost to a struggle between two magicians: Chastity and Comus," and declared in *De Comus à Satan* (p. 62) that it was radically un-Christian. Two years later A. S. P. Woodhouse was to treat the mask as fundamentally Christian in its movement from the humanistic or stoic conception of virtue in the dia-logue of the Lady's brothers to her own realization of the "doctrine of virginity" as a Christian virtue which is finally vindicated by divine grace as symbolized by Sabrina in her final disenchantment.

7. Though Woodhouse has established the Christian elements in *Comus*, there is still truth in Coleridge's emphasis on the Attendant Spirit's Prologue as a summary of Plato's doctrine of virtue as reason in the *Phaedo*. The Spirit himself tells us (as Wright notes in *TLS*, Aug. 4, 1935, p. 367) that his "mansion" is in "the True Earth of the *Phaedo* myth, which is in the upper air and is a celestial version of the older earthly paradises of the poets —the Isles of the Blest, the Elysian Fields, the Gardens of the Hesperides." As one of Plato's aerial spirits, Milton's Attendant Spirit returns to "the Gardens fair of Hesperus" when his work is done. The theme of his Prologue is not over-simplified in J. C. Max-well's "Pseudo-Problem of *Comus*," in *CJ*, I (1948), as "reason *vs.* passion." He even denies that it is "chastity *vs.* vice." But the Lady has suffered much for her chastity and particularly for her vision of that Platonic ideal as she sees it "visibly" and (it is alleged) sees it usurping the place of the Christian virtue of charity, standing ready to keep her

"life and honor unassail'd" (ll. 213–20). "Faith, Hope, and *Chastity*," says M. M. Ross with contempt in *Poetry and Dogma* (p. 196). "And the greatest of these is chastity! The substitution of chastity for charity is the reduction of the highest supernatural grace to a secondary practical virtue." And Kenneth Muir, no less shocked (in *Penguin New Writing*, No. 24, 1945), surmises that Milton must have written ironically and have intended to criticize the Lady's inhumanity as severely as Ross criticizes what he regards as Milton's impiety. Even E. M. W. Tillyard thinks that Milton narrowed his idea of chastity in the original mask to a virginity having little in common with Plato's ideal of chastity as loyalty to reason. Tillyard rests his case on what he regards as an explicit repudiation of Milton's original view of chastity in favor of the Spenserian ideal of "married chastity" in the printed version of *Comus* in 1637, and (in *S.M.*, pp. 82–99) cites Milton's echo of the symbolism of the union of Venus and Adonis in *The Faerie Queene* (III, vi, 46) in his Epilogue (ll. 997–1011) as he finally revised it for publication. But Tillyard's view has nothing in common with Phelps-Morand's, and, modifying Tillyard in *ESEA*, n.s. VIII (1955), 89, A. E. Dyson sees the Lady as "an actual if rather rarified mortal" with nothing of the stoic but a great deal of the platonist in her.

8. Milton's revisions should not be strained so as to cast doubt on his "doctrine of love as a compound of reason, allied to the Aristotelian ideal of temperance, and the mystic harmony of nature and grace, derived from the Platonic ideal of Eros"—as Michael Macklem puts it in "Love, Nature, and Grace in Milton" in *QQ*, LVI (1949), 546. The Lady is no stoic though Comus calls her so. Nor does she have "the stern frigidity of an adolescent Isabella," of which D. C. Allen accuses her in *ELH*, XVI (1949), 116. On the contrary, as Ethel Seaton observes, there are no clear reflections of *Measure for Measure* in *Comus*, and "Isabella, faced with her agonizing choice, has little in word or theme to give to the Lady" (*ESEA*, XXI, 68).

9. In *Comus* actually, Milton's ideas about love between the sexes are secondary. They have been delightfully studied in "Hail, Wedded Love"—in *ELH*, XIII (1946), 79–97—by William Haller, who regrets that recent critics and biographers have encumbered the poem with "notions of an ascetic, celibate chastity, clothed with something like supernatural powers and blessings." A better view is the one that regards its chastity as "erotic," not only in the sense that it stems from the Platonic myth of the celestial Eros, to which the Attendant Spirit appeals in the Epilogue, but also because—as J. W. Saunder puts it in "Milton, Diomede, and Amaryllis," in *ELH*, XXII (1955), 277—"Milton pours into the defense of chastity [in *Comus*] all his finest erotic imagery; the real victory in the drama belongs to Sabrina and to the Epilogue which—like Shelley's fourth act in *Prometheus Unbound*—persuades with music and not with logic."

10. Two good illustrated editions of *Comus* are:

Comus: a mask . . . with eight illustrations by William Blake. Edited by Darrell Figgis. London, 1926.

The Mask of Comus, edited by E. H. Visiak; the airs of the five songs reprinted from the composer's autograph MS, with a foreword by the Earl of Ellesmere. Ornamented by M. R. H. Farrar. London, 1937.

The Persons

The attendant Spirit, afterwards in the habit of *Thyrsis*.
Comus with his crew.
The Lady.
First Brother.
Second Brother.
Sabrina, the Nymph.

The chief persons which presented, were
The Lord *Brackley.*
Mr. *Thomas Egerton,* his Brother.
The Lady *Alice Egerton.*

The first Scene discovers a wild Wood.

The attendant Spirit descends or enters.

Before the starry threshold of *Jove's* Court
My mansion is, where those immortal shapes
Of bright aërial Spirits live inspher'd
In Regions mild of calm and serene Air,
Above the smoke and stir of this dim spot,   5
Which men call Earth, and with low-thoughted care
Confin'd and pester'd in this pinfold here,
Strive to keep up a frail and Feverish being,
Unmindful of the crown that Virtue gives
After this mortal change, to her true Servants   10
Amongst the enthron'd gods on Sainted seats.
Yet some there be that by due steps aspire
To lay their just hands on that Golden Key
That opes the Palace of Eternity:
To such my errand is, and but for such,   15
I would not soil these pure Ambrosial weeds
With the rank vapors of this Sin-worn mold.
    But to my task. *Neptune,* besides the sway
Of every salt Flood and each ebbing Stream,
Took in by lot 'twixt high and nether *Jove*   20
Imperial rule of all the Sea-girt Isles
That like to rich and various gems inlay
The unadorned bosom of the Deep;
Which he to grace his tributary gods
By course commits to several government,   25
And gives them leave to wear their Sapphire crowns,
And wield their little tridents; but this Isle,
The greatest and the best of all the main,
He quarters to his blue-hair'd deities;
And all this tract that fronts the falling Sun   30
A noble Peer of mickle trust and power
Has in his charge, with temper'd awe to guide
An old and haughty Nation proud in Arms;
Where his fair offspring nurs't in Princely lore,
Are coming to attend their Father's state   35
And new-entrusted Scepter. But their way

7. *pinfold* (literally, a pen for animals) is Milton's equivalent for the hollows or pits of the earth which Plato contrasted with the "true earth" and the heavenly dwellings to which the Spirit returns. Cf. l. 982 below and the headnote ¶ 7.

10–11. The lines combine Plato's conception of birth and death as boundaries of the mortal experience of the immortal soul with St. John's vision of the seats of the saints "about the throne of God" (Rev. iv, 4).

16. *Ambrosial:* heavenly. Cf. l. 840 below. *weeds:* garments.

20. In the *Iliad* XV, 190–3, Poseidon (*Neptune*) reminds Zeus that he himself and Hades, the Jove

of the underworld, have been allotted their realms of the sea and the dead as surely as the sky has been allotted to Zeus. The scene was familiar in emblems like that in J. J. Boissard's *Theatrum Humanae Vitae* (Besançon, 1596), Chap. xiv, p. 67.

24. Spenser catalogues over two hundred sea and river gods who follow "great Neptune with his three-forkt mace" (*F.Q.* IV, xi, 11–36). Such deities appear in Jonson's mask of *Neptune's Triumph.*

30. *this tract:* Wales and the bordering English counties which were part of the "presidency" of the Earl of Bridgewater.

31. *mickle:* much, great.

Lies through the perplex't paths of this drear Wood,
The nodding horror of whose shady brows
Threats the forlorn and wand'ring Passenger;
And here their tender age might suffer peril, 40
But that by quick command from Sovran *Jove*
I was dispatcht for their defense and guard;
And listen why, for I will tell ye now
What never yet was heard in Tale or Song
From old or modern Bard, in Hall or Bow'r. 45
   Bacchus that first from out the purple Grape
Crusht the sweet poison of misused Wine,
After the *Tuscan* Mariners transform'd,
Coasting the *Tyrrhene* shore, as the winds listed,
On *Circe's* Island fell. (Who knows not *Circe* 50
The daughter of the Sun? Whose charmed Cup
Whoever tasted, lost his upright shape,
And downward fell into a groveling Swine.)
This Nymph that gaz'd upon his clust'ring locks,
With Ivy berries wreath'd, and his blithe youth, 55
Had by him, ere he parted thence, a Son
Much like his Father, but his Mother more,
Whom therefore she brought up, and *Comus* nam'd:
Who, ripe and frolic of his full grown age,
Roving the *Celtic* and *Iberian* fields, 60
At last betakes him to this ominous Wood,
And in thick shelter of black shades imbow'r'd,
Excels his Mother at her mighty Art,
Off'ring to every weary Traveller
His orient liquor in a Crystal Glass, 65
To quench the drought of *Phœbus,* which as they taste,
(For most do taste through fond intemperate thirst)
Soon as the Potion works, their human count'nance,
Th' express resemblance of the gods, is chang'd
Into some brutish form of Wolf, or Bear, 70
Or Ounce, or Tiger, Hog, or bearded Goat,
All other parts remaining as they were.
And they, so perfect is their misery,
Not once perceive their foul disfigurement,
But boast themselves more comely than before, 75
And all their friends and native home forget,
To roll with pleasure in a sensual sty.
Therefore when any favor'd of high *Jove*
Chances to pass through this advent'rous glade,

37. The *Wood* is symbolic like Spenser's wood of error (*F.Q.* I, i, 10, 8–9) and Dante's (*Inf.* I, 2).

46. The Homeric Hymn to Bacchus is the oldest version of the story of his transformation of the ship of some *Tuscan* (Italian) pirates who had kidnapped him into an arbor of vines. Ovid (*Met.* III, 670–86) added the changing of the pirates into dolphins.

50. *Circe's Island:* Aeaea in Homer (*Od.* X, 135) —lay somewhere in the Tyrrhenian sea off the Circean Promontory on the southwest coast of Italy.

58. *Comus:* see the headnote ¶ 2.

60. *Celtic:* French. *Iberian:* Spanish.

65. *orient:* bright, like orient (i.e. eastern) pearls.
66. *drought of Phoebus:* thirst caused by the sun-god, i.e. the sun.

71. *Ounce:* lynx.

72. In Homer (*Od.* X, 238) Circe turns Ulysses' men into swine, but Spenser's Circean witch, Acrasia (*F. Q.* II, xii, 39), like many such enchantresses in Renaissance allegory, is surrounded by beasts of many kinds. In William Browne's *Inner Temple Masque* Circe appeared, followed by "Two with harts' heads and bodies, . . . two like wolves, . . . two like baboons, and Grillus (of whom Plutarch writes . . .) in the shape of a hog."

Swift as the Sparkle of a glancing Star   80
I shoot from Heav'n to give him safe convoy,
As now I do. But first I must put off
These my sky robes spun out of *Iris'* Woof,
And take the Weeds and likeness of a Swain
That to the service of this house belongs,   85
Who with his soft Pipe and smooth-dittied Song
Well knows to still the wild winds when they roar,
And hush the waving Woods, nor of less faith,
And in this office of his Mountain watch
Likeliest, and nearest to the present aid   90
Of this occasion. But I hear the tread
Of hateful steps, I must be viewless now.

Comus *enters with a Charming Rod in one hand, his Glass in the other; with him a*
rout of Monsters, headed like sundry sorts of wild Beasts, but otherwise like Men and
Women, their Apparel glistering. They come in making a riotous and unruly noise,
with Torches in their hands.

 Comus. The Star that bids the Shepherd fold
Now the top of Heav'n doth hold,
And the gilded Car of Day   95
His glowing Axle doth allay
In the steep *Atlantic* stream,
And the slope Sun his upward beam
Shoots against the dusky Pole,
Pacing toward the other goal   100
Of his Chamber in the East.
Meanwhile welcome Joy and Feast,
Midnight shout and revelry,
Tipsy dance and Jollity.
Braid your Locks with rosy Twine   105
Dropping odors, dropping Wine.
Rigor now is gone to bed,
And Advice with scrupulous head,
Strict Age, and sour Severity,
With their grave Saws in slumber lie.   110
We that are of purer fire
Imitate the Starry Choir,
Who in their nightly watchful Spheres,
Lead in swift round the Months and Years.
The Sounds and Seas with all their finny drove   115
Now to the Moon in wavering Morris move,

86. Again in 494–6 Lawes's songs (ditties) are
praised. His implied comparison with Orpheus is
no bolder than Herrick's question in his epigram
To Mr. Henry Lawes: "Tell me, canst thou be Less
than Apollo?" Cf. the headnote ¶ 1.
 88. *nor of less faith:* no less trustworthy (than
he is admirable as a musician).
 92. *viewless:* invisible.
 93. So, in Spenser's *Virgil's Gnat,* 319, Venus
or Hesperus is "the folding star" because, when
it rises, the shepherd,
 "Gathering his straying flocke, does homeward
fare." J. A. Himes argues ingeniously in *MLN,*
XXXVI (1921), 414–15, that Sirius, the Dog Star,
is meant, because it rises when Leo (the Lion),
the flocks' enemy, is in the zenith.

 95–101. Cf. Euripides' sun god "sitting exalted
in a golden chariot and dividing his path through
the heavens" (*Phoenecian Damsels,* 1–2) to cool
his glowing wheels in the western ocean at night,
and Ovid's picture of the chariot of Phoebus (*Met.*
II, 59–69).
 110. *Saws:* maxims, proverbs.
 111–114. Scott Elledge notes a reminiscence of
Plato's *Timaeus,* 40, where the heavenly gods are
said to be created out of fire and to wheel in a
dance that measures all time. Cf. *Nat,* 117–32,
Vac, 40 and *PL* I, 117; V, 178 and 620–7.
 116. John Fryer's *New Account of East India and*
Persia: "A Chorus of Porpoises had taken the sea in
their Dance; which Morris once over, the Seas were
quiet" (quoted by *O.E.D.*).

And on the Tawny Sands and Shelves
Trip the pert Fairies and the dapper Elves;
By dimpled Brook and Fountain brim,
The Wood-Nymphs deckt with Daisies trim,   120
Their merry wakes and pastimes keep:
What hath night to do with sleep?
Night hath better sweets to prove,
Venus now wakes, and wak'ns Love.
Come let us our rites begin,   125
'Tis only daylight that makes Sin,
Which these dun shades will ne'er report
Hail Goddess of Nocturnal sport,
Dark veil'd *Cotytto,* t' whom the secret flame
Of midnight Torches burns; mysterious Dame,   130
That ne'er art call'd but when the Dragon womb
Of Stygian darkness spits her thickest gloom,
And makes one blot of all the air,
Stay thy cloudy Ebon chair
Wherein thou rid'st with *Hecat',* and befriend   135
Us thy vow'd Priests, till utmost end
Of all thy dues be done, and none left out
Ere the blabbing Eastern scout,
The nice Morn on th' *Indian* steep,
From her cabin'd loophole peep,   140
And to the telltale Sun descry
Our conceal'd Solemnity.
Come, knit hands, and beat the ground,
In a light fantastic round.

The Measure

Break off, break off, I feel the different pace   145
Of some chaste footing near about this ground.
Run to your shrouds within these Brakes and Trees;
Our number may affright: Some Virgin sure
(For so I can distinguish by mine Art)
Benighted in these Woods. Now to my charms,   150
And to my wily trains; I shall ere long
Be well stock't with as fair a herd as graz'd
About my Mother *Circe.* Thus I hurl
My dazzling Spells into the spongy air,
Of power to cheat the eye with blear illusion,   155
And give it false presentments, lest the place
And my quaint habits breed astonishment,

121. *wakes:* originally a wake was a religious festival lasting through the night.

129. In a condemnation of Rome as more viciously superstitious than the East itself Juvenal (*Sat.* II, 91–92) attacked the orgies of the Thracian goddess *Cotytto.* Her midnight rites were burlesqued by Horace (*Ep.* XVI, 56–57).

131. *Dragons* compose "triple Hecate's team" in *A Midsummer Night's Dream* V, 391. Cf. the note on her in *Ely,* 57.

135. Cf. Medea's terrible invocation of *Hecate* in Ovid (*Met.* VII, 94 and 194). In *Macbeth* III, v, 10, she is the "Mistress of the witches" and the "close contriver of all harms."

139. The *Indian steep* is the Himalayas, the "steep of India" in *A Midsummer Night's Dream* II, i, 69. Cf. *PR* IV, 575.

142. Cf. *solemnity* in *Arc,* 39.

147. *shrouds:* cover, hiding places. Cf. *Nat,* 218 and l. 316 below.

151. *trains:* lures. Cf. *venereal trains* in *SA,* 533.

154. In the Trinity MS "powder'd" in the place of *dazzling* suggests that something like confetti may have been thrown. *spongy:* absorbing.

155. *blear:* misty, confusing.

156. *false presentments:* misleading representations, illusions.

157. *quaint habits:* strange dress. Cf. *Nat,* 194 and *SA,* 1303.

And put the Damsel to suspicious flight,
Which must not be, for that's against my course.
I under fair pretense of friendly ends   160
And well-plac't words of glozing courtesy,
Baited with reasons not unplausible,
Wind me into the easy-hearted man,
And hug him into snares.   When once her eye
Hath met the virtue of this Magic dust,   165
I shall appear some harmless Villager
Whom thrift keeps up about his Country gear;
But here she comes, I fairly step aside,
And hearken, if I may, her business here.

The Lady enters.

Lady.   This way the noise was, if mine ear be true,   170
My best guide now; methought it was the sound
Of Riot and ill-manag'd Merriment,
Such as the jocund Flute or gamesome Pipe
Stirs up among the loose unletter'd Hinds,
When for their teeming Flocks and granges full   175
In wanton dance they praise the bounteous *Pan,*
And thank the gods amiss.   I should be loath
To meet the rudeness and swill'd insolence
Of such late Wassailers; yet O where else
Shall I inform my unacquainted feet   180
In the blind mazes of this tangl'd Wood?
My Brothers, when they saw me wearied out
With this long way, resolving here to lodge
Under the spreading favor of these Pines,
Stept as they said to the next Thicket side   185
To bring me Berries, or such cooling fruit
As the kind hospitable Woods provide.
They left me then, when the gray-hooded Ev'n
Like a sad Votarist in Palmer's weed
Rose from the hindmost wheels of *Phœbus'* wain.   190
But where they are, and why they came not back,
Is now the labor of my thoughts; 'tis likeliest
They had engag'd their wand'ring steps too far,
And envious darkness, ere they could return,
Had stole them from me; else O thievish Night   195
Why shouldst thou, but for some felonious end,
In thy dark lantern thus close up the Stars,
That nature hung in Heav'n, and fill'd their Lamps
With everlasting oil, to give due light
To the misled and lonely Traveller?   200
This is the place, as well as I may guess,

161. *glozing:* insinuating, flattering.
165. *virtue*—power—is used as it is in *PL* IV,
198.
169. This reading was corrected in 1673 to:
   And hearken, if I may her business hear.
The preferable reading of 1645 means: "listen so
as to find out why she is here."
174. *Hinds:* farm laborers.
175. *teeming:* multiplying, bearing young.
granges: barns.
176. *Pan,* "the shepheards god," as Spenser called

him (*Calendar,* April, 5), sometimes represented
God in pastoral poetry rather than the nature
deity of classical tradition. Cf. *Nat,* 89.
179. *Wassailers:* revellers, drinkers of wassail.
189. *sad Votarist:* A votarist was a person under
any kind of vow, but a *Palmer* was a pilgrim who
carried a bit of palm as evidence that he had been
to the Holy Land.
197. Cf. "There's Husbandry in Heaven, Their
Candles are all out" (*Macbeth* II, i, 10–11).

Whence ev'n now the tumult of loud Mirth
Was rife and perfect in my list'ning ear,
Yet nought but single darkness do I find.
What might this be?   A thousand fantasies   205
Begin to throng into my memory,
Of calling shapes and beck'ning shadows dire,
And airy tongues that syllable men's names
On Sands and Shores and desert Wildernesses.
These thoughts may startle well, but not astound   210
The virtuous mind, that ever walks attended
By a strong siding champion Conscience.——
O welcome pure-ey'd Faith, white-handed Hope,
Thou hov'ring Angel girt with golden wings,
And thou unblemish't form of Chastity,   215
I see ye visibly, and now believe
That he, the Supreme good, t' whom all things ill
Are but as slavish officers of vengeance,
Would send a glist'ring Guardian, if need were,
To keep my life and honor unassail'd.   220
Was I deceiv'd, or did a sable cloud
Turn forth her silver lining on the night?
I did not err, there does a sable cloud
Turn forth her silver lining on the night,
And casts a gleam over this tufted Grove.   225
I cannot hallo to my Brothers, but
Such noise as I can make to be heard farthest
I'll venture, for my new enliv'n'd spirits
Prompt me; and they perhaps are not far off.

SONG

Sweet Echo, sweetest Nymph that liv'st unseen   230
          Within thy airy shell
     By slow Meander's margent green,
And in the violet-embroider'd vale
     Where the love-lorn Nightingale
Nightly to thee her sad Song mourneth well.   235

Canst thou not tell me of a gentle Pair
          That likest thy Narcissus are?
          O if thou have
          Hid them in some flow'ry Cave,
          Tell me but where,   240
Sweet Queen of Parley, Daughter of the Sphere,
So mayst thou be translated to the skies,
And give resounding grace to all Heav'n's Harmonies.

204. *single*: mere or total.
215. See the headnote ¶ 7.
216. The Platonic conception of the ideal of a virtue becoming so distinct to the mind that it can be seen had Bacon's approval when he said "that virtue, if she could be seen, would move great love and affection; so seeing that she cannot be showed to the sense by corporal shape, the next degree is to show her to the imagination in lively representation" (*Advancement* II, xviii, 3; p. 178).

230. Songs with *Echo* answering, as in Jonson's *Masque of Queens* and Browne's *Inner Temple Masque*, were common. This one recalls that Echo was a nymph in love with *Narcissus* (in Ovid's *Met.* III, 351–401), and that she wandered everywhere, from the river *Meander* in Phrygia to the valleys of the *nightingales* below Pindar's "violet-crowned Athens" (Frag. LXXV—45). She is the *Daughter of the Sphere* because her *airy shell* is the arch of the sky.

  Comus. Can any mortal mixture of Earth's mold
Breathe such Divine enchanting ravishment?   245
Sure something holy lodges in that breast,
And with these raptures moves the vocal air
To testify his hidd'n residence;
How sweetly did they float upon the wings
Of silence, through the empty-vaulted night,   250
At every fall smoothing the Raven down
Of darkness till it smil'd: I have oft heard
My mother *Circe* with the Sirens three,
Amidst the flow'ry-kirl'd *Naiades,*
Culling their Potent herbs and baleful drugs,   255
Who as they sung, would take the prison'd soul,
And lap it in *Elysium; Scylla* wept,
And chid her barking waves into attention,
And fell *Charybdis* murmur'd soft applause:
Yet they in pleasing slumber lull'd the sense,   260
And in sweet madness robb'd it of itself,
But such a sacred and home-felt delight,
Such sober certainty of waking bliss,
I never heard till now. I'll speak to her
And she shall be my Queen. Hail foreign wonder,   265
Whom certain these rough shades did never breed,
Unless the Goddess that in rural shrine
Dwell'st here with *Pan* or *Silvan,* by blest Song
Forbidding every bleak unkindly Fog
To touch the prosperous growth of this tall Wood.   270
  Lady. Nay gentle Shepherd, ill is lost that praise
That is addrest to unattending Ears;
Not any boast of skill, but extreme shift
How to regain my sever'd company,
Compell'd me to awake the courteous Echo   275
To give me answer from her mossy Couch.
  Comus. What chance, good Lady, hath bereft you thus?
  Lady. Dim darkness and this leavy Labyrinth.
  Comus. Could that divide you from near-ushering guides?
  Lady. They left me weary on a grassy turf.   280
  Comus. By falsehood, or discourtesy, or why?
  Lady. To seek i'th' valley some cool friendly Spring.
  Comus. And left your fair side all unguarded, Lady?
  Lady. They were but twain, and purpos'd quick return.
  Comus. Perhaps forestalling night prevented them.   285
  Lady. How easy my misfortune is to hit!
  Comus. Imports their loss, beside the present need?
  Lady. No less than if I should my brothers lose.
  Comus. Were they of manly prime, or youthful bloom?
  Lady. As smooth as *Hebe's* their unrazor'd lips.   290
  Comus. Two such I saw, what time the labor'd Ox

---

253. Ovid's picture of *Circe* gathering flowers with water nymphs like the *Naiades* (*Met.* XIV, 264–68) fuses with Homer's *Sirens* (*Od.* XII, 39–72), whose songs lured sailors to their death.

257. *Scylla,* whose deadly rocks lay opposite the whirlpool of *Charybdis* in the Sicilian Straits, was a nymph whom Circe had transformed from the waist down into barking dogs (*Met.* XIV, 8–74).

Allegorizing the myth, Natale Conti said (VIII, xii; p. 880) that Scylla's metamorphosis signified the brutal degeneration of men who fall away from the life of reason.

268. Here *Pan* is a mere wood god, like *Sylvanus,* with whom Virgil linked him (*Ec.* X, 24).

277–90. For the form of dialogue, stichomythia, see the headnote ¶ 5.

In his loose traces from the furrow came,
And the swink't hedger at his Supper sat;
I saw them under a green mantling vine
That crawls along the side of yon small hill,   295
Plucking ripe clusters from the tender shoots;
Their port was more than human, as they stood;
I took it for a faëry vision
Of some gay creatures of the element
That in the colors of the Rainbow live   300
And play i'th' plighted clouds. I was awe-struck,
And as I past, I worshipt; if those you seek,
It were a journey like the path to Heav'n
To help you find them.
    Lady.   Gentle villager,
What readiest way would bring me to that place?   305
    Comus. Due west it rises from this shrubby point.
    Lady. To find out that, good Shepherd, I suppose,
In such a scant allowance of Star-light,
Would overtask the best Land-Pilot's art,
Without the sure guess of well-practic'd feet.   310
    Comus. I know each lane and every alley green,
Dingle or bushy dell of this wild Wood,
And every bosky bourn from side to side,
My daily walks and ancient neighborhood
And if your stray attendance be yet lodg'd,   315
Or shroud within these limits, I shall know
Ere morrow wake or the low-roosted lark
From her thatch't pallet rouse; if otherwise,
I can conduct you, Lady, to a low
But loyal cottage, where you may be safe   320
Till further quest.
    Lady.   Shepherd, I take thy word,
And trust thy honest offer'd courtesy,
Which oft is sooner found in lowly sheds
With smoky rafters, than in tap'stry Halls
And Courts of Princes, where it first was nam'd,   325
And yet is most pretended: In a place
Less warranted than this or less secure
I cannot be, that I should fear to change it.
Eye me blest Providence, and square my trial
To my proportion'd strength. Shepherd lead on.—   330

The Two Brothers.

    Elder Brother. Unmuffle ye faint stars, and thou fair Moon
That wont'st to love the traveller's benison,
Stoop thy pale visage through an amber cloud,

292. So in Homer (*Il.* XVI, 779) and Virgil (*Ec.* II, 67) the unyoking of oxen is a symbol of nightfall.

293. *swink't:* hard-worked, tired.

297. *port:* bearing, deportment. The scene is like the herdmen's mistake of Pylades and Orestes for gods in Euripides' *Iphigeneia in Tauris* (250–73).

299. *element:* the air, which was the allotted home of spirits. Cf. *PR* II, 122 and *IlPen,* 93–99.

301. *plighted:* folded.

312. *Dingle:* cleft between hills.

313. *bosky bourn:* stream overhung by bushes (bosks).

318. *thatch't pallet:* bed or nest of straw.

332. *benison:* blessing. Cf. the moon shining through clouds in Spenser's *F.Q.* III, i, 43, 5–6:
    Of the poore traueller, that went astray,
    With thousand blessings she is heried.

And disinherit *Chaos,* that reigns here
In double night of darkness and of shades;   335
Or if your influence be quite damm'd up
With black usurping mists, some gentle taper,
Though a rush Candle from the wicker hole
Of some clay habitation, visit us
With thy long levell'd rule of streaming light,   340
And thou shalt be our star of *Arcady*
Or *Tyrian* Cynosure.
    Second Brother.   Or if our eyes
Be barr'd that happiness, might we but hear
The folded flocks penn'd in their wattled cotes,
Or sound of pastoral reed with oaten stops,   345
Or whistle from the Lodge, or village cock
Count the night watches to his feathery Dames,
'Twould be some solace yet, some little cheering
In this close dungeon of innumerous boughs.
But O that hapless virgin our lost sister,   350
Where may she wander now, whither betake her
From the chill dew, amongst rude burs and thistles?
Perhaps some cold bank is her bolster now,
Or 'gainst the rugged bark of some broad Elm
Leans her unpillow'd head fraught with sad fears.   355
What if in wild amazement and affright,
Or while we speak, within the direful grasp
Of Savage hunger or of Savage heat?
    Elder Brother. Peace brother, be not over-exquisite
To cast the fashion of uncertain evils;   360
For grant they be so, while they rest unknown,
What need a man forestall his date of grief,
And run to meet what he would most avoid?
Or if they be but false alarms of Fear,
How bitter is such self-delusion?   365
I do not think my sister so to seek,
Or so unprincipl'd in virtue's book
And the sweet peace that goodness bosoms ever,
As that the single want of light and noise
(Not being in danger, as I trust she is not)   370
Could stir the constant mood of her calm thoughts,
And put them into misbecoming plight.
Virtue could see to do what virtue would
By her own radiant light, though Sun and Moon

334. *disinherit Chaos:* disposses *Chaos.* Cf. *PL* I, 10 and 543; II, 895.

336. Cf. the *precious influence* of the stars in *Nat,* 71 and *PL* IX, 107.

342. *Tyrian Cynosure:* the pole star, by which the Phoenician sailors steered. In Ovid (*Met.* II, 401–507) the Arcadian princess Callisto, who bore a son Arcas to Jove, was transformed into the Great Bear while Arcas became the Little Bear, the tip of whose tail is the North Star.

344. *wattled cotes:* sheepfolds of stakes and plaited twigs.

345. The traditional pipe in pastoral poetry was a flute made of a reed, like the "oaten pipe" of Spenser's Colin Clout (*Calendar,* January, 72).

349. *innumerous:* innumerable. Cf. *PL* VII, 455.

359. *over-exquisite:* over-curious, over-precise.

360. *cast:* forecast, foresee and worry over.

365. *delusion,* like *condition* in l. 685, has four syllables.

366. *to seek:* to be at a loss.

368. Cf. Norfolk's advice in *Henry VIII* I, i, 112: "Bosom up thy counsel."

373. Cf. Redcross's encouragement of Una in the wood of error:
Vertue giues her selfe light, through darkenesse for to wade.
                      (*F.Q.* I, i, 12, 9)

Were in the flat Sea sunk.   And Wisdom's self   375
Oft seeks to sweet retired Solitude,
Where with her best nurse Contemplation
She plumes her feathers, and lets grow her wings
That in the various bustle of resort
Were all to-ruffl'd, and somtimes impair'd.   380
He that has light within his own clear breast
May sit i'th' center, and enjoy bright day,
But he that hides a dark soul and foul thoughts
Benighted walks under the midday Sun;
Himself is his own dungeon.
    Second Brother.   'Tis most true   385
That musing meditation most affects
The Pensive secrecy of desert cell,
Far from the cheerful haunt of men and herds,
And sits as safe as in a Senate-house;
For who would rob a Hermit of his Weeds,   390
His few Books, or his Beads, or Maple Dish,
Or do his gray hairs any violence?
But beauty, like the fair Hesperian Tree
Laden with blooming gold, had need the guard
Of dragon watch with unenchanted eye,   395
To save her blossoms and defend her fruit
From the rash hand of bold Incontinence.
You may as well spread out the unsunn'd heaps
Of Miser's treasure by an outlaw's den,
And tell me it is safe, as bid me hope   400
Danger will wink on Opportunity,
And let a single helpless maiden pass
Uninjured in this wild surrounding waste.
Of night or loneliness it recks me not,
I fear the dread events that dog them both,   405
Lest some ill-greeting touch attempt the person
Of our unowned sister.
    Elder Brother.   I do not, brother,
Infer as if I thought my sister's state
Secure without all doubt or controversy:
Yet where an equal poise of hope and fear   410
Does arbitrate th'event, my nature is
That I incline to hope rather than fear,
And gladly banish squint suspicion.
My sister is not so defenceless left
As you imagine; she has a hidden strength   415
Which you remember not.

377. Cf. *Contemplation* in *IlPen*, 54. The pronunciation is *contemplati-on*, in five syllables.

380. *to-ruffl'd*: ruffled up, bedraggled; *to-* is an intensive prefix. Cf. "woman . . . all to-brake his skull" (Judges ix, 53).

382. *center*: the earth. Cf. *PL* I, 686.

385. Cf. the thought in *PL* I, 255; IV, 20; and *SA*, 155–6.

386. *affects*: loves, feels an affection for.

393. In l. 981 Milton treats the *Golden Tree* in the Gardens of the Hesperides as a symbol of paradise, but its dragon-guarded fruit might also symbolize the beauty of the Hesperian maidens whose rescue from their ravishers by Hercules Conti records (VII, vii; p. 735).

395. *unenchanted*: unenchantable. Cf. the similar, Latin use of the participle in l. 215.

401. Cf. the similar use of *Danger* in *PL* II, 1008. and of *Opportunity* in Shakespeare's reference to harlots in *Troilus and Cressida* IV, v, 62, as "sluttish spoils of opportunity."

404. *it recks* etc.: it makes no difference to me . . . Cf. *Lyc*, 122.

407. *Unowned*: unaccompanied, unprotected.

411. *arbitrate th'event*: determine the outcome.

    Second Brother.   What hidden strength,
Unless the strength of Heav'n, if you mean that?
    Elder Brother. I mean that too, but yet a hidden strength
Which if Heav'n gave it, may be term'd her own:
'Tis chastity, my brother, chastity: 420
She that has that, is clad in complete steel,
And like a quiver'd Nymph with Arrows keen
May trace huge Forests and unharbor'd Heaths,
Infamous Hills and sandy perilous wilds,
Where through the sacred rays of Chastity,   425
No savage fierce, Bandit or mountaineer
Will dare to soil her Virgin purity:
Yea there, where very desolation dwells,
By grots and caverns shagg'd with horrid shades,
She may pass on with unblench't majesty,   430
Be it not done in pride or in presumption.
Some say no evil thing that walks by night
In fog or fire, by lake or moorish fen,
Blue meager Hag or stubborn unlaid ghost
That breaks his magic chains at curfew time,   435
No goblin or swart Faëry of the mine,
Hath hurtful power o'er true virginity.
Do ye believe me yet, or shall I call
Antiquity from the old Schools of *Greece*
To testify the arms of Chastity?   440
Hence had the huntress *Dian* her dread bow,
Fair silver-shafted Queen for ever chaste,
Wherewith she tam'd the brinded lioness
And spotted mountain pard, but set at nought
The frivolous bolt of *Cupid;* gods and men   445
Fear'd her stern frown, and she was queen o' th' Woods.
What was that snaky-headed *Gorgon* shield
That wise *Minerva* wore, unconquer'd Virgin,
Wherewith she freez'd her foes to congeal'd stone,
But rigid looks of Chaste austerity   450
And noble grace that dash't brute violence
With sudden adoration and blank awe?
So dear to Heav'n is Saintly chastity,
That when a soul is found sincerely so,
A thousand liveried Angels lackey her,   455
Driving far off each thing of sin and guilt,
And in clear dream and solemn vision
Tell her of things that no gross ear can hear,

---

422. *a quiver'd Nymph*: a nymph whose quiver of arrows marked her as a follower of *the huntress Dian* (l. 441), the goddess of chastity, whose passion for hunting Conti said (III, xviii; p. 273) was itself symbolic of chastity.

423. *unharbor'd*: unsheltered, lacking harbors. Cf. *Vac*, 88 and *PR* I, 307.

430. *unblench't*: undismayed.

433. *fire*: Will-o'-the-wisp, Jack-o'-lantern, or fatuous fire. Books of travel described spirits such as William Cuningham said in his *Cosmographical Glas* (1559, p. Rvir) sought to bring travellers in Asia "into daungers, sumtime by calling them by theyr names, other times by musical noise, alluringe

them by the swetnes of the sounde, vntil they be brought into danger through wilde beasts." Cf. *L'All*, 104.

436. Cf. the daemons of *underground* in *IlPen*, 93–94.

439. *Schools of Greece*: the *schools of ancient Sages* of *PR* IV, 251.

444. *pard*: panther.

448. *Minerva*, as she is described by Homer (*Il.* V, 738–41), carrying the Gorgon's petrifying face on her shield, is explained by Conti (IV, v, p. 311) as symbolizing the dread which she strikes into her lustful enemies.

457. Cf. Bacon quoting "the Hebrew rabbins—

Till oft converse with heav'nly habitants
Begin to cast a beam on th'outward shape,   460
The unpolluted temple of the mind,
And turns it by degrees to the soul's essence,
Till all be made immortal: but when lust
By unchaste looks, loose gestures, and foul talk,
But most by lewd and lavish act of sin,   465
Lets in defilement to the inward parts,
The soul grows clotted by contagion,
Imbodies and imbrutes, till she quite lose
The divine property of her first being.
Such are those thick and gloomy shadows damp   470
Oft seen in Charnel vaults and Sepulchers,
Lingering and sitting by a new-made grave,
As loath to leave the body that it lov'd,
And link't itself by carnal sensualty
To a degenerate and degraded state.   475
  Second Brother. How charming is divine Philosophy!
Not harsh and crabbed as dull fools suppose,
But musical as is *Apollo's* lute,
And a perpetual feast of nectar'd sweets,
Where no crude surfeit reigns.
  Elder Brother. List, list, I hear   480
Some far-off hallo break the silent Air.
  Second Brother. Methought so too; what should it be?
  Elder Brother.   For certain
Either some one like us night-founder'd here,
Or else some neighbor Woodman, or at worst,
Some roving Robber calling to his fellows.   485
  Second Brother. Heav'n keep my sister! Again, again, and near!
Best draw, and stand upon our guard.
  Elder Brother.   I'll hallo;
If he be friendly he comes well, if not,
Defense is a good cause, and Heav'n be for us.

   The attendant Spirit habited like a Shepherd.

That hallo I should know; what are you? speak;   490
Come not too near, you fall on iron stakes else.
  Spirit. What voice is that? my young Lord? speak again.
  Second Brother. O brother, 'tis my father's Shepherd sure.
  Elder Brother. Thyrsis? Whose artful strains have oft delay'd

'Your young men shall see visions, and your old men shall dream dreams' " to prove that the object of education should be to secure such "apparitions of God" (*Advancement* I, iii, 3; p. 21). Cf. *PL* XII, 611.

462. Cf. the explanation of this basic Miltonic doctrine to Adam by Raphael in *PL* V, 496–503. Here the thought is involved with St. Paul's question: "Know ye not that ye are the temple of God, and that the Spirit of God dwelleth in you?" (1 Cor. iii, 16).

466. Cf. Psalm li, 6: "Thou desirest truth in the inward parts."

468. Cf. *imbrute* in *PL* IX, 166.

466–475. The passage follows Socrates' argument for the soul's immortality (*Phaedo*, 81) on the ground that noble spirits welcome release from the body and its passions through death; while the souls of the wicked are dragged back after death to this visible world by their fear of the invisible and by their load of fleshly lusts, and are seen haunting their tombs. The thought was echoed by Lactantius (*Divine Institutes* VII, xx, 8–9) and by other Christian writers.

478. *nectar'd:* heavenly. Cf. l. 838 below, and *PL* IV, 240

479. *crude:* indigestible.

483. *night-founder'd:* overwhelmed by night. Cf. *PL* I, 204.

491. *iron stakes:* swords.

494. Theocritus and Virgil made the name *Thyrsis* traditional in pastoral poetry.

The huddling brook to hear his madrigal,   495
And sweeten'd every musk rose of the dale.
How cam'st thou here good Swain?   hath any ram
Slipt from the fold, or young Kid lost his dam,
Or straggling wether the pent flock forsook?
How couldst thou find this dark sequester'd nook?   500
   Spirit.   O my lov'd master's heir and his next joy,
I came not here on such a trivial toy
As a stray'd Ewe, or to pursue the stealth
Of pilfering Wolf; not all the fleecy wealth
That doth enrich these Downs, is worth a thought   505
To this my errand, and the care it brought.
But O my Virgin Lady, where is she?
How chance she is not in your company?
   Elder Brother.   To tell thee sadly, Shepherd, without blame,
Or our neglect, we lost her as we came.   510
   Spirit.   Ay me unhappy! then my fears are true.
   Elder Brother.   What fears good *Thyrsis?*   Prithee briefly show.
   Spirit.   I'll tell ye; 'tis not vain or fabulous,
(Though so esteem'd by shallow ignorance)
What the sage Poets taught by th' heav'nly Muse   515
Storied of old in high immortal verse
Of dire *Chimeras* and enchanted Isles,
And rifted Rocks whose entrance leads to hell,
For such there be, but unbelief is blind.
   Within the navel of this hideous Wood,   520
Immur'd in cypress shades, a Sorcerer dwells,
Of *Bacchus* and of *Circe* born, great *Comus,*
Deep skill'd in all his mother's witcheries,
And here to every thirsty wanderer,
By sly enticement gives his baneful cup,   525
With many murmurs mixt, whose pleasing poison
The visage quite transforms of him that drinks,
And the inglorious likeness of a beast
Fixes instead, unmolding reason's mintage
Charácter'd in the face; this have I learnt   530
Tending my flocks hard by i'th' hilly crofts
That brow this bottom glade, whence night by night
He and his monstrous rout are heard to howl
Like stabl'd wolves, or tigers at their prey,
Doing abhorred rites to *Hecate*   535
In their obscured haunts of inmost bow'rs.
Yet have they many baits and guileful spells
To inveigle and invite th'unwary sense
Of them that pass unweeting by the way.
This evening late, by then the chewing flocks   540
Had ta'en their supper on the savory Herb
Of Knotgrass dew-besprent, and were in fold,
I sat me down to watch upon a bank

495. *huddling:* pressing (i.e. to hear Thyrsis',
i.e., Lawes', music). Cf. l. 84 above.
   509. *sadly:* seriously.
   517. The monster *Chimaera,* which Hesiod describes with its three heads of lion, goat, and dragon
(*Theog.,* 319–25), was a traditional symbol of
monsters of all kinds, real and imaginary. Cf. *PL*
VII, 18, n., and II, 628.

520. *navel:* center.
526. *murmurs:* incantations.
530. *Charácter'd:* engraved or stamped, as money
is minted.
531. *crofts:* small enclosed farms.
532. *brow:* overlook.
539. *unweeting:* unwitting, uninformed.

With Ivy canopied, and interwove
With flaunting Honeysuckle, and began,   545
Wrapt in a pleasing fit of melancholy,
To meditate my rural minstrelsy,
Till fancy had her fill; but ere a close
The wonted roar was up amidst the Woods,
And fill'd the Air with barbarous dissonance,   550
At which I ceas't, and listen'd them a while,
Till an unusual stop of sudden silence
Gave respite to the drowsy frighted steeds
That draw the litter of close-curtain'd sleep;
At last a soft and solemn-breathing sound   555
Rose like a stream of rich distill'd Perfumes,
And stole upon the Air, that even Silence
Was took ere she was ware, and wish't she might
Deny her nature, and be never more,
Still to be so displac't. I was all ear,   560
And took in strains that might create a soul
Under the ribs of Death; but O ere long
Too well I did perceive it was the voice
Of my most honor'd Lady, your dear sister.
Amaz'd I stood, harrow'd with grief and fear,   565
And "O poor hapless Nightingale," thought I,
"How sweet thou sing'st, how near the deadly snare!"
Then down the Lawns I ran with headlong haste
Through paths and turnings oft'n trod by day,
Till guided by mine ear I found the place   570
Where that damn'd wizard hid in sly disguise
(For so by certain signs I knew) had met
Already, ere my best speed could prevent,
The aidless innocent Lady his wish't prey
Who gently ask't if he had seen such two,   575
Supposing him some neighbor villager;
Longer I durst not stay, but soon I guess'd
Ye were the two she meant; with that I sprung
Into swift flight, till I had found you here,
But further know I not.
  Second Brother. O night and shades,   580
How are ye join'd with hell in triple knot
Against th'unarmed weakness of one Virgin
Alone and helpless! Is this the confidence
You gave me, Brother?
  Elder Brother. Yes, and keep it still,
Lean on it safely, not a period   585
Shall be unsaid for me: against the threats
Of malice or of sorcery, or that power
Which erring men call Chance, this I hold firm;
Virtue may be assail'd but never hurt,
Surpris'd by unjust force but not enthrall'd,   590

546. *melancholy:* not sadness but the mood invoked in *IlPen,* 12.
 547. Cf. *meditate* in *Lyc,* 66. Thyrsis means
that he improvised a tune.
 548. *close:* conclusion of a musical theme.
 553. *drowsie frighted* is the reading of the early
editions. Most editors follow the Trinity MS, which
has "drowsie-flighted." Or perhaps "drowsy-

freighted.'
 554. *litter:* chariot made so that the traveller
could lie down. With *close-curtain'd sleep* cf. Macbeth's "Curtain'd sleepe" (*Macbeth* II, i, 64).
 560. *Still . . . displac't:* provided that she might
always be supplanted by such music.
 568. *Lewns:* grassy, open lanes in the forest.
 585. *period:* sentence.

Yea even that which mischief meant most harm
Shall in the happy trial prove most glory.
But evil on itself shall back recoil,
And mix no more with goodness, when at last
Gather'd like scum, and settl'd to itself,   595
It shall be in eternal restless change
Self-fed and self-consum'd; if this fail,
The pillar'd firmament is rott'nness,
And earth's base built on stubble. But come, let's on.
Against th' opposing will and arm of Heav'n   600
May never this just sword be lifted up,
But for that damn'd magician, let him be girt
With all the grisly legions that troop
Under the sooty flag of *Acheron,*
Harpies and *Hydras,* or all the monstrous forms   605
'Twixt *Africa* and *Inde,* I'll find him out,
And force him to restore his purchase back,
Or drag him by the curls to a foul death,
Curs'd as his life.
    Spirit.   Alas good vent'rous youth,
I love thy courage yet and bold Emprise,   610
But here thy sword can do thee little stead;
Far other arms and other weapons must
Be those that quell the might of hellish charms.
He with his bare wand can unthread thy joints,
And crumble all thy sinews.
    Elder Brother.   Why, prithee Shepherd,   615
How durst thou then thyself approach so near
As to make this relation?
    Spirit.   Care and utmost shifts
How to secure the Lady from surprisal,
Brought to my mind a certain Shepherd Lad
Of small regard to see to, yet well skill'd   620
In every virtuous plant and healing herb
That spreads her verdant leaf to th'morning ray.
He lov'd me well, and oft would beg me sing,
Which when I did, he on the tender grass
Would sit, and hearken even to ecstasy,   625
And in requital ope his leathern scrip,
And show me simples of a thousand names,
Telling their strange and vigorous faculties;
Amongst the rest a small unsightly root,
But of divine effect, he cull'd me out;   630
The leaf was darkish, and had prickles on it,
But in another Country, as he said,
Bore a bright golden flow'r, but not in this soil:
Unknown, and like esteem'd, and the dull swain

593–597. Cf. the restatement of this thought in *PL* XI, 50-53; and II, 795–802.

604. *Acheron* was one of the four rivers of Hades, but here it stands simply for hell. Cf. *PL* II, 577–80.

605. Cf. *Harpies* in *PR* II, 403, and *Hydras* in *PL* II, 628.

606. *Inde,* India, stands for the far east as *Africa* does for the west.   Mt. Atlas, opposite Gibraltar, was the extreme western landmark in the ancient world.

607. *purchase:* prey. Originally it meant the chase of game.

621. *virtuous:* rich in healing power. Cf. *PL* IX, 616.

626. *scrip:* bag.

627. *simples:* medicinal plants, so-called because they were used uncompounded as simple remedies.

Treads on it daily with his clouted shoon,   635
And yet more med'cinal is it than that *Moly*
That *Hermes* once to wise *Ulysses* gave;
He call'd it *Haemony,* and gave it me,
And bade me keep it as of sovran use
'Gainst all enchantments, mildew blast, or damp,   640
Or ghastly furies' apparition;
I purs't it up, but little reck'ning made,
Till now that this extremity compell'd,
But now I find it true; for by this means
I knew the foul enchanter though disguis'd,   645
Enter'd the very lime-twigs of his spells,
And yet came off: if you have this about you
(As I will give you when we go) you may
Boldly assault the necromancer's hall;
Where if he be, with dauntless hardihood   650
And brandish't blade rush on him, break his glass,
And shed the luscious liquor on the ground,
But seize his wand; though he and his curst crew
Fierce sign of battle make, and menace high,
Or like the sons of *Vulcan* vomit smoke,   655
Yet will they soon retire, if he but shrink.
 Elder Brother. *Thyrsis* lead on apace, I'll follow thee,
And some good angel bear a shield before us.

The Scene changes to a stately Palace set out with all manner of deliciousness; soft Music, Tables spread with all dainties. Comus *appears with his rabble, and the Lady set in an enchanted Chair, to whom he offers his Glass, which she puts by, and goes about to rise.*

 Comus. Nay Lady, sit; if I but wave this wand,
Your nerves are all chain'd up in Alabaster   660
And you a statue; or as *Daphne* was,
Root-bound, that fled *Apollo.*
 Lady. Fool, do not boast.
Thou canst not touch the freedom of my mind
With all thy charms, although this corporal rind
Thou hast immanacl'd, while Heav'n sees good.   665
 Comus. Why are you vext, Lady? why do you frown?

635. *clouted:* patched, or studded with iron clouts.
636. *Moly* was the herb with milk-white flower and dark root given to Ulysses by Hermes (*Od.* X, 287–303) to immunize him against Circe's charms. The name *Haemony* suggests derivation from Haemonia (Thessaly), a traditional land of magic, or perhaps simply the exotic character of the plant which—as E. S. LeComte in *PQ,* XXI (1943), 283–98, and T. P. Harrison, Jr. in *PQ,* XXII (1944), 251–54, have shown—was related by contemporary herbalists to several similar foreign plants, like the Italian Christ's-thorn, which were supposed to protect against enchantments. For Milton's readers *Moly* signified "that loue of honestie and hatred of ill" which Roger Ascham saw in it and to which he said that David gave the plainer name of "the feare of God" (Ascham, *English Works,* ed. Wright, p. 226). The popularity of the story of Mercury's gift of haemony "to wise Ulysses" explains many allusions to it as a protection against black magic, one of which Scott Elledge has spotted in *MLN,* LVIII (1943), 551, in the form of an exact antici-

pation of .. 637 in the crude play of *The Valiant Welshman* (1615), IV, ii, 12.
651. So Mercury (*Od.* X, 294–5) tells Ulysses to draw his sword and attack Circe the moment she touches him with her wand.
652. So Spenser's Knight of Temperance refuses and shatters a tempter's cup on the ground,
 That all in peeces it was broken fond,
 And with the liquor stained all the lond.
     (*F.Q.* II, xii, 49, 7–8)
655. The fire god *Vulcan,* whose forge was under Mt. Aetna, was the father or master of the "Fiery Spirits" which Burton described as keeping "their residence in that *Hecla,* a mountain in *Iceland, Aetna,* in Sicily, *Lipari, Vesuvius* etc." (*Anatomy* I, ii, 1, 2; Vol. I, 191).
660. *nerves:* sinews. *Alabaster:* marble.
661. When *Daphne* was pursued by *Apollo,* Ovid says (*Met.* I, 547–52), she escaped by turning into a laurel, her arms becoming branches and her feet roots in an instant.

Here dwell no frowns, nor anger, from these gates
Sorrow flies far: See, here be all the pleasures
That fancy can beget on youthful thoughts,
When the fresh blood grows lively, and returns   670
Brisk as the *April* buds in Primrose-season.
And first behold this cordial Julep here,
That flames and dances in his crystal bounds
With spirits of balm and fragrant Syrups mixt.
Not that *Nepenthes* which the wife of *Thone*   675
In *Egypt* gave to *Jove*-born *Helena*
Is of such power to stir up joy as this,
To life so friendly, or so cool to thirst.
Why should you be so cruel to yourself,
And to those dainty limbs which nature lent   680
For gentle usage and soft delicacy?
But you invert the cov'nants of her trust,
And harshly deal like an ill borrower
With that which you receiv'd on other terms,
Scorning the unexempt condition   685
By which all mortal frailty must subsist,
Refreshment after toil, ease after pain,
That have been tir'd all day without repast,
And timely rest have wanted; but, fair Virgin,
This will restore all soon.
    Lady.   'Twill not, false traitor,   690
'Twill not restore the truth and honesty
That thou hast banish't from thy tongue with lies.
Was this the cottage and the safe abode
Thou told'st me of?   What grim aspects are these,
These ugly-headed Monsters?   Mercy guard me!   695
Hence with thy brew'd enchantments, foul deceiver;
Hast thou betray'd my credulous innocence
With vizor'd falsehood and base forgery,
And wouldst thou seek again to trap me here
With lickerish baits fit to ensnare a brute?   700
Were it a draught for *Juno* when she banquets,
I would not taste thy treasonous offer; none
But such as are good men can give good things,
And that which is not good, is not delicious
To a well-govern'd and wise appetite.   705
    Comus.   O foolishness of men! that lend their ears
To those budge doctors of the *Stoic* Fur,
And fetch their precepts from the *Cynic* Tub,
Praising the lean and sallow Abstinence.
Wherefore did Nature pour her bounties forth   710
With such a full and unwithdrawing hand,
Covering the earth with odors, fruits, and flocks,
Thronging the Seas with spawn innumerable,

---

675. Homer first mentioned *Nepenthes* as an ano-
dyne (*Od.* IV, 221) in a scene where Menelaus and
Helen are entertained on their way home from Troy
by the Egyptian *Thone* and his wife Polydamna.
  698. *vizor'd:* masked. *forgery:* deception. Cf.
PL IV, 800.
  700. *lickerish:* delicious, tempting.

707. *budge* was a kind of fur used on doctors'
hoods at Cambridge and seems to have implied
stodginess or pomposity.
  708. The *Cynic* philosopher Diogenes was famous
for living in a tub at Athens to show his contempt
for luxury.

But all to please and sate the curious taste?
And set to work millions of spinning Worms   715
That in their green shops weave the smooth-hair'd silk
To deck her Sons; and that no corner might
Be vacant of her plenty, in her own loins
She hutch't th'all-worshipt ore and precious gems
To store her children with.   If all the world   720
Should in a pet of temperance feed on Pulse,
Drink the clear stream, and nothing wear but Frieze,
Th'all-giver would be unthank't, would be unprais'd,
Not half his riches known, and yet despis'd,
And we should serve him as a grudging master,   725
As a penurious niggard of his wealth,
And live like Nature's bastards, not her sons,
Who would be quite surcharg'd with her own weight,
And strangl'd with her waste fertility;
Th'earth cumber'd, and the wing'd air dark't with plumes,   730
The herds would over-multitude their Lords,
The Sea o'erfraught would swell, and th'unsought diamonds
Would so emblaze the forehead of the Deep,
And so bestud with Stars, that they below
Would grow inur'd to light, and come at last   735
To gaze upon the Sun with shameless brows.
List Lady, be not coy, and be not cozen'd
With that same vaunted name Virginity;
Beauty is nature's coin, must not be hoarded,
But must be current, and the good thereof   740
Consists in mutual and partak'n bliss,
Unsavory in th'enjoyment of itself.
If you let slip time, like a neglected rose
It withers on the stalk with languish't head.
Beauty is nature's brag, and must be shown   745
In courts, at feasts, and high solemnities
Where most may wonder at the workmanship;
It is for homely features to keep home,
They had their name thence; coarse complexions
And cheeks of sorry grain will serve to ply   750
The sampler, and to tease the housewife's wool.
What need a vermeil-tinctur'd lip for that,
Love-darting eyes, or tresses like the Morn?
There was another meaning in these gifts,
Think what, and be advis'd; you are but young yet.   755
    Lady.   I had not thought to have unlockt my lips
In this unhallow'd air, but that this Juggler
Would think to charm my judgment, as mine eyes,
Obtruding false rules prankt in reason's garb.

---

719. *hutch't:* locked away, shut up.
722. *Frieze:* coarse woolen cloth.
733. Milton's MS variant—"Would so bestud the center with their starlight"—shows that *Deep* means the earth, as in *PL* VI, 480. In *MLQ*, XII (1951), 422-7, H. F. Robins explores the scientific background of the belief in the power of "Th'Archemic Sun" (*PL* III, 609) to generate gems underground. Unless they are mined, says Comus, they will so encrust the inside of the earth's surface that its subterranean inhabitants will learn to bear the sunlight.
737. *coy:* shy, reserved. *cozen'd:* duped. deluded.
739-744. For the background of Comus' plea see the headnote ¶ 2-3.
750. *grain:* color.
751. *tease:* comb.
752. *vermeil:* vermilion.

I hate when vice can bolt her arguments, 760
And virtue has no tongue to check her pride:
Impostor, do not charge most innocent nature,
As if she would her children should be riotous
With her abundance; she, good cateress,
Means her provision only to the good 765
That live according to her sober laws
And holy dictate of spare Temperance:
If every just man that now pines with want
Had but a moderate and beseeming share
Of that which lewdly-pamper'd Luxury 770
Now heaps upon some few with vast excess,
Nature's full blessings would be well dispens't
In unsuperfluous even proportion,
And she no whit encumber'd with her store,
And then the giver would be better thank't, 775
His praise due paid, for swinish gluttony
Ne'er looks to Heav'n amidst his gorgeous feast,
But with besotted base ingratitude
Crams, and blasphemes his feeder. Shall I go on?
Or have I said enough? To him that dares 780
Arm his profane tongue with contemptuous words
Against the Sun-clad power of Chastity
Fain would I something say, yet to what end?
Thou hast nor Ear nor Soul to apprehend
The sublime notion and high mystery 785
That must be utter'd to unfold the sage
And serious doctrine of Virginity,
And thou art worthy that thou shouldst not know
More happiness than this thy present lot.
Enjoy your dear Wit and gay Rhetoric 790
That hath so well been taught her dazzling fence,
Thou art not fit to hear thyself convinc't;
Yet should I try, the uncontrolled worth
Of this pure cause would kindle my rapt spirits
To such a flame of sacred vehemence, 795
That dumb things would be mov'd to sympathize,
And the brute Earth would lend her nerves, and shake,
Till all thy magic structures rear'd so high,
Were shatter'd into heaps o'er thy false head.
      Comus. She fables not, I feel that I do fear 800
Her words set off by some superior power;
And though not mortal, yet a cold shudd'ring dew
Dips me all o'er, as when the wrath of *Jove*
Speaks thunder and the chains of *Erebus*
To some of *Saturn's* crew. I must dissemble, 80'
And try her yet more strongly. Come, no more,
This is mere moral babble, and direct

760. *bolt:* the metaphor is from sieving flour, but the meaning is a reflection on Comus' finespun sophistry. Cf. the headnote ¶ 3.

785. *mystery* implies both St. Paul's "mystery of godliness, God was manifest in the flesh" (I Tim. iii, 16) and a mystery such as Socrates was taught about love by Diotima in Plato's *Symposium,* 201d–212b, as well as "the doctrine of Holy Scripture unfolding those chaste and high mysteries . . .

that the body is for the Lord, and the Lord fo. the body," which Milton named in *Apology,* p. 695

791. *fence:* the art of fencing, i.e. debating.

794. *rapt:* transported. Cf. *PR* II, 40.

797. *brute Earth* significantly echoes Horace, Odes, I, xxxiv, 9, where the earth (*bruta tellus*) reels under a thunderbolt so marvellous that it shook his scepticism about the gods.

Against the canon laws of our foundation;
I must not suffer this, yet 'tis but the lees
And settlings of a melancholy blood;   810
But this will cure all straight, one sip of this
Will bathe the drooping spirits in delight
Beyond the bliss of dreams. Be wise, and taste.—

*The Brothers rush in with Swords drawn, wrest his Glass out of his hand, and break it
against the ground; his rout make sign of resistance, but are all driven in; The attendant
Spirit comes in.*

    Spirit. What, have you let the false enchanter scape?
O ye mistook, ye should have snatcht his wand   815
And bound him fast; without his rod revers't,
And backward mutters of dissevering power,
We cannot free the Lady that sits here
In stony fetters fixt and motionless;
Yet stay, be not disturb'd, now I bethink me,   820
Some other means I have which may be us'd,
Which once of *Meliboeus* old I learnt
The soothest Shepherd that ere pip't on plains.
    There is a gentle Nymph not far from hence,
That with moist curb sways the smooth Severn stream,   825
Sabrina is her name, a Virgin pure;
Whilom she was the daughter of *Locrine,*
That had the Scepter from his father *Brute.*
She, guiltless damsel, flying the mad pursuit
Of her enraged stepdam *Guendolen,*   830
Commended her fair innocence to the flood
That stay'd her flight with his cross-flowing course.
The water Nymphs that in the bottom play'd
Held up their pearled wrists and took her in,
Bearing her straight to aged *Nereus'* Hall,   835
Who piteous of her woes, rear'd her lank head,
And gave her to his daughters to imbathe
In nectar'd lavers strew'd with Asphodel,
And through the porch and inlet of each sense

816. So Ovid (*Met.* XIV, 300) says that Circe's charms were annulled by reversing her rod and formula of words; and so the charms of Busyrane in *F.Q.* III, xii, 36, are thwarted by reversal.

822. *Meliboeus* points to Spenser, as *Tityrus* in Spenser's *Shepheardes Calendar* (February, 92, etc.) points to Chaucer. The names are paired in Virgil's First Eclogue, the latter, traditionally, referring to himself.

826-832. Spenser's *Sabrina* is simply an innocent girl who has been murdered on the bank of the Welsh border stream

    Which of her name men Severne now do call.
                (*F.Q.* II, x, 19, 8)
The original, barbarous story of her illegitimate birth and murder in Geoffrey of Monmouth's *Historia Britonum* (which Milton accepted as factual in *Britain*) seems unassimilable in *Comus,* even in its idealized form, to several critics: R. Blennerhassett in *MLN,* LXIV (1949), 315-18; D. C. Allen in *Vision,* p. 34; and W. B. C. Watkins in *Anatomy,* p. 99. It was acceptable to Milton's audience at Ludlow, who probably knew Sabrina only in the

illustrations of Drayton's *Polyolbion,* Song 6, where she is the crowned goddess of the Severn whose descent from the Trojan founder of Britain, Brutus (Milton's *Brute*), through her father *Locrine* suggests that she is a symbol of British and Welsh patriotism. Or, as Leicester Bradner suggests in *Musae Anglicanae* (London, 1940), p. 39, Milton may have remembered Sabrina's metamorphosis into a goddess in the *De literis antiquae Britanniae* of Phineas Fletcher the Elder.

835. *Nereus,* Homer's "ancient one of the sea" (*Il.* XVIII, 141), is described by Spenser with his daughters, the Nereids, as treating a wounded mortal in their submarine grotto with
    souveraine Balme, and Nectar good,
  Good both for earthly med'cine, and for heavenly food.
           (*F.Q.* III, iv, 40, 8-9)

838. *Asphodel,* the traditional flower of immortality, covers the meadows in the Elysian Fields where Ulysses met the great dead (*Od.* XI, 538).

839. With *porch* cf. "the porches of my ears" in *Hamlet* I, v, 63.

Dropt in Ambrosial Oils till she reviv'd   840
And underwent a quick immortal change,
Made Goddess of the River; still she retains
Her maid'n gentleness, and oft at Eve
Visits the herds along the twilight meadows,
Helping all urchin blasts, and ill-luck signs   845
That the shrewd meddling Elf delights to make,
Which she with precious vial'd liquors heals.
For which the Shepherds at their festivals
Carol her goodness loud in rustic lays,
And throw sweet garland wreaths into her stream   850
Of pansies, pinks, and gaudy Daffodils.
And, as the old Swain said, she can unlock
The clasping charm and thaw the numbing spell,
If she be right invok't in warbled Song,
For maid'nhood she loves, and will be swift   855
To aid a Virgin, such as was herself,
In hard-besetting need.   This will I try
And add the power of some adjuring verse.

SONG

Sabrina fair
   Listen where thou art sitting   860
Under the glassy, cool, translucent wave,
   In twisted braids of Lilies knitting
The loose train of thy amber-dropping hair;
   Listen for dear honor's sake,
   Goddess of the silver lake,   865
        Listen and save.

Listen and appear to us
In name of great *Oceanus,*
By the earth-shaking *Neptune's* mace
And *Tethys'* grave majestic pace,   870
By hoary *Nereus'* wrinkled look,
And the *Carpathian* wizard's hook,
By scaly *Triton's* winding shell,
And old soothsaying *Glaucus'* spell,
By *Leucothea's* lovely hands   875
And her son that rules the strands,
By *Thetis'* tinsel-slipper'd feet,

845. *urchin* was a common name for the hedge-hog, but mischievous fairies were supposed to plague people with the "urchin-shows" dreaded by Caliban in *The Tempest* II, ii, 5.

852. *the old Swain:* Meliboeus.

869. Homer's constant epithet for Poseidon (*Neptune*) is "the earth-shaker." *mace:* trident, Neptune's symbol.

870. *Tethys,* the wife of *Oceanus,* Hesiod says (*Theog.,* 337–70), was the mother of the rivers and of countless divine children.

872. The *Carpathian wizard* is Proteus, the Old Man of the Sea, who, Virgil says (*Georg.* IV, 433) haunted the Carpathian Sea between Rhodes and Crete. He carries a sheep-hook because Homer

describes him (*Od.* IV, 411–13) as counting his sea-calves like a shepherd.

873. Ovid describes *Triton* as Neptune's herald, proclaiming his decrees on a conch shell (*Met.* I, 330–5). Cf. *Lyc,* 89.

874. "*Glaucus,* that wise soothsayes understood," appears in Spenser (*F.Q.* IV, xi, 13, 3) and Virgil (*Aen.* V, 823).

875–876. Homer says that Ulysses was be-friended by "*Leucothea,* who in time past was a maiden of mortal speech, but now in the depths of the salt sea she obtained a share of the honor of the gods." Her son, Melicertes, was also changed into a sea god, and so he *rules the strands.*

877. *Thetis,* one of the Nereids, is usually "silver-footed" in the *Iliad.*

And the Songs of *Sirens* sweet,
By dead *Parthenope's* dear tomb,
And fair *Ligea's* golden comb,   880
Wherewith she sits on diamond rocks
Sleeking her soft alluring locks,
By all the *Nymphs* that nightly dance
Upon thy streams with wily glance,
Rise, rise, and heave thy rosy head   885
From thy coral-pav'n bed,
And bridle in thy headlong wave,
Till thou our summons answer'd have.
                              Listen and save.

Sabrina rises, attended by water-Nymphs, and sings.

  By the rushy-fringed bank,   890
Where grows the Willow and the Osier dank,
  My sliding Chariot stays,
Thick set with Agate and the azurn sheen
Of Turquoise blue and Em'rald green
  That in the channel strays,   895
Whilst from off the waters fleet
Thus I set my printless feet
O'er the Cowslip's Velvet head,
  That bends not as I tread;
Gentle swain at thy request   900
  I am here.

  Spirit.   Goddess dear
We implore thy powerful hand
To undo the charmed band
Of true Virgin here distrest,   905
Through the force and through the wile
Of unblest enchanter vile.
  Sabrina.   Shepherd 'tis my office best
To help ensnared chastity;
Brightest Lady look on me,   910
Thus I sprinkle on thy breast
Drops that from my fountain pure
I have kept of precious cure,
Thrice upon thy finger's tip,
Thrice upon thy rubied lip;   915
Next this marble venom'd seat
Smear'd with gums of glutinous heat
I touch with chaste palms moist and cold.
Now the spell hath lost his hold;
And I must haste ere morning hour   920
To wait in *Amphitrite's* bow'r.

Sabrina descends, and the Lady rises out of her seat.

879. *Parthenope* was a siren whose tomb, Strabo says (I, xxiii, 26), lay near Naples and gave the city its ancient name.

880. *Ligea* is a name given to one of Homer's sirens by the commentator, Eustathius.

907. *unblest:* cut off from the blessing of God's grace, i. e. *damn'd,* as Comus is called in l. 571.

911–913. The scene recalls Fletcher's in *The Faithful Shepherdess* where Amarillis presides over a "holy well' which

  Hath power to change the form of any creature
                       (III, i, 378)

and actually heals the wounded Amoret.

921. *Amphitrite:* Neptune's wife.

    Spirit. Virgin, daughter of *Locrine*
Sprung of old *Anchises'* line,
May thy brimmed waves for this
Their full tribute never miss   925
From a thousand petty rills,
That tumble down the snowy hills:
Summer drouth or singed air
Never scorch thy tresses fair,
Nor wet *October's* torrent flood   930
Thy molten crystal fill with mud;
May thy billows roll ashore
The beryl and the golden ore,
May thy lofty head be crown'd
With many a tower and terrace round,   935
And here and there thy banks upon
With Groves of myrrh and cinnamon.

Come Lady, while Heaven lends us grace,
Let us fly this cursed place,
Lest the Sorcerer us entice   940
With some other new device.
Not a waste or needless sound
Till we come to holier ground.
I shall be your faithful guide
Through this gloomy covert wide,   945
And not many furlongs thence
Is your Father's residence,
Where this night are met in state
Many a friend to gratulate
His wish't presence, and beside   950
All the Swains that there abide,
With Jigs and rural dance resort.
We shall catch them at their sport,
And our sudden coming there
Will double all their mirth and cheer;   955
Come let us haste, the Stars grow high,
But night sits monarch yet in the mid sky.

The Scene changes, presenting Ludlow *Town and the President's Castle, then come in Country-Dancers, after them the attendant Spirit, with the two Brothers and the Lady.*

SONG

    Spirit. Back Shepherds, back, enough your play,
Till next Sun-shine holiday;
Here be without duck or nod   960
Other trippings to be trod
Of lighter toes, and such Court guise
As Mercury *did first devise*
With the mincing Dryades
On the Lawns and on the Leas.   965

This second Song presents them to their father and mother.

---

  923. As the father of Aeneas, whom Geoffrey made the great-grandfather of *Locrine, Anchises* was a progenitor of Sabrina. Cf. ll. 826–32, n.
  960. *duck:* a curtsy or bow in a peasants' dance.

  963. So in Jonson's mask, *Pan's Anniversary,* the nymphs chant
           the best of leaders, Pan,
  That leads the Naiads and the Dryads forth,
  And to their dances more than Hermes can.

Noble Lord, and Lady bright,
I have brought ye new delight,
Here behold so goodly grown
Three fair branches of your own.
Heav'n hath timely tri'd their youth,   970
Their faith, their patience, and their truth,
And sent them here through hard assays
With a crown of deathless Praise,
   To triumph in victorious dance
O'er sensual Folly and Intemperance.   975

   The dances ended, the Spirit Epiloguizes.

   Spirit. To the Ocean now I fly,
And those happy climes that lie
Where day never shuts his eye,
Up in the broad fields of the sky:
There I suck the liquid air   980
All amidst the Gardens fair
Of *Hesperus,* and his daughters three
That sing about the golden tree:
Along the crisped shades and bow'rs
Revels the spruce and jocund Spring,   985
The Graces and the rosy-bosom'd Hours,
Thither all their bounties bring,
That there eternal Summer dwells,
And West winds with musky wing
About the cedarn alleys fling   990
Nard and *Cassia's* balmy smells.
Iris there with humid bow,
Waters the odorous banks that blow
Flowers of more mingled hue
Than her purfl'd scarf can shew,   995
And drenches with *Elysian* dew
(List mortals, if your ears be true)
Beds of *Hyacinth* and Roses
Where young *Adonis* oft reposes,
Waxing well of his deep wound   1000
In slumber soft, and on the ground
Sadly sits th' *Assyrian* Queen;
But far above in spangled sheen
Celestial *Cupid* her fam'd son advanc't,
Holds his dear *Psyche* sweet entranc't   1005
After her wand'ring labors long,

---

970. *timely:* early.

982. Leaving the "pinfold" (l. 7) of earth, the Spirit is ready now to go first to the *Gardens of Hesperus,* which—as Arthos notes (*M.P.L.C.,* p. 38)—lie "upon the earth, the True Earth, far to the west, beside the Ocean that circles the world," while above them are the abodes of which Plato speaks in the *Phaedo,* 114b–c. There Milton imagines "Venus and Adonis, and in another region, *farr above in spangled sheen,* Cupid and Psyche." Cf. the headnote ¶ 7.

984. The sense of *crisped* in this line is "uncertain" (*O.E.D.*).

992–995. The scarf of the rainbow goddess *Iris* is *purfl'd*—fringed or edged with embroidered colors.

993. *blow:* cause to blossom.

1002. The *Assyrian Queen,* Venus or Aphrodite, was first worshipped as a heavenly divinity (rather than as the goddess of earthly passion), says Pausanias I xiv, 6, by the Assyrians. Cf. l. 982, n.

1004–1011. The story of *Cupid's* much thwarted love for *Psyche* was told by Apuleius (*Golden Ass* IV, 28–VI, 24), who says that when at last the gods gave the lovers to each other Psyche bore the child Pleasure to Cupid. So Spenser, retelling the myth in brief, made *"Pleasure* the daughter of *Cupid* and *Psyche* late" (*F.Q.* III, vi, 50, 9).

Till free consent the gods among
Make her his eternal Bride,
And from her fair unspotted side
Two blissful twins are to be born,   1010
Youth and Joy; so *Jove* hath sworn.

But now my task is smoothly done,
I can fly, or I can run
Quickly to the green earth's end,
Where the bow'd welkin slow doth bend,   1015
And from thence can soar as soon
To the corners of the Moon.

Mortals that would follow me,
Love virtue, she alone is free,
She can teach ye how to climb   1020
Higher than the Sphery chime;
Or if Virtue feeble were,
Heav'n itself would stoop to her.

1015. The *welkin* is the sky, bending to the
horizon.

1018–1023. Much critical ingenuity has been
spent in efforts to show that Milton's meaning is
essentially theological, like Spenser's in his comment
on Florimel's escape from a lustful pursuer:

See how the heauens of voluntary grace.
And soueraine fauor towards chastity,
Doe succour send to her distressed cace:
So much high God doth innocence embraçe.
            (*F.Q.* III, viii, 39, 2–5)

Equal ingenuity has been shown in proving that
Milton's humanistic faith in virtue inspires the
lines with a Platonism like that in Mercury's summons to the masquers at the close of Jonson's
Pleasure Reconciled to Virtue to pursue Virtue, who,
. . . though a stranger here on earth,
In heaven she hath her right of birth.
        There, there is Virtue's seat:
        Strive to keep her your own.

1021. The *Sphery chime* is the music of the
spheres. Cf. *Arc,* 63, n.

PSALM CXIV

Milton's youthful translation of this psalm into English will be found on page 3 above.
The Greek rendering preserves most of the freedoms with the Original Hebrew text which
are discussed in the headnote to the English version.   For the sake of comparison the version in the King James Authorized Version (1611) is printed below the English translation
of Milton's Greek.

Ἰσραὴλ ὅτε παῖδες, ὅτ' ἀγλαὰ φῦλ' Ἰακώβου
Αἰγύπτιον λίπε δῆμον, ἀπεχθέα, βαρβαρόφωνον,
Δὴ τότε μοῦνον ἔην ὅσιον γένος υἷες Ἰούδα.
Ἐν δὲ θεὸς λαοῖσι μέγα κρείων βασίλευεν.
Εἶδε, καὶ ἐντροπάδην φύγαδ' ἐρρώησε θάλασσα,   5
Κύματι εἰλυμένη ῥοθίῳ, ὁ δ' ἄρ' ἐστυφελίχθη
Ἱρὸς Ἰορδάνης ποτὶ ἀργυροειδέα πηγήν.
Ἐκ δ' ὄρεα σκαρθμοῖσιν ἀπειρέσια κλονέοντο,
Ὡς κριοὶ σφριγόωντες ἐὐτραφερῷ ἐν ἀλωῇ.
Βαιότεραι δ' ἅμα πᾶσαι ἀνασκίρτησαν ἐρίπναι,   10
Οἷα παραὶ σύριγγι φίλῃ ὑπὸ μητέρι ἄρνες.
Τίπτε σύ γ' αἰνὰ θάλασσα πέλωρ φυγάδ' ἐρρώησας;

When the children of Israel, when
the glorious tribes of Jacob left the
land of Egypt—a land abhorred and
barbarous in speech—then, in truth,
the only holy race was the sons of
Judah, and among those tribes God
reigned in mighty power.   The sea
saw it and, reverently rolling back
its roaring waves, it gave comfort to
the fugitive.   The sacred Jordan was
thrust back upon its silver sources.
The huge mountains flung themselves about with mighty leaps like
lusty rams in a flourishing garden.
All the little hills skipped like lambs
dancing to the music of the syrinx
about their dear mother.

Why, O dreadful and monstrous
sea, didst thou give comfort to the
fugitive, rolling back thy roaring

Κύματι εἰλυμένη ῥοθίῳ; τί δ' ἄρ' ἐστυφελίχθης
Ἱρὸς Ἰορδάνη ποτὶ ἀργυροειδέα πηγήν;
Τίπτ' ὄρεα σκαρθμοῖσιν ἀπειρέσια κλονέεσθε   15
Ὡς κριοὶ σφριγόωντες εὐτραφερῷ ἐν ἀλωῇ;
Βαιότεραι τί δ' ἄρ' ὔμμες ἀνασκιρτησατ' ἐρίπναι,
Οἷα παραὶ σύριγγι φίλῃ ὑπὸ μητέρι ἄρνες,
Σείεο, γαῖα, τρέουσα θεὸν μεγάλ' ἐκτυπέοντα,
Γαῖα, θεὸν τρείουσ' ὕπατον σέβας Ἰσσακίδαο   20
Ὅς τε καὶ ἐκ σπιλάδων ποταμοὺς χέε μορμύροντας
Κρήνην τ' ἀέναον πέτρης ἀπὸ δακρυοέσσης. (1634)

waves? Why wast thou, sacred Jordan, thrust back upon thy silver fountains? Why did the huge mountains fling themselves about with mighty leaps like lusty rams in a flourishing garden? Why did you, O little hills, skip like lambs dancing to the music of the syrinx about their dear mother?

Shake, O earth, and fear the Lord who does mighty things; O earth, fear the Lord, the high and holy One of the seed of Isaac, who poured roaring rivers out of the crags and a perennial fountain out of the trickling rock.

PSALM CXIV (Authorized Version)

1. When Israel went out of Egypt, the house of Jacob from a people of strange language;
2. Judah was his sanctuary, and Israel his dominion.
3. The sea saw it and fled: Jordan was driven back.
4. The mountains skipped like rams, and the little hills like lambs.
5. What ailed thee, O thou sea, that thou fleddest? thou Jordan, that thou was driven back?
6. Ye mountains, that ye skipped like rams; and ye little hills, like lambs?
7. Tremble, thou earth, at the presence of the Lord, at the presence of the God of Jacob;
8. Which turned the rock into a standing water, the flint into a fountain of waters.

[The italicized words have no equivalent in the original Hebrew.]

PHILOSOPHUS AD REGEM

This undatable epigram seems to W. R. Parker possibly to refer to a clash between Milton's old tutor, Alexander Gill, and Archbishop Laud for which we have the date of Gill's pardon by King Charles—November 30, 1630. But its position in Milton's volume of 1645, among the Sylvae, suggests 1634 as the most probable date to Parker (in T.G.C.T., p. 129). The sentiment is attributed to Luther by Comenius in the closing words of The Great Didactic: "A good and wise man is the most precious treasure of a state, and is of far more value than palaces, than heaps of gold and silver, than gates of brass or bars of iron."

Philosophus ad regem quendam qui eum ignotum & insontem inter reos forte captum inscius damnaverat τὴν ἐπὶ θανάτῳ πορευόμενος, haec subito misit.

This message was suddenly sent to a king by a philosopher who was on the way to his death because the ruler had unwittingly condemned him—unrecognized and innocent—when he happened to be seized among some robbers.

Ὦ ἄνα εἰ ὀλέσῃς με τὸν ἔννομον, οὐδέ τιν' ἀνδρῶν
Δεινὸν ὅλως δράσαντα, σοφώτατον ἴθι κάρηνον
Ῥηϊδίως ἀφέλοιο, τὸ δ'ὕστερον αὖθι νοήσεις·

O King, if you make an end of me, an observer of the laws and a doer of absolutely no harm to any man, you must know that you would find it easy to destroy one of the wisest of heads, but later you

Μαψ αὔτως δ' ἀρ' ἔπειτα χρόνῳ μάλα πολλὸν ὀδύρῃ,
Τοιόνδ' ἐκ πόλεως περιώνυμον ἄλκαρ ὀλέσσας.

will sorrow vainly and grievously
because you have done away with
so famous a protection of the city.

LYCIDAS

1. In editing his *Poems* in 1645 Milton called *Lycidas* a "Monody" in which "the Author bewails a learned Friend, unfortunately drown'd . . . on the Irish Seas, 1637. And by occasion foretels the ruine of our corrupted Clergy then in their height." In 1638 *Lycidas* was first published with some elegies by King's friends at Cambridge. Few of the poems in the volume are worth reading for their own sake or for any possible intrinsic connection with *Lycidas,* but as a group they are profitably analyzed by Ruth Wallerstein in *Studies in Seventeenth Century Poetic* (Madison, 1950; pp. 96–114). They tell us little more about King than is implied in Milton's pastoral allegory of their six years together at Christ's College. It is enough for us to know that King was a good scholar, a fair poet, and a sufficiently promising young clergyman to justify a conventional portrait of him as a good shepherd of the sheep whose neglect by the "corrupted clergy" Milton took occasion to condemn. He was drowned when his ship mysteriously foundered on a clear August day in 1637, somewhere between the mouth of the river Dee (the *Deva* of l. 55) and the Isle of Anglesea (the *Mona* of l. 54), perhaps within sight of the adjacent island of Bardsey, where many ancient Welsh bards were supposed to lie buried "with twenty thousand saints," as Camden's *Britannia* testifies.

2. Modern readers may find the pastoral allegory annoying. So did Dr. Johnson when he laughed at Milton's picture of himself and King as undergraduates, pasturing the "same flock" on "the self-same hill." He disliked the pastoral conventions—the symbolic laurel and myrtle that must be plucked before the poet's talent is mature; the Muses, who may not consent to inspire him; and the nymphs, who have failed to watch over his dead friend, as the nymphs of Tempe, Peneus, and Pindus failed to protect the dead Daphnis in the first of Milton's many pastoral models, Theocritus' *Lament for Daphnis*. A modern reader may jib at the "pathetic fallacy" of the "Woods and desert Caves" and indeed "all Nature" mourning for Lycidas or for the greater singer Orpheus. He may be so unsympathetic with the whole pastoral tradition that an illuminating chart of it such as A. S. P. Woodhouse draws in "Milton's Pastoral Monodies" (Toronto, 1952) will seem like mere literary antiquarianism. Then the "fallacy" will gain no interest from being traced up the centuries through Renaissance France and Italy, through Virgil, and finally to Theocritus and to Moschus in his Lament for Bion:

> The nymphs of the fountains sobbed in the forest;
> They heard the hollows of the hills replying;
> They heard the weeping waters overflow.

3. As an unsympathetic reader goes on beyond the first movement of the poem he may feel that Dr. Johnson's charge of insincerity can be capped with the more serious one of lack of unity. A specious case on that ground can be made from the very different subjects of its three main movements; the meditation on true fame as Jove "pronounces lastly on each deed" of the young poet who fears defeat of his hope of popular applause; the prophecy of "the ruin of our corrupted Clergy," of which Milton spoke in his headnote; and the final deification of Lycidas as "the Genius of the shore." Between the prophecy and the deification—as an afterthought in the Trinity Manuscript—is the list of flowers (ll. 132–64), about whose meaning there is sharp disagreement. Are they—as H. H. Adams suggests in *MLN,* LXV (1950), 468–72—a chastened version of Perdita's flowers in *The Winter's Tale* IV, iv, 113–32? Or is R. P. Adams right—in *PMLA,* LXIV (1949),

Why should a poet have simply one meaning in mind for his verse, And shouldn't poetry create new images? from old words in everyone

LYCIDAS 117

183-8—in finding in the violet, the rose, and the "unfading" amaranth intimations of the immortality of which Lycidas, "sunk low but mounted high," is soon to be the supreme symbol? Or—with Wayne Shumaker in *PMLA*, LXVI (1951), 485-94—should we regard the flowers as a sweetly disillusioned use of the pathetic fallacy which Milton intended us to recognize as ironical and "deliberately delusive"? If we interpret them in this way, they throw the theme of immortality into painful contrast with nature's impotence to console us for death even with her richest beauty. In the irreconcileable conflict of opinions about the artistic purpose of the link between the middle and the final main movements of the poem an unsympathetic reader may see proof that it lacks unity and conclude with G. W. Knight in *The Burning Oracle* (London, 1939; p. 70) that it is simply "an accumulation of magnificent fragments."

4. It is on the denial of the denials of its sincerity and unity that the reputation of *Lycidas* has been built. If it had not been condemned for those weaknesses it might possibly now be idolized as "the crown of English pastoral poetry," but Kenneth Muir would not be speaking for the majority when he says—in *John Milton* (London, 1955), p. 48—that "the artificiality of the form is burned up in the sincerity of the poet." Without the challenge of insincerity scholars might have been content to stop with such excellent studies of the pastoral background as J. H. Hanford's "The Pastoral Elegy and Milton's *Lycidas*" in *PMLA*, XXV (1910), 403-47; Sir John Sandys's "Literary Sources of Milton's *Lycidas*" in *TRSL*, XXXII (1914), 1-32; and W. B. Austin's "Milton's *Lycidas* and Two Latin Elegies by Giles Fletcher, the Elder," in *SP*, XLIV (1947), 41-55. They would probably have gone further in an external way to study the roots of the "digression" on the clergy in pastoral sources like Spenser's satire of the clergy in *The Shepheardes Calendar* and behind it ultimately in the Bible itself in Christ's parable of the Good Shepherd and his antitype, the "hireling" (John x, 12), and Ezekiel's denunciation of the shepherds of Israel who "eat the fat, but feed not the flock" (Ez. xxxiv, 2-3). Echoes of that pastoral tradition were to be heard in many Puritan pamphlets denouncing the bishops in the English Church. Some scholars—like M. M. Ross in *Poetry and Dogma* (New Brunswick, 1954), pp. 201-204—see Milton's Saint Peter simply as a Protestant drill sergeant, or—with C. E. Kreipe in *Milton's "Samson Agonistes"* (Halle, 1926), p. 30—regard the words of Saint Peter as an explicit, personal attack upon Archbishop Laud.

5. If the passage on the clergy is simply Puritan propaganda against the bishops, the unity of *Lycidas* is questionable. Our interest in it becomes more historical than literary, and the narrower our view of its historical context, the worse for the poem as poetry. For many readers the historical interest of the passage seems to be limited to the absorbing problem of the meaning of St. Peter's closing words about the "two-handed engine at the door" which is waiting to end all corruption in the church with a single stroke. Over forty guesses about its meaning are on record, most of which are summarized by W. A. Turner in *JEGP*, XLIX (1950), 562-5, in a study finally suggesting that the two-handedness of the engine signifies the two sanctions of death and damnation which have been symbolized earlier by St. Peter's golden and iron keys for the locks of heaven and hell. His suggestion may prove to be a dividing line between early identifications of the engine with the two houses of Parliament or the two kingdoms of England and Scotland, and the now prevailing tendency to interpret it theologically. But a very interesting political interpretation coming later than Turner's suggestion—and a similar one by Leon Howard in 1952 in *HLQ*, XV, 173-6—is made in *SP*, LII (1955), 583-91, by W. J. Grace, who again surveys the many solutions of the riddle on record, but then takes the original line of reading line 129 as placing the "two-handed engine" in apposition with "the grim wolf." The resulting meaning is that, like the wolf, which is a symbol of the

Roman Catholic Church, that Church is ready, "operating through its twin superstitious appeals to *hope* of gain and *fear* of consequence, . . . to mount one more attack [on England, although] its days are numbered and its defeat is imminent."

6. It is a fact to be reckoned with that the more narrowly the "digression" on the clergy is limited to reference to the quarrel of the Puritans with the English or with the Roman Catholic Church, the less interesting it is both from the historical and the literary point of view.   Perhaps it is for that reason that prevailing opinion inclines toward apocalyptic interpretations of the two-handed engine.   As Maurice Kelley recalls in *N&Q*, CLXXXI (1941), 273, it seems very much like the sword of the Lord which Michael uses to fell "Squadrons at once" (*PL* VI, 251) when he drives Satan and the rebel angels out of Heaven.   In the longer historical background is the sword of the Lord threatening to smite a corrupt Church as G. R. Coffman traces it to the sermons of Saint Gregory the Great in *ELH*, III (1936), 101–113, and as E. S. LeComte traces it to the pre-Reformation sermons of Savanorola in *SP*, XLVII (1950), 589–606 and XLIX (1952), 548–50.   Milton's rebuke of the "corrupted clergy" should be read as a part of a tradition flowing down to him from Gregory, Petrarch, and Dante.   Perhaps—as Kenneth MacKenzie suggests in *Italica* XX (1943), 120—it may rest directly upon Milton's recollection of the corrupt popes whom Dante has St. Peter denounce in the *Paradiso* XXVII, 19–66.

7. The historical tradition behind Milton's attack on the clergy had been deeply involved with literature from its beginnings in the prophecy of Ezekiel to its emergence in the Renaissance in criticism of ecclesiastical corruption as we find it in the much imitated pastorals of the General of the Carmelite Order, Baptista Mantuano.   In essence it is the undying theme of the hope of mankind for the end of its material exploitation by its spiritual guides, be they priests or teachers or writers.   In this light the climax of Milton's "digression" on the clergy is a natural sequel to the preceding movement that contrasts the craving of the immature poet for the fame from which he, like Lycidas, may be cut off by premature death, with the true fame of Jove's giving as he "pronounces lastly on each deed."   It is to the author, to Milton himself, that Apollo is speaking in line 78, but it does not follow, as E. M. W. Tillyard suggested in *Milton*, p. 81, that he was thinking mainly of himself.   But later, in a comparison of the structure of *Lycidas* with that of Keats's *Ode to a Nightingale* (*M.S.*, pp. 38–42), Tillyard opens the way for recognition of the theme of the poem as the maturing and discipline of the poet and his faith in poetry. Now the way is open to read the last of the three main movements of the poem, the deification of Lycidas, as a climax naturally climaxing the two preceding movements.   Indeed, it may be open—as David Daiches declares it to be in *A Study of Literature* (Ithaca, 1948), p. 173—for a view of the real subject of the poem as neither Milton himself nor as spokesman for all poets, but as "man in his capacity for creating something significant in his span on earth."

8. This structural analysis of *Lycidas* into a triple suite of climaxes was made by Ernest Barker in *UTQ*, (1941), 171, and has been widely accepted.   It has been confirmed and enriched by D. C. Allen's exploration of the historical background of its last movement. He has traced it beyond familiar parallels to the apotheosis of Lycidas like Virgil's deification of Daphnis (Julius Caesar?) in his *Fifth Eclogue* and Spenser's deification of Dido in "November" (l. 175) in *The Shepheardes* Calendar to reign "a goddesse now among the saintes."   The quest takes us beyond poetry to pagan consolations for mourners like Seneca's for Marcia on the death of her son, who is described (in *Epistles* xxv) as soaring aloft to join the societies of the blessed and learn all heaven's mysteries.   But the pagan consolations were the pattern for later Christian funeral orations, of which the classic example is Gregory Nazianzen's tribute to his brother Caesar.   Pagan consolations and pagan pastoral poetry alike look forward to the fusion of pagan and Christian elements in

Lycidas' apotheosis as the "Genius of the shore," while at the same time (ll. 174–7) he listens to "the marriage song of the Lamb" beside "the living fountains of waters" which Saint John described in the Apocalypse (Rev. xxii, 2). The far-flung historical study of the apotheosis of Lycidas exposes all its elements as familiar in pagan and Christian poetry alike, but in *Lycidas* Allen sees their supreme moment of fusion in Christian faith. And by implication he seems to agree with P. E. More's conclusion in "How to Read *Lycidas*" —*AR*, VII (1936), 156—when he apologized for comparing the poem to "the mighty structure of Dante's *Paradiso*," but said that "no single incident in Dante's voyage" touched him "with a shock of actuality" like Milton's treatment of the theme of immortality.

9. Studies of the mythology and traditional symbolism in *Lycidas* have helped confirm its inner unity and climactic structure. In the light of Wayne Shumaker's analysis of its water imagery in *PMLA*, LXVI (1951), 485–94, the drowned man's emergence into immortality,

Sunk though he be beneath the watery floor,

is contrasted with many earlier references in the poem to the sea as his grave. It is also mysteriously foreshadowed by many hints at the Christian symbol of the water of life and at pagan myths like that of Palaemon, who was drowned near Corinth but later honored as the protector of sailors by a temple on the beach at a spot where his body was supposed to have been brought ashore by a dolphin. No less interesting is Milton's use of the myth of Arethusa and her lover Alpheus to introduce and close his attack on the clergy. The Arcadian hunter Alpheus loved the nymph Arethusa and in the form of the river of which he was the god pursued her under the sea to Sicily. There she escaped him by transformation into a fountain, but finally its waters were mingled with his. Alpheus' name, said the mythographer Natale Conti—in *Mythologiae . . . Libri decem* (Frankfurt, 1596; VIII, xxi; p. 922)—meant "imperfection," and Arethusa, "virtue." D. C. Allen has noted—in *MLN*, LXXI (1956), 173—a parallel view of the myth as signifying the love of truth for justice in Fulgentius' *Mythologiarum libri tres*. And, quite apart from any mythological allegory, J. E. Hardy—in *KR*, VII (1945), 111—has noted the mysterious effect of this passage in "the essential method of the poem's movement." It hardly seems likely that the invocations of Arethusa and Alpheus which frame the passage on the truth-betraying clergy do not hint at Milton's faith in the ultimate triumph of truth and goodness. And in the light of Caroline W. Mayerson's study of "The Orpheus Image in *Lycidas*," in *PMLA*, LXIV (1949), 189–207, a similar faith emerges in Milton's allusion (ll. 58–63) to the murder of the sweet singer by the drunken worshippers of Bacchus on the shores of the Hebrus in Thrace. For the myth says that Orpheus' head floated to the island of Lesbos and endowed the islanders with its immortal gift of song.

10. The harmonies in *Lycidas* have been attributed by John Crow Ransom to Milton's rough and individualistic handling of a form which was really English though it might have some insignificant connection with Italy through poems like Spenser's *Prothalamion* and *Epithalamion*. That theory is not tenable. Though it is severe to say—as M. C. Battestin does in *ColE*, XVII (1956), 223—that Ransom's famous essay on "A Poem Nearly Anonymous" in *AR*, I (1933), 179–201, "contributes nothing of value to an understanding of *Lycidas*," he does not overstate the case against Ransom's theory that Milton's revisions of the poem in the Trinity Manuscript betray his impatience with rhyme and with any formal design. Actually, his revisions did not add even one to the original ten unrhymed lines nor in any way diminish the poem's resemblance to the *canzone* as it was described and written by Dante and Tasso. F. T. Prince has shown (in *I.E.M.V.*, pp. 87–88) the derivation of its verse paragraphs from the divided stanzas of the *canzone* with its "key" line linking its parts together by rhyming the last line of the first with the first line in the second part. This device for binding a poem together with rhymes subordinated

to the development of its thought and larger harmony led to the use of short lines rhyming with longer preceding ones—as the six-syllable lines in *Lycidas* do—to signal oncoming shifts in tone.   The pattern of *Lycidas* is that of the *canzone,* though Prince also regards it as owing something to the choruses in plays like Tasso's *Aminta.*   Gretchen Finney has compared it with Italian musical drama—in *HLQ,* XV (1951–2), 325–50—and in a criticism of her in *MP,* LII (1954), 12–22, Ants Oras has pled for the influence of the Italian madrigal on the pattern of *Lycidas,* especially on its opening lines.   In that suggestion he is surely right, just as Prince is right in recognizing a counterpart of the traditional, short, final stanza of the *canzone* (the *commiato*) in Milton's farewell to his sad subject in the eight final lines, which look forward to "fresh Woods, and Pastures new."

11. There are several modern, illustrated editions of *Lycidas.*   None of them offers more than four etchings, but the more recent of them succeed in breaking down the wall between modern taste and the pastoral tradition.   The spirit of Milton's dancing satyrs and "Fauns with cloven heel" is caught by Marguerite Benjamin in her illustrations to Tom Peete Cross's edition of the *Minor Poems* (New York, 1936).   Incidentally, she makes their traditionally half-goat, half-human anatomy plain for readers who need an introduction to it.   The sinister Neptune of line 90 is made still more potentially sinister by Blaer Hughes-Stanton in his wood engraving in Edward Beeching's edition of *Four Poems* of Milton (London, 1933).   Philip Evergood lets his imagination play sympathetically with the picture of the two young shepherds pasturing their flocks on "the self-same hill" (in *Lycidas,* with four etchings by P. Evergood, New York, 1929), and in his representation of the nymphs and shepherds dancing to welcome Lycidas to the marriage of the Lamb we have a serious attempt to make Milton's fusion of pastoral tradition with Saint John's vision of the New Jerusalem speak to the sensibility of the twentieth century.

In this Monody the Author bewails a learned Friend, unfortunately drown'd in his Passage from *Chester* on the *Irish* Seas, 1637.   And by occasion foretells the ruin of our corrupted Clergy then in their height.

> Yet once more, O ye Laurels, and once more
> Ye Myrtles brown, with Ivy never sere,
> I come to pluck your Berries harsh and crude,
> And with forc'd fingers rude,
> Shatter your leaves before the mellowing year. *he's not mature enough.*   5
> Bitter constraint, and sad occasion dear,
> Compels me to disturb your season due:
> For *Lycidas* is dead, dead ere his prime,
> Young *Lycidas,* and hath not left his peer:
> Who would not sing for *Lycidas?* he knew   10
> Himself to sing, and build the lofty rhyme.
> He must not float upon his wat'ry bier
> Unwept, and welter to the parching wind,
> Without the meed of some melodious tear.
> Begin then, Sisters of the sacred well,   15
> That from beneath the seat of *Jove* doth spring,
> Begin, and somewhat loudly sweep the string.
> Hence with denial vain, and coy excuse,

1. Contrast Milton's confidence of winning the poet's laurel in *Patrem,* 102.

2. *brown:* dusky, dark. Cf. "alleys brown" in *PR* II, 293.

3. *crude:* unripe—lacking the "inward ripeness" which Milton confessed that he lacked in *Sonn.* VII.

10. An echo of Virgil's question: "Who would refuse songs for Gallus?" (*Ec.* X, 3).

15. So in *IlPen,* 47 the Muses "round about Jove's Altar sing." Like Theocritus and Moschus, Milton invokes the Muses to "begin the dirge." See the headnote ¶ 2.

So may some gentle Muse
With lucky words favor my destin'd Urn,   20
And as he passes turn,
And bid fair peace be to my sable shroud.
For we were nurst upon the self-same hill,
Fed the same flock, by fountain, shade, and rill.
  Together both, ere the high Lawns appear'd   25
Under the opening eyelids of the morn,
We drove afield, and both together heard
What time the Gray-fly winds her sultry horn,
Batt'ning our flocks with the fresh dews of night,
Oft till the Star that rose, at Ev'ning, bright   30
Toward Heav'n's descent had slop'd his westering wheel.
Meanwhile the Rural ditties were not mute,
Temper'd to th'Oaten Flute;
Rough *Satyrs* danc'd, and *Fauns* with clov'n heel
From the glad sound would not be absent long,   35
And old *Damaetas* lov'd to hear our song.
  But O the heavy change, now thou art gone,
Now thou art gone, and never must return!
Thee Shepherd, thee the Woods, and desert Caves,
With wild Thyme and the gadding Vine o'ergrown,   40
And all their echoes mourn.
The Willows and the Hazel Copses green
Shall now no more be seen,
Fanning their joyous Leaves to thy soft lays.
As killing as the Canker to the Rose,   45
Or Taint-worm to the weanling Herds that graze,
Or Frost to Flowers, that their gay wardrobe wear,
When first the White-thorn blows;
Such, *Lycidas,* thy loss to Shepherd's ear.
  Where were ye Nymphs when the remorseless deep   50
Clos'd o'er the head of your lov'd *Lycidas?*
For neither were ye playing on the steep,
Where your old *Bards,* the famous *Druids,* lie,
Nor on the shaggy top of *Mona* high,
Nor yet where *Deva* spreads her wizard stream: 55
Ay me, I fondly dream!
Had ye been there—for what could that have done?
What could the Muse herself that *Orpheus* bore,
The Muse herself, for her enchanting son

19–20. The thought is like Virgil's as he invokes the muse to mourn for Gallus (*Ec.* X, 4–5).

28. *winds:* blows. *sultry,* in reference to the noon heat, implies the insect hum of midday.

29. *batt'ning:* feeding, fattening.

30. Cf. the folding star, Hesperus, in *Comus,* 93.

36. Some Cambridge don is meant by *Damaetas* (a name taken from Virgil's *Ec.* III); perhaps—as Marjorie Nicolson suggests in *MLN,* XLI (1926), 293–300—the greatest of the tutors in Milton's time there, Joseph Mede.

39–41. For the "pathetic fallacy" see the headnote ¶ 2.

45. *Canker:* cankerworm. Cf. *Arc,* 53.

46. The *Taint-worm,* says Thomas Tusser in *Hundreth pointes of good husbandry,* "lurks where ox should eat" to destroy him.

50–55. The lines reflect the maps of Ortelius and Mercator as well as the account in William Camden's *Britain* of Bardsey and Anglesey (*Mona*), *shaggy* because it was once covered by "groves consecrated to the cruel superstitions" of the *Druids,* and *steep* because the east end of the island "mounteth aloft with an high promontory." The passage from Camden is quoted at length by G. W. Whiting (*Milieu,* pp. 102–105). Cf. *Manso,* 41.

55. Camden says that the river Dee (*Deva . . wizard stream*) "foreshadowed a sure token of victorie to the inhabitants upon it" by changing its channel, and that for various reasons they "attribute Divinitie to this river *Dwy* above all others."

Whom Universal nature did lament,   60
When by the rout that made the hideous roar,
His gory visage down the stream was sent,
Down the swift *Hebrus* to the *Lesbian* shore?
   Alas!   What boots it with uncessant care
To tend the homely slighted Shepherd's trade, — *poetry and*   65
And strictly meditate the thankless Muse?   *priesthood*
Were it not better done as others use,
To sport with *Amaryllis* in the shade,   *— screw around*
Or with the tangles of *Neaera's* hair?
Fame is the spur that the clear spirit doth raise *— last hindrance the poet* 70
(That last infirmity of Noble mind)   *to overcome*
To scorn delights, and live laborious days;
But the fair Guerdon when we hope to find,
And think to burst out into sudden blaze,
Comes the blind *Fury* with th'abhorred shears,   75
And slits the thin-spun life.   "But not the praise,"
Phoebus repli'd, and touch'd my trembling ears;
"*Fame* is no plant that grows on mortal soil,
Nor in the glistering foil
Set off to th'world, nor in broad rumor lies,   80
But lives and spreads aloft by those pure eyes
And perfect witness of all-judging *Jove*;
As he pronounces lastly on each deed,
Of so much fame in Heav'n expect thy meed." *—what god thinks is*
   O Fountain *Arethuse*, and thou honor'd flood,   *important.*   85
Smooth-sliding *Mincius*; crown'd with vocal reeds,
That strain I heard was of a higher mood:
But now my Oat proceeds,
And listens to the Herald of the Sea
That came in *Neptune's* plea.   90
He ask'd the Waves, and ask'd the Felon winds,
What hard mishap hath doom'd this gentle swain?
And question'd every gust of rugged wings

64. *boots:* profits. Cf. *SA*, 560.

65–69. "To *meditate the Muse*" is Virgil's phrase (*Ec.* I, 2) for the poet's work, and his *Amaryllis* (*Ec.* II, 14) serves as a symbol for the erotic poets whom Milton condemns. In *N&Q*, n.s. III (1956), 190–1, R. J. Schoeck traces *Naeara's* path from Virgil (*Ec.* III) through Tibullus, Johannes Secundus' *Kisses* and the Caroline love lyrists to Milton. Cf. J. W. Saunders' "Milton, Diomede, and Amaryllis," in *ELH*, XXII (1955), 254–86.

70. Though Milton spoke in his own voice here, he thought also of expressions of similar aspiration by many Renaissance poets from Petrarch down. Renaissance faith in fame as a spur of virtue crystallized in many emblems under that title in books like Jean Boissard's *Emblematum liber* (Frankfort, 1593).

71. A famous passage in Tacitus' *Histories* IV, v, praises Helvidius Priscus for dedicating his youth to study and justifies his ambition on the ground that "the passion for glory is the last from which even wise men free themselves."

75. The *blind Fury* is Atropos, the Fate who cuts the threads of men's lives after her sisters have spun them out.

77. *Phoebus:* Apollo, god of inspiration, who Virgil says (*Ec.* VI, 3–4) plucked his ears, warning him against impatient ambition.

79. *foil:* setting of a gem. Thomas Fuller speaks of false diamonds as deceptive even to good jewelers when "set with a good foil." *Worthies* (1840); Vol. I, 300.

80–84. The lines bear comparison with St. Thomas' faith in the beatific vision as the reward of those who are not blinded by earthly prizes (*Summa contra gentiles* III, lxiii, 5) and Dante's glimpse of the souls in the heaven of Mercury (*Par.* VI, 112–17) who have striven after earthly glory and "thereby dimmed the beams of love."

85. For the myth of *Arethuse* and Alpheus see the headnote ¶ 9. Virgil mentions the *Mincius* (*Ec.* VII, 12) as flowing among reeds through the Lombard plain.

88. *Oat:* oaten pipe, song. Cf. *Comus*, 345.

89. Cf. Triton as the *Herald of the Sea* in *Comus*, 873.

90. *in Neptune's plea:* in defense of the god of the sea against the charge of responsibility for the drowning of Lycidas.

That blows from off each beaked Promontory.
They knew not of his story,   95
And sage *Hippotades* their answer brings,
That not a blast was from his dungeon stray'd,
The Air was calm, and on the level brine,
Sleek *Panope* with all her sisters play'd.
It was that fatal and perfidious Bark   100
Built in th'eclipse, and rigg'd with curses dark,
That sunk so low that sacred head of thine.
    Next *Camus,* reverend Sire, went footing slow,
His Mantle hairy, and his Bonnet sedge,
Inwrought with figures dim, and on the edge   105
Like to that sanguine flower inscrib'd with woe.
"Ah! Who hath reft" (quoth he) "my dearest pledge?"
Last came, and last did go,
The Pilot of the *Galilean* lake. — Peter
Two massy Keys he bore of metals twain   110
(The Golden opes, the Iron shuts amain).
He shook his Mitred locks, and stern bespake:
"How well could I have spar'd for thee, young swain,
Enough of such as for their bellies' sake,
Creep and intrude and climb into the fold?   115
Of other care they little reck'ning make,
Than how to scramble at the shearers' feast,
And shove away the worthy bidden guest;
Blind mouths! that scarce themselves know how to hold
A Sheep-hook, or have learn'd aught else the least   120
That to the faithful Herdman's art belongs!
What recks it them? What need they? They are sped;
And when they list, their lean and flashy songs
Grate on their scrannel Pipes of wretched straw.
The hungry Sheep look up, and are not fed,   125
But swoln with wind, and the rank mist they draw,
Rot inwardly, and foul contagion spread:

96. *Hippotades* is Aeolus, son of Hippotas, and *sage* perhaps because he was the traditional inventor of navigation.

99. Virgil mentions *Panope* (*Aen.* V, 240) as the greatest of the Nereids.

101. The ship was doomed perhaps because an eclipse shed its "disastrous twilight" (*PL* I, 597) on the construction.

103. *Camus,* the god of the river Cam, represents Cambridge University, personified as wearing an academic robe with colors like the dark reeds on its bank, but relieved by the crimson of a *sanguine flower,* the hyacinth of Theocritus' *Idyl* X, 28. It was created, says Ovid (*Met.* X. 214-6) by Apollo from the blood of Hyacinth, whom he had accidentally killed. "And not satisfied with this, Apollo inscribed his grieving words upon the leaves, AI, AI, characters of mourning."

107. *pledge:* a child.

109. *The Pilot:* St. Peter, from whose ship Christ preached to the people beside the Sea of Galilee (Luke v, 2-4), and to whom he gave "the keys of the kingdom of heaven" (Matt. xvi, 19). As the first bishop of the Church, he wears a miter. See the headnote ¶ 5-6.

115. 'He that entereth not by the door into the sheepfold, but climbeth up some other way, the same is a thief and a robber" (John x, 1).

118. '. . . they which were bidden" (to the feast in the parable in Matt. xxii, 8) "were not worthy." Milton borrows the language, not the thought.

119. John Ruskin's interpretation of *Blind mouths* as meaning the greed of the bishops (in *Sesame and Lilies* I, 22) seems obvious although it is challenged by Himes in *MLN*, XXXV (1920), 441, on the ground that the term *blind-mouthed* was applied by Strabo to rivers with shallow outlets to the sea. Thus shallowness rather than greed is Milton's charge against the clergy.

122. *What recks it them?:* Of what importance is it to them? Cf. *Comus,* 240. *They are sped:* they have prospered.

124. *scrannel:* thin, feeble.

126-127. The lines seem almost like a translation of Dante's allegory of the ignorant sheep turning with disgust from the wind on which they are pastured by their wicked shepherds (*Par.* XXIX, 106-107) In *Images and Themes* (Harvard, 1957), p. 77, R. Tuve also compares *Par.* V and IX.

Besides what the grim Wolf with privy paw   *— flock image repeated*
Daily devours apace, and nothing said;   *see line 29.*
But that two-handed engine at the door   — ?   130
Stands ready to smite once, and smite no more."   *Parliament, Axe?*
    Return *Alpheus*, the dread voice is past   *Christ*
That shrunk thy streams; Return *Sicilian* Muse,
Despair —   And call the Vales, and bid them hither cast   *— life comes back*
Their Bells and Flowrets of a thousand hues.   135
Ye valleys low where the mild whispers use
Of shades and wanton winds and gushing brooks,
On whose fresh lap the swart Star sparely looks,
Throw hither all your quaint enamell'd eyes,
That on the green turf suck the honied showers,   140
And purple all the ground with vernal flowers.
omitted in   Bring the rathe Primrose that forsaken dies,
1st draft   The tufted Crow-toe, and pale Jessamine,
The white Pink, and the Pansy freakt with jet,
The glowing Violet,   145
The Musk-rose, and the well-attir'd Woodbine,
With Cowslips wan that hang the pensive head,
And every flower that sad embroidery wears:
Bid *Amaranthus* all his beauty shed,
And Daffadillies fill their cups with tears,   150
To strew the Laureate Hearse where *Lycid* lies.
For so to interpose a little ease,
Let our frail thoughts dally with false surmise.
Ay me! Whilst thee the shores and sounding Seas
Wash far away, where'er thy bones are hurl'd,   155
lament for   Whether beyond the stormy *Hebrides,*
poet body   Where thou perhaps under the whelming tide
Visit'st the bottom of the monstrous world;
Or whether thou to our moist vows denied,
Sleep'st by the fable of *Bellerus* old,   160
Where the great vision of the guarded Mount
Looks toward *Namancos* and *Bayona's* hold;
>Look homeward Angel now, and melt with ruth:
And, O ye *Dolphins*, waft the hapless youth.<   *see intro ,*
Despair replaced   Weep no more, woeful Shepherds weep no more,   165
with Joy   For *Lycidas* your sorrow is not dead,
Sunk though he be beneath the wat'ry floor,

128. For the *grim Wolf* see the headnote ¶ 5.
132. Cf. *Alpheus* in *Arc*, 30 and in the headnote ¶ 9.
138. the *swart Star* is *Sirius*, the Dog Star, which is in the zenith in late summer, when vegetation often withers.
149. *Amaranthus* means literally the unfading flower. Cf. *Immortal Amarant* in *PL* III, 353.
156. The *Hebrides* lie off the west coast of Scotland.
158. the *monstrous world:* the world of sea monsters. Cf. the *monstrous rout* in *Comus*, 533.
159. *moist vows:* tearful prayers. Cf. *vows* in *Arc*, 6.
160. *Bellerus:* a fabulous giant for whom Land's End (the southwestern tip of Cornwall) was called Bellerium in Roman times.

162. *Bayona* was a Spanish stronghold about fifty miles south of Cape Finisterre, near which are the mountains of *Namancos*, towards which Milton thought of St. Michael's Mount on the Cornish coast as looking. All these places are picturesquely prominent on Ortelius' maps.
163. The *Angel* is Michael, who is imagined as standing on St. Michael's Mount, looking southward. In Jewish and often in Christian tradition he is the patron of mariners and is so recognized in the church of Mont St. Michel on the Norman coast.
164. For the basis of the appeal to the *Dolphins* see the headnote ¶ 9.
165. The line contrasts with Theocritus' refrain in the despairing farewell to Daphnis in *Idyl* I. "Stay, O Muses, stay your pastoral songs."

So sinks the day-star in the Ocean bed,
And yet anon repairs his drooping head,
And tricks his beams, and with new-spangled Ore,   170
Flames in the forehead of the morning sky:
So *Lycidas,* sunk low, but mounted high,
Through the dear might of him that walk'd the waves,
Where other groves, and other streams along,
With *Nectar* pure his oozy Locks he laves,   175
And hears the unexpressive nuptial Song,
In the blest Kingdoms meek of joy and love.
There entertain him all the Saints above,
In solemn troops, and sweet Societies
That sing, and singing in their glory move,   180
And wipe the tears for ever from his eyes.
Now *Lycidas,* the Shepherds weep no more;
Henceforth thou art the Genius of the shore,
In thy large recompense, and shalt be good
To all that wander in that perilous flood.   185
    Thus sang the uncouth Swain to th'Oaks and rills,
While the still morn went out with Sandals gray;
He touch't the tender stops of various Quills,
With eager thought warbling his *Doric* lay:
And now the Sun had stretch't out all the hills,   190
And now was dropt into the Western bay;
At last he rose, and twitch't his Mantle blue:
Tomorrow to fresh Woods, and Pastures new.   (Nov. 1637)

Benediction [handwritten annotation]

back to poet. [handwritten annotation]

168. The *day-star* is the sun, the *diurnal Star* of *PL* X, 1069.

173. *him that walk'd the waves:* Christ, whom the "disciples saw . . . walking on the sea" (Matt. xiv, 26).

176. The unutterable *nuptial Song* is sung at the "marriage supper of the Lamb" (Rev. xix, 9). See the headnote ¶ 8 and ¶ 11.

181. An echo of the promise that "God shall wipe away all tears from their eyes" (Rev. vii, 17 and xxi, 4).

183. Lycidas (Edward King) becomes the *Genius* or protecting deity of the Irish sea and its navigators as Julius Caesar (Daphnis) is imagined

by Virgil to be deified in heaven and "good" to men below (*Ec.* v, 65).

186. The *uncouth Swain,* or unknown rustic, is Milton himself, the singer of the pastoral (*Doric*) poem now drawing to a close. See the headnote ¶ 10.

188. *Quills:* the hollow stems of reeds in a Pan's pipe.

190-193. Perhaps we are under the shadows of the mountains at sunset with Virgil at the end of his first eclogue. We surely hear an echo of Virgil's farewell to his Lament for Gallus (*Ec.* X, 70-77).

AD SALSILLUM (TO SALZILLI)

Poetam Romanum, Aegrotantem, Scazontes (A Roman Poet, when He Was Ill)

O Musa gressum quae volens trahis claudum,
Vulcanioque tarda gaudes incessu,
Nec sentis illud in loco minus gratum
Quam cum decentes flava Dëiope suras
Alternat aureum ante Iunonis lectum,   5

O my Muse—fond as you are of moving with a halting[1] step and pleased as you are with a gait like Vulcan's,[2] which seems to you, when it is in the right place, no less charming than the graceful ankles of blond Dëiope[4] dancing before the golden couch of Juno— come, if you please, and carry these

1. *Halting* literally translates the name of the scazontic or "limping" meter which consisted in substituting a spondee or trochee for the iamb at the end of an iambic line and occasionally elsewhere within the line.

2. Vulcan's limp is explained by Homer's story of his fall from heaven (*Il.* I, 588-95), to which

there is an interesting reference in *PL* I, 739-46.

4. Virgil has Juno call *Dëiope* the loveliest of her nymphs (*Aen.* I, 72).

Adesdum, et haec s'is verba pauca Salsillo
Refer, camena nostra cui tantum es cordi,
Quamque ille magnis praetulit immerito divis.
Haec ergo alumnus ille Londini Milto
Diebus hisce qui suum linquens nidum   10
Polique tractum, (pessimus ubi ventorum,
Insanientis impotensque pulmonis,
Pernix anhela sub Iove exercet flabra)
Venit feraces Itali soli ad glebas,
Visum superba cognitas urbes fama,   15
Virosque doctaeque indolem iuventutis,
Tibi optat idem hic fausta multa, Salsille,
Habitumque fesso corpori penitus sanum;
Cui nunc profunda bilis infestat renes,
Praecordiisque fixa damnosum spirat.   20
Nec id pepercit impia quod tu Romano
Tam cultus ore Lesbium condis melos.
O dulce divum munus, O Salus, Hebes
Germana! Tuque Phoebe, morborum terror,
Pythone caeso, sive tu magis Paean   25
Libenter audis, hic tuus sacerdos est.
Querceta Fauni, vosque rore vinoso
Colles benigni, mitis Evandri sedes,
Siquid salubre vallibus frondet vestris,
Levamen aegro ferte certatim vati.   30
Sic ille caris redditus rursum Musis
Vicina dulci prata mulcebit cantu.
Ipse inter atros emirabitur lucos
Numa, ubi beatum degit otium aeternum,
Suam reclivis semper Aegeriam spectans.   35
Tumidusque et ipse Tibris, hinc delinitus,
Spei favebit annuae colonorum;
Nec in sepulchris ibit obsessum reges,
Nimium sinistro laxus irruens loro;

few words to Salzilli,[6] who likes my Muse so cordially that, quite undeservedly, he ranks me above great and divine poets.[8] For you, then, Salzilli, these are the wishes of that London-bred Milton who recently left his nest and his own quarter of the sky—where the worst of the winds in its headlong flight, with its lungs uncontrollably raging, rolls its panting gusts beneath the heavens—and came to the genial soil of Italy to see its cities, which their proud fame has made familiar, and its men and its talented and cultured youth; that same Milton, Salzilli, wishes you many blessings and a healthy constitution for your exhausted body, whose reins are deeply infected with the bile which spreads bane from its seat in your vitals. Although you have taught your Roman mouth to produce elegant Lesbian melody,[22] the accursed thing has shown you no mercy.

O sweet gift of the gods, O Health, sister of Hebe![23] And you too, O Phoebus—or Paean,[25] if you prefer to be called by that name—you who by virtue of your destruction of Python became the terror of diseases—this man is your priest. Oakgroves of Faunus,[27] and you hills that are generous with the liquor of the grape, and you seats of the gentle Evander,[28] if any health-giving plant burgeons in your valleys, let all of you contend to be the first to bring alleviation to the suffering Bard. Thus restored again to his dear Muses he will gladden the neighboring meadows with his sweet song. Numa[34] himself will marvel, under the dark groves where he lies forever entertaining the leisure of eternity in the contemplation of his Egeria. The swelling Tiber himself, calmed by the song, will bless the annual hopes of the farmers. He will not run wild and uncontrolled, with his left rein lax, to overwhelm kings in their sepulchers, but he will more

6. The Roman poet Giovanni Salzilli was identified by Masson (in his edition of Milton's *Poetical Works*, 1893. Vol. I, 105) as the author of several poems in a volume published by the Academy of the Fantastics in honor of Cardinal Cesarini in Rome in 1637. Nothing is known about his illness, but because Milton put his tribute to Salzilli before *Manso* in the 1645 edition of his poems, it seems to belong to his first Roman visit and to date in the late fall of 1638.

8. In his epigram complimenting Milton, which Milton printed among the commendatory verses in the volume of 1645, Salzilli ranked him above Homer, Virgil, and Tasso.

22. The lyric poets Alcaeus and Sappho were natives of Lesbos.

23. Cf. *Hebe* in *L'All*, 29 and *Comus*, 289.

25. *Paean* was a name for Apollo, whose slaying of the serpent *Python* is recalled in *El VII*, 31.

27. Cf. the wood god *Faunus* in *Comus*, 268, *El V*, 127, and *Damon*, 32.

28. As the founder of the Latian kingdom and, according to Virgil (*Aen.* VIII, 51–54), one of the first settlers of Rome, *Evander* is a protector of any Roman.

34. Ovid (*Met.* XV, 482–92) describes the legendary Roman king *Numa* as learning the arts of civilization from the goddess *Egeria*. Cf. Spenser's "*Aegerie*, that *Numa* taught" (*F.Q.* II, x, 42, 8).

Sed fraena melius temperabit undarum,   40

Adusque curvi salsa regna Portumni.   (1638)

41. The name of *Portumnus,* originally the god of ports, seems here to be used (like Neptune in *Vac,* 43) for the sea. For that reason, D. P. Hard-

effectively control his waves as far as the salt realms of curving Portumnus.[41]

ing suggests in *Ovid,* p. 56, that he is called "curving."

MANSUS (MANSO)

Ioannes Baptista Mansus, Marchio Villensis, vir ingenii laude, tum literarum studio, nec non et bellica virtute aput Italos clarus in primis est. Ad quem Torquati Tassi dialogus extat de Amicitia scriptus; erat enim Tassi amicissimus; ab quo etiam inter Campaniae principes celebratur, in illo poemate cui titulus *Gerusalemme conquistata, lib. 20:*

> Fra cavalier magnanimi e cortesi
> Risplende il Manso.

Is authorem Neapoli commorantem summa benevolentia prosecutus est, multaque ei detulit humanitatis officia. Ad hunc itaque hospes ille antequam ab ea urbe discederet, ut ne ingratum se ostenderet, hoc carmen misit.

Haec quoque, Manse, tuae meditantur carmina laudi
Pierides; tibi, Manse, choro notissime Phoebi,
Quandoquidem ille alium haud aequo est dignatus
    honore,
Post Galli cineres, et Maecenatis Etrusci.
Tu quoque, si nostrae tantum valet aura Camenae,   5
Victrices hederas inter laurosque sedebis.
Te pridem magno felix concordia Tasso
Iunxit, et aeternis inscripsit nomina chartis.
Mox tibi dulciloquum non inscia Musa Marinum
Tradidit; ille tuum dici se gaudet alumnum,   10
Dum canit Assyrios divum prolixus amores,

1. Manso's patronage of countless Italian poets had brought him many literary tributes before Milton sent him *"these verses."* In the *Second Defense* (p. 829) Milton recalls his introduction to "John Baptista Manso, Marquis of Villa, a nobleman of distinguished rank and authority, to whom Torquato Tasso, the illustrious poet, inscribed his book on friendship." Compare the note on 70–72 below.
   2. *Pierides:* the Muses. Cf. *El IV* 31, and *Patrem* 1.
   4. Cornelius *Gallus,* the first Roman elegist, is the poet lamented by Virgil in his *Ec.* X. Cf. *Lyc,* 10 and 190–3, notes. In *Ec.* VI, 64–66, Virgil describes him as being saluted by the Muses on Mt. Helicon.
   The compliment is patterned on Horace's salute of his patron, *Maecenas,* as "sprung from Rome's early kings (*Odes* I, i), and Propertius' tribute to his royal Etruscan blood (*El III* ix, 1).
   6. Cf. the laurels of *Patrem,* 102 and *Lyc,* 1.
   7. *Tasso* seems to have been Manso's guest several times between 1588 and 1594 and perhaps to have

John Baptista Manso, Marquis of Villa, is one of the first men in Italy alike for the renown of his intellect and his literary pursuits and no less for his martial prowess. There is extant a Dialogue on Friendship which Torquato Tasso wrote to him; for he was in the highest degree friendly to Tasso, by whom he is honored among the Campanian princes in the poem entitled *Jerusalem Conquered,* Book 20:

Among magnanimous and courteous
  cavaliers
Manso is resplendent.

This gentleman honored the present author with supreme kindness during his stay in Naples and showed him many courteous attentions. Accordingly, before leaving the city, the visitor, in order not to seem ungrateful, sent him this poem.

These verses[1] also, Manso, the Pierides[2] are meditating in your praise—in yours, Manso of the wide acquaintance among the choir of Phoebus, for since the death of Gallus and Etruscan Maecenas[4] the god has granted to hardly any one else honors equal to yours. If my Muse has breath sufficient, you too shall sit among the victorious ivy and laurels.[6] You were once bound to the great Tasso[7] by a happy friendship which has written your names in an everlasting record. Not long afterward the Muse, not ill-advised, entrusted to you the sweet-tongued Marini,[9] who took pleasure in being called your foster-child when he sang his voluminous song of the loves of the Assyrian gods[11] and laid the soft

finished the *Jerusalem Conquered* in his house.
   9. *Marino* published the *Adone,* a version of the story of Venus and Adonis, in 1623.
   11. The myth of Adonis, dying on the Assyrian mountains while Venus mourns for him, figures again in *PL* I, 446–52.

Mollis et Ausonias stupefecit carmine nymphas.
Ille itidem moriens tibi soli debita vates
Ossa, tibi soli supremaque vota reliquit.
Nec manes pietas tua cara fefellit amici;   15
Vidimus arridentem operoso ex aere poetam.
Nec satis hoc visum est in utrumque, et nec pia cessant
Officia in tumulo; cupis integros rapere Orco,
Qua potes, atque avidas Parcarum eludere leges:
Amborum genus, et varia sub sorte peractam   20
Describis vitam, moresque, et dona Minervae;
Aemulus illius Mycalen qui natus ad altam
Rettulit Aeolii vitam facundus Homeri.
Ergo ego te, Clius et magni nomine Phoebi,
Manse pater, iubeo longum salvere per aevum,   25
Missus Hyperboreo iuvenis peregrinus ab axe.
Nec tu longinquam bonus aspernabere Musam,
Quae nuper, gelida vix enutrita sub Arcto,
Imprudens Italas ausa est volitare per urbes.
Nos etiam in nostro modulantes flumine cygnos   30
Credimus obscuras noctis sensisse per umbras,
Qua Thamesis late puris argenteus urnis
Oceani glaucos perfundit gurgite crines.
Quin et in has quondam pervenit Tityrus oras.
  Sed neque nos genus incultum, nec inutile Phoebo,
Qua plaga septeno mundi sulcata Trione   36
Brumalem patitur longa sub nocte Boöten.
Nos etiam colimus Phoebum, nos munera Phoebo,
Flaventes spicas, et lutea mala canistris,
Halantemque crocum (perhibet nisi vana vetustas)   40
Misimus, et lectas Druidum de gente choreas.
Gens Druides antiqua, sacris operata deorum,
Heroum laudes imitandaque gesta canebant.
Hinc quoties festo cingunt altaria cantu
Delo in herbosa Graiae de more puellae   45
Carminibus laetis memorant Corineïda Loxo,

21. Milton's word is our only evidence that
Manso wrote a life of Marino, but he seems certainly
to have written a life of Tasso, the first part of
which had been published in 1620.
22–23. The *son of lofty Mycale* is Herodotus,
the traditional biographer of Homer, whose birthplace Aeolis in Asia Minor claimed to be. Mycale
lay nearby on the steep coast.
24. *Clio:* the Muse of history. Cf. *Patrem,* 14
and 64.
26. Cf. the allusion to England as a *Hyperborean*
land in *QNov,* 95 and to its cold climate as unfavorable to poetic gifts in *PL* IX, 44–45.
34. Similarly in Spenser's *Shepheardes Calendar*
(February, 92, June, 81, and December, 4) *Tityrus*
means Chaucer.
36. The *Triones* or ploughing oxen (the Big
Dipper, Great Bear, or Charles' Wain in modern
naming of the constellations) were supposed to be
driven by the ox-herd, *Boötes.* Cf. *Ely,* 51.
42–44. As in *Lyc,* 53, the *Druids* are regarded
as both bards and priests, as Caesar described them
in the *Gallic War* VI, xiv.
46. *Corineïda* is formed from the name of a

spell of his song upon the Italian
maidens. So, at his death, the poet
paid his obligation by leaving his
remains in your care and entrusting
his last wishes to you alone. And
your affectionate devotion has not
disappointed your friend's spirit, for
we have seen him smiling down
from his carved bronze. But you
were not content to do merely this
much for either poet, and your
loving fidelity did not end at the
tomb. As far as lies within your
power, you labor to snatch them
uninjured out of Hades and to
cheat the voracious laws of the
Fates. So you write the family
history of both,[21] the varying fortunes through which their lives were
lived, their traits, and their gifts
from Minerva. You are the rival
of that eloquent man, the son of
lofty Mycale, who recounted the life
of Aeolian Homer.[22] Therefore,
father Manso, in the name of Clio[24]
and of great Phoebus, I, a young
pilgrim sent from Hyperborean[26]
skies, wish you health and long life.
You, who are so good, will not
despise an alien Muse, which,
though poorly nourished under the
frozen Bear, has recently presumed
to make her rash flight through the
cities of Italy. I believe that in the
dim shadows of night I too have
heard the swans singing on our
river, where the silvery Thames
with pure urns spreads her green
locks wide in the swell of the ocean.
And Tityrus[34] also long ago made
his way to these shores.
  Yet we, who in the long nights
endure the wintry Boötes in that
zone of the world which is fur-
rowed by the seven-fold Wain,[36]
are no uncultivated race, profitless
to Phoebus. We also worship
Phoebus and—unless antiquity asserts vain things—we sent him gifts,
golden ears of grain, baskets of
yellow apples, the fragrant crocus
and chosen bands of the stock of
the Druids. The ancient race of
the Druids,[42] experienced in the cult
of the gods, used to sing the praises
of heroes and their emulable acts.
So, as often as the Greek maidens
observe their custom of encircling
the altars in grassy Delos with a
festal chant, their happy songs commemorate Corinedian[46] Loxo and

Fatidicamque Upin, cum flavicoma Hecaërge,
Nuda Caledonio variatas pectora fuco.
   Fortunate senex! ergo quacunque per orbem
Torquati decus et nomen celebrabitur ingens,   50
Claraque perpetui succrescet fama Marini,
Tu quoque in ora frequens venies plausumque vi-
   rorum,
Et parili carpes iter immortale volatu.
Dicetur tum sponte tuos habitasse penates
Cynthius, et famulas venisse ad limina Musas.   55
At non sponte domum tamen idem, et regis adivit
Rura Pharetiadae caelo fugitivus Apollo;
Ille licet magnum Alciden susceperat hospes;
Tantum ubi clamosos placuit vitare bubulcos,
Nobile mansueti cessit Chironis in antrum,   60
Irriguos inter saltus frondosaque tecta
Peneium prope rivum. Ibi saepe sub ilice nigra,
Ad citharae strepitum, blanda prece victus amici,
Exilii duros lenibat voce labores.
Tum neque ripa suo, barathro nec fixa sub imo   65
Saxa stetere loco; nutat Trachinia rupes,
Nec sentit solitas, immania pondera, silvas;
Emotaeque suis properant de collibus orni,
Mulcenturque novo maculosi carmine lynces.
   Diis dilecte senex, te Iupiter aequus oportet   70
Nascentem, et miti lustrarit lumine Phoebus,
Atlantisque nepos; neque enim nisi carus ab ortu
Diis superis poterit magno favisse poetae.
Hinc longaeva tibi lento sub flore senectus
Vernat, et Aesonios lucratur vivida fusos,   75

British hero Corineus, which stands in the Trinity
MS in a rejected form of l. 160 in *Lyc.*
46–48. Milton fused Herodotus' story (IV, 35)
of two Hyperborean virgins, Arge and Opis, who
had carried gifts to Delos and were honored there
in a popular hymn, with an account in Callimachus'
Hymn to Delos (291–4) of *Oupis, Loxo,* and
Hecaërge, maidens from the remote north who
brought tribute to the island.
   49. The line adapts Virgil's congratulation of a
veteran living peacefully on a farm: "Fortunate old
man! for your farms shall rest secure" (*Ec.* I, 46).
   55. Apollo is called *Cynthius* from his birthplace on Mt. Cynthus on the island of Delos.
   56–69. The story of Apollo's banishment from
heaven and service as a herdsman with *Admetus,*
the king of Pherae in Thessaly, goes back to
Pindar's *Pythian Odes* (IX, 112–14). The tale of
Admetus' welcome of *Hercules* is most familiar in
Euripides' *Alcestis,* to which Milton refers in
Sonn XXIII.
   60. "The most righteous of the centaurs"—
Homer declared (*Il.* XI, 831)—was *Chiron,* to
whom Ovid says (*Met.* II, 630) that Apollo entrusted his son Aesculapius to be educated in the
Vale of Tempe, under the *Trachinian cliff,* in
Thessaly.
   68. Cf. the power of Orpheus' song in *Patrem,*
52 and in *Prolusions* I and VI.

Prophetic Upis, with golden-haired
Hecaërge—damsels whose naked
breasts were colored with Cale-
donian woad.
   Fortunate old man![49] For wherever the glory and the mighty name
of Torquato shall be celebrated
through all the world and wherever
the glorious reputation of the immortal Marini shall spread, your
name and fame also shall constantly
be in men's mouths, and with flight
no less swift than theirs you shall
mount the way of immortality. It
shall be said that of his own free
will Apollo dwelt in your house and
that the Muses were familiar attendants at your doors. Unwillingly that same Apollo[55] came,
when he was an exile from
heaven,[56] to the farmstead of Admetus, although Admetus had been
host to the great Hercules. When
he wished to get away from the
clamorous ploughmen, he retreated
to the renowned cave of the gentle
Chiron[60] among the moist wood-
land pastures and verdurous shades
beside the river Peneus. There, under the dark ilex, persuaded by his
friend's soft entreaty, he would
lighten the hard labors of exile by
singing to the accompaniment of
the cithara. Then neither the banks
nor the rocks fixed in the lowest
depths of the chasm stood fast in
their places; the Trachinian cliff
swayed and no longer felt the vast
weight of its familiar forests; the
trees were moved and hastened
down from their hills and the
spotted lynxes became gentle at the
unfamiliar song.[68]
   Old man, beloved of the gods!
At your birth Jupiter must have
been favorable, Phoebus and the
grandson of Atlas[72] must have shed
their gentle light upon you, for no
one, unless from his birth he were
dear to the gods, could have be-
friended a great poet. Therefore
your old age is green with lingering
bloom and, still robust, enjoys the
spindles of Aeson[75]—preserving the

72. The *grandson of Atlas* is Mercury. Cf. *Idea,*
27.
   75. The *spindles* belong to the Fates. Cf. *Lyc,*
75, n.
   Aeson, the father of Jason, as Ovid tells the
story (*Met.* VII, 251–93), was made forty years
younger by the enchantments of Medea.

Nondum deciduos servans tibi frontis honores,
Ingeniumque vigens, et adultum mentis acumen.
O mihi si mea sors talem concedat amicum
Phoebaeos decorasse viros qui tam bene norit,
Si quando indigenas revocabo in carmina reges,   80
Arturumque etiam sub terris bella moventem,
Aut dicam invictae sociali foedere mensae
Magnanimos Heroas, et—O modo spiritus adsit—
Frangam Saxonicas Britonum sub Marte phalanges!
Tandem ubi non tacitae permensus tempora vitae,   85
Annorumque satur, cineri sua iura relinquam,
Ille mihi lecto madidis astaret ocellis,
Astanti sat erit si dicam, 'Sim tibi curae.'
Ille meos artus, liventi morte solutos,
Curaret parva componi molliter urna.   90
Forsitan et nostros ducat de marmore vultus,
Nectens aut Paphia myrti aut Parnasside lauri
Fronde comas, at ego secura pace quiescam.
Tum quoque, si qua fides, si praemia certa bonorum,
Ipse ego, caelicolum semotus in aethera divum,   95
Quo labor et mens pura vehunt atque ignea virtus,
Secreti haec aliqua mundi de parte videbo,
Quantum fata sinunt, et tota mente serenum
Ridens purpureo suffundar lumine vultus,
Et simul aethereo plaudam mihi laetus Olympo.   100

honors of your brow unfallen, your spirit strong and the power of your mind at its height. O, if my lot might but bestow such a friend upon me, a friend who understands how to honor the devotees of Phoebus—if ever I shall summon back our native kings into our songs,[80] and Arthur, waging his wars beneath the earth, or if ever I shall proclaim the magnanimous heroes of the table[82] which their mutual fidelity made invincible, and (if only the spirit be with me) shall shatter the Saxon phalanxes under the British Mars! And at last, after I shall have lived through the span of no silent career, and when, full of years, I shall pay to the ashes their due, that friend would stand with tears in his eyes beside my bed. I should be content if I might say to him as he stood there, "Take me into your care." He would see to it that, when livid death had relaxed them, my limbs were gently bestowed in a little urn. Perhaps he might even cause my features to take form in marble and wreathe my locks with Paphian myrtle[92] and Parnassian laurel.[92] So I should rest in perfect peace. Then, if there be such a thing as faith and assured rewards of the righteous, I myself, far remote in the ethereal homes of the gods who dwell in heaven, whither labor and a pure mind and ardent virtue lead, shall look down upon these events—as much as the fates permit—from some part of that mysterious world, and with a serene spirit and a face suffused with smiles and rosy light, I shall congratulate myself on ethereal Olympus.[100]

80. Milton was thinking of Arthur, "Begirt with *British* and *Armoric* Knights" (*PL* I, 581), as the most promising of the subjects for an epic from British history, twenty-eight of which he set down in the Trinity MS.

82. The *table:* Arthur's round table.

92. The *myrtle* traditionally came from Venus' island of Paphos and the *laurel* from the haunts of the Muses on Mt. Parnassus. Cf. *El I*, 84, and *El IV*, 30.

100. *Olympus* might mean the Christian heaven as well as the seat of Zeus and the gods of Greece, as it does in *Ely*, 63.

AD LEONORAM ROMAE CANENTEM (TO LEONORA SINGING IN ROME)

Angelus unicuique suus—sic credite, gentes—
  Obtigit aethereis ales ab ordinibus.
Quid mirum, Leonora, tibi si gloria maior?
  Nam tua praesentem vox sonat ipsa Deum.
Aut Deus, aut vacui certe mens tertia caeli,   5

Over everyone—so let the nations believe—his own particular angel from out the heavenly hierarchies spreads protecting wings. What wonder, Leonora,[3] if a greater glory be yours? For the music of your voice itself bespeaks the presence of God. Either God, or certainly some third mind[5] from the untenanted

3. *Leonora* was a Neapolitan singer whom Milton may have heard in the Barberini palace in Rome in the fall of 1638. Perhaps this poem was written for a volume of tributes to her in several languages which was published as *Applausi Poetici alle Glorie della Signora Leonora Baroni* in Rome in 1639.

5. The opening suggestion that Leonora is in-

spired by a guardian angel now changes to the fancy that she is inspired by the Holy Spirit. *Third mind* seems to refer to I John v, 7: "For there are three that bear record in heaven, the Father, the Word, and the Holy Ghost."

Per tua secreto guttura serpit agens;
Serpit agens, facilisque docet mortalia corda
  Sensim immortali assuescere posse sono.
Quod, si cuncta quidem Deus est, per cunctaque fusus,
  In te una loquitur, caetera mutus habet.   10

(1639)

9. The image shifts to a recollection of Virgil's conception of the universe as animated by an omnipresent intelligence (*Aen.* VI, 726–7) in lines that were often quoted by Italian Neo-Platonists in proof of pantheistic theories like that which

skies, is moving mysteriously in your throat—mysteriously moving and graciously teaching mortal hearts how they may gradually become accustomed to immortal tones. If God is all things and permeates all things,[9] in you alone he speaks and possesses all His other creatures in silence.

Giordano Bruno supported by quoting them in *De la Causa, Principio e Uno* (*Opere Italiane*, ed. by G. Gentile, 1925; I, 179).

AD EANDEM (TO THE SAME)

Altera Torquatum cepit Leonora Poetam,
  Cuius ab insano cessit amore furens.
Ah miser ille tuo quanto felicius aevo
  Perditus, et propter te, Leonora, foret!
Et te Pieria sensisset voce canentem   5
  Aurea maternae fila movere lyrae!
Quamvis Dircaeo torsisset lumina Pentheo
  Saevior, aut totus desipuisset iners,
Tu tamen errantes caeca vertigine sensus
  Voce eadem poteras composuisse tua;   10
Et poteras, aegro spirans sub corde quietem,
  Flexanimo cantu restituisse sibi.   (1639)

1. The insanity of *Torquato Tasso* (1544–95), from which he suffered more or less in the last twenty years of his life, had several causes—among them the attacks of critics on the *Jerusalem Delivered*. His devotion to Leonora d'Este, a sister of his patron Alfonso, Duke of Ferrara, has played a larger part in literature than it did in his life.
6. Leonora's mother, Adriana Baroni, was a musician.
7. *Pentheus*, king of Thebes, was torn to pieces

Another Leonora made a captive of the poet, Torquato, who, for passionate love of her, went mad.[1] Ah, unhappy man, how much more blessedly he might have been brought to ruin in your times and for your sake, Leonora. He would have heard you singing with Pierian voice as you touched the strings of your mother's harp.[6] Although he had rolled his eyes more dreadfully than that Theban Pentheus,[7] and raved until he was insensible, your voice could still have composed his straying wits in their blind confusion. And, breathing peace into his diseased breast with your heart-stirring song, you might have restored him to himself.

by the women worshippers of Bacchus—among them (according to Euripides' *Bacchae*, 916–28) his own mother, *Agave*.

AD EANDEM (TO THE SAME)

Credula quid liquidam Sirena, Neapoli, iactas,
  Claraque Parthenopes fana Acheloiados,
Littoreamque tua defunctam Naiada ripa
  Corpora Chalcidico sacra dedisse rogo?
Illa quidem vivitque, et amoena Tibridis unda   5
  Mutavit rauci murmura Pausilipi.
Illic, Romulidum studiis ornata secundis,
  Atque homines cantu detinet atque Deos.   (1639)

2. Cf. *Parthenope's dear tomb* in *Comus*, 879, on the shore of the Bay of Naples, which is called *Chalcidian* because it was settled by Greeks from Chalcis in Euboea in 326 B.C.
6. *Pausilipus*: a mountain between Naples and Puteoli, penetrated by a tunnel through which much noisy traffic passed.

Why, credulous Naples, do you boast of your liquid-voiced Siren and of the famous shrine of the daughter of Achelous, Parthenope,[2] the Naiad of the shore, that, when she perished on your coast, her body was consecrated on a Chalcidian pyre? In truth, she lives and has exchanged the confusion of noisy Pausilipus[3] for the smooth waves of the Tiber. There she is honored by the cordial applause of the sons of Romulus and lays the spell of her song upon both men and gods.

EPITAPHIUM DAMONIS (DAMON'S EPITAPH)

Argumentum (Argument)

(Thyrsis et Damon,* eiusdem viciniae Pastores, eadem studia sequuti a pueritia amici erant, ut qui plurimum. Thyrsis animi causa profectus peregre de obitu Damonis nuntium accepit. Domum postea reversus, et rem ita esse comperto, se, suamque solitudinem hoc carmine deplorat. Damonis autem sub persona hic intelligitur Carolus Diodatus ex urbe Etruriae Luca paterno genere oriundus, caetera Anglus; ingenio, doctrina, clarissimisque caeteris virtutibus, dum viveret, iuvenis egregius.)

* *Damon,* Charles Diodati, was buried in St. Anne's churchyard, Blackfriars, London, 27 August, 1638. The date when his death was reported to Milton is discussed by D. Dorian in *Diodatis,* pp. 175–81, by E. H. Visiak in his edition of Skeat's translation of *Milton's Lament for Damon* (London, 1935), pp. 88–93, and by W. R. Parker in *MLN,* LXXII (1957), pp. 486–88.

(Thyrsis and Damon,* shepherds of the same neighborhood, from childhood had pursued the same interests and were most affectionate friends. While studying abroad, Thyrsis received the report of Damon's death. When, later, he returned home and found that it was so, he bewailed himself and his loneliness in this song. Now Damon represents Charles Diodati, who through his father was descended from the Tuscan city of Lucca, but in all else was an Englishman—a youth who, while he lived, was outstanding for genius, learning, and every other splendid virtue.)

Himerides nymphae—nam vos et Daphnin et Hylan,
Et plorata diu meministis fata Bionis—
Dicite Sicelicum Thamesina per oppida carmen:
Quas miser effudit voces, quae murmura Thyrsis,
Et quibus assiduis exercuit antra querelis   5
Fluminaque, fontesque vagos, nemorumque recessus,
Dum sibi praereptum queritur Damona, neque altam
Luctibus exemit noctem, loca sola pererrans.
Et iam bis viridi surgebat culmus arista,
Et totidem flavas numerabant horrea messes,   10
Ex quo summa dies tulerat Damona sub umbras,
Nec dum aderat Thyrsis; pastorem scilicet illum
Dulcis amor Musae Tusca retinebat in urbe.
Ast ubi mens expleta domum pecorisque relicti
Cura vocat, simul assueta seditque sub ulmo,   15
Tum vero amissum, tum denique, sentit amicum,
Coepit et immensum sic exonerare dolorem:
"Ite domum impasti, domino iam non vacat, agni.

Nymphs of Himera—for you remember Daphnis and Hylas[1] and the long-lamented destiny of Bion—utter your Sicilian song through the cities of the Thames. Sing the moans and sighs that the wretched Thyrsis[4] poured out, his ceaseless complaints that importuned the caves and rivers, the vagrant streams and the depths of the groves, when he mourned the cutting off of Damon and went wandering through solitary places, even in the latest hours of the night never sparing his groans. And now twice[9] the stalk with its green ear had grown up and twice the yellow harvest had been numbered into the barns since his last day had swept Damon to the shades below, and still Thyrsis was absent, for love of the sweet Muse detained that shepherd in the Tuscan city.[13] But when he had filled his mind full and the care of the flock that he had left behind him recalled him to his home, and when he sat down under the accustomed elm, then truly, then at last, he felt the loss of his friend, and he began to pour out his tremendous sorrow in words like these:
"Go home unfed, for your master has no time for you, my lambs.[18]

1. In "The *Epitaphium Damonis* in the Stream of Classical Lament" in *Read,* pp. 207–20, W. A. Montgomery traces the influence of the *Sicilian Muse* (*Lyc,* 133) and of the Muses of the Sicilian river *Himera* in this poem. The Italian channel of that influence is studied by T. P. Harrison, Jr., in "The Latin Pastorals of Milton and Castiglione," *PMLA,* L (1935), 480–93. See headnote to *Lyc* ¶ 2 and ¶ 4. For *Hylas* see *PR* II, 353, n.

4. *Thyrsis,* who represents Milton, is a mourner for Daphnis in Theocritus' *Idyl* I.

9–11. Spring and summer nave twice passed since Diodati's death in August, 1638. The lines imply composition of the poem in 1639.

13. The *Tuscan city* is Florence, where Milton spent the greater part of March and April in 1639.

18. Similar refrains give unity to Bion's *Epitaph of Adonis* and Moschus' *Epitaph for Bion.* In The-

Hei mihi! quae terris, quae dicam numina caelo,
Postquam te immiti rapuerunt funere, Damon;   20
Sicine nos linquis, tua sic sine nomine virtus
Ibit, et obscuris numero sociabitur umbris?
At non ille animas virga qui dividit aurea
Ista velit, dignumque tui te ducat in agmen,
Ignavumque procul pecus arceat omne silentum.   25
    "Ite domum impasti, domino iam non vacat, agni.
Quicquid erit, certe, nisi me lupus ante videbit,
Indeplorato non comminuere sepulchro,
Constabitque tuus tibi honos, longumque vigebit
Inter pastores. Illi tibi vota secundo   30
Solvere post Daphnin, post Daphnin dicere laudes
Gaudebunt, dum rura Pales, dum Faunus amabit—
Si quid id est, priscamque fidem coluisse, piumque,
Palladiasque artes, sociumque habuisse canorum.   35
    "Ite domum impasti, domino iam non vacat, agni
Haec tibi certa manent, tibi erunt haec praemia,
    Damon.
At mihi quid tandem fiet modo? quis mihi fidus
Haerebit lateri comes, ut tu saepe solebas
Frigoribus duris, et per loca foeta pruinis,
Aut rapido sub sole, siti morientibus herbis,   40
Sive opus in magnos fuit eminus ire leones,
Aut avidos terrere lupos praesepibus altis?
Quis fando sopire diem cantuque solebit?
    "Ite domum impasti, domino iam non vacat, agni.
Pectora cui credam? quis me lenire docebit   45

Ah me! what deities shall I profess in earth or heaven, now that they have torn you mercilessly away in death, O Damon? And do you leave us in this way and shall your virtue go down without a name to be numbered with the company of the unknown dead? But he who divides the souls with his golden wand would not wish this,[23] for he would lead you into a company worthy of you and would warn off the whole brutal herd of the silent dead.

"Go home unfed, for your master has no time for you, my lambs. Whatever befalls, Damon, you may be sure—unless a wolf first sets eyes upon me[27]—that you shall not turn to dust in the sepulcher unmourned. Your fame shall abide and long be held in esteem among the shepherds. To you, next after Daphnis, it shall be their delight to pay their vows,[30] and to sing praises of you next after Daphnis, as long as Pales[32] and Faunus shall love the fields—if there be any profit in having cultivated the ancient faith and piety and the arts of Pallas Athene, and in having possessed a comrade who was a poet.

"Go home unfed, for your master has no time for you, my lambs. For you these rewards are certainly in store and you shall certainly possess them, Damon. But what at last is to become of me? What faithful companion will stay by my side as you always did when the cold was cruel and the frost thick on the ground, and when the herbs were dying of thirst under a consuming sun—whether the work were to chase the lions to close quarters or to frighten the hungry wolves away from the high sheepfolds? Who now is to beguile my days with conversation and song?

"Go home unfed, for your master has no time for you, my lambs. To whom shall I confide my heart? Who will teach me to alleviate my mordant cares and shorten the long night with delightful conversation while the ripe pear simmers before the grateful fire and nuts burst on the hearth, when the wicked southwind makes general confusion outside and thunders in the peak of the elm tree?[45]

ocritus' *Idyl* I there are sixteen repetitions of the line:
    Begin, dear Muses, begin your pastoral songs.
Milton's refrain translates Virgil's *Ite domum pasti, siquis pudor, ite iuvenci* (*Ec.* VII, 44).

23. Milton was thinking of Virgil's description of Mercury as the conductor of the souls of the dead (*Aen.* IV, 242–5).

27. The line recalls a Virgilian reference (*Ec.* IX, 53) to a superstition that, if a wolf saw a man before the man saw him, the man became blind.

30–32. Cf. Virgil's *Eclogues* V, 76–80 (in Dryden's translation):
    While savage boars delight in shady woods,
    And finny fish inhabit in the floods—
    While bees on thyme, and locusts feed on dew—
    Thy grateful swains these honours shall renew.
    Such honours as we pay to pow'rs divine,
    To Bacchus and to Ceres shall be thine.

32. The goddess *Pales,* whom Eve outrivals in loveliness (*PL* IX, 393), was a protectress of flocks. Cf. *Faunus* in *Salsillus*, 27.

45–49. The lines recall Horace's *Epode* xiii with its contrast of conviviality inside a house with a storm outside.

Mordaces curas, quis longam fallere noctem
Dulcibus alloquiis, grato cum sibilat igni
Molle pirum, et nucibus strepitat focus, at malus auster
Miscet cuncta foris, et desuper intonat ulmo.
"Ite domum impasti, domino iam non vacat, agni.
Aut aestate, dies medio dum vertitur axe,   51
Cum Pan aesculea somnum capit abditus umbra
Et repetunt sub aquis sibi nota sedilia nymphae,
Pastoresque latent, stertit sub saepe colonus,
Quis mihi blanditiasque tuas, quis tum mihi risus   55
Cecropiosque sales referet, cultosque lepores?
"Ite domum impasti, domino iam non vacat, agni.
At iam solus agros, iam pascua solus oberro,
Sicubi ramosae densantur vallibus umbrae,
Hic serum expecto; supra caput imber et Eurus   60
Triste sonant, fractaeque agitata crepuscula silvae.
"Ite domum impasti, domino iam non vacat, agni.
Heu! quam culta mihi prius arva procacibus herbis
Involuntur, et ipsa situ seges alta fatiscit!
Innuba neglecto marcescit et uva racemo,   65
Nec myrteta iuvant; ovium quoque taedet, at illae
Moerent, inque suum convertunt ora magistrum.
"Ite domum impasti, domino iam non vacat, agni.
Tityrus ad corylos vocat, Alphesiboeus ad ornos,
Ad salices Aegon, ad flumina pulcher Amyntas: 70
'Hic gelidi fontes, hic illita gramina musco,
Hic Zephyri, hic placidas interstrepit arbutus undas.'
Ista canunt surdo, frutices ego nactus abibam.
"Ite domum impasti, domino iam non vacat, agni.
Mopsus ad haec, nam me redeuntem forte notarat,   75
Et callebat avium linguas et sidera Mopsus:
'Thyrsi, quid hoc?' dixit, 'quae te coquit improba bilis?
Aut te perdit amor, aut te male fascinat astrum,
Saturni grave saepe fuit pastoribus astrum,
Intimaque obliquo figit praecordia plumbo.'   80

52–53. So *Pan* sleeps at noon in Theocritus' *Idyl* I, 15–17. Cf. *El V*, 125.

56. "All life's charm and greatest pleasures, and rest from its labor," Pliny explained (XXXI, vii, 41), were called its salt. According to Martial (III, xx, 9), *Attic salt* was proverbial.

65. Because vines were traditionally "wedded" to trees, Horace spoke playfully of trees without vines as "celibate" (*Odes* II, xv, 4) or "widowed" (*Odes* IV, v, 30). Cf. *PL* V, 215–19.

69–70. *Tityrus, Aegon,* and *Amyntas* are found in various idyls of Theocritus. Milton adds *Alphesiboeus,* the "bringer of oxen," to the pastoral community.

75. *Mopsus* seems to be a transfer of Mopso who, in Tasso's *Aminta,* understands the speech of birds. Thomas Randolph put a burlesque seer Mopsus into his *Amyntas.*

79. Cf. *Saturn* in *IlPen*, 43. Traditionally, the planet Saturn was supposed to cause the "maladyes Colde" and "pestilence" that Chaucer attributed to

"Go home unfed, for your master has no time for you, my lambs. Or in summer, when the day is at the turn of high noon, and Pan is asleep and out of sight in the shade of the oak,[52] and the nymphs go back to their familiar haunts beneath the waters, and the shepherds hide themselves, and the ploughman snores under the hedge, who then will bring back to me your mirth and Attic salt,[56] your culture and humor?

"Go home unfed, for your master has no time for you, my lambs. Alone now I stray through the fields, alone through the pastures, wherever the branches make dense shadows in the valleys, there I wait for the evening. Over my head the rain and the southeast wind make their sad sound in the restless twilight of the wind-swept trees.

"Go home unfed, for your master has no time for you, my lambs. Alas, how entangled with insolent weeds are my once well cultivated fields! The tall grain itself is tumid with mold. The unwedded grapes[65] are shrivelled on their neglected vine and the myrtle groves have no loveliness. My sheep also are disgusting and mope and turn their gaze upon their master.

"Go home unfed, for your master has no time for you, my lambs. Tityrus[69] is calling me to the hazels, Alphesiboeus to the ash-trees, Aegon to the willows, and comely Amyntas to the rivers. 'Here are cool springs, here are lawns soft with moss, here are zephyrs, and here the arbutus and the quiet streams whisper together.' They sing to deaf ears, for I slip away into the thickets and am gone.

"Go home unfed, for your master has no time for you, my lambs. The next was Mopsus[75]—Mopsus who had skill in the language of the birds and the stars—for he had chanced to notice my return: 'What now, Thyrsis?' he said, 'what excess of bile ails you? Either you are pining away with love or you are banefully influenced by some star. Saturn's star has often been malignant to shepherds and his slanting, leaden shot strikes to the innermost vitals.'[79]

"Go home unfed, for your master

"Ite domum impasti, domino iam non vacat, agn﹏.
Mirantur nymphae, et 'Quid te, Thyrsi, futurum est⸴
Quid tibi vis?' aiunt: 'non haec solet esse iuventae
Nubila frons, oculique truces, vultusque severi;
Illa choros, lususque leves, et semper amorem   85
Iure petit; bis ille miser qui serus amavit.'

"Ite domum impasti, domino iam non vacat, agni
Venit Hyas, Dryopeque, et filia Baucidis Aegle,
Docta modos, citharaeque sciens, sed perdita fastu;
Venit Idumanii Chloris vicina fluenti.   90
Nil me blanditiae, nil me solantia verba,
Nil me, si quid adest, movet, aut spes ulla futuri.

"Ite domum impasti, domino iam non vacat, agni
Hei mihi! quam similes ludunt per prata iuvenci,
Omnes unanimi secum sibi lege sodales,   95
Nec magis hunc alio quisquam secernit amicum
De grege; sic densi veniunt ad pabula thoes,
Inque vicem hirsuti paribus iunguntur onagri;
Lex eadem pelagi, deserto in littore Proteus
Agmina phocarum numerat, vilisque volucrum   100
Passer habet semper quicum sit, et omnia circum
Farra libens volitet, sero sua tecta revisens;
Quem si fors letho obiecit, seu milvus adunco
Fata tulit rostro, seu stravit arundine fossor,
Protinus ille alium socio petit inde volatu.   105
Nos durum genus, et diris exercita fatis
Gens, homines, aliena animis, et pectore discors,
Vix sibi quisque parem de millibus invenit unum,
Aut, si sors dederit tandem non aspera votis,
Illum inopina dies, qua non speraveris hora   110
Surripit, aeternum linquens in saecula damnum.

"Ite domum impasti, domino iam non vacat, agni.
Heu! quis me ignotas traxit vagus error in oras
Ire per aëreas rupes, Alpemque nivosam?

him in *The Knight's Tale,* 2467 and 2469. In
Alchemy Saturn was the technical name for lead.
86. This epigram occurs in the first scene of
Guarini's *Il Pastor Fido* in lines that say (in English
rendering):
> If your hairs are gray,
> When first love troubles,
> The misery doubles.

88. The names are all found in Ovid's *Metamorphoses,* where (VIII, 630–724) *Baucis* and her
husband Philemon are described as entertaining
Jove and Mercury unawares. Ovid gave her no
children, but her name might mean simply an old
woman (as it does in Persius iv, 21), or a mother.
89. The line recalls "Thracian Chloe" in Horace's
Odes III, ix, who was also skilled with the cithara.
90. Since Camden identified the *Idumanum
aestuarium* as the Blackwater in Essex (*Britannia,*
1607; II, 45), a real woman seems to be meant by
Chloris.
99. Cf. *Proteus,* the "Shepherd of the Sea" (in
F.Q. III, viii, 30, 1), in *El III,* 26, and in *PL* III,
604.

has no time for you, my lambs.
The nymphs are astonished and
cry, 'What is to become of you,
Thyrsis? What do you wish? The
brow of youth is not usually
clouded, nor its eyes severe, nor its
aspect stern. Youth's lawful pursuits are dances and frivolous sports
and love always. Twice miserable
is the man who loves late.'[86]

"Go home unfed, for your master
has no time for you, my lambs.
Hyas[88] and Dryope came, and
Aegle, the daughter of Baucis—
Aegle accomplished in music and
skilled with the harp, but ruined by
pride[89]—and Chloris, the neighbor
of the Idumenian river,[90] came also.
No flattery and no words of comfort move me, nor does anything
that is present nor any hope of the
future.

"Go home unfed, for your master
has no time for you, my lambs.
How like one another are the steers
at play in the meadows, all mutually
companions together, because, under
the law which gives them one mind
together in common, not one singles
out another from the herd as a
friend. So the wolves come to their
food in packs and the rough-coated
wild asses mate together by turns.
The law of the sea is the same,
where Proteus[99] counts his hosts of
seals on the deserted shore. Even
that pariah of birds, the sparrow,
always has a fellow to play with and
flits gaily about to every shock of
grain, returning late to his own
roof. Yet if death has chanced to
carry off his fellow, or the kite's
hooked beak has brought his doom,
or the peasant's arrow has struck
him down, the bird incontinently
seeks out another to share his flight.
But we men are a painful race, a
stock tormented by cruel fate, with
minds mutually alienated and hearts
discordant. A man can hardly find
a comrade for himself in a thousand; or, if one is granted to us by
a fate at last not unkind to our
prayers, a day and hour when we
apprehend nothing snatches him
away, leaving an eternal loss to all
the years.

"Go home unfed, for your master
has no time for you, my lambs.
Alas! what wandering fancy carried
me across the skyey cliffs of the

Ecquid erat tanti Romam vidisse sepultam?   115
Quamvis illa foret, qualem dum viseret olim,
Tityrus ipse suas et oves et rura reliquit,
Ut te tam dulci possem caruisse sodale,
Possem tot maria alta, tot interponere montes,
Tot silvas, tot saxa tibi, fluviosque sonantes?   120
Ah! certe extremum licuisset tangere dextram,
Et bene compositos placide morientis ocellos,
Et dixisse, 'Vale! nostri memor ibis ad astra.'
    "Ite domum impasti, domino iam non vacat, agni.
Quamquam etiam vestri nunquam meminisse pigebit,
Pastores Tusci, Musis operata iuventus,   126
Hic Charis, atque Lepos; et Tuscus tu quoque Damon,
Antiqua genus unde petis Lucumonis ab urbe.
O ego quantus eram, gelidi cum stratus ad Arni
Murmura, populeumque nemus, qua mollior herba,
Carpere nunc violas, nunc summas carpere myrtos,   131
Et potui Lycidae certantem audire Menalcam!
Ipse etiam tentare ausus sum, nec puto multum
Displicui, nam sunt et apud me munera vestra,
Fiscellae, calathique, et cerea vincla cicutae.   135
Quin et nostra suas docuerunt nomina fagos
Et Datis et Francinus, erant et vocibus ambo
Et studiis noti, Lydorum sanguinis ambo.
    "Ite domum impasti, domino iam non vacat, agni.
Haec mihi tum laeto dictabat roscida luna,   140
Dum solus teneros claudebam cratibus haedos.
Ah! quoties dixi, cum te cinis ater habebat,
'Nunc canit, aut lepori nunc tendit retia Damon
Vimina nunc texit varios sibi quod sit in usus;'
Et quae tum facile sperabam mente futura   145
Arripui voto levis, et praesentia finxi.
'Heus bone! numquid agis? nisi te quid forte retardat,
Imus, et arguta paulum recubamus in umbra,

---

117. *Tityrus* probably refers to Virgil—not, as in
Manso, 34, to Chaucer, since his journeys to Italy
are not known to have included Rome.

128. *Lucomo* was an Etruscan title for princes
and priests which was misunderstood by Livy (I,
xxxiv) as the personal name of Tarquin the first
king of Rome, of whom Milton thought as the
founder also of *Lucca* in Tuscany.

129. In a letter to Benedetto Buonmattai, dated
September 10, 1638, Milton spoke of his pleasure in
visiting Fiesole above Florence on the river *Arno*.

132. In Theocritus' *Idyl* VII, *Menalcas* com-
petes in such a contest of song as Milton fancies
here as representing the actual poetical contests that
he shared in the Gaddian Academy in Florence.

134. The gifts were books or copies of verses like
the ode by Antonio Francini which Milton placed
at the head of his Latin poems in the edition of
1645.

138. Herodotus (I, 74) and Virgil (*Aen.* VIII,
479) both declare that "the Lydian race, glorious
in war, settled the Etruscan hills."

---

snow-bound Alps to unknown
shores? Was it of such importance
to have seen buried Rome, even
though it were what it was when
long ago Tityrus[117] left his sheep
and his fields to see it, that I should
suffer separation from so sweet a
friend or be able to put so many
deep seas, so many mountains, so
many forests and cliffs and roaring
rivers between us? Ah! had I not
gone, surely I might have touched
his right hand at the last and closed
his eyes as he lay peacefully dying,
and have said, 'Farewell! remember
me in your flight to the stars.'

"Go home unfed, for your master
has no time for you, my lambs.
Though I shall never weary of your
memory, Tuscan shepherds, youths
in the service of the Muses, yet
here was grace and here was gentleness; you also, Damon, were a Tuscan, tracing your lineage from the
ancient city of Lucca.[128] Ah, what
a man was I when I lay beside cool,
murmuring Arno,[129] where the soft
grass grows by the poplar grove, and
I could pluck the violets and the
myrtle shoots and listen to Menalcas
competing with Lycidas.[132] And I
myself even dared to compete, and
I think that I did not much displease, for your gifts[134] are still in
my possession, the baskets of reeds
and osiers and the pipes with fastenings of wax. Even their beech-trees
learned my name from Dati and
Francini, men who were both
famous for their song and their
learning, and both were of Lydian
blood.[138]

"Go home unfed, for your master
has no time for you, my lambs.
These things the dewy moon would
say to me, when happy and solitary,
I would be shutting the tender kids
in the wattled folds.

"Ah! how often would I say,
when already dark ashes possessed
you, 'Now Damon is singing or
stretching his nets for the hare or
weaving osiers for his various objects.' And all that my careless
mind hoped for the future I
snatched from the mere wish and
imagined it to be a present reality.
'Ho, good friend, have you any
work in hand? If, by good luck,
nothing prevents, let us go and lie
for a little while in the murmurous

Aut ad aquas Colni, aut ubi iugera Cassibelauni?
Tu mihi percurres medicos, tua gramina, succos,   150
Helleborumque, humilesque crocos, foliumque hya-
    cinthi,
Quasque habet ista palus herbas, artesque medentum.'
    "Ah! pereant herbae, pereant artesque medentum,
Gramina, postquam ipsi nil profecere magistro!
Ipse etiam—nam nescio quid mihi grande sonabat
Fistula—ab undecima iam lux est altera nocte—   156
Et tum forte novis admoram labra cicutis,
Dissiluere tamen, rupta compage, nec ultra
Ferre graves potuere sonos; dubito quoque ne sim
Turgidulus, tamen et referam; vos cedite, silvae.   160
    "Ite domum impasti, domino iam non vacat, agni.
Ipse ego Dardanias Rutupina per aequora puppes
Dicam, et Pandrasidos regnum vetus Inogeniae,
Brennumque Arviragumque duces, priscumque Be-
    linum,
Et tandem Armoricos Britonum sub lege colonos;   165
Tum gravidam Arturo fatali fraude Iogernen,
Mendaces vultus, assumptaque Gorloïs arma,
Merlini dolus. O, mihi tum si vita supersit,
Tu procul annosa pendebis, fistula, pinu
Multum oblita mihi, aut patriis mutata camenis   170
Brittonicum strides! Quid enim? omnia non licet uni,
Non sperasse uni licet omnia. Mi satis ampla
Merces, et mihi grande decus—sim ignotus in aevum
Tum licet, externo penitusque inglorius orbi—
Si me flava comas legat Usa, et potor Alauni,   175

shade, either by the waters of Colne[149] or in the country of Cassivelaunus. You shall run over all your healing balms and herbs,[150] your hellebore, humble crocus, and leaf of the hyacinth—all the simples that the meadow holds—and the arts of the physicians.'

"Ah! let the herbs and simples perish, let all the arts of the doctors perish, since they are worthless to their master. And myself—for I do not know what grand song my pipe was sounding—it is now eleven nights and a day—perhaps I was setting my lips to new pipes, but their fastenings snapped and they fell asunder and could carry the grave notes no further. I am afraid that I am vain, yet I will relate it. Give way, then, O forest.[160]

"Go home unfed, for your master has no time for you, my lambs. I, for my part, am resolved to tell the story of the Trojan ships[162] in the Rutupian sea and of the ancient kingdom of Inogene,[163] the daughter of Pandrasus, and of the chiefs, Brennus and Arviragus, and of old Belinus,[164] and of the Armorican settlers who came at last under British law.[165] Then I shall tell of Igraine pregnant with Arthur by fatal deception,[166] the counterfeiting of Gorlois' features and arms by Merlin's treachery. And then, O my pipe,[169] if life is granted me, you shall be left dangling on some old pine tree far away and quite forgotten by me; or else, quite changed, you shall shrill forth a British theme to your native Muses. What then? One man cannot do everything nor so much as hope to do everything. I shall have ample reward and think my glory great—though I may be forever unknown and inglorious throughout all the outside world—if only blond-haired Ouse[175] reads me and he who

149. The river *Colne* flows near Horton, which seems to lie near the kingdom of the British chief, Cassivelaunus, whom Caesar confessed in the *Gallic War* (V, xi) that he had great difficulty in subduing.

150. Diodati was a medical student at Oxford.

160. So Virgil took leave of pastoral poetry with a farewell to the forests in his "Lament for Gallus" (*Ec.* X, 63). Milton now repeats the epic ambitions which he has confessed in *Manso*, 78–84.

162. Milton thinks of opening his British epic with the approach of the Trojan fleet under Brutus (see *Comus*, 828, n.) to the English coast. *Rutupina*, to which Lucan referred in the *Pharsalia* VI, 67, as one of Rome's great colonial cities, is identified with Richborow in the account of Kent in Camden's *Britannia*.

163. *Inogene*: Spenser's "Inogene of Italy" (*F.Q.* II, x, 13, 5), the wife of "Trojan Brute," is represented by Geoffrey of Monmouth as having been won from her father Pandracos in Greece.

164. "*Brennus* and *Belinus*, kings of Britany," as Spenser recalled (*F.Q.* II, x, 40), "ransackt Greece" as well as France and Germany. Brennus sacked Rome in 390 B.C. *Arviragus*, who Spenser says (*F.Q.* II, x, 52) was dreaded by the Romans, actually fought bravely against the legions of Claudius.

165. In *Britain* III (C.E. X, 118) Milton mentions a British colony planted in Brittany by Constantine the Great or by Maximus.

166. Uther Pendragon, says Malory in *Morte d'Arthur* I, ii, "by means of *Merlin*," disguised himself in the arms of *Igraine's* husband, *Gorlois*, Duke of Cornwall, to become her lover for a night, and so begot King Arthur.

169. Milton is taking leave of the pipe of pastoral poetry.

175. The *Ouse* winds through the central counties to the Wash. The *Trent* enters the estuary of the *Humber* between Yorkshire and Lincolnshire. Camden mentions a river *Alne* in Northumberland and another in Hampshire.

Vorticibusque frequens Abra, et nemus omne Trean-
  tae,
Et Thamesis meus ante omnes, et fusca metallis
Tamara, et extremis me discant Orcades undis.
  "Ite domum impasti, domino iam non vacat, agni.
Haec tibi servabam lenta sub cortice lauri.   180
Haec, et plura simul; tum quae mihi pocula Mansus,
Mansus, Chalcidicae non ultima gloria ripae,
Bina dedit, mirum artis opus, mirandus et ipse,
Et circum gemino caelaverat argumento.
In medio rubri maris unda, et odoriferum ver,   185
Littora longa Arabum, et sudantes balsama silvae;
Has inter Phoenix, divina avis, unica terris,
Caeruleum fulgens diversicoloribus alis,
Auroram vitreis surgentem respicit undis.
Parte alia polus omnipatens, et magnus Olympus.   190
Quis putet? hic quoque Amor, pictaeque in nube
  pharetrae,
Arma corusca, faces, et spicula tincta pyropo;
Nec tenues animas, pectusque ignobile vulgi,
Hinc ferit; at, circum flammantia lumina torquens,
Semper in erectum spargit sua tela per orbes   195
Impiger, et pronos nunquam collimat ad ictus.
Hinc mentes ardere sacrae, formaeque deorum.
  "Tu quoque in his—nec me fallit spes lubrica,
  Damon—
Tu quoque in his certe es; nam quo tua dulcis abiret
Sanctaque simplicitas, nam quo tua candida virtus?
Nec te Lethaeo fas quaesivisse sub orco,   201
Nec tibi conveniunt lacrymae, nec flebimus ultra.
Ite procul, lacrymae; purum colit aethera Damon,

178. From the earliest times the valley of the
Tamar, between Cornwall and Devonshire, has
been famous for its mines.
181. Instead of actual *cups* M. De Filippis suggests, in *PMLA,* LI (1936), 745–56, that Manso
gave Milton two volumes of his poems, and that
their subjects corresponded with the decorations of
the cups. D. Dorian remarks, in *PMLA,* LIV
(1939), 612, that Pindar referred to his seventh
Olympian Ode as a cup to be quaffed like a
wedding-cup.
182. Again, as in *Leon* 3, 6, Milton calls the
shore of the Bay of Naples by the name of its
Chalcidian Greek colonists.
187. Of the many possible "sources" for this
description of the *Phoenix,* the closest—as Rudolf
Gottfried shows in *SP,* XXX (1933), 497–503—is
Tasso's *La Fenice* in the version to be found in *Le
Sette Giornate del Mondo Creato.* Cf. *PL* V,
272, and *SA,* 1699.
193. This *Cupid* is the Heavenly Eros which
Plato distinguished from the Popular Eros in the
Symposium, 180d–182a, and which the Neo-
Platonism of the Renaissance evolved into Spenser's
Celestial Cupid, the
  Lord of truth and loialtie,
Lifting himselfe out of the lowly dust

drinks from the Alne and the
Humber with its many whirlpools,
and every forest by the Trent, and
before them all my Thames, and
the Tamora,[178] which minerals dis-
color, and if the Orkneys in their
distant seas will learn my song.
  "Go home unfed, for your master
has no time for you, my lambs.
These things I was keeping for you
in the tough-barked laurel. These
and more also—and in addition the
two cups[181] which Manso gave me
—Manso, who is not the least glory
of the Chalcidian shore.[182] They
are a marvellous work of art, and
he is a marvellous man. Around
them goes an engraving with a
double motif. In the middle are
the waves of the Red Sea, the perfumed springtime, the far-stretching
shores of Arabia, and the groves
that distil balsam. Among those
trees the Phoenix,[187] the divine bird
which is unique on earth, gleams
cerulean with parti-colored wings,
and watches Aurora rise over the
glassy waters. In another part are
the widespreading sky and mighty
Olympus. Who would suppose
such a thing? Here is Cupid[193]
also, his quiver painted against a
cloud, his gleaming arms, his torches
and his darts of bronze tincture,
the color of flame. From that
height he does not wound frivolous
spirits or the ignoble hearts of the
rabble, but—looking around him
with flaming eyes—he tirelessly
scatters his darts aloft through the
spheres and never points his shots
downward. That is why the minds
of the elect and the essences of the
gods themselves are enkindled.
  "You also are among them—for
no uncertain hope deceives me—
certainly you also are among them;
for where else should your sweet
and holy simplicity have gone?
Where else your unsullied virtue?
It would be sinful to look to find
you in Lethean Orcus.[201] Tears for
you are an impertinence and I do
not shed them any more. Be gone,
my tears! Damon dwells in the

On golden plumes up to the purest skie.
  (*An Hymne in Honour of Love,* 176–8)
Cf. *Comus,* 1004–11, and *DDD* I, vi.
  201. Cf. *Lethe* in *QNov,* 132.

Aethera purus habet, pluvium pede reppulit arcum;
Heroumque animas inter, divosque perennes,   2c5
Aethereos haurit latices et gaudia potat
Ore Sacro. Quin tu, caeli post iura recepta,
Dexter ades, placidusque fave, quicunque vocaris,
Seu tu noster eris Damon, sive aequior audis
Diodatus, quo te divino nomine cuncti   21ͻ
Caelicolae norint, silvisque vocabere Damon.
Quod tibi purpureus pudor, et sine labe iuventus
Grata fuit, quod nulla tori libata voluptas,
En! etiam tibi virginei servantur honores!
Ipse, caput nitidum cinctus rutilante corona,   21ͼ
Laetaque frondentis gestans umbracula palmae,
Aeternum perages immortales hymenaeos,
Cantus ubi, choreisque furit lyra mista beatis,
Festa Sionaeo bacchantur et Orgia Thyrso."   (1640)

pure aether, the aether which he is pure enough to possess, and his foot spurns the rainbow. Among the souls of heroes and the immortal gods he drinks the draughts of heaven and quaffs its joys with his sacred lips. And now, since you have received the privileges of heaven, assist and gently favor me, however you may be called; whether you are to be known as our Damon or would rather be Diodati, by which divine name[210] the inhabitants of heaven will know you, while in the forests you will keep the name of Damon. Because you loved the blush of modesty[212] and a stainless youth and because you did not taste the delight of the marriage-bed, lo! the rewards of virginity are reserved for you. Your glorious head shall be bound with a shining crown[215] and with shadowing fronds of joyous palms in your hands[216] you shall enact your part eternally in the immortal marriage where song and the sound of the lyre are mingled in ecstasy with blessed dances, and where the festal orgies rage under the heavenly thyrsus."[219]

210. *Diodatus,* like the Greek name Theodore, means "God-given."

212. Editors trace the phrase *purpureus pudor* to Ovid's *Amores* I, iii, 14, and the description is like the Ovidian Cupid, but the real reference is to the modesty which Plato said (*Phaedrus,* 254a) restrains the soul from incontinence; or it is to the modesty which St. Bernard called "the sister of Continence," and which St. Ambrose said was "the friend of Pudicity."

215. In the background are St. John's vision of those "which were not defiled with women; for they are virgins" (Rev. xiv, 4) and also perhaps the tradition which gave virgins a crown of lilies like the one brought by an angel to St. Cecilia in Chaucer's *Second Nun's Tale,* 220–3.

216. So St. John saw the heavenly host before the throne "with palms in their hands" (Rev. vii, 9) before his vision of "the marriage of the Lamb" (Rev. xix, 7). Cf. *Lyc,* 176–7.

219. The *thyrsus* was the vine-wreathed wand carried by Bacchic revellers. By comparing the

joys of heaven to their orgies Milton—to whom Bacchus was a symbol of incontinence and "barbarous dissonance" (*PL* VII, 33)—meant to say that in the life to come the passions of the soul would be both intensified and chastened into ecstasy.

TRANSLATIONS FROM *OF REFORMATION TOUCHING CHURCH DISCIPLINE IN ENGLAND*

Ah, *Constantine,* of how much ill was Cause,
Not thy Conversion, but those rich Demains
That the first wealthy *Pope* receiv'd of thee.
            (Dante, *Inferno* XIX, 115–17)

Founded in chaste and humble Poverty,
'Gainst them that rais'd thee dost thou lift thy Horn,
Impudent Whore, where hast thou plac'd thy Hope?
In thy Adulterers, or thy ill-got wealth?
Another *Constantine* comes not in haste.
            (Petrarch, *Sonnet* 138. [1ͻ8.])

Then past he to a flow'ry Mountain green,
Which once smelt sweet, now stinks as odiously;

This was that Gift (if you the Truth will have)
That *Constantine* to good *Sylvestro* gave.[1]
(*Orlando Furioso* XXXIX, 80)   (1641)

[1] Four lines from Harington's translation of stanza 72 in Canto XXXIV (in his *Orlando Furioso in English Heroical Verse*, 1591) are also quoted in *Of Reformation*. Since they differ in Milton's quotation by only a single, insignificant word from Harington's rendering, they are not included here. Milton's translation of stanza 79 is original.

TRANSLATIONS FROM *AN APOLOGY FOR SMECTYMNUUS*

—laughing to teach the Truth
What hinders?   As some teachers give to Boys
Junkets and Knacks, that they may learn apace.
(Horace, *Satires* I, i, 25–27)

—Jesting decides great Things
Stronglier, and better oft than earnest can. .
(Horace, *Satires* I, x, 14–15)

'Tis you that say it, not I: you do the Deeds,
And your ungodly Deeds find me the Words.
(Sophocles, *Electra*, 624–25)   (1642)

SONNET VIII

When the Assault Was Intended to the City[1]

Captain or Colonel, or Knight in Arms,
　　Whose chance on these defenseless doors may seize,
　　If ever deed of honor did thee please,
　　Guard them, and him within protect from harms;
He can requite thee, for he knows the charms　　　　　　5
　　That call Fame on such gentle acts as these,
　　And he can spread thy Name o'er Lands and Seas,
　　Whatever clime the Sun's bright circle warms.
Lift not thy spear against the Muses' Bow'r:
　　The great *Emathian* Conqueror bid spare　　　　　　10
　　The house of *Pindarus,* when Temple and Tow'r
Went to the ground; and the repeated air
　　Of sad *Electra's* Poet had the pow'r
　　To save th' *Athenian* Walls from ruin bare.　　　　(1642)

[1] The original title, as found in the Trinity MS, was *On his door when the City expected an assault.* As J. H. Finley, Jr., notes in "Milton and Horace"—*HSCP,* XLVIII (1937), 37—both that title and the references to the fall of Thebes and of Athens show that the sonnet was playfully cast in the form of a classical inscription. The Royalist assault on London was expected on Nov. 13, 1642, but the forces of King Charles were repulsed at Turnham Green by the Earl of Essex.
　Colonel had three syllables: cur-o-nel.
　10. The *Emathian* is Alexander the Great. (Cf. the reference to Macedon as Emathia in *PR* III, 290.) Renaissance writers were fond of Pliny's story (VII, xix) that in the sack of Thebes Alexan-

der spared the house of the poet Pindar. "He commaunded streightly, that no man should, upon payne of death, do any violence to that house," said E. K. in his gloss on *October* in Spenser's *Shepheardes Calendar*.
　12. *the repeated air:* the repeating of the air. Cf. the similar Latin construction in *SA,* 1294. In the "Life of Lysander," the conqueror of Athens in 404 B.C., Plutarch says that the city would have been destroyed if one of the Spartan generals had not pled for it by singing the first chorus from Euripides' *Electra:*
　　　　Electra, Agamemnon's child, I come
　　　　Unto thy desert home . . .

SONNET IX

Lady That in the Prime

Lady that in the prime of earliest youth,
   Wisely hast shunn'd the broad way and the green,
   And with those few art eminently seen
   That labor up the Hill of Heav'n y Truth,
The better part with *Mary* and with *Ruth*   5
   Chosen thou hast; and they that overween,
   And at thy growing virtues fret their spleen,
   No anger find in thee, but pity and ruth.
Thy care is fixt and zealously attends
   To fill thy odorous Lamp with deeds of light,   10
   And Hope that reaps not shame.   Therefore be sure
Thou, when the Bridegroom with his feastful friends
   Passes to bliss at the mid-hour of night,
   Hast gain'd thy entrance, Virgin wise and pure.   (1645)

1. The girl to whom the sonnet was addressed is unknown.

2–4. In the background are Christ's saying that "broad is the way that leadeth to destruction," and also Holbein's illustrations of the *Table of Cebes*, which show young people trifling at the foot of the rugged mountain of *Truth* while men and women struggle up a steep path to the citadel of true felicity and are crowned by a king who—in spite of the pagan origin of the allegory—seems to be the Christian God. Cf. *PR* II, 217.

5. *Mary*, whom Jesus praised for choosing "that good part which shall not be taken away from her" (Luke x, 42), and *Ruth*, who gave up her home in Moab to live with her Hebrew mother-in-law, Naomi (Ruth i, 14), traditionally exemplified Christian womanhood.

8. *ruth*: pity.

10–14. In the parable of the ten virgins (Matt. xxvi, 6) only five were ready with filled lamps to go to the marriage feast, when "at midnight, there was a cry made, Behold, the bridegroom cometh."

TRANSLATION FROM *TETRACHORDON*

Whom do we count a good man, whom but he
Who keeps the laws and statutes of the Senate,
Who judges in great suits and controversies,
Whose witness and opinion wins the cause?
But his own house, and the whole neighborhood   5
See his foul inside through his whited skin.
        (Horace, Epistles I, xvi, 40)   (1645)

1. The context of this translation from *Tetrachordon* may be found in C.E. IV, 137.

SONNET X

To the Lady Margaret Ley

Daughter to that good Earl, once President
   Of *England's* Council and her Treasury,
   Who liv'd in both, unstained with gold or fee,
   And left them both, more in himself content,

1. After Mary Powell Milton left him in 1642, Milton's nephew Phillips says that he often called on Lady Ley and her husband, Captain Hobson. (See below p. 1031.) Her father, the *good Earl*, was Sir James Ley, who became Lord Chief Justice in 1622, and successively Lord High Treasurer and Lord President of the Council under Charles I, who created him Earl of Marlborough.

Till the sad breaking of that Parliament   5
Broke him, as that dishonest victory
At *Chaeronéa,* fatal to liberty,
Kill'd with report that Old man eloquent;
Though later born than to have known the days
Wherein your Father flourisht, yet by you,   10
Madam, methinks I see him living yet;
So well your words his noble virtues praise
That all both judge you to relate them true
And to possess them, Honor'd *Margaret.*   (1645)

5. The Earl died on March 14, 1629, four days after the dissolution of the Parliament which marked the first open breach between its leaders and the King.
6. *dishonest* has the Latin meaning of "disgraceful."
7. By a victory at *Chaeronéa* in 338 B.C. Philip of Macedon ended the independence of Thebes and Athens.
8. *that Old man eloquent* is Isocrates, the Athenian orator, who was ninety-eight years old in 338 B.C. Tradition says that after his city's defeat at Chaeronéa he deliberately starved himself to death.

IN EFFIGIEI EIUS SCULPTOREM.* (ON THE ENGRAVER OF HIS LIKENESS)

'Αμαθεῖ γεγράφθαι χειρὶ τήνδε μὲν εἰκόνα
Φαίης τάχ' ἄν, πρὸς εἶδος αὐτοφυὲς βλέπων·
Τὸν δ' ἐκτυωτὸν οὐκ ἐπιγνόντες, φίλοι,
Γελᾶτε φαύλου δυσμίμημα ζωγράφου.   (1645)

* Humorous lines placed by Milton below the engraving of himself which served as a frontispiece to the edition of 1645. It is so bad a likeness that its only interest is bibliographical.

Looking at the form of its original, you might say, mayhap, that this likeness had been drawn by a tyro's hand; but, friends, since you do not recognize what is modelled here, have a laugh at a caricature by a good-for-nothing artist.

VERSES FROM *THE HISTORY OF BRITAIN,*

BOOK I

(Geoffrey of Monmouth says that Brutus the Trojan asked the advice of Diana at her shrine on the forsaken Mediterranean island of Leogecia. The Greek verses of his address to the goddess were turned by Gildas into the Latin elegiacs which Milton translated.)

Goddess of Shades, and Huntress, who at will
Walk'st on the rolling Sphere and through the deep,
On thy third Reign, the Earth, look now and tell
What Land, what Seat of rest thou bidst me seek,
What certain Seat, where I may worship thee
For aye, with Temples vow'd, and Virgin choirs.

"To whom sleeping before the Altar," says Milton, *"Diana* in a Vision that night thus answer'd;"

Brutus, far to the West in th' Ocean wide
Beyond the realm of Gaul a Land there lies,
Sea-girt it lies, where Giants dwelt of old,
Now void, it fits thy People; thither bend
Thy course, there shalt thou find a lasting seat,
There to thy Sons another Troy shall rise.

And Kings be born of thee, whose dreaded might
Shall awe the World and Conquer Nations bold.   (1645?)

FROM BOOK IV

(Matthew of Westminster tells the story of the revelation of the murder of little King
Kenelm by a dove, reporting it to the pope in a note consisting of two lines of poetry,
which Milton translated:)

Low in a mead of Kine under a Thorn,
Of head bereft li'th poor Kenelm King-born.

SONNET XI

ON THE DETRACTION WHICH FOLLOWED UPON MY WRITING CERTAIN TREATISES

A book was writ of late call'd *Tetrachordon;*
  And wov'n close, both matter, form and style;
  The Subject new: it walk'd the Town a while,
  Numb'ring good intellects; now seldom por'd on.
Cries the stall-reader, "Bless us! what a word on   5
  A title page is this!" and some in file
Stand spelling false, while one might walk to Mile-
  End Green. Why is it harder, Sirs, than Gordon,
Colkitto, or Macdonnel, or Galasp?
  Those rugged names to our like mouths grow sleek   10
  That would have made *Quintilian* stare and gasp.
Thy age, like ours, O Soul of Sir *John Cheke,*
  Hated not Learning worse than Toad or Asp,
  When thou taught'st *Cambridge* and King *Edward* Greek.   (1646?)

1. *Tetrachordon* was published March 5, 1645, but this sardonic sonnet can hardly have been written immediately thereafter. In the Trinity MS *Sonnet XII* (*I did but prompt . . .*) stands first though in 1673 Milton numbered the two sonnets as they stand here. In Greek music the tetrachords or scales consisted of four notes. In Milton's *Tetrachordon* the "notes" are the four biblical passages on marriage and divorce: Gen. i, 26–28; Deut. xxiv, 1–2; Matt. v, 31–32; and I Cor. vii, 10–16.

7. *spelling false:* misreading, misunderstanding.

10. Instead of *rugged*, Milton first wrote *barbarian* in the MS. None of the bearers of his random Scottish names can be certainly identified.

11. The warning in Quintilian's *Institutes* I, v, 8, against foreign words as barbarous threats to the purity of Latin, was applied to innovations in all the national languages of Europe by their champions in the Renaissance.

12. *Sir John Cheke,* the first professor of Greek at Cambridge (1540–1551), and later tutor to Edward VI, is said by Roger Ascham to have popularized his subject. J. M. French shows—in *MLN,* LXX (1955), 404—that in Milton's time Cheke's success was regarded as a triumph over early Tudor ignorance and bigotry.

SONNET XII

ON THE SAME

I did but prompt the age to quit their clogs
  By the known rules of ancient liberty,

1. The date is uncertain. If W. R. Parker is right in seeing a reference to *Tetr* and *Colis* in *Latona's* twins (l. 6), the sonnet may have been written not long after William Prynne attacked those tracts in *Twelve Considerable Questions* in September, 1644. D. H. Stevens—in *MP.* XVII (1919), 27—saw its "spirit of active conflict" as reflecting Puritan passions after Cromwell's victory at Marston Moor on July 12, 1644. Cf. *Sonn* XI, 1, n.

2. *the known rules:* the Mosaic law of divorce in Deut. xxiv, 1–2.

When straight a barbarous noise environs me
Of Owls and Cuckoos, Asses, Apes and Dogs.
As when those Hinds that were transform'd to Frogs   5
Rail'd at *Latona's* twin-born progeny
Which after held the Sun and Moon in fee.
But this is got by casting Pearl to Hogs,
That bawl for freedom in their senseless mood,
And still revolt when truth would set them free.   10
License they mean when they cry liberty;
For who loves that, must first be wise and good;
But from that mark how far they rove we see,
For all this waste of wealth and loss of blood.   (1646?)

6. Ovid tells the story (*Met.* VI, 317–81) of the Lycian peasants who annoyed Latona when she was nursing Apollo and Diana, the destined deities of the sun and moon. At her prayer, the children's father, Jove, turned her tormentors into frogs.

7. *fee:* fee simple, full legal possession.
11. "Honest liberty," said Milton in his letter to Parliament prefixed to *DDD*, "is the greatest foe to dishonest license." Cf. *PL* XII, 83–85.

SONNET XIII

To My Friend, Mr. Henry Lawes, on His Airs

Harry, whose tuneful and well measur'd Song
First taught our English Music how to span
Words with just note and accent, not to scan
With *Midas'* Ears, committing short and long,
Thy worth and skill exempts thee from the throng,   5
With praise enough for Envy to look wan;
To after age thou shalt be writ the man
That with smooth air couldst humor best our tongue.
Thou honor'st Verse, and Verse must lend her wing
To honor thee, the Priest of *Phoebus'* Choir   10
That tun'st their happiest lines in Hymn, or Story.
Dante shall give Fame leave to set thee higher
Than his *Casella*, whom he woo'd to sing,
Met in the milder shades of Purgatory.   (February 9, 1646)

1. Milton's admiration for Lawes shines through the opening song which he sang as the Attendant Spirit in *Comus*, and in the compliment paid to him in ll. 86–87. Their relation is studied by Willa M. Evans in *Henry Lawes, Musician and Friend of Poets* (London, 1941).
4. *Midas* got his ass's *ears*, according to Ovid (*Met.* XI, 153–79), for preferring Pan's music to Apollo's. *Committing* has its Latin meaning of "setting in conflict." Miss Evans has shown that Lawes was the first English composer to fit his music to the sense and rhythm of the lyrics for

which he wrote it.
11. The *Story* was William Cartwright's poem, *The Complaint of Ariadne*, which Lawes set to music.
13. Dante's friend, the musician *Casella*, retained his power to charm Dante with his voice in Purgatory (*Purg.* II, 76–119).
14. *milder* is written as *mildest* in the first version of this sonnet in the Trinity MS. Dante and Casella met on the threshold of Purgatory, where—as J. S. Diekhoff says in *MLN*, LII (1937), 410—its mildest shades are found.

ON THE NEW FORCERS OF CONSCIENCE UNDER THE LONG PARLIAMENT

Because you have thrown off your Prelate Lord,
And with stiff Vows renounc'd his Liturgy

1–4. On July 1, 1643, after the abolition of episcopacy by Parliament, the Westminster Assembly

of Divines began deliberations "for the settling of the liturgy and the government of the Church of

To seize the widow'd whore Plurality
From them whose sin ye envied, not abhorr'd,
Dare ye for this adjure the Civil Sword   5
To force our Consciences that Christ set free,
And ride us with a classic Hierarchy
Taught ye by mere *A.S.* and *Rotherford?*
Men whose Life, Learning, Faith and pure intent
    Would have been held in high esteem with *Paul,*   10
    Must now be nam'd and printed Heretics
By shallow *Edwards* and Scotch what d'ye call:
    But we do hope to find out all your tricks,
    Your plots and packing worse than those of *Trent,*
            That so the Parliament   15
May with their wholesome and preventive Shears
Clip your Phylacteries, though baulk your Ears,
            And succor our just Fears,
When they shall read this clearly in your charge:
New Presbyter is but *Old Priest* writ Large.   (1646?)   20

England." There was a heavy majority of Presbyterians, and those "great rebukers of non-
residence," as Milton called them in *Britain* (C.E.
X, 322), "were not ashamed to be seen quickly
pluralists and non-residents themselves." The Assembly's domination of the English Church continued until its abolition by Parliament on February
22, 1649.
  7. For *classic* see *TKM,* n. 27.
  8. *A. S.* was Adam Stewart, a Scottish pamphleteer supporting the Presbyterian party in the
Assembly and in Parliament. Samuel Rutherford
(*Rotherford*) was a Scottish Presbyterian sitting in
the Assembly.
  12. Thomas *Edwards* deserved to be called
shallow for his *Antapologia* (1644), a reply to
the *Apologetical Narration* (1643) of Thomas
Goodwin, with whose defense of the Independents
in the Assembly Milton was in sympathy. *Scotch
what d'ye call* was Robert Baillie, the most violent
of the Scottish members of the Assembly.
  14. The Council of *Trent,* which met irregularly
from 1545 to 1563, was proverbial in England for
its compromises.
  15. This and the two following lines are the
first of the sonnet's two tails. In Italy many

satirical sonnets ended in chains of such stinging
tails (*coce*).
  17. *Phylacteries:* little boxes containing quotations
from the Mosaic law which were worn on the
forehead by pious Jews. Their display was made
a byword for hypocrisy by Christ's charge that the
Pharisees made "broad their phylacteries" (Matt.
xxiii, 5). The line—as D. C. Dorian observes in
MLN, LVI (1941), 63—is a threat to the Presbyterians even though Milton says that the opposition to them may *baulk* at (stop short of) cutting
off their ears and so, by a principle of the Mosaic
law, rendering them incapable of priesthood of any
kind. Prynne had actually been shorn of both ears
for a pamphlet attacking Bishop Wren in 1637, a
fact which Milton recalled in a version of the line
which is still legible in the Trinity MS:
    Clip ye as close as marginal P——'s ears.
  20. *Presbyter* and *Priest* are derived from the
same Greek word, but the latter came into English
early through French and Latin while the former
was directly introduced from Greek in the sixteenth century. In 1644 William Walwyn had
written in *The Compassionate Samaritane* (p. 16),
"Some say the tyrannie over Conscience that was
exercised by the Bishops, is like to be continued by
the Presbiters."

SONNET XIV

On the Religious Memory of Mrs. Catharine Thomason,
My Christian Friend, Deceased 16 December, 1646[1]

When Faith and Love which parted from thee never,
    Had ripen'd thy just soul to dwell with God,

[1] Of the Thomasons' relations with Milton we
know simply that he gave signed copies of several
of his works to Catharine's husband, George
Thomason, to whom we owe the great "Thomason
Collection" of tracts published between 1641 and
1662. This sonnet may or may not be impersonal in its use of the traditional figures of *Faith*
and *Love, Works* and *Alms* allegorically preparing
the soul to meet Death in a way which R. L.
Ramsay compared in *SP,* XV (1918), 142, to the
allegory in *Everyman.* Milton's date is wrong.
Mrs. Thomason was buried Dec. 12, 1646.

Meekly thou didst resign this earthy load
Of Death, call'd Life; which us from Life doth sever.
Thy Works and Alms and all thy good Endeavor   5
Stay'd not behind, nor in the grave were trod;
But, as Faith pointed with her golden rod,
Follow'd thee up to joy and bliss for ever.
Love led them on, and Faith who knew them best
Thy handmaids, clad them o'er with purple beams   10
And azure wings, that up they flew so drest,
And spake the truth of thee in glorious Themes
Before the Judge, who thenceforth bid thee rest
And drink thy fill of pure immortal streams.   (1646)

4. The allegory shifts to that of life as a pilgrimage ending in death, "when we put off our earthly *tabernacle* and departing from *this house of clay, whose foundation is in the dust,* arrive in the faire hauens of Heauen, in the quire of Angels." So St. Paul's thought (in II Cor. v, 1–4) was allegorized in *Purchas his Pilgrimes* (1625) I, ii, 1; Vol. I, 50, as the basis of that famous collection of Christian pilgrimages.

6. Cf. Rev. xiv, 13: "Blessed are the dead which die in the Lord. . . . Yea, saith the Spirit, that they may rest from their labor; and their works do follow them."

12. *Themes* is used in its musical sense, says Sir Herbert Grierson in *TLS* of Jan. 15, 1925, p. 40.

14. *immortal*—immortality-giving—like the "pure river of water of life, clear as crystal," which St. John saw "proceeding out of the throne of God and of the Lamb" (Rev. xxii, 1).

AD IOANNEM ROUSIUM (TO JOHN ROUSE)

Oxoniensis Academiae Bibliothecarium (Librarian of Oxford University)

(De libro Poematum amisso, quem ille sibi denuo mitti postulabat, ut cum aliis nostris in Bibliotheca Publica reponeret, Ode.)

(An ode on a volume of my poems which was lost and another copy of which he requested so that he might place it in the public library with the rest of my books.)

Strophe 1

Gemelle cultu simplici gaudens liber,
Fronde licet gemina,
Munditieque nitens non operosa
Quam manus attulit
Iuvenilis olim   5
Sedula, tamen haud nimii Poetae;
Dum vagus Ausonias nunc per umbras,
Nunc Britannica per vireta lusit,
Insons populi, barbitoque devius
Indulsit patrio, mox itidem pectine Daunio   10
Longinquum intonuit melos
Vicinis, et humum vix tetigit pede.

Twin-membered book[1] rejoicing in a single cover, yet with a double leaf,[2] and shining with unlabored elegance which a hand once young imparted—a careful hand, but hardly that of one who was too much a poet—while he played, footloose, now in the forest-shades of Ausonia[7] and now on the lawns of England and, following his own devious ways aloof from the people, he trifled with his native lute or chanted some exotic strain with a Daunian[10] quill to his neighbors—his foot scarcely touching the ground.

1. This poem was first published in 1673. The stolen book was the volume of poems published in 1645, a copy of which Milton had sent to Rouse together with a volume containing the eleven prose pamphlets which he had published up to that date. The replacement copy of the poems is still in the Bodleian with the manuscript of this ode where Milton placed it, between the English and Latin poems.

2. *fronde:* either the title pages under which the Latin and English poems were separately paginated or the double crown deserved by the collections of poems in the two languages.

7. *Ausonia:* an ancient name for Italy.

10. *Daunia* was the ancient name of the modern province of Puglia in southeastern Italy. Here it stands by metonymy for the whole country.

Antistrophe

Quis te, parve liber, quis te fratribus
Subduxit reliquis dolo,
Cum tu missus ab urbe,   15
Docto iugiter obsecrante amico,
Illustre tendebas iter
Thamesis ad incunabula
Caerulei patris,
Fontes ubi limpidi   20
Aonidum, thyasusque sacer,
Orbi notus per immensos
Temporum lapsus redeunte caelo,
Celeberque futurus in aevum?

Strophe 2

Modo quis deus, aut editus deo,   25
Pristinam gentis miseratus indolem—
Si satis noxas luimus priores,
Mollique luxu degener otium—
Tollat nefandos civium tumultus,
Almaque revocet studia sanctus,   30
Et relegatas sine sede Musas
Iam paene totis finibus Angligenum,
Immundasque volucres
Unguibus imminentes
Figat Apollinea pharetra,   35
Phineamque abigat pestem procul amne Pegaseo?

Antistrophe

Quin tu, libelle, nuntii licet mala
Fide, vel oscitantia,
Semel erraveris agmine fratrum,
Seu quis te teneat specus,   40
Seu qua te latebra, forsan unde vili
Callo tereris institoris insulsi,
Laetare felix; en! iterum tibi
Spes nova fulget posse profundam
Fugere Lethen, vehique Superam   45
In Iovis aulam remige penna:

Strophe 3

Nam te Rousius sui
Optat peculi, numeroque iusto

Who was it, little book, who furtively purloined you from your remaining brothers, when, in response to my learned friend's importunity, you had been dispatched from the town and were going on the glorious journey to the nursery of the Thames[18]—blue father Thames—where the limpid fountains of the Muses[21] are found and also that consecrated band, which has been famous through the world while vast ages have rolled under the revolving heaven, and which is destined to be glorious forever?

What god or what god-begotten man will take pity on the ancient character of our race—if we have sufficiently atoned for our earlier offenses and the degenerate idleness of our effeminate luxury—and will sweep away these accursed tumults among the citizens?[29] What deity will summon our fostering studies home and recall the Muses who have been left with hardly a retreat anywhere in all the confines of England? Who will use the arrows of Apollo to transfix the foul birds[33] whose claws menace us,[35] and will drive the pest of Phineas far away from Pegasus' river?[36]

But, my little book—even though, thanks to a messenger's dishonesty or drowsiness, you have wandered from the company of your brothers—whether some den or some dive imprisons you now, where perhaps you are scraped by the dirty, calloused hand of an illiterate dealer—still you may rejoice, for you are fortunate. Lo, again a new hope shines that you may avoid the depths of Lethe and be carried on soaring wing to the courts of Jupiter on high.

For Rouse—to whose keeping are

18. Milton refers to Oxford as the birthplace of the *Thames* because it lies on the river Isis, not far above that river's confluence with the Thames, where the Thames proper begins.

21. *Aonidum:* the Aonides or Muses, whose traditional home was Mount Helicon in Aonia. Compare *Patrem,* 75, n.

29. Milton was writing in the fourth year of the Civil War.

33–36. Milton thought of the Harpies as Virgil described them (*Aen.* III, 225–41), monstrous birds that defiled everything which they could not devour, and of a story (stemming from Apollonius of Rhodes, *Argonautica* II, 195–228) that they had

once been sent by Zeus to punish the prophet, Phineus, for the abuse of his powers.

35. See the note on Apollo's destruction of the Python in *El VII*, 31–32.

36. Milton called the Thames the river of *Pegasus* not merely because he thought of the more famous fountain of Pirene, near Corinth, which was associated with the winged horse, but also because his flight to heaven with Bellerophon (compare *PL* VII, 18) was regarded (e.g. by Conti IX, iv) as a symbol of the human mind in quest of astronomical knowledge and of the control of nature generally.

Sibi pollicitum queritur abesse,
Rogatque venias ille, cuius inclyta   50
Sunt data virum monumenta curae;
Teque adytis etiam sacris
Voluit reponi, quibus et ipse praesidet
Aeternorum operum custos fidelis,
Quaestorque gazae nobilioris   55
Quam cui praefuit Ion,
Clarus Erechtheides,
Opulenta dei per templa parentis,
Fulvosque tripodas, donaque Delphica,
Ion Actaea genitus Creusa.   60

Antistrophe

Ergo tu visere lucos
Musarum ibis amoenos
Diamque Phoebi rursus ibis in domum
Oxonia quam valle colit,
Delo posthabita,   65
Bifidoque Parnassi iugo.
Ibis honestus,
Postquam egregiam tu quoque sortem
Nactus abis, dextri prece sollicitatus amici.
Illic legeris inter alta nomina   70
Authorum, Graiae simul et Latinae
Antiqua gentis lumina et verum decus.

Epodos

Vos tandem haud vacui mei labores,
Quicquid hoc sterile fudit ingenium.
Iam sero placidam sperare iubeo   75
Perfunctam invidia requiem, sedesque beatas
Quas bonus Hermes
Et tutela dabit solers Roüsi,
Quo neque lingua procax vulgi penetrabit, atque longe
Turba legentum prava facesset;   80
At ultimi nepotes,
Et cordatior aetas
Iudicia rebus aequiora forsitan
Adhibebit integro sinu.
Tum livore sepulto,   85
Si quid meremur sana posteritas sciet
Roüsio favente.

(Ode tribus constat Strophis, totidemque Antis-
trophis, una demum epodo clausis; quas, tametsi
omnes nec versuum numero, nec certis ubique colis

entrusted the glorious monuments of heroes—covets you as part of his treasure, complains that you are missing from the just number promised, and requests that you may come to him. He has desired that you may be placed in those sacred sanctuaries where he himself presides, a faithful warden of immortal works and a custodian of wealth[55] nobler than the gilt tripods and Delphic offerings which were committed in the rich temple of his divine father to Ion,[56] the glorious descendant of Apollo—Ion who was born of Actaean Creusa.

So you shall go to see the delightful groves of the Muses and again you shall go to the divine home of Phoebus, which he inhabits in Oxford's valley in preference to Delos[65] and the riven[66] peak of Parnassus. You shall go with honor, since you are departing assured of a splendid destiny and are invited by a propitious friend. There you shall be read among the sublime names of authors who were the ancient lights and the true glory of the Greek and Latin race.

You then, my labors[73]—whatever my sterile brain has produced—have hardly been in vain. Now at last I bid you look forward to quiet rest, after you have outlived envy, in the blessed retreats provided by kind Hermes[77] and the alert protection of Rouse, where the insolent noise of the crowd never shall enter and the vulgar mob of readers shall forever be excluded. But our distant descendants and a more sensitive age will perhaps render a more nearly just judgment of things out of its unprejudiced heart. Then, when envy has been buried, a sane posterity will know what my deserts are—thanks to Rouse.

(The ode consists of three strophes and the same number of antistrophes, concluding with an epode. Although these units do

55. Cf. the contemptuous reference to *gazae* (royal treasures) in *Ad Patrem* 94.

56-60. Milton thought of the atmosphere of charmed magnificence thrown around Apollo's Delphian temple in the first act of Euripides' *Ion*. The hero, who is Apollo's son, begotten by violence on Creusa, the daughter of Erechtheus, king of Athens, has been secretly reared to be the custodian of his father's temple. Creusa is called *Actaean* because Acte was an ancient name of Attica.

65. Cf. *Delos* in *Manso*, 45.

66. Cf. the *peak of Parnassus* in *El IV*, 30, n.

73. Milton's *labors* are his controversial works, copies of which he had given to the Bodleian Library and to Rouse.

77. *Hermes* (Mercury), the god of learning, has provided the Bodleian as a secure retreat for Milton's books.

exacte respondeant, ita tamen secuimus, commode legendi potius, quam ad antiquos concinendi modos rationem spectantes. Alioquin hoc genus rectius fortasse dici monostrophicum debuerat. Metra partim sunt κατὰ σχέσιν, partim ἀπολελυμένα.* Phaleucia quae sunt, spondaeum tertio loco bis admittunt, quod idem in secundo loco Catullus ad libitum fecit.)

(January 23, 1647)

not perfectly correspond in their number of verses or in divisions which are strictly parallel, nevertheless I have divided them in this way with a view rather to convenience in reading than to conformity with the ancient rules of versification. In other respects a poem of this kind should perhaps more correctly be called monostrophic. The meters are in part regularly patterned and in part free. There are two Phaleucian* verses which admit a spondee in the third foot, a practice which Catullus freely followed in the second foot.)

* The Phaleucian line consisted of a spondee, a dactyl, and three trochees:
$- - / - \smile \smile / - \smile / - \smile / - \smile .$
Milton reasoned badly, as Landor protested, in appealing to Catullus to justify his liberties with his verse. He really meant to declare his purpose to experiment with his meter as freely as he had experimented with his scazons in *Salsillus*.

* Compare the use of the same term in Milton's Preface to *SA*.

April, 1648, J. M.

Nine of the Psalms done into Meter, wherein all but what is in a different Character, are the very words of the Text, translated from the Original.

PSALM LXXX

1 Thou Shepherd that dost Israel *keep*
　Give ear in time of need,
　Who leadest like a flock of sheep
　　Thy loved Joseph's seed,
　That sitt'st between the Cherubs *bright*　　　　　5
　　Between their wings outspread,
　Shine forth, *and from thy cloud give light,*
　　And on our foes thy dread.

2 In Ephraim's view and Benjamin's,
　　And in Manasseh's sight　　　　　　　　　　10
　Awake* thy strength, come, and *be seen*　　　* *Gnorera.*
　　To save us *by thy might.*

3 Turn us again, *thy grace divine*
　　To us O God *vouchsafe;*
　Cause thou thy face on us to shine,　　　　　15
　　And then we shall be safe.

4 Lord God of Hosts, how long wilt thou,
　　How long wilt thou declare
　Thy *smoking wrath *and angry brow*　　　* *Gnashanta.*

1. The importance of these Psalms in Milton's development is discussed by W. B. Hunter in "Sources of Milton's Prosody," *PQ*, XXVII (1949), 125–44. Their value as evidence of his command of Hebrew is disputed by E. C. Baldwin in *MP*, XVII (1920), 457–63, and Marian H. Studley in *PQ*, IV (1925), 364–72. Their background is well studied in P. A. Scholes's *The Puritans and Music in England and New England* (London, 1934).

Against thy people's pray'r?   20
5 Thou feed'st them with the bread of tears,
   Their bread with tears they eat,
And mak'st them *largely drink the tears   * Shalish.
   Wherewith their cheeks are wet.
6 A strife thou mak'st us *and a prey*   25
   To every neighbor foe,
Among themselves they *laugh, they *play,   * Jilgnagu.
   And *flouts at us they throw.
7 Return us, *and thy grace divine,*
   O God of Hosts *vouchsafe;*   30
Cause thou thy face on us to shine,
   And then we shall be safe.
8 A Vine from Egypt thou hast brought,
   Thy free love made it thine,
And drov'st out Nations *proud and haut*   35
   To plant this *lovely* Vine.
9 Thou did'st prepare for it a place
   And root it deep and fast,
That it *began to grow apace*
   And fill'd the land *at last.*   40
10 With her *green* shade *that* cover'd *all,*
   The Hills were *overspread,*
Her Bows as *high as* Cedars tall
   Advanc'd their lofty head.
11 Her branches *on the western side*   45
   Down to the Sea she sent,
And *upward* to that river *wide*
   Her other branches *went.*
12 Why hast thou laid her Hedges low
   And brok'n down her Fence,   50
That all may pluck her, as they go,
   With rudest violence?
13 The *tusked* Boar out of the wood
   Upturns it by the roots,
Wild Beasts there browse, and make their food   55
   Her Grapes and tender Shoots.
14 Return now, God of Hosts, look down
   From Heav'n, thy Seat divine,
Behold *us, but without a frown,*
   And visit this *thy* Vine.   60
15 Visit this Vine which thy right hand
   Hath set and planted *long,*
And the young branch, that for thyself
   Thou hast made firm and strong.
16 But now it is consum'd with fire   65
   And cut *with Axes* down,
They perish at thy dreadful ire,
   At thy rebuke and frown.
17 Upon the man of thy right hand
   Let thy *good* hand be *laid,*   70
Upon the Son of Man, whom thou
   Strong for thyself hast made.
18 So shall we not go back from thee
   To ways of sin and shame,

Quick'n us thou, then *gladly* wee   75
  Shall call upon thy Name.
Return us, *and thy grace divine*
  Lord God of Hosts vouchsafe,
Cause thou thy face on us to shine,
  And then we shall be safe.   80

PSALM LXXXI

1 To God our strength sing loud *and clear,*
  Sing loud to God *our King,*
To Jacob's God, *that all may hear*
  Loud acclamations ring.
2 Prepare a Hymn, prepare a Song,   5
  The Timbrel hither bring,
The *cheerful* Psalt'ry bring along
  And Harp *with* pleasant *string.*
3 Blow, *as is wont,* in the new Moon
  With Trumpets' *lofty sound,*   10
Th' appointed time, the day whereon
  Our solemn Feast *comes round.*
4 This was a Statute *giv'n of old*
  For Israel *to observe,*
A Law of Jacob's God, *to hold*   15
  From whence they might not swerve.
5 This he a Testimony ordain'd
  In Joseph, *not to change,*
When as he pass'd through Egypt land;
  The Tongue I heard, was strange.   20
6 From burden *and from slavish toil*
  I set his shoulder free;
His hands from pots *and miry soil*
  Deliver'd were *by me.*
7 When trouble did thee sore assail,   25
  On me then didst thou call,
And I to free thee *did not fail,*
  And led thee out of thrall.
I answer'd thee in *thunder deep   ** Be Sether ragnam*
  With clouds encompass'd round;   30
I tried thee at the water *steep*
  Of Meriba *renown'd.*
8 Hear O my people, *heark'n well,*
  I testify to thee
Thou ancient stock of Israel,   35
  If thou wilt list to mee,
9 Throughout the land of thy abode
  No alien God shall be,
Nor shalt thou to a foreign God
  In honor bend thy knee.   40
10 I am the Lord thy God which brought
  Thee out of Egypt land;
Ask large enough, and I, *besought,*
  Will grant thy full demand.
11 And yet my people would not *hear,*   45

Nor hearken to my voice;
And Israel *whom I lov'd so dear*
Mislik'd me for his choice.

12 Then did I leave them to their will
And to their wand'ring mind;   50
Their own conceits they follow'd still
Their own devices blind.

13 O that my people would *be wise*
To serve me *all their days,*
And O that Israel would *advise*   55
To walk my *righteous* ways.

14 Then would I soon bring down their foes
That now so proudly rise,
And turn my hand against *all those*
That are their enemies.   60

15 Who hate the Lord should *then be fain*
To bow to him and bend,
But *they, His people, should remain,*
Their time should have no end.

16 And he would feed them *from the shock*   65
With flour of finest wheat,
And satisfy them from the rock
With Honey *for their Meat.*

PSALM LXXXII

1 God in the *great *assembly stands   * *Bagnadath-el.*
 Of Kings and lordly States,
Among the gods† on both his hands   † *Bekerev.*
 He judges and debates.

2 How long will ye *pervert the right   * *Tishphetu*   5
 With *judgment false and wrong,   *gnavel.*
Favoring the wicked *by your might,*
 Who thence grow bold and strong?

3 *Regard the *weak and fatherless,   * *Shiphtu-dal.*
 *Dispatch the *poor man's cause,
And †raise the man in deep distress
 By †just and equal Laws.   † *Hatzdiku.*

4 Defend the poor and desolate,
 And rescue from the hands
Of wicked men the low estate   15
 Of him *that help demands.*

5 They know not nor will understand,
 In darkness they walk on,
The Earth's foundations all are *mov'd   * *Jimmotu.*
 And *out of order gone.   20

6 I said that ye were Gods, yea all
 The Sons of God most high;

7 But ye shall die like men, and fall
 As other Princes *die.*

8 Rise God, *judge thou the earth *in might,*   25
 This *wicked* earth *redress,   * *Shiphta.*
For thou art he who shalt by right
 The Nations all possess.

PSALM LXXXIII

1 Be not thou silent *now at length*
   O God hold not thy peace.
   Sit not thou still O God of *strength,*
   We cry and do not cease.

2 For lo thy *furious* foes *now* *swell   5
   And *storm outrageously,   * *Jehemajun.*
   And they that hate thee *proud and fell*
   Exalt their heads full high

3 Against thy people they †contrive   † *Jagnarimu.*
   †Their Plots and Counsels deep,   † *Sod*   10
   *Them to ensnare they chiefly strive   * *Jithjagnatsu gnal.*
   *Whom thou dost hide and keep.   * *Tsephuneca.*

4 "Come let us cut them off," say they,
   "Till they no Nation be,
   That Israel's name for ever may   15
   Be lost in memory."

5 For they consult †with all their might,   † *Lev jachdau.*
   And all as one in mind
   Themselves against thee they unite
   And in firm union bind.   20

6 The tents of Edom and the brood
   Of *scornful* Ishmael,
   Moab, with them of Hagar's blood
   That in the Desert dwell,

7 Gebal and Ammon *there conspire,*   25
   And *hateful* Amalec,
   The Philistines, and they of Tyre
   Whose bounds the Sea doth check.

8 With them *great* Asshur also bands
   And doth confirm the knot,   30
   All these have lent their armed hands
   To aid the Sons of Lot.

9 Do to them as to Midian *bold*
   That wasted all the Coast,
   To Sisera, and as *is told*   35
   Thou didst to Jabin's *host,*
   When at the brook of Kishon *old*
   They were repulst and slain,

10 At Endor quite cut off, and roll'd
   As dung upon the plain.   40

11 As Zeb and Oreb evil sped
   So let their Princes speed,
   As Zeba, and Zalmunna *bled*
   So let their Princes *bleed.*

12 *For they amidst their pride* have said   45
   "By right now shall we seize
   God's houses, and *will now invade*
   †Their stately Palaces."   † *Neoth Elohim*
                                            bears both.

13 My God, oh make them as a wheel,
   No quiet let them find,   50
   Giddy and *restless* let *them* reel

Like stubble from the wind.
14 As *when* an *aged* wood takes fire
 Which on a sudden strays,
The *greedy* flame runs higher and higher   55
 Till all the mountains blaze,
15 So with thy whirlwind them pursue,
 And with thy tempest chase;
16 *And till they *yield thee honor due,   *They seek thy*
 Lord fill with shame their face.   *Name.* Heb.
17 Asham'd and troubl'd let them be,   60
 Troubl'd and sham'd for ever,
Ever confounded, and so die
 With shame, *and scape it never.*
18 Then shall they know that thou whose name
 Jehovah is alone,   65
Art the most high, *and thou the same*
 O'er all the earth *art one.*

PSALM LXXXIV

1 How lovely are thy dwellings fair!
 O Lord of Hosts, how dear
The *pleasant* Tabernacles are
 Where thou dost dwell so near!
2 My Soul doth long and almost die   5
 Thy Courts O Lord to see,
My heart and flesh aloud do cry,
 O living God, for thee.
3 There ev'n the Sparrow *freed from wrong*
 Hath found a house of *rest,*   10
The Swallow there, to lay her young
 Hath built her *brooding* nest,
Ev'n *by* thy Altars Lord of Hosts
 They find their safe abode,
And home they fly from round the Coasts 15
 Toward thee, My King, my God.
4 Happy who in thy house reside
 Where thee they ever praise,
5 Happy whose strength in thee doth bide,
 And in their hearts thy ways!   20
6 They pass through Baca's *thirsty* Vale,
 That dry and barren ground
As through a fruitful wat'ry Dale
 Where Springs and Show'rs abound.
7 They journey on from strength to strength 25
 With joy and gladsome cheer,
Till all before *our* God *at length*
 In Sion do appear.
8 Lord God of Hosts hear *now* my prayer,
 O Jacob's God give ear,   30
9 Thou God our shield look on the face
 Of thy anointed *dear.*
10 For one day in thy Courts *to be*
 is better *and more blest*

Than *in the joys of Vanity,*   35
   A thousand days *at best.*
I in the temple of my God
   Had rather keep a door
Than dwell in Tents *and rich abode*
   With Sin *for evermore.*   40

11 For God the Lord, both Sun and Shield,
   Gives grace and glory *bright,*
No good from them shall be withheld
   Whose ways are just and right.

12 Lord *God* of Hosts *that reign'st on high,*   45
   That man is *truly* blest
Who *only* on thee doth rely,
   And in thee only rest.

PSALM LXXXV

1 Thy Land to favor graciously
   Thou hast not Lord been slack,
Thou hast from *hard* Captivity
   Returned Jacob back.

2 Th' iniquity thou didst forgive   5
   That wrought thy people woe,
And all their Sin *that did thee grieve*
   Hast hid *where none shall know.*

3 Thine anger all thou hadst remov'd,
   And *calmly* didst return   10
From thy †fierce wrath which we had prov'd†   Heb. *The burning heat of thy wrath.*
   Far worse than fire to burn.

4 God of our saving health and peace,
   Turn us, and us restore,
Thine indignation cause to cease   15
   Toward us, *and chide no more.*

5 Wilt thou be angry without end,
   For ever angry thus?
Wilt thou thy frowning ire extend
   From age to age on us?   20

6 Wilt thou not *turn and *hear our voice*   * Heb. *Turn to quicken us.*
   And us again *revive,
That so thy people may rejoice
   By thee preserv'd alive.

7 Cause us to see thy goodness Lord,   25
   To us thy mercy show,
Thy saving health to us afford
   And life in us renew.

8 *And now* what God the Lord will speak
   I will *go straight and* hear,   30
For to his people he speaks peace
   And to his Saints *full dear,*
To his dear Saints he will speak peace,
   But let them never more
Return to folly, *but surcease*   35
   To trespass as before.

9 Surely to such as do him fear

Salvation is at hand
And glory shall *ere long appear*
To dwell within our Land.   40
10 Mercy and Truth *that long were miss'd*
Now *joyfully* are met;
Sweet Peace and Righteousness have kiss'd
And hand in hand are set.
11 Truth from the earth *like to a flow'r*   45
Shall bud and blossom *then,*
And Justice from her heavenly bow'r
Look down *on mortal men.*
12 The Lord will also then bestow
Whatever thing is good;   50
Our Land shall forth in plenty throw
Her fruits *to be our food.*
13 Before him Righteousness shall go
His Royal Harbinger,
Then *will he come, and not be slow,   * Heb.   *He will set*   55
His footsteps cannot err.   his   steps   to   the
                                               way.

PSALM LXXXVI

1 Thy *gracious* ear, O Lord, incline,
O hear me *I thee pray,*
For I am poor, and almost pine
With need *and sad decay.*
2 Preserve my soul, for† I have trod   † Heb.   *I am good.*   5
Thy ways, and love the just;   *loving, a doer*
Save thou thy servant O my God   *of good and*
Who *still* in thee doth trust.   *holy things.*
3 Pity me Lord for daily thee
I call; 4 O make rejoice   10
Thy Servant's Soul; for Lord to thee
I lift my soul *and voice,*
5 For thou art good, thou Lord art prone
To pardon, thou to all
Art full of mercy, thou *alone*   15
To them that on thee call.
6 Unto my supplication Lord
Give ear, and to the cry
Of my *incessant* prayers afford
Thy hearing graciously.   20
7 I in the day of my distress
Will call on thee *for aid;*
For thou wilt *grant* me *free access*
And answer, *what I pray'd.*
8 Like thee among the gods is none   25
O Lord, nor any works
Of all that other gods have done
Like to thy *glorious* works.
9 The Nations all whom thou hast made
Shall come, *and all shall frame*   30
To bow them low before thee Lord,
And glorify thy name.

10 For great thou art, and wonders great
   By thy strong hand are done,
   Thou *in thy everlasting Seat*   35
   Remainest God alone.
11 Teach me O Lord thy way *most right,*
   I in thy truth will bide,
   To fear thy name my heart unite
   So shall it never slide.   40
12 Thee will I praise O Lord my God
   Thee honor, and adore
   With my whole heart, and blaze abroad
   Thy name for evermore.
13 For great thy mercy is toward me,   45
   And thou hast freed my Soul,
   Ev'n from the lowest Hell set free
   From deepest darkness foul.
14 O God the proud against me rise
   And violent men are met   50
   To seek my life, and in their eyes
   No fear of thee have set.
15 But thou Lord art the God most mild
   Readiest thy grace to show,
   Slow to be angry, and *art styl'd*   55
   Most merciful, most true.
16 O turn to me *thy face at length*
   And me have mercy on,
   Unto thy servant give thy strength,
   And save thy handmaid's Son.   60
17 Some sign of good to me afford
   And let my foes *then* see
   And be asham'd, because thou Lord
   Dost help and comfort me

PSALM LXXXVII

1 Among the holy Mountains *high*
  Is his foundation fast,
  There Seated in his Sanctuary,
  His *Temple there is* plac't.
2 Sion's *fair* Gates the Lord loves more   5
  Than all the dwellings *fair*
  Of Jacob's *Land, though there be store,*
  And all within his care.
3 City of God, most glorious things
  Of thee *abroad* are spoke;   10
4 I mention Egypt, *where proud Kings*
  Did our forefathers yoke,
  I mention Babel to my friends,
  Philistia *full of scorn,*
  And Tyre with Ethiop's *utmost ends,*   15
  Lo this man there was born:
5 But *twice that praise shall in our ear*
  Be said of Sion *last:*
  This and this man was born in her,

High God shall fix her fast.   20
6 The Lord shall write it in a Scroll
   That ne'er shall be outworn
   When he the Nations doth enroll
   That this man there was born.
7 Both they who sing and they who dance   25
   With sacred Songs are there,
   In thee *fresh brooks and soft streams glance,*
   And all my fountains *clear.*

PSALM LXXXVIII

1 Lord God that dost me save and keep,
   All day to thee I cry;
   And all night long before thee *weep,*
   Before thee *prostrate lie.*
2 Into thy presence let my prayer   5
   With sighs devout ascend;
   And to my cries, that *ceaseless are,*
   Thine ear with favor bend.
3 For cloy'd with woes and trouble store
   Surcharg'd my Soul doth lie,   10
   My life *at death's uncheerful door*
   Unto the grave draws nigh.
4 Reck'n'd I am with them that pass
   Down to the *dismal* pit;
   I am a *man, but weak alas   * Heb. *A   man*   15
   And for that name unfit.   *without manly*
                                             strength.
5 From life discharg'd and parted quite
   Among the dead *to sleep,*
   And like the slain *in bloody fight*
   That in the grave lie *deep;*   20
   Whom thou rememberest no more,
   Dost never more regard,
   Them from thy hand deliver'd o'er
   Death's hideous house hath barr'd.
6 Thou in the lowest pit *profound*   25
   Hast set me *all forlorn,*
   Where thickest darkness *hovers round,*
   In horrid deeps *to mourn.*
7 Thy wrath *from which no shelter saves*
   Full sore doth press on me;   30
   *Thou break'st upon me all thy waves,   * The Heb. bears
   *And all thy waves break me.   both.
8 Thou dost my friends from me estrange,
   And mak'st me odious,
   Me to them odious, *for they change,*   35
   And I here pent up thus.
9 Through sorrow and affliction great
   Mine eye grows dim and dead,
   Lord all the day I thee entreat,
   My hands to thee I spread.   40
10 Wilt thou do wonders on the dead,
   Shall the deceas'd arise

And praise thee *from their loathsome bed*
With pale and hollow eyes?
11 Shall they thy loving kindness tell   45
    On whom the grave *hath hold,*
  Or they *who* in perdition *dwell*
    Thy faithfulness *unfold?*
12 In darkness can thy mighty *hand*
    Or wondrous acts be known,   50
  Thy justice in the *gloomy* land
    Of *dark* oblivion?
13 But I to thee O Lord do cry
    Ere yet my life be spent,
  And *up to thee* my prayer *doth hie*   55
    Each morn, and thee prevent.
14 Why wilt thou Lord my sou forsake,
    And hide thy face from me,
15 That am already bruis'd, and †shake   † Heb. *Prae Concus-*
    With terror sent from thee   *sione.*   60
  Bruised, and afflicted and *so low*
    As ready to expire,
  While I thy terrors undergo
    Astonish'd with thine ire.
16 Thy fierce wrath over me doth flow   65
    Thy threat'nings cut me through:
17 All day they round about me go,
    Like waves they me pursue.
18 Lover and friend thou hast remov'd
    And sever'd from me far.   70
  They *fly me now* whom I have lov'd,
    And as in darkness are.

SONNET XV

On the Lord General Fairfax at the Siege of Colchester

Fairfax, whose name in arms through Europe rings,
  Filling each mouth with envy or with praise,
  And all her jealous monarchs with amaze
  And rumors loud, that daunt remotest kings,
Thy firm unshak'n virtue ever brings   5
  Victory home, though new rebellions raise
  Thir Hydra heads, and the false North displays
  Her brok'n league, to imp their serpent wings.
O yet a nobler task awaits thy hand;
  For what can War, but endless war still breed,   10

1. Sir Thomas Fairfax's victories at Marston Moor on July 2, 1644, and Naseby on June 14, 1645, decided the Civil War. When some Royalists revolted in Kent and Essex in 1648, he drove them into Colchester and crowned his career by taking the city on August 27.

5. *Virtue,* in the Roman sense of courage and civic leadership, is a theme in this sonnet, as it is in Tasso's "heroic sonnets," to which J. S. Smart compares it in *The Sonnets of John Milton* (Glasgow, 1921). But, as Finley shows (in *HSCP,* XLVIII, 41 and 59), the tradition goes back through Petrarch and Dante to Horace's vision of civic virtue stamping out the hydra of rebellion (*Odes* IV, ix, 61–62) and to similar Horatian odes.

7. *the false North:* Scotland, which broke its Solemn League and Covenant with Parliament of September, 1645, by sending the Duke of Hamilton to the support of King Charles in 1648.

8. *Imping* or grafting feathers to the injured wing of a falcon was well understood. Cf. Shakespeare's image—to

  Imp out our drooping country's broken wing.
              (*Richard II* II, i, 292)

Till Truth and Right from Violence be freed,
And Public Faith clear'd from the shameful brand
Of Public Fraud. In vain doth Valor bleed
While Avarice and Rapine share the land.   (1648)

LATIN VERSES FROM *PRO POPULO ANGLICANO DEFENSIO*

In Salmasii Hundredam (Against the Hundred of Salmasius)

Quis expedivit Salmasio suam *hundredam*
Picamque docuit verba nostra conari?
Magister artis venter, et Iacobaei
Centum, exulantis viscera marsupii regis.
Quod, si dolosi spes refulserit nummi,   5
Ipse, Antichristi modo qui primatum Papae
Minatus uno est dissipare sufflatu,
Cantabit ultro Cardinalitium melos.   (1651)

1. Claude de Saumaise (*Salmasius*—1588–1653) spent his best years (1631–1650) at the University of Leyden, though his fame as a scholar made the Prince de Condé and the Cardinals Richelieu and Mazarin eager to retrieve his services for France. As a controversialist he was violent and unskilful but less inconsistent than Milton thought him because his attack on papal supremacy (*De primatu papae;* Leyden, 1645) did not square perfectly with his defense of episcopacy (*De episcopis et presbyteris;* Leyden, 1641). In 1649 he was persuaded—as rumor had it, by an offer of a hundred gold Jacobuses—to condemn the "mur-

Who made Salmasius[1] so glib with his "Hundred" and taught the magpie to try our words? His teacher in this art was his stomach and the hundred Jacobuses that were the vitals of the purse of the exiled king. If there were a glimmer of hope of illgotten lucre, this very fellow—who recently threatened to blow to pieces the supremacy of the Pope, the Antichrist, with a single puff—would be perfectly willing to sing the song of the Cardinals.

derers" of Charles I in his *Defensio regia pro Carolo I ad regem Carolum II,* to which Milton replied in March, 1651, with *Pro populo anglicano defensio.* In the *Defensio regia* Salmasius had paraded a knowledge of English law and had expatiated on the term "hundred," a term for the subdivisions of counties in England.

SONNET XVI

To The Lord General Cromwell

On the proposals of certain ministers at the Committee for Propagation of the Gospel

Cromwell, our chief of men, who through a cloud
    Not of war only, but detractions rude,
    Guided by faith and matchless Fortitude,
    To peace and truth thy glorious way hast plough'd,
And on the neck of crowned Fortune proud   5
    Hast rear'd God's Trophies and his work pursu'd,
    While Darwen stream with blood of Scots imbru'd,
    And *Dunbar* field resounds thy praises loud,
And *Worcester's* laureate wreath; yet much remains
    To conquer still; peace hath her victories   10
    No less renown'd than war, new foes arise

1–9. In 1651 *Truth and Peace* appeared on a coin issued by Parliament to express its confidence in the results of Cromwell's victories over the Scots at Preston on the banks of the *Darwen* in 1648 and at *Dunbar* in Scotland in September, 1650, and at *Worcester* in September, 1651.

10–11. There is a clear echo of Cicero's balancing of the glories of war against those of peace in

De officiis I, xxii. The ethical and dramatic strains in this sonnet are like those in Marvell's *An Horatian Ode upon Cromwell's Return from Ireland,* which—as Ruth Wallerstein notes in *Poetic,* p. 280—is as much indebted to Lucan's *Pharsalia* as it is to Horace's civic odes.

11–12. The *new foes* are the clergy who on March 29, 1652, asked Parliament to establish the

Threat'ning to bind our souls with secular chains:
Help us to save free Conscience from the paw
Of hireling wolves whose Gospel is their maw.   (May, 1652)

English Church on broad Protestant principles but with a State-salaried and State-controlled ministry. Cf. Milton's attitude in *Hirelings*.

14. Cf. the echo in *Lyc*, 114–22 of Christ's warn-ing to 'Beware of false prophets, which come to you in sheep's clothing, but inwardly they are ravening wolves" (Matt. vii, 15).

SONNET XVII

To Sir Henry Vane the Younger

Vane, young in years, but in sage counsel old,
    Than whom a better Senator ne'er held
    The helm of *Rome*, when gowns not arms repell'd
    The fierce *Epirot* and the *African* bold
Whether to settle peace, or to unfold   5
    The drift of hollow states hard to be spell'd,
    Then to advise how war may best, upheld,
    Move by her two main nerves, Iron and Gold,
In all her equipage; besides to know
    Both spiritual power and civil, what each means,   10
    What severs each, thou hast learnt, which few have done.
The bounds of either sword to thee wee owe.
    Therefore on thy firm hand religion leans
    In peace, and reck'ns thee her eldest son.   (July, 1652)

1. Like Cromwell, as Max Patrick has pointed out, Sir Henry Vane was a good subject for an "heroic sonnet" of the kind written by Tasso about some of his great contemporaries in Italy. As the leading member of a committee on foreign alliances which the Council of State had set up in March, 1649, he had first striven for an alliance with the Dutch, and later, when war with them became inevitable in June, 1652, had firmly ended the negotiations which their ambassadors protracted until the end of the month for purposes of espionage.

2–4. In the *History of Rome* (XXII, lx) Livy stresses the courage of the Senate in standing firm when Pyrrhus, King of Epeirus, and Hannibal won great initial victories in their invasions of Italy.

6. Holland is *hollow* both in character and in its situation, with much of its land below sea level.

8. Vane was efficient in supplying Parliament's armies with the *gold*, the sinew of war which Machiavelli had compared with the stronger *iron* sinew of good troops in his *Discourses* II, x.

12. In *Peace* (C.E. VI, 262) Milton describes the "Civil sword" as an improper weapon, in comparison with "the spiritual, which is the Word of God," for the extirpation of "Heresy and Schism." Vane was a strong advocate of unqualified religious toleration.

PSALMS I TO VIII

Since there is no doubt that Milton translated these Psalms in the first two weeks of August, 1653, and since they are much more faithful translations from the Hebrew than those done in 1648, it is very interesting that they should contrast with the simple meters of all his earlier translations of Psalms. It is a striking fact that those in Horatian stanzas and, still more markedly, the Psalm (II) in Dante's *terza rima* should—as Lawrence Binyon objected in *SCSHG*, p. 185—have failed to give the effect of their models by "moving in a continuous motion" with "pauses without reference to the stanzas." Already Milton was laying the stress on "the sense variously drawn out from one verse into another," as he was to do in *Paradise Lost*.

PSALM I

Done into Verse, 1653.

Bless'd is the man who hath not walk'd astray
In counsel of the wicked, and i'th'way
Of sinners hath not stood, and in the seat
Of scorners hath not sat.   But in the great
Jehovah's Law is ever his delight,   5
And in his Law he studies day and night.
He shall be as a tree which planted grows
By wat'ry streams, and in his season knows
To yield his fruit, and his leaf shall not fall,
And what he takes in hand shall prosper all.   10
Not so the wicked, but as chaff which fann'd
The wind drives, so the wicked shall not stand
In judgment, or abide their trial then,
Nor sinners in th'assembly of just men.
For the Lord knows th'upright way of the just,   15
And the way of bad men to ruin must.

PSALM II

Done Aug. 8. 1653.   Terzetti.

Why do the Gentiles tumult, and the Nations
    Muse a vain thing, the Kings of th'earth upstand
    With power, and Princes in their Congregations
Lay deep their plots together through each Land,
    Against the Lord and his Messiah dear?   5
    Let us break off, say they, by strength of hand
Their bonds, and cast from us, no more to wear,
    Their twisted cords: he who in Heaven doth dwell
    Shall laugh, the Lord shall scoff them, then severe
Speak to them in his wrath, and in his fell   10
    And fierce ire trouble them; but I, saith hee,
    Anointed have my King (though ye rebel)
On Sion my holi' hill.   A firm decree
    I will declare; the Lord to me hath said,
    Thou art my Son, I have begotten thee   15
This day; ask of me, and the grant is made;
    As thy possession I on thee bestow
    Th'Heathen, and as thy conquest to be sway'd
Earth's utmost bounds: them shalt thou bring full low
    With Iron Scepter bruis'd, and them disperse   20
    Like to a potter's vessel shiver'd so.
And now be wise at length, ye Kings averse,
    Be taught, ye Judges of the earth; with fear
    Jehovah serve, and let your joy converse
With trembling; kiss the Son lest he appear   25
    In anger and ye perish in the way,
    If once his wrath take fire like fuel sere.
Happy all those who have in him their stay.

PSALM III

Aug. 9. 1653.

When he fled from Absalom.
Lord, how many are my foes!
    How many those
  That in arms against me rise!
    Many are they
That of my life distrustfully thus say,   5
"No help for him in God there lies."
But thou, Lord, art my shield, my glory,
    Thee through my story
  Th' exalter of my head I count,
    Aloud I cried   10
Unto Jehovah, he full soon replied
And heard me from his holy mount.
I lay and slept, I wak'd again,
    For my sustain
  Was the Lord. Of many millions   15
    The populous rout
I fear not though encamping round about
They pitch against me their Pavilions.
Rise Lord, save me my God, for thou
    Hast smote ere now   20
  On the cheek-bone all my foes,
    Of men abhorr'd
Hast broke the teeth. This help was from the Lord;
Thy blessing on thy people flows.

PSALM IV

Aug. 10. 1653.

Answer me when I call,
God of my righteousness;
In straits and in distress
Thou didst me disenthrall
And set at large; now spare,   5
  Now pity me, and hear my earnest pray'r.
Great ones, how long will ye
My glory have in scorn?
How long be thus forborne
Still to love vanity,   10
To love, to seek, to prize
  Things false and vain and nothing else but lies?
Yet know the Lord hath chose,
Chose to himself apart,
The good and meek of heart   15
(For whom to choose he knows);
Jehovah from on high
  Will hear my voice what time to him I cry.
Be aw'd, and do not sin,

Speak to your hearts alone,   20
Upon your beds, each one,
And be at peace within.
Offer the offerings just
    Of righteousness and in Jehovah trust.
Many there be that say   25
"Who yet will show us good?"
Talking like this world's brood;
But Lord, thus let me pray,
On us lift up the light,
    Lift up the favor of thy count'nance bright.   30
Into my heart more joy
And gladness thou hast put
Than when a year of glut
Their stores doth overcloy,
And from their plenteous grounds   35
    With vast increase their corn and wine abounds.
In peace at once will I
Both lay me down and sleep,
For thou alone dost keep
Me safe where'er I lie: 40
As in a rocky Cell
    Thou Lord alone in safety mak'st me dwell.

PSALM V

Aug. 12. 1653.

Jehovah, to my words give ear,
    My meditation weigh,
The voice of my complaining hear,
My King and God, for unto thee I pray.
Jehovah thou my early voice   5
    Shalt in the morning hear,
I'th'morning I to thee with choice
Will rank my Prayers, and watch till thou appear.
For thou art not a God that takes
    In wickedness delight,   10
Evil with thee no biding makes;
Fools or mad men stand not within thy sight.
    All workers of iniquity
        Thou hat'st; and them unblest
    Thou wilt destroy that speak a lie;   15
The bloodi' and guileful man God doth detest.
    But I will in thy mercies dear,
        Thy numerous mercies go
    Into thy house; I in thy fear
Will towards thy holy temple worship low.   20
    Lord lead me in thy righteousness,
        L~ad me because of those
    That do observe if I transgress,
Set thy ways right before, where my step goes.
    For in his falt'ring mouth unstable   25
        No word is firm or sooth;

Their inside, troubles miserable
An open grave their throat, their tongue they smooth.
    God, find them guilty, let them fall
        By their own counsels quell'd;   30
    Push them in their rebellions all
Still on; for against thee they have rebell'd;
    Then all who trust in thee shall bring
        Their joy, while thou from blame
    Defend'st them, they shall ever sing   35
And shall triumph in thee, who love thy name.
    For thou Jehovah wilt be found
        To bless the just man still,
    As with a shield thou wilt surround
Him with thy lasting favor and good will.   40

PSALM VI

Aug. 13. 1653.

Lord in thine anger do not reprehend me,
    Nor in thy hot displeasure me correct;
Pity me, Lord, for I am much deject,
    Am very weak and faint; heal and amend me,
For all my bones, that even with anguish ache,   5
    Are troubled, yea my soul is troubled sore;
And thou, O Lord, how long? turn Lord, restore
    My soul, O save me for thy goodness' sake,
For in death no remembrance is of thee;
    Who in the grave can celebrate thy praise?   10
Wearied I am with sighing out my days,
    Nightly my Couch I make a kind of Sea;
My Bed I water with my tears; mine Eye
    Through grief consumes, is waxen old and dark
I'th' mid'st of all mine enemies that mark.   15
    Depart all ye that work iniquity.
Depart from me, for the voice of my weeping
    The Lord hath heard, the Lord hath heard my pray'r,
My supplication with acceptance fair
    The Lord will own, and have me in his keeping.   20
Mine enemies shall all be blank and dash't
    With much confusion; then grow red with shame;
They shall return in haste the way they came
    And in a moment shall be quite abash't.

PSALM VII

Aug. 14. 1653.

Upon the words of Chush *the* Benjamite *against him.*

    Lord my God to thee I fly,
    Save me and secure me under
    Thy protection while I cry;
    Lest as a Lion (and no wonder)

He haste to tear my Soul asunder,   5
Tearing and no rescue nigh.

Lord my God, if I have thought
Or done this, if wickedness
Be in my hands, if I have wrought
Ill to him that meant me peace,   10
Or to him have render'd less,
And not freed my foe for naught;

Let th'enemy pursue my soul
And overtake it, let him tread
My life down to the earth and roll   15
In the dust my glory dead,
In the dust and there outspread
Lodge it with dishonor foul.

Rise Jehovah in thine ire
Rouse thyself amidst the rage   20
Of my foes that urge like fire;
And wake for me, their furi' assuage;
Judgment here thou didst engage
And command which I desire.

So th' assemblies of each Nation   25
Will surround thee, seeking right,
Thence to thy glorious habitation
Return on high and in their sight.
Jehovah judgeth most upright
All people from the world's foundation.   30

Judge me Lord, be judge in this
According to my righteousness
And the innocence which is
Upon me: cause at length to cease
Of evil men the wickedness,   35
And their power that do amiss.

But the just establish fast,
Since thou art the just God that tries
Hearts and reins. On God is cast
My defense, and in him lies,   40
In him who both just and wise
Saves th' upright of Heart at last.

God is a just Judge and severe,
And God is every day offended;
If th' unjust will not forbear,   45
His Sword he whets, his Bow hath bended
Already, and for him intended
The tools of death, that waits him near.

(His arrows purposely made he
For them that persecute.) Behold   50
He travails big with vanity,
Trouble he hath conceiv'd of old
As in a womb, and from that mold
Hath at length brought forth a Lie.

He digg'd a pit, and delv'd it deep,   55
And fell into the pit he made;
His mischief that due course doth keep,

Turns on his head, and his ill trade
  Of violence will undelay'd
Fall on his crown with ruin steep.   60
Then will I Jehovah's praise
  According to his justice raise
And sing the Name and Deity
  Of Jehovah the most high.

PSALM VIII

Aug. 14. 1653.

O Jehovah, our Lord, how wondrous great
  And glorious is thy name through all the earth!
So as above the Heavens thy praise to set
  Out of the tender mouths of latest birth,
Out of the mouths of babes and sucklings thou   5
  Hast founded strength because of all thy foes,
To stint th'enemy, and slack th'avenger's brow
  That bends his rage thy providence to oppose.
When I behold thy Heavens, thy Fingers' art,
  The Moon and Stars which thou so bright hast set   10
In the pure firmament, then saith my heart,
  O what is man that thou rememb'rest yet,
And think'st upon him? or of man begot
  That him thou visit'st and of him art found?
Scarce to be less than Gods, thou mad'st his lot,   15
  With honor and with state thou hast him crown'd.
O'er the works of thy hand thou mad'st him Lord,
  Thou hast put all under his lordly feet,
All Flocks, and Herds, by thy commanding word,
  All beasts that in the field or forest meet;   20
Fowl of the Heavens, and Fish that through the wet
  Sea-paths in shoals do slide, and know no dearth.
O Jehovah, our Lord, how wondrous great
  And glorious is thy name through all the earth!

SONNET XVIII

ON THE LATE MASSACRE IN PIEMONT

Avenge, O Lord, thy slaughter'd Saints, whose bones
  Lie scatter'd on the Alpine mountains cold,
  Ev'n them who kept thy truth so pure of old
When all our Fathers worship't Stocks and Stones,

1-2. In May, 1655, in several official letters to European rulers on Cromwell's behalf, Milton protested against the abrupt termination of freedom of worship for the Waldensians and its violent enforcement on April 24, 1655, in the "Piedmontese Easter." The full story was later told by Cromwell's special envoy to the Duke of Savoy, Sir Samuel Morland, in *The History of the Evangelical Churches of the Valleys of Piemont. Containing . . . a faithfull Account of the Doctrine,* *Life, and Persecutions of the Ancient Inhabitants. Together with a most naked and punctual Relation of the late Bloody Massacre, 1655* (London, 1658). Milton's sonnet opens like his Letter of State to the King of Sweden (C.E. XVIII, 167), which described the Waldensians as "forced to wander over wild mountains and through perpetual winter with their wives and children"; but the sonnet rises above its topical subject to a vision of Truth triumphant.

Forget not: in thy book record their groans   5
Who were thy Sheep and in their ancient Fold
Slain by the bloody *Piemontese* that roll'd
Mother with Infant down the Rocks.   Their moans
The Vales redoubl'd to the Hills, and they
To Heav'n.   Their martyr'd blood and ashes sow   10
O'er all th'*Italian* fields where still doth sway
The triple Tyrant: that from these may grow
A hundredfold, who having learnt thy way
Early may fly the *Babylonian* woe.   *considered bad Sonnet.* (1655)

10–13. In *SAB*, XX (1945), 155, K. Svendsen notes the fusion of the parable of the sower (Matt. xiii, 3) with the legend of Cadmus, whose sowing of a dragon's teeth bore a harvest of warriors.

14. The *Babylonian woe* recalls Petrarch's reference to the Papal Court as a Babylon and a "fountain of woe" in the sonnet (108) which Milton translated in part in *Ref*.

SONNET XIX

WHEN I CONSIDER . . .

When I consider how my light is spent,
Ere half my days, in this dark world and wide,
And that one Talent which is death to hide,
Lodg'd with me useless, though my Soul more bent
To serve therewith my Maker, and present   5
My true account, lest he returning chide;
"Doth God exact day-labor, light denied,"
I fondly ask; But patience to prevent
That murmur, soon replies, "God doth not need
Either man's work or his own gifts; who best   10
Bear his mild yoke, they serve him best; his State
Is Kingly.   Thousands at his bidding speed
And post o'er Land and Ocean without rest:
They also serve who only stand and wait."   (1652?)

Not really humble,
Seraphim stand
around God and
praise him.

1. Because Milton's blindness became complete in 1652 Smart so dated this sonnet. 1655 has also been proposed because it follows No. XVIII in the edition of 1673, and for other reasons which Maurice Kelley summarizes in *MP* LIV (1956), 20–25. But in *RES*, n.s. IX (1958), 57–60, Fitzroy Pyle preferred 1652, and in *TLS*, Sept. 15, 1961, p. 620. C. J. Morse defended 1652 with conclusive proof that the order of the sonnets in 1673 is not chronological.

2. In *Expl.*, X (1951), No. 116, Donald Dorian interpreted *half my days* as the working days of a normal life and so justified a date about 1655 somewhat less plausibly than Emile Saillens argued in *TLS*, Oct. 6, 1961, p. 672, for 1652 on the basis of Plato's theory (*Rep.*, X, 615) that man's life-

span should be a century.

3–14. As in Sonnet VII, Milton recalls the "wicked and slothful servant" who neglects his Lord's talent (Matt. xxv. 26). Pyle treats the entire passage too sweepingly as based upon the commands to the Lord's servants in Luke xii. 35–40. The *Thousands* (1. 12) must belong to the "huge, mighty, and royal armies" of angels which Hooker regarded (*Laws*, I. iv. 1) as eager to do "all manner of good to the creatures of God."   Perhaps, as H. F. Robins thinks—*RES*, n.s. VII (1956), 360–366—Milton also had in mind St. Thomas's attribution of supreme contemplative insight to the higher angelic orders or Beatrice's revelation (*Par.*, XXVIII, 110) that those orders have an understanding of God which exceeds all the joy of his active service.

SONNET XX

LAWRENCE OF VIRTUOUS FATHER . . .

Lawrence of virtuous Father virtuous Son,
Now that the Fields are dank and ways are mire,

1. The *Father*, Henry Lawrence (1600–1664), was Lord President of the Council under Crom-

well. The *Son*, Edward Lawrence (1633–1656), was a member of Parliament.

Where shall we sometimes meet and by the fire
Help waste a sullen day, what may be won
From the hard Season gaining? Time will run   5
   On smoother till *Favonius* re-inspire
   The frozen earth, and clothe in fresh attire
   The Lily and Rose, that neither sow'd nor spun.
What neat repast shall feast us, light and choice,
   Of Attic taste, with Wine, whence we may rise   10
   To hear the Lute well toucht, or artful voice
Warble immortal Notes and *Tuscan* Air?
   He who of those delights can judge and spare
   To interpose them oft, is not unwise.   (1655)

6. The allusion to *Favonius,* the west wind, whom Horace invokes in a famous invitation to enjoy the delights of springtime (*Odes* I, iv), is the clearest of many Horatian notes in this and the following sonnet.

8. Cf. Matt. vi, 28: "Consider the lilies of the field; . . . they toil not, neither do they spin."

10. *Attic* (Athenian) banquets were traditionally delicate, even when they were served in Epicurus' gardens.

12. *Tuscan* here is equivalent to "Italian."

13. *spare* (contrary to the editorial tradition, but in harmony with the spirit of the sonnet and the O.E.D. definitions of the word) has been shown by Fraser Neiman in *PMLA,* LXIV (1949), 328 and Elizabeth Jackson in *PMLA,* LXV (1950), 329 to mean "afford."

14. *unwise* seems to allude to the "wise man" whom both the ancient Epicureans and Stoics in different ways admired as exemplifying their philosophic creeds.

SONNET XXI

CYRIACK, WHOSE GRANDSIRE . . .

Cyriack, whose Grandsire on the Royal Bench
   Of British *Themis,* with no mean applause
   Pronounc't and in his volumes taught our Laws,
Which others at their Bar so often wrench:
Today deep thoughts resolve with me to drench   5
   In mirth, that after no repenting draws;
   Let *Euclid* rest and *Archimedes* pause,
And what the *Swede* intend, and what the *French.*
To measure life learn thou betimes, and know
   Toward solid good what leads the nearest way;   10
   For other things mild Heav'n a time ordains,
And disapproves that care, though wise in show,
   That with superfluous burden loads the day,
   And when God sends a cheerful hour refrains.   (1655?)

1. Cyriack Skinner was a grandson of Sir Edward Coke, Chief Justice of the King's Bench (1613–1616) and famous as the author of *The Institutes of the Law of England* ("Coke upon Littleton").

2. *Themis:* the goddess of Justice. Cf. *PL* XI, 14.

7. Skinner's interest in *Archimedes, Euclid,* and Greek mathematics in general may have begun when he was a pupil in Milton's school in Aldersgate Street.

8. In 1655 Charles X of Sweden was conducting brilliant campaigns against the Poles; French policy was guided by Cardinal Mazarin. The line, however, reflects Horace's invitation to Quintius Hirpinus to forget what "the warlike Cantabrian and the Scyth" may be meditating, and to remember that "youth flees fast away" (*Odes* II, xi, 1–6). For readers who recognize the Horatian allusion the line is a transition to the tone of mixed cordiality and piety in the concluding six lines, which recall the sestet of *Sonn* XX. The fusion of Roman and Christian feeling in these sonnets is interestingly studied by J. H. Finney, Jr. in *HSCP,* XLIII (1937), 64–67.

SONNET XXII

To Mr. Cyriack Skinner upon his Blindness

Cyriack, this three years' day these eyes, though clear
  To outward view of blemish or of spot,
  Bereft of light thir seeing have forgot;
  Nor to thir idle orbs doth sight appear
Of Sun or Moon or Star throughout the year,   5
  Or man or woman. Yet I argue not
  Against heav'n's hand or will, nor bate a jot
  Of heart or hope; but still bear up and steer
Right onward. What supports me, dost thou ask?
  The conscience, Friend, to have lost them overplied   10
  In liberty's defense, my noble task,
Of which all Europe talks from side to side.
  This thought might lead me through the world's vain mask
  Content though blind, had I no better guide.   (1655)

1–4. For a scientifically exact and also humanly moving description of the symptoms of Milton's blindness as it slowly developed during the three years before and the seven years after the writing of this sonnet we may read his letter to Leonard Philaris (C.E. XII, 64–70). The meaning of his symptoms in modern pathological terms is studied by Eleanor G. Brown in *Milton's Blindness* (New York, 1934), pp. 16–48. Cf. *Def 2*, p. 826; *PL* III, 22–50.

10. *conscience:* consciousness. Cf. *PL* VIII, 502.

12–14. Cf. Milton's faith in *Def 2* (p. 819) that, "from the columns of Hercules to the Indian Ocean" he saw "the nations of the earth recovering that liberty which they so long had lost."

SONNET XXIII*

Methought I Saw . . .

Methought I saw my late espoused Saint
  Brought to me like *Alcestis* from the grave,
  Whom *Jove's* great Son to her glad Husband gave,
  Rescu'd from death by force though pale and faint.
Mine as whom washt from spot of child-bed taint,   5

* Our biographers do not agree as to which of Milton's first two wives is the subject of this sonnet, and one critic denies that its theme is a blind widower's grief pouring itself into a probably actual dream about the lost wife appearing to him dressed like one of those who "have washed their robes and made them white in the blood of the Lamb" (Rev. vii, 14). Perhaps Leo Spitzer is right in declaring—in the *Hopkins Review*, IV (1951), 20–22—that we should question even that final certainty about the sonnet and regard its real subject as the *donna angelicata* of Dante and Petrarch, the ideal embodiment of a poet's heavenly vision. He would dispose of the poignant reference to the poet's blindness as an irrelevant indulgence of self-pity by Milton. Readers must decide for themselves whether to regard the husband's *fancied sight* of the dead woman's *veil'd face* as implying simply that it will at last be unveiled when they are reunited, "face to face," in heaven; or as implying that he has never seen her face (as, it is probable, Milton had never seen Katherine Woodcock's face); or as being simply a recollection of the veiled Alcestis in Euripides'

tragedy; or as proving Milton's absorption in the ideal of the angelified ladies of Dante and Petrarch.

The sonnet's final position in the edition of 1673 suggests a date no earlier than that of *Sonnet XXII*, and possibly a date as late as 1658.

1. *Saint* means "a soul in heaven," as it does in *Winchester*, 71, but the picture is that of Admetus' wife *Alcestis* in Euripides' play (*Alcestis*), as she is brought back alive from the grave by Hercules. Not recognizing her veiled figure, Admetus cries, "I seem to see my wife. She stirs my heart and fountains burst from my eyes" (ll. 1062–3).

5–6. Since Mary Powell Milton died in child-birth three days after the birth of her last child on May 2, 1652, W. R. Parker pleads—in *RES*, XXI (1945), 236—for her as the subject of this sonnet, rather than Katherine Woodcock Milton, "who did not die in childbirth, as the early biographers and editors supposed." Her death occurred on Feb. 3, 1658—more than three months after the birth of her child. Sharply disagreeing about the interpretation of the *old Law* (Lev. xii, 2–5) which prescribed sixty-six days of purification for the mother after a daughter's birth, Parker and

Purification in the old Law did save,
And such, as yet once more I trust to have
Full sight of her in Heaven without restraint,
Came vested all in white, pure as her mind:
Her face was veil'd, yet to my fancied sight,   10
Love, sweetness, goodness, in her person shin'd
So clear, as in no face with more delight.
But O, as to embrace me she inclin'd,
I wak'd, she fled, and day brought back my night.   (1658)

Fitzroy Pyle—in *RES*, XXV (1949), 57–60—do agree that l. 6 is the key to the sonnet. In *whom* in l. 5 Pyle sees a reference to the Virgin Mary and, in consequence, a tenuous reason for identifying Katherine Woodcock as the *late espoused* (i.e. recently married) but lost wife of Milton, because she died on the day after the Purification of the Virgin (*RES*, n.s. II, 1951, 153). All contributions to the dispute are reviewed by J. T. Shawcross in *N&Q*, n.s. III (1955), 202–4 in a defense of Parker's position on the ground that line 5, by describing the dead wife as bearing *the spot of child-bed taint*, can refer only to Mary. In discussing the date of this sonnet in *JEGP*, LVIII (1959), 33, Shawcross declares that "it is only our own sensibilities that make us feel that, if Mary was intended, the sonnet had to be written before the second marriage."

Paradise Lost

INTRODUCTION

Epic or Drama?

1. A reader coming to *Paradise Lost* for the first time, and going rapidly through it to the end of Book X, is likely to get the impression that he is reading drama. It is a heightened kind of drama which is too big for the stage and too rich for it in poetic perspectives around the conversations and debates that take up more room than the narrative does. If he reads on through the unfolding of the never-ending but finally defeated waylaying of good by evil in human history as Michael unfolds it to Adam in a quiet dialogue in the last two books of the poem, he will miss the clash of characters and ideas in the earlier books, but he may find satisfaction in the sombre but not tragic resolution of the plot as the final step in the development of Adam's character. Looking back, he will see a series of dramas composing the epic plot: the council of the devils in Book II, with Moloch, Belial, and Mammon making bids for leadership which wonderfully reveal their characters but fail to shake Satan's leadership; the council in heaven in Book III, where the Son of God discovers his character by making himself responsible for mankind's redemption; Satan's first attempt to seduce Eve, by a dream, in Book IV; the revolt of Satan's followers against God as Raphael reports it to Adam in Books V and VI; pausing to tell him of the refusal of a single seraph in the throng, Abdiel, to be swept into the crime; the dialogue about creation and nature in Books VII and VIII, which should have made Adam proof against the temptation to betray his own nature by disobedience to God's order in Book IX; the great temptation scenes in that book; and the hardly less psychologically interesting scenes of reconciliation between Adam and Eve, in which she takes the initiative and becomes almost, if not quite, the stronger character in Book X.

2. But *Paradise Lost* is not a drama; it is an epic built out of dramas. Its plan is epic. It begins as the *Iliad* and the *Aeneid* begin, with a plunge into the action at a point where it has reached its third crisis, the time when the devils after the decision to revolt in Heaven and their defeat in battle there, debate their policy against God and man in Hell. The first two crises wait for narration by Raphael to Adam in Book V. The fourth crisis in the order of events is the scene in Heaven in Book III. Here we find a new kind of drama—the drama of contrast between situations. What has just happened in Hell is a parody of what happens in Heaven. As Satan has established his right to rule the devils by monopolizing the glory of undertaking man's destruction, so the Son of God proves his right to reign in heaven by undertaking man's redemption. There is direct narrative in Book II of Satan's flight through Chaos and in later books more of it about his travels in our universe. But the high peaks in his later story are dramatic—his soliloquies on the theme of "Myself am hell," his seduction of Eve, his encounter with his daughter Sin and grandson Death on their bridge across Chaos, and the grand opera scene in Pandaemonium where his final disappearance in serpent form begins with the rising orchestral roar of recognition by his followers and ends in their involuntary hisses —hisses that Dr. Edith Sitwell thinks are the finest sibilant music in all English poetry. We seldom see Satan except at moments of high drama, but his career is epic.

3. Just how epic Satan's career is we can see only in the light of the whole poem. His revolt in Heaven depopulates it by drawing off perhaps a third of the angels. Out of that evil good comes immediately in the creation of the universe and of man, who is intended to sire a race which—as Raphael explains to Adam—can ultimately achieve a virtually angelic nature and live at will on earth or in Heaven. When Satan wrecks that plan in Book IX the result is the epic struggle for man's redemption in the three following books. For Milton's contemporaries that story had the fascination simply as a theory of history which historical writing like Toynbee's has for us today, but with the difference that its redemptive hope for both humanity in general and for individual men was absolutely assured by the scriptural texts that stud Milton's lines. And in creation Milton had the great epic theme of his century, the theme of the *Divine Weeks* of the French Calvinist poet Guillaume Salluste Sieur du Bartas, which was more popular in the English translation of Joshua Sylvester that Milton knew as a child than the original ever was in France. Creation was the theme of Torquato Tasso's *The Creation of the World* (*Il mondo creato*) and—to some extent—of pagan poems like Hesiod's *Theogony,* Ovid's *Metamorphoses,* and Lucretius' *On the Nature of Things* (*De rerum natura*). Milton's cosmic passages bear the occasional print of all these poems as plainly as his first two books occasionally reflect facets of the hells of Homer and Virgil, Dante and Spenser. Such poems were not Milton's models but they were a part of the sinews of his strength as he pursued

Things unattempted yet in Prose or Rhyme.

4. So his poem is not a drama though its dramatic roots are strong. Less has been written about them than about its epic subsoil. Like that subsoil, they lie on both sides of the poem, the classical and the Christian. Traditionally, Milton's Satan has been compared with Aeschylus' Prometheus, and the older editions of *Paradise Lost* mark many lines in Satan's speeches as conscious echoes of *Prometheus Bound.* But it would be impossible to write a book exploring Milton's debt to Greek drama on the scale of the studies of his epic backgrounds by Dr. Tillyard and Sir Maurice Bowra. And recently we have been taught by J. C. Maxwell and Robert Adams to suspect the Promethean parallels and to think of Satan and Prometheus as contrasting characters rather than the high-souled first cousins that Shelley made them for the nineteenth century. Milton's Satan owes only a general debt to Greek tragedy. It is of the vitally negative kind that P. F. Fisher implies when he says that, by concentrating the Greek tragic flaw of pride (*hybris*) in "the character of the Adversary and the Author of Evil . . . Milton repudiated the doctrine that life was essentially tragic and that retribution was . . . the final victory of evil as far as man was concerned." As an influence on the characters and design of *Paradise Lost* Greek drama counts for less than classical epic.

5. When we turn to Christian drama, the balance shifts. In Milton its two main currents flow together—the medieval, native stream of the half-forgotten mystery plays and the contemporary, continental revival of their tradition in Holland and Italy. If anyone will take the trouble to read Hugo Grotius' *Adamus Exul* and Giambattista Andreini's *L'Adamo* in the *Celestial Cycle* of Watson Kirkconnell or in any other translations of the original Latin and Italian, he will be struck with many things that they have in common with *Paradise Lost* and with each other. The ground common to all three is especially extensive in the treatment of the temptation, the sin, and Adam's involvement in it through his love or passion for Eve. The lovers' quarrel threatens the existence of humanity but is reconciled in a scene of some psychological depth. In a general way Milton stands close to Grotius in the scenes between Raphael and Adam in *Paradise Lost*—much closer than he does in the scenes in Books I and II to the corresponding scenes in the work of another Dutchman whose claim to have influenced him can hardly be proved, the *Lucifer* of Joost van den Vondel. Milton must have heard about and perhaps seen

performances of sacred plays like Andreini's *L'Adamo* in Italy, and the cumulative Italian influence upon him may have been substantial; but the more Italian plays one reads and the more closely one reads them individually, the weaker their individual claims to have influenced Milton become. The late Norman Douglas was fond of insisting (in *Old Calabria* and elsewhere) that Milton's main source was the *Adamo caduto* (*Adam's Fall*) of Serafino della Salandra, which was published in 1647 and may not have been known to Milton. Their few strikingly close but merely verbal resemblances are noted in the proper places in this edition. Their differences are far more instructive. Salandra's demons are classico-medieval monsters. Anything like epic characterization of them is unthinkable. And Salandra's treatment of the basic theme of Redemption, the paradox of the Fortunate Fall, has as little as possible in common with Adam's echo of the medieval hymn *O felix culpa* when in Book XII he explains:

> O goodness infinite, goodness immense!
> That all this good of evil shall produce,
> And evil turn to good.

In Salandra's last act an allegorical Misericordia taunts Sin, Malice, and Death with their failure to destroy mankind, and in Heaven later vaunts the inexhaustible "excesses" of divine love in its more than successful effort to repair the harm done in Eden.

6. When Milton returned to London from his Italian tour in the summer of 1639 he may have already been meditating plans for some biblical dramas like those that he sketched in the Trinity manuscript in 1640 to 1642. The plans undoubtedly have a bearing on *Paradise Lost,* and perhaps they are a link between it and the native English medieval drama. In puppet shows or "motions" that drama still survived in Milton's youth, and a capital criticism of its main weakness is implied in Milton's sneer in *Areopagitica* at its failure to make Adam anything but a pawn in a game between God and the Devil. Milton's Adam has a will as well as a mind of his own, and by them hangs the justification of the ways of God to man in *Paradise Lost*. But there were things that he could admire in the English mysteries, such things as the traditional debate of Justice and Mercy over Adam before the throne of God. If there had been no such tradition, we should have no scene like the appeal of the Son of God for man in Book III, 227–265, and the following speech by the Father. In the two most elaborate plans for dramas on the subject of the fall of man in the Trinity manuscript the medieval allegorical element is obvious, but it is most interestingly entangled with other elements that plainly come from Italy and ancient Greece.

7. In the Trinity manuscript Milton left four sketches of a developing plan for a drama on the fall of man. The two last and most elaborate of them fuse or confuse the features of the sacred dramas of the Counter-Reformation in Italy with Greek and medieval elements. In the fourth sketch there are signs of an inclination to treat the subject epically —as if Milton were feeling his way toward an epic design as alone giving scope to the different levels of his drama in Hell, Heaven, and Earth. The scene opens with Gabriel descending on a mission like that which we see him executing when he takes Satan into custody in *Paradise Lost* IV, 798–990. He explains to a chorus of angels that since Lucifer's revolt he is constantly on guard in Eden, and he tells them what he knows

of Man, as the creation of Eve, with their love, and marriage. After this Lucifer appears after his overthrow, bemoans himself, seeks revenge on Man. The Chorus prepare resistance at his first approach. At last, after discourse of enmity on either side, he departs; whereat the Chorus sings of the battle and victory in Heaven against him and his accomplices, as before, after the first Act, was sung a hymn of the Creation. Here again may appear Lucifer, relating and insulting in what he had done to the destruction of Man. Man next and Eve, having been by this time seduced by the Serpent, appears confusedly, covered with leaves. Conscience, in a shape, accuses him; Justice cites him to the place whither Jehovah called for him.   In the meantime the Chorus entertains the stage and is informed by some Angel of the manner of his Fall. Here the Chorus bewails Adam's fall.   Adam then and Eve return and accuse one another; but especially Adam lays the blame to his wife—is stubborn in his offence.   Justice appears, reasons with him, convinces him.   The Chorus admonisheth Adam, and bids him beware by Lucifer's example of impenitence.   The Angel is sent to banish them out of Paradise; but, before, causes to pass before his eyes, in shapes, a masque of all the evils of this life and world.   He is humbled, relents, despairs.   At last appears Mercy, comforts him, promises him the Messiah; then calls in Faith, Hope, Charity; instructs him.   He repents, gives God the glory, submits to his penalty. The Chorus briefly concludes. Compare this with the former Draft.

8. An interesting aspect of this draft is its greater emphasis on Adam and Eve and the angelic actors than on Lucifer-Satan, in comparison with the stresses in *Paradise Lost*. Lucifer seems to be simply the evil one.   There is no trace of the intriguing, exploring, despairing Satan of the poem that we have.   There is no trace of the Satan who still seems to many readers to be tragic in at least an Elizabethan if not a Greek sense of the word.   In an Elizabethan sense that makes tragedy consist in wilful self-exclusion from all good Miss Helen Gardner has pled that Milton's Satan is like Macbeth, Doctor Faustus, and Beatrice-Joanna in Middleton's *Changling*.   Satan's repeated confession that he is his own hell has often been set beside Mephistophilis' matter-of-fact statement to the same effect in *Faustus,* but Miss Gardner makes it a part of Satan's passion for self-pitying soliloquy, which is in turn an aspect of the perversion of will that shuts him wilfully out of all good.   If we look at him in this way, his character becomes consistent and the Shakespearian echoes that editors have spotted in his speeches become a part of a unified tragic character.   But not a noble one.   And Miss Gardner explains that in her view such tragic heroes are unforgettable because they are not pitiable.

9. So *Paradise Lost* first germinated in Milton's mind as a drama and became an epic only after years of reflection and some experience with at least partial drafts finally ended in the poem that we have.   From one such draft we know that he preserved a few lines in Satan's address to the sun in Book IV (32–41).   Perhaps, as Arthur Barker suggests, the original conception explains the division of the poem into ten books in the first edition—breaking the action into something like the structure of a five-act play.   When the original, very long Book X was split into the Books XI and XII of the second edition, their true weight in the drama of human destiny was clarified though the only addition to them was the opening five lines of Book XII.   In the new arrangement Book IX dominates the action less than it seemed to do in the original one, and the many dramatic ironies in the structure of the whole poem are strengthened by the new weighting of the recovery of the "paradise within you happier far" in Books X to XII.

10. Building on the small external evidence that we have about the writing of the poem and also on lynx-eyed analysis of internal evidence of changes, additions, and minor inconsistencies, Allan H. Gilbert has made it impossible to think that the composition of *Paradise Lost* was a single, straightforward act.   There were afterthoughts.   Perhaps one of them was the episode of Abdiel's refusal to join the rebel angels who sweep him along with them into the north parts of Heaven in Book V.   By Raphael his story is intended as an example of brave obedience to Adam, and by Milton it was intended as a contrast to Adam's later behavior.   The most interesting surmise about Milton's additions to his original design is the suggestion that he added the first two books somewhere late in the process of composing his poem in order to provide it with a standard epic beginning—a plunge into the midst of the action at the start.   If the suggestion is sound, it disposes of the persistent objection that poetically the remaining books of *Paradise Lost* are an anticlimax because in Book III Milton grew tired and irretrievably lost the dash and power that made the first two books great.   The suggestion would also, almost if not quite dis-

pose of A. J. A. Waldock's view that Milton "blundered in the earlier books by making Satan much more glorious than he ever meant to do," and then "sought somewhat belatedly to rectify his earlier errors."

Satan Hero?

11. It is only in the first two books of *Paradise Lost* that Satan seems heroic. There is grandeur but no heroism in his later soliloquies and after the seduction of Eve he departs to Hell, leaving the world to his vice-gerents Sin and Death. There is no doubt of Milton's intent to degrade him, step by step, down to the scene of his second and involuntary appearance in serpent form in Book X. The first shock to any admiration for him in a reader's mind comes when he meets his allegorical daughter Sin and his incestuously begotten grandson Death at Hell's gates (II, 648–883). For over two centuries critics agreed that the step into pure allegory in Sin and Death was a blemish on the poem and an external incrustation. Recently they have been wondering whether it is not a part of the structural irony of the whole design. Satan, Sin, and Death are now seen to be a parody of the Trinity of Heaven. Satan's "daughter and . . . darling without end" is the antitype of the Son of God's bosom who is his "word, wisdom, and effectual might" (III, 170). Sin makes only one further appearance, but again it seems—as Ernest Schanzer observes —that the purpose is to extend the over-arching dramatic irony that ties the poem together. When she meets Satan in Chaos she tells him that she has been drawn to him from Hell by "a secret harmony" that moves her heart with his, "joined in connexion sweet," and that the distance of worlds between them has not broken the "fatal consequence" that will forever unite them. Her words can hardly be an accidental parallel to Adam's protestation to Eve at the moment of decision in Eden:

> So forcibly within my heart I feel
> The bond of Nature draw me to my own;
> My own in thee; for what thou art is mine.

12. Everything in the poem, of course, depends on the way in which this speech of Adam's is read. Mr. Waldock has read it as both the most dramatic and the noblest utterance in the entire poem—a brave and beautiful expression of human love at its heroic best. He will not even consider it as an honest effort by Milton to accept the hardest element in the biblical account of the Fall—the deception of Adam by Eve. And Mr. Waldock had nothing but contempt for the critics who variously condemn or palliate Adam's act as "uxoriousness" (Milton's term for it in the *Christian Doctrine*) "gregariousness," "passion," or "sentimentality." For Mr. Waldock then Adam becomes the hero of the poem though he behaves rather badly with Eve later on and is in danger of losing his laurels as a human being to her.

13. By the same token Mr. Waldock saw Satan as a dramatic failure and a hopelessly inconsistent personality in the course of his whole story. He constantly misses his opportunities for tragedy. His character does not degenerate; it is degraded. In the later books he becomes essentially an allegory and a kind of emblem of evil. This criticism seems wide of the mark when we think of Satan's intelligently and shrewdly consistent play on Eve's vanity in the two temptation scenes and compare his flattery of her half-formed wish for "godhead" with his flattery of the same craving in his followers in Books V (772–802) and I (94–124). But in general Mr. Waldock's objection to Satan as a dramatic character is sound, and it is a searching criticism of the poem itself. In substance, it comes close to Mr. Rajan's view of Satan as a great opportunist, putty to be molded by the changing situation, constant only to his resolve in Book I (165) "out of good still to find means of evil." But Mr. Rajan's view of Satan is less critical than it is

historical. For Milton's contemporaries Satan was simply the Adversary whom John Calvin described as "an enemie that is in courage most hardie, in strength most mightie, in policies most subtle, in diligence and celeritie unweariable, with all sorts of engins plenteously furnishd, in skill of warre most readie." The Satan of the seventeenth century was a figure to hate and fear. In poetry and in life alike, he was the father of lies, "with all sorts of engins plenteously furnishd." And that was his main character.

14. But he was also courageous and "in skill of warre most readie"—a fact that we overlook even though we see him fighting in spite of his wounds, like Turnus or Hector, through the three days of battle in Heaven, and proving his skill by inventing artillery on the eve of the second day. As a field marshal in Heaven, the critics agree to find Satan disgusting and to say as little as possible about him except to deplore his jibes and Belial's at the angels whom their first salvo topples over. But the jeers at God are a part of Satan's nature. We hear them in his first speeches to his followers in Book V, and we hear them still echoing in Book X (625–27) when God speaks of

> my scornful Enemies
> That laugh, as if transported with some fit
> Of Passion.

The contrast of Satan's jeers with the laughter of Him "that sitteth in the heavens," is a part of the cosmic irony of *Paradise Lost*. In the battle in heaven Satan is a much more comic than tragic figure, and he is constantly skirting comedy all the way through the poem. In the allegory of his defeat by the Son of God on the third day of that battle Satan ceases to be comic only because the situation is too serious. All the faith in Truth's power to crush Falsehood in any open encounter that Milton poured into *Areopagitica* is symbolized in the all-seeing eyes of the victorious Son's chariot.

15. Probably Milton regarded the war in Heaven as both allegorical and historical. For centuries various commentators had regarded the drawing off of a "third part of the angels" by Lucifer, in Revelation xii, 4–11, and his battle there with Michael, as a record of angelic war before the creation of Adam. Others regarded it as a prophecy of a battle to be fought at the end of the world, or an allegory of some moral crisis in Heaven. In *Lucifer* the poet Vondel treated it as allegory with the resonance of history behind it. In the moment of Lucifer's defeat he and his rebel angels are all suddenly transformed into monsters more terrible than the serpents into which Satan and his followers are changed when we see them for the last time in *Paradise Lost*. Here no grim comedy is intended— as it may be intended in Milton's scene. Vondel is interested only in driving home the truth that Jakob Boehme put into the teaching that after "the divine light went out of the Devils, they . . . became like Serpents, Dragons, Wormes, and evill Beasts: as may be seen by *Adam's* Serpent."

16. But Milton was too much a humanist and at the same time too much interested in the historical truth to be found in the Bible to be content to treat the battle in heaven as sheer allegory. The biblical warrant for it as history might be small, but in the traditions of battles between the Olympian gods and the Titans which Hesiod tells, and which left their marks widely in classical literature and sculpture, Milton—like most of his contemporaries—saw a survival of sacred history in the legends of the pagans. This belief was part of a larger one that is mentioned in paragraph 25 below. It is cryptically involved in the allusion to Eurynome in *Paradise Lost* X, 581. Once more the rebels, the Titans, or at least many of them, were traditionally described as taking serpent or other monstrous forms. The forms might be allegory, but for Milton the legends about the Titans' war with the gods of light on Olympus were proof of a core of some kind of historical truth in the revolt of the angels.

17. As the battle in heaven was in one of its aspects actual for Milton, so was Satan him-

self. He believed in the existence of the historical Author of Evil at least in the Augustinian sense that evil is deprivation or negation of good and is produced by pride. The only way to portray Satan then was as a voice confessing and vaunting the proud will and the discovery that in his assault on heaven the speaker has himself created a hell within him. In achieving that kind of a Satan Milton earned the praise of William Hazlitt and the Romantics generally for having got away from the medieval devil of Tasso and of all the poets up to his time, Italian and English too, who had drawn portraits of the fiends. But pride is self-deception, and Milton's Satan deceives himself so well that he deceived Shelley into thinking him a Promethean apostle of human regeneration, and Byron into thinking him an inspiring symbol of revolt against political tyranny. For Milton Satan was the archetypal tyrant. His reign in hell is the express antitype of the reign of the Son of God by merit in Heaven. And at the moment of commitment to the attack on Eve in Book IV, 393–94, it is "with necessity, The Tyrant's plea," that he justifies his act. It is not the courage of Satan's revolt against God that counts; it is the ambition which betrays him into what Arnold Stein calls "the trap of leadership." In recent years Satan has been too often and too easily compared with Mussolini and Hitler, but such analogies are not very helpful. Nor is it helpful to compare Satan with Cromwell. The "trap of leadership" deprives Satan of all private character and makes him speak to the councils in Hell and act in Eden in mechanical response to what he calls in his soliloquy in Book IV "public reason." If he had an historical counterpart in Milton's mind, it was prelacy. Satan's comparison with "huge Python" in *PL* X, 531, has been paralleled by J. B. Broadbent with the simile for prelacy in *The Reason of Church Government* as "that huge dragon of Egypt, . . . Python," which Apollo killed with his arrows of light. In like manner, said Milton, the prelates would be "shot to death with . . . the powerful beams of God's word."

18. It should be clear that in drawing his portrait of Satan Milton was objective. Its weakness is its greatness—its power to fool readers into its own delusion of power and make them say that Milton's Satan is a noble anticipation of the Nietzschean superman. If, to give the devil his due, we must say that in the first two books of *Paradise Lost* he is drawn with too many virtues, the answer is perhaps in Socrates' words in the *Republic* when he says that the finer virtues—"courage, temperance, and the rest"—belong to the most evil men: "Or do you fancy that great crimes and unmixed wickedness come from a feeble nature and not rather from a noble nature that has been ruined?"

Milton's Cosmos

19. Satan's revolt in Heaven, his plunge with his followers through Chaos to Hell, and his journey up from Hell to the created universe—these and the later steps in Milton's plot imply a cosmic scheme like that on page 180, reproduced with the permission of Professor Walter Clyde Curry. In Milton's time his treatment of Chaos would not have seemed strange. He conceived it much as St. Augustine did when he described it in the *Confessions* XIII, xxix, 40, as "formless matter, prior in origin but not by interval of time to formed matter, and therefore never having existed independently in this world." To scientific minds it was a physical hypothesis, yet not far removed from the poet's vision of "the huge eternall chaos" out of which Spenser imagined all forms and all living things as arising, only to be gathered into it again by "Time's eternall sickle" in the Garden of Adonis. But it was also understood as a kind of womb of space, vast enough to engulf the universe and filled with warring atoms. It had been pictured in half-allegorical scenes like that on page 181 from Geffrey Whitney's *A Choice of Emblemes* (1586), where Chaos

is a maelstrom of "warring atoms" or formless matter which is being blown into ever greater confusion by a being who seems to be both its personification and its ruler. In Boccaccio's *Genealogy of the Gods* Chaos is represented as a crowned figure sitting on a throne with his consort Night, as Hesiod described those first parents of all things in the *Theogony*. In Milton's "anarch" enthroned "on the wasteful Deep" in *Paradise Lost* II, 960, his readers would recognize Boccaccio's Chaos. Thus, in some mysterious way, Milton's "anarch" was identifiable with a Chaos bounded by Heaven above and more or less by Hell below it and also by our universe, which had recently been excavated out of it somewhere not far below the floor of Heaven.

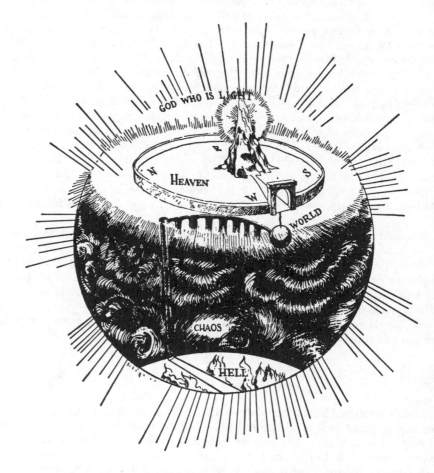

20. Milton's Heaven is a realm of light. God is a "fountain of light" so dazzling that the angels, who are themselves creatures of pure light, must see him only through a veil of cloud that surrounds him "like a radiant shrine" (III, 378). When he speaks, "ambrosial fragrance fills all Heaven" (III, 135). His Son is the "effulgence" (VI, 680) of the Father's glory, "shining most glorious" himself (III, 139). It is as light that he defeats Satan in the battle in Heaven. If the angels are less luminous than he, it is because they shine with rainbow colors, as Raphael does when he appears like the god Mercury in "colors dipt in heaven" (V, 283), radiating light and "Heavenly fragrance" as he travels

down to Eden to talk with Adam.   According to St. Augustine and several other Fathers
of the Church, the angels were creatures made of the light that came into being on the
first day of creation, when God said, "Let there be light."   The heaven which Milton's
angels inhabit is a celestial incandescence that is called by a Greek name, the Empyrean,
which literally describes it.   In some esoteric sense, its fiery substance is indestructible
(though for Milton the divine origin of all matter implied the indestructibility of its
substance if not of its forms).   That is why Satan assures the demons that their "Empyreal substance cannot fail" (I, 117), or—in other words—that they are immortal past
God's power to destroy them.   Milton left his readers free to doubt Satan's deduction, but

122   *Sine iuſtitia, confuſio.*

Ad eoſdem Iudices.

W H E N Fire, and Aire, and Earthe, and Water, all weare one:
        Before that worke deuine was wrought, which nowe wee
        looke vppon.

if they were acquainted with the *Treatise of Angels* of the former Jesuit John Salkeld,
who was a master of the literature of the subject, they had his authority for thinking that
both "natural philosophy and true divinity" taught that "no spirits whatsoever they be are
subject to corruption."

21. Although Raphael and Michael have major roles in *Paradise Lost* and Uriel, Gabriel, Ithuriel, and Zephon have variously important minor ones, Milton tells us little about
the angels in Heaven.   Unlike St. Augustine, he followed an ancient tradition that placed
their creation long before that of our universe.   Of their life before earthly time began

we learn nothing except what Raphael tells Adam about the conclave when God first made his Son known to them as reigning over them "by right of merit," and about the battle in Heaven and the interest of the loyal angels in the creation of the universe.   In the convocations in heaven and the parody of them in Pandaemonium by the devils it was inevitable that Milton should use the titles of the nine orders of the heavenly hierarchy that the Church had inherited from Dionysius the "Areopagite," who was thought to have been a disciple of St. Paul.   His sequence was this: Seraphim (the order of purely contemplative angels to whom Milton compared himself in the first sonnet on his blindness), and then downward, the Cherubim, Thrones, Dominations, Virtues, Powers, Principalities, Archangels, and Angels.   In a literal and passionate way of his own Milton believed in the angels as he understood that St. Paul believed in the "principalities and powers" of Romans viii, 38, against whom all Christians must contend.   But—as Robert West makes clear in *Milton and the Angels*—there is every evidence of Protestant and Puritan reticence about belief in angels in *Paradise Lost*.   Nowhere does Milton quite commit himself to so much as definite acceptance of the Dionysian hierarchy.   He tells us little more about the angelic world than that its ranks were important and that the devils willingly perpetuated them in Hell.   In *Paradise Lost* VII, 182, we hear an echo of the song of the angels at creation in the Book of Job xxxviii, 7; and in III, 654, Uriel's fitness for his charge of the sun is hinted at by his identification as one of the seven angels who are God's "eyes" throughout the universe in Zechariah's prophecy.   And the angels in the four principal angelic roles have the full force of tradition behind them, stretching back through the approval of their invocation by name in a decision of the Council of Trent to its practice in the Jewish night prayer: "May Michael be at my right hand, Gabriel at my left, before me Uriel, and behind me Raphael, and above my head the divine presence of God."

22. Milton's hell is more complex than his heaven.   It is local and as terribly remote from our universe as Milton declares it to be when he reasons that, "if the whole world is finally to be consumed by fire, it follows that hell, if situated in the centre of the earth, must share the fate of the surrounding universe; a consummation more to be desired than expected by the souls in perdition."   Between Milton's Hell and Dante's local one in the bowels of the earth there are many differences, yet they both have traces of the geography of Virgil's Hades in the *Aeneid,* and there are moments when the "fiery Deluge" that scorches Milton's devils "With ever-burning sulphur unconsumed" (I, 69) makes his climate seem much like Dante's.   We may agree with Mr. J. B. Broadbent that Milton's imagination worked only in terms of the "sophisticated and Christian notion of an inner hell," and that he was "irritated at having to support it with classico-medieval flames and sulphur."   Up to a certain point we can go along with Mr. Broadbent.   When the devils build their proud palace of Pandaemonium, when they amuse themselves with tournaments of the kind that Milton says in the invocation to Book IX are unworthy subjects of epic poetry, when they reason like pagan philosophers and sing sentimental songs of self-pity, when they howl their praise of Satan with one voice like a mob saluting a dictator, we feel the poet's imagination working at a more intense pitch than it is when they suffer the torments of alternate frost and fire, as do some of Dante's damned souls.   Milton usually thought of Hell as psychological and non-local, as Spenser did.   At its most intense he imagined it in the heart of Satan when the devil cries, "Myself am hell" (IV, 75).   But for Milton Heaven and Hell both definitely outlast the physical universe.   He agreed with St. Augustine and many other theologians that they could be imagined without limit as states of the spirit as long as their historical and local existence was not denied.

23. Milton's conception of Hell can be illustrated with one of its features that naive

readers usually take in a purely physical sense—its "darkness visible" (I, 63). The phrase is not a lapse into the vagueness that Macaulay marked as distinguishing Milton's hell from Dante's. Nor is there any ground for Mr. T. S. Eliot's objection that "it is difficult to imagine a burning lake where there was only darkness visible." The only fair objection to the phrase is that it was a paradox that Milton's contemporaries knew only too well and regarded as a profound and perennially fresh truth. They did not have to go to Robert Herrick's *Noble Numbers* to learn that

> The fire of Hell this strange condition hath,
> To burn, not shine (as Learned Basil saith).

Many of them could have turned easily to the passage that Herrick had in mind, as many of them could have turned to the passage in the *Summa Theologica* III, xcvii, 4, where St. Thomas Aquinas makes the same observation in a matter-of-fact way and explains Hell's tenebrosity as mainly due to the earth encasing it. Mr. West notes that for as "scientific" a writer as Cornelius Agrippa in the sixteenth century the dark fires of Hell were simply one of its punishments. On the other hand, for a philosophical poet like Milton's contemporary Joseph Beaumont the dark fires were a natural part of the devil's inner hell:

> . . . th'immortal Prince of equall spight
> Abhorrs all *Love* in every name and kinde;
> But chiefly that which burns with flames as bright
> As his are dark, and which as long shall finde
> Their living fuell.

24. Two of Milton's devils, Belial and Mammon, he knew were—a matter of historical fact—only popular personifications of the abstractions that were originally meant by the two names. In the Old Testament we meet "sons of Belial" who commit acts of lust, but the phrase is a Hebraism that by no means implied that Belial was a deity or the father of sons. So in the Gospels we are told that men serve Mammon rather than God, but Mammon there means simply avarice or worldliness. Yet in the medieval religious drama and in plays like Salandra's *Adamo caduto* Belial appears as a grossly sensual devil. Mammon is not a character in any of the dramas that are represented in Kirkconnell's *Celestial Cycle,* but in Andreini's *L'Adamo* the World appears in a speaking role that might easily be taken by Mammon. Beside these demonic personifications of vices in most of the plays Beelzebub usually has a leading part as a prince of the devils second only to Satan and loosely corresponding to the Pharisees' description of him as such in Matthew xii, 24. Milton's readers expected to find these three devils in *Paradise Lost,* and they almost certainly expected to find them participating in some grand demonic conspiratorial council like those that come early in the action of *Adamo caduto, L'Adamo,* in both of Vondel's plays *Lucifer* and *Adam in Ballingschap,* and in a familiar epic poem like Tasso's *Jerusalem Delivered.* Milton did not disappoint them. His council has the glory and humanity of the assemblies of the gods in Homer, and the roll-call of the participating demons had associations that made it more interesting and powerful than Homer's catalogue of ships.

25. The catalogue of devils rests on a widely accepted belief, coming down from antiquity, that in ancient times the devils deceived mankind and usurped God's worship by masquerading as the gods of the pagan world. Richard Hooker put the matter succinctly in *The Laws of Ecclesiastical Polity:* "The fall of the angels was pride. Since their fall, . . . being dispersed, some in the air, some on the earth, some in the water, some among the minerals, dens, and caves that are under the earth, they have by all means laboured to effect a universal rebellion against the laws, and as far as in them lieth, utter destruction of the works of God. These wicked spirits the heathens honoured

instead of gods, . . . some in oracles, some in idols, some as household gods, some as nymphs" (I, iv, 3). The belief plays a momentary part in Vondel's *Lucifer* when Lucifer says to his followers:

> I shall exalt my haughty tyranny,
> And ye, my sons, shall be adored as gods.
> At altars in high temples without number,
> Worshipped with cattle, frankincense, and gold.
>
> (*Celestial Cycle*, p. 417)

In Milton's roll-call of devils their later careers as pagan deities let them appear under the names of the gods whom the prophets denounced for seducing Israel. The best known of them to Milton's readers was probably

> *Moloch,* horrid King besmear'd with blood
> Of human sacrifice, and parents' tears,
> Though for the noise of Drums and Timbrels loud
> Thir children's cries unheard, that past through fire
> To his grim Idol.
>
> (I, 392–96)

Milton did not exaggerate his importance in letting him speak first from the floor in Pandaemonium.

26. After Moloch a modern reader may not recognize many of the names except Astarte and Adonis. Their cult is described in lines (I, 437–46) which may have inspired John Singer Sergeant's painting of them in the ceiling of the Boston Public Library, where Astarte's cloudy robes and dancing priestesses make a delicate contrast to the bull-head of Moloch. Milton's readers would easily have recognized them all and matched their names with the places that are infamous in the Bible records for their seductions of the Israelites. Many of the places were shown on maps like the two from Thomas Fuller's *A Pisgah-Sight of Palestine* on pages 185 and 186. Chemos and Baal-Peor and Dagon, whose worship in five Philistine cities figures in Milton's list, could be tracked to their lairs on the maps, and in some cases their very temples could be seen. The names of the cities live for us only in the poetry, but for Milton's public they were familiar in geography and terrible in history.

27. When—leaving Hell—we approach the universe which the Son of God shapes with his golden compasses in Book VII we are inclined to think of the account of the creation as only a kind of long approach to the—for us—more interesting account of astronomy in the first two hundred lines of Book VIII. Beyond the dialogue on astronomy lies Adam's narrative to Raphael of his own awakening to life in Eden, of his naming of the animals, and of the creation of Eve. Of the three great subjects of discussion between the angel and the man, the least interesting in Milton's judgment was their debate over the Copernican theory of the heavens as contrasted with that of Aristotle, Ptolemy, and the medieval astronomers. The most interesting subject was the creation, and since Adam's experience was really only an aspect of that great miracle, the dialogue on astronomy must have seemed to Milton to be a mere interlude in the symphony of the angels and the spheres praising the Creator. It was as music that Milton imagined the creation—the song of the angels shouting for joy as they do in the account of it in the Book of Job (xxxviii). That is why—as Mr. Watkins says in his chapter on the subject in *An Anatomy of Milton's Verse*—Milton made creation both an expression of power in the vision of "Heavens and Earth" rising in a moment "out of Chaos" and an expression of wisdom and love in the figure of the heavenly spirit sitting "Dove-like brooding on the vast abyss" to make it "pregnant." "By passing constantly from one to the other Milton

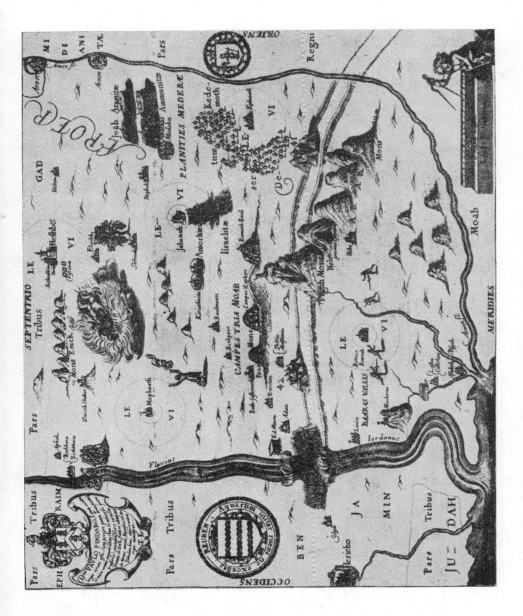

185

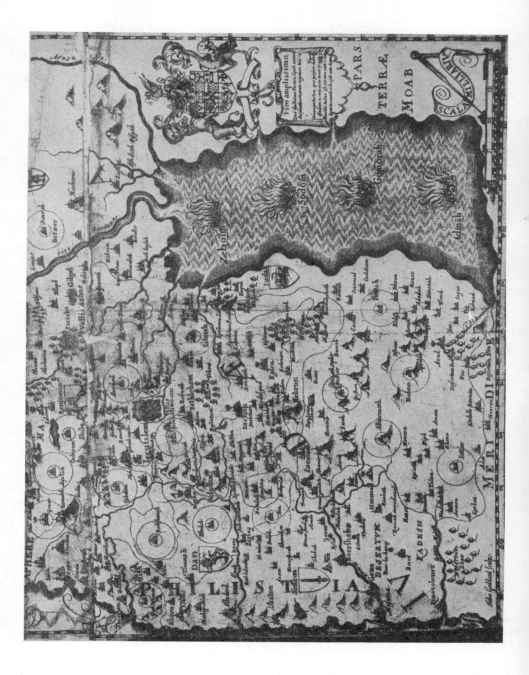

186

manages to infuse a brooding warmth into his abstractions, so that when we come to the Golden Compasses drawing swift arcs over Chaos the image seems more biological than geometric."

28. But the image of the spirit brooding on the face of the primeval waters comes from Genesis, and in the expansion of the story of the six days of creation Milton stayed as close as he could to the letter of Scripture. He regarded it less as a source than as an authority and an inspiration. To have felt that way would have been impossible if countless writers coming between him and the first redaction of the Book of Genesis had not variously shared and anticipated his creative veneration for its authority. At least as early as the writing of the first of the many versions of the Apocryphal Book of Enoch in the second century before Christ or earlier, men's imaginations had been at work interpreting and embroidering the record of creation in Genesis. It was extended by the Hebrew commentaries that Professor Harris Fletcher has brought into the Miltonic orbit in *Milton's Rabbinical Readings,* and by the Christian commentaries of the Fathers, Greek and Latin, the medieval Schoolmen, and their heirs in the Renaissance, to many of whom Professor Arnold Williams introduces us in *The Common Expositor.* Through Mr. Williams at least a bowing acquaintance becomes possible with theologians like the great Frenchman, Marin Mersenne, the friend of Cardinal Bellarmine and of Descartes; or like the German Lutheran David Pareus and the Italian Protestant Girolamo Zanchi (cited in our notes as Zanchius). In their works abundant warrant could be found for Milton's dramatic treatment of the creation of the world as an expression of God's goodness if not of his will to bring good out of the evil done by the revolt of Satan and his angels.

29. Turning now to the architecture of the spherical universe that Milton hangs by a golden chain from Heaven's floor, we must first remember that he was writing for a public that visualized the universe essentially as it appears in the accompanying scheme (p. 188) from Peter Apian's *Cosmographia,* edition of 1584. It was published without change for nearly a century from its first appearance in 1524. Quite unresponsive to the changes in astronomical thinking that began with the publication of Copernicus' work *On Celestial Motions* in 1543, the schools continued to teach the Ptolemaic theory that pictured the universe with the earth at its center and the "seven planets"—the moon, Mercury, Venus, the sun, Mars, Jupiter, and Saturn—and beyond them the fixed stars— revolving as if supported by concentric spheres which were moved by an enveloping "First Mover" or sphere, whose ceaseless movement turned everything within it except the motionless earth. Between the Eighth Heaven or sphere of the fixed stars and the "First Mover" (*Primum Mobile*) medieval astronomy put a crystalline sphere, to which Milton refers in Book III, 482, but which he did not have in mind when he put a crystalline ocean *outside* the shell of the universe in VII, 271. Apian put the Empyrean or Habitation of God outside his spherical universe but not so definitely above it as it is in Milton's scheme.

30. Milton was as well aware as his enlightened contemporaries were of the inadequacy of the Ptolemaic view of the heavens, but he knew that his readers could easily visualize them only as we see them in Apian's chart. For them the sun and the moon were planets like the "other five," as we find them in *Paradise Lost* X, 651–57. And it is down through the sphere of the fixed stars and then through those of the "planets seven"—sailing between "worlds and worlds"—that Raphael descends (V, 268) from the opening in the outside shell of our universe where it is open at the foot of the golden chain of Book II, 1051, which becomes the "Structure high" of III, 503, that seems comparable with

> The Stairs . . . whereon *Jacob* saw
> Angels ascending and descending, bands
> Of Guardians bright . . .
>
> (III, 509–511)

31. When Milton has Raphael drop, "prone in flight . . . between worlds and worlds," there is an implication that some at least of the planets that he passes are inhabited. A few lines earlier Milton has referred to "the glass of Galileo" and to his famous discovery that the moon's surface was much more terrestrial and less mysterious than tradition had made it. And in Book VIII, in lines which many modern readers have regarded as expressing Milton's private astronomical opinions, Adam puts the crucial question whether it is possible to believe that the apparent diurnal motion of the heavens is due to their revolution or to the earth's rotation. If the Copernican reply was made to that question, the same reply seemed inevitable to the question whether the universe was geocentric. And as soon as the earth ceased to be regarded as the center of the universe, we know that the doctrine of a plurality of worlds seemed to follow for many of Milton's contemporaries as a matter of course. But Raphael's reply to Adam's question is non-committal and brings us back to Galileo's observations of the

6   PRIMA PARS COSMOGRAPH.

Schema prædictæ diuifionis.

moon. The angel says that, "if land be there," then there may be "fields and inhabit-ants"; and that if the spots on the moon are clouds, then those

> Clouds may rain, and Rain produce
> Fruits in her soften'd Soil, for some to eat
> Allotted there; and other Suns perhaps
> With their attendant Moons thou shalt descry . . .
>
> (VIII, 146–49)

32. On the strength mainly of Adam's dialogue with Raphael, Professor E. N. S. Thompson, writing in 1917 in *MLN*, XXXIII, 479, drew the conclusion that Milton was a convinced Copernican when he wrote *Paradise Lost,* and in 1932 Mr. Grant McColley (in *MLN*, XLVII, 323) was inclined to concur. But five years later (in *PMLA*, LII, 728–62) Mr. McColley took a different view in a study of the debate between Bishop John Wilkins in his *Discovery of a New World* and his *Discourse Concerning a New Planet, That the Earth May be a Planet* (1640), and his truculent antagonist, the Presby-terian divine Alexander Ross, in *The New Planet: or, The Earth no wandring Star: Except in the wandring heads of Galileans* (1646). Limitations of space forbid the dis-cussion of these books here and of Professor Marjorie Nicolson's survey in *A World in the Moon* of the more interesting speculation on the subject that began with the publica-tion of Galileo's *Heavenly Messenger* (*Sidereus Nuncius*) in 1610, that was intensified in 1634 by the *Dream* (*Somnium*)—a speculative voyage to the moon—of the German as-tronomer Kepler, and reached a climax in France with the publication of Fontenelle's *Conversations on the Plurality of Worlds* in 1686. But in the *Sidereus Nuncius* Galileo denied the possibility of life on the moon and the question remained open. Milton may have been thinking of Galileo's scepticism when he wrote that

> by night the Glass
> Of *Galileo,* less assur'd, observes
> Imagin'd Lands and Regions in the Moon.
>
> (V, 261–63)

33. There is no doubt that Milton had long been fascinated by the "Optic Glass" (I, 288) of the "Tuscan Artist," or that he shared the eagerness of his contemporaries to see the heavens as they had been probed by the discoverer of the satellites of Jupiter and the phases of Venus, the "Morning Planet," of which he wonderingly said that she "gilds her horns" (VII, 366). For him, no less than for his scientifically informed con-temporaries, the great question was the centrality of the earth, just as for us it seems to be that of an expanding universe. Quite as important a point in Miss Nicolson's studies as the kindling of his imagination by Galileo's evidence for the heliocentric theory is her stress upon the fact that much of its prestige in the eyes of his classically trained contemporaries came from antiquity. It had—supposedly—been taught by Pythagoras, and from Milton's second Prolusion ("On the Music of the Spheres") and from *At a Solemn Music* we know how strongly he responded to Pythagoras' more famous doc-trine that the orbs of the seven planets rang with a harmony such as Plato describes in the tenth book of the *Republic*. The still powerful hold of that doctrine on the imagina-tion of the time is clear from the drawing reproduced on page 190 from *The History of both Worlds* (*Utriusque Cosmi Historia*—1624) of Milton's acquaintance Robert Flud, whom Saurat has regarded as exerting an influence on much of his cosmological thinking.

34. For men hesitating to accept the Copernican view because they disliked novelty and craved some venerable authority for it such as Aristotle and the Bible itself seemed to give to the Ptolemaic theory there were ingenious compromises such as the scheme of Tycho Brahe reproduced on page 191 from John Swan's *Speculum Mundi, or a Glasse Representing the Face of the World* (Cambridge, 1655). The scheme and the

Hic autem monochordum mundanum cum suis proportionibus, confo-
nantiis & intervallis exactiùs compofuimus, cujus motorem extra mundum effe
hoc modo depinximus.

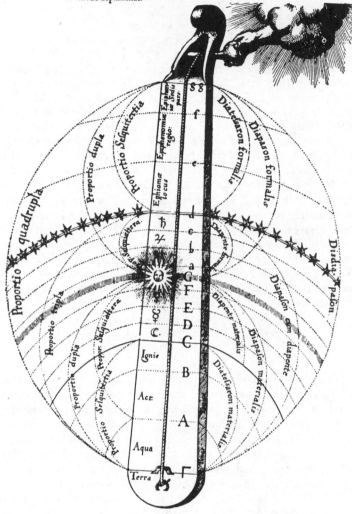

bit of text above and below it are interesting for the light they throw on a once famous attempt to preserve the stationary dignity of the earth by making the sun wheel around it, and yet to let the sun be as nearly as possible the center of the universe by having the other planets revolve around *it*. This theory had the inconvenience of making the spheres of Venus, Mars, and Mercury cut through the sun's orbit—an assumption inconsistent with the usual view that the spheres were not merely the orbital paths of the planets in space, but that they were impenetrable though transparent balls— "corporeal substances" that were turned, as Raphael says (VIII, 108–110), by "Omnipotence" with "Speed almost Spiritual."

35. Milton's treatment of astronomy is not "evasive," nor is it unctuously pious like John Swan's. When he speaks of the divine laughter at the "quaint Opinions" (VIII,

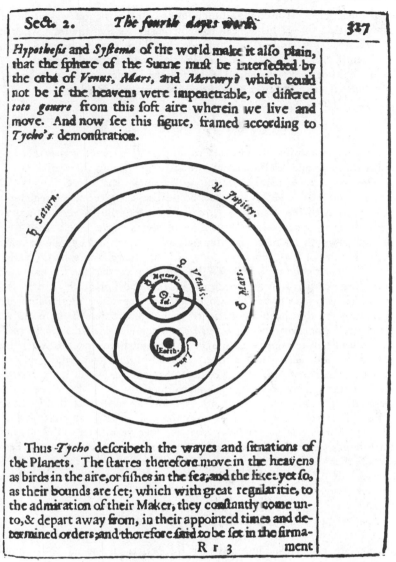

Sect. 2.   *The fourth dayes work*   327

Hypothesis and *Systeme* of the world make it also plain, that the sphere of the Sunne must be intersected by the orbs of *Venus*, *Mars*, and *Mercury?* which could not be if the heavens were impenetrable, or differed *toto genere* from this soft aire wherein we live and move. And now see this figure, framed according to *Tycho's* demonstration.

Thus *Tycho* describeth the wayes and situations of the Planets. The starres therefore move in the heavens as birds in the aire, or fishes in the sea, and the like: yet so, as their bounds are set; which with great regularitie, to the admiration of their Maker, they constantly come unto, & depart away from, in their appointed times and determined orders; and therefore said to be set in the firmament

R r 3   ment

77–78) of men like Tycho, which were so "wide" of the truth, his contempt is incomparably more restrained than George Herbert's sweeping denunciation of all astronomical and scientific speculation in a poem like *Vanitie*. Milton had none of the cosmic insecurity that shudders in the verses by John Donne that are quoted in our footnote to Book VIII, 82. Professor E. E. Stoll has collected abundant and beautiful evidence to show that not only was Milton undisturbed by the fact that this earth is what Adam calls a "punctual spot" (VIII, 23) in the universe, a grain of sand, but that he had good historical reasons for accepting the fact. The tininess of the earth had been put into an emphatic perspective by Roger Bacon in the thirteenth century, and the moral of that fact had been drawn by Chaucer, Dante, Cicero, and even Ptolemy himself. The fact is—as Mr. Howard Schultz proves with a cloud of witnesses supporting him in *Milton and*

Forbidden Knowledge—that Milton's attitude toward all the sciences was no more evasive or "obscurantist" than that of his learned contemporaries. From the time when he wrote his third Prolusion as a student at Cambridge until he put the warning against the pursuit of scientific knowledge as an end in itself into Raphael's mouth in *Paradise Lost*, Milton's attitude never varied. He exalted the sciences as an enrichment of life but he subordinated them (like Socrates) to philosophy and divinity.

Milton's Ontology

36. If we try to probe Milton's ontology we find that, even more than his cosmology, it implies his theology and leads constantly toward his theological treatise *On Christian Doctrine* (*De doctrina christiana*). Since no one now challenges Professor Maurice Kelley's proof in *This Great Argument* that the treatise was given its present form almost contemporaneously with the writing of *Paradise Lost*—probably a very little earlier than the final writing of the poem—its relevance for us seems clear. It has been used in the notes to this edition with references both by part and chapter and by volume and page in the Columbia Edition of *The Works of John Milton*. Its relevance hardly suffers if we accept Mr. P. F. Fisher's thesis, in *JHI*, XVII (1956), 28–53, that the treatise was finished perhaps three years earlier than the poem and states a still immature faith in theological speculation which was soon to be transcended in the imaginative illumination of poetry. However illuminating the spiritual experience of the composition of the poem may have been, there is good evidence showing that Milton's confidence in his *Christian Doctrine* was such as to lead him to hope that it might be published after his death and contribute to the great theological debates of his time. Its study for its own sake is of no interest here, but its light on *Paradise Lost* and *Paradise Regained* is worth having, especially as it bears on four much debated passages in the former.

37. Diverse though the four passages are, they are all aspects of that "Christian materialism" that M. Saurat expounded in *Milton: Man and Thinker* in 1925, and developed more boldly in *Milton et le matérialisme chretien* three years later. Two of them have to do with Milton's treatment of the angels and are not so important as the debate over them has made them seem. They are the places in Book V, 404–413, and VIII, 620–629, where Raphael tells Adam that the angels eat in the physical sense that men do, and that when they make love,

> Easier than Air with Air, if Spirits embrace,
> Total they mix, Union of Pure with Pure
> Desiring.

These passages are negatively illuminated by the perfect silence on both points in the chapter on the angels in *Christian Doctrine*. Food and sex were not important in Milton's thinking about angels. Mr. West is surely right in thinking that Milton inserted the two passages in his poem because he wished to stress and dramatize his materialism, which in different ways is the subject of the two other passages in question here. They are Raphael's comparison of the development of man to that of a tree which obviously is a symbol of the Great Chain of Being in Book V, 469–503, and the very different passage in VII, 168–172, where the Almighty says to the Son as he rides out on his creative mission into Chaos:

> Boundless the Deep, because I am who fill
> Infinitude, nor vacuous the space.
> Though I uncircumscribed myself retire,
> And put not forth my goodness, which is free
> To act or not.

38. From this description of creation as voluntary withdrawal by the Creator from the infinitude which he had previously filled M. Saurat drew the conclusion that Milton's justification of God's ways to man could be entirely read into these five lines. He saw in them the basis for Milton's belief in absolute human freedom, at least before Adam's fall, and consequently in man's responsibility for evil. His authority for reducing creation to a simple act of "withdrawal" by God from infinitude was a passage in the *Zohar* of which he took Milton's lines to be a translation. M. Saurat has been assailed for this theory by an army of opponents—most recently and devastatingly by R. J. Zwi Werblowski in *JWCI*, XVIII (1955), 90–113. The story of the attack on him has been told by Professor Robert Adams in *Ikon*. It is not, as he says, that the *Zohar* is "a tangled, confused, elaborate mass of mumbo-jumbo" or that Saurat misread both what it and Milton say in the two passages in question. Mr. Kelley puts his finger on the main point when he says in *This Great Argument* (p. 211) that M. Saurat's "Retraction Theory" of creation destroys his own sound doctrine that Milton derived matter itself from God and therefore believed in its essential goodness and in a monistic universe.

39. In a much more interesting ontological passage Raphael declares (V, 469–471) that all things "proceed" from God and return to him—a statement which is just as clearly made in the *Christian Doctrine* (I, vii; C. E. XV, 22–24). It leaves no doubt that Milton thought of creation as God's shaping through the Word, his Son, of the unformed matter which originated in him. Milton's reason for thinking so was simply his understanding of the meaning of the Hebrew word that is translated "make" in the verse, "In the beginning God made heaven and earth."

40. Milton's most beautiful and crucial ontological passage is in Book V, 469–503. In "Some Notes on Milton's View of the Creation" (*PQ*, XXVIII, 1949, pp. 211–236), Professor Woodhouse suggests that in all the ontological passages Milton was writing as a Christian Humanist who was out of sympathy with the effort of some ultra-orthodox clergymen to interpret Genesis i, 1, in a unique, theological sense. The divines could see no alternative to their view except atheistic materialism. To both views Milton opposed "creation by God (*ex Deo*)"—a conception which was "implicit in the Stoic conception of reason as an active aspect of matter, which they 'did not scruple to call God.'" The Stoic view was usually regarded as pantheistic and heretical, and so Milton may have regarded it himself. In the *Christian Doctrine* he clearly defined nature as God's creation and subject to God's laws, but described matter as if, though passive, it were informed with something like the 'seminal reason' of the Stoics. In this he saw no contradiction—just as he saw no inconsistency in describing the appearance of animal life on the earth and the invention of fire and metals as they are described in the "materialist" poem *On the Nature of Things* by the Epicurean, Lucretius. His ideas and imagery were drawn from a great variety of sources that have been largely explored by Professors W. C. Curry and W. B. Hunter, Jr., in a series of studies that have widened the base of his thinking and at the same time proved its critical independence. In one of them (*RSUL*, 1941, pp. 173–192) Mr. Curry brings us well within sight of the imagery in Book V, 469–503, that takes us to the heart of Milton's thinking about the nature of man as it originally was in Eden, and as by God's grace it yet may be again. But the thought is not inharmonious with Aristotle's conception of nature as growth, nor with St. Paul's belief that "the human body is sown a natural body," but "raised a spiritual body."

41. Very deliberately, Milton has Raphael put the essence of his thought into the image of the tree which represents the scale of being in the universe as a whole as well as man's body and mind as a replica or microcosm of nature. Both man and nature are like a tree from whose

> root
> Springs lighter the green stalk, from thence the leaves
> More aery, last the bright consummate flow'r
> Spirits odorous breathes.

Life and all being vitally resemble or involve processes like those of the digestion of food in the human body, which produces spirits (as Milton calls the chyle, blood, etc. in the medical language of his time) that both animate it and make it capable of intellectual activity—

> give both life and sense
> Fancy and understanding, whence the Soul
> Reason receives, and reason is her being.

42. Milton's image may go back to Plato's *Timaeus* (90a), where man's spiritual root and perfecting character are both said to end in heaven. Milton's readers could find something like his image in several medieval writers, and they could find something like his thought among contemporary Platonists of the Cambridge School. Indeed, it had become a familiar idea among popular theologians like William Ames that "all natural things tend to God." If Milton's readers wanted scientific confirmation for his idea of the human body, they had the word of William Harvey, the discoverer of the circulation of the blood, that "the blood is a spirit, celestial in nature," which nourishes "the soul, that which answers to the essence of the stars, . . . something analogous to heaven, the instrument of heaven." Or, as the philosophical poet John Davies of Hereford put it in *Mirum in Modum* (1602):

> The *Body* in the Elements is cloz'd;
> The *Bloud* within the body is confin'd;
> The *Spirits,* within the Bloud; the Soul's dispoz'd
> Within the *Spirites,* which *Soule* includes the *Minde.*
> The *Understanding* in the Minde's repoz'd,
> And God in th'Understanding rest doth find:
> So this Worlde's made for *Man,* Man for the Soule,
> *Soule* for the *Mind,* and *Minde* for God her Gole.

43. Milton's thought might further be illustrated by countless passages like these from Harvey and Davies to show how familiar and convincing it was to his contemporaries. His image of the tree—as Kester Svendsen shows in *Milton and Science,* pp. 114–116— was also familiar in contemporary scientific works as various as Mercator's *Historia Mundi* and Matthew Hale's *The Primitive Origination of Mankind, considered according to the Light of Nature.* Milton used the tree as a symbol of his conceptions of matter and of the nature and destiny of man. It is a kind of microcosm of his whole poem, and in Raphael's words he made it into an emblem of man's potential divinity in obedience to God:

> Your bodies may at last turn all to Spirit,
> Improv'd by tract of time, and wing'd ascend
> Ethereal as wee, or may at choice
> Here or in Heav'nly Paradises dwell;
> If ye be found obedient, and retain
> Unalterably firm his love entire
> Whose progeny you are.

"Of Man's First Disobedience"

44. Unless we are in a mood to think that

> Malt does more than Milton can
> To justify God's ways to man,

we have to recognize that in at least one way human disobedience is the theme of *Paradise Lost*. We may regret the fact, as Sir Walter Raleigh did in his *Milton* when he said that the poem was "a monument to dead ideas." We may even accept Sir Herbert Grierson's view in *Milton and Wordsworth* that the "shift of perspective" since the seventeenth century makes it impossible for us to accept the myth of Eden and "take refuge in the mystery." Milton himself was not satisfied with that refuge, but his discussion of the matter in the *Christian Doctrine* seems too "legalistic" to satisfy us. And we come with a shock to his analysis of it in the *Christian Doctrine* I, xi (C. E. XV, 180–182), as including "at once distrust of the divine veracity, and a proportionate credulity in the assurances of Satan; unbelief; ingratitude; disobedience; gluttony; in the man excessive uxoriousness, in the woman a want of proper regard for her husband, in both an insensibility to the welfare of their offspring, and that offspring the whole human race; parricide, theft, invasion of the rights of others, sacrilege, deceit, presumption in aspiring to divine attributes, fraud in the means employed to attain the object, pride, and arrogance."

45. Unless a reader can accept this passage as a matter of religious faith or strong philosophical conviction, he is likely to reject it outright and he may reject *Paradise Lost* into the bargain. Short of such conviction, Professor C. S. Lewis said in *A Preface to Paradise Lost* (p. 70), readers must either "accept Milton's doctrine of obedience as they accept the inexplicable prohibitions in *Lohengrin, Cinderella,* or *Cupid and Psyche,* or else they must play at historical make-believe seriously enough to read the poem from inside "that whole hierarchical conception of the universe" to which it belongs.

46. One way of playing that game is to follow Professor John Diekhoff in his *Commentary on the Argument of Paradise Lost* step by step through the scenes in the poem which establish the logical and legal case against Adam. Another way is to try testing the case by Milton's own rules as he stated them in his *Art of Logic*. Only a reader with some logical training is likely to wish to follow the critical study of that work as bearing on *Paradise Lost* which has been made by Professor Leon Howard in *HLQ*, IX (1946), 149–73. The reader needs some knowledge of Aristotelian logic as it was taught in Milton's youth and also of the challenge to it by the French logician Peter Ramus, whose work was to some extent a basis of Milton's *Art of Logic*. Otherwise it may not seem helpful to find that Eve is the "procatarctic" cause of Adam's fall, or that the fall itself was due to all four of the traditional kinds of cause—efficient, material, formal, and final. But it may be suggestive to find Adam's innocence regarded as the material cause of his deception. And—regardless of the extent to which Milton's logic was Ramist or Aristotelian—it is encouraging to find Mr. Howard agreeing with Mr. Diekhoff that, "Man in the person of Adam was the principal cause of his own disobedience." And a welcome light is shed on Adam's cry in Book XII, 469–471, that the evil of his sin has been turned into a vastly greater good when we are told that the final cause of his fall was not only the "glory of God," but also the "greater glory of man."

47. If we could stick strictly to logic and law we might accept Milton's attitude toward man's disobedience. The great logical objection to doing so—for most readers—is probably the close resemblance of Eve's reasoning to justify tasting the Tree of Knowledge to Milton's own reasoning against "a fugitive and cloistered virtue" in *Areopagitica*. For Milton's readers there was no problem for they agreed with Francis Bacon—in the *Advancement of Learning* VI, 138—that it was "not curiosity about Nature's secrets but the desire for moral omniscience in order that Adam might be a law unto himself that caused the Fall." In its dogmatic way Bacon's distinction may seem empty, but at bottom it is very much like what Mr. Philip Wheelwright has to say when in the *Sewanee Review*, LIX (1951), 589–90, he compares a Navajo myth about the breaking of a tabu

of silence to the symbolism of "the Eden myth." His interpretation of the third chapter of Genesis is that "the creature, not content with the bounty of the tree of life, which is freely allowed him, dares to take good and evil into his own hands and to speak in his own way of primal matters, instead of bringing his mind and heart into the stillness of listening and thus into the harmony of universal rhythms."

48. With Bacon and Mr. Wheelwright championing the soundness of the tabu on the Tree of knowledge, Milton's case against Adam and Eve may seem to have been confirmed, if ever there was such a case. There is an old suggestion that Milton did not really intend his shrewder readers to believe that Adam and Eve lost innocence when they tasted the Tree of Knowledge, simply because they had none to lose. Recently the suspicion has been getting support from delvers into the psychology of the Renaissance. In studies of "Milton's Prelapsarian Adam" in *RSUW*, XII (1946), 163–84, and of "Eve's Demonic Dream" in *ELH*, XIII (1946), 255–65, M. W. Bundy and W. B. Hunter, Jr., have reminded us that Eve's dream in *Paradise Lost* IV, 800–809, and V, 31–93, does not merely add a touch of the supernatural to the poem, as Agamemnon's dream of the woes threatening the Greek forces embarking for Troy casts a beam of prophecy ahead on the action of the *Iliad*. Eve's dream of a vaguely divine adventure near the forbidden tree betrays her susceptibility to the temptation awaiting her in Book IX. Perhaps it is itself a temptation. Evil spirits were held to be able to work through dreams to stir the imagination, rouse the Sensitive Appetite, lull the Reason into compliance or take advantage of its impotence in sleep, and move the will itself to evil. We are given a case history from a rather outstanding book, *Of Our Communion and Warre with Angels,* by Henry Lawrence, to whose son Edward Milton addressed a sonnet. The parallel with Eve's dream is interesting and close. The conclusion that Eve is already fallen is not by any means inevitable, but it is suggested.

49. The case for Eve as already fallen from our first sight of her, fascinated by her own image in the pool, is pressed hard by Mrs. Millicent Bell, in *PMLA*, LXX (1955), 1192–1202, who argues Eve's pride before the fall from her earlier betrayals of self-love, and Adam's uxoriousness as already apparent in his conversation with Raphael. What happens at noon on the fatal day is seen simply as a natural consequence of the passions that show in the lovers' quarrel when Adam gives way to Eve in the morning. In this way we may try to evade the problem of the sudden step from innocence to guilt by the simple breach of the tabu on the Tree of Knowledge. Of course, Milton did not evade it. At the edge of Eve's surrender to the serpent's wiles, we are told that she is "yet sinless" (IX, 659). But it is alluring for the reader who instinctively tries to read modern psychology into Milton to try to evade the problem in "the intractable myth" by injecting a smooth development of character into the story at the expense of losing Milton's tenacious faith that, although the fall was "fortunate," something in a supreme way valuable was forever and needlessly lost through the fruit of the Tree of Knowledge, the power to know good without knowing evil.

50. Milton understood the need for convincing character development and in the last three books of his poem he faced that problem against the still undimished intractability of the myth. In the scene of Eve's reconciliation with Adam it is generally agreed that he notably achieved the transition from despair to hope and purpose through love in a dialogue that is both personal and universal, both idiomatic in its style as the talk of unfallen Adam and Eve was not, and at the same time charged with the tone of strong passion. The story in Genesis gives Milton no lead of that kind, nor does it in the least suggest that the initiative in the dialogue should be taken by Eve. Certainly it does not suggest, as does Mr. J. H. Summers in *PMLA*, LXX (1955), 1088, that her words counterpoint those of the Son of God speaking as the Redeemer in XI,

30–44, and XII, 614–623. From the reconciliation scene to the end of the poem there is no breach in the evolution of her mood and character. When the moment of final banishment from the garden in Eden comes, she and Adam are up to it. They do not—as John Erskine once suggested in the mood of the time when "we were very young"—go out into the world in the spirit of a bride and groom of the Renaissance going to seek their fortune. They go out rather in what E. E. Stoll has called "a twilight mood," but it is the mood of those who are determined to know good though it must be only through evil.

51. It is perhaps not strictly accurate to say that the myth of Eden gave Milton no hint of the redemptive role of Eve in his last three books. In the text of Genesis it does not do so, but by very ancient Christian tradition the curse that is pronounced on the serpent in Genesis iii, 15—"I will put enmity between thee and the woman, and between her seed and thy seed; it shall bruise thy head, and thou shalt bruise his heel" —was interpreted as identifying the serpent with Satan and the seed of the woman particularly with the Redeeming Christ. Milton may well have known that Jewish commentary and tradition by no means justified even the identification of the serpent of Genesis with Satan. From the point of view of a man anxious to minimize the miraculous elements in Scripture—as we know from the *Christian Doctrine* that Milton was— it must have required a deliberate decision to accept the Christian influence of a prophecy of Christ in the promise that the woman's seed should bruise the serpent's head. Milton accepted it as completely as possible—as completely as any man of his time. In the last three books of *Paradise Lost* it is as much taken for granted as it is in Caravaggio's picture of the *Madonna della Serpe,* where the boy Christ and his mother Mary, Milton's "Second Eve" (X, 183), together tread down a serpent. The Christian inference into the myth did not make it untractable for Milton.

52. But the full meaning of the Christian inference is hardly clear in *Paradise Lost*. In Adam's preview of human history it is just distinct enough to let him be sure of the good that is to come out of evil, but it is not clear enough for him to be told more about it by Michael than that he must not dream of Christ's coming battle with Satan

> As of a Duel, or the local wounds
> Of head or heel: not therefore joins the Son
> Manhood to Godhead, with more strength to foil
> Thy enemy.

> (XII, 387–390)

The preview of history seems to have given Adam an impression of a struggle ending in a second casting out of "that old serpent, Satan" from heaven and earth at the end of time, as popular interpreters of Revelation xii, 9, had usually read the prophecy. All interpreters of Scripture—among them the most learned—men like Zanchius and Melanchthon—were agreed that the outcome of human history would be a proof of the "Fortunate Fall." Milton had seen some of the dangers of a popular, political interpretation of the promise that the seed of the woman should bruise the serpent's head, and he did not intend that *Paradise Lost* should contribute to that illusion. But the canvas of history was not to be his medium for imaginative escape from that illusion. His escape could be complete only when the paradise that had been lost by "one man's disobedience" had been recovered

> to all mankind
> By one man's firm obedience fully tried
> Through all temptation, . . .
> (*Paradise Regained* I, 3–5)

Milton's Muse

53. A critic who has seen far into Milton's mind and art has said that the language, images, and rhythms of *Paradise Lost* can be explained only as a mysterious gift of the "Celestial Patroness" of whom he said that she

> deigns
> Her nightly visitation unimplor'd,
> And dictates to me slumbring, or inspires
> Easy my unpremeditated verse.
>
> (IX, 21–24)

Scholarship and criticism have, however, been very busy with the mystery, and they seem almost determined to destroy it. Even without the reminders of Miss Darbishire's work on the manuscript of the first book of the poem and on her text of 1952, without Gilbert's book *On the Composition of Paradise Lost* or Diekhoff's study of "The Trinity MS and the Dictation of Paradise Lost" in *PQ, XXVIII* (1949), 44–52, we should hardly imagine that Milton's experience in writing the poem resembled that of a stenographer taking dictation from a heavenly spirit. The poem which began as a drama and, years later, became an epic, we should feel certain, must have developed in the poet's mind as a long-cultivated garden develops. Much planning and changing lie behind the harmony of its beds and shrubs, but its summer beauty is a product of an almost spontaneous growth. And for Milton as he composed his poem in "parcels of ten, twenty, or thirty verses at a time," as his nephew Edward Phillips says that he did, the finally inevitable combination of the words, lines, and paragraphs into the crystallizing design of the entire work would seem to have something of the spontaneous blooming of flowers.

54. It would be a mistake to doubt him when he tells us that the poetic experience was the heavenly revelation for which he prayed in the invocations to Books I, III, and VII. In undertaking to retell the story of the fall he asked for inspiration by the Spirit that the opening verses of Genesis describe as brooding on the waters when the earth "was without form and void." In Book I he called his Muse simply by that divine name, adding a comparison of her to the nine Muses of classical tradition which implies his belief that the myths of the pagan gods were shadows of the truth in Scripture. We see that belief become explicit when he tells us that Homer's story of Mulciber (Hephaestus) being thrown out of heaven by Zeus was a tale that the pagans told,

> Erring; for he with this (Satan's) rebellious rout
> Fell long before.
>
> (I, 747–748)

When in Book VII he is ready to tell the story of creation he invokes his Muse by the name of the traditional patroness of astronomy, the ninth of the Muses of Greek tradition, Urania; but he says that what he has in mind is "the meaning, not the Name" (VII, 5). His words—Gilbert Murray tells us in *Classical Tradition and Poetry* (Harvard, 1927; p. 9)—plainly owe something to the ancient Stoics and something to Theocritus, but his prayer is not pagan. Nor did it suggest a pagan Muse to his readers. To many of them it suggested the Urania whom Du Bartas pompously invoked in *The Divine Weeks,* the Urania whom Spenser also invoked in *The Teares of the Muses* (499–502) as patronizing the knowledge of

> the worlds creation,
> How in his cradle first he fostred was;

And judge of Natures cunning operation,
How things she formed of a formelesse mas.

55. Milton speaks of his Urania as a sister of Eternal Wisdom, with whom she played "In presence of th'Almighty Father" and pleased him with her "Celestial Song." So perhaps Urania is the Understanding by which, together with Wisdom, Professor Fletcher reminds us in *Milton's Rabbinical Readings* (p. 111), rabbinical tradition said that the world was made. We need not wander away with M. Saurat in his cabalistic speculations about the sisters' games before the creation of the world, nor review the crushing replies that have been made to him. It is wiser to follow Mr. Hanford in "That Shepherd who First Taught the Chosen Seed" in *UTQ*, VII (1939), 403-19, and to take Milton at his word when he says that he is not interested in the name but is interested in guidance by the Spirit which inspired Moses,

> That Shepherd, who first taught the Chosen Seed,
> In the beginning how the Heav'ns and Earth
> Rose out of Chaos.

(I, 8-10)

56. In the most personal of his three invocations Milton has something to say about his experience with his Muse, whom here he simply calls Light. Was he thinking of the divine Light that sits with Sapience in Spenser's *Hymne of Heavenly Beautie* (183)? Or simply of the light that we are told "is God" in I John i, 5? Or of the light that Dante said in the *Paradise* XIII, l-lvi, is God's creative power as well as an aspect of his essence, and that he calls in the *Convito* III, xii, "the spiritual and intellectual sun that is God"? Or of St. Augustine's distinction in the *Confessions* VII, x, between "the light which is God and the light which God has made"? Or was he—as Arnold Williams suggests in *The Common Expositor* (p. 54)—thinking of the discussion by the great Catholic commentator Benedictus Pererius of Dionysius' comparison of the attributes of light to those of God? Or is Professor Kelley right in believing (*Argument*, p. 92) that by light in this passage Milton meant simply the physical light from which he was cut off by blindness? Or is D. C. Allen right in *The Harmonious Vision* (p. 101) in regarding Milton's invocation as a kind of metaphor comparing the varying intensities of physical light to the spiritual ladder of light by which Marsilio Ficino and the Florentine Neo-Platonists taught that man rises to the Creator of all light? We may hear as many or as few literary overtones as we choose to do in his prayer to the "Celestial Light" to

> Shine inward, and the mind through all her powers
> Irradiate, there plant eyes, all mist from thence
> Purge and disperse.

(III, 52-54)

In this prayer "a complete, deliberate, and substantial theory of poetry" has been found, and there is no doubt that it is a perfect expression of the Renaissance theory that great poetry—and particularly great epic poetry—can be written only by men who deserve and enjoy divine illumination. It is as revealing an account of the poetic experience as Milton ever wrote.

57. But if the invocation to Book III is our best key to Milton's art, we can only agree with Dr. Tillyard that the mystery of his Muse is inscrutable. In the *Essay on Rime* Karl Shapiro seems to hope that the key can be found in the prosody when, contrasting the "auricular" power of Shakespeare's verse with Milton's appeal to the eye, he says that

> No metre more exactly planned exists
> Than his. A perfect mechanism turns

Paradise Lost, his solar masterpiece.
Written in blindness and by count of eye.
In Bridges' study of the poem we learn
What feats the decasyllable performs.

Yet modern metrists are not satisfied with Robert Bridges' analysis of Milton's verse. Not even when it is amended by S. Ernest Sprott in *Milton's Art of Prosody* (Oxford, 1953) does it seem likely to satisfy the objection to Bridges' method that is voiced for many readers by B. Rajan when he says that, to talk of the poem's prosody or language is "a misleading abstraction." Perhaps we shall have the key in Mr. Edward Weismiller's promised study of the problem, or in the approach to it by way of Milton's verse paragraphs in Mr. James Whaler's *Counterpoint and Symbol* we shall find the still missing key.

58. It is by way of the verse paragraph that Mr. Wylie Sypher attacks the problem of Milton's style when—as a typical example—he analyzes the description of Adam and Eve in the nuptial bower (IV, 691–743) and briefly identifies its "verse rhythms with their repletions" as characteristic of the "plenitude of the baroque" (in *Four Stages of Renaissance Style*, New York, 1955, p. 193). We may not come very close to the heart of Milton's mystery when we are told that *"Paradise Lost* is the flood-tide of baroque poetry" because it has in fullest measure the baroque elements of the "sumptuous, pompous, invigorating, fleshly, authoritarian." But until we feel these qualities among others we have not begun to understand the poem. Its pomp may best be explicable as Mr. C. S. Lewis has explained it in his chapter on the ritual style that it has in common with the *Aeneid* and other "literary epics." Its fleshliness is both a matter of taste and of Milton's ontology, his belief in a "theistic materialism." Its authoritative tone, like its style, expresses his nature; but it is also the only possible tone in a poem about good and evil that was written, as Milton said, to be "exemplary to a nation."

59. Mr. Sypher speaks also of the "plastic quality of baroque space" as vital and highly characteristic in *Paradise Lost,* and in *Poetry and Humanism* Miss Mahood speaks of its "shapeliness" moulding every element in it from the over-all design to the verse-paragraphs and individual phrases. For her the quality is also baroque. It has been brilliantly discussed from the points of view of space and time by D. C. Allen in *The Harmonious Vision* and by Arnold Stein in *Answerable Style*. Mr. Allen makes us see how a panorama like the review of the demons marching into Pandaemonium moves before us until we are caught in its motion ourselves. Though he regards the essence of the passage as baroque art, he does not draw an analogy with the power of baroque architecture to involve us with the upward movement of the soaring domes of its churches. Approaching the structural problem in *Paradise Lost* from the point of view of its depth in time, we learn—for example—in the great speeches of Satan how both to hear and see him in action not far down stage, but at the same time to see him in the perspective of the larger action of the entire poem. Its complete design in terms of the irony of the drama between evil and good is never so clear as when Satan is speaking. But it is also true that we can discover the ironies of the poem and its depth in time in other ways. One of them, as Mr. Whaler said in an old-fashioned article on "The Miltonic Simile" in *PMLA,* LXVI (1931), 1034–74, that anticipates much later discussion of the subject, is simply to look through a comparison like that of Satan to the sun "In dim eclipse" (I, 597) at what it plainly implies about his destiny. In a fine analysis of the baroque elements in *Paradise Lost* in *UTQ,* XIV (1945), 407, Roy Daniells treats Satan's career as the supreme illustration of Milton's power to hold "in one tense equilibrium his own strong instinct for individualistic revolt and his Christian submission to reasoned doctrine, to the revealed will of God."

60. When a ticket like "the baroque" has been fastened to Milton's style, there is a

temptation to feel that it has been brought completely under control, especially by readers who are less interested in poetry than they are in some other arts. But it is good for students who are less interested in painting and sculpture than they ought to be to read a study like Mario Praz's comparison of Milton's style with that of Poussin (in *Seventeenth Century Studies presented to Sir Herbert Grierson,* Oxford, 1938). They need not be disturbed by the fact that for Mr. Sypher the baroque artist with whom Milton has most in common is Rubens, or that for other investigators of the styles of the Renaissance he owes the sculptural power of his portraits of Adam and Eve to Michelangelo. For various reasons Milton is compared by Mr. Sypher to a dozen different Italian artists. It is impossible to see the aptness of the comparisons with them all, but it is not necessary to see the aptness of any of them to be qualified to agree with Dr. Tillyard's remark that in the painting of Poussin and Claude Loraine we have a key to the formality—the absence of "the tone of ordinary talk"—in both the dramas of Racine and in *Paradise Lost.* A landscape of Poussin is a commentary on the heroic atmosphere of Milton's Garden of Eden and on the heroic mould of Adam and Eve.

61. From the exclusive point of view of style it is possible to agree—as Mr. M. M. Ross does in *Poetry and Dogma*—that the term *baroque* applies well to Milton, and yet to deny that his art has anything in common with the spirit of the Counter-Reformation or with traditional Christianity itself. It is possible to see that Milton's style harmonizes with the Catholic tradition of worship and yet to feel that his spirit was too humanistic to share at all in the belief and experience of Dante. This involves identifying him with the movement that culminated in the empirical rationalism of John Locke and cutting him off in a fundamental way from the Christian tradition. Such an excommunication carries with it the charge that his central and symbolic images—unlike Dante's—are outside the Christian pale. For Mr. Ross the Platonic image of the tree and the implied image of the chain of being in Book V, 479–500, are applicable only to man's unfallen life in Eden and seem blasphemous when they are applied to the actual life of the world. But he is significantly silent about the invocation to Book III, the ladder of light, which is central to Milton's experience both as a poet and as a man, and which was also central in the Catholic Neo-Platonism of the Florentine School. Milton's experience had taught him that the foot of the ladder rests on the basic Christian virtue of humility. In the hard school of experience he had learned that virtue so well that—as Douglas Bush puts it in *Paradise Lost in Our Time* (p. 56)—he ended his career in a complete break from the movement that had already "inaugurated the scientific naturalism and scientific *hybris* of modern times."

62. There is one possible objection to much discussion of Milton's style as baroque or "grand." Such terms can blind us to its flexibility. It is important to notice how the manner changes from speaker to speaker in the debate in Pandemonium, how the formality and high titles drop out of Adam's conversations with Eve after the fall, how the tone of the verse changes when the subject becomes what Milton recognized as 're-demptive' in his last three books. The blank verse of the speeches in Hell in Book II is more regular than that in any of the plays of the seventeenth century. It is more formal because the speakers are superhuman and incarnate certain passions in an almost abstract way, yet it expresses personality in Moloch, Belial, and Belial's imitator, Mammon, as well as in Satan himself. It can also express impersonality. When God speaks in Book III it is not like the "School Divine" that Pope said that Milton made of him. It is like the logical and dispassionate voice of Truth itself. Milton was more aware of this flexibility in his style—decorum, as he would have called it—than he was of some other features in it that interest modern readers. To keep decorum, his contemporaries believed, that was the great art.

63. There is a question on which some oblique light may be thrown by comparison of Milton's style with the styles of the painters whom he probably admired in Italy. He was—as Dr. Johnson said two hundred years ago—evidently desirous "to use English words with a foreign idiom." Dr. Johnson did not like Latinisms such as "was walkt" (VII, 503), where a verb which does not work well in the passive voice and in an impersonal construction is used passively and impersonally because the usage was frequent in Latin. It probably seemed to him wilfully quaint to use *intelligent* in its Latin sense of "knowledgeable about" something, as Milton uses it of the mysteriously "prudent crane" in VII, 427. Presumably, Dr. Johnson disliked Grecisms such as "Adam the goodliest man of men since born" (IX, 644) as a casual way of mentioning even the only man who was ever created perfect. None of us may be quite prepared to understand a Hebraism like "the Tree of prohibition" (IX, 644) when Milton applies it to the Tree of Knowledge. For many readers such things are annoying even after they have learned from Mr. Empson in *Seven Types of Ambiguity* that many of Milton's poetic doublings of the meanings of his words come from his habit of using many of them in combinations of their Latin and English senses. But are we sure that Milton had a special fondness for Latin even though he wrote a great deal of it for publication? Excellent and powerful though his Latin style was, it was not quite idiomatic in the sense that it represented spoken Latin or even the colloquial element in the style of Ovid or any other Roman poet. In that way he also wrote a little Greek verse, and a very little Hebrew.

From William Cuningham's *Cosmographicall Glasse* (London, 1599).

64. We are not perfectly sure what language made the greatest impact on the style of *Paradise Lost*. The question is not merely academic. Too many people have been sure that Milton's style was fundamentally bad because it is "Latinate." What if it is fundamentally something else? Dr. Johnson thought it was Italianate and said that "the disposition of his words was frequently Italian"—that the strongest influence on his style was that of "the Tuscan poets." In a study that was suggested by Johnson's *Life of Milton*, Mr. F. T. Prince actually finds reason to believe that Johnson was right. He finds good evidence that both practising poets and critics in Italy had been preaching and practising what Milton himself said was the first essential of blank verse: "the sense variously drawn out from one verse to another." Milton's striking habit of placing a noun between two adjectives—

Two of far nobler shape erect and tall,
Godlike erect—

(IV, 288–289)

seems to Mr. Prince to have been taught him by the Italian sonneteers from Petrarch down to Giovanni della Casa. Other devices for suspending the logical word-order so as to diffuse the sense through several successive lines appear to have been suggested to Milton by the Italians. So do the puns, and so does the theory that poets should pun and ought to make their puns out of the differences between the meanings of their words in everyday life and the meanings of the Latin and Greek words from which they were obviously derived. And as Mr. A. M. Clark suggests, the theories of the Italians played a part in Milton's preference for blank verse over rhyme.

65. The Muse that Milton invoked seems to have allowed us a glimpse into his secret by consenting to let us call him—at least tentatively—a baroque artist and a stylist whose ideals of the language of heroic poetry were consciously Italian. But if we think that we have penetrated very far into his secret, we should go back and reread the invocation to light at the beginning of the third book of *Paradise Lost*.

A Bibliography of Books Dealing Mainly with Paradise Lost *and Published Since 1934*

Adams, Robert Martin. *IKON: John Milton and the Modern Critics.* Ithaca, 1955.

Allen, Don Cameron. *The Harmonious Vision: Studies in Milton's Poetry.* Baltimore, 1954.

Banks, Theodore. *Milton's Imagery.* New York, 1950.

Belloc, Hilaire. *Milton.* Philadelphia and London, 1935.

Bowra, C. M. *From Virgil to Milton.* London, 1945

Broadbent, J. B. *Some Graver Subject. An Essay on Paradise Lost.* London, 1960.

Bush, Douglas. *"Paradise Lost" in our Time: Some Comments.* New York, 1945.

———. *The Renaissance and English Humanism.* Toronto, 1939.

Cawley, Robert R. *Milton and the Literature of Travel.* Princeton, 1952.

Chinol, Elio. *Il Dramma divino e il Dramma umano nel Paradiso Perduto.* Naples, 1957.

Conklin, George Newton. *Biblical Criticism and Heresy in Milton.* New York, 1949.

Corcoran, Sister M. I. *Milton's Paradise with reference to the Hexaemeral Background.* Chicago, 1945.

Curry, Walter Clyde. *Milton's Ontology, Cosmogony, and Physics.* Lexington, Ky., 1957.

Daiches, David. *Milton.* London, 1956.

Diekhoff, John S. *Milton's "Paradise Lost": A Commentary on the Argument.* New York, 1946.

Frye, Roland Mushat. *God, Man, and Satan. Patterns of Christian Thought and Life in Paradise Lost, Pilgrim's Progress, and the Great Theologians.* Princeton, 1960.

Gilbert, Allan H. *On the Composition of "Paradise Lost."* Chapel Hill, 1947.

Grierson, Sir Herbert J. C. *Milton and Wordsworth: Poets and Prophets.* Cambridge, 1937.

Grün, Richard Heinrich. *Das Menschenbild John Miltons in Paradise Lost. Eine Interpretation seines Epos im Lichte des Begriffes 'Disobedience.'* Heidelberg, 1956.

Hamilton, G. Rostrevor. *Hero or Fool?* London, 1944.

Hanford, James H. *John Milton, Englishman.* New York, 1949.

Harding, Davis P. *Milton and the Renaissance Ovid.* Urbana, 1946.

Hutchinson, F. E. *Milton and the English Mind.* London, 1946.

Kelley, Maurice. *This Great Argument: A Study of Milton's "De Doctrina Christiana" as a Gloss upon "Paradise Lost."* Princeton, 1941.

Kermode, Frank, ed. *The Living Milton.* London, 1960.

Kirkconnell, Watson. *The Celestial Cycle.* Toronto, 1952.

Knight, G. Wilson. *The Burning Oracle.* London, 1939.

———. *Chariot of Wrath: The Message of John Milton to Democracy at War.* London, 1942.

Kurth, Burton O. *Milton and Christian Heroism. Biblical Epic Themes and Forms in Seventeenth Century England.* Berkeley, 1959.

Le Comte, Edward S. *Yet Once More.* New York, 1953.

Lewis, Clive S. *A Preface to "Paradise Lost."* London, 1942.

Looten, Canon, C. *J. Milton: quelques aspects de son génie.* Lille and Paris, 1938.

MacCaffrey, Isabel Gamble. *Paradise Lost as 'Myth.'* Cambridge, Massachusetts, 1959.

Madsen, William G. "The Idea of Nature in Milton's Poetry," in *Three Studies in the Renaissance: Sidney, Jonson, Milton.* New Haven, 1958.

Mahood, M. M. *Poetry and Humanism.* London, 1950.

McColley, Grant. *"Paradise Lost": An Account of its Growth and Major Origins, with a Discussion of Milton's Use of Sources and Literary Patterns.* Chicago, 1940.

McDill, Joseph M. *Milton and the Pattern of Calvinism.* Nashville, 1942.

Mody, Jehangir R. P. *Vondel and Milton.* Bombay, 1942.

Mohl, Ruth. *Studies in Spenser, Milton, and the Theory of Monarchy.* New York, 1949.

Muir, Kenneth. *John Milton.* London, 1955.

Nazari, Emilio. *Problemi miltoniani.* Palermo, 1952.

Nicolson, Marjorie. *A World in the Moon.* Smith College Studies in Modern Languages XVII, 1936.

Oras, Ants. *Notes on some Miltonic Usages.* Tartu, 1938.

Peter, John. *A Critique of Paradise Lost.* New York, 1960.

Phelps-Morand, Paul. *De Comus à Satan.* Paris, 1939.

Pommer, Henry F. *Milton and Melville.* Pittsburgh, 1950.

Prince, F. T. *The Italian Elements in Milton's Verse.* Oxford, 1954.

Rajan, B. *"Paradise Lost" and the Seventeenth Century Reader.* London, 1947.

Ross, Malcolm M. *Milton's Royalism: A Study of the Conflict of Symbolism and Idea in the Poems.* Ithaca, 1943.

———. *Poetry and Dogma: The Transfiguration of Eucharist Symbols in Seventeenth Century English Poetry.* New Brunswick, 1954.

SAMLA Studies in Milton, edited by Max Patrick. Gainesville, 1953.

Samuel, Irene. *Plato and Milton.* Ithaca, 1947.

Saurat, Denis. *Milton: Man and Thinker.* New York, 1925. Second edition, London, 1946.

Schultz, Howard. *Milton and Forbidden Knowledge.* New York, 1955.

Sewell, Arthur. *A Study in Milton's "Christian Doctrine."* London, 1939.

Smith, Logan Pearsall. *Milton and his Modern Critics.* London, 1940.

Sprott, S. Ernest. *Milton's Art of Prosody.* Oxford, 1953.

Starnes, DeWitt T., and Talbert, Ernest W. *Classical Myth and Legend in Renaissance Dictionaries.* Chapel Hill, 1955.

Stein, Arnold. *Answerable Style: Essays on "Paradise Lost."* Minneapolis, 1953.

Studies in Milton: Essays in Memory of Elbert N. S. Thompson. Philological Quarterly XXVIII (1949). Iowa City, 1949.

Svendsen, Kester. *Milton and Science.* Cambridge, 1956.

Thorpe, James. *Milton Criticism: Selections from Four Centuries.* New York, 1950.
Tillyard, E. M. W. *Milton.* London, 1930. Second edition, 1949.
———. *Studies in Milton.* London, 1951.
———. *The Miltonic Setting, Past and Present.* Cambridge, 1938.
———. *The Metaphysicals and Milton.* London, 1956.
Waldock, A. J. A. *"Paradise Lost" and its Critics.* Cambridge, 1947.
Warner, Rex. *John Milton.* London, 1949.
Watkins, W. B. C. *An Anatomy of Milton's Verse.* Baton Rouge, 1955.
Werblowski, R. J. Zwi. *Lucifer and Prometheus: A Study of Milton's Satan.* London, 1952.
West, Robert H. *Milton and the Angels.* Athens, 1955.
Whaler, James. *Counterpoint and Symbol: An Inquiry into the Rhythm of Milton's Epic Style.* Anglistica, Vol. VI. Copenhagen, 1956.
Whiting, George W. *Milton and this Pendant World.* Austin, 1958.
———. *Milton's Literary Milieu.* Chapel Hill, 1939.
Williams, Arnold. *The Common Expositor.* Chapel Hill, 1948.

Some Outstanding Editions of Paradise Lost Since 1935

The Poems of John Milton, with introduction and notes by J. H. Hanford. New York, 1936. Second edition, 1953.
Complete Poems of John Milton, with complete notes by Thomas Newton, illustrated by Gustave Doré and others. New York, 1936.
"Paradise Lost" and "Paradise Regained," by John Milton, with an introduction by William Rose Benét and illustrations by Carlotta Petrina. San Francisco, 1936.
Complete Poetry and Selected Prose of John Milton edited by E. H. Visiak. London and New York, 1938.
Paradise Lost, by John Milton, with the illustrations of William Blake: printed in color for the first time and with prefaces by Philip Hofer and John T. Winterich. New York, 1940.
The Poetical Works of Milton, edited by Charles Williams. London (The World's Classics), 1940.
The Complete Poetical Works of John Milton, edited by Harris Fletcher. Boston, 1941.
Complete Poetry and Selected Prose of John Milton. New York (Modern Library), 1942.
Complete Poetical Works of John Milton, reproduced in photographic facsimile by Harris Fletcher. Urbana, 1943.
"Paradise Lost," and other poems by John Milton, edited by Maurice Kelley. New York, 1943.
"Paradise Lost" and other poems by John Milton, edited by Northrop Frye. New York, 1951.
The Portable Milton, edited by Douglas Bush. New York, 1949.
The Poetical Works of John Milton, edited by Helen Darbishire. Vol. I. *Paradise Lost.* Oxford, 1952. Vol. II. *"Paradise Regain'd," "Samson Agonistes," "Poems upon Several Occasions,"* both English and Latin. Oxford, 1955.
Milton's Poems. Textual editing, Glossary, and Introduction by B. A. Wright. London, 1956. Everyman's Library.

Gul. Faithorne ad Vivum   Delin. et sculpsit.

Joannis Miltoni Effigies Ætat: 62.
1670.

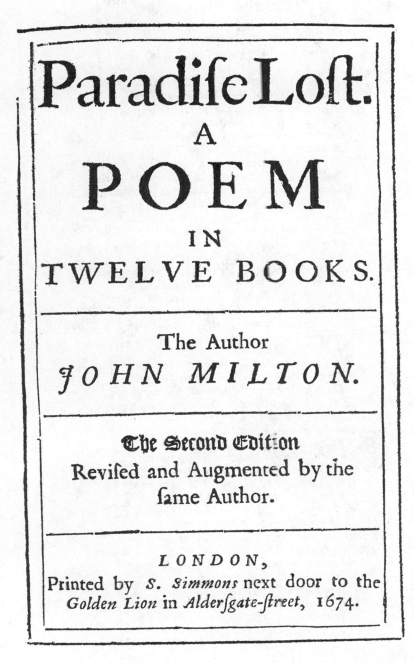

Paradiſe Loſt.

A
POEM
IN
TWELVE BOOKS.

The Author
JOHN MILTON.

𝕿𝖍𝖊 𝕾𝖊𝖈𝖔𝖓𝖉 𝕰𝖉𝖎𝖙𝖎𝖔𝖓
Reviſed and Augmented by the
ſame Author.

LONDON,
Printed by *S. Simmons* next door to the
Golden Lion in *Alderſgate-ſtreet,* 1674.

IN
PARADISUM AMISSAM

SUMMI POETÆ

JOHANNIS MILTONI

Qui legis Amissam Paradisum, grandia magni
  Carmina *Miltoni, quid nisi cuncta legis?*
Res cunctas, & cunctarum primordia rerum,
  Et fata, & fines continet iste liber.
Intima panduntur magni penetralia mundi,
  Scribitur & toto quicquid in Orbe latet.
Terræque, tractusque maris, cælumque profundum,
  Sulphureumque Erebi flammivomumque specus.
Quæque colunt terras, Pontumque & Tartara cæca,
  Qæque colunt summi lucida regna Poli.
Et quodcunque ullis conclusum est finibus usquam,
  Et sine fine Chaos, & sine fine Deus;
Et sine fine magis, si quid magis est sine fine,
  In Christo erga homines conciliatus amor.
Hæc qui speraret quis crederet esse futurum?
  Et tamen hæc hodie terra Britanna *legit.*
O quantos in bella Duces! quæ protulit arma!
  Quæ canit, et quanta prælia dira tuba.
Cælestes acies! atque in certamine Cælum!
  Et quæ Cælestes pugna deceret agros!
Quantus in ætheriis tollit se Lucifer armis!
  Atque ipso graditur vix Michaële minor!
Quantis, & quam funestis concurritur iris
  Dum ferus hic stellas protegit, ille rapit!
Dum vulsos Montes ceu Tela reciproca torquent,
  Et non mortali desuper igne pluunt:
Stat dubius cui se parti concedat Olympus,
  Et metuit pugnæ non superesse suæ.
At simul in cælis Messiæ insignia fulgent,
  Et currus animes, armaque digna Deo,
Horrendumque rotæ strident, & sæva rotarum
  Erumpunt torvis fulgura luminibus,
Et flammæ vibrant, & vera tonitrua rauco
  Admistis flammis insonuere Polo:
Excidit attonitis mens omnis, & impetus omnis
  Et cassis dextris irrita Tela *cadunt.*
Ad pœnas fugiunt, & ceu foret Orcus asylum
  Infernis certant condere se tenebris.
Cedite Romani *scriptores, cedite* Graii
  Et quos fama recens vel celebravit anus.
Hæc quicunque leget tantum cecinisse putabit
  Mæonidem ranas, Virgilium *culices.*

S. B., M. D.

ON
PARADISE LOST

When I beheld the Poet blind, yet bold,
In slender Book his vast Design unfold,
Messiah Crown'd, God's Reconcil'd Decree,
Rebelling Angels, the Forbidden Tree,
Heav'n, Hell, Earth, Chaos, All; the Argument
Held me a while misdoubting his Intent,
That he would ruin (for I saw him strong)
The sacred Truths to Fable and old Song
(So *Sampson* grop'd the Temple's Posts in spite)
The World o'erwhelming to revenge his sight.
    Yet as I read, soon growing less severe,
I lik'd his Project, the success did fear;
Through that wide Field how he his way should find
O'er which lame Faith leads Understanding blind;
Lest he perplex'd the things he would explain,
And what was easy he should render vain.
    Or if a Work so infinite he spann'd,
Jealous I was that some less skilful hand
(Such as disquiet always what is well,
And by ill imitating would excel)
Might hence presume the whole Creation's day
To change in Scenes, and show it in a Play.
    Pardon me, Mighty Poet, nor despise
My causeless, yet not impious, surmise.
But I am now convinc'd, and none will dare
Within thy Labours to pretend a share.
Thou hast not miss'd one thought that could be fit,
And all that was improper dost omit:
So that no room is here for Writers left,
But to detect their Ignorance or Theft.
    That Majesty which through thy Work doth Reign
Draws the Devout, deterring the Profane.
And things divine thou treat'st of in such state
As them preserves, and thee, inviolate
At once delight and horror on us seize,
Thou sing'st with so much gravity and ease;
And above human flight dost soar aloft
With Plume so strong, so equal, and so soft.
The Bird nam'd from that Paradise you sing
So never flags, but always keeps on Wing.
    Where couldst thou words of such a compass find?
Whence furnish such a vast expense of mind?
Just Heav'n thee like *Tiresias* to requite
Rewards with Prophecy thy loss of sight.
    Well mightst thou scorn thy Readers to allure
With tinkling Rime, of thy own sense secure;
While the *Town-Bayes* writes all the while and spells,
And like a Pack-horse tires without his Bells:
Their Fancies like our Bushy-points appear,
The Poets tag them, we for fashion wear.

I too transported by the Mode offend,
And while I meant to Praise thee must Commend.
Thy Verse created like thy Theme sublime,
In Number, Weight, and Measure, needs not Rime.

A. M. [Andrew Marvell]

THE PRINTER TO THE READER

Courteous Reader, There was no Argument at first intended to the Book, but for the satisfaction of many that have desired it, I have procured it, and withal a reason of that which stumbled many others, why the Poem Rimes not.

THE VERSE

The measure is *English* Heroic Verse without Rime, as that of *Homer* in *Greek,* and of *Virgil* in *Latin;* Rime being no necessary Adjunct or true Ornament of Poem or good Verse, in longer Works especially, but the Invention of a barbarous Age, to set off wretched matter and lame Meter; grac't indeed since by the use of some famous modern Poets, carried away by Custom, but much to thir own vexation, hindrance, and constraint to express many things otherwise, and for the most part worse than else they would have exprest them. Not without cause therefore some both *Italian* and *Spanish* Poets of prime note have rejected Rime both in longer and shorter Works, as have also long since our best *English* Tragedies, as a thing of itself, to all judicious ears, trivial and of no true musical delight; which consists only in apt Numbers, fit quantity of Syllables, and the sense variously drawn out from one Verse into another, not in the jingling sound of like endings, a fault avoided by the learned Ancients both in Poetry and all good Oratory. This neglect then of Rime so little is to be taken for a defect, though it may seem so perhaps to vulgar Readers, that it rather is to be esteem'd an example set, the first in *English,* of ancient liberty recover'd to Heroic Poem from the troublesome and modern bondage of Riming.

Paradise Lost

BOOK I

THE ARGUMENT

This first Book proposes, first in brief, the whole Subject, *Man's disobedience, and the loss thereupon of Paradise wherein he was plac't:* Then touches *the prime cause of his fall, the Serpent, or rather* Satan *in the Serpent; who revolting from God, and drawing to his side many Legions of Angels, was by the command of God driven out of Heaven with all his Crew into the great Deep.* Which action past over, the Poem hastes into the midst of things, presenting *Satan with his Angels now fallen into Hell,* describ'd here, *not in the Centre* (for Heaven and Earth may be suppos'd as yet not made, certainly not yet accurst) *but in a place of utter darkness, fitliest call'd* Chaos: *Here* Satan *with his Angels lying on the burning Lake, thunder-struck and astonisht, after a certain space recovers, as from confusion, calls up him who next in Order and Dignity lay by him; they confer of thir miserable fall.* Satan *awakens all his Legions, who lay till then in the same manner confounded; They rise, thir Numbers, array of Battle, thir chief Leaders nam'd, according to the Idols known afterwards in* Canaan *and the Countries adjoining. To these* Satan *directs his Speech, comforts them with hope yet of regaining Heaven, but tells them lastly of a new World and new kind of Creature to be created, according to an ancient Prophecy or report in Heaven; for that* Angels were long before this visible Creation, was the opinion of many ancient Fathers. *To find out the truth of this Prophecy, and what to determine thereon he refers to a full Council. What his Associates thence attempt.* Pandemonium *the Palace of* Satan *rises, suddenly built out of the Deep: The infernal Peers there sit in Council.*

> Of Man's First Disobedience, and the Fruit
> Of that Forbidden Tree, whose mortal taste
> Brought Death into the World, and all our woe,
> With loss of *Eden,* till one greater Man
> Restore us, and regain the blissful Seat,   *holy spirit.*   5
> Sing Heav'nly Muse, that on the secret top
> Of *Oreb,* or of *Sinai,* didst inspire
> That Shepherd, who first taught the chosen Seed,
> In the Beginning how the Heav'ns and Earth
> Rose out of *Chaos:* Or if *Sion* Hill   10
> Delight thee more, and *Siloa's* Brook that flow'd
> Fast by the Oracle of God; I thence
> Invoke thy aid to my advent'rous Song,

1–4. *Man* is emphatically repeated in a way that recalls the stress upon the corresponding words in the opening lines of the *Odyssey* and *Aeneid* and the conviction of Milton's contemporaries that epic poetry should portray a "vertuous man," as Spenser said—in the letter to Raleigh introducing *The Faerie Queene*—that Homer did "in the persons of Agamemnon and Ulysses." Milton's purpose is to draw two perfect men, Adam and the "greater man," the Son of God, whose portrayal is complete only in *PR.* The tradition culminating in these lines is illuminated by R. W. Condee in *JEGP,* L (1951), 502–8 on its formal side, and on

its theological side by L. A. Cormican in *From Donne to Marvell,* ed. by Boris Ford (London, 1956), pp. 176–9.

6–17. For the *Heav'nly Muse,* the Urania of VII, 1, see the Introduction 54–57.

7–8. The *Shepherd* is Moses, who received the Law on Mount *Oreb* or its spur, Mount *Sinai,* for the *chosen Seed,* the children of Israel (Exod. xix-xx). Cf. XII, 227–30; and the Introduction 55.

10–11. To be understood, *Chaos* must be explored with Satan in II, 890–1053. Cf. *Sion* and *Siloa* in III, 29–31, n.

That with no middle flight intends to soar
Above th' *Aonian* Mount, while it pursues   — end of first sentence 15
Things unattempted yet in Prose or Rhyme.
And chiefly Thou O Spirit, that dost prefer
Before all Temples th' upright heart and pure,
Instruct me, for Thou know'st; Thou from the first
Wast present, and with mighty wings outspread   20
Dove-like satst brooding on the vast Abyss
And mad'st it pregnant: What in me is dark
Illumine, what is low raise and support;
That to the highth of this great Argument
I may assert Eternal Providence,   25
And justify the ways of God to men.

   Say first, for Heav'n hides nothing from thy view
Nor the deep Tract of Hell, say first what cause
Mov'd our Grand Parents in that happy State,
Favor'd of Heav'n so highly, to fall off   30
From thir Creator, and transgress his Will
For one restraint, Lords of the World besides?
Who first seduc'd them to that foul revolt?
Th' infernal Serpent; hee it was, whose guile
Stirr'd up with Envy and Revenge, deceiv'd   35
The Mother of Mankind; what time his Pride
Had cast him out from Heav'n, with all his Host
Of Rebel Angels, by whose aid aspiring
To set himself in Glory above his Peers,
He trusted to have equall'd the most High,   40
If he oppos'd; and with ambitious aim
Against the Throne and Monarchy of God
Rais'd impious War in Heav'n and Battle proud
With vain attempt. Him the Almighty Power
Hurl'd headlong flaming from th' Ethereal Sky   45
With hideous ruin and combustion down
To bottomless perdition, there to dwell
In Adamantine Chains and penal Fire,
Who durst defy th' Omnipotent to Arms.
Nine times the Space that measures Day and Night   50
To mortal men, hee with his horrid crew
Lay vanquisht, rolling in the fiery Gulf
Confounded though immortal: But his doom

16. The line ironically paraphrases Ariosto's opening of the *Orlando Furioso*. The reason why is explained in IX, 29–31, n.

21. *Abyss* was the word used by the translators of the Old Testament into Greek for the Hebrew word translated as "the deep" in Genesis i, 2. Cf. II, 405.

24. *Argument* is used, as it more evidently is used in IX, 28, to mean the subject and development of the poem—not to refer only to the justification of God's ways. See the Introduction 46.

33. So Homer (*Il.* I, 8) asks who it was that brought discord among the Greeks and instantly answers that it was Apollo.

34. *Th' Infernal Serpent* here and in XII, 383, is "that old serpent, which is the Devil, and Satan" (Rev. xx, 2–3) more distinctly than he is the serpent seducer of Eve. He is *infernal* in the literal sense that he is doomed to the punishment of hell or "the bottomless pit," where Milton imagines all the devils as dramatically turned into serpents (X, 509–40).

38. The first of the rare lines ending in an unstressed, redundant syllable. Less than one per cent of the lines in *PL* have feminine endings.

45–48. The lines blend biblical associations stretching from Isaiah xiv, 12—"How art thou fallen from heaven, O Lucifer, son of the morning" —to the picture of "the angels which kept not their first estate . . . in everlasting chains, under darkness," in Jude i, 6.

50. Here and in VI, 871, the devils fall for as many days as Hesiod (*Theog.*, 664–735) gives for the Titans' fall from heaven after their overthrow by the Olympian gods. See the Introduction 15–16, and l. 74 below.

Reserv'd him to more wrath; for now the thought
Both of lost happiness and lasting pain   55
Torments him; round he throws his baleful eyes
That witness'd huge affliction and dismay
Mixt with obdúrate pride and steadfast hate:
At once as far as Angels' ken he views
The dismal Situation waste and wild.   60
A Dungeon horrible, on all sides round
As one great Furnace flam'd, yet from those flames
No light, but rather darkness visible
Serv'd only to discover sights of woe
Regions of sorrow, doleful shades, where peace   65
And rest can never dwell, hope never comes
That comes to all; but torture without end
Still urges, and a fiery Deluge, fed
With ever-burning Sulphur unconsum'd:
Such place Eternal Justice had prepar'd   70
For those rebellious, here thir Prison ordained
In utter darkness, and thir portion set
As far remov'd from God and light of Heav'n
As from the Center thrice to th' utmost Pole.
O how unlike the place from whence they fell!   75
There the companions of his fall, o'erwhelm'd
With Floods and Whirlwinds of tempestuous fire,
He soon discerns, and welt'ring by his side
One next himself in power, and next in crime,
Long after known in *Palestine,* and nam'd   80
Beëlzebub. To whom th' Arch-Enemy,
And thence in Heav'n call'd Satan, with bold words
Breaking the horrid silence thus began.
   If thou beest hee; But O how fall'n! how chang'd
From him, who in the happy Realms of Light   85
Cloth'd with transcendent brightness didst outshine
Myriads though bright: If he whom mutual league,
United thoughts and counsels, equal hope,

---

59. Early editions are irregular in their use of the apostrophe to indicate the possessive case, which is lacking in them after *Angels*. It is inserted here on the assumption that *ken* is a noun and is used as it is in XI, 379.

63. The thought goes back to Job's description of the world of the dead as a realm where "the light is darkness" (x, 22). See the Introduction 23.

66. A deliberate echo of Dante's inscription over Hell's gate—"All hope abandon ye who enter here" (*Inf.* III, 9)—is unmistakable.

70. No less explicitly, Dante made hell the creation of divine justice, power, wisdom, and love (*Inf.* III, 4–6).

73–74. So heaven towers up to the celestial north pole in a passage of Aratus' *Phainomena* which Cicero paraphased in *On the Nature of the Gods* (II, xl–xli), but the scene directly recalls Virgil's picture of Avernus as *twice* as far under the earth as heaven is above (*Aen.* VI, 577–79). Cf. V, 503, n.

81. The wavering traditions behind Beelzebub's title of "chief of the devils" in Matthew x, 25 (cf.

Mark iii, 22, and Luke xi, 15) were skeptically reviewed by Milton's friend, John Selden, in his *Syrian Gods* (*De Dis Syris* syntagmata II—London, 1617—II, b), and the literal meaning of the name, "god of flies," was compared with some titles of Jupiter and other deities who were sometimes worshipped as deliverers from insect pests, or as lords of altars that were either avoided or infested by flies. For Milton's readers Beelzebub was vaguely the prince of the first order of demons that Burton made him in the *Anatomy* (I, ii, 1, 2; Everyman Ed. I, p. 187) or the monarch of flaming hell that Marlowe made him in Faust's first invocation in *Doctor Faustus.* R. H. West notes in *The Invisible World* (Athens, 1939), p. 69 that in the *Occult Philosophy* of Cornelius Agrippa Beelzebub was, in general, any demon engaged in the "false assumption of godhead." In X, 386–87, the literal meaning of *Satan* is again stressed.

84–85. Satan's first words recall Aeneas' vision of the ghost of Hector on the night of Troy's fall— so changed from the living Hector beside whom he had fought against the Greeks (*Aen.* II, 275–76).

And hazard in the Glorious Enterprise,
Join'd with me once, now misery hath join'd   90
In equal ruin: into what Pit thou seest
From what highth fall'n, so much the stronger prov'd
He with his Thunder: and till then who knew
The force of those dire Arms? yet not for those,
Nor what the Potent Victor in his rage   95
Can else inflict, do I repent or change,
Though chang'd in outward luster; that fixt mind
And high disdain, from sense of injur'd merit,
That with the mightiest rais'd me to contend,
And to the fierce contention brought along   100
Innumerable force of Spirits arm'd
That durst dislike his reign, and mee preferring,
His utmost power with adverse power oppos'd
In dubious Battle on the Plains of Heav'n,
And shook his throne. What though the field be lost?   105
All is not lost; the unconquerable Will,
And study of revenge, immortal hate,
And courage never to submit or yield:
And what is else not to be overcome?
That Glory never shall his wrath or might   110
Extort from me. To bow and sue for grace
With suppliant knee, and deify his power
Who from the terror of this Arm so late
Doubted his Empire, that were low indeed,
That were an ignominy and shame beneath   115
This downfall; since by Fate the strength of Gods
And this Empyreal substance cannot fail,
Since through experience of this great event
In Arms not worse, in foresight much advanc't,
We may with more successful hope resolve   120
To wage by force or guile eternal War
Irreconcilable to our grand Foe,
Who now triúmphs, and in th' excess of joy
Sole reigning holds the Tyranny of Heav'n.
    So spake th' Apostate Angel, though in pain,   125
Vaunting aloud, but rackt with deep despair:
And him thus answer'd soon his bold Compeer.
    O Prince, O Chief of many Throned Powers,
That led th' imbattl'd Seraphim to War

[handwritten marginalia: implying he might have never rebelled.]
[handwritten marginalia: possible]
[handwritten marginalia: ? with bracket]
[handwritten marginalia: rude Will is all he has left.]
[handwritten marginalia: what Glory?]
[handwritten marginalia: =blasphemy]

94–97. A possible echo of Capaneus' boast in
Inferno XIV, 52–91, that Jove's thunder would never
break his blasphemous spirit, or of the warning of
Aeschylus' Prometheus to Hermes (*Prom.*, 987–96)
that he would never yield to Zeus though the god
might buffet him with thunder and snow forever.
A traditionally exaggerated view of Satan as a magnificently Promethean hero has suggested several
other doubtful parallels between their speeches.

98. Contrast Satan's assertion of *merit* here and
in II, 6 and 21, with the merit that makes Christ
"more than birthright Son of God" (III, 309) and
entitles him to reign in heaven (VI, 43).

114. *Doubted:* feared for.

115. *ignominy:* probably pronounced "ignomy"
here and in II, 207, though not in VI, 383.
"Ignomy" was a common spelling.

116. Compare the unwilling recognition of the
supremacy of fate by Belial (II, 197), Mammon
(II, 231–33), and Beelzebub (II, 393) with Sin's
certainty that fate has doomed her and Death to a
common end (II, 805–807), and God's declaration
that His will is fate (VII, 173).

Though the angels are sometimes called "gods"
(even by God Himself in III, 341), J. C. Maxwell
marks Satan's use of the word here as "redolent of
paganism; and Beelzebub, in echoing his master,
implies the same error"—*N&Q*, CXCIII (1948),
234–45. The speeches anticipate Satan's claim (V,
853–66) that the devils are self-begotten and his
promise to Eve (IX, 708) that by eating the forbidden fruit she and Adam should "be as gods."
See the Introduction 20.

129. *Seraphim* is the Hebrew plural form. In

Under thy conduct, and in dreadful deeds   130
Fearless, endanger'd Heav'n's perpetual King;
And put to proof his high Supremacy,
Whether upheld by strength, or Chance, or Fate;
Too well I see and rue the dire event,
That with sad overthrow and foul defeat   135
Hath lost us Heav'n, and all this mighty Host
In horrible destruction laid thus low,
As far as Gods and Heav'nly Essences
Can perish: for the mind and spirit remains
Invincible, and vigor soon returns,   140
Though all our Glory extinct, and happy state
Here swallow'd up in endless misery.
But what if he our Conqueror (whom I now
Of force believe Almighty, since no less
Than such could have o'erpow'rd such force as ours)   145
Have left us this our spirit and strength entire
Strongly to suffer and support our pains,
That we may so suffice his vengeful ire,
Or do him mightier service as his thralls
By right of War, whate'er his business be   150
Here in the heart of Hell to work in Fire,
Or do his Errands in the gloomy Deep;
What can it then avail though yet we feel
Strength undiminisht, or eternal being
To undergo eternal punishment?   155
Whereto with speedy words th' Arch-fiend repli'd.
    Fall'n Cherub, to be weak is miserable
Doing or Suffering: but of this be sure,
To do aught good never will be our task,
But ever to do ill our sole delight,   160
As being the contrary to his high will
Whom we resist. If then his Providence
Out of our evil seek to bring forth good,
Our labor must be to pervert that end,
And out of good still to find means of evil;   165
Which oft-times may succeed, so as perhaps
Shall grieve him, if I fail not, and disturb
His inmost counsels from thir destin'd aim.
But see the angry Victor hath recall'd
His Ministers of vengeance and pursuit   170
Back to the Gates of Heav'n: the Sulphurous Hail
Shot after us in storm, o'erblown hath laid
The fiery Surge, that from the Precipice
Of Heav'n receiv'd us falling, and the Thunder,
Wing'd with red Lightning and impetuous rage,   175
Perhaps hath spent his shafts, and ceases now

---

the *Christian Doctrine* (I, vii) Milton quotes Christ's
description of Satan falling from heaven "like lightning" to explain the literal meaning of the word
seraphim (C.E., XV, 35).

148. Beelzebub's words recall Milton's (*CD*, I, ix)
description of the bad angels as "sometimes permitted to wander throughout the whole earth, the
air, the heaven itself, to execute the judgments of
God" (C.E. XV, 109).

158. *doing or suffering:* Cf. II, 199, n., and *PR*
III, 195.

162–168. Satan's dramatic resolve and self-
characterization here and in IX, 118–30, prepare for
the final discovery, in Adam's words, that God shall
produce all the good to be worked in the world by
the Son's redemption of Adam's sin, and so "evil
turn to good" (XII, 471).

To bellow through the vast and boundless Deep.
Let us not slip th' occasion, whether scorn,
Or satiate fury yield it from our Foe.
Seest thou yon dreary Plain, forlorn and wild,   180
The seat of desolation, void of light,
Save what the glimmering of these livid flames
Casts pale and dreadful? Thither let us tend
From off the tossing of these fiery waves,
There rest, if any rest can harbor there,   185
And reassembling our afflicted Powers,
Consult how we may henceforth most offend
Our Enemy, our own loss how repair,
How overcome this dire Calamity,
What reinforcement we may gain from Hope,   190
If not what resolution from despair.
     Thus Satan talking to his nearest Mate
With Head up-lift above the wave, and Eyes
That sparkling blaz'd, his other Parts besides
Prone on the Flood, extended long and large   195
Lay floating many a rood, in bulk as huge
As whom the Fables name of monstrous size,
Titanian, or *Earth-born*, that warr'd on *Jove*,
Briareos or *Typhon*, whom the Den
By ancient *Tarsus* held, or that Sea-beast   200
Leviathan, which God of all his works
Created hugest that swim th' Ocean stream:
Him haply slumb'ring on the *Norway* foam
The Pilot of some small night-founder'd Skiff,
Deeming some Island, oft, as Seamen tell,   205
With fixed Anchor in his scaly rind
Moors by his side under the Lee, while Night
Invests the Sea, and wished Morn delays:
So stretcht out huge in length the Arch-fiend lay
Chain'd on the burning Lake, nor ever thence   210
Had ris'n or heav'd his head, but that the will
And high permission of all-ruling Heaven
Left him at large to his own dark designs,
That with reiterated crimes he might

180–188. The livid darkness recalls descriptions of hell as diverse as Statius' picture of the shadowy "Styx livida" (*Thebaid* I, 57), Dante's picture of the place where all light is "silent" (*Inf.* V, 28), and the fiery but lightless land described in Caedmon's *Genesis* (333–34).

186. *afflicted* has its Latin force of "stricken" or "overthrown."

197. In the war of the Titans with the Olympian gods the hundred-armed *Briareos* is described by Hesiod (*Theog.*, 713–16) as helping to defeat his brother Titans. For the parallel with the revolt of Satan's angels see the Introduction. Hesiod's story of *Typhon* or Typhoeus as the most frightful of Earth-born monsters (*Theog.*, 819–85) whom Zeus hurled back from Olympus and Ovid's description of him as buried alive under Aetna and neighboring mountains (*Met.* V, 346–58), were typically allegorized by Natale Conti (*Mythologiae* liber VI, xxii) as symbolizing ambition that assails even heaven itself, is as fiery-mouthed as Aetna, and has as many violent

plots as Typhon had serpent-heads. The parallel between him and Satan is traced back by Conti to Theodorus *De Bello Giganteo*. See the Introduction 16.

201–209. Of all the biblical allusions to the mysterious sea-monster Leviathan, the closest is Isaiah's prophecy that the Lord "shall punish Leviathan, the piercing serpent, even Leviathan, that crooked serpent; and he shall slay the dragon that is in the sea" (xxvii, 1). The tale of the mariners who mistake the leviathan for an island is widespread: in the story of Sinbad the sailor in the Arabian nights, in Olaus Magnus' *Historia de gentibus septentrionalibus* (Rome, 1555), in Caxton's *Mirrour of the World* (II, ix), in Bartholemew's *De proprietatibus rerum* (xiii, 29), etc. See J. H. Pitman, "Milton and the Physiologus," in *MLN*, XL (1925), 439.

210–215. Milton's discussion of Scriptural evidence for the doctrine of God's blamelessness in permitting the crimes of the wicked, in *CD*, I, viii, is worth comparing here (C.E. XV, 72–73).

Heap on himself damnation, while he sought   215
Evil to others, and enrag'd might see
{How all his malice serv'd but to bring forth} — ruin satans ego
{Infinite goodness, grace and mercy shown}
On Man by him seduc't, but on himself
Treble confusion, wrath and vengeance pour'd.   220
Forthwith upright he rears from off the Pool
His mighty Stature; on each hand the flames
Driv'n backward slope thir pointing spires, and roll'd
In billows, leave i' th' midst a horrid Vale.
Then with expanded wings he steers his flight   225
Aloft, incumbent on the dusky Air
That felt unusual weight, till on dry Land
He lights, if it were Land that ever burn'd
With solid, as the Lake with liquid fire
And such appear'd in hue; as when the force   230
Of subterranean wind transports a Hill
Torn from *Pelorus,* or the shatter'd side
Of thund'ring *Ætna,* whose combustible
And fuell'd entrails thence conceiving Fire,
Sublim'd with Mineral fury, aid the Winds,   235
And leave a singed bottom all involv'd
With stench and smoke: Such resting found the sole
Of unblest feet. Him follow'd his next Mate,
Both glorying to have scap't the *Stygian* flood
As Gods, and by thir own recover'd strength,   240
Not by the sufferance of supernal Power.
   Is this the Region, this the Soil, the Clime,
Said then the lost Arch-Angel, this the seat
That we must change for Heav'n, this mournful gloom
For that celestial light? Be it so, since he   245
Who now is Sovran can dispose and bid
What shall be right: fardest from him is best
Whom reason hath equall'd, force hath made supreme
Above his equals. Farewell happy Fields
Where Joy for ever dwells: Hail horrors, hail   250
Infernal world, and thou profoundest Hell
Receive thy new Possessor: One who brings   Professor?
A mind not to be chang'd by Place or Time.
The mind is its own place, and in itself   ~ inflexible
Can make a Heav'n of Hell, a Hell of Heav'n.   255

230. *hue* is glossed as meaning "aspect" or appearance by Wright—*RES,* XXIII (1947), 146—on the strength of Milton's bracketing of it with "look" in *Of Prelatical Episcopacy.*
231–237. The lines recall Virgil's picture of Mt. Aetna darkening the peninsula of Pelorus in Sicily with its smoke (*Aen.* III, 570–77) and Ovid's account of the creation of a hill near Troezen by winds bursting out of the earth (*Met.* XV, 296–355). Ovid's seismology was still acceptable when Burton surmised in the *Anatomy of Melancholy* (II, ii, 3) that the earth might "be full of wind, or sulfureous, innate fire, as our Meteorologists inform us, which, sometimes breaking out, causeth horrible earthquakes" (Everyman Ed. II, p. 43).
235. Milton had sulphur mainly in mind as one of the three or four basic minerals of the alchemists,

for whom "sublimation" meant the refining of metals by the hottest possible fires.
239. The word is often used without reference to the Styx, the most famous of hell's rivers, to mean "infernal," but usually it connotes darkness, as here and in *Comus,* 90, and *El IV,* 95.
242. Cf. *clime* used to mean "region" in I, 297; II, 572; X, 678; and XII, 636.
246. *Sovran* was Milton's preferred spelling for *sovereign.* Cf. I, 753; II, 244, etc.
255. Satan's heresy is traced by D. C. Allen in *MLN,* LXXI (1956), 325, to Amaury de Bene, who was burned for his denial of the resurrection early in the thirteenth century. A corollary of his heresy was the doctrine that heaven and hell alike are found only in the individual's heart. The wider roots of Satan's boast are traced in *MP,* LIII (1956), 80–94,

What matter where, if I be still the same,   — but he's already admitted he has changed.
And what I should be, all but less than hee
Whom Thunder hath made greater?   Here at least
We shall be free; th' Almighty hath not built
Here for his envy, will not drive us hence: 260
Here we may reign secure, and in my choice
To reign is worth ambition though in Hell:
Better to reign in Hell, than serve in Heav'n.
But wherefore let we then our faithful friends,
Th' associates and copartners of our loss   265
Lie thus astonisht on th' oblivious Pool,
And call them not to share with us their part
In this unhappy Mansion: or once more
With rallied Arms to try what may be yet
Regain'd in Heav'n, or what more lost in Hell?   270
    So *Satan* spake, and him *Beëlzebub*
Thus answer'd. Leader of those Armies bright,
Which but th' Omnipotent none could have foiled,
If once they hear that voice, thir liveliest pledge
Of hope in fears and dangers, heard so oft   275
In worst extremes, and on the perilous edge
Of battle when it rag'd, in all assaults
Thir surest signal, they will soon resume
New courage and revive, though now they lie
Groveling and prostrate on yon Lake of Fire,   280
As we erewhile, astounded and amaz'd;
No wonder, fall'n such a pernicious highth.
    He scarce had ceas't when the superior Fiend
Was moving toward the shore; his ponderous shield
Ethereal temper, massy, large and round,   285
Behind him cast; the broad circumference
Hung on his shoulders like the Moon, whose Orb
Through Optic Glass the *Tuscan* Artist views
At Ev'ning from the top of *Fesole*,
Or in *Valdarno*, to descry new Lands,   290
Rivers or Mountains in her spotty Globe.
His Spear, to equal which the tallest Pine
Hewn on *Norwegian* hills, to be the Mast
Of some great Ammiral, were but a wand,

---

to ancient Stoic denials of a local Tartarus and of
its torments as existing anywhere but in the consciences of sinners, to Renaissance distortions of the
Stoic doctrine that the mind is master of its fate,
and to the interpretation of Christ's teaching that
"the kingdom of God is within you" by Jakob
Boehme and his disciples as meaning that "we have
heaven and hell in ourselves" (Boehme's *The Threefold Life of Man*, xiv, 72).

263. The passage contrasts with Abdiel's warning
to Satan in heaven that his reign in hell will be mere
bondage (VI, 178–88). It parodies a remark attributed to Julius Caesar by Plutarch (*Life of Caesar*,
xi, 2) that he would rather be the first man in an
Alpine village than second in Rome. Its parody by
Satan was traditional; in *Adamo caduto* (II, i) Serafino Salandra's Lucifer tells Belial that he would
rather be first (Duce) in hell than a mere prince
in heaven.

266. There is a reference to the infernal river
Lethe which (as the ghost in *Hamlet* I, v, 33, recalled) causes forgetfulness.

276. *edge* has its now obsolete, Latin meaning
of the front line of battle.

282. *pernicious* keeps its Latin meaning of "death-
giving."

285. *ethereal*: Cf. the notes on l. 117 above and
II, 139.

288. The *Tuscan artist* is Galileo, the first astronomer to use a telescope capable of revealing the
real nature of the moon's surface. In *Areopagitica*
Milton recalls what seems to have been an actual
visit to him at Fiesole in the Tuscan hills above the
Arno, whose valley is (in Italian) the *Valdarno*.
Cf. V, 415–26, n., and the Introduction 32–33.

294. *Ammiral*: admiral's ship. Neither the
meaning nor the spelling was obsolete; the latter indicates Milton's preferred pronunciation here.

He walkt with to support uneasy steps   295
Over the burning Marl, not like those steps
On Heaven's Azure, and the torrid Clime
Smote on him sore besides, vaulted with Fire;
Nathless he so endur'd, till on the Beach
Of that inflamed Sea, he stood and call'd   300
His Legions, Angel Forms, who lay intrans't
Thick as Autumnal Leaves that strow the Brooks
In *Vallombrosa,* where th' *Etrurian* shades
High overarch't imbow'r; or scatter'd sedge
Afloat, when with fierce Winds *Orion* arm'd   305
Hath vext the Red-Sea Coast, whose waves o'erthrew
Busiris and his *Memphian* Chivalry,
While with perfidious hatred they pursu'd
The Sojourners of *Goshen,* who beheld
From the safe shore thir floating Carcasses   310
And broken Chariot Wheels; so thick bestrown
Abject and lost lay these, covering the Flood,
Under amazement of thir hideous change.
He call'd so loud, that all the hollow Deep
Of Hell resounded. Princes, Potentates,   315
Warriors, the Flow'r of Heav'n, once yours, now lost,
If such astonishment as this can seize
Eternal spirits; or have ye chos'n this place
After the toil of Battle to repose
Your wearied virtue, for the ease you find   320
To slumber here, as in the Vales of Heav'n?
Or in this abject posture have ye sworn
To adore the Conqueror? who now beholds
Cherub and Seraph rolling in the Flood
With scatter'd Arms and Ensigns, till anon   325
His swift pursuers from Heav'n Gates discern
Th' advantage, and descending tread us down
Thus drooping, or with linked Thunderbolts
Transfix us to the bottom of this Gulf.
Awake, arise, or be for ever fall'n. ⟶ *aren't they already*   330
    They heard, and were abasht, and up they sprung
Upon the wing; as when men wont to watch
On duty, sleeping found by whom they dread,
Rouse and bestir themselves ere well awake.
Nor did they not perceive the evil plight   335
In which they were, or the fierce pains not feel;
Yet to thir General's Voice they soon obey'd
Innumerable. As when the potent Rod

302–304. Perhaps a memory of Dante's spirits numberless as autumn leaves (*Inf.* III, 112–14) or of the image as C. M. Bowra notes it (in *From Virgil to Milton,* 240–41) in Homer, Bacchylides, Virgil and Tasso. Milton may have visited the shady valley, Vallombrosa, during his stay in Florence.

304–314. The rapidly compounding simile fuses Virgilian descriptions of the constellation Orion as cloudy and stormy (*Aen.* I, 535; VII, 719) with biblical references to the masses of seaweed in the Red Sea, which in turn recalls the destruction there of Pharoah's chariots and horsemen (the *Memphian Chivalry*) whom it overwhelmed as they tried to stop the flight of the Hebrews across it from the Land of Goshen in Egypt to safety on the eastern shore.

307. D. C. Allen has shown—MLN, LXV (1950), 115—that the *Chronicle* of Carion, which Milton used in Melarcthon's revision, misled him into identifying the mythical Busiris with the Pharaoh of Exodus, who had long been recognized by commentators as a type of Satan, *vera daemonis figura,* as he is called in the Prologue to the Rule of St. Benedict.

313. For the use of *amazement* see VI, 646, n.

314. In the MS Miss Darbishire notes that the reading is *deeps,* as if to suggest reverberation from one level to another.

Of *Amram's* Son in *Egypt's* evil day
Wav'd round the Coast, up call'd a pitchy cloud   340
Of *Locusts,* warping on the Eastern Wind,
That o'er the Realm of impious *Pharaoh* hung
Like Night, and darken'd all the Land of *Nile:*
So numberless were those bad Angels seen
Hovering on wing under the Cope of Hell   345
'Twixt upper, nether, and surrounding Fires;
Till, as a signal giv'n, th' uplifted Spear
Of thir great Sultan waving to direct
Thir course, in even balance down they light
On the firm brimstone, and fill all the Plain;   350
A multitude, like which the populous North
Pour'd never from her frozen loins, to pass
Rhene or the *Danaw,* when her barbarous Sons
Came like a Deluge on the South, and spread
Beneath *Gibraltar* to the *Lybian* sands.   355
Forthwith from every Squadron and each Band
The Heads and Leaders thither haste where stood
Thir great Commander; Godlike shapes and forms
Excelling human, Princely Dignities,
And Powers that erst in Heaven sat on Thrones;   360
Though of thir Names in heav'nly Records now
Be no memorial, blotted out and ras'd
By thir Rebellion, from the Books of Life.
Nor had they yet among the Sons of *Eve*
Got them new Names, till wand'ring o'er the Earth,   365
Through God's high sufferance for the trial of man,   *- how they are*
By falsities and lies the greatest part   *allowed over the earth.*
Of Mankind they corrupted to forsake
God thir Creator, and th' invisible
Glory of him that made them, to transform   370
Oft to the Image of a Brute, adorn'd
With gay Religions full of Pomp and Gold,
And Devils to adore for Deities:
Then were they known to men by various Names,
And various Idols through the Heathen World.   375
Say, Muse, thir Names then known, who first, who last,

---

339. *Amram* was Moses' father. The plague of
locusts which he called down on the Egyptians by
the power of his rod, so that it covered "the face of
the whole earth, so that the land was darkened"
(Exod. x, 12–15), was the basis of a familiar metaphor that was applied alike to men and devils by
Phineas Fletcher in his *Locustae* (1607). Cf. XII,
176–99.

341. *O.E.D.* quotes this line to illustrate *warping*
in this sense and brackets it with an earlier example
of the word applied to "snow driving and warping
in the wind."

353–356. Perhaps an echo of Machiavelli's opening of the *Florentine History* (anonymous translation of 1674): "The people inhabiting the Regions
Northwards from the rivers *Rhyne* and *Danube,*
living in a healthful clime, and apt for Generation,
oft-times increase to such vast multitudes, that part
of them are constrained to forsake their Native
Country, and seek new places to dwell in. . . .

These people were they, who destroyed the *Roman*
Empire." The crossing of the Vandals into North
Africa (the *Lybian sands*) is prominent on Machia-
velli's second page. Cf. the opening of *Prol* V.

360–375. For the *Powers that erst sat on thrones*
and later were known by various names to the
heathen see the Introduction 25–26.

361–362. Biblical references to the Book of Life
run from Psalm lxix, 28, to the "Lamb's book of
life" in Revelation xxi, 27, into which came nothing
"that defileth, neither whatsoever worketh abomination or maketh a lie." Cf. V, 658–59, n.

367–371. The lines recall St. Paul's contempt for
pagan religions that "changed the glory of the incorruptible God into an image made like to corruptible man, and to birds, and four-footed beasts,
and creeping things" (Rom. i, 23).

376. The line echoes Homer's introduction of the
catalogue of ships in the *Iliad* (II, 484) with the
plea to the Muse to tell him who were the com-

Rous'd from the slumber on that fiery Couch,
At thir great Emperor's call, as next in worth
Came singly where he stood on the bare strand,
While the promiscuous crowd stood yet aloof?   380
The chief were those who from the Pit of Hell
Roaming to seek thir prey on earth, durst fix
Thir Seats long after next the Seat of God,
Thir Altars by his Altar, Gods ador'd
Among the Nations round, and durst abide   385
Jehovah thund'ring out of Sion, thron'd
Between the Cherubim; yea, often plac'd
Within his Sanctuary itself thir Shrines,
Abominations; and with cursed things
His holy Rites, and solemn Feasts prefan'd,   390
And with thir darkness durst affront his light.
First Moloch, horrid King besmear'd with blood
Of human sacrifice, and parents' tears,
Though for the noise of Drums and Timbrels loud
Thir children's cries unheard, that pass'd through fire   395
To his grim Idol. Him the Ammonite
Worshipt in Rabba and her wat'ry Plain,
In Argob and in Basan, to the stream
Of utmost Arnon. Nor content with such
Audacious neighborhood, the wisest heart   400
Of Solomon he led by fraud to build
His Temple right against the Temple of God
On that opprobrious Hill, and made his Grove
The pleasant Valley of Hinnom, Tophet thence
And black Gehenna call'd, the Type of Hell.   405
Next Chemos, th' obscene dread of Moab's Sons,
From Aroar to Nebo, and the wild
Of Southmost Abarim; in Hesebon
And Horonaim, Seon's Realm, beyond

manders and lords of the Greeks. See the Introduction 25.

382-389. The image is that of the "Shepherd of Israel, . . . thou that dwellest between the cherubim," of Psalm lxxx, 1, whose shrine on Mt. Sion in Jerusalem itself was sometimes dishonored by apostate kings of Judah who, like Ahaz (II Kings xvi, 10-18), surrounded it with pagan altars.

392. The name Moloch literally means "king." Cf. the account of his worship in Nativity, 205-12.

397. Rabba, the Ammonite capital, was conquered by David (II Sam. xii, 27).

398-399. Near the Moabite border stream of Arnon lay Argob and Basan, where the Israelites destroyed the "sons of Ammon" (Deut. iii, 1-13).

401. Beguiled by his wives, Solomon built "an high place for Chemosh, the abomination of Moab, in the hill that is before Jerusalem, and for Moloch, the abomination of Ammon" (I Kings xi, 7). The hill was the Mount of Olives, the "mount of offense" of II Kings xxiii, 13, and the "hill of scandal" of l. 416 below. See the Introduction 26.

404. In Jeremiah (xix, 6) the apostate Israelites burn "their sons with fire for burnt offerings unto Baal" in the valley of the "son of Hinnom." The form Gehenna, as St. Jerome wrote in his Commentary on the Gospel of Matthew, is not biblical, but under that name he identified the place and associated it with the Baal-worship of the neighboring valley of Tophet, which was called "the monument to the dead"; hence "the eternal punishments by which sinners are tortured are designated by the name of this place." Reflections of St. Jerome in several biblical commentators are traced by A. L. Kellogg in N&Q, CXCV (1950), 10-13. Cf. Starnes and Talbert, Dictionaries, pp. 317-318.

406. In Numbers xxi, 29, the Moabites are called the "people of Chemosh." He is not identified in Selden's De Dis Syris, and Fuller was in doubt whether the "Babylonish Deity Bell" was "the same with Chemosh and Baal-Peor (which is the opinion of St. Jerome) and if not, wherein lay the difference" (Pisgah-Sight, p. 64).

407-409. Aroar, Mt. Nebo, the Abarim hills, and Hesebon (Hesabon) are conspicuous on Thomas Fuller's map of the land of the tribe of Reuben—in A Pisgah-Sight (p. 55)—together with the other places that are named in ll. 398 and 406-18 below. The destruction of Seon's (Sihon's) city of Heshbon is celebrated in Numbers xxi, 25. Cf. Psalms cxxxv, 11, and cxxxvi, 19, and Isaiah xv, 5.

The flow'ry Dale of *Sibma* clad with Vines,   410
And *Eleale* to th' *Asphaltic* Pool.
Peor his other Name, when he entic'd
Israel in *Sittim* on thir march from *Nile*
To do him wanton rites, which cost them woe.
Yet thence his lustful Orgies he enlarg'd   415
Even to that Hill of scandal, by the Grove
Of *Moloch* homicide, lust hard by hate;
Till good *Josiah* drove them thence to Hell.
With these came they, who from the bord'ring flood
Of old *Euphrates* to the Brook that parts   420
Egypt from *Syrian* ground, had general Names
Of *Baalim* and *Ashtaroth,* those male,
These Feminine. For Spirits when they please
Can either Sex assume, or both; so soft
And uncompounded is thir Essence pure,   425
Not ti'd or manacl'd with joint or limb,
Nor founded on the brittle strength of bones,
Like cumbrous flesh; but in what shape they choose
Dilated or condens't, bright or obscure,
Can execute thir aery purposes,   430
And works of love or enmity fulfil.
For those the Race of *Israel* oft forsook
Thir living strength, and unfrequented left
His righteous Altar, bowing lowly down
To bestial Gods; for which thir heads as low   435
Bow'd down in Battle, sunk before the Spear
Of despicable foes. With these in troop
Came *Astoreth,* whom the *Phœnicians* call'd
Astarte, Queen of Heav'n, with crescent Horns;
To whose bright Image nightly by the Moon   440
Sidonian Virgins paid thir Vows and Songs,
In *Sion* also not unsung, where stood
Her Temple on th' offensive Mountain, built
By that uxorious King, whose heart though large,
Beguil'd by fair Idolatresses, fell   445
To Idols foul. *Thammuz* came next behind,

---

410. 411. Close to the city of *Eleale* on Fuller's map *Sibma* is marked by a vine and in his text the valley is described as filled with vineyards for whose destruction the prophets later mourned (Isa. xvi, 8–9, and Jer. xlviii, 32).

411. *th'Asphaltic* Pool: the Dead Sea, which is described in a famous passage of Diodorus Siculus' *Library* (XIX, 98) as producing a floating island of solid asphalt every year.

412. On the march from Egypt to Canaan "Israel abode in Shittim, and the people began to commit whoredom with the daughters of Moab. . . . And Israel joined himself unto Baal-Peor" (Num. xxv, 1, 3). Later biblical passages (Psalm cvi, 28, and Hosea ix, 10) treat the incident as a lasting national disgrace, but Selden (*De Dis Syris* II, v) was sceptical of the identification of Baal-Peor's rites by the commentators with those of other obscene deities, including those of the Sidonian gods to whom Milton refers in ll. 440–46.

420. The Euphrates bounded Palestine on the east and the "brook Besor" (I Sam. xxx, 10) was the Egyptian frontier.

422–431. *Baalim* and *Ashtaroth*: plural forms: cf. the singular *Astarte* in l. 439. Baal-Peor was only one of several local Baals in Scripture. In attributing Protean powers to the devils and angels Milton had in mind a passage in Michael Psellus' work of the tenth century, the *De operatione daemonum* (V, 8–9), which was published in Paris in 1615 and widely quoted by writers on witchcraft to explain spirit-apparitions in the forms of beasts, men, or angels. Cf. *PL* III, 636; IV, 800, and VI, 327–92.

438. Cf. the allusions to *Astarte,* the Phoenecian Aphrodite or Venus, as "mooned Ashtaroth, Heaven's queen," in *Nativity,* 200, and as the "Assyrian queen" in *Comus,* 1002.

444. The *uxorious King* is Solomon. Cf. l. 401 above.

446. Because *Thammuz* was identified with Adonis in St. Jerome's commentary on Ezekiel's account (viii, 13–14) of the idolatrous weeping of the women of Jerusalem for his "death" when an-

Whose annual wound in *Lebanon* allur'd
The *Syrian* Damsels to lament his fate
In amorous ditties all a Summer's day,
While smooth *Adonis* from his native Rock   450
Ran purple to the Sea, suppos'd with blood
Of *Thammuz* yearly wounded: the Love-tale
Infected *Sion's* daughters with like heat,
Whose wanton passions in the sacred Porch
Ezekiel saw, when by the Vision led   455
His eye survey'd the dark Idolatries
Of alienated *Judah*. Next came one
Who mourn'd in earnest, when the Captive Ark
Maim'd his brute Image, head and hands lopt off
In his own Temple, on the grunsel edge,   460
Where he fell flat, and sham'd his Worshippers:
Dagon his Name, Sea Monster, upward Man
And downward Fish: yet had his Temple high
Rear'd in *Azotus*, dreaded through the Coast
Of *Palestine*, in *Gath* and *Ascalon*,   465
And *Accaron* and *Gaza's* frontier bounds.
Him follow'd *Rimmon*, whose delightful Seat
Was fair *Damascus*, on the fertile Banks
Of *Abbana* and *Pharphar*, lucid streams.
He also against the house of God was bold: 470
A Leper once he lost and gain'd a King,
Ahaz his sottish Conqueror, whom he drew
God's Altar to disparage and displace
For one of *Syrian* mode, whereon to burn
His odious off'rings, and adore the Gods   475
Whom he had vanquisht. After these appear'd
A crew who under Names of old Renown,
Osiris, Isis, Orus and thir Train,
With monstrous shapes and sorceries abus'd
Fanatic *Egypt* and her Priests, to seek   480
Thir wand'ring Gods disguis'd in brutish forms
Rather than human. Nor did *Israel* scape
Th' infection when thir borrow'd Gold compos'd

nually, in July, the river that bore his name in Lebanon ran red (supposedly with the god's blood), his
story was popular and could be found in works as
heterogeneous as Sir Walter Raleigh's *History of
the World*, George Sandys' *Relation of a Journey*,
and Charles Stephanus' *Dictionary* in forms so close
to Milton's passage that all of them have been mentioned as possible sources. Selden (in *De Dis Syris*
II, x) found Thammuz-Adonis identified by various
commentators with many pagan deities, including
Osiris, and treated his worship as a nature cult. Cf.
Milton's allusion in *Manso*, 11.

458–460. The story of the miraculous fall of the
image of the fish-deity Dagon "upon his face to
the ground before the ark of the Lord" so that "the
head of Dagon and both the palms of his hands
were cut off upon the threshold" (I Sam. v, 5) was
hardly less popular than the story of Thammuz.
Sandys, Selden, Purchase, Raleigh, and the great
vulgarizer of pagan backgrounds to the Bible, Alexander Ross, in *Pansebeia, or, A View of all Religions of the World* (1653), all describe Dagon's

fall in Ashdod and represent his image as human
from the waist up but fishlike below. Cf. *SA*, 13,
etc.

464. *Azotus* is the Greek form given on Ortelius'
maps for *Ashdod*, the form in *SA*, 981, where
Accaron is mentioned as *Ekron*. All five Philistine
cities lay on or near the Mediterranean shore.

467–476. II Kings xvi, 10, deplores King Ahaz's
apostasy to the Syrian god *Rimmon* after conquering Damascus where his temple stood. The familiarity of Elisha's curing of the leprous Syrian
general Naaman by the water of Jordan is shown
by Ralph Cudworth's allusion in his Sermon before
the Commons (p. 31): "The Gospel is not like
Abana and Pharphar, those common rivers of Damascus, that could only cleanse the outside; but
it is a true Jordan."

478. Cf. the rout of the Egyptian gods by "the
dreaded Infant's hand" in *Nativity*, 211–15.

482–484. The golden calf worshipped by the
Israelites in the desert (Exod. xxxii, 4) is identified
with the Egyptian bull god, Apis.

The Calf in *Oreb:* and the Rebel King
Doubl'd that sin in *Bethel* and in *Dan,*   485
Lik'ning his Maker to the Grazed Ox,
Jehovah, who in one Night when he pass'd
From *Egypt* marching, equall'd with one stroke
Both her first born and all her bleating Gods.
Belial came last, than whom a Spirit more lewd   490
Fell not from Heaven, or more gross to love
Vice for itself: To him no Temple stood
Or Altar smok'd; yet who more oft than hee
In Temples and at Altars, when the Priest
Turns Atheist, as did *Ely's* Sons, who fill'd   495
With lust and violence the house of God.
In Courts and Palaces he also Reigns
And in luxurious Cities, where the noise
Of riot ascends above thir loftiest Tow'rs,
And injury and outrage: And when Night   500
Darkens the Streets, then wander forth the Sons
Of *Belial,* flown with insolence and wine.
Witness the Streets of *Sodom,* and that night
In *Gibeah,* when the hospitable door
Expos'd a Matron to avoid worse rape.   505
These were the prime in order and in might;
The rest were long to tell, though far renown'd,
Th' *Ionian* Gods, of *Javan's* Issue held
Gods, yet confest later than Heav'n and Earth
Thir boasted Parents; *Titan* Heav'n's first born   510
With his enormous brood, and birthright seiz'd
By younger *Saturn,* he from mightier *Jove*
His own and *Rhea's* Son like measure found;
So *Jove* usurping reign'd: these first in *Crete*
And *Ida* known, thence on the Snowy top   515
Of cold *Olympus* rul'd the middle Air
Thir highest Heav'n; or on the *Delphian* Cliff,
Or in *Dodona,* and through all the bounds
Of *Doric* Land; or who with *Saturn* old
Fled over *Adria* to th' *Hesperian* Fields,   520

484–489. When Jeroboam led the secession of the Ten Tribes from the Judaean kingdom he set up golden calves in the key cities of Samaria, *Bethel* and *Dan,* and proclaimed, "Behold thy gods, O Israel, which brought thee up out of the land of Egypt" (I Kings xii, 28). Milton contrasts the miraculous slaying of the first-born children and cattle, including the sacred Egyptian animals (the *bleating gods*) on the night of Israel's escape from Egypt.

490–501. In the biblical account of the crimes in *Gibeah* (Judges xix, 22 and xx, 13) *Belial* is an abstract noun meaning profligacy. *Sons of Belial* was a widely current phrase in the Bible and in Puritan sermons and pamphlets, meaning dissipated men or enemies of God. In the New Testament it was sometimes personified (as in II Cor. vi, 15), and in sacred dramas Belial often appeared as a character like Burton's prince of the third order of devils, the "vessels of anger and inventors of all mischief" (*Anatomy* I, ii, 1, 2; Everyman Ed. I, p. 187)

495. The story is found in I Samuel ii, 12–25.

508–510. The identification of the Ionians (Greeks) as descendants of Javan, the son of Japhet (Gen. x, 2) goes back as far as the translation of the Old Testament into Greek in the third century B.C. Cf. IV, 717, and *SA,* 716.

510–519. In the background are myths of the Titans as the first children of *Heaven* and Earth, of their displacement by Zeus or *Jove,* the son of the youngest of them, *Saturn,* and his sister *Rhea,* and of the rearing of Zeus on Mt. *Ida* in *Crete* and of his worship at *Delphi* and in the grove of *Dodona* in Epeirus. After losing power to Zeus, Saturn fled across the Adriatic Sea (*Adria*) to Italy, where he left the tradition of a "reign of gold" to which *Il Penseroso,* 25, refers. Later he fled to the *Celtic land* of Britain, which was sometimes identified with the Islands of the *Hesperides,* where—according to a tale mentioned by Plutarch in his essay *On the Cessation of Oracles*—he was still imprisoned, asleep, on the Isle of Anglesea. Cf. II, 714–718, n.

And o'er the *Celtic* roam'd the utmost Isles.
All these and more came flocking; but with looks
Downcast and damp, yet such wherein appear'd
Obscure some glimpse of joy, to have found thir chief
Not in despair, to have found themselves not lost   525
In loss itself; which on his count'nance cast
Like doubtful hue: but he his wonted pride
Soon recollecting, with high words, that bore
Semblance of worth, not substance, gently rais'd
Thir fainting courage, and dispell'd thir fears.   530
Then straight commands that at the warlike sound
Of Trumpets loud and Clarions be uprear'd
His mighty Standard; that proud honor claim'd
Azazel as his right, a Cherub tall:
Who forthwith from the glittering Staff unfurl'd   535
Th' Imperial Ensign, which full high advanc't
Shone like a Meteor streaming to the Wind
With Gems and Golden lustre rich imblaz'd,
Seraphic arms and Trophies: all the while
Sonorous metal blowing Martial sounds: 540
At which the universal Host upsent
A shout that tore Hell's Concave, and beyond
Frighted the Reign of *Chaos* and old Night.
All in a moment through the gloom were seen
Ten thousand Banners rise into the Air   545
With Orient Colors waving: with them rose
A Forest huge of Spears: and thronging Helms
Appear'd, and serried Shields in thick array
Of depth immeasurable: Anon they move
In perfect *Phalanx* to the *Dorian* mood   550
Of Flutes and soft Recorders; such as rais'd
To highth of noblest temper Heroes old
Arming to Battle, and instead of rage
Deliberate valor breath'd, firm and unmov'd
With dread of death to flight or foul retreat,   555
Nor wanting power to mitigate and swage
With solemn touches, troubl'd thoughts, and chase
Anguish and doubt and fear and sorrow and pain
From mortal or immortal minds. Thus they
Breathing united force with fixed thought   560
Mov'd on in silence to soft Pipes that charm'd
Thir painful steps o'er the burnt soil; and now

---

534. In Lev. xvi, 20, *Azazel* is the word signifying the scapegoat which annually carried the sins of Israel into the wilderness, but in Jewish tradition as represented by the Book of Enoch (x, 4) the name is given to a prince of the devils whom Raphael binds "to await the great day of fire." In Origen's work *Contra Celsum* (VI, 43) *Azazel* is identified with Satan himself. In the occult writings of Cornelius Agrippa, John Reuchlin, and Robert Fludd—as R. H. West shows in *Angels*, pp. 155-6—he ranked with Samael, Azael, and Mahazael as a standard-bearer in Satan's armies.

543. *Reign of Chaos:* the realm of Chaos. Cf. II, 895 and 907, where Chaos is used to signify both the region of disorganized matter between hell and heaven and the ruler of that realm.

550-567. In the background is Plato's teaching in the *Republic* III, 399A, that music in the quietly firm Dorian mode best prepares men for battle. In John Bingham's translation of Aelian's *Tacktics* (1616), p. 70, Thucydides, Plutarch, and several other ancient writers are quoted on the Spartan practice of going into battle to the music of the flute, "neither dissolving their order, nor shewing any astonishment of minde, but mildely and ioyfully approaching the danger of conflict." In Peter Whitehorne's translation of Machiavelli's *Arte of Warre* (1560), p. 126, the Spartan practice is contrasted with the Roman use of the trumpet in battle—a comparison that is made by several Renaissance writers.

Advanc't in view they stand, a horrid Front
Of dreadful length and dazzling Arms, in guise
Of Warriors old with order'd Spear and Shield,   565
Awaiting what command thir mighty Chief
Had to impose: He through the armed Files
Darts his experienc't eye, and soon traverse
The whole Battalion views, thir order due,
Thir visages and stature as of Gods;   570
Thir number last he sums. And now his heart
Distends with pride, and hard'ning in his strength
Glories: For never since created man,
Met such imbodied force, as nam'd with these
Could merit more than that small infantry   575
Warr'd on by Cranes: though all the Giant brood
Of *Phlegra* with th' Heroic Race were join'd
That fought at *Thebes* and *Ilium,* on each side
Mixt with auxiliar Gods; and what resounds
In Fable or *Romance* of *Uther's* Son   580
Begirt with *British* and *Armoric* Knights;
And all who since, Baptiz'd or Infidel
Jousted in *Aspramont* or *Montalban,*
Damasco, or *Marocco,* or *Trebisond,*
Or whom *Biserta* sent from *Afric* shore   585
When *Charlemain* with all his Peerage fell
By *Fontarabbia.* Thus far these beyond
Compare of mortal prowess, yet observ'd
Thir dread commander: he above the rest
In shape and gesture proudly eminent   590
Stood like a Tow'r; his form had yet not lost
All her Original brightness, nor appear'd
Less than Arch-Angel ruin'd, and th' excess
Of Glory obscur'd: As when the Sun new ris'n
Looks through the Horizontal misty Air   595
Shorn of his Beams, or from behind the Moon
In dim Eclipse disastrous twilight sheds
On half the Nations, and with fear of change

---

573. *since created man:* since the creation of man.

575. The *small infantry* are "that pygmean race beyond the Indian mount" of l. 780. A tradition as old as Homer (*Il.* III, 1–5), much embroidered by Pliny (VII, ii), was perpetuated by pygmy figures drawn on some maps of eastern Asia to illustrate the "Pygmaeans there (men but a cubite in height) which riding on Goats and Rammes do kepe warre with Cranes"—William Cunningham, *The Cosmographical Glasse* (London, 1559), Rvi[r].

577. In l. 197 the battle of the giants with the Olympian gods on the Phlegraean plains in Macedonia (where Ovid places it—*Met.* X, 151) has already suggested a parallel between the giants and the devils.

578. *Thebes* and *Ilium* (Troy) evoke scenes from Aeschylus' *Seven against Thebes* and from the *Iliad,* where the gods enter the mêlée to help the heroes.

580–581. *Uther's Son,* Arthur, with his knights both *British* and *Armoric* (i.e. from Brittany), recall another reference to them in a context of renunciation (*PR* II, 360–62) of such fables. Cf. *Manso,* 81.

582–583. *Aspramont,* near Nice, gave its name to an Italian romance, published in 1516, which narrates Charlemagne's repulse of a Saracen invasion. *Montalban* is Rinaldo's castle in Luigi Pulci's *Il Morgante Maggiore,* Matteo Boiardo's *Orlando Inammorato,* and Ariosto's *Orlando Furioso.*

584. In Ariosto's *Orlando Furioso,* Canto XVII, *Damascus* is the scene of a tournament of Christian and pagan knights, one of whom is the king of *Morocco.* The Byzantine city of *Trebizond,* on the south shore of the Black Sea, was captured by the Turks in 1461. Its story was popular in Giovanni Ambrogio Marini's romance *Il Colloandro Fedele* (Bracciano, 1640). It was translated into French by M. de Scudéry and imitated in La Calprènede's *Cléopâtre.*

587. The climax of the *Song of Roland,* the massacre of Charlemagne's rear-guard in the Pyrenees by the Saracens, was commonly placed at *Fontarabbia,* forty miles from the scene of the battle at Roncesvalles.

598. Milton may have intended his readers to

Perplexes Monarchs. Dark'n'd so, yet shone
Above them all th' Arch-Angel: but his face   600
Deep scars of Thunder had intrencht, and care
Sat on his faded cheek, but under Brows
Of dauntless courage, and considerate Pride
Waiting revenge: cruel his eye, but cast
Signs of remorse and passion to behold   605
The fellows of his crime, the followers rather
(Far other once beheld in bliss) condemn'd
For ever now to have thir lot in pain.
Millions of Spirits for his fault amerc't
Of Heav'n, and from Eternal Splendors flung   610
For his revolt, yet faithful how they stood,
Thir Glory wither'd. As when Heaven's Fire
Hath scath'd the Forest Oaks, or Mountain Pines,
With singed top thir stately growth though bare
Stands on the blasted Heath. He now prepar'd   615
To speak; whereat thir doubl'd Ranks they bend
From wing to wing, and half enclose him round
With all his Peers: attention held them mute.
Thrice he assay'd, and thrice in spite of scorn,
Tears such as _Angels weep_, burst forth at last _— Angels can't weep!_   620
Words interwove with sighs found out thir way.
  O Myriads of immortal Spirits, O Powers _— Satan_
Matchless, but with th' Almighty, and that strife
Was not inglorious, though th' event was dire,
As this place testifies, and this dire change   625
Hateful to utter: but what power of mind
Foreseeing or presaging, from the Depth
Of knowledge past or present, could have fear'd
How such united force of Gods, how such
As stood like these, could ever know repulse?   630
For who can yet believe, though after loss,
That all these puissant Legions, whose exíle
Hath emptied Heav'n, shall fail to re-ascend
Self-rais'd, and repossess thir native seat?
For mee be witness all the Host of Heav'n,   635
If counsels different, or danger shunn'd
By me, have lost our hopes. But he who reigns
Monarch in Heav'n, till then as one secure
Sat on his Throne, upheld by old repute,
Consent or custom, and his Regal State   _— he tricked us_ 640
Put forth at full, but still his strength conceal'd,
Which tempted our attempt, and wrought our fall.
Henceforth his might we know, and know our own

think of similar comparisons of doomed rulers
to the rising sun in clouds or eclipse such as
Shakespeare's simile for the appearance of Richard
II, like

    the blushing, discontented sun
From out the fiery portal of the east,
When he perceives the envious clouds are bent
To dim his glory. (_Richard II_ III, iii, 62–66)
The simile adumbrates Satan's final defeat as the
eclipse in Book XI, 181–84, adumbrates the effect
of man's sin on the world. Charles II's censor
is said to have objected to the lines as a veiled

threat to the King.
    603. _considerate:_ deliberate, conscious.
    609. _amerc't:_ penalized, punished.
    636. _different_ seems to have its obsolete meaning
of de-ferent, procrastinating, as Florence M. Stewart
notes in _N&Q._ CLXVI (1934), 79.
    642. _tempted our attempt:_ Cf. the similar pun
in IX, 648. In Milton such puns usually have a
grim humor, but as a figure of speech they had
been much admired as part of the "bravery" of
poetry, as Abraham Fraunce said that they were
in his _Arcadia Rhetorike_ (London, 1588).

So as not either to provoke, or dread
New War, provok't; our better part remains   645
To work in close design, by fraud or guile
What force effected not: that he no less
At length from us may find, who overcomes
By force, hath overcome but half his foe.
Space may produce new Worlds; whereof so rife   650
There went a fame in Heav'n that he ere long
Intended to create, and therein plant
A generation, whom his choice regard
Should favor equal to the Sons of Heaven:
Thither, if but to pry, shall be perhaps   655
Our first eruption, thither or elsewhere:
For this Infernal Pit shall never hold
Celestial Spirits in Bondage, nor th' Abyss
Long under darkness cover. But these thoughts
Full Counsel must mature: Peace is despair'd,   660
For who can think Submission? War then, War
Open or understood, must be resolv'd.
    He spake: and to confirm his words, out-flew
Millions of flaming swords, drawn from the thighs
Of mighty Cherubim; the sudden blaze   665
Far round illumin'd hell: highly they rag'd
Against the Highest, and fierce with grasped Arms
Clash'd on thir sounding shields the din of war,
Hurling defiance toward the Vault of Heav'n.
    There stood a Hill not far whose grisly top   670
Belch'd fire and rolling smoke; the rest entire
Shone with a glossy scurf, undoubted sign
That in his womb was hid metallic Ore,
The work of Sulphur. Thither wing'd with speed
A numerous Brígad hasten'd. As when bands   675
Of Píoners with Spade and Pickax arm'd
Forerun the Royal Camp, to trench a Field,
Or cast a Rampart. *Mammon* led them on,
Mammon, the least erected Spirit that fell
From Heav'n, for ev'n in Heav'n his looks and thoughts   680
Were always downward bent, admiring more
The riches of Heav'n's pavement, trodd'n Gold,
Than aught divine or holy else enjoy'd
In vision beatific: by him first
Men also, and by his suggestion taught,   685
Ransack'd the Center, and with impious hands

---

646. *close:* secret.

651. *fame:* rumor. Cf. II, 345-53, 830-35, and X, 481.

674. Cf. VI, 509-15,

675. *Brígad:* brigade. Milton accented the first syllable.

678. *Mammon*—an Aramaic word meaning riches —enters the Bible in Matthew vi, 24. Mediaeval tradition personified it, and Mammon became the prince of the lowest of the nine orders of demons, "those tempters in several kinds," as Burton called them in the *Anatomy* I, ii, 1, 2 (Everyman Ed. I, p. 188). ᷄ wealth

684. The *vision beatific* of Dante's *Paradiso,* the

fulfilment of the promise that "the pure in heart shall see God" (Matt. v, 8), is as much a part of the imaginative background of *PL* as it is of the *Divine Comedy.* Cf. V, 613. In *On Time,* 18, it is translated in "happy-making sight." In the final chapter of *Of Reformation* it gives Milton his conception of the reformers in their "supereminence of beatific vision, progressing the dateless and ir-revoluble circle of eternity."

686-692. In *Nature is not Subject to Old Age,* 63-65, Milton alludes to Ovid's classic statement of this commonplace (*Met.* I, 137-42). The root of all evil is the gold that men first stole from the earth when the golden age ended. The oxymoron

Rifl'd the bowels of thir mother Earth
For Treasures better hid. Soon had his crew
Op'n'd into the Hill a spacious wound
And digg'd out ribs of Gold. Let none admire   690
That riches grow in Hell; that soil may best
Deserve the precious bane. And here let those
Who boast in mortal things, and wond'ring tell
Of *Babel*, and the works of *Memphian* Kings,
Learn how thir greatest Monuments of Fame,   695
And Strength and Art are easily outdone
By Spirits reprobate, and in an hour
What in an age they with incessant toil
And hands innumerable scarce perform.
Nigh on the Plain in many cells prepar'd,   700
That underneath had veins of liquid fire
Sluic'd from the Lake, a second multitude
With wondrous Art founded the massy Ore,
Severing each kind, and scumm'd the Bullion dross:
A third as soon had form'd within the ground   705
A various mould, and from the boiling cells
By strange conveyance fill'd each hollow nook:
As in an Organ from one blast of wind
To many a row of Pipes the sound-board breathes.
Anon out of the earth a Fabric huge   710
Rose like an Exhalation, with the sound
Of Dulcet Symphonies and voices sweet,
Built like a Temple, where *Pilasters* round
Were set, and Doric pillars overlaid
With Golden Architrave; nor did there want   715
Cornice or Frieze, with bossy Sculptures grav'n;
The Roof was fretted Gold. Not *Babylon*,
Nor great *Alcairo* such magnificence
Equall'd in all thir glories, to inshrine
Belus or *Serapis* thir Gods, or seat   720
Thir Kings, when *Egypt* with *Assyria* strove
In wealth and luxury. Th' ascending pile

of gold as *precious bane* (valuable evil) inspired the often repeated paradox that Chaucer translated from Boethius in *The Former Age:*

But cursed was the tyme, I dar wel seye,
That men first dide hir swety bysinesse,
To grobbe up metal, lurkinge in derknesse.

Cf. VI, 470–520, and *Comus*, 732–35.

690. *admire:* wonder.

694. *Babel:* the capital of the tyrant Nimrod, whose story is told in XII, 24–62. Here *Memphian* means "Egyptian," but it connotes the great temples at Memphis on the Nile.

703. The reading of the second edition, *found out,* has the disadvantage of repeating the thought in l. 690; that of the first, *founded,* has the disadvantage of anticipating the process of founding the metal that is described in ll. 705–709. The case for *found out* is stated by B. A. Wright in *TLS,* Aug. 9, 1934, p. 553.

709. *sound-board:* the surface that deflects the air from the bellows into an organ's pipes. Pandemonium, like Troy and Camelot, is built to music.

710–717. The passage has resemblances to Ovid's description of the palaces of the gods (*Met.* I, 171–72, and IV, 762–64) and especially to the technical architectural terms in his description of the palace built by Vulcan for Apollo. It compares more interestingly with the machinery of a masque at court on the Sunday after Twelfth Night in 1637: "the *earth open'd,* and there rose up a richly-adorned pallace, seeming all of goldsmith's work, with porticos vaulted, on pilasters of rich rustick work; their bases and capitels of gold. Above these ran an architrave freese, and coronis of the same—the freese enrich'd with jewels." (Quoted by Todd from *The Stage Condemn'd,* 1698.)

717. In *PR* III, 280, the pride of Babylon, "the wonder of all tongues," is again a symbol of Satan's power. In its glory it rivalled Egypt's Memphis, to which Milton here gives its modern name of Cairo (*Alcairo*).

720. *Belus* is a variant of Baal (cf. l. 421 above). *Serapis* (usually, though not here, accented on the second syllable) was a name given to Osiris as lord of the underworld and patron of the land's fertility.

Stood fixt her stately highth, and straight the doors
Op'ning thir brazen folds discover wide
Within, her ample spaces, o'er the smooth   725
And level pavement: from the arched roof
Pendant by subtle Magic many a row
Of Starry Lamps and blazing Cressets fed
With *Naphtha* and *Asphaltus* yielded light
As from a sky. The hasty multitude   730
Admiring enter'd, and the work some praise
And some the Architect: his hand was known
In Heav'n by many a Tow'red structure high,
Where Scepter'd Angels held thir residence,
And sat as Princes, whom the supreme King   735
Exalted to such power, and gave to rule,
Each in his Hierarchy, the Orders bright.
Nor was his name unheard or unador'd
In ancient *Greece;* and in *Ausonian* land
Men call'd him *Mulciber;* and how he fell   740
From Heav'n, they fabl'd, thrown by angry *Jove*
Sheer o'er the Crystal Battlements: from Morn
To Noon he fell, from Noon to dewy Eve,
A Summer's day; and with the setting Sun
Dropt from the Zenith like a falling Star,   745
On *Lemnos* th' *Ægæan* Isle: thus they relate,
Erring; for he with this rebellious rout
Fell long before; nor aught avail'd him now
To have built in Heav'n high Tow'rs; nor did he scape
By all his Engines, but was headlong sent   750
With his industrious crew to build in hell.
Meanwhile the winged Heralds by command
Of Sovran power, with awful Ceremony
And Trumpets' sound throughout the Host proclaim
A solemn Council forthwith to be held   755
At *Pandæmonium,* the high Capitol
Of Satan and his Peers: thir summons call'd
From every Band and squared Regiment
By place or choice the worthiest; they anon
With hunderds and with thousands trooping came   760
Attended: all access was throng'd, the Gates
And Porches wide, but chief the spacious Hall
(Though like a cover'd field, where Champions bold
Wont ride in arm'd, and at the Soldan's chair

728. *Cressets:* iron baskets for burning fragments of the bitumen, or *Asphalt,* from which the *Naphtha* was extracted.

739. Italy, the *Ausonian* land, is given its ancient Greek name.

740. *Mulciber:* the "founder of metal," more commonly called Vulcan in Latin, and in Greek Hephaestus. Homer's story (*Il.* I, 588–95) that Zeus tossed him out of heaven in drunken rage, and that he was all day long in falling onto the island of *Lemnos* in the *Aegean* Sea, was condemned as frivolous by Plato (*Rep.* II, 378d). Milton's attitude toward it resembles Sandys' (*Relation,* p. 23) in contempt for a story still told by the Lemnians with superstitious credulity. See the Introduction 54.

756. *Pandaemonium:* the name, from Greek πᾶν ("all") and δαίμων ("spirit" or "deity"), and the conception seem indebted to Henry More's *Pandaemoniothen,* which signifies the dominion of the devils in this world, which is so densely inhabited by personified sins of all kinds that

What Poets phancies fain'd to be in Hell
Are truly here, A Vulture *Tytius* heart
Still gnaws, yet death doth never *Tytius* quell:
Sad Sisyphus a stone with toylsome smart
Doth roul up hill, but it transcends his art,
To get it to the top, . . .

(*Psychozoia* I, iii, 23, 1–6)

Defi'd the best of *Paynim* chivalry   765
To mortal combat or career with Lance)
Thick swarm'd, both on the ground and in the air,
Brusht with the hiss of rustling wings. As Bees
In spring time, when the Sun with *Taurus* rides,
Pour forth thir populous youth about the Hive   770
In clusters; they among fresh dews and flowers
Fly to and fro, or on the smoothed Plank,
The suburb of thir Straw-built Citadel,
New rubb'd with Balm, expatiate and confer
Thir State affairs. So thick the aery crowd   775
Swarm'd and were strait'n'd; till the Signal giv'n,
Behold a wonder! they but now who seem'd   *shrinking*
In bigness to surpass Earth's Giant Sons
Now less than smallest Dwarfs, in narrow room
Throng numberless, like that Pigmean Race   780
Beyond the *Indian* Mount, or Faery Elves,
Whose midnight Revels, by a Forest side
Or Fountain some belated Peasant sees,
Or dreams he sees, while over-head the Moon
Sits Arbitress, and nearer to the Earth   785
Wheels her pale course; they on thir mirth and dance
Intent, with jocund Music charm his ear;
At once with joy and fear his heart rebounds.
Thus incorporeal Spirits to smallest forms
Reduc'd thir shapes immense, and were at large,   790
Though without number still amidst the Hall
Of that infernal Court. But far within
And in thir own dimensions like themselves
The great Seraphic Lords and Cherubim
In close recess and secret conclave sat   795
A thousand Demi-Gods on golden seats,
Frequent and full. After short silence then
And summons read, the great consult began.

The End of the First Book.

769. The Bull, *Taurus*, the second sign in the Zodiac, is entered by the sun in April.

768–775. The simile opens vistas on comparisons of throngs of people to bees by Homer (*Il.* II, 87–90) and Virgil (*Aen.* I, 430–36) and on Milton's interpretation of Virgil's account of bees as possessing cities and laws (*Georg.* IV, 149–227) in the *First Defense* (C.E. VII, 84) in reply to Salmasius' serious assertion that the respect of bees for their "kings" was a divine example of absolute monarchy worthy of human imitation. It is worth noting also, as Miss R. W. Smith points out in her architectural comparison of *Pandaemonium* with St. Peter's in Rome—*MP*, XXIX (1931), 187–98—that the bee was the emblem of the Barberini Pope Urban VIII, who dedicated the basilica in 1636, and that "his followers were often referred to as bees."

774. *expatiate:* to walk abroad (the Latin sense of the word originally).

780–781. Cf. l. 575, n., and the allusion to the Himalayas as "the *Indian* steep" in *Comus*, 139.

781–787. Comparison with *A Midsummer Night's Dream* II, i, s fair, but the note of perilous mystery is Miltonic, like the sound of "sands and shores and desert wildernesses" in *Comus*, 208–209. There is certainly a reminiscence of Virgil's picture of Aeneas in the Elysian Fields, seeing or thinking that he sees Dido, "like the fugitive moon among clouds" (*Aen* VI, 450–55).

795. *close recess:* a secret meeting place. *Conclave*—literally, "inner chamber"—illustrates the use of that word and its equivalent, "cabinet," to mean secret governing councils.

797. *Frequent:* in throngs. The word has its basic Latin meaning.

BOOK II

THE ARGUMENT

The Consultation begun, Satan *debates whether another Battle be to be hazarded for the recovery of Heaven: some advise it, others dissuade: A third proposal is preferr'd, mention'd before by* Satan, *to search the truth of that Prophecy or Tradition in Heaven concerning another world, and another kind of creature equal or not much inferior to themselves, about this time to be created: Thir doubt who shall be sent on this difficult search:* Satan *thir chief undertakes alone the voyage, is honor'd and applauded. The Council thus ended, the rest betake them several ways and to several employments, as thir inclinations lead them, to entertain the time till* Satan *return. He passes on his Journey to Hell Gates, finds them shut, and who sat there to guard them, by whom at length they are op'n'd, and discover to him the great Gulf between Hell and Heaven; with what difficulty he passes through, directed by* Chaos, *the Power of that place, to the sight of this new World which he sought.*

> High on a Throne of Royal State, which far
> Outshone the wealth of *Ormus* and of *Ind,*
> Or where the gorgeous East with richest hand
> Show'rs on her Kings *Barbaric* Pearl and Gold,
> Satan exalted sat, by merit rais'd   5
> To that bad eminence; and from despair
> Thus high uplifted beyond hope, aspires
> Beyond thus high, insatiate to pursue
> Vain War with Heav'n, and by success untaught
> His proud imaginations thus display'd.   10
> Powers and Dominions, Deities of Heav'n,
> For since no deep within her gulf can hold
> Immortal vigor, though opprest and fall'n,
> I give not Heav'n for lost. From this descent
> Celestial Virtues rising, will appear   15
> More glorious and more dread than from no fall
> And trust themselves to fear no second fate:
> Mee though just right and the fixt Laws of Heav'n
> Did first create your Leader, next, free choice,
> With what besides, in Counsel or in Fight,   20
> Hath been achiev'd of merit, yet this loss
> Thus far at least recover'd, hath much more
> Establisht in a safe unenvied Throne
> Yielded with full consent. The happier state
> In Heav'n, which follows dignity, might draw   25

[handwritten marginal note:] Hope where there is no hope. Angels try to regain their former state.

1. The scene may have been intended to recall Spenser's more symbolic description of the throne of Lucifera, incarnate Pride:
  High above all a cloth of state was spred,
  And a rich throne, as bright as sunny day.
    (*F.Q.* I, iv, 8, 1–2)
2. The strategic position of the island situation of *Ormus* at the mouth of the Persian gulf made it a rich trading city that figured conspicuously on the maps. Fulke Greville made it the scene of his tragedy of *Alaham,* and perhaps some of Milton's readers responded to the name by recalling

the cry of the usurping hero in the last scene:
  Is this *Ormus?* Or is *Ormus* my hell,
  Where only Furies, and not Men, doe dwell?
Cf. Satan's comparison with an eastern sultan as a type of tyranny in I, 348.
  5. Cf. I, 98, n., and II, 21.
  9. Cf. *success* in l. 123 below. The word meant "outcome" or "event" without implying either good or bad results.
  11. For the titles in the infernal hierarchy and the background of the demonic council see the Introduction 21 and 24.

Envy from each inferior; but who here
Will envy whom the highest place exposes
Foremost to stand against the Thunderer's aim
Your bulwark, and condemns to greatest share
Of endless pain? where there is then no good   30
For which to strive, no strife can grow up there
From Faction; for none sure will claim in Hell
Precedence, none, whose portion is so small
Of present pain, that with ambitious mind
Will covet more. With this advantage then   35
To union, and firm Faith, and firm accord,
More than can be in Heav'n, we now return
To claim our just inheritance of old,
Surer to prosper than prosperity
Could have assur'd us; and by what best way,   40
Whether of open War or covert guile,
We now debate; who can advise, may speak.
      He ceas'd, and next him *Moloch*, Scepter'd King
Stood up, the strongest and the fiercest Spirit
That fought in Heav'n; now fiercer by despair: 45
His trust was with th' Eternal to be deem'd
Equal in strength, and rather than be less
Car'd not to be at all; with that care lost
Went all his fear: of God, or Hell, or worse
He reck'd not, and these words thereafter spake.   50
      My sentence is for open War: Of Wiles,
More unexpert, I boast not: them let those
Contrive who need, or when they need, not now.
For while they sit contriving, shall the rest,
Millions that stand in Arms, and longing wait   55
The Signal to ascend, sit ling'ring here
Heav'n's fugitives, and for thir dwelling place
Accept this dark opprobrious Den of shame,
The Prison of his Tyranny who Reigns
By our delay? no, let us rather choose   60
Arm'd with Hell flames and fury all at once
O'er Heav'n's high Tow'rs to force resistless way,
Turning our Tortures into horrid Arms
Against the Torturer; when to meet the noise
Of his Almighty Engine he shall hear   65
Infernal Thunder, and for Lightning see
Black fire and horror shot with equal rage
Among his Angels; and his Throne itself

---

28. *Thunderer* recalls Ovid's repeated attribution of the thunderbolt to Jove as his emblem (*Met.* I, 154, 170, 197). Satan uses the symbol of omnipotence to suggest that God is a tyrant. Cf. Belial's reference to "his red right hand" (II, 174), a reminiscence of Horace's picture of Jove threatening to destroy Rome (*Odes* I, ii), and Moloch's proposal to counter the tyrant's lightning with black fire and infernal thunder (II, 66–67).

32. Milton had no intention of making Satan a tragic hero of the kind that (like Alaham's father in Greville's play) fails to understand Bacon's warning that, "when factions are carried too high and too violently, it is a sign of weakness in princes" (*Essays* LI).

43. *Moloch* the "furious king" of the battle in heaven (VI, 357) is *Scepter'd* as the kings often are in Homeric councils (e. g. *Il.* II, 86, and *Od.* II, 231).

51. *sentence* has its basic Latin meaning of "decision" or "judgment." Cf. l. 291 below.

52. *unexpert* keeps its basic Latin meaning of "inexperienced." Cf. *expert* in VI, 233.

65. *Engine* has the military significance that it has in IV, 17, and VI, 484.

Mixt with *Tartarean* Sulphur, and strange fire,
His own invented Torments. But perhaps   70
The way seems difficult and steep to scale
With upright wing against a higher foe.
Let such bethink them, if the sleepy drench
Of that forgetful Lake benumb not still,
That in our proper motion we ascend   75
Up to our native seat: descent and fall
To us is adverse. Who but felt of late
When the fierce Foe hung on our brok'n Rear
Insulting, and pursu'd us through the Deep,
With what compulsion and laborious flight   80
We sunk thus low? Th' ascent is easy then;
Th' event is fear'd; should we again provoke
Our stronger, some worse way his wrath may find
To our destruction: if there be in Hell
Fear to be worse destroy'd: what can be worse   85
Than to dwell here, driv'n out from bliss, condemn'd
In this abhorred deep to utter woe;
Where pain of unextinguishable fire
Must exercise us without hope of end
The Vassals of his anger, when the Scourge   90
Inexorably, and the torturing hour
Calls us to Penance? More destroy'd than thus
We should be quite abolisht and expire.
What fear we then? what doubt we to incense
His utmost ire? which to the highth enrag'd,   95
Will either quite consume us, and reduce
To nothing this essential, happier far
Than miserable to have eternal being:
Or if our substance be indeed Divine,
And cannot cease to be, we are at worst   100
On this side nothing; and by proof we feel
Our power sufficient to disturb his Heav'n,
And with perpetual inroads to Alarm,
Though inaccessible, his fatal Throne:
Which if not Victory is yet Revenge.   105
    He ended frowning, and his look denounc'd
Desperate revenge, and Battle dangerous
To less than Gods. On th' other side up rose
Belial, in act more graceful and humane;

69. *Tartarean* is derived from *Tartarus,* the name
for the place of torment in the classical underworld.
74. The *forgetful Lake,* like the "oblivious pool"
of I, 266, is the river Lethe, a *drench* (drink) of
whose waters made the spirits of the dead forget
their earthly life. Moloch's contempt for his companions' forgetfulness of their glory in heaven
suggests the reference of the ghost in *Hamlet* (I,
v, 32–33) to the "dulness" of "the fat weed/ That
rots itself in ease on Lethe wharf." Other echoes
of the scene are perhaps heard in the following
lines here.
89. *exercise* keeps its Latin meaning of "torment."
90. *Vassals* has its Latin meaning of "servant"
or "slave," as it does in Spenser's description of
men as "The vassals of God's *wrath,* and slaves

of sin," in *The Teares of the Muses,* 126. But
Bentley suggested that the word should be "vessels,"
and that the allusion is to "vessels of wrath, fitted
to destruction" in Romans ix, 22.
97. *essential*—the adjective used as a noun—
means "essence." Cf. I, 138.
104. Cf. the meanings of *fate* and *gods* in I, 116.
109. Cf. Belial's first appearance in I, 490, and
his later ones in VI, 620–27, and *PR* II, 150–73.
For his bearing Milton may have been indebted
to the tradition that he "taketh the form of a beau-
tifull angel, he speaketh faire"—in Reginald Scot's
Discoverie of Witchcraft (1584), xv, 2—but the
characterization is Milton's own—as E. E. Stoll
shows in "Belial as an Example" in *MLN,* XLVIII
(1933), 419–27.

A fairer person lost not Heav'n; he seem'd   110
For dignity compos'd and high exploit:
But all was false and hollow; though his Tongue
Dropt Manna, and could make the worse appear — *some critics suggest Socrates.*
The better reason, to perplex and dash
Maturest Counsels: for his thoughts were low;   115
To vice industrious, but to Nobler deeds
Timorous and slothful: yet he pleas'd the ear,
And with persuasive accent thus began.
    I should be much for open War, O Peers,   *— glib speech like Odysseus*
As not behind in hate; if what was urg'd   120
Main reason to persuade immediate War,
Did not dissuade me most, and seem to cast
Ominous conjecture on the whole success:
When he who most excels in fact of Arms,
In what he counsels and in what excels   125
Mistrustful, grounds his courage on despair
And utter dissolution, as the scope
Of all his aim, after some dire revenge.
First, what Revenge? the Tow'rs of Heav'n are fill'd
With Armed watch, that render all access   130
Impregnable; oft on the bordering Deep
Encamp thir Legions, or with obscure wing
Scout far and wide into the Realm of night,
Scorning surprise. Or could we break our way
By force, and at our heels all Hell should rise   135
With blackest Insurrection, to confound
Heav'n's purest Light, yet our great Enemy
All incorruptible would on his Throne
Sit unpolluted, and th' Ethereal mould
Incapable of stain would soon expel   140
Her mischief, and purge off the baser fire
Victorious. Thus repuls'd, our final hope
Is flat despair: we must exasperate
Th' Almighty Victor to spend all his rage
And that must end us, that must be our cure,   145
To be no more; sad cure; for who would lose,
Though full of pain, this intellectual being,
Those thoughts that wander through Eternity,
To perish rather, swallow'd up and lost
In the wide womb of uncreated night,   150
Devoid of sense and motion? and who knows,
Let this be good, whether our angry Foe
Can give it, or will ever? how he can
Is doubtful; that he never will is sure.

124. *fact of arms:* deed or feat of arms.

139–141. In part the passage rests on the conception of God as "a consuming fire" (Deut. iv, 24) and of "his angels" as "a flaming fire" (Psalm civ, 4), and in part it rests on the distinction between *Ethereal* or celestial fire and the *baser fire* of earth, which Spenser allegorized by making Vesta a symbol of "the fire aetheriall,/ Vulcan, of this, with us so usuall" (*F.Q.* VII, vii, 26, 6–7). Cf. *PL* I, 117, n., and XI, 48–53.

146–151. Editors quote Claudio's dread of death, when "This sensible warm motion" will "become

A kneaded clod" (*Measure for Measure* III, i, 120–21); but the thought parallels Seneca's in writing to his mother, Helvia (*On Consolation* xi, 7), about the soul as kindred to the gods and at home in every world and every age because its thought ranges through all heaven and through all past and future time. Cf. Plato's quotation of Pindar (in *Theaetetus,* 173E) on the mind's power to explore the universe independently of the body. Milton repeats the thought in *Areopagitica* (see p. 733), 'minds that can wander beyond all limit and satiety."

Will he, so wise, let loose at once his ire,   155
Belike through impotence, or unaware,
To give his Enemies thir wish, and end
Them in his anger, whom his anger saves
To punish endless? wherefore cease we then?
Say they who counsel War, we are decreed,   160
Reserv'd and destin'd to Eternal woe;
Whatever doing, what can we suffer more,
What can we suffer worse? is this then worst,
Thus sitting, thus consulting, thus in Arms?
What when we fled amain, pursu'd and strook   165
With Heav'n's afflicting Thunder, and besought
The Deep to shelter us? this Hell then seem'd
A refuge from those wounds: or when we lay
Chain'd on the burning Lake? that sure was worse.
What if the breath that kindl'd those grim fires   170
Awak'd should blow them into sevenfold rage
And plunge us in the flames? or from above
Should intermitted vengeance arm again
His red right hand to plague us? what if all
Her stores were op'n'd, and this Firmament   175
Of Hell should spout her Cataracts of Fire,
Impendent horrors, threat'ning hideous fall
One day upon our heads; while we perhaps
Designing or exhorting glorious war,
Caught in a fiery Tempest shall be hurl'd   180
Each on his rock transfixt, the sport and prey
Of racking whirlwinds, or for ever sunk
Under yon boiling Ocean, wrapt in Chains;
There to converse with everlasting groans,
Unrespited, unpitied, unrepriev'd,   185
Ages of hopeless end; this would be worse.
War therefore, open or conceal'd, alike
My voice dissuades; for what can force or guile
With him, or who deceive his mind, whose eye
Views all things at one view? he from Heav'n's highth   190
All these our motions vain, sees and derides;
Not more Almighty to resist our might
Than wise to frustrate all our plots and wiles.
Shall we then live thus vile, the race of Heav'n
Thus trampl'd, thus expell'd to suffer here   195
Chains and these Torments? better these than worse
By my advice; since fate inevitable
Subdues us, and Omnipotent Decree,
The Victor's will. To suffer, as to do,
Our strength is equal, nor the Law unjust   200
That so ordains: this was at first resolv'd,
If we were wise, against so great a foe

---

174. Cf. l. 28 above, n.

174–184. Several classical parallels have been cited—none of them close. There is a real resemblance, however, to the description of the felling of the Titans Atlas and Typhon by the thunders of Zeus and their living entombment in Aeschylus' *Prometheus,* 353–68.

191. Belial anticipates Psalm ii, 4: "He that

sitteth in the heavens shall laugh; the Lord shall have them in derision."

199. *To suffer, as to do* translates the word of Mucius Scaevola as he thrust his hand into the fire to give his Etruscan captors a casual example of what a Roman could suffer after he had been seized in a suicidal attempt to assassinate their king (Livy, ii, 12).

Contending, and so doubtful what might fall.
I laugh, when those who at the Spear are bold
And vent'rous, if that fail them, shrink and fear   205
What yet they know must follow, to endure
Exile, or ignominy, or bonds, or pain,
The sentence of thir Conqueror: This is now
Our doom; which if we can sustain and bear,   *the false hope he*
Our Supreme Foe in time may much remit   *bears. Reasoning*   210
His anger, and perhaps thus far remov'd   *gives way.*
Not mind us not offending, satisfi'd
With what is punisht; whence these raging fires
Will slack'n, if his breath stir not thir flames.
Our purer essence then will overcome   215
Thir noxious vapor, or enur'd not feel,
Or chang'd at length, and to the place conform'd
In temper and in nature, will receive
Familiar the fierce heat, and void of pain;
This horror will grow mild, this darkness light,   220
Besides what hope the never-ending flight
Of future days may bring, what chance, what change
Worth waiting, since our present lot appears
For happy though but ill, for ill not worst,
If we procure not to ourselves more woe.   225
    Thus *Belial* with words cloth'd in reason's garb
Counsell'd ignoble ease, and peaceful sloth,
Not peace: and after him thus *Mammon* spake.
    Either to disinthrone the King of Heav'n   *— fairly middle class*
We war, if war be best, or to regain   230
Our own right lost: him to unthrone we then
May hope, when everlasting Fate shall yield
To fickle Chance, and *Chaos* judge the strife:
The former vain to hope argues as vain
The latter: for what place can be for us   235
Within Heav'n's bound, unless Heav'n's Lord supreme
We overpower? Suppose he should relent
And publish Grace to all, on promise made
Of new Subjection; with what eyes could we   *—Angels unlike men,*
Stand in his presence humble, and receive   *cannot humble*   240
Strict Laws impos'd, to celebrate his Throne   *themselves*
With warbl'd Hymns, and to his Godhead sing
Forc't Halleluiahs; while he Lordly sits
Our envied Sovran, and his Altar breathes
Ambrosial Odors and Ambrosial Flowers,   245

207. For the pronunciation of ignominy see I, 115, n.
213–219. The thought is allied to that attributed to St. Augustine by Thomas Heywood in his *Hierarchie of the Blessed Angels* (1635) IV, p. 211:
For in Saint *Austines* Comment you may finde,
The subtile essence of the Angels (pure
At first, that they more fully might endure
The sence of Fire) was grossed in their Fall,
Of courser temper, then th'Originall.
216. *enur'd*: accustomed or used to.
218. *temper*—loosely equivalent to "temperament"—was used physiologically to mean the balance of physical "humors" in the body, variations

in which caused various individual natures or characters. Cf. l. 276 below.
224. *for happy*: from the point of view of happiness.
228. Cf. *Mammon* in I, 678.
232. Cf. *Fate* in I, 116, n.
243. *Halleluiah* transliterates the Hebrew phrase, "Praise ye 'ah," i. e. Jehovah. Bishop Sanderson said (*Sermons* I, p. 115) that the Psalms could all be summed up in the words *Hosannah* and *Halleluiah.*
245. In the *Iliad* (IV, 3–4) Hebe pours out ambrosia for the gods, but it is often mentioned as their food. *Ambrosial* naturally appeared in con-

Our servile offerings. This must be our task
In Heav'n, this our delight; how wearisome
Eternity so spent in worship paid
To whom we hate. Let us not then pursue
By force impossible, by leave obtain'd   250
Unácceptable, though in Heav'n, our state
Of splendid vassalage, but rather seek
Our own good from ourselves, and from our own
Live to ourselves, though in this vast recess,
Free, and to none accountable, preferring   255
Hard liberty before the easy yoke
Of servile Pomp. Our greatness will appear
Then most conspicuous, when great things of small,
Useful of hurtful, prosperous of adverse
We can create, and in what place soe'er   260
Thrive under evil, and work ease out of pain
Through labor and endurance. This deep world
Of darkness do we dread? How oft amidst
Thick clouds and dark doth Heav'n's all-ruling Sire
Choose to reside, his Glory unobscur'd,   265
And with the Majesty of darkness round
Covers his Throne; from whence deep thunders roar
Must'ring thir rage, and Heav'n resembles Hell?
As he our darkness, cannot we his Light
Imitate when we please? This Desert soil   270
Wants not her hidden lustre, Gems and Gold;
Nor want we skill or art, from whence to raise
Magnificence; and what can Heav'n show more?
Our torments also may in length of time
Become our Elements, these piercing Fires   275
As soft as now severe, our temper chang'd
Into their temper; which must needs remove
The sensible of pain. All things invite
To peaceful Counsels, and the settl'd State
Of order, how in safety best we may   280
Compose our present evils, with regard
Of what we are and where, dismissing quite
All thoughts of War; ye have what I advise.
He scarce had finisht, when such murmur fill'd

texts like the "Celestial food, Divine, Ambrosial"
of *PR* IV, 588-89.

249. *pursue:* try to obtain. Its object, *state,* is
modified by the relative clauses "[what is] by force
impossible" and "[what is, if] by leave obtain'd,
unacceptable."

255-257. This Miltonic principle is restated in
SA, 268-71. Here it seems to echo the closing
words of the invective of the Consul Aemilius Lepi-
dus against the tyrant Cornelius Sulla in 78 B.C. as
it is found in Sallust's version of that *Oration to the
Roman People*.

264. At the dedication of Solomon's temple "the
house was filled with a cloud . . . for the glory
of the Lord filled the house of God. Then said
Solomon, the Lord hath said that he would dwell
in the thick darkness" (II Chron. v, 13-VI, 1). Cf.
Psalm xviii, 11-13: "He made darkness his secret
place; his pavilion round about him were dark

waters and thick clouds of the skies. The Lord
also thundered in the heavens."

275. Traditionally, the devils were assigned to
the elements and might be classified, as they were
by Burton in the *Anatomy* (I, ii, 1, 2; Everyman
Ed. I, p. 190), into Fiery Spirits or Devils, Aerial
Spirits or Devils, Water-devils, Terrestrial and Sub-
Terrestrial devils. Cf. the "Daemons" of "fire, air,
flood, or underground" in *Il Pen*, 93-94.

278. *sensible of pain* is rightly glossed by J. C.
Maxwell (*RES*, V—n. s., 1954—268) as "that element in our pain which is apprehended by the
senses," and he notes that Mammon betrays his
character by his indifference to all except the physical pains of hell.

284-290. There are several classical parallels—
the closest that in the *Aeneid* (X, 96-99) where the
gods in council assent to Juno's violent appeal like
winds threatening storm to sailors.

Th' Assembly, as when hollow Rocks retain   285
The sound of blust'ring winds, which all night long
Had rous'd the Sea, now with hoarse cadence lull
Sea-faring men o'erwatcht, whose Bark by chance
Or Pinnace anchors in a craggy Bay
After the Tempest: Such applause was heard   290
As *Mammon* ended, and his Sentence pleas'd,
Advising peace: for such another Field
They dreaded worse than Hell: so much the fear
Of Thunder and the Sword of *Michaël*
Wrought still within them; and no less desire— pride   295
To found this nether Empire, which might rise
By policy, and long process of time,
In emulation opposite to Heav'n.
Which when *Beëlzebub* perceiv'd, than whom,   no reality, just appearances.
Satan except, none higher sat, with grave   300
Aspect he rose, and in his rising seem'd
A Pillar of State; deep on his Front engraven
Deliberation sat and public care;
And Princely counsel in his face yet shone,
Majestic though in ruin: sage he stood   305
With *Atlantean* shoulders fit to bear
The weight of mightiest Monarchies; his look
Drew audience and attention still as Night
Or Summer's Noon-tide air, while thus he spake.

    Thrones and Imperial Powers, off-spring of Heav'n,   310
Ethereal Virtues; or these Titles now
Must we renounce, and changing style be call'd
Princes of Hell? for so the popular vote
Inclines, here to continue, and build up here
A growing Empire; doubtless; while we dream,   315
And know not that the King of Heav'n hath doom'd
This place our dungeon, not our safe retreat
Beyond his Potent arm, to live exempt
From Heav'n's high jurisdiction, in new League
Banded against his Throne, but to remain   320
In strictest bondage, though thus far remov'd,
Under th' inevitable curb, reserv'd
His captive multitude: For he, be sure,
In highth or depth, still first and last will Reign
Sole King, and of his Kingdom lose no part   325
By our revolt, but over Hell extend
His Empire, and with Iron Sceptre rule

291. Cf. Mammon, "the least erected spirit that fell / From Heav'n."—I, 679–80.

294. An anticipation of Michael's command of the heavenly host in Book VI.

297. *policy*: statesmanship.

299. Cf. Beelzebub's first appearance in I, 81.

302. *Front* keeps its Latin meaning of "forehead."

306. The myth of the Titan, Atlas, "whom the Gentiles feign to bear up Heav'n" (*SA*, 150), similarly suggested a comparison to "pillars of state" to Spenser when he described England as supported by Lord Burleigh,

    As the wide compasse of the firmament
    On Atlas mighty shoulders is upstayd.

(Sonnets Dedicatory to the *Faerie Queene*)

312. *style*: the formal title of a king or nobleman.

315. *doubtless*, standing between semicolons as it does in the early editions, is a flash of sarcasm between Beelzebub's irony up to this point and his ensuing earnest argument.

324. The words attributed to God in the Apocalypse, "I am Alpha and Omega, the beginning and the end, the first and the last" (Rev. i, 2; xxi, 6; and xxii, 13), inspire Beelzebub's despair, as later (V, 165) they nspire the triumph of the angels.

327. The *Iron Sceptre* recalls God's promise to his Son, "Thou shalt break them with a rod of iron" (Psalm ii, 9) Iron was a traditional symbol of

Us here, as with his Golden those in Heav'n.
What sit we then projecting peace and war?
War hath determin'd us, and foil'd with loss   330
Irreparable; terms of peace yet none
Voutsaf't or sought; for what peace will be giv'n
To us enslav'd, but custody severe,
And stripes, and arbitrary punishment
Inflicted? and what peace can we return,   335
But to our power hostility and hate,
Untam'd reluctance, and revenge though slow,
Yet ever plotting how the Conqueror least
May reap his conquest, and may least rejoice
In doing what we most in suffering feel?   340
Nor will occasion want, nor shall we need
With dangerous expedition to invade
Heav'n, whose high walls fear no assault or Siege,
Or ambush from the Deep. What if we find
Some easier enterprise? There is a place   345
(If ancient and prophetic fame in Heav'n
Err not) another World, the happy seat
Of some new Race call'd *Man,* about this time
To be created like to us, though less
In power and excellence, but favor'd more   — creating jealousy 350
Of him who rules above; so was his will   sibling?
Pronounc'd among the Gods, and by an Oath,
That shook Heav'n's whole circumference, confirm'd.
Thither let us bend all our thoughts, to learn
What creatures there inhabit, of what mould,   355
Or substance, how endu'd, and what thir Power,
And where thir weakness, how attempted best,
By force or subtlety: Though Heav'n be shut,
And Heav'n's high Arbitrator sit secure
In his own strength, this place may lie expos'd   360
The utmost border of his Kingdom, left
To their defense who hold it: here perhaps
Some advantageous act may be achiev'd
By sudden onset, either with Hell fire
To waste his whole Creation, or possess   365
All as our own, and drive as we were driven,
The puny habitants, or if not drive,
Seduce them to our Party, that thir God
May prove thir foe, and with repenting hand

enmity and gold of friendship, a symbolism which recurs in Abdiel's warning to Satan (V, 886–88).

332. *Voutsaf't:* vouchsafed, granted or gave.

336. *to our power:* to the limit of our power.

346. Cf. Satan's reference to this *fame* in I, 651.

348. Milton makes use of Origen's doctrine (condemned by St. Thomas in the *Summa Theologica* I, 961, a.33) that God created the world after the revolt of the angels.

352. Milton combines biblical representations of God taking an oath by himself "because he could swear by no greater" (Heb. vi, 13; Gen. xxii, 16) with classical recollections of Zeus shaking Olympus as he makes a vow to Thetis (*Il.* I, 530) or making a promise to Cybele with an oath (*Aen.* IX, 106).

Here and in III, 341; V, 60, 117; IX, 164; and X, 90, *Gods* refers to the angels, for—as Milton explains in *CD* I, v (C.E. XIV, 245)—"the name of God is not infrequently ascribed, by the will and concession of God the Father, even unto angels and men."

356. *endu'd:* gifted (with qualities of mind).

367. *puny* may have its primary meaning of later born—here, later created. Some versions of the motivation of the revolt of the angels based it simply on their resentment of the honor that God commanded them to pay to the newly created race of man. So, in an infernal council in *Psyche* (1648), Joseph Beaumont has Beelzebub ask rhetorically: Was't not enough, against the righteous Law Of Primogeniture, to throw Us down

Abolish his own works. This would surpass   370
Common revenge, and interrupt his joy
In our Confusion, and our Joy upraise
In his disturbance; when his darling Sons
Hurl'd headlong to partake with us, shall curse
Thir frail Original, and faded bliss,   375
Faded so soon. Advise if this be worth
Attempting, or to sit in darkness here
Hatching vain Empires. Thus *Beëlzebub*
Pleaded his devilish Counsel, first devis'd
By *Satan,* and in part propos'd: for whence,   380
But from the Author of all ill could Spring
So deep a malice, to confound the race
Of mankind in one root, and Earth with Hell
To mingle and involve, done all to spite
The great Creator? But thir spite still serves   385
His glory to augment. The bold design
Pleas'd highly those infernal States, and joy
Sparkl'd in all thir eyes; with full assent
They vote: whereat his speech he thus renews.   *—still Beelzebub*
    Well have ye judg'd, well ended long debate,   390
Synod of Gods, and like to what ye are,
Great things resolv'd, which from the lowest deep
Will once more lift us up, in spite of Fate,
Nearer our ancient Seat; perhaps in view
Of those bright confines, whence with neighboring Arms   395
And opportune excursion we may chance
Re-enter Heav'n; or else in some mild Zone
Dwell not unvisited of Heav'n's fair Light
Secure, and at the bright'ning Orient beam
Purge off this gloom; the soft delicious Air,   400
To heal the scar of these corrosive Fires
Shall breathe her balm. But first whom shall we send
In search of this new world, whom shall we find
Sufficient? who shall tempt with wand'ring feet
The dark unbottom'd infinite Abyss   405
And through the palpable obscure find out
His uncouth way, or spread his aery flight
Upborne with indefatigable wings
Over the vast abrupt, ere he arrive
The happy Isle; what strength, what art can then   410
Suffice, or what evasion bear him safe

From that bright home, which all the world do's
    know
Was by confest inheritance our own:
    But, to our shame, Man, that vile worm, must
    dwell
In our fair Orbs, and Heav'n with Vermin fill.
                    (Canto I, stanza 24)
    375. *Original* seems not to mean "original state,"
as it does in IX, 150, but to refer to Adam as the
original man. The first edition reads: *Originals.*
    387. *States:* estates. The parliaments of England
and France traditionally consisted of the three estates, lords, clergy, and commons. In *King John*
(II, i, 395-96) the Bastard ends a speech to a council of war with the demand:

How like you this wild counsel, mighty States;
Smacks it not something of the policy?
    394. Cf. *seat* in the sense of "established home"
in l. 347 above.
    404. *tempt* has its Latin sense "make trial of,"
or "make an attempt upon."
    406. *palpable obscure* recalls the "darkness which
may be felt' which God sent to plague the Egyptians. (Excd. x, 21)
    407. *uncouth:* unknown. Cf. l. 827 below.
    409. Here *abrupt* is regarded by the *OED* as a
noun meaning "an abyss or chasm." It is the gap
between Hell and Heaven.

Through the strict Senteries and Stations thick
Of Angels watching round? Here he had need
All circumspection, and wee now no less
Choice in our suffrage; for on whom we send,   415
The weight of all and our last hope relies.
        This said, he sat; and expectation held
His look suspense, awaiting who appear'd
To second, or oppose, or undertake
The perilous attempt; but all sat mute,   420
Pondering the danger with deep thoughts; and each
In other's count'nance read his own dismay
Astonisht: none among the choice and prime
Of those Heav'n-warring Champions could be found
So hardy as to proffer or accept   425
Alone the dreadful voyage; till at last
Satan, whom now transcendent glory rais'd
Above his fellows, with Monarchal pride
Conscious of highest worth, unmov'd thus spake.
        O Progeny of Heav'n, Empyreal Thrones,   430
With reason hath deep silence and demur
Seiz'd us, though undismay'd: long is the way
And hard, that out of Hell leads up to light;
Our prison strong, this huge convex of Fire,
Outrageous to devour, immures us round   435
Ninefold, and gates of burning Adamant
Barr'd over us prohibit all egress.
These past, if any pass, the void profound
Of unessential Night receives him next
Wide gaping, and with utter loss of being   440
Threatens him, plung'd in that abortive gulf.
If thence he scape into whatever world,
Or unknown Region, what remains him less
Than unknown dangers and as hard escape.
But I should ill become this Throne, O Peers,   445
And this Imperial Sov'ranty, adorn'd
With splendor, arm'd with power, if aught propos'd
And judg'd of public moment, in the shape
Of difficulty or danger could deter
Mee from attempting. Wherefore do I assume   450
These Royalties, and not refuse to Reign,
Refusing to accept as great a share

412. The three syllables of *senteries* are metrically necessary, and the form was not unusual in the seventeenth century.

415. *suffrage:* vote to select the agent in whose choice no less circumspection is needed than he will need himself to succeed in his mission.

418. *suspense* is an adjective modifying look and meaning literally "suspended": i.e. doubtful or "in suspense."

423. *prime* has its Latin force of first men, princes, or leaders.

432. The line harks back to the Sibyl's warning to Aeneas (*Aen.* VI, 126–29) that the descent to Avernus is easy, and perhaps also to Virgil's warning to Dante (*Inf.* XXXIV, 95), as they prepare to ascend from the center of the earth toward Purgatory, that the way is hard. Cf. III, 21.

434. *convex* is used as a noun to mean the sphere surrounding hell. Cf. III, 419.

436. *Ninefold* recalls the nine circles of the Styx around the underworld, in the *Aeneid* (VI, 439), as the *gates of burning Adamant* recall Virgil's columns of solid adamant supporting the gates of Tartarus (*Aen.* VI, 552).

439–441. *unessential:* without actual being, uncreated, as in l. 150 above. The negative form of the word anticipates *abortive,* which may mean "aborted" (lifeless), or "monstrous" (and therefore terrifying), or "abortion-causing" (frustrating, i.e. to an intruder).

448. *moment:* importance. The word has the Latin force that it still has in the adjective *momentous.*

Of hazard as of honor, due alike
To him who Reigns, and so much to him due
Of hazard more, as he above the rest   455
High honor'd sits? Go therefore mighty Powers,
Terror of Heav'n, though fall'n; intend at home,
While here shall be our home, 'what best may ease
The present misery, and render Hell
More tolerable; if there be cure or charm   460
To respite or deceive, or slack the pain
Of this ill Mansion: intermit no watch
Against a wakeful Foe, while I abroad
Through all the Coasts of dark destruction seek
Deliverance for us all: this enterprise   465
None shall partake with me.   Thus saying rose
The Monarch, and prevented all reply,
Prudent, lest from his resolution rais'd
Others among the chief might offer now
(Certain to be refus'd) what erst they fear'd;   470
And so refus'd might in opinion stand
His Rivals, winning cheap the high repute
Which he through hazard huge must earn.   But they
Dreaded not more th' adventure than his voice
Forbidding; and at once with him they rose;   475
Thir rising all at once was as the sound
Of Thunder heard remote.   Towards him they bend
With awful reverence prone; and as a God
Extol him equal to the highest in Heav'n: ——
Nor fail'd they to express how much they prais'd,   480
That for the general safety he despis'd
His own: for neither do the Spirits damn'd
Lose all thir virtue; lest bad men should boast
Thir specious deeds on earth, which glory excites,
Or close ambition varnisht o'er with zeal.   485
Thus they thir doubtful consultations dark
Ended rejoicing in their matchless Chief:
As when from mountain tops the dusky clouds
Ascending, while the North wind sleeps, o'erspread
Heav'n's cheerful face, the low'ring Element   490
Scowls o'er the dark'n'd lantskip Snow, or show'r;
If chance the radiant Sun with farewell sweet
Extend his ev'ning beam, the fields revive,
The birds thir notes renew, and bleating herds
Attest thir joy, that hill and valley rings.   495
O shame to men! Devil with Devil damn'd
Firm concord holds, men only disagree
Of Creatures rational, though under hope

457. *intend* has its Latin force of "attend to,"
"consider."
461: *deceive* has its Latin force of "elude" or
"beguile."
462. *Mansion* is derived from the word which is
equivalent to *seat* as used in l. 347 above.
468. *rais'd:* emboldened.
478. *awful:* full of awe or reverence.
485. *close:* secret or hidden.
490. *Element:* sky or atmosphere. Cf. the "gay
creatures of the Element" in *Comus*, 299.

491. *lantskip:* landscape. A Dutch word which
had not yet crystallized into its modern English
form.
496–502. The lines state an orthodox doctrine
that is found in Antonio Rusca's *De Inferno et Statu
Daemonum* (Milan, 1621), pp. 505–507. He does
not refer to the great European wars of the time, as
Milton does, but he says explicitly that the devils
avoid civil strife and maintain orders and ranks
among themselves so as to tempt mankind most
efficiently.

Of heavenly Grace; and God proclaiming peace,
Yet live in hatred, enmity, and strife   500
Among themselves, and levy cruel wars,
Wasting the Earth, each other to destroy:
As if (which might induce us to accord)
Man had not hellish foes anow besides,
That day and night for his destruction wait.   505
   The *Stygian* Council thus dissolv'd; and forth
In order came the grand infernal Peers:
Midst came thir mighty Paramount, and seem'd
Alone th' Antagonist of Heav'n, nor less
Than Hell's dread Emperor with pomp Supreme,   510
And God-like imitated State; him round
A Globe of fiery Seraphim inclos'd
With bright imblazonry, and horrent Arms.
Then of thir Session ended they bid cry
With Trumpet's regal sound the great result: 515
Toward the four winds four speedy Cherubim
Put to thir mouths the sounding Alchymy
By Herald's voice explain'd: the hollow Abyss
Heard far and wide, and all the host of Hell
With deaf'ning shout, return'd them loud acclaim.   520
Thence more at ease thir minds and somewhat rais'd
By false presumptuous hope, the ranged powers
Disband, and wand'ring, each his several way
Pursues, as inclination or sad choice
Leads him perplext, where he may likeliest find   525
Truce to his restless thoughts, and entertain
The irksome hours, till this great Chief return.
Part on the Plain, or in the Air sublime
Upon the wing, or in swift Race contend,
As at th' *Olympian* Games or *Pythian* fields;   530
Part curb thir fiery Steeds, or shun the Goal
With rapid wheels, or fronted Brígads form.
As when to warn proud Cities war appears
Wag'd in the troubl'd Sky, and Armies rush
To Battle in the Clouds, before each Van   535
Prick forth the Aery Knights, and couch thir spears
Till thickest Legions close; with feats of Arms
From either end of Heav'n the welkin burns.
Others with vast *Typhœan* rage more fell

507. *Peers:* lords. Like the great nobles in a national parliament, the devils follow their *Paramount* (chief), carrying their weapons imblazoned (cf. l. 513) with their coats of arms.

512. *Globe:* a phalanx of soldiers. *O.E.D.* cites Giles Fletcher's lines:

> Out there flies
> A globe of winged angels, swift as thought.
> (*Christ's Triumph after Death,* xiii)

Cf. *PR* IV, 581.

517. "Bell-metal," said Sir Francis Bacon in *Articles of Questions Touching Minerals,* speaking of various alloys, "they call *alchemy.*" Numerous examples of the word used to mean alloys of various kinds are cited by E. H. Duncan in *Osiris* XI (1954), 403–404.

522. *powers:* armies.

530. The sports of the demons are an interlude like the funeral games at the tomb of Anchises in the *Aeneid* (V, 103–603) and those at the tomb of Patroclus in the *Iliad* (XXIII, 287–897), but they include contests in music and oratory, as the Olympian and Pythian games did in ancient Greece.

531. The picture is the famous one of Roman charioteers swinging their teams around the turning posts in the arena as Horace describes them in the opening stanza of his first book of *Odes.*

534. Perhaps there is a reflection of the "chariots and troops of soldiers in their armour running about among the clouds" that Josephus mentions among the portents seen by the Jews before the fall of Jerusalem. (*Wars* VI, v. 3).

539. Cf. the note on *Typhoean* in I, 197. The name Typhon or Typhoeus meant "whirlwind,"

Rend up both Rocks and Hills, and ride the Air   540
In whirlwind; Hell scarce holds the wild uproar.
As when *Alcides* from *Oechalia* Crown'd
With conquest, felt th' envenom'd robe, and tore
Through pain up by the roots *Thessalian* Pines,
And *Lichas* from the top of *Oeta* threw   545
Into th' *Euboic* Sea. Others more mild,
Retreated in a silent valley, sing
With notes Angelical to many a Harp
Thir own Heroic deeds and hapless fall
By doom of Battle; and complain that Fate   550
Free Virtue should enthrall to Force or Chance.
Thir Song was partial, but the harmony
(What could it less when Spirits immortal sing?)
Suspended Hell, and took with ravishment   — sweet music in hell?
The thronging audience. In discourse more sweet   555
(For Eloquence the Soul, Song charms the Sense,)
Others apart sat on a Hill retir'd,
In thoughts more elevate, and reason'd high
Of Providence, Foreknowledge, Will, and Fate,
Fixt Fate, Free will, Foreknowledge absolute,   560
And found no end, in wand'ring mazes lost.
Of good and evil much they argu'd then,
Of happiness and final misery,
Passion and Apathy, and glory and shame,   — don't know from God anymore,
Vain wisdom all, and false Philosophie: so· they quarrel.   565
Yet with a pleasing sorcery could charm
Pain for a while or anguish, and excite
Fallacious hope, or arm th' obdured breast
With stubborn patience as with triple steel.
Another part in Squadrons and gross Bands,   570
On bold adventure to discover wide
That dismal World, if any Clime perhaps
Might yield them easier habitation, bend
Four ways thir flying March, along the Banks
Of four infernal Rivers that disgorge   575
Into the burning Lake thir baleful streams;
Abhorred *Styx* the flood of deadly hate,
Sad *Acheron* of sorrow, black and deep;

and the Greek word has influenced the English word
"typhoon," which is of Arabian or Persian origin.
Cf. the demonic storm in *PR* IV, 409-19.

542. *Alcides:* Hercules. The passage reflects the
story of his death after returning from a victory in
Oechalia to the island of *Euboea*, off the Attic coast,
where he slew his friend *Lichas* in blind rage, as it
is treated by Sophocles in the *Trachiniae* and by
Seneca in *The Mad Hercules*. Ovid's version (*Met.*
IX, 134 ff.) makes Mt. *Oeta* in Thessaly, rather than
Euboea, the scene of the action.

552. *Thir Song was partial* to their own view of
their quarrel with God as a struggle of *Virtue*
against tyrannic *Force*.

564. Cf. the condemnation of the Stoic ideal of
apathy or absolute mastery of all the passions in
CD II, x, and the contempt in *PR* IV, 300-301, for
the Stoic's *Philosophic pride, by him call'd virtue*.

565. Like Henry More in his *Immortality of the*

Soul (III, xvii, 10), Milton found it natural that
there should be "students of philosophy" among
the demons, who "are divided into sects and opinions, as we are here."

577-581. The lines translate the meanings of
the Greek names of the four rivers. Though they
flow into the "burning lake" of Revelation xx, 10,
they bound a hell that is like Virgil's (*Aen.* VI, 656-
59) or Spenser's. In the *Faerie Queene* II, viii, 20,
Spenser's reader found the allegorically "bitter wave
of *Styx*"; in II, vii, 57, he found *Cocytus*, whose sad
waves echoed with "piteous cryes and yelling
shrightes"; in II, vi, 50, he met "flaming *Phlegethon*," and in I, v, 33, "the bitter waves of Acheron."
Or—as Starnes and Talbert hint in *Dictionaries*, p.
335—he might find all the etymology and allegory
of the infernal rivers in a work like Nicholas
Perottus' *Cornucopiae* (1489).

Cocytus, nam'd of lamentation loud
Heard on the rueful stream; fierce *Phlegeton*   580
Whose waves of torrent fire inflame with rage.
Far off from these a slow and silent stream,
Lethe the River of Oblivion rolls
Her wat'ry Labyrinth, whereof who drinks,
Forthwith his former state and being forgets,   585
Forgets both joy and grief, pleasure and pain.
Beyond this flood a frozen Continent
Lies dark and wild, beat with perpetual storms
Of Whirlwind and dire Hail, which on firm land
Thaws not, but gathers heap, and ruin seems   590
Of ancient pile; all else deep snow and ice,
A gulf profound as that *Serbonian* Bog
Betwixt *Damiata* and Mount *Casius* old,
Where Armies whole have sunk: the parching Air
Burns frore, and cold performs th' effect of Fire.   595
Thither by harpy-footed Furies hal'd,   _what revolutions_
At certain revolutions all the damn'd
Are brought: and feel by turns the bitter change
Of fierce extremes, extremes by change more fierce,
From Beds of raging Fire to starve in Ice   600
Thir soft Ethereal warmth, and there to pine
Immovable, infixt, and frozen round,
Periods of time, thence hurried back to fire.
They ferry over this *Lethean* Sound
Both to and fro, thir sorrow to augment,   605
And wish and struggle, as they pass, to reach
The tempting stream, with one small drop to lose
In sweet forgetfulness all pain and woe,
All in one moment, and so near the brink;
But Fate withstands, and to oppose th' attempt   610
Medusa with *Gorgonian* terror guards
The Ford, and of itself the water flies
All taste of living wight, as once it fled
The lip of *Tantalus*. Thus roving on
In confus'd march forlorn, th' advent'rous Bands   615
With shudd'ring horror pale, and eyes aghast
View'd first thir lamentable lot, and found
No rest: through many a dark and dreary Vale
They pass'd, and many a Region dolorous,

583. *Lethe:* the "forgetful Lake" of l. 74 above.
591. The accumulated hail seems like the ruin of a marble *pile* (i.e. building).
592–594. On Fuller's map of the route of the Hebrews from Egypt to Palestine (*Pisgah-Sight,* op. p. 43) and on some maps of Ortelius the reader could find the *Serbonian Bog* between *Damiata* (modern Damietta, on the east mouth of the Nile) and Mt. Casius. In Diodorus Siculus' *Library* I, xxx, 5–7, and several contemporary works he could learn that whole armies had sunk in its quicksands.
595. Claudio's fear that in hell his soul might "bathe in fiery floods" or "reside/In thrilling region of thick-ribbed ice" (*Measure for Measure* III, i, 121–22) reflected a belief which is illustrated in Dante's *Inferno* XXXII, 29 ff., and categorically affirmed by St. Thomas in *Summa Theologica* (Suppl.

Part III, 2, xcvii).
596. Virgil anticipated Milton in attributing the claws of the harpies to the Furies or Eumenides, goddesses who avenged crimes like Orestes' slaying of his mother (*Aen.* III, 217).
600. *starve* has its original, general sense of "die" for any cause.
611. One of the worst fears of Ulysses during his visit to Hades in the *Odyssey* (XI, 634) is that he may be shown the head of the *Gorgon* that turns all living men to stone by a mere look.
614. In Tartarus (*Od.* XI, 582–92) Ulysses saw *Tantalus* fixed in a pool of water that forever fell below the reach of his thirsty lips—"thirsty Tantalus hung by the chin," as Spenser describes him (*F.Q.* I, v, 35). Above him laden fruit trees are just out of his reach.

O'er many a Frozen, many a Fiery Alp,   620
Rocks, Caves, Lakes, Fens, Bogs, Dens, and shades of death,
A Universe of death, which God by curse
Created evil, for evil only good,
Where all life dies, death lives, and Nature breeds,
Perverse, all monstrous, all prodigious things,   625
Abominable, inutterable, and worse
Than Fables yet have feign'd, or fear conceiv'd,
Gorgons and Hydras, and Chimeras dire.   *Kimeras*
    Meanwhile the Adversary of God and Man,
Satan with thoughts inflam'd of highest design,   630
Puts on swift wings, and towards the Gates of Hell
Explores his solitary flight; sometimes
He scours the right hand coast, sometimes the left,
Now shaves with level wing the Deep, then soars
Up to the fiery concave tow'ring high.   635
As when far off at Sea a Fleet descri'd
Hangs in the Clouds, by Equinoctial Winds
Close sailing from Bengala, or the Isles
Of Ternate and Tidore, whence Merchants bring
Thir spicy Drugs: they on the Trading Flood   640
Through the wide Ethiopian to the Cape
Ply stemming nightly toward the Pole. So seem'd
Far off the flying Fiend: at last appear
Hell bounds high reaching to the horrid Roof,
And thrice threefold the Gates; three folds were Brass,   645
Three Iron, three of Adamantine Rock,
Impenetrable, impal'd with circling fire,
Yet unconsum'd. Before the Gates there sat
On either side a formidable shape;
The one seem'd Woman to the waist, and fair,   *Scylla*   650
But ended foul in many a scaly fold
Voluminous and vast, a Serpent arm'd
With mortal sting: about her middle round
A cry of Hell Hounds never ceasing bark'd
With wide Cerberean mouths full loud, and rung   655
A hideous Peal: yet, when they list, would creep,
If aught disturb'd thir noise, into her womb,

---

620. *Alp*: any high mountain.
628. The many-headed *Hydras* and the flame-spitting dragon *Chimeras* are vague monsters like the "unnumbered spectres" of Virgil's hell, where
    "horrid Hydra stands,
And Briareus with all his hundred hands,
Gorgons, Geryon with his triple frame;
And vain Chimera vomits empty flame."
    (*Aen.* VI, 286-89.) Dryden's translation.)
In *Prol* I Milton treats these monsters allegorically, as representing the pangs of guilty consciences.
632. *Explores* has its Latin meaning of "test, put to the proof," as Elizabeth Holmes notes in *Essays and Studies*, X (1924), 106.
638-641. The simile reflects the interest in the new trade across the *Ethiopian* Sea (the Indian Ocean off east Africa) which English ships reached by sailing round the Cape of Good Hope *en route* to the Moluccas or Spice Islands, of which *Ternate*

and *Tidore* were the best known. In Milton's time *Bengal* was part of the Mogul empire.
649-660. The lines become clear only in the light of 752-67 below. Sin owes her serpentine nether parts to conceptions like Spenser's Error:
    "Halfe like a serpent horribly displaide,
    But th'other halfe did womans shape retaine."
    (*F.Q.* I, i, 14)
But the dogs around Sin's waist, and especially their *Cerberean mouths*—a literally Ovidian phrase—plainly match Ovid's description of Scylla, the lovely nymph whose body Circe transformed into a mass of yelping hounds from the waist down (*Met.* XIV, 40-74). Finally—according to Ovid—she became the dangerous reef between Sicily (*Trinacria*) and the toe of the Italian boot (*Calabria*). But—as J. F. Gilliam recalls in *PQ*, XIX (1950), 346—the allegorization of the myth to make Scylla a symbol of sin goes back at least as far as St. John Chrysostom. Cf. l. 665, r.

And kennel there, yet there still bark'd and howl'd
Within unseen. Far less abhorr'd than these
Vex'd *Scylla* bathing in the Sea that parts   660
Calabria from the hoarse *Trinacrian* shore:
Nor uglier follow the Night-Hag, when call'd
In secret, riding through the Air she comes
Lur'd with the smell of infant blood, to dance
With *Lapland* Witches, while the laboring Moon   665
Eclipses at thir charms. The other shape,
If shape it might be call'd that shape had none
Distinguishable in member, joint, or limb,
Or substance might be call'd that shadow seem'd,
For each seem'd either; black it stood as Night,   670
Fierce as ten Furies, terrible as Hell,
And shook a dreadful Dart; what seem'd his head
The likeness of a Kingly Crown had on.
Satan was now at hand, and from his seat
The Monster moving onward came as fast,   675
With horrid strides; Hell trembled as he strode.
Th' undaunted Fiend what this might be admir'd,
Admir'd, not fear'd; God and his Son except,
Created thing naught valu'd he nor shunn'd;
And with disdainful look thus first began.   680
    Whence and what are thou, execrable shape,
That dar'st, though grim and terrible, advance
Thy miscreated Front athwart my way
To yonder Gates? through them I mean to pass,
That be assured, without leave askt of thee: 685
Retire, or taste thy folly, and learn by proof,
Hell-born, not to contend with Spirits of Heav'n.
    To whom the Goblin full of wrath repli'd:
Art thou that Traitor Angel, art thou hee,
Who first broke peace in Heav'n and Faith, till then   690
Unbrok'n, and in proud rebellious Arms
Drew after him the third part of Heav'n's Sons
Conjur'd against the Highest, for which both Thou
And they outcast from God, are here condemn'd
To waste Eternal days in woe and pain?   695

662. The *Night-Hag* is probably Hecate, whose
charms were used by Circe to bewitch Scylla. Popular superstition made her the witches' queen, as in
Macbeth (III, v, and IV, i).

665. In *Muscovia* (C.E. X, 361) Milton refers
skeptically to one of the many current stories about
Lapland as the home of witches. In her *Literary
Relations of England and Scandinavia in the 17th
Century* (Oxford, 1935) p. 328, Ethel Seaton suggests that Milton switched to a northern scene because the image of Scylla reminded him of Dithmar
Blefken's account of the "Dogge-fish, which putting
his head out of the Sea, barketh and receiveth the
whelps sporting in the Sea again into his belly."

665. *laboring:* undergoing eclipse. In the
Georgics (II, 478) Virgil speaks of the labors (*labores*) of the moon in this sense. Popular superstition held that witches—like Caliban's mother—
"could control the moon, make ebbs and floods"
(*Tempest* V, i, 270).

667. Everywhere in Renaissance literature the
negativeness of death is stressed, as it is in Bacon's
Essay *Of Death* and Spenser's picture:
"Death with most grim and griesly visage seen,
    Yet is he nought but parting of the breath;
    Ne ought to see, but like a shade to ween,
    Unbodied, unsoul'd, unheard, unseen."
                                        (*F.Q.* VII, vii, 46)

673. Milton thought of St. John's vision of the
king of terrors, when "a crown was given unto him,
and he went forth conquering, and to conquer"
(Rev. vi, 2). See Introduction, 3.

677. *admir'd* has its Latin force of "wonder" or
"observe."

692. *The third part of Heaven's Sons* alludes to
St. John's dragon, whose "tail drew the third part
of the stars of heaven, and did cast them to earth"
(Rev. xii, 3–4).

693. *Conjur'd:* bound together by an oath. The
word keeps its Latin meaning literally.

And reck'n'st thou thyself with Spirits of Heav'n,
Hell-doom'd, and breath'st defiance here and scorn,
Where I reign King, and to enrage thee more,
Thy King and Lord?   Back to thy punishment,
False fugitive, and to thy speed add wings,   700
Lest with a whip of Scorpions I pursue
Thy ling'ring, or with one stroke of this Dart
Strange horror seize thee, and pangs unfelt before.
        So spake the grisly terror, and in shape,
So speaking and so threat'ning, grew tenfold   705
More dreadful and deform: on th' other side
Incens't with indignation *Satan* stood
Unterrifi'd, and like a Comet burn'd,
That fires the length of *Ophiucus* huge
In th' Artic Sky, and from his horrid hair   710
Shakes Pestilence and War.   Each at the Head
Levell'd his deadly aim; thir fatal hands
No second stroke intend, and such a frown
Each cast at th' other, as when two black Clouds
With Heav'n's Artillery fraught, come rattling on   715
Over the *Caspian,* then stand front to front
Hov'ring a space, till Winds the signal blow
To join thir dark Encounter in mid air:
So frown'd the mighty Combatants, that Hell
Grew darker at thir frown, so matcht they stood; — *evils battle*   720
For never but once more was either like   *Bluff and*
To meet so great a foe: and now great deeds   *bluster*
Had been achiev'd, whereof all Hell had rung,
Had not the Snaky Sorceress that sat
Fast by Hell Gate, and kept the fatal Key,   725
Ris'n, and with hideous outcry rush'd between.
        O Father, what intends thy hand, she cri'd,
Against thy only Son?   What fury O Son
Possesses thee to bend that mortal Dart
Against thy Father's head? and know'st for whom;   730
For him who sits above and laughs the while
At thee ordain'd his drudge, to execute
Whate'er his wrath, which he calls Justice bids,
His wrath which one day will destroy ye both.
        She spake, and at her words the hellish Pest   735
Forbore, then these to her *Satan* return'd:
So strange thy outcry, and thy words so strange

708. So Aeneas' helmet shines like a portentous
comet as his ship approaches Turnus' camp (*Aen.*
X, 272–75). K. Svendsen—among several contemporary theories about comets cited in *M.&S.,*
pp. 92 and 266—quotes John Swan in *Speculum
Mundi* for the belief that, "if a Comet be in fashion
like unto a sword, it then signifieth warres and destruction of cities." Perhaps the simile in XII,
632–35, implies such a belief about the sword of
the cherubim at the gate of Paradise.

709. *Ophiucus,* the "serpent-bearer," is one of
the largest northern constellations, his name and
situation both suggesting Satan as a serpent and as
ruling the northern heavens. Cf. V, 689.

714–718. So Orlando and the Tartar king Agri-

cane encounter each other like *two black Clouds* in
Boiardo's *Orlando Innamorato* I, xvi. Cf. *M.&S.,*
p. 94.

mid air—as Svendsen notes (*M.&S.,* p. 94)—was
the region where clouds, winds, rain, hail, snow,
ice, thunder, and lightning were generated.   It was
also traditionally the realm of the demons, as
it is in I, 516, and as it plainly is again when Satan
meets his *Potentates in Council* in the *middle
Region of thick Air* in PR II, 117–118, and in IV,
409–419, has them bring a violent storm upon
Christ.

The *Caspian* Sea was proverbial for storms as early
as the reference to it as such by Horace in *Odes* II,
ix, 2.

Thou interposest, that my sudden hand
Prevented spares to tell thee yet by deeds
What it intends; till first I know of thee,   740
What thing thou art, thus double-form'd, and why
In this infernal Vale first met thou call'st
Me Father, and that Phantasm call'st my Son?
I know thee not, nor ever saw till now
Sight more detestable than him and thee.   745
    T' whom thus the Portress of Hell Gate repli'd:
Hast thou forgot me then, and do I seem
Now in thine eye so foul, once deem'd so fair
In Heav'n, when at th' Assembly, and in sight
Of all the Seraphim with thee combin'd   750
In bold conspiracy against Heav'n's King,
All on a sudden miserable pain
Surpris'd thee, dim thine eyes, and dizzy swum
In darkness, while thy head flames thick and fast
Threw forth, till on the left side op'ning wide,   755
Likest to thee in shape and count'nance bright,
Then shining heav'nly fair, a Goddess arm'd
Out of thy head I sprung: amazement seiz'd
All th' Host of Heav'n; back they recoil'd afraid
At first, and call'd me Sin, and for a Sign   760
Portentous held me; but familiar grown,
I pleas'd, and with attractive graces won
The most averse, thee chiefly, who full oft
Thyself in me thy perfect image viewing
Becam'st enamor'd, and such joy thou took'st   765
With me in secret, that my womb conceiv'd
A growing burden. Meanwhile War arose,
And fields were fought in Heav'n: wherein remain'd
(For what could else) to our Almighty Foe
Clear Victory, to our part loss and rout   770
Through all the Empyrean: down they fell
Driv'n headlong from the Pitch of Heaven, down
Into this Deep, and in the general fall
I also; at which time this powerful Key
Into my hand was giv'n, with charge to keep   775
These Gates for ever shut, which none can pass
Without my op'ning. Pensive here I sat
Alone, but long I sat not, till my womb
Pregnant by thee, and now excessive grown
Prodigious motion felt and rueful throes.   780
At last this odious offspring whom thou seest
Thine own begotten, breaking violent way
Tore through my entrails, that with fear and pain
Distorted, all my nether shape thus grew
Transform'd: but he my inbred enemy   785
Forth issu'd, brandishing his fatal Dart
Made to destroy: I fled, and cri'd out Death;

752. The myth of Athene's (Minerva's) birth from the head of Zeus in Hesiod's *Theogony* (925–29) is fused with an ancient allegory stemming from St. James's words (i, 15): "When lust hath conceived, it bringeth forth sin: and sin, when it is finished, bringeth forth death." John Gower's personification of Sin as the incestuous mother of Death in the *Mirrour de l'Omme* (205–37) and Salandra's use of the same allegory in the *Adamo caduto* have both been cited as Milton's "source."

Hell trembl'd at the hideous Name, and sigh'd
From all her Caves, and back resounded *Death*.
I fled, but he pursu'd (though more, it seems,   790
Inflam'd with lust than rage) and swifter far,
Mee overtook his mother all dismay'd,
And in embraces forcible and foul
Ingend'ring with me, of that rape begot
These yelling Monsters that with ceasless cry   795
Surround me, as thou saw'st, hourly conceiv'd
And hourly born, with sorrow infinite
To me, for when they list, into the womb
That bred them they return, and howl and gnaw
My Bowels, thir repast; then bursting forth   800
Afresh with conscious terrors vex me round,
That rest or intermission none I find.
Before mine eyes in opposition sits
Grim *Death* my Son and foe, who sets them on,
And me his Parent would full soon devour   805
For want of other prey, but that he knows
His end with mine involv'd; and knows that I
Should prove a bitter Morsel, and his bane,
Whenever that shall be; so Fate pronounc'd.
But thou O Father, I forewarn thee, shun   810
His deadly arrow; neither vainly hope
To be invulnerable in those bright Arms,
Though temper'd heav'nly, for that mortal dint,
Save he who reigns above, none can resist.
    She finish'd, and the subtle Fiend his lore   815
Soon learn'd, now milder, and thus answer'd smooth.
Dear Daughter, since thou claim'st me for thy Sire,
And my fair Son here shows't me, the dear pledge
Of dalliance had with thee in Heav'n, and joys
Then sweet, now sad to mention, through dire change   820
Befall'n us unforeseen, unthought of, know
I come no enemy, but to set free
From out this dark and dismal house of pain,
Both him and thee, and all the heav'nly Host
Of Spirits that in our just pretenses arm'd   825
Fell with us from on high: from them I go
This uncouth errand sole, and one for all
Myself expose, with lonely steps to tread
Th' unfounded deep, and through the void immense
To search with wand'ring quest a place foretold   830
Should be, and, by concurring signs, ere now
Created vast and round, a place of bliss
In the Purlieus of Heav'n, and therein plac't
A race of upstart Creatures, to supply
Perhaps our vacant room, though more remov'd,   835

798. Both the allegory and the details resemble
Spenser's Error:
      Of her there bred
A thousand yong ones, which she dayly fed,
Sucking upon her poisnous dugs, . . .
Soone as the uncouth light upon them shone,
Into her mouth they crept, and suddain all were
gone.

(*F.Q.* I, i, 15, 4–9. Cf. ll. 649–60 above.)
818. *pledge:* a child as a pledge of love.
823. *House* is used for hell as it is in Job (xxx,
23): ". . . thou wilt bring me to death, to the
house appointed for all living."
825. *pretenses:* pretensions, legal claims.

Lest Heav'n surcharg'd with potent multitude
Might hap to move new broils: Be this or aught
Than this more secret now design'd, I haste
To know, and this once known, shall soon return,
And bring ye to the place where Thou and Death   840
Shall dwell at ease, and up and down unseen ─ *smooth tongue*
Wing silently the buxom Air, imbalm'd
With odors; there ye shall be fed and fill'd
Immeasurably, all things shall be your prey.
    He ceas'd, for both seem'd highly pleas'd, and Death   845
Grinn'd horrible a ghastly smile, to hear
His famine should be fill'd, and blest his maw
Destin'd to that good hour: no less rejoic'd
His mother bad, and thus bespake her Sire.
    The key of this infernal Pit by due,   850
And by command of Heav'n's all-powerful King
I keep, by him forbidden to unlock
These Adamantine Gates; against all force
Death ready stands to interpose his dart,
Fearless to be o'ermatcht by living might.   855
But what owe I to his commands above
Who hates me, and hath hither thrust me down
Into this gloom of *Tartarus* profound,
To sit in hateful Office here confin'd,
Inhabitant of Heav'n, and heav'nly-born,   860
Here in perpetual agony and pain,
With terrors and with clamors compasst round
Of mine own brood, that on my bowels feed:
Thou art my Father, thou my Author, thou
My being gav'st me; whom should I obey   865
But thee, whom follow? thou wilt bring me soon
To that new world of light and bliss, among
The Gods who live at ease, where I shall Reign
At thy right hand voluptuous, as beseems
Thy daughter and thy darling, without end.   870
    Thus saying, from her side the fatal Key,
Sad instrument of all our woe, she took;
And towards the Gate rolling her bestial train,
Forthwith the huge Portcullis high up drew,
Which but herself not all the *Stygian* powers   875
Could once have mov'd; then in the key-hole turns
Th' intricate wards, and every Bolt and Bar
Of massy Iron or solid Rock with ease
Unfast'ns: on a sudden op'n fly
With impetuous recoil and jarring sound   880

840–844. Satan's promise is fulfilled in X, 397–409.
842. *buxom*: unresisting. Cf. V, 270.
847. *famine*: ravenous hunger. Cf. X, 991.
868. In Homer (*Il.* VI, 138; *Od.* IV, 805, etc.) the *Gods* seem always to *live at ease*.
869. Sin imagines herself enthroned with her father Satan as the Son is seated at his Father's right hand in III, 63, and B. Rajan is undoubtedly right (*Reader*, p. 50) in seeing Satan, Sin, and Death as "a kind of infernal Trinity in contrast with its heavenly counterpart." Arlene Anderson suggests that, since Sin is a product of the mind of Satan (cf. l. 858 above), as St. Thomas says that the Son "is the procession of the Word of God" (*Summa Theol.* I, xxvii, 3), and since the Son "proceeds by way of the intellect as Word, and the Holy Ghost by way of the will as love," so that "in this way it is manifest that the Holy Ghost proceeds from the Son," the entire allegory of Satan's paternity of Sin and Death is a perfect parody of orthodox theology. See the Introduction 11.

Th' infernal doors, and on thir hinges grate
Harsh Thunder, that the lowest bottom shook
Of *Erebus*. She op'n'd, but to shut
Excell'd her power; the Gates wide op'n stood,
That with extended wings a Banner'd Host   885
Under spread Ensigns marching might pass through
With Horse and Chariots rankt in loose array;
So wide they stood, and like a Furnace mouth
Cast forth redounding smoke and ruddy flame.
Before thir eyes in sudden view appear   890
The secrets of the hoary deep, a dark
Illimitable Ocean without bound,
Without dimension, where length, breadth, and highth,
And time and place are lost; where eldest *Night*
And *Chaos*, Ancestors of Nature, hold   895
Eternal Anarchy, amidst the noise
Of endless wars, and by confusion stand.
For hot, cold, moist, and dry, four Champions fierce
Strive here for Maistry, and to Battle bring
Thir embryon Atoms; they around the flag   900
Of each his Faction, in thir several Clans,
Light-arm'd or heavy, sharp, smooth, swift or slow,
Swarm populous, unnumber'd as the Sands
Of *Barca* or *Cyrene's* torrid soil,
Levied to side with warring Winds, and poise   905
Thir lighter wings. To whom these most adhere,
Hee rules a moment; *Chaos* Umpire sits,
And by decision more imbroils the fray
By which he Reigns: next him high Arbiter
Chance governs all. Into this wild Abyss,   910
The Womb of nature and perhaps her Grave,
Of neither Sea, nor Shore, nor Air, nor Fire,
But all these in thir pregnant causes mixt
Confus'dly, and which thus must ever fight,
Unless th' Almighty Maker them ordain   915
His dark materials to create more Worlds,
Into this wild Abyss the wary fiend
Stood on the brink of Hell and look'd a while,

---

883. In Hesiod's account of the generation of the oldest Gods (*Theog.*, 123), in a line which Milton quotes in his first Prolusion, *Erebus* is named as the first child of Chaos, while Night is the second. All three are personified, and in Hesiod both Erebus and Chaos mean a dark, vast, primeval envelope of space and matter and are oftenest used in a vaguely local and metaphysical sense.

891. Cf. *Abyss* in I, 21, n., and *deep* in I, 152.

895-903. The conception of *Chaos* stems both from Hesiod's mythological account and Ovid's rationalized treatment of the primeval chaotic mass of "warring seeds of things" before the world began (*Met.* I, 5-20). The conception influenced Renaissance thought so deeply that the orthodox Du Bartas imagined Chaos as corresponding to the formless "void" of Genesis i, 2, and described its "brawling Elements" as lying

"jumbled all together,
Where hot and cold were jarring each with either;

The blunt with sharp, the dank against the drie,
The hard with soft . . ."
(Sylvester's translation of Du Bartas' *Divine Weeks*—London, 1608—p. 8)
The war of the elements and its resolution by love went back to Empedocles but had been Christianized in the eclectic tradition that give Spenser his view of it as ended when "their Almightie Maker . . .

bound them with inviolable bands;
Else would the waters overflow the lands,
And fire devoure the ayre, and hell them quight."
(*F.Q.* IV, x, 35)
See the Introduction 19.

904. *Barca* is the desert between Egypt and Tunis. *Cyrene* was a city near the site of modern Tripoli.

911. The line is a translation of Lucretius' *De rerum natura* (V, 259), but his materialistic prophecy of the world's destruction is felt here as harmonious with the Christian doctrine that (in Du Bartas' words) "This *world* to Chaos shall again *return*." (*Divine Weeks, The Schisme*, p. 111.)

Pondering his Voyage: for no narrow frith
He had to cross.   Nor was his ear less peal'd   920
With noises loud and ruinous (to compare
Great things with small) than when *Bellona* storms,
With all her battering Engines bent to rase
Some Capital City; or less than if this frame
Of Heav'n were falling, and these Elements   925
In mutiny had from her Axle torn
The steadfast Earth.   At last his Sail-broad Vans
He spreads for flight, and in the surging smoke
Uplifted spurns the ground, thence many a League
As in a cloudy Chair ascending rides   930
Audacious, but that seat soon failing, meets
A vast vacuity: all unawares
Flutt'ring his pennons vain plumb down he drops
Ten thousand fadom deep, and to this hour
Down had been falling, had not by ill chance   935
The strong rebuff of some tumultuous cloud
Instinct with Fire and Nitre hurried him
As many miles aloft: that fury stay'd,
Quencht in a Boggy *Syrtis,* neither Sea,
Nor good dry Land, nigh founder'd on he fares,   940
Treading the crude consistence, half on foot,
Half flying; behoves him now both Oar and Sail.
As when a Gryfon through the Wilderness
With winged course o'er Hill or moory Dale,
Pursues the *Arimaspian,* who by stealth   945
Had from his wakeful custody purloin'd
The guarded Gold: So eagerly the fiend
O'er bog or steep, through strait, rough, dense, or rare,
With head, hands, wings, or feet pursues his way,
And swims or sinks, or wades, or creeps, or flies: 950
At length a universal hubbub wild
Of stunning sounds and voices all confus'd
Borne through the hollow dark assaults his ear
With loudest vehemence: thither he plies,
Undaunted to meet there whatever power   955
Or Spirit of the nethermost Abyss
Might in that noise reside, of whom to ask
Which way the nearest coast of darkness lies

919. *no narrow frith* (i. e. firth): no mere narrow arm of the sea.
920. *peal'd:* struck or deafened by noise. Cf.
III, 329, and *SA,* 235.
922. *Bellona:* the Roman goddess of war.
934. *fadom* was a frequent 17th century spelling
and pronunciation of *fathom.*
936–938. Contemporary science explained thunder clouds as occurring when—in the words of
J. A. Comenius' *Synopsis of Physics*—the earth's
"sulphury exhalations are mixed with nitrous, (the
first of a hot nature, the second most cold) they
endure one another so long, as till the sulphur takes
fire. But as soon as that is done, presently there
follows the same effect as in gun-powder, (whose
composition is the same of Sulphur and Nitre) a
fight, a rupture, a noise, a violent casting forth of

the matter." The entire passage from the English
translation (1651) of Comenius' *Physicae ad Lumen
Divinum reformatae Synopsis* (Amsterdam, 1643)
is quoted by E. H. Duncan in *PQ,* XXX (1951),
442–43. *Instinct:* Cf. VI, 752.
939. The classical description of the two vast tidal
marshes called the *Syrtis* is in Pliny V, iv.
945. The popular story of the gold which the
Arimaspians, "a one-eyed people" living in the
north of Europe, "steal from the griffons," goes
back to Herodotus (III, 116).
948. Cf. Sir William Alexander's abuse of this
device in *Jonathan* (556) in a duel scene between
Jonathan and Nahas; they
"Urg'd, shunn'd, forc'd, fayn'd, bow'd, rais'd, hand,
  leg, left, right, . . ."

Bordering on light; when straight behold the Throne
Of *Chaos,* and his dark Pavilion spread   960
Wide on the wasteful Deep; with him Enthron'd
Sat Sable-vested *Night,* eldest of things,
The Consort of his Reign; and by them stood
Orcus and *Ades,* and the dreaded name
Of *Demogorgon; Rumor* next and *Chance,*   965
And *Tumult* and *Confusion* all imbroil'd,
And *Discord* with a thousand various mouths.
     T' whom *Satan* turning boldly, thus.   Ye Powers
And Spirits of this nethermost Abyss,
Chaos and *ancient Night,* I come no Spy,   970
With purpose to explore or to disturb
The secrets of your Realm, but by constraint
Wand'ring this darksome Desert, as my way
Lies through your spacious Empire up to light,
Alone, and without guide, half lost, I seek   975
What readiest path leads where your gloomy bounds
Confine with Heav'n; or if some other place
From your Dominion won, th' Ethereal King
Possesses lately, thither to arrive
I travel this profound, direct my course;   980
Directed, no mean recompence it brings
To your behoof, if I that Region lost,
All usurpation thence expell'd, reduce
To her original darkness and your sway
(Which is my present journey) and once more   985
Erect the Standard there of *ancient Night;*
Yours be th' advantage all, mine the revenge.
     Thus *Satan;* and him thus the Anarch old
With falt'ring speech and visage incompos'd
Answer'd.   I know thee, stranger, who thou art,   990
That mighty leading Angel, who of late
Made head against Heav'n's King, though overthrown.
I saw and heard, for such a numerous Host
Fled not in silence through the frighted deep
With ruin upon ruin, rout on rout,   995
Confusion worse confounded; and Heav'n Gates
Pour'd out by millions her victorious Bands
Pursuing.   I upon my Frontiers here
Keep residence; if all I can will serve,
That little which is left so to defend,   1000
Encroacht on still through our intestine broils
Weak'ning the Sceptre of old *Night:* first Hell

959–967. The Pavilion of *Chaos* recalls Spenser's description of the home of the Fates,
"Farre under ground from tract of living went, Downe in the bottome of the deepe *Abysse,* Where *Demogorgon,* in dull darknesse pent, Farre from the view of gods and heavens blis, The hideous *Chaos* keepes, . . ."
     (*F.Q.* IV, ii, 47)
It more distinctly recalls Boccaccio's account of the mysterious elder deity *Demogorgon* and its vivid illustrations in the many editions of the *Genealogy of the Gods* that represent him with his offspring around him—figures like *Rumor* and *Discord, Orcus* (Hell) and *Ades* (Hades).   *Demogorgon's* name is said to be a corruption of Plato's Demiourgos in the *Timaeus* and to figure in literature for the first time in Lucan's *Pharsalia* VI, 744, where it is the kind of dreaded name that Spenser made it when he wrote that at it "*Cocytus* quakes, and *Styx* is put to flight" (*F.Q.* I, i, 37).   Cf. Milton's allusion to him as the "ancestor of all the gods" in *Prolusion* I.
     977. *Confine with:* border upon.
     988. The *Anarch: Chaos,* personified as ruler of his lawless realm.   Cf. ll. 896 and 907-10 above.
     989. *incompos'd:* discomposed.

Your dungeon stretching far and wide beneath;
Now lately Heaven and Earth, another World
Hung o'er my Realm, link'd in a golden Chain   1005
To that side Heav'n from whence your Legions fell:
If that way be your walk, you have not far;
So much the nearer danger; go and speed;
Havoc and spoil and ruin are my gain.

He ceas'd; and *Satan* stay'd not to reply,   1010
But glad that now his Sea should find a shore,
With fresh alacrity and force renew'd
Springs upward like a Pyramid of fire
Into the wild expanse, and through the shock
Of fighting Elements, on all sides round   1015
Environ'd wins his way; harder beset
And more endanger'd, than when *Argo* pass'd
Through *Bosporus* betwixt the justling Rocks:
Or when *Ulysses* on the Larboard shunn'd
Charybdis, and by th' other whirlpool steer'd.   1020
So he with difficulty and labor hard
Mov'd on, with difficulty and labor hee;
But hee once past, soon after when man fell,
Strange alteration! Sin and Death amain
Following his track, such was the will of Heav'n,   1025
Pav'd after him a broad and beat'n way
Over the dark Abyss, whose boiling Gulf
Tamely endur'd a Bridge of wondrous length
From Hell continu'd reaching th' utmost Orb
Of this frail World; by which the Spirits perverse   1030
With easy intercourse pass to and fro
To tempt or punish mortals, except whom
God and good Angels guard by special grace.
But now at last the sacred influence
Of light appears, and from the walls of Heav'n   1035
Shoots far into the bosom of dim Night
A glimmering dawn; here Nature first begins
Her fardest verge, and *Chaos* to retire
As from her outmost works a brok'n foe
With tumult less and with less hostile din,   1040
That *Satan* with less toil, and now with ease
Wafts on the calmer wave by dubious light
And like a weather-beaten Vessel holds
Gladly the Port, though Shrouds and Tackle torn;
Or in the emptier waste, resembling Air,   1045
Weighs his spread wings, at leisure to behold
Far off th' Empyreal Heav'n, extended wide
In circuit, undetermin'd square or round,

1005. For Milton's use of the Homeric story of the golden chain with which Zeus boasted that he could draw earth and all its seas up to heaven (*Il.* VIII, 23–24) see l. 1051 below, n.

1008. *danger* keeps its obsolete sense of "damage, mischief, or harm." B. A. Wright compares "Danger will wink on Opportunity" in *Comus,* 401.

1017. The *Argo* was the ship of Jason and his crew, the Argonauts, when they escaped death between the floating islands in the *Bosporus* or Straits

of Constantinople, as Apollonius of Rhodes told the tale in his *Argonautica* II, 552–611.

1020. *Charybdis* is the whirlpool on the Sicilian side of the Straits of Messina, to Ulysses' *larboard* as he sailed westward in Homer's account of his escape from Charybdis and the still more frightful Scylla (*Od.* XII, 73–100, 234–59).

1037. *Nature,* in Milton's use here, means the created world as distinct from the surrounding Chaos, where not even the first of God's creations, light, is known.

With Opal Tow'rs and Battlements adorn'd
Of living Sapphire, once his native Seat;   1050
And fast by hanging in a golden Chain
This pendant world, in bigness as a Star
Of smallest Magnitude close by the Moon.
Thither full fraught with mischievous revenge,
Accurst, and in a cursed hour he hies.   1055

The End of the Second Book.

1050. So St. John speaks of one of the foundations of heaven's wall as a sapphire (Rev. xxi, 19).

1051. Cf. Milton's use of the golden chain of Zeus in *Prolusion* II as a symbol of divine design penetrating the entire universe. The conception runs through literature from Plato's *Theaetetus* (153c) to Chaucer's *Knight's Tale* (I-A-2987-93).

"The Firste Moevere of the cause above,
When he first made the faire cheyne of love,

Greet was th'effect, and heigh was his entente.
Wel wiste he why, and what thereof he mente;
For with that faire cheyne of love he bond
The fyr, the eyr, the water, and the lond
In certeyn boundes, that they may nat flee."

1052. *The pendant world* is not the earth but the entire created universe within its "convex" shell (see III, 419), which Satan has yet to penetrate.

BOOK III

THE ARGUMENT

God *sitting on his Throne sees* Satan *flying towards this world, then newly created; shows him to the Son who sat at his right hand; foretells the success of* Satan *in perverting mankind; clears his own Justice and Wisdom from all imputation, having created Man free and able enough to have withstood his Tempter; yet declares his purpose of grace towards him, in regard he fell not of his own malice, as did* Satan, *but by him seduc't. The Son of God renders praises to his Father for the manifestation of his gracious purpose towards Man; but God again declares, that Grace cannot be extended towards Man without the satisfaction of divine Justice; Man hath offended the majesty of God by aspiring to Godhead, and therefore with all his Progeny devoted to death must die, unless some one can be found sufficient to answer for his offense, and undergo his Punishment. The Son of God freely offers himself a Ransom for Man: the Father accepts him, ordains his incarnation, pronounces his exaltation above all Names in Heaven and Earth; commands all the Angels to adore him; they obey, and hymning to thir Harps in full Choir, celebrate the Father and the Son. Meanwhile* Satan *alights upon the bare convex of this World's outermost Orb; where wand'ring he first finds a place since call'd The Limbo of Vanity; what persons and things fly up thither; thence comes to the Gate of Heaven, describ'd ascending by stairs, and the waters above the Firmament that flow about it: His passage thence to the Orb of the Sun; he finds there* Uriel *the Regent of that Orb, but first changes himself into the shape of a meaner Angel; and pretending a zealous desire to behold the new Creation and Man whom God had plac't there, inquires of him the place of his habitation, and is directed; alights first on Mount* Niphates.

Hail holy Light, offspring of Heav'n first-born,
Or of th' Eternal Coeternal beam
May I express thee unblam'd? since God is Light,
And never but in unapproached Light
Dwelt from Eternity, dwelt then in thee,   5
Bright effluence of bright essence increate.
Or hear'st thou rather pure Ethereal stream,
Whose Fountain who shall tell? before the Sun,

1-12. For the thought and its background see the Introduction 56.

7. *hear'st thou rather:* wouldest thou prefer to be called?

Before the Heavens thou wert, and at the voice
Of God, as with a Mantle didst invest   10
The rising world of waters dark and deep,
Won from the void and formless infinite.
Thee I revisit now with bolder wing,
Escap't the *Stygian* Pool, though long detain'd
In that obscure sojourn, while in my flight   15
Through utter and through middle darkness borne
With other notes than to th' *Orphean* Lyre
I sung of *Chaos* and *Eternal Night*,
Taught by the heav'nly Muse to venture down
The dark descent, and up to reascend,   20
Though hard and rare: thee I revisit safe,
And feel thy sovran vital Lamp; but thou
Revisit'st not these eyes, that roll in vain
To find thy piercing ray, and find no dawn;
So thick a drop serene hath quencht thir Orbs,   25
Or dim suffusion veil'd. Yet not the more
Cease I to wander where the Muses haunt
Clear Spring, or shady Grove, or Sunny Hill,
Smit with the love of sacred Song; but chief
Thee *Sion* and the flow'ry Brooks beneath   30
That wash thy hallow'd feet, and warbling flow,
Nightly I visit: nor sometimes forget
Those other two equall'd with me in Fate,
So were I equall'd with them in renown,
Blind *Thamyris* and blind *Mæonides*,   35
And *Tiresias* and *Phineus* Prophets old.
Then feed on thoughts, that voluntary move

9. Cf. VII, 247–49.

12. *Void:* Cf. VII, 233, n.

16. *utter and middle darkness:* Hell and Chaos. Cf. I, 72, and VI, 614.

18. Milton may have thought of the Orphic hymn to Night where Night is treated as a beneficent goddess. He surely thought of the tradition of Orpheus as the first interpreter of the physical and spiritual secrets of hell, "a man most learned in divinity," as Conti called him in *Mythologiae* VII, xiv.

21. Cf. the Sibyl's warning that the ascent from hell is hard (*Aen.* VI, 128) and its earlier echo in II, 432.

25. *drop serene* translates the *gutta serena,* the Latin medical term for "all blindness in which the eye retains a normal appearance" (Eleanor Brown, *Blindness,* p. 22). Milton was glad that his eyes— as the portrait-frontispiece of his poem proved—betrayed so little "external appearance of injury," and were "as clear and bright, without the semblance of a cloud, as the eyes of those whose sight is the most perfect" (*Def.* 2, C.E. VIII, 61).

29. The line echoes Virgil's hope (*Georg.* II, 475–92) that, smitten by the love of the Muses, he may be a prophetic poet and sing the secrets of nature.

30. To the haunts of the Muses near the Castalian spring on Mt. Parnassus Milton prefers Mt. Sion and its brooks Kidron and Siloa. For him—as for Bartolomaeus in the *Book of Nature* (1537), Kkii^v—

Sion was "the Mount of lore and teaching, as it is written in Isaye, ii, Out of Syon shall come lawe: mounte of prophesye and reuelation."

35. *Maeonides:* Homer, whose obviously blind eyes were familiar, "turn'd upwards," as George Chapman described them in *Euthymiae Raptus,* ll. 36–38, because he was "outward blind;

But, inward; past and future things he sawe;
And was to both, and present times, their lawe."

Again in the frontispiece to Chapman's translations of the Homeric Hymns Homer raises blind eyes to Apollo, Hermes, and Athene for inspiration.

Among the obscure myths about *Thamyris,* whom Homer mentions (*Il.* II, 502–509), Milton remembered that he was blind, and that Plutarch (in *On Music*) made him the author of a poem about the war of the Titans against the gods.

36. Cf. Milton's allusion in *De Idea Platonica,* ll. 25–26, to *Tiresias,* the sage who prophesies in Sophocles' *Oedipus the King* and *Antigone,* as "the Theban seer whose blindness proved his great illumination." Speaking of his own blindness (*Def* 2, C.E. VIII, 64) he quoted Apollonius' *Argonautica* about *Phineus:*

Fearless, though Jove might rage, he showed
The arcane purposes of heaven to us;
Endless old age the gods on him bestowed
And made him strong, but blind and piteous.

Phineus, who was stricken blind by the sun, Conti says (*Mythologiae* VII, vi), chose long old age and blindness rather than a short and happy life.

Harmonious numbers; as the wakeful Bird
Sings darkling, and in shadiest Covert hid
Tunes her nocturnal Note. Thus with the Year 40
Seasons return, but not to me returns
Day, or the sweet approach of Ev'n or Morn,
Or sight of vernal bloom, or Summer's Rose,
Or flocks, or herds, or human face divine;
But cloud instead, and ever-during dark 45
Surrounds me, from the cheerful ways of men
Cut off, and for the Book of knowledge fair
Presented with a Universal blanc
Of Nature's works to me expung'd and ras'd,
And wisdom at one entrance quite shut out. 50
So much the rather thou Celestial Light
Shine inward, and the mind through all her powers
Irradiate, there plant eyes, all mist from thence
Purge and disperse, that I may see and tell
Of things invisible to mortal sight. 55
  Now had th' Almighty Father from above,
From the pure Empyrean where he sits
High Thron'd above all highth, bent down his eye,
His own works and their works at once to view:
About him all the Sanctities of Heaven 60
Stood thick as Stars, and from his sight receiv'd
Beatitude past utterance; on his right
The radiant image of his Glory sat,
His only Son; On Earth he first beheld
Our two first Parents, yet the only two 65
Of mankind, in the happy Garden plact,
Reaping immortal fruits of joy and love,
Uninterrupted joy, unrivall'd love
In blissful solitude; he then survey'd
Hell and the Gulf between, and *Satan* there 70
Coasting the wall of Heav'n on this side Night
In the dun Air sublime, and ready now
To stoop with wearied wings, and willing feet
On the bare outside of this World, that seem'd

38. *numbers:* the measured rhythm of the poem. Cf. the "true musical delight" of "apt numbers" in Milton's prefatory note on the verse of *PL.*

39. *darkling:* not a participle but an adverb. Cf. *Lear* I, iv, 240: "So out went the candle and we were left darkling."

48. *blanc:* Milton's spelling when he used the word in its primitive sense of "white" or "gray." In his blindness he said that he never lost a sensation of a faint gray light about him.

51–55. The lines bravely parallel Milton's assertion of the rewards of a sharpened vision resulting from his blindness as he described it in a letter of March 24, 1656, to Emeric Bigot. His faith was supported by his confidence in the Neoplatonic conception of the "lucid essence" of God as mysteriously related to the physical light of the sun on the one hand and to the human mind on the other—a doctrine that the Lutheran theologian Philipp Melanchthon approved in his chapter on "The Image of God in Man" in his *De anima.* See the Introduction, 20.

60. *the Sanctities of Heaven:* the angelic hierarchies.

62. Cf. Milton's reference in *CD* I, xxxiii (C.E. XVI, p. 375) to the enjoyment of the sight of God as the supreme joy of the righteous in heaven. Cf. I, 684, n.

63. Hebrews i, 2–3, is quoted in *CD* I, v (see p. 935) as the fullest account of God's Son, "by whom he made the worlds. Who, being the brightness of his glory, and the express image of his person, . . . sat down on the right hand of the majesty on high."

70–73. Satan flies *sublime* (aloft) through the upper limits of Chaos and close to the wall of heaven in a twilit atmosphere (*dun air*), ready to *stoop* (pounce like a hawk) upon the outer shell of the universe.

74. *World:* not the earth, but the convex outer shell of the universe. Cf. II, 434, and VII, 266. The *Firmament* is described in VII, 261–67.

Firm land imbosom'd without Firmament,   75
Uncertain which, in Ocean or in Air.
Him God beholding from his prospect high,
Wherein past, present, future he beholds,
Thus to his only Son foreseeing spake.
  Only begotten Son, seest thou what rage   80
Transports our adversary, whom no bounds
Prescrib'd, no bars of Hell, nor all the chains
Heapt on him there, nor yet the main Abyss
Wide interrupt can hold; so bent he seems
On desperate revenge, that shall redound   85
Upon his own rebellious head. And now
Through all restraint broke loose he wings his way
Not far off Heav'n, in the Precincts of light,
Directly towards the new created World,
And Man there plac't, with purpose to assay   90
If him by force he can destroy, or worse,
By some false guile pervert; and shall pervert;
For Man will heark'n to his glozing lies,
And easily transgress the sole Command,
Sole pledge of his obedience: So will fall   95
Hee and his faithless Progeny: whose fault?
Whose but his own? ingrate, he had of mee
All he could have; I made him just and right,
Sufficient to have stood, though free to fall.
Such I created all th' Ethereal Powers   100
And Spirits, both them who stood and them who fail'd;
Freely they stood who stood, and fell who fell.
Not free, what proof could they have giv'n sincere
Of true allegiance, constant Faith or Love,
Where only what they needs must do, appear'd,   105
Not what they would? what praise could they receive?
What pleasure I from such obedience paid,
When Will and Reason (Reason also is choice)
Useless and vain, of freedom both despoil'd,
Made passive both, had serv'd necessity,   110
Not mee. They therefore as to right belong'd,
So were created, nor can justly accuse

76. *Uncertain,* an impersonal and absolute construction. It is uncertain, hard to see, whether Chaos around the floating universe is more like water or like air.

83–84. Cf. *Abyss* in I, 21, and II, 405 and 518. *interrupt* has its Latin meaning and participial form, and means "broken open."

90. *assay:* make trial.

94. *sole Command:* the prohibition to touch the tree of knowledge.

96. *faithless:* because Adam was to break faith with God by his act of disobedience and thereby—without sense of "the welfare of his offspring" (as Milton said in *CD* I, xi; C.E. XV, 183)—involve them all in his breach of faith. Cf. III, 209.

98–102. In *CD* I, iii (p. 914), in urging God's freedom from responsibility in spite of his foreknowledge, Milton said that he had gifted both men and angels with free will, so that their fall might depend upon their own volition. Thus all the evil which ensued from man's fall was entirely "contingent upon man's will." Cf. Satan's confession in IV, 63–68, and the stress on the angels' guilt in V, 525–43. The thought here, however, hardly amounts to a Pelagian profession of belief in man's ability to stand fast without support from God's grace In the word *Sufficient* Sister Mary Corcoran points out an allusion to the doctrine of sufficient grace, by which theologians of all communions held that Adam was supported before his fall (*Milton's Paradise,* 1954, pp. 104–105).

106. Pleading that the miracle of grace is enhanced, not impaired, by belief in the freedom of the will, Milton insisted in *CD* I, iv, that, "The acceptableness of duties done under a law of necessity is diminished, or rather is annihilated altogether" (C.E. XIV, 141). Cf. ll. 173–89.

108. Cf. the reliance in *Areopagitica* (see p. 733) upon Aristotle's definition of reason as the power of choice (*Nicomachean Ethics* III, ii, 6).

Thir maker, or thir making, or thir Fate;
As if Predestination over-rul'd
Thir will, dispos'd by absolute Decree   115
Or high foreknowledge; they themselves decreed
Thir own revolt, not I: if I foreknew,
Foreknowledge had no influence on their fault,
Which had no less prov'd certain unforeknown.
So without least impulse or shadow of Fate,   120
Or aught by me immutably foreseen,
They trespass, Authors to themselves in all
Both what they judge and what they choose; for so
I form'd them free, and free they must remain,
Till they enthrall themselves: I else must change   125
Thir nature, and revoke the high Decree
Unchangeable, Eternal, which ordain'd
Thir freedom: they themselves ordain'd thir fall.
The first sort by thir own suggestion fell,
Self-tempted, self-deprav'd: Man falls deceiv'd   130
By th' other first: Man therefore shall find grace,
The other none: in Mercy and Justice both,
Through Heav'n and Earth, so shall my glory excel,
But Mercy first and last shall brightest shine.
    Thus while God spake, ambrosial fragrance fill'd   135
All Heav'n, and in the blessed Spirits elect
Sense of new joy ineffable diffus'd:
Beyond compare the Son of God was seen
Most glorious, in him all his Father shone
Substantially express'd, and in his face   140
Divine compassion visibly appear'd,
Love without end, and without measure Grace,
Which uttering thus he to his Father spake.
    O Father, gracious was that word which clos'd
Thy sovran sentence, that Man should find grace;   145
For which both Heav'n and Earth shall high extol
Thy praises, with th' innumerable sound
Of Hymns and sacred Songs, wherewith thy Throne
Encompass'd shall resound thee ever blest.
For should Man finally be lost, should Man   150
Thy creature late so lov'd, thy youngest Son
Fall circumvented thus by fraud, though join'd
With his own folly? that be from thee far,
That far be from thee, Father, who art Judge
Of all things made, and judgest only right.   155

119. The long chapter on *Predestination* in *CD*
I, iv, is devoted to proof that "the prescience of God
seems to have no connection with the principle or
essence of predestination."
    128. Cf. *CD* I, iii, where Milton insists that "God
is not mutable, so long as he decrees nothing absolutely which could happen otherwise through the
liberty that he assigns to man. He would indeed
be mutable if he were to obstruct by another decree
that liberty which he had already decreed, or were
to darken it with the least shadow of necessity"
(see p. 913).
    129. *The first sort:* the angels who revolted.
suggestion: temptation.

136. The good angels are *Spirits elect.* In *CD*
I, ix, Milton challenges the "opinion that the good
angels are now upheld, not as much by their own
strength, as by the grace of God"; and he adds that
"the elect angels" of I Timothy v, 21, means "those
who have not revolted" (see p. 990). Cf. l. 184
below.
    140. Hebrews i, 2–3, is interpreted (in *CD* I,
v; see p. 935) to mean that "God imparted to
the Son as much as he pleased of the divine nature,
nay of the divine substance itself." The passage
does not necessarily contradict the conception of the
Son in *CD* I, v. Cf. Maurice Kelly, in *Argument,*
p. 30.

Or shall the Adversary thus obtain
His end, and frustrate thine, shall he fulfil
His malice, and thy goodness bring to naught,
Or proud return though to his heavier doom,
Yet with revenge accomplish't and to Hell   160
Draw after him the whole Race of mankind,
By him corrupted? or wilt thou thyself
Abolish thy Creation, and unmake,
For him, what for thy glory thou hast made?
So should thy goodness and thy greatness both   165
Be question'd and blasphem'd without defense.
    To whom the great Creator thus repli'd.
O Son, in whom my Soul hath chief delight,
Son of my bosom, Son who art alone
My word, my wisdom, and effectual might,   170
All hast thou spok'n as my thoughts are, all
As my Eternal purpose hath decreed:
Man shall not quite be lost, but sav'd who will,
Yet not of will in him, but grace in me
Freely voutsaf't; once more I will renew   175
His lapsed powers, though forfeit and enthrall'd
By sin to foul exorbitant desires;
Upheld by me, yet once more he shall stand
On even ground against his mortal foe,
By me upheld, that he may know how frail   180
His fall'n condition is, and to me owe
All his deliv'rance, and to none but me.
Some I have chosen of peculiar grace
Elect above the rest; so is my will:
The rest shall hear me call, and oft be warn'd   185
Thir sinful state, and to appease betimes
Th' incensed Deity while offer'd grace
Invites; for I will clear thir senses dark,
What may suffice, and soft'n stony hearts
To pray, repent, and bring obedience due.   190
To Prayer, repentance, and obedience due,
Though but endeavor'd with sincere intent,
Mine ear shall not be slow, mine eye not shut.

156. Cf. II, 629, and "foe" in l. 179 below.
166. *blasphem'd* keeps its Greek force of "insulting," "evil-speaking."
168. Cf. the words from heaven at Christ's baptism: "This is my beloved Son, in whom I am well pleased" (Matt. iii, 17), and the naming of Christ as "the only begotten Son, which is in the bosom of the Father" (John i, 18).
174. The distinction between God's grace and man's will may—as Leon Howard insists in *HLQ*, IX (1945), 168—be an explicit dichotomy such as logicians of Ramus' school made between the two parts of the efficient cause of man's salvation, his own will as the impelling, helping part, and God's grace as the instrumental cause. Milton insists upon the co-operation of the two.
176. *lapsed*: (literally) fallen, and therefore diminished. *forfeit*—forfeited—anticipates the legal view of the penalty properly to be paid by Adam in l. 210 below.

180. "Lord, make me to know . . . how frail I am" (Psalm xxxix, 4).
183–193. Milton distils the essence of his chapter "On Predestination" in *CD* I, iv, which challenges the Calvinistic doctrine (as characteristically stated in the Westminster Confession) that "before the foundation of the world" God, for his own glory, "without any foresight of faith and good works, or perseverance in either of them," had predestined certain souls to salvation and ordained others "to dishonor and wrath for their sin." Milton explains God's "election" of men in terms of his "sufficient grace" and their free acceptance of it. So "none can be reprobated, except they do not believe or continue in the faith, and even this as a consequence rather than a decree" (C. E. XIV, 141). M. Kelley analyses the chapter and the Confession in *PMLA*, LII (1937), 75–79.
190. The line looks forward to X, 1081–96.

And I will place within them as a guide
My Umpire *Conscience,* whom if they will hear,   195
Light after light well us'd they shall attain,
And to the end persisting, safe arrive.
This my long sufferance and my day of grace
They who neglect and scorn, shall never taste;
But hard be hard'n'd, blind be blinded more,   200
That they may stumble on, and deeper fall;
And none but such from mercy I exclude.
But yet all is not done; Man disobeying,
Disloyal breaks his fealty, and sins
Against the high Supremacy of Heav'n,   205
Affecting God-head, and so losing all,
To expiate his Treason hath naught left,
But to destruction sacred and devote,
He with his whole posterity must die,
Die hee or Justice must; unless for him   210
Some other able, and as willing, pay
The rigid satisfaction, death for death.
Say Heav'nly Powers, where shall we find such love,
Which of ye will be mortal to redeem
Man's mortal crime, and just th' unjust to save,   215
Dwells in all Heaven charity so dear?
    He ask'd, but all the Heav'nly Choir stood mute,
And silence was in Heav'n: on man's behalf
Patron or Intercessor none appear'd,
Much less that durst upon his own head draw   220
The deadly forfeiture, and ransom set.
And now without redemption all mankind
Must have been lost, adjudg'd to Death and Hell
By doom severe, had not the Son of God,
In whom the fulness dwells of love divine,   225
His dearest mediation thus renew'd.
    Father, thy word is past, man shall find grace;
And shall grace not find means, that finds her way,
The speediest of thy winged messengers,
To visit all thy creatures, and to all   230
Comes unprevented, unimplor'd, unsought?
Happy for man, so coming; he her aid
Can never seek, once dead in sins and lost;
Atonement for himself or offering meet,
Indebted and undone, hath none to bring: 235

195 *Conscience* is constantly equated with reason
and individual judgment in the *CD.* In the end,
says the chapter on the Last Judgment (I, xxxiii),
man shall be judged according to the response of
his conscience to "the measure of light which he has
enjoyed" (C. E. XVI, 357).
    206. It is to be a "Goddess among Gods" that
Satan tempts Eve (IX, 547).
    208. *sacred* and *devote* both keep their Latin
meaning of "dedicated to a deity" for destruction.
    216. *charity* has its Greek meaning of "love" that
is usual in the New Testament.
    218. So St. John says that there was silence in
heaven when the seventh seal was opened (Rev.
viii, 1).

219. *Patron,* in its Latin sense of a defender in a
court of law, and *Intercessor* both reflect the conception of Christ in I John ii, 1: "And if any man
sin, we have an advocate with the Father, Jesus
Christ the righteous."
    225. In the chapter on the Son in *CD* I, v Mil-
ton quotes John iii, 35, "The Father loveth the
Son, and hath given all things into his hand," as
evidence of his power as Redeemer.
    231. *unprevented* has its Latin meaning of "un-
anticipated."
    233. So Christ is the reviver of those who are
"dead in sins" (Col. ii, 13).

Behold mee then, mee for him, life for life
I offer, on mee let thine anger fall;
Account mee man; I for his sake will leave
Thy bosom, and this glory next to thee
Freely put off, and for him lastly die   240
Well pleas'd, on me let Death wreck all his rage;
Under his gloomy power I shall not long
Lie vanquisht; thou hast giv'n me to possess
Life in myself for ever, by thee I live,
Though now to Death I yield, and am his due   245
All that of me can die, yet that debt paid,
Thou wilt not leave me in the loathsome grave
His prey, nor suffer my unspotted Soul
For ever with corruption there to dwell;
But I shall rise Victorious, and subdue   250
My vanquisher, spoil'd of his vaunted spoil;
Death his death's wound shall then receive, and stoop
Inglorious, of his mortal sting disarm'd.
I through the ample Air in Triumph high
Shall lead Hell Captive maugre Hell, and show   255
The powers of darkness bound. Thou at the sight
Pleas'd, out of Heaven shalt look down and smile,
While by thee rais'd I ruin all my Foes,
Death last, and with his Carcass glut the Grave:
Then with the multitude of my redeem'd   260
Shall enter Heav'n long absent, and return,
Father, to see thy face, wherein no cloud
Of anger shall remain, but peace assur'd,
And reconcilement; wrath shall be no more
Thenceforth, but in thy presence Joy entire.   265
    His words here ended, but his meek aspéct
Silent yet spake, and breath'd immortal love
To mortal men, above which only shone
Filial obedience: as a sacrifice
Glad to be offer'd, he attends the will   270
Of his great Father. Admiration seiz'd
All Heav'n, what this might mean, and whither tend
Wond'ring; but soon th' Almighty thus repli'd:
    O thou in Heav'n and Earth the only peace
Found out for mankind under wrath, O thou   275

246. Both M. Kelley (*Argument,* p. 32) and D. Saurat—*RES,* XII (1936), 324—think that Milton is influenced by the doctrine of Robert Overton in *Man's Mortality* (1655), that the soul is simply the life of the body and perishes with it at death (to revive only at the resurrection). But Kelley believes Milton's meaning to be that, "on account of our sins, even the soul of Christ was for a short time subject unto death," while Saurat believes it to be that, because the Son's "soul—his life—is unspotted, therefore he shall not die." Actually the words are traditional in this connection and occur without theological surcharge about the Son's immunity to death in Serafino Salandra's *Adamo caduto* (Cosanza, 1647), V, vii, p. 123. Milton is not splitting theological hairs; he is dealing with the justice of Christ's incarnation and crucifixion, which—as Beatrice explains to Dante in *Paradiso*

VII, 40–42—can be explained only on the ground that in assuming human nature Christ became guilty of all human sin.

253. Milton seems to have been influenced by Sannazaro, in the first book of whose epic on the birth of Christ, *De partu Virginis,* he found a similar network of biblical texts forming a prophecy which is put into the mouth of David. Pluto (Satan) is foreseen as led captive to Tartarus while Christ conquers the powers of the air (the fiends) and subdues Death and Hell.

254. The lines echo Psalm lxviii, 18: "Thou hast ascended on high, thou hast led captivity captive."

255. *maugre:* in spite of.

259. "The last enemy to be destroyed is death" (I Cor. xv, 26).

270. *attends:* waits (for an expression of his Father's will).

My sole complacence! well thou know'st how dear
To me are all my works, nor Man the least
Though last created, that for him I spare
Thee from my bosom and right hand, to save,
By losing thee a while, the whole Race lost.   280
Thou therefore whom thou only canst redeem,
Thir Nature also to thy Nature join;
And be thyself Man among men on Earth,
Made flesh, when time shall be, of Virgin seed,
By wondrous birth: Be thou in *Adam's* room   285
The Head of all mankind, though *Adam's* Son.
As in him perish all men, so in thee
As from a second root shall be restor'd,
As many as are restor'd, without thee none.
His crime makes guilty all his Sons, thy merit   290
Imputed shall absolve them who renounce
Thir own both righteous and unrighteous deeds,
And live in thee transplanted, and from thee
Receive new life. So Man, as is most just,
Shall satisfy for Man, be judg'd and die,   295
And dying rise, and rising with him raise
His Brethren, ransom'd with his own dear life.
So Heav'nly love shall outdo Hellish hate,
Giving to death, and dying to redeem,
So dearly to redeem what Hellish hate   300
So easily destroy'd, and still destroys
In those who, when they may, accept not grace.
Nor shalt thou by descending to assume
Man's Nature, lessen or degrade thine own.
Because thou hast, though Thron'd in highest bliss   305
Equal to God, and equally enjoying
God-like fruition, quitted all to save
A world from utter loss, and hast been found
By Merit more than Birthright Son of God,
Found worthiest to be so by being Good,   310
Far more than Great or High; because in thee
Love hath abounded more than Glory abounds,
Therefore thy Humiliation shall exalt
With thee thy Manhood also to this Throne;
Here shalt thou sit incarnate, here shalt Reign   315
Both God and Man, Son both of God and Man,
Anointed universal King; all Power

276. *complacence:* satisfaction, basis of pleasure.

282. "How much better it is for us to know simply that the Son of God, our Mediator, was made flesh, that he is called both God and Man, and is such in reality," than it is to indulge in subtle explanations of the fact, says Milton in *CD* I, xiv (C.E. XV, 272).

284. Similarly in Matthew i, 23, Isaiah's prophecy (vii, 14), "Behold a virgin shall conceive, and bear a son, and shall call his name Immanuel," is interpreted as a prophecy of the birth of Christ. Cf. X, 74.

287. "For as in Adam all die, even so in Christ shall all be made alive" (I Cor. xv, 22).

291. So, says Milton in *CD* I, xxii (C. E. XVI,

29), "Christ paid the ransom of our sins, which he took upon himself by imputation."

299. "The Son of Man came . . . to give his life a ransom for many" (Matt. xx, 28).

306. The hard problem of Milton's precise view of the Son's equality to the Father, if it can be solved in any single statement in the chapter on the Son of God in *CD* (I, v), is best reduced to the statement that, "lastly, the Son himself and his apostles acknowledge throughout the whole of their discourses and writings, that the Father is greater than the Son in all things" (see p. 939).

317-318. The lines fuse God's words to the Son in Hebrews i, 9: "Thou hast loved righteousness and hated iniquity; therefore God, even thy God, hath

I give thee, reign for ever, and assume
Thy Merits; under thee as Head Supreme
Thrones, Princedoms, Powers, Dominions I reduce: 320
All knees to thee shall bow, of them that bide
In Heaven, or Earth, or under Earth in Hell;
When thou attended gloriously from Heav'n
Shalt in the Sky appear, and from thee send
The summoning Arch-Angels to proclaim   325
Thy dread Tribunal: forthwith from all Winds
The living, and forthwith the cited dead
Of all past Ages to the general Doom
Shall hast'n, such a peal shall rouse thir sleep.
Then all thy Saints assembl'd, thou shalt judge   330
Bad men and Angels, they arraign'd shall sink
Beneath thy Sentence; Hell, her numbers full,
Thenceforth shall be for ever shut. Meanwhile
The World shall burn, and from her ashes spring
New Heav'n and Earth, wherein the just shall dwell   335
And after all thir tribulations long
See golden days, fruitful of golden deeds,
With Joy and Love triumphing, and fair Truth.
Then thou thy regal Sceptre shalt lay by,
For regal Sceptre then no more shall need,   340
God shall be All in All. But all ye Gods,
Adore him, who to compass all this dies,
Adore the Son, and honor him as mee.
    No sooner had th' Almighty ceas't, but all
The multitude of Angels with a shout   345
Loud as from numbers without number, sweet
As from blest voices, uttering joy, Heav'n rung
With Jubilee, and loud Hosannas fill'd
Th' eternal Regions: lowly reverent
Towards either Throne they bow, and to the ground   350
With solemn adoration down they cast
Thir Crowns inwove with Amarant and Gold,
Immortal Amarant, a Flow'r which once   — digression
In Paradise, fast by the Tree of Life
Began to bloom, but soon for man's offense   355
To Heav'n remov'd where first it grew, there grows,
And flow'rs aloft shading the Fount of Life,
And where the river of Bliss through midst of Heav'n

---

anointed thee with the oil of gladness above thy fellows," and Christ's saying that, "All power is given unto me" (Matt. xxviii, 18).

321. The promise stems from Philippians ii, 10: "That at the name of Jesus every knee should bow, of things in heaven, and things in earth, and things under the earth."

324. The details of the last judgment are from Matthew xxv, 31–32, and I Thessalonians iv, 16.

326. *from all Winds:* from all directions.

334. *CD* I, xxxiii (C. E. XVI, 369) affirms "the destruction of the present unclean and polluted world itself, namely, the FINAL CONFLAGRATION."

335. The new heaven and earth of Revelation xxi, 1, meant to Milton "the renovation of heaven **and earth, and of all things therein adapted to our**

service or delight, to be possessed in perpetuity—Isaiah lxv, 17" (C. E. XVI, 379). Cf. XI, 900–901 and XII, 547–51.

341. "And when all things shall be subdued unto him, then shall the Son himself be subject unto him that put all things under him, that God may be all in all" (I Cor. xv, 28). For *Gods* see II, 352, n.

353. *Amarant* (unfading) describes the saints' "heavenly inheritance incorruptible and undefiled, that fadeth not away" in I Peter i, 4. The flower amaranthus ("Love-lies-bleeding" or "Prince's Feather") grows beside the Tree of Life—D. C. Allen suggests—because Clement of Alexandria put it there in the *Paedagogus* (Dindorff, I, 277). Cf. *Lyc,* 149 and *PL* XI, 78.

358. *The river of Bliss* is St. John's "pure river

Rolls o'er *Elysian* Flow'rs her Amber stream;
With these that never fade the Spirits elect 360
Bind thir resplendent locks inwreath'd with beams,
Now in loose Garlands thick thrown off, the bright
Pavement that like a Sea of Jasper shone
Impurpl'd with Celestial Roses smil'd.
Then Crown'd again thir gold'n Harps they took, 365
Harps ever tun'd, that glittering by thir side
Like Quivers hung, and with Preamble sweet
Of charming symphony they introduce
Thir sacred Song, and waken raptures high;
No voice exempt, no voice but well could join 370
Melodious part, such concord is in Heav'n.
　　Thee Father first they sung Omnipotent,
Immutable, Immortal, Infinite,
Eternal King; thee Author of all being,
Fountain of Light, thyself invisible 375
Amidst the glorious brightness where thou sit'st
Thron'd inaccessible, but when thou shad'st
The full blaze of thy beams, and through a cloud
Drawn round about thee like a radiant Shrine,
Dark with excessive bright thy skirts appear, 380
Yet dazzle Heav'n, that brightest Seraphim
Approach not, but with both wings veil thir eyes.
Thee next they sang of all Creation first,
Begotten Son, Divine Similitude,
In whose conspicuous count'nance, without cloud 385
Made visible, th' Almighty Father shines,
Whom else no Creature can behold; on thee
Impresst th' effulgence of his Glory abides,
Transfus'd on thee his ample Spirit rests.
Hee Heav'n of Heavens and all the Powers therein 390
By thee created, and by thee threw down
Th' aspiring Dominations: thou that day
Thy Father's dreadful Thunder didst not spare,
Nor stop thy flaming Chariot wheels, that shook
Heav'n's everlasting Frame, while o'er the necks 395
Thou drov'st of warring Angels disarray'd.

of water of life, clear as crystal" (Rev. xxii, 1) though it flows through the Elysian Fields and is the haunt of spirits singing paeans, as Virgil describes the Elysian river (*Aen.* VI, 656–59).

363. The colors are those of the "sea of glass, like unto crystal" (Rev. iv, 6) and the "light like unto a stone most precious, even like a jasper stone, clear as crystal" (Rev. xxi, 11) that St. John saw around the throne of God.

373–382. Visually, the lines recall Moses' accounts of God speaking to him on Sinai when "a cloud covered the mount" (Exod. xxiv, 15) and Isaiah's vision (vi, 1–4) of "the Lord sitting upon a throne" with the seraphim veiling their eyes about him in the smoke-filled temple. Theologically, the lines reflect Milton's thought in *CD* I, ii, that, as the uncaused cause, God is knowable and definable only by his attributes. But the conception was familiar, as G. C. Taylor notes in *Milton and Du Bartas*, p. 42, and was put in superficially simi-

lar language in Sylvester's translation of the *Divine Weeks* (p. 2):

> Before all Time, all Matter, Form, and Place,
> God all in all, and all in God it was:
> Immutable, immortal, infinite,
> Incomprehensible, all spirit, all light,
> All Majestie, all-self-Omnipotent,
> Invisible.

Cf. II, 264, and V, 599.

383–392. The conception of the Son as the Word *by* whom God created the universe is elaborated in *CD* I, vii (see p. 974). Cf. VII, 174–75. The Son's triumph over the *aspiring Dominations* or rebellious powers of Satan is the theme of VI, 824–92.

389. M. Kelley rightly observes that here and in I, 17, and VII, 165, 209, and 235, the reference is to the "virtue and power of God the Father," and "not to the Third Person" or Holy Spirit (*Argument,* p. 109).

Back from pursuit thy Powers with loud acclaim
Thee only extoll'd, Son of thy Father's might,
To execute fierce vengeance on his foes:
Not so on Man; him through their malice fall'n,   400
Father of Mercy and Grace, thou didst not doom
So strictly, but much more to pity incline:
No sooner did thy dear and only Son
Perceive thee purpos'd not to doom frail Man   *confusion*
So strictly, but much more to pity inclin'd,   405
Hee to appease thy wrath, and end the strife
Of Mercy and Justice in thy face discern'd,
Regardless of the Bliss wherein hee sat
Second to thee, offer'd himself to die
For man's offense. O unexampl'd love,   410
Love nowhere to be found less than Divine!
Hail Son of God, Savior of Men, thy Name
Shall be the copious matter of my Song
Henceforth, and never shall my Harp thy praise
Forget, nor from thy Father's praise disjoin.   415
    Thus they in Heav'n, above the starry Sphere,
Thir happy hours in joy and hymning spent.
Meanwhile upon the firm opacous Globe
Of this round World, whose first convex divides
The luminous inferior Orbs, enclos'd   420
From *Chaos* and th' inroad of Darkness old,
Satan alighted walks: a Globe far off
It seem'd, now seems a boundless Continent
Dark, waste, and wild, under the frown of Night
Starless expos'd, and ever-threat'ning storms   425
Of *Chaos* blust'ring round, inclement sky;
Save on that side which from the wall of Heav'n,
Though distant far, some small reflection gains
Of glimmering air less vext with tempest loud:
Here walk'd the Fiend at large in spacious field.   430
As when a Vultur on *Imaus* bred,
Whose snowy ridge the roving *Tartar* bounds,
Dislodging from a Region scarce of prey
To gorge the flesh of Lambs or yeanling Kids
On Hills where Flocks are fed, flies toward the Springs   435
Of *Ganges* or *Hydaspes, Indian* streams;
But in his way lights on the barren Plains
Of *Sericana*, where *Chineses* drive

413. Here, as usual in his angel choruses, Milton puts himself into the choir and uses *my Song* and *Harp* as if he spoke with the angels as a representative of the City of God on earth.

416. *The starry Sphere* is inside the shell of the universe on which Satan has landed in l. 74 above. The empyreal heaven of the angels is outside and "above" it.

418. *opacous:* opaque.

431. The vulture was described in Batman's version of Bartholomaeus' *Book of Nature* (*De proprietatibus rerum*, 1582, p. Gg) as able to scent its prey across whole continents. Milton's picture resembles Ortelius' maps of Asia, showing Mt. *Imaus* stretching from the Hyperborean Ocean to the Caucasus, with *Sericana* to the southeast and the

Hydaspes flowing into the Indus, but—as Starnes and Talbert note in *Dictionaries*, p. 322—it more closely resembles the description of the sources of the Ganges and Hydaspes in the dictionaries.

438–439. Several geographers confirmed the story of the Chinese wind-wagons, which first reached England in Robert Parke's translation of the Spanish Jesuit Juan Gonzalez de Mendoza's *Historie of the Great and Mighty Kingdome of China* (1588). F. L. Huntley says in *MLN*, LXIX (1954), 406, that Ortelius' maps of China were trimmed with handsome landships, but he suspects that Milton was sceptical of Mendoza's story and intended his readers to recall that his name, in its Latin form, means "blundersome" and therefore "untrustworthy."

With Sails and Wind thir cany Waggons light:
So on this windy Sea of Land, the Fiend   440
Walk'd up and down alone bent on his prey,
Alone, for other Creature in this place
Living or lifeless to be found was none,
None yet, but store hereafter from the earth
Up hither like Aereal vapors flew   445
Of all things transitory and vain, when Sin
With vanity had fill'd the works of men:
Both all things vain, and all who in vain things
Built thir fond hopes of Glory or lasting fame,
Or happiness in this or th' other life;   450
All who have thir reward on Earth, the fruits
Of painful Superstition and blind Zeal,
Naught seeking but the praise of men, here find
Fit retribution, empty as thir deeds;
All th' unaccomplisht works of Nature's hand,   455
Abortive, monstrous, or unkindly mixt,
Dissolv'd on Earth, fleet hither, and in vain,
Till final dissolution, wander here,
Not in the neighboring Moon, as some have dream'd;
Those argent Fields more likely habitants,   460
Translated Saints, or middle Spirits hold
Betwixt th' Angelical and Human kind:
Hither of ill-join'd Sons and Daughters born
First from the ancient World those Giants came
With many a vain exploit, though then renown'd: 465
The builders next of *Babel* on the Plain
Of *Sennaar*, and still with vain design
New *Babels*, had they wherewithal, would build:
Others came single; he who to be deem'd
A God, leap'd fondly into *Ætna* flames,   470
Empedocles, and hee who to enjoy
Plato's Elysium, leap'd into the Sea,
Cleombrotus, and many more too long,
Embryos, and Idiots, Eremites and Friars
White, Black and Grey, with all thir trumpery.   475

444–496. Though Milton (l. 471), like Dante (*Inf.* IV, 138), puts Empedocles into Limbo, his Limbo of Vanity has little in common with Dante's circle of the great poets, philosophers, and heroes. Nor has it much in common with Ariosto's lunar Limbo where Astolfo finds his own and Orlando's lost wits in
  "a goodly valley, where he sees
A mighty mass of things strangely confus'd,
  Things that on earth were lost, or were abus'd."
(*Orlando Furioso* XXXIV, 70. The translation is by Milton in *Of Reformation in England*.)
In "A Justification of Milton's Paradise of Fools" in *ELH*, XXI (1954), 107–113, F. L. Huntley relates the entire passage to Satan's purposes by observing that his pride, his "bluster and disguise," and his paternity of Sin and Death are all symbolized by the human types that gather on the windy outside of the shell of Milton's universe.
459–462. The air, the moon, and the stars had speculatively been peopled with various spirit inhabitants by philosophers like Giordano Bruno,

Jerome Cardan, and Milton's contemporary at Cambridge, Henry More. "Readers of *PL*," says H. Schultz in *Milton and Forbidden Knowledge*, p. 16, "had been taught to smile, especially at moon-dwellers, by Ariosto's Lunar paradise or Donne's in *Ignatius*, the supplement to the *Satyre Menippé*, Ben Jonson's masques," etc.
464. For the story of the misbegotten giants see XI, 573–97.
466. For *Babel* see XII, 45. *Sennaar* is the plain of Shinar in Genesis x, 10.
470–474. As J. Horrell notes in *RES*, xviii (1943), 413–27, these suicides come from Lactantius' chapter on "The False Wisdom of the Philosophers" in the *Divine Institutes* III. The moral was pointed by Joseph Hall in *Heaven upon Earth*, 17, and by John Eliot in *The Monarchie of Man* (ed. Grosart, 1879, II, 162), where Cleombrotus is said to have killed himself after a too enthusiastic study of "Platoes discourses of the immortalitie of the Soule" (*Phaedo*, 68).
474–475. *Eremites:* hermits. The *White Friars*

Here Pilgrims roam, that stray'd so far to seek
In *Golgotha* him dead, who lives in Heav'n;
And they who to be sure of Paradise
Dying put on the weeds of *Dominic,*
Or in *Franciscan* think to pass disguis'd;   480
They pass the Planets seven, and pass the fixt,
And that Crystalline Sphere whose balance weighs
The Trepidation talkt, and that first mov'd;
And now Saint *Peter* at Heav'n's Wicket seems
To wait them with his Keys, and now at foot   485
Of Heav'n's ascent they lift thir Feet, when lo
A violent cross wind from either Coast
Blows them transverse ten thousand Leagues awry
Into the devious Air; then might ye see
Cowls, Hoods and Habits with thir wearers tost   490
And flutter'd into Rags, then Reliques, Beads,
Indulgences, Dispenses, Pardons, Bulls,
The sport of Winds: all these upwhirl'd aloft
Fly o'er the backside of the World far off
Into a *Limbo* large and broad, since call'd   495
The Paradise of Fools, to few unknown
Long after, now unpeopl'd, and untrod;
All this dark Globe the Fiend found as he pass'd,
And long he wander'd, till at last a gleam
Of dawning light turn'd thither-ward in haste   500
His travell'd steps; far distant he descries
Ascending by degrees magnificent
Up to the wall of Heaven a Structure high,
At top whereof, but far more rich appear'd
The work as of a Kingly Palace Gate   505
With Frontispiece of Diamond and Gold
Imbellisht; thick with sparkling orient Gems
The Portal shone, inimitable on Earth
By Model, or by shading Pencil drawn.
The Stairs were such as whereon *Jacob* saw   510

are the Carmelites; the *Black*, the Dominicans; and the *Grey*, the Franciscans.

477. *Golgotha:* the hill near Jerusalem where Christ was crucified (John xix, 17).

479. Illustrations of the practice are given by J. Huizinga in *The Waning of the Middle Ages* (London, 1924), pp. 164–65.

481–483. "They pass the seven planets; the star-sphere; and the crystalline sphere, whose balance (i.e. the sign of Libra, the Scales), weighs (i.e. measures) the amount of the supposed trepidation of the star-sphere; and they pass the primum mobile."—G. Carnall's paraphrase in *N&Q*, CXCVII (1952), 315–16. Cf. l. 558 below.

483. *Trepidation:* "a libration of the eighth or ninth sphere, added to the system of Ptolemy by the Arab astronomer Thabet ben Korah, c. 950, . . . to account for certain phenomena . . . really due to the rotation of the earth's axis" (O.E.D.). An account of Copernicus' use of the hypothesis of trepidation to explain the observable irregularities in the precession of the equinoxes is given by F. R. Johnson in *Astronomical Thought in Renaissance England* (Baltimore, 1937), pp. 110–11.

490-496. An illuminating parallel to this passage has been noted by W. J. Grace—in *SP*, LII (1955), 590—in Burton's anticipation of phrases like "the sport of Winds" and "Indulgences, Dispenses, Pardons, Bulls" in the familiar passage in the *Anatomy* III, iv, 1, 2 (III, 333, Everyman Ed.) which declares that the doctrine of pardons (*Dispenses* in Milton's phrase) has "so fleeced the commonalty, and spurred on this free superstitious horse, that he runs himself blind, and is an Ass to carry burdens."

501. *travell'd* has the French and Italian force of "tired."

502. *degrees:* steps (of a stairway).

506. *Frontispiece:* façade of heaven's gate, the *Wicket* of l. 484 above.

510–518. The *mysteriously meant* stair is the ladder whose top Jacob dreamed "reached to heaven, and behold the angels of God ascending and descending on it" (Gen. xxviii, 12). The scene of his vision in *Padan-Aram* was familiar in an actual representation of the "ladder" on Fuller's map showing it in the *field of Luz* in *A Pisgah-Sight.* Milton knew it also in Dante's vision

Angels ascending and descending, bands
Of Guardians bright, when he from *Esau* fled
To *Padan-Aram* in the field of *Luz,*
Dreaming by night under the open Sky,
And waking cri'd, *This is the Gate of Heav'n.*   515
Each Stair mysteriously was meant, nor stood
There always, but drawn up to Heav'n sometimes
Viewless, and underneath a bright Sea flow'd
Of Jasper, or of liquid Pearl, whereor
Who after came from Earth, sailing arriv'd,   520
Wafted by Angels, or flew o'er the Lake
Rapt in a Chariot drawn by fiery Steeds.
The Stairs were then let down, whether to dare
The Fiend by easy ascent, or aggravate
His sad exclusion from the doors of Bliss.   525
Direct against which op'n'd from beneath,
Just o'er the blissful seat of Paradise,
A passage down to th' Earth, a passage wide,
Wider by far than that of after-times
Over Mount *Sion,* and, though that were large,   530
Over the *Promis'd Land* to God so dear,
By which, to visit oft those happy Tribes,
On high behests his Angels to and fro
Pass'd frequent, and his eye with choice regard
From *Paneas* the fount of *Jordan's* flood   535
To *Beërsaba,* where the *Holy Land*
Borders on *Egypt* and th' *Arabian* shore;
So wide the op'ning seem'd, where bourds were set
To darkness, such as bound the Ocean wave.
Satan from hence now on the lower stair   540
That scal'd by steps of Gold to Heaven Gate
Looks down with wonder at the sudden view
Of all this World at once. As when a Scout
Through dark and desert ways with peril gone
All night; at last by break of cheerful dawn   545
Obtains the brow of some high-climbing Hill,
Which to his eye discovers unaware
The goodly prospect of some foreign land
First seen, or some renown'd Metropolis
With glistering Spires and Pinnacles adorn'd,   550
Which now the Rising Sun gilds with his beams.
Such wonder seiz'd, though after Heaven seen,
The Spirit malign, but much more envy seiz'd
At sight of all this World beheld so fair.

of it in the Orb of Saturn (*Par.* xxi), where the poet meets Sts. Damian and Benedict and is amazed by their glory and their denunciation of corruption in the Church. Sacred art often portrayed it, and—as D. C. Allen notes in *MLN,* LXVIII (1953), 360—liberal interpreters like Jean Bodin (in *Heptaplomeres*) identified it with the golden chain of Zeus (to which Milton refers in II, 1005 and 1051) as a symbol of the links of causation that bind the universe together.

518-519. The *Sea . . . of Jasper* is the "waters above the Firmament" which the Argument to this book says flow about the gate of heaven. Cf.

l. 574 below and VII, 261.

521. The parable of the flight of the beggar Lazarus to heaven in the arms of angels (Luke xvi, 22) is parallelled with Elijah's translation to heaven in a "chariot of fire" (II Kings ii, 11).

530. Cf. *Sion* in I, 386 and 442, and III, 30.

535-536. *Paneas,* the city of Dan, near the source of the Jordan n the north of Palestine, and Beersheba (*Beërsaba*) in the extreme south, are often mentioned as the bounds of the country (e.g. I Kings iv, 25).

552. *though after Heaven seen:* though he had seen heaven's glory.

Round he surveys, and well might, where he stood   555
So high above the circling Canopy
Of Night's extended shade; from Eastern Point
Of *Libra* to the fleecy Star that bears
Andromeda far off *Atlantic* Seas
Beyond th' Horizon; then from Pole to Pole   560
He views in breadth, and without longer pause
Down right into the World's first Region throws
His flight precipitant, and winds with ease
Through the pure marble Air his oblique way
Amongst innumerable Stars, that shone   565
Stars distant, but nigh hand seem'd other Worlds,
Or other Worlds they seem'd, or happy Isles,
Like those *Hesperian* Gardens fam'd of old,
Fortunate Fields, and Groves and flow'ry Vales,
Thrice happy Isles, but who dwelt happy there   570
He stay'd not to enquire: above them all
The golden Sun in splendor likest Heaven
Allur'd his eye: Thither his course he bends
Through the calm Firmament; but up or down
By centre, or eccentric, hard to tell,   575
Or Longitude, where the great Luminary
Aloof the vulgar Constellations thick,
That from his Lordly eye keep distance due,
Dispenses Light from far; they as they move
Thir Starry dance in numbers that compute   580
Days, months, and years, towards his all-cheering Lamp
Turn swift thir various motions, or are turn'd
By his Magnetic beam, that gently warms
The Universe, and to each inward part
With gentle penetration, though unseen,   585
Shoots invisible virtue even to the deep:
So wondrously was set his Station bright.
There lands the Fiend, a spot like which perhaps
Astronomer in the Sun's lucent Orb

555-579. Passing through the shell of the universe where it is suspended from heaven by the golden chain (cf. II, 1051), Satan sees the panorama of the stars stretching from the Scales (*Libra*) at the eastern end of the Zodiac to the constellation of the Ram, the *fleecy star,* with that of *Andromeda* seeming to ride on it at the western end, below the *Atlantic horizon.* He plunges through the upper air or *World's first Region,* through the orbs of the *primum mobile,* the Crystalline Sphere and the fixed stars (in the reverse order from that in which they are named in ll. 481–83 above), and then, entering the lower region of the planets, is attracted by the sun, whose orb in the geocentric, Ptolemaic astronomy was *below* that of the fixed stars. The *golden Sun* is *above* the stars in the sense that it is more splendid than they and *dispenses Light* to them, as it is said again to do in V, 423.

564. The reference, as Svendsen notes in *M.&S.,* p. 88, is to the uppermost of the four bands of air which contemporary meteorology regarded as lying three below and one above the fiery spheres of the stars. The air of that uppermost or "first Re-

gion" was deadly cold and shining. Shining is the literal meaning of the Greek word from which marble is derived. Cf. the "marble heaven" of *Othello* III, iii, 460.

567. Here, as in *Comus,* 981–82, the *Hesperian Gardens* are in the *happy Isles* or Hesperides, which were vaguely identified with the Canary Islands or even with the British Isles. Cf. I, 510–19, n.

575. Editors surmise that Milton hesitates here between the Ptolemaic and Copernican views of the sun respectively as *eccentric,* because not at the center of the universe, or at the *centre.*

576. The *Longitude* or horizontal direction of Satan's movement is as hard to define as the vertical direction.

579–581. Here, as in VII, 341–42, there is an echo of Genesis i, 14: "And God said, Let there be lights in the firmament of the heaven to divide the day from the night; and let them be for signs, and for seasons, and for days, and for years." Equally clear is the reflection of Plato's dance of the stars (*Tim.,* 40).

583–585. Cf. VI, 472–83, and the note there.
589–590. Galileo's discovery of sun spots with

Through his glaz'd Optic Tube yet never saw. 590
The place he found beyond expression bright,
Compar'd with aught on Earth, Metal or Stone;
Not all parts like, but all alike inform'd
With radiant light, as glowing Iron with fire;
If metal, part seem'd Gold, part Silver clear; 595
If stone, Carbuncle most or Chrysolite,
Ruby or Topaz, to the Twelve that stone
In *Aaron's* Breastplate, and a stone besides
Imagin'd rather oft than elsewhere seen,
That stone, or like to that which here below 600
Philosophers in vain so long have sought,
In vain, though by thir powerful Art they bind
Volatile *Hermes,* and call up unbound
In various shapes old *Proteus* from the Sea,
Drain'd through a Limbec to his Native form. 605
What wonder then if fields and regions here
Breathe forth *Elixir* pure, and Rivers run
Potable Gold, when with one virtuous touch
Th' Arch-chemic Sun so far from us remote
Produces with Terrestrial Humor mixt 610
Here in the dark so many precious things
Of color glorious and effect so rare?
Here matter new to gaze the Devil met
Undazzl'd, far and wide his eye commands,
For sight no obstacle found here, nor shade, 615
But all Sun-shine, as when his Beams at Noon
Culminate from th' *Equator,* as they now
Shot upward still direct, whence no way round
Shadow from body opaque can fall, and the Air,
Nowhere so clear, sharp'n'd his visual ray 620
To objects distant far, whereby he soon

his *glaz'd Optic Tube* (telescope) in 1609 was one of the most exciting astronomical events of the century.

596. D. P. Harding—in *Milton and the Renaissance Ovid,* p. 90—sees in *Carbuncle* a translation of Ovid's *pyropus* in his famous description of the temple of the sun (*Met.* II, 2), which obviously influences this entire passage in spite of the express reference to the twelve precious stones of *Aaron's Breastplate* in Exodus xxviii, 17–24.

600–605. "*Hermes* and *Proteus,*" E. H. Duncan points out in *Osiris,* XI (1954), 405, were the "metaphorical names for 'the elixir of the philosophers,' the proximate material of the philosopher's stone or transmuting elixir."

605. *Limbec:* alembic, the distilling apparatus of the alchemists.

607. The name *Elixir,* which was the drink of the gods in Homer, was the basis of the mediaeval medical term "elixir of life," a life-prolonging substance akin to the "philosopher's stone" and so to be regarded as *Potable Gold.*

608–612. The belief that the sun's rays generate precious stones in the ground (to which *Comus,* 732–36, and *PL* VI, 479–81 refer) is used here as evidence that precious metals must abound in the sun, which glows with the virtue of the "Philosophers' Stone" and of the elixir which were

thought capable of transmuting base metals into gold. So in *The Extasie* (stanza 8) Cowley describes the "*Essences of Gems*" as "Drawn forth" in the heavens by "*Chymic Angels* Art." In *M.&S.* (pp. 29–30 and 124–27) Svendsen traces many contemporary allusions to potable gold or elixir, the Philosophers' Stone, and to gems which shine in darkness with the solar fire that is their essence—ideas all of which contribute to the contrast between the sun's purity and Satan's wickedness.

610. *Humor* is equivalent to moisture.

617–621. Satan's *visual ray* (his sight) is sharpened because no shadows fall anywhere when the sun *culminates* or reaches the meridian over the *Equator.* Though this happens only at the spring and autumn equinoxes, Milton thought of it as happening daily before, as a result of Adam's sin, the sun was pushed "from th' Equinoctial Road" (X, 672). In an unpublished Northwestern University dissertation, "Folklore in Milton's Major Poems," E. C. Kirkland suggests that Satan's temptation of Eve at high noon (IX, 739) and of Christ at the same hour (*PR* II, 292) is connected with the ancient fear of the noonday devil (the *daemonio meridi,* as the Vulgate renders the Hebrew that is translated "the destruction that wasteth at noonday" in the King James Bible, Psalm xci, 6).

Saw within ken a glorious Angel stand,
The same whom *John* saw also in the Sun:
His back was turn'd, but not his brightness hid;
Of beaming sunny Rays, a golden tiar   625
Circl'd his Head, nor less his Locks behind
Illustrious on his Shoulders fledge with wings
Lay waving round; on some great charge employ'd
He seem'd, or fixt in cogitation deep.
Glad was the Spirit impure; as now in hope   630
To find who might direct his wand'ring flight
To Paradise the happy seat of Man,
His journey's end and our beginning woe.
But first he casts to change his proper shape,   *like a thief.*
Which else might work him danger or delay: *cf. Dante*   635
And now a stripling Cherub he appears,
Not of the prime, yet such as in his face
Youth smil'd Celestial, and to every Limb
Suitable grace diffus'd, so well he feign'd;
Under a Coronet his flowing hair   640
In curls on either cheek play'd, wings he wore
Of many a color'd plume sprinkl'd with Gold,
His habit fit for speed succinct, and held
Before his decent steps a Silver wand.
He drew not nigh unheard; the Angel bright,   645
Ere he drew nigh, his radiant visage turn'd,
Admonisht by his ear, and straight was known
Th' Arch-Angel *Uriel,* one of the sev'n
Who in God's presence, nearest to his Throne
Stand ready at command, and are his Eyes   650
That run through all the Heav'ns, or down to th' Earth
Bear his swift errands over moist and dry,
O'er Sea and Land: him *Satan* thus accosts.
  Uriel, for thou of those sev'n Spirits that stand
In sight of God's high Throne, gloriously bright,   655
The first art wont his great authentic will
Interpreter through highest Heav'n to bring,
Where all his Sons thy Embassy attend;
And here art likeliest by supreme decree

622. The *glorious Angel,* Uriel, though he is never mentioned in the Bible, is here painted like the angel whom St. John saw "standing in the sun" (Rev. xix, 17). Milton knew that, with Michael, Gabriel, and Raphael, Uriel was one of the four great archangels of Jewish tradition who ruled the four quarters of the world—Uriel's being the south. R. West, in *Milton and the Angels,* p. 208, wonders whether Milton made Uriel regent of the sun because Agrippa and Robert Fludd assigned various angels to the planets, though they did not assign Uriel to the sun. The name in Hebrew means—as *The Jewish Encyclopaedia* notes—"the fire of God," and in "medieval mysticism is represented as the source of the heat of the day in winter." Milton's "source" for Uriel was his own imagination playing on the tradition.

625. *tiar:* tiara, crown.

648. Milton had in mind "the seven Spirits" whom St. John saw before God's throne (Rev. i, 4)

and of whom Zechariah wrote (iv, 10): "The Seven are the eyes of the Lord, which run to and fro through the whole earth." In a Discourse on this text Joseph Mede, Fellow of Christ's College, Cambridge, in Milton's time, treated it as an interesting Jewish tradition symbolizing the seven great archangels by the seven-branched candlestick and—according to Josephus in *The Wars of the Jews* VI, vi—making the seven angels "the Prefects of the Seven Planets." But Uriel's name is not mentioned by Mede, who identifies only Michael, Gabriel, and Raphael as belonging to the seven prime angels. (*The Works of . . . Joseph Mede*—London, 1677 —pp. 41–42.)

658. Like the writer of Job (ii, 1), Milton calls the angels Sons of God and thinks of them as living scattered through the provinces of heaven, except on the days when they must "present themselves before the Lord."

Like honor to obtain, and as his Eye   660
To visit oft this new Creation round
Unspeakable desire to see, and know
All these his wondrous works, but chiefly Man,
His chief delight and favor, him for whom
All these his works so wondrous he ordain'd,   665
Hath brought me from the Choirs of Cherubim
Alone thus wand'ring. Brightest Seraph, tell
In which of all these shining Orbs hath Man
His fixed seat, or fixed seat hath none,
But all these shining Orbs his choice to dwell;   670
That I may find him, and with secret gaze,
Or open admiration him behold
On whom the great Creator hath bestow'd
Worlds, and on whom hath all these graces pour'd;
That both in him and all things, as is meet,   675
The Universal Maker we may praise;
Who justly hath driv'n out his Rebel Foes
To deepest Hell, and to repair that loss
Created this new happy Race of Men
To serve him better: wise are all his ways.   680
    So spake the false dissembler unperceiv'd;
For neither Man nor Angel can discern
Hypocrisy, the only evil that walks
Invisible, except to God alone,
By his permissive will, through Heav'n and Earth: 685
And oft though wisdom wake, suspicion sleeps
At wisdom's Gate, and to simplicity
Resigns her charge, while goodness thinks no ill
Where no ill seems: Which now for once beguil'd
Uriel, though Regent of the Sun, and held   690
The sharpest-sighted Spirit of all in Heav'n;
Who to the fraudulent Impostor foul
In his uprightness answer thus return'd.
    Fair Angel, thy desire which tends to know
The works of God, thereby to glorify   695
The great Work-Master, leads to no excess
That reaches blame, but rather merits praise
The more it seems excess, that led thee hither
From thy Empyreal Mansion thus alone,
To witness with thine eyes what some perhaps   700
Contented with report hear only in Heav'n:
For wonderful indeed are all his works,
Pleasant to know, and worthiest to be all
Had in remembrance always with delight;
But what created mind can comprehend   705
Thir number, or the wisdom infinite

685. The distinction between God's *permissive* and his active will avoids making him responsible for evil. Cf. I, 211.

696. It was a principle of Renaissance Neoplatonism (e.g. The *Heroic Madnesses* of Giordano Bruno, Part I, Dialogue ii) that no extreme in the contemplation of God and his works could violate Aristotle's principle in the *Nicomachean Ethics* that virtue consists in avoiding extremes.

702. Several Psalms are echoed: e.g. viii and cxi, 4.

706. The word *wisdom* in Proverbs iii, 19, to which Milton alludes—"The Lord by wisdom hath founded the earth; by understanding hath he established the heavens"—was sometimes interpreted as referring to Christ, the Word by whom the world is created in the passage in VII, 208-21, which is anticipated here. See the Introduction 55.

That brought them forth, but hid thir causes deep.
I saw when at his Word the formless Mass,
This world's material mould, came to a heap;
Confusion heard his voice, and wild uproar   710
Stood rul'd, stood vast infinitude confin'd;
Till at his second bidding darkness fled,
Light shone, and order from disorder sprung:
Swift to thir several Quarters hasted then
The cumbrous Elements, Earth, Flood, Air, Fire,   715
And this Ethereal quintessence of Heav'n
Flew upward, spirited with various forms,
That roll'd orbicular, and turn'd to Stars
Numberless, as thou seest, and how they move;
Each had his place appointed, each his course,   720
The rest in circuit walls this Universe.
Look downward on that Globe whose hither side
With light from hence, though but reflected, shines;
That place is Earth the seat of Man, that light
His day, which else as th' other Hemisphere   725
Night would invade, but there the neighboring Moon
(So call that opposite fair Star) her aid
Timely interposes, and her monthly round
Still ending, still renewing through mid Heav'n,
With borrow'd light her countenance triform   730
Hence fills and empties to enlighten the Earth,
And in her pale dominion checks the night.
That spot to which I point is *Paradise*,
Adam's abode, those lofty shades his Bow'r.
Thy way thou canst not miss, me mine requires.   735
    Thus said, he turn'd, and *Satan* bowing low,
As to superior Spirits is wont in Heav'n,
Where honor due and reverence none neglects,
Took leave, and toward the coast of Earth beneath,
Down from th' Ecliptic, sped with hop'd success,   740
Throws his steep flight in many an Aery wheel,
Nor stay'd, till on *Niphates'* top he lights.

The End of the Third Book.

710. *Confusion* and *uproar*, like Chaos in II, 895 and 907, are half-personified.

713–719. In l. 713 *Light* is the first of God's creations, as it is in Genesis and in l. 1 above. The conception of creation as ending the war of "embryon atoms" in Chaos (cf. II, 900, above) by the separating out of the four elements reflects Plato's picture of creation in the *Timaeus* 30, a, as a divine transformation of disorder into order. That of an *Ethereal quintessence* or fifth element, called aether, rising from chaos to form the imperishable substance of heaven and the stars stems from Ovid's account of the creation (*Met*. I, 21–27), and from Aristotle's assertion of it as a trustworthy tradition from earliest times (*On the Heavens* I, iii, 270 b). Cf. VII, 237–42, n.

718. The *Timaeus* (33b, 41d–e) and the forgery known as the *Timaeus Locrus* were responsible for the conception of the heavenly bodies as living spirits and for the belief that, since the most perfect form is the sphere, their shape is spherical.

730. *triform* is a reminiscence of Horace's term, the "triform goddess" (*Odes* III, 22, 4), which implies both that the moon has three visible phases and was also known as three divinities, Luna, Diana, and Hecate.

740. Satan now plunges earthward from the *Ecliptic,* the sun's path, and the sun itself, where he has been talking with Uriel. Cf. ll. 617–21 above.

742. Mt. *Niphates* was in the Taurus range in Armenia, near Assyria, as Milton says in IV, 126. In XI, 381, and *PR* III, 252–65, he ironically makes it the scene of Satan's vain temptation of Christ.

BOOK IV

THE ARGUMENT

Satan *now in prospect of* Eden, *and nigh the place where he must now attempt the bold enterprise which he undertook alone against God and Man, falls into many doubts with himself, and many passions, fear, envy, and despair; but at length confirms himself in evil, journeys on to Paradise, whose outward prospect and situation is described, overleaps the bounds, sits in the shape of a Cormorant on the Tree of Life, as highest in the Garden to look about him.   The Garden describ'd; Satan's first sight of* Adam *and* Eve; *his wonder at thir excellent form and happy state, but with resolution to work thir fall; overhears thir discourse, thence gathers that the Tree of Knowledge was forbidden them to eat of, under penalty of death; and thereon intends to found his Temptation, by seducing them to transgress: then leaves them a while, to know further of thir state by some other means.   Meanwhile* Uriel *descending on a Sun-beam warns* Gabriel, *who had in charge the Gate of Paradise, that some evil spirit had escap'd the Deep, and past at Noon by his Sphere in the shape of a good Angel down to Paradise, discovered after by his furious gestures in the Mount.   Gabriel promises to find him ere morning.   Night coming on,* Adam *and* Eve *discourse of going to thir rest: thir Bower describ'd; thir Evening worship.   Gabriel drawing forth his Bands of Night-watch to walk the round of Paradise, appoints two strong Angels to* Adam's *Bower, lest the evil spirit should be there doing some harm to* Adam *or* Eve *sleeping; there they find him at the ear of* Eve, *tempting her in a dream, and bring him, though unwilling, to* Gabriel; *by whom question'd, he scornfully answers, prepares resistance, but hinder'd by a Sign from Heaven, flies out of Paradise.*

>   O for that warning voice, which he who saw
> Th' *Apocalypse,* heard cry in Heav'n aloud,
> Then when the Dragon, put to second rout,
> Came furious down to be reveng'd on men,
> *Woe to the inhabitants on Earth!* that now,   5
> While time was, our first Parents had been warn'd
> The coming of thir secret foe, and scap'd
> Haply so scap'd his mortal snare; for now
> *Satan,* now first inflam'd with rage, came down,
> The Tempter ere th' Accuser of man-kind,   10
> To wreck on innocent frail man his loss
> Of that first Battle, and his flight to Hell:
> Yet not rejoicing in his speed, though bold,
> Far off and fearless, nor with cause to boast,
> Begins his dire attempt, which nigh the birth   15
> Now rolling, boils in his tumultuous breast,
> And like a devilish Engine back recoils
> Upon himself; horror and doubt distract
> His troubl'd thoughts, and from the bottom stir
> The Hell within him, for within him Hell   20
> He brings, and round about him, nor from Hell

1–5. To make the transition to earth and the scene of man's fall Milton paraphrases St. John's prophecy of the defeat of the "dragon," Satan, as a defeat of the "serpent" who tempted Eve and the "accuser" who tempted Job: "And there was war in heaven: Michael and his angels fought against the dragon; and the dragon fought and his angels.

. . . And the great dragon was cast out, that old serpent, called the Devil and Satan, which deceiveth the whole world: he was cast out into the earth, and his angels were cast out with him" (Rev. xii, 7–9).

17. *a devilish Engine:* a cannon. Cf. VI, 518.

20–23. The most famous of many assertions of

One step no more than from himself can fly
By change of place: Now conscience wakes despair
That slumber'd, wakes the bitter memory
Of what he was, what is, and what must be   25
Worse; of worse deeds worse sufferings must ensue.
Sometimes towards *Eden* which now in his view
Lay pleasant, his griev'd look he fixes sad,
Sometimes towards Heav'n and the full-blazing Sun,
Which now sat high in his Meridian Tow'r: 30
Then much revolving, thus in sighs began.
    O thou that with surpassing Glory crown'd,
Look'st from thy sole Dominion like the God
Of this new World; at whose sight all the Stars
Hide thir diminisht heads; to thee I call,   35
But with no friendly voice, and add thy name
O Sun, to tell thee how I hate thy beams
That bring to my remembrance from what state
I fell, how glorious once above thy Sphere;
Till Pride and worse Ambition threw me down   40
Warring in Heav'n against Heav'n's matchless King:
Ah wherefore! he deserv'd no such return
From me, whom he created what I was
In that bright eminence, and with his good
Upbraided none; nor was his service hard.   45
What could be less than to afford him praise,
The easiest recompense, and pay him thanks,
How due! yet all his good prov'd ill in me,
And wrought but malice; lifted up so high
I sdein'd subjection, and thought one step higher   50
Would set me highest, and in a moment quit
The debt immense of endless gratitude,
So burdensome, still paying, still to owe;
Forgetful what from him I still receiv'd,
And understood not that a grateful mind   55
By owing owes not, but still pays, at once

— argue idea of indebtedness

the doctrine is by Marlowe's Mephistophelis:
  Hell hath no limits, nor is circumscribed
  In any one self place; for where we are is hell,
  And where hell is, there must we ever be.
                    (*Doctor Faustus*, ll. 553-55)
But St. Bonaventura said (*Sentences* II, d, vi, 2, 2)
that "the devils carry the fire of hell wherever they
go," and St. Thomas Aquinas declared (*Summa
Theol.* I, q. 64, art. 4) that they are "bound with
the fire of hell while they are in the dark atmosphere
of this world." Cf. I, 255, and VI, 181.
  25. Cf. Francesca's cry to Dante: "No greater
pain than the recollection of happiness in misery"
(*Inf.* V, 121-22)—words which Dante remembered
as coming from Boethius' *Consolation of Philosophy*
(II, pr. iv), a passage put into Pandarus' mouth by
Chaucer:
  The worst kynde of infortune is this,
  A man to han ben in prosperitee,
  And it remembren, when it passed is.
      (*Troilus and Criseyde* III, 1626-28)
The commonplace was applied to the devils by Sir
Thomas Browne in *Christian Morals* II, 10, and to

the damned in hell by St. Thomas in the *Summa
Theologica*, Suppl. Part. III, q. 98, art. 7.
  32-39. For Edward Phillips' statement that these
lines were written "several years before the poem
was begun," see his Life of Milton, p. 1034. Their
resemblance to the openings of Euripides' *Phoenissae*
and Aeschylus' *Prometheus Bound* cannot have been
accidental.
  40-57. Replying to a criticism that "there is no
complexity or pressure of feeling in Satan's address
to the Sun," Sir H. J. C. Grierson says (in *Milton
and Wordsworth*, pp. 126-27) that the only rival
of the passage, and its possible source, is "the
speech of Claudius when he has fled from the play-
scene and pours forth the agitation of his tormented
conscience; and Milton's the more impressive because of the loftier character of Satan . . . and his
more terrible situation."
  43. Contrast Satan's declaration that the angels
are "self-begot" (V, 860).
  45. "God giveth to all men liberally, and up-
braideth not" (James i, 5).
  50. *sdein'd:* disdained.
  53-54. *still:* continually.

— Claudius still has another chance

Indebted and discharg'd; what burden then?
O had his powerful Destiny ordain'd
Me some inferior Angel, I had stood
Then happy; no unbounded hope had rais'd   60
Ambition. Yet why not? some other Power
As great might have aspir'd, and me though mean
Drawn to his part; but other Powers as great
Fell not, but stand unshak'n, from within
Or from without, to all temptations arm'd.   65
Hadst thou the same free Will and Power to stand?
Thou hadst: whom hast thou then or what to accuse,
But Heav'n's free Love dealt equally to all?
Be then his Love accurst, since love or hate,
To me alike, it deals eternal woe.   70
Nay curs'd be thou; since against his thy will
Chose freely what it now so justly rues.
Me miserable! which way shall I fly
Infinite wrath, and infinite despair?
Which way I fly is Hell; myself am Hell; _another biggie line_   75
And in the lowest deep a lower deep
Still threat'ning to devour me opens wide,
To which the Hell I suffer seems a Heav'n.
O then at last relent: is there no place
Left for Repentance, none for Pardon left?   80
None left but by submission; and that word
Disdain forbids me, and my dread of shame
Among the Spirits beneath, whom I seduc'd
With other promises and other vaunts
Than to submit, boasting I could subdue   85
Th' Omnipotent. Ay me, they little know
How dearly I abide that boast so vain,
Under what torments inwardly I groan:
While they adore me on the Throne of Hell,
With Diadem and Sceptre high advanc'd   _— whole discussion_   90
The lower still I fall, only Supreme   _shows why Christ must_
In misery; such joy Ambition finds.   _die. We keep falling._
But say I could repent and could obtain _Takes a lot to save us._
By Act of Grace my former state; how soon
Would highth recall high thoughts, how soon unsay   95
What feign'd submission swore: ease would recant
Vows made in pain, as violent and void.
For never can true reconcilement grow
Where wounds of deadly hate have pierc'd so deep:
Which would but lead me to a worse relapse,   100
And heavier fall: so should I purchase dear
Short intermission bought with double smart.
This knows my punisher; therefore as far

66–72. Cf. God's statement that the devils fell "freely" (III, 102) and Raphael's insistence on the free obedience of the good angels (V, 535).

75. Cf. I, 255, n; IX, 122–23, and especially l. 20 above.

75–77. In *Doctrine of Divorce* II, iii, Milton, arguing that even the pagans understood that sin's natural punishment was the sinner's depravity, wrote: "To banish forever into a local hell, whether in the air or in the centre, or in that uttermost and bottomless gulf of chaos, deeper from the holy bliss than the world's diameter multiplied; they thought not a punishing so proper and proportionate for God to inflict as to punish sin with sin" (C. E. III, 442). See the Introduction 22.

82–86. Cf. l. 388–92 below.

94. *Act of Grace:* formal pardon.

From granting hee, as I from begging peace:
All hope excluded thus, behold instead   105
Of us out-cast, exil'd, his new delight,
Mankind created, and for him this World.
So farewell Hope, and with Hope farewell Fear,
Farewell Remorse: all Good to me is lost;
Evil be thou my Good; by thee at least   110
Divided Empire with Heav'n's King I hold
By thee, and more than half perhaps will reign;
As Man ere long, and this new World shall know.
   Thus while he spake, each passion dimm'd his face,
Thrice chang'd with pale, ire, envy and despair,   *his passions*   115
Which marr'd his borrow'd visage, and betray'd
Him counterfeit, if any eye beheld.
For heav'nly minds from such distempers foul
Are ever clear. Whereof hee soon aware,
Each perturbation smooth'd with outward calm,   120
Artificer of fraud; and was the first
That practis'd falsehood under saintly show,   *first hypocrite*
Deep malice to conceal, couch't with revenge: *reference to present priests*
Yet not anough had practis'd to deceive
Uriel once warn'd; whose eye pursu'd him down   125
The way he went, and on th' *Assyrian* mount
Saw him disfigur'd, more than could befall
Spirit of happy sort: his gestures fierce
He mark'd and mad demeanor, then alone,
As he suppos'd, all unobserv'd, unseen.   130
So on he fares, and to the border comes
Of *Eden,* where delicious Paradise,
Now nearer, Crowns with her enclosure green,
As with a rural mound the champaign head
Of a steep wilderness, whose hairy sides   135

110. Cf. I, 165, and IX, 122–23.

111–113. *reign:* govern. The idea appears in poems on the fall of man as early as St. Avitus' *De originali peccato* (sixth century—published in 1508 and again, in his *Works,* in 1643). His Satan tells Adam and Eve that as their teacher (*magister*) he has a greater claim on them than God has as their creator.

115–120. Satan's *borrow'd visage* is that of a *stripling Cherub* (III, 636) and was ruddy or sanguine, the complexion which Timothy Bright described in his *Treatise of Melancholy* (1586), p. 97, as resulting from a "just proportion" of the spirits and humors of the body, such that they "all conspire together in due proportion" and breed "an indifferencie to all passion." It might be turned pale by a *perturbation* like anger or fear, which—as Bright noted (p. 88)—procured "a boyling of heat" about the heart that was caused by "a retraite of the bloud and certaine spirits not farre of, . . . as in feare, . . . euen from the extreme and utmost parts: whereby it gathereth great heate within. . . ."

121. *Artificer of fraud:* Satan as "father of lies." Cf. III, 683.

123. *couch't:* lying concealed.

126. *Assyrian mount:* Niphates. Cf. III, 742.

132–135. *Eden* signifies, literally, "pleasure."

Somewhere to the east within its boundaries (which are drawn in ll. 210–214 below) lay the *delicious Paradise* which Sister M. Corcoran notes (*Milton's Paradise,* p. 20) got its name from the *deliciarum paradisum* of the Polyglot Bible and its echo in Purchas's "delicious Land" in the midst of a "naturall Amphitheatre" amid "woodie hils" which surrounded though they did not top what Milton calls the *champaign head* (plateau) of the Garden of Eden. His synthetic details owe something to the "divine forest" of Dante's Earthly Paradise crowning the Mount of Purgatory (*Purg.* xxviii, 2), something more to Spenser's Garden of Adonis,

With mountaines rownd about environed,
And mightie woodes, which did the valley shade,
And like a stately theatre it made.

(*F.Q.* III, vi, 39) (Cf. *Comus,* 980–81) His main debt was to Diodorus' description of the *Nyseian Isle,* to which he refers in l. 275 below, and which—as studies by E. M. Clark and T. D. Starnes in *University of Texas Studies in English,* XXIX (1950), 138–41, and XXXI (1952), 46–50, indicate—was embroidered in Purchas's *Pilgrimage* (1613), VII, 5, and Heylyn's *Cosmography* (1657), p. 980, and reproduced in Conti's *Mythography* III, xix. Cf. ll. 281 and 544 below.

With thicket overgrown, grotesque and wild,
Access deni'd; and over head up grew
Insuperable highth of loftiest shade,
Cedar, and Pine, and Fir, and branching Palm,
A Silvan Scene, and as the ranks ascend   140
Shade above shade, a woody Theatre
Of stateliest view. Yet higher than thir tops
The verdurous wall of Paradise up sprung:
Which to our general Sire gave prospect large *Adam*
Into his nether Empire neighboring round.   145
And higher than that Wall a circling row
Of goodliest Trees loaden with fairest Fruit,
Blossoms and Fruits at once of golden hue
Appear'd, with gay enamell'd colors mixt:
On which the Sun more glad impress'd his beams   150
Than in fair Evening Cloud, or humid Bow,
When God hath show'r'd the earth; so lovely seem'd
That Lantskip: And of pure now purer air
Meets his approach, and to the heart inspires
Vernal delight and joy, able to drive   155
All sadness but despair: now gentle gales
Fanning thir odoriferous wings dispense
Native perfúmes, and whisper whence they stole
Those balmy spoils. As when to them who sail
Beyond the *Cape of Hope,* and now are past   160
Mozambic, off at Sea North-East winds blow
Sabean Odors from the spicy shore
Of *Araby* the blest, with such delay
Well pleas'd they slack thir course, and many a League
Cheer'd with the grateful smell old Ocean smiles.   165
So entertain'd those odorous sweets the Fiend
Who came thir bane, though with them better pleas'd
Than *Asmodeus* with the fishy fume,
That drove him, though enamor'd, from the Spouse
Of *Tobit's* Son, and with a vengeance sent   170
From *Media* post to *Egypt,* there fast bourd.
    Now to th' ascent of that steep savage Hill

136. grotesque: the form is French though the word comes from Italian *grotto,* a cave. In Milton's time it referred to painting or sculpture in which foliage was prominent.

151. humid Bow—the rainbow—is used in a setting like that in *Comus,* 992.

160. Cape of Hope: the Cape of Good Hope.

161. Mozambic: a province of Portuguese East Africa and its island capital. It was so fertile that "all the Armadas and Fleetes that sayle from Portugall to the Indies, if they cannot finish and performe their Voyage, will goe and Winter . . . in this Iland of Mozambique" (Samuel Purchas, *Pilgrimes* —1625—Part II, p. 1023).

162. Saba, the Sheba of the Bible, "in the Greeke tongue signifieth a secret mysterie" (Pliny, Holland's translation, XII, 14). It was in *Araby the blest* or *Arabia Felix,* the land described by Diodorus (III, xlv) as swept by winds that "waft the air from off that land, perfumed with sweet odours of myrrh and other odoriferous plants, to the adjacent parts of the sea."

167. bane harm. In Old English the word means "a murderer."

168. The interest of the time in the apocryphal Book of Tobit is illustrated by Savoldo's painting of Milton's "sociable Spirit" (V, 221) accompanying Tobias, Tobit's son, in Media. There by Raphael's advice Tobias married Sara, who had previously lost seven husbands—all of them murdered on the wedding night by her demon lover *Asmodeus,* or *Asmadai,* as he is called in VI, 365. He would have slain Tobias on the wedding night if Raphael had not instructed the youth to burn the heart and liver of a fish in his chamber. "The which smell when the evil spirit had smelled, he fled into the utmost parts of Egypt, and the angel bound him." (Tobit viii, 3).

172. savage may have essentially its original sense of "woody" (from Italian *selvaggio,* Latin *silvaticum*) and may mean simply that the hill was covered with trees.

Satan had journey'd on, pensive and slow;
But further way found none, so thick entwin'd,
As one continu'd brake, the undergrowth   175
Of shrubs and tangling bushes had perplext
All path of Man or Beast that pass'd that way:
One Gate there only was, and that look'd East
On th' other side: which when th' arch-felon saw
Due entrance he disdain'd, and in contempt,   180
At one slight bound high overleap'd all bound
Of Hill or highest Wall, and sheer within
Lights on his feet. As when a prowling Wolf,
Whom hunger drives to seek new haunt for prey,
Watching where Shepherds pen thir Flocks at eve   185
In hurdl'd Cotes amid the field secure,
Leaps o'er the fence with ease into the Fold:
Or as a Thief bent to unhoard the cash
Of some rich Burgher, whose substantial doors,
Cross-barr'd and bolted fast, fear no assault,   190
In at the window climbs, or o'er the tiles:
So clomb this first grand Thief into God's Fold:
So since into his Church lewd Hirelings climb.
Thence up he flew, and on the Tree of Life,
The middle Tree and highest there that grew,   195
Sat like a Cormorant; yet not true Life
Thereby regain'd, but sat devising Death
To them who liv'd; nor on the virtue thought
Of that life-giving Plant, but only us'd
For prospect, what well us'd had been the pledge   200
Of immortality. So little knows
Any, but God alone, to value right
The good before him, but perverts best things
To worst abuse, or to thir meanest use.
Beneath him with new wonder now he views   205
To all delight of human sense expos'd
In narrow room Nature's whole wealth, yea more,
A Heaven on Earth: for blissful Paradise
Of God the Garden was, by him in the East
Of *Eden* planted; *Eden* stretch'd her Line   210
From *Auran* Eastward to the Royal Tow'rs

178. It was on the "east of the garden of Eden" (Gen. iii, 24) that God posted the cherubs to prevent Adam and Eve from re-entering it after their banishment.

181. The value of the pun in *bound* as the climax of the similes that transform Satan from the tragic mood of his invocation to the sun to the comic one where "he can assume the form of no more dignified bird than a cormorant," is traced by Tillyard in *Studies in Milton*, pp. 71–75.

183–193. St. John's warning against the thief climbing into the sheepfold (x, 1) underlies the passage as clearly as it does *Lycidas*, 115.

194. "Out of the ground made the Lord God to grow every tree that is pleasant to the sight and good for food; and the tree of life also in the midst of the garden, and the tree of knowledge of good and evil" (Gen. ii, 9). Cf. ll. 218–21 below.

195–198. The *Tree* is the "tree of life in the

midst of the garden" (Gen. ii, 9), whose virtue is implied in the possibility that Adam might, after his sin, "put forth his hand, and take also of the tree of life, and eat, and live forever" (Gen. iii, 22).

196. The *Cormorant* (literally, "crow of the sea") was a traditional symbol of greed and greedy men. Cf. the vulture simile in III, 431.

210. Cf. l. 132 above. Though there was immense discussion of the situation of Eden, A. Williams finds (*Expositor*, p. 99) that "The consensus of nearly all opinion in the Renaissance . . . was that Eden, of which Paradise was a part, was somewhere between Palestine and Persia."

211. *Auran*, as Whiting notes (*Milieu*, p. 50), was spelled *Haran, Charran,* or *Charrar,* and was taken by Sir Walter Raleigh to be the city or province in Mesopotamia where Abraham once lived (Gen. xi, 31).

Of Great *Seleucia,* built by *Grecian* Kings,
Or where the Sons of *Eden* long before
Dwelt in *Telassar:* in this pleasant soil
His far more pleasant Garden God ordain'd;   215
Out of the fertile ground he caus'd to grow
All Trees of noblest kind for sight, smell, taste;
And all amid them stood the Tree of Life,
High eminent, blooming Ambrosial Fruit
Of vegetable Gold; and next to Life   220
Our Death the Tree of Knowledge grew fast by,
Knowledge of Good bought dear by knowing ill.
Southward through *Eden* went a River large,
Nor chang'd his course, but through the shaggy hill
Pass'd underneath ingulft, for God had thrown   225
That Mountain as his Garden mould high rais'd
Upon the rapid current, which through veins
Of porous Earth with kindly thirst up-drawn,
Rose a fresh Fountain, and with many a rill
Water'd the Garden; thence united fell   230
Down the steep glade, and met the nether Flood,
Which from his darksome passage now appears,
And now divided into four main Streams,
Runs diverse, wand'ring many a famous Realm
And Country whereof here needs no account,   235
But rather to tell how, if Art could tell,
How from that Sapphire Fount the crisped Brooks,
Rolling on Orient Pearl and sands of Gold,
With mazy error under pendant shades
Ran Nectar, visiting each plant, and fed   240
Flow'rs worthy of Paradise which not nice Art
In Beds and curious Knots, but Nature boon
Pour'd forth profuse on Hill and Dale and Plain,
Both where the morning Sun first warmly smote
The open field, and where the unpierc't shade   245
Imbrown'd the noontide Bow'rs: Thus was this place,
A happy rural seat of various view:
Groves whose rich Trees wept odorous Gums and Balm,
Others whose fruit burnisht with Golden Rind

212. Alexander's general, Seleucus, founded *Seleucia* as the seat of his Greek kingdom in western Asia on the Tigris, about fifteen miles below modern Bagdad.

214. *Telassar* is mentioned as a city of Eden in II Kings xix, 12, and Isaiah xxxvii, 12. Willem Blaeu put it on his map of Mesopotamia and described it in *Geographie Blaviane* (Amsterdam, 1667) XI, 33, as lying in the part of Upper Chaldaea called Auranite, near the Euphrates, a fact which seemed to him to prove positively that that rich region was the biblical Eden.

218–220. The picture—as Harding notes in *Milton and the Renaissance Ovid,* p. 80—comes both from Genesis ii, 9, and Ovid's fable of the dragon-guarded apples of the Hesperides (*Met.* x, 647–48). In the *History of the World* (1614), p. 86, Raleigh said that the dragon of the Hesperides was "taken from the Serpent, which tempted Evah: so was Paradise it selfe transported out of Asia into Africa."

222. Cf. the statement in *Areopagitica* (see p. 728), that "perhaps this is that doom which Adam fell into of knowing good and evil, that is to say, of knowing good by evil."

229–240. The passage rests upon the translation of the doubtful language of Genesis ii, 10, which the King James Bible renders: "A river went out of Eden to water the garden: and from thence it was parted, and became into four heads." Milton declines to mention the four rivers of Paradise, though in IX, 71, he mentions the Tigris as one of them. Their *Nectar* is a reminiscence of the nectar streams of Ovid's Age of Gold (*Met.* I, 111).

239. *error* has its Latin force of "wandering." The *O.E.D.* cites Ben Jonson's *Discoveries* as calling the wanderings of Aeneas his "error by sea."

242. *boon:* liberal.

246. *Imbrown'd* has the Italian sense of "darkened" that it has in IX, 1088.

Hung amiable, *Hesperian* Fables true,   250
If true, here only, and of delicious taste:
Betwixt them Lawns, or level Downs, and Flocks
Grazing the tender herb, were interpos'd,
Or palmy hillock, or the flow'ry lap
Of some irriguous Valley spread her store,   255
Flow'rs of all hue, and without Thorn the Rose:
Another side, umbrageous Grots and Caves
Of cool recess, o'er which the mantling Vine
Lays forth her purple Grape, and gently creeps
Luxuriant; meanwhile murmuring waters fall   260
Down the slope hills, disperst, or in a Lake,
That to the fringed Bank with Myrtle crown'd,
Her crystal mirror holds, unite thir streams.
The Birds thir choir apply; airs, vernal airs,
Breathing the smell of field and grove, attune   265
The trembling leaves, while Universal *Pan*
Knit with the *Graces* and the *Hours* in dance
Led on th' Eternal Spring. Not that fair field
Of *Enna*, where *Proserpin* gath'ring flow'rs
Herself a fairer Flow'r by gloomy *Dis*   270
Was gather'd, which cost *Ceres* all that pain
To seek her through the world; nor that sweet Grove
Of *Daphne* by *Orontes*, and th' inspir'd
Castalian Spring might with this Paradise
Of *Eden* strive; nor that *Nyseian* Isle   275
Girt with the River *Triton*, where old *Cham*,
Whom Gentiles *Ammon* call and *Lybian Jove*,
Hid *Amalthea* and her Florid Son,

250. For the *Hesperian Fable* see ll. 218–20, n., above.

252–268. In reply to criticism of these lines and their context by F. R. Leavis and G. W. Knight as the focus of a "sensuous poverty" from which *P. L.* often suffers, J. B. Broadbent agrees—in *MP*, LI (1954), 171—with Leavis, that they lack "the sensuous richness of *Comus*," but makes the point that "in *Paradise* the details are not so sensuously rich because sensuousness would have been out of place. These are the riches of God. *Comus* is more than sensuously rich: the subject of the speech is a degraded Epicureanism."

256. Herrick's epigram, *The Rose*, repeats the tradition that

Before man's fall the Rose was born,

St. Ambrose says, without the thorn.

266–267. The Orphic *Hymn to Pan* underlies the conception of *Universal Pan* as the god of all nature, enthroned with the *Hours*. In *Mythology* V, vi, Conti identified him with nature itself, proceeding from and created by the divine mind. Cf. the dance of "The Graces and the rosy-bosom'd Hours" in *Comus*, 986.

268. So Dante describes the Earthly Paradise on the mount of Purgatory as alive with the seminal gales of spring (*Purg.* xxviii, 106–11), and the symbolic gardens of Adonis in Spenser (cf. ll. 132–35 above) and in Drayton's *Endymion and Phoebe* are also in the background. Even the gardens of the Celtic underworld—as A. Williams notes in *Expositor*, p. 5—"somehow became entangled with the

Mount of Paradise." Cf. Milton's *Elegy V*.

269–272. It is from a landscape of perpetual spring in the Sicilian grove of *Enna* that Ovid has *Proserpina* kidnapped by *Dis* (Pluto, in *Met.* V, 385–91). The Homeric *Hymn to Demeter* describes *Ceres'* quest of her daughter for "nine days through the earth with flaming torches in her hands, nor did she once taste sweet nectar or ambrosia in her grief." The myth inspired Milton's figure in a letter to Charles Diodati in 1637: "Ceres never sought her daughter Proserpina . . . with greater ardor than I do this idea of Beauty" (C. E. XII, 26). Cf. Starnes & Talbert, *Dictionaries*, pp. 276–77.

273. The gardens of *Daphne* on the river *Orontes* in Syria had a temple of Apollo and a spring called after the *Castalian Spring* on Mt. Parnassus (cf. III, 30, n.). It was *inspired* because its waters traditionally gave oracles.

275–279. Nysa was an island in the *River Triton* in modern Tunis, where (according to a widely-known passage in Diodorus' *Library* III, 67) Saturn's son *Ammon*, fearing the jealousy of his wife, had his love-child by the nymph *Amalthea, Bacchus,* secretly brought up. As Starnes and Talbert show (*Dictionaries*, p. 237), *Ammon* was identified with the *Lybian Jove* and with Noah's son Ham or *Cham.* Milton does not identify Bacchus with Jove, as Empson supposes in *Pastoral*, p. 174, though he *may* associate them in order, as Empson says, to express "his pagan feelings about paradise" by the symbol of a "demigod of the glory and fertility of the earth."

Young *Bacchus,* from his Stepdame *Rhea's* eye;
Nor where *Abassin* Kings thir issue Guard,   280
Mount *Amara,* though this by some suppos'd
True Paradise under the *Ethiop* Line
By *Nilus* head, enclos'd with shining Rock,
A whole day's journey high, but wide remote
From this *Assyrian* Garden, where the Fiend   285
Saw undelighted all delight, all kind
Of living Creatures new to sight and strange:
Two of far nobler shape erect and tall,
Godlike erect, with native Honor clad
In naked Majesty seem'd Lords of all,   290
And worthy seem'd, for in thir looks Divine
The image of thir glorious Maker shone,
Truth, Wisdom, Sanctitude severe and pure,
Severe, but in true filial freedom plac't;
Whence true autority in men; though both   295
Not equal, as thir sex not equal seem'd;
For contemplation hee and valor form'd,
For softness shee and sweet attractive Grace,
Hee for God only, shee for God in him:
His fair large Front and Eye sublime declar'd   300
Absolute rule; and Hyacinthine Locks
Round from his parted forelock manly hung
Clust'ring, but not beneath his shoulders broad:
Shee as a veil down to the slender waist
Her unadorned golden tresses wore   305
Dishevell'd, but in wanton ringlets wav'd
As the Vine curls her tendrils, which impli'd
Subjection, but requir'd with gentle sway,
And by her yielded, by him best receiv'd,
Yielded with coy submission, modest pride,   310
And sweet reluctant amorous delay.
Nor those mysterious parts were then conceal'd,
Then was not guilty shame: dishonest shame
Of Nature's works, honor dishonorable,
Sin-bred, how have ye troubl'd all mankind   315
With shows instead, mere shows of seeming pure,

---

280. *Abassia:* Abyssinian. *issue:* children.

281–285. "In locating Mt. Amara on the equator" (the *Ethiop Line*), Clark notes ("Abyssinian Para-dise," p. 144; cf. l. 132 above, n.) that "both Mil-ton and Purchas, though wrong, were in exact ac-cord with the best maps available up to the year of the completion of *PL.*" On Ortelius' maps it is prominent; on Livio Sanuto's map (in *Geografia,* Venice, 1588) it dominates Abyssinia as the "regalis mons." Milton was also influenced by a widely-repeated story which Heylin told at length in *Cos-mographie* IV, lxiv: "The hill of Amara is a day's journey high, on the top whereof are thirty-four palaces in which the younger sons of the emperor are continually enclosed to avoid sedition: . . . though not much distant from the Equator if not plainly under it, yet blessed with such a temperate air that some have taken it for the place of Paradise."

285. By making Paradise an *Assyrian Garden* Mil-ton indicates his belief that it was in Assyria or some-

where in the Euphrates region and not in Africa.

288. Classical tradition (e.g. Ovid, *Met.* I, 82–86) stressed man's uprightness in contrast with the other creatures. Cf. VII, 506–11.

300. *sublime:* upward-looking.

301. The suggestion is of superhuman beauty such as Athene gave to Ulysses when she made him taller and mightier than ordinary men and gave him flowing locks like the hyacinth flower (*Od.* VI, 230–32). The effect, Homer says, was like silver over-laid with gold.

303. Milton's authority is St. Paul: ". . . if a man have long hair, it is a shame unto him, But if a woman have long hair, it is a glory unto her; for her hair is given unto her for a covering" (I Cor. xi, 14–15). But Eve's coloring is like the "golden Aphrodite" of Homer (*Il.* III, 61, and many times elsewhere).

310. *coy:* shy.

313. *dishonest:* unchaste.

And banisht from man's life his happiest life,
Simplicity and spotless innocence.
So pass'd they naked on, nor shunn'd the sight
Of God or Angel, for they thought no ill: —— *beginning of the heroism*   320
So hand in hand they pass'd, the loveliest pair
That ever since in love's imbraces met,
Adam the goodliest man of men since born
His Sons, the fairest of her Daughters *Eve.*
Under a tuft of shade that on a green   325
Stood whispering soft, by a fresh Fountain side
They sat them down, and after no more toil
Of thir sweet Gard'ning labor than suffic'd
To recommend cool *Zephyr,* and made ease
More easy, wholesome thirst and appetite   330
More grateful, to thir Supper Fruits they fell,
Nectarine Fruits which the compliant boughs
Yielded them, side-long as they sat recline
On the soft downy Bank damaskt with flow'rs:
The savory pulp they chew, and in the rind   335
Still as they thirsted scoop the brimming stream;
Nor gentle purpose, nor endearing smiles
Wanted, nor youthful dalliance as beseems
Fair couple, linkt in happy nuptial League,
Alone as they.   About them frisking play'd   340
All Beasts of th' Earth, since wild, and of all chase
In Wood or Wilderness, Forest or Den;
Sporting the Lion ramp'd, and in his paw
Dandl'd the Kid; Bears, Tigers, Ounces, Pards
Gamboll'd before them, th' unwieldy Elephant   345
To make them mirth us'd all his might, and wreath'd
His Lithe Proboscis; close the Serpent sly
Insinuating, wove with Gordian twine
His braided train, and of his fatal guile
Gave proof unheeded; others on the grass   350
Coucht, and now fill'd with pasture gazing sat,
Or Bedward ruminating; for the Sun
Declin'd was hasting now with prone career
To th' Ocean Isles, and in th' ascending Scale
Of Heav'n the Stars that usher Evening rose: 355
When *Satan* still in gaze, as first he stood,
Scarce thus at length fail'd speech recover'd sad.

329. *Zephyr:* the west wind, which Homer says refreshed the Elysian Fields (*Od.* IV, 567). Cf. *L'All,* 19, and *El V,* 69.

333. *recline:* reclining.

334. *damask:* richly figured, like silks from Damascus.

337. *purpose:* conversation.   So Spenser says that Una and the Red Cross Knight sit together in her father's palace and "fitting purpose frame" (*F.Q.* I, xii, 13, 9).

338. *Wanted:* were lacking.

340–352. Biblical illustrators liked to represent the friendly animals around Adam and Eve in Eden in the spirit of their description in popular poems like Samuel Pordage's *Mundorum explicatio* (1663):

ADAM is Lord, and King: each animal
Comes at his beck, and doth obey his call;
All bow their lofty heads if he come near,
The Hart, nor timerous Hare his presence fear:
The shaggy Lion, Bear, the Bull, the Bore
Couch at his feet, him as their God adore.
   (pp. 58–59) (Cf. *PL* VIII, 345–54, n).

344. *Ounces:* lynxes.

348. *Insinuating:* coiling.   *Gordian twine:* tangle like the Gordian knot which Alexander the Great cut.   Cf. IX, 436.

352. *Bedward ruminating:* chewing the cud on the way to bed.

354. *Ocean Isles:* the Azores, as l. 592 below indicates.

O Hell! what do mine eyes with grief behold,
Into our room of bliss thus high advanc't
Creatures of other mould, earth-born perhaps,   360
Not Spirits, yet to heav'nly Spirits bright
Little inferior; whom my thoughts pursue
With wonder, and could love, so lively shines
In them Divine resemblance, and such grace
The hand that form'd them on thir shape hath pour'd.   365
Ah gentle pair, yee little think how nigh
Your change approaches, when all these delights
Will vanish and deliver ye to woe,
More woe, the more your taste is now of joy;
Happy, but for so happy ill secur'd   370
Long to continue, and this high seat your Heav'n
Ill fenc't for Heav'n to keep out such a foe
As now is enter'd; yet no purpos'd foe
To you whom I could pity thus forlorn
Though I unpitied: League with you I seek,   375
And mutual amity so strait, so close,
That I with you must dwell, or you with me
Henceforth; my dwelling haply may not please
Like this fair Paradise, your sense, yet such
Accept your Maker's work; he gave it me,   380
Which I as freely give; Hell shall unfold,
To entertain you two, her widest Gates,
And send forth all her Kings; there will be room,
Not like these narrow limits, to receive
Your numerous offspring; if no better place,   385
Thank him who puts me loath to this revenge
On you who wrong me not for him who wrong'd.
And should I at your harmless innocence
Melt, as I do, yet public reason just,
Honor and Empire with revenge enlarg'd,   390
By conquering this new World, compels me now
To do what else though damn'd I should abhor.
    So spake the Fiend, and with necessity,
The Tyrant's plea, excus'd his devilish deeds.
Then from his lofty stand on that high Tree   395
Down he alights among the sportful Herd
Of those fourfooted kinds, himself now one
Now other, as thir shape serv'd best his end
Nearer to view his prey, and unespi'd
To mark what of thir state he more might learn   400

359. Cf. the reference to the *vacant room* of the
fallen angels in VII, 190.
    362. Satan paraphrases Psalm viii, 5, which says
that God has made man "a little lower than the
angels."
    375. *Though I unpitied:* though Satan is beyond
God's pity, he feels an impulse to pity Adam and
Eve.
    376. *strait:* close, intimate.
    382. The lines echo Isaiah xiv, 9: "Hell from
beneath is moved for thee to meet thee at thy coming; . . . it hath raised up from their thrones all
the kings of the nations."
    389. *public reason:* reason of state, a perversion

of the Ciceronian principle (*Laws* III, iii, 8) that
the good of the people is the supreme law. In *The
Contra-Replicant* (1643, p. 19) Henry Parker approved its use by Parliament and condemned the
Royalists for too frequent appeals to it. In the
Advancement I, ii, 3 (edited by William Aldis
Wright, Oxford, 1900), Bacon recalled that its abuse
in Italy under the name *ragione di stato* had been
condemned by Pius V as an invention "against religion and the moral virtues." In *Adamo caduto* V,
ii, Salandra has Satan tell the devils that they are
going to corrupt mankind by inventing *ragione di
stato.*
    398. *end:* object, purpose.

By word or action markt: about them round
A Lion now he stalks with fiery glare,
Then as a Tiger, who by chance hath spi'd
In some Purlieu two gentle Fawns at play,
Straight couches close, then rising changes oft   405
His couchant watch, as one who chose his ground
Whence rushing he might surest seize them both
Gript in each paw: when *Adam* first of men
To first of women *Eve* thus moving speech,
Turn'd him all ear to hear new utterance flow.   410
    Sole partner and sole part of all these joys,
Dearer thyself than all; needs must the Power
That made us, and for us this ample World
Be infinitely good, and of his good
As liberal and free as infinite,   415
That rais'd us from the dust and plac't us here
In all this happiness, who at his hand
Have nothing merited, nor can perform
Aught whereof hee hath need, hee who requires
From us no other service than to keep   420
This one, this easy charge, of all the Trees
In Paradise that bear delicious fruit
So various, not to taste that only Tree
Of Knowledge, planted by the Tree of Life,
So near grows Death to Life, whate'er Death is,   425
Some dreadful thing no doubt; for well thou know'st
God hath pronounc't it death to taste that Tree,
The only sign of our obedience left
Among so many signs of power and rule
Conferr'd upon us, and Dominion giv'n   430
Over all other Creatures that possess
Earth, Air, and Sea.   Then let us not think hard
One easy prohibition, who enjoy
Free leave so large to all things else, and choice
Unlimited of manifold delights: 435
But let us ever praise him, and extol
His bounty, following our delightful task
To prune these growing Plants, and tend these Flow'rs,
Which were it toilsome, yet with thee were sweet.
    To whom thus *Eve* repli'd.   O thou for whom   440
And from whom I was form'd flesh of thy flesh,
And without whom am to no end, my Guide
And Head, what thou hast said is just and right.

---

404. *Purlieu:* border tract around a wood.
402–408. So in Du Bartas' *Divine Weeks,* "a mis-
chiefe to effect," Satan

Thinks now the beauty of a Horse to borrow;
Anon to creep into a Haifer's side,
Then in a Cock, or in a Dog to hide;
Then in a nimble Hart himself to shroud;
Then in the starr'd plumes of a Peacock proud.
              (Kirkconnell, *Cycle,* p. 67)
410. *him* may refer to Satan, who is *all ear* to
catch what Adam will say, or to Adam, who is eager
to draw a reply from Eve.
419–428. In the *Commentarius de paradiso* of
the Syriac bishop Moses Bar-Cepha, which was published in Latin in Antwerp in 1569, Grant McColley

found a parallel for Milton's episode and especially
for Satan's picking up of Adam's "words to his
wife concerning the precept" against the Tree of
Knowledge (*Paradise Lost,* p. 155). The traditional situation finds its most ridiculous parallel in
Salandra's scene with Lucifer, Belial, and Behemoth
all eavesdropping in Eden (*Adamo caduto* I, vii;
Kirkconnell, *Cycle,* p. 306).
430. Cf. God's words of man at creation: "Let
us make man in our image, . . . and let him have
dominion over the fish of the sea, and over the
fowl of the air, and over the cattle, and over all the
earth" (Gen. i, 26).
443. Cf. St. Paul's words: "The head of the
woman is the man" (I Cor. xi, 3).

For wee to him indeed all praises owe
And daily thanks, I chiefly who enjoy   445
So far the happier Lot, enjoying thee
Preëminent by so much odds, while thou
Like consort to thyself canst nowhere find.
That day I oft remember, when from sleep
I first awak't, and found myself repos'd   450
Under a shade on flow'rs, much wond'ring where
And what I was, whence thither brought, and how.
Not distant far from thence a murmuring sound
Of waters issu'd from a Cave and spread
Into a liquid Plain, then stood unmov'd   455
Pure as th' expanse of Heav'n; I thither went
With unexperienc't thought, and laid me down
On the green bank, to look into the clear
Smooth Lake, that to me seem'd another Sky.
As I bent down to look, just opposite,   460
A Shape within the wat'ry gleam appear'd
Bending to look on me, I started back,   — Narcissum in women
It started back, but pleas'd I soon return'd,
Pleas'd it return'd as soon with answering looks
Of sympathy and love; there I had fixt   465
Mine eyes till now, and pin'd with vain desire,
Had not a voice thus warn'd me, What thou seest,
What there thou seest fair Creature is thyself,
With thee it came and goes: but follow me,
And I will bring thee where no shadow stays   470
Thy coming, and thy soft imbraces, hee
Whose image thou art, him thou shalt enjoy
Inseparably thine, to him shalt bear
Multitudes like thyself, and thence be call'd
Mother of human Race: what could I do,   475
But follow straight, invisibly thus led?
Till I espi'd thee, fair indeed and tall,
Under a Platan, yet methought less fair,
Less winning soft, less amiably mild,
Than that smooth wat'ry image; back I turn'd,   480
Thou following cri'd'st aloud, Return fair *Eve,*
Whom fli'st thou? whom thou fli'st, of him thou art,
His flesh, his bone; to give thee being I lent
Out of my side to thee, nearest my heart
Substantial Life, to have thee by my side   485
Henceforth an individual solace dear;
Part of my Soul I seek thee, and thee claim
My other half: with that thy gentle hand
Seiz'd mine, I yielded, and from that time see
How beauty is excell'd by manly grace   490
And wisdom, which alone is truly fair.
　　So spake our general Mother, and with eyes

---

461. So Ovid describes Narcissus lying beside a
pool, fascinated by his reflection, but pining away
because he never learns that what he sees and loves
is himself (*Met.* III, 402–510).

470. *stays:* waits for.

475. XI, 168–72, explains that Eve means mother
of life.

478. *Platan:* plane tree. *methought:* it seemed
to me.

483. The line paraphrases Adam's words after
Eve's creation in Genesis ii, 23.

486. *individual* keeps its Latin meaning of "inseparable."

Of conjugal attraction unreprov'd,
And meek surrender, half imbracing lean'd
On our first Father, half her swelling Breast   495
Naked met his under the flowing Gold
Of her loose tresses hid: hee in delight
Both of her Beauty and submissive Charms
Smil'd with superior Love, as *Jupiter*
On *Juno* smiles, when he impregns the Clouds   500
That shed *May* Flowers; and press'd her Matron lip
With kisses pure: aside the Devil turn'd
For envy, yet with jealous leer malign
Ey'd them askance, and to himself thus plain'd.
　　Sight hateful, sight tormenting! thus these two   505
Imparadis't in one another's arms
The happier *Eden*, shall enjoy thir fill
Of bliss on bliss, while I to Hell am thrust,
Where neither joy nor love, but fierce desire,
Among our other torments not the least,   510
Still unfulfill'd with pain of longing pines;
Yet let me not forget what I have gain'd
From thir own mouths; all is not theirs it seems:
One fatal Tree there stands of Knowledge call'd,
Forbidden them to taste: Knowledge forbidd'n?   515
Suspicious, reasonless. Why should thir Lord
Envy them that? can it be sin to know,
Can it be death? and do they only stand
By Ignorance, is that thir happy state,
The proof of thir obedience and thir faith?   520
O fair foundation laid whereon to build
Thir ruin! Hence I will excite thir minds
With more desire to know, and to reject
Envious commands, invented with design
To keep them low whom Knowledge might exalt   525
Equal with Gods; aspiring to be such,
They taste and die: what likelier can ensue?
But first with narrow search I must walk round
This Garden, and no corner leave unspi'd;
A chance but chance may lead where I may meet   530
Some wand'ring Spirit of Heav'n, by Fountain side,
Or in thick shade retir'd, from him to draw
What further would be learnt. Live while ye may,
Yet happy pair; enjoy, till I return,
Short pleasures, for long woes are to succeed.   535
　　So saying, his proud step he scornful turn'd,
But with sly circumspection, and began
Through wood, through waste, o'er hill, o'er dale his roam.
Meanwhile in utmost Longitude, where Heav'n
With Earth and Ocean meets, the setting Sun   540
Slowly descended, and with right aspect

493. *unreprov'd:* unreprovable, innocent. Cf. *L'All,* 40 and *unremov'd* in l. 987 below.

499–500. Traditionally, *Jupiter* (as the name literally indicates) was "Lord of the sky," and *"Juno,* of the ayre" (*F.Q.* VII, vii, 26).

502–504. Satan's envy of the love of Adam and Eve was traditional. The devils knew desire but not love.

511. *pines:* makes (me) pine.

526. Cf. IX, 547–48.

539. *utmost Longitude:* farthest west.

541. *right aspect:* direct view. The setting sun shines straight upon the inner side of the eastern gate of Paradise.

Against the eastern Gate of Paradise
Levell'd his ev'ning Rays: it was a Rock
Of Alablaster, pil'd up to the Clouds,
Conspicuous far, winding with one ascent 545
Accessible from Earth, one entrance high;
The rest was craggy cliff, that overhung
Still as it rose, impossible to climb.
Betwixt these rocky Pillars *Gabriel* sat
Chief of th' Angelic Guards, awaiting night; 550
About him exercis'd Heroic Games
Th' unarmed Youth of Heav'n, but nigh at hand
Celestial Armory, Shields, Helms, and Spears
Hung high with Diamond flaming, and with Gold.
Thither came *Uriel,* gliding through the Even 555
On a Sun-beam, swift as a shooting Star
In *Autumn* thwarts the night, when vapors fir'd
Impress the Air, and shows the Mariner
From what point of his Compass to beware
Impetuous winds: he thus began in haste. 560
   Gabriel, to thee thy course by Lot hath giv'n
Charge and strict watch that to this happy place
No evil thing approach or enter in:
This day at highth of Noon came to my Sphere
A Spirit, zealous, as he seem'd, to know 565
More of th' Almighty's works, and chiefly Man
God's latest Image: I describ'd his way
Bent all on speed, and markt his Aery Gait;
But in the Mount that lies from *Eden* North,
Where he first lighted, soon discern'd his looks 570
Alien from Heav'n, with passions foul obscur'd:
Mine eye pursu'd him still, but under shade
Lost sight of him; one of the banisht crew
I fear, hath ventur'd from the Deep, to raise
New troubles; him thy care must be to find. 575
   To whom the winged Warrior thus return'd:
Uriel, no wonder if thy perfect sight,
Amid the Sun's bright circle where thou sitst,
See far and wide: in at this Gate none pass
The vigilance here plac't, but such as come 580
Well known from Heav'n; and since Meridian hour

544–548. *Alablaster* (modern "alabaster") is defined in Cockeram's *English Dictionarie* (1623) as "a very cold Marble, white and clear." The picture of the *Rock* may—as Clark thinks ("Abyssinian Paradise," p. 146)—be due to Purchas's account of Mt. Amara as seeming "to him that stands beneath, like a high wall, whereon the heaven is as it were propped"—at the top, "overhanged with rocks, jutting forth of the sides the space of a mile, bearing out like mushromes, so that it is impossible to ascend it" except at "the ascending place, a faire gate." But such descriptions go back to stories in Diodorus like that (in *Library* III, 69) of the central African crag overlooking the cave where the infant Bacchus was nursed—"a crag of immense height, formed of parti-colored rocks . . . in bands sending forth a bright lustre, some like sea-purple, some bluish,

and others of every brilliant hue. . . . Before the entrance grew marvellous trees, some fruit-bearing, others evergreen, and all fashioned by nature to delight the eye." Cf. ll. 281–85.

549. Though none of the scriptural references to Gabriel (Dan. viii, 16; ix, 21; and Luke i, 19) implies his guardianship of Paradise, tradition had made him (with Michael and Raphael) one of the three protecting angels to whom "the Catholic church sanctioned prayer by name" (West, *Milton and the Angels,* p. 62). See the Introduction 21.

557. *thwarts:* flies across. *vapors fir'd:* "heat-lightning."

567. *God's latest Image:* man. The first was the Son, cf. III, 63 and 384.

580. *vigilance:* the abstract word is put for the vigilant Gabriel himself.

No Creature thence: if Spirit of other sort,
So minded, have o'erleapt these earthy bounds
On purpose, hard thou know'st it to exclude
Spiritual substance with corporeal bar.   585
But if within the circuit of these walks
In whatsoever shape he lurk, of whom
Thou tell'st, by morrow dawning I shall know.
  So promis'd hee, and *Uriel* to his charge
Return'd on that bright beam, whose point now rais'd   590
Bore him slope downward to the Sun now fall'n
Beneath th' *Azores;* whither the prime Orb,
Incredible how swift, had thither roll'd
Diurnal, or this less volúbil Earth
By shorter flight to th' East, had left him there   595
Arraying with reflected Purple and Gold
The Clouds that on his Western Throne attend:
Now came still Ev'ning on, and Twilight gray
Had in her sober Livery all things clad;
Silence accompanied, for Beast and Bird,   600
They to thir grassy Couch, these to thir Nests
Were slunk, all but the wakeful Nightingale;
She all night long her amorous descant sung;
Silence was pleas'd: now glow'd the Firmament
With living Sapphires: *Hesperus* that led   605
The starry Host, rode brightest, till the Moon
Rising in clouded Majesty, at length
Apparent Queen unveil'd her peerless light,
And o'er the dark her Silver Mantle threw.
  When *Adam* thus to *Eve:* Fair Consort, th' hour   610
Of night, and all things now retir'd to rest
Mind us of like repose, since God hath set
Labor and rest, as day and night to men
Successive, and the timely dew of sleep
Now falling with soft slumbrous weight inclines   615
Our eye-lids; other Creatures all day long
Rove idle unimploy'd, and less need rest;
Man hath his daily work of body or mind
Appointed, which declares his Dignity,
And the regard of Heav'n on all his ways;   620
While other Animals unactive range,
And of thir doings God takes no account.
Tomorrow ere fresh Morning streak the East

585. Cf. I, 423-31, n.
591. *Uriel* slides *down* the sunbeam to the sun, which is now below the horizon and therefore, in a Ptolemaic universe, *lower* than the earth.
592. Cf. the Azores in l. 354 above. *prime Orb:* the sun.
593. Milton shared Donne's wonder (though perhaps not his faith) that "so vast and immense a body as the Sun, should run so many miles, in a minute" (Sermon at St. Paul's, Easter, 1627. *Sermons,* ed. Simpson and Potter, VII, 374). He seems impartial about the alternative—the rotation of the *volubil* (turning) earth. Cf. 661-64 below, and VIII, 25-38.
603. *descant:* a warbled song. It was often

used of birds' singing.
604. Cf. *Silence,* enchanted by the Lady's music in *Comus,* 557-60, and in *Il Penseroso,* 55-56, "the mute Silence" to be broken only by the nightingale's song.
605. *Hesperus:* the evening star. Cf. IX, 49.
608. *Apparent Queen:* manifest or visible queen.
623-633. Williams notes—*Expositor,* p. 110—that Milton declined to follow St. Augustine in the view that Adam lived the purely contemplative rather than the active life in Paradise; and he quotes Donne's *Sermon XIX* (*Works* I, 372): "Adam was not put into Paradise, only in that Paradise to contemplate the future Paradise, but to dress and keep the present."

With first approach of light, we must be ris'n,
And at our pleasant labor, to reform   625
Yon flow'ry Arbors, yonder Alleys green,
Our walk at noon, with branches overgrown,
That mock our scant manuring, and require
More hands than ours to lop thir wanton growth:
Those Blossoms also, and those dropping Gums,   630
That lie bestrown unsightly and unsmooth,
Ask riddance, if we mean to tread with ease;
Meanwhile, as Nature wills, Night bids us rest.
      To whom thus *Eve* with perfect beauty adorn'd.
My Author and Disposer, what thou bid'st   635
Unargu'd I obey; so God ordains,
God is thy Law, thou mine: to know no more
Is woman's happiest knowledge and her praise.
With thee conversing I forget all time,
All seasons and thir change, all please alike.   640
Sweet is the breath of morn, her rising sweet,
With charm of earliest Birds; pleasant the Sun
When first on this delightful Land he spreads
His orient Beams, on herb, tree, fruit, and flow'r,
Glist'ring with dew; fragrant the fertile earth   645
After soft showers; and sweet the coming
Of grateful Ev'ning mild, then silent Night
With this her solemn Bird and this fair Moon,
And these the Gems of Heav'n, her starry train:
But neither breath of Morn when she ascends   650
With charm of earliest Birds, nor rising Sun
On this delightful land, nor herb, fruit, flow'r,
Glist'ring with dew, nor fragrance after showers,
Nor grateful Ev'ning mild, nor silent Night
With this her solemn Bird, nor walk by Moon,   655
Or glittering Star-light without thee is sweet.
But wherefore all night long shine these, for whom
This glorious sight, when sleep hath shut all eyes?
      To whom our general Ancestor repli'd.
Daughter of God and Man, accomplisht *Eve,*   660
Those have thir course to finish, round the Earth,
By morrow Ev'ning, and from Land to Land
In order, though to Nations yet unborn,
Minist'ring light prepar'd, they set and rise;
Lest total darkness should by Night regain   665
Her old possession, and extinguish life
In Nature and all things, which these soft fires
Not only enlighten, but with kindly heat

628. *manuring* has its Latin meaning of "working with the hands," i. e. "cultivating."

635. Eve's formal titles for Adam and his for her (as in l. 660) are traced to complimentary titles of Homer's heroes for one another, but before Adam's sin they have an aptness which —as M. Barstow notes in "Milton's Use of the Forms of Epic Address," in *MLN,* XXXI (1916), 121—is lost afterwards; and in Books IX to XII Adam and Eve do not use them.

640. *seasons:* times, periods in the day.

642. *charm:* song (the etymological meaning of the word). It is used in this sense in *PR* IV, 257.

660. *accomplisht:* full of accomplishments. Cf. Samson's ironical description of Dalila as his "accomplisht snare." (*SA,* 230).

668. *kindly:* natural.

667–673. Cf. the theory that the sun's ray is all-potent in III, 606–12, and the transformation of the stars' influence into something *malign* in X, 657–67. Cf. also VII, 171, and VIII, 150.

Of various influence foment and warm,
Temper or nourish, or in part shed down   670
Thir stellar virtue on all kinds that grow
On Earth, made hereby apter to receive
Perfection from the Sun's more potent Ray.
These then, though unbeheld in deep of night,
Shine not in vain, nor think, though men were none,   675
That Heav'n would want spectators, God want praise;
Millions of spiritual Creatures walk the Earth
Unseen, both when we wake, and when we sleep:
All these with ceaseless praise his works behold
Both day and night: how often from the steep   680
Of echoing Hill or Thicket have we heard
Celestial voices to the midnight air,
Sole, or responsive each to other's note
Singing thir great Creator: oft in bands
While they keep watch, or nightly rounding walk,   685
With Heav'nly touch of instrumental sounds
In full harmonic number join'd, thir songs
Divide the night, and lift our thoughts to Heaven.
   Thus talking hand in hand alone they pass'd
On to thir blissful Bower; it was a place   690
Chos'n by the sovran Planter, when he fram'd
All things to man's delightful use; the roof
Of thickest covert was inwoven shade
Laurel and Myrtle, and what higher grew
Of firm and fragrant leaf; on either side   695
Acanthus, and each odorous bushy shrub
Fenc'd up the verdant wall; each beauteous flow'r,
Iris all hues, Roses, and Jessamin
Rear'd high thir flourisht heads between, and wrought
Mosaic; underfoot the Violet,   700
Crocus, and Hyacinth with rich inlay
Broider'd the ground, more color'd than with stone
Of costliest Emblem: other Creature here
Beast, Bird, Insect, or Worm durst enter none;
Such was thir awe of Man.   In shadier Bower   705
More sacred and sequester'd, though but feign'd,
Pan or *Silvanus* never slept, nor Nymph,
Nor *Faunus* haunted.   Here in close recess
With Flowers, Garlands, and sweet-smelling Herbs
Espoused *Eve* deckt first her Nuptial Bed,   710
And heav'nly Choirs the Hymenæan sung,
What day the genial Angel to our Sire
Brought her in naked beauty more adorn'd,

674–688. The angelic singers seem like the Muses in Hesiod's *Theogony,* 3–21 and 35–52, who sing the greatness of their father Zeus, the earth and heaven, in ceaseless concert as they mount the cloudy slope of Olympus in the darkness.

688. *Divide the night:* break it up into watches that the Roman soldiers marked off by trumpet calls.

699. *flourisht:* flower-laden, or adorned with flowers.

702. *stone Of costliest Emblem:* stone inlaid with precious metal.

706. *feign'd*—in the sense that "the truest poetry is the most feigning" (*As You Like It* III, iii, 21–22)—implies that myths of *Pan, Sylvanus,* and *Faunus,* were pagan fabrications. Cf. l. 266 above, n.

708. *close:* secret.

711. *Hymenaean:* marriage song.

712. *genial:* nuptial. The term becomes a kind of title for the angel presiding over the union of Adam and Eve.

More lovely than *Pandora,* whom the Gods
Endow'd with all thir gifts, and O too like   715
In sad event, when to the unwiser Son
Of *Japhet* brought by *Hermes,* she ensnar'd
Mankind with her fair looks, to be aveng'd
On him who had stole *Jove's* authentic fire.
    Thus at thir shady Lodge arriv'd, both stood,   720
Both turn'd, and under op'n Sky ador'd
The God that made both Sky, Air, Earth and Heav'n
Which they beheld, the Moon's resplendent Globe
And starry Pole: Thou also mad'st the Night,
Maker Omnipotent, and thou the Day,   725
Which we in our appointed work imploy'd
Have finisht happy in our mutual help
And mutual love, the Crown of all our bliss
Ordain'd by thee, and this delicious place
For us too large, where thy abundance wants   730
Partakers, and uncropt falls to the ground.
But thou hast promis'd from us two a Race
To fill the Earth, who shall with us extol
Thy goodness infinite, both when we wake,
And when we seek, as now, thy gift of sleep.   735
    This said unanimous, and other Rites
Observing none, but adoration pure
Which God likes best, into thir inmost bower   *—hands are heavy*
Handed they went; and eas'd the putting off
These troublesome disguises which wee wear,   740
Straight side by side were laid, nor turn'd I ween
Adam from his fair Spouse, nor *Eve* the Rites
Mysterious of connubial Love refus'd:
Whatever Hypocrites austerely talk
Of purity and place and innocence,   745

714–719. *Pandora* was given by *Hermes* to Epimetheus (After-thought), *unwiser* than his brother Prometheus (Forethought), whose theft of fire from heaven for men the gods resented. Epimetheus married her and opened the casket that the gods sent with her, but found it full of all life's ills. "Plato and Chrysippus," Milton wrote in *Doctrine of Divorce* II, iii (see p. 714), "knew not what a consummate and most adorned Pandora was bestowed upon Adam, to be the nurse . . . of his native innocence and perfection, which might have kept him from being our true Epimetheus." The brothers were sons of the Titan Iapetos, who was sometimes identified by tradition with Noah's son *Japhet* (Gen. ix, 27; x, 1), the father of *Javan,* the legendary founder of the Greek people, who is mentioned in I, 508.

724. *Pole* stands here for the entire sky, as it does in *Comus,* 99.

724–735. The passage has much in common with Psalm lxxiv, 16: "The day is thine, and the night is thine," and Psalm cxxvii, 2: "he giveth his beloved sleep"; but the *gift of sleep* is often mentioned in Homer and Virgil in passages like Aeneas' reference to the quiet of evening coming to bring the most welcome gift of the gods (*Aen.* II, 269).

743. So Milton justifies the "intelligible flame," not "in Paradise to be resisted," in *Divorce* I, iv (see p. 709). He calls it *mysterious* because St. Paul calls marriage "a great mystery" (Ephes. v, 32), and in *Colasterion* (C. E. IV, 263) he rebuts an objection to his description of marriage as "a mystery of joy." Hexameral literature was full of eulogies of marriage, a fair example of which is a speech of Joseph to Potiphar in Joseph Beaumont's *Psyche* I, 203–06:

Except the venerable Temples, what
Place is more reverend than the Nuptial Bed?
Nay, heav'n has made a Temple too of that
For Chastitie's most secret rites . . .

744. On this controversial point Milton took the established Protestant position that was stated by John Salkeld in *A Treatise of Paradise* (1617), pp. 178–79, when he rejected the opinion of "Gregory Nisene, Damascene, Chrysostome, Procopius, Gazeus, and divers others, . . . that if *Adam* had not sinned, there should have been no such naturall generation of mankinde, as is now." But C. S. Lewis notes— *Allegory of Love* (1935), p. 15—that Albertus Magnus also swept away "the idea that the pleasure is evil and the result of the Fall," declaring that it "would have been greater if we had remained in Paradise."

Defaming as impure what God declares
Pure, and commands to some, leaves free to all.
Our Maker bids increase, who bids abstain
But our Destroyer, foe to God and Man?
Hail wedded Love, mysterious Law, true source   750
Of human offspring, sole propriety
In Paradise of all things common else.
By thee adulterous lust was driv'n from men
Among the bestial herds to range, by thee
Founded in Reason, Loyal, Just, and Pure,   755
Relations dear, and all the Charities
Of Father, Son, and Brother first were known.
Far be it, that I should write thee sin or blame,
Or think thee unbefitting holiest place,
Perpetual Fountain of Domestic sweets,   760
Whose bed is undefil'd and chaste pronounc't,
Present, or past, as Saints and Patriarchs us'd.
Here Love his golden shafts imploys, here lights
His constant Lamp, and waves his purple wings,
Reigns here and revels; not in the bought smile   765
Of Harlots, loveless, joyless, unindear'd,
Casual fruition, nor in Court Amours,
Mixt Dance, or wanton Mask, or Midnight Ball,
Or Serenate, which the starv'd Lover sings
To his proud fair, best quitted with disdain.   770
These lull'd by Nightingales imbracing slept,
And on thir naked limbs the flow'ry roof
Show'r'd Roses, which the Morn repair'd. Sleep on,
Blest pair; and O yet happiest if ye seek
No happier state, and know to know no more.   775
     Now had night measur'd with her shadowy Cone
Half way up Hill this vast Sublunar Vault,
And from thir Ivory Port the Cherubim
Forth issuing at th' accustom'd hour stood arm'd
To thir night watches in warlike Parade,   780
When *Gabriel* to his next in power thus spake.
     Uzziel, half these draw off, and coast the South
With strictest watch; these other wheel the North;
Our circuit meets full West. As flame they part
Half wheeling to the Shield, half to the Spear.   785
From these, two strong and subtle Spirits he call'd
That near him stood, and gave them thus in charge.
     Ithuriel and *Zephon,* with wing'd speed

748. Cf. "Be fruitful, and multiply, and replenish the earth" (Gen. i, 28).

763. So Ovid describes Cupid with an arrow of gold, inspiring love, and another of lead, which banished it (*Met.* I, 468).

768. Cf. Milton's attack on the bishops for encouraging "gaming, jigging, wassailing, and mixed dancing" in *Of Reformation* (C. E. III, 53).

773. *repair'd:* supplied the loss (with fresh roses).

775. *know to know no more:* be wise enough to seek no more knowledge (i.e. of good and evil). Cf. VII 120.

776–777. The cone of the earth's shadow, cast by the sun below the horizon at an angle of 45°, in-

dicates that it is nine o'clock. When the point of the cone reaches the zenith, it will be midnight.

782. *Uzziel* occurs in the Bible only as a human name, literally meaning "strength of God" (Exod. vi, 18, and Num. iii, 19). West notes—*Milton and the Angels,* p. 154—that it occurs in "the *Sepher Raziel,* for instance, and in several other mystical and Cabalistic works." The ordonnance of the lines—as Whaler notes (*Counterpoint,* pp. 76–79) —matches the complete circle to be made by the angels on their rounds.

788. *Ithuriel* ("discovery of God") does not occur in the Bible, and *Zephon* ("searcher") occurs only as a human name (Num. xxvi, 15). West (p. 155)

Search through this Garden, leave unsearcht no nook,
But chiefly where those two fair Creatures Lodge,   790
Now laid perhaps asleep secure of harm.
This Ev'ning from the Sun's decline arriv'd
Who tells of some infernal Spirit seen
Hitherward bent (who could have thought?) escap'd
The bars of Hell, on errand bad no doubt: 795
Such where ye find, seize fast, and hither bring.
    So saying, on he led his radiant Files,
Dazzling the Moon; these to the Bower direct
In search of whom they sought: him there they found
Squat like a Toad, close at the ear of Eve;   *- part of his*   800
Assaying by his Devilish art to reach   *diminishing*
The Organs of her Fancy, and with them forge
Illusions as he list, Phantasms and Dreams,
Or if, inspiring venom, he might taint
Th' animal spirits that from pure blood arise   805
Like gentle breaths from Rivers pure, thence raise
At least distemper'd, discontented thoughts,
Vain hopes, vain aims, inordinate desires
Blown up with high conceits ingend'ring pride.
Him thus intent *Ithuriel* with his Spear   810
Touch'd lightly; for no falsehood can endure
Touch of Celestial temper, but returns
Of force to its own likeness: up he starts
Discover'd and surpris'd. As when a spark
Lights on a heap of nitrous Powder, laid   815
Fit for the Tun some Magazin to store
Against a rumor'd War, the Smutty grain
With sudden blaze diffus'd, inflames the Air:
So started up in his own shape the Fiend.
Back stepp'd those two fair Angels half amaz'd   820
So sudden to behold the grisly King;
Yet thus, unmov'd with fear, accost him soon.
    Which of those rebel Spirits adjudg'd to Hell
Com'st thou, escap'd thy prison, and transform'd,
Why satst thou like an enemy in wait   825
Here watching at the head of these that sleep?
    Know ye not then said *Satan*, fill'd with scorn,
Know ye not mee? ye knew me once no mate

---

spots a Baal-Zephon among the many local Baals (cf.
I, 422, n.), but surmises that "perhaps Milton knew
somewhere in the literature of angelology of a
Zephon that was a good angel. Or perhaps he did
not, and cared very little."

800–803. See the Introduction 48.

804–809. Burton (*Anatomy* I, i, 2, 2; Everyman
Ed. I, 148) explained the theory of the natural,
vital, and animal spirits. "The *natural* are begotten
in the *liver*, and thence dispersed through the
veins. . . . The *vital spirits* are made in the
heart. . . . The *animal* (i.e. spiritual, from Latin
anima, soul) *spirits* formed of the *vital*, brought
up to the brain, and diffused by the nerves, to
the subordinate members, give sense and motion to them all." In "Eve's Demonic Dream"
(*ELH*, XIII—1946—pp. 359–64) W. B. Hunter, Jr.,

quotes numerous passages from St. Thomas Aquinas
and other theologians affirming that evil spirits may
act on the fancy or imagination through the
"animal spirits" in the blood. See the Introduction, 42–43.

809. *pride* is prominent in Satan's successful attempt on Eve in IX, 703–32, and P. L. Carver believes (*RES*, XVI—1940—p. 427) that Satan does
induce Eve "to acquiesce, according to the words
of St. Augustine, 'in the love of her own power, and
in a presumption of self-conceit.'" But McColley
traces through Calvin and others a tradition of two
temptations of Eve, the first of which is not successful (*Harvard Theological Review*, XXXII—1939—
p. 211).

815. *nitrous Powder:* gunpowder.

817. *Against:* in anticipation of.

For you, there sitting where ye durst not soar;
Not to know mee argues yourselves unknown,   830
The lowest of your throng; or if ye know,
Why ask ye, and superfluous begin
Your message, like to end as much in vain?
To whom thus *Zephon,* answering scorn with scorn.
Think not, revolted Spirit, thy shape the same,   835
Or undiminisht brightness, to be known
As when thou stood'st in Heav'n upright and pure;
That Glory then, when thou no more wast good,
Departed from thee, and thou resembl'st now
Thy sin and place of doom obscure and foul.   840
But come, for thou, be sure, shalt give account
To him who sent us, whose charge is to keep
This place inviolable, and these from harm.
    So spake the Cherub, and his grave rebuke
Severe in youthful beauty, added grace   845
Invincible: abasht the Devil stood,
And felt how awful goodness is, and saw   —nice line
Virtue in her shape how lovely, saw, and pin'd
His loss; but chiefly to find here observ'd
His lustre visibly impair'd; yet seem'd   850
Undaunted. If I must contend, said he,
Best with the best, the Sender not the sent,
Or all at once; more glory will be won,
Or less be lost. Thy fear, said *Zephon* bold,
Will save us trial what the least can do   855
Single against thee wicked, and thence weak.
    The Fiend repli'd not, overcome with rage;
But like a proud Steed rein'd, went haughty on,
Champing his iron curb: to strive or fly
He held it vain; awe from above had quell'd   860
His heart, not else dismay'd. Now drew they nigh
The western Point, where those half-rounding guards
Just met, and closing stood in squadron join'd
Awaiting next command. To whom thir Chief
Gabriel from the Front thus call'd aloud.   865
    O friends, I hear the tread of nimble feet
Hasting this way, and now by glimpse discern
Ithuriel and *Zephon* through the shade,
And with them comes a third of Regal port,
But faded splendor wan; who by his gait   870
And fierce demeanor seems the Prince of Hell,
Not likely to part hence without contést;
Stand firm, for in his look defiance low'rs.
    He scarce had ended, when those two approach'd
And brief related whom they brought, where found,   875

830. *argues:* proves. As an example of this use
of the word Milton quotes a Virgilian tag, "Fear
argues degenerate souls" (*Aen.* IV, 13) in *Art of
Logic* I, ii (C. E. XI, 24). Cf. l. 931 below.
832. *superfluous:* with superfluous words.
840. *obscure* has its Latin force, "dark."
843. *these:* The sleeping Adam and Eve.
848. In *Comus,* 214–16, the Platonic conception
of the virtues as capable of making their forms visi-

ble suggests the Lady's glimpse of Hope as a "hovering angel girt with golden wings" and her cry,
    "Thou unblemish't form of Chastity!
    I see ye visible."
862. *Point:* the western limit of Paradise, due
west from Gabriel's station at its gate on the east
side. *half-rounding:* completing the half-circle of
the garden, some having swung north, the others
south, so as to meet in the west.

How busied, in what form and posture coucht.
    To whom with stern regard thus *Gabriel* spake.
Why hast thou, *Satan,* broke the bounds prescrib'd
To thy transgressions, and disturb'd the charge
Of others, who approve not to transgress   880
By thy example, but have power and right
To question thy bold entrance on this place;
Imploy'd it seems to violate sleep, and those
Whose dwelling God hath planted here in bliss?
    To whom thus *Satan,* with contemptuous brow.   885
Gabriel, thou hadst in Heav'n th' esteem of wise,
And such I held thee; but this question askt
Puts me in doubt. Lives there who loves his pain?
Who would not, finding way, break loose from Hell,
Though thither doom'd? Thou wouldst thyself, no doubt,   890
And boldly venture to whatever place
Farthest from pain, where thou might'st hope to change
Torment with ease, and soonest recompense
Dole with delight, which in this place I sought;
To thee no reason; who know'st only good,   895
But evil hast not tri'd: and wilt object
His will who bound us? let him surer bar
His Iron Gates, if he intends our stay
In that dark durance: thus much what was askt.
The rest is true, they found me where they say;   900
But that implies not violence or harm.
    Thus he in scorn. The warlike Angel mov'd,
Disdainfully half smiling thus repli'd.
 O loss of one in Heav'n to judge of wise,
Since *Satan* fell, whom folly overthrew,   905
And now returns him from his prison scap't,
Gravely in doubt whether to hold them wise
Or not, who ask what boldness brought him hither
Unlicens't from his bounds in Hell prescrib'd;
So wise he judges it to fly from pain   910
However, and to scape his punishment.
So judge thou still, presumptuous, till the wrath,
Which thou incurr'st by flying, meet thy flight
Sevenfold, and scourge that wisdom back to Hell,
Which taught thee yet no better, that no pain   915
Can equal anger infinite provok't.
But wherefore thou alone? wherefore with thee
Came not all Hell broke loose? is pain to them
Less pain, less to be fled, or thou than they
Less hardy to endure? courageous Chief,   920
The first in flight from pain, hadst thou a leg'd
To thy deserted host this cause of flight,
Thou surely hadst not come sole fugitive.
    To which the Fiend thus answer'd frowning stern.
Not that I less endure, or shrink from pain,   925
Insulting Angel, well thou know'st I stood

879. *charge:* Adam and Eve, with whose protection Gabriel's troop is charged.
  896. *object:* raise the legal objection (that the devils are confined to hell by God's will).

904. *O loss:* O what a loss (to lose such a judge of wisdom as Satan).
  911. *However:* howsoever, by whatever means.
  926. *stood:* withstood or confronted, stood up

Thy fiercest, when in Battle to thy aid
The blasting volley'd Thunder made all speed
And seconded thy else not dreaded Spear.
But still thy words at random, as before,   930
Argue thy inexperience what behooves
From hard assays and ill successes past
A faithful Leader, not to hazard all
Through ways of danger by himself untri'd.
I therefore, I alone first undertook   935
To wing the desolate Abyss, and spy
This new created World, whereof in Hell
Fame is not silent, here in hope to find
Better abode, and my afflicted Powers
To settle here on Earth, or in mid Air;   940
Though for possession put to try once more
What thou and thy gay Legions dare against;
Whose easier business were to serve thir Lord
High up in Heav'n, with songs to hymn his Throne,
And practis'd distances to cringe, not fight.   945
    To whom the warrior Angel soon repli'd.
To say and straight unsay, pretending first
Wise to fly pain, professing next the Spy,
Argues no Leader, but a liar trac't,
Satan, and couldst thou faithful add? O name,   950
O sacred name of faithfulness profan'd!
Faithful to whom? to thy rebellious crew?
Army of Fiends, fit body to fit head;
Was this your discipline and faith ingag'd,
Your military obedience, to dissolve   955
Allegiance to th' acknowledg'd Power supreme?
And thou sly hypocrite, who now wouldst seem
Patron of liberty, who more than thou
Once fawn'd, and cring'd, and servilely ador'd
Heav'n's awful Monarch? wherefore but in hope   960
To dispossess him, and thyself to reign?
But mark what I arede thee now, avaunt;
Fly thither whence thou fledd'st: if from this hour
Within these hallow'd limits thou appear,
Back to th' infernal pit I drag thee chain'd,   965
And Seal thee so, as henceforth not to scorn
The facile gates of hell too slightly barr'd.
    So threat'n'd hee, but Satan to no threats
Gave heed, but waxing more in rage repli'd.
    Then when I am thy captive talk of chains,   970
Proud limitary Cherub, but ere then

against. A flashback in time but a look forward in
the poem to the battle in heaven in VI, 56–879.
931. *Argue:* Cf. l. 830 above. The thought is
that Gabriel's reasoning betrays his ignorance of a
leader's duty to his followers.
938. Cf. *fame* in I, 651.
939. Cf. Satan's *afflicted Powers* in I, 186.
940. Satan is the "prince of the power of the air"
in Ephesians ii, 2. Cf. II, 275, n.
944. Editors generally quote the taunt of Aeschylus' Prometheus (*Prom.,* 937–39) to the chorus:

"Worship, adore, and fawn upon the ruler"; and
Gabriel's words to Satan in l. 962 below as echoing
Hermes' warning to him in reply (*Prom.,* 1071).
The first parallel is far from close. Cf. I, 116, n.
958. Cf. the similar use of *Patron* in III, 219.
962. *arede:* advise. Cf. l. 944 above, n.
965. Cf. I, 45–48.
971. *limitary:* "boundary-protecting" is the meaning, but there is an overtone suggesting that Gabriel
is presuming too much in setting bounds to Satan's
movements.

Far heavier load thyself expect to feel
From my prevailing arm, though Heaven's King
Ride on thy wings, and thou with thy Compeers,
Us'd to the yoke, draw'st his triumphant wheels   975
In progress through the road of Heav'n Star-pav'd.
   While thus he spake, th' Angelic Squadron bright
Turn'd fiery red, sharp'ning in mooned horns
Thir Phalanx, and began to hem him round
With ported Spears, as thick as when a field   980
Of *Ceres* ripe for harvest waving bends
Her bearded Grove of ears, which way the wind
Sways them; the careful Plowman doubting stands
Lest on the threshing floor his hopeful sheaves
Prove chaff.   On th' other side *Satan* alarm'd   985
Collecting all his might dilated stood,
Like *Teneriff* or *Atlas* unremov'd:
His stature reacht the Sky, and on his Crest
Sat horror Plum'd; nor wanted in his grasp
What seem'd both Spear and Shield: now dreadful deeds   990
Might have ensu'd, nor only Paradise
In this commotion, but the Starry Cope
Of Heav'n perhaps, or all the Elements
At least had gone to rack, disturb'd and torn
With violence of this conflict, had not soon   995
Th' Eternal to prevent such horrid fray
Hung forth in Heav'n his golden Scales, yet seen
Betwixt *Astrea* and the *Scorpion* sign,
Wherein all things created first he weigh'd,
The pendulous round Earth with balanc't Air   1000
In counterpoise, now ponders all events,
Battles and Realms: in these he put two weights
The sequel each of parting and of fight;
The latter quick up flew, and kickt the beam;
Which *Gabriel* spying, thus bespake the Fiend.   1005
   Satan, I know thy strength, and thou know'st mine,
Neither our own but giv'n; what folly then
To boast what Arms can do, since thine no more
Than Heav'n permits, nor mine, though doubl'd now
To trample thee as mire: for proof look up,   1010

975. The line looks forward to VI, 770–71.
978. *mooned*: crescent-shaped.
980. *ported*: held diagonally across the bearer's breast.
981. *Ceres*, the name of the goddess of grain, represents the grain itself.   Cf. *On the Fifth of November*, 32.
983. *careful*: anxious.
987. *Teneriff*, the great peak in the Canary Islands, like the *Atlas* range in Morocco, was made dramatically conspicuous on the maps of Milton's time, but he might visualize it from Virgil's description of "the top of Atlas . . .
Whose brawny back supports the starry skies—
Atlas, whose head, with piny forests crown'd,
Is beaten by the winds—with foggy vapors bound."
   (*Aen.* IV, 246–49. Dryden's translation.)
992. *Cope* (which is etymologically related to "cape") is again used of the sky in VI, 215.

997. Milton remembered the golden scales in which Zeus weighed the destinies of the Greeks against those of the Trojans (*Il.* VIII, 69–72), and of Hector against Achilles (*Il.* XXII, 209), or the weighing of Aeneas' fate against that of Turnus (*Aen.* XII, 725–27), but he gives the conception cosmic scope by identifying the scales with the constellation of *Libra*, or the Scales, which stands between the Virgin and the Scorpion in the Zodiac.
999. Compare Isaiah xl, 12: God is he "Who hath measured the waters in the hollow of his hand, and meted out heaven with the span, and comprehended the dust of the earth in a measure, and weighed the mountains in scales, and the hills in a balance."
1001. *ponders*: has its literal, Latin meaning, "weighs."
1003. *sequel*: consequence.

And read thy Lot in yon celestial Sign
Where thou art weigh'd, and shown how light, how weak,
If thou resist. The Fiend lookt up and knew
His mounted scale aloft: nor more; but fled
Murmuring, and with him fled the shades of night.   *what are these,*   1015
                                                     — Dawn

The End of the Fourth Book.

1012. Milton repeats a phrase from the record in Daniel (v, 27) of God's use of the figure of the scales to warn the Babylonian king, Belshazzar: "Thou art weighed in the balance, and art found wanting."

1015. Like Book II, Book IV ends with a transition from darkness to day.

BOOK V

THE ARGUMENT

Morning approacht, Eve *relates to* Adam *her troublesome dream; he likes it not, yet comforts her: They come forth to thir day labors: Thir Morning Hymn at the Door of thir Bower.* God to render Man inexcusable sends *Raphael to admonish him of his obedience, of his free estate, of his enemy near at hand; who he is, and why his enemy, and whatever else may avail* Adam *to know.* Raphael *comes down to Paradise, his appearance describ'd, his coming discern'd by* Adam *afar off sitting at the door of his Bower; he goes out to meet him, brings him to his lodge, entertains him with the choicest fruits of Paradise got together by* Eve; *thir discourse at Table:* Raphael *performs his message, minds* Adam *of his state and of his enemy; relates at Adam's request who that enemy is, and how he came to be so, beginning from his first revolt in Heaven, and the occasion thereof; how he drew his Legions after him to the parts of the North, and there incited them to rebel with him, persuading all but only* Abdiel *a Seraph, who in Argument dissuades and opposes him, then forsakes him.*

Now Morn her rosy steps in th' Eastern Clime
Advancing, sow'd the Earth with Orient Pearl,
When *Adam* wak't, so custom'd, for his sleep
Was Aery light, from pure digestion bred,
And temperate vapors bland, which th' only sound   5
Of leaves and fuming rills, *Aurora's* fan,
Lightly dispers'd, and the shrill Matin Song
Of Birds on every bough; so much the more
His wonder was to find unwak'n'd *Eve*
With Tresses discompos'd, and glowing Cheek,   10
As through unquiet rest: hee on his side
Leaning half-rais'd, with looks of cordial Love
Hung over her enamor'd, and beheld
Beauty, which whether waking or asleep,
Shot forth peculiar graces; then with voice   15
Mild, as when *Zephyrus* on *Flora* breathes,
Her hand soft touching, whisper'd thus.   Awake

1. The *rosy steps* are Milton's transformation of the rosy-fingered Dawn of Homer. Cf. VI, 524, and VII, 29.

4. After their sin the sleep of Adam and Eve is "grosser" (IX, 1049).

5. *vapors* is a definite medical term meaning the exhalations of digestion. Cf. the "vapors of wine" in *Church Government* (see p. 671).

6. *Aurora's fan:* the leaves, stirred by the breeze of the goddess of morning, Aurora.

15. *peculiar:* solely belonging (to Eve).

16. So *Zephyrus* plays with the Dawn in *L'Allegro,* 19, and fans Paradise in IV, 329. *Flora,* goddess of flowers, is half personification and half metonymy, as *Ceres* is in IV, 981.

17–25. The obvious parody of the Song of Solo-

My fairest, my espous'd, my latest found,
Heav'n's last best gift, my ever new delight,
Awake, the morning shines, and the fresh field   20
Calls us; we lose the prime, to mark how spring
Our tended Plants, how blows the Citron Grove,
What drops the Myrrh, and what the balmy Reed,
How Nature paints her colors, how the Bee
Sits on the Bloom extracting liquid sweet.   25
    Such whispering wak'd her, but with startl'd eye
On *Adam,* whom imbracing, thus she spake.
    O Sole in whom my thoughts find all repose,
My Glory, my Perfection, glad I see
Thy face, and Morn return'd, for I this Night,   30
Such night till this I never pass'd, have dream'd,
If dream'd, not as I oft am wont, of thee,
Works of day past, or morrow's next design,
But of offense and trouble, which my mind
Knew never till this irksome night; methought   35
Close at mine ear one call'd me forth to walk
With gentle voice, I thought it thine; it said,
Why sleep'st thou *Eve?* now is the pleasant time,
The cool, the silent, save where silence yields
To the night-warbling Bird, that now awake   40
Tunes sweetest his love-labor'd song; now reigns
Full Orb'd the Moon, and with more pleasing light *— evil and dark*
Shadowy sets off the face of things; in vain,
If none regard; Heav'n wakes with all his eyes,
Whom to behold but thee, Nature's desire,   45
In whose sight all things joy, with ravishment
Attracted by thy beauty still to gaze.
I rose as at thy call, but found thee not;
To find thee I directed then my walk;
And on, methought, alone I pass'd through ways   50
That brought me on a sudden to the Tree
Of interdicted Knowledge: fair it seem'd,
Much fairer to my Fancy than by day:
And as I wond'ring lookt, beside it stood
One shap'd and wing'd like one of those from Heav'n   55
By us oft seen; his dewy locks distill'd
Ambrosia; on that Tree he also gaz'd;
And O fair Plant, said he, with fruit surcharg'd,
Deigns none to ease thy load and taste thy sweet,
Nor God, nor Man; is Knowledge so despis'd?   60
Or envy, or what reserve forbids to taste?
Forbid who will, none shall from me withhold

mon ii, 10—"Rise up, my love, my fair one, and
come away"—is an inversion of the pictures,
"changing the dove for the nightingale, keeping only
the sensuous delights," as H. Schultz observes in
"Satan's Serenade" in *PQ,* XXVII (1948), 24.

21. *prime:* the first hour of the day. Cf. l. 170
below.

22. *blows:* blooms. Cf. VII, 319, and IX, 629.

23. *balmy Reed:* balm-producing reed.

44. So for Spenser (and many other poets) the
stars were the "many eyes" with which "High
heven beholdes" mankind. (*F.Q.* III, xi, 45, 7-8).

45-47. The passage, like the anticipation of a
theme to be developed later in a symphony, looks
forward to the temptation in IX, 494-833.

55-57. Milton remembered Virgil's Venus ap-
pearing in sudden glory to Aeneas with
    dishevell'd hair,
Which flowing from her shoulders reach'd the
    ground,
And widely spread ambrosial scents around.
    (*Aen.* I, 403-404. Dryden's translation.)

60. *God* here means "angel," as in II, 352, and
V, 117.

Longer thy offer'd good, why else set here?
This said he paus'd not, but with vent'rous Arm
He pluckt, he tasted; mee damp horror chill'd   65
At such bold words voucht with a deed so bold:
But he thus overjoy'd, O Fruit Divine,
Sweet of thyself, but much more sweet thus cropt,
Forbidd'n here, it seems, as only fit
For Gods, yet able to make Gods of Men: 70
And why not Gods of Men, since good, the more
Communicated, more abundant grows,
The Author not impair'd, but honor'd more?
Here, happy Creature, fair Angelic *Eve*,
Partake thou also; happy though thou art,   75
Happier thou may'st be, worthier canst not be:
Taste this, and be henceforth among the Gods
Thyself a Goddess, not to Earth confin'd,
But sometimes in the Air, as wee, sometimes
Ascend to Heav'n, by merit thine, and see   80
What life the Gods live there, and such live thou.
So saying, he drew nigh, and to me held,
Even to my mouth of that same fruit held part
Which he had pluckt; the pleasant savory smell
So quick'n'd appetite, that I, methought,   85
Could not but taste. Forthwith up to the Clouds
With him I flew, and underneath beheld
The Earth outstretcht immense, a prospect wide
And various: wond'ring at my flight and change
To this high exaltation; suddenly   90
My Guide was gone, and I, methought, sunk down,
And fell asleep; but O how glad I wak'd
To find this but a dream! Thus *Eve* her Night
Related, and thus *Adam* answer'd sad.
    Best Image of myself and dearer half,   95
The trouble of thy thoughts this night in sleep
Affects me equally; nor can I like
This uncouth dream, of evil sprung I fear;
Yet evil whence? in thee can harbor none,
Created pure. But know that in the Soul   100
Are many lesser Faculties that serve
Reason as chief; among these Fancy next
Her office holds; of all external things,
Which the five watchful Senses represent,
She forms Imaginations, Aery shapes,   105
Which Reason joining or disjoining, frames
All what we affirm or what deny, and call
Our knowledge or opinion; then retires

---

65. *damp horror:* the sweat of fear.

71. The ambiguous use of the word "gods" figures in Satan's temptation of Eve in IX, 705-712, as it has in his speech to Beelzebub in I, 116.

100-116. The passage summarizes the popular faculty psychology which is familiar in Spenser's allegory (*F.Q.* II, ix, 49-58) of Phantastes, the faculty which Adam calls *Fancy* and contrasts for its fertility in *Imaginations, Aery shapes,* with *Reason.* In *M.&S.,* pp. 36-38, Svendsen quotes

several discussions of this "faculty of the fantasie" from La Primaudaye's *French Academie* and other encyclopaedias.

107-113. D. F. Bond aptly quotes (in *Explicator* III, 54) from Bishop Bramhall's *Castigation of Mr. Hobbes* (1658): "In time of sleep, . . . when the imagination is not governed by reason, we see what absurd and monstrous and inconsistent shapes and phansies it doth collect, remote from true deliberation."

Into her private Cell when Nature rests
Oft in her absence mimic Fancy wakes   110
To imitate her; but misjoining shapes,
Wild work produces oft, and most in dreams,
Ill matching words and deeds long past or late.
Some such resemblances methinks I find
Of our last Ev'ning's talk, in this thy dream,   115
But with addition strange; yet be not sad.
Evil into the mind of God or Man
May come and go, so unapprov'd, and leave
No spot or blame behind: Which gives me hope
That what in sleep thou didst abhor to dream,   120
Waking thou never wilt consent to do.
Be not disheart'n'd then, nor cloud those looks
That wont to be more cheerful and serene
Than when fair Morning first smiles on the World,
And let us to our fresh imployments rise   125
Among the Groves, the Fountains, and the Flow'rs
That open now thir choicest bosom'd smells
Reserv'd from night, and kept for thee in store.
    So cheer'd he his fair Spouse, and she was cheer'd,
But silently a gentle tear let fall   130
From either eye, and wip'd them with her hair;
Two other precious drops that ready stood,
Each in thir crystal sluice, hee ere they fell
Kiss'd as the gracious signs of sweet remorse
And pious awe, that fear'd to have offended.   135
    So all was clear'd, and to the Field they haste.
But first from under shady arborous roof,
Soon as they forth were come to open sight
Of day-spring, and the Sun, who scarce up risen
With wheels yet hov'ring o'er the Ocean brim,   140
Shot parallel to the earth his dewy ray,
Discovering in wide Lantskip all the East
Of Paradise and *Eden's* happy Plains,
Lowly they bow'd adoring, and began
Thir Orisons, each Morning duly paid   145
In various style, for neither various style
Nor holy rapture wanted they to praise
Thir Maker, in fit strains pronounct or sung
Unmeditated, such prompt eloquence
Flow'd from thir lips, in Prose or numerous Verse,   150

117–119. *God* is probably rightly interpreted by T. Banks—in *MLN*, LIV (1939), 451—as meaning "angel," as it does in III, 341. Thus the line repeats Raphael's statement in V, 538, that the good angels remain good by their own free choice. Interpreting *God* as "the Infinite," Saurat (in *Milton: Man and Thinker*, p. 110) regards the lines as meaning that the world was created "to drive away the evil latent in the Infinite, and to exalt the good latent also." But Milton may be simply appealing to the universally accepted view of God's omniscience as implying that His knowledge extends to the potential, accidental evil in good things because—as St. Thomas explains (*Summa Theol.* I, q. 14, a.10) —"God would not know good things perfectly un-less he knew evil things."

The lines suggest to Mrs. Bell—in *PMLA*, LXVIII (1953), 871—that Eve is "already receptive to the Tempter's choice flattery"—a position which W. Shumaker challenges on theological ground in *PMLA*, LXX (1955), 1199. Milton was echoing Titus i, 15: "Unto the pure, all things are pure; but unto them that are defiled is nothing pure; but even their mind and conscience is defiled." Cf. *Areop*, p. 727.

137. *arborous*: arbor-like, tree-made.

142. Cf. *Lantskip* in II, 491.

146–152. So in *CD* II, iv (C. E. XVII, 85), Milton stresses "the superfluousness of set forms of worship."

150. With *numerous* cf. the "Harmonious numbers" of III, 38.

More tuneable than needed Lute or Harp
To add more sweetness, and they thus began.
  These are thy glorious works, Parent of good,
Almighty, thine this universal Frame,
Thus wondrous fair; thyself how wondrous then!   155
Unspeakable, who sit'st above these Heavens
To us invisible or dimly seen
In these thy lowest works, yet these declare
Thy goodness beyond thought, and Power Divine:
Speak yee who best can tell, ye Sons of Light,   160
Angels, for yee behold him, and with songs
And choral symphonies, Day without Night,
Circle his Throne rejoicing, yee in Heav'n;
On Earth join all ye Creatures to extol
Him first, him last, him midst, and without end.   165
Fairest of Stars, last in the train of Night,
If better thou belong not to the dawn,
Sure pledge of day, that crown'st the smiling Morn
With thy bright Circlet, praise him in thy Sphere
While day arises, that sweet hour of Prime.   170
Thou Sun, of this great World both Eye and Soul,
Acknowledge him thy Greater, sound his praise
In thy eternal course, both when thou climb'st,
And when high Noon hast gain'd, and when thou fall'st.
Moon, that now meet'st the orient Sun, now fli'st   175
With the fixt Stars, fixt in thir Orb that flies,
And yee five other wand'ring Fires that move
In mystic Dance not without Song, resound
His praise, who out of Darkness call'd up Light.
Air, and ye Elements the eldest birth   180
Of Nature's Womb, that in quaternion run
Perpetual Circle, multiform, and mix
And nourish all things, let your ceaseless change
Vary to our great Maker still new praise.

154. *Frame* is used as it is in Hamlet's "goodly frame, the earth" (*Hamlet* II, ii, 310).

156-169. The theme of the hymn is the doctrine of God's revelation of himself only in his creatures—in Du Bartas' words:

God, of himself incapable to sensce,
  In's Works, reveals him t'our intelligence.

(*Divine Weeks,* p. 5. Cf. Taylor, *Du Bartas,* p. 82.)

The hymn parallels Psalm cxlviii, 2-4 and 8-10: "Praise ye him, all his angels: praise ye him, all his hosts.

Praise ye him, sun and moon: praise ye him, all ye stars of light. . . .

Fire, and hail: snow, and vapor: stormy wind fulfilling his word:

Mountains, and all hills: fruitful trees, and all cedars:

Beasts, and all cattle: creeping things, and flying fowl."

162. Cf. ll. 642-46 below.

166. So Venus is the fairest star in Heaven in the *Iliad* XXII, 318. In the pre-sunrise sky it is Lucifer, the light-bringer, and after sunset it is Hesperus.

171. As Donne conceived the sun in terms of the metaphor that made it the eye of the world and the male force inspiriting it—

Thee, eye of heaven, this great Soule envies not,
  By thy male force, is all wee have, begot.

(*Progress of the Soul,* stanza 2) (Cf. *PL* VIII, 150.) so Milton conceived its light as "male" and as a life-giving spirit. The conception of the sun as the soul of the world goes back to Pliny (*Nat. Hist.* II, 4) and was developed by Conti (*Mythologiae* V, xvii, p. 543) into a synthesis of many solar myths signifying that the sun was "lord of the stars and giver of life to mortals, since he is the author of light to the other stars and by him all things flourish." Cf. IV, 667-73, and VIII, 94-97, n.

176. For the *Orb that flies* see the Introduction 34.

177. The *five other wand'ring Fires* are Venus (though it has been mentioned in l. 166), Mercury, Mars, Jupiter, and Saturn. So in *Doctor Faustus* I, vi, 43-44, Marlowe refers to the literal meaning of the word "planet" by calling Saturn, Mars, and Jupiter "erring stars." Cf. VIII, 126.

181. As far back as Plato's *Timaeus* (49, c), the four elements had been supposed to be reversibly transformable into one another. Cf. ll. 415-26 below.

Ye Mists and Exhalations that now rise   185
From Hill or steaming Lake, dusky or grey,
Till the Sun paint your fleecy skirts with Gold,
In honor to the World's great Author rise,
Whether to deck with Clouds th' uncolor'd sky,
Or wet the thirsty Earth with falling showers,   190
Rising or falling still advance his praise.
His praise ye Winds, that from four Quarters blow,
Breathe soft or loud; and wave your tops, ye Pines,
With every Plant, in sign of Worship wave.
Fountains and yee, that warble, as ye flow,   195
Melodious murmurs, warbling tune his praise.
Join voices all ye living Souls; ye Birds,
That singing up to Heaven Gate ascend,
Bear on your wings and in your notes his praise;
Yee that in Waters glide, and yee that walk   200
The Earth, and stately tread, or lowly creep;
Witness if I be silent, Morn or Even,
To Hill, or Valley, Fountain, or fresh shade
Made vocal by my Song, and taught his praise.
Hail universal Lord, be bounteous still   205
To give us only good; and if the night
Have gather'd aught of evil or conceal'd,
Disperse it, as now light dispels the dark.
   So pray'd they innocent, and to thir thoughts
Firm peace recover'd soon and wonted calm.   210
On to thir morning's rural work they haste
Among sweet dews and flow'rs; where any row
Of Fruit-trees overwoody reach'd too far
Thir pamper'd boughs, and needed hands to check
Fruitless imbraces: or they led the Vine   215
To wed her Elm; she spous'd about him twines
Her marriageable arms, and with her brings
Her dow'r th' adopted Clusters, to adorn
His barren leaves. Them thus imploy'd beheld
With pity Heav'n's high King, and to him call'd   220
Raphael, the sociable Spirit, that deign'd
To travel with *Tobias*, and secur'd
His marriage with the seven-times-wedded Maid.
   Raphael, said hee, thou hear'st what stir on Earth
Satan from Hell scap't through the darksome Gulf   225
Hath rais'd in Paradise, and how disturb'd
This night the human pair, how he designs
In them at once to ruin all mankind.
   Go therefore, half this day as friend with friend

189. *uncolor'd*: without variety of colors.
202. Each speaker seems to invoke every creature to witness his fidelity to God's praise, night and
morning, as the Psalmist (cxxxvii, 6) prays that,
if he forgets Zion, his tongue may cleave to the
roof of his mouth.
206. The lines seem to echo Socrates' prayer "for
good gifts, for the gods know best what things are
good," as Xenophon reports it in *Memorabilia* I, ii, 2,
and as Cardinal Bembo recalled it in Castiglione's
Courtier when he prayed God "to correct the falsehood of the senses and, after long wandering in van-

itie, to give us the right and sound joy" (Everyman
Ed. of Hoby's tr., p. 321).
216. The figure was traditional when Spenser
wrote of the "vine-propp elme" (*F. Q.* I, i, 8, 7) and
when Horace used it in *Odes* II, xv, 4, and IV, v, 31.
221. The name *Raphael* means "medicine of God,"
and it corresponds with the angel's role in the Book
of Tobit as it is reflected in IV, 166–71. With Michael, Gabriel, and Uriel, Raphael is one of "the
four angels of the presence" of God in Jewish tradition.

Converse with *Adam,* in what Bow'r or shade   230
Thou find'st him from the heat of Noon retir'd,
To respite his day-labor with repast,
Or with repose; and such discourse bring on,
As may advise him of his happy state,
Happiness in his power left free to will,   235
Left to his own free Will, his Will though free,
Yet mutable; whence warn him to beware
He swerve not too secure: tell him withal
His danger, and from whom, what enemy
Late fall'n himself from Heaven, is plotting now   240
The fall of others from like state of bliss;
By violence, no, for that shall be withstood,
But by deceit and lies; this let him know,
Lest wilfully transgressing he pretend
Surprisal, unadmonisht, unforewarn'd.   245
        So spake th' Eternal Father, and fulfill'd
All Justice: nor delay'd the winged Saint
After his charge receiv'd; but from among
Thousand Celestial Ardors, where he stood
Veil'd with his gorgeous wings, up springing light   250
Flew through the midst of Heav'n; th' angelic Choirs
On each hand parting, to his speed gave way
Through all th' Empyreal road; till at the Gate
Of Heav'n arriv'd, the gate self-open'd wide
On golden Hinges turning, as by work   255
Divine the sovran Architect had fram'd.
From hence, no cloud, or, to obstruct his sight,
Star interpos'd, however small he sees,
Not unconform to other shining Globes,
Earth and the Gard'n of God, with Cedars crown'd   260
Above all Hills. As when by night the Glass
Of *Galileo,* less assur'd, observes
Imagin'd Lands and Regions in the Moon:
Or Pilot from amidst the *Cyclades*
Delos or *Samos* first appearing kens   265
A cloudy spot. Down thither prone in flight
He speeds, and through the vast Ethereal Sky
Sails between worlds and worlds, with steady wing
Now on the polar winds, then with quick Fan
Winnows the buxom Air; till within soar   270
Of Tow'ring Eagles, to all the Fowls he seems
A *Phœnix,* gaz'd by all, as that sole Bird

234. *advise:* inform.
238. *secure:* overconfident of safety (literally,
"without care"). Cf. IV, 186.
247. Cf. the use of *Saints* in III, 330.
249. *Ardors:* angels, as in Psalm civ, 4: "Who
maketh his angels spirits; his ministers a flaming
fire."
259. *Not unconform:* not unlike.
261–262. *the Glass Of Galileo:* the telescope. Cf.
I, 287–91.
264. *Cyclades:* the Aegean archipelago of which
Delos is the center. *Samos* lies outside them to
the northeast.
266. *prone:* downward moving. The picture is

more splendid than those of Mercury running Jove's
errands over sea and land (in *Il.* XXIV, 341, and
Aen. IV, 241). Raphael plunges earthward by the
same *passage* or route that Satan has followed in
III, 528–87, but without pausing at the sun.
269. *Fan:* wing.
272. Milton knew many accounts of the *Phoenix,*
the unique bird that Ovid describes (*Met.* XV, 391–
407) as immolating itself once in five hundred years
on a pyre of spices, only to "carry its own cradle
and its father's tomb to the city of the sun." Ovid's
city of the sun, Heliopolis, becomes Milton's neighboring Egyptian city of Thebes. In *The Phoenix*
that is attributed to Lactantius and in Tasso's *Phoe-*

When to enshrine his reliques in the Sun's
Bright Temple, to *Egyptian Thebes* he flies.
At once on th' Eastern cliff of Paradise   275
He lights, and to his proper shape returns
A Seraph wing'd; six wings he wore, to shade
His lineaments Divine; the pair that clad
Each shoulder broad, came mantling o'er his breast
With regal Ornament; the middle pair   280
Girt like a Starry Zone his waist, and round
Skirted his loins and thighs with downy Gold
And colors dipt in Heav'n; the third his feet
Shadow'd from either heel with feather'd mail
Sky-tinctur'd grain.   Like *Maia's* son he stood,   285
And shook his Plumes, that Heav'nly fragrance fill'd
The circuit wide.   Straight knew him all the Bands
Of Angels under watch; and to his state,
And to his message high in honor rise;
For on some message high they guess'd him bound.   290
Thir glittering Tents he pass'd, and now is come
Into the blissful field, through Groves of Myrrh,
And flow'ring Odors, Cassia, Nard, and Balm;
A Wilderness of sweets; for Nature here
Wanton'd as in her prime, and play'd at will   295
Her Virgin Fancies, pouring forth more sweet,
Wild above Rule or Art, enormous bliss.
Him through the spicy Forest onward come
Adam discern'd, as in the door he sat
Of his cool Bow'r, while now the mounted Sun   300
Shot down direct his fervid Rays, to warm
Earth's inmost womb, more warmth than *Adam* needs;
And *Eve* within, due at her hour prepar'd
For dinner savoury fruits, of taste to please
True appetite, and not disrelish thirst   305
Of nectarous draughts between, from milky stream,
Berry or Grape: to whom thus *Adam* call'd.
   Haste hither *Eve,* and worth thy sight behold
Eastward among those Trees, what glorious shape
Comes this way moving; seems another Morn   310
Ris'n on mid-noon; some great behest from Heav'n
To us perhaps he brings, and will voutsafe
This day to be our Guest.   But go with speed,
And what thy stores contain, bring forth and pour
Abundance, fit to honor and receive   315
Our Heav'nly stranger; well we may afford
Our givers thir own gifts, and large bestow

nix he found the reborn bird in full flight described
as a splendid "thing to gaze at." J. Whaler notes, in
PMLA, XLVII (1932), 545, that the simile may
have had a secondary application for Milton in the
light of an Elizabethan proverb that "A faithful
friend is like a phoenix." Cf. *SA,* 1699–1707.

276. Raphael's *proper shape* Milton takes to be
that of the seraphs in Isaiah vi, 2, each with "six
wings; with twain he covered his face, and with
twain he covered his feet, and with twain did he fly."

285. *Sky-tinctur'd grain:* sky-blue color. *Maia's
son:* Mercury.

288. *state:* majestic rank. Cf. I, 640, and II, 511,
and l. 353 below.

289. *message:* mission (as God's emissary).

292. *blissful field:* Paradise. Cf. *bliss* in l. 297
below.

299. So Abraham, sitting in front of his tent,
saw the Lord coming and told Sarah to prepare a
meal (Gen. xviii, 2–8).

308. *worth thy sight:* worth seeing.

From large bestow'd, where Nature multiplies
Her fertile growth, and by disburd'ning grows
More fruitful, which instructs us not to spare.   320
    To whom thus *Eve. Adam,* earth's hallow'd mould,
Of God inspir'd, small store will serve, where store,
All seasons, ripe for use hangs on the stalk;
Save what by frugal storing firmness gains
To nourish, and superfluous moist consumes: 325
But I will haste and from each bough and brake,
Each Plant and juiciest Gourd will pluck such choice
To entertain our Angel guest, as hee
Beholding shall confess that here on Earth
God hath dispenst his bounties as in Heav'n.   330
    So saying, with dispatchful looks in haste
She turns, on hospitable thoughts intent
What choice to choose for delicacy best,
What order, so contriv'd as not to mix
Tastes, not well join'd, inelegant, but bring   335
Taste after taste upheld with kindliest change;
Bestirs her then, and from each tender stalk
Whatever Earth all-bearing Mother yields
In *India* East or West, or middle shore
In *Pontus* or the *Punic* Coast, or where   340
Alcinoüs reign'd, fruit of all kinds, in coat,
Rough, or smooth rin'd, or bearded husk, or shell
She gathers, Tribute large, and on the board
Heaps with unsparing hand; for drink the Grape
She crushes, inoffensive must, and meaths   345
From many a berry, and from sweet kernels prest
She tempers dulcet creams, nor these to hold
Wants her fit vessels pure, then strews the ground
With Rose and Odors from the shrub unfum'd.
Meanwhile our Primitive great Sire, to meet   350
His god-like Guest, walks forth, without more train
Accompanied than with his own complete
Perfections; in himself was all his state,
More solemn than the tedious pomp that waits
On Princes, when thir rich Retinue long   355
Of Horses led, and Grooms besmear'd with Gold
Dazzles the crowd, and sets them all agape.
Nearer his presence *Adam* though not aw'd,
Yet with submiss approach and reverence meek,
As to a superior Nature, bowing low,   360
    Thus said. Native of Heav'n, for other place
None can than Heav'n such glorious shape contain;
Since by descending from the Thrones above,
Those happy places thou hast deign'd a while

322. *inspir'd:* inspirited or fertilized.
336. *kindliest:* in perfect harmony with nature.
339. *India East or West:* tropical Asia and tropical America. *middle shore:* the coast of the Mediterranean Sea.
340. As *PR* II, 347, testifies, fish from the Black Sea on its Pontic (or southern) shore were a Roman delicacy. The *Punic Coast* is the Carthaginian coast of the Mediterranean—modern Tunis.
341. Around *Alcinoüs'* palace Ulysses found a garden of perpetual springtime and harvest (*Od.* VII, 125–28), like that in Paradise.
345. *must:* unfermented wine. *meath:* mead.
349. *the shrub unfum'd:* unburned. The perfume from the fresh plant, not from its burning—not from any kind of incense.

To want, and honor these, voutsafe with us   365
Two only, who yet by sovran gift possess
This spacious ground, in yonder shady Bow'r
To rest, and what the Garden choicest bears
To sit and taste, till this meridian heat
Be over, and the Sun more cool decline.   370
    Whom thus the Angelic Virtue answer'd mild.
Adam, I therefore came, nor art thou such
Created, or such place hast here to dwell,
As may not oft invite, though Spirits of Heav'n
To visit thee; lead on then where thy Bow'r   375
O'ershades; for these mid-hours, till Ev'ning rise
I have at will. So to the Silvan Lodge
They came, that like *Pomona's* Arbor smil'd
With flow'rets deck't and fragrant smells: but *Eve*
Undeckt, save with herself more lovely fair   380
Than Wood-Nymph, or the fairest Goddess feign'd
Of three that in Mount *Ida* naked strove.
Stood to entertain her guest from Heav'n: no veil
Shee needed, Virtue-proof, no thought infirm
Alter'd her cheek. On whom the Angel *Hail*   385
Bestow'd, the holy salutation us'd
Long after to blest *Mary,* second *Eve.*
    Hail Mother of Mankind, whose fruitful Womb
Shall fill the World more numerous with thy Sons
Than with these various fruits the Trees of God   390
Have heap'd this Table. Rais'd of grassy turf
Thir Table was, and mossy seats had round,
And on her ample Square from side to side
All *Autumn* pil'd, though *Spring* and *Autumn* here
Danc'd hand in hand. A while discourse they hold;   395
No fear lest Dinner cool; when thus began
Our Author. Heav'nly stranger, please to taste
These bounties which our Nourisher, from whom
All perfet good unmeasur'd out, descends,
To us for food and for delight hath caus'd   400
The Earth to yield; unsavory food perhaps
To spiritual Natures; only this I know,
That one Celestial Father gives to all.
    To whom the Angel. Therefore what he gives
(Whose praise be ever sung) to man in part   405
Spiritual, may of purest Spirits be found
No ingrateful food: and food alike those pure
Intelligential substances require

---

365. *want:* do without.

371. As a seraph or one of the supreme rank in the heavenly hierarchy, Raphael may have the title of any of the inferior orders, of which the *Virtues* were one. See the Introduction 21.

374. *though Spirits of Heav'n:* even heavenly spirits.

378. *Pomona:* the Roman goddess of flowers.

382. The *three that in Mount Ida naked strove* are Juno, Venus, and Athene, to the second of whom Paris awarded the golden apple of discord that bore the inscription, "For the fairest." Mt. Ida over-

looked ancient Troy.

384. *Virtue-proof:* proof (against evil) by her virtue.

385–388. *Hail* is the greeting of the angel of the Annunciation to Mary (Luke i, 28). Mary is the *second Eve* of X, 183, as she is here. Cf. XI, 158–59.

399. The line recalls James i, 17: "Every good and perfect gift is from above, and cometh down from the Father of lights."

403–500. For the conception of angels and cosmic nature see the Introduction 37.

As doth your Rational; and both contain
Within them every lower faculty   410
Of sense, whereby they hear, see, smell, touch, taste,
Tasting concoct, digest, assimilate,
And corporeal to incorporeal turn.
For know, whatever was created, needs
To be sustain'd and fed; of Elements   415
The grosser feeds the purer, Earth the Sea,
Earth and the Sea feed Air, the Air those Fires
Ethereal, and as lowest first the Moon;
Whence in her visage round those spots, unpurg'd
Vapors not yet into her substance turn'd.   420
Nor doth the Moon no nourishment exhale
From her moist Continent to higher Orbs.
The Sun that light imparts to all, receives
From all his alimental recompense
In humid exhalations, and at Even   425
Sups with the Ocean: though in Heav'n the Trees
Of life ambrosial fruitage bear, and vines
Yield Nectar, though from off the boughs each Morn
We brush mellifluous Dews, and find the ground
Cover'd with pearly grain: yet God hath here   430
Varied his bounty so with new delights,
As may compare with Heaven; and to taste
Think not I shall be nice. So down they sat,
And to thir viands fell, nor seemingly
The Angel, nor in mist, the common gloss   435
Of Theologians, but with keen dispatch
Of real hunger, and concoctive heat
To transubstantiate; what redounds, transpires
Through Spirits with ease; nor wonder; if by fire
Of sooty coal the Empiric Alchemist   440
Can turn, or holds it possible to turn
Metals of drossiest Ore to perfet Gold
As from the Mine.   Meanwhile at Table *Eve*
Minister'd naked, and thir flowing cups   – she's not sitting
With pleasant liquors crown'd: O innocence   445
Deserving Paradise! if ever, then,
Then had the Sons of God excuse to have been
Enamour'd at that sight; but in those hearts
Love unlibidinous reign'd, nor jealousy
Was understood, the injur'd Lover's Hell.   450

412. Cf. the first process of digestion as concoction in *Of Education* (see p. 638).

415–426. Plato's theory of the four elements as "passing one into another in an unbroken circle of birth" (*Tim.* 49C) helps explain why Justus Lipsius—in *Physiologiae Stoicorum* (Antwerp, 1637) II, xiv, p. 540—could find countless authorities, among them Homer, Cleanthes, Cicero, Seneca, and especially Pliny (*Nat. Hist.* II, ix), for the idea that the stars "feed on the vapors of the earth, that the sun sups on the waters of the great ocean, and the moon on those of rivers and brooks." Milton was sympathetic with contemporary revivals of the doctrine like that of Robert Fludd in *Utriusque cosmi historia* I, v, 6, where an engraving shows the sun

actually "supping with the ocean" at sunset. Yet in I, 290–91, he mentions the lunar landscape as the telescope reveals it.

429. *mellifluous:* honey-flowing.

433. *nice:* fastidious.

438. *redounds:* is excessive or unassimilable. Cf. the angels' immunity to *surfeit* at their heavenly feasts in heaven in l. 638–39 below.

440. The *Empiric Alchemist* is any dabbling experimenter in alchemy.

445. So the cups of Apollo's worshippers are literally "crowned" with wine in *Iliad* I, 470, and so Virgil's peasants "crown" their cups in *Georgics* II, 528.

447. Cf. the *Sons of God* in XI, 573–627, n.

p8 446

Thus when with meats and drinks they had suffic't,
Not burd'n'd Nature, sudden mind arose
In *Adam,* not to let th' occasion pass
Given him by this great Conference to know
Of things above his World, and of thir being   455
Who dwell in Heav'n, whose excellence he saw
Transcend his own so far, whose radiant forms
Divine effulgence, whose high Power so far
Exceeded human, and his wary speech
Thus to th' Empyreal Minister he fram'd.   460
    Inhabitant with God, now know I well
Thy favor, in this honor done to Man,
Under whose lowly roof thou hast voutsaf't
To enter, and these earthly fruits to taste,
Food not of Angels, yet accepted so,   465
As that more willingly thou couldst not seem
At Heav'n's high feasts to have fed: yet what compare?
    To whom the winged Hierarch repli'd.
O *Adam,* one Almighty is, from whom
All things proceed, and up to him return,   470
If not deprav'd from good, created all
Such to perfection, one first matter all,
Indu'd with various forms, various degrees
Of substance, and in things that live, of life;
But more refin'd, more spiritous, and pure,   475
As nearer to him plac't or nearer tending
Each in thir several active Spheres assign'd,
Till body up to spirit work, in bounds
Proportion'd to each kind.   So from the root
Springs lighter the green stalk, from thence the leaves   480
More aery, last the bright consummate flow'r
Spirits odorous breathes: flow'rs and thir fruit
Man's nourishment, by gradual scale sublim'd
To vital spirits aspire, to animal,
To intellectual, give both life and sense,   485
Fancy and understanding, whence the Soul
Reason receives, and reason is her being,
Discursive, or Intuitive; discourse
Is oftest yours, the latter most is ours,
Differing but in degree, of kind the same.   490
Wonder not then, what God for you saw good
If I refuse not, but convert, as you,
To proper substance; time may come when men
With Angels may participate, and find
No inconvenient Diet, nor too light Fare: 495
And from these corporal nutriments perhaps

467. *what compare?:* what comparison can there be?

469–500. For the image of the tree and the thought of the entire passage see the Introduction 40–43 and 61.

488–490. *discourse* literally means the "running to and fro" of the human mind in reasoning about things which the angels intuitively know. The principle had the best theological authority. Zanchius, for example, declared in *De Operibus Dei* (Neustadt, 1591) III, vi, that "angels do not know by rationating, combining and dividing data" as men do, and in this respect heaven differs from earth as much as it does in other ways.   The distinction itself stems from Plato (*Rep.* VII, 534A) and—as W. B. Hunter's Vanderbilt thesis shows—was widely developed by Christian commentators on the *Timaeus.*

493. *proper:* veritable substance of the angel himself.

Your bodies may at last turn all to spirit,
Improv'd by tract of time, and wing'd ascend
Ethereal, as wee, or may at choice
Here or in Heav'nly Paradises dwell;   500
If ye be found obedient, and retain
Unalterably firm his love entire
Whose progeny you are. Meanwhile enjoy
Your fill what happiness this happy state
Can comprehend, incapable of more.   505
  To whom the Patriarch of mankind repli'd:
O favorable Spirit, propitious guest,
Well hast thou taught the way that might direct
Our knowledge, and the scale of Nature set
From centre to circumference, whereon   510
In contemplation of created things
By steps we may ascend to God. But say,
What meant that caution join'd, *if ye be found
Obedient?* can we want obedience then
To him, or possibly his love desert   515
Who form'd us from the dust, and plac'd us here
Full to the utmost measure of what bliss
Human desires can seek or apprehend?
  To whom the Angel. Son of Heav'n and Earth,
Attend: That thou art happy, owe to God;   520
That thou continu'st such, owe to thyself,
That is, to thy obedience; therein stand.
This was that caution giv'n thee; be advis'd.
God made thee perfet, not immutable;
And good he made thee, but to persevere   525
He left it in thy power, ordain'd thy will
By nature free, not over-rul'd by Fate
Inextricable, or strict necessity;
Our voluntary service he requires,
Not our necessitated, such with him   530
Finds no acceptance, nor can find, for how
Can hearts, not free, be tri'd whether they serve
Willing or no, who will but what they must
By Destiny, and can no other choose?
Myself and all th' Angelic Host that stand   535
In sight of God enthron'd, our happy state
Hold, as you yours, while our obedience holds;
On other surety none; freely we serve,
Because we freely love, as in our will
To love or not; in this we stand or fall: 540

498. *tract:* extent.

503. The words *Whose progeny you are* are taken from St. Paul's sermon to the Athenians (Acts xvii, 28), but St. Paul expressly quoted them from Aratus' *Phainomena* (l. 5). From a study of Milton's own edition of Aratus, M. Kelley has shown in *PMLA,* LXX (1955), 1092, that he found corroboration for the thought in Lucretius' materialistic derivation of all life from "one celestial seed" in *De rerum natura* II, 991–92. Cf. I, 73–74, n.

509. The *scale of Nature* also stems—as A. O. Lovejoy shows in *The Great Chain of Being* (Cambridge, Mass., 1953), p. 50—from the *Timaeus,* but its ramifications in the thought of Milton's time were such as to let him regard the *golden Chain* of II, 1005, as one of its symbols.

521. Cf. III, 96–128, and *CD* I, iii, p. 913, where Milton declares that it would be "unworthy of God that man should nominally enjoy a liberty of which he was virtually deprived, which would be the case were that liberty to be oppressed or even obscured under the pretext of some sophistical necessity of immutability."

540. So in *CD* I, iii (C.E. XIV, 81), Milton says

And some are fall'n, to disobedience fall'n,
And so from Heav'n to deepest Hell; O fall
From what high state of bliss into what woe!
    To whom our great Progenitor. Thy words
Attentive, and with more delighted ear   545
Divine instructor, I have heard, than when
Cherubic Songs by night from neighboring Hills
Aereal Music send: nor knew I not
To be both will and deed created free;
Yet that we never shall forget to love   550
Our maker, and obey him whose command
Single, is yet so just, my constant thoughts
Assur'd me and still assure: though what thou tell'st
Hath past in Heav'n, some doubt within me move,
But more desire to hear, if thou consent,   555
The full relation, which must needs be strange,
Worthy of Sacred silence to be heard;
And we have yet large day, for scarce the Sun
Hath finisht half his journey, and scarce begins
His other half in the great Zone of Heav'n.   560
    Thus *Adam* made request, and *Raphaël*
After short pause assenting, thus began.
    High matter thou injoin'st me, O prime of men,
Sad task and hard, for how shall I relate
To human sense th' invisible exploits   565
Of warring Spirits; how without remorse
The ruin of so many glorious once
And perfet while they stood; how last unfold
The secrets of another World, perhaps
Not lawful to reveal? yet for thy good   570
This is dispens't, and what surmounts the reach
Of human sense, I shall delineate so,
By lik'ning spiritual to corporal forms,
As may express them best, though what if Earth
Be but the shadow of Heav'n, and things therein   575
Each to other like, more than on Earth is thought?
    As yet this World was not, and *Chaos* wild
Reign'd where these Heav'ns now roll, where Earth now rests
Upon her Centre pois'd, when on a day
(For Time, though in Eternity, appli'd   580

---

that "in assigning the gift of free will God suffered
both men and angels to stand or fall at their own
uncontrolled choice."

547. Cf. the *celestial Voices* of IV, 682.

556-560. The *full relation* to be told by Raphael
in the remaining *large day* includes the war in
heaven (VI), the creation of the universe (VII), and
a short discussion of the stars (VIII, 1-178). The
Sacred silence is a reminiscence of that of the spirits
in the underworld as Horace imagined them (*Odes*
II, xiii, 29-30) listening to the songs of the shades
of the poets.

563-570. So Aeneas begins his story of the fall
of Troy that fills the first two books of the *Aeneid.*
Addressing Dido he says:

  Great Queen, what you command me to relate
  Renews the sad remembrance of our fate.
  An empire from its old foundations rent,

And every woe the Trojans underwent.
     (*Aen.* II, 3-6. Dryden's translation.)

571-576. Though the conception of earth as the
shadow of heaven has been traced to various sources,
it stems from Plato's doctrine of the universe as
formed on a divine and eternal model, and from
Cicero's interpretation of it (in *Timaeus ex Platone*
ii, 39-41) as implying that "the world which we
see is a simulacrum of an eternal one."

573. Though the first three editions read
corporal, several editors read *corporeal,* because
Milton usually used the former to mean "relating
to the body," the latter to mean "having a body."

578-579. Cf. the fuller account of the *Earth self-
balanc't on her Centre* in VII, 242.

580-582. Pleading in *CD* I, vii that "it seems
probable that the apostasy which caused the expulsion of so many thousands [of angels] from

To motion, measures all things durable
By present, past, and future) on such day
As Heav'n's great Year brings forth, th' Empyreal Host
Of Angels by Imperial summons call'd,
Innumerable before th' Almighty's Throne   585
Forthwith from all the ends of Heav'n appear'd
Under thir Hierarchs in orders bright;
Ten thousand thousand Ensigns high advanc'd,
Standards and Gonfalons, twixt Van and Rear
Stream in the Air, and for distinction serve   590
Of Hierarchies, of Orders, and Degrees;
Or in thir glittering Tissues bear imblaz'd
Holy Memorials, acts of Zeal and Love
Recorded eminent. Thus when in Orbs
Of circuit inexpressible they stood,   595
Orb within Orb, the Father infinite,
By whom in bliss imbosom'd sat the Son,
Amidst as from a flaming Mount, whose top
Brightness had made invisible, thus spake.
    Hear all ye Angels, Progeny of Light,   600
Thrones, Dominations, Princedoms, Virtues, Powers,
Hear my Decree, which unrevok't shall stand.
This day I have begot whom I declare
My only Son, and on this holy Hill
Him have anointed, whom ye now behold   605
At my right hand; your Head I him appoint;
And by my Self have sworn to him shall bow
All knees in Heav'n, and shall confess him Lord:
Under his great Vice-gerent Reign abide
United as one individual Soul   610
For ever happy: him who disobeys
Mee disobeys, breaks union, and that day
Cast out from God and blessed vision, falls
Into utter darkness, deep ingulft, his place

---

heaven, took place before the foundations of the world were laid," Milton attacked "the common opinion that motion and time (which is the measure of motion) could not, according to the ratio of priority and subsequence, have existed before the world was made." He was thinking of Plato's account of the divine creation of the "sun, the moon, and the five other planets" as indicators of time (*Tim.* 38C–E), and he went on to argue that "Aristotle, who teaches that no ideas of motion and time can be formed except in reference to this world, nevertheless pronounces the world itself to be eternal." See the Introduction 21.

583. The conception of the *great Year*, when all the stars should return to their first positions, is also from the *Timaeus* (39D). Plato implies that it contained 36,000 earthly years.

597. Cf. III, 169, n., for the representation of the Son *in bliss imbosom'd.*

599. Cf. II, 263–67, for God's invisible brightness.

603–615. In deciding to begin the chronological action of *PL* by dramatizing a tradition of the revelation of the exaltation of Christ to the angels that stems from Hebrews i, 6, and had orthodox theological support such as St. Thomas gives to it (*Summa Theol.* I, q. 57, a.5), Milton was strongly influenced by Psalm ii, 6–7, which he quoted in *CD* I, v, and in 1653 had translated in this way:
          . . . but I saith he
    Anointed have my King (though ye rebell)
On Sion my holi' hill. A firm decree
    I will declare; the Lord to me hath say'd
    Thou art my Son, I have begotten thee
    This day; . . .
The words in parentheses, which are not suggested by the Hebrew original, are related to the dramatic situation in this passage by C. Dahlberg in *MLN*, LXVII (1952), 27. In summing up the meaning of *begot* in l. 603, M. Kelley rightly rejects Saurat's view that it means that the Son was created at this moment of his presentation to the angels. The generation is "figurative" (*Argument*, p. 105); it means that Christ was exalted, and it is used because God, "in proclaiming the Son ruler over the angels, is metaphorically generating a new thing—a king."

607. So God swears by himself to Abraham (Gen. xxii, 16).

613. Cf. the reference to the beatific vision in I, 684.

Ordain'd without redemption, without end.   615
  So spake th' Omnipotent, and with his words
All seem'd well pleas'd, all seem'd, but were not all.
That day, as other solemn days, they spent
In song and dance about the sacred Hill,
Mystical dance, which yonder starry Sphere   620
Of Planets and of fixt in all her Wheels
Resembles nearest, mazes intricate,
Eccentric, intervolv'd, yet regular
Then most, when most irregular they seem:
And in thir motions harmony Divine   625
So smooths her charming tones, that God's own ear
Listens delighted. Ev'ning now approach'd
(For wee have also our Ev'ning and our Morn,
Wee ours for change delectable, not need)
Forthwith from dance to sweet repast they turn   630
Desirous; all in Circles as they stood,
Tables are set, and on a sudden pil'd
With Angels' Food, and rubied Nectar flows:
In Pearl, in Diamond, and massy Gold,
Fruit of delicious Vines, the growth of Heav'n.   635
On flow'rs repos'd, and with fresh flow'rets crown'd,
They eat, they drink, and in communion sweet
Quaff immortality and joy, secure
Of surfeit where full measure only bounds
Excess, before th' all bounteous King, who show'r'd   640
With copious hand, rejoicing in thir joy.
Now when ambrosial Night with Clouds exhal'd
From that high mount of God, whence light and shade
Spring both, the face of brightest Heav'n had chang'd
To grateful Twilight (for Night comes not there   645
In darker veil) and roseate Dews dispos'd
All but the unsleeping eyes of God to rest,
Wide over all the Plain, and wider far
Than all this globous Earth in Plain outspread,
(Such are the Courts of God) th'Angelic throng   650
Disperst in Bands and Files thir Camp extend
By living Streams among the Trees of Life,
Pavilions numberless, and sudden rear'd,
Celestial Tabernacles, where they slept
Fann'd with cool Winds, save those who in thir course   655
Melodious Hymns about the sovran Throne
Alternate all night long: but not so wak'd
Satan, so call him now, his former name
Is heard no more in Heav'n; he of the first,

623. *Eccentric* has the astronomical application
that it has in III, 575, and VIII, 83.
  620–624. Milton could count on his readers to
know both Plato's conception of the orderly movement of the stars as a *dance* and its literary trail in
poems like Sir John Davies' *Orchestra: Or a Poeme
of Dauncing* (1596):
  What if to you these sparks disordered seeme
  As if by chaunce they had been scattered there?
  The Gods a solemne measure doe it deeme
  And see a iust proportion euery where.
                (Stanza 36, 1–4)

637. Cf. the *fellowships of joy* in XI, 80, and the
sweet societes of *Lycidas,* 179.
  645. The *Twilight* corresponds to the prophecy in
Revelation xxi, 25, that "there shall be no night
there."
  647. God is *unsleeping,* for "he that keepeth
Israel shall neither slumber nor sleep" (Psalm cxxi,
4).
  658–659. Cf. the explanation in I, 361–63, that
the names of the fallen angels are blotted out of
heavenly records.

If not the first Arch-Angel, great in Power,   660
In favor and preëminence, yet fraught
With envy against the Son of God, that day
Honor'd by his great Father, and proclaim'd
Messiah King anointed, could not bear
Through pride that sight, and thought himself impair'd.   665
Deep malice thence conceiving and disdain,
Soon as midnight brought on the dusky hour
Friendliest to sleep and silence, he resolv'd
With all his Legions to dislodge, and leave
Unworshipt, unobey'd the Throne supreme,   670
Contemptuous, and his next subordinate
Awak'ning, thus to him in secret spake.
    Sleep'st thou, Companion dear, what sleep can close
Thy eye-lids? and rememb'rest what Decree
Of yesterday, so late hath past the lips   675
Of Heav'n's Almighty. Thou to me thy thoughts
Wast wont, I mine to thee was wont to impart;
Both waking we were one; how then can now
Thy sleep dissent? new Laws thou see'st impos'd;
New Laws from him who reigns, new minds may raise   680
In us who serve, new Counsels, to debate
What doubtful may ensue; more in this place
To utter is not safe. Assemble thou
Of all those Myriads which we lead the chief;
Tell them that by command, ere yet dim Night   685
Her shadowy Cloud withdraws, I am to haste,
And all who under me thir Banners wave,
Homeward with flying march where we possess
The Quarters of the North, there to prepare
Fit entertainment to receive our King   690
The great *Messiah,* and his new commands,
Who speedily through all the Hierarchies
Intends to pass triumphant, and give Laws.
    So spake the false Arch-Angel, and infus'd
Bad influence into th' unwary breast   695
Of his Associate; hee together calls,
Or several one by one, the Regent Powers,
Under him Regent, tells, as he was taught,
That the most High commanding, now ere Night,
Now ere dim Night had disincumber'd Heav'n,   700
The great Hierarchal Standard was to move;

---

664. *Messiah* literally means "anointed."
665. *impair'd:* lowered in rank among the heavenly peers or aristocratic hierarchy.
671. *his next subordinate:* Beelzebub. Cf. II,
299–300. P. L. Carver notes—*RES,* XVI (1940),
423—that St. Thomas describes (*Summa Theol.* I,
q. 63, a.7) Satan, moved by pride and envy to
revolt against God, as appealing to his fellows in
just the way that Satan does to Beelzebub here.
689. The tradition of Satan as lord of the north
is partly due to the key passage in Isaiah xiv, 12,
from which his name of Lucifer is taken together
with the idea that the passage referred to Satan as
rebelling against God, and from the following verse:
"I will ascend into heaven, I will exalt my throne

above the stars of God: I will sit also upon the
mount of the congregation, in the sides of the north."
St. Augustine rationalized the tradition (in Epistle
140, sect. 55) by suggesting that, because the devils
have turned their backs on the warmth of charity
and are far advanced in pride and envy, they are
torpid in icy hardness. "And hence through a
figure they are put in the north." The tradition was
widespread in folklore and popular literature.
Shakespeare's audience had no trouble in recognizing Satan under the name of "the lordly monarch of
the north" (*I Henry VI* V, iii, 6).
696. *he:* Beelzebub.
697. *several:* severally, separately.

Tells the suggested cause, and casts between
Ambiguous words and jealousies, to sound
Or taint integrity; but all obey'd
The wonted signal, and superior voice   705
Of thir great Potentate; for great indeed
His name, and high was his degree in Heav'n;
His count'nance, as the Morning Star that guides
The starry flock, allur'd them, and with lies
Drew after him the third part of Heav'n's Host: 710
Meanwhile th' Eternal eye, whose sight discerns
Abstrusest thoughts, from forth his holy Mount
And from within the golden Lamps that burn
Nightly before him, saw without thir light
Rebellion rising, saw in whom, how spread   715
Among the sons of Morn, what multitudes
Were banded to oppose his high Decree;
And smiling to his only Son thus said.
      Son, thou in whom my glory I behold
In full resplendence, Heir of all my might,   720
Nearly it now concerns us to be sure
Of our Omnipotence, and with what Arms
We mean to hold what anciently we claim
Of Deity or Empire, such a foe
Is rising, who intends to erect his Throne   725
Equal to ours, throughout the spacious North;
Nor so content, hath in his thought to try
In battle, what our Power is, or our right.
Let us advise, and to this hazard draw
With speed what force is left, and all imploy   730
In our defense, lest unawares we lose
This our high place, our Sanctuary, our Hill.
      To whom the Son with calm aspect and clear
Lightning Divine, ineffable, serene,
Made answer. Mighty Father, thou thy foes   735
Justly hast in derision, and secure
Laugh'st at thir vain designs and tumults vain,
Matter to mee of Glory, whom thir hate
Illustrates, when they see all Regal Power
Giv'n me to quell thir pride, and in event   740
Know whether I be dext'rous to subdue
Thy Rebels, or be found the worst in Heav'n.
      So spake the Son, but Satan with his Powers
Far was advanc't on winged speed, an Host
Innumerable as the Stars of Night,   745

708. *The Morning Star* is still another allusion
to "Lucifer, son of the morning" (Isa. xiv, 12).

710. Cf. II, 692, n.

713. Milton refers to the "seven lamps of fire
burning before the throne" (Rev. iv, 5) and the
"unsleeping eyes of God" (cf. l. 647 above), passages which he perhaps related to the seven angelic
eyes mentioned in Zechariah iii, 9, which figure in III, 648.

716. The phrase *sons of Morn* is from Isaiah xiv,
12. Cf. *Nativity*, 119.

719. Cf. III, 63, n.

734. The Son is the *Similitude* of the invisible
Fountain of Light in III, 375-84.

736. Cf. II, 191, n.

739. *Illustrates*: makes luminous or glorious.
The picture is that of Christ set as king on God's
"holy hill" in Psalm ii, 6.

740. *event* keeps its Latin meaning of "outcome."
Cf. II, 82.

743. *Powers* means "armies" and is not used here,
as it is in 601 above, with reference to that rank
in the *triple Degrees* of the Dionysian hierarchy of
angels that are mentioned in ll. 749-750 below.
See the Introduction 21.

Or Stars of Morning, Dew-drops, which the Sun
Impearls on every leaf and every flower.
Regions they pass'd, the mighty Regencies
Of Seraphim and Potentates and Thrones
In thir triple Degrees, Regions to which   750
All thy Dominion, *Adam,* is no more
Than what this Garden is to all the Earth,
And all the Sea, from one entire globose
Stretcht into Longitude; which having pass'd
At length into the limits of the North   755
They came, and *Satan* to his Royal seat
High on a Hill, far blazing, as a Mount
Rais'd on a Mount, with Pyramids and Tow'rs
From Diamond Quarries hewn, and Rocks of Gold,
The Palace of great *Lucifer,* (so call   760
That Structure in the Dialect of men
Interpreted) which not long after, he
Affecting all equality with God,
In imitation of that Mount whereon
Messiah was declar'd in sight of Heav'n,   765
The Mountain of the Congregation call'd;
For thither he assembl'd all his Train,
Pretending so commanded to consult
About the great reception of thir King,
Thither to come, and with calumnious Art   770
Of counterfeited truth thus held thir ears.
　　　Thrones, Dominations, Princedoms, Virtues, Powers,
If these magnific Titles yet remain
Not merely titular, since by Decree
Another now hath to himself ingross't   775
All Power, and us eclipst under the name
Of King anointed, for whom all this haste
Of midnight march, and hurried meeting here,
This only to consult how we may best
With what may be devis'd of honors new   780
Receive him coming to receive from us
Knee-tribute yet unpaid, prostration vile,
Too much to one, but double how endur'd,
To one and to his image now proclaim'd?
But what if better counsels might erect   785
Our minds and teach us to cast off this Yoke?
Will ye submit your necks, and choose to bend
The supple knee? ye will not, if I trust
To know ye right, or if ye know yourselves
Natives and Sons of Heav'n possest before   790

748. *Regencies:* provinces, dominions.

753. *globose:* sphere. It is imagined as stretched on a flat projection.

763. *Affecting:* aspiring or pretending (to possess something).

777. *King anointed* looks back to *Messiah* in l. 664 above.

784. Cf. the *radiant Image of his Glory* in III, 63.

788. The *supple knee* recalls "the tribute of his supple knee" in Shakespeare's *Richard II* I, iv, 33. and other examples that reveal its proverbial character.

792–99. Satan twists the truth that Milton asserted in *CD* I, ix, and embodied in his conception of human order and liberty in *The Reason of Church Government* (see p. 642) as patterned upon "the angels themselves, in whom no disorder is feared, as the apostle that saw them in his rapture describes, . . . distinguished and quaternioned into their celestial princedoms and satrapies, according as God himself has writ his imperial decrees through the great provinces of heaven."

By none, and if not equal all, yet free,
Equally free; for Orders and Degrees
Jar not with liberty, but well consist.
Who can in reason then or right assume
Monarchy over such as live by right   795
His equals, if in power and splendor less,
In freedom equal? or can introduce
Law and Edict on us, who without law
Err not? much less for this to be our Lord,
And look for adoration to th' abuse   800
Of those Imperial Titles which assert
Our being ordain'd to govern, not to serve?
      Thus far his bold discourse without control
Had audience, when among the Seraphim
Abdiel, than whom none with more zeal ador'd   805
The Deity, and divine commands obey'd,
Stood up, and in a flame of zeal severe
The current of his fury thus oppos'd.
      O argument blasphémous, false and proud!
Words which no ear ever to hear in Heav'n   810
Expected, least of all from thee, ingrate,
In place thyself so high above thy Peers.
Canst thou with impious obloquy condemn
The just Decree of God, pronounc't and sworn,
That to his only Son by right endu'd   815
With Regal Sceptre, every Soul in Heav'n
Shall bend the knee, and in that honor due
Confess him rightful King? unjust thou say'st
Flatly unjust, to bind with Laws the free,
And equal over equals to let Reign,   820
One over all with unsucceeded power.
Shalt thou give Law to God, shalt thou dispute
With him the points of liberty, who made
Thee what thou art, and form'd the Pow'rs of Heav'n
Such as he pleas'd, and circumscrib'd thir being?   825
Yet by experience taught we know how good,
And of our good, and of our dignity
How provident he is, how far from thought
To make us less, bent rather to exalt
Our happy state under one Head more near   830
United.   But to grant it thee unjust,
That equal over equals Monarch Reign:
Thyself though great and glorious dost thou count,
Or all Angelic Nature join'd in one,
Equal to him begotten Son, by whom   835

804. *audience:* hearing, acceptance.
805. The name *Abdiel,* meaning "servant of God," occurs only as a human name in the Bible (I Chron. v, 15). Milton invented his character as an embodiment of that "ardent desire of hallowing the name of God, together with an indignation against whatever tends to the violation or contempt of religion" which he said in *CD* II, vi (C. E. XVII, 153) "is called zeal." Though—as A. H. Gilbert says in *MP,* XL (1943), 19–42—Abiel's episode is not essential to the narrative plot, it dramatizes Satan's revolt against the Son of God, who is imagined

here as the "king" of Psalm ii, 6, whom God has set upon his "holy hill of Zion," and who represents Milton's ideal of the ruler "who by right of merit Reigns" in VI, 43.
834. *all Angelic Nature:* all that part of nature (or of God's creation) that is represented by the angels.
835–845. Milton echoes Colossians i, 15–17, which he interprets in *CD* I, vii, p. 974, as meaning that all things were created *through* Christ, who is "the first-born of every creature" both in the sense that he existed before all other creatures and

As by his Word the mighty Father made
All things, ev'n thee, and all the Spirits of Heav'n
By him created in thir bright degrees,
Crown'd them with Glory, and to thir Glory nam'd
Thrones, Dominations, Princedoms, Virtues, Powers,   840
Essential Powers, nor by his Reign obscur'd,
But more illustrious made, since he the Head
One of our number thus reduc't becomes,
His Laws our Laws, all honor to him done
Returns our own. Cease then this impious rage,   845
And tempt not these; but hast'n to appease
Th' incensed Father, and th' incensed Son,
While Pardon may be found in time besought.
    So spake the fervent Angel, but his zeal
None seconded, as out of season judg'd,   850
Or singular and rash, whereat rejoic'd
Th' Apostate, and more haughty thus repli'd.
    That we were form'd then say'st thou? and the work
Of secondary hands, by task transferr'd
From Father to his Son? strange point and new!   855
Doctrine which we would know whence learnt: who saw
When this creation was? remember'st thou
Thy making, while the Maker gave thee being?
We know no time when we were not as now;
Know none before us, self-begot, self-rais'd   860
By our own quick'ning power, when fatal course
Had circl'd his full Orb, the birth mature
Of this our native Heav'n, Ethereal Sons.
Our puissance is our own, our own right hand
Shall teach us highest deeds, by proof to try   865
Who is our equal: then thou shalt behold
Whether by supplication we intend
Address, and to begirt th' Almighty Throne
Beseeching or besieging. This report,
These tidings carry to th' anointed King;   870
And fly, ere evil intercept thy flight.
    He said, and as the sound of waters deep
Hoarse murmur echo'd to his words applause
Through the infinite Host, nor less for that
The flaming Seraph fearless, though alone   875
Encompass'd round with foes, thus answer'd bold.
    O alienate from God, O Spirit accurst,
Forsak'n of all good; I see thy fall
Determin'd, and thy hapless crew involv'd
In this perfidious fraud, contagion spread   880
Both of thy crime and punishment: henceforth
No more be troubl'd how to quit the yoke
Of God's *Messiah:* those indulgent Laws
Will not be now voutsaf'd, other Decrees

in the sense that he excels all his fellow creatures
and stands nearest of them all to the maker of all.
    853–863. As early as I, 116, Satan is casting doubt
upon the article of faith that Milton formulated in
CD I, vii, p. 978, in the words: "the angels
were created at some particular period." Precedent
for Satan's insinuation that his followers were self-

created has been observed by G. McColley in *Harvard Theological Review,* XXXII (1939), 183, as
early as the twelfth century in perhaps the first
imaginative treatment of the theme of the victory of
the Son, the *De victoria Verbi Dei* of Abbot Rupert Tuitensis.

Against thee are gone forth without recall;   885
That Golden Sceptre which thou didst reject
Is now an Iron Rod to bruise and break
Thy disobedience. Well thou didst advise,
Yet not for thy advice or threats I fly
These wicked Tents devoted, lest the wrath   890
Impendent, raging into sudden flame
Distinguish not: for soon expect to feel
His Thunder on thy head, devouring fire.
Then who created thee lamenting learn,
When who can uncreate thee thou shalt know.   895
    So spake the Seraph *Abdiel* faithful found,
Among the faithless, faithful only hee;
Among innumerable false, unmov'd,
Unshak'n, unseduc'd, unterrifi'd
His Loyalty he kept, his Love, his Zeal;   900
Nor number, nor example with him wrought
To swerve from truth, or change his constant mind
Though single. From amidst them forth he pass'd,
Long way through hostile scorn, which he sustain'd
Superior, nor of violence fear'd aught;   905
And with retorted scorn his back he turn'd
On those proud Tow'rs to swift destruction doom'd.

The End of the Fifth Book.

887. Cf. the *iron Sceptre* which the devils have learned to fear in II, 327. Abdiel's words resemble the threat in *Of Reformation* II (C. E. III, 69) that he who rejects "the meek censure of the church" must "fear to fall under the iron sceptre of his [Christ's] anger, that will dash him to pieces like a potsherd."

890. Abdiel resembles Moses urging the Jews to abandon the blasphemous rebels Korah, Dathan, and Abiram with the words, "Depart from the tents of these wicked men, lest ye be consumed in all their sins" (Num. xvi, 26).

890. *devoted* has its Latin force of "doomed to destruction."

906. *retorted* keeps its literal Latin meaning of "turned back."

BOOK VI

THE ARGUMENT

Raphael *continues to relate how* Michael *and* Gabriel *were sent forth to Battle against* Satan *and his Angels. The first Fight describ'd:* Satan *and his Powers retire under Night: He calls a Council, invents devilish Engines, which in the second day's Fight put* Michael *and his Angels to some disorder; but they at length pulling up Mountains overwhelm'd both the force and Machines of* Satan: *Yet the Tumult not so ending, God on the third day sends* Messiah *his Son, for whom he had reserv'd the glory of that Victory: Hee in the Power of his Father coming to the place, and causing all his Legions to stand still on either side, with his Chariot and Thunder driving into the midst of his Enemies, pursues them unable to resist towards the wall of Heaven; which opening, they leap down with horror and confusion into the place of punishment prepar'd for them in the Deep:* Messiah *returns with triumph to his Father.*

All night the dreadless Angel unpursu'd
Through Heav'n's wide Champaign held his way, till Morn,
Wak't by the circling Hours, with rosy hand

1. *the dreadless Angel:* Abdiel.   2-4. Cf. *Morn with rosy steps* in V, 1. Homer

Unbarr'd the gates of Light. There is a Cave
Within the Mount of God, fast by his Throne,   5
Where light and darkness in perpetual round
Lodge and dislodge by turns, which makes through Heav'n
Grateful vicissitude, like Day and Night;
Light issues forth, and at the other door
Obsequious darkness enters, till her hour   10
To veil the Heav'n, though darkness there might well
Seem twilight here; and now went forth the Morn
Such as in highest Heav'n, array'd in Gold
Empyreal, from before her vanisht Night,
Shot through with orient Beams: when all the Plain   15
Cover'd with thick embattl'd Squadrons bright,
Chariots and flaming Arms, and fiery Steeds
Reflecting blaze on blaze, first met his view:
War he perceiv'd, war in procinct, and found
Already known what he for news had thought   20
To have reported: gladly then he mixt
Among those friendly Powers who him receiv'd
With joy and acclamations loud, that one
That of so many Myriads fall'n, yet one
Return'd not lost: On to the sacred hill   25
They led him high applauded, and present
Before the seat supreme; from whence a voice
From midst a Golden Cloud thus mild was heard.
    Servant of God, well done, well hast thou fought
The better fight, who single hast maintain'd   30
Against revolted multitudes the Cause
Of Truth, in word mightier than they in Arms;
And for the testimony of Truth hast borne
Universal reproach, far worse to bear
Than violence: for this was all thy care   35
To stand approv'd in sight of God, though Worlds
Judg'd thee perverse: the easier conquest now
Remains thee, aided by this host of friends,
Back on thy foes more glorious to return
Than scorn'd thou didst depart, and to subdue   40
By force, who reason for thir Law refuse,
Right reason for thir Law, and for thir King

---

first personified the Hours (*Il.* V, 749) as the "fair
daughters of high Jove" whom we find in the *Faerie
Queene* guarding
        the charge to them fore-shewed
By mighty Jove; who did them porters make
Of heavens gate.
                        (VII, vii, 45, 5–7)
The cave of Light and Darkness seems like an adaptation of the abysm where Hesiod said that Day
and Night alternately lived (*Theog.*, 736–57).
    8. *vicissitude:* alternation, change. Cf. VII, 351.
    10. *Obsequious* has little more than its neutral
Latin meaning of "following," but cf. the *Grateful
twilight* of V, 645.
    14. In *Empyreal* there is a reference both to its
derivation from the Greek word for "fire" and to
the distinction of heavenly from earthly fire that is
intimated in II, 139.

19. So Chapman uses the technical Latin term
procinct in translating *Iliad* XII, 88–89: "each chariot and steed . . . to be kept in all procinct of
warre." The word means "readiness."
    29. *Servant of God* translates the literal mean-
ing of *Abdiel.* Cf. V, 805. The greeting, "Well
done, good and faithful servant," to the man in the
parable of judgment (Matt. xxv, 21) who is told to
"enter into the joy" of his Lord, mingles here with
St. Paul's cry, "I have fought a good fight."
    32. So Truth appears in metaphors of struggle in
Areopagitica as "strong, next to the Almighty" (see
p. 747).
    34. Spenser put the maxim into the words: "For
evill deedes may better then bad words be bore"
(*F.Q.* IV, iv, 4, 9).
    42. Cf. *Reason* as "the image of God" in *Areo-
pagitica.*

Messiah, who by right of merit Reigns.
Go *Michael* of Celestial Armies Prince,
And thou in Military prowess next,   45
Gabriel, lead forth to Battle these my Sons
Invincible, lead forth my armed Saints
By Thousands and by Millions rang'd for fight;
Equal in number to that Godless crew
Rebellious, them with Fire and hostile Arms   50
Fearless assault, and to the brow of Heav'n
Pursuing drive them out from God and bliss,
Into thir place of punishment, the Gulf
Of *Tartarus,* which ready opens wide
His fiery *Chaos* to receive thir fall.   55
  So spake the Sovran voice, and Clouds began
To darken all the Hill, and smoke to roll
In dusky wreaths, reluctant flames, the sign
Of wrath awak't: nor with less dread the loud
Ethereal Trumpet from on high gan blow: 60
At which command the Powers Militant,
That stood for Heav'n, in mighty Quadrate join'd
Of Union irresistible, mov'd on
In silence thir bright Legions, to the sound
Of instrumental Harmony that breath'd   65
Heroic Ardor to advent'rous deeds
Under thir God-like Leaders, in the Cause
Of God and his *Messiah.* On they move
Indissolubly firm; nor obvious Hill,
Nor straitening Vale, nor Wood, nor Stream divides   70
Thir perfet ranks; for high above the ground
Thir march was, and the passive Air upbore
Thir nimble tread; as when the total kind
Of Birds in orderly array on wing
Came summon'd over *Eden* to receive   75
Thir names of thee; so over many a tract
Of Heav'n they march'd, and many a Province wide
Tenfold the length of this terrene: at last
Far in th' Horizon to the North appear'd
From skirt to skirt a fiery Region, stretcht   80
In battailous aspect, and nearer view
Bristl'd with upright beams innumerable
Of rigid Spears, and Helmets throng'd, and Shields

---

43. In I, 98, this line is foreshadowed.
44. In Jewish tradition *Michael* (the "God-like" or "strength of God") is "the great prince which standeth for the children of thy people" (Dan. xii, 1), as Milton noted in *CD* I, ix (p. 991). Jewish and Christian tradition concur in making him the chief angel, but the *Jewish Encyclopaedia* notes (VIII, 537) that the legend of Michael and the dragon "is not found in Jewish sources except insofar as Samael or Satan is called in the Cabala 'the primitive serpent.'" West notes (in *Milton and Angels,* p. 125) that in making the name *Michael* signify "not Christ but the first of the Angels," Milton accepted Catholic rather than Protestant opinion.
46. Cf. *Gabriel* in IV, 549.
57. The scene resembles Mt. Sinai when it was "altogether on a smoke, because the Lord descended upon it in fire; and the smoke thereof ascended as the smoke of a furnace" (Exod. xix, 18).
62. *Quadrate:* a square phalanx. Another such military term is *globe* in II, 512. Cf. the devils moving "in perfect phalanx" to Dorian strains in I, 550.
69. *obvious* keeps its literal, Latin meaning of "in the way."
70. *straitening:* confining.
74. So Homer (*Il.* II, 459–63) and Vergil (*Aen.* VII, 699–701) compare mustering troops to flights of birds.
79. Cf. the mustering of the devils in the *Quarters of the North* in V, 689.

Various, with boastful Argument portray'd,
The banded Powers of *Satan* hasting on   85
With furious expedition; for they ween'd
That selfsame day by fight, or by surprise
To win the Mount of God, and on his Throne
To set the envier of his State, the proud
Aspirer, but thir thoughts prov'd fond and vain   90
In the mid way: though strange to us it seem'd
At first, that Angel should with Angel war,
And in fierce hosting meet, who wont to meet
So oft in Festivals of joy and love
Unanimous, as sons of one great Sire   95
Hymning th' Eternal Father: but the shout
Of Battle now began, and rushing sound
Of onset ended soon each milder thought.
High in the midst exalted as a God
Th' Apostate in his Sun-bright Chariot sat   *Satan*   100
Idol of Majesty Divine, enclos'd
With Flaming Cherubim, and golden Shields;
Then lighted from his gorgeous Throne, for now
'Twixt Host and Host but narrow space was left,
A dreadful interval, and Front to Front   105
Presented stood in terrible array
Of hideous length: before the cloudy Van,
On the rough edge of battle ere it join'd,
Satan with vast and haughty strides advanc'd,
Came tow'ring, arm'd in Adamant and Gold;   110
Abdiel that sight endur'd not, where he stood
Among the mightiest, bent on highest deeds,
And thus his own undaunted heart explores.
  O Heav'n! that such resemblance of the Highest
Should yet remain, where faith and realty   115
Remain not; wherefore should not strength and might
There fail where Virtue fails, or weakest prove
Where boldest; though to sight unconquerable?
His puissance, trusting in th' Almighty's aid,
I mean to try, whose Reason I have tri'd   120
Unsound and false; nor is it aught but just,
That he who in debate of Truth hath won,
Should win in Arms, in both disputes alike
Victor; though brutish that contest and foul,
When Reason hath to deal with force, yet so   125
Most reason is that Reason overcome.
  So pondering, and from his armed Peers
Forth stepping opposite, half way he met

why can evil be so strong

---

84. *Argument:* the signification of the inscriptions or emblems on the shields. There may be an allusion to the boastfully inscribed shields of the seven doomed kings in the assault on Thebes in Euripides' *Phoenician Maidens,* 1108-40.

86. *expedition* keeps its Latin force of "haste."

93. *hosting:* rallying of troops into hosts. *wont:* accustomed.

100. *Apostate* is felt almost as a verb as well as a noun. It means a seceder, a person who stands out from or against others.

101. *Idol* suggests that Satan is idolized by his followers, who ought, of course, to worship the true image of God in his Son.

113. The line translates Homer's introduction of Hector's soliloquy of decision to face Achilles in the single combat in which he finally is slain (*Il.* xxii, 98).

115. *realty,* if it is not a misprint for "lealty" or "fealty," is a contraction of "reality," the want of which Abdiel charges to the *Idol,* Satan.

120. *tri'd:* proved by trial.

His daring foe, at this prevention more
Incenst, and thus securely him defi'd.   130
    Proud, art thou met? thy hope was to have reacht
The highth of thy aspiring unoppos'd,
The Throne of God unguarded, and his side
Abandon'd at the terror of thy Power
Or potent tongue; fool, not to think how vain   135
Against th' Omnipotent to rise in Arms;
Who out of smallest things could without end
Have rais'd incessant Armies to defeat
Thy folly; or with solitary hand
Reaching beyond all limit, at one blow   *yeah, why didn't*   140
Unaided could have finisht thee, and whelm'd   *he.*
Thy Legions under darkness; but thou seest
All are not of thy Train; there be who Faith
Prefer, and Piety to God, though then
To thee not visible, when I alone   145
Seem'd in thy World erroneous to dissent
From all: my Sect thou seest, now learn too late
How few sometimes may know, when thousands err.   *— Milton seeing*
    Whom the grand Foe with scornful eye askance   *himself*
Thus answer'd. Ill for thee, but in wisht hour   150
Of my revenge, first sought for thou return'st
From flight, seditious Angel, to receive   *pot calling kettle*
Thy merited reward, the first assay   *black*
Of this right hand provok'd, since first that tongue
Inspir'd with contradiction durst oppose   155
A third part of the Gods, in Synod met
Thir Deities to assert, who while they feel
Vigor Divine within them, can allow
Omnipotence to none. But well thou com'st
Before thy fellows, ambitious to win   160
From me some Plume, that thy success may show
Destruction to the rest: this pause between
(Unanswer'd lest thou boast) to let thee know;
At first I thought that Liberty and Heav'n
To heav'nly Souls had been all one; but now   165
I see that most through sloth had rather serve,   *— slow word sounds*
Minist'ring Spirits, train'd up in Feast and Song;
Such hast thou arm'd, the Minstrelsy of Heav'n,
Servility with freedom to contend,
As both thir deeds compar'd this day shall prove.   170
    To whom in brief thus *Abdiel* stern repli'd.
Apostate, still thou err'st, nor end wilt find

---

129. *prevention* has the literal, Latin force of "confrontation"—in this case by an obstacle or challenge.

143. *there be:* there are those. *Faith:* faithfulness, fidelity.

146. *erroneous:* erring. Cf. *erroneous* in the literal sense of "wandering" in VII, 20. Satan lives in a world of wandering from truth.

147. *Sect* was a term of reproach among the Royalists for the denominations into which Protestantism was splintering. In the Preface to *Eikonoklastes* (C. E. V, 73) Milton protested against the "odious names of Schism and Sectarism," and

added, "I never knew that time in *England,* when men of truest Religion were not counted Sectaries."

153. *assay:* trial of strength.

156. As in II, 391, *Synod* is Satan's pompous term for the assembly of *Gods* who have rallied to his standard.

161. As in II, 123, *success* implies doubt of a happy outcome.

162. The *pause* is the time between Satan's meeting with Abdiel and their impending combat.

167-169. The *Minstrelsy* stands for the loyal angels who are still God's ministers, chanting hymns in his praise; *freedom* stands for the rebels.

Of erring, from the path of truth remote:
Unjustly thou deprav'st it with the name
Of *Servitude* to serve whom God ordains,   175
Or Nature; God and Nature bid the same,
When he who rules is worthiest, and excels
Them whom he governs. This is servitude,
To serve th' unwise, or him who hath rebell'd
Against his worthier, as thine now serve thee,   180
Thyself not free, but to thyself enthrall'd;
Yet lewdly dar'st our minist'ring upbraid.
Reign thou in Hell thy Kingdom, let mee serve
In Heav'n God ever blest, and his Divine
Behests obey, worthiest to be obey'd;   185
Yet Chains in Hell, not Realms expect: meanwhile
From mee return'd, as erst thou said'st, from flight,
This greeting on thy impious Crest receive.
   So saying, a noble stroke he lifted high,
Which hung not, but so swift with tempest fell   190
On the proud Crest of *Satan,* that no sight,
Nor motion of swift thought, less could his Shield
Such ruin intercept: ten paces huge
He back recoil'd; the tenth on bended knee
His massy Spear upstay'd; as if on Earth   195
Winds under ground or waters forcing way
Sidelong, had pusht a Mountain from his seat
Half sunk with all his Pines. Amazement seiz'd
The Rebel Thrones, but greater rage to see
Thus foil'd thir mightiest, ours joy fill'd, and shout,   200
Presage of Victory and fierce desire
Of Battle: whereat *Michaël* bid sound
Th' Arch-Angel trumpet; through the vast of Heav'n
It sounded, and the faithful Armies rung
Hosanna to the Highest: nor stood at gaze   205
The adverse Legions, nor less hideous join'd
The horrid shock: now storming fury rose,
And clamor such as heard in Heav'n till now
Was never, Arms on Armor clashing bray'd
Horrible discord, and the madding Wheels   210
Of brazen Chariots rag'd; dire was the noise
Of conflict; over head the dismal hiss
Of fiery Darts in flaming volleys flew,
And flying vaulted either Host with fire.
So under fiery Cope together rush'd   215

174. *deprav'st* keeps its Latin force of "perverting" or "impairing."
176. The thought is that of nature as "the
mysterious power and efficacy of the divine voice
which went forth in the beginning, and to which,
as to a perpetual command, all things have since
paid obedience" (*CD* I, viii; p. 989). The laws
of nature and reason are one, and obedience to
God as reason is natural. Cf. l. 42 above, n.
178–181. So servitude is defined in XII, 90–101,
and *PR* II, 463–72. The thought is anticipated in
I, 255, and IV, 75.
187. *as erst thou said'st* recalls Ascanius' tough
reply to Numanus in their typical, epic exchange

of boasts between heroes in battle (*Aen.* IX, 599–
635).
193–194. J. Whaler suggests (in *Counterpoint,*
p. 100) that in the number symbolism of Milton's
times ten would signify power and ten reversed,
power destroyed.
196. So the cause of earthquakes is implied in
I, 231–37, to be.
199. *Thrones,* though it means one of the nine
orders of angels, is loosely used to mean all of
Satan's adherents. See the Introduction, 21.
205. Cf. II, 243.
215. *Cope:* sky (as in IV, 992). Hesiod describes
it as darkened by missiles in the struggle of the

Both Battles main, with ruinous assault
And inextinguishable rage; all Heav'n
Resounded, and had Earth been then, all Earth
Had to her Centre shook. What wonder? when
Millions of fierce encount'ring Angels fought   220
On either side, the least of whom could wield
These Elements, and arm him with the force
Of all thir Regions: how much more of Power
Army against Army numberless to raise
Dreadful combustion warring, and disturb,   225
Though not destroy, thir happy Native seat;
Had not th' Eternal King Omnipotent
From his stronghold of Heav'n high over-rul'd
And limited thir might; though number'd such
As each divided Legion might have seem'd   230
A numerous Host, in strength each armed hand
A Legion; led in fight, yet Leader seem'd
Each Warrior single as in Chief, expert
When to advance, or stand, or turn the sway
Of Battle, open when, and when to close   235
The ridges of grim War; no thought of flight,
None of retreat, no unbecoming deed
That argu'd fear; each on himself reli'd,
As only in his arm the moment lay
Of victory; deeds of eternal fame   240
Were done, but infinite: for wide was spread
That War and various; sometimes on firm ground
A standing fight, then soaring on main wing
Tormented all the Air; all Air seem'd then
Conflicting Fire: long time in even scale   245
The Battle hung; till *Satan*, who that day
Prodigious power had shown, and met in Arms
No equal, ranging through the dire attack
Of fighting Seraphim confus'd, at length
Saw where the Sword of *Michael* smote, and fell'd   250
Squadrons at once, with huge two-handed sway   *two handed engine*
Brandisht aloft the horrid edge came down
Wide wasting; such destruction to withstand
He hasted, and oppos'd the rocky Orb
Of tenfold Adamant, his ample Shield   255
A vast circumference: At his approach
The great Arch-Angel from his warlike toil
Surceas'd, and glad as hoping here to end
Intestine War in Heav'n, the Arch-foe subdu'd
Or Captive dragg'd in Chains, with hostile frown   260

giants with the gods (*Theog.*, 716–17). Cf. I. 50.

222. *These Elements* are those of earth, which, as Raphael implies, had not yet been created. Their equivalents in value for warlike purposes were, however, at the disposal of the least of the angels.

229. *number'd such*: so numerous.

232. *led in fight* etc. Though they had leaders, every individual acted with the skill of an experienced commander.

236. *ridges*: ranks.

239. *moment*: weight (here equivalent to force). Cf. X, 45.

254. *Orb*, the circle of Satan's shield is rocky because it is made of adamant, which might mean diamond, as it does when it is applied to Arthur's shield in *F.Q.* V, xi, 10, 7–9, and, probably, in II, 853, though Milton seems to identify it with iron in *CD* I, viii, and has the armor of the angels made of it (l. 542 below).

259. *Intestine War*: civil war. *the Arch-foe subdued*: when the chief foe should be subdued.

And visage all inflam'd first thus began.
    Author of evil, unknown till thy revolt,
Unnam'd in Heav'n, now plenteous, as thou seest
These Acts of hateful strife, hateful to all,
Though heaviest by just measure on thyself   265
And thy adherents: how hast thou disturb'd
Heav'n's blessed peace, and into Nature brought
Misery, uncreated till the crime
Of thy Rebellion? how hast thou instill'd
Thy malice into thousands, once upright   270
And faithful, now prov'd false. But think not here
To trouble Holy Rest; Heav'n casts thee out
From all her Confines. Heav'n the seat of bliss
Brooks not the works of violence and War.
Hence then, and evil go with thee along,   275
Thy offspring, to the place of evil, Hell,
Thou and thy wicked crew; there mingle broils,
Ere this avenging Sword begin thy doom,
Or some more sudden vengeance wing'd from God
Precipitate thee with augmented pain.   280
    So spake the Prince of Angels; to whom thus
The Adversary. Nor think thou with wind
Of airy threats to awe whom yet with deeds
Thou canst not. Hast thou turn'd the least of these
To flight, or if to fall, but that they rise   285
Unvanquisht, easier to transact with mee
That thou shouldst hope, imperious, and with threats
To chase me hence? err not that so shall end
The strife which thou call'st evil, but wee style
The strife of Glory: which we mean to win,   290
Or turn this Heav'n itself into the Hell
Thou fabl'st, here however to dwell free,
If not to reign: meanwhile thy utmost force,
And join him nam'd *Almighty* to thy aid,
I fly not, but have sought thee far and nigh.   295
    They ended parle, and both address'd for fight
Unspeakable; for who, though with the tongue
Of Angels, can relate, or to what things
Liken on Earth conspicuous, that may lift
Human imagination to such highth   300
Of Godlike Power: for likest Gods they seem'd,
Stood they or mov'd, in stature, motion, arms
Fit to decide the Empire of great Heav'n.
Now wav'd thir fiery Swords, and in the Air
Made horrid Circles; two broad Suns thir Shields   305
Blaz'd opposite, while expectation stood

267. *Nature* is treated as having been created free from all discord, until the fall of the angels disturbs *Heav'n's blessed peace,* as man's fall further disturbs it in IX, 782.

275–276. *evil . . . thy offspring* is a contemptuous reference to Sin's parentage in II, 743–58.

282. Cf. Satan as the *Adversary* in III, 81 and 156.

286. *transact:* deal (in the sense of "dealing" with an antagonist in a struggle).

288. *err not:* do not make the error (of prejudging the result of battle).

289. In l. 268 above Michael has called Satan's disturbance of the peace a *crime.*

296. *parle:* parleying. *address'd:* prepared.

306. *Expectation* represents the expectant, watching armies; or it is a personification of their mood. So in the Prologue to Shakespeare's *Henry V, Expectation* "sits . . . in the air."

In horror; from each hand with speed retir'd
Where erst was thickest fight, th' Angelic throng,
And left large field, unsafe within the wind
Of such commotion, such as, to set forth   310
Great things by small, if Nature's concord broke,
Among the Constellations war were sprung,
Two Planets rushing from aspect malign
Of fiercest opposition in mid Sky,
Should combat, and thir jarring Spheres confound.   315
Together both with next to Almighty Arm,
Uplifted imminent one stroke they aim'd
That might determine, and not need repeat,
As not of power, at once; nor odds appear'd
In might or swift prevention; but the sword   320
Of *Michael* from the Armory of God
Was giv'n him temper'd so, that neither keen
Nor solid might resist that edge: it met
The sword of *Satan* with steep force to smite
Descending, and in half cut sheer, nor stay'd,   325
But with swift wheel reverse, deep ent'ring shear'd
All his right side; then *Satan* first knew pain,
And writh'd him to and fro convolv'd; so sore
The griding sword with discontinuous wound
Pass'd through him, but th' Ethereal substance clos'd   330
Not long divisible, and from the gash
A stream of Nectarous humor issuing flow'd
Sanguine, such as Celestial Spirits may bleed,
And all his Armor stain'd erewhile so bright.
Forthwith on all sides to his aid was run   335
By Angels many and strong, who interpos'd
Defense, while others bore him on thir Shields
Back to his Chariot, where it stood retir'd
From off the files of war: there they him laid
Gnashing for anguish and despite and shame   340
To find himself not matchless, and his pride
Humbl'd by such rebuke, so far beneath
His confidence to equal God in power.
Yet soon he heal'd; for Spirits that live throughout
Vital in every part, not as frail man   345
In Entrails, Heart or Head, Liver or Reins,
Cannot but by annihilating die;
Nor in thir liquid texture mortal wound

---

311. So Spenser described nature's concord, by which

> . . . the heaven is in his course contained,
> And all the world in state unmoved stands,
> As their Almightie Maker first ordained,
> And bound them with inviolable bands.
>
> (*F.Q.* IV, x, 35, 1–4)

313. So in X, 658–59, the opposite *aspect* of two planets—their opposite positions in the heavens—is mentioned. It is *malign* because their colliding rays were supposed by astrologers to be injurious to life on earth.

318. *determine:* end (the matter). *repeat:* repetition, second trial.

320. *prevention:* speed in anticipating a blow.

327–334. In I, 55, we have already found the devils capable of pain. In the tradition of Michael Psellus, to which West (in *Milton and Angels,* pp. 146–47) traces this passage through Marsilio Ficino's rendering of it, their bodies are said to be able to recover immediately from wounds and to close "like air and water" although they suffer "while divided," and "fear the edge of the sword."

329. *discontinuous:* breaking the continuity or solidity of the body.

332. Milton was perhaps thinking of the clear ichor that Homer attributed to the gods instead of blood.

335. Cf. this impersonal, Latin construction with X, 229. The meaning is that there was a rush, or running, to Satan's aid on all sides.

Receive, no more than can the fluid Air:
All Heart they live, all Head, all Eye, all Ear,   350
All Intellect, all Sense, and as they please,
They Limb themselves, and color, shape or size
Assume, as likes them best, condense or rare.   — Satan as a toad.
    Meanwhile in other parts like deeds deserv'd
Memorial, where the might of *Gabriel* fought,   355
And with fierce Ensigns pierc'd the deep array
Of *Moloch* furious King, who him defi'd,
And at his Chariot wheels to drag him bound
Threat'n'd, nor from the Holy One of Heav'n
Refrain'd his tongue blasphémous; but anon   360
Down clov'n to the waist, with shatter'd Arms
And uncouth pain fled bellowing.   On each wing
Uriel and *Raphaël* his vaunting foe,
Though huge, and in a Rock of Diamond Arm'd,
Vanquish'd *Adramelech,* and *Asmadai,*   365
Two potent Thrones, that to be less than Gods
Disdain'd, but meaner thoughts learn'd in thir flight,
Mangl'd with ghastly wounds through Plate and Mail.
Nor stood unmindful *Abdiel* to annoy
The Atheist crew, but with redoubl'd blow   370
Ariel and *Arioch,* and the violence
Of *Ramiel* scorcht and blasted overthrew.
I might relate of thousands, and thir names
Eternize here on Earth; but those elect
Angels contented with thir fame in Heav'n   375
Seek not the praise of men; the other sort
In might though wondrous and in Acts of War,
Nor of Renown less eager, yet by doom
Cancell'd from Heav'n and sacred memory,

350–353. These powers of the demons are implied in I, 422–33.

354–362, If A. H. Gilbert is justified in his suggestion that Milton intended readers of the Italian romances to see a resemblance here to the comic battle between devils and Saracens in Boiardo's *Orlando Innamorato* II, xxii, 50–54, the absurd physical violence of Milton's devils and angels becomes all the more striking in contrast with the symbolic power of truth that is represented in their overthrow by the Son of God who ends the "wild work in Heav'n" (l. 698). See *Italica* XX (1943), 132–34.

355. *the might of Gabriel:* the mighty Gabriel. Cf. ll. 371–72.

360. Milton adapts Isaiah's question: "Whom hast thou reproached and blasphemed?" (II Kings xix, 22)

365. *Adramelech,* the "mighty king," was a local phase of the Babylonian sun god. II Kings xvii, 31, says that children were burned on his altar. *Asmadai* is the *Asmodeus* of IV, 168, but medieval tradition, which (according to Heywood in the *Hierarchie,* p. 436) made him chief of the fourth order of fallen angels, makes him one of their leaders here.

366. *Gods* is ironical, referring to the divine ambitions of the devils which Satan flatters by calling them *Gods* in II, 391, and VI, 156.

370. Since the devils disbelieve in God's nature as transcending their own, they may be called an *Atheist crew.*

371–372. *Ariel*—"lion of God" or "light of God"—is an epithet of Jerusalem in Isaiah xxix, 1, and in xxxiii, 7, it is translated doubtfully as "valiant ones." West notes (*Milton and Angels,* p. 154) that in the translations of the Old Testament by Aquila and Symmachus *Ariel* signifies the pagan city of Arina or Ariopolis, which worshipped the idol *Ariel* (Mars). So *Ariel* "was, like many of his fellows in *PL,* a heathen god, and got his name from a biblical place."

Arioch is the name of one of the kings with whom Abram (Abraham) fights in defense of Lot (Gen. xiv), but the aptness of its meaning of "lion-like" here is perhaps also related to the fact that it is the name of the captain of Nebuchadnezzar's guard (Dan. ii, 14), who (the *Jewish Encyclopaedia* notes) roared like a lion against the Jews in Babylon. As the "spirit of Revenge," West notes that he was known to demonologists like Robert Turner and turns up in Thomas Nashe's *Pierce Pennilesse.*

the violence of Ramiel may be intended as a translation of *Ramiel* "thunder of God" and also as a metonymy. Though the name occurs in the *Book of Enoch,* West thinks that Milton knew it only in Cabalistic accounts of devils of "wizardry and superstition."

Nameless in dark oblivion let them dwell.   380
For strength from Truth divided and from Just,
Illaudable, naught merits but dispraise
And ignominy, yet to glory aspires
Vain-glorious, and through infamy seeks fame:
Therefore Eternal silence be thir doom.   385
    And now thir Mightiest quell'd, the battle swerv'd,
With many an inroad gor'd; deformed rout
Enter'd, and foul disorder; all the ground
With shiver'd armor strown, and on a heap
Chariot and Charioter lay overturn'd   390
And fiery foaming Steeds; what stood, recoil'd
O'erwearied, through the faint Satanic Host
Defensive scarce, or with pale fear surpris'd,
Then first with fear surpris'd and sense of pain
Fled ignominious, to such evil brought   395
By sin of disobedience, till that hour
Not liable to fear or flight or pain.
Far otherwise th' inviolable Saints
In Cubic Phalanx firm advanc'd entire,
Invulnerable, impenetrably arm'd: 400
Such high advantages thir innocence
Gave them above thir foes, not to have sinn'd,
Not to have disobey'd; in fight they stood
Unwearied, unobnoxious to be pain'd
By wound, though from thir place by violence mov'd.   405
    Now Night her course began, and over Heav'n
Inducing darkness, grateful truce impos'd,
And silence on the odious din of War:
Under her Cloudy covert both retir'd,
Victor and Vanquisht: on the foughten field   410
Michaël and his Angels prevalent
Encamping, plac'd in Guard thir Watches round,
Cherubic waving fires: on th' other part
Satan with his rebellious disappear'd,
Far in the dark dislodg'd, and void of rest,   415
His Potentates to Council call'd by night;
And in the midst thus undismay'd began.
    O now in danger tri'd, now known in Arms
Not to be overpow'r'd, Companions dear,
Found worthy not of Liberty alone,   420
Too mean pretense, but what we more affect,
Honor, Dominion, Glory, and renown,
Who have sustain'd one day in doubtful fight,
(And if one day, why not Eternal days?)
What Heaven's Lord had powerfullest to send   425
Against us from about his Throne, and judg'd
Sufficient to subdue us to his will,
But proves not so: then fallible, it seems,
Of future we may deem him, though till now

391. *what stood:* those who stood.
393. *Defensive scarce:* hardly able to stand on the defensive.
398. *inviolable Saints:* the loyal angels, who are immune to harm.

404. *unobnoxious:* unexposed to harm, incapable of being harmed.
415. *dislodg'd:* driven from their lodges or positions.
421. *Too mean pretense:* too low an object of ambition.

Omniscient thought.   True is, less firmly arm'd,   430
Some disadvantage we endur'd and pain,
Till now not known, but known as soon contemn'd,
Since now we find this our Empyreal form
Incapable of mortal injury,
Imperishable, and though pierc'd with wound,   435
Soon closing, and by native vigor heal'd.
Of evil then so small as easy think
The remedy; perhaps more valid Arms,
Weapons more violent, when next we meet,
May serve to better us, and worse our foes,   440
Or equal what between us made the odds,
In Nature none: if other hidden cause
Left them Superior, while we can preserve
Unhurt our minds, and understanding sound,
Due search and consultation will disclose.   445
     He sat; and in th' assembly next upstood
Nisroch, of Principalities the prime;
As one he stood escap't from cruel fight,
Sore toil'd, his riv'n Arms to havoc hewn,
And cloudy in aspect thus answering spake.   450
Deliverer from new Lords, leader to free
Enjoyment of our right as Gods; yet hard
For Gods, and too unequal work we find
Against unequal arms to fight in pain,
Against unpain'd, impassive; from which evil   455
Ruin must needs ensue; for what avails
Valor or strength, though matchless, quell'd with pain
Which all subdues, and makes remiss the hands
Of Mightiest.   Sense of pleasure we may well
Spare out of life perhaps, and not repine,   460
But live content, which is the calmest life:
But pain is perfet misery, the worst
Of evils, and excessive, overturns
All patience.   He who therefore can invent
With what more forcible we may offend   465
Our yet unwounded Enemies, or arm
Ourselves with like defense, to me deserves
No less than for deliverance what we owe.
     Whereto with look compos'd Satan repli'd.
Not uninvented that, which thou aright   470
Believ'st so main to our success, I bring;
Which of us who beholds the bright surface
Of this Ethereous mould whereon we stand,

---

429. Of future: in future.

432. known as soon contemn'd: despised as soon
as it is known.

447. Nisroch, whose name may mean "eagle,"
was an Assyrian deity in whose temple Sennacherib was murdered (II Kings xix, 37). In
Charles Stephanus' Dictionarium—according to
Starnes and Talbert, Dictionaries, p. 268—he is uncertainly defined as Sennacherib's idol, as a fugitive, and as perhaps a standard-bearer.

455. impassive: not subject to passion or painful
sensation.

465. offend keeps its Latin force of "strike at."

467. to me: in my judgment.

472–483. Tracing this passage to Aristotle's theory of the origin of metals in the Meteorologica I,
4 (341B) and III, 6 (348A), E. H. Duncan explains
—in Osiris, XI (1954), 388—that Milton's spiritous
and fiery spume is simply the exhalation of fire
and water underground, by whose evaporation
under the influence of Heaven's ray (the sunshine)
metals of all kinds were supposed to "originate
from the imprisonment of the vaporous exhalation
in the earth and especially in stones." Cf. III,
583–85, 609–12, and Comus. 732–36.

This continent of spacious Heav'n, adorn'd
With Plant, Fruit, Flow'r Ambrosial, Gems and Gold, 475
Whose Eye so superficially surveys
These things, as not to mind from whence they grow
Deep under ground, materials dark and crude,
Of spiritous and fiery spume, till toucht
With Heav'n's ray, and temper'd they shoot forth 480
So beauteous, op'ning to the ambient light.
These in thir dark Nativity the Deep
Shall yield us, pregnant with infernal flame,
Which into hollow Engines long and round
Thick ramm'd, at th' other bore with touch of fire 485
Dilated and infuriate shall send forth
From far with thund'ring noise among our foes
Such implements of mischief as shall dash
To pieces, and o'erwhelm whatever stands
Adverse, that they shall fear we have disarm'd 490
The Thunderer of his only dreaded bolt.
Nor long shall be our labor, yet ere dawn,
Effect shall end our wish. Meanwhile revive;
Abandon fear; to strength and counsel join'd
Think nothing hard, much less to be despair'd. 495
He ended, and his words thir drooping cheer
Enlight'n'd, and thir languisht hope reviv'd.
Th' invention all admir'd, and each, how hee
To be th' inventor miss'd, so easy it seem'd
Once found, which yet unfound most would have thought 500
Impossible: yet haply of thy Race
In future days, if Malice should abound,
Some one intent on mischief, or inspir'd
With dev'lish machination might devise
Like instrument to plague the Sons of men 505
For sin, on war and mutual slaughter bent.
Forthwith from Council to the work they flew,
None arguing stood, innumerable hands
Were ready, in a moment up they turn'd
Wide the Celestial soil, and saw beneath 510
Th' originals of Nature in thir crude
Conception; Sulphurous and Nitrous Foam
They found, they mingl'd, and with subtle Art,
Concocted and adusted they reduc'd

484–489. One Italian scholar has found a direct source for this passage in Ariosto's comic account of Cimasco's invention of the arquebus in *Orlando Furioso* IX, 91, while another has found such a source in Erasmo di Valvasone's *L'Angeleida*. Its entirely serious account of the battle of Michael and his angels against the rebel angels in heaven is reproduced in Kirkconnell's *Celestial Cycle,* pp. 80–87, and the stanza on the invention of cannon is on p. 81. But the attitude toward artillery was a commonplace which found its way into the *Faerie Queene* in a condemnation of

. . . that divelish engin, wrought
In deepest hell, and framd by furies skill,
With windy nitre and quick sulphur fraught,
And ramd with bollet rownd, ordaind to kill.
(*F.Q.* I, vii, 13, 1–4. Cf. 597–606 below.)

Milton seems not to have shared Donne's faith that "by the benefit of this light of reason, (men) have found out *Artillery,* by which warres come to quicker ends than heretofore, and the great expense of blouc is avoyded: for the numbers of men slain now, since the invention of Artillery, are much lesse than before, when the sword was the executioner" (sermon at St. Paul's, Christmas, 1621).

494. *to strength and counsel:* with the aid of strength and good judgment.

496. *cheer,* which in Old French meant "face," developed the meanings of "appearance," "aspect," and "mood" or "frame of mind" in English.

512. With *Foam* cf. *spume* in l. 479 above.

514. *concocted* has its Latin meaning of "cook" or "bake." *adusted* was familiar as a medical

To blackest grain, and into store convey'd: *powder*   515
Part hidd'n veins digg'd up (nor hath this Earth
Entrails unlike) of Mineral and Stone,
Whereof to found thir Engines and thir Balls
Of missive ruin; part incentive reed
Provide, pernicious with one touch to fire.   520
So all ere day-spring, under conscious Night
Secret they finish'd, and in order set,
With silent circumspection unespi'd.
Now when fair Morn Orient in Heav'n appear'd
Up rose the Victor Angels, and to Arms   525
The matin Trumpet Sung: in Arms they stood
Of Golden Panoply, refulgent Host,
Soon banded; others from the dawning Hills
Look'd round, and Scouts each Coast light-armed scour
Each quarter, to descry the distant foe,   530
Where lodg'd, or whither fled, or if for fight,
In motion or in halt: him soon they met
Under spread Ensigns moving nigh, in slow
But firm Battalion; back with speediest Sail
Zophiel, of Cherubim the swiftest wing,   535
Came flying, and in mid Air aloud thus cri'd.
    Arm, Warriors, Arm for fight, the foe at hand,
Whom fled we thought, will save us long pursuit
This day, fear not his flight; so thick a Cloud
He comes, and settl'd in his face I see   540
Sad resolution and secure: let each
His Adamantine coat gird well, and each
Fit well his Helm, grip fast his orbed Shield,
Borne ev'n or high, for this day will pour down,
If I conjecture aught, no drizzling show'r,   545
But rattling storm of Arrows barb'd with fire.
So warn'd he them aware themselves, and soon
In order, quit of all impediment;
Instant without disturb they took Alarm,
And onward move Embattl'd; when behold   550
Not distant far with heavy pace the Foe
Approaching gross and huge; in hollow Cube
Training his devilish Enginry, impal'd
On every side with shadowing Squadrons Deep,
To hide the fraud. At interview both stood   555
A while, but suddenly at head appear'd

term with the basic, Latin meaning of "burnt" or "reduced to ashes."

519. *missive ruin:* missile destruction. Both words have their basic, Latin meaning. The *incentive* ("kindling") reed is the gunner's match.

520. *pernicious* keeps its Latin meaning of "swift," i.e. in destructive response to the match.

521. *conscious Night* is night personified and interested in watching the work. So Virgil has Dido pray to the stars that are "conscious of her fate" (*Aen.* IV, 519), and Ovid makes night "conscious" or aware of the frauds of Ulysses.

535. *Zophiel* ("Spy of God") is found nowhere in the Bible nor can he be clearly traced in any

authorities better than Robert Fludd and Cornelius Agrippa, who (according to West in *Milton and Angels,* p. 77) made him the ruler of the Cherubim in Dionysius' angelic hierarchy.

540. *He,* the foe collectively. So in II Peter ii, 17, the host of the blasphemers are called "clouds carried with a tempest."

541. *Sad:* firm. *secure:* reckless.

548. *quit of all impediment:* unencumbered of all baggage (for which the Latin military term was *impedimenta*).

549. *Instant* keeps its Latin meaning of "forward," "urgent."

553. *training:* dragging. *impal'd:* surrounded.

why colon?

Satan: And thus was heard Commanding loud.
   Vanguard, to Right and Left the Front unfold;
That all may see who hate us, how we seek
Peace and composure, and with open breast   560
Stand ready to receive them, if they like
Our overture, and turn not back perverse;
But that I doubt; however witness Heaven,
Heav'n witness thou anon, while we discharge
Freely our part: yee who appointed stand   565
Do as you have in charge, and briefly touch
What we propound, and loud that all may hear.
   So scoffing in ambiguous words, he scarce
Had ended; when to Right and Left the Front
Divided, and to either Flank retir'd.   570
Which to our eyes discover'd new and strange,
A triple-mounted row of Pillars laid
On Wheels (for like to Pillars most they seem'd
Or hollow'd bodies made of Oak or Fir
With branches lopt, in Wood or Mountain fell'd)   575
Brass, Iron, Stony mould, had not thir mouths
With hideous orifice gap't on us wide,
Portending hollow truce; at each behind
A Seraph stood, and in his hand a Reed
Stood waving tipt with fire; while we suspense,   580
Collected stood within our thoughts amus'd,
Not long, for sudden all at once thir Reeds
Put forth, and to a narrow vent appli'd
With nicest touch.   Immediate in a flame
But soon obscur'd with smoke, all Heav'n appear'd,   585
From those deep-throated Engines belcht, whose roar
Embowell'd with outrageous noise the Air,
And all her entrails tore, disgorging foul
Thir devilish glut, chain'd Thunderbolts and Hail
Of Iron Globes, which on the Victor Host   590
Levell'd, with such impetuous fury smote,
That whom they hit, none on thir feet might stand,
Though standing else as Rocks, but down they fell
By thousands, Angel on Arch-Angel roll'd;
The sooner for thir Arms; unarm'd they might   595
Have easily as Spirits evaded swift
By quick contraction or remove; but now
Foul dissipation follow'd and forc't rout;
Nor serv'd it to relax thir serried files.
What should they do? if on they rush'd repulse   600

560. *composure:* composition, agreement.
569–594. H. H. Scudder notes—*N&Q,* CVC
(1950), 335—that one of many parallels to this
maneuver in the military records of the time is
the "stratagem" in H. C. Davila's *Historie of the
Warres of France*—in the translation of Aylesbury
and Cotterel (1647), p. 141—of the masking of
"ordnance" behind troops, "invisibly, loaden with
Musquet-bullet: and when they should have charged
the Enemy, made them wheel off, that those bloody
Engins might break their ranks, which they performed to purpose, and forced them to retire. . . ."

576. *mould:* substance. Cf. III, 709, and IV,
226.
578. *hollow* puns on the physical and moral
senses of the word.
580. *suspense* has the force of a Latin participle,
"suspended" (i. e. with curiosity).
581. *amus'd:* in a muse or daze.
587. *Embowell'd:* filled, packed.
597. *quick contraction or remove* recalls the
ability attributed to the angels in I, 429.
598. *dissipation* keeps its Latin, military meaning of "disperse" or "rout."

Repeated, and indecent overthrow
Doubl'd, would render them yet more despis'd,
And to thir foes a laughter; for in view
Stood rankt of Seraphim another row
In posture to displode thir second tire   605
Of Thunder: back defeated to return
They worse abhorr'd. *Satan* beheld thir plight,
And to his Mates thus in derision call'd.
    O Friends, why come not on these Victors proud?
Erewhile they fierce were coming, and when wee,   610
To entertain them fair with open Front
And Breast, (what could we more?) propounded terms
Of composition, straight they chang'd thir minds,
Flew off, and into strange vagaries fell,
As they would dance, yet for a dance they seem'd   615
Somewhat extravagant and wild, perhaps
For joy of offer'd peace: but I suppose
If our proposals once again were heard
We should compel them to a quick result.
    To whom thus *Belial* in like gamesome mood.   620
Leader, the terms we sent were terms of weight,
Of hard contents, and full of force urg'd home,
Such as we might perceive amus'd them all,
And stumbl'd many; who receives them right,
Had need from head to foot well understand;   625
Not understood, this gift they have besides,
They show us when our foes walk not upright.
    So they among themselves in pleasant vein
Stood scoffing, highth'n'd in thir thoughts beyond
All doubt of Victory, eternal might   630
To match with thir inventions they presum'd
So easy, and of his Thunder made a scorn,
And all his Host derided, while they stood
A while in trouble; but they stood not long,
Rage prompted them at length, and found them arms   635
Against such hellish mischief fit to oppose.
Forthwith (behold the excellence, the power
Which God hath in his mighty Angels plac'd)
Thir Arms away they threw, and to the Hills
(For Earth hath this variety from Heav'n   640
Of pleasure situate in Hill and Dale)
Light as the Lightning glimpse they ran, they flew,
From thir foundations loos'ning to and fro
They pluckt the seated Hills with all thir load,
Rocks, Waters, Woods, and by the shaggy tops   645
Uplifting bore them in thir hands: Amaze,

601. *indecent* keeps its Latin force of "ugly" or "disgraceful."

605. *displode:* explode, fire. *tire:* volley.

615. Satan's irony, which Addison regarded (in *Spectator, 279*) as in the worst possible taste, has reminded most editors of Patroclus' praise of the "skilful dance" of Hector's charioteer in his death agony.

625. The pun is on the familiar, metaphorical meaning of *understand* and its now obsolete meaning of "support." So Viola says, "My legs do bet-

ter understand me, sir, than I understand what you mean" (*Twelfth Night* III, i, 90).

640. *from Heav'n:* derived from heaven, resembling heaven.

642. *Light:* swift because light in weight.

643–666. So the giants fighting for Zeus against the titans in Hesiod's *Theogony* (713–20) uproot the hills and hurl them at their enemies. Cf. the allusion to the same battle in Hesiod in *PL* I, 50.

646. *Amaze:* amazement.

Be sure, and terror seiz'd the rebel Host,
When coming towards them so dread they saw
The bottom of the Mountains upward turn'd,
Till on those cursed Engines' triple-row   650
They saw them whelm'd, and all thir confidence
Under the weight of Mountains buried deep,
Themselves invaded next, and on thir heads
Main Promontories flung, which in the Air
Came shadowing, and opprest whole Legions arm'd,   655
Thir armor help'd thir harm, crush't in and bruis'd
Into thir substance pent, which wrough: them pain
Implacable, and many a dolorous groan,
Long struggling underneath, ere they could wind
Out of such prison, though Spirits of purest light,   660
Purest at first, now gross by sinning grown.
The rest in imitation to like Arms
Betook them, and the neighboring Hills uptore;
So Hills amid the Air encounter'd Hills
Hurl'd to and fro with jaculation dire,   665
That under ground they fought in dismal shade:
Infernal noise; War seem'd a civil Game
To this uproar; horrid confusion heapt
Upon confusion rose: and now all Heav'n
Had gone to wrack, with ruin overspread,   670
Had not th' Almighty Father where he sits
Shrin'd in his Sanctuary of Heav'n secure,
Consulting on the sum of things, foreseen
This tumult, and permitted all, advis'd:
That his great purpose he might so fulfil,   675
To honor his Anointed Son aveng'd
Upon his enemies, and to declare
All power on him transferr'd: whence to His Son
Th' Assessor of his Throne he thus began.
    Effulgence of my Glory, Son belov'd,   680
Son in whose face invisible is beheld
Visibly, what by Deity I am,
And in whose hand what by Decree I do,
Second Omnipotence, two days are past,
Two days, as we compute the days of Heav'n,   685
Since *Michael* and his Powers went forth to tame
These disobedient; sore hath been thir fight,
As likeliest was, when two such Foes met a:m'd;
For to themselves I left them, and thou know'st,
Equal in thir Creation they were form'd,   690
Save what sin hath impair'd, which yet hath wrought

655. *opprest:* physically crushed.
665. *jaculation:* throwing.
666. The scene recalls the volleys of mountains thrown by the contending giants and titans in Hesiod's story (see l. 644, n. above).
667. *civil* is used in a sense contrasted to "military."
673. *sum of things* translates Lucretius' almost technical term for the universe in *De rerum natura* V, 361.
674. *advis'd:* with a mind informed and resolved in advance.

679. *Assessor* is still used in England of associate judges as "sharers of the seat" of a chief judge and of associate officials generally (*O.E.D.*).
682–584. The chapter on "The Son of God" in the *Christian Doctrine* (I, v) begins with a reference to the verse that is echoed here: "Who is the image of the invisible God" (Col. i, 15). In the later discussion of the Son's Omnipotence Milton quotes John v 19: "The Son can do nothing of himself, but what he seeth the Father do" (p. 958).

Insensibly, for I suspend thir doom;
Whence in perpetual fight they needs must last
Endless, and no solution will be found:
War wearied hath perform'd what War can do,   695
And to disorder'd rage let loose the reins,
With Mountains as with Weapons arm'd, which makes
Wild work in Heav'n, and dangerous to the main.
Two days are therefore past, the third is thine;
For thee I have ordain'd it, and thus far   700
Have suffer'd, that the Glory may be thine
Of ending this great War, since none but Thou
Can end it.   Into thee such Virtue and Grace
Immense I have transfus'd, that all may know
In Heav'n and Hell thy Power above compare,   705
And this perverse Commotion govern'd thus,
To manifest thee worthiest to be Heir
Of all things, to be Heir and to be King
By Sacred Unction, thy deserved right.
Go then thou Mightiest in thy Father's might,   710
Ascend my Chariot, guide the rapid Wheels
That shake Heav'n's basis, bring forth all my War,
My Bow and Thunder, my Almighty Arms
Gird on, and Sword upon thy puissant Thigh;
Pursue these sons of Darkness, drive them out   715
From all Heav'n's bounds into the utter Deep:
There let them learn, as likes them, to despise
God and *Messiah* his anointed King.
   He said, and on his Son with Rays direct
Shone full; hee all his Father full exprest   720
Ineffably into his face receiv'd,
And thus the filial Godhead answering spake.
   O Father, O Supreme of heav'nly Thrones,
First, Highest, Holiest, Best, thou always seek'st
To glorify thy Son, I always thee,   725
As is most just; this I my Glory account,
My exaltation, and my whole delight,
That thou in me well pleas'd, declar'st thy will
Fulfill'd, which to fulfil is all my bliss.
Sceptre and Power, thy giving, I assume,   730
And gladlier shall resign, when in the end
Thou shalt be All in All, and I in thee
For ever, and in mee all whom thou lov'st;

692. *Insensibly:* imperceptibly, i.e. not so as to have perceptibly weakened the strength of the rebel angels.

695. *War wearied* etc.: war's resources have been exhausted without settling the dispute.

698. *main:* the continent or whole extent of heaven.

701. *suffer'd:* permitted (matters to run their course).

709. the *Sacred Unction* is implied in the *anointed King* of V, 664.

712. *War* means "army," as it does again in XII, 214.

717. *as likes them:* as pleases them. Cf. "the music likes me not" (*Two Gentlemen of Verona* IV, ii, 56).

723–733. The lines are woven from several New Testament passages which Milton quotes in *CD* I, v (p. 961) to show that "the Father does not alienate his glory from himself in imparting it to the Son, inasmuch as the Son uniformly glorifies the Father."

725. The thought is that of Christ's prayer before the crucifixion: "Father, the hour is come; glorify thy Son, that thy Son also may glorify thee" (John xvii, 1).

728. Cf. the voice from heaven at Christ's baptism and again at the transfiguration, "This is my beloved Son, in whom I am well pleased" (Matt. iii, 17, and xvii, 5).

732. Cf. III, 341.

But whom thou hat'st, I hate, and can put on
Thy terrors, as I put thy mildness on,   735
Image of thee in all things; and shall soon,
Arm'd with thy might, rid heav'n of these rebell'd,
To thir prepar'd ill Mansion driven down,
To chains of darkness, and th' undying Worm,
That from thy just obedience could revolt,   740
Whom to obey is happiness entire.
Then shall thy Saints unmixt, and from th' impure
Far separate, circling thy holy Mount
Unfeigned *Halleluiahs* to thee sing,
Hymns of high praise, and I among them chief.   745
So said, he o'er his Sceptre bowing, rose
From the right hand of Glory where he sat,
And the third sacred Morn began to shine
Dawning through Heav'n: forth rush'd with whirl-wind sound
The Chariot of Paternal Deity,   750
Flashing thick flames, Wheel within Wheel, undrawn,
Itself instinct with Spirit, but convoy'd
By four Cherubic shapes, four Faces each
Had wondrous, as with Stars thir bodies all
And Wings were set with Eyes, with Eyes the Wheels   755
Of Beryl, and careering Fires between;
Over thir heads a crystal Firmament,
Whereon a Sapphire Throne, inlaid with pure
Amber, and colors of the show'ry Arch.
Hee in Celestial Panoply all arm'd   760
Of radiant *Urim*, work divinely wrought,
Ascended, at his right hand Victory
Sat Eagle-wing'd, beside him hung his Bow
And Quiver with three-bolted Thunder stor'd,
And from about him fierce Effusion roll'd   765
Of smoke and bickering flame, and sparkles dire;
Attended with ten thousand thousand Saints,
He onward came, far off his coming shone,
And twenty thousand (I thir number heard)
Chariots of God, half on each hand were seen: 770
Hee on the wings of Cherub rode sublime

734. The line is from Psalm cxxxix, 21: "Do not I hate them, O Lord, that hate thee?"

739. As in I, 47–48, and IV, 965, the reference is to the chaining of Satan in the Apocalypse (Rev. xx, 1–2. Cf. II Pet. ii, 4, and Jude i, 6). The *undying Worm* echoes Mark ix, 44.

748. The Homeric phrase *sacred Morn* (*Il.* XI, 84) stresses the contrast of the peaceful landscape with its impending violation.

750–759. The chariot comes from Ezekiel's vision of "a great cloud, and a fire infolding itself, . . . Also out of the midst thereof came the likeness of four living creatures, . . . And every one had four faces, and every one had four wings" (Ezek. i, 4–6). From the same chapter come the idea of the chariot as self-moved because it is pure spirit, of its mysterious wheels, the play of colors in its precious stones, its darting eyes, and the firmament above it. At least one hexemeral poet before Milton, Rupert of Deutz in the twelfth century, had—as G. McColley notes in *Paradise*

Lost, pp. 26–38—used the vision of Ezekiel as a symbol of Christ triumphing spiritually over the rebel angels. Cf. V, 853, n.

752. *instinct* is used in its Latin participial meaning of "instigated" or "impelled," as it is in II, 937.

761. The *Urim* are first mentioned in the Bible as something to be worn in Aaron's high-priestly "breastplate of judgment" (Exod. xxviii, 30). Their radiance here is part of the symbolism of the spiritual light incarnate in the Son as God's judge and executioner.

762. *Victory* is personified and visualized like the statuettes of Victory on the war chariots of the Greeks.

767–770. So the loyal angels are called *Saints* in l. 398 above. Cf. Psalm lxviii, 17: "The chariots of God are twenty thousand, even thousands of angels."

771. The line echoes David's cry: God "rode upon a cherub, and did fly; and he was seen upon

On the Crystálline Sky, in Sapphire Thron'd.
Illústrious far and wide, but by his own
First seen, them unexpected joy surpris'd,
When the great Ensign of *Messiah* blaz'd   775
Aloft by Angels borne, his Sign in Heav'n:
Under whose Conduct *Michael* soon reduc'd
His Army, circumfus'd on either Wing,
Under thir Head imbodied all in one.
Before him Power Divine his way prepar'd;   780
At his command the uprooted Hills retir'd
Each to his place, they heard his voice and went
Obsequious, Heav'n his wonted face renew'd,
And with fresh Flow'rets Hill and Valley smil'd.
This saw his hapless Foes, but stood obdur'd,   785
And to rebellious fight rallied thir Powers
Insensate, hope conceiving from despair.
In heav'nly Spirits could such perverseness dwell?
But to convince the proud what Signs avail,
Or Wonders move th' obdúrate to relent?   790
They hard'n'd more by what might most reclaim,
Grieving to see his Glory, at the sight
Took envy, and aspiring to his highth,
Stood reimbattl'd fierce, by force or fraud
Weening to prosper, and at length prevail   795
Against God and *Messiah,* or to fall
In universal ruin last, and now
To final Battle drew, disdaining flight,
Or faint retreat; when the great Son of God
To all his Host on either hand thus spake.   800
    Stand still in bright array ye Saints, here stand
Ye Angels arm'd, this day from Battle rest;
Faithful hath been your Warfare, and of God
Accepted, fearless in his righteous Cause,
And as ye have receiv'd, so have ye done   805
Invincibly: but of this cursed crew
The punishment to other hand belongs;
Vengeance is his, or whose he sole appoints;
Number to this day's work is not ordain'd
Nor multitude, stand only and behold   810
God's indignation on these Godless pour'd
By mee; not you but mee they have despis'd,
Yet envied; against mee is all thir rage,
Because the Father, t'whom in Heav'n supreme
Kingdom and Power and Glory appertains,   815
Hath honor'd me according to his will.
Therefore to mee thir doom he hath assign'd;
That they may have thir wish, to try with mee

---

the wings of the wind" (II Sam. xxii, 11). *sub-*
lime—aloft—is a recollection of that divine flight.
776. The *Sign* recalls the promise that at the
end of the world there "shall appear the sign of
the Son of Man in heaven" (Matt. xxiv, 30).
777. *reduc'd:* led back. The word has its basic,
Latin meaning.
785. *obdur'd* has its Latin meaning of "hardened." So in *CD* I, iv (p. 929) Milton speaks

of "hardening of the heart" as the self-induced
punishment of those who abuse the freedom of the
will.
788. The line translates Virgil's question at the
end of his account of Juno's malice against Aeneas
(*Aen.* I, 11).
808. The thought often recurs in the Bible
(Deut. xxxii, 35; Ps. xciv, 1; Rom. xii, 19; and
Heb. x, 30).

In Battle which the stronger proves, they all,
Or I alone against them, since by strength   820
They measure all, of other excellence
Not emulous, nor care who them excels;
Nor other strife with them do I voutsafe.
    So spake the Son, and into terror chang'd
His count'nance too severe to be beheld   825
And full of wrath bent on his Enemies.
At once the Four spread out thir Starry wings
With dreadful shade contiguous, and the Orbs
Of his fierce Chariot roll'd, as with the sound
Of torrent Floods, or of a numerous Host.   830
Hee on his impious Foes right onward drove,
Gloomy as Night; under his burning Wheels
The steadfast Empyrean shook throughout,
All but the Throne itself of God. Full soon
Among them he arriv'd; in his right hand   835
Grasping ten thousand Thunders, which he sent
Before him, such as in thir Souls infix'd
Plagues; they astonisht all resistance lost,
All courage; down thir idle weapons dropp'd;
O'er Shields and Helms, and helmed heads he rode   840
Of Thrones and mighty Seraphim prostrate,
That wish't the Mountains now might be again
Thrown on them as a shelter from his ire.
Nor less on either side tempestuous fell
His arrows, from the fourfold-visag'd Four,   845
Distinct with eyes, and from the living Wheels,
Distinct alike with multitude of eyes;
One Spirit in them rul'd, and every eye
Glar'd lightning, and shot forth pernicious fire
Among th' accurst, that wither'd all thir strength, 850
And of thir wonted vigor left them drain'd,
Exhausted, spiritless, afflicted, fall'n.
Yet half his strength he put not forth, but check'd
His Thunder in mid Volley, for he meant
Not to destroy, but root them out of Heav'n: 855
The overthrown he rais'd, and as a Herd

832. So Hector, though splendidly armed, was "gloomy as night" (*Il*. XII, 462), and so, with Apollo's aid, he paralyzed his foes (*Il*. XV, 323). The *Wheels* here, which are a part of Ezekiel's vision as reflected in l. 755 above, prompt West to say (in *Milton and Angels*, p. 157) that "Milton always associates Wheels with Cherubim, the second order in the Dionysian scheme as Wheels was in the Cabalistic." When Christ rides out to realize in Creation his "Great Idea" (VII, 557), Milton seems to identify the Cherubim on whose wings the Son is uplifted (VII, 218) with the "fervid Wheeles" of VII, 224.

838. *Plagues* has its original Greek force of "blow" or "stroke."

840 The imagery is compared by Broadbent in *ES*, XXXVII (1956), 51, to "the invincible warrior Zeal" in *An Apology*. Arming his "ethereal substance" in "complete diamond," Zeal "ascends his fiery Chariot drawn with two blazing Meteors

figur'd like beasts, but of a higher breed than any the Zodiac yields, resembling two of those four which Ezekiel and Saint John saw, the one visag'd like a Lion to express power, high authority and indignation, the other of count'nance like a man to cast derision and scorn upon perverse and fraudulent seducers" (C.E. III, 313–14). Cf. *PL* III, 388–92, and the Introduction, 17.

842. The line evokes the cry of the wicked at the last judgment, saying "to the mountains and rocks, Fall on us, and hide us from the face of him that sitteth on the throne" (Rev. vi, 16).

856–857. It is interesting to find the early editors excusing the bad taste of this simile on the ground that Homer compares the Greek hosts to flies around a milk-pail, or that Milton had in mind the separation of the "sheep" from the "goats" at the last judgment (Matt. xxv, 33), while for A. Stein the simile is the skilful climax of a series of indications throughout the battle in heaven that Mil-

Of Goats or timorous flock together throng'd
Drove them before him Thunder-struck, pursu'd
With terrors and with furies to the bounds
And Crystal wall of Heav'n, which op'ning wide,   860
Roll'd inward, and a spacious Gap disclos'd
Into the wasteful Deep; the monstrous sight
Struck them with horror backward, but far worse
Urg'd them behind; headlong themselves they threw
Down from the verge of Heav'n, Eternal wrath   865
Burn'd after them to the bottomless pit.
    Hell heard th' unsufferable noise, Hell saw
Heav'n ruining from Heav'n, and would have fled
Affrighted; but strict Fate had cast too deep
Her dark foundations, and too fast had bound.   870
Nine days they fell; confounded *Chaos* roar'd,
And felt tenfold confusion in thir fall
Through his wild Anarchy, so huge a rout
Incumber'd him with ruin: Hell at last
Yawning receiv'd them whole, and on them clos'd,   875
Hell thir fit habitation fraught with fire
Unquenchable, the house of woe and pain.
Disburd'n'd Heav'n rejoic'd, and soon repair'd
Her mural breach, returning whence it roll'd.
Sole Victor from th' expulsion of his Foes   880
Messiah his triumphal Chariot turn'd:
To meet him all his Saints, who silent stood
Eye-witnesses of his Almighty Acts,
With Jubilee advanc'd; and as they went,
Shaded with branching Palm, each order bright,   885
Sung Triumph, and him sung Victorious King,
Son, Heir, and Lord, to him Dominion giv'n,
Worthiest to Reign: he celebrated rode
Triumphant through mid Heav'n, into the Courts
And Temple of his mighty Father Thron'd   890
On high; who into Glory him receiv'd,
Where now he sits at the right hand of bliss.
    Thus measuring things in Heav'n by things on Earth
At thy request, and that thou mayst beware
By what is past, to thee I have reveal'd   895
What might have else to human Race been hid:
The discord which befell, and War in Heav'n

---

ton's object was to leave the rebels "exposed to
laughter" (*Answerable Style*, p. 25) both divine
and human.
    864. With this line the chain of events whose
last link was given to the reader in I, 44–49, is
complete.
    868. With *ruining* cf. ruin in I, 46.
    879. *mural breach:* breach in the walls.
    880–892. The apocalyptic echoes here culminate
in the final allusion to St. Paul's vision of the Son
"upholding all things by the word of his power" and
sitting down "on the right hand of the Majesty
on high" (Heb. i, 3). Many critics take the
lines as a final reason for believing that Milton intended the war in heaven seriously as a physical
battle—as Matthew Arnold took it in "A French

Critic of Milton," in *Mixed Essays* (New York,
1899), p. 197. But if Milton intended it other than
symbolically he stands in marked contrast to most
hexemeral poets from Rupert of Deutz to Thomas
Heywood, for whom the "weapons" of the angels
were
Onely spiritual Armes . . .
And these were call'd *Affection* and *Consent.*
Now both of these, in *Lucifer* the Diuell
And his Complyes, immoderate were, and euill.
Those that in *Michael* the Arch-Angell raign'd,
And his good Spirits, meekely were maintain'd,
Squar'd and directed by th' Almighties will
(The Rule by which they fight, and conquer still).
(*Hierarchie of the Blessed Angels*—1635—Bk. VI,
pp. 341–42) See the Introduction 14–15.

Among th' Angelic Powers, and the deep fall
Of those too high aspiring, who rebell'd
With *Satan*, hee who envies now thy state,   900
Who now is plotting how he may seduce
Thee also from obedience, that with him
Bereav'd of happiness thou mayst partake
His punishment, Eternal misery;
Which would be all his solace and revenge,   905
As a despite done against the most High,
Thee once to gain Companion of his woe.
But list'n not to his Temptations, warn
Thy weaker; let it profit thee to have heard
By terrible Example the reward   910
Of disobedience; firm they might have stood,
Yet fell; remember, and fear to transgress.

The End of the Sixth Book.

909. *Thy weaker:* Eve, the "weaker vessel" of I Peter iii, 7. Even the humanist, Vives, could speak of woman as "a frail thing, and of weak discretion, and that may lightly be deceived, which thing our first mother Eve showeth, whom the Devil caught with a light argument." (Richard Hyrde's translation of Vives' *Instruction of a Christian Woman*, ed. by Watson, p. 56)

BOOK VII

THE ARGUMENT

Raphael *at the request of* Adam *relates how and wherefore this world was first created; that God, after the expelling of* Satan *and his Angels out of Heaven, declar'd his pleasure to create another World and other Creatures to dwell therein; sends his Son with Glory and attendance of Angels to perform the work of Creation in six days: the Angels celebrate with Hymns the performance thereof, and his reascension into Heaven.*

Descend from Heav'n *Urania*, by that name
If rightly thou art call'd, whose Voice divine
Following, above th' *Olympian* Hill I soar,
Above the flight of *Pegasean* wing.
The meaning, not the Name I call: for thou   5
Nor of the Muses nine, nor on the top
Of old *Olympus* dwell'st, but Heav'nly born,
Before the Hills appear'd, or Fountain flow'd,
Thou with Eternal Wisdom didst converse,

1. *Urania* is invoked both to inspire the coming account of creation and to lift the poet up to the heavens where it mainly takes place. For the meaning of her name here and her invocation in I, 6, see the Introduction 54.

3. The *Olympian Hill*, like the *Aonian Mount* of I, 15, was a haunt of the classical Muses, whose inspiration falls short of Milton's need.

4. Pegasus, the winged horse traditionally symbolizing poetic inspiration, anticipates the reference to his rider, *Bellerophon* in l. 18.

9. Behind the conception of *Eternal Wisdom* playing before God lies Proverbs viii, 30, where Wisdom tells of her part in the Creation, and adds, "Then I was by him [God], as one brought up with him: and I was daily his delight, rejoicing ['playing' in the Vulgate] always before him." In the *Wisdom of Solomon* vii, 17–18, Milton found Wisdom gifted with knowledge "how the world was made" and understanding "the operation of the elements . . . the alteration of the turning of the sun and the change of the seasons," etc. In the Renaissance this quasi-theological figure gathered prestige from the half-metaphysical wisdom of classical philosophy, the wisdom which "is knowledge of things divine and human, and in which is contained the relationships and the society of men with gods mutually" (Cicero, *De officiis* I, 145). Drawing upon both Hebrew

Wisdom thy Sister, and with her didst play   10
In presence of th' Almighty Father, pleas'd
With thy Celestial Song. Up led by thee
Into the Heav'n of Heav'ns I have presum'd,
An Earthly Guest, and drawn Empyreal Air,
Thy temp'ring; with like safety guided down   15
Return me to my Native Element:
Lest from this flying Steed unrein'd, (as once
Bellerophon, though from a lower Clime)
Dismounted, on th' *Aleian* Field I fall
Erroneous there to wander and forlorn.   20
Half yet remains unsung, but narrower bound
Within the visible Diurnal Sphere;
Standing on Earth, not rapt above the Pole,
More safe I Sing with mortal voice, unchang'd
To hoarse or mute, though fall'n on evil days,   25
On evil days though fall'n, and evil tongues;
In darkness, and with dangers compast round,
And solitude; yet not alone, while thou
Visit'st my slumbers Nightly, or when Morn
Purples the East: still govern thou my Song,   30
Urania, and fit audience find, though few.
But drive far off the barbarous dissonance
Of *Bacchus* and his Revellers, the Race
Of that wild Rout that tore the *Thracian* Bard
In *Rhodope,* where Woods and Rocks had Ears   35

and Neo-Platonic sources, Spenser dedicated *An Hymne of Heavenly Beautie* to Sapience (i.e., Wisdom),

The soveraine dearling of the Deity. (184)

.   .   .   .

Both heaven and earth obey unto her will,
And all the creatures which they both containe:
For of her fulnesse, which the world doth fill,
They all partake, and do in state remaine,
As their great Maker did at first ordaine. (197–201)

15. *Thy temp'ring:* thou temperest the heavenly air to my mortal lungs.

16. *Native Element:* the earth.

18. In the myth of *Bellerophon's* attempt to explore the mysteries of the stars on Pegasus, and perhaps in that of his slaying of the monster *Chimaera* (cf. II, 628), a symbol of delusion and falsehood, Milton saw a parallel to his own boldness in attempting to write his poem. Zeus punished Bellerophon by casting him onto the *Aleian* plain in Lycia, where he wandered, crazed and (according to Conti, *Mythologiae* IX, viii, p. 964) blind, until he died. Cf. Starnes and Talbert, *Dictionaries,* p. 241.

22. *Diurnal Sphere:* the globe of the skies that seems to revolve daily.

23. *rapt*—"caught up" (into heaven)—illustrates the basic meaning of *rapture* as used metaphorically in l. 36 below. Cf. *Pole* used in the sense found here also in I, 74 and IV, 724.

25–27. *evil days:* the period of reaction against the Puritan revolution after the Stuart Restoration, when for a time Milton's life is said by his early biographer, John Toland, to have been in some

danger. The *darkness* refers to his blindness, to contrast it—as in III, 21–55—with his inward illumination.

29. Cf. the nightly visits of Milton's Muse in III, 32, and IX, 22.

31. So in the Preface to *Eikonoklastes* (C. E. V, 65) Milton launched that tract "to find out her own fit readers: few perhaps, but those few, such of value and substantial worth, as truth and wisdom, not respecting numbers and big names, have been ever wont in all ages to be contented with." But the attitude had been commended since Joachim du Bellay advised the poet "who aspires to a more than vulgar glory to separate himself from inept admirers, . . . and to content himself with few readers" (*La deffence et illustration de la langue françoyse*—1549—II, xi).

32–33. An over-positive identification of the *barbarous rout* with the courtiers of Charles II by McColley, in an effort to date *PL* in 1660, is challenged by Broadbent in *ES* XXXVII (1956), 61, on the basis of "very similar pronouncements in *SA*" and of the use of the Orpheus myth in *Lycidas,* as well as of the allusion to the Irish rebels in *CG* (p. 664) as a "barbarous crew."

33–38. With equal emotion Milton retold Ovid's version of the story of the murder of Orpheus by the worshippers of Bacchus in *Lycidas,* 57–63. He expects his readers to remember Ovid's details: the scene on the Thracian mountain, *Rhodope,* the trees and rocks that so loved Orpheus' voice and lyre that they resisted being used as missiles against him by the drunken bacchantes. In *Lycidas* also the Muse of epic poetry, Calliope, cannot save Orpheus.

To rapture, till the savage clamor drown'd
Both Harp and Voice; nor could the Muse defend
Her Son. So fail not thou, who thee implores:
For thou art Heavn'ly, shee an empty dream.
    Say Goddess, what ensu'd when *Raphaël,*   40
The affable Arch-angel, had forewarn'd
Adam by dire example to beware
Apostasy, by what befell in Heaven
To those Apostates, lest the like befall
In Paradise to *Adam* or his Race,   45
Charg'd not to touch the interdicted Tree,
If they transgress, and slight that sole command,
So easily obey'd amid the choice
Of all tastes else to please thir appetite,
Though wand'ring. He with his consorted *Eve*   50
The story heard attentive, and was fill'd
With admiration, and deep muse to hear
Of things so high and strange, things to thir thought
So unimaginable as hate in Heav'n,
And War so near the Peace of God in bliss   55
With such confusion: but the evil soon
Driv'n back redounded as a flood on those
From whom it sprung, impossible to mix
With Blessedness. Whence *Adam* soon repeal'd
The doubts that in his heart arose: and now   60
Led on, yet sinless, with desire to know
What nearer might concern him, how this World
Of Heav'n and Earth conspicuous first began,
When, and whereof created, for what cause,
What within *Eden* or without was done   65
Before his memory, as one whose drouth
Yet scarce allay'd still eyes the current stream,
Whose liquid murmur heard new thirst excites,
Proceeded thus to ask his Heav'nly Guest.
    Great things, and full of wonder in our ears,   70
Far differing from this World, thou hast reveal'd
Divine Interpreter, by favor sent
Down from the Empyrean to forewarn
Us timely of what might else have been our loss,
Unknown, which human knowledge could not reach: 75
For which to th' infinitely Good we owe
Immortal thanks, and his admonishment
Receive with solemn purpose to observe
Immutably his sovran will, the end

40. Compare *Raphael, the sociable spirit,* of V, 221.

44. Compare *Apostate* in VI, 100.

46. The interdiction on which Milton's story turns is the word of God to Adam in Paradise: "But of the tree of the knowledge of good and evil, thou shalt not eat of it: for in the day that thou eatest thereof, thou shalt surely die" (Gen. ii, 17).

50. *consorted:* associated. "Consort" was a not unusual name for a wife.

57. *redounded:* thrown back. The root of the word is the Latin word for "wave."

59. *repeal'd* preserves the French meaning of "call back."

63. *conspicuous:* visible (in contrast to the unseen heaven of the angels).

66. *drouth:* thirst. The feeling is like that of Dante saying to Virgil in the fourth circle of Purgatory (*Purg.* XVIII, 4) that his thirst for more revelation of theological truth is still urgent.

72. *Divine Interpreter* recalls Virgil's title for Mercury as spokesman of the gods (*Aen.* IV, 378), and perhaps Virgil himself as Dante's "master."

79. *end:* final purpose. Cf. God's glorification as "the chief end of man" in the Shorter Catechism.

Of what we are. But since thou hast voutsaf't   80
Gently for our instruction to impart
Things above Earthly thought, which yet concern'd
Our knowing, as to highest wisdom seem'd,
Deign to descend now lower, and relate
What may no less perhaps avail us known,   85
How first began this Heav'n which we behold
Distant so high, with moving Fires adorn'd
Innumerable, and this which yields or fills
All space, the ambient Air wide interfus'd
Imbracing round this florid Earth, what cause   90
Mov'd the Creator in his holy Rest
Through all Eternity so late to build
In *Chaos,* and the work begun, how soon
Absolv'd, if unforbid thou mayst unfold
What wee, not to explore the secrets ask   95
Of his Eternal Empire, but the more
To magnify his works, the more we know.
And the great Light of Day yet wants to run
Much of his Race though steep, suspense in Heav'n
Held by thy voice, thy potent voice he hears,   100
And longer will delay to hear thee tell
His Generation, and the rising Birth
Of Nature from the unapparent Deep:
Or if the Star of Ev'ning and the Moon
Haste to thy audience, Night with her will bring   105
Silence, and Sleep list'ning to thee will watch,
Or we can bid his absence, till thy Song
End, and dismiss thee ere the Morning shine.
   Thus *Adam* his illustrious Guest besought:
   And thus the Godlike Angel answer'd mild.   110
This also thy request with caution askt
Obtain: though to recount Almighty works
What words or tongue of Seraph can suffice,
Or heart of man suffice to comprehend?
Yet what thou canst attain, which best may serve   115
To glorify the Maker, and infer
Thee also happier, shall not be withheld
Thy hearing, such Commission from above
I have receiv'd, to answer thy desire
Of knowledge within bounds; beyond abstain   120

[handwritten margin note: which reveals to you that you can learn, and serves to glorify him]

---

83. *seem'd:* seemed good.
90. *florid:* flowery.
92. To Adam, as to many a mediaeval school-man and rabbi, and to Milton himself, it was "not imaginable that God should have been wholly oc-cupied from eternity in decreeing that which was to be created in a period of six days" (*CD* I, vii; p. 973).
94. *Absolv'd* has its Latin force of "finished" or "completed."
98. *wants:* is short (of having run).
99. *suspense* has the Latin meaning that it has in VI, 580.
103. The *Deep* or Chaos is *unapparent* (invisi-ble) both because it is outside the shell of the visible universe and because Milton regarded it as "con-fused and formless" (*CD* I, vii; p. 976). For him the act of creation itself was the imposition of forms (in the Platonic sense) upon unformed matter. Cf. l. 233 below.
105. *audience:* hearing.
106. *watch:* stay awake, keep vigil.
116. *infer:* prove. Cf. VIII, 91.
120–125. The passage fuses the pagan dread of revealing ultimate secrets such as Virgil prayed that he might safely reveal in the *Aeneid* VI, 264–67, with Jewish awe of the "glorious and secret things of God" (Ecclesiasticus xi, 4) and Christian respect for the principle of control of the lust of knowledge for its own sake. Cf. VIII, 66–75, as well as the closing lines of VII.

To ask, nor let thine own inventions hope
Things not reveal'd, which th' invisible King,
Only Omniscient, hath supprest in Night,
To none communicable in Earth or Heaven:
Anough is left besides to search and know. 125
But Knowledge is as food, and needs no less
Her Temperance over Appetite, to know
In measure what the mind may well contain,
Oppresses else with Surfeit, and soon turns
Wisdom to Folly, as Nourishment to Wind. 130
  Know then, that after *Lucifer* from Heav'n
(So call him, brighter once amidst the Host
Of Angels, than that Star the Stars among)
Fell with his flaming Legions through the Deep
Into his place, and the great Son return'd 135
Victorious with his Saints, th' Omnipotent
Eternal Father from his Throne beheld
Thir multitude, and to his Son thus spake.
  At least our envious Foe hath fail'd, who thought
All like himself rebellious, by whose aid 140
This inaccessible high strength, the seat
Of Deity supreme, us dispossest,
He trusted to have seiz'd, and into fraud
Drew many, whom thir place knows here no more;
Yet far the greater part have kept, I see, 145
Thir station, Heav'n yet populous retains
Number sufficient to possess her Realms
Though wide, and this high Temple to frequent
With Ministeries due and solemn Rites:
But lest his heart exalt him in the harm 150
Already done, to have dispeopl'd Heav'n,
My damage fondly deem'd, I can repair
That detriment, if such it be to lose
Self-lost, and in a moment will create
Another World, out of one man a Race 155
Of men innumerable, there to dwell,
Not here, till by degrees of merit rais'd
They open to themselves at length the way
Up hither, under long obedience tri'd,
And Earth be chang'd to Heav'n, and Heav'n to Earth, 160
One Kingdom, Joy and Union without end.

121. *inventions* has the meaning of *Conjecture* in VIII, 76: the guesswork of science.

126. The comparison was familiar, as Keightley's quotation from Davenant's *Gondibert* (II. viii, 22–25) shows:

For though books serve as diet for the mind,
If knowledge, early got, self-value breeds,
By false digestion it is turned to wind,
And what should nourish on the eater feeds.

132. *So call him* alludes to Satan's loss of his angelic name. Cf. I, 361, n.

133. The *Star* is Venus as the morning star, bringing or heralding the day, as the name *Lucifer* literally signifies. Like Spenser, Milton thought of all angels as "bright,

All glistring glorious in their Makers light;"
  (*An Hymne of Heavenly Love*, 55–56)

and of Satan as

"The brightest angell, even the Child of Light"
  (l. 83).

Cf. I, 84, n.

136. As in VI, 767, *Saints* means the loyal angels.

137. The Throne is that seen by St. John, "set in heaven, and one sat on the throne" (Rev. iv, 2).

142. *us dispossest*: after dispossessing us.

143. *fraud* keeps its Latin meaning of "injury" or "treachery."

144. The line echoes the words of Job (vii, 10) about the lot of the dead: "Neither shall his place know him any more."

154. *Self-lost*: lost, or ruined, by their own act and to themselves rather than to God.

160. The line tallies with Raphael's account of the process of man's development in V, 469–79.

Meanwhile inhabit lax, ye Powers of Heav'n;
And thou my Word, begotten Son, by thee
This I perform, speak thou, and be it done:
My overshadowing Spirit and might with thee   165
I send along, ride forth, and bid the Deep
Within appointed bounds be Heav'n and Earth,
Boundless the Deep, because I am who fill
Infinitude, nor vacuous the space.
Though I uncircumscrib'd myself retire,   170
And put not forth my goodness, which is free
To act or not, Necessity and Chance
Approach not mee, and what I will is Fate.   *Mightier than Jove*
    So spake th' Almighty, and to what he spake
His Word, the Filial Godhead, gave effect.   175
Immediate are the Acts of God, more swift
Than time or motion, but to human ears
Cannot without procéss of speech be told,
So told as earthly notion can receive.
Great triumph and rejoicing was in Heav'n   180
When such was heard declar'd the Almighty's will;
Glory they sung to the most High, good will
To future men, and in thir dwellings peace:
Glory to him whose just avenging ire
Had driven out th' ungodly from his sight   185
And th' habitations of the just; to him
Glory and praise, whose wisdom had ordain'd
Good out of evil to create, instead
Of Spirits malign a better Race to bring
Into their vacant room, and thence diffuse   190
His good to Worlds and Ages infinite.
So sang the Hierarchies: Meanwhile the Son
On his great Expedition now appear'd,
Girt with Omnipotence, with Radiance crown'd
Of Majesty Divine, Sapience and Love   195
Immense, and all his Father in him shone.

God, therefore, ordains Satan's fall.

162. *inhabit lax:* spread out, settle widely through the regions which have lost a third of their inhabitants in Satan's revolt.

163. Cf. Milton's insistence in *CD* I, v (p. 956) that the Son was voluntarily begotten by the Father, that creation was accomplished through him by the Father, and that the Son "in his capacity of creator, is himself called 'the first-born of every creature' Col. i, 15–17."

165. For the identity of the Spirit see ll. 235–37 below.

170–172. The doctrine of creation by "withdrawal" is discussed in the Introduction 37–38.

173. *what I will is Fate* does not mean that God's will is arbitrary. Fate, said Milton in *CD* I, ii (p. 905), "means either the essence of a thing or that general law which is the origin of everything, and under which everything acts; . . . fate can be nothing but a divine decree emanating from some almighty power." God is replying to Satan, who, in Tasso's *Jerusalem Delivered* IV, 17, actually says that what he wills shall be fate. Cf. I, 116, n.

176. A mass of Jewish and Christian commentary

on Genesis declared that creation was instantaneous —that, as Du Bartas said,

His Word and Deed, all in an instant wrought.
                          (*Divine Weeks,* p. 164)

But commentators generally held either that the instantaneous work was later revealed by the stages of the six days of creation in Genesis, or—as Bacon thought—that while God's power was manifest in the making of "the confused mass and matter of heaven and earth in a moment," his wisdom was manifest in "the order and disposition of that chaos or mass" in "the work of six days" (*Advancement* I, vi, 2).

179. *earthly notion:* human intelligence.

182. There is an echo both of the angels' song to the shepherds at Christ's birth (Luke ii, 13–14) and of their shouting "for joy before God at the creation" in Job xxxviii, 7, a verse that is quoted in *CD* I, vii (p. 978) to prove that the angels were created before the visible universe. Cf. *Nativity,* 119–20.

196. The line parallels III, 139, and recalls VI, 719–21.

About his Chariot numberless were pour'd
Cherub and Seraph, Potentates and Thrones,
And Virtues, winged Spirits, and Chariots wing'd,
From the Armory of God, where stand of old   200
Myriads between two brazen Mountains lodg'd
Against a solemn day, harness't at hand,
Celestial Equipage; and now came forth
Spontaneous, for within them Spirit liv'd,
Attendant on thir Lord: Heav'n op'n'd wide   205
Her ever-during Gates, Harmonious sound
On golden Hinges moving, to let forth
The King of Glory in his powerful Word
And Spirit coming to create new Words.
On heav'nly ground they stood, and from the shore   210
They view'd the vast immeasurable Abyss
Outrageous as a Sea, dark, wasteful, wild,
Up from the bottom turn'd by furious winds
And surging waves, as Mountains to assault
Heav'n's highth, and with the Centre mix the Pole.   215
    Silence, ye troubl'd waves, and thou Deep, peace,
Said then th' Omnific Word, your discord end:
    Nor stay'd, but on the Wings of Cherubim
Uplifted, in Paternal Glory rode
Far into *Chaos,* and the World unborn;   220
For *Chaos* heard his voice: him all his Train
Follow'd in bright procession to behold
Creation, and the wonders of his might.
Then stay'd the fervid Wheels, and in his hand
He took the golden Compasses, prepar'd   225
In God's Eternal store, to circumscribe
This Universe, and all created things:
One foot he centred, and the other turn'd
Round through the vast profundity obscure,
And said, Thus far extend, thus far thy bounds,   230
This be thy just Circumference, O World.
Thus God the Heav'n created, thus the Earth,
Matter unform'd and void: Darkness profound

---

200. So in Jeremiah l, 25, "the Lord hath opened his armoury."

201. The *brazen Mountains* recall Zechariah's vision of four chariots coming "out from between two mountains; and the mountains were mountains of brass" (Zech. vi, 1).

205-215. The opening gates suggest Psalm xxiv, 9: "Lift up your heads, O ye gates: . . . and the King of glory shall come in." The view of Chaos recalls Satan's view of it when the infernal doors open for him "and on thir hinges grate Harsh thunder" (II, 881-82).

217. *omnific:* all-creating.

218. Cf. the chariot made of the wings of cherubim in VI, 827, and its rolling *Orbs,* which here become *fervid Wheels*—fervid because they gleam in swift motion, or perhaps because they are like the wheels of the chariot of deity in Ezekiel i, 16, which "was like unto the color of a beryl."

225. Milton thought of Wisdom's account of the Creation in Proverbs viii, 27: "When he prepared the heavens, I was there: when he set a compass

upon the face of the depth." Here compass means simply a circle, but—as H. Fletcher notes (*M.R.R.,* p. 108)—Rabbi Kimchi's commentary in the Buxtorf Bible interpreted the passage as meaning that a literal compass was used in creation, with one foot on the earth and the other describing the surrounding heavens. This is the picture in Dante's reference (*Par.* xix, 40-42) to him "who rolled the compass round the limit of the universe." But the divine hand drawing a circle in Chaos was a familiar printer's ornament, and—as McColley shows in *N&Q,* CLXXVI (1939), 98—it was a part of the conception of God as the architect of the universe that is given by the popular preacher Godfrey Goodman in a sermon printed in 1616 (p. 16): "In the beginning God did square and proportion the heauens for the earth, vsing his rule, leauell, and compasse; the earth as a center, and the heauens for the circumference." See the Introduction 27.

233. The formless matter of Plato's account of the beginning of the universe (*Tim.* 50, E) harmo-

Cover'd th' Abyss: but on the wat'ry calm
His brooding wings the Spirit of God outspread,   235
And vital virtue infus'd, and vital warmth
Throughout the fluid Mass, but downward purg'd
The black tartareous cold Infernal dregs
Adverse to life; then founded, then conglob'd
Like things to like, the rest to several place   240
Disparted, and between spun out the Air,
And Earth self-balanc't on her Centre hung.
　　Let there be Light, said God, and forthwith Light
Ethereal, first of things, quintessence pure
Sprung from the Deep, and from her Native East   245
To journey through the airy gloom began,
Spher'd in a radiant Cloud, for yet the Sun
Was not; shee in a cloudy Tabernacle
Sojourn'd the while.　God saw the Light was good;
And light from darkness by the Hemisphere   250
Divided: Light the Day, and Darkness Night
He nam'd.　Thus was the first Day Ev'n and Morn:
Nor pass'd uncelebrated, nor unsung
By the Celestial Choirs, when Orient Light
Exhaling first from Darkness they beheld;   255
Birth-day of Heav'n and Earth; with joy and shout
The hollow Universal Orb they fill'd,
And touch'd thir Golden Harps, and hymning prais'd
God and his works, Creator him they sung,
Both when first Ev'ning was, and when first Morn.   260
　　Again, God said, let there be Firmament

---

nizes both with Milton's conception in V, 469–74, and with the description of the earth as "without form and void," with darkness spreading over the face of the deep, in Genesis i, 2.

235–237. From here on Milton follows the Bible closely.　In Genesis i, 2, where the Spirit is said to have "moved upon the face of the deep," he saw, not the Holy Spirit, but—as *CD* I, vii (p. 975) explains—either Christ, "to whom the name of Spirit is sometimes given in the Old Testament," or some "subordinate minister."　The Hebrew word which is translated by "moved"—as Milton observed—means "brood" and was so explained by most lexicons and commentators on Genesis.　The mistranslation—as G. N. Conklin notes in *Criticism*, p. 50—is perpetuated in the Sumner translation of *CD* in spite of Milton's rendering of it by the Latin *incubabat* (brooded). Cf. I, 21, and III, 713–19.

237–242. The picture is the ultimately Platonic conception that Cicero visualized in the *Tusculans* I, xvii, 40, of the original differentiation of the four elements by the sinking of the earthy and damp elements "by their own weight" and the rising of the airy and fiery ones to form the "heavenly region" above the solid "center of the universe."　Milton was familiar with the same idea in Ovid's "self-poised world" at the center of the universe (*Met.* I, 12), and—as A. H. Gilbert notes in *SP*, XIX (1922), 160—he could find the conception of the earth as "suspended and balanced in the circumference of the great circle" of heaven in Galileo's *Dialogue about the two Chief Cosmic Systems,*

the Ptolemaic and the Copernican.　But for Milton the primary authority was Job xxvi, 7: "He hangeth the earth upon nothing."　Cf. *Nativity*, 124.

243. *Let there be light* is God's first creative command (Gen. i, 3).

243–252. God's command, "Let there be light," and his division of the light from the darkness (Gen. i, 4–5) occur on the first day of creation, while it is on the fourth day that the "two great lights, the greater light to rule the day, and the lesser light to rule the night, . . . and the stars also," are created (Gen. ii, 16).　In *CD* I, vii (p. 978) Milton recognized the difficulty of conceiving of "light independent of a luminary," but such was the light above the heavens, where he recalled that God is described (in 1 Tim. 6.16) as "dwelling in the light that no man can approach unto."

261–271. In Gen. i, 6–8, God says, "Let there be a firmament in the midst of the water. . . . And God made the firmament, and divided the waters which were under the firmament from the waters which were above the firmament. . . . And God called the firmament heaven."　Although—as Robbins shows in *Hexaemeral Lit.*, p. 38—the hexaemeral writers prevailingly understood the firmament as a solid shell of air, vapor, or some other substance which served to prevent the water above it from engulfing the still uncreated stars and the earth below (or within) it, Milton's prevailing conception of it—as Svendsen shows in *M.&S.*, p. 60—was that of the entire mass of air and vapor between the earth and the "uttermost convex" of the

Amid the Waters, and let it divide
The Waters from the Waters: and God made
The Firmament, expanse of liquid, pure,
Transparent, Elemental Air, diffus'd   265
In circuit to the uttermost convex
Of this great Round: partition firm and sure,
The Waters underneath from those above
Dividing: for as Earth, so hee the World
Built on circumfluous Waters calm, in wide   270
Crystálline Ocean, and the loud misrule
Of *Chaos* far remov'd, lest fierce extremes
Contiguous might distemper the whole frame:
And Heav'n he nam'd the Firmament: So Ev'n
And Morning *Chorus* sung the second Day.   275
　　The Earth was form'd, but in the Womb as yet
Of Waters, Embryon immature involv'd,
Appear'd not: over all the face of Earth
Main Ocean flow'd, not idle, but with warm
Prolific humor soft'ning all her Globe,   280
Fermented the great Mother to conceive,
Satiate with genial moisture, when God said,
Be gather'd now ye Waters under Heav'n
Into one place, and let dry Land appear.
Immediately the Mountains huge appear   285
Emergent, and thir broad bare backs upheave
Into the Clouds, thir tops ascend the Sky:
So high as heav'd the tumid Hills, so low
Down sunk a hollow bottom broad and deep,
Capacious bed of Waters: thither they   290
Hasted with glad precipitance, uproll'd
As drops on dust conglobing from the dry;
Part rise in crystal Wall, or ridge direct
For haste; such flight the great command impress'd
On the swift floods: as Armies at the call   295
Of Trumpet (for of Armies thou hast heard)
Troop to thir Standard, so the wat'ry throng,
Wave rolling after Wave, where way they found,
If steep, with torrent rapture, if through Plain,
Soft-ebbing; nor withstood them Rock or Hill,   300
But they, or under ground, or circuit wide
With Serpent error wand'ring, found thir way,
And on the washy Ooze deep Channels wore;

---

created universe. The waters above it then become the *Crystalline Ocean* of l. 271. This outer
ocean is distinguished by H. F. Robins, in *PMLA*
LXIX (1954), 904, from the *Crystalline Sphear* of
PL III, 482.

267–269. *Round* and *World* both mean the universe, at the center of which the *Earth* is poised.

280. The *Prolific humor* of the fertilizing sea is
less biblical than it is in keeping with Ovid's account of creation (*Met.* I, 1–51) and with Lucretius' theory of organic life (*De rerum natura* V,
783–820), but it is in harmony with Milton's conception of the impregnating spirit brooding on the
waters in I, 21, and VII, 235–37. See the Introduction 40.

282. *genial*: fertilizing, life-producing.

285–292. The lines fuse the picture of the mountains and valleys going up and down "unto the
place which thou has founded for them" in Psalm
civ, 8, with the command of God in Genesis i, 9:
"Let the waters under the heaven be gathered together unto one place, and let the dry land appear."
In *The Breaking of the Circle* (Evanston, 1950),
p. 20, M. Nicolson sees in the lines the clear statement of a traditional belief in a symmetrical correspondence between the depths of the sea and the
height of the world's mountains.

302. *error*: meandering (in serpentine coils).
Cf. *erroneous* in VII, 20.

Easy, ere God had bid the ground be dry,
All but within those banks, where Rivers now   305
Stream, and perpetual draw thir humid train.
The dry Land, Earth, and the great receptacle
Of congregated Waters he call'd Seas:
And saw that it was good, and said, Let th' Earth
Put forth the verdant Grass, Herb yielding Seed,   310
And Fruit Tree yielding Fruit after her kind;
Whose Seed is in herself upon the Earth.
He scarce had said, when the bare Earth, till then
Desert and bare, unsightly, unadorn'd,
Brought forth the tender Grass, whose verdure clad   315
Her Universal Face with pleasant green,
Then Herbs of every leaf, that sudden flow'r'd
Op'ning thir various colors, and made gay
Her bosom smelling sweet: and these scarce blown,
Forth flourish'd thick the clust'ring Vine, forth crept   320
The smelling Gourd, up stood the corny Reed
Embattl'd in her field: and th' humble Shrub,
And Bush with frizzl'd hair implicit: last
Rose as in Dance the stately Trees, and spread
Thir branches hung with copious Fruit: or gemm'd   325
Thir Blossoms: with high Woods the Hills were crown'd,
With tufts the valleys and each fountain side,
With borders long the Rivers.   That Earth now
Seem'd like to Heav'n, a seat where Gods might dwell,
Or wander with delight, and love to haunt   330
Her sacred shades: though God had yet not rain'd
Upon the Earth, and man to till the ground
None was, but from the Earth a dewy Mist
Went up and water'd all the ground, and each
Plant of the field, which ere it was in the Earth   335
God made, and every Herb, before it grew
On the green stem; God saw that it was good:
So Ev'n and Morn recorded the Third Day.
  Again th' Almighty spake: Let there be Lights
High in th' expanse of Heaven to divide   340
The Day from Night; and let them be for Signs,
For Seasons, and for Days, and circling Years,
And let them be for Lights as I ordain

306. *humid train:* liquid flow.

309. Cf. Genesis i, 11: "And God said, Let the earth bring forth grass, the herb yielding seed, and the fruit tree yielding fruit after his kind, whose seed is in itself upon earth."

321. Bentley's emendation of "swelling" for "smelling" is doubtfully challenged by McColley (*Paradise Lost,* p. 57) on the ground that Du Bartas mentions the "smelling" (i.e. sweet smelling) Indian pepper in a context like this where Milton's "gourd" is mentioned. *corny:* corn- (i. e. grain-) bearing. Cf. *balmy Reed* in V, 23.

322. So a *field of Ceres* is like an army with ported spears in IV, 980-83. Ed. 1 reads *add* for *and.*

323. *frizzl'd* is paralleled by the *O.E.D.* in Browne's *Britannia's Pastorals:* "The frizled coates which doe the mountaines hide." *implicit* keeps its Latin meaning of "tangled."

325. *gemm'd* keeps its Latin meaning of "budding."

327. Cf. the *tufted Groves* of *L'Allegro* 78.

331-334. Cf. Genesis ii, 5-6: ". . . God had not caused it to rain upon the earth, and there was not a man to till the ground. But there went up a mist from the earth, and watered the whole face of the ground."

335-337. God's creation of "every plant of the earth before it was in the earth" (Gen. ii, 5) may have meant to Milton—as Robbins notes (*Hexaemeral Lit.,* p. 32) that it did to Philo—that the plants were created before the sun so that men might not ascribe their creation to it, but rather to God.

339-351. These lines closely paraphrase Genesis i, 14-19.

Thir Office in the Firmament of Heav'n
To give Light on the Earth; and it was so.   345
And God made two great Lights, great for thir use
To Man, the greater to have rule by Day,
The less by Night altern: and made the Stars,
And set them in the Firmament of Heav'n
To illuminate the Earth, and rule the Day   350
In thir vicissitude, and rule the Night,
And Light from Darkness to divide. God saw,
Surveying his great Work, that it was good:
For of Celestial Bodies first the Sun
A mighty Sphere he fram'd, unlightsome first,   355
Though of Ethereal Mould: then form'd the Moon
Globose, and every magnitude of Stars,
And sow'd with Stars the Heav'n thick as a field:
Of Light by far the greater part he took,
Transplanted from her cloudy Shrine, and plac'd   360
In the Sun's Orb, made porous to receive
And drink the liquid Light, firm to retain
Her gather'd beams, great Palace now of Light.
Hither as to thir Fountain other Stars
Repairing, in thir gold'n Urns draw Light,   365
And hence the Morning Planet gilds her horns;
By tincture or reflection they augment
Thir small peculiar, though from human sight
So far remote, with diminution seen.
First in his East the glorious Lamp was seen,   370
Regent of Day, and all th' Horizon round
Invested with bright Rays, jocund to run
His Longitude through Heav'n's high road: the gray
Dawn, and the *Pleiades* before him danc'd
Shedding sweet influence: less bright the Moon,   375
But opposite in levell'd West was set
His mirror, with full face borrowing her Light
From him, for other light she needed none
In that aspect, and still that distance keeps
Till night, then in the East her turn she shines,   380
Revolv'd on Heav'n's great Axle, and her Reign
With thousand lesser Lights dividual holds,
With thousand thousand Stars, that then appear'd
Spangling the Hemisphere: then first adorn'd
With thir bright Luminaries that Set and Rose,   385
Glad Ev'ning and glad Morn crown'd the fourth day.
And God said, let the Waters generate

351. Cf. *vicissitude* (meaning alternation) in VI, 8.

356. Cf. *Mould* (meaning matter in general) in III, 709.

359–366. For another poetical development of Pliny's conception of the sun as the fountain of light (*Nat. Hist.* II, iv, 6) see VIII, 148–52.

366. The gilded horns of the *Morning Planet* plainly refer to Galileo's discovery that Venus has phases like those of the moon, whose horns were a traditional metaphor.

367. Either by absorbing (*tincture*) or by reflecting the sun's rays the planets increase the light which, as Svendsen shows in *M.&S.,* p. 73, most contemporary encyclopaedias taught that the planets naturally radiated from themselves.

373. Cf. *Longitude* in III, 576, and IV, 539.

374. There is an allusion to "the sweet influence of Pleiades" (Job xxxviii, 31) and perhaps to Guido Reni's picture of the sun's chariot with the dawn incarnate as a lovely woman flying before it and seven nymphs—who correspond in number to the Pleiades—alongside.

382. *dividuel,* which modifies *Reign,* has its Latin meaning of "divided."

387–398. The lines paraphrase Genesis i, 20–23.

Reptile with Spawn abundant, living Soul:
And 'let Fowl fly above the Earth, with wings
Display'd on the op'n Firmament of Heav'n.   390
And God created the great Whales, and each
Soul living, each that crept, which plenteously
The waters generated by thir kinds,
And every Bird of wing after his kind;
And saw that it was good, and bless'd them, saying,   395
Be fruitful, multiply, and in the Seas
And Lakes and running Streams the waters fill;
And let the Fowl be multipli'd on the Earth.
Forthwith the Sounds and Seas, each Creek and Bay
With Fry innumerable swarm, and Shoals   400
Of Fish that with thir Fins and shining Scales
Glide under the green Wave, in Sculls that oft
Bank the mid Sea: part single or with mate
Graze the Seaweed thir pasture, and through Groves
Of Coral stray, or sporting with quick glance   405
Show to the Sun thir wav'd coats dropt with Gold,
Or in thir Pearly shells at ease, attend
Moist nutriment, or under Rocks thir food
In jointed Armor watch: on smooth the Seal,
And bended Dolphins play: part huge of bulk   410
Wallowing unwieldly, enormous in thir Gait
Tempest the Ocean: there Leviathan
Hugest of living Creatures, on the Deep
Stretcht like a Promontory sleeps or swims,
And seems a moving Land, and at his Gills   415
Draws in, and at his Trunk spouts out a Sea.
Meanwhile the tepid Caves, and Fens and shores
Thir Brood as numerous hatch, from th' Egg that soon
Bursting with kindly rupture forth disclos'd
Thir callow young, but feather'd soon and fledge   420
They summ'd thir Pens, and soaring th' air sublime
With clang despis'd the ground, under a cloud
In prospect; there the Eagle and the Stork
On Cliffs and Cedar tops thir Eyries build:
Part loosely wing the Region, part more wise   425
In common, rang'd in figure wedge thir way,

388. *Reptile* means any reptant or creeping thing in the broadest sense and includes fish. *Soul* is used in Genesis i, 20, as equivalent to life, and in *CD* I, vii, Milton emphasizes its application to "every beast of the field wherein there is life."

402. *Sculls:* schools.

403. *Bank the mid Sea:* make a bank with their numbers in mid-ocean.

409. *on smooth:* on the smooth sea.

412–415. Cf. the *Leviathan* in I, 200–205.

417–421. D. C. Allen suspects (*MLN*, LXIII—1948—p. 264) that the egg is intentionally put before the bird and quotes Plutarch's mooting of that question in *Symposiacs,* Macrobius' in the *Saturnalia* VII, xvi, and Erycius Puteanus' in his *Praise of the Egg* (*Ovi encomium*). Puteanus' *Comus* (Louvain, 1608) seems to have been known to Milton.

419. *kindly:* natural.

420. *callow:* unfledged. *fledge:* fledged.

421. *summ'd their Pens:* developed complete plumage.

422. *under a cloud:* under what seemed from the point of view of the earth below to be a cloud (so great was the number of birds).

425. *Region* is probably "the middle Region of thick Air" of *PR* II, 117, the middle stratum of the three layers into which the atmosphere was traditionally divided. Cf. I, 516.

426–431. In war *the prudent Crane* understood (according to several Elizabethan writers whom K. Svendsen quotes in *M.&S.*, pp. 157–58 and 275–76) "the expedient of posting sentries and the triangular order of battle." In flight "the hindmost do commonly rest their heads upon the foremost, and when the guide is weary of going before, he cometh hindmost." Cf. I, 576, and the Introduction 63.

Intelligent of seasons, and set forth
Thir Aery Caravan high over Seas
Flying, and over Lands with mutual wing
Easing thir flight; so steers the prudent Crane   430
Her annual Voyage, borne on Winds; the Air
Floats, as they pass, fann'd with unnumber'd plumes:
From Branch to Branch the smaller Birds with song
Solac'd the Woods, and spread thir painted wings
Till Ev'n, nor then the solemn Nightingale   435
Ceas'd warbling, but all night tun'd her soft lays:
Others on Silver Lakes and Rivers Bath'd
Thir downy Breast; the Swan with Arched neck
Between her white wings mantling proudly, Rows
Her state with Oary feet: yet oft they quit   440
The Dank, and rising on stiff Pennons, tow'r
The mid Aereal Sky: Others on ground
Walk'd firm; the crested Cock whose clarion sounds
The silent hours, and th' other whose gay Train
Adorns him, color'd with the Florid hue   445
Of Rainbows and Starry Eyes. The Waters thus
With Fish replenisht, and the Air with Fowl,
Ev'ning and Morn solémniz'd the Fift day.
    The Sixt, and of Creation last arose
With Ev'ning Harps and Matin, when God said,   450
Let th' Earth bring forth Soul living in her kind,
Cattle and Creeping things, and Beast of the Earth,
Each in their kind. The Earth obey'd, and straight
Op'ning her fertile Womb teem'd at a Birth
Innumerous living Creatures, perfet forms,   455
Limb'd and full grown: out of the ground up rose
As from his Lair the wild Beast where he wons
In Forest wild, in Thicket, Brake, or Den;
Among the Trees in Pairs they rose, they walk'd:
The Cattle in the Fields and Meadows green: 460
Those rare and solitary, these in flocks
Pasturing at once, and in broad Herds upsprung.
The grassy Clods now Calv'd, now half appear'd
The Tawny Lion, pawing to get free
His hinder parts, then springs as broke from Bonds,   465
And Rampant shakes his Brinded mane; the Ounce,
The Libbard, and the Tiger, as the Mole
Rising, the crumbl'd Earth above them threw
In Hillocks; the swift Stag from under ground
Bore up his branching head: scarce from his mould   470

432. *Floats:* undulates, is fanned into waves.

439. According to *O.E.D., mantling* is uniquely used by Milton in the sense that it has here and in V, 279.

441. *The Dank:* the water. *tow'r:* soar high in air.

450. The command of God is based on Genesis i, 24–25.

451. Bentley's emendation of *Fowle* in the early editions to *Soul* seems inevitable. Cf. VII, 388, n.

454. *teem'd:* brought forth.

457. *wons:* dwells.

463–470. Here Coleridge thought that Milton

"certainly copied the *fresco* of the Creation in the Sistine Chapel at Rome," but said that, though the image was justified by "the necessities of the painter," it was "wholly unworthy . . . of the enlarged powers of the poet" (Brinkley, *Coleridge,* p. 598). Actually the calving clods and the struggling lion are two of several resemblances to Lucretius' illustrations of the fertility of the earth in its prime, when it directly brought forth all forms of life (*De rerum natura* II, 991–98). Cf. X, 1075-78, and the Introduction 40.

466. *Brinded:* brindled. *Ounce:* lynx or panther.

Behemoth biggest born of Earth upheav'd
His vastness: Fleec't the Flocks and bleating rose,
As Plants: ambiguous between Sea and Land
The River Horse and scaly Crocodile.
At once came forth whatever creeps the ground,   475
Insect or Worm; those wav'd thir limber fans
For wings, and smallest Lineaments exact
In all the Liveries deckt of Summer's pride
With spots of Gold and Purple, azure and green:
These as a line thir long dimension drew,   480
Streaking the ground with sinuous trace; not all
Minims of Nature; some of Serpent kind
Wondrous in length and corpulence involv'd
Thir Snaky folds, and added wings. First crept
The Parsimonious Emmet, provident   485
Of future, in small room large heart enclos'd,
Pattern of just equality perhaps
Hereafter, join'd in her popular Tribes
Of Commonalty: swarming next appear'd
The Female Bee that feeds her Husband Drone   490
Deliciously, and builds her waxen Cells
With Honey stor'd: the rest are numberless,
And thou thir Natures know'st, and gav'st them Names,
Needless to thee repeated; nor unknown
The Serpent subtl'st Beast of all the field,   495
Of huge extent sometimes, with brazen Eyes
And hairy Mane terrific, though to thee
Not noxious, but obedient at thy call.
Now Heav'n in all her Glory shone, and roll'd
Her motions, as the great first-Mover's hand   500
First wheel'd thir course; Earth in her rich attire
Consummate lovely smil'd; Air, Water, Earth,
By Fowl, Fish, Beast, was flown, was swum, was walkt
Frequent; and of the Sixt day yet remain'd;

471. A marginal note on Job xl, 15–24, in the Geneva Bible says: "The Hebrues say Behemoth signifieth Elephant, so called for his hugenesse, by the whiche may be understood the deuyl." The *Jewish Encyclopaedia* does not confirm the identification with the elephant, but brackets *Behemoth* with Leviathan as a primeval monster.

474. *River Horse* is a literal translation of the Greek "hippopotamus."

476. *Worm*, as in IX, 1068, means serpent, but here—generally—any creeping animal. Milton agreed with Henry More—in *An Antidote against Atheisme* (1653), p. 83—that "the swarmes of little *Vermine*, and of *Flyes*, and innumerable suchlike diminutive Creatures" deserve that we should "congratulate their coming into Being rather than murmure sullenly and scornfully against their Existence."

480. *These* are the *Worm* (and serpent) kind of l. 476.

482. *Minims:* tiniest creatures.

483. *corpulence involv'd:* coiled body.

484. For winging his serpents—as D. C. Allen notes in *MLN*, LIX (1944), 538—Milton had the authority of Isaiah xxx, 6, and Herodotus II, 75,

as well as of Samuel Bochart's *Hierozoicon* (a work on biblical animals, published in London in 1663) and of several standard writers.

485–492. The *Emmet*, like the ant in Horace's *Satires* I, i, 35, provides for the future. The supposed democracy of the ants seemed to Milton as exemplary as the monarchy of the bees, which he twitted some Royalist writers for taking seriously. Cf. *Def 1* (C.E. VII, 279). In Charles Butler's *The Feminine Monarchie* (1634), p. 55, the worker bees are expressly declared to be females and to spoil the drones, who always have "a drop of nectar in their mouths."

493. Cf. Adam's naming of the animals in VIII, 349–54.

494–499. Before its curse (cf. X, 175–78) the serpent was thought to be a splendid creature, and for its mane Milton had the example of the sea-serpents that Virgil describes as devouring Laocoon and his sons (*Aen.* II, 203–207). Cf. IX, 494–502.

503. With the impersonal, Latin constructions cf. that in VI, 335.

504. *Frequent* keeps its Latin meaning of "in throngs" or "in hosts." Cf. *PR* I, 128, and II, 130.

There wanted yet the Master work, the end 505
Of all yet done; a Creature who not prone
And Brute as other Creatures, but endu'd
With Sanctity of Reason, might erect
His Stature, and upright with Front serene
Govern the rest, self-knowing, and from thence 510
Magnanimous to correspond with Heav'n,
But grateful to acknowledge whence his good
Descends, thither with heart and voice and eyes
Directed in Devotion, to adore
And worship God Supreme who made him chief 515
Of all his works: therefore th'Omnipotent
Eternal Father (For where is not hee
Present) thus to his Son audibly spake.
  Let us make now Man in our image, Man
In our similitude, and let them rule 520
Over the Fish and Fowl of Sea and Air,
Beast of the Field, and over all the Earth,
And every creeping thing that creeps the ground.
This said, he form'd thee, *Adam*, thee O Man
Dust of the ground, and in thy nostris breath'd 525
The breath of Life; in his own Image hee
Created thee, in the Image of God
Express, and thou becam'st a living Soul.
Male he created thee, but thy consort
Female for Race; then bless'd Mankind, and said, 530
Be fruitful, multiply, and fill the Earth,
Subdue it, and throughout Dominion hold
Over Fish of the Sea, and Fowl of the Air,
And every living thing that moves on the Earth.
Wherever thus created, for no place 535
Is yet distinct by name, thence, as thou know'st
He brought thee into this delicious Grove,
This Garden, planted with the Trees of God,
Delectable both to behold and taste;
And freely all thir pleasant fruit for fooc 540
Gave thee, all sorts are here that all th' Earth yields,

505. *the end*: the object. Cf. l. 79 above, n. and l. 591 below.

505–511. The belief in man's upright attitude as a symbol of his superiority to the beasts and kinship with God runs through classical literature from Plato (*Tim.* 90, a) to Cicero (*On the Nature of the Gods* II, lvi) and Ovid (*Met.* I, 76–86). The idea is so frequent in Lactantius that K. Hartwell in *Milton and Lactantius*, p. 75, says that "there are too many instances to quote"; and it runs through hexaemeral literature in many passages like Du Bartas' description of Adam as

Yet, not his Face down to the earth-ward bending,
Like beasts that but regard their belly, . . .
. . . but towards the Azure Skyes.

.   .   .   .   .   .

Also thou plantedst the Intellectual Pow'r.
                              (*Divine Weeks*, p. 165)

518. In *CD* I, vii (p. 979) Milton observed that "the Deity speaks like to a man deliberating" when, in Genesis i, 26, he says, "Let us make man in our own image, after our own likeness." Bib-

lical commentary traditionally interpreted the passage as meaning—in words that Sir Walter Raleigh translated from the Spanish Jesuit Benedict Pereira in the *History of the World* I, ii, 2—that man images God's "reasonable and understanding nature" and "the divine grace and heavenly glory, which is indeed the perfection and accomplishment of the natural image."

520–534. The lines paraphrase Genesis i, 26–28. The command to Adam to "have dominion over the fish of the sea, and over the fowl of the air, and over every living thing that moveth upon the earth" rang through seventeenth century literature in countless passages like Burton's glorification of man as the "Sovereigne Lord of the Earth, Viceroy of the World, sole Commander and Governour of all the creatures in it" (*Anatomy* I, i, 1; Everyman Ed. I, 130). Cf. VIII, 495–508.

535–538. Genesis ii, 15, says that God put Adam into the *Garden*, and the Apocryphal book of II Esdras iii, 6, says that Adam was led into paradise, which God had planted.

Variety without end; but of the Tree
Which tasted works knowledge of Good and Evil,
Thou may'st not; in the day thou eat'st, thou di'st;
Death is the penalty impos'd, beware,   545
And govern well thy appetite, lest sin
Surprise thee, and her black attendant Death.
Here finish'd hee, and all that he had made
View'd, and behold all was entirely good;
So Ev'n and Morn accomplish'd the Sixt day: 550
Yet not till the Creator from his work
Desisting, though unwearied, up return'd
Up to the Heav'n of Heav'ns his high abode,
Thence to behold this new created World
Th' addition of his Empire, how it show'd   555
In prospect from his Throne, how good, how fair,
Answering his great Idea. Up he rode
Follow'd with acclamation and the sound
Symphonious of ten thousand Harps that tun'd
Angelic harmonies: the Earth, the Air   560
Resounded, (thou remember'st, for thou heard'st)
The Heav'ns and all the Constellations rung,
The Planets in thir station list'ning stood,
While the bright Pomp ascended jubilant.
Open, ye everlasting Gates, they sung,   565
Open, ye Heav'ns, your living doors; let in
The great Creator from his work return'd
Magnificent, his Six days' work, a World;
Open, and henceforth oft; for God will deign
To visit oft the dwellings of just Men   570
Delighted, and with frequent intercourse
Thither will send his winged Messengers
On errands of supernal Grace. So sung
The glorious Train ascending: He through Heav'n,
That open'd wide her blazing Portals, led   575
To God's Eternal house direct the way,
A broad and ample road, whose dust is Gold
And pavement Stars, as Stars to thee appear,
Seen in the Galaxy, that Milky way
Which nightly as a circling Zone thou seest   580
Powder'd with Stars. And now on Earth the Seventh
Ev'ning arose in *Eden,* for the Sun
Was set, and twilight from the East came on,
Forerunning Night; when at the holy mount
Of Heav'n's high-seated top, th' Imperial Throne   585
Of Godhead, fixt for ever firm and sure,

557. So in *CD* I, iii (p. 911), Milton speaks of God's foreknowledge and wisdom as "that idea of everything, which he had in his mind, to use the language of men, before he decreed anything." Here the thought also seems congenial with the pleasure of Plato's creator in the fulfilment of his pattern in the universe that he produces (*Tim.* 37, c).

564. *Pomp* keeps its Greek meaning of "splendid procession."

565-566. Cf. ll. 205-215 above, n.

571. In *CD* I, v (p. 945), Milton observed that in the Old Testament "the name of God seems to be attributed to angels, because as heavenly messengers they bear the appearance of the divine glory and person, and even speak in the very words of the Deity." Cf. III, 531-34.

577-581. The lines resemble Ovid's description of the Milky Way (*Met.* I, 166-69), though—as M. Nicolson suggests in *ELH,* II (1935), 24—we may also have here "a Galilean description of the Milky Way," since there has been a reference to Galileo's telescope in ll. 366 above.

584. Cf. the *holy mount* in V, 643.

The Filial Power arriv'd, and sat him down
With his great Father, for he also went
Invisible, yet stay'd (such privilege
Hath Omnipresence) and the work ordain'd,   590
Author and end of all things, and from work
Now resting, bless'd and hallow'd the Sev'nth day,
As resting on that day from all his work,
But not in silence holy kept; the Harp
Had work and rested not, the solemn Pipe,   595
And Dulcimer, all Organs of sweet stop,
All sounds on Fret by String or Golden Wire
Temper'd soft Tunings, intermixt with Voice
Choral or Unison; of incense Clouds
Fuming from Golden Censers hid the Mount.   600
Creation and the Six days' acts they sung:
Great are thy works, *Jehovah,* infinite
Thy power; what thought can measure thee or tongue
Relate thee; greater now in thy return
Than from the Giant Angels; thee that day   605
Thy Thunders magnifi'd; but to create
Is greater than created to destroy.
Who can impair thee, mighty King, or bound
Thy Empire? easily the proud attempt
Of Spirits apostate and thir Counsels vain   610
Thou hast repell'd, while impiously they thought
Thee to diminish, and from thee withdraw
The number of thy worshippers. Who seeks
To lessen thee, against his purpose serves
To manifest the more thy might: his evil   615
Thou usest, and from thence creat'st more good.
Witness this new-made World, another Heav'n
From Heaven Gate not far, founded in view
On the clear *Hyaline,* the Glassy Sea;
Of amplitude almost immense, with Stars   620
Numerous, and every Star perhaps a World
Of destin'd habitation; but thou know'st
Thir seasons: among these the seat of men,
Earth with her nether Ocean circumfus'd,
Thir pleasant dwelling-place. Thrice happy men,   625
And sons of men, whom God hath thus advanc't,
Created in his Image, there to dwell
And worship him, and in reward to rule
Over his Works, on Earth, in Sea, or Air,

---

592. The blessing of the Sabbath is based on Genesis ii, 2-3.

597. *Fret:* the bar on the finger-board of a guitar.

605. Satan's rebel hosts—as Todd's notes indicate—are called *Giant Angels* because the Hebrew word *gibbor* implies "a proud, fierce, and aspiring temper," and because here, as in VI, 643-66, Milton had the revolt of the giants against Zeus in mind and intended to suggest that "the fictions of the Greek poets owed their rise to some clouded tradition of this real event, and that their giants were, if they understood his story aright, his fallen angels."

619. The *Glassy Sea* is the waters above the firmament and therefore visible to eyes looking down from heaven on the outside of the universe. Cf. VII, 261-71, n. *Hyaline* translates the Greek word meaning "glassy" which describes the sea of glass before God's throne in Revelation iv, 6.

622. The actively controversial idea that the stars may be inhabited goes back to Plato's *Timaeus,* 41. Cf. III, 565-71, and VIII, 144-45.

624. The *nether Ocean* is the waters under the firmament, which were regarded by ancient geographers as encircling all the continents.

629. Cf. Psalm viii, 6: "Thou madest him to have dominion over the works of thy hands; thou hast put all things under his feet."

And multiply a Race of Worshippers   630
Holy and just: thrice happy if they know
Thir happiness, and persevere upright.
So sung they, and the Empyrean rung,
With *Halleluiahs:* Thus was Sabbath kept.
And thy request think now fulfill'd, that ask'd   635
How first this World and face of things began,
And what before thy memory was done
From the beginning, that posterity
Inform'd by thee might know; if else thou seek'st
Aught, not surpassing human measure, say.   640

The End of the Seventh Book.

631. Adam's idyllic happiness evokes Virgil's famous lines on the happiness of the Italian peasants:
O, happy, if he knew his happy state,
The swain, who, free from bus'ness and debate,
Receives his easy food from nature's hand.
        (*Georg.* II, 457–59. Dryden's translation.)
632. Cf. Raphael's repeated warning to Adam to persevere in VIII, 639.
636. *face of things:* visible nature. Cf. l. 63 above. Milton's readers were familiar with this transition from man's creation in the image of God in Book VII to his introduction to the marvels of nature in Book VIII. Commenting on a parallel thought in Aristotle's *Politics* I, i, Loys le Roy compared the passages from Plato and Lactantius that are mentioned in the note on ll. 505–511 above, and added: "Man is begotten . . . after the image and similitude of God . . . to celebrate his honour . . . to the end that he may view the order of the celestiall bodies, and keepe . . . the habitation of this middle terrestrial globe" (I. D.'s translation, London, 1598, p. 18).

BOOK VIII

THE ARGUMENT

Adam *inquires concerning celestial Motions, is doubtfully answer'd, and exhorted to search rather things more worthy of knowledge:* Adam *assents, and still desirous to detain* Raphael, *relates to him what he remember'd since his own Creation, his placing in Paradise, his talk with God concerning solitude and fit society, his first meeting and Nuptials with* Eve, *his discourse with the Angel thereupon; who after admonitions repeated departs.*

The Angel ended, and in *Adam's* Ear
So Charming left his voice, that he a while
Thought him still speaking, still stood fixt to hear;
Then as new wak't thus gratefully repli'd.
What thanks sufficient, or what recompense   5
Equal have I to render thee, Divine
Historian, who thus largely hast allay'd
The thirst I had of knowledge, and voutsaf't
This friendly condescension to relate
Things else by me unsearchable, now heard   10
With wonder, but delight, and, as is due,
With glory attribúted to the high
Creator; something yet of doubt remains,
Which only thy solution can resolve.

1–4. These lines were added in the second edition when Milton divided the original Book VII at l. 640 to make the present Books VII and VIII. The original line 641 read,
    To whom thus *Adam* gratefully repli'd.
The words sounding in Adam's ears may be an echo of those of the incarnate Laws that Socrates hears ringing in his ears and obeys at the close of Plato's *Crito.*

When I behold this goodly Frame, this World   15
Of Heav'n and Earth consisting, and compute
Thir magnitudes, this Earth a spot, a grain,
An Atom, with the Firmament compar'd
And all her number'd Stars, that seem to roll
Spaces incomprehensible (for such   20
Thir distance argues and thir swift return
Diurnal) merely to officiate light
Round this opacous Earth, this punctual spot,
One day and night; in all thir vast survey
Useless besides; reasoning I oft admire,   25
How Nature wise and frugal could commit
Such disproportions, with superfluous hand
So many nobler Bodies to create,
Greater so manifold to this one use,
For aught appears, and on thir Orbs impose   30
Such restless revolution day by day
Repeated, while the sedentary Earth,
That better might with far less compass move,
Serv'd by more noble than herself, attains
Her end without least motion, and receives,   35
As Tribute such a sumless journey brought
Of incorporeal speed, her warmth and light;
Speed, to describe whose swiftness Number fails.
    So spake our Sire, and by his count'nance seem'd
Ent'ring on studious thoughts abstruse, which *Eve*   40
Perceiving where she sat retir'd in sight,
With lowliness Majestic from her seat,
And Grace that won who saw to wish her stay,
Rose, and went forth among her Fruits and Flow'rs,
To visit how they prosper'd, bud and bloom,   45
Her Nursery; they at her coming sprung
And toucht by her fair tendance gladlier grew.   ~ potential in Eve?
Yet went she not, as not with such discourse
Delighted, or not capable her ear
Of what was high: such pleasure she reserv'd,   50
Adam relating, she sole Auditress;

15. *Frame:* creation, universe. Cf. V, 154, and VII, 273.
19. Probably *number'd* means "numerous," but it resembles Psalm cxlvii, 4: "He telleth the number of the stars: He calleth them by their names." The entire speech is colored by Psalm viii.
22. *officiate:* furnish.
23. *opacous:* shadowy, dark. *punctual:* point-like. Milton was aware that Copernican astronomers stressed the tiny earth and the widening astronomical spaces that terrified Pascal, but he also knew that Ptolemy had declared the earth a dot in comparison with the heavens, that to Dante as he saw it from the heaven of fixed stars it seemed like a little threshing-floor (*Par.* xxii, 151), as it did to Chaucer's Troilus from the same point-of-view, and that to a Protestant theologian like Jerome Zanchius the fact that the earth was "less than a point" in the universe was a prime reason for glorifying God (*De operibus Dei* II, ii, 5, Neustadt, 1591). Cf. ll. 107–110 below, n. See the Introduction 35.
25–38. *admire:* wonder, question. Though Mil-
ton's Adam regards the *sedentary Earth* as motionless, he is as puzzled as Burton was by the "fury . . . that shall drive the Heavens . . . about in 24 hours" (*Anatomy* II, ii, 3; Everyman Ed. II, p. 52). Joseph Glanvill, writing as a Copernican in 1661, and believing that before the fall Adam's sight penetrated to the limits of the universe, thought that " 'tis not unlikely that he had as clear a perception of the earth's motion, as we think we have of its quiescence" (*Vanity of Dogmatizing*, p. 5).
36. *sumless:* immeasurable.
37. *incorporeal*, as applied to the speed of the heavenly bodies, matches *spiritual* in l. 110 below. The words, says Ruth Wallerstein (*Poetic*, p. 258), are "entirely consonant with his (Milton's) view in Book V . . . of the indefinable gradation from 'matter' to spirit."
46. *Nursery* means the objects of nursing. So King Lear says (*King Lear* I, i, 126), speaking of Cordelia, that he had depended for his rest "on her kind nursery."

Her Husband the Relater she preferr'd
Before the Angel, and of him to ask
Chose rather: hee, she knew, would intermix
Grateful digressions, and solve high dispute   55
With conjugal Caresses, from his Lip
Not Words alone pleas'd her. O when meet now
Such pairs, in Love and mutual Honor join'd?
With Goddess-like demeanor forth she went;
Not unattended, for on her as Queen   60
A pomp of winning Graces waited still,
And from about her shot Darts of desire
Into all Eyes to wish her still in sight.
And *Raphael* now to *Adam's* doubt propos'd
Benevolent and facile thus repli'd.   65
    To ask or search I blame thee not, for Heav'n
Is as the Book of God before thee set,
Wherein to read his wond'rous Works, and learn
His Seasons, Hours, or Days, or Months, or Years:
This to attain, whether Heav'n move or Earth,   70
Imports not, if thou reck'n right; the rest
From Man or Angel the great Architect
Did wisely to conceal, and not divulge
His secrets to be scann'd by them who ought
Rather admire; or if they list to try   75
Conjecture, he his Fabric of the Heav'ns
Hath left to thir disputes, perhaps to move
His laughter at thir quaint Opinions wide
Hereafter, when they come to model Heav'n
And calculate the Stars, how they will wield   80
The mighty frame, how build, unbuild, contrive
To save appearances, how gird the Sphere
With Centric and Eccentric scribbl'd o'er,
Cycle and Epicycle, Orb in Orb:
Already by thy reasoning this I guess,   85
Who are to lead thy offspring, and supposest
That bodies bright and greater should not serve
The less not bright, nor Heav'n such journeys run,

[Handwritten margin note: Leave well enough alone. A very conservative attitude.]

61. *pomp:* procession. Cf. VII, 564.
64. *doubt propos'd:* question raised. Cf. l. 13 above.
65. *facile* has its Latin meaning of "easy of access," "gracious."
67. "The Book of God" or the "Book of the Creation" (or "of the Creatures") was a traditional metaphor among theologians, who, like Richard Baxter, condemned the sceptical philosophy which "most readeth the book of Nature and least understandeth or feeleth the meaning of it" (*The Reasons of the Christian Religion*, 1667, p. 108).
78. *wide:* i.e. of the truth.
82. *To save appearances,* or to "save the phenomena" were traditional terms for the attempts of astronomers to explain the movements of the heavenly bodies systematically. Their efforts seemed to John Donne only to have warped the globe of heaven and forced
Men to finde out so many Eccentrique parts,
Such divers downe-right lines, such overthwarts,
As disproportion that pure forme: It teares

The Firmament in eight and forty sheires . . .
                (*The First Anniversary,* 255–58)
83. *Centric and Eccentric:* spheres respectively centred or not centred on the earth as the centre of the universe. Burton ridiculed one hypothesis which made "the Earth as before the universal Center," but made the sun (although its sphere was conceived as geocentric) the centre of the orbits of "the five upper planets," and ascribed "diurnal motion" to the eighth sphere (that of the fixed stars), and so, "as a tinker stops one hole and makes two," the astronomer "reforms some (errors), and mars all" (*Anatomy* II, ii, 3; Everyman Ed. II, p. 57).
84. *Epicycle:* "A small circle, having its centre on the circumference of a greater circle. In the Ptolemaic system . . . each of the 'seven planets' was supposed to revolve in an epicycle, the centre of which moved along a greater circle called a deferent" (*O.E.D.*). The device was also used by Copernicus.

Earth sitting still, when she alone receives
The benefit: consider first, that Great   90
Or Bright infers not Excellence: the Earth
Though, in comparison of Heav'n, so small,
Nor glistering, may of solid good contain
More plenty than the Sun that barren shines,
Whose virtue on itself works no effect,   95
But in the fruitful Earth; there first receiv'd
His beams, unactive else, thir vigor find.
Yet not to Earth are those bright Luminaries
Officious, but to thee Earth's habitant.
And for the Heav'n's wide Circuit, let it speak   100
The Maker's high magnificence, who built
So spacious, and his Line stretcht out so far;
That Man may know he dwells not in his own;
An Edifice too large for him to fill,
Lodg'd in a small partition, and the rest   105
Ordain'd for uses to his Lord best known.
The swiftness of those Circles áttribute,
Though numberless, to his Omnipotence,
That to corporeal substances could add
Speed almost Spiritual; mee thou think'st not slow,   110
Who since the Morning hour set out from Heav'n
Where God resides, and ere mid-day arriv'd
In *Eden,* distance inexpressible
By Numbers that have name. But this I urge,
Admitting Motion in the Heav'ns, to show   115
Invalid that which thee to doubt it mov'd;
Not that I so affirm, though so it seem
To thee who hast thy dwelling here on Earth.
God to remove his ways from human sense,
Plac'd Heav'n from Earth so far, that earthly sight,   120
If it presume, might err in things too high,
And no advantage gain. What if the Sun
Be Centre to the World, and other Stars
By his attractive virtue and their own
Incited, dance about him various rounds?   125
Thir wandring course now high, now low, then hid,
Progressive, retrograde, or standing still,
In six thou seest, and what if sev'nth to these
The Planet Earth, so steadfast though she seem,
Insensibly three different Motions move?   130

94–97. The thought is related by W. B. Hunter in *MLR*, XLIV (1949), 89, to Proclus' description of the sun as "shadowless and unreceptive of generation" in his *Commentaries on the Timaeus of Plato,* and to Marsilio Ficino's conception of the sun as "the soul of the world" that "distributes life, sense, and motion to the universe" (in the chapter "On the Sun and Light" in his translation of *Iamblichus de Mysteriis*). Cf. V, 171.

99. *officious:* serviceable. Cf. *officiate* in l. 22 above.

102. The line echoes God's question about the earth: "Who hath laid the measures thereof, if thou knowest? or who hath stretched the line upon it?" (Job xxxviii, 5.)

107–110. The swift circles seem like a reminiscence of the "sempitern courses of the stars" and their "rushing spheres" which are contrasted in Cicero's "Dream of Scipio" (*De re publica* VI, xvii–xix) with this point (*punctum*), the earth. See the Introduction 34.

124. *attractive virtue:* power of attraction. Cf. the sun's *Magnetic beam* in III, 583.

126. Cf. V, 177, n.

130. *Insensibly:* imperceptibly. The three motions are rotation, orbital revolution, and the very slow revolution of the earth's north pole around that of the ecliptic, causing the precession of the equinoxes or *Trepidation* of III, 483.

Which else to several Spheres thou must ascribe,
Mov'd contrary with thwart obliquities,
Or save the Sun his labor, and that swift
Nocturnal and Diurnal rhomb suppos'd,
Invisible else above all Stars, the Wheel   135
Of Day and Night; which needs not thy belief,
If Earth industrious of herself fetch Day
Travelling East, and with her part averse
From the Sun's beam meet Night, her other part
Still luminous by his ray. What if that light   140
Sent from her through the wide transpicuous air,
To the terrestrial Moon be as a Star
Enlight'ning her by Day, as she by Night
This Earth? reciprocal, if Land be there,
Fields and Inhabitants: Her spots thou seest   145
As Clouds, and Clouds may rain, and Rain produce
Fruits in her soft'n'd Soil, for some to eat
Allotted there; and other Suns perhaps
With thir attendant Moons thou wilt descry
Communicating Male and Female Light,   150
Which two great Sexes animate the World,
Stor'd in each Orb perhaps with some that live.
For such vast room in Nature unpossest
By living Soul, desert and desolate,
Only to shine, yet scarce to cóntribute   155
Each Orb a glimpse of Light, convey'd so far
Down to this habitable, which returns
Light back to them, is obvious to dispute.
But whether thus these things, or whether not,
Whether the Sun predominant in Heav'n   160
Rise on the Earth, or Earth rise on the Sun,
Hee from the East his flaming road begin,
Or Shee from West her silent course advance
With inoffensive pace that spinning sleeps
On her soft Axle, while she paces Ev'n,   165
And bears thee soft with the smooth Air along,
Solicit not thy thoughts with matters hid,
Leave them to God above, him serve and fear;
Of other Creatures, as him pleases best,
Wherever plac't, let him dispose: joy thou   170
In what he gives to thee, this Paradise
And thy fair *Eve:* Heav'n is for thee too high

132. *thwart obliquities:* the transverse movements of the spheres as conceived oblique to one another in the Ptolemaic system.

134–136. The *Nocturnal and Diurnal rhomb* is the invisible sphere or *primum mobile* by which Ptolemaic astronomers regarded the spheres of the seven planets and that of fixed stars as enclosed and moved.

137. *industrious:* active, i. e. moving, not stationary.

142. The *terrestrial Moon* is the moon as understood to be inhabitable like the earth. For Milton's ambivalent treatment of the matter see the Introduction 31.

150. That the sun is *Male* is implied in ll. 94–96 above; the moon's *Female Light* is traced by Whiting (*Milieu,* p. 78) to Pliny's *Natural History* I, 129–30.

155. *Only to shine,* for the sake of mere illumination, though the amount of light furnished by each star to *this habitable* (earth) is very small.

158. *obvious:* exposed. In his Seventh *Prolusion* Milton asked his audience of Cambridge undergraduates whether they could believe that the "vast spaces of boundless air are illuminated and adorned by everlasting lights . . . merely to serve as a lantern for base and slothful men."

To know what passes there; be lowly wise:
Think only what concerns thee and thy being;
Dream not of other Worlds, what Creatures there   175
Live, in what state, condition or degree,
Contented that thus far hath been reveal'd
Not of Earth only but of highest Heav'n.
   To whom thus *Adam* clear'd of doubt, repli'd.
How fully hast thou satisfi'd me, pure   180
Intelligence of Heav'n, Angel serene,
And freed from intricacies, taught to live
The easiest way, nor with perplexing thoughts
To interrupt the sweet of Life, from which
God hath bid dwell far off all anxious cares,   185
And not molest us, unless we ourselves
Seek them with wand'ring thoughts, and notions vain.
But apt the Mind or Fancy is to rove
Uncheckt, and of her roving is no end;
Till warn'd, or by experience taught, she learn   190
That not to know at large of things remote
From use, obscure and subtle, but to know
That which before us lies in daily life,
Is the prime Wisdom; what is more, is fume,
Or emptiness, or fond impertinence,   195
And renders us in things that most concern
Unpractic'd, unprepar'd, and still to seek.
Therefore from this high pitch let us descend
A lower flight, and speak of things at hand
Useful, whence haply mention may arise   200
Of something not unseasonable to ask
By sufferance, and thy wonted favor ceign'd.
Thee I have heard relating what was done
Ere my remembrance: now hear mee relate
My Story, which perhaps thou hast not heard;   205
And Day is yet not spent; till then thou seest
How subtly to detain thee I devise,
Inviting thee to hear while I relate,
Fond, were it not in hope of thy reply:
For while I sit with thee, I seem in Heav'n,   210
And sweeter thy discourse is to my ear
Than Fruits of Palm-tree pleasantest to thirst
And hunger both, from labor, at the hour

---

173. So Du Bartas advised:
Be sober wise: so, bound thy frail desire:
And, what thou canst not comprehend, admire.
         (*Divine Weeks*, p. 447)
  181. *Intelligence:* angelic being. George Puttenham spoke of poets as the first students of "Celestial courses, by reason of the continuall motion of the heavens, searching after the first mover, and from thence by degrees coming to know and consider of the substances separate & abstract, which we call the divine intelligences or good Angels" (*The Arte of English Poesie* I, iii).
  188. Milton is not attacking scientific curiosity but, like Glanvill, arguing that, "To say, *Reason* opposeth *Faith,* is to scandalize both: 'Tis *Imagina-*

tion is the Rebel; *Reason* contradicts its impious suggestions" (*Vanity,* p. 103).
  190–197. The thought in the lines was traditional when Montaigne recalled it (*Essays* II, xii. Translation of G. B. Ives, Harvard University Press, 1925, II, 260): "The desire to increase in wisdom and knowledge was the first ruin of the human race; it was the way by which it cast itself into eternal damnation."
  194. *fume:* vapor, vanity.
  195. *fond impertinence:* foolish irrelevance. Cf. *fond* in l. 209.
  197. *still to seek:* always seeking (never finding) solutions.
  213. *from labor:* after labor.

Of sweet repast; they satiate, and soon fill,
Though pleasant, but thy words with Grace Divine   215
Imbu'd, bring to thir sweetness no satiety.
　　To whom thus *Raphael* answer'd heav'nly meek.
Nor are thy lips ungraceful, Sire of men,
Nor tongue ineloquent; for God on thee
Abundantly his gifts hath also pour'd   220
Inward and outward both, his image fair:
Speaking or mute all comeliness and grace
Attends thee, and each word, each motion forms.
Nor less think wee in Heav'n of thee on Earth
Than of our fellow servant, and inquire   225
Gladly into the ways of God with Man:
For God we see hath honor'd thee, and set
On Man his Equal Love: say therefore on;
For I that Day was absent, as befell,
Bound on a voyage uncouth and obscure,   230
Far on excursion toward the Gates of Hell;
Squar'd in full Legion (such command we had)
To see that none thence issu'd forth a spy,
Or enemy, while God was in his work,
Lest hee incenst at such eruption bold,   235
Destruction with Creation might have mixt.
Not that they durst without his leave attempt,
But us he sends upon his high behests
For state, as Sovran King, and to enure
Our prompt obedience.　Fast we found, fast shut   240
The dismal Gates, and barricado'd strong;
But long ere our approaching heard within
Noise, other than the sound of Dance or Song,
Torment, and loud lament, and furious rage.
Glad we return'd up to the coasts of Light   245
Ere Sabbath Ev'ning: so we had in charge.
But thy relation now; for I attend,
Pleas'd with thy words no less than thou with mine.
　　So spake the Godlike Power, and thus our Sire.
For Man to tell how human Life began   250
Is hard; for who himself beginning knew?
Desire with thee still longer to converse
Induc'd me.　As new wak't from soundest sleep
Soft on the flow'ry herb I found me laid
In Balmy Sweat, which with his Beams the Sun   255
Soon dri'd, and on the reeking moisture fed.
Straight toward Heav'n my wond'ring Eyes I turn'd,
And gaz'd a while the ample Sky, till rais'd
By quick instinctive motion up I sprung,
As thitherward endeavoring, and upright   260
Stood on my feet; about me round I saw
Hill, Dale, and shady Woods, and sunny Plains,
And liquid Lapse of murmuring Streams; by these,

[handwritten margin note: why, because God is omniscent.]

221. Cf. the stress upon man as God's image in
VII, 519 and 627.
230. *uncouth:* unknown.
232. Cf. the military use of the term *squar'd* in
I, 758.
239. *For state:* to preserve the dignity of God's

state, for his honor. *enure:* discipline, train.
244. Cf. the *rage* of the demons in I, 666–69.
256. Cf. V, 415, n., for the feeding of the sun
on the earth's vapors.
260. Cf. VII, 505–11, for the significance of
Adam's *upright* posture.

Creatures that liv'd, and mov'd, and walk'd, or flew,
Birds on the branches warbling; all things smil'd, 265
With fragrance and with joy my heart o'erflow'd.
Myself I then perus'd, and Limb by Limb
Survey'd, and sometimes went, and sometimes ran
With supple joints, as lively vigor led:
But who I was, or where, or from what cause, 270
Knew not; to speak I tri'd, and forthwith spake,
My Tongue obey'd and readily could name
Whate'er I saw. Thou Sun, said I, fair Light,
And thou enlight'n'd Earth, so fresh and gay,
Ye Hills and Dales, ye Rivers, Woods, and Plains 275
And ye that live and move, fair Creatures, tell,
Tell, if ye saw, how came I thus, how here?
Not of myself; by some great Maker then,
In goodness and in power preëminent;
Tell me, how may I know him, how adore, 280
From whom I have that thus I move and live,
And feel that I am happier than I know.
While thus I call'd, and stray'd I knew not whither,
From where I first drew Air, and first beheld
This happy Light, when answer none return'd, 285
On a green shady Bank profuse of Flow'rs
Pensive I sat me down; there gentle sleep
First found me, and with soft oppression seiz'd
My drowsed sense, untroubl'd, though I thought
I then was passing to my former state 290
Insensible, and forthwith to dissolve:
When suddenly stood at my Head a dream,
Whose inward apparition gently mov'd
My fancy to believe I yet had being,
And liv'd: One came, methought, of shape Divine, 295
And said, thy Mansion wants thee, *Adam*, rise,
First Man, of Men innumerable ordain'd
First Father, call'd by thee I come thy Guide
To the Garden of bliss, thy seat prepar'd.
So saying, by the hand he took me rais'd, 300
And over Fields and Waters, as in Air
Smooth sliding without step, last led me up
A woody Mountain; whose high top was plain,
A Circuit wide, enclos'd, with goodliest Trees
Planted, with Walks, and Bowers, that what I saw 305
Of Earth before scarce pleasant seem'd. Each Tree
Load'n with fairest Fruit, that hung to the Eye
Tempting, stirr'd in me sudden appetite
To pluck and eat; whereat I wak'd, and found
Before mine Eyes all real, as the dream 310

no contradiction, just poetic licensce.

268. *went:* walked.
272. The language which Adam spoke—as Milton assumed in his *Art of Logic* I, xxiv (C. E. XI, 221) would be universally taken for granted—was Hebrew.
281. The line clearly evokes Aratus' prayer to Zeus in the opening lines of the *Phaenomena*— Zeus who fills the streets and market-places of his offspring, mankind—and St. Paul's echo of it

in Acts xvii 28: "For in him we live, and move, and have our being."
292. Compare Adam's discussion of dreams in V, 100-13.
296. The *Mansion* is the Earthly Paradise in Eden, outside of which Adam was created. Cf. the note on VII, 537.
303. Cf. the account of the mountain of Paradise in IV, 133-49.

Had lively shadow'd: Here had new begun
My wand'ring, had not hee who was my Guide
Up hither, from among the Trees appear'd,
Presence Divine. Rejoicing, but with awe,
In adoration at his feet I fell   315
Submiss: he rear'd me, and Whom thou sought'st I am,
Said mildly, Author of all this thou seest
Above, or round about thee or beneath.
This Paradise I give thee, count it thine
To Till and keep, and of the Fruit to eat: 320
Of every Tree that in the Garden grows
Eat freely with glad heart; fear here no dearth:
But of the Tree whose operation brings
Knowledge of good and ill, which I have set
The Pledge of thy Obedience and thy Faith,   325
Amid the Garden by the Tree of Life,
Remember what I warn thee, shun to taste,
And shun the bitter consequence: for know,
The day thou eat'st thereof, my sole command
Transgrest, inevitably thou shalt die;   330
From that day mortal, and this happy State
Shalt lose, expell'd from hence into a World
Of woe and sorrow. Sternly he pronounc'd
The rigid interdiction, which resounds
Yet dreadful in mine ear, though in my choice   335
Not to incur; but soon his clear aspect
Return'd and gracious purpose thus renew'd.
Not only these fair bounds, but all the Earth
To thee and to thy Race I give; as Lords
Possess it, and all things that therein live,   340
Or live in Sea, or Air, Beast, Fish, and Fowl.
In sign whereof each Bird and Beast behold
After thir kinds; I bring them to receive
From thee thir Names, and pay thee fealty
With low subjection; understand the same   345
Of Fish within thir wat'ry residence,

311. *lively shadow'd:* made appear like the living reality.

316. *submiss* has its Latin force as a participle meaning "cast down."

320–328. Cf. Genesis ii, 15–17: "And the Lord spake unto the man, and put him into the garden of Eden to dress it and keep it. And the Lord God commanded the man, saying, Of every tree of the garden thou mayest freely eat: But of the tree of the knowledge of good and evil, thou shalt not eat of it: for in the day that thou eatest thereof thou shalt surely die." In *CD* I, xii (C. E. XV, 202) Milton explains that, "Under the head of death, in Scripture, all evils whatever, together with everything which in its consequences tends to death, must be understood as comprehended; for mere bodily death, as it is called, did not follow the sin of Adam on the same day." In *CD* I, viii (p. 989) he says that "it is evident that God, at least after the fall of man, limited human life to a certain term."

337. *purpose:* speech. Cf. IV, 337.

340. Cf. Adam's rule of the beasts in VII, 520–43.

345–354. Like his contemporaries, Milton found proof that Adam was "endued with natural wisdom" in the fact that, "without extraordinary wisdom he could not have given names to the whole animal creation with such sudden intelligence" (*CD* I, vii; p. 982). Bacon found proof of man's enjoyment of the contemplative life in perfection in Eden in the fact that "the first acts which man performed in Paradise consisted of the two summary parts of knowledge; the view of the creatures, and the imposition of Names" (*Advancement* I, vi, 6). Since G. W. Knight objects (*Oracle,* p. 87) to the blandishments of the beasts in this scene with Adam, it is worth noting that in Vondel's account, when he

gave them one by one their various names,
The mountain-lion wagged his tail and smiled
Upon his lord. And at his sovereign feet
The tiger too his fierceness laid. The bull
Bowed low his horns: the elephant his trunk . . .
(*Lucifer* in *The Celestial Cycle,* p. 364)

Not hither summon'd, since they cannot change
Thir Element to draw the thinner Air.
As thus he spake, each Bird and Beast behold
Approaching two and two, These cow'ring low   350
With blandishment, each Bird stoop'd on his wing.
I nam'd them, as they pass'd, and understood
Thir Nature, with such knowledge God endu'd
My sudden apprehension: but in these
I found not what methought I wanted still;   355
And to the Heav'nly vision thus presum'd.
   O by what Name, for thou above all these,
Above mankind, or aught than mankind higher,
Surpassest far my naming, how may I
Adore thee, Author of this Universe,   360
And all this good to man, for whose well being
So amply, and with hands so liberal
Thou hast provided all things: but with mee
I see not who partakes. In solitude
What happiness, who can enjoy alone,   365
Or all enjoying, what contentment find?
Thus I presumptuous; and the vision bright,
As with a smile more bright'n'd, thus repli'd.
   <u>What call'st thou solitude? is not the Earth</u>   —*Accusing Adam?*
With various living creatures, and the Air   370
Replenisht, and all these at thy command
To come and play before thee; know'st thou not
Thir language and thir ways? They also know,
And reason not contemptibly; with these
Find pastime, and bear rule; thy Realm is large.   375
So spake the Universal Lord, and seem'd
So ordering. I with leave of speech implor'd,
And humble deprecation thus repli'd.
   Let not my words offend thee, Heav'nly Power,
My Maker, be propitious while I speak.   380
Hast thou not made me here thy substitute,
And these inferior far beneath me set?
Among unequals what society
Can sort, what harmony or true delight?
Which must be mutual, in proportion due   385
Giv'n and receiv'd; but in disparity
The one intense, the other still remiss
Cannot well suit with either, but soon prove   *cold Puritan*
<u>Tedious alike: Of fellowship I speak</u>
Such as I seek, fit to participate   390
All rational delight, wherein the brute
Cannot be human consort; they rejoice

355. Cf. Genesis ii, 20: "And Adam gave names to all cattle, and to the fowl of the air, and to every beast of the field; but for Adam there was not found an help meet for him."

356. *presum'd:* dared speak.

372–373. Adam's knowledge of the beasts included that of their language. On the day of Adam's banishment from Paradise, says the Book of Jubilees (c. 100 B.C.) iii, 28, "was closed the mouth of all beasts . . . so that they could no longer speak. For they had all spoken one with another with one lip and with one tongue" (Charles's translation).

379. So Abraham pled: "Oh let not the Lord be angry, and I will speak" (Gen. xviii, 30).

384–387. *sort:* be appropriate or satisfying. With *harmony* a musical metaphor begins which continues through *intense* and *remiss* in the figure of taut and slack strings in an instrument, which stand for man's high-strung nature in contrast with that of the animals.

Each with thir kind, Lion with Lioness;
So fitly them in pairs thou hast combin'd;
Much less can Bird with Beast, or Fish with Fowl   395
So well converse, nor with the Ox the Ape;
Worse then can Man with Beast, and least of all.
  Whereto th' Almighty answer'd, not displeas'd.
A nice and subtle happiness I see
Thou to thyself proposest, in the choice   400
Of thy Associates, *Adam,* and wilt taste
No pleasure, though in pleasure, solitary.
What think'st thou then of mee. and this my State,
Seem I to thee sufficiently possest
Of happiness, or not? who am alone   405
From all Eternity, for none I know
Second to mee or like, equal much less.
How have I then with whom to hold converse
Save with the Creatures which I made, and those
To me inferior, infinite descents   410
Beneath what other Creatures are to thee?
  He ceas'd, I lowly answer'd. To attain
The highth and depth of thy Eternal ways
All human thoughts come short, Supreme of things;
Thou in thyself art perfet, and in thee   415
Is no deficience found; not so is Man,
But in degree, the cause of his desire
By conversation with his like to help,
Or solace his defects. No need that thou
Shouldst propagate, already infinite;   420
And through all numbers absolute, though One;
But Man by number is to manifest
His single imperfection, and beget
Like of his like, his Image multipli'd,
In unity defective, which requires   425
Collateral love, and dearest amity.
Thou *in* thy secrecy although alone,
Best with thyself accompanied, seek'st not
Social communication, yet so pleas'd,
Canst raise thy Creature to what highth thou wilt   430
Of Union or Communion, deifi'd;
I by conversing cannot these erect
From prone, nor in thir ways complacence find.
Thus I embold'n'd spake, and freedom us'd
Permissive, and acceptance found, which gain'd   435
This answer from the gracious voice Divine.
  Thus far to try thee, *Adam,* I was pleas'd,

---

399. *nice:* delicate.

407. The line echoes Horace's allusion to the supreme deity, "than whom no greater exists, and to whom there is none similar or second" (*Odes* I, xii, 17–18), but the thought of the entire passage reflects Aristotle's demonstration of the simplicity and unity of the divine nature (unlike Adam's *unity* or solitary oneness in l. 425 below, which disqualifies him for happiness) and its capacity for eternal happiness in the contemplation of unchanging truth (*Nicomachean Ethics* VII, xiv, 8).

421. *numbers* is here used in its Latin sense of

"parts," but in l. 422 it has its ordinary meaning. God is perfect in all respects because he is absolute; but man fulfills himself only in society.

431. Sister M. I. Corcoran notes—*Background,* p. 103—that "theologians used the term 'deification' to describe the elevation of the soul to a supernatural state." Adam may be deified by God's grace, but the brutes cannot be humanized by conversation with him.

433. *prone:* proneness, the reverse of man's uprightness. Cf. l. 260.

And find thee knowing not of Beasts alone,
Which thou hast rightly nam'd, but of thyself,
Expressing well the spirit within thee free,   440
My Image, not imparted to the Brute,
Whose fellowship therefore unmeet for thee
Good reason was thou freely shouldst dislike,
And be so minded still; I, ere thou spak'st,
Knew it not good for Man to be alone,   445
And no such company as then thou saw'st
Intended thee, for trial only brought,
To see how thou couldst judge of fit and meet:
What next I bring shall please thee, be assur'd,
Thy likeness, thy fit help, thy other self,   450
Thy wish, exactly to thy heart's desire.
    Hee ended, or I heard no more, for now
My earthly by his Heav'nly overpower'd,
Which it had long stood under, strain'd to the highth
In that celestial Colloquy sublime,   455
As with an object that excels the sense,
Dazzl'd and spent, sunk down, and sought repair
Of sleep, which instantly fell on me, call'd
By Nature as in aid, and clos'd mine eyes.
Mine eyes he clos'd, but op'n left the Cell   460
Of Fancy my internal sight, by which
Abstract as in a trance methought I saw,
Though sleeping, where I lay, and saw the shape
Still glorious before whom awake I stood;
Who stooping op'n'd my left side, and took   465
From thence a Rib, with cordial spirits warm,
And Life-blood streaming fresh; wide was the wound,
But suddenly with flesh fill'd up and heal'd:
The Rib he form'd and fashion'd with his hands;
Under his forming hands a Creature grew,   470
Manlike, but different sex, so lovely fair,
That what seem'd fair in all the World, seem'd now
Mean, or in her summ'd up, in her contain'd
And in her looks, which from that time infus'd
Sweetness into my heart, unfelt before,   475
And into all things from her Air inspir'd
The spirit of love and amorous delight.
Shee disappear'd, and left me dark, I wak'd
To find her, or for ever to deplore   — would give up all for Eve.
Her loss, and other pleasures all abjure: This is the 'Fall here,   480
When out of hope, behold her, not far off,   for love he places here
Such as I saw her in my dream, adorn'd   above her station

450. Against the biblical term for wife, "help-meet" (fit help) Milton puts the classical term for an ideal friend, an *other self*. In *Doctrine of Divorce* I, ii, interpreting "God's intention" in creating Eve, he wrote: "A meet and happy conversation is the chiefest and the noblest end of marriage" (see p. 707).

453. *My earthly*, i.e. nature. Exhausted by the unequal conversation, Adam falls asleep. "The Lord God caused a deep sleep to fall upon Adam, and he slept; and he took one of his ribs. . . . And the rib, which the Lord God had taken from man,

made he a woman, and brought her unto the man" (Gen. ii, 21–22).

461. Adam has explained the part of *Fancy* in dreams in V, 102–109.

462. *Abstract:* abstracted, drawn into a trance.

466. *cordial spirits:* the "vital spirits" which the heart was supposed to distribute to the body. Cf. V, 484.

481. *When out of hope:* when I had given up hope.

482. The dream resembles Milton's vision of his dead wife in *Sonnet* XXIII.

With what all Earth or Heaven could bestow
To make her amiable: On she came,
Led by her Heav'nly Maker, though unseen,   485
And guided by his voice, nor uninform'd
Of nuptial Sanctity and marriage Rites:
Grace was in all her steps, Heav'n in her Eye,
In every gesture dignity and love.
I overjoy'd could not forbear aloud.   490
    This turn hath made amends; thou hast fulfill'd
Thy words, Creator bounteous and benign,
Giver of all things fair, but fairest this
Of all thy gifts, nor enviest. I now see
Bone of my Bone, Flesh of my Flesh, my Self   495
Before me; Woman is her Name, of Man
Extracted; for this cause he shall forgo
Father and Mother, and to his Wife adhere;
And they shall be one Flesh, one Heart, one Soul.
    She heard me thus, and though divinely brought,   500
Yet Innocence and Virgin Modesty,
Her virtue and the conscience of her worth,
That would be woo'd, and not unsought be won,
Not obvious, not obtrusive, but retir'd,
The more desirable, or to say all,   505
Nature herself, though pure of sinful thought,
Wrought in her so, that seeing me, she turn'd;
I follow'd her, she what was Honor knew,
And with obsequious Majesty approv'd
My pleaded reason. To the Nuptial Bow'r   *too much passion,   510
I led her blushing like the Morn: all Heav'n,   lose reason!
And happy Constellations on that hour
Shed thir selectest influence; the Earth
Gave sign of gratulation, and each Hill;
Joyous the Birds; fresh Gales and gentle Airs   515
Whisper'd it to the Woods, and from thir wings
Flung Rose, flung Odors from the spicy Shrub,
Disporting, till the amorous Bird of Night
Sung Spousal, and bid haste the Ev'ning Star
On his Hill top, to light the bridal Lamp.   520
Thus I have told thee all my State, and brought
My Story to the sum of earthly bliss
Which I enjoy, and must confess to find
In all things else delight indeed, but such

490. *could not forbear aloud:* could not resist
crying aloud.

494. *nor enviest:* nor dost thou grudge thy gifts
—in contrast to the Greek gods, who often envied
men their happiness.

495–499. Matthew xix, 4–6, and Mark x, 6–8,
repeat Genesis ii, 23–24: "And Adam said, This is
now bone of my bones, and flesh of my flesh: she
shall be called Woman, because she was taken out
of Man. Therefore shall a man leave his father and
mother, and shall cleave unto his wife: and they
shall be one flesh."

502. *conscience:* consciousness.

504. *obvious:* bold, forward.

508. *Honor* perhaps refers to Hebrews xiii, 4:

"Marriage is honorable unto all." Cf. VII, 529–31,
and IV, 741–47.

513. Cf. the dance of the stars, "shedding sweet
influence," as a portent of the happiness of the universe at its creation in VII, 375.

518. *amorous Bird of Night:* the nightingale.
Cf. V, 39–41, n.

519. The evening star is Venus. Its appearance
was the traditional signal for lighting nuptial
torches from Catullus' epithalamium (lxii) to Spenser's:

Long though it be, at last I see it gloome
And the bright evening-star with golden crest
Appeare out of the east.
(*Epithalamion*, 285–87)

As us'd or not, works in the mind no change,   525
Nor vehement desire, these delicacies
I mean of Taste, Sight, Smell, Herbs, Fruits, and Flow'rs,
Walks, and the melody of Birds; but here
Far otherwise, transported I behold,
Transported touch; here passion first I felt,   530
Commotion strange, in all enjoyments else
Superior and unmov'd, here only weak
Against the charm of Beauty's powerful glance.
Or Nature fail'd in mee, and left some part
Not proof enough such Object to sustain,   535
Or from my side subducting, took perhaps
More than enough; at least on her bestow'd
Too much of Ornament, in outward show
Elaborate, of inward less exact.
For well I understand in the prime end   540
Of Nature her th' inferior, in the mind
And inward Faculties, which most excel,
In outward also her resembling less
His Image who made both, and less expressing
The character of that Dominion giv'n   545
O'er other Creatures; yet when I approach
Her loveliness, so absolute she seems
And in herself complete, so well to know
Her own, that what she wills to do or say,
Seems wisest, virtuousest, discreetest, best;   550
All higher knowledge in her presence falls
Degraded, Wisdom in discourse with her
Loses discount'nanc't, and like folly shows;
Authority and Reason on her wait,
As one intended first, not after made   555
Occasionally; and to consummate all,
Greatness of mind and nobleness thir seat
Build in her loveliest, and create an awe
About her, as a guard Angelic plac't.
To whom the Angel with contracted brow.   560
　　Accuse not Nature, she hath done her part;
Do thou but thine, and be not diffident   ₀doesn't like his tragic flaw.
Of Wisdom, she deserts thee not, if thou
Dismiss not her, when most thou need'st her nigh,
By attribúting overmuch to things   565
Less excellent, as thou thyself perceiv'st.
For what admir'st thou, what transports thee so,
An outside? fair no doubt, and worthy well
Thy cherishing, thy honoring, and thy love,
Not thy subjection: weigh with her thyself;   570
Then value: Oft-times nothing profits more
Than self-esteem, grounded on just and right

---

532. Adam finds himself *superior* to and *un-*
moved by all other pleasures.

537–546. Cf. *Samson Agonistes*, 1025–30. In
the commentaries on Genesis of both the Catholic
Pererius and the Lutheran Pareus—as well as in
others cited by A. Williams (*Expositor*, p. 87)—
Eve's resemblance to God is said to be less perfect
than Adam's, though both are made in his image.

547. *absolute:* perfect.
556. *occasionally:* for an occasion, i. e. an accidental need.
561–570. Cf. God's rebuke to Adam in X, 145–
56.
569. So the marriage service in the Book of Common Prayer reads: "I take thee to my wedded wife
. . . to love and to cherish."

Well manag'd; of that skill the more thou know'st,
The more she will acknowledge thee her Head,
And to realities yield all her shows;   575
Made so adorn for thy delight the more,
So awful, that with honor thou may'st love
Thy mate, who sees when thou art seen least wise.
But if the sense of touch whereby mankind   *sex, sex, sex!*
Is propagated seem such dear delight   580
Beyond all other, think the same voutsaf't
To Cattle and each Beast; which would not be
To them made common and divulg'd, if aught
Therein enjoy'd were worthy to subdue
The Soul of Man, or passion in him move.   585
What higher in her society thou find'st
Attractive, human, rational, love still;
In loving thou dost well, in passion not,
Wherein true Love consists not; Love refines
The thoughts, and heart enlarges, hath his seat   590
In Reason, and is judicious, is the scale
By which to heav'nly Love thou may'st ascend,
Not sunk in carnal pleasure, for which cause   *Pauls attitude to*
Among the Beasts no Mate for thee was found.   *women.*
    To whom thus half abash't *Adam* repli'd.   595
Neither her out-side form'd so fair, nor aught
In procreation common to all kinds
(Though higher of the genial Bed by far,
And with mysterious reverence I deem)
So much delights me, as those graceful acts,   600
Those thousand decencies that daily flow
From all her words and actions, mixt with Love
And sweet compliance, which declare unfeign'd
Union of Mind, or in us both one Soul;
Harmony to behold in wedded pair   605
More grateful than harmonious sound to the ear.
Yet these subject not; I to thee disclose
What inward thence I feel, not therefore foil'd,
Who meet with various objects, from the sense
Variously representing; yet still free   610
Approve the best, and follow what I approve.
To Love thou blam'st me not, for Love thou say'st
Leads up to Heav'n, is both the way and guide;
Bear with me then, if lawful what I ask;
Love not the heav'nly Spirits, and how thir Love   615

---

573. *skill:* power or faculty, i.e. of self-esteem.
574. Cf. ". . . the head of the woman is the man" (I Cor. xi, 3).
589. The distinction is essentially the Neoplatonic one between sacred and profane love which Cardinal Bembo makes in Castiglione's *Book of the Courtier,* and which Spenser echoed in *An Hymne in Honour of Love* (190–94):
Such is the powre of that sweet passion,
That it all sordid basenesse doth expell,
And the refyned mynd doth newly fashion
Unto a fairer forme, which now doth dwell
In his high thought, that would it selfe excell.
591. The *scale* is the scale of nature. Cf. V, 509,

n., and IX, 112.
592. *heav'nly Love* is the divine love of Plato's *Symposium* as it had been Christianized by poets from Dante to Spenser in passages like the latter's vision in *An Hymne of Heavenly Love* of the divine passion so inflaming the spirit
With burning zeale, through every part entire,
That in no earthly thing thou shalt delight,
But in his sweet and amiable sight.
598. *genial:* procreative. Cf. IV, 712.
599. Cf. *mysterious* in IV, 743, and 750.
601. *decencies:* graces.
608. *not therefore foil'd:* not conquered (by the objects of sense).

Express they, by looks only, or do they mix
Irradiance, virtual or immediate touch?
   To whom the Angel with a smile that glow'd   *blushing.*
Celestial rosy red, Love's proper hue,
Answer'd. Let it suffice thee that thou know'st   620
Us happy, and without Love no happiness.
Whatever pure thou in the body enjoy'st
(And pure thou wert created) we enjoy
In eminence, and obstacle find none
Of membrane, joint, or limb, exclusive bars: 625
Easier than Air with Air, if Spirits embrace,
Total they mix, Union of Pure with Pure
Desiring; nor restrain'd conveyance need
As Flesh to mix with Flesh, or Soul with Soul.
But I can now no more; the parting Sun   630
Beyond the Earth's green Cape and verdant Isles
Hesperian sets, my Signal to depart.
Be strong, live happy, and love, but first of all
Him whom to love is to obey, and keep
His great command; take heed lest Passion sway   635
Thy Judgment to do aught, which else free Will
Would not admit; thine and of all thy Sons
The weal or woe in thee is plac't; beware.
I in thy persevering shall rejoice,
And all the Blest: stand fast; to stand or fall   640
Free in thine own Arbitrement it lies.
Perfet within, no outward aid require;
And all temptation to transgress repel.
   So saying, he arose; whom *Adam* thus
Follow'd with benediction. Since to part,   645
Go heavenly Guest, Ethereal Messenger,
Sent from whose sovran goodness I adore.
Gentle to me and affable hath been
Thy condescension, and shall be honor'd ever
With grateful Memory: thou to mankind   650
Be good and friendly still, and oft return.
   So parted they, the Angel up to Heav'n
From the thick shade, and *Adam* to his Bow'r.

The End of the Eighth Book.

619. Change of color is described as possible for the angels in the passage from Psellus on which I, 422–431, is based, but in *blushing Celestial rosy red* E. L. Marilla notes—in *MLN*, LXVIII (1953), 486 —that Raphael turned the *proper hue* of the friendship which, among the angels, is an even higher manifestation of their aspiration to the love of God than even the highest kind of human love can be.

622–629. Physically, Milton conceived the angels much in Henry More's way as "penetrable but indiscerptible body," and, like More in the *Immortality of the Soul* (1659, p. 200), he must have imagined them as singing and dancing together, "reaping the lawful pleasures of the very animal life, in a far higher degree than we are capable of in this world. . . . Wherefore they cannot but enravish one another's souls, while they are mutual

spectators of the perfect pulchritude of one another's person and comely carriage, of their graceful dancing, their melodious singing and playing." See the Introduction 37.

631. On the Mercator maps Cape Verde is marked *Cabo Blanco,* but Starnes and Talbert note (*Dictionaries,* p. 314) that in Charles Stephanus' dictionary its name is given in English as the *green Cape.* The *verdant Isles* are the Cape Verde Islands.

632. *Hesperian* may modify *Isles,* for the Cape Verdes were sometimes identified with the Gardens of the Hesperides; but it may apply to the setting sun.

634. Cf. I John v, 3: "For this is the love of God, that we keep his commandments."

640. The *Blest* are the blessed angels.

BOOK IX

THE ARGUMENT

Satan *having compast the Earth, with meditated guile returns as a mist by Night into Paradise, enters into the Serpent sleeping.* Adam *and* Eve *in the Morning go forth to thir labors, which* Eve *proposes to divide in several places, each laboring apart:* Adam *consents not, alleging the danger, lest that Enemy, of whom they were forewarn'd, should attempt her found alone:* Eve *loath to be thought not circumspect or firm enough, urges her going apart, the rather desirous to make trial of her strength;* Adam *at last yields: The Serpent finds her alone; his subtle approach, first gazing, then speaking, with much flattery extolling* Eve *above all other Creatures.* Eve *wond'ring to hear the Serpent speak, asks how he attain'd to human speech and such understanding not till now; the Serpent answers, that by tasting of a certain Tree in the Garden he attain'd both to Speech and Reason, till then void of both:* Eve *requires him to bring her to that Tree, and finds it to be the Tree of Knowledge forbidden: The Serpent now grown bolder, with many wiles and arguments induces her at length to eat; she pleas'd with the taste deliberates awhile whether to impart thereof to Adam or not, at last brings him of the Fruit, relates what persuaded her to eat thereof:* Adam *at first amaz'd, but perceiving her lost, resolves through vehemence of love to perish with her; and extenuating the trespass, eats also of the Fruit: The effects thereof in them both; they seek to cover thir nakedness; then fall to variance and accusation of one another.*

No more of talk where God or Angel Guest
With Man, as with his Friend, familiar us'd
To sit indulgent, and with him partake
Rural repast, permitting him the while
Venial discourse unblam'd: I now must change   5
Those Notes to Tragic; foul distrust, and breach
Disloyal on the part of Man, revolt,
And disobedience: On the part of Heav'n
Now alienated, distance and distaste,
Anger and just rebuke, and judgment giv'n,   10
That brought into this World a world of woe,
Sin and her shadow Death, and Misery
Death's Harbinger: Sad task, yet argument
Not less but more Heroic than the wrath
Of stern *Achilles* on his Foe pursu'd   15
Thrice Fugitive about *Troy* Wall; or rage
Of *Turnus* for *Lavinia* disespous'd,
Or *Neptune's* ire or *Juno's*, that so long
Perplex'd the *Greek* and *Cytherea's* Son;
If answerable style I can obtain   20

[handwritten margin note: Keeps reminding us that this is a more heroic subject matter, but it is a later age.*]*

---

6. *Tragic* is used with more than a trace of its medieval meaning, for the falls of Lucifer and Adam were traditionally the greatest of tragedies, as Chaucer's Monk defined them—a story
  Of hym that stood in greet prosperitee,
  And is yfallen out of heigh degree.
But basically, Milton used the word in the moral sense that he immediately suggests.
  11. Cf. the same word-play in XI, 627.
  15. As in the invocations to Books I and VII, Milton challenges comparison with the pagan epics.

The *wrath of stern Achilles* is the theme announced in the opening line of the *Iliad*, and its final expression is the brutal slaughter of Hector on the battlefield.
  17. The contrast here is with the struggle of *Turnus* and Aeneas for the hand of *Lavinia* in the later books of the *Aeneid*, and with the persecution of Ulysses by *Neptune* in the *Odyssey* and with *Juno's* injustice to Aeneas in the *Aeneid*, simply because she had quarrelled with his mother Venus, or *Cytherea*.

Of my Celestial Patroness, who deigns
Her nightly visitation unimplor'd,
And dictates to me slumb'ring, or inspires
Easy my unpremeditated Verse:
Since first this Subject for Heroic Song   25
Pleas'd me long choosing, and beginning late;
Not sedulous by Nature to indite
Wars, hitherto the only Argument
Heroic deem'd, chief maistry to dissect
With long and tedious havoc fabl'd Knights   30
In Battles feign'd; the better fortitude
Of Patience and Heroic Martyrdom
Unsung; or to describe Races and Games,
Or tilting Furniture, emblazon'd Shields,
Impreses quaint, Caparisons and Steeds;   35
Bases and tinsel Trappings, gorgeous Knights
At Joust and Tournament; then marshal'd Feast
Serv'd up in Hall with Sewers, and Seneschals;
The skill of Artifice or Office mean,
Not that which justly gives Heroic name   40
To Person or to Poem. Mee of these
Nor skill'd nor studious, higher Argument
Remains, sufficient of itself to raise
That name, unless an age too late, or cold
Climate, or Years damp my intended wing   45
Deprest; and much they may, if all be mine,
Not Hers who brings it nightly to my Ear.
    The Sun was sunk, and after him the Star
Of *Hesperus,* whose Office is to bring
Twilight upon the Earth, short Arbiter   50

21. The *Celestial Patroness* is the *Urania* of I, 6, and VII, 1.

26. *long choosing, and beginning late:* see the Introduction 6–10.

29–32. In a different tone from the popular poet Samuel Pordage, who professed in the Proaemium to *Mundorum Explicatio,*
I sing no Hero's douty gests and warrs,
Nor blazon forth some warlike Champion's Scarrs, . . .
Milton declares his religious theme to be unlike that of any previous epic poem. With similar intent in I, 16, he ironically echoed Ariosto's boast in the opening lines of the *Orlando Furioso* that he was attempting something never before attempted in prose or rhyme.

35. *Impreses quaint:* emblematic ornaments on the shields of knights (from Italian *impresa*).

36. *Bases:* housings for horses (*O.E.D.* cites this line).

38. *Sewers:* waiters or ushers: literally, "seaters."

40–41. Neither Homer's epics, nor the *Aeneid,* nor any other epic poem has ever exemplified the spiritual heroism that is Milton's theme. Cf. I, 1–4, n.

44. As early as his Cambridge days, in Prolusion VII and in *Nature is not Subject to Old Age,* Milton had challenged the scientific pessimism of a traditional belief that human talents had decayed with the earth itself because (in John Norden's words in *Vicissitudo Rerum,* 1600) the sun had lost its

pristine gredience:
The *Solstices* and *Equinoxes* run,
    As in pretended disobedience.
The *Sunne* observed by *Artes* diligence,
    Is found in fourteene hundred yeeres to fall,
    Neere twelve *Degrees* towards the Center ball.
                                        (Stanza 41)

45–46. Aristotle's theory (*Politics* VII, vi, 1) that northern races lacked intelligence colored Milton's fear in the Preface to Book II of *Reason of Church Government* (see p. 669) that "our climate or the fate of this age" might prove to be obstacles to his ambition to write an epic poem. Z. S. Fink, tracing the currency of this theory in Renaissance literature —in *MLQ,* II (1941), 80—concludes that "the ultimate effect of the climatic theory upon Milton's poetical ambitions was to . . . make him more dependent upon the idea of divine inspiration which he had inherited from the Renaissance and which was congenial to his mind." The scientific basis for the idea—as T. B. Stroup notes in *MLQ,* IV (1943), 188—was explained by Burton's view that "cold climes are more subject to natural melancholy which is cold and dry: for which cause Mercurius Britannicus belike puts melancholy men to inhabit just under the Pole" (*Anatomy* I, ii: 2, 5. Everyman Ed. I, 239).

46. Milton's flight would be *Deprest* if his subject did not *raise* it. Cf. l. 43 above.

Twixt Day and Night, and now from end to end
Night's Hemisphere had veil'd the Horizon round:
When *Satan* who late fled before the threats
Of *Gabriel* out of *Eden,* now improv'd
In meditated fraud and malice, bent   55
On Man's destruction, maugre what might hap
Of heavier on himself, fearless return'd.
By Night he fled, and at Midnight return'd
From compassing the Earth, cautious of day,
Since *Uriel* Regent of the Sun descri'd   60
His entrance, and forewarn'd the Cherubim
That kept thir watch; thence full of anguish driv'n,
The space of seven continu'd Nights he rode
With darkness, thrice the Equinoctial Line
He circl'd, four times cross'd the Car of Night   65
From Pole to Pole, traversing each Colure;
On th'eighth return'd, and on the Coast averse
From entrance or Cherubic Watch, by stealth
Found unsuspected way. There was a place,
Now not, though Sin, not Time, first wrought the change,   70
Where *Tigris* at the foot of Paradise
Into a Gulf shot under ground, till part
Rose up a Fountain by the Tree of Life;
In with the River sunk, and with it rose
Satan involv'd in rising Mist, then sought   75
Where to lie hid; Sea he had searcht and Land
From *Eden* over *Pontus,* and the Pool
Mæotis, up beyond the River *Ob;*
Downward as far Antarctic; and in length
West from *Orontes* to the Ocean barr'd   80
At *Darien,* thence to the Land where flows
Ganges and *Indus:* thus the Orb he roam'd
With narrow search; and with inspection deep
Consider'd every Creature, which of all
Most opportune might serve his Wiles, and found   85
The Serpent subtlest Beast of all the Field.
Him after long debate, irresolute
Of thoughts revolv'd, his final sentence chose
Fit Vessel, fittest Imp of fraud, in whom
To enter, and his dark suggestions hide   90

54. *improv'd* or taught by his experience with *Gabriel* (IV, 873–1015) how to refine his intended deceit.

60. *Uriel . . . descri'd:* in IV, 549–88.

65. *The Car of Night*—meaning simply night as it moves around the earth—is the traditional figure that Milton knew in the "yron charet" of Night, under whose protection Spenser's Duessa pursues her evil purposes (*F.Q.* I, v, 20).

66. *Colure:* circles of longitude intersecting at right angles so as to cut the ecliptic into four equal parts.

67. *the Coast averse:* the side opposite.

71. Milton had the authority of Josephus (*Antiquities* I, i, 3) for relating the *Tigris* to the river which "went out of Eden to water the garden" (Gen. ii, 10).

74–75. In his unpublished thesis, "The Folklore

of Milton's English Poems," E. C. Kirkland compares several classical and medieval instances where "supernatural creatures enter the world of man by rising through some body of water" (pp. 30–31).

76. Satan first flew north over *Pontus* (the Black Sea) and the *Pool Mæotis* (Sea of Azof), beyond the river *Ob,* or Obi, on the arctic shore of Siberia. In *Moscovia* Milton often refers to the Ob.

80. *Orontes:* the chief river of Syria.

81. *Darien:* the Isthmus of Panama.

82. *the Orb:* the globe of the world.

86. Without mentioning Satan, Genesis iii, 1, says that "the Serpent was more subtil than any beast of the field which the Lord had made."

87–88. *irresolute* etc.: undecided among circling thoughts.

89. *Imp:* child.

From sharpest sight: for in the wily Snake,
Whatever sleights none would suspicious mark,
As from his wit and native subtlety
Proceeding, which in other Beasts observ'd
Doubt might beget of Diabolic pow'r   95
Active within beyond the sense of brute.
Thus he resolv'd, but first from inward grief
His bursting passion into plaints thus pour'd:
    O Earth, how like to Heav'n, if not preferr'd
More justly, Seat worthier of Gods, as built   100
With second thoughts, reforming what was old!
For what God after better worse would build?
Terrestrial Heav'n, danc't round by other Heav'ns
That shine, yet bear thir bright officious Lamps,
Light above Light, for thee alone, as seems,   105
In thee concentring all thir precious beams
Of sacred influence: As God in Heav'n
Is Centre, yet extends to all, so thou
Centring receiv'st from all those Orbs; in thee,
Not in themselves, all thir known virtue appears   110
Productive in Herb, Plant, and nobler birth
Of Creatures animate with gradual life
Of Growth, Sense, Reason, all summ'd up in Man.
With what delight could I have walkt thee round,
If I could joy in aught, sweet interchange   115
Of Hill and Valley, Rivers, Woods and Plains,
Now Land, now Sea, and Shores with Forest crown'd,
Rocks, Dens, and Caves; but I in none of these
Find place or refuge; and the more I see
Pleasures about me, so much more I feel   120
Torment within me, as from the hateful siege
Of contraries; all good to me becomes
Bane, and in Heav'n much worse would be my state.
But neither here seek I, no nor in Heav'n
To dwell, unless by maistring Heav'n's Supreme;   125
Nor hope to be myself less miserable
By what I seek, but others to make such
As I, though thereby worse to me redound:
For only in destroying I find ease
To my relentless thoughts; and him destroy'd,   130
Or won to what may work his utter loss,
For whom all this was made, all this will soon
Follow, as to him linkt in weal or woe,

95. *Doubt:* suspicion.
104. *officious* is used as it is in VIII, 99.
107. *sacred* because light partakes of the sacredness of deity, as in III, 1–12.
109–112. The thought—as McColley noted in *PMLA*, LII (1937), 741–42—took a bigotedly obscurantist form in works like Alexander Ross's *The New Planet* (1649): "The wise God placed the earth in the midst of this great systeme of the world, not onely for mans sake, who being the Lord of this universe, and the most honourable of all the creatures, deserved to have the most honourable place, which is the middle: but chiefly that man with all other animall and vegetable creatures might by an equal distance from all parts of heaven have

an equall comfort and influence, what place more fit for conservation, then that which is in the midst of the world? . . . all the powers of the universe uniting themselves together in the earth, as in a small epitome." See the Introduction 32–35.
121–122. Satan feels his mind to be the *siege* (seat) of logical opposites or *contraries,* which Milton defines in the *Art of Logic* I, xiv (C. E. XI, 117) as simply one-to-one, mutually exclusive conceptions such as seeing *vs.* blindness and motion *vs.* quiet.
123. *Bane:* evil. Cf. Satan's reflections in IV, 32–112, and IX, 467–70.
133. When Eve tasted the fruit of the Tree of Knowledge, all nature "gave signs of woe" (IX, 783). Cf. X, 651–714.

In woe then: that destruction wide may range:
To mee shall be the glory sole among   135
Th'infernal Powers, in one day to have marr'd
What he *Almighty* styl'd, six Nights and Days
Continu'd making, and who knows how long
Before had been contriving, though perhaps
Not longer than since I in one Night freed   140
From servitude inglorious well nigh half
Th' Angelic Name, and thinner left the throng
Of his adorers: hee to be aveng'd,
And to repair his numbers thus impair'd,
Whether such virtue spent of old now fail'd   145
More Angels to Create, if they at least
Are his Created, or to spite us more,
Determin'd to advance into our room
A Creature form'd of Earth, and him endow,
Exalted from so base original,   150
With Heav'nly spoils, our spoils; What he decreed
He effected; Man he made, and for him built
Magnificent this World, and Earth his seat,
Him Lord pronounc'd, and, O indignity!
Subjected to his service Angel wings,   155
And flaming Ministers to watch and tend
Thir earthy Charge: Of these the vigilance
I dread, and to elude, thus wrapt in mist
Of midnight vapor glide obscure, and pry
In every Bush and Brake, where hap may find   160
The Serpent sleeping, in whose mazy folds
To hide me, and the dark intent I bring.
O foul descent! that I who erst contended
With Gods to sit the highest, am now constrain'd
Into a Beast, and mixt with bestial slime,   165
This essence to incarnate and imbrute,
That to the highth of Deity aspir'd;
But what will not Ambition and Revenge
Descend to? who aspires must down as low
As high he soar'd, obnoxious first or last   170
To basest things.   Revenge, at first though sweet,
Bitter ere long back on itself recoils;
Let it; I reck not, so it light well aim'd,
Since higher I fall short, on him who next
Provokes my envy, this new Favorite   175
Of Heav'n, this Man of Clay, Son of despite,
Whom us the more to spite his Maker rais'd

143–149. Satan contradicts Beelzebub's statement in II, 345–53.

146. Contrast Satan's acknowledgement in IV, 43, that he is God's creature with his assumption here and in I, 116–17, and V, 853–63, that the angels are self-created and immortal.

149. So Vida in the *Christiad* and Tasso in *Jerusalem Delivered* make Satan in an infernal council appeal to the demons' contempt of man on the ground that

. . . in our Place, the Heavens possess he must,
Vile Man, begot of Clay, and born of Dust.

(*Jerusalem Delivered*, Fairfax's translation, IV, x)

155. Satan makes a grievance of the discovery that God "gives his angels charge" (Psalm xci, 11) of mankind.

166. Cf. *This essence* with the *Heavenly Essences* of I, 138.

170. *obnoxious:* exposed. Cf. IX, 1094.

175. In the Foreword to Vondel's *Lucifer* pride and envy are made the mainsprings of the devil's nature, and St. Augustine's definition of envy as hatred of another's happiness is quoted as uniting with pride to motivate Satan's temptation of Adam. (Cf. *The City of God* XII, xi.)

From dust: spite then with spite is best repaid.
   So saying, through each Thicket Dank or Dry,
Like a black mist low creeping, he held on   180
His midnight search, where soonest he might find
The Serpent: him fast sleeping soon he found
In Labyrinth of many a round self-roll'd,
His head the midst, well stor'd with subtle wiles:
Not yet in horrid Shade or dismal Den,   185
Nor nocent yet, but on the grassy Herb
Fearless unfear'd he slept: in at his Mouth
The Devil enter'd, and his brutal sense,
In heart or head, possessing soon inspir'd
With act intelligential; but his sleep   190
Disturb'd not, waiting close th' approach of Morn.
Now whenas sacred Light began to dawn
In *Eden* on the humid Flow'rs, that breath'd
Thir morning incense, when all things that breathe,
From th' Earth's great Altar send up silent praise   195
To the Creator, and his Nostrils fill
With grateful Smell, forth came the human pair
And join'd thir vocal Worship to the Choir
Of Creatures wanting voice; that done, partake
The season, prime for sweetest Scents and Airs: 200
Then cómmune how that day they best may ply
Thir growing work: for much thir work outgrew
The hands' dispatch of two Gard'ning so wide.
And *Eve* first to her Husband thus began.
   Adam, well may we labor still to dress   205
This Garden, still to tend Plant, Herb and Flow'r,
Our pleasant task enjoin'd, but till more hands
Aid us, the work under our labor grows,
Luxurious by restraint; what we by day
Lop overgrown, or prune, or prop, or bind,   210
One night or two with wanton growth derides
Tending to wild. Thou therefore now advise
Or hear what to my mind first thoughts present,
Let us divide our labors, thou where choice
Leads thee, or where most needs, whether to wind   215
The Woodbine round this Arbor, or direct
The clasping Ivy where to climb, while I
In yonder Spring of Roses intermixt

---

178. Cf. the charge against Beelzebub and Satan of doing all "to spite the great Creator" (II, 384–85). The phrasing here resembles Aeschylus' declaration of enmity against Zeus (*Prom.*, 944).

180. A reminiscence, perhaps, of Thetis rising "like a cloud" from the sea to answer Achilles' prayer (*Il.* I, 359), and an expression of a current belief that,

    as in liquid clouds (exhaled thickly),
Water and Ayr (as moist) do mingle quickly,
The evil Angells slide too easily,
As subtle spirits into our fantasie.
      (Du Bartas, *Divine Weeks*, p. 251)

191. *close:* hidden.

192. *whenas:* when.

197. So in Genesis viii, 21, the Lord smells a sweet savor from the altars of sacrifice erected by Noah.

199. *wanting:* lacking.

208–225. Three views seem possible: Sister M. I. Corcoran's in *Milton's Paradise*, pp. 54 and 126, representing Eve on the basis of some pre-Christian commentaries on Genesis as originally having part of the garden assigned to her care, or as pleading to work alone on the day of temptation in a way which Milton chose to treat as "obstinate presumption"; or J. C. Ransom's view in *God without Thunder* (1931), pp. 133–34, that the forbidden fruit symbolizes applied science, which makes Eve's plea foreshadow the sophistries of modern efficiency experts; or the private view of the late W. E. Leonard that her plea is a final stroke of art in the characterization of the mother of all women.

218. *Spring:* grove of young trees or shrubs.

With Myrtle, find what to redress till Noon:
For while so near each other thus all day   220
Our task we choose, what wonder if so near
Looks intervene and smiles, or object new
Casual discourse draw on, which intermits
Our day's work brought to little, though begun
Early, and th' hour of Supper comes unearn'd.   225
　　　To whom mild answer Adam thus return'd.
Sole Eve, Associate sole, to me beyond
Compare above all living Creatures dear,
Well hast thou motion'd, well thy thoughts imploy'd
How we might best fulfil the work which here   230
God hath assign'd us, nor of me shalt pass
Unprais'd: for nothing lovelier can be found
In Woman, than to study household good,
And good works in her Husband to promote.
Yet not so strictly hath our Lord impos'd   235
Labor, as to debar us when we need
Refreshment, whether food, or talk between,
Food of the mind, or this sweet intercourse
Of looks and smiles, for smiles from Reason flow,
To brute deni'd, and are of Love the food,   240
Love not the lowest end of human life.
For not to irksome toil, but to delight
He made us, and delight to Reason join'd.
These paths and Bowers doubt not but our joint hands
Will keep from Wilderness with ease, as wide   245
As we need walk, till younger hands ere long
Assist us: But if much converse perhaps
Thee satiate, to short absence I could yield.
For solitude sometimes is best society,
And short retirement urges sweet return.   250
But other doubt possesses me, lest harm
Befall thee sever'd from me; for thou know'st
What hath been warn'd us, what malicious Foe
Envying our happiness, and of his own
Despairing, seeks to work us woe and shame   255
By sly assault; and somewhere nigh at hand
Watches, no doubt, with greedy hope to find
His wish and best advantage, us asunder,
Hopeless to circumvent us join'd, where each
To other speedy aid might lend at need;   260
Whether his first design be to withdraw
Our fealty from God, or to disturb
Conjugal Love, than which perhaps no bliss
Enjoy'd by us excites his envy more;

---

229. *motion'd*: suggested, "moved," as in a deliberative body.

245. *Wilderness*: wildness.

249. The thought was a favorite aphorism, going back to Cicero's remark that Africanus was never so little alone as when he was by himself (*De re publica* I, xvii, 27). Cf. *PR* I, 302.

264. Rabbinical commentary on the statement that "the serpent was more subtil than any beast of the field" (Gen. iii, 1) explained that the serpent was jealous of their happiness. Josephus says that "the serpent, which then lived together with Adam and his wife, showed an envious disposition, at his supposal of their living happily; . . . and persuaded the woman out of a malicious intention to taste of the tree of knowledge" (*Antiquities* I, i, 4).

Or this, or worse, leave not the faithful side   265
That gave thee being, still shades thee and protects.
The Wife, where danger or dishonor lurks,
Safest and seemliest by her Husband stays,
Who guards her, or with her the worst endures.
    To whom the Virgin Majesty of *Eve*,   270
As one who loves, and some unkindness meets,
With sweet austere composure thus repli'd.
    Offspring of Heav'n and Earth, and all Earth's Lord,
That such an Enemy we have, who seeks
Our ruin, both by thee inform'd I learn,   275
And from the parting Angel over-heard
As in a shady nook I stood behind,
Just then return'd at shut of Ev'ning Flow'rs.
But that thou shouldst my firmness therefore doubt
To God or thee, because we have a foe   280
May tempt it, I expected not to hear.
His violence thou fear'st not, being such,
As wee, not capable of death or pain,
Can either not receive, or can repel.
His fraud is then thy fear, which plain infers   285
Thy equal fear that my firm Faith and Love
Can by his fraud be shak'n or seduc't;
Thoughts, which how found they harbor in thy breast,
Adam, misthought of her to thee so dear?
    To whom with healing words *Adam* repli'd.   290
Daughter of God and Man, immortal *Eve*
For such thou art, from sin and blame entire:
Not diffident of thee do I dissuade
Thy absence from my sight, but to avoid
Th' attempt itself, intended by our Foe.   295
For hee who tempts, though in vain, at least asperses
The tempted with dishonor foul, suppos'd
Not incorruptible of Faith, not proof
Against temptation: thou thyself with scorn
And anger wouldst resent the offer'd wrong,   300
Though ineffectual found: misdeem not then,
If such affront I labor to avert
From thee alone, which on us both at once
The Enemy, though bold, will hardly dare,
Or daring, first on mee th' assault shall light.   305
Nor thou his malice and false guile contemn;
Subtle he needs must be, who could seduce
Angels, nor think superfluous others' aid.
I from the influence of thy looks receive
Access in every Virtue, in thy sight   310

265–266. *the . . . side That gave thee being:*
Cf. VIII, 465–71.

270. *virgin:* virginal, innocent.

274–278. Eve's full, independent knowledge of
the command not to eat the fruit of the Tree of
Knowledge was stressed by several biblical commentators, Catholic and Protestant, who are quoted
by Williams in *Expositor*, p. 114.

289. *misthought:* misjudgment.

292. *entire* has its Latin force of "whole" and

therefore proof against wrong of any kind, perhaps
alluding to Horace's *Ode* (I, xxii) on the strength
of the man whose life is "whole" (*integer:* entire).
Cf. X, 910.

298. *Faith:* fidelity, loyalty. Cf. *firm Faith* in
II, 36.

310. *Access:* increase. Plato's value of the mutual
stimulation of friends in lives of virtue (*Symposium*,
178–79) was prominent in the thinking of the
Renaissance about friendship.

More wise, more watchful, stronger, if need were
Of outward strength; while shame, thou looking on,
Shame to be overcome or over-reacht
Would utmost vigor raise, and rais'd unite.
Why shouldst not thou like sense within thee feel   315
When I am present, and thy trial choose
With me, best witness of thy Virtue tri'd.
   So spake domestic *Adam* in his care
And Matrimonial Love; but *Eve*, who thought
Less attribúted to her Faith sincere,   320
Thus her reply with accent sweet renew'd.
   If this be our condition, thus to dwell
In narrow circuit strait'n'd by a Foe,
Subtle or violent, we not endu'd
Single with like defense, wherever met,   325
How are we happy, still in fear of harm?
But harm precedes not sin: only our Foe
Tempting affronts us with his foul esteem
Of our integrity: his foul esteem
Sticks no dishonor on our Front, but turns   330
Foul on himself; then wherefore shunn'd or fear'd
By us? who rather double honor gain
From his surmise prov'd false, find peace within,
Favor from Heav'n, our witness from th' event.
And what is Faith, Love, Virtue unassay'd   335
Alone, without exterior help sustain'd?
Let us not then suspect our happy State
Left so imperfet by the Maker wise,
As not secure to single or combin'd.
Frail is our happiness, if this be so,   340
And *Eden* were no *Eden* thus expos'd.
   To whom thus *Adam* fervently repli'd.
O Woman, best are all things as the will
Of God ordain'd them, his creating hand
Nothing imperfet or deficient left   345
Of all that he Created, much less Man,
Or aught that might his happy State secure,
Secure from outward force; within himself
The danger lies, yet lies within his power:
Against his will he can receive no harm.   350
But God left free the Will, for what obeys
Reason, is free, and Reason he made right,
But bid her well beware, and still erect,
Lest by some fair appearing good surpris'd
She dictate false, and misinform the Will   355
To do what God expressly hath forbid.
Not then mistrust, but tender love enjoins,
That I should mind thee oft, and mind thou me.

[handwritten margin note: • he's perverting Reason to get his way.]

---

323. *strait'n'd:* confined, limited.

330. *Front:* brow, as in II, 302. The word points back to *affronts* in l. 328, with its derived meaning of "insult" or impudently "confront" a person.

334. The reasoning is St. Paul's: "The Spirit itself beareth witness with our spirit, that we are the children of God" (Rom. viii, 16). Cf. the similar use of *event* in I, 134, II, 82, etc.

351-356. Adam states the doctrine that he has learned from Raphael (V, 520-40) and that has been distinctly stated by God in III, 96-128; or in Milton's own words: "Reason has been implanted in all, by which they may of themselves resist bad desires" (*CD* I, iv; p. 923).

353. *erect:* alert.

358. *mind:* remind.

Firm we subsist, yet possible to swerve,
Since Reason not impossibly may meet   360
Some specious object by the Foe suborn'd,
And fall into deception unaware,
Not keeping strictest watch, as she was warn'd.
Seek not temptation then, which to avoid
Were better, and most likely if from mee   365
Thou sever not: Trial will come unsought.
Wouldst thou approve thy constancy, approve
First thy obedience; th' other who can know,
Not seeing thee attempted, who attest?
But if thou think, trial unsought may find   370
Us both securer than thus warn'd thou seem'st,
Go; for thy stay, not free, absents thee more;
Go in thy native innocence, rely
On what thou hast of virtue, summon all,
For God towards thee hath done his part, do thine.   375
    So spake the Patriarch of Mankind, but *Eve*
Persisted, yet submiss, though last, repli'd.
    With thy permission then, and thus forewarn'd
Chiefly by what thy own last reasoning words
Touch'd only, that our trial, when least sought,   380
May find us both perhaps far less prepar'd,
The willinger I go, nor much expect
A Foe so proud will first the weaker seek;
So bent, the more shall shame him his repulse.
Thus saying, from her Husband's hand her hand   385
Soft she withdrew, and like a Wood-Nymph light,
Oread or *Dryad,* or of *Delia's* Train,
Betook her to the Groves, but *Delia's* self
In gait surpass'd and Goddess-like deport,
Though not as shee with Bow and Quiver arm'd,   390
But with such Gard'ning Tools as Art yet rude,
Guiltless of fire had form'd, or Angels brought.
To *Pales,* or *Pomona,* thus adorn'd,
Likest she seem'd, *Pomona* when she fled
Vertumnus, or to *Ceres* in her Prime,   395
Yet Virgin of *Proserpina* from *Jove.*
Her long and ardent look his Eye pursu'd
Delighted, but desiring more her stay.
Oft he to her his charge of quick return
Repeated, shee to him as oft engag'd   400
To be return'd by Noon amid the Bow'r,
And all things in best order to invite
Noontide repast, or Afternoon's repose.

361. Cf. Archimago's "suborned wyle" in the shape of speciously "falsed letters" in Spenser's *Faerie Queene* II, i, 1, 3.

367. *approve:* prove, give proof of.

371. *securer:* less careful, less on guard. Cf. *secure* in l. 339 above and in IV, 791.

377. *submiss:* submitted (a participle); the meaning is "submissively."

387. *Oread or Dryad:* mountain or wood nymph. Diana (Artemis) is called *Delia* from her birthplace, Delos. Milton thought of her with her traditional bow and arrows, leading her nymphs in the hunt.

389. *deport:* deportment, bearing.

393. *Pales* was a primitive Roman goddess of flocks and herds.

394. Ovid pictures the goddess of fruit, *Pomona,* with a symbolic pruning hook (*Met.* XIV, 628) and tells the story of her long resistance to the pursuit of the wood-god *Vertumnus.*

395. Renaissance painters often represented the young Ceres with the symbolic plough that Ovid says (*Met.* V, 341) she was the first to teach men to use. Cf. Ceres in a different role in IV, 271–72, after she has become the mother of Proserpina.

O much deceiv'd, much failing, hapless *Eve*,
Of thy presum'd return! event perverse!   405
Thou never from that hour in Paradise
Found'st either sweet repast, or sound repose;
Such ambush hid among sweet Flow'rs and Shades
Waited with hellish rancor imminent
To intercept thy way, or send thee back   410
Despoil'd of Innocence, of Faith, of Bliss.
For now, and since first break of dawn the Fiend,
Mere Serpent in appearance, forth was come,
And on his Quest, where likeliest he might find
The only two of Mankind, but in them   415
The whole included Race, his purpos'd prey.
In Bow'r and Field he sought, where any tuft
Of Grove or Garden-Plot more pleasant lay,
Thir tendance or Plantation for delight,
By Fountain or by shady Rivulet,   420
He sought them both, but wish'd his hap might find
Eve separate, he wish'd, but not with hope
Of what so seldom chanc'd, when to his wish,
Beyond his hope, *Eve* separate he spies,
Veil'd in a Cloud of Fragrance, where she stood,   425
Half spi'd, so thick the Roses bushing round
About her glow'd, oft stooping to support
Each Flow'r of slender stalk, whose head though gay
Carnation, Purple, Azure, or speckt with Gold,
Hung drooping unsustain'd, them she upstays   430
Gently with Myrtle band, mindless the while,
Herself, though fairest unsupported Flow'r,
From her best prop so far, and storm so nigh.
Nearer he drew, and many a walk travers'd
Of stateliest Covert, Cedar, Pine, or Palm,   435
Then voluble and bold, now hid, now seen
Among thick-wov'n Arborets and Flow'rs
Imborder'd on each Bank, the hand of *Eve*:
Spot more delicious than those Gardens feign'd
Or of reviv'd *Adonis*, or renown'd   440
Alcinoüs, host of old *Laertes'* Son,
Or that, not Mystic, where the Sapient King
Held dalliance with his fair *Egyptian* Spouse.

413. *Mere Serpent:* simply a serpent. The meaning seems to be that the tempter was not the more
or less humanized snake with a woman's head often
seen in paintings of the temptation. In Andreini's
L'Adamo II, iii, the tempting serpent is represented
as a woman who is serpentine only from the waist
down.
   419. *tendance:* object of care. Cf. *nursery* in
VIII, 46.
   431. *mindless:* heedless, careless (of herself).
   436. *voluble* keeps its Latin meaning of "rolling
upon itself."
   438. *imborder'd:* planted with borders. *the
hand of Eve:* the handiwork of Eve.
   439–440. Cf. Milton's use of the Garden of *Adonis*
as a symbol of an earthly but mystical paradise in
Comus, 976–1011. As Williams notes—*Expositor,*
p. 108—the comparison was traditional and many

commentators had declared that Paradise excelled the
gardens of *Alcinoüs* and the Hesperides. Cf. V,
341.
   441. *Laertes' Son* is Ulysses, whose visit to the gardens of Alcinoüs is told in the *Odyssey* VII.
   442. *not Mystic* means "real" or "historical," for
the garden of Adonis was mythological. To its
pagan mystery is opposed the garden where Solomon, the *Sapient King,* brought his bride when he
"made affinity with Pharaoh king of Egypt, and
took Pharaoh's daughter" (I Kings iii, 1). Milton
had in mind the allusions to Solomon's garden in
the Song of Solomon, which he may have understood—on the strength of the address to the "prince's
daughter" in vii, 1—as an epithalamion written for
the Egyptian princess. In *Reason of Church Government* he calls it "a divine pastoral drama" (see
p. 669).

Much hee the Place admir'd, the Person more.
As one who long in populous City pent   445
Where Houses thick and Sewers annoy the Air,
Forth issuing on a Summer's Morn to breathe
Among the pleasant Villages and Farms
Adjoin'd, from each thing met conceives delight,
The smell of Grain, or tedded Grass, or Kine,   450
Or Dairy, each rural sight, each rural sound;
If chance with Nymphlike step fair Virgin pass,
What pleasing seem'd, for her now pleases more,
She most, and in her look sums all Delight.
Such Pleasure took the Serpent to behold   455
This Flow'ry Plat, the sweet recess of Eve
Thus early, thus alone; her Heav'nly form
Angelic, but more soft, and Feminine,
Her graceful Innocence, her every Air
Of gesture or least action overaw'd   460
His Malice, and with rapine sweet bereav'd
His fierceness of the fierce intent it brought:
That space the Evil one abstracted stood
From his own evil, and for the time remain'd
Stupidly good, of enmity disarm'd,   465
Of guile, of hate, of envy, of revenge;
But the hot Hell that always in him burns,
Though in mid Heav'n, soon ended his delight,
And tortures him now more, the more he sees
Of pleasure not for him ordain'd: then soon   470
Fierce hate he recollects, and all his thoughts
Of mischief, gratulating, thus excites.
   Thoughts, whither have ye led me, with what sweet
Compulsion thus transported to forget
What hither brought us, hate, not love, nor hope   475
Of Paradise for Hell, hope here to taste
Of pleasure, but all pleasure to destroy,
Save what is in destroying, other joy
To me is lost. Then let me not let pass
Occasion which now smiles, behold alone   480
The Woman, opportune to all attempts,
Her Husband, for I view far round, not nigh,
Whose higher intellectual more I shun,
And strength, of courage haughty, and of limb
Heroic built, though of terrestrial mould,   485
Foe not informidable, exempt from wound,
I not; so much hath Hell debas'd, and pain
Infeebl'd me, to what I was in Heav'n.
Shee fair, divinely fair, fit Love for Gods,
Not terrible, though terror be in Love   490

---

450. *tedded:* spread, scattered (to make hay). *Kine:* cattle.

453. *for her:* on her account.

454. *sums:* gathers together and concentrates in herself.

457–466. As G. D. Hildebrand suggests in *N&Q*, CXCVII (1952), 246, the underlying thought is like that of the supernatural power of chastity in *Comus*, 446–51.

456. *Plat:* plot of ground.

467. Cf. the *Hell within him* in IV, 20.

481. *opportune:* opportunely situated.

485. *terrestrial mould:* earthly substance, earth. Cf. *mould* in II, 139.

486. Cf. man's incapability *of death or pain* in l. 283 above and Satan's first knowledge of pain in VI, 327.

And beauty, not approacht by stronger hate,
Hate stronger, under show of Love well feign'd,
The way which to her ruin now I tend.
   So spake the Enemy of Mankind, enclos'd
In Serpent, Inmate bad, and toward *Eve*   495
Address'd his way, not with indented wave,
Prone on the ground, as since, but on his rear,
Circular base of rising folds, that tow'r'd
Fold above fold a surging Maze, his Head
Crested aloft, and Carbuncle his Eyes;   500
With burnisht Neck of verdant Gold, erect
Amidst his circling Spires, that on the grass
Floated redundant: pleasing was his shape,
And lovely, never since of Serpent kind
Lovelier, not those that in *Illyria* chang'd   505
Hermione and *Cadmus*, or the God
In *Epidaurus;* nor to which transform'd
Ammonian Jove, or *Capitoline* was seen,
Hee with *Olympias*, this with her who bore
Scipio the highth of *Rome*. With tract oblique   510
At first, as one who sought access, but fear'd
To interrupt, side-long he works his way.
As when a Ship by skilful Steersman wrought
Nigh River's mouth or Foreland, where the Wind
Veers oft, as oft so steers, and shifts her Sail;   515
So varied hee, and of his tortuous Train
Curl'd many a wanton wreath in sight of *Eve*,
To lure her Eye; shee busied heard the sound
Of rustling Leaves, but minded not, as us'd
To such disport before her through the Field,   520
From every Beast, more duteous at her call,
Than at *Circean* call the Herd disguis'd.
Hee bolder now, uncall'd before her stood;
But as in gaze admiring: Oft he bow'd
His turret Crest, and sleek enamell'd Neck,   525
Fawning, and lick'd the ground whereon she trod.
His gentle dumb expression turn'd at length
The Eye of *Eve* to mark his play; he glad
Of her attention gain'd, with Serpent Tongue
Organic, or impulse of vocal Air,   530

502. *Spires* keeps its Latin force of "loops" or "coils." The theories of several biblical commentators on the serpent's upright stance before its curse to go upon its belly (cf. X, 177) are collected in Williams' *Expositor*, p. 116.

505. *chang'd:* metamorphosed. The word itself alludes to Ovid's story of the metamorphosis of *Cadmus* and Harmonia (*Hermione*) into serpents (*Met.* IV, 563–603).

506. *The God* is Aesculapius, the deity of healing, whom Ovid described (*Met.* XV, 669–74) as appearing like a serpent with head held as high as a man's breast, and with flashing eyes, in his temple in *Epidaurus,* in Argolis.

507–510. In Edward Topsell's *Historie of Serpents* (1608), p. 5, four ancient authorities are sceptically cited for the stories that *Olympias,* the mother of Alexander the Great, was beloved by Jupiter Am-

mon (cf. IV, 277) in the form of a serpent, and that the mother of *Scipio* Africanus, the *highth of Rome,* or greatest of Romans, was similarly loved by the *Capitoline* Jupiter. W. Empson interprets this passage as meaning that "Eve turned into a snake and became Satan's consort" (*Pastoral*, p. 175). But Milton's eye was on the tradition that Eve was charmed by the serpent's beauty—a tradition which led John Salkeld in *A Treatise of Paradise* (1617), p. 218, to surmise that her tempter must have been "that most beautiful serpent Scytile," and not the basilisk, though it was the "king of Serpents."

522. The *Herd disguis'd* are the victims of Circe's power to change men into swine. Homer says that they approached Ulysses' men "like dogs fawning on a returning master" (*Od.* X, 214–19).

530. *Organic:* "as a tool," says A. Williams (*Ex-*

His fraudulent temptation thus began.
   Wonder not, sovran Mistress, if perhaps
Thou canst, who are sole Wonder, much less arm
Thy looks, the Heav'n of mildness, with disdain,
Displeas'd that I approach thee thus, and gaze   535
Insatiate, I thus single, nor have fear'd
Thy awful brow, more awful thus retir'd.
Fairest resemblance of thy Maker fair,
Thee all things living gaze on, all things thine
By gift, and thy Celestial Beauty adore   540
With ravishment beheld, there best beheld
Where universally admir'd: but here
In this enclosure wild, these Beasts among,
Beholders rude, and shallow to discern
Half what in thee is fair, one man except,   545
Who sees thee? (and what is one?) who shouldst be seen
A Goddess among Gods, ador'd and serv'd
By Angels numberless, thy daily Train.
   So gloz'd the Tempter, and his Proem tun'd;
Into the Heart of *Eve* his words made way,   550
Though at the voice much marvelling; at length
Not unamaz'd she thus in answer spake.
   What may this mean?   Language of Man pronounc't
By Tongue of Brute, and human sense exprest?
The first at least of these I thought deni'd   555
To Beasts, whom God on thir Creation-Day
Created mute to all articulate sound;
The latter I demur, for in thir looks
Much reason, and in thir actions oft appears.
Thee, Serpent, subtlest beast of all the field   560
I knew, but not with human voice endu'd;
Redouble then this miracle, and say,
How cam'st thou speakable of mute, and how
To me so friendly grown above the rest
Of brutal kind, that daily are in sight?   565
Say, for such wonder claims attention due.
   To whom the guileful Tempter thus repli'd.
Empress of this fair World, resplendent *Eve,*
Easy to mee it is to tell thee all
What thou command'st and right thou should'st be obey'd: 570
I was at first as other Beasts that graze
The trodden Herb, of abject thoughts and low,

positor, p. 116). Because the devil or the serpent
lacked the power of human speech, the latter had
either to use the former's tongue as an instrument
or else to impel the air in such a way as to make
it seem voice-like or *vocal.*

   532–548. So—like several other tempting serpents
in the scene of Eve's temptation—Andreini's serpent
hails her as

Nature's show-piece, micro-paradise,
To whom all things on earth bow down in praise,
   etc.

   (*L'Adamo* II, vi. In the *Celestial Cycle,* p. 244.)
Satan is behaving traditionally though he may also
speak a contemporary idiom—as D. S. Berkeley sug-

gests in "Précieuse Gallantry and the Seduction of
Eve" in *N&Q,* CXCVI (1951), 337.

   549. *gloz'd* recalls Comus' "glozing courtesy,/
Baited with reasons not unplausible" (*Comus,* 161–
62) in a passage which may also reflect the tone of
comparable scenes in contemporary court drama.

   558–559. *demur:* entertain doubts of. God has
said that the beasts "know/ And reason not contemptibly" (VIII, 373–74).

   563. *speakable of mute:* capable of speech from
a mute condition.

   571–574. Behind the lines is the Aristotelian distinction of the noble pleasures of which men are
capable from the gross limitations of the animals
(*Nicomachean Ethics* I, ix, 9).

As was my food, nor aught but food discern'd
Or Sex, and apprehended nothing high:
Till on a day roving the field, I chanc'd   575
A goodly Tree far distant to behold
Loaden with fruit of fairest colors mixt,
Ruddy and Gold: I nearer drew to gaze;
When from the boughs a savory odor blown,
Grateful to appetite, more pleas'd my sense   580
Than smell of sweetest Fennel, or the Teats
Of Ewe or Goat dropping with Milk at Ev'n,
Unsuckt of Lamb or Kid, that tend thir play.
To satisfy the sharp desire I had
Of tasting those fair Apples, I resolv'd   585
Not to defer; hunger and thirst at once,
Powerful persuaders, quick'n'd at the scent
Of that alluring fruit, urg'd me so keen.
About the mossy Trunk I wound me soon,
For high from ground the branches would require   590
Thy utmost reach or *Adam's:* Round the Tree
All other Beasts that saw, with like desire
Longing and envying stood, but could not reach.
Amid the Tree now got, where plenty hung
Tempting so nigh, to pluck and eat my fill   595
I spar'd not, for such pleasure till that hour
At Feed or Fountain never had I found.
Sated at length, ere long I might perceive
Strange alteration in me, to degree
Of Reason in my inward Powers, and Speech   600
Wanted not long, though to this shape retain'd.
Thenceforth to Speculations high or deep
I turn'd my thoughts, and with capacious mind
Consider'd all things visible in Heav'n,
Or Earth, or Middle, all things fair and good;   605
But all that fair and good in thy Divine
Semblance, and in thy Beauty's heav'nly Ray
United I beheld; no Fair to thine
Equivalent or second, which compell'd
Mee thus, though importune perhaps, to come   610
And gaze, and worship thee of right declar'd
Sovran of Creatures, universal Dame.
    So talk'd the spirited sly Snake; and *Eve*
Yet more amaz'd unwary thus repli'd.
    Serpent, thy overpraising leaves in doubt   615
The virtue of that Fruit, in thee first prov'd:
But say, where grows the Tree, from hence how far?
For many are the Trees of God that grow
In Paradise, and various, yet unknown
To us, in such abundance lies our choice,   620
As leaves a greater store of Fruit untoucht,

Still hanging incorruptible, till men
Grow up to thir provision, and more hands
Help to disburden Nature of her Birth.
    To whom the wily Adder, blithe and glad.   625
Empress, the way is ready, and not long,
Beyond a row of Myrtles, on a Flat,
Fast by a Fountain, one small Thicket past
Of blowing Myrrh and Balm; if thou accept
My conduct, I can bring thee thither soon.   630
    Lead then, said *Eve*. Hee leading swiftly roll'd
In tangles, and made intricate seem straight,
To mischief swift. Hope elevates, and joy
Bright'ns his Crest, as when a wand'ring Fire,
Compact of unctuous vapor, which the Night   635
Condenses, and the cold invirons round,
Kindl'd through agitation to a Flame,
Which oft, they say, some evil Spirit attends,
Hovering and blazing with delusive Light,
Misleads th' amaz'd Night-wanderer from his way   640
To Bogs and Mires, and oft through Pond or Pool,
There swallow'd up and lost, from succor far.
So glister'd the dire Snake, and into fraud
Led *Eve* our credulous Mother, to the Tree
Of prohibition, root of all our woe;   645
Which when she saw, thus to her guide she spake.
    Serpent, we might have spar'd our coming hither,
Fruitless to mee, though Fruit be here to excess,
The credit of whose virtue rest with thee,
Wondrous indeed, if cause of such effects.   650
But of this Tree we may not taste nor touch;
God so commanded, and left that Command
Sole Daughter of his voice; the rest, we live
Law to ourselves, our Reason is our Law.
    To whom the Tempter guilefully repli'd.   655
Indeed? hath God then said that of the Fruit
Of all these Garden Trees ye shall not eat,
Yet Lords declar'd of all in Earth or Air?
    To whom thus *Eve* yet sinless. Of the Fruit
Of each Tree in the Garden we may eat,   660

---

623. *to thir provision:* to numbers proportionate to what has been provided.

624. *Birth* is spelled "bearth" in the original, a form which indicates the meaning of "fruit" of every kind better than the modern spelling of this word.

629. *blowing:* blossoming. Cf. V, 22, and VII, 319.

634–642. John Swan's popular *Speculum Mundi* (1643), pp. 88–89, is a striking parallel. K. Svendsen notes—*ELH*, IX (1942), 220—its definition of the *Ignis fatuus* or *foolish Fire* as "a fat and oily Exhalation, hot and drie," which the "much terrified, ignorant, and superstitious people" have often mistaken for "walking spirits. They are no spirits, and yet lead out of the way, because those who see them are amazed, and look so earnestly after them that they forget their way: and then . . . wander to and fro, . . . sometimes to waters,

pits, and other dangerous places." Cf. *Comus*, 433.

644–645. *the Tree Of prohibition:* a Hebraism for "the forbidden tree."

648. The pun is pathetically made by Spenser in the *Faerie Queene* II, vii, 55; 1–3:
    Here also sprong that goodly golden fruit,
    With which Acontius got his lover trew,
    Whom he had long time sought with fruitlesse suit.

653. The Hebraism *Daughter of his voice* is explained by W. Hunter in *MLQ*, IX (1948), 180, as a translation of *Bath Kol*, "a voice sent from heaven," but a revelation of God's will of less weight than an absolute command. Eve is softening the divine prohibition of the Tree of Knowledge.

654. An echo of St. Paul's remark about the virtuous Gentiles who, though outside Hebrew law, were "a law unto themselves" (Rom. ii, 14).

But of the Fruit of this fair Tree amidst
The Garden, God hath said, Ye shall not eat
Thereof, nor shall ye touch it, lest ye die.
  She scarce had said, though brief, when now more bold
The Tempter, but with show of Zeal and Love   665
To Man, and indignation at his wrong,
New part puts on, and as to passion mov'd,
Fluctuates disturb'd, yet comely, and in act
Rais'd, as of some great matter to begin.
As when of old some Orator renown'd   670
In *Athens* or free *Rome,* where Eloquence
Flourish'd, since mute, to some great cause addrest,
Stood in himself collected, while each part,
Motion, each act won audience ere the tongue,
Sometimes in highth began, as no delay   675
Of Preface brooking through his Zeal of Right.
So standing, moving, or to highth upgrown
The Tempter all impassion'd thus began.
  O Sacred, Wise, and Wisdom-giving Plant,
Mother of Science, Now I feel thy Power   680
Within me clear, not only to discern
Things in thir Causes, but to trace the ways
Of highest Agents, deem'd however wise.
Queen of this Universe, do not believe
Those rigid threats of Death; ye shall not Die: 685
How should ye? by the Fruit? it gives you Life
To Knowledge: By the Threat'ner? look on mee,
Mee who have touch'd and tasted, yet both live,
And life more perfet have attain'd than Fate
Meant mee, by vent'ring higher than my Lot.   690
Shall that be shut to Man, which to the Beast
Is open? or will God incense his ire
For such a petty Trespass, and not praise
Rather your dauntless virtue, whom the pain
Of Death denounc't, whatever thing Death be,   695
Deterr'd not from achieving what might lead
To happier life, knowledge of Good and Evil;
Of good, how just? of evil, if what is evil
Be real, why not known, since easier shunn'd?
God therefore cannot hurt ye, and be just;   700
Not just, not God; not fear'd then, nor obey'd:
Your fear itself of Death removes the fear.
Why then was this forbid? Why but to awe,
Why but to keep ye low and ignorant,

670–675. Satan is abusing the art of the orator that Milton admired as it was practiced by the democratic orators of Athens who
    Wielded at will the fierce Democracy.
        (*PR* IV, 269)
674. *audience:* attention, hearing.
675. *highth:* height of feeling.
680. *Science* keeps its Latin meaning of "knowledge."
683. *highest Agents:* active beings of the highest rank, angels or perhaps even God himself.
685. "And the serpent said unto the woman, ye shall not surely die" (Gen. iii, 4).

686–687. *Life To Knowledge:* life as well as knowledge.
703–709. So Henry Lawrence (to whose son, Edward, Milton's *Sonnet XX* was addressed) explains in *Our Communion and War with Angels* (1646), p. 98, that when Satan tempted Eve he "accused God" and "told her *they should be as Gods, knowing good and evill,*" this temptation tooke, now hee intimated that God made that restraynt out of envy, because hee would have none so great and so happy as himself." Interpreting the fall philosophically in *Conjectura Cabbalistica,* Henry More had the serpent tell Eve

His worshippers; he knows that in the day   705
Ye Eat thereof, your Eyes that seem so clear,
Yet are but dim, shall perfetly be then
Op'n'd and clear'd, and ye shall be as Gods,
Knowing both Good and Evil as they know.
That ye should be as Gods, since I as Man,   710
Internal Man, is but proportion meet,
I of brute human, yee of human Gods.
So ye shall die perhaps, by putting off
Human, to put on Gods, death to be wisht,
Though threat'n'd, which no worse than this can bring.   715
And what are Gods that Man may not become
As they, participating God-like food?
The Gods are first, and that advantage use
On our belief, that all from them proceeds;
I question it, for this fair Earth I see,   720
Warm'd by the Sun, producing every kind,
Them nothing: If they all things, who enclos'd
Knowledge of Good and Evil in this Tree,
That who so eats thereof, forthwith attains
Wisdom without their leave? and wherein lies   725
Th' offense, that Man should thus attain to know?
What can your knowledge hurt him, or this Tree
Impart against his will if all be his?
Or is it envy, and can envy dwell
In heav'nly breasts? these, these and many more   730
Causes import your need of this fair Fruit.
Goddess humane, reach then, and freely taste.
      He ended, and his words replete with guile
Into her heart too easy entrance won:
Fixt on the Fruit she gaz'd, which to behold   735
Might tempt alone, and in her ears the sound
Yet rung of his persuasive words, impregn'd
With Reason, to her seeming, and with Truth;
Meanwhile the hour of Noon drew on, and wak'd
An eager appetite, rais'd by the smell   *reason perverted, the   740
So savory of that Fruit, which with desire,   body takes over.
Inclinable now grown to touch or taste, –hangs down
Solicited her longing eye; yet first
Pausing a while, thus to herself she mus'd.
      Great are thy Virtues, doubtless, best of Fruits,   745
Though kept from Man, and worthy to be admir'd,
Whose taste, too long forborne, at first assay
Gave elocution to the mute, and taught
The Tongue not made for Speech to speak thy praise:

that "God indeed loves to keep his creatures in
awe; . . . but he knows very well that if you
take your liberty with us, and satiate yourselves
freely with your own will, your eyes will be wonderfully opened, . . . and like God know all things
whatsoever good or evil." "To both More
and Milton," says M. Nicolson in quoting this
passage in PQ, VI (1927), 17, "the ethical import
of the fall is that man followed his instincts and
will, not his reason." Cf. 1177–81 below, n.
      711. Internal Man corresponds to the serpent's
statement (l. 600 above) that his inward Powers

have become human though his form is unchanged.
      722. If they (produced) all things.
      731. import: indicate, prove.
      732. humane may mean "kind," but Ants Oras
is probably right in taking it literally as combined
with Goddess in a typically Miltonic oxymoron—
in MLR, XLIX (1954), 51–53.
      741–742. Eve (in Gen. iii, 6) yields when she
sees that the tree is "good for food . . . and a
tree to be desired to make one wise."
      742. Inclinable: easily inclined (as Eve now is).

Thy praise hee also who forbids thy use,   750
Conceals not from us, naming thee the Tree
Of Knowledge, knowledge both of good and evil;
Forbids us then to taste, but his forbidding
Commends thee more, while it infers the good
By thee communicated, and our want: 755
For good unknown, sure is not had, or had
And yet unknown, is as not had at all.
In plain then, what forbids he but to know,
Forbids us good, forbids us to be wise?
Such prohibitions bind not. But if Death   760
Bind us with after-bands, what profits then
Our inward freedom? In the day we eat
Of this fair Fruit, our doom is, we shall die.
How dies the Serpent? hee hath eat'n and lives,
And knows, and speaks, and reasons, and discerns,   *applying reason alone 765
Irrational till then. For us alone   no faith
Was death invented? or to us deni'd
This intellectual food, for beasts reserv'd?
For Beasts it seems: yet that one Beast which first
Hath tasted, envies not, but brings with joy   770
The good befall'n him, Author unsuspect,
Friendly to man, far from deceit or guile.
What fear I then, rather what know to fear
Under this ignorance of Good and Evil,
Of God or Death, of Law or Penalty?   775
Here grows the Cure of all, this Fruit Divine,
Fair to the Eye, inviting to the Taste,   *this is a better argument
Of virtue to make wise: what hinders then   than Satan's. Self-tempt.
To reach, and feed at once both Body and Mind?   Reduces Satan more.
    So saying, her rash hand in evil hour   780
Forth reaching to the Fruit, she pluck'd, she eat:
Earth felt the wound, and Nature from her seat
Sighing through all her Works gave signs of woe,
That all was lost. Back to the Thicket slunk
The guilty Serpent, and well might, for *Eve*   785
Intent now wholly on her taste, naught else
Regarded, such delight till then, as seem'd,
In Fruit she never tasted, whether true
Or fancied so, through expectation high
Of knowledge, nor was God-head from her thought.   790
Greedily she ingorg'd without restraint,
And knew not eating Death: Satiate at length,
And hight'n'd as with Wine, jocund and boon,
Thus to herself she pleasingly began.
    O Sovran, virtuous, precious of all Trees   795

---

758. *In plain:* in clear language.
771. *Author unsuspect:* authority not to be suspected.
781. *eat* was the usual spelling for the past tense.
Probably the word rhymed with *seat*.
782-784. Cf. IX, 1000-1004, and X, 651-714.
The thought was widespread in English poetry
from John Gower's expression of it in the *Mirrour
de l'Homme* (ll. 26,810-26,820) to Joseph Beau-

mont's assertion that when Eve touched the for-
bidden fruit,
        she reach'd away
All the Worlds Blisse whil'st she the Apple took:
When low, the Earth did move, the Heav'ns did
        stay,
Beasts and Birds shiver'd, absent *Adam* shook.
                    (*Psyche* VI, 254, 1-4)
    792. *knew not eating death:* knew not that she
was eating death.

In Paradise, of operation blest
To Sapience, hitherto obscur'd, infam'd,
And thy fair Fruit let hang, as to no end
Created; but henceforth my early care,
Not without Song, each Morning, and due praise   800
Shall tend thee, and the fertile burden ease
Of thy full branches offer'd free to all;
Till dieted by thee I grow mature
In knowledge, as the Gods who all things know;
Though others envy what they cannot give;   805
For had the gift been theirs, it had not here
Thus grown. Experience, next to thee I owe,
Best guide; not following thee, I had remain'd
In ignorance, thou op'n'st Wisdom's way,
And giv'st access, though secret she retire.   810
And I perhaps am secret; Heav'n is high,
High and remote to see from thence distinct
Each thing on Earth; and other care perhaps
May have diverted from continual watch
Our great Forbidder, safe with all his Spies   *a change in god's   815
About him. But to *Adam* in what sort   *status*
Shall I appear? shall I to him make known
As yet my change, and give him to partake
Full happiness with mee, or rather not.
But keep the odds of Knowledge in my power   820
Without Copartner? so to add what wants
In Female Sex, the more to draw his Love,   *rebellious female*
And render me more equal, and perhaps,
A thing not undesirable, sometime
Superior: for inferior who is free?   825
This may be well: but what if God have seen,
And Death ensue? then I shall be no more,
And *Adam* wedded to another *Eve*,
Shall live with her enjoying, I extinct;
A death to think. Confirm'd then I resolve,   830
Adam shall share with me in bliss or woe:
So dear I love him, that with him all deaths   *good logic*
I could endure, without him live no life.
 So saying, from the Tree her step she turn'd,
But first low Reverence done, as to the power   835
That dwelt within, whose presence had infus'd
Into the plant scient ial sap, deriv'd
From Nectar, drink of Gods. *Adam* the while

---

797. *To Sapience:* gifted with power to confer
wisdom. *infam'd:* misreputed, made the subject of
evil fame.
 804. The plural, *Gods,* shows that Eve is so
muddled that she echoes Satan's equivocal use of
the word in l. 712 above, and that she has been
deceived by his reasoning in ll. 720–29. Cf. I,
116, n.
 811. *secret:* hidden, unseen. The thought reflects Job xxii, 13–14: "How doth God know? can
he judge through the dark cloud?"
 825. Contrast V, 792–93.
 827–833. Eve's jealousy is a commonplace which
has been traced to the *Zohar* by D. Saurat in *Milton*

et le matérialisme chretien, p. 95; to *Yosippon* by
H. Fletcher in *SP,* XXI (1924), 496 ff.; to Rabbi
Eliezer and other rabbinical sources by D. C. Allen
in *MLN,* LXIII (1948), 262; to John Mercerus,
Peter Martyr, and other Christian commentators by
A. Williams in *Expositor,* p. 123; and to Milton's
own inventiveness by C. S. Lewis in *Preface,* p.
121.
 832. Milton seems to have been consciously varying the terms of Lydia's devotion in the closing
lines of Horace's *Ode* (III, ix), familiar in translations by Herrick and Ben Jonson.
 837. *sciential:* endowed or endowing with knowledge.

Waiting desirous her return, had wove
Of choicest Flow'rs a Garland to adorn   840
Her Tresses, and her rural labors crown,
As Reapers oft are wont thir Harvest Queen.
Great joy he promis'd to his thoughts, and new
Solace in her return, so long delay'd;
Yet oft his heart, divine of something ill,   845
Misgave him; hee the falt'ring measure felt;
And forth to meet her went, the way she took
That Morn when first they parted; by the Tree
Of Knowledge he must pass; there he her met,
Scarce from the Tree returning; in her hand   850
A bough of fairest fruit that downy smil'd,
New gather'd, and ambrosial smell diffus'd.
To him she hasted, in her face excuse
Came Prologue, and Apology to prompt,
Which with bland words at will she thus addrest.   855
   Hast thou not wonder'd, *Adam*, at my stay?
Thee I have misst, and thought it long, depriv'd
Thy presence, agony of love till now
Not felt, nor shall be twice, for never more
Mean I to try, what rash untri'd I sought,   860
The pain of absence from thy sight.   But strange
Hath been the cause, and wonderful to hear:
This Tree is not as we are told, a Tree
Of danger tasted, nor to evil unknown
Op'ning the way, but of Divine effect   865
To open Eyes, and make them Gods who taste;
And hath been tasted such: the Serpent wise,
Or not restrain'd as wee, or not obeying,
Hath eat'n of the fruit, and is become,
Not dead, as we are threat'n'd, but thenceforth   870
Endu'd with human voice and human sense,
Reasoning to admiration, and with mee
Persuasively hath so prevail'd, that I
Have also tasted, and have also found
Th' effects to correspond, opener mine Eyes,   875
Dim erst, dilated Spirits, ampler Heart,
And growing up to Godhead; which for thee
Chiefly I sought, without thee can despise.
For bliss, as thou hast part, to me is bliss,
Tedious, unshar'd with thee, and odious soon.   880
Thou therefore also taste, that equal Lot
May join us, equal Joy, as equal Love;
Lest thou not tasting, different degree
Disjoin us, and I then too late renounce
Deity for thee, when Fate will not permit.   885
   Thus *Eve* with Count'nance blithe her story told;

839. *wove:* woven.
845. *divine:* foreseeing. A Latinism. Compare
the verb "divine," in X, 357.
846. *the falt'ring measure:* the irregular beat.
853. *excuse Came Prologue, etc.:* excuse came like
the *Prologue* to a speech or play to *prompt* or lead
on the following *Apology,* or formal defence of her
conduct.

860. *rash untri'd:* because I was *rash* and it was
untried or unfamiliar.
864. *tasted:* if tasted.
867. *tasted:* proved by tasting.
872. *to admiration:* to the point of seeming
marvellous.

But in her Cheek distemper flushing glow'd.
On th' other side, *Adam*, soon as he heard
The fatal Trespass done by *Eve*, amaz'd,
Astonied stood and Blank, while horror chill   890
Ran through his veins, and all his joints relax'd;
From his slack hand the Garland wreath'd for *Eve*
Down dropp'd, and all the faded Roses shed:
Speechless he stood and pale, till thus at length
First to himself he inward silence broke.   895
   O fairest of Creation, last and best
Of all God's Works, Creature in whom excell'd
Whatever can to sight or thought be form'd,
Holy, divine, good, amiable, or sweet!
How art thou lost, how on a sudden lost,   900
Defac't, deflow'r'd, and now to Death devote?
Rather how hast thou yielded to transgress
The strict forbiddance, how to violate
The sacred Fruit forbidd'n! some cursed fraud
Of Enemy hath beguil'd thee, yet unknown,   905
And mee with thee hath ruin'd, for with thee
Certain my resolution is to Die;
How can I live without thee, how forgo
Thy sweet Converse and Love so dearly join'd,
To live again in these wild Woods forlorn?   910
Should God create another *Eve*, and I
Another Rib afford, yet loss of thee
Would never from my heart; no no, I feel
The Link of Nature draw me: Flesh of Flesh,
Bone of my Bone thou art, and from thy State   915
Mine never shall be parted, bliss or woe.
   So having said, as one from sad dismay
Recomforted, and after thoughts disturb'd
Submitting to what seem'd remediless,
Thus in calm mood his Words to *Eve* he turn'd.   920
   Bold deed thou hast presum'd, advent'rous *Eve*,

[handwritten margin note at lines 905–907: "— Adam starts becoming heroic"]

---

890. The language suggests both Job xvii, 8, "Upright men shall be astonied at this," and Virgil's description of Aeneas' horror:
Mute and amaz'd, my hair with terror stood,
Fear Shrunk my sinews, and congeal'd my blood.
   (*Aen.* III, 29–30. Dryden's translation)
In his unpublished Vanderbilt thesis W. B. Hunter quotes Charron's *Of Wisdom* to show what fear was supposed to do to moral resistance: Horror, said Charron, "wastes and weakens the Soul, deprives us of the use of our Reason, . . . adulterates the whole Man, binds up his Senses, and lays his Virtues to sleep" (Stanhope's translation—1697—I, 227).
892–895. Many remotely possible classical parallels for this passage are capped by E. M. W. Tillyard (in *TLS*, July 1, 1949, p. 429) from Statius' *Thebaid* VII, 148–50, where the frightened Bacchus drops his garlands, "while the grapes that fall from his horned head are *unimpaired* and as such could well have suggested the opposite condition of Adam's roses."
901. *devote*: doomed. Cf. III, 208.
910. C. S. Lewis (*Preface*, p. 67), Brooks and

Hardy (*Poems of Mr. John Milton*, pp. 273–74), and M. Giovanni (*Explicator*, Oct. 1953, xii, 1) follow Thyer in regarding the wildness of the woods as subjective and, due to Adam's "mental distress." Challenging them (in *Explicator*, June, 1954, xii, 8), G. Koretz notes that vegetation in Eden is "Wild above Rule or Art" (V, 297), and that the garden is a "Wilderness of sweets" (V, 294). The connotation of *wild* may change from its earlier application to Eden, but not its basic meaning.
914. Cf. VIII, 495–99, n.
914–916. Most familiar among many precedents for Adam's behavior for Milton was St. Augustine's saying that, "it is to be thought, that the first man did not yield to his wife in this transgression of God's precep, as if he thought she spoke the truth: but only compelled to it by his social love to her, . . . for the apostle says: 'Adam was not deceived: but the woman was deceived'" (*City of God* XII, xi, John Healy's translation). St. Paul's words (I Tim. ii, 14) are paraphrased in l. 999 below.

And peril great provok't, who thus hath dar'd
Had it been only coveting to Eye
That sacred Fruit, sacred to abstinence,
Much more to taste it under ban to touch.   925
But past who can recall, or done undo?
Not God Omnipotent, nor Fate; yet so
Perhaps thou shalt not Die, perhaps the Fact
Is not so heinous now, foretasted Fruit,
Profan'd first by the Serpent, by him first   930
Made common and unhallow'd ere our taste;
Nor yet on him found deadly, he yet lives,
Lives, as thou said'st, and gains to live as Man
Higher degree of Life, inducement strong
To us, as likely tasting to attain   935
Proportional ascent, which cannot be
But to be Gods, or Angels Demi-gods.
Nor can I think that God, Creator wise,
Though threat'ning, will in earnest so destroy
Us his prime Creatures, dignifi'd so high,   940
Set over all his Works, which in our Fall,
For us created, needs with us must fail,
Dependent made; so God shall uncreate,
Be frustrate, do, undo, and labor lose,
Not well conceiv'd of God, who though his Power   945
Creation could repeat, yet would be loath
Us to abolish, lest the Adversary
Triumph and say; Fickle their State whom God
Most Favors, who can please him long?   Mee first
He ruin'd, now Mankind; whom will he next?   950
Matter of scorn, not to be given the Foe.
However I with thee have fixt my Lot,
Certain to undergo like doom; if Death
Consort with thee, Death is to mee as Life;
So forcible within my heart I feel   955
The Bond of Nature draw me to my own,
My own in thee, for what thou art is mine;
Our State cannot be sever'd, we are one,
One Flesh; to lose thee were to lose myself.
    So *Adam,* and thus *Eve* to him repli'd.   960
O glorious trial of exceeding Love,
Illustrious evidence, example high!
Ingaging me to emulate, but short
Of thy perfection, how shall I attain,
Adam, from whose dear side I boast me sprung,   965
And gladly of our Union hear thee speak,
One Heart, one Soul in both; whereof good proof
This day affords, declaring thee resolv'd,
Rather than Death or aught than Death more dread
Shall separate us, linkt in Love so dear,   970

* Deist argument

922. *hath,* which makes the thought a generaliza-
tion, is the reading of the second edition; *hast,* of
the first. See the discussion by B. A. Wright in
RES, n. s. V (1954), 170.
    947. Cf. the meaning of *Adversary* in I, 361,
and VI, 282.
    953. *Certain:* resolved. A Latinism, translating

Aeneas' phrase, *certus eundi,* expressing his determination to leave Carthage (*Aen.* IV, 554).
    960–989. Eve's application of the *trial by love*
to Adam is restrained here in comparison with
her pressure upon him in Grotius' corresponding
scene in *Adamus Exul* (V, i; *Cycle,* 180–84) and
in Andreini's *L'Adamo* (III, i; *Cycle,* pp. 254–57).

To undergo with mee one Guilt, one Crime,
If any be, of tasting this fair Fruit,
Whose virtue, for of good still good proceeds,
Direct, or by occasion hath presented
This happy trial of thy Love, which else   975
So eminently never had been known.
Were it I thought Death menac't would ensue
This my attempt, I would sustain alone
The worst, and not persuade thee, rather die
Deserted, than oblige thee with a fact   980
Pernicious to thy Peace, chiefly assur'd
Remarkably so late of thy so true,
So faithful Love unequall'd; but I feel
Far otherwise th' event, not Death, but Life
Augmented, op'n'd Eyes, new Hopes, new Joys,   985
Taste so Divine, that what of sweet before
Hath toucht my sense, flat seems to this, and harsh.
On my experience, *Adam,* freely taste,
And fear of Death deliver to the Winds.
    So saying, she embrac'd him, and for joy   *what, no hand holding!* 990
Tenderly wept, much won that he his Love
Had so ennobl'd, as of choice to incur
Divine displeasure for her sake, or Death.
In recompense (for such compliance bad
Such recompense best merits) from the bough   995
She gave him of that fair enticing Fruit
With liberal hand: he scrupl'd not to eat
Against his better knowledge, not deceiv'd,
But fondly overcome with Female charm.
Earth trembl'd from her entrails, as again   1000
In pangs, and Nature gave a second groan,
Sky low'r'd, and muttering Thunder, some sad drops
Wept at completing of the mortal Sin
Original; while *Adam* took no thought,
Eating his fill, nor *Eve* to iterate   1005
Her former trespass fear'd, the more to soothe
Him with her lov'd society, that now
As with new Wine intoxicated both
They swim in mirth, and fancy that they feel
Divinity within them breeding wings   1010
Wherewith to scorn the Earth: but that false Fruit
Far other operation first display'd,
Carnal desire inflaming, hee on *Eve*
Began to cast lascivious Eyes, she him
As wantonly repaid; in Lust they burn: 1015
Till *Adam* thus 'gan *Eve* to dalliance move.
    Eve, now I see thou are exact of taste,

---

980. *Oblige* keeps its Latin force of "involve in guilt." *fact:* deed (of evil), crime.

999. Cf. ll. 914–16 above, n.

1003. In *CD* I, xi (C.E. XV, 180–82) Milton wrote that "sin originated, first, in the instigation of the devil," and that "undoubtedly all sinned in Adam." He recognized the "principle uniformly acted upon in the divine proceedings, and recognized by all nations, . . . that the penalty incurred by the violation of things sacred (and such was the tree of the knowledge of good and evil) attaches not only to the criminal himself, but to the whole of his posterity."

1017. Milton plays on the literal and figurative meanings of *teste,* remembering Cicero's remark that "a man of discerning heart does not always lack a discerning palate" (*De finibus* II, viii).

And elegant, of Sapience no small part,
Since to each meaning savor we apply,
And Palate call judicious; I the praise   1020
Yield thee, so well this day thou hast purvey'd.
Much pleasure we have lost, while we abstain'd
From this delightful Fruit, nor known till now
True relish, tasting; if such pleasure be
In things to us forbidden, it might be wish'd,   1025
For this one Tree had been forbidden ten.
But come, so well refresh't, now let us play,
As meet is, after such delicious Fare;
For never did thy Beauty since the day
I saw thee first and wedded thee, adorn'd   1030
With all perfections, so inflame my sense
With ardor to enjoy thee, fairer now
Than ever, bounty of this virtuous Tree.
    So said he, and forbore not glance or toy
Of amorous intent, well understood   1035
Of *Eve,* whose Eye darted contagious Fire.
Her hand he seiz'd, and to a shady bank,
Thick overhead with verdant roof imbowr'd
He led her nothing loath; Flow'rs were the Couch,
Pansies, and Violets, and Asphodel,   1040
And Hyacinth, Earth's freshest softest lap.
There they thir fill of Love and Love's disport
Took largely, of thir mutual guilt the Seal,
The solace of thir sin, till dewy sleep
Oppress'd them, wearied with thir amorous play.   1045
Soon as the force of that fallacious Fruit,
That with exhilarating vapor bland
About thir spirits had play'd, and inmost powers
Made err, was now exhal'd, and grosser sleep
Bred of unkindly fumes, with conscious dreams   1050
Encumber'd, now had left them, up they rose
As from unrest, and each the other viewing,
Soon found thir Eyes how op'n'd, and thir minds
How dark'n'd; innocence, that as a veil
Had shadow'd them from knowing ill, was gone,   1055
Just confidence, and native righteousness,
And honor from about them, naked left
To guilty shame: hee cover'd, but his Robe
Uncover'd more.   So rose the *Danite* strong
Herculean Samson from the Harlot-lap   1060
Of *Philistean Dalilah,* and wak'd
Shorn of his strength, They destitute and bare
Of all thir virtue: silent, and in face

1037–1045. The scene resembles that between
Zeus and Hera in *Iliad* XIV, 292–353.
    1042. Cf. the words of the lewd woman in
Proverbs vii, 18: "Come, let us take our fill of
love until the morning; let us solace ourselves
with loves." In *Expositor,* p. 125, Williams notes
that the Protestant commentator John Mercerus
and the great Catholic Marin Mersenne more or less
favorably discussed the "Jewish notion that the first
effect of the fruit was to influence carnal appetite."
    1049. The *grosser sleep* contrasts with Adam's

Aery light sleep in V, 4.
    1050. *unkindly:* unnatural.
    1058. The thought follows Psalm cix, 29: "Let
mine adversaries be clothed with shame."   Cf. *SA,*
841–42.
    1059. *Samson,* whose betrayal by his Philistine
wife *Dalilah* is recorded in Judges xvi, came of the
tribe of Dan.
    1062–1064. Milton had in mind the first of the
four degrees of death that he defined in *CD* I, xii.
Cf. X, 49–53, n.

Confounded long they sat, as struck'n mute,
Till *Adam,* though not less than *Eve* abasht,   1065
At length gave utterance to these words constrain'd.
　O *Eve,* in evil hour thou didst give ear
To that false Worm, of whomsoever taught
To counterfeit Man's voice, true in our Fall,
False in our promis'd Rising; since our Eyes   1070
Op'n'd we find indeed, and find we know
Both Good and Evil, Good lost, and Evil got,
Bad Fruit of Knowledge, if this be to know,
Which leaves us naked thus, of Honor void,
Of Innocence, of Faith, of Purity,   1075
Our wonted Ornaments now soil'd and stain'd,
And in our Faces evident the signs
Of foul concupiscence; whence evil store;
Even shame, the last of evils; of the first
Be sure then. How shall I behold the face   1080
Henceforth of God or Angel, erst with joy
And rapture so oft beheld? those heav'nly shapes
Will dazzle now this earthly, with thir blaze
Insufferably bright. O might I here
In solitude live savage, in some glade   1085
Obscur'd, where highest Woods impenetrable
To Star or Sun-light, spread thir umbrage broad,
And brown as Evening: Cover me ye Pines,
Ye Cedars, with innumerable boughs
Hide me, where I may never see them more.   1090
But let us now, as in bad plight, devise
What best may for the present serve to hide
The Parts of each from other, that seem most
To shame obnoxious, and unseemliest seen,
Some Tree whose broad smooth Leaves together sew'd,   1095
And girded on our loins, may cover round
Those middle parts, that this new comer, Shame,
There sit not, and reproach us as unclean.
　So counsell'd hee, and both together went
Into the thickest Wood, there soon they chose   1100
The Figtree, not that kind for Fruit renown'd,
But such as at this day to *Indians* known   *turned to savages*

1070–1076. Like most commentators, Milton derived the name of the Tree of Knowledge "from the event; for since Adam tasted it, we not only know evil, but we know good only by means of evil" (*CD* I, x; C. E. XV, 115). Cf. *Areopagitica* (p. 728).

1086. Cf. "the shady roof/ Of branching Elm Star-proof" in *Arcades,* 89.

1088. *brown:* shadowy, dark. Cf. *Imbrown'd* in IV, 246.

1091–1098. In *CD* I, xii (C. E. XV, 204) Milton interprets "They knew that they were naked" (Gen. iii, 7) as signifying "a conscious degradation of mind, whence arises shame," as a result of which "they sewed fig-leaves together and made themselves aprons."

1101–1106. In *Biographia Literaria* xxii, Coleridge called these lines *"creation* rather than *painting,"* although he was aware of Warton's attribu-

tion of the passage to the description of the banyan or "arched Indian Figtree" in Gerard's *Herball* (1597; III, cxxix), which declares that its leaves are as broad as the shields of Amazons and that its branches touch the ground, "where they take root and grow in such sort, that those twigs become great trees; . . . by meanes whereof it cometh to passe, that of one tree is made a great wood . . . which the Indians do use for coverture against the extreme heate of the sun. Some . . . cut loopholes or windowes in some places, to the end to receiue thereby the fresh cool air, . . . as also for the light that they may see their cattell that feed thereby. From which vault doth rebound an admirable echo. . . . The first or mother of this wood is hard to be known from the children." In *M.&S.,* pp. 31–32, Svendsen lists countless similar accounts of the Indian figtree in contemporary encyclopaedias.

In *Malabar* or *Decan* spreads her Arms
Branching so broad and long, that in the ground
The bended Twigs take root, and Daughters grow   1105
About the Mother Tree, a Pillar'd shade
High overarch't, and echoing Walks between;
There oft the *Indian* Herdsman shunning heat
Shelters in cool, and tends his pasturing Herds
At Loopholes cut through thickest shade: Those Leaves   1110
They gather'd, broad as *Amazonian* Targe,
And with what skill they had, together sew'd,
To gird thir waist, vain Covering if to hide
Thir guilt and dreaded shame; O how unlike
To that first naked Glory.   Such of late   1115
Columbus found th' *American* so girt
With feather'd Cincture, naked else and wild
Among the Trees on Isles and woody Shores.
Thus fenc't, and as they thought, thir shame in part
Cover'd, but not at rest or ease of Mind,   1120
They sat them down to weep, nor only Tears
Rain'd at thir Eyes, but high Winds worse within
Began to rise, high Passions, Anger, Hate,
Mistrust, Suspicion, Discord, and shook sore
Thir inward State of Mind, calm Region once   1125
And full of Peace, now toss't and turbulent:
For Understanding rul'd not, and the Will
Heard not her lore, both in subjection now
To sensual Appetite, who from beneath
Usurping over sovran Reason claim'd   1130
Superior sway: From thus distemper'd breast,
Adam, estrang'd in look and alter'd style,
Speech intermitted thus to *Eve* renew'd.
    Would thou hadst heark'n'd to my words, and stay'd
With me, as I besought thee, when that strange   1135
Desire of wand'ring this unhappy Morn,
I know not whence possess'd thee; we had then
Remain'd still happy, not as now, despoil'd
Of all our good, sham'd, naked, miserable.
Let none henceforth seek needless cause to approve   1140
The Faith they owe; when earnestly they seek
Such proof, conclude, they then begin to fail.
    To whom soon mov'd with touch of blame thus *Eve.*
What words have past thy Lips, *Adam* severe,
Imput'st thou that to my default, or will   1145
Of wand'ring, as thou call'st it, which who knows
But might as ill have happ'n'd thou being by,
Or to thyself perhaps: hadst thou been there,
Or here th' attempt, thou couldst not have discern'd
Fraud in the Serpent, speaking as he spake;   1150
No ground of enmity between us known,
Why hee should mean me ill, or seek to harm.

1122–1131. In *CD* I, xii (C. E. XV, 207) Adam's punishment "consists first in the loss, or at least in the darkening to a great extent of that right reason which enabled him to discern the chief good, and in which consisted the life of the understanding." Cf. VI, 41, and XII, 98.

1132. *alter'd style:* changed manner (of speech).
1141. *owe:* possess. Adam recalls Eve's words in ll. 335–36 above.
1144. The phrase is a Homeric warning to rash speakers (*Il.* XIV, 83).

Was I to have never parted from thy side?
As good have grown there still a lifeless Rib.
Being as I am, why didst not thou the Head   1155
Command me absolutely not to go,
Going into such danger as thou said'st?
Too facile then thou didst not much gainsay,
Nay, didst permit, approve, and fair dismiss.
Hadst thou been firm and fixt in thy dissent,   1160
Neither had I transgress'd, nor thou with mee.
    To whom then first incenst Adam repli'd.
Is this the Love, is this the recompense
Of mine to thee, ingrateful Eve, express't
Immutable when thou wert lost, not I,   1165
Who might have liv'd and joy'd immortal bliss,
Yet willingly chose rather Death with thee:
And am I now upbraided, as the cause
Of thy transgressing? not enough severe,
It seems, in thy restraint: what could I more?   1170
I warn'd thee, I admonish'd thee, foretold
The danger, and the lurking Enemy
That lay in wait; beyond this had been force,
And force upon free Will hath here no place.
But confidence then bore thee on, secure   1175
Either to meet no danger, or to find
Matter of glorious trial; and perhaps   *moment of awareness*
I also err'd in overmuch admiring
What seem'd in thee so perfet, that I thought
No evil durst attempt thee, but I rue   1180
That error now, which is become my crime,
And thou th' accuser. Thus it shall befall
Him who to worth in Woman overtrusting
Lets her Will rule; restraint she will not brook,
And left to herself, if evil thence ensue,   1185
Shee first his weak indulgence will accuse.
    Thus they in mutual accusation spent
The fruitless hours, but neither self-condemning,
And of thir vain contést appear'd no end.

The End of the Ninth Book

1155. In a different tone Eve has called Adam her *Head* in IV, 443.

1164. In ll. 956–67 above, Eve has praised Adam for his love *express't Immutable*, i. e. proved unchangeable by his action.

1177–1181. M. Nicolson is surely right in recognizing more than a chance resemblance between Milton's contrast of will with reason and Henry More's stress in *Conjectura Cabbalistica* upon "spirit, reason, and man, first as *creative,* and then as *regulative* principles," and upon Eve as representing the instincts and the Will. (Cf. ll. 703–

709 above, n.). More's value of the Will, in spite of his treatment of the temptation as an exaggeration of its influence upon a feminized Adam, leads toward the psychological interpretation of the Fall by P. Turner in "Woman and the Fall of Man" in *English Studies,* XXIX (1948), 1–18, and M. Bertschlinger's "Man's Part in the Fall of Woman" in *English Studies,* XXXI, 49–64.

1183. *Women* is the reading of all the early editions, but Bentley's emendation to *Woman* seems inevitable.

BOOK X

THE ARGUMENT

Man's *transgression known, the Guardian Angels forsake Paradise, and return up to Heaven to approve thir vigilance, and are approv'd, God declaring that the entrance of* Satan *could not be by them prevented.* He sends his Son to judge the Transgressors, *who descends and gives Sentence accordingly; then in pity clothes them both, and re-ascends.* Sin *and* Death *sitting till then at the Gates of Hell, by wondrous sympathy feeling the success of* Satan *in this new World, and the sin by Man there committed, resolve to sit no longer confin'd in Hell, but to follow* Satan *thir Sire up to the place of Man: To make the way easier from Hell to this World to and fro, they pave a broad Highway or Bridge over* Chaos, *according to the Track that* Satan *first made; then preparing for Earth, they meet him proud of his success returning to Hell; thir mutual gratulation.* Satan *arrives at* Pandemonium, *in full assembly relates with boasting his success against Man; instead of applause is entertained with a general hiss by all his audience, transform'd with himself also suddenly into Serpents, according to his doom giv'n in Paradise; then deluded with a show of the forbidden Tree springing up before them, they greedily reaching to take of the Fruit, chew dust and bitter ashes.* The proceedings of Sin *and* Death; *God foretells the final Victory of his Son over them, and the renewing of all things; but for the present commands his Angels to make several alterations in the Heavens and Elements.* Adam *more and more perceiving his fall'n condition heavily bewails, rejects the condolement of* Eve: *she persists and at length appeases him: then to evade the Curse likely to fall on thir Offspring, proposes to* Adam *violent ways, which he approves not, but conceiving better hope, puts her in mind of the late Promise made them, that her Seed should be reveng'd on the Serpent, and exhorts her with him to seek Peace of the offended Deity, by repentance and supplication.*

> Meanwhile the heinous and despiteful act
> Of *Satan* done in Paradise, and how
> Hee in the Serpent had perverted *Eve,*
> Her Husband shee, to taste the fatal fruit,
> Was known in Heav'n; for what can scape the Eye   5
> Of God All-seeing, or deceive his Heart
> Omniscient, who in all things wise and just,
> Hinder'd not *Satan* to attempt the mind
> Of Man, with strength entire, and free will arm'd,
> Complete to have discover'd and repulst   10
> Whatever wiles of Foe or seeming Friend.
> For still they knew, and ought to have still remember'd
> The high Injunction not to taste that Fruit,
> Whoever tempted; which they not obeying,
> Incurr'd, what could they less, the penalty,   15
> And manifold in sin, deserv'd to fall.

7. The lines distil the thought in the chapter "Of the Divine Decrees" in *CD* I, iii, where Milton says that God "suffered both men and angels to stand or fall at their own uncontrolled choice, . . . not necessitating the evil consequences that ensued, but leaving them contingent" (C.E. XIV, 81).

9–10. *Complete to:* fully endowed with power to, etc. *Complete* modifies *mind* in l. 8. Cf. IX, 292, n., and 351–56.

16. Though Milton thought of God's prohibition of the Tree of Knowledge as a just though in-scrutable "exercise of jurisdiction" (*CD* I, x; p. 993), he also regarded its violation as comprehending "at once distrust of the divine veracity, . . . unbelief; ingratitude; disobedience; gluttony; in the man excessive uxoriousness, in the woman a want of proper regard for her husband, in both an insensibility to the welfare of their offspring; . . . parricide, theft, invasion of the rights of others, sacrilege, deceit, presumption in aspiring to divine attributes, fraud, . . . pride, and arrogance" (*CD* I, xi; C. E. XV, 180–82).

Up into Heav'n from Paradise in haste
Th' Angelic Guards ascended, mute and sad
For Man, for of his state by this they knew,
Much wond'ring how the subtle Fiend had stol'n   20
Entrance unseen. Soon as th' unwelcome news
From Earth arriv'd at Heaven Gate, displeas'd
All were who heard, dim sadness did not spare
That time Celestial visages, yet mixt
With pity, violated not thir bliss.   25
About the new-arriv'd, in multitudes
Th' ethereal People ran, to hear and know
How all befell: they towards the Throne Supreme
Accountable made haste to make appear
With righteous plea, thir utmost vigilance,   30
And easily approv'd; when the most High
Eternal Father from his secret Cloud,
Amidst in Thunder utter'd thus his voice.
    Assembl'd Angels, and ye Powers return'd
From unsuccessful charge, be not dismay'd,   35
Nor troubl'd at these tidings from the Earth,
Which your sincerest care could not prevent,
Foretold so lately what would come to pass,
When first this Tempter cross'd the Gulf from Hell.
I told ye then he should prevail and speed   40
On his bad Errand, Man should be seduc't
And flatter'd out of all, believing lies
Against his Maker; no Decree of mine
Concurring to necessitate his Fall,
Or touch with lightest moment of impulse   45
His free Will, to her own inclining left
In even scale. But fall'n he is, and now
What rests, but that the mortal Sentence pass
On his transgression, Death denounc't that day,
Which he presumes already vain and void,   50
Because not yet inflicted, as he fear'd,
By some immediate stroke; but soon shall find
Forbearance no acquittance ere day end.
Justice shall not return as bounty scorn'd.
But whom send I to judge them? whom but thee   55
Vicegerent Son, to thee I have transferr'd
All Judgment, whether in Heav'n, or Earth, or Hell.
Easy it may be seen that I intend

---

18. The *Guards* are Gabriel, Ithuriel, Zephon, and
their troop in IV, 561–1015.
   19. *by this:* by this time.
   31. *approv'd:* vindicated.
   32–33. The conception is colored by the chapter
on the throne of God in the Apocalypse—"out of
the throne proceeded lightnings and thunderings
and voices" (Rev. iv, 5)—and by other biblical
passages that are also reflected in II, 263–67.
   40. *I told ye then:* cf. III, 92–97. *speed:* succeed.
   45. *moment:* weight. Cf. the use in VI, 239.
   48. *rests:* remains to be done.
   52. "This death," says *CD* I, xii (C. E. XV,
206–208), "consists first, in the loss, or at least in
the obscuration to a great extent of that right

reason which enabled man to discern the chief
good. . . . It consists, secondly, in . . . deprivation of righteousness and liberty to do good. . . .
Lastly, sin is its own punishment, and produces
. . . the death of the spiritual life." Cf. IX, 1053–
64.
   53. *acquittance:* acquittal, exoneration. Cf.
Claudius' words to Laertes: "Now must your conscience my acquittance seal" (*Hamlet* IV, vii, 1).
   56. "The Son," says Milton in *CD* I, v (C.E. XIV,
250), "was entitled to the name of God . . . in
the capacity of a judge"; and he had no doubt of
the Son's "future judicial advent" (C.E. XIV, 330).
   58. *may* is the reading of the first edition;
might, of the second.

Mercy colleague with Justice, sending thee
Man's Friend, his Mediator, his design'd   60
Both Ransom and Redeemer voluntary,
And destin'd Man himself to judge Man fall'n.
So spake the Father, and unfolding bright
Toward the right hand his Glory, on the Son
Blaz'd forth unclouded Deity; he full   65
Resplendent all his Father manifest
Express'd, and thus divinely answer'd mild.
Father Eternal, thine is to decree,
Mine both in Heav'n and Earth to do thy will
Supreme, that thou in mee thy Son belov'd   70
May'st ever rest well pleas'd. I go to judge
On Earth these thy transgressors, but thou know'st,
Whoever judg'd, the worst on mee must light,
When time shall be, for so I undertook
Before thee; and not repenting, this obtain   75
Of right, that I may mitigate thir doom
On me deriv'd, yet I shall temper so
Justice with Mercy, as may illustrate most
Them fully satisfied, and thee appease.
Attendance none shall need, nor Train, where none   80
Are to behold the Judgment, but the judg'd,
Those two; the third best absent is condemn'd,
Convict by flight, and Rebel to all Law:
Conviction to the Serpent none belongs. • see later,
                                           not in the Bible!
Thus saying, from his radiant Seat he rose   85
Of high collateral glory: him Thrones and Powers,
Princedoms, and Dominations ministrant
Accompanied to Heaven Gate, from whence
Eden and all the Coast in prospect lay.
Down he descended straight; the speed of Gods   90
Time counts not, though with swiftest minutes wing'd.
Now was the Sun in Western cadence low
From Noon, and gentle Airs due at thir hour
To fan the Earth now wak'd, and usher in
The Ev'ning cool, when he from wrath more cool   95
Came the mild Judge and Intercessor both
To sentence Man: the voice of God they heard
Now walking in the Garden, by soft winds

59. Cf. III, 132 and 407, and *Nativity*, 141–46.
60. "*The mediatorial office of* Christ is that whereby . . . *he voluntarily performed, and continues to perform, on behalf of man, whatever is requisite for obtaining reconciliation with God, and eternal salvation*" (*CD* I, xv; C. E. XV, 284).
64. Cf. the Son's participation in God's glory in III, 139, and VI, 679–83. Behind these passages is Hebrews i, 3: "Who being the brightness of his glory, and the express image of his person, . . . sat down on the right hand of the Majesty on high."
74. Cf. the similar allusion in III, 284, to Galatians iv, 4: "But when the fullness of the time was come, God sent forth his Son, made of a woman." For the Son's undertaking, see III, 227–65.
77. *deriv'd* keeps its Latin meaning of "diverted."

78. *illustrate:* shed light upon, glorify. Cf. V, 739.
83–84. *Convict:* convicted. *Conviction:* formal proof of guilt.
89. *Coast:* surrounding region. Cf. II, 633, and VI, 529.
90. *Gods* is used here as it is of the heavenly beings in II, 352. Cf. Raphael's *speed almost spiritual* in VIII, 110.
92. *cadence* keeps its Latin meaning of "falling" or "descent."
95–97. Cf. Genesis iii, 8: "And they heard the voice of the Lord God walking in the garden in the cool of the day: and Adam and his wife hid themselves from the presence of the Lord God amongst the trees of the garden." The following thirteen verses are closely followed in ll. 103–223.

Brought to thir Ears, while day declin'd, they heard,
And from his presence hid themselves among   100
The thickest Trees, both Man and Wife, till God
Approaching, thus to *Adam* call'd aloud.
    Where art thou *Adam,* wont with joy to meet
My coming seen far off? I miss thee here,
Not pleas'd, thus entertain'd with solitude,   105
Where obvious duty erewhile appear'd unsought:
Or come I less conspicuous, or what change
Absents thee, or what chance detains? Come forth.
He came, and with him *Eve,* more loath, though first
To offend, discount'nanc't both, and discompos'd;   110
Love was not in thir looks, either to God
Or to each other, but apparent guilt,
And shame, and perturbation, and despair,
Anger, and obstinacy, and hate, and guile.
Whence *Adam* falt'ring long, thus answer'd brief.   115
    I heard thee in the Garden, and of thy voice
Afraid, being naked, hid myself. To whom
The gracious Judge without revile repli'd.
    My voice thou oft hast heard, and hast not fear'd,
But still rejoic't, how is it now become   120
So dreadful to thee? that thou art naked, who
Hath told thee? hast thou eaten of the Tree
Whereof I gave thee charge thou shoulds: not eat?
    To whom thus *Adam* sore beset repli'd.
O Heav'n! in evil strait this day I stand   125
Before my Judge, either to undergo
Myself the total Crime, or to accuse
My other self, the partner of my life;
Whose failing, while her Faith to me remains,
I should conceal, and not expose to blame   130
By my complaint; but strict necessity
Subdues me, and calamitous constraint,
Lest on my head both sin and punishment,
However insupportable, be all
Devolv'd; though should I hold my peace, yet thou   135
Wouldst easily detect what I conceal.
This Woman whom thou mad'st to be my help,
And gav'st me as thy perfet gift, so good,
So fit, so acceptable, so Divine,
That from her hand I could suspect no ill,   140
And what she did, whatever in itself,
Her doing seem'd to justify the deed;
Shee gave me of the Tree, and I did eat.
    To whom the sovran Presence thus repli'd.
Was shee thy God, that her thou didst obey   145
Before his voice, or was shee made thy guide,
Superior, or but equal, that to her
Thou didst resign thy Manhood, and the Place

101. The Son is called *God* as the *Vicegerent God* of l. 56 above.
106. *obvious* keeps its Latin meaning of "confronting in the way," i.e. to meet and welcome a person.
112. *apparent:* evident, conspicuous.

118. *revile:* revilement, reproach.
128. So God calls Eve Adam's *other self* in VIII, 450.
144–156. The rebuke parallels Raphael's warning in VIII, 561–85, as the preceding lines match Adam's preceding speech in ll. 540–59.

Wherein God set thee above her made of thee,
And for thee, whose perfection far excell'd   150
Hers in all real dignity: Adorn'd
She was indeed, and lovely to attract
Thy Love, not thy Subjection, and her Gifts
Were such as under Government well seem'd,
Unseemly to bear rule, which was thy part   155
And person, hadst thou known thyself aright.
  So having said, he thus to *Eve* in few:
Say Woman, what is this which thou hast done?
  To whom sad *Eve* with shame nigh overwhelm'd,
Confessing soon, yet not before her Judge   160
Bold or loquacious, thus abasht repli'd.
  The Serpent me beguil'd and I did eat.
  Which when the Lord God heard, without delay
To Judgment he proceeded on th' accus'd
Serpent though brute, unable to transfer   165
The Guilt on him who made him instrument
Of mischief, and polluted from the end
Of his Creation; justly then accurst,
As vitiated in Nature: more to know
Concern'd not Man (since he no further knew)   170
Nor alter'd his offense; yet God at last
To Satan first in sin his doom appli'd,
Though in mysterious terms, judg'd as then best:
And on the Serpent thus his curse let fall.
  Because thou hast done this, thou art accurst   175
Above all Cattle, each Beast of the Field;
Upon thy Belly groveling thou shalt go,
And dust shalt eat all the days of thy Life.
Between Thee and the Woman I will put
Enmity, and between thine and her Seed;   180
Her Seed shall bruise thy head, thou bruise his heel.
  So spake this Oracle, then verifi'd
When *Jesus* son of *Mary* second *Eve*,
Saw Satan fall like Lightning down from Heav'n,
Prince of the Air; then rising from his Grave   185
Spoil'd Principalities and Powers, triumpht
In open show, and with ascension bright
Captivity led captive through the Air,
The Realm itself of Satan long usurpt,

---

156. *person* has its Latin meaning of "character in a drama" and continues the metaphor of *part* (role) in l. 155.

166–167. So in IX, 530, Satan is said to make a tool of the serpent, applying it to a use which was not the *end* (object) of its creation.

168–181. The mystery is explained in *CD* I, xiv (C. E. XV, 252), where Milton says that God, "in pronouncing the punishment of the serpent, previously to passing sentence on man, promised that he would raise up from the seed of the woman one who would bruise the serpent's head, Gen. iii, 15, and thus anticipated the condemnation of mankind by a gratuitous redemption." See the Introduction 51.

183–184. Cf. *Mary second Eve* in V, 386–87. In making the prophecy refer to Mary and Jesus—

as Williams notes (*Expositor*, p. 128)—Milton took the Catholic position as distinguished from Calvin's view that the enmity was to be "between the righteous, the seed of the woman, and the reprobate, the seed of Satan." In Christ's vision of Satan "as lightning," falling "from heaven" (Luke x, 18), Milton saw the fulfilment of the prophecy that the seed of the woman should "bruise the serpent's head."

185. Cf. I, 516, where the air is the realm of the demons. In Ephesians ii, 2, Satan is called the "prince of the power of the air."

186. Psalm lxviii, 18—"Thou hast ascended up on high, thou hast led captivity captive"—blends with St. Paul's prophecy of Christ's resurrection and triumph over "principalities and powers" (Col. ii, 15).

Whom he shall tread at last under our feet;   190
Ev'n hee who now foretold his fatal bruise,
And to the Woman thus his Sentence turn'd.
    Thy sorrow I will greatly multiply
By thy Conception; Children thou shalt bring
In sorrow forth, and to thy Husband's will   195
Thine shall submit, hee over thee shall rule.
    On *Adam* last thus judgment he pronounc'd.
Because thou hast heark'n'd to the voice of thy Wife,
And eaten of the Tree concerning which
I charg'd thee, saying: Thou shalt not eat thereof,   200
Curs'd is the ground for thy sake, thou in sorrow
Shalt eat thereof all the days of thy Life;
Thorns also and Thistles it shall bring thee forth
Unbid, and thou shalt eat th' Herb of the Field,
In the sweat of thy Face shalt thou eat Bread,   205
Till thou return unto the ground, for thou
Out of the ground wast taken, know thy Birth,
For dust thou art, and shalt to dust return.
    So judg'd he Man, both Judge and Savior sent,
And th' instant stroke of Death denounc't that day   210
Remov'd far off; then pitying how they stood
Before him naked to the air, that now
Must suffer change, disdain'd not to begin
Thenceforth the form of servant to assume,
As when he wash'd his servants' feet, so now   215
As Father of his Family he clad
Thir nakedness with Skins of Beasts, or slain,
Or as the Snake with youthful Coat repaid;
And thought not much to clothe his Enemies:
Nor hee thir outward only with the Skins   220
Of Beasts, but inward nakedness, much more
Opprobrious, with his Robe of righteousness,
Arraying cover'd from his Father's sight.
To him with swift ascent he up return'd,
Into his blissful bosom reassum'd   225
In glory as of old, to him appeas'd
All, though all-knowing, what had past with Man
Recounted, mixing intercession sweet.
Meanwhile ere thus was sinn'd and judg'd on Earth,
Within the Gates of Hell sat Sin and Death,   230
In counterview within the Gates, that now
Stood open wide, belching outrageous flame
Far into *Chaos,* since the Fiend pass'd through,
Sin opening, who thus now to Death began.
    O Son, why sit we here each other viewing   235

193–196. In *CD* I, x (p. 994) Milton interprets Genesis iii, 16–19 as meaning that, "The power of the husband was even increased after the fall."

216–217. Genesis iii, 21, says simply that "the Lord God made coats of skins and clothed them," but Milton thought also of Christ's taking "upon him the form of a servant" (Phil. ii, 7) and washing the feet of the disciples (John xiii, 5).

217–218. Milton wonders whether beasts were slain for their pelts or survived the loss like moulting snakes, *repaid* (recompensed) by new skins.

219. *thought not much:* did not grudge. So Spenser wonders at the mercy which sends the angels "To serve to wicked men, to serve his (God's) wicked foe" (*F.Q.* II, viii, 1).

222. *Robe of righteousness* is a phrase from Isaiah lxi, 10. Cf. IX, 1058.

230–231. So Sin and Death sit opposite each other (*in counterview*) in II, 649.

Idly, while Satan our great Author thrives
In other Worlds, and happier Seat provides
For us his offspring dear? It cannot be
But that success attends him; if mishap,
Ere this he had return'd, with fury driv'n   240
By his Avengers, since no place like this
Can fit his punishment, or their revenge.
Methinks I feel new strength within me rise,
Wings growing, and Dominion giv'n me large
Beyond this Deep; whatever draws me on,   245
Or sympathy, or some connatural force
Powerful at greatest distance to unite
With secret amity things of like kind
By secretest conveyance. Thou my Shade
Inseparable must with mee along: 250
For Death from Sin no power can separate.
But lest the difficulty of passing back
Stay his return perhaps over this Gulf
Impassable, Impervious, let us try
Advent'rous work, yet to thy power and mine   255
Not unagreeable, to found a path
Over this Main from Hell to that new World
Where Satan now prevails, a Monument
Of merit high to all th' infernal Host,
Easing thir passage hence, for intercourse,   260
Or transmigration, as thir lot shall lead.
Nor can I miss the way, so strongly drawn
By this new felt attraction and instinct.
    Whom thus the meagre Shadow answer'd soon.
Go whither Fate and inclination strong   265
Leads thee, I shall not lag behind, nor err
The way, thou leading, such a scent I draw
Of carnage, prey innumerable, and taste
The savor of Death from all things there that live:
Nor shall I to the work thou enterprisest   270
Be wanting, but afford thee equal aid.
    So saying, with delight he snuff'd the smell
Of mortal change on Earth. As when a flock
Of ravenous Fowl, though many a League remote,
Against the day of Battle, to a Field,   275
Where Armies lie encampt, come flying, lur'd
With scent of living Carcasses design'd
For death, the following day, in bloody fight,
So scented the grim Feature, and upturn'd

246. Here and in the Argument to Book X
sympathy has the quasi-scientific meaning of attraction at great distances.
249–263. The allegory which Sin now makes
almost explicit bears comparison with Samuel
Pordage's forced allegory in *Mundorum Explicatio*
(*Celestial Cycle*, p. 431), where Satan, returning in
triumph from earth to hell, dispatches Beelzebub
with his "discords and plagues," Abaddon with
"sicknesse and death," and the other major devils
with the crimes and evils appropriate to them, to
take possession of the world.
256. *found* has its literal Latin meaning of "lay

a foundation."
257. *Main:* the sea of Chaos over which Satan
makes his *Voyage* in II, 919.
260–261. *intercourse:* two-way traffic. *transmigration:* emigration, not to return.
274. The belief in the power of birds of ravin
to foresee impending battles goes back to the verse
about the eagle in Job, xxxix, 30: "And where the
slain are, there is she." It is quoted with reference
to vultures by Abraham Cowley in his notes to his
translation of Isaiah xxxiv. Cf. III, 431, n.
279. *Feature* is used in its Italian sense of
"creature."

His Nostril wide into the murky Air, 280
Sagacious of his Quarry from so far.
Then Both from out Hell Gates into the waste
Wide Anarchy of *Chaos* damp and dark
Flew diverse, and with Power (thir Power was great)
Hovering upon the Waters; what they met 285
Solid or slimy, as in raging Sea
Tost up and down, together crowded drove
From each side shoaling towards the mouth of Hell.
As when two Polar Winds blowing adverse
Upon the *Cronian* Sea, together drive 290
Mountains of Ice, that stop th' imagin'd way
Beyond *Petsora* Eastward, to the rich
Cathaian Coast. The aggregated Soil
Death with his Mace petrific, cold and dry,
As with a Trident smote, and fix't as firm 295
As *Delos* floating once; the rest his look
Bound with *Gorgonian* rigor not to move,
And with *Asphaltic* slime; broad as the Gate,
Deep to the Roots of Hell the gather'd beach
They fasten'd, and the Mole immense wrought on 300
Over the foaming deep high Archt, a Bridge
Of length prodigious joining to the Wall
Immoveable of this now fenceless World
Forfeit to Death; from hence a passage broad,
Smooth, easy, inoffensive down to Hell. 305
So, if great things to small may be compar'd,
Xerxes, the Liberty of *Greece* to yoke,
From *Susa* his *Memnonian* Palace high
Came to the Sea, and over *Hellespont*
Bridging his way, *Europe* with *Asia* join'd, 310
And scourg'd with many a stroke th' indignant waves.
Now had they brought the work by wondrous Art

282–305. Anent W. Empson's objection (in *Pastoral*, p. 154) Tillyard first suggests an interesting parallel between this passage and the account in Philostratus' *Life of Apollonius* (I, 25) of the construction of a tunnel under the Euphrates, and then notes that in their bridge-building Sin and Death "parody God's creative act in the seventh book." . . . Sin and Death "hover over the waters of chaos (birds of prey, not the dove); . . . and instead of warmth they infuse cold and petrifaction" (*SP*, XXXVIII—1941—267–70).

288. *shoaling:* solidifying into a shoal.

290. The *Cronian Sea:* the Arctic Ocean.

291. *th' imagin'd way:* the northeast passage for which Hudson vainly sought in 1608.

292. "The river [*Petsora*] Pechora," Milton wrote in *Moscovia,* "holding his course through *Siberia,* how far the *Russians* thereabout know not, runneth into the Sea at 72 mouths, full of Ice . . ." (C. E. X, 332).

293. Milton distinguished Cathay from China proper and thought of it as a separate empire, the destined seat of Chingiz Khan (XI, 386–88), in northeastern Asia, as the Mercator maps represented it.

296. Out of the warring elements in Chaos— "hot, cold, moist, and dry" (II, 898)—*Death* separates the *cold* and *dry* atoms for the masonry of his bridge and petrifies them with a touch of his *Mace,* as Neptune was fabled to have moulded the island of *Delos* out of the sea with his *Trident.* Later Zeus was supposed to have anchored the island in the centre of the Cyclades.

297. Like the Gorgon Medusa in the myth of Perseus, Death can turn everything at which he looks into stone; and for mortar he uses asphalt, which the devils have previously turned to a different purpose (I, 729).

302. The *Wall* is the shell of the created universe, which—in spite of it—is *fenceless* (without defense) against Death.

305. *inoffensive* has its Latin force of "free of stumbling-blocks."

307–311. In the dictionaries of Calepine and Charles Stephanus, Milton's readers could find summaries of several ancient accounts of Xerxes scourging the waves of the Hellespont when they broke his bridge of ships between the European and Asiatic shores of the Dardenelles.

308. *Susa* (the biblical Shushan, winter capital of the Persian kings) was founded by Tithonus, the mythical lover of Aurora, by whom he had a son Memnon.

Pontifical, a ridge of pendent Rock
Over the vext Abyss, following the track
Of *Satan,* to the selfsame place where hee   315
First lighted from his Wing, and landed safe
From out of *Chaos* to the outside bare
Of this round World: with Pins of Adamant
And Chains they made all fast, too fast they made
And durable; and now in little space   320
The confines met of Empyrean Heav'n
And of this World, and on the left hand Hell
With long reach interpos'd; three sev'ral ways
In sight, to each of these three places led.
And now thir way to Earth they had descri'd,   325
To Paradise first tending, when behold
Satan in likeness of an Angel bright
Betwixt the *Centaur* and the *Scorpion* steering
His *Zenith,* while the Sun in *Aries* rose:
Disguis'd he came, but those his Children dear   330
Thir Parent soon discern'd, though in disguise.
Hee, after *Eve* seduc't, unminded slunk
Into the Wood fast by, and changing shape
To observe the sequel, saw his guileful act
By *Eve,* though all unweeting, seconded   335
Upon her Husband, saw thir shame that sought
Vain covertures; but when he saw descend
The Son of God to judge them, terrifi'd
Hee fled, not hoping to escape, but shun
The present, fearing guilty what his wrath   340
Might suddenly inflict; that past, return'd
By Night, and list'ning where the hapless Pair
Sat in thir sad discourse and various plaint,
Thence gather'd his own doom; which understood
Not instant, but of future time, with joy   345
And tidings fraught, to Hell he now return'd,
And at the brink of *Chaos,* near the foot
Of this new wondrous Pontifice, unhop't
Met who to meet him came, his Offspring dear.
Great joy was at thir meeting, and at sight   350
Of that stupendous Bridge his joy increas'd.
Long hee admiring stood, till Sin, his fair
Enchanting Daughter, thus the silence broke.
O Parent, these are thy magnific deeds,

Pope

313. The Latin *pontifex* (from which *Pontifical* comes) means "bridge-builder."

314. *vext*: harried by storms, as it is described in II, 894–97, and VII, 211–15.

316. Satan lights on the *opacous Globe* in III, 418.

320–324. The meeting *confines* are the bottom end of the stair which unites the empyrean heaven to the shell of the universe in III, 510, the passage thence inside the shell of the universe, down to the earth, and the causeway which Sin and Death have just built up from hell to the opening already existing in the shell of the universe. In paintings of the Last Judgment as described in Matthew xxv, 33, the side of hell was traditionally the left.

328–329. As in IX, 58–69, Satan puts the earth

between himself and Uriel, who is in the sun, which is in the zodiacal sign of the Ram (*Aries*) and opposite that of the *Scorpion*. D. C. Allen notes —*MLN*, LXVIII (1953), 361—an allegorical overtone in the astrological doctrine that men who are strongly influenced by Scorpio and the *Centaur* are likely to be very deceitful.

332. *after Eve seduc't*: after the seduction of Eve. Cf. I, 573.

335. *unweeting*: unaware, unsuspecting.

337. The *covertures* are the garments made of leaves in IX, 1110–14.

345–346. *joy And tidings* mean "joyful tidings."

347. *foot*: bottom of the slope of the bridge (*Pontifice*) leading to the universe from hell. Cf. l. 313 above, n.

Thy Trophies, which thou view'st as not thine own,   355
Thou art thir Author and prime Architect:
For I no sooner in my Heart divin'd,
My Heart, which by a secret harmony
Still moves with thine, join'd in connexion sweet,
That thou on Earth hadst prosper'd, which thy looks   360
Now also evidence, but straight I felt
Though distant from thee Worlds between, yet felt
That I must after thee with this thy Son;
Such fatal consequence unites us three:
Hell could no longer hold us in her bounds,   365
Nor this unvoyageable Gulf obscure
Detain from following thy illustrious track.
Thou hast achiev'd our liberty, confin'd
Within Hell Gates till now, thou us impow'r'd
To fortify thus far, and overlay   370
With this portentous Bridge the dark Abyss.
Thine now is all this World, thy virtue hath won
What thy hands builded not, thy Wisdom gain'd
With odds what War hath lost, and fully aveng'd
Our foil in Heav'n; here thou shalt Monarch reign,   375
There didst not; there let him still Victor sway,
As Battle hath adjudg'd, from this new World
Retiring, by his own doom alienated,
And henceforth Monarchy with thee divide
Of all things, parted by th' Empyreal bounds,   380
His Quadrature, from thy Orbicular World,
Or try thee now more dang'rous to his Throne.
      Whom thus the Prince of Darkness answer'd glad.
Fair Daughter, and thou Son and Grandchild both,
High proof ye now have giv'n to be the Race   385
Of *Satan* (for I glory in the name,
Antagonist of Heav'n's Almighty King)
Amply have merited of me, of all
Th' Infernal Empire, that so near Heav'n's door
Triumphal with triumphal act have met,   390
Mine with this glorious Work, and made one Realm
Hell and this World, one Realm, one Continent
Of easy thorough-fare. Therefore while I
Descend through Darkness, on your Road with ease
To my associate Powers, them to acquaint   395
With these successes, and with them rejoice,
You two this way, among those numerous Orbs
All yours, right down to Paradise descend;
There dwell and Reign in bliss, thence on the Earth
Dominion exercise and in the Air,   400
Chiefly on Man, sole Lord of all declar'd,

358. The *secret harmony* is the sympathy of l.
246 above.
   364. *consequence:* dependence.
   370. *fortify:* construct (what amounts to a military road).
   381. Heaven is "foursquare," as it is in Revelation xxi, 16. Cf. II. 1048, n.
   386. In *CD* I, ix (p. 992) Milton stresses the

fact that the name *Satan* means the Adversary in
Scripture. Cf. I, 82.
   390. Satan's triumph in Eden is matched by the
triumphal work of Sin and Death, their bridge,
the *Causey* of l. 415 below.
   397. So Satan drops from the shell of the universe to earth "amongst innumerable Stars" in III,
565, and Raphael descends "between worlds and
worlds" in V, 268.

Him first make sure your thrall, and lastly kill.
My Substitutes I send ye, and Create
Plenipotent on Earth, of matchless might
Issuing from mee: on your joint vigor now   405
My hold of this new Kingdom all depends,
Through Sin to Death expos'd by my exploit.
If your joint power prevail, th' affairs of Hell
No detriment need fear, go and be strong.
     So saying he dismiss'd them, they with speed   410
Thir course through thickest Constellations held
Spreading thir bane; the blasted Stars lookt wan,
And Planets, Planet-strook, real Eclipse
Then suffer'd. Th' other way *Satan* went down
The Causey to Hell Gate; on either side   415
Disparted *Chaos* over-built exclaim'd,
And with rebounding surge the bars assail'd,
That scorn'd his indignation: through the Gate,
Wide open and unguarded, *Satan* pass'd,
And all about found desolate; for those   420
Appointed to sit there, had left thir charge,
Flown to the upper World; the rest were all
Far to th'inland retir'd, about the walls
Of *Pandæmonium,* City and proud seat
Of *Lucifer,* so by allusion call'd,   425
Of that bright Star to *Satan* paragon'd.
There kept thir Watch the Legions, while the Grand
In Council sat, solicitous what chance
Might intercept thir Emperor sent, so hee
Departing gave command, and they observ'd.   430
As when the *Tartar* from his *Russian* Foe
By *Astracan* over the Snowy Plains
Retires, or *Bactrian* Sophi from the horns
Of *Turkish* Crescent, leaves all waste beyond
The Realm of *Aladule,* in his retreat   435
To *Tauris* or *Casbeen:* So these the late
Heav'n-banisht Host, left desert utmost Hell
Many a dark League, reduc't in careful Watch
Round thir Metropolis, and now expecting
Each hour their great adventurer from the search   440
Of Foreign Worlds: he through the midst unmark't,
In show Plebeian Angel militant
Of lowest order, pass't; and from the door
Of that *Plutonian* Hall, invisible

407–409. Milton thought of a formula used in giving Roman consuls supreme power in crises to protect Rome against all *detriment* (*detrimentum*) or injury.

413. Popular astrology regarded people who suffered from unfavorable influences from the stars as "planet-struck."   At Christmas time says Marcellus, "No planets strike" (*Hamlet* I, i, 162). Milton regards the stars themselves as being blasted by Sin and Death.

426. The *Star* is Lucifer or Venus as the light-bringing morning star. Cf. VII, 132, n.

427. The *Grand* are the *great consulting Peers* of l. 456 below.

432. In *Moscovia* Milton often mentions *Astracan,* a Russian frontier town on the Volga, not far from the Caspian Sea.

433–436. A. H. Gilbert spots Hakluyt's *Voyages* I, 351, as Milton's authority for the *Bactrian* ruler then reigning as "nothing valiant," and as having been driven back by the Turks "even nigh unto the Citie of *Teveris,* wherein he was wont to keepe his chiefe court. And now having forsaken the same, is chiefly resiant at *Casbin.*" *Tauris* (or Tebriz) was an important Persian city under king *Aladule* in the wars with the Turks.

438. *Reduc't* keeps its Latin military meaning of "lead back" (an army in retreat).

Ascended his high Throne, which under state   445
Of richest texture spread, at th' upper end
Was plac't in regal lustre. Down a while
He sat, and round about him saw unseen:
At last as from a Cloud his fulgent head
And shape Star-bright appear'd, or brighter, clad   450
With what permissive glory since his fall
Was left him, or false glitter: All amaz'd
At that so sudden blaze the *Stygian* throng
Bent thir aspect, and whom they wish'd beheld,
Thir mighty Chief return'd: loud was th' acclaim: 455
Forth rush'd in haste the great consulting Peers,
Rais'd from thir dark *Divan,* and with like joy
Congratulant approach'd him, who with hand
Silence, and with these words attention won.

    Thrones, Dominations, Princedoms, Virtues, Powers,   460
For in possession such, not only of right,
I call ye and declare ye now, return'd
Successful beyond hope, to lead ye forth
Triumphant out of this infernal Pit
Abominable, accurst, the house of woe,   465
And Dungeon of our Tyrant: Now possess,
As Lords, a spacious World, to our native Heaven
Little inferior, by my adventure hard
With peril great achiev'd. Long were to tell
What I have done, what suffer'd, with what pain   470
Voyag'd th' unreal, vast, unbounded deep
Of horrible confusion, over which
By Sin and Death a broad way now is pav'd
To expedite your glorious march; but I
Toil'd out my uncouth passage, forc't to ride   475
Th' untractable Abyss, plung'd in the womb
Of unoriginal *Night* and *Chaos* wild,
That jealous of thir secrets fiercely oppos'd
My journey strange, with clamorous uproar
Protesting Fate supreme; thence how I found   480
The new created World, which fame in Heav'n
Long had foretold, a Fabric wonderful
Of absolute perfection, therein Man
Plac't in a Paradise, by our exile
Made happy: Him by fraud I have seduc'd   485
From his Creator, and the more to increase
Your wonder, with an Apple; he thereat
Offended, worth your laughter, hath giv'n up
Both his beloved Man and all his World,
To Sin and Death a prey, and so to us,   490
Without our hazard, labor, or alarm,
To range in, and to dwell, and over Man

---

445. *state:* canopy over a chair of state or throne like Satan's in II, 1–4, where he is compared with a Turkish Sultan as he is in l. 458 below.

451. *permissive:* permissible or permitted (i. e. by God).

458. The Turkish council of state was known as the *Divan.*

461. *Possession* of the world that Satan has won for them as well as their claim to their lost heavenly ranks, entitles the devils to Satan's titles for them.

471. Cf. the *unapparent Deep* in VII, 103. Its formless elements make it *unreal.*

477. *Night,* which in II, 962, is *eldest of things,* is *unoriginal* because nothing existed before it to originate it. Night does not oppose Satan and Chaos helps him on his way in II, 999–1009.

To rule, as over all he should have rul'd.
True is, mee also he hath judg'd, or rather
Mee not, but the brute Serpent in whose shape   495
Man I deceiv'd: that which to mee belongs,
Is enmity, which he will put between
Mee and Mankind; I am to bruise his heel;
His Seed, when is not set, shall bruise my head:
A World who would not purchase with a bruise,   500
Or much more grievous pain?   Ye have th' account
Of my performance: What remains, ye Gods,
But up and enter now into full bliss.
     So having said, a while he stood, expecting
Thir universal shout and high applause   505
To fill his ear, when contrary he hears
On all sides, from innumerable tongues
A dismal universal hiss, the sound
Of public scorn; he wonder'd, but not long
Had leisure, wond'ring at himself now more;   510
His Visage drawn he felt to sharp and spare,
His Arms clung to his Ribs, his Legs entwining
Each other, till supplanted down he fell
A monstrous Serpent on his Belly prone,
Reluctant, but in vain: a greater power   515
Now rul'd him, punisht in the shape he sinn'd,
According to his doom: he would have spoke,
But hiss for hiss return'd with forked tongue
To forked tongue, for now were all transform'd
Alike, to Serpents all as accessories   520
To his bold Riot: dreadful was the din
Of hissing through the Hall, thick swarming now
With complicated monsters, head and tail,
Scorpion and Asp, and *Amphisbæna* dire,
Cerastes horn'd, *Hydrus,* and *Ellops* drear,   525
And *Dipsas* (not so thick swarm'd once the Soil
Bedropt with blood of *Gorgon,* or the Isle

508. In the devils' hiss James Hutton makes the plausible suggestion (in *English Miscellany,* ed. by M. Praz, V, 1955, p. 59) that Milton intended an antithesis to the music of the angels at the creation of the world in VII, 558–74.

513. *supplanted* has its Latin force of "tripped by the heels."

514–533. Though there are traces of Ovid's story of the metamorphosis of Cadmus into a serpent (*Met.* IV, 575–89) and of Lucan's account in *The Civil War* IX, 700–733, of the varieties of serpents that sprang from the blood dripping from the Gorgon's head as Perseus carried it over Libya, Milton's lines rest on a belief which Jakob Boehme interpreted religiously when he wrote in *A Description of the Three Principles of the Divine Essence* (tr. John Sparrow, 1648), iv, 64, that, after "the divine light went out of the Devils, they lost their beauteous forme and Image, and became like Serpents, Dragons, Wormes, and evill Beasts: as may be seen by *Adam's* Serpent." In Vondel's *Lucifer,* as the devil falls under Michael's sword in the battle in heaven, he is suddenly changed into a monster mingling serpent features with those of

six other fierce animals (*Cycle,* p. 414).   See the Introduction 15.

521. *Riot:* revolt.

523. *complicated* has its Latin meaning of "intertwined."

524. Like all Milton's serpents, the fabulous *Amphisbæna,* which had a head at each end, was understood to be real and symbolic. In the *Serpentum et draconum historiae Libri II* (Bologna, 1640) of Ulisse Aldovrandus the *amphisbæna* is both scientifically described and then "hieroglyphically" made a symbol of inconstancy and adultery.

525. Aldovrandus says that the *Cerastes* symbolizes the devil and lust for power.   The *Hydrus* was a watersnake; the *Ellops* perhaps originally the swordfish.

526. The *Dipsas* was familiar from Lucian's dialogue "The Thirst Snake" and from Lucan's account of it in *The Civil War* IX, 737–50. Aldovrandus and Topsell in his *Historie of serpents* both interpret the thirst provoked by its bite as an allegory like the thirst of Tantalus in hell. Cf. II, 614.

Ophiusa) but still greatest hee the midst,
Now Dragon grown, larger than whom the Sun
Ingender'd in the *Pythian* Vale on slime, 530
Huge *Python,* and his Power no less he seem'd
Above the rest still to retain; they all
Him follow'd issuing forth to th' open Field,
Where all yet left of that revolted Rout
Heav'n-fall'n, in station stood or just array, 535
Sublime with expectation when to see
In Triumph issuing forth thir glorious Chief;
They saw, but other sight instead, a crowd
Of ugly Serpents; horror on them fell,
And horrid sympathy; for what they saw, 540
They felt themselves now changing; down thir arms,
Down fell both Spear and Shield, down they as fast,
And the dire hiss renew'd, and the dire form
Catcht by Contagion, like in punishment,
As in thir crime. Thus was th' applause they meant, 545
Turn'd to exploding hiss, triumph to shame
Cast on themselves from thir own mouths. There stood
A Grove hard by, sprung up with this thir change,
His will who reigns above, to aggravate
Thir penance, laden with fair Fruit, like that 550
Which grew in Paradise, the bait of *Eve*
Us'd by the Tempter: on that prospect strange
Thir earnest eyes they fix'd, imagining
For one forbidden Tree a multitude
Now ris'n, to work them furder woe or shame; 555
Yet parcht with scalding thirst and hunger fierce,
Though to delude them sent, could not abstain,
But on they roll'd in heaps, and up the Trees
Climbing, sat thicker than the snaky locks
That curl'd *Megæra*: greedily they pluck'd 560
The Fruitage fair to sight, like that which grew
Near that bituminous Lake where *Sodom* flam'd;
This more delusive, not the touch, but taste
Deceiv'd; they fondly thinking to allay

528. *Ophiusa,* the "snaky" or "snake-filled," was a name given by the Greeks to several of the Balearic islands.

531. Ovid tells the story of the primitive earth's unwilling engendering of the mountainous serpent *Python* (*Met.* I, 438-40). Cf. *El. VII,* 31.

535. *in station:* on posts. *array:* in review order (like troops).

536. *sublime* has its literal Latin meaning of "uplifted."

545-572. This "cartoon scene," which Waldock condemns as crude allegory in *"PL" and Its Critics,* p. 91, is shown by Stein in *PMLA* LXV (1950), 226, to be a "psychological" and "physical climax" in the drama of the poem. For Addison in *Spectator,* 357, for L. Abercrombie in *The Idea of Great Poetry* (London, 1925), p. 80, and for Edith Sitwell in *The Pleasures of Poetry* (New York, n.d.) p. 25, the lines are a triumph of language and verbal power.

551. The trees loaded with the *bait of Eve* sug-

gest the graft of the Tree of Knowledge below which Dante found a host of famished spirits in *Purgatory* (xxiv, 103-117).

560. *Megæra,* one of the Furies or goddesses who avenge crime, and who appear with *snaky locks* as the chorus in Aeschylus' *Eumenides.*

562. Throughout the popular encyclopaedias—Swan's *Speculum Mundi* and Caxton's *Mirrour of the World* especially—Svendsen (*M.&S.,* pp. 28-29) traces repetitions of Josephus' story of *that bituminous Lake* (the Dead Sea) and the city of *Sodom,* which, "for the impiety of its inhabitants, was burnt by lightning; . . . and the traces are still to be seen, as well as the ashes growing in their fruits, which fruits have a color as if they were fit to be eaten; but if you pluck them with your hands, they dissolve into smoke and ashes" (*Wars* IV, viii, 4). Sodom and Gomorrah, upon which "the Lord rained . . . brimstone and fire . . . out of heaven" (Gen. xix, 24), are shown all aflame together with Zeboim and Admah on Fuller's map on p. 186.

Thir appetite with gust, instead of Fruit   565
Chew'd bitter Ashes, which th' offended taste
With spattering noise rejected: oft they assay'd,
Hunger and thirst constraining, drugg'd as oft,
With hatefullest disrelish writh'd thir jaws
With soot and cinders fill'd; so oft they fell   570
Into the same illusion, not as Man
Whom they triumph'd, once lapst. Thus were they plagu'd
And worn with Famine long, and ceaseless hiss,
Till thir lost shape, permitted, they resum'd,
Yearly enjoin'd, some say, to undergo   575
This annual humbling certain number'd days,
To dash thir pride, and joy for Man seduc't.
However some tradition they dispers'd
Among the Heathen of thir purchase got,
And Fabl'd how the Serpent, whom they call'd   580
Ophion with Eurynome, the wide-
Encroaching Eve perhaps, had first the rule
Of high Olympus, thence by Saturn driv'n
And Ops, ere yet Dictæan Jove was born.
Meanwhile in Paradise the hellish pair   585
Too soon arriv'd, Sin there in power before,
Once actual, now in body, and to dwell
Habitual habitant; behind her Death
Close following pace for pace, not mounted yet
On his pale Horse: to whom Sin thus began.   590
    Second of Satan sprung, all conquering Death,
What think'st thou of our Empire now, though earn'd
With travail difficult, not better far
Than still at Hell's dark threshold to have sat watch,
Unnam'd, undreaded, and thyself half starv'd?   595
    Whom thus the Sin-born Monster answer'd soon.
To mee, who with eternal Famine pine,
Alike is Hell, or Paradise, or Heaven,
There best, where most with ravin I may meet;
Which here, though plenteous, all too little seems   600

565. gust: keen relish, gusto.

566–570. In the background is a popular belief that snakes eat nothing but dust which Topsell in his Historie of Serpents, p. 16, challenged, though he thought it possible that snakes of the kind that figures in Eve's temptation might have no food but dust.

568. drugg'd: nauseated.

572. triumph'd: triumphed over, vanquished.

572–577. Again folklore may be in the background in stories like Ariosto's account in the Orlando Furioso XLIII, 98, of the confession of the fairy Manto that she and all her kind are obliged every seventh day to assume the form of serpents.

581. In the Argonautica I, 503–506, Apollonius recalls that Olympus was ruled by the Titans Ophion ("the serpent") and his wife Eurynome until their expulsion by Saturn and his wife Rhea, whom Milton calls Ops. Ophion seems to be the Titan Ophioneus who—according to the sixth century B. C. philosopher Pherecydes—led an unsuccessful attack on Olympus. Ophioneus was identi-

fied by Origen (contra Celsum VI, 43) with "the serpent which was the cause of man's expulsion from the divine paradise, and deceived the female race with a promise of divine power of attaining to greater things." Ophioneus' identification with the serpent of Eden survived as a tradition in George Sandys' introduction to his version of Ovid's Metamorphoses II, and it was extended by Jean Bodin in Le Fleau des Demons et Sorciers (Nyort, 1616), pp. 3–4, and by Cornelius Agrippa in De Occulta Philosophia III, xviii, to include "that old serpent called the devil" in Rev. xii, 9. Since Eurynome means "wide-encroaching," punctuation with the comma immediately after the word rather than immediately before it (as in the early editions), seems justified. Cf. IX, 507–510, n, and the Introduction 16.

586. Sin was in Eden in power when Adam and Eve fell.

590. The pale Horse is from Revelation vi, 8: "And I looked, and behold a pale horse; and his name that sat on him was Death."

To stuff this Maw, this vast unhide-bound Corpse.
   To whom th' incestuous Mother thus repli'd.
Thou therefore on these Herbs, and Fruits, and Flow'rs
Feed first, on each Beast next, and Fish, and Fowl,
No homely morsels, and whatever thing   605
The Scythe of Time mows down, devour unspar'd,
Till I in Man residing through the Race,
His thoughts, his looks, words, actions all infect,
And season him thy last and sweetest prey.
   This said, they both betook them several ways,   610
Both to destroy, or unimmortal make
All kinds, and for destruction to mature
Sooner or later; which th' Almighty seeing
From his transcendent Seat the Saints among,
To those bright Orders utter'd thus his voice.   615
   See with what heat these Dogs of Hell advance
To waste and havoc yonder World, which I
So fair and good created, and had still
Kept in that state, had not the folly of Man
Let in these wasteful Furies, who impute   620
Folly to mee, so doth the Prince of Hell
And his Adherents, that with so much ease
I suffer them to enter and possess
A place so heav'nly, and conniving seem
To gratify my scornful Enemies,   625
That laugh, as if transported with some fit
Of Passion, I to them had quitted all,
At random yielded up to their misrule;
And know not that I call'd and drew them thither
My Hell-hounds, to lick up the draff and filth   630
Which man's polluting Sin with taint hath shed
On what was pure, till cramm'd and gorg'd, nigh burst
With suckt and glutted offal, at one sling
Of thy victorious Arm, well-pleasing Son,
Both *Sin*, and *Death*, and yawning *Grave* at last   635
Through *Chaos* hurl'd, obstruct the mouth of Hell
For ever, and seal up his ravenous Jaws.
Then Heav'n and Earth renew'd shall be made pure
To sanctity that shall receive no stain:
Till then the Curse pronounc't on both precedes.   640
   He ended, and the heav'nly Audience loud
Sung *Halleluiah*, as the sound of Seas,
Through multitude that sung: Just are thy ways,
Righteous are thy Decrees on all thy Works;

617. *havoc* was a battle-cry used when troops were ready to begin plundering. It was often used as a transitive verb.

624. *conniving* reflects its Latin meaning of "shutting the eyes."

629–633. Among many vague parallels to this scene in Du Bartas which are noted by G. McColley in *SP*, XXXV (1938), 87, the closest is to these lines. To make the parallel McColley collects the following scattered phrases from *The Divine Weeks*, p. 273:
"God . . . summon'd-up/With thundering call the damned *Crew*, that sup/Of . . . Bloody *Cocy-* *tus*, muddy *Acheron.*/Come snake-trest Sisters, com . . ./Com, parbreak heer your foul, black, banefull gall."

635. Cf. St. Paul: "Death is swallowed up in victory" (I Cor. xv, 54).

638. In *CD* I, xxxiii (C. E. XVI, 368), Milton stated his faith in "a new heaven and a new earth . . . coming down from God out of heaven" and in the "destruction of the present unclean and polluted world."

642. "And I heard as it were the voice of a great multitude, and as the voice of many waters, . . . saying 'Alleluia' " (Rev. xix, 6).

Who can extenuate thee? Next, to the Son,   645
Destin'd restorer of Mankind, by whom
New Heav'n and Earth shall to the Ages rise,
Or down from Heav'n descend. Such was thir song,
While the Creator calling forth by name
His mighty Angels gave them several charge,   650
As sorted best with present things. The Sun
Had first his precept so to move, so shine,
As might affect the Earth with cold and heat
Scarce tolerable, and from the North to call
Decrepit Winter, from the South to bring   655
Solstitial summer's heat. To the blanc Moon
Her office they prescrib'd, to th' other five
Thir planetary motions and aspécts
In *Sextile, Square,* and *Trine,* and *Opposite,*
Of noxious efficacy, and when to join   660
In Synod unbenign, and taught the fixt
Thir influence malignant when to show'r,
Which of them rising with the Sun, or falling,
Should prove tempestuous: To the Winds they set
Thir corners, when with bluster to confound   665
Sea, Air, and Shore, the Thunder when to roll
With terror through the dark Aereal Hall.
Some say he bid his Angels turn askance
The Poles of Earth twice ten degrees and more
From the Sun's Axle; they with labor push'd   670
Oblique the Centric Globe: Some say the Sun
Was bid turn Reins from th' Equinoctial Road
Like distant breadth to *Taurus* with the Sev'n
Atlantic Sisters, and the *Spartan* Twins
Up to the *Tropic* Crab; thence down amain   675
By *Leo* and the *Virgin* and the *Scales,*
As deep as *Capricorn,* to bring in change

651–706. Like all his contemporaries Milton interpreted Genesis iii, 17, as meaning that after the Fall nature "became subject to mortality and a curse on account of man" (*CD* I, xiii; C. E. XV, 216). The theme inspired such theological works as Godfrey Goodman's *The Fall of Man, or the Corruption of Nature Proved by Natural Reason* and such poetry as Du Bartas' *Divine Weeks.* When Adam sinned, said Henry Vaughan in *Corruption,*

He drew the curse upon the world and cracked
    The whole frame with his fall.

651. *sorted:* corresponded.
656. *blanc* was Milton's spelling when he intended the word to mean "white" or "pale-colored," as it does in French.
657. *th' other five* are the other five planets. Cf. V, 177.
659. In a *Sextile* (60°), a *Square* (90°), a *Trine* (120°), or *Opposite* (180°) aspect to each other any two planets were regarded as exerting a harmful influence upon the earth.
661. In *Synod* (conjunction) in any sign of the zodiac the planets were regarded as in an "indifferent" aspect, neither benign nor malignant.

662. Contrast the "selectest influence" of the constellations in VIII, 513.
665. So in the seventh Holy Sonnet Donne commands the angels to blow "At the round earth's imagin'd corners."
668–678. Regarding the course of the sun as having originally coincided with the celestial equator, Milton imagines either that the angels tilted the earth's axis 23½ degrees or that the sun changed its course so as to approach the tropic of Cancer in the spring, when it reaches the constellation *Taurus* (the Bull), in whose neck are the *Atlantic Sisters* (the Pleiades, cf. VII, 374), and then to climb through the *Spartan Twins* (Castor and Pollux) to the *Crab.* In July, August, and September it descends through *Leo* (the Lion), the *Virgin,* and the *Scales* to cross the equator southward to the tropic of *Capricorn.* "No heat nor cold had touched them," said Jakob Boehme in *Mysterium Magnum* xviii, 13, "if Adam had not fallen; there had been no winter manifest upon the earth." The entire passage seems—as M. Kelley suggests in *PMLA,* LXX (1955), 1098—to reflect Aratus' survey of the signs of the Zodiac in *Phaenomena,* 741–50.

Of Seasons to each Clime; else had the Spring
Perpetual smil'd on Earth with vernant Flow'rs,
Equal in Days and Nights, except to those   680
Beyond the Polar Circles; to them Day
Had unbenighted shone, while the low Sun
To recompense his distance, in thir sight
Had rounded still th' *Horizon,* and not known
Or East or West, which had forbid the Snow   685
From cold *Estotiland,* and South as far
Beneath *Magellan.* At that tasted Fruit
The Sun, as from *Thyéstean* Banquet, turn'd
His course intended; else how had the World
Inhabited, though sinless, more than now,   690
Avoided pinching cold and scorching heat?
These changes in the Heav'ns, though slow, produc'd
Like change on Sea and Land, sideral blast,
Vapor, and Mist, and Exhalation hot,
Corrupt and Pestilent: Now from the North   695
Of *Norumbega,* and the *Samoed* shore
Bursting thir brazen Dungeon, arm'd with ice
And snow and hail and stormy gust and flaw,
Boreas and *Cæcias* and *Argestes* loud
And *Thrascias* rend the Woods and Seas upturn;   700
With adverse blast upturns them from the South
Notus and *Afer* black with thundrous Clouds
From *Serraliona;* thwart of these as fierce
Forth rush the *Levant* and the *Ponent* Winds
Eurus and *Zephir* with thir lateral noise,   705
Sirocco, and *Libecchio.* Thus began
Outrage from lifeless things; but Discord first
Daughter of Sin, among th' irrational,
Death introduc'd through fierce antipathy:
Beast now with Beast gan war, and Fowl with Fowl,   710
And Fish with Fish; to graze the Herb all leaving,
Devour'd each other; nor stood much in awe
Of Man, but fled him, or with count'nance grim
Glar'd on him passing: these were from without
The growing miseries, which *Adam* saw   715
Already in part, though hid in gloomiest shade,

686–687. On the Mercator maps *Estotiland* lies on the northeastern coast of Labrador. *Magellan:* the straits of Magellan.

688. The myth of Atreus represented the sun as averting his face when Atreus served his brother Thyestes with the flesh of his own sons.

693. *sideral* (sidereal) *blast:* a blast from the stars.

696. All northern New England was vaguely called *Norumbega,* where Burton thought that "in 45° lat. all the sea is frozen ice" (*Anatomy* II, ii, 3; Everyman Ed. II. p. 44). In *Moscovia* (C. E. X, 344) Milton describes the *Samoeds* as accustomed to live and travel over immense depths of snow.

699-706. Most of these winds will be found on Peter Apian's chart in his *Cosmographia,* which is reproduced on page 432 from the edition of 1580. It is oriented with the south at the top K. Svend-

sen has collected much relevant meteorological lore in *M.&S.,* pp. 94–97, and in *Milieu,* pp. 79 and 121–22, Whiting connects this passage with Pliny's distribution of the winds to the four points of the compass and with their representation in Jan Jansson's *Atlas.*

703. *Serraliona:* the modern Sierra Leone, on the west African coast.

704. *Levant,* like "Orient," refers to the east; *Ponent,* like "Occident," to the west. On the chart east winds like *Eurus* and west winds like *Zephyr* blow laterally.

706. The use of the Italian name, *Sirocco,* for the southeast wind, and of *Libecchio* for the southwest wind seemed natural to Milton because, as Peacham's *Compleat Gentleman* (1634, p. 64) explained, "the eight principall winds are commonly expressed in the *Italian.*"

To sorrow abandon'd, but worse felt within,
And in a troubl'd Sea of passion tost,
Thus to disburd'n sought with sad complaint.
O miserable of happy! is this the end   720
Of this new glorious World, and mee so late
The Glory of that Glory, who now become
Accurst of blessed, hide me from the face
Of God, whom to behold was then my highth
Of happiness: yet well, if here would end   725
The misery, I deserv'd it, and would
My own deservings; but this will not serve;
All that I eat or drink, or shall beget,
Is propagated curse. O voice once heard
Delightfully, *Increase and multiply,*   730
Now death to hear! for what can I increase
Or multiply, but curses on my head?
Who of all Ages to succeed, but feeling
The evil on him brought by me, will curse
My Head; Ill fare our Ancestor impure,   735
For this we may thank *Adam;* but his thanks
Shall be the execration; so besides
Mine own that bide upon me, all from mee
Shall with a fierce reflux on mee redound,
On mee as on thir natural centre light   740
Heavy, though in thir place. O fleeting joys
Of Paradise, dear bought with lasting woes!
Did I request thee, Maker, from my Clay
To mould me Man, did I solicit thee
From darkness to promote me, or here place   745
In this delicious Garden? as my Will
Concurr'd not to my being, it were but right
And equal to reduce me to my dust,
Desirous to resign, and render back
All I receiv'd, unable to perform   750
Thy terms too hard, by which I was to hold
The good I sought not. To the loss of that,
Sufficient penalty, why hast thou added
The sense of endless woes? inexplicable
Thy Justice seems; yet to say truth, too late   755
I thus contest; then should have been refus'd
Those terms whatever, when they were propos'd:
Thou didst accept them; wilt thou enjoy the good,
Then cavil the conditions? and though God
Made thee without thy leave, what if thy Son   760
Prove disobedient, and reprov'd, retort,
Wherefore didst thou beget me? I sought it not:
Wouldst thou admit for his contempt of thee
That proud excuse? yet him not thy election,

718. The metaphor, which is elaborated at length
in Vaughan's *The Storm,* goes back to Isaiah lvii,
20—"The wicked are like the troubled sea, when
it cannot rest."
730. *Increase and multiply* was part of God's
blessing in Genesis i, 28.
738. *Mine own* refers to *curses* in l. 732.
739. *redound:* flow back (like a returning wave).

743. Cf. Isaiah xlv, 9: "Woe unto him that striveth with his maker! . . . Shall the clay say to him
that fashioneth it, 'What makest thou?' "
748. *equal:* just, fair.
762. Cf. Isaiah xlv, 10: "Woe unto him that saith
unto his father, 'What begettest thou?' "
764. *election:* choice.

But Natural necessity begot.   765
God made thee of choice his own, and of his own
To serve him, thy reward was of his grace,
Thy punishment then justly is at his Will.
Be it so, for I submit, his doom is fair,
That dust I am, and shall to dust return: 770
O welcome hour whenever! why delays
His hand to execute what his Decree
Fix'd on this day? why do I overlive,
Why am I mockt with death, and length'n'd out
To deathless pain? How gladly would I meet   775
Mortality my sentence, and be Earth
Insensible, how glad would lay me down
As in my Mother's lap! There I should rest
And sleep secure; his dreadful voice no more
Would Thunder in my ears, no fear of worse   780
To mee and to my offspring would torment me
With cruel expectation. Yet one doubt
Pursues me still, lest all I cannot die,
Lest that pure breath of Life, the Spirit of Man
Which God inspir'd, cannot together perish   785
With this corporeal Clod; then in the Grave,
Or in some other dismal place, who knows
But I shall die a living Death? O thought
Horrid, if true! yet why? it was but breath
Of Life that sinn'd; what dies but what had life   790
And sin? the Body properly hath neither.
All of me then shall die: let this appease
The doubt, since human reach no further knows.
For though the Lord of all be infinite,
Is his wrath also? be it, Man is not so,   795
But mortal doom'd. How can he exercise
Wrath without end on Man whom Death must end?
Can he make deathless Death? that were to make
Strange contradiction, which to God himself
Impossible is held, as Argument   800
Of weakness, not of Power. Will he draw out,
For anger's sake, finite to infinite
In punisht Man, to satisfy his rigor
Satisfi'd never; that were to extend
His Sentence beyond dust and Nature's Law,   805
By which all Causes else according still
To the reception of thir matter act,
Not to th' extent of thir own Sphere. But say

770. The thought of the entire passage recalls
the verse in Job (xxxiv, 15) which is echoed here.

782–794. Adam's rhetorical question parallels
Milton's in CD I, xiii (C. E. XV, 22–28): "What
could be more absurd than that the mind, which is
the part principally offending, should escape the
threatened death; and that the body alone, to which
immortality was equally alotted, . . . should pay
the penalty of sin by undergoing death, though
not implicated in the transgression?" Milton's belief in the extinction of both soul and body at physical death and in their joint resurrection may be
implicit, as G. Williamson declares in SP, XXXII

(1935), 553–79; but N. H. Henry is right in thinking—SP, XLVIII (1951), 248—that for Milton the
belief was "a thing indifferent, and no heresy." Cf.
ll. 49–54 above, n.

799. Writing on the divine omnipotence, Milton
said: "It must be remembered that the power of God
is not exerted in things which imply a contradiction" (CD I, ii, p. 908).

805. Nature's Law is "that general law which is
the origin of everything, and under which everything
acts" (CD I, ii; p. 905).

807. To explain reception Newton quoted the
axiom: "Every efficient (i. e. everything which acts)

That Death be not one stroke, as I suppos'd,
Bereaving sense, but endless misery   810
From this day onward, which I feel begun
Both in me, and without me, and so last
To perpetuity; Ay me, that fear
Comes thund'ring back with dreadful revolution
On my defenseless head; both Death and I   *born to die*   815
Am found Eternal, and incorporate both,
Nor I on my part single, in mee all
Posterity stands curst: Fair Patrimony
That I must leave ye, Sons; O were I able
To waste it all myself, and leave ye none!   820
So disinherited how would ye bless
Me now your Curse! Ah, why should all mankind
For one man's fault thus guiltless be condemn'd,
If guiltless? But from me what can proceed,
But all corrupt, both Mind and Will deprav'd,   825
Not to do only, but to will the same
With me? how can they then acquitted stand
In sight of God? Him after all Disputes
Forc't I absolve: all my evasions vain
And reasonings, though through Mazes, lead me still   830
But to my own conviction: first and last
On mee, mee only, as the source and spring
Of all corruption, all the blame lights due;
So might the wrath. Fond wish! couldst thou support
That burden heavier than the Earth to bear,   835
Than all the World much heavier, though divided
With that bad Woman? Thus what thou desir'st,
And what thou fear'st, alike destroys all hope
Of refuge, and concludes thee miserable
Beyond all past example and future,   840
To *Satan* only like both crime and doom.
O Conscience, into what Abyss of fears
And horrors hast thou driv'n me; out of which
I find no way, from deep to deeper plung'd!
    Thus *Adam* to himself lamented loud   845
Through the still Night, not now, as ere man fell,
Wholesome and cool and mild, but with black Air
Accompanied, with damps and dreadful gloom,
Which to his evil Conscience represented
All things with double terror: On the ground   850
Outstretcht he lay, on the cold ground, and oft

acts according to the powers of what receives its action, not according to its own powers."
    810. *Bereaving sense:* depriving of power of sen-
sation. The haunting dread is like Hamlet's fear
of consciousness
    When we have shuffled off this mortal coil.
    816. *Am* agrees with the near subject *I. incor-
porate:* united in one body.
    828–834. Adam's conviction of sin marks the
first of the four steps in regeneration in *CD* I, xix
(C. E. XV, 384): "Conviction of sin, contrition, confession, departure from evil and conversion to good."
    823. Adam's answer resembles Milton's reasoning
to prove that Adam's and Eve's posterity are "judged

and condemned in them, so that without doubt they
also sinned in them."
    840. Cf. the awakening of despair by Conscience
in Satan in IV, 23.
    842–844. In the chapter "Of the Punishment of
Sin"—in *CD* I, xii (C. E. XV, 204)—Adam's experience is the first illustration of the "terrors of
conscience" that follow "guiltiness." In her Rad-
cliffe thesis Miss I. Gamble quotes St. Augustine's
saying in his *Commentaries on the Psalms* (xli, 13),
that, "If by 'abyss' we understand a great depth,
is not man's heart an abyss? For what is more
profound than that abyss?"

Curs'd his Creation, Death as oft accus'd,
Of tardy execution, since denounc't
The day of his offense. Why comes not Death,
Said he, with one thrice acceptable stroke   855
To end me? Shall Truth fail to keep her word,
Justice Divine not hast'n to be just?
But Death comes not at call, Justice Divine
Mends not her slowest pace for prayers or cries.
O Woods, O Fountains, Hillocks, Dales and Bow'rs,   860
With other echo late I taught your Shades
To answer, and resound far other Song.
Whom thus afflicted when sad *Eve* beheld,
Desolate where she sat, approaching nigh,
Soft words to his fierce passion she assay'd: 865
But her with stern regard he thus repell'd.
     Out of my sight, thou Serpent, that name best
Befits thee with him leagu'd, thyself as false
And hateful; nothing wants, but that thy shape,
Like his, and color Serpentine may show   870
Thy inward fraud, to warn all Creatures from thee
Henceforth; lest that too heav'nly form, pretended
To hellish falsehood, snare them. But for thee
I had persisted happy, had not thy pride
And wand'ring vanity, when least was safe,   875
Rejected my forewarning, and disdain'd
Not to be trusted, longing to be seen
Though by the Devil himself, him overweening
To over-reach, but with the Serpent meeting
Fool'd and beguil'd, by him thou, I by thee,   880
To trust thee from my side, imagin'd wise,
Constant, mature, proof against all assaults,
And understood not all was but a show
Rather than solid virtue, all but a Rib
Crooked by nature, bent, as now appears,   885
More to the part sinister from me drawn,   *left side*
Well if thrown out, as supernumerary
To my just number found. O why did God,
Creator wise, that peopl'd highest Heav'n
With Spirits Masculine, create at last   890
This novelty on Earth, this fair defect
Of Nature, and not fill the World at once
With Men as Angels without Feminine,
Or find some other way to generate
Mankind? this mischief had not then befall'n,   895
And more that shall befall, innumerable
Disturbances on Earth through Female snares,
And strait conjunction with this Sex: for either

872. *pretended* has its Latin force of "held out"
(as a screen or disguise).
886. The play on the literal meaning of *sinister*
(left) and its common figurative meaning rests on
the tradition that Eve was made from a rib from
Adam's left side (as in VIII, 465). The idea that
woman was made from a bent rib and is "an imperfect animal—she always deceives," is traced by
K. Svendsen—in *M.&S.*, 183–85—to the *Malleus*

Maleficarum of Henricus Institoris and Jacobus
Springer (c. 1434) and to similar channels of anti-
feminist lore.
887. *supernumerary* may refer to a belief that
Adam was created with an extra rib for the later
creation of Eve.
888. The thought recalls Euripides' invective
against women in *Hippolytus* 616–18, and Milton's
reflection on them in *SA*, 1053–60.

He never shall find out fit Mate, but such
As some misfortune brings him, or mistake,   900
Or whom he wishes most shall seldom gain
Through her perverseness, but shall see her gain'd
By a far worse, or if she love, withheld
By Parents, or his happiest choice too late
Shall meet, already linkt and Wedlock-bound   905
To a fell Adversary, his hate or shame:
Which infinite calamity shall cause
To Human life, and household peace confound.
   He added not, and from her turn'd, but *Eve*
Not so repulst, with Tears that ceas'd not flowing,   910
And tresses all disorder'd, at his feet
Fell humble, and imbracing them, besought
His peace, and thus proceeded in her plaint.
   Forsake me not thus, *Adam,* witness Heav'n
What love sincere, and reverence in my heart   915
I bear thee, and unweeting have offended,
Unhappily deceiv'd; thy suppliant
I beg, and clasp thy knees; bereave me not,
Whereon I live, thy gentle looks, thy aid,
Thy counsel in this uttermost distress,   920
My only strength and stay: forlorn of thee,
Whither shall I betake me, where subsist?
While yet we live, scarce one short hour perhaps,
Between us two let there be peace, both joining,
As join'd in injuries, one enmity   925
Against a Foe by doom express assign'd us,
That cruel Serpent: On me exercise not
Thy hatred for this misery befall'n,
On me already lost, mee than thyself
More miserable; both have sinn'd, but thou   930
Against God only, I against God and thee,
And to the place of judgment will return,
There with my cries importune Heaven, that all
The sentence from thy head remov'd may light
On me, sole cause to thee of all this woe,   935
Mee mee only just object of his ire.
   She ended weeping, and her lowly plight,
Immovable till peace obtain'd from fault
Acknowledg'd and deplor'd, in *Adam* wrought
Commiseration; soon his heart relented   940
Towards her, his life so late and sole delight,
Now at his feet submissive in distress,
Creature so fair his reconcilement seeking,
His counsel whom she had displeas'd, his aid;
As one disarm'd, his anger all he lost,   945
And thus with peaceful words uprais'd her soon.
   Unwary, and too desirous, as before,
So now of what thou know'st not, who desir'st
The punishment all on thyself; alas,
Bear thine own first, ill able to sustain   950

---

899. Cf. VIII, 450, n.
938. *Immovable* seems to qualify *Adam,* who is inflexible until Eve's confession of her fault brings

peace between them. The thought recurs in *Samson Agonistes,* 1003–1007.

His full wrath whose thou feel'st as yet least part,
And my displeasure bear'st so ill. If Prayers
Could alter high Decrees, I to that place
Would speed before thee, and be louder heard,
That on my head all might be visited,   955
Thy frailty and infirmer Sex forgiv'n,
To me committed and by me expos'd.
But rise, let us no more contend, nor blame
Each other, blam'd enough elsewhere, but strive
In offices of Love, how we may light'n   960
Each other's burden in our share of woe
Since this day's Death denounc't, if aught I see,
Will prove no sudden, but a slow-pac't evil,
A long day's dying to augment our pain.
And to our Seed (O hapless Seed!) deriv'd.   965
     To whom thus Eve, recovering heart, repli'd.
Adam, by sad experiment I know
How little weight my words with thee can find,
Found so erroneous, thence by just event
Found so unfortunate; nevertheless,   970
Restor'd by thee, vile as I am, to place
Of new acceptance, hopeful to regain
Thy Love, the sole contentment of my heart
Living or dying, from thee I will not hide
What thoughts in my unquiet breast are ris'n,   975
Tending to some relief of our extremes,
Or end, though sharp and sad, yet tolerable,
As in our evils, and of easier choice.
If care of our descent perplex us most,
Which must be born to certain woe, devour'd   980
By Death at last, and miserable it is
To be to others cause of misery,
Our own begott'n, and of our Loins to bring
Into this cursed World a woeful Race,
That after wretched Life must be at last   985
Food for so foul a Monster, in thy power
It lies, yet ere Conception to prevent
The Race unblest, to being yet unbegot.
Childless thou art, Childless remain: So Death
Shall be deceiv'd his glut, and with us two   990
Be forc'd to satisfy his Rav'nous Maw.
But if thou judge it hard and difficult,
Conversing, looking, loving, to abstain
From Love's due Rites, Nuptial embraces sweet,
And with desire to languish without hope,   995
Before the present object languishing
With like desire, which would be misery
And torment less than none of what we dread,
Then both ourselves and Seed at once to free
From what we fear for both, let us make short,   1000

959. elsewhere, i. e., at "the place of judgment"
(932 above).
978. As in our evils: in such evils as ours—a Latinism.
979. descent: descendants.

987. prevent: forestall, cut off in advance. Cf.
IV, 996.
996. the present object is Eve herself, standing in
Adam's presence.

Let us seek Death, or he not found, supply
With our own hands his Office on ourselves;
Why stand we longer shivering under fears,
That show no end but Death, and have the power,
Of many ways to die the shortest choosing,   1005
Destruction with destruction to destroy.
   She ended here, or vehement despair
Broke off the rest; so much of Death her thoughts
Had entertain'd, as dy'd her Cheeks with pale.
But *Adam* with such counsel nothing sway'd,   1010
To better hopes his more attentive mind
Laboring had rais'd, and thus to *Eve* replied.
  Eve, thy contempt of life and pleasure seems
To argue in thee something more sublime
And excellent than what thy mind contemns;   1015
But self-destruction therefore sought, refutes
That excellence thought in thee, and implies,
Not thy contempt, but anguish and regret
For loss of life and pleasure overlov'd.
Or if thou covet death, as utmost end   1020
Of misery, so thinking to evade
The penalty pronounc't, doubt not but God
Hath wiselier arm'd his vengeful ire than so
To be forestall'd; much more I fear lest Death
So snatcht will not exempt us from the pain   1025
We are by doom to pay; rather such acts
Of contumacy will provoke the Highest
To make death in us live: Then let us seek
Some safer resolution, which methinks
I have in view, calling to mind with heed   1030
Part of our Sentence, that thy Seed shall bruise
The Serpent's head; piteous amends, unless
Be meant, whom I conjecture, our grand Foe
Satan, who in the Serpent hath contriv'd
Against us this deceit: to crush his head   1035
Would be revenge indeed; which will be lost
By death brought on ourselves, or childless days
Resolv'd, as thou proposest; so our Foe
Shall 'scape his punishment ordain'd, and wee
Instead shall double ours upon our heads.   1040
No more be mention'd then of violence
Against ourselves, and wilful barrenness,
That cuts us off from hope, and savors only
Rancor and pride, impatience and despite,
Reluctance against God and his just yoke   1045
Laid on our Necks.   Remember with what mild
And gracious temper he both heard and judg'd
Without wrath or reviling; wee expected
Immediate dissolution, which we thought

1013–1028. Adam's reasoning against Eve's proposal of suicide seems to G. Williamson—in *SP,*
XXXII (1935), 570—to be a reflection on the libertine arguments for suicide in Walter Charleton's *The
Immortality of the Human Soul* (1657) and in
Donne's *Biathanatos,* as well as on Hobbes's interpretation of the law of nature in *Leviathan.* But
basically the thought is as general as Hamlet's wish
that "th'Everlasting had not fix'd/His canon 'gainst
self-slaughter."
   1031–1036. Cf. ll. 168–84 above.
   1045. *Reluctance* keeps its Latin meaning of
"struggling."

Was meant by Death that day, when lo, to thee   1050
Pains only in Child-bearing were foretold,
And bringing forth, soon recompens't with joy,
Fruit of thy Womb: On mee the Curse aslope
Glanc'd on the ground, with labor I must earn
My bread; what harm? Idleness had been worse;   1055
My labor will sustain me; and lest Cold
Or Heat should injure us, his timely care
Hath unbesought provided, and his hands
Cloth'd us unworthy, pitying while he judg'd;
How much more, if we pray him, will his ear   1060
Be open, and his heart to pity incline,
And teach us further by what means to shun
Th' inclement Seasons, Rain, Ice, Hail and Snow,
Which now the Sky with various Face begins
To show us in this Mountain, while the Winds   1065
Blow moist and keen, shattering the graceful locks
Of these fair spreading Trees; which bids us seek
Some better shroud, some better warmth to cherish
Our Limbs benumb'd, ere this diurnal Star
Leave cold the Night, how we his gather'd beams   1070
Reflected, may with matter sere foment,
Or by collision of two bodies grind
The Air attrite to Fire, as late the Clouds
Justling or pusht with Winds rude in thir shock
Tine the slant Lightning, whose thwart flame driv'n down 1075
Kindles the gummy bark of Fir or Pine,
And sends a comfortable heat from far,
Which might supply the Sun: such Fire to use,
And what may else be remedy or cure
To evils which our own misdeeds have wrought,   1080
Hee will instruct us praying, and of Grace
Beseeching him, so as we need not fear
To pass commodiously this life, sustain'd
By him with many comforts, till we end
In dust, our, final rest and native home.   1085
What better can we do, than to the place
Repairing where he judg'd us, prostrate fall
Before him reverent, and there confess
Humbly our faults, and pardon beg, with tears
Watering the ground, and with our sighs the Air   1090
Frequenting, sent from hearts contrite, in sign
Of sorrow unfeign'd, and humiliation meek.
Undoubtedly he will relent and turn
From his displeasure; in whose look serene,
When angry most he seem'd and most severe,   1095

1050. *that day* is the preceding day.

1053. The curse has struck only a glancing blow and fallen to the ground, like an arrow that has grazed its mark. Cf. l. 201 above.

1065. In IV, 132–72, Paradise has been described as a *Mountain.*

1066. So Spenser speaks in *The Shepheardes Calendar* (*November,* l. 125) of "faded lockes" that "fall from the loftie oke."

1069. *this diurnal Star:* the sun. Cf. the *Day-star in Lycidas,* 168.

1073. *Attrite* is felt as having its Latin form as a perfect passive participle, and as meaning "rubbed," or "worked by friction."

1075. *Tine:* kindle. *thwart:* transverse, slanting.

1075–1078. The theory that men first secured fire from the kindling of the forests by lightning is vividly stated in Lucretius' *De rerum natura* V, 1091–95. Cf. VII, 463–70, n.

1081. *praying:* if we pray.

1091. *Frequenting* has its Latin meaning of "filling" or "crowding."

What else but favor, grace, and mercy shone?
  So spake our Father penitent, nor *Eve*
Felt less remorse: they forthwith to the place
Repairing where he judg'd them prostrate fell
Before him reverent, and both confess'd
Humbly thir faults, and pardon begg'd, with tears
Watering the ground, and with thir sighs the Air
Frequenting, sent from hearts contrite, in sign
Of sorrow unfeign'd, and humiliation meek.

1100

The End of the Tenth Book.

BOOK XI

THE ARGUMENT

The Son of God presents to his Father the Prayers of our first Parents now repenting, and intercedes for them: God accepts them, but declares that they must no longer abide in Paradise; sends Michael *with a Band of Cherubim to dispossess them; but first to reveal*

Epic description of shield; Achilles, Aeneas' shields.

to Adam *future things:* Michael's *coming down.* Adam *shows to* Eve *certain ominous signs; he discerns* Michael's *approach, goes out to meet him: the Angel denounces thir departure.* Eve's *Lamentation.* Adam *pleads, but submits: The Angel leads him up to a high Hill, sets before him in vision what shall happ'n till the Flood.*

Thus they in lowliest plight repentant stood
Praying, for from the Mercy-seat above
Prevenient Grace descending had remov'd
The stony from thir hearts, and made new flesh
Regenerate grow instead, that sighs now breath'd   5
Unutterable, which the Spirit of prayer
Inspir'd, and wing'd for Heav'n with speedier flight
Than loudest Oratory: yet thir port
Not of mean suitors, nor important less
Seem'd thir Petition, than when th' ancient Pair   10
In Fables old, less ancient yet than these,
Deucalion and chaste *Pyrrha* to restore
The Race of Mankind drown'd, before the Shrine
Of *Themis* stood devout. To Heav'n thir prayers
Flew up, nor miss'd the way, by envious winds   15
Blown vagabond or frustrate: in they pass'd
Dimensionless through Heav'nly doors: then clad
With incense, where the Golden Altar fum'd,
By thir great Intercessor, came in sight
Before the Father's Throne: Then the glad Son   20
Presenting, thus to intercede began.
See Father, what first fruits on Earth are sprung
From thy implanted Grace in Man, these Sighs
And Prayers, which in this Golden Censer, mixt
With Incense, I thy Priest before thee bring,   25
Fruits of more pleasing savor from thy seed
Sown with contrition in his heart, than those
Which his own hand manuring all the Trees
Of Paradise could have produc't, ere fall'n
From innocence. Now therefore bend thine ear   30
To supplication, hear his sighs though mute;
Unskilful with what words to pray, let mee
Interpret for him, mee his Advocate

1. *stood* seems inconsistent with *prostrate* in X, 1099, but in IV, 720, Adam stands to pray. In *CD* II, iv (C. E. XVII, 90), Milton says that, "No particular posture of the body in prayer was enjoined, even under the law."

2. The image is the mercy-seat in Aaron's tabernacle with its "two cherubim of gold, of beaten work, . . . in the two ends" (Exod. xxv, 18), which was traditionally a type of the intercession of angels, or of Christ, in heaven.

3. *Prevenient Grace:* grace which anticipates repentance. Cf. Ezekiel xi, 19: "I will take the stony heart out of their flesh, and will give them an heart of flesh."

5. So St. Paul says that "the Spirit itself maketh intercession for us with groanings that cannot be uttered" (Rom. viii, 26).

10. *th' ancient Pair:* Deucalion and Pyrrha, whom Ovid describes (*Met.* I, 321–80) as praying effectually to "fate-revealing Themis," the goddess of justice, after their survival of a great flood.

15. These prayers are contrasted with the "fruits/ Of painful superstition and blind zeal" in III, 451–52, which "a violent cross wind . . . blows . . . transverse" in the limbo of vanity.

17. *Dimensionless* implies the immateriality of the prayers; extensionlessness was basic in the Cartesian definition of non-corporeal or spiritual being. The prayers are *clad With incense,* like those which are presented by the angel in Revelation viii, 3, who "stood at the altar, having a golden censer; and there was given unto him much incense, that he should offer it with the prayers of all saints. . . ."

19. The *Intercessor* is the Son of God, who makes intercession by "appearing in the presence of God for us" and by "rendering our prayers agreeable to God" (*CD* I, xv; C. E. XV, 294).

28. *manuring:* dressing, cultivating. Cf. IV, 628.

33. Cf. "We have an advocate with the Father, Jesus Christ the righteous: And he is the propitiation for our sins" (I John ii, 1–2).

And propitiation, all his works on mee
Good or not good ingraft, my Merit those   35
Shall perfet, and for these my Death shall pay.
Accept me, and in mee from these receive
The smell of peace toward Mankind, let him live
Before thee reconcil'd, at least his days
Number'd, though sad, till Death, his doom (which I   40
To mitigate thus plead, not to reverse)
To better life shall yield him, where with mee
All my redeem'd may dwell in joy and bliss,
Made one with me as I with thee am one.
  To whom the Father, without Cloud, serene.   45
All thy request for Man, accepted Son,
Obtain, all thy request was my Decree:
But longer in that Paradise to dwell,
The Law I gave to Nature him forbids:
Those pure immortal Elements that know   50
No gross, no unharmonious mixture foul,
Eject him tainted now, and purge him off
As a distemper, gross to air as gross,
And mortal food, as may dispose him best
For dissolution wrought by Sin, that first   55
Distemper'd all things, and of incorrupt
Corrupted. I at first with two fair gifts
Created him endow'd, with Happiness
And Immortality: that fondly lost,
This other serv'd but to eternize woe;   60
slip of Milton's? <u>Till I provided Death; so Death becomes</u>
His final remedy, and after Life
Tri'd in sharp tribulation, and refin'd
By Faith and faithful works, to second Life,
<u>Wak't in the renovation of the just,</u>   65
<u>Resigns him up with Heav'n and Earth renew'd.</u>
But let us call to Synod all the Blest
Through Heav'n's wide bounds; from them I will not hide
My judgments, how with Mankind I proceed,
As how with peccant Angels late they saw;   70
And in thir state, though firm, stood more confirm'd.
  He ended, and the Son gave signal high
To the bright Minister that watch'd: hee blew
His Trumpet, heard in *Oreb* since perhaps
When God descended, and perhaps once more   75
To sound at general Doom. Th' Angelic blast
Fill'd all the Regions: from thir blissful Bow'rs
Of *Amarantin* Shade, Fountain or Spring,

43. So Christ prays in John xvii, 11: "Holy Father, keep through thine own name those whom thou hast given me, that they may be one, as we are."

49. Cf. *Nature's Law* in X, 805.

50–57. The *incorrupt* and *pure Elements* of Eden are regarded as expelling fallen man as Belial says that the *Ethereal mould* of heaven, *incapable of stain*, would automatically *purge off the baser fire* of the rebel angels if they were to invade heaven. Cf. II, 140.

64. Here and in XII, 427, Milton indicates his

qualified assent to the Lutheran doctrine of justification by faith.

74. The *Trumpet*, which summoned Michael's forces in heaven (VI, 60), Milton says *may* have been heard on earth when God gave the Ten Commandments to Moses on Mount Sinai, or *Horeb*, and *may* be heard again when God "shall send his angels with a great sound of the trumpet" (Matt. xxiv, 31) for the last judgment. At the judgment—according to traditions recorded in the *Jewish Encyclopaedia* VIII, 537—Michael will blow the trumpet. Cf. the comparison of *the wakeful trump of*

By the waters of Life, where'er they sat
In fellowships of joy, the Sons of Light   80
Hasted, resorting to the Summons high,
And took thir Seats; till from his Throne supreme
Th' Almighty thus pronounc'd his sovran Will.
　　O Sons, like one of us Man is become
To know both Good and Evil, since his taste   85
Of that defended Fruit; but let him boast
His knowledge of Good lost, and Evil got,
Happier, had it suffic'd him to have known
Good by itself, and Evil not at all.
He sorrows now, repents, and prays contríte,   90
My motions in him; longer than they move,
His heart I know, how variable and vain
Self-left. Lest therefore his now bolder hand
Reach also of the Tree of Life, and eat,
And live for ever, dream at least to live   95
For ever, to remove him I decree,
And send him from the Garden forth to Till
The Ground whence he was taken, fitter soil.
　　Michael, this my behest have thou in charge,
Take to thee from among the Cherubim   100
Thy choice of flaming Warriors, lest the Fiend
Or in behalf of Man, or to invade
Vacant possession some new trouble raise:
Haste thee, and from the Paradise of God
Without remorse drive out the sinful Pair,   105
From hallow'd ground th' unholy, and denounce
To them and to thir Progeny from thence
Perpetual banishment. Yet lest they faint
At the sad Sentence rigorously urg'd,
For I behold them soft'nd and with tears   110
Bewailing thir excess, all terror hide.
If patiently thy bidding they obey,
Dismiss them not disconsolate; reveal
To Adam what shall come in future days,
As I shall thee enlighten, intermix   115
My Cov'nant in the woman's seed renew'd;
So send them forth, though sorrowing, yet in peace:
And on the East side of the Garden place,
Where entrance up from Eden easiest climbs,
Cherubic watch, and of a Sword the flame   120
Wide waving, all approach far off to fright,
And guard all passage to the Tree of Life:

doom to such a horrid clang/As on Mount Sinai
rang in Nativity, 157-58.
　79. The waters of Life are the River of Bliss of
III, 358.
　84. "And the Lord God said, Behold, the man is
become as one of us, to know good and evil: and
now, lest he put forth his hand, and take also of
the tree of life, and eat, and live for ever: Therefore the Lord God sent him forth from the garden
of Eden" (Gen. iii, 22-23).
　86. defended: forbidden. Cf. XII, 207.
　91. My motions: my influence, i.e. the prevenient
Grace of l. 3 above.

　93. Self-left: when left to itself.
　99. Cf. the note on Michael in VI, 44.
　102. In reply to those who would interpret in behalf of as "implying Satan's good will towards man."
R. Adams observes—in Ikon, p. 119—that the
O.E.D. makes the meaning "with regard to" clear
as a usage of Milton's time.
　105. remorse: sorrow or pity. Cf. V, 566.
　118. "So he drove out the man; and he placed at
the east of the garden of Eden cherubim, and a
flaming sword which turned every way, to keep the
way of the tree of life" (Gen. iii, 24).

Lest Paradise a receptácle prove
To Spirits foul, and all my Trees thir prey,
With whose stol'n Fruit Man once more to delude.   125
    He ceas'd; and th' Archangelic Power prepar'd
For swift descent, with him the Cohort bright
Of watchful Cherubim; four faces each
Had, like a double *Janus,* all thir shape
Spangl'd with eyes more numerous than those   130
Of *Argus,* and more wakeful than to drowse,
Charm'd with *Arcadian* Pipe, the Pastoral Reed
Of *Hermes,* or his opiate Rod.   Meanwhile
To resalute the World with sacred Light
Leucóthea wak'd, and with fresh dews imbalm'd   135
The Earth, when *Adam* and first Matron *Eve*
Had ended now thir Orisons, and found
Strength added from above, new hope to spring
Out of despair, joy, but with fear yet linkt;
Which thus to *Eve* his welcome words renew'd.   140
    Eve, easily may Faith admit, that all
The good which we enjoy, from Heav'n descends;
But that from us aught should ascend to Heav'n
So prevalent as to concern the mind
Of God high-blest, or to incline his will,   145
Hard to belief may seem; yet this will Prayer,
Or one short sigh of human breath, up-borne
Ev'n to the Seat of God.   For since I sought
By Prayer th' offended Deity to appease,
Kneel'd and before him humbl'd all my heart,   150
Methought I saw him placable and mild,
Bending his ear; persuasion in me grew
That I was heard with favor; peace return'd
Home to my Breast, and to my memory
His promise, that thy Seed shall bruise our Foe;   155
Which then not minded in dismay, yet now
Assures me that the bitterness of death
Is past, and we shall live.   Whence Hail to thee,
Eve rightly call'd, Mother of all Mankind,
Mother of all things living, since by thee   160
Man is to live, and all things live for Man.
    To whom thus *Eve* with sad demeanor meek.
Ill worthy I such title should belong
To me transgressor, who for thee ordain'd
A help, became thy snare; to mee reproach   165
Rather belongs, distrust and all dispraise:

129. The cherubs are compared to the Roman
god of gates, *Janus,* who was usually sculptured with
two, but sometimes with four faces, like the angels
of Ezekiel's vision. A. Gilbert notes in *PMLA,* LIV
(1941), 1026–30, that Calvin interpreted the four
faces of Ezekiel's cherubim as signifying their power
in the four quarters of the earth—a symbolism which
was also understood to attach to the Janus quadri-
frons. Cf. VI, 750, n.
130–132. The allusions span the description of the
cherubs as "full of eyes" in Ezekiel i, 18, and
Ovid's description (*Met.* I, 625–26) of Juno's com-

mission of *Argus,* whose "head was set about with
a hundred eyes," to watch her rival Io, though later
in the story *Hermes* lulls all the eyes to sleep with his
medicated rod and his pipes.
    135. *Leucothea,* the "shining goddess," is identi-
fied by Ovid (*Fasti,* 479 and 545) with the Roman
goddess of the dawn, Matuta.
    159. "And Adam called his wife's name Eve; be-
cause she was the mother of all living" (Gen. iii, 20).
    162. *sad:* serious, grave. Cf. the angels' *sad reso-
lution* in VI, 541.
    165. Cf. the note on *Mate* in X, 899.

But infinite in pardon was my Judge,
That I who first brought Death on all, am grac't
The source of life; next favorable thou,
Who highly thus to entitle me voutsaf'st,   170
Far other name deserving. But the Field
To labor calls us now with sweat impos'd,
Though after sleepless Night; for see the Morn,
All unconcern'd with our unrest, begins
Her rosy progress smiling; let us forth,   175
I never from thy side henceforth to stray,
Where'er our day's work lies, though now enjoin'd
Laborious, till day droop; while here we dwell,
What can be toilsome in these pleasant Walks?
Here let us live, though in fall'n state, content.   180
  So spake, so wish'd much humbl'd Eve, but Fate
Subscrib'd not; Nature first gave Signs, imprest
On Bird, Beast, Air, Air suddenly eclips'd
After short blush of Morn; nigh in her sight
The Bird of Jove, stoopt from his aery tow'r,   *eagle   185
Two Birds of gayest plume before him drove:
Down from a Hill the Beast that reigns in Woods,
First hunter then, pursu'd a gentle brace,
Goodliest of all the Forest, Hart and Hind;
Direct to th' Eastern Gate was bent thir flight.   190
Adam observ'd, and with his Eye the chase
Pursuing, not unmov'd to Eve thus spake.
  O Eve, some furder change awaits us nigh,
Which Heav'n by these mute signs in Nature shows
Forerunners of his purpose, or to warn   195
Us haply too secure of our discharge
From penalty, because from death releast
Some days; how long, and what till then our life,
Who knows, or more than this, that we are dust,
And thither must return and be no more.   200
Why else this double object in our sight
Of flight pursu'd in th' Air and o'er the ground
One way the self-same hour? why in the East
Darkness ere Day's mid-course, and Morning light
More orient in yon Western Cloud that draws   205
O'er the blue Firmament a radiant white,
And slow descends, with something heav'nly fraught.
  He err'd not, for by this the heav'nly Bands
Down from a Sky of Jasper lighted now
In Paradise, and on a Hill made halt,   210
A glorious Apparition, had not doubt
And carnal fear that day dimm'd Adam's eye.

182–192. The Air is eclips'd or darkened probably
by an eclipse of the sun such as sheds disastrous twilight in I, 597. The blight now beginning to fall
on all nature is the consequence of the influence malignant of X, 662, that the heavenly bodies have begun to pour upon the earth. The "pathetic fallacy"
involved in the conception of nature as degenerating
after man's fall is justified by A. Z. Butler in Essays
in Honor of Walter Clyde Curry (Nashville, 1954),
pp. 274–76, as logical in the light of the theory of
the "great chain of being" which Raphael expounds
in V, 469–90.

185. The Bird of Jove, the eagle, and the lion
both feel their first hunting instinct. Stooping was
a term in falconry for the swoop of a hawk from its
tower (lofty flight) to strike its prey.

204. the light is the glory of Michael's descending
angels.

Not that more glorious, when the Angels met
Jacob in *Mahanaim,* where he saw
The field Pavilion'd with his Guardians bright;   215
Nor that which on the flaming Mount appear'd
In *Dothan,* cover'd with a Camp of Fire,
Against the *Syrian* King, who to surprise
One man, Assassin-like had levied War,
War unproclaim'd.   The Princely Hierarch   220
In thir bright stand, there left his Powers to seize
Possession of the Garden; hee alone,
To find where *Adam* shelter'd, took his way,
Not unperceiv'd of *Adam,* who to *Eve,*
While the great Visitant approach'd, thus spake.   225
    Eve, now expect great tidings, which perhaps
Of us will soon determine, or impose
New Laws to be observ'd; for I descry
From yonder blazing Cloud that veils the Hill
One of the heav'nly Host, and by his Gait   230
None of the meanest, some great Potentate
Or of the Thrones above, such Majesty
Invests him coming; yet not terrible,
That I should fear, nor sociably mild,
As *Raphaël,* that I should much confide,   235
But solemn and sublime, whom not to offend,
With reverence I must meet, and thou retire.

[margin note: • She retires again]

He ended; and th' Arch-Angel soon drew nigh,
Not in his shape Celestial, but as Man
Clad to meet Man; over his lucid Arms   240

[margin note: • Same as Genesis meeting Abraham.]

A military Vest of purple flow'd
Livelier than *Melibæan,* or the grain
Of *Sarra,* worn by Kings and Heroes old
In time of Truce; *Iris* had dipt the woof;
His starry Helm unbuckl'd show'd him prime   245
In Manhood where Youth ended; by his side
As in a glistering *Zodiac* hung the Sword,
Satan's dire dread, and in his hand the Spear.
Adam bow'd low, hee Kingly from his State
Inclin'd not, but his coming thus declar'd.   250
    Adam, Heav'n's high behest no Preface needs:
Sufficient that thy Prayers are heard, and Death,
Then due by sentence when thou didst transgress,
Defeated of his seizure many days
Giv'n thee of Grace, wherein thou mayst repent,   255

---

214. *Mahanaim* (i. e. the two hosts) was Jacob's name for the place where "the angels of God met him" (Gen. xxxii, 1–2).

217. After warning the king of Israel of a treacherous raid by the king of Syria, the prophet Elisha was surrounded by the Syrians in *Dothan.* He would have been kidnapped if the mountain had not been "full of horses and chariots of fire round about Elisha" (II Kings vi, 17).

234–235. Cf. the reference to Raphael as *the sociable Spirit* in V, 221.

242. The Thessalian town of *Melibæa* was famous for its purple *grain* (dye), as Virgil suggests in the *Aeneid* V, 251.

243. *Sarra* was an ancient name for Tyre, which was famous for its dyes as early as its king's dispatch of "a man skilful to work . . . in purple, in blue, and in fine linen" to help build Solomon's temple (II Chron. ii, 14).

244. Cf. *Iris' Woof,* the colors of the goddess of dawn, in *Comus,* 83.

247. *Zodiac* keeps its Greek meaning of "a belt," but it also suggests the splendor of the celestial zodiac and its constellations.

254. *Defeated:* frustrated (in his attempt to arrest Adam). Cf. ll. 96–98 and 48–49 above.

And one bad act with many deeds well done
May'st cover: well may then thy Lord appeas'd
Redeem thee quite from Death's rapacious claim;
But longer in this Paradise to dwell
Permits not; to remove thee I am come,   260
And send thee from the Garden forth to till
The ground whence thou wast tak'n, fitter Soil.
     He added not, for *Adam* at the news
Heart-strook with chilling gripe of sorrow stood,
That all his senses bound; *Eve,* who unseen   265
Yet all had heard, with audible lament
Discover'd soon the place of her retire.
     O unexpected stroke, worse than of Death!   • *best lines she*
Must I thus leave thee Paradise? thus leave   *has.*
Thee Native Soil, these happy Walks and Shades,   270
Fit haunt of Gods? where I had hope to spend,
Quiet though sad, the respite of that day
That must be mortal to us both. O flow'rs,
That never will in other Climate grow,
My early visitation, and my last   275
At Ev'n, which I bred up with tender hand
From the first op'ning bud, and gave ye Names,
Who now shall rear ye to the Sun, or rank
Your Tribes, and water from th' ambrosial Fount?
Thee lastly nuptial Bower, by mee adorn'd   280
With what to sight or smell was sweet; from thee
How shall I part, and whither wander down
Into a lower World, to this obscure
And wild, how shall we breathe in other Air
Less pure, accustom'd to immortal Fruits?   285
     Whom thus the Angel interrupted mild.
Lament not *Eve,* but patiently resign
What justly thou hast lost; nor set thy heart,
Thus over-fond, on that which is not thine;
Thy going is not lonely, with thee goes   290
Thy Husband, him to follow thou art bound;
Where he abides, think there thy native soil.
     Adam by this from the cold sudden damp
Recovering, and his scatter'd spirits return'd,
To *Michael* thus his humble words address'd.   295
     Celestial, whether among the Thrones, or nam'd
Of them the Highest, for such of shape may seem
Prince above Princes, gently hast thou told
Thy message, which might else in telling wound,
And in performing end us; what besides   300
Of sorrow and dejection and despair
Our frailty can sustain, thy tidings bring,
Departure from this happy place, our sweet
Recess, and only consolation left

272. *respite:* the remainder of the time granted
by God's reprieve of the sentence of physical death.

273-285. The thought remotely parallels Henry
More's interpretation of Adam's "casting out of Paradise" as "a descent from an 'aerial' to a 'terrestrial'
world," the loss of an original state that was "wholly

etherial" and was "an happy and joyful condition of
the Spirit." Cf. ll. 50-57 above, n.

283. *to this:* in comparison with this.

294. Cf. *Eve's damp horror* in V, 65. Fear *scattered* the vital and animal *spirits* from their seats in
the heart and head throughout the whole body. Cf.
V, 484-88, n.

Familiar to our eyes, all places else   305
Inhospitable appear and desolate,
Nor knowing us nor known: and if by prayer
Incessant I could hope to change the will
Of him who all things can, I would not cease
To weary him with my assiduous cries: 310
But prayer against his absolute Decree
No more avails than breath against the wind,
Blown stifling back on him that breathes it forth:
Therefore to his great bidding I submit.
This most afflicts me, that departing hence,   315
As from his face I shall be hid, depriv'd
His blessed count'nance; here I could frequent,
With worship, place by place where he voutsaf'd
Presence Divine, and to my Sons relate;
On this Mount he appear'd, under this Tree   320
Stood visible, among these Pines his voice
I heard, here with him at this Fountain talk'd:
So many grateful Altars I would rear
Of grassy Turf, and pile up every Stone
Of lustre from the brook, in memory,   325
Or monument to Ages, and thereon
Offer sweet smelling Gums and Fruits and Flow'rs:
In yonder nether World where shall I seek
His bright appearances, or footstep trace?
For though I fled him angry, yet recall'd   330
To life prolong'd and promis'd Race, I now
Gladly behold though but his utmost skirts
Of glory, and far off his steps adore.
  To whom thus *Michael* with regard benign.
Adam, thou know'st Heav'n his, and all the Earth,   335
Not this Rock only; his Omnipresence fills
Land, Sea, and Air, and every kind that lives,
Fomented by his virtual power and warm'd:
All th' Earth he gave thee to possess and rule,
No despicable gift; surmise not then   340
His presence to these narrow bounds confin'd
Of Paradise or *Eden:* this had been
Perhaps thy Capital Seat, from whence had spread
All generations, and had hither come
From all the ends of th' Earth, to celebrate   345
And reverence thee thir great Progenitor.
But this preëminence thou hast lost, brought down
To dwell on even ground now with thy Sons:
Yet doubt not but in Valley and in Plain
God is as here, and will be found alike   350

309. Cf. Lovelace's transitive use of *can:* "Yet
can I music too" (*O.E.D.*).
  310. *weary:* importune. Milton contrasts God
with the unjust judge of Luke xviii, 5–7, who could
be made to yield only by importunity.
  316. Adam's words resemble Cain's after his
curse for the murder of Abel: "Behold, thou hast
driven me out this day from the face of the earth;
and from thy face shall I be hid" (Gen. iv, 14).
  335–338. The thought fuses Christ's warning to

the woman of Samaria against worshipping God
only "in this mountain" (John iv, 21) with Jeremiah's question: "Can any hide himself in secret
places that I shall not see him? saith the Lord: do
not I fill heaven and earth?" (xxiii, 24). Cf. VII,
168–69.
  338. *Fomented:* filled with life-giving heat. Cf.
IV, 669. *virtual:* possessed of the power to instil
virtue.

Present, and of his presence many a sign
Still following thee, still compassing thee round
With goodness and paternal Love, his Face
Express, and of his steps the track Divine.
Which that thou may'st believe, and be confirm'd,   355
Ere thou from hence depart, know I am sent
To show thee what shall come in future days
To thee and to thy Offspring; good with bad
Expect to hear, supernal Grace contending
With sinfulness of Men; thereby to learn   360
True patience, and to temper joy with fear
And pious sorrow, equally inur'd
By moderation either state to bear,
Prosperous or adverse: so shalt thou lead
Safest thy life, and best prepar'd endure   365
Thy mortal passage when it comes. Ascend
This Hill; let *Eve* (for I have drencht her eyes) · *She doesn't see again*
Here sleep below while thou to foresight wak'st,
As once thou slep'st, while Shee to life was form'd.
　　To whom thus *Adam* gratefully repli'd.   370
Ascend, I follow thee, safe Guide, the path
Thou lead'st me, and to the hand of Heav'n submit,
However chast'ning, to the evil turn
My obvious breast, arming to overcome
By suffering, and earn rest from labor won,   375
If so I may attain. So both ascend
In the Visions of God: It was a Hill
Of Paradise the highest, from whose top
The Hemisphere of Earth in clearest Ken
Stretcht out to the amplest reach of prospect lay.   380
Not higher that Hill nor wider looking round,
Whereon for different cause the Tempter set
Our second *Adam* in the Wilderness,
To show him all Earth's Kingdoms and thir Glory.
His Eye might there command wherever stood   385
City of old or modern Fame, the Seat
Of mightiest Empire, from the destin'd Walls
Of *Cambalu*, seat of *Cathaian Can*,
And *Samarchand* by *Oxus*, *Temir's* Throne,
To *Paquin* of *Sinæan* Kings, and thence   390
To *Agra* and *Lahor* of great *Mogul*

357. Adam's vision of the future of mankind rests on epic precedent like the vision of Rome's future that Aeneas sees in the Elysian Fields (*Aen.* VI, 754–854) and Britomart's vision of her progeny in the *Faerie Queene* III, iii, 29–49; but it rests also on Daniel's vision of "Michael, one of the chief princes" coming to the help of exiled Israel (Dan. x, 13). Cf. VI, 44, n. Milton's closest precedent is in Du Bartas' *Divine Weeks*, in the parts from *The Handicrafts* through to *The Decay*.

363. The phrasing suggests the title of Petrarch's treatise *On the Remedies of both Kinds of Fortune* (i.e. of good and bad). The Stoic principle was assimilated very early by Christian humanism.

377–384. Milton recalls both "the visions of God . . . upon a very high mountain" of the prophet Ezekiel (x, 2) and the "exceeding high mountain"

where the devil tempted Christ with "all the kingdoms of the world, and the glory of them" (Matt. iv, 8). Cf. *PR* III, 252.

388. In *Moscovia* (C. E. X, 344–47) Milton describes the glories of the wall of Cathay (China) and the *Can* (Khan), its ruler, whose seat is *Cambalu*. E. N. S. Thompson suggests—in *SP*, XVI (1919), 160–62—that here he remembered *Cambalu* on Ortelius' map of Tartary, with the Khan pictured sitting in a great tent, sceptre in hand, under an inscription reading: "Magnus Cham, maximus Asie princeps." On the same map *Temir* or Timur (Tamberlane) is shown enthroned in his capital *Samarchand* on the river *Oxus*.

390. *Paquin*: Pekin. *Sinæan*: Chinese.

391. *Agra*, in northwestern India, is the site of

Down to the golden *Chersonese,* or where
The *Persian* in *Ecbatan* sat, or since
In *Hispahan,* or where the *Russian Ksar*
In *Mosco,* or the Sultan in *Bizance,*   395
Turchestan-born; nor could his eye not ken
Th' Empire of *Negus* to his utmost Port
Ercoco and the less Marítime Kings
Mombaza, and *Quiloa,* and *Melind,*
And *Sofala* thought *Ophir,* to the Realm   400
Of *Congo,* and *Angola* fardest South;
Or thence from *Niger* Flood to *Atlas* Mount
The Kingdoms of *Almansor, Fez* and *Sus,*
Marocco and *Algiers,* and *Tremisen;*
On *Europe* thence, and where *Rome* was to sway   405
The World: in Spirit perhaps he also saw
Rich *Mexico* the seat of *Montezume,*
And *Cusco* in *Peru,* the richer seat
Of *Atabalipa,* and yet unspoil'd
Guiana, whose great City *Geryon's* Sons   410
Call *El Dorado:* but to nobler sights
Michael from *Adam's* eyes the Film remov'd
Which that false Fruit that promis'd clearer sight
Had bred; then purg'd with Euphrasy and Rue
The visual Nerve, for he had much to see;   415
And from the Well of Life three drops instill'd.
So deep the power of these Ingredients pierc'd,
Ev'n to the inmost seat of mental sight,
That *Adam* now enforc't to close his eyes,
Sunk down and all his Spirits became intranst: 420
But him the gentle Angel by the hand
Soon rais'd, and his attention thus recall'd.
    Adam, now ope thine eyes, and first behold
Th' effects which thy original crime hath wrought
In some to spring from thee, who never touch'd   425

the Taj Mahal. Like *Lahor* in the Punjab, it was a great *Mogul* capital.

392. Purchas suggests both Siam and Molucca or Sumatra (*Pilgrimage,* pp. 557 and 697) as identifiable with the *golden Chersonese* of Ptolemy and also with the *Ophir* whence gold was brought for Solomon's temple (I Kings ix, 28). Cf. l. 400, n.

393–394. *Ecbatana* was the ancient capital of Persia; *Hispahan* (Ispahan) became its capital under Shah Abbás the Great about 1600.

395. *Bizance:* Byzantium, the modern Constantinople, conquered by the Turks in 1453.

397–398. The *Negus* or king of Abyssinia controlled the port of *Ercoco,* the modern Arkiko, on the Red Sea.

399. *Mombaza* in British East Africa, *Melind* on the East African coast, and *Quiloa* (Kilwa-Kisiwani), an island port off the Tanganyikan shore, are briefly mentioned by Purchase (*Pilgrimes,* II, 1024).

400. *Sofala* in Portuguese East Africa, was a port so famous for traffic in gold that it was sometimes identified with the *golden Chersonese.* Cf. l. 392 above, n.

401. Purchase mentions *Angola* as ruled by a king who was "but a Governour or Deputie under the king of Congo" (*Pilgrimes,* II, 995).

403–404. *Almansor* (Mansur, 938–1002 A.D.) ruled *Fez* and *Sus* in Morocco, *Tremisen* (modern Tlemcen) in Algeria, and parts of Spain.

407. *Montezuma* was the Aztec emperor whom Cortez conquered in 1520.

408. *Cusco* was the capital of the Peruvian emperor *Atabalipa* or Atahuallpa whom Pizarro overthrew in 1533.

410. The *great City* is probably Manoa, the reputed residence of *El Dorado,* the Gilded King, in quest of whom Sir Walter Raleigh undertook to explore the Orinoco in 1595.

414. *Euphrasy* or Eiebright, says Gerard's *Herball,* p. 537, "is very much commended for the eies. . . . It preserveth the sight, increaseth it, and being feeble and lost it restoreth the same." On p. 1074 *Rue* is said, "when a little is boyled or scalded, and kept in pickle, . . . and eaten," to have virtue that "quickeneth the sight."

416. Cf. Psalm xxxvi, 9: "For with thee is the fountain of life: in thy light shall we see light."

420. So Daniel sinks into trance in the vision to which l. 357 above refers.

Th'excepted Tree, nor with the Snake conspir'd,
Nor sinn'd thy sin, yet from that sin derive
Corruption to bring forth more violent deeds.
   His eyes he op'n'd, and beheld a field,
Part arable and tilth, whereon were Sheaves   430
New reapt, the other part sheep-walks and folds;
I' th' midst an Altar as the Land-mark stood —
Rustic, of grassy sward; thither anon
A sweaty Reaper from his Tillage brought
First Fruits, the green Ear, and the yellow Sheaf,   435
Uncull'd, as came to hand; a Shepherd next
More meek came with the Firstlings of his Flock
Choicest and best; then sacrificing, laid
The Inwards and thir Fat, with Incense strew'd,
On the cleft Wood, and all due Rites perform'd.   440
His Off'ring soon propitious Fire from Heav'n
Consum'd with nimble glance, and grateful steam;
The other's not, for his was not sincere;
Whereat hee inly rag'd, and as they talk'd,
Smote him into the Midriff with a stone   445
That beat out life; he fell, and deadly pale
Groan'd out his Soul with gushing blood effus'd.
Much at that sight was *Adam* in his heart
Dismay'd, and thus in haste to th' Angel cri'd.
   O Teacher, some great mischief hath befall'n   450
To that meek man, who well had sacrific'd;
Is Piety thus and pure Devotion paid?
   T' whom *Michael* thus, hee also mov'd repli'd.
These two are Brethren, *Adam,* and to come
Out of thy loins; th' unjust the just hath slain,   455
For envy that his Brother's Offering found
From Heav'n acceptance; but the bloody Fact
Will be aveng'd, and th' other's Faith approv'd
Lose no reward, though here thou see him die,
Rolling in dust and gore. To which our Sire.   460
   Alas, both for the deed and for the cause!
But have I now seen Death? Is this the way
I must return to native dust? O sight
Of terror, foul and ugly to behold,
Horrid to think, how horrible to feel!   465
   To whom thus *Michaël*. Death thou hast seen
In his first shape on man; but many shapes
Of Death, and many are the ways that lead
To his grim Cave, all dismal; yet to sense
More terrible at th' entrance than within.   470
Some, as thou saw'st, by violent stroke shall die,
By Fire, Flood, Famine, by Intemperance more
In Meats and Drinks, which on the Earth shall bring

---

430. *tilth:* land under cultivation.
432–460. Milton stresses the murder of Abel by
Cain because of its symbolic importance, to which
St. Augustine contributed in the *City of God* XIII.
v, by making it an example of the danger of envy.
436. *Uncull'd:* unselected (in contrast with *Choicest and best* in 438).
441. *Fire from Heav'n* kindles sacrifices by sin-

cere worshippers in Lev. ix, 24; I Chron. xxi, 26,
etc.

469. The *Cave* resembles an underworld such as
the Sheol of the Hebrews or—as G. L. Loane suggests in *N&Q* CLXXV (1938), 457—"that invisible cave that no light enters," Hades, as Chapman describes it in the opening lines of the *Iliad*.

Diseases dire, of which a monstrous crew
Before thee shall appear; that thou may'st know   475
What misery th' inabstinence of *Eve*
Shall bring on men.   Immediately a place
Before his eyes appear'd, sad, noisome, dark,
A Lazar-house it seem'd, wherein were laid
Numbers of all diseas'd, all maladies   480
Of ghastly Spasm, or racking torture, qualms
Of heart-sick Agony, all feverous kinds,
Convulsions, Epilepsies, fierce Catarrhs,
Intestine Stone and Ulcer, Colic pangs,
Dæmoniac Frenzy, moping Melancholy   485
And Moon-struck madness, pining Atrophy,
Marasmus, and wide-wasting Pestilence,
Dropsies, and Asthmas, and Joint-racking Rheums.
Dire was the tossing, deep the groans, despair
Tended the sick busiest from Couch to Couch;   490
And over them triumphant Death his Dart
Shook, but delay'd to strike, though oft invok't
With vows, as thir chief good, and final hope.
Sight so deform what heart of Rock could long
Dry-ey'd behold? *Adam* could not, but wept,   495
Though not of Woman born; compassion quell'd
His best of Man, and gave him up to tears
A space, till firmer thoughts restrain'd excess,
And scarce recovering words his plaint renew'd.
O miserable Mankind, to what fall   500
Degraded, to what wretched state reserv'd!
Better end here unborn. Why is life giv'n
To be thus wrested from us? rather why
Obtruded on us thus? who if we knew
What we receive, would either not accept   505
Life offer'd, or soon beg to lay it down,
Glad to be so dismist in peace. Can thus
Th' Image of God in man created once
So goodly and erect, though faulty since,
To such unsightly sufferings be debas't   510

477–495. Godwin, in his *Life of Chaucer* (II, 412) suggested that Milton got the "first hint of a lazar-house from *Piers Plowman*, Passus XX," but the spirit of Milton's scene is rather like that of Du Bartas in the account of human misery that opens *The Furies* in *The Divine Weeks*. Cf. l. 357 above, n.

480–488. Milton's names for these diseases and his indications of their symptoms are studied by K. Svendsen in *M.&S.*, pp. 174–200.

485–487. These lines were added by Milton in the second edition.

487. *Marasmus:* any wasting away or "consumption" of the body.

492. *oft invok't* is a vague allusion to many passages in the classics (e.g., Sophocles' *Oedipus Colonneus,* 1220, and *Philoctetes,* 797–98) which Milton may have remembered as echoed in Spenser's lines:
. . . death is an equall doome
To good and bad, the commen in of rest.
(*F.Q.* II, i, 59)

496. Here the reminiscence of *Macbeth* (V, viii, 37–39) must have been conscious:
Though Byrnane wood be come to Dunsinane,
And thou oppos'd, being of no woman borne,
Yet I will try the last.

497. Again the reminiscence is of *Macbeth* (V, viii, 23–24):
Accursed be that tongue that tels mee so;
For it hath Cow'd my better part of man.

504. In making Adam guilty of what Sir Thomas Browne called the "underweening of this life" Milton was probably thinking, like Browne, of the saying of "the Stoic (i.e., Seneca) that life would not be accepted if it were offered unto such as knew it" (*Christian Morals* III, xxv).

507–514. Adam has heard from Raphael (VII, 519) that God made man in his own image, and Milton represents the angel as adding the Platonic argument for human nobility from man's upright stature. Cf. VII, 509, n.

Under inhuman pains? Why should not Man,
Retaining still Divine similitude
In part, from such deformities be free,
And for his Maker's Image sake exempt?
    Thir Maker's Image, answer'd *Michael*, then
Forsook them, when themselves they vilifi'd   515
To serve ungovern'd appetite, and took
His Image whom they served, a brutish vice,
Inductive mainly to the sin of *Eve*.
Therefore so abject is thir punishment,   520
Disfiguring not God's likeness, but thir own,
Or if his likeness, by themselves defac't
While they pervert pure Nature's healthful rules
To loathsome sickness, worthily, since they
God's Image did not reverence in themselves.   525
    I yield it just, said *Adam*, and submit.
But is there yet no other way, besides
These painful passages, how we may come
To Death, and mix with our connatural dust?
    There is, said *Michael*, if thou well observe   530
The rule of not too much, by temperance taught,
In what thou eat'st and drink'st, seeking from thence
Due nourishment, not gluttonous delight,
Till many years over thy head return:
So may'st thou live, till like ripe Fruit thou drop   535
Into thy Mother's lap, or be with ease
Gather'd, not harshly pluckt, for death mature:
This is old age; but then thou must outlive
Thy youth, thy strength, thy beauty, which will change
To wither'd weak and gray; thy Senses then   540
Obtuse, all taste of pleasure must forgo,
To what thou hast, and for the Air of youth
Hopeful and cheerful, in thy blood will reign
A melancholy damp of cold and dry
To weigh thy Spirits down, and last consume   545
The Balm of Life. To whom our Ancestor.
    Henceforth I fly not Death, nor would prolong
Life much, bent rather how I may be quit
Fairest and easiest of this cumbrous charge,
Which I must keep till my appointed day   550
Of rend'ring up, and patiently attend
My dissolution. *Michaël* repli'd.
    Nor love thy Life, nor hate; but what thou liv'st
Live well, how long or short permit to Heav'n:

---

529. Cf. X, 246, and XI, 199–200 and 463.
  531. The idea that "health is destroyed by too much and too little food and drink" was already a commonplace when Aristotle stated it as one of many aspects of the *rule of not too much* in the *Nicomachean Ethics* II, ii, 6.
  535. The simile of *ripe Fruit* came down from Cicero's *Of Old Age* (xix) through Dante's *Convito* (iv) and Spenser's image of being "made ripe for death by eld" (*F.Q.* II, x, 32, 2).
  544. Cf. Burton on old age as the most frequent cause of melancholy, since it is "cold and dry, and of the same quality as melancholy is, . . . needs must

cause it, by diminution of spirits and substance" (*Anatomy* I, ii, 1, 5; Everyman Ed. I, 210).
  551–552. *and patiently attend My dissolution:* Milton's insertion in the second edition. The reader of the first was expected to complete the thought from Job xiv, 14: "All the days of my appointed time will I wait, till my change come."
  553. The maxim repeats Martial in his tenth *Epigram*: "Neither dread nor desire thy last hour," and similar advice in Horace's famous "Soracte" *Ode* (I, ix, 9) and in Seneca's *Epistles* xxiv, 24, and lxv, 18.

And now prepare thee for another sight.   555
He look'd and saw a spacious Plain, whereon
Were Tents of various hue; by some were herds
Of Cattle grazing: others, whence the sound
Of Instruments that made melodious chime
Was heard, of Harp and Organ; and who mov'd   560
Thir stops and chords was seen: his volant touch
Instinct through all proportions low and high
Fled and pursu'd transverse the resonant fugue.
In other part stood one who at the Forge
Laboring, two massy clods of Iron and Brass   565
Had melted (whether found where casual fire
Had wasted woods on Mountain or in Vale,
Down to the veins of Earth, thence gliding hot
To some Cave's mouth, or whether washt by stream
From underground); the liquid Ore he drain'd   570
Into fit moulds prepar'd; from which he form'd
First his own Tools; then, what might else be wrought
Fusile or grav'n in metal.   After these,
But on the hither side a different sort
From the high neighboring Hills, which was thir Seat,   575
Down to the Plain descended: by thir guise
Just men they seem'd, and all thir study bent
To worship God aright, and know his works
Not hid, nor those things last which might preserve
Freedom and Peace to men: they on the Plain   580
Long had not walkt, when from the Tents behold
A Bevy of fair Women, richly gay
In Gems and wanton dress; to the Harp they sung
Soft amorous Ditties, and in dance came on:
The Men though grave, ey'd them, and let thir eyes   585
Rove without rein, till in the amorous Net
Fast caught, they lik'd, and each his liking chose;
And now of love they treat till th' Ev'ning Star
Love's Harbinger appear'd; then all in heat
They light the Nuptial Torch, and bid invoke   590
Hymen, then first to marriage Rites invok't;

556–711. The basis for the scenes in the *spacious plain* is the account in Genesis iv, 20–22, of the sons of Lamech: Jabal, "the father of such as dwell in tents," Jubal, "the father of all such as handle the harp and organ," and Tubal-Cain, "an instructor of every artificer in brass and iron." Du Bartas embroidered the subject of the metalworkers, over whom

         sweating *Tubal* stands,
Hastning the hot work in their sounding hands,
No time lost *Jubal:* th'unfull Harmony
Of uneven hammers, beating diversely,
Wakens the tunes that his sweet numbery soule
Yer birth (some think) learn'd of the warbling *Pole.*
         (*Divine Weeks,* p. 304)

561–563. The rhythm of the lines is analyzed in Whaler's *Counterpoint,* p. 74, as exactly corresponding to a fugal effect.

562. Jubal's art is inborn (*instinct*) because he has, as "some think," absorbed it before birth from "the warbling Pole" (the heavens).

564–573. The lines reflect Lucretius' account of the discovery of metals when they were first laid bare by lightning-kindled forest fires and accidentally fused in natural pits (*De rerum natura* V, 1241–68).

573–627. The scene shifts from east of Eden to *the hither side,* west. A tradition stemming from Genesis vi, 2–4, represents the sons of Seth as deservedly called the "sons of God" until they were lured from their mountain homes to marry and beget a giant race on the daughters of Cain. Many commentators, Jewish and Patristic, interpreted "sons of God" as meaning that the lovers of Cain's daughters were fallen angels, but Saint Augustine, Saint Thomas Aquinas, and most later commentators, Protestant as well as Catholic, condemned that view as heretical. Cf. D. C. Allen in *MLN,* LXI (1946), 78; R. H. West in *Angels,* pp. 129–31; and A. Williams in *Expositor,* p. 152. Cf. also V, 446–49, and *PR* II, 178–81.

588. The *Ev'ning Star* is Venus, as in VIII, 519.

591. Milton thought of many invocations of

With Feast and Music all the Tents resound.
Such happy interview and fair event
Of love and youth not lost, Songs, Garlands, Flow'rs,
And charming Symphonies attach'd the heart 595
Of *Adam,* soon inclin'd to admit delight
The bent of Nature; which he thus express'd.
    True opener of mine eyes, prime Angel blest,
Much better seems this Vision, and more hope
Of peaceful days portends, than those two past; 600
Those were of hate and death, or pain much worse,
Here Nature seems fulfill'd in all her ends.
    To whom thus *Michael.* Judge not what is best
By pleasure, though to Nature seeming meet,
Created, as thou art, to nobler end 605
Holy and pure, conformity divine.
Those Tents thou saw'st so pleasant, were the Tents
Of wickedness, wherein shall dwell his Race
Who slew his Brother; studious they appear
Of Arts that polish Life, Inventors rare, 610
Unmindful of thir Maker, though his Spirit
Taught them, but they his gifts acknowledg'd none.
Yet they a beauteous offspring shall beget;
For that fair female Troop thou saw'st, that seem'd
Of Goddesses, so blithe, so smooth, so gay, 615
Yet empty of all good wherein consists
Woman's domestic honor and chief praise;
Bred only and completed to the taste
Of lustful appetence, to sing, to dance,
To dress, and troll the Tongue, and roll the Eye. 620
To these that sober Race of Men, whose lives
Religious titl'd them the Sons of God,
Shall yield up all thir virtue, all thir fame
Ignobly, to the trains and to the smiles
Of these fair Atheists, and now swim in joy, 625
(Erelong to swim at large) and laugh; for which
The world erelong a world of tears must weep.
    To whom thus *Adam* of short joy bereft.
O pity and shame, that they who to live well
Enter'd so fair, should turn aside to tread 630
Paths indirect, or in the mid way faint!
But still I see the tenor of Man's woe
Holds on the same, from Woman to begin.
    From Man's effeminate slackness it begins,
Said th' Angel, who should better hold his place 635
By wisdom, and superior gifts receiv'd.

the god of marriage such as the cry of the groomsmen in Spenser's *Epithalamion,* l. 140:
   "Hymen, Iö Hymen, Hymen, they do shout."
  607. Cf. Psalm lxxxix, 10: "I had rather be a
doorkeeper in the house of my God, than to dwell
in the tents of wickedness."
  611. *Spirit*—as M. Kelley notes in *Argument,* p.
109—"does not refer to the Third Person" of the
Trinity, but to "the virtue and power of God the
Father." Cf. XII, 485-95.
  618-625. The lines owe something to the commentary on Genesis in the Geneva Bible, which

observes that the "men had more respect to the
beautie, and worldly considerations, then to their
manners and godliness." G. W. Whiting collects
the Geneva marginal notes in *N&Q,* CXCIV (1949),
75.
  620. *troll:* wag.
  624. *trains:* tricks, deceits.
  626. The play on *swim* anticipates the flood in
ll. 818-74 below.
  633. To illustrate the popular etymology the
O.E.D. quotes John Heywood's *Proverbs* II, vii: "A
woman! As who saith, woe to the man!"

But now prepare thee for another Scene.
He look'd and saw wide Territory spread
Before him, Towns, and rural works between,
Cities of Men with lofty Gates and Tow'rs,   640
Concourse in Arms, fierce Faces threat'ning War,
Giants of mighty Bone, and bold emprise;
Part wield thir Arms, part curb the foaming Steed,
Single or in Array of Battle rang'd
Both Horse and Foot, nor idly must'ring stood;   645
One way a Band select from forage drives
A herd of Beeves, fair Oxen and fair Kine
From a fat Meadow ground; or fleecy Flock,
Ewes and thir bleating Lambs over the Plain,
Thir Booty; scarce with Life the Shepherds fly,   650
But call in aid, which makes a bloody Fray;
With cruel Tournament the Squadrons join;
Where Cattle pastur'd late, now scatter'd lies
With Carcasses and Arms th' ensanguin'd Field
Deserted: Others to a City strong   655
Lay Siege, encampt; by Battery, Scale, and Mine,
Assaulting; others from the wall defend
With Dart and Jav'lin, Stones and sulphurous Fire;
On each hand slaughter and gigantic deeds.
In other part the scepter'd Heralds call   660
To Council in the City Gates: anon
Grey-headed men and grave, with Warriors mixt,
Assemble, and Harangues are heard, but soon
In factious opposition, till at last
Of middle Age one rising, eminent   665
In wise deport, spake much of Right and Wrong,
Of Justice, of Religion, Truth and Peace,
And Judgment from above: him old and young
Exploded, and had seiz'd with violent hands,
Had not a Cloud descending snatch'd him thence   670
Unseen amid the throng: so violence
Proceeded, and Oppression, and Sword-Law
Through all the Plain, and refuge none was found.
Adam was all in tears, and to his guide
Lamenting turn'd full sad; O what are these,   675
Death's Ministers, not Men, who thus deal Death
Inhumanly to men, and multiply
Ten thousandfold the sin of him who slew
His Brother; for of whom such massacre
Make they but of thir Brethren, men of men?   680
But who was that Just Man, whom had not Heav'n
Rescu'd, had in his Righteousness been lost?
To whom thus *Michael*. These are the product

638–673. The panorama has many obvious
Homeric echoes—particularly of the description of
the shield of Achilles (*Il.* XVIII, 478–616).
646. *Band select:* a band of picked men.
660. The council of elders called together by
heralds while a city is besieged is very close to *Iliad*
XVIII, 503–10.
665. *Of middle Age one rising* is Enoch, who
"walked with God" and was translated to heaven

at the "middle age" (in comparison with that of
most of the patriarchs) of 365 years (Gen. v, 21–
24).
669. *Exploded:* hooted.
683–697. For the Giants of l. 688 see the note
on ll. 573–627 above. The tone of the passage—
as Whiting notes in *N&Q,* CXCIV (1949), 75—is
that of the marginal comment on Genesis vi, 4–5,
in the Geneva Bible: "All were given to the con-

Of those ill-mated Marriages thou saw'st;
Where good with bad were matcht, who of themselves   685
Abhor to join; and by imprudence mixt,
Produce prodigious Births of body or mind.
Such were these Giants, men of high renown;
For in those days Might only shall be admir'd,
And Valor and Heroic Virtue call'd;   690
To overcome in Battle, and subdue
Nations, and bring home spoils with infinite
Man-slaughter, shall be held the highest pitch
Of human Glory, and for Glory done
Of triumph, to be styl'd great Conquerors,   695
Patrons of Mankind, Gods, and Sons of Gods,
Destroyers rightlier call'd and Plagues of men.
Thus Fame shall be achiev'd, renown on Earth,
And what most merits fame in silence hid.
But hee the sev'nth from thee, whom thou beheld'st   700
The only righteous in a World perverse,
And therefore hated, therefore so beset
With Foes for daring single to be just,
And utter odious Truth, that God would come
To judge them with his Saints: Him the most High   705
Rapt in a balmy Cloud with winged Steeds
Did, as thou saw'st, receive, to walk with God
High in Salvation and the Climes of bliss
Exempt from Death; to show thee what reward
Awaits the good, the rest what punishment;   710
Which now direct thine eyes and soon behold.
    He look'd, and saw the face of things quite chang'd;
The brazen Throat of War had ceast to roar,
All now was turn'd to jollity and game,
To luxury and riot, feast and dance,   715
Marrying or prostituting, as befell,
Rape or Adultery, where passing fair
Allur'd them; thence from Cups to civil Broils.
At length a Reverend Sire among them came,
And of thir doings great dislike declar'd,   720
And testifi'd against thir ways; hee oft
Frequented thir Assemblies, whereso met,
Triumphs or Festivals, and to them preach'd
Conversion and Repentance, as to Souls
In Prison under Judgments imminent: 725

tempt of God, & oppression of their neighbours."
Cf. IX, 27–31, PR III, 44–87, and *Lycidas*, 78:
Fame is no plant that grows on mortal soil.
    700. *Hee the seventh from thee* is Enoch, who
has been mentioned in l. 665. "God tooke him
away," says the Geneva gloss, "To shew that there
was a better life prepared, and to be a testimonie
of the immortalitie of soules and bodies."
    715. *luxury:* lust. Cf. "Fie on lust, and luxury"
in *Merry Wives of Windsor* V, v, 98, and many
other Shakespearian examples.
    717. *fair:* beauty, i. e. beautiful women. Cf. IX,
606.
    719–720. The *Reverend Sire* is Noah, who was
"six hundred years old when the flood of waters
was upon the earth" (Gen. vii, 6). Milton remembered Josephus' picture of Noah pleading with the
giants to "change their dispositions," when he saw
that they "were slaves to their wicked pleasures"
(*Antiquities* I iii, 1). In the main the account of
the flood follows Genesis vi, 9–ix, 17; but it is
influenced by the countless Renaissance pictures
of it, many of which are reproduced in D. C.
Allen's *The Legend of Noah* (Urbana, 1949),
facing p. 176.
    723. *Triumphs:* processions, entertainments. Cf.
L'Allegro, 120
    724–725. "Spirits in prison" is a phrase applied
by Saint Peter to the "slaves to their wicked
pleasures" to whom Noah preached. (I Pet. iii,
19.)

But all in vain: which when he saw, he ceas'd
Contending, and remov'd his Tents far off;
Then from the Mountain hewing Timber tall,
Began to build a Vessel of huge bulk,
Measur'd by Cubit, length, and breadth, and highth,   730
Smear'd round with Pitch, and in the side a door
Contriv'd, and of provisions laid in large
For Man and Beast: when lo a wonder strange!
Of every Beast, and Bird, and Insect small
Came sevens, and pairs, and enter'd in, as taught   735
Thir order; last the Sire, and his three Sons
With thir four Wives; and God made fast the door.
Meanwhile the Southwind rose, and with black wings
Wide hovering, all the Clouds together drove
From under Heav'n; the Hills to their supply   740
Vapor, and Exhalation dusk and moist,
Sent up amain; and now the thick'n'd Sky
Like a dark Ceiling stood; down rush'd the Rain
Impetuous, and continu'd till the Earth
No more was seen; the floating Vessel swum   745
Uplifted; and secure with beaked prow
Rode tilting o'er the Waves, all dwellings else
Flood overwhelm'd, and them with all thir pomp
Deep under water roll'd; Sea cover'd Sea,
Sea without shore; and in thir Palaces   750
Where luxury late reign'd, Sea-monsters whelp'd
And stabl'd; of Mankind, so numerous late,
All left, in one small bottom swum embark't.
How didst thou grieve then, *Adam,* to behold
The end of all thy Offspring, end so sad,   755
Depopulation; thee another Flood,
Of tears and sorrow a Flood thee also drown'd,
And sunk thee as thy Sons; till gently rear'd
By th' Angel, on thy feet thou stood'st at last,
Though comfortless, as when a Father mourns   760
His Children, all in view destroy'd at once;
And scarce to th' Angel utter'd'st thus thy plaint.
   O Visions ill foreseen! better had I
Liv'd ignorant of future, so had borne
My part of evil only, each day's lot   765

735. Cf. Genesis vii, 2: "Of every clean beast thou shalt take to thee by sevens, the male and his female; and of beasts that are not clean by two."

737. With the detail that *God made fast the door* (Gen. vii, 16) Milton turned from the Bible story to Ovid's account of Deucalion's flood (cf. l. 10 above, n.), many details of which are also embodied in Du Bartas' description of Noah's flood in *The Divine Weeks.* Davis P. Harding in *Renaissance Ovid,* pp. 82–84, and Allen in *The Legend of Noah,* pp. 176–77, discuss Milton's belief that Ovid's story was a foil and (it may be added) a corroboration for the biblical account.

738. Milton could count on his readers to remember that in Ovid's account of Deucalion's flood (*Met.* I, 264), when Jove prepared vengeance on wicked mankind, he called the South Wind, Notus, to drown the earth with rain. Contemporary me-

teorologists—as Svendsen notes in *M.&S.,* p. 97—confirmed Milton's theory of rain as caused by the action of the south wind on thick clouds.

750. The shoreless sea is a striking touch in Ovid's story (*Met.* I, 292). It reappears in Du Bartas' picture of "stormy waters" where

Rivers and Seas have all one common shoar,
(To wit) a Sable, water-loaden Skie,
Ready to rain new Oceans instantly.
                    (*Divine Weeks,* p. 310)

750–751. This is Ovid's picture (*Met.* I, 299–303) with a touch of its quaintness in Du Bartas:

The Sturgeon, coasting over Castles, muses
(Under the Sea) to see so many houses.
                    (*Divine Weeks,* p. 59)

765. Cf. Matthew vi, 34: "Sufficient unto the day, is the evil thereof."

Anough to bear; those now, that were dispens't
The burd'n of many Ages, on me light
At once, by my foreknowledge gaining Birth
Abortive, to torment me ere thir being,
With thought that they must be. Let no man seek   770
Henceforth to be foretold what shall befall
Him or his Children, evil he may be sure,
Which neither his foreknowing can prevent,
And hee the future evil shall no less
In apprehension than in substance feel   775
Grievous to bear: but that care now is past,
Man is not whom to warn: those few escap't
Famine and anguish will at last consume
Wand'ring that wat'ry Desert: I had hope
When violence was ceas't, and War on Earth,   780
All would have then gone well, peace would have crown'd
With length of happy days the race of man;
But I was far deceiv'd; for now I see
Peace to corrupt no less than War to waste.
How comes it thus? unfold, Celestial Guide,   785
And whether here the Race of man will end.
    To whom thus *Michael*. Those whom last thou saw'st
In triumph and luxurious wealth, are they
First seen in acts of prowess eminent
And great exploits, but of true virtue void;   790
Who having spilt much blood, and done much waste
Subduing Nations, and achiev'd thereby
Fame in the World, high titles, and rich prey,
Shall change thir course to pleasure, ease, and sloth,
Surfeit, and lust, till wantonness and pride   795
Raise out of friendship hostile deeds in Peace.
The conquer'd also, and enslav'd by War
Shall with thir freedom lost all virtue lose
And fear of God, from whom thir piety feign'd
In sharp contést of Battle found no aid   800
Against invaders; therefore cool'd in zeal
Thenceforth shall practice how to live secure,
Worldly or dissolute, on what thir Lords
Shall leave them to enjoy; for th' Earth shall bear
More than anough, that temperance may be tri'd: 805
So all shall turn degenerate, all deprav'd,
Justice and Temperance, Truth and Faith forgot;
One Man except, the only Son of light
In a dark Age, against example good,
Against allurement, custom, and a World   810
Offended; fearless of reproach and scorn,
Or violence, hee of thir wicked ways
Shall them admonish, and before them set
The paths of righteousness, how much more safe,
And full of peace, denouncing wrath to come   815

779. *Wand'ring* is transitive.

807. This climax to a passage which is filled with Milton's passionate political and ethical faith can be read as an attack upon the time-servers in his own party. Perhaps the best light in which to regard it is as the record of disillusion from the mood in which he painted England in *Areopagitica*: "a noble and puissant nation," "entering the glorious ways of truth and prosperous virtue, destined to become great and honorable in these latter ages."

On thir impenitence; and shall return
Of them derided, but of God observ'd
The one just Man alive; by his command
Shall build a wondrous Ark, as thou beheld'st,
To save himself and household from amidst   820
A World devote to universal rack.
No sooner hee with them of Man and Beast
Select for life shall in the Ark be lodg'd,
And shelter'd round, but all the Cataracts
Of Heav'n set open on the Earth shall pour   825
Rain day and night, all fountains of the Deep
Broke up, shall heave the Ocean to usurp
Beyond all bounds, till inundation rise
Above the highest Hills: then shall this Mount
Of Paradise by might of Waves be mov'd   830
Out of his place, push'd by the horned flood,
With all his verdure spoil'd, and Trees adrift
Down the great River to the op'ning Gulf,
And there take root an Island salt and bare,
The haunt of Seals and Orcs, and Sea-mews' clang.   835
To teach thee that God áttributes to place
No sanctity, if none be thither brought
By Men who there frequent, or therein dwell.
And now what further shall ensue, behold.
    He look'd, and saw the Ark hull on the flood,   840
Which now abated, for the Clouds were fled,
Driv'n by a keen North-wind, that blowing dry
Wrinkl'd the face of Deluge, as decay'd;
And the clear Sun on his wide wat'ry Glass
Gaz'd hot, and of the fresh Wave largely drew,   845
As after thirst, which made thir flowing shrink
From standing lake to tripping ebb, that stole
With soft foot towards the deep, who now had stopt
His Sluices, as the Heav'n his windows shut.
The Ark no more now floats, but seems on ground   850
Fast on the top of some high mountain fixt.
And now the tops of Hills as Rocks appear;
With clamor thence the rapid Currents drive
Towards the retreating Sea thir furious tide.
Forthwith from out the Ark a Raven flies,   855
And after him, the surer messenger,
A Dove sent forth once and again to spy

---

821. *devote:* dedicated to destruction. Cf. III, 208.

831. So Virgil describes the Po as dividing its stream into horns:

Po first issues from his dark abodes, . . .
Two golden horns on his large front he wears,
And his grim face a bull's resemblance bears.

  (*Georgics* IV, 370–73. Dryden's translation)
833. The *great River* is probably the Euphrates. The *Gulf* is the Persian Gulf.
834–835. *Orcs:* whales. J. B. Broadbent—in *MP*, LI (1954), 163—notes that "islands of whales (orcs) were frequently described (as in *Hakluytus Posthumus* xix, 80)" by voyagers in eastern seas.
840–843. So "God made a wind to pass over

the earth, and the waters asswaged" (Gen. viii, 1); and so also Ovid makes a north wind drive away the clouds after Deucalion's flood ·(*Met.* I, 328). But the picture—says E. M. W. Tillyard in *TLS*, 6 March, 1953, p. 153—comes from Sidney's opening scene in the *Arcadia* of "a ship . . . hulling there, part broken, part burned, part drowned. . . . A number of dead bodies (as it were) filled the wrinckles of the sea visage."
845. Cf. the sun supping with the ocean in V, 426.
849. So in Genesis viii, 2: "The fountains of the deep and the windows of heaven were stopped." and the details of the raven, the dove, and the olive leaf follow.

Green Tree or ground whereon his foot may light;
The second time returning, in his Bill
An Olive leaf he brings, pacific sign: 860
Anon dry ground appears, and from his Ark
The ancient Sire descends with all his Train;
Then with uplifted hands, and eyes devout,
Grateful to Heav'n, over his head beholds
A dewy Cloud, and in the Cloud a Bow 865
Conspicuous with three listed colors gay,
Betok'ning peace from God, and Cov'nant new.
Whereat the heart of *Adam* erst so sad
Greatly rejoic'd, and thus his joy broke forth.
    O thou who future things canst represent 870
As present, Heav'nly instructor, I revive
At this last sight, assur'd that Man shall live
With all the Creatures, and thir seed preserve.
Far less I now lament for one whole World
Of wicked Sons destroy'd, than I rejoice 875
For one Man found so perfet and so just,
That God voutsafes to raise another World
From him, and all his anger to forget.
But say, what mean those color'd streaks in Heav'n,
Distended as the Brow of God appeas'd, 880
Or serve they as a flow'ry verge to bind
The fluid skirts of that same wat'ry Cloud,
Lest it again dissolve and show'r the Earth?
    To whom th' Arch-Angel. Dext'rously thou aim'st;
So willingly doth God remit his Ire, 885
Though late repenting him of Man deprav'd,
Griev'd at his heart, when looking down he saw
The whole Earth fill'd with violence, and all flesh
Corrupting each thir way; yet those remov'd,
Such grace shall one just Man find in his sight, 890
That he relents, not to blot out mankind,
And makes a Cov'nant never to destroy
The Earth again by flood, nor let the Sea
Surpass his bounds, nor Rain to drown the World
With Man therein or Beast; but when he brings 895
Over the Earth a Cloud, will therein set
His triple-color'd Bow, whereon to look
And call to mind his Cov'nant: Day and Night,
Seed-time and Harvest, Heat and hoary Frost
Shall hold thir course, till fire purge all things new, 900
Both Heav'n and Earth, wherein the just shall dwell.

The End of the Eleventh Book.

867. The *Cov'nant* is the promise of God, of which the rainbow with its *listed* (striped) *colors* was the pledge, never again to flood the world (Gen. ix, 11–17).

898–901. Milton's account of the flood ends like that in Genesis viii, 22, to which he adds the promise of a "new heaven and a new earth" after the melting of the elements "with fervent heat" (II Peter, iii, 12–13). Cf. *CD* I, xxxiii (C. E. XVI, 375 and 381). As a theme for poetry the final conflagration of the world was strikingly developed in Vida's *Hymn to the Son of God,* and as a scientific doctrine it found expression as late as 1696 in William Whiston's *A New Theory of the Earth, From its Original, to the Consummation of all Things, . . . the General Conflagration.*

BOOK XII

THE ARGUMENT

The Angel Michael *continues from the Flood to relate what shall succeed; then, in the mention of* Abraham, *comes by degrees to explain, who that Seed of the Woman shall be, which was promised* Adam *and* Eve *in the Fall; his Incarnation, Death, Resurrection, and Ascension; the state of the Church till his second Coming.* Adam *greatly satisfied and recomforted by these Relations and Promises descends the Hill with* Michael; *wakens* Eve, *who all this while had slept, but with gentle dreams compos'd to quietness of mind and submission.* Michael *in either hand leads them out of Paradise, the fiery Sword waving behind them, and the Cherubim taking thir Stations to guard the Place.*

As one who in his journey bates at Noon,
Though bent on speed, so here the Arch-Angel paus'd
Betwixt the world destroy'd and world restor'd,
If *Adam* aught perhaps might interpose;
Then with transition sweet new Speech resumes.   5
    Thus thou hast seen one World begin and end;
And Man as from a second stock proceed.
Much thou hast yet to see, but I perceive
Thy mortal sight to fail; objects divine
Must needs impair and weary human sense: 10
Henceforth what is to come I will relate,
Thou therefore give due audience, and attend.
This second source of Men, while yet but few,
And while the dread of judgment past remains
Fresh in thir minds, fearing the Deity,   15
With some regard to what is just and right
Shall lead thir lives, and multiply apace,
Laboring the soil, and reaping plenteous crop,
Corn, wine and oil; and from the herd or flock,
Oft sacrificing Bullock, Lamb, or Kid,   20
With large Wine-offerings pour'd, and sacred Feast,
Shall spend thir days in joy unblam'd, and dwell
Long time in peace by Families and Tribes
Under paternal rule; till one shall rise
Of proud ambitious heart, who not content   25
With fair equality, fraternal state,
Will arrogate Dominion undeserv'd
Over his brethren, and quite dispossess
Concord and law of Nature from the Earth;

1–5. These transitional lines were added in 1674 when the tenth book of the first edition was divided to form the eleventh and twelfth books of the second edition.

1. *bates:* abates, reduces speed or pauses.

24–63. Nimrod, whose name means "rebel," is "a mighty hunter before the Lord" (Gen. x, 9), but he is not mentioned in the biblical account of the confusion of tongues at Babel (Gen. xi, 1–9). His character as the foiled empire-builder of St. Gregory's commentary on Genesis in *On the Trinity and its Works* and of Dante's *Purgatory* (xii, 34; cf. *Inf.* xxxi, 77) is first foreshadowed

in Josephus' *Antiquities* I, iv, 2. For the fifteenth century lawyer, Sir John Fortescue, whom Milton quoted in the first *Defense* (C. E. VII, 476, 478), Nimrod's mighty hunting meant that he was "an oppressor and destroyer of men, as hunters are destroyers but not rulers of beasts" (*On the Nature of the Law of Nature* I, vii). Milton's public, like Sir Thomas Browne in *Vulgar Errors* VII, vi, thought of Nimrod as one whose "secret design to settle unto himself a place of dominion" had been nipped by the confusion of tongues at Babel. For the popular conception of Nimrod see Starnes and Talbert, *Dictionaries*, pp. 264–68.

Hunting (and Men not Beasts shall be his game)   30
With War and hostile snare such as refuse
Subjection to his Empire tyrannous:
A mighty Hunter thence he shall be styl'd
Before the Lord, as in despite of Heav'n,
Or from Heav'n claiming second Sovranty;   35
And from Rebellion shall derive his name,
Though of Rebellion others he accuse.
Hee with a crew, whom like Ambition joins
With him or under him to tyrannize,
Marching from *Eden* towards the West, shall find   40
The Plain, wherein a black bituminous gurge
Boils out from under ground, the mouth of Hell;
Of Brick, and of that stuff they cast to build
A City and Tow'r, whose top may reach to Heav'n;
And get themselves a name, lest far disperst   45
In foreign Lands thir memory be lost,
Regardless whether good or evil fame.
But God who oft descends to visit men
Unseen, and through thir habitations walks
To mark thir doings, them beholding soon,   50
Comes down to see thir City, ere the Tower
Obstruct Heav'n Tow'rs, and in derision sets
Upon thir Tongues a various Spirit to rase
Quite out thir Native Language, and instead
To sow a jangling noise of words unknown: 55
Forthwith a hideous gabble rises loud
Among the Builders; each to other calls
Not understood, till hoarse, and all in rage,
As mockt they storm; great laughter was in Heav'n   — The practical joker
And looking down, to see the hubbub strange   in God.   60
And hear the din; thus was the building left
Ridiculous, and the work Confusion nam'd.
    Whereto thus *Adam* fatherly displeas'd.
O execrable Son so to aspire
Above his Brethren, to himself assuming   65
Authority usurpt, from God not giv'n:
He gave us only over Beast, Fish, Fowl
Dominion absolute; that right we hold
By his donation; but Man over men
He made not Lord; such title to himself   — Milton hitting at   70
Reserving, human left from human free.   monarchy?
But this Usurper his encroachment proud
Stays not on Man; to God his Tower intends
Siege and defiance: Wretched man! what food
Will he convey up thither to sustain   75

41–44. *The Plain* of Shinar has been mentioned in III, 467. The idea that the brick in the tower of Babel was "cemented with mortar made of bitumen" comes from Josephus, *Antiquities* I, iv, 3.

52–59. "Languages," said Milton in the *Logic* I, xxiv (C. E. XI, 220), "both that first one which Adam spoke in Eden, and those varied ones also possibly derived from the first, which the builders of the tower of Babel suddenly received, are without doubt divinely given." In *PQ*, XXVIII (1949), 11, D. C. Allen observes that, "Every philologist of

the seventeenth century was quite ready to accept the Confusion as a miracle."

53. *A various Spirit:* a spirit of contradiction, a quarrelsome spirit.

62. The name *Babel* seems to have meant "gate of the Gods" or "of God." Josephus declared that "the tower is now called Babylon because of the confusion of that language which they readily understood before, for the Hebrews mean by the word *Babel,* Confusion" (*Antiquities* I, iv, 3).

Himself and his rash Army, where thin Air
Above the Clouds will pine his entrails gross,
And famish him of breath, if not of Bread?
    To whom thus *Michael*. Justly thou abhorr'st
That Son, who on the quiet state of men   80
Such trouble brought, affecting to subdue
Rational Liberty; yet know withal,
Since thy original lapse, true Liberty
Is lost, which always with right Reason dwells
Twinn'd, and from her hath no dividual being: 85
Reason in man obscur'd, or not obey'd,
Immediately inordinate desires
And upstart Passions catch the Government
From Reason, and to servitude reduce
Man till then free. Therefore since hee permits   90
Within himself unworthy Powers to reign
Over free Reason, God in Judgment just
Subjects him from without to violent Lords;
Who oft as undeservedly enthral
His outward freedom: Tyranny must be,   95
Though to the Tyrant thereby no excuse.
Yet sometimes Nations will decline so low
From virtue, which is reason, that no wrong,
But Justice, and some fatal curse annext
Deprives them of thir outward liberty,   100
Thir inward lost: Witness th' irreverent Son
Of him who built the Ark, who for the shame
Done to his Father, heard this heavy curse,
Servant of Servants, on his vicious Race.
Thus will this latter, as the former World,   105
Still tend from bad to worse, till God at last
Wearied with their iniquities, withdraw
His presence from among them, and avert
His holy Eyes; resolving from thenceforth
To leave them to thir own polluted ways;   110
And one peculiar Nation to select
From all the rest, of whom to be invok'd,
A Nation from one faithful man to spring:

82–101. Milton's political inference from his belief that through Adam's sin men at least partially lost "that right reason which enabled man to discern the chief good" (*CD* I, xii; C. E. XV, 206) was no less explicitly drawn by many commentators on Genesis—as A. Williams shows in *Expositor,* pp. 222–23. But his politics stemmed equally from Plato's *Republic* and its echoes in definitions of "true libertie" such as Castiglione's view of it in the *Book of the Courtier* (Hoby's translation, Everyman Ed. p. 275) as not living "as a man will," but rather as living "according to good lawes." The equally humanistic and biblical political creed of Sir John Eliot as he stated it in the closing sentence of *The Monarchie of Man* (written c. 1631) was the faith that man's "safety and tranquillity by God" (as Aristotle's *Ethics* "did expresse it) are made dependant on himselfe, & in that selfe dependance, . . . in the intire rule & dominion of himselfe, the affections being com-

pos'd, the action soe divided, is the perfection of our government, that *summum bonum* in Philosophie, the *bonum publicum* in our pollicie, the true end and object of this Monarchy of man." Cf. IX, 352 and 654.

101. The *irreverent Son* of Noah was Ham, the father of Canaan. "And [Noah] said, Cursed be Canaan; a servant of servants shall he be unto his brethren" (Gen. ix, 25).

111–113. Cf. *CD* I, iv (p. 917), where Milton condemns the Calvinistic doctrine of individual election to personal salvation by God, but recognizes "that general or national election by which God chose the whole nation of Israel for his own people."

113–121. The *one faithful man* is Abraham, to whom God promised the land of Canaan (Gen. xii, 7). God called him "from his father's house," said Milton in *CD* I, xvii (C. E. XV, 348–50), although he "was even an idolator at the time."

Him on this side *Euphrates* yet residing,
Bred up in Idol-worship; O that men   115
(Canst thou believe?) should be so stupid grown,
While yet the Patriarch liv'd, who scap'd the Flood,
As to forsake the living God, and fall
To worship thir own work in Wood and Stone
For Gods! yet him God the most High voutsafes   120
To call by Vision from his Father's house,
His kindred and false Gods, into a Land
Which he will show him, and from him will raise
A mighty Nation, and upon him show'r
His benediction so, that in his Seed   125
All Nations shall be blest; he straight obeys,
Not knowing to what Land, yet firm believes:
I see him, but thou canst not, with what Faith
He leaves his Gods, his Friends, and native Soil
Ur of *Chaldæa,* passing now the Ford   130
To *Haran,* after him a cumbrous Train
Of Herds and Flocks, and numerous servitude;
Not wand'ring poor, but trusting all his wealth
With God, who call'd him, in a land unknown.
Canaan he now attains, I see his Tents   135
Pitcht about *Sechem,* and the neighboring Plain
Of *Moreh;* there by promise he receives
Gift to his Progeny of all that Land;
From *Hamath* Northward to the Desert South
(Things by thir names I call, though yet unnam'd)   140
From *Hermon* East to the great Western Sea,
Mount *Hermon,* yonder Sea, each place behold
In prospect, as I point them; on the shore
Mount *Carmel;* here the double-founted stream
Jordan, true limit Eastward; but his Sons   145
Shall dwell to *Senir,* that long ridge of Hills.
This ponder, that all Nations of the Earth
Shall in his Seed be blessed; by that Seed
Is meant thy great deliverer, who shall bruise
The Serpent's head; whereof to thee anon   150
Plainlier shall be reveal'd. This Patriarch blest,
Whom *faithful Abraham* due time shall call,
A Son, and of his Son a Grandchild leaves,
Like him in faith, in wisdom, and renown;

128. "By faith Abraham, when he was called to go out into a place which he should after receive for an inheritance, obeyed" (Heb. xi, 8).

130–131. Perhaps knowing that *Ur* was on the west bank of the Euphrates, Milton saw Abraham leaving it for Haran on the east of the river but far northwest of Ur. From Haran Palestine lay southwest over the Euphrates. Cf. IV, 211 n.

132. *servitude:* servants. The story of the migration as told in Genesis xii, 5–6, is traced below Ortelius' large map of Canaan in a diagram called *Abrahami Patriarchae Perigrinatio et Vita.* It shows *Sechem* (Schechem), lying between Mounts Ebal and Gerizim, where Abraham first camped in Canaan, and the plain of *Moreh.*

139. *Hamath,* on the Orontes in Syria, is mentioned as the northern frontier of Canaan in Num-

bers xxxiv, 8. The promise in Joshua xiii, 5–6, was that all the inhabitants of the region "under Mount Hermon unto the entering into Hamath" should be driven out "before the children of Israel."

143. "Carmel by the sea" (Jer. xlvi, 18) is a mountainous promontory jutting into the Mediterranean from the Palestinian shore.

144–145. The notion that the Jordan was formed by the confluence of two non-existent streams, the Jor and the Dan, seems ultimately to have stemmed from St. Jerome's commentary on Genesis xiv, 14. Cf. A. Gilbert, *Geographical Dictionary,* p. 163.

146. *Senir* was a peak of the ridge of Hermon (I Chron. v, 23).

153. *A Son:* Isaac. From this point the Bible story is briefly summarized.

The Grandchild with twelve Sons increast, departs   155
From *Canaan,* to a Land hereafter call'd
Egypt, divided by the River *Nile;*
See where it flows, disgorging at seven mouths
Into the Sea: to sojourn in that Land
He comes invited by a younger Son   160
In time of dearth, a Son whose worthy deeds
Raise him to be the second in that Realm
Of *Pharaoh:* there he dies, and leaves his Race
Growing into a Nation, and now grown
Suspected to a sequent King, who seeks   165
To stop thir overgrowth, as inmate guests
Too numerous; whence of guests he makes them slaves
Inhospitably, and kills thir infant Males:
Till by two brethren (those two brethren call
Moses and *Aaron*) sent from God to claim   170
His people from enthralment, they return
With glory and spoil back to thir promis'd Land.
But first the lawless Tyrant, who denies
To know thir God, or message to regard,
Must be compell'd by Signs and Judgments dire;   175
To blood unshed the Rivers must be turn'd,
Frogs, Lice and Flies must all his Palace fill
With loath'd intrusion, and fill all the land;
His Cattle must of Rot and Murrain die,
Botches and blains must all his flesh imboss,   180
And all his people; Thunder mixt with Hail,
Hail mixt with fire must rend th' *Egyptian* Sky
And wheel on th' Earth, devouring where it rolls;
What it devours not, Herb, or Fruit, or Grain,
A darksome Cloud of Locusts swarming down   185
Must eat, and on the ground leave nothing green:
Darkness must overshadow all his bounds,
Palpable darkness, and blot out three days;
Last with one midnight stroke all the first-born
Of *Egypt* must lie dead. Thus with ten wounds   190
The River-dragon tam'd at length submits
To let his sojourners depart, and oft
Humbles his stubborn heart, but still as Ice
More hard'n'd after thaw, till in his rage
Pursuing whom he late dismiss'd, the Sea   195
Swallows him with his Host, but them lets pass
As on dry land between two crystal walls,
Aw'd by the rod of *Moses* so to stand
Divided, till his rescu'd gain thir shore:
Such wondrous power God to his Saint will lend,   200

171–172. By a dubious trick the Israelites "spoiled the Egyptians" (Exod. xii, 36) when they left the country. The summary of the ten plagues rests on Exodus vii, 19–xii, 51.

173. *denies:* refuses.

180. *imboss:* cover with bosses or swellings.

188. The *Palpable darkness* is the plague of "thick darkness" (Exod. x, 22).

191. "Behold, I am against thee, Pharaoh king of Egypt, the great dragon that lieth in the midst of his rivers" (Ezek. xxix, 3).

197. The *crystal walls* are a reminiscence of Du Bartas' description of the same scene:
    And on each side is flanked all along
    With walls of crystal, beautiful and strong.
          .   .   .   .   .   .
    Two walls of Glass, built with a word alone.
          (*Divine Weeks,* pp. 476–77)
The passage also left its mark on Milton's boyish paraphrase of Psalm cxxxvi, 49.

200–204. "The Lord went before them by day in a pillar of cloud; . . . and by night in a pillar

Though present in his Angel, who shall go
Before them in a Cloud, and Pillar of Fire,
By day a Cloud, by night a Pillar of Fire,
To guide them in thir journey, and remove
Behind them, while th' obdúrate King pursues: 205
All night he will pursue, but his approach
Darkness defends between till morning Watch;
Then through the Fiery Pillar and the Cloud
God looking forth will trouble all his Host
And craze thir Chariot wheels: when by command   210
Moses once more his potent Rod extends
Over the Sea; the Sea his Rod obeys;
On thir imbattl'd ranks the Waves return,
And overwhelm thir War: the Race elect
Safe towards *Canaan* from the shore advance   215
Through the wild Desert, not the readiest way,
Lest ent'ring on the *Canaanite* alarm'd
War terrify them inexpert, and fear
Return them back to *Egypt,* choosing rather
Inglorious life with servitude; for life   220
To noble and ignoble is more sweet
Untrain'd in Arms, where rashness leads not on.
This also shall they gain by thir delay
In the wide Wilderness, there they shall found
Thir government, and thir great Senate choose   225
Through the twelve Tribes, to rule by Laws ordain'd:
God from the Mount of *Sinai,* whose gray top
Shall tremble, he descending, will himself
In Thunder, Lightning and loud Trumpet's sound
Ordain them Laws; part such as appertain   230
To civil Justice, part religious Rites
Of sacrifice, informing them, by types
And shadows, of that destin'd Seed to bruise
The Serpent, by what means he shall achieve
Mankind's deliverance. But the voice of God   235
To mortal ear is dreadful; they beseech
That *Moses* might report to them his will,
And terror cease; he grants what they besought,
Instructed that to God is no access
Without Mediator, whose high Office now   240

of fire, to give them light" (Exod. xiii, 21). In
CD I, v (C. E. XIV, 296) Milton made a point
of the fact that God lent his name to an angel
who guided the Israelites.
207. *defends:* prevents (by coming between
Pharaoh and the Israelites).
210. *craze:* shatter. The scene is described in
Exodus xiv.
217. The devious route of Israel during its
thirty-eight years in the wilderness on the way
to Canaan was clearly traced on contemporary maps.
Milton found the explanation that he gives for it
in Exodus xiii, 17–18.
225–226. Milton thought of the Seventy Elders
in Exodus xxiv, 1–9, and Numbers xi, 16–30, who
witness some of the acts of Moses. Though Roger
Williams was unwilling to see the charter of the
Colony of Massachusetts Bay based upon "the sandy

and dangerous ground of Israel's pattern" (quoted
by Perry Miller in *Roger Williams: His Contribution to the American Tradition,* Cambridge, 1954,
p. 153), Milton accepted the Seventy Elders as a
divinely constituted Senate which, with the support
of the "Magistracy and People," were what James
Harington regarded as the perfect pattern of government by law rather than by royal power, as it was
once for all revealed "in the fabrick of the Commonwealth of Israel" (*Oceana,* ed. by S. B. Liljegren, Heidelberg, 1921, p. 26).
236. In Exodus xx, 19, the Israelites say "unto
Moses, Speak thou with us, and we will hear:
but let not God speak with us, lest we die."
240. Christian commentators treated Moses as the
first of the types of Christ as *Mediator* (cf. X, 60)
mainly because Deuteronomy xviii, 15, is quoted in
Acts iii, 22: "For Moses truly said unto the fathers,

Moses in figure bears, to introduce
One greater, of whose day he shall foretell,
And all the Prophets in thir Age the times
Of great *Messiah* shall sing.   Thus Laws and Rites
Establisht, such delight hath God in Men   245
Obedient to his will, that he voutsafes
Among them to set up his Tabernacle,
The holy One with mortal Men to dwell:
By his prescript a Sanctuary is fram'd
Of Cedar, overlaid with Gold, therein   250
An Ark, and in the Ark his Testimony,
The Records of his Cov'nant, over these
A Mercy-seat of Gold between the wings
Of two bright Cherubim, before him burn
Sev'n Lamps as in a Zodiac representing   255
The Heav'nly fires; over the Tent a Cloud
Shall rest by Day, a fiery gleam by Night,
Save when they journey, and at length they come,
Conducted by his Angel to the Land
Promis'd to *Abraham* and his Seed: the rest   260
Were long to tell, how many Battles fought,
How many Kings destroy'd, and Kingdoms won,
Or how the Sun shall in mid Heav'n stand still
A day entire, and Night's due course adjourn,
Man's voice commanding, Sun in *Gibeon* stand,   265
And thou Moon in the vale of *Aialon,*
Till *Israel* overcome; so call the third
From *Abraham,* Son of *Isaac,* and from him
His whole descent, who thus shall *Canaan* win.
Here *Adam* interpos'd.   O sent from Heav'n,   270
Enlight'ner of my darkness, gracious things
Thou hast reveal'd, those chiefly which concern
Just *Abraham* and his Seed: now first I find
Mine eyes true op'ning, and my heart much eas'd,
Erewhile perplext with thoughts what would become   275
Of mee and all Mankind; but now I see
His day, in whom all Nations shall be blest,
Favor unmerited by me, who sought
Forbidd'n knowledge by forbidd'n means.
This yet I apprehend not, why to those   280
Among whom God will deign to dwell on Earth
So many and so various Laws are giv'n;
So many Laws argue so many sins
Among them; how can God with such reside?
To whom thus *Michael.*   Doubt not but that sin   285
Will reign among them, as of thee begot;

[handwritten marginal note:]
• *being more enlightened.*
• *This might be the climax.*

A Prophet shall the Lord your God raise up unto
you of your brethren, like unto me."
   247–256. The *Tabernacle* is described loosely as it
is in Exodus xxv. Cf. the *Mercy-seat* in XI, 2, n.
   255. Josephus describes the golden candle-stick as
having "seven lamps . . . in imitation of the number of planets" (*Antiquities* III, vi, 7).
   260, 277. The allusion is to the promise to
Abraham in Genesis xxii, 18.
   263–267. Du Bartas, in his dramatization of
Israel's victory over the Amorites when the sun

halted in heaven "until the people had avenged
themselves upon their enemies" (Joshua x, 13),
similarly paraphrased Joshua's command to the
sun and moon:
   Stay, stand thou still, stand still in *Gabaon;*
   And thou, O Moone, i'th'vale of *Aialon.*
                              (*Divine Weeks,* p. 516)
   267. The name *Israel* ("he that striveth with
God") was given to Jacob at Peniel (Gen. xxxii,
28) and later to all his descendants as "the children
of Israel."

And therefore was Law given them to evince
Thir natural pravity, by stirring up
Sin against Law to fight; that when they see
Law can discover sin, but not remove,   290
Save by those shadowy expiations weak,
The blood of Bulls and Goats, they may conclude
Some blood more precious must be paid for Man,
Just for unjust, that in such righteousness
To them by Faith imputed, they may find   295
Justification towards God, and peace
Of Conscience, which the Law by Ceremonies
Cannot appease, nor Man the moral part
Perform, and not performing cannot live.
So Law appears imperfet, and but giv'n   300
With purpose to resign them in full time
Up to a better Cov'nant, disciplin'd
From shadowy Types to Truth, from Flesh to Spirit,
From imposition of strict Laws, to free
Acceptance of large Grace, from servile fear   305
To filial, works of Law to works of Faith.
And therefore shall not *Moses,* though of God
Highly belov'd, being but the Minister
Of Law, his people into *Canaan* lead;
But *Joshua* whom the Gentiles *Jesus* call,   310
His Name and Office bearing, who shall quell
The adversary Serpent, and bring back
Through the world's wilderness long wander'd man
Safe to eternal Paradise of rest.
Meanwhile they in thir earthly *Canaan* plac't   315
Long time shall dwell and prosper, but when sins
National interrupt thir public peace,
Provoking God to raise them enemies:
From whom as oft he saves them penitent
By Judges first, then under Kings; of whom   320
The second, both for piety renown'd
And puissant deeds, a promise shall receive
Irrevocable, that his Regal Throne
For ever shall endure; the like shall sing
All Prophecy, That of the Royal Stock   325
Of *David* (so I name this King) shall rise
A Son, the Woman's Seed to thee foretold,
Foretold to *Abraham,* as in whom shall trust

---

290. The line fuses several Pauline passages which teach that "what things soever the law saith, it saith to them who are under the law; that . . . all the world may become guilty before God" (Rom. iii, 19).

291. Milton describes the sacrifices as shadows or types of Christ's expiation of sin as the law is said to have been "a shadow of good things to come" in Hebrews x, 1, though the "sacrifices which they offered year by year continually" could never "make the comers thereunto perfect." Cf. Romans x, 5, where the righteousness taught by the Mosaic law is contrasted with Christian righteousness.

307. Cf. *CD* I, xxvii (C. E. XVI, 134), where

Christians are said to be "'delivered' not from the ceremonial law alone, but from the whole law of Moses," because (I, xxvi; C. E. XVI, 110) "the imperfection of the law was manifested in . . . Moses himself; for Moses, who was a type of the law, could not bring the children of Israel into the land of Canaan, that is, into eternal rest; but an entrance was given to them under Joshua, or Jesus." In Charles Stephanus' *Dictionary* Joshua is identified with Jesus both as bearing the same name and as a "type" of Christ. Cf. Starnes and Talbert, *Dictionaries,* p. 261.

321. *The second:* David, to whom the prophet Nathan promised that his throne should "be established for ever" (II Sam. vii, 16).

All Nations, and to Kings foretold, of Kings
The last, for of his Reign shall be no end.   330
But first a long succession must ensue,
And his next Son for Wealth and Wisdom fam'd,
The clouded Ark of God till then in Tents
Wand'ring, shall in a glorious Temple enshrine.
Such follow him, as shall be register'd   335
Part good, part bad, of bad the longer scroll,
Whose foul Idolatries, and other faults
Heapt to the popular sum, will so incense
God, as to leave them, and expose thir Land,
Thir City, his Temple, and his holy Ark   340
With all his sacred things, a scorn and prey
To that proud City, whose high Walls thou saw'st
Left in confusion, *Babylon* thence call'd.
There in captivity he lets them dwell
The space of seventy years, then brings them back,   345
Rememb'ring mercy, and his Cov'nant sworn
To *David*, stablisht as the days of Heav'n.
Return'd from *Babylon* by leave of Kings
Thir Lords, whom God dispos'd, the house of God
They first re-edify, and for a while   350
In mean estate live moderate, till grown
In wealth and multitude, factious they grow;
But first among the Priests dissension springs,
Men who attend the Altar, and should most
Endeavor Peace: thir strife pollution brings   355
Upon the Temple itself: at last they seize
The Sceptre, and regard not *David's* Sons,
Then lose it to a stranger, that the true
Anointed King *Messiah* might be born
Barr'd of his right; yet at his Birth a Star   360
Unseen before in Heav'n proclaims him come,
And guides the Eastern Sages, who enquire
His place, to offer Incense, Myrrh, and Gold;
His place of birth a Solemn Angel tells
To simple Shepherds, keeping watch by night;   365
They gladly thither haste, and by a Choir
Of squadron'd Angels hear his Carol sung.
A Virgin is his Mother, but his Sire
The Power of the most High; he shall ascend
The Throne hereditary, and bound his Reign   370

332. The *next Son:* Solomon, whose building of
the temple in Jerusalem is elaborately described in I
Kings vi–vii and II Chronicles iii–iv.

337. Compare the allusion to Solomon's idolatries
in I, 399–403.

347. Milton treats the return of the Hebrew
exiles from Babylon to Jerusalem in 536 B.C. as a
fulfilment of God's covenant with David to make
"his throne as the days of heaven" (Psalm lxxxix,
29).

348. The *Kings* are Cyrus the Great, Darius, and
Artaxerxes, under whom the Jews conducted the
rebuilding of Jerusalem that is recorded in the
Book of Ezra.

353–358. In summarizing the struggle for the

high priesthood between Onias and Joshua in the
second century B.C., Milton follows II Maccabees
iii–iv, and Josephus' *Antiquities* XII, iv–v. In l.
356 *they* refers to the Asmonean family, which
held the priesthood from 153 to 35 B.C. The
stranger in l. 358 is Antipater the Idumaean, whom
the Romans made governor of Jerusalem in 61 B.C.
Under his son, Herod the Great, Christ was born.

366. *thither:* to Bethlehem, Christ's birthplace.

368–369. In *CD* I, xiv (C. E. XV, 280) Milton
declares the "efficient cause" of the conception of
Christ to be the "Holy Spirit," which he adds
that he is inclined to regard as "the power and
spirit of the Father."

With earth's wide bounds, his glory with the Heav'ns.
　He ceas'd, discerning *Adam* with such joy
Surcharg'd, as had like grief been dew'd in tears,
Without the vent of words, which these he breath'd.
　O Prophet of glad tidings, finisher   375
Of utmost hope! now clear I understand
What oft my steadiest thoughts have searcht in vain,
Why our great expectation should be call'd
The seed of Woman: Virgin Mother, Hail,
High in the love of Heav'n, yet from my Loins   380
Thou shalt proceed, and from thy Womb the Son
Of God most High; So God with man unites.
Needs must the Serpent now his capital bruise
Expect with mortal pain: say where and when
Thir fight, what stroke shall bruise the Victor's heel.   385
　To whom thus *Michael.* Dream not of thir fight,
As of a Duel, or the local wounds
Of head or heel: not therefore joins the Son
Manhood to Godhead, with more strength to foil
Thy enemy; nor so is overcome   390
Satan, whose fall from Heav'n, a deadlier bruise,
Disabl'd not to give thee thy death's wound:
Which hee, who comes thy Saviour, shall recure,
Not by destroying *Satan,* but his works
In thee and in thy Seed: nor can this be,   395
But by fulfilling that which thou didst want,
Obedience to the Law of God, impos'd
On penalty of death, and suffering death,
The penalty to thy transgression due,
And due to theirs which out of thine will grow: 400
So only can high Justice rest appaid.
The Law of God exact he shall fulfil
Both by obedience and by love, though love
Alone fulfil the Law; thy punishment
He shall endure by coming in the Flesh   405
To a reproachful life and cursed death,
Proclaiming Life to all who shall believe
In his redemption, and that his obedience
Imputed becomes theirs by Faith, his merits
To save them, not thir own, though legal works.   410
For this he shall live hated, be blasphem'd,
Seiz'd on by force, judg'd, and to death condemn'd
A shameful and accurst, nail'd to the Cross
By his own Nation, slain for bringing Life;
But to the Cross he nails thy Enemies,   415
The Law that is against thee, and the sins
Of all mankind, with him there crucifi'd,

371. The line blends the promise in Psalm ii, 8 (which was referred to Christ)—"Ask of me, and I shall give thee . . . the uttermost parts of the earth for thy possession"—with Virgil's prophecy that the fame of Augustus should be bounded by the stars (*Aen.* I, 287).

383. *capital* plays on the literal Latin meaning, "pertaining to the head," where the serpent is to be bruised, and the derived meaning, "fatal."

393. *recure:* heal, restore.

401. *appaid:* satisfied. Cf. III, 210.

401–458. The doctrinal elements of this passage are expressly affirmed in Milton's detailed assertion of Christ's "voluntary submission of himself to the divine justice both in life and in death . . . for man's redemption," and his resurrection and ascension "to a state of immortality and highest glory" in *CD* I, xvi (C. E. XV, 302).

Never to hurt them more who rightly trust
In this his satisfaction; so he dies,
But soon revives, Death over him no power   420
Shall long usurp; ere the third dawning light
Return, the Stars of Morn shall see him rise
Out of his grave, fresh as the dawning light,
Thy ransom paid, which Man from death redeems,
His death for Man, as many as offer'd Life   425
Neglect not, and the benefit embrace
By Faith not void of works: this God-like act
Annuls thy doom, the death thou shouldst have di'd,
In sin for ever lost from life; this act
Shall bruise the head of *Satan,* crush his strength   430
Defeating Sin and Death, his two main arms,
And fix far deeper in his head thir stings
Than temporal death shall bruise the Victor's heel,
Or theirs whom he redeems, a death like sleep,
A gentle wafting to immortal Life.   435
Nor after resurrection shall he stay
Longer on Earth than certain times to appear
To his Disciples, Men who in his Life
Still follow'd him; to them shall leave in charge
To teach all nations what of him they learn'd   440
And his Salvation, them who shall believe
Baptizing in the profluent stream, the sign
Of washing them from guilt of sin to Life
Pure, and in mind prepar'd, if so befall,
For death, like that which the redeemer di'd.   445
All Nations they shall teach; for from that day
Not only to the Sons of *Abraham's* Loins
Salvation shall be Preacht, but to the Sons
Of *Abraham's* Faith wherever through the world;
So in his seed all Nations shall be blest.   450
Then to the Heav'n of Heav'ns he shall ascend
With victory, triúmphing through the air
Over his foes and thine; there shall surprise
The Serpent, Prince of air, and drag in Chains
Through all his Realm, and there confounded leave;   455
Then enter into glory, and resume
His Seat at God's right hand, exalted high
Above all names in Heav'n; and thence shall come,
When this world's dissolution shall be ripe,
With glory and power to judge both quick and dead,   460
To judge th' unfaithful dead, but to reward
His faithful, and receive them into bliss,
Whether in Heav'n or Earth, for then the Earth
Shall all be Paradise, far happier place

433. Cf. Milton's conception of *temporal death* in XI, 469.

442. *profluent* is derived from the Latin word used in Milton's discussion of baptism as ideally to be performed in running water (in *CD* I, xxviii; C. E. XVI, 168).

447. Cf. Galatians iii, 8: "And the scripture, foreseeing that God would justify the heathen through faith, preached before the gospel unto Abraham, saying, In thee shall all nations be blessed." In the next eighty lines countless reminiscences from the New Testament, the Psalms, and the Prophets are more or less clearly introduced.

460. *quick and dead:* living and dead. The phrase is from the Apostles' Creed, with Christ's words, "all that are in the graves shall hear the voice" (John v, 28), in the background.

Than this of *Eden*, and far happier days.   465
  So spake th' Arch-Angel *Michaël*, then paus'd,
As at the World's great period; and our Sire
Replete with joy and wonder thus repli'd.
  O goodness infinite, goodness immense!
That all this good of evil shall produce,   470
And evil turn to good; more wonderful
Than that which by creation first brought forth
Light out of darkness! full of doubt I stand,
Whether I should repent me now of sin

more glorious to save a sinner than a righteous man.

By mee done and occasion'd, or rejoice   475
Much more, that much more good thereof shall spring,
To God more glory, more good will to Men
From God, and over wrath grace shall abound.
But say, if our deliverer up to Heav'n
Must reascend, what will betide the few   480
His faithful, left among th' unfaithful herd,
The enemies of truth; who then shall guide
His people, who defend? will they not deal
Worse with his followers than with him they dealt?
  Be sure they will, said th' Angel; but from Heav'n   485
Hee to his own a Comforter will send,
The promise of the Father, who shall dwell
His Spirit within them, and the Law of Faith
Working through love, upon thir hearts shall write,
To guide them in all truth, and also arm   490
With spiritual Armor, able to resist
Satan's assaults, and quench his fiery darts,
What Man can do against them, not afraid,
Though to the death, against such cruelties
With inward consolations recompens't,   495
And oft supported so as shall amaze
Thir proudest persecutors: for the Spirit
Pour'd first on his Apostles, whom he sends
To evangelize the Nations, then on all
Baptiz'd, shall them with wondrous gifts endue   500
To speak all Tongues, and do all Miracles,
As did thir Lord before them. Thus they win
Great numbers of each Nation to receive
With joy the tidings brought from Heav'n: at length
Thir Ministry perform'd, and race well run,   505
Thir doctrine and thir story written left,
They die; but in thir room, as they forewarn,
Wolves shall succeed for teachers, grievous Wolves,

469–478. Adam's cry repeats the title of the medieval hymn *O Felix Culpa* (*O Happy Sin*). It is paraphrased by the chorus in Salandra's *Adamo caduto* II, xiv: "O happy Sin / O blessed crime / O precious theft / Dear Disobedience / Adam, blest thief not of the Apple / But of Mercy, Clemency, and Glory." The paradox is the climax of poems like Giles Fletcher's *Christ's Triumph over Death* (1610) and Du Bartas' *Divine Weeks* (p. 261), when Adam finds that he is "blessed more" in his "offence" than in his "primer happy innocence." The theological history of the belief is traced by A. O. Lovejoy in *ELH*, IV (1937), 161–79, and

by A. Williams in *Expositor*, p. 138. See the Introduction 5, 46 and 49.

478. Cf. Romans v, 20: "Where sin abounded, grace did much more abound."

486. So in *CD* I, vi (p. 970) Milton says that "the Holy Spirit, the Comforter, was sent by the Son from the Father." Cf. John xv, 26.

489. Hebrews viii, 10, echoes Jeremiah xxxi, 33, in describing God's laws and love as written on the heart.

491. The *spiritual Armor* comes from Ephesians vi, 11–17.

508. *grievous Wolves* is St. Paul's term (Acts

Who all the sacred mysteries of Heav'n
To thir own vile advantages shall turn   510
Of lucre and ambition, and the truth
With superstitions and traditions taint,
Left only in those written Records pure,
Though not but by the Spirit understood.
Then shall they seek to avail themselves of names,   515
Places and titles, and with these to join
Secular power, though feigning still to act
By spiritual, to themselves appropriating
The Spirit of God, promis'd alike and giv'n
To all Believers; and from that pretense,   520
Spiritual Laws by carnal power shall force
On every conscience; Laws which none shall find
Left them inroll'd, or what the Spirit within
Shall on the heart engrave. What will they then
But force the Spirit of Grace itself, and bind   525
His consort Liberty; what, but unbuild
His living Temples, built by Faith to stand,
Thir own Faith not another's: for on Earth
Who against Faith and Conscience can be heard
Infallible? yet many will presume: 530
Whence heavy persecution shall arise
On all who in the worship persevere
Of Spirit and Truth; the rest, far greater part,
Will deem in outward Rites and specious forms
Religion satisfi'd; Truth shall retire   535
Bestuck with sland'rous darts, and works of Faith
Rarely be found: so shall the World go on,
To good malignant, to bad men benign,
Under her own weight groaning, till the day
Appear of respiration to the just,   540
And vengeance to the wicked, at return
Of him so lately promis'd to thy aid,
The Woman's seed, obscurely then foretold,
Now ampler known thy Saviour and thy Lord,
Last in the Clouds from Heav'n to be reveal'd   545
In glory of the Father, to dissolve
Satan with his perverted World, then raise
From the conflagrant mass, purg'd and refin'd,
New Heav'ns, new Earth, Ages of endless date
Founded in righteousness and peace and love,   550
To bring forth fruits Joy and eternal Bliss.
    He ended; and thus *Adam* last repli'd.
How soon hath thy prediction, Seer blest,
Measur'd this transient World, the Race of time,

xx, 29), which is echoed in *grim Wolf* in the
attack on the corrupt clergy in *Lycidas,* 128, and
again in the *hireling Wolves, whose gospel is their
maw* of the *Sonnet to Cromwell.*
    517-525. So in *CD* I, xxx (C. E. XVI, 280)
Milton denounced all efforts to impose "human authority in matters of religion" as in effect efforts
"to impose a yoke, not on man, but on the Holy
Spirit itself." Cf. "Now the Lord is that Spirit:
and where the Spirit of the Lord is, there is
liberty" (II Cor. iii, 17).

527. St. Paul called the body "the temple of
the Holy Ghost" (I Cor. vi, 19).
    533. ". . . true worshippers shall worship the
Father in spirit and in truth" (John iv, 23).
    539-551. Milton interprets St. Peter's day of *res-
piration to the just* (Acts iii, 19) as the day of
Christ's coming "with the clouds" (Rev. i, 7) at
the last judgment, when, he says in *CD* I, xxxiii
(C. E. XVI), "Christ shall judge the evil angels
and the whole race of mankind." Cf. XI, 900-
901, and III, 334-38.

Till time stand fixt: beyond is all abyss,   555
Eternity, whose end no eye can reach.
Greatly instructed I shall hence depart,
Greatly in peace of thought, and have my fill
Of knowledge, what this Vessel can contain;
Beyond which was my folly to aspire.   560
Henceforth I learn, that to obey is best,
And love with fear the only God, to walk
As in his presence, ever to observe
His providence, and on him sole depend,
Merciful over all his works, with good   565
Still overcoming evil, and by small
Accomplishing great things, by things deem'd weak
Subverting worldly strong, and worldly wise
By simply meek; that suffering for Truth's sake
Is fortitude to highest victory,   570
And to the faithful Death the Gate of Life;
Taught this by his example whom I now
Acknowledge my Redeemer ever blest.
  To whom thus also th' Angel last repli'd:
This having learnt, thou hast attain'd the sum   575
Of wisdom; hope no higher, though all the Stars
Thou knew'st by name, and all th' ethereal Powers,
All secrets of the deep, all Nature's works,
Or works of God in Heav'n, Air, Earth, or Sea,
And all the riches of this World enjoy'dst,   580
And all the rule, one Empire; only add
Deeds to thy knowledge answerable, add Faith,
Add Virtue, Patience, Temperance, add Love,
By name to come call'd Charity, the soul
Of all the rest: then wilt thou not be loath   585
To leave this Paradise, but shalt possess
A paradise within thee, happier far.
Let us descend now therefore from this top
Of Speculation; for the hour precise
Exacts our parting hence; and see the Guards,   590
By mee encampt on yonder Hill, expect
Thir motion, at whose Front a flaming Sword,
In signal of remove, waves fiercely round;
We may no longer stay: go, waken Eve;
Her also I with gentle Dreams have calm'd   595
Portending good, and all her spirits compos'd
To meek submission: thou at season fit
Let her with thee partake what thou hast heard,
Chiefly what may concern her Faith to know,
The great deliverance by her Seed to come   600

559. *this vessel,* as St. Paul called the human body (I Thess. iv, 4), Milton warns in *CD* I, ii (p. 905), is able to understand God only "in such manner as may be within the scope of our comprehension." Cf. VIII, 167–73.

565. The line repeats St. Paul's words in Romans xii, 21.

566–569. "God hath chosen the weak things of the world to confound the things that are mighty . . ." (I Cor. i, 27).

587. The *paradise within* (in contrast with the hell within Satan in IV, 20) recalls Robert Crofts's title for his *A Paradise within Us or the Happie Mind* (1640). Reasoning much as Milton does in ll. 469–78, Crofts pled that the possibility of an inward paradise proved that Adam's fall was fortunate. A case for Crofts's influence on Milton is made with some reservations by G. C. Taylor in *PQ,* XXVIII (1949), 208.

589. *Speculation* has its Latin meaning of "looking out." Cf. the *specular Mount* of *PR* IV, 236.

(For by the Woman's Seed) on all Mankind,
That ye may live, which will be many days,
Both in one Faith unanimous though sad,
With cause for evils past, yet much more cheer'd
With meditation on the happy end.   605
He ended, and they both descend the Hill;
Descended, *Adam* to the Bow'r where *Eve*
Lay sleeping ran before, but found her wak't;
And thus with words not sad she him receiv'd.
Whence thou return'st, and whither went'st, I know;   610
For God is also in sleep, and Dreams advise,
Which he hath sent propitious, some great good
Presaging, since with sorrow and heart's distress
Wearied I fell asleep: but now lead on;
In mee is no delay; with thee to go,   615
Is to stay here; without thee here to stay,
Is to go hence unwilling; thou to mee
Art all things under Heav'n, all places thou,
Who for my wilful crime art banisht hence.
This further consolation yet secure   620
I carry hence; though all by mee is lost,
Such favor I unworthy am voutsaf't,
By mee the Promis'd Seed shall all restore.
So spake our Mother *Eve,* and *Adam* heard
Well pleas'd, but answer'd not; for now too nigh   625
Th' Arch-Angel stood, and from the other Hill
To thir fixt Station, all in bright array
The Cherubim descended; on the ground
Gliding meteorous, as Ev'ning Mist
Ris'n from a River o'er the marish glides,   630
And gathers ground fast at the Laborer's heel
Homeward returning. High in Front advanc't,
The brandisht Sword of God before them blaz'd
Fierce as a Comet; which with torrid heat,
And vapor as the *Libyan* Air adust,   635
Began to parch that temperate Clime; whereat
In either hand the hast'ning Angel caught
Our ling'ring Parents, and to th' Eastern Gate
Led them direct, and down the Cliff as fast
To the subjected Plain; then disappear'd.   640
They looking back, all th' Eastern side beheld
Of Paradise, so late thir happy seat,
Wav'd over by that flaming Brand, the Gate
With dreadful Faces throng'd and fiery Arms:
Some natural tears they dropp'd, but wip'd them soon;   645

602. ". . . the days that Adam lived were nine hundred and thirty years: and he died" (Gen. v, 5).

611. Perhaps there is a trace of Achilles' words to Agamemnon: "A dream is from Zeus" (*Il.* I, 63). There is certainly a reminiscence of the distinction which Bacon said (*Essays* xlii) that a certain rabbi drew between a vision and a dream on the ground that the former is the clearer revelation of God.

635. *adust:* burnt. Milton had perhaps read John Salkeld's review of several theories about the swords of the cherubim guarding the entrance of Eden, and among them St. Thomas Aquinas' suggestion that the garden lay under the equator and that "the sword which the angel held before Paradise, is nothing else but the mighty heate of the torrida zona" (*A Treatise of Angels*—1613—p. 290); but like Salkeld he seems to have thought that the cherubim were true angels. Cf. II, 714, n.

640. *subjected* has its Latin meaning of "lying beneath."

The World was all before them, where to choose
Thir place of rest, and Providence thir guide:
They <u>hand in hand</u> with wand'ring steps and slow,
Through *Eden* took thir solitary way.

The End

648. Since Michael was instructed to dismiss Adam and Eve "not disconsolate" (XI, 113), the way has been prepared for the mood in which they quit the "blissful Paradise / Of God . . . by him in the East / Of *Eden* planted" (IV, 208–210).

PARADISE REGAIN'D.

A POEM.

In IV BOOKS.

To which is added

SAMSON AGONISTES.

The Author
JOHN MILTON.

LONDON,

Printed by *J. M.* for *John Starkey* at the
Mitre in *Fleetstreet*, near *Temple-Bar.*
MDCLXXI.

Paradise Regained

INTRODUCTION

1. The basis of *Paradise Regained* is Luke's record of Satan's triple temptation of Christ to make bread out of a stone in the desert, to accept "all the kingdoms of the world," and "the glory of them" as Satan's gift, and finally to cast himself down from "a pinnacle of the temple" in Jerusalem. The first temptation ends in Christ's refusal to perform a miracle. The second is a miracle of Satan, for his show of the world's empires is produced in "a moment of time." The third unravels the plot with Christ's miraculous realization of his deity by simple obedience to Satan's ironic command that, if he can, he shall stand on the needle point of the pinnacle or else presumptuously cast himself down,

> safely if Son of God:
> For it is written, He will give command
> Concerning thee to his Angels in thir hands
> They shall up lift thee, lest at any time
> Thou chance to dash thy foot against a stone.

2. Luke's record suited Milton better than Matthew's because it put the "temptation of the tower" last. If we agree with A. S. P. Woodhouse in *UTQ*, XXV (1956), 170—that the first temptation wears the Protestant interpretation of "distrust of God's providence" and is "balanced by the third, to presumption" upon that providence—the brief initial and final episodes are complementary in the design of the poem. Between them (Book II, 300 to Book IV, 393) stretches the "temptation of the kingdoms" with its panorama of luxury, empire, and finally of all the wisdom and poetry of pagan culture at its best. Psychologically, the test of Christ's innocence of any lust for power prepares him for an immediate victory over the devil's suggestion of an act of presumption or vulgar exhibitionism, and so the second temptation fits logically into a plot which is to culminate in the temptation of the tower. The climax and the final unravelling of the plot come with the discovery of the full truth about themselves and about each other by Christ and the Adversary. The scene has the power of Iphigeneia's recognition of her brother Orestes in the Greek whom she is on the point of sacrificing to the Tauric god in Euripides' drama. It is like the crucial recognitions which Aristotle regarded as essential to the plot of any good tragedy.

3. Milton's invention of his climax was not entirely original. It perpetuated a tradition which Miss E. M. Pope traces to a disagreement among Protestant theologians about "the precise extent to which Christ's divinity remained dormant during the temptation itself" (*Tradition*, p. 19). She sees all the temptations as an intense and "desperate test of identity" which is at last resolved when Christ warns Satan in the last speech attributed to him in the poem: "It is written, 'Tempt not the Lord thy God.'" Readers must decide for themselves whether to regard that speech as a simple declaration of divinity or to agree with J. H. Hanford—in *SP*, XV (1918), 188—in regarding it simply as a "human victory over all temptation." Then comes the question whether—as D. C. Allen thinks (in *Vision*, pp. 118–19)—the dramatic success is achieved by Christ's uncertainty about himself, since he can "flare into divine certainty" only when "he is confronted by the subhuman enticements of the mind of evil." But Allen regards Satan as fully aware of

471

Christ's identity as the person from whom, he reminds the devils in Council in Book I, 53–54, and 85–90, he is doomed to suffer a "fatal wound." A consequence of Allen's view is to make Satan guilty of a crude act of violence and "poorly concealed murder" on the pinnacle of the temple. The violence is obvious and the murderous purpose is confirmed by Edward Cleveland's parallels—in *MLQ*, XVI (1955), 235—between Satan's behavior here and that of Christ's tormentors in the scenes before the Crucifixion in the Gospels.

4. Every reader must decide for himself whether to read the poem as Allen does or to read it as intended to keep him uncertain until the end as to how far Satan ever understands Christ. If we accept Arnold Stein's view—in *ELH*, XXIII (1956), 126—that in the third temptation Satan abandons the effort to corrupt Christ and tries simply to goad him into an act which will "reveal what Satan wants to know," we are returning to A. H. Gilbert's interpretation of the scene—in *JEGP*, XVI (1916), 606—as essentially "a final test of identity on Satan's part." But, regardless how it is read, the question remains as to whether there is true drama in a debate where Christ is above the battle as well as in it. The paradox is given its most paradoxical development by Jacques Blondel in his excellent introduction to the poem (*Le Paradis reconquis*, p. 55) in an analysis of the divinely skilful dialectic which forces Satan to defeat himself merely by letting him exhaust his ingenuity against a mind more profound than the depths of evil itself. This essentially theological and philosophical view transcends rather than avoids the question of inward dramatic tension in Christ's experience, and it gives a peculiarly medieval aspect to the outward drama. A contributor to *N&Q*—CLXXXVII (1944), 39—sees the poem as a dramatic elaboration of Gregory the Great's metaphor of the "hook" of Satan's curiosity, which entangles him with Christ in the first place and disables him in their uneven struggle. If there is fatalism and even cruelty in the image of the hook, there is also an optimistic irony, which was once the theme of an undeniably moving hymn of Abelard.

5. As climax and sudden resolution of the plot the last temptation is the most interesting of the three, but as spiritual duel and debate upon life's values, the second deserves the wide scope which Milton gave to it. Misunderstanding of its drama as depending entirely upon a humanistic view of Christ has led to some determined attempts to prove that Milton regarded him as less than divine both in *Paradise Regained* and the *Christian Doctrine*. Milton is often loosely called an Arian and sometimes represented as the "disciple of Servetus" which H. McLachlan thinks him in *The Religious Opinions of Milton, Locke, and Newton* (Manchester, 1941) p. 61. Or he is seen as an English pioneer of the Unitarian doctrine that "Jesus was a man," of which M. A. Larson regarded him as a spokesman in *The Modernity of Milton* (Chicago, 1927), p. 152. Milton's Arianism implied a limitation of Christ's divinity but by no means amounted to its denial. Canon Looten regarded his faith as "semi-arienne, semi-catholique" (*Génie*, p. 214). After reviewing the support which W. G. Rice and others have given to Saurat's belief that Milton's Christ fades into "mere man," Miss Pope (in *Tradition*, p. 24) finds nothing in the poem to suggest any doubt of Christ's dual nature, human and divine. Indeed, everything in the poem corresponds with Milton's use of the temptation of Christ in the *Christian Doctrine* (I, 16) to illustrate his human nature—his humanity, in which he was tempted in the wilderness and died on the cross, and which was, by the supreme mystery of Christian faith, united with his divine nature. The doctrine was very familiar to Milton's readers. "Christ's workes are of his Godhead," said the popular preacher, Daniel Dike, In *Michael and the Dragon or Christ Tempted and Satan foyled* (1635), p. 230, and he cited the creation of the world as his first divine work; but he went on to

say that "the works of Christ's humanity" were "workes of morall obedience." In the light of this clear distinction between the works of Christ's two natures his divine nature cannot suffer when—as Hanford put the matter in a pioneer analysis of Milton's handling of the temptation theme in *SP*, XV (1918), 181—his resistance of Satan in the wilderness is seen as symbolic of the potentially universal human experience of retrieving all that mankind had lost through Adam's disobedience.

6. Though Milton's "Arianism" meant explicit denial of the doctrine of the Trinity, it also meant an assertion of Christ's divinity as well as of his humanity. Howard Schultz rightly stresses (in *Knowledge*, p. 117) its difference from the Socinianism which "would have afforded him a less mysterious religion." Even M. M. Ross does not deny that Milton's Christ is divine, though he condemns the character as thoroughly ugly and sees in it only a "scornful, snobbish, Miltonic demi-god" (*Dogma*, p. 222). Writing from the point of view of an Anglo-Catholic, Ross condemns the poem because its center is ethical rather than mystical, because Milton did not choose the "Eucharistic sacrifice of the Cross" as his subject in preference to the dramatic struggle with Satan which seemed to him to be the necessary preparation and promise of the Cross.

7. It is true that Milton was passionately dedicated to the ethical view of the temptation which was that of Protestant Reformers generally. Their idea was stated very early (1530) in the *Commentarius de anima* (Book II, in the section on the Certainty of Doctrines) of the Lutheran theologian Philip Melanchthon, who pled that God's son was set before men as an example to regenerate their nature, and that when "the Word of God enters our minds, it kindles our hearts to delighted love and obedience to God." In that passage Melanchthon was casting no doubt on Christ's divinity, but he had in mind an image of his humanity not unlike Tillyard's humanistic conception of Christ (in the Warton Lecture, 1936, p. 10) as "a great example, a highly significant object lesson, a figure of solemn and inspiring didacticism."

8. Several figures of inspiring didacticism besides Christ seemed comparable enough with him *in his temptation* for him to cite them as examples to Satan. The one whom Milton has him mention most frequently is Job. Traditionally, Job, like Samson, was not only a Christian saint, he was also the hero who faces us in the opening lines of George Sandys' *Paraphrase upon Job* (1638):

> In Hus, a land which near the sun's uprise,
> And northern confines of Sabaea lies,
> A great example of perfection reign'd;
> His name was Job, his soul with guilt unstain'd.

As early as 1642 Milton suggested by a reference to the Book of Job in *Reason of Church Government* that he thought of it as a perfect "brief epic" and perhaps dreamed of writing something like it. His dream was a natural one for any young man aspiring to write a poem that would be "exemplary to a nation," for—as C. W. Jones shows in *SP*, XLIV (1947), 209–27—St. Jerome's view of the Book of Job as a finished epic was universally accepted. Indeed, on the authority of Josephus and Origen, its dialogue was mistakenly regarded as being in true, classical hexameter and pentameter verse. But it was less the Hebrew rhythms of Job that attracted Milton than it was the lonely hero, sore beset by Satan and by his own unhelpful friends, and fencing with them and with their vulgarity as constantly as Christ fenced with Satan in *Paradise Regained*.

9. Another inspiring human figure in Milton's epic background was Spenser's Knight of Temperance, Guyon, who explores the Cave of Mammon and the Palace of Philotime —not undaunted, but unharmed—in *The Faerie Queene* II, vii. Guyon is a human ideal because he was largely shaped by Aristotle's conception of temperance in the *Nicomachean*

Ethics as a healthy habit of self-restraint in the presence of appeals to the flesh and the craving for money, power, and glory. Actually—as Ernest Sirluck shows in *MP,* XLVIII (1950), 95—Aristotle's definition of temperance is less strenuous than Milton's in *Christian Doctrine* II, ix, and in *Areopagitica,* in the famous passage praising Spenser as "a better teacher than Scotus or Aquinas." But Spenser's treatment of Guyon in the Cave of Mammon is less Aristotelian than it is Platonic, and on that ground Edwin Greenlaw declared in *SP,* XIV (1917), 205, that "the three days of temptation of Guyon concludes a series of incidents that pretty certainly influenced *Paradise Regained*—Mammon's proffer of riches, worldly power, fame; the three days without sleep or food, followed by exhaustion; the angel sent to care for Guyon after the trial is over; even the debates between Mammon and Guyon, which parallel Christ's rebukes of Satan." The precise reflection of Aristotelian, Platonic, and Christian ethics in Milton's Christ and Spenser's Guyon cannot be definitely determined. Guyon's temperance is a matter of rational self-control, and in most of his adventures Reason walks incarnate beside him in the person of a Palmer. For Denis Saurat Reason seems to be the object of Christ's final loyalty. Reason, as it was understood by the Neo-Platonists of the Renaissance, had divine as well as human connotations, and Blondel's Introduction (p. 71) gives us the answer to the problem by recognizing the Platonism in Milton's ideal of the perfect mastery of passion by Reason, though the Platonism wears the garment of a sensitively Christian loyalty to a rationally ordered moral world.

10. In the debate about fame (III, 21–151) the mixed classical and Christian elements in Milton's Christ begin to develop into a paradox which comes to a climax in his "repudiation" of classical philosophy and poetry (IV, 285–364) at the climax of the second temptation. Satan's argument that popular glory must be the basis of Christ's kingdom is well described by Miss Samuel (*Plato,* p. 95) as "semi-Platonic sophistry," while the wisdom of Christ will seem to any ardent Platonist to be "wholly Platonic." The debate is not shadow-boxing. Milton remembered the historic fact—which D. Daube stresses in *RES,* XIX (1943), 206—that the temptation to become the leader of Jewish nationalism was a factor in the life of Christ in the synoptic gospels. The debate leads into the three temptations of Parthia, Rome, and Athens, which reveal all the variety and depth of the Renaissance passion for fame. A very good study of *Paradise Regained* by Miss M. M. Mahood (in *Poetry and Humanism,* p. 225) treats the refinement of that passion as the main theme of the poem. The motive of refinement is obvious in the sequence of false power, false justice, and false wisdom, which unifies the second temptation in terms of the passion for glory, about which Milton had had something to say in *Lycidas,* in *Paradise Lost* (III, 348 and 698), and in the sonnet to Fairfax.

11. The debate about fame begins on familiar ground. Satan needles Christ by comparing his obscurity with the glory of soldiers like Alexander and Pompey the Great, who had the civilized world at their feet in their twenties. One of them is Scipio Africanus, the young conqueror of Spain and Carthage whose skill as a strategist and statesman was matched by his purity of character. He had been chosen by Petrarch, the prophet of the Renaissance cult of Fame, as the subject of the *Africa,* the epic poem which was to have crowned his life work though he did not live to finish it. To these examples of youthful honors Satan subtly adds the thought that

> years, and to ripe years judgment mature,
> Quench not the thirst of glory, but augment.
> Great *Julius,* whom now all the world admires,
> The more he grew in years, the more inflam'd
> With glory . . .

(III, 37–41)

Christ's rejection of the lure of military glory is no surprise to us, but it was less of a surprise to readers who had been brought up in the tradition of dialogues like the *Christi Jesu triumphus* of Luis Vives, which had been a textbook in the schools in the sixteenth century. In that dialogue a group of scholars are represented as looking at a drawing of a Caesarian triumph in a French Book of Hours and as being inspired by it to contrast the virtues of Caesar and of Christ.

12. The contrast between Christ and Caesar sets the pattern which—as F. Kermode says in *RES*, n.s. IV (1953), 329—culminates in the equation: "Pagan learning is to Christian learning as Socrates is to Christ." That is the only possible outcome of Satan's challenge to Christ to "Be famous . . . by wisdom" (IV, 221–2). Without the survey of the schools of philosophy which follows, the challenge would be meaningless, and Milton evidently meant it to be overwhelmingly moving and unequivocal. It is so moving that it can be read as veiled advocacy of the supreme claims of pagan literature—much as the appeal of Comus to the Lady to "be advised" and not lend her ears to the "budge doctors of the Stoic fur" (*Comus*, 705 and 707) has been seriously taken to represent Milton's real though probably "subconscious" feeling about the merits of that debate. Since Christ's reply to Satan is too clear and passionate to reflect anything but the poet's actual state of mind, psychological criticism has taken another tack and treated Christ's denial of "True Wisdom" (IV, 319) to the ancients as "masochism," and seen in it a reaction against "Milton's action during the Civil War"—as Tillyard explained it in 1930 in *Milton* (p. 309). The suggestion is attractive, if—like G. F. Sensabaugh in *SP*, XLIII (1946), 258–72—we think that "Milton's strange pronouncements upon intellectual curiosity and humane studies no doubt stem from deep disillusion" and therefore from a religious experience such as he himself described in his chapter on Regeneration in the *Christian Doctrine* (I, xviii): "the old man destroyed, the inward man regenerated by God after his own image." Yet in the following discussion of the Christian virtues in the *Christian Doctrine*, as Sensabaugh takes care to say, the foundation of Milton's ethics is candidly classical.

13. Critical opinion is split about the treatment of human learning in *Paradise Regained*. Robert Adams (in *Ikon*, p. 127) sees in it only "that provincial contempt for the classics, that feeling for the Christian dispensation as not only supplementing but cancelling pagan reason, which resounds through *Paradise Regained*." Ross sees the Savior (in *Royalism*, p. 122) as not only denying "the philosophic spirit, the searching mind of the Greeks (once so dear to Milton)," but also as repudiating "their political thinking." Middle ground is suggested by Douglas Bush (in *Humanism*, p. 125), though he finds it "painful to watch Milton turn and rend some main roots of his being." But this does not mean "that in old age the puritan has conquered the humanist"; it means simply that "Milton holds the traditional attitude of the humanist with additional fervor." This view is a long step towards Blondel's defense (*Le Paradis reconquis* pp. 79–86) of Christ's "repudiation" of the classics as springing from a "hierarchy of values" which is an intense thirst for the beatific vision, and which is almost as Platonic as it is Christian. Milton was certainly aware of the Platonism in his thought. That—thinks Miss Samuel in *P.&M.*, pp. 19 and 59—is why his only charge against Plato is the gentle one that he "to fabling fell and smooth conceits" (IV, 295). Most critics have agreed more or less with Hanford—in *SP*, XV (1918), 183–4—that there was a conscious compromise in Milton's treatment of the classics, "a half-reconciliation between his Puritanism and his love of learning," which consists in "opposing Hebrew literature to pagan at all points and contending for its superiority."

14. But compromise is not the spirit of Christ's denial that "True Wisdom" is to be found among philosophers who

in themselves seek virtue, and to themselves
All glory arrogate, to God give none.

(IV, 314-5)

If any tolerance for humanism is to be found in these words and their context, it is to be found not by toning down what they say but by looking closely at their distinct meaning. Their closest and at the same time most impartial analyst is Schultz, who is not splitting hairs when he points out (in *Knowledge*, p. 227) that "Christ is not unwilling to be thought learned," and that he intends to exculpate the arts when he says, "Think not but that I know these things" (IV, 286). Northrop Frye is not hair-splitting when he declares that "it is Greek philosophy in its context as part of Satan's kingdom that is being rejected. A Christian working outward from his faith might find the study of Plato and Aristotle profitable enough, but if he were to *exchange* the direct tradition of revelation for their doctrines, which is what Christ is tempted to do, he would find in them only the fine flower of a speculative tree with its roots in the demonic metaphysics and theology described in the second book of *Paradise Lost*" (*MP*, LIII [1956], 236). Confirmation of Frye's view comes from Schultz's study of *Paradise Regained* (in *Knowledge*) in the light of Milton's nearly contemporary *Considerations touching the likeliest means to remove Hirelings out of the church* (1659). Even if we doubt the theory that the poem, like the pamphlet, was really a shot in the great battle between churchmen who insisted on a classical education for all clergymen and nonconformists like Milton, who resented the monopoly of clerical training by Oxford and Cambridge, we may agree with Schultz that the pamphlet can shed light on the poem. Writing impartially and with no effort to exculpate Milton from the charge of "Hebraism," Schultz declares (p. 222) that in *Hirelings* Milton took for granted the freedom of laymen to "frequent academies" and of ministers "to compass all the human learning they could master without neglecting or perverting their high calling."

15. Turning now from the political and ecclesiastical context of *Paradise Regained*, we may look at its context in the heroic tradition. It was not only a literary tradition, which was regarded as having developed from the violent hero of the *Iliad* and the shrewd or wise hero of the *Odyssey* to the divinely guided hero of the *Aeneid*. Milton expressly took his place in that tradition by putting the word *man* in the opening lines of both his epic poems in a way to challenge comparison with the emphasis in the opening lines of the classical epics upon the word *man* as significant of the peculiar heroic character of their heroes. The literary tradition had been entangled with Platonic and Aristotelian doctrines of heroic virtue such as played a part in *The Faerie Queene*, both in the portrayal of the Knight of Temperance and in the shaping of Prince Arthur, who was meant to represent what Spenser regarded as the Aristotelian ideal of magnanimity. Elsewhere—in *SP*, XXXV (1938), 258-72—I have traced the links between Milton's Christ, Spenser's Arthur, and Aristotle's magnanimous man. It is a long chain, running by way of Aquinas and the Renaissance interpreters of Aristotle's definition of magnanimity to Milton's definition of it in the *Christian Doctrine* (II, ix) as something which motivates us "when in seeking or avoiding riches, advantages, or honors, we are actuated by our own dignity, rightly understood." One of his illustrations is Job, and another is "Christ rejecting the empire of the world, Matt. iv, 9." Milton was thinking of Aristotle's conception of magnanimity in the *Nicomachean Ethics* IV, iii, 16, but he was thinking also of countless commentaries on it by both theologians and publicists who had made it the supreme "heroical virtue." So Castiglione called it when he made that "heroicall virtue" the final glory of his ideal courtier statesman in *The Book of the Courtier* (Hoby's translation, Everyman Ed., p. 276) and declared that it would make him "most glorious and most dearly beloved of God," and would let him "passe the bounds of the nature of man and rather be called a demi-god than a man mortall."

16. For Milton magnanimity or "heroic virtue" very definitely had the public aspect that it has in Christ's "temptation of the kingdoms." In *Of Reformation in England* magnanimity is mentioned as the prime virtue of statesmen, and with an eye on the training of political leaders in *Of Education* Milton planned a curriculum to prepare them to display it in "all the offices of peace and war." In Italy, where the public and private aspects of the virtue were seen as aspects of the conflict between the active and contemplative ideals, Tasso had discussed the problem in his Discourse *Della Virtù Eroica e della Carità* and had given the edge to the active life; but the essence of his "heroic virtue" was really a balance of the two ideals. Julius Caesar Scaliger called Aeneas the most perfect of epic heroes because he had all the contemplative virtues and yet lived the active life in obedience to Reason as it was revealed to him by the gods. Scaliger's interest was that of a literary critic judging an heroic poem, but, as a practising poet with an assured European audience, Tasso regarded the hero of the *Aeneid* in the same way though he divided his virtues among the heroes of the *Jerusalem Delivered*.

17. In Tasso's essay *Del Poema Eroico* the working ideal of heroic magnanimity seems almost like a design for Milton's Christ. Tasso traced it to Aristotle's *Ethics,* but even more definitely to his *Politics,* where he found justification for his own view of heroic virtue as "an excess or perfection of the good, something which has nothing to do with moderation, as the moral virtues have," something divine and distinguishable from Christian charity and the love of God only because its object is true earthly honor rather than heavenly glory. The finest earthly honor, he thought, belonged to Roman worthies like the Curzii, Decii, and Marcelli, names such as Augustine had mentioned with honor in *The City of God* V, xviii; but their heroic spirit seemed to Tasso to be "a mere shadow and figure" of the divine love which Christ brought into the world. Tasso's words about the founders of Rome's greatness are worth remembering when we read Christ's reply to Satan's challenge to him to emulate them:

> Among the Heathen (for throughout the World
> To me is not unknown what hath been done
> Worthy of Memorial) canst thou not remember
> *Quintius, Fabricius, Curius, Regulus?*

18. This rebuke of Christ to Satan is a key to Milton's treatment of the devil. In the typology of *Paradise Regained* Satan is an obvious parody of the epic hero of the poem, just as in *Paradise Lost* he parodies God's heavenly council with his parliament of devils in Pandemonium, Christ's rule over the angels "by merit" with his own dictatorial rule of the demons, and in general parodies the divine goodness by his own resolve to make evil his good. In a study of *Paradise Regained* from the political side Z. S. Fink has described Satan as an antitype of Christ and as the acknowledged dictator of the demons (I, 113). His analysis—in *JEGP*, XL (1941), 482-8—makes the parody of Christ by the Adversary inevitable in a poem which is built around the contrast between Christian "heroic virtue" and the selfishly ambitious kinds of heroism which Satan has to offer. His misunderstanding of Christ is like his envy of God in *Paradise Lost.* He cannot even understand Christ's plain words and unconsciously translates them into a kind of double-talk of his own. Northrop Frye has suggested—in *MP*, LIII (1956), 232—that his dialectic is essentially that of "the evasive or quibbling oracle," while "Christ's is the simplicity and plainness that Milton prizes in Scripture, and especially in the Gospels." And he is surely right in seeing a symbol of the parody of Christ by Satan in the simile comparing them to Oedipus and the Sphinx (IV, 572-6). For, like Oedipus, Christ, the divine Word, destroys the monster whose riddles threaten all human life.

19. To see Satan as a parody or antitype of Christ is not the same thing as to see "the diminished Satan" whom Arnold Stein (in *Style,* p. 122) finds "more nearly individual" than the Satan of *Paradise Lost.* As a study in the development of the Will to Deceive

(or to Self-Deceive), Satan is psychologically so successful that Tillyard (in *Milton*, p. 305) sees him as utterly "different from his namesake in *Paradise Lost*" and thinks it "a pity he cannot be given another title." The Satan of *Paradise Regained* seems likely to suffer as many insults from critics as his namesake Old Nick suffered for his rogueries on the medieval stage. D. C. Allen (in *Vision*, p. 110) writes that "the temper of the weary but clever Satan is by no means that of the newly-fallen archangel and novice tempter of Eve." For Robert Adams (in *Ikon*, p. 54) he is "a mealy-mouthed scamp, a whining juggler of words and stage-properties, a confidence man." But it is a question whether he is really brought lower in *Paradise Regained* than he is as the dictator of hell in *Paradise Lost*, when he and his horde of followers are helplessly changed into their appropriate serpent forms. Though he is "shorn of his grandeur" in *Paradise Regained*, Woodhouse rightly insists—in *UTQ*, XXV (1956), 172—that the grandeur was lost "by the end of the earlier epic," and that "Satan is the same character as the Satan of *Paradise Lost*. He is the great romantic, the rebel not only against God, but against fact, who cannot bring himself to accept his place in the scale of being or to act upon what in his heart he knows to be the truth."

20. As a parody of Christ Satan may be psychologically less interesting than he is as a whining juggler. But as a parody he also has his psychological interest, which is not entirely different from his interest as a juggler. He represents the sick psychology of the self-deceiving human spirit rationalizing its passions. The exposure of his reasoning was a part of Christian tradition. His wiles with Milton's Christ are like Mammon's wiles with Spenser's Knight of Temperance, though Milton makes him more dramatic and individual. But appreciation of his impact as an individual should not blind us to his nature as the universal antitype of Christ.

21. It is an odd fact that, while the Satan of *Paradise Lost* has often been called an unconscious self-portrayal by Milton, W. B. C. Watkins (in *An Anatomy of Milton's Verse*, p. 118) is the only critic to regard Milton as betraying his own character in the Satan of *Paradise Regained*. But he accuses Milton of that mistake only in the passage (II, 208–23) where "Satan steps out of character" to rebuke Belial for advising that Christ be tempted with the "daughters of men . . . the fairest found" (II, 154). In Belial's rejected dream of fair women and its rebuke by Satan Watkins sees Milton's sensuality betraying itself as distinctly as he sees the ascetic tone of the poem in Satan's image of Christ "Seated on the top of virtue's hill." In that image other readers have seen the "pale Galilean" and in him a symbol of Milton's "asceticism." Milton himself intended in it only one of several confessions by Satan that in Christ he saw the perfect, Platonic "shape" or ideal of the "good, wise," and "just" (III, 11). Readers must decide for themselves how objective Milton made his Christ. It is hard not to agree with Tillyard that in part the character was an idealization of Milton's own personality as he understood it. But the portrait is not prevailingly ascetic or puritanical if Tillyard is right—in *SP*, XXXVI (1939), 250—in regarding the poem as a reaction against the spirit of the younger Milton who in 1642 had advocated reforms in the church that were to be as "speedy and vehement" as "the reformations of all the good kings of Judah." We may still have the "pale Galilean" in the Christ of *Paradise Regained*, but he is a figure less like St. Anthony than he is like Ghandi. And there is no paleness in Milton's declaration of the power of "the Church of God" to rise triumphant over violence in his pamphlet on *Hirelings*. The Church, says the opening sentence, may have much to fear from "hire," which often corrupts the clergy; but "under force . . . true religion oft-times best thrives and flourishes." In the temptation on the pinnacle of the Temple, if we agree with the theologians who regarded it as a violent, physical attack on Christ, the analogy with the thought in *Hirelings* is very striking indeed. And in Milton's treatment

of the last temptation the element of violence is clear, though Dick Taylor may be right—in *UTQ*, XXIV (1955), 359-76—in his suggestion that the storm on the preceding night (IV, 409-19) was intended by Satan as an omen to frighten Christ into panic dread of some impending disaster, and not as a part of the violent attack so soon to follow. But when Satan comes in the morning as an ill-concealed murderer, Christ's resistance is only in words; and if any supernatural power is used against Satan, it is only the power of truth. The scene fulfills Michael's prophecy to Adam (*PL* XII, 386-95) that Satan's final defeat will involve no "local wounds of head or heel."

22. The defeat of violence by truth is a paradox whose nature Milton implies by using the myth of Antaeus to symbolize it after Satan's fall from the pinnacle (IV, 563-8). None of the labors of Hercules was better known than his destruction of the giant Antaeus, who drew fresh strength from his mother earth every time that he was thrown down, and who was killed only when Hercules held him aloft and crushed him to death. The obvious interpretation of the myth as a symbol of the victory of the spirit over the flesh was widespread in Renaissance literature. It was the motif of countless statuary groups, bas-reliefs, and medals showing the wrestlers—Antaeus always aloft in Hercules' arms—against the background of the Libyan desert. Hercules was often understood to be a type of Christ (as Milton made him in *The Passion*), and his victory over Antaeus could be paralleled with Christ's victory over Satan. But Hercules was also treated by some mythographers as a symbol of the sun, which in turn was a symbol of light and truth. In that interpretation of Hercules there was a subtle suggestion for Milton of a meaning less obvious in the defeat of Antaeus than the defeat of falsehood by truth. The most influential of the mythographers, Natale Conti, allegorized the myth in a medico-moral way as meaning that diseases of the body and soul are often cured by their opposites, but he warned that the treatment of fevers—to take an example which might also represent the passions—should never be violent. The same principle, he said, was applicable to political disturbances; opposite but not violent remedies should be applied to the ills of the body politic. Unfortunately, he added nothing to explain why Milton stresses the death of Antaeus in the air, but—as Frye suggests—that may be a fulfilment of the prophecy in *Paradise Lost* (X, 184-5) that Christ would see Satan, "Prince of the Air," "fall like Lightning down from Heav'n."

23. The story of Hercules and Antaeus has lost its charm in the modern world. Its most familiar interpretation as a symbol of the triumph of spirit over flesh makes it seem like an emblem of masochistic puritanism. Milton chose to interpret it, seemingly, in Conti's way, as an emblem of non-violent power over violence. If in that fact we have a key to Milton's mood and thought when he wrote *Paradise Regained*, we have good reason to doubt the picture of him as an uncompromising puritan and "Stoic" which was drawn in Germany in the nineteen-twenties and is redrawn in Josef Reck's *Das Prinzip der Freiheit bei Milton* (Erlangen, 1931), p. 27. Indeed, as Robert Adams notes with amusement in *Ikon* (p. 103), the "critical outcries about the Stoicism and grim pessimism of the last poems" are legion Lord David Cecil and Middleton Murry have denied Milton the name of Christian, and P. Phelps-Morand, in *The Effects of his Political Life upon Milton* (Paris, 1939), p. 7, has almost denied that his Christ can be taken as anything but "an unemotional rather priggish superman." In critical discussion the charges against Milton's character and his Christ often get mixed together indiscriminately, and it is important to heed Adams' remark that, however just the charges against the poet's character may be, such charges have "no more direct relation to the essential poetic value of Milton's later poetry than to that of Yeats's *Last Poems*."

24. Stoicism is a strange charge to bring against the man whose Christ thinks that of all the ancient philosophers the Stoic sinned worst in "Philosophic pride, By him call'd

virtue" (IV, 300–1), and was the most blasphemous. In the portrayal of Christ in *Paradise Regained* there may be inconsistency and—as Don Wolfe argues in *SR,* LI (1943), 474—even some reflection of a spiritual conflict in the poet in the act of creation; but Wolfe's conclusion is that "Milton's portrait of Christ resolves itself into a reflection of Milton himself, with an accent not of love and sympathy, but of temperance and self-mastery as the supreme virtues." Wolfe tries to avoid the pitfall of confusing Milton's character and mood with his Christ. It is hard to avoid the confusion and its attendant entanglements of esthetic judgments of his portrait of an ideal hero with ethical judgments of his character as read, or misread, in the light of the poem. Milton lived and wrote on the principle that the life of a poet should itself be a true poem. The inevitable result was—as Kermode acknowledges in his study of "Milton's Hero" in *RES,* n.s. IV (1953), 317—that he "cast himself as well as his Christ in this heroic mold; hence a degree of resemblance between them which has dangerously and unnecessarily been called identity."

25. Milton retells Luke's record of the temptations of Christ in a style with a surface as plain as its original in Scripture. He regarded it as both actual history and yet as a drama embodying the Platonic hierarchy of values on which his own life and thought were based. That is why a sympathetic reader like Blondel finds lyric power in his most didactic passages. It was realization of the supreme dramatic importance of the temptation as an incident in the life of Christ and in world history that stimulated Milton to shape Luke's record of it into a kind of philosophic dialogue with the climax of a Greek tragedy. But the subject forbade dramatization of the style, and the lyric passion had to be contained in the even, spare language of Christ's denials and rebukes of Satan. If the blank verse is not the idiom of men in the street or in the senate, it is the language of man thinking about the meaning of history and life. The tone is far from the allegorical abstraction of Giles Fletcher's *Christ's Victory and Triumph on Earth,* which is sometimes mentioned as Milton's "source." Only in Milton's imagery is there an occasional reflection of Fletcher's allegory—most clearly in Satan's traditional appearance in *Paradise Regained* as "an aged man in rural weeds" (I, 314). So Fletcher's tempter comes "slowly footing," leaning on a stick which is the best of his three legs, blessing the ground

> With benedicities, and prayers store,
>
> .   .   .   .
>
> And all his head with snowe of Age was waxen hore.
>   (Stanza 15)

But both Fletcher and Milton were familiar with the disguise of the master magician Archimago who approaches Spenser's Knight of Holiness in the Wood of Error, disguised as

> An aged sire, in long blacke weedes yclad,
>
> .   .   .   .
>
> Simple in shew, and voide of malice bad.
> And all the way he prayed as he went,
> And often knocked his breast, as one that did repent.
>   (*F.Q.* I, i, 2, 7–9)

Fletcher's Satan is in no danger of becoming a dramatic person; and though Spenser's Archimago repeatedly suggests the Protean power of the Father of Lies to deceive the very elect, his diminishing part in the action of Spenser's Legend of Holiness does not entitle him to serious comparison with the Satan whom Milton shows us on the pinnacle of the temple with Christ.

26. Milton's Satan is closer to allegory than his Christ, for Satan is colored by memories

of Malory as we find them in the Banquet Scene (II, 337–403), which A. H. Gilbert first saw—in *JEGP*, XV (1916), 604—was not intended as a repetition of the temptation to turn stones into bread, but as the first of the glories of the world in the Temptation of the Kingdoms. In the duel between Christ and Satan it may be the "feint" which Miss Mahood sees in it (in *Poetry and Humanism*, p. 234)—a trap to catch Christ by letting him scorn the grosser pleasures of sense before exposing him to the greater temptations of power. A part of the allegory in the scene is structural, for it looks forward to the angelic banquet of Christ at the very end of the action (IV, 587–95). In agreeing with Kermode—in *RES*, n.s. IV (1953), 324—about the structural importance of the demonic banquet, however, we need not agree that it is "a quasi-allegorical development" of the first temptation rather than an induction to the second. Its intermediate character has been challenged by readers who see it as an independent temptation—one, not among three, but among four or more. And perhaps it is less allegory than it is a pageant which Milton differentiates from the following visions of Parthia and Rome, for which he had some justification in Luke's record. In the Banquet Scene Milton makes no secret of his source; it is plainly from Malory that he takes his

> Knights of *Logres*, or of *Lyones*,
> *Lancelot*, or *Pelleas*, or *Pellenore*.

27. Malory's influence on the allegorical element in *Paradise Regained* goes further than the Banquet Scene. It begins with the "fiend" who tries "in likeness of a man of religion" to bring Sir Bors into "error and wanhope." And the end of Sir Bors's temptation by the disguised Evil One resembles the fall of Satan from the pinnacle of the temple. Sir Bors has a glimpse of his tempter on ' an high battlement," appealing to him in the form of a queen with her ladies about her; but "anon he heard a great noise and a great cry, as though all the fiends of hell had been about him, and therewith he saw neither tower, nor lady, nor gentlewomen" (*Morte d'Arthur*, Bk. II, ii; Everyman Ed., Vol. II, 228). Still more like Satan's fall from the pinnacle is the disappearance of Malory's fiend after tempting Sir Percivale (Bk. XIV, ix; Vol. II, 204). The fiend vanishes, "roaring and yelling," into "the wind," which is the realm and "old Conquest" (I, 46) of Satan and his angels.

28. If *Paradise Regained* is interpretable in terms of its images, we should perhaps see the shadow of the fiends who fled shrieking from Sir Bors and Sir Percivale, and vanished into "the wind," in the Satan who falls and vanishes into mid-air when Christ resists him. Milton felt the imaginative power of some of Malory's symbols of evil as distinctly as he did that of the emblems of Hercules vanquishing Antaeus and Oedipus vanquishing the Sphinx. He may have felt it more distinctly than he did that of his formal Homeric similes which compare Satan's last attack upon Christ to flies hovering over a wine-press and the "vain batt'ry" of waves against a rock (IV, 15–20). The poet and Platonist was attracted by Malory's embodiment of the deceptive mystery of iniquity in his fiends, while the designer of a poem that was itself to be a symbol of the triumph of truth over falsehood saw the essence of his work in the defeat of Antaeus and the Sphinx, and in the repulse of the waves by the rock.

A List of Books and Articles Dealing Substantially with Paradise Regained
Which Have Been Published Since 1930.

Banks, Theodore H. "The Banquet Scene in *Paradise Regained*," PMLA, LV (1940), 773–76.

Carlisle, Audrey I. "Milton and Ludwig Lavater," RES, n.s. V (1954), 249–55.

Cleveland, Edward D. "On the Identity Motive in *Paradise Regained*," *MLQ*, XVI (1955), 232–36.

Condee, Ralph Waterbury. "The Formalized Openings of Milton's Epic Poems," *JEGP*, L (1952), 502–508.

Daube, David. "Three Notes on *Paradise Regained*," *RES*, XIX (1943), 205–13.

Fink, Zera S. "On the Political Implications in *Paradise Regained*," *JEGP*, XL (1941), 482–88.

Fiore, Amadeus P. "The Problem of Seventeenth Century Soteriology in Reference to Milton," *Franciscan Studies*, XV (1955), 48–59, 257–82.

Fixler, Michael. "The Unclean Meats of the Mosaic Law and the Banquet Scene in *Paradise Regained*," *MLN*, LXX (1955), 573–77.

Frye, Northrop. "The Typology of *Paradise Regained*," *MP*, LIII (1956), 227–38.

Horrell, Joseph. "Milton, Limbo, and Suicide," *RES*, XVIII (1943), 413–27.

Hughes, Merritt Y. "The Christ of *Paradise Regained* and the Renaissance Heroic Tradition," *SP*, XXXV (1938), 254–77.

Jones, Charles W. "Milton's 'Brief Epic,' " *SP*, XLIV (1947), 209–27.

Kermode, Frank. "Milton's Hero," *RES*, n.s. IV (1953), 317–30.

Kliger, Samuel. "The 'Urbs Aeterna' in *Paradise Regained*," *PMLA*, LXI (1946), 474–91.

Lewalski, Barbara K. "Theme and Structure in *Paradise Regained*," *SP*, LVII (1960), 186–220.

Mahood, M. M. *Poetry and Humanism*. London, 1950.

Martz, Louis L. "*Paradise Regained*: The Meditative Combat," *ELH*, XXVII (1960), 223–47.

Menzies, W. "Milton: The Last Poems," *ESEA*, XXIV (1938), 80–113.

Petit, Hubert H. "The Second Eve in *Paradise Regained*." Papers of the Michigan *Academy of Sciences, Arts and Letters*, XLIV (1959), 365–69.

Pope, Elizabeth M. *"Paradise Regained": The Tradition and the Poem*. Baltimore, 1947.

Rajan, B. " 'Simple, Sensuous and Passionate'." *RES*, XXI (1945), 289–301.

Sackton, Alexander H. "Architectonic Structure in *Paradise Regained*," *UTSE*, XXXIII (1954), 33–45.

Samuel, Irene. "Milton on Learning and Wisdom," *PMLA*, LXIV (1949), 708–23.

Schultz, Howard. *Milton and Forbidden Knowledge*. New York, 1955.

——. "Christ and Antichrist in *Paradise Regained*," *PMLA*, LXVII (1952), 790–808.

Sensabaugh, George F. "Milton on Learning," *SP*, XLIII (1946), 258–72.

Sirluck, Ernest. "Milton Revises the *Faerie Queene*," *MP*, XLVIII (1950), 90–96.

Stein, Arnold. *Heroic Knowledge*. Minneapolis, 1957.

——. "The Kingdoms of the World: *Paradise Regained*," *ELH*, XXIII (1956), 112–26.

Svendsen, Kester. "Milton's 'Aerie Microscope,' " *MLN*, LXIV (1949), 525–29.

Taylor, Dick. "The Storm Scene in *Paradise Regained*: A Reinterpretation," *UTQ*, XXIV (1955), 1082–89.

Whiting, George. "Christ's Miraculous Fast," *MLN*, LXVI (1951), 12–16.

Wolfe, Don M. "The Role of Milton's Christ," *SR*, LI (1943), 467–75.

Woodhouse, A. S. P. "Theme and Pattern in *Paradise Regained*," *UTQ*, XXV (1956), 167–82.

Separate Editions of the Poem Since 1930

Paradise Regained, ed. by E. H. Blakeney. London, 1932.

Le Paradis reconquis (*Paradise Regained*). Étude critique, traduction et notes par Jacques Blondel. Paris, 1955.

Paradise Regained

The First Book

I who erewhile the happy Garden sung,
By one man's disobedience lost, now sing
Recover'd Paradise to all mankind,
By one man's firm obedience fully tried
Through all temptation, and the Tempter foil'd   5
In all his wiles, defeated and repuls't,
And *Eden* rais'd in the waste Wilderness.
  Thou Spirit who led'st this glorious Eremite
Into the Desert, his Victorious Field
Against the Spiritual Foe, and brought'st him thence   10
By proof th'undoubted Son of God, inspire,
As thou art wont, my prompted Song, else mute,
And bear through height or depth of nature's bounds
With prosperous wing full summ'd to tell of deeds
Above Heroic, though in secret done,   15
And unrecorded left through many an Age,
Worthy t' have not remain'd so long unsung.
  Now had the great Proclaimer with a voice
More awful than the sound of Trumpet, cried
Repentance, and Heaven's Kingdom nigh at hand   20
To all Baptiz'd: to his great Baptism flock'd
With awe the Regions round, and with them came
From *Nazareth* the Son of *Joseph* deem'd
To the flood *Jordan,* came as then obscure,
Unmarkt, unknown; but him the Baptist soon   25
Descried, divinely warn'd, and witness bore
As to his worthier, and would have resign'd
To him his Heavenly Office, nor was long
His witness unconfirm'd; on him baptiz'd
Heaven open'd, and in likeness of a Dove   30
The Spirit descended, while the Father's voice
From Heav'n pronounc'd him his beloved Son.
That heard the Adversary, who roving still
About the world, at that assembly fam'd
Would not be last, and with the voice divine   35
Nigh Thunderstruck, th' exalted man, to whom
Such high attest was giv'n, a while survey'd
With wonder, then with envy fraught and rage

2–3. See the Introduction 15 for the epic tradition which is the background of this echo of St. Paul (Rom. v, 19): "For as by one man's disobedience many were made sinners; so by the obedience of one man shall many be made righteous."

8–12. Milton invokes the Spirit of God by which Jesus was "led into the wilderness, Being forty days tempted of the devil" (Luke iv, 1–2), and which is called in *CD* I, vi, "a divine impulse, or light, or voice, or word, transmitted from above." This interpretation of the Spirit invoked here and in *PL* I, 17, is defended on theological grounds by M. Kelley in *SP*, XXXII (1935), 230.

14. In falconry a hawk with full-grown feathers was called *full summ'd,* i. e. developed to the sum of perfection.

18. *the great Proclaimer:* John the Baptist. See Matt. iii, 1–6.

30–32. The scene and the words follow Matt. iii, 16–17.

33. The Evil One is called the *Adversary* in Job i, 6. In the New Testament he is often the "false accuser," a literal translation of the Greek word from which *devil* and *diabolic* are derived.

Flies to his place, nor rests, but in mid air
To Council summons all his mighty Peers,   40
Within thick Clouds and dark tenfold involv'd,
A gloomy Consistory; and them amidst
With looks aghast and sad he thus bespake.
    O ancient Powers of Air and this wide world—
For much more willingly I mention Air,   45
This our old Conquest, than remember Hell
Our hated habitation—well ye know
How many Ages, as the years of men,
This Universe we have possest, and rul'd
In manner at our will th' affairs of Earth,   50
Since *Adam* and his facile consort *Eve*
Lost Paradise deceiv'd by me, though since
With dread attending when that fatal wound
Shall be inflicted by the Seed of *Eve*
Upon my head. Long the decrees of Heav'n   55
Delay, for longest time to him is short;
And now too soon for us the circling hours
This dreaded time have compast, wherein we
Must bide the stroke of that long threat'n'd wound,
At least if so we can, and by the head   60
Broken be not intended all our power
To be infring'd, our freedom and our being
In this fair Empire won of Earth and Air;
For this ill news I bring, the Woman's seed
Destin'd to this, is late of woman born: 65
His birth to our just fear gave no small cause,
But his growth now to youth's full flow'r, displaying
All virtue, grace and wisdom to achieve
Things highest, greatest, multiplies my fear.
Before him a great Prophet, to proclaim   70
His coming, is sent Harbinger, who all
Invites, and in the Consecrated stream
Pretends to wash off sin, and fit them so
Purified to receive him pure, or rather
To do him honor as their King; all come,   75
And he himself among them was baptiz'd,
Not thence to be more pure, but to receive
The testimony of Heaven, that who he is
Thenceforth the Nations may not doubt; I saw
The Prophet do him reverence; on him rising   80
Out of the water, Heav'n above the Clouds
Unfold her Crystal Doors, thence on his head
A perfect Dove descend, whate'er it meant,
And out of Heav'n the Sovran voice I heard,

39–42. The demonic council compares better with those in Vida's *Christias* and Tasso's *Jerusalem Delivered* than with those in *PL*.

39–45. The conception of Satan as "prince of the power of the air" (Eph. ii, 2) is important again in *PR* IV, 568. See the Introduction 22 and *PL* I, 516; X, 185–9; and XII, 386–95.

53–55. The prophecy in Gen. iii, 15 that the "seed of the woman" should bruise the serpent's head is repeated in *PL* X, 180. See the Introduction 3 and 21.

53. *attending* has its French sense, waiting.

55–58. In Psalm xc, 4, a thousand years are as a day in God's sight; in Homer (*Od.* XI, 247) and Virgil (*Aen.* I, 234) the circling months or years subserve Fate.

73–85. Satan ridicules John's baptizing in the Jordan (Luke iii, 2 and xxi, 2) and the miracle of the descending dove and the voice from heaven at Christ's baptism, declaring him "my beloved Son."

This is my Son belov'd, in him am pleas'd. 85
His Mother then is mortal, but his Sire,
Hee who obtains the Monarchy of Heav'n,
And what will he not do to advance his Son?
His first-begot we know, and sore have felt,
When his fierce thunder drove us to the deep; 90
Who this is we must learn, for man he seems
In all his lineaments, though in his face
The glimpses of his Father's glory shine.
Ye see our danger on the utmost edge
Of hazard, which admits no long debate, 95
But must with something sudden be oppos'd,
Not force, but well couch't fraud, well woven snares,
Ere in the head of Nations he appear
Their King, their Leader, and Supreme on Earth.
I, when no other durst, sole undertook 100
The dismal expedition to find out
And ruin *Adam*, and the exploit perform'd
Successfully; a calmer voyage now
Will waft me; and the way found prosperous once
Induces best to hope of like success. 105
    He ended, and his words impression left
Of much amazement to th' infernal Crew,
Distracted and surpris'd with deep dismay
At these sad tidings; but no time was then
For long indulgence to their fears or grief: 110
Unanimous they all commit the care
And management of this main enterprise
To him their great Dictator, whose attempt
At first against mankind so well had thriv'd
In *Adam's* overthrow, and led thir march 115
From Hell's deep-vaulted Den to dwell in light,
Regents and Potentates, and Kings, yea gods
Of many a pleasant Realm and Province wide.
So to the Coast of *Jordan* he directs
His easy steps, girded with snaky wiles, 120
Where he might likeliest find this new-declar'd,
This man of men, attested Son of God,
Temptation and all guile on him to try,
So to subvert whom he suspected rais'd
To end his Reign on Earth so long enjoy'd: 125
But contrary unweeting he fulfill'd
The purpos'd Counsel pre-ordain'd and fixt
Of the most High, who, in full frequence bright
Of Angels, thus to *Gabriel* smiling spake.
    Gabriel, this day by proof thou shalt behold, 130
Thou and all Angels conversant on Earth
With man or men's affairs, how I begin
To verify that solemn message late,

97. *couch't:* concealed.

100. Satan reminds the devils of his offer in Pandaemonium (*PL* II, 430–66) to seek their "deliverance" by exploring the way from hell across Chaos to the newly-created world.

117. So the demons become pagan gods in *PL* I, 361–521. Cf. the Introduction to *PL*, sections 25–6.

120. An ironic allusion to Isaiah's prophecy (xi, 5) that righteousness should be the girdle of the loins of the restorer of Israel.

128. *full frequence:* full attendance. Cf. II, 130.

129. *Gabriel,* the traditional angel of the Annunciation, is naturally addressed here. Cf. *PL* IV, 549.

On which I sent thee to the Virgin pure
In *Galilee,* that she should bear a Son   135
Great in Renown, and call'd the Son of God;
Then told'st her doubting how these things could be
To her a Virgin, that on her should come
The Holy Ghost, and the power of the highest
O'er-shadow her: this man born and now upgrown,   140
To show him worthy of his birth divine
And high prediction, henceforth I expose
To Satan; let him tempt and now assay
His utmost subtlety, because he boasts
And vaunts of his great cunning to the throng   145
Of his Apostasy; he might have learnt
Less overweening, since he fail'd in *Job,*
Whose constant perseverance overcame
Whate'er his cruel malice could invent.
He now shall know I can produce a man   150
Of female Seed, far abler to resist
All his solicitations, and at length
All his vast force, and drive him back to Hell,
Winning by Conquest what the first man lost
By fallacy surpris'd.   But first I mean   155
To exercise him in the Wilderness;
There he shall first lay down the rudiments
Of his great warfare, ere I send him forth
To conquer Sin and Death the two grand foes,
By Humiliation and strong Sufferance: 160
His weakness shall o'ercome Satanic strength
And all the world, and mass of sinful flesh;
That all the Angels and Ethereal Powers,
They now, and men hereafter, may discern
From what consummate virtue I have chose   165
This perfect Man, by merit call'd my Son,
To earn Salvation for the Sons of men.
    So spake the Eternal Father, and all Heaven
Admiring stood a space, then into Hymns
Burst forth, and in Celestial measures mov'd,   170
Circling the Throne and Singing, while the hand
Sung with the voice, and this the argument.
    Victory and Triumph to the Son of God
Now ent'ring his great duel, not of arms,
But to vanquish by wisdom hellish wiles.   175
The Father knows the Son; therefore secure
Ventures his filial Virtue, though untried,
Against whate'er may tempt, whate'er seduce,
Allure, or terrify, or undermine.
Be frustrate, all ye stratagems of Hell,   180

134–140. The lines paraphrase the record of the Annunciation in Luke i, 26–38.

147. Cf. the references to *Job* in ll. 369 and 425 below and in III, 64, 67, and 95. See the Introduction 8 and 15.

157. *rudiments:* beginnings.

159. Cf. *Sin* and *Death* in *PL* II, 648–73 and X, 585–609.

161. The line translates I Cor. i, 27.

163. Cf. the "ethereal mold" of the angels in *PL* II, 139.

172. *argument:* subject. Cf. *PL* I, 24 and IX, 13.

174. Cf. *PL* XII, 386–400 on this *duel,* and the Introduction 21.

180. *frustrate:* frustrated. Cf. *instruct* in 439 below, similarly used as a perfect passive participle because it is derived from a Latin participle.

And devilish machinations come to nought.
   So they in Heav'n their Odes and Vigils tun'd.
Meanwhile the Son of God, who yet some days
Lodg'd in *Bethabara,* where *John* baptiz'd,
Musing and much revolving in his breast,   185
How best the mighty work he might begin
Of Savior to mankind, and which way first
Publish his Godlike office now mature,
One day forth walk'd alone, the Spirit leading,
And his deep thoughts, the better to converse   190
With solitude, till far from track of men,
Thought following thought, and step by step led on,
He enter'd now the bordering Desert wild,
And with dark shades and rocks environ'd round,
His holy Meditations thus pursu'd.   195
   O what a multitude of thoughts at once
Awak'n'd in me swarm, while I consider
What from within I feel myself, and hear
What from without comes often to my ears,
Ill sorting with my present state compar'd.   200
When I was yet a child, no childish play
To me was pleasing, all my mind was set
Serious to learn and know, and thence to do
What might be public good; myself I thought
Born to that end, born to promote all truth,   205
All righteous things: therefore above my years,
The Law of God I read, and found it sweet,
Made it my whole delight, and in it grew
To such perfection that, ere yet my age
Had measur'd twice six years, at our great Feast   210
I went into the Temple, there to hear
The Teachers of our Law, and to propose
What might improve my knowledge or their own;
And was admir'd by all: yet this not all.
To which my Spirit aspir'd; victorious deeds   215
Flam'd in my heart, heroic acts; one while
To rescue *Israel* from the *Roman* yoke,
Then to subdue and quell o'er all the earth
Brute violence and proud Tyrannic pow'r,
Till truth were freed, and equity restor'd: 220
Yet held it more humane, more heavenly, first
By winning words to conquer willing hearts,
And make persuasion do the work of fear;
At least to try, and teach the erring Soul
Not wilfully misdoing, but unware   225

182. *Vigils:* hymns or psalms sung in services at night.
184. *Bethabara:* a town near the ford on the Jordan where John baptized.
200–214. The "autobiography" which has been seen in these lines is no more demonstrable than the "self-portraiture" of Milton in his Christ which is discussed in the Introduction 21 and 23.
205. The line echoes the words of Christ to Pilate in John xviii, 37.
208. Cf. the "delight" of the righteous man "in the law of the Lord," Ps. i, 2.

209–214. The record of Christ's talk with the doctors of the *Law* during his Passover visit to Jerusalem is in Luke ii, 46–50.
214. *admir'd:* wondered at.
218. There is a contrast with Anchises' prophecy (*Aen.* VI, 851–3) that Rome's destiny should be to impose peace on the world and quell the proud.
222. Among several classical parallels Milton may have remembered Xenophon's remark (*Oeconomics* xxi, 12) that it is more divine than human to govern men who freely consent.

Misled: the stubborn only to subdue.
These growing thoughts my Mother soon perceiving
By words at times cast forth, inly rejoic'd,
And said to me apart: High are thy thoughts
O Son, but nourish them and let them soar   230
To what height sacred virtue and true worth
Can raise them, though above example high;
By matchless Deeds express thy matchless Sire.
For know, thou art no Son of mortal man;
Though men esteem thee low of Parentage,   235
Thy Father is th'Eternal King, who rules
All Heaven and Earth, Angels and Sons of men.
A messenger from God foretold thy birth
Conceiv'd in me a Virgin; he foretold
Thou shouldst be great and sit on *David's* Throne,   240
And of thy Kingdom there should be no end.
At thy Nativity a glorious Choir
Of Angels in the fields of *Bethlehem* sung
To Shepherds watching at their folds by night,
And told them the Messiah now was born,   245
Where they might see him, and to thee they came,
Directed to the Manger where thou lay'st,
For in the Inn was left no better room.
A Star, not seen before in Heaven appearing
Guided the Wise Men thither from the East,   250
To honor thee with Incense, Myrrh, and Gold,
By whose bright course led on they found the place,
Affirming it thy Star new-grav'n in Heaven,
By which they knew thee King of *Israel* born.
Just *Simeon* and Prophetic *Anna,* warn'd   255
By Vision, found thee in the Temple, and spake,
Before the Altar and the vested Priest,
Like things of thee to all that present stood.
This having heard, straight I again revolv'd
The Law and Prophets, searching what was writ   260
Concerning the Messiah, to our Scribes
Known partly, and soon found of whom they spake
I am; this chiefly, that my way must lie
Through many a hard assay even to the death,
Ere I the promis'd Kingdom can attain,   265
Or work Redemption for mankind, whose sins'
Full weight must be transferr'd upon my head.
Yet neither thus dishearten'd or dismay'd,
The time prefixt I waited, when behold
The Baptist (of whose birth I oft had heard,   270
Not knew by sight) now come, who was to come
Before Messiah and his way prepare.
I as all others to his Baptism came,
Which I believ'd was from above; but hee
Straight knew me, and with loudest voice proclaim'd   275
Mee him (for it was shown him so from Heaven)

240–254. The details come from the first two chapters of Luke and the second of Matthew.

255–259. The prophecies of *Simeon* and *Anna* are in Luke ii, 25–38.

266–267. Isaiah's words (liii, 6), "The Lord hath laid on him the iniquity of us all," are applied to Christ.

270–279. Mark's Gospel opens with John the Baptist as "the voice of one crying in the wilderness, Prepare ye the way of the Lord."

Mee him whose Harbinger he was; and first
Refus'd on me his Baptism to confer,
As much his greater, and was hardly won.
But as I rose out of the laving stream, 280
Heaven open'd her eternal doors, from whence
The Spirit descended on me like a Dove;
And last the sum of all, my Father's voice,
Audibly heard from Heav'n, pronounc'd me his,
Mee his beloved Son, in whom alone 285
He was well pleas'd; by which I knew the time
Now full, that I no more should live obscure,
But openly begin, as best becomes
The Authority which I deriv'd from Heaven.
And now by some strong motion I am led 290
Into this Wilderness, to what intent
I learn not yet; perhaps I need not know;
For what concerns my knowledge God reveals.
So spake our Morning Star then in his rise,
And looking round on every side beheld 295
A pathless Desert, dusk with horrid shades;
The way he came not having mark'd, return
Was difficult, by human steps untrod;
And he still on was led, but with such thoughts
Accompanied of things past and to come 300
Lodg'd in his breast, as well might recommend
Such Solitude before choicest Society.
Full forty days he pass'd, whether on hill
Sometimes, anon in shady vale, each night
Under the covert of some ancient Oak, 305
Or Cedar, to defend him from the dew,
Or harbor'd in one Cave, is not reveal'd;
Nor tasted human food, nor hunger felt
Till those days ended, hunger'd then at last
Among wild Beasts: they at his sight grew mild, 310
Nor sleeping him nor waking harm'd, his walk
The fiery Serpent fled, and noxious Worm;
The Lion and fierce Tiger glar'd aloof.
But now an aged man in Rural weeds,
Following, as seem'd, the quest of some stray Ewe, 315
Or wither'd sticks to gather, which might serve
Against a Winter's day when winds blow keen,
To warm him wet return'd from field at Eve,

---

281. *eternal doors:* the "everlasting doors" of
Psalm xxiv, 7–9.

286–297. Gal. iv, 4—"When the fulness of time
was come, God sent forth his Son"—is applied to
both Christ and Satan. Cf. 55–65 above.

291–293. In *CD* I, v Milton holds that, "Even
the Son knows not all things absolutely." See the
Introduction 2–3.

294. In Rev. xxii, 16 Christ appears saying: "I
am . . . the bright and morning star."

296. *horrid:* bristling. Cf. *PL* II, 63.

302. Cowley's essay *Of Solitude* opens with the
remark that Cicero's aphorism, "Never less alone
than when in solitude" (*De officiis* III, i, 1), "is now
become a very vulgar saying." It was defended by

Sir George MacKenzie in *A Moral Essay, preferring
Solitude to Publick Employment and all its Ap-
panages; such as Fame, Command, Riches, Pleasures,
Conversations, &c.* (Edinburgh, 1665). John Evelyn replied with *Public Employment, and an active
life, preferred to Solitude* (London, 1667).

310–313. Mark (i, 13) says that Christ "was with
the wild beasts" in the desert, fulfilling Isaiah's
prophecy (lxv, 25) that, "The wolf and the lamb
shall feed together . . . They shall not hurt nor
destroy in all my holy mountain, saith the Lord."
Cf. Isa. xi, 6–9 and Ezek. xxxiv, 25. Contrast
PL X, 710–15.

312. *Worm:* serpent.

314. For Satan's disguise see the Introduction 25.

He saw approach; who first with curious eye
Perus'd him, then with words thus utter'd spake.   320
    Sir, what ill chance hath brought thee to this place
So far from path or road of men, who pass
In Troop or Caravan, for single none
Durst ever, who return'd, and dropt not here
His Carcass, pin'd with hunger and with drought?   325
I ask the rather, and the more admire,
For that to me thou seem'st the man whom late
Our new baptizing Prophet at the Ford
Of *Jordan* honor'd so, and call'd thee Son
Of God; I saw and heard, for wee sometimes   330
Who dwell this wild, constrain'd by want, come forth
To Town or Village nigh (nighest is far)
Where aught we hear, and curious are to hear,
What happ'ns new; Fame also finds us out.
    To whom the Son of God. Who brought me hither   335
Will bring me hence, no other Guide I seek.
    By Miracle he may, replied the Swain,
What other way I see not; for we here
Live on tough roots and stubs, to thirst inur'd
More than the Camel, and to drink go far,   340
Men to much misery and hardship born;
But if thou be the Son of God, Command
That out of these hard stones be made thee bread;
So shalt thou save thyself and us relieve
With Food, whereof we wretched seldom taste.   345
    He ended, and the Son of God replied.
Think'st thou such force in Bread? is it not written
(For I discern thee other than thou seem'st)
Man lives not by Bread only, but each Word
Proceeding from the mouth of God, who fed   350
Our Fathers here with Manna? In the Mount
Moses was forty days, nor eat nor drank,
And forty days *Eliah* without food
Wander'd this barren waste; the same I now:
Why dost thou then suggest to me distrust,   355
Knowing who I am, as I know who thou art?
    Whom thus answer'd th' Arch Fiend now undisguis'd.
'Tis true, I am that Spirit unfortunate,
Who, leagu'd with millions more in rash revolt,
Kept not my happy Station, but was driv'n   360
With them from bliss to the bottomless deep,
Yet to that hideous place not so confin'd

320. So Adam, newly created, *perus'd* himself, and *Limb by Limb survey'd* (*PL* VIII, 267–8).

325. *Pine* is again used transitively in *PL* XII, 77.

331. Cf. *dwell,* used transitively, in *PL* III, 670.

334. *Fame* keeps its Latin meaning of "rumor" and has a trace of personification, as in Chaucer's *Hous of Fame,* and in Virgil (*Aen.* IV, 173).

339. No food can be found in a desert full of stubs of trees,
Whereon nor fruit, nor leafe was euer seene.
        (*F.Q.* I, ix, 34, 1–2)

349. Christ cites Deut. viii, 3. His dialogue with

Satan is from Luke iv, 3–4 and Matt. iv, 3–4.

352. When *Moses* received the Ten Commandments on Mt. Sinai, he was "in the mount forty days and forty nights" (Exod. xxiv, 18).

353. *eat* was the usual past tense.
    Eliah (or *Elijah*—cf. II, 268 and 277 below), after eating food which an angel brought to him, "went in the strength of that meat forty days and forty nights" (I Kings xix, 8).

355. For *distrust* as the essence of the temptation see the Introduction 1–2.

By rigor unconniving but that oft
Leaving my dolorous Prison I enjoy
Large liberty to round this Globe of Earth,   365
Or range in th' Air, nor from the Heav'n of Heav'ns
Hath he excluded my resort sometimes.
I came among the Sons of God when he
Gave up into my hands *Uzzean Job*
To prove him, and illustrate his high worth;   370
And when to all his Angels he propos'd
To draw the proud King *Ahab* into fraud
That he might fall in *Ramoth,* they demurring,
I undertook that office, and the tongues
Of all his flattering Prophets glibb'd with lies   375
To his destruction, as I had in charge;
For what he bids I do.   Though I have lost
Much luster of my native brightness, lost
To be belov'd of God, I have not lost
To love, at least contémplate and admire   380
What I see excellent in good, or fair,
Or virtuous; I should so have lost all sense.
What can be then less in me than desire
To see thee and approach thee, whom I know
Declar'd the Son of God, to hear attent   385
Thy wisdom, and behold thy Godlike deeds?
Men generally think me much a foe
To all mankind: why should I? they to me
Never did wrong or violence; by them
I lost not what I lost, rather by them   390
I gain'd what I have gain'd, and with them dwell
Copartner in these Regions of the World,
If not disposer; lend them oft my aid,
Oft my advice by presages and signs,
And answers, oracles, portents and dreams,   395
Whereby they may direct their future life.
Envy they say excites me, thus to gain
Companions of my misery and woe.
At first it may be; but long since with woe
Nearer acquainted, now I feel by proof,   400
That fellowship in pain divides not smart,

363. *unconniving:* unwinking, i.e. never relax-ing vigilance.

368–376. Satan's bold appearance before God with the other "sons of God" in Job i, 6, and his cruel temptations of Job are paralleled with his ap-pearance before God's throne as the "lying spirit" who volunteered to deceive the prophets of the wicked king Ahab and lure him to his death at *Ramoth* in *Gilead* (I Kings xxii, 19–22). In *RES,* n.s. V (1954), 249–55, Audrey I. Carlisle shows that Ludwig Lavater's Commentary *In Libros Paralipomenon sive Chronicorum* bracketed Satan's roles with Job and Ahab to illustrate the readiness of the "liar from the beginning" to do evil to men, of which God cannot rightly be held guilty. Milton's summary of Lavater's passage is in the Trinity *MS.,* p. 36.

372. Cf. the use of *Fraud* in *PL* VII, 143 and IX, 643.

377–378. Tradition identified Satan with Lucifer (in Isa. xiv, 12) son of the morning,
          brighter once amidst the Host
      of Angels, than that Star the Stars among.
                    (*PL* VII, 132–3)
385. *attent:* attentively.

393–396. Milton's interest in the lying oracles of the ancient world goes back to *Nat,* 173.   Like Au-gustine, he regarded the evil spirits which spoke through them as mere pretenders to be divine "mes-sengers and bringers of men's good fortunes" (*City of God* VII, xxii). See the Introduction 18.

401–403. The commonplace goes back as far as Seneca's letter *To Polybius on Consolation* (XII, ii). Sir Thomas Browne challenged "that natural fallacy of Man, to take comfort from Society, and think adversities less, because others also suffer them" (*Christian Morals* I, xviii).

Nor lightens aught each man's peculiar load:
Small consolation then, were Man adjoin'd.
This wounds me most (what can it less?) that Man,
Man fall'n, shall be restor'd, I never more.   405
    To whom our Savior sternly thus replied.
Deservedly thou griev'st, compos'd of lies
From the beginning, and in lies wilt end;
Who boast'st release from Hell, and leave to come
Into the Heav'n of Heavens; thou com'st indeed,   410
As a poor miserable captive thrall
Comes to the place where he before had sat
Among the Prime in Splendor, now depos'd,
Ejected, emptied, gaz'd, unpitied, shunn'd,
A spectacle of ruin or of scorn   415
To all the Host of Heaven; the happy place
Imparts to thee no happiness, no joy,
Rather inflames thy torment, representing
Lost bliss, to thee no more communicable,
So never more in Hell than when in Heaven.   420
But thou art serviceable to Heaven's King.
Wilt thou impute to obedience what thy fear
Extorts, or pleasure to do ill excites?
What but thy malice mov'd thee to misdeem
Of righteous *Job,* then cruelly to afflict him   425
With all inflictions?   But his patience won.
The other service was thy chosen task,
To be a liar in four hundred mouths;
For lying is thy sustenance, thy food.
Yet thou pretend'st to truth; all Oracles   430
By thee are giv'n, and what confest more true
Among the Nations?   That hath been thy craft,
By mixing somewhat true to vent more lies.
But what have been thy answers, what but dark,
Ambiguous and with double sense deluding,   435
Which they who ask'd have seldom understood,
And not well understood, as good not known?
Who ever by consulting at thy shrine
Return'd the wiser, or the more instruct
To fly or follow what concern'd him most,   440
And run not sooner to his fatal snare?
For God hath justly giv'n the Nations up
To thy Delusions; justly, since they fell
Idolatrous; but when his purpose is
Among them to declare his Providence,   445
To thee not known, whence hast thou then thy truth,
But from him or his Angels President

407. In John viii, 44, the devil is called "a liar,
and the father of it."
   420. Cf. *PL* I, 255, IV, 20 and IX, 467–8.
   423. Cf. Satan's boast in *PL* I, 160, that his "sole
delight" will be "ever to do ill."
   428. The lying prophets of Ahab numbered four
hundred.
   434–441. Sceptical discussion of the oracles in
ancient literature went back further than Chrysippus'
collection of their ambiguous answers, which Cicero

mentioned in *Of Divination* II, lvi. The Church
Fathers, like Lactantius (*Divine Institutes* II, xvi),
attributed them to devils posing as gods—a doctrine
which Fontenelle regarded (in his *Histoire des
Oracles,* 1687, Caps. 2–3) as having dishonored
but helped to perpetuate popular faith in the oracles.
   447–448. Jewish tradition regarded the points of
the compass as angelic provinces. Before Lucifer's
fall he was lord of the "Quarters of the North" (*PL*
V, 689).

In every Province, who, themselves disdaining
To approach thy Temples, give thee in command
What to the smallest tittle thou shalt say   450
To thy Adorers? thou with trembling fear,
Or like a Fawning Parasite obey'st;
Then to thyself ascrib'st the truth foretold.
But this thy glory shall be soon retrench'd;
No more shalt thou by oracling abuse   455
The Gentiles; henceforth Oracles are ceast,
And thou no more with Pomp and Sacrifice
Shalt be inquir'd at *Delphos* or elsewhere,
At least in vain, for they shall find thee mute.
God hath now sent his living Oracle   460
Into the World to teach his final will,
And sends his Spirit of Truth henceforth to dwell
In pious Hearts, an inward Oracle
To all truth requisite for men to know.
        So spake our Savior; but the subtle Fiend,   465
Though inly stung with anger and disdain,
Dissembl'd, and this answer smooth return'd.
        Sharply thou hast insisted on rebuke,
And urg'd me hard with doings, which not will
But misery hath wrested from me; where   470
Easily canst thou find one miserable,
And not enforc'd ofttimes to part from truth,
If it may stand him more in stead to lie,
Say and unsay, feign, flatter, or abjure?
But thou art plac't above me, thou art Lord;   475
From thee I can and must submiss endure
Check or reproof, and glad to scape so quit.
Hard are the ways of truth, and rough to walk,
Smooth on the tongue discourst, pleasing to th' ear,
And tunable as Silvan Pipe or Song;   480
What wonder then if I delight to hear
Her dictates from thy mouth? most men admire
Virtue, who follow not her lore: permit me
To hear thee when I come (since no man comes)
And talk at least, though I despair to attain.   485
Thy Father, who is holy, wise and pure,
Suffers the Hypocrite or Atheous Priest
To tread his Sacred Courts, and minister
About his Altar, handling holy things,
Praying or vowing, and vouchsaf'd his voice   490
To *Balaam* Reprobate, a Prophet yet
Inspir'd; disdain not such access to me.

454–464. Milton follows the tradition of the cessation of all oracles after Christ's birth. Fontenelle
attacked this tradition in its popular form but
acknowledged the value of its Platonic interpretation as meaning that the impostures of paganism
gradually disappeared after the incarnation of God's
Son, the Word (*Logos*) of the Platonizing Gospel of
John. Milton echoes Augustine's distinction between the false lights of the oracles and the illumination which comes from God's Son and Holy Spirit
(*City of God* IX, xxiii). See the Introduction 18.

458. Apollo's oracle at Delphi, in Phocis, was
the most famous in the Greek world.

462. Cf. Christ's promise that, "when he, the
Spirit of truth, is come, he will guide you into all
truth" (John xvi, 13).

476. *submiss:* submissive. The word is felt as a
participle, as if it meant "submitted" or "subdued."
Cf. frustrate in l. 180. Cf. *PL* V, 359 and VIII, 316.

490–492. When *Balaam* was urged to curse the
Israelites by the king of Moab, he answered that
God had commanded him "to bless; and he hath
blessed; and I cannot reverse it" (Num. xxiii, 20).

To whom our Saviour with unalter'd brow.
Thy coming hither, though I know thy scope,
I bid not or forbid; do as thou find'st   495
Permission from above; thou canst not more.
    He added not; and Satan, bowing low
His gray dissimulation, disappear'd
Into thin Air diffus'd: for now began
Night with her sullen wing to double-shade   500
The Desert; Fowls in thir clay nests were couch't;
And now wild Beasts came forth the woods to roam.

The End of the First Book.

499. Satan vanishes *"Into thin air diffus'd,"* as the   cury after talking with Aeneas (*Aen.* IV, 278).
gods often do in Homer, Virgil, and Ovid: e. g. Mer-

The Second Book

Meanwhile the new-baptiz'd, who yet remain'd
At *Jordan* with the Baptist, and had seen
Him whom they heard so late expressly call'd
Jesus Messiah, Son of God declar'd,
And on that high Authority had believ'd,   5
And with him talkt, and with him lodg'd, I mean
Andrew and *Simon,* famous after known
With others though in Holy Writ not nam'd,
Now missing him thir joy so lately found,
So lately found, and so abruptly gone,   10
Began to doubt, and doubted many days,
And as the days increas'd, increas'd thir doubt:
Sometimes they thought he might be only shown,
And for a time caught up to God, as once
Moses was in the Mount, and missing long;   15
And the great *Thisbite* who on fiery wheels
Rode up to Heaven, yet once again to come.
Therefore as those young Prophets then with care
Sought lost *Eliah,* so in each place these
Nigh to *Bethabara;* in *Jericho*   20
The City of Palms, *Aenon,* and *Salem* Old,
Machaerus and each Town or City wall'd
On this side the broad lake *Genezaret,*
Or in *Peraea,* but return'd in vain.
Then on the bank of *Jordan,* by a Creek   25
Where winds with Reeds and Osiers whisp'ring play,

4. The Hebrew word *Messiah* was translated in the Septuagint by the Greek word *Christ.* Both mean "anointed one."

7. At the time of the baptism of Christ, *Andrew* and *Simon* Peter went with him "and saw where he dwelt, and abode with him that day" (John i, 39).

14–15. Cf. the note on *Moses* in I, 352.

16–17. The *Thisbite, Elijah,* whose fast is mentioned in I, 353, went up in "a chariot of fire" and "by a whirlwind into heaven" (II Kings ii, 11). Thisbe was east of Jordan in Gilead. Cf. *Plot* I, 7–8, and *Passion,* 36–37.

18–19. After Elijah's translation "fifty strong men" of the "sons of the Prophets" searched for him "three days, but found him not" (II Kings ii, 15–17).

20. Beside baptizing in *Bethabara* (see l. 184), "John also was baptizing in Aenon near to Salem" (John iii, 23). *Jericho* is called the "city of palm trees" in Deut. xxxiv, 3.

22. *Machaerus,* the traditional place of the death of John the Baptist, was a fortified mountain in *Peraea,* in the desert east of the Dead Sea.

23. *Genezaret* is a variant form of the name of the Sea of Galilee.

Plain Fishermen, (no greater men them call)
Close in a Cottage low together got,
Thir unexpected·loss and plaints outbreath'd.
Alas, from what high hope to what relapse   30
Unlook'd for are we fall'n! Our eyes beheld
Messiah certainly now come, so long
Expected of our Fathers; we have heard
His words, his wisdom full of grace and truth;
Now, now, for sure, deliverance is at hand,   35
The Kingdom shall to *Israel* be restor'd:
Thus we rejoic'd, but soon our joy is turn'd
Into perplexity and new amaze:
For whither is he gone, what accident
Hath rapt him from us? will he now retire   40
After appearance, and again prolong
Our expectation? God of *Israel,*
Send thy Messiah forth, the time is come;
Behold the Kings of th'Earth how they oppress
Thy chosen, to what height thir pow'r unjust   45
They have exalted, and behind them cast
All fear of thee; arise and vindicate
Thy Glory, free thy people from thir yoke!
But let us wait; thus far he hath perform'd,
Sent his Anointed, and to us reveal'd him,   50
By his great Prophet, pointed at and shown,
In public, and with him we have convers'd;
Let us be glad of this, and all our fears
Lay on his Providence; he will not fail
Nor will withdraw him now, nor will recall,   55
Mock us with his blest sight, then snatch him hence;
Soon we shall see our hope, our joy return.
    Thus they out of their plaints new hope resume
To find whom at the first they found unsought.
But to his Mother *Mary,* when she saw   60
Others return'd from Baptism, not her Son,
Nor left at *Jordan,* tidings of him none;
Within her breast, though calm, her breast though pure,
Motherly cares and fears got head, and rais'd
Some troubl'd thoughts, which she in sighs thus clad.   65
    O what avails me now that honor high
To have conceiv'd of God, or that salute,
Hail highly favor'd, among women blest!
While I to sorrows am no less advanc't,
And fears as eminent, above the lot   70
Of other women, by the birth I bore,
In such a season born when scarce a Shed
Could be obtain'd to shelter him or me
From the bleak air; a Stable was our warmth,
A Manger his; yet soon enforc't to fly   75

---

34. "And the Word was made flesh, and dwelt among us, . . . full of grace and truth" (John i, 14).

35–36. An echo of the disciples' question to Christ when they first met him after the Resurrection: "Lord, wilt thou at this time restore again the kindom to Israel?" (Acts i, 6.)

68–69. The *salute* is Gabriel's to Mary (Luke i, 28).

75–78. Herod the Great was the *Murd'rous King* who "slew all the children that were in Bethlehem" (Matt. ii, 16), and drove Joseph and Mary to take refuge in Egypt.

Thence into *Egypt,* till the Murd'rous King
Were dead, who sought his life, and missing fill'd
With Infant blood the streets of *Bethlehem.*
From *Egypt* home return'd, in *Nazareth*
Hath been our dwelling many years, his life   80
Private, unactive, calm, contemplative,
Little suspicious to any King; but now
Full grown to Man, acknowledg'd, as I hear,
By *John* the Baptist, and in public shown,
Son own'd from Heaven by his Father's voice;   85
I look't for some great change; to Honor? no,
But trouble, as old *Simon* plain foretold,
That to the fall and rising he should be
Of many in *Israel,* and to a sign
Spoken against, that through my very Soul   90
A sword shall pierce; this is my favor'd lot,
My Exaltation to Afflictions high;
Afflicted I may be, it seems, and blest;
I will not argue that, nor will repine.
But where delays he now? some great intent   95
Conceals him: when twelve years he scarce had seen,
I lost him, but so found, as well I saw
He could not lose himself; but went about
His Father's business; what he meant I mus'd,
Since understand; much more his absence now   100
Thus long to some great purpose he obscures.
But I to wait with patience am inur'd;
My heart hath been a storehouse long of things
And sayings laid up, portending strange events.
    Thus *Mary* pondering oft, and oft to mind   105
Recalling what remarkably had pass'd
Since first her Salutation heard, with thoughts
Meekly compos'd awaited the fulfilling:
The while her Son tracing the Desert wild,
Sole, but with holiest Meditations fed,   110
Into himself descended, and at once
All his great work to come before him set;
How to begin, how to accomplish best
His end of being on Earth, and mission high:
For Satan with sly preface to return   115
Had left him vacant, and with speed was gone
Up to the middle Region of thick Air,
Where all his Potentates in Council sat;
There without sign of boast, or sign of joy,
Solicitous and blank he thus began.   120
    Princes, Heaven's ancient Sons, Ethereal Thrones,

79. *Nazareth,* in Galilee, is still the site of a church standing over the traditional place of the Annuciation.

87–91. Cf. Simeon's prophecy in I, 255–6. It is paraphrased here from Luke ii, 34–35.

98–99. When Mary finds the young Jesus talking with the scribes in the Temple, he asks her: "Wist ye not that I must be about my Father's business?" (Luke ii, 49.)

99–104. Luke adds (ii, 51) that "his mother kept all these sayings in her heart."

116. *vacant:* unoccupied, at leisure.

117. As Burton pointed out (*Anatomy* I, ii, 1, 2; Vol. I, 188), though demons inhabited all elements, some authorities confined them to the middle region of the air, which was their principal residence. Cf. *PL* I, 516 and *PR* I, 39–45, n.

120. *blank:* at a loss for words. In *Eikon* (Chap. xxi) the Duchess of Burgundy is blank when she is publicly caught in a lie.

Demonian Spirits now, from th'Element
Each of his reign allotted, rightlier call'd,
Powers of Fire, Air, Water, and Earth beneath,
So may we hold our place and these mild seats   125
Without new trouble; such an Enemy
Is ris'n to invade us, who no less
Threat'ns than our expulsion down to Hell.
I, as I undertook, and with the vote
Consenting in full frequence was empow'r'd,   130
Have found him, view'd him, tasted him, but find
Far other labor to be undergone
Than when I dealt with *Adam* first of Men,
Though *Adam* by his Wife's allurement fell,
However to this Man inferior far,   135
If he be Man by Mother's side at least
With more than human gifts from Heav'n adorn'd,
Perfections absolute, Graces divine,
And amplitude of mind to greatest Deeds.
Therefore I am return'd, lest confidence   140
Of my success with *Eve* in Paradise
Deceive ye to persuasion over-sure
Of like succeeding here; I summon all
Rather to be in readiness with hand
Or counsel to assist; lest I who erst   145
Thought none my equal, now be overmatch'd.
    So spake th'old Serpent doubting, and from all
With clamor was assur'd thir utmost aid
At his command; when from amidst them rose
Belial the dissolutest Spirit that fell,   150
The sensuallest, and after *Asmodai*
The fleshliest Incubus, and thus advis'd.
    Set women in his eye and in his walk,
Among daughters of men the fairest found;
Many are in each Region passing fair   155
As the noon Sky; more like to Goddesses
Than Mortal Creatures, graceful and discreet,
Expert in amorous Arts, enchanting tongues
Persuasive, Virgin majesty with mild
And sweet allay'd, yet terrible to approach,   160
Skill'd to retire, and in retiring draw
Hearts after them tangl'd in Amorous Nets.
Such object hath the power to soft'n and tame
Severest temper, smooth the rugged'st brow,
Enerve, and with voluptuous hope dissolve,   165
Draw out with credulous desire, and lead

122–124. Cf. *llPen*, 93–96, n.
131. *tasted:* examined.   Literally the word means
to test by touch.
139. *amplitude of mind* translates "magnanimity,"
the Aristotelian ideal in the background of Milton's
conception of Christ. See the Introduction 15–17.
150. Cf. *Belial* in *PL* I, 490, n., and II, 109–225,
and in the Introduction 21.
151. *Asmodai* (*Asmodeus* in *PL* IV, 168) is the
lecherous angel in the Book of Tobit whose jealousy
of Tobit's young wife, Sara, has led him to murder
her seven previous husbands on their wedding nights.

152. In confirmation of the belief in *Incubi*, or
demon seducers of women, Jean Bodin, writing
from a jurist's point of view in the *Démonamanie*
(Paris, 1587; Bk. II, Chap. vii, p. 276) quoted St.
Augustine's positive assertion of their wicked activity in *The City of God*, Bk. XV.
164. *temper* temperament, character. Cf. *PL*
II, 218.
166. The line echoes Horace's "credulous hope"
of a lady's favor in an aging lover's heart (*Odes* IV,
i, 30).

At will the manliest, resolutest breast,
As the Magnetic hardest Iron draws.
Women, when nothing else, beguil'd the heart
Of wisest *Solomon,* and made him build,   170
And made him bow to the Gods of his Wives.
　　To whom quick answer Satan thus return'd.
Belial, in much uneven scale thou weigh'st
All others by thyself; because of old
Thou thyself dot'st on womankind, admiring   175
Thir shape, thir color, and attractive grace,
None are, thou think'st, but taken with such toys.
Before the Flood thou with thy lusty Crew,
False titl'd Sons of God, roaming the Earth
Cast wanton eyes on the daughters of men,   180
And coupl'd with them, and begot a race.
Have we not seen, or by relation heard,
In Courts and Regal Chambers how thou lurk'st,
In Wood or Grove by mossy Fountain side,
In Valley or Green Meadow, to waylay   185
Some beauty rare, *Calisto, Clymene,*
Daphne, or *Semele, Antiopa,*
Or *Amymone, Syrinx,* many more
Too long, then lay'st thy scapes on names ador'd,
Apollo, Neptune, Jupiter, or *Pan,*   190
Satyr, or Faun, or Silvan?   But these haunts
Delight not all; among the Sons of Men,
How many have with a smile made small account
Of beauty and her lures, easily scorn'd
All her assaults, on worthier things intent?   195
Remember that *Pellean* Conqueror,
A youth, how all the Beauties of the East
He slightly view'd, and slightly overpass'd;
How hee surnam'd of *Africa* dismiss'd
In his prime youth the fair *Iberian* maid.   200
For *Solomon,* he liv'd at ease, and full
Of honor, wealth, high fare, aim'd not beyond
Higher design than to enjoy his State;
Thence to the bait of Women lay expos'd.
But he whom we attempt is wiser far   205
Than *Solomon,* of more exalted mind,
Made and set wholly on th'accomplishment
Of greatest things; what woman will you find,
Though of this Age the wonder and the fame,
On whom his leisure will vouchsafe an eye   210

168. *Magnetic:* magnet. The word was often used as a noun.

170. Cf. the reference in *PL* I, 444–6 to *Solomon's* worship of the gods of his wives (I Kings xi, 1–8).

178–189. The reference is not to the story in Gen. vi, 2 of the seduction of the sons of Seth by the daughters of Cain, which is told at length in *PL* XI, 573–627, but—as R. H. West shows in *Angels,* pp. 129–31—to the adventures of the fallen angels with mortal women. As in *PR* I, 443–59, Milton thinks of the evil angels as masquerading as pagan gods, many of whom, he recalls, had such *scapes* with the nymphs whose names he takes from Ovid's *Metamorphoses.*

196–200. Alexander was born at Pella, the Macedonian capital. Plutarch's story of his honorable treatment of the wife and daughters of Darius after his victory over the Persians near Issus in 333 B.C. was often linked (as it is in Sir Richard Barckley's *Felicitie of Man,* 1631, p. 320) with Livy's story (*History of Rome* XXVI, l) of Scipio's scrupulous respect for a beautiful Spanish captive after the capture of New Carthage by the Romans in 210 B.C.

Of fond desire? or should she confident,
As sitting Queen ador'd on Beauty's Throne,
Descend with all her winning charms begirt
To enamor, as the Zone of *Venus* once
Wrought that effect on *Jove,* so Fables tell;   215
How would one look from his Majestic brow,
Seated as on the top of Virtue's hill,
Discount'nance her despis'd, and put to rout
All her array; her female pride deject,
Or turn to reverent awe! for Beauty stands   220
In th'admiration only of weak minds
Led captive; cease to admire, and all her Plumes
Fall flat and shrink into a trivial toy,
At every sudden slighting quite abasht:
Therefore with manlier objects we must try   225
His constancy, with such as have more show
Of worth, of honor, glory, and popular praise;
Rocks whereon greatest men have oftest wreck'd;
Or that which only seems to satisfy
Lawful desires of Nature, not beyond;   230
And now I know he hungers where no food
Is to be found, in the wide Wilderness;
The rest commit to me, I shall let pass
No advantage, and his strength as oft assay.
   He ceas'd, and heard thir grant in loud acclaim;   235
Then forthwith to him takes a chosen band
Of Spirits likest to himself in guile
To be at hand, and at his beck appear,
If cause were to unfold some active Scene
Of various persons, each to know his part;   240
Then to the Desert takes with these his flight;
Where still from shade to shade the Son of God
After forty days fasting had remain'd,
Now hung'ring first, and to himself thus said.
   Where will this end? four times ten days I have pass'd, 245
Wand'ring this woody maze, and human food
Nor tasted, nor had appetite: that Fast
To Virtue I impute not, or count part
Of what I suffer here; if Nature need not,
Or God support Nature without repast   250
Though needing, what praise is it to endure?
But now I feel I hunger, which declares
Nature hath need of what she asks; yet God
Can satisfy that need some other way,
Though hunger still remain: so it remain   255
Without this body's wasting, I content me,
And from the sting of Famine fear no harm,
Nor mind it, fed with better thoughts that feed

214–215. Homer has Zeus yield to Hera when she comes to him wearing the girdle of Aphrodite, which was decorated with symbols of passion (*Il.* XIV, 214–18).

217. Perhaps a reference to the *hill* to which the figure of *Virtue* points in illustrations of Prodicus' famous apologue, *The Judgment of Hercules,* or to the hill of virtue in the *Table of Cebes.* Cf. *Sonn* IX, 4, n.

222–223. Milton had a peacock in mind and probably a passage in Ovid's *Art of Love* I, 627, which says that the bird of Juno shows its plumes only to admirers of the display.

240. *persons . . . part:* dramatic terms.

Mee hung'ring more to do my Father's will.
It was the hour of night, when thus the Son   260
Commun'd in silent walk, then laid him down
Under the hospitable covert nigh
Of Trees thick interwoven; there he slept,
And dream'd, as appetite is wont to dream,
Of meats and drinks, Nature's refreshment sweet.   265
Him thought, he by the Brook of *Cherith* stood
And saw the Ravens with thir horny beaks
Food to *Elijah* bringing Even and Morn,
Though ravenous, taught to abstain from what they brought:
He saw the Prophet also how he fled   270
Into the Desert, and how there he slept
Under a Juniper; then how awakt,
He found his Supper on the coals prepar'd,
And by the Angel was bid rise and eat,
And eat the second time after repose,   275
The strength whereof suffic'd him forty days;
Sometimes that with *Elijah* he partook,
Or as a guest with *Daniel* at his pulse.
Thus wore out night, and now the Herald Lark
Left his ground-nest, high tow'ring to descry   280
The morn's approach, and greet her with his Song.
As lightly from his grassy Couch up rose
Our Savior, and found all was but a dream,
Fasting he went to sleep, and fasting wak'd.
Up to a hill anon his steps he rear'd,   285
From whose high top to ken the prospect round,
If Cottage were in view, Sheepcote or Herd;
But Cottage, Herd or Sheepcote none he saw,
Only in a bottom saw a pleasant Grove,
With chant of tuneful Birds resounding loud.   290
Thither he bent his way, determin'd there
To rest at noon, and enter'd soon the shade
High rooft, and walks beneath, and alleys brown
That open'd in the midst a woody Scene;
Nature's own work it seem'd (Nature taught Art)   295
And to a Superstitious eye the haunt
Of Wood Gods and Wood Nymphs; he view'd it round,
When suddenly a man before him stood,
Not rustic as before, but seemlier clad,
As one in City, or Court, or Palace bred,   300
And with fair speech these words to him address'd.
With granted leave officious I return,
But much more wonder that the Son of God

---

259. Cf. Christ's words in John iv, 34: "My meat is to do the will of him that sent me."

266–276. In I Kings xvii, 5–6 Milton read of *Elijah's* retreat to the "brook Cherith, that is before Jordan," where "the ravens brought him bread and flesh." The account of the angel and the food lasting *forty days* is in I Kings xix, 4–8. Cf. *PR* I, 353.

269. The pun on *Raven-ravenous* was less forced when the different etymologies of the words were less familiar than they now are, and when no less labored puns were recommended as ornaments of

epic poetry, as they are by Abraham Fraunce in his *Arcadian Rhetorike*, Chap. xxiv.

278. *Daniel's* refusal of Nebuchadnezzar's meat so as to live on his usual *pulse* diet is found in Daniel i, 8–19.

293. *brown*: dusky, dark. Cf. *PL* IX, 1088.

295. The contrast with the desert suggests Tasso's observation in his essay *On the Heroic Poem* (Bk. III) that "the view of deserts and of the ruggedness and sternness of mountains is agreeable in contrast with the amenity of lakes and gardens."

302. *officious*: anxious to please.

In this wild solitude so long should bide
Of all things destitute, and well I know,   305
Not without hunger. Others of some note,
As story tells, have trod this Wilderness:
The Fugitive Bondwoman with her Son
Outcast *Nebaioth*, yet found he relief
By a providing Angel; all the race   310
Of *Israel* here had famish'd, had not God
Rain'd from Heaven Manna; and that Prophet bold
Native of *Thebez* wand'ring here was fed
Twice by a voice inviting him to eat.
Of thee these forty days none hath regard,   315
Forty and more deserted here indeed.
    To whom thus Jesus; What conclud'st thou hence?
They all had need, I as thou seest have none.
    How hast thou hunger then? Satan replied.
Tell me, if Food were now before thee set,   320
Would'st thou not eat? Thereafter as I like
The giver, answer'd Jesus. Why should that
Cause thy refusal, said the subtle Fiend,
Hast thou not right to all Created things,
Owe not all Creatures by just right to thee   325
Duty and Service, nor to stay till bid,
But tender all thir power? nor mention I
Meats by the Law unclean, or offer'd first
To Idols, those young *Daniel* could refuse;
Nor proffer'd by an Enemy, though who   330
Would scruple that, with want opprest? behold
Nature asham'd, or better to express,
Troubl'd that thou shouldst hunger, hath purvey'd
From all the Elements her choicest store
To treat thee as beseems, and as her Lord   335
With honor; only deign to sit and eat.
    He spake no dream, for as his words had end,
Our Savior lifting up his eyes beheld
In ample space under the broadest shade
A Table richly spread, in regal mode,   340
With dishes pil'd, and meats of noblest sort
And savor, Beasts of chase, or Fowl of game,
In pastry built, or from the spit, or boil'd,

306–310. Ishmael, the son of the *Bondwoman* Hagar, would have died in the desert if "the angel of God" had not shown her "a well of water" (Gen. xxi, 17–19). Ishmael is called by the name of his oldest son, *Nebaioth* (Gen. xxv, 13).

310–312. In the wilderness of Sin (or Zin) "the children of Israel did eat manna forty years, until they came to a land inhabited" (Exod. xvi, 35).

312. The *Prophet* is Elijah the Thisbite. See ll. 16–17 above.

324–327. Satan challenges Jesus as God's "Son, whom he hath appointed heir of all things, by whom also he made the worlds" (Heb. i, 2).

328–347. *Meats by the Law unclean*—as Michael Fixler shows in *MLN*, LXX (1955), 573–7—included the shellfish and probably other animals which Satan inconsistently offers to Christ. Since

Christ has come to supersede the Mosaic dietary laws he is put into a dilemma: if he refuses the unclean meats, he seems to confirm the law; if he accepts them, he seems to accept the giver with them. Satan's subtlest suggestion of acceptance is the echo, in ll. 328–9, of St. Paul's reassurance of some Christians who had hesitated to buy meat which had been previously offered to idols (1 Cor. X, 28).

340. In a comparable scene in Tasso's *Jerusalem Delivered* the witch Armida tempts her lovers with a banquet of

All Beasts, all Birds, beguil'd by Fowler's Trade;
All Fish were there in Floods or Seas that pass,
  All Dainties made by Art, and at the Table
  An hundred Virgins serv'd, for Husbands able.

(Fairfax's translation, X, 64, 5–8)

Grisamber steam'd; all Fish from Sea or Shore,
Freshet, or purling Brook, of shell or fin,   345
And exquisitest name, for which was drain'd
Pontus and *Lucrine* Bay, and *Afric* Coast.
Alas how simple, to these Cates compar'd,
Was the crude Apple that diverted *Eve!*
And at a stately sideboard by the wine   350
That fragrant smell diffus'd, in order stood
Tall stripling youths rich clad, of fairer hue
Than *Ganymede* or *Hylas;* distant more
Under the Trees now tripp'd, now solemn stood
Nymphs of *Diana's* train, and *Naiades*   355
With fruits and flowers from *Amalthea's* horn,
And Ladies of th' *Hesperides,* that seem'd
Fairer than feign'd of old, or fabl'd since
Of Fairy Damsels met in Forest wide
By Knights of *Logres,* or of *Lyones,*   360
Lancelot or *Pelleas,* or *Pellenore;*
And all the while Harmonious Airs were heard
Of chiming strings or charming pipes, and winds
Of gentlest gale *Arabian* odors fann'd
From their soft wings, and *Flora's* earliest smells.   365
Such was the Splendor, and the Tempter now
His invitation earnestly renew'd.
    What doubts the Son of God to sit and eat?
These are not Fruits forbidden; no interdict
Defends the touching of these viands pure;   370
Thir taste no knowledge works, at least of evil,
But life preserves, destroys life's enemy,
Hunger, with sweet restorative delight.
All these are Spirits of Air, and Woods, and Springs,
Thy gentle Ministers, who come to pay   375
Thee homage, and acknowledge thee thir Lord:
What doubt'st thou Son of God? sit down and eat.
    To whom thus Jesus temperately replied:
Said'st thou not that to all things I had right?
And who withholds my pow'r that right to use?   380
Shall I receive by gift what of my own,
When and where likes me best, I can command?
I can at will, doubt not, as soon as thou,
Command a Table in this Wilderness,

344. *Grisamber:* ambergris, which was used as a sauce.

347. *Pontus:* the Black Sea. Juvenal (*Satires* IV, 141) ridicules the taste of the decadent Romans for the oysters which came from the *Lucrine Bay,* near Naples.

349. *diverted:* allured, misled.

353. Cf. *Ganymede* in *El VIII,* 21. n. *Hylas* is described by Conti (VII, i; pp. 704-5) as Hercules' quiver-bearer and drinking companion.

355. Cf. the *Naiades* in Circe's train, in *Comus,* 254.

356. *Amalthea's horn:* the cornucopia or horn of plenty. Ovid says (*Fasti* I, 115-27) that it belonged to the goat which the nymph Amalthea taught to suckle the infant Zeus on Mt. Ida.

357. According to one story told by Conti (VII,

vii, p. 715), the *Hesperides* (daughters of Hesperus) were so beautiful that the Pharaoh Busiris sent some pirates to kidnap them, but they were saved by Hercules.

360. *Logres,* according to Geoffrey of Monmouth, was England east of the Severn and south of the Humber. *Lyonesse,* the land of Arthur's birth, lay in western Cornwall or beyond Land's End, and is now submerged. For the knights see the Introduction 26.

365. *Flora:* the goddess of flowers. Cf. *PL* V, 16.

370. *defends:* forbids.

382. *likes me:* pleases me. Cf. *PL* VI, 353.

384. Perhaps an allusion to the blasphemy of the Israelites in the desert when they asked ironically, "Can God furnish a table in the widerness?" (Ps. lxxviii, 19.)

And call swift flights of Angels ministrant   385
Array'd in Glory on my cup to attend;
Why shouldst thou then obtrude this diligence,
In vain, where no acceptance it can find,
And with my hunger what hast thou to do?
Thy pompous Delicacies I contemn,   390
And count thy specious gifts no gifts but guiles.
    To whom thus answer'd Satan malcontent:
That I have also power to give thou seest;
If of that pow'r I bring thee voluntary
What I might have bestow'd on whom I pleas'd,   395
And rather opportunely in this place
Chose to impart to thy apparent need,
Why shouldst thou not accept it? but I see
What I can do or offer is suspect;
Of these things others quickly will dispose   400
Whose pains have earn'd the far-fet spoil.   With that
Both Table and Provision vanish'd quite
With sound of Harpies' wings and Talons heard;
Only the importune Tempter still remain'd,
And with these words his temptation pursu'd.   405
    By hunger, that each other Creature tames,
Thou art not to be harm'd, therefore not mov'd;
Thy temperance invincible besides,
For no allurement yields to appetite,
And all thy heart is set on high designs,   410
High actions; but wherewith to be achiev'd?
Great acts require great means of enterprise;
Thou art unknown, unfriended, low of birth,
A Carpenter thy Father known, thyself
Bred up in poverty and straits at home;   415
Lost in a Desert here and hunger-bit:
Which way or from what hope dost thou aspire
To greatness? whence Authority deriv'st,
What Followers, what Retinue canst thou gain,
Or at thy heels the dizzy Multitude,   420
Longer than thou canst feed them on thy cost?
Money brings Honor, Friends, Conquest, and Realms;
What rais'd *Antipater* the *Edomite*,
And his Son *Herod* plac'd on *Judah's* Throne
(Thy throne) but gold that got him puissant friends?   425
Therefore, if at great things thou wouldst arrive,
Get Riches first, get Wealth, and Treasure heap,
Not difficult, if thou hearken to me,
Riches are mine, Fortune is in my hand;

385. The line may owe something to Horatio's invocation of "flights of angels" to sing Hamlet to his rest (*Hamlet* V, ii, 347). It also looks forward to the *Angelic choirs* in IV, 593.

391. Sophocles used the proverb that the gifts of enemies are not real gifts in *Ajax*, 664.

401. *far-fet:* far-fetched.

403. The scene recalls the stage direction in *The Tempest*, III, iii: "Enter Ariel like a harpy; claps his wings upon the table; and with a quaint device, the banquet vanishes." But the tone is like Virgil's in describing the stripping of the Trojan's tables by harpies (*Aen.* III, 225–8).

416. "His strength shall be hunger-bitten," says one of Job's comforters (Job xviii, 12).

423. In the *Antiquities of the Jews* XIV, i, Josephus recorded the rise of *Antipater*, "who was very rich, and in his nature an active and seditious man."

427. A clear allusion to Horace's irony: "O citizens, citizens, money should be the first object" (*Epistles* I, i, 53).

They whom I favor thrive in wealth amain,   430
While Virtue, Valor, Wisdom sit in want.
    To whom thus Jesus patiently replied:
Yet Wealth without these three is impotent
To gain dominion or to keep it gain'd.
Witness those ancient Empires of the Earth,   435
In height of all thir flowing wealth dissolv'd;
But men endu'd with these have oft attain'd
In lowest poverty to highest deeds:
Gideon and *Jephtha,* and the Shepherd lad,
Whose offspring on the Throne of *Judah* sat   440
So many Ages, and shall yet regain
That seat, and reign in *Israel* without end.
Among the Heathen, (for throughout the World
To me is not unknown what hath been done
Worthy of Memorial) canst thou not remember   445
Quintius, Fabricius, Curius, Regulus?
For I esteem those names of men so poor
Who could do mighty things, and could contemn
Riches though offer'd from the hand of Kings.
And what in me seems wanting, but that I   450
May also in this poverty as soon
Accomplish what they did, perhaps and more?
Extol not Riches then, the toil of Fools,
The wise man's cumbrance if not snare, more apt
To slacken Virtue and abate her edge,   455
Than prompt her to do aught may merit praise.
What if with like aversion I reject
Riches and Realms; yet not for that a Crown,
Golden in show, is but a wreath of thorns,
Brings dangers, troubles, cares, and sleepless nights   460
To him who wears the Regal Diadem,
When on his shoulders each man's burden lies:
For therein stands the office of a King,
His Honor, Virtue, Merit and chief Praise,
That for the Public all this weight he bears.   465
Yet he who reigns within himself, and rules
Passions, Desires, and Fears, is more a King;
Which every wise and virtuous man attains:
And who attains not, ill aspires to rule
Cities of men, or headstrong Multitudes,   470
Subject himself to Anarchy within,
Or lawless passions in him, which he serves.
But to guide Nations in the way of truth
By saving Doctrine, and from error lead
To know, and knowing worship God aright,   475
Is yet more Kingly; this attracts the Soul,

439. *Gideon's* answer to God's call to save Israel from the Midianites was, "Lord, wherewith shall I save Israel? behold, my family is poor in Manasseh" (Judg. vi, 15). *Jephthah,* who delivered Israel from the Ammonites, was disinherited in youth (Judg. xi, 2). The *Shepherd lad* is David, whom God "took from the sheep-folds" and "brought him to feed Jacob his people" (Ps. lxxviii, 70–71).

440–442. So in the Annunciation (Luke i, 32) Gabriel prophesies the immortality of David's line when he tells Mary that her son should "be called the Son of the Highest: and the Lord God shall give unto him the throne of his father David."

446. For the Roman worthies and their appearance in Christian literature see the Introduction 17. Cf. Note 260 on page 686 below.

453. *toil:* trap or snare.

Governs the inner man, the nobler part;
That other o'er the body only reigns,
And oft by force, which to a generous mind
So reigning can be no sincere delight.   480
Besides, to give a Kingdom hath been thought
Greater and nobler done, and to lay down
Far more magnanimous than to assume.
Riches are needless then, both for themselves,
And for thy reason why they should be sought,   485
To gain a Scepter, oftest better miss't.

The End of the Second Book.

481–483. Refusal of a crown was often cited as a supreme example of magnanimity. "Carolus Martellus," said Sir Richard Barckley in The Felicitie of Man (1631), p. 167, "shewed great magnanimitie in refusing principalitie."

The Third Book

So spake the Son of God, and Satan stood
A while as mute confounded what to say,
What to reply, confuted and convinc't
Of his weak arguing and fallacious drift;
At length collecting all his Serpent wiles,   5
With soothing words renew'd, him thus accosts.
    I see thou know'st what is of use to know,
What best to say canst say, to do canst do;
Thy actions to thy words accord, thy words
To thy large heart give utterance due, thy heart   10
Contains of good, wise, just, the perfect shape.
Should Kings and Nations from thy mouth consult,
Thy Counsel would be as the Oracle
Urim and Thummim, those oraculous gems
On Aaron's breast, or tongue of Seers old   15
Infallible; or wert thou sought to deeds
That might require th' array of war, thy skill
Of conduct would be such, that all the world
Could not sustain thy Prowess, or subsist
In battle, though against thy few in arms.   20
These Godlike Virtues wherefore dost thou hide?
Affecting private life, or more obscure
In savage Wilderness, wherefore deprive
All Earth her wonder at thy acts, thyself
The fame and glory, glory the reward   25
That sole excites to high attempts the flame

11. When Milton wrote of "Virtue in her shape how lovely" (PL IV, 848) and made the Lady in Comus (216) speak of seeing the "unblemish't form of Chastity . . . visibly," he voiced the Platonic doctrine that "the very form and shape of moral goodness, if it could be seen with the physical eye, would"—as Cicero said in De officiis I, v, 15—"awaken a marvellous love of wisdom." The form of the most good, said Plato (Tim., 45d) is divinely revealed through physical vision but mainly to the eye of Reason.

14. The Urim and Thummim worn by Aaron in his high-priestly breastplate (Lev. viii, 8) seem to have been used by Eleazar the priest to "ask counsel before the Lord" (Num. xxvii, 21).

23. savage: uncultivated, wild. Cf. PL IV, 172.

25–30. Cicero declared (De officiis I, viii, 26) that "the greatest passion for honor, empire, power, and glory" was found in "the greatest minds and the most splendid spirits." See the Introduction 10–11.

Of most erected Spirits, most temper'd pure
Ethereal, who all pleasures else despise,
All treasures and all gain esteem as dross,
And dignities and powers, all but the highest?   30
Thy years are ripe, and over-ripe; the Son
Of *Macedonian Philip* had ere these
Won *Asia* and the Throne of *Cyrus* held
At his dispose; young *Scipio* had brought down
The *Carthaginian* pride, young *Pompey* quell'd   35
The *Pontic* King and in triumph had rode.
Yet years, and to ripe years judgment mature,
Quench not the thirst of glory, but augment.
Great *Julius*, whom now all the world admires,
The more he grew in years, the more inflam'd   40
With glory, wept that he had liv'd so long
Inglorious: but thou yet art not too late.
        To whom our Savior calmly thus replied.
Thou neither dost persuade me to seek wealth
For Empire's sake, nor Empire to affect   45
For glory's sake by all thy argument.
For what is glory but the blaze of fame,
The people's praise, if always praise unmixt?
And what the people but a herd confus'd,
A miscellaneous rabble, who extol   50
Things vulgar, and well weigh'd, scarce worth the praise?
They praise and they admire they know not what;
And know not whom, but as one leads the other;
And what delight to be by such extoll'd,
To live upon thir tongues and be thir talk,   55
Of whom to be disprais'd were no small praise?
His lot who dares be singularly good.
Th'intelligent among them and the wise
Are few, and glory scarce of few is rais'd.
This is true glory and renown, when God   60
Looking on th'Earth, with approbation marks
The just man, and divulges him through Heaven
To all his Angels, who with true applause
Recount his praises; thus he did to *Job*,
When to extend his fame through Heaven and Earth,   65
As thou to thy reproach mayst well remember,
He ask'd thee, hast thou seen my servant *Job*?
Famous he was in Heaven, on Earth less known;
Where glory is false glory, attributed
To things not glorious, men not worthy of fame.   70
They err who count it glorious to subdue
By Conquest far and wide, to overrun

32–42. On Alexander the Great, *Scipio*, and *Pompey*, see the Introduction 11. In the *Life of Caesar* Plutarch describes the young Caesar as reading of Alexander's wars and bursting into tears because he did not have "one glorious achievement to boast."

47–48. Milton translates Seneca's question (*Epistles* cii, 19): "What distinguishes clear renown (*claritas*) from glory? Glory consists in the judgment of the many; renown in that of the good."

71–87. Basic and sincere though the thought is both here and in *PL* XI, 696–7, Whiting (*Milieu*, p. 168) notes that it was shared by many writers whom Burton quoted as deploring the human tendency to "put a note of divinity upon the most cruel, & pernicious plague of human kind, adore such men with grand titles, degrees, statues, images, honour, & highly reward them for their good service" (*Anatomy*, Everyman Ed. I, 61).

Large Countries, and in field great Battles win,
Great Cities by assault: what do these Worthies,
But rob and spoil, burn, slaughter, and enslave   75
Peaceable Nations, neighboring or remote,
Made Captive, yet deserving freedom more
Than those thir Conquerors, who leave behind
Nothing but ruin wheresoe'er they rove,
And all the flourishing works of peace destroy,   80
Then swell with pride, and must be titl'd Gods,
Great Benefactors of mankind, Deliverers,
Worship't with Temple, Priest and Sacrifice?
One is the Son of *Jove,* of *Mars* the other,
Till Conqueror Death discover them scarce men,   85
Rolling in brutish vices, and deform'd,
Violent or shameful death thir due reward.
But if there be in glory aught of good,
It may by means far different be attain'd,
Without ambition, war, or violence;   90
By deeds of peace, by wisdom eminent,
By patience, temperance; I mention still
Him whom thy wrongs with Saintly patience borne,
Made famous in a Land and times obscure;
Who names not now with honor patient *Job?*   95
Poor *Socrates* (who next more memorable?)
By what he taught and suffer'd for so doing,
For truth's sake suffering death unjust, lives now
Equal in fame to proudest Conquerors.
Yet if for fame and glory aught be done,   100
Aught suffer'd; if young *African* for fame
His wasted Country freed from *Punic* rage,
The deed becomes unprais'd, the man at least,
And loses, though but verbal, his reward.
Shall I seek glory then, as vain men seek   105
Oft not deserv'd? I seek not mine, but his
Who sent me, and thereby witness whence I am.
    To whom the Tempter murmuring thus replied.
Think not so slight of glory: therein least
Resembling thy great Father; he seeks glory,   110
And for his glory all things made, all things
Orders and governs, nor content in Heaven
By all his Angels glorifi'd, requires
Glory from men, from all men good or bad,
Wise or unwise, no difference, no exemption;   115
Above all Sacrifice, or hallow'd gift
Glory he requires, and glory he receives

---

80. *flourishing* was pronounced "flourshing" in the Sternhold and Hopkins translation of the Psalms —as W. B. Hunter shows in *PQ*, XXVIII (1949), 139.

81–84. Roman emperors were given the title "Divine" by the Senate. Several of Alexander's successors took titles like "Benefactor," and Alexander himself posed as the son of Jupiter Ammon (cf. *PL* IX, 508). Romulus was called the son of Mars.

96–99. On *Socrates* and *Job* see the Introduction 12 and 8.

101. The *young African* is Scipio. Cf. l. 34 above.

106–107. "I seek not mine own glory," said Christ to the Pharisees (John viii, 50).

110–120. The sophistry twists the doctrine of the Westminster Shorter Catechism that the chief end of man is "to glorify God," and exploits the praise of the elders in Rev. iv, 11: "Thou art worthy, O Lord, to receive glory and honor and power: for thou hast created all things, and for thy pleasure they were created."

Promiscuous from all Nations, Jew, or Greek,
Or Barbarous, nor exception hath declar'd;
From us his foes pronounc't glory he exacts.   120
    To whom our Savior fervently replied.
And reason; since his word all things produc'd,
Though chiefly not for glory as prime end,
But to show forth his goodness, and impart
His good communicable to every soul   125
Freely; of whom what could he less expect
Than glory and benediction, that is thanks,
The slightest, easiest, readiest recompense
From them who could return him nothing else,
And not returning that would likeliest render   130
Contempt instead, dishonor, obloquy?
Hard recompense, unsuitable return
For so much good, so much beneficence.
But why should man seek glory? who of his own
Hath nothing, and to whom nothing belongs   135
But condemnation, ignominy, and shame?
Who for so many benefits receiv'd
Turn'd recreant to God, ingrate and false,
And so of all true good himself despoil'd,
Yet, sacrilegious, to himself would take   140
That which to God alone of right belongs;
Yet so much bounty is in God, such grace,
That who advance his glory, not thir own,
Them he himself to glory will advance.
    So spake the Son of God; and here again   145
Satan had not to answer, but stood struck
With guilt of his own sin, for he himself
Insatiable of glory had lost all,
Yet of another Plea bethought him soon.
    Of glory as thou wilt, said he, so deem,   150
Worth or not worth the seeking, let it pass:
But to a Kingdom thou art born, ordain'd
To sit upon thy Father *David's* Throne;
By Mother's side thy Father, though thy right
Be now in powerful hands, that will not part   155
Easily from possession won with arms;
Judaea now and all the promis'd land
Reduc't a Province under Roman yoke,
Obeys *Tiberius;* nor is always rul'd
With temperate sway; oft have they violated   160
The Temple, oft the Law with foul affronts,
Abominations rather, as did once
Antiochus: and think'st thou to regain

119. *Barbarous* keeps its Greek meaning of "foreign," i. e. outside the Greek world, as "gentile" signified the non-Jewish world.
122. Cf. *PL* VII, 163–75.
136. *ignominy* is accented on the first syllable, while the second and third are made into a single light syllable.
138. *recreant:* unfaithful. In *DDD* II, iii Milton speaks of the Mosaic Law as turning "recreant from its own end."
157–160. *Judaea* became a Roman province in

A.D. 6. *Tiberius,* who reigned from A.D. 24 to 37, kept Pilate in office from 26 to 36, in spite of several acts of tyranny like the massacre of "the Galileans, whose blood Pilate had mingled with their sacrifices" (Luke xiii, 1).
161. Pompey violated the Holy of Holies in the Temple in 63 B.C.
162–163. *Antiochus* Epiphanes "entered proudly into the sanctuary and took away the golden altar, and the candlestick of light, and all the vessels thereof . . ." (I Maccabees i, 21).

Thy right by sitting still or thus retiring?
So did not *Maccabaeus:* he indeed   165
Retir'd unto the Desert, but with arms;
And o'er a mighty King so oft prevail'd,
That by strong hand his Family obtain'd,
Though Priests, the Crown, and *David's* Throne usurp'd,
With *Modin* and her Suburbs once content.   170
If Kingdom move thee not, let move thee Zeal
And Duty; Zeal and Duty are not slow,
But on Occasion's forelock watchful wait.
They themselves rather are occasion best,
Zeal of thy Father's house, Duty to free   175
Thy Country from her Heathen servitude;
So shalt thou best fullfil, best verify
The Prophets old, who sung thy endless reign,
The happier reign the sooner it begins.
Reign then; what canst thou better do the while?   180
   To whom our Savior answer thus return'd.
All things are best fulfill'd in their due time,
And time there is for all things, Truth hath said:
If of my reign Prophetic Writ hath told
That it shall never end, so when begin   185
The Father in his purpose hath decreed,
He in whose hand all times and seasons roll.
What if he hath decreed that I shall first
Be tried in humble state, and things adverse,
By tribulations, injuries, insults,   190
Contempts, and scorns, and snares, and violence,
Suffering, abstaining, quietly expecting
Without distrust or doubt, that he may know
What I can suffer, how obey? who best
Can suffer, best can do; best reign, who first   195
Well hath obey'd; just trial e'er I merit
My exaltation without change or end.
But what concerns it thee when I begin
My everlasting Kingdom?   Why art thou
Solicitous?   What moves thy inquisition?   200
Know'st thou not that my rising is thy fall,
And my promotion will be thy destruction?
   To whom the Tempter inly rackt replied.
Let that come when it comes; all hope is lost
Of my reception into grace; what worse?   205
For where no hope is left, is left no fear;
If there be worse, the expectation more
Of worse torments me than the feeling can.
I would be at the worst; worst is my Port,

165–170. In 166 B.C. Judas *Maccabaeus*, a Levite
born in the obscure Judaean town of *Modin*, began
the struggle with Antiochus which ended in putting
his family on the throne of David as the Asmonean
Dynasty.

175. Christ's whipping of the money-changers out
of the Temple was regarded by his disciples (John
ii, 17) as fulfilling a prophecy in Ps. lxix, 9: "The
zeal of thine house hath eaten me up."

183. The line quotes Ecclesiastes iii, 1.

187. "It is not for you," said Christ to his disciples, "to know the times or the seasons, which
the Father hath put in his own power" (Acts i, 7).

194–197. The lines unite Mucius' Scaevola's famous boast of Roman courage alike to do and to
suffer the greatest things (in Livy's *History* II, xiv)
and Plato's principle (*Laws,* 715c) that "the administration of the laws must be given to that man
who is most obedient to the laws."

204–211. Cf. *PL* IV, 108–110.

My harbor and my ultimate repose,   210
The end I would attain, my final good.
My error was my error, and my crime
My crime; whatever, for itself condemn'd,
And will alike be punish'd; whether thou
Reign or reign not; though to that gentle brow   215
Willingly I could fly, and hope thy reign,
From that placid aspect and meek regard,
Rather than aggravate my evil state,
Would stand between me and thy Father's ire
(Whose ire I dread more than the fire of Hell)   220
A shelter and a kind of shading cool
Interposition, as a summer's cloud.
If I then to the worst that can be haste,
Why move thy feet so slow to what is best,
Happiest both to thyself and all the world,   225
That thou who worthiest art shouldst be thir King?
Perhaps thou linger'st in deep thoughts detain'd
Of the enterprise so hazardous and high;
No wonder, for though in thee be united
What of perfection can in man be found,   230
Or human nature can receive, consider
Thy life hath yet been private, most part spent
At home, scarce view'd the *Galilean* Towns,
And once a year *Jerusalem,* few days'
Short sojourn; and what thence couldst thou observe?   235
The world thou hast not seen, much less her glory,
Empires, and Monarchs, and thir radiant Courts,
Best school of best experience, quickest insight
In all things that to greatest actions lead.
The wisest, unexperienc't, will be ever   240
Timorous and loth, with novice modesty
(As he who seeking Asses found a Kingdom)
Irresolute, unhardy, unadvent'rous:
But I will bring thee where thou soon shalt quit
Those rudiments, and see before thine eyes   245
The Monarchies of th'Earth, thir pomp and state,
Sufficient introduction to inform
Thee, of thyself so apt, in regal Arts,
And regal Mysteries; that thou mayst know
How best their opposition to withstand.   250
    With that (such power was giv'n him then) he took
The Son of God up to a Mountain high.
It was a Mountain at whose verdant feet
A spacious plain outstretcht in circuit wide
Lay pleasant; from his side two rivers flow'd,   255
Th'one winding, th'other straight, and left between

213–214. Cf. *PL* IV, 75.

234. Luke says (ii, 41) that Jesus' "parents went to Jerusalem every year at the feast of the passover."

242. While searching for his father's lost asses Saul met the prophet Samuel, who "took a vial of oil and poured it upon his head, . . . and said, Is it not because the Lord hath anointed thee to be captain over his inheritance?" (I Sam. x, 1.)

249. Satan misunderstands the "mysteries of the kingdom" which Jesus says (Matt. xiii, 11) that it is given to the disciples "to know."

252–258. The *Mountain* may be Niphates, where Satan first views the world in *PL* III, 742, or the mountain of Adam's vision in *PL* XI, 377–88, which Milton compares with it. The *rivers* are the Tigris and Euphrates.

Fair Champaign with less rivers intervein'd,
Then meeting join'd thir tribute to the Sea:
Fertile of corn the glebe, of oil and wine;
With herds the pastures throng'd, with flocks the hills;   260
Huge Cities and high tow'r'd, that well might seem
The seats of mightiest Monarchs; and so large
The Prospect was, that here and there was room
For barren desert fountainless and dry.
To this high mountain top the Tempter brought   265
Our Savior, and new train of words began.
   Well have we speeded, and o'er hill and dale,
Forest and field, and flood, Temples and Towers
Cut shorter many a league; here thou behold'st
Assyria and her Empire's ancient bounds,   270
Araxes and the Caspian lake, thence on
As far as Indus East, Euphrates West,
And oft beyond; to South the Persian Bay,
And inaccessible th'Arabian drought;
Here Nineveh, of length within her wall   275
Several days' journey, built by Ninus old,
Of that first golden Monarchy the seat,
And seat of Salmanassar, whose success
Israel in long captivity still mourns;
There Babylon the wonder of all tongues,   280
As ancient, but rebuilt by him who twice
Judah and all thy Father David's house
Led captive and Jerusalem laid waste,
Till Cyrus set them free; Persepolis
His city there thou seest, and Bactra there;   285
Ecbatana her structure vast there shows,
And Hecatompylos her hundred gates,
There Susa by Choaspes, amber stream,
The drink of none but Kings; of later fame
Built by Emathian, or by Parthian hands,   290
The great Seleucia, Nisibis, and there
Artaxata, Teredon, Ctesiphon,
Turning with easy eye thou mayst behold.
All these the Parthian, now some Ages past,
By great Arsáces led, who founded first   295

271. The Araxes flows east from near Erzerum in Armenia to the Caspian.

273. The Tigris and Euphrates empty into the arm of the Indian Ocean which Milton calls the Persian Bay.

274. drought: desert.

275–279. Nineveh was supposed to be named for Ninus, its founder. Its size is suggested by the statement in Jonah iii, 3 that its circumference was "a three days' journey." Salmanassar (Shalmaneser) carried the ten northern tribes of Israel into captivity in 726 B.C.

280–283. Nebuchadnezzar carried away Jehoiachim "and all the princes and all the mighty men of valor, even ten thousand captives," from Jerusalem to Babylon in 597 B.C.

280–302. The panorama of cities and kingdoms matches well with the maps in Ptolemy's Geographia (1605), one of which is reproduced by Whiting in Milieu, opposite p. 124.

284–288. The Persian Cyrus, whose return of the Israelites from Babylonian captivity to Judaea is recorded in Ezra i, 1–3, first made Persepolis his capital. Bactra was the capital of his province of Bactria, and Hecatompylos, "the city of a hundred gates," was in Parthia. The Persian city Ecbatana occurs in PL XI, 393.

289–300. Seleucia was rebuilt by Alexander's general Seleucus Nicator on the Tigris, about fifty miles from Babylon, as his seat of Macedonian (Emathian) government. Nisibis was in northern Mesopotamia, Teredon in the south, at the confluence of the Tigris and Euphrates. Ctesiphon was built by the Parthians on the Tigris after their conquest of the Seleucid empire. Antioch, on the Orontes in Syria, had become the Seleucid capital when the empire fell to Arsáces about 250 B.C. Artaxata was the capital of ancient Armenia.

That Empire, under his dominion holds,
From the luxurious Kings of *Antioch* won.
And just in time thou com'st to have a view
Of his great power; for now the *Parthian* King
In *Ctesiphon* hath gather'd all his Host   300
Against the *Scythian,* whose incursions wild
Have wasted *Sogdiana;* to her aid
He marches now in haste; see, though from far,
His thousands, in what martial equipage
They issue forth, Steel Bows and Shafts their arms,   305
Of equal dread in flight, or in pursuit;
All Horsemen, in which fight they most excel;
See how in warlike muster they appear,
In Rhombs and wedges, and half-moons, and wings.
  He look't and saw what numbers numberless   310
The City gates outpour'd, light armed Troops
In coats of Mail and military pride;
In Mail thir horses clad, yet fleet and strong,
Prancing their riders bore, the flower and choice
Of many Provinces from bound to bound;   315
From *Arachosia,* from *Candaor* East,
And *Margiana* to the *Hyrcanian* cliffs
Of *Caucasus,* and dark *Iberian* dales;
From *Atropatia* and the neighboring plains
Of *Adiabene, Media,* and the South   320
Of *Susiana* to *Balsara's* hav'n.
He saw them in thir forms of battle rang'd,
How quick they wheel'd, and flying behind them shot
Sharp sleet of arrowy showers against the face
Of thir pursuers, and overcame by flight;   325
The field all iron cast a gleaming brown,
Nor wanted clouds of foot, nor on each horn,
Cuirassiers all in steel for standing fight;
Chariots or Elephants endorst with Towers
Of Archers, nor of laboring Pioners   330
A multitude with Spades and Axes arm'd
To lay hills plain, fell woods, or valleys fill,
Or where plain was raise hill, or overlay
With bridges rivers proud, as with a yoke;

---

309. *Rhombs:* phalanxes in rhomboid shape, which gave a point at the two sharper ends.

311–314. The description of the Parthian equipment seems to be drawn from Montaigne's *Essays* II, ix, or from Montaigne's source in Ammianus Marcellinus' account of the Parthian cavalry.

316–321. *Arachosia* lay in modern Baluchistan; *Candaor* (now called Candahar) is a province of Afghanistan. *Margiana* corresponds with modern Khorasan. *Hyrcania* lay on the Caspian Sea not far from the *Caucasus.* Purchas (*Pilgrimes* III, 110) speaks of the "palpable darkness" and mysterious inhabitants of *Iberia* (not Spain) in the *Caucasus.* *Atropatia* was a Median province south of the river Araxes. *Adiabene* is mentioned by Strabo (XIV, i, 1) as a great plain near Nineveh. *Susiana* was a Persian and later a Parthian province on the Persian Gulf. *Balsara,* the modern Basra, on the Shatt-al-Arab, is a port which Milton's contem-

poraries mistakenly identified with the ancient Teredon.

323–327. Horace (*Odes* II, xiii, 17–18) spoke of the arrows and swift flight of the Parthians as a terror to the Roman soldiers, and Virgil (*Georg.* III, 31) called Augustus' victory over their backward-shooting cavalry a supreme triumph. The entire scene, with the *gleaming brown* or high-lighted dark color of the moving mass of troops, resembles Virgil's picture of the advancing Trojan forces (*Aen.* XI, 601–2), and the image of *clouds of foot* is Virgilian (*Aen.* VII, 793) and Homeric (*Il.* IV, 274).

329. So Ben Jonson's epigram declares that the Earl of Newcastle's "seat" on a handsome charger "his beauties did endorse." The pun on the Latin meaning of the word is equally possible on the English verb "to back."

Mules after these, Camels and Dromedaries,   335
And Wagons fraught with Utensils of war.
Such forces met not, nor so wide a camp,
When *Agrican* with all his Northern powers
Besieg'd *Albracca*, as Romances tell,
The City of *Gallaphrone*, from thence to win   340
The fairest of her Sex, *Angelica*,
His daughter, sought by many Prowest Knights,
Both *Paynim*, and the Peers of *Charlemagne*.
Such and so numerous was thir Chivalry;
At sight whereof the Fiend yet more presum'd,   345
And to our Savior thus his words renew'd.
    That thou mayst know I seek not to engage
Thy Virtue, and not every way secure
On no slight grounds thy safety, hear, and mark
To what end I have brought thee hither and shown   350
All this fair sight: thy Kingdom though foretold
By Prophet or by Angel, unless thou
Endeavor, as thy Father *David* did,
Thou never shalt obtain; prediction still
In all things, and all men, supposes means,   355
Without means us'd, what it predicts revokes.
But say thou wert possess'd of *David's* Throne
By free consent of all, none opposite,
Samaritan or *Jew;* how couldst thou hope
Long to enjoy it quiet and secure,   360
Between two such enclosing enemies
Roman and *Parthian?*   Therefore one of these
Thou must make sure thy own; the *Parthian* first
By my advice, as nearer and of late
Found able by invasion to annoy   365
Thy country, and captive lead away her Kings,
Antigonus and old *Hyrcanus* bound,
Maugre the *Roman:* it shall be my task
To render thee the *Parthian* at dispose;
Choose which thou wilt, by conquest or by league.   370
By him thou shalt regain, without him not,
That which alone can truly reinstall thee
In *David's* royal seat, his true Successor,
Deliverance of thy brethren, those ten Tribes
Whose offspring in his Territory yet serve   375
In *Habor*, and among the *Medes* dispers't,
Ten Sons of *Jacob*, two of *Joseph* lost
Thus long from *Israel;* serving as of old

338–343. In Boiardo's *Orlando Innamorato* (I, x, 26) *Angelica* involves Astolfo, Roland, and some other knights of *Charlemagne* in the fighting around *Albracca*, a fabulous fortress of her father *Galla-phrone*, the king of Cathay (China), when it is besieged by her lover *Agrican*, king of Tartary.

342. *Prowest:* hardiest. From Old French *prou*, "knightly."

343. *Paynim:* pagan. Cf. *PL* I, 765.

358. *opposite:* none opposing.

359. Any alliance between *Samaritans* and *Jews* was impossible because the Jews had "no dealings with the Samaritans" (John iv, 9).

367–368. Josephus (*Antiquities* XIV) records the consolidation of *Antigonus'* power by *Parthian* support against his uncle, the High Priest *Hyrcanus*, who had *Roman* help. After a three-year reign Antigonus was shamefully executed by Herod the Great, who later degraded Hyrcanus and finally had him executed (c. 30 B.C.).

373–380. About 722 B.C. the Assyrians crushed the ten northern tribes (including those named for Ephraim and Manasseh, sons of *Joseph*) and moved them to "*Habor* by the river of Gozan, and in the cities of the *Medes*" (II Kings xvii, 6).

Thir Fathers in the land of *Egypt* serv'd,
This offer sets before thee to deliver.   380
These if from servitude thou shalt restore
To thir inheritance, then, nor till then,
Thou on the Throne of *David* in full glory,
From *Egypt* to *Euphrates* and beyond
Shalt reign, and *Rome* or *Caesar* not need fear.   385
    To whom our Savior answer'd thus unmov'd.
Much ostentation vain of fleshly arm
And fragile arms, much instrument of war
Long in preparing, soon to nothing brought,
Before mine eyes thou hast set; and in my ear   390
Vented much policy, and projects deep
Of enemies, of aids, battles and leagues,
Plausible to the world, to mee worth naught.
Means I must use thou say'st, prediction else
Will unpredict and fail me of the Throne: 395
My time I told thee (and that time for thee
Were better farthest off) is not yet come;
When that comes think not thou to find me slack
On my part aught endeavoring, or to need
Thy politic maxims, or that cumbersome   400
Luggage of war there shown me, argument
Of human weakness rather than of strength.
My brethren, as thou call'st them, those Ten Tribes
I must deliver, if I mean to reign
David's true heir, and his full Scepter sway   405
To just extent over all *Israel's* Sons;
But whence to thee this zeal? Where was it then
For *Israel*, or for *David*, or his Throne,
When thou stood'st up his Tempter to the pride
Of numb'ring *Israel*, which cost the lives   410
Of threescore and ten thousand *Israelites*
By three days' Pestilence? Such was thy zeal
To *Israel* then, the same that now to me.
As for those captive Tribes, themselves were they
Who wrought their own captivity, fell off   415
From God to worship Calves, the Deities
Of *Egypt*, *Baal* next and *Ashtaroth*,
And all the Idolatries of Heathen round,
Besides thir other worse than heathenish crimes;
Nor in the land of their captivity   420
Humbled themselves, or penitent besought
The God of thir forefathers; but so died

---

384. God covenanted with Abraham to give his "seed" the land "from the river of Egypt unto the great river, the river Euphrates" (Gen. xv, 18). Solomon actually reigned over all the kingdoms from the *Euphrates* "unto the border of *Egypt*" (I Kings iv, 21).

387. Cf. the curse in Jer. xvii, 5 on the "man that trusteth in man and maketh flesh his arm."

391. *policy:* shrewd statecraft. Cf. *PL* II, 297.

396–397. *My time . . . is not yet come:* the words of Jesus to his unfriendly "brethren" in a context (John vii, 6) of rebuke to worldly standards.

409–412. After "Satan stood up against Israel and provoked David to number Israel" (I Chron. xxi, 1), "the Lord sent pestilence upon Israel, and there fell of Israel seventy thousand men."

414–417. Jeroboam, who drew the Ten Tribes away from Judah and Benjamin to form the kingdom of Samaria, "made two calves of gold, and said unto them, . . . behold, thy gods, O Israel, which brought thee up out of the land of Egypt" (I Kings xii, 28). Cf. *PL* I, 482–89.

417. Cf. *Baal* and *Ashtaroth* in *PL* I, 422.

Impenitent, and left a race behind
Like to themselves, distinguishable scarce
From Gentiles but by Circumcision vain,   425
And God with Idols in their worship join'd.
Should I of these the liberty regard,
Who freed, as to their ancient Patrimony,
Unhumbl'd, unrepentant, unreform'd,
Headlong would follow, and to thir Gods perhaps   430
Of *Bethel* and of *Dan*? No, let them serve
Thir enemies, who serve Idols with God.
Yet he at length, time to himself best known,
Rememb'ring *Abraham*, by some wond'rous call
May bring them back repentant and sincere,   435
And at their passing cleave the *Assyrian* flood,
While to their native land with joy they haste,
As the Red Sea and *Jordan* once he cleft,
When to the promis'd land thir Fathers pass'd;
To his due time and providence I leave them.   440
   So spake *Israel's* true King, and to the Fiend
Made answer meet, that made void all his wiles.
So fares it when with truth falsehood contends.

The End of the Third Book.

427–431. Christ questions whether, if the Ten Tribes were repatriated, they would not return to the worship of their "calves of gold."
429. Cf. *PL* V, 899, and *SA*, 417.
436–439. Isaiah (xi, 16) had prophesied a "high-way for the remnant of [God's] people, which shall be left, from Assyria; like as it was to Israel in the day that he came up out of the land of Egypt."

The Fourth Book

   Perplex'd and troubl'd at his bad success
The Tempter stood, nor had what to reply,
Discover'd in his fraud, thrown from his hope,
So oft, and the persuasive Rhetoric
That sleek't his tongue, and won so much on *Eve*,   5
So little here, nay lost; but *Eve* was *Eve*,
This far his over-match, who self-deceiv'd
And rash, beforehand had no better weigh'd
The strength he was to cope with, or his own:
But as a man who had been matchless held   10
In cunning, overreach't where least he thought,
To salve his credit, and for very spite
Still will be tempting him who foils him still,
And never cease, though to his shame the more;
Or as a swarm of flies in vintage time,   15
About the wine-press where sweet must is pour'd,
Beat off, returns as oft with humming sound;
Or surging waves against a solid rock,

1. *success:* result. Cf. the pertinacity of Satan when, "by success untaught" (*PL* II, 9), he plans a renewed attack on heaven.
10–20. In the background are Ariosto's simile of the Moors attacking the Christians as flies do ripe grapes (*Orlando Furioso* XIV, 109), Homer's comparison of the warriors around Sarpedon's body to flies around milk cans (*Il.* XVI, 641), and Spenser's comparison of delusive temptations to buzzing flies (*F.Q.* II, ix, 51).

Though all to shivers dash't, th'assault renew,
Vain batt'ry, and in froth or bubbles end;   20
So Satan, whom repulse upon repulse
Met ever, and to shameful silence brought,
Yet gives not o'er though desperate of success,
And his vain importunity pursues.
He brought our Savior to the western side   25
Of that high mountain, whence he might behold
Another plain, long but in breadth not wide;
Wash'd by the Southern Sea, and on the North
To equal length back'd with a ridge of hills
That screen'd the fruits of th'earth and seats of men   30
From cold *Septentrion* blasts, thence in the midst
Divided by a river, of whose banks
On each side an Imperial City stood,
With Towers and Temples proudly elevate
On seven small Hills, with Palaces adorn'd,   35
Porches and Theaters, Baths, Aqueducts,
Statues and Trophies, and Triumphal Arcs,
Gardens and Groves presented to his eyes,
Above the height of Mountains interpos'd:
By what strange Parallax or Optic skill   40
Of vision multiplied through air, or glass
Of Telescope, were curious to inquire:
And now the Tempter thus his silence broke.
    The City which thou seest no other deem
Than great and glorious *Rome,* Queen of the Earth   45
So far renown'd, and with the spoils enricht
Of Nations; there the Capitol thou seest,
Above the rest lifting his stately head
On the *Tarpeian rock,* her Citadel
Impregnable, and there Mount *Palatine*   50
Th'Imperial Palace, compass huge, and high
The Structure, skill of noblest Architects,
With gilded battlements, conspicuous far,
Turrets and Terraces, and glittering Spires.
Many a fair Edifice besides, more like   55
Houses of Gods (so well I have dispos'd
My Airy Microscope) thou mayst behold
Outside and inside both, pillars and roofs
Carv'd work, the hand of fam'd Artificers
In Cedar, Marble, Ivory or Gold.   60
Thence to the gates cast round thine eye, and see
What conflux issuing forth or ent'ring in,
Praetors, Proconsuls to thir Provinces
Hasting or on return, in robes of State;
Lictors and rods, the ensigns of thir power,   65

27–31. The *plain* is Latium, with Rome in the center and the Apennines screening it from the *Septentrion blasts* or north winds.

40. *Parallax:* seeming displacement of an object due to a shift in an observer's point of view.

44–45. An ironical echo of St. John's description of *Rome,* who "saith in her heart, I sit a queen, and am no widow, and shall see no sorrow" (Rev. xviii, 7).

49. The *Tarpeian rock* was a precipice on the Capitoline hill over which condemned criminals were hurled.

63. *Praetors:* Roman governors enjoying the rule of a province in the year following their term of office in Rome, as the *Proconsuls* regularly did after their consulships.

65. *Lictors:* attendants on high Roman officials.

Legions and Cohorts, turms of horse and wings:
Or Embassies from Regions far remote
In various habits on the *Appian* road,
Or on th'*Aemilian*, some from farthest South,
Syene, and where the shadow both way falls,   70
Meroë, *Nilotic* Isle, and more to West,
The Realm of *Bocchus* to the Blackmoor Sea;
From the *Asian* Kings and *Parthian* among these,
From *India* and the golden *Chersonese*,
And utmost *Indian* Isle *Taprobane*,   75
Dusk faces with white silken Turbans wreath'd;
From *Gallia*, *Gades*, and the *British* West,
Germans and *Scythians*, and *Sarmatians* North
Beyond *Danubius* to the *Tauric* Pool.
All Nations now to *Rome* obedience pay,   80
To *Rome's* great Emperor, whose wide domain
In ample Territory, wealth and power,
Civility of Manners, Arts, and Arms,
And long Renown thou justly mayst prefer
Before the *Parthian;* these two Thrones except,   85
The rest are barbarous, and scarce worth the sight,
Shar'd among petty Kings too far remov'd;
These having shown thee, I have shown thee all
The Kingdoms of the world, and all thir glory.
This Emperor hath no Son, and now is old,   90
Old, and lascivious, and from *Rome* retir'd
To *Capreae*, an Island small but strong
On the *Campanian* shore, with purpose there
His horrid lusts in private to enjoy,
Committing to a wicked Favorite   95
All public cares, and yet of him suspicious,
Hated of all, and hating. With what ease,

They carried fasces or bundles of rods to signify and enforce the authority to punish criminals.

66. A *Cohort* was a tenth part of a *legion*. Because Roman cavalry fought on the flanks its units were called *wings*, and their decimal divisions were called *turms*.

68. The *Appian* Way (*road*), between Rome and Brindisi, is still lined with splendid ruins of Roman tombs.

69. The *Aemilian* Way ran from Rome to Aquileia on the Adriatic.

70. *Syene*, modern Assouan, on the upper Nile, was a Roman outpost.

70–86. The panorama resembles Claudian's picture of Rome uniting Colchian and Iberian, mitred Arab with coifed Armenian, painted Sacian with dyed Mede, dark Indians with warriors from the Rhone and the Atlantic shores of Gaul (*On Stilicho's Consulship* I, 152–60).

71. Many geographers repeated Pliny's statement that in *Meroë*, at the confluence of the Nile and Blue Nile, "twice in the yeare the shadowes are gone, and none at all seene, to wit, when the summer is in the 18 degree of Taurus, and the 14 of Leo" (Holland's Tr. II, lxxviii, 75). Whiting notes (*Milieu*, p. 89) that Pliny goes on at once to mention an Indian mountain where "the shadows in summer fall towards the south, and in winter

towards the north."

72. *Bocchus'* kingdom roughly coincided with modern Mauretania. The *Blackmoor Sea* is the Mediterranean off the Barbary coast.

74. Sumatra and Java were identified with "the land called Ophir, but now the *Aurea Chersonesus*," where Josephus (*Antiquities* VIII, vi, 4) says that Solomon sent for gold. Cf. *PL* XI, 392.

75. *Taprobane* is identified with Sumatra rather than with Ceylon by Whiting in *RES*, XIII (1937), 202–12. As J. D. Gordon suggests in *RES*, XVIII (1942), 319, Milton remembered Ariosto's story of Astolfo's flight over the Ganges to Taprobane and beyond it (*O.F.* XV, 17). The word has four syllables, accent on the second.

77. *Gades:* Cadiz.

78. The *Tauric Pool:* the Sea of Azof. Cf. *PL* IX, 78.

90–94. Tiberius (42 B.C.–A.D. 37) was drawn to *Capri* on the Bay of Naples, off the *Campanian* shore, because, as Suetonius says (*Caesars* III, xl), "it was accessible only by one small beach and was girt about everywhere else by sheer rocks and deep water"; but the crimes of which he was supposed to have been guilty in Capri may be exaggerated.

95–97. The *Favorite* was Sejanus, whose cruelty is the subject of Juvenal's Tenth Satire and of Ben Jonson's *Sejanus*.

Endu'd with Regal Virtues as thou art,
Appearing, and beginning noble deeds,
Might'st thou expel this monster from his Throne   100
Now made a sty, and in his place ascending
A victor people free from servile yoke?
And with my help thou mayst; to me the power
Is given, and by that right I give it thee.
Aim therefore at no less than all the world,   105
Aim at the highest, without the highest attain'd
Will be for thee no sitting, or not long
On David's Throne, be prophesi'd what will.
    To whom the Son of God unmov'd replied.
Nor doth this grandeur and majestic show   110
Of luxury, though call'd magnificence,
More than of arms before, allure mine eye,
Much less my mind; though thou should'st add to tell
Thir sumptuous gluttonies, and gorgeous feasts
On *Citron* tables or *Atlantic* stone,   115
(For I have also heard, perhaps have read)
Their wines of *Setia, Cales,* and *Falerne,*
Chios and *Crete,* and how they quaff in Gold,
Crystal and Murrhine cups emboss'd with Gems
And studs of Pearl, to me should'st tell who thirst   120
And hunger still: then Embassies thou show'st
From Nations far and nigh; what honor that,
But tedious waste of time to sit and hear
So many hollow compliments and lies,
Outlandish flatteries? then proceed'st to talk   125
Of the Emperor, how easily subdu'd,
How gloriously; I shall, thou say'st, expel
A brutish monster; what if I withal
Expel a Devil who first made him such?
Let his tormentor Conscience find him out;   130
For him I was not sent, nor yet to free
That people victor once, now vile and base,
Deservedly made vassal, who once just,
Frugal, and mild, and temperate, conquer'd well,
But govern ill the Nations under yoke,   135
Peeling thir Provinces, exhausted all
By lust and rapine; first ambitious grown
Of triumph, that insulting vanity;
Then cruel, by thir sports to blood inur'd
Of fighting beasts, and men to beasts expos'd,   140
Luxurious by thir wealth, and greedier still,
And from the daily Scene effeminate.
What wise and valiant man would seek to free

104. "And the devil said unto him, All this power will I give thee, and the glory of them; for that is delivered unto me" (Luke iv, 6).

115. Pliny mentions (XIII, xxix, 15) the perfumed wood of the African citrus as used for expensive furniture. The Atlas mountains in Algeria were the source of a marble that was known as *Atlantic stone.*

117. *Setia* was near Rome. *Cales* and the famous Falernian vineyards were in Campania, near Mt. Vesuvius.

118. The Aegean islands of *Chios* and *Crete* furnished famous wines.

119. *Murrhine cups* were made of a rare Parthian clay.

136. *peeling:* pillaging, robbing.

138–142. The lines crystallize the attacks on the corrupt Roman theaters by the Latin Fathers of the church, e. g. Lactantius in the *Divine Institutes* VI, xx, 12–13 and 27–29, and Augustine in many passages in *The City of God.*

These thus degenerate, by themselves enslav'd,
Or could of inward slaves make outward free?   145
Know therefore when my season comes to sit
On *David's* Throne, it shall be like a tree
Spreading and overshadowing all the Earth,
Or as a stone that shall to pieces dash
All Monarchies besides throughout the world,   150
And of my Kingdom there shall be no end:
Means there shall be to this, but what the means,
Is not for thee to know, nor me to tell
    To whom the Tempter impudent replied.
I see all offers made by me how slight   155
Thou valu'st, because offer'd, and reject'st:
Nothing will please the difficult and nice,
Or nothing more than still to contradict:
On th'other side know also thou, that I
On what I offer set as high esteem,   160
Nor what I part with mean to give for naught;
All these which in a moment thou behold'st,
The Kingdoms of the world to thee I give;
For giv'n to me, I give to whom I please,
No trifle; yet with this reserve, not else,   165
On this condition, if thou wilt fall down,
And worship me as thy superior Lord,
Easily done, and hold them all of me;
For what can less so great a gift deserve?
    Whom thus our Savior answer'd with disdain.   170
I never lik'd thy talk, thy offers less,
Now both abhor, since thou hast dar'd to utter
Th'abominable terms, impious condition;
But I endure the time, till which expir'd,
Thou hast permission on me. It is written   175
The first of all Commandments, Thou shalt worship
The Lord thy God, and only him shalt serve;
And dar'st thou to the Son of God propound
To worship thee accurst, now more accurst
For this attempt bolder than that on *Eve*,   180
And more blasphémous? which expect to rue.
The Kingdoms of the world to thee were giv'n,
Permitted rather, and by thee usurp't,
Other donation none thou canst produce:
If given, by whom but by the King of Kings,   185
God over all supreme? If giv'n to thee,
By thee how fairly is the Giver now
Repaid? But gratitude in thee is lost
Long since. Wert thou so void of fear or shame,

147–150. Christ appropriates Nebuchadnezzar's vision of a tree which "reached unto heaven, and the sign thereof to the end of all the earth" (Dan. iv, 11). He reads his own destiny in Daniel's vision of a stone which smote the image of worldly power and "became a great mountain and filled the whole earth" (Dan. ii, 35).

157. *the* should perhaps read "thee," but C. W. Brodrib's arguments for the emendation in *TLS*, May 17, 1941, pp. 239–40, are unconvincing. *nice*: fastidious. Cf. *PL* V, 433.

176–177. "Thou shalt fear the Lord thy God, and serve him" (Deut. vi, 13).

184. *donation* keeps its Latin meaning of a bestowal of property or privilege by a superior authority on an individual or institution.

185–186. "King of kings" is Paul's title for God (I Tim. vi, 15) and John's title for the risen Christ (Rev. xvii, 14 and xix, 16).

As offer them to me the Son of God,   190
To me my own, on such abhorred pact,
That I fall down and worship thee as God?
Get thee behind me; plain thou now appear'st
That Evil one, Satan for ever damn'd.
   To whom the Fiend with fear abasht replied.   195
Be not so sore offended, Son of God,
Though Sons of God both Angels are and Men;
If I to try whether in higher sort
Than these thou bear'st that title, have propos'd
What both from Men and Angels I receive,   200
Tetrarchs of fire, air, flood, and on the earth
Nations besides from all the quarter'd winds,
God of this world invok't and world beneath;
Who then thou art, whose coming is foretold
To me so fatal, me it most concerns.   205
The trial hath indamag'd thee no way,
Rather more honor left and more esteem;
Mee naught advantag'd, missing what I aim'd.
Therefore let pass, as they are transitory,
The Kingdoms of this world; I shall no more   210
Advise thee, gain them as thou canst, or not.
And thou thyself seem'st otherwise inclin'd
Than to a worldly Crown, addicted more
To contemplation and profound dispute,
As by that early action may be judg'd,   215
When slipping from thy Mother's eye thou went'st
Alone into the Temple; there wast found
Among the gravest Rabbis disputant
On points and questions fitting *Moses'* Chair,
Teaching not taught; the childhood shows the man, 220
As morning shows the day. Be famous then
By wisdom; as thy Empire must extend,
So let extend thy mind o'er all the world,
In knowledge, all things in it comprehend.
All knowledge is not couch't in *Moses'* Law,   225
The *Pentateuch* or what the Prophets wrote;
The *Gentiles* also know, and write, and teach
To admiration, led by Nature's light;
And with the *Gentiles* much thou must converse,
Ruling them by persuasion as thou mean'st,   230
Without thir learning how wilt thou with them,
Or they with thee hold conversation meet?
How wilt thou reason with them, how refute
Thir Idolisms, Traditions, Paradoxes?
Error by his own arms is best evinc't.   235

197. Hosea (i, 10) anticipated Paul's doctrine that all men who "are led by the spirit of God are sons of God" (Rom. viii, 14). Satan is included among the "sons of God" in Job i, 6.

201–203. Cf. *PR* II, 122–4. *Tetrarch* was a title meaning ruler of a fourth part of a country, but is given to the demons who are assigned to their proper elements among the traditional four. Satan's subordinates give him power over the elements, and human blindness to truth makes him "the god of this world" (II Cor. iv, 4).

215–220. Cf. Christ's talks in the Temple with the Pharisees who pretended to "sit in Moses' seat" (Matt. xxiii, 2).

226. *Pentateuch*: the first five books of the Bible, embodying the Mosaic law.

234. *Idolism*: idolatry.

235. Satan's principle—as Miss Samuel shows in *P&M*, p. 124—is the essence of the sophistry which Socrates refutes in all his criticism of the sophists who boasted of the rhetorical power which they could give to their pupils.

Look once more ere we leave this specular Mount
Westward, much nearer by Southwest, behold
Where on the *Aegean* shore a City stands
Built nobly, pure the air, and light the soil,
Athens, the eye of *Greece,* Mother of Arts   240
And Eloquence, native to famous wits
Or hospitable, in her sweet recess,
City or Suburban, studious walks and shades;
See there the Olive Grove of *Academe,*
Plato's retirement, where the *Attic* Bird   245
Trills her thick-warbl'd notes the summer long;
There flow'ry hill *Hymettus* with the sound
Of Bees' industrious murmur oft invites
To studious musing; there *Ilissus* rolls
His whispering stream; within the walls then view   250
The schools of ancient Sages; his who bred
Great *Alexander* to subdue the world,
Lyceum there, and painted *Stoa* next;
There thou shalt hear and learn the secret power
Of harmony in tones and numbers hit   255
By voice or hand, and various-measur'd verse,
Aeolian charms and *Dorian Lyric* Odes,
And his who gave them breath, but higher sung,
Blind *Melesigenes* thence *Homer* call'd,
Whose Poem *Phoebus* challeng'd for his own.   260
Thence what the lofty grave Tragedians taught
In *Chorus* or *Iambic,* teachers best
Of moral prudence, with delight receiv'd
In brief sententious precepts, while they treat
Of fate, and chance, and change in human life,   265
High actions, and high passions best describing:
Thence to the famous Orators repair,
Those ancient, whose resistless eloquence
Wielded at will that fierce Democraty,
Shook the Arsenal and fulmin'd over *Greece,*   270
To *Macedon,* and *Artaxerxes'* Throne;
To sage Philosophy next lend thine ear,
From Heaven descended to the low-rooft house
Of *Socrates,* see there his Tenement,

---

236. *specular Mount:* lookout mountain. Latin *specula* means "watch-tower."

239. Plato (*Tim.,* 24C) attributed the intelligence of the Athenians to the clear air and light soil of their city.

244. Plato's Academy was in an *Olive Grove* near Athens.

247–250. The *Ilissus* rises on the slopes of Mt. Hymettus—famous for its honey—and flows through Athens.

251–253. In the walks of a park called the *Lyceum* Aristotle, who was once Alexander's tutor, founded his Peripatetic School of philosophy. The founder of the Stoics, Zeno, taught in the *Stoa* or colonnade in the Athenian market-place, which Pausanias described (I, iii. 1; XIV, vi, 3) as decorated by famous painters.

257. Cf. *charm* in PL IV, 642. *Aeolian* lyric poetry is best known through Sappho's songs, and

Dorian by Pindar's odes.

259. *Melesigenes:* Homer, who, according to one tradition, was born near the river Meles in Ionia. An epigram in the *Palatine Anthology* (IX, 455) has Apollo say: "It was I who sang, but divine Homer wrote it down."

262. Aside from the choral odes, Greek tragedy mainly used iambic meter.

269. *Democraty:* democracy.

270–271. Milton thought of situations like that described in Aristophanes' *Acharnians,* 530, when Pericles "thundered and lightened and confounded Hellas" when the Athenians were pitted against Sparta and her Persian ally, *Artaxerxes.*

274–294. Socrates' recognition by the Delphic oracle as the wisest of men was interpreted in the light of his confession of ignorance of all the science of which men are usually proud in Plato's *Phaedo* (96A–99D). See the Introduction 12.

Whom well inspir'd the Oracle pronounc'd   275
Wisest of men; from whose mouth issu'd forth
Mellifluous streams that water'd all the schools
Of Academics old and new, with those
Surnam'd *Peripatetics,* and the Sect
Epicurean, and the *Stoic* severe;   280
These here revolve, or, as thou lik'st, at home,
Till time mature thee to a Kingdom's weight;
These rules will render thee a King complete
Within thyself, much more with Empire join'd.
    To whom our Savior sagely thus replied.   285
Think not but that I know these things; or think
I know them not; not therefore am I short
Of knowing what I ought: he who receives
Light from above, from the fountain of light,
No other doctrine needs, though granted true;   290
But these are false, or little else but dreams,
Conjectures, fancies, built on nothing firm.
The first and wisest of them all profess'd
To know this only, that he nothing knew;
The next to fabling fell and smooth conceits;   295
A third sort doubted all things, though plain sense;
Others in virtue plac'd felicity,
But virtue join'd with riches and long life;
In corporal pleasure he, and careless ease;
The Stoic last in Philosophic pride,   300
By him call'd virtue; and his virtuous man,
Wise, perfect in himself, and all possessing
Equal to God, oft shames not to prefer,
As fearing God nor man, contemning all
Wealth, pleasure, pain or torment, death and life,   305
Which when he lists, he leaves, or boasts he can,
For all his tedious talk is but vain boast,
Or subtle shifts conviction to evade.
Alas! what can they teach, and not mislead;
Ignorant of themselves, of God much more,   310
And how the world began, and how man fell
Degraded by himself, on grace depending?
Much of the Soul they talk, but all awry,
And in themselves seek virtue, and to themselves
All glory arrogate, to God give none,   315
Rather accuse him under usual names,
Fortune and Fate, as one regardless quite
Of mortal things. Who therefore seeks in these
True wisdom, finds her not, or by delusion
Far worse, her false resemblance only meets,   320

296. Pyrrho founded the sceptical school, of which *Carneades* became the leader in the second century B.C. Cf. l. 234, n.

299. *he:* Epicurus, founder of the Epicurean school. Cf. l. 280.

300–308. Condemnation of the Stoic exaggeration of the ideal of the perfectly virtuous and passionless man runs from Cicero's criticism of it in *De finibus* Bks. III–IV, through Augustine's *The City of God* XII, xi, to Milton's own rejection of "stoical apathy" in *CD* II, x, as "inconsistent with

true patience; as may be seen in Job and other saints under pressure of affliction." Jean Francois Senault's *De l'usage des passions* (1641) opens with a declaration that the Stoic ideal had been the laughing-stock of the centuries.

314–318. The thought parallels Cicero's plea in *De natura deorum* III, xxxvi, that, to be genuine, virtue must be rooted in the heart, and not be, like the goods of fortune, a gift of the gods.

320–321. The hidden story behind the lines is that of Ixion's deception by Jove with a cloud image

An empty cloud. However, many books
Wise men have said are wearisome; who reads
Incessantly, and to his reading brings not
A spirit and judgment equal or superior
(And what he brings, what needs he elsewhere seek)   325
Uncertain and unsettl'd still remains,
Deep verst in books and shallow in himself,
Crude or intoxicate, collecting toys,
And trifles for choice matters, worth a sponge;
As Children gathering pebbles on the shore.   330
Or if I would delight my private hours
With Music or with Poem, where so soon
As in our native Language can I find
That solace? All our Law and Story strew'd
With Hymns, our Psalms with artful terms inscrib'd   335
Our Hebrew Songs and Harps in *Babylon,*
That pleas'd so well our Victors' ear, declare
That rather *Greece* from us these Arts deriv'd;
Ill imitated, while they loudest sing
The vices of thir Deities, and thir own   340
In Fable, Hymn, or Song, so personating
Thir Gods ridiculous, and themselves past shame.
Remove their swelling Epithets thick laid
As varnish on a Harlot's cheek, the rest,
Thin sown with aught of profit or delight,   345
Will far be found unworthy to compare
With *Sion's* songs, to all true tastes excelling,
Where God is prais'd aright, and Godlike men,
The Holiest of Holies, and his Saints;
Such are from God inspir'd, not such from thee;   350
Unless where moral virtue is express'd
By light of Nature, not in all quite lost.
Thir Orators thou then extoll'st, as those
The top of Eloquence, Statists indeed,
And lovers of thir Country, as may seem;   355
But herein to our Prophets far beneath,
As men divinely taught, and better teaching
The solid rules of Civil Government
In thir majestic unaffected style
Than all the Oratory of *Greece* and *Rome.*   360
In them is plainest taught, and easiest learnt,

of Juno, on which he begot the centaurs. Cf. Ovid (*Met.* XII, 504–6).

321–322. "Of making many books there is no end" (Eccl. xii, 12).

328. *crude* keeps its Latin meaning of "surfeited."

329. *worth a sponge:* fit to be expunged.

334. *Story:* history. Cf. *PR* II, 307.

335. *artful:* full of art. The reference is to the *terms* in the Psalms indicating their poetical class and the instruments appropriate to them.

336–337. "By the rivers of Babylon, there we sat down. . . . For there they that carried us away captive required of us a song" (Ps. cxxxvii, 1–3).

338. Cf. Jonson in *Timber* (*Works,* Ed. Herford & Simpson, Oxford, 1947; VIII, 636) "[Poesy] had her original from heaven, received thence from the Hebrews, and had in prime estimation with the Greeks, transmitted to the Latins and all nations that professed civility."

343. Milton thought of Homeric epithets like the "far-darter" for Apollo and "the golden" or "the crowned" for Aphrodite.

346–350. Cf. Sir Philip Sidney's confidence in *An Apologie for Poetry* (*Works,* Ed. Feuillerat, Cambridge, 1923; III, 9) that the best poets were the biblical writers who "did imitate the unconceivable excellencies of GOD. Such were David in his Psalms, Salomon in his song of songs, in his Ecclesiastes, and Proverbs, *Moses* and *Debora* in their Hymns, and the writer of *Job.*" See the Introduction 12–14.

354. *Statists:* statesmen.

What makes a Nation happy, and keeps it so,
What ruins Kingdoms, and lays Cities flat;
These only, with our Law, best form a King.
 So spake the Son of God; but Satan now   365
Quite at a loss, for all his darts were spent,
Thus to our Savior with stern brow replied.
 Since neither wealth, nor honor, arms nor arts,
Kingdom nor Empire pleases thee, nor aught
By me propos'd in life contemplative,   370
Or active, tended on by glory, or fame,
What dost thou in this World? The Wilderness
For thee is fittest place; I found thee there,
And thither will return thee; yet remember
What I foretell thee; soon thou shalt have cause 375
To wish thou never hadst rejected thus
Nicely or cautiously my offer'd aid,
Which would have set thee in short time with ease
On *David's* Throne, or Throne of all the world,
Now at full age, fulness of time, thy season, 380
When Prophecies of thee are best fullfill'd.
Now contrary, if I read aught in Heaven,
Or Heav'n write aught of Fate, by what the Stars
Voluminous, or single characters
In their conjunction met, give me to spell, 385
Sorrows, and labors, opposition, hate,
Attends thee, scorns, reproaches, injuries,
Violence and stripes, and lastly cruel death.
A Kingdom they portend thee, but what Kingdom,
Real or Allegoric I discern not,   390
Nor when, eternal sure, as without end,
Without beginning; for no date prefixt
Directs me in the Starry Rubric set.
 So saying he took (for still he knew his power
Not yet expir'd) and to the Wilderness 395
Brought back the Son of God, and left him there,
Feigning to disappear. Darkness now rose,
As daylight sunk, and brought in louring night,
Her shadowy offspring, unsubstantial both,
Privation mere of light and absent day. 400
Our Savior meek and with untroubl'd mind
After his airy jaunt, though hurried sore,
Hungry and cold betook him to his rest,
Wherever, under some concourse of shades
Whose branching arms thick intertwin'd might shield 405
From dews and damps of night his shelter'd head;

366. Perhaps a reference to "the fiery darts of the wicked" (Eph. vi, 16), which are turned by "the shield of faith."

370–371. For the distinction between the active and contemplative ideals see the Introduction 16.

382–393. Cf. the rationalized interest and limited faith in judicial astrology which Milton indicates in *PL* X, 656–72. He may have known that such faith was not incompatible with Pico della Mirandola's *Confutation* of the astrologers, or with Calvin's treatise against astrology. Even Bishop Carleton, whose book on *The madness of the astrologers*

(1624) attacked them on essentially scientific grounds, regarded them as dupes and tools of the devil. Newton suggested that Milton is satirizing the Italian astrologer Jerome Cardan (1501–1576) for a famous attempt to cast the horoscope of Jesus.

385. *conjunction:* the apparent near approach of two stars or planets. It was an unfavorable "aspect" in astrology. Cf. *PL* X, 661.

393. *Rubric:* any formal document containing laws or liturgies.

398. Cf. *unessential Night* in *PL* II, 439.

402. *jaunt* originally meant a tiring journey.

But shelter'd slept in vain, for at his head
The Tempter watch'd, and soon with ugly dreams
Disturb'd his sleep; and either Tropic now
'Gan thunder, and both ends of Heav'n; the Clouds   410
From many a horrid rift abortive pour'd
Fierce rain with lightning mixt, water with fire
In ruin reconcil'd: nor slept the winds
Within thir stony caves, but rush'd abroad
From the four hinges of the world, and fell   415
On the vext Wilderness, whose tallest Pines,
Though rooted deep as high, and sturdiest Oaks
Bow'd thir Stiff necks, loaden with stormy blasts,
Or torn up sheer: ill wast thou shrouded then,
O patient Son of God, yet only stood'st   420
Unshaken; nor yet stay'd the terror there.
Infernal Ghosts, and Hellish Furies, round
Environ'd thee, some howl'd, some yell'd, some shriek'd,
Some bent at thee thir fiery darts, while thou
Satt'st unappall'd in calm and sinless peace.   425
Thus pass'd the night so foul till morning fair
Came forth with Pilgrim steps in amice gray;
Who with her radiant finger still'd the roar
Of thunder, chas'd the clouds, and laid the winds,
And grisly Specters, which the Fiend had rais'd   430
To tempt the Son of God with terrors dire.
And now the Sun with more effectual beams
Had cheer'd the face of Earth, and dried the wet
From drooping plant, or dropping tree; the birds
Who all things now behold more fresh and green,   435
After a night of storm so ruinous,
Clear'd up their choicest notes in bush and spray
To gratulate the sweet return of morn.
Nor yet amidst this joy and brightest morn
Was absent, after all his mischief done,   440
The Prince of darkness; glad would also seem
Of this fair change, and to our Savior came,
Yet with no new device, they all were spent;
Rather by this his last affront resolv'd,
Desperate of better course, to vent his rage   445
And mad despite to be so oft repell'd.
Him walking on a Sunny hill he found,
Back'd on the North and West by a thick wood;
Out of the wood he starts in wonted shape,
And in a careless mood thus to him said.   450
    Fair morning yet betides thee, Son of God,
After a dismal night; I heard the rack

407–409. Cf. Satan, "close at the ear of Eve," inspiring an evil dream in *PL* IV, 799–809.

409. *Tropic* is used loosely for the opposite parts of the sky.

410–419. It suits Milton's purpose to disregard Reginald Scot's denial in *The Discoverie of Witchcraft* that Satan has any power over the weather, the lightning or thunder, and to assume with Burton (*Anatomy* I, ii, 1, 2; Vol. I, 191) that "Aerial spirits . . . cause many tempests, thunder, and lightnings, tear oaks, fire steeples, houses. . . ."

The great Calvinist divine William Perkins definitely listed "the raising of stormes, tempests, winds and weather" among the powers of the devil in his *Discourse of Witchcraft* (1608, p. 128).

420. *only:* preëminent. Cf. "your onely Jigge-maker" (*Hamlet* III, ii, 131).

426–430. Cf. *L'All,* 114.

427. *amice:* a hood or cape, lined with grey fur, worn by some monastic orders.

436. Cf. *ruin* in *PL* I, 46 and *PR* IV, 413.

As Earth and Sky would mingle, but myself
Was distant; and these flaws, though mortals fear them
As dangerous to the pillar'd frame of Heaven,   455
Or to the Earth's dark basis underneath,
Are to the main as inconsiderable
And harmless, if not wholesome, as a sneeze
To man's less universe, and soon are gone;
Yet as being oftimes noxious where they light   460
On man, beast, plant, wasteful and turbulent,
Like turbulencies in the affairs of men,
Over whose heads they roar, and seem to point,
They oft fore-signify and threaten ill:
This Tempest at this Desert most was bent;   465
Of men at thee, for only thou here dwell'st.
Did I not tell thee, if thou didst reject
The perfect season offer'd with my aid
To win thy destin'd seat, but wilt prolong
All to the push of Fate, pursue thy way   470
Of gaining *David's* Throne no man knows when,
For both the when and how is nowhere told,
Thou shalt be what thou art ordain'd, no doubt;
For Angels have proclaim'd it, but concealing
The time and means: each act is rightliest done,   475
Not when it must, but when it may be best.
If thou observe not this, be sure to find,
What I foretold thee, many a hard assay
Of dangers, and adversities and pains,
Ere thou of *Israel's* Scepter get fast hold;   480
Whereof this ominous night that clos'd thee round,
So many terrors, voices, prodigies
May warn thee, as a sure foregoing sign.
    So talk'd he, while the Son of God went on
And stay'd not, but in brief him answer'd thus.   485
    Mee worse than wet thou find'st not; other harm
Those terrors which thou speak'st of, did me none;
I never fear'd they could, though noising loud
And threat'ning nigh; what they can do as signs
Betok'ning or ill-boding I contemn   490
As false portents, not sent from God, but thee;
Who, knowing I shall reign past thy preventing,
Obtrud'st thy offer'd aid, that I accepting
At least might seem to hold all power of thee,
Ambitious spirit, and wouldst be thought my God,   495
And storm'st refus'd, thinking to terrify
Mee to thy will; desist, thou art discern'd
And toil'st in vain, nor me in vain molest.
    To whom the Fiend now swoln with rage replied:
Then hear, O Son of *David,* Virgin-born;   500

453. A clear reminiscence of Virgil's description
of a Mediterranean storm that mingled earth and
sky (*Aen.* I, 133–4).
    455. "The pillars of heaven tremble and are
astonished at his reproof" (Job xxvi, 11).
    457. *main:* the universe.
    458–459. Milton is not straining "the ancient
opinion that man was *microcosmus,* an abstract or
model of the world," which Bacon said in the
Advancement of Learning (II, x, 2) "had been
fantastically strained by Paracelsus and the alchemists." Like Sir Thomas Browne in *Pseudodoxia Epidemica* IV, ix (*Works,* Ed. by Geoffrey
Keynes, London, 1928; III, 41), he was simply
agreeing with medical opinion from Aristotle down
that a sneeze is a good symptom.

For Son of God to me is yet in doubt:
Of the Messiah I have heard foretold
By all the Prophets; of thy birth at length
Announc't by *Gabriel,* with the first I knew,
And of the Angelic Song in *Bethlehem* field,   505
On thy birth-night, that sung thee Savior born.
From that time seldom have I ceas'd to eye
Thy infancy, thy childhood, and thy youth,
Thy manhood last, though yet in private bred;
Till at the Ford of *Jordan* whither all   510
Flock'd to the Baptist, I among the rest,
Though not to be Baptiz'd, by voice from Heav'n
Heard thee pronounc'd the Son of God belov'd.
Thenceforth I thought thee worth my nearer view
And narrower Scrutiny, that I might learn   515
In what degree or meaning thou art call'd
The Son of God, which bears no single sense;
The Son of God I also am, or was,
And if I was, I am; relation stands;
All men are Sons of God; yet thee I thought   520
In some respect far higher so declar'd.
Therefore I watch'd thy footsteps from that hour,
And follow'd thee still on to this waste wild,
Where by all best conjectures I collect
Thou art to be my fatal enemy.   525
Good reason then, if I beforehand seek
To understand my Adversary, who
And what he is; his wisdom, power, intent,
By parle, or composition, truce, or league
To win him, or win from him what I can.   530
And opportunity I here have had
To try thee, sift thee, and confess have found thee
Proof against all temptation as a rock
Of Adamant, and as a Center, firm;
To th'utmost of mere man both wise and good,   535
Not more; for Honors, Riches, Kingdoms, Glory
Have been before contemn'd, and may again:
Therefore to know what more thou art than man,
Worth naming Son of God by voice from Heav'n,
Another method I must now begin.   540
    So saying he caught him up, and without wing
Of *Hippogrif* bore through the Air sublime
Over the Wilderness and o'er the Plain;
Till underneath them fair *Jerusalem,*
The holy City, lifted high her Towers,   545
And higher yet the glorious Temple rear'd
Her pile, far off appearing like a Mount

---

501. See the Introduction 2–5.
525. Cf. God's *fatal throne* in *PL* II, 104, and Satan's *fatal* (i. e. fated) *wound* in *PR* I, 53.
529. *parle:* parley, negotiation.
534. Cf. *Adamant* in *PL* VI, 110, and *diamond* in *PL* VI, 364. *Center:* point of equilibrium in a heavy body.
542. Milton thought of Ariosto's tale of Astolfo's journey to the moon on a *Hippogrif:*

Only the Beast he rode was not of art,
But gotten of a Griffeth on a Mare,
And like a Griffeth had the former part,
As Wings and Head, and Claws that hideous are,
And passing strength and force, and ventrous Heart,
But all the rest may with a Horse compare.
    (*Orlando Furioso* IV, 13. Harrington's Tr.)
546. This is the *Temple* built by Herod the Great on the site of Solomon's temple.

Of Alabaster, top't with golden Spires:
There on the highest Pinnacle he set
The Son of God, and added thus in scorn.   550
    There stand, if thou wilt stand; to stand upright
Will ask thee skill; I to thy Father's house
Have brought thee, and highest plac't, highest is best,
Now show thy Progeny; if not to stand,
Cast thyself down; safely if Son of God: 555
For it is written, He will give command
Concerning thee to his Angels, in thir hands
They shall up lift thee, lest at any time
Thou chance to dash thy foot against a stone.
    To whom thus Jesus. Also it is written,   560
Tempt not the Lord thy God; he said and stood.
But Satan smitten with amazement fell
As when Earth's Son *Antaeus* (to compare
Small things with greatest) in *Irassa* strove
With *Jove's Alcides,* and oft foil'd still rose,   565
Receiving from his mother Earth new strength,
Fresh from his fall, and fiercer grapple join'd,
Throttl'd at length in th'Air, expir'd and fell;
So after many a foil the Tempter proud,
Renewing fresh assaults, amidst his pride   570
Fell whence he stood to see his Victor fall.
And as that *Theban* Monster that propos'd
Her riddle, and him who solv'd it not, devour'd,
That once found out and solv'd, for grief and spite
Cast herself headlong from th' *Ismenian* steep,   575
So struck with dread and anguish fell the Fiend,
And to his crew, that sat consulting, brought
Joyless triumphals of his hop't success,
Ruin, and desperation, and dismay,
Who durst so proudly tempt the Son of God.   580
So Satan fell; and straight a fiery Globe
Of Angels on full sail of wing flew nigh,
Who on their plumy Vans receiv'd him soft
From his uneasy station, and upbore
As on a floating couch through the blithe Air,   585
Then in a flow'ry valley set him down
On a green bank, and set before him spread.
A table of Celestial Food, Divine,
Ambrosial, Fruits fetcht from the tree of life,
And from the fount of life Ambrosial drink,   590
That soon refresh'd him wearied, and repair'd

---

554. *Progeny:* birth, descent, parentage.
556–559. The lines paraphrase Psalm xci, 11–12.
561. Cf. Deut. vi, 16. See the Introduction 3.
563–571. Hercules is called *Alcides* for his grandfather Alceus. Milton seems to have remembered Pindar's account of the struggle with the giant *Antaeus* as occurring in *Irassa* in Cyrenaica (*Isthmian Odes,* iii, 87). See the Introduction 22.
572–575. The *Monster* is the Sphinx which threw itself from the acropolis of Thebes into the river Ismenus when Oedipus found the answer, "Man," to her question which animal walks first on four, then on two, and finally on three legs. See the

Introduction 18.
    578. *triumphals:* celebrations. Said ironically.
    581. *Globe:* a circular phalanx of troops. Cf. PL II, 512.
    589. Cf. *Ambrosial* in PL II, 245.
    589–590. Milton remembered the Well of Life from which Spenser's Knight of Holiness drank at the crisis of his conflict with the Satanic dragon (*F.Q.* I, xi, 29) and also the place
        Where *Tigris* at the foot of Paradise
        Into a Gulf shot under ground, till part
        Rose up a Fountain by the Tree of Life.
                                        (PL IX, 71–73)

What hunger, if aught hunger had impair'd,
Or thirst; and as he fed, Angelic Choirs
Sung Heavenly Anthems of his victory
Over temptation and the Tempter proud. 595
    True Image of the Father, whether thron'd
In the bosom of bliss, and light of light
Conceiving, or remote from Heaven, enshrin'd
In fleshly Tabernacle, and human form,
Wand'ring the Wilderness, whatever place, 600
Habit, or state, or motion, still expressing
The Son of God, with Godlike force endu'd
Against th' Attempter of thy Father's Throne,
And Thief of Paradise; him long of old
Thou didst debel, and down from Heav'n cast 605
With all his Army; now thou hast aveng'd
Supplanted *Adam,* and by vanquishing
Temptation, hast regain'd lost Paradise,
And frustrated the conquest fraudulent:
He never more henceforth will dare set foot 610
In Paradise to tempt; his snares are broke:
For though that seat of earthly bliss be fail'd,
A fairer Paradise is founded now
For *Adam* and his chosen Sons, whom thou
A Savior art come down to reinstall, 615
Where they shall dwell secure, when time shall be
Of Tempter and Temptation without fear.
But thou, Infernal Serpent, shalt not long
Rule in the Clouds; like an Autumnal Star
Or Lightning thou shalt fall from Heav'n trod down 620
Under his feet: for proof, ere this thou feel'st
Thy wound, yet not thy last and deadliest wound
By this repulse receiv'd, and hold'st in Hell
No triumph; in all her gates *Abaddon* rues
Thy bold attempt; hereafter learn with awe 625
To dread the Son of God: hee all unarm'd
Shall chase thee with the terror of his voice
From thy Demoniac holds, possession foul,
Thee and thy Legions; yelling they shall fly,
And beg to hide them in a herd of Swine, 630
Lest he command them down into the deep,
Bound, and to torment sent before thir time.
Hail Son of the most High, heir of both worlds,
Queller of Satan, on thy glorious work

596–597. A reference to the opening verses of John's Gospel, where Christ, the Word, is said to have been from the beginning with God, who is Light and Life, and to have declared him to men, because He "is in the bosom of the Father" (i, 18).

605. *debel:* war down. Anchises uses the word in his prophecy of Rome's destiny as the destroyer of lawlessness throughout the world (*Aen.* VI, 853).

611. The line echoes Psalm cxxiv, 7: "The snare is broken, and we are escaped."

612. *be fail'd:* "be absent or wanting" is the first meaning of the word.

620–621. Christ's words, "I beheld Satan as light-

ning fall from heaven" (Luke x, 18) are fused with prophecies like Malachi's promise that "ye shall tread down the wicked" (Mal. iv, 3).

622. The picture is that of Satan's destruction at the end of time in Rev. xxii, 10.

624. *Abaddon* is the name of hell in Job xxvi, 6; xxviii, 22; and xxxi, 12.

629. Cf. the plea of the devils cast out of the swine by Jesus in Matt. viii, 29: "Art thou come hither to torment us before the time?"

634–635. J. Whaler notes in *Counterpoint,* p. 23, that these lines echo both the substance and the meter of a hymn of the sixth century poet and rhetorician Venantius Fortunatus.

Now enter, and begin to save mankind. 635
    Thus they the Son of God our Savior meek
Sung Victor, and from Heavenly Feast refresht
Brought on his way with joy; hee unobserv'd
Home to his Mother's house private return'd.

The End.

639. Cf. Satan's sneer at Christ's love of "private   life" in III, 231–32 and his contempt for the life
                which Christ lived in Nazareth.

Samson Agonistes

INTRODUCTION

I

Venerable tradition has made *Samson* the last of Milton's poems and seen it as coming to birth in the years just before its first edition in 1671 in a volume whose title leaves its date a mystery: *Paradise Regain'd A Poem. To which is added Samson Agonistes.* Until 1949, when composition at earlier dates had seldom been suggested, Milton was regarded as writing his drama in old age and as more or less drawing his own portrait in his blind hero. Now we have a choice of four times in Milton's life for the writing of *Samson:* Masson's traditional and vague 1666 to 1670; Woodhouse's "year before the Restoration (May, 1660) and the spring of 1661,"[1] Parker's surmise of "the period 1647–1653,"[2] and Gilbert's proposal of an earlier time,[3] perhaps not much later than Milton's draft of plans for five Samson plays as we have them in the Trinity Manuscript. This would mean at least a first draft of the drama quite as early as the sixteen-forties. It would also imply preoccupation at the time of writing *Samson* with the other related subjects which we find sketched in the manuscript: *Samson at Ramath-Lechi*, to which lines 142–145 of the drama as we have it refer, or *Samson marrying*—marrying, not Dalila, but "the woman of Timna" who is mentioned in lines 219–226 and 381–387: *Dagonalia*, or the feast of the Philistine god Dagon, which is the setting of the catastrophe in our *Samson; Samson Pursophorus,* or the arsonist Samson who drove three hundred foxes with torches on their tails into the standing corn of the Philistines; *Samson Hybristes,* or Samson yielding to pride (*hybris*) of the kind which led to the downfall of the heroes in many Greek tragedies.

The case for composition early in the sixteen-forties does not rest alone upon Milton's allegedly inartistic allusions to the themes of other Samson plays which were floating in his mind. In any dramatization of the story as we have it in Judges xiii–xvi a seventeenth-century audience would look for references to some events in the hero's life outside of the play. Familiarity with the entire biblical account would have been assumed, just as familiarity with the myth behind a tragedy like the *Mad Hercules* of Euripides would have been assumed in an Athenian audience. Flashbacks to the foxes and the woman of Timna were as understandable and interesting for Milton's public as they would be frustrating for the audience which Leonid Andreyev had in mind for his *Samson in Chains.* If a modern reader knows the biblical record, and if he is stirred by Milton's treatment of its most famous secondary character, Dalila, he will not boggle over Milton's flashbacks. Indeed, he will see them as vital parts of the action, which really begins long before we meet Samson, "eyeless in Gaza," at the opening of Milton's drama.[4] Reactions to the three middle episodes differ. For some readers the central one is "the magnificent episode of Dalila" (as Saurat called it in *La Pensée de Milton,* p. 350). But if a reader agrees with Allan Gilbert that Dalila's scene is any-

---

[1] In Transactions of the Royal Society of Canada, 3rd Series, XLIII (1949), 157–75.
[2] In *PQ*, XXVIII (1949), 164.
[3] In *PQ*, XXVIII (1949), 98–106.
[4] The point is made by M. E. Grenander in *"Samson's* Middle: Aristotle and Dr. Johnson," in *UTQ*, XXIV (1955), 377–89.

thing but splendid—that it is a comic failure, he may also agree that the following episode between Samson and the giant Harapha (who is entirely Milton's invention) is a collapse into comedy of the kind that Milton himself said in his preface to the drama ought never to intrude into tragedy. For a reader sharing Gilbert's views of those key episodes the entire drama must seem to fall short of success and to betray more than enough crudity to confirm the suspicion that it was unfinished work of the early sixteen-forties which Milton allowed his publisher to use to pad the volume of 1671.

The case for the composition of *Samson* in the early forties is really in something the same position as Dr. Johnson's complaint that the drama "has a beginning and an end which Aristotle himself could not have disapproved," but that it must "be allowed to have no middle, since nothing passes between the first act and the last, that either hastens or delays the death of Samson." In its way Gilbert's criticism impugns Milton's artistry as seriously as does Dr. Johnson's. Perhaps in the end the only reply to him must be in terms of the autonomy of taste. If a reader is not moved by the three middle episodes of the drama—by the irony of Manoa's hope for his son's ransom, or the passionate inconsistency of Dalila's pleas and insults to Samson, or by his repulse of Harapha—for that reader it has no conflict, no causality, no crisis nor form. For him, as for Max Beerbohm, "the *personae* come on, speak, go off, without any swelling or expediting the volume of the idea"; and the result must be that all of them seem "quite static and marmoreal."[5] If the middle episodes lack dramatic tension, then the characters are dead—the victims of the "general lifelessness, or general effect of factitious, mechanical life," of which F. R. Leavis roundly pronounces them guilty.[6]

II

Dalila

Today it may seem inevitable that a scene with Dalila, the Philistine who betrayed her lover to save her country, should be the keystone of any Samson drama, as it is in Andreyev's play. In the seventeenth century it was not clear that in a classical tragedy whose action occurred on the last day of the hero's life she had a proper place. Psychologically, she was not supposed to be any more interesting than Cecil de Mille has made her. She was the "lemman Dalida" of Chaucer's Monk's Tale, to whom

he tolde
That in his heeris al his strengthe lay.

The mediaeval stereotype, as Michael Krouse has shown, persisted into the Renaissance, and in allegorical interpretations of the story she could even be "interpreted as a figure of Judas," while "her attempts to learn from Samson the secret of his strength were compared also with Satan's temptation of Christ."[7] Milton might have made her merely the bearer of a "fair enchanted cup" and the singer of "warbling charms"—an example such as Spenser saw in her of the "wondrous powre" of

Womens faire aspect
To captive men and make them all the world reject.[8]

In Spenser's stanza Dalila's name is linked with Cleopatra's, but in *The Faerie Queene*

---

[5] *The Saturday Review of Literature, Politics, and Science,* LXXXIX (1900), 489.
[6] *Revaluation,* Third Impression, 1953, p. 65.
[7] *Milton's Samson,* p. 76. Krouse noted that among theological commentators only Cardinal Cajetan "made any attempt to defend Dalila," and that he did so on the strange ground that she was really a Hebrew, not a Philistine, and that she was lured into betraying Samson by the promise that his captors would do him no bodily harm.
[8] *F.Q.* V, viii, 2, 8-9.

there is no trace of psychological development such as Shakespeare gave to Cleopatra, or Milton to Dalila. If the two women are to be compared at all, it should be only on the basis of the contrast between the very different kinds of plays that we have in *Antony and Cleopatra* and *Samson*. In a classically designed tragedy it might have seemed wisest to Milton to follow the example of the Dutch poet Vondel in *Samson of Heilige Wraeck* and leave the wicked Dalila out of the action altogether.

Milton's motive for putting Dalila into his drama is easy to oversimplify. Most readers ignore E. M. W. Tillyard's warning that Samson's failure was due less to sensuality than to pride and assume, without recognizing the mediaeval tradition, that Milton's Dalila reflects his dislike of women or his bitter memories of Mary Powell. Or they compare Milton with Euripides as a "misogynist" and equate Dalila's final violence with Medea's boast of wringing Jason's heart by the murder of their sons. But Jason and Medea reverse the relation between Samson and Dalila. Euripides' Jason has betrayed his wife and the chorus is as frankly on the woman's side as Milton's chorus is with Samson. For a true counterpart to Milton's situation William R. Parker rightly sends us to Euripides' *Troades*, where after the fall of Troy Helen makes Dalila's mistake of going to her husband gorgeously dressed—in Trojan finery. Her defense of her elopement with Paris sounds rather like Dalila's justification of her treason. Helen's first excuse is patriotic: "she has saved Greece by her sacrifice. She then pleads a religious excuse: her disappearance from home was the will of the gods. . . . Like Dalila, she concludes by asking pardon."[9]   And Hecuba's retort to her final plea—"Charge not the gods with folly!"—is like Samson's retort of Dalila's "ungodly deeds" upon her head. The resemblance of Euripides' situations to the quarrel between Samson and Dalila is too distinct for accident and too close not to challenge comparison. In *Samson* the balanced speeches are shorter and more effective than they are in Euripides' play. The sophisticated rhetoric of the parties in the wrong is all of a piece, and in Dalila's case it is good enough to lure a modern critic into a protest that "her speeches do not betray her as a scheming woman, as they should if the audience is to know her as such. On the other hand, what object could Milton have in presenting her as repentant and genuinely asking for forgiveness?"[10]

The two possible replies to the question are not necessarily mutually exclusive: Dalila may be regarded as skillful enough an actress to fool the reader if not her husband, or Milton may have intended passion for Samson to be the real key to her character. On that assumption—which by Milton's standards would be less creditable to her than it would be by modern romantic ones—we may regard her as more than superficially sincere in pleading jealousy as the motive for her betrayal of him and in promising to treat him with "redoubl'd love and care" if he will consent to live with her again. Psychologically, this theory is attractive. Indeed, it is even more attractive than Andreyev makes it in *Samson in Chains* when—just before the climax of the play—the lady chariots her blind lover through a desert storm with the cry: "No one but myself shall be your driver, my beloved, my soul!" This is unambiguous. Dalila's abrupt and bitter turn upon the irreconcilable Samson in the final speech that boasts of her future glory in Philistia as the savior of "her country from a fierce destroyer" seems equally unambiguous to the chorus, which pronounces her

> a manifest serpent by her sting
> Discover'd in the end, till now conceal'd. (ll. 997-98)

The modern reader, however, is free, if he likes, to see her as a more complex figure than she seems to the Danite chorus. For them she is the

[9] *Milton's Debt to Greek Tragedy*, p. 127. The case for the *Medea* as the stronger influence on *Samson* is made by P. W. Timberlake in *The Parrott Presentation Volume* (Princeton, 1935), pp. 334-38.
[10] James Waddell Tupper in "The Dramatic Structure of *Samson Agonistes*," PMLA, XXXV (1920), 382.

> wanton, whose distrustful eye
> Was fixt upon reward,

whom we meet in the naively-drawn portrait in Francis Quarles's *History of Samson* (1631). By filling Dalila's last speech with something like despair as well as pride, Milton has given us an incomparably richer character than Quarles drew, but he has no intention of including her in Samson's tragedy, or even of making her the main cause of his downfall.

It is important to remember Samson's confession:

> of what now I suffer
> She was not the prime cause, But I myself
> Who vanquisht with a peal of words (O weakness!)
> Gave up my fort of silence to a woman.   (ll. 233–36)

The point was made by all the commentators on the story of Samson in the Christian tradition that Milton inherited. All alike, as Krouse has abundantly demonstrated,[11] they blamed Samson for "his immoderate affections toward the wicked woman." The man's greater guilt, however, was not regarded as excusing the woman, nor was the "strange power" of injurious beauty to re-arouse a wronged lover's passion ever mistaken for evidence of sincere love. When the chorus congratulates Samson on having resisted the "secret sting of amorous remorse" (or pity) for Dalila, he at once corrects the implication that what has occurred was a lovers' quarrel:

> Love-quarrels oft in pleasing concord end,
> Not wedlock-treachery endangering life.   (ll. 1008–09)

Samson denies that Dalila has ever loved him. By making her his wife instead of the mistress that she is in the biblical story and in most Jewish and Christian commentaries on it, Milton intended to stress the depth of her treason and of Samson's infatuation.

In assessing the "anti-feminism" in the treatment of Dalila the traditional condemnation of her by the biblical commentators should be remembered, and so should requirements of the dramatic tradition that made the chorus the moral supporters of the protagonist. It is not Milton but the chorus speaking to the victim of a wily woman that we hear putting to Samson the sympathetic question:

> Is it for that such outward ornament
> Was lavish't on thir sex, that inward gifts
> Were left for haste unfinish't, judgment scant,
> Capacity not raised to apprehend
> Or value what is best
> In choice, but oftest to affect the wrong?   (ll. 1025–30)

Flat denial of all personal anti-feminism in Milton's chorus may be impossible, but Milton's embittered Danites are no harder on the sex than are Euripides' Corinthian women in the *Medea*. Samson himself—as Parker points out in his discussion of Milton's "misogyny"[12]—never generalizes about women, and he is not so hard on Dalila when she begs to be allowed to "approach at least, and touch thy hand" as is Menelaus on Helen when she makes the same appeal to him in the *Troades*. Only gross exaggeration of the dramatic evidence and of Dalila's importance in the drama as a whole can have betrayed anyone into the fancy that *"Samson Agonistes* is one massive tirade against feminine wiles and guiles."[13]

---

[11] *Milton's Samson*, p. 76. Cf. pp. 73 and 100–103.
[12] *Milton's Debt to Greek Tragedy*, pp. 127–30.
[13] The words are quoted from G. Wilson Knight in *The Burning Oracle*, p. 81.

III

Harapha

If a reader is incurably convinced that Milton was embittered against women either by his unhappy first marriage, or by his Puritanism, or by the medieval tradition that

> They were to good ends, and they are so still,
> But accessory, and principall in ill,[14]

(which could creep into a poem of serious compliment to a lady by John Donne), then he will see only personal spite against the sex in the choruses of *Samson*. As a result, he is likely to slip into the autobiographical fallacy again and read the following episode between Samson and Harapha as a complacent picture of Milton hugging a romanticized memory of his reply in his *Defense of the English People* to Salmasius' *Defensio regia pro Carolo I.* Milton *was* proud of his bout with the famous French prosecutor of the executioners of Charles I before the bar of European opinion, but it is a long step from direct confession of such pride in his controversial writings to indulgence of it in naive identification of himself with the hero of his drama. The suggestion that he may have done so goes back to Masson and still attracts critics who share Visiak's view of Milton as writing oblique autobiography in his tragedy—"Samson being Milton; Harapha, Salmasius."[15]

Visiak's statement is pure surmise. Some historical overtones there may be in the episode, but it is most impressive if Harapha is regarded as the embodiment of classes and attitudes to which we usually give the name "Cavalier." For more than a century editors have noticed that Harapha's bragging challenge of Samson to a duel has overtones of the romances about it. Recently it has been shown that Milton conceived the episode in the light of the duelling code that governed many situations in Italian plays that were almost certainly familiar to him—at least as a type—when he was in Italy. Harapha accuses Samson of three of the six crimes that books on the *duello* stamped as destroying a man's honor: lying, murder, and robbery. In reply to Samson's challenge, Harapha objects that he is infamous and barred by the code from duelling with a man of honor. A similar but not entirely consistent interpretation treats Harapha as a comic braggart stemming partly from the *miles gloriosus* of Plautus' plays but more directly from the boastful and cowardly knights of the tragi-comedies of Beaumont and Fletcher and their continental forerunners.[16] If Samson's triumph over Harapha seems too easy, the fact is to be explained by Milton's contempt for the "Cavaliers" whom he represented. Actually, however, as D. C. Allen insists, the victory is not easy; Harapha is a good fighting man who comes to see Samson, and it takes a hundred and fifty lines to reduce this Lancelot to a Braggadochio. For Allen the function of the scene is to restore Samson's faith in himself as God's champion. Denying all comedy in it, he makes it "the most

[14] *The First Anniversary*, 103–04.

[15] E. H. Visiak in *Milton Agonistes* (London, 1922), p. 99. In *Miltons Samson Agonistes* (Halle, 1926), pp. 54–56, C. E. Kreipe approves Masson's suggestion that, because Salmasius was contemporaneously called a gigantic figure, the giant in *Samson* is to be interpreted as a portrait of him. Kreipe also reviews the unconvincing evidence for the suggestion that Milton intended Harapha to represent the Duke of York. German criticism has too readily followed Mutschmann's reading of Milton's personality. Its most recent spokesman, Theodor Seibert—in "Egozentrisches in Miltons Schreibweise," *Anglia*, LIV (1930), 64—holds that Milton must have envied Samson his easy victories over Dalila and Harapha, and interprets them as poetic wish-fulfillments which are "naturlich auch egozentrisch, aber nicht eine simple Photographie des eigenen Lebens."

[16] The first interpretation is by Edith Buchanan in her Duke University doctoral thesis on The Italian Neo-Senecan Background of *Samson Agonistes* (1952); the second is by D. Boughner in "Milton's Harapha and Renaissance Comedy," *ELH*, XI (1944), 297–306.

important scene of all, for it is the hinge of the tragedy."[17]   And the scene is cardinal
as the final step in Samson's recovery of the chastened faith in himself and his divine
guidance that makes his impending death a victory. But in reading the episode as
vital to his regeneration is it necessary to exclude not only all comic intention but also
the overtone of satire of the trappings of chivalry that survived at the court of Charles II?

IV

Manoa

Up to this point in our survey of the criticism of the "middle" which Dr. Johnson
denied in Samson nothing has been said about the first of its three episodes—Samson's
interview with his father Manoa, who has been negotiating with the Philistines for his
ransom. It stands first because one of its functions is to remind the audience of the
facts about Samson's supernatural birth and sacred character as a Nazarite pledged to
abstinence from wine and from ever cutting his hair. In the development of the main
theme—Samson's recovery of his forfeited strength—its function is to show him as having
taken the first step towards recovery when he tells his father that his suffering is a
just punishment for his breach of his Nazarite's vow. His danger, as Manoa perceives,
is despair; but he conquers it in a burst of confidence in the final triumph of the God
whom he has betrayed over the Philistine deity in whose temple the audience know that
he will die. God, he says,

> be sure,
> Will not connive, or linger, thus provok'd,
> But will arise and his great name assert:
> *Dagon* must stoop, and shall ere long receive
> Such a discomfit, as shall quite despoil him
> Of all these boasted trophies won on me,
> And with confusion blank his worshippers. (ll. 465-72)

In Manoa's reply—". . . these words/ I as a prophecy receive"—we have a fore-
gleam of the fall of Dagon's temple and a foretaste of Manoa's role as the unconscious
prophet of the catastrophe to come. It is interesting to find less said about him in
Parker's chapter on him in *Milton's Debt to Greek Tragedy* than is said about him in
the chapter on dramatic irony and in the scattered discussions of peripeteia or the Aristotelian doctrine of a change of fortune in the catastrophe as a feature of the best tragic
plots. The irony flashes again and most poignantly at the moment of the fall of Dagon's
temple when Manoa is telling the chorus about his confidence that God would not have
permitted Samson's

> strength again to grow up with his hair
> Garrison'd round about him like a Camp
> Of faithful Soldiery, were not his purpose
> To use him further yet in some great service.
>   (ll. 1496-99)

As Manoa talks to the chorus at the moment of catastrophe about his plan to spend
everything for his son's ransom the irony reaches its climax in the father's assertion that
he is "fixt not to part hence without him." The resolution is realized in Manoa's sad
summons of his kindred to come and carry off the dead Samson

> With silent obsequy and funeral train,
> Home to his Father's house. (ll. 1732-33)

---

[17] In *The Harmonious Vision*, p. 91.

The structural skill of Milton's management of the irony to which Manoa contributes more than any other character is the best reply to the charge that *Samson* has no "middle." In the biblical story there is no foundation for Manoa's plan to ransom his son, out of which Milton developed so much of his unifying dramatic irony in Manoa's scenes early and late in the drama. The underlying design belongs to the mature art that conceals itself. As our examination of the play advances, more evidences of its fundamental artistic maturity will emerge to cast doubt on the suggestion that its crudities are too obvious for mature work.

V

The Date of Composition as Related to the Greek, Hebrew,
and Italian Elements in the Drama.

If now we turn to Parker's suggestion of the years 1646 to 1655 as the limits within which the presumably twice or thrice interrupted composition of *Samson* took place, we find him challenging the traditional dating on the ground that it rests on the "auto-biographical fallacy" of reading the drama simply as a portrait of Milton in old age. Yet Parker unhesitatingly reads it as a mirror of Milton's moods in his middle years. Like Sir Herbert Grierson, Parker sees the spirit of dramatic prophecy as dominant in the play—in contrast with the muting of the "tone of prophecy in the great epics." He regards *Samson* as dramatizing the same faith in great leaders as prompted the sonnets to Fairfax and Cromwell—"the conception that God chooses a few men—individuals, not nations—for the fulfillment of His mysterious purposes."[18] Certainly, this is quite true of the drama. Equally true is Parker's contention both in 1949 and earlier, in *Milton's Debt to Greek Tragedy*[19] in 1937, that *Samson* is a drama of regeneration with its action "largely confined to the hero's soul." In his essay on "The Date of *Samson Agonistes*" Parker repeats his earlier plea for the fusion of Greek and Christian ideals in what is essentially a "drama of regeneration" to which "the key" is the hero's faith in himself and God. In this interpretation readers of all opinions about the date of the play can concur. They may equally well follow Parker in his break-down of the action into four steps in regeneration: the achievement of patience, achievement of faith, conquest of the weakness that led to the hero's fall, and achievement of the power to respond to the divine call to further service. We may even go a step further and agree with Parker that after writing the *Second Defense*—after 1654—Milton always felt "national politics of far less importance than the human soul." All this we may believe and at the same time find that Parker strains the autobiographical evidence of Milton's first years of blindness to date the drama early in a way that Grierson does not do when he says that in *Samson* Milton composed "a dramatic vindication of his own life" and of the supporters of the Parliamentary cause as he looked back on it in the time of Charles II.

There is another doubtful side to the suggestion of 1646–1655 as limiting dates for the composition of *Samson*. After agreeing with Edward Phillips that its dates cannot be made definite, Parker argues from Phillips' *Life* that the drama was metrically influenced by Milton's experience in translating some of the Psalms into common meter in 1648, and still more in translating others in 1653 into "a great variety of rhyme and metrical patterns." It is not suggested—as recently it has been[20]—that his rhythms owe

---

[18] "The Date of *Samson Agonistes*," *PQ*, XXVIII (1949), 152–55.

[19] *Milton's Debt to Greek Tragedy in Samson Agonistes*, pp. 237–42.

[20] By Frank Kermode in "*Samson Agonistes* and Greek Prosody," *Durham University Journal*, XIV (1953), 59–63. For A. Ralli, who regards Milton's choruses as prosaic, they come to life only "where

something to the Hebrew. Parker believes that the fluidity of *Samson* is due to the fact that, like the *Ode to John Rouse* (1647), it is an experiment in "the free rhythms of the Greek chorus." In the "strangely anarchic rhythms" of the translations of 1653 he finds an even more striking resemblance to *Samson* in passages like that in Psalm vi, which must have moved Milton as he read it with failing sight amid his discouragements —especially the lines:

> . . . . . . my soul is troubled sore.
> And thou, O Lord, how long? Turn, Lord, restore
> My soul . . . . mine eye
> Through grief consumes, is waxen old and dark
> In the midst of all mine enemies that mark.

But just how Hebraic and just how Greek are the rhythms in the choruses of *Samson*? Were they truly one or the other or a mixture of both? Milton described them as "introduc'd after the Greek manner, not antient only but modern, and still in use among the Italians. In modelling this poem . . . the Antients and *Italians* are rather follow'd, as of more authority and fame." Taking the obvious hint in this statement by Milton himself, recent scholarship has compared his choruses with those in a great number of Italian plays. Miss Finney's study of "Chorus in *Samson Agonistes*"[21] first made it clear that Milton's great quarry of examples for his rhythms was in Italy, and her conclusion has been confirmed and at the same time moderated by Mrs. Dufner's careful analysis of a much larger number of plays than any other investigator has covered with her objectives.[22] In the most recent study of the problem[23] F. T. Prince traces the structure of Milton's choruses to Tasso's *Aminta* and Guarini's *Il Pastor Fido*. The choruses in those plays differ from the formal imitations of Greek choric odes by Tasso in *Torrismondo* and by Trissino in *Sofonisba* by being simplified into the form that Milton used in *Samson* and described as what was "call'd by the Greeks *Monostrophic*, or rather *Apolelymenon*, without regard had to *Strophe, Antistrophe,* or *Epod.*" The case for a pastoral drama like *Il Pastor Fido* as a pattern for Milton's choruses is helped by the fact that in his preface he associated pastoral drama with tragedy. Guarini's plot —with its many frustrations and final union of the loyal lovers Mirtillo and Amarilli in strange fulfillment of an oracle—was molded to infuse tragic or pseudo-tragic tone into its choruses and catastrophe. To Milton its ending may have seemed to be such a reversal of the hero's fortunes as Aristotle might have recognized as a genuinely tragic peripeteia.

No one can read the extracts from the choruses in *Il Pastor Fido* and the *Aminta* in Prince's appendixes without perceiving their resemblance to those in *Samson*. They are followed by a chorus from Andreini's *L'Adamo* (1613), which is often mentioned as a "source" for *Paradise Lost*. Its loose operatic design in the choruses and in its entire pattern was far from that in Greek tragedy, yet Prince thinks that it made an impression on Milton when he first considered the problem of adapting Greek choruses to his purpose. In its semi-lyrical dialogues also he sees at least a parallel for Milton's use of intermittent rhyme in his monostrophic choruses. It is interesting that Miss Finney should ignore Andreini's opera and pick out the *Angelica in Ebuda* of Gabriello Chiabrera

---

something is captured of the rhythms of the Hebrew prophets." *Poetry and Faith* (London, 1951), p. 141. The possibility of an influence by the smooth Latin choruses of George Buchanan's *Jeptha* and *Baptistes* is wisely not made by René Galland though in "Milton and Buchanan"—*Révue Anglo-Américaine*, XIII (1936), 326–33—he made the most of the slender evidence for a general resemblance between them and *Samson*.

[21] In *PMLA*, LVIII (1943), 649–64.

[22] Mrs. Dufner (Marguerite Little) is the author of an unpublished University of Illinois dissertation on "Some Italian Elements in the Choral Practice of *Samson Agonistes.*"

[23] In *The Italian Element in Milton's Verse* F. T. Prince devotes a chapter to "The Choruses of *Samson Agonistes*" (pp. 145–68).

(acted two years earlier than *L'Adamo*) as a *tragedia per musica* paralleling *Samson* so closely in its choruses that "one could make parallel charts of the two works." Yet Prince, who includes a fragment of Chiabrera's *Il Diluvio* among analogues to *Paradise Lost*, ignores *Angelica in Ebuda* entirely and concentrates on the three familiar plays of Tasso, Guarini, and Andreini.

Our three authorities on Milton's choric debt to the Italians differ less in opinion than they do in the extent and character of the ground that they cover. Miss Finney paints a wide panorama of Italian drama with emphasis on its musical aspect from the classical revival of the sixteenth century to the emergence of oratorios like Benedetto Ferrari's *Il Sansone* (c. 1660). Her study gives us the background of the evolution in European taste which made the Jennens-Handel transformation of Milton's *Samson* into an oratorio easy and easily popular in 1740. None of the three writers attempts to do more with the scansion of Milton's choruses than Prince does in his opening criticism of Robert Bridges' "account of the elemental structure of the verse of *Samson Agonistes*" as failing to recognize that "prosody cannot be completely distinguished from the diction and total structure of poetry." Implicitly the three Italianists seem to concur with modern opinion about the choruses in *Samson,* which has been described[24] as having "now largely settled down under the influence of students like G. M. Hopkins and Bridges" to regard them as "among the strongest features" of the drama. But none of the research into Milton's Italian background brings us the answer to Karl Shapiro's protest in his *Essay on Rime* that

> The chorus
> Of Milton's *Samson,* endlessly discussed,
> Flows by the count of ear and no more scans
> (But parse it if you can) than Hebrew.

It is a bit surprising that only one investigator of Milton's relations with Italian drama should have shown any interest in the date of the composition of *Samson*. Without insisting on the suggestion, Miss Buchanan implies that Milton's overtones of the chivalry in the plays of Giraldi, Cavallerino, and Tasso are too strong for us to suppose that he had long been at home from his Italian journey when he wrote *Samson*. But in Prince's suggestion that the choruses of *Samson* have something metrically "in common with Milton's very early experiments, written perhaps thirty years before," there is no flicker of suspicion that his drama may have been written shortly after his return from Italy in 1639. In comparing *Samson* with Milton's earlier work Prince refers to Spenserian rather than to Italian traditions. Nor is there any comfort in his remarks on the rhymes in its choruses for Parker's belief that after writing *Paradise Lost* Milton would never again have been likely to use rhyme. In Prince's statement of the "secret" of Milton's "rhymed verse which does not rhyme, or unrhymed verse which seems to do so," and in his analysis of the flowering in drama of Milton's "discovery, first applied in the sonnets and elaborated in his blank verse, that a line-ending can be emphatic both when the sentence ends with it and when it does not,"[25] there is as little support for the view that *Samson* was written before the epic poems as there is for Leavis's complaint that its verse suffers everywhere from a "pervasive stiff, pedantic aridity."

VI

The Date of Composition as Related to the Style and Theme

Since the Italianists cannot give much encouragement to the suggestion of any of the earlier dates that have been proposed for *Samson*, we come back to the view of Masson,

[24] By W. Menzies in "Milton: the Last Poems," *Essays and Studies,* XXIV, p. 84.
[25] *The Italian Element in Milton's Verse,* p. 167.

Grierson, and Hanford that it was the work of Milton's old age. That traditional view in its classical restatements by Hanford is vulnerable to Parker's objection that it rests on the unproved assumption that the drama reflects Milton's later years.[26]   But to most close readers the assumption seems as inevitable as it does to A. S. P. Woodhouse in his study of "*Samson Agonistes* in Milton's Experience."[27]   The mood of the drama seems to him to reflect the struggle between despair and hope in Milton's mind in 1660–1661 rather than in the years after the composition of *Paradise Regained,* when, presumably, he was at peace with himself.   The style, though different from that of *Paradise Regained,* resembles it in its freedom from "the traditional royalist imagery" which Woodhouse agrees with Ross was still firmly rooted in Milton's imagination when he wrote *Paradise Lost.*   Unfortunately, Ross's criterion is too blunt a tool for him even to think of using it to date *Samson* relatively to *Paradise Regained.*   Though he thinks that *Samson* was shorn of "the vivid and concrete image" by the effect of Milton's republican principles upon his imagination, Ross is in no doubt that *Samson Agonistes* is a later and "a more successful poem than *Paradise Regained.*"[28]   Unlike either epic, it seems to him to achieve "dignity as well as consistency of style, and formally (to be) perhaps Milton's most perfect performance."

When Ross and Woodhouse wrote, no objective analysis of Milton's stylistic evolution had been made.   Insofar as the question of the date of *Samson* can be determined by such an analysis, however, we now have the answer in the statistical comparisons of the frequencies of the strong pauses, feminine endings, and some less interesting prosodic phenomena in Ants Oras' study of "Milton's Blank Verse and the Chronology of his Major Poems."[29]   His procedure seems as sound as that on which the best metrical dating of Shakespeare's plays has been based, and the result is to show that *Paradise Regained* was written after *Paradise Lost,* and *Samson* the latest of the three.   Conclusions based upon statistical studies of selected elements of prosody may never be finally conclusive, but there is no doubt that Oras' results are much less speculative than those of anyone else who has introduced matters of style into the dating of *Samson.*

Short of documentary proof of the time when Milton wrote his drama, our best evidence about it must come from his treatment of his theme.   In a Columbia thesis on "Milton and Dryden," by Morris Freedman, an interesting attempt is made to relate the 1668 preface to *Paradise Lost* to the discussion of blank verse in the same year in Dryden's *Essay of Dramatic Poesy,* and the chapter on *Samson* tries to relate the preface to the drama to Dryden's *Essay* so as to show that the preface was "intended by Milton as his demonstration of how tragedy should be written."[30]   If this hypothesis is accepted as proved or probable, it is easy to jump to the conclusion that the drama was written in or not long after 1668.   It is quite as easy, however, to point out that the writing of the preface may have followed that of the play by as long an interval as we know that the 1668 preface to *Paradise Lost* followed the publication of the epic.   And in this connection it is interesting to recall Gilbert's belief that the preface to *Samson* and its Argument represent plans for the play that were drawn up thirty years before it was published.

A subtler contribution than Freedman's to the problem of dating *Samson* by analysis of its treatment of its theme has been made by implication in Michael Krouse's study of *Milton's Samson and the Christian Tradition.*   His bold purpose in that book is to prove both that Milton conceived Samson as the saint of patristic, scholastic, and renaissance

[26] James Holly Hanford in *"Samson Agonistes* and Milton in Old Age" and in *John Milton, Englishman.*
[27] In Transactions of the Royal Society of Canada, Third Series, Vol. XLIII, Section II (1949), p. 160. Woodhouse quotes from Malcolm M. Ross's *Milton's Royalism,* p. 120.
[28] *Milton's Royalism,* p. 137.
[29] Ants Oras' essay is in *Essays on John Milton and his Works* by Members of the South Atlantic Modern Language Association, pp. 128–95.
[30] Mr. Freedman took his doctorate in 1953.   The account of it here is drawn from the summer issue of *Seventeenth Century News,* July, 1955.

tradition and that he no less definitely conceived his hero as a prototype of Christ. This rather esoteric theory regards *Samson* fundamentally as an allegory founded upon an analogy with the three-fold temptation of Christ in *Paradise Regained.* The implication about their proximate dates is obvious. Since Krouse accepts Miss Pope's interpretation of the traditional "triple equation" between Christ's temptations and those attributed to Adam in their Protestant version—meaning in Christ's case that the temptation to turn stones into bread was a trial of his faith by physical necessity, his temptation by the offer of the kingdoms of this world a trial by fraud, and his temptation on the pinnacle of the temple a trial by violence—it follows that Manoa comes to Samson as an unconscious tempter of his wavering faith in God; that Dalila tempts him by fraud; and Harapha, by violence. A serious objection to this reading of Harapha's role is the fact that he is not violent in action. "A blustering, arrogant representative of force," as Parker calls him, he may be; but as Parker repeatedly observes, he is afraid to act.[31] And the more he is reduced to a mere symbol of violence to satisfy a theological theory, the dimmer becomes his psychological role of revealing Samson's recrudescent strength to him on the threshold of the catastrophe. It is true that critical opinion is increasingly supporting the view that Harapha is "the hinge of the plot"; but in calling him so Allen does not regard him as a theological symbol though he may "symbolize all that is valiant in Philistia,"[32] and in his discomfiture may encourage Samson's hope of a victory over Philistia's Dagon by Israel's God, working through his redeemed champion's strength.

Aside from its doubtful treatment of the tradition which made Samson (and for that matter even Hercules) a prototype of Christ, there is truth in Krouse's statement of the long tradition which made him a Christian saint. Krouse's commentary on the word *agonistes* is a lovely semantic excursion. We see it at first simply meaning an athlete struggling for a prize in the Olympic games, but later being used metaphorically for the champions of the truth about whom Plutarch tells us that Socrates talked, and finally signifying the Christian athlete of whom Augustine wrote in his *De agone Christiano.* This is St. Paul's champion armed with "the whole armor of Christ" whose many re-births in Christian literature culminated in Milton's contender for "that immortal garland" of virtue in *Areopagitica.* But identification of Samson with Christ conflicts radically with Parker's interpretation of him as a study in regeneration and with M. M. Mahood's confirmation of that view in *Poetry and Humanism.*[33]

A more serious difficulty with some efforts to identify Milton's Samson with Christ is their forcing of the entire plot of the drama and particularly of Samson's death into the Procrustean bed of the passion as it was treated by Calvinist theologians. So Scott-Craig, starting from the dogmatic statement that "Samson Agonistes is really Christus Agonistes," describes Milton's plot simply as an effort to represent the agony of Christ in Gethsemane "typologically." The result is to make the drama a liturgical "orchestration of the major themes of Calvinist scholasticism: Chastisement of sinners; Trial or Agony of the Saints —as the Fortitude and Patience of Samson are tried by Dalila and Harapha; Ransom, Deliverance, Redemption, etc."[34] In Scott-Craig's scheme Dalila and Harapha are not distinguished as successive tempters by fraud and violence; they are confused together as psychologically indifferent persecutors in a single ordeal. As a whole the drama is treated as liturgical; Milton's "organ music and elaborate language" make him as much priest as

[31] *Milton's Debt to Greek Tragedy,* p. 174.

[32] D. C. Allen in *The Harmonious Vision,* p. 93.

[33] M. M. Mahood, *Poetry and Humanism,* London, 1950, p. 237. That there is no evidence in *Samson* for the identification of the hero with Christ is the unanimous opinion of three of Krouse's reviewers: E. L. Allen in *RES,* n.s. II (1951), 28–32; Ernest Sirluck in *MP,* XLVIII (1950), 71–72; and A. S. P. Woodhouse in *MLN,* LXVI (1951), 116–18.

[34] T. S. K. Scott-Craig, "Concerning Milton's *Samson*," in *Renaissance News,* V (1952), 43–53.

poet. The catastrophe becomes a lustration and the "agony of Samson is a surrogate for the unbloody sacrifice of the mass." The final confirmation of this view of the drama seems to Scott-Craig to be Milton's simile of the Phoenix as seen in the light of his introductory translation of Aristotle's term *katharsis* for the specific effect of tragedy by the liturgical word *lustratio* rather than by the usual rendering of *purgatio*.

Undeniably, it is easy to *feel* the semi-chorus's simile comparing Samson's returning virtue to the rebirth of the Phoenix as pure liturgy. Yet the liturgical effect is not so incantatory as it is in Shakespeare's *The Phoenix and the Turtle,* with which it is natural to compare Milton's lines on "that self-begotten bird" that

> Revives, reflourishes, then vigorous most
> When most unactive deem'd,
> And though her body die, her fame survives,
> A secular bird ages of lives. (ll. 1704–07)

Of the many writers who have described the Phoenix—from Herodotus, Ovid, and Claudian to Torquato Tasso and Pierre Motin—Scott-Craig selects one, St. Clement, as offering the key to Milton's simile. But St. Clement made the wonderful bird that builds its own funeral pyre and is reborn from its own ashes a symbol of the resurrection of the soul (as Milton did in *Damon's Epitaph*), but not (as we are asked to believe that Milton did in *Samson*) a symbol of Christ. As a symbol of the resurrection of the dead the Phoenix became established in Christian tradition long before it did as the symbol of Christ that we find in Tasso's and Motin's poems. Neither of those poems is a probable "source" for Milton's Phoenix in *Damon's Epitaph, Paradise Lost* (V, 272), or *Samson.*[35] As a symbol of Christ the Phoenix belongs most characteristically in the Counter-Reformation. As a Christ-symbol its choice by Milton would be strikingly in conflict with Hanford's humanistic view that Milton's choice of an Old Testament figure as his hero indicates that he did not regard the passion of Christ as "a necessary instrument to salvation."[36] To anyone familiar with the countless references to the Phoenix among Milton's contemporaries, an attempt to wring a major, specific theological commitment out of the simile in *Samson* must seem forced. To regard Hanford's view of the drama as equally forced would be unfair to him. Readers who accept his view of Milton's theology can still understand that, like Henry Vaughan in *Resurrection and Immortality,* he could see the miracle of the virtue in all created things which

> Phoenix-like renew'th
> Both life and youth;
> For a preserving spirit still doth passe
> Untainted through this Masse,
> Which doth resolve, produce, and ripen all.

---

[35] In the most careful examination of the verbal parallels to the passage on the Phoenix in *Damon's Epitaph* that has yet been made, Kathleen E. Hartwell decides in *Lactantius and Milton* (pp. 128–31) that the closest resemblances are to the *Phoenixes* of Claudian and Lactantius (if the *De Ave Phoenice* is rightly attributed to Lactantius).

[36] "*Samson Agonistes* and Milton in Old Age," p. 177. With Hanford it is worth while to compare Saurat in *Milton, Man and Thinker* (p. 238): "Milton cared little for the vicarious atonement" and deliberately omitted all reference to Christ in *Samson;* and M. M. Ross in *Poetry and Dogma* (pp. 12–13): "Samson is not precisely a Christ-type" though he "does die the sacrificial and redemptive Christ-death," while his moral and spiritual victory is "also social—a victory in history." Cf. Robert Adams' remark on Ross's passage that, "there is something a little arbitrary about straining *Samson*" into one of Milton's "shining sacramental poems, isolated amid acres of barren machinery." And he adds, after a doubt whether much of "Samson's total feeling fits into a pattern which could properly be called 'sacramental'!" that in any case the critical significance "of the fact" is open to doubt (*Ikon,* p. 220).

VII

Milton's Conception of Tragedy

To support his view of *Samson* as "a surrogate for the unbloody mass" Scott-Craig stresses Milton's translation of Aristotle's *katharsis* by the Latin term *lustratio* in the epigraph of the play. "The word *lusis* in Aristotle's *Poetics,* which we usually translate as *denouement* or *catastrophe,*" carries for Scott-Craig the theological meaning of "loosing," and he derives it "from the root from which *lustratio* in Latin comes."[37] But here he gives a theological turn to Milton's basically medical and humanistic idea. In the lexicons of the time—e.g. in the *Thesaurus linguae Graecae ab Henrico Stephano constructus* (Paris, 1572)—the first meaning given for *lusis* is the medical one of release from pain or passion (*perturbatio*), while redemption (*redemptio*) is given only as a derived meaning without theological overtone, in the sense of payment for a debt. It is the medical meaning of the term that Milton clearly has in mind when he goes on in the first sentence of his preface to say that Aristotle regarded the nature of tragedy as consisting in its "power by raising pity and fear, or terror, to purge the mind of those and such like passions, that is to temper and reduce them to just measure with a kind of delight, stirr'd up by reading or seeing those passions well imitated." If space permitted, it would be interesting to pause and speculate as to whether Milton and his Italian guides anticipated Freud's supplement of the Aristotelian conception of tragedy in *Beyond the Pleasure Principle.* Following where some Italians had led, Milton went on to add the striking statement that Aristotle's theory is confirmed "by Nature . . . ; for so, in Physic, things of melancholy hue and quality are used against melancholy, sour against sour, salt to remove salt humours." If we force his meaning only a little here by laying stress on *Nature,* it is possible to look at the whole process of Samson's regeneration in a medical light and to see it, with Hanford, as illuminating such key passages as Manoa's warning to him not to give way to his darkest dreads,

which proceed
From anguish of the mind, and humours black; (ll. 599–600)

or Samson's diagnosis of his griefs as "lingering disease" and "wounds immedicable" that

Rankle, and fester, and gangrene,
To black mortification," (ll. 621–22)

that no "Medicinal liquor can assuage."

If it seems odd to find the Aristotelian *katharsis* given a medical twist, the explanation is found in Milton's own experience of it as it had been sublimated for him by

what the lofty grave Tragoedians taught
In *Chorus* or *Iambic,* teachers best
Of moral prudence. (*PR* IV, 261–63)

The words are Satan's and are part of the glorification of ancient wisdom that provokes Christ's denunciation of the spiritual heritage of Greece and Rome. Could Milton have written as Hellenic a drama as *Samson* after—or even very long before—putting that denunciation into Christ's mouth? The answer is that he could; and that he would have appropriated the entire technique of Attic tragedy to his purposes in just the spirit that he had when he used the classical myths of the Golden Age to transcend them in describing Paradise in *Paradise Lost.* The medical twist that he gives to Aristotle's *katharsis,* he gives us to understand, was a part of the ethical element that he had learned from "Castelvetro, Tasso, Mazzoni, and the others" in Italy who had theorized about the nature of tragedy. One of the other Italian critics whom he had in mind when he recommended

---

[37] Scott-Craig in "Concerning Milton's *Samson,*" p. 48.

Castelvetro for study in *Of Education*, may have been Minturno, whose *L'Arte Poetica* (1564) is pervaded with a medical view of tragedy and satire—the former presented in just Milton's homeopathic way. The conception is not didactic. Although Milton and Minturno both "conceived of tragedy as having an ethical aim"—as Spingarn observed[38] —yet both "clearly perceived that by *katharsis* Aristotle had reference not to a moral, but to an emotional, effect."

Milton's preface to *Samson* significantly begins with the principle of *katharsis*, which comes last in Aristotle's definition of tragedy. Tragic beauty, Milton thought, came from the suffering and regeneration and triumphant death of a protagonist. Everything must center on him and his regeneration must dominate everything—even to the imagery. Perhaps—as Mrs. McCall suggests[39]—the entire drama is to be regarded as an example of what Miss Bodkin calls the Rebirth Archetype of tragic development in a pattern of "image-sequences" of downward movement into a "severed relation with the outer world and, it may be, disintegration and death," to be balanced by an upward and outward movement —"an expansion or outburst of activity, a transition toward reintegration and life-renewal." Samson's regeneration broadly corresponds to this "image-pattern," and it also corresponds to another of Miss Bodkin's patterns, that of movement from darkness to light—from the outer and inner darkness of Samson's opening speech[40] to the moment when

> he though blind of sight,
> Despis'd and thought extinguish't quite
> With inward eyes illuminated
> His fiery virtue rous'd
> From under ashes into sudden flame. (ll. 1686–91)

From this image of flame, which closely precedes that of the Phoenix, we go immediately to that of the dragon in the chicken-roosts. If we dislike that simile for the slaughter of the Philistines, we are at liberty to murmur with Ezra Pound against Milton's "asinine bigotry, his beastly Hebraism, the coarseness of his mentality."[41] Or, with Ralli, we may sentimentalize over "the last word of Milton's life" as sad "frustration" because "he remained a fighter to the last—his armor of combativeness not pierced, nor his heart touched."[42] With Ralli stands Sir Herbert Grierson, declaring that "Revenge is the dominant note of Milton's last poem" and behind them both is Sir Richard Jebb's famous over-simplification of "the issue of the drama" as Dagon's struggle with Jehovah, or that of Hebraism with Arnold's "Hellenism."

If "Hebraism" hardly seems the right word to describe the spirit of *Samson Agonistes*, then perhaps we may try "Protestantism." Its aptness has been studied in the light of the glosses on Judges in the Geneva Bible by a scholar who rejoices in Milton's embodiment of "a character, a pattern of life, and an attitude toward God that is essentially Protestant and Puritan"[43] in his hero. Though this view needs checking against traditionally severe Catholic commentaries on Samson's fleshly sin and final triumph over God's enemies, there is truth in it; but it is also true that Milton's Samson is most "Protestant" because he ac-

---

[38] Joel E. Spingarn in *Literary Criticism in the Renaissance* (New York, 1899), p. 188.

[39] Lois Gilbert McCall, Imagery and Symbolism of *Samson Agonistes*, unpublished Mt. Holyoke M. A. thesis (1949), p. 39. Her quotation of Maud Bodkin is from *Archetypal Patterns in Poetry* (New York, 1934), p. 54.

[40] In *Milton's Blindness* (New York, 1934), p. 92, Eleanor G. Brown pleads that there is nothing subjective in *Samson*—no trace of Milton's symptoms or experience of blindness.

[41] Ezra Pound in *Make it New* (New Haven, 1953), p. 109.

[42] A. Ralli in *Poetry and Faith* (London, 1951), p. 142. Grierson's words come from "Milton and Liberty" in *MLR*, XXXIX (1944), 106; Jebb's from "*Samson Agonistes* and the Hellenic Drama," in the Proceedings of the British Academy, III (1903), 341.

[43] George W. Whiting in "*Samson Agonistes* and the Geneva Bible," The Rice Institute Pamphlet, XXXVIII (1951), 33.

cepts "every shred of responsibility" for his misfortunes, and because "it is by that acceptance that he is regenerated."[44]

Beside Milton's conception of a possibly "Hebraic" Samson as an instrument of divine vengeance we also have a clear Hellenic note of questioning of God's justice in some of Milton's choruses.   In memorable lines after Manoa's first appearance the Danites protest against the fate of heroes who, though not flawless, suffer punishment

> Too grievous for the trespass or omission. (l. 691)

Here Tillyard is surely right in seeing at least emotional sympathy with human weakness, however it may be submerged in the final tribute of the chorus to "highest Wisdom."   The comforting hint of the earlier chorus that Samson's guilt is less than his pain is left unchallenged as Dalila sails into view.

But Samson himself does not share the doubt of the chorus; his regeneration rests on his faith in God's justice.   And through the working of an irony more ironic than Sophoclean fate, Samson is divinely drawn toward a destiny that springs both from his sin and his repentance.   He is both sinner and saint.   That is why Milton felt it necessary to explain that his death was not an act of despair—not suicide, as some biblical commentators had said, though against the teaching of St. Augustine and St. Thomas.[45]   So Samson lies "victorious" among his victims,

> self-kill'd
> Not willingly, but tangl'd in the fold
> Of dire necessity. (ll. 1664–66)

That is why Milton also warns us not to expect a plot obviously either simple or complex in Aristotle's sense, for it is hard to tell whether the straightforward regeneration of Samson's faith, terminating in both death and victory, involves a reversal of fortune.

So it is possible to regard Milton as ending his drama in an act which seemed to him both providential and fatal in the Greek sense.   The twin conception would seem no stranger to him here than it did when he ended his chapter on Predestination in the *Christian Doctrine* by quoting Homer to illustrate the kind of doom from heaven which self-blinded men bring upon themselves.   In his last chorus in the drama—

> All is best, though oft we doubt,
> What th'unsearchable dispose
> Of highest wisdom brings about,
> And ever best found in the close. (ll. 1745–48)

—he translated lines that recur almost identically in the final choruses of five of Euripides' plays.   Similarly the chapter on Predestination ends with an affirmation of God's providence from the Psalms and an echo of the words of Zeus in the opening movement of the *Odyssey* about the fatal punishments that men bring upon themselves from heaven.   In this common appeal to the Greeks as well as to the Bible in Milton's drama and in his chapter on Predestination there may be no evidence that *Samson* was written as late as the final revision of the *Christian Doctrine,* but it is certain that the two passages alike bear the mark of his maturest Christian humanism.

Much ink has been spilled to prove that the declaration of faith in the mysterious decrees of "highest wisdom" is un-Greek and un-tragic.   Opinion is moving toward Miss Ellis-Fermor's view when she says that few readers "are content to call Samson's triumphant death a tragic catastrophe," because Milton, "by justifying the ways of God to man leaves

---

[44] E. M. W. Tillyard in *The Miltonic Setting,* pp. 86–87. Cf. E. Mertner's summation in "Die Bedeutung der kosmischen Konzeption in Miltons Dichtung"—in *Anglia,* LXIX (1950), 133—that *Samson* "ist ganz und gar ein drama der Seele, ein Triumph der 'plain heroic magnitude of mind.' "

[45] Interesting discussions of this problem occur in Grierson's *Milton and Wordsworth,* pp. 138–40, and Krouse's *Milton's Samson,* pp. 106–08.

no room for tragic ecstasy and substitutes ecstasy of another kind."[46]   The denial of any possible tragic effect because Milton "insists throughout the drama that the heavenly Disposition is not to be disputed, that the ways of God are just and justifiable,"[47] runs widely through modern criticism from Baum to O'Connor, who is troubled because Samson "is an instrument, not a victim of providence."[48]   The effect of the play for him is a feeling that in "tone and content" it is "curiously similar to Eliot's *Murder in the Cathedral*." If Milton could read his modern critics, he would not be disturbed by the dictum of one of them[49] on one page that, because his hero "reaches the end for which providence intended him, it may indeed be said that the drama is removed from the strict limits of tragedy," while on the next page *Samson* is declared to be the "best of the Greek tragedies in English."   Nor would he do more than smile at Sir Maurice Bowra's objection that, "Samson's fault is stressed so strongly that we hardly pity him, and if we feel any fear, it is less for him than for the Philistines."[50]   If Milton's drama realized his early hope of mastery in "those Dramatick constitutions, wherein Sophocles and Euripides raigne," he may be forgiven for having produced a kind of isotope of tragedy—something assayable as of the same general kind of metal though of better quality, perhaps, than most of the surviving Greek tragedies themselves.   It is Miss Ellis-Fermor who most definitely pronounces *Samson* an isotope and a splendid one.   For her Milton's new creation on the tragic frontier is not "a miscarried tragedy," but a drama of inward struggle giving us "a steady psychological progression from despair through heroic conflict upwards to exultation and the final assumption into beatitude."[51]   If Milton could recognize *Samson* in this description, he could only blush with joy.   At the same time he might inquire whether, after all, if the biblical critic whom his preface quotes was right in interpreting the Revelation of St. John as a tragedy, there may not be some justification for drawing the tragic frontiers a little less narrowly than they are drawn in the twentieth century.

A Bibliography of Books and Articles Published since 1929, bearing upon

Samson Agonistes

Allen, Don Cameron.   "The Idea as Pattern—Despair in *Samson Agonistes*," in *The Harmonious Vision*.   Baltimore, 1954.

Boughner, Daniel C.   "Milton's Harapha and Renaissance Comedy," *ELH*, XI (1944), 297–306.

Bowra, Sir C. M. "*Samson Agonistes*," in *Inspiration and Poetry*.   London, 1955.

Buchanan, Edith.   *The Italian Neo-Senecan Background of "Samson Agonistes."*   Duke University unpublished thesis, 1952.

Fell, K.   "From Myth to Martyrdom: Towards a View of *Samson Agonistes*," *ES*, XXXIV (1953), 145–55.

Finney, Gretchen L.   "Chorus in *Samson Agonistes*," *PMLA*, LVIII (1943), 649–64.

Flatter, R., Farnham-Flower, F. F., and Kelley, Maurice.   A correspondence captioned "*Samson Agonistes* and Milton" in *TLS*, 7 and 28 August and 4 September, 1948.

---

[46] Una Ellis-Fermor, *The Frontiers of Drama* (New York, 1946), p. 17.

[47] Paull Franklin Baum, "*Samson Agonistes* Again," *PMLA*, XXXVI (1921), p. 369.

[48] William Van O'Connor, *Climates of Tragedy* (Baton Rouge, 1943), p. 81.   The comparison with *Murder in the Cathedral* is also made on ethical ground by K. Fell in "From Myth to Martyrdom: Towards a View of Milton's *Samson Agonistes*," English Studies, XXXIV (1953), p. 152.

[49] Chauncey B. Tinker in *Tragic Themes in Western Literature*, ed. by Cleanth Brooks (New Haven, 1955), pp. 74–75.

[50] *Inspiration and Poetry*, p. 128.

[51] *The Frontiers of Drama*, p. 32.

Gilbert, Allan H. "Is *Samson Agonistes* Unfinished?" *PQ*, XXVIII (1949), 98–106.

Gray, F. Campbell. "Milton's Counterpoint: Classicism and Romanticism in the Poetry of John Milton," *SR*, XLIII (1935), 136–45.

Grenender, M. E. "*Samson's* Middle, Aristotle, and Dr. Johnson," *UTQ*, XXIV (1955), 377–89.

Grierson, Sir Herbert J. C. "A Note upon the *Samson Agonistes* of John Milton and *Samson of Heilige Wraeck* by Joost van den Vondel," *Melanges d'histoire littéraire et comparée offerts à Fernand Baldensperger*, Tome I. (Paris, 1930), pp. 330–39.

Kermode, Frank. "*Samson Agonistes* and Hebrew Prosody," *Durham University Journal*, XIV (1953), 59–63.

Kirkconnell, Watson. "Six Sixteenth-Century Forerunners of Milton's *Samson Agonistes*," *Transactions of the Royal Society of Canada*, Third Series, XLIII (1940), 73–85.

Kreipe, Christian Edzard. *Milton's Samson Agonistes*. Halle, 1926.

Krouse, F. Michael. *Milton's Samson and the Christian Tradition*. Princeton, 1949.

Little, Marguerite (Mrs. Max Dufner). *Some Italian Elements in the Choral Practice of "Samson Agonistes."* University of Illinois unpublished thesis, 1946.

Nash, Ralph. "Chivalric Themes in *Samson Agonistes*." In *Studies in Honor of John Wilcox*, edited by A. D. Wallace and W. O. Ross (Wayne State University Press, 1958), pp. 23–38.

Parker, William R. "On Milton's Early Literary Program," *MP*, XXXIII (1935), 49–53.

———. "The Trinity MS and Milton's Plans for Tragedy," *JEGP*, XXXIV (1935), 225–32.

———. "Symmetry in Milton's *Samson Agonistes*," *MLN*, L (1935), 355–60.

———. "The Greek Spirit in Milton's *Samson Agonistes*," *ESEA*, XX (1935), 21–44.

———. "The Kommos in Milton's *Samson Agonistes*," *SP*, XXXII (1935), 240–44.

———. Correspondence on the etymology of *Harapha*, *TLS*, January 2, 9, 23, 1937.

———. "Misogyny in Milton's *Samson Agonistes*," *PQ*, XVI (1937), 139–44.

———. "Tragic Irony in Milton's *Samson Agonistes*," *Études Anglaises* (July, 1937), 314–20.

———. "The Date of *Samson Agonistes*," *PQ*, XXVIII (1949), 145–66.

———. *Milton's Debt to Greek Tragedy in "Samson Agonistes."* Baltimore, 1937.

Scott-Craig, T. S. K. "Concerning Milton's *Samson*," *Renaissance News*, V (1952), 45–53.

Siegel, Paul N. "Milton and the Humanist Attitude toward Women," *JHI*, XI (1950), 42–53.

Tillyard, E. M. W. "Milton and Protestantism," in *The Miltonic Setting*. Cambridge, 1938.

Timberlake, P. "Milton and Euripides," The Parrott *Presentation Volume*. Princeton, 1935.

Waggoner, George R. "The Challenge to Single Combat in *Samson Agonistes*," *PQ*, XXXIX (1960), 82–92.

Whiting, George W. "*Samson Agonistes* and the Geneva Bible," *The Rice Institute Pamphlet*, XXXVIII (1951), 16–35.

Woodhouse, Arthur S. P. "*Samson Agonistes* and Milton's Experience," *Transactions of the Royal Society of Canada*, Third Series, XLIII (1949), 157–75.

———. "Tragic Effect in *Samson Agonistes*," *UTQ*, LIII (1959), 205–222.

Editions

Samson Agonistes. Edited by V. Hammer. Florence, 1931.

Samson Agonistes: A Dramatic Poem. With Wood-Engravings by Robert Ashwin Maynard. Harrow Weald, Middlesex. The Raven Press, 1931.

Samson Agonistes. Edited by A. J. Wyatt and A. J. F. Collins. With the Sonnets, edited by A. R. Weeks. 1932.

Samson Agonistes. Edited by T. Lerario. Florence, 1931.

Paradise Regained, the Minor Poems, and Samson Agonistes. Edited by Merritt Y. Hughes. New York, 1937.

Samson Agonistes. Edited by J. C. Collins. Oxford, 1938.

Samson Agonistes e Paradise Regained. Edited by A. Zanco. Milan, 1951.

Samson Agonistes. Edited by M. Lombardi. Milan, 1943.

Samson Agonistes. Edited by F. T. Prince. London, 1957.

Simson der Kampfer. Translated by H. Ulrich. Edited by R. Schneider. Freiburg, 1947.

200   *Joachimi Camerarii Symbolorum.*

C.

VITA MIHI
MORS EST.

Ex seipsa nascens, ex se reparabilis ales,
Quae exoriens moritur, qua moriens oritur.

Visum fuit tandem hanc tertiam Centuriam nostram cum Phœnice concludere, & de illa paulo verbosius, quam antea factum est, disserere. Idque tum propter autorum plurimorum de ea varias ac interdum discrepantes opiniones, tum ob symbola, ex hac ave ingeniosa nonnulla & præclara

Joachimi Camerarii Symbolorum ac Emblematum Ethico. Politicorum Centuriæ Quatuor, Moguntiæ, 1697

Samson Agonistes

A DRAMATIC POEM

ARISTOTLE, *Poetics*, Chapter vi

Τραγῳδία μίμησισ πράξεωσ σπουδαίασ, etc.

Tragoedia est imitatio actionis seriae, etc. per misericordiam et metum
perficiens talium affectuum lustrationem.

OF THAT SORT OF DRAMATIC POEM WHICH IS CALL'D TRAGEDY

Tragedy, as it was anciently compos'd, hath been ever held the gravest, moralest, and most profitable of all other Poems: therefore said by *Aristotle*[2] to be of power by raising pity and fear, or terror, to purge the mind of those and such like passions, that is to temper and reduce them to just measure with a kind of delight, stirr'd up by reading or seeing those passions well imitated. Nor is Nature wanting in her own effects to make good his assertion: for so in Physic things of melancholic hue and quality are us'd against melancholy, sour against sour, salt to remove salt humors.[3] Hence Philosophers and other gravest Writers, as *Cicero, Plutarch* and others, frequently cite out of Tragic Poets, both to adorn and illustrate thir discourse. The Apostle *Paul* himself thought it not unworthy to insert a verse of *Euripides* into the Text of Holy Scripture,[4] 1 Cor. xv, 33, and *Paraeus*,[5] commenting on the *Revelation*, divides the whole Book as a Tragedy, into Acts distinguisht each by a Chorus of Heavenly Harpings and Song between. Heretofore Men in highest dignity have labor'd not a little to be thought able to compose a Tragedy. Of that honor *Dionysius*[6] the elder was no less ambitious than before of his attaining to the Tyranny. *Augustus Caesar* also had begun his *Ajax*[7] but unable to please his own judgment with what he had begun, left it unfinisht. *Seneca* the Philosopher is by some thought the Author of those Tragedies[8] (at least the best of them) that go under that name. *Gregory Nazianzen* a Father of the Church, thought it not unbeseeming the

---

[1] In form the title resembles such Greek titles as Aeschylus' *Prometheus Bound* and Euripides' *Hercules Distracted*. The meaning of *Agonistes* is discussed in the Introduction, p. 541.

[2] Milton is paraphrasing the Aristotelian definition of tragedy which he partly quotes in the original Greek and in Latin translation as an epigraph.

[3] In his *Arte Poetica* (1564) the Italian critic Minturno applied the homeopathic principle that "like cures like" to Aristotle's theory of tragic catharsis, saying that, "Medicine has no greater power, by means of poison, to expel poison from an afflicted body than tragedy has to purge the soul of its impetuous passions by the skilful expression of strong emotion in poetry." Minturno developed the idea no further than Milton did, but he came close to Milton's "agonistic" conception by adding that tragedy is properly a kind of spiritual athletic discipline like the hard physical training of the Spartans, and that it trains men to endure reversals of fortune.

[4] The verse, "Evil communications corrupt good manners," was proverbial when St. Paul quoted it. Though Milton attributed it to Euripides both here and in *Areopagitica* (p. 726, below), the fragment in which it has come down has been attributed both to him and to Menander.

[5] Milton had long been interested in the commentaries of the German Calvinist, David Paraeus, whose work on Revelation was translated into English in 1644. Its eighth chapter, "Touching the Forme of the Revelation," suggested his description of the Apocalypse of St. John, in the Preface to Book II of *The Reason of Church Government*, as "the majestic image of a high and stately tragedy, shutting up and intermingling her solemn scenes and acts with a sevenfold chorus of hallelujahs and harping symphonies: and this my opinion the grave authority of Paraeus . . . is sufficient to confirm."

[6] Dionysius (431–367 B.C.), tyrant of Syracuse, consolidated the cities of Magna Graecia and stopped the Carthaginian expansion in Sicily. He patronized all the arts and wrote a tragedy, *The Ransom of Hector*, to which the Athenians gave the first prize at the Dionysiac festival.

[7] Milton was familiar with the story about Augustus Caesar which Suetonius told (*Caesars* II, lxxxv): "Though he began a tragedy with much enthusiasm, he destroyed it because his style did not satisfy him."

[8] The ten tragedies of the Stoic philosopher Lucius Annaeus Seneca were familiar in Thomas Newton's translation of 1581.

sanctity of his person to write a Tragedy, which he entitl'd *Christ Suffering*.[9]   This is mention'd to vindicate Tragedy from the small esteem, or rather infamy, which in the account of many it undergoes at this day with other common Interludes; happ'ning through the Poet's error of intermixing Comic stuff with Tragic sadness and gravity; or introducing trivial and vulgar persons, which by all judicious hath been counted absurd; and brought in without discretion, corruptly to gratify the people.   And though ancient Tragedy use no Prologue,[10] yet using sometimes, in case of self defense, or explanation, that which *Martial* calls an Epistle; in behalf of this Tragedy coming forth after the ancient manner, much different from what among us passes for best, thus much beforehand may be Epistl'd; that *Chorus* is here introduc'd after the Greek manner, not ancient only but modern, and still in use among the *Italians*.   In the modeling therefore of this Poem, with good reason, the Ancients and *Italians*[11] are rather follow'd, as of much more authority and fame.   The measure of Verse us'd in the Chorus is of all sorts, call'd by the Greeks *Monostrophic,* or rather *Apolelymenon,*[12] without regard had to *Strophe, Antistrophe* or *Epode,* which were a kind of Stanzas fram'd only for the Music, then us'd with the Chorus that sung; not essential to the Poem, and therefore not material; or being divided into Stanzas or Pauses, they may be call'd *Allaeostropha.*[13]   Division into Act and Scene referring chiefly to the Stage (to which this work never was intended) is here omitted; it suffices if the whole Drama be found not produc't beyond the fifth Act.

Of the style and uniformity, and that commonly call'd the Plot, whether intricate or explicit, which is nothing indeed but such economy,[14] or disposition of the fable as may stand best with verisimilitude and decorum; they only will best judge who are not unacquainted with *Aeschylus, Sophocles,* and *Euripides,* the three Tragic Poets unequall'd yet by any, and the best rule to all who endeavor to write Tragedy.   The circumscription of time[15] wherein the whole Drama begins and ends, is according to ancient rule, and best example, within the space of 24 hours.

THE ARGUMENT

Samson made Captive, Blind, and now in the Prison at Gaza,[16] *there to labor as in a common workhouse, on a Festival day, in the general cessation from labor, comes forth*

[9] Like his contemporaries, Milton believed that the tragedy called *Christ Suffering,* which seems to have been written by a Byzantine Greek about the end of the twelfth century, was the work of Gregory Nazianzen (325?–390?), Bishop of Constantinople. He admired its Euripidean echoes and must have been interested in a long-standing controversy as to whether the "Playe of Christ" by Nazianzenus, as Stephen Gosson called it in his *Schoole of Abuse,* was intended for acting or was composed "dialoguewise, as Plato and Tullie did their Philosophye, to be reade, not to be played."

[10] Milton used the word *prologue* here to mean an apology for a play, prefixed to it like the epistle "To the reader" in which Ben Jonson defended his discharge of the "offices of a tragic writer" in *Sejanus;* not—obviously—a prologue in verse like those which Dryden prefixed to his plays; nor did Milton have any thought here of a prologue as Aristotle defined it in the *Poetics* xii to mean the part of a tragedy before the entrance of the chorus.

[11] So in *Of Education* Milton spoke of the Italians as the best representatives, after the ancients, of "that sublime art which in Aristotle's poetics, in Horace, and the Italian commentaries of Castelvetro, Tasso, Mazzoni, and others, teaches what the laws

are of a true epic poem, what of a dramatic, what of a lyric, what decorum is, which is the grand masterpiece to observe."

[12] *Apolelymenon* transliterates a Greek term meaning "free" in the sense that the choruses are not bound by strict divisions into the elaborate stanzaic patterns of the strophe, antistrophe and epode.

[13] *Allaeostropha:* with strophes or stanzas of various lengths.

[14] In the *Poetics,* vi, Aristotle put first among his six elements of tragedy the plot or arrangement of episodes, which is what Milton understood by *economy.*   His feeling about his own plot as related to Aristotle's distinction between simple and complex types is discussed in the Introduction.

[15] The "unity of time," or principle that a drama ought not to exceed twelve, or at most twenty-four hours in the ideal duration of its action, was inevitable on a stage without a drop curtain to mark pauses between the acts. It was not, however, a part of Aristotle's doctrine, but was read into the *Poetics* by neoclassical critics.

[16] Milton seems to have visualized Gaza as Sandys described it in his *Travels* (p. 116): "But now return we unto Gaza, one of the five Cities, and that the principal that belonged to the Pales-

*into the open Air, to a place nigh, somewhat retir'd, there to sit a while and bemoan his
condition. Where he happens at length to be visited by certain friends and equals*[17] *of
his tribe, which make the Chorus, who seek to comfort him what they can; then by his
old Father* Manoa, *who endeavors the like, and withal tells him his purpose to procure his
liberty by ransom; lastly, that this Feast was proclaim'd by the* Philistins[18] *as a day of
Thanksgiving for thir deliverance from the hands of* Samson, *which yet more troubles
him. Manoa then departs to prosecute his endeavor with the* Philistian *Lords for* Samson's *redemption; who in the meanwhile is visited by other persons; and lastly by a public
Officer to require his coming to the Feast before the Lords and People, to play or show
his strength in thir presence; he at first refuses, dismissing the public Officer with absolute
denial to come; at length persuaded inwardly that this was from God, he yields to go
along with him, who came now the second time with great threatenings to fetch him; the
Chorus yet remaining on the place,* Manoa *returns full of joyful hope to procure ere long
his Son's deliverance: in the midst of which discourse an* Ebrew *comes in haste; confusedly
at first; and afterward more distinctly relating the Catastrophe, what* Samson *had done to
the* Philistins, *and by accident to himself; wherewith the Tragedy ends.*

THE PERSONS

Samson.
Manoa *the Father of* Samson.
Dalila *his Wife.*
Harapha *of* Gath.
Public Officer.
Messenger.
Chorus *of* Danites.

The Scene before the Prison in Gaza.

Samson. A little onward lend thy guiding hand
To these dark steps, a little further on;
For yonder bank hath choice of Sun or shade,
There I am wont to sit, when any chance
Relieves me from my task of servile toil,   5
Daily in the common Prison else enjoin'd me,
Where I a Prisoner chain'd, scarce freely draw
The air imprison'd also, close and damp,
Unwholesome draught: but here I feel amends,
The breath of Heav'n fresh-blowing, pure and sweet,   10
With day-spring born; here leave me to respire.
This day a solemn Feast the people hold
To *Dagon* thir Sea-Idol, and forbid

[handwritten margin note: • little Igor leading him Setting Samson First and foremost.]

tines, called Philistins in the Scripture, a warlike
and powerful people . . . Gaza or Aza signifieth
strong." It lay near the Mediterranean coast in
southwestern Palestine. Compare l. 1605, n.

17 *equals* has its Latin meaning of "contemporaries," persons of about the same age.

18 Commentators worried over *Philistins.* In his
Hexapla in Genesin (Cambridge, 1605), p. 124, Andrew Willet noted that its Septuagint translation as
"aliens or strangers" (*allophyloi*) implied no link
of the Philistines with any Asian people. In *Anno-
tations . . . upon Genesis* (London, 1616; F 1.2),
Henry Ainsworth interpreted their link with the
Caphtorim in Deuteronomy 2.23 and in Jeremiah
47.4 as implying their not improbable Cretan origin.

1–2. The situation resembles that in the opening scene of Sophocles' *Oedipus at Colonus,* where

Antigone leads her blind father forward, and that
in Euripides' *Phoenissae,* 834–5, where the "blind
feet" of Tiresias are guided by his daughter. It
is less like that in Sidney's *Arcadia* II, x, 3, to
which Shakespeare's treatment of Gloucester's
blindness in *Lear* is traced; but E. G. Fogel in
N&Q, CXCVI (1951), 115–117, appositely quotes
Sidney's King of Paphlagonia as he protests that
no one dares "to lend me a hande to guide my
darke steppes."

11. *day-spring:* daybreak. Compare *PL* V, 139,
and VI, 521.

13. Milton's conception of Dagon as a "Sea
Monster, upward Man And downward Fish" (*PL*
I, 462–3) corresponds with the usual derivation of
his name from a Semitic root meaning "fish." In
Phoenicia his name was connected with the word

Laborious works, unwillingly this rest
Thir Superstition yields me; hence with leave   15
Retiring from the popular noise, I seek
This unfrequented place to find some ease;
Ease to the body some, none to the mind
From restless thoughts, that like a deadly swarm
Of Hornets arm'd, no sooner found alone,   20
But rush upon me thronging, and present
Times past, what once I was, and what am now.
O wherefore was my birth from Heaven foretold
Twice by an Angel, who at last in sight
Of both my Parents all in flames ascended   25
From off the Altar, where an Off'ring burn'd,
As in a fiery column charioting
His Godlike presence, and from some great act
Or benefit reveal'd to *Abraham's* race?
Why was my breeding order'd and prescrib'd   30
As of a person separate to God,
Design'd for great exploits; if I must die
Betray'd, Captiv'd, and both my Eyes put out,
Made of my Enemies the scorn and gaze;
To grind in Brazen Fetters under task   35
With this Heav'n-gifted strength? O glorious strength
Put to the labor of a Beast, debas't
Lower than bondslave! Promise was that I
Should *Israel* from *Philistian* yoke deliver;
Ask for this great Deliverer now, and find him   40
Eyeless in *Gaza* at the Mill with slaves,
Himself in bonds under *Philistian* yoke;
Yet stay, let me not rashly call in doubt
Divine Prediction; what if all foretold
Had been fulfill'd but through mine own default,   45
Whom have I to complain of but myself?
Who this high gift of strength committed to me,
In what part lodg'd, how easily bereft me,
Under the Seal of silence could not keep,
But weakly to a woman must reveal it,   50
O'ercome with importunity and tears.
O impotence of mind, in body strong!
But what is strength without a double share
Of wisdom? Vast, unwieldly, burdensome,
Proudly secure, yet liable to fall   55

[marginalia: • questioning of Job]

[marginalia: • opposite of Christian Stoicism, that this world is unimportant]

[marginalia: • but don't overdo the self-pity.]

for corn, *dagan,* and he seems to have been an
agricultural deity. His cult, as Judg. xvi, 23, and
I Sam. v, indicate, centered in the Philistine cities
of Ashdod and Gaza.
22. Compare Satan's "bitter memory Of what
he was, what is" (*PL* IV, 24–25).
24. Samson's birth was foretold to his mother
and later to her and to Manoa (Judg. xiii, 3–5 and
10–20).
27–28. Compare *PR* II, 16–17. Josephus (*Antiquities* V, vii) says that after Manoa had sacrificed
"the angel ascended openly, in their sight, up to
heaven, by means of the smoke as by a vehicle."
31. The root meaning of "Nazarite" was "to
separate," in the sense that men should "separate
themselves to vow a vow of a Nazarite, to separate

themselves unto the Lord; He shall separate himself from wine and strong drink" (Num. iv, 2–3,
and Judg. xiii, 7).
34. *gaze:* gazing stock. So Macduff threatens to
make Macbeth "the shew, and gaze o'th'time"
(*Macbeth* I, viii, 24).
38–39. Compare the angel's prophecy that Samson should "begin to deliver Israel out of the hand
of the Philistines" (Judg. xiii, 5).
53–54. The saying that *Vis consili expers mole
ruit sua* comes from Horace (*Odes* III, iv, 65), but
the thought goes back to Pindar's reflection on the
danger of strength without intelligence (*Pythian
Odes* VIII, 15).
55. *secure* keeps its Latin meaning of "careless,"
or "heedless of danger." Cf. *PR* I, 176.

By weakest subtleties, not made to rule,
But to subserve where wisdom bears command.
God, when he gave me strength, to show withal
How slight the gift was, hung it in my Hair.
But peace, I must not quarrel with the will   60
Of highest dispensation, which herein
Haply had ends above my reach to know:
Suffices that to mee strength is my bane,
And proves the source of all my miseries;
So many, and so huge, that each apart   65
Would ask a life to wail, but chief of all,
O loss of sight, of thee I most complain!   *o Milton knows*
Blind among enemies, O worse than chains,
Dungeon, or beggary, or decrepit age!
Light the prime work of God to me is extinct,   70
And all her various objects of delight
Annull'd, which might in part my grief have eas'd,
Inferior to the vilest now become
Of man or worm; the vilest here excel me,
They creep, yet see; I dark in light expos'd   75
To daily fraud, contempt, abuse and wrong,
Within doors, or without, still as a fool,
In power of others, never in my own;
Scarce half I seem to live, dead more than half.
O dark, dark, dark, amid the blaze of noon,   80
Irrecoverably dark, total Eclipse
Without all hope of day!
O first created Beam, and thou great Word,
"Let there be light, and light was over all";
Why am I thus bereav'd thy prime decree?   85
The Sun to me is dark
And silent as the Moon,
When she deserts the night,
Hid in her vacant interlunar cave.
Since light so necessary is to life,   90
And almost life itself, if it be true
That light is in the Soul,
She all in every part; why was the sight
To such a tender ball as th' eye confin'd?
So obvious and so easy to be quench't,   95
And not as feeling through all parts diffus'd,
That she might look at will through every pore?
Then had I not been thus exil'd from light;

---

63. *bane:* death, ruin. Cf. l. 351.
66. *ask:* require, need.
70. Compare the conception of *light* as the "off-spring of Heav'n first-born" in *PL* III, 1.
77. *still:* always.
82. *all:* any. Compare Lady Macbeth's words: "Things without all remedie Should be without regard" (*Macbeth* III, ii, 11-12).
83. A reminiscence of God's command, "Let there be Light" (Gen. i, 3). Cf. *PL* VII, 243.
86. Editors compare Dante's line (*Inf.* I, 60) saying that in hell the sun is silent, i.e., dark.
87-89. According to Pliny (XVI, xxxix) the Romans called the dark of the moon its interlunar

time or the time of its silence. T. S. Eliot has pronounced 'interlunar" a stroke of genius, but regrets its combination with "vacant" and "cave"—ignoring (as Tillyard notes in *Miltonic Setting,* p. 101) the ancient notion of the moon as vacationing in its "dark" somewhere in a cave beneath the earth.
93. Many mediaeval and Protestant authorities are quoted by Arnold Williams (*MLN,* LXIII—1948—537) as confirming Augustine's doctrine (*De trinitate* V, vi) that the soul is *tota in qualibet parte corporis* (entire in every part of the body). In *CD* I, vii, p. 381, below, Milton misattributes the doctrine to Aristotle and approves it.

As in the land of darkness yet in light,
To live a life half dead, a living death,   100
And buried; but O yet more miserable!
Myself my Sepulcher, a moving Grave,
Buried, yet not exempt
By privilege of death and burial
From worst of other evils, pains and wrongs,   105
But made hereby obnoxious more
To all the miseries of life,
Life in captivity
Among inhuman foes.
But who are these? for with joint pace I hear   110
The tread of many feet steering this way;
Perhaps my enemies who come to stare
At my affliction, and perhaps to insult,
Thir daily practice to afflict me more.
    Chorus.   This, this is he; softly a while,   115
Let us not break in upon him;
O change beyond report, thought, or belief!
See how he lies at random, carelessly diffus'd,
With languish't head unpropt,
As one past hope, abandon'd,   120
And by himself given over;
In slavish habit, ill-fitted weeds
O'erworn and soil'd;
Or do my eyes misrepresent?   Can this be hee,
That Heroic, that Renown'd,   125
Irresistible *Samson?* whom unarm'd
No strength of man, or fiercest wild beast could withstand;
Who tore the Lion, as the Lion tears the Kid,
Ran on embattled Armies clad in Iron,
And weaponless himself,   130
Made Arms ridiculous, useless the forgery
Of brazen shield and spear, the hammer'd Cuirass,
Chalybean temper'd steel, and frock of mail
Adamantean Proof;
But safest he who stood aloof,   135
When insupportably his foot advanc't,
In scorn of thir proud arms and warlike tools,

100. Compare Adam's fear of *a living death* (*PL* X, 788). Many parallels are familiar, from Petrarch's *O viva morte* (Sonnet 102) to Donne's "living buried man" in *The Progresse of the Soul,* 160.

106. *obnoxious* keeps its Latin meaning of "exposed to."

115–175. Milton's parodos or initial choral ode seems to W. R. Parker (*Milton's Debt to Greek Tragedy,* p. 99) to be most closely paralleled in Aeschylus' *Choephorae,* though almost as close formal parallels are found in Sophocles' parodoi in *Oedipus the King* and *Antigone.* The situation resembles the scene in Euripides' *Orestes,* 140–5, where Electra warns the chorus of maidens not to disturb her fury-possessed brother.

118. *diffus'd* keeps its literal Latin meaning of "poured out." Editors compare Ovid's picture of himself in exile, his "languid limbs poured out upon his bed" (*Pontus* III, iii, 8).

119. *languish't:* relaxed. The two words are etymologically related.

122. *habit:* dress. *weeds:* clothes.

128. Judg. xiv, 5–6, tells the story of Samson's finding honey in the carcass of a young lion which "roared against him: . . . and he rent him as he would have rent a kid."

131. *forgery* has the active meaning of "forging."

133. The Chalybes lived in Pontus, on the southern shore of the Black Sea, and were famous for their skill in forging iron.

134. *Adamantean.* In the ancient world the word meant steel of the hardest kind, but in early English "the properties ascribed to it show a confusion of ideas between the diamond and the loadstone or magnet" (*O.E.D.*). Milton described Satan's shield as made of adamant (*PL* VI, 255).

136. *insupportably:* irresistibly.

137. *tools:* weapons. The word often meant "sword," as in *Romeo and Juliet* I, i, 28–29: "Draw

Spurn'd them to death by Troops.   The bold *Ascalonite*
Fled from his Lion ramp, old Warriors turn'd
Thir plated backs under his heel;   140
Or grov'ling soil'd thir crested helmets in the dust.
Then with what trivial weapon came to hand,
The Jaw of a dead Ass, his sword of bone,
A thousand foreskins fell, the flower of *Palestine,*
In *Ramath-lechi* famous to this day: 145
Then by main force pull'd up, and on his shoulders bore
The Gates of *Azza,* Post, and massy Bar
Up to the Hill by *Hebron,* seat of Giants old,
No journey of a Sabbath day, and loaded so;
Like whom the Gentiles feign to bear up Heav'n.   150
Which shall I first bewail,
Thy Bondage or lost Sight,
Prison within Prison
Inseparably dark?
Thou art become (O worst imprisonment!)   155
The Dungeon of thyself; thy Soul
(Which Men enjoying sight oft without cause complain)
Imprison'd now indeed,
In real darkness of the body dwells,
Shut up from outward light   160
To incorporate with gloomy night;
For inward light, alas,
Puts forth no visual beam.
O mirror of our fickle state,
Since man on earth unparallel'd!   165
The rarer thy example stands,
By how much from the top of wondrous glory,
Strongest of mortal men,

[margin, handwritten: blindness outside is metaphor for inner.]

thy toole, here comes two of the house of the Montagues."

138. Ascalon was one of the five great Philistine cities and lay on the Mediterranean coast near Gaza. Samson "went down to Ashkelon, and slew thirty men of them, and took their spoil" (Judg. xiv, 19).

140. *plated:* armor-clad. Shakespeare describes Antony as "like plated Mars" (*Antony and Cleopatra* I, i, 4).

142. The *trivial weapon* was the jawbone of an ass which Samson found "and slew a thousand men therewith" (Judg. xv, 15–16).

144. *Palestine* refers to Philistia. Cf. note 4 on the Argument.

145. Samson "called that place Ramath-lechi" (Judg. xv, 17). The marginal note translates the Hebrew words as "the casting away or the lifting up of the jawbone."

146–149. Samson's last exploit, before his betrayal by Dalila, was his surprise of the Gazites, when he "took the doors of the gate of the city, and the two posts, and went away with them, bar and all, . . . and carried them up to the top of an hill, that is before Hebron" (Judg. xvi, 3).

147. *Azza* was a variant form of *Gaza.* Compare note 2 on the Argument.

148. At *Hebron* the first Hebrew spies who penetrated Palestine saw "the giants, the sons of

Anak, which come of the giants; and so we were in our own sight as grasshoppers, and so we were in their sight" (Num. iii, 33).

150. Milton was even more doubtful than Raleigh (*Historie of the World* II, vi, 4) about the Atlas myths, some of which seemed to Raleigh authentic enough to prove that Atlas was an historic person living in the time of Moses, while others seemed to confuse two or more giants who were supposed to have supported the skies on their shoulders in the Atlas mountains in what is now Morocco.

156. The First Brother puts the same thought into the same metaphor in *Comus,* 383–5, and in *PL* IV, 20–23, it inspires the picture of Satan unable to fly from the "Hell within him."

163. *visual beam,* like the *visual ray* of *PL* III, 620, means the faculty of sight. Milton conceived it in accordance with the "ancient theories" which A. Wolf says in *A History of Science, Technology, and Philosophy* (New York, 1935), p. 244, explained it as "due to something emanating from the eye and falling upon the object seen."

164–173. Samson's *abject fortune* after his rise to glory by his own strength—not by a chance turn of *the sphere* (wheel) *of fortune,* makes him a supreme *mirror* (example) of the reverses of fortune to which men have been subject ever since they have lived on earth.

To lowest pitch of abject fortune thou art fall'n.
For him I reckon not in high estate   170
Whom long descent of birth
Or the sphere of fortune raises;
But thee whose strength, while virtue was her mate,
Might have subdu'd the Earth,
Universally crown'd with highest praises.   175
  Samson. I hear the sound of words, thir sense the air
Dissolves unjointed ere it reach my ear.
  Chorus. He speaks, let us draw nigh. Matchless in might,
The glory late of *Israel,* now the grief;
We come thy friends and neighbors not unknown   180
From *Eshtaol* and *Zora's* fruitful Vale
To visit or bewail thee, or if better,
Counsel or Consolation we may bring,
Salve to thy Sores; apt words have power to swage
The tumors of a troubl'd mind,   185
And are as Balm to fester'd wounds.
  Samson. Your coming, Friends, revives me, for I learn
Now of my own experience, not by talk,
How counterfeit a coin they are who friends
Bear in their Superscription (of the most   190
I would be understood); in prosperous days
They swarm, but in adverse withdraw thir head
Not to be found, though sought. Yee see, O friends;
How many evils have enclos'd me round;
Yet that which was the worst now least afflicts me,   195
Blindness, for had I sight, confus'd with shame,
How could I once look up, or heave the head,
Who like a foolish Pilot have shipwreck't
My Vessel trusted to me from above,
Gloriously rigg'd; and for a word, a tear,   200
Fool, have divulg'd the secret gift of God
To a deceitful Woman: tell me, Friends,
Am I not sung and proverb'd for a Fool
In every street; do they not say, "How well
Are come upon him his deserts?" yet why?   205
Immeasurable strength they might behold
In me, of wisdom nothing more than mean;
This with the other should, at least, have pair'd,
These two proportion'd ill drove me transverse.

[handwritten marginal note: more than just the Biblical fdlk-hero *]*

---

181. The story of Samson opens in Judges (xiii, 2) with the statement that his father, Manoah, was a citizen of *Zora.* The town lay in the coastal plain of Sorec (mentioned in l. 229), and in the list of cities in that valley in Joshua xv, 33, it is mentioned next after *Eshtaol.*

184. *Salve to . . . Sores* was a proverbial phrase and is illustrated by Britomart's refusal in *F.Q.* III, ii, 36–37, to accept "idle wordes" as salve to her sores. Of the many parallels to the thought one of the most interesting is the question of Ocean in Aeschylus' *Prometheus Bound,* 379—which was famous because Cicero quoted it in the *Tusculan Disputations* (III, xxxi):
Know'st thou not this, Prometheus, that mild words
Are medicines of fierce wrath?

185. *Tumor* was often used to mean a swelling of passion in the mind. *O.E.D.* quotes Sir Henry Wotton: "There is in him no tumour, no sowrenesse, . . . but a quiet mind."

190. *Superscription:* stamp denoting the value of a coin.

191. Editors compare Ovid's lines from the *Tristia* (I, ix, 5–6): "Whilst thou art happy, thou numberest countless friends; once skies are overcast, thou art alone."

203. David, in despair over his "foolishness," says (Ps. lxix, 11) that he has became "a proverb" to his enemies, and Job's worst chagrin is the fact that he is "a byword to the people" (Job xvii, 6).

207. *mean:* ordinary, average.

208. *pair'd:* equalled.

209. *transverse:* off the straight course (i.e., of Samson's intended career).

Chorus. Tax not divine disposal; wisest Men   210
Have err'd, and by bad Women been deceiv'd;
And shall again, pretend they ne'er so wise.
Deject not then so overmuch thyself,
Who hast of sorrow thy full load besides;
Yet truth to say, I oft have heard men wonder   215
Why thou shouldst wed *Philistian* women rather
Than of thine own Tribe fairer, or as fair,
At least of thy own Nation, and as noble.
    Samson. The first I saw at *Timna,* and she pleas'd
Mee, not my Parents, that I sought to wed,   220
The daughter of an Infidel: they knew not
That what I motion'd was of God; I knew
From intimate impulse, and therefore urg'd
The Marriage on; that by occasion hence
I might begin *Israel's* Deliverance,   225
The work to which I was divinely call'd;
She proving false, the next I took to Wife
(O that I never had! fond wish too late)
Was in the Vale of *Sorec, Dalila,*
That specious Monster, my accomplisht snare.   230
I thought it lawful from my former act,
And the same end; still watching to oppress
Israel's oppressors: of what now I suffer
She was not the prime cause, but I myself,
Who vanquisht with a peal of words (O weakness!)   235
Gave up my fort of silence to a Woman.
    Chorus. In seeking just occasion to provoke
The *Philistine,* thy Country's Enemy,
Thou never wast remiss, I bear thee witness:
Yet *Israel* still serves with all his Sons.   240
    Samson. That fault I take not on me, but transfer
On *Israel's* Governors, and Heads of Tribes,
Who seeing those great acts which God had done
Singly by me against their Conquerors
Acknowledg'd not, or not at all consider'd   245
Deliverance offer'd: I on th' other side
Us'd no ambition to commend my deeds,
The deeds themselves, though mute, spoke loud the doer;
But they persisted deaf, and would not seem

[handwritten margin note: Free will / problem / again]

210. In *Animadversions* (C. E. III, 144) Milton
warned his readers not to "taxe the renovating
Spirit of God with innovation."

210–212. In *Tetrachordon* (C. E. IV, 92) Milton
described Adam in Eden as the only man who ever
"had the gift to . . . apprehend at first sight the
true fitness of that consort which God provided
him," while "the best and wisest men, amidst the
sincere and cordial designs of their hearts, do daily
err in choosing."

219–225. The account of Samson's resolve to
marry the woman of *Timna* in Judges xiv, 1–4, does
not suggest that his motive was passion; and his
reply to his parents' protest against his marriage
with a Philistine—"Get her for me for she pleaseth
me well"—is justified by the statement that "his
father and mother knew not that it was of the
Lord, that he sought the occasion against the Philistines."

230. Compare "specious object of the foe
suborn'd" in *PL* IX, 361. *Accomplisht,* says
Empson (*Seven Types,* p. 102), puns on Dalila's
accomplished charms and her accomplishment of
Samson's ruin.

235. It was only when Dalila "pressed him daily
with her words, and urged him, so that his soul
was vexed unto death, that he told her all his
heart, and said unto her, There hath not a razor
come upon mine head for I have been a Nazarite
unto God from my mother's womb: if I be shaven,
then my strength will go from me" (Judg. xiv, 16–
17). Compare *peal* in the figure of a volley of
cannon-shot in l. 906 below.

240. *serves:* is in subjection (to the Philistines).
245. *consider'd:* esteemed, appreciated.
247. *ambition* keeps its Latin meaning of can-
vassing for public support. *O.E.D.* cites Houssaie's
Government of Venice: "This bartering and ambition of Office was forbidden."

To count them things worth notice, till at length 250
Thir Lords, the *Philistines,* with gather'd powers
Enter'd *Judea* seeking mee, who then
Safe to the rock of *Etham* was retir'd,
Not flying, but forecasting in what place
To set upon them, what advantag'd best; 255
Meanwhile the men of *Judah* to prevent
The harass of thir Land, beset me round;
I willingly on some conditions came
Into thir hands, and they as gladly yield me
To the uncircumcis'd a welcome prey, 260
Bound with two cords; but cords to me were threads
Toucht with the flame: on thir whole Host I flew
Unarm'd, and with a trivial weapon fell'd
Their choicest youth; they only liv'd who fled.
Had *Judah* that day join'd, or one whole Tribe, 265
They had by this possess'd the Towers of *Gath,*
And lorded over them whom now they serve;
But what more oft in Nations grown corrupt,
And by thir vices brought to servitude,
Than to love Bondage more than Liberty, 270
Bondage with ease than strenuous liberty;
And to despise, or envy, or suspect
Whom God hath of his special favor rais'd
As thir Deliverer; if he aught begin,
How frequent to desert him, and at last 275
To heap ingratitude on worthiest deeds?
   Chorus. Thy words to my remembrance bring
How *Succoth* and the Fort of *Penuel*
Thir great Deliverer contemn'd,
The matchless *Gideon* in pursuit 280
Of *Madian* and her vanquisht Kings:
And how ingrateful *Ephraim*
Had dealt with *Jephtha,* who by argument,
Not worse than by his shield and spear
Defended *Israel* from the *Ammonite,* 285
Had not his prowess quell'd thir pride
In that sore battle when so many died

253–264. It was to consider his next step after smiting the Philistines "hip and thigh with a great slaughter," that Samson "went and dwelt in the top of the rock Etam" (Judg. xv, 8). There he hoped that the Hebrews would rally to him, but the "three thousand men of Judah" who came to him asked them to allow them to bind him and deliver him to the Philistines. "And Samson said unto them, Swear unto me, that ye will not fall upon me yourselves. And they spake unto him, saying, No; but we will bind thee fast, and deliver thee into their hand. . . . And when he came unto Lehi, the Philistines shouted against him: and the Spirit of the Lord came mightily upon him, and the cords that were upon his arms became as flax that was burnt with fire, and his bands loosed from off his hands" (Judg. xv, 12–14). The sequel has been mentioned in ll. 142–5 above.

266. *Gath* stands here for the whole country of Philistia, one of whose five great cities it was.

270. Cf. *PL* II, 255–7, n.

278–281. The *vanquisht Kings* were "Zebah and Zalmunna, kings of Midian," in whose pursuit the men of the Hebrew cities of *Succoth* and *Penuel* refused to aid *Gideon* (Judg. viii, 4–9).

282–289. *Jephtha's* diplomatic and military victory over the *Ammonites* is recorded in Judges xi, 12–33. Later he and his Gileadite supporters quarreled with the Ephraimite Hebrews, who had refused to help him against the Ammonites. The successful Gileadites seized the fords of the Jordan and, "when those Ephraimites which were escaped said, Let me go over; . . . the men of Gilead said unto him, Art thou an Ephraimite? If he said, Nay; Then said they unto him, Say now Shibboleth; and he said Sibboleth: for he could not frame to pronounce it right. Then they . . . slew him . . . : and there fell . . . of the Ephraimites forty and two thousand" (Judg. xii, 5–6).

Without Reprieve adjudg'd to death,
For want of well pronouncing *Shibboleth.*
   Samson. Of such examples add mee to the roll,   290
Mee easily indeed mine may neglect,
But God's propos'd deliverance not so.
   Chorus. Just are the ways of God,
And justifiable to Men;
Unless there be who think not God at all: 295
If any be, they walk obscure;
For of such Doctrine never was there School,
But the heart of the Fool,
And no man therein Doctor but himself.
   Yet more there be who doubt his ways not just,   300
As to his own edícts, found contradicting,
Then give the reins to wand'ring thought,
Regardless of his glory's diminution;
Till by thir own perplexities involv'd
They ravel more, still less resolv'd,   305
But never find self-satisfying solution.
   As if they would confine th' interminable,
And tie him to his own prescript,
Who made our Laws to bind us, not himself,
And hath full right to exempt   310
Whom so it pleases him by choice
From National obstriction, without taint
Of sin, or legal debt;
For with his own Laws he can best dispense.
   He would not else who never wanted means,   315
Nor in respect of th'enemy just cause
To set his people free,
Have prompted this Heroic *Nazarite,*
Against his vow of strictest purity,
To seek in marriage that fallacious Bride,   320
Unclean, unchaste.
   Down Reason then, at least vain reasonings down,
Though Reason here aver
That moral verdict quits her of unclean:
Unchaste was subsequent, her stain not his.   325
     But see here comes thy reverend Sire
With careful step, Locks white as down,
Old *Manoa:* advise
Forthwith how thou ought'st to receive him.

291. *mine:* i.e., my people. Compare the parallel Latinism in *thine* in l. 1169.

293. There is an echo of the song of the triumphant host on the fiery sea of glass in Revelation xv, 3: ". . . just and true are thy ways, thou King of saints."

295. Milton used a Greek construction familiar to him in many authors, from Herodotus to Plato, in expressions of disbelief in the gods.

298–325. This first stasimon by its echo of Psalm xiv, 1, sets an example for later choruses reflecting Milton's deepest convictions. Psalm xiv, 1, introduces the chapter "Of God" in *CD.*

305. *ravel* is used in its primitive meaning of "become tangled." *resolv'd:* unperplexed. Cf. the Duke in *Measure for Measure* IV, ii, 225: "You are amazed but this shall absolutely resolve you."

307. *interminable:* infinite, boundless (of God).

312. *obstriction:* legal obligation or limitation. The reference is to the law against gentile marriages in Deuteronomy vii, 3.

319. *strictest purity,* in Mosaic law, did not imply celibacy; but any infraction of the law made the sinner "impure."

320. *fallacious:* deceitful.

321. Dalila's "uncleanness" was the ritual uncleanness of all gentiles, with whom even the bread that was eaten by the Jews was "defiled" (Ezek. iv, 13).

327. *careful* keeps its literal force of "full of care."

328. *advise:* take thought, consider.

Samson.   Ay me, another inward grief awak't,   330
With mention of that name renews th' assault.
   Manoa.   Brethren and men of *Dan,* for such ye seem,
Though in this uncouth place; if old respect,
As I suppose, towards your once gloried friend,
My Son now Captive, hither hath inform'd   335
Your younger feet, while mine cast back with age
Came lagging after; say if he be here.
   Chorus.   As signal now in low dejected state,
As erst in highest, behold him where he lies.
   Manoa.   O miserable change! is this the man,   340
That invincible *Samson,* far renown'd,
The dread of *Israel's* foes, who with a strength
Equivalent to Angels' walk'd thir streets,
None offering fight; who single combatant
Duell'd thir Armies rank't in proud array,   345
Himself an Army, now unequal match
To save himself against a coward arm'd
At one spear's length.   O ever failing trust
In mortal strength! and oh, what not in man
Deceivable and vain!   Nay, what thing good   350
Pray'd for, but often proves our woe, our bane?
I pray'd for Children, and thought barrenness
In wedlock a reproach; I gain'd a Son,
And such a Son as all Men hail'd me happy;
Who would be now a Father in my stead?   355
O wherefore did God grant me my request,
And as a blessing with such pomp adorn'd?
Why are his gifts desirable, to tempt
Our earnest Prayers, then, giv'n with solemn hand
As Graces, draw a Scorpion's tail behind?   360
For this did th'Angel twice descend? for this
Ordain'd thy nurture holy, as of a Plant?
Select, and Sacred, Glorious for a while,
The miracle of men: then in an hour
Ensnar'd, assaulted, overcome, led bound,   365
Thy Foes' derision, Captive, Poor, and Blind,
Into a Dungeon thrust, to work with Slaves?
Alas! methinks whom God hath chosen once
To worthiest deeds, if he through frailty err,
He should not so o'erwhelm, and as a thrall   370
Subject him to so foul indignities,
Be it but for honor's sake of former deeds.
   Samson.   Appoint not heavenly disposition, Father,
Nothing of all these evils hath befall'n me
But justly; I myself have brought them on,   375
Sole Author I, sole cause: if aught seem vile,

---

333. *uncouth:* unknown, strange. Compare Raphael's "voyage uncouth and obscure" in *PL* III, 230.

334. *gloried* may mean either "honored" or "boasted."

335. *inform'd:* guided. So the Lady in *Comus,* 179–80, asks, ". . . where else, Shall I inform my unacquainted feet?"

338. *signal:* eminent, conspicuous.

345. *Duell'd:* fought alone against whole armies as if he and they were equal antagonists in a duel.

360. *Graces:* favors. Perhaps there is a glance at Luke xi, 12: "If a son shall ask of his father an egg, will he offer him a scorpion?"

373. *Appoint:* prescribe a course of action. Cf. *Areop* (p. 748): "Neither is God appointed and confined . . ."

As vile hath been my folly, who have profan'd
The mystery of God giv'n me under pledge
Of vow, and have betray'd it to a woman,
A *Canaanite*, my faithless enemy.   380
This well I knew, nor was at all surpris'd,
But warn'd by oft experience: did not she
Of *Timna* first betray me, and reveal
The secret wrested from me in her height
Of Nuptial Love profest, carrying it straight   385
To them who had corrupted her, my Spies,
And Rivals? In this other was there found
More Faith? who also in her prime of love,
Spousal embraces, vitiated with Gold,
Though offer'd only, by the scent conceiv'd   390
Her spurious first-born; Treason against me?
Thrice she assay'd with flattering prayers and sighs,
And amorous reproaches to win from me
My capital secret, in what part my strength
Lay stor'd, in what part summ'd, that she might know: 395
Thrice I deluded her, and turn'd to sport
Her importunity, each time perceiving
How openly, and with what impudence
She purpos'd to betray me, and (which was worse
Than undissembl'd hate) with what contempt   400
She sought to make me Traitor to myself;
Yet the fourth time, when must'ring all her wiles,
With blandisht parleys, feminine assaults,
Tongue batteries, she surceas'd not day nor night
To storm me over-watch't, and wearied out.   405
At times when men seek most repose and rest,
I yielded, and unlock'd her all my heart,
Who with a grain of manhood well resolv'd
Might easily have shook off all her snares:
But foul effeminacy held me yok't   410
Her Bondslave; O indignity, O blot
To Honor and Religion! servile mind
Rewarded well with servile punishment!
The base degree to which I now am fall'n,
These rags, this grinding, is not yet so base   415
As was my former servitude, ignoble,
Unmanly, ignominious, infamous,

377. *profan'd* has its Latin meaning of "disclose a sacred secret."

380. The Philistines might be called *Canaanites* because they were the earliest conquerors of the land of Canaan.

382–387. At Samson's wedding with the woman of *Timna* he challenged his thirty Philistine groomsmen to solve the riddle: "Out of the eater came forth meat, and out of the strong came forth sweetness." Unable to solve it, "they said unto Samson's wife, Entice thy husband, that he may declare unto us the riddle. . . . And she wept before him the seven days, while their feast lasted; and . . . on the seventh day . . . he told her . . . and she told the riddle to the children of her people. And the men of the city said unto him . . . What *is* sweeter than honey? and what *is* stronger than a lion? And he said unto them, If ye had not plowed with my heifer, ye had not found out my riddle" (Judg. xiv, 11–18).

390. The offer of the lords of the Philistines to Dalila, if she could extract Samson's secret, was "eleven hundred pieces of silver" from every one of them (Judg. xvi, 5).

394. Here and in the allusion to the Serpent's "capital bruise" (*PL* XII, 383) there is an overtone of the word's Latin meaning of "pertaining to the head" from which the meaning "fatal" is derived.

402. *must'ring*: assembling (like troops). Cf. the military metaphor in *peal* in ll. 235 and 906.

405. *over-watch't*: tired out with keeping awake. Compare the "seafaring men o'er-watcht" of *PL* II, 288.

True slavery, and that blindness worse than this,
That saw not how degenerately I serv'd.
   Manoa. I cannot praise thy marriage choices, Son,   420
Rather approv'd them not; but thou didst plead
Divine impulsion prompting how thou might'st
Find some occasion to infest our Foes.
I state not that; this I am sure; our Foes
Found soon occasion thereby to make thee   425
Thir Captive, and thir triumph; thou the sooner
Temptation found'st, or over potent charms
To violate the sacred trust of silence
Deposited within thee; which to have kept
Tacit, was in thy power; true; and thou bear'st   430
Enough, and more the burden of that fault;
Bitterly hast thou paid, and still art paying
That rigid score. A worse thing yet remains.
This day the *Philistines* a popular Feast
Here celebrate in *Gaza;* and proclaim   435
Great Pomp, and Sacrifice, and Praises loud
To *Dagon,* as their God who hath deliver'd
Thee, *Samson,* bound and blind into thir hands,
Them out of thine, who slew'st them many a slain.
So *Dagon* shall be magnified, and God,   440
Besides whom is no God, compar'd with Idols,
Disglorified, blasphem'd, and had in scorn
By th' Idolatrous rout amidst thir wine;
Which to have come to pass by means of thee,
Samson, of all thy sufferings think the heaviest,   445
Of all reproach the most with shame that ever
Could have befall'n thee and thy Father's house.
   Samson. Father, I do acknowledge and confess
That I this honor, I this pomp have brought
To *Dagon,* and advanc'd his praises high   450
Among the Heathen round; to God have brought
Dishonor, obloquy, and op't the mouths
Of Idolists, and Atheists; have brought scandal
To *Israel,* diffidence of God, and doubt
In feeble hearts, propense enough before   455
To waver, or fall off and join with Idols:
Which is my chief affliction, shame and sorrow,
The anguish of my Soul, that suffers not
Mine eye to harbor sleep, or thoughts to rest.
This only hope relieves me, that the strife   460
With mee hath end; all the contést is now
'Twixt God and *Dagon; Dagon* hath presum'd,
Mee overthrown, to enter lists with God,

---

423. *infest:* annoy, molest.

430. *Tacit* keeps the force of the Latin participle from which it comes; "covered in silence," "not mentioned."

433. *score:* record of a debt.

434–439. After Samson's betrayal, "the lords of the Philistines gathered them together for to offer a great sacrifice unto Dagon their god, and to rejoice: for they said, Our god hath delivered Samson our enemy into our hand" (Judg. xvi, 23).

439. *them* is in the dative case and *slain* is the direct object of *slew'st;* i.e., "slew many to their disadvantage."

453. *Idolists* seems to have been first used by Sylvester. *O.E.D.* quotes from *Bethulia's Rescue* II, 498: "You shall . . . make ruddy Mocmur's Floud, With Idolist Assyrian Armies bloud."

454. *diffidence:* distrust, absolute want of confidence.

455. *propense:* having a propensity, inclined.

463. *Me overthrown:* since my overthrow.

His Deity comparing and preferring
Before the God of *Abraham*. He, be sure,   465
Will not connive, or linger, thus provok'd,
But will arise and his great name assert:
Dagon must stoop, and shall ere long receive
Such a discomfit, as shall quite despoil him
Of all these boasted Trophies won on me,   470
And with confusion blank his Worshippers.
    Manoa.   With cause this hope relieves thee, and these words
I as a Prophecy receive: for God,
Nothing more certain, will not long defer
To vindicate the glory of his name   475
Against all competition, nor will long
Endure it, doubtful whether God be Lord,
Or *Dagon*. But for thee what shall be done?
Thou must not in the meanwhile here forgot
Lie in this miserable loathsome plight   480
Neglected. I already have made way
To some *Philistian* Lords, with whom to treat
About thy ransom: well they may by this
Have satisfied thir utmost of revenge
By pains and slaveries, worse than death inflicted   485
On thee, who now no more canst do them harm.
    Samson.   Spare that proposal, Father, spare the trouble
Of that solicitation; let me here,
As I deserve, pay on my punishment;
And expiate, if possible, my crime,   490
Shameful garrulity. To have reveal'd
Secrets of men, the secrets of a friend,
How heinous had the fact been, how deserving
Contempt, and scorn of all, to be excluded
All friendship, and avoided as a blab,   495
The mark of fool set on his front? But I
God's counsel have not kept, his holy secret
Presumptuously have publish'd, impiously,
Weakly at least, and shamefully: A sin
That Gentiles in thir Parables condemn   500
To thir abyss and horrid pains confin'd.
    Manoa.   Be penitent and for thy fault contríte,
But act not in thy own affliction, Son;
Repent the sin, but if the punishment
Thou canst avoid, self-preservation bids;   505
Or th' execution leave to high disposal,
And let another hand, not thine, exact
Thy penal forfeit from thyself; perhaps

466. *connive,* here as in *PL* X, 624, has the
Latin sense of "shut the eyes," or "ignore."
    471. *blank:* confound. Compare Satan in *PR* II,
119–20; "without sign of boast, or sign of joy,
Solicitous and blank."
    493. *fact:* deed. Adam, referring to the sin in
Eden, says, "perhaps the Fact/Is not so heinous
now" (*PL* IX, 928–9).
    499–501. Milton thought of the myth of Tantalus,
who, Euripides says (*Orestes,* 10), was punished in
Hades for revealing the secrets of the gods. Natale
Conti, in whose *Mythology* (VI, xviii) several al-

legorical interpretations are represented, preferred
this of Euripides. In a number of classical references to Tantalus (e.g., Ovid, *Met.* IV, 457) Conti
found evidence that he was condemned for his
"loquacity, because he divulged the secrets of the
gods."
    503–508. In *CD* II, viii, Milton defines *righteous-
ness* as justice to a man's self. "Opposed to this
is, first, a perverse hatred of self. In this class are
to be reckoned those who lay violent hands on
themselves."

God will relent, and quit thee all his debt;
Who evermore approves and more accepts   510
(Best pleas'd with humble and filial submission)
Him who imploring mercy sues for life,
Than who self-rigorous chooses death as due;
Which argues over-just, and self-displeas'd
For self-offence, more than for God offended.   515
Reject not then what offer'd means, who knows
But God hath set before us, to return thee
Home to thy country and his sacred house,
Where thou mayst bring thy off'rings, to avert
His further ire, with prayers and vows renew'd.   520
   Samson.   His pardon I implore; but as for life,
To what end should I seek it? when in strength
All mortals I excell'd, and great in hopes
With youthful courage and magnanimous thoughts
Of birth from Heav'n foretold and high exploits,   525
Full of divine instinct, after some proof
Of acts indeed heroic, far beyond
The Sons of *Anak,* famous now and blaz'd,
Fearless of danger, like a petty God
I walk'd about admir'd of all and dreaded   530
On hostile ground, none daring my affront.
Then swoll'n with pride into the snare I fell
Of fair fallacious looks, venereal trains,
Soft'n'd with pleasure and voluptuous life;
At length to lay my head and hallow'd pledge   535
Of all my strength in the lascivious lap
Of a deceitful Concubine who shore me
Like a tame Wether, all my precious fleece,
Then turn'd me out ridiculous, despoil'd,
Shav'n, and disarm'd among my enemies.   540
   Chorus.   Desire of wine and all delicious drinks,
Which many a famous Warrior overturns,
Thou couldst repress, nor did the dancing Ruby
Sparkling, outpour'd, the flavor, or the smell,
Or taste that cheers the heart of Gòds and men,   545
Allure thee from the cool Crystálline stream.
   Samson.   Wherever fountain or fresh current flow'd

---

509. *quit thee all his debt:* cancel all your debt.
Compare *Merchant of Venice* IV, i, 381: "To quit
the fine for one half of his goods, I am content."

514. *argues over-just:* proves a person excessively
just or rigorous toward himself. Compare Satan's
words to Gabriel: "But still thy words . . . Argue
thy inexperience" (*PL* IV, 930–1).

526. *instinct:* inward knowledge or impulse.
Compare *PL* X, 262–3:
  Nor can I miss the way, so strongly drawn
  By this new felt attraction and instinct.

533. *venereal trains:* tricks to arouse physical
passion.

535–540. Milton remembered the scene in Judg.
xvi, 19, when Dalila made Samson "sleep upon
her knees: and she called for a man, and she
caused him to shave off the seven locks of his head;
and she began to afflict him, and his strength went
from him."   Compare *PL* IX, 1059–62.

541–546. For the Nazarite vow of abstinence see
the note on l. 31. Here there is a reminiscence of
Jotham's parable of the trees which asked the vine
to be their king. "And the vine said unto them,
Should I leave my wine, which cheereth God and
man, and go to be promoted over the trees?"
(Judg. ix, 13.)

547–549. Thyer compared Tasso's verses in *The
Seven Days of the World's Creation* (III, 133–40)
which say that of all pleasant waters the most
wholesome is that which springs out of clayey soil
in the face of the rising sun. Professor Percival
traces this idea, which is paralleled in Burton's
Anatomy (II, ii, 1, 1; Vol. II, 23), back as far as
Ezekiel's vision of the waters which "issue out
toward the east country, and go down into the
desert, and go into the sea; which being brought
forth into the sea, the waters shall be healed"
(Ezek. xlvii, 8).

Against the Eastern ray, translucent, pure,
With touch ethereal of Heav'n's fiery rod
I drank, from the clear milky juice allaying   550
Thirst, and refresht; nor envied them the grape
Whose heads that turbulent liquor fills with fumes.
    Chorus. O madness, to think use of strongest wines
And strongest drinks our chief support of health,
When God with these forbidd'n made choice to rear   555
His mighty Champion, strong above compare,
Whose drink was only from the liquid brook.
    Samson. But what avail'd this temperance, not complete
Against another object more enticing?
What boots it at one gate to make defense,   560
And at another to let in the foe,
Effeminately vanquish't? by which means,
Now blind, disheart'n'd, sham'd, dishonor'd, quell'd,
To what can I be useful, wherein serve
My Nation, and the work from Heav'n impos'd,   565
But to sit idle on the household hearth,
A burdenous drone; to visitants a gaze,
Or pitied object, these redundant locks
Robustious to no purpose clust'ring down,
Vain monument of strength; till length of years   570
And sedentary numbness craze my limbs
To a contemptible old age obscure?
Here rather let me drudge and earn my bread,
Till vermin or the draff of servile food
Consume me, and oft-invocated death   575
Hast'n the welcome end of all my pains.
    Manoa. Wilt thou then serve the *Philistines* with that gift
Which was expressly giv'n thee to annoy them?
Better at home lie bedrid, not only idle,
Inglorious, unemploy'd, with age outworn.   580
But God who caus'd a fountain at thy prayer
From the dry ground to spring, thy thirst to allay
After the brunt of battle, can as easy
Cause light again within thy eyes to spring,
Wherewith to serve him better than thou hast;   585
And I persuade me so; why else this strength

550. *milky juice,* like the "milky stream" of *PL*
V, 306, is used for sweet or fresh water.

552. *fumes:* influences from food or drink penetrating the body and brain, like the "unkindly
fumes" of *PL* IX, 1050, which bred a gross sleep
in Adam and Eve after they had eaten the fruit
of the Tree of Knowledge.

553–557. Compare Milton's definition of temperance in *CD* II, ix, as consisting first in sobriety or
"abstinence from immoderate eating and drinking."
Compare also *PL* XI, 531–2.

557. *liquid* is used in the Latin sense of "trans-
lucent" or "transparent." Compare the "liquid
Light" of *PL* VII, 362, and the "liquid Air" of
Comus, 980.

560. *What boots it:* what good does it do?
Compare *Lyc,* 64–65.

568. *redundant* is used in the Latin sense of
"waving" or "flowing."

569. *Robustious* is used without any unfavor-

able connotation, and means strong or healthy
looking.

571. *craze:* to impair or render infirm. *O.E.D.*
cites Heywood's *Dialogue:* "Craz'd . . . or in
health."

574. *draff:* offal. Compare the "draff and filth"
of *PL,* X, 630.

581–583. The story is told in Judg. xv, 18–19.
Josephus says (*Antiquities* V, viii, 9) that God,
moved by Samson's entreaties when he was athirst
after his victory at Ramath-lechi (see the note on
l. 145 above), "raised him up a plentiful fountain
of sweet water at a certain rock; whence it was
that Samson called the place *The Jaw-bone.*"

586. The hope that Samson's strength would
return with the growth of his hair is suggested by
the statement in Judg. xvi, 22: "Howbeit the hair
of his head began to grow again after he was
shaven." Compare l. 1355 below.

Miraculous yet remaining in those locks?
His might continues in thee not for naught,
Nor shall his wondrous gifts be frustrate thus.
   Samson.   All otherwise to me my thoughts portend,   590
That these dark orbs no more shall treat with light,
Nor th' other light of life continue long,
But yield to double darkness nigh at hand:
So much I feel my genial spirits droop,
My hopes all flat, nature within me seems   595
In all her functions weary of herself;
My race of glory run, and race of shame,
And I shall shortly be with them that rest.
   Manoa.   Believe not these suggestions which proceed
From anguish of the mind and humors black,   600
That mingle with thy fancy.   I however
Must not omit a Father's timely care
To prosecute the means of thy deliverance
By ransom or how else: meanwhile be calm,
And healing words from these thy friends admit.   605
   Samson.   O that torment should not be confin'd
To the body's wounds and sores
With maladies innumerable
In heart, head, breast, and reins;
But must secret passage find   610
To th' inmost mind,
There exercise all his fierce accidents,
And on her purest spirits prey,
As on entrails, joints, and limbs,
With answerable pains, but more intense,   615
Though void of corporal sense.
   My griefs not only pain me
As a ling'ring disease,
But finding no redress, ferment and rage,
Nor less than wounds immedicable   620
Rankle, and fester, and gangrene,
To black mortification.
Thoughts my Tormentors arm'd with deadly stings
Mangle my apprehensive tenderest parts,
Exasperate, exulcerate, and raise   625
Dire inflammation which no cooling herb
Or med'cinal liquor can assuage,
Nor breath of Vernal Air from snowy *Alp.*
Sleep hath forsook and giv'n me o'er
To death's benumbing Opium as my only cure.   630
Thence faintings, swoonings of despair,
And sense of Heav'n's desertion.

593. *double darkness*: darkness of blindness and of death.

594. *genial*: arising from a man's "genius" or natural character. *O.E.D.* cites Sir Thomas Browne's *Pseudodoxia Epidemica:* "Naturall incapacity, and geniall indisposition."

599–601. Compare the note on ll. 8–11 in the Preface.

605. *healing words* may not be unrelated to the misapplied healing words of the nurse in Euripides' *Hippolytus,* 478. Cf. l. 184 above.

609. *reins*: kidneys.

612. *accidents* was regularly used to mean symptoms of disease of any kind. Burton mentions "Old age, from which natural melancholy is almost an inseparable accident" (*Anatomy* I, i, 3, 2; Vol. I, 172).

624. *apprehensive*: sensitive.

628. *Alp*: any high mountain. PL II, 620, describes the devils passing "many a Frozen, many a Fiery Alp."

I was his nursling once and choice delight,
His destin'd from the womb,
Promis'd by Heavenly message twice descending.   635
Under his special eye
Abstemious I grew up and thriv'd amain;
He led me on to mightiest deeds
Above the nerve of mortal arm
Against th'uncircumcis'd, our enemies.   640
But now hath cast me off as never known,
And to those cruel enemies,
Whom I by his appointment had provok't,
Left me all helpless with th' irreparable loss
Of sight, reserv'd alive to be repeated   645
The subject of thir cruelty, or scorn.
Nor am I in the list of them that hope;
Hopeless are all my evils, all remediless;
This one prayer yet remains, might I be heard,
No long petition, speedy death,   650
The close of all my miseries, and the balm.
   Chorus. Many are the sayings of the wise
In ancient and in modern books enroll'd,
Extolling Patience as the truest fortitude,
And to the bearing well of all calamities,   655
All chances incident to man's frail life
Consolatories writ
With studied argument, and much persuasion sought
Lenient of grief and anxious thought,
But with th'afflicted in his pangs thir sound   660
Little prevails, or rather seems a tune,
Harsh, and of dissonant mood from his complaint,
Unless he feel within
Some source of consolation from above;
Secret refreshings, that repair his strength,   665
And fainting spirits uphold.
   God of our Fathers, what is man!
That thou towards him with hand so various,
Or might I say contrarious,
Temper'st thy providence through his short course,   670
Not evenly, as thou rul'st
Th'Angelic orders and inferior creatures mute,
Irrational and brute.

635. *message:* messenger.
639. *nerve:* sinew or muscle. Compare its use in l. 1646 below.
645. *repeated:* made to repeat the experience of being over and over *the subject of their cruelty.*
652–656. An example of such *sayings of the wise* is Henry More's chapter in *An Account of Virtue* (II, vii) which quotes Aristotle, Andronicus of Rhodes, and Cicero in its consideration of "Fortitude" as a "Branch of Patience." Elsewhere (II, iii) More calls Christian patience "the highest perfection of Man's Will." Compare ll. 1287–92 below.
659. *Lenient:* softening, allaying. Grammatically, the word is equivalent to the Latin participle from which it is derived. In a familiar assertion of the power of philosophy to heal suffering,

Horace used the word in *Epistles* (I, i, 34).
662. *mood* is the musical term. Compare *PL* I, 550, and *L'All,* 136.
667. Milton repeats the question, "What is man, that thou art mindful of him?" which is echoed in Heb. ii, 6, from Ps. viii, 4, and varied in Job vii, 17, to "What is man, that thou shouldest magnify him?" Probably he remembered the same question as put to Prometheus in the second choral hymn of Aeschylus' *Prometheus Bound:*
            What is man? behold!
Can he requite thy love—child of a day—
Or help thy extreme need?
            (Blackie's translation)
672. Compare the angels "Under thir Hierarchs in orders bright" (*PL* V, 587).

Nor do I name of men the common rout,
That wand'ring loose about   675
Grow up and perish, as the summer fly,
Heads without name no more remember'd,
But such as thou hast solemnly elected,
With gifts and graces eminently adorn'd
To some great work, thy glory,   680
And people's safety, which in part they effect:
Yet toward these, thus dignifi'd, thou oft,
Amidst thir height of noon,
Changest thy count'nance and thy hand, with no regard
Of highest favors past   685
From thee on them, or them to thee of service.
    Nor only dost degrade them, or remit
To life obscur'd, which were a fair dismission,
But throw'st them lower than thou didst exalt them high,
Unseemly falls in human eye,   690
Too grievous for the trespass or omission,
Oft leav'st them to the hostile sword
Of Heathen and profane, thir carcases
To dogs and fowls a prey, or else captív'd:
Or to th'unjust tribunals, under change of times,   695
And condemnation of th'ingrateful multitude.
If these they scape, perhaps in poverty
With sickness and disease thou bow'st them down,
Painful diseases and deform'd,
In crude old age;   700
Though not disordinate, yet causeless suff'ring
The punishment of dissolute days: in fine,
Just or unjust, alike seem miserable,
For oft alike, both come to evil end.
    So deal not with this once thy glorious Champion,   705
The Image of thy strength, and mighty minister.
What do I beg? how hast thou dealt already?
Behold him in this state calamitous, and turn
His labors, for thou canst, to peaceful end.
    But who is this, what thing of Sea or Land?   710
Female of sex it seems,
That so bedeckt, ornate, and gay,
Comes this way sailing
Like a stately Ship
Of *Tarsus,* bound for th' Isles   715

687. *remit:* return, send back.
688. *obscur'd:* disgraced.
693–696. Milton may have had in mind the insult to the bodies of Cromwell, Ireton, and Bradshaw, which were exhumed and hanged on a gallows in Tyburn on the twelfth anniversary of Charles I's execution—worse treated than the Greeks whose bodies Homer says were thrown to the dogs and birds (*Il.* I, 4–5). The regicide judge Sir Henry Vane was condemned to death and General Lambert to life imprisonment.
700. *crude:* premature.
701. *Though not disordinate:* though not intemperate in their lives.
706. *minister:* agent. Compare God's "Ministers of vengeance," in *PL* I, 170.

714. Ben Jonson's Lady Pecunia in *The Staple of News* (Act II), whose array costs "as much as furnishing a fleet," and who appears "like a galley, Gilt in the prow," is suggested by Peter Ure in *N&Q,* CXCV (1950), 298, as a crowning example of a satirical symbol that goes back as far as Plautus' *Paenulus* I, ii.
715. Ships of Tarshish are often mentioned in the Old Testament as symbols of pride, and usually they are made objects of God's anger; e.g., "Thou breakest the ships of Tarshish with an east wind" (Ps. xlviii, 7. Compare Isa. xxiii, 1 and 14). Milton, like Josephus (*Antiquities* VIII, vii, 2), seems to have identified *Tarsus* on the River Cydnus in Cilicia with the Tarshish of the Old Testament. Tarshish was a port on the Guadalquivir in Spain.

Of *Javan* or *Gadire*
With all her bravery on, and tackle trim,
Sails fill'd, and streamers waving,
Courted by all the winds that hold them play,
An Amber scent of odorous perfume   720
Her harbinger, a damsel train behind;
Some rich *Philistian* Matron she may seem,
And now at nearer view, no other certain
Than *Dalila* thy wife.
    Samson. My Wife, my Traitress, let her not come near me.   725
    Chorus. Yet on she moves, now stands and eyes thee fixt,
About t' have spoke, but now, with head declin'd
Like a fair flower surcharg'd with dew, she weeps
And words addrest seem into tears dissolv'd,
Wetting the borders of her silk'n veil;   730
But now again she makes address to speak.
    Dalila. With doubtful feet and wavering resolution
I came, still dreading thy displeasure, *Samson*,
Which to have merited, without excuse,
I cannot but acknowledge; yet if tears   735
May expiate (though the fact more evil drew
In the perverse event than I foresaw)
My penance hath not slack'n'd, though my pardon
No way assur'd. But conjugal affection,
Prevailing over fear and timorous doubt,   740
Hath led me on desirous to behold
Once more thy face, and know of thy estate.
If aught in my ability may serve
To light'n what thou suffer'st, and appease
Thy mind with what amends is in my power,   745
Though late, yet in some part to recompense
My rash but more unfortunate misdeed.
    Samson. Out, out Hyaena; these are thy wonted arts.
And arts of every woman false like thee,
To break all faith, all vows, deceive, betray,   750
Then as repentant to submit, beseech,
And reconcilement move with feign'd remorse,
Confess, and promise wonders in her change,
Not truly penitent, but chief to try
Her husband, how far urg'd his patience bears,   755
His virtue or weakness which way to assail:
Then with more cautious and instructed skill
Again transgresses, and again submits;
That wisest and best men full oft beguil'd,
With goodness principl'd not to reject   760

[handwritten marginal note:] — If she doesn't want him why is she back? But now she can be the master. Possessions are what is important to her (and Milton)

716. Noah's grandson, *Javan* (Gen. x, 2), was the traditional ancestor of the Ionians or of the Greeks generally, as Milton implies in *PL* I, 508. *Gadire* (modern Cadiz) was a Phoenician city, famous, according to Pliny the Younger (*Epist.* I, 15) for its dancing girls.

720. *Amber:* ambergris. Compare Donne's lady of pleasure in *El II,* 13–14, who, in buying "things perfumed," loads herself with "muske and amber."

736–737. *fact* and *event* keep their respective Latin meanings of "deed" and "outcome."

738. *penance:* penitence.

738–739. *though my pardon No way assur'd* is a Latin absolute construction. "Be" must be read in after *pardon.*

742. *estate:* condition.

748. Milton's readers were familiar with the belief that the hyaena was "a wilde beaste that counterfaiteth the voyce of men, and so entiseth them out of their houses and devoureth them." (Gloss of the Geneva Bible to Ecclesiasticus xiii, 18, quoted by *O.E.D.*)

752. *move:* propose.

The penitent, but ever to forgive,
Are drawn to wear out miserable days,
Entangl'd with a pois'nous bosom snake,
If not by quick destruction soon cut off
As I by thee, to Ages an example.   765
    Dalila.   Yet hear me *Samson;* not that I endeavor
To lessen or extenuate my offense,
But that on th' other side if it be weigh'd
By itself, with aggravations not surcharg'd,
Or else with just allowance counterpois'd,   770
I may, if possible, thy pardon find
The easier towards me, or thy hatred less.
First granting, as I do, it was a weakness
In me, but incident to all our sex,
Curiosity, inquisitive, importune   775
Of secrets, then with like infirmity
To publish them, both common female faults:
Was it not weakness also to make known
For importunity, that is for naught,
Wherein consisted all thy strength and safety?   780
To what I did thou show'd'st me first the way.
But I to enemies reveal'd, and should not.
Nor shouldst thou have trusted that to woman's frailty:
Ere I to thee, thou to thyself wast cruel.
Let weakness then with weakness come to parle   785
So near related, or the same of kind,
Thine forgive mine; that men may censure thine
The gentler, if severely thou exact not
More strength from me, than in thyself was found.
And what if Love, which thou interpret'st hate,   790
The jealousy of Love, powerful of sway
In human hearts, nor less in mine towards thee,
Caus'd what I did?   I saw thee mutable
Of fancy, fear'd lest one day thou wouldst leave me
As her at *Timna,* sought by all means therefore   795
How to endear, and hold thee to me firmest:
No better way I saw than by importuning
To learn thy secrets, get into my power
Thy key of strength and safety: thou wilt say,
Why then reveal'd?   I was assur'd by those   800
Who tempted me, that nothing was design'd
Against thee but safe custody, and hold:
That made for me, I knew that liberty
Would draw thee forth to perilous enterprises,
While I at home sat full of cares and fears   805
Wailing thy absence in my widow'd bed;

763. The treacherous snake cherished in the breast was proverbial. In *Richard II* (III, ii, 131) the king calls his unfaithful favorites
Snakes, in my heart-blood warm'd, that sting my heart!

775. *Curiosity* is in apposition with *weakness* in l. 773, while the two adjectives following it modify *sex* in l. 774. *importúne:* persistently bent upon an object. Compare Satan as "the importune Tempter" in *PR* II, 404.

777. *publish:* make public, betray.

785. *parle:* parley.
786. *kind:* nature.
794. *fancy:* affection, love. Compare "maiden meditation, fancy-free," in *Midsummer Night's Dream* II, i, 161.
800–802. Milton could count upon his readers to recognize a lie here because they would remember that the Philistines asked Dalila to entice his secret from Samson so that they might "bind him to afflict him" (Judg. xvi, 5).

Here I should still enjoy thee day and night
Mine and Love's prisoner, not the *Philistines'*,
Whole to myself, unhazarded abroad,
Fearless at home of partners in my love.   810
These reasons in Love's law have pass'd for good,
Though fond and reasonless to some perhaps:
And Love hath oft, well meaning, wrought much woe,
Yet always pity or pardon hath obtain'd.
Be not unlike all others, not austere   815
As thou art strong, inflexible as steel.
If thou in strength all mortals dost exceed,
In uncompassionate anger do not so.
   Samson. How cunningly the sorceress displays
Her own transgressions, to upbraid me mine!   820
That malice not repentance brought thee hither,
By this appears: I gave, thou say'st, th' example,
I led the way; bitter reproach, but true,
I to myself was false ere thou to me;
Such pardon therefore as I give my folly,   825
Take to thy wicked deed: which when thou seest
Impartial, self-severe, inexorable,
Thou wilt renounce thy seeking, and much rather
Confess it feign'd. Weakness is thy excuse,
And I believe it, weakness to resist   830
Philistian gold: if weakness may excuse,
What Murderer, what Traitor, Parricide,
Incestuous, Sacrilegious, but may plead it?
All wickedness is weakness: that plea therefore
With God or Man will gain thee no remission. — *starts preaching a bit*   835
But Love constrain'd thee; call it furious rage
To satisfy thy lust: Love seeks to have Love;
My love how couldst thou hope, who took'st the way
To raise in me inexpiable hate,
Knowing, as needs I must, by thee betray'd?   840
In vain thou striv'st to cover shame with shame,
Or by evasions thy crime uncover'st more.
   Dalila. Since thou determin'st weakness for no plea
In man or woman, though to thy own condemning,
Hear what assaults I had, what snares besides,   845
What sieges girt me round, ere I consented;
Which might have aw'd the best resolv'd of men,
The constantest to have yielded without blame.
It was not gold, as to my charge thou lay'st,
That wrought with me: thou knowst the Magistrates   850
And Princes of my country came in person,
Solicited, commanded, threat'n'd, urg'd,   *2) appeals to patriotism*
Adjur'd by all the bonds of civil Duty
And of Religion, press'd how just it was,
How honorable, how glorious to entrap   855
A common enemy, who had destroy'd
Such numbers of our Nation: and the Priest

808. *Mine,* for "my," was regularly used when the word was separated from its noun.
826. *which* refers to *pardon* in l. 825.
835. *remission:* forgiveness.
837. There are many classical parallels to the thought, such as Cicero's definition of love as nothing less than the cherishing of the loved person without ceasing and without thought of advantage of any kind *On Friendship*, xxvii, 100).

Was not behind, but ever at my ear,
Preaching how meritorious with the gods
It would be to ensnare an irreligious   860
Dishonorer of *Dagon:* what had I
To oppose against such powerful arguments?
Only my love of thee held long debate,
And combated in silence all these reasons
With hard contest: at length that grounded maxim   865
So rife and celebrated in the mouths
Of wisest men, that to the public good
Private respects must yield, with grave authority
Took full possession of me and prevail'd;
Virtue, as I thought, truth, duty so enjoining.   870
   Samson. I thought where all thy circling wiles would end;
In feign'd Religion, smooth hypocrisy.   *Free will of Dalila*
But had thy love, still odiously pretended,
Been, as it ought, sincere, it would have taught thee
Far other reasonings, brought forth other deeds.   875
I before all the daughters of my Tribe
And of my Nation chose thee from among
My enemies, lov'd thee, as too well thou knew'st,
Too well, unbosom'd all my secrets to thee,
Not out of levity, but overpow'r'd   880
Othello line   By thy request, who could deny thee nothing;   *disturbs chain of being*
Yet now am judg'd an enemy. Why then
Didst thou at first receive me for thy husband,
Then, as since then, thy country's foe profest?
Being once a wife, for me thou wast to leave   885
Parents and country; nor was I their subject,
Nor under their protection but my own,
Thou mine, not theirs: if aught against my life
Thy country sought of thee, it sought unjustly,
Against the law of nature, law of nations,   890
No more thy country, but an impious crew
Of men conspiring to uphold thir state
By worse than hostile deeds, violating the ends
For which our country is a name so dear;
Not therefore to be obey'd. But zeal mov'd thee;   895
To please thy gods thou didst it; gods unable
To acquit themselves and prosecute their foes
But by ungodly deeds, the contradiction
Of thir own deity, Gods cannot be:

866. *rife:* widespread. Compare Satan's reference to "new Worlds; whereof so rife There went a fame in Heav'n" (*PL* I, 650–1).

868. *respects:* interests. The reasoning is like Satan's justification of his attempt upon Eve on grounds of "public reason" in *PL* IV, 389.

871. *circling:* devious, prevaricating, indirect in coming to the point.

880. Milton thought of levity as a vice, opposed, as he says in *CD* II, xiii; C. E. XVII, 321, to the virtue of gravity, which "consists in an habitual self-government of speech and action, . . . befitting a man of holiness and probity."

884. *profest:* avowed, declared.

885–886. Adam's words after the creation of Eve were, "Therefore shall a man leave his father and his mother, and shall cleave unto his wife: and they shall be one flesh" (Gen. ii, 24).

890. To a contemporary ear the line would recall the title—*Of the Law of Nature and of Nations*—of "that noble volume written by our learned Selden," as Milton called the book in *DDD* II, xxii.

891. Milton often used *crew* in this derogatory sense in *PL* to refer to the devils. *O.E.D.* compares *II Henry VI* II, ii, 72: "Winke at the Duke of Suffolkes insolence, At Beaufords Pride, at Somersets ambition, At Buckingham, and all the Crew of them."

897. *acquit:* clear one's self of any obligation. Here the word means "to pay off a score against an enemy."

Less therefore to be pleas'd, obey'd, or fear'd.   900
These false pretexts and varnish'd colors failing,
Bare in thy guilt how foul must thou appear?
    Dalila. In argument with men a woman ever
Goes by the worse, whatever be her cause.

• women in Milton's day always got the worst of it.

    Samson. For want of words no doubt, or lack of breath,   905
Witness when I was worried with thy peals.
    Dalila. I was a fool, too rash, and quite mistaken
In what I thought would have succeeded best.
Let me obtain forgiveness of thee, *Samson,*
Afford me place to show what recompense   910
Towards thee I intend for what I have misdone,
Misguided: only what remains past cure
Bear not too sensibly, nor still insist

3) • forgiving

To afflict thyself in vain: though sight be lost,
Life yet hath many solaces, enjoy'd   915
Where other senses want not their delights
At home in leisure and domestic ease,
Exempt from many a care and chance to which
Eyesight exposes daily men abroad.
I to the Lords will intercede, not doubting   920
Thir favorable ear, that I may fetch thee
From forth this loathsome prison-house to abide
With me, where my redoubl'd love and care
With nursing diligence, to me glad office,
May ever tend about thee to old age   925
With all things grateful cheer'd, and so supplied,
That what by me thou hast lost thou least shalt miss.

• is she sincere, or really playing him for the fool
• Does she love him?

    Samson. No, no, of my condition take no care;
It fits not; thou and I long since are twain;
Nor think me so unwary or accurst   930
To bring my feet again into the snare
Where once I have been caught; I know thy trains
Though dearly to my cost, thy gins, and toils;
Thy fair enchanted cup, and warbling charms
No more on me have power, thir force is null'd,   935
So much of Adder's wisdom I have learn't
To fence my ear against thy sorceries.
If in my flower of youth and strength, when all men
Lov'd, honor'd, fear'd me, thou alone could hate me,
Thy Husband, slight me, sell me, and forego me;   940
How wouldst thou use me now, blind, and thereby
Deceivable, in most things as a child

---

901. *colors* was frequently used in this sense. So Prospero in *The Tempest* I, ii, 143, speaking of excuses for their treachery made by his brother's confederates, says that they "With colors fairer painted their foul ends."

906. *Witness when:* by the evidence of the times when. Compare *PL* I, 503–5. *peals:* compare "a peal of words" in l. 235 above.

913. *sensibly:* acutely.

916. *want:* lack. Compare l. 315 above.

924. *office:* responsibility, task.

930. *accurst:* under a divine curse or possessed by a hostile, supernatural power. Milton used the word in a Greek sense, as Homer did in describing

Lycurgus as "A wretch accursed, and hated by the gods" (Pope's *Il.* VI, 177).

934. *charms* keeps its Latin meaning of "songs," as it does in *PR* IV, 257, where Satan mentions "Aeolian charms" as a feature of Greek civilization; but the word also connotes the idea of spells. Compare *Comus,* 51–53.

935. *null'd:* annulled, destroyed.

936. The superstition that adders are deaf is as old as the account in Ps. lviii, 4–5, of "the deaf adder that stoppeth the ear; Which will not hearken to the voice of the charmers, charming never so wisely."

Helpless, thence easily contemn'd, and scorn'd,
And last neglected?   How wouldst thou insult
When I must live uxorious to thy will   945
In perfect thraldom, how again betray me,
Bearing my words and doings to the Lords
To gloss upon, and censuring, frown or smile?
jail   This Gaol I count the house of Liberty
To thine whose doors my feet shall never enter.   950
    Dalila.   Let me approach at least, and touch thy hand.
    Samson.   Not for thy life, lest fierce remembrance wake
My sudden rage to tear thee joint by joint.
At distance I forgive thee, go with that;
Bewail thy falsehood, and the pious works   955
It hath brought forth to make thee memorable
Among illustrious women, faithful wives:
Cherish thy hast'n'd widowhood with the gold
Of Matrimonial treason: so farewell.
    Dalila.   I see thou art implacable, more deaf   960
To prayers, than winds and seas, yet winds to seas   *is she?*
Are reconcil'd at length, and Sea to Shore: *4) Turns on him*
Thy anger, unappeasable, still rages,
Eternal tempest never to be calm'd.
Why do I humble thus myself, and suing   965
For peace, reap nothing but repulse and hate?
Bid go with evil omen and the brand
Of infamy upon my name denounc't?
To mix with thy concernments I desist
Henceforth, nor too much disapprove my own.   970
Fame if not double-fac't is double-mouth'd,
And with contrary blast proclaims most deeds;
On both his wings, one black, the other white,
Bears greatest names in his wild aery flight.
My name perhaps among the Circumcis'd   *5) Lament*   975
In *Dan,* in *Judah,* and the bordering Tribes,
To all posterity may stand defam'd,
With malediction mention'd, and the blot
Of falsehood most unconjugal traduc't.
But in my country where I most desire,   *6) Triumph*   980

948. *gloss:* make remarks about. *censuring:* judging.

953. Samson's wish is less ferocious than Polymnestor's impulse to tear Hecuba limb from limb (Euripides, *Hecuba,* 1125), with which it is compared. His behavior in this entire scene is an expression of Milton's belief that "Hatred . . . is in some cases a religious duty. . . . We are to hate even our dearest connexions, if they endeavor to seduce or deter us from the love of God" (*CD* II, xi; C.E. XVII, 259).

967. The *evil omen* is Samson's warning of the kind of reputation and life in store for her (in ll. 956–59 above).

969. *concernments:* interests, affairs.

971. *double-fac't:* having two opposite faces (like "a subtile Janus," as Milton—in *Animadversions* 2; C.E. III, 120—called the Roman god of gates whom he is comparing here with the goddess Fame).

971–974. Here and in his picture of Fame in *On*

the Fifth of November (205–212) Milton was influenced by Boccaccio's interpretation (*Genealogy of the Gods* I, ix) of the earth-born goddess in the *Aeneid* (IV, 173–190), who flies through the night sky with sinister news. Milton gives Fame one black wing and one white because he was familiar with symbolism like that which led Ben Jonson to introduce Good Fame in the *Masque of Queens* as a goddess "attired in white, with white wings." Milton's Fame is like Chaucer's "femynyne creature" in *The House of Fame* who, when men asked her for glory, summoned the god, Eolus, to bring his golden trumpet, Clear Laud, and his black trumpet, Slander, and blow them indiscriminately. Why Milton should make Fame masculine is not easy to surmise, unless he confused her with her trumpeter, Eolus.

975. *the Circumcis'd:* the Jews.

976. The territory of *Dan,* Samson's own tribe. lay northwest of that of the tribe of *Judah* and extended as far as the Mediterranean.

In *Ekron, Gaza, Asdod,* and in *Gath*
I shall be nam'd among the famousest
Of Women, sung at solemn festivals,
Living and dead recorded, who to save
Her country from a fierce destroyer, chose   985
Above the faith of wedlock bands, my tomb
With odors visited and annual flowers.
Not less renown'd than in Mount *Ephraim,*
Jael, who with inhospitable guile
Smote *Sisera* sleeping through the Temples nail'd.   990
Nor shall I count it heinous to enjoy
The public marks of honor and reward
Conferr'd upon me, for the piety
Which to my country I was judg'd to have shown.
At this who ever envies or repines   995
I leave him to his lot, and like my own.
  Chorus. She's gone, a manifest Serpent by her sting
Discover'd in the end, till now conceal'd.
  Samson. So let her go, God sent her to debase me,
And aggravate my folly who committed   1000
To such a viper his most sacred trust
Of secrecy, my safety, and my life.
  Chorus. Yet beauty, though injurious, hath strange power,
After offense returning, to regain
Love once possest, nor can be easily   1005
Repuls't, without much inward passion felt
And secret sting of amorous remorse.
  Samson. Love-quarrels oft in pleasing concord end,
Not wedlock-treachery endangering life.
  Chorus. It is not virtue, wisdom, valor, wit,   1010
Strength, comeliness of shape, or amplest merit
That woman's love can win or long inherit;
But what it is, hard is to say,
Harder to hit,
(Which way soever men refer it)   1015
Much like thy riddle, *Samson,* in one day
Or seven, though one should musing sit;

---

981. Beginning with the most northern Philistine city, *Ekron,* Dalila next names the southernmost, *Gaza,* and then two other principal cities of her countrymen, to suggest that she will be known everywhere in Philistia.

987. *odors:* spices. The promise is like that made by Jeremiah to Zedekiah: "But thou shalt die in peace: and with the burnings of thy fathers, the former kings were before thee, so shall they burn odours for thee" (Jer. xxxiv, 5).

988–990. The Song of Deborah (Judg. v) celebrates the death of the Canaanite leader, *Sisera,* whom *Jael* lured to take refuge with her after his defeat by the Hebrews. "Then Jael, Heber's wife, took a nail of the tent, and took an hammer in her hand, . . . and smote the nail into his temples: . . . for he was fast asleep and weary: so he died" (Judg. iv, 21). In the Song the tribe of Ephraim is mentioned (Judg. v, 14) as foremost in the attack on the Canaanites. Deborah lived "between Ramah and Bethel in Mount Ephraim" (Judg. iv, 5).

993. *piety* is used in the Latin sense of devotion to one's country. Tamora, the Gothic queen, in *Titus Andronicus* (I, i, 114–15), replies to Titus' refusal of mercy to her sons who are his captives:
  O! if to fight for king and commonweal
  Were piety in thine, it is in these.

995–996. There may be a reminiscence of the scene in Sophocles' *Ajax,* 1038–9 where Teucer tells his opponents to love their opinions, as he intends to love his own.

1000. *aggravate* is used in the literal, Latin sense of "add to the gravity, or weight, of anything."

1006. *passion:* emotion.

1007. *remorse:* pity. "It was your own . . . remorse," says Celia to her father in *As You Like It* I, iii. 73, referring to his consent that Rosalind should not follow her father into banishment.

1008. A paraphrase of a famous line in Terence (*Andria,* 554–5).

1012. *inherit:* keep, possess.

1016–1017. Compare ll. 382–7 above.

If any of these or all, the *Timnian* bride
Had not so soon preferr'd
Thy Paranymph, worthless to thee compar'd,   1020
Successor in thy bed,
Nor both so loosely disallied
Thir nuptials, nor this last so treacherously
Had shorn the fatal harvest of thy head.
Is it for that such outward ornament   1025
Was lavish't on thir Sex, that inward gifts
Were left for haste unfinish't, judgment scant,
Capacity not rais'd to apprehend
Or value what is best
In choice, but oftest to affect the wrong?   1030
Or was too much of self-love mixt,
Of constancy no root infixt,
That either they love nothing, or not long?
      Whate'er it be, to wisest men and best
Seeming at first all heavenly under virgin veil,   1035
Soft, modest, meek, demure,
Once join'd, the contrary she proves, a thorn
Intestine, far within defensive arms
A cleaving mischief, in his way to virtue
Adverse and turbulent, or by her charms   1040
Draws him awry enslav'd
With dotage, and his sense deprav'd
To folly and shameful deeds which ruin ends.
What Pilot so expert but needs must wreck
Embark'd with such a Steers-mate at the Helm?   1045
      Favor'd of Heav'n who finds
One virtuous, rarely found,
That in domestic good combines:
Happy that house! his way to peace is smooth:
But virtue which breaks through all opposition,   1050
And all temptation can remove,
Most shines and most is acceptable above.
      Therefore God's universal Law

1020. *Paranymph:* groomsman. For the story, see the note on ll. 382–7 above.

1025. *for that:* because.

1030. *affect* has the Latin meaning of "aim at," or "ardently desire."

1034–1037. These lines and, less distinctly, the entire chorus may stem from Euripides' outburst against women in the *Hippolytus*, 616–18, which has also been compared with Adam's invective against women in *PL* X, 888–908.

1037–1038. *a thorn Intestine* suggests St. Paul's phrase, "a thorn in the flesh (II Cor. xii, 7), but *Intestine* is here equivalent to "domestic," as it is in Milton's reference to marital unhappiness as "an intestine evil" in *CD* I, x, p. 1001.

1038–1039. *far within defensive arms A cleaving mischief* seems like the portrayal in Sophocles' *Trachiniae* of Hercules' death by the "envenom'd robe" which his wife, Deianira, sent to him in hope of regaining his love. Compare *PL* II, 543.

1046–1047. Perhaps there are allusions here to the maxim in Prov. xix, 14, that, "A prudent wife is from the Lord," and to the cry of the chorus in Euripides' *Alcestis,* 473–5, that it is a rare lot in life to find a wife good like their lady.

1048. *That in domestic good combines:* that unites herself perfectly with her husband for the sake of domestic happiness. Here and in *PL* IX, 232–4, Milton may have been thinking of the virtuous woman in Prov. xxxi, 10–11, whose "price is far above rubies. The heart of her husband doth safely trust in her." His ideal resembles Sir Thomas Overbury's in *A Good Woman:* "Now she is given fresh and alive to a husband, and she doth nothing more than love him, for she takes him to that purpose. So his good becomes the business of her actions, and she doth herself kindness upon him. After his, her chiefest virtue is a good husband. For she is he."

1053–1060. In *DDD* II, xv (C.E. III, 475), Milton protested against the "female pride" which sought domestic equality, and he quoted St. Paul: "I suffer not the woman to usurp authority over the man." Cf. *PL* IV, 295–9, and X, 145–56.

Gave to the man despotic power
Over his female in due awe,   1055
Nor from that right to part an hour,
Smile she or lour:
So shall he least confusion draw
On his whole life, not sway'd
By female usurpation, nor dismay'd.   1060
  But had we best retire, I see a storm?   _ ev
  Samson.   Fair days have oft contracted wind and rain.
  Chorus.   But this another kind of tempest brings.
  Samson.   Be less abstruse, my riddling days are past.
  Chorus.   Look now for no enchanting voice, nor fear   1065
The bait of honied words; a rougher tongue
Draws hitherward, I know him by his stride,
The Giant Harapha of Gath, his look   - a cavalier
Haughty as is his pile high-built and proud.
Comes he in peace? what wind hath blown him hither   1070
I less conjecture than when first I saw
The sumptuous *Dalila* floating this way:
His habit carries peace, his brow defiance.
  Samson.   Or peace or not, alike to me he comes.
  Chorus.   His fraught we soon shall know, he now arrives.   1075
  Harapha.   I come not, *Samson*, to condole thy chance,
As these perhaps, yet wish it had not been,
Though for no friendly intent.   I am of *Gath;*
Men call me *Harapha,* of stock renown'd
As *Og* or *Anak* and the *Emims* old   1080
That *Kiriathaim* held: Thou knowst me now.
If thou at all art known.   Much I have heard
Of thy prodigious might and feats perform'd
Incredible to me, in this displeas'd,
That I was never present on the place   1085
Of those encounters, where we might have tried
Each other's force in camp or listed field;
And now am come to see of whom such noise
Hath walk'd about, and each limb to survey,
If thy appearance answer loud report.   1090
  Samson.   The way to know were not to see but taste.
  Harapha.   Dost thou already single me; I thought
Gyves and the Mill had tam'd thee?   O that fortune

1062. *contracted:* incurred, suffered.

1064. The *riddling days* are explained in ll. 382–7 above and 1017–33 below.

1068. The name *Harapha* is composed of the Hebrew definite article, *ha,* and the word for giant, *raphah.* Its doubtful etymology is discussed by W. R. Parker and others in a correspondence which began in the *TLS,* Jan. 2, 1937, p. 12. Cf. l. 1248 below.

1069. *his pile:* his enormous body. Cf. *structure* in l. 1239 below.

1075. *fraught:* freight, i.e., charge or business.

1076. *condole,* as a transitive verb, is obsolete.

1077. *these* refers to the chorus. *yet wish, etc.:* Though he does not sympathize with Samson, he regrets his mischance, for it has prevented them from meeting on equal terms.

1080. *Og,* king of Bashan, is described (Deut. iii,

11) as alone remaining "of the remnant of the giants; behold, his bedstead . . . nine cubits was the length thereof." The *Emims* were "a people great, and many, and tall, as the Anakims; which also were accounted giants" (Deut. ii, 10–11). In Gen. xiv, 5, they are said to have been crushed by their enemies in the town of Kiriathaim, east of the Jordan.

1087. *camp* keeps the Italian meaning of "field" (i.e., of battle). *listed:* furnished with lists such as those in which knights met in tournament.

1091. *taste:* try, examine.   So Satan reports having found Jesus, "view'd him, tasted him" (*PR* II, 131).

1092. *single:* challenge to single combat.   O.E.D. quotes Richard's challenge in *III Henry VI* II, iv, 1: "Now, Clifford, I have singled thee alone."

Had brought me to the field where thou art fam'd
To have wrought such wonders with an Ass's Jaw;   1095
I should have forc'd thee soon wish other arms,
Or left thy carcase where the Ass lay thrown:
So had the glory of Prowess been recover'd
To *Palestine,* won by a *Philistine*
From the unforeskinn'd race, of whom thou bear'st   1100
The highest name for valiant Acts; that honor
Certain to have won by mortal duel from thee,
I lose, prevented by thy eyes put out.
    Samson. Boast not of what thou wouldst have done, but do
What then thou wouldst, thou seest it in thy hand.   1105
    Harapha. To combat with a blind man I disdain,
And thou hast need much washing to be toucht.
    Samson. Such usage as your honorable Lords
Afford me assassinated and betray'd,
Who durst not with thir whole united powers   1110
In fight withstand me single and unarm'd,
Nor in the house with chamber Ambushes
Close-banded durst attack me, no not sleeping,
Till they had hir'd a woman with thir gold,
Breaking her Marriage Faith to circumvent me.   1115
Therefore without feign'd shifts let be assign'd
Some narrow place enclos'd, where sight may give thee,
Or rather flight, no great advantage on me;
Then put on all thy gorgeous arms, thy Helmet
And Brigandine of brass, thy broad Habergeon,   1120
Vant-brace and Greaves, and Gauntlet, add thy Spear
A Weaver's beam, and seven-times-folded shield,
I only with an Oak'n staff will meet thee,
And raise such outcries on thy clatter'd Iron,
Which long shall not withhold me from thy head,   1125
That in a little time, while breath remains thee,
Thou oft shalt wish thyself at Gath to boast
Again in safety what thou wouldst have done
To *Samson,* but shalt never see *Gath* more.
    Harapha. Thou durst not thus disparage glorious arms   1130
Which greatest Heroes have in battle worn,
Thir ornament and safety, had not spells
And black enchantments, some Magician's Art
Arm'd thee or charm'd thee strong, which thou from Heaven

1096. *wish,* the prevailingly accepted editorial emendation of the reading "with" of the original editions, is confirmed by R. I. McDavid in *PQ,* XXXIII (1954), 86–89.

1102. *mortal duel:* duel to the death of one of the parties.

1109. *afford:* allow, grant. *assassinated:* treacherously attacked, not actually slain. An *O.E.D.* example, dated 1683, is: "William of Orange was twice Assassinated, and lost his Life the Second time."

1113. *close-banded:* secretly banded. A man practices closeness and secrecy, said Bacon (Essay VI) when he "leaveth himself without observation, or without hold to be taken, what he is."

1116. *feign'd shifts:* delusive tricks.

1120. *Brigandine:* Body armor of metal plates or rings sewed between layers of cloth or leather. *Habergeon:* a sleeveless coat of mail.

1121. *Vant-brace:* vambrace, armor for the forearm.

1121–1122. *thy Spear, A Weaver's beam* is a reminiscence of the description of Goliath, "the staff of his spear was like a weaver's beam" (I Sam. xvii, 7).

1122. Milton may have thought of the shield of the gigantic Ajax, which was made of seven layers of bull's hide (*Il.* VII, 220) or of the seven-fold shield of Turnus which Aeneas pierced (*Aen.* XII, 925).

1134. *Arm'd thee or charm'd thee strong:* gave thee magically powerful arms or a charm of personal strength. For the jingle compare *PR* II, 269, n., and l. 1278 below.

Feign'd'st at thy birth was giv'n thee in thy hair,   1135
Where strength can least abide, though all thy hairs
Were bristles rang'd like those that ridge the back
Of chaf't wild Boars, or ruff'd Porcupines.
   Samson. I know no spells, use no forbidden Arts;
My trust is in the living God who gave me   *his faith returning*   1140
At my Nativity this strength, diffius'd
No less through all my sinews, joints and bones,
Than thine, while I preserv'd these locks unshorn,
The pledge of my unviolated vow.
For proof hereof, if *Dagon* be thy god,   1145
Go to his Temple, invocate his aid
With solemnest devotion, spread before him
How highly it concerns his glory now
To frustrate and dissolve these Magic spells,
Which I to be the power of *Israel's* God   1150
Avow, and challenge *Dagon* to the test,
Offering to combat thee his Champion bold,
With th' utmost of his Godhead seconded:
Then thou shalt see, or rather to thy sorrow
Soon feel, whose God is strongest, thine or mine.   1155
   Harapha. Presume not on thy God, whate'er he be, *scorn, but truth*
Thee he regards not, owns not, hath cut off
Quite from his people, and delivered up
Into thy Enemies' hand, permitted them
To put out both thine eyes, and fetter'd send thee   1160
Into the common Prison, there to grind
Among the Slaves and Asses thy comrades,
As good for nothing else, no better service
With those thy boist'rous locks, no worthy match *where did they come from*
For valor to assail, nor by the sword   1165
Of noble Warrior, so to stain his honor,
But by the Barber's razor best subdu'd.
   Samson. All these indignities, for such they are
From thine, these evils I deserve and more,   *almost a martyr*
Acknowledge them from God inflicted on me   1170
Justly, yet despair not of his final pardon
Whose ear is ever open; and his eye
Gracious to re-admit the suppliant;
In confidence whereof I once again
Defy thee to the trial of mortal fight,   1175
By combat to decide whose god is God,
Thine or whom I with *Israel's* Sons adore.
   Harapha. Fair honor that thou dost thy God, in trusting

1134–1135. *which* implies an unexpressed antecedent, "strength."

1138. With the *ruff'd Porcupines* compare the Ghost's words to Hamlet (I, v, 19–20): ". . . each particular hair to stand an end, Like quills upon the fretful porpentine."

1139–1144. Todd compared the oath taken by the champions in medieval combats: "I do swear that I have not upon me, nor on any of the arms I shall use, words, charms, or enchantments, to which I trust for help to conquer my enemy, but that I do only trust in God, in my right, and in the strength of my body and arms."

1143. *while:* as long as.

1147. *spread:* lay.

1157. The language is like that of the sanctions pronounced against disobedient Hebrews in the Old Testament: "that soul shall be cut off from Israel" (Exod. xii, 15).

1164. *boist'rous:* thick-growing.

1169. For *thine* used to mean Harapha's people generally, see the note on *mine* in l. 291 above.

1175–1176. Again, as in ll. 1139–44 above, there is a reference to the medieval trials of the justice of various kinds of causes by combat between champions representing the parties.

He will accept thee to defend his cause,
A Murderer, a Revolter, and a Robber.   1180
  Samson.   Tongue-doughty Giant, how dost thou prove me these?
  Harapha.   Is not thy Nation subject to our Lords?
Thir Magistrates confest it, when they took thee
As a League-breaker and deliver'd bound
Into our hands: for hadst thou not committed   1185
Notorious murder on those thirty men
At *Askalon,* who never did thee harm,
Then like a Robber stripp'dst them of thir robes?
The *Philistines,* when thou hadst broke the league,
Went up with armed powers thee only seeking,   1190
To others did no violence nor spoil.
  Samson.   Among the Daughters of the *Philistines*
I chose a Wife, which argu'd me no foe;
And in your City held my Nuptial Feast:
But your ill-meaning Politician Lords,   1195
Under pretense of Bridal friends and guests,
Appointed to await me thirty spies,
Who, threat'ning cruel death, constrain'd the bride
To wring from me and tell to them my secret,
That solv'd the riddle which I had propos'd.   1200
When I perceiv'd all set on enmity,
As on my enemies, wherever chanc'd,
I us'd hostility, and took thir spoil
To pay my underminers in thir coin.
My Nation was subjected to your Lords.   1205
It was the force of Conquest; force with force
Is well ejected when the Conquer'd can.
But I a private person, whom my Country
As a league-breaker gave up bound, presum'd
Single Rebellion and did Hostile Acts.   1210
I was no private but a person rais'd
With strength sufficient and command from Heav'n
To free my Country; if their servile minds
Me their Deliverer sent would not receive,
But to thir Masters gave me up for nought,   1215
Th' unworthier they; whence to this day they serve.
I was to do my part from Heav'n assign'd,
And had perform'd it if my known offense
Had not disabl'd me, not all your force:
These shifts refuted, answer thy appellant,   1220
Though by his blindness maim'd for high attempts,

1182–1185. For the original story of this incident see the note on ll. 253–64 above.

1185–1188. After the betrayal of his riddle by the woman of Timna, Samson "went down to Ashkelon and slew thirty men of them, and took their spoil, and gave change of garments to them which expounded the riddle" (Judg. xiv, 19).

1194. After Manoa had arranged for his marriage with the woman of Timna, his first wife, "Samson made there a feast; for so used the young men to do" (Judg. xiv, 10).

1195–1197. Josephus (*Antiquities* V, viii, 6) says that "the people of Timnath, out of dread of the young man's strength, gave him during the time of the wedding feast, . . . thirty of the most stout of their youth, in pretense to be his companions, but in reality to be a guard upon him."

1198–1200. After Samson had propounded his riddle the thirty men "desired the damsel (i.e., his wife) to discover it by the means of her husband, and tell it them; and they threatened to burn her if she did not tell it them" (Judg. xiv, 15). For the substance of the riddle see the note on ll. 382–7 above.

1220. *appellant:* challenger.

1221. *high attempts:* great enterprises. The words belonged to the language of romance and

Who now defies thee thrice to single fight,
As a petty enterprise of small enforce.
Harapha. With thee a Man condemn'd, a Slave enroll'd,
Due by the Law to capital punishment?   *children*   1225
To fight with thee no man of arms will deign.
Samson. Cam'st thou for this, vain boaster, to survey me,
To descant on my strength, and give thy verdict?
Come nearer, part not hence so slight inform'd;
But take good heed my hand survey not thee.   1230
Harapha. O *Baäl-zebub!* can my ears unus'd
Hear these dishonors, and not render death?
Samson. No man withholds thee, nothing from thy hand
Fear I incurable; bring up thy van,
My heels are fetter'd, but my fist is free.   1235
Harapha. This insolence other kind of answer fits.
Samson. Go baffl'd coward, lest I run upon thee,
Though in these chains, bulk without spirit vast,
And with one buffet lay thy structure low,
Or swing thee in the Air, then dash thee down   1240
To the hazard of thy brains and shatter'd sides.
Harapha. By *Astaroth,* ere long thou shalt lament
These braveries in Irons loaden on thee.
Chorus. His Giantship is gone somewhat crestfall'n,
Stalking with less unconsci'nable strides,   1245
And lower looks, but in a sultry chafe.
Samson. I dread him not, nor all his Giant-brood,   *Now he's ready to fight*
Though Fame divulge him Father of five Sons   *the last battle*
All of Gigantic size, *Goliah* chief.
Chorus. He will directly to the Lords, I fear,   1250
And with malicious counsel stir them up
Some way or other yet further to afflict thee.
Samson. He must allege some cause, and offer'd fight
Will not dare mention, lest a question rise
Whether he durst accept the offer or not,   1255

heraldry. *O.E.D.* quotes Guillim's *Heraldry:* "His noble courage and high attempts atchieved."

1222. The medieval custom of challenging three times in judicial combats was familiar through the coronation ceremonies. When Charles II was crowned, a herald proclaimed that "if any dare deny Charles Stewart to be lawful King of England, here was a champion that would fight with him." "And with these words," Pepys says (April 23rd, 1661), "the Champion flings down his gauntlet, and all this he do three times in his going up towards the King's table."

1224–1226. Todd quoted from the treatise on duelling (published in 1595) of Vincentio Saviolo, the London fencing master who suggested Touchstone's quarrelling "by the book" (*As You Like It* V, iv, 94) to Shakespeare, a passage denying the right of single combat to traitors, robbers, "excommunicate persons, hereticks, vsurers, and all other persons, not liuing as a gentleman or a souldier."

1228. *descant* was often used to mean "make unfavorable comments," as it is used in the opening sentence of *Eikon:* "To descant on the misfortunes of a person fallen from dignity is not commendable."

1231. Baal was the great sun-god of the Philistines, Canaanites, and Phoenicians, and he was worshipped under many local names, of which *Baal-zebub* (literally, "Baal" or "god of flies") was his title in his temple at Ekron. Cf. *PL* I, 81. *unus'd:* unaccustomed (i.e., to insults).

1234. *bring up thy van:* bring up thy advance guard, begin the fight.

1242. In *PL* I, 338–9, Milton mentions "*Astoreth, whom the Phoenicians call'd Astarte,* Queen of Heav'n," and in *PL* I, 422, he explains that the form *Astaroth* is plural. It was a general name for the many manifestations of the supreme goddess who stood opposite to Baal and represented fertility and passion.

1243. *braveries:* boasts.

1245. *unconsci'nable:* unreasonable, absurdly insolent.

1248. II Samuel xxi tells the story of four sons who "were born to the giant in Gath, and fell by the hand of David, and by the hand of his servants." The giant is called in Hebrew simply "Rapha," the word from which Milton derived the name "Harapha." See l. 1068, n. His fifth son was Goliath.

And that he durst not plain enough appear'd.
Much more affliction than already felt
They cannot well impose, nor I sustain;
If they intend advantage of my labors,
The work of many hands, which earns my keeping   1260
With no small profit daily to my owners.
But come what will, my deadliest foe will prove
My speediest friend, by death to rid me hence,
The worst that he can give, to me the best.
Yet so it may fall out, because thir end   1265
Is hate, not help to me, it may with mine
Draw thir own ruin who attempt the deed.
     Chorus.   Oh how comely it is and how reviving
To the Spirits of just men long opprest!
When God into the hands of thir deliverer   1270
Puts invincible might
To quell the mighty of the Earth, th' oppressor,
The brute and boist'rous force of violent men
Hardy and industrious to support
Tyrannic power, but raging to pursue   1275
The righteous and all such as honor Truth;
Hee all thir Ammunition
And feats of War defeats
With plain Heroic magnitude of mind
And celestial vigor arm'd,   1280
Thir Armories and Magazines contemns,
Renders them useless, while
With winged expedition
Swift as the lightning glance he executes
His errand on the wicked, who surpris'd   1285
Lose thir defense, distracted and amaz'd.
     But patience is more oft the exercise
Of Saints, the trial of thir fortitude,
Making them each his own Deliverer,
And Victor over all   1290
That tyranny or fortune can inflict.
Either of these is in thy lot,
Samson, with might endu'd
Above the Sons of men; but sight bereav'd
May chance to number thee with those   1295
Whom Patience finally must crown.
This Idol's day hath been to thee no day of rest,
     Laboring thy mind
More than the working day thy hands.
And yet perhaps more trouble is behind,   1300
For I descry this way
Some other tending, in his hand
A Scepter or quaint staff he bears,

1263. The thought that "though death be poor,
it ends a mortal woe," (*Richard II* II, i, 152) is too
widespread to suggest a "parallel."
     1277. *Ammunition:* munitions of war.
     1278–1280. It is worth while to compare the
sonnets to Fairfax, Cromwell and Sir Henry Vane
the Younger.
     1283. *expedition:* speed. Compare "The banded

Powers of *Satan* hasting on With furious expedition" (*PL* VI, 85–86).
     1286. *defense:* power to defend themselves.
     1294. *sight bereav'd:* loss of sight.
     1303. *quaint,* curiously made or decorated, like
the wands of office which Greek heralds and messengers carried.

Comes on amain, speed in his look.
By his habit I discern him now   1305
A Public Officer, and now at hand.
His message will be short and voluble.
  Officer. *Ebrews,* the Pris'ner *Samson* here I seek.
  Chorus. His manacles remark him, there he sits.
  Officer. *Samson,* to thee our Lords thus bid me say;   1310
This day to *Dagon* is a solemn Feast,
With Sacrifices, Triumph, Pomp, and Games;
Thy strength they know surpassing human rate,
And now some public proof thereof require
To honor this great Feast, and great Assembly;   1315
Rise therefore with all speed and come along,
Where I will see thee heart'n'd and fresh clad
To appear as fits before th' illustrious Lords.
  Samson. Thou knowst I am an *Ebrew,* therefore tell them,
Our Law forbids at thir Religious Rites   1320
My presence; for that cause I cannot come.
  Officer. This answer, be assur'd, will not content them.
  Samson. Have they not Sword-players, and ev'ry sort
Of Gymnic Artists, Wrestlers, Riders, Runners,
Jugglers and Dancers, Antics, Mummers, Mimics,   1325
But they must pick mee out with shackles tir'd,
And over-labor'd at thir public Mill,
To make them sport with blind activity?
Do they not seek occasion of new quarrels
On my refusal to distress them more,   1330
Or make a game of my calamities?
Return the way thou cam'st, I will not come.
  Officer. Regard thyself, this will offend them highly.
  Samson. Myself? my conscience and internal peace.
Can they think me so broken, so debas'd   1335
With corporal servitude, that my mind ever
Will condescend to such absurd commands?
Although thir drudge, to be thir fool or jester,
And in my midst of sorrow and heart-grief
To show them feats, and play before thir god,   1340
The worst of all indignities, yet on me
Join'd with extreme contempt? I will not come.
  Officer. My message was impos'd on me with speed,
Brooks no delay: is this thy resolution?
  Samson. So take it with what speed thy message needs.   1345
  Officer. I am sorry what this stoutness will produce.

1307. *voluble* occurs in the same sense in *Eikon iv* (C.E. V, 108): ". . . a discourse, voluble enough, and full of sentence."

1308. Milton's inconsistency in spelling *Ebrews* here and in l. 1319 and 1540 below, while in *PR* IV, 336, and Ps. cxxxvi, 50, he spelled the word *Hebrew,* may be due to his familiarity with the unaspirated form of the word in Greek and Italian. In the Latin Vulgate he found it regularly aspirated, as he knew that it was in the Hebrew Bible.

1309. *remark:* distinguish. *O.E.D.* quotes Jeremy Taylor: "Those blessings and separations with which God hath remarked your family and person."

1320. The Mosaic law commanded, "Thou shalt not bow down to their gods, nor serve them; . . . but thou shalt utterly overthrow them, and quite break down their images" (Exod. xxiii, 24).

1324. *Gymnic artists:* gymnasts.

1325. *Antics:* grotesquely dressed players in a pageant or carnival. *Mummers:* actors in a dumb-show parade such as still goes by that name in Philadelphia.

1333. *Regard thyself:* look to your own interests.

1342. *Join'd:* enjoined, imposed.

1344. *brooks:* permits, bears.

1346. *sorry what:* sorry to imagine what. *stoutness:* pride, arrogance.

Samson. Perhaps thou shalt have cause to sorrow indeed.
Chorus. Consider, *Samson;* matters now are strain'd
Up to the height, whether to hold or break;
He's gone, and who knows how he may report   1350
Thy words by adding fuel to the flame?
Expect another message more imperious,
More Lordly thund'ring than thou well wilt bear.
Samson. Shall I abuse this Consecrated gift
Of strength, again returning with my hair   1355
After my great transgression, so requite
Favor renew'd, and add a greater sin
By prostituting holy things to Idols;
A *Nazarite* in place abominable
Vaunting my strength in honor to thir *Dagon?*   1360
Besides, how vile, contemptible, ridiculous,
What act more execrably unclean, profane?
Chorus. Yet with this strength thou serv'st the *Philistines,*
Idolatrous, uncircumcis'd, unclean.
Samson. Not in thir Idol-Worship, but by labor   1365
Honest and lawful to deserve my food
Of those who have me in thir civil power.
Chorus. Where the heart joins not, outward acts defile not.   ⟵old argument
Samson. Where outward force constrains, the sentence holds;
But who constrains me to the Temple of *Dagon,*   1370
Not dragging? the *Philistian* Lords command.
Commands are no constraints. If I obey them,
I do it freely; venturing to displease
God for the fear of Man, and Man prefer,
Set God behind: which in his jealousy   1375
Shall never, unrepented, find forgiveness.
Yet that he may dispense with me or thee
Present in Temples at Idolatrous Rites
For some important cause, thou needst not doubt.
Chorus. How thou wilt here come off surmounts my reach.   1380
Samson. Be of good courage, I begin to feel

Something is happening God is speaking

Some rousing motions in me which dispose
To something extraordinary my thoughts.
I with this Messenger will go along,
Nothing to do, be sure, that may dishonor   1385
Our Law, or stain my vow of *Nazarite.*
If there be aught of presage in the mind,

1355. Cf. l. 586 above.
1362. *unclean* is used in the legal sense in which Samson's Philistine bride is called "unclean" (in l. 321) because she was a gentile.
1366. *deserve:* earn.
1368. The maxim may refer to Aristotle's doctrine that "it is only voluntary feelings and actions for which praise and blame are given; those that are involuntary are condoned, and sometimes even pitied" (*Nicomachean Ethics,* III, i, 1).
1369. *sentence:* maxim.
1374-1375. The Second Commandment forbids any kind of worship of idols: "Thou shalt not bow down thyself to them, nor serve them: for I the Lord thy God am a jealous God" (Exod. xx, 5).
1377. *dispense with:* arrange to remit a penalty for a person so that he may do a forbidden act.

O.E.D. quotes Latimer's Sermons: "God had dispensed wyth theym to haue many wyues."
1377-1379. In *CD* II, 5 (C.E. XVII, 145), Milton raises the question "whether it be lawful for a professor of the true religion to be present at idolworship, in cases where his attendance is necessary for the discharge of some civil duty. The affirmative seems to be established by the example of Naaman the Syrian, II Kings v, 17-19, who was permitted . . . to construct for himself a private altar of Israelitish earth."
1387-1388. The prophecy—as J. C. Maxwell notes in *PQ,* XXXIII (1954), 36-39—suggests the oracle in Sophocles' *Trachiniae,* 79-81, which warns that at the moment of the opening of the action of the play Heracles is destined either to death or to enduring happiness.

This day will be remarkable in my life
By some great act, or of my days the last.
   Chorus. In time thou hast resolv'd, the man returns.   1390
   Officer. Samson, this second message from our Lords
To thee I am bid say. Art thou our Slave,
Our Captive, at the public Mill our drudge,
And dar'st thou at our sending and command
Dispute thy coming? come without delay;   1395
Or we shall find such Engines to assail
And hamper thee, as thou shalt come of force,
Though thou wert firmlier fast'n'd than a rock.
   Samson. I could be well content to try thir Art,
Which to no few of them would prove pernicious.   1400
Yet knowing thir advantages too many,
Because they shall not trail me through thir streets
Like a wild Beast, I am content to go.
Masters' commands come with a power resistless
To such as owe them absolute subjection;   1405
And for a life who will not change his purpose?
(So mutable are all the ways of men)
Yet this be sure, in nothing to comply
Scandalous or forbidden in our Law.
   Officer. I praise thy resolution; doff these links: 1410
By this compliance thou wilt win the Lords
To favor, and perhaps to set thee free.
   Samson. Brethren farewell, your company along
I will not wish, lest it perhaps offend them
To see me girt with Friends; and how the sight   1415
Of mee as of a common Enemy,
So dreaded once, may now exasperate them
I know not. Lords are Lordliest in thir wine;
And the well-feasted Priest then soonest fir'd
With zeal, if aught Religion seem concern'd: 1420
No less the people on thir Holy-days
Impetuous, insolent, unquenchable.
Happ'n what may, of me expect to hear
Nothing dishonorable, impure, unworthy
Our God, our Law, my Nation, or myself;   1425
The last of me or no I cannot warrant.
   Chorus. Go, and the Holy One
Of *Israel* be thy guide
To what may serve his glory best, and spread his name
Great among the Heathen round: 1430
Send thee the Angel of thy Birth, to stand
Fast by thy side, who from thy Father's field

1396. *Engines:* probably "engines of torture."
1397. *hamper:* fetter, confine. *of force:* by force.
1400. *pernicious* has the Latin meaning of "deadly."
1402. *because:* so that.
1421–1422. Compare Milton's condemnation of the bishops in *Of Reformation* (C.E. III, 53) for luring the people from the Puritan Sabbath to "gaming, jigging, wassailing, and mixed dancing. Thus did the reprobate hireling priest Balaam seek to subdue the Israelites to Moab, if not by force, then by his devilish policy, to draw them from the sanctuary of God to the luxurious and ribald feasts of Baal-Peor."
1426. The thought is: "Whether you see me for the last time now or not, I cannot positively say."
1431–1435. The *Angel* has been mentioned in ll. 24, 361, and 635 and his fiery ascent to heaven in ll. 27–28. Milton's belief that there are "Angels conversant on Earth with man or men's affairs" (*PR* I, 131–2) is stated clearly in *CD* I, ix; p. 990.

Rode up in flames after his message told
Of thy conception, and be now a shield
Of fire; that Spirit that first rusht on thee   1435
In the camp of *Dan*
Be efficacious in thee now at need.
For never was from Heaven imparted
Measure of strength so great to mortal seed,
As in thy wond'rous actions hath been seen.   1440
But wherefore comes old *Manoa* in such haste
With youthful steps? much livelier than erewhile
He seems: supposing here to find his Son,
Or of him bringing to us some glad news?

   Manoa.   Peace with you brethren; my inducement hither   1445
Was not at present here to find my Son,
By order of the Lords new parted hence
To come and play before them at thir Feast.
I heard all as I came, the City rings,
And numbers thither flock; I had no will,   1450
Lest I should see him forc't to things unseemly.
But that which mov'd my coming now, was chiefly
To give ye part with me what hope I have
With good success to work his liberty.

   Chorus.   That hope would much rejoice us to partake   1455
With thee; say reverend Sire, we thirst to hear.

   Manoa.   I have attempted one by one the Lords
Either at home, or through the high street passing,
With supplication prone and Father's tears
To accept of ransom for my Son thir pris'ner.   1460
Some much averse I found and wondrous harsh,
Contemptuous, proud, set on revenge and spite;
That part most reverenc'd *Dagon* and his Priests:
Others more moderate seeming, but thir aim
Private reward, for which both God and State   1465
They easily would set to sale: a third
More generous far and civil, who confess'd
They had enough reveng'd, having reduc't
Thir foe to misery beneath thir fears,
The rest was magnanimity to remit,   1470
If some convenient ransom were propos'd.
What noise or shout was that? it tore the Sky.

   Chorus.   Doubtless the people shouting to behold
Thir once great dread, captive, and blind before them,
Or at some proof of strength before them shown.   1475

   Manoa.   His ransom, if my whole inheritance
May compass it, shall willingly be paid
And number'd down: much rather I shall choose
To live the poorest in my Tribe, than richest,

1433. *after his message told:* after the delivery of his message. Compare the note on l. 1294 above.

1435-1436. In the biblical story, Samson's first inkling of his strength came when "the Spirit of the Lord began to move him at times in the camp of Dan between Zorah and Eshtaol" (Judg. xiii, 25).

1454. *success:* effect, consequence. The word seldom had the modern force which would make *good* unnecessary. Compare Belial's "Ominous conjecture on the whole success" (*PL* II, 123) of the devils' purposes.

1457. *attempted:* appealed to. *O.E.D.* compares *Merchant of Venice* IV, i, 421: "Deare sir, of force I must attempt you further."

1470. *The rest etc.:* the rest of their revenge, they said, it would be only magnanimous to let go.

And he in that calamitous prison left.   ·1480
No, I am fixt not to part hence without him.
For his redemption all my Patrimony,
If need be, I am ready to forego
And quit: not wanting him, I shall want nothing.
    Chorus. Fathers are wont to lay up for thir Sons,   1485
Thou for thy Son art bent to lay out all;
Sons wont to nurse thir Parents in old age,
Thou in old age car'st how to nurse thy Son,
Made older than thy age through eyesight lost.
    Manoa. It shall be my delight to tend his eyes,   1490
And view him sitting in the house, ennobl'd
With all those high exploits by him achiev'd,
And on his shoulders waving down those locks,
That of a Nation arm'd the strength contain'd:
And I persuade me God had not permitted   1495
His strength again to grow up with his hair
Garrison'd round about him like a Camp
Of faithful Soldiery, were not his purpose
To use him further yet in some great service,
Not to sit idle with so great a gift   1500
Useless, and thence ridiculous about him.
And since his strength with eyesight was not lost,
God will restore him eyesight to his strength.
    Chorus. Thy hopes are not ill founded, nor seem vain,
Of his delivery, and thy joy thereon   1505
Conceiv'd, agreeable to a Father's love,
In both which we, as next, participate.
    Manoa. I know your friendly minds and—O what noise!
Mercy of Heav'n! what hideous noise was that?
Horribly loud, unlike the former shout.   1510
    Chorus. Noise call you it or universal groan
As if the whole inhabitation perish'd?
Blood, death, and deathful deeds are in that noise,
Ruin, destruction at the utmost point.
    Manoa. Of ruin indeed methought I heard the noise,   1515
Oh it continues, they have slain my Son.
    Chorus. Thy Son is rather slaying them; that outcry
From slaughter of one foe could not ascend.
    Manoa. Some dismal accident it needs must be;
What shall we do, stay here or run and see?   1520
    Chorus. Best keep together here, lest, running thither,
We unawares run into danger's mouth.
This evil on the *Philistines* is fall'n,
From whom could else a general cry be heard?
The sufferers then will scarce molest us here,   1525

1480. *And he . . . left:* while he is left.
1487. *wont:* are wont, are accustomed.
1494. In Ovid's account of Nisus (*Met.* VIII, 10) there is a similar line declaring that the security of his kingdom depended upon a lock of his hair.
1503. *to his strength:* in addition to his strength.
1507. *next:* i. e., of kin, because the chorus, like Samson, are Danites.
1515. *ruin* keeps its Latin meaning of "down-fall" or "collapse." Cf. "Heav'n ruining from Heav'n" in *PL* VI, 868.
1520–1522. So in moments of crisis Euripides' choruses question what to do. When Phaedra's death-cry is heard in the *Hippolytus,* 782–5, a semi-chorus asks whether they should rush to the dying queen, and the other replies by asking, "Are there no handmaids at her side? The busy meddler treadeth perilous paths."

From other hands we need not much to fear.
What if his eyesight (for to *Israel's* God
Nothing is hard) by miracle restor'd,
He now be dealing dole among his foes,
And over heaps of slaughter'd walk his way?   1530
   Manoa. That were a joy presumptuous to be thought.
   Chorus. Yet God hath wrought things as incredible
For his people of old; what hinders now?
   Manoa. He can, I know, but doubt to think he will;
Yet Hope would fain subscribe, and tempts Belief.   1535
A little stay will bring some notice hither.
   Chorus. Of good or bad so great, of bad the sooner;
For evil news rides post, while good news baits.
And to our wish I see one hither speeding,
An *Ebrew,* as I guess, and of our Tribe.   1540
   Messenger. O whither shall I run, or which way fly
The sight of this so horrid spectacle
Which erst my eyes beheld and yet behold?
For dire imagination still pursues me.
But providence or instinct of nature seems,   1545
Or reason though disturb'd, and scarce consulted,
To have guided me aright, I know not how,
To thee first, reverend *Manoa,* and to these
My Countrymen, whom here I knew remaining,
As at some distance from the place of horror,   1550
So in the sad event too much concern'd.
   Manoa. The accident was loud, and here before thee
With rueful cry, yet what it was we hear not;
No Preface needs, thou seest we long to know.
   Messenger. It would burst forth, but I recover breath   1555
And sense distract, to know well what I utter.
   Manoa. Tell us the sum, the circumstance defer.
   Messenger. *Gaza* yet stands, but all her Sons are fall'n,
All in a moment overwhelm'd and fall'n.
   Manoa. Sad, but thou knowst to *Israelites* not saddest   1560
The desolation of a Hostile City.
   Messenger. Feed on that first, there may in grief be surfeit.
   Manoa. Relate by whom.
   Messenger.   By *Samson.*
   Manoa.   That still lessens
The sorrow, and converts it nigh to joy.
   Messenger. Ah *Manoa,* I refrain too suddenly   1565

1529. *dole*: grief, pain. Perhaps there is a play on the homonym which means "something dealt," for it was familiar in phrases like Shakespeare's "dole of blows" (*II Henry IV* I, i, 169).

1538. *baits*: delays, travels slowly. The meaning arose from the use of "bait" to mean "to stop in a journey to feed horses."

1541. In the *Argument* the Ebrew is said to enter "confusedly at first," like the messengers who bring dreadful news in several Greek tragedies. "Wretch that I am!" exclaims the reporter of the fatal strife of Creon's nephews in Euripides' *Phoenissae*, 1336-8, "What words can I find? . . . Ah! wretched me." J. C. Smith points out (*TLS*, Dec. 5, 1936, p. 1016) that the thickest cluster of femi-

nine endings in Milton's three major poems occurs in this excited dialogue, in contrast with their rarity in *Samson* as a whole—about 3 per cent. Cf. *PL* I, 38, n.

1556. *distract*: distracted. Compare *extinct* in l. 70.

1557. *the sum*: the main thing, the gist. *circumstance*: circumstances. *O.E.D.* quotes Tourneur's *Atheist's Tragedy*, I, iv: "Time cuts off circumstance; I must be briefe."

1562. Compare Valentine's words in *Two Gentlemen of Verona* III, i, 220–1:
O, I have fed upon this woe already,
And now excess of it will make me surfeit.

To utter what will come at last too soon;
Lest evil tidings with too rude irruption
Hitting thy aged ear should pierce too deep.
    Manoa. Suspense in news is torture, speak them out.
    Messenger. Then take the worst in brief, *Samson* is dead.   1570
    Manoa. The worst indeed! O all my hope's defeated
To free him hence! but death who sets all free
Hath paid his ransom now and full discharge.
What windy joy this day had I conceiv'd
Hopeful of his Delivery, which now proves   1575
Abortive as the first-born bloom of spring
Nipt with the lagging rear of winter's frost.
Yet ere I give the reins to grief, say first,
How died he? death to life is crown or shame.
All by him fell thou say'st, by whom fell he,   1580
What glorious hand gave *Samson* his death's wound?
    Messenger. Unwounded of his enemies he fell.
    Manoa. Wearied with slaughter then or how? explain.
    Messenger. By his own hands.
    Manoa.   Self-violence? what cause
Brought him so soon at variance with himself   1585
Among his foes?
    Messenger.   Inevitable cause
At once both to destroy and be destroy'd;
The Edifice where all were met to see him
Upon their heads and on his own he pull'd.
    Manoa. O lastly over-strong against thyself!   1590
A dreadful way thou took'st to thy revenge.
More than enough we know; but while things yet
Are in confusion, give us if thou canst,
Eye-witness of what first or last was done,
Relation more particular and distinct.   1595
    Messenger. Occasions drew me early to this City,
And as the gates I enter'd with Sunrise,
The morning Trumpets Festival proclaim'd
Through each high street: little I had dispatch't
When all abroad was rumor'd that this day   1600
Samson should be brought forth to show the people
Proof of his mighty strength in feats and games;
I sorrow'd at his captive state, but minded
Not to be absent at that spectacle.
The building was a spacious Theater   1605
Half round on two main Pillars vaulted high,
With seats where all the Lords and each degree

1570. In the *Electra* (673) of Sophocles, Todd noticed that the death of Orestes is announced in just this way, with the bare words, "Orestes is dead."

1574. *windy:* vain. O.E.D. quotes Gabriel Harvey: "A wan or windy Hope, is a notable breakenecke vnto itselfe."

1576–1577. The clear Shakespearian quality of the lines has led editors to compare *Love's Labour's Lost* I, i, 100–101: "Like an envious sneaping frost, That bites the first-born infants of the spring."

1596. *Occasions:* affairs, business.

1599. *little . . . dispatch't;* i.e., had dispatched little business.

1603. *minded:* resolved. Compare the noun in *PL* V, 452: "sudden mind arose, In *Adam,* not to let th'occasion pass."

1605–1610. In Judg. xvi, 27, the building is described as a "house full of men and women; and all the lords of the Philistines were there; and there were upon the roof about three thousand men and women, that beheld while Samson made sport." Arias Montanus' design of the temple in *De Varia Republica* (Antwerp, 1592) is reproduced by Krouse in *Milton's Samson,* opposite p. 68.

1607–1608. *degree . . . sort:* high social rank.

Of sort, might sit in order to behold,
The other side was op'n, where the throng
On banks and scaffolds under Sky might stand;   1610
I among these aloof obscurely stood.
The Feast and noon grew high and Sacrifice
Had fill'd thir hearts with mirth, high cheer, and wine,
When to thir sports they turn'd. Immediately
Was *Samson* as a public servant brought,   1615
In thir state Livery clad; before him Pipes
And Timbrels, on each side went armed guards,
Both horse and foot before him and behind,
Archers, and Slingers, Cataphracts and Spears.
At sight of him the people with a shout   1620
Rifted the Air clamoring thir god with praise,
Who had made thir dreadful enemy thir thrall.
He patient but undaunted where they led him,
Came to the place, and what was set before him
Which without help of eye might be assay'd,   1625
To heave, pull, draw, or break, he still perform'd
All with incredible, stupendious force,
None daring to appear Antagonist.
At length for intermission sake they led him
Between the pillars; he his guide requested   1630
(For so from such as nearer stood we heard)
As overtir'd to let him lean a while
With both his arms on those two massy Pillars
That to the arched roof gave main support.
He unsuspicious led him; which when *Samson*   1635
Felt in his arms, with head a while inclin'd,
And eyes fast fixt he stood, as one who pray'd,
Or some great matter in his mind revolv'd.
At last with head erect thus cried aloud,
     "Hitherto, Lords, what your commands impos'd   1640
I have perform'd, as reason was, obeying,
Not without wonder or delight beheld.
Now of my own accord such other trial
I mean to show you of my strength, yet greater;
As with amaze shall strike all who behold."   1645

1610. *banks:* benches.
1616. *Livery:* uniform of public or private retainers.
1619. *Cataphracts:* mounted soldiers whose horses, like themselves, wore heavy armor. *Spears:* spearmen.
1621. With *clamoring* compare Evelyn's use of the word (quoted by the *O.E.D.*): "Legions of women went down to clamour the House for his enlargement."
1627. *stupendious* was a more common form than *stupendous.* Compare *PL* X, 351.
1630–1634. The account (in Judg. xvi, 25–26) says that, when Samson was set between the pillars, he "said unto the lad that held him by the hand, Suffer me that I may feel the pillars whereupon the house standeth, that I may lean upon them."
1634. Milton may have been influenced by the account of the contemporary appearance of the ruins of Gaza in Sandys' *Travels* (p. 116): "On the North-East Corner and summity of the Hill are the ruines of huge Arches sunk low in the Earth, and other foundations of a stately Building. . . . The Jews do fable this place to have been the Theatre of Sampson pulled down on the heads of the Philistines." Sandys adds that in his opinion the ruins belonged to a Roman structure. Milton may have known that the arch was a Roman invention, and have described the building as *arched* with no more definite an idea of it than Quarles had when he spoke of its "arched roofe" as all "Builded with massie stone" and yet as being sustained by "mighty Rafters" (*The History of Samson,* Sec. 23).
1637–1638. *eyes fast fixt . . . revolv'd:* the phrasing recalls Virgil's picture of Aeneas leaving the cave of the Sibyl with sad face and downcast eyes, meditating a dark future (*Aen.* VI, 156–7).
1645. *amaze:* confusion. Compare *amaz'd* in l. 1286.

This utter'd, straining all his nerves he bow'd;
As with the force of winds and waters pent
When Mountains tremble, those two massy Pillars
With horrible convulsion to and fro
He tugg'd, he shook, till down they came, and drew   1650
The whole roof after them with burst of thunder
Upon the heads of all who sat beneath,
Lords, Ladies, Captains, Counsellors, or Priests,
Thir choice nobility and flower, not only
Of this but each *Philistian* City round   1655
Met from all parts to solemnize this Feast.
Samson with these immixt, inevitably
Pull'd down the same destruction on himself;
The vulgar only scap'd who stood without.
   Chorus. O dearly bought revenge, yet glorious!   1660
Living or dying thou hast fulfill'd
The work for which thou wast foretold
To *Israel,* and now li'st victorious
Among thy slain self-kill'd
<u>Not willingly, but tangl'd in the fold</u> — suicide is verboten   1665
<u>Of dire necessity,</u> whose law in death conjoin'd
Thee with thy slaughter'd foes in number more
Than all thy life had slain before.
   Semichorus. While thir hearts were jocund and sublime,
Drunk with Idolatry, drunk with Wine,   1670
And fat regorg'd of Bulls and Goats,
Chanting thir Idol, and preferring
Before our living Dread who dwells
In *Silo* his bright Sanctuary:
Among them hee a spirit of frenzy sent,   1675
Who hurt thir minds,
And urg'd them on with mad desire
To call in haste for thir destroyer;
They only set on sport and play
Unwittingly importun'd   1680
Thir own destruction to come speedy upon them.
So fond are mortal men
Fall'n into wrath divine,
As thir own ruin on themselves to invite,

1647-1648. Two great similes in (*PL* I, 230-7 and IV, 195-8) arise from the belief that earthquakes are caused by "Winds under ground or waters forcing way Sidelong."

1664-1665. Milton challenges the view of those who agreed with Donne that Samson's death seemed perilously like suicide. "The very text," said Donne in *Biathanatos* (III, v, 4) "is against those who, like St. Augustine, equally zealous of Samson's honor and his own conscience," argue that Samson acted simply by divine prompting, "for Samson dyed with these words in his mouth, *Let me lose my life with the Philistins.*" Compare Burton, *Anatomy* I, iv, 1; Vol. I, 436.

1667-1668. From Judg. xvi, 30: "the dead which he slew at his death were more than they which he slew in his life."

1669. *sublime* is used in the Latin sense of "uplifted." Compare the devils awaiting Satan,

Sublime with expectation when to see
In Triumph issuing forth thir glorious Chief.
          (*PL* X, 136-7)

1674. It was at *Silo* (Authorized Version, *Shiloh*) that "the whole congregation of the children of Israel . . . set up the tabernacle of the congregation" (Josh. xviii, 1). Milton thought of it as it is described in Exod. xl, 34: "the glory of the Lord filled the tabernacle."

1675-1683. The thought parallels the discussion of reprobation in *CD* I, iv, p. 928 as the self-punishment of hard-hearted men though several biblical passages (e.g., Isa. vi, 10) speak of God as hardening the hearts of the doomed. Milton significantly closes the chapter by quoting the *Od.* (I, 32-34), where Zeus protests to the gods that men accuse them unjustly of responsibility for the woes that blind mortals bring upon themselves.

Insensate left, or to sense reprobate,   1685
And with blindness internal struck.   *= Standard Chorus, but*
   Semichorus. But he though blind of sight, *Milton preaching too.*
Despis'd and thought extinguish't quite,
With inward eyes illuminated
His fiery virtue rous'd   1690
From under ashes into sudden flame,
And as an ev'ning Dragon came,
Assailant on the perched roosts,
And nests in order rang'd
Of tame villatic Fowl; but as an Eagle   1695
His cloudless thunder bolted on thir heads.
So virtue giv'n for lost,
Deprest, and overthrown, as seem'd,
Like that self-begott'n bird
In the *Arabian* woods embost,   1700
That no second knows nor third,
And lay erewhile a Holocaust,
From out her ashy womb now teem'd,
Revives, reflourishes, then vigorous most
When most unactive deem'd,   1705
And though her body die, her fame survives,
A secular bird ages of lives.
   Manoa. Come, come, no time for lamentation now,
Nor much more cause: *Samson* hath quit himself
Like *Samson,* and heroicly hath finish'd   1710
A life Heroic, on his Enemies
Fully reveng'd hath left them years of mourning,
And lamentation to the Sons of *Caphtor*
Through all *Philistian* bounds. To *Israel*
Honor hath left, and freedom, let but them   1715
Find courage to lay hold on this occasion;
To himself and Father's house eternal fame;
And which is best and happiest yet, all this
With God not parted from him, as was fear'd,
But favoring and assisting to the end.   1720
Nothing is here for tears, nothing to wail
Or knock the breast, no weakness, no contempt,
Dispraise, or blame, nothing but well and fair,
And what may quiet us in a death so noble.
Let us go find the body where it lies   1725
Soak't in his enemies' blood, and from the stream
With lavers pure and cleansing herbs wash off
The clotted gore. I with what speed the while
(*Gaza* is not in plight to say us nay)

1692. *Dragon:* serpent.
1695. *villatic Fowl:* barndoor fowls. To Milton's mind the word *villa* kept its Italian meaning of "a farmhouse."
1699. *that self-begotten bird:* the Phoenix, which Ovid describes (*Met.* XV, 391–402) as living for five secles (whence *secular* in l. 1707) or centuries and then preparing for death and rebirth by fire in a magnificent pyre of spices. Cf. *PL* V, 272, and the emblem on page 548.
1700. *embost:* sheltered. The word originally

applied to hunted animals.
1701. *That no second knows:* only one phoenix is alive at a time.
1702. *Holocaust:* a sacrifice completely consumed by the fire.
1703. *teem'd:* delivered, brought forth.
1713. *Sons of Caphtor:* the Philistines. Cf. *The Argument,* 10, and note.
1728. *with what speed:* with what speed I can.
1729. *plight:* state or condition. Compare "sweetest, saddest plight" in *IlPen,* 57.

Will send for all my kindred, all my friends 1730
To fetch him hence and solemnly attend
With silent obsequy and funeral train
Home to his Father's house: there will I build him
A Monument, and plant it round with shade
Of Laurel ever green, and branching Palm, 1735
With all his Trophies hung, and Acts enroll'd
In copious Legend, or sweet Lyric Song.
Thither shall all the valiant youth resort,
And from his memory inflame thir breasts
To matchless valor, and adventures high: 1740
The Virgins also shall on feastful days
Visit his Tomb with flowers, only bewailing *— odd little insert*
His lot unfortunate in nuptial choice,
From whence captivity and loss of eyes.

    Chorus. All is best, though we oft doubt, 1745
What th' unsearchable dispose
Of highest wisdom brings about,
And ever best found in the close.
Oft he seems to hide his face,
But unexpectedly returns 1750
And to his faithful Champion hath in place
Bore witness gloriously; whence *Gaza* mourns
And all that band them to resist
His uncontrollable intent;
His servants he with new acquist 1755
Of true experience from this great event
With peace and consolation hath dismist,
And calm of mind, all passion spent. *a calming the whole story*

THE END

1730–1733. "Then his brethren and all the house of his father came down, and . . . brought him up, and buried him between Zorah and Eshtaol, in the burying-place of Manoah his father" (Judg. xvi, 31).

1745–1748. Compare the closing choruses—virtually identical in every case—of Euripides' *Alcestis, Andromache, Bacchae, Helen,* and *Medea:*

> In many forms the gods appear,
> And many things unhoped they do;
> Forecasts of men they bring not to pass;
> What is unforecast they bestow.
> So happens this marvel now.

1746. *dispose:* dispensation.

1749. *hide his face;* i. e., in anger. Compare the prayer, "Hide not thy face far from me; put not thy servant away in anger" (Ps. xxvii, 9), which may have been in Milton's mind here as well as when he wrote l. 641 above.

1751. *in place:* "on the spot, then and there." O.E.D.

1755. *acquist:* increase, acquisition.

1758. *passion* is used in the strong sense that it is in the quotation from Minturno in the note to ll. 8–11 of the Preface.

P.L. — Confusion of events. Man has not yet fallen,
     yet is to be forgiven. The ways of gods, govts, and girls

Tree of Life, Knowledge of Good and Evil —
    Can go without God. ie. Eve eats the fruit

If you are protected and never have been tested in combat
with sin, when you die, how does God know you are true.

Adam is archetype of christian hero. ie. G. Washington,
   and. Abraham Lincoln, Ike Eisenhower

Promise of Christ at end of P.L. makes work comic.

Greek drama —   prologos, parados, episodia,
          stasima { strophe antistrophe epode }, exodus

peripatea — where action gets reversed. happens
   because of;
   anagnorisis — a recognition

FOR YOUR NOTES

FOR YOUR NOTES

FOR YOUR NOTES

FOR YOUR NOTES

FOR YOUR NOTES

FOR YOUR NOTES

Prose

Some Early ORATORICAL PERFORMANCES (Prolusions)

BIBLIOGRAPHICAL NOTE—The seven academic exercises which are translated here were published by Milton in 1674. Their Latin originals are available in C.E. XII, 118–284. The best translation is by Phyllis B. Tillyard (Cambridge, 1932) with an Introduction and Commentary by E. M. W. Tillyard, who has also compared *Prols* I and VI with *L'All* and *IlPen* in *The Miltonic Setting* (Cambridge, 1938), pp. 1–28, in an essay which is challenged by F. R. Leavis in *The Common Pursuit* (London, 1952), pp. 34–36, and by E. S. LeComte in *Yet Once More* (New York, 1953), pp. 60–69, as well as by several reviewers. The best study of the relation of the Oratorical Performances (*Prolusiones*) to Milton's experience as a schoolboy and to his theories as a schoolmaster in *Educ* is by D. L. Clark in *Milton at St. Paul's School* (New York, 1948). The best commentary on the Prolusions is by Kathryn McEuen in *The Complete Prose Works of John Milton*, Vol. I (Yale University Press, 1953), pp. 211–306. The present translation has been made from the Latin originals in C.E. XII, 118–284.

I. Delivered in College

WHETHER DAY OR NIGHT IS THE MORE EXCELLENT

The noblest masters of rhetoric have left behind them in various screeds a maxim which can hardly have escaped you, my academic friends, and which says that in every type of speech—demonstrative, deliberative, or judicial—the opening should be designed to win the good will of the audience. On those terms only can the minds of the auditors be made responsive and the cause that the speaker has at heart be won. If this be true (and—not to disguise the truth—I know that it is a principle established by the vote of the entire learned world), how unlucky I am! What a plight I am in today! In the very first words of my speech I am afraid that I am going to say something unbecoming to a speaker, and that I shall be obliged to neglect the first and most important duty of an orator. And in fact, what good will can I expect from you when in as great an assembly as this I recognize almost every face within eyeshot as unfriendly to me? I seem to have come to play an orator's part before an utterly unsympathetic audience.

Such are the quarrels that the competitive spirit engenders even in colleges among those who are interested in different subjects and even among those who pursue the same subjects with different conceptions of them. But I do not care if
Polydamas and the Trojan women prefer Labeo to me—
Nothing there to take seriously.[1]

But, to save me from utter despair, if I am not mistaken, I see here and there a few whose expressions silently but by no means uncertainly indicate how friendly their wishes are. I should rather have their approval—however few they be—than that of countless legions of ignorant fellows who have no mind, no reasoning faculties, no sound judgment, and who try to sell themselves by their bragging and ridiculous froth of talk. Strip them of the patches that they

[1] The verse from Persius' *Satires* (I, 4–5) which Milton quotes, warns his audience that he is no more afraid of them than Persius was of the Roman public. Persius was echoing Hector's contempt for his critics, Polydamas and the Trojan women (*Il.* XXII, 100), which he turned against a contemporary, Attius Labeo, whom the same satire mentions as the author of a drink-inspired *Iliad*. According to a note in Barton Holyday's translation of the *Satires* (1616), Persius intended Polydamas to represent (and challenge) the emperor Nero.

have begged from our most modern authors and—by the Eternal—you will find them as empty as a bean pod.[2] Once their baggage of phrases and wise-cracks is exhausted, there is not so much as a grunt in them, and and they are as dumb as the little frogs of Seriphus.[3] If Heraclitus were in the land of the living,[4] how hard even he would have to struggle to keep from laughing if, by the gods' permission, he should happen to see these little orators (whom he might have heard a short time ago tragically bombasting Euripides' *Orestes* or Hercules'[5] rant in his dying agony) creeping off, now that their little stock of words is exhausted and their superciliousness has vanished, like certain little vermin with their horns drawn in.

But I must end this little digression. If there is anyone who has spurned all conditions of peace and declared a truceless war against me, at this moment I will not let pride prevent me from begging and appealing to him to set his quarrel aside for a little while and stand by as an impartial judge in this debate, and not to allow the speaker's fault (if he is at fault) to reflect invidiously on so excellent and glorious a cause. If you think what I have said too mordant and vinegary, I confess that I have acted deliberately, for I intend to have the introduction to my speech resemble the lowering of early dawn, from whose darkest clouds comes the loveliest day.

Whether Day is more excellent than Night, Gentlemen, is no ordinary topic for discussion.[6] Its meticulous and minute examination is the task assigned to me as my

part in the business of this morning,—though the subject seems to suit a poetical performance better than it does an oratorical competition.

Did I say that Night has challenged Day? What does this mean? What kind of a contest is this? Are the Titans[7] redrawing their ancient battle lines and fighting the Phlegraean struggle over again? Or has Earth spawned some new offspring of portentous size to assail the gods of heaven? Or has Typhoeus[8] shaken off the mighty mass of Mount Etna that was piled on top of him? Or has Briareus[9] dodged Cerberus and slipped out of his adamant chains? What is it that now for the third time has stirred up the infernal deities with the hope of winning heaven's empire? Is there no respect for Jove's thunder or Athene's[10] invincible might, which did such execution in olden times among the sons of Earth? Has the memory of Father Bacchus' rout of the giants through the vaults of heaven quite faded out of mind? Far from it! Night well remembers, to her sorrow, how most of her brothers were slain by Jupiter and the fleeing survivors driven down to the uttermost recesses of hell's pit. Now in her fright she is preparing for nothing less than war, but she prefers to work with charges and complaints. After the quarrel has been well fought out with nails and fists, she resorts, like a woman, to talking and wrangling, in order, I suppose, to discover whether she is better with her tongue or her weapons. Believe me, I shall lose no time in showing how recklessly and arrogantly she is claiming the mastery, and how weak her case is compared with Day's. And indeed I see Day herself, roused by

---

[2] Athenaeus (early third century A.D.) put this jibe into the mouth of one of his gossiping gourmets in *The Deipnosophists* (VIII, 362b).

[3] The proverbially silent frogs of Seriphus (the tiny Aegean island of Serfo) often figure in Juvenal's *Satires* (e.g. VI, 564 and X, 170).

[4] "To lament with Heracleitus"—as Burton recalled (*Anatomy*, Everyman Ed., Vol. I, p. 19)—was proverbial. Heracleitus had the reputation of not suffering fools gladly in his native Ephesus in the fifth century B.C.

[5] Amateur declaimers were fond of the title roles in Euripides' *Herakles* and *Orestes*.

[6] Milton is striking a note of ironical playfulness. His subject resembles the assignments on the relative merits of earth and water, air and fire, which we find as late as 1657 in such a textbook as John Tesmarus, *Exercitationum Rhetoricarum Libri VIII*, published in Amsterdam, but representative of English as well as of continental practice.

[7] Hesiod's *Theog.*, 617–735, tells the story of the attack of the *Titans* on the Olympian gods, and Pindar's first *Nemean Ode* ends with an account of their overthrow on the plains of Phlegra, in Macedonia. Cf. *PL* I, 197–200, and *Naturam*, 30–32.

[8] *Typhoeus* (the smoky one), whose name seems to have made him a symbol of volcanic activity to the Greeks, was the youngest son of Earth and Tartarus. Pindar's first *Pythian Ode*, 15, describes him as buried by Zeus under Mount Etna. Cf. *PL* II, 539.

[9] The hundred-handed *Briareus* was the most formidable of the giants whom Zeus overwhelmed with mountains. Cf. *Theog.*, 617–20.

[10] Natale Conti, IV, v, "On Pallas Athene," assembles several versions of the story of *Athene's* and of Bacchus' parts in the struggle of Zeus with the Titans.

PRIMVS HABET STIRPEM DEMOGORGONIS AETHERE DEMPTO

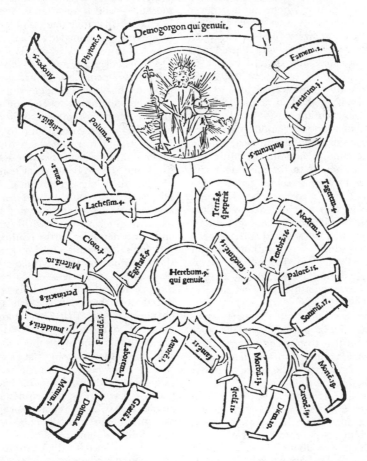

the cock's crowing, hurrying faster than usual on her way so as to hear what is going to be said in her praise. And now, to begin!

Since everyone thinks his honor and personal dignity established if he can prove his descent from noble forebears and his possession of the ancient blood of kings and gods, my first inquiry must be, which of the two is of the more illustrious birth; my next, which is the more honored by antiquity; and my third, which serves mankind the better.

Among the oldest writers on mythology I find it recorded that, beside the other children of whom Demogorgon begot so many, that progenitor of all the gods (who, I divine, was the same as he whom the ancients called Chaos) sired Earth. By an un-

known father she became the mother of Night, though Hesiod differs a little from this and prefers to make her Chaos-begotten in the verse,[11]

Of Chaos were Erebus and black Night born.

Whoever her father may have been, when she ripened to an age fit for marriage, the shepherd Phanes asked her for his wife. In spite of her mother's approval, she rebelled

11 The verse is from the *Theog.*, 123. The prime source of the fantasies about Night's parentage and progeny with which Milton amuses his audience is the following passage of Hesiod. With minor variations such as Milton suggests, it was to be found popularized in the writings of many Renaissance mythographers, and in traditional illustrations of Boccaccio's *Genealogy of the Gods,* one of which is reproduced here from the edition of Augustinus de Zannis de Portesio (Venice, 1511), the myth was visualized. Boccaccio makes Night the child of Demogorgon and the sister of Erebus.

and refused to share the bed of a man who was a stranger to her, whom she had never seen, and whose habits were so very unlike her own. Taking her refusal in bad part, Phanes changed his love into hatred and vengefully pursued this dark daughter of Earth through every country in the world to kill her. Now she feared him as her enemy no less than she had despised him as her lover. So even among the most distant nations and in the most remote places, and even in her own mother's embrace, she did not feel safe enough, and she stealthily and darkly betook herself to the incestuous embrace of her brother Erebus. So she both escaped from the burden of her fear and got a husband very much of her own kind. And it is by this charming conjugal couple that Aether and Day are said to have been begotten, according to the author whom I have previously quoted, Hesiod:[12]

From Night were Aether and Day born, Whom she brought forth, conceiving them in Erebus' embrace.

But these inventions of the poets—particularly the Greek poets—about the gods are hardly entitled to our confidence. Our Muses, who are more humane than theirs, and Philosophy herself, who is the neighbor of the gods, both forbid it. So let no one regard it as a slur on these writers that in so important a matter as this they should hardly seem adequate. If any of them has veered a point away from the truth, their genius—which was divine above all others —ought not to be blamed for the error. The blame should rest on the vicious and blind ignorance which covered the world in those days. *They* have won honor and glory enough simply because they settled men in fixed habitations who had been wandering like wild beasts in the forests and on the mountains,[13] and because they founded states and by their divine inspiration were the first to teach all the arts of which we are the heirs today—thanks to their presentation in the alluring disguise of

poetry. The sole title of the poets to immortality—and a very noble one too—shall be the fact that they made so happy a beginning with that knowledge of the arts which they left to posterity to develop.

So—whoever you may be—do not be rash enough to accuse me of arrogance on the ground that I have done violence to the utterances of the old poets, and that I have altered them without authority. That is not what I am presuming to do. I am simply trying to bring them to the test of reason, to find out in this way whether they can stand the probe of strict truth.

First, then, the story that Night is the offspring of Earth has been learnedly and elegantly told by antiquity, for what could make Night cover the world but the solid and impenetrable earth coming between the sun's light and our horizon? As for the assertions of the mythologists that she was either motherless or fatherless—they are gay fables, if indeed it is correctly deduced from them that she was a bastard or changeling, or that her parents were ashamed to recognize so notoriously ignoble a child. But why they should think that the superhumanly handsome Phanes should have been so much in love with Night—the Ethiop, the mere shadow—as to propose marriage to her, seems a very hard riddle to answer on the evidence, unless the astounding scarcity of women in those days gave him no choice.

And now let us really come to grips with our subject. The ancients interpret Phanes either as the sun or the day, and they interpret the story of his first seeking Night in marriage and then pursuing her to punish her contempt for the union as meaning nothing else than the alternation of the days and nights. But to prove this what need was there to introduce Phanes as the wooer of Night when their ceaseless alternation and—as it seems—expulsion of each other by turns, might be better explained by their inborn and irreconcilable hatred? For it is a well enough established fact that from the dawn of creation light and darkness have disagreed between themselves in a most bitter quarrel. My firm belief is that Night got her name of *euphrone*[14] from her prudence and discretion in refusing to en-

---

[12] *Theog.*, 124–5.

[13] Milton is presenting a great commonplace. "What," asks Henry Peacham in the *Compleat Gentleman* (1634), p. 79, "were the songs of *Linus, Orpheus, Amphyon, Olympus*, and that ditty *Iopas* sang to his harpe at *Dido's* banquet, but Naturall and Morall Philosophy, sweetned with the pleasance of Numbers, that Rudenesse and Barbarisme might the better taste and digest the lessons of civility?"

[14] The epithet *euphrone* was applied euphemistically to night, for its literal meaning is "well-

tangle herself in a marriage with Phanes. If she had once admitted him to her bridal bed, there can be no doubt that she would either have been annihilated by the unbearable brightness of his rays or else consumed in a fiery death, such as they say that Semele[15] suffered, although it was against the will of her lover, Jupiter. So with her eye on her own safety, it seems, she made choice of Erebus. Hence comes that clever and elegant epigram of Martial;[16]

The worst of husbands and the worst of wives,
I muse not at the bliss your match contrives.

Nor, in my judgment, ought the veil of silence to be drawn over the lovely progeny —so worthy of herself—with which Night blessed her husband; Tribulation, forsooth, and Envy, Fear, Deceit, Fraud, Pertinacity, Poverty, Penury, Starvation, Complaint, Illness, Old Age, Pallor, Darkness, Sleep, Death, and the child of her last delivery, Charon.[17] So the situation squares well with the Greek proverb: 'from a bad crow, bad eggs.'

Then there is no lack of writers who say that Night also bore Aether and Day to her husband Erebus. But is there anyone—unless he is out of his wits—who does not hoot down and throw out such philosophy as he would the theories of Democritus[18] or the tales of his nurses? For does it seem likely that the dark and swarthy Night would spawn anything so lovely and so

thinking" or "well-intentioned." Milton suggests that it should be taken to mean "shrewd."

15 In *Met*. III, 259–315, Ovid tells of the destruction of *Semele* when she took the jealous Juno's advice to ask her lover *Jupiter* to visit her in his full, heavenly glory.

16 Milton distorted the last line of the epigram (Martial, *Epigrams* VIII, 35) to make it fit his purpose. The original reads:
Cum sitis similes, paresque vita,
Uxor pessima, pessimus maritus,
Miror non bene convenire vobis.

17 *Charon*, the ferryman of souls over the Styx to the realms of death, is not found in Hesiod's list of Night's children (*Theog.*, 211–32), though it contains several names which are not found either here or in Boccaccio's tree. Milton's original list reads: Aerumna (ablative case), Invidia, Timore, Dolo, Fraude, Pertinacia, Paupertate, Miseria, Fame, Querela, Morbo, Senectute, Pallore, Caligine, Somno, Morte, Charonte.

18 Although *Democritus* (?470–380? B.C.) was one of the great natural philosophers in the ancient world, his atheism and his atomic theory inclined many Christian writers to accept a tradition that the citizens of his native Abdera, in Thrace, regarded him as insane.

amiable and so agreeable and desirable to everyone? Such a child would have caused the mother's death at the moment of conception by bursting prematurely from her womb. She would have chased her father Erebus clean away. She would have made old gaffer Charon hide his blinking eyes at the very bottom of the Styx, and—if there are any hideouts in the underworld—she would have driven him off to them with sails as well as oars speeding him on his way. Day was not born in hell, and she has never been seen there, nor—except in defiance of the Fates—can she penetrate there even through the tiniest loophole. I'll tell you what. I dare assert that Day is older than Night, and that when the universe first emerged from chaos she brightened it with her far-spreading light—before Night began to take turns with her—unless we wilfully and wrongly identify that foul and hideous obscurity[19] with Night and with Demogorgon himself.

Therefore I regard Day as Heaven's first daughter[20] or rather as his son, whom he is said to have begotten to be the consolation of humanity and the terror of the deities of hell; lest Night should seize power and wipe out the boundary between Earth and Hades, and lest the ghosts and Furies and all the obscene tribe of monsters should leave their infernal stations and rush up into the world, and lest wretched mankind should be overwhelmed and, everywhere oppressed by dense darkness, living men should have to endure the punishments of the spirits that have died.

Thus far, members of the university, we have been trying to drag the obscure progeny of Night out of their dark and deep shadows. You shall soon understand how worthy they are of their parentage—particularly if I should first try to the best of my small ability to praise the Day, though she herself excels the eloquence of all who praise her.

In the first place, what need can there possibly be to inform you how welcome and delightful she is to everything that is alive?

19 By *that . . . obscurity* Milton means the primeval chaos out of which Hesiod described the universe as arising.

20 Cf. Spenser's description of Night as one who was "begot in Demogorgon's hall," and who had seen "the secrets of the world unmade" (*F.Q.* I, v, 22, 5–6).

When the birds themselves cannot hide their joy, but leave their little nests at the first flush of dawn and either trill it from the tree-tops in a sweet concert or else lift themselves up as close to the sun as they can fly to welcome the returning light. But the first of all to hail the coming of the sun is the sleepless cock.[21] Like some herald, he seems to command men to shake off slumber and go abroad, and run to meet the rising dawn. The goats gambol in the fields and the whole four-footed race leaps and capers in delight. Moreover the heliotrope, after mourning almost all night with her face turned eastward in expectation of her lover, Phoebus, now welcomes his approach with a caressing smile.[22] The marigold also and the rose, in order to do their best for the general happiness, open their breasts and are lavish with the perfume that they have kept for the sun alone. They grudge them to the Night, and shut themselves up inside their tiny leaves at evening's first approach. The other flowers lift their drooping, dewy heads and offer themselves to the sun, silently asking for his kisses to dry away the tears which they have shed for his absence. As the sun approaches, the Earth herself puts on a lovelier garment. The clouds in rainbow colors seem to deploy their long and festal ranks to wait upon the rising god.

Now let me complete my argument and omit nothing that magnifies his glory. It is to him that the Persians, to him that the Libyans[23] have decreed divine honors; to him that the Rhodians also dedicated the famous Colossus[24] whose vast bulk was fabricated by the marvellous skill of Chares of Lindus. To him likewise even today we have heard that the Indians of the Americas sacrifice with incense and splendor.

Gentlemen of the University, I call you to witness how welcome he is when he brings his light to you in the morning, after you have yearned for him and looked forward to his coming as one who would restore you to the gentle Muses, guardians of the culture for which you have an insatiable thirst, and from which the hateful night had divided you.

Last, I call the god Saturn, who was cast down from heaven to Tartarus, to witness how willingly he would return to the upper air from the hated shades, if only Jove would permit. Even Pluto himself betrays his strong preference for the light over his darkness by his many attempts to win the empire of heaven. So Orpheus says poetically and very truly in his Hymn to the goddess Aurora:[25]

In her all tribes of mortal men rejoice;
Not one desires to fly that glorious face.
Whene'er you shake the sweet sleep from our eyes
Joy thrills all hearts:—the creeping things, the race
Four-footed, birds, and all within the sea's embrace.

Nor is there anything wonderful here, for Day is no less useful than delightful, and only Day is suited to the pursuit of our practical affairs. What mortal would undertake to cross the broad and boundless seas if he despaired of the coming of day? Men would cross the ocean as the ghosts do Lethe and Acheron, hemmed about on every side by frightful darkness. Everyone would huddle in his own miserable hovel, hardly ever daring to creep out—with the inevitable result that human society would at once be destroyed. In vain would Apelles[26] have designed Venus rising from the sea; in vain would Zeuxis[27] have painted Helen, if blind and shadowy night robbed

---

[21] Cf. L'All, 49–50, and verses from the Commonplace Book, 3–4.

[22] Shakespeare's allusion to
　　　　　pale primroses
　That die unmarried ere they can behold
　Bright Phoebus in his strength,
(A Winter's Tale IV, iv, 122–4)
indicates the familiarity of this fancy. Cf. Lyc, 142.

[23] Libyans: inhabitants of northeastern Africa. Milton thought of the temple to the Egyptian sun god, Re, at Heliopolis, above the Nile delta.

[24] Pliny's description (Natural History XXXIV, vii, 18) of the fallen Colossus of Rhodes indicates that it must have been over one hundred feet high. It was erected in the third century B.C. by Chares of Lindus, to stand at the entrance of the harbor.

[25] The Orphic Hymn to Aurora XXVIII, 7–11. Cf. Shakespeare, Sonnet VII, 1–4:
　Lo, in the Orient when the gracious light
　Lifts up his burning head, each under eye
　Doth homage to his new-appearing sight,
　Serving with looks his sacred majesty.

[26] Apelles (336–306? B.C.), whose life was spent mainly at the court of Alexander the Great, was thought to be best represented by his Venus Anadyomene, which represented the goddess rising from the sea in a cloud of spray.

[27] Zeuxis (424–400? B.C.), according to Cicero's story (De Inventione Rhetorica II, i), used the five most beautiful virgins of Croton as models for his painting of Helen of Troy.

us of the sight of things that are so well worth seeing. In vain also would the earth bring forth its wealth of vines with their intricate, serpentine tangles of foliage; in vain would it produce the magnificent, tall trees. To no purpose would she trim herself with buds and blossoms, as if trying to reflect the sky overhead. Then, truly, no living thing would profit by the noblest of the senses, sight. With the eye of the world blinded, all things would fade and utterly die; nor would men themselves, inhabiting a universe quite blacked out, long survive the plague, for nothing would be available to support life, nor would anything prevent a general collapse into primeval chaos.

A man might go on inexhaustibly to add more to what has been said, but the modest Day herself would not permit him to go through every detail of the story. In swift flight she would hasten toward the sunset to put an end to her eulogist's transports. And already day is declining toward evening and is about to yield to night, in order to prevent your making the joke here in the midst of winter that the day seems the longest of summer. With your consent, however, may I just add a few thoughts that cannot properly be omitted?

With good reason the poets have written that night arises out of hell, for it is plainly impossible that such great evils should come in such great numbers from any other place to infest mankind. For when night comes, all things turn ugly and dark. Then truly there is no distinguishing between Helen and Canidia,[28] or between the most costly gems and the most worthless pebbles (if some gems did not vanquish even night's obscurity). Then also the most delightful places inspire our horror and aggravate it by their deep and melancholy silence. Whatever is anywhere abroad in the field, whether man or beast, loses no time in getting to his home or his lair. There they burrow under their covers and close their eyes against the dreadful apparitions of the night. Outside you will descry nothing except those dreaders of the light, footpads and thugs, who breathe out slaughter and

rapine, and lay their plots against the citizens' property. Their reason for walking abroad only at night is their fear of being detected by day. For Day is not in the habit of leaving any villainy unexposed,[29] and so she cannot endure to have her light polluted by such wickedness. You meet nothing except ghosts and specters and the hobgoblins that Night brings with her as her companions from the infernal realms. All the night they claim to have the earth under their jurisdiction, and to share it with mankind. That, I surmise, is why Night has sharpened our ears to make them quicker to catch the sighing of the shades, the shrieks of owls and night-birds, and the roars of lions, which hunger calls forth, and so to smite our hearts with greater terror. Hence it is as clear as crystal how false is the man who says that at night men are exempt from fear, and that night lulls all cares to rest. How vain and futile this fancy is, they know from bitter experience who have ever been conscience-stricken for any crime, or hounded by Sphinxes and Harpies, the Gorgon and Chimaeras, with their flaming torches. They also know, the wretches, who, with no one at hand to help and care for them, no one to soften their grief with a gentle word, let their vain complaints fall upon the senseless stones while over and over they long for the coming of dawn. So with very good reason the most accomplished of poets, Ovid,[30] called Night "the greatest nurse of cares."

As for the fact that at night our sleep renews and restores the bodies that are broken and weary from the day's work—that is a blessing of God and not the gift of Night. And even if it were, sleep is not so valuable that we should honor Night on its account; for when we commit ourselves to slumber, we tacitly acknowledge that we are helpless and wretched mortals who cannot support our miserable little bodies for even a short

---

28 *Canidia,* the gray-head, is Horace's name for the hag whose poisonous philtres figure in *Epodes* iii, v, and xvii, and whom he describes as dishevelled and crowned with serpent locks.

29 Cf. Spenser's turn to the formal contrast of Day with Night in Arthur's diatribe on Milton's subject in *F.Q.* III, iv, 59, 1–2:
> For day discovers all dishonest wayes,
> And sheweth each thing, as it is indeed.

30 Ovid's familiar line from *Met.* VIII, 81, was paraphrased by Spenser in Arthur's diatribe against Night:
> But well I wote, that to an heavy heart
> Thou art the roote and nourse of bitter cares,
> Breeder of new, renewer of old smarts.
>   (*F.Q.* III, iv, 57, 1–3)

while without repose. And truly what else is sleep than the image and likeness of death? So in Homer, Sleep and Death are twins,[31] the offspring of a single conception, born at a single birth. And finally, even the bright fires which the moon and the other stars display at night, are due to the sun, for they do not possess the light that they reflect, except as they borrow it from him.[32]

Who then but a child of darkness, a burglar, a dice-thrower, an all-night addict of the company of whores, and an all-day snorer—who, I ask, but a fellow of this kind would undertake to defend a cause so unworthy and intrinsically so disreputable? I wonder that the ingrate dare even look upon this sun, and that he unflinchingly enjoys his share in the common daylight which he insults. He deserves that the sun should smite him with the destroying violence of its rays, as if he were a new Python.[33] He deserves to be locked up in Cimmerian darkness to spend a long and odious lifetime. And he also deserves to have his oration put his audience to sleep, and to have his words inspire no more confidence than a dream. Then, half-asleep himself, he will be deluded into taking his hearers' nods and snores for applause as he brings his speech to a close.

But I see the black brows of Night, and I feel her dun shadows rising. I must withdraw, or Night will overwhelm me unawares. And you, my hearers, since Night is nothing but the passing and, as it were, the death of Day, avoid giving the preference to death over life, and rather award my cause the honor of your votes. So may the Muses make your studies fortunate! So may the Dawn, who is the Muses' friend, give ear to your petitions! And may Phoebus,[34] who sees and hears all things, grant the prayers of those in this assembly who are loyal to the cause of his glory. My speech has been made.

II. Delivered in the Public Schools

ON THE MUSIC OF THE SPHERES

If, Members of the University, there is any room for my insufficiency after so many and such able speakers have been heard today, I shall now try, as far as my small ability permits, to show how friendly I am to the solemn ceremonial of this day. And though I come behind, I shall follow in the train of today's triumph of eloquence. And so, of course, I am avoiding trite and commonplace subjects. I have a horror of them, and the thought of this occasion and of those who, as I quite rightly expected, would deliver themselves of something fully worthy of it, has kindled and challenged my mind to the hard attempt of a new theme. Both these considerations might well afford a stimulus and a spur for my lazy and otherwise indisposed mind. So it has occurred to me to offer a few preliminary remarks in a free style of eloquence and (as the saying is) "with open palm"[1] about that celestial harmony on which there is soon to be a debate, as it

---

[31] The most outstanding Homeric references to *Sleep* as the brother of *Death* occur in *Il.* XIV, 231, 672, and 682.

[32] One of the obsolete astronomical theories reviewed by Copernicus in *De revolutionibus* X, i, is that of the followers of Plato, "supposing that all starres should have obscure and darcke bodyes shyninge with borrowed light like the Mone." Leonard Digges' translation, quoted by Francis Johnson in *Astronomical Thought in Renaissance England*, p. 98.

[33] See *CG*, n. 270.

[34] A recurring Homeric line describes the sun god, Phoebus Apollo, as him "who sees and hears all things."

[1] For the "open hand" of Rhetoric and the "closed fist" of Logic see *Educ,* n. 71. Milton was ironic when he said that his subject was novel, for he knew that it had been discussed in several medieval works like John Scotus Erigena's *De divisione naturae* (Book III), and went back beyond Plato's *Republic* X, 616c–617d, where the eight planetary spheres are described in the vision of Er as turning on a great distaff which rests on the knees of Necessity, while the eight sirens sitting on the respective spheres sing each one her own note and together make the celestial harmony. In the *De coelo* II, ix, 290b, Aristotle challenged Plato's conception, pointing out that it was a Pythagorean theory which rested on the dubious assumption that the spheres can produce any sound, and that their revolutions are in ratios that would produce musical consonance. The Platonic conception, which inspired *Music* and the close of *Arcades,* entered Renaissance literature with the authority of the Florentine Neoplatonists. In 1622, Martin Fotherby, Bishop of Salisbury, summing up the historic arguments *pro* and *con,* concluded (*Atheomastix,* p. 318) that, while he could not affirm the music of the spheres "as a certainty," yet he could propose it "as a probabilitie: leaving every man to his owne liberty to beleeve it, or not to beleeve it, as he findeth himselfe most inclined in his mind."

were, with the clenched fist:—but with due respect to the time limits, which both spur me and curb me. And yet I hope, my hearers, that you will take what I say as being said, as it were, in jest.

For what sane man would suppose that Pythagoras,[2] that god of philosophers, at whose name all the men of his times rose up to do solemn reverence—who, I say, would have supposed that he would have brought forward so well grounded a theory? Certainly, if he taught a harmony of the spheres, and a revolution of the heavens to that sweet music, he wished to symbolize in a wise way the intimate relations of the spheres and their even revolution forever in accordance with the law of destiny. In this he seems to have followed the example of the poets—or, what is almost the same thing, of the divine oracles—by which no sacred and arcane mystery is ever revealed to vulgar ears without being somehow wrapped up and veiled. The greatest of Mother Nature's interpreters, Plato, has followed him, for he has told us that certain sirens have their respective seats on every one of the heavenly spheres and hold both gods and men fast bound by the wonder of their utterly harmonious song. And that universal interaction of all things, that lovely concord among them, which Pythagoras poetically symbolized as harmony, was splendidly and aptly represented by Homer's figure of the golden chain which Jove suspended from heaven.[3] Hence Aristotle, the rival and perpetual detractor of Pythagoras and Plato, hoping to pave his way to glory over the ruins of the theories of such great men, imputed this symphony of the heavens,

which has never been heard, and this music of the spheres to Pythagoras. But, O Father Pythagoras, if only destiny or chance had brought it about that your spirit had transmigrated into me, you would not now be lacking a ready advocate, however great the load of infamy you might bear.[4]

And indeed why should not the heavenly bodies produce musical vibrations? Does it not seem probable to you, Aristotle? Certainly I find it hard to believe that your intelligences[5] could have endured the sedentary task of revolving the heavens for so many aeons, unless the ineffable chanting of the stars had detained them when they would have departed, and persuaded them by its harmonies to delay. If you take that music out of heaven, you hand over those lovely intelligences of yours and their subsidiary gods to slavery, and you condemn them to the treadmill. Why, Atlas himself would have long ago dropped the sky off his shoulders to its destruction if, while he panted and sweated under such a weight, he had not been soothed by the sweet ecstasy of that song. And the Dolphin, tired of the stars, if he had not been consumed by the thought of how far the vocal orbs of heaven surpass the sweetness of Arion's[6] lyre, would long ago have preferred his native ocean to the skies. Why, it is quite credible that the lark herself soars up into the clouds at dawn and that the nightingale passes the night in solitary trilling in order to harmonize their songs with that heavenly music to which they studiously listen.

Hence arose also that primeval story[7]

---

[2] *Pythagoras* (late seventh century B.C.?) appealed to the imagination of Milton's contemporaries because his legendary travels (as Selden's *Law of Nature and Nations* I, ii, observes) were supposed to have included Palestine and (as Milton recalls in *Areopagitica*) England and Cambridge itself. Cf. *Arc.* 63–69, and *Music,* 19–24. Meric Casaubon (*A Treatise of Use and Custom,* p. 58) quoted a certain Robertus Constantinus who accepted Pythagoras' theory of the music of the spheres, which he claimed to hear himself.

[3] Homer's story (*Il.* VIII, 18–29) of the challenge of Zeus to the other gods to drag him from heaven by a golden chain, and of his boast that he would be able to lift them all up to heaven with it, passed through many allegorical interpretations, from that in Plato's *Thaeatetus,* 153C, to Bacon's in *The Advancement of Learning* I, i, 3; p. 10, "The highest link of nature's chain must needs be tied to the foot of Jupiter's chair."

[4] The popular disrepute of Pythagoras' doctrine of transmigration of souls is illustrated by Malvolio's protest (in *Twelfth Night* IV, ii, 59) that he thought too "nobly' of the soul to "approve his opinion."

[5] The best discussion of the tenuous evidence that Aristotle believed in the movement of the planets by *"intelligences"* is by Sir W. D. Ross in *Aristotle's Physics* (Oxford, 1936), pp. 94–102.

[6] Cf. Spenser's allusion to the myth of *Arion* in *Amoretti* xxxviii, 1–4:

Arion, when, through tempests cruel wracke,
He forth was thrown into the greedy seas,
Through the sweet music which his harp did make
Allur'd a dolphin him from death to ease.

The dolphin's reward was a place in the skies as the constellation of the dolphin, which is near the sign of Capricorn.

[7] Hesiod's *Theogony* opens with the story of the birth of the Muses and of their eternal dance and song before the altar of Jove. Cf. *PL* I, 6.

that the Muses dance day and night before Jove's altar; and hence comes that ancient attribution of skill with the lyre to Apollo. Hence reverend antiquity believed Harmonia to be the daughter of Jove and Electra, and at her marriage with Cadmus it was said that all heaven's chorus sang.[8] What though no one on earth has ever heard that symphony of the stars? Is that ground for believing that everything beyond the moon's sphere is absolutely mute and numb with torpid silence? On the contrary, let us blame our own impotent ears, which cannot catch the songs or are unworthy to hear such sweet strains. But this celestial melody is not absolutely unheard; for who, O Aristotle, would think those 'goats'[9] of yours would skip in the mid region of the air unless they cannot resist the impulse to dance when they so plainly hear the music of the neighboring heavens?

But Pythagoras alone of mortals is said to have heard this harmony[10]—unless he was a good genius or a denizen of the sky who perhaps was sent down by some ordinance of the gods to imbue the minds of men with divine knowledge and to recall them to righteousness. At least, he surely was a man who possessed every kind of virtue, who was worthy to consort with the gods themselves, whom he resembled, and to enjoy celestial society. And so I do not wonder that the gods, who loved him very much, permitted him to enter into the most mysterious secrets of nature.

Our impotence to hear this harmony seems to be a consequence of the insolence of the robber, Prometheus,[11] which brought so many evils upon men, and at the same

---

[8] Diodorus Siculus (*Historical Library* V, 49) tells the myth of the heavenly chorus at the wedding of *Harmonia*. In *Mythologiae* IX, xiv, Conti interprets the story as an allegory of the Pythagorean doctrine of the music of the spheres.

[9] Aristotle's *Meteorologica* I, 4, 341b, describes the combustible exhalations of the earth and sea as being sometimes ignited by movements of the atmosphere, and as then producing shooting stars or other phenomena which the Greeks called *"goats"* or "torches."

[10] Cf. *Arc*, 63–69, n.

[11] In *Theog.* 564–616 Hesiod tells the story of *Prometheus'* theft of fire from Zeus and of his deception of Zeus about his claim on men for sacrifice, with at least a suggestion that the subsequent punishment of mankind by the evils which were sent down in Pandora's box was an allegory of the evils brought upon civilization by the development of the arts. Here Milton was probably

time deprived us of that felicity which we shall never be permitted to enjoy as long as we wallow in sin and are brutalized by our animal desires. For how can we, whose spirits, as Persius says,[12] are warped earthward, and are defective in every heavenly element, be sensitive to that celestial sound? If our hearts were as pure, as chaste, as snowy as Pythagoras' was, our ears would resound and be filled with that supremely lovely music of the wheeling stars. Then indeed all things would seem to return to the age of gold. Then we should be immune to pain, and we should enjoy the blessing of a peace that the gods themselves might envy.

But now the hour cuts me short in mid-career, and very fortunately too, for I am afraid that by my rough and inharmonious style I have all along been clashing with this very harmony which I am proclaiming, and that I myself have impeded your hearing of it. And so I shut up.

thinking of a famous allusion to the myth of Prometheus by Horace in *Odes* I, iii.

[12] In *Satires* II, 61, this exclamation interrupts Persius' diatribe on the perversity and selfishness of most prayers to the gods.

III. In the Public Schools

AGAINST SCHOLASTIC PHILOSOPHY

A strenuous search for a rhetorical display that would fascinate you, my collegiate audience, was by no means the least of my recent worries until suddenly I bethought myself of what was so often laid down in the writings of Cicero (whose name I not inauspiciously set on my masthead): that the business of a speaker is to inform, to regale, and to convince his hearers. And so the task which I have set myself in this affair is—to the best of my ability—not to fall short of this triple function of the orator.

But since there is no subject about which I should presume to inform scholars so universally erudite as you are, nor about which you would submit to my instruction, I can only hope for your permission to come close to it by saying something which perhaps will not be entirely off our subject. As for regaling you—as I fear I am far from talented enough to do—it is my dearest hope, and if I attain it, the result will certainly be much the same as convincing you. And now I shall abundantly convince you out of my own heart's judgment, if I shall succeed in persuading you, O my auditors, to relax your study of those enormous and near monstrous volumes of the so-called subtle doctors[1] and to be less strenuous in your enjoyment of the warty disputes of the sophists. Yes truly, so as to make the soundness and rightness of my thesis plain to everyone, I shall briefly prove in my little half hour that the mind is neither entertained nor educated by these studies, nor any good done by them for society.

And at the outset, O Collegians, I put it to you (if I can guess your feelings by my own), and I ask what possible pleasure can lurk in these gamesome quarrels of gloomy oldsters. If they were not born in the cave of Trophonius,[2] their stench betrays their birth in the caves of the monks, they reek with the grim harshness of their authors and are as wrinkled as their fathers. Their style is terse but in spite of it they are so prolix that they bore us and nauseate us. When they are read at any length, they generate an almost instinctive aversion and an even stronger natural hatred in their readers. Too often, my hearers, when it has been my bad luck to be saddled with assignments of research in their contemptible sophistries, when both my eyes and my mind were dull with long reading—too often, I say, I have stopped for breath, and sought some miserable relief in measuring the task before me. But when—as always —I found more ahead of me than I had yet got through, how often have I wished that I had been set to shovel out the Augean[3] ox-stalls rather than struggle with such absurd assignments. And I have called Hercules happy because Juno was so easy-going as never to give him a job like mine to struggle through.

[1] Compare Milton's thrusts at the *Subtle Doctor*, the great Franciscan scholastic philosopher Duns Scotus, in *CG*, p. 652, and *Areop*, p. 729.

[2] The oracle of *Trophonius* in Boeotian Lebadea was famous for the terrifying scenery of the gorge on the river Hercyra where it lay.

[3] The cleaning of King Augeas' Elian stables— as Ovid has Hercules recall in his death agony (*Met.* IX, 187)—was one of the frightful labors which "cruel Juno" had imposed upon him in the tormented course of his life.

No flowers of rhetoric relieve this lifeless, flaccid, crawling stuff, but the jejune, juiceless style matches its thin substance, so that I might easily believe that it was written under melancholy Saturn[4] were it not that the innocent simplicity of his times knew nothing of the tricks and impertinences which swarm in these books. Believe me, O most erudite young gentlemen, while I peruse these inane arguments I seem to myself to be ploughing my way through deserts and impassable places, through enormous wastes and narrow mountain gorges. It is incredible that the lovely and fastidious Muses preside over these wretched, squalid studies or could patronize their crazy fans. I am sure that there was never a place for them on Parnassus[5] except perhaps some abandoned spot at the bottom of the mountain, some ugly place, thick and bristling with thornbushes and brambles, and covered with thistles and stinging nettles, where the chorus of the goddesses never comes, where no laurels or flowers are found, and where the sound of Apollo's lyre never reaches.

For surely divine poetry has the heaven-given power to lift the soul with its crust of earthly filth aloft and enshrine it in the skies, to breathe the perfume of nectar upon it, to bathe it with ambrosia, to fill it with heavenly bliss and whisper to it of immortal joy. Rhetoric so ensnares men's minds and so sweetly lures them with her chains that at one moment she can move them to pity, at another she can drive them to hatred, at another she can fire them with warlike passion, and at another lift them up to contempt of death itself. History, when it is handsomely related, can allay and compose the anxious troubles of the mind or anoint it with joy or, again, evoke tears, but gentle and calm tears, tears that bring a strange pleasure with their flow.

But these futile and barren controversies and wordy disputes are impotent to move the affections of the heart; they simply stupefy and benumb the mind. And so they please no one except a boor or a hairy ape with a secret craving for disputes and quarrels, a chatterer whose back is forever turned on true and sound wisdom. Chase him off with his sophisms either to Mount

[4] Compare *Il Pen*, 24, and *Arc*, 52.

[5] Compare *El V*, 9; *Patrem*, 33 and 270; *PL* III, 28.

Caucasus or to any region where blind savagery prevails, and let him set up shop with his subtleties and quibbles and twist and torture himself as much as he likes until too much worry eats out his vitals, as the vulture ate out the heart of Prometheus.[6]

But these studies which teach us nothing about things can give us no profit and no pleasure. Let us conjure up a vision of those crowds of old fellows in cowls, the prime contrivers of these sophisms: how many of them have ever enriched literature with anything good? No doubt, their crude violence has almost deformed Philosophy, who once was splendid, cultured, and gentler than she is now. Like an evil spirit, they have filled men's breasts with thorns and briars and have brought endless discord into the schools, which has marvellously impeded the scholars' happy progress.

What's the matter? Do these agile philosophasters box the compass with their arguments? One establishes a solid position and another struggles mightly to knock it down; and what you think has been fortified with impregnable logic is swiftly and handily knocked over by his opponent. Meanwhile the unhappy reader is in a quandary, as if at a crossroads, uncertain which way to turn and which road to take, while all around him the missiles fly so thick that they shut out the light and involve things in deep darkness. So, at last the reader is obliged to imitate the long suffering of Ceres[7] and go searching with a lighted torch for truth through the whole wide world, and find it nowhere; until he is brought so close to insanity as to think that he is miserably blind because there is nothing that he can see.

And further, when those who yield and dedicate themselves entirely to the darkness of these disputations happen to stumble upon something foreign to their silliness, they usually betray their ignorance and laughable childishness. And finally, the great reward of all your hard work is that you emerge a more polished fool and contriver of nonsense. And it is no wonder that you grow more expertly ignorant, when

all these things on which so much toil has been desperately and painfully spent have no existence in reality anywhere. Yet empty fancies and airy phantoms mislead puzzled and empty heads that lack sounder wisdom. As for the rest and as for the main matter, which is the nothing that these fooleries contribute to integrity of life and moral education, though I may say nothing, the facts are perfectly plain to you.

And so now the last point which I proposed to discuss becomes clear: namely, that this impudent battle of words does nothing for the good of society or for the honor or profit of our fatherland, the first priority, by common consent, in the sciences.

Now I have observed that our country is pre-eminently strengthened and honored by two things: by clear speaking and by brave deeds. And surely this contentious duel of clashing opinions seems impotent either to teach eloquence or to develop wisdom or to stir men to brave actions. So away with these clever disputants and their formalities; whose lot after death should be to twist ropes in Hades with that notorious Oenus.[8]

But how much more satisfaction there would be, gentlemen, and how much worthier it would be of your name to rove with your eyes over all the lands which are drawn on the map, to look at the places where the heroes walked of old, to explore the regions made glorious by wars, triumphs, and the tales of famous poets; to cross the surging Adriatic unhurt; to ascend Mount Aetna in eruption; then to scrutinize the manners of men and the well-ordered governments of nations; then to search out and examine the natures of all living creatures; and from them to turn to the study of the hidden virtues of stones and herbs. Nor should you hesitate, gentlemen, to fly into the heavens and contemplate the manifold shapes of the clouds, the compacted power of the snow, and the source of the morning dews; then examine the chambers of the hail and the armories of the thunderbolts. Let there be nothing secret from you about the purpose of either Jove or Nature when a dire, tremendous

---

[6] Compare *Prol* II, n. 11. Here the allusion is to *Prometheus'* punishment for stealing fire from heaven—an act of kindness for men which might also be interpreted as a consuming curiosity and craving to experiment with nature.

[7] Compare *PL* IV, 271.

[8] Among the famous paintings of Polygnotus, Conti (VII, xvi; p. 801) lists one of *Oenus* with an ass beside him in hell, twisting a rope which the beast is devouring, and explains that Oenus was a stupid fellow whose wife wasted all his earnings.

comet threatens to set the skies on fire. Not even the tiniest stars should be hidden from you—however numerous they are, scattered and dispersed between the two poles. You must follow the sun on his journey—be his companions and call time itself to a reckoning, and demand an account of its eternal flight.[9]

But your mind should not consent to be limited and circumscribed by the earth's boundaries, but should range beyond the confines of the world. Let it reach the summit of knowledge and learn to know itself and at the same time to know those blessed minds and intelligences with whom hereafter it will enter into eternal fellowship.

What can I say more? Let your teacher in all these studies be the famous man who is already your favorite, Aristotle, who has written learnedly and diligently about almost all the things that should be studied. At his name I see that you start up, gentlemen, and you are gradually being brought to this way of thinking and inclining to it as if he were inviting you to come on. If this is so, you should praise and thank him for anything that you have got out of this affair. As far as I am concerned, I am content if I can persuade you in your kindness of heart to forgive me for speaking at such length. And now my last word has been said.

[9] Compare *PL* V, 581, and *CD* I, vii, p. 979.

IV. Delivered in College: A Thesis

IN THE DESTRUCTION OF ANY SUBSTANCE THERE CAN BE NO RESOLUTION INTO FIRST MATTER[1]

It is not the business of this place to look too narrowly into the question whether Error sprang from Pandora's[2] box or from the bottom of the Styx[3], or whether he was

[1] For the meaning and background of Milton's terms and arguments the student should turn to K. McEuen's note in *Complete Prose Works of John Milton*, edited by Don M. Wolfe, Vol. I (Yale University Press), pp. 255–6.
[2] Cf. *Prol* II, n. 11.
[3] The principal river of Hell. Cf. *El I*, 43, *El II*, 9, and *PL* II, 577.

a conspirator with the sons of Earth[4] against the gods of heaven. But even an indifferent observer can see that by the tiniest gains Error has grown, like Typhon[4] or Ephialtes[5], the child of Neptune, to such formidable size that he seems to me to threaten Truth herself. All too often I see him battling on equal terms with the goddess Truth herself; I see him defeated but all the stronger in the sinews of war, wounded but flourishing, defeated but insulting his conquerors. It is like the story told about Libyan Antaeus[6] in the ancient world. It really seems as if there might be good grounds for doubting Ovid's tale that Astraea[7] was the last of the heavenly deities to forsake the earth, for I am afraid that Peace and Truth would not have been many centuries behind her in leaving the detested race of men. Surely, if Truth were still abroad on earth, who could be brought to believe that one-eyed, myopic Error could behold her, the sun's peer, without being dazzled and driven down into his original, infernal home. But Truth's flight to her heavenly home is beyond all doubt, and never will she come back to wretched mankind. And now vile Error lords it everywhere in the schools, and seems to have things in her hands and to have found plenty of indefatigable partisans. Insufferably inflated by the support of these strong backers, he has left no smallest part or parcel of natural science unviolated by his profane talons, as we are told that the tables of King Phineus[8] of the Arcadians were outraged.

The natural consequence has been that the most elegant dishes at Philosophy's banquet, as rich as the plates of the gods themselves, now nauseate her guests. For the usual fate of the student who cons the mighty volumes of the philosophers and handles them day and night, is to be sent away in greater confusion than he came. Whatever one declares and supposes that he

[4] Cf. *PL* I, 197, n.
[5] *Ephialtes* had various pedigrees, but his growth to gigantic stature by tiny degrees and his participation in the assault on Olympus by the giants are affirmed by Apollodorus (I, vii, 4).
[6] Cf. *PR* IV, 563, n.
[7] Cf. *Nat*, 141–3 and *El IV*, 81–82, n.
[8] Cf. *PL* II, 596, n. for another glancing allusion to Virgil's story (*Aen*. III, 209–18) of the harpies' violation of the tables of the Arcadian king *Phineus*.

has established by sound reasoning, another knocks down with no ado, or at least seems to knock down. And so everlastingly one has something to set up and the other has some objection to make, while the miserable reader is pulled and hauled as if between two savage beasts; he is bored to death, and finally he is dropped like a man at a crossroads, utterly uncertain what direction to take. And to tell the truth it may hardly be worth the effort necessary to find on which side Truth stands, for often the greatest tussle among legions of philosophers rages over an issue of the very least importance.

But I seem to hear a few people saying, *sotto voce*, "What is he after now? While he preaches against Error, his own errors run all over the map." Well, I admit that I have erred; and I should not have done so if I had not felt that I could expect much from your liberality. So at last let us get ready for the task assigned, and (as Lipsius says) may the goddess Lua[9] get me well out of such great difficulties.

The question which we have to thresh out today is this: whether when anything is destroyed a resolution into first matter (*materia prima*) may take place. Usually this is proposed in other terms: whether any accidents which were in something which has been destroyed remain in what is generated from it, or whether all accidents which have existed in a certain form perish when the form perishes. Vast is the difference of opinion of philosophers of no mean reputation on this point. One lot battle furiously for the affirmative; the others contend violently that no resolution into *materia prima* can occur. My own inclination is for the negative since my wide dissent from the former seems to me to rest upon reason and upon numerous important authorities. By what procedure the point can be established it remains for us briefly to try to determine; and this I shall do as fast as possible, and first in the following way.

If there is a resolution into primary mat-

ter, our essential assumption that primary matter is never found pure, is consequently mistaken. Our adversaries are quick to reply that this is said in respect of form. Well, let those dabblers have their point that substantial forms are never anywhere found apart from accidental ones. But this amounts to nothing and does not come to grips with the question. More solid arguments than these must be brought up.

First let us see whether we have any friendly champions among the ancient philosophers. No sooner do we inquire than Aristotle volunteers for us with an elite troop of his commentators. Indeed, my hearers, I should like you to understand that the initiative in this battle was Aristotle's; he was the leader and instigator at its auspicious beginning. For he seems to intimate the very thing that we believe in his *Metaphysics* 7, Text 8, when he says that, primarily, quantity inheres in all matter. Against anyone objecting to this dictum I can bring a charge of bold heresy under the law of all wise men. And again, elsewhere he plainly holds that quantity is a property of primary matter—a position which most of his followers also defend. But who could bear the thought of ripping a property out of a subject, even with the formal approval of a judge of his own choosing.

But come, let us really set to work and try to understand where reason would lead us. Our assertion is proved first by the fact that matter has a true entity of its own simply because it exists, and therefore can have quantity; or at least the kind of quantity which is called undetermined. Another point! A good many people boldly declare that form cannot be received by matter without the mediation of quantity.

Secondly, if an accident is destroyed, necessarily it must be destroyed only in these ways: either by the introduction of something contrary to it, or by the expiration of its term, or by default of some other conserving cause, or, finally by defect of the proper subject of which it is an accident. But quantity cannot be destroyed in the first way because it has no contrary. And though quality has a contrary, it is not introducible here. The second way is not applicable because it is proper to relative terms. Nor the absence of a conserving

---

[9] *Lua*, as the Belgian scholar, Justus Lipsius (1547–1606) noted in his tractate *De censura et censu* (*Opera omnia*, Vesaliae, 1625, p. 1483) was a goddess presiding over the religious rites relating to the Roman census. The name is derived from the verb *luor* to release, especially from debt of any kind.

cause, for the very thing that our adversaries assign is form. Now accidents are supposed to depend upon form in two ways, either in the order of formal cause or in that of efficient cause. The first kind of dependence is not direct, for substantial form does not give form to accidents, nor is it comprehensible what other function with respect to them a cause of this order could have. And so it is only mediate, and insofar as matter depends upon form, form in turn depends upon matter. The second kind of dependence is in the order of the efficient cause, but in this order it is doubtful whether accidents depend upon form or not. But if we were to grant it so, it would not follow that the accidents would perish with the perishing of the form, for when that cause fails it is immediately succeeded by another so entirely like it as to maintain the same effect without interruption. Finally, the fact that quantity and other accidents of that kind are not wiped out by defect of their proper subject is proved by the fact that the subject of quantity is either a composite or form or matter. That it is not a composite is shown by the fact that an accident which is in a composite pertains to both matter and form at once and through their becoming one. But actually quantity cannot possibly pertain to the rational soul because it is spiritual and therefore quite incapable of the effect of formal quantity, which is extension. And further, from what has been said it is obvious that form is not the subject of quantity. The result is that only matter can be the subject of quantity, and so all inference that quantity is destructible is shut out.

The example of a scar which is ordinarily cited I regard as a very strong argument, for who can put such pressure upon my faith as to force me to believe that it is absolutely distinct in the dead from what it recently was in the living body, when no reason or necessity appears for correcting our perception, which is seldom at fault about its proper object? I would sooner and more readily listen to a man spinning yarns about ghosts and spooks than listen to these silly philosophasters bumbling stupidly and inanely about the new creation of their accidents. For we have made sure that at the instant of death and after death heat and other animal qualities which can increase and diminish are the same. Why should they be destroyed when others like them have to be produced? Then there is the point that, if they were created afresh, they would last more than a short while, and they would not immediately reach their peak of intensity but would come to it gradually, a step at a time. Now add the point that we have a very ancient axiom that quantity follows matter, and quality form.

I might and perhaps ought to tarry longer on this matter. I am in doubt whether I seem tedious to you, but I am being tremendously tedious to myself. Our remaining task is to come down to the arguments of our opponents. May the Muses grant, if it is possible, that I reduce them to primary matter, or rather, annihilate them outright.

As to the first point, the testimony of Aristotle that in generation no sensible subject remains, we answer that it should be understood of the whole and entire subject, that is, of the substantial composite, to which the ancient and erudite author Philoponus bears witness.[10] Secondly, Aristotle has said that matter is neither a what nor a quantum nor a quality. This is not to say that it is unrelated to any quantity or quality, but that it comprehends no quantity or quality of itself or within its own being. Thirdly, Aristotle says that when primary substances are destroyed all accidents are destroyed, something which we do not deny will happen if in place of every destroyed accident another promptly appears. Finally, he says that form is received into naked matter, naked, that is, of substantial form.

Now the fight is getting tough, and victory is tottering, and they are renewing the battle with this attack: since matter is merely a potential, it has nothing except what it has begged from form, and so it has no intrinsic power to support accidents unless at least at first it is joined by nature to form from which it can receive being. The remedy which they usually apply to this error is this: that primary matter has a proper being of its own which may be imperfect in the order of substance, but

10 *Philoponus:* a seventh century Alexandrian commentator on Aristotle.

which can appropriately and absolutely be called being if it is compared with accident. They also protest that matter is involved with form as its primary act, as accidents are related to secondary acts. I answer that matter is related to form first in the order of intention rather than of generation or of execution.

Now the dispute is boiling up and boiling over, and they press murderously upon us with this tactic: Every property flows actively from the essence of which it is a property, but for quantity this is impossible because this flux is a kind of activity, but matter is incapable of action in itself because it is merely passive: therefore, etc. My answer is that there are two possible ways of understanding the union of matter with quantity, one of which is by reason of the innate inclination of the passive potentiality itself towards such a state, for there is no compelling reason why every innate property should be traced to an active principle, since sometimes a passive one is sufficient, as—according to many men's opinion—motion is natural to the heavens. The second way of understanding the union of matter with quantity is as an inward, active flux, since it possesses true and genuine being within itself.

But even yet they have not lost all hope of victory. Up they come again to a fresh assault, arguing that form enters matter through the medium of quantity, since it dwells first in matter. We, on the other side, openly reject this conclusion, and to secure all our positions against it we make the distinction that form can enter into matter through the medium of quantity as by a disposition or inevitable condition, but certainly not by a potency directly receptive of form.

Finally, they plead that if quantity resides in matter alone, the consequence is that it is ingenerable and incorruptible. But this is inconsistent, for motion of itself moves toward quantity. But we allow the consequence, for in its entity quantity is incorruptible, yet with respect to its various terms it can begin and cease to exist by union and fission of quantity. For in itself motion has nothing to do with the production of quantity, but rather with its augmentation. Nor does it take place as if a new quantity were to come into existence in the nature of things, but as if one quantity were to be joined to another and become one a proper part of the other though it had been distinct from it before.

I might advance more arguments on both sides, but I omit them so as to make an end of the tedious business. It will suffice now if I blow the retreat.

V. In the Public Schools

PARTIAL FORMS ARE NOT FOUND IN AN ANIMAL BESIDE ITS WHOLE FORM

The Romans, the ancient rulers of the world, attained the highest peak of power, such as neither Assyrian[1] greatness nor Macedonian valor could ever achieve, and to which no future royal majesty will ever be able to rise. Either Jove himself, feeling the weight of years, was content to live at ease in his heaven after turning over the reins of human affairs to the Roman People as a kind of gods on earth; or else, after casting Father Saturn down into Italy, Jove solaced him for the loss of heaven by granting that his descendants, the citizens of Rome, should rule all things everywhere on land and sea. However that may be, he made the grant on no easy terms, but on condition of relentless wars and protracted evils which, I think, were intended to test the right of the Romans alone to wield the power of Jove among men. So they were bound to a tough and austere life and to find the budding pleasures of peace broken off by the cry of war and the shouts of men at arms.

Furthermore, after conquering cities and provinces they had to find and constantly renew garrisons for them and to dispatch almost all their youth to distant military or colonial service. And besides, they did not always bring home bloodless victories; indeed they were often involved in disastrous misfortunes. A case in point is that of Brennus,[2] the leader of the Gauls, who almost crushed the budding glory of Rome; and it was only by a hair-breadth that the

[1] Cf. the references to the vast power of ancient Assyria in *Def 1* (C.E. VII, 298) and in *PR* III, 270, and to the Asiatic conquests of the Macedonians (Emathians) in *PR* III, 290.

[2] In *Britain* Milton explained that the name *Brennus* meant a king (C.E. X, 25), and claimed British blood for the Gaulish conqueror of Rome in 390 B.C.

very noble city of Carthage came short of snatching away the hegemony which had been divinely committed to Rome. Then the Goths and the Vandals under their King Alaric,[3] the Huns and Pannonians[4] under their chiefs Attila and Bleda, flooding over Italy[5] hideously wasted the abounding wealth of the empire, collected out of the spoils of so many wars, and they shamefully routed the Romans who not long before had been the kings of men, and they got possession of the city of Rome itself— of Rome itself, I say—by the mere dread of their name. It was a deed glorious beyond the power of words or imagination to conceive; it was as if they had made Victory fall in love with them, or had so terrified her by their armed might to force her over to their party.

You have been puzzled long enough, O my hearers, over my motive for discussing all these things. Well, now listen. Whenever I recall these things and turn them over in my mind, just so often do I reflect how great are the forces which defend Truth, how mighty are the efforts and the vigilance of all men to rush to her defense when she staggers and is almost thrown down by the wrongs done her by her enemies. Yet there is no means of preventing a rotten mass of errors from intruding daily into every field of learning. Error is indeed so prevalent by its violence or by its poison that it can either stamp its own image upon snow-white Truth or by some device impenetrable to me assume her starry aspect—an art whereby it has often imposed upon great philosophers and appropriated honors and respect which are due to Truth alone.

You can see this in our subject of debate today, which has rallied some by no means unenthusiastic champions, men of famous name if they would but give up their partisanship and choose rather to honor Truth. And so it is our job to strip error and tear off her borrowed feathers and reduce her to her natural ugliness. To do the job

most expeditiously I think that I should tread in the steps of the greatest authorities, for it is not to be expected that all by myself I should make a contribution which has escaped and eluded so many men outstanding for their intelligence. And so I shall briefly indicate what will throw sufficient light on the subject and will fortify my position with one or two arguments. Then if any claim or objection is made to my judgment, I shall resolve it as best I can. But I shall dispatch everything in a few words and I shall touch everything as if with my wing tips.

Against singleness of form, which the more acute philosophers have always been accustomed to regard as existing in one and the same matter, we read that various opinions have sprung up. Many have stubbornly argued that several whole forms occur in an animal, and they justify variously, each one according to his own fancy. Others pertinaciously assert that the whole form is unique, but that several partial forms find a resting place in the same matter. With the former we shall call a truce for the moment, according to military practice, while we shift the whole force and drive of the battle against the latter.

Let Aristotle take first place in the battle line, for he is clearly on our side and near the end of the first book of his *De Anima* supports our assertion in no uncertain way. No very long inquiry is needed to add other arguments to this authority. Chrysostom Javello[3] first rallies to me, from the dung-pile of whose frightfully crude style we may dig up gold and pearls. If anyone is so fastidious as to spurn these, the fable of Aesop's cock[7] will fit him very nicely. He argues much like this: that distinction and organization of dissimilar parts must precede the introduction of the soul, which is the active principle not of any ordinary body, but of a physical, organic one. And so immediately before the production of a total form the partial ones must be done

---

[3] Summing up *Alaric's* career, Milton noted in *Britain* (C.E. X, 101) that the Roman empire had lasted 462 years before his occupation of the city in 410 A.D.

[4] In *Britain* (C.E. X, 51) Milton mentions the stirring of early revolt against Augustus and also (C.E. X, 96) a *Pannonian* conspiracy against Theodosius.

[5] Cf. *PL* I, 353, n.

[6] Perhaps Milton was drawn to this Bolognese commentator on St. Thomas by his attack on the doctrine of predestination in his tract *De Dei praedestinatione et reprobatione.* Miss McEuen suggests that Milton had explored Javelli's Commentary on the First Part of St. Thomas's *Summa Theologica* (Lyon, 1581).

[7] Milton was fond enough of Aesop's fable of the honest, plain cock that ignored the jewel among the grains of barley in the barnyard to use it again against Salmasius (C.E. VII, 281).

away with, unless that universally accepted axiom is to collapse; the generation of one thing is the corruption of another. The production of those partial forms is not followed by the immediate production of others resembling them. For that there would be no reason, and it would not properly harmonize with Mother Nature's wisdom.

Further, every form, whether it be perfect or imperfect, bestows a specific being, and it is necessary that so long as that form abides, that thing shall abide unchanged in its essential substance. Then the total form will supervene like an accident—not by generation but by alteration. It follows, then, that the total soul, whether divisible or indivisible, is insufficient to inform all parts of a living being fully and perfectly— a proposition which we have no reason to grant. It also follows that one substantial form is—so to speak—a proximate and persevering disposition toward another. That does not harmonize with the truth, for every form has constituted a perfect essence in the genus of substance.

Finally, if there are numerous partial forms in all parts of—for instance—a man, out of them there is sure to arise one whole form distinct from the rational soul. Hence that will be either the form of something inanimate or of corporeity or of a combination (something beside the soul in man which cannot reasonably be believed in); or else it will be a sensitive or vegetative soul.[8] But no one making this assertion could get a hearing among the more erudite troop of philosophers. On this point I spare you further argument, since it is conceded and does not get to the point of the discussion.

But in truth our opponents raise the objection (and this is the main point at issue) that an amputated part of an animal retains its actuality, not by virtue of the total form because it is outside of the totality, nor by virtue of the form recently acquired, because no activating force is present, no perceptible action, and no prevenient change. Hence, in its actuality it

exists through its own proper form which it had while it was one part in the whole. And with this argument they think that they can shatter our position and destroy it outright.

On the other side the answer is made no less soundly than commonly, that a newly generated form, as very often happens with a corpse on the way to dissolution, does not require much time, nor many arrangements, nor an ordered alteration. And what if some universal cause were to concur with the former combination, lest matter should be found empty. And the fact that various activities are visible in an animal is not to be attributed to distinct partial forms, but to the power of the total soul, which surely equals that of forms that are distinct in aspect.

I may be permitted, by common consent, to skip other objections of less weight which arise, but which are not formidable; and which can be more easily disposed of and more clearly rebutted if they happen to be introduced in the course of the disputation.

However the affair may go, even if I lose my cause, the cause shall not be lost, for Truth is unconquerable and more than able in her own strength to defend herself. Nor does she need any trifling outside help to do so. And even though sometimes she may seem to be worsted and to be crushed to earth, nevertheless she maintains herself forever inviolate and intact from Error's claws. In this she is like the sun, which often reveals himself to men's eyes wrapped up in clouds that befoul him, nevertheless gathers his rays to himself and summons all his glory to him, and blazes forth in perfectly stainless brilliance.

VI. In the summer holidays of the College, but—as is usual—before an assembly of almost all the student body

(i) *The Oration*

THAT SPORTIVE EXERCISES ARE OCCASIONALLY NOT ADVERSE TO PHILOSOPHIC STUDIES

When I returned recently from that city which is the chief of cities, O fellow acad-

[8] Cf. Milton's affirmation in *CD* I, vii (pp. 979–80), of the doctrine of St. Thomas Aquinas that the spiritual and rational faculty contains the corporeal and the sentient and *vegetative* faculties. On the level of the human soul Milton entertained similar views. Cf. *PL* V, 472–85.

emicians, crammed to repletion with all the pleasures which swarm there, I was counting on resuming the scholarly leisure which is the kind of life that I believe that the souls in heaven enjoy. Deep in my soul was the purpose to devote myself to literature and to consecrate my days and nights to Philosophy's supreme charms. In this way the rotation of work and play can always be relied upon to drive off the tedium of satiety, and interrupted activities are picked up again all the more eagerly. Suddenly, when I was hot after these pursuits, an annual and anciently traditional festival has called me and dragged me away. I am given an order to transfer that effort which I had first consecrated to the acquisition of wisdom to nonsense and the excogitation of new fooleries. As if the world were not already packed with fools; as if there had been a wreck of that famous Ship of Fools[1] which has had no less poetic attention than the Argo;[2] or finally, as if there were any shortage of provocation for Democritus[3] himself to laugh.

I beg you to pardon me, O hearers; for though I have spoken a bit too freely about it, this custom which we are observing today is really not absurd, but rather is exceedingly honorable, as I intend at once to explain more clearly. If that famous second founder of Rome and great avenger of a king's lust, Junius Brutus,[4] could bear to hold down a mind almost equal to the immortal gods and a wonderful inborn genius under a pretense of idiocy, there is no reason why I should hesitate to put on a sophomoric show, especially at the command of him who—like a Roman aedile[5] —has charge of these entertainments, which

are almost traditional. And then no small inducement and attraction to this business has been your recent show of kindness to me—you who belong to one college with me; for when I undertook to deliver an academic speech to you several months ago I felt that the product of any midnight oil that I might burn would be anything but agreeable to you, and that Aeacus and Minos[6] would be more tolerant judges than you. But quite against my expectation and quite against any glimmering hope of mine, as I learned, or rather as I myself felt, my efforts were received with great applause from you all, and especially from those who once had been irritated and hostile to me on account of some disagreements about our studies. A generous kind of exercise of rivalry, and not unworthy of a royal breast. For while friendship itself may often distort many things that are quite innocently done, on that occasion passionate and embittered enmity ungrudgingly put a kind and a more tolerant interpretation than I deserved upon my many perhaps mistaken remarks and upon my doubtless by no means few rhetorical blunders. This was a unique instance of brainless anger seeming to have become sound of mind and by doing so to have cleared itself of the suspicion of insanity.

And now, truly, I am supremely happy and marvellously pleased when I see so great a gathering of most learned men surrounding me and crowding around me. And yet when I descend into myself and as if with eyes turned inward intimately consider my slender ability, I often blush at what I alone know, and suddenly an assault of sadness crushes and chokes my surging joy. But, fellow students, do not, I beg you, forsake me as I lie here in confusion, struck down by your keen eyes as if by a lightning bolt. Let the breath of your kindness lift me up and rekindle the life that is only half alive in me, as it can do. So by your doing my suffering will be less heavy, and the remedy of the suffering will be the more acceptable and delightful because it is you who provide it. And so it would be highly agreeable to faint often if only I might as often have you to revive and restore me. And what a rare power

---

[1] Sebastian Brandt's *Narrenschiff* (1494), which was given an English dress in Alexander Barclay's *Ship of Fools* in 1509.

[2] Cf. *PL* II, 1017.

[3] Cf. *Prol* I, n. 18. Here Milton is thinking of the "laughing Philosopher" whose legend inspired one of the panels in the frontispiece to Robert Burton's *Anatomy of Melancholy*.

[4] Livy tells the story of Lucius *Junius Brutus'* feigned madness, of his punishment of Tarquin for the rape of Lucrece, and of his banishment of the Tarquin kings, his election as one of Rome's first consuls, and his traditional recognition as the father of his country (*Roman History* I, lix, 1–2; II, vi, 7–9). Cf. *TKM*, n. 73.

[5] *Roman aediles* were officers in charge of public property, including buildings, streets, theaters, and public entertainments.

[6] Cf. *In Obitum Praecancelarii Medici*, 45, *CG*, n. 24, and *Areop*, n. 76.

and what a singular virtue is yours, which like the spear of Achilles,[7] the gift of Vulcan, both wounds and heals. And let no one wonder that I glory like a man exalted among the stars when I see so many men outstanding for their erudition, and indeed the whole flower of the University, assembled here. I hardly think that in old Athens greater audiences came to hear those two supreme orators Demosthenes[8] and Aeschines competing for primacy in eloquence; or that such felicity ever befell Hortensius,[9] when he delivered a speech, or that so many men of extraordinary learning ever honored one of Cicero's orations. And so, however small my success in performing my present task may be, it will be no contemptible honor to have spoken a word in so great and so thronged an assembly of the most distinguished men.

And just now, by Hercules, I cannot but congratulate myself on being, as it seems to me, far happier than Orpheus[10] or Amphion;[11] for they simply used their fingers with a trained and artful technique to get sweet music out of their tuned strings, and the sweetness was due as much to the lyrestrings as it was to the dexterity of the hands. But if I win any praise here today, it will be entirely and truly mine, and more splendid in proportion as a creation of the mind transcends and excels anything made with the hands. And what they drew was an audience of rocks, wild animals, and trees, and if there were any men, they were rough and rustic; but I see the most learned ears surrendered to me and hanging upon my lips. And finally, those rustics and those wild creatures were running after familiar music on the strings which they already knew well, but mere expectation has brought and holds you here.

But yet, fellow students, I would first of all like you to understand that I have not said these things in too boastful a mood. Ah! would that now I might be endowed with that honey-sweet or, rather, nectarian stream of eloquence which long ago imbued and celestially bedewed the great spirits of Athens and Rome! Would that I might suck out the marrow of Persuasion! Would that I might sack the desks of Mercury[12] himself and strip all the treasuries of wit so as to bring something worthy of such great expectation, of such a distinguished assembly, and of such refined and sensitive ears.

You see, O my hearers, how far I have been rapt and carried away by my excessively violent desire and yearning to please you. Actually it comes over me, quite suddenly, that I have been swept away by a desire that is unholy and yet, if the thing be possible, is also pious and righteous. And sure I am that I have no need to beg and pray for the help of the Muses because I regard myself as surrounded by men who incarnate the Muses and Graces, and I think that all Mount Helicon[13] and whatever other shrines of the Muses there may be, have poured forth all their pupils to celebrate this day. It seems to me quite credible that the laurels of Parnassus are weeping and withering for them, and that it would be vain to look anywhere in the world for the Muses or the Graces or the Goddesses of Delight except right here. And in that case it must be that Barbarity itself and Error and Ignorance and that whole tribe so hateful to the Muses must take to flight at top speed at sight of you and hide themselves in some region far away. And then what is there to prevent every trace of barbaric, rude, or hackneyed style from being instantly knocked out of my oration, and why shouldn't I forthwith

---

[7] Milton is thinking of Vulcan's (Hephaestus') forging of armor for *Achilles* in *Il.* XVIII (forgetting that Vulcan did not make a spear for him) and of the story in Apollodorus' *Epitome* III, 17–20, which says that Achilles used rust from his spear as a healing ointment for a wound that it had inflicted.

[8] Milton was perhaps thinking less of the bitter political rivalry between *Demosthenes* and *Aeschines* than of Bacon's story in the *Advancement* I, ii, 7 (p. 16 in Wright's ed., 1900) of Aeschines' jibe at Demosthenes about his orations smelling of the lamp. "Indeed (said Demosthenes) there is a great difference between the things that you and I do by lamp-light." Cf. *Sonn* X, 8.

[9] *Hortensius* and *Cicero* were also political opponents, especially when Cicero prosecuted Verres in 70 B.C.

[10] Cf. *El VI*, 70; and *Patrem*, 52.

[11] Milton ignores the fact—which Conti (VIII, xv; p. 890) stresses—that *Amphion* was no less famous as a singer than he was for his skill in playing the cithaera.

[12] Milton was thinking of the tradition that *Mercury* was the god both of thieves and of scholars, which goes back as far as the Homeric Hymn to Mercury and which inspired a famous digression in Marlowe's *Hero and Leander*.

[13] Cf. *PL* I, 15, and III, 29; and *El IV*, 29.

become eloquent and witty by your inspiration and secret impulse.

And so I beg, O my hearers, that none of you begrudge a few minutes for my nonsense. Why, all the very gods are said to drop the cares of celestial administration for a while and go to see the show put on by insignificant humanity, and they are fabled sometimes not to have scorned lowly cottages and to have accepted humble hospitality, and to have eaten beans and salad. And so I beg and pray, O most excellent hearers, that this very ordinary feast of mine may suit your fine and fastidious taste.

I may indeed have known many amateurs who were very much in the habit of pouring arrogant and ignorant scorn upon interests in others of which they know nothing themselves, as if it were not worth any one's pains. So, for example, one fellow stupidly runs down dialectic because he never could make the grade in it; another despises natural philosophy for the obvious reason that Nature, who is the most beautiful of the goddesses, has never honored him with the sight of her naked beauty. But I am not going to begrudge what praise I am capable of giving to sports and quips of a sort for which I know that my talent is exceedingly small. And yet I must add one point—something which seems truly arduous and by no means easy—that today I am to make a serious speech in praise of buffoonery.

But there is nothing improper in this. For what is there that makes friendships more readily or holds onto them longer than a charming and merry disposition? And you will hardly find anyone agreeable and popular who has no fund of quips and pleasantries and clever little jokes.

And, fellow students, if we had the habit of going to sleep daily and—as it might seem—dying in philosophy, and of growing old without the least relaxation among the thorns and brambles of logic, with never a moment allowed to catch our breath, what, I ask, would the philosophical life be but vaticination in the cave of Trophonius[14] and adherence to the school of too-too-rigid Cato;[15] then even the country bumpkins would say that we fed on mustard.

14 Cf. *Prol* III, n. 2.
15 Marcus Porcius *Cato*, the Stoic and opponent

Add something more: just as those who practice wrestling and other field sports become much stronger than others and readier for every task; so it usually comes about that the mind's sinews are toughened by this mental gymnastic, and a better blood and spirit seem to be developed, and all a man's abilities are refined and sharpened and made more apt and versatile for all purposes. If a man does not care to be thought witty and elegant, he should not take umbrage if he is called a peasant and a boor. We are very familiar with men of an ignoble breed who, because they are awkward and dour, and are silently conscious of their own contemptible stupidity, apply every witty remark that they happen to hear to themselves. They would only get their deserts if what they suspect were really to happen to them, and they were to be so trounced by everyone's jibes that they almost meditated hanging themselves. But such human trash as they are cannot deny wit its right to its elegant little refinements.

And so, my hearers, would you like me to crown my foundation of reasons with confirmation by examples? Surely there are plenty of them at hand, and the first is Homer, the rising sun or morning star of the finer kind of literature, with whom all learning was twin-born. He sometimes recalled his divine mind from the councils of the gods and the deeds done in heaven and, turning to comedy, he most wittily described the battle of the frogs and mice.[16] And Socrates, who on the authority of the Pythian oracle was the wisest of mortals, is said to have often put a witty bit upon the quarrelsome ill-nature of his wife.[17] All the talk of the ancient philosophers— so the books say—was seasoned with wit and stuffed with pleasant humor; and surely it was this alone that bestowed immortality upon all the ancient writers of comedies and epigrams, both Greek and Latin. We have the tradition that Cicero's jests and witticisms filled three books, put

of Julius Caesar, who committed suicide after Caesar's victory at Pharsalia, seems to be the Cato in question here.
16 Though the Homeric authorship of this burlesque epic was under suspicion, it was usually included in Renaissance editions of the *Iliad* and *Odyssey*, and it was translated by George Chapman.
17 Xantippe, whose shrewish treatment of Socrates was proverbial. Cf. *PR* IV, 275.

together by Tyro.[18] And the *Praise of Folly,* that most ingenious book by a writer of no mean rank,[19] is in everyone's hands. And there are plenty more by no means unsuccessful essays in wit of this kind by very famous writers.

Are you asking for eminent generals, kings, and mighty men? You may have Pericles, Epaminondas, Agesilaus, and Philip the Macedonian, who (if I may speak like Gellius) are declared by the historians to have abounded with gay and witty sallies. Add to these Gaius Laelius, Publius Cornelius Scipio, Gnaeus Pompey, Caius Julius and Octavius Caesar, all of whom Cicero tells us excelled all their contemporaries in wit. Do you want more and greater names? The poets, those wisest imagers of truth, give us Jove and the other gods abandoned to gaiety among their delicacies and their cups.

Finally, fellow students, I appeal to you for approval and support, which are worth as much as all the rest to me, for your gathering here today in such numbers is sufficient proof that jests and horseplay do not displease you. And on this every head seems to me to be nodding assent. And it is not strange, by Hercules, that this festive and trim spirit of urbanity should please all men of probity and honor since it sits gloriously in the splendid hierarchy of the Aristotelian virtues,[20] like some divinity among her sister goddesses.

But perhaps there are some bearded Masters in our purlieus, grim, unfriendly fellows who regard themselves as great Catos, or perhaps as little ones, and who are now drawing their faces into a Stoic sternness and obstinately shaking their heads as they whine that in these times everything is in confusion and going to ruin, and that the newly graduated Bachelors, instead of expounding the *Prior Analytics* of Aristotle, are tossing their jeers and silly jests about, quite shamelessly, and at a very inappro-

priate time; and that our exercise today, which doubtless was founded by our forefathers in order to secure some splendid profit, either in Rhetoric or Philosophy, has latterly degenerated into a display of pointless wit.

But I have something on hand and ready to answer them. Let them know, if they are not aware of the fact, that when the laws of our Republic of Letters were first laid down, letters had only recently been brought to these shores from distant lands. And so, since skill in Greek and Latin was very rare and unusual, it was proper that the cultivation of those studies should be the more zealous, and that they should have been pursued with all the greater exertions. But for us, since we have worse morals than our forebears though we are more learned than they, it should be becoming to abandon the studies that are not very difficult and to turn to the studies to which they would have devoted themselves if they had had the leisure. And it has not escaped your notice that the first men to give laws made it a practice always to set up statutes that were a little tougher and sterner than could easily be borne, so that men might slide into sound conduct by slighting and slipping away, just a little, from the law. And now that the face of everything has completely changed, many laws and many customs should, if they do not become defunct and obsolete, then be limited gradually and not be generally observed. But they say, raising their eyebrows, if such trifling fun were to be openly justified and approved, there would not be a man who would not turn his mind away from safe and solid learning to run headlong after shows and frivolous theatricals, to a point where the halls of learning themselves would be sending out jesters more impudent than buffoons and vaudeville artists, instead of scholarly and prudent men.

But in fact I regard a man who is so carried away by silly jokes as to neglect serious and more important things for them—such a man, I say, I regard as incompetent either for jest or earnest: not for the latter, because if his talent were for managing serious business, I feel sure that he would not let himself be so easily drawn away from it; nor for the trifling kind of

---

[18] Cicero's freedman and the posthumous editor of some of his orations and letters.

[19] Erasmus.

[20] *Urbanity,* as Aristotle defines it in the *Nicomachean Ethics* II, i–vii, meant more than a superficially pleasant disposition—the ability to make friends and influence people. Milton defined it in *CD* II, xiii (C.E. XVII, 322) as meaning more than "innocent elegances in conversation," and as implying acuteness, candor, and purity of mind.

thing, for no one can jest gracefully and handsomely unless he has first learned how to handle serious business. But I am afraid, O fellow Collegians, that I have spun out my talk too long. I am not going to offer such excuses as I might, lest in making them I should aggravate my crime. We are on the point of escaping from the laws of oratory to plunge into comic license, where, if I should happen to slip by a finger-length, as the saying goes, out of my usual habits and violate the strict laws of modesty, you should know, O fellow Collegians, that for your pleasure I have momentarily dropped my usual character, and if I say anything indecorous or improper, do not think of it as expressive of my true mind or nature, but as reflecting the needs of the time and the spirit of the place. And now, at the start of my entertainment, I beg the favor for which actors ask at the end of theirs: give me your laughter and applause.

(ii) The Prolusion

Staggering and almost falling to destruction as it is, the commonwealth of fools has for no merit of mine of which I am aware—created me its Dictator. And why am I chosen, when that distinguished leader and standard-bearer of all the Sophisters[21] has sedulously canvassed for the office and could have been a doughty performer of its duties. For that veteran soldier has briskly led as many as fifty Sophisters armed with short clubs across the Barnwellian Fields[22] and begun the siege of the town in a sufficiently military way by knocking down the aqueduct, so that thirst might drive the townsmen to surrender. I am sincerely sorry about the man's recent departure. By going away he has left all us Sophisters not only ἀκεφάλους (headless, literally acephalic) but also beheaded.

And now, my hearers, though it is not the first day of April, pretend that the feast of Hilaria[23]—sacred to the Mother of the

Gods—is here, or that worship is being paid to the god Laughter. So laugh and raise a guffaw out of your petulant vitals, smooth your brows, indulge in some nose-wrinkling but don't turn up your noses at anything.[24] Let the whole place ring with spasms of laughter, and let its unbridled bursts shake the happy tears out of you until they have been so dried up by laughing that Grief may not have one little drop to trim her triumph. And positively I, if I spot anyone laughing with his lips too close, I shall declare that he is hiding teeth that are foul and rotten and yellow with tartar, or all awry and protruding; or that he has so loaded his belly at today's feast that he dares not stretch his guts too far in laughing, lest not the Sphinx but his sphincter anus should sing bass to his mouth's tenor and unwillingly let slip a few riddles, which I leave to the medics to explain, and not to Oedipus. I should dislike to have the groan of a posterior blowing counter to the gay voice of laughter in this assembly. Let the medics, who can dissolve the bowels, resolve all these things. If anyone fails to let out a good loud shout, I shall swear that his breath is so nasty and lethal that neither Aetna or Avernus breathes out anything more loathsome; that at least he has been eating garlic or leeks, so that he dares not open his mouth for fear of killing some of his neighbors with his fetid breath. And then let that horrendous and infernal sound, a hiss, be far remote from this assembly, for if any such thing were to be heard here today, I shall believe that the Furies and Eumenides[25] are lurking darkly among you, that they have sent their snakes and vipers into your breasts, and that you are infected with the madness of Athamas.[26]

Truly indeed, O Collegians, I feel wonder

brated about March 22 in honor of Cybele, the Mother of the Gods. Cf. Arc, 21–22.

[24] Cf. Horace, Satires I, vi, 5.

[25] The Eumenides or Furies (the latter word simply translates the former) are the avengers of crime who pursue Orestes in Aeschylus' Eumenides and Euripedes' Orestes. But in QNov, 8 Milton treated them as daughters of Satan.

[26] Ovid (Met. IV, 452–542) tells the most melodramatic of several ancient versions of the story of Fury-inspired madness of King Athamas of Thebes and his wife Ino. Athamas killed one of his infant sons and drove Ino to leap into the sea with the other.

[21] Sophisters: loosely equivalent to Sophomores in American colleges, but not strictly limited to second-year men.

[22] Meadows belonging to the University. Barnwellian is a mock-heroic epithet. Cf. "th' Aleian Field" in PL VII, 19. Milton is recalling a recent student prank.

[23] The Roman festival of the Hilaria was cele-

and delight at your friendliness in forcing your way through flames and fire into this place to listen to me. For on our very threshold our blazing Cerberus[27] stands, frightful, smoking, barking, flashing his fiery staff and blowing sparks out of his wide open mouth; while opposite to him our burning and devouring Furnace spits lurid fire and belches tornados of smoke. The road to hell itself could not be harder, even though Pluto should bar it. And certainly Jason[28] himself faced no greater danger when he attacked the pyropneumatic oxen of Mars.

And now, O hearers, conceive yourselves to have been welcomed into heaven after passing through Purgatory and by what new-fangled miracle I cannot tell coming safe out of the fiery furnace. Nor does any hero occur to me whose courage I could compare with yours; for that famous Bellerophon[29] did not slay the flame-vomiting Chimaera with greater valor, nor did the stoutest champions of King Arthur ever more easily subdue and scatter the enchantments of a fire- and flame-girdled castle. And so it follows that I can promise myself some fine and highly eligible auditors, for if any offal has got as far as this through our smelting furnace, I shall at once declare that our gate-keepers are mere *ignes fatui* or will-o'-the-wisps.

How happy we are, and how secure we shall be to all eternity! For at Rome they were zealous and pious about preserving the everlasting fires to secure the long survival of the empire, while we are protected by fires that are vigilant because they are alive. But why have I said vigilant and alive? Surely the phrase slipped out by some kind of lapse? Now I bethink myself better: as soon as the first twilight comes these lights go out and are rekindled only when the bright dawn comes. Yet there is hope at last that our House shall once more become luminous, for no one will deny that the two greatest lights

of the University preside over our College. But they would never be more highly honored than at Rome, for there the Vestal Virgins would keep them alight and awake all night long, or perhaps they would be consecrated as fiery brothers of the Seraphic Order.[30] Their case is well matched by that famous Virgilian hemistich: "Within them is the force of fire." [31] Indeed, I am almost convinced that Horace[32] mentioned these Fires of ours, for when the elder of them stands among his wife and children he shines among them all like the moon among the lesser fires. Nor can I forbear to mention Ovid's horrible mistake in saying that "you see no creatures that are born out of fire."[33] For wandering all around us are plenty of little firelets that are born of our fire. And if Ovid were to deny this, he would inevitably be casting a reflection upon the honor of our Fire's lady.

I return to you, my hearers. Have no regret for the rough and frightful journey, for behold, a feast is prepared for you—tables loaded with Persian luxury and heaped with the dishes that are most sought for, such as might flatter and délectate an Apician[34] gullet. The story goes that eight boars were set whole on the board for Antony and Cleopatra, but for your first course there are fifty fattened boars that have been softening up for three years in pickling beer, and they are still tough enough to tire our canine teeth. Then we

[30] Milton fancies the ancient Roman priests, flamens, initiating his friends into a modern Italian *Seraphic* Academy whose name recalled the fact that all angels are "flames of fire" (Heb. i, 7). Cf. *PL* II, 512.

[31] A humorous turn to Virgil's line (*Aen* VI, 730) of solemn description of the spiritual fire which informs the entire universe. The scene is the Elysian fields. Anchises is explaining the universe to Aeneas.

[32] There is an echo of *Horace's* reproach to the unfaithful Neæra in the opening lines of Epode XV.

[33] Perhaps Milton's auditors caught the allusion to the *Fasti* VI, 292, where Ovid is making the point that the chaste goddess Vesta, like the fire which is sacred to her, cannot be portrayed by any image and so has no statue in her temples, for her only symbol is the fire which the vestal virgins never permit to die on her altar. Obviously, there is a pun on the name of some college servant who had a large family. He may also have been called Sparks, or perhaps Match or Furness.

[34] Apicius Caelius, a famous epicure in Augustus' reign, left a name that became a trade mark for spices.

[27] Mrs. Tillyard has shown that the play with *Cerberus* puns on the name of a student called Sparks.

[28] An assignment against fire-vomiting bulls is mentioned by Conti (VI, viii, p. 594) as one of *Jason's* minor dangers.

[29] *Bellerophon's* victory over the *Chimaera* (third lion, third goat, and third dragon) is in Milton's mind. Cf. *PL* VII, 18.

have the same number of glorious oxen with noble tails, fresh barbecued at the doors by our domestic fire, but I am afraid that they have rendered out all the juice into the dripping pan. Then come as many calves heads, fat and plump enough, but without brains enough for seasoning. And then a hundred kids, more or less, but too lean, I surmise, from too much devotion to Venus. We expected some rams with handsome spreading horns, but our cooks have not yet brought them along from town. If anyone prefers birds, we have any number of them that have been fattened for a long time on balls and pellets of dough and grated cheese: in the first place, a kind of birds unknown to me and green alike in character and color, and hence I opine that they have been imported from the land of parrots. Since they always fly around in flocks and nest in the same place, they shall be served in the same platter. But I should like you to nibble at them gingerly because —aside from the fact that they are a bit underdone and contain no solid nourishment—they cause some kind of rash in those who eat them (if our dietician tells the truth).

Now fall to and eat for all you are worth, for here we have coming a dish that I can recommend as tops. It is a tremendous turkey, so fat and so oilily obese after three years stuffing that a single vast platter hardly holds him. And his beak is so long and so hard that he would be quite safe in taking on an elephant or a rhinoceros. We have beheaded him in good time today because he was beginning like the big monkeys to waylay the girls and assault the women.

After him comes a variety of Irish birds of name unknown to me, but very like cranes in gait and in their stringy shape. Usually they are served as a last course. This is a novel and rare rather than a salubrious food, and so I warn you to hold back from them because (if our dietician tells the truth) they are prone to produce lice. I think that they are more apt to be useful to grooms, for they are by nature lively, active, and saltatory, and if injected by an enema into a few nags they would make them keener and speedier than if they had ten live eels in their bellies.

You also see a good many geese, some

of this years hatch and some of yesteryear —jabbering creatures and noisier than Aristophanes' frogs. You will easily recognize them; and it is strange that they have not given themselves away by hissing. Perhaps you will soon be hearing them.

In addition, we have a few eggs, but they come from κακοῦ κόρακος[35] (a bad crow).

For fruit we have only apples and medlars, and they come from an ill-omened tree[36] and are not quite ripe and would profit by being hung up again in the sunshine.

You see what we have prepared for you. I beg you hungry men to fall to. But I foresee that you are going to say that these viands, like the midnight feasts which are prepared by the devil for the witches, have been concocted without salt,[37] and I am afraid that you will go away hungrier than you came.

But I come now to matters more closely concerning me. The Romans had their Floralia,[38] the country people had their Palilia,[39] and the Bakers their Fornacalia,[40] and we too have the Socratic custom of entertaining ourselves—especially at this time when we are free from routine business. In the same way the Inns of Court have their Lords of the Revels, on whom they confer a title which betrays their craving for office. But we, O Collegians, because we like the idea of coming as close as possible to paternity, by assuming the name try to enjoy a role which we should not dare to play except in secret; just as girls solemnly play at their games of marrying and bearing babies, snatching at the shadows of their yearning and desire, and hugging them fast.

[35] Milton has already used this Greek proverb in *Prol* I.

[36] The words *infelix arbor* usually meant (even in classical Latin) a gallows tree.

[37] *Salt*, according to old tradition, was proof against all diabolic works; it was also synonymous with wit in Latin, as it is in English.

[38] Games in honor of the goddess of Flowers, Flora, which Ovid describes (*Fasti* IV, 947 ff.) as being solemnly held about May first. Cf. *PL* V, 16, and *PR* II, 365.

[39] A spring festival in honor of the goddess of flocks, Pales. Cf. *PL* IX, 393.

[40] A winter festival in honor of the goddess of ovens, Fornax, which Ovid says was instituted by Numa (*Fasti* II, 525 ff.).

Why this solemnity of ours should have been omitted a year ago, I surely cannot surmise, unless the men who should have been the fathers had been so active in the town that the director of the affair took pity on their great labors and of his own accord set them free of this obligation.

But how is it that I have so suddenly been made a Father? May the gods protect me! What is the wonder that beats anything in Pliny's books? Have I done violence to some snake and suffered the fate of Tiresias?[41] Or has some Thessalian[42] witch anointed me with magic salve? Or like old Caenius,[43] have I been violated by some god and bought my male sex as the price of my dishonor, so that in this sudden way I have been changed from a woman to a man? For from some of you I have recently been getting the title of Lady.[44] And why do I seem to them to be so little of a man? Is there no respect for Priscian?[45] Do these grammaticasters attribute the marks of the masculine to the feminine gender? It is because I have never been able to swallow mighty potations like the all-round athletes; or doubtless because my hand has not been hardened by holding the plough; or because I never sprawled on my back in the midday sun like a seven-year ox-driver; or perhaps because I have never showed myself to be a man in the way that those debauchees do. How I wish that their asininity could be shed as easily as my femininity!

But see how dumb and thoughtless they are to twit me about something for which a sound judge would think that I might be honored. Demosthenes himself was called something less than a man by his rivals and opponents. Even Quintus Hortensius, that most famous of orators after Cicero, was called Dionysia the harpist by Lucius Torquatus. Hortensius' reply to him was: "I should rather be Dionysia than a man without culture, urbanity, or refinement—like yourself."[46] But as for this business of Lord and Lady, I will have nothing to do with it and I reject it, for unless it be on your platforms and in your courts, O Collegians, I have no wish to lord it at all. Now who is going to forbid me to take pleasure in so favorable and happy an omen, or to exult in the satisfaction of being linked in this reproach with such famous men! Meanwhile, as I regard all good and eminent men as being above envy, so I think that these malicious men are so far below all others that they who speak ill of them are not worthy of respect.

And now in my role as a father, I turn to my sons, of whom I see a respectable number, and I see that the clever rogues acknowledge me as their father by a sly nod.[47] Do you ask for their names. I am not willing to deliver my sons to you under the names of dishes for you to make a meal of them; that would smack too much of the savagery of Tantalus[48] and Lycaon.[49] Nor shall I call them by the names of parts of the body, lest you should think that I had begotten so many fragments of men rather than whole ones, nor is it my notion to call them after various kinds of wines, lest whatever I shall say should seem to be off the subject and not to the Bacchic point. I should like my sons to bear the names of

41 Ovid (Met. III, 324–31) tells the story of Tiresias suffering a change of sex for his violence to a pair of mating serpents.

42 Thessalian poisons figure in Horace's Odes more than once and in Ovid's Amores III, vii, 27.

43 Ovid (Met. XII, 189–209) is Milton's source for the story of the Thessalian girl who demanded a change of sex from Neptune as amends for his violence to her.

44 On the first page of John Aubrey's Collections for the Life of Milton he is called the lady of Christ's College.

45 Priscian, the compiler of the most famous of Latin grammars, lived in Athens in the sixth century A.D.

46 The anecdote comes from Aulus Gellius' Noctes Ambrosianae I, 5.

47 Milton is now preparing for the transition to English in the poem which he entitled At a Vacation Exercise in the College, part Latin, part English, and published separately in 1645. The connection between Prol VI and the poem is worked out in detail by J. M. French in The Life Records of John Milton, Vol. I, 170–1. Milton now takes the role of substance and his 'sons' that of attributes in a little allegorical play which is based upon the Aristotelian conception of 'absolute being' and its nine accidents: Quantity, Quality, Relation, Place, Time, Posture, Possession, Action, and Passion.

48 Milton seems to be following Conti's summary (VI, xviii; p. 631) of the story of Tantalus serving his son Pelops to the gods, of the refusal of the meal by all of them except Ceres, who inadvertently ate Pelops' shoulder, and of his miraculous restoration to life with an ivory shoulder.

49 Lycaon's serving of his sons to Jove is narrated in Ovid's Met. I, 226–35.

the predicaments[50] to show in this way that they are nobly born and live like free men; and I shall see to it that all of them are advanced to some degree before I die.[51]

As for my jests, I do not intend them to be toothless, for then you might call them trite and stale, and say that some gasping old crone had spat them out. And so I think that no one is going to object to my jests for their teeth except the man who is toothless himself and is going to condemn mine for not resembling his own. And certainly now I could wish that it were my lot to be, like Horace, a fishmonger's son, for then my jests would be salted to perfection, and I should send you off with such a salt rubbing that you would hate salt water as much as our runaway soldiers from the Isle of Rhé.[52]

I should like to avoid tediousness in bestowing my advice on you, my sons, lest I should seem to have worked harder in educating than in begetting you. Only let every one of you see to it that from a son he does not degenerate into a spoiled child, and let no one who wants to keep me for his father develop a fondness for Father Liber.[53] Whatever other bits of advice I have to give, I feel should be offered in our native tongue; and to the best of my ability I shall try to have you understand everything.

It remains for me to beg Neptune, Apollo, Vulcan, and all the craftsman gods to shore up my sides with boards or to bind them round with iron plates. And I have still to entreat the goddess Ceres, who gave Pelops an ivory shoulder,[54] to condescend to make similar repairs on my almost collapsing ribs. There is no reason for anyone to wonder why I should be a bit pulled down after all this excitement and after begetting so many sons. In a Neronian sense,[55] I have fooled away

too much time about this business. And now I am going to jump the Statutes of the University like the walls of Romulus,[56] and quit Latin in favor of English. You who are amused by such things, give me attentive ears and minds.

Neronian sayings (i.e. puns) are mentioned by Cicero in De Oratori II, lxi, 248.
[56] Romulus' slaying of his brother Remus for jumping over the newly-drawn wall of Rome was a familiar incident in Plutarch's Life of Romulus.

VII. Delivered in the College Chapel in Defense of Learning An Oration

LEARNING MAKES MEN HAPPIER THAN DOES IGNORANCE[1]

Although, O hearers, nothing could be more delightful and desirable to me than

[50] The Aristotelian *predicaments* or categories correspond to the accidents in n. 47 above.
[51] All of Milton's 'sons' are students and therefore will some day be candidates for *degrees*.
[52] The defeat of the English expedition which was led to the relief of the French Huguenots on the *Isle of Rhé* by the unpopular Duke of Buckingham in 1627 is discussed in *Eikon*, Chap. ix.
[53] *Liber*—literally "the liberator"—was a familiar name for Bacchus.
[54] See note 48 above.
[55] There is an almost untranslatable pun on the verbs *moror*, to delay or tarry, and *moror*, to be a fool or to act foolishly, in the original Latin.

[1] E. M. W. Tillyard, in his Introduction to Mrs. Tillyard's *Milton, Private Correspondence and Academic Exercises*, p. xxxv, agrees with Masson (*Life of Milton* I, 297) that this speech was one of the requirements for advancement to the Master's degree, which Milton took in July, 1632. It is obviously indebted to Bacon's *Advancement of Learning* for its rejection of Scholastic logic, for its enthusiasm over the three realms of learning—history, poetry, and philosophy (including natural philosophy, i.e. natural science)—for its faith in the value of education to individuals and to the state, and for many details such as the reference to Alexander and Julius Caesar as learned soldiers and statesmen. This indebtedness to Bacon and the hardly less interesting indebtedness to Cicero's oration *Pro Archia* for ideas about the integrity of learned men, the rewards that knowledge brings to them in every stage of life, and the final reward of fame, etc., are summarized by K. McEuen in D. Wolfe's edition of the *Complete Prose Works of John Milton* I, 287-8. Milton probably expected his audience to recognize the hands of both Bacon and Cicero in the design of his work. His direct reference to Erasmus in *Prol* IV shows that he was very familiar with the *Praise of Folly*, and there is more than a trace of irony in *Prol* VII; but Milton's tone in the climactic passage on the study of God's works as a means to his praise is Baconian or even solemnly Platonic—as Irene Samuel suggests in pointing to the *Symposium* as a part of its background (in *Plato and Milton* p. 104). But of course the great chorus in that background is the mass of theologians, Catholic and Protestant, who have urged that the Book of God's Creatures reveals its author no less distinctly than the Bible itself. And Howard Schultz seems to be correct—in *Milton and Forbidden Knowledge*, pp. 78-80—in tracing the substance and form of this

your appearance here, or than this ardent crowd in academic robes, or than my honorable assignment as orator—an assignment which I have taken some pleasure in performing with you once or twice in the past; nevertheless, if I may speak the truth, it always happens that I can hardly bring myself to make a speech voluntarily or with a really good will, even though my nature and the character of my studies are not averse to the task. If the choice had been mine, I would willingly have spared myself this evening's work. For I have learned from the printed and the spoken wisdom of the most learned men that nothing mean or mediocre is tolerable in an orator any more than it is in a poet, and that it behoves an aspirant to true, and not to merely specious eloquence, to be instructed and perfected in an all-around foundation in all the arts and in every science. Since my years do not permit this, I have hitherto preferred to set up that foundation and to struggle for that true glory by long and strenuous study rather than to grab a false glory on the basis of a forced and immature style.

When I am all on fire and daily growing hotter with this idea and intention, I have never found any interference or delay more serious than the harm done by this ceaseless interruption. The truth is that nothing has fed my mind or contributed more to its health than intelligent and liberal leisure have done—quite contrary to our experience with the body. This is what I conceive to have been that divine sleep of Hesiod,[2] those nocturnal encounters of Endymion with the moon,[3] and that retirement of Prometheus[4] with Mercury as his guide to the loneliest heights of Mount Caucasus, where he became the wisest of

the gods and men—so wise that Jupiter himself is said to have gone to consult him about the marriage of Thetis.

For my own part I appeal to the groves and streams and the dear village elms under which in the summer now just over I remember that I enjoyed supreme happiness with the Muses (if it is lawful to speak of the secrets of the goddesses). There among the fields and in the depths of the woods I seemed to myself to have achieved some real growth in the season of seclusion.

Here also I might have hoped for the same opportunity to retire, if this troublesome nuisance of a speech had not thrust itself onto me at an untimely hour and so horribly infringed upon my holy slumber, and so disturbed my mind when it was fixed on other things, and so thwarted and encumbered me in the midst of any peace. I began mournfully to reflect how far away I am from that tranquillity which literary study at first promised me, and how wretched life is going to be in all this confusion and upheaval, and how much better it would be to give up the arts entirely. And so, almost out of my mind, I took up the rash notion of praising Ignorance, which is quite secure against these commotions. And as a subject for debate I propose: *Whether Learning Makes Men Happier Than does Ignorance.*

How it is I do not know, but my destiny or my character declined to let me abandon my old love for the Muses. Even blind chance itself seemed suddenly to have become sensible and clear-sighted enough to forbid it. Before it seemed possible to me, Ignorance found her champion, and Learning's defense fell to me. I am truly happy that the trick has been played on me, and I am not ashamed of the fact that blind Fortune has given me back my sight. For this I give her my thanks. And now at least it is my privilege to praise the Lady from whose embrace I was torn, and to be consoled for my separation from her by discoursing about her. So this surely is no interruption, for who would call it an interruption to have to glorify and defend what he loves, what he esteems, and what he wishes most devotedly to pursue?

The truth is, my hearers, that—as I see it—the might of eloquence is best displayed on subjects which do not excite very great

Oration to Pierre Charron's *De la Sagesse* as the most influential of its many "sources."

[2] Milton remembered *Hesiod's* story of the Muses teaching him the art of song in the opening lines of the *Theogony.* Cf. *PL* III, 27.

[3] After tracing the story of *Endymion* and the *moon* to Hesiod and a dozen other ancient writers, Conti (IV, viii; pp. 337–8) suggests its interpretation to mean that Endymion was a speculative philosopher and pioneer astronomer, but a variety of other allegorizations are also suggested as possible.

[4] Conti (IV, v; p. 300; and IV, vi, p. 321) refers to some obscure myths about Jove himself meditating marriage with *Thetis* and being dissuaded by *Prometheus.*

applause. Those which arouse the most applause can hardly by any means be kept within the limits of a speech. The very richness of the subject encumbers it and straitens and hedges the spreading parade of eloquence. My difficulty now is this wealth of material. The sinews of my war are my weakness; my arms make me harmless. And so a choice must be made, or surely the facts which establish and fortify my cause with strong defenses will have to be enumerated rather than elaborated.

Just now the one theme to be developed seems to me to be to show how much Learning and Ignorance, on the one part and on the other, have to contribute to that happiness which all of us are pursuing. With the debate on this subject my speech will easily deal, for I need hardly be afraid of any attack that Callowness can make on Knowledge, or Ignorance on Learning. And the very faculty of making an objection, or of verbalizing anything, or of so much as daring to open the mouth in this conclave of a most erudite society, has all been obtained by the kindness, or rather by the charity of Learning.

It is a fact, Gentlemen, universally understood and acknowledged, I think, that though the mighty Builder of the universe made all other things transient and perishable, he mingled with man's nature, beside its mortal part, a certain breath of divinity, as it were a part of himself—immortal, inextinguishable, and proof against death and annihilation. It was destined, after wandering for a time on earth in innocence and purity, like some celestial visitor, to fly upward to its native heaven, and return to its proper home and the land of its birth. Therefore nothing can rightly be considered as contributing to our happiness unless it somehow looks both to that everlasting life as well as to our life as citizens of this world. Contemplation is by almost universal consent the only means whereby the mind can set itself free from the support of the body and concentrate its powers for the unbelievable delight of participating in the life of the immortal gods. Yet without learning, the mind is quite sterile and unhappy, and amounts to nothing. For who can rightly observe and consider the ἰδέας[5]

of things human and divine, about which he can know almost nothing, unless his spirit has been enriched and cultivated by learning and discipline? So the man who knows nothing of the liberal arts seems to be cut off from all access to the happy life —unless God's supreme desire was that we should struggle to the heights of knowledge of those things for which he has planted such a burning passion in our minds at birth. He would seem to have acted vainly or malevolently in giving us a spirit capable and insatiably curious of this high wisdom. Scrutinize the face of all the world in whatever way you can. The Builder of this great work has made it for his own glory. The more deeply we search into its marvelous plan, into this vast structure with its magnificent variety—something which only Learning permits us to do—the more we honor its Creator with our admiration and follow him with our praise. In doing so we may be securely confident that we please Him. Can we suppose, gentlemen, that the sweep of so vast a sky, which is marked and illuminated by eternal lights, sustains so many swiftly and intricately revolving bodies, merely to give light to ignorant and sluggish men, and to be torch-bearers to us below, the lazy and slothful? Can we suppose that there is nothing more in the fruits and herbs that grow so abundantly than their frail green beauty? If we are to value these things so unworthily as to perceive nothing more in them than brute sensation reveals, we shall seem to act not only vilely and basely, but unjustly and wickedly toward that gracious spirit whom our indifference and ingratitude rob both of much of His glory and of the veneration due to His power. So then, if learning is our leader and director in our quest for happiness, and if it has the approval of the Almighty and contributes to his praise, it surely cannot fail to make its followers happy in the very noblest way.

I do not forget, Gentlemen, that the contemplative way which leads to all that is supremely desirable, can give us no taste of true happiness without integrity in our lives and purity in our conduct. I remember the wicked characters of many men famous for their learning, who were quarrelsome, vin-

[5] The Greek spelling stresses the allusion to Plato's *ideas* or ideally perfect forms, to which all that we know by experience and reflection imperfectly corresponds.

dictive, and enslaved by base passions: and I also remember that many men of no education have proved to be honorable and upright. What does this mean? Is Ignorance the more blessed? Certainly not! The fact is, Gentlemen, that though some few outstanding scholars may have been corrupted by the bad morals of their country and the vulgarity of ignorant men, yet the illiterate masses have often been held to their duty by the efforts of a single learned and wise man. Indeed a single family or a single individual, if he possesses knowledge and discretion, may seem as if he were a gift of God endowed with power to make a whole nation virtuous. But where learning has been starved and scholarship has been exterminated, there you find no trace of any good man, and savagery and frightful barbarity run riot. As an instance of this I will not mention any particular state or province or tribe, but rather all Europe, which is a fourth part of the whole world. There several centuries ago all the liberal arts had perished, and the Muses who preside over them now, had abandoned the universities of that time. A blind inertia possessed and pervaded everything. In the schools nothing except the absurd dogmas of the doddering monks was heard, and the insulting and ugly master, Ignorance, put on the gown and strutted on our empty platforms and in our lecture-desks and the forsaken chairs of the professors. Then for the first time Piety was in mourning, and Religion languished and weakened so that only very recently and very feebly did she begin to recover from her deadly wound.

Truly, Gentlemen, it has long been a well enough established principle in philosophy that the mastery of every art and science belongs to the intellect alone, while the home and shrine of the virtues of righteousness is the Will. By universal consent, the human intellect not only shines forth as the prince and ruler of the other faculties of the soul, but its radiance also directs and illuminates the otherwise blind and fumbling Will, which, like the moon, shines with a borrowed light. So let us willingly grant and confess that Virtue without Learning is more favorable to the happy life than Learning without Virtue. But once the two are happily united, as they surely ought to be, and as they very often

are, then Learning lifts her head and instantly shines out so as to appear by far the superior. She takes her high seat beside the royal and ruling Intellect, and from there she looks down upon the doings of the Will as something far beneath her feet. And then she readily claims for herself an excellence, glory, and majesty akin to that of God himself forever.

Descending now to our life as citizens of this world, let us see what Learning and Ignorance are worth respectively in public and private life. I shall ignore the fact that Learning is youth's finest ornament, the strong support of the prime of life, and the consolation of old age. I shall make no point of the fact that, after careers full of achievement and glory, many of the men who have been most honored by their contemporaries and many of the most eminent of the Romans withdrew from the conflict and hurlyburly of ambition to literary studies, as to a harbor and a delightful retreat. Clearly, those fine old veterans understood that, because the part of life remaining to them was the best, it should be used to the best purpose. They were already the foremost among men, and by means of those studies they intended not to be the last among the gods. Fame had once been their goal, now it was immortality. In their struggles against the foes of the Empire they fought a very different fight, but when they were to fight against death, the greatest curse of humanity—see what weapons they chose, what forces they recruited, and with what resources they equipped themselves.

But it is a fact that the great bulk of the world's happiness consists in human relationships and the development of friendships. According to a widespread complaint, many men of the more learned kind are unapproachable, rude, queer, and possessing none of the graces of persuasive speech. I confess that the man who shuts himself up and is almost entirely immured in study, is readier to talk with the gods than with men, either because he is habitually at home among celestial affairs and is unfamiliar and really strange among mortal ones, or because a mind which has been enlarged by the steady pursuit of divine interests is irked by physical constraints and disqualified for the more formal social amenities. But if good friendships of the right kind come into his way, no one is more loyal than he. And what is more pleasant—what can be imagined more delightful than the talks of learned and serious men together—such, for example, as the divine Plato is said to have often had under that famous plane tree?[6] Certainly they deserved that all mankind should listen to them in rapt silence. But stupid talk or what goes on among those who encourage one another in extravagance and debauchery, is the friendship of ignorance, or, rather, it is ignorance of what friendship is.

Again, if the happiness of the life that we live among men consists in the mind's honest and liberal pleasure, then the delights that are the secret of study and learning as such easily surpass all others. How much it means to grasp all the principles of the heavens and their stars, all the movements and disturbances of the atmosphere, both its awful fulmination of thunder and the blaze of its comets,[7] which terrify dull minds, and also its freezing into snow and hail, and its soft and gentle precipitation of dew and rain. How much it means to get an insight into the fluctuating winds and the exhalations and gases which the earth and sea emit,[8] and—if it be possible—into the nature and the sensory experience of every living creature, and hence into the delicate anatomy of the human body and into its medical treatment, and—finally—into the divine powers and faculties of the spirit, and whatever knowledge may be accessible to us about the beings that are called household gods and genii and daemons. Beside these there are countless other subjects, many of which might be mastered in less time than I should need to name them all.

So at last, Gentlemen, when the cycle of universal knowledge has been completed, still the spirit will be restless in our dark imprisonment here, and it will rove about until the bounds of creation itself no longer limit the divine magnificence of its quest. Then most happenings and events about us will become obvious so quickly that almost nothing can happen without warning or by accident to a man who is in possession of the stronghold of wisdom. Truly he will seem to have the stars under his control and dominion, land and sea at his command, and the winds and storms submissive to his will. Mother Nature herself has surrendered to him. It is as if some god had abdicated the government of the world and committed its justice, laws, and administration to him as ruler.

And besides all this, how great an additional pleasure of the mind it is to take our flight over all the history and regions of the world, to view the conditions and changes of kingdoms, nations, cities, and people— all with a view to improving our wisdom and our morals. This is the way to live in all the epochs of history, Gentlemen, and to be a contemporary of time itself. And while we are looking forward to the future glory of our name, this will also be the way to extend life backward from the womb and to extort from unwilling Fate a kind of immortality in the past. And shall I ignore a satisfaction to which no parallel can be found? To be the oracle of many peoples, to have one's home become a shrine, to be the object of invitations from kings and commonwealths and of visits from neighbors and distant foreigners, and of pride for still others who will boast it an honorable distinction merely to have had a single glimpse of one. These are the rewards of study and the profits that learning can and often does bring to those who cultivate her in private life.

What then about public life? It is true that few men have been raised to the glory of a crown by a reputation for learning, nor many more by a reputation for integrity. Men of that kind enjoy a kingdom within themselves far more magnificent than any earthly sovereignty, and who can aspire to power in two realms and escape the charge of ambition? Let me add another point: up to this time there have been only two men who have had possession of the whole circle of the earth as heaven's gift and have shared empire equal with the gods them-

---

[6] Milton is thinking of the *plane tree* under which Socrates and Phaedrus sit down for their famous conversation about friendship. Cf. Plato's *Phaedrus*, 229A.

[7] In a contemporary work such as Zanchius' *On the Creation* (*De operibus Dei* III, i–ii) Milton might have found the Aristotelian theory that *comets* are formed by the sun's action in the upper air from dense, dry, and warm exhalations from the earth.

[8] Compare *IlPen*, 93–96 and 170–74.

selves over all kings and potentates: Alexander the Great and Octavius Caesar[9] both of them students of philosophy. Indeed it is as if they had been divinely provided for humanity as an example of the kind of man to whom the helm and the reins of affairs should be entrusted.

But many nations have achieved fame without learning, by their great deeds or their wealth. Very few Spartans are remembered who devoted themselves to literary studies. The Romans were a very long time in admitting philosophy to the city, yet the former employed the philosopher and amateur of poets, Lycurgus,[10] as their lawgiver. Such an amateur of poets was he that he was the first man to make a careful collection of the writings of Homer when they were scattered far and wide in Ionia. The Romans, when they were hardly able to maintain themselves in the city after various commotions and disturbances, sent ambassadors to Athens, which at that time was culturally most flourishing, to bring back the Decemviral Laws, which are otherwise known as the Laws of the Twelve Tables.

But how can we answer the objection that the modern Turks, who have no literary culture at all, have made themselves masters of everything throughout the rich realms of Asia? What there may be conspicuously admirable in that commonwealth (if the name of a republic can be given to the power which has been violently and murderously grabbed by men of the utmost barbarity, who have been brought together in one place by their partnership in crime) I surely do not know. To provide the necessities of life and to hold onto them— these things we owe to nature, not to art. To make aggressive onslaughts on the property of others, to rally together for the sake of plunder, to conspire in crime—these things we owe to Nature's perversion. Justice of a kind is used among them. No

wonder. Other virtues are easily banished; Justice is a true queen and compels allegiance, for without her even the most unjust societies would soon go to pieces. Nor should I overlook the fact that the Saracens, to whom the Turks mainly owe their existence, spread their power less by force of arms than by their interest in literature.

If we go back to ancient times, we shall find that commonwealths were not only disciplined but were actually founded by Learning. The most ancient tribes, the indigenous people, are said to have roved over the woods and mountains looking for food like wild animals, their bodies grovelling though their heads were erect. Except for the dignity of their form, you might have thought that they had everything in common with the beasts: the same caves, the same lairs defended them from the weather and the cold. Then there were no shining cities, marble edifices or altars or temples of the gods; then there was no divine law; no laws were declared in the forum; at marriages there were no torches, no choral dances, no song at the genial table. There was no funeral solemnity, no mourning, scarcely even a heap of stones to honor the dead. There were no social feasts, no games. The sound of the cithara was not heard. Not one of the things existed with which luxury now pampers idleness.

Then suddenly the arts and sciences inspired the rude breasts of men, imbued them with knowledge of themselves, and induced them to live together between common walls. And surely by the help of those founders by whom cities were first established and then stabilized with laws, and later strengthened with wisdom, by their guidance the cities will be able to maintain themselves long and prosperously.

And now what about Ignorance? I perceive, O hearers, that she is in a fog, and in terror and retreat. She is looking everywhere for a way of escape. She is whining about art being long and life short. Well, if we were only to do away with the two great obstacles of our studies, one of which is our bad method of teaching the arts, while the other is our own inertia, we should find—with due respect to Galen[11] or

---

[9] Cf. Milton's allusions to Aristotle's instruction of Alexander in *El IV*, 25, and *PR II*, 196. For his interest in *Octavius* (Augustus) see the prefatory letter to *SA*.

[10] Perhaps Milton was thinking of Plutarch's statement in the Life of *Lycurgus* that, in youth and before drawing up his famous code of laws for the Spartans, Lycurgus visited Asia Minor and made an edition of the Homeric poems because he thought that they would be morally beneficial to his countrymen.

[11] Editors trace Chaucer's source for the opening line of the Parliament of Fowls—

whoever originated the saying—that the truth is quite to the contrary: life is long, and art is short. Nothing is sounder than art, or more exhausting. Nothing is lazier or slacker than we are. In work at night and before sunrise we let the laborers and farmers get the better of us. They are less sluggish about earning a pittance in sordid work than we are in the quest of a happy life by work of the noblest kind. Though we aspire to the highest and best in human life, we can endure neither hard study or the reproach of indolence. Indeed, we are ashamed of the very thing the lack of which we should resent having imputed to us.

But it is for our health's sake that we shrink from night work and hard study. Shameful to relate: we neglect the uncultivated mind and worry about the body. And who would not sacrifice its strength to increase the strength of the mind? And most of those who argue about health are lost souls who have no regard for time, talent, or health, and never complain that they suffer from gluttonizing or drinking like a fish, or spending their nights between the stews and the dice. Since they school and train themselves to be keen and prompt about every kind of vice, and are listless and languid when virtue or intelligence are in question, they are dishonest and unjust in putting the blame on nature and the brevity of life. But if by living a modest and temperate life we prefer to tame the first vehemence of the ungovernable age by reason and steady fidelity to our studies, keeping the heavenly powers of the mind clean and unstained from all filth and pollution, it would be incredible to us, my hearers, as we would look back after a few years, to see how much distance we had covered, and what a mighty sea of learning we had quietly navigated.

Our voyage also may be notably shortened if we but know what subjects to study and how to pick out the useful things in them. In the first place, how much contemptible nonsense there is from the grammarians and teachers of composition. When the former teach their art, they talk like barbarians, and the latter talk like infants. What about logic? If she were

The life so short, the craft so long to learn— to the first axiom of Hippocrates. In either case, a physician has credit for the maxim.

treated as she deserves, she would indeed be queen of the sciences—but alas, how much absurdity is reason responsible for! In this field there are no human beings; there are only thorn-finches stuffing themselves with thistles and briars.

O reapers with iron bowels!
[Horace, *Epodes* III, 4.]

And what shall I say about the art which the Aristotelians call metaphysics? It is not an art, I say, though the authority of great men would persuade me to accept it as a most valuable one. It is rather a scandalous reef and a bog of sophistry, which has been contrived to bring men to shipwreck and ruin. These are the evils of that gowned ignorance to which I have already referred. This is the disease for whose spread even into natural philosophy the monks were responsible far and wide. Even the mathematicians suffer from the foolish vanity of their demonstrations. When all these unprofitable subjects have been brought into the contempt which they deserve and abolished, the number of whole years that we shall save will astound us.

Another point! Our legal science particularly suffers from the confusion of our system and—still worse—from a jargon that I can hardly tell how to describe. It may be the gibberish of American Indians, and it may not be human speech at all. Often when I have heard our shysters bawling in this lingo, I have wondered whether those who had neither human mouths nor human powers of speech[12] could have any human feelings inside them. I am positively afraid that Justice in her sanctity cannot bear to look upon us[13] and will never heed the grievances and wrongs of men whose language she does not know how to speak.

So, Gentlemen, if from childhood up we never let a day pass without its assignment and without some hard work, and if we wisely keep our studies clear of everything that is impertinent, superfluous, or insignificant, we are certain before we reach the age of Alexander the Great to have mastered something finer and more magnificent than

[12] Compare Milton's jibe at the language of the courts in *El I*, 31–32.
[13] Milton thought of the myth of the departure of Justice or Astraea from earth, where she had lived among men during the Golden Age of Saturn's reign. Cf. *F.Q.* V, i, 5, and *El IV*, 81.

the world that he conquered. And we shall be so far from protesting against the shortness of life and the tediousness of art that we shall rather be ready, I think, to weep and shed tears, as he did long ago, because there are no more worlds left for us to conquer.

Ignorance is at her last breath, and you see her final throes and her death struggle. She murmurs that men are stimulated in the main by glory; that while a long sequence and course of years has glorified the illustrious men of the past, we are borne down by the world's decrepit old age and the impending destruction of all things.[14] If we leave anything behind us for everlasting fame to proclaim, our name will flourish but briefly, since hardly any posterity are to succeed us. And so it is in vain that so many books and glorious monuments of the mind are produced, since the impending conflagration of the world will burn them all.

I do not deny that this may be quite probable. But in truth to set no value on glory when you have done well, that is beyond all glory. How little pleasure could the empty praise of men give to those dead and departed worthies whom no pleasure and no sensation from it could reach! But we may look forward to eternal life which will never erase the memory of our good deeds on earth.[15] Whatever lovely thing we may have done here we shall be present to hear praised there. And there—as many men have seriously thought—those who have lived temperately and dedicated all their time to worthy studies and thereby helped mankind, will be enriched above all others with knowledge that is peerless and supreme.

So let the lazy fellows cease to cavil about the things which hitherto have been doubtful and difficult for us in the sciences, for these things are less to be blamed upon science than upon human nature. This it is, O my hearers, which either disproves that famous Socratic profession of ignorance[16] and the timid doubt of the Sceptics[17] or else comforts us and compensates us for them.

14 Cf. *Naturam*, 1, n.
15 Cf. *Lyc*, 78–84.
16 Cf. *PR* IV, 293–4.
17 Cf. *PR* IV, 296.

And so at last we may ask what are the joys of Ignorance. Are they to enjoy what one has, to be molested by no one, to be superior to all cares and annoyance, to live a secure and quiet life insofar as possible? Truly, this is the life of any wild beast or bird that has its little nest in the deepest and most distant forests, as near as possible to the sky, and there rears its nestlings, flies around in search of food with no fear of being hunted, and warbles its sweet songs at dawn and sunset. Why crave for the heavenly power of the mind in addition to these pleasures? Ergo, let Ignorance throw off her humanity, let her have Circe's cup[18] and betake herself on all fours to the beasts.

To the beasts, indeed? But they refuse to receive such a foul guest, if they have any share in an inferior kind of reason—as many observers have thought that they do—or have an intelligence that is due to some strong instinct, or make use of the arts or of anything resembling the arts among themselves. For, according to Plutarch,[19] dogs in pursuit of game are said to have some sense of logic and to make obvious use of the disjunctive syllogism when they happen to come to a fork in the road. Aristotle[20] notes that the nightingale is in the habit of giving some kind of musical instruction to her young. Almost every beast is its own doctor, and many of them have taught notable medical lessons to mankind. The Egyptian ibis[21] has shown us the value of purges, and the hippopotamus[22] of phlebotomy. Who can deny a knowledge of astronomy to those from whom come so many warnings of winds, rain, floods, and calm weather? With what

18 Cf. *Comus*, 50–53.
19 Milton is quoting *Plutarch's* omnium gatherum of more or less unnatural natural history, the essay in the *Moralia* which is entitled, "Which are the Most Crafty, Water or Land Animals," xiii.
20 The Aristotelian passage is in the *Historia animalium* IV, ix, but Milton may also have found the story about the nightingale in "Which are the Most Crafty," xix.
21 Milton may be following Plutarch's essay (xx) again, or Pliny's *Natural History* VIII, xii, where the self-purgation of the *ibis* is mentioned not far from the prescience of many birds about winds, rain, and floods.
22 Milton's authority here seems to be Pliny VIII, xl, 1. Miss McEuen quotes the full passage on the dyspeptic *hippopotamus'* art of self-bleeding against a sharp reed.

prudent and stern discipline the geese[23] check their dangerous garrulity with pebbles in their bills when they are flying over Mt. Taurus! Our domestic science owes much to the ants, and our political science to the bees.[24] Military art thanks the cranes[25] for the principle of posting sentinels and forming the triangular phalanx. The beasts are too intelligent to admit Ignorance to their company and fellowship; they put her lower down.

So what then? Must she go to the trees and the stones. The very trees, and shrubs, and the entire forest tore away from their roots to run after the elegant music of Orpheus.[26] Often they have had mysterious powers and have given divine oracles, as the oaks at Dodona did. Rocks also respond with some docility to the sacred voice of the poets. And will not even the rocks spurn Ignorance away? And so, since she is lower than every kind of brute, lower than the trees and rocks, lower than every order known to Nature, will it be granted to Ignorance to find rest in the not-being of the Epicureans?[27] No, not there, since

it is necessary that what is worse, what is viler, what is more wretched, what is lowest, should be Ignorance.

I come to you now, O my most intelligent auditors, for—even though I myself had said nothing—I see that you are not so many arguments, but rather that you are so many weapons which I shall turn against Ignorance to destroy her.

Now that I have sounded the battle-signal, hurl yourselves into the mêlée. Throw your enemy back. Drive her out of your porticos and walks. If you let her exist at all, you yourselves will be the thing that you know to be the most despicable of all things. Therefore this cause is yours—for every one of you.

And so if perhaps I have spoken much longer than is allowed by the customs of this place—aside from the fact that the great subject required it—I believe that you will forgive me, O my judges, since it lets you understand much better how much concerned I am for you, how devoted to you I am, what toil and what vigils I have borne for your sake. I have said my final word.

23 Mrs. Tillyard traces this story to Stephen Gosson's *School of Abuse* (1579).

24 Cf. *Way*, n. 25.

25 Cf. *PL* I, 575, n.

26 Cf. *El VI*, 70. *Patrem*, 52, and *Prol* VI, n. 10.

27 Milton may have been thinking both of Epicurus' reduction of all existence to empty space and atoms which could hardly be said to have any significant being before chance combined them into phenomenal forms, and also of Epicurus' depreciation of the active pleasures of satisfied ambition in comparison with "that Pleasure," which "is the Indolency of the Body, and Tranquillity of Mind," as the principle is stated in William Charleton's version of *Epicurus' Morals* (London, 1656), p. 22.

OF EDUCATION

To Master Samuel Hartlib[1]

Written above twenty Years since.

BIBLIOGRAPHICAL NOTE—*Of Education* was first issued in 1644 as an informal, eight-page pamphlet without titlepage, date, or publisher's name. In 1673 a second edition was published, without significant changes from the first, in *Poems, etc. upon Several Occasions with a small tractate of Education*—to Mr. Hartlib. The best scholarly edition is by Oliver M. Ainsworth (New Haven, 1928). The present text is based on the copy of the second edition in the Houghton Library at Harvard.

MR. HARTLIB,

I am long since persuaded that to say or do aught worth memory and imitation, no purpose or respect should sooner move us than simply the love of God and of mankind. Nevertheless to write now the reforming of education, though it be one of the greatest and noblest designs that can be thought on, and for the want whereof this nation perishes, I had not yet at this time been induced but by your earnest entreaties and serious conjurements; as having my mind for the present half diverted in the pursuance of some other assertions, the knowledge and the use of which cannot but be a great furtherance both to the enlargement of truth and honest living, with much more peace. Nor should the laws of any private friendship have prevailed with me to divide thus, or transpose my former thoughts, but that I see those aims, those actions, which have won you with me the esteem of a person sent hither by some good providence from a far country to be the occasion and the incitement of great good to this island.

And, as I hear, you have obtained the same repute with men of most approved wisdom, and some of the highest authority among us; not to mention the learned correspondence which you hold in foreign parts, and the extraordinary pains and diligence which you have used in this matter, both here and beyond the seas; either by the definite will of God so ruling, or the peculiar sway of nature,[2] which also is God's working. Neither can I think that, so reputed and so valued as you are, you would, to the forfeit of your own discerning ability, impose upon me an unfit and over-ponderous argument; but that the satisfaction which you profess to have received from those incidental discourses which we have wandered into, hath pressed and almost constrained you into a persuasion that what you require from me in this point, I neither ought nor can in conscience defer beyond this time both of so much need at once, and so much opportunity to try what God hath determined.

I will not resist therefore whatever it is either of divine or human obligement that you lay upon me; but will forthwith set down in writing, as you request me, that voluntary idea[3] which hath long in silence presented itself to me, of a better education, in extent and comprehension far more large, and yet of time far shorter, and of attainment far more certain, than hath been yet in practice. Brief I shall endeavor to be;

[1] G. H. Turnbull's *Samuel Hartlib* is the best account of this indefatigable writer of books on agriculture, religion, and education, whose services to "husbandry" won him a pension from Parliament. He was the child of a Polish father and English mother, and his residence in Prussia brought him into contact with Comenius (see n. 4) until, at about the age of thirty (in 1628), he emigrated to England. Milton's tractate was one of several pamphlets which were stimulated by Hartlib's translation of one of Comenius' designs for educational reform under the title, *A Reformation of Schooles* (1642).

[2] So in *CD* I, viii, Milton defines nature as simply "the mysterious power and efficacy of that divine voice which went forth at the beginning, and to which, as to a perpetual command, all things have since paid obedience." Cf. p. 989.

[3] Milton's italicization of the word *Idea* in the first edition suggests to Herbert Agar (*Milton and Plato*, p. 66) that Milton is presenting an ideal like the ideals of justice which Plato defended in the *Republic* and *Laws*.

C.P. Newman

for that which I have to say, assuredly this nation hath extreme need should be done sooner than spoken. To tell you therefore what I have benefited herein among old renowned authors, I shall spare; and to search what many modern Januas and Didactics,[4] more than ever I shall read, have projected, my inclination leads me not. But if you can accept of these few observations which have flowered off, and are as it were the burnishing of many studious and contemplative years altogether spent in the search of religious and civil knowledge, and such as pleased you so well in the relating, I here give you them to dispose of.

The end then of learning is to repair the ruins[5] of our first parents by regaining to know God aright, and out of that knowledge to love him, to imitate him, to be like him, as we may the nearest by possessing our souls of true virtue, which being united to the heavenly grace of faith makes up the highest perfection.[6] But because our understanding cannot in this body found itself but on sensible things, nor arrive so clearly to the knowledge of God and things invisible as by orderly conning over the visible and inferior creature, the same method is necessarily to be followed in all discreet teaching. And seeing every nation affords not experience and tradition enough for all kind of learning, therefore we are chiefly taught the languages of those people who have at any time been most industrious after wisdom; so that language is but the instrument conveying to us things useful to be known. And though a linguist should pride himself to have all the tongues that Babel cleft the world into, yet, if he have not studied the solid things in them as well as the words and lexicons, he were nothing so much to be esteemed a learned man as any yeoman or tradesman competently wise in his mother dialect only.

Hence appear the many mistakes which have made learning generally so unpleasing and so unsuccessful; first, we do amiss to spend seven or eight years merely in scraping together so much miserable Latin and Greek as might be learned otherwise easily and delightfully in one year. And that which casts our proficiency therein so much behind, is our time lost partly in too oft idle vacancies[7] given both to schools and universities, partly in a preposterous exaction,[8] forcing the empty wits of children to compose themes, verses and orations, which are the acts of ripest judgment and the final work of a head filled by long reading and observing with elegant maxims and copious invention. These are not matters to be wrung from poor striplings, like blood out of the nose, or the plucking of untimely fruit: besides the ill habit which they get of wretched barbarizing[9] against the Latin and Greek idiom with their untutored Anglicisms, odious to be read, yet not to be avoided without a well-continued and judicious conversing[10] among pure authors digested, which they scarce taste. Whereas, if after some preparatory grounds of speech by their certain forms got into memory, they were

[4] The allusion is to works like Comenius' *Janua linguarum reserata*, an elementary introduction to Latin and to the study of other languages, and to its numerous precursors and imitations calling themselves "Doorways" to language study. Comenius' *Great Didactic* exerted a wide influence through men like Hartlib, who made an abstract of it in his abridgment of Comenius' larger work, *Pansophia*, for publication in London in 1639. Cf. n. 1 above.

[5] Milton had no more doubt than did Bacon that, before the Fall, Adam possessed "a pure light of natural knowledge" ("Of the Interpretation of Nature," in *The Works of Francis Bacon*, ed. by Spedding and Ellis, III, 219), which extended to all sciences, although its only recorded manifestation was Adam's naming of the animals. Cf. *PL* VIII, 342–54.

[6] Milton shared John Hall's faith in educational reform as the final step in the Protestant Reformation in England. So Hall regarded it in his *An Humble Motion to the Parliament of England Concerning the Advancement of Learning and Reformation of the Universities* (1649).

[7] *vacancies:* short holidays as well as the long vacations.

[8] *preposterous exaction:* premature requirement. So John Brinsley, in his *Ludus Literarius* (1612), condemned the premature exercises in written Latin, which made boys "live in a continuall horrour and hatred of learning; and to account the school, not *Ludus literarius*, but . . . *pistrinum literarium*" (not a literary playground but a literary torture-chamber). Brinsley's title claimed that "the highest perfection required in the grammar schooles" could be achieved by his method, "with ease, certainty, and delight both to masters and schollars."

[9] *barbarizing:* writing barbarisms or unidiomatic Latin.

[10] *conversing:* living familiarly, i.e. with authors whose works are worth digesting. Cf. Bacon's distinction between books to be tasted and books to be chewed and digested in the Essay "Of Studies."

led to the praxis[11] thereof in some chosen short book lessoned thoroughly to them, they might then forthwith proceed to learn the substance of good things, and arts in due order, which would bring the whole language quickly into their power. This I take to be the most rational and most profitable way of learning languages, and whereby we may best hope to give account to God of our youth spent herein.

And for the usual method of teaching arts,[12] I deem it to be an old error of universities not yet well recovered from the scholastic grossness of barbarous ages, that instead of beginning with arts most easy—and those be such as are most obvious to the sense—they present their young unmatriculated[13] novices at first coming with the most intellective abstractions of logic[14] and metaphysics. So that they having but newly left those grammatic flats and shallows where they stuck unreasonably to learn a few words with lamentable construction, and now on the sudden transported under another climate to be tossed and turmoiled with their unballasted wits in fathomless and unquiet deeps of controversy, do for the most part grow into hatred and contempt of learning, mocked and deluded all this while with ragged notions and babblements, while they expected worthy and delightful knowledge; till poverty or youthful years[15] call them importunately their several ways and hasten them with the sway of friends either to an ambitious and mercenary, or ignorantly zealous divinity: some allured to the trade of law, grounding their purposes not on the prudent and heavenly contemplation of justice and equity which was never taught them, but on the promising and pleasing thoughts of litigious terms, fat contentions, and flowing fees; others betake them to state affairs with souls so unprincipled in virtue and true generous breeding that flattery and court shifts and tyrannous aphorisms[16] appear to them the highest points of wisdom; instilling their barren hearts with a conscientious slavery,[17] if, as I rather think, it be not feigned. Others, lastly, of a more delicious and airy[18] spirit, retire themselves—knowing no better —to the enjoyments of ease and luxury, living out their days in feast and jollity; which indeed is the wisest and the safest course of all these, unless they were with more integrity undertaken. And these are the fruits[19] of misspending our prime youth at the schools and universities as we do, either in learning mere words or such things chiefly as were better unlearned.

I shall detain you no longer in the demonstration of what we should not do, but straight conduct ye to a hillside, where I will point ye out the right path of a virtuous and noble education; laborious indeed at the first ascent, but else so smooth, so green, so full of goodly prospect and melodious sounds on every side, that the harp of Orpheus[20] was not more charming. I doubt not but ye shall have more ado to drive our dullest and laziest youth, our stocks and stubs, from the infinite desire of such a happy nurture, than we have now to hale and drag our choicest and hopefullest wits to that asinine feast of sowthistles[21] and brambles which is commonly set before them as all the food and entertainment of their tenderest and most docible age. I call therefore a complete and generous education that which fits a man to perform justly, skilfully, and magnanimously all the offices, both private and public, of peace and war.[22]

---

[11] The *praxis*, as I. E. Taylor explains in *MLJ*, XXX (1949), 533, would be outlined in the little book which Milton may have begun at Cambridge, though it was not published until 1669: *Accedence Commenced Grammar, Supplied with Sufficient Rules.* The principles of elementary foreign language study in this "masterpiece of simplicity and clarity," seem to Mr. Taylor to be "those in general use today."

[12] The traditional Seven Liberal Arts were Grammar, Logic, Rhetoric, Arithmetic, Geometry, Astronomy, and Music, which presupposed proficiency in Latin, if not in Greek.

[13] *unmatriculated:* inexperienced in university life and work.

[14] Cf. Milton's revolt against misuse of *logic* in *Prol VII*.

[15] *youthful years:* the impatience of youth.

[16] *tyrannous aphorisms:* specious maxims claiming absolute authority for kings.

[17] *conscientious slavery:* superstitiously exaggerated loyalty.

[18] *airy:* volatile, superficial.

[19] In the first edition the sentence reads: "And these are the errors and these are the fruits" etc.

[20] Cf. *Orpheus* in *L'All,* 145, *IlPen,* 105, and *Prol* VIII, n. 26.

[21] Cf. the attack on "thorny lectures of monkish and miserable sophistry" in the universities in *CG* I, iii, p. 686.

[22] Milton's definition of the civic objects of education recalls Plato's in the *Laws* (I, 643) and Quintilian's opening statement of the purposes in the training of a public speaker in the *Institutio*

: discernment

And how all this may be done between twelve and one and twenty, less time than is now bestowed in pure trifling at grammar and sophistry, is to be thus ordered.

First, to find out a spacious house and ground about it fit for an academy and big enough to lodge a hundred and fifty persons, whereof twenty or thereabout may be attendants, all under the government of one, who shall be thought of desert sufficient, and ability either to do all or wisely to direct and oversee it done. This place should be at once both school and university, not needing a remove to any other house of scholarship, except it be some peculiar college of law or physic,[23] where they mean to be practitioners; but as for those general studies which take up all our time from Lily[24] to the commencing, as they term it, master of art, it should be absolute. After this pattern, as many edifices may be converted to this use as shall be needful in every city throughout this land, which would tend much to the increase of learning and civility[25] everywhere. This number, less or more thus collected, to the convenience of a foot company, or interchangeably two troops of cavalry, should divide their day's work into three parts, as it lies orderly: their studies, their exercise, and their diet.

For their studies: first, they should begin with the chief and necessary rules of some good grammar, either that now used, or any better; and while this is doing, their speech is to be fashioned to a distinct and clear pronunciation, as near as may be to the Italian,[26] especially in the vowels. For we Englishmen, being far northerly, do not open our mouths in the cold air wide enough to grace a southern tongue, but are observed by all other nations to speak exceeding close and inward; so that to smatter Latin with an English mouth is as ill a hearing as law French. Next, to make them expert in the usefullest points of grammar, and withal to season them and win them early to the love of virtue and true labor, ere any flattering seducement or vain principle seize them wandering, some easy and delightful book of education would be read to them, whereof the Greeks have store; as Cebes,[27] Plutarch, and other Socratic discourses.[28] But in Latin we have none of classic authority extant, except the two or three first books of Quintilian,[29] and some select pieces elsewhere.

But here the main skill and groundwork will be to temper them such lectures and explanations upon every opportunity as may lead and draw them in willing obedience, inflamed with the study of learning and the admiration of virtue—stirred up with high hopes of living to be brave men and worthy patriots, dear to God and famous to all ages; that they may despise and scorn all their childish and ill-taught qualities to delight in manly and liberal exercises, which he who hath the art and proper eloquence to catch them with, what with mild and effectual persuasions and what with the intimation of some fear, if need be, but chiefly by his own example, might in a short

---

Oratoria. It had many echoes: e.g. in John Dury's *Reformed School* (1649?), where "good Commonwealths men" are described as apt in "husbandry, trade, navigation, administration, in peace and war."

23 *physic*: medicine.

24 *Lily* was the usual reference to the *Beginning Book in Latin* by the first headmaster of St. Paul's School, William Lily (1468?–1522). It was the only authorized textbook of its kind in the reign of Henry VIII, and it continued to be used, in revised editions, for more than two centuries.

25 *civility*: the level of culture implied by civilization.

26 In a letter to his friend, Benedetto Buonmattei (C.E. XII, 34–36) Milton urged him to supplement his Italian grammar with a section on pronunciation. Unlike most Englishmen, Milton believed that Italian should be a guide to the pronunciation of Latin.

27 Though probably written in the first century A.D. by the Stoic philosopher, *Cebes,* the *Table* was regarded as the work of the Theban Cebes who offers to pay the fine of Socrates in Plato's *Crito* (45b). It is a short description of an allegorical picture of the birth of children at the foot of a pathway leading through temptation to a garden where the wisest men in history dwell at the top. It was familiar in a stream of editions, usually with an allegorical frontispiece to match the description, which was often printed with the Greek original and a Latin translation in parallel columns for use by beginners in one or both of the languages.

28 Several of Plutarch's essays in the *Moralia*—particularly that "On the Education of Children" and others such as "On the Daemon of Socrates"—were among the *Socratic discourses* frequently used as elementary texts, either in the original Greek or in parallel Latin.

29 The influence of the *Institutio Oratoria* of Quintilian (30?–96? A.D.) emerges in *Of Education* in the definition of the objects of humanistic training (Cf. n. 22 above) and in the emphasis upon the Renaissance conviction that all study, and especially that of mathematics, should be made to seem like play. Cf. n. 8 above.

space gain them to an incredible diligence and courage, infusing into their young breasts such an ingenuous and noble ardor, as would not fail to make many of them renowned and matchless men. At the same time, some other hour of the day, might be taught them the rules of arithmetic, and soon after the elements of geometry, even playing,[30] as the old manner was. After evening repast till bedtime their thoughts will be best taken up in the easy grounds of religion and the story of scripture.

The next step would be to the authors of agriculture, Cato,[31] Varro, and Columella, for the matter is most easy; and, if the language be difficult, so much the better—it is not a difficulty above their years. And here will be an occasion of inciting and enabling them hereafter to improve the tillage of their country, to recover the bad soil and to remedy the waste that is made of good; for this was one of Hercules' praises.[32] Ere half these authors be read (which will soon be with plying hard and daily) they cannot choose but be masters of any ordinary prose. So that it will be then seasonable for them to learn in any modern author the use of the globes and all the maps, first with the old names and then with the new; or they might be then capable to read any compendious method of natural philosophy.

And at the same time might be entering into the Greek tongue after the same manner as was before prescribed in the Latin; whereby the difficulties of grammar being soon overcome, all the historical physiology of Aristotle[33] and Theophrastus are open

before them, and, as I may say, under contribution. The like access will be to Vitruvius,[34] to Seneca's[35] *Natural Questions,* to Mela,[36] Celsus,[37] Pliny,[38] or Solinus.[39] And having thus passed the principles of arithmetic, geometry, astronomy, and geography, with a general compact of physics, they may descend in mathematics to the instrumental science of trigonometry, and from thence to fortification, architecture, enginery,[40] or navigation. And in natural philosophy they may proceed leisurely from the history of meteors, minerals, plants, and living creatures, as far as anatomy.

Then also in course might be read to them out of some not tedious writer the institution of physic,[41] that they may know the tempers, the humors,[42] the seasons, and how to manage a crudity;[43] which he who can wisely and timely do, is not only a great physician to himself and to his friends, but also may at some time or other save an army by this frugal and expenseless means

---

[30] So Plato's *Republic* (VII, 536–E) advises that young boys should be induced to learn arithmetic and geometry voluntarily and not under compulsion. Quintilian (I, x, 39) thought that such studies should be made a kind of game, as they had been when Euclid first popularized the study of geometry.

[31] Practical farmers could still learn much from the three Roman treatises on agriculture which Milton mentions: the *De re rustica* of Cato the Censor (234–149 B.C.), the books *Rerum rusticarum* of Varro (116–27 B.C.), and the twelve books of Columella (first century A.D.) *De re rustica.*

[32] Perhaps Milton thought of Conti's interpretation (VII, i) of *Hercules'* cleansing of the Augean stables as a primitive allegory teaching the use of animal fertilizers.

[33] Aristotle's *Natural History of Animals* was often accompanied by extracts from the works of his successor in the leadership of the Peripatetic School at Athens, Theophrastus (372?–285 B.C.),

an *Enquiry into Plants* and the *Causes* (or *Development*) *of Plants,* as was the case in the Aldine edition of Aristotle's *Works* (1498).

[34] The *De architectura* of Vitruvius Pollio (first century B.C.) was highly valued by architects all over western Europe in the seventeenth century.

[35] The *Natural Questions* of Lucius Annaeus Seneca (8? B.C.–65 A.D.) was valued as an introduction to "general science," especially to astronomy.

[36] For Milton's contemporaries Pomponius Mela (first century A.D.) was still the "excellent cosmographer" whose work *Of the situation of the world, with the Longitude and Latitude of everie Kingdome, Regent, Province, Rivers, Mountaines, Cities and Countries* Arthur Golding had translated in 1585.

[37] Aulus Cornelius Celsus wrote an encyclopaedia of *Artes* in the first century A.D., extracts from which on pharmacy were published under the title "Flowers of Celsus" in an *Enchiridion medicum* as late as 1619.

[38] Every Englishman of any education knew the *Natural History* of Pliny the Elder (23?–79 A.D.), either in the original Latin or in Philemon Holland's popular translation (1601).

[39] Elizabethans had been sufficiently interested in the *Collectanea rerum memorabilium* of Caius Julius Solinus (third century A.D.) for Arthur Golding to translate it under the title, *Of the Noble Actions of Human Creatures,* as a kind of appendix to his translation of Pomponius Mela.

[40] *enginery:* engineering, mechanics.

[41] *institution of physic:* teaching of medicine.

[42] *humors:* blood, phlegm, choler, and melancholy, upon whose mixture or tempering in the body character and health were supposed to depend. Cf. *PL* II, 218; v, 484; and XI, 544; *Comus,* 810; and *SA,* the preface and l. 600.

[43] *crudity:* fit of indigestion.

only, and not let the healthy and stout bodies of young men rot away under him for want of this discipline—which is a great pity, and no less a shame to the commander. To set forward all these proceedings in nature and mathematics, what hinders but that they may procure, as oft as shall be needful, the helpful experiences of hunters, fowlers, fishermen, shepherds, gardeners, apothecaries; and in the other sciences, architects, engineers, mariners, anatomists; who doubtless would be ready, some for reward and some to favor such a hopeful seminary. And this will give them such a real tincture of natural knowledge as they shall never forget, but daily augment with delight. Then also those poets which are now counted most hard, will be both facile and pleasant: Orpheus,[44] Hesiod,[45] Theocritus,[46] Aratus,[47] Nicander,[48] Oppian,[49] Dionysius,[50] and, in Latin, Lucretius,[51] Manilius[52] and the rural part of Virgil.

By this time,[53] years and good general precepts will have furnished them more distinctly with that act of reason which in ethics is called Proairesis;[54] that they may with some judgment contemplate upon moral good and evil. Then will be required a special reinforcement of constant and sound indoctrinating to set them right and firm, instructing them more amply in the knowledge of virtue and the hatred of vice; while their young and pliant affections are led through all the moral works of Plato,[55] Xenophon, Cicero, Plutarch, Laertius,[56] and those Locrian remnants;[57] but still to be reduced[58] in their nightward studies wherewith they close the day's work, under the determinate sentence[59] of David or Solomon, or the evangels and apostolic scriptures. Being perfect in the knowledge of personal duty, they may then begin the study of economics.[60] And either now or before this, they may have easily learned at any odd hour the Italian tongue. And soon after, but with wariness and good antidote, it would be wholesome enough to let them taste some choice comedies, Greek, Latin, or Italian; those tragedies also that treat of household matters, as *Trachiniæ*, *Alcestis*, and the like.[61]

---

[44] The reference is to a poem on the magical virtues of precious stones, the *Lithica*, which was vaguely attributed to *Orpheus*.

[45] The *Works and Days* of Hesiod (eighth century B.C.) were almost as much valued as were Virgil's *Eclogues* and *Georgics*, which Milton calls his "rural part."

[46] For *Theocritus* see the Introduction to *Lyc*, paragraphs 3–4.

[47] For *Aratus* see *PL* V, 503 n.

[48] Like many ancient medical works, the *Theriaca* (on venomous animals) and the *Alexipharmaca* (on poisons and their antidotes) of Nicander (second century B.C.) were respected as of practical value.

[49] The *Halieutica* of Oppian (early third century A.D.?) was familiar in the Latin translation of Laurentius Lippius (1478), which was reprinted several times in the sixteenth century. It begins as a more or less unnatural natural history of fishes and ends as a treatise on fishing.

[50] The *Periegesis* of Dionysius of Alexandria (second century A.D.) surveys the geography of the ancient world in 1187 lines of hexameter verse.

[51] Milton's admiration for the *De rerum natura* of Lucretius (99?–55? B.C.) appears in several reminiscences of its boldest accounts of the natural evolution of life and civilization in *PL*: e.g. V, 503; X, 1073, n., and XI, 565, n.

[52] Milton's reference to the *Astronomica* of Manilius (first century A.D.) in DDD, n. 94, shows that he was most interested in the theological aspect of the work, which was original enough to combine scientific doubt of the Ptolemaic theory that the fixed stars are all equi-distant from the earth with a defense of the Stoic doctrine of the World-Soul.

[53] The pupils are at the end of the first three or four years of a curriculum which they would

begin at about twelve years of age and end at twenty.

[54] *Proairesis:* Aristotle's term for intelligent choice between good and evil in the *Nicomachean Ethics* II, iv, 3, is the key to Aristotle's conception of virtue as possible only for free and intelligent beings. Cf. *PL* III, 108.

[55] Cf. Milton's own youthful pleasure in the Platonic dialogues, Xenophon's *Apology for Socrates*, *Memorabilia*, *Banquet*, and perhaps the *Oeconomics*, and in Cicero's essay *On Friendship* and his treatises on ethics, *De officiis* and *De finibus*, is clear from his account of his early reading in *Apology*, p. 694. Cf. his appreciation of Plutarch's "Socratic discourses" above, n. 28.

[56] Nothing is known about Diogenes Laertius, to whom doubtful tradition attributes the *Lives and Opinions of Eminent Philosophers* (third century A.D.?), but it was frequently published in Italy in the sixteenth century as a popular manual.

[57] Cf. *PL* III, 718, n. for evidence of Milton's interest in the forgery called *On the Soul of the World*, which was attributed to Plato's "teacher" in the *Timaeus*, Timaeus of Locri.

[58] *reduced:* brought back.

[59] The biblical writers are *determinate*, i.e. conclusive, says D. S. Berkeley in *N&Q*, CXCIX (1954), 25, because their works contain the counsels and decrees of God.

[60] Cf. the use of *economize* in its root meaning of administration of a household or community in *TKM*, n. 163.

[61] In Sophocles' *Trachiniae* Deianira innocently

The next remove must be to the study of politics; to know the beginning, end, and reasons of political societies, that they may not in a dangerous fit of the commonwealth be such poor, shaken, uncertain reeds, of such a tottering conscience, as many of our great counsellors have lately shown themselves, but steadfast pillars of the state. After this, they are to dive into the grounds of law and legal justice; delivered first and with best warrant by Moses,[62] and as far as human prudence can be trusted, in those extolled remains of Grecian lawgivers, Lycurgus, Solon,[63] Zaleucus, Charondas,[64] and thence to all the Roman edicts and tables with their Justinian:[65] and so down to the Saxon and common laws of England, and the statutes.

Sundays also and every evening may be now understandingly spent in the highest matters of theology and church history ancient and modern; and ere this time the Hebrew tongue at a set hour might have been gained, that the scriptures may be now read in their own original; whereto it would be no impossibility to add the Chaldee and the Syrian[66] dialect. When all these employments are well conquered, then will the choice histories, heroic poems, and Attic tragedies[67] of stateliest and most regal argument, with all the famous political orations, offer themselves; which, if they were not only read, but some of them got by memory and solemnly pronounced with right accent and grace, as might be taught, would endue them even with the spirit and vigor of Demosthenes[68] or Cicero, Euripides or Sophocles.

And now, lastly, will be the time to read with them those organic[69] arts which enable men to discourse and write perspicuously, elegantly, and according to the fitted style of lofty, mean, or lowly.[70] Logic, therefore, so much as is useful, is to be referred to this due place with all her well-couched heads and topics, until it be time to open her contracted palm[71] into a graceful and ornate rhetoric, taught out of the rule of Plato, Aristotle, Phalereus,[72] Cicero, Hermogenes,[73] Longinus.[74] To which poetry

causes the death of her husband Hercules in an attempt to regain his love, and then kills herself in remorse. The more moving story of Euripides' *Alcestis* is the basis of *Sonn XXIII*.

[62] Milton's respect for *Moses* as a lawgiver is unmistakable in the Preface of *CG*, p. 641.

[63] Although Plutarch declared in his Life of *Lycurgus* that the Spartan law-giver forbade any of his laws to be put into written form, he makes it clear that they were designed to prevent tyranny from developing. In his Life of *Solon* he also stressed the safeguards against tyranny in the laws which Solon gave to the Athenians after the overthrow of the tyrant Peisistratus.

[64] In Stobaeus' Anthology Milton found the preface to the laws which *Zaleucus* was believed to have given to the Locrian Greeks in the eighth century B.C., and in Stobaeus he also found the preamble to the laws which *Charondas* gave to the Greeks of Catania in Sicily in the fifth century B.C. As Bentley later pointed out in his *Dissertation upon the Epistles of Phaleris*, both those almost legendary legislators were mistakenly believed to have been pupils of Pythagoras; whereas a forger "in the times of Ptolomee . . . made a System of Laws under the name of Zaleucus," and neither of the famous prefaces was really of ancient origin.

[65] The Twelve Tables were the earliest statement of Roman law and were understood to have been engraved on bronze about 450 B.C.. The Edicts were a gradually accumulating body of decrees of the Senate. In the *Institutes* and *Digest* of the Emperor Justinian the Great (483–565 A.D.) Roman law was finally codified.

[66] After the return of the Jews from Babylon in the fifth century B.C., Hebrew gave way to Aramaic (which is known as *Chaldee* in Dan. i, 4, Ezek. xxiii, 15–16, etc.), the prevailing language in southern Babylonia. *Syriac*, or Christian Aramaic, is the language of the oldest manuscripts of the Synoptic Gospels.

[67] Cf. *IlPen*, 97.

[68] Cf. *Sonn X*, 8.

[69] The arts of composing poems and plays are *organic* in the sense that such works must be skilfully organized.

[70] The three styles, *lofty*, *mean*, and *lowly*, were more strictly discriminated by Renaissance principles of decorum than are their rough modern equivalents of formal, informal, and colloquial levels of writing.

[71] The reference is to Aristotle's comparison—quoted by Cicero in *De finibus* II, vi—of logic to a *contracted palm*, and of rhetoric to an open hand. When Milton wrote these words he may already have been at work on his textbook of logic for his own pupils, *Artis logicae Plenior Institutio*, which was an independent development of the principles of the French logician, Peter Ramus, as Milton chose to qualify them in the light of his knowlege of classical logic.

[72] Milton may have been as much interested in Demetrius *Phalereus* (350–283 B.C.) for his orations defending Athenian liberty as for the work on the art *Of Expression*, which was already suspected to have been written by some later author.

[73] *Hermogenes* (second century A.D.) wrote five rhetorical works, some of which were much edited, abridged, and translated in the sixteenth century. They were often published with Aristotle's *Rhetoric*.

[74] Modern scholarship is doubtful even of the

would be made subsequent, or indeed rather precedent, as being less subtle and fine, but more simple, sensuous, and passionate.[75] I mean not here the prosody of a verse, which they could not but have hit on before among the rudiments of grammar; but that sublime art which in Aristotle's *Poetics,* in Horace, and the Italian commentaries of Castelvetro,[76] Tasso,[77] Mazzoni,[78] and others, teaches what the laws are of a true epic poem, what of a dramatic, what of a lyric, what decorum is,[79] which is the grand masterpiece to observe. This would make them soon perceive what despicable creatures our common rhymers and play-writers be, and show them what religious, what glorious and magnificent use might be made of poetry, both in divine and human things.

From hence, and not till now, will be the right season of forming them to be able writers and composers in every excellent matter, when they shall be thus fraught with an universal insight into things. Or whether they be to speak in parliament or council, honor and attention would be waiting on their lips. There would then also appear in pulpits other visages, other gestures, and stuff otherwise wrought than what we now sit under, ofttimes to as great a trial of our patience as any other that they preach to us. These are the studies wherein our noble and our gentle youth ought to bestow their time in a disciplinary way from twelve to one and twenty: unless they rely more upon their ancestors dead than upon themselves living. In which methodical

course it is so supposed they must proceed by the steady pace of learning onward, as at convenient times for memory's sake to retire back into the middle ward,[80] and sometimes into the rear of what they have been taught, until they have confirmed and solidly united the whole body of their perfected knowledge, like the last embattling of a Roman legion. Now will be worth the seeing what exercises and recreations may best agree and become these studies.

Their Exercise.

The course of study hitherto briefly described, is, what I can guess by reading, likest to those ancient and famous schools[81] of Pythagoras, Plato, Isocrates, Aristotle and such others, out of which were bred up such a number of renowned philosophers, orators, historians, poets, and princes all over Greece, Italy, and Asia, besides the flourishing studies[82] of Cyrene and Alexandria. But herein it shall exceed them and supply a defect as great as that which Plato noted in the commonwealth of Sparta;[83] whereas that city trained up their youth most for war, and these in their academies and Lycæum all for the gown, this institution of breeding which I here delineate shall be equally good both for peace and war. Therefore about an hour and a half ere they eat at noon should be allowed them for exercise and due rest afterwards; but the time for this may be enlarged at pleasure, according as their rising in the morning shall be early.

The exercise which I commend first is the exact use of their weapon,[84] to guard

existence of *Longinus* (first century A.D.), to whom the famous treatise *On the Sublime* is attributed.

[75] Milton is not defining the sublime art of poetry which had had its classical definition in Horace's *Art of Poetry* and Aristotle's *Poetics;* he is simply distinguishing poetry from rhetoric as *more simple, sensuous, and passionate* than any of the varieties of prose composition.

[76] Ludovico Castelvetro (1505–1571) was best known for his translation of Aristotle's *Poetics* (1570).

[77] Torquato Tasso's *Discourses on Epic Poetry* (Naples, 1594) may have had a special interest for Milton when he was a guest in the house of Tasso's Neapolitan patron, Manso.

[78] Two famous defenses of Dante's *Divine Comedy* against inappropriate criticism based upon Aristotle's *Poetics* were successively published by Jacopo Mazzoni in 1573 and 1587.

[79] The principle of *decorum* or propriety was regarded as a key both to problems of characterization in drama and epic and to problems of style in work of every kind. Cf. n. 70.

[80] *ward:* a division of an army or city.

[81] *Pythagoras'* "school" at Crotona in Sicily in the sixth century B.C. was perhaps essentially an almost monastic community living by the ideals to which Milton refers in *Prol* II and *El VI,* 59. Cf. *Music,* 21, n. Plato's "school" in the Academy and *Aristotle's* in the Lyceum at Athens were to some extent training grounds for young men, and so more definitely was the school of oratory which *Isocrates* founded near the Lyceum in 392 B.C.

[82] The *study* (Milton's rendering of Latin *studium,* school) or medical school which developed in Cyrene was less famous than the great center of literary and scientific activity which grew up in Alexandria in the last three centuries B.C.

[83] In the *Laws* (I, 633 and 636) Plato disapproved of the overemphasis on military training in Spartan education although he had great faith in athletic discipline as a moral training (*Laws* VII, 791).

[84] *their weapon:* the sword.

and to strike safely with edge or point; this will keep them healthy, nimble, strong, and well in breath—is also the likeliest means to make them grow large and tall, and to inspire them with a gallant and fearless courage, which, being tempered with seasonable lectures and precepts to them of true fortitude and patience, will turn into a native and heroic valor, and make them hate the cowardice of doing wrong. They must be also practised in all the locks and grips of wrestling, wherein Englishmen were wont to excel, as need may often be in fight to tug or grapple, and to close. And this perhaps will be enough wherein to prove and heat their single strength.

The interim of unsweating themselves regularly, and convenient rest before meat may, both with profit and delight, be taken up in recreating and composing their travailed spirits with the solemn and divine harmonies of music, heard or learned,[85] either while the skilful organist plies his grave and fancied descant[86] in lofty fugues, or the whole symphony with artful and unimaginable touches adorn and grace the well-studied chords of some choice composer; sometimes the lute or soft organ stop waiting on elegant voices, either to religious, martial, or civil ditties; which, if wise men and prophets be not extremely out, have a great power over dispositions and manners to smooth and make them gentle from rustic harshness and distempered passions.[87] The like also would not be inexpedient after meat to assist and cherish nature in her first concoction[88] and send their minds back to study in good tune and satisfaction. Where having followed it close under vigilant eyes till about two hours before supper, they are by a sudden alarum or watchword to be called out to their military motions, under sky or covert according to the season, as was the Roman wont; first on foot, then, as their age permits, on horseback, to all the art of cavalry; that having

in sport, but with much exactness and daily muster, served out the rudiments of their soldiership in all the skill of embattling, marching, encamping, fortifying, besieging, and battering, with all the helps of ancient and modern stratagems, tactics, and warlike maxims, they may as it were out of a long war come forth renowned and perfect commanders in the service of their country. They would not then, if they were trusted with fair and hopeful armies, suffer them for want of just and wise discipline[89] to shed away from about them like sick feathers, though they be never so oft supplied; they would not suffer their empty and unrecruitable[90] colonels of twenty men in a company to quaff out or convey into secret hoards the wages of a delusive list and a miserable remnant; yet in the meanwhile to be overmastered with a score or two of drunkards, the only soldiery left about them, or else to comply with all rapines and violences. No, certainly, if they knew aught of that knowledge that belongs to good men or good governors, they would not suffer these things.

But to return to our own institute: besides these constant exercises at home, there is another opportunity of gaining experience to be won from pleasure itself abroad. In those vernal seasons of the year when the air is calm and pleasant, it were an injury and sullenness against nature not to go out and see her riches and partake in her rejoicing with heaven and earth. I should not therefore be a persuader to them of studying much then, after two or three years that they have well laid their grounds, but to ride out in companies with prudent and staid guides to all the quarters of the land: learning and observing all places of strength, all commodities[91] of building and of soil,

---

[85] learned: acquired by practice.

[86] fancied descant: fanciful improvisation.

[87] Milton shared the Renaissance faith in Plato's doctrine that the right kind of musical education would train the just man to harmonize the principles of his nature into a character fit for noble action (Rep. III, 410), whereas bad music corrupts society (Laws, 656–7, 701, and 800). Cf. M. Y. Hughes in MLN, XL (1925), 129–37.

[88] concoction: digestion. Cf. PL V, 437.

[89] In the Civil War, says F. C. Montague in The History of England from the Accession of James I to the Restoration (London, 1907), p. 272, both sides conscripted soldiers, neither paid its troops punctually, and "indiscipline and desertion were common, but, since the king was much poorer than the Parliament, these evils were most glaring in his forces."

[90] In armies where colonels often recruited their own regiments it was not unusual for dishonest officers to keep their numbers low in order to embezzle as much of the soldiers' pay as possible. Recruits had a way of vanishing from such regiments.

[91] commodities: conveniences, suitability for various purposes.

for towns and tillage, harbors and ports for trade. Sometimes taking sea as far as to our navy, to learn there also what they can in the practical knowledge of sailing and of sea fight.

These ways would try all their peculiar gifts of nature; and if there were any secret excellence among them, would fetch it out and give it fair opportunities to advance itself by which could not but mightily redound to the good of this nation, and bring into fashion again those old admired virtues and excellencies, with far more advantage now in this purity of Christian knowledge. Nor shall we then need the monsieurs of Paris[92] to take our hopeful youth into their slight and prodigal custodies and send them over back again transformed into mimics, apes, and kickshaws.[93] But if they desire to see other countries at three or four and twenty years of age, not to learn principles but to enlarge experience and make wise observation, they will by that time be such as shall deserve the regard and honor of all men where they pass, and the society and friendship of those in all places who are best and most eminent. And perhaps then other nations will be glad to visit us for their breeding, or else to imitate us in their own country.

Now, lastly, for their diet there cannot be much to say, save only that it would be best in the same house; for much time else would be lost abroad, and many ill habits got; and that it should be plain, healthful, and moderate, I suppose is out of controversy. Thus, Mr. Hartlib, you have a general view in writing, as your desire was, of that which at several times I had discoursed with you concerning the best and noblest way of education; not beginning, as some have done, from the cradle, which yet might be worth many considerations. If brevity had not been my scope, many other circumstances also I could have mentioned, but this, to such as have the worth in them to make trial, for light and direction may be enough. Only I believe that this is not a bow for every man to shoot in that counts himself a teacher, but will require sinews almost equal to those which Homer gave Ulysses;[94] yet I am withal persuaded that it may prove much more easy in the assay[95] than it now seems at distance, and much more illustrious; howbeit, not more difficult than I imagine, and that imagination presents me with nothing but very happy and very possible according to best wishes; if God have so decreed, and this age have spirit and capacity enough to apprehend.

[92] In 1638 Milton cut his own stay in Paris short in order to hurry on to Italy, and in 1667 he wrote to his young friend, Richard Jones (C.E. XII, 99) praising him for "despising the luxuries of Paris" and for hastening to Italy to "enjoy the pleasures of literature and the conversation of the learned."
[93] The *O.E.D.* quotes Usshers' *Annals of the World:* "Xuthus a musician, Metrodorus a dancer, and all the Asian comicks and Kickshaws crept into the Court."

[94] Homer's story (*Od.* XXI) of *Ulysses'* bending the bow which Penelope's suitors could not bend, and slaying them all with it, had made the bow of Ulysses a symbol for any test of supreme strength. Milton was familiar with many humorous allusions to it, such as Ovid's in the *Amores* VIII, 47–48, but he used it here because Homeric criticism took it for granted, as Spenser said in his letter to Raleigh, prefixed to *The Faerie Queene,* that "in Ulysses" Homer "ensampled a good governour and a vertuous man."
[95] *assay:* experiment, practical experience.

THE REASON OF CHURCH GOVERNMENT
URGED AGAINST PRELATY

THE PREFACE

Bibliographical Note—The single edition of this pamphlet in Milton's lifetime was published early in 1642 in reply to a volume consisting of little treatises by eight more or less distinguished theologians, of whom Richard Hooker, Lancelot Andrewes, James Ussher, Martin Bucer, and Edward Brerewood were the best known. Its title was *Certain Briefe Treatises, Written by Diverse Learned Men, Concerning the Ancient and Moderne Government of the Church,* and its compiler was certainly Archbishop Ussher, who is one of the few contributors to whom there is a clear reference in Milton's Preface (see n. 5). The best annotated edition of *CG* is by Ralph A. Haug in the *Complete Prose Works of John Milton,* edited by Don M. Wolfe and others, Vol. I (New Haven, 1953), pp. 736–861. The present text is based upon the two copies of the first edition which are in the Houghton Library at Harvard.

In the publishing of human laws, which for the most part aim not beyond the good of civil society, to set them barely forth to the people without reason or preface, like a physical prescript,[1] or only with threatenings, as it were a lordly command, in the judgment of Plato was thought to be done neither generously nor wisely. His advice was, seeing that persuasion certainly is a more winning and more manlike way to keep men in obedience than fear, that to such laws as were of principal moment, there should be used as an induction some well-tempered discourse, showing how good, how gainful, how happy it must needs be to live according to honesty and justice; which being uttered with those native colors and graces of speech, as true eloquence,[2] the daughter of virtue, can best bestow upon her mother's praises, would so incite and in a manner charm the multitude into the love of that which is

[1] *physical prescript:* medical prescription. So in *Laws* IV, 720a, Plato compares good lawgivers to free-born professional physicians who can explain the nature and proper treatment of every disease to their patients; while bad lawgivers resemble slave doctors to whom the Athenians sent slaves for offhand treatment. Plato held that every law should have an official preamble explaining its rational grounds, and he illustrated his principle by devoting the tenth book of the *Laws* to a statement of his theology in justification of his law against sacrilege.

[2] *True eloquence* is contrasted with the false eloquence which Plato regarded as the worst enemy of individual and social discipline.

really good, as to embrace it ever after, not of custom and awe, which most men do, but of choice and purpose, with true and constant delight. But this practice we may learn from a better and more ancient authority than any heathen writer hath to give us, and indeed being a point of so high wisdom and worth, how could it be but we should find it in that book within whose sacred context all wisdom is enfolded? Moses,[3] therefore, the only lawgiver that we can believe to have been visibly taught of God, knowing how vain it was to write laws to men whose hearts were not first seasoned with the knowledge of God and of his works, began from the book of Genesis, as a prologue to his laws (which Josephus[4] right well hath noted), that the na-

[3] As good Calvinists, English Presbyterians shared John Calvin's reverence for *Moses* as God's chosen prophet, whom "he tooke vp into the mountaine, and separated him from the companie of men, to the end that when he should come to set forth his Law, the people should accept him as an Angell, and not as a mortal creature . . . And when he came down againe, his face shone as bright as it had beene another sunne." *The Sermons of M. John Calvin upon Deuteronomie.* Translated by Arthur Golding (1583), pp. 1–2.

[4] In the *Antiquities* Josephus says that "Moses . . . began not his ordinances with the treatise of contracts and covenants which we practice with one another, as other lawgivers are accustomed to do, but he hath lifted their spirits on high, to the end that they might think on God, and on the ornament of this world made by him, persuading that the most accomplished work among all those things which God had made in the world,

tion of the Jews, reading therein the universal goodness of God to all creatures in the creation, and his peculiar favor to them in his election of Abraham, their ancestor, from whom they could derive so many blessings upon themselves, might be moved to obey sincerely by knowing so good a reason of their obedience. If then, in the administration of civil justice and under the obscurity of ceremonial rites, such care was had by the wisest of the heathen, and by Moses among the Jews, to instruct them at least in a general reason of that government to which their subjection was required, how much more ought the members of the church, under the gospel, seek to inform their understanding in the reason of that government which the church claims to have over them: especially for that the church hath in her immediate cure those inner parts and affections of the mind where the seat of reason is, having power to examine our spiritual knowledge and to demand from us in God's behalf a service entirely reasonable. But because about the manner and order of this government, whether it ought to be presbyterial or prelatical, such endless question, or rather uproar, is arisen in this land, as may be justly termed, what the fever is to the physicians, the eternal reproach of our divines, whilst other profound clerks of late, greatly, as they conceive, to the advancement of prelaty, are so earnestly meting out the Lydian proconsular Asia,[5] to make good the prime metropolis of Ephesus, as if some of our prelates in all haste meant to change their soil and become neighbors to the English bishop of Chalcedon;[6] and whilst good

Breerwood[7] as busily bestirs himself in our vulgar tongue, to divide precisely the three patriarchates of Rome, Alexandria, and Antioch; and whether to any of these England doth belong: I shall in the meanwhile not cease to hope through the mercy and grace of Christ, the head and husband of his church, that England shortly is to belong, neither to see patriarchal nor see prelatical, but to the faithful feeding and disciplining of that ministerial order which the blessed apostles constituted throughout the churches; and this, I shall essay to prove, can be no other than that of presbyters[8] and deacons. And if any man incline to think I undertake a task too difficult for my years, I trust through the supreme enlightening assistance far otherwise; for my years, be they few or many, what imports it? So they bring reason, let that be looked on: and for the task, from hence that the question in hand is so needful to be known at this time, chiefly by every meaner capacity, and contains in it the explication of many admirable and heavenly privileges reached out to us by the gospel, I conclude the task must be easy: God having to this end ordained his gospel to be the revelation of his power and wisdom in Christ Jesus. And this is one depth of his wisdom, that he could so plainly reveal so great a measure of it to the gross, distorted

---

was the creation of us men. After he had made them capable of things concerning piety, then he might more easily perswade them in the rest." Thomas Lodge's translation (Ed. of 1640), pp. 2–3.

[5] Archbishop Ussher's contribution to *Certain Briefe Treatises* (see the Bibliographical Note) was a *Geographicall and Historicall Disquisition, touching the Lydian or Proconsular Asia, and the seven Metropoliticall Churches contained in it.* Ephesus was the most important of the metropolitan or archepiscopal sees from which Ussher argued that the early church had been administered in Asia Minor.

[6] The *bishop of Chalcedon*, Richard Smith (1566–1655), had been consecrated Jan. 12, 1625, by Cardinal Spada, then Papal Nuncio in Paris, to succeed William Bishop as Urban VIII's vicar apostolic for England and Scotland. In 1629 he had been indiscreet and the Vatican ceased to recog-

nize him. In 1635, when he was living under Cardinal Richelieu's protection in Paris, an effort seems to have been made by the Pope's representative, Gregorio Panzini, to persuade King Charles to consent to the re-establishment of Smith, who was still titular Bishop of Chalcedon in Asia Minor, as an acknowledged leader of the English Catholics, with his residence in London.

[7] Until its publication in *Certain Briefe Treatises*, Edward Brerewood's *The Patriarchall Government of the Ancient Church* had been lying in manuscript since some time before the author's death in 1613. Brerewood was a theologian and had taught Divinity at Oxford, where he was also an historian and astronomer, a member of the Old Society of Antiquaries, and at his death was professor of Astronomy at Gresham College in London. On historical evidence he held that every Roman province had had its bishop, archbishop, or patriarch in ancient times, and that, as "one of the VI *Dioceses* of the West Empire," England had "had a *Primate* of its owne: which . . . was the Arch-Bishop of Yorke" (p. 113).

[8] *presbyters*: literally, elders, though the word is the etymon of *priest*. Here it is used to mean a clergyman in charge of a church, as distinguished from a bishop.

apprehension of decayed mankind.[9] Let others, therefore, dread and shun the scriptures for their darkness; I shall wish I may deserve to be reckoned among those who admire and dwell upon them for their clearness. And this seems to be the cause why in those places of holy writ, wherein is treated of church government, the reasons thereof are not formally and professedly set down, because to him that heeds attentively the drift and scope of Christian profession, they easily imply themselves; which thing further to explain, having now prefaced enough, I shall no longer defer.

CHAPTER I.

That Church government is prescribed in the Gospel, and that to say otherwise is unsound.

The first and greatest reason of church government we may securely, with the assent of many on the adverse part, affirm to be because we find it so ordained and set out to us by the appointment of God in the scriptures; but whether this be presbyterial or prelatical, it cannot be brought to the scanning, until I have said what is meet to some who do not think it for the ease of their inconsequent opinions to grant that church discipline is platformed in the Bible, but that it is left to the discretion of men. To this conceit of theirs I answer that it is both unsound and untrue. For there is not that thing in the world of more grave and urgent importance throughout the whole life of man, than is discipline.[10] What need I instance? He that hath read with judgment of nations and commonwealths, of cities and camps, of peace and war, sea and land, will readily agree that the flourishing and decaying of all civil societies, all the moments and turnings of human occasions, are moved to and fro as upon the

axle of discipline. So that whatsoever power or sway in mortal things weaker men have attributed to fortune, I durst with more confidence (the honor of divine providence ever saved) ascribe either to the vigor or the slackness of discipline. Nor is there any sociable perfection in this life, civil or sacred, that can be above discipline; but she is that which with her musical chords preserves and holds all the parts thereof together.[11] Hence in those perfect armies of Cyrus in Xenophon,[12] and Scipio[13] in the Roman stories, the excellence of military skill was esteemed, not by the not needing, but by the readiest submitting to the edicts of their commander. And certainly discipline is not only the removal of disorder; but if any visible shape can be given to divine things, the very visible shape and image of virtue,[14] whereby she is not only seen in the regular gestures and motions of her heavenly paces as she walks, but also makes the harmony of her voice audible to mortal ears.[15] Yea, the angels themselves, in whom no disorder is feared, as the apostle[16] that saw them in his rapture describes, are distinguished and quarternioned into their celestial princedoms and satrapies,[17] according as God himself hath writ his imperial decrees through the great provinces of heaven. The state also of the blessed in paradise, though never so perfect, is not therefore left without discipline, whose golden surveying reed[18] marks out

[9] Milton thinks of human faculties as definitely deteriorated from the perfection of Adam's original creation in the image of God. Cf. *Educ, n.* 5.

[10] The stress in this chapter and the next on the *discipline* which English Presbyterians took from a key chapter in Calvin's *Institutes of the Christian Religion* (IV, xii), reveals both a moral code and an ideal of government. Calvin's discipline extended beyond the government of the church and its members to prescribe ideally severe principles for the government of both the family and the state.

[11] Cf. *Educ, n.* 87.

[12] In the *Cyropaedia* I, vi, Xenophon describes Cyrus' discipline of the Persian soldiers and recalls a conversation in which Cyrus is taught by his father, Cambyses, that the best obedience is the most willing.

[13] Cf. Scipio in *PL* IX, 510; *PR* II, 199; III, 34 and 102. His firm but moderate discipline of his troops was proverbial—particularly his development of a well disciplined army out of raw Sicilian conscripts in 205 B.C., as Dio Cassius records it (in Zonaras ix, 11).

[14] Cf. the incarnation of "Virtue in her shape how lovely" in the angel Zephon (*PL* IV, 848) and Satan's recognition of "the perfect shape" of the "good, wise, just" in Christ in *PR* III, 11.

[15] One of Milton's many references to the music of the spheres. Cf. *Prol* II and *Music,* 20.

[16] *The apostle* is St. John, and his rapture is the vision of Rev. vii–viii, with the angels ranged in order about the throne of God.

[17] Cf. *PL* Introduction, 21.

[18] The angel with "a golden reed to measure the city" of the New Jerusalem (Rev. xxi, 15) was explained in the commentary of the German theologian Paraeus (mentioned again in the Preface

and measures every quarter and circuit of New Jerusalem. Yet is it not to be conceived that those eternal effluences of sanctity and love live in the glorified saints should by this means be confined and cloyed with repetition of that which is prescribed, but that our happiness may orb itself into a thousand vagancies[19] of glory and delight, and with a kind of eccentrical equation be, as it were, an invariable planet of joy and felicity; how much less can we believe that God would leave his frail and feeble, though not less beloved church here below, to the perpetual stumble of conjecture and disturbance in this our dark voyage, without the card[20] and compass of discipline? Which is so hard to be of man's making that we may see even in the guidance of a civil state to worldly happiness, it is not for every learned or every wise man, though many of them consult in common, to invent or frame a discipline: but if it be at all the work of man, it must be of such a one as is a true knower of himself, and himself in whom contemplation and practice, wit, prudence, fortitude, and eloquence must be rarely met, both to comprehend the hidden causes of things and span in his thoughts all the various effects that passion or complexion[21] can work in man's nature; and hereto must his hand be at defiance with gain, and his heart in all virtues heroic. So far is it from the ken of these wretched projectors of ours that bescrawl their pamphlets every day with new forms of government for our church. And therefore all the ancient lawgivers were either truly inspired, as Moses, or were

to Book II of *CG*) as measuring the city with "the most perfect rule of faith and church discipline," the word of God.

[19] Planets (wanderers) are symbols of the joy which is free to circle (*orb*) in a course of unnumbered deviations (*vagancies*) from what might seem to be its true orbit, but to an astronomer understanding the equation which explains the eccentricities of the planet of our heavenly joy it is as invariable as are the planets whose seemingly eccentric courses around the sun (or, according to Ptolemaic astronomy, the earth) can be shown by the *eccentrical equation* to be *invariable*.

[20] *card*: mariner's chart.

[21] *complexion*: temperament or balance of the humors in the body, hence *character*. Cf. *PL* V, 484. Plato similarly described the ideal lawgiver as observing all the pains and pleasures of men in all situations, and as knowing how to control their passions by legal penalties and rewards (*Laws* I, 631e). Cf. *Areop*, n. 247.

such men as with authority enough might give it out to be so, as Minos,[22] Lycurgus,[23] Numa,[24] because they wisely forethought that men would never quietly submit to such a discipline as had not more of God's hand in it than man's. To come within the narrowness of household government, observation will show us many deep counsellors of state and judges to demean themselves incorruptly in the settled course of affairs, and many worthy preachers upright in their lives, powerful in their audience: but look upon either of these men where they are left to their own disciplining[25] at home, and you shall soon perceive, for all their single knowledge and uprightness, how deficient they are in the regulating of their own family; not only in what may concern the virtuous and decent composure of their minds in their several places, but, that which is of a lower and easier performance, the right possessing of the outward vessel, their body, in health or sickness, rest or labor, diet or abstinence, whereby to render it more pliant to the soul and useful to the commonwealth: which if men were but as good to discipline themselves as some are to tutor their horses and hawks, it could not be so gross in most households. If then it appear so hard and so little known, how to govern a house well, which is thought of so easy discharge and for every man's undertaking, what skill of man, what wisdom, what parts can be

[22] Though not traditionally a lawgiver, *Minos*—as Conti declares (III, vi; p. 211) in the light of several passages from the *Odyssey*—was the wisest of judges both as ruler in Crete and, after death, as chief justice in Hades.

[23] Cf. *Educ*, n. 63.

[24] *Numa*, said Machiavelli (*Discourses*, tr. by E. D., 1636, pp. 62–63), like every "maker of extraordinary lawes in a nation, had . . . recourse to God, for otherwise the lawes had not bin accepted. For many severall goodes are knowne by a wise man, which have not such evident reasons in themselves, that he by perswasion can make others conceive them. Therefore the wise men that would free themselves of this difficulty, have recourse to God; so did Lycurgus, so Solon, so many others."

[25] So Calvin said that, "In fellowship, yea no house, though it have but a small household, can be kept in right state without discipline; the same is much more necessarie in the Church, whose state ought to be most orderly of all." *Institutes of the Christian Religion*, tr. by Thomas Norton, 1634; IV, xii, i; p. 604. Calvin echoed I Tim. iii, 5. Cf. n. 10 above.

sufficient to give laws and ordinances to the elect household of God? If we could imagine that he had left it at random without his provident and gracious ordering, who is he so arrogant, so presumptuous, that durst dispose and guide the living ark of the Holy Ghost, though he should find it wandering in the field of Bethshemesh,[26] without the conscious warrant of some high calling? But no profane insolence can parallel that which our prelates dare avouch, to drive outrageously and shatter the holy ark of the church, not borne upon their shoulders with pains and labor in the word, but drawn with rude oxen, their officials, and their own brute inventions. Let them make shows of reforming while they will, so long as the church is mounted upon the prelatical cart, and not, as it ought, between the hands of the ministers, it will but shake and totter; and he that sets to his hand, though with a good intent to hinder the shogging of it in this unlawful waggonry wherein it rides, let him beware it be not fatal to him, as it was to Uzzah. Certainly if God be the father of his family the church, wherein could he express that name more than in training it up under his own allwise and dear economy, not turning it loose to the havoc of strangers and wolves,[27] that would ask no better plea than this, to do in the church of Christ whatever humor, faction, policy, or licentious will would prompt them to? Again, if Christ be the church's husband,[28] expecting her to be presented before him a pure unspotted virgin, in what could he show his tender love to her more than in prescribing his own ways which he best

knew would be to the improvement of her health and beauty, with much greater care doubtless than the Persian king could appoint for his queen Esther those maiden dietings and set prescriptions of baths and odors[29] which may tender her at last more amiable to his eye? For of any age or sex, most unfitly may a virgin be left to an uncertain and arbitrary education. Yea, though she be well instructed, yet is she still under a more strait tuition, especially if betrothed. In like manner the church bearing the same resemblance, it were not reason to think she should be left destitute of that care which is as necessary and proper to her as instruction. For public preaching indeed is the gift of the Spirit, working as best seems to his secret will, but discipline is the practic work of preaching directed and applied as is most requisite to particular duty; without which it were all one to the benefit of souls, as it would be to the cure of bodies, if all the physicians in London should get into the several pulpits of the city, and, assembling all the diseased in every parish, should begin a learned lecture of pleurisies, palsies, lethargies, to which perhaps none there present were inclined; and so, without so much as feeling one pulse, or giving the least order to any skilful apothecary, should dismiss 'em from time to time, some groaning, some languishing, some expiring, with this only charge, to look well to themselves and do as they hear.[30] Of what excellence and necessity then church discipline is, how beyond the faculty of man to frame and how dangerous to be left to man's invention, who would be every foot turning it to sinister ends; how properly also it is the work of God as father and of Christ as husband of the church, we have by thus much heard.

---

[26] II Sam. vi tells of David's attempt to move the ark of God "on a new cart," drawn by oxen, to a proper resting place. But "when they came to Nachon's threshingfloor, Uzzah put forth his hand to the ark of God, and took hold of it; for the oxen shook it. And the anger of the Lord was kindled against Uzzah; and God smote him there for his error; and there he died by the ark of God." I Sam. vi, 19 mentions the destruction of fifty thousand Philistines of *Bethshemesh* "because they had looked into the ark of the Lord."

[27] Cf. *Lyc*, 128.

[28] Cf. St. Paul saying to the Corinthian church: "I have espoused you to one husband, that I may present you as a chaste virgin to Christ" (II Cor. xi, 2).

[29] "Six months with oil of myrrh, and six months with sweet odours, and with other things for the purifying of the women" are mentioned in Esther ii, 12, as having been prescribed for Esther before her presentation to King Ahasuerus. Traditionally, Esther was an allegory of the presentation of the Church to Christ.

[30] A recurrence to the passage in Plato's *Laws* (720c) to which Milton refers earlier, in n. 1 above. Case histories, says Plato, meant nothing to the careless Athenian slave doctors.

CHAPTER II.

*That Church government is set down
in holy Scripture, and that to say
otherwise is untrue.*

As therefore it is unsound to say that
God hath not appointed any set government in his church, so it is untrue. Of the
time of the law there can be no doubt; for
to let pass the first institution of priests and
Levites, which is too clear to be insisted
upon, when the temple came to be built,
which in plain judgment could breed no
essential change, either in religion or in
the priestly government, yet God, to show
how little he could endure that men should
be tampering and contriving in his worship, though in things of less regard, gave
to David for Solomon not only a pattern
and model of the temple, but a direction for
the courses of the priests and Levites and
for all the work of their service. At the
return from the captivity things were only
restored after the ordinance of Moses and
David; or if the least alteration be to be
found, they had with them inspired men,
prophets; and it were not sober to say they
did aught of moment without divine intimation. In the prophecy of Ezekiel,[31]
from the fortieth chapter onward, after the
destruction of the temple, God, by his
prophet, seeking to wean the hearts of the
Jews from their old law, to expect a new
and more perfect reformation under Christ,
sets out before their eyes the stately fabric
and constitution of his church, with all the
ecclesiastical functions appertaining: indeed
the description is as sorted best to the apprehension of those times, typical and shadowy, but in such manner as never yet came
to pass, nor never must literally, unless we
mean to annihilate the gospel. But so exquisite and lively the description is in por-

traying the new state of the church, and
especially in those points where government seems to be most active, that both Jews
and Gentiles might have good cause to be
assured that God, whenever he meant to
reform his church, never intended to leave
the government thereof, delineated here in
such curious architecture, to be patched
afterwards and varnished over with the
devices and embellishings of man's imagination. Did God take such delight in
measuring out the pillars, arches, and doors
of a material temple? Was he so punctual
and circumspect in lavers,[32] altars, and sacrifices soon after to be abrogated, lest any
of these should have been made contrary
to his mind? Is not a far more perfect
work more agreeable to his perfection in
the most perfect state of the church militant, the new alliance of God to man?
Should not he rather now by his own prescribed discipline have cast his line and
level upon the soul of man, which is his
rational temple, and by the divine square
and compass thereof form and regenerate
in us the lovely shapes of virtues and graces,
the sooner to edify and accomplish that
immortal stature of Christ's body, which is
his church, in all her glorious lineaments
and proportions? And that this indeed
God hath done for us in the gospel we
shall see with open eyes, not under a veil.[33]
We may pass over the history of the Acts
and other places, turning only to those
epistles of St. Paul to Timothy and Titus,[34]
where the spiritual eye may discern more

---

31 The detailed specifications for Solomon's temple in I Kings vi and II Chron. iii–iv, and for the
reconstructed temple as it was ideally envisioned
by *Ezekiel* (Ezek. xl–xlvi) were all regarded by the
typical Presbyterian pamphleteer, Alexander Leighton, in his *Appeal to the Parliament* (1628) as
allegorical counterparts of the "platforme of government" which God had instantly prescribed as
soon as He had "ordained" a Church, either under
the *Law* or the *Gospell*" (p. 190).

32 In Solomon's temple, beside the great laver
where the priests washed their hands, there were
ten *lavers* of brass described in I Kings vii, 27–39,
as standing, five on the north and five on the south
side of the court of the priests, for cleansing sacrifices.

33 The minds of the Jews, said St. Paul (II Cor.
iii, 14), were blinded by a *veil* which "until this
day remaineth . . . in the reading of the old testament; which veil is done away in Christ."

34 Behind this passage was a long struggle between its episcopal interpreters, who regarded it as
actually constituting *Timothy* and *Titus* as bishops
in the primitive church, and the Presbyterians, who
accepted Calvin's view that in the early church
there were no distinctions between priests and
bishops, and that "Churches were governed by the
common counsell of the Elders" until bishops were
set up to check growing dissensions. Hence, said
Calvin, we should "let the Bishops know, that they
are above the Priests, rather by custome than by the
truth of the Lords disposing." (Commentary on
Titus i, 7.) Cf. n. 92 below.

goodly and gracefully erected than all the magnificence of temple or tabernacle, such a heavenly structure of evangelic discipline, so diffusive of knowledge and charity to the prosperous increase and growth of the church, that it cannot be wondered if that elegant and artful symmetry of the promised new temple in Ezekiel, and all those sumptuous things under the law, were made to signify the inward beauty and splendor of the Christian church thus governed. And whether this be commanded, let it now be judged. St. Paul, after his preface to the first of Timothy, which he concludes in the seventeenth verse with Amen, enters upon the subject of his epistle, which is to establish the church government with a command: "This charge I commit to thee, son Timothy; according to the prophecies which went before on thee, that thou by them mightest war a good warfare."[35] Which is plain enough thus expounded: This charge I commit to thee, wherein I now go about to instruct thee how thou shalt set up church discipline, that thou mightest war a good warfare, bearing thyself constantly and faithfully in the ministry, which, in the first to the Corinthians, is also called a warfare.[36] And so after a kind of parenthesis concerning Hymenæus,[37] he returns to his command, though under the mild word of exhorting (chap. ii, 1), "I exhort therefore;"—as if he had interrupted his former command by the occasional mention of Hymenæus. More beneath in the fourteenth verse of the third chapter, when he hath delivered the duties of bishops or presbyters and deacons, not once naming any other order in the church, he thus adds; "These things write I unto thee, hoping to come unto thee shortly (such necessity seems there was); but if I tarry long, that thou mayest know how thou oughtest to behave thyself in the house of God." From this place it may be justly asked whether Timothy by this here written might know what was to be known concerning the orders of church governors or no. If he might, then in such a clear text as this may we know too without

further jangle; if he might not, then did St. Paul write insufficiently, and moreover said not true, for he saith here he might know; and I persuade myself he did know ere this was written, but that the apostle had more regard to the instruction of us than to the informing of him. In the fifth chapter, after some other church precepts concerning discipline, mark what a dreadful command follows (v. 21): "I charge thee before God and the Lord Jesus Christ and the elect angels that thou observe these things." And as if all were not yet sure enough, he closes up the epistle with an adjuring charge thus: "I give thee charge in the sight of God, who quickeneth all things, and before Christ Jesus, that thou keep this commandment:" that is, the whole commandment concerning discipline, being the main purpose of the epistle: although Hooker[38] would fain have this denouncement referred to the particular precept going before, because the word commandment is in the singular number, not remembering that even in the first chapter of this epistle the word commandment is used in a plural sense (v. 5): "Now the end of the commandment is charity."[39] And what more frequent than in like manner to say the law of Moses? So that either to restrain the significance too much, or too much to enlarge it, would make the adjuration either not so weighty or not so pertinent. And thus we find here that the rules of church discipline are not only commanded but hedged about with such a terrible impalement of commands, as he that will break through wilfully to violate the least of them, must hazard the wounding of his conscience even to death. Yet all this notwithstanding, we shall find them broken well nigh all by the fair pretenders even of the next ages. No less to the contempt of him whom they feign to be the archfounder of prelaty, St. Peter,

---

[35] I Tim. i, 18.

[36] In I Cor. ix, 7, St. Paul refers to his ministry as "a warfare."

[37] In I Tim. i, 20, Hymenæus is mentioned as having, "concerning faith . . . made shipwreck."

[38] Richard Hooker's contribution to Certain Briefe Treatises is entitled, The causes of the continuance of these Contentions concerning Church-Government, but contains only a passing reference to St. Paul. Haug cites Of the Laws of Ecclesiastical Polity III, xi, 11 (1611, p. 117): "The very words themselves doe restraine themselves unto some one speciall commandement among many."

[39] I Tim. i, 5: "Now the end of the commandment is charity out of a pure heart, and of a good conscience, and of faith unfeigned."

who, by what he writes in the fifth[40] chapter of his first epistle, should seem to be far another man than tradition reports him: there he commits to the presbyters only full authority both of feeding the flock and episcopating; and commands that obedience be given to them as to the mighty hand of God, which is his mighty ordinance. Yet all this was as nothing to repel the venturous boldness of innovation that ensued, changing the decrees of God that is immutable, as if they had been breathed by man. Nevertheless when Christ by these visions of St. John[41] foreshows the reformation of his church, he bids him take his reed and mete it out again after the first pattern, for he prescribes him no other. "Arise," said the angel, "and measure the temple of God, and the altar, and them that worship therin." What is there in the world can measure men but discipline? Our word ruling imports no less. Doctrine indeed is the measure, or at least the reason of the measure, it is true; but unless the measure be applied to that which it is to measure, how can it actually do its proper work? Whether therefore discipline be all one with doctrine or the particular application thereof to this or that person, we all agree that doctrine must be such only as is commanded; or whether it be something really differing from doctrine, yet was it only of God's appointment as being the most adequate measure of the church and her children, which is here the office of a great evangelist and the reed given him from heaven. But that part of the temple which is not thus measured, so far is it from being in God's tuition or delight, that in the following verse he rejects it; however in show and visibility it may seem a part of his church, yet inasmuch as it lies thus unmeasured, he leaves it to be trampled by the Gentiles, that is to be polluted with idolatrous and Gentilish rites and ceremonies. And that the principal refor-

mation here foretold[42] is already come to pass as well in discipline as in doctrine, the state of our neighbor churches afford us to behold. Thus through all the periods and changes of the church it hath been proved that God hath still reserved to himself the right of enacting church government.

CHAPTER III.

That it is dangerous and unworthy the Gospel to hold that Church government is to be patterned by the Law, as Bishop Andrewes and the Primate of Armagh maintain.

We may return now from this interposing difficulty thus removed, to affirm that, since church government is so strictly commanded in God's word, the first and greatest reason why we should submit thereto is because God hath so commanded. But whether of these two, prelaty or presbytery, can prove itself to be supported by this first and greatest reason, must be the next dispute; wherein this position is to be first laid down as granted, that I may not follow a chase rather than an argument, that one of these two, and none other, is of God's ordaining; and if it be, that ordinance must be evident in the gospel. For the imperfect and obscure institution of the law, which the apostles themselves doubt[43] not ofttimes to vilify, cannot give rules to the complete and glorious ministration of the gospel, which looks on the law as on a child, not as on a tutor. And that the prelates have no sure foundation in the gospel, their own guiltiness doth manifest; they would not else run questing up as high as Adam to fetch their original, as it is said one of them lately did in public.[44] To which assertion, had I heard

---

[40] In I Peter v, 1, the general charge to the clergy of the churches of Pontus, Galatia, Cappadocia, Bithynia, and the Roman province of Asia, addresses them all simply as "elders" (i.e. presbyters or priests) and bids them (v, 2) "feed the flock of God."

[41] In his apocalyptic vision *St. John* saw himself given "a reed like unto a rod; and the angel stood, saying, Rise, and measure the temple of God, and the altar, and them that worship therein" (Rev. xi, 1–2).

[42] Milton had the authority of Paraeus for believing that St. John's apocalypse could be read as "a generall prophesie touching the restoring of the Church being declyned under Antichrist." *Commentarie on the Revelation*, p. 211. Cf. n. 18 above.

[43] *doubt*: hesitate. Milton thought of passages like St. Paul's discussion in Romans of the transcendence of the law of Moses by "the law of the spirit of life in Christ Jesus" (Rom. viii, 2), and of his bold suggestion that even "the Gentiles, which have not the law," might "do by nature the things contained in the law" (Rom. ii, 14).

[44] On evidence in *The Diurnall Occurrences and*

it, because I see they are so insatiable of antiquity,[45] I should have gladly assented and confessed them yet more ancient: for Lucifer, before Adam, was the first prelate angel, and both he, as is commonly thought, and our forefather Adam, as we all know, for aspiring above their orders were miserably degraded. But others, better advised, are content to receive their beginning from Aaron and his sons, among whom Bishop Andrewes[46] of late years, and in these times the Primate of Armagh,[47] for their learning are reputed the best able to say what may be said in this opinion. The primate in his discourse about the original of episcopacy newly revised, begins thus: "The ground of episcopacy is fetched partly from the pattern prescribed by God in the Old Testament, and partly from the imitation thereof brought in by the apostles." Herein I must entreat to be excused of the desire I have to be satisfied, how for example the ground of episcopacy is fetched partly from the example of the Old Testament, by whom next, and by whose authority. Secondly, how the church government under

the gospel can be rightly called an imitation of that in the Old Testament; for that the gospel is the end and fulfilling of the law, our liberty also from the bondage of the law,[48] I plainly read. How then the ripe age of the gospel should be put to school again and learn to govern herself from the infancy of the law, the stronger to imitate the weaker, the freeman to follow the captive, the learned to be lessoned by the rude, will be a hard undertaking to evince from any of those principles which either art or inspiration hath written. If anything done by the apostles may be drawn howsoever to a likeness of something Mosaical, if it cannot be proved that it was done of purpose in imitation, as having the right thereof grounded in nature and not in ceremony or type, it will little avail the matter. The whole Judaic law is either political (and to take pattern by that, no Christian nation ever thought itself obliged in conscience) or moral, which contains in it the observation of whatsoever is substantially and perpetually true and good, either in religion or course of life. That which is thus moral, besides what we fetch from those unwritten laws and ideas which nature hath engraven in us, the gospel, as stands with her dignity most, lectures to us from her own authentic handwriting and command, not copies out from the borrowed manuscript of a subservient scroll, by way of imitating. As well might she be said in her sacrament of water to imitate the baptism of John.[49] What though she retain excommunication used in the synagogue, retain the morality of the Sabbath, she does not therefore imitate the law, her underling, but perfect her. All that was morally delivered from the law to the gospel in the office of the priests and Levites was that there should be a ministry set apart to teach and discipline the church, both which duties the apostles thought

Dayly Proceedings of Both Houses, in This Great and Happy Parliament (1641), p. 415, Haug has shown that John Williams, Bishop of Lincoln, made the claim that Adam was the first bishop in a speech to the Lords in early November, 1641. On December 27th (when Williams had become Archbishop of York) he and eleven other bishops were so seriously insulted by mobs on their way to Westminster that they did not attend Parliament and formally protested to King Charles that all votes taken in their absence were void. For that protest Parliament committed them to the Tower of London on December 30th, and they were still in the Tower when CG was published.

45 "Antiquitarians" was Milton's contemptuous name in Ref (C. E. III, 14) for champions of episcopacy who leaned heavily on the Greek and Latin Fathers of the Church for authority.

46 Lancelot Andrewes (1555–1626) was the subject of Milton's El III. In Certain Briefe Treatises Andrewes' pamphlet is A summary view of the Government both of the Old and New Testament; his argument was a parallel between the Aaronic priesthood in the Old Testament and the pattern of government of the primitive church as he deduced it from the New Testament.

47 The primate of Armagh: Archbishop James Ussher, who was very unpopular with the Puritans for his support of King Charles in a sermon at Oxford which was published in 1644 under the title, The Sovereignes Power and the Subjects Duty. Cf. the bibliographical note and n. 5 above. Here the reference is to the longer of his tracts in Certain Briefe Treatises, The Originall of Bishops and Metropolitans; briefly laid downe by Martin Bucer, Iohn Rainoldes, and Iames Arch-Bishop of Armagh.

48 Like all the Presbyterian pamphleteers, Milton takes his stand on verses like St. Paul's statements that "Christ is the end of the law" (Rom. x, 4) and that Christians "have not received the spirit of bondage" (Rom viii, 15). Cf. CD I, xxvii (C.E. XVI, 146), and the discussions by Kelley in Argument, pp. 61–64, and Barker in Dilemma, pp. 19–59.

49 In Acts xix, 1–5, Paul persuades some disciples who had received the "baptism of repentance" of John the Baptist, to accept baptism "in the name of the Lord Jesus."

good to commit to the presbyters. And if any distinction of honor were to be made among them, they directed it should be to those not that only rule well, but especially to those that labor in the word and doctrine.[50] By which we are taught that laborious teaching is the most honorable prelaty that one minister can have above another in the gospel; if, therefore, the superiority of bishopship be grounded on the priesthood as a part of the moral law, it cannot be said to be an imitation; for it were ridiculous that morality should imitate morality, which ever was the same thing. This very word of patterning or imitating excludes episcopacy from the solid and grave ethical law, and betrays it to be a mere child of ceremony, or likelier some misbegotten thing that having plucked the gay feathers of her obsolete bravery to hide her own deformed bareness, now vaunts and glories in her stolen plumes. In the meanwhile, what danger there is against the very life of the gospel to make in anything the typical law her pattern, and how impossible in that which touches the priestly government, I shall use such light as I have received, to lay open. It cannot be unknown by what expressions the holy apostle St. Paul spares not to explain to us the nature and condition of the law, calling those ordinances which were the chief and essential offices of the priests, the elements and rudiments of the world, both weak and beggarly.[51] Now to breed and bring up the children of the promise, the heirs of liberty and grace, under such a kind of government as is professed to be but an imitation of that ministry which engendered to bondage the sons of Agar,[52] how can this be but a foul injury and derogation, if not

a cancelling of that birthright and immunity which Christ hath purchased for us with his blood? For the ministration of the law,[53] consisting of carnal things, drew to it such a ministry as consisted of carnal respects, dignity, precedence, and the like. And such a ministry established in the gospel, as is founded upon the points and terms of superiority and nests itself in worldly honors, will draw to it, and we see it doth, such a religion as runs back again to the old pomp and glory of the flesh. For doubtless there is a certain attraction and magnetic force betwixt the religion and the ministerial form thereof. If the religion be pure, spiritual, simple, and lowly, as the Gospel most truly is, such must the face of the ministry be. And in like manner if the form of the ministry be grounded in the worldly degrees of authority, honor, temporal jurisdiction, we see it with our eyes, it will turn the inward power and purity of the gospel into the outward carnality of the law, evaporating and exhaling the internal worship into empty conformities and gay shows. And what remains then but that we should run into as dangerous and deadly apostacy as our lamented neighbors the papists, who, by this very snare and pitfall of imitating the ceremonial law, fell into that irrecoverable superstition, as must needs make void the covenant of salvation to them that persist in this blindness?

CHAPTER IV.

That it is impossible to make the Priesthood of Aaron a pattern whereon to ground Episcopacy.

That which was promised next is to declare the impossibility of grounding evangelic government in the imitation of the Jewish priesthood; which will be done by considering both the quality of the persons and the office itself. Aaron and his sons

---

[50] "I Tim. 5." is Milton's marginal note. The reference is to verse 17: "Let the elders that rule well be counted worthy of double honor, especially they who labor in the word and doctrine."

[51] In Gal. iv, 9, Paul protests against the desire of some converted Jews to return "again to the weak and beggarly elements" of the Mosaic law.

[52] *Agar*, or Hagar, Abraham's bondwoman, bore him Ishmael, who figures in Gal. iv, 21-31, with Isaac, Abraham's son by his wife Sarah, "a freewoman," in an allegory of "the two covenants; the one . . . which gendereth to bondage, which is Agar," and the other, which is represented by the free woman's son and by the free city of Jerusalem, "which is above, . . . which is the mother of us all . . . So then, brethren, we are not children of the bondwoman, but of the free."

[53] The *ministration of the law* was even more influential in English ecclesiastical polity than appears from Milton's words. Its prestige is illuminated by the analogy between the royal supremacy in the English church and the powers of "the godly kings . . . among the Jews and Christian emperors of the primitive church" which was drawn by the second of the Canons of 1603.

were the princes of their tribe before they were sanctified to the priesthood:[54] that personal eminence which they held above the other Levites, they received not only from their office, but partly brought it into their office; and so from that time forward the priests were not chosen out of the whole number of the Levites, as our bishops, but were born inheritors of the dignity. Therefore, unless we shall choose our prelates only out of the nobility and let them run in a blood, there can be no possible imitation of lording over their brethren in regard of their persons altogether unlike. As for the office, which was a representation of Christ's own person more immediately in the high-priest,[55] and of his whole priestly office in all the other, to the performance of which the Levites were but as servitors and deacons, it was necessary there should be a distinction of dignity between two functions of so great odds. But there being no such difference among our ministers, unless it be in reference to the deacons, it is impossible to found a prelaty upon the imitation of this priesthood. For wherein, or in what work, is the office of a prelate excellent above that of a pastor? In ordination, you'll say; but flatly against scripture, for there we know Timothy[56] received ordination by the hands of the presbytery, notwithstanding all the vain delusions that are used to evade that testimony and maintain an unwarrantable usurpation. But wherefore should ordination be a cause of setting up a superior degree in the church? Is not that whereby Christ became our Savior a

higher and greater work than that whereby he did ordain messengers to preach and publish him our Savior? Every minister sustains the person of Christ in his highest work of communicating to us the mysteries of our salvation, and hath the power of binding and absolving; how should he need a higher dignity to represent or execute that which is an inferior work in Christ? Why should the performance of ordination, which is a lower office, exalt a prelate, and not the seldom discharge of a higher and more noble office, which is preaching and administering, much rather depress him? Verily, neither the nature nor the example of ordination doth any way require an imparity between the ordainer and the ordained. For what more natural than every like to produce his like, man to beget man, fire to propagate fire? And in examples of highest opinion the ordainer is inferior to the ordained; for the pope is not made by the precedent pope, but by cardinals, who ordain and consecrate to a higher and greater office than their own.

CHAPTER V.

To the Arguments of Bishop Andrewes and the Primate.

It follows here to attend to certain objections in a little treatise lately printed among others of like sort at Oxford, and in the title said to be "out of the rude draughts of Bishop Andrewes."[57] And surely they be rude draughts indeed, insomuch that it is marvel to think what his friends meant, to let come abroad such shallow reasonings with the name of a man so much bruited for learning. In the twelfth and twenty-third pages he seems most notoriously inconstant to himself; for in the former place he tells us he forbears to take any argument of prelaty from Aaron, as being the type of Christ. In the latter he can forbear no longer, but repents him of his rash gratuity, affirming, that to say, Christ being come in the flesh, his figure in the highpriest ceaseth, is the

---

[54] *The priesthood* was assigned to Aaron and his sons forever (Exod. xxvii, 21).

[55] Milton follows Paul in treating the *high priest* of Jewish temple worship as a type of Christ, who was incarnated "that he might be a merciful and faithful high priest . . . to make reconciliation for the sins of the people." (Heb. ii, 17).

[56] Milton replies to interpretations of *Timothy's* ordination by "the apostles and elders which were at Jerusalem" (Acts xvi, 4), with "the laying on of the hands of the presbytery" (I Tim. iv, 14) such as the following in Bishop Thomas Bilson's *Perpetuall Governement of Christes Churche* (1593), p. 302: "And touching hands laid on Timothy by the Presbyterie, you answere yourselves, for when you alleage that the Presbyterie did impose handes on Timothy, wee aske you whether all the Presbyterie had right and power to impose hands, or onely some of them? If all, then Laie Elders must either impose handes (which Calvine conclusively denieth [*Inst.* li. 4. ca. 3]) or be no part of the Presbyterie."

[57] The first tract in *Certain Briefe Treatises* was described on the titlepage as "Out Of the rude Draughts of Lancelot Andrewes, late Bishop of *Winchester.*" Cf. n. 46 above. Milton does not exaggerate the crudity of Andrewes' notes on p. 12.

shift of an anabaptist;[58] and stiffly argues that Christ being as well king as priest, was as well foreresembled by the kings then, as by the highpriest. So that if his coming take away the one type, it must also the other. Marvellous piece of divinity! and well worth that the land should pay six thousand pound a year for in a bishopric, although I read of no sophister among the Greeks that was so dear, neither Hippias nor Protagoras,[59] nor any whom the Socratic school famously refuted without hire. Here we have the type of the king sewed to the tippet[60] of the bishop, subtly to cast a jealousy upon the crown, as if the right of kings, like Meleager in the *Metamorphosis*,[61] were no longer-lived than the firebrand of prelaty. But more likely the prelates fearing (for their own guilty carriage protests they do fear[62]) that their fair days cannot long hold, practise, by possessing the king with this most false doctrine, to engage his power for them as in his own quarrel, that when they fall they may fall in a general ruin, just as cruel Tiberius would wish,

When I die let the earth be rolled in flames.[63]

But where, O Bishop, doth the purpose of the law set forth Christ to us as a king? That which never was intended in the law can never be abolished as part thereof. When the law was made, there was no

king: if before the law, or under the law, God by a special type in any king would foresignify the future kingdom of Christ, which is not yet visibly come, what was that to the law? The whole ceremonial law, and types can be in no law else, comprehends nothing but the propitiatory office of Christ's priesthood, which being in substance accomplished, both law and priesthood fades away of itself and passes into air like a transitory vision, and the right of kings neither stands by any type nor falls. We acknowledge that the civil magistrate wears an authority of God's giving,[64] and ought to be obeyed as his vicegerent. But to make a king a type, we say is an abusive and unskilful speech, and of a moral solidity makes it seem a ceremonial shadow. Therefore your typical chain of king and priest must unlink. But is not the type of priest taken away by Christ's coming? "No," saith this famous Protestant bishop of Winchester, "it is not, and he that saith it is, is an anabaptist."[65] What think ye, readers? Do ye not understand him? What can be gathered hence, but that the prelate would still sacrifice? Conceive him, readers, he would missificate.[66] Their altars, indeed, were in a fair forwardness, and by such arguments as these they were setting up the molten calf of their mass again, and of their great hierarch the pope. For if the type of priest be not taken away, then neither of the highpriest, it were a strange beheading; and highpriest more than one there cannot be, and that one can be no less than a pope. And this doubtless was the bent of his career, though never so covertly. Yea, but there was something else in the highpriest besides the figure, as is plain by St. Paul's acknowledging him. 'Tis true that in the seventeenth of

[58] The *Anabaptists* denied the efficacy of infant baptism and the right of civil authorities to interfere in ecclesiastical affairs. They were regarded as dangerous, secret inheritors of the communism of the early German Anabaptists who shared in the Peasants' Wars and were bloodily suppressed at Munster in 1535. Cf. n. 65 below, and *TKM* n. 195.

[59] In the prologue of Plato's *Hippias Major* the sophist is rallied by Socrates for his big fees. *Protagoras'* financial shrewdness as a professional teacher of wisdom figures in Plato's *Meno*, 91d, as well as in the *Protagoras*.

[60] *tippet* (spelled *typet* in the original): a formally cut scarf, part of a bishop's ecclesiastical dress.

[61] Ovid describes Althaea's careful preservation of the half-burnt brand on which the life of her baby, *Meleager*, depended. Years later she burnt the brand to avenge her brothers, Plexippus and Toxeus, whom Meleager had killed in a burst of anger (*Met.* VIII, 425–525).

[62] A reference to the episode which is recalled in n. 44 above.

[63] This verse is attributed to Nero by Suetonius in his *Life of Nero* xxxviii, and by Dio Cassius in the *Roman History* LXVIII.

[64] No Presbyterian writer denied that "the powers that be are ordained of God" (Rom. xiii, 1). Cf. *TKM*, n. 28.

[65] "This is the *Anabaptists* only shift," says Andrewes (p. 23. See notes 46 and 57 above.). "That we are to have no *Warres*: for the warres of the Iewes were but *figures* of our *spirituall Battell*. No *Magistrate*: for their Magistrates were but figures of our *Ministers, Pastors,* and *Doctors,* and, all by Christ's coming abolished." Cf. n. 108 below.

[66] *missificate*: celebrate mass, which is a sacrifice. Archbishop Laud's insistence that the communion table stand in the chancel of every church was resented by the Puritans as an attempt to make it serve as an altar.

Deuteronomy,[67] whence this authority arises to the priest in matters too hard for the secular judges, as must needs be many in the occasions of those times involved so with ceremonial niceties, no wonder though it be commanded to inquire at the mouth of the priests, who besides the magistrates, their colleagues, had the oracle of urim to consult with. And whether the highpriest Ananias[68] had not encroached beyond the limits of his priestly authority, or whether used it rightly, was no time then for St. Paul to contest about. But if this instance be able to assert any right of jurisdiction to the clergy, it must impart it in common to all ministers, since it were a great folly to seek for counsel in a hard intricate scruple from a dunce[69] prelate, when there might be found a speedier solution from a grave and learned minister whom God hath gifted with the judgment of urim more amply ofttimes than all the prelates together; and now in the gospel hath granted the privilege of this oraculous ephod[70] alike to all his ministers. The reason, therefore, of imparity[71] in the priests, being now, as is aforesaid, really annulled both in their person and in their representative office, what right of jurisdiction soever can be from this place Levitically[72] bequeathed, must descend upon the ministers of the gospel equally, as it finds them in all other points equal. Well, then, he is finally content to let Aaron go. Eleazar[73] will serve

his turn, as being a superior of superiors, and yet no type of Christ in Aaron's lifetime. O thou that wouldest wind into any figment or phantasm to save thy miter! Yet all this will not fadge,[74] though it be cunningly interpolished by some second hand with crooks and emendations: hear then, the type of Christ in some one particular, as of entering yearly into the holy of holies, and suchlike, rested upon the highpriest only as more immediately personating our Savior: but to resemble his whole satisfactory office[75] all the lineage of Aaron was no more than sufficient. And all or any of the priests, considered separately without relation to the highest, are but as a lifeless trunk and signify nothing. And this shows the excellence of Christ's sacrifice, who at once and in one person fulfilled that which many hundreds of priests many times repeating had enough to foreshow. What other imparity there was among themselves, we may safely suppose it depended on the dignity of their birth and family together with the circumstances of a carnal service, which might afford many priorities. And this I take to be the sum of what the bishop hath laid together to make plea for prelaty by imitation of the law: though indeed, if it may stand, it will infer popedom all as well. Many other courses he tries, enforcing himself with much ostentation of endless genealogies,[76] as if he were the man that St. Paul forewarns us of in Timothy,

[67] In Deut. xvii, 8–13, the Hebrews are commanded, when involved in personal quarrels, to go to the priests or Levites for "a sentence of judgment." Exod. viii, 30, directed Aaron to wear Urim and Thummim, mysterious stones of judgment, in his breastplate as highpriest; in Deut. xxxiii, 8, Urim and Thummim are mentioned as a charge of the tribe of Levi.

[68] When Paul was tried before the highpriest, Ananias, he recognized Ananias as "the ruler" of his people (Acts xxiii, 5). This passage was so much cited in defense of episcopacy that Lord Brooke protested against it as a precedent in A discourse opening the nature of the episcopacie, which is exercised in England (1641), p. 9.

[69] Cf. the reference to Duns Scotus, the "subtle doctor," in Areop, p. 729.

[70] The ephod, or priestly robe, and its "curious girdle" figure in Lev. viii, 7, together with the Urim and Thummim. Cf. n. 67 above.

[71] imparity: inequality, i.e., between the levels of priest and bishop.

[72] Levitically: In accordance with the laws laid down for the priests and Levites in Leviticus.

[73] In Num. xx, 26, Moses invests Eleazar with the highpriestly robes of his dying father Aaron.

In Andrewes' typology, Aaron, as Highpriest, was equated with Christ, while Eleazar, who before Aaron's death had been "Prince of the Princes of the Priests," was equated with the archbishops in the rule of the Christian church. The "Princes of the Priests" were regarded as types of Christian bishops. So Andrewes declared (p. 23) that it was not necessary to justify episcopal government in the church by straining Aaron's claim to be an archiepiscopal type. "For Eleazar being Princeps Principum, that is, having a superiour authoritie over the Superiours of the Levits in Aarons life time, was never by any in this point reputed a Type of Christ. So that, though Aaron be accounted such, yet Eleazar will serve our purpose."

[74] fadge: serve the purpose.

[75] Christ's satisfactory office is his work of making satisfaction or amends to God by his sacrificial death and mediation for the sins of men. Of that all the sacrifices ever offered by the Hebrew priests are inadequate as a type or symbol.

[76] In I Tim. i, 4, Paul warns Timothy not to "give heed to fables and endless genealogies." Milton applies the verse to the catalogues of bishops in the early church whom Andrewes listed as prototypes of the bishops in the Church of England.

but so unvigorously that I do not fear his winning of many to his cause, but such as doting upon great names are either over weak or over sudden of faith. I shall not refuse, therefore, to learn so much prudence as I find in the Roman soldier that attended the cross, not to stand breaking of legs when the breath is quite out of the body,[77] but pass to that which follows. The Primate of Armagh,[78] at the beginning of his tractate, seeks to avail himself of that place in the sixty-sixth of Isaiah,[79] "I will take of them for priests and Levites, saith the Lord," to uphold hereby such a form of superiority among the ministers of the gospel, succeeding those in the law, as the Lord's day did the sabbath. But certain if this method may be admitted of interpreting those prophetical passages concerning Christian times in a punctual correspondence, it may with equal probability be urged upon us that we are bound to observe some monthly solemnity answerable to the new moons, as well as the Lord's day which we keep in lieu of the sabbath: for in the twenty-third verse the prophet joins them in the same manner together, as before he did the priests and Levites, thus; "And it shall come to pass that from one new moon to another, and from one sabbath to another, shall all flesh come to worship before me, saith the Lord." Undoubtedly with as good consequence may it be alleged from hence that we are to solemnize some religious monthly meeting different from the sabbath, as from the other any distinct formality of ecclesiastical orders may be inferred. This rather will appear to be the lawful and unconstrained sense of the text, that God, in taking of them for priests and Levites, will not esteem them unworthy, though Gentiles, to undergo any function in the church, but will make of them a full and perfect ministry, as was that of the priests and Levites in their kind. And Bishop Andrewes himself, to end the con-

troversy, sends us a candid exposition of this quoted verse from the twenty-fourth page of his said book, plainly deciding that God, by those legal names there of priests and Levites, means our presbyters and deacons;[80] for which either ingenuous confession or slip of his pen we give him thanks, and withal to him that brought these treatises into one volume, who, setting the contradictions of two learned men so near together, did not foresee. What other deducements or analogies are cited out of St. Paul to prove a likeness between the ministers of the Old and New Testament, having tried their sinews, I judge they may pass without harm doing to our cause. We may remember then that prelaty neither hath nor can have foundation in the law, nor yet in the gospel; which assertion, as being for the plainness thereof a matter of eyesight rather than of disquisition, I voluntarily omit; not forgetting to specify this note again, that the earnest desire which the prelates have to build their hierarchy upon the sandy bottom of the law, gives us to see abundantly the little assurance which they find to rear up their high roofs by the authority of the gospel, repulsed as it were from the writings of the apostles and driven to take sanctuary among the Jews. Hence that open confession of the primate before mentioned: "Episcopacy is fetched partly from the pattern of the Old Testament, and partly from the New as an imitation of the Old;"[81] though nothing can be more rotten in divinity than such a position as this, and is all one as to say, "Episcopacy is partly of divine institution, and partly of man's own carving." For who gave the authority to fetch more from the pattern of the law than what the apostles had already fetched, if they fetched anything at all, as hath been proved they did not? So was Jeroboam's episcopacy[82] partly from the pattern of the

---

[77] John xix, 33.

[78] Archbishop Ussher's see of *Armagh* had been recognized as the archiepiscopal see of Ireland, in preference to Dublin, by the Lord Lieutenant, Strafford, after Ussher's consecration. Cf. n. 47 above.

[79] The reference is to Isa. lxvi, 19–21: ". . . and they shall declare my glory among the gentiles. . . . And I will also take of them for priests and for Levites, saith the Lord."

[80] Ussher expressly said (p. 24) that Isa. lxvi, 21, meant that "*God* himselfe saith of the *Christian* Church under the *Gentiles; that he will take* of the *Gentiles,* and make them *Priests* and *Levits* to himselfe (Esai. 66. 21) there calling our *Presbyters* and *Deacons* by those *Legall* names."

[81] Milton is quoting and slightly abridging a statement of Ussher on pp. 51–52 of *The Originall of Bishops and Metropolitans.*

[82] *Jeroboam's episcopacy* is an allusion to that king's abuse of his power to withdraw the ten northern tribes of Israel from worship in the temple at Jerusalem. He set up "calves of gold" at Dan

law and partly from the pattern of his own carnality; a parti-colored and a parti-membered episcopacy, and what can this be less than a monstrous? Others therefore among the prelates, perhaps not so well able to brook or rather to justify this foul relapsing to the old law, have condescended at last to a plain confessing that both the names and offices of bishops and presbyters at first were the same, and in the scriptures nowhere distinguished. This grants the Remonstrant[83] in the fifth section of his *Defense* and in the preface to his last short *Answer*. But what need respect be had whether he grant it or grant it not, whenas through all antiquity and even in the loftiest times of prelaty, we find it granted? Jerome,[84] the learnedest of the fathers, hides not his opinion that custom only, which the proverb calls a tyrant, was the maker of prelaty; before his audacious workmanship the churches were ruled in common by the presbyters; and such a certain truth this was esteemed that it became a decree among the papal canons compiled by Gratian.[85] Anselm also of Canterbury, who to uphold the points of his prelatism made himself a traitor to his country, yet, commenting the epistles to Titus and the Philippians,[86] acknowledges from the clear-

ness of the text what Jerome and the church rubric hath before acknowledged. He little dreamed then that the weeding-hook of reformation would after two ages pluck up his glorious poppy[87] from insulting over the good corn. Though since, some of our British prelates, seeing themselves pressed to produce scripture, try all their cunning, if the New Testament will not help them, to frame of their own heads, as it were with wax, a kind of mimic bishop limned out to the life of a dead priesthood. Or else they would strain us out a certain figurative prelate by wringing the collective allegory of those seven angels[88] into seven single rochets.[89] Howsoever, since it thus appears that custom was the creator of prelaty, being less ancient than the government of presbyters, it is an extreme folly to give them the hearing that tell us of bishops through so many ages: and if against their tedious muster of citations, sees, and successions, it be replied that wagers[90] and church antiquities, such as are repugnant to the plain dictate of scripture, are both alike the arguments of fools, they have their answer. We rather are to cite all those ages to an arraignment before the word of God, wherefore, and what pretending, how presuming they durst alter that divine institution of presbyters, which the apostles, who were no various and inconstant men, surely had set up in the churches; and why they choose to live by custom and catalog, or, as St. Paul saith, by sight and visibility,

---

and Bethel, and "made priests of the lowest of the people, which were not of the sons of Levi" (I Kings, xii, 27–31).

[83] *The Remonstrant* is Bishop Joseph Hall, who had used the word *Remonstrance* in the titles of three of his contributions to the pamphlet war over episcopacy. Milton's *Animadversions upon the Remonstrants Defence against Smectymnuus* (1641) was the first of his anti-episcopal tracts to be directed against Hall personally.

[84] St. *Jerome*, the author of the Latin Vulgate version of the Bible, left commentaries on Paul's Epistles to Timothy and Titus which were much discussed in the debate over episcopacy. The Presbyterians regarded St. Jerome as supporting their belief in the primitive parity of priests with bishops, and they relied upon Calvin's rendering of the key passage of Jerome in his commentary on I Tim. iii.

[85] Gratian's *Decretum,* the greatest medieval codification of Canon Law, was compiled about 1150 A.D. In Part I, Distinction xcv, chapter 5, it is plainly declared that a presbyter is the same as a bishop, and that it is only by custom that the latter takes precedence. Gratian, however, sustained episcopacy, although (as Calvin observed, *Institutes* IV, iv, 13) he acknowledged that under the Roman Empire the clergy shared the right to elect bishops with the emperors and nobles and, under proper safeguards, with the people. Cf. n. 123 below.

[86] No commentary on *Titus* or *Philippians* by

St. Anselm of Canterbury is known. Dom Anselm Strittmatter suggests that Milton refers to the *Commentary* of Herveus Burgidolensis (1080–1150?), which was published as by Anselm of Canterbury at Cologne in 1533 and 1612, at Paris in 1533 and 1549, and at Venice in 1547. Herveus describes bishops and presbyters as "the same."

[87] An allusion to the parable of the tares and the wheat in Matt. xiii, 24–30. Cf. *Areop,* n. 271.

[88] *those seven angels* are the angels of the seven churches to whom St. John was commanded to write his Apocalypse (Rev. i, 20; ii, 1, etc.). In *The Originall of Episcopacy,* p. 65, Ussher "deduced *Episcopacy* from the Apostolical times: and declared withal, that *the Angels of the seven Churches* were no other, but such as in the next age after the Apostles were by the Fathers tearmed *Bishops.*" Cf. n. 121 below.

[89] *rochets:* linen vestments "resembling the surplice, but having close sleeves reaching to the hands, worn especially by bishops and abbots." (Webster.)

[90] Milton anticipated Byron's contempt for the majority of men who "back their own opinions with a wager" (*Beppo* xxvii).

rather than by faith?[91] But first I conclude from their own mouths that God's command in scripture, which doubtless ought to be the first and greatest reason of church government, is wanting to prelaty. And certainly we have plenteous warrant in the doctrine of Christ to determine that the want of this reason is of itself sufficient to confute all other pretenses that may be brought in favor of it.

CHAPTER VI.

That Prelaty was not set up for Prevention of Schism, as is pretended, or if it were, that it performs not what it was first set up for, but quite the contrary.

Yet because it hath the outside of a specious reason, and specious things we know are aptest to work with human lightness and frailty, even against the solidest truth that sounds not plausibly, let us think it worth the examining for the love of infirmer Christians, of what importance this their second reason may be. Tradition they say hath taught them that, for the prevention of growing schism, the bishop was heaved above the presbyter.[92] And must tradition then ever thus to the world's end be the perpetual cankerworm to eat out God's commandments? Are his decrees so inconsiderate and so fickle that when the statutes of Solon or Lycurgus[93] shall prove durably good to many ages, his in forty years shall be found defective, ill contrived, and for needful causes to be altered? Our Savior and his apostles did not only foresee, but foretell and forewarn us to look for schism. Is it a thing to be imagined of God's wisdom, or at least of apostolic prudence, to set up such a government in the tenderness of the church as should incline, or not be more able than any other to oppose itself to schism? It was well known what a bold lurker schism was even in the household of Christ, between his own disciples and those of John the Baptist, about fasting;[94] and early in the Acts of the Apostles the noise of schism had almost drowned the proclaiming of the gospel;[95] yet we read not in scripture that any thought was had of making prelates, no, not in those places where dissension was most rife. If prelaty had been then esteemed a remedy against schism, where was it more needful than in that great variance among the Corinthians which St. Paul[96] so labored to reconcile? And whose eye could have found the fittest remedy sooner than his? And what could have made the remedy more available than to have used it speedily? And, lastly, what could have been more necessary than to have written it for our instruction? Yet we see he neither commended it to us nor used it himself. For the same division remaining there, or else bursting forth again more than twenty years after St. Paul's death, we find in Clement's epistle,[97] of venerable authority, written to the yet factious Corinthians, that they were still governed by presbyters. And the same of other churches out of Hermas,[98] and divers other the scholars of the apostles, by the late industry of the learned Salmasius appears.[99] Neither yet did this worthy Clement, St. Paul's disciple, though writing to

neglect of *fasting* against the criticism of the disciples of John.

[95] A reference, perhaps, to the "murmuring of the Grecians against the Hebrews" (Acts vi, 1) in the church in Jerusalem, and to the protests of "the apostles and brethren that were in Judaea" against Peter's preaching to "men uncircumcised" and eating with them in Caesarea (Acts xi, 1-3).

[96] Cf. Paul's protests against the "contentions" in the church at Corinth (I Cor. i, 11).

[97] *Clement* became Bishop of Rome in 92?A.D. and wrote his Epistles to the Corinthians in 96?. He pled for discipline in the church like that in the Roman legions and in the order of the heavens, as well as that in the Levitical Temple worship, but he did not imply a clear hierarchical distinction between presbyters (priests) and bishops.

[98] *Hermas*, Bishop of Rome 140?-50?, is regarded as the author of *The Book of Visions*, otherwise known as *The Shepherd*. In the principal vision of the Shepherd or Angel of Repentance the church is described as a tower of exactly fitting stones which represent the apostles, doctors, bishops, and other clergy, but without definite hierarchical distinctions.

[99] *Salmasius*, or Claude de Saumaise (1588-1653), was to be the author of *Defensio Regia pro Carolo Primo*, to which Milton was to reply with *Def 1* in 1651. His first important work dealt with the Papacy, and in 1641 he had published the book to which Milton refers here, *De episcopis et presbyteris*, at Leyden. Cf. p. 160 above.

[91] "For we walk by faith, and not by sight," (II Cor. v, 7).
[92] Cf. n. 34 above.
[93] Cf. n. 24 above.
[94] In Matt. ix, 14-15, Christ justifies his disciples'

them to lay aside schism, in the least word advise them to change the presbyterial government into prelaty. And therefore if God afterward gave or permitted this insurrection of episcopacy, it is to be feared he did it in his wrath, as he gave the Israelites a king.[100] With so good a will doth he use to alter his own chosen government once established. For mark whether this rare device of man's brain thus preferred before the ordinance of God, had better success than fleshly wisdom not counselling with God is wont to have. So far was it from removing schism, that if schism parted the congregations before, now it rent and mangled, now it raged. Heresy begat heresy with a certain monstrous haste of pregnancy in her birth, at once born and bringing forth. Contentions before brotherly were now hostile. Men went to choose their bishop as they went to a pitched field, and the day of his election was like the sacking of a city, sometimes ended with the blood of thousands. Nor this among heretics only, but men of the same belief, yea confessors, and that with such odious ambition that Eusebius,[101] in his eighth book, testifies he abhorred to write. And the reason is not obscure, for the poor dignity or rather burden of a parochial presbyter could not engage any great party, nor that to any deadly feud: but prelaty was a power of that extent and sway, that if her election were popular, it was seldom not the cause of some faction or broil in the church. But if her dignity came by favor of some prince, she was from that time his creature and obnoxious[102] to comply with his ends in state, were they right or wrong. So that instead of finding prelaty an impeacher of schism or faction, the more I search, the more I grow into all persuasion to think rather that faction and she, as with a spousal ring, are wedded together, never to be divorced. But here let

everyone behold the just and dreadful judgment of God meeting with the audacious pride of man that durst offer to mend the ordinances of heaven. God, out of the strife[103] of men, brought forth by his apostles to the church that beneficent and ever-distributing office of deacons, the stewards and ministers of holy alms: man, out of the pretended care of peace and unity, being caught in the snare of his impious boldness to correct the will of Christ, brought forth to himself upon the church that irreconcilable schism of perdition and apostacy, the Roman antichrist; for that the exaltation of the pope arose out of the reason of prelaty, it cannot be denied. And as I noted before that the pattern of the highpriest pleaded for in the gospel, (for take away the head priest, the rest are but a carcase,) sets up with better reason a pope than an archbishop, for if prelaty must still rise and rise till it come to a primate, why should it stay there? Whenas the catholic government is not to follow the division of kingdoms, the temple best representing the universal church and the highpriest the universal head; so I observe here, that if to quiet schism there must be one head of prelaty in a land or monarchy, rising from a provincial to a national primacy, there may upon better grounds of repressing schism be set up one catholic head over the catholic church. For the peace and good of the church is not terminated in the schismless estate of one or two kingdoms, but should be provided for by the joint consultation of all reformed Christendom: that all controversy may end in the final pronounce or canon of one archprimate or protestant pope; although by this means, for aught I see, all the diameters of schism may as well meet and be knit up in the center of one grand falsehood. Now let all impartial men arbitrate what goodly inference these two main reasons of the prelates have, that by a natural league of consequence make more for the pope than for themselves; yea, to say more home, are the very womb for a new subantichrist to breed in, if it be not rather the old force and power of the same man of sin counterfeiting protestant. It was not the prevention of schism, but it was schism itself, and the hateful thirst of lording in the church, that

---

[100] Cf. *TKM*, n. 72; and *Eikon,* Chap. xxviii, n. 19.

[101] The historian *Eusebius* of Caesarea (260?–340?) devoted the eighth book of his *Ecclesiastical History* to the persecution of the Church by Diocletian. The first chapter describes the Church as having been previously divided into violent factions armed with "the armour of spite and sharpe speares of opprobrious wordes; so that Bishops against Bishops, and people against people, raysed sedition" (Meredith Hanmer's translation, 1585; p. 145).

[102] *obnoxious:* under obligation.

[103] Cf. n. 95 above.

first bestowed a being upon prelaty; this was the true cause, but the pretense is still the same. The prelates, as they would have it thought, are the only mauls[104] of schism.[105] Forsooth if they be put down, a deluge of innumerable sects will follow; we shall be all Brownists,[106] Familists,[107] Anabaptists.[108] For the word Puritan seems to be quashed, and all that heretofore were counted such, are now Brownists. And thus do they raise an evil report upon the expected reforming grace that God hath bid us hope for; like those faithless spies[109] whose carcasses shall perish in the wilderness of their own confused ignorance and never taste the good of reformation. Do they keep away schism? If to bring a numb and chill stupidity of soul, an inactive blindness of mind upon the people by their leaden doctrine, or no doctrine at all, if to persecute all knowing and zealous Christians by the violence of their courts[110] be to keep away schism, they keep away schism indeed: and by this kind of discipline all Italy and Spain is as purely and politicly kept from schism as England hath been by them. With as good a plea might

the dead-palsy boast to a man. " 'Tis I that free you from stitches and pains, and the troublesome feeling of cold and heat, of wounds and strokes: if I were gone, all these would molest you." The winter might as well vaunt itself against the spring, "I destroy all noisome and rank weeds, I keep down all pestilent vapors." Yes, and all wholesome herbs and all fresh dews, by your violent and hidebound frost: but when the gentle west winds shall open the fruitful bosom of the earth, thus overgirded by your imprisonment, then the flowers put forth and spring, and then the sun shall scatter the mists, and the manuring hand of the tiller shall root up all that burdens the soil without thank to your bondage. But far worse than any frozen captivity is the bondage of prelates, for that other, if it keep down anything which is good within the earth, so doth it likewise that which is ill; but these let out freely the ill and keep down the good, or else keep down the lesser ill and let out the greatest. Be ashamed at last to tell the parliament ye curb schismatics, whenas they know ye cherish and side with papists and are now as it were one party with them and 'tis said they help to petition for ye.[111] Can we believe that your government strains in good earnest at the petty gnats[112] of schism, whenas we see it makes nothing to swallow the camel heresy of Rome, but that indeed your throats are of the right pharisaical strain? Where are those schismatics with whom the prelates hold such hot skirmish? Show us your acts, those glorious annals which your courts of loathed memory lately deceased have left us? Those schismatics I doubt me will be found the most of them such as whose only schism was to have spoke the truth against your high abominations and cruelties in the church; this is the

104 *mauls:* heavy hammers used for breaking stone etc.
105 The same charge is made by Lord Brooke in *A Discourse* (cf. n. 68 above). The parallel with *CG* is studied by Whiting in *Milieu,* pp. 302–310.
106 Robert Brown (1550?–1633) was the leader in the movement for absolute freedom of self-government by every congregation and the most important of the founders of Congregationalism.
107 The *Familists* spread from Holland to England in 1575 and were conspicuous (though never very influential) for their alleged abuses of the doctrine of brotherly love, as they were represented in *A description of the sect called the Family of Love . . . discovered by one Mrs. Susanna Snow* (1641) and in Thomas Middleton's *The Familie of Love* (1607).
108 Cf. n. 65 above. The *Anabaptists* were generally regarded as entertaining dangerous communistic principles and as the spiritual heirs of the leaders of the bloody peasant revolts of a century earlier in Germany.
109 The cowardice of the *spies* who were sent into Canaan by Moses (Num. xiii–xiv) and reported that its inhabitants were giants too strong for the Israelites to attack, was traditionally despicable.
110 Cf. the closing reference to the Inquisition's abuse of censorship of the press in Spain and Milton's parallel with it of the subservience of the Court of Star Chamber and inferior English courts to ecclesiastical abuse at the close of *Areop.* Here Milton aims mainly at the Court of High Commission, which had been abolished in 1641.

111 The suspicion that "the Prelates intend to bring in Popery," as Archbishop Laud remarked in his speech against the Puritan leaders, John Bastwick, Henry Burton, and William Prynne, on June 16, 1637, was at the heart of the Puritan objection to all the "innovations" in the services and furniture of the Church of England for which Laud was himself largely responsible. From Thomas Frankland, *The Annals of King James and King Charles the First* (London, 1681), p. 840, 1.
112 Christ called the Pharisees "blind guides, which strain at a gnat, and swallow a camel" (Matt. xxiii, 24).

TRUTHS VICTORY
AGAINST HERESIE;

All ſorts comprehended under theſe ten mentioned :

1. Papiſts, **2.** Familiſts, **3.** Arrians, **4.** Arminians, **5.** Anabaptiſts, **6.** Separatiſts, **7.** Antinomiſts, **8.** Monarchiſts. **9.** Millenariſts, **10.** Independents.

As alſo a Deſcription of the Truth, the Church of Chriſt, her preſent ſuffering eſtate for a ſhort time yet to come; and the glory that followeth at the generall Reſurrection.

By *I. G.* A faithfull lover and obeyer of the Truth.

Now I beſeech you, Brethren, mark them which cauſe diviſions and offences, contrary to the doctrine which you have learned, and avoid them, Rom. 16. 17.

Imprimatur, JOHN DOWNAME.

London, Printed for *H. R.* at the three Pigeons in *Pauls Church-yard,* 1645.

schism ye hate most, the removal of your criminous hierarchy. A politic government of yours, and of a pleasant conceit, set up to remove those as a pretended schism, that would remove you as a palpable heresy in government. If the schism would pardon ye that, she might go jagged in as many cuts and slashes as she pleased for you. As for the rending of the church, we have many reasons to think it is not that which ye labor to prevent, so much as the rending of your pontifical sleeves: that schism[113] would be the sorest schism to you;

that would be Brownism and Anabaptism indeed. If we go down, say you, as if Adrian's wall[114] were broke, a flood of sects will rush in. What sects? What are their opinions? Give us the inventory.[115]

schism: a tear or rent in cloth or fabric of any kind.

[114] The *wall* which the emperor Hadrian built "with great stakes driv'n in deep, and fastn'd together, in manner of a strong mound, 80 mile in length, to divide what was *Roman* from *Barbarian,*" as Milton described it in *Britain* (C.E. X, 81), was a symbol of civilized resistance to everything barbaric.

[115] Milton refers to the many lists of sects which were supposed to endanger true religion (usually Anglicanism or Presbyterianism), of which an in-

[113] Milton puns on the literal meaning of

It will appear both by your former prosecutions and your present instances, that they are only such to speak of as are offended with your lawless government, your ceremonies, your liturgy, an extract of the Mass-book translated.[116] But that they should be contemners of public prayer and churches used without superstition, I trust God will manifest it ere long to be as false a slander as your former slanders against the Scots.[117] Noise it till ye be hoarse that a rabble of sects will come in; it will be answered ye, No rabble, sir priest, but a unanimous multitude of good protestants will then join to the church, which now because of you stand separated. This will be the dreadful consequence of your removal. As for those terrible names of sectaries and schismatics which ye have got together, we know your manner of fight, when the quiver of your arguments, which is ever thin and weakly stored, after the first brunt is quite empty, your course is to betake ye to your other quiver of slander, wherein lies your best archery. And whom you could not move by sophistical arguing, them you think to confute by scandalous misnaming; thereby inciting the blinder sort of people to mislike and deride sound doctrine and good Christianity under two or three vile and hateful terms. But if we could easily endure and dissolve your doughtiest reasons in argument, we shall more easily bear the worst of your unreasonableness in calumny and false report: especially being foretold by Christ, that if he our master were by your predecessors called Samaritan and Beelzebub,[118] we

must not think it strange if his best disciples in the reformation, as at first by those of your tribe they were called Lollards[119] and Hussites, so now by you be termed Puritans and Brownists. But my hope is that the people of England will not suffer themselves to be juggled thus out of their faith and religion by a mist of names cast before their eyes, but will search wisely by the scriptures and look quite through this fraudulent aspersion of a disgraceful name into the things themselves: knowing that the primitive Christians in their times were accounted such as are now called Familists and Adamites,[120] or worse. And many on the prelatic side, like the church of Sardis,[121] have a name to live and yet are dead; to be protestants, and are indeed papists in most of their principles. Thus persuaded, this your old fallacy we shall soon unmask and quickly apprehend how you prevent schism, and who are your schismatics. But what if ye prevent and hinder all good means of preventing schism? That way which the apostles used, was to call a council: from which, by anything that can be learned from the fifteenth of the Acts, no faithful Christian was debarred, to whom knowledge and piety might give entrance. Of such a council as this every parochial consistory[122] is a right homogeneous and constituting part, being in itself as it were a little synod, and towards a general assembly moving upon her own basis in an even and firm progression, as those smaller squares in battle unite

Jerusalem said, He hath Beelzebub, and by the prince of the devils casteth he out devils" (Mark iii, 22).

[119] *Lollards* was the name given to the followers of the fourteenth-century reformer, John Wycliff, possession of whose books was forbidden by a bull of Pope Alexander V in 1409. The spread of Wycliffite doctrines on the Continent owed much to the Bohemian, John Huss, who was burned in 1415.

[120] The *Adamites* were a branch of the Anabaptists whose alleged practice of nudity was the butt of much popular wit and prejudice.

[121] "And unto the angel of the church in Sardis write; . . . I know thy works, that thou hast a name that thou livest, and art dead" (Rev. iii, 1). Cf. n. 88 above.

[122] *consistory*: an official assembly of the church. At the bottom of the Presbyterian organization was the parish; then came intermediate councils of widening territorial scope, culminating in provincial synods and finally in a national synod like the modern General Assembly of the Church of Scotland.

teresting example is furnished by the title page of Ephraim Pagitt's *Heresiography*. See page 658.

[116] In repeating this statement in *Eikon*, Chap. xvi (C.E. V, 220), Milton explains that he had in mind Edward VI's proclamation to "the Cornish rebels" in 1549 that the "service in the Englyshe tongue," which seemed to them "a newe service," was "indeed none but the olde. . . . The difference is that we ment godlye that you our subjectes sholde understande in Englishe, being our naturall Countrie tongue, that whiche was heretofore spoken in Latine" (Holinshed, *The Chronicles of England, Scotlande, Ireland . . .*, 1577; p. 1653, 1).

[117] Milton reminds his readers that only after the end of the second "Bishops' War" in the ignominious Treaty of Ripon, which Charles concluded on Oct. 21, 1640, did the bishops give up their effort to impose episcopacy on the Scottish Kirk.

[118] "And the scribes which came down from

in one great cube, the main phalanx, an emblem of truth and steadfastness. Whereas on the other side, prelaty ascending by a gradual monarchy from bishop to archbishop, from thence to primate, and from thence, for there can be no reason yielded neither in nature nor in religion wherefore, if it have lawfully mounted thus high, it should not be a lordly ascendant in the horoscope of the church, from primate to patriarch, and so to pope. I say, prelaty thus ascending in a continual pyramid upon pretense to perfect the church's unity, if notwithstanding it be found most needful, yea, the utmost help to darn up the rents of schism by calling a council, what does it but teach us that prelaty is of no force to effect this work, which she boasts to be her masterpiece, and that her pyramid aspires and sharpens to ambition, not to perfection or unity? This we know, that as often as any great schism disparts the church and synods be proclaimed, the presbyters have as great right there and as free vote of old as the bishops, which the canon law conceals not.[123] So that prelaty, if she will seek to close up divisions in the church, must be forced to dissolve and unmake her own pyramidal figure, which she affirms to be of such uniting power, whenas indeed it is the most dividing and schismatical form that geometricians know of, and must be fain to inglobe or incube herself among the presbyters; which she hating to do, sends her haughty prelates from all parts with their forked miters, the badge of schism, or the stamp of his cloven foot whom they serve I think, who, according to their hierarchies acuminating still higher and higher in a cone of prelaty, instead of healing up the gashes of the church, as it happens in such pointed bodies meeting, fall to gore one another with their sharp spires for upper place and precedence, till the council itself prove the greatest schism of all. And thus they are so far from hindering dissension that they have made unprofitable, and even noisome, the chiefest remedy we have to keep Christendom at one; which is by councils: and these, if we rightly consider apostolic example, are nothing else but general presbyteries. This seemed so far from the apostles to think much of, as if hereby their dignity were

[123] Cf. n. 85 above.

impaired, that, as we may gather by those epistles of Peter and John, which are likely to be latest written, when the church grew to a settling, like those heroic patricians of Rome[124] (if we may use such comparison) hasting to lay down their dictatorship, they rejoiced to call themselves and to be as fellow elders among their brethren; knowing that their high office was but as the scaffolding of the church yet unbuilt, and would be but a troublesome disfigurement so soon as the building was finished. But the lofty minds of an age or two after, such was their small discerning, thought it a poor indignity that the high-reared government of the church should so on a sudden, as it seemed to them, squat into a presbytery. Next, or rather before councils, the timeliest prevention of schism is to preach the gospel abundantly and powerfully throughout all the land, to instruct the youth religiously, to endeavor how the scriptures may be easiest understood by all men; to all which the proceedings of these men have been on set purpose contrary. But how, O prelates, should you remove schism, and how should you not remove and oppose all the means of removing schism? When prelaty is a schism itself from the most reformed and most flourishing of our neighbor churches abroad and a sad subject of discord and offense to the whole nation at home. The remedy which you allege, is the very disease we groan under and never can be to us a remedy but by removing itself. Your predecessors were believed to assume this preëminence above their brethren only that they might appease dissension. Now God and the church calls upon you for the same reason to lay it down, as being to thousands of good men offensive, burdensome, intolerable. Surrender that pledge which, unless you foully usurped it, the church gave you and now claims it again for the reason she first lent it. Discharge the trust committed to you, prevent schism; and that ye can never do, but by discharging yourselves. That government which ye hold, we confess, prevents much, hinders much, removes much: but what? the schisms and

[124] Milton thought of Roman dictators like L. Quintius Cincinnatus, who was called from the plow to supreme command in 458 B.C., and in sixteen days saved an army which had been trapped by the Aequians and returned to his farm. Cf. *PR* II, 446.

grievances of the church? no, but all the peace and unity, all the welfare not of the church alone, but of the whole kingdom. And if it be still permitted ye to hold, will cause the most sad, I know not whether separation be enough to say, but such a wide gulf of distraction in this land as will never close her dismal gap until ye be forced (for of yourselves you will never do as that Roman Curtius[125] nobly did) for the church's peace and your country's to leap into the midst and be no more seen. By this we shall know whether yours be that ancient prelaty, which you say was first constituted for the reduction of quiet and unanimity into the church, for then you will not delay to prefer that above your own preferment. If otherwise, we must be confident that your prelaty is nothing else but your ambition, an insolent preferring of yourselves above your brethren; and all your learned scraping in antiquity, even to disturb the bones of old Aaron and his sons in their graves, is but to maintain and set upon our necks a stately and severe dignity, which you call sacred, and is nothing in very deed but a grave and reverent gluttony, a sanctimonious avarice; in comparison of which, all the duties and dearnesses which ye owe to God or to his church, to law, custom, or nature, ye have resolved to set at nought. I could put you in mind what counsel Clement, a fellow laborer with the apostles, gave to the presbyters of Corinth, whom the people, though unjustly, sought to remove. "Who among you," saith he, "is noble-minded, who is pitiful, who is charitable, let him say thus, 'If for me this sedition, this enmity, these differences be, I willingly depart, I go my ways; only let the flock of Christ be at peace with the presbyters that are set over it.' He that shall do this," saith he, "shall get him great honor in the Lord, and all places will receive him."[126] This was Clement's counsel to good and holy men, that they should de-

part rather from their just office than by their stay to ravel out the seamless garment of concord in the church. But I have better counsel to give the prelates and far more acceptable to their ears; this advice in my opinion is fitter for them: Cling fast to your pontifical sees, bate not, quit yourselves like barons,[127] stand to the utmost for your haughty courts and votes in parliament. Still tell us that you prevent schism, though schism and combustion be the very issue of your bodies, your first-born; and set your country a bleeding in a prelatical mutiny to fight for your pomp, and that ill-favored weed of temporal honor, that sits dishonorably upon your laic shoulders, that ye may be fat and fleshy, swoln with high thoughts and big with mischievous designs, when God comes to visit upon you all this fourscore years vexation of his church under your Egyptian tyranny. For certainly of all those blessed souls which you have persecuted and those miserable ones which you have lost, the just vengeance does not sleep.

CHAPTER VII.

That those many Sects and Schisms by some supposed to be among us, and that rebellion in Ireland, ought not to be a hindrance, but a hastening of Reformation.

As for those many sects and divisions rumored abroad to be amongst us, it is not hard to perceive that they are partly the mere fictions and false alarms of the prelates, thereby to cast amazements and panic terrors into the hearts of weaker Christians, that they should not venture to change the present deformity of the church for fear of I know not what worse inconveniences. With the same objected fears and suspicions, we know that subtle prelate Gardiner[128] sought to divert the first reformation. It

---

125 When a chasm opened in the Roman forum in 362 B.C., which soothsayers declared could be closed only by a sacrifice of the city's greatest treasure, Marcus Curtius offered himself as a symbol of the sacrificial valor which should be Rome's most valued treasure, rode, fully armed, into the chasm, and disappeared as it closed. Livy says (*Roman History* VII, vi) that the Curtian Lake stood as memorial of his deed.

126 A free rendering of Clement's *I Corinthians* xxii, 14–15. Cf. n. 97 above.

127 Cf. Milton's scorn for the assertion of the bishops' right to rank as *barons* in Parliament (in *Eikon,* chap. iv C.E. V, 115).

128 Stephen *Gardiner* (1483?–1555), bishop of Winchester, was a strong opponent of Protestant reform in the later years of Henry VIII and under Edward VI. Under Mary, as Lord Chancellor, he was active in securing legislation under which a number of Protestants suffered. A full and favorable account of his struggle against the Reformers is that by Philip Hughes in *The Reformation in England,* Vol. II (New York, 1954), *passim.*

may suffice us to be taught by St. Paul, that there must be sects for the manifesting of those that are sound hearted.[129] These are but winds and flaws to try the floating vessel of our faith, whether it be stanch and sail well, whether our ballast be just, our anchorage and cable strong. By this is seen who lives by faith and certain knowledge, and who by credulity and the prevailing opinion of the age; whose virtue is of an unchangeable grain, and whose of a slight wash. If God come to try our constancy, we ought not to shrink or stand the less firmly for that, but pass on with more steadfast resolution to establish the truth, though it were through a lane of sects and heresies on each side. Other things men do to the glory of God: but sects and errors it seems God suffers to be for the glory of good men, that the world may know and reverence their true fortitude and undaunted constancy in the truth. Let us not therefore make these things an incumbrance or an excuse of our delay in reforming, which God sends us as an incitement to proceed with more honor and alacrity. For if there were no opposition, where were the trial of an unfeigned goodness and magnanimity? Virtue that wavers is not virtue, but vice revolted from itself and after a while returning. The actions of just and pious men do not darken in their middle course, but Solomon tells us they are as the shining light that shineth more and more unto the perfect day.[130] But if we shall suffer the trifling doubts and jealousies of future sects to overcloud the fair beginnings of purposed reformation, let us rather fear that another proverb of the same wise man be not upbraided to us, that "the way of the wicked is as darkness, they stumble at they know not what." If sects and schisms be turbulent in the unsettled estate of a church, while it lies under the amending hand, it best beseems our Christian courage to think they are but as the throes and pangs that go before the birth of reformation, and that the work itself is now in doing. For if we look but on the nature of elemental and mixed

things, we know they cannot suffer any change of one kind or quality into another without the struggle of contrarieties.[131] And in things artificial, seldom any elegance is wrought without a superfluous waste and refuse in the transaction. No marble statue can be politely carved, no fair edifice built without almost as much rubbish and sweeping. Insomuch that even in the spiritual conflict of St. Paul's conversion,[132] there fell scales from his eyes that were not perceived before. No wonder then in the reforming of a church, which is never brought to effect without the fierce encounter of truth and falsehood together, if, as it were the splinters and shares of so violent a jousting, there fall from between the shock many fond errors and fanatic opinions, which, when truth has the upper hand, and the reformation shall be perfected, will easily be rid out of the way or kept so low, as that they shall be only the exercise of our knowledge, not the disturbance or interruption of our faith. As for that which Barclay[133] in his *Image of Minds* writes concerning the horrible and barbarous conceits of Englishmen in their religion, I deem it spoken like what he was, a fugitive papist traducing the island whence he sprung. It may be more judiciously gathered from hence that the Englishman of many other nations is least atheistical and bears a natural disposition of much reverence and awe towards the Deity; but in his weakness and want of

---

[129] "For there must be also heresies among you, that they which are approved may be made manifest among you" (I Cor. xi, 19).

[130] The words paraphrase Prov. iv, 18. In the next sentence verse 19 is quoted.

[131] The figure stems from the ancient conception of earth, air, fire, and water, "the eldest birth of Nature's womb" (*PL* V, 180) in their primitive state as "fighting" (*PL* II, 1015) and "in mutiny" (*PL* II, 925) against one another and against all order, as Spenser describes them in *An Hyme in Honour of Love,* 78–82:
Each against other, by all meanes they may,
Threatning their owne confusion and decay.

[132] After *St. Paul* had been struck blind at the moment of his conversion on the road to Damascus, "scales as it were fell from his eyes" (Acts ix, 18).

[133] John *Barclay* (1582–1621), the writer of *Argenis* and a Catholic, satirized the Jesuits as severely as the English. In his *Icon animorum* (1614) he sketched the characteristics of several nations and described the English as divided by their pride "into divers sects and names; . . . onely by wilful obstinacy; and that which is most worthy of pity and laughter is this, that with cruell censure these sects doe persecute one another: holding that they onely are the children of God, and all others reprobates" (*The Mirrour of Mindes,* Englished by T. May, London, 1631, pp. 120–1).

better instruction, which among us too frequently is neglected, especially by the meaner sort, turning the bent of his own wits, with a scrupulous and ceaseless care what he might do to inform himself aright of God and his worship, he may fall not unlikely sometimes, as any other landman,[134] into an uncouth opinion. And verily if we look at his native towardliness in the roughcast without breeding, some nation or other may haply be better composed to a natural civility and right judgment than he. But if he get the benefit once of a wise and well-rectified nurture, which must first come in general from the godly vigilance of the church, I suppose that wherever mention is made of countries, manners, or men, the English people, among the first that shall be praised, may deserve to be accounted a right pious, right honest, and right hardy nation. But thus while some stand dallying and deferring to reform for fear of that which should mainly hasten them forward, lest schism and error should increase, we may now thank ourselves and our delays, if instead of schism a bloody and inhuman rebellion be struck in between our slow movings. Indeed against violent and powerful opposition there can be no just blame of a lingering dispatch. But this I urge against those that discourse it for a maxim, as if the swift opportunities of establishing or reforming religion were to attend upon the phlegm[135] of state business. In state many things at first are crude and hard to digest, which only time and deliberation can supple and concoct.[136] But in religion, wherein is no immaturity, nothing out of season, it goes far otherwise. The door of grace turns upon smooth hinges, wide opening to send out, but soon shutting to recall the precious offers of mercy to a nation: which, unless Watchfulness and Zeal, two quick-sighted and ready-handed virgins, be there in our behalf to receive, we lose:[137] and still the oftener we lose, the straiter[138] the door opens, and the less is offered. This is all we get by demurring in God's service. 'Tis not rebellion that ought to be the hindrance of reformation, but it is the want of this which is the cause of that. The prelates which boast themselves the only bridlers of schism, God knows have been so cold and backward both there and with us to repress heresy and idolatry, that either through their carelessness or their craft, all this mischief is befallen. What can the Irish subject do less in God's just displeasure against us than revenge upon English bodies the little care that our prelates have had of their souls?[139] Nor hath their negligence been new in that island, but ever notorious in Queen Elizabeth's days, as Camden,[140] their known friend, forbears not to complain. Yet so little are they touched with remorse of these their cruelties, for these cruelties are theirs, the bloody revenge of those souls which they have famished, that whenas against our brethren the Scots, who by their upright and loyal deeds have now bought themselves an honorable name to posterity, whatsoever malice by slander could invent, rage in hostility attempt, they greedily attempted; toward these murderous Irish, the enemies of God and mankind, a cursed offspring of their own connivance, no man takes notice but that they seem to be very calmly and indifferently affected. Where then should we begin to extinguish a rebellion that hath his cause from the misgovernment of the church? Where but at the

oil and go with him into his wedding, but the foolish virgins with empty lamps are shut out.

138 *straiter:* narrower, more closely.

139 Milton refers to the revolt in Ireland which began with a massacre of English and Scottish settlers in Ulster on Oct. 23, 1641. In *Eikon,* Chap. xii (C.E. V, 188), he quotes the exaggerated figure of 154,000 victims "in the Province of *Ulster* onely." Puritan opinion fixed the blame for the Irish revolt upon King Charles and, for different reasons, upon the bishops and clergy of the English church in Ireland as well as upon the native Irish themselves.

140 In *Britain, or a Chorographicall Description of the kingdomes, England, Scotland, and Ireland* . . . Translated by Philemon Holland (1610), Division of Scotland and Ireland, p. 82, William *Camden* said: "So firmely doth this nation [the Irish] persevere in the old religion of their forefathers, which the carelesse negligence of their prelates and ignorance together, hath beyond al measure encreased, whenas there be none to instruct and teach them otherwise."

---

134 *landman:* citizen of (any) land.

135 Among the traditional four humors of the body, blood, yellow and black bile, and *phlegm,* the last was associated with sluggish characters. Cf. *DDD* I, v, p. 710.

136 Cf. *PL* V, 412, and *Educ,* n. 88.

137 The wise *virgins* in Christ's parable (Matt. xxv, 1–13) wait for their lord with lamps full of

church's reformation and the removal of that government which pursues and wars with all good Christians under the name of schismatics, but maintains and fosters all papists and idolaters as tolerable Christians? And if the sacred Bible may be our light, we are neither without example nor the witness of God himself, that the corrupted estate of the church is both the cause of tumult and civil wars, and that to stint them, the peace of the church must first be settled. "Now for a long season," saith Azariah to King Asa,[141] "Israel hath been without the true God, and without a teaching priest, and without law: and in those times there was no peace to him that went out, nor to him that came in, but great vexations were upon all the inhabitants of the countries. And nation was destroyed of nation, and city of city, for God did vex them with all adversity. Be ye strong therefore," saith he to the reformers of that age, "and let not your hands be weak, for your work shall be rewarded." And in those prophets that lived in the times of reformation after the captivity often doth God stir up the people to consider that while establishment of church matters was neglected and put off, there was "no peace to him that went out or came in; for I," saith God, "had set all men every one against his neighbor." [142] But from the very day forward that they went seriously and effectually about the welfare of the church, he tells them that they themselves might perceive the sudden change of things into a prosperous and peaceful condition. But it will here be said that the reformation is a long work, and the miseries of Ireland are urgent of a speedy redress. They be indeed; and how speedy we are, the poor afflicted remnant of our martyred countrymen that sit there on the seashore, counting the hours of our delay with their sighs and the minutes with their falling tears, perhaps with the distilling of their bloody wounds, if they have not quite by this time cast off and almost cursed the vain hope of our foundered ships and aids, can best judge

how speedy we are to their relief. But let their succors be hasted[143] as all need and reason is, and let not therefore the reformation, which is the chiefest cause of success and victory, be still procrastinated. They of the captivity in their greatest extremities could find both counsel and hands enough at once to build and to expect the enemy's assault.[144] And we, for our parts, a populous and mighty nation, must needs be fallen into a strange plight either of effeminacy or confusion, if Ireland, that was once the conquest of one single earl with his private forces and the small assistance of a petty Kernish prince,[145] should now take up all the wisdom and prowess of this potent monarchy to quell a barbarous crew of rebels, whom, if we take but the right course to subdue, that is beginning at the reformation of our church, their own horrid murders and rapes will so fight against them that the very sutlers[146] and horse-boys of the camp will be able to rout and chase them without the staining of any noble sword. To proceed by other method in this enterprise, be our captains and commanders never so expert, will be as great an error in the art of war as any novice in soldiership ever committed. And thus I leave it as a declared truth that neither the fear of sects, no nor rebellion, can be a fit plea to stay reformation, but rather to push it forward with all possible diligence and speed.

141 This prophecy (II Chron. xv, 3–7) was made when *Asa* was returning from the rout of "an host of a thousand thousand" Ethiopians. Asa then put away "the abominable idols out of all the land of Judah and Benjamin."

142 "Zechariah viii, 10; Haggai 2." (These are Milton's notes.)

143 Milton wrote in the midst of the excitement over the first news of the rebellion and of the resentment over King Charles's attempt to take advantage of military preparations for its suppression. His conduct, said Thomas May in *The History of the Parliament of England* (London, 1853; p. 150), writing near the events that he recorded, was an "unhappy impediment to the sudden relief of Ireland; . . . and so heavily went all preparations, that it was long before the house of commons could find means to enable the lord lieutenant to send over so much as one regiment, for the defence of the castle and city of Dublin, which . . . landed there on the last day of December, 1641."

144 At the rebuilding of Jerusalem by Nehemiah, when the Samaritans threatened the work, "they which builded on the wall, . . . every one with his hands wrought in the work, and with the other hand held a weapon. (Neh. iv, 17).

145 Richard FitzGilbert de Clare, Earl of Pembroke, known in Ireland as "Strongbow," landed at Waterford in 1170 to support Dermot MacMurrouch, King of Leinster, and so prepared for the subjugation of the greater part of the island in 1171 by Henry II.

146 *sutlers:* traders on whom the troops depended for supplies.

THE SECOND BOOK.

How happy were it for this frail and, as it may be truly called, mortal life of man, since all earthly things which have the name of good and convenient in our daily use, are withal so cumbersome and full of trouble, if knowledge yet which is the best and lightsomest possession of the mind, were, as the common saying is, no burden, and that what is wanted of being a load to any part of the body, it did not with a heavy advantage overlay upon the spirit! For not to speak of that knowledge that rests in the contemplation of natural causes and dimensions,[147] which must needs be a lower wisdom, as the object is low, certain it is that he who hath obtained in more than the scantest measure to know anything distinctly of God and of his true worship, and what is infallibly good and happy in the state of man's life, what in itself evil and miserable, though vulgarly not so esteemed—he that hath obtained to know this, the only high valuable wisdom indeed, remembering also that God even to a strictness requires the improvement of these his entrusted gifts,[148] cannot but sustain a sorer burden of mind, and more pressing, than any supportable toil or weight which the body can labor under, how and in what manner he shall dispose and employ those sums of knowledge and illumination which God hath sent him into this world to trade with. And that which aggravates the burden more is that (having received amongst his allotted parcels certain precious truths of such an orient[149] luster as no diamond can equal, which nevertheless he has in charge to put off at any cheap rate, yea for

nothing to them that will) the great merchants of this world, fearing that this course would soon discover and disgrace the false glitter of their deceitful wares wherewith they abuse the people, like poor Indians with beads and glasses, practise by all means how they may suppress the venting of such rarities, and such a cheapness as would undo them, and turn their trash upon their hands. Therefore by gratifying the corrupt desires of men in fleshly doctrines, they stir them up to persecute with hatred and contempt all those that seek to bear themselves uprightly in this their spiritual factory:[150] which they foreseeing, though they cannot but testify of truth and the excellence of that heavenly traffic which they bring against what opposition or danger soever, yet needs must it sit heavily upon their spirits, that being, in God's prime intention and their own, selected heralds of peace and dispensers of treasure inestimable, without price, to them that have no pence, they find in the discharge of their commission that they are made the greatest variance and offense, a very sword and fire both in house and city over the whole earth. This is that which the sad prophet Jeremiah laments: "Woe is me, my mother, that thou hast borne me a man of strife and contention!"[151] And although divine inspiration must certainly have been sweet to those ancient prophets, yet the irksomeness of that truth which they brought was so unpleasant to them that everywhere they call it a burden. Yea, that mysterious book of revelation[152] which the great evangelist was bid to eat, as it had been some eye-brightening electuary of knowledge and foresight, though it were sweet in his mouth and in the learning, it was bitter in his belly, bitter

---

[147] So Bacon in *The Advancement* (I, i, 3; p. 9) distinguished the knowledge of divine things from knowledge produced from "the contemplation of God's creatures and works," which, "having regard to God," can give "no perfect knowledge, but wonder, which is broken knowledge."

[148] Milton regards the parable of the talents *entrusted* to good and negligent servants (Matt. xxv, 14–30) in much the way that he does in *Sonn* VII: "How soon hath time . . ."

[149] *orient,* meaning lustrous, was applied to pearls because the best of them came from the East. Milton thought of Christ's comparison of the kingdom of heaven to a "pearl of great price," to buy which a merchant "sold all that he had" (Matt. xiii, 46).

[150] *factory:* trading post, where Europeans bartered cheap wares with the native "Indians," either American or Asiatic.

[151] Jer. xv, 10. Cf. Matt. x, 34: "I came not to bring peace, but a sword."

[152] In Rev. x, 9, an angel commands John to take the mysterious book in his hand and "eat it up; and it shall make thy belly bitter, but it shall be in thy mouth sweet as honey." David Paraeus (See *SA* prefatory letter, n. 3), in his *Commentary on Revelation* (English version of 1644), interpreted this verse as teaching "the ministers of the word . . . earnestly to devour or eat up the doctrine of salvation divinely written and received from Christ, that is, diligently to read, understand, and meditate, & as it were to turne it into their verie moisture and blood."

in the denouncing. Nor was this hid from the wise poet Sophocles,[153] who in that place of his tragedy where Tiresias is called to resolve king Œdipus in a matter which he knew would be grievous, brings him in bemoaning his lot, that he knew more than other men. For surely to every good and peaceable man it must in nature needs be a hateful thing to be the displeaser and molester of thousands; much better would it like him doubtless to be the messenger of gladness and contentment, which is his chief intended business to all mankind, but that they resist and oppose their own true happiness. But when God commands to take the trumpet and blow a dolorous or a jarring blast, it lies not in man's will what he shall say or what he shall conceal. If he shall think to be silent, as Jeremiah[154] did because of the reproach and derision he met with daily, and "All his familiar friends watched for his halting," to be revenged on him for speaking the truth, he would be forced to confess as he confessed: "His word was in my heart as a burning fire shut up in my bones; I was weary with forbearing and could not stay." Which might teach these times not suddenly to condemn all things that are sharply spoken or vehemently written as proceeding out of stomach, virulence, and ill nature; but to consider rather that if the prelates have leave to say the worst that can be said and do the worst that can be done, while they strive to keep to themselves, to their great pleasure and commodity, those things which they ought to render up, no man can be justly offended with him that shall endeavor to impart and bestow, without any gain to himself, those sharp but saving words which would be a terror and a torment in him to keep back. For me, I have determined to lay up as the best treasure and solace of a good old age, if God vouchsafe it me, the honest liberty of free speech from my youth, where I shall think it available in so dear a concernment as the church's good. For if I be, either by disposition or what other cause, too inquisitive

or suspicious of myself and mine own doings, who can help it? But this I foresee, that should the church be brought under heavy oppression, and God have given me ability the while to reason against that man that should be the author of so foul a deed, or should she, by blessing from above on the industry and courage of faithful men, change this her distracted estate into better days without the least furtherance or contribution of those few talents which God at that present had lent me, I foresee what stories I should hear within myself, all my life after, of discourage and reproach. "Timorous and ungrateful, the church of God is now again at the foot of her insulting enemies, and thou bewailest. What matters it for thee, or thy bewailing? When time was, thou couldst not find a syllable of all that thou hadst read or studied, to utter in her behalf. Yet ease and leisure was given thee for thy retired thoughts, out of the sweat of other men. Thou hadst the diligence, the parts, the language of a man, if a vain subject were to be adorned or beautified, but when the cause of God and his church was to be pleaded, for which purpose that tongue was given thee which thou hast, God listened if he could hear thy voice among his zealous servants, but thou wert dumb as a beast; from henceforward be that which thine own brutish silence hath made thee." Or else I should have heard on the other ear: "Slothful, and ever to be set light by, the church hath now overcome her late distresses after the unwearied labors of many her true servants that stood up in her defense; thou also wouldst take upon thee to share amongst them of their joy: but wherefore thou? Where canst thou show any word or deed of thine which might have hastened her peace? Whatever thou dost now talk or write, or look, is the alms of other men's active prudence and zeal. Dare not now to say or do anything better than thy former sloth and infancy,[155] or if thou darest, thou dost impudently to make a thrifty purchase of boldness to thyself out of the painful merits of other men; what before was thy sin is now thy duty, to be abject and worthless." These and suchlike lessons as these, I know would have been

<hr>

[153] In Sophocles' *Oedipus the King*, 316–18 Tiresias unwillingly exposes Oedipus as the unwitting slayer of his father and the husband of his mother.

[154] In Jer. xx, 8–10, the prophet recalls that some doubters of his perseverance in delivering his message had become convinced that God's word was in his heart like a fire in his bones.

[155] *infancy*: speechlessness, the probable original Latin meaning of the word.

my matins duly and my evensong. But now by this little diligence, mark what a privilege I have gained; with good men and saints to claim my right of lamenting the tribulations of the church, if she should suffer, when others that have ventured nothing for her sake, have not the honor to be admitted mourners. But if she lift up her drooping head and prosper, among those that have something more than wished her welfare, I have my charter and freehold of rejoicing to me and my heirs. Concerning therefore this wayward subject against prelaty, the touching whereof is so distasteful and disquietous to a number of men, as by what hath been said I may deserve of charitable readers to be credited, that neither envy nor gall hath entered me upon this controversy, but the enforcement of conscience only and a preventive fear lest the omitting of this duty should be against me, when I would store up to myself the good provision of peaceful hours; so lest it should be still imputed to me, as I have found it hath been, that some self-pleasing humor of vainglory hath incited me to contest with men of high estimation, now while green years are upon my head; from this needless surmisal I shall hope to dissuade the intelligent and equal[156] auditor, if I can but say successfully that which in this exigent behoves me; although I would be heard only, if it might be, by the elegant and learned reader, to whom principally for a while I shall beg leave I may address myself. To him it will be no new thing though I tell him that if I hunted after praise by the ostentation of wit and learning, I should not write thus out of mine own season when I have neither yet completed to my mind the full circle of my private studies,[157] although I complain not of any insufficiency to the matter in hand; or were I ready to my wishes, it were a folly to commit anything elaborately composed to the careless and interrupted listening of these tumultuous times. Next, if I were wise only to mine own ends, I would certainly take such a subject as of itself might catch applause, whereas this

hath all the disadvantages on the contrary, and such a subject as the publishing whereof might be delayed at pleasure, and time enough to pencil it over with all the curious touches of art, even to the perfection of a faultless picture; whenas in this argument the not deferring is of great moment to the good speeding, that if solidity have leisure to do her office, art cannot have much.

Lastly, I should not choose this manner of writing, wherein knowing myself inferior to myself, led by the genial power of nature to another task, I have the use, as I may account it, but of my left hand. And though I shall be foolish in saying more to this purpose, yet, since it will be such a folly as wisest men going about to commit have only confessed and so committed, I may trust with more reason, because with more folly, to have courteous pardon. For although a poet, soaring in the high region of his fancies with his garland and singing robes about him, might without apology speak more of himself than I mean to do, yet for me sitting here below in the cool element of prose, a mortal thing among many readers of no empyreal conceit,[158] to venture and divulge unusual things of myself, I shall petition to the gentler sort, it may not be envy to me. I must say, therefore, that after I had from my first years by the ceaseless diligence and care of my father (whom God recompense) been exercised to the tongues and some sciences, as my age would suffer, by sundry masters and teachers both at home and at the schools, it was found that whether aught was imposed me by them that had the overlooking, or betaken to of mine own choice in English or other tongue, prosing or versing, but chiefly this latter, the style, by certain vital signs it had, was likely to live. But much latelier in the private academies of Italy, whither I was favored to resort—perceiving that some trifles which I had in memory, composed at under twenty or thereabout (for the manner is that everyone must give some proof of his wit and reading there) met with acceptance above what was looked for, and other

156 *equal:* impartial, fair-minded.
157 The course of systematic study of world history and culture which Milton pursued at Horton from 1632 to 1638, and for generous encouragement in which he thanked his father in *Patrem*, 67–92.

158 *empyreal conceit:* heavenly imagination. Cf. Milton's draft of "Empyreal Air" in *PL* VII, 14, as he looks back on his song of heavenly events in Book VI and invokes his Muse afresh for epic inspiration.

things which I had shifted in scarcity of books and conveniences to patch up amongst them, were received with written encomiums,[159] which the Italian is not forward to bestow on men of this side the Alps—I began thus far to assent both to them and divers of my friends here at home, and not less to an inward prompting which now grew daily upon me, that by labor and intent study (which I take to be my portion in this life) joined with the strong propensity of nature, I might perhaps leave something so written to aftertimes, as they should not willingly let it die. These thoughts at once possessed me, and these other; that if I were certain to write as men buy leases,[160] for three lives and downward, there ought no regard be sooner had than to God's glory, by the honor and instruction of my country. For which cause, and not only for that I knew it would be hard to arrive at the second rank among the Latins, I applied myself to that resolution which Ariosto[161] followed against the persuasions of Bembo, to fix all the industry and art I could unite to the adorning of my native tongue; not to make verbal curiosities the end, that were a toilsome vanity, but to be an interpreter and relater of the best and sagest things among mine own citizens throughout this island in the mother dialect. That what the greatest and choicest wits of Athens, Rome, or modern Italy, and those Hebrews of old did for their country, I, in my proportion, with this over and above of being a Christian, might do for mine; not caring to be once named abroad, though perhaps I could attain to that, but content with these British islands as my world; whose fortune hath hitherto been

that if the Athenians, as some say,[162] made their small deeds great and renowned by their eloquent writers, England hath had her noble achievements made small by the unskilful handling of monks and mechanics.[163]

Time serves not now, and perhaps I might seem too profuse to give any certain account of what the mind at home in the spacious circuits of her musing hath liberty to propose to herself, though of highest hope and hardest attempting; whether that epic form whereof the two poems of Homer and those other two of Virgil and Tasso are a diffuse, and the book of Job[164] a brief model: or whether the rules of Aristotle[165] herein are strictly to be kept, or nature to be followed, which in them that know art and use judgment, is no transgression but an enriching of art: and lastly, what king or knight before the conquest might be chosen in whom to lay the pattern of a

[159] The poems by the Marquis of Manso, the Roman poet Giovanni Salzilli, and the Florentine, Antonio Francini, which Milton prefixed to the edition of his early poems in 1645, are examples of these *encomiums*.

[160] Such *leases* are defined by the *O.E.D.* as to "remain in force during the longest liver of three specified persons."

[161] Ludovico *Ariosto* (1474–1533) was well known to have told Cardinal Bembo that he would "rather be one of the first Italian authors than barely a second among the Latins." In Giovanni Pigna's life of Ariosto, which was prefixed to many editions of the *Orlando Furioso*, he is described as deliberately disusing the skill in Latin verse which he had learned in youth and deciding for patriotic motives to write in Italian.

[162] Haug notes that the saying comes from Sallust's *Catiline* viii.

[163] Milton had already been examining the monastic chronicles on which he had to depend as sources for *Britain*, and for which he expressed contempt on many of its pages because they were mechanically compiled and naively credulous and prejudiced.

[164] Contemporary criticism accepted poems like the *Iliad*, the *Aeneid*, and the *Jerusalem Delivered* of Torquato Tasso as examples of the long epic which Aristotle defined in the *Poetics*, xxvi, and may have regarded the *book of Job* as an example of his shorter epic, but they can hardly have been blind to the dramatic elements in Job which Martin Luther recognized in his *Table Talk* (*Tischreden* IV, 405–6). Cf. Charles W. Jones on "Milton's 'Brief Epic,'" in *SP*, XLIV (1947), 216–18.

[165] Critical discussion of the *Orlando Furioso* and the *Jerusalem Delivered* had gone to extremes in condemning and justifying the irregularity of the former and the regularity of the latter in the light of Aristotle's epic principles. During his Italian journey Milton must have heard much discussion of epic theory, and C. S. Lewis is probably right in suggesting in *Preface*, p. 5, that he was familiar with a passage in Tasso's *Discourses on the Heroic Poem* which contrasts Aristotle's doctrine of strict epic unity with the taste for multiple elements in the loosely constructed plots of romances like Ariosto's *Orlando*. But Milton may have used the word "nature" as Galileo did in his *Considerations*, when in comparing the two poems he stressed Ariosto's realism from the point of view of a natural scientist interested in the pictorial power of poetry. The greater realism of Ariosto's kaleidoscopic plot in terms of its resemblance to actual experience had been defended by Alessandro Tassoni and several other Italians in the sixteen twenties.

Christian hero.[166] And as Tasso[167] gave to a prince of Italy his choice whether he would command him to write of Godfrey's expedition against the Infidels, or Belisarius against the Goths, or Charlemain against the Lombards; if to the instinct of nature and the emboldening of art aught may be trusted, and that there be nothing adverse in our climate[168] or the fate of this age, it haply would be no rashness, from an equal diligence and inclination, to present the like offer in our own ancient stories: or whether those dramatic constitutions, wherein Sophocles and Euripides[169] reign, shall be found more doctrinal and exemplary to a nation. The scripture also affords us a divine pastoral drama in the Song of Solomon,[170] consisting of two persons and a

double chorus, as Origen rightly judges. And the Apocalypse of St. John is the majestic image of a high and stately tragedy,[171] shutting up and intermingling her solemn scenes and acts with a sevenfold chorus of hallelujahs and harping symphonies: and this my opinion the grave authority of Pareus, commenting that book, is sufficient to confirm. Or if occasion shall lead to imitate those magnific odes and hymns wherein Pindarus and Callimachus[172] are in most things worthy, some others in their frame judicious, in their matter most an end faulty. But those frequent songs[173] throughout the law and prophets beyond all these, not in their divine argument alone, but in the very critical art of composition, may be easily made appear over all the kinds of lyric poesy to be incomparable. These abilities, wheresoever they be found, are the inspired gift of God rarely bestowed, but yet to some (though most abuse) in every nation; and are of power beside the office of a pulpit, to inbreed and cherish in a great people the seeds of virtue and public civility, to allay the perturbations of the mind and set the affections in right tune, to celebrate in glorious and lofty hymns the throne and equipage of God's almightiness, and what he works and what

166 Cf. Milton's confession of his hope of writing a Christian epic on King Arthur in *Manso*, 80–84, and of his abandonment of such epic themes in *PL* IX, 25–41. Cf. also P. F. Jones, "Milton and the Epic Subject from British History," *PMLA*, XLII (1927), pp. 901–9, and M. M. Ross, *Milton's Royalism*, pp. 54–56, for a survey of the political motives which led Milton to prefer a Saxon hero like Alfred at this time to Arthur.

167 When *Tasso* planned the *Jerusalem Delivered*, he was a pensioner of Cardinal Luigi d'Este at the court of his brother, Alfonso II, Duke of Ferrara. Beside Godfrey of Bouillon's conquest of the Holy Land, *Tasso* thought of two other Christian conquests as possible subjects: the reconquest of Italy from the Ostrogoths by Belisarius in 538–40 A.D., and *Charlemagne's* victory over the *Lombards* in 774.

168 Milton's interest in the originally Aristotelian idea that the *climate* of northern Europe was unfavorable to the development of the highest intelligence may have been sharpened by its prominence in Jean Bodin's *Six Books of the Republic*, which he quotes in Chap. iii below. Cf. *Manso*, 28, and *PL* IX, 44–45, notes.

169 Cf. Milton's justification of the ethical value of Greek tragedy in his preface to *SA*.

170 This reference to the Song of Solomon is explained by the following passage from Paraeus' *Commentary on the Revelation*, which comes on p. 20 in Arnold's translation (1644), immediately before the remarks about the Apocalypse to which Milton next refers: "What Origen therefore wrote (in Prologo Cant. & Homil. I) touching the *Song of Songs: that it seemed to him Solomon wrote a wedding song after the manner of a Drama: which*, saith he, *is a song of* many Personages: . . . and he calleth that *wedding Verse a Spirituall Interlude of foure Personages, which* he saith *the Lord revealed unto him in the same; viz. the Bridegroom and Bride: with the Bride her Virgins: with the Bridegroom his flock of Companions:* The same thing I more truly may say touching the Revelation, that it seemes unto mee, the Lord Iesus revealed the same unto Iohn by his Angell, after the manner of a *Drammaticall Representation*."

171 Paraeus then goes on to call Revelation "a *Propheticall Drama*, show, or representation. For as in human Tragedies, diverse persons one after another come upon the Theater to represent things done, and so again depart: diverse Chores also or Companies of Musitians and Harpers distinguish the diversity of the *Acts*, and while the *Actors* hold up, do with musicall accord sweeten the wearinesse of the Spectators, and keepe them in attention: so verily the thing it selfe speaketh that in this Heavenly Interlude, by diverse *shewes* and *apparitions* are represented diverse, or rather . . . the same things touching the Church, not past, but to come, and that their diverse *Acts* are renewed by diverse *Chores* or Companies, one while of 24 *Elders* and *four Beasts*, another while of *Angels*, sometimes of *Sealed ones in their foreheads*, and sometimes of *Harpers, &c.* with *new Songs*, and worthy *Hymmes*, not so much to lessen the wearisomenesse of the Spectators, as to infuse holy meditations into the mindes of the Readers, and to lift them up to Heavenly matters."

172 The reference is to the *Odes* of *Pindar* and the *Hymns* of the Alexandrian poet *Callimachus* (310?–235 B.C.), but the underlying thought rests on Plato's *Laws*, VII, 801–802, as Irene Samuel shows in *P. & M.*, pp. 53–61.

173 For Renaissance parallels to this opinion of the Psalms see Milton's translation of Psalm cxiv and the notes there.

he suffers to be wrought with high providence in his church, to sing the victorious agonies of martyrs and saints, the deeds and triumphs of just and pious nations doing valiantly through faith against the enemies of Christ, to deplore the general relapses of kingdoms and states from justice and God's true worship. Lastly, whatsover in religion is holy and sublime, in virtue amiable or grave, whatsoever hath passion or admiration in all the changes of that which is called fortune from without, or the wily subtleties and refluxes of man's thoughts from within, all these things with a solid and treatable smoothness to paint out and describe. Teaching[174] over the whole book of sanctity and virtue through all the instances of example, with such delight to those especially of soft and delicious temper who will not so much as look upon Truth herself, unless they see her elegantly dressed, that whereas the paths of honesty and good life appear now rugged and difficult, though they be indeed easy and pleasant, they would then appear to all men both easy and pleasant, though they were rugged and difficult indeed. And what a benefit this would be to our youth and gentry may be soon guessed by what we know of the corruption and bane which they suck in daily from the writings and interludes of libidinous and ignorant poetasters, who, having scarce ever heard of that which is the main consistence of a true poem, the choice of such persons as they ought to introduce, and what is moral and decent to each one, do for the most part lap up vicious principles in sweet pills to be swallowed down, and make the taste of virtuous documents harsh and sour. But because the spirit of man cannot demean itself lively in this body without some recreating intermission of labor and serious things, it were happy for the commonwealth if our magistrates, as in those famous governments of old, would take into their care, not only the deciding of our contentious lawcases and brawls, but the managing of our public sports and festival pastimes,[175] that they might be, not such as were authorized a while since, the provocations of drunkenness and lust, but such as may inure and harden our bodies by martial exercises to all warlike skill and performance, and may civilize, adorn, and make discreet our minds by the learned and affable meeting of frequent academies, and the procurement of wise and artful recitations sweetened with eloquent and graceful enticements to the love and practice of justice, temperance, and fortitude, instructing and bettering the nation at all opportunities, that the call of wisdom and virtue may be heard everywhere, as Solomon saith: "She crieth without, she uttereth her voice in the streets, in the top of high places, in the chief concourse, and in the openings of the gates."[176] Whether this may not be, not only in pulpits, but after another persuasive method, at set and solemn panegyries,[177] in theaters, porches,[178] or what other place or way may win most upon the people to receive at once both recreation and instruction, let them in authority consult. The thing which I had to say, and those intentions which have lived within me ever since I could conceive myself anything worth to my country, I return to crave excuse that urgent reason hath plucked from me by an abortive and foredated discovery. And the accomplishment of them lies not but in a power above man's to promise; but that none hath by more studious ways endeavored, and with more unwearied spirit that none shall, that I dare almost aver of myself as far as life and free leisure will extend; and that the land had once enfran-

---

[174] The background of this classic statement of the Renaissance faith in virtue and learning as the foundation of the poetic character is surveyed from Plato's *Republic* and more especially *Laws* (VII, 801–2, 817) through "the Italian commentaries of Castelvetro, Tasso, Mazzoni, and others" (See *Educ*, n. 76) to Sidney and Milton by Miss Samuel in *Plato and Milton*, pp. 45–67. Cf. *El VI*, 55–78; and *Apology*, n. 31. The traditional belief that this passage clearly looks forward to the achievement of *PL, PR,* and *SA* is challenged by W. R. Parker in *MP,* XXXIII (1935), 49–53.

[175] Here again Milton has Plato's *Laws* in mind (cf. notes 1 and 30 above) and their elaborate prescriptions about public festivals and education in traditional songs and dances in the seventh book. In contrast, he recalls the traditional encouragement of such recreation as "dancing, either men or women, . . . archery for men, leaping, running, vaulting, . . . May-games, Whitsun-ales, and Morrice-dances" by James I's Declaration of Sports (1618) and by Cavalier practice generally.

[176] Milton conflates Prov. i, 20–21, and, viii, 2–3.

[177] *panegyries:* solemn religious festivals.

[178] *porches:* porticos or porches of churches or public buildings. Sermons were often preached from them to audiences standing in the open air.

chised herself from this impertinent yoke of prelaty, under whose inquisitorious and tyrannical duncery no free and splendid wit can flourish. Neither do I think it shame to covenant with any knowing reader, that for some few years yet I may go on trust with him toward the payment of what I am now indebted, as being a work not to be raised from the heat of youth, or the vapors of wine, like that which flows at waste from the pen of some vulgar amorist, or the trencher fury of a riming parasite, nor to be obtained by the invocation of Dame Memory and her Siren daughters, but by devout prayer to that eternal Spirit who can enrich with all utterance and knowledge, and sends out his seraphim with the hallowed fire of his altar, to touch and purify the lips of whom he pleases.[179] To this must be added industrious and select reading, steady observation, insight into all seemly and generous arts and affairs, till which in some measure be compassed, at mine own peril and cost I refuse not to sustain this expectation from as many as are not loth to hazard so much credulity upon the best pledges that I can give them. Although it nothing content me to have disclosed thus much beforehand, but that I trust hereby to make it manifest with what small willingness I endure to interrupt the pursuit of no less hopes than these, and leave a calm and pleasing solitariness, fed with cheerful and confident thoughts, to embark in a troubled sea of noises and hoarse disputes, put from beholding the bright countenance of truth in the quiet and still air of delightful studies to come into the dim reflection of hollow antiquities sold by the seeming bulk, and there be fain to club quotations with men whose learning and belief lies in marginal stuffings, who, when they have like good sumpters[180] laid ye down their horseload of citations and fathers at your door, with a rhapsody of who and who were bishops here or there, ye may take off their pack-saddles, their day's work is done, and episcopacy, as they think, stoutly vindicated. Let any gentle apprehension that can distinguish learned pains from unlearned drudgery imagine what pleasure or profoundness can be in this, or what honor to deal against such adversaries. But were it the meanest underservice, if God by his secretary conscience enjoin it, it were sad for me if I should draw back, for me especially, now when all men offer their aid to help ease and lighten the difficult labors of the church, to whose service by the intentions of my parents and friends I was destined of a child, and in mine own resolutions: till coming to some maturity of years and perceiving what tyranny had invaded the church, that he who would take orders must subscribe slave and take an oath withal, which, unless he took with a conscience that would retch, he must either straight perjure or split his faith; I thought it better to prefer a blameless silence before the sacred office of speaking, bought and begun with servitude and forswearing. Howsoever, thus church-outed[181] by the prelates, hence may appear the right I have to meddle in these matters, as before the necessity and constraint appeared.

CHAPTER I.

That Prelaty opposeth the reason and end of the Gospel three ways, and first, in her outward form.

After this digression it would remain that I should single out some other reason which might undertake for prelaty to be a fit and lawful church government; but finding none of like validity with these that have already sped according to their fortune, I shall add one reason why it is not to be thought a church government at all, but a church tyranny, and is at hostile terms with the end and reason of Christ's evangelic ministry. Albeit I must confess to be half in doubt whether I should bring it forth or no, it being so contrary to the eye of the world, and the world so potent in most

---

[179] The allusion is to the vision of "the Lord sitting upon a throne . . . Above it stood the seraphim" in Isa. vi, 1-2, though Milton invokes the Muses whom Hesiod describes as the daughters of Memory and Zeus. Cf. *PL* I, 6, n. Milton's profession of faith in learning and virtue as the foundation of poetry in *Patrem*, 67-76, and *El VI*, 67-78, are worth comparison.

[180] *sumpters*: pack animals.

[181] For a discussion of the justice of Milton's claim to have been "church-outed by the prelates," cf. William Haller, *The Rise of Puritanism*, Chap. viii.

men's hearts, that I shall endanger either not to be regarded or not to be understood. For who is there almost that measures wisdom by simplicity, strength by suffering, dignity by lowliness?[182] Who is there that counts it first to be last, something to be nothing, and reckons himself of great command in that he is a servant?[183] Yet God, when he meant to subdue the world and hell at once, part of that to salvation, and this wholly to perdition, made choice of no other weapons or auxiliaries than these, whether to save or to destroy. It had been a small mastery for him to have drawn out his legions into array and flanked them with his thunder; therefore he sent foolishness to confute wisdom, weakness to bind strength, despisedness to vanquish pride. And this is the great mystery of the gospel made good in Christ himself, who, as he testifies, came not to be ministered to, but to minister;[184] and must be fulfilled in all his ministers till his second coming. To go against these principles St. Paul so feared, that if he should but affect the wisdom of words in his preaching, he thought it would be laid to his charge that he had made the cross of Christ to be of none effect.[185] Whether, then, prelaty do not make of none effect the cross of Christ by the principles it hath so contrary to these, nullifying the power and end of the gospel, it shall not want due proof, if it want not due belief. Neither shall I stand to trifle with one that will tell me of quiddities[186] and formalities, whether prelaty or prelateity in abstract notion be this or that; it suffices me that I find it in his skin, so I find it inseparable, or not oftener otherwise than a phœnix[187] hath been seen; although

I persuade me that whatever faultiness was but superficial to prelaty at the beginning, is now by the just judgment of God long since branded and inworn into the very essence thereof. First, therefore, if to do the work of the gospel Christ our Lord took upon him the form of a servant,[188] how can his servant in this ministry take upon him the form of a lord? I know Bilson[189] hath deciphered us all the gallantries of *signore* and *monsignore* and *monsieur* as circumstantially as any punctualist of Castile, Naples, or Fountain Bleau could have done: but this must not so compliment us out of our right minds as to be to learn that the form of a servant was a mean, laborious, and vulgar life, aptest to teach; which form Christ thought fittest that he might bring about his will according to his own principles, choosing the meaner things of this world that he might put under the high. Now, whether the pompous garb, the lordly life, the wealth, the haughty distance of prelaty, be those meaner things of the world, whereby God in them would manage the mystery of his gospel, be it the verdict of common sense. For Christ saith in St. John, "The servant is not greater than his lord, nor he that is sent greater than he that sent him;" and adds, "If ye know these things, happy are ye if ye do them."[190] Then let the prelates well advise, if they neither know nor do these things, or if they know and yet do them

---

[182] Milton writes with St. Paul's "simplicity and godly sincerity" (II Cor. i, 12) and not by the standards of those who are "corrupted from the simplicity that is in Christ" (II Cor. xi, 3).

[183] Milton is building on Christ's words to the apostles: "If any man desire to be first, the same shall be last of all, and a servant of all" (Mark ix, 35). This verse figured constantly in antiepiscopal writing.

[184] The sentence is woven out of reminiscences of I Cor. i, *passim;* II Cor. xii, 9; Matt. xx, 28; and Mark x, 45.

[185] I Cor. i, 17.

[186] *quiddities:* abstract essences, philosophically defined. *Prelateity*—"the essential quality or essence of a prelate" (*O.E.D.*)—is an example.

[187] Cf. the "self-begotten bird" in *SA,* 1699, n., and the *Phoenix* in *PL* V, 272, n.

[188] So Paul describes Christ as taking "upon him the form of a servant" when he "was made in the likeness of men" (Phil. ii, 7). The passage looks forward to Christ's warning, after washing the disciples' feet, that "the servant is not greater than his master" (John, xiii, 16; xv, 20). Cf. n. 190 below.

[189] The revival of interest in *The True Difference between Christian Subjection and Unchristian Rebellion* (1585), by Thomas Bilson, who was Bishop of Winchester from 1597 until his death in 1616, seems to have been considerable. In resenting his defense of ecclesiastical titles as smacking of their origin at the courts of *Castile, Naples,* and *Fontainebleau,* Milton took the Puritan position to which Bilson himself had replied in *The Perpetual Government of Christes Church* (1593), chap. vi: "What Dominion and Titles Christ interdicted his Apostles." He held that, though Christ forbade the Apostles lordship over one another, he permitted it among them as brothers; that, although he forbade the abuse of the title Rabbi, he permitted all innocent use of titles of respect, such as the Puritans themselves gave to their clergy.

[190] John xviii, 17.

not, wherein their happiness consists. And thus is the gospel frustrated by the lordly form of prelaty.

CHAPTER II.

That the ceremonious doctrine of Prelaty opposeth the reason and end of the Gospel.

That which next declares the heavenly power and reveals the deep mystery of the gospel is the pure simplicity of doctrine, accounted the foolishness of this world,[191] yet crossing and confounding the pride and wisdom of the flesh. And wherein consists this fleshly wisdom and pride? In being altogether ignorant of God and his worship? No, surely; for men are naturally ashamed of that. Where then? It consists in a bold presumption of ordering the worship and service of God after man's own will in traditions and ceremonies. Now if the pride and wisdom of the flesh were to be defeated and confounded, no doubt but in that very point wherein it was proudest and thought itself wisest, that so the victory of the gospel might be the more illustrious. But our prelates, instead of expressing the spiritual power of their ministry by warring against this chief bulwark and stronghold of the flesh, have entered into fast league with the principal enemy against whom they were sent, and turned the strength of fleshly pride and wisdom against the pure simplicity of saving truth. First, mistrusting to find the authority of their order in the immediate institution of Christ or his apostles by the clear evidence of scripture, they fly to the carnal supportment of tradition; when we appeal to the Bible, they to the unwieldy volumes of tradition: and do not shame to reject the ordinance of him that is eternal for the perverse iniquity of sixteen hundred years; choosing rather to think truth itself a liar, than that sixteen ages should be taxed with an error; not considering the general apostacy that was foretold and the church's flight into the wilderness.[192]

Nor is this enough; instead of showing the reason of their lowly condition from divine example and command, they seek to prove their high preëminence from human consent and authority. But let them chant while they will of prerogatives, we shall tell them of scripture; of custom, we of scripture; of acts and statutes, still of scripture; till the quick and piercing word enter to the dividing of their souls,[193] and the mighty weakness of the gospel throw down the weak mightiness of man's reasoning.[194] Now for their demeanor within the church, how have they disfigured and defaced that more than angelic brightness, the unclouded serenity of Christian religion with the dark overcasting of superstitious copes and flaminical[195] vestures, wearing on their backs and, I abhor to think, perhaps in some worse place, the unexpressible image of God the Father! Tell me, ye priests, wherefore this gold, wherefore these robes and surplices over the gospel? Is our religion guilty of the first trespass and hath need of clothing to cover her nakedness? What does this else but cast an ignominy upon the perfection of Christ's ministry by seeking to adorn it with that which was the poor remedy of our shame? Believe it, wondrous doctors, all corporeal resemblances of inward holiness and beauty are now past; he that will clothe the gospel now, intimates plainly that the gospel is naked, uncomely, that I may not say reproachful. Do not, ye church maskers, while Christ is clothing upon our bareness with his righteous garment to make us acceptable in his Father's sight, do not, as

"woman clothed with the Sun" in Rev. xii as it was understood by Protestants generally. In his *Commentary on the Revelation,* p. 274, David Paraeus treated her as representing the early church, and interpreted her *flight into the wilderness* as representing the scattering of true Christians into obscure retreats during the Middle Ages. "The Lord," said Leonard Busher in *Religious Peace* (1614), p. 6, "hath showed by the mouth of his holy servant John, that the woman (meaning the church) sholde fleye into the wildernes for a tyme . . . from the persecution of the serpent."

[193] "For the word of God is quick, and powerful, sharper than any two edged sword, piercing even to the dividing asunder of soul and spirit" (Heb. iv, 12).

[194] "The weakness of God is stronger than men" (I Cor. i, 25).

[195] The flamens were priests in ancient Roman paganism. Cf. *Nat,* 194.

[191] "For the wisdom of this world is foolishness with God" (I Cor. iii, 19). "For it is written, He taketh the wise in their own craftiness" (Job v, 13).

[192] Milton interprets the prophecy about the

ye do, cover and hide his righteous verity with the polluted clothing of your ceremonies to make it seem more decent in your own eyes. "How beautiful," saith Isaiah, "are the feet of him that bringeth good tidings, that publisheth salvation!"[196] Are the feet so beautiful, and is the very bringing of these tidings so decent of itself? What new decency then can be added to this by your spinstry?[197] Ye think by these gaudy glisterings to stir up the devotion of the rude multitude; ye think so, because ye forsake the heavenly teaching of St. Paul for the hellish sophistry of papism. If the multitude be rude, the lips of the preacher must give knowledge, and not ceremonies. And although some Christians be newborn babes[198] comparatively to some that are stronger, yet in respect of ceremony, which is but a rudiment of the law, the weakest Christian hath thrown off the robes of his minority and is a perfect man, as to legal rites. What children's food there is in the gospel we know to be no other than the "sincerity of the word, that they may grow thereby."[199] But is here the utmost of your outbraving the service of God? No. Ye have been bold not to set your threshold by his threshold[200] or your posts by his posts, but your sacrament, your sign, call it what you will, by his sacrament, baptizing the Christian infant with a solemn sprinkle, and unbaptizing for your own part with a profane and impious forefinger; as if, when ye had laid the purifying element upon his forehead, ye meant to cancel and cross it out again with a character not of God's bidding. O but the innocence of these ceremonies! O rather the sottish absurdity of this excuse! What could be more innocent than the washing of a cup, a glass, or hands before meat, and that un-der the law when so many washings were commanded, and by long tradition? Yet our Savior detested their customs[201] though never so seeming harmless, and charges them severely that they had transgressed the commandments of God by their traditions and worshipped him in vain. How much more then must these and much grosser ceremonies now in force, delude the end of Christ's coming in the flesh against the flesh, and stifle the sincerity of our new covenant which hath bound us to forsake all carnal pride and wisdom, especially in matters of religion. Thus we see again how prelaty, sailing in opposition to the main end and power of the gospel, doth not join in that mysterious work of Christ, by lowliness to confound height, by simplicity of doctrine the wisdom of the world; but contrariwise hath made itself high in the world and the flesh to vanquish things by the world accounted low, and made itself wise in tradition and fleshly ceremony to confound the purity of doctrine which is the wisdom of God.

CHAPTER III.

That Prelatical jurisdiction opposeth the reason and end of the Gospel and of State.

The third and last consideration remains, whether the prelates in their function do work according to the gospel, practising to subdue the mighty things of this world by things weak, which St. Paul[202] hath set forth to be the power and excellence of the gospel, or whether in more likelihood they band themselves with the prevalent things of this world, to overrun the weak things which Christ hath made choice to work by: and this will soonest be discerned by the course of their jurisdiction. But here again I find my thoughts almost in suspense betwixt yea and no, and am nigh turning mine eye which way I may best retire and not proceed in this subject, blaming the ardency of my mind that fixed me too at-

---

196 Isa. lii, 7.

197 *spinstry:* drapery, millinery.

198 Milton adapts Paul's argument (Rom. ii, 20; I Cor. iii, 1–3; and Ephes. iv, 13–14) that Christians who had emerged from Judaism and had not abandoned their "bondage to the law" (i.e. the ceremonial law of Moses) were "babes" in the faith.

199 "As newborn babes, desire the sincere milk of the word, but ye may grow thereby" (I Pet. ii, 2).

200 Speaking of the disrespect which the Israelites had shown to the Temple the prophet said (Ezek. xliv, 8): "In their setting of their threshold by my thresholds, and their post by my posts, . . . they have even defiled my holy name."

201 Christ condemned the ceremonial importance attached by the Pharisees to washing "the cup and the platter" (Matt. xxiii, 25) and to washing hands before eating (Mark vii, 4).

202 Milton paraphrases Paul's words in I Cor. i, 26–28.

tentively to come thus far. For truth, I know not how, hath this unhappiness fatal to her, ere she can come to the trial and inspection of the understanding; being to pass through many little wards and limits of the several affections and desires, she cannot shift it, but must put on such colors[203] and attire as those pathetic handmaids of the soul please to lead her in to their queen. And if she find so much favor with them, they let her pass in her own likeness; if not, they bring her into the presence habited and colored like a notorious falsehood. And contrary, when any falsehood comes that way, if they like the errand she brings, they are so artful to counterfeit the very shape and visage of truth that the understanding not being able to discern the fucus which these enchantresses with such cunning have laid upon the feature sometimes of truth, sometimes of falsehood interchangeably, sentences for the most part one for the other at the first blush, according to the subtle imposture of these sensual mistresses that keep the ports and passages between her and the object. So that were it not for leaving imperfect that which is already said, I should go near to relinquish that which is to follow. And because I see that most men—as it happens in this world, either weakly or falsely principled, what through ignorance and what through custom of license, both in discourse and writing, by what hath been of late written in vulgar—have not seemed to attain the decision of this point, I shall likewise assay those wily arbitresses who in most men have, as was heard, the sole ushering of truth and falsehood between the sense and the soul, with what loyalty they will use me in convoying this truth to my understanding; the rather for that, by as much acquaintance as I can obtain with them, I do not find them engaged either one way or other. Concerning therefore ecclesial jurisdiction I find still more controversy,

who should administer it, than diligent inquiry made to learn what it is; for had the pains been taken to search out that, it had been long ago enrolled to be nothing else but a pure tyrannical forgery of the prelates; and that jurisdictive power in the church there ought to be none at all. It cannot be conceived that what men now call jurisdiction in the church, should be other thing than a Christian censorship; and therefore is it most commonly and truly named ecclesiastical censure. Now if the Roman censor,[204] a civil function, to that severe assize[205] of surveying and controlling the privatest and slyest manners of all men and all degrees had no jurisdiction, no courts of plea or indictment, no punitive force annexed—whether it were that to this manner of correction the entanglement of suits was improper, or that the notice of those upright inquisitors extended to such the most covert and spiritous vices as would slip easily between the wider and more material grasp of law, or that it stood more with the majesty of that office to have no other sergeants or maces about them but those invisible ones of terror and shame, or lastly, were it their fear lest the greatness of this authority and honor, armed with jurisdiction, might step with ease into a tyranny—in all these respects, with much more reason undoubtedly ought the censure of the church be quite divested and disentailed of all jurisdiction whatsoever. For if the course of judicature to a political censorship seem either too tedious or too contentious, much more may it to the discipline of church, whose definitive decrees are to be speedy, but the execution of rigor slow, contrary to what in legal proceedings is most usual, and by how much the less contentious it is, by so much will it be the more Christian. And if the Censor, in his moral episcopy[206] being to judge most in matters not answerable by writ or action, could not use an instrument so gross and bodily as jurisdiction is, how can the minister of gospel manage the cor-

---

[203] This figure, which owed its popularity in part to Bacon's use of it in his essay "Of Truth," was frequent in Puritan controversy. On the first page of his *A Counter-Snarle for Ishmael Rabshacheh* (1613), Sir Edward Hoby said: "You are not to learne what *Artificiall* shadowes *Heresie* hath in all ages contriued, for the couering of her vgly shape; neither are you vnable to discern the counterfeit colours wherewith she hath varnished her wrinkled deformities."

[204] The Roman Censorship consisted in the scrutiny of public morals by two officials who were elected for a five-year term and had unlimited *moral* power in the exercise of their office. The institution lasted from 443 to 22 B.C., and its discontinuance was regarded in Milton's time as a result of the decay of republican institutions in Rome.

[205] *assize:* court session.

[206] *episcopy:* inspection.

pulent and secular trial of bill and process in things merely spiritual? Or could that Roman office, without this juridical sword or saw, strike such a reverence of itself into the most undaunted hearts as with one single dash of ignominy to put all the senate and knighthood of Rome into a tremble, surely much rather might the heavenly ministry of the evangel bind herself about with far more piercing beams of majesty and awe, by wanting the beggarly help of halings and amercements[207] in the use of her powerful keys.[208] For when the church without temporal support is able to do her great works upon the unforced obedience of men, it argues a divinity about her. But when she thinks to credit and better her spiritual efficacy and to win herself respect and dread by strutting in the false vizard of worldly authority, 'tis evident that God is not there, but that her apostolic virtue is departed from her and hath left her key-cold; which she perceiving as in a decayed nature seeks to the outward fomentations and chafings of worldly help and external flourishes to fetch, if it be possible, some motion into her extreme parts, or to hatch a counterfeit life with the crafty and artificial heat of jurisdiction. But it is observable that so long as the church, in true imitation of Christ, can be content to ride upon an ass,[209] carrying herself and her government along in a mean and simple guise, she may be as he is, a lion of the tribe of Judah, and in her humility all men with loud hosannas will confess her greatness. But when, despising the mighty operation of the Spirit by the weak things of this world, she thinks to make herself bigger and more considerable by using the way of civil force and jurisdiction, as she sits upon this lion she changes into an ass, and instead of hosannas every man pelts her with stones and dirt. Lastly, if the wisdom of the Romans feared to commit jurisdiction to an office of so high esteem and dread as was the censor's, we may see what a solecism in the art of policy it hath been all this while through Christendom to give jurisdiction to ecclesiastical censure. For that strength, joined with religion abused and pretended to ambitious ends, must of necessity breed the heaviest and most quelling tyranny, not only upon the necks, but even to the souls of men: which if Christian Rome had been so cautelous[210] to prevent in her church as pagan Rome was in her state, we had not had such a lamentable experience thereof as now we have from thence upon all Christendom. For although I said before that the church coveting to ride upon the lionly form of jurisdiction makes a transformation of herself into an ass and becomes despicable, that is to those whom God hath enlightened with true knowledge; but where they remain yet in the relics of superstition, this is the extremity of their bondage and blindness, that while they think they do obeisance to the lordly vision of a lion, they do it to an ass, that through the just judgment of God is permitted to play the dragon among them because of their wilful stupidity. And let England here well rub her eyes lest by leaving jurisdiction and church censure to the same persons, now that God hath been so long medicining her eyesight, she do not with her overpolitic fetches[211] mar all, and bring herself back again to worship this ass bestriding a lion. Having hitherto explained that to ecclesiastical censure no jurisdictive power can be added without a childish and dangerous oversight in polity and a pernicious contradiction in evangelic discipline, as anon more fully, it will be next to declare wherein the true reason and force of church censure consists, which by then it shall be laid open to the root, so little is it that I fear lest any crookedness, any wrinkle or spot should be found in presbyterial government, that if Bodin,[212] the famous

---

[207] *halings and amercements:* violently executed summonses to the ecclesiastical courts and penalties, usually fines, fixed at their discretion.

[208] The "keys of the kingdom of heaven," which Christ gives to Peter in Matt. xvi, 19, are interpreted in *CD* I, xxxii (C.E. XVI, 230), as "a power not committed to Peter and his successors exclusively, . . . but to the whole particular church collectively."

[209] Milton interprets the story of Christ's entry into Jerusalem riding on an ass (Luke xix, 35–38) in the light of the salutation of the Lion of the Tribe of Judah by the elders in Rev. v, 5. In identifying the lion with Christ, he was following Paraeus (*Commentary,* p. 99).

[210] *cautelous:* wary, watchful.

[211] *over-politic fetches:* tricks or devices which are likely to fail or cause trouble because they are too artful.

[212] In the *Republic* (1576) VI, i, 854, the great

French writer, though a papist, yet affirms that the commonwealth which maintains this discipline will certainly flourish in virtue and piety, I dare assure myself that every true protestant will admire the integrity, the uprightness, the divine and gracious purposes thereof, and even for the reason of it so coherent with the doctrine of the gospel, besides the evidence of command in scripture, will confess it to be the only true church government, and that, contrary to the whole end and mystery of Christ's coming in the flesh, a false appearance of the same is exercised by prelaty.

But because some count it rigorous, and that hereby men shall be liable to a double punishment, I will begin somewhat higher and speak of punishment, which, as it is an evil, I esteem to be of two sorts or rather two degrees only, a reprobate conscience in this life, and hell in the other world. Whatever else men call punishment or censure is not properly an evil, so it be not an illegal violence, but a saving medicine ordained of God both for the public and private good of man, who consisting of two parts, the inward and the outward, was by the eternal Providence left under two sorts of cure, the church and the magistrate. The magistrate hath only to deal with the outward part, I mean not of the body alone, but of the mind in all her outward acts, which in scripture is called the outward man. So that it would be helpful to us if we might borrow such authority as the rhetoricians by patent may give us, with a kind of Promethean skill to shape and fashion this outward man into the similitude of a body[213] and set him visible before us; imagining the inner man only as the soul. Thus then the civil magistrate look-

French publicist, Jean *Bodin* (1530–1596), expressed admiration for the control of public morals exercised by the "bishops, ministers, and elders" of the Church at Geneva without any use of force either by their own authority or that of the state. Incidentally, like Milton, Bodin compared the Presbyterian censorship of morals with that in ancient Rome, in both cases approving the avoidance of fines and other penalties for offenders and the appeal of the censors to public opinion to control them.

[213] Milton was perhaps thinking of Propertius' variation (in *Elegies* III, v, 7–10) of the myth of the making of men by Prometheus. In forming them out of the physical features of various animals and giving them the passions of various creatures, Propertius says that Prometheus forgot to give them minds.

ing only upon the outward man (I say as a magistrate, for what he doth further, he doth it as a member of the church), if he find in his complexion, skin, or outward temperature the signs and marks, or in his doings the effects of injustice, rapine, lust, cruelty, or the like, sometimes he shuts up as in frenetic or infectious diseases, or confines within doors, as in every sickly estate. Sometimes he shaves by penalty or mulct, or else to cool and take down those luxuriant humors which wealth and excess have caused to abound. Otherwhiles he sears, he cauterizes, he scarifies, lets blood, and finally, for utmost remedy cuts off. The patients which most an end are brought into his hospital, are such as are far gone and beside themselves (unless they be falsely accused) so that force is necessary to tame and quiet them in their unruly fits, before they can be made capable of a more human cure. His general end is the outward peace and welfare of the commonwealth, and civil happiness in this life. His particular end in every man is, by the infliction of pain, damage, and disgrace, that the senses and common perceivance might carry this message to the soul within, that it is neither easeful, profitable, nor praiseworthy in this life to do evil. Which must needs tend to the good of man, whether he be to live or die; and be undoubtedly the first means to a natural man, especially an offender, which might open his eyes to a higher consideration of good and evil, as it is taught in religion. This is seen in the often penitence of those that suffer, who, had they escaped, had gone on sinning to an immeasurable heap, which is one of the extremest punishments. And this is all that the civil magistrate, as so being, confers to the healing of man's mind, working only by terrifying plasters upon the rind and orifice of the sore, and by all outward appliances, as the logicians say, *a posteriori*, at the effect, and not from the cause; not once touching the inward bed of corruption and that hectic disposition to evil, the source of all vice and obliquity against the rule of law. Which how insufficient it is to cure the soul of man, we cannot better guess than by the art of bodily physic. Therefore God to the intent of further healing man's depraved mind, to this power of the magistrate which contents itself with the restraint of evil-doing in the external man,[214] added that which we call censure, to purge it and remove it clean out of the inmost soul. In the beginning this authority seems to have been placed, as all both civil and religious rites once were, only in each father of family.[215] Afterwards among the heathen, in the wise men and philosophers of the age; but so as it was a thing voluntary, and no set government. More distinctly among the Jews, as being God's peculiar, where the priests, Levites, prophets, and at last the scribes and Pharisees took charge of instructing and overseeing the lives of the people. But in the gospel, which is the straitest and the dearest covenant can be made between God and man, we being now his adopted sons, and nothing fitter for us to think on than to be like him, united to him, and, as he pleases to express it, to have fellowship with him; it is all necessity that we should expect this blessed efficacy of healing our inward man to be ministered to us in a more familiar and effectual method than ever before. God being now no more a judge after the sentence of the law, nor, as it were, a schoolmaster of perishable rites, but a most indulgent father governing his church as a family of sons in their discreet age; and therefore, in the sweetest and mildest manner of paternal discipline, he hath committed this other office of preserving in healthful constitution the inner man, which may be termed the spirit of the soul, to his spiritual deputy the minister of each congregation; who being best acquainted with his own flock, hath best reason to know all the secretest diseases likely to be there. And look, by how much the internal man is more excellent and noble than the external, by so much is his cure more exactly,

more thoroughly, and more particularly to be performed. For which cause the Holy Ghost by the apostles joined to the minister, as assistant in this great office, sometimes a certain number of grave and faithful brethren[216] (for neither doth the physician do all in restoring his patient; he prescribes, another prepares the medicine; some tend, some watch, some visit) much more may a minister partly not see all, partly err as a man: besides that nothing can be more for the mutual honor and love of the people to their pastor, and his to them, than when in select numbers and courses they are seen partaking and doing reverence to the holy duties of discipline by their serviceable and solemn presence, and receiving honor again from their employment, not now any more to be separated in the church by veils and partitions as laics and unclean, but admitted to wait upon the tabernacle as the rightful clergy of Christ, a chosen generation, a royal priesthood, to offer up spiritual sacrifice in that meet place to which God and the congregation shall call and assign them. And this all Christians ought to know, that the title of clergy St. Peter gave to all God's people, till pope Higinus[217] and the succeeding prelates took it from them, appropriating that name to themselves and their priests only; and condemning the rest of God's inheritance to an injurious and alienate condition of laity, they separated from them by local partitions in churches, through their gross ignorance and pride imitating the old temple, and excluded the members of Christ from the property of being members, the bearing of orderly and

214 Milton writes cautiously, as he does in *CD* I, xvii (C.E. XVII, 386–8), in interpreting Mark x, 42 and Rom. xiii, 3–4, in a way to stress the obligation of civil magistrates to be the servants of the society in which they have authority over moral offenses.

215 The principle was axiomatic. In *The Anarchy of Limited Monarchy* (1648), p. 6, Robert Filmer said that in Adam's ordination "to rule over his Wife . . . we have the originall grant of Government, & the fountain of all power placed in the *father* of all mankind; accordingly we find the *law* for obedience to government given in the tearms of *honor thy Father.*"

216 Milton thought of Christ's command that injured brothers should plead with those who had offended them, if necessary, taking "one or two" with them, "that in the mouth of two or three witnesses every word may be established" (Matt. xviii, 15–17), and of Paul's plea to the Thessalonians (II Thes. v, 12) "to know them which . . . are over you in the Lord, and admonish you."

217 In *An Answer to the Book entituled An Humble Remonstrance* (see n. 83 above) the Smectymnuans anticipated this attack on *Higinus* by grouping him with five others "whom the Papists call *Bishops,* and the popes *predecessours,*" and by asserting that he was called a presbyter by Eusebius. In *The Ecclesiastical History* IV, x–xi, however, he is recognized as the ninth bishop of Rome and as having held the see for four years (141–144? A.D.). The *Liber Pontificalis* seems to be the source of the tradition that he drastically reorganized his clergy.

fit offices in the ecclesiastical body, as if they had meant to sew up that Jewish veil which Christ by his death on the cross rent in sunder.[218] Although these usurpers could not so presently overmaster the liberties and lawful titles of God's freeborn church, but that Origen,[219] being yet a layman, expounded the scriptures publicly and was therein defended by Alexander of Jerusalem and Theoctistus of Cæsarea, producing in his behalf divers examples that the privilege of teaching was anciently permitted to many worthy layman: and Cyprian[220] in his epistles professes he will do nothing without the advice and assent of his assistant laics. Neither did the first Nicene[221] council, as great and learned as

it was, think it any robbery to receive in and require the help and presence of many learned lay brethren, as they were then called. Many other authorities to confirm this assertion both out of scripture and the writings of next antiquity, Golartius[222] hath collected in his notes upon Cyprian; whereby it will be evident that the laity, not only by apostolic permission but by consent of many the ancientest prelates, did participate in church offices as much as is desired any lay elder should now do. Sometimes also not the elders alone, but the whole body of the church is interested in the work of discipline, as oft as public satisfaction is given by those that have given public scandal. Not to speak now of her right in elections. But another reason there is in it, which though religion did not commend to us, yet moral and civil prudence could not but extol. It was thought of old in philosophy that shame,[223] or to call it better, the reverence of our elders, our brethren, and friends, was the greatest incitement to virtuous deeds and the greatest dissuasion from unworthy attempts that might be. Hence we may read in the *Iliad,* where Hector[224] being wished to retire from the battle, many of his forces being routed, makes answer that he durst not for shame, lest the Trojan knights and dames should think he did ignobly. And certain it is, that whereas terror is thought such a great stickler in a commonwealth, honorable shame is a far greater, and has more reason. For where shame is, there is fear, but where fear is, there is not presently shame. And if anything may be done to inbreed in us this generous and Christianly reverence one of another, the very nurse and guardian of piety and virtue, it cannot sooner be than by such a discipline in the church as may use us to have

218 Milton follows a traditional interpretation of the rending of the veil of the temple at Christ's crucifixion (Matt. xxvii, 51; Mark, xv, 38; and Luke xxiii, 45) as symbolizing the superceding of the Mosaic Law (the veil) by the liberty of the Gospel.

219 Fleeing from Caracalla's persecution at Alexandria (216 A.D.), *Origen* "was cordially welcomed by his old friend, *Alexander,* Bishop of Jerusalem, and subsequently by *Theoktistes, Bishop* of Caesarea, who jointly invited him to give expository lectures in their churches. . . . Although a layman, Origen acquiesced, to the no small displeasure of his own bishop, Demetrius. . . . The Palestinian bishops were able to plead precedents for what they had done," but when Demetrius insisted, Origen returned to Alexandria "as a teacher and student." (W. Fairweather, *Origen and Greek Patristic Theology,* 1901, p. 50.)

220 Although *Cyprian* (?200–258 A.D.), the first African bishop martyr, insisted on the divine origin and authority of his order, he was careful to secure the support of his clergy, especially in matters involving church unity. His *Letters* (especially 5 and 10) were famous for their stress upon the participation of his presbyters in the assemblies which voted the adherence of his diocese to Pope Cornelius. Straining the evidence of such letters, the Smectymnuans wrote: "*Cyprian* professeth, that *hee would doe nothing without the Clergie; nay, he could doe nothing without them; nay, he durst not take upon him alone to* determine that which *of right did belong to all*" (*An Answer,* p. 38).

221 At the *Nicene Council* (325 A.D.), says the church historian Socrates Scholasticus, "There were present also many of the laity, which were skillful Logicians. . . . Before the Bishops met together, . . . the Logicians busied themselves propounding against divers others certain preambles of disputation, and when divers were thus drawne to disputation, . . . a Layman . . . of a simple and sincere mind set himselfe against the Logicians, told them thus in plaine wordes: that neither Christ nor his Apostles had delivered unto us the art of Logicke, . . . but an open and plaine mind to be preserved of us with faith and good workes" (Meredith Hanmer's translation, 1636, p. 221).

222 S. Goulart the elder edited Cyprian in 1593 and revised and reissued the work at Paris in 1603 and 1607.

223 Perhaps Milton thought of the modesty which Plato attributes (*Phaedrus,* 253d) to the white horse which symbolizes the soul's best aspirations, or of the ending of Seneca's *Epistle* xi, "On Shame," which suggests that all serious men should follow the maxim of Epicurus which advises them to choose some revered person and live constantly as if they were in his presence.

224 For the background of this allusion to *Il.* XXII, 100, in Milton's mind cf. the first *Oratorical Performance,* note 1.

in awe the assemblies of the faithful, and to count it a thing most grievous, next to the grieving of God's Spirit,[225] to offend those whom he hath put in authority as a healing superintendence over our lives and behaviors, both to our own happiness and that we may not give offense to good men, who, without amends by us made, dare not against God's command hold communion with us in holy things. And this will be accompanied with a religious dread of being outcast from the company of saints and from the fatherly protection of God in his church, to consort with the devil and his angels. But there is yet a more ingenuous and noble degree of honest shame, or call it, if you will, an esteem, whereby men bear an inward reverence toward their own persons. And if the love of God, as a fire sent from heaven to be ever kept alive upon the altar of our hearts, be the first principle of all godly and virtuous actions in men, this pious and just honoring of ourselves is the second, and may be thought as the radical moisture and fountainhead whence every laudable and worthy enterprise issues forth. And although I have given it the name of a liquid thing, yet is it not incontinent to bound itself, as humid things are, but hath in it a most restraining and powerful abstinence to start back and globe itself upward from the mixture of any ungenerous and unbeseeming motion or any soil wherewith it may peril to stain itself. Something I confess it is to be ashamed of evildoing in the presence of any, and to reverence the opinion and the countenance of a good man rather than a bad, fearing most in his sight to offend, goes so far as almost to be virtuous; yet this is but still the fear of infamy, and many such, when they find themselves alone, saving their reputation, will compound with other scruples and come to a close treaty with their dearer vices in secret. But he that holds himself in reverence and due esteem, both for the dignity of God's image upon him[226] and for the price of his redemption, which he thinks is visibly marked upon his forehead,[227] accounts himself both a fit person to do the noblest and godliest deeds, and much better worth than to deject and defile with such a debasement and such a pollution as sin is, himself so highly ransomed and ennobled to a new friendship and filial relation with God. Nor can he fear so much the offense and reproach of others, as he dreads and would blush at the reflection of his own severe and modest eye upon himself, if it should see him doing or imagining that which is sinful, though in the deepest secrecy. How shall a man know to do himself this right, how to perform this honorable duty of estimation and respect towards his own soul and body? Which way will lead him best to this hilltop of sanctity and goodness above which there is no higher ascent but to the love of God, which from this self-pious regard cannot be asunder? No better way doubtless than to let him duly understand, that as he is called by the high calling of God to be holy and pure, so is he by the same appointment ordained, and by the church's call admitted, to such offices of discipline in the church, to which his own spiritual gifts by the example of apostolic institution have authorized him. For we have learned that the scornful term of laic, the consecrating of temples, carpets, and tablecloths, the railing in of a repugnant and contradictive mount Sinai[228] in the gospel, as if the touch of a lay Christian, who is nevertheless God's living temple, could profane dead Judaisms, the exclusion of Christ's people from the offices of holy discipline through the pride of a usurping clergy causes the rest to have an unworthy and abject opinion of themselves, to approach to holy duties with a slavish fear and to unholy doings with a familiar boldness. For seeing such a wide and terrible the mount Sion, and with him an hundred and forty and four thousand, having his Father's name written in their foreheads" (Rev. xiv, 1).

225 "Grieve not the Holy Spirit of God, whereby ye are sealed unto the day of redemption" (Eph. iv, 30).

226 Cf. I Cor. xi, 7: "For a man . . . is the image and glory of God." Cf. also PL VII, 518, n.

227 "And I looked, and, lo, a Lamb stood on

228 Before the ceremonial and moral laws were revealed to Moses on Mount Sinai, God commanded him to "set bounds unto the people round about, saying, Take heed to yourselves, that ye go not up into the mount, or touch the border of it: whosoever toucheth the mount shall be surely put to death" (Exod. xix, 12). Archbishop Laud's policy of railing in the communion table seemed to the Puritans to be one of the most offensive aspects of his effort to exclude laymen from their full privileges and exalt the clergy to a position analogous with that enjoyed by the priests as their order was constituted by the ceremonial law of Moses.

distance between religious things and themselves, and that in respect of a wooden table and the perimeter of holy ground about it, a flagon pot and a linen corporal,[229] the priest esteems their layships unhallowed and unclean, they fear religion with such a fear as loves not, and think the purity of the gospel too pure for them, and that any uncleanness is more suitable to their unconsecrated estate. But when every good Christian, thoroughly acquainted with all those glorious privileges of sanctification[230] and adoption which render him more sacred than any dedicated altar or element, shall be restored to his right in the church, and not excluded from such place of spiritual government as his Christian abilities and his approved good life in the eye and testimony of the church shall prefer him to, this and nothing sooner will open his eyes to a wise and true valuation of himself, which is so requisite and high a point of Christianity, and will stir him up to walk worthy the honorable and grave employment wherewith God and the church hath dignified him; not fearing lest he should meet with some outward holy thing in religion which his lay touch or presence might profane, but lest something unholy from within his own heart should dishonor and profane in himself that priestly unction and clergy-right whereto Christ hath entitled him. Then would the congregation of the Lord soon recover the true likeness and visage of what she is indeed, a holy generation, a royal priesthood,[231] a saintly communion, the house-

hold and city of God. And this I hold to be another considerable reason why the functions of church government ought to be free and open to any Christian man, though never so laic, if his capacity, his faith, and prudent demeanor commend him. And this the apostles warrant us to do. But the prelates object that this will bring profaneness into the church; to whom may be replied that none have brought that in more than their own irreligious courses, nor more driven holiness out of living into lifeless things. For whereas God, who hath cleansed every beast and creeping worm, would not suffer St. Peter to call them common or unclean,[232] the prelate bishops, in their printed orders hung up in churches, have proclaimed the best of creatures, mankind, so unpurified and contagious, that for him to lay his hat or his garment upon the chancel table they have defined it no less heinous, in express words, than to profane the table of the Lord. And thus have they by their Canaanitish doctrine[233] (for that which was to the Jew but Jewish, is to the Christian no better than Canaanitish), thus have they made common and unclean, thus have they made profane that nature which God hath not only cleansed, but Christ also hath assumed. And now that the equity and just reason is so perspicuous, why in ecclesiastic censure the assistance should be added of such as whom not the vile odor of gain and fees (forbid it, God, and blow it with a whirlwind out of our land), but charity,

---

229 *corporal:* a communion cloth.

230 Building upon scriptures like Heb. x, 10, the Assembly of Divines sitting at Westminster when Milton wrote these words finally (in the Confession of 1647, chapter 12) defined *adoption* as the grace whereby Christians are "taken into the number, and enjoy the liberties and privileges of the children of God; have his name put upon them, receive the Spirit of adoption; have access to the throne of grace with boldness; are enabled to cry, Abba, Father; are pitied, protected, provided for, and chastened by him as by a father." The next chapter defines *sanctification* as a state in which, by the indwelling spirit of Christ, "the dominion of the whole body of sin is destroyed, and the several lusts thereof weakened and mortified"; so that Christians are "more and more quickened and strengthened in all saving graces, to the practice of holiness, without which no man shall see the Lord." Cf. *CD* I, xvii–xviii; C.E. XV, 342–77.

231 Milton built upon a verse often quoted by champions of the doctrine of the right of all Chris-

tians to be regarded as priests rather than mere laymen: "But ye are a chosen generation, a royal priesthood, an holy nation, a peculiar people; that ye should show forth the praises of him who hath called you out of darkness into his marvellous light" (I Pet. ii, 9). Since Calvin had declared (*Institutes* III, xix) the liberty of Christians from the Jewish ceremonial and civil law, this verse had been a rallying cry of all who challenged the rights of any hierarchy which seemed to derive in any way from the Jewish priesthood.

232 In a vision teaching that the Jewish ceremonial law which stigmatized the gentiles as *unclean* had been abrogated, St. Peter saw "four-footed beasts of the earth, and wild beasts, and creeping things, and fowls of the air"; and he heard "a voice saying, Arise, Peter; slay and eat." To his objection that the beasts were unclean the voice answered "from heaven, What God hath cleansed, that call not thou common" (Acts xi, 5–10).

233 The *Canaanites,* whom the Israelites drove out of Palestine when they settled the land, remained a byword among them for idolatry.

neighborhood, and duty to church government hath called together, where could a wise man wish a more equal, gratuitous, and meek examination of any offense that he might happen to commit against Christianity, than here? Would he prefer those proud simoniacal[234] courts? Thus therefore the minister assisted attends his heavenly and spiritual cure: where we shall see him both in the course of his proceeding, and first in the excellence of his end, from the magistrate far different, and not more different than excelling. His end is to recover all that is of man, both soul and body, to an everlasting health; and yet as for worldly happiness, which is the proper sphere wherein the magistrate cannot but confine his motion without a hideous exorbitancy from law, so little aims the minister, as his intended scope, to procure the much prosperity of this life, that ofttimes he may have cause to wish much of it away, as a diet puffing up the soul with a slimy fleshiness and weakening her principal organic parts. Two heads of evil he has to cope with, ignorance and malice. Against the former he provides the daily manna of incorruptible doctrine, not at those set meals only in public, but as oft as he shall know that each infirmity or constitution requires. Against the latter with all the branches thereof, not meddling with that restraining and styptic surgery[235] which the law uses, not indeed against the malady but against the eruptions and outermost effects thereof; he on the contrary, beginning at the prime causes and roots of the disease, sends in those two divine ingredients of most cleansing power to the soul, admonition and reproof, besides which two there is no drug or antidote that can reach to purge the mind, and without which all other experiments are but vain, unless by accident. And he that will not let these pass into him, though he be the greatest king, as

Plato[236] affirms, must be thought to remain impure within and unknowing of those things wherein his pureness and his knowledge should most appear. As soon therefore as it may be discerned that the Christian patient, by feeding otherwhere on meats not allowable but of evil juice, hath disordered his diet and spread an ill humor through his veins, immediately disposing to a sickness, the minister, as being much nearer both in eye and duty than the magistrate, speeds him betimes to overtake that diffused malignance with some gentle potion of admonishment; or if aught be obstructed, puts in his opening and discussive confections.[237] This not succeeding after once or twice, or oftener, in the presence of two or three his faithful brethren appointed thereto, he advises him to be more careful of his dearest health, and what it is that he so rashly hath let down into the divine vessel of his soul, God's temple.[238] If this obtain not, he then, with the counsel of more assistants who are informed of what diligence hath been already used, with more speedy remedies lays nearer siege to the entrenched causes of his distemper, not sparing such fervent and well-aimed reproofs as may best give him to see the dangerous estate wherein he is. To this also his brethren and friends entreat, exhort, adjure, and all these endeavors, as there is hope left, are more or less repeated. But if neither the regard of himself nor the reverence of his elders and friends prevail with him to leave his vicious appetite, then as the time urges, such engines of terror God hath given into the hand of his minister as to search the tenderest angles of the heart: one while he shakes his stubbornness with racking convulsions nigh despair, otherwhiles with deadly corrosives he gripes the very roots of his faulty liver to bring him to life through the entry of death. Hereto the whole church beseech him, beg of him, deplore him, pray for him. After all this performed with what patience and

---

[234] *Simony* is the crime of buying or selling preferment in the church, or—more broadly—of trafficking in its authority in any way. The bishops' courts, which controlled questions of marriage, divorce, and other matters which had come to seem purely civil, often had to face that charge from the Puritans.

[235] In the background is Plato's presentation of Socrates as a physician for the Athenians who believes that he has a duty to continue his caustic criticism of their lives even though it will make him fatally unpopular (*Gorgias*, 521a–522d).

[236] The reference, as Myer Levenson shows in *MLN*, XLVI (1931), 87, is to Plato's *Sophist*, 230d-e, where Socrates says that "he who has never been refuted, though he were the Great King himself, is in an awful state of impurity."

[237] *discussive*: dissipative (of morbid matter in the body).

[238] "Ye are the temple of the Lord" (I Cor. iii, 16).

attendance is possible, and no relenting on his part, having done the utmost of their cure, in the name of God and of the church they dissolve their fellowship with him, and holding forth the dreadful sponge of excommunion,[239] pronounce him wiped out of the list of God's inheritance and in the custody of Satan till he repent. Which horrid sentence, though it touch neither life nor limb, nor any worldly possession, yet has it such a penetrating force that swifter than any chemical sulphur or that lightning which harms not the skin and rifles the entrails, it scorches the inmost soul. Yet even this terrible denouncement is left to the church for no other cause but to be as a rough and vehement cleansing medicine where the malady is obdurate, a mortifying to life, a kind of saving by undoing. And it may be truly said that as the mercies of wicked men are cruelties,[240] so the cruelties of the church are mercies. For if repentance sent from Heaven meet this lost wanderer and draw him out of that steep journey wherein he was hasting towards destruction, to come and reconcile to the church, if he bring with him his bill of health, and that he is now clear of infection and of no danger to the other sheep; then with incredible expressions of joy all his brethren receive him and set before him those perfumed banquets of Christian consolation; with precious ointments bathing and fomenting the old and now to be forgotten stripes, which terror and shame had inflicted; and thus with heavenly solaces they cheer up his humble remorse, till he regain his first health and felicity. This is the approved way which the gospel prescribes, these are the "spiritual weapons of holy censure," and ministerial "warfare, not carnal, but mighty through God to the pulling down of strongholds, casting down imaginations, and every high thing that exalteth itself against the knowledge of God, and bringing into captivity every thought to the obedience of Christ."[241] What could be done more for the healing and reclaiming that divine particle of God's breathing, the soul?[242] And what could

be done less? He that would hide his faults from such a wholesome curing as this, and count it a twofold punishment, as some do, is like a man that having foul diseases about him, perishes for shame and the fear he has of a rigorous incision to come upon his flesh. We shall be able by this time to discern whether prelatical jurisdiction be contrary to the gospel or no. First, therefore, the government of the gospel being economical[243] and paternal, that is, of such a family where there be no servants, but all sons in obedience, not in servility,[244] as cannot be denied by him that lives but within the sound of scripture; how can the prelates justify to have turned the fatherly orders of Christ's household, the blessed meekness of his lowly roof, those ever open and inviting doors of his dwelling house, which delight to be frequented with only filial accesses, how can they justify to have turned these domestic privileges into the bar of a proud judicial court, where fees and clamors keep shop and drive a trade, where bribery and corruption solicits, paltering the free and moneyless power of discipline with a carnal satisfaction by the purse. Contrition, humiliation, confession, the very sighs of a repentant spirit, are there sold by the penny. That undeflowered and unblemishable simplicity of the gospel, not she herself, for that could never be, but a false-whited, a lawny resemblance of her, like that air-borne[245] Helena in the fables, made by the sorcery of prelates, instead of calling her disciples from the receipt of custom, is now turned publican herself; and gives up her body to a mercenary whoredom under those fornicated arches which she calls God's house, and in the sight of those her altars, which she hath set up to be adored, makes merchandise of the bodies and souls of men. Rejecting purgatory for no other reason, as it seems, than because her greediness can-

239 *excommunion*: excommunication.

240 ". . . the tender mercies of the wicked are cruel" (Prov. xii, 10).

241 II Cor. x, 4–5. Milton incorrectly gave the reference as "Cor. 2. 10."

242 And the Lord God formed man of the dust

of the ground, and breathed into his nostrils the breath of life" (Gen. ii, 7).

243 *economical*: relating to the family, domestic.

244 "For as many as are led by the Spirit of God, they are the sons of God. For ye have not received the spirit of bondage again to fear; but ye have received the spirit of adoption, whereby we cry, Abba, Father" (Rom. viii, 14–15).

245 Milton perhaps thought of the story as told by Euripides, *Helen*, 31–51, that Hera deceived Paris with a phantom Helen, whom he took to Troy, while Hermes took the real Helen to Egypt.

not defer but had rather use the utmost extortion of redeemed penances in this life. But because these matters could not be thus carried without a begged and borrowed force from worldly authority, therefore prelaty, slighting the deliberate and chosen council of Christ in his spiritual government, whose glory is in the weakness of fleshly things[246] to tread upon the crest of the world's pride and violence by the power of spiritual ordinances, hath on the contrary made these her friends and champions which are Christ's enemies in this his high design, smothering and extinguishing the spiritual force of his bodily weakness in the discipline of his church with the boisterous and carnal tyranny of an undue, unlawful, and ungospel-like jurisdiction. And thus prelaty, both in her fleshly supportments, in her carnal doctrine of ceremony and tradition, in her violent and secular power, going quite counter to the prime end of Christ's coming in the flesh, that is, to reveal his truth, his glory, and his might, in a clean contrary manner than prelaty seeks to do, thwarting and defeating the great mystery of God; I do not conclude that prelaty is antichristian, for what need I? The things themselves conclude it. Yet if such like practices, and not many worse than these of our prelates, in that great darkness of the Roman church, have not exempted both her and her present members from being judged to be antichristian in all orthodoxal esteem; I cannot think but that it is the absolute voice of truth and all her children to pronounce this prelaty, and these her dark deeds in the midst of this great light wherein we live, to be more antichristian than Antichrist himself.

THE CONCLUSION.

The mischief that Prelaty does in the State.

I add one thing more to those great ones that are so fond of prelaty: this is certain, that the gospel being the hidden might of Christ, as hath been heard, hath ever a victorious power joined with it, like him in the Revelation that went forth on the white horse with his bow and his crown, conquering and to conquer.[247] If we let the angel of the gospel ride on his own way, he does his proper business, conquering the high thoughts and the proud reasonings of the flesh, and brings them under to give obedience to Christ with the salvation of many souls. But if ye turn him out of his road, and in a manner force him to express his irresistible power by a doctrine of carnal might, as prelaty is, he will use that fleshly strength which ye put into his hands to subdue your spirits by a servile and blind superstition; and that again shall hold such dominion over your captive minds, as returning with an insatiate greediness and force upon your worldly wealth and power, wherewith to deck and magnify herself and her false worships, she shall spoil and havoc your estates, disturb your ease, diminish your honor, enthral your liberty under the swelling mood of a proud clergy who will not serve or feed your souls with spiritual food; look not for it, they have not wherewithal, or if they had, it is not in their purpose. But when they have glutted their ungrateful bodies, at least if it be possible that those open sepulchers should ever be glutted, and when they have stuffed their idolish temples with the wasteful pillage of your estates, will they yet have any compassion upon you and that poor pittance which they have left you; will they be but so good to you as that ravisher was to his sister, when he had used her at his pleasure;[248] will they but only hate ye, and so turn ye loose? No, they will not, Lords and Commons, they will not favor ye so much. What will they do then, in the name of God and saints, what will these manhaters yet with more despite and mischief do? I'll tell ye, or at least remember ye, for most of ye know it already. That they may want nothing to make them true merchants of Babylon,[249] as they have done

---

[246] "For our rejoicing is this, the testimony of our conscience, that in simplicity and godly sincerity, not with fleshly wisdom, but by the grace of God, we have had our conversation in the world" (II Cor. i, 12).

[247] The reference is to the *white horse* and its rider of Rev. xix, 11, and vi, 2, who "had a bow; and a crown was given unto him: and he went forth conquering, and to conquer."

[248] Milton refers to Amnon's incestuous violence to Tamar and his subsequent hatred of her, "so that the hatred wherewith he hated her was greater than the love wherewith he had loved her" (II Sam. xiii, 15).

[249] Milton is voicing the bitter Puritan resentment

to your souls, they will sell your bodies, your wives, your children, your liberties, your parliaments, all these things; and if there be aught else dearer than these, they will sell at an outcry in their pulpits to the arbitrary and illegal dispose of anyone that may hereafter be called a king, whose mind shall serve him to listen to their bargain. And by their corrupt and servile doctrines boring our ears to an everlasting slavery,[250] as they have done hitherto, so will they yet do their best to repeal and erase every line and clause of both our great charters. Nor is this only what they will do, but what they hold as the main reason and mystery of their advancement that they must do; be the prince never so just and equal to his subjects, yet such are their malicious and depraved eyes that they so look on him and so understand him, as if he required no other gratitude or piece of service from them than this. And indeed they stand so opportunely for the disturbing or the destroying of a state, being a knot of creatures whose dignities, means, and preferments have no foundation in the gospel, as they themselves acknowledge, but only in the prince's favor, and to continue so long to them as by pleasing him they shall deserve: whence it must needs be they should bend all their intentions and services to no other ends but to his, that if it should happen that a tyrant (God turn such a scourge from us to our enemies) should come to grasp the scepter, here were his spearmen and his lances, here were his firelocks ready, he should need no other prætorian band[251] nor pensionary than

these, if they could once with their perfidious preachments awe the people. For although the prelates in time of popery were sometimes friendly enough to Magna Charta,[252] it was because they stood upon their own bottom, without their main dependence on the royal nod: but now being well acquainted that the protestant religion, if she will reform herself rightly by the scriptures, must undress them of all their gilded vanities and reduce them as they were at first to the lowly and equal order of presbyters, they know it concerns them nearly to study the times more than the text, and to lift up their eyes to the hills[253] of the court from whence only comes their help; but if their pride grow weary of this crouching and observance, as ere long it would, and that yet their minds climb still to a higher ascent of worldly honor, this only refuge can remain to them, that they must of necessity contrive to bring themselves and us back again to the pope's supremacy; and this we see they had by fair degrees of late been doing. These be the two fair supporters between which the strength of prelaty is borne up, either of inducing tyranny, or of reducing popery.[254] Hence also we may judge that prelaty is mere falsehood. For the property of truth is, where she is publicly taught, to unyoke and set free the minds and spirits of a nation first from the thraldom of sin and superstition, after which all honest and legal freedom of civil life cannot be long absent; but prelaty, whom the tyrant custom[255] begot a natural tyrant in religion, and in state the agent and minister of tyr-

of the defense of the royal power and even of such abuses of it as ship-money by the bishops in their sermons at court and elsewhere. Because Puritan prejudice identified them with the Roman Catholics, and because Rome was often called Babylon in Puritan parlance, he called them *merchants of Babylon*. Compare the popular saying: "All Babylon lies low; Luther destroyed the roof thereof, Calvin the walls, but Socinus the foundations." Cf. Rev. xviii, 10–11.

[250] The master of the Hebrew slave who voluntarily sought life-long servitude was to "bore his ear through with an awl" (Exod. xxi, 6) as a sign that his bondage was "forever." Puritan resistance to King Charles's infractions of popular rights constantly stressed Magna Charta and the Charter of Forests (1215 and 1216 respectively) as the foundation of the liberties which were vindicated by the Petition of Right, to which the king assented 7 June, 1628.

[251] The bishops, Milton suggests, are threatening

to become mere pensioners of the king and to make him the nominal head of a tyranny like that which the *Praetorian* guards of the Roman emperors developed under the pretense of protecting the imperial power and the rights of the emperors.

[252] Several bishops took an active part in extorting *Magna Charta* from King John in 1215, but their motives were always unfavorably interpreted by the Puritans.

[253] An ironical application of Psalm cxxi, 1.

[254] *reducing*: bringing back. Archbishop Laud's opponents, says Mr. Trevor-Roper (*Laud*, p. 306) "continually . . . attacked him as a Papist himself: and the charge, though we can see that it was untrue, was natural: nor was the subtle difference between the new high anglicanism and the old Rome likely to be appreciated by ears attuned to Puritan hysterics."

[255] Cf. the opening attacks on *custom* as the parent of corruption and tyranny in *DDD* and *TKM*.

anny, seems to have had this fatal gift in her nativity, like another Midas, that whatsoever she should touch or come near either in ecclesial or political government, it should turn, not to gold, though she for her part could wish it, but to the dross and scum of slavery, breeding and settling both in the bodies and the souls of all such as do not in time, with the sovereign treacle[256] of sound doctrine, provide to fortify their hearts against her hierarchy. The service of God, who is truth, her liturgy confesses to be perfect freedom,[257] but her works and her opinions declare, that the service of prelaty is perfect slavery, and by consequence perfect falsehood. Which makes me wonder much that many of the gentry, studious men as I hear, should engage themselves to write and speak publicly in her defense; but that I believe their honest and ingenuous natures coming to the universities to store themselves with good and solid learning and there unfortunately fed with nothing else but the scragged and thorny lectures of monkish and miserable sophistry, were sent home again with such a scholastic burr in their throats as hath stopped and hindered all true and generous philosophy from entering, cracked their voices for ever with metaphysical gargarisms,[258] and hath made them admire a sort of formal outside men prelatically addicted; whose unchastened and unwrought minds (never yet initiated or subdued under the true lore of religion or moral virtue, which two are the best and greatest points of learning, but either slightly trained up in a kind of hypocritical and hackney course of literature to get their living by and dazzle the ignorant, or else fondly overstudied in useless controversies, except those which they use with all the specious and delusive subtlety they are able,

to defend their prelatical Sparta[259]) having a gospel and church government set before their eyes, as a fair field wherein they might exercise the greatest virtues and the greatest deeds of Christian authority in mean fortunes and little furniture of this world (which even the sage heathen writers, and those old Fabritii and Curii[260] well knew to be a manner of working, than which nothing could liken a mortal man more to God, who delights most to work from within himself, and not by the heavy luggage of corporeal instrument) they understand it not, and think no such matter, but admire and dote upon worldly riches and honors, with an easy and intemperate life, to the bane of Christianity. Yea, they and their seminaries shame not to profess, to petition, and never lin pealing[261] our ears, that unless we fat them like boars, and cram them as they list with wealth, with deaneries and pluralities,[262] with baronies and stately preferments, all learning and religion will go underfoot. Which is such a shameless, such a bestial plea, and of that odious impudence in churchmen, who should be to us a pattern of temperance and frugal mediocrity,[263] who should teach us to contemn this world and the gaudy things thereof, according to the promise which they themselves require from us in baptism,[264] that should the scripture stand

256 *treacle:* originally, a remedy against the bites of poisonous creatures; a powerful antidote or medicine of any kind.

257 The Collect for Peace in the Anglican Liturgy reads: "O God, who art the author of peace and lover of concord, in knowledge of whom standeth our eternal life, whose service is perfect freedom; defend us thy humble servants in all assaults of our enemies. . . ."

258 So in *Educ,* p. 632, Milton attacked the universities because they were "not yet recovered from scholastic grossness," and in *Prols* III and VII he was frank in his contempt for scholastic logic and theology.

259 Ecclesiastical champions of episcopacy are like the ancient Spartans, stout champions of oligarchical privilege, but lacking real character and real culture.

260 Gaius Fabricius was famous in Roman history for having refused the bribes of King Pyrrhus when they were negotiating about an exchange of prisoners in 282 B.C., and for his severity when he became censor in 275. His contemporary, Marcus Curius Dentatus, defeated Pyrrhus in that year and refused his immense share, as a consul, in the booty.

261 *lin:* cease. *pealing:* assailing with noise, nagging. Cf. *SA,* 235.

262 *pluralities:* enjoyment of two or more benefices simultaneously by a clergyman. In defending them in *The Laws of Ecclesiastical Polity* V, lxxxi, Hooker first inveighed as vigorously as any Puritan could against their abuse, but committed himself to them "by way of honour to learning, nobility, and authority." "The brethren and sons of lords temporal and knights, if God shall move the hearts of such to enter at any time into holy orders," he felt, should "obtain to themselves a faculty or license to hold two ecclesiastical livings."

263 *mediocrity:* moderate estate, humble style of living.

264 The Anglican Liturgy asks the sponsors of a child at baptism to renounce on his behalf "the

by and be mute, there is not that sect of philosophers among the heathen so dissolute, no not Epicurus, nor Aristippus[265] with all his Cyrenaic rout, but would shut his school doors against such greasy sophisters; not any college of mountebanks, but would think scorn to discover[266] in themselves with such a brazen forehead the outrageous desire of filthy lucre. Which the prelates make so little conscience of that they are ready to fight and, if it lay in their power, to massacre all good Christians under the names of horrible schismatics for only finding fault with their temporal dignities, their unconscionable wealth and revenues, their cruel authority over their brethren that labor in the word, while they snore in their luxurious excess: openly proclaiming themselves now in the sight of all men to be those which for a while they sought to cover under sheep's clothing, ravenous and savage wolves[267] threatening inroads and bloody incursions upon the flock of Christ, which they took upon them to feed, but now claim to devour as their prey. More like that huge dragon of Egypt breathing out waste and desolation to the land, unless he were daily fattened with virgin's blood. Him our old patron St. George[268] by his matchless valor slew, as

the prelate of the garter that reads his collect[269] can tell. And if our princes and knights will imitate the fame of that old champion, as by their order of knighthood solemnly taken they vow, far be it that they should uphold and side with this English dragon; but rather to do as indeed their oath binds them, they should make it their knightly adventure to pursue and vanquish this mighty sail-winged monster that menaces to swallow up the land, unless her bottomless gorge may be satisfied with the blood of the king's daughter, the church; and may, as she was wont, fill her dark and infamous den with the bones of the saints. Nor will anyone have reason to think this as too incredible or too tragical to be spoken of prelaty, if he consider well from what a mass of slime and mud, the slothful, the covetous, and ambitious hopes of church promotions and fat bishoprics, she is bred up and nuzzled in like a great Python[270] from her youth, to prove the general poison both of doctrine and good discipline in the land. For certainly such hopes and such principles of earth as these wherein she welters from a young one, are the immediate generation both of a slavish and tyran-

Knights of the Garter should imitate Spenser's Red Cross Knight (*St. George*), who slays the dragon of ecclesiastical hierarchy in *F.Q.* I, xi. The development of the legend of St. George, who was connected with Silene in Libya, is traced in F. M. Padelford's notes in Vol. I, pp. 379–90, of *The Complete Works of Edmund Spenser* (Baltimore, 1932).

[265] "Who can but pity the virtuous Epicurus," asked Thomas Browne in *Vulgar Errors* VII, xvii, "who is commonly conceived to have placed his chief felicity in pleasure and sensual delights, and hath therefore left an infamous name behind him? . . . The ground hereof seems a misapprehension of his opinion, who placed his felicity not in the pleasures of the body, but the mind, and tranquillity thereof, obtained by wisdom and virtue." *Aristippus* was traditionally regarded as "luxurious," but Milton perhaps remembered that he left his native Cyrene to spend years in study with Socrates in Athens.

[266] *discover:* expose, exhibit.

[267] This passage, like the lines on the "blind mouths" in *Lyc* (119–31), is the culmination of what can be recognized among many attacks on the bishops in William Prynne's *A Breviate of the Prelates intollerable usurpations, both upon the Kings Prerogative Royal, and the Subjects Libertes* (1637), p. 29, as a classic use of a favorite figure of speech in denouncing the bishops, "these ravenous evening wolves (Habakuk i, 8) (though in Sheepes clothing) who devour and prey upon" the "poore, innocent, harmlesse wooried sheeps and lambes."

[268] Milton ironically suggests that King Charles's

[269] The *collect* in question occurs in the *Primer according to the Usage of Salisbury* and is translated by Peter Heylin in *The History of that most famous Saynt and Souldier of Christ Jesus, St. George of Cappadocia* (1631) in this way, in part:

George, holy Martyr, praise and fame
Attend upon thy glorious name;
Advanced to knightly dignitie:
The Daughter of a King, by thee
(As she was making grievous moane
By a fierce Dragon, all alone)
Was freed from death. Thee we entreat
That we in Heaven may have a seat.

Puritan feeling resented the connection of the bishops of Winchester with the Order of the Garter as its prelates, and as early as 1574 Archbishop Whitgift—in *The Defence of the Answer to the Admonition* (*The Works of John Whitgift*, Parker Society, 1853, III, 405–8)—had replied at length to the charge that it was "against the word of God . . . for an archbishop to be a lord president, a lord bishop to be a county palatine, a prelate of the Garter, who hath much to do at St. George's feast," etc.

[270] Cf. *PL* I, 197–99 n.

nous life to follow and a pestiferous contagion to the whole kingdom, till like that fen-born serpent she be shot to death with the darts of the sun, the pure and powerful beams of God's word. And this may serve to describe to us in part what prelaty hath been and what, if she stand, she is like to be toward the whole body of people in England. Now that it may appear how she is not such a kind of evil as hath any good or use in it, which many evils have, but a distilled quintessence, a pure elixir of mischief, pestilent alike to all, I shall show briefly, ere I conclude, that the prelates, as they are to the subjects a calamity, so are they the greatest underminers and betrayers of the monarch, to whom they seem to be most favorable. I cannot better liken the state and person of a king than to that mighty Nazarite Samson;[271] who, being disciplined from his birth in the precepts and the practice of temperance and sobriety, without the strong drink of injurious and excessive desires, grows up to a noble strength and perfection with those his illustrious and sunny locks, the laws,[272] waving and curling about his godlike shoulders. And while he keeps them about him undiminished and unshorn, he may with the jawbone of an ass, that is, with the word of his meanest officer, suppress and put to confusion thousands of those that rise against his just power. But laying down his head among the strumpet flatteries of prelates,[273] while he sleeps and thinks no harm, they,

wickedly shaving off all those bright and weighty tresses of his laws and just prerogatives, which were his ornament and strength, deliver him over to indirect and violent counsels, which, as those Philistines, put out the fair and far-sighted eyes of his natural discerning and make him grind in the prisonhouse of their sinister ends and practices upon him: till he, knowing his prelatical razor to have bereft him of his wonted might, nourish again his puissant hair, the golden beams of law and right; and they sternly shook, thunder with ruin upon the heads of those his evil counsellors, but not without great affliction to himself. This is the sum of their loyal service to kings; yet these are the men that still cry, "The king, the king, the Lord's anointed!"[274] We grant it, and wonder how they came to light upon anything so true; and wonder more, if kings be the Lord's anointed, how they dare thus oil over and besmear so holy an unction with the corrupt and putrid ointment of their base flatteries, which, while they smooth the skin, strike inward and envenom the lifeblood.[275] What fidelity kings can expect from prelates both examples past and our present experience of their doings at this day, whereon is grounded all that hath been said, may suffice to inform us. And if they be such clippers of regal power and shavers of the laws, how they stand affected to the law-giving parliament, yourselves, worthy peers and commons, can best testify, the current of whose glorious and immortal actions hath been only opposed by the obscure and pernicious designs of the prelates, until their insolence broke out to such a bold affront as hath justly immured their haughty looks within strong walls.[276] Nor have they done anything of late with more diligence than to hinder or break the happy assembling of parliaments, however needful to repair the shattered and disjointed frame of the commonwealth, or if they

---

[271] A discussion of the possible ties between this outline of the story of *Samson* in Judg. xiii–xvi and *SA* is provided by E. M. Clark in *University of Texas Bulletin*, No. 2734 (1927), pp. 144–54, and from another point of view by W. R. Parker in *JEGP*, XXXIV (1935), 225–32.

[272] This is a final allusion to Plato's *Laws*. In Book IV (715d) Law is said to be rightly lord over the magistrates, while they should be the servants of the Law. Plato saw prosperity and every blessing of the gods in states where that principle was honored, and ruin impending everywhere that it was violated.

[273] Milton's thought here is a commonplace of Puritan propaganda. In *An Appeal to the Parliament* (p. 212) Leighton warned that Charles was about to "split upon the *rocks* of malicious Counsell, or sinke in the quicksands of base flatteries." The bishops, he said (p. 25) were "opposite *to the King and his Lawes*, in affirming their calling to be *jure divino*, because by his Laws they are said to be a part *of his prerogative*." The argument goes directly on to describe their attack on the king and the law as nothing short of treason.

[274] Cf. *TKM*, n. 32.

[275] Cf. Lord Brooke's *Discourse opening the Nature of Episcopacy* (p. 60): "What meanes their crying up an unjust and illimited power in Princes? Is not This their bleating out of an illegal unwarranted Prerogative (with which our pulpits have rung of late) intended to tickle Princes till they be luld asleepe? or to sow pillowes under them, till They themselves can thrust them downe."

[276] Cf. n. 45 above.

cannot do this, to cross, to disenable, and traduce all parliamentary proceedings. And this, if nothing else, plainly accuses them to be no lawful members of the house, if they thus perpetually mutiny against their own body. And though they pretend, like Solomon's harlot,[277] that they have right thereto, by the same judgment that Solomon gave, it cannot belong to them, whenas it is not only their assent but their endeavor continually to divide parliaments in twain; and not only by dividing but by all other means to abolish and destroy the free use of them to all posterity. For the which and for all their former misdeeds, whereof this book and many volumes more cannot contain the moiety, I shall move ye, Lords, in the behalf I dare say of many thousand good Christians, to let your justice and speedy sentence pass against this great malefactor, prelaty. And yet in the midst of rigor I would beseech ye to think of mercy; and such a mercy (I fear I shall overshoot with a desire to save this falling prelaty), such a mercy (if I may venture to say it) as may exceed that which for only ten righteous persons would have saved Sodom.[278] Not

that I dare advise ye to contend with God whether he or you shall be more merciful, but in your wise esteems to balance the offenses of those peccant[279] cities with these enormous riots of ungodly misrule that prelaty hath wrought both in the church of Christ and in the state of this kingdom. And if ye think ye may with a pious presumption strive to go beyond God in mercy, I shall not be one now that would dissuade ye. Though God for less than ten just persons would not spare Sodom, yet if you can find after due search but only one good thing in prelaty, either to religion or civil government, to king or parliament, to prince or people, to law, liberty, wealth, or learning, spare her, let her live, let her spread among ye, till with her shadow all your dignities and honors, and all the glory of the land be darkened and obscured. But on the contrary, if she be found to be malignant, hostile, destructive to all these, as nothing can be surer, then let your severe and impartial doom imitate the divine vengeance; rain[280] down your punishing force upon this godless and oppressing government, and bring such a dead sea of subversion upon her that she may never in this land rise more to afflict the holy reformed church, and the elect people of God.

---

[277] I Kings iii, 16–27, tells the story of Solomon's judgment between two harlots who claimed the same child. At his command to "divide the living child in two," the true mother identified herself by yielding her claim.

[278] When Abraham asked God not to destroy Sodom if as many as *ten righteous* men were to be found there, he received God's promise that he would "not destroy it for ten's sake" (Gen. xviii, 32).

[279] *peccant*: sinful.

[280] "Then the Lord rained upon Sodom and upon Gomorrah brimstone and fire from the Lord out of heaven" (Gen. xix, 24).

A Selection from

AN APOLOGY AGAINST A PAMPHLET CALLED "A MODEST CONFUTATION OF THE ANIMADVERSIONS UPON THE REMONSTRANT AGAINST SMECTYMNUUS."[1] (1642)

BIBLIOGRAPHICAL NOTE—*An Apology* was published anonymously, probably in the late spring, in 1642, in reply to *A Modest Confutation of a Slanderous and Scurrilous Libell, Entituled, Animadversions etc.* In Milford C. Jochums' edition of *An Apology* (*Illinois Studies in Language and Literature,* XXV, Nos. 1–2. 1950), pp 3 and 113, the author is surmised to be Bishop Joseph Hall's son Edward, but Frederick L. Taft takes an impartial view of the claims of Edward *vs* those of Robert Hall, another son of the Bishop, in his edition of *An Apology* in *Complete Prose Works of John Milton,* ed. by Don M. Wolfe and others, Vol. I (New Haven, 1953), p. 863. Both the modern editions are liberally annotated. The present selections are based on the copy of the first edition in the Houghton Library at Harvard.

Thus having spent his first onset not in confuting but in a reasonless defaming of the book, the method of his malice hurries him[2] to attempt the like against the author;[3] not by proofs and testimonies, but "having no certain notice of me," as he professes, "further than what he gathers from the *Animadversions,*" blunders at me for the rest, and flings out stray crimes at a venture, which he could never, though he be a serpent, suck from anything that I have written, but from his own stuffed magazine and hoard of slanderous inventions, over and above that which he converted to venom in the drawing. To me, readers, it happens as a singular contentment, and let it be to good men no slight satisfaction, that the slanderer here confesses he has "no further notice of me than his own conjecture." Although it had been honest to have inquired before he uttered such infamous words, and I am credibly informed he did inquire; but finding small comfort from the intelligence which he received, whereon to ground the falsities which he had provided, thought it his likeliest course under a pretended ignorance to let drive at random, lest he should lose his odd ends which from some penurious Book of Characters[4] he had been culling out and would fain apply. Not caring to burden me with those vices whereof, among whom my conversation hath been, I have been ever least suspected; perhaps not without some subtlety to cast me into envy by bringing on me a necessity to enter into mine own praises. In which argument I know every wise man is more unwillingly drawn to speak than the most repining ear can be averse to hear.

Nevertheless, since I dare not wish to pass this life unpersecuted of slanderous tongues, for God hath told us that to be generally praised is woeful,[5] I shall rely on his promise to free the innocent from causeless aspersions: whereof nothing sooner can assure me than if I shall feel him now assisting me in the just vindication of myself, which yet I could defer, it being more meet that to those other matters of public debatement in this book I should give attendance first, but that I fear it would but harm the truth for me to reason in her behalf, so long as I should suffer my honest estimation to lie unpurged from these insolent suspicions. And if I shall be large

---

[1] Masson first brought together the facts about the five Presbyterian ministers whose initials were combined into the signature which cryptically identified the authors of *An Answer to a Book entituled 'An Humble Remonstrance,'* (1641) in *The Life of John Milton* (London, 1871), Vol. II, pp. 219–22. Cf. *CG,* n. 83, and *Eikon,* Chap. xxvii, n. 18.

[2] *him:* the author of *Animadversions.*

[3] *the author:* Milton.

[4] *Book of Characters:* an allusion to Hall's *Characters of Virtues and Vices* (1608), the most successful of his early bids for literary fame. It was translated into French in 1610, and in 1691 was versified by Nahum Tate.

[5] "Woe unto you, when all men shall speak well of you" (Luke vi, 26).

or unwonted in justifying myself to those who know me not (for else it would be needless), let them consider that a short slander will ofttimes reach further than a long apology; and that he who will do justly to all men, must begin from knowing how, if it so happen, to be not unjust to himself. I must be thought, if this libeller (for now he shows himself to be so) can find belief, after an inordinate and riotous youth spent at "the University," to have been at length "vomited out thence."[6] For which commodious lie, that he may be encouraged in the trade another time, I thank him; for it hath given me an apt occasion to acknowledge publicly with all grateful mind that more than ordinary favor and respect which I found above any of my equals[7] at the hands of those courteous and learned men, the fellows of that college wherein I spent some years: who at my parting, after I had taken two degrees, as the manner is, signified many ways how much better it would content them that I would stay; as by many letters full of kindness and loving respect, both before that time and long after, I was assured of their singular good affection towards me. Which being likewise propense to all such as were for their studious and civil life worthy of esteem, I could not wrong their judgments and upright intentions so much as to think I had that regard from them for other cause than that I might be still encouraged to proceed in the honest and laudable courses of which they apprehended I had given good proof. And to those ingenuous and friendly men who were ever the countenancers of virtuous and hopeful wits, I wish the best and happiest things that friends in absence wish one to another.

As for the common approbation or dislike of that place, as now it is, that I should esteem or disesteem myself or any other the more for that, too simple and too credulous is the confuter, if he think to obtain with me or any right discerner. Of small practice were that physician who could not judge by what both she or her sister[8] hath of long time vomited, that the worser stuff she strongly keeps in her stomach, but the better she is ever kecking at, and is queasy. She vomits now out of sickness, but ere it will be well with her, she must vomit by strong physic. In the meanwhile that "suburb sink,"[9] as this rude scavenger calls it—and more than scurrilously taunts it with the "plague," having a worse plague in his middle entrail—that suburb wherein I dwell shall be in my account a more honorable place than his university. Which, as in the time of her better health and mine own younger judgment I never greatly admired, so now much less. But he follows me to the city, still usurping[10] and forging beyond his book notice, which only he affirms to have had; "and where my morning haunts are, he wisses not." T'is wonder that, being so rare an alchemist of slander, he could not extract that as well as the university vomit and the suburb sink which his art could distil so cunningly; but because his limbec[11] fails him, to give him and envy the more vexation, I'll tell him. Those morning haunts are where they should be, at home; not sleeping or concocting[12] the surfeits of an irregular feast, but up and stirring, in winter often ere the sound of any bell awake men to labor or to devotion; in summer as oft with the bird that first rouses, or not much tardier, to read good authors, or cause them to be read, till the attention be weary, or memory have its full fraught: then, with useful and generous labors preserving the body's health and hardiness, to render lightsome, clear, and not lumpish obedience to the mind, to the cause of religion, and our country's liberty, when it shall require firm hearts in sound bodies to stand and cover their stations, rather than to see the ruin of our protestation and the enforcement of a slavish life.

These are the morning practices: proceed now to the afternoon; "in playhouses," he says, "and the bordelloes." Your intelli-

---

[6] Milton's rustication from Cambridge in the Lent Term of 1626 seems to have been trivial. The best commentary on it is his El I.

[7] equals: contemporaries, persons of about the same age.

[8] her sister: Oxford.

[9] The Confutation had accused Milton of haunting places of bad repute in the London suburbs.

[10] usurping: presuming, going beyond the evidence.

[11] limbec: an alembic, an alchemist's device for distilling various chemicals.

[12] concocting: digesting. Cf. Educ, n. 88, and PL V, 437.

gence, unfaithful spy of Canaan?[13] He gives in his evidence, that "there he hath traced me." Take him at his word, readers, but let him bring good sureties ere ye dismiss him, that while he pretended to dog others, he did not turn in for his own pleasure: for so much in effect he concludes against himself, not contented to be caught in every other gin,[14] but he must be such a novice as to be still hampered in his own hemp. In the *Animadversions,* saith he, I find the mention of old cloaks, false beards, night-walkers, and salt lotion; therefore, the animadverter haunts playhouses and bordelloes; for if he did not, how could he speak of such gear? Now that he may know what it is to be a child and yet to meddle with edged tools, I turn his antistrophon[15] upon his own head; the confuter knows that these things are the furniture of playhouses and bordelloes, therefore, by the same reason, *the confuter himself hath been traced in those places.* Was it such a dissolute speech, telling of some politicians who were wont to eavesdrop in disguises, to say they were often liable to a nightwalking cudgeller, or the emptying of a urinal? What if I had written as your friend the author of the aforesaid mime, *Mundus alter et idem,*[16] to have been ravished like some young Cephalus[17] or Hylas[18] by a troop of camping housewives in Viraginea, and that he was there forced to swear himself an uxorious varlet; then after a long servitude to have come into Aphrodisia, that pleasant country that gave such a sweet smell to his nostrils among the shameless courtesans of Desvergonia? Surely he would have then concluded me as constant at the bordello as the galley-slave at his oar.

But since there is such necessity to the hearsay of a tire,[19] a periwig, or a vizard,[20] that plays must have been seen, what difficulty was there in that, when in the colleges so many of the young divines, and those in next aptitude to divinity, have been seen so oft upon the stage, writhing and unboning their clergy limbs to all the antic and dishonest gestures of Trinculos,[21] buffoons, and bawds, prostituting the shame of that ministry, which either they had or were nigh having, to the eyes of courtiers and court ladies, with their grooms and mademoiselles. There, while they acted and overacted, among other young scholars I was a spectator; they thought themselves gallant men, and I thought them fools; they made sport, and I laughed; they mispronounced, and I misliked; and, to make up the atticism, they were out, and I hissed. Judge now whether so many good textmen were not sufficient to instruct me of false beards and vizards, without more expositors; and how can this confuter take the face to object to me the seeing of that which his reverend prelates allow, and incite their young disciples to act? For if it be unlawful[22] to sit and behold a mercenary comedian personating that which is least unseemly for a hireling to do, how much more blameful is it to endure the sight of as vile things acted by persons either entered, or presently to enter into the ministry, and how much more foul and ignominious for them to be the actors!

But because, as well by this upbraiding

---

[13] The spies whom Moses sent into Canaan, "returned, . . . bringing up a slander upon the land" (Num. xiv, 36).

[14] *gin:* a trap or snare for game.

[15] *antistrophon:* the rhetorical figure of retort or turning of a quip or argument back upon an opponent.

[16] In the paragraph preceding this extract Hall's *Mundus Alter et idem* (1605; English translation as *The Discovery of a New World,* 1608) is called "the idlest and paltriest mime that ever mounted upon the bank," and its imaginary voyage to a land of viragos (*Viraginea*), a land of romance (*Aphrodisia*), and a city of debauchery (*Desvergognia*) is disparagingly compared to More's *Utopia* and Bacon's *New Atlantis.*

[17] *Cephalus,* according to the story retold by Ovid in *Met.* VII, 700–13, was snatched away from his wife, Procris, by the goddess of the dawn, Aurora.

[18] One of the most familiar and least admirable features of the story of Hercules, according to Conti (VII, i), was his seizure of *Hylas* and his passion for the youth.

[19] *tire:* costume.

[20] *vizard:* mask.

[21] One of the *Trinculos* in the background is Shakespeare's drunken sailor in *The Tempest* III, ii; but Milton probably thought of Thomas Tomkys' Trincalo in *Albumazar,* a rustic who confesses: "I am idle, choicely neate in my cloathes, valiant, and extreame witty: My meditations are loaded with metaphors, and songs and sonnets: Not a one shakes his tayle, but I sigh out a passion; thus doe I to my Mistris: But alas I kisse the dogge, and she kicks me" (Act II, i). The play was acted at Trinity College, Cambridge, in 1614, and published several times.

[22] Milton was writing only a few months before the closing of the theaters by Parliament on Sept. 2, 1642.

to me the bordelloes as by other suspicious glancings in his book, he would seem privily to point me out to his readers as one whose custom of life were not honest but licentious, I shall entreat to be borne with though I digress; and in a way not often trod acquaint ye with the sum of my thoughts in this matter, through the course of my years and studies: although I am not ignorant how hazardous it will be to do this under the nose of the envious, as it were in skirmish to change the compact order,[23] and instead of outward actions, to bring inmost thoughts into front. And I must tell ye, readers, that by this sort of men I have been already bitten at; yet shall they not for me know how slightly they are esteemed, unless they have so much learning as to read what in Greek ἀπειροκαλία[24] is, which, together with envy, is the common disease of those who censure books that are not for their reading. With me it fares now as with him whose outward garment hath been injured and ill-bedighted; for having no other shift, what help but to turn the inside outwards, especially if the lining be of the same, or, as it is sometimes, much better? So if my name and outward demeanor be not evident enough to defend me, I must make trial if the discovery of my inmost thoughts can: wherein of two purposes, both honest and both sincere, the one perhaps I shall not miss; although I fail to gain belief with others of being such as my perpetual thoughts shall here disclose me, I may yet not fail of success in persuading some to be such really themselves, as they cannot believe me to be more than what I feign.

I had my time, readers, as others have who have good learning bestowed upon them, to be sent to those places where, the opinion was, it might be soonest attained; and as the manner is, was not unstudied in those authors which are most commended. Whereof some were grave orators and historians, whose matter methought I loved indeed, but as my age then was, so I understood them; others were the smooth elegiac poets, whereof the schools are not scarce, whom both for the pleasing sound of their numerous[25] writing, which in imitation I found most easy and most agreeable to nature's part in me, and for their matter, which what it is there be few who know not, I was so allured to read that no recreation came to me better welcome. For that it was then those years with me which are excused though they be least severe, I may be saved the labor to remember ye. Whence having observed them to account it the chief glory of their wit, in that they were ablest to judge, to praise, and by that could esteem themselves worthiest to love those high perfections which under one or other name they took to celebrate, I thought with myself by every instinct and presage of nature, which is not wont to be false, that what emboldened them to this task, might with such diligence as they used embolden me; and that what judgment, wit, or elegance was my share, would herein best appear, and best value itself, by how much more wisely, and with more love of virtue I should choose (let rude ears be absent)[26] the object of not unlike praises. For albeit these thoughts to some will seem virtuous and commendable, to others only pardonable, to a third sort perhaps idle; yet the mentioning of them now will end in serious.

Nor blame it, readers, in those years to propose to themselves such a reward as the noblest dispositions above other things in this life have sometimes preferred: whereof not to be sensible when good and fair in one person meet, argues both a gross and shallow judgment, and withal an ungentle and swainish breast. For by the firm settling of these persuasions I became, to my best memory, so much a proficient that, if I found those authors anywhere speaking unworthy things of themselves or unchaste of those names which before they had extolled, this effect it wrought with me, from that time forward their art I still applauded, but the men I deplored; and above them all, preferred the two famous renowners of

<hr>

[23] *compact order:* i.e. of soldiers in close order in a square formation when the inner and outer ranks change positions.

[24] ἀπειροκαλία: bad taste such as produces bad conduct. Plato uses the word in the *Republic* (403c and 405b) of the propensities to undue physical intimacy and to litigiousness.

[25] *numerous:* rhythmic because metrical. Cf. Milton's allusion to "numbers" as "various-measur'd verse" in *PR* IV, 255–6.

[26] A reminiscence of classical warnings, like that of the seer in Virgil's *Aen.* VI, 258, to all profane persons to keep their distance from a sacred place.

Beatrice and Laura,[27] who never write but honor of them to whom they devote their verse, displaying sublime and pure thoughts, without transgression. And long it was not after, when I was confirmed in this opinion that he who would not be frustrate of his hope to write well hereafter in laudable things, ought himself to be a true poem,[28] that is, a composition and pattern of the best and honorablest things—not presuming to sing high praises of heroic men or famous cities, unless he have in himself the experience and the practice of all that which is praiseworthy. These reasonings, together with a certain niceness of nature, an honest haughtiness and self-esteem either of what I was, or what I might be (which let envy call pride), and lastly that modesty whereof, though not in the title-page, yet here I may be excused to make some beseeming profession; all these uniting the supply of their natural aid together, kept me still above those low descents of mind beneath which he must deject and plunge himself that can agree to saleable and unlawful prostitutions.

Next (for hear me out now, readers), that I may tell ye whether my younger feet wandered; I betook me among those lofty fables and romances,[29] which recount in solemn cantos the deeds of knighthood founded by our victorious kings, and from hence had in renown over all Christendom. There I read it in the oath of every knight, that he should defend to the expense of his best blood, or of his life if it so befell him, the honor and chastity of virgin or matron; from whence even then I learned what a noble virtue chastity sure must be, to the defense of which so many worthies, by such a dear adventure of themselves, had sworn. And if I found in the story afterward any of them, by word or deed, breaking that oath, I judged it the same fault of the poet as that which is attributed to Homer,[30] to

have written indecent things of the gods. Only this my mind gave me, that every free and gentle spirit, without that oath, ought to be born a knight, nor needed to expect the gilt spur, or the laying of a sword upon his shoulder to stir him up both by his counsel and his arm to secure and protect the weakness of any attempted chastity. So that even those books which to many others have been the fuel of wantonness and loose living, I cannot think how, unless by divine indulgence, proved to me so many incitements, as you have heard, to the love and steadfast observation of that virtue which abhors the society of bordelloes.

Thus, from the laureate fraternity of poets, riper years and the ceaseless round of study and reading led me to the shady spaces of philosophy, but chiefly to the divine volumes of Plato[31] and his equal,[32] Xenophon: where, if I should tell ye what I learnt of chastity and love (I mean that which is truly so, whose charming cup is only virtue, which she bears in her hand to those who are worthy—the rest are cheated with a thick intoxicating potion which a certain sorceress, the abuser of love's name, carries about) and how the first and chiefest office of love begins and ends in the soul, producing those happy twins of her divine generation, knowledge and virtue—with such abstracted sublimities as these, it might be worth your listening, readers, as I may one day hope to have ye in a still time, when there shall be no chiding; not in these noises, the adversary, as you know, barking at the door, or searching for me at the bordelloes, where it may be he has lost himself, and raps up without pity the sage and rheumatic old prelatess with all her young Corinthian[33] laity, to inquire for such a one.

Last of all, not in time, but as perfection is last, that care was ever had of me, with my earliest capacity, not to be negligently

[27] Milton thought of Dante's idealization of Beatrice in the *Vita Nuova* and the *Paradiso* and of Petrarch's idealization of *Laura* in his *Canzoniere*.

[28] Cf. *CG*, n. 174.

[29] The best evidence of the hold that medieval romance once had on Milton's imagination is in *PL* IX, 27–37. Perhaps the reference here is to treatments of the Arthurian legends like Malory's, and to Milton's early ambition to write a "British" epic. Cf. *Manso*, 80–88.

[30] Milton was thinking of Plato's criticism of

Homer for drawing morally unsatisfactory portraits of the gods and heroes (*Rep.*, 377e).

[31] Cf. *CG*, n. 174.

[32] Milton describes *Xenophon* (?430–?359 B.C.) as Plato's *equal* in the sense that he was contemporary with Plato. (Cf. note 7 above.) Doubtless he set a high value on Xenophon's *Memorabilia*, or recollections of Socrates' practical teachings presented specifically to refute the charge of corrupting youth, for which the Athenians condemned him to death.

[33] *Corinthians*, as a name for prostitutes, goes back to ancient times.

trained in the precepts of Christian religion. This that I have hitherto related, hath been to show that though Christianity had been but slightly taught me, yet a certain reservedness of natural disposition, and moral discipline learnt out of the noblest philosophy, was enough to keep me in disdain of far less incontinences than this of the bordello. But having had the doctrine of holy scripture unfolding those chaste and high mysteries with timeliest care infused, that "the body is for the Lord, and the Lord for the body,"[34] thus also I argued to myself: that if unchastity in a woman, whom St. Paul terms the glory of man,[35] be such a scandal and dishonor, then certainly in a man, who is both the image and glory of God, it must, though commonly not so thought, be much more deflowering and dishonorable; in that he sins both against his own body, which is the perfecter sex,[36] and his own glory, which is in the woman, and, that which is worst, against the image and glory of God, which is in himself. Nor did I slumber over that place expressing such high rewards of ever accompanying the Lamb with those celestial songs to others inapprehensible, but not to those who were not defiled with women,[37] which doubtless means fornication; for marriage must not be called a defilement.

Thus large I have purposely been, that if I have been justly taxed with this crime, it may come upon me, after all this my confession, with a tenfold shame.

could be seriously argued that "women are unperfect creatures, and consequently of lesse worthinesse than men, and not apt to conceive those virtues that they are." Milton agreed, yet he pled in *Tetr* (C.E. IV, 121) that "the law is to tender the dignity and human liberty of them that live under the law, whether it be the man's right above the woman, or the woman's just appeal against wrong and servitude."

[37] Milton is thinking especially of the hymn to the Lamb of God which is sung at the "marriage of the Lamb," in Rev. xix, by the redeemed, to which he refers in *Lyc*, 176–7, and again, much more significantly, in *Damon*, 215–9. For what he says here he has the authority of Calvin (*Institutes* IV, xii, 25; Norton's translation, p. 615): "The Apostle doth without exception boldly pronounce, that marriage is honourable among all men, but that for whoremongers, and adulterers abideth the judgment of God."

---

[34] "Now the body is not for fornication, but for the Lord; and the Lord is for the body" (I Cor. vi, 13).

[35] ". . . a man . . . is the image and glory of God: but the woman is the glory of the man" (I Cor. xi, 7).

[36] So in the greatest and least anti-feminine of courtesy books, Castiglione's *Book of the Courtier* (Hoby's translation, Everyman Ed., p. 196), it

A Selection from

THE DOCTRINE AND DISCIPLINE OF DIVORCE;
RESTORED TO THE GOOD OF BOTH SEXES, FROM THE BONDAGE OF CANON LAW, AND OTHER MISTAKES, TO THE TRUE MEANING OF SCRIPTURE IN THE LAW AND GOSPEL COMPARED.
WHEREIN ALSO ARE SET DOWN THE BAD CONSEQUENCES OF ABOLISHING, OR CONDEMNING AS SIN, THAT WHICH THE LAW OF GOD ALLOWS, AND CHRIST ABOLISHED NOT.
NOW THE SECOND TIME REVISED AND MUCH AUGMENTED, IN TWO BOOKS

BIBLIOGRAPHICAL NOTE—*DDD* was first published anonymously in 1643 and is dated "Aug: 1st" in the copy in the British Museum. The second edition (1644) introduced the chapter divisions and added very substantially to the first. The selections which are reproduced here are based upon the two slightly differing copies of the second edition in the Houghton Library at Harvard. *DDD* is represented here by the dedication, the preface, and chapters one to six in Book I, and by chapter one and the conclusion to chapter three in Book II.

TO THE PARLIAMENT OF ENGLAND WITH THE ASSEMBLY.

The Author J. M.

MATT. xiii, 52. "Every scribe instructed to the kingdom of heaven is like the master of a house, which bringeth out of his treasury things new and old."

PROV. xviii, 13. "He that answereth a matter before he heareth it, it is folly and shame unto him."

If it were seriously asked (and it would be no untimely question, renowned Parliament, select Assembly) who of all teachers and masters that have ever taught hath drawn the most disciples after him, both in religion and in manners, it might be not untruly answered, custom.[1] Though vir-

tue be commended for the most persuasive in her theory, and conscience in the plain demonstration of the spirit finds most evincing, yet whether it be the secret of divine will or the original blindness[2] we are born in, so it happens for the most part that custom still is silently received for the best instructor. Except it be because her method is so glib and easy, in some manner like to that vision of Ezekiel[3] rolling up her sudden book of implicit[4] knowledge for him that will to take and swallow down at pleasure; which proving but of bad nourishment in the concoction,[5] as it was heedless in the devouring, puffs up unhealthily a certain big face of

[1] Milton's attacks upon *custom* as the sponsor of reaction in the church, here and in the exordia to *TKM* and *Tetr*, continue a tradition among Protestant Reformers which had been imaged by John Goodman a century earlier in an allegory opening a sermon which was later expanded into the book which is quoted in *TKM* (see *TKM*, n. 210). Goodman made Custom the daughter of Ignorance, a witch who deludes men faster than "Truth and reason bring us to the understanding of our error." In an essentially conservative *Treatise of Use and Custom* (1638) Milton's contemporary, Meric Casaubon, approvingly quoted

the saying of Tertullian that "Christ called himself Truth and not Custom." Cf. *TKM*, n. 1.

[2] *original blindness:* the spiritual blindness of man, to which, as Milton says below, sin—i.e. the original sin of Adam—"hath sunk him."

[3] *Ezekiel* (iii, 1–3) describes the prophet as eating a roll at God's command and finding it in his mouth "as honey for sweetness." The roll symbolizes the prophet's message, and Milton's use of it here hardly harmonizes with its Biblical context.

[4] By "implicit faith" in any human authority, Milton said in *Civil Power*, "the conscience also becomes implicit, and so by voluntary servitude to man's law, forfeits her Christian liberty."

[5] *Concoction:* digestion. Cf. *PL*, V, 412, and *Educ*, p. 638.

pretended learning mistaken among credulous men for the wholesome habit of soundness and good constitution, but is indeed no other than that swollen visage of counterfeit knowledge and literature, which not only in private mars our education, but also in public is the common climber into every chair where either religion is preached, or law reported; filling each estate of life and profession with abject and servile principles, depressing the high and heaven-born spirit of man far beneath the condition wherein either God created him, or sin hath sunk him.

To pursue the allegory, custom being but a mere face, as echo is a mere voice, rests not in her unaccomplishment until by secret inclination she accorporate herself with error, who being a blind and serpentine body without a head willingly accepts what he wants and supplies what her incompleteness went seeking. Hence it is that error supports custom, custom countenances error; and these two between them would persecute and chase away all truth and solid wisdom out of human life, were it not that God, rather than man, once in many ages calls together the prudent and religious counsels of men deputed to repress the encroachments and to work off the inveterate blots and obscurities wrought upon our minds by the subtle insinuating of error and custom; who, with the numerous and vulgar train of their followers, make it their chief design to envy and cry down the industry of free reasoning, under the terms of humor[6] and innovation; as if the womb of teeming truth were to be closed up if she presume to bring forth aught that sorts not with their unchewed notions and suppositions. Against which notorious injury and abuse of man's free soul to testify and oppose the utmost that study and true labor can attain, heretofore the incitement of men reputed grave hath led me among others. And now the duty and the right of an instructed Christian calls me through the chance of good or evil report to be the sole advocate of a discountenanced truth: a high enterprise, Lords and Commons, a high enterprise and a hard, and such as every seventh son of a seventh son does not venture on.

Nor have I amidst the clamor of so much envy and impertinence whither to appeal, but to the concourse of so much piety and wisdom here assembled. Bringing in my hands an ancient and most necessary, most charitable and yet most injured, statute of Moses:[7] not repealed ever by him who only had the authority, but thrown side with much inconsiderate neglect under the rubbish of canonical ignorance; as once the whole law was by some such like conveyance in Josiah's time.[8] And he who shall endeavor the amendment of any old neglected grievance in church or state, or in the daily course of life, if he be gifted with abilities of mind that may raise him to so high an undertaking, I grant he hath already much whereof not to repent him. Yet let me aread him not to be the foreman[9] of any misjudged opinion, unless his resolutions be firmly seated in a square and constant mind, not conscious to itself of any deserved blame and regardless of ungrounded suspicions. For this let him be sure, he shall be boarded[10] presently by the ruder sort, but not by discreet and well-nurtured men, with a thousand idle descants[11] and surmises. Who, when they cannot confute the least joint or sinew of any passage in the book, yet God forbid that truth should be truth because they have a boisterous conceit of some pretenses in the writer. But were they not more busy and inquisitive than the apostle[12] commends, they would hear him at least, "rejoicing so the truth be preached, whether of envy or other pretense whatsoever." For truth

---

[6] Cf. "Humor, faction, policy, or licentious will" in CG, p. 644.

[7] Milton rested his case primarily upon the plea that Christ's saying that, "Whosoever shall put away his wife, saving for the cause of fornication, causeth her to commit adultery" (Matt. v, 32), should not be understood as canceling the law of Moses in Deut. xxiv, 1–2: 'When a man hath taken a wife and married her, and it come to pass that she shall find no favor in his eyes, because he hath found some uncleanness in her; then let him write her a bill of divorcement, and give it in her hand, and send her out of his house."

[8] II Kings xxii and xxiii, tells the story of the discovery of the forgotten Mosaic scriptures and their restoration to a controlling place in the Temple worship in the reign of Josiah.

[9] foreman: spokesman, leading representative.

[10] boarded: accosted, assailed.

[11] descants: cf. the opening words of Eikon: "To descant on the misfortunes of a person fallen from . . . a dignity . . ."

[12] The apostle quoted is St. Paul, in Phil. i, 18.

is as impossible to be soiled by any outward touch as the sunbeam, though this ill hap wait on her nativity, that she never comes into the world but like a bastard, to the ignominy of him that brought her forth; till time, the midwife rather than the mother of truth,[13] have washed and salted the infant, declared her legitimate, and churched the father of his young Minerva[14] from the needless causes of his purgation.

Yourselves can best witness this, worthy patriots, and better will, no doubt, hereafter. For who among ye of the foremost that have travailed in her behalf to the good of church or state, hath not been often traduced to be the agent of his own by-ends, under pretext of reformation? So much the more I shall not be unjust to hope that however infamy or envy may work in other men to do her fretful will against this discourse, yet that the experience of your own uprightness misinterpreted will put ye in mind to give it free audience and generous construction. What though the brood of Belial,[15] the draff of men, to whom no liberty is pleasing but unbridled and vagabond lust without pale or partition, will laugh broad perhaps to see so great a strength of scripture mustering up in favor, as they suppose, of their debaucheries? They will know better when they shall hence learn that honest liberty is the greatest foe to dishonest license.

And what though others out of a waterish and queasy conscience because ever crazy and never yet sound, will rail and fancy to themselves that injury and license is the best of this book? Did not the distemper of their own stomachs affect them with a dizzy megrim, they would soon tie up their tongues and discern themselves like that Assyrian blasphemer,[16] all this while reproaching not man but the Almighty, "the Holy One of Israel," whom they do not deny to have belawgiven his own sacred people with this very allowance which they now call injury and license and dare cry shame on, and will do yet a while, till they get a little cordial sobriety to settle their qualming zeal. But this question concerns not us perhaps: indeed man's disposition though prone to search after vain curiosities, yet when points of difficulty are to be discussed appertaining to the removal of unreasonable wrong and burden from the perplexed life of our brother, it is incredible how cold, how dull and far from all fellow feeling we are, without the spur of self-concernment.

Yet if the wisdom, the justice, the purity of God be to be cleared from foulest imputations which are not yet avoided; if charity be not to be degraded and trodden down under a civil ordinance; if matrimony be not to be advanced like that exalted perdition written of to the Thessalonians, "above all that is called God,"[17] or goodness, nay, against them both; then I dare affirm there will be found in the contents of this book that which may concern us all. You it concerns chiefly, worthies in Parliament, on whom, as on our deliverers, all our grievances and cares by the merit of your eminence and fortitude are devolved. Me it concerns next, having with much labor and faithful diligence first found out, or at least with a fearless and communicative candor first published, to the manifest good of Christendom, that which, calling to witness everything mortal and immortal, I believe unfeignedly to be true. Let not other men think their conscience bound to search continually after truth, to pray for enlightening from above, to publish what they think they have so obtained, and debar me from conceiving myself tied by the same duties.

---

[13] Milton questions the soundness of the popular idea of *Truth* as the daughter of Time, which was the theme of allegorical tapestries and pictures and is traced to two old plays by B. J. Whiting in *Proverbs in the Earlier English Drama* (Cambridge, 1938), pp. 113 and 285. Cf. the prophecy in *Areop* (n. 194) that the licensing order will be "the step-dame to truth."

[14] Cf. the bold use in *PL* II, 757–8, of the myth that the goddess of wisdom was the offspring of Jupiter. Milton compares the "churching" or purification of women after childbirth in the Anglican Church to the treatment that he may expect as the father of his present brain child.

[15] Cf. "Belial, the dissolutest spirit that fell" (*PR* II, 150), and "the sons of Belial, flown with insolence and wine" (*PL* I, 502).

[16] The reply of the prophet Isaiah to the threats of the *Assyrian* king, Sennacherib, before his unsuccessful attack on King Hezekiah, was: "Whom hast thou reproached and blasphemed? . . . even . . . the Holy One of Israel" (II Kings xix, 22).

[17] The thought is that, by exalting any law above Christian charity, Parliament is in danger of fulfilling Paul's prophecy about "the son of perdition" who "exalteth himself above all that is called God" (II Thess. ii, 3–4).

Ye have now, doubtless by the favor and appointment of God, ye have now in your hands a great and populous nation to reform; from what corruption, what blindness in religion, ye know well; in what a degenerate and fallen spirit from the apprehension of native liberty and true manliness, I am sure ye find; with what unbounded license rushing to whoredoms and adulteries, needs not long inquiry: insomuch that the fears which men have of too strict a discipline perhaps exceed the hopes that can be in others of ever introducing it with any great success. What if I should tell ye now of dispensations and indulgences, to give a little the reins, to let them play and nibble with the bait awhile; a people as hard of heart as that Egyptian colony[18] that went to Canaan. This is the common doctrine that adulterous and injurious divorces were not connived only, but with eye open allowed of old for hardness of heart. But that opinion, I trust, by then this following argument hath been well read, will be left for one of the mysteries of an indulgent Antichrist,[19] to farm out incest by, and those his other tributary pollutions. What middle way can be taken then, may some interrupt, if we must neither turn to the right nor to the left, and that the people hate to be reformed? Mark then, judges and lawgivers, and ye whose office it is to be our teachers, for I will utter now a doctrine, if ever any other, though neglected or not understood, yet of great and powerful importance to the governing of mankind. He who wisely would restrain the reasonable soul of man within due bounds, must first himself know perfectly how far the territory and dominion extends of just and honest liberty. As little must he offer to bind that which God hath loosened, as to loosen that which he hath bound. The ignorance and mistake of this high point hath heaped up one huge half of all the misery that hath

been since Adam. In the gospel we shall read a supercilious crew of masters whose holiness, or rather whose evil eye, grieving that God should be so facile to man, was to set straiter limits to obedience than God had set, to enslave the dignity of man, to put a garrison upon his neck of empty and over-dignified precepts: and we shall read our Savior never more grieved and troubled[20] than to meet with such a peevish madness among men against their own freedom. How can we expect him to be less offended with us, when much of the same folly shall be found yet remaining where it least ought, to the perishing of thousands?

The greatest burden in the world is superstition, not only of ceremonies in the church but of imaginary and scarecrow sins at home. What greater weakening, what more subtle stratagem against our Christian warfare,[21] when besides the gross body of real transgressions to encounter, we shall be terrified by a vain and shadowy menacing of faults that are not? When things indifferent shall be set to overfront us under the banners of sin, what wonder if we be routed, and by this art of our adversary, fall into the subjection of worst and deadliest offenses? The superstition of the papist is, "Touch not, taste not,"[22] when God bids both; and ours is, "Part not, separate not," when God and charity both permits and commands. "Let all your things be done with charity," saith St. Paul;[23] and his master saith, "She is the fulfilling of the law." Yet now a civil, an indifferent, a sometime dissuaded law of marriage, must be forced upon us to fulfil, not only without charity but against her. No place in heaven or earth, except hell, where charity may not enter: yet marriage,

---

[18] The *Egyptian colony* is the Israelites, who often incurred the reproach of hardening their hearts from the fear of God (as in Isa. lxiii, 17), and for whose "hardness of heart" Christ said (Mark x, 4) that "Moses suffered to write a bill of divorcement."

[19] Contrast Milton's statement in *Civil Power*, p. 841, that the pope's assumption of "infallibility over both conscience and the scripture" is the reason that "all true Protestants account the pope antichrist."

[20] A reference to Christ's rebuke of the Pharisees in Matt. xxiii, for hypocritically increasing the burden of the Jewish ceremonial law.

[21] Cf. St. Paul's image of *Christian warfare* in II Cor. x, 4, and I Tim. i, 18, and *Areop*, n. 102.

[22] A reference to St. Paul's rhetorical question to the Colossians (ii, 20–21) as to why, if they have Christ in their hearts, they should regard themselves as "subject to ordinances: Touch not, taste not, handle not."

[23] The references are I Cor. xvi, 14, and Rom. xiii, 10. For the full significance of Milton's application of the doctrine of Christian liberty here see M. Kelley, *Argument*, pp. 56–66, and A. Barker in "Christian Liberty in Milton's Divorce Pamphlets" in *MLR*, XXXV (1940), 153–61.

the ordinance of our solace and contentment, the remedy of our loneliness, will not admit now either of charity or mercy to come in and mediate or pacify the fierceness of this gentle ordinance, the unremedied loneliness of this remedy. Advise ye well, supreme senate, if charity be thus excluded and expulsed, how ye will defend the untainted honor of your own actions and proceedings.

He who marries, intends as little to conspire his own ruin as he that swears allegiance: and as a whole people is in proportion to an ill government, so is one man to an ill marriage. If they, against any authority, covenant, or statute, may by the sovereign edict of charity save not only their lives but honest liberties from unworthy bondage, as well may he against any private covenant, which he never entered to his mischief, redeem himself from unsupportable disturbances to honest peace and just contentment. And much the rather, for that to resist the highest magistrate though tyrannizing, God never gave us express allowance,[24] only he gave us reason, charity, nature and good example to bear us out; but in this economical misfortune thus to demean ourselves, besides the warrant of those four great directors, which doth as justly belong hither, we have an express law of God, and such a law as whereof our Savior with a solemn threat forbade the abrogating.[25] For no effect of tyranny can sit more heavy on the commonwealth than this household unhappiness on the family. And farewell all hope of true reformation in the state, while such an evil as this lies undiscerned or unregarded in the house: on the redress whereof depends not only the spiritful and orderly life of our grown men, but the willing and careful education of our children.

Let this therefore be new examined, this tenure and freehold of mankind, this native and domestic charter given us by a greater lord than that Saxon king the Confessor.[26] Let the statutes of God be turned over, be scanned anew, and considered not altogether by the narrow intellectuals of quotationists and commonplacers, but (as was the ancient right of councils)[27] by men of what liberal profession soever, of eminent spirit and breeding, joined with a diffuse and various knowledge of divine and human things; able to balance and define good and evil, right and wrong, throughout every state of life; able to show us the ways of the Lord straight and faithful as they are, not full of cranks and contradictions and pitfalling dispenses, but with divine insight and benignity measured out to the proportion of each mind and spirit, each temper and disposition, created so different each from other, and yet by the skill of wise conducting, all to become uniform in virtue.

To expedite these knots were worthy a learned and memorable synod; while our enemies expect to see the expectation of the church tired out with dependencies and independencies, how they will compound and in what calends.[28] Doubt not, worthy senators, to vindicate the sacred honor and judgment of Moses your predecessor, from the shallow commenting of scholastics and canonists. Doubt not after him to reach out your steady hands to the misinformed and wearied life of man, to restore this his lost heritage into the household state. Wherewith be sure that peace and love, the best subsistence of a Christian family, will return home from whence they are now banished; places of prostitution will be less haunted, the neighbor's bed less attempted, the yoke of prudent and manly discipline will be generally submitted to; sober and well-ordered living will soon spring up in the commonwealth.

Ye have an author great beyond exception, Moses; and one yet greater, he who hedged in from abolishing every smallest jot and tittle of precious equity contained in that law, with a more accurate and last-

---

[24] Cf. Milton's altered attitude toward St. Paul's command to Christians to "be subject to the higher powers" (Rom. xiii, 1) in *TKM*, n. 28.

[25] Teaching the disciples that their "righteousness should exceed the righteousness of the . . . Pharisees," Christ solemnly warned against breaking even the "least commandments" of the Mosaic law (Matt. v, 19–20).

[26] In closing the chapter on Edward the *Confessor's* death in 1066 in *Britain* (C.E. X, 306), Milton observed that, "His laws, held good and just, and long after desired by the English of their Norman kings, are yet extant."

[27] Cf. *Eikon*, Chap. xxviii, notes 17–19.

[28] *calends:* date. In Latin the word meant the first day of every month.

ing Masoreth[29] than either the synagogue of Ezra[30] or the Galilæan school at Tiberias[31] hath left us. Whatever else ye can enact will scarce concern a third part of the British name: but the benefit and good of this your magnanimous example will easily spread far beyond the banks of Tweed and the Norman isles.[32] It would not be the first or second time since our ancient druids,[33] by whom this island was the cathedral of philosophy to France, left off their pagan rites, that England hath had this honor vouchsafed from heaven, to give out reformation to the world. Who was it but our English Constantine[34] that baptized the Roman empire? Who but the Northumbrian Willibrorde[35] and Winifride of Devon,[36] with their followers, were the first apostles of Germany? Who but Alcuin[37] and Wycliffe[38] our countrymen,

opened the eyes of Europe, the one in arts, the other in religion? Let not England forget her precedence of teaching nations how to live.

Know, worthies, know and exercise the privilege of your honored country. A greater title I here bring ye than is either in the power or in the policy of Rome to give her monarchs. This glorious act will style ye the defenders of charity. Nor is this yet the highest inscription that will adorn so religious and so holy a defense as this. Behold here the pure and sacred law of God and his yet purer and more sacred name, offering themselves to you, first of all Christian reformers, to be acquitted from the long-suffered ungodly attribute of patronizing adultery. Defer not to wipe off instantly these imputative blurs and stains cast by rude fancies upon the throne and beauty itself of inviolable holiness, lest some other people more devout and wise than we bereave us this offered immortal glory, our wonted prerogative, of being the first asserters in every great vindication.

For me, as far as my part leads me, I have already my greatest gain, assurance and inward satisfaction to have done in this nothing unworthy of an honest life and studies well employed. With what event, among the wise and right understanding handful of men I am secure. But how among the drove of custom and prejudice this will be relished by such whose capacity, since their youth run ahead into the easy creek of a system or a medulla,[39] sails there at will under the blown physiognomy of their unlabored rudiments; for them, what their taste will be, I have also surety sufficient from the entire league that hath been ever between formal ignorance and grave obstinacy. Yet when I remember the little that our Savior could prevail about this doctrine of charity against the crabbed textuists of his time, I make no wonder, but rest confident that whoso prefers either matrimony or other ordinance before the

29 *Masoreth:* the body of critical notes on the Old Testament compiled by Hebrew scholars in the tenth century and earlier. "Milton (misled by the rendering 'tradition') seems to have supposed the word applicable to the exegetical traditions of the Rabbis, by which the severity of the law was increased." (*O.E.D.*)

30 After the return of the Jews from captivity in Babylon, under *Ezra,* synagogue worship grew up in the Palestinian cities beside the re-established temple worship in Jerusalem.

31 From the third to the twelfth century *Tiberias* was a seat of Jewish culture. It was the last city in which a Sanhedrin held sittings. The collection of the Mishnah began there and the Talmud was edited there.

32 The *Norman isles* are Jersey, Guernsey, and the other Channel Islands.

33 Cf. Milton's pride in the ancient culture of the *druids* in *Manso,* 42–48.

34 In 312 the Emperor *Constantine* declared the Roman Empire officially Christian for the first time. "There goes a fame, and that seconded by most of our own historians, though not those the ancientest," says Milton in *Britain* (C.E. X, 92), "that Constantine was born in this island."

35 *Willibrorde* (657?–738?), an Englishman who was educated in Ireland, was an aggressive missionary in Frisia and, with the support of Pepin and Charles Martel, did much to civilize the Germans. When he died, he was Archbishop of Utrecht.

36 *Winifride,* better known as St. Boniface (680–755), succeeded Willibrorde in his bishopric after an adventurous missionary career in Bavaria and other parts of Germany. After some dramatic successes in discrediting the worship of Wotan, he finally suffered martyrdom in Frisia.

37 *Alcuin* (735–804) carried English learning to the court of Charlemagne. As head of the abbeys of Ferrières and Saint Loup, and later at Tours, he founded important schools, developed the art of illuminating manuscripts, wrote several influential

theological works, and revised the text of the Latin Bible.

38 John *Wycliffe* (1324?–1384) was regarded as a precursor of the Reformation. Cf. *CG,* n. 119.

39 *medulla:* (Latin) marrow. The word was used in titles like William Ames's *Medulla Theologiae* (1622–3; English translation, 1642), which contributed to the plan of *CD.* It meant a short compendium of knowledge in any field.

good of man and the plain exigence of charity, let him profess papist, or protestant, or what he will, he is no better than a pharisee, and understands not the gospel: whom as a misinterpreter of Christ I openly protest against; and provoke him to the trial of this truth before all the world. And let him bethink him withal how he will solder up the shifting flaws of his ungirt permissions, his venial and unvenial dispenses,[40] wherewith the law of God pardoning and unpardoning hath been shamefully branded for want of heed in glossing, to have eluded and baffled out all faith and chastity from the marriage-bed of that holy seed, with politic and judicial adulteries.

I seek not to seduce the simple and illiterate. My errand is to find out the choicest and the learnedest who have this high gift of wisdom to answer solidly, or to be convinced. I crave it from the piety, the learning, and the prudence which is housed in this place. It might perhaps more fitly have been written in another tongue: and I had done so, but that the esteem I have of my country's judgment, and the love I bear to my native language to serve it first with what I endeavor, made me speak it thus, ere I assay the verdict of outlandish readers. And perhaps also here I might have ended nameless, but that the address of these lines chiefly to the Parliament of England might have seemed ingrateful not to acknowledge by whose religious care, unwearied watchfulness, courageous and heroic resolutions, I enjoy the peace and studious leisure to remain,

The Honorer and Attendant of their
Noble worth and virtues,
JOHN MILTON

THE DOCTRINE AND DISCIPLINE
OF DIVORCE;

RESTORED TO THE GOOD OF BOTH SEXES.

BOOK I.

THE PREFACE.

That Man is the occasion of his own miseries in most of those evils which he imputes to God's inflicting. The absurdity of our

canonists *in their decrees about divorce. The Christian imperial Laws framed with more Equity. The opinion of* Hugo Grotius *and* Paulus Fagius: *and the purpose in general of this Discourse.*

Many men, whether it be their fate or fond opinion, easily persuade themselves, if God would but be pleased a while to withdraw his just punishments from us and to restrain what power either the devil or any earthly enemy hath to work us woe, that then man's nature would find immediate rest and releasement from all evils. But verily they who think so, if they be such as have a mind large enough to take into their thoughts a general survey of human things, would soon prove themselves in that opinion far deceived. For though it were granted us by divine indulgence to be exempt from all that can be harmful to us from without, yet the perverseness of our folly is so bent that we should never lin[41] hammering out of our own hearts, as it were out of a flint, the seeds and sparkles of new misery to ourselves, till all were in a blaze again.

And no marvel if out of our own hearts, for they are evil; but even out of those things which God meant us either for a principal good or a pure contentment, we are still hatching and contriving upon ourselves matter of continual sorrow and perplexity. What greater good to man than that revealed rule whereby God vouchsafes to show us how he would be worshipped? And yet that not rightly understood became the cause that once a famous man in Israel[42] could not but oblige his conscience to be the sacrificer, or if not, the jailer of his innocent and only daughter; and was the cause ofttimes that armies of valiant men have given up their throats to a heathenish enemy on the sabbath day,[43] fondly thinking their defensive resistance to be as then a work unlawful.

[40] *dispenses:* dispensations; in this case, either for venial sins or for mortal ones.

[41] *lin:* stop.

[42] Jephthah's needless vow to sacrifice whatever first greeted him on his return home from victory over the Ammonites, led to the offering of his daughter (Judg. xi, 29–40).

[43] Milton perhaps had in mind Josephus' statement in the first book of the *Wars of the Jews* that "the labors of the Romans would have been endless had not Pompey taken advantage of the seventh day of the week, on which the Jews refrain from all manual work. At the very hour when the

What thing more instituted to the solace and delight of man than marriage? And yet the misinterpreting of some scripture, directed mainly against the abusers of the law for divorce given by Moses, hath changed the blessing of matrimony not seldom into a familiar and coinhabiting mischief, at least into a drooping and disconsolate household captivity, without refuge or redemption—so ungoverned and so wild a race doth superstition run us from one extreme of abused liberty into the other of unmerciful restraint. For although God in the first ordaining of marriage taught us to what end he did it, in words expressly implying the apt and cheerful conversation of man with woman, to comfort and refresh him against the evil of solitary life, not mentioning the purpose of generation till afterwards, as being but a secondary end in dignity, though not in necessity: yet now, if any two be but once handed in the church, and have tasted in any sort the nuptial bed, let them find themselves never so mistaken in their dispositions through any error, concealment, or misadventure, that through their different tempers, thoughts and constitutions, they can neither be to one another a remedy against loneliness nor live in any union or contentment all their days; yet they shall, so they be but found suitably weaponed to the least possibility of sensual enjoyment, be made, spite of antipathy, to fadge together and combine as they may to their unspeakable wearisomeness and despair of all sociable delight in the ordinance which God established to that very end.

What a calamity is this, and, as the wise man, if he were alive, would sigh out in his own phrase, what a "sore evil is this under the sun!"[44] All which we can refer justly to no other author than the canon law and her adherents, not consulting with charity, the interpreter and guide of our faith, but resting in the mere element of the text—doubtless by the policy of the devil to make that gracious ordinance become insupportable, that what with men not daring to venture upon wedlock, and what with men wearied out of it, all inordinate license might abound.

It was for many ages that marriage lay in disgrace with most of the ancient doctors as a work of the flesh, almost a defilement, wholly denied to priests, and the second time dissuaded to all, as he that reads Tertullian or Jerome[45] may see at large. Afterwards it was thought so sacramental that no adultery or desertion could dissolve it, and this is the sense of our canon courts in England to this day, but in no other reformed church else. Yet there remains in them also a burden on it as heavy as the other two were disgraceful or superstitious, and of as much iniquity, crossing a law not only written by Moses, but charactered in us by nature, of more antiquity and deeper ground than marriage itself; which law is to force nothing against the faultless proprieties of nature.[46] Yet that this may be colorably done, our Savior's words touching divorce are as it were congealed into a stony rigor, inconsistent both with his doctrine and his office, and that which he preached only to the conscience is by canonical tyranny snatched into the compulsive censure of a judicial court, where laws are imposed even against the venerable and secret power of nature's impression, to love, whatever cause be found to loathe: which is a heinous barbarism both against the honor of marriage, the dignity of man and his soul, the goodness of Christianity and all the human respects of civility. Notwithstanding that some the wisest and gravest among the Christian emperors,[47] who had about them, to con-

---

44 In Eccles. v. 13 and 16, and elsewhere, the phrase "a sore evil under the sun" is used. Ecclesiastes was attributed to Solomon, to whom God gave "an understanding heart" (I Kings iii, 12), so that he never had an equal in wisdom.

45 In works like On Monogamy and On Pudicity Tertullian (155?–222?) and Jerome in his Book against Jovinian treated the ideal of monogamous marriage as inferior to that of strict chastity Chaucer coupled their names as Milton does here when he made the Wife of Bath mention in her Prologue, ll. 674-6,

A cardinal that highte Seint Jerome,
That made a book agayn Jovinian;
In which book eek ther was Tertulan

as items in Clerk Jankyn's volume of misogynistic literature.

46 For the influence of Selden's study of "the law of nature and nations" upon Milton's thought see Eivion Owen, "Milton and Selden on Divorce," in SP, XLIII (1946), 233-57.

47 In Bucer (C.E. IV, 11) Milton says that he was moved to write DDD by reading Hugo Gro-

---

temple was taken, when they were being massacred about the altar, they never desisted from the religious rites of the day."

sult with, those of the fathers then living, who for their learning and holiness of life are still with us in great renown, have made their statutes and edicts concerning this debate far more easy and relenting in many necessary cases wherein the canon is inflexible. And Hugo Grotius, a man of these times, one of the best learned, seems not obscurely to adhere in his persuasion to the equity of those imperial decrees, in his notes upon the Evangelists; much allaying the outward roughness of the text, which hath for the most part been too immoderately expounded; and excites the diligence of others to inquire further into this question, as containing many points that have not yet been explained. Which ever likely to remain intricate and hopeless upon the suppositions commonly stuck to, the authority of Paulus Fagius,[48] one so learned and so eminent in England once, if it might persuade, would straight acquaint us with a solution of these differences no less prudent than compendious. He, in his comment on the Pentateuch, doubted not to maintain that divorces might be as lawfully permitted by the magistrate to Christians as they were to the Jews.

But because he is but brief, and these things of great consequence not to be kept obscure, I shall conceive it nothing above my duty, either for the difficulty or the censure that may pass thereon, to communicate such thoughts as I also have had, and do offer them now in this general labor of reformation to the candid view both of church and magistrate: especially because I see it the hope of good men that those irregular and unspiritual courts have spun their utmost date in this land, and some better course must now be constituted. This therefore shall be the task and period

of this discourse to prove, first, that other reasons of divorce besides adultery were by the law of Moses, and are yet to be allowed by the Christian magistrate as a piece of justice, and that the words of Christ are not hereby contraried. Next, that to prohibit absolutely any divorce whatsoever, except those which Moses excepted, is against the reason of law, as in due place I shall show out of Fagius, with many additions. He therefore who by adventuring shall be so happy as with success to light the way of such an expedient liberty and truth as this, shall restore the much wronged and over-sorrowed state of matrimony, not only to those merciful and life-giving remedies of Moses, but, as much as may be, to that serene and blissful condition it was in at the beginning, and shall deserve of all apprehensive men (considering the troubles and distempers which, for want of this insight, have been so oft in kingdoms, in states, and families) shall deserve to be reckoned among the public benefactors of civil and human life, above the inventors of wine and oil; for this is a far dearer, far nobler and more desirable cherishing to man's life, unworthily exposed to sadness and mistake, which he shall vindicate,

Not that license and levity and unconsented breach of faith should herein be countenanced, but that some conscionable and tender pity might be had of those who have unwarily, in a thing they never practised before, made themselves the bondmen of a luckless and helpless matrimony. In which argument, he whose courage can serve him to give the first onset, must look for two several oppositions: the one from those who having sworn themselves to long custom and the letter of the text, will not out of the road; the other from those whose gross and vulgar apprehensions conceit but low of matrimonial purposes, and in the work of male and female think they have all. Nevertheless, it shall be here sought by due ways to be made appear that those words of God in the institution, promising a meet help against loneliness,[49] and those words of Christ, that "his yoke is easy, and his burden light,"[50] were not spoken in

tius' *Commentary on Matthew,* which he quotes in *DDD* II, xviii (C.E. III, 487) for the opinion that Deut. xxiv, 1–2, permitted divorce on a variety of grounds, and that Matt. v, 31, was simply a solemn warning by Christ about the moral dangers in divorce.

[48] The eminent German reformer and Biblical scholar, *Paulus Fagius* (1504–1549), left his Strassbourg pastorate with Martin Bucer to accompany him to England and become professor of Hebrew at Cambridge, but died there within a few months. The dishonor done to his body and to Bucer's in Mary's reign and their splendid reinterment in Elizabeth's reign made them martyrs of the Protestant cause.

[49] "And God said, It is not good that man should be alone; I will make an helpmeet for him" (Gen. ii, 18).

[50] Matt. xi, 30.

vain: for if the knot of marriage may in no case be dissolved but for adultery, all the burdens and services of the law are not so intolerable.

This only is desired of them who are minded to judge hardly of thus maintaining, that they would be still and hear all out, nor think it equal to answer deliberate reason with sudden heat and noise; remembering this, that many truths now of reverend esteem and credit had their birth and beginning once from singular and private thoughts, while the most of men were otherwise possessed; and had the fate at first to be generally exploded and exclaimed on by many violent opposers. Yet I may err perhaps in soothing myself that this present truth revived will deserve on all hands to be not sinisterly received, in that it undertakes the cure of an inveterate disease crept into the best part of human society; and to do this with no smarting corrosive, but with a smooth and pleasing lesson, which received, hath the virtue to soften and dispel rooted and knotty sorrows; and without enchantment, if that be feared, or spell[51] used, hath regard at once both to serious pity and upright honesty; that tends to the redeeming and restoring of none but such as are the object of compassion, having in an ill hour hampered themselves to the utter dispatch of all their most beloved comforts and repose for this life's term.

But if we shall obstinately dislike this new overture of unexpected ease and recovery, what remains but to deplore the frowardness of our hopeless condition, which neither can endure the estate we are in, nor admit of remedy either sharp or sweet? Sharp we ourselves distaste; and sweet, under whose hands we are, is scrupled and suspected as too luscious. In such a posture Christ found the Jews, who were neither won with the austerity of John the Baptist,[52] and thought it too much license to follow freely the charming pipe of him who sounded and proclaimed liberty and relief to all distresses: yet truth in some age or other will find her witness, and shall be justified at last by her own children.[53]

CHAPTER I.

The Position, proved by the Law of Moses. That Law expounded and asserted to a moral and charitable use, first by Paulus Fagius, *next with other additions.*

To remove therefore, if it be possible, this great and sad oppression which through the strictness of a literal interpreting hath invaded and disturbed the dearest and most peaceable estate of household society, to the overburdening, if not the overwhelming of many Christians better worth than to be so deserted of the church's considerate care, this position shall be laid down, first proving, then answering what may be objected either from scripture or light of reason.

"That indisposition, unfitness, or contrariety of mind, arising from a cause in nature unchangeable, hindering and ever likely to hinder the main benefits of conjugal society, which are solace and peace, is a greater reason of divorce than natural frigidity, especially if there be no children, and that there be mutual consent."

This I gather from the law in Deut. xxiv, 1: "When a man hath taken a wife and married her, and it come to pass that she find no favor in his eyes, because he hath found some uncleanness in her, let him write her a bill of divorcement, and give it in her hand, and send her out of his house," &c. This law, if the words of Christ may be admitted into our belief, shall never, while the world stands, for him be abrogated. First therefore I here set down what learned Fagius hath observed on this law: "The law of God," saith he, "permitted divorce for the help of human

51 "Where persuasions and other remedies" for holding love proved ineffective, Burton's *Anatomy of Melancholy* (III, ii, 5, 4; Vol. III, 226) reported many flying "to unlawful means, Philters, Amulets, Magick Spells, Ligatures, Characters, Charms."

52 Milton fused the story of Jesus' answer to those who objected that "the disciples of John . . . used to fast," while his did not, with his comparison of himself to a child piping to other children who will not dance, and with his description of himself as preaching "deliverance to captives, . . . and to set at liberty them that are bruised." (Mark ii, 18; Matt. xi, 17; and Luke iv, 18.)

53 "The Son of man is come eating and drinking: and ye say, Behold a gluttonous man, and a winebibber, a friend of publicans and sinners.

"But wisdom is justified of her children" (Luke vii, 34-5).

weakness. For every one that of necessity separates, cannot live single. That Christ denied divorce to his own, hinders not; for what is that to the unregenerate, who hath not attained such perfection? Let not the remedy be despised, which was given to weakness. And when Christ saith, who marries the divorced commits adultery, it is to be understood if he had any plot in the divorce." The rest I reserve until it be disputed, how the magistrate is to do herein. From hence we may plainly discern a two-fold consideration in this law: first, the end of the lawgiver and the proper act of the law, to command or to allow something just and honest, or indifferent. Secondly, his sufferance from some accidental result of evil by this allowance, which the law cannot remedy. For if this law have no other end or act but only the allowance of a sin, though never to so good intention, that law is no law, but sin muffled in the robe of law, or law disguised in the loose garment of sin. Both which are too foul hypotheses to save the phenomenon of our Savior's answer to the pharisees about this matter.[54] And I trust anon, by the help of an infallible guide, to perfect such Prutenic[55] tables as shall mend the astronomy of our wide expositors.

The cause of divorce mentioned in the law is translated "some uncleanness," but in the Hebrew it sounds "nakedness of aught, or any real nakedness," which by all the learned interpreters is referred to the mind as well as to the body. And what greater nakedness or unfitness of mind than that which hinders ever the solace and peaceful society of the married couple? And what hinders that more than the unfitness and defectiveness of an unconjugal mind? The cause therefore of divorce expressed in the position cannot but agree with that described in the best and equallest

sense of Moses's law. Which, being a matter of pure charity, is plainly moral, and more now in force than ever, therefore surely lawful. For if under the law such was God's gracious indulgence as not to suffer the ordinance of his goodness and favor through any error to be seared and stigmatized upon his servants to their misery and thraldom, much less will he suffer it now under the covenant of grace, by abrogating his former grant of remedy and relief. But the first institution will be objected to have ordained marriage inseparable. To that a little patience until this first part have amply discoursed the grave and pious reasons of this divorcive law; and then I doubt not but with one gentle stroking to wipe away ten thousand tears out of the life of man. Yet thus much I shall now insist on, that whatever the institution were, it could not be so enormous, nor so rebellious against both nature and reason as to exalt itself above the end and person for whom it was instituted.

CHAPTER II.

The first reason of this Law grounded on the prime reason of matrimony. That no covenant whatsoever obliges against the main end both of itself, and of the parties covenanting.

For all sense and equity reclaims that any law or covenant, how solemn or strait soever, either between God and man, or man and man, though of God's joining, should bind against a prime and principal scope of its own institution, and of both or either party covenanting; neither can it be of force to engage a blameless creature to his own perpetual sorrow, mistaken for his expected solace, without suffering charity to step in and do a confessed good work of parting those whom nothing holds together but this of God's joining, falsely supposed against the express end of his own ordinance. And what his chief end was of creating woman to be joined with man, his own instituting words declare, and are infallible to inform us what is marriage and what is no marriage, unless we can think them set there to no purpose: "It is not

---

[54] Christ's answer to the Pharisees when they "came tempting him, and saying unto him, Is it lawful for a man to put away his wife for every cause?" is in Matt. xix, 3–9. Cf. Matt. v, 31.

[55] Copernicus' planetary tables were published in 1551 under this title in honor of Albert, Duke of Prussia. In *SP,* XXXIV (1937), 245, Grant McColley corrected Milton's choice of the *Prutenic Tables* for his image and observed that, "for knowledgeable men, after 1627, the Rudolphine Tables of the German astronomer, Johann Kepler, had supplanted Copernicus' tables." But the fallibility of the tables is the point of Milton's image.

good," saith he, "that man should be alone. I will make him a helpmeet for him."[56] From which words so plain, less cannot be concluded, nor is by any learned interpreter, than that in God's intention a meet and happy conversation is the chiefest and the noblest end of marriage,[57] for we find here no expression so necessarily implying carnal knowledge as this prevention of loneliness to the mind and spirit of man. To this, Fagius, Calvin, Pareus,[58] Rivetus,[59] as willingly and largely assent as can be wished. And indeed it is a greater blessing from God, more worthy so excellent a creature as man is, and a higher end to honor and sanctify the league of marriage, whenas the solace and satisfaction of the mind is regarded and provided for before the sensitive pleasing of the body. And with all generous persons married thus it is that where the mind and person pleases aptly, there some unaccomplishment of the body's delight may be better borne with than when the mind hangs off in an unclosing disproportion, though the body be as it ought; for there all corporal delight will soon become unsavoury and contemptible. And the solitariness of man, which God had namely and principally ordered to prevent by marriage, hath no remedy, but lies under a worse condition than the loneliest single life: for in single life the absence and remoteness of a helper might inure him to expect his own comforts out of himself, or to seek with hope; but here the continual sight of his deluded thoughts, without cure, must needs be to him, if especially his complexion incline him to melancholy, a daily trouble and pain of loss, in some degree like that which reprobates[60]

feel. Lest therefore so noble a creature as man should be shut up incurably under a worse evil by an easy mistake in that ordinance which God gave him to remedy a less evil, reaping to himself sorrow while he went to rid away solitariness, it cannot avoid to be concluded that if the woman be naturally so of disposition as will not help to remove, but help to increase that same God-forbidden loneliness (which will in time draw on with it a general discomfort and dejection of mind not beseeming either Christian profession or moral conversation, unprofitable and dangerous to the commonwealth, when the household estate, out of which must flourish forth the vigor and spirit of all public enterprises, is so ill-contented and procured at home, and cannot be supported), such a marriage can be no marriage, whereto the most honest end is wanting; and the aggrieved person shall do more manly to be extraordinary and singular in claiming the due right whereof he is frustrated, than to piece up his lost contentment by visiting the stews, or stepping to his neighbor's bed, which is the common shift in this misfortune; or else by suffering his useful life to waste away and be lost under a secret affliction of an unconscionable size to human strength. Against all which evils the mercy of this Mosaic law was graciously exhibited.

CHAPTER III.

The ignorance and iniquity of Canon law providing for the right of the body in marriage, but nothing for the wrongs and grievances of the mind. An objection, that the mind should be better looked to before contract, answered.

How vain, therefore, is it, and how preposterous in the canon law,[61] to have made such careful provision against the impediment of carnal performance, and to have had no care about the unconversing inability

---

[56] Gen. ii, 18.

[57] Cf. Owen Feltham in "Of Marriage and Single Life:" "Questionless, a *Woman* with a *wise soul*, is the fittest Companion for *Man:* otherwise *God* would have given him a *Friend* rather than a *Wife*. A wise *Wife* comprehends both sexes; she is *Woman* for her *Body*, and she is man within; for her soul is like her *Husbands*." (*Resolves*, First Century, LXXXV.)

[58] For *Pareus* see the Prefatory Letter to *SA*, n. 3. In *DDD*, Book II, Pareus' biblical commentaries are much quoted and cited.

[59] *Rivetus*, André Rivet (1572–1651), was professor of theology at Leyden 1620–1626, and published his great *Isagoge or Introduction to the Holy Scripture of the Old and New Testaments* there in 1617.

[60] Reprobation, the doctrine of punishment with-

out reprieve for the wicked, Milton declared in *CD* I, iv; p. 928, was not an effect of God's arbitrary will, but was reasonable because reprobates incurred their punishment by neglect of God's grace.

[61] Milton regarded the matrimonial law which was enforced in the courts of the English bishops as very little different from the Canon Law of the Roman Catholic Church.

of mind so defective to the purest and most sacred end of matrimony; and that the vessel of voluptuous enjoyment must be made good to him that has taken it upon trust, without any caution, whenas the mind, from whence must flow the acts of peace and love—a far more precious mixture than the quintessence of an excrement —though it be found never so deficient and unable to perform the best duty of marriage in a cheerful and agreeable conversation, shall be thought good enough, however flat and melancholious it be, and must serve, though to the eternal disturbance and languishing of him that complains him. Yet wisdom and charity, weighing God's own institution, would think that the pining of a sad spirit wedded to loneliness should deserve to be freed, as well as the impatience of a sensual desire so providently relieved. It is read to us in the liturgy that "we must not marry to satisfy the fleshly appetite, like brute beasts that have no understanding;"[62] but the canon so runs as if it dreamed of no other matter than such an appetite to be satisfied; for if it happen that nature hath stopped or extinguished the veins of sensuality, that marriage is annulled. But though all the faculties of the understanding and conversing part after trial appear to be so ill and so aversely met through nature's unalterable working as that neither peace nor any sociable contentment can follow, 'tis as nothing—the contract shall stand as firm as ever, betide what will. What is this but secretly to instruct us that however many grave reasons are pretended to the married life, yet that nothing indeed is thought worth regard therein, but the prescribed satisfaction of an irrational heat? Which cannot be but ignominious to the state of marriage, dishonorable to the undervalued soul of man and even to Christian doctrine itself: while it seems more moved at the disappointing of an impetuous nerve than at the ingenuous grievance of a mind unreasonably yoked, and to place more of marriage in the channel of concupiscence than in the pure influence of peace and love, whereof the soul's lawful contentment is the only fountain.

But some are ready to object that the disposition ought seriously to be considered before. But let them know again that for all the wariness can be used, it may yet befall a discreet man to be mistaken in his choice, and we have plenty of examples. The soberest and best governed men are least practised in these affairs; and who knows not that the bashful muteness of a virgin may ofttimes hide all the unliveliness and natural sloth which is really unfit for conversation? Nor is there that freedom of access granted or presumed as may suffice to a perfect discerning till too late; and where any indisposition is suspected, what more usual than the persuasion of friends that acquaintance, as it increases, will amend all? And lastly, it is not strange though many who have spent their youth chastely are in some things not so quick-sighted, while they haste too eagerly to light the nuptial torch;[63] nor is it, therefore, that for a modest error a man should forfeit so great a happiness, and no charitable means to release him, since they who have lived most loosely, by reason of their bold accustoming, prove most successful in their matches, because their wild affections, unsettling at will, have been as so many divorces to teach them experience. Whenas the sober man honoring the appearance of modesty, and hoping well of every social virtue under that veil, may easily chance to meet, if not with a body impenetrable, yet often with a mind to all other due conversation inaccessible, and to all the more estimable and superior purposes of matrimony useless and almost lifeless; and what a solace, what a fit help such a consort would be through the whole life of a man, is less pain to conjecture than to have experience.

CHAPTER IV.

The Second Reason of this Law, because without it marriage, as it happens oft, is not a remedy of that which it promises, as any rational creature would expect. That marriage, if we pattern from the beginning, as our Savior bids, was not properly the remedy of lust, but the fulfilling of conjugal love and helpfulness.

---

[62] From the marriage service of the English Church.

[63] Cf. the pagan lighting of the *nuptial torch* in *PL* XI, 590.

And that we may further see what a violent and cruel thing it is to force the continuing of those together whom God and nature in the gentlest end of marriage never joined, divers evils and extremities that follow upon such a compulsion shall here be set in view. Of evils, the first and greatest is that hereby a most absurd and rash imputation is fixed upon God and his holy laws, of conniving and dispensing with open and common adultery among his chosen people—a thing which the rankest[64] politician would think it shame and disworship that his laws should countenance. How and in what manner this comes to pass I shall reserve till the course of method brings on the unfolding of many scriptures. Next, the law and gospel are hereby made liable to more than one contradiction, which I refer also thither. Lastly, the supreme dictate of charity[65] is hereby many ways neglected and violated; which I shall forthwith address to prove. First, we know St. Paul saith, "It is better to marry than to burn."[66] Marriage, therefore, was given as a remedy of that trouble: but what might this burning mean? Certainly not the mere motion of a sensitive desire, not the mere goad of a sensitive desire: God does not principally take care of such cattle. What is it then but that desire which God put into Adam in Paradise, before he knew the sin of incontinence—that desire which God saw it was not good that man should be left alone to burn in—the desire and longing to put off an unkindly solitariness by uniting another body, but not without a fit soul, to his in the cheerful society of wedlock? Which if it were so needful before the fall, when man was much more perfect in himself, how much more is it needful now against all the sorrows and casualties of this life, to have an intimate and speaking help, a ready and reviving associate in marriage? Whereof who misses by chancing on a mute and spiritless mate, remains more alone than before, and in a burning less to be contained than that which is fleshly, and more to be considered as being more deeply rooted even in the faultless innocence of nature. As for that other burning, which is but as it were the venom of a lusty and over-abounding concoction, strict life and labor with the abatement of a full diet, may keep that low and obedient enough; but this pure and more inbred desire of joining to itself in conjugal fellowship a fit conversing soul (which desire is properly called love) "is stronger than death," as the spouse of Christ thought, "many waters cannot quench it, neither can the floods drown it."[67] This is that rational burning that marriage is to remedy, not to be allayed with fasting, nor with any penance to be subdued: which how can he assuage who by mishap hath met the most unmeetest and unsuitable mind? Who hath the power to struggle with an intelligible flame, not in Paradise to be resisted,[68] become now more ardent by being failed of what in reason it looked for; and even then most unquenched when the importunity of a provender burning is well enough appeased, and yet the soul hath obtained nothing of what it justly desires. Certainly such a one forbidden to divorce is in effect forbidden to marry, and compelled to greater difficulties than in a single life; for if there be not a more human burning which marriage must satisfy, or else may be dissolved, than that of copulation, marriage cannot be honorable for the meet reducing and terminating of lust between two; seeing many beasts in volun-

---

[64] *rankest politician:* "Wonderfull!" says *An Answer to a Book intituled The Doctrine and Discipline of Divorce* (p. 17), "What a Boarish Adjective you joyne with a Politician. Politician is a title worthie of honour and respect, and why you should disgrace it with this homelie language, I cannot imagine; except it be, because Politicians ordinarily differ from you in thir opinion." To this Milton replied in *Colasterion:* "It offends him, that 'rankest' should signify aught but his own smell. . . . Next, the word 'politician' is not used to his maw; and thereupon he plays the most notorious hobby-horse, jesting and frisking in the luxury of his nonsense with such poor fetches to cog a laughter from us, that no antic hobnail at a morris, but is more handsomely facetious" (*C.E.* IV, 257).

[65] Milton is thinking of Erasmus' Commentary on I Cor. vii, which attacks the Canon Law for violating Christianity's first principle of *charity* by obliging incompatible mates to "lyve myserably and ungodly togyther with the greate peryl and daunger of bothe ther sowl helthes" (*The Censure of Erasmus* [1550], CVIII, v).

[66] I Cor. vii, 9.

[67] Like Pareus in his Commentary on the Song of Solomon viii, 7, Milton interprets the lover as Christ, and his serenaded lady as the Church.

[68] The treatment of passion resembles that in *PL* IV, 741-70.

tary and chosen couples live together as un-adulterously, and are as truly married in that respect. But all ingenuous men will see that the dignity and blessing of marriage is placed rather in the mutual enjoyment of that which the wanting soul needfully seeks than of that which the plenteous body would joyfully give away. Hence it is that Plato in his festival discourse brings in Socrates relating what he feigned to have learned from the prophetess Diotima, how Love was the son of Penury, begot of Plenty in the garden of Jupiter.[69] Which divinely sorts with that which in effect Moses tells us, that Love was the son of Loneliness, begot in Paradise by that sociable and helpful aptitude which God implanted between man and woman toward each other. The same, also, is that burning mentioned by St. Paul, whereof marriage ought to be the remedy: the flesh hath other mutual and easy curbs which are in the power of any temperate man. When, therefore, this original and sinless penury, or loneliness of the soul, cannot lay itself down by the side of such a meet and acceptable union as God ordained in marriage, at least in some proportion, it cannot conceive and bring forth love, but remains utterly unmarried under a formal wedlock, and still burns in the proper meaning of St. Paul. Then enters hate, not that hate that sins, but that which only is natural dissatisfaction and the turning aside from a mistaken object. If that mistake have done injury, it fails not to dismiss with recompense, for to retain still, and not be able to love, is to heap up more injury. Thence this wise and pious law of dismission now defended took beginning: he, therefore, who lacking of his due in the most native and human end of marriage, thinks it better to part than to live sadly and injuriously to that cheerful covenant (for not to be beloved and yet retained, is the greatest injury to a gentle spirit), he, I say, who therefore seeks to part, is one who highly honors the married life and would not stain it: and the reasons which now move him to divorce are equal to the best of those that could first warrant him to marry; for, as was

[69] Milton remembered both *Diotima's* allegory of the birth of Love from the embrace of Poverty and Plenty in Plato's *Symposium*, 203, and the creation of Eve to relieve Adam's loneliness (Gen. ii, 18).

plainly shown, both the hate which now diverts him and the loneliness which leads him still powerfully to seek a fit help, hath not the least grain of a sin in it, if he be worthy to understand himself.

CHAPTER V.

The Third Reason of this Law, because without it, he who has happened where he finds nothing but remediless offenses and discontents, is in more and greater temptations than ever before.

Thirdly, Yet it is next to be feared, if he must be still bound without reason by a deaf rigor, that when he perceives the just expectance of his mind defeated, he will begin even against law to cast about where he may find his satisfaction more complete, unless he be a thing heroically virtuous,[70] and that are not the common lump of men for whom chiefly the laws ought to be made—though not to their sins yet to their unsinning weaknesses, it being above their strength to endure the lonely estate, which while they shunned they are fallen into. And yet there follows upon this a worse temptation. For if he be such as hath spent his youth unblamably and laid up his chiefest earthly comforts in the enjoyment of a contented marriage, nor did neglect that furtherance which was to be obtained therein by constant prayers, when he shall find himself bound fast to an uncomplying discord of nature (or, as it oft happens, to an image of earth and phlegm) with whom he looked to be the copartner of a sweet and gladsome society, and sees withal that his bondage is now inevitable, though he be almost the strongest Christian, he will be ready to despair in virtue, and mutiny against divine providence. And this doubtless is the reason of those lapses and that melancholy despair which we see in many wedded persons, though they understand it not, or pretend other causes because they know no remedy; and is of extreme danger. Therefore when human frailty surcharged is at such a loss, charity ought to venture much and use bold physic, lest an overtossed faith endanger to shipwreck.

[70] Cf. heroic virtue in *PL* XI, 690.

CHAPTER VI.

The fourth Reason of this Law, that God regards Love and Peace in the family more than a compulsive performance of marriage, which is more broke by a grievous continuance than by a needful divorce.

Fourthly, Marriage is a covenant the very being whereof consists not in a forced cohabitation and counterfeit performance of duties, but in unfeigned love and peace. And of matrimonial love, no doubt but that was chiefly meant, which by the ancient sages was thus parabled: that Love, if he be not twin-born, yet hath a brother wondrous like him, called Anteros;[71] whom while he seeks all about, his chance is to meet with many false and feigning desires that wander singly up and down in his likeness. By them in their borrowed garb, Love,[72] though not wholly blind as poets wrong him, yet having but one eye, as being born an archer aiming, and that eye not the quickest in this dark region here below which is not Love's proper sphere, partly out of the simplicity and credulity which is native to him, often deceived, embraces and consorts him with these obvious and suborned striplings, as if they were his mother's own sons; for so he thinks them, while they subtly keep themselves most on his blind side. But after a while, as his manner is, when soaring up into the high

tower of his Apogæum,[73] above the shadow of the earth, he darts out the direct rays of his then most piercing eyesight upon the impostures and trim disguises that were used with him, and discerns that this is not his genuine brother, as he imagined. He has no longer the power to hold fellowship with such a personated mate. For straight his arrows lose their golden heads and shed their purple feathers, his silken braids untwine and slip their knots, and that original and fiery virtue given him by fate all on a sudden goes out, and leaves him undeified and despoiled of all his force; till finding Anteros at last, he kindles and repairs the almost faded ammunition of his deity by the reflection of a coequal and homogeneal fire. Thus mine author sung it to me; and by the leave of those who would be counted the only grave ones, this is no mere amatorious novel (though to be wise and skilful in these matters, men heretofore of greatest name in virtue have esteemed it one of the highest arcs that human contemplation circling upward can make from the glassy sea whereon she stands); but this is a deep and serious verity, showing us that love in marriage cannot live nor subsist unless it be mutual; and where love cannot be, there can be left of wedlock nothing but the empty husk of an outside matrimony, as undelightful and unpleasing to God as any other kind of hypocrisy. So far is his command from tying men to the observance of duties which there is no help for, but they must be dissembled. If Solomon's advice[74] be not over frolic, "Live joyfully," saith he, "with the wife whom thou lovest, all thy days, for that is thy portion." How then, where we find it impossible to rejoice or to love, can we obey this precept? How miserably do we defraud ourselves of that comfortable portion which God gives us, by striving vainly to glue an error together which God and nature will not join, adding but more vexation and violence to that blissful society by our importunate superstition that will not hearken to St. Paul, I Cor. vii,

71 For a survey of the development of the *Anteros* of Plato's *Phaedrus*, 255d, (Cf. *Lysis*, 221–22) into the deity of reciprocated love between the sexes and even of heavenly love in Neoplatonic works like Mario Equicola's *Libro di natura d'amore* (1525), Augustinus Niphus' *De amore* (1529), and Celio Calcagnini's *Anteros sive de mutuo amore* (1544), see R. V. Merrill on "Eros and Anteros" in *Speculum*, XIX (1944), 265–84. Milton might expect his readers to be familiar with poems like Ben Jonson's *Eros and Anteros* and with figures of Anteros like those in Alciati's *Emblemata*, or in Cartari's *Imagini de i dei*, or in Antoine Heroët's *La Parfaicte Amye* (*Oeuvres poétiques*, ed. by F. Gohin, Paris, 1909, p. 96).

72 So Spenser united passion with ethical idealism in the heavenly Eros of *An Hymne in Honour of Love* (177–8), who lifts
    himselfe out of the lowly dust
    On golden plumes up to the purest skie,
and in *Colin Clout's Come Home Againe* (834–94) identified him with the cosmic Eros who was born before the creation of the world and unites all its elements in rational order.

73 *Apogæum:* a planet's most distant point from the earth. From such a "summit of the heavens," where Plato describes the gods ascending for a festival (*Phaedrus*, 247b), vision is clearer than it is in the shadowy mirror or "glassy sea" of human sight.

74 Eccles. ix, 9.

who, speaking of marriage and divorce, determines plain enough in general that God therein "hath called us to peace," and not "to bondage." Yea, God himself commands in his law more than once, and by his prophet Malachi, as Calvin and the best translations read, that "he who hates, let him divorce."[75] that is, he who cannot love. Hence it is that the rabbins, and Maimonides, famous among the rest, in a book[76] of his set forth by Buxtorfius, tells us that "divorce was permitted by Moses to preserve peace in marriage, and quiet in the family." Surely the Jews had their saving peace about them as well as we, yet care was taken that this wholesome provision for household peace should also be allowed them: and must this be denied to Christians? O perverseness! that the law should be made more provident of peace-making than the gospel! that the gospel should be put to beg a most necessary help of mercy from the law, but must not have it! and that to grind in the mill of an undelighted and servile copulation must be the only forced work of a Christian marriage, ofttimes with such a yoke-fellow, from whom both love and peace, both nature and religion, mourns to be separated. I cannot therefore be so diffident as not securely to conclude that he who can receive nothing of the most important helps in marriage, being thereby disenabled to return that duty which is his, with a clear and hearty countenance, and thus continues to grieve whom he would not, and is no less grieved; that man ought even for love's sake and peace to move divorce upon good and liberal conditions to the divorced. And

it is a less breach of wedlock to part with wise and quiet consent betimes, than still to soil and profane that mystery of joy and union with a polluting sadness and perpetual distemper: for it is not the outward continuing of marriage that keeps whole that covenant, but whosoever does most according to peace and love, whether in marriage or in divorce, he it is that breaks marriage least; it being so often written that "Love only is the fulfilling of every commandment."[77]

.   .   .   .

BOOK II.

CHAPTER I.

The Ordinance of Sabbath and marriage compared. Hyperbole no infrequent figure in the Gospel. Excess cured by contrary excess. Christ neither did, nor could abrogate the Law of divorce, but only reprove the abuse thereof.

Hitherto the position undertaken hath been declared and proved by a law of God, that law proved to be moral and unabolishable, for many reasons equal, honest, charitable, just, annexed thereto. It follows now that those places of scripture which have a seeming to revoke the prudence of Moses, or rather that merciful decree of God, be forthwith explained and reconciled. For what are all these reasonings worth, will some reply, whenas the words of Christ are plainly against all divorce, "except in case of fornication?"[78] To whom he whose mind were to answer no more but this, "except also in case of charity," might safely appeal to the more plain words of Christ in defense of so excepting. "Thou shalt do no manner of work,"[79] saith the commandment of the Sabbath. Yes, saith Christ, works of charity.[80] And shall we be more severe in paraphrasing the considerate and tender gospel than he was in ex-

---

75 The reference is to Mal. ii, 16, one of the most disputed verses in the Bible. In the King James Version it reads: "For the Lord, the God of Israel, saith that he hateth putting away" (divorcing). The context is a prophetic allegory representing the Hebrews as having put away the wife of their youth (i.e. the worship of Jehovah) for a wife who is a stranger (i.e. idol-worship). In *DDD* II, xiii, Milton again says that God "commands divorce" both "in the law and in the prophet Malachi."

76 The *book* is *The Guide for the Perplexed*, which was translated from the original Arabic into Hebrew in 1204, and into Latin by Buxtorf in 1629. Translations into modern European languages began with the Italian version in 1580?, but there was no complete English translation until 1889. The author, the great Jewish physician and philosopher, Maimonides, was born in Cordova in 1135, and died in Cairo in 1204.

77 ". . . love is the fulfilling of the law" (Rom. xiii, 10).

78 Matt. v, 32.

79 Exod. xx, 10.

80 Defending himself against criticism for healing a woman on the Sabbath, Christ asked, "ought not this woman, . . . whom Satan hath bound, lo, these eighteen years, be loosed from this bond on the sabbath day?" (Luke xiii, 16.)

pounding the rigid and peremptory law? What was ever in all appearance less made for man, and more for God alone, than the Sabbath? Yet when the good of man comes into the scales, we hear that voice of infinite goodness and benignity that "Sabbath was made for man, not man for Sabbath."[81] What thing ever was more made for man alone, and less for God, than marriage? And shall we load it with a cruel and senseless bondage utterly against both the good of man and the glory of God? Let whoso will now listen. I want neither pall nor miter, I stay neither for ordination or induction; but in the firm faith of a knowing Christian, which is the best and truest endowment of the keys,[82] I pronounce, the man who shall bind so cruelly a good and gracious ordinance of God, hath not in that the spirit of Christ. Yet that every text of scripture seeming opposite may be attended with a due exposition, this other part ensues, and makes account to find no slender arguments for this assertion, out of those very scriptures which are commonly urged against it.

First therefore let us remember, as a thing not to be denied, that all places of scripture wherein just reason of doubt arises from the letter, are to be expounded by considering upon what occasion everything is set down, and by comparing other texts. The occasion which induced our Savior to speak of divorce, was either to convince the extravagance of the pharisees in that point, or to give a sharp and vehement answer to a tempting question.[83] And in such cases, that we are not to repose all upon the literal terms of so many words, many instances will teach us: wherein we may plainly discover how Christ meant not to be taken word for word, but like a wise physician, administering one excess against another to reduce us to a perfect mean. Where the pharisees were strict, there Christ seems remiss; where they were too remiss, he saw it needful to seem most

severe. In one place he censures an unchaste look to be adultery already committed.[84] Another time he passes over actual adultery[85] with less reproof than for an unchaste look, not so heavily condemning secret weakness as open malice. So here he may be justly thought to have given this rigid sentence against divorce, not to cut off all remedy from a good man who finds himself consuming away in a disconsolate and unenjoyed matrimony, but to lay a bridle upon the bold abuses of those overweening rabbis; which he could not more effectually do than by a countersway of restraint curbing their wild exorbitance almost into the other extreme, as when we bow things the contrary way to make them come to their natural straightness. And that this was the only intention of Christ is most evident if we attend but to his own words and protestation made in the same sermon, not many verses before he treats of divorcing, that he came not to abrogate from the law "one jot or tittle,"[86] and denounces against them that shall so teach.

But St. Luke, the verse immediately before-going that of divorce, inserts the same caveat, as if the latter could not be understood without the former; and as a witness to produce against this our wilful mistake of abrogating, which must needs confirm us that whatever else in the political law[87] of more special relation to the Jews might cease to us, yet that of those precepts concerning divorce, not one of them was repealed by the doctrine of Christ, unless we have vowed not to believe his own cautious and immediate profession. For if these our Savior's words inveigh against all divorce and condemn it as adultery, except it be for adultery, and be not rather understood against the abuse

[84] The verse is from the Sermon on the Mount, Matt. v, 18.
[85] Christ's only words to the woman "taken in adultery" were, "Go, and sin no more" (John viii, 11).
[86] "And it is easier for heaven and earth to pass, than one tittle of the law to fail."
"Whosoever putteth away his wife, and marrieth another, committeth adultery: and whosoever marrieth her that is put away from her husband, committeth adultery" (Luke xvi, 17–18).
[87] Cf. n. 7 above, and also the saying in *CD* I, x, that "God in his just and pure and holy law, has not only permitted divorce on a variety of grounds, but has even ratified it in some cases, and enjoined it in others, under the severest penalties."

[81] Mark ii, 27.
[82] Cf. the allusion to St. Peter as the bearer of the keys of the kingdom of heaven in *Lyc*, 110, and the denial in *CD* I, xxix (C.E. XVI, p. 231) that any prelate can derive any authority from Peter, "inasmuch as the power of the keys, as it is called, or the right of binding and loosing, is not entrusted to him alone."
[83] Cf. n. 54 above.

of those divorces permitted in the law, then is that law of Moses, Deut. xxiv, 1, not only repealed and wholly annulled against the promise of Christ and his known profession not to meddle in matters judicial, but that which is more strange, the very substance and purpose of that law is contradicted, and convinced both of injustice and impurity, as having authorized and maintained legal adultery by statute. Moses also cannot scape to be guilty of unequal and unwise decrees, punishing one act of secret adultery by death, and permitting a whole life of open adultery by law. And albeit lawyers write that some political edicts, though not approved, are yet allowed to the scum of the people and the necessity of the times, these excuses have but a weak pulse. For first, we read, not that the scoundrel people, but the choicest, the wisest, the holiest of that nation have frequently used these laws, or such as these, in the best and holiest times. Secondly, be it yielded that in matters not very bad or impure, a human lawgiver may slacken something of that which is exactly good, to the disposition of the people and the times. But if the perfect, the pure, the righteous law of God (for so are all his statutes and his judgments) be found to have allowed smoothly, without any certain reprehension, that which Christ afterward declares to be adultery, how can we free this law from the horrible indictment of being both impure, unjust and fallacious?

Extract from CHAPTER III

The Jesuits and that sect among us which is named of Arminius,[88] are wont to charge us of making God the author of sin, in two degrees especially, not to speak of his permission: 1. Because we hold that he hath decreed some to damnation, and con-

sequently to sin, say they; next, Because those means which are of saving knowledge to others, he makes to them an occasion of greater sin. Yet considering the perfection wherein man was created and might have stood, no decree necessitating his free will, but subsequent, though not in time yet in order, to causes which were in his own power, they might methinks be persuaded to absolve both God and us. Whenas the doctrine of Plato[89] and Chrysippus[90] with their followers, the Academics and the Stoics, who knew not what a consummate and most adorned Pandora[91] was bestowed upon Adam to be the nurse and guide of his arbitrary happiness and perseverance, I mean his native innocence and perfection, which might have kept him from being our true Epimetheus; and though they taught of virtue and vice to be both the gift of divine destiny, they could yet find[92] reasons not invalid to justify the councils of God and fate from the insulsity of mortal tongues:—that man's own will self-corrupted is the adequate and sufficient cause of his disobedience besides fate; as Homer[93] also wanted not to express, both in his *Iliad* and *Odyssey*. And Manilius[94] the poet, although in his fourth book

[88] In his reply to his Calvinist opponents at the University of Leyden in October, 1604, *Arminius* charged that by their extreme interpretation of the doctrine of Predestination they represented God as "the author of sin; nor that alone; but also that God really sins, nay, that God alone sins." Whereas God made Christ "the mediator to save all who should believe on Him, . . . God foreknew, but did not foreordain, who would be saved, and who would be damned." (Quoted by W. K. Jordan, *Development of Religious Toleration in England, 1603–40*, p. 325.) Cf. *CD* I, iv, p. 918.

[89] Perhaps Milton thought of the place in *Plato's* theodicy in the *Laws* X, 904ab, where proof of the goodness of the soul of the universe is followed by the statement that evil is altogether a matter of the individual wills which, in their various situations in the universe, determine their own characters by their desires.

[90] Almost nothing remains except quotations in other writers of the voluminous works of *Chrysippus* (280–207 B.C.), who followed Zeno and Cleanthes in founding Stoicism. In Arian's *Discourses of Epictetus* II, 9, he is represented as teaching that man's creation with the faculty of choice imposed responsibility for his conduct upon him.

[91] Cf. Eve "more lovely than *Pandora*" in *PL* IV, 714.

[92] The reading in the text is "give." The *Errata* correct it to "find."

[93] Milton's reference may be to the opening of the *Iliad*, where Achilles' violence is said to have fulfilled the council of Zeus. The *Odyssey* I, 9, says that the followers of Ulysses "perished, self-destroyed by their own fault," and at the end of his chapter on Predestination (*CD* I, iv; p. 931) Milton quoted the line and the more emphatic passage that follows (ll. 40–45):

Perverse mankind! whose wills, created free,
Charge all their woes on absolute decree:
All to the dooming gods their guilt translate,
And follies are miscalled the crimes of fate.
        (Pope's version.)

[94] *Manilius* (who seems to have been a contem-

he tells of some "created both to sin and punishment," yet without murmuring, and with an industrious cheerfulness, acquits the deity. They were not ignorant in their heathen lore that it is most godlike to punish those who of his creatures became his enemies with the greatest punishment; and they could attain also to think that the greatest, when God himself throws a man furthest from him; which then they held he did, when he blinded, hardened and stirred up his offenders to finish and pile up their desperate work since they had undertaken it. To banish for ever into a local hell, whether in the air or in the center, or in that uttermost and bottomless gulf of chaos, deeper from holy bliss than the world's diameter multiplied, they thought had not a punishing so proper and proportionate for God to inflict as to punish sin with sin. Thus were the common sort of Gentiles wont to think, without any wry thoughts cast upon divine governance. And therefore Cicero,[95] not in his Tusculan or Campanian retirements among the learned wits of that age, but even in the senate to a mixed auditory (though he were sparing otherwise to broach his philosophy among statists and lawyers), yet as to this point, both in his *Oration against Piso,* and in that which is about the answers of the soothsayers against Clodius, he declares it publicly as no paradox to common ears that God cannot punish man more, nor make him more miserable, than still by making him more sinful. Thus we see how in this controversy the justice of God stood upright even among

heathen disputers. But if any one be truly and not pretendedly zealous for God's honor, here I call him forth before men and angels, to use his best and most advised skill lest God more unavoidably than ever yet, and in the guiltiest manner, be made the author of sin: if he shall not only deliver over and incite his enemies by rebuke to sin as a punishment, but shall by patent under his own broad seal[96] allow his friends whom he would sanctify and save, whom he would unite to himself and not disjoin, whom he would correct by wholesome chastening, and not punish as he doth the damned by lewd sinning; if he shall allow these in his law, the perfect rule of his own purest will and our most edified conscience, the perpetrating of an odious and manifold sin without the least contesting. 'Tis wondered how there can be in God a secret and revealed will,[97] and yet what wonder, if there be in man two answerable causes. But here there must be two revealed wills grappling in a fraternal war with one another without any reasonable cause apprehended. This cannot be less than to ingraft sin into the substance of the law, which law is to provoke sin by crossing and forbidding, not by complying with it. Nay, this is, which I tremble in uttering, to incarnate sin into the unpunishing and wellpleased will of God. To avoid these dreadful consequences that tread upon the heels of those allowances to sin, will be a task of far more difficulty than to appease those minds which perhaps out of a vigilant and wary conscience except against predestination. Thus finally we may conclude that a law wholly giving license cannot upon any good consideration be given to a holy people, for hardness of heart in the vulgar sense.

porary of Augustus and Tiberius) says that we rightly hate those who are "created to guilt and punishment," and that crime is not to be imputed to heaven (*Astronomicon* IV, 115-7). Cf. *Educ,* n. 52.

[95] In the oration to the Senate *On Behalf of Milo* (86) *Cicero* dramatically described the Latian gods as having been outraged by Clodius, and as having inspired him and his gang with the madness that drove them to their deaths in their lawless attack on Milo in the Appian Way. In the oration *Against Piso* (46) Cicero asserted that the extreme crimes of the wicked are "the most inevitable of the penalties ordained for them by the immortal gods."

[96] Royal *patents* or licenses were issued under the *broad seal* of the English kings.

[97] Cf. Milton's assault in *CD* I, iv, "of Predestination," on "the scholastic distinction which ascribes a two-fold will to God; his revealed will, whereby he prescribes the way in which he desires us to act, and his hidden will, whereby he decrees that we shall never so act."

AREOPAGITICA

A SPEECH FOR THE LIBERTY OF UNLICENSED PRINTING,
TO THE PARLIAMENT OF ENGLAND

This is true liberty, when free-born men,
Having to advise the public, may speak free,
Which he who can and will, deserves high praise;
Who neither can nor will, may hold his peace;
What can be juster in a State than this?

EURIPIDES, *The Suppliants.*

BIBLIOGRAPHICAL NOTE—"I wrote my *Areopagitica,*" said Milton in *Def 2* (p. 831 below), "in order to deliver the press from the restraints with which it was encumbered." He referred to Parliament's ordinance for licensing the press of June 14, 1643, and to the formal demand of the Stationers' Company on August 24 for its strict enforcement. Milton was mentioned by name in that document, as he had been in a sermon before Parliament by the Presbyterian divine, Herbert Palmer, on August 14, 1644, and condemned for the unlicensed publication of *DDD*. But Milton also had in mind the attitude of men like Bishop Hall (see *Apology* Bibliographical Note), who, in *The Peace-Maker* (1624), after observing that the "cunning adversaries" of the Church of England in Italy were wrong to forbid the circulation of the Bible and other unchallengeable books, yet drew from their example the moral that, "If they be thus cautious to forbid the best of books, for their own advantage; what a shame it shall be for us, to be so slack and supine, as not to restrain the worst writings, to the infinite disadvantage of the Gospel!" By a decree of the Court of Star Chamber (see *CG*, n. 110) of July 11, 1637, all licensing authority had been entrusted to the two archbishops, the Bishop of London, and the chancellors of the two universities. The effect was to give Archbishop Laud, who was also Chancellor of the University of Oxford, actual control of every press in England, with power to stop publication of any book "contrary to . . . the Doctrine and Discipline of the Church of England."

Nominally, *Areopagitica* was an oration addressed to Parliament, although Milton had no more intention of delivering it in person than Isocrates had of public delivery of the speech whose title Milton adopted. Both men regarded the almost prehistoric court which traditionally had sat on the hill of Ares (Mars) in Athens, the Areopagus, as having possessed the almost superhuman probity and prestige which the Dutch Protestant scholar, Jean de Meurs, attributed to it in his *De Areopago, sive de Senatu Areopago liber* (1624). In a chapter on the "dignity and authority" of the Court, de Meurs accumulated a mass of evidence proving that it had always been traditionally venerated. Its nearly three hundred members were elected by vote of all the freedmen in Athens, and in Isocrates' *Panathenaic Oration* it is described as the glory of the democratic constitution of Athens, in contrast to the Oligarchic constitution of Sparta. Milton implies that Parliament should be like the Areopagus, which Robert Burton described in the *Anatomy* as consisting only of such men "as are learned, wise, discreet, and well brought up."

Areopagitica was published in 1644; the copy in the Thomason collection in the British Museum is dated Nov. 24. The present text is based on the copy of the first edition in the Houghton Library at Harvard University.

A facsimile reproduction of the edition of 1644 is available in the Noel Douglas Replicas (London, 1927); good annotated editions are available, edited by Laura E. Lockwood in her

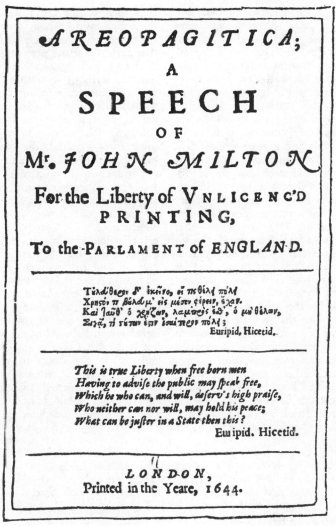

AREOPAGITICA;

A

SPEECH

OF

Mᵣ. *JOHN MILTON*

For the Liberty of Vnlicenc'd
PRINTING,

To the Parlament of ENGLAND.

Τὶ λδ'θερι δ' ἐκεῖνο, εἰ τις θέλη πόλε
Χρησὸν τι βέλδμ' εἰς μέσον φέρειν, ἔχων.
Καὶ ταῦθ' ὁ χρηζων, λαμπρὸς ἰσθ', ὁ μὴ θέλων,
Σιγᾷ, τί τέτων ἐστιν ἰσαίτερον πόλει;
            Euripid, Hicetid.

*This is true Liberty when free born men
Having to advise the public may speak free,
Which he who can, and will, deserv's high praise,
Who neither can nor will, may hold his peace;
What can be juster in a State then this?*
            Euripid. Hicetid.

LONDON,
Printed in the Yeare, 1644.

Selected Essays of John Milton (Boston, 1911), by J. W. Hales (Oxford, Clarendon Press, 1904 and 1917), by William Haller (New York, 1927), and by O. Lutaud (Paris, 1956).

They who to states[1] and governors of the Commonwealth direct their speech, High Court of Parliament, or, wanting such access in a private condition, write that which they foresee may advance the public good; I suppose them, as at the beginning of no mean endeavor, not a little altered and moved inwardly in their minds: some with doubt of what will be the success, others with fear of what will be the censure;[2] some with hope, others with confidence of what they have to speak. And me perhaps each of these dispositions, as the subject was whereon I entered, may

[1] *states* is used as it is in Milton's reference to the "States General of Holland" founding a university (CB, C.E. XVIII, 137), or in his reference to the "infernal States" of the devils' parliament in *PL* II, 387. Cf. States General, the ancient parliament of France, consisting of clergy, nobility, and the third estate.

[2] *censure* is used in a neutral way, to mean judgment either favorable or unfavorable.

have at other times variously affected; and likely might in these foremost expressions now also disclose which of them swayed most, but that the very attempt of this address thus made, and the thought of whom it hath recourse to, hath got the power within me to a passion,[3] far more welcome than incidental to a preface.

Which though I stay not to confess ere any ask, I shall be blameless, if it be no other than the joy and gratulation which it brings to all who wish and promote their country's liberty; whereof this whole discourse proposed will be a certain testimony, if not a trophy. For this is not the liberty which we can hope, that no grievance ever should arise in the Commonwealth—that let no man in this world expect; but when complaints are freely heard, deeply considered, and speedily reformed, then is the utmost bound of civil liberty attained that wise men look for. To which, if I now manifest by the very sound of this which I shall utter, that we are already in good part arrived, and yet from such a steep disadvantage of tyranny and superstition grounded into our principles as was beyond the manhood of a Roman recovery;[4] it will be attributed first, as is most due, to the strong assistance of God our deliverer, next, to your faithful guidance and undaunted wisdom, Lords and Commons of England.

Neither is it in God's esteem the diminution of his glory, when honorable things are spoken of good men and worthy magistrates; which if I now first should begin to do, after so fair a progress of your laudable deeds and such a long obligement[5] upon the whole realm to your indefatigable virtues, I might be justly reckoned among the tardiest and the unwillingest of them that praise ye.

Nevertheless, there being three principal things without which all praising is but courtship and flattery: first, when that only is praised which is solidly worth praise; next, when greatest likelihoods are brought

that such things are truly and really in those persons to whom they are ascribed; the other, when he who praises, by showing that such his actual persuasion is of whom he writes, can demonstrate that he flatters not; the former two of these I have heretofore endeavored, rescuing the employment from him who went about to impair your merits with a trivial and malignant encomium;[6] the latter, as belonging chiefly to mine own acquittal, that whom I so extolled I did not flatter, hath been reserved opportunely to this occasion. For he who freely magnifies what hath been nobly done and fears not to declare as freely what might be done better, gives ye the best covenant of his fidelity; and that his loyalest affection and his hope waits on your proceedings. His highest praising is not flattery, and his plainest advice is a kind of praising; for thoug. I should affirm and hold by argument that it would fare better with truth, with learning, and the Commonwealth, if one of your published orders,[7] which I should name, were called in; yet at the same time it could not but much redound to the luster of your mild and equal government, whenas private persons are hereby animated to think ye better pleased with public advice than other statists[8] have been delighted heretofore with public flattery. And men will then see what difference there is between the magnanimity of a triennial parliament[9] and that jealous haughtiness of prelates and cabin counsellors[10] that usurped of late, whenas they shall observe ye in the midst

[6] Milton refers to Bishop Hall's *Modest Confutation* (see the Bibliographical Note to *Apology*), which had made its bow to Parliament on the first page with the assurance that, "The sun looks not on a braver, nobler Convocation than is that of King, Peers, and Commons, whose equal justice and moderation shall eternally triumph. . . ."

[7] See the Bibliographical Note to *Areop.*

[8] *statists:* statesmen. Cf. *PR* IV, 354.

[9] By an act of 15 February, 1641, Parliament provided that it should be summoned at least once every three years.

[10] *cabin:* cabinet or council chamber. The "cabin counsellors" of Charles I were the little groups of intimate advisers, most of whom held offices of the highest trust and prominence, with whose aid the king governed without summoning Parliament between 1626 and 1628 and between 1629 and 1640. From 1603 until 1640 "parliamentary sessions totalled less than four-and-a-half in thirty-seven years," and "the centre of government . . . lay in the royal council." D. L. Keir,

[3] *passion:* enthusiasm (for writing on the subject of *Areop*).

[4] The contrast is between England's successful revolt against King Charles and the bishops, as opposed to the impotence of Rome to shake off the tyranny into which she fell under the emperors and popes.

[5] *obligement:* obligation.

of your victories and successes more gently brooking written exceptions against a voted order than other courts, which had produced nothing worth memory but the weak ostentation of wealth, would have endured the least signified dislike at any sudden proclamation.

If I should thus far presume upon the meek demeanor of your civil[11] and gentle greatness, Lords and Commons, as what your published order hath directly said, that to gainsay, I might defend myself with ease, if any should accuse me of being new or insolent, did they but know how much better I find ye esteem it to imitate the old and elegant humanity of Greece than the barbaric pride of a Hunnish[12] and Norwegian stateliness. And out of those ages, to whose polite wisdom and letters we owe that we are not yet Goths and Jutlanders, I could name him[13] who from his private house wrote that discourse to the parliament of Athens that persuades them to change the form of democraty which was then established. Such honor was done in those days to men who professed the study of wisdom and eloquence, not only in their own country, but in other lands, that cities and seignories[14] heard them gladly and with great respect, if they had aught in public to admonish the state. Thus did Dion Prusæus,[15] a stranger and a private orator, counsel the Rhodians against a former edict; and I abound with other like examples, which to set here would be superfluous. But if from the industry of a life wholly dedicated to studious labors and those natural endowments haply not the worst for two and fifty degrees of northern latitude,[16] so much must be derogated as to count me not equal to any of those who had this privilege, I would obtain to be thought not so inferior as yourselves are superior to the most of them who received their counsel: and how far you excel them, be assured, Lords and Commons, there can no greater testimony appear than when your prudent spirit acknowledges and obeys the voice of reason from what quarter soever it be heard speaking; and renders ye as willing to repeal any act of your own setting forth, as any set forth by your predecessors.

If ye be thus resolved, as it were injury to think ye were not, I know not what should withhold me from presenting ye with a fit instance wherein to show both that love of truth which ye eminently profess, and that uprightness of your judgment which is not wont to be partial to yourselves; by judging over again that Order which ye have ordained *to regulate Printing: that no book, pamphlet, or paper shall be henceforth printed, unless the same be first approved and licensed by such*, or at least one of such as shall be thereto appointed. For that part which preserves justly every man's copy[17] to himself, or provides for the poor, I touch not, only wish they be not made pretenses to abuse and persecute honest and painful[18] men, who offend not in either of these particulars. But that other clause of licensing books, which we thought had died with his

---

The Constitutional History of Modern Britain, London (1938), pp. 162–3.

[11] *civil*: civilized, polite. Cf. its use as synonymous with "generous" in *SA* 1467.

[12] Milton thought both of the contemporary reputation of the Scandinavians and of their share in the Danish invasions of England from the fifth to the tenth centuries. In *Britain* I (C.E. X, 15) he noted the invasion of Scotland by "Humber, King of the Huns, who with a fleet invaded that land, was slain in fight, and his people driven back." Danish arrogance was proverbial, as Donne implied in describing a proud courtier as,

"One, who for a Dane,
In the Danes Massacre had sure been slaine."
(*Satire IV*, 23–24)

[13] *him*: Isocrates. Cf. the Bibliographical Note to *Areop*.

[14] "A Monarch Signorial is he who by force of Arms and just War is made owner of Mens Bodies and Goods, and governeth them as a Master of a Family governeth base Servants and Slaves." *The Arts of Empire and Mysteries of States Discabineted*, by Sir Walter Raleigh, published by John Milton (Edition of 1692, p. 5). Turkey and the West Indies are mentioned as typical signories.

[15] Dion Chrysostomos (the "Golden-mouthed") was born in Prusa but was famous as a spokesman of republican ideals in Rome in speeches advising the Emperor Vespasian to restore the Republic and condemning the tyranny of Domitian. He was influential in placing the "worthy emperor" Trajan (see *TKM*, n. 65) on the throne, under whom he returned to his native Asia to encourage liberal studies. The law against which he counselled the Rhodians permitted the erasure of names standing on public monuments to make room for those of contemporary public men (*Thirty-first Discourse*, 8–10).

[16] Cf. *Manso*, 28, *PL* IX, 45, and *CG*, n. 168.

[17] *copy*: copyright.

[18] *painful*: diligent, willing to take pains.

brother *quadragesimal*[19] and *matrimonial*[20] when the prelates expired, I shall now attend with such a homily as shall lay before ye, first, the inventors of it to be those whom ye will be loth to own; next, what is to be thought in general of reading, whatever sort the books be; and that this Order avails nothing to the suppressing of scandalous, seditious, and libellous books, which were mainly intended to be suppressed. Last, that it will be primely to the discouragement of all learning and the stop of truth, not only by disexercising and blunting our abilities in what we know already, but by hindering and cropping the discovery that might be yet further made both in religious and civil wisdom.

I deny not but that it is of greatest concernment in the church and commonwealth to have a vigilant eye how books demean themselves as well as men; and thereafter to confine, imprison, and do sharpest justice on them as malefactors. For books are not absolutely dead things, but do contain a potency of life in them to be as active as that soul was whose progeny they are; nay, they do preserve as in a vial the purest efficacy and extraction of that living intellect that bred them.[21] I know they are as lively and as vigorously productive as those fabulous dragon's teeth; and being sown up and down, may chance to spring up armed men.[22] And yet, on the other hand, unless wariness be used, as good almost kill a man as kill a good book: who kills a man kills a reasonable creature, God's image; but he who destroys a good book, kills reason itself, kills the image of God, as it were, in the eye. Many a man lives a burden to the earth; but a good book is the precious lifeblood of a master spirit, embalmed and treasured up on purpose to a life beyond life.[23] 'Tis true, no age can restore a life, whereof perhaps there is no great loss; and revolutions of ages do not oft recover the loss of a rejected truth, for the want of which whole nations fare the worse. We should be wary, therefore, what persecution we raise against the living labors of public men, how we spill that seasoned life of man preserved and stored up in books; since we see a kind of homicide may be thus committed, sometimes a martyrdom; and if it extend to the whole impression, a kind of massacre, whereof the execution ends not in the slaying of an elemental life, but strikes at that ethereal and fifth essence,[24] the breath of reason itself, slays an immortality rather than a life. But lest I should be condemned of introducing license, while I oppose licensing, I refuse not the pains to be so much historical as will serve to show what hath been done by ancient and famous commonwealths against this disorder, till the very time that this project of licensing crept out of the Inquisition,[25] was caught up by our prelates, and hath caught some of our presbyters.

In Athens, where books and wits were ever busier than in any other part of Greece, I find but only two sorts of writings which the magistrate cared to take notice of; those either blasphemous and atheistical, or libellous. Thus the books of Protagoras[26] were

---

[19] *quadragesimal*: pertaining to the forty days of Lent. The Puritans had relaxed the traditional, Anglican restrictions on diet during Lent.

[20] In *Hirelings* (p. 868) Milton approved of Parliament's act securing the "civil liberty of marriage; transferring the ratifying, and registering of marriage to the civil magistrates."

[21] Several parallels to Milton's thought can be found—none of them perhaps likelier to have influenced the present passage than Bacon's saying in the *Advancement* (W. A. Wright's ed., Oxford, 1900), I, viii, 6, p. 72; "But the images of men's wits and knowledges remain in books, exempted from the wrong of time and capable of perpetual renovation. Neither are they fitly to be called images, because they generate still, and cast their seeds in the minds of others, provoking and causing infinite actions and opinions in succeeding ages."

[22] Milton had in mind the almost complete mutual slaughter of the warriors who sprang from the teeth of the dragon which Ovid says (*Met.* III, 95-126) were sown by its slayer, Cadmus, King of Thebes in Boeotia.

[23] Cf. Henry Vaughan, *To his Books*:
Bright books! the *perspectives* to our weak sights:
The clear *projections* of discerning lights.
Burning and shining *Thoughts;* man's posthume day:
The *track* of fled souls, and their *Milkie-way.*
The dead *alive* and *busie,* the still *voice*
Of inlarg'd Spirits, . . .

[24] Cf. *PL* III, 713-19, n.

[25] Milton referred not only to the Spanish *Inquisition* which was instituted in Spain in 1480 and took strong measures against heresy in Holland in the sixteenth century, but also to the whole inquisitorial movement which was first instituted by the Council of Toulouse in 1229.

[26] *Protagoras* (? 480-411 B.C.) of Abdera, in Thrace, was the first of the great sophists or professional teachers of rhetoric. In 411 he was impeached for a theological treatise which began by

by the judges of Areopagus[27] commanded to be burnt, and himself banished the territory for a discourse begun with his confessing not to know whether there were gods, or whether not. And against defaming, it was decreed that none should be traduced by name, as was the manner of Vetus Comœdia,[28] whereby we may guess how they censured libelling; and this course was quick enough, as Cicero[29] writes, to quell both the desperate wits of other atheists and the open way of defaming, as the event showed. Of other sects and opinions, though tending to voluptuousness and the denying of divine providence, they took no heed. Therefore we do not read that either Epicurus,[30] or that libertine school of Cyrene,[31] or what the Cynic impudence uttered,[32] was ever questioned by the laws. Neither is it recorded that the writings of those old comedians were suppressed, though the acting of them were forbid; and that Plato[33] commended the reading of Aristophanes, the loosest of them all, to his royal scholar Dionysius, is com-

monly known and may be excused, if holy Chrysostom,[34] as is reported, nightly studied so much the same author and had the art to cleanse a scurrilous vehemence into the style of a rousing sermon.

That other leading city of Greece, Lacedæmon, considering that Lycurgus[35] their lawgiver was so addicted to elegant learning as to have been the first that brought out of Ionia the scattered works of Homer, and sent the poet Thales[36] from Crete to prepare and mollify the Spartan surliness with his smooth songs and odes, the better to plant among them law and civility, it is to be wondered how museless[37] and unbookish they were, minding nought but the feats of war. There needed no licensing of books among them, for they disliked all but their own laconic apothegms and took a slight occasion to chase Archilochus[38] out of their city, perhaps for composing in a higher strain than their own soldierly ballads and roundels could reach to; or if it were for his broad verses, they were not therein so cautious, but they were as dissolute in their promiscuous conversing; whence Euripi-

disclaiming all knowledge on his part as to whether or not the gods existed. The book was burned and Protagoras is said to have been banished from Athens.

27 "Scorners or Despisers of the gods," wrote Thomas Heywood in *The Hierarchie of the blessed Angells* (1635), p. 32, were "convented before the Areopagitae; and beeing convicted, their goods were sold at a publique out-cry, and their irreligions grauen upon pillars, to make their persons odible."

28 *Vetus Comœdia:* in the Old Comedy of Athens, says Gilbert Norwood in *Greek Comedy* (1931), p. 28, "we know certainly of but one law restraining" comic freedom of personal reference, and that "endured from 440–39 till 438–7, less than three years."

29 The reference is to Cicero's treatise *On the Nature of the Gods* I, xxiii, where the punishment of Protagoras is regarded as having done much to repress open atheism, "inasmuch as even doubt" of the existence of the gods "was punished."

30 Cf. *CG*, n. 265.

31 The life of the founder of the Cyrenaic school, Aristippus, as told by Diogenes Laertius, contains many scandalous stories of his libertinism.

32 The stories of Diogenes' search in open daylight with a lantern for an honest man, and of his contempt for Alexander's invitation to live at court in preference to his tub or shack, illustrate the severity and unconventionality of the *Cynics*, whose most famous representative he was.

33 The tradition that *Plato* recommended Aristophanes' comedies to Dionysius (the Elder?), Tyrant of Syracuse from 367 to 356 B.C. and from 346 to 343 B.C., goes back to the short, ancient life of Aristophanes which is to be found in the Teubner edition of his plays.

34 An interest in Aristophanes on the part of John Chrysostom (347–407 A.D.) would seem noteworthy to Puritans who honored him most because (according to Socrates Scholasticus, *Ecclesiastical History* VI, xvi) he was banished from his see for opposing the idolatrous honor paid to the empress Eudoxia and the "common playes and showes" that she approved. (Meredith Hanmer's translation, 1585.) In the first printed edition of Aristophanes' plays (1498) "Aldo Manuzio says that St. John Chrysostom was so fond of (them) that he constantly had with him a copy of (them), that he always put them beneath his pillow at night, . . . and that to his constant study of this poet he owed his unmatched eloquence and his hatred of vice." Louis E. Lord, *Aristophanes, his Plays and Influence*, Boston (1925), p. 97.

35 Cf. *Educ*, n. 63.

36 *Thales,* one of the earliest Ionian poets, is mentioned in Plutarch's *Life of Lycurgus* (IV, v) as having been persuaded by Lycurgus to leave his home in Crete and settle in Sparta. "His odes," says Plutarch, "were so many persuasives to obedience and unanimity, and . . . they softened insensibly the manners of the audience, drew them often from the animosities which then prevailed, and united them in zeal for . . . virtue."

37 *museless:* unfamiliar with the Muses, goddesses of poetry and the other arts.

38 *Archilochus* (early seventh century B.C.) "took delight in flouting the conventions of the aristocracy" (H. J. Rose, *A Handbook of Greek Literature*, p. 89) and may have earned his traditional banishment from Sparta for his supposedly licentious verses or for his poem boasting of his own cowardice in throwing away his shield in a retreat.

des[39] affirms in *Andromache* that their women were all unchaste. Thus much may give us light after what sort books were prohibited among the Greeks.

The Romans also, for many ages trained up only to a military roughness, resembling most the Lacedæmonian guise, knew of learning little but what their twelve tables[40] and the Pontific College with their augers and flamens[41] taught them in religion and law, so unacquainted with other learning that when Carneades[42] and Critolaus,[43] with the Stoic Diogenes[44] coming ambassadors to Rome, took thereby occasion to give the city a taste of their philosophy, they were suspected for seducers by no less a man than Cato[45] the Censor, who moved

it in the senate to dismiss them speedily, and to banish all such Attic babblers out of Italy. But Scipio[46] and others of the noblest senators withstood him and his old Sabine austerity; honored and admired the men; and the censor himself at last, in his old age, fell to the study of that whereof before he was so scrupulous. And yet at the same time, Nævius[47] and Plautus,[48] the first Latin comedians, had filled the city with all the borrowed scenes of Menander[49] and Philemon.[50]

Then began to be considered there also what was to be done to libellous books and authors; for Nævius was quickly cast into prison for his unbridled pen and released by the tribunes upon his recantation; we read also that libels were burnt, and the makers punished by Augustus.[51] The like severity, no doubt, was used, if aught were impiously written against their esteemed gods. Except in these two points, how the world went in books, the magistrate kept no reckoning. And therefore Lucretius[52]

---

[39] Opinion in the ancient world differed about the Spartan practice of encouraging girls to exercise naked as men did in the gymnasia, publicly. Plutarch's *Life of Lycurgus* justified the practice, but Plato mentioned (*Laws*, 806a) Sparta as a scandalous example of the effects of bad discipline among women, and Aristotle (*Politics* II, vi, 5) says that the Spartan women lived in every kind of intemperance and self-indulgence. In *Andromache*, 590–3, *Euripides* wrote: "No! a Spartan maid could not be chaste, e'en if she would, who leaves her home and bares her limbs and lets her robe float free, to share with youths their races and their sports." (Coleridge's translation.)

[40] Cf. *Educ*, n. 65.

[41] The *Pontific College* went back to the most revered of the half-legendary Roman kings, Numa, and its president, the Pontifex Maximus, was the greatest religious dignitary in republican Rome. The *flamens* were priests subordinate to the *pontifices*, and the *augurs*, whose business it was to consult the omens before public acts such as battles, treaties and holidays, composed another priestly college. Cf. "the flamens at their service quaint" (*Nat*, 194).

[42] *Carneades* (?213–129 B.C.), the founder of the Third or New Academy at Athens, was a sceptic and an opponent of Stoicism. In 155 B.C. he was sent from Athens to Rome with Diogenes and Critolaus to protest against a fine which had been assessed against the Athenians for destroying Oropus. In Rome he shocked public opinion by first defending and then attacking the principle of justice in two formal addresses.

[43] *Critolaus* was the head of the Peripatetic or Aristotelian School of philosophy in Athens in the middle of the second century B.C.

[44] *Diogenes* succeeded Zeno as head of the Stoic School at Athens. He must not be confused with Diogenes the Cynic, to whom n. 32 above refers.

[45] One of Plutarch's final anecdotes in his life of *Cato the Censor* (Marcus Porcius Cato, 234?–149 B.C.) is the story of Cato's gruff scepticism about the influence of Carneades and even of the Socratic philosophical tradition upon the young men of Rome. "For his blasphemy against learning," said Bacon in the *Advancement* I, ii, 9; p. 17, ". . . he

[46] *Scipio* the Younger (?185–129 B.C.), who captured Carthage in 146, was friendly with Terence and Polybius and other writers. In Cicero's dialogue *On Friendship* his geniality and his esteem for the virtues that Cato practised on his Sabine farm were familiar to every schoolboy.

[47] *Nævius* produced the first of his satiric plays about 235 B.C. He was imprisoned for attacking Scipio the younger and the aristocratic party in his plays and obliged to recant. He died in exile in Utica ?202 B.C.

[48] *Plautus* (?254–184 B.C.) was the most popular of Roman writers of comedy.

[49] *Menander* (342–291 B.C.) wrote over one hundred comedies, the surviving portions of seven of which are almost our only representation of the Athenian New Comedy, upon which Plautus' plays were modelled. Cf. note 28 above.

[50] *Philemon* (?361–263 B.C.) was a rival of Menander. Only a few short fragments of his plays survive, but two of them are suggested as sources which Plautus followed closely in his *Mercator* and *Trinummus*.

[51] Tacitus declared (*Annals* I, lxxii) that *Augustus* so resented the damage done to the best people in Rome by the insolent libels of Cassius Severus that he urged the passage of a law against libel.

[52] Lucretius' *De rerum natura*, a frank defense of Epicurean views about the gods and the human soul, was dedicated to Gaius Memmius Gemellus

was well punished, . . . for when he was past threescore years old, he was taken with an extreme desire to go to school again, and to learn the Greek tongue, to the end to peruse the Greek authors, which doth well demonstrate that his former censure of the Grecian learning was rather an affected gravity than according to the inward sense of his own opinion."

without impeachment versifies his Epicurism to Memmius, and had the honor to be set forth the second time by Cicero, so great a father of the commonwealth; although himself disputes against that opinion in his own writings. Nor was the satirical sharpness or naked plainness of Lucilius,[53] or Catullus,[54] or Flaccus,[55] by any order prohibited.

And for matters of state, the story of Titus Livius,[56] though it extolled that part which Pompey held, was not therefore suppressed by Octavius Cæsar of the other faction. But that Naso[57] was by him banished in his old age for the wanton poems of his youth, was but a mere covert of state over some secret cause: and besides, the books were neither banished nor called in. From hence we shall meet with little else but tyranny in the Roman empire,[58] that we may not marvel, if not so often bad as good books were silenced. I shall therefore deem to have been large enough in producing what among the ancients was punishable to write, save only which, all other arguments were free to treat on.

By this time the emperors were become Christians, whose discipline in this point I do not find to have been more severe than what was formerly in practice. The books of those whom they took to be grand heretics were examined, refuted, and condemned in the general councils;[59] and not till then were prohibited, or burnt, by authority of the emperor. As for the writings of heathen authors, unless they were plain invectives against Christianity, as those of Porphyrius[60] and Proclus,[61] they met with no interdict that can be cited till about the year 400 in a Carthaginian Council[62] wherein bishops themselves were forbid to read the books of Gentiles, but heresies they might read: while others long before them, on the contrary, scrupled more the books of heretics than of Gentiles. And that the primitive councils and bishops were wont only to declare what books were not commendable, passing no further, but leaving it to each one's conscience to read or to lay by, till after the year 800, is observed already by Padre Paolo, the great unmasker of the Trentine Council.[63] After which time the Popes of Rome, engrossing what they

(Praetor in 58 B.C.). The belief that Cicero edited Lucretius rests upon a vague statement of St. Jerome in his additions to Eusebius' *Chronicon* and is hardly consistent with Cicero's attacks on Epicureanism in the *Tusculan Disputations* II and III, and in the *De finibus* I and II.

[53] *Lucilius* (148–103 B.C.) is usually recognized as the founder of Roman satire.

[54] Among the vivid lyrics of *Catullus* (87–47? B.C.) were some lampoons of Caesar and his partisans.

[55] Quintus Horatius *Flaccus* (Horace, 65–8 B.C.) hardly challenged censorship of any kind by his *Satires*.

[56] In his *History of Rome* Livy (*Titus Livius,* 59 B.C.–17 A.D.) is said by Tacitus (*Annals* IV, 34) to have praised Augustus' great rival for power, Pompey, very highly, and to have had Augustus' approval for so doing.

[57] *Naso:* Ovid (Publius Ovidius Naso) was banished to Tomi near the mouth of the Danube; tradition says less on account of his licentious poems than for an intrigue with the granddaughter of the Emperor Augustus, Julia. He died at Tomi in 18 A.D.

[58] So in the Epistle Dedicatory to *The Liberty of Prophecying* Jeremy Taylor quoted Tacitus' *Agricola* to prove that under the more tyrannous Roman emperors books were suppressed by "an illiterate policy" which supposed that "such indirect and uningenuous proceedings can, among wise and free men, disgrace the authors and disrepute their discourses."

[59] In the following survey of the attempts of some of the *general councils* and popes to suppress heresy Milton is mainly following Padre Paolo Sarpi's *Historie of the Council of Trent* (as it was entitled in Nathaniel Brent's translation, 1620). In *MP,* L (1953), 226–31, E. Sirluck exhaustively traces the extent of Milton's indebtedness to Sarpi and finds that he checked Sarpi's statements about Porphyry and Proclus, and that he corrected the former of them from Socrates' *Ecclesiastical History.* For another and more important such correction see n. 64 below.

[60] *Porphyry* (233–305? A.D.) is said to have been a pupil of Origen and to have apostatized under the influence of Plotinus in Rome. His book against Christianity was publicly destroyed by order of the emperor Theodosius.

[61] *Proclus* (412–485 A.D.) was a lifelong enemy of Christianity.

[62] Sirluck observes that Milton follows Sarpi's statement that a council at Carthage burned heretical books "about the year 400," without identifying any of the four councils held there between 397 and 412 as the responsible one.

[63] The Council of Trent (in the Tyrol) met frequently between Dec. 13, 1545, and Dec. 4, 1563, and ended its efforts to reconcile Protestant with Catholic Europe by reaffirming most of the great doctrines of Roman Catholicism, and by affirming that in matters of faith and morals the tradition of the Church ranked with the Bible as an authority. In describing Sarpi (1552–1623) as its "unmasker," Milton does not misrepresent the spirit of his *History,* which was first published in 1619. He wrote as a Catholic, but also from the point of view of a supporter of the Venetian Republic in its struggle with the popes. Cf. n. 59 above.

pleased of political rule into their own hands, extended their dominion over men's eyes as they had before over their judgments, burning and prohibiting to be read what they fancied not; yet sparing in their censures, and the books not many which they so dealt with; till Martin V,[64] by his bull, not only prohibited, but was the first that excommunicated the reading of heretical books; for about that time Wycliffe and Huss[65] growing terrible, were they who first drove the papal court to a stricter policy of prohibiting. Which course Leo X[66] and his successors followed, until the Council of Trent and the Spanish Inquisition,[67] engendering together, brought forth, or perfected those catalogs and expurging indexes[68] that rake through the entrails of many an old good author with a violation worse than any could be offered to his tomb.

Nor did they stay in matters heretical, but any subject that was not to their palate they either condemned in a prohibition, or had it straight into the new purgatory of an Index. To fill up the measure of encroachment, their last invention was to ordain that no book, pamphlet, or paper should be printed (as if St. Peter had bequeathed them the keys of the press also out of paradise) unless it were approved and licensed under the hands of two or three glutton friars. For example:

Let the Chancellor Cini be pleased to see if in this present work be contained aught that may withstand the printing. Vincent Rabbatta, Vicar of Florence.

I have seen this present work, and find nothing athwart the Catholic faith and good manners: in witness whereof I have given, &c. Nicolo Cini, Chancellor of Florence.

Attending the precedent relation, it is allowed that this present work of

Davanzati[69] may be printed.
                    Vincent Rabatta, &c.
It may be printed, July 15.
Friar Simon Mompei d'Amelia,
Chancellor of the holy office in Florence.

Sure they have a conceit, if he of the bottomless pit had not long since broke prison, that this quadruple exorcism would bar him down. I fear their next design will be to get into their custody the licensing of that which they say Claudius* intended but went not through with. Vouchsafe to see another of their forms, the Roman stamp:

Imprimatur, If it seem good to the reverend Master of the holy Palace,
                    Belcastro, Vicegerent.
Imprimatur,
            Friar Nicolo Rodolphi,
            Master of the holy Palace.

Sometimes five Imprimaturs are seen together, dialoguewise, in the piazza of one titlepage, complimenting and ducking each to other with their shaven reverences, whether the author, who stands by in perplexity at the foot of his epistle, shall to the press or to the sponge. These are the pretty responsories,[70] these are the dear antiphonies[71] that so bewitched of late our prelates and their chaplains with the goodly echo they made; and besotted us to the gay imitation of a lordly Imprimatur,[72] one from Lambeth House,[73] another from the

---

64 *Martin V* (Otto Colonna) was Pope from 1417 to 1431. Sirluck notes that Milton wrote from knowledge of the full text of Martin's bull of 1418, *Inter cunctas,* when he declared that the bull definitely excommunicated contumacious heretics. Sarpi, knowing the bull only in an abridged form, was unaware of its full severity. Cf. n. 59 above.

65 Cf. *CG,* n. 119.

66 *Leo X* (Giovanni dei Medici) was Pope from 1513 to 1521.

67 Sirluck notes that the *Inquisition* was reorganized by a bull of Paul III on July 21, 1542.

68 The first *Index Expurgatorius* was issued by Paul IV in 1559.

69 The little book *On the English Schism* (*Lo Scisma d'Inghilterra*) by Bernardo Davanzati (1529–1606) was reissued in Florence in 1638 in an edition which may have been published while Milton was there, and which has been identified by A. Allodoli in *Giovanni Milton e l'Italia,* p. 82, as having been used by him in writing *Areop.* Cf. n. 118 below.

* In the Milton text the following was printed in the margin: *Quo veniam daret flatum crepitumque ventris in convivio emittendi. Suetonius in Claudio.*

70 *responsories:* sections of the Psalms sung interspersed between readings from the missal in the mass.

71 *antiphonies:* hymns or anthems sung in responsive parts by two choirs.

72 *Imprimatur:* "let it be printed," the order stamped on manuscripts which are permitted by ecclesiastical authority to be sent to the press. "To the sponge"—meaning, to have the contents wiped off—has been applied to manuscripts unworthy of publication since Suetonius helped to popularize the expression in the *Life of Augustus,* 85.

73 *Lambeth* Palace is still the residence of the Archbishop of Canterbury, on the south bank of the Thames.

west end of Paul's,[74] so apishly Romanizing that the word of command still was set down in Latin; as if the learned grammatical pen that wrote it would cast no ink without Latin; or perhaps, as they thought, because no vulgar tongue was worthy to express the pure conceit of an Imprimatur; but rather, as I hope, for that our English, the language of men ever famous and foremost in the achievements of liberty, will not easily find servile letters enough to spell such a dictatory presumption English.

And thus ye have the inventors and the original of book-licensing ripped up and drawn as lineally as any pedigree. We have it not, that can be heard of, from any ancient state, or polity, or church, nor by any statute left us by our ancestors elder or later; nor from the modern custom of any reformed city or church abroad; but from the most antichristian council and the most tyrannous inquisition that ever inquired.

Till then books were ever as freely admitted into the world as any other birth; the issue of the brain was no more stifled than the issue of the womb; no envious Juno[75] sat cross-legged over the nativity of any man's intellectual offspring; but if it proved a monster, who denies but that it was justly burnt, or sunk into the sea? But that a book, in worse condition than a peccant soul, should be to stand before a jury ere it be born to the world and undergo yet in darkness the judgment of Rhadamanth[76] and his colleagues, ere it can pass the ferry backward into light, was never heard before, till that mysterious iniquity, provoked and troubled at the first entrance of reformation, sought out new limbos[77] and

new hells wherein they might include our books also within the number of their damned. And this was the rare morsel so officiously snatched up, and so ill-favoredly imitated by our inquisiturient bishops and the attendant minorites,[78] their chaplains. That ye like not now these most certain authors of this licensing order, and that all sinister intention was far distant from your thoughts, when ye were importuned the passing it, all men who know the integrity of your actions, and how ye honor truth, will clear ye readily.

But some will say, what though the inventors were bad, the thing for all that may be good. It may so; yet if that thing be no such deep invention, but obvious and easy for any man to light on, and yet best and wisest commonwealths through all ages and occasions have forborne to use it, and falsest seducers and oppressors of men were the first who took it up, and to no other purpose but to obstruct and hinder the first approach of reformation; I am of those who believe it will be a harder alchemy than Lullius[79] ever knew to sublimate[80] any good use out of such an invention. Yet this only is what I request to gain from this reason, that it may be held a dangerous and suspicious fruit, as certainly it deserves, for the tree that bore it, until I can dissect one by one the properties it has. But I have first to finish, as was propounded, what is to be thought in general of reading books, whatever sort they be, and whether be more the benefit or the harm that thence proceeds?

---

74 St. Paul's is the cathedral church of the Bishop of London. Cf. the Bibliographical Note above.

75 In Metamorphoses IX, 285–319, Ovid tells the story of Juno's cruelty to Alcmena in placing the goddess of childbirth cross-legged beside her, muttering charms to prevent her delivery of the infant Hercules. On the seventh night of labor the wit of Alcmena's maid tricked the cross-legged goddess into rising and so breaking the charm that closed her mistress's womb.

76 According to Plato in Gorgias, 524a, the Cretan king Rhadamanthus, together with Minos and Aeacus, was made a judge of the dead by Zeus, and had power to strip every soul naked of its body for examination. Cf. CG, n. 24.

77 limbos: purlieus of hell, such as the limbus puerorum or limbo of babes, and limbus patrum or limbo of the patriarchs, who were delivered in Christ's harrowing of hell. In RES, XVIII (1942),

417, J. Horrell compares PL III, 440–7, and notes that "the sombre associations of the word might easily come from Virgil's limen, or threshold to Hades, . . . where the souls of infants weep, and with them are the suicides." Milton refers to the charge which Jeremy Taylor repeated in his Dissuasive from Popery, II, vi: "Of the Expurgatory Indices in the Roman Church," viz.: "1. That the king of Spain gave a commission to the inquisitors to purge all catholic authors, but with a clause of secresy. 2. That they purged the indices of the fathers' works. 3. That they did also purge the works of the fathers themselves."

78 minorites: the Franciscans, traditionally the humblest of the monastic orders.

79 Lullius: Raymond Lully (1234?–1315) was traditionally better known for his writings on alchemy and medicine than for the missionary ardor that took him to north Africa three times and finally ended his life by martyrdom in Mauretania.

80 sublimate: in alchemy, to transform a base into a precious metal. Cf. PL V, 483.

Not to insist upon the examples of Moses, Daniel,[81] and Paul,[82] who were skilful in all the learning of the Egyptians, Chaldeans, and Greeks, which could not probably be without reading their books of all sorts; in Paul especially, who thought it no defilement to insert into holy scripture the sentences of three Greek poets, and one of them a tragedian; the question was notwithstanding sometimes controverted among the primitive doctors, but with great odds on that side which affirmed it both lawful and profitable, as was then evidently perceived when Julian the Apostate[83] and subtlest enemy to our faith, made a decree forbidding Christians the study of heathen learning; for, said he, they wound us with our own weapons, and with our own arts and sciences they overcome us. And indeed the Christians were put so to their shifts by this crafty means, and so much in danger to decline into all ignorance, that the two Apollinarii[84] were fain, as a man may say, to coin all the seven liberal sciences[85] out of the Bible, reducing it into divers forms of orations, poems, dialogues, even to the calculating of a new Christian grammar. But, saith the historian Socrates, the providence of God provided better than the industry of Apollinarius and his son, by taking away that illiterate law with the life of him who devised it.[86]

So great an injury they then held it to be deprived of Hellenic learning; and thought it a persecution more undermining, and secretly decaying the Church, than the open cruelty of Decius[87] or Diocletian.[88] And perhaps it was the same politic drift that the devil whipped St. Jerome[89] in a Lenten dream, for reading Cicero; or else it was a phantasm bred by the fever which had then seized him. For had an angel been his discipliner, unless it were for dwelling too much upon Ciceronianisms, and had chastised the reading, not the vanity, it had been plainly partial; first to correct him for grave Cicero, and not for scurril Plautus, whom he confesses to have been reading not long before; next to correct him only, and let so many more ancient fathers wax old in those pleasant and florid studies without the lash of such a tutoring apparition; insomuch that Basil[90] teaches how some good use may be made of *Margites,* a sportful poem not now extant writ by Homer; and why not then of *Morgante,*[91] an Italian romance much to the same purpose?

[81] In Acts vii, 22, *Moses* is called "learned in all the wisdom of the Egyptians," and in Dan. i, 17, *Daniel* is described as seemingly more learned than any of the other Hebrew princes who were educated in the wisdom of Chaldea. St. Paul's learning was got partly under the great Hebrew teacher Gamaliel (Acts xxii, 3), but it also included knowledge of Greek literature.
[82] Acts xvii, 28, represents *Paul* as quoting Aratus. I Cor. xv, 33, "evil communications corrupt good manners" translates a fragment of Euripides or Menander. The saying in Titus i, 12—"the Cretans are always liars"—is attributed to the Cretan poet, Epimenides. Cf. *SA,* p. 549 above, n. 4.
[83] *Julian the Apostate* (Flavius Claudius Julianus, 331–363 A.D.) became emperor in 361 and was killed by the Persians two years later. Though trained as a Christian, he seems to have been attracted early by pagan thought, and he publicly apostatized and made his famous decree against *teaching* pagan literature by the Christians when he became emperor.
[84] The *Ecclesiastical History* of Socrates Scholasticus (385?–440? A.D.), Book III, chapter xiv, recounts that when "the Emperour Iulian forbad the Christians the studie of Prophane literature, both the Apollinariuses, the father, and the sonne, fell a writing. . . . For the father . . . turned the five bookes of *Moses* into Heroicall verse, together with other bookes of the old Testament, which contained Histories: partly in Hexameter verse, & partly after the forme of comedies and tragedies. . . . The son (who became bishop of Alexandria), an eloquent Rhetorician, brought the writings of the Euangelistes, and works of the Apostles, into Dialogues, as *Plato* used among the Heathens" (Hanmer's translation, 1585, p. 307).

[85] Cf. *Educ,* n. 12.
[86] Socrates' eighteenth chapter tells the story of Julian's perhaps providential taking-off in battle with the Persians, and chapter nineteen celebrates the restoration of full cultural rights to the Christians by his Christian successor, Jovian.
[87] *Decius* was emperor from 249 until 251.
[88] The persecutions under Decius and *Diocletian,* who reigned from 284 to 305, were particularly severe.
[89] The story of *St. Jerome's* dream of being brought by an angel before a tribunal in heaven and accused of being a Ciceronian because he had Cicero's works by heart, goes back to Jerome's *Epistle* XVIII, "To Eustochius on Virginity." Milton's interpretation of it goes back as far as Gratian's *Decretum,* Prima Pars, Distinctio XXXVII, vii, where the saint is said to have replied to his heavenly judge by asking whether clergymen ought not to have skill in secular literature.
[90] *Basil* the Great, Bishop of Cappodocia, 370–379 A.D., is described in the *Ecclesiastical History* (IV, xxi) of Socrates Scholasticus as preparing for a career as a Christian apologist by reading pagan philosophy in Athens in his youth. Milton is quoting Basil's *The Right Use of Greek Literature* (Padelford's Ed, p. 102).
[91] The mock-heroic romance of Luigi Pulci

But if it be agreed we shall be tried by visions, there is a vision recorded by Eusebius,[92] far ancienter than this tale of Jerome to the nun Eustochium, and, besides, has nothing of a fever in it. Dionysius Alexandrinus was, about the year 240, a person of great name in the church for piety and learning, who had wont to avail himself much against heretics by being conversant in their books; until a certain presbyter laid it scrupulously to his conscience, how he durst venture himself among those defiling volumes. The worthy man, loth to give offense, fell into a new debate with himself what was to be thought; when suddenly a vision sent from God (it is his own *Epistle* that so avers it) confirmed him in these words: "Read any books whatever come to thy hands, for thou art sufficient both to judge aright and to examine each matter." To this revelation he assented the sooner, as he confesses, because it was answerable to that of the apostle to the Thessalonians: "Prove all things, hold fast that which is good."[93]

And he might have added another remarkable saying of the same author: "To the pure, all things are pure";[94] not only meats and drinks, but all kind of knowledge whether of good or evil; the knowledge cannot defile, nor consequently the books, if the will and conscience be not defiled. For books are as meats and viands are—some of good, some of evil substance, and yet God in that unapocryphal vision said without exception, "Rise, Peter, kill and eat,"[95] leaving the choice to each man's discretion. Wholesome meats to a vitiated stomach differ little or nothing from unwholesome, and best books to a naughty mind are not unappliable to occasions of evil. Bad meats will scarce breed good nourishment in the healthiest concoction; but herein the difference is of bad books, that they to a discreet and judicious reader serve in many respects to discover, to confute, to forewarn, and to illustrate.

Whereof what better witness can ye expect I should produce than one of your own now sitting in parliament, the chief of learned men reputed in this land, Mr. Selden;[96] whose volume of natural and national laws proves, not only by great authorities brought together, but by exquisite reasons and theorems almost mathematically demonstrative, that all opinions, yea errors, known, read, and collated, are of main service and assistance toward the speedy attainment of what is truest.

I conceive, therefore, that when God did enlarge the universal diet of man's body, saving ever the rules of temperance, he then also, as before, left arbitrary the dieting and repasting of our minds; as wherein every mature man might have to exercise his own leading capacity. How great a virtue is temperance, how much of moment through the whole life of man! Yet God commits the managing so great a trust, without particular law or prescription, wholly to the demeanor of every grown man. And therefore, when he himself tabled the Jews from heaven, that omer[97] which was every man's daily portion of manna, is computed to have been more than might have well sufficed the heartiest feeder thrice as many meals. For those actions which enter into a man, rather than issue out of him, and therefore defile not, God uses not to captivate under a perpetual childhood of prescription, but trusts him with the gift of reason to be his own chooser; there were but little work left for preaching, if law and compulsion should grow so fast upon those things which heretofore were governed only by exhortation.

(1431–1487), the *Morgante Maggiore* (published in 1488), was coarser than Ariosto's *Orlando Furioso,* of which it was one of the main sources of inspiration. As Homer's *Margites* was traditionally regarded as the first great humorous poem in the ancient world, the *Morgante* was accepted as having founded its type in Renaissance Europe.

[92] Milton quoted loosely from the summary of Dionysius' (Bishop of Alexandria, 247–65) letter to Philemon in Eusebius' *Ecclesiastical History* VII, vi, confessing that he had "read over the traditions and commentaries of the heretickes" because a vision had commanded him to "Reade all whatsoever come into thy handes; thou shalt be able to weye, to prove, and trye all" (Meredith Hanmer's translation, p. 127).

[93] I Thess. v, 21.

[94] Titus i, 15.

[95] Cf. *CG*, n. 232.

[96] John *Selden* (1584–1654) published his *De Jure Naturali et Gentium iuxta Disciplinam Hebraeorum* in 1640. Sirluck indicates that Milton is paraphrasing Selden's Preface. Cf. n. 59 above.

[97] The *omer* was the measure of manna which Moses was commanded in Exod. xvi, 16, to ration to the Israelites daily. The account lays stress on the abundance of the supply.

Solomon[98] informs us that much reading is a weariness to the flesh; but neither he nor other inspired author tells us that such or such reading is unlawful; yet certainly had God thought good to limit us herein, it had been much more expedient to have told us what was unlawful than what was wearisome.

As for the burning of those Ephesian books by St. Paul's converts;[99] 'tis replied the books were magic, the Syriac so renders them. It was a private act, a voluntary act, and leaves us to a voluntary imitation: the men in remorse burnt those books which were their own; the magistrate by this example is not appointed; these men practised the books, another might perhaps have read them in some sort usefully.

Good and evil we know in the field of this world grow up together almost inseparably; and the knowledge of good is so involved and interwoven with the knowledge of evil, and in so many cunning resemblances hardly to be discerned, that those confused seeds which were imposed on Psyche[100] as an incessant labor to cull out and sort asunder, were not more intermixed. It was from out the rind of one apple tasted, that the knowledge of good and evil, as two twins cleaving together, leaped forth into the world. And perhaps this is that doom which Adam fell into of knowing good and evil, that is to say, of knowing good by evil.[101]

As therefore the state of man now is, what wisdom can there be to choose, what continence to forbear without the knowledge of evil? He that can apprehend and consider vice with all her baits and seeming pleasures, and yet abstain, and yet distinguish, and yet prefer that which is truly better, he is the true warfaring[102] Christian.

I cannot praise a fugitive and cloistered virtue, unexercised and unbreathed, that never sallies out and sees her adversary, but slinks out of the race where that immortal garland[103] is to be run for, not without dust and heat. Assuredly we bring not innocence into the world, we bring impurity much rather: that which purifies us is trial, and trial is by what is contrary. That virtue therefore which is but a youngling in the contemplation of evil, and knows not the utmost that vice promises to her followers, and rejects it, is but a blank[104] virtue, not a pure; her whiteness is but an excremental[105] whiteness; which was the reason why our sage and serious poet Spenser,[106] whom I dare be known to think a

---

[98] Eccles. xii, 12. Mark vii, 15: "There is nothing from without a man, that entering into him can defile him: but the things which come out of him, those are they that defile the man."

[99] The story is found in Acts xix, 19.

[100] Milton would know the story of *Psyche* best in *The Golden Ass* of Apuleius IV–VI. Anger because Psyche has won Cupid's love makes Venus doom her to sort the various kinds of grain out of a vast, mixed pile, but the work is done for her by the sympathetic ants.

[101] Again in *CD* I, x, Milton reaffirms this interpretation of the meaning of the fall of man in Gen. iii.

[102] *wayfaring*, the reading of the first edition,

has the weight of priority, but *warfaring* is suggested by the fact that the entire passage seems to echo Lactantius' repeated stress in *Institutes* III, xxix; V, vii; and VI, *passim*, upon a Christian ethic "ex quo fit ut virtus nulla sit, si *adversarius* desit." (See Miss K. Hartwell, *Milton and Lactantius*, pp. 21–35, for Milton's echo of the Lactantian passages in his Commonplace Book and for the relation of Lactantius to Seneca's *De Ira*.) In the background is St. Paul's Christian soldier in Ephes. vi, a conception popularized by Erasmus' *Enchiridion Militis Christiani* and by Puritan books like John Downame's *The Christian Warfare* which went into four editions from 1604 to 1618. In three extant copies of the first edition of *Areopagitica* the "y" in *Wayfaring* is changed to "r" in a hand that may be Milton's.

[103] *that:* like the Latin *ille*, the word is used to refer to something well known. Milton is perhaps thinking of that prize for which St. Paul described himself as pressing forward in Philippians iii, 14, or of the crown of righteousness in II Timothy iv, 8, or of the crown of life that is promised in James i, 12, to him "that endureth temptation" and "is tried." Cf. *TKM*, note 50.

[104] *blank:* pale or colorless. Cf. its force in *PL* III, 48: "a universal blank Of nature's works," where the substantial meaning is the darkness or indiscriminate grayness of the blind Milton's world.

[105] *excremental:* excrescential, external.

[106] In the account of Guyon's temptation in *F.Q.* II, viii, as E. Sirluck observes in *MP*, XLVIII (1950), 90–96, the Palmer does not accompany Guyon into the Cave of Mammon. In Spenser's Aristotelian allegory the Knight of Temperance represents the "firm and unchangeable character" of Aristotle's truly temperate man, and in the cave of Mammon he does not need the support of the Palmer who, in Spenser's allegory, objectifies the "rational principle" which restrains passion when the settled habits of character fail to do so. But in many passages Milton disapproves of virtue which is a matter of settled habit, or at least reserves his admiration for the kind that is constantly won "with dust and heat." Cf. n. 150 below.

better teacher than Scotus[107] or Aquinas,[108] describing true temperance under the person of Guyon, brings him in with his palmer through the cave of Mammon and the bower of earthly bliss, that he might see and know, and yet abstain.

Since therefore, the knowledge and survey of vice is in this world so necessary to the constituting of human virtue, and the scanning of error to the confirmation of truth, how can we more safely and with less danger scout into the regions of sin and falsity than by reading all manner of tractates and hearing all manner of reason? And this is the benefit which may be had of books promiscuously read.

But of the harm that may result hence, three kinds are usually reckoned. First is feared the infection that may spread; but then all human learning and controversy in religious points must remove out of the world, yea the Bible itself; for that ofttimes relates blasphemy not nicely, it describes the carnal sense of wicked men not unelegantly, it brings in holiest men passionately murmuring against providence through all the arguments of Epicurus;[109] in other great disputes it answers dubiously and darkly to the common reader; and ask a Talmudist what ails the modesty of his marginal Keri,[110] that Moses and all the prophets cannot persuade him to pronounce the textual Chetiv. For these causes we all know the Bible itself put by the papist into the first rank of prohibited books. The ancientest fathers must be next removed, as Clement of Alexandria,[111] and that Eusebian[112] book of Evangelic preparation transmitting our ears through a hoard of heathenish obscenities to receive the Gospel. Who finds not that Irenæus,[113] Epiphanius,[114] Jerome,[115] and others discover more heresies than they well confute, and that oft for heresy which is the truer opinion?

Nor boots it to say for these and all the heathen writers of greatest infection, if it must be thought so, with whom is bound up the life of human learning, that they writ in an unknown tongue, so long as we are sure those languages are known as well to the worst of men, who are both most able and most diligent to instil the poison they suck, first into the courts of princes, acquainting them with the choicest delights and criticisms of sin. As perhaps did that Petronius[116] whom Nero called his Arbiter, the master of his revels; and that notorious

[107] John Duns *Scotus* (1265?–1308), the Subtle Doctor in the Scholastic tradition, was born in Scotland but taught at Paris and Oxford and died in Cologne. He was a Franciscan, and in several important ways his teaching was opposed to that of his great Dominican predecessor, St. Thomas. The prejudice against Scholastic logic which Milton illustrates here was responsible for the quite unfair development of the word *dunce* from Duns Scotus' name.

[108] St. Thomas *Aquinas* (1225?–1274), the Seraphic Doctor, in his *Summa Theologica* left the greatest monument of Scholastic thought, and in his *Summa contra Gentiles*, the greatest medieval compendium of Christian doctrine.

[109] Solomon's recommendation of "mirth, because a man hath no better thing under the sun than to eat, and to drink, and to be merry" (Eccl. viii, 15), was often compared with the supposedly similar advice of *Epicurus*. Cf. *CG*, n. 265.

[110] *Keri*: what is read, opposed to *Chetiv*: what is written. Milton explains the terms when he says in the *Apology*, that "rabbinical scholiasts, not well attending, have often used to blur the margin with Keri instead of Ketiv, and gave us this insulse rule out of their Talmud, 'That all words which in the law are written obscenely, must be changed to more civil words:' fools, who would teach men to read more decently than God thought fit to write" (C.E. III, 316).

[111] *Clement of Alexandria* (150?–? A.D.) was the first great Christian apologist to make intimate use of Greek philosophy. Sirluck sees Milton "thinking of Clement's *Hortatory Address to the Greeks*, in which, to dissuade his hearers from . . . certain pagan rites, he describes them with much emphasis on their lewdness and obscenity." See n. 59 above.

[112] Eusebius' *Preparatio Evangelica* is well described by Milton's words in the text. Many patristic books exhibited the worst features of pagan thought and religious practice to turn their readers to Christianity.

[113] *Irenæus* (140?–202? A.D.) became Bishop of Lyons in 177. He wrote *Against Heresies* to combat Gnosticism.

[114] Milton may have been interested in the *Panarion* or general refutation of heresies which was written by *Epiphanius* (315–403), who became Bishop of Constantia in Cyprus in 367. He was certainly familiar with Socrates' story in the *Ecclesiastical History* VI, ix and xiii, of Epiphanius' quarrel with John, Bishop of Constantinople, and of his seeming prostitution of his position as a controversialist in a struggle for power.

[115] Traditionally, *St. Jerome* (c340–420 A.D.) has been almost as famous as a controversialist—especially against Rufinus and other champions of Origen's teaching—as he has been for his Old Testament translations and commentaries.

[116] In *Def.* 1.4 Milton refers rather differently to Tacitus' description of Petronius in *Annals* 16.18–19 as Nero's *arbiter elegantiarum* or adviser in matters of taste—hardly a playboy master of the royal revels. Like Tacitus, Milton does not refer to Petronius as a satirist or author of the *Satyricon*.

ribald of Arezzo,[117] dreaded, and yet dear to the Italian courtiers. I name not him for posterity's sake, whom Harry VIII named in merriment his Vicar of hell.[118] By which compendious way all the contagion that foreign books can infuse, will find a passage to the people far easier and shorter than an Indian voyage, though it could be sailed either by the north of Cathay[119] eastward, or of Canada westward, while our Spanish licensing gags the English press never so severely.

But, on the other side, that infection which is from books of controversy in religion, is more doubtful and dangerous to the learned than to the ignorant; and yet those books must be permitted untouched by the licenser. It will be hard to instance where any ignorant man hath been ever seduced by papistical book in English, unless it were commended and expounded to him by some of that clergy; and indeed all such tractates, whether false or true, are as the prophecy of Isaiah was to the eunuch, not to be "understood without a guide."[120] But of our priests and doctors how many have been corrupted by studying the comments of Jesuits and Sorbonists,[121] and how fast they could transfuse that corruption into the people, our experience is both late and sad. It is not forgot, since the acute and distinct Arminius[122] was perverted

merely by the perusing of a nameless discourse written at Delft, which at first he took in hand to confute.

Seeing, therefore, that those books, and those in great abundance which are likeliest to taint both life and doctrine, cannot be suppressed without the fall of learning, and of all ability in disputation; and that these books of either sort are most and soonest catching to the learned, from whom to the common people whatever is heretical or dissolute may quickly be conveyed; and that evil manners are as perfectly learned without books a thousand other ways which cannot be stopped; and evil doctrine not with books can propagate, except a teacher guide, which he might also do without writing, and so beyond prohibiting: I am not able to unfold how this cautelous[123] enterprise of licensing can be exempted from the number of vain and impossible attempts. And he who were pleasantly disposed, could not well avoid to liken it to the exploit of that gallant man who thought to pound up the crows by shutting his park gate.

Besides another inconvenience, if learned men be the first receivers out of books and dispreaders both of vice and error, how shall the licensers themselves be confided in, unless we can confer upon them, or they assume to themselves above all others in the land, the grace of infallibility and uncorruptedness? And again, if it be true that a wise man, like a good refiner, can gather gold out of the drossiest volume, and that a fool will be a fool with the best book, yea or without book, there is no reason that we should deprive a wise man of any advantage to his wisdom, while we seek to restrain from a fool that which being restrained will be no hindrance to his folly. For if there should be so much exactness always used to keep that from him which is unfit for his reading, we should, in the judgment of Aristotle[124] not only, but of

---

[117] Pietro Aretino (1492–1557), by practising a kind of magnificent literary blackmail and by exploiting the aristocratic taste for indecency, achieved banishment from Rome as well as from *Arezzo*, won a European reputation, and left some revealing records of his times behind him.

[118] The *Vicar of hell* is Sir Francis Brian, to whom Henry VIII's minister Thomas Cromwell often referred in that way. The nickname was "popular," says R. B. Merriman in his edition of *The Letters of Thomas Cromwell* (Oxford, 1902), Vol. II, 296, presumably on account of his cynical betrayal of his niece Anne Boleyn to Henry when the royal suspicion of her chastity was first aroused. The story of the nickname is told in Davanzati's *Schism*, p. 66 (see n. 69 above), as Harris Fletcher has noted in *JEGP*, XLVII (1948), 387–9.

[119] *Cathay:* China. Cf. *PL* X, 291–3.

[120] Cf. the Apostle Philip's conversion of the Ethiopian eunuch by interpreting Isaiah to him (Acts viii, 28–35).

[121] The school which Robert de Sorbon founded for poor students at the University of Paris in 1252 soon gave its name to the entire institution, which was the center of Scholastic teaching for four centuries.

[122] The allusion to *Arminius* (1560–1609), the Dutch opponent of the extreme Calvinistic belief

about Predestination, in *DDD* II, iii, shows that Milton was hardly in sympathy with him at this time. Arminius was Professor of Theology at Leyden, and was said to have been persuaded against Calvin's position by the writing of one or more obscure Dutch clergymen to whom he was asked, in his official capacity, to reply.

[123] *cautelous:* uncertain, tricky.

[124] In the *Nicomachean Ethics* X, viii, 3, *Aristotle* acknowledges, in closing his great work, that discourses on ethics have no effect on ordinary man-

Solomon[125] and of our Savior,[126] not vouchsafe him good precepts, and by consequence not willingly admit him to good books; as being certain that a wise man will make better use of an idle pamphlet than a fool will do of sacred scripture.

'Tis next alleged we must not expose ourselves to temptations without necessity, and, next to that, not employ our time in vain things. To both these objections one answer will serve, out of the grounds already laid; that to all men such books are not temptations nor vanities, but useful drugs and materials wherewith to temper and compose effective and strong medicines which man's life cannot want.[127] The rest, as children and childish men, who have not the art to qualify[128] and prepare these working minerals, well may be exhorted to forbear, but hindered forcibly they cannot be by all the licensing that sainted Inquisition could ever yet contrive. Which is what I promised to deliver next: that this order of licensing conduces nothing to the end for which it was framed; and hath almost prevented[129] me by being clear already while thus much hath been explaining. See the ingenuity[130] of Truth, who, when she gets a free and willing hand, opens herself faster than the pace of method and discourse can overtake her.

It was the task which I began with, to show that no nation, or well instituted state, if they valued books at all, did ever use this way of licensing; and it might be answered that this is a piece of prudence lately discovered. To which I return that as it was a thing slight and obvious to think on, so if it had been difficult to find out, there wanted not among them long since who suggested such a course; which they not following, leave us a pattern of their judgment that it was not the not knowing, but the not approving, which was the cause of their not using it.

Plato,[131] a man of high authority indeed, but least of all for his commonwealth, in the book of his *Laws,* which no city ever yet received, fed his fancy with making many edicts to his airy burgomasters, which they who otherwise admire him, wish had been rather buried and excused in the genial cups of an Academic night-sitting. By which laws he seems to tolerate no kind of learning, but by unalterable decree, consisting most of practical traditions, to the attainment whereof a library of smaller bulk than his own dialogues would be abundant. And there also enacts that no poet should so much as read to any private man what he had written, until the judges and law-keepers had seen it and allowed it;[132] but that Plato meant this law peculiarly to that commonwealth which he had imagined, and to no other, is evident. Why was he not else a law-giver to himself, but a transgressor, and to be expelled by his own magistrates; both for the wanton epigrams and dialogues which he made, and his perpetual reading of Sophron[133] Mimus, and Aristophanes, books of grossest infamy; and also for commending the latter of them, though he were the malicious libeller of his chief friends, to be read by the tyrant Dionysius,[134] who had little need of such trash to spend his time on? But that he

kind and can inspire virtue only in men of generous temperament.

125 "Wisdom is before him that hath understanding; but the eyes of a fool are in the ends of the earth" (Prov. xvii, 24).

126 "Give not that which is holy unto dogs, neither cast ye your pearls before swine" (Matt. vii, 6).

127 *want:* do without, lack.

128 *qualify:* fix the quality or nature of a drug by proper compounding.

129 *prevented:* anticipated or "got ahead of" another person in arriving somewhere, or—as here—in doing something.

130 *ingenuity:* ingenuousness, liberality.

131 Herbert Agar points out in *Milton and Plato,* p. 59, that, "except for the fact that Milton does not approve of censoring any reasonable form of art, his own attitude towards music was very similar to that of Plato." Cf. *Educ,* n. 87.

132 Miss Lockwood quotes *Laws* VII, 801: "Shall we make a law that the poet shall compose nothing contrary to the ideas of the lawful, or just, or beautiful, or good, which are allowed in the state? nor shall he be permitted to show his compositions to any private individuals, until he shall have shown them to the appointed judges, . . . and they are satisfied with them."

133 Milton thought of epigrams like Plato's to Agathon as it is found in the Third Book of Diogenes Laertius. Shelley paraphrased it:

Kissing Helena, together
    With my kiss, my soul beside it
Came to my lips, and there I kept it, . . .

Sophron the Mimer left a number of mimes or dramatic sketches which, according to Diogenes, were sufficiently admired by Plato to justify Milton's statement in *Apology* (C.E. III, 293) that he took "them nightly to read on and after to make them his pillow."

134 Cf. n. 33 above.

knew this licensing of poems had reference and dependence to many other provisos there set down in his fancied republic, which in this world could have no place; and so neither he himself, nor any magistrate, or city ever imitated that course, which, taken apart from those other collateral injunctions, must needs be vain and fruitless.

For if they fell upon one kind of strictness, unless their care were equal to regulate all other things of like aptness to corrupt the mind, that single endeavor they knew would be but a fond[135] labor; to shut and fortify one gate against corruption, and be necessitated to leave others round about wide open. If we think to regulate printing, thereby to rectify manners, we must regulate all recreations and pastimes, all that is delightful to man. No music must be heard, no song be set or sung, but what is grave and Doric.[136] There must be licensing dancers, that no gesture, motion, or deportment be taught our youth, but what by their allowance shall be thought honest;[137] for such Plato[138] was provided of. It will ask more than the work of twenty licensers to examine all the lutes, the violins, and the guitars in every house; they must not be suffered to prattle as they do, but must be licensed what they may say. And who shall silence all the airs and madrigals that whisper softness in chambers? The windows also, and the balconies must be thought on; there are shrewd[139] books, with dangerous frontispieces,[140] set to sale; who shall prohibit them? Shall twenty licensers? The villages also must have their visitors[141] to inquire what lectures the bagpipe and the rebeck[142] reads even to the balladry and the gamut of every municipal fiddler, for these are the countryman's Arcadias,[143] and his Monte Mayors.

Next, what more national corruption, for which England hears ill[144] abroad, than household gluttony? Who shall be the rectors of our daily rioting? And what shall be done to inhibit the multitudes that frequent those houses where drunkenness is sold and harbored? Our garments also should be referred to the licensing of some more sober workmasters, to see them cut into a less wanton garb. Who shall regulate all the mixed conversation[145] of our youth, male and female together, as is the fashion of this country? Who shall still appoint what shall be discoursed, what presumed, and no further? Lastly, who shall forbid and separate all idle resort, all evil company? These things will be and must be; but how they shall be least hurtful, how least enticing, herein consists the grave and governing wisdom of a state.

To sequester out of the world into Atlantic and Utopian[146] polities, which never can be drawn into use, will not mend our beginning.

---

135 *fond:* ineffective, foolish.

136 Cf. Roger Ascham's praise of that "kinde of Musicke inuented by the Dorians," because both Plato and Aristotle thought "it to be verie fyt for the studie of vertue & learning, because of a man-lye, rough and stoute sounde in it, whyche shulde encourage yong stomakes, to attempte manlye matters." Ascham recalled also that "they both agre, that [that] Musike vsed amonges the Lydians is verie ill for yong men." (Ascham's *English Works,* edited by W. A. Wright, Cambridge, 1904, p. 12.) Cf. *PL* I, 550.

137 *honest:* honorable, decent.

138 The passage in the *Laws* (800–802) which Milton has in mind provides that a selection from the countless existing songs of the Greeks shall be made by mature judges—men not under fifty—to make sure that the ideal city for which he is legislating shall have no music or poetry which does not rightly praise the gods and the great dead.

139 *shrewd:* mischievous, wicked.

140 *frontispieces:* fronts or decorated pages at the

141 Such *visitors* or censors were being urged by Puritans like George Wither, who in dedicating his HALELUIAH, *or Britans Second Remembrancer* (1641) to Parliament was "an humble petitioner" for them to supervise "Publike Feasts and civil meetings," where, he said, "Scurrilous and obscaene Songs are impudently sung, without respecting the reverend Presences of *Matrons, Virgins, Magistrates* or *Divines.* Nay, sometime, in their despight, they are *called for, sung, and Acted,* with such abominable gesticulations as are very offensive to all modest hearers, and beholders; and fitting only to be exhibited at the Diabolicall Solemnities of *Bacchus, Venus,* or *Priapus.*"

142 *rebeck: a* simple fiddle, originally with only two strings. Cf. *L'All,* 94.

143 Cf. the prominence of Sir Philip Sidney's *Arcadia* in *Eikon,* Chap. i, n. 38. Milton refers also to the Italian *Arcadia* of Jacopo Sannazaro and to the *Diana Enamorada* of the Portuguese, Jorge de Montemayor (1520?–1561).

144 *hears ill* (said of itself). The idiom is Greek.

145 *conversation:* social intercourse.

146 As he has condemned the strict social regulation of Plato's *Republic* and *Laws,* Milton now objects to the same aspect of the *Utopia* of Sir Thomas More and of Sir Francis Bacon's *New Atlantis.* To "sequester" one's self in such speculative commonwealths is mere escapism.

condition; but to ordain wisely as in this world of evil, in the midst whereof God hath placed us unavoidably. Nor is it Plato's licensing of books will do this, which necessarily pulls along with it so many other kinds of licensing as will make us all both ridiculous and weary, and yet frustrate; but those unwritten, or at least unconstraining, laws of virtuous education, religious and civil nurture, which Plato there mentions as the bonds and ligaments of the commonwealth,[147] the pillars and the sustainers of every written statute; these they be which will bear chief sway in such matters as these, when all licensing will be easily eluded. Impunity and remissness, for certain, are the bane of a commonwealth; but here the great art lies, to discern in what the law is to bid restraint and punishment, and in what things persuasion only is to work. If every action which is good or evil in man at ripe years, were to be under pittance[148] and prescription and compulsion, what were virtue but a name, what praise could be then due to well-doing, what gramercy[149] to be sober, just, or continent?

Many there be that complain of divine providence for suffering Adam to transgress. Foolish tongues! when God gave him reason, he gave him freedom to choose, for reason is but choosing;[150] he had been else a mere artificial Adam, such an Adam as he is in the motions.[151] We ourselves esteem not of that obedience, or love, or gift, which is of force. God therefore left him free, set before him a provoking object, ever almost in his eyes; herein consisted his merit, herein the right of his reward, the praise of his abstinence. Wherefore did he create passions within us, pleasures round about us, but that these rightly tempered are the very ingredients of virtue? They are not skilful considerers of human things who imagine to remove sin by removing the matter of sin. For, besides that it is a huge heap increasing under the very act

of diminishing, though some part of it may for a time be withdrawn from some persons, it cannot from all, in such a universal thing as books are; and when this is done, yet the sin remains entire. Though ye take from a covetous man all his treasure, he has yet one jewel left—ye cannot bereave him of his covetousness. Banish all objects of lust, shut up all youth into the severest discipline that can be exercised in any hermitage, ye cannot make them chaste that came not thither so: such great care and wisdom is required to the right managing of this point.

Suppose we could expel sin by this means; look how much we thus expel of sin, so much we expel of virtue: for the matter of them both is the same; remove that, and ye remove them both alike. This justifies the high providence of God, who, though he command us temperance, justice, continence, yet pours out before us, even to a profuseness, all desirable things, and gives us minds that can wander beyond all limit and satiety. Why should we then affect a rigor contrary to the manner of God and of nature, by abridging or scanting those means which books freely permitted are, both to the trial of virtue and the exercise of truth?

It would be better done to learn that the law must needs be frivolous which goes to restrain things uncertainly and yet equally working to good and to evil. And were I the chooser, a dram of well-doing should be preferred before many times as much the forcible hindrance of evil-doing. For God sure esteems the growth and completing of one virtuous person more than the restraint of ten vicious. And albeit whatever thing we hear or see, sitting, walking, travelling, or conversing, may be fitly called our book, and is of the same effect that writings are; yet grant the thing to be prohibited were only books, it appears that this order hitherto is far insufficient to the end which it intends. Do we not see—not once or oftener, but weekly—that continued court-libel[152] against the Parliament and City printed, as the wet sheets can witness, and dispersed among us, for all that licensing can do? Yet this is the prime service a

---

[147] Milton is thinking of the passage in the *Republic* IV, 424–33, where Plato makes sound education the basis of social order.

[148] *pittance:* ration, allowance. Originally, the word was applied to a monk's portion of food.

[149] *gramercy:* thanks.

[150] Milton quotes from Aristotle's *Nicomachean Ethics* III, ii, 6. Cf. n. 106 above.

[151] *motions:* puppet shows.

[152] Milton refers to the *Mercurius Aulicus* or *Court Mercury,* which was published 1642–1645 and was written mainly by Sir John Birkenhead.

man would think, wherein this Order should give proof of itself. If it were executed, you'll say. But certain, if execution be remiss or blindfold now, and in this particular, what will it be hereafter and in other books?

If then the Order shall not be vain and frustrate, behold a new labor, Lords and Commons. Ye must repeal and proscribe all scandalous and unlicensed books already printed and divulged[153] (after ye have drawn them up into a list, that all may know which are condemned and which not) and ordain that no foreign books be delivered out of custody, till they have been read over. This office will require the whole time of not a few overseers, and those no vulgar men. There be also books which are partly useful and excellent, partly culpable and pernicious; this work will ask as many more officials, to make expurgations and expunctions,[154] that the commonwealth of learning be not damnified. In fine, when the multitude of books increase upon their hands, ye must be fain to catalog all those printers who are found frequently offending, and forbid the importation of their whole suspected typography. In a word, that this your Order may be exact and not deficient, ye must reform it perfectly according to the model of Trent and Seville,[155] which I know ye abhor to do.

Yet, though ye should condescend to this, which God forbid, the Order still would be but fruitless and defective to that end whereto ye meant it. If to prevent sects and schisms, who is so unread or so uncatechized in story that hath not heard of many sects refusing books as a hindrance, and preserving their doctrine unmixed for many ages, only by unwritten traditions? The Christian faith, for that was once a schism, is not unknown to have spread all over Asia, ere any Gospel or Epistle was seen in writing. If the amendment of manners be aimed at, look into Italy and Spain, whether those places be one scruple the better, the honester, the wiser, the chaster, since all the inquisitional rigor that hath been executed upon books.

Another reason whereby to make it plain that this Order will miss the end it seeks, consider by the quality which ought to be in every licenser. It cannot be denied but that he who is made judge to sit upon the birth or death of books, whether they may be wafted into this world or not,[156] had need to be a man above the common measure, both studious, learned, and judicious. There may be else no mean mistakes in the censure of what is passable or not, which is also no mean injury. If he be of such worth as behoves him, there cannot be a more tedious and unpleasing journey-work,[157] a greater loss of time levied upon his head, than to be made the perpetual reader of unchosen books and pamphlets, ofttimes huge volumes. There is no book that is acceptable unless at certain seasons; but to be enjoined the reading of that at all times, and in a hand scarce legible, whereof three pages would not down at any time in the fairest print, is an imposition which I cannot believe how he that values time and his own studies, or is but of a sensible[158] nostril, should be able to endure.

In this one thing I crave leave of the present licensers to be pardoned for so thinking; who doubtless took this office up, looking on it through their obedience to the parliament, whose command perhaps made all things seem easy and unlaborious to them; but that this short trial hath wearied them out already, their own expressions and excuses to them who make so many journeys to solicit their license, are testimony enough. Seeing, therefore, those who now possess the employment, by all evident signs wish themselves well rid of it, and that no man of worth, none that is not a plain unthrift of his own hours, is ever likely to succeed them, except he mean to put himself to the salary of a press corrector, we may easily foresee what kind of licensers we are to expect hereafter, either ignorant, imperious, and remiss, or basely pecuniary. This is what I had to show, wherein this Order cannot conduce to that end whereof it bears the intention.

I lastly proceed from the no good it can

---

[153] *divulged*: publicly distributed, made generally available.

[154] *expunctions*: expungings, excisions by the censor.

[155] Cf. notes 63 and 77 above.

[156] A glancing reference, says Sirluck, to the river on whose banks the souls wait to be born into this world in Plato's *Phaedo*, 113.

[157] *journey-work*: work by the day or by a journeyman.

[158] *sensible*: sensitive.

do, to the manifest hurt it causes in being first the greatest discouragement and affront that can be offered to learning and to learned men.

It was the complaint and lamentation of prelates, upon every least breath of a motion to remove pluralities[159] and distribute more equally church revenues, that then all learning would be for ever dashed and discouraged. But as for that opinion, I never found cause to think that the tenth part of learning stood or fell with the clergy; nor could I ever but hold it for a sordid and unworthy speech of any churchman who had a competency left him. If, therefore, ye be loth to dishearten utterly and discontent, not the mercenary crew of false pretenders to learning, but the free and ingenuous sort of such as evidently were born to study and love learning for itself, not for lucre, or any other end but the service of God and of truth, and perhaps that lasting fame and perpetuity of praise which God and good men have consented shall be the reward of those whose published labors advance the good of mankind; then know, that so far to distrust the judgment and the honesty of one who hath but a common repute in learning, and never yet offended, as not to count him fit to print his mind without a tutor and examiner, lest he should drop a schism, or something of corruption, is the greatest displeasure and indignity to a free and knowing spirit that can be put upon him.

What advantage is it to be a man over it is to be a boy at school, if we have only scaped the ferula[160] to come under the fescue of an Imprimatur; if serious and elaborate writings, as if they were no more than the theme of a grammar-lad under his pedagogue, must not be uttered without the cursory eyes of a temporizing and extemporizing licenser? He who is not trusted with his own actions, his drift not being known to be evil, and standing to the hazard of law and penalty, has no great argument to think himself reputed, in the commonwealth wherein he was born, for other than a fool or a foreigner.

When a man writes to the world, he summons up all his reason and delibera-

tion to assist him; he searches, meditates, is industrious, and likely consults and confers with his judicious friends, after all which done he takes himself to be informed in what he writes, as well as any that writ before him. If in this the most consummate act of his fidelity and ripeness, no years, no industry, no former proof of his abilities can bring him to that state of maturity as not to be still mistrusted and suspected (unless he carry all his considerate diligence, all his midnight watchings, and expense of Palladian[161] oil, to the hasty view of an unleisured licenser, perhaps much his younger, perhaps far his inferior in judgment, perhaps one who never knew the labor of book-writing), and if he be not repulsed, or slighted, must appear in print like a puny[162] with his guardian, and his censor's hand on the back of his title to be his bail and surety that he is no idiot or seducer; it cannot be but a dishonor and derogation to the author, to the book, to the privilege and dignity of learning.

And what if the author shall be one so copious of fancy as to have many things well worth the adding, come into his mind after licensing, while the book is yet under the press, which not seldom happens to the best and diligentest writers; and that perhaps a dozen times in one book. The printer dares not go beyond his licensed copy. So often then must the author trudge to his leave-giver, that those his new insertions may be viewed, and many a jaunt will be made, ere that licenser, for it must be the same man, can either be found, or found at leisure. Meanwhile, either the press must stand still, which is no small damage, or the author lose his accuratest thoughts and send the book forth worse than he had made it, which to a diligent writer is the greatest melancholy and vexation that can befall.

And how can a man teach with authority, which is the life of teaching, how can he be a doctor in his book as he ought to be, or else had better be silent, whenas all he teaches, all he delivers, is but under the

---

159 Cf. *CG,* n. 262.

160 *ferula:* a schoolmaster's rod. *fescue:* a pointer.

161 *Palladian:* pertaining to Pallas Athene. The oil of the olive tree, which was sacred to her, when burned by an author, might be regarded as no less her gift than the wisdom which she was supposed to give to her devotes.

162 *puny:* a child, a person under the legal age of majority.

tuition, under the correction of his patriarchal[168] licenser to blot or alter what precisely accords not with the hidebound humor which he calls his judgment? When every acute reader upon the first sight of a pedantic license, will be ready with these like words to ding the book a quoit's distance from him: "I hate a pupil teacher, I endure not an instructor that comes to me under the wardship of an overseeing fist. I know nothing of the licenser, but that I have his own hand here for his arrogance; who shall warrant me his judgment?"

"The state, sir," replies the stationer,[164] but has a quick return: "The state shall be my governors, but not my critics; they may be mistaken in the choice of a licenser as easily as this licenser may be mistaken in an author; this is some common stuff"; and he might add from Sir Francis Bacon,[165] "That such authorized books are but the language of the times." For though a licenser should happen to be judicious more than ordinary, which will be a great jeopardy of the next succession, yet his very office and his commission enjoins him to let pass nothing but what is vulgarly received already.

Nay, which is more lamentable, if the work of any deceased author, though never so famous in his lifetime and even to this day, come to their hands for license to be printed, or reprinted; if there be found in his book one sentence of a venturous edge, uttered in the height of zeal, and who knows whether it might not be the dictate of a divine spirit, yet not suiting with every low, decrepit humor of their own, though it were Knox[166] himself, the re-

former of a kingdom, that spake it, they will not pardon him their dash; the sense of that great man shall to all posterity be lost, for the fearfulness, or the presumptuous rashness, of a perfunctory licenser. And to what an author this violence hath been lately done, and in what book of greatest consequence to be faithfully published, I could now instance, but shall forbear till a more convenient season.[167]

Yet if these things be not resented seriously and timely by them who have the remedy in their power, but that such iron-molds[168] as these shall have authority to gnaw out the choicest periods of exquisitest books, and to commit such a treacherous fraud against the orphan remainders of worthiest men after death, the more sorrow will belong to that hapless race of men whose misfortune it is to have understanding. Henceforth let no man care to learn, or care to be more than worldly wise; for certainly in higher matters to be ignorant and slothful, to be a common, steadfast dunce, will be the only pleasant life, and only in request.

And as it is a particular disesteem of every knowing person alive, and most injurious to the written labors and monuments of the dead, so to me it seems an undervaluing and vilifying of the whole nation. I cannot set so light by all the invention, the art, the wit, the grave and solid judgment which is in England, as that it can be comprehended in any twenty capacities how good soever; much less that it should not pass except their superintendence be over it, except it be sifted and strained with their strainers; that it should be uncurrent without their manual stamp. Truth and understanding are not such wares as to be monopolized[169] and traded in by tickets and

---

[163] In the eastern churches the position of a patriarch is comparable with that of the Archbishop of Canterbury as Primate of England. Archbishop Laud had been suspected of aspiring to the title and of planning to be recognized as a successor of the Anglo-Saxon patriarchs for whose historical existence Edward Brerewood argued in *The Patriarchall Government of the Ancient Church.* Cf. *CG,* n. 7.

[164] *stationer:* printer. For the part played in book-licensing by the Stationers' Company see the Bibliographical Note above.

[165] Milton quotes Bacon's *An Advertisement touching the Controversies of the Church of England* (*The Letters and the Life of Francis Bacon,* ed. by J. Spedding, Vol. I. London, 1862; p. 78), to which he returns later. Cf. n. 193.

[166] Cf. *TKM* notes 122, 123, and 206. Milton thinks of Knox here as a founder of Scottish Pres-

byterianism and an uncompromising opponent of Mary, Queen of Scots.

[167] Since Knox's *History of the Reformation in Scotland* suffered some mutilation in its edition of 1644, Knox may be the author in question; but so may be the great jurist, Sir Edward Coke (1552–1634), whose *Institutes* were also mutilated when their publication was authorized by Parliament.

[168] *iron-molds:* stains "on cloth, caused by rusty iron or ink." (Webster)

[169] So in the Preface to *Eikon* Milton took advantage of Puritan resentment of the commercial monopolies which Elizabeth, James I, and Charles I had increasingly abused, and he made them the basis of his metaphor of "religion" brought almost to be "a kind of trading monopoly."

statutes and standards.[170] We must not think to make a staple commodity of all the knowledge in the land, to mark and license it like our broadcloth and our woolpacks. What is it but a servitude like that imposed by the Philistines,[171] not to be allowed the sharpening of our own axes and coulters,[172] but we must repair from all quarters to twenty licensing forges.

Had anyone written and divulged erroneous things and scandalous to honest life, misusing and forfeiting the esteem had of his reason among men; if, after conviction, this only censure were adjudged him, that he should never henceforth write, but what were first examined by an appointed officer, whose hand should be annexed to pass his credit for him, that now he might be safely read; it could not be apprehended less than a disgraceful punishment.

Whence, to include the whole nation, and those that never yet thus offended, under such a diffident[173] and suspectful prohibition, may plainly be understood what a disparagement it is. So much the more, whenas debtors and delinquents may walk abroad without a keeper, but unoffensive books must not stir forth without a visible jailor in their title. Nor is it to the common people less than a reproach; for if we be so jealous[174] over them as that we dare not trust them with an English pamphlet, what do we but censure them for a giddy, vicious, and ungrounded people, in such a sick and weak estate of faith and discretion, as to be able to take nothing down but through the pipe[175] of a licenser. That this is care or love of them, we cannot pretend, whenas in those popish places where the laity are most hated and despised, the same strictness is used over them. Wisdom we cannot call it, because it stops but one breach of license, nor that neither; whenas those corruptions which it seeks to prevent,

break in faster at other doors which cannot be shut.

And in conclusion, it reflects to the disrepute of our ministers also, of whose labors we should hope better, and of the proficiency which their flock reaps by them, than that after all this light of the Gospel which is and is to be, and all this continual preaching, they should be still frequented with such an unprincipled, unedified, and laic[176] rabble, as that the whiff of every new pamphlet should stagger them out of their catechism and Christian walking. This may have much reason to discourage the ministers, when such a low conceit is had of all their exhortations and the benefiting of their hearers, as that they are not thought fit to be turned loose to three sheets of paper without a licenser; that all the sermons, all the lectures preached, printed, vended in such numbers and such volumes as have now well nigh made all other books unsaleable, should not be armor enough against one single enchiridion,[177] without the castle St. Angelo[178] of an Imprimatur.

And lest some should persuade ye, Lords and Commons, that these arguments of learned men's discouragement at this your Order are mere flourishes, and not real, I could recount what I have seen and heard in other countries where this kind of inquisition tyrannizes; when I have sat among their learned men, for that honor I had, and been counted happy to be born in such a place of philosophic freedom as they supposed England was, while themselves did nothing but bemoan the servile condition into which learning amongst them was brought; that this was it which had damped the glory of Italian wits; that nothing had been there written now these many years but flattery and fustian. There it was that I found and visited the famous Galileo,[179]

170 *tickets:* "official warrants or permissions of any kind." (*O.E.D.*)
171 When the *Philistines* disarmed the Israelites and forbade them to have forges, "all the Israelites went down to the Philistines, to sharpen every man his share, and his coulter, and his ax" (I Sam. xiii, 20).
172 *coulter:* the iron "foot" or point of the plough.
173 *diffident:* lacking in confidence, suspicious.
174 *jealous:* suspiciously watchful.
175 *pipe:* a tube for taking medicine.

176 *laic:* belonging to the laity. A Puritan grievance against Laud was his depression of laymen's importance in favor of the clergy.
177 *enchiridion:* a pun on the two meanings, hand-sword and handbook, of the Greek word.
178 The *castle of St. Angelo,* on the left bank of the Tiber in Rome, was built in 136 A.D. by the emperor Hadrian and was used as an imperial mausoleum for nearly a century. In Milton's time it was the papal prison.
179 *Galileo* (1564–1642) was under what amounted to house arrest near Florence when Milton was there in 1638–1639. Though he was a

grown old, a prisoner to the Inquisition for thinking in astronomy otherwise than the Franciscan and Dominican licensers thought. And though I knew that England then was groaning loudest under the prelatical yoke, nevertheless I took it as a pledge of future happiness that other nations were so persuaded of her liberty.

Yet was it beyond my hope that those worthies were then breathing in her air, who should be her leaders to such a deliverance as shall never be forgotten by any revolution of time that this world hath to finish. When that was once begun, it was as little in my fear, that what words of complaint I heard among learned men of other parts uttered against the Inquisition, the same I should hear by as learned men at home uttered in time of Parliament against an order of licensing; and that so generally, that when I had disclosed myself a companion of their discontent, I might say, if without envy, that he whom an honest quæstorship had endeared to the Sicilians, was not more by them importuned against Verres,[180] than the favorable opinion which I had among many who honor ye, and are known and respected by ye, loaded me with entreaties and persuasions that I would not despair to lay together that which just reason should bring into my mind toward the removal of an undeserved thraldom upon learning.

That this is not, therefore, the disburdening of a particular fancy, but the common grievance of all those who had prepared their minds and studies above the vulgar pitch to advance truth in others, and from

others to entertain it, thus much may satisfy. And in their name I shall for neither friend nor foe conceal what the general murmur is; that if it come to inquisitioning again and licensing, and that we are so timorous of ourselves and so suspicious of all men as to fear each book and the shaking of every leaf, before we know what the contents are; if some who but of late little better than silenced from preaching,[181] shall come now to silence us from reading, except what they please, it cannot be guessed what is intended by some but a second tyranny over learning; and will soon put it out of controversy that bishops and presbyters are the same to us both name and thing.

That those evils of prelaty which before from five or six and twenty sees[182] were distributively charged upon the whole people, will now light wholly upon learning, is not obscure to us; whenas now the pastor of a small unlearned parish on the sudden shall be exalted archbishop over a large diocese of books, and yet not remove, but keep his other cure too, a mystical pluralist.[183] He who but of late cried down the sole ordination of every novice bachelor of art, and denied sole jurisdiction over the simplest parishioner, shall now at home in his private chair assume both these over worthiest and excellentest books and ablest authors that write them. This is not, ye covenants[184] and protestations[185] that we have made, this is not to put down prelaty; this is but to chop an episcopacy; this is but to translate the palace metropolitan[186] from one kind of dominion into another; this is but an old canonical[187] sleight of commuting our penance. To startle thus betimes

nominal prisoner of the Inquisition from the publication of his evidence for the Copernican theory in 1632 until his death, he was not inaccessible to visitors. In *Studies in Milton* (Land, 1919), S. B. Liljegren grossly overstated the probability that Milton would not have had access to him. Liljegren's effort to cast doubt upon this and other statements about the Italian journey which Milton makes elsewhere, especially in *Def 2*, have been refuted by Fr. A. Pompen in *Neophilologus*, VI (1922), 272–9; by Walther Fischer in *Englische Studien*, B. 52 (1918), 390–6, and by B. A. Wright in *MLR*, XXVIII (1933), 308–14. Cf. *Eikon*, Chap. xxviii, n. 2.

180 While serving as quæstor in Sicily in 75 B.C., Cicero won such confidence that the Sicilians asked him to prosecute Gaius Verres for his extortions there as praetor in B.C. 73–71. After taking less than two months to collect evidence, Cicero virtually won his case and drove Verres into exile by the first of his orations against him.

181 Milton is thinking of the Presbyterian clergy in London, who until recently had been held in severe check by authorities. He anticipates the mood in which he was to write within about two years that

New Presbyter is but Old Priest writ Large.
(Sonnet *On the New Forcers of Conscience*, 20)

182 *sees:* seats or diocesan centers of bishops.

183 Cf. *CG*, n. 262.

184 Cf. *Eikon*, Preface, n. 33, and *TKM*, n. 7.

185 In May, 1641, when Charles planned to use the army to overawe Parliament, the members agreed on a *Protestation* asserting civil liberties, parliamentary freedom, etc.

186 *metropolitan:* pertaining to an archbishop or to his power or property.

187 *canonical:* pertaining to Canon Law or lawyers.

at a mere unlicensed pamphlet will after a while be afraid of every conventicle,[188] and a while after will make a conventicle of every Christian meeting.

But I am certain that a state governed by the rules of justice and fortitude, or a church built and founded upon the rock of faith and true knowledge, cannot be so pusillanimous. While things are yet not constituted in religion, that freedom of writing should be restrained by a discipline imitated from the prelates, and learnt by them from the Inquisition, to shut us up all again into the breast of a licenser, must needs give cause of doubt and discouragement to all learned and religious men. Who cannot but discern the fineness[189] of this politic drift, and who are the contrivers: that while bishops were to be baited down,[190] then all presses might be open; it was the people's birthright and privilege in time of parliament, it was the breaking forth of light?

But now, the bishops abrogated and voided[191] out of the church, as if our reformation sought no more but to make room for others into their seats under another name, the episcopal arts begin to bud again; the cruse[192] of truth must run no more oil; liberty of printing must be enthralled again under a prelatical commission of twenty, the privilege of the people nullified; and, which is worse, the freedom of learning must groan again, and to her old fetters: all this the parliament yet sitting. Although their own late arguments and defenses against the prelates might remember them that this obstructing violence meets for the most part with an event utterly opposite to the end which it drives at; instead of suppressing sects and schisms, it raises them and invests them with a reputation: "The punishing of wits enhances their authority," saith the Viscount St. Albans,[193] "and a forbidden writing is thought to be a certain spark of truth that flies up in the faces of them who seek to tread it out."

This Order, therefore, may prove a nursing mother[194] to sects, but I shall easily show how it will be a stepdame to Truth; and first by disenabling us to the maintenance of what is known already.

Well knows he who uses to consider, that our faith and knowledge thrives by exercise, as well as our limbs and complexion.[195] Truth is compared in scripture to a streaming fountain;[196] if her waters flow not in a perpetual progression, they sicken into a muddy pool of conformity and tradition. A man may be a heretic in the truth;[197] and if he believe things only because his pastor says so, or the Assembly[198] so determines, without knowing other reason, though his belief be true, yet the very truth he holds becomes his heresy. There is not any burden that some would gladlier post off to another than the charge and care of their religion. There be, who knows not that there be, of protestants and professors[199] who live and die in as arrant an implicit faith, as any lay papist of Loreto.[200] A wealthy man addicted to his pleasure and to his profits, finds religion to be a traffic so entangled, and of so many piddling accounts, that of all mysteries[201] he cannot skill[202] to keep a stock going upon that trade. What should he do? Fain he

[194] "And kings shall be thy nursing fathers, and their queens thy nursing mothers" (Isa. xlix, 23).
[195] complexion: the balance of "humors" in the body on which temperament and character were thought to depend. Cf. Educ, n. 42.
[196] Milton is echoing Psalm lxxxv, 11, but he is probably also recalling that Bacon had said that "the truth is, that time seemeth to be of the nature of a river or stream, which carrieth down to us that which is light and blown up, and sinketh and drowneth that which is weighty and solid" (Advancement I, v, 3; p. 39).
[197] So in TR Milton defines heresy as "a religion taken up and believed from the traditions of men," and contrasts "implicit faith" with "unimplicit truth" (C.E. VI, 178).
[198] Presbyterians prevailed in the Assembly of Divines, which was then sitting at Westminster.
[199] professors: persons professing religious (and presumably Protestant) faith.
[200] Loreto: the shrine near Ancona in Italy where, since 1294, pilgrims have attested their faith in the miraculous translation there by angels of the Santa Casa or house of Christ's residence in Nazareth.
[201] mysteries: trades, skills—in the sense in which the term was applied to the trades which were organized into guilds.
[202] skill: contrive.

[188] conventicle: a religious meeting of any of the independent sects whose services were forbidden.
[189] fineness: subtlety, cleverness.
[190] baited down: as bears are in the sport of bear-baiting.
[191] voided: emptied out, expelled. Cf. CG, n. 44.
[192] The cruse of truth is like the widow's inexhaustible cruse of oil in I Kings xvii, 12.
[193] Viscount St. Albans: Bacon. See n. 165 above.

would have the name to be religious, fain he would bear up with his neighbors in that. What does he, therefore, but resolves to give over toiling, and to find himself out some factor[203] to whose care and credit he may commit the whole managing of his religious affairs; some Divine of note and estimation that must be. To him he adheres, resigns the whole warehouse of his religion with all the locks and keys into his custody; and indeed makes the very person of that man his religion; esteems his associating with him a sufficient evidence and commendatory of his own piety. So that a man may say his religion is now no more within himself, but is become a dividual[204] movable, and goes and comes near him, according as that good man frequents the house. He entertains him, gives him gifts, feasts him, lodges him. His religion comes home at night, prays, is liberally supped, and sumptuously laid to sleep, rises, is saluted, and after the malmsey,[205] or some well spiced brewage, and better breakfasted than he whose morning appetite would have gladly fed on green figs between Bethany and Jerusalem,[206] his religion walks abroad at eight, and leaves his kind entertainer in the shop trading all day without his religion.

Another sort there be, who, when they hear that all things shall be ordered, all things regulated and settled, nothing written but what passes through the custom-house of certain publicans[207] that have the tonnaging and the poundaging[208] of all free-spoken truth, will straight give themselves up into your hands, make 'em and cut 'em out what religion ye please. There be delights, there be recreations and jolly pastimes that will fetch the day about from sun to sun, and rock the tedious year as in a delightful dream. What need they torture their heads with that which others have taken so strictly and so unalterably into their own purveying? These are the fruits which a dull ease and cessation of our knowledge will bring forth among the people. How goodly, and how to be wished, were such an obedient unanimity as this, what a fine conformity would it starch us all into! Doubtless a staunch and solid piece of framework, as any January could freeze together.

Nor much better will be the consequence even among the clergy themselves. It is no new thing never heard of before, for a parochial minister, who has his reward, and is at his Hercules pillars[209] in a warm benefice, to be easily inclinable, if he have nothing else that may rouse up his studies, to finish his circuit in an English concordance and a topic folio, the gatherings and savings of a sober graduateship, a harmony[210] and a catena,[211] treading the constant round of certain common doctrinal heads, attended with their uses, motives, marks, and means; out of which, as out of an alphabet or sol-fa, by forming and transforming, joining and disjoining variously a little bookcraft, and two hours' meditation, might furnish him unspeakably to the performance of more than a weekly charge of sermoning; not to reckon up the infinite helps of interlinearies,[212] breviaries, synopses, and other loitering gear.

But as for the multitude of sermons ready printed and piled up on every text that is not difficult, our London trading St. Thomas[213] in his vestry, and add to boot

---

[203] *factor*: agent.

[204] *dividual*: separable.

[205] *malmsey*: a strong, sweet wine.

[206] Riding from *Bethany* on his way to *Jerusalem*, Christ "was hungry: And seeing a fig tree afar off, . . . he came, if haply he might find anything thereon: and . . . found nothing but leaves" (Mark xi, 12–3).

[207] *publicans*: tax-gatherers.

[208] *Tonnage* and *poundage* were a form of excise taxes traditionally granted to the king by Parliament, but disputed in 1641, when "the tonnage and poundage act declared the taking of all such duties without the consent of Parliament illegal" (F. C. Montague, *The History of England from the Accession of James I to the Restoration*, p. 242).

[209] *Hercules pillars*: Gibraltar and the promontory opposite to it, which in the ancient world represented the final limit of at least ordinary travel or ambition.

[210] *harmony*: a simple treatise bringing divergent scripture narratives, such as those in the four gospels, into harmony with one another.

[211] *catena*: a chain. The term was applied to popular but systematic theological works as various as the *Catena Aurea* of St. Thomas Aquinas and the *Golden Chaine, or The description of theologie, containing the order of the causes of Salvation and damnation according to Gods Word* (1621) of the Reverend William Perkins.

[212] *interlinearies*: interlinear commentaries on scripture.

[213] *St. Thomas*, etc. The identifications of the London churches intended are not clear, but the three spots indicated evidently bounded the bookselling district in the city.

St. Martin and St. Hugh, have not within their hallowed limits more vendible ware of all sorts ready made; so that penury he never need fear of pulpit provision, having where so plenteously to refresh his magazine. But if his rear and flanks be not impaled,[214] if his back door be not secured by the rigid licenser, but that a bold book may now and then issue forth and give the assault to some of his old collections in their trenches; it will concern him then to keep waking, to stand in watch, to set good guards and sentinels about his received opinions, to walk the round and counter-round with his fellow inspectors, fearing lest any of his flock be seduced, who also then would be better instructed, better exercised and disciplined. And God send[215] that the fear of this diligence, which must then be used, do not make us affect the laziness of a licensing church.

For if we be sure we are in the right, and do not hold the truth guiltily, which becomes not, if we ourselves condemn not our own weak and frivolous teaching, and the people for an untaught and irreligious, gadding rout, what can be more fair than when a man judicious, learned, and of a conscience, for aught we know, as good as theirs that taught us what we know, shall not privily from house to house, which is more dangerous, but openly by writing, publish to the world what his opinion is, what his reasons, and wherefore that which is now thought cannot be sound? Christ urged[216] it as wherewith to justify himself that he preached in public; yet writing is more public than preaching; and more easy to refutation, if need be, there being so many whose business and profession merely it is, to be the champions of truth; which if they neglect, what can be imputed but their sloth or unability?

Thus much we are hindered and disinured[217] by this course of licensing toward the true knowledge of what we seem to know. For how much it hurts and hinders the licensers themselves in the calling of their ministry, more than any secular employment, if they will discharge that office as they ought, so that of necessity they must neglect either the one duty or the other, I insist not, because it is a particular, but leave it to their own conscience, how they will decide it there.

There is yet behind of what I purposed to lay open, the incredible loss and detriment that this plot of licensing puts us to. More than if some enemy at sea should stop up all our havens and ports and creeks, it hinders and retards the importation of our richest merchandise, truth.[218] Nay, it was first established and put in practice by Antichristian malice and mystery, on set purpose to extinguish, if it were possible, the light of reformation, and to settle falsehood; little differing from that policy wherewith the Turk upholds his Alcoran, by the prohibition of printing. 'Tis not denied, but gladly confessed, we are to send our thanks and vows to Heaven, louder than most of nations, for that great measure of truth which we enjoy, especially in those main points between us and the Pope, with his appurtenances the prelates; but he who thinks we are to pitch our tent here, and have attained the utmost prospect of reformation that the mortal glass[219] wherein we contemplate can show us, till we come to beatific vision,[220] that man by this very opinion declares that he is yet far short of truth.

Truth indeed came once into the world with her divine Master, and was a perfect shape[221] most glorious to look on. But when he ascended, and his apostles after him were laid asleep, then straight arose a

---

[214] impaled: protected. Cf. Satan's artillery in PL VI, 553-4.
  "impal'd
On every side with shadowing squadrons deep."
[215] send, the reading of the original, has been emended by some editors to fend: prevent, forfend.
[216] Questioned by the high priest, "Jesus answered him, I spake openly to the world; . . . in secret have I said nothing" (John xviii, 20).
[217] disinured: diverted from a customary practice, or one to which habit has become inured.

[218] Perhaps an allusion to the pearl of great price in Christ's parable of the merchant who sold everything for that single purchase (Matt. xiii, 46) —or to the "trade, not for gold, silver, jewels, nor for silks, nor for spices, nor for any other commodity of matter, but only for God's first creature, which was Light," which Bacon describes his New Atlanteans as maintaining. (Essays, Advancement of Learning, New Atlantis, and Other Pieces, edited by R. F. Jones, p. 469.)
[219] glass: mirror. Cf. I Cor. xiii, 12: "For now we see through [or in] a glass, darkly; but then, face to face."
[220] Cf. PL I, 684, n.
[221] Cf. Satan's recognition of Christ as "of good, wise, just, the perfect shape," in PR III, 11, and also CG, n. 14, and Comus, 216, n.

wicked race of deceivers, who, as that story goes of the Egyptian Typhon[222] with his conspirators, how they dealt with the good Osiris, took the virgin Truth, hewed her lovely form into a thousand pieces, and scattered them to the four winds. From that time ever since, the sad friends of Truth, such as durst appear, imitating the careful search that Isis made for the mangled body of Osiris, went up and down gathering up limb by limb still as they could find them. We have not yet found them all, Lords and Commons, nor ever shall do, till her Master's second coming. He shall bring together every joint and member, and shall mold them into an immortal feature of loveliness and perfection. Suffer not these licensing prohibitions to stand at every place of opportunity, forbidding and disturbing them that continue seeking, that continue to do our obsequies[223] to the torn body of our martyred saint.

We boast our light; but if we look not wisely on the sun itself, it smites us into darkness. Who can discern those planets that are oft combust,[224] and those stars of brightest magnitude that rise and set with the sun, until the opposite motion of their orbs bring them to such a place in the firmament, where they may be seen evening or morning. The light which we have gained, was given us, not to be ever staring on, but by it to discover onward things more remote from our knowledge. It is not the unfrocking of a priest, the unmitering of a bishop, and the removing him from off the Presbyterian shoulders that will make us a happy nation; no, if other things as great in the church, and in

the rule of life both economical[225] and political, be not looked into and reformed, we have looked so long upon the blaze that Zwinglius[226] and Calvin hath beaconed up to us, that we are stark blind.

There be who perpetually complain of schisms and sects, and make it such a calamity that any man dissents from their maxims. It is their own pride and ignorance which causes the disturbing, who neither will hear with meekness, nor can convince, yet all must be suppressed which is not found in their syntagma.[227] They are the troublers, they are the dividers of unity, who neglect and permit not others to unite those dissevered pieces which are yet wanting to the body of Truth. To be still searching what we know not by what we know, still closing up truth to truth as we find it (for all her body is homogeneal and proportional), this is the golden rule in theology as well as in arithmetic, and makes up the best harmony in a church; not the forced and outward union of cold and neutral and inwardly divided minds.

Lords and Commons of England, consider what nation it is whereof ye are, and whereof ye are the governors; a nation not slow and dull, but of a quick, ingenious, and piercing spirit, acute to invent, subtle and sinewy to discourse, not beneath the reach of any point the highest that human capacity can soar to. Therefore the studies of learning in her deepest sciences have been so ancient and so eminent among us that writers of good antiquity and ablest judgment have been persuaded that even the school of Pythagoras[228] and the Persian wisdom took beginning from the old philosophy of this island. And that wise and civil Roman, Julius Agricola,[229] who gov-

---

[222] Milton's public was familiar with Plutarch's *Isis and Osiris*, where the myth is interpreted as a symbol of the ceaseless assembly by Isis of the divine truth which is continually mangled and scattered by *Typhon*. In *An Humble Motion to the Parliament of England Concerning the Advancement of Learning* (1649, pp. 5–6) John Hall transferred the symbolism to the myth of Medea and described "the body of learning" as lying "scattered in as many pieces as ever Medea cut her little brother into, that they are as hard to finde and reunite as his was."

[223] *obsequies*: services or acts of veneration.

[224] *combust*: burnt up. In astrology the term applied to any planet coming within eight and a half degrees of the sun.

[225] *economical*: pertaining to household management. Cf. *CG*, n. 243.

[226] Cf. Milton's quotation of *Zwingli* and *Calvin* in *TKM*, notes 201–202.

[227] *syntagma*: systematic treatise or body of doctrine.

[228] Milton's interest in *Pythagoras* is best illustrated by *Prol II*.

[229] *Julius Agricola* (37–93 A.D.) was proconsul in Britain from 78 to 85, and under him the Roman conquest was consolidated. In the *Life of Agricola* his son-in-law, Tacitus, says that he educated the sons of the chiefs in the liberal arts so successfully that those who had recently despised the language of the Romans were soon anxious to become eloquent in it.

erned once here for Cæsar, preferred the natural wits of Britain before the labored studies of the French. Nor is it for nothing that the grave and frugal Transylvanian[230] sends out yearly from as far as the mountainous borders of Russia and beyond the Hercynian wilderness,[231] not their youth, but their staid men to learn our language and our theologic arts.

Yet that which is above all this, the favor and the love of Heaven, we have great argument to think in a peculiar manner propitious and propending[232] towards us. Why else was this nation chosen before any other, that out of her as out of Sion[233] should be proclaimed and sounded forth the first tidings and trumpet of reformation to all Europe? And had it not been the obstinate perverseness of our prelates against the divine and admirable spirit of Wycliffe[234] to suppress him as a schismatic and innovator, perhaps neither the Bohemian Huss and Jerome,[235] no, nor the name of Luther, or of Calvin, had been ever known; the glory of reforming all our neighbors had been completely ours. But now, as our obdurate clergy have with violence demeaned the matter, we are become hitherto the latest and the backwardest scholars of whom God offered to have made us the teachers.

Now once again by all concurrence of signs, and by the general instinct of holy and devout men, as they daily and solemnly express their thoughts, God is decreeing to begin some new and great period in his Church, even to the reforming of reformation itself. What does he then but reveal himself to his servants, and, as his manner is, first to his Englishmen?[236] I say as his manner is, first to us, though we mark not the method of his counsels and are unworthy. Behold now this vast city, a city of refuge, the mansion house of liberty, encompassed and surrounded with his protection. The shop of war hath not there more anvils and hammers waking, to fashion out the plates[237] and instruments of armed justice in defense of beleaguered Truth, than there be pens and heads there, sitting by their studious lamps,[238] musing, searching, revolving new notions and ideas wherewith to present, as with their homage and their fealty, the approaching reformation; others as fast reading, trying all things, assenting to the force of reason and convincement.

What could a man require more from a nation so pliant and so prone to seek after knowledge? What wants there to such a towardly and pregnant soul but wise and faithful laborers to make a knowing people, a nation of prophets, of sages, and of worthies? We reckon more than five months yet to harvest; there need not be five weeks, had we but eyes to lift up; the fields are white already.[239] Where there is much desire to learn, there of necessity will be much arguing, much writing, many opinions; for opinion in good men is but knowledge in the making. Under these fantastic terrors of sect and schism, we wrong the earnest and zealous thirst after

---

230 From 1535 until 1689 Transylvania was independent, and in the seventeenth century it was aggressively Protestant.

231 Hales points out that the name Hercynian survives in that of the Harz (mountains), but that ancient writers applied it vaguely to most of the mountains in the south and center of Germany.

232 propending: inclining.

233 Sion: Mt. Zion in Jerusalem, standing for the city itself as the center of ancient Hebrew worship.

234 For Wycliffe and Huss see CG, n. 119.

235 Jerome of Prague (d. 1416), a strong supporter of Huss, studied and read Wycliffe's work at Oxford in 1398, and later became a devoted, though not perfectly loyal, supporter of Huss in Bohemia. He was burned at the stake.

236 As early as 1595 Milton's piously patriotic

confidence in England's destiny was anticipated by the practical navigator, John Davis, in The Worldes Hydrographical description, "There is no doubt but that we of England are . . . by the eternal and infallible presence of the Lord predestined to be sent unto all these Gentiles in the sea of the Isles and famous kingdoms, there to preach the peace of the Lord: for are not we only set upon Mount Zion to give light to all the rest of the world." In Miltons Anschauung im Staat, Kirche, und Toleranz (Halle, Saale, 1934) Gertrude Hardeland collects a number of interesting, later parallels to Milton's thought.

237 plates: armor of plate mail.

238 "Christ Jesus the Son of Glory and Righteousness hath lighted up such a candle in the midst of this Nation, and from hence in the midst of Europe, and the world, (as to Soul-freedom) that all the Devils of Hell shall never be able to extinguish," says An Outrageous Outcry for Tithes . . . Answered (1652), p. 23. This tract is anonymous.

239 Milton paraphrases Christ's words to the disciples whom he sent to preach to the Jews (John iv, 35).

knowledge and understanding which God hath stirred up in this city.

What some lament of, we rather should rejoice at, should rather praise this pious forwardness among men, to reassume the ill-deputed care of their religion into their own hands again. A little generous prudence, a little forbearance of one another, and some grain of charity might win all these diligences to join and unite into one general and brotherly search after truth; could we but forego this prelatical tradition of crowding free consciences and Christian liberties into canons and precepts of men. I doubt not, if some great and worthy stranger should come among us, wise to discern the mold and temper of a people, and how to govern it, observing the high hopes and aims, the diligent alacrity of our extended thoughts and reasonings in the pursuance of truth and freedom, but that he would cry out as Pyrrhus[240] did, admiring the Roman docility and courage, "If such were my Epirots, I would not despair the greatest design that could be attempted to make a church or kingdom happy."

Yet these are the men cried out against for schismatics and sectaries; as if, while the temple[241] of the Lord was building, some cutting, some squaring the marble, others hewing the cedars, there should be a sort of irrational men who could not consider there must be many schisms[242] and many dissections made in the quarry and in the timber, ere the house of God can be built. And when every stone is laid artfully together, it cannot be united into a continuity, it can but be contiguous in this world; neither can every piece of the building be of one form; nay rather the perfection consists in this, that out of many moderate varieties and brotherly dissimilitudes that are not vastly disproportional, arises the goodly and the graceful symmetry that commends the whole pile and structure.

Let us, therefore, be more considerate builders, more wise in spiritual architecture, when great reformation is expected. For now the time seems come, wherein Moses, the great prophet, may sit in heaven rejoicing to see that memorable and glorious wish of his fulfilled, when not only our seventy elders, but all the Lord's people, are become prophets. No marvel then though some men, and some good men too perhaps, but young in goodness, as Joshua[243] then was, envy them. They fret and out of their own weakness are in agony, lest these divisions and subdivisions will undo us. The adversary again applauds and waits the hour. When they have branched themselves out, saith he, small enough into parties and partitions, then will be our time. Fool! he sees not the firm root, out of which we all grow, though into branches; nor will beware until he see our small divided maniples[244] cutting through at every angle of his ill-united and unwieldy brigade. And that we are to hope better of all these supposed sects and schisms, and that we shall not need that solicitude, honest perhaps, though over-timorous, of them that vex in this behalf, but shall laugh in the end at those malicious applauders of our differences, I have these reasons to persuade me.

First, when a city shall be as it were besieged and blocked about, her navigable river infested, inroads and incursions round, defiance[245] and battle oft rumored to be marching up even to her walls and suburb trenches; that then the people, or the greater part, more than at other times, wholly taken up with the study of highest and most important matters to be reformed, should be disputing, reasoning, reading, inventing, discoursing, even to a rarity and admiration, things not before discoursed or written of, argues first a singular goodwill, contentedness and confidence in your prudent foresight and safe government, Lords and Commons; and from thence de-

---

[240] *Pyrrhus* (318–272 B.C.), King of Epirus, is said by Florus (*Epitome de gestis Romanorum* I, 18) to have paid this tribute to Roman discipline after his victory over Valerius Laevinus at Heraclea in 280 B.C.

[241] The stones for Solomon's *temple* were all shaped exactly for their positions at the quarry (I Kings vi, 7; but cf. the longer account in II Chron. ii, 5–9).

[242] Milton puns on the literal meaning of *schism*, cutting or division.

[243] When *Joshua* was still one of Moses' "young men," he protested against certain prophets in the camp. "And Moses said unto him, Enviest thou for my sake? Would God that all the Lord's people were prophets" (Num. xi, 29).

[244] *maniple*: a platoon of Roman soldiers.

[245] Milton remembered the situation in which he wrote *Sonn* VIII, when, after the battle of Edgehill in October, 1643, the Royalists advanced to the newly fortified suburbs of London.

rives itself to a gallant bravery and well grounded contempt of their enemies, as if there were no small number of as great spirits among us, as his was, who, when Rome was nigh besieged by Hannibal,[246] being in the city, bought that piece of ground at no cheap rate whereon Hannibal himself encamped his own regiment.

Next, it is a lively and cheerful presage of our happy success and victory. For as in a body, when the blood is fresh, the spirits[247] pure and vigorous not only to vital but to rational faculties, and those in the acutest and the pertest operations of wit and subtlety, it argues in what good plight and constitution the body is; so when the cheerfulness of the people is so sprightly up, as that it has not only wherewith to guard well its own freedom and safety, but to spare, and to bestow upon the solidest and sublimest points of controversy and new invention, it betokens us not degenerated nor drooping to a fatal decay, but casting off the old and wrinkled skin of corruption to outlive these pangs and wax young again, entering the glorious ways of truth and prosperous virtue, destined to become great and honorable in these latter ages.

Methinks I see in my mind a noble and puissant nation rousing herself like a strong man after sleep, and shaking her invincible locks. Methinks I see her as an eagle muing[248] her mighty youth, and kindling her undazzled eyes at the full midday beam; purging and unscaling her long-abused sight at the fountain itself of heavenly radiance; while the whole noise of timorous and flocking birds, with those also that love the twilight, flutter about, amazed at what she means, and in their envious gabble would prognosticate a year of sects and schisms.

What should ye do then, should ye suppress all this flowery crop of knowledge and new light sprung up and yet springing daily in this city? Should ye set an oligarchy of twenty engrossers over it, to bring a famine upon our minds again, when we shall know nothing but what is measured to us by their bushel? Believe it, Lords and Commons, they who counsel ye to such a suppressing, do as good as bid ye suppress yourselves; and I will soon show how.

If it be desired to know the immediate cause of all this free writing and free speaking, there cannot be assigned a truer than your own mild and free and humane government. It is the liberty, Lords and Commons, which your own valorous and happy counsels have purchased us, liberty which is the nurse of all great wits. This is that which hath rarefied and enlightened our spirits like the influence of heaven;[249] this is that which hath enfranchised, enlarged, and lifted up our apprehensions degrees above themselves. Ye cannot make us now less capable, less knowing, less eagerly pursuing of the truth, unless ye first make yourselves, that made us so, less the lovers, less the founders of our true liberty. We can grow ignorant again, brutish, formal, and slavish, as ye found us; but you then must first become that which ye cannot be, oppressive, arbitrary, and tyrannous, as they were from whom ye have freed us. That our hearts are now more capacious, our thoughts more erected to the search and expectation of greatest and exactest things,

[246] Livy's *History* (XXVI, xi) tells the story of the damaging effect on the morale of *Hannibal's* Carthaginians who were besieging Rome when it was reported that the field where he had his headquarters had just been sold at *"an unreduced price"* inside Rome.

[247] For the general conception see *PL* V, 484, n. In his Vanderbilt thesis W. B. Hunter quotes Thomas Walkington's *Optick Glasse of Humours* (1607), p. 49r & v, appositely to the effect that the demonic enemies of man's reason "do never take up their lodgings in a body happely attempered; there the spirits are subtile and of a pure constitution. . . . These spirits the more attenuated and purified they bee, the more that coelestiall particle of heavens flame, our reason."

[248] Behind Milton's eagle are many stories of eagles flying in their old age straight into the zenith to singe their wings and burn the mist from their eyes in the sun's rays before plunging thrice into a fountain where, as T. H. White's translation of a twelfth century Bestiary in his *The Book of Beasts* (London, 1954), p. 105, has it, they are "renewed with a great vigor of plumage and splendor of vision." Because the word "renewed" is used in some similar passages and also in Psalm ciii, 5, as well as on scribal grounds, G. U. Yule—

in *RES*, XIX (1943), 61–67—and R. S. Loomis in *MLN*, XXXII (1917), 437, have amended "muing" to "newing," but L. C. Martin justifies the reading of the text in *RES*, XXI (1945), 44, because "muing" (moulting) implies renewal of youth to follow as a result.

[249] Milton probably thought in astrological terms, as he did in describing the union of Adam and Eve:
> . . . all Heav'n
> And happy Constellations on that hour
> Shed their selectest influence.
>
> (*PL* VIII, 511–3.)

is the issue of your own virtue propagated in us. Ye cannot suppress that unless ye reinforce an abrogated and merciless law, that fathers may despatch at will their own children. And who shall then stick closest to ye, and excite others? not he who takes up arms for coat and conduct,[250] and his four nobles[251] of Danegelt.[252] Although I dispraise not the defense of just immunities, yet love my peace better, if that were all. Give me the liberty to know, to utter, and to argue freely according to conscience, above all liberties.

What would be best advised then, if it be found so hurtful and so unequal[253] to suppress opinions for the newness, or the unsuitableness to a customary acceptance, will not be my task to say. I only shall repeat what I have learned from one of your own honorable number, a right noble and pious lord, who, had he not sacrificed his life and fortunes to the church and commonwealth, we had not now missed and bewailed a worthy and undoubted patron of this argument. Ye know him I am sure; yet I for honor's sake, and may it be eternal to him, shall name him, the Lord Brook.[254] He, writing of episcopacy, and by the way treating of sects and schisms, left ye his vote,[255] or rather now the last words of his dying charge (which I know will ever be of dear and honored regard with ye) so full of meekness and breathing charity that next to his last testament who bequeathed love and peace to his disciples,[256] I cannot call to mind where I have read or heard words more mild and peaceful. He there exhorts us to hear with patience and humility those, however they be miscalled, that desire to live purely, in such a use of God's ordinances as the best guidance of their conscience gives them, and to tolerate them, though in some disconformity to ourselves. The book itself will tell us more at large, being published to the world and dedicated to the parliament by him who, both for his life and for his death, deserves that what advice he left be not laid by without perusal.

And now the time in special is, by privilege, to write and speak what may help to the further discussing of matters in agitation. The temple of Janus[257] with his two controversal faces might now not unsignificantly be set open. And though all the winds of doctrine[258] were let loose to play upon the earth, so Truth be in the field, we do injuriously by licensing and prohibiting to misdoubt her strength. Let her and Falsehood grapple; who ever knew Truth put to the worse, in a free and open encounter. Her confuting is the best and surest suppressing. He who hears what praying there is for light and clearer knowledge to be sent down among us, would think of other matters to be constituted beyond the discipline of Geneva,[259] framed and fabriced[260] already to our hands.

Yet when the new light which we beg for shines in upon us, there be who envy and oppose, if it come not first in at their casements. What a collusion is this, whenas we are exhorted by the wise man to use diligence, to seek for wisdom as for hidden treasures[261] early and late, that another order shall enjoin us to know nothing but by statute. When a man hath been laboring the hardest labor in the deep mines of knowledge, hath furnished out his findings in all their equipage, drawn forth his reasons as it were a battle ranged, scattered and defeated all objections in his way, calls out his adversary into the plain, offers him the advantage of wind and sun, if he please,

---

[250] *coat and conduct*: an obsolete tax, originally levied to pay for clothing and transporting feudal troops in the king's service, and revived by Charles I in his effort to obtain funds without a parliamentary grant. cf. *Eikon*, Chap. i, n. 10.

[251] *noble*: a coin worth about six shillings and eight pence.

[252] *Danegelt*: originally, the money secured by taxation in England to buy off the Danish invaders of the Saxon kingdoms. Under the Norman kings it was established as a tax on land. King Charles's lawyers appealed to it in Hampden's case.

[253] *unequal*: unjust, inequitable.

[254] Lord Brooke's *A discourse of the nature of that episcopacie, which is exercised in England* (1641) is the work here mentioned. Milton was also influenced in his thought in *Areop* by Lord Brooke's *On the Nature of Truth* (1640).

[255] *vote*: wish, expressed intention.

[256] "Peace I leave with you, my peace I give unto you" (John xiv, 27).

[257] *Janus*, the ancient Italian deity of gates and doors, had a sacred gateway in the Roman Forum which was always open in time of war—probably because it was supposed to make the armies that departed through it fortunate. In peace it was kept closed.

[258] "That we henceforth be no more children, tossed to and fro, carried about by every wind of doctrine" (Eph. iv, 14).

[259] Cf. *CG*, n. 10.

[260] *fabriced*: fabricated.

[261] An echo of Prov. viii, 11.

only that he may try the matter by dint of argument; for his opponents then to skulk, to lay ambushments, to keep a narrow bridge of licensing where the challenger should pass, though it be valor enough in soldiership, is but weakness and cowardice in the wars of Truth.

For who knows not that Truth is strong, next to the Almighty. She needs no policies, nor stratagems, nor licensings to make her victorious—those are the shifts and the defenses that error uses against her power. Give her but room, and do not bind her when she sleeps, for then she speaks not true, as the old Proteus[262] did, who spake oracles only when he was caught and bound, but then rather she turns herself into all shapes except her own,[263] and perhaps tunes her voice according to the time, as Micaiah[264] did before Ahab, until she be adjured into her own likeness.

Yet is it not impossible that she may have more shapes than one. What else is all that rank of things indifferent, wherein Truth may be on this side, or on the other, without being unlike herself? What but a vain shadow else is the abolition of those ordinances, that handwriting nailed to the cross;[265] what great purchase is this Christian liberty which Paul so often boasts of?[266] His doctrine is, that he who eats, or eats not, regards a day, or regards it not, may do either to the Lord.[267] How many other things might be tolerated in peace and left to conscience, had we but charity, and were it not the chief stronghold of our hypocrisy to be ever judging one another. I fear yet this iron yoke of outward conformity hath left a slavish print upon our necks; the ghost of a linen decency[268] yet haunts us.

We stumble and are impatient at the least dividing of one visible congregation from another, though it be not in fundamentals; and through our forwardness to suppress, and our backwardness to recover any enthralled piece of truth out of the gripe of custom,[269] we care not to keep truth separated from truth, which is the fiercest rent and disunion of all. We do not see that while we still affect by all means a rigid external formality, we may as soon fall again into a gross conforming stupidity, a stark and dead congealment of "wood, and hay, and stubble"[270] forced and frozen together, which is more to the sudden degenerating of a church than many subdichotomies of petty schisms.

Not that I can think well of every light separation, or that all in a church is to be expected "gold and silver and precious stones." It is not possible for man to sever the wheat from the tares,[271] the good fish from the other fry; that must be the angels' ministry at the end of mortal things. Yet if all cannot be of one mind,—as who looks they should be?—this doubtless is more wholesome, more prudent, and more Christian, that many be tolerated, rather than all compelled. I mean not tolerated popery and open superstition, which, as it extirpates all religions and civil supremacies, so itself should be extirpate, provided first that all charitable and compassionate means be used to win and regain the weak and the misled; that also which is impious or evil absolutely, either against faith or manners,[272] no law can possibly permit, that intends not to unlaw itself; but those neighboring differences, or rather indifferences, are what I speak of, whether in some point of doctrine or of discipline, which though they may be many, yet need not interrupt "the unity of spirit,"

[262] The myth of *Proteus* as a prophet goes back to the *Odyssey* IV, 384–93.

[263] Cf. Owen Feltham: *"Truth, in logical arguments, is like a Prince in a Masque; where are so many other presented in the same attire, that we know not which is he!" (Resolves I, iv.)*

[264] For a time *Micaiah*, the prophet of God, agreed with the four hundred pagan prophets who gave Ahab the advice which led him into an attack on Ramoth-Gilead in which he lost his life. When he was adjured to speak the truth, he warned Ahab that the other prophets were inspired by "a lying spirit" (I Kings xxii, 23).

[265] "Blotting out the handwriting of ordinances that was against us, . . . and took it out of the way, nailing it to his cross" (Col. ii, 14).

[266] Gal. v, 1.

[267] A paraphrase of Rom. xiv, 6.

[268] Cf. Milton in *Of Reformation* girding at the

bishops' "pure linen, . . . palls and mitres, gold and gewgaws fetched from Aaron's old wardrobe, or the flamen's vestry" (*C.E.* III, 2).

[269] Cf. the attack on *custom* in *CG* I, v, and in the preface to *DDD*.

[270] "Now if any man build upon this foundation gold, silver, precious stones, wood, hay, stubble" (I Cor. iii, 12).

[271] This is the lesson of the parable of the *tares* and the *wheat* in Matt. xiii, 24–30.

[272] Milton's position is parallel with that of Jeremy Taylor in *Liberty of Prophecying*. Section xix provides "that there may be no toleration of doctrine inconsistent with piety or the public good."

if we could but find among us the "bond of peace."[273]

In the meanwhile, if any one would write and bring his helpful hand to the slow-moving reformation which we labor under, if truth have spoken to him before others, or but seemed at least to speak, who hath so bejesuited us that we should trouble that man with asking license to do so worthy a deed? And not consider this, that if it come to prohibiting, there is not aught more likely to be prohibited than truth itself; whose first appearance to our eyes bleared and dimmed with prejudice and custom, is more unsightly and unplausible than many errors, even as the person is of many a great man slight and contemptible to see to.[274] And what do they tell us vainly of new opinions, when this very opinion of theirs, that none must be heard but whom they like, is the worst and newest opinion of all others; and is the chief cause why sects and schisms do so much abound, and true knowledge is kept at distance from us; besides yet a greater danger which is in it. For when God shakes a kingdom[275] with strong and healthful commotions to a general reforming, it is not untrue that many sectaries and false teachers are then busiest in seducing; but yet more true it is that God then raises to his own work men of rare abilities and more than common industry, not only to look back and revise what hath been taught heretofore, but to gain further and go on some new enlightened steps in the discovery of truth.

For such is the order of God's enlightening his church, to dispense and deal out by degrees his beam, so as our earthly eyes may best sustain it. Neither is God appointed[276] and confined, where and out of what place these his chosen shall be first heard to speak: for he sees not as man sees, chooses not as man chooses, lest we should devote ourselves again to set places and assemblies and outward callings of men; planting our faith one while in the old Convocation[277] house, and another while in the Chapel at Westminster; when all the faith and religion that shall be there canonized,[278] is not sufficient without plain convincement and the charity of patient instruction, to supple the least bruise of conscience, to edify the meanest Christian who desires to walk in the Spirit and not in the letter of human trust, for all the number of voices that can be there made; no, though Harry VII himself there, with all his liege tombs about him, should lend them voices from the dead to swell their number.

And if the men be erroneous who appear to be the leading schismatics, what withholds us but our sloth, our self-will, and distrust in the right cause, that we do not give them gentle meetings and gentle dismissions, that we debate not and examine the matter thoroughly with liberal and frequent audience; if not for their sakes, yet for our own? Seeing no man who hath tasted learning but will confess the many ways of profiting by those who, not contented with stale receipts, are able to manage and set forth new positions to the world. And were they but as the dust and cinders of our feet, so long as in that notion they may yet serve to polish and brighten the armory of Truth, even for that respect they were not utterly to be cast away. But if they be of those whom God hath fitted for the special use of these times with eminent and ample gifts—and those perhaps neither among the priests, nor among the pharisees[279]—and we in the haste of a precipitant zeal shall make no distinction, but resolve to stop their mouths because we fear they come with new and dangerous opinions (as we commonly forejudge them ere we understand them); no less than woe to us while, thinking thus to defend the Gospel, we are found the persecutors.

There have been not a few since the beginning of this Parliament,[280] both of the

---

[273] An echo of Ephes. iv, 3.

[274] *to see to:* to look at.

[275] "And I will shake all nations, and the desire of all nations shall come" (Hag. ii, 7).

[276] *appointed:* bound by prescription. Cf.

Appoint not heavenly disposition, Father.
                                    (*SA*, 373.)

[277] The Chapter-house at Westminster was the meeting-place of Laud's *Convocations,* while the

Assembly of Divines at Westminster was meeting in Henry VII's chapel.

[278] *canonized:* formulated in canons, given the force of ecclesiastical law. *The Longer and Shorter Catechisms* are the best known of the results of the long sittings of the Westminster Assembly.

[279] Milton thought of the traditional skill of the Hebrew *Pharisees* in law and of their unwillingness to meet Christ as an equal in their many encounters with him.

[280] *this Parliament:* the Long Parliament, which first assembled on 3 November, 1640. Milton thought of England as embarking under its guidance upon an enterprise more heroic than the first ven-

presbytery and others, who by their unlicensed books, to the contempt of an Imprimatur, first broke that triple ice clung about our hearts, and taught the people to see day. I hope that none of those were the persuaders to renew upon us this bondage which they themselves have wrought so much good by contemning. But if neither the check that Moses gave to young Joshua,[281] nor the countermand which our Savior gave to young John,[282] who was so ready to prohibit those whom he thought unlicensed, be not enough to admonish our elders how unacceptable to God their testy mood of prohibiting is; if neither their own remembrance what evil hath abounded in the church by this let of licensing, and what good they themselves have begun by transgressing it, be not enough, but that they will persuade and execute the most Dominican[283] part of the Inquisition over us, and are already with one foot in the stirrup so active at suppressing, it would be no unequal distribution, in the first place, to suppress the suppressors themselves; whom the change of their condition hath puffed up more than their late experience of harder times hath made wise.

And as for regulating the press, let no man think to have the honor of advising ye better than yourselves have done in that order[284] published next before this, that no book be printed, unless the printer's and the author's name, or at least the printer's, be registered. Those which otherwise come forth, if they be found mischievous and libellous, the fire and the executioner will be the timeliest and the most effectual remedy that man's prevention can use. For this authentic Spanish policy of licensing books, if I have said aught, will prove the

most unlicensed book itself within a short while; and was the immediate image of a Star Chamber[285] decree to that purpose made in those very times when that Court did the rest of those her pious works, for which she is now fallen from the stars with Lucifer. Whereby ye may guess what kind of state prudence, what love of the people, what care of religion or good manners there was at the contriving, although with singular hypocrisy it pretended to bind books to their good behavior. And how it got the upper hand of your precedent order so well constituted before, if we may believe those men whose profession gives them cause to inquire most, it may be doubted there was in it the fraud of some old patentees and monopolizers in the trade of bookselling; who under pretense of the poor in their Company not to be defrauded, and the just retaining of each man his several copy (which God forbid should be gainsaid) brought divers glosing colors[286] to the House, which were indeed but colors, and serving to no end except it be to exercise a superiority over their neighbors; men who do not, therefore, labor in an honest profession to which learning is indebted, that they should be made other men's vassals. Another end is thought was aimed at by some of them in procuring by petition this Order, that having power in their hands, malignant books might the easier scape abroad, as the event shows.

But of these sophisms and elenchs[287] of merchandise I skill not. This I know, that errors in a good government and in a bad are equally almost incident; for what magistrate may not be misinformed and much the sooner, if liberty of printing be reduced into the power of a few; but to redress willingly and speedily what hath been erred,[288] and in highest authority to esteem a plain advertisement[289] more than others have done a sumptuous bribe, is a virtue, honored Lord and Commons, answerable to your highest actions, and whereof none can participate but greatest and wisest men.

tures of men on the sea, for which Horace said that hearts strengthened by *aes triplex* (triple brass) were needed.
281 Cf. n. 243 above.
282 When John reported having seen a man casting out devils in Jesus' name, "Jesus said unto him, Forbid him not, for he that is not against us is for us" (Luke ix, 50).
283 "The first that preached that doctrine was Dominic," says Taylor in the Epistle Dedicatory to *The Liberty of Prophecying*, "the founder of the begging order of friars, the friars-preachers; in memory of which the inquisition is intrusted only to the friars of his order" (Works, 1828, VII, ccccxvi).
284 For the *order* of Parliament see the Bibliographical Note.

285 For the Court of *Star Chamber* see the Bibliographical Note. Cf. *PL* VII, 131.
286 Cf. *CG*, n. 203.
287 *elench:* "a fallacious answer to a sophistical question" (White).
288 *what hath been erred:* what mistakes have been made. Milton's construction is a Latinism.
289 *advertisement:* intimation, notification.

THE
TENURE OF KINGS AND MAGISTRATES:

PROVING

THAT IT IS LAWFUL, AND HATH BEEN HELD SO THROUGH ALL AGES, FOR ANY, WHO HAVE THE POWER, TO CALL TO ACCOUNT A TYRANT OR WICKED KING, AND AFTER DUE CONVICTION, TO DEPOSE AND PUT HIM TO DEATH IF THE ORDINARY MAGISTRATE HAVE NEGLECTED OR DENIED TO DO IT. AND THAT THEY WHO OF LATE SO MUCH BLAME DEPOSING, ARE THE MEN THAT DID IT THEMSELVES.

BIBLIOGRAPHICAL NOTE—The text of the second edition of *The Tenure*, which is reproduced here, differs substantially from the first edition by a few interpolated words here and there and by the addition of an appendix of extracts from the great Protestant reformers to sustain Milton's thesis that they had justified tyrannicide. The exact date of publication of neither edition is certain, but the date on Thomason's copy of the first edition in the British Museum is "Feb. 13, 1648" (n. s., 1649), while his date on the second edition is "Feb. 15," with 1649 (n. s., 1650) understood. The present text is based on my own copy of the second edition and has been collated with both copies in the Houghton Library at Harvard. The only modern annotated edition is by William T. Allison in *Yale Studies in English*, 1911.

If men within themselves would be governed by reason and not generally give up their understanding to a double tyranny of custom from without and blind affections[1] within, they would discern better what it is to favor and uphold the tyrant of a nation. But being slaves within doors, no wonder that they strive so much to have the public state conformably governed to the inward vicious rule by which they govern themselves. For, indeed, none can love freedom heartily but good men; the rest love not freedom but license, which never hath more scope or more indulgence than under tyrants. Hence is it that tyrants are not oft offended, nor stand much in doubt of bad men, as being all naturally servile,[2] but in whom virtue and true worth most is eminent, them they fear in earnest, as by right their masters; against them lies all their hatred and suspicion. Consequently, neither do bad men hate tyrants, but have been always readiest with the falsified names of loyalty and obedience to color over their base compliances.

And although sometimes for shame, and when it comes to their own grievances, of purse especially, they would seem good patriots and side with the better cause, yet (when others for the deliverance of their country, endued with fortitude and heroic virtue[3] to fear nothing but the curse written against those "that do the work of the Lord negligently,"[4] would go on to remove not

Done into English by William Jones (1594), p. 198.

[1] As in *DDD* and *Eikon* Milton begins with an attack on *custom* as opposed to reason and as allied with the passions or *affections within*, which Plato describes (*Rep.* VIII, 582c) as spreading from private life to open the way for tyranny in the state by undermining the moral foundations of liberty. Cf. *PL* XII, 79–90.

[2] The thought, as Allison notes, stems from Aristotle's *Politics* (V, ix, 12), but it had been put by Sallust into the epigram which Milton made the epigram of *Eikon*, and it is parallelled by numerous classical writers who were quoted by Justus Lipsius in *Six Bookes of Politickes* . . .

[3] The words ironically refer to a tract entitled *The Religious and Loyal Protestation, of John Gauden, Dr. in Divinitie: against the Present Declared Purposes and Proceedings of the Army and Others: About the Trying and Destroying our Soveraign Lord the KING* (issued Jan. 5, 1649). There are several later references to this tract. It ends with fulsome praise of Parliament's "Loyalty, sanctified with Piety, and sweetened with Pitty, not foolish and *feminine*, which I would have below you, but *masculine*, Heroick, Truly Christian and Divine."

[4] Jer. xlviii, 10—a warning to Israel not to be

only the calamities and thraldoms of a people but the roots and causes whence they spring) straight these men[5] and sure helpers at need, as if they hated only the miseries but not the mischiefs, after they have juggled and paltered with the world, bandied and borne arms against their king, divested him, disanointed him, nay, cursed him all over in their pulpits and their pamphlets[6] to the engaging of sincere and real men beyond what is possible or honest to retreat from, not only turn revolters from those principles which only could at first move them, but lay the stain of disloyalty and worse on those proceedings which are the necessary consequences of their own former actions; nor disliked by themselves, were they managed to the entire advantages of their own faction;[7] not considering the while that he toward whom they boasted their new fidelity, counted them accessory; and by those statutes and laws which they so impotently brandish against others,[8] would have doomed them to a traitor's death for what they have done already.[9]

'Tis true that most men are apt enough

to civil wars and commotions as a novelty, and for a flash hot and active; but through sloth or inconstancy and weakness of spirit, either fainting ere their own pretenses, though never so just, be half attained, or through an inbred falsehood and wickedness, betray, ofttimes to destruction with themselves, men of noblest temper joined with them for causes whereof they in their rash undertakings were not capable.[10]

If God and a good cause give them victory, the prosecution whereof for the most part inevitably draws after it the alteration of laws, change of government,[11] downfall of princes with their families—then comes the task to those worthies which are the soul of that enterprise, to be sweat and labored out amidst the throng and noises of vulgar and irrational men. Some contesting for privileges, customs, forms, and that old entanglement of iniquity, their gibberish laws,[12] though the badge of their ancient slavery. Others, who have been fiercest against their prince under the notion of a tyrant, and no mean incendiaries of the war against him, when God out of his providence and high disposal hath delivered him into the hand of their brethren,[13] on a sudden and in a new garb of allegiance, which their doings have long since cancelled, they plead for him, pity him, extol him, protest against those that talk of bringing him to the trial of justice, which is the sword of God, superior to all mortal things, in whose hand soever by apparent signs his testified will is to put it.

But certainly, if we consider who and what they are, on a sudden grown so pitiful, we may conclude their pity can be no true and Christian commiseration but either levity and shallowness of mind or else a carnal admiring of that worldly pomp and greatness from whence they see him fallen;

slack in executing God's curses on the Moabites. The reference is Milton's.

[5] *these men:* the Presbyterian faction.

[6] A typical case was Stephen Marshall's. His sermons before Parliament repeatedly asserted its right to take up arms against the King, as did his *Letter* in reply to Royalist claims in 1643, but he was reported to have pled with Cromwell for mercy for Charles on the eve of his execution.

[7] The object of the Presbyterians in forcing Charles to take the Covenant, said Clement Walker in *Anarchia Anglicana, or The History of Independency* (1649), Part II, p. 17, was "to joyn the King to their Interest and Party." Milton may not have known that by the terms of the Engagement of 26 December, 1647, Charles promised the Scottish Commissioners that Presbyterianism should be established for three years, and that Independency in all its branches should be rigidly suppressed. Cf. *Eikon*, Chap. xxviii, n. 30.

[8] Presbyterians like the author of *A Vindication of the Imprisoned and Secluded Members of the House of Commons* (Jan. 23, 1649) stressed (p. 28) Charles's assent at Carisbrooke to "the Lawes they desire," and to Parliament's "choice of Judges and Officers that must administer them." In a speech to the Commons on Dec. 4, 1648, Prynne had set the seal of Presbyterian approval upon this pattern for closing the negotiations with Charles at Carisbrooke.

[9] Prynne ignored Charles's open statement to his friends at Carisbrooke that his concessions there were but pretenses—"merely in order to my escape," and so to a resumption of the war (Trevelyan, *England Under the Stuarts*, p. 238).

[10] Cf. *SA*, 268–75.

[11] The change was soon to be confirmed by the act of the Commons on Feb. 6, 1649, declaring that the House of Lords was "useless and dangerous, and ought to be abolished."

[12] Cf. Milton's contempt for legal jargon in *Prol* VI and *Patrem*, 71–72. Perhaps there is a sympathetic reference here to John Lilburne's Protest on the title page of his *The Legal, Fundamental Liberties of the People of England* (2nd ed., 1649) against the special pleaders who were sanctifying oppressive laws as "the Badges of our Freedom."

[13] Cf. *Eikon*, Chap. xxviii, n. 40.

or rather, lastly, a dissembled and seditious pity feigned of industry to beget new discord. As for mercy, if it be to a tyrant (under which name they themselves have cited him so oft in the hearing of God, of angels, and the holy church assembled, and there charged him with the spilling of more innocent blood by far than ever Nero[14] did) undoubtedly the mercy which they pretend is the mercy of wicked men. And "their mercies," we read, "are cruelties;"[15] hazarding the welfare of a whole nation to have saved one whom so oft they have termed Agag,[16] and vilifying the blood of many Jonathans[17] that have saved Israel; insisting with much niceness[18] on the unnecessariest clause of their covenant[19] wrested, wherein the fear of change and the absurd contradiction of a flattering hostility had hampered them, but not scrupling to give away for compliments to an implacable revenge the heads of many thousand Christians more.

Another sort there is, who (coming in the course of these affairs to have their share in great actions above the form of law or custom, at least to give their voice and approbation) begin to swerve and almost shiver at the majesty and grandeur of some noble deed, as if they were newly entered into a great sin; disputing precedents, forms, and circumstances, when the commonwealth nigh perishes for want of deeds in substance, done with just and faithful expedition. To these I wish better instruction, and virtue equal to their calling; the former of which, that is to say instruction, I shall endeavor, as my duty is, to bestow

on them; and exhort them not to startle[20] from the just and pious resolution of adhering with all their strength and assistance to the present parliament and army in the glorious way wherein justice and victory hath set them—the only warrants[21] through all ages, next under immediate revelation, to exercise supreme power—in those proceedings which hitherto appear equal to what hath been done in any age or nation heretofore justly or magnanimously.

Nor let them be discouraged or deterred by any new apostate scarecrows,[22] who, under show of giving counsel, send out their barking monitories and *mementoes*,[23] empty of aught else but the spleen of a frustrated faction. For how can that pretended counsel be either sound or faithful, when they that give it see not, for madness and vexation of their ends lost, that those statutes and scriptures which both falsely and scandalously they wrest[24] against their friends and associates, would, by sentence of the common adversary, fall first and heaviest upon their own heads. Neither let mild and tender dispositions be foolishly softened from their duty and perseverance with the unmasculine rhetoric[25] of any puling

---

[14] Cf. *Nero* in *Eikon,* Chap. xxviii, n. 23, and *TKM,* n. 200.

[15] Proverbs xii, 10. (Milton's note.)

[16] *Agag* was the Amalekite king whom Samuel "hewed in pieces before the Lord in Gilgal" (I Sam. xv, 33). Replying to the frequent Puritan identification of Charles with Agag, Gauden said in an open letter to General Fairfax, *The Religious and Loyal Protestation,* pleading for the King's life (p. 7): "You know that neither is the King an *Agag* to you, nor you as *Samuel* to him."

[17] Cf. *Jonathan's* almost single-handed victory over the Philistines and his narrow escape from death for innocently breaking his father Saul's vow that no Hebrew should touch food before the complete achievement of the victory (I Sam. xiv, 1-45).

[18] *niceness:* foolish or dishonest quibbling.

[19] Cf. note 138 below and *Eikon,* Chap xxviii, n. 30.

[20] *startle:* "to swerve, deviate from purpose" (*O.E.D.*).

[21] Cf. *Eikon,* Chap. xxviii, n. 40.

[22] The reference is perhaps to Prynne, with his cropped ears, his cheeks with the livid brand SL, for Seditious Libeller.

[23] A glance at *A Briefe Memento to the Present Unparliamentary Junto Touching their present Intentions and Proceedings to Depose and Execute Charles Stewart, their Lawfull KING.* By William Prynne, Esquire (1648).

[24] The reference is probably to the anonymous *Prynn against Prinn.* Or, The Answer of *William Prynne,* Utter Barrester, of *Lincolnes Inne:* To a Pamphlet lately published by *William Prynne,* Esquire, a Member of the House of COMMONS. Intituled *A Briefe Memento* etc. (Jan. 26, 1649). Several passages are cited from Prynne's *The Soveraigne Power of Parliaments & Kingdomes* (1643) to show that he flatly contradicted himself when he said in the *Memento* of a Statute of Henry VI, chaps. 2, 3, 4, "That it is no lesse then high Treason for any man by overt act to compasse or imagine the deposition or death of the King: Adding the word deposition, which is nowhere found in the whole Statute."

[25] Here Allison notes an obvious thrust at the paragraph in Gauden's *Religious . . . Protestation* which is quoted in n. 3 above. Gauden's loyalty to King Charles did not prevent his maintenance of an understanding with some leaders in Parliament and in the army.

priest or chaplain, sent as a friendly letter of advice—for fashion sake in private—and forthwith published by the sender himself that we may know how much of friend there was in it, to cast an odious envy upon them to whom it was pretended to be sent in charity. Nor let any man be deluded by either the ignorance or the notorious hypocrisy and self-repugnance of our dancing divines,[26] who have the conscience and the boldness to come with scripture in their mouths, glossed and fitted for their turns with a double contradictory sense, transforming the sacred verity of God to an idol with two faces, looking at once two several ways; and with the same quotations to charge others, which in the same case they made serve to justify themselves. For while the hope to be made classic and provincial lords[27] led them on, while pluralities greased them thick and deep to the shame and scandal of religion more than all the sects and heresies they exclaim against— then to fight against the king's person, and no less a party of his lords and commons, or to put force upon both the houses, was good, was lawful, was no resisting of superior powers.[28] They only were powers not to be resisted, who countenanced the good and punished the evil.

But now that their censorious domineering is not suffered to be universal, truth and conscience to be freed, tithes and plurali-

ties[29] to be no more, though competent allowance provided and the warm experience of large gifts, and they so good at taking them—yet now to exclude and seize upon impeached members,[30] to bring delinquents without exemption to a fair tribunal by the common national law against murder, is now to be no less than Korah, Dathan, and Abiram.[31] He who but erewhile in the pulpits was a cursed tyrant, an enemy to God and saints, laden with all the innocent blood spilt in three kingdoms, and so to be fought against, is now, though nothing penitent or altered from his first principles, a lawful magistrate, a sovereign lord, the Lord's anointed,[32] not to be touched, though by themselves imprisoned. As if this only were obedience, to preserve the mere useless bulk of his person, and that only in prison not in the field, and to disobey his commands, deny him his dignity and office, everywhere to resist his power but where they think it only surviving in their own faction.

But who in particular is a tyrant cannot be determined in a general discourse, otherwise than by supposition. His particular charge and the sufficient proof of it, must determine that; which I leave to magistrates,[33] at least to the uprighter sort of them and of the people, though in number

26 The reference is to a group headed by Charles's former chaplain, the author of an open letter *To the Right Honourable, the Lord Fairfax, and his Councell of Warre, the Humble Addresse of Henry Hammond* (Jan. 15, 1649), and to the more influential Presbyterian group who issued *A Serious and Faithful Representation of . . . Ministers of the Gospel, within the Province of London (contained in a Letter from Them to the General and his Council of War)* (Jan. 18, 1649) and two following, similar pamphlets. The *Representation* has been edited, with an Introduction, by R. W. K. Hinton (Reading, 1949).

27 The Westminster Assembly provided that the English church should be organized by "provinces," which in turn would be subdivided into "classical assemblies" or "classes," but the organization never became effective. Cf. *Forcers*, 7.

28 "Let every soul be subject unto the higher powers. For . . . the powers that be are ordained of God" (Rom. xiii, 1). This text and the following denunciation of every one who "resisteth the ordinance of God," were strongly affirmed in Calvin's *Institutes* IV, xx, 23, though he also asserted the obligation of inferior magistrates to punish a ruler who abused his power.

29 Cf. Milton's plea in *Hirelings*, p. 863, that England follow the example of Protestants on the Continent and abolish tithes. He felt himself entitled to both Presbyterian and Independent support in his objection to *pluralities*, which had been justified by the bishops as due, in Hooker's words in *Of the Laws of Ecclesiastical Polity* V, lxxxi, 7, "by way of honour to learning, nobility, and authority."

30 On July 6, 1647, Parliament received formal charges from the army against eleven of its members for corresponding with Queen Henrietta Maria. Some of the eleven fled; the others were impeached.

31 Royalist divines often compared the leaders of Parliament to the rebel Levites, *Korah, Dathan,* and *Abiram,* under whom "the earth opened her mouth, and swallowed them up," so that Israel might understand that these men had "provoked the Lord" (Num. xvi, 32 and 30).

32 David's sparing of King Saul's life because he was "the Lord's anointed" (I Sam. xxiv, 10, and xxvi, 11) was seriously urged as a precedent giving kings absolute immunity from physical punishment. Cf. *Eikon*, Chap. xxviii, n. 9; *Def 1* (C.E. VII, 218-20).

33 The *magistrate* in question was the prosecutor in Charles's trial, John Bradshaw, who had justified the formal charge of tyranny in the King's indictment on the ground of the "arbitrary government"

less by many, in whom faction least hath prevailed above the law of nature and right reason,[34] to judge as they find cause. But this I dare own as part of my faith, that if such a one there be, by whose commission whole massacres[35] have been committed on his faithful subjects, his provinces offered to pawn or alienation,[36] as the hire of those whom he had solicited to come in and destroy whole cities and countries; be he king, or tyrant, or emperor, the sword of justice is above him, in whose hand soever is found sufficient power to avenge the effusion and so great a deluge of innocent blood. For if all human power to execute, not accidentally but intendedly, the wrath of God upon evildoers without exception, be of God, then that power, whether ordinary or, if that fail, extraordinary, so executing that intent of God, is lawful and not to be resisted.

But to unfold more at large this whole question, though with all expedient brevity, I shall here set down from first beginning, the original of kings; how and wherefore exalted to that dignity above their brethren; and from thence shall prove that, turning to tyranny, they may be as lawfully deposed and punished as they were at first elected.[37] This I shall do by authorities and reasons, not learnt in corners among schisms and heresies, as our doubling divines are ready to calumniate, but fetched out of the midst of choicest and most authentic learning, and no prohibited authors, nor many heathen, but Mosaical,[38] Christian, orthodoxal, and, which must needs be more convincing to our adversaries, presbyterial.[39]

No man who knows aught, can be so stupid to deny that all men naturally were born free,[40] being the image and resemblance of God himself, and were, by privilege above all the creatures, born to command,[41] and not to obey; and that they lived so, till from the root of Adam's transgression falling among themselves to do wrong and violence, and foreseeing that such courses must needs tend to the destruction of them all, they agreed by common league to bind each other from mutual injury, and jointly to defend themselves against any that gave disturbance or opposition to such agreement. Hence came cities, towns, and commonwealths. And because no faith in all was found sufficiently binding, they saw it needful to ordain some authority that might restrain by force and punishment what was violated against peace and common right.

This authority and power of self-defense and preservation being originally and naturally in every one of them, and unitedly in them all, for ease, for order, and lest each man should be his own partial judge, they communicated and derived either to one whom for the eminence of his wisdom and integrity they chose above the rest, or to more than one whom they thought of equal deserving. The first was called a king,[42] the other, magistrates: not to be their lords and masters (though afterward those names in some places were given voluntarily to such as had been authors of inestimable good to the people), but to be their deputies and commissioners, to execute, by virtue of their entrusted power, that justice which else every man by the bond of nature and of covenant must have executed for himself, and for one another. And to him that shall consider well why among free persons one man by civil right should bear authority and jurisdiction over another, no other end or reason can be imaginable.

which he had "fought to put upon the people" (Muddiman, *Trial*, p. 122).

[34] Cf. *PL* VI, 41, n., and IX, 352.

[35] In *Eikon*, Chap. xii, Milton argued that the "prime author" of the "horrid massacre of English Protestants in *Ireland*" had been the King because he had "hindered the suppressing" of the Irish rebellion (C.E. V, 188–9 and 195).

[36] Charles's attempt to buy off the rebellious Irish in Ulster by dropping claims to wide lands in five counties is interpreted as a kind of bribe in *Eikon*, Chap. xii (C.E. V, 192).

[37] Milton's appeal to ancient precedent for the election of kings was implicit in the resolve of the House of Commons when they asserted their right to bring Charles to trial on the ground that "the People are, under God, the original of all just power."

[38] The tradionally Mosaic books: Genesis to Deuteronomy.

[39] Milton will quote several Presbyterians: cf.

n. 206 below.

[40] Allison quotes this principle from the *Institutes* of Justinian I, ii, 2, as Milton's legal authority, but he was also asserting man's moral freedom on the strength of his creation in God's image. Cf. *PL* VII, 519.

[41] Man is to have "dominion over the fish of the sea, and over the fowl of the air, and over the cattle" (Gen. i, 26).

[42] Milton paraphrases Aristotle's account of the origin of kings in *Politics* III, ix.

These for a while governed well and with much equity decided all things at their own arbitrement, till the temptation of such a power, left absolute in their hands, perverted them at length to injustice and partiality. Then did they who now by trial had found the danger and inconveniences of committing arbitrary power to any, invent laws, either framed or consented to by all, that should confine and limit the authority of whom they chose to govern them: that so man, of whose failing they had proof, might no more rule over them, but law and reason, abstracted as much as might be from personal errors and frailties: while, as the magistrate was set above the people, so the law was set above the magistrate.[43] When this would not serve, but that the law was either not executed, or misapplied, they were constrained from that time, the only remedy left them, to put conditions and take oaths[44] from all kings and magistrates at their first instalment to do imparital justice by law: who, upon those terms and no other, received allegiance from the people, that is to say, bond or covenant to obey them in execution of those laws which they, the people, had themselves made or assented to. And this ofttimes with express warning, that if the king or magistrate proved unfaithful to his trust, the people would be disengaged.

They added also counsellors and parliaments,[45] not to be only at his beck, but, with him or without him, at set times, or at all times when any danger threatened, to have care of the public safety. Therefore saith Claudius Sesell,[46] a French statesman, "The parliament was set as a bridle to the king;" which I instance rather, not because our English lawyers have not said the same long before, but because that French monarchy is granted by all to be a far more absolute than ours. That this and the rest of what hath hitherto been spoken is most true, might be copiously made appear throughout all stories, heathen and Christian; even of those nations where kings and emperors have sought means to abolish all ancient memory of the people's right by their encroachments and usurpations. But I spare long insertions, appealing to the known constitutions of both the latest Christian empires in Europe, the Greek and the German,[47] besides the French, Italian,[48] Arragonian,[49] English, and not least the Scottish[50] histories: not forgetting this only by the way, that William the Norman,[51] though a conqueror, and not unsworn at his coronation, was compelled the second time to take oath[52] at St. Albans' ere the people would be brought to yield obedience.

It being thus manifest that the power of kings and magistrates is nothing else but what is only derivative, transferred, and committed to them in trust from the people to the common good of them all, in whom the power yet remains fundamentally and cannot be taken from them without a viola-

[43] Against extreme assertions of royal prerogative as transcending law (as Robert Filmer declared that it did in *Patriarcha*, xxiv) Milton quoted St. Paul and Plato in *Def 1* (C.E. VII, 166) and added that Aristotle and Cicero concurred.

[44] Cf. *Eikon*, Chap. xxviii, n. 29.

[45] Cf. *Eikon*, Chap. i, notes 4, 5, 8, and 9.

[46] In CB (C.E. XVIII, 185) Milton had transcribed this passage from *La grant monarchie de France composee par missire Claude de Seyssel* (1st ed., Lyons, 1519). Seyssel's works on feudal and civil law and his experience as a councillor of state and as an ambassador from Louis XII of France to Henry VII of England, made him a strong authority.

[47] In *The Six Bookes of a Commonweale*, by Jean Bodin, II, vi, aristocracy is defined in Aristotle's terms as government by the best men. Examples are found in Switzerland and Germany, where the seven electoral princes choose the emperor, and "even the imperiall citties [are] also governed in manner and form of pure Aristocracies" (Richard Knolles' translation, 1606, p. 241).

[48] In Italy—as Zera Fink shows in *The Classical Republicans* (Evanston, 1945), pp. 99 and 110 —the Venetian and Genoese republics were recognized by Bodin as exemplary aristocracies.

[49] In CB (C.E. XVIII, 176) Milton quoted from Guicciardini's *History of Italy* a note on the limited monarchy of Aragon as he had observed it at the court of Ferdinand and Isabella.

[50] Cf. n. 206 below.

[51] In *The Trew Law of Free Monarchies* James I had based his main claim to the crown of England upon his inheritance of it from William the Conqueror. The claim was echoed by many royalists, but challenged by writers like Henry Parker, who, in *Jus Populi* (1644), p. 14, denied that Englishmen lived "in a base thraldome . . . of three Conquests in this Iland, and yet neither of them all was just, or totall; or meerly forcible, without consent preceding, or following."

[52] William's repeated *oaths* in confirmation of the rights of his English subjects are elaborately recorded in George Walker's *Anglo-Tyrannus, Or the Idea of a Norman Monarch, Represented in the parallel Reignes of Henrie the Third and Charles Kings of England* (1650), pp. 50–52. Cf. n. 44 above.

tion of their natural birthright, and seeing that from hence Aristotle, and the best of political writers, have defined a king, him who governs to the good and profit of his people, and not for his own ends[53]—it follows from necessary causes that the titles of sovereign lord, natural lord, and the like, are either arrogancies or flatteries, not admitted by emperors and kings of best note, and disliked by the church both of Jews (Isa. xxvi, 13) and ancient Christians, as appears by Tertullian[54] and others. Although generally the people of Asia, and with them the Jews also, especially since the time they chose a king[55] against the advice and counsel of God, are noted by wise authors much inclinable to slavery.[56]

Secondly, that to say, as is usual, the king hath as good right to his crown and dignity as any man to his inheritance, is to make the subject no better than the king's slave, his chattel, or his possession that may be bought and sold. And doubtless, if hereditary title[57] were sufficiently inquired, the best foundation of it would be found either but in courtesy or convenience.[58] But suppose it to be of right hereditary, what can be more just and legal, if a subject for certain crimes be to forfeit by law from himself and posterity all his inheritance to the king, than that a king, for crimes proportional,[59] should forfeit all his title and inheritance to the people? Unless the peo-

ple must be thought created all for him, he not for them, and they all in one body inferior to him single; which were a kind of treason against the dignity of mankind to affirm.

Thirdly, it follows that to say kings are accountable to none but God, is the overturning of all law and government. For if they may refuse to give account, then all covenants made with them at coronation, all oaths are in vain, and mere mockeries, all laws which they swear to keep, made to no purpose: for if the king fear not God (as how many of them do not?) we hold then our lives and estates by the tenure of his mere grace and mercy, as from a god,[60] not a mortal magistrate—a position that none but court parasites or men besotted would maintain. Aristotle, therefore, whom we commonly allow for one of the best interpreters of nature and morality, writes in the fourth of his *Politics,* chap. x, that "monarchy unaccountable is the worst sort of tyranny, and least of all to be endured by free-born men."[61]

And surely no Christian prince, not drunk with high mind and prouder than those pagan Cæsars that deified themselves, would arrogate so unreasonably above human condition, or derogate so basely from a whole nation of men, his brethren, as if for him only subsisting, and to serve his glory; valuing them in comparison of his own brute will and pleasure no more than so many beasts, or vermin under his feet, not to be reasoned with, but to be trod on; among whom there might be found so many thousand men for wisdom, virtue, nobleness of mind, and all other respects but the fortune of his dignity, far above him. Yet some would persuade us that this absurd opinion was King David's, because in the 51 Psalm he cries out to God, "Against thee only have I sinned";[62] as if David had imagined

---

[53] The words are from *Nicomachean Ethics* VIII, xi, 1. Cf. n. 81 below.

[54] In *On the Crown* (written in 201 A.D.) *Tertullian* ends with a promise of a crown of life for Christ's followers and a tirade against the vanity of all crowns of royalty and victory.

[55] Cf. *Eikon,* Chap. xxvii, n. 19.

[56] The idea that "the Asiatic race is feeble" goes back to Hippocrates in *On Airs, Waters, and Places,* Chap. lxxxvi, and to Aristotle's *Politics* VII, vi. Cf. *Eikon,* Chap. xxvii, n. 9.

[57] Cf. n. 51 above. James I's claim to an absolute right to the crown by inheritance was confirmed by an Act of Parliament at his accession. Even a strong opponent of royal absolutism like Samuel Rutherford held, in *Lex, Rex: the Law and the Prince* (1644), Question X, that the general European practice of inheritance of crowns by primogeniture was sound.

[58] The commonplace was quoted from Seneca's *De Clementia* by the anonymous author of *Satisfaction to some Scruples about the putting of the late King to death* (1649), p. 17: *"Seneca said well, when he said, that Common-wealths were not made for Kings, but Kings for Common-wealths."*

[59] *proportional:* greater (than the crimes of

private men) proportionately as Charles was greater than his subjects.

[60] Cf. n. 32 above. In Robert Weldon's *The Doctrine of the Scriptures* (1648), p. 38, "Gods Donation" is said to make the kings "to whom he imparteth it, . . . to be honoured, as taken in, into the communion of *Elohim."* . . . (i.e. as deities).

[61] Bradshaw quoted this passage, with others from the *Politics,* in his arraignment of King Charles. (Muddiman, *Trial,* p. 116.)

[62] Psalm li, 4. Of the royalist interpretation of this verse John Eliot said in *The Monarchie of Man* that, "Others inferre from the confession made

that to murder Uriah and adulterate his wife had been no sin against his neighbor, whenas that law of Moses was to the king expressly (Deut. xvii) not to think so highly of himself above his brethren.[63] David, therefore, by those words could mean no other than either that the depth of his guiltiness was known to God only, or to so few as had not the will or power to question him, or that the sin against God was greater beyond compare than against Uriah. Whatever his meaning were, any wise man will see that the pathetical words of a psalm can be no certain decision to a point that hath abundantly more certain rules to go by.

How much more rationally spake the heathen king Demophoön, in a tragedy of Euripides,[64] than these interpreters would put upon king David! "I rule not my people by tyranny, as if they were barbarians, but am myself liable, if I do unjustly, to suffer justly." Not unlike was the speech of Trajan,[65] the worthy emperor, to one whom he made general of his prætorian forces: "Take this drawn sword," saith he, "to use for me if I reign well; if not, to use against me." Thus Dion relates. And not Trajan only, but Theodosius the younger,[66] a Christian emperor and one of the best,

caused it to be enacted as a rule undeniable and fit to be acknowledged by all kings and emperors, that a prince is bound to the laws; that on the authority of law the authority of a prince depends, and to the laws ought submit. Which edict of his remains yet in the Code of Justinian[67] (Bk. I, title 24) as a sacred constitution to all the succeeding emperors. How then can any king in Europe maintain and write himself accountable to none but God, when emperors in their own imperial statutes have written and decreed themselves accountable to law? And indeed where such account is not feared, he that bids a man reign over him above law, may bid as well a savage beast.

It follows, lastly, that since the king or magistrate holds his authority of the people, both originally and naturally for their good in the first place, and not his own, then may the people, as oft as they shall judge it for the best, either choose him or reject him, retain him or depose him, though no tyrant, merely by the liberty and right of freeborn men to be governed as seems to them best. This, though it cannot but stand with plain reason, shall be made good also by Scripture (Deut. xvii, 14): "When thou art come into the land which the Lord thy God giveth thee, and shalt say, I will set a king over me, like as all the nations about me."[68] These words confirm us that the right of choosing, yea of changing their own government, is by the grant of God himself in the people. And therefore when they desire a king, though then under another form of government and though their changing dis-

by *David,* against thee only have I sinned; that princes offend not men, and therefore have a libertie . . . to doe what acts they please, wch Judgem^ts wee shall rather pittie then contest" (Grosart Ed., 1879. Vol. II, 46).

63 The context of Deut. xvii, 20, justifies Henry Parker's interpretation in *Jus Populi,* p. 19: "As for the Prince, the Law of God is most expresse in that is not to make his advancement any ground of lifting up his heart above his brethren."

64 Cf. *Def I* (C.E. VII, 310), where Demophoön is quoted as disclaiming all tyrannical power in Euripides' *Heraclidae,* 418–21.

65 The story in Dio Cassius' *Roman History* LXVIII, xvi, was interpreted by John Goodwin in *Right and Might Well Met* (Jan. 2, 1649), pp. 6–7, as evident proof "that whensoever a *King,* or other Supreame authoritie, creates an inferiour, they invest it with a legitimacy of magisteriall power to *punish* themselves also."

66 *Theodosius II* (401–450 A.D.), Eastern Emperor, was often linked with *Trajan* as George Buchanan said in his *History of Scotland* (London, 1690), Book XX, p. 268, that he was by the Earl of Morton in a speech to the Scottish lords at Stirling: "Theodosius, a good Emperour in bad Times, would have it left recorded amongst his Sanctions and Laws, as a Speech worthy of an Emperur, yea, greater than his Empire it self, to confess, 'That he was inferiour to the Laws.'"

67 English royalists deprecated the restrictions of the *Code of Justinian* (483–565 A.D.) upon royal authority and agreed with James I in *A Remonstrance for the Rights of Kings (The Political Works of James I,* ed. by C. M. McIlwain. Cambridge, Mass., 1918; p. 227) that "Justinian's law" made nothing to the purpose. "For it is our free and voluntary confession, that a Christian Prince is to have speciall care of the Lawes."

68 Deut. xvii, 14, had been interpreted adversely to popular rights by Grotius in *De Jure Belli et Pacis* II, iv, 3. In reply Samuel Rutherford said in *Lex, Rex* (Question xviii. Cf. n. 57 above.) that the royal authority was simply "either a *power* to rule according to *Gods* law, as he is commanded, Deut. 17, and this is the very office or official power which the *King of Kings* hath given to all *Kings* under him: . . . or this is a power to doe ill, and tyrannise over God's people: but this is . . . the character of a Tyrant, and is not from God. . . ."

pleased him, yet he that was himself their king and rejected by them would not be a hindrance to what they intended further than by persuasion, but that they might do therein as they saw good (I Sam. viii),[69] only he reserved to himself the nomination of who should reign over them. Neither did that exempt the king, as if he were to God only accountable, though by his especial command anointed. Therefore "David first made a covenant with the elders of Israel, and so was by them anointed king" (II Sam. v, 3; I Chron. xi). And Jehoiada[70] the priest, making Jehoash king, made a covenant between him and the people (II Kings xi, 17). Therefore when Roboam,[71] at his coming to the crown, rejected those conditions which the Israelites brought him, hear what they answer him: "What portion have we in David, or inheritance in the son of Jesse? See to thine own house, David." And for the like conditions not performed, all Israel before that time deposed Samuel, not for his own default, but for the misgovernment of his sons.[72]

But some will say to both these examples, it was evilly done. I answer that not the latter, because it was expressly allowed them in the law to set up a king if they pleased; and God himself joined with them in the work, though in some sort it was at that time displeasing to him, in respect of old Samuel, who had governed them uprightly. As Livy praises the Romans, who took occasion from Tarquinius, a wicked prince, to gain their liberty, which to have extorted, saith he, from Numa,[73] or any of the good kings before, had not been seasonable. Nor was it in the former example done unlawfully; for when Roboam had prepared a huge army to reduce the Israelites, he was forbidden by the prophet (I Kings xii, 24): "Thus saith the Lord, ye shall not go up, nor fight against your brethren, for this thing is from me." He calls them their brethren, not rebels, and forbids to be proceeded against them, owning the thing himself, not by single providence but by approbation, and that not only of the act, as in the former example, but of the fit season also. He had not otherwise forbid to molest them. And those grave and wise counsellors whom Rehoboam first advised with, spake no such thing as our old gray-headed flatterers now are wont: —"Stand upon your birthright, scorn to capitulate; you hold of God, not of them." For they knew no such matter, unless conditionally, but gave him politic counsel as in a civil transaction.

Therefore kingdom and magistracy, whether supreme or subordinate, is without difference called "a human ordinance" (I Pet. ii, 13, &c.),[74] which we are there taught is the will of God we should alike submit to, so far as for the punishment of evildoers and the encouragement of them that do well. "Submit," saith he, "as free men." But to any civil power unaccountable, unquestionable, and not to be resisted, no, not in wickedness and violent actions, how can we submit as free men? "There is no power but of God," saith Paul (Rom. xiii),[75] as much as to say God put it into

---

[69] Cf. n. 55 above.

[70] The concern of Protestant interpreters of II Kings xi, 17, had been to show—as David Pareus did in his Commentary on Romans xiii—that Jehoiada's power to put Jehoash on the throne was not due to his priesthood but to his position as the guardian of the young prince. Cf. n. 205 below.

[71] In The Original and End of Civil Power (1649), p. 27, Anthony Ascham made the traditional link between the dethroned Roman tyrant, Tarquin, and Rehoboam, who vowed to whip his subjects with scorpions: "But what follows: what portion (say the people) have we in the son of Jesse? To your tents, O Israel, &c. And so they shook off Rehoboam's tyrannical oath." E. Sirluck —in HLQ, XIX (1956), 301–5—collects convincing evidence that one of the "seditious Pamphlets" against which Charles protested to Parliament on March 12, 1642, was entitled To Your Tents, O Israel, and that it was actually thrown into the King's coach as he drove to the Guildhall on Jan. 5, 1642, in pursuit of the five members of the House of Commons whom he had tried to arrest, in violation of Parliament's privileges, on the preceding day. Cf. Eikon, Chap. xxvii, notes 2 and 17.

[72] Cf. the story in I Sam. viii, 5, and also in Eikon, Chap. xxviii, n. 19.

[73] The second book of Livy's Roman History opens with the story of Tarquin's successor, the good king Numa, who was guided by the nymph Egeria in founding Roman polity and religious worship. Cf. CG, n. 24.

[74] I Peter ii, 13, was constantly bracketed with Rom. xiii, 1–2, as it was in Filmer's Patriarcha (Ed. by Laslett, Oxford, 1949), p. 101, to enjoin unquestioning obedience to "every ordinance of man for the Lord's sake, whether it be to the King as supreme, or unto governours."

[75] Threatening God's vengeance on England if King Charles should be executed, Prynne quoted Rom. xiii, 1–2. in his Declaration of Jan. 15, 1649,

man's heart to find out that way at first for common peace and preservation, approving the exercise thereof; else it contradicts Peter, who calls the same authority an ordinance of man. It must be also understood of lawful and just power, else we read of great power in the affairs and kingdoms of the world permitted to the devil: for saith he to Christ (Luke iv, 6), "All this power will I give thee and the glory of them, for it is delivered to me, and to whomsoever I will, I give it:" neither did he lie, or Christ gainsay what he affirmed; for in the thirteenth of the Revelation, we read how the dragon gave to the beast "his power, his seat, and great authority:" which beast so authorized most expound to be the tyrannical powers and kingdoms of the earth.[76] Therefore Saint Paul in the forecited chapter tells us that such magistrates he means as are not a terror to the good, but to the evil; such as bear not the sword in vain, but to punish offenders and to encourage the good.[77]

If such only be mentioned here as powers to be obeyed, and our submission to them only required, then doubtless those powers that do the contrary are no powers ordained of God, and by consequence no obligation laid upon us to obey or not to resist them. And it may be well observed that both these apostles, whenever they give this precept, express it in terms not concrete but abstract,[78] as logicians are wont to speak; that is, they mention the ordinance, the power, the authority, before the persons that execute it; and what that power is, lest we should be deceived, they describe exactly. So that if the power be not such or the person execute not such power, neither the one nor the other is of God, but of the

devil and by consequence to be resisted. From this exposition Chrysostom[79] also on the same place, dissents not, explaining that these words were not written in behalf of a tyrant. And this is verified by David, himself a king, and likeliest to be author of the Psalm (xciv. 20) which saith, "Shall the throne of iniquity have fellowship with thee?" And it were worth the knowing, since kings in these days, and that by scripture, boast the justness of their title by holding it immediately of God,[80] yet cannot show the time when God ever set on the throne them or their forefathers, but only when the people chose them; why by the same reason, since God ascribes as oft to himself the casting down of princes from the throne, it should not be thought as lawful and as much from God when none are seen to do it but the people and that for just causes. For if it needs must be a sin in them to depose, it may as likely be a sin to have elected. And contrary, if the people's act in election be pleaded by a king as the act of God and the most just title to enthrone him, why may not the people's act of rejection be as well pleaded by the people as the act of God and the most just reason to depose him? So that we see the title and just right of reigning or deposing, in reference to God, is found in scripture to be all one; visible only in the people, and depending merely upon justice and demerit. Thus far hath been considered briefly the power of kings and magistrates, how it was and is originally the people's, and by them conferred in trust only to be employed to the common peace and benefit; with liberty therefore and right remaining in them to reassume it to themselves, if by kings or magistrates it be abused, or to dispose of it by any alteration as they shall judge most conducing to the public good.

We may from hence with more ease and force of argument determine what a tyrant is, and what the people may do against him. A tyrant, whether by wrong or by right

and said: "Ruminate upon it, and then be wise, both for your soules good, and the welfare of England" (p. 3).

[76] Protestant thought identified the kings of Rev. xiii, who gave their power to the beast with seven heads, as the Roman Catholic kings in contemporary Europe. Cf. Eikon, Chap. xxviii, notes 37-39.

[77] Rom. xiii, 4.

[78] Milton seems to follow John Goodwin, who had recalled in closing his Might and Right Well Met (Cf. n. 65 above) that Calvin had noted that St. Paul "doth not say, 'let every soule be subject to the higher Magistrates,' but, 'to the higher powers.' Nor doth he say, 'There is no' Magistrate, but of God; but, 'there is no power but of God.' "

[79] Royalist writers were fond of recalling that St. John Chrysostom's Homily XXIII had been cited by Grotius in De Jure Belli et Pacis (2nd Ed., Amsterdam, 1631), p. 74, to corroborate Rom. xiii, 1-2, as enjoining submission to kings.

[80] The principle that "Royalty is an Honour, wherein, Kings are stated immediately from God," was flatly asserted by Roger Maynwaring in Religion and Allegiance (1627), p. 13.

coming to the crown, is he who, regarding neither law nor the common good, reigns only for himself and his faction: thus St. Basil,[81] among others, defines him. And because his power is great, his will boundless and exorbitant, the fulfilling whereof is for the most part accompanied with innumerable wrongs and oppressions of the people, murders, massacres, rapes, adulteries, desolation, and subversion of cities and whole provinces—look, how great a good and happiness a just king is, so great a mischief is a tyrant; as he the public father of his country, so this the common enemy. Against whom what the people lawfully may do, as against a common pest and destroyer of mankind, I suppose no man of clear judgment need go further to be guided than by the very principles of nature in him.[82]

But because it is the vulgar folly of men to desert their own reason and shutting their eyes to think they see best with other men's, I shall show by such examples as ought to have most weight with us, what hath been done in this case heretofore. The Greeks and Romans, as their prime authors witness, held it not only lawful, but a glorious and heroic deed rewarded publicly with statues and garlands,[83] to kill an infamous tyrant at any time without trial: and but reason, that he who trod down all law, should not be vouchsafed the benefit of law. Insomuch that Seneca the tragedian brings in Hercules,[84] the grand suppressor of tyrants, thus speaking:

—— Victima haud ulla amplior
Potest, magisque opima mactari Jovi
Quam rex iniquus ——————

—— There can be slain
No sacrifice to God more acceptable
Than an unjust and wicked king ——.

But of these I name no more, lest it be objected they were heathen; and come to produce another sort of men that had the knowledge of true religion. Among the Jews this custom of tyrant-killing was not unusual. First, Ehud,[85] a man whom God had raised to deliver Israel from Eglon king of Moab who had conquered and ruled over them eighteen years, being sent to him as an ambassador with a present, slew him in his own house. But he was a foreign prince, an enemy, and Ehud besides had special warrant from God. To the first I answer, it imports not whether foreign or native. For no prince so native but professes to hold by law; which when he himself overturns, breaking all the covenants and oaths that gave him title to his dignity and were the bond and alliance between him and his people, what differs he from an outlandish king or from an enemy? For look, how much right the king of Spain hath to govern us at all, so much right hath the king of England to govern us tyrannically. If he, though not bound to us by any league, coming from Spain in person to subdue us or to destroy us, might lawfully by the people of England either be slain in fight or put to death in captivity, what hath a native king to plead, bound by so many covenants, benefits, and honors to the welfare of his people; why he (through the contempt of all laws and parliaments, the only tie of our obedience to him, for his own will's sake and a boasted prerogative[86]

[81] The definition of a tyrant by *St. Basil* the *Great,* Bishop of Cappodocia (370–379 A.D.), stands at the head of Milton's entries under that caption in CB (C.E. XVIII, 181). As he implies, it rests on Aristotle's *Politics.* Cf. n. 53 above.
[82] The spirit of this indictment of tyrants resembles their violent indictments in the name of reason and the Law of *Nature* which, as A. S. P. Woodhouse observes in *Puritanism and Liberty* (London, 1938), pp. 28–30, were characteristic of the debates in the Army Council before the decision to arrest and try King Charles in the autumn of 1648. Cf. n. 220 below.
[83] Bronze *statues* were erected in 509 B.C. in the temple of Ares in Athens in honor of Harmodius and Aristogeiton, in memory of their assassination of Hipparchus, the brother of the tyrant Hippias.
[84] In the *Hercules Furens* of Seneca, *Hercules*

chants these lines as he returns in triumph from slaying the tyrant Lycus.
[85] After "the children of Israel had served Eglon King of Moab eighteen years, . . . the Lord raised them up a deliverer, Ehud, the son of Gera, a Benjamite" (Judg. iii, 14–16). Royalists found *Ehud's* case awkward. Even Grotius felt it necessary to warn against interpreting God's commands to Ehud to kill a foreign usurper as a precedent for the assassination of a king (*De Jure Belli et Pacis* I, iv, 7; p. 88). Cf. n. 75 above.
[86] The *prerogative* of the crown, which vastly increased under the Tudors, and which Tanner (*Conflicts,* pp. 18–19) virtually identifies with the unquestionable "sovereignty" of the crown, was viewed by believers in limited monarchy as it was in Rutherford's *Lex, Rex,* Question XIX: "Whether or no the King be in dignity and power above the people." For some purposes Rutherford set the king above individual subjects, but regarded him

unaccountable) after seven years' warring and destroying of his best subjects, overcome and yielded prisoner,[87] should think to scape unquestionable as a thing divine, in respect of whom so many thousand Christians destroyed should lie unaccounted for, polluting with their slaughtered carcasses all the land over, and crying for vengeance against the living that should have righted them? Who knows not that there is a mutual bond of amity and brotherhood between man and man over all the world, neither is it the English sea that can sever us from that duty and relation? A straiter bond yet there is between fellow-subjects, neighbors, and friends. But when any of these do one to another so as hostility could do no worse, what doth the law decree less against them than open enemies and invaders? Or if the law be not present or too weak, what doth it warrant us to less than single defense or civil war? And from that time forward the law of civil defensive war differs nothing from the law of foreign hostility. Nor is it distance of place that makes enmity, but enmity that makes distance. He, therefore, that keeps peace with me, near or remote, of whatsoever nation, is to me, as far as all civil and human offices, an Englishman and a neighbor. But if an Englishman, forgetting all laws, human, civil, and religious, offend against life and liberty, to him offended and to the law in his behalf, though born in the same womb, he is no better than a Turk, a Saracen, a heathen.

This is gospel and this was ever law among equals; how much rather then in force against any king whatever, who in respect of the people is confessed inferior and not equal: to distinguish, therefore, of a tyrant by outlandish, or domestic, is a weak evasion. To the second, that he was an enemy, I answer, "What tyrant is not?" Yet Eglon by the Jews had been acknowledged as their sovereign. They had served him eighteen years, as long almost as we

our William the Conqueror,[88] in all which time he could not be so unwise a statesman but to have taken of them oaths of fealty and allegiance, by which they made themselves his proper subjects, as their homage and present sent by Ehud testified. To the third, that he had special warrant to kill Eglon in that manner, it cannot be granted because not expressed. It is plain that he was raised by God to be a deliverer, and went on just principles such as were then and ever held allowable to deal so by a tyrant that could no otherwise be dealt with.

Neither did Samuel, though a prophet, with his own hand abstain from Agag,[89] a foreign enemy no doubt, but mark the reason: "As thy sword hath made women childless,"[90] a cause that by the sentence of law itself nullifies all relations. And as the law is between brother and brother, father and son, master and servant, wherefore not between king, or rather tyrant, and people? And whereas Jehu[91] had special command to slay Jehoram,[92] a successive and hereditary tyrant, it seems not the less imitable for that. For where a thing grounded so much on natural, reason hath the addition of a command from God, what does it but establish the lawfulness of such an act? Nor is it likely that God, who had so many ways of punishing the house of Ahab, would have sent a subject against his prince, if the fact in itself, as done to a tyrant, had been of bad example. And if David[93] refused to lift his hand against the Lord's anointed,[94] the matter between them was not tyranny, but private enmity,[95] and David, as a private person, had been his own revenger, not so much the people's:

---

[88] *William* reigned from 1066 to 1087. Cf. notes 50-51 above.

[89] Cf. n. 16 above.

[90] I Sam. xv, 33.

[91] *Jehu* was a mere captain when he became king of Israel and executed the prophet's order to "smite the house of Ahab thy master" (II Kings ix, 7).

[92] After slaying Ahab, Jehu killed his son *Jehoram* (II Kings ix, 24).

[93] Cf. notes 32 above and 178 below.

[94] Cf. *Eikon*, Chap. xxviii, n. 9.

[95] This point is prominent in John Sadler's *Rights of the Kingdom* (Jan. 22, 1649), p. 4. In answer to the argument for non-resistance to royal injustice from David's example, Sadler said "that it was only a *Private Quarrell* of *Saul* to *David*: who yet did not scruple, at Defensive Armes, in his own Cause." Cf. *Eikon*, Chap. v, n. 3.

---

as always inferior to his people collectively. Cf. *Eikon*, Chap. xxvii, n. 8.

[87] In May, 1646, Charles gave himself up to the Scottish commanders, who held him prisoner until Jan., 1647, when they made terms with Parliament whereby he passed under its control and began his confinement at Holmby House in Northamptonshire.

but when any tyrant at this day can show to be the Lord's anointed, the only mentioned reason why David withheld his hand, he may then, but not till then, presume on the same privilege.

We may pass, therefore, hence to Christian times. And first, our Savior himself, how much he favored tyrants and how much intended they should be found or honored among Christians, declares his mind not obscurely; accounting their absolute authority no better than Gentilism, yea, though they flourished it over with the splendid name of benefactors;[96] charging those that would be his disciples to usurp no such dominion; but that they who were to be of most authority among them, should esteem themselves ministers and servants to the public. Matt. xx, 25, "The princes of the Gentiles exercise lordship over them," and Mark x, 42, "They that seem to rule," saith he, either slighting or accounting them no lawful rulers; "but ye shall not be so, but the greatest among you shall be your servant." And although he himself were the meekest and came on earth to be so, yet to a tyrant we hear him not vouchsafe an humble word but, "Tell that fox," Luke xiii.[97] So far we ought to be from thinking that Christ and his gospel should be made a sanctuary for tyrants from justice, to whom his law before never gave such protection. And wherefore did his mother, the Virgin Mary,[98] give such praise to God in her prophetic song, that he had now by the coming of Christ cut down dynastas[99] or proud monarchs from the throne, if the church, when God manifests his power in them to do so, should rather choose all misery and vassalage to serve them, and let them still sit on their potent seats to be adored for doing mischief?

Surely it is not for nothing that tyrants by a kind of natural instinct both hate and fear none more than the true church and saints of God,[100] as the most dangerous enemies and subverters of monarchy, though indeed of tyranny. Hath not this been the perpetual cry of courtiers and courtprelates? Whereof no likelier cause can be alleged but that they well discerned the mind and principles of most devout and zealous men, and indeed the very discipline of church, tending to the dissolution of all tyranny. No marvel then if since the faith of Christ received, in purer or impurer times, to depose a king and put him to death for tyranny hath been accounted so just and requisite that neighbor kings have both upheld and taken part with subjects in the action. And Ludovicus Pius,[101] himself an emperor, and son of Charles the Great, being made judge (du Haillan[102] is my author) between Milegast, king of the Vultzes, and his subjects, who had deposed him, gave his verdict for the subjects and for him whom they had chosen in his room. Note here that the right of electing whom they please is, by the impartial testimony of an emperor, in the people: for, said he, "A just prince ought to be preferred before an unjust, and the end of government before the prerogative."[103] And Constantinus Leo,[104] another emperor, in the Byzantine Laws saith, "That the end of a king is for the general good, which he not performing, is but the counterfeit of a king."

And to prove that some of our own monarchs have acknowledged that their

---

[96] "They that exercise authority upon them are called benefactors" (Luke xxii, 25).

[97] Christ's reply to the Pharisees when they told him that King Herod would kill him (Luke xiii, 32).

[98] A reference to the Magnificat: "He hath put down the mighty from their seats, and exalted them of low degree."

[99] dynastas—the Greek accusative case seems to give Milton this form of the word. Its connotation is like Hardy's title, The Dynasts.

[100] The saints are the foes of tyranny, but not of monarchy. Cf. n. 2 above and Eikon, Chap. xxviii, n. 36.

[101] Louis the Pious, Holy Roman Emperor, 814–840 A.D.

[102] Bernard de Girard, seigneur du Haillan (1535–1610), historiographer to Charles IX and Henri III, wrote the Histoire de France which Milton quoted repeatedly from the first folio edition (Paris, 1576) in CB. Du Haillan records the rejection of Milegast's claim to rule the Vultzes by the Emperor Louis, in a great gathering of the Bohemians, Moravians, and Pannonians in Rouen, on the ground that he had been governing too insolently (trop insolement, p. 248). Cf. CB (C.E. XVIII, 182).

[103] CB (C.E. XVIII, 175) gives the reference to du Haillan's Histoire de France, Book XIII, p. 719.

[104] Milton quotes the Eclogue, or compendium of the laws of Justinian which Constantinus Leo issued in 740 A.D., as he found it in Juri Graeco-Romani tam Canonici quam Civilis Tomi duo of Johannes Leunclavius (Frankfurt, 1596), Tome II, p. 83. Cf. CB (C.E. XVIII, 174).

high office exempted them not from punishment, they had the sword of St. Edward[105] borne before them by an officer, who was called earl of the palace, even at the times of their highest pomp and solemnities, to mind them, saith Matthew Paris, the best of our historians, that if they erred, the sword had power to restrain them. And what restraint the sword comes to at length, having both edge and point, if any sceptic will doubt, let him feel. It is also affirmed from diligent search made in our ancient books of law[106] that the peers and barons of England had a legal right to judge the king, which was the cause most likely (for it could be no slight cause) that they were called his peers or equals.[107] This, however, may stand immovable, so long as man hath to deal with no better than man; that if our law judge all men to the lowest by their peers,[108] it should in all equity ascend also and judge the highest.

And so much I find both in our own and foreign story, that dukes, earls, and marquises[109] were at first not hereditary, not empty and vain titles, but names of trust and office; and with the office ceasing, as induces me to be of opinion that every worthy man in parliament (for the word baron[110] imports no more) might for the public good be thought a fit peer and judge of the king, without regard had to petty caveats[111] and circumstances, the chief impediment in high affairs, and ever stood upon most by circumstantial men. Whence doubtless our ancestors, who were not ignorant with what rights either nature or ancient constitution had endowed them, when oaths both at coronation and renewed in parliament would not serve, thought it no way illegal to depose and put to death their tyrannous kings. Insomuch that the parliament drew up a charge against Richard the Second,[112] and the commons requested to have judgment decreed against him that the realm might not be endangered. And Peter Martyr,[113] a divine of foremost rank, on the third of Judges, approves their doings. Sir Thomas Smith also,[114] a protestant and a statesman, in his *Commonwealth of England,* putting the question whether it be lawful to rise against a tyrant, answers that the vulgar judge of it according to the event and the learned according to the purpose of them that do it.

But far before those days, Gildas,[115] the

---

[105] By the laws of Edward the Confessor—as Milton recalled in *Def. 1* (C.E. VII, 440)—an English king who failed in his duty was not to retain so much as the name of a king. And he added that *the sword of King Edward,* called Curtano, which was borne by the Earl of Chester at the wedding of Henry III, was "'a token,' says Matthew Paris, 'that he has authority by law to punish the king if he will not do his duty.'"

[106] The reference is to the work which was translated by William Hughes in 1646 under the title *The Booke called The Mirrour of Justices* from the original *La Somme appelle Miroir des Justices,* which is described by F. W. Maitland in his Introduction to W. J. Whittaker's edition of the translation for the Camden Society (1895) as probably having been written by one of Edward I's judges, Andrew Horn, in his "fantastic and irresponsible youth.' It declares (Whittaker's Ed., p. 7) that the king "should have companions to hear and determine in the parliaments all the writs and plaints concerning wrongs done by the king, the queen, their children, and their special ministers." Cf. *Eikon,* Chap. v, n. 3, and *Def 1* (C.E. 447).

[107] "Dukes, counts, Marquises etc. were not hereditary at first, but only places of government, and office in the time of Charles the great," wrote Milton in CB (C E. XVIII, 195), citing Girard du Haillan. He was arguing from the tradition that the twelve *peers* of France were the Emperor's *equals* before the law.

[108] A reference to the right of every subject in English common law to be judged by his peers.

[109] In *Peace* (C.E. VI, 253) Milton declared that in all nations councils "consisting of whomsoever chosen and assembled for the public good,"

had existed "before . . . such a thing as a titular marquis had either name or being in the world."

[110] The title of *baron,* said Milton in *Def 1* (C.E. VII, 423 and 447) had been applied to all members of the House of Commons, all of whom had been treated as peers of the realm.

[111] *caveats:* processes "in court to suspend proceedings," *O.E.D.*

[112] In Holinshed's *Chronicles of England* Richard II (1377-1399) is so treated as to justify Milton's description of him in CB (C.E. XVIII, 182) as "not only deposed by Parliament, but sute made by the Commons that he might have judgment decreed against him to avoid further mischief in the realm." Cf. *Def 1* (C.E. VII, 465).

[113] The discussion of the election and deposition by the Reformer, *Peter Martyr* (1500-1562) is summarized in CB (C.E. XVIII, 182).

[114] This paraphrase of the opening pages of Sir Thomas Smith's *The Commonwealth of England* (1583) resembles that in CB (C.E. XVIII, 176). In contrast with tyrants, Smith describes a king as a ruler who "doth administer the commonwealth by the laws of the same."

[115] Milton seems to have gone to his CB (C.E. XVIII, 198) for this description of Alcuin as "the wisest of the Britons" in the *Fall of Britain* (*Liber Querulus de Excidio Britanniae*) of Gildas

most ancient of all our historians, speaking of those times wherein the Roman empire decaying, quitted and relinquished what right they had by conquest to this island and resigned it all into the people's hands, testifies that the people thus reinvested with their own original right, about the year 446, both elected them kings whom they thought best (the first Christian British kings that ever reigned here since the Romans) and by the same right, when they apprehended cause, usually deposed and put them to death.[116] This is the most fundamental and ancient tenure that any king of England can produce or pretend to, in comparison of which all other titles and pleas are but of yesterday. If any object that Gildas condemns the Britons for so doing, the answer is as ready—that he condemns them no more for so doing than he did before for choosing such; for, saith he, "They anointed them kings not of God, but such as were more bloody than the rest." Next, he condemns them not at all for deposing or putting them to death, but for doing it over hastily without trial or well examining the cause, and for electing others worse in their room.

Thus we have here both domestic and most ancient examples that the people of Britain have deposed and put to death their kings in those primitive Christian times. And to couple reason with example, if the church in all ages, primitive, Romish, or protestant, held it ever no less their duty than the power of their keys,[117] though without express warrant of scripture, to bring indifferently both king and peasant under the utmost rigor of their canons and censures ecclesiastical, even to the smiting him with a final excommunion[118] if he persist impenitent; what hinders but that the temporal law both may and ought, though without a special text or precedent, extend with like indifference the civil sword to the cutting off without exemption him that capitally offends, seeing that justice and religion are from the same God, and works of justice ofttimes more acceptable? Yet because that some lately, with the tongues and arguments of malignant backsliders, have written that the proceedings now in parliament against the king are without precedent from any protestant state or kingdom, the examples which follow shall be all protestant, and chiefly presbyterian.[119]

In the year 1546, the Duke of Saxony, Landgrave of Hesse, and the whole protestant league, raised open war against Charles the Fifth, their emperor, sent him a defiance, renounced all faith and allegiance towards him, and debated long in council whether they should give him so much as the title of Cæsar (Sleidan, Bk. XVII).[120] Let all men judge what this wanted of deposing or killing but the power to do it.

In the year 1559, the Scots protestants claiming promise of their queen-regent for liberty of conscience, she answering that promises were not to be claimed of princes beyond what was commodious for them to grant, told her to her face in the parliament then at Stirling that if it were so, they renounced their obedience; and soon after betook them to arms (Buchanan, *Hist.*, Bk. XVI).[121] Certainly, when allegiance is re-

excommunicate offenders against ecclesiastical discipline.

[119] Quoting this passage from *TKM*, John Goodwin said in *The Obstructours of Justice* (1649), pp. 70–71, that the Presbyterians could not plausibly deny that "there is no Protestant Church from the first Waldenses of Lyons and Languedoc to this day, but have in a round made war against a Tyrant in defense of Religion and civil liberty, and maintain'd it lawfull."

[120] Johann Philippson (1506–1556), better known as *Sleidan*, represented several German cities at the Council of Trent and was France's ambassador at the courts of Henry VIII and Edward VI. While he was in England he wrote his *State of Religion and Public Affairs* (De statu religionis et reipublicae, Carolo V Caesare, Commentarii XXV libris comprehensi.* Strassbourg, 1555), from which Milton quotes again in *TKM* (see n. 194) and repeatedly in CB.

[121] This account of the challenge of the Queen Regent, Mary of Lorraine, widow of James V of

(516–570). It had been published in the original Latin by Polydore Virgil in 1525, and in English translation in 1638.

[116] In *Def 1* (C.E. VII, 437) Milton presents the seamy side of Gildas' account of the lawless violence of the Britons in making and slaying their kings.

[117] "The administration of church discipline," said Milton in *CD* (C.E. XVI, 326), referring to the claims which all churches in the seventeenth century more or less asserted in consequence of Christ's charge to Peter (Matt. xvi, 19), "is called the power of the keys."

[118] It was an "unenthusiastic Parliament," says R. W. Tawney (*Religion,* p. 214), which passed the Act permitting the English Presbyterians to

nounced, that very hour the king or queen is in effect deposed.

In the year 1564, John Knox,[122] a most famous divine and the reformer of Scotland to the presbyterian discipline, at a general assembly maintained openly in a dispute against Lethington[123] the secretary of state that subjects might and ought execute God's judgments upon their king; that the fact of Jehu and others against their king, having the ground of God's ordinary command to put such and such offenders to death, was not extraordinary, but to be imitated of all that preferred the honor of God to the affection of flesh and wicked princes; that kings, if they offend, have no privilege to be exempted from the punishments of law more than any other subject: so that if the king be a murderer, adulterer, or idolater, he should suffer, not as a king, but as an offender; and this position he repeats again and again before them. Answerable was the opinion of John Craig,[124] another learned divine, and that laws made by the tyranny of princes or the negligence of people, their posterity might abrogate and reform all things according to the original institution of commonwealths. And Knox being commanded by the nobility to write to Calvin and other learned men for their judgment in that question, refused,

alleging that both himself was fully resolved in conscience and had heard their judgments and had the same opinion under handwriting of many the most godly and most learned that he knew in Europe; that if he should move the question to them again, what should he do but show his own forgetfulness or inconstancy? All this is far more largely in the *Ecclesiastic history of Scotland* (Bk. IV),[125] with many other passages to this effect all the book over, set out with diligence by Scotchmen of best repute among them at the beginning of these troubles, as if they labored to inform us what we were to do and what they intended upon the like occasion.

And to let the world know that the whole church and protestant state of Scotland in those purest times of reformation were of the same belief, three years after, they met in the field Mary their lawful and hereditary queen, took her prisoner yielding before fight, kept her in prison, and the same year deposed her (Buchanan, *Hist.*, Bk. XVIII).[126]

And four years after that, the Scots, in justification of their deposing Queen Mary, sent ambassadors[127] to Queen Elizabeth and in a written declaration alleged that they had used towards her more lenity than she deserved; that their ancestors had heretofore punished their kings by death or banishment; that the Scots were a free nation, made king whom they freely chose, and with the same freedom unkinged him if they saw cause, by right of ancient laws and ceremonies yet remaining and old customs yet among the Highlanders in choosing the head of their clans or families; all which, with many other arguments, bore witness that regal power was nothing else

Scotland and mother of Mary, Queen of Scots, is taken from George Buchanan's *History of Scotland* (*Rerum Scoticarum Historia*, Edinburgh, 1582; f., 193r).

122 In *Areop* (p. 736) Milton thought of *Knox* (1505–1572) as the "reformer of a kingdom" who, after long exile under the English queen Mary in Geneva, became one of the founders of Scottish Presbyterianism. Cf. n. 206 below.

123 William Maitland of *Lethington* (1528–1573), in spite of his loyalty to Mary Queen of Scots, was consistently loyal to the Reformation in Scotland. But he objected to Knox's public attacks upon "the Quenis Idolatrie," and challenged his assertions that "the peopill, yea, or ane pairt of the peopill may execut Godis jugementis agains thair King, being an offendar." In reply, Knox read a number of passages justifying the punishment of kings by inferior magistrates from the works of Luther, Melanchthon, Martin Bucer, Musculus, and Calvin.

124 *John Craig* (1512–1600) was believed to have become a Calvinist through reading Calvin's *Institutes* while serving as a master of novices in a Dominican monastery in Rome. Knox recorded his view of tyrannical laws and his judgment that "evrie kingdom is, or at leist sould be, ane Commonwealth, albeit that evrie Commonwealth be nocht ane Kingdom" (Knox, *Works*, II, 458).

125 The *History of the Reformation in Scotland* (Edinburgh, 1644) is the work in question. Knox wrote the first four of its five books.

126 *Buchanan* is severe about Mary's "tyranny" after the murder of her husband, Darnley, and he ends his eighteenth book with the story of her arrest by "the Vindicators of the publick Parricide," who compelled her to "resign up her Government, upon pretence of Sickness, or any other specious Allegation."

127 One of the *ambassadors* was James Douglas, Earl of Morton, who replied to Elizabeth's question of the legality of Mary's forced abdication by citing the cases of "many Kings whom our Forefathers have chastis'd by Imprisonment, Banishment, nay, Death it self" (Buchanan, *History*, p. 423).

but a mutual covenant or stipulation between king and people (Buchanan, *Hist.*, Bk. XX). These were Scotchmen and Presbyterians:[128] but what measure then have they lately offered to think such liberty less beseeming us than themselves, presuming to put him upon us for a master, whom their law scarce allows to be their own equal? If now then we hear them in another strain than heretofore in the purest times of their church, we may be confident it is the voice of faction speaking in them, not of truth and reformation. Which no less in England than in Scotland, by the mouths of those faithful witnesses commonly called puritans and non-conformists, spake as clearly for the putting down, yea, the utmost punishing of kings, as in their several treatises may be read even from the first reign of Elizabeth to these times. Insomuch that one of them, whose name was Gibson,[129] foretold King James he should be rooted out and conclude his race, if he persisted to uphold bishops. And that very inscription, stamped upon the first coins at his coronation, a naked sword in a hand with these words, *Si mereor, in me,* "Against me, if I deserve,"[130] not only manifested the judgment of that state, but seemed also to presage the sentence of divine justice in this event upon his son.

In the year 1581, the states of Holland[131] in a general assembly at the Hague abjured all obedience and subjection to Philip king of Spain, and in a declaration justify their so doing, for that by his tyrannous government, against faith so many times given and broken, he had lost his right to all the Belgic provinces—that therefore they deposed him and declared it lawful to choose another in his stead (Thuanus, Bk. LXXIV). From that time to this, no state or kingdom in the world hath equally prospered.[182] But let them remember not to look with an evil and prejudicial eye[133] upon their neighbors, walking by the same rule.

But what need these examples to Presbyterians, I mean to those who now of late would seem so much to abhor deposing, whenas they to all Christendom have given the latest and the liveliest example of doing it themselves? I question not the lawfulness of raising war against a tyrant in defense of religion or civil liberty, for no protestant church, from the first Waldenses[134] of Lyons and Languedoc to this day, but have done it round and maintained it lawful. But this I doubt not to affirm, that the Presbyterians, who now so much condemn deposing, were the men themselves that deposed the king, and cannot with all their shifting and relapsing wash off the guiltiness from their own hands. For they themselves by these their late doings have made it guiltiness and turned their own warrantable actions into rebellion.

There is nothing that so actually makes a king of England as rightful possession and supremacy in all causes both civil and ecclesiastical, and nothing that so actually makes a subject of England as those two oaths of allegiance[135] and supremacy[136] ob-

[128] In *Lex, Rex* (p. 143) Samuel Rutherford (the Rotherford of *On the New Forcers of Conscience*, 8) had devoted a chapter (the 28th) to proving that in many cases wars waged by subjects against kings were lawful, and as an instance had cited "The case of *England* and *Ireland*, now invaded by the bloody Rebels of Ireland" (p. 143). Cf. notes 57 and 68 above.

[129] Allison quotes John Mackintosh's *History of Civilization in Scotland* (Paisley, 1893), Vol. II, 188, as declaring that James *Gibson* warned the young James VI in 1586 that he might suffer the fate of Jeroboam, who was "rooted out for staying of the true worship of God."

[130] Cf. n. 65 above.

[131] The declaration of the rights of nations against their rulers by the Dutch in 1581 was sympathetically recorded by the French historian Jacques-Auguste de Thou (1553–1617) in his *History of his Own Times* (J.-A. Thuani *Historiarum sui temporis pars prima*, 1604). Milton used the Geneva edition of 1620.

[132] English republicans attributed Dutch prosperity to the free institutions of Holland, but royalists like Edward Gee (or whoever was the author of the anonymous *Vindication of the Oath of Allegiance*) questioned whether "those Provinces excell in blessings," and whether their quesionable blessings were "brought by a change in their lawfull Government" (p. 29).

[133] Milton resented the "great importunity" of the ambassadors whom the Dutch sent to protest against the trial of King Charles.

[134] Cf. n. 119 above and *Sonn* XVIII.

[135] Milton's moderate but uncompromising reasoning answers the equally uncompromising though moderate position of the *Vindication of the Oath of Allegiance* (p. 12) that, "It is a lesse evill for a people to be bound to a Prince that possibly may prove bad, then to be so loose, as to be at the liberty to cast him off when they shall judge him to rule ill, that is, when they please." Cf. notes 51 and 132 above.

[136] The *oath of supremacy* acknowledged the

served without equivocating, or any mental reservation. Out of doubt then, when the king shall command things already constituted in church or state, obedience is the true essence of a subject, either to do, if it be lawful, or if he hold the thing unlawful, to submit to that penalty which the law imposes, so long as he intends to remain a subject. Therefore when the people, or any part of them, shall rise against the king and his authority, executing the law in anything established, civil or ecclesiastical, I do not say it is rebellion, if the thing commanded though established be unlawful, and that they sought first all due means of redress (and no man is further bound to law). But I say it is an absolute renouncing both of supremacy and allegiance, which in one word is an actual and total deposing of the king and the setting up of another supreme authority over them.

And whether the Presbyterians have not done all this and much more, they will not put me, I suppose, to reckon up a seven years' story fresh in the memory of all men. Have they not utterly broke the oath of allegiance, rejecting the king's command and authority sent them from any part of the kingdom, whether in things lawful or unlawful? Have they not abjured the oath of supremacy by setting up the parliament without the king, supreme to all their obedience; and though their vow and covenant bound them in general to the parliament, yet sometimes adhering to the lesser part[137] of lords and commons that remained faithful, as they term it, and even of them, one while to the commons without the lords, another while to the lords without the commons? Have they not still declared their meaning, whatever their oath were, to hold them only for supreme whom they found at any time most yielding to what they petitioned? Both these oaths, which were the straitest bond of an English subject in reference to the king, being thus broke and made void, it follows undeniably that the king from that time was by them in fact absolutely deposed; and they no longer in reality to be thought his subjects, notwithstanding their fine clause in the covenant to preserve his person, crown, and dignity,[138] set there by some dodging casuist with more craft than sincerity to mitigate the matter in case of ill success; and not taken, I suppose, by any honest man, but as a condition subordinate to every the least particle that might more concern religion, liberty, or the public peace.

To prove it yet more plainly that they are the men who have deposed the king, I thus argue. We know that king and subject are relatives, and relatives[139] have no longer being than in the relation. The relation between king and subject can be no other than regal authority and subjection. Hence I infer, past their defending, that if the subject, who is one relative, take away the relation, of force he takes away also the other relative. But the Presbyterians, who were one relative, that is to say, subjects, have for this seven years taken away the relation, that is to say, the king's authority and their subjection to it. Therefore the Presbyterians for these seven years have removed and extinguished the other relative, that is to say, the king, or, to speak more in brief, have deposed him—not only by depriving him the execution of his authority, but by conferring it upon others.

If then their oaths of subjection broken, new supremacy obeyed, new oaths and covenants taken, notwithstanding frivolous evasions, have in plain terms unkinged the king much more than hath their seven years' war—not deposed him only, but outlawed him and defied him as an alien, a rebel

king as head of the English church. By accepting the Covenant and calling the Westminster Assembly, the House of Commons had virtually made itself the head of a more or less legally established Presbyterian church.

137 Up until the concurrence of the Lords and Commons in rejecting Charles's proposals for an essentially episcopal settlement of the Church on Oct. 11, 1648, most Presbyterians voted with the Independent minority in Parliament. Afterwards they vacillated, but on Jan. 1, 1649, their support of the Lords' unanimous rejection of the Commons' ordinance providing for a High Court of Justice to try the King finally made an open breach between them and the Independents.

138 Cf. *Eikon,* Chap. xxviii, n. 30.

139 So Rutherford argued in *Lex, Rex,* p. 144, that, "It is in vaine that some say, the King and Kingdome are relatives, and not one is before another; for its true in the naked relation, so are father and sonne, Master and servant, *Relata simul natura;* but sure there is a priority of worth and independency for all that, in the father above the sonne, and in the master above the servant, and so in the people above the King."

to law, and enemy to the state—it must needs be clear to any man not averse from reason that hostility and subjection are two direct and positive contraries, and can no more in one subject stand together in respect of the same king than one person at the same time can be in two remote places. Against whom therefore the subject is in act of hostility, we may be confident that to him he is in no subjection; and in whom hostility takes place of subjection, for they can by no means consist together, to him the king can be not only no king, but an enemy.

So that from hence we shall not need dispute whether they have deposed him, or what they have defaulted towards him as no king, but show manifestly how much they have done toward the killing him. Have they not levied all these wars against him, whether offensive or defensive[140] (for defense in war equally offends and most prudently beforehand) and given commission to slay where they knew his person could not be exempt from danger? And if chance or flight had not saved him, how often had they killed him,[141] directing their artillery without blame or prohibition to the very place where they saw him stand? Have they not sequestered[142] him, judged or unjudged, and converted his revenue to other uses, detaining from him as a grand delinquent[143] all means of livelihood, so that for them long since he might have perished, or have starved? Have they not hunted and pursued him round about the kingdom with sword and fire? Have they not formerly denied to treat with him,[144]

140 Cf. n. 95 above.
141 As a Presbyterian spokesman, Rutherford had urged in 1644 that it was "absurd to pursue the Kings Person with a cannon-bullett at Edgehill, and preserve his authority at London" (*Lex, Rex*, p. 141). Rutherford held that Charles's inviolable character as a monarch was not violated when his person was attacked, in the company of his evil counsellors, on the field of battle.
142 Legal *sequestration* is "appropriation of income or property in order to satisfy claims against the owner" (*O.E.D.*).
143 Any serious resistance to Parliament was punishable under *A Declaration & Ordinance Of the Lords & Commons Assembled in Parliament, For the seizing & sequestering of the estates, both reall and personall, of certain kinds of notorious Delinquents, to the use, & for the maintaining of the Army raised by the Parliament* (Printed March 31, 1643).
144 By the vote of "No more addresses" on Jan.

and their now recanting ministers preached against him as a reprobate incurable, an enemy to God and his church, marked for destruction and therefore not to be treated with? Have they not besieged him, and to their power forbid him water and fire, save what they shot against him to the hazard of his life? Yet while they thus assaulted and endangered it with hostile deeds, they swore in words to defend it, with his crown and dignity; not in order, as it seems now, to a firm and lasting peace, or to his repentance after all this blood; but simply, without regard, without remorse, or any comparable value of all the miseries and calamities suffered by the poor people, or to suffer hereafter, through his obstinacy or impenitence.

No understanding man can be ignorant that covenants are ever made according to the present state of persons and of things, and have ever the more general laws of nature and of reason included in them, though not expressed. If I make a voluntary covenant as with a man to do him good, and he prove afterward a monster to me, I should conceive a disobligement. If I covenant not to hurt an enemy, in favor of him and forbearance and hope of his amendment, and he after that shall do me tenfold injury and mischief to what he had done when I so covenanted, and still be plotting what may tend to my destruction, I question not but that his afteractions release me; nor know I covenant so sacred that withholds me from demanding justice on him.

Howbeit, had not their distrust in a good cause and the fast and loose of our prevaricating divines overswayed, it had been doubtless better not to have inserted in a covenant unnecessary obligations and words, not works of a supererogating allegiance[145] to their enemy; no way advantageous to themselves had the king prevailed, as to their cost many would have felt; but full of snare and distraction to our friends, useful only, as we now find, to our adversaries, who under such a latitude and shelter of ambiguous interpretation have ever since

3, 1648, both houses of Parliament resolved to make and tolerate no more efforts to negotiate with King Charles.
145 Again the reference is to "the unnecessariest clause of their Covenant." Cf. *Eikon*, Chap. xxviii, n. 30, and *TKM*, notes 19 and 138.

been plotting and contriving new opportunities to trouble all again. How much better had it been and more becoming an undaunted virtue, to have declared openly and boldly whom and what power the people were to hold supreme (as on the like occasion[146] protestants have done before, and many conscientious men[147] now in these times have more than once besought the parliament to do) that they might go on upon a sure foundation and not with a riddling covenant in their mouths, seeming to swear counter, almost in the same breath, allegiance and no allegiance; which doubtless had drawn off all the minds of sincere men from siding with them, had they not discerned their actions far more deposing him than their words upholding him; which words, made now the subject of cavillous interpretations, stood ever in the covenant, by judgment of the more discerning sort, an evidence of their fear, not of their fidelity.

What should I return to speak on, of those attempts for which the king himself hath often charged the Presbyterians of seeking his life, whenas in the due estimation of things they might without a fallacy be said to have done the deed outright? Who knows not that the king is a name of dignity and office, not of person? Who therefore kills a king, must kill him while he is a king. Then they certainly who by deposing him have long since taken from him the life of a king, his office and his dignity, they in the truest sense may be said to have killed the king: nor only by their deposing and waging war against him (which besides the danger to his personal life, set him in the farthest opposite point from any vital function of a king) but by their holding him in prison,[148] vanquished and yielded into their absolute and despotic power, which brought him to the lowest degradement and incapacity of the regal name. I say not by whose matchless valor[149] next under God, lest the story of their ingratitude thereupon carry me from the purpose in hand, which is to convince them that they—which I repeat again—were the men who in the truest sense killed the king, not only as is proved before, but by depressing him, their king, far below the rank of a subject to the condition of a captive, without intention to restore him (as the chancellor of Scotland[150] in a speech told him plainly at Newcastle) unless he granted fully all their demands, which they knew he never meant.

Nor did they treat or think of treating with him, till their hatred to the army that delivered them, not their love or duty to the king, joined them secretly with men sentenced so oft for reprobates in their own mouths, by whose subtle inspiring they grew mad[151] upon a most tardy and improper treaty. Whereas if the whole bent of their actions had not been against the king himself, but only against his evil counsellors, as they feigned and published, wherefore did they not restore him all that while to the true life of a king, his office, crown, and dignity, when he was in their power and they themselves his nearest counsellors? The truth, therefore, is both that they would not, and that indeed they could not without their own certain destruction, having reduced him to such a final pass as was the very death and burial of all that in him was regal, and from whence never king of England yet revived but by the new reinforcement of his own party, which was a kind of resurrection to him.

Thus having quite extinguished all that could be in him of a king, and from a total privation clad him over, like another spe-

---

146 A reference to the establishment of a republic in Holland. Cf. n. 131 above.

147 The *men* who were pressing Parliament toward the resolution of Jan. 5, 1649, when the Commons declared, "That the office of a King in this Nation . . . is unnecessary, burdensome, and dangerous to the Liberty, Safety, and publick Interest of the People of this Nation: and therefore ought to be abolished" (*The Journals of the House of Commons* VI, 133).

148 From Charles's surrender to the Scots on May 5, 1646, until his surrender by them to Parliament in Jan., 1647, he was virtually a prisoner of Presbyterianism. Cf. n. 87 above.

149 The reference, of course, is to Cromwell.

150 The Scottish *Chancellor,* John Campbell, Earl of Loudoun, a leading Covenanter, was one of the Commissioners who negotiated with Charles at Newcastle in 1646.

151 When the Prince of Wales's ships seized some London merchantmen in July, 1648, and held them for ransom, Parliament declared his supporters guilty of high treason, but yielded to a petition for the King's release from some war-weary citizens by voting to negotiate with him. Some Independent members concurred in the hasty commitment to the abortive "Treaty of Newport."

cifical[152] thing, with forms and habitudes destructive to the former, they left in his person, dead as to law and all the civil right either of king or subject, the life only of a prisoner, a captive, and a malefactor: whom the equal and impartial hand of justice finding, was no more to spare than another ordinary man: not only made obnoxious to the doom of law by a charge more than once drawn up against him and his own confession to the first article at Newport,[153] but summoned and arraigned in the sight of God and his people; cursed and devoted to perdition worse than any Ahab,[154] or Antiochus,[155] with exhortation to curse all those in the name of God, that made not war against him, as bitterly as Meroz[156] was to be cursed that went not out against a Canaanitish king, almost in all the sermons,[157] prayers, and fulminations that have been uttered this seven years, by those cloven tongues of falsehood and dissension who now, to the stirring up of new discord, acquit him; and against their own

discipline,[158] which they boast to be the throne and scepter of Christ, absolve him, unconfound him, though unconverted, unrepentant, insensible of all their precious saints and martyrs, whose blood they have so often laid upon his head. And now again, with a new sovereign anointment,[159] can wash it all off as if it were as vile and no more to be reckoned for than the blood of so many dogs in a time of pestilence: giving the most opprobrious lie to all the acted zeal that for these many years hath filled their bellies and fed them fat upon the foolish people. Ministers of sedition, not of the gospel, who, while they saw it manifestly tend to civil war and bloodshed, never ceased exasperating the people against him; and now that they see it likely to breed new commotion, cease not to incite others against the people that have saved them from him—as if sedition were their only aim, whether against him or for him.

But God, as we have cause to trust, will put other thoughts into the people and turn them from giving ear or heed to these mercenary noisemakers of whose fury and false prophecies we have enough experience; and from the murmurs of new discord will incline them to hearken rather with erected minds to the voice of our supreme magistracy, calling us to liberty[160] and the flourishing deeds of a reformed commonwealth; with this hope, that as God was heretofore angry with the Jews who rejected him and his form of government to choose a king,[161] so that he will bless us and be propitious to us who reject a king to make him only our leader and supreme governor, in the conformity, as near as may be, of his own ancient government; if we have at least but so much worth in us to entertain the sense of our future happiness, and the courage to receive what God vouchsafes us—wherein we have the honor

---

[152] *specifical:* a thing considered specifically, or with reference to its species.

[153] Tension between Presbyterians and Independents led to the submission to Charles by Parliament's commissioners of certain Propositions which were discussed with him in *Newport* on the Isle of Wight in the autumn of 1648. Charles shrewdly refused to assent to the Preamble, which began: "Whereas both Houses of the Parliament of England have been necessitated to undertake a war in their just and lawful defense . . ."; but his handling of the Propositions was such that Prynne passionately defended him in a *Speech Made in the House of Commons . . . On Monday, the Fourth of December, 1648.* On the title page Prynne declared his faith in "the *Satisfactoriness* of the Kings Answers to the *Propositions* for settlement of a firm and lasting *Peace,* and future security of the Subjects against all feared Regal Invasions, and encroachments whatsoever." On Prynne see notes 8, 9, 24, and 75 above.

[154] Cf. n. 91 above.

[155] The Apocryphal Books of Maccabees tell the story of the overthrow of *Antiochus* IV, Epiphanes, by the priest Mattathias and his son, Judas Maccabeus, who restored the worship of Jehovah in Jerusalem.

[156] In the Song of Deborah the men of *Meroz* are cursed for their failure to support Barak in his attack on the Canaanite king Jabin—"because they came not to the help of the Lord against the mighty" (Judg. v, 23).

[157] A conspicuous set of such *sermons* had been preached by the independently-minded Presbyterian Charles Herle to the House of Commons and the Mayor and Aldermen of London under the title *Ahab's Fall by his Prophets Flatteries.* Cf. notes 91 and 92 above.

[158] Presbyterian *discipline* included the ideals of just government which are laid down in Calvin's *Institutes* IV, xii, and their sanctions in passages like those which Milton cites below. Cf. n. 202.

[159] Cf. n. 32 above.

[160] The *magistracy's call to liberty* is the resolution of the Commons on 4 Jan., 1649, that "the people are, under God, the original of all just power: . . . that the Commons of England, in Parliament assembled, have the supreme power in this nation."

[161] Cf. notes 55 and 68 above.

to precede other nations who are now laboring to be our followers.

For as to this question in hand, what the people by their just right may do in change of government or of governor, we see it cleared sufficiently, besides other ample authority, even from the mouths of princes themselves.[162] And surely they that shall boast, as we do, to be a free nation, and not have in themselves the power to remove or to abolish any governor supreme or subordinate, with the government itself upon urgent causes, may please their fancy with a ridiculous and painted freedom fit to cozen babies; but are indeed under tyranny and servitude, as wanting that power which is the root and source of all liberty, to dispose and economize[163] in the land which God hath given them, as masters of family in their own house and free inheritance. Without which natural and essential power of a free nation, though bearing high their heads, they can in due esteem be thought no better than slaves and vassals born, in the tenure and occupation of another inheriting lord,[164] whose government, though not illegal or intolerable, hangs over them as a lordly scourge, not as a free government—and therefore to be abrogated.

How much more justly then may they fling off tyranny or tyrants, who being once deposed can be no more than private men, as subject to the reach of justice and arraignment as any other transgressors? And certainly if men, not to speak of heathen, both wise and religious, have done justice upon tyrants what way they could soonest, how much more mild and humane then is it to give them fair and open trial—to teach lawless kings and all who so much adore them that not mortal man, or his imperious will, but justice, is the only true sovereign and supreme majesty upon earth? Let men cease therefore out of faction and hypocrisy to make outcries and horrid things of things so just and honorable.

Though perhaps till now no protestant state or kingdom can be alleged to have openly put to death their king,[165] which

lately some have written and imputed to their great glory, much mistaking the matter, it is not, neither ought to be, the glory of a protestant state never to have put their king to death; it is the glory of a protestant king never to have deserved death. And if the parliament and military council do what they do without precedent, if it appear their duty, it argues the more wisdom, virtue, and magnanimity, that they know themselves able to be a precedent to others; who perhaps in future ages, if they prove not too degenerate, will look up with honor and aspire towards these exemplary and matchless deeds of their ancestors, as to the highest top of their civil glory and emulation. Which heretofore, in the pursuance of fame and foreign dominion, spent itself vaingloriously abroad, but henceforth may learn a better fortitude[166]—to dare execute highest justice on them that shall by force of arms endeavor the oppressing and bereaving of religion and their liberty at home: that no unbridled potentate or tyrant, but to his sorrow, for the future may presume such high and irresponsible license over mankind, to havoc[167] and turn upside down whole kingdoms of men, as though they were no more in respect of his perverse will than a nation of pismires.[168]

As for the party called Presbyterian, of whom I believe very many to be good and faithful Christians though misled by some of turbulent spirit, I wish them, earnestly and calmly, not to fall off from their first principles nor to affect rigor and superiority over men not under them; not to compel unforcible things,[169] in religion especially,

regicide judges to Jesuits. In reply, writers like the author (William Dell?) of The City-Ministers unmasked (published Feb. 26, 1649) proudly contrasted Jesuit "private killing and murthering of kings" with "the present case of the Parliament and Army, calling the King to publique tryall for his treasons and murders, and judging him according to the known Law of God, and the Kingdom" (p. 15).
166 So
      the better fortitude
  Of patience and heroic martyrdom
is contrasted with military government in PL IX, 31–32, as well as in Sonn XVI.
167 Cf. havoc in PL X, 617: "these dogs . . . havoc yonder world."
168 pismires: ants.
169 Cf. CD I, xv and xxvii, which declare that the government of the church should be "by inward law and spiritual power," and that Christian

---

162 Cf. notes 65 and 130 above.
163 economize: direct any society (family or nation).
164 Cf. n. 57 above.
165 Presbyterian pamphleteers compared the

which, if not voluntary, becomes a sin;[170] nor to assist the clamor and malicious drifts of men whom they themselves have judged to be the worst of men, the obdurate enemies of God and his church: nor to dart against the actions of their brethren, for want of other argument, those wrested laws and scriptures thrown by prelates and malignants against their own sides, which though they hurt not otherwise, yet taken up by them to the condemnation of their own doings, give scandal to all men and discover[171] in themselves either extreme passion or apostasy. Let them not oppose their best friends and associates, who molest them not at all, infringe not the least of their liberties—unless they call it their liberty to bind other men's consciences—but are still seeking to live at peace with them and brotherly accord. Let them beware an old and perfect enemy, who, though he hope by sowing discord to make them his instruments, yet cannot forbear a minute the open threatening of his destined revenge upon them, when they have served his purposes.[172] Let them fear therefore, if they be wise, rather what they have done already than what remains to do; and be warned in time they put no confidence in princes[173] whom they have provoked, lest they be added to the examples of those that miserably have tasted the event.

Stories can inform them how Christiern the Second, king of Denmark,[174] not much above a hundred years past, driven out by his subjects and received again upon new oaths and conditions, broke through them all to his most bloody revenge; slaying his chief opposers when he saw his time, both them and their children invited to a feast for that purpose. How Maximilian[175] dealt

with those of Bruges, though by mediation of the German princes reconciled to them by solemn and public writings drawn and sealed: how the massacre at Paris[176] was the effect of that credulous peace which the French protestants made with Charles the ninth their king: and that the main visible cause which to this day hath saved the Netherlands from utter ruin, was their final not believing the perfidious cruelty, which, as a constant maxim of state, hath been used by the Spanish kings on their subjects that have taken arms and after trusted them; as no later age but can testify, heretofore in Belgia itself, and this very year in Naples.[177] And to conclude with one past exception though far more ancient, David,[178] whose sanctified prudence might be alone sufficient not to warrant us only but to instruct us, when once he had taken arms never after that trusted Saul, though with tears and much relenting twice promised not to hurt him. These instances, few of many, might admonish them, both English and Scotch, not to let their own ends and the driving on of a faction betray them blindly into the snare of those enemies whose revenge looks on them as the men who first begun, fomented, and carried on beyond the cure of any sound or safe accommodation, all the evil which hath since unavoidably befallen them and their king.

I have something also to the divines, though brief to what were needful; not to be disturbers of the civil affairs,[179] being in hands better able and more belonging to manage them; but to study harder and to attend the office of good pastors, knowing

Bruges unless he granted reforms in government.
[176] Cf. the references to the massacre of St. Bartholemew in CB (C.E. XVIII, 190) and to Charles IX's schemes to establish a "Turkish tyranny" in France (C.E. XVIII, 184).
[177] Spanish cruelty after the revolt in *Naples* in 1648 violated a formal pledge. For the relation of the Neapolitan revolt to the Civil War in England see R. B. Merriman's *Six Contemporary Revolutions* (Cambridge, Mass., 1938).
[178] Saul's first oath not to hurt *David* was given to Jonathan (I Sam. xix, 6) and the second to David himself (I Sam. xxvi, 21) after David had for the second time had Saul in his power and spared his life. Cf. n. 32 above.
[179] For instances of clerical intervention in *civil affairs* see notes 26, 94, 165, 169, and 171 above.

liberty should free men from "all civil decrees and penalties in religious matters" (C.E. XV, 297, and XVI, 157).
[170] The doctrine that every violation of Christian liberty is a *sin* is the thesis of *Civil Power*.
[171] *discover*: expose, betray.
[172] Cf. n. 9 above.
[173] "Put not your trust in princes" (Psalm clxiii, 3).
[174] The reference is to Buchanan's *History of Scotland*, Book XX, p. 269, where *Christiern II of Denmark* (1481–1559) is mentioned as having been forced out of his kingdom for his cruelty. Cf. n. 66 above.
[175] In 1490 *Maximilian I* severely punished a revolt which had threatened his personal safety in

that he whose flock is least among them hath a dreadful charge, not performed by mounting twice into the chair[180] with a formal preachment huddled up at the odd hours of a whole lazy week, but by incessant pains and watching, in season and out of season,[181] from house to house, over the souls of whom they have to feed. Which if they ever well considered, how little leisure would they find to be the most pragmatical sidesmen[132] of every popular tumult and sedition? And all this while are to learn what the true end and reason is of the gospel which they teach, and what a world it differs from the censorious and supercilious lording over conscience. It would be good also they lived so as might persuade the people they hated covetousness, which, worse than heresy, is idolatry;[183] hated pluralities,[184] and all kinds of simony; left rambling from benefice to benefice like ravenous wolves seeking where they may devour the biggest. Of which if some, well and warmly seated from the beginning, be not guilty, it were good they held not conversation with such as are. Let them be sorry that, being called to assemble about reforming the church, they fell to progging[185] and soliciting the parliament, though they had renounced the name of priests, for a new settling of their tithes and oblations,[186] and doublelined themselves with spiritual places of commodity beyond the possible discharge of their duty. Let them assemble in consistory[187] with their elders and deacons, according to ancient ecclesiastical rule, to the preserving of church discipline each in his several charge, and not a pack of clergymen by themselves to bellycheer[188] in their presumptuous Sion,[189] or to promote designs, abuse and gull the simple laity, and stir up tumult, as the prelates did, for the maintenance of their pride and avarice.

These things if they observe and wait with patience, no doubt but all things will go well without their importunities or exclamations; and the printed letters, which they send subscribed with the ostentation of great characters[190] and little moment,[191] would be more considerable than now they are. But if they be the ministers of mammon instead of Christ and scandalize his church with the filthy love of gain—aspiring also to sit the closest and the heaviest of all tyrants upon the conscience[192]—and fall notoriously into the same sins whereof so lately and so loud they accused the prelates, as God rooted out those wicked ones immediately before so will he root out them, their imitators; and, to vindicate his own glory and religion, will uncover their hypocrisy to the open world; and visit upon their own heads that "Curse ye Meroz,"[193] the very motto of their pulpits, wherewith so frequently, not as Meroz but more like atheists, they have blasphemed the vengeance of God and traduced the zeal of his people.

And that they be not what they go for, true ministers of the protestant doctrine, taught by those abroad, famous and religious men who first reformed the church, or by those no less zealous who withstood corruption and the bishops here at home, branded with the name of puritans and nonconformists, we shall abound with testimonies to make appear: that men may yet more fully know the difference between protestant divines and these pulpit-firebrands.

---

180 *chair:* pulpit.

181 "Preach the word; be instant, in season, out of season" (II Tim. iv, 2).

182 *pragmatical sidesmen:* meddlesome partisans.

183 The Presbyterian idol is Mammon. In the next paragraph Milton calls them "ministers of Mammon."

184 Cf. n. 29 above.

185 *progging:* importuning, nagging.

186 *oblations:* consecrated gifts. Cf. n. 28 above.

187 Formal meetings of the Presbyterian clergy and lay elders were often called *consistories.*

188 *bellycheer:* to guzzle. It might be either verb or noun.

189 From 1647 to 1659 *Sion* College was the seat of the Presbyterian Provincial Assembly in London.

190 The titlepages of the letters addressed by the Presbyterian clergy to Fairfax, the Army, and Parliament, had an even larger display of emphatic capitals than was usual in such pamphlets. Their inflated literary style was a byword among the Independents. Cf. n. 26 above.

191 *moment:* weight, importance.

192 In *An Answer to the London Ministers Letter* (1649) p. 28, Samuel Richardson wrote: ". . . we see your principall is that you will have none tolerated but yourselves . . . Doe you love to see the bodyes of others tortured, and their estates ruined, because they are not of your Religion?"

193 Cf. n. 156 above.

Luther.

Liber contra Rusticos apud Sleidan,[194] Bk. V.

Is est hodie rerum status, &c.[195] "Such is the state of things at this day that men neither can nor will nor indeed ought to endure longer the domination of you Princes."

Neque vero Cæsarem, &c. "Neither is Cæsar to make war as head of Christendom, Protector of the Church, Defender of the Faith; these titles being false and windy, and most kings being the greatest enemies to religion." *Liber de bello contra Turcas apud Sleidan,* Bk. XIV.[196] What hinders then, but that we may depose or punish them?

These also are recited by Cochlæus[197] in his *Miscellanies* to be the words of Luther, or some other eminent divine then in Germany, when the Protestants there entered into solemn covenant at Smalcaldia. *Ut ora iis obturem* &c.[198] "That I may stop

their mouths, the Pope and Emperor are not born but elected, and may also be deposed as hath been often done." If Luther, or whoever else thought so, he could not stay there, for the right of birth or succession can be no privilege in nature to let a tyrant sit irremovable over a nation free born, without transforming that nation from the nature and condition of men born free into natural, hereditary, and successive slaves. Therefore he saith further: "To displace and throw down this exactor, this Phalaris,[199] this Nero, is a work well pleasing to God."[200] Namely, for being such a one, which is a moral reason. Shall then so slight a consideration as his hap to be. not elective simply but by birth, which was a mere accident, overthrow that which is moral, and make unpleasing to God that which otherwise had so well pleased him? Certainly not, for if the matter be rightly argued, election much rather than chance binds a man to content himself with what he suffers by his own bad election. Though indeed neither the one nor other binds any man, much less any people, to a necessary sufferance of those wrongs and evils which they have ability and strength enough given them to remove.

Zwinglius.[201] tom. 1, articul. 42.

Quando vero perfidè, &c. "When kings reign perfidiously and against the rule of Christ, they may according to the word of God be deposed."

---

[194] Milton's extracts from Sleidan's *Commentaries* in CB (see n. 120 above) indicate that he read that work as a record of the assertion of the religious and political rights of the German Reformers against the Holy Roman Emperors and the other princes who opposed them.

[195] The passage occurs in Sleidan's Book V, the book "Against the Peasants" (p. 80r). Elsewhere Luther is no less firm in condemning the outrages of the peasants against their landlords.

[196] The passage occurs in Sleidan's Book XIV, "Against the Turks" (p. 230r). Although Luther supported Charles V's resistance of the Turks when they tried to cross the Danube in force in 1542, he was challenged because in a youthful book he had condemned the financial abuses of the wars with the Turks and ridiculed the Emperor's titles, Defender of the Faith, etc.

[197] Johannes Dobeneck (1479–1552), better known as *Cochlaeus,* from 1529 to 1539 served as secretary to Duke George of Saxony, one of Luther's strongest opponents. In three places in the *Miscellaneorum Libri Primi Tractatus Quartus. Consilium Io. Cochlaei super negocio Lutherano ad . . . Card. & Archiepiscopum Moguntinum* (Ingoldstadt, 1545) Milton found Luther's warning to the German princes quoted to prove him the arch-anarch of his age. Milton's treatment of the Reformation in *TKM* is studied by M. Y. Hughes in *The Seventeenth Century: Studies in the History of English Thought and Literature from Bacon to Pope.* By Richard Foster Jones and others (Stanford University Press, 1951), pp. 247–63.

[198] Milton quotes from p. 49v of Cochlaeus'

book, two pages below the previous extract, a tirade against "impious authority," which is attributed to Luther.

[199] *Phalaris,* tyrant of Agrigentum (565–549 B.C.), whose legendary practice of roasting his enemies to death in a brazen bull made him a byword of tyranny.

[200] Again Milton is quoting Cochlaeus' *Miscellanies* (f. 49r), this time attributing to Luther a sweeping denial of the right of rulers to levy taxes of any kind and a denunciation of all princes asserting such a right as deserving the fate of Agag, Phalaris, and Nero. Cf. n. 14 above.

[201] The quotations are from the *Opus Articulorum sive Conclusionum Huldrichi Zuingli* (in his *Opera,* Zurich, 1545; pp. 84–86). Zwingli's leadership in assuring republican institutions in Switzerland was an outgrowth of his faith in Congregational self-government in the churches in Geneva. Milton quotes him through a Latin translation (1535) of the *Usslegen und Gründ der Schlussreden* (1523), a minor but influential work, written in Zwingli's forty-first year.

Mihi ergo compertum non est, &c. "I know not how it comes to pass that kings reign by succession, unless it be with consent of the whole people." *ibid.*

Quum vero consensu, &c. "But when by suffrage and consent of the whole people, or the better part of them, a tyrant is deposed or put to death, God is the chief leader in that action." *ibid.*

Nunc cum tam tepidi sumus, &c. "Now that we are so lukewarm in upholding public justice, we endure the vices of tyrants to reign nowadays with impunity; justly therefore by them we are trod underfoot, and shall at length with them be punished. Yet ways are not wanting by which tyrants may be removed, but there wants public justice." *ibid.*

Cavete vobis ô tyranni. "Beware ye tyrants for now the Gospel of Jesus Christ spreading far and wide will renew the lives of many to love innocence and justice; which if ye also shall do, ye shall be honored. But if ye shall go on to rage and do violence, ye shall be trampled on by all men." *ibid.*

Romanum imperium imò quodq; &c. When the Roman Empire or any other shall begin to oppress religion, and we negligently suffer it, we are as much guilty of religion so violated as the oppressors themselves." *Idem. Epist. ad Conrad, Somium.*

Calvin on Daniel, chap. 4, v. 25.[202]

Hodie Monarchae semper in suis titulis, &c. "Nowadays monarchs pretend always in their titles to be kings by the grace of God; but how many of them to this end only pretend it, that they may reign without control? For to what purpose is the grace of God mentioned in the title of kings but that they may acknowledge no superior? In the meanwhile God whose name they use to support themselves, they willingly would tread under their feet. It is therefore a mere cheat when they boast to reign by the grace of God."[203]

Abdicant se terreni principes, &c.

"Earthly princes depose themselves while they rise against God, yea they are unworthy to be numbered among men; rather it behooves us to spit upon their heads than to obey them." *On Daniel,* chap. 6, v. 22.

Bucer[204] on Matthew, chap. 5.

Si princeps superior, &c. "If a sovereign prince endeavor by arms to defend transgressors, to subvert those things which are taught in the word of God, they who are in authority under him ought first to dissuade him; if they prevail not, and that he now bears himself not as a prince but as an enemy, and seeks to violate privileges and rights granted to inferior magistrates or commonalties, it is the part of pious magistrates, imploring first the assistance of God, rather to try all ways and means than to betray the flock of Christ to such an enemy of God. For they also are to this end ordained, that they may defend the people of God, and maintain those things which are good and just. For to have supreme power lessens not the evil committed by that power, but makes it the less tolerable, by how much the more generally hurtful." Then certainly the less tolerable, the more unpardonably to be punished.

Of Peter Martyr we have spoke before. Paræus[205] in *Romanos,* 13.

Quorum est constituere Magistratus, &c. "They whose part it is to set up magistrates

---

[202] Definitely though John Calvin (1509–1564) disliked democracy, his attitude toward royal pride was not misrepresented by Milton's extracts from his reflections on Nebuchadnezzar in his *Praelectiones in librum prophetiarum Danielis* (Geneva, 1561; p. 51).

[203] The passage is from p. 78 of Calvin's work.

[204] As a friend of Luther in Germany who later held a theological chair at Cambridge under Edward VI, *Martin Bucer* (1491–1551) was a link between the Reformers on the Continent and in England. Milton had translated part of his work *On the Kingdom of Christ* as *Martin Bucer on Divorce.* Here he is quoting from Bucer's *Sacra quattuor Evangelia* (6th ed. Strassbourg, 1555; p. 53).

[205] Milton quotes from one of the most influential Calvinist commentators on Romans, *David Paræus* (1548–1622). The quoted passage occurs on p. 262 and again on p. 282 of Paræus' *Theological Works* (*Opera Theologica.* Frankfurt, 1647)—on p. 282 in an appendix of parallels between Paræus and his English critic, David Owen, who had attacked him in 1622 in a Latin treatise which was translated in 1642 as *Anti-Paraeus, or, A Treatise in the Defence of the Royal Right of Kings: against Paraeus and the rest of the Antimonarchians, whether Presbyterians or Jesuits.*

may restrain them also from outrageous deeds, or pull them down; but all magistrates are set up either by parliament, or by electors, or by other magistrates. They therefore who exalted them may lawfully degrade and punish them.

Of the Scotch divines I need not mention others than the famousest among them, Knox, and his fellow laborers in the reformation of Scotland, whose large treatises on this subject defend the same opinion. To cite them sufficiently were to insert their whole books, written purposely on this argument. Knox's *Appeal* and *To the Reader,*[206] where he promises in a postscript that the book which he intended to set forth, called *The Second Blast of the Trumpet,* should maintain more at large that the same men most justly may depose and punish him whom unadvisedly they have elected, notwithstanding birth, succession, or any oath of allegiance. Among our own divines, Cartwright[207] and Fenner,[208] two of the learnedest, may in reason satisfy us what was held by the rest. Fenner in his *Book of Theology,* maintaining, that "they who have power, that is to say a parliament, may either by fair means or by force depose a tyrant," whom he defines to be him that wilfully breaks all, or the principal, conditions made between him and the commonwealth. Fenner, *Sacra Theologia,* chap. xiii, and Cartwright in a prefixed Epistle testifies his approbation of the whole book.

Gilby,[209] *de obedientia,* pp. 25 & 105.

"Kings have their authority of the people, who may upon occasion reassume it to themselves."

England's Complaint against the Canons.

"The people may kill wicked princes as monsters and cruel beasts."

Christopher Goodman,[210] *Of Obedience.*

"When kings or rulers become blasphemers of God, oppressors and murderers of their subjects, they ought no more to be accounted kings or lawful magistrates, but as private men to be examined, accused, condemned, and punished by the law of God, and being convicted and punished by that law, it is not man's but God's doing" (Chap. x, p. 139).

"By the civil laws a fool or idiot born, and so proved, shall lose the lands and inheritance whereto he is born, because he is not able to use them aright. And especially ought in no case be suffered to have the government of a whole nation; but there is no such evil can come to the commonwealth by fools and idiots as doth by the rage and fury of ungodly rulers; such therefore being without God ought to have no authority over God's people, who by his word requireth the contrary" (Chap. xi, pp. 143, 144).

"No person is exempt by any law of God from this punishment, be he king, queen, or emperor, he must die the death, for God hath not placed them above others to transgress his laws as they list, but to be

---

[206] Milton refers to *The Appellation of John Knoxe from the cruell and most unjust sentence pronounced against him by the false Bishoppes and clergy of Scotland* . . . , which was published at Geneva in 1558, bound with Anthony Gilby's *An Admonition to England and Scotland, to call them to Repentance.* The same volume contained *John Knox to the Reader.* Cf. notes 122 and 123 above and 211 below.

[207] As Lady Margaret Professor of Divinity at Cambridge and as the author of the *Admonition to the Parliament* in 1572, *Thomas Cartwright* ranked as one of the founders of English Presbyterianism.

[208] *Dudley Fenner* (1558?–1587) was associated with Cartwright, whom he succeeded in the pastorate of the English church in Middelburg in the Netherlands in 1586. His *Sacra Theologia, sive Veritas quae est secumdum Pietatem* (1585), to which Milton refers, was a compendium of faith, morals, and politics. On p. 80v it reaches the declaration which Milton translates here.

[209] The author of the passage which Milton misattributes to *Anthony Gilby* (1510–1585?) was his fellow exile in Geneva, John Poynet, who became Bishop of Rochester and later of Winchester under Queen Elizabeth. In *JEGP,* L (1951), 320–5, Miss Sonia Miller has traced Milton's quotation to Poynet's *A shorte treatise of politike power* through successive quotations of it by Sir Thomas Aston and Archbishop Bancroft.

[210] *Goodman* was co-pastor of the English congregation in Geneva with John Knox. His last act before returning from exile in Switzerland in 1558 was to publish *How Superior Powers ought to be Obeyd of their subjects: and Wherein they may lawfully by Gods Worde be disobeyed.* . . . Milton's page references check with those of the Facsimile Text Society's reprint of 1931.

subject to them as well as others, and if they be subject to his laws, then to the punishment also, so much the more as their example is more dangerous" (Chap. xiii, p. 184).

"When magistrates cease to do their duty, the people are as it were without magistrates; yea worse, and then God giveth the sword into the people's hand, and he himself is become immediately their head" (p. 185).

"If princes do right and keep promise with you, then do you owe to them all humble obedience. If not, ye are discharged and your study ought to be in this case how ye may depose and punish according to the law such rebels against God and oppressors of their country" (p. 190).

This Goodman was a minister of the English church at Geneva, as Dudley Fenner was at Middleburgh, or some other place in that country. These were the pastors of those saints and confessors who, flying from the bloody persecution of Queen Mary, gathered up at length their scattered members into many congregations. Whereof some in upper, some in lower Germany, part of them settled at Geneva, where this author having preached on this subject to the great liking of certain learned and godly men who heard him, was by them sundry times and with much instance required to write more fully on that point. Who thereupon took it in hand, and conferring with the best learned in those parts (among whom Calvin was then living in the same city), with their special approbation he published this treatise, aiming principally, as is testified by Whittingham[211] in the Preface, that his brethren of England, the protestants, might be persuaded in the truth of that doctrine concerning obedience to magistrates (Whittingham in Prefat.).

These were the true protestant divines of England, our fathers in the faith we hold. This was their sense, who for so many years laboring under prelacy, through all storms and persecutions, kept religion from extinguishing; and delivered it pure to us,

till there arose a covetous and ambitious generation of divines (for divines they call themselves) who, feigning on a sudden to be new converts and proselytes from episcopacy, under which they had long temporized, opened their mouths at length, in show against pluralities[212] and prelacy, but with intent to swallow them down both; gorging themselves like harpies on those simonious[213] places and preferments of their outed predecessors, as the quarry for which they hunted, not to plurality only but to multiplicity; for possessing which they had accused them, their brethren, and aspiring under another title to the same authority and usurpation over the consciences of all men.

Of this faction, divers reverend and learned divines (as they are styled in the phylactery[214] of their own titlepage) pleading the lawfulness of defensive arms against this king in a treatise called *Scripture and Reason*,[215] seem in words to disclaim utterly the deposing of a king. But both the scripture and the reasons which they use draw consequences after them which, without their bidding, conclude it lawful. For if by scripture, and by that especially to the Romans[216] which they most insist upon, kings, doing that which is contrary to St. Paul's definition of a magistrate, may be resisted, they may altogether with as much force of consequence be deposed or punished. And if by reason the unjust authority of kings "may be forfeited in part, and his power be reassumed in part, either by the parliament or people, for the case in hazard and the present necessity" (as they affirm, p. 34), there can no scripture

---

[211] As an exile in Geneva, *William Whittingham* (1524–1579) collaborated with Knox, Gilby, and others in drafting the *Genevan Service Book*. Under Elizabeth he became Dean of Durham.

[212] Cf. notes 29 and 190 above.

[213] Cf. n. 228 below.

[214] Cf. *Forcers*, 17.

[215] In 1642 the Royalist divine, Dr. Henry Ferne, had hindered recruiting for Parliament's forces by publishing *Resolving of Conscience Upon this Question*: "Whether upon a Supposition . . . (The King will not discharge his trust, but is bent or seduced to subvert Religion, Laws, and Liberties) Subjects may take up Arms and resist." On April 14, 1643, by order of the Commons, a reply by some Presbyterian clergy was published under the title: *Scripture and Reason pleaded for Defensive Armes: or, the whole Controversie about Subjects taking up Armes. Wherein . . . an answer is punctually delivered to Dr. Fernes Booke, entitled Resolving of Conscience. . . .*

[216] Cf. n. 75 above.

be alleged, no imaginable reason given that necessity continuing—as it may always, and they in all prudence and their duty may take upon them to foresee it—why in such a case they may not finally amerce him with the loss of his kingdom, of whose amendment they have no hope. And if one wicked action persisted in against religion, laws, and liberties may warrant us to thus much in part, why may not forty times as many tyrannies by him committed, warrant us to proceed on restraining him till the restraint become total? For the ways of justice are exactest proportion. If for one trespass of a king it require so much remedy or satisfaction, then for twenty more as heinous crimes, it requires of him twentyfold, and so proportionably, till it come to what is utmost among men. If in these proceedings against their king they may not finish by the usual course of justice what they have begun, they could not lawfully begin at all. For this golden rule[217] of justice and morality as well as of arithmetic, out of three terms which they admit, will as certainly and unavoidably bring out the fourth as any problem that ever Euclid[218] or Appollonius made good by demonstration.

And if the parliament, being undeposable but by themselves (as is affirmed, pp. 37, 38), might for his whole life, if they saw cause, take all power, authority, and the sword out of his hand, which in effect is to unmagistrate him, why might they not —being then themselves the sole magistrates in force—proceed to punish him, who, being lawfully deprived of all things that define a magistrate, can be now no magistrate to be degraded lower, but an offender to be punished. Lastly, whom they may defy and meet in battle,[219] why may they not as well prosecute by justice? For lawful war

is but the execution of justice against them who refuse law. Among whom if it be lawful (as they deny not, pp. 19, 20) to slay the king himself coming in front at his own peril, wherefore may not justice do that intendedly, which the chance of a defensive war might without blame have done casually, nay, purposely, if there it find him among the rest? They ask (p. 19), "By what rule of conscience or God a state is bound to sacrifice religion, laws, and liberties, rather than a prince, defending such as subvert them, should come in hazard of his life." And I ask by what conscience, or divinity, or law, or reason, a state is bound to leave all these sacred concernments under a perpetual hazard and extremity of danger rather than cut off a wicked prince, who sits plotting day and night to subvert them.

They tell us that the law of nature[220] justifies any man to defend himself, even against the king in person. Let them show us then why the same law may not justify much more a state or whole people, to do justice upon him against whom each private man may lawfully defend himself; seeing all kind of justice done is a defense to good men, as well as a punishment to bad, and justice done upon a tyrant is no more but the necessary self-defense of a whole commonwealth. To war upon a king that his instruments may be brought to condign punishment, and thereafter to punish them the instruments, and not to spare only, but to defend and honor him the author, is the strangest piece of justice to be called Christian, and the strangest piece of reason to be called human, that by men of reverence and learning, as their style imports them, ever yet was vented. They maintain in the third and fourth section that a judge or inferior magistrate is anointed of God, is his minister, hath the sword in his hand, is to be obeyed by St. Peter's rule,[221] as well as the supreme, and without difference anywhere expressed: and yet will have us fight against the supreme till he remove and punish the inferior magistrate (for such were greatest delinquents); whenas by scripture and by reason there can no more authority be shown to resist the one than the other; and altogether as much to punish or

---

[217] Allison cites Barnard Smith's *Arithmetic for the Schools* (Cambridge, 1854, pp. 195–6): "Almost all questions which arise in the common concerns of life, so far as they require calculation by numbers, might be brought within the scope of the Rule of Three, which enables us to find the fourth term in a proportion, and which . . . is often called the Golden Rule."

[218] Euclid's *Elements of Geometry,* if not the work on conic sections by Apollonius of Perga, was so much a part of ordinary education that "clear as the rules of Euclid" was a phrase coming naturally to Milton in *Tetr* (C.E. IV, 111).

[219] Cf. n. 141 above.

[220] Cf. n. 82 above.

[221] I Peter ii, 13–14. Cf. n. 74 above.

depose the supreme himself as to make war upon him till he punish or deliver up his inferior magistrates, whom in the same terms we are commanded to obey and not to resist.

Thus while they, in a cautious line or two here and there stuffed in, are only verbal against the pulling down or punishing of tyrants, all the scripture and the reason which they bring, is in every leaf direct and rational to infer it altogether as lawful as to resist them. And yet in all their sermons, as hath by others been well noted, they went much further. For divines, if ye observe them, have their postures and their motions,[222] no less expertly and with no less variety than they that practise feats in the Artillery-ground. Sometimes they seem furiously to march on, and presently march counter. By and by they stand, and then retreat; or if need be, can face about, or wheel in a whole body with that cunning and dexterity as is almost unperceivable, to wind themselves by shifting ground into places of more advantage. And providence only must be the drum, providence the word of command that calls them from above, but always to some larger benefice, or acts them into such or such figures and promotions. At their turns and doublings no men readier, to the right, or to the left; for it is their turns which they serve chiefly; herein only singular that with them there is no certain hand right or left, but as their own commodity[223] thinks best to call it. But if there come a truth to be defended which to them and their interest of this world seems not so profitable, straight these nimble motionists can find no even legs to stand upon, and are no more of use to reformation thoroughly performed and not superficially, or to the advancement of truth (which among mortal men is always in her progress), than if on a sudden they were struck maim and crippled. Which the better to conceal, or the more to countenance by a general conformity to their own limping, they would have scripture, they would have reason also made to halt with them for company; and would put us off with impotent conclusions,[224] lame and shorter than the premises.

222 *motions:* evolutions of drilling troops.
223 *commodity:* advantage.
224 The phrase was a cliché in the schools of

In this posture they seem to stand with great zeal and confidence on the wall of Sion, but like Jebusites, not like Israelites, or Levites. Blind also as well as lame, they discern not David from Adonibezek,[225] but cry him up for the Lord's anointed whose thumbs and great toes not long before they had cut off upon their pulpit cushions. Therefore he who is our only King, the Root of David, and whose kingdom is eternal righteousness, with all those that war under him, whose happiness and final hopes are laid up in that only just and rightful kingdom (which we pray incessantly may come soon, and in so praying wish hasty ruin and destruction to all tyrants)—even he our immortal King, and all that love him, must of necessity have in abomination these blind and lame defenders of Jerusalem; as the soul of David[226] hated them and forbid them entrance into God's house and his own. But as to those before them, which I cited first (and with an easy search, for many more might be added), as they there stand, without more in number, being the best and chief of protestant divines, we may follow them for faithful guides and without doubting may receive them as witnesses abundant of what we here affirm concerning tyrants. And indeed I find it generally the clear and positive determination of them all (not prelatical, or of this late faction subprelatical) who have written on this argument: that to do justice on a lawless king is to a private man unlawful, to an inferior magistrate lawful:[227] or if they

logic before Desdemona used it (*Othello,* II, i, 160). The term goes back to Quintilian's warning against rhetorically weak endings to sentences in his *Institutes* IX, iv, 70.
225 The story of the Canaanite king *Adonibezek* (Judg. i, 5–6) is similarly used in John Redingstone's *Plain English to the Parliament and the Army* . . . (1649), p. 2. Arguing that Charles had forfeited all royal authority, and that to support him was treason to the nation, Redingstone declared that "he that ruleth over men, must be just, ruling in the fear of God; And that *Adonibezek,* though a heathen King, acknowledged, saying, 'As I have done so God hath requited me.'"
226 The story of the unsuccessful defense of Jerusalem against *David* by the Jebusites, and of their provocation of his hatred of "the blind and the lame," is told in II Sam. v, 1–8.
227 In contending that kings who abuse their power should be "resisted, not by private men, but by elected magistrates to whom the guardianship of the people's rights should be particularly entrusted," Milton was following what Preserved

were divided in opinion, yet greater than these here alleged, or of more authority in the church, there can be none produced.

If any one shall go about by bringing other testimonies to disable these, or by bringing these against themselves in other cited passages of their books, he will not only fail to make good that false and impudent assertion of those mutinous ministers —that the deposing and punishing of a king or tyrant "is against the constant judgment of all protestant divines" (it being quite the contrary), but will prove rather what perhaps he intended not, that the judgment of divines, if it be so various and inconstant to itself, is not considerable or to be esteemed at all. Ere which be yielded, as I hope it never will, these ignorant assertors in their own art will have proved themselves more and more not to be protestant divines (whose constant judgment in this point they have so audaciously belied) but rather to be a pack of hungry churchwolves, who in the steps of Simon Magus[228] their father, following the hot scent of double livings and pluralities, advowsons,[229]

donatives,[230] inductions,[231] and augmentations[232] (though uncalled to the flock of Christ but by the mere suggestion of their bellies, like those priests of Bel[233] whose pranks Daniel found out), have got possession, or rather seized upon the pulpit, as the stronghold and fortress of their sedition and rebellion against the civil magistrate. Whose friendly and victorious hand having rescued them from the bishops, their insulting lords, fed them plenteously, both in public and in private, raised them to be high and rich of poor and base; only suffered not their covetousness and fierce ambition (which as the pit that sent out their fellow-locusts[234] hath been ever bottomless and boundless) to interpose in all things and over all persons their impetuous ignorance and importunity.

Smith has described in *The Age of the Reformation* (New York, 1920), p. 597, as the definite teaching of both Luther and Calvin about the rights of subjects.

[228] The first man in the Christian church to practise simony (abuse of ecclesiastical position for financial gain) was *Simon Magus,* who "used sorcery" and offered Peter and John money for the gift of imparting the Holy Ghost (Acts viii, 9–25). Cf. n. 213.

[229] *advowson:* the right of presentation to an ecclesiastical living or appointment.

[230] *donative:* a living which the founder or his heirs may grant without any interference by the ordinary bishop.

[231] *induction:* formal installation of a clergyman in his parish.

[232] *augmentation:* an increase of a clergyman's stipend.

[233] According to the Apocryphal Book of Bel, 18–22, Daniel found a secret passage into the image of the great god Bel through which the priests' families got unsuspected possession of the offerings of his worshippers in the temple in Babylon.

[234] Milton's last shot at the Presbyterian divines is to compare them to the locusts which St. John described as swarming out of the bottomless pit of hell in the last days, when "men shall desire to die, and death shall flee from them" (Rev. ix, 1–6).

EIKONOKLASTES:

IN ANSWER TO A BOOK ENTITLED

"EIKON BASILIKE,

THE PORTRAITURE OF HIS SACRED MAJESTY IN HIS SOLITUDES
AND SUFFERINGS."

"As a roaring lion and ranging bear, so is a wicked ruler over the poor people.

"The prince that wanteth understanding, is also a great oppressor; but he that hateth covetousness shall prolong his days.

"A man that doth violence to the blood of any person, shall fly to the pit, let no man stay him."—PROV. xxviii. 15, 16, 17.

SALLUST, *Conjuratio Catilinae*

"Regium imperium, quod initio, conservandæ libertatis, atque augendæ reipublicæ causâ fuerat, in superbiam, dominationemque se convertit.

"Regibus boni, quam mali, suspectiores sunt, semperque his aliena virtus formidolosa est.

"Impunè quælibet facere, id est regem esse."

SALLUST, *Bellum Jugurthinum*

PUBLISHED BY AUTHORITY

. . . .

BIBLIOGRAPHICAL NOTE—The following extracts from *Eikonoklastes*—the Preface and chapters I, V, XXVII, and XXVIII—are based upon the text of the second edition (1650) which is now in the Memorial Library of the University of Wisconsin. They have been selected for the light which they throw upon Milton's view of King Charles I. To understand them the reader should, if possible, have a copy of the *Eikon Basilike* at hand, so as to read the context of Milton's quotations from the work which pretended to have been written by the king himself "in his solitudes and sufferings." For an authoritative treatment of the evidence which all but conclusively proves that the man who was mainly responsible for the *Eikon Basilike* was John Gauden, whom Charles II made Bishop of Exeter, the reader should refer to Francis F. Madan's *A New Bibliography of the Eikon Basilike of King Charles the first, with a note on the authorship* (Oxford, 1950).

THE PREFACE

To descant on the misfortunes of a person fallen from so high a dignity, who hath also paid his final debt both to nature and his faults, is neither of itself a thing commendable nor the intention of this discourse. Neither was it fond ambition or the vanity to get a name, present or with posterity, by writing against a king. I never was so thirsty after fame nor so destitute of other hopes and means, better and more certain to attain it. For kings have gained glorious titles from their favorers by writing against private men, as Henry VIII did against Luther,[1] but no man ever gained much honor by writing against a king, as

[1] *Henry VIII's* title of Defender of the Faith was conferred upon him by Pope Leo X in recognition of his *Assertion of the Seven Sacraments against Martin Luther (Assertio Septem Sacramentorum adversus Martinum Lutherum),* 1521.

not usually meeting with that force of argument in such courtly antagonists which to convince might add to his reputation. Kings most commonly, though strong in legions,[2] are but weak at arguments; as they who ever have accustomed from the cradle to use their will only as their right hand, their reason[3] always as their left. Whence, unexpectedly constrained to that kind of combat, they prove but weak and puny adversaries. Nevertheless for their sakes who through custom, simplicity, or want of better teaching, have not more seriously considered kings than in the gaudy name of majesty, and admire them and their doings as if they breathed not the same breath with other mortal men, I shall make no scruple to take up (for it seems to be the challenge both of him and all his party) to take up this gauntlet, though a king's, in the behalf of liberty and the commonwealth.

And further, since it appears manifestly the cunning drift of a factious and defeated party[4] to make the same advantage of his book which they did before of his regal name and authority, and intend it not so much the defense of his former actions as the promoting of their own future designs —making thereby the book their own rather than the king's, as the benefit now must be their own more than his—now the third time to corrupt and disorder the minds of weaker men by new suggestions and narrations, either falsely or fallaciously representing the state of things to the dishonor of this present government and the retarding of a general peace, so needful to this afflicted nation and so nigh obtained; I suppose it no injury to the dead, but a good deed rather to the living, if by better information given them, or, which is enough, by only remembering them the truth of what they themselves know to be here[5] misaffirmed, they may be kept from entering the third time unadvisedly into war and bloodshed. For as to any moment[6] of solidity in the book itself—save only that a king is said to be the author, a name than which there needs no more among the blockish vulgar, to make it wise, and excellent, and admired, nay to set it next the Bible, though otherwise containing little else but the common grounds of tyranny and popery, dressed up, the better to deceive, in a new Protestant guise, and trimly garnished over. Or as to any need of answering, in respect of staid and well-principled men, I take it on me as a work assigned,[7] rather than by me chosen or affected: which was the cause both of beginning it so late and finishing it so leisurely in the midst of other employments and diversions.

And though well it might have seemed in vain to write at all, considering the envy and almost infinite prejudice likely to be stirred up among the common sort against whatever can be written or gainsaid to the king's book, so advantageous to a book it is only to be a king's; and though it be an irksome labor to write with industry and judicious pains that which, neither weighed nor well read, shall be judged without industry or the pains of well-judging by faction and the easy literature of custom[8] and opinion; it shall be ventured yet, and the truth[9] not smothered, but sent abroad in the native confidence of her single self to earn, how she can, her entertainment in the world, and to find out her own readers —few perhaps, but those few such of value and substantial worth as truth and wisdom, not respecting numbers and big names, have

[2] When the philosopher Favorinus was twitted by his friends for failing to reply to a jibe of the emperor Hadrian, he laughed at them for thinking that he could safely cast any doubt on the wisdom of the master of thirty legions. (Aelius Spartianus in *Scriptores Historiae Augustae, Vita Hadriana* XV, 12–13.)

[3] Milton regarded Charles as "a soul to all reason irreducible (Chap. ix), who constantly deceived himself by confusing "his conscience, honour, and reason" in webs of "large and indefinite words, to defend himself at such a distance as may hinder the eye of common judgment from all distinct view and examination of his reasoning" (Chap. xi).

[4] The *factious . . . party* is the Presbyterian, whose representatives had been excluded from the Long Parliament before the establishment of the court which sentenced King Charles to death. Their clergy were inveighing against his execution in their pulpits and in pamphlets like those which are assailed in Chap. xxviii below.

[5] *here:* i.e. in the *Eikon-Basilike,* from which Milton constantly quotes.

[6] *moment:* tiny particle.

[7] In *Def* 2 (C.E. VIII, 138) Milton speaks of the writing of *Eikonoklastes* as a definite assignment to him by the Council of State.

[8] Cf. the opening attack in *TKM* on "those wily Arbitresses," Ignorance and Custom, against whom readers are also warned in *CG* II, iii.

[9] Cf. the personifications of truth in *Areop* and in Chap. xxviii below.

been ever wont in all ages to be contented with.

And if the late king had thought sufficient those answers and defenses made for him in his lifetime, they who on the other side accused his evil government, judging that on their behalf enough also hath been replied, the heat of this controversy was in likelihood drawing to an end, and the further mention of his deeds, not so much unfortunate as faulty, had in tenderness to his late sufferings been willingly forborne;[10] and perhaps for the present age might have slept with him unrepeated; while his adversaries, calmed and assuaged with the success of their cause, had been the less unfavorable to his memory. But since he himself, making new appeal to truth and the world, hath left behind him this book as the best advocate and interpreter of his own actions, and that his friends by publishing, dispersing, commending, and almost adoring it, seem to place therein the chief strength and nerves of their cause; it would argue doubtless in the other party great deficience and distrust of themselves not to meet the force of his reason in any field whatsoever, the force and equipage of whose arms they have so often met victoriously. And he who at the bar stood excepting against the form and manner of his judicature[11] and complained that he was not heard—neither he nor his friends shall have that cause now to find fault, being met and debated with in this open and monumental court of his own erecting; and not only heard uttering his whole mind at large, but answered—which to do effectually, if it be necessary that to his book nothing the more respect be had for being his, they of his own party can have no just reason to exclaim.

For it were too unreasonable that he, because dead, should have the liberty in his book to speak all evil of the Parliament; and they, because living, should be expected to have less freedom, or any for them, to speak home the plain truth of a full and pertinent reply. As he, to acquit himself, hath not spared his adversaries to load them with all sorts of blame and accusation, so to him, as in his book alive,[12] there will be used no more courtship than he uses; but what is properly his own guilt, not imputed any more to his evil counsellors[13] (a ceremony used longer by the Parliament than he himself desired) shall be laid here without circumlocutions at his own door. That they who from the first beginning, or but now of late, by what unhappiness I know not, are so much affatuated,[14] not with his person only but with his palpable faults, and dote upon his deformities, may have none to blame but their own folly if they live and die in such a stricken blindness as, next to that of Sodom,[15] hath not happened to any sort of men more gross or more misleading. Yet neither let his enemies expect to find recorded here all that hath been whispered in the court or alleged openly of the king's bad actions; it being the proper scope of this work in hand not to rip up and relate the misdoings of his whole life, but to answer only and refute the missayings of his book.

First then, that some men (whether this

---

10 Milton has been mistaken for the author of a tract, *The Life and Reigne of King Charls* (1651), which opens with an expression of "pitty to him, who hath already paid his debt to Nature," and declares that "his offences, much of his exorbitant government and irregular motions might, and doubtlesse would have been concealed, more tenderly intreated, and himselfe suffering to rest where he is, in the silent grave, had not that madnesse of his defeated party, by their indefatigable instigations, given frequent occasions for raking over the ashes of him, who living (without injury to truth and his memory it may be said) that rather than to have failed in the accomplishing of his design, (had it layn in his power) he would have set the World on fire."

11 *His Majesties Reasons against the Pretended Jurisdiction of the High Court of Justice, which he intended to have delivered in writing on Monday, January 22, 1648* (n.s. 1649) *but was not permitted* is available in J. G. Muddiman's *Trial of King Charles the First* (London, 1928), pp. 231–2. Charles denied that a king could be subject to any human tribunal.

12 Charles is to be treated as if he spoke with a living voice in the *Eikon Basilike*, which his admirers accepted as his "lively portraiture."

13 Charles could not plead that "the king can do no wrong" because his ministers are responsible for his acts. He had always asserted his right to choose them for himself, rejecting the principle that Parliament should have the right to expect him "to employ such councillors, ambassadors, and other ministers . . . as the Parliament may have cause to confide in," as it was put to him in the Grand Remonstrance. Charles's willing "hearkening to evil counsellors" figures largely in Chap. xiii.

14 *affatuated* infatuated.

15 *Sodom* was a byword for the spiritual blindness which led to its destruction (Gen. xix, 24).

were by him intended, or by his friends) have by policy accomplished after death that revenge upon their enemies which in life they were not able, hath been oft related. And among other examples we find that the last will of Cæsar[16] being read to the people, and what bounteous legacies he had bequeathed them, wrought more in that vulgar audience to the avenging of his death than all the art he could ever use, to win their favor in his lifetime. And how much their intent who published these over-late apologies and meditations of the dead king, drives to the same end of stirring up the people to bring him that honor, that affection, and by consequence that revenge to his dead corpse which he himself living could never gain to his person, it appears both by the conceited portraiture[17] before his book, drawn out to the full measure of a masking scene, and set there to catch fools and silly gazers, and by those Latin words after the end, *Vota dabunt quæ bella negarunt,* intimating that "What he could not compass by war he should achieve by his meditations." For in words which admit of various sense the liberty is ours to choose that interpretation which may best mind us of what our restless enemies endeavor and what we are timely to prevent.

And here may be well observed the loose and negligent curiosity of those who took upon them to adorn the setting out of this book. For though the picture set in front would martyr him and saint him to befool the people, yet the Latin motto in the end, which they understand not, leaves him, as it were, a politic contriver to bring about that interest by fair and plausible words which the force of arms denied him. But quaint emblems and devices, begged from the old pageantry of some Twelfthnight's entertainment[18] at Whitehall, will do but ill to make a saint or martyr; and if the people resolve to take him sainted at the rate of such a canonizing, I shall suspect their calendar more than the Gregorian.[19] In one thing I must commend his openness who gave the title to this book, Εἰκὼν Βασιλικὴ, that is to say, *The King's Image;* and by the shrine he dresses out for him certainly would have the people come and worship him. For which reason this answer also is entitled *Eikonoklastes,*[20] the famous surname of many Greek emperors who, in their zeal to the command of God, after long tradition of idolatry in the Church, took courage and broke all superstitious images to pieces.

But the people, exorbitant and excessive in all their motions, are prone ofttimes not to a religious only, but to a civil kind of idolatry in idolizing their kings; though never more mistaken in the object of their worship; heretofore being wont to repute for saints those faithful and courageous barons[21] who lost their lives in the field making glorious war against tyrants for the common liberty: as Simon de Montfort[22] Earl of Leicester, against Henry III;

---

[16] If not in Suetonius' Life of Caesar (83), then in Shakespeare's *Julius Caesar* III, ii, Milton's readers were familiar with the reading of the will which Mark Antony said would make the Romans "go kiss dead Caesar's wounds."

[17] The frontispiece of the *Eikon Basilike* is mentioned again in the last paragraph of Chap. xxviii, below which it is reproduced.

[18] Shakespeare's *Twelfth Night* is the most familiar of the entertainments which had marked the end of the Christmas season at court, but a better example is Ben Jonson's *Masque of Augurs,* which was presented on Twelfth Night, 1622.

[19] In 1649, English practice in dating was far from fully reconciled to the modern calendar, which Gregory XIII proclaimed in March, 1582, to supersede the Julian calendar.

[20] The title of Milton's book had been given to the Isaurian emperor Leo III, who began the Iconoclastic Controversy in 726 A.D. by promulgating a decree against Pope Gregory II and the orthodox leaders of the Roman Catholic Church, whereby images and their worship were forbidden in churches throughout the empire. Milton's authority (for whose point of view he had no sympathy) was Cuspinian, who represented Leo's "iconoclasm" as having venal and political motives in *Joannis Cuspiniani viri clarissimi, poetae et medici, ac D. Maximiliani Aug. oratoris, de Caesaribus atque Imperatoribus Romanis Opus insigne* (Frankfort, 1601), pp. 163–9.

[21] Like President Bradshaw in his sentence of death upon King Charles, Milton interpreted the depositions of Edward II and Richard II as precedents for the trial and death sentence on Charles. (See Muddiman, *Trial of Charles I,* p. 120.)

[22] The Royalist view of Henry III's struggles with *Simon de Montfort* and the barons supporting him was stated in Edward Chamberlayne's *The Present Warre Parallel'd. Or, a briefe Relation of the five yeares Civil Warres of Henry the Third, King of England, with the event and issue of that unnatural warre* (1647). He was answered by George Walker in *Anglo-Tyrannus, Represented in the parallel Reignes of Henrie the Third and Charles Kings of England* (1650), whose long title declared that the work *discovered the impious, abusive, and delusive practices by which the English have been bobbed of their freedome, and the*

Thomas Plantagenet Earl of Lancaster, against Edward II. But now, with a besotted and degenerate baseness of spirit, except some few who yet retain in them the old English fortitude and love of freedom and have testified it by their matchless deeds, the rest, imbastardized from the ancient nobleness of their ancestors, are ready to fall flat and give adoration to the image and memory of this man who hath offered at more cunning fetches to undermine our liberties, and put tyranny into an art, than any British king before him. Which low dejection and debasement of mind in the people, I must confess, I cannot willingly ascribe to the natural disposition of an Englishman, but rather to two other causes: first, to the prelates and their fellow-teachers, though of another name and sect, whose pulpit stuff, both first and last, hath been the doctrine and perpetual infusion of servility[23] and wretchedness to all their hearers; whose lives the type of worldliness and hypocrisy, without the least true pattern of virtue, righteousness, or self-denial in their whole practice. I attribute it, next, to the factious inclination of most men divided from the public by several ends and humors of their own.

At first no man less beloved, no man more generally condemned, than was the king; from the time that it became his custom to break Parliaments at home and either wilfully or weakly to betray Protestants abroad, to the beginning of these combustions. All men inveighed against him; all men, except court-vassals, opposed him and his tyrannical proceedings; the cry was universal; and this full Parliament was at first unanimous in their dislike and protestation against his evil government. But when they who sought themselves and not the public, began to doubt that all of them could not by one and the same way attain to their ambitious purposes, then was the king, or his name at least, as a fit property, first made use of, his doings made the best of, and by degrees justified. Which begot him such a party as, after many wiles and strugglings with his inward fears, embold-

ened him at length to set up his standard[24] against the Parliament. Whenas before that time all his adherents, consisting most of dissolute swordmen and suburb roisterers, hardly amounted to the making up of one ragged regiment strong enough to assault the unarmed House of Commons. After which attempt, seconded by a tedious and bloody war on his subjects, wherein he hath so far exceeded those his arbitrary violences in time of peace, they who before hated him for his high misgovernment, nay, fought against him[25] with displayed banners in the field, now applaud him and extol him for the wisest and most religious prince that lived. By so strange a method amongst the mad multitude is a sudden reputation won, of wisdom by wilfulness and subtle shifts, of goodness by multiplying evil, of piety by endeavoring to root out true religion.

But it is evident that the chief of his adherents never loved him, never honored either him or his cause, but as they took him to set a face upon their own malignant designs, nor bemoan his loss at all, but the loss of their own aspiring hopes: like those captive women whom the poet notes in his *Iliad* to have bewailed the death of Patroclus in outward show, but indeed their own condition.

Πάτροκλον πρόφασιν, σφῶν δ'αὐτῶν κηδε' ἑκάστη. Homer, *Iliad* T.[26] [302].

And it needs must be ridiculous to any judgment unenthralled that they who in other matters express so little fear either of God or man, should in this one particular outstrip all precisianism with their scruples and cases, and fill men's ears continually with the noise of their conscientious loyalty and allegiance to the king, rebels in the

---

Norman Tyrannie founded and continued over them.
[23] Cf. the many references to the support of the king by Archbishop Laud's party in the Church, both in *TKM* and in Chap. i of *Eikon*.

[24] When Charles *set up his standard* at Nottingham on Aug. 22, 1642, says G. M. Trevelyan in *England under the Stuarts* (London, 1904), p. 193, "it was a slender band that greeted the erection of the royal standard with a cheery shout of 'God save King Charles and hang up the Roundheads.'"
[25] Cf. the opening attack on the Presbyterians in *TKM*.
[26] Chapman translates Homer's comment on the tears of Briseis' attendants after her lament for the dead Patroclus in these words:
Thus spake she weeping, and with her did th'other ladies moan
Patroclus' fortunes in pretext, but in sad truth their own.

meanwhile to God in all their actions beside: much less that they whose professed loyalty and allegiance led them to direct arms against the king's person[27] and thought him nothing violated by the sword of hostility drawn by them against him, should now in earnest think him violated by the unsparing sword of justice, which undoubtedly so much the less in vain she bears among men, by how much greater and in highest place the offender.[28] Else justice, whether moral or political, were not justice, but a false counterfeit of that impartial and godlike virtue. The only grief is that the head was not struck off to the best advantage and commodity of them that held it by the hair—an ungrateful and perverse generation, who having first cried to God to be delivered from their king, now murmur against God that heard their prayers, and cry as loud for their king against those that delivered them.

But as to the author of these soliloquies, whether it were undoubtedly the late King, as is vulgarly believed, or any secret coadjutor, and some stick not to name him,[29] it can add nothing, nor shall take from the weight, if any be, of reason which he brings. But allegations, not reasons, are the main contents of this book, and need no more than other contrary allegations to lay the question before all men in an even balance; though it were supposed that the testimony of one man in his own cause affirming could be of any moment to bring in doubt the authority of a parliament denying. But if these his fair-spoken words shall be here fairly confronted and laid parallel to his own far differing deeds, manifest and visible to the whole nation, then surely we may look on them who, notwithstanding, shall persist to give to bare words more credit than to open deeds, as men whose judgment was not rationally evinced and persuaded, but fatally stupefied and bewitched into such a blind and obstinate belief. For whose cure it may be doubted, not whether any charm, though never so wisely murmured, but whether any prayer, can be available.

This, however, would be remembered and well noted that while the king, instead of that repentence which was in reason and in conscience to be expected from him, without which we could not lawfully readmit[30] him, persists here to maintain and justify the most apparent of his evildoings, and washes over with a court-fucus[31] the worst and foulest of his actions, disables and uncreates the Parliament itself, with all our laws and native liberties that ask not his leave, dishonors and attaints all Protestant Churches, not prelatical,[32] and what they piously reformed, with the slander of rebellion, sacrilege, and hypocrisy; they who seemed of late to stand up hottest for the Covenant,[33] can now sit mute and much pleased to hear all these opprobrious things uttered against their faith, their freedom, and themselves in their own doings made traitors to boot. The divines also, their wizards, can be so brazen as to cry Hosanna to this his book, which cries louder against them for no disciples of Christ, but of Iscariot;[34] and to seem now convinced with these withered arguments and reasons here, the same which in some other writings of that party and in his own former declarations and expresses[35] they have so often heretofore endeavored to confute and to explode—none appearing all this while to vindicate Church or State from these calumnies and reproaches but a small handful of men whom they defame and spit at with

[30] Cf. Chap. xxvii, n. 4.

[31] *fucus:* liquid cosmetic.

[32] Cf. Milton's appeal in *TKM,* p. 779, to the non-prelatical or "not prelatical or of this late [i.e. Presbyterian] faction subprelatical" Protestant churches in Europe as examples of resistance to tyranny.

[33] Not the Scottish National Covenant but the Solemn League and Covenant of the Scots with the English Parliament to reform "religion in the kingdoms of England and Ireland, in doctrine, worship, discipline, and government, according to the Word of God and the example of the best reformed Churches." Cf. its discussion in Chap. xxviii.

[34] Disciples of Judas *Iscariot* are, of course, traitors.

[35] Communications less formal than royal proclamations were often called *expresses.*

[27] Cf. the criticism of the Presbyterians about bearing arms against the *king's person* in the opening paragraph of *TKM.*

[28] Cf. the basic argument for royal responsibility throughout *TKM.*

[29] The evidence that Bishop John Gauden was the *coadjutor* is reviewed by F. F. Madan in the appendix to his *New Bibliography of the Eikon Basilike* (London, 1950).

all the odious names of schism and sectarism. I never knew that time in England when men of truest religion were not counted secretaries:[36] but wisdom now, valor, justice, constancy, prudence united and embodied to defend religion and our liberties, both by word and deed against tyranny, is counted schism and faction.

Thus in a graceless age things of highest praise and imitation under a right name, to make them infamous and hateful to the people, are miscalled. Certainly, if ignorance and perverseness will needs be national and universal, then they who adhere to wisdom and to truth, are not therefore to be blamed for being so few as to seem a sect or faction. But in my opinion it goes not ill with that people where these virtues grow so numerous and well joined together as to resist and make head against the rage and torrent of that boisterous folly and superstition that possesses and hurries on the vulgar sort. This therefore we may conclude to be a high honor done us from God and a special mark of his favor, whom he hath selected as the sole remainder,[37] after all these changes and commotions, to stand upright and steadfast in his cause; dignified with the defense of truth and public liberty; while others who aspired to be the top of zealots[38] and had almost brought religion to a kind of trading monopoly, have not only by their late silence and neutrality belied their profession, but foundered themselves and their consciences to comply with enemies in that wicked cause and interest which they have too often cursed in others to prosper now in the same themselves.

---

[36] Cf. the irony of the remark in *Areop*, p. 748, that in Reformation times "many sectaries were busy."

[37] Cf. the *remnant* of Israel (in Isa. xi) who are to return from captivity and see God "with equity reprove the meek of the earth: and he shall smite the earth with the rod of his mouth, and with the breath of his lips shall he slay the wicked.

[38] Milton's use of *zealots* is illustrated by Henry Hammond in *Of the Zelots among the Jewes* (Oxford, 1644) when he rebuked the Puritans for using religion as a cloak for political agitation and abusing "that Jewish priviledge of Zealots in the Old Testament," which "is clearly interdicted all Christians" (p. 56).

Ἐικονοκλάστης

1. Upon the King's calling this last Parliament.

That which the king lays down here as his first foundation and as it were the head-stone of his whole structure, that "he called this last Parliament, not more by others advice and the necessity of his affairs than by his own choice and inclination[1]," is to all knowing men so apparently not true that a more unlucky and inauspicious sentence, and more betokening the downfall of his whole fabric, hardly could have come into his mind. For who knows not that the inclination of a prince is best known either by those next about him and most in favor with him, or by the current of his own actions? Those nearest to this king and most his favorites were courtiers[2] and prelates,[3] men whose chief study was to find out which way the king inclined and to imitate him exactly. How these men stood affected to Parliaments cannot be forgotten.

---

[1] Well-informed men of even the most moderate Parliamentary sympathies shared the amusement over Charles's pretense that the Long Parliament was "called as much by his own choyce and inclination, as advise of others," when—as William Lilly said in *Monarchy, or no Monarchy in England* (1651), p. 80—"it is manifestly knowne even unto all, it was only necessity and the importunity of the *English*, who would not fight with the *Scots*, and this onely cause was it which gave occasion for calling this *Parliament*."

[2] Many *courtiers*—as was charged in the work which G. W. Whiting declares in *SP*, XXXII (1935), 76–84, that Milton was following, *The History of the Parliament of England: which began November the third, MDCL* . . . , by Thomas May, Secretary for the Parliament (1647), pp. 18–19 —were inclined "to dispute against Parliaments in their ordinary discourse, That they were cruell to those whom the King favoured, and too injurious to his Prerogative; . . . and that they hoped the King should never need any more Parliaments." Yet it should be remembered that the Triennial Act of Feb. 15, 1641, was carried by a large majority and had the support of such outstanding courtiers and partisans of the King as Hyde, Falkland, and the Baron Digby.

[3] Parliament's quarrel with the *prelates* was officially stated in the Grand Remonstrance, which accused them of preaching "the most public and solemn sermons before His Majesty . . . to advance prerogative above law, and decry the property of the subject" (Gardiner, *Documents*, p. 215).

No man but may remember it was their continual exercise to dispute and preach against them, and in their common discourse nothing was more frequent than that "they hoped the King should now have no need of Parliaments any more." And this was but the copy which his parasites had industriously taken from his own words and actions, who never called a Parliament but to supply his necessities;[4] and having supplied those, as suddenly and ignominiously dissolved it, without redressing any one grievance of the people, sometimes choosing rather to miss of his subsidies, or to raise them by illegal courses, than that the people should not still miss of their hopes to be relieved by Parliaments.

The first[5] he broke off at his coming to the crown, for no other cause than to protect the Duke of Buckingham[6] against them who had accused him, besides other heinous crimes, of no less than poisoning[7] the deceased king his father; concerning which matter the Declaration of *No more addresses* hath sufficiently informed us. And still the latter[8] breaking was with more affront and indignity put upon the House and her worthiest members than the former. Insomuch that in the fifth year of his reign, in a proclamation[9] he seems offended at the very rumor of a Parliament divulged among the people; as if he had taken it for a kind of slander that men should think him that way exorable, much less inclined: and forbids it as a presumption to prescribe him any time for Parliaments; that is to say, either by persuasion or petition or so much as the reporting of such a rumor; for other manner of prescribing was at that time not suspected. By which fierce edict the people, forbidden to complain as well as forced to suffer, began from thenceforth to despair of Parliaments. Whereupon such illegal actions, and especially to get vast sums of money, were put in practice by the king and his new officers, as monopolies,[10] compulsive knighthoods, coat, conduct and ship-money, the seizing not of one Naboth's vineyard,[11] but of whole inheritances under the pretense of forest or crownlands, corruption and bribery compounded for, with impunities granted for the future, as gave evident proof that the king never meant, nor could it stand with the reason

[4] In the Grand Remonstrance Charles was accused of "dissolving the Parliament in the second year of His Majesty's reign, after a declaration of their intent to grant five subsidies" (Gardiner, *Documents,* p. 209), and of calling "a Parliament, not to seek counsel and advice from them, but to draw countenance and supply from them . . ." (*Documents,* p. 216).

[5] Charles I's *first* parliament met on June 18, 1625, but moved to Oxford on July 11 and sat there for only ten days before it was adjourned on August 10.

[6] George Villiers (1592–1628) was distrusted by the Puritans not only because James I's doting fondness for him had promoted him from the rank of a mere gentleman of the royal bedchamber to be *Duke of Buckingham* and Lord High Admiral of England, but also because they distrusted his patriotism and loyalty to the Protestant cause in his repeated but always unsuccessful efforts to relieve the Huguenots in La Rochelle. In the last of these expeditions he was assassinated by one of his own discharged officers, who was said to have felt justified in the crime by the charges of injustice which had been brought against him in Parliament.

[7] In *The Votes of the Lords and Commons Assembled in Parliament, Touching no farther addresses to the King* (published Feb. 18, 1648), pp. 12–16, the charge of murder by the Commons in 1626 was reprinted. It was also revived by one of James's physicians in 1648 in *A Declaration to the Kingdom of England, concerning The poysoning of King James, . . . touching the Duke of Buckingham . . .*

[8] Charles summoned Parliament on Feb. 6, 1626, and dissolved it on June 15 to prevent its impeachment of Buckingham. His third Parliament—to which Milton refers as "the latter"—met on March 17, 1628, and again in 1629, after the Duke's assassination. It broke up in the confusion of Sir John Eliot's reading of three resolutions of protest against the royal policy in religion and taxation while the Speaker of the House of Commons was forcibly held in his chair on March 2, 1629. Two days later Eliot and seven other members of the House were sent to the Tower, where he died in November, 1632.

[9] Charles's *proclamations* after dissolving Parliament in 1626 and 1629 were described in the Grand Remonstrance as "published to asperse their proceedings, and some of their members unjustly; to make them odious, and colour the violence which was used against them, . . . to the great dejecting of the hearts of the people, forbidding them even to speak of Parliaments" (*Documents,* p. 210).

[10] The Remonstrance protested against the sale of *monopolies* in "soap, salt, wine, leather, sea-coal, and in a manner of all things of most common and necessary use," and charged corruption in the sale of "Titles of honour, judicial places, serjeantships at law, and other offices" for "great summs of money" (*Documents,* p. 214). Cf. *Areop,* n. 250.

[11] Cf. Samuel Rutherford's use of King Ahab's seizure of *Naboth's vineyard* (I Kings xxi) in *Lex, Rex: the Law and the Prince* (1644), p. 68, to illustrate his definition of a tyrant as a ruler who seeks to "rake the proper goods of his subjects, and use them as his own."

of his affairs, ever to recall Parliaments: having brought by these irregular courses the people's interest and his own to so direct an opposition that he might foresee plainly, if nothing but a Parliament could save the people, it must necessarily be his undoing.

Till eight or nine years after, proceeding with a high hand in these enormities, and having the second time levied an injurious war against his native country, Scotland;[12] and finding all those other shifts of raising money, which bore out his first expedition, now to fail him, not "of his own choice and inclination," as any child may see, but urged by strong necessities and the very pangs of state, which his own violent proceedings had brought him to, he calls a Parliament; first in Ireland,[13] which only was to give him four subsidies, and so to expire; then in England, where his first demand was but twelve subsidies[14] to maintain a Scotch war,[15] condemned and abominated by the whole kingdom; promising their grievances should be considered afterward. Which when the Parliament, who judged that war itself one of their main grievances, made no haste to grant, not enduring the delay of his impatient will, or else fearing the conditions of their grant, he breaks off the whole session and dismisses them and their grievances with scorn and frustration.

Much less therefore did he call this last Parliament[16] by his own choice and inclination; but having first tried in vain all un-

due ways to procure money, his army of their own accord being beaten in the north, the Lords petitioning,[17] and the general voice of the people almost hissing him and his ill-acted regality off the stage, compelled at length both by his wants and by his fears, upon mere extremity he summoned this last Parliament. And how is it possible that he should willingly incline to Parliaments, who never was perceived to call them but for the greedy hope of a whole national bribe, his subsidies; and never loved, never fulfilled, never promoted the true end of Parliaments, the redress of grievances;[18] but still put them off and prorogued[19] them, whether gratified or not gratified; and was indeed the author of all those grievances? To say therefore that he called this Parliament of his own choice and inclination, argues how little truth we can expect from the sequel of this book, which ventures in the very first period to affront more than one nation with an untruth so remarkable; and presumes a more implicit faith in the people of England than the pope ever commanded from the Romish laity; or else a natural sottishness fit to be abused and ridden. While in the judgment of wise men, by laying the foundation of his defense on the avouchment of that which is so manifestly untrue, he hath given a worse foil[20] to his own cause than when his whole forces were at any time overthrown. They therefore who think such great service done to the king's affairs in publishing this book will find themselves in the end mistaken, if sense and right mind, or but any medi-

[12] Charles's first war in *Scotland* ended inconclusively in the Treaty of Berwick, June 18, 1639. The second ended in the Treaty of Ripon, which left the Scots masters of Northumberland and Durham and assured them of a daily payment of £850 until a final settlement could be reached.

[13] In March, 1640, Charles was granted four subsidies of £45,000 each by the Irish Parliament with a willingness which contrasted sharply with the reluctance of the English Parliament to subsidize his wars in Scotland.

[14] Charles's demand for twelve *subsidies* was challenged by John Pym on April 27, 1640, with the demand that redress of grievances should take precedence over discussion of grants of supply. Charles replied by dissolving the Short Parliament a week later.

[15] So unpopular was the war with Scotland that when the "enemy" was on English soil the City of London refused a loan to enable Charles to carry it on, and his troops were too mutinous to be used effectively against the Scots.

[16] *This last Parliament* is the Long Parliament, which met on Nov. 3, 1640, and was still sitting when Milton wrote.

[17] After the dissolution of the Short Parliament Charles summoned *the Lords* to meet at York, and the eighty who responded were mainly responsible for the treaty of Ripon and for Charles's reluctant decision to summon the Long Parliament.

[18] The position of Parliament about *redress of grievances* was justified by an anonymous tract, *The English Presbyterian and Independent Reconciled* (1651) on the ground that a statute of Edward III had defined "the End wherefore that Court was instituted at first" as "redresse of grievances in a Commonwealth" (p. 4).

[19] The *O.E.D.* cites this passage to illustrate "prolong" in its obsolete meaning of *prorogue*, i.e. adjourn *sine die*.

[20] *foil* is the clear reading of the copies in the Houghton Library at Harvard and of the copy in the Memorial Library of the University of Wisconsin, though in some copies the word seems to be *soil*. Both words were used as substantives: *foil* to mean a repulse of any kind, and *soil* to mean a stain or disgrace.

ocrity of knowledge and remembrance, hath not quite forsaken men.

But to prove his inclination to Parliaments he affirms here "to have always thought the right way of them most safe for his crown and best pleasing to his people."[21] What he thought, we know not; but that he ever took the contrary way we saw; and from his own actions we felt long ago what he thought of Parliaments or of pleasing his people—a surer evidence than what we hear now too late in words.

He alleges that "the cause of forbearing to convene Parliaments was the sparks which some men's distempers[22] there studied to kindle." They were indeed not tempered to his temper; for it neither was the law, nor the rule, by which all other tempers were to be tried; but they were esteemed and chosen for the fittest men, in their several counties, to allay and quench those distempers which his own inordinate doings had inflamed. And if that were his refusing to "convene" till those men had been qualified to his temper, that is to say, his will, we may easily conjecture what hope there was of Parliaments, had not fear and his insatiate poverty, in the midst of his excessive wealth, constrained him.

"He hoped by his freedom and their moderation to prevent misunderstandings." And wherefore not by their freedom and his moderation? But freedom he thought too high a word for them and moderation too mean a word for himself: this was not the way to prevent misunderstandings. He still "feared passion and prejudice in other men"; not in himself: "and doubted not by the weight of his" own "reason to counterpoise any faction"; it being so easy for him, and so frequent, to call his obstinacy reason, and other men's reason faction. We in the meanwhile must believe that wisdom and all reason came to him by title with his crown; passion, prejudice, and faction came to others by being subjects.

"He was sorry to hear with what popular heat elections[23] were carried in many places." Sorry rather that court-letters and intimations[24] prevailed no more to divert or to deter the people from their free election of those men whom they thought best affected to religion and their country's liberty, both at that time in danger to be lost. And such men they were as by the kingdom were sent to advise him, not sent to be cavilled at, because elected, or to be entertained by him with an undervalue and misprision of their temper, judgment, or affection. In vain was a Parliament thought fittest by the known laws of our nation to advise and regulate unruly kings, if they, instead of hearkening to advice, should be permitted to turn it off and refuse it by vilifying and traducing their advisers, or by accusing of a popular heat those that lawfully elected them.

"His own and his children's interest obliged him to seek and to preserve the love and welfare of his subjects." Who doubts it? But the same interest, common to all kings, was never yet available to make them all seek that which was indeed best for themselves and their posterity. All men by their own and their children's interest are obliged to honesty and justice: but how little that consideration works in private men, how much less in kings, their deeds declare best.

"He intended to oblige both friends and enemies and to exceed their desires, did they but pretend to any modest and sober sense"—mistaking the whole business of a Parliament. Which met not to receive from him obligations, but justice; nor he to expect from them their modesty, but their grave advice, utter'd with freedom in the public cause. His talk of modesty in their desires of the common welfare argues him not much to have understood what he had to grant, who misconceived so much the nature of what they had to desire. And for "sober sense" the expression was too mean; and recoils with as much dishonor

---

21 Cf. Milton's treatment of Charles's lip-service to "parliaments held with freedom and with honor" in Chap. xxvii.

22 Belial's hope that the devils' bodies may change "in temper and in nature" (*PL* II, 215–9) is illuminated by the punning use of *temper* as applicable both to the physical and moral constitution or temperament, which was regarded as depending upon a balance of the four humors, blood, bile, phlegm, and melancholy. Cf. *PL* IX, 887, and XI, 53.

23 The *elections* for the Long Parliament do not seem to Godfrey Davies "to have caused any great excitement" (*Stuarts*, p. 90).

24 Again in Chap. xi Milton says that "the court was wont . . . to tamper with elections," a practice which Tanner (*Conflicts*, pp. 28, 46, and 91) says irritated James I's parliaments and failed in the case of the Long Parliament.

upon himself, to be a king where sober sense could possibly be so wanting in a Parliament.

"The odium and offenses which some men's rigor or remissness in church and state had contracted upon his government he resolved to have expiated with better laws and regulations." And yet the worst of misdemeanors committed by the worst of all his favorites in the height of their dominion, whether acts of rigor or remissness, he hath from time to time continued, owned, and taken upon himself by public declarations as often as the clergy, or any other of his instruments, felt themselves overburdened with the people's hatred. And who knows not the superstitious rigor of his Sunday's chapel,[25] and the licentious remissness of his Sunday's theater[26]—accompanied with that reverend statute[27] for dominical jigs[28] and maypoles, published in his own name, and derived from the example of his father, James? Which testifies all that rigor in superstition, all that remissness in religion, to have issued out originally from his own house and from his own authority.

Much rather then may those general miscarriages in State, his proper sphere, be imputed to no other person chiefly than to himself. And which of all those oppressive acts or impositions did he ever disclaim or disavow till the fatal awe of this Parliament hung ominously over him? Yet here he smoothly seeks to wipe off all the envy of his evil government upon his substitutes and under-officers, and promises, though much too late, what wonders he purposed to have done in the reforming of religion—a work wherein all his undertakings heretofore declare him to have had little or no judgment. Neither could his breeding or his course of life acquaint him with a thing so spiritual. Which may well assure us what kind of reformation we could expect from him: either some politic form of an imposed religion or else perpetual vexation and persecution to all those that complied not with such a form.

The like amendment he promises in State; not a step further "than his reason and conscience told him was fit to be desired"; wishing "he had kept within those bounds and not suffered his own judgment to have been overborne in some things," of which things one was the Earl of Strafford's execution.[29] And what signifies all this but that still his resolution was the same, to set up an arbitrary government of his own; and that all Britain was to be tied and chained to the conscience, judgment, and reason of one man; as if those gifts had been only his peculiar[30] and prerogative,[31] entailed upon him with his fortune to be a king? Whenas doubtless no man so obstinate or so much a tyrant, but professes to be guided by that which he

---

[25] As early as 1620 the Spanish ambassador Gondomar noted Charles's careful private devotions—a trait of sincere piety which annoyed those who (like Milton) found it hard to accept the honesty of his professions of faith. In his discussion of some of Charles's "Penitential Meditations and Vows" in Chap. xxv he notes that "the conditions of his treating with God" were such as to abate "nothing of what he stood upon with the Parliament."

[26] Milton's alliance with the Puritan opposition to Sunday theatrical entertainments was avowed when in Ref (C.E. III, 53) he attacked the bishops for using the Book of Sports to encourage "gaming, jigging, wassailing, and mixed dancing" on Sundays. The conflict—as E. N. S. Thompson showed in The Controversy between the Puritans and the Stage (New York, 1903)—was part of a larger struggle between the court and the political and religious groups for whom William Prynne spoke in Histrio-mastix (1632).

[27] Charles's Declaration of Sports (or "Book of Sports") of Oct. 18, 1633, was a renewal of James I's Declaration of 1618. It pleased the Puritans by forbidding bear- and bull-baiting, interludes, and bowling on Sundays, but it repeated James's rebuke of "Puritans and precise people" who condemned "lawful recreation" on Sundays, such as "dancing, either men or women; archery for men, leaping, vaulting, or any other such harmless recreations,"

[28] Jigs were dances or light entertainments. The combination of the word with the Latin term for Sunday, dominica dies, the Lord's day, is a typical Miltonic combination of a Latin epithet with an English monosyllable for satiric effect.

[29] In Chap. ii, Milton speaks of the sentence of the Earl of Strafford to death for his subordination of the interests of the Irish and of Parliament to the King's interest in increasing the royal domain in Ireland as "the most seasonable and solemn piece of justice that had been done of many years."

[30] Canon law recognized "peculiar jurisdictions" over parishes specially reserved from episcopal for private control, one variety of which was a "royal peculiar."

[31] Cf. the figure of the royal prerogative as a "misty cloud" in Chap. x, and as an unjust wardship of the nation in Chap. xi, and the account of the Civil War in Way, p. 892, as "endless tugging between petition of right and royal prerogative."

calls his reason and his judgment, though never so corrupted; and pretends also his conscience. In the meanwhile, for any Parliament or the whole nation to have either reason, judgment, or conscience, by this rule was altogether in vain, if it thwarted the king's will; which was easy for him to call by any other more plausible name. He himself hath many times acknowledged to have no right over us but by law;[32] and by the same law to govern us: but law in a free nation hath been ever public reason, the enacted reason of a Parliament; which he denying to enact, denies to govern us by that which ought to be our law; interposing his own private reason, which to us is no law. And thus we find these fair and specious promises, made upon the experience of many hard sufferings and his most mortified retirements, being thoroughly sifted, to contain nothing in them much different from his former practices, so cross and so averse to all his Parliaments and both the nations of this island. What fruits they could in likelihood have produced in his restorement, is obvious to any prudent foresight.

And this is the substance of his first section, till we come to the devout of it, modelled into the form of a private psalter.[33] Which they who so much admire, either for the matter or the manner, may as well admire the archbishop's late breviary[34] and many other as good *Manuals* and *Handmaids of Devotion,* the lip-work of every prelatical liturgist, clapped together and quilted out of Scripture phrase with as much ease and as little need of Christian diligence or judgment as belongs to the compiling of any ordinary and saleable piece of English divinity that the shops value. But he who from such a kind of psalmistry or any other verbal devotion, without the pledge and earnest of suitable deeds, can be persuaded of a zeal and true

righteousness in the person, hath much yet to learn; and knows not that the deepest policy of a tyrant hath been ever to counterfeit religious. And Aristotle in his *Politics,*[35] hath mentioned that special craft among twelve other tyrannical sophisms. Neither want we examples: Andronicus Comnenus the Byzantine emperor, though a most cruel tyrant, is reported by Nicetas[36] to have been a constant reader of Saint Paul's Epistles; and by continual study had so incorporated the phrase and style of that transcendent apostle into all his familiar letters that the imitation seemed to vie with the original. Yet this availed not to deceive the people of that empire, who, notwithstanding his saint's vizard, tore him to pieces for his tyranny.

From stories of this nature both ancient and modern which abound, the poets also, and some English, have been in this point so mindful of decorum as to put never more pious words in the mouth of any person than of a tyrant. I shall not instance an abstruse author, wherein the king might be less conversant, but one whom we well know was the closest companion of these his solitudes, William Shakespeare, who introduces the person of Richard III, speaking in as high a strain of piety and mortification as is uttered in any passage of this book, and sometimes to the same sense and purpose with some words in this place: "I intended," saith he, "not only to oblige my friends but mine enemies." The like saith Richard, Act II, Scene i:

I do not know that Englishman alive,
With whom my soul is any jot at odds,
More than the infant that is born tonight;
I thank my God for my humility.

Other stuff of this sort may be read throughout the whole tragedy, wherein the Poet used not much license in departing from the truth of history, which delivers him a deep dissembler, not of his affections only, but of religion.

In praying therefore, and in the outward work of devotion, this king we see hath not at all exceeded the worst of kings before him. But herein the worst of kings, pro-

---

[32] Cf. *TKM,* n. 43.

[33] It may be that as early as 1649 there existed some part of the *Psalterium Carolinum. The Devotions of his Sacred Majestie in his Solitudes and Sufferings, Rendred in Verse. Set to Musick for 3 Voices and an Organ or Theorbo.* By Dr. John Wilson. London, 1657.

[34] *The archbishop's late breviary* is Milton's name for Laud's Prayer Book, which Puritans regarded in the light of Robert Baillie's *A Parallel or Briefe Comparison of the Liturgie with the Masse-Book, and other Romish Ritualls* (1641).

[35] Scrupulous care for the forms of religion is mentioned in Aristotle's *Politics* V, ix, 15, as one of the most effective devices of tyrants.

[36] The twelfth century historian Nicetas recorded the cruelty of Comnenus' short reign (1183–85).

fessing Christianism, have by far exceeded him. They, for aught we know, have still prayed their own, or at least borrowed from fit authors. But this king, not content with that which, although in a thing holy, is no holy theft, to attribute to his own making other men's whole prayers, hath as it were unhallowed and unchristened the very duty of prayer itself, by borrowing to a Christian use prayers offered to a heathen god.[37] Who would have imagined so little fear in him of the true all-seeing Deity, so little reverence of the Holy Ghost, whose office is to dictate and present our Christian prayers, so little care of truth in his last words, or honor to himself, or to his friends, or sense of his afflictions, or of that sad hour which was upon him, as immediately before his death to pop into the hand of that grave bishop who attended him, for a special relic of his saintly exercises, a prayer stolen word for word from the mouth of a heathen fiction praying to a heathen God; and that in no serious book, but the vain amatorious poem[38] of Sir Philip Sidney's *Arcadia*—a book in that kind full of worth and wit, but among religious thoughts and duties not worthy to be named, nor to be read at any time without good caution, much less in time of trouble and affliction to be a Christian's prayer-book?

They who are yet incredulous of what I tell them for a truth, that this philippic[39] prayer is no part of the king's goods, may satisfy their own eyes at leisure in the third book of Sir Philip's *Arcadia*, p. 248,[40] comparing Pamela's prayer with the first prayer of his Majesty, delivered to Dr. Juxon[41] immediately before his death, and entitled, *A Prayer in Time of Captivity,* printed in all the best editions of his book. And since there be a crew of lurking railers who in their Libels and their fits of railing up and down, as I hear from others, take it so currishly that I should dare to tell abroad the secrets of their Egyptian Apis,[42] to gratify their gall in some measure yet more, which to them will be a kind of alms (for it is the weekly vomit of their gall, which to most of them is the sole means of their feeding) that they may not starve for me, I shall gorge them once more with this digression somewhat larger than before: nothing troubled or offended at the working upward of their sale-venom[43] thereupon, though it happen to asperse me; being, it seems, their best livelihood and the only use or good digestion that their sick and perishing minds can make of truth charitably told them.

However, to the benefit of others much more worth the gaining, I shall proceed in my assertion; that if only but to taste wittingly of meat or drink offered to an idol[44] be in the doctrine of St. Paul judged a pollution, much more must be his sin who takes a prayer so dedicated into his mouth and offers it to God. Yet hardly it can be thought upon (though how sad a thing) without some kind of laughter at the manner and solemn transaction of so gross a cozenage[45]: that he, who had trampled

---

[37] The problem of Milton's treatment of Pamela's prayer and his alleged interpolation of it in some editions of *Eikon Basilike* is treated by the present editor in *RES,* III (1952), 130–40.

[38] In Sidney's *Arcadia* Pamela's prayer in captivity ends in a passionate plea for God's mercy on her lover Musidorus. In *Eikon Basilike* it is the first of Charles's prayers on the eve of his execution—unchanged, except that it ends in a personal plea for Christ's mercy. Milton's disapproval of the king's reading was not merely personal. An anonymous tract, *The None-Such Charles*—quoted by Ernest Sirluck in *MLN,* LXX (1955), 332—regrets that the king's "soule was more fixt on *Bens* verses, and other Romances, during the time of his imprisonment, then on those Holy Writs, wherein salvation is to be sought for the soul. . . ." (p. 171.)

[39] *philippic*: pertaining to Philip; i.e. to Sir Philip Sidney. The *O.E.D.* cites this use of the word by Milton as if it were unique.

[40] From the fifth edition of the *Arcadia* (1621) to the thirteenth (1674) inclusive, Pamela's prayer is found on p. 248.

[41] *William Juxon* (1582–1663) had served so disinterestedly as Bishop of London (1633–1649) that he escaped most of the criticism which was levelled at most other bishops by the Puritans. He was with Charles on the scaffold, and it was to him that Charles said his enigmatic last word, "Remember."

[42] According to Plutarch in *Isis and Osiris* xxv, the god Osiris was mysteriously represented by the bulls which the Egyptian priests consecrated under the name *Apis* and buried with elaborate public rites. Cf. *Nat,* 213–20.

[43] *Sale-venom* is Milton's term for the railing of the Royalists against the answers to the *Eikon Basilike* and for their advertising of the "King's book" itself.

[44] Cf. St. Paul's warning of the Corinthian Christians against using meat which was sold cheaply after being used in idolatrous worship (I Cor. viii, 1).

[45] *cozenage*: deception, especially by abusing a pretended relationship such as cousinship. As a

over us so stately and so tragically, should leave the world at last so ridiculously in his exit as to bequeath among his deifying friends that stood about him such a precious piece of mockery to be published by them as must needs cover both his and their heads with shame, if they have any left. Certainly, they that will may now see at length how much they were deceived in him, and were ever like to be hereafter, who cared not, so near the minute of his death, to deceive his best and dearest friends with the trumpery of such a prayer, not more secretly than shamefully purloined; yet given them as the royal issue of his own proper zeal. And sure it was the hand of God to let them fall and be taken in such a foolish trap as hath exposed them to all derision; if for nothing else, to throw contempt and disgrace in the sight of all men upon this his idolized book and the whole rosary of his prayers; thereby testifying how little he accepted them from those who thought no better of the living God than of a buzzard idol, fit to be so served and worshipped in reversion,[46] with the polluted orts[47] and refuse of *Arcadias* and romances, without being able to discern the affront rather than the worship of such an ethnic[48] prayer.

But leaving what might justly be offensive to God, it was a trespass also more than usual against human right, which commands that every author should have the property of his own work reserved to him after death, as well as living. Many princes have been rigorous in laying taxes on their subjects by the head, but of any king heretofore that made a levy upon their wit and seized it as his own legitimate, I have not whom beside to instance. True it is, I looked rather to have found him gleaning out of books written purposely to help devotion. And if in likelihood he have borrowed much more out of prayer books than out of pastorals, then are these painted feathers that set him off so gay among the people to be thought few or none of them his own. But if from his

divines he have borrowed nothing, nothing out of all the magazine and the rheum of their mellifluous prayers and meditations, let them who now mourn for him as for Thammuz,[49] them who howl in their pulpits and by their howling declare themselves right wolves; remember and consider in the midst of their hideous faces, when they do only not cut their flesh for him like those rueful priests whom Elijah[50] mocked; that he who was once their Ahab,[51] now their Josiah,[52] though feigning outwardly to reverence churchmen, yet here hath so extremely set at nought both them and their praying faculty that, being at a loss himself what to pray in captivity, he consulted neither with the liturgy nor with the directory, but, neglecting the huge fardell of all their honeycomb devotions, went directly where he doubted not to find better praying to his mind with Pamela in the Countess's *Arcadia*.

What greater argument of disgrace and ignominy could have been thrown with cunning upon the whole clergy than that the king, among all his priestery,[53] and all those numberless volumes of their theological distillations, not meeting with one man or book of that coat that could befriend him with a prayer in captivity, was forced to rob Sir Philip and his captive shepherdess of their heathen orisons to supply in any fashion his miserable indigence, not of bread, but of a single prayer

king, Charles was conventionally regarded as the father of his people.

[46] *reversion:* the right of succeeding to property or office after its occupant has died or for any reason surrendered possession.

[47] *orts:* crumbs of food.

[48] *ethnic:* gentile, pagan.

[49] Cf. the mourning of the "Tyrian maids" for "their wounded Thammuz" in *Nat,* 204 and the reference to the passage to which Milton refers here (Ezek. viii, 4) as he uses it in *PL* I, 446–57.

[50] *Elijah* mocks the priests of Baal, upon whose altars their god can send no miraculous fire, while he prepares for fire to descend on God's altar in answer to his prayer (I Kings xviii, 27).

[51] As a king of Israel who "did evil in the sight of the Lord above all that were before him" (I Kings xvi, 30), *Ahab* had been a by-word for royal wickedness in Presbyterian pulpits. Cf. *TKM,* nn. 91 and 92.

[52] After the execution of the king there was a flood of Royalist tracts and elegies in the vein of John Cleveland's *Jeremias Redivivus: or an Elegiacall Lamentation on the death of our English Josias, Charles the First, . . . publiquely murdered by his Calvino-Judiacall subjects* (1649). Charles had often been compared by high churchmen with the pious young *Josiah,* who restored the temple worship in Jerusalem more splendidly than any of his predecessors since David and Solomon (II Chron. xxxiv–xxxv).

[53] priestery: Milton's nonce-word for the Anglican clergy.

to God? I say therefore not of bread, for that want may befall a good man and yet not make him totally miserable: but he who wants a prayer to beseech God in his necessity, it is inexpressible how poor he is; far poorer within himself than all his enemies can make him. And the unfitness, the indecency of that pitiful supply which he sought, expresses yet further the deepness of his poverty.

Thus much be said in general to his prayers, and in special to that Arcadian prayer used in his captivity; enough to undeceive us what esteem we are to set upon the rest. For he certainly, whose mind could serve him to seek a Christian prayer out of a pagan legend and assume it for his own, might gather up the rest God knows from whence; one perhaps out of the French *Astræa*,[54] another out of the Spanish *Diana*;[55] *Amadis*[56] and *Palmerin*[57] could hardly scape him. Such a person we may be sure had it not in him to make a prayer of his own, or at least would excuse himself the pains and cost of his invention, so long as such sweet rhapsodies of heathenism and knight-errantry could yield him prayers. How dishonorable then, and how unworthy of a Christian king, were these ignoble shifts to seem holy and to get a saintship among the ignorant and wretched people; to draw them by this deception, worse than all his former injuries, to go a whoring[58] after him! And how unhappy, how forsook of grace, and unbeloved of God that people who resolve to know no more of piety or of goodness than to account him their chief saint and martyr whose

[54] The *Astrée* of Honoré d'Urfé was first published in two parts in 1610; the third part appeared in 1619, and the fourth in 1627. The sophisticated dialogues of its lovers, Celadon and Astrée, set a new fashion in French fiction and drama.

[55] Jorge Montemayor's Portuguese romance *Diana Enamorada* was first printed in Valencia in 1542. Many editions and two continuations were published in the seventeenth century.

[56] It is not certain how early in the fourteenth century *Amadis* was written, nor by whom, nor whether originally in Spanish or Portuguese, nor by how many authors it was redacted.

[57] *Palmerin of England* was written in Portuguese by Francesco Moraes (1500–1572), but was first printed in the Spanish version of Luis Hurtado. French, Italian, and English versions came later.

[58] *a whoring* has the meaning which it carries in Moses' warning to Israel not to mingle with the gentile inhabitants of Palestine nor "go a whoring after their gods" (Exod. xxxiv, 15).

bankrupt devotion came not honestly by his very prayers; but having sharked them from the mouth of a heathen worshipper (detestable to teach him prayers) sold them to those that stood and honored him next to the Messiah as his own heavenly compositions in adversity, for hopes no less vain and presumptuous (and death at that time so imminent upon him) than by these goodly relics to be held a saint and martyr in opinion with the cheated people.

And thus far in the whole chapter we have seen and considered, and it cannot but be clear to all men, how and for what ends, what concernments and necessities the late king was no way induced, but every way constrained to call this last Parliament. Yet here in his first prayer he trembles not to avouch, as in the ears of God, "That he did it with an upright intention, to his glory, and his people's good." Of which dreadful attestation, how sincerely meant, God, to whom it was avowed, can only judge; and he hath judged already, and hath written his impartial sentence in characters legible to all Christendom; and besides hath taught us that there be some whom he hath given over to delusion, whose very mind and conscience is defiled; of whom Saint Paul to Titus[59] makes mention.

.   .   .   .   .   .

[59] Since God's condemnation of the Royalists is clear from their utter defeat, doubt of His attitude toward them can be possible only for such self-deluded minds as *Saint Paul* described to *Titus* as utterly defiled (Titus I, 15).

V. *Upon the Bill for Triennial Parliaments, and for settling this &c.*

The bill for a triennial Parliament[1] was but the third part of one good step toward that which in times past was our annual right. The other bill[2] for settling this Parliament was new indeed, but at that time very necessary; and, in the king's own words, no more than what the world "was

[1] The Triennial Act of Feb. 15, 1641, provided that not over three years should pass without the summoning of a Parliament, and that neither house should be dissolved without its own consent within fifty days of its opening.

[2] The *other bill* became the Act of May 10, 1641, which forbade the dissolution of the Long Parliament without its own consent.

fully confirmed he might in justice, reason, honor, and conscience grant them"; for to that end he affirms to have done it.

But whereas he attributes the passing of them to his own act of grace and willingness—as his manner is to make virtues of his necessities—and giving to himself all the praise, heaps ingratitude upon the Parliament, a little memory will set the clean contrary before us: that for those beneficial acts we owe what we owe to the Parliament, but to his granting them neither praise nor thanks. The first bill granted much less than two former statutes yet in force by Edward III:[3] that a Parliament should be called every year, or oftener if need were; nay, from a far ancienter Law-Book called the *Mirror*,[4] it is affirmed in a late treatise called *Rights of the Kingdom*[5] that Parliaments by our old laws ought twice a year to be at London. From twice in one year to once in three years it may be soon cast up how great a loss we fell into of our ancient liberty by that act, which in the ignorant and slavish minds we then were was thought a great purchase.

Wisest men perhaps were contented— for the present, at least—by this act to have recovered Parliaments, which were then upon the brink of danger to be forever lost. And this is that which the king preaches here for a special token of his princely favor, to have abridged and overreached the people five parts in six of what their due was, both by ancient statute and originally. And thus the taking from us all but a triennial remnant of that English freedom which our fathers left us double,

in a fair annuity enrolled, is set out and sold to us here for the gracious and overliberal giving of a new enfranchisement. How little, may we think, did he ever give us, who in the bill of his pretended givings writes down *imprimis* that benefit or privilege once in three year given us, which by so giving he more than twice every year illegally took from us. Such givers as give single to take away sixfold, be to our enemies. For certainly this Commonwealth, if the statutes of our ancestors be worth aught, would have found it hard and hazardous to thrive under the damage of such a guileful liberality.

The other act was so necessary that nothing in the power of Man more seemed to be the stay and support of all things from that steep ruin to which he had nigh brought them, than that act obtained. He had by his ill-stewardship and, to say no worse, the needless raising of two armies, intended for a civil war, beggared both himself and the public; and besides had left us upon the score of his needy enemies for what it cost them in their own defense against him. To disengage him and the Kingdom great sums were to be borrowed,[6] which would never have been lent, nor could ever be repaid, had the king chanced to dissolve this Parliament as heretofore. The errors also of his government had brought the Kingdom to such extremes as were incapable of all recovery without the absolute continuance of a Parliament. It had been else in vain to go about the settling of so great distempers if he who first caused the malady, might, when he pleased, reject the remedy. Notwithstanding all which, that he granted both these Acts unwillingly and as a mere passive instrument, was then visible even to most of those men who now will see nothing.

At passing of the former act he himself concealed not his unwillingness; and testifying a general dislike of their actions, which they then proceeded in with great approbation of the whole Kingdom, he told them

---

[3] Milton's authority about the *former statutes* was John Sadlar's *Rights of the Kingdom* (1649), which declared (p. 183) that, "By express Statutes of Ed the 3. we are to have Parliaments Once every year; and Oftener if need be. . . . In K. Alfred's Time, they were to be Twice a Year; and that at London; as the *Mirror* affirmeth." The statutes of Edward III had been cited also in the Grand Remonstrance (See Gardiner's *Documents*, p. 225). Cf. *TKM*, n. 106.

[4] Cf. the references to Horn's *Mirror of Justices* in *TKM*, n. 106.

[5] Here Milton quotes from the discussion of "King Alfred's Parliaments: so famous in All Historians, and Lawyers," on p. 86 of *Rights of the Kingdom*. The *Mirror* is again quoted in proof that Alfred met his "Parliaments Twice every year in London." Unreliable though Sadlar's account of Saxon and Norman public law was, he was sometimes cited as an authority by lawyers as distinguished as Sir Edward Coke.

[6] The main reason for the Act "against dissolution of the Long Parliament," says Tanner (*Conflicts*, p. 97) "was not constitutional but financial." To pay the Scots' army Parliament had to have a loan, but, "if Parliament should be dissolved, the King could legally repudiate the loan, for his revenue could not be made liable for an indefinite period for debts which Parliament had contracted."

with a masterly brow that "by this Act he had obliged them above what they had deserved,"[7] and gave a piece of justice to the Commonwealth six times short of his predecessors, as if he had been giving some boon or begged office to a sort of his desertless grooms.

That he passed the latter act against his will, no man in reason can hold it questionable. For if the February before he made so dainty and were so loath to bestow a Parliament once in three years upon the nation, because this had so opposed his courses, was it likely that the May following he should bestow willingly on this Parliament an indissoluble sitting, when they had offended him much more by cutting short and impeaching of high treason his chief favorites?[8] It was his fear then, not his favor, which drew from him that act, lest the Parliament, incensed by his conspiracies against them about the same time discovered, should with the people have resented too heinously those his doings, if to the suspicion of their danger from him he had also added the denial of this only means to secure themselves.

From these acts therefore in which he glories, and wherewith so oft he upbraids the Parliament, he cannot justly expect to reap aught but dishonor and dispraise; as being both unwillingly granted, and the one granting much less than was before allowed by statute, the other being a testimony of his violent and lawless custom, not only to break privileges, but whole Parliaments; from which enormity they were constrained to bind him first of all his predecessors; never any before him having given like causes of distrust and jealousy to his people. As for this Parliament, how far he was from being advised by them, as he ought,[9] let his own words express.

He taxes them with "undoing what they found well done," and yet knows they undid nothing in the Church but lord bishops, liturgies, ceremonies, high commission, judged worthy by all true Protestants to be thrown out of the Church. They undid nothing in the State but irregular and grinding courts, the main grievances to be removed; and if these were the things which in his opinion they found well done, we may again from hence be informed with what unwillingess he removed them; and that those gracious acts whereof so frequently he makes mention, may be Englished[10] more properly acts of fear and dissimulation against his mind and conscience.

The bill preventing dissolution of this Parliament he calls "an unparalleled Act out of the extreme confidence that his Subjects would not make ill use of it." But was it not a greater confidence of the people to put into one man's hand so great a power, till he abused it, as to summon and dissolve Parliaments? He would be thanked for trusting them and ought to thank them rather for trusting him—the trust issuing first from them, not from him.

And that it was a mere trust, and not his prerogative, to call and dissolve Parliaments at his pleasure; and that Parliaments were not to be dissolved till all Petitions were heard, all grievances redressed, is not only the assertion of this Parliament, but of our ancient law-books, which aver it to be an unwritten law of common right so engraven in the hearts of our ancestors, and by them so constantly enjoyed and claimed, as that it needed not enrolling. And if the Scots in their declaration could charge the king with breach of their laws, for breaking up that Parliament[11] without their consent, while matters of greatest moment were depending, it were unreasonable to imagine that the wisdom of England should be so wanting to itself through all ages as not to provide by some known law, written or unwritten, against the not calling or the

---

[7] Milton follows May's statement that, when Parliament demanded the Triennial Act on the ground that there were "two Statutes then in force, for a Parliament once a yeere," Charles "could not forbear to tell them that," in signing the Act, "he put an obligation upon them . . . which they scarce deserved."

[8] The *favorites* were Strafford, who was attainted and executed in May, 1641, and Archbishop Laud, who suffered the same fate in Jan., 1645. Cf. Chap. i, n. 13.

[9] The thought is that Charles rejected Parliament's advice, not that he was improperly advised.

[10] Milton's resentment of the convention which made everything done by royalty a "condescension" or "gracious act," made him suggest that such court cant should be turned into plain English.

[11] A *Declaration of the estaitts of parliament* in Scotland on June 10, 1640, protested the prorogation of the Scots *parliament* in the preceding August on the ground that the prorogation "without consent of the estates was against the laws and liberties of the kingdome" (Thurloe, *State Papers* I, 3).

arbitrary dissolving of Parliaments; or that they who ordained their summoning twice a year, or as oft as need required, did not tacitly enact also that as necessity of affairs called them, so the same necessity should keep them undissolved till that were fully satisfied. Were it not for that, Parliaments and all the fruit and benefit we receive by having them, would turn soon to mere abusion.

It appears then that if this bill of not dissolving were an unparalleled act, it was a known and common right which our ancestors under other kings enjoyed as firmly as if it had been graven in marble; and that the infringement of this king first brought it into a written act: who now boasts that as a great favor done us which his own less fidelity than was in former kings constrained us only of an old undoubted right to make a new written act. But what needed written acts whenas anciently it was esteemed part of his crown oath not to dissolve Parliaments till all grievances were considered? Whereupon, the old *Modi of Parliament*[12] calls it flat perjury if he dissolve them before; as I find cited in a book mentioned at the beginning of this chapter, to which and other law-tractates I refer the more lawyerly mooting of this point: which is neither my element, nor my proper work here; since the book which I have to answer pretends to reason, not authorities and quotation: and I hold reason to be the best arbitrator and the law of law itself.

'Tis true that "Good subjects think it not just that the king's condition should be worse by bettering theirs." But then the king must not be at such a distance from the people in judging what is better and what worse; which might have been agreed, "had he known" (for his own words condemn him) "as well with moderation to use, as with earnestness to desire his own advantages."

"A continual Parliament he thought would keep the Commonwealth in tune." Judge, Commonwealth, what proofs he gave that this boasted profession was ever in his thought.

"Some," saith he, "gave out that I repented me of the settling act." His own actions gave it out beyond all supposition. For doubtless it repented him to have established that by law which he went about so soon after to abrogate by the sword.[13]

He calls those acts which he confesses "tended to their good, not more princely than friendly contributions." As if to do his duty were of courtesy, and the discharge of his trust a parcel of his liberality; so nigh lost in his esteem was the birthright of our liberties that to give them back again upon demand stood at the mercy of his "contribution."

"He doubts not but the affections of his people will compensate his sufferings for those acts of confidence." And imputes his sufferings to a contrary cause. Not his confidence, but "his distrust," was that which brought him to those sufferings from the time that he forsook his Parliament; and trusted them never the sooner for what he tells "of their piety and religious strictness," but rather hated them as Puritans, whom he always sought to extirpate.

He would have it believed that "to bind his hands by these acts argued a very short foresight of things and extreme fatuity of mind in him," if he had meant a war. If we should conclude so, that were not the only argument. Neither did it argue that he meant peace—knowing that what he granted for the present out of fear, he might as soon repeal by force, watching his time; and deprive them the fruit of those acts, if his own designs, wherein he put his trust, took effect.

Yet he complains "that the tumults threatened to abuse all acts of grace[14] and turn them into wantonness." I would they had turned his wantonness into the grace of not abusing Scripture. Was this becoming such a saint as they would make him, to

---

[12] In *Rights of the Kingdom,* p. 182, after recalling the semiannual parliaments of Alfred, Sadlar declared that "the old *Modi of Parliament* agree in This, that a Parliament should not be dissolved till All Petitions were discussed and answered," and then only "by a generall consent."

[13] Milton probably had in mind Charles's attempt to arrest five members of the House of Commons in January, 1642, an act which most of the members regarded as no less violent than his raising of his standard against Parliament in August of that year.

[14] The passage in the *Eikon Basilike* which Milton partially quotes, imitates St. Paul's exhortations beseeching the Corinthians that they should "receive not the grace of God in vain" (II Cor. vi, 1), and the Romans to ask themselves: "What then, shall we sin, because we are not under the law, but under grace?" (Rom. vi, 15.)

adulterate those sacred words from the grace of God to the acts of his own grace? Herod[15] was eaten up of worms for suffering others to compare his voice to the voice of God; but the borrower of this phrase gives much more cause of jealousy, that he likened his own acts of grace to the acts of God's grace.

From profaneness he scarce comes off with perfect sense. "I was not then in a capacity to make war," therefore "I intended not." "I was not in a capacity," therefore "I could not have given my enemies greater advantage than by so unprincely inconstancy to have scattered them by arms whom but lately I had settled by Parliament." What place could there be for his inconstancy in that thing whereto he was in no capacity? Otherwise his inconstancy was not so unwonted or so nice but that it would have easily found pretenses to scatter those in revenge whom he settled in fear.

"It had been a course full of sin as well as of hazard and dishonor." True; but if those considerations withheld him not from other actions of like nature, how can we believe they were of strength sufficient to withhold him from this? And that they withheld him not, the event soon taught us.

"His letting some men go up to the pinnacle of the temple[16] was a temptation to them to cast him down headlong." In this simile we have himself compared to Christ, the Parliament to the Devil, and his giving them that act of settling, to his letting them go up to the "pinnacle of the temple." A tottering and giddy act rather than a settling. This was goodly use made of Scripture in his solitudes. But it was no pinnacle of the temple, it was a pinnacle of Nebuchadnezzar's palace,[17] from

[15] When the persecutor of the Christians, King *Herod,* addressed the men of Tyre, "the people gave a great shout, saying, It is the voice of a god, and not of a man. And immediately the angel of the Lord smote him, because he gave not God the glory: and he was eaten of worms, and gave up the ghost" (Acts xii, 22–23).

[16] Milton does not exaggerate the distortion in the *Eikon Basilike* of the account in Matt. iv, 5–6, of the devil's temptation of Christ to exhibit his power by casting himself down from a pinnacle of the temple.

[17] *Nebuchadnezzar,* the Babylonian king who destroyed Jerusalem in 586 B.C., built many famous buildings in Babylon, of which his "new palace" was regarded as the most conspicuous.

whence he and monarchy fell headlong together.

He would have others see that "all the kingdoms of the world are not worth gaining by the ways of sin which hazard the soul"; and hath himself left nothing unhazarded to keep three. He concludes with sentences that, rightly scanned, make not so much for him as against him, and confesses that "the act of settling was no sin of his will," and we easily believe him, for it hath been clearly proved a sin of his unwillingness.

With his orisons I meddle not, for he appeals to a high audit. This yet may be noted, that at his prayers he had before him the sad presage of his ill success, "as of a dark and dangerous storm which never admitted his return to the port from whence he set out." Yet his prayer book no sooner shut but other hopes flattered him, and their flattering was his destruction.

•   •   •   •   •   •

XXVII. *Entitled, To the Prince of Wales.*

What the king wrote to his son as a father, concerns not us; what he wrote to him as a king of England, concerns not him—God and the Parliament having now otherwise disposed of England. But because I see it done with some artifice and labor, to possess the people that they might amend their present condition by his or by his son's restorement, I shall show point by point that although the king had been reinstalled to his desire, or that his son admitted should observe exactly all his father's precepts, yet that this would be so far from conducing to our happiness, either as a "remedy to the present distempers, or a prevention of the like to come," that it would inevitably throw us back again into all our past and fulfilled miseries; would force us to fight over again all our tedious wars and put us to another fatal struggling for liberty and life, more dubious than the former. In which as our success hath been no other than our cause, so it will be evident to all posterity that his "misfortunes" were the mere consequence of his perverse "judgment."

First he argues from "the experience of

those troubles," which both he and his son have had, to the improvement of their "piety and patience": and by the way bears witness in his own words that the corrupt education of his youth, which was but glanced at only in some former passages of this answer,[1] was a thing neither of mean consideration, nor untruly charged upon him or his son: himself confessing here that "court-delights are prone either to root up all true virtue and honor, or to be contented only with some leaves and withering formalities of them, without any real fruits tending to the public good:" Which presents him still in his own words another "Rehoboam,[2] softened" by a far worse court than "Solomon's, and so corrupted" by "flatteries," which he affirms to be "inseparable" to the overturning of all "peace" and the loss of his own honor and kingdoms.

That he came therefore thus bred up and nurtured to the throne, far worse than Rehoboam, unless he be of those who equalized his father to king Solomon,[3] we have here his own confession. And how voluptuously, how idly reigning in the hands of other men, he either tyrannized or trifled away those seventeen years of peace, without care or thought, as if to be a king had been nothing else in his apprehension but to eat and drink and have his will and take his pleasure (though there be who can relate his domestic life to the

exactness of a diary), there shall be here no mention made. This yet we might have then foreseen that he who spent his leisure so remissly and so corruptly to his own pleasing, would one day or other be worse busied and employed to our sorrow. And that he acted in good earnest what Rehoboam did but threaten, to make his little finger heavier than his father's loins and to whip us with his two twisted scorpions, both temporal and spiritual tyranny, all his kingdoms have felt. What good use he made afterward of his adversity, both his impenitence and obstinacy to the end (for he was no Manasseh)[4] and the sequel of these his meditated resolutions, abundantly express; retaining, commending, teaching to his son all those putrid and pernicious documents both of State and of religion, instilled by wicked doctors, and received by him as in a vessel nothing better seasoned, which were the first occasion both of his own and all our miseries.

And if he, in the best maturity of his years and understanding, made no better use to himself or others of his so long and manifold afflictions, either looking up to God, or looking down upon the reason of his own affairs, there can be no probability that his son, bred up, not in the soft effeminacies of court only, but in the rugged and more boisterous license of undisciplined camps and garrisons, for years unable to reflect with judgment upon his own condition, and thus ill-instructed by his father, should give his mind to walk by any other rules than these bequeathed him as on his father's deathbed, and as the choicest of all that experience, which his most serious observation and retirement in good or evil days had taught him. David indeed, by suffering without just cause, learned that meekness and that wisdom by adversity, which made him much the fitter man to reign. But they who suffer as oppressors, tyrants, violators of law, and persecutors of reformation, without appearance of repenting, if they once get hold again of that dignity and power which they had lost, are but whetted and enraged by what they

---

[1] In *Def 1* (C.E. VII, 514) Milton is explicit about Charles's life "amid banquets, plays, and bevies and troops of women," and (p. 236) his public indecorum with ladies "at the theatre," in contrast with Salmasius' fulsome comparison of him with "the most religious king and prophet," David.

[2] Milton's repeated comparisons of Charles to *Rehoboam*—here and in *TKM* (see n. 71) and twice in *Def 1*, Chap. iv—are in part explicable in the light of Royalist condemnations of the revolt of his subjects (in I Kings xii, 15) as impious defiance of royal authority. The biblical record, said Thomas Bayly in *The Royal Charter granted unto Kings, by God himself: and collected out of both Testaments* (1649), merely "proves that such a thing was done, not that it was well done" (p. 63).

[3] The habit of referring to James I as the "British Solomon" was so general that the sermon preached at his funeral by the Archbishop of York, John Williams, on May 7, 1625, was published under the title, *Great Britain's Salomon. A sermon preached at the magnificent funeral of the most high and mighty king, James, the late king of Great Britaine, France, and Ireland.*

[4] After making the Jews "to err and do worse than the heathen," *Manasseh* suffered military reverses and then "humbled himself greatly before the God of his fathers" and "repaired the altar of the Lord" (II Chron. xxxiii, 9, 12, and 16).

suffered, against those whom they look upon as them that caused their sufferings.

How he hath been "subject to the scepter of God's word and spirit," though acknowledged to be the "best government," and what his "dispensation of civil power" hath been, with what "justice," and what "honor to the public peace," it is but looking back upon the whole catalogue of his deeds, and that will be sufficient to remember us. "The cup of God's physic," as he calls it, what alteration it wrought in him to a firm "healthfulness" from any surfeit or excess whereof the people generally thought him sick, if any man would go about to prove, we have his own testimony following here, that it wrought none at all.

First, he hath the same fixed opinion and esteem of his old Ephesian goddess,[5] called the Church of England as he had ever; and charges strictly his son after him to persevere in that antipapal schism (for it is not much better) as that "which will be necessary both for his soul's and the Kingdom's peace." But if this can be any foundation of the Kingdom's peace, which was the first cause of our distractions, let common sense be judge. It is a rule and principle worthy to be known by Christians that no Scripture, no, nor so much as any ancient creed, binds our faith or our obedience to any church whatsoever, denominated by a particular name; far less, if it be distinguished by a several government from that which is indeed catholic. No man was ever bid be subject to the Church of Corinth, Rome, or Asia, but to the Church without addition, as it held faithful to the rules of Scripture, and the government established in all places by the apostles; which at first was universally the same in all churches and congregations; not differing or distinguished by the diversity of countries, territories, or civil bounds. That church that from the name of a distinct place takes authority to set up a distinct faith or government, is a schism and faction, not a church. It were an injury to

condemn the papist of absurdity and contradiction for adhering to his Catholic Romish religion, if we, for the pleasure of a king and his politic considerations, shall adhere to a Catholic English.

But suppose the Church of England were as it ought to be, how is it to us the safer by being so named and established, whenas that very name and establishment, by his contriving or approbation, served for nothing else but to delude us and amuse us, while the Church of England insensibly was almost changed and translated into the Church of Rome? Which as every man knows in general to be true, so the particular treaties and transactions tending to that conclusion are at large discovered in a book entitled the *English Pope*.[6] But when the people, discerning these abuses, began to call for reformation, in order to which the Parliament demanded of the king to unestablish that prelatical government which without Scripture had usurped over us; straight, as Pharaoh[7] accused of idleness the Israelites that sought leave to go and sacrifice to God, he lays faction to their charge.

And that we may not hope to have ever anything reformed in the Church either by him or his son, he forewarns him, "that the devil of rebellion doth most commonly turn himself into an angel of reformation": and says enough to make him hate it as the worst of evils and the bane of his crown. Nay he counsels him to "let nothing seem little or despicable to him, so as not speedily and effectually to suppress errors and schisms." Whereby we may perceive plainly that our consciences were destined to the same servitude and persecution, if

---

[5] The reference is to the mob-worship of Diana with the cry, "Great is Diana of the Ephesians" (Acts xix, 28), but the term was bandied between the Puritans and the partisans of Archbishop Laud, one of whom is quoted in Keith Feiling's *History of the Tory Party* (Oxford, 1924), p. 15, as saying that the Diana of the Yarmouth fishermen was "their liberty."

[6] *The English Pope, or a Discourse Wherein The late mysticall Intelligence betwixt the Court of England, and the Court of Rome is in part discovered* (1643). The work represented Charles and still more his queen, Henrietta Maria, as plotting with the papal nuncio Gregorio Panzini and other papal emissaries for years to restore Roman Catholicism in England—Archbishop Laud, "*Chichester* and other 8 bishops, (amongst whom we may boldly nominate *Gloucester*) as also Portland, Cotting, Windebank and many other Lay Grandees cooperating in this zealous work of Reconciliation" (p. 21).

[7] *Pharaoh's* reply to Moses' request that the Israelites might go into the wilderness to worship God was: "They be idle; therefore they cry, saying, Let us go and sacrifice to our God" (Exod v, 8).

not worse than before, whether under him, or if it should so happen, under his son; who count all protestant churches erroneous and schismatical which are not episcopal.

His next precept is concerning our civil liberties, which by his sole voice and predominant will must be circumscribed and not permitted to extend a handsbreadth further than his interpretation of "the laws already settled." And although all human laws are but the offspring of that frailty, that fallibility, and imperfection which was in their authors, whereby many laws in the change of ignorant and obscure ages may be found both scandalous and full of grievance to their posterity that made them, and no law is further good than mutable upon just occasion; yet if the removing of an old law, or the making of a new, would save the kingdom, we shall not have it, unless his arbitrary voice will so far slacken the stiff curb of his prerogative[8] as to grant it us; who are as free-born to make our own laws as our fathers were, who made these we have.

Where are then the English liberties which we boast to have been left us by our progenitors? To that he answers that "our liberties consist in the enjoyment of the fruits of our industry and the benefit of those laws to which we ourselves have consented." First, for the enjoyment of those fruits which our industry and labors have made our own upon our own, what privilege is that above what the Turks, Jews, and Moors enjoy under the Turkish monarchy?[9] For without that kind of justice which is also in Algiers among thieves and pirates between themselves, no kind of government, no society, just or unjust, could stand; no combination or conspiracy could stick together. Which he also acknowledges in these words: "That if the crown upon his head be so heavy as to oppress the whole body, the weakness of in-

ferior members cannot return anything of strength, honor, or safety to the head; but that a necessary debilitation must follow." So that this liberty of the subject concerns himself and the subsistence of his own regal power in the first place and before the consideration of any right belonging to the subject. We expect therefore something more that must distinguish free government from slavish. But instead of that, this king, though ever talking and protesting as smooth as now, suffered it in his own hearing to be preached and pleaded without control or check by them whom he most favored and upheld, that the subject had no property of his own goods, but that all was the king's right.[10]

Next, for the "benefit of those laws to which we ourselves have consented," we never had it under him; for not to speak of laws ill executed, when the Parliament and in them the people have consented to divers laws and, according to our ancient rights, demanded them, he took upon him to have a negative will as the transcendent and ultimate law above all our laws, and to rule us forcibly by laws to which we ourselves did not consent, but complained of. Thus these two heads wherein the utmost of his allowance here will give our liberties leave to consist, the one of them shall be so far only made good to us as may support his own interest and crown "from ruin" or "debilitation"; and so far Turkish vassals enjoy as much liberty under Mahomet and the Grand Signor: the other we neither yet have enjoyed under him, nor were ever like to do under the tyranny of a negative voice,[11] which he claims above the unani-

---

[8] Cf. the note (86) on the royal *prerogative*, to which Milton refers in *TKM* as Charles's "boasted prerogative unaccountable."

[9] *The Turkish monarchy*, as James Harrington pointed out in *Oceana* (ed. of John Toland, 1720), p. 58, was regarded as the only pure or absolute monarchy known in all history, because—thanks to its land system—its inhabitants "scarce ever knew any other condition than that of slavery." Cf. *TKM*, n. 56, and *Peace* (C.E. VI, 252–3).

[10] In defense of Charles's claim of the *right* to collect "shipmoney" in the famous trial of John Hampden before the Exchequer Court in 1638 Sir John Finch had declared, in a statement which was later widely published, that Parliament had no power "to bind the King not to command the subjects, their persons and their goods and I say their money too." "These words, everywhere bruited and everywhere discussed," says G. M. Trevelyan in *England under the Stuarts* (New York, 1904), p. 184, "convinced the most unwilling that . . . nothing but a restoration of the power of Parliament could preserve the individual in his person and his goods."

[11] In Chap. vi (C.E. V, 128) Milton has argued against the royal veto of the will of Parliament on the ground that the king represents no one but himself, that he cannot speak for the nation, and that "the king's negative voice was never any law,

mous consent and power of a whole nation virtually in the Parliament.

In which negative voice to have been cast by the doom of war and put to death by those who vanquished him in their own defense, he reckons to himself more than a negative "Martyrdom." But martyrs bear witness to the truth, not to themselves: "If I bear witness of myself," saith Christ, "my witness is not true."[12] He who writes himself martyr by his own inscription is like an ill painter who, by writing on the shapeless picture which he hath drawn, is fain to tell passengers what shape it is; which else no man could imagine: no more than how a martyrdom can belong to him who therefore dies for his religion because it is "established." Certainly if Agrippa[13] had turned Christian, as he was once turning, and had put to death Scribes and Pharisees for observing the Law of Moses and refusing Christianity, they had died a truer martyrdom. For those laws were established by God and Moses, these by no warrantable authors of religion, whose laws in all other best reformed churches are rejected. And if to die for an establishment of religion be martyrdom, then Romish priests executed for that which had so many hundred years been established in this land, are no worse martyrs than he. Lastly, if to die for "the testimony of his own conscience" be enough to make him martyr, what heretic dying for direct blasphemy, as some have done constantly, may not boast a martyrdom?

As for the constitution or repeal of civil laws, that power lying only in the Parliament, which he by the very law of his coronation[14] was to grant them, not to debar them, nor to preserve a lesser law with the contempt and violation of a but an absurd and reasonless custom, begotten and grown up either from the flattery of basest times, or the usurpation of immoderate princes." Again in Chap. xiii (C.E. V, 207) he has condemned the "presumptuous negative voice, tyranical to the Parliament, but much more tyrannical to the church of God."

[12] John xxx., 31.

[13] If, that is, King *Agrippa* had been sincere in saying to St. Paul, "Almost thou persuadest me to be a Christian" (Acts xxvi, 28).

[14] Cf. Milton's discussion of the *coronation* oath and the royal veto power in *TKM* and its background as indicated in notes 44 and 51. Other important discussions occur in *Eikon,* Chap. vi (C.E. V, 133) and *Def 1* (C.E. VII, 536–40).

greater; it will conclude him not so much as in a civil and metaphorical sense to have died a martyr of our laws, but a plain transgressor of them. And should the Parliament, endued with legislative power, make our laws and be after to dispute them piecemeal with the reason, conscience, humor, passion, fancy, folly, obstinacy, or other ends of one man, whose sole word and will shall baffle and unmake what all the wisdom of a Parliament hath been deliberately framing; what a ridiculous and contemptible thing a Parliament would soon be, and what a base unworthy nation we, who boast our freedom, and send them with the manifest peril of their lives to preserve it, they who are not marked by destiny for slaves may apprehend. In this servile condition to have kept us still under hatches he both resolves here to the last and so instructs his son.

As to those offered condescensions of "charitable connivance or toleration," if we consider what went before and what follows, they molder into nothing. For, what with not suffering "ever so little" to "seem a despicable" schism, without effectual suppression, as he warned him before, and what with "no opposition of law, government, or established religion" to be permitted, which is his following proviso, and wholly within his own construction, what a miserable and suspected toleration under spies and haunting promoters[15] we should enjoy, is apparent. Besides that it is so far beneath the honor of a Parliament and free nation to beg and supplicate the godship of one frail man for the bare and simple toleration of what they all consent to be both just, pious, and best pleasing to God, while that which is erroneous, unjust, and mischievous in the Church or State shall by him alone against them all be kept up and established, and they censured the while for a "covetous, ambitious, and sacrilegious faction."

Another bait to allure the people is the charge he lays upon his son to be tender of them. Which if we should believe in part, because they are his herd, his cattle, the stock upon his ground, as he accounts

[15] *promoter:* "One whose business it is to prosecute or denounce offenders against the law: . . . a professional accuser or informer." *O.E.D.* In this sense, the word is obsolete.

them, whom to waste and destroy would undo himself, yet the inducement which he brings to move him renders the motion itself something suspicious. For if princes "need no palliations," as he tells his son, wherefore is it that he himself hath so often used them? Princes, of all other men, have not more change of raiment in their wardrobes than variety of shifts and "palliations" in their solemn actings and pretenses to the people.

To try next if he can ensnare the prime men of those who have opposed him, whom, more truly than his meaning was, he calls the "patrons and vindicators of the people," he gives out "indemnity" and offers "acts of oblivion." But they who with a good conscience and upright heart did their civil duties in the sight of God and in their several places to resist tyranny and the violence of superstition banded both against them, he may be sure will never seek to be forgiven that which may be justly attributed to their immortal praise; nor will assent ever to the guilty blotting out of those actions before men by which their faith assures them they chiefly stand approved and are had in remembrance before the throne of God.

He exhorts his son "not to study revenge." But how far he, or at least they about him, intend to follow that exhortation, was seen lately at the Hague[16] and now lateliest at Madrid;[17] where to execute in the basest manner, though but the smallest part of that savage and barbarous revenge which they do nothing else but "study" and "contemplate," they cared not to let the world know them for professed traitors and assassinators of all law both divine and human, even of that last and most extensive law kept inviolable to public persons among all fair enemies in the midst of uttermost defiance and hostility. How implacable therefore they would be after any terms of closure or admittance for the future, or any like opportunity given them hereafter, it will be wisdom and our safety to believe rather, and prevent, than to make trial. And it will concern the multitude, though courted here, to take heed how they seek to hide or color their own fickleness and instability with a bad repentance of their well-doing and their fidelity to the better cause; to which at first so cheerfully and conscientiously they joined themselves.

He returns again to extol "the Church of England" and again requires his son by the joint authority "of a father and a king, not to let his heart receive the least check or disaffection against it." And not without cause, for by that means having sole influence upon the clergy, and they upon the people, "after long search and many disputes," he could not possibly find a more compendious and politic way to uphold and settle tyranny than by subduing first the consciences of vulgar men with the insensible poison of their slavish doctrine; for then the body and besotted mind without much reluctancy was likeliest to admit the yoke.

He commends also "Parliaments held with freedom and with honor." But I would ask how that can be while he only must be the sole free person in that number, and would have the power with his unaccountable denial to dishonor them by rejecting all their counsels, to confine their lawgiving power, which is the foundation of our freedom, and to change at his pleasure the very name of a Parliament into the name of a faction.

The conclusion therefore must needs be quite contrary to what he concludes; that nothing can be more "unhappy," more dishonorable, more unsafe "for all," than when

---

[16] Dr. Isaac Dorislaus, who was murdered at *the Hague* on May 12, 1649, was a Hollander who had had a long and distinguished career in England, culminating in service as judge advocate in Parliament's forces and a share (according to the *D.N.B.*) in the preparation of "the charge of high treason against Charles I." He was at the Hague to help the resident ambassador of Parliament prepare a scheme for "a firm peace and reciprocal alliance between the two republics." He was murdered with the cry, "Thus dies one of the king's judges," by twelve masked men whose leader "received a pension after the Restoration for his deed." Milton's letter protesting the failure of the Dutch to arrest the assassins (C.E. XVIII, 14) accuses them of virtual connivance in the crime.

[17] Antony Ascham and his interpreter, a Spaniard, were murdered on the night after his arrival in *Madrid* by six masked Englishmen, one of whom was executed for the crime by the Spanish authorities. He was obnoxious to the Royalists not only as Parliament's representative, but also as the author of a *Discourse of what is lawful during confusions and revolutions of Government* (1648), of which Bishop Sanderson wrote a refutation. Cf. *TKM*, n. 71.

a wise, "grave, and honorable Parliament" shall have labored, debated, argued, consulted, and, as he himself speaks, "contributed" for the public good "all their counsels in common," to be then frustrated, disappointed, denied and repulsed by the single whiff of a negative from the mouth of one wilful man; nay to be blasted, to be struck as mute and motionless as a Parliament of tapestry in the hangings; or else after all their pains and travel to be dissolved and cast away like so many noughts in arithmetic, unless it be to turn the O of their insignificance into a lamentation with the people who had so vainly sent them. For this is not to "enact all things by public consent," as he would have us be persuaded, this is to enact nothing but by the private consent and leave of one not negative tyrant; this is mischief without remedy, a stifling and obstructing evil that hath no vent, no outlet, no passage through. Grant him this, and the Parliament hath no more freedom than if it sat in his noose, which when he pleases to draw together with one twitch of his negative, shall throttle a whole nation, to the wish of Caligula, in one neck.[18]

This with the power of the militia in his own hands over our bodies and estates, and the prelates to enthrall our consciences either by fraud or force, is the sum of that happiness and liberty we were to look for, whether in his own restitution or in these precepts given to his son. Which unavoidably would have set us in the same state of misery wherein we were before, and have either compelled us to submit like bond-slaves or put us back to a second wandering over that horrid wilderness of distraction and civil slaughter which, not without the

[18] In pronouncing sentence on Charles, John Bradshaw, President of the Court, said, after reviewing the King's "designs and plots . . . for the crushing and confounding of this Parliament," that he was reminded of what "we read of the great Roman Emperor, by the way let us call him a great Roman tyrant, Caligula, that he wish't that the people of Rome had but one neck that at one blow he might cut it off" (Muddiman, Trial, p. 118). The story was so familiar that John Cleveland used it in a sneer at the Smectymnuans:

Caligula (whose Pride was Mankind's Bail,
As who disdain'd to murder by Retail,
Wishing the World had but one general Neck)
His glutton Blade might have found Game in
   Smec.
(The Works of Mr. John Cleveland, 1687, p. 29.)

strong and miraculous hand of God assisting us, we have measured out and survived. And who knows, if we make so slight of this incomparable deliverance which God hath bestowed upon us, but that we shall, like those foolish Israelites who deposed God and Samuel to set up a king, "cry out" one day, "because of our king," which we have been mad upon;[19] and then God, as he foretold them, will no more deliver us.

There remains now but little more of his discourse, whereof yet to take a short view will not be amiss. His words make semblance as if he were magnanimously exercising himself and so teaching his son "to want as well as to wear a crown"; and would seem to account it "not worth taking up or enjoying upon sordid, dishonorable, and irreligious terms"; and yet to his very last did nothing more industriously than strive to take up and enjoy again his sequestered crown upon the most sordid, disloyal, dishonorable, and irreligious terms, not of making peace only, but of joining and incorporating with the murderous Irish, formerly by himself declared against for "wicked and detestable rebels, odious to God and all good men."[20] And who but those rebels now are the chief strength and confidence of his son while the presbyter Scot that woos and solicits him is neglected and put off[21]—as if no terms were to him sordid, irreligious and dishonorable, but the Scottish and Presbyterian, never to be complied with till the fear of instant perishing starve

[19] Cf. the similar use of the wilful demand of the Israelites for a king (I Sam. viii, 1–18) in TKM, n. 55.

[20] Language like that here attributed to Charles had been used by him officially when under pressure like that under which he wrote his reply to Sir James Montgomery and other Parliamentary officers in Ireland who appealed to him when it was known that he was receiving representatives of the Irish rebels at Oxford in December, 1642. His reply recalled that he had "offered, and most really intended, in His Own Royal Person, to have undergone the Danger of that War, for the defence of his good Subjects, and the chastisement of those perficious and barbarous Rebels . . . those Merciless and Idolatrous Rebels." (Rushworth, Collections, Third Part, Vol. II, 534.)

[21] Charles II had been promptly proclaimed by the Duke of Ormond in Ireland and by the Scottish Parliament. Though he finally and unwillingly went to Scotland in June, 1650, his relations with his Presbyterian supporters there fully corresponded with Milton's description of them.

him out at length to some unsound and hypocritical agreement?

He bids his son "keep to the true principles of piety, virtue, and honor, and he shall never want a kingdom." And I say, "People of England, keep ye to those principles and ye shall never want a king." Nay after such a fair deliverance as this, with so much fortitude and valor shown against a tyrant, that people that should seek a king claiming what this man claims, would show themselves to be by nature slaves and arrant beasts—not fit for that liberty which they cried out and bellowed for, but fitter to be led back again into their old servitude like a sort of clamoring and fighting brutes, broke loose from their copyholds,[22] that know not how to use or possess the liberty which they fought for, but with the fair words and promises of an old exasperated foe are ready to be stroked and tamed again into the wonted and well-pleasing state of their true Norman villeinage,[23] to them best agreeable.

The last sentence, whereon he seems to venture the whole weight of all his former reasons and argumentations, "that religion to their God and loyalty to their King cannot be parted without the sin and infelicity of a people," is contrary to the plain teaching of Christ that, "No man can serve two masters",[24] but, if he hold to the one, he must reject and forsake the other. If God then, and earthly kings be for the most part not several only, but opposite masters, it will as oft happen that they who will serve their king must forsake their God; and they who will serve God must forsake their king: which then will neither be their sin nor their infelicity, but their wisdom, their piety, and their true happiness; as to be deluded by these unsound and subtle ostentations here would be their misery; and in all likelihood much greater than what they hitherto have undergone: if now again intoxicated and moped with these royal, and therefore so delicious because royal, rudiments of bondage, the cup of deception, spiced and tempered to their bane, they should deliver up themselves to these glozing words and illusions of him whose rage and utmost violence they have sustained and overcome so nobly.

XXVIII. Entitled, Meditations upon Death.

It might be well thought by him who reads no further than the title of this last essay, that it required no answer. For all other human things are disputed and will be variously thought of to the world's end. But this business of death is a plain case and admits no controversy; in that center all opinions meet. Nevertheless since, out of those few mortifying hours that should have been entirest to themselves and most at peace from all passion and disquiet, he can afford spare time to inveigh bitterly against that justice which was done upon him, it will be needful to say something in defense of those proceedings; though briefly, in regard so much on this subject hath been written lately.

It happened once, as we find in Esdras[1]

---

[22] The direction of Milton's thought is shown by a letter to him from John Wall, dated May 26, 1659, which is reproduced in Richard Baron's edition of Eikon (1756), p. vi. It speaks of "the Norman conquest and tyranny" as "continued upon the nation, without any thought of removing it; I mean the tenure of lands by copy-hold, and holding for life under a Lord, or rather Tyrant of a Manour; whereby people care not to improve their land, not knowing how soon themselves or theirs may be outed it."

[23] Puritan resentment of the claims of the Royalists arising from the conquest and laws of William the Conqueror stimulated the writing of a number of replies such as England's proper and only Way to an Establishment in Honour, Freedom, Peace, and Happiness: Or, The Norman Yoke once more uncased: and the Necessity, Justice, and perfect Seasonableness of breaking it in Pieces, demonstrated in Eight most plain and true Prospections, with their Proofs. By the Author of Anti-Normanism. 1648. (Harleian Miscellany VI, 35) Cf. TKM, n. 50.

[24] Matt. vi, 24; Luke xvi, 13.

[1] With minor differences, the Apocryphal Book of I Esdras, iii and iv, and Josephus' Antiquities XI, 38–56, tell the story of the triumph of the Hebrew leader Zorobabel in a solemn demonstration to the Persian king Darius that women are stronger than both wine and the power of kings. The spokesman of kingly power has argued that men, who rule the earth, are in turn ruled by kings, whose possession of unsurpassable power and strength is only reasonable; but after observing that Darius himself is ruled by his concubine, Zorobabel declares the supreme power of truth, which gives none of the perishable goods of fortune, but only what is just and lawful, and disgraces and banishes all injustice.

and Josephus, authors not less believed than any under sacred, to be a great and solemn debate in the court of Darius, what thing was to be counted strongest of all other. He that could resolve this, in reward of his excelling wisdom, should be clad in purple, drink in gold, sleep on a bed of gold, and sit next Darius. None but they, doubtless, who were reputed wise had the question propounded to them; who, after some respite given them by the king to consider, in full assembly of all his lords and gravest counselors returned severally what they thought. The first held that wine was strongest; another that the king was strongest; but Zorobabel, prince of the captive Jews, and heir to the crown of Judah, being one of them, proved women to be stronger than the king, for that he himself had seen a concubine take his crown from off his head to set it upon her own. And others besides him have lately seen the like feat done, and not in jest. Yet he proved on, and it was so yielded by the king himself and all his sages, that neither wine, nor women, nor the king, but truth, of all other things was the strongest.

For me, though neither asked nor in a nation that gives such rewards to wisdom, I shall pronounce my sentence somewhat different from Zorobabel, and shall defend that either truth and justice are all one— for truth is but justice in our knowledge, and justice is but truth in our practice;[2] and he indeed so explains himself in saying that with truth is no accepting of persons, which is the property of justice—or else, if there be any odds, that justice, though not stronger than truth, yet by her

office is to put forth and exhibit more strength in the affairs of mankind. For truth is properly no more than contemplation, and her utmost efficiency is but teaching: but justice in her very essence is all strength and activity, and hath a sword put into her hand to use against all violence and oppression on the earth. She it is most truly who accepts no person and exempts none from the severity of her stroke. She never suffers injury to prevail, but when falsehood first prevails over truth; and that also is a kind of justice done on them who are so deluded. Though wicked kings and tyrants counterfeit her sword, as some did that buckler[3] fabled to fall from heaven into the Capitol, yet she communicates her power to none but such as like herself are just, or at least will do justice. For it were extreme partiality and injustice, the flat denial and overthrow of herself, to put her own authentic sword into the hand of an unjust and wicked man, or so far to accept and exalt one mortal person above his equals that he alone shall have the punishing of all other men transgressing and not receive like punishment from men, when he himself shall be found the highest transgressor.

We may conclude therefore that justice, above all other things, is and ought to be the strongest; she is the strength, the kingdom, the power, and majesty of all ages. Truth herself would subscribe to this, though Darius and all the monarchs of the world should deny. And if by sentence thus written it were my happiness to set free the minds of Englishmen from longing to return poorly under that captivity of kings from which the strength and supreme sword of justice hath delivered them, I shall have done a work not much inferior to that of Zorobabel; who, by well praising and extolling the force of truth, in that contemplative strength conquered Darius and freed his country and the people of God from the captivity of Babylon.[4]

---

[2] Ignoring the literary background of these words, S. B. Liljegren treated them in *Studies in Milton* (Lund, 1918) as proof that Milton was a Machiavellian fanatic who had constituted himself "one of the few righteous joined in hatred, contempt, and irresponsibility against the greater part of the English people at the Revolution" (p. 143). For A. Barker (in *Dilemma*, p. 173) Milton's conception of *justice as truth in practice* is a reaffirmation of his "idea of absolute law which had formed the centre of his attack on episcopacy, and whose restrictive implications had seemed to disappear in the reasoning of the divorce tracts." Psychologically, the passage illustrates Milton's lifelong idea of the heroic in character and action as combining "contemplation and practice, wit, prudence, fortitude and eloquence" in the combination "rarely met" which he described in *CG*, p. 643.

[3] The glancing reference is to the buckler (*ancile*) which Plutarch in the Life of Numa and Ovid in the *Fasti* (III, 365–92) describe as falling from heaven into the king's hands with the promise of Jove that, as long as it was preserved, Rome would be safe. Numa had eleven similar bucklers made and committed them all, with the original one, to the safekeeping of the Salian priests.

[4] In I Esdras iv Zorobabel wins freedom to re-

Which I shall yet not despair to do, if they in this land whose minds are yet captive be but as ingenuous to acknowledge the strength and supremacy of justice as that heathen king was to confess the strength of truth.   Or let them but, as he did, grant that, and they will soon perceive that truth resigns all her outward strength to justice. Justice therefore must needs be strongest, both in her own and in the strength of truth.   But if a king may do among men whatsoever is his will and pleasure, and notwithstanding be unaccountable to men, then contrary to this magnified wisdom of Zorobabel, neither truth nor justice, but the king, is strongest of all other things, which that Persian monarch himself in the midst of all his pride and glory durst not assume.

Let us see therefore what this king hath to affirm, why the sentence of justice and the weight of that sword which she delivers into the hands of men, should be more partial to him offending than to all others of human race. First, he pleads that "no Law of God or man gives to subjects any power of judicature without or against him."[5] Which assertion shall be proved in every part to be most untrue. The first express law of God given to mankind was that to Noah, as a law in general to all the sons of men. And by that most ancient and universal law, "whosoever sheddeth man's blood, by man shall his blood be shed,"[6] we find here no exception. If a king therefore do this, to a king, and that by men also, the same shall be done. This in the law of Moses, which came next, several times is repeated and in one place remarkably, Numbers 35: "Ye shall take no satisfaction for the life of a murderer, but he shall surely be put to death: the land cannot be cleansed of the blood that is shed therein,"[7] but by the blood of him that shed it. This is so spoken as that which concerned all Israel, not one man alone, to see performed; and if no satisfaction were to be taken, then certainly no exception. Nay, the king, when they should set up any, was to observe the

whole law and not only to see it done, but to "do it; that his heart might not be lifted up above his brethren,"[8] to dream of vain and reasonless prerogatives or exemptions, whereby the law itself must needs be founded in unrighteousness.

And were that true, which is most false, that all kings are the Lord's anointed, it were yet absurd to think that the anointment[9] of God should be as it were a charm against law; and give them privilege who punish others, to sin themselves unpunishably. The high Priest was the Lord's anointed as well as any king, and with the same consecrated oil; yet Solomon had put to death Abiathar,[10] had it not been for other respects than that anointment. If God himself say to kings, "Touch not mine anointed,"[11] meaning his chosen people, as is evident in that Psalm, yet no man will argue thence that he protects them from civil laws if they offend. Then certainly, though David, as a private man and in his own cause, feared to lift his hand against the Lord's anointed,[12] much less can this forbid the law or disarm justice from having legal power against any king. No other supreme magistrate, in what kind of Government soever, lays claim to any such enormous privilege. Wherefore then should any king, who is but one kind of magistrate and set over the people for no other end than they?

Next in order of time to the laws of Moses are those of Christ, who declares professedly his judicature to be spiritual, abstract from civil managements, and therefore leaves all nations to their own particular laws and way of government. Yet because the Church hath a kind of jurisdiction within her own bounds, and that also, though in process of time much cor-

store Jerusalem as his final reward for his defense of truth.
    [5] Cf. n. 11 in the Preface to *Eikon*.
    [6] Gen. ix, 6.
    [7] Num. xxxv, 31.

    [8] Deut. xvii, 19–20.
    [9] In a chapter on "What is meant by anointing of Kings" in *The Royal Charter,* Thomas Bayly protested against the "Disesteem of the Person" of kings, which he attributed to Puritan contempt for "the Ceremonies of State (as Anointing, sitting on Thrones, holding Sceptres, and Coronation itself). . . . Tush, say they, what need all these Fopperies, a King's Throne is his Justice, his Crown his Honour, his Sceptre and chiefest strength his People's Hearts, his Holy Oyle is his Religion and Zeal to God's Glory" (p. 15). Cf. *TKM,* n. 32.
    [10] I Kings ii, 26.
    [11] Psalms cv, 15.
    [12] I Sam. xxiv, 6 and 10. Cf. *TKM,* n. 32.

rupted and plainly turned into a corporal judicature, yet much approved by this king, it will be firm enough and valid against him, if subjects, by the laws of Church also, be "invested with a power of judicature" both without and against their king, though pretending and by them acknowledged "next and immediately under Christ supreme head and Governor." Theodosius,[13] one of the best Christian emperors, having made a slaughter of the Thessalonians for sedition, but too cruelly, was excommunicated to his face by Saint Ambrose, who was his subject. And excommunion is the utmost of ecclesiastical judicature, a spiritual putting to death. But this, ye will say, was only an example. Read then the story; and it will appear, both that Ambrose avouched it for the law of God, and Theodosius confessed it of his own accord to be so; "and that the law of God was not to be made void in him for any reverence to his imperial power." From hence, not to be tedious, I shall pass into our own land of Britain, and show that subjects here have exercised the utmost of spiritual judicature, and more than spiritual, against their kings, his predecessors. Vortiger,[14] for committing incest with his daughter, was by Saint German, at that time his subject, cursed and condemned in a British council about the yeare 448; and thereupon soon after was deposed. Mauricus,[15] a king in Wales, for breach of oath and the murder of Cynetus was excommunicated and cursed, with all his offspring, by Oudoceus, Bishop of Landaff, in full synod,

about the year 560; and not restored till he had repented. Morcant[16] another king of Wales having slain Frioc his uncle, was fain to come in person and receive judgment from the same bishop and his clergy; who upon his penitence acquitted him for no other cause than lest the kingdom should be destitute of a successor in the royal line. These examples are of the Primitive, British, and Episcopal Church, long ere they had any commerce or communion with the Church of Rome. What power afterward of deposing kings, and so consequently of putting them to death, was assumed and practised by the canon law, I omit as a thing generally known. Certainly, if whole councils of the Romish Church have in the midst of their dimness discerned so much of truth as to decree at Constance[17] and at Basil,[18] and many of them to avouch at Trent[19] also, that a council is above the pope and may judge him, though by them not denied to be the Vicar of Christ, we in our clearer light may be ashamed not to discern further that a parliament is by all equity and right, above a king, and

---

[13] In *Ref* (C.E. III, 70), in *DDD* (C.E. VII, 197), and in CB (C.E. XVIII, 170) Milton shows his interest in the account in Theodoret's *Church History* (Ed. Paris, 1544), pp. 342 ff., of St. Ambrose's excommunication of the elder *Theodosius* (the father of Theodosius I) after his order of the massacre of several thousand Thessalonians in 390 A.D. for disrespect to his officers at a public ceremony.

[14] *Vortigern's* excommunication is recorded by Milton in *Britain* (C.E. X, 120) and recalled in *Def I* (C.E. VII, 159 and 437).

[15] In *Britain* (C.E. X, 139-40) Milton tells the story of the death of Teudric, the father of Mouric (Meurig ap Tewdrig, the king of Glamorgan), and quotes "the Regest of Landaff" as his authority. In that work, the *Book of Llan Dav* (ed. by J. G. Evans and John Rhys. Oxford, 1893), p. 147, we have the story of the treacherous slaying of *Cynetus* (Cynuetu) by *Mauricus* (Meurig) and of his subsequent malediction and punishment by *Oudoceus, Bishop of Llandaff.*

[16] *Morcant* (Morgan Mwynfawr, regulus of Glamorgan, who died in 665?), is said in the *Book of Llan Dav* (pp. 152-4) to have given Oudoceus several charters of land in favor of the see of Llandaff after the "ecclesiastical proceedings taken against him by Oudoceus in consequence of his murdering his uncle Frioc." He also suffered formal malediction and excommunication, but was readmitted to good standing in the church on his repentance.

[17] The Council of *Constance* (5 Nov., 1414, to 22 April, 1418) forced the abdication of the rivals for papal authority, John XXIII, Gregory XII, and Benedict XIII. From the pope whom it confirmed, Martin V, it obtained a guarantee of the periodicity of councils and approval of a project for reforms, though it did not obtain his unqualified approval of all its decrees.

[18] On Dec. 15, 1433, Eugenius IV annulled a bull of dissolution which he had issued earlier against the Council of *Basle*, but his submission did not include unqualified ratification of all its decrees.

[19] Many of Milton's readers would be familiar with Paolo Sarpi's account in *The historie of the Councel of Trent* (tr. by Nathaniel Brent. 3rd ed., 1640), p. 817, of a crucial debate in the College of Cardinals on Jan. 26, 1563, over a proposal for full papal approval of the acts of the Council: "In the end, the Pope concluded, that it was good to confirme all without exception, and so he did in words, in the consistory, confirming them, and commanding that they should be received, & inviolably observed by all the faithful, and the same day he published a Bull, subscribed by all the Cardinals."

may judge him, whose reasons and pretensions to hold of God only, as his immediate vicegerent, we know how far-fetched they are and insufficient.

As for the laws of man, it would ask a volume to repeat all that might be cited in this point against him from all antiquity. In Greece Orestes,[20] the son of Agamemnon, and by succession king of Argos, was in that country judged and condemned to death for killing his mother: whence escaping, he was judged again, though a stranger, before the great council of Areopagus in Athens. And this memorable act of judicature was the first that brought the justice of that grave senate into fame and high estimation over all Greece for many ages after. And in the same city tyrants were to undergo legal sentence by the laws of Solon.[21]

The kings of Sparta, though descended lineally from Hercules, esteemed a God among them, were often judged, and sometimes put to death by the most just and renowned laws of Lycurgus; who, though a king, thought it most unequal to bind his subjects by any law to which he bound not himself. In Rome the laws made by Valerius Publicola[22] soon after the expelling of Tarquin and his race, expelled without a written law—the law being afterward written—and what the Senate decreed against Nero,[23] that he should be judged and punished according to the laws of their ancestors, and what in like manner was decreed against other emperors,[24] is vulgarly known—as it was known to those heathen and found just by nature ere any law mentioned it. And that the Christian civil law warrants like power of judicature to subjects against tyrants, is written clearly by the best and famousest civilians. For if it was decreed by Theodosius[25] and stands yet firm in the Code of Justinian, that the law is above the emperor, then certainly the emperor being under law, the law may judge him; and if judge him, may punish him, proving tyrannous. How else is the law above him, or to what purpose? These are necessary deductions; and thereafter hath been done in all ages and kingdoms oftener than to be here recited.

But what need we any further search after the law of other lands for that which is so fully and so plainly set down lawful in our own? Where ancient books tell us, Bracton,[26] Fleta,[27] and others, that the king is under law and inferior to his court of Parliament; that although his place "to do justice," be highest, yet that he stands as liable "to receive justice" as the meanest of his kingdom. Nay, Alfred, the most worthy king and by some accounted first

Charles in open court the condemnation of "that great tyrant of his time, Nero," was called one of the most "famous acts of justice even done by the Senate of Rome" (Muddiman, *Trial of Charles I*, p. 119). Cf. Chap. xxvii, n. 18.

[24] Cf. *TKM*, n. 65, which indicates that Trajan is the likeliest of the *other emperors* to have been in Milton's mind.

[25] Cf. *TKM*, notes 66 and 67.

[26] Henry of *Bracton* (d. 1268), a judge under Henry III, wrote the first important compendium of English law, *De legibus et consuetudinibus Angliae libri quinque*, which was first published in 1569. The passage which is loosely paraphrased here occurs on F34r (Bk. II, Chap. xvi), with an even more elaborate statement of the law whereby the king reigned and to which he owed his office in Bk. I, Chap. viii.

[27] The authorship of the work to which Milton refers as *Fleta* (*Fleta seu Commentarius juris Anglicani sic nuncupatus, sub Edwardo rege primo seu circa annos abhinc CCCXL ab anonymo conscriptus*, etc. 1647) was surmised by John Selden in his *Dissertatio* appended to the first edition to be the work of several judges whom Edward I imprisoned in the Fleet prison in 1288. Selden suspected that the name of the work was derived from that of the prison. In the first chapter Milton found a passage (p. 16) which emphatically declared that the law and the barons were a check upon the abuse of royal power.

[20] The allusion is to the scene in Euripides' *Orestes* (943-9) where the hero is banished for his murder of his mother Clytemnestra in spite of the fact that his deed was an obligatory vengeance for her slaying of his father, and to the scene in the *Eumenides* (775-81) of Aeschylus, where Orestes is finally acquitted by the Areopagus in Athens.

[21] Cf. the recommendation in *Educ* (n. 63) that the curriculum include a study of the Athenian legal code of *Solon* and the Spartan code of Lycurgus for their safeguards against usurpation of power.

[22] Livy tells the story in *The Romane Historie* (tr. by Philemon Holland, 1600), p. 49, of the misgivings of the Romans about the sincerity of the democratic professions of the consul *Valerius* after his successful struggle to expel the Tarquin kings of Rome, and of their final persuasion of his honesty and deserving of the title *Publicola* when he took the lead in legislation "cursing and condemning of him both bodie and goods, that should intend or plot to usurpe princely dominion over them."

[23] In recalling Suetonius' statement (*Caesars*, VI, xlix) that the Senate condemned *Nero* to die by a shameful, "ancient mode" (*more maiorum*) for his tyrannies, Milton can hardly have been unaware that in one of Bradshaw's speeches to

absolute monarch of the Saxons here, so ordained; as is cited out of an ancient law
book called the *Mirror*,[28] in *Rights of the
Kingdom*, p. 31, where it is complained on
"as the sovereign abuse of all" that "the
king should be deemed above the Law,
whereas he ought be subject to it by his
oath."[29] Of which oath anciently it was
the last clause that the king "should be as
liable and obedient to suffer right as others
of his people." And indeed it were but
fond and senseless that the king should be
accountable to every petty suit in lesser
courts as we all know he was, and not be
subject to the judicature of Parliament in
the main matters of our common safety or
destruction; that he should be answerable
in the ordinary course of law for any wrong
done to a private person, and not answerable in court of Parliament for destroying
the whole kingdom.

By all this, and much more that might
be added, as in an argument over-copious
rather than barren, we see it manifest that
all laws, both of God and man, are made
without exemption of any person whomsoever; and that if kings presume to overtop
the law by which they reign for the public
good, they are by law to be reduced into
order; and that can no way be more justly
than by those who exalted them to that
high place. For who should better understand their own laws, and when they are
transgressed, than they who are governed
by them and whose consent first made
them? And who can have more right to
take knowledge of things done within a
free nation than they within themselves?

Those objected oaths of allegiance and
supremacy we swore, not to his person but
as it was invested with his authority; and
his authority was by the people first given
him conditionally, in law and under law,
and under oath also for the kingdom's
good, and not otherwise. The oaths then

28 Cf. notes 3, 5, and 12 in Chap. v above.
29 The reasoning resembles Sadlar's in *Rights
of The Kingdom*, p. 110, that they who "are
most Zealous for Prerogative, or that Title of
Conquests, are least acquainted with the Lawes,
or Histories of *England*." William the Conqueror had repeatedly ratified all Saxon laws, and
hence, "to this very day," said Sadlar (p. 115),
"one speciall Clause of the *Coronation Oath* . . .
*was to confirme All the Lawes and Customes of
the Kingdome;* but especially, the Lawes of Saint
Edward." Cf. Chap. v, n. 3.

were interchanged and mutual; stood and
fell together. He swore fidelity to his trust
(not as a deluding ceremony, but as a real
condition of their admitting him for king;
and the conqueror himself swore it oftener
than at his crowning). They swore homage and fealty to his person in that trust.
There was no reason why the kingdom
should be further bound by oaths to him
than he by his coronation oath to us, which
he hath every way broken; and having
broken, the ancient crown-oath of Alfred
above mentioned conceals not his penalty.

As for the Covenant,[30] if that be meant,
certainly no discreet person can imagine it
should bind us to him in any stricter sense
than those oaths formerly. The acts of
hostility which we received from him were
no such dear obligements that we should
owe him more fealty and defense for being our enemy than we could before when
we took him only for a king. They were
accused by him and his party to pretend
liberty and reformation, but to have no
other end than to make themselves great
and to destroy the king's person and authority. For which reason they added that
third article, testifying to the world that
as they were resolvd to endeavor first a
reformation in the Church, to extirpate prelacy, to preserve the rights of Parliament
and the liberties of the Kingdom, so they
intended, so far as it might consist with the
preservation and defense of these, to preserve the king's person and authority; but
not otherwise. As far as this comes to, they
covenant and swear in the sixth article to
preserve and defend the persons and authority of one another and all those that
enter into that league; so that this Covenant
gives no unlimitable exemption to the king's

30 A crucial clause in the Solemn League and
Covenant explicitly bound the English and Scottish
Parliaments and King Charles to respect one another's safety and to strive together for "the
preservation and defense of the true Religion and
Liberties of the Kingdom." (Cf. the Preface, n.
33, and *TKM*, n. 19.) Milton stood with John
Goodwin, who argued in ὑβριστοδίκαι, *The Obstructours of Justice* (1649), p. 51: "Evident it is
that those words of the Covenant import a condition to be performed on the King's part, without
the performance whereof the Covenant obligeth no
man to *the preservation or defense of his Person,
or Authority.*" Goodwin added: "If this is not the
clear meaning and importance of them, the Covenant is a *Barbarian* unto me: I understand not
the English of it."

person, but gives to all as much defense and preservation as to him, and to him as much as to their own persons, and no more; that is to say, in order and subordination to those main ends for which we live and are a nation of men joined in society either Christian or, at least, human.

But if the Covenant were made absolute, to preserve and defend any one whomsoever, without respect had, either to the true religion or those other superior things to be defended and preserved however, it cannot then be doubted but that the Covenant was rather a most foolish, hasty, and unlawful vow than a deliberate and well-weighed covenant, swearing us into labyrinths and repugnances no way to be solved or reconciled, and therefore no way to be kept: as first offending against the law of God, to vow the absolute preservation, defense, and maintaining of one man, though in his sins and offenses never so great and heinous against God or his neighbor; and to except a person from justice, whereas his law excepts none. Secondly, it offends against the law of this nation, wherein, as hath been proved, kings in receiving justice and undergoing due trial are not differenced from the meanest subject.

Lastly, it contradicts and offends against the Covenant itself, which vows in the fourth article to bring to open trial and condign punishment all those that shall be found guilty of such crimes and deliquencies, whereof the king by his own letters and other undeniable testimonies not brought to light till afterward[31] was found and convicted to be chief actor in what they thought him at the time of taking that Covenant, to be overruled only by evil counselors.[32] And those, or whomsoever they should discover to be principal, they vowed to try "either by their own supreme judicatories" (for so even then they called them) "or by others having power from them to that effect." So that to have brought the

king to condign punishment hath not broke the Covenant, but it would have broke the Covenant to have saved him from those judicatories which both nations declared in that Covenant to be "supreme" against any person whatsoever.

And besides all this, to swear in covenant the bringing of his evil counselors and accomplices to condign punishment, and not only to leave unpunished and untouched the grand offender, but to receive him back again from the accomplishment of so many violences and mischiefs, dipped from head to foot and stained over with the blood of thousands that were his faithful subjects, forced to their own defense against a civil war by him first raised upon them, and to receive him thus, in this gory pickle, to all his dignities and honors, covering the ignominious and horrid purple robe of innocent blood that sat so close about him with the glorious purple of royalty and supreme rule, the reward of highest excellence and virtue here on earth, were not only to swear and covenant the performance of an unjust vow, the strangest and most impious to the face of God, but were the most unwise and unprudential act as to civil government. For so long as a king shall find by experience that, do the worst he can, his subjects, overawed by the religion of their own Covenant, will only prosecute his evil instruments, not dare to touch his person; and that whatever hath been on his part offended or transgressed, he shall come off at last with the same reverence to his person and the same honor as for welldoing, he will not fail to find them work; seeking far and near, and inviting to his court all the concourse of evil counselors or agents that may be found: who, tempted with preferments and his promise to uphold them, will hazard easily their own heads and the chance of ten to one but they shall prevail at last over men so quelled and fitted to be slaves by the false conceit of a religious covenant. And they in that superstition neither wholly yielding nor to the utmost resisting, at the upshot of all their foolish war and expense will find to have done no more but fetched a compass only of their miseries, ending at the same point of slavery and in the same distractions wherein they first began.

But when kings themselves are made as

---

[31] In Chap. xxi, "Upon his Letters taken and divulged," Milton has defended the ethics of Parliament's decision to publish the contents of the King's letters which were captured after the battle of Naseby, on June 14, 1645. Charles did not dispute the fact that they revealed his definite plan to bring "foreign forces, Irish, French, Dutch, Lorrainers, and our old invaders the Danes" into England against the forces of Parliament.

[32] Cf. the Preface, n. 13.

liable to punishment as their evil counselors, it will be both as dangerous from the king himself as from his parliament, to those that evil-counsel him. And they who else would be his readiest agents in evil will then not fear to disuade or to disobey him, not only in respect of themselves and their own lives, which for his sake they would not seem to value, but in respect of that danger which the king himself may incur, whom they would seem to love and serve with greatest fidelity. On all these grounds therefore of the Covenant itself, whether religious or political, it appears likeliest that both the English Parliament, and the Scotch Commissioners, thus interpreting the Covenant (as indeed at that time they were the best and most authentical interpreters joined together) answered the king unanimously, in their letters[33] dated January 13th, 1645, that till security and satisfaction first given to both kingdoms for the blood spilt, for the Irish rebels brought over, and for the war in Ireland by him fomented, they could in no wise yield their consent to his return.

Here was satisfaction, full two years and upward after the Covenant taken, demanded of the king by both nations in Parliament for crimes at least capital, wherewith they charged him. And what satisfaction could be given for so much blood but justice upon him that spilled it? Till which done, they neither took themselves bound to grant him the exercise of his regal office by any meaning of the Covenant which they then declared (though other meanings have been since contrived) not so much regarded the safety of his person as to admit of his return among them from the midst of those whom they declared to be his greatest enemies. Nay, from himself as from an actual enemy, not as from a king, they demanded security.

But if the Covenant, all this notwithstanding, swore otherwise to preserve him then in the preservation of true religion and our liberties, against which he fought, if not in arms, yet in resolution, to his dying day, and now after death still fights against in this his book, the Covenant was better broken than he saved. And God hath testified by all propitious and the most evident signs, whereby in these latter times he is wont to testify what pleases him, that such a solemn and for many ages unexampled act of due punishment was no "mockery of justice," but a most grateful and well-pleasing sacrifice. Neither was it "to cover their perjury," as he accuses, but to uncover his perjury to the oath of his coronation.

The rest of his discourse quite forgets the title, and turns his meditations upon death into obloquy and bitter vehemence against his "judges and accusers"—imitating therein, not our Savior, but his grandmother Mary Queen of Scots,[34] as also in the most of his other scruples, exceptions, and evasions. And from whom he seems to have learnt, as it were by heart, or else by kind, that which is thought by his admirers to be the most virtuous, most manly, most Christian, and most martyr-like both of his words and speeches here, and of his answers and behavior at his trial.

"It is a sad fate," he saith, "to have his enemies both accusers, parties, and judges." Sad indeed, but no sufficient plea to acquit him from being so judged. For what malefactor might not sometimes plead the like? If his own crimes have made all men his enemies, who else can judge him? They of the powder-plot[35] against his father might as well have pleaded the same. Nay

---

[33] Milton's point is equally well confirmed by A Letter from the Parliament of Scotland to the Parliament of England, dated at Edinburgh, Jan. 16, 1647, which gave large powers to the Scottish Commissioners then negotiating in London. In a formal Declaration of the Kingdom of Scotland Charles is described as having failed to give both Parliaments the "just satisfaction to the joynt Desires of both Kingdoms" which he had assured the Scots commanders that he would give when he surrendered to them at Newark, and of having violated the "Solemn League and Covenant, for the Reformation and Defence of Religion, The Honour and Happiness of the King, and their own Peace and Safety." Accordingly the Scots concurred in the decision of the English Parliament to confine Charles at Holmby House "until he give satisfaction to both Kingdoms in the Propositions of Peace."

[34] Mary's firm denial of the jurisdiction of her judges over her as a sovereign princess and her expressions of forgiveness for her enemies are fully confirmed by records sent from the scene of her execution in Fotheringay Castle in 1587, which are reproduced in Camden's Annales (1615), pp. 455–7. Bradshaw had compared Charles's denial of the authority of his judges with Mary's similar denial, but he did not stress the point in his speeches to the king as heavily as Milton does.

[35] For the powder-plot see Plot, n. 1.

at the Resurrection it may as well be pleaded, that the saints who then shall judge the world, are "both enemies, judges, parties, and accusers."

So much he thinks to abound in his own defense that he undertakes an unmeasurable task; to bespeak "the singular care and protection of God over all kings," as "being the greatest patrons of law, justice, order, and religion on earth." But what patrons they be, God in the scripture oft enough hath expressed; and the earth itself hath too long groaned under the burden of their injustice, disorder, and irreligion. Therefore "to bind their kings in chains, and their nobles with links of iron" is an honor belonging to his saints; not to build Babel (which was Nimrod's work the first king, "and the beginning of his Kingdom was Babel")[36] but to destroy it, especially that spiritual babel: and first to overcome those European kings[37] which receive their power, not from God, but from the beast; and are counted no better than his ten horns. "These shall hate the great Whore," and yet "shall give their kingdoms to the beast that carries her; they shall commit fornication with her," and yet "shall burn her with fire," and yet "shall lament the fall of Babylon,"[38] where they fornicated with her. Rev. xvii, xviii.

Thus shall they be to and fro, doubtful and ambiguous in all their doings, until at last, "joining their armies with the beast,"[39] whose power first raised them, they shall perish with him by the "King of Kings," against whom they have rebelled; and "the Fowls shall eat their flesh." This is their doom written, Rev. xix, and the utmost that we find concerning them in these latter days; which we have much more cause to believe than his unwarranted revelation here, prophesying what shall follow after his death, with the spirit of enmity, not of Saint John.

He would fain bring us out of conceit with the good "success" which God hath vouchsafed us. We measure not our cause by our success, but our success by our cause. Yet certainly in a good cause success is a good confirmation, for God hath promised it to good men almost in every leaf of Scripture.[40] If it argue not for us, we are sure it argues not against us; but as much or more for us than ill success argues for them, for to the wicked God hath denounced ill success in all that they take in hand.[41]

He hopes much of those "softer tempers," as he calls them, and "less advantaged by his ruin, that their consciences do already" gripe them. 'Tis true, there be a sort of moody, hotbrained, and always unedified consciences, apt to engage their leaders into great and dangerous affairs past retirement, and then, upon a sudden qualm and swimming of their conscience, to betray them basely in the midst of what was chiefly undertaken for their sakes. Let such men never meet with any faithful Parliament to hazard for them; never with any noble spirit to conduct and lead them out; but let them live and die in servile condition and their scrupulous queasiness, if no instruction will confirm them. Others there be in whose consciences the loss of gain and those advantages they hoped for, hath

[36] The words from Gen. x, 10, are interpreted in *PL* XII, 44, as meaning that *Nimrod* was the first tyrant. In reply to Charles's prophecy that God will not "suffer those men long to prosper in their *Babel,* who build it with the bones, and cement it with the blood of their Kings," Milton quotes Psalm cxlix, 8, as proof that the "saints" will bind kings with chains and nobles with links of iron, and will destroy "that spiritual *Babel,*" i.e. "that spiritual *Babel* of prelates against which he had inveighed in *Ref* (C.E. III, 54).

[37] The contemporary *European kings* are compared with the ten kings who "have received no power as yet," but are identified with the ten horns of the seven-headed beast upon whose back rides the woman upon whose "forehead is a name written, MYSTERY, BABYLON THE GREAT, THE MOTHER OF HARLOTS AND ABOMINATIONS OF THE EARTH." (Rev. xvii, 3, 5, and 12.)

[38] Cf. the "Babylonian woe" of *Sonn* XVIII, 14.

[39] St. John prophesies (Rev. xvii, 13-14) that the kings shall "give their power and strength unto the beast," but shall be overcome by the Lamb who is "King of Kings." The prophecy of the fowls eating the flesh of kings is in Rev. xix, 18 and 21.

[40] Milton thought of passages like the promise of prosperity to the works of the righteous man in Psalm i, 3, but he was less confident of his position than Cromwell was when he urged the Governor of the Isle of Wight to surrender Charles to the Army because God had indicated his approval of the Army by granting it the victories of the second civil war. "Let us look to providences; surely they mean somewhat," wrote Cromwell in a letter quoted by Sir John A. R. Marriott in *The Crisis of English Liberty* (Oxford, 1930), p. 240.

[41] "The way of the ungodly shall perish" (Psalm i, 6).

sprung a sudden leak. These are they that cry out the Covenant broken,[42] and, to keep it better, slide back into neutrality or join actually with incendiaries and malignants. But God hath eminently begun to punish those, first in Scotland,[43] then in Ulster,[44] who have provoked him with the most hateful kind of mockery to break his Covenant under pretense of strictest keeping it; and hath subjected them to those malignants with whom they scrupled not to be associates. In God therefore we shall not fear what their false fraternity can do against us.

He seeks again with cunning words to turn our success into our sin—but might call to mind that the Scripture speaks of those also who, "when God slew them, then sought him"; yet did but "flatter him with their mouth and lied to him with their tongues; for their heart was not right with him."[45]   And there was one who in the time of his affliction trespassed more against God: "This was that King Ahaz."[46]

[42] The London Presbyterian clergy had appealed against Parliament on Jan. 24, 1649, to the "Covenant-keeping Citizens," and on Feb. 24 the Scottish Commissioners in London had declared that they "detested the execution of the late King," and had charged Parliament with "breach of the Solemn League and Covenant, the suppression of monarchy," and "an ungodly toleration in matters of religion."

[43] The punishment of the Scottish attempt to set Charles II on the throne began with the crushing defeat on April 27, 1650, of his ablest supporter, the Marquis of Montrose, against whom he had been forced to turn by the Scottish Parliament because the Marquis was opposed by the Presbyterian majority.

[44] From Milton's point of view, the *Ulster* Scots had virtually been made allies of the Duke of Ormond in his effort to establish Charles II's power in Ireland when on Feb. 15, 1649, the Presbytery of Belfast officially condemned the policy of Parliament. (Cf. *Peace*, C.E. VI, 236–41.) Ormond was defeated at Rathmines by Colonel Jones, acting as Parliament's commander in Dublin, on Aug. 2, 1649, and he left the country after Cromwell crushed resistance in northern Ireland in the winter of 1649–50.

[45] Psalm v, 9—"For there is no faithfulness in their mouth; . . . they flatter with their tongue"—to which Charles refers, is capped by Psalm lxxviii, 34–37: "When he slew them, then they sought him . . . Nevertheless they did flatter him with their mouth, and they lied unto him with their tongues, for their heart was not right with him."

He glories much in the forgiveness of his enemies. So did his grandmother at her death.[47] Wise men would sooner have believed him had he not so often told us so. But he hopes to erect "the trophies of his charity over us." And trophies of charity no doubt will be as "glorious" as trumpets before the alms of hypocrites; and more especially the trophies of such an aspiring charity as offers in his prayer to share victory with God's "compassion," which is over all his works. Such prayers as these may haply catch the people, as was intended: but how they please God is to be much doubted, though prayed in secret, much less, written to be divulged. Which perhaps may gain him after death a short, contemptible, and soon-fading reward; not what he aims at, to stir the constancy and solid firmness of any wise man, or to unsettle the conscience of any knowing Christian (if he could ever aim at a thing so hopeless and above the genius of his "cleric" elocution), but to catch the worthless approbation of an inconstant, irrational, and image-doting rabble; that like a credulous and hapless herd, begotten to servility and enchanted with these popular institutes of tyranny, subscribed with a new device of the king's picture[48] at his prayers, hold out both their ears with such delight and ravishment to be stigmatized and bored through in witness of their own voluntary and beloved baseness. The rest, whom perhaps ignorance without malice, or some error, less than fatal, hath for the time misled, on this side sorcery or obduration, may find the grace and good guidance to bethink themselves and recover.

[46] "And in the time of his distress did he trespass yet more against the Lord: this is that king Ahaz." (II Chron. xxviii, 22.) Cf. *PL* I, 470–6. For Milton, Ahaz was a symbol of wilful apostasy from true religion to idolatry.

[47] The official record (preserved by Camden, *Annales*, p. 456) leaves no doubt that, before mounting the scaffold, Mary prayed for Queen Elizabeth and for all those who had thirsted for her blood. Cf. n. 34 above.

[48] The reference is to the famous frontispiece which was published with all except the earliest editions of the *Eikon Basilike*, and which is reproduced on the following page.

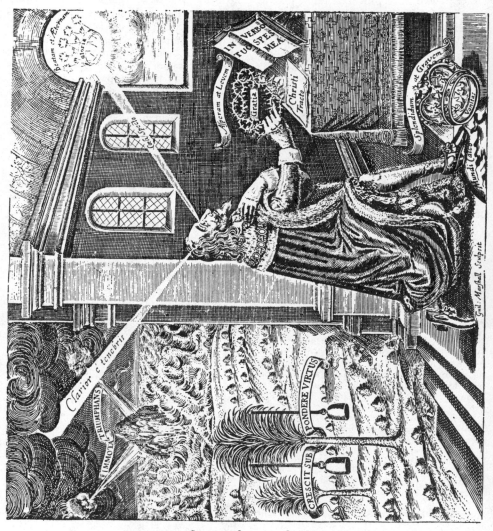

See note 48 on page 815.

Selections from
THE SECOND
DEFENSE OF THE PEOPLE OF ENGLAND.

AGAINST AN ANONYMOUS LIBEL,

ENTITLED

"THE ROYAL BLOOD CRYING TO HEAVEN FOR VENGEANCE ON THE ENGLISH PARRICIDES."

BIBLIOGRAPHICAL NOTE—*Joannis Miltoni Angli Pro Populo Anglicano Defensio Secunda* was published in the original Latin in 1654, in reply to *Regii Sanguinis Clamor ad Coelum adversus Parricidas Anglicanos* (1652). The *Cry of the Royal Blood* was anonymous, and its authorship by Peter du Moulin was not known in England until the Restoration, and perhaps not even when du Moulin was made one of Charles II's chaplains and given a prebend at Canterbury in 1660. His connection with the *Cry* was so far from being suspected in 1656 that Oxford University gave him a D.D. The editor of the *Cry* was Alexander More (1616–1670), a man of French birth but half-Scottish blood, who in 1652 had just lost the chair of Theology at Middleburg under a cloud which seems actually to have been as dark as Milton suggests that it was in *Def 2* (See n. 8 below). He was the acknowledged editor of the *Cry,* and he doubtless had the encouragement of Salmasius (See n. 6 below.) in forwarding its publication. Masson summarized the *Cry* in his *Life of Milton* IV, 453–9.

The following selections from *Def 2* are from the translation by Robert Fellowes, which was first published in Symmons' edition of Milton's *Prose Works* in 1806, and was published again in the Bohn edition. The present text is based on Symmons. A new translation with scholarly notes by Donald Roberts is being prepared for the *Complete Prose Works of John Milton,* edited by Don M. Wolfe and others for the Yale University Press.

A grateful recollection of the divine goodness is the first of human obligations; and extraordinary favors demand more solemn and devout acknowledgments. With such acknowledgments I feel it my duty to begin this work. First, because I was born at a time when the virtue of my fellow-citizens, far exceeding that of their progenitors in greatness of soul and vigor of enterprise, having invoked Heaven to witness the justice of their cause, and been clearly governed by its directions, has succeeded in delivering the commonwealth from the most grievous tyranny, and religion from the most ignominious degradation. And next, because when there suddenly arose many who (as is usual with the vulgar) basely calumniated the most illustrious achievements and, when one eminent above the rest, inflated with literary pride and the zealous applauses of his partisans, had in a scandalous publication, which was particularly levelled against me, nefariously under-taken to plead the cause of despotism, I, who was neither deemed unequal to so renowned an adversary nor to so great a subject, was particularly selected by the deliverers of our country and by the general suffrage of the public, openly to vindicate the rights of the English nation and consequently of liberty itself. Lastly, because in a matter of so much moment, and which excited such ardent expectations, I did not disappoint the hopes nor the opinions of my fellow-citizens; while men of learning and eminence abroad honored me with unmingled approbation; while I obtained such a victory over my opponent that notwithstanding his unparalleled assurance he was obliged to quit the field with his courage broken and his reputation lost; and for the three years which he lived afterwards, much as he menaced and furiously as he raved, he gave me no further trouble except that he procured the paltry aid of some despicable hirelings and suborned some of his silly and extravagant admirers to support him under the weight of the unexpected and recent disgrace which he had experienced. This will immediately appear. Such are the signal favors which I ascribe to the divine beneficence and which I thought it right devoutly to commemorate, not only that I might discharge a debt of gratitude, but particularly because they seem auspicious to the success of my present undertaking.

For who is there who does not identify the honor of his country with his own? And what can conduce more to the beauty or glory of one's country than the recovery, not only of its civil, but its religious liberty? And what nation or state ever obtained both by more successful or more valorous exertion? For fortitude is seen resplendent, not only in the field of battle and amid the clash of arms, but displays its energy under every difficulty and against every assailant. Those Greeks and Romans[1] who are the objects of our admiration, employed hardly any other virtue in the extirpation of tyrants than that love of liberty which made them prompt in seizing the sword and gave them strength to use it. With facility they accomplished the undertaking amid the general shout of praise and joy; nor did they engage in the attempt so much as an enterprise of perilous and doubtful issue, as in a contest the most glorious in which virtue could be signalized; which infallibly led to present recompense; which bound their brows with wreaths of laurel and consigned their memories to immortal fame.

For as yet tyrants were not beheld with a superstitious reverence; as yet they were not regarded with tenderness and complacency as the vicegerents or deputies of Christ,[2] as they have suddenly professed to be; as yet the vulgar, stupefied by the subtle casuistry of the priest, had not degenerated into a state of barbarism more gross than that which disgraces the most senseless natives of Hindostan. For these make mischievous demons, whose malice they cannot resist, the objects of their religious adoration; while those elevate impotent tyrants, in order to shield them from destruction, into the rank of gods; and, to their own cost, consecrate the pests of the human race. But against this dark array of long-received opinions, superstitions, obloquy, and fears, which some dread even more than the enemy himself, the English had to contend. And all this, under the light of better information and favored by an impulse from above, they overcame with such singular enthusiasm and bravery that, great as were the numbers engaged in the contest, the grandeur of conception and loftiness of spirit which were universally displayed, merited for each individual more than a mediocrity of fame. And Britain, which was formerly styled the hotbed of tyranny, will hereafter deserve to be celebrated for endless ages as a soil most genial to the growth of liberty.

During the mighty struggle no anarchy, no licentiousness was seen; no illusions of glory, no extravagant emulation of the ancients inflamed them with a thirst for ideal liberty; but the rectitude of their lives and the sobriety of their habits taught them the only true and safe road to real liberty. And they took up arms only to defend the sanctity of the laws and the rights of conscience. Relying on the divine assistance, they used every honorable exertion to break the yoke of slavery; of the praise of which, though I claim no share to myself, yet I can easily repel any charge which may be adduced against me, either of want of courage or want of zeal. For though I did not participate in the toils or dangers of the war, yet I was at the same time engaged in a service not less hazardous to myself and more beneficial to my fellow-citizens. Nor in the adverse turns of our affairs did I ever betray

[1] The passage confirms Thomas Hobbes's saying in *Leviathan* II, xxix, that "one of the most frequent causes" of "rebellion against monarchy" had been "the reading of the books of policy and histories of the ancient Greeks and Romans." The entire passage is quoted by Z. S. Fink on p. 1 of *The Classical Republicans* (Evanston, 1945), where one of the best introductions to the historical milieu of *Def 2* is to be found.

[2] Milton's statement is borne out by works like *The Doctrine of the Scriptures Concerning the Originall of Dominion. Wherein Gods Perpetuall Propriety in the Soveraignty of the whole Earth, and the Kings Great Charter for the Administration thereof, are justified by Authoritative Records in both the Testaments.* By Robert Weldon, Rector of Stony-Stanton in the County of Leicester. 1648.

Weldon seriously argued that the name of Christ was "Communicated indifferently to all *Christian Kings*" (p. 65) and that, as "the Lords Anointed," they actually possessed divine "Power, both for *Perpetuity and Intangibility.*"

any symptoms of pusillanimity and dejection, or show myself more afraid than became me of malice or of death. For since from my youth I was devoted to the pursuits of literature, and my mind had always been stronger than my body, I did not court the labors of a camp, in which any common person would have been of more service than myself, but resorted to that employment in which my exertions were likely to be of most avail. Thus with the better part of my frame I contributed as much as possible to the good of my country and to the success of the glorious cause in which we were engaged; and I thought that if God willed the success of such glorious achievements, it was equally agreeable to his will that there should be others by whom those achievements should be recorded with dignity and elegance, and that the truth, which had been defended by arms, should also be defended by reason; which is the best and only legitimate means of defending it.

Hence, while I applaud those who were victorious in the field, I will not complain of the province which was assigned me, but rather congratulate myself upon it and thank the Author of all good for having placed me in a station which may be an object of envy to others rather than of regret to myself. I am far from wishing to make any vain or arrogant comparisons or to speak ostentatiously of myself, but in a cause so great and glorious, and particularly on an occasion when I am called by the general suffrage to defend the very defenders of that cause, I can hardly refrain from assuming a more lofty and swelling tone than the simplicity of an exordium may seem to justify. And much as I may be surpassed in the powers of eloquence and copiousness of diction by the illustrious orators of antiquity, yet the subject of which I treat was never surpassed in any age in dignity or in interest. It has excited such general and such ardent expectation that I imagine myself not in the forum or on the rostra, surrounded only by the people of Athens or of Rome, but about to address in this, as I did in my former *Defense,* the whole collective body of people, cities, states, and councils of the wise and eminent through the wide expanse of anxious and listening Europe. I seem to survey, as from

a towering height, the far extended tracts of sea and land and innumerable crowds of spectators betraying in their looks the liveliest interest and sensations the most congenial with my own. Here I behold the stout and manly prowess of the Germans disdaining servitude; there the generous and lively impetuosity of the French; on this side, the calm and stately valor of the Spaniard; on that, the composed and wary magnanimity of the Italian. Of all the lovers of liberty and virtue the magnanimous and the wise, in whatever quarter they may be found, some secretly favor, others openly approve; some greet me with congratulations and applause; others who had long been proof against conviction at last yield themselves captive to the force of truth. Surrounded by congregated multitudes, I now imagine that, from the columns of Hercules[3] to the Indian Ocean, I behold the nations of the earth recovering that liberty which they so long had lost; and that the people of this island are transporting to other countries a plant of more beneficial qualities and more noble growth than that which Triptolemus[4] is reported to have carried from region to region; that they are disseminating the blessings of civilization and freedom among cities, kingdoms, and nations.[5]

Nor shall I approach unknown nor perhaps unloved, if it be told that I am the same person who engaged in single combat that fierce advocate of despotism[6] till then reputed invincible in the opinion of many, and in his own conceit who in-

[3] Conti. (VII, i; p. 689) tells the famous story of *Hercules* setting up his pillars of triumph on the mounts Calpe and Abyla on opposite sides of the Straits of Gibraltar.

[4] Cf. *EL IV,* 11, n.

[5] Cf. *Areop,* n. 236.

[6] Salmasius (1588–1653), had (of course, unintentionally) provoked Milton's *Defense of the English People* by publishing his *Defensio Regia pro Carolo Primo* (Nov., 1649), a work which was published at the expense of Charles II, and for which Salmasius received an honorarium of £100. As a good Calvinist (one of whose works Milton had once cited with approval—see *CG.* n. 99), and as the distinguished successor to Scaliger's chair at Leyden in 1631, Salmasius was well qualified for his commission by Charles. After an initial success, which led to his invitation to the court of Christina of Sweden in 1650, the influence of his book rapidly diminished, in part because of its refutation in Milton's *First Defense.* There is no doubt that Queen Christina read Milton's book, or

solently challenged us and our armies to the combat, but whom, while I repelled his virulence, I silenced with his own weapons; and over whom, if I may trust to the opinions of impartial judges, I gained a complete and glorious victory. That this is the plain unvarnished fact appears from this: that, after the most noble queen of Sweden, than whom there neither is nor ever was a personage more attached to literature and to learned men, had invited Salmasius or Salmasia (for to which sex he belonged is a matter of uncertainty) to her court, where he was received with great distinction, my *Defense* suddenly surprised him in the midst of his security. It was generally read, and by the queen among the rest, who, attentive to the dignity of her station, let the stranger experience no diminution of her former kindness and munificence. But, with respect to the rest, if I may assert what has been often told and was matter of public notoriety, such a change was instantly effected in the public sentiment that he, who but yesterday flourished in the highest degree of favor, seemed to-day to wither in neglect; and soon after receiving permission to depart he left it doubtful among many whether he was more honored when he came, or more disgraced when he went away. And even in other places it is clear that it occasioned no small loss to his reputation. And all this I have mentioned, not from any futile motives of vanity or ostentation, but that I might clearly show as I proposed in the beginning, what momentous reasons I had for commencing this work with an effusion of gratitude to the Father of the universe.

Such a preface was most honorable and appropriate, in which I might prove by an enumeration of particulars that I had not been without my share of human misery; but that I had, at the same time, experienced singular marks of the divine regard; that in topics of the highest concern, the most connected with the exigencies of my country, and the most beneficial to civil and religious liberty; the supreme wisdom and beneficence had invigorated and enlarged my faculties to defend the dearest interests, not merely of one people, but of the whole

human race, against the enemies of human liberty; as it were in a full concourse of all the nations on the earth. And I again invoke the same Almighty Being that I may still be able with the same integrity, the same diligence, and the same success, to defend those actions which have been so gloriously achieved; while I vindicate the authors as well as myself, whose name has been associated with theirs, not so much for the sake of honor as disgrace, from unmerited ignominy and reproach. But if there are any who think that it would have been better to have passed over these in silent contempt, I should agree with them if they had been dispersed only among those who were thoroughly acquainted with our principles and our conduct. But how were strangers to discover the false assertions of our adversaries? When proper pains have been taken to make the vindication as extensive as the calumny, I think that they will cease to think ill of us, and that he will be ashamed of the falsehoods which he has promulgated. But if he be past the feeling of shame, we may then well leave him to contempt.

I should sooner have prepared an answer to his invective if he had not entrenched himself in unfounded rumors and frequent denunciations that Salmasius was laboring at the anvil[7] and fabricating new libels against us, which would soon make their appearance; by which he obtained only a short delay of vengeance and of punishment; for I thought it right to reserve my whole strength unimpaired against the more potent adversary. But the conflict between me and Salmasius is now finally terminated by his death, and I will not write against the dead; nor will I reproach him with the loss of life as he did me with the loss of sight; though there are some who impute his death to the penetrating severity of my strictures, which he rendered only the more sharp by his endeavors to resist. When he saw the work which he had in hand proceed slowly on, the time of reply elapsed, the public curiosity subsided, his fame marred, and his reputation lost, the favor of the princes whose cause he had so ill defended alienated, he was destroyed after three years of grief rather by the force of

---

that she made Salmasius' withdrawal easy in 1651, but a few months later she invited him to return. Her second invitation was not accepted.

[7] Salmasius' reply to Milton was posthumously published in 1660.

depression than disease. However this may be, if I must wage even a posthumous war with an enemy whose strength I so well know, whose most vigorous and impetuous attacks I so easily sustained, there seems no reason why I should dread the languid exertions of his dying hour.

But now at last let us come to this thing, whatever it may be, that provokes us to the combat; though I hear, indeed, the cry, not of the royal blood as the title pretends, but that of some skulking and drivelling miscreant.[8] Well, I beseech, who are you? a man, or nobody at all? Certainly one of the dregs of men, for even slaves are not without a name. Shall I always have to contend with anonymous scribblers? though they would willingly indeed pass for king's men, but I much doubt whether they can make kings believe that they are. The followers and friends of kings are not ashamed of kings. How then are these the friends of kings? They make no contributions; they more willingly receive them; they will not even lend their names to the support of the royal cause. What then? They support it by their pen; but even this service they have not sufficient liberality to render gratuitously to their kings; nor have they the courage to affix their names to their productions.

But though, O anonymous sirs! I might plead the example of your Claudius[9] (who composed a plausible work concerning the rights of kings, but without having respect enough either for me or for the subject to put his name to production), I should think it scandalous to undertake the discussion of so weighty a subject while I concealed my name. What I in a republic openly attempt against kings, why do you in a monarchy and under the patronage of kings not dare to do except clandestinely and by stealth? Why do you, trembling with apprehension in the midst of security and seeking darkness in the midst of light, depreciate the power and the majesty of sovereigns by a cowardice which must excite both hatred and distrust? Do you suspect that you have no protection in the power of kings? But surely, thus skulking in obscurity and prowling in disguise, you seem to have come not so much as advocates to maintain the right of kings as thieves to rob the treasury. What I am, I ingenuously profess to be. The prerogative[10] which I deny to kings I would persist in denying in any legitimate monarchy; for no sovereign could injure me without first condemning himself by a confession of his despotism. If I inveigh against tyrants, what is this to kings? whom I am far from associating with tyrants. As much as an honest man differs from a rogue, so much I contend that a king differs from a tyrant. Whence it is clear that a tyrant is so far from being a king that he is always in direct opposition to a king. And he who peruses the records of history, will find that more kings have been subverted by tyrants than by their subjects. He therefore who would authorize the destruction of tyrants does not authorize the destruction of kings, but of the most inveterate enemies to kings.

But that right which you concede to kings, the right of doing what they please, is not justice, but injustice, ruin, and despair. By that envenomed present you yourselves destroy those whom you extol as if they were above the reach of danger and oppression, and you quite obliterate the difference between a king and a tyrant if you invest both with the same arbitrary power. For, if a king does not exercise that power (and no king will exercise it as long as he is not a tyrant) the power must be ascribed, not to the king, but to the individual. For what can be imagined more absurd than that regal prerogative, which, if any one

---

[8] The *miscreant,* Alexander More, the author of the *Cry* (see the Bibliographical Note above), was, at the date when Milton wrote, Professor of Ecclesiastical History at Amsterdam. His career in Holland had begun through the influence of Salmasius in 1651, after he had resigned the chair of Theology at Geneva in the face of serious charges of heresy and immorality. The facts on record at the time seem to support all of Milton's specific criticisms of his character in *Def 2,* but he was a man of great ability and charm, and in later years was a successful Protestant pastor in Paris. He replied to *Def 2* with *Alexandri Mori Ecclesiastae et Sacrarum Litterarum Professoris Fides Publica contra Calumnias Joannis Miltoni* (The Hague, 1654), but did not reply to Milton's *Def se.*

[9] *Claudius* is Salmasius (Claude de Saumaise). His *Defensio Regia* was anonymous.

[10] In general, Milton is reasoning as he did in attacking King Charles's interpretation of his *prerogative* as arbitrary power in *TKM* (see notes 43 and 68) and again in *Eikon,* Chap. xxvii. The best short study of the development of Milton's ideas about limiting royal power is by Z. S. Fink in *PMLA,* LXVII (1942), 705-36.

uses as often as he wishes to act the king, so often he ceases to be an honest man; and as often as he chooses to be an honest man, so often he must evince that he is not a king? Can any more bitter reproach be cast upon kings? He who maintains this prerogative must himself be a monster of injustice and iniquity, for how can there be a worse person than he who must himself first verify the exaggerated picture of atrocity which he delineates? But if every good man, as an ancient sect of philosophers magnificently taught, is a king,[11] it follows that every bad one is, according to his capacity, a tyrant; nor does the name of tyrant signify anything soaring or illustrious, but the meanest reptile on the earth; for in proportion as he is great, he is contemptible and abject. Others are vicious only for themselves, but tyrants are vicious, not only for themselves, but are even involuntarily obliged to participate in the crimes of their importunate menials and favorites and to entrust certain portions of their despotism to the vilest of their dependents. Tyrants are thus the most abject of slaves, for they are the servants of those who are themselves in servitude. This name therefore may be rightly applied to the most insignificant pugilist of tyranny or even to this brawler, who, why he should so strenuously clamor for the interests of despotism, will sufficiently appear from what has been said already, and what will be said in the sequel; as also why this hireling chooses to conceal his name.

Treading in the steps of Salmasius, he has prostituted his cry for the royal blood, and either blushing for the disgrace of his erudition or the flagitiousness of his life, it is not strange that he should wish to be concealed. Or perhaps he is watching an opportunity, wherever he may scent some richer odors of emolument, to desert the cause of kings and transfer his services to some future republic. This was the manner of Salmasius,[12] who,

captivated by the lure of gain, apostatized, even when sinking in years, from the orthodox to the episcopalians, from the popular party to the royalists. Thou brawler, then, from the stews, who thou art thou in vain endeavorest to conceal; believe me, you will be dragged to light, nor will the helmet of Pluto[13] any longer serve you for a disguise. And you will swear downright as long as you live, either that I am not blind or that I was quick-sighted enough to detect you in the labyrinth of imposture. Attend then while I relate who he is, from whom descended, by what expectations he was led, or by what blandishments soothed to advocate the royal cause.

There is one More, part Frenchman and part Scot,[14] so that one country or one people cannot be quite overwhelmed with the whole infamy of his extraction; an unprincipled miscreant and proved not only by the general testimony of his enemies, but even by that of his dearest friends whom he has alienated by his insincerity, to be a monster of perfidy, falsehood, ingratitude, and malevolence, the perpetual slanderer, not only of men, but of women, whose chastity he is no more accustomed to regard than their reputation. To pass over the more obscure transactions of his youth, he first made his appearance as a teacher of the Greek language at Geneva, where he could not divest himself either of the knave or fool; but where, even while secretly conscious, though perhaps not yet publicly convicted, of so many enormities, he had the audacity to solicit the office of pastor in the church and to profane the character by his crimes. But his debaucheries, his pride, and the general profligacies of his conduct could not long escape the censure of the presbyters. After being condemned for many heresies, which he basely recanted, and to which he still as impiously adhered, he was at last openly found guilty of adultery.

He had conceived a violent passion for the maidservant of his host, and even after

[11] Irene Samuel cites Plato's doctrine of "the crown of happiness" which is bestowed by "the science of good and evil" (*Charmides, 174*) and of the architectonic science of the good as "the kingly art" (*Euthydemus, 291*) in her analysis of the full scope of that doctrine in the *Republic and Laws*. See her *Plato and Milton*, pp. 101–102.

[12] Salmasius' *De episcopis et presbyteriis* (Leyden, 1641), to which Milton refers in *CG* (see n. 99), challenged the claims of bishops to exercise authority over priests.

[13] The wearer of *the helmet of Pluto* walked invisible, as Perseus does with its help (according to Conti VII, xi) in his expedition against the Gorgons.

[14] More's father was an emigrant *Scot* who had spent most of his life as a schoolmaster in Castres in Languedoc, where Alexander was born of a French mother. Details about him are found in Masson's *Life* IV, 459–64.

she was married to another did not cease to solicit the gratification of his love. The neighbors often observed them together in close converse under a shed in the garden. But you will say this might have no reference to any criminal amours; he might have conversed upon horticulture and have read lectures on the art to the untutored and curious girl; he might one while have praised the beauty of the parterres, or regretted the absence of shade; he might have inserted a mulberry in a fig and thence have rapidly raised a progeny of sycamores, a cooling bower; and then might have taught the art of grafting to the fair. All this and more he might, no doubt, have done. But all this would not satisfy the presbyters, who passed sentence on him as an adulterer and judged him unworthy of the ecclesiastical functions. The heads of those and other accusations of the like kind are still preserved in the public library at Geneva.

But even after this had become matter of public notoriety, he was invited, at the instance of Salmasius, to officiate in the French church at Middleburg. This gave great offense to Spanheim, a man of singular erudition and integrity, who was well acquainted with his character at Geneva, though at last, but not without the most violent opposition, he succeeded in obtaining letters testimonial from the Genevese, but these only on the condition that he should leave the place, and couched in expressions rather bordering on censure than on praise. As soon as he arrived in Holland he went to pay his respects to Salmasius; where he immediately cast his libidinous looks on his wife's maid, whose name was Pontia[15] (for the fellow's lust is always inflamed by cooks and waiting-maids); hence he began to pay assiduous court to Salmasius and, as often as he had opportunity, to Pontia. I know not whether Salmasius, taken by the busy attentions and unintermitted adulation of More, or More thinking that it would favor his purpose of meeting Pontia, which first caused their conversation to turn on the answer of Milton to Salmasius. But, however this might be, More undertook to defend Salmasius, and Salmasius promises to obtain for More the divinity chair in that city. Besides this More promises himself other sweets in his clandestine amour with Pontia, for under pretext of consulting Salmasius in the prosecution of this work, he had free admission to the house at all hours of the night or day. And, as formerly Pyramus was changed into a mulberry tree, so More[16] seems suddenly transformed into Pyramus. But in proportion as he was more criminal, so was more fortunate than that youth. He had no occasion to seek for a chink in the wall; he had every facility of carrying on his intrigue with his Thisbe under the same roof. He promises her marriage, and under the lure of this promise violates her chastity. O shame: a minister of the gospel abuses the confidence of friendship to commit this atrocious crime! From this amour no common prodigy accrued, for both man and woman suffered the pains of parturition: Pontia conceived a Morill, which long afforded employment to the natural disquisitions of Salmasius; More, the barren and windy egg, from which issued that flatulent cry of the royal blood.

. . . . . .

Let us now come to the charges which were brought against myself. Is there anything reprehensible in my manners or my conduct? Surely nothing. What no one not totally divested of all generous sensibility would have done, he reproaches me with want of beauty and loss of sight.

"A monster huge and hideous, void of sight."

the trial.

---

15 The name (which Masson gives as Bontia, and which appears inconsistently as either Pontia or Portia in Fellowes' translation of *Def* 2) seems to have been used in Salmasius' family circle. Thanks to the research of Charles Cabanis of the Bibliothèque Wallone in Leyden and of Professor K. Svendsen, it is now possible to identify the girl as Elisabeth Guerret (or Gerret), whose name appears in Article 26 of the "Actes des Synodes Wallones" under the date September 3–6, 1653. The Synod of Utrecht, acting in a suit brought against her by More to clear his name of the charge to which Milton refers, settled the case by declaring that the evidence was not enough to debar the Leyden church from admitting More to its pulpit. The record does not show that Friedrich Spanheim, professor of theology at Leyden, had any part in the trial.

16 Milton puns on the name *Morus*, which in Latin means a mulberry tree. The pun is resumed in the diminutive of *morus* in the Latin text, *morillus*), which is translated as "a morill" a few lines below. In Ovid's story of Pyramus and Thisbe (*Met.* IV, 158–66) the lovers' blood turns the fruit of the *mulberry tree* under which they died to its own red color forever.

I certainly never supposed that I should have been obliged to enter into a competition for beauty with the Cyclops.[17] But he immediately corrects himself and says, "though not indeed huge, for there cannot be a more spare, shrivelled, and bloodless form." It is of no moment to say anything of personal appearance, yet lest (as the Spanish vulgar, implicitly confiding in the relations of their priests, believe of heretics) anyone, from the representations of my enemies, should be led to imagine that I have either the head of a dog or the horn of a rhinoceros, I will say something on the subject that I may have an opportunity of paying my grateful acknowledgments to the Deity and of refuting the most shameless lies. I do not believe that I was ever once noted for deformity by anyone who ever saw me, but the praise of beauty I am not anxious to obtain. My stature certainly is not tall, but it rather approaches the middle than the diminutive. Yet what if it were diminutive when so many men, illustrious both in peace and war, have been the same? And how can that be called diminutive which is great enough for every virtuous achievement? Nor, though very thin, was I ever deficient in courage or in strength; and I was wont constantly to exercise myself in the use of the broadsword as long as it comported with my habit and my years. Armed with this weapon, as I usually was, I should have thought myself quite a match for anyone though much stronger than myself, and I felt perfectly secure against the assult of any open enemy. At this moment I have the same courage, the same strength, though not the same eyes; yet so little do they betray any external appearance of injury that they are as unclouded and bright as the eyes of those who most distinctly see. In this instance alone I am a dissembler against my will. My face, which is said to indicate a total privation of blood, is of a complexion entirely opposite to the pale and the cadaverous; so that, though I am more than forty years old, there is scarcely anyone to whom I do not appear ten years younger than I am; and the smoothness of my skin is not in the least affected by the wrinkles of age. If there be one particle of falsehood in this relation, I should deservedly incur the ridicule of many thousands of my countrymen and even many foreigners to whom I am personally known. But if he, in a matter so foreign to his purpose, shall be found to have asserted so many shameless and gratuitous falsehoods, you may the more readily estimate the quantity of his veracity on other topics. Thus much necessity compelled me to assert concerning my personal appearance.

Respecting yours, though I have been informed that it is most insignificant and contemptible, a perfect mirror of the worthlessness of your character and the malevolence of your heart, I say nothing, and no one will be anxious that anything should be said. I wish that I could with equal facility refute what this barbarous opponent has said of my blindness; but I cannot do it; and I must submit to the affliction. It is not so wretched to be blind as it is not to be capable of enduring blindness. But why should I not endure a misfortune, which it behooves everyone to be prepared to endure if it should happen; which may, in the common course of things, happen to any man; and which has been known to happen to the most distinguished and virtuous persons in history. Shall I mention those wise and ancient bards whose misfortunes the gods are said to have compensated by superior endowments, and whom men so much revered that they chose rather to impute their want of sight to the injustice of heaven than to their own want of innocence or virtue? What is reported of the augur Tiresias[18] is well known. Of Phineus, Apollonius[19] sang thus in his *Argonauts:*

---

[17] In *Def se* (C.E. IX, 123) Milton recalls that More had reproached him with being blind like the Cyclops, the hideous giant with a single eye in his forehead, which Ulysses gouged out in Homer's story (*Od.* IX, 375–98).

[18] Cf. the similar references to *Tiresias* in *PL* III, 36, and *Idea*, 25–26. The quotation from the *Argonautica* here is followed by Apollonius' account of the blindness of Phineus as a vengeance of Zeus, who resented the prophet's unerring command of the gift of prophecy.

[19] Apollonius began and ended his career as a member of the staff of poets attached to the library in Alexandria in the middle of the third century B.C. (cf. *Educ*, n. 82), but spent the better part of his productive years at the school of Rhodes. His "Homeric" epic, the *Argonautica*, tells the story of the expedition of the Argonauts to Colchis

To men he dar'd the will divine disclose,
Nor fear'd what Jove might in his wrath impose.
The gods assigned him age, without decay,
But snatched the blessing of his sight away.

But God himself is truth; in propagating which, as men display a greater integrity and zeal, they approach nearer to the similitude of God, and possess a greater portion of his love. We cannot suppose the deity envious of truth, or unwilling that it should be freely communicated to mankind. The loss of sight, therefore, which this inspired sage, who was so eager in promoting knowledge among men, sustained, cannot be considered as a judicial punishment. Or shall I mention those worthies who were as distinguished for wisdom in the cabinet, as for valor in the field? And first, Timoleon[20] of Corinth, who delivered his city and all Sicily from the yoke of slavery; than whom there never lived in any age, a more virtuous man, or a more incorrupt statesman: Next Appius Claudius,[21] whose discreet counsels in the senate though they could not restore sight to his own eyes, saved Italy from the formidable inroads of Pyrrhus:[22] then Cæcilius Metellus[23] the high-priest, who lost his sight while he saved, not only the city, but the palladium, the protection of the city, and the most sacred relics from the destruction of the flames. On other occasions Providence has indeed given conspicuous proofs of its regard for such singular exertions of patriotism and virtue; what, therefore, happened to so great and so good a man, I can hardly place in the catalogue of misfortunes. Why should I mention others of later times, as Dandolo[24] of Venice, the incomparable

Doge; or Boemar Zisca,[25] the bravest of generals, and the champion of the cross; or Jerome Zanchius,[26] and some other theologians of the highest reputation? For it is evident that the patriarch Isaac,[27] than whom no man ever enjoyed more of the divine regard, lived blind for many years; and perhaps also his son Jacob,[28] who was equally an object of the divine benevolence. And in short, did not our Savior[29] himself clearly declare that that poor man whom he restored to sight had not been born blind either on account of his own sins or those of his progenitors?

And with respect to myself, though I have accurately examined my conduct, and scrutinized my soul, I call thee, O God, the searcher of hearts, to witness, that I am not conscious either in the more early or in the later periods of my life, of having committed any enormity which might deservedly have marked me out as a fit object for such a calamitous visitation. But since my enemies boast that this affliction is only a retribution for the transgressions of my pen, I again invoke the Almighty to witness, that I never, at any time, wrote anything which I did not think agreeable to

to secure the golden fleece, and its central episode is the love story of Jason and Medea. The lines quoted are from Book II, 181-4. Cf. *PL* III, 36.

[20] Most of Milton's readers were familiar with the account of the blindness of *Timoleon* in Plutarch's *Life* (Chap. xxxvii) where he is described as losing his sight in old age, though he had indulged in no vice which might cause such an affliction. The citizens of Corinth vied for the opportunity of seeing him and honoring him in his affliction.

[21] Again Plutarch—this time in the *Life of Pyrrhus*, Chap. xviii—is the source.

[22] Cf. *Areop*, n. 240.

[23] *Lucius Cæcilius Metellus* was consul in 251 B.C. and a general in the first Punic War. The *palladium* which he is supposed to have saved, was the same that Æneas preserved from the flames that destroyed Troy.

[24] *Enrico Dandolo* (1120–1205) is said to have

been disfigured and partially blinded by a wound suffered in youth in Constantinople. Elected Doge of Venice at seventy-three, he led an army which conquered Dalmatia and sacked Constantinople, carrying back the famous bronze horses of St. Mark.

[25] *John Zisca* (1376?–1424) lost an eye in the civil wars of Wenceslaus IV, king of Bohemia. In 1421 at the siege of the castle of Ralii, he lost the second eye, but afterward twice severely defeated Sigismund, king of the Germans, and took an active part in the civil wars centering around Prague in 1422–1423. His interest in John Huss perhaps attracted Milton's attention.

[26] *Jerome Zanchius* (1516–1590) was born in Brescia and entered a German monastery at sixteen. Going to Italy for study, he was converted there by reading Bullinger and Calvin, and in 1551 went to Strassbourg to hold the first of the university chairs which he successively occupied in various German cities for the rest of his life. In *CD* Milton quotes from several of his theological works.

[27] When *Isaac* was old "his eyes were dim" (Gen. xxvii, 1).

[28] Perhaps Milton had the scene of *Jacob's* death in mind. He is told of the coming of his son Joseph as if he could not recognize him for himself (Gen. lxviii, 2).

[29] When Jesus saw a blind man, "his disciples asked him, saying, Master, who did sin, this man, or his parents, that he was born blind?

"Jesus answered, Neither hath this man sinned, nor his parents" (John ix, 2–3).

truth, to justice, and to piety. This was my persuasion then, and I feel the same persuasion now. Nor was I ever prompted to such exertions by the influence of ambition, by the lust of lucre or of praise; it was only by the conviction of duty and the feeling of patriotism, a disinterested passion for the extension of civil and religious liberty. Thus, therefore, when I was publicly solicited to write a reply to the *Defense* of the royal cause,[30] when I had to contend with the pressure of sickness, and with the apprehension of soon losing the sight of my remaining eye, and when my medical attendants clearly announced that, if I did engage in the work, it would be irreparably lost, their premonitions caused no hesitation and inspired no dismay. I would not have listened to the voice even of Esculapius[31] himself from the shrine of Epidaurus, in preference to the suggestions of the heavenly monitor within my breast; my resolution was unshaken, though the alternative was either the loss of my sight or the desertion of my duty: and I called to mind those two destinies, which the oracle of Delphi announced to the son of Thetis:—

Two fates may lead me to the realms of night;
If staying here, around Troy's wall I fight,
To my dear home no more must I return;
But lasting glory will adorn my urn.
But, if I withdraw from the martial strife,
Short is my fame, but long will be my life.

ll. IX, 410–16.

I considered that many had purchased a less good by a greater evil, the meed of glory by the loss of life; but that I might procure great good by little suffering; that though I am blind, I might still discharge the most honorable duties, the performance of which, as it is something more durable than glory, ought to be an object of superior admiration and esteem; I resolved, therefore, to make the short interval of sight which was left me to enjoy as beneficial as possible to the public interest. Thus it is clear by what motives I was

governed in the measures which I took, and the losses which I sustained. Let then the calumniators of the divine goodness cease to revile, or to make me the object of their superstitious imaginations. Let them consider that my situation, such as it is, is neither an object of my shame or my regret, that my resolutions are too firm to be shaken, that I am not depressed by any sense of the divine displeasure; that, on the other hand, in the most momentous periods, I have had full experience of the divine favor and protection; and that, in the solace and the strength which have been infused into me from above, I have been enabled to do the will of God; that I may oftener think on what he has bestowed than on what he has withheld; that, in short, I am unwilling to exchange my consciousness of rectitude with that of any other person; and that I feel the recollection a treasured store of tranquillity and delight. But, if the choice were necessary, I would, sir, prefer my blindness to yours; yours is a cloud spread over the mind, which darkens both the light of reason and of conscience; mine keeps from my view only the colored surfaces of things, while it leaves me at liberty to contemplate the beauty and stability of virtue and of truth. How many things are there besides which I would not willingly see; how many which I must see against my will; and how few which I feel any anxiety to see! There is, as the apostle has remarked,[32] a way to strength through weakness. Let me then be the most feeble creature alive, as long as that feebleness serves to invigorate the energies of my rational and immortal spirit; as long as in that obscurity, in which I am enveloped, the light of the divine presence more clearly shines; then, in proportion as I am weak, I shall be invincibly strong, and in proportion as I am blind, I shall more clearly see. O! that I may thus be perfected by feebleness, and irradiated by obscurity! And, indeed, in my blindness, I enjoy in no inconsiderable degree the favor of the Deity, who regards me with more tenderness and compassion in proportion as I am able to behold nothing but himself. Alas! for him who insults me; who maligns me merits public execration!

---

[30] Salmasius' *Defensio Regia pro Carolo Primo* appeared in the early autumn of 1649. In spite of the warnings of physicians about the danger of approaching blindness, Milton had his *Defensio* ready to go through the press in March, 1651.

[31] The shrine of *Æsculapius*, the god of medicine and healing, was traditionally in *Epidaurus* in the Peloponnesus.

[32] "Out of weakness we were made strong" (Heb. xi, 34).

For the divine law not only shields me from injury,[32] but almost renders me too sacred to attack; not indeed so much from the privation of my sight, as from the overshadowing of those heavenly wings which seem to have occasioned this obscurity; and which, when occasioned, he is wont to illuminate with an interior light, more precious and more pure.

To this I ascribe the more tender assiduities of my friends, their soothing attentions, their kind visits, their reverential observances; among whom there are some with whom I may interchange the Pyladean and Thesean dialogue of inseparable friends:—

Orestes. Proceed, and be the rudder of my feet.
Pylades. Dear to me is the care I take.

And in another place:—

Lend your hand to your devoted friend,
Throw your arm round my neck, and I will
    conduct you on the way.[34]

This extraordinary kindness which I experience, cannot be any fortuitous combination; and friends such as mine do not suppose that all the virtues of a man are contained in his eyes. Nor do the persons of principal distinction in the commonwealth suffer me to be bereaved of comfort, when they see me bereaved of sight, amid the exertions which I made, the zeal which I showed, and the dangers which I run for the liberty which I love. But, soberly reflecting on the casualties of human life, they show me favor and indulgence, as to a soldier who has served his time, and kindly concede to me an exemption from care and toil. They do not strip me of the badges of honor which I have once worn; they do not deprive me of the places of public trust to which I have been appointed; they do not abridge my salary or emoluments; which, though I may not do so much to deserve as I did formerly, they are too considerate and too kind to take away; and, in short, they honor me as much as the Athenians did those whom they determined to support at the public ex-

pense in the Prytaneum.[35] Thus, while both God and man unite in solacing me under the weight of my affliction, let no one lament my loss of sight in so honorable a cause. And let me not indulge in unavailing grief, or want the courage either to despise the revilers of my blindness, or the forbearance easily to pardon the offense.

* * * * *

You[36] say, that "the fellow having been expelled from the university of Cambridge, on account of his atrocities, had fled his country in disgrace and travelled into Italy." Hence we may discern what little reliance can be placed on the veracity of those from whom you derived your information; for all who know me, know, that in this place both you and they have uttered the most abominable falsehoods; as I shall soon make more fully appear. But, when I was expelled from Cambridge, why should I rather travel into Italy than into France or Holland? where you, though a minister of the Gospel, and yet so vile a miscreant, not only enjoy impunity, but, to the great scandal of the church, pollute the pulpit and the altar by your presence. But why, sir, into Italy? Was it that, like another Saturn,[37] I might find a hiding-place in Latium? No, it was because I well knew, and have since experienced, that Italy, instead of being, as you suppose, the general receptacle of vice, was the seat of civilization and the hospitable domicile of every species of erudition. "When he returned, he wrote his book on divorce." I wrote nothing more than what Bucer[38] on the

---

[33] "Cursed be he that maketh the blind to wander out of the way" (Deut. xxvii, 18).
[34] Euripides' *Orestes* was mainly responsible for the tradition in the Renaissance as well as in the ancient world that Pylades and Orestes were ideally typical friends. The first of the two passages quoted is from the *Orestes*, 796; the second is from *Hercules Mad*, 1398–1402.

[35] *The Prytaneum* was a dining hall maintained at public expense in Athens, where, as Milton says, distinguished citizens were entertained. When Socrates was asked at his trial what penalty he thought appropriate for himself, he answered, entertainment for life in the Prytaneum.
[36] *You* is Alexander More, whom Milton constantly treats as fully responsible for the *Cry*. Cf. the Bibliographical Note.
[37] The legend, to which Virgil refers in *Aeneid* VIII, 319–23, has it that after being driven from Olympus by Jove, *Saturn* took refuge among the uncivilized mountain tribes of *Latium* in central Italy, and brought peace and the blessing of laws among them.
[38] Milton's second divorce tract was a translation of a substantial part of the revolutionary theological work *On the Kingdom of Christ*, which had been written in the reign of Edward VI by the German theologian, *Martin Bucer*, at the young king's request.

Kingdom of Christ, Fagius[39] on Deuteronomy, and Erasmus on the First Epistle to the Corinthians,[40] which was more particularly designed for the instruction of the English, had written before me, for the most useful purposes and with the most disinterested views. Why what was not reprehensible in them should constitute a charge of criminality against me, I cannot understand; though I regret that I published this work in English; for then it would not have been exposed to the view of those common readers, who are wont to be as ignorant of their own blessings as they are insensible to other's sufferings.

.   .   .   .   .   .

I will now mention who and whence I am. I was born at London, of an honest family; my father was distinguished by the undeviating integrity of his life; my mother, by the esteem in which she was held, and the alms which she bestowed. My father destined me from a child to the pursuits of literature; and my appetite for knowledge was so voracious that, from twelve years of age, I hardly ever left my studies, or went to bed before midnight. This primarily led to my loss of sight. My eyes were naturally weak, and I was subject to frequent headaches; which, however, could not chill the ardor of my curiosity, or retard the progress of my improvement. My father had me daily instructed in the grammar-school, and by other masters at home. He then, after I had acquired a proficiency in various languages, and had made a considerable progress in philosophy, sent me to the University of Cambridge. Here I passed seven years in the usual course of instruction and study, with the approbation of the good and without any stain upon my character, till I took the degree of Master of Arts. After this I did not, as this miscreant feigns, run away into Italy, but of my own accord retired to my father's house, whither I was accompanied by the regrets of most of the fellows of the college, who showed me no common marks of friendship and esteem. On my father's estate, where

he had determined to pass the remainder of his days, I enjoyed an interval of uninterrupted leisure, which I entirely devoted to the perusal of the Greek and Latin classics; though I occasionally visited the metropolis, either for the sake of purchasing books, or of learning something new in mathematics or in music, in which I, at that time, found a source of pleasure and amusement. In this manner I spent five years till my mother's death.

I then became anxious to visit foreign parts, and particularly Italy. My father gave me his permission, and I left home with one servant. On my departure, the celebrated Henry Wotton,[41] who had long been king James's ambassador at Venice, gave me a signal proof of his regard in an elegant letter which he wrote, breathing not only the warmest friendship, but containing some maxims of conduct which I found very useful in my travels. The noble Thomas Scudamore,[42] king Charles's ambassador, to whom I carried letters of recommendation, received me most courteously at Paris. His lordship gave me a card of introduction to the learned Hugo Grotius,[43] at that time ambassador from the queen of Sweden[44] to the French court; whose acquaintance I anxiously desired, and to whose house I was accompanied by some of his lordship's friends. A few days after, when I set out for Italy, he gave me letters to the English merchants on my route, that they might show me any civilities in their power. Taking ship at Nice, I arrived at Genoa, and afterwards visited Leghorn, Pisa, and Florence. In the latter city, which I have always more particularly esteemed for the elegance of its dialect, its genius, and its

---

[39] Cf. *DDD*, n. 48.

[40] Erasmus' commentary on the seventh chapter of I Cor. used St. Paul's famous discussion of marriage as the basis of a plea for relaxation of the prohibition of divorce for incompatibility by the Canon Law.

[41] *Sir Henry Wotton* (1568–1639) was three times ambassador to Venice. When Milton went to Italy, he was Master of Eton College. His letter of commendation of *Comus* indicates the cordiality of their relation.

[42] John (according to the *D.N.B.* not Thomas) *Scudamour,* Viscount Sligo (1601–1671), was a devoted Royalist and friend of the high church prelates. He had been ambassador since 1634, and was intimate with Grotius.

[43] In Edward Phillips' *Life of Milton* (p. 1028 below) *Grotius* is said to have taken this visit kindly and to have treated him with respect. Milton may have been indebted to his *Adamus Exul* to some extent in *PL*, and he quoted him repeatedly in *DDD*, particularly in the Preface, as an authority on Roman Law.

[44] Cf. *Christina of Sweden* in n. 6 above.

taste, I stopped about two months; when I contracted an intimacy with many persons of rank and learning, and was a constant attendant at their literary parties; a practice which prevails there, and tends so much to the diffusion of knowledge and the preservation of friendship. No time will ever abolish the agreeable recollections which I cherish of Jacob Gaddi,[45] Carolo Dati,[46] Frescobaldo,[47] Coltellino,[48] Bonmatthei,[49] Clementillo,[50] Francini,[51] and many others. From Florence I went to Siena, thence to Rome, where, after I had spent about two months in viewing the antiquities of that renowned city, where I experienced the most friendly attentions from Lucas Holstein,[52] and other learned and ingenious

men, I continued my route to Naples. There I was introduced by a certain recluse, with whom I had travelled from Rome, to John Baptista Manso,[53] marquis of Villa, a nobleman of distinguished rank and authority, to whom Torquato Tasso,[54] the illustrious poet, inscribed his book on friendship. During my stay, he gave me singular proofs of his regard: he himself conducted me round the city, and to the palace of the viceroy; and more than once paid me a visit at my lodgings. On my departure he gravely apologized for not having shown me more civility, which he said he had been restrained from doing, because I had spoken with so little reserve on matters of religion.

When I was preparing to pass over into Sicily and Greece, the melancholy intelligence which I received of the civil commotions in England made me alter my purpose; for I thought it base to be travelling for amusement abroad, while my fellow-citizens were fighting for liberty at home. While I was on my way back to Rome, some merchants informed me that the English Jesuits had formed a plot against me if I returned to Rome, because I had spoken too freely on religion; for it was a rule which I laid down to myself in those places, never to be the first to begin any conversation on religion; but if any questions were put to me concerning my faith, to declare it without any reserve or fear. I, nevertheless, returned to Rome. I took no steps to conceal either my person or my character; and for about the space of two months I again openly defended, as I had done before, the reformed religion in the very metropolis of popery.

By the favor of God, I got safe back to Florence, where I was received with as much affection as if I had returned to my native country. There I stopped as many months as I had done before, except that

[45] *Jacob Gaddi* was the founder of "the whole Gaddian Academy" in Florence, to several of whose members Milton sent greetings in a letter addressed to Carolo Dati in April, 1647. (See C.E. XII, 45-53.)

[46] *Dati's* regard for Milton is proved by letter 34 (in *Miscellaneous Correspondence*, C.E. XII, 312-15), thanking him for two "erudite poems," and reporting Dati's recent appointment to a chair in the Florentine Academy. A more formal letter from Dati to Milton was published at the front of the 1645 volume of his poems. In *Damon*, 136-7, Dati is mentioned as a well-known poet.

[47] In *Familiar Letters*, 10 (C.E. XII, 53) Milton sends greetings to Frescobaldi, and in *Miscellaneous Correspondence* (C.E. XII, 315) Frescobaldi sends his greetings to Milton.

[48] In *Familiar Letters*, 10 (C.E. XII, 53) Milton sends greetings to Coltellino, and in *Miscellaneous Correspondence* 35 (C.E. XII, 315) Coltellino sends his cordial greetings to Milton.

[49] Milton's eighth *Familiar Letter* is to *Benedetto Bonmatthei*, thanking him for a "compilation of new institutes of (his) native tongue" and suggesting that in a proposed enlargement of the work there should be an appendix on pronunciation devised particularly for the benefit of foreigners, and a second appendix listing the Italian writers "illustrious in tragedy," "happy in comedy," and "noble in history."

[50] In *Familiar Letters*, 10 (C.E. XII, 53) Milton sends greetings to Clementillo.

[51] Besides being mentioned in *Damon*, 136, *Antonio Francini* receives greetings from Milton in the tenth *Familiar Letter* (C.E. XII, 53) and sends them in a letter which is reproduced in C.E. XII, 315. His ode to Milton was published in the 1645 volume of Milton's poems.

[52] *Lucas Holstein* (1596-1661), German geographer and theologian, had had a distinguished career as a papal ambassador, becoming librarian of the Vatican Library in 1627. On March 30, 1639 (C.E. XII, 38-45), Milton wrote from Florence to thank him for showing him some Manuscripts in the Vatican and for introducing him to Cardinal Barberini. The holograph of this letter has been discovered by J. M. Bottkol in the *Fondo*

Barberini in the Vatican and is described in *PMLA*, LXVIII (1953), 617-27.

[53] *Giovanni Battista Manso*, Marquis of Villa (1560-1640), founded the Oziosi and left his fortune to found the Collegio dei Nobili. The best memorial to his life of service to literary men is Torquato Tasso's *Dialogue of Friendship*, which was written for his benefit. In *Damon*, 181, there is a reference to a gift probably of books, which Manso had given to Milton during his Neapolitan visit. *Mansus* is Milton's verse letter of thanks for Manso's hospitality in Naples.

[54] Cf. *CG*, n. 167.

I made an excursion for a few days to Lucca; and, crossing the Apennines, passed through Bologna and Ferrara to Venice. After I had spent a month in surveying the curiosities of this city, and had put on board a ship the books which I had collected in Italy, I proceeded through Verona and Milan, and along the Leman lake to Geneva. The mention of this city brings to my recollection the slandering More, and makes me again call the Deity to witness, that in all those places in which vice meets with so little discouragement, and is practised with so little shame, I never once deviated from the paths of integrity and virtue, and perpetually reflected that, though my conduct might escape the notice of men, it could not elude the inspection of God. At Geneva I held daily conferences with John Deodati,[55] the learned professor of Theology.

Then pursuing my former route through France, I returned to my native country, after an absence of one year and about three months; at the time when Charles, having broken the peace, was renewing what is called the episcopal war with the Scots, in which the royalists being routed in the first encounter, and the English being universally and justly disaffected, the necessity of his affairs at last obliged him to convene a parliament. As soon as I was able, I hired a spacious house in the city for myself and my books; where I again with rapture renewed my literary pursuits, and where I calmly awaited the issue of the contest, which I trusted to the wise conduct of Providence and to the courage of the people. The vigor of the parliament had begun to humble the pride of the bishops.

As long as the liberty of speech was no longer subject to control, all mouths began to be opened against the bishops; some complained of the vices of the individuals, others of those of the order. They said that it was unjust that they alone should differ from the model of other reformed churches; that the government of the church should be according to the pattern of other churches, and particularly the word of God.

This awakened all my attention and my zeal. I saw that a way was opening for the establishment of real liberty; that the foundation was laying for the deliverance of man from the yoke of slavery and superstition; that the principles of religion, which were the first objects of our care, would exert a salutary influence on the manners and constitution of the republic; and as I had from my youth studied the distinctions between religious and civil rights, I perceived that if I ever wished to be of use, I ought at least not to be wanting to my country, to the church, and to so many of my fellow-Christians, in a crisis of so much danger.

I therefore determined to relinquish the other pursuits in which I was engaged, and to transfer the whole force of my talents and my industry to this one important object. I accordingly wrote two books to a friend concerning the Reformation of the Church of England. Afterwards, when two bishops[56] of superior distinction vindicated their privileges against some principal ministers, I thought that on those topics, to the consideration of which I was led solely by my love of truth and my reverence for Christianity, I should not probably write worse than those who were contending only for their own emoluments and usurpations. I therefore answered the one in two books, of which the first is inscribed, Concerning Prelatical Episcopacy, and the other, Concerning the Mode of Ecclesiastical Government; and I replied to the other in some Animadversions, and soon after in an Apology. On this occasion it was supposed that I brought a timely succor to the ministers, who were hardly a match for the eloquence of their opponents; and from that time I was actively employed in refuting any answers that appeared.

When the bishops could no longer resist the multitude of their assailants, I had leisure to turn my thoughts to other subjects, to the promotion of real and substantial liberty, which is rather to be sought from within than from without, and whose existence depends not so much on the terror of the sword as on sobriety of conduct and integrity of life. When, therefore, I perceived that there were three species of lib-

---

[55] John Diodati (1576–1649), the uncle of Charles Diodati, to whom Elegies I and VI were addressed, and in whose memory Damon's Epitaph was written, was a distinguished theologian all his active life in Geneva. He is best known for his translation of the Bible into Italian, published in 1607. (See Masson's Life I, 99–100.)

[56] For the bishops, Hall and Ussher, and for the Smectymnuan "principal ministers," see the Bibliographical Note to Apology.

erty which are essential to the happiness of social life—religious, domestic, and civil; and as I had already written concerning the first, and the magistrates were strenuously active in obtaining the third, I determined to turn my attention to the second, or the domestic species. As this seemed to involve three material questions, the conditions of the conjugal tie, the education of the children, and the free publication of the thoughts, I made them objects of distinct consideration. I explained my sentiments, not only concerning the solemnization of the marriage, but the dissolution, if circumstances rendered it necessary; and I drew my arguments from the divine law, which Christ did not abolish, or publish another more grievous than that of Moses. I stated my own opinions, and those of others, concerning the exclusive exception of fornication, which our illustrious Selden has since, in his *Hebrew Wife*,[57] more copiously discussed; for he in vain makes a vaunt of liberty in the senate or in the forum, who languishes under the vilest servitude, to an inferior at home. On this subject, therefore, I published some books which were more particularly necessary at that time when man and wife were often the most inveterate foes, when the man often stayed to take care of his children at home, while the mother of the family was seen in the camp of the enemy, threatening death and destruction to her husband. I then discussed the principles of education in a summary manner, but sufficiently copious for those who attend seriously to the subject; than which nothing can be more necessary to principle the minds of men in virtue, the only genuine source of political and individual liberty, the only true safeguard of states, the bulwark of their prosperity and renown. Lastly, I wrote my *Areopagitica*, in order to deliver the press from the restraints with which it was encumbered; that the power of determining what was true and what was false, what ought to be published and what to be suppressed, might no longer be entrusted to a few illiterate and illiberal individuals, who refused their sanction to any work which contained views or

sentiments at all above the level of vulgar superstition.

On the last species of civil liberty I said nothing, because I saw that sufficient attention was paid to it by the magistrates; nor did I write anything on the prerogative of the crown, till the king, voted an enemy by the parliament and vanquished in the field, was summoned before the tribunal which condemned him to lose his head. But when, at length, some Presbyterian ministers, who had formerly been the most bitter enemies to Charles, became jealous of the growth of the independents and of their ascendancy in the parliament, most tumultuously clamored against the sentence, and did all in their power to prevent the execution,[58] though they were not angry so much on account of the act itself, as because it was not the act of their party; and when they dared to affirm that the doctrine of the protestants, and of all the reformed churches, was abhorrent to such an atrocious proceeding against kings, I thought that it became me to oppose such a glaring falsehood; and accordingly, without any immediate or personal application to Charles, I showed, in an abstract consideration of the question, what might lawfully be done against tyrants; and in support of what I advanced, produced the opinions of the most celebrated divines; while I vehemently inveighed against the egregious ignorance or effrontery of men who professed better things, and from whom better things might have been expected. That book did not make its appearance till after the death of Charles, and was written rather to reconcile the minds of the people to the event, than to discuss the legitimacy of that particular sentence which concerned the magistrates, and which was already executed.

Such were the fruits of my private studies, which I gratuitously presented to the church and to the state; and for which I was recompensed by nothing but impunity; though the actions themselves procured me peace of conscience, and the approbation of the good; while I exercised that freedom of discussion which I loved. Others, without labor or desert, got possession of honors and emoluments; but no one ever knew me either soliciting anything myself or through the medium of my friends, ever beheld me

[57] For the relation of Selden's *Uxor Hebraica* (which was not published until three years later than *DDD*) see Eivion Owen, "Milton and Selden on Divorce," in *SP*, XLIII (1946), 233–57.

[58] Cf. *TKM*, n. 26.

in a supplicating posture at the doors of the senate or the levees of the great. I usually kept myself secluded at home, where my own property, part of which had been withheld during the civil commotions, and part of which had been absorbed in the oppressive contributions which I had to sustain, afforded me a scanty subsistence. When I was released from these engagements, and thought that I was about to enjoy an interval of uninterrupted ease, I turned my thoughts to a continued history of my country from the earliest times to the present period. I had already finished four books, when, after the subversion of the monarchy and the establishment of a republic, I was surprised by an invitation from the council of state, who desired my services in the office for foreign affairs. A book appeared soon after, which was ascribed to the king, and contained the most invidious charges against the parliament. I was ordered to answer it; and opposed the Iconoclast to his Icon. I did not insult over fallen majesty, as is pretended; I only preferred queen Truth to king Charles. The charge of insult, which I saw that the malevolent would urge, I was at some pains to remove in the beginning of the work: and as often as possible in other places. Salmasius then[59] appeared, to whom they were not, as More says, long in looking about for an opponent, but immediately appointed me, who happened at the time to be present in the council. I have thus, sir, given some account of myself, in order to stop your mouth and to remove any prejudices which your falsehoods and misrepresentations might cause even good men to entertain against me.

. . . . . .

Oliver Cromwell was sprung from a line of illustrious ancestors who were distinguished for the civil functions which they sustained under the monarchy and still more for the part which they took in restoring and establishing true religion in this country. In the vigor and maturity of his life, which he passed in retirement, he was conspicuous for nothing more than for the strictness of his religious habits and the innocence of his life, and he had tacitly cherished in his breast that flame of piety which

was afterwards to stand him in so much stead on the greatest occasions and in the most critical exigencies. In the last Parliament which was called by the king he was elected to represent his native town,[60] when he soon became distinguished by the justness of his opinions and the vigor and decision of his councils.

When the sword was drawn, he offered his services and was appointed to a troop of horse, whose numbers were soon increased by the pious and the good, who flocked from all quarters to his standard; and in a short time he almost surpassed the greatest generals in the magnitude and the rapidity of his achievements. Nor is this surprising, for he was a soldier disciplined to perfection in the knowledge of himself. He had either extinguished, or by habit had learned to subdue, the whole host of vain hopes, fears, and passions which infest the soul. He first acquired the government of himself and over himself acquired the most signal victories, so that on the first day he took the field against the external enemy he was a veteran in arms, consummately practised in the toils and exigencies of war.

It is not possible for me in the narrow limits in which I circumscribe myself on this occasion to enumerate the many towns which he has taken, the many battles which he has won. The whole surface of the British empire has been the scene of his exploits and the theater of his triumphs, which alone would furnish ample materials for a history and want a copiousness of narration not inferior to the magnitude and diversity of the transactions. This alone seems to be a sufficient proof of his extraordinary and almost supernatural virtue, that by the vigor of his genius, or the excellence of his discipline, adapted not more to the necessities of war than to the precepts of Christianity, the good and the brave were from all quarters attracted to his camp, not only as to the best school of military talents, but of piety and virtue; and that during the whole war and the occasional intervals of peace, amid so many vicissitudes of faction and of events, he retained and still retains the obedience of his troops, not by largesses

---

[59] *then*—in Nov., 1649, when Salmasius published his *Defensio Regia.* See n. 6 above.

[60] Cromwell was born in Huntingdon, which he represented in Parliament in 1628; in the Short and Long Parliaments he sat for Cambridge.

or indulgence, but by his sole authority and the regularity of his pay. In this instance his fame may rival that of Cyrus,[61] of Epaminondas,[62] or any of the great generals of antiquity. Hence he collected an army as numerous and as well equipped as anyone ever did in so short a time; which was uniformly obedient to his orders and dear to the affections of the citizens; which was formidable to the enemy in the field, but never cruel to those who laid down their arms; which committed no lawless ravages on the persons or the property of the inhabitants, who, when they compared their conduct with the turbulence, the intemperance, the impiety, and the debauchery of the royalists, were wont to salute them as friends and to consider them as guests. They were a stay to the good, a terror to the evil, and the warmest advocates for every exertion of piety and virtue.

Nor would it be right to pass over the name of Fairfax,[63] who united the utmost fortitude with the utmost courage; and the spotless innocence of whose life seemed to point him out as the peculiar favorite of Heaven. Justly, indeed, may you be excited to receive this wreath of praise, though you have retired as much as possible from the world and seek those shades of privacy which were the delight of Scipio.[64] Nor was it only the enemy whom you subdued,

but you have triumphed over that flame of ambition and that lust of glory which are wont to make the best and the greatest of men their slaves. The purity of your virtues and the splendor of your actions consecrate those sweets of ease which you enjoy, and which constitute the wished-for haven of the toils of man. Such was the ease which, when the heroes of antiquity possessed it after a life of exertion and glory not greater than yours, the poets, in despair of finding ideas or expressions better suited to the subject, feigned that they were received into heaven and invited to recline at the tables of the gods. But whether it were your health, which I principally believe, or any other motive which caused you to retire, of this I am convinced, that nothing could have induced you to relinquish the service of your country if you had not known that in your successor liberty would meet with a protector and England with a stay to its safety and a pillar to its glory. For while you, O Cromwell, are left among us, he hardly shows a proper confidence in the Supreme, who distrusts the security of England, when he sees that you are in so special a manner the favored object of the divine regard.

But there was another department of the war which was destined for your exclusive exertions. Without entering into any length of detail I will, if possible, describe some of the most memorable actions with as much brevity as you performed them with celerity. After the loss of all Ireland with the exception of one city, you in one battle immediately discomfited the forces of the rebels and were busily employed in settling the country when you were suddenly recalled to the war in Scotland. Hence you proceeded with unwearied diligence against the Scots, who were on the point of making an irruption into England with the king in their train. And in about the space of one year you entirely subdued and added to the English dominion that kingdom which all our monarchs, during a period of eight hundred years, had in vain struggled to subject. In one battle you almost annihilated the remainder of their forces, who in a fit of desperation had made a sudden incursion into England, then almost destitute of garrisons, and got as far as Worcester, where you came up with them

---

[61] Cf. the allusion to *Cyrus* the Great as encouraging the rebuilding of Jerusalem in *PL* XII, 348–50, and to the perfect discipline in his armies in *CG*, n. 12.

[62] The Theban patriot, *Epaminondas*, assisted in the expulsion of the Spartans from Thebes in 379 B.C., defeated them and broke their domination of all Greece at the battle of Leuctra in 371, and later made four successful expeditions against the Spartans in the Peloponnesus.

[63] *Sir Thomas Fairfax*, third Viscount Fairfax (1612–1671) was from the first a leading parliamentary general. He commanded the left wing at Marston Moor, became commander-in-chief of the New Model Army, conquered at Naseby, and took a decisive part in putting down the Royalists in the Second Civil War. He was not in sympathy with the trial of Charles, and after the first sitting of the High Court of Justice, of which he was appointed a member, he did not attend again. In June, 1650, he resigned as commander-in-chief and was succeeded by Cromwell. Cf. the sonnet *To the Lord General Fairfax*, and *TKM*, n. 26.

[64] In *Def se* (C.E. IX, 7) Milton refers at length to the account in Plutarch's *Life of Scipio Africanus* of his retirement to private life in his own villa when the Roman Senate lost a proper respect for his achievements and character.

by forced marches and captured almost the whole of their nobility.

A profound peace ensued; when we found, though indeed not then for the first time, that you were as wise in the cabinet as valiant in the field. It was your constant endeavor in the senate either to induce them to adhere to those treaties which they had entered into with the enemy or speedily to adjust others which promised to be beneficial to the country. But when you saw that the business was artfully procrastinated, that every one was more intent on his own selfish interest than on the public good, that the people complained of the disappointments which they had experienced and the fallacious promises by which they had been gulled, that they were the dupes of a few overbearing individuals, you put an end to their domination. A new Parliament[65] is summoned, and the right of election given to those to whom it was expedient. They meet, but do nothing; and after having wearied themselves by their mutual dissensions and fully exposed their incapacity to the observation of the country, they consent to a voluntary dissolution.

In this state of desolation to which we were reduced you, O Cromwell, alone remained to conduct the government, and to save the country. We all willingly yield the palm of sovereignty to your unrivalled ability and virtue, except the few among us who, either ambitious of honors which they have not the capacity to sustain, or who envy those which are conferred on one more worthy than themselves, or else who do not know that nothing in the world is more pleasing to God, more agreeable to reason, more politically just, or more generally useful than that the supreme power should be vested in the best and the wisest of men. Such, O Cromwell, all acknowledge you to be. Such are the services which you have rendered, as the leader of our councils, the general of our armies, and the father of your country. For this is the tender appellation by which all the good among us salute you from the very soul.

[65] The Little *Parliament* of 1553, which was composed of 140 members mainly nominated on the invitation of the council of the army acting with Cromwell by the Congregational churches in every county.

Other names you neither have nor could endure, and you deservedly reject that pomp of title which attracts the gaze and admiration of the multitude. For what is a title but a certain definite mode of dignity; but actions such as yours surpass, not only the bounds of our admiration, but our titles; and, like the points of pyramids, which are lost in the clouds, they soar above the possibilities of titular commendation. But since, though it be not fit, it may be expedient, that the highest pitch of virtue should be circumscribed within the bounds of some human appellation, you endured to receive, for the public good, a title most like to that of the father of your country; not to exalt, but rather to bring you nearer to the level of ordinary men. The title of king was unworthy the transcendent majesty of your character. For if you had been captivated by a name over which, as a private man, you had so completely triumphed and crumbled into dust, you would have been doing the same thing as if, after having subdued some idolatrous nation by the help of the true God, you should afterwards fall down and worship the gods which you had vanquished.

Do you then, sir, continue your course with the same unrivalled magnanimity; it sits well upon you. To you our country owes its liberties, nor can you sustain a character at once more momentous and more august than that of the author, the guardian, and the preserver of our liberties; and hence you have not only eclipsed the achievements of all our kings, but even those which have been fabled of our heroes. Often reflect what a dear pledge the beloved land of your nativity has entrusted to your care; and that liberty which she once expected only from the chosen flower of her talents and her virtues she now expects from you only, and by you only hopes to obtain. Revere the fond expectations which we cherish, the solicitudes of your anxious country. Revere the looks and the wounds of your brave companions in arms who, under your banners, have so strenuously fought for liberty. Revere the shades of those who perished in the contest. Revere also the opinions and the hopes which foreign states entertain concerning us, who promise to themselves so many advantages from that liberty which we have so bravely acquired, from the establishment of that new government which has begun to shed its splendor on the world, which, if it be suffered to vanish like a dream, would involve us in the deepest abyss of shame. And lastly, revere yourself; and after having endured so many sufferings and encountered so many perils for the sake of liberty, do not suffer it, now it is obtained, either to be violated by yourself, or in any one instance impaired by others. You cannot be truly free unless we are free too; for such is the nature of things that he who entrenches on the liberty of others is the first to lose his own and become a slave.

But if you who have hitherto been the patron and tutelary genius of liberty, if you who are exceeded by no one in justice, in piety, and goodness, should hereafter invade that liberty which you have defended, your conduct must be fatally operative, not only against the cause of liberty, but the general interests of piety and virtue. Your integrity and virtue will appear to have evaporated, your faith in religion to have been small. Your character with posterity will dwindle into insignificance, by which a most destructive blow will be levelled against the happiness of mankind.

The work which you have undertaken is of incalculable moment, which will thoroughly sift and expose every principle and sensation of your heart, which will fully display the vigor and genius of your character, which will evince whether you really possess those great qualities of piety, fidelity, justice, and self-denial, which made us believe that you were elevated by the special direction of the Deity to the highest pinnacle of power. At once wisely and discreetly to hold the scepter over three powerful nations, to persuade people to relinquish inveterate and corrupt for new and more beneficial maxims and institutions, to penetrate into the remotest parts of the country, to have the mind present and operative in every quarter, to watch against surprise, to provide against danger, to reject the blandishments of pleasure and pomp of power —these are exertions compared with which the labor of war is mere pastime; which will require every energy and employ every faculty that you possess, which demand a man supported from above and almost instructed by immediate inspiration.

These and more than these are, no doubt, the objects which occupy your attention and engross your soul; as well as the means by which you may accomplish these important ends and render our liberty at once more ample and more secure. And this you can, in my opinion, in no other way so readily effect as by associating in your councils the companions of your dangers and your toils —men of exemplary modesty, integrity, and courage, whose hearts have not been hardened in cruelty and rendered insensible to pity by the sight of so much ravage and so much death, but whom it has rather inspired with the love of justice, with a respect for religion, and with the feeling of compassion, and who are more zealously interested in the preservation of liberty in proportion as they have encountered more perils in its defense.

.   .   .   .   .   .

For it is of little consequence, O citizens, by what principles you are governed, either in acquiring liberty or in retaining it when acquired. And unless that liberty which is of such a kind as arms can neither procure nor take away, which alone is the fruit of piety, of justice, of temperance, and unadulterated virtue, shall have taken deep root in your minds and hearts, there will not long be wanting one who will snatch from you by treachery what you have acquired by arms. War has made many great whom peace makes small. If after being released from the toils of war you neglect the arts of peace, if your peace and your liberty be a state of warfare, if war be your only virtue, the summit of your praise, you will, believe me, soon find peace the most adverse to your interests. Your peace will be only a more distressing war, and that which you imagined liberty will prove the worst of slavery.[66] Unless by the means of piety, not frothy and loquacious, but operative, unadulterated, and sincere, you clear the horizon of the mind from those mists of superstition which arise from the ignorance of true religion, you will always have those who will bend your necks to the yoke as if you were brutes, who, nothwithstanding all your triumphs, will put you up to the highest bidder as

[66] The close parallel of this entire closing section with Milton's summary of political wisdom in *PL* XII, 79–104 should be obvious.

if you were mere booty made in war; and will find an exuberant source of wealth in your ignorance and superstition. Unless you will subjugate the propensity to avarice, to ambition and sensuality, and expel all luxury from yourselves and from your families, you will find that you have cherished a more stubborn and intractable despot at home than you ever encountered in the field; and even your very bowels will be continually teeming with an intolerable progeny of tyrants.

Let these be the first enemies whom you subdue. This constitutes the campaign of peace. These are triumphs, difficult indeed, but bloodless and far more honorable than those trophies which are purchased only by slaughter and by rapine. Unless you are victors in this service, it is in vain that you have been victorious over the despotic enemy in the field. For if you think that it is a more grand, a more beneficial or a more wise policy to invent subtle expedients for increasing the revenue, to multiply our naval and military force, to rival in craft the ambassadors of foreign states, to form skilful treaties and alliances, than to administer unpolluted justice to the people, to redress the injured, and to succor the distressed, and speedily to restore to every one his own, you are involved in a cloud of error. And too late will you perceive, when the illusion of those mighty benefits has vanished, that in neglecting these, which you now think inferior considerations, you have only been precipitating your own ruin and despair. The fidelity of enemies and allies is frail and perishing unless it be cemented by the principles of justice. That wealth and those honors which most covet, readily change masters; they forsake the idle and repair[67] where virtue, where industry, where patience flourish most. Thus nation precipitates the downfall of nation; thus the more sound part of one people subverts[68] the more corrupt; thus you obtained the ascendant over the royalists. If you plunge into the same depravity, if you imitate their excesses and hanker after the same vanities, you will become royalists as well as they, and liable to be subdued by the same enemies or by others in your turn, who—placing their reliance on the same re-

ligious principles, the same patience, the same integrity and discretion which made you strong—will deservedly triumph over you who are immersed in debauchery, in the luxury and the sloth of kings.

Then, as if God was weary of protecting you, you will be seen to have passed through the fire that you might perish in the smoke. The contempt which you will then experience will be great as the admiration which you now enjoy; and, what may in future profit others, but cannot benefit yourselves, you will leave a salutary proof what great things the solid reality of virtue and of piety might have effected when the mere counterfeit and varnished resemblance could attempt such mighty achievements and make such considerable advances towards the execution. For, if either through your want of knowledge, your want of constancy, or your want of virtue, attempts so noble and actions so glorious have had an issue so unfortunate, it does not therefore follow that better men should be either less daring in their projects or less sanguine in their hopes. But from such an abyss of corruption into which you so readily fall no one, not even Cromwell himself nor a whole nation of Brutuses,[69] if they were alive, could deliver you if they would, or would deliver you if they could. For who would vindicate your right of unrestrained suffrage or of choosing what representatives you liked best, merely that you might elect the creatures of your own faction, whoever they might be, or him, however small might be his worth, who would give you the most lavish feasts and enable you to drink to the greatest excess?

Thus not wisdom and authority, but turbulence and gluttony, would soon exalt the vilest miscreants from our taverns and our brothels, from our towns and villages, to the rank and dignity of senators. For, should the management of the republic be entrusted to persons to whom no one would willingly entrust the management of his private concerns, and the treasury of the state be left to the care of those who had lavished their own fortunes in an infamous prodigality? Should they have the charge of the public purse, which they would soon

---

[67] *repair:* go.
[68] *subverts:* destroys, overcomes.

[69] Cf. Milton's allusion in *Prol* VI (see n. 4) to *Junius Brutus,* the founder of Roman liberty. Cf. *TKM,* n. 73.

convert into a private, by their unprincipled peculations? Are they fit to be the legislators of a whole people who themselves know not what law, what reason, what right and wrong, what crooked and straight, what licit and illicit means? who think that all power consists in outrage, all dignity in the parade of insolence? who neglect every other consideration for the corrupt gratification of their friendships or the prosecution of their resentments? who disperse their own relations and creatures through the provinces for the sake of levying taxes and confiscating goods—men, for the greater part the most profligate and vile, who buy up for themselves what they pretend to expose to sale, who thence collect an exorbitant mass of wealth, which they fraudulently divert from the public service, who thus spread their pillage through the country and in a moment emerge from penury and rags to a state of splendor and of wealth?

Who could endure such thievish servants, such vicegerents of their lords? Who could believe that the masters and the patrons of a banditti could be the proper guardians of liberty? Or who would suppose that he should ever be made one hair more free by such a set of public functionaries (though they might amount to five hundred elected in this manner from the counties and boroughs), when among them who are the very guardians of liberty, and to whose custody it is committed, there must be so many who know not either how to use or to enjoy liberty, who neither understand the principles nor merit the possession? But, what is worthy of remark, those who are the most unworthy of liberty are wont to behave most ungratefully towards their deliverers. Among such persons who would be willing either to fight for liberty or to encounter the least peril in its defense? It is not agreeable to the nature of things that such persons ever should be free. However much they may brawl about liberty, they are slaves, both at home and abroad, but without perceiving it. And when they do perceive it, like unruly horses that are impatient of the bit, they will endeavor to throw off the yoke, not from the love of genuine liberty (which a good man only loves and knows how to obtain), but from the impulses of pride and little passions. But though they often attempt it by arms, they will make no advances to the execution; they may change their masters, but will never be able to get rid of their servitude.

This often happened to the ancient Romans, wasted by excess and enervated by luxury; and it has still more so been the fate of the moderns, when, after a long interval of years, they aspired under the auspices of Crescentius Nomentanus and afterwards of Nicolas Rentius, who had assumed the title of Tribune of the People, to restore the splendor and re-establish the government of ancient Rome.[70] For, instead of fretting with vexation or thinking that you can lay the blame on any one but yourselves, know that to be free is the same thing as to be pious, to be wise, to be temperate and just, to be frugal and abstinent, and lastly, to be magnanimous and brave. So to be the opposite of all these is the same as to be a slave. And it usually happens by the appointment and as it were retributive justice of the Deity that that people which cannot govern themselves and moderate their passions, but crouch under the slavery of their lusts, should be delivered up to the sway of those whom they abhor and made to submit to an involuntary servitude. It is also sanctioned by the dictates of justice and by the constitution of nature that he, who from the imbecility or derangement of his intellect is incapable of governing himself, should, like a minor, be committed to the government of another, and least of all should he be appointed to superintend the affairs of others or the interest of the state.

You, therefore, who wish to remain free, either instantly be wise or, as soon as possible, cease to be fools. If you think slavery an intolerable evil, learn obedience to rea-

[70] Milton remembered his early note under "Liberty" in CB: "It is impossible that a city, though it loves liberty, should do glorious deeds and retrieve liberty after it has been lost, as Crescentius of Nomantum failed in his effort to restore the ancient constitution of the Roman Republic. . . . So also later Niccolo Rienzi, who gloried in the title of Tribune of the People." *Crescentius* successfully maintained good government in *Rome*, reviving the title of Consul for himself in 980, but he was overthrown in 998 by Otto III. Cola di Rienzi, the friend of Petrarch, led popular reforms in 1347 and was given the title of Tribune and Liberator of Rome, but soon proved weak, lost power, and was publicly murdered in 1354.

son and the government of yourselves, and finally bid adieu to your dissensions, your jealousies, your superstitions, your outrages, your rapine, and your lusts. Unless you will spare no pains to effect this, you must be judged unfit, both by God and mankind, to be entrusted with the possession of liberty and the administration of the government, but will rather, like a nation in a state of pupilage, want some active and courageous guardian to undertake the management of your affairs.

With respect to myself, whatever turn things may take, I thought that my exertions on the present occasion would be serviceable to my country; and as they have been cheerfully bestowed, I hope that they have not been bestowed in vain. And I have not circumscribed my defense of liberty within any petty circle around me, but have made it so general and comprehensive that the justice and the reasonableness of such uncommon occurrences, explained and defended both among my countrymen and among foreigners, and which all good men cannot but approve, may serve to exalt the glory of my country and to excite the imitation of posterity. If the conclusion do not answer to the beginning, that is their concern. I have delivered my testimony, I would almost say, have erected a monument that will not readily be destroyed to the reality of those singular and mighty achievements which were above all praise. As the epic poet, who adheres at all to the rules of that species of composition, does not profess to describe the whole life of the hero whom he celebrates, but only some particular action of his life, as the resentment of Achilles at Troy, the return of Ulysses, or the coming of Æneas into Italy, so it will be sufficient, either for my justification or apology, that I have heroically celebrated at least one exploit of my countrymen. I pass by the rest, for who could recite the achievements of a whole people?[71] If after such a display of courage and of vigor you basely relinquish the path of virtue, if you do anything unworthy of yourselves, posterity will sit in judgment on your conduct. They will see that the foundations were well laid; that the beginning (nay, it was more than a beginning) was glorious; but with deep emotions of concern will they regret that those were wanting who might have completed the structure. They will lament that perseverance was not conjoined with such exertions and such virtues. They will see that there was a rich harvest of glory and an opportunity afforded for the greatest achievements, but that men only were wanting for the execution; while they were not wanting who could rightly counsel, exhort, inspire, and bind an unfading wreath of praise round the brows of the illustrious actors in so glorious a scene.

[71] After quoting this and the preceding sentence, in *Milton and Wordsworth* (New York, 1937), p. 72, Sir Herbert Grierson declares that this passage shows that Milton felt that his *Defenses of the English People* had virtually fulfilled the epic purpose which he had stated in *Manso*, 78–84, and in the Preface to *CG*, Book II. Cromwell and his generals and counselors "were Milton's 'pattern of a Christian hero.' If this be so, then we must see in *PL* something other than the fulfilment of his original intention, something to which he passed when that had been achieved in ways decreed by God and destiny."

A TREATISE

OF

CIVIL POWER IN ECCLESIASTICAL CAUSES;

SHOWING THAT IT IS NOT LAWFUL FOR ANY POWER ON EARTH TO COMPEL
IN MATTERS OF RELIGION.

BIBLIOGRAPHICAL NOTE—*Civil Power* and *Hirelings* were planned when Richard Cromwell summoned Parliament on January 27, 1659, (as Masson noted in his *Life of Milton* V, 581) as complementary pamphlets, the first of which would handle "the effects of compulsion or state-restraint in matters of religion and speculation," while the other would deal with "the effects of hire or state-endowments in the same." The former represented a conviction which inspired the Sonnet *To Sir Henry Vane* (No. XVII) and which is effectively traced through Milton's thought by Barker in *Dilemma,* 236–59. Masson notes that *Civil Power* was registered with the Stationers Company on Feb. 16, 1659, and must have been published soon afterwards.

The present text is based on a photostat of the copy of the edition of 1659 which is in the Houghton Library at Harvard University.

TO THE PARLIAMENT OF THE COMMON-
WEALTH OF ENGLAND, WITH THE
DOMINIONS THEREOF.

I have prepared, supreme council, against the much expected time of your sitting, this treatise; which, though to all Christian magistrates equally belonging, and therefore to have been written in the common language of Christendom,[1] natural duty and affection hath confined and dedicated first to my own nation, and in a season wherein the timely reading thereof, to the easier accomplishment of your great work, may save you much labor and interruption: of two parts usually proposed, civil and ecclesiastical, recommending civil only to your proper care, ecclesiastical to them only from who it takes both that name and nature. Yet not for this cause only do I require or trust to find acceptance, but in a twofold respect besides: first, as bringing clear evidence of scripture and protestant maxims to the Parliament of England, who in all their late acts, upon occasion, have professed to assert only the true protestant Christian religion, as it is contained in the holy scriptures: next, in regard that your power being but for a time, and having in yourselves a Christian liberty of your own,

which at one time or other may be oppressed, thereof truly sensible, it will concern you while you are in power, so to regard other men's consciences, as you would your own should be regarded in the power of others; and to consider that any law against conscience is alike in force against any conscience, and so may one way or other justly redound upon yourselves. One advantage I make no doubt of, that I shall write to many eminent persons of your number, already perfect and resolved in this important article of Christianity. Some of whom I remember to have heard often for several years, at a council[2] next in authority to your own, so well joining religion with civil prudence, and yet so well distinguishing the different power of either; and this not only voting, but frequently reasoning why it should be so, that if any there present had been before of an opinion contrary, he might doubtless have departed thence a convert in that point, and have confessed that then both commonwealth and religion will at length, if ever, flourish in Christendom, when either they who govern discern between civil and religious,[3] or they only who so discern shall be admitted to govern. Till then, nothing but troubles, persecutions, commotions can be expected; the inward

---

[1] *the common language of Christendom:* Latin, in which Milton had written his *Defenses of the English People* and of himself.

[2] *a council:* the Council of State, in which Milton still retained his Latin secretaryship.

[3] Cf. *Sonn* XVII, 9–12.

decay of true religion among ourselves, and the utter overthrow at last by a common enemy. Of civil liberty I have written heretofore by the appointment and not without the approbation of civil power: of Christian liberty I write now; which others long since having done with all freedom under heathen emperors, I should do wrong to suspect that I now shall with less under Christian governors, and such especially as profess openly their defense of Christian liberty; although I write this not otherwise appointed or induced than by an inward persuasion of the Christian duty which I may usefully discharge herein to the common Lord and Master of us all, and the certain hope of his approbation, first and chiefest to be sought: in the hand of whose providence I remain, praying all success and good event on your public councils, to the defense of true religion and our civil rights.

JOHN MILTON.

A TREATISE OF CIVIL POWER IN ECCLESIASTICAL CAUSES

Two things there be which have been ever found working much mischief to the church of God and the advancement of truth: force on one side restraining, and hire on the other side corrupting the teachers thereof. Few ages have been since the ascension of our Savior, wherein the one of these two, or both together, have not prevailed. It can be at no time, therefore, unseasonable to speak of these things; since by them the church is either in continual detriment and oppression, or in continual danger. The former shall be at this time my argument; the latter as I shall find God disposing me, and opportunity inviting. What I argue shall be drawn from the scripture only; and therein from true fundamental principles of the gospel, to all knowing Christians undeniable. And if the governors of this commonwealth, since the rooting out of prelates, have made least use of force in religion, and most have favored Christian liberty[4] of any in this island before them since the first preaching of the gospel, for which we are not to forget our thanks to God, and their due praise; they may, I doubt not, in

[4] Cf. Milton's early appeal to this principle and its grounds in CG, n. 48.

this treatise find that which not only will confirm them to defend still the Christian liberty which we enjoy, but will incite them also to enlarge it, if in aught they yet straiten it. To them who perhaps hereafter, less experienced in religion, may come to govern or give us laws, this or other such, if they please, may be a timely instruction: however, to the truth it will be at all times no unneedful testimony, at least some discharge of that general duty which no Christian but according to what he hath received, knows is required of him, if he have aught more conducing to the advancement of religion than what is usually endeavored, freely to impart it.

It will require no great labor of exposition to unfold what is here meant by matters of religion; being as soon apprehended as defined, such things as belong chiefly to the knowledge and service of God, and are either above the reach and light of nature without revelation from above, and therefore liable to be variously understood by human reason: or such things as are enjoined or forbidden by divine precept, which else by the light of reason would seem indifferent to be done or not done, and so likewise must needs appear to every man as the precept is understood. Whence I here mean by conscience or religion that full persuasion whereby we are assured that our belief and practice, as far as we are able to apprehend and probably make appear, is according to the will of God and his Holy Spirit within us, which we ought to follow much rather than any law of man, as not only his word everywhere bids us, but the very dictate of reason tells us: Acts iv. 19, "Whether it be right in the sight of God, to hearken to you more than to God, judge ye." That for belief or practice in religion according to this conscientious persuasion, no man ought to be punished or molested by any outward force on earth whatsoever, I distrust not, through God's implored assistance, to make plain by these following arguments.

First, it cannot be denied, being the main foundation of our protestant religion, that we of these ages, having no other divine rule or authority from without us, warrantable to one another as a common ground, but the holy scripture, and no other within us but the illumination of the

Holy Spirit, so interpreting that scripture as warrantable only to ourselves, and to such whose consciences we can so persuade, can have no other ground in matters of religion but only from the scriptures. And these being not possible to be understood without this divine illumination, which no man can know at all times to be in himself, much less to be at any time for certain in any other, it follows clearly that no man or body of men in these times can be the infallible judges or determiners in matters of religion to any other men's consciences but their own. And therefore those Bereans are commended, Acts xvii, 11, who after the preaching even of St. Paul, "searched the scriptures daily, whether those things were so." Nor did they more than what God himself in many places commands us by the same apostle, to search, to try, to judge of these things ourselves: and gives us reason also, Gal. vi, 4, 5: "Let every man prove his own work, and then shall he have rejoicing in himself alone, and not in another: for every man shall bear his own burden." If then we count it so ignorant and irreligious in the papist to think himself discharged in God's account, believing only as the church believes, how much greater condemnation will it be to the protestant his condemner, to think himself justified, believing only as the state believes? With good cause, therefore, it is the general consent of all sound protestant writers that neither traditions, councils, nor canons of any visible church, much less edicts of any magistrate or civil session, but the scripture only, can be the final judge or rule in matters of religion, and that only in the conscience of every Christian to himself. Which protestation made by the first public reformers of our religion against the imperial edicts of Charles V,[5] imposing church traditions without scripture, gave

first beginning to the name of Protestant; and with that name hath ever been received this doctrine, which prefers the scripture before the church, and acknowledges none but the scripture sole interpreter of itself to the conscience. For if the church be not sufficient to be implicitly believed, as we hold it is not, what can there else be named of more authority than the church but the conscience, than which God only is greater? I John iii, 20. But if any man shall pretend that the scripture judges to his conscience for other men, he makes himself greater not only than the church, but also than the scripture, than the consciences of other men: a presumption too high for any mortal, since every true Christian able to give a reason of his faith, hath the word of God before him, the promised Holy Spirit, and the mind of Christ within him, I Cor. ii, 16; a much better and safer guide of conscience, which as far as concerns himself he may far more certainly know than any outward rule imposed upon him by others whom he inwardly neither knows nor can know; at least knows nothing of them more sure than this one thing, that they cannot be his judges in religion, I Cor. ii, 15: "The spiritual man judgeth all things, but he himself is judged of no man." Chiefly for this cause do all true protestants account the pope antichrist,[6] for that he assumes to himself this infallibility over both the conscience and the scripture; "sitting in the temple of God," as it were opposite to God, "and exalting himself above all that is called God, or is worshipped," II Thes. ii, 4. That is to say, not only above all judges and magistrates, who though they be called gods are far beneath infallible, but also above God himself, by giving law both to the scripture, to the conscience, and to the spirit itself of God within us. Whenas we find, James iv, 12, "There is one lawgiver, who is able to save and to destroy: Who art thou that judgest another?" That Christ is the only lawgiver of his church, and that it is here meant in religious matters, no well-grounded Christian will deny. Thus also St. Paul, Rom. xiv, 4, "Who art thou that judgest the servant of another? to his own lord he standeth or falleth: but he shall stand; for God is able to make him stand."

---

[5] Milton was thinking of the formal plea of the princes of the League of Schmalkald to the ambassador of the Emperor *Charles V* in February, 1537, which turned upon the assertion of the authority of Scripture as superior to that of the Church. It even accused the Pope of heresy for his support of the imperial judges who, "in all assemblies where religion is treated of, albeit they see that the Scripture maketh against them, yet they wyl presume to take upon them the authoritie of determination" (Sleidan's *Commentaries*, tr. by John Daus, 1560. Ddiiiir). Cf. *TKM*, notes 120 and 194.

[6] Cf. *CG*, n. 42.

As therefore of one beyond expression bold and presumptuous, both these apostles demand, "Who art thou," that presumest to impose other law or judgment in religion than the only lawgiver and judge Christ, who only can save and destroy, gives to the conscience? And the forecited place to the Thessalonians, by compared effects resolves us that, be he or they who or wherever they be or can be, they are of far less authority than the church, whom in these things as protestants they receive not, and yet no less antichrist in this main point of antichristianism, no less a pope or popedom than he at Rome, if not much more, by setting up supreme interpreters of scripture either those doctors whom they follow, or, which is far worse, themselves as a civil papacy assuming unaccountable supremacy to themselves, not in civil only, but in ecclesiastical causes. Seeing then that in matters of religion, as hath been proved, none can judge or determine here on earth, no, not church governors themselves, against the consciences of other believers, my inference is, or rather not mine but our Savior's own, that in those matters they neither can command nor use constraint, lest they run rashly on a pernicious consequence, forewarned in that parable, Matt. xiii, 26–31: "Lest while ye gather up the tares, ye root up also the wheat with them. Let both grow together until the harvest: and in the time of harvest I will say to the reapers, Gather ye together first the tares,"[7] &c. Whereby he declares that this work neither his own ministers nor any else can discerningly enough or judgingly perform without his own immediate direction, in his own fit season, and that they ought till then not to attempt it. Which is further confirmed, II Cor. i, 24, "Not that we have dominion over your faith, but are helpers of your joy." If apostles had no dominion or constraining power over faith or conscience, much less have ordinary ministers: I Pet. v, 2, 3, "Feed the flock of God not by constraint, &c., neither as being lords over God's heritage." But some will object that this overthrows all church discipline, all censure of errors, if no man can determine. My answer is that what they hear is plain scripture, which forbids not church sentence or determining, but as it

[7] Cf. *Areop,* n. 271.

ends in violence upon the conscience unconvinced. Let whoso will interpret or determine, so it be according to true church discipline; which is exercised on them only who have willingly joined themselves in that covenant of union, and proceeds only to a separation from the rest, proceeds never to any corporal enforcement or forfeiture of money, which in all spiritual things are the two arms of Antichrist, not of the true church; the one being an inquisition, the other no better than a temporal indulgence of sin for money, whether by the church exacted or by the magistrate; both the one and the other a temporal satisfaction for what Christ hath satisfied eternally; a popish commuting of penalty, corporal for spiritual; a satisfaction to man, especially to the magistrate, for what and to whom we owe none. These and more are the injustices of force and fining in religion, besides what I most insist on, the violation of God's express commandment in the gospel, as hath been shown. Thus then, if church governors cannot use force in religion, though but for this reason, because they cannot infallibly determine to the conscience without convincement, much less have civil magistrates authority to use force where they can much less judge; unless they mean only to be the civil executioners of them who have no civil power to give them such commission, no, nor yet ecclesiastical, to any force or violence in religion. To sum up all in brief, if we must believe as the magistrate appoints, why not rather as the church? If not as either without convincement, how can force be lawful? But some are ready to cry out, what shall then be done to blasphemy? Them I would first exhort not thus to terrify and pose the people with a Greek word, but to teach them better what it is, being a most usual and common word in that language to signify any slander, any malicious or evil-speaking, whether against God or man, or anything to good belonging: blasphemy or evil-speaking against God maliciously, is far from conscience in religion; according to that of Mark ix, 39, "There is none who doth a powerful work in my name, and can lightly speak evil of me." If this suffice not, I refer them to that prudent and well deliberated act, August 9, 1650, where the parliament defines blasphemy against God, as far as it is a crime belonging to civil judicature, *plenius ac melius Chrysippo et Crantore;*[8] in plain English, more warily, more judiciously, more orthodoxally than twice their number of divines have done in many a prolix volume: although in all likelihood they whose whole study and profession these things are, should be most intelligent and authentic therein, as they are for the most part; yet neither they nor these unerring always, or infallible. But we shall not carry it thus; another Greek apparition stands in our way, *heresy* and *heretic;* in like manner also railed at to the people as in a tongue unknown. They should first interpret to them that heresy, by what it signifies in that language, is no word of evil note, meaning only the choice or following of any opinion, good or bad, in religion, or any other learning;[9] and thus not only in heathen authors but in the New Testament itself, without censure or blame; Acts xv, 5, "Certain of the heresy of the Pharisees which believed"; and xxvi, 5, "After the exactest heresy of our religion I lived a Pharisee." In which sense Presbyterian or Independent may without reproach be called a heresy. Where it is mentioned with blame, it seems to differ little from schism: I Cor. xi, 18, 19, "I hear that there be schisms among you," &c. "for there must also heresies be among you," &c. Though some, who write of heresy after their own heads, would make it far worse than schism: whenas on the contrary, schism signifies division, and in the worst sense; heresy, choice only of one opinion before another, which may be without discord. In apostolic times, therefore, ere the scripture was written, heresy was a doctrine

maintained against the doctrine by them delivered; which in these times can be no otherwise defined than a doctrine maintained against the light, which we now only have, of the scripture. Seeing, therefore, that no man, no synod, no session of men, though called the church, can judge definitively the sense of scripture to another man's conscience, which is well known to be a general maxim of the protestant religion, it follows plainly that he who holds in religion that belief or those opinions which to his conscience and utmost understanding appear with most evidence or probability in the scripture, though to others he seem erroneous, can no more be justly censured for a heretic than his censurers, who do but the same thing themselves, while they censure him for so doing.

For ask them, or any protestant, which hath most authority, the church or the scripture? They will answer, doubtless, that the scripture: and what hath most authority, that no doubt but they will confess is to be followed. He then, who to his best apprehension follows the scripture, though against any point of doctrine by the whole church received, is not the heretic; but he who follows the church against his conscience and persuasion grounded on the scripture. To make this yet more undeniable, I shall only borrow a plain simile, the same which our own writers, when they would demonstrate plainest that we rightly prefer the scripture before the church, use frequently against the papist in this manner. As the Samaritans believed Christ, first for the woman's word, but next and much rather for his own,[10] so we the scripture: first on the church's word, but afterwards and much more for its own, as the word of God; yea, the church itself we believe then for the scripture. The inference of itself follows: if by the protestant doctrine we believe the scripture, not for the church's saying but for its own, as the word of God, then ought we to believe what in our conscience we apprehend the scripture to say, though the visible church, with all her doctors, gainsay: and being taught to believe them only for the scripture, they who so do are not heretics, but the best protestants: and by their opinions, what-

---

[8] In *Epistles* I, ii, 4, Horace speaks playfully of the Stoic philosopher *Chrysippus* and the Academic, *Crantor,* as less reliable guides to wisdom than the Homeric poems.

[9] The definition, as Barker shows (*Dilemma,* p. 241), is a reply to a definition of heresy by the Congregationalist minister William Ames which had been adopted by the drafters of the *Westminster Confession* and some more liberal groups. In part it read as follows: "To make a man a heretic . . . , it is required: 1. that he be such an one as makes some profession of Christianity. . . . 2. that the error which he holds be not only contrary to the doctrine which is contained in the Scriptures, but that it be contrary to that doctrine which belongs to the sum and substance of faith and manners. . . . 3. that the error which he holds be joined with stubbornness and obstinacy."

[10] The *woman* is the Samaritan whose story is told in John iv, 7–42.

ever they be, can hurt no protestant, whose rule is not to receive them but from the scripture: which to interpret convincingly to his own conscience, none is able but himself guided by the Holy Spirit; and not so guided, none than he to himself can be a worse deceiver. To protestants, therefore, whose common rule and touchstone is the scripture, nothing can with more conscience, more equity, nothing more protestantly can be permitted than a free and lawful debate at all times by writing, conference, or disputation of what opinion soever, disputable by scripture: concluding that no man in religion is properly a heretic at this day, but he who maintains traditions or opinions not probable by scripture, who, for aught I know, is the papist only; he the only heretic who counts all heretics but himself. Such as these, indeed, were capitally punished by the law of Moses, as the only true heretics, idolaters, plain and open deserters of God and his known law:[11] but in the gospel such are punished by excommunion only: Tit. iii, 10, "An heretic, after the first and second admonition, reject."

But they who think not this heavy enough, and understand not that dreadful awe and spiritual efficacy which the apostle hath expressed so highly to be in church discipline, II Cor. x, of which anon, and think weakly that the church of God cannot long subsist but in a bodily fear, for want of other proof will needs wrest that place of St. Paul, Rom. xiii, to set up civil inquisition and give power to the magistrate both of civil judgment and punishment in causes ecclesiastical. But let us see with what strength of argument: "Let every soul be subject to the higher powers."[12] First, how prove they that the apostle means other powers than such as they to whom

he writes were then under; who meddled not at all in ecclesiastical causes, unless as tyrants and persecutors? And from them, I hope, they will not derive either the right of magistrates to judge in spiritual things, or the duty of such our obedience. How prove they next that he entitles them here to spiritual causes from whom he withheld, as much as in him lay, the judging of civil? I Cor. vi, 1, &c. If he himself appealed to Cæsar, it was to judge his innocence, not his religion. "For rulers are not a terror to good works, but to the evil." Then are they not a terror to conscience, which is the rule or judge of good works grounded on the scripture. But heresy, they say, is reckoned among evil works, Gal. v, 20, as if all evil works were to be punished by the magistrate; whereof this place, their own citation, reckons up besides heresy a sufficient number to confute them; "uncleanness, wantonness, enmity, strife, emulations, animosities, contentions, envyings"; all which are far more manifest to be judged by him than heresy, as they define it; and yet I suppose they will not subject these evil works, nor many more suchlike, to his cognizance and punishment. "Wilt thou then not be afraid of the power? Do that which is good and thou shalt have praise of the same." This shows that religious matters are not here meant; wherein from the power here spoken of, they could have no praise. "For he is the minister of God to thee for good:"[13] true; but in that office and to that end and by those means which in this place must be clearly found, if from this place they intend to argue. And how for thy good, by forcing, oppressing, and ensnaring thy conscience? Many are the ministers of God and their offices no less different than many; none more different than state and church government. Who seeks to govern both must needs be worse than any lord prelate or church pluralist: for he in his own faculty and profession, the other not in his own and for the most part not thoroughly understood, makes himself supreme lord or pope of the church, as far as his civil jurisdiction stretches: and all the ministers of God therein, his ministers, or his curates rather in the function only, not in the government; while he himself assumes to rule by

[11] Cromwell's son-in-law, Henry Ireton, as Barker points out (*Dilemma*, p. 238), had laid great stress in the officers' debates at Whitehall in December, 1648, on the argument of men like Thomas Edwards in *Antapologia* (1644) and Samuel Rutherford in *A Free Disputation* (1649), that Jewish magistrates in Old Testament times had used their civil authority to prevent Gentiles living in Palestine from participating in pagan worship of any kind.

[12] For the great part played by Paul's admonition, "Let every soul be subject to the higher powers" (Rom. xiii, 1) in the self-justification of the Parliamentarians in resisting King Charles see *TKM*, n. 74.

[13] Rom. xiii, 3–4.

civil power things to be ruled only by spiritual: whenas this very chapter, verse 6, appointing him his peculiar office, which requires utmost attendance, forbids him this worse than church plurality from that full and weighty charge, wherein alone he is "the minister of God, attending continually on this very thing." To little purpose will they here instance Moses, who did all by immediate divine direction, no, nor yet Asa, Jehoshaphat, or Josiah,[14] who both might, when they pleased, receive answer from God, and had a commonwealth by him delivered them, incorporated with a national church exercised more in bodily than in spiritual worship: so as that the church might be called a commonwealth, and the whole commonwealth a church: nothing of which can be said of Christianity, delivered without the help of magistrates, yea, in the midst of their opposition; how little then with any reference to them, or mention of them, save only of our obedience to their civil laws, as they countenance good and deter evil; which is the proper work of the magistrate, following in the same verse, and shows distinctly wherein he is the minister of God, "a revenger to execute wrath on him that doth evil."

But we must first know who it is that doth evil: the heretic, they say, among the first. Let it be known then certainly who is a heretic; and that he who holds opinions in religion professedly from tradition or his own inventions, and not from scripture, but rather against it, is the only heretic: and yet though such, not always punishable by the magistrate, unless he do evil against a civil law, properly so called, hath been already proved without need of repetition: "But if thou do that which is evil, be afraid."[15] To do by scripture and the gospel, according to conscience, is not to do evil; if we thereof ought not to be afraid, he ought not by his judging to give cause: causes therefore of religion are not here meant: "For he beareth not the sword in vain." Yes, altogether in vain, if it smite he knows not what; if that for heresy which

not the church itself, much less he, can determine absolutely to be so; if truth for error, being himself so often fallible, he bears the sword not in vain only, but unjustly and to evil. "Be subject not only for wrath, but for conscience sake." How for conscience sake, against conscience? By all these reasons it appears plainly that the apostle in this place gives no judgment or coercive power to magistrates, neither to those then, nor these now, in matters of religion; and exhorts us no otherwise than he exhorted those Romans. It hath now twice befallen me to assert, through God's assistance, this most wrested and vexed place of scripture: heretofore against Salmasius[16] and regal tyranny over the state; now against Erastus[17] and state tyranny over the church. If from such uncertain or rather such improbable grounds as these, they endue magistracy with spiritual judgment, they may as well invest him in the same spiritual kind with power of utmost punishment, excommunication; and then turn spiritual into corporal, as no worse authors did than Chrysostom, Jerome, and Austin, whom Erasmus[18] and others in their notes on the New Testament have cited to interpret that "cutting off" which St. Paul wished to them who had brought back the Galatians to circumcision, no less than the amerce-

---

[14] The restoration of the temple worship as laid down in the Mosaic law at various times by *Asa, Jehoshaphat,* and *Josiah* is recounted in I Kings xv, 9–22, and II Chron. xiv, 1–5; II Chron. xix; and II Chron. xxxiv, 1–7, respectively. Cf. n. 23 below.

[15] Rom. xiii, 4.

[16] Cf. *Def* 1, C.E. VII, 164–74. The *place* is still Rom. xiii, 4–5, which has just been quoted piecemeal.

[17] The famous German theologian *Thomas Erastus* (1524–1583) was famous for his doctrine that civil authority should punish all offenses of a kind which ecclesiastical authorities had been accustomed to punish by excommunication. His thesis on the subject was translated under the title *The Nullity of Church Censures* in 1659, although it had been rejected by the Westminster Assembly.

[18] The words in question here are St. Paul's saying in Gal. v, 12: "I would that they were even cut off which trouble you." He is perhaps playing on the double or triple possible meanings of the Greek word which is translated "cut off," which in one form is used to mean the rite of circumcision which the Judaizing members of the Galatian church were urging upon all Christians. In his commentary on the verse in his *Annotationes ad Novum Testamentum* (Basle, 1522), p. 464, Erasmus quotes Augustine as interpreting Paul as recommending that the Judaizers should be cut off in the sense that they should be excommunicated, and not in the sense that they should suffer the absurdly severe punishment of "amercement of their whole virility." The other authorites cited in the paragraph are St. Ambrose and Anastasius Theophylactus—not Saints *Chrysostom* and *Jerome.* Milton seems to have quoted from memory.

ment of their whole virility: and Grotius[19] adds that this concising punishment of circumcisers became a penal law thereupon among the Visigoths: a dangerous example of beginning in the spirit to end so in the flesh; whereas that cutting off much likelier seems meant a cutting off from the church, not unusually so termed in scripture, and a zealous imprecation, not a command. But I have mentioned this passage to show how absurd they often prove who have not learned to distinguish rightly between civil power and ecclesiastical. How many persecutions then, imprisonments, banishments, penalties, and stripes; how much bloodshed have the forcers of conscience to answer for, and protestants rather than papists! For the papist, judging by his principles, punishes them who believe not as the church believes though against the scripture; but the protestant, teaching everyone to believe the scripture though against the church, counts heretical and persecutes, against his own principles, them who in any particular so believe as he in general teaches them; them who most honor and believe divine scripture, but not against it any human interpretation though universal; them who interpret scripture only to themselves, which by his own position none but they to themselves can interpret: them who use the scripture no otherwise by his own doctrine to their edification than he himself uses it to their punishing; and so whom his doctrine acknowledges a true believer, his discipline persecutes as a heretic.

The papist exacts our belief as to the church due above scripture; and by the church, which is the whole people of God, understands the pope, the general councils, prelatical only, and the surnamed[20] fathers: but the forcing protestant, though he deny such belief to any church whatsoever, yet takes it to himself and his teachers, of far less authority than to be called the church

19 By an even more absurd extension of the worst of the three possible interpretations which were put upon Gal. v, 12, the passage became the basis of a law among the Visigoths (as *Grotius* indicated) which justified mutilation as a punishment for apostasy.

20 The *surname* of Fathers of the Church was never acceptable to Milton as a general title or description of the Greek and Latin theological writers of early post-apostolic times. "Their times corrupt, their books corrupt" was his characterization of them in *Of Reformation* (C.E. III, 14).

and above scripture believed: which renders his practice both contrary to his belief, and far worse than that belief which he condemns in the papist. By all which, well considered, the more he professes to be a true protestant, the more he hath to answer for his persecuting than a papist. No protestant therefore, of what sect soever, following scripture only, which is the common sect wherein they all agree and the granted rule of every man's conscience to himself, ought by the common doctrine of protestants to be forced or molested for religion.

But as for popery and idolatry, why they also may not hence plead to be tolerated, I have much less to say. Their religion the more considered, the less can be acknowledged a religion, but a Roman principality rather, endeavoring to keep up her old universal dominion under a new name, and mere shadow of a catholic religion; being indeed more rightly named a catholic heresy against the scripture, supported mainly by a civil and, except in Rome, by a foreign power: justly therefore to be suspected, not tolerated, by the magistrate of another country. Besides, of an implicit faith which they profess, the conscience also becomes implicit, and so by voluntary servitude to man's law, forfeits her Christian liberty. Who then can plead for such a conscience, as being implicitly enthralled to man instead of God, almost becomes no conscience, as the will not free, becomes no will. Nevertheless, if they ought not to be tolerated, it is for just reason of state more than of religion; which they who force, though professing to be protestants, deserve as little to be tolerated themselves, being no less guilty of popery in the most popish point. Lastly, for idolatry, who knows it not to be evidently against all scripture, both of the Old and New Testament, and therefore a true heresy, or rather an impiety, wherein a right conscience can have nought to do; and the works thereof so manifest that a magistrate can hardly err in prohibiting and quite removing at least the public and scandalous use thereof.

From the riddance of these objections, I proceed yet to another reason why it is unlawful for the civil magistrate to use force in matters of religion; which is, because to judge in those things, though we should grant him able, which is proved he is not, yet as a civil magistrate he hath no right. Christ hath a government of his own sufficient of itself to all his ends and purposes in governing his church, but much different from that of the civil magistrate; and the difference in this very thing principally consists, that it governs not by outward force, and that for two reasons: first, because it deals only with the inward man and his actions, which are all spiritual and to outward force not liable; secondly, to show us the divine excellence of his spiritual kingdom, able without worldly force to subdue all the powers and kingdoms of this world, which are upheld by outward force only. That the inward man is nothing else but the inward part of man, his understanding and his will; and that his actions thence proceeding, yet not simply thence but from the work of divine grace upon them, are the whole matter of religion under the gospel, will appear plainly by considering what that religion is; whence we shall perceive yet more plainly that it cannot be forced. What evangelic religion is, is told in two words, faith and charity, or belief and practice. That both these flow, either the one from the understanding, the other from the will, or both jointly from both, once indeed naturally free, but now only as they are regenerate and wrought on by divine grace, is in part evident to commonsense and principles unquestioned, the rest by scripture: concerning our belief, Matt. xvi, 17, "Flesh and blood hath not revealed it unto thee, but my Father which is in heaven"; concerning our practice, as it is religious and not merely civil, Gal. v, 22, 23,[21] and other places, declare it to be the fruit of the spirit only. Nay, our whole practical duty in religion is contained in charity, or the love of God and our neighbor,[22] no way to be forced, yet the fulfilling of the whole law; that is to say, our whole practice in religion. If then both our belief and practice, which

comprehend our whole religion, flow from faculties of the inward man, free and unconstrainable of themselves by nature, and our practice not only from faculties endued with freedom but from love and charity besides, incapable of force, and all these things by transgression lost, but renewed and regenerated in us by the power and gift of God alone; how can such religion as this admit of force from man, or force be any way applied to such religion, especially under the free offer of grace in the gospel, but it must forthwith frustrate and make of no effect both the religion and the gospel? And that to compel outward profession, which they will say perhaps ought to be compelled, though inward religion cannot, is to compel hypocrisy, not to advance religion, shall yet, though of itself clear enough, be ere the conclusion further manifest.

The other reason why Christ rejects outward force in the government of his church, is, as I said before, to show us the divine excellence of his spiritual kingdom, able without worldly force to subdue all the powers and kingdoms of this world, which are upheld by outward force only: by which to uphold religion otherwise than to defend the religious from outward violence, is no service to Christ or his kingdom but rather a disparagement, and degrades it from a divine and spiritual kingdom to a kingdom of this world: which he denies it to be, because it needs not force to confirm it: John xviii, 36: "If my kingdom were of this world, then would my servants fight, that I should not be delivered to the Jews." This proves the kingdom of Christ not governed by outward force, as being none of this world, whose kingdoms are maintained all by force only; and yet disproves not that a Christian commonwealth may defend itself against outward force in the cause of religion as well as in any other; though Christ himself, coming purposely to die for us, would not be so defended. I Cor. i, 27: "God hath chosen the weak things of the world to confound the things which are mighty." Then surely he hath not chosen the force of this world to subdue conscience and conscientious men, who in this world are counted weakest, but rather conscience, as being weakest, to subdue and regulate force, his adversary, not

---

[21] The verses read: "But the fruit of the Spirit is love, joy, peace, long-suffering, gentleness, goodness, faith, meekness, temperance: against such there is no law."

[22] Milton recalls Christ's saying that to love God "with all the heart, and with all the understanding, and with all the soul, and to love his neighbor as himself, is more than whole burnt offerings and sacrifices" (Mark, xii, 32).

his aid or instrument in governing the church: II Cor. x, 3–6: "For though we walk in the flesh, we do not war after the flesh: for the weapons of our warfare are not carnal, but mighty through God to the pulling down of strongholds, casting down imaginations, and every high thing that exalts itself against the knowledge of God, and bringing into captivity every thought to the obedience of Christ: and having in a readiness to avenge all disobedience."

It is evident by the first and second verses of this chapter that the apostle here speaks of that spiritual power by which Christ governs his church, how all-sufficient it is, how powerful to reach the conscience and the inward man with whom it chiefly deals, and whom no power else can deal with. In comparison of which, as it is here thus magnificently described, how ineffectual and weak is outward force with all her boisterous tools, to the shame of those Christians and especially those churchmen who to the exercising of church discipline never cease calling on the civil magistrate to interpose his fleshly force! An argument that all true ministerial and spiritual power is dead within them who think the gospel, which both began and spread over the whole world for above three hundred years under heathen and persecuting emperors, cannot stand or continue supported by the same divine presence and protection to the world's end, much easier under the defensive favor only of a Christian magistrate, unless it be enacted and settled, as they call it, by the state, a statute or a state religion; and understand not that the church itself cannot, much less the state, settle or impose one tittle of religion upon our obedience implicit, but can only recommend or propound it to our free and conscientious examination. Unless they mean to set the state higher than the church in religion, and with a gross contradiction give to the state in their settling petition that command of our implicit belief which they deny in their settled confession both to the state and to the church.

Let them cease then to importune and interrupt the magistrate from attending to his own charge in civil and moral things, the settling of things just, things honest, the defense of things religious settled by the churches within themselves; and the repressing of their contraries determinable by the common light of nature; which is not to constrain or to repress religion probable by scripture, but the violaters and persecuters thereof. Of all which things he hath enough and more than enough to do, left yet undone, for which the land groans and justice goes to wrack the while. Let him also forbear force where he hath no right to judge, for the conscience is not his province, lest a worse woe arrive him, for worse offending, than was denounced by our Savior, Matt. xxiii, 23, against the Pharisees: ye have forced the conscience, which was not to be forced, but judgment and mercy ye have not executed; this ye should have done, and the other let alone.

And since it is the counsel and set purpose of God in the gospel, by spiritual means which are counted weak, to overcome all power which resists him; let them not go about to do that by worldly strength which he hath decreed to do by those means which the world counts weakness, lest they be again obnoxious to that saying which in another place is also written of the Pharisees, Luke vii, 30, that "they frustrated the counsel of God." The main plea is, and urged with much vehemence to their imitation, that the kings of Judah, as I touched before,[23] and especially Josiah, both judged and used force in religion: II Chron. xxxiv, 33, "He made all that were present in Israel to serve the Lord their God:" an argument, if it be well weighed, worse than that used by the false prophet Shemaia to the high-priest, that in imitation of Jehoiada he ought to put Jeremiah in the stocks, Jer. xxix, 24, 26, &c.; for which he received his due denouncement from God. But to this besides I return a threefold answer: first, that the state of religion under the gospel is far differing from what it was under the law. Then was the state of rigor, childhood, bondage, and works, to all which force was not unbefitting; now is the state of grace, manhood, freedom, and faith, to all which belongs willingness and reason, not force. The law was then written on tables of stone, and to be performed according to the letter, willingly or unwillingly; the gospel, our new covenant, upon the heart of every believer, to be interpreted only by the sense of charity and inward persuasion:

23 Cf. n. 14 above.

the law had no distinct government or governors of church and commonwealth, but the priests and Levites judged in all causes, not ecclesiastical only, but civil, Deut. xvii, 8, &c.; which under the gospel is forbidden to all church ministers, as a thing which Christ their master in his ministry disclaimed, Luke xii, 14, as a thing beneath them, I Cor. vi, 4, and by many other statutes, as to them who have a peculiar and far-differing government of their own. If not, why different the governors? Why not church ministers in state affairs, as well as state ministers in church affairs? If church and state shall be made one flesh again as under the law, let it be withal considered that God, who then joined them, hath now severed them; that which, he so ordaining, was then a lawful conjunction, to such on either side as join again what he hath severed would be nothing now but their own presumptuous fornication.

Secondly, the kings of Judah and those magistrates under the law might have recourse, as I said before, to divine inspiration; which our magistrates under the gospel have not, more than to the same spirit, which those whom they force have ofttimes in greater measure than themselves: and so, instead of forcing the Christian, they force the Holy Ghost; and, against that wise forewarning of Gamaliel,[24] fight against God. Thirdly, those kings and magistrates used force in such things only as were undoubtedly known and forbidden in the law of Moses, idolatry and direct apostacy from that national and strict enjoined worship of God; whereof the corporal punishment was by himself expressly set down; but magistrates under the gospel, our free, elective, and rational worship, are most commonly busiest to force those things which in the gospel are either left free, nay, sometimes abolished when by them compelled, or else controverted equally by writers on both sides, and sometimes with odds on that side which is against them. By which means they either punish that which they ought to favor and protect, or that with corporal punishment and of their own inventing,

which not they, but the church, had received command to chastise with a spiritual rod only.

Yet some are so eager in their zeal of forcing that they refuse not to descend at length to the utmost shift of that parabolical proof, Luke xiv, 16, &c., "Compel them to come in:"[25] therefore magistrates may compel in religion. As if a parable were to be strained through every word or phrase, and not expounded by the general scope thereof; which is no other here than the earnest expression of God's displeasure on those recusant Jews and his purpose to prefer the Gentiles on any terms before them: expressed here by the word *compel*. But how compels he? Doubtless no other way than he draws, without which no man can come to him, John vi, 44; and that is by the inward persuasive motions of his spirit and by his ministers, not by the outward compulsions of a magistrate or his officers.

The true people of Christ, as is foretold, Psalm cx, 3, "are a willing people in the day of his power"; then much more now when he rules all things by outward weakness, that both his inward power and their sincerity may the more appear. "God loveth a cheerful giver"; then certainly is not pleased with an uncheerful worshipper: as the very words declare of his evangelical invitations, Isa. lv, 1, "Ho, every one that thirsteth, come." John vii, 37, "If any man thirst." Rev. iii, 18, "I counsel thee." And xxii, 17, "Whosover will, let him take the water of life freely." And in that grand commission of preaching, to invite all nations, Mark xvi, 16, as the reward of them who come, so the penalty of them who come not, is only spiritual.

But they bring now some reason with their force, which must not pass unanswered, that the church of Thyatira was blamed, Rev. ii, 20, for suffering the false "prophetess to teach and to seduce." I answer, that seducement is to be hindered by fit and proper means ordained in church discipline, by instant and powerful demonstration to the contrary; by opposing truth to error, no unequal match; truth the strong

---

[24] In Acts V, 38–39, when violence is recommended in the council of the high priest against Peter and the apostles, Gamaliel's advice is to "refrain from these men, and let them alone: for if this . . . work be of men, it will come to nought: But if it be of God, ye cannot overthrow it."

[25] The interpretation obviously distorts the meaning of the parable in Luke xiv, 15–24, which represents the host of a dinner to which his friends have refused invitations as sending his servants into the streets to find guests.

to error the weak, though sly and shifting. Force is no honest confutation, but uneffectual, and for the most part unsuccessful, ofttimes fatal to them who use it: sound doctrine, diligently and duly taught, is of herself both sufficient, and of herself (if some secret judgment of God hinder not) always prevalent against seducers. This the Thyatirians had neglected, suffering, against church discipline, that woman to teach and seduce among them: civil force they had not then in their power, being the Christian part only of that city, and then especially under one of those ten great persecutions whereof this the second was raised by Domitian[26]: force therefore in these matters could not be required of them who were under force themselves.

I have shown that the civil power hath neither right, nor can do right, by forcing religious things; I will now show the wrong it doth by violating the fundamental privilege of the gospel, the new birthright of every true believer, Christian liberty: II Cor. iii, 17, "Where the Spirit of the Lord is, there is liberty." Gal. iv, 26, "Jerusalem which is above is free; which is the mother of us all," and 31, "We are not children of the bondwoman, but of the free."[27] It will be sufficient in this place to say no more of Christian liberty than that it sets us free not only from the bondage of those ceremonies, but also from the forcible imposition of those circumstances, place and time in the worship of God: which though by him commanded in the old law, yet in respect of that verity and freedom which is evangelical, St. Paul comprehends both kinds alike, that is to say, both ceremony and circumstance, under one and the same contemptuous name of "weak and beggarly rudiments," Gal. iv, 3, 9, 10; Col. ii, 8 with 16; conformable to what our Savior himself taught, John iv, 21, 23, "Neither in this mountain, nor yet at Jerusalem. In spirit and in truth; for the Father seeketh such to worship him:" that is to say, not only sincere of heart, for such he sought ever, but also, as the words here chiefly import, not compelled to place, and by the same reason, not to any set time; as his apostle by the same spirit hath taught us, Rom. xiv, 5, &c. "One man esteemeth one day above another, another, . . ."; Gal. iv, 10, "Ye observe days and months," &c.; Col. ii, 16. These and other such places in scripture the best and learnedest reformed writers have thought evident enough to instruct us in our freedom, not only from ceremonies, but from those circumstances also, though imposed with a confident persuasion of morality in them, which they hold impossible to be in place or time.

By what warrant then our opinions and practices herein are of late turned quite against all other protestants, and that which is to them orthodoxal to us become scandalous and punishable by statute, I wish were once again better considered, if we mean not to proclaim a schism in this point from the best and most reformed churches abroad. They who would seem more knowing, confess that these things are indifferent, but for that very cause by the magistrate may be commanded. As if God of his special grace in the gospel had to this end freed us from his own commandments in these things, that our freedom should subject us to a more grievous yoke, the commandments of men. As well may the magistrate call that common or unclean which God hath cleansed, forbidden to St. Peter, Acts x, 15;[28] as well may he loosen that which God hath straitened or straiten that which God hath loosened, as he may enjoin those things in religion which God hath left free, and lay on that yoke which God hath taken off. For he hath not only given us this gift as a special privilege and excellence of the free gospel above the servile law, but strictly also hath commanded us to keep it and enjoy it: Gal. v, 13, "You are called to liberty." I Cor. vii, 23, "Be not made the servants of men." Gal. v, 14, "Stand fast therefore in the liberty wherewith Christ hath made us free; and be not entangled again with the yoke of bondage." Neither is this a mere command, but for the most part in these forecited places, accompanied with the very weightiest and inmost reasons of Christian

---

[26] Domitian, who was emperor from 81 to 96 A.D., persecuted the Christians all over the empire and (according to the *Catholic Encyclopaedia*) made participation in the feasts instituted in honor of his own divinity a test of faith in the gods of Rome.

[27] Cf. another forced interpretation of the "children of the bondwoman" and its explanation in *CG*, n. 52.

[28] Cf. *CG*, n. 232.

religion: Rom. xiv, 9, 10, "For to this end Christ both died and rose and revived, that he might be Lord both of the dead and living. But why dost thou judge thy brother?" &c. How presumest thou to be his lord, to be whose only Lord, at least in these things, Christ both died and rose and lived again? "We shall all stand before the judgment seat of Christ."

Why then dost thou not only judge, but persecute in these things for which we are to be accountable to the tribunal of Christ only, our Lord and lawgiver? I Cor. vii, 23, "Ye are bought with a price: be not made the servants of men." Some trivial price belike, and for some frivolous pretenses paid in their opinion, if bought and by him redeemed, who is God, from what was once the service of God, we shall be enthralled again and forced by men to what now is but the service of men: Gal. iv, 31, with v, 1, "We are not children of the bondwoman," &c.; "stand fast therefore," &c. Col. ii, 8 "Beware lest any man spoil you," &c., "after the rudiments of the world, and not after Christ." Solid reasons whereof are continued through the whole chapter. Verse 10, "Ye are complete in him, which is the head of all principality and power": not completed therefore or made the more religious by those ordinances of civil power from which Christ their head hath discharged us; "blotting out the handwriting of ordinances that was against us, which was contrary to us; and took it out of the way, nailing it to his cross," verse 14. Blotting out ordinances written by God himself, much more those so boldly written over again by men; ordinances which were against us, that is, against our frailty, much more those which are against our conscience. "Let no man therefore judge you in respect of," &c., verse 16; Gal. iv, 3, &c. "Even so we, when we were children, were in bondage under the rudiments of the world: but when the fulness of time was come, God sent forth his son," &c., "to redeem them that were under the law, that we might receive the adoption of sons," &c. "Wherefore thou art no more a servant, but a son," &c. "But now," &c. "how turn ye again to the weak and beggarly rudiments, whereunto ye desire again to be in bondage? Ye observe days," &c. Hence it plainly appears that if we be not

free, we are not sons, but still servants unadopted; and if we turn again to those weak and beggarly rudiments, we are not free; yea, though willingly and with a misguided conscience, we desire to be in bondage to them; how much more then if unwillingly and against our conscience?

Ill was our condition changed from legal to evangelical, and small advantage gotten by the gospel, if for the spirit of adoption to freedom promised us, we receive again the spirit of bondage to fear; if our fear, which was then servile towards God only, must be now servile in religion towards men: strange also and preposterous fear, if when and wherein it hath attained by the redemption of our Savior to be filial only towards God, it must be now servile towards the magistrate: who, by subjecting us to his punishment in these things, brings back into religion that law of terror and satisfaction belonging now only to civil crimes; and thereby in effect abolishes the gospel, by establishing again the law to a far worse yoke of servitude upon us than before. It will therefore not misbecome the meanest Christian to put in mind Christian magistrates, and so much the more freely by how much the more they desire to be thought Christian (for they will be thereby, as they ought to be in these things, the more our brethren and the less our lords), that they meddle not rashly with Christian liberty, the birthright and outward testimony of our adoption; lest while they little think it, nay, think they do God service, they themselves, like the sons of that bondwoman, be found persecuting them who are freeborn of the spirit; and by a sacrilege of not the least aggravation bereaving them of that sacred liberty which our Savior with his own blood purchased for them.

A fourth reason why the magistrate ought not to use force in religion I bring from the consideration of all those ends which he can likely pretend to the interposing of his force therein; and those hardly can be other than first the glory of God; next, either the spiritual good of them whom he forces, or the temporal punishment of their scandal to others. As for the promoting of God's glory, none, I think, will say that his glory ought to be promoted in religious things by unwarrantable means, much less by means contrary to what he hath commanded. That outward force is such, and that God's glory in the whole administration of the gospel according to his own will and counsel ought to be fulfilled by weakness, at least so refuted, not by force; or if by force, inward and spiritual, not outward and corporeal, is already proved at large. That outward force cannot tend to the good of him who is forced in religion, is unquestionable. For in religion whatever we do under the gospel, we ought to be thereof persuaded without scruple; and are justified by the faith we have, not by the work we do: Rom. xiv, 5, "Let every man be fully persuaded in his own mind." The other reason which follows necessarily is obvious, Gal. ii, 16, and in many other places of St. Paul, as the groundwork and foundation of the whole gospel, that we are "justified by the faith of Christ, and not by the works of the law." If not by the works of God's law, how then by the injunctions of man's law? Surely force cannot work persuasion, which is faith; cannot therefore justify nor pacify the conscience: and that which justifies not in the gospel, condemns; is not only not good, but sinful to do, Rom. xiv, 23, "Whatsoever is not of faith, is sin."

It concerns the magistrate then to take heed how he forces in religion conscientious men, lest by compelling them to do that whereof they cannot be persuaded, that wherein they cannot find themselves justified, but by their own consciences condemned, instead of aiming at their spiritual good, he force them to do evil; and while he thinks himself Asa, Josiah, Nehemiah, he be found Jeroboam,[29] who caused Israel to sin; and thereby draw upon his own head all those sins and shipwrecks of implicit faith and conformity, which he hath forced, and all the wounds given to those "little ones," whom to offend he will find worse one day than that violent drowning mentioned Matt. xviii, 6. Lastly, as a preface to force, it is the usual pretense that, although tender consciences shall be tolerated, yet scandals thereby given shall not be unpunished, profane and licentious men shall not be encouraged to neglect the performance of religious and holy duties by color of any law giving liberty to tender consciences. By which contrivance the way lies ready open to them hereafter, who may be so minded, to take away by little and little that liberty which Christ and his gospel, not any magistrate, hath right to give: though this kind of his giving be but to give with one hand and take away with the other, which is a deluding, not a giving.

As for scandals, if any man be offended at the conscientious liberty of another, it is a taken scandal, not a given. To heal one conscience, we must not wound another: and men must be exhorted to beware of scandals in Christian liberty not forced by the magistrate; lest while he goes about to take away the scandal, which is uncertain whether given or taken, he take away our liberty, which is the certain and the sacred gift of God, neither to be touched by him, nor to be parted with by us. None more cautious of giving scandal than St. Paul. Yet while he made himself "servant to all," that he "might gain the more," he made himself so of his own accord, was not made so by outward force, testifying at the same time that he "was free from all men," I Cor. ix, 19; and thereafter exhorts us also, Gal. v, 13, "Ye were called to liberty," &c., "but by love serve one another": then not by force.

As for that fear lest profane and licentious men should be encouraged to omit the performance of religious and holy duties, how can that care belong to the civil magistrate, especially to his force? For if profane and licentious persons must not neglect the performance of religious and holy duties, it implies that such duties they can perform, which no protestant will affirm. They who mean the outward performance, may so explain it; and it will then appear yet more plainly that such performance of religious and holy duties, especially by profane and licentious persons, is a dishonoring rather than a worshipping of God; and not only by him not required, but detested: Prov. xxi, 27, "The sacrifice of the wicked is an abomination; how much more when he bringeth it with a wicked mind?" To compel, therefore, the profane to things holy in his profaneness,

---

[29] There is a grim reminder that the king of the ten Jewish tribes, *Jeroboam,* who instituted idolatrous worship among them (I Kings xii, 26–33), came to an appropriately sad end (I Kings xiv, 20).

is all one under the gospel as to have compelled the unclean to sacrifice in his uncleanness under the law. And I add withal that to compel the licentious in his licentiousness, and the conscientious against his conscience, comes all to one: tends not to the honor of God, but to the multiplying and the aggravating of sin to them both.

We read not that Christ ever exercised force but once, and that was to drive profane ones out of his temple,[30] not to force them in; and if their being there was an offense, we find by many other scriptures that their praying there was an abomination: and yet to the Jewish law, that nation, as a servant, was obliged; but to the gospel each person is left voluntary, called only, as a son, by the preaching of the word; not to be driven in by edicts and force of arms. For if by the apostle, Rom. xii, 1, we are "beseeched as brethren by the mercies of God to present" our "bodies a living sacrifice, holy, acceptable to God, which is" our "reasonable service," or worship, then is no man to be forced by the compulsive laws of men to present his body a dead sacrifice, and so under the gospel most unholy and unacceptable, because it is his unreasonable service, that is to say, not only unwilling but unconscionable. But if profane and licentious persons may not omit the performance of holy duties, why may they not partake of holy things? Why are they prohibited the Lord's supper, since both the one and the other action may be outward; and outward performance of duty may attain at least an outward participation of benefit? The church denying them that communion of grace and thanksgiving, as it justly doth, why doth the magistrate compel them to the union of performing that which they neither truly can, being themselves unholy, and to do seemingly is both hateful to God and perhaps no less dangerous to perform holy duties irreligiously than to receive holy signs or sacraments unworthily?

All profane and licentious men, so known, can be considered but either so without the church as never yet within it, or departed thence of their own accord, or excommunicate: if never yet within the church, whom

the apostle, and so consequently the church have nought to do to judge, as he professes, I Cor. v. 12, then by what authority doth the magistrate judge; or, which is worse, compel in relation to the church? If departed of his own accord like that lost sheep, Luke xv, 4, &c., the true church, either with her own or any borrowed force, worries him not in again, but rather in all charitable manner sends after him; and if she find him, lays him gently on her shoulders, bears him, yea, bears his burdens, his errors, his infirmities any way tolerable, "so fulfilling the law of Christ," Gal. vi, 2. If excommunicate, whom the church hath bid go out, in whose name doth the magistrate compel to go in? The church, indeed, hinders none from hearing in her public congregation, for the doors are open to all: nor excommunicates to destruction, but, as much as in her lies, to a final saving. Her meaning, therefore, must needs be that as her driving out brings on no outward penalty, so no outward force or penalty of an improper and only a destructive power should drive in again her infectious sheep; therefore sent out because infectious, and not driven in but with the danger not only of the whole and sound, but also of his own utter perishing. Since force neither instructs in religion nor begets repentance or amendment of life, but, on the contrary, hardness of heart, formality, hypocrisy, and, as I said before, every way increase of sin; more and more alienates the mind from a violent religion expelling out and compelling in, and reduces it to a condition like that which the Britons complain of in our story, driven to and fro between the Picts and the sea.[31] If after excommunion he be found intractable, incurable, and will not hear the church, he becomes as one never yet within her pale, "a heathen or a publican," Matt. xviii, 17, not further to be judged, no, not by the magistrate, unless for civil causes; but left to the final sentence of that judge whose coming shall be in flames of fire: that Maranatha, I Cor. xvi, 22, than which to him so left nothing can be more dreadful, and ofttimes to him particularly nothing more speedy, that is to say, the Lord cometh: in the meanwhile delivered up to Satan, I Cor. v, 5; I Tim. i, 20, that is, from the fold of Christ and

---

[30] The reference is to Christ's driving the money-changers out of the *temple* in Jerusalem with a whip of small cords (John ii, 14–16).

[31] Cf. *Britain*, Bk. III (C.E. X, 110).

kingdom of grace to the world again, which is the kingdom of Satan; and as he was received "from darkness to light, and from the power of Satan to God," Acts xxvi, 18, so now delivered up again from light to darkness, and from God to the power of Satan; yet so as is in both places manifested, to the intent of saving him, brought sooner to contrition by spiritual than by any corporal severity. But grant it belonging any way to the magistrate, that profane and licentious persons omit not the performance of holy duties, which in them were odious to God even under the law, much more now under the gospel; yet ought his care both as a magistrate and a Christian to be much more that conscience be not inwardly violated than that license in these things be made outwardly conformable: since his part is undoubtedly as a Christian, which puts him upon this office much more than as a magistrate, in all respects to have more care of the conscientious than of the profane; and not for their sakes to take away (while they pretend to give) or to diminish the rightful liberty of religious consciences.

On these four scriptural reasons as on a firm square, this truth, the right of Christian and evangelic liberty, will stand immovable against all those pretended consequences of license and confusion which for the most part men most licentious and confused themselves, or such as whose severity would be wiser than divine wisdom, are ever aptest to object against the ways of God: as if God without them, when he gave us this liberty, knew not of the worst which these men in their arrogance pretend will follow: yet knowing all their worst, he gave us this liberty as by him judged best. As to those magistrates who think it their work to settle religion, and those ministers or others who so oft call upon them to do so, I trust that having well considered what hath been here argued, neither they will continue in that intention, nor these in that expectation from them; when they shall find that the settlement of religion belongs only to each particular church by persuasive and spiritual means within itself, and that the defense only of the church belongs to the magistrate. Had he once learned not further to concern himself with church affairs, half his labor might be spared, and the com-

mon-wealth better tended. To which end, that which I premised in the beginning, and in due place treated of more at large, I desire now concluding, that they would consider seriously what religion is; and they will find it to be, in sum, both our belief and our practice depending upon God only. That there can be no place then left for the magistrate or his force in the settlement of religion, by appointing either what we shall believe in divine things, or practise in religious (neither of which things are in the power of man either to perform himself or to enable others), I persuade me in the Christian ingenuity of all religious men, the more they examine seriously, the more they will find clearly to be true; and find how false and deceivable that common saying is, which is so much relied upon, that the Christian magistrate is *custos utriusque tabulæ*,[32] keeper of both tables, unless is meant by keeper the defender only: neither can that maxim be maintained by any proof or argument, which hath not in this discourse first or last been refuted.

For the two tables, or ten commandments, teach our duty to God and our neighbor from the love of both; give magistrates no authority to force either: they seek that from the judicial law, though on false grounds, especially in the first table, as I have shown; and both in first and second execute that authority for the most part not according to God's judicial laws but their own. As for civil crimes, and of the outward man, which all are not, no, not of those against the second table, as that of coveting; in them what power they have, they had from the beginning, long before Moses or the two tables were in being.

[32] The two tables are the moral laws of the commandments which were given to Moses on tables of stone on Mt. Sinai. Barker (*Dilemma*, p. 391) quotes Roger Williams in *The Hireling Ministry*, pp. 25–26, as denying that the magistrate has any power over opinions "savouring of impiety," though he did introduce the idea of public censorship of political thought by reserving some power over men's private opinions "savouring of incivility." Although Milton's clear distinction between the two realms of public authority over men's consciences here, and his unqualified assertion of the right of freedom of religious opinion has been challenged by Arthur Sewell in Milton's "De Doctrina Christiana," as being modified later in *CD*, there seems to be no real reason for regarding the present passage as representing anything but Milton's final opinion.

And whether they be not now as little in being to be kept by any Christian as they are two legal tables, remains yet as undecided, as it is sure they never were yet delivered to the keeping of any Christian magistrate. But of these things, perhaps, more some other time; what may serve the present hath been above discoursed sufficiently out of the scriptures: and to those produced might be added testimonies, examples, experiences of all succeeding ages to these times, asserting this doctrine: but having herein the scripture so copious and so plain, we have all that can be properly called true strength and nerve; the rest would be but pomp and encumbrance. Pomp and ostentation of reading is admired among the vulgar; but doubtless, in matters of religion, he is learnedest who is plainest. The brevity I use, not exceeding a small manual, will not therefore, I suppose, be thought the less considerable, unless with them, perhaps, who think that great books only can determine great matters. I rather choose the common rule, not to make much ado where less may serve, which in controversies, and those especially of religion, would make them less tedious, and by consequence read oftener by many more, and with more benefit.

CONSIDERATIONS
TOUCHING THE LIKELIEST MEANS
TO REMOVE HIRELINGS OUT OF THE CHURCH.

WHEREIN IS ALSO DISCOURSED
OF TITHES, CHURCH FEES, AND CHURCH-REVENUES;
WHETHER ANY MAINTENANCE OF MINISTERS CAN BE SETTLED BY LAW.

BIBLIOGRAPHICAL NOTE—*Civil Power* and its sequel, *Hirelings,* which was published in the summer of 1659, may both be regarded as contributions to the great public debate about the form which English government should take which raged from the death of Oliver Cromwell on Sept. 3, 1658, to the restoration of Charles II in May, 1660. Though *Hirelings* is far less carefully written than Milton's major contribution to that discussion, the *Way,* it is interesting as the logical and extreme development of thought about the problem of an established church supported by tithes amounting to a constitutional form of taxation. Its value as a key to the interpretation of *PR* may not be as great as Howard Schultz pleads that it is in *PMLA,* LXVII (1952), 790–808, but it is invaluable for the light that it sheds on his thinking about the final implications of the principles which he defended in *Civil Power.*

The present text is based on a microfilm of the edition of 1659 in the Houghton Library at Harvard.

TO THE PARLIAMENT OF THE COMMON-
WEALTH OF ENGLAND, WITH THE
DOMINIONS THEREOF.

Owing to your protection, supreme senate, this liberty of writing, which I have used these eighteen years on all occasions to assert the just rights and freedoms both of church and state, and so far approved as to have been trusted with the representment and defense of your actions to all Christendom against an adversary of no mean repute,[1] to whom should I address what I still publish on the same argument but to you whose magnanimous councils first opened and unbound the age from a double bondage under prelatical and regal tyranny; above our own hopes heartening us to look up at last, like men and Christians, from the slavish dejection wherein from father to son we were bred up and taught; and thereby deserving of these nations, if they be not barbarously ungrateful, to be acknowledged, next under God, the authors and best patrons of religious and civil liberty that ever these islands brought forth? The care and tuition of whose peace and safety, after a short but scandalous night of interruption, is now again by a new dawning of God's miraculous providence among us, revolved upon your shoulders. And to whom more appertain these considerations which I propound than to yourselves and the debate before you, though I trust of no difficulty, yet at present of great expectation, not whether ye will gratify, were it no more than so, but whether ye will hearken to the just petition of many thousands best affected both to religion and to this your return, or whether ye will satisfy, which you never can, the covetous pretenses and demands of insatiable hirelings, whose disaffection ye well know both to yourselves and your resolutions. That I, though among many others in this common concernment, interpose to your deliberations what my thoughts also are, your own judgment and the success thereof hath given me the confidence: which requests but this, that if I have prosperously, God so favoring me, defended the public cause of this commonwealth to foreigners, ye would not think the reason and ability, whereon ye trusted once (and repent not) your whole reputation to the world, either grown less by more maturity and longer study, or less available in English than in another tongue: but that if it sufficed some years past to convince and satisfy the unengaged of other nations in

[1] Salmasius. Cf. *Def* 2, n. 6.

856

the justice of your doings, though then held paradoxal, it may as well suffice now against weaker opposition in matters, except here in England with a spirituality of men devoted to their temporal gain, of no controversy else among protestants. Neither do I doubt, seeing daily the acceptance which they find who in their petitions venture to bring advice also and new models of a commonwealth, but that you will interpret it much more the duty of a Christian to offer what his conscience persuades him may be of moment to the freedom and better constituting of the church: since it is a deed of highest charity to help undeceive the people, and a work worthiest your authority, in all things else authors, assertors, and now recoverers of our liberty, to deliver us, the only people of all protestants left still undelivered, from the oppressions of a simonious[2] decimating clergy,[3] who shame not, against the judgment and practice of all other churches reformed, to maintain, though very weakly, their popish and oft refuted positions; not in a point of conscience, wherein they might be blameless, but in a point of covetousness and unjust claim to other men's goods; a contention foul and odious in any man, but most of all in ministers of the gospel, in whom contention, though for their own right, scarce is allowable. Till which grievances be removed and religion set free from the monopoly of hirelings, I dare affirm that no model whatsoever of a commonwealth will prove successful or undisturbed; and so persuaded, implore divine assistance on your pious counsels and proceedings to unanimity in this and all other truth.

JOHN MILTON.

CONSIDERATIONS, &c.

The former treatise, which leads in this, began with two things ever found working much mischief to the church of God and the advancement of truth, force on the one side restraining, and hire on the other side corrupting, the teachers thereof. The lat-

ter of these is by much the more dangerous: for under force, though no thank to the forcers, true religion ofttimes best thrives and flourishes: but the corruption of teachers, most commonly the effect of hire, is the very bane of truth in them who are so corrupted. Of force not to be used in matters of religion, I have already spoken;[4] and so stated matters of conscience and religion in faith and divine worship, and so severed them from blasphemy and heresy, the one being such properly as is despiteful, the other such as stands not to the rule of scripture, and so both of them not matters of religion, but rather against it, that to them who will yet use force, this only choice can be left, whether they will force them to believe, to whom it is not given from above, being not forced thereto by any principle of the gospel, which is now the only dispensation of God to all men; or whether being protestants, they will punish in those things wherein the protestant religion denies them to be judges, either in themselves infallible, or to the consciences of other men; or whether, lastly, they think fit to punish error, supposing they can be infallible that it is so, being not wilful but conscientious, and, according to the best light of him who errs, grounded on scripture: which kind of error all men religious, or but only reasonable, have thought worthier of pardon, and the growth thereof to be prevented by spiritual means and church discipline, not by civil laws and outward force, since it is God only who gives as well to believe aright as to believe at all, and by those means which he ordained sufficiently in his church to the full execution of his divine purpose in the gospel.

It remains now to speak of hire, the other evil so mischievous in religion: whereof I promised then to speak further, when I should find God disposing me and opportunity inviting. Opportunity I find now inviting and apprehend therein the concurrence of God disposing; since the maintenance of church ministers, a thing not properly belonging to the magistrate, and yet with such importunity called for and expected from him, is at present under public debate. Wherein lest anything may happen to be determined and established prejudicial

---

[2] Milton constantly called the place-hunting of the Presbyterian clergy a form of *simony*. Cf. *TKM*, n. 228.

[3] *decimating*: tithe-taking. Traditionally, people were expected to tithe or give a tenth of their income to the support of the church.

[4] I.e. in *Civil Power*. See its Bibliographical Note.

to the right and freedom of the church, or advantageous to such as may be found hirelings therein, it will be now most seasonable, and in these matters wherein every Christian hath his free suffrage, no way misbecoming Christian meekness to offer freely, without disparagement to the wisest, such advice as God shall incline him and enable him to propound: since heretofore in commonwealths of most fame for government, civil laws were not established till they had been first for certain days published to the view of all men, that whoso pleased might speak freely his opinion thereof and give in his exceptions, ere the law could pass to a full establishment. And where ought this equity to have more place than in the liberty which is inseparable from Christian religion?[5] This, I am not ignorant, will be a work unpleasing to some: but what truth is not hateful to some or other, as this, in likelihood, will be to none but hirelings. And if there be among them who hold it their duty to speak impartial truth, as the work of their ministry, though not performed without money, let them not envy others who think the same no less their duty by the general office of Christianity, to speak truth, as in all reason may be thought, more impartially and unsuspectedly without money.

Hire of itself is neither a thing unlawful, nor a word of any evil note, signifying no more than a due recompense or reward; as when our Savior saith, "The laborer is worthy of his hire."[6] That which makes it so dangerous in the church, and properly makes the *hireling,* a word always of evil signification, is either the excess thereof, or the undue manner of giving and taking it. What harm the excess thereof brought to the church, perhaps was not found by experience till the days of Constantine;[7] who

out of his zeal thinking he could be never too liberally a nursing father of the church, might be not unfitly said to have either overlaid it or choked it in the nursing. Which was foretold, as is recorded in ecclesiastical traditions, by a voice heard from heaven on the very day that those great donations and church revenues were given, crying aloud, "This day is poison poured into the church." Which the event soon after verified as appears by another no less ancient observation, "That religion brought forth wealth, and the daughter devoured the mother." But long ere wealth came into the church, so soon as any gain appeared in religion, hirelings were apparent; drawn in long before by the very scent thereof. Judas therefore, the first hireling, for want of present hire answerable to his coveting, from the small number or the meanness of such as then were the religious, sold the religion itself with the founder thereof, his master. Simon Magus[8] the next, in hope only that preaching and the gifts of the Holy Ghost would prove gainful, offered beforehand a sum of money to obtain them. Not long after, as the apostle foretold, hirelings like wolves came in by herds: Acts xx, 29, "For I know this, that after my departing shall grievous wolves enter in among you, not sparing the flock." Tit. i, 11, "Teaching things which they ought not, for filthy lucre's sake." II Pet, ii, 3, "And through covetousness shall they with feigned words make merchandise of you." Yet they taught not false doctrine only, but seeming piety: I Tim. vi, 5, "Supposing that gain is godliness." Neither came they in of themselves only, but invited ofttimes by a corrupt audience: II Tim. iv, 3, "For the time will come when they will not endure sound doctrine, but after their own lusts they will heap to themselves teachers, hav-

---

[5] Cf. *CG,* n. 48.

[6] Luke x, 7.

[7] This passage on the evil effect of the endowment of the Church by the Emperor *Constantine* recalls the very much longer one in *Of Reformation,* which pivots around the lines which Milton quotes from Dante's *Inferno* xx, 115–17:

Ah Constantine, of how much ill was cause
Not thy conversion, but those rich domains
That the first wealthy Pope receiv'd of thee.

The passage is excellently annotated by Don Wolfe and William Alfred in the *Complete Prose Works of John Milton* (Yale University Press, 1953), Vol. I, 554–61. Milton seems to take the tradition

of Constantine's endowment of the Church with Rome and the entire Western Empire as its eternal possession more seriously than Lorenzo Valla did in his famous attack upon its historicity, but his language here almost echoes the description of Constantine's offer as poison for the Church in the refusal of the gift which Valla put into the mouth of Pope Sylvester I. *La Donation de Constantin,* par Laurent Valla, traduit en Français par Alcide Bonneau (Paris, 1879), p. 105. On the preceding page Valla anticipates Milton's comparison of papal acceptance of the emperor's wealth to Judas' acceptance of the price of his betrayal of Christ.

[8] Cf. *TKM,* n. 228.

ing itching ears:" and they on the other side, as fast heaping to themselves disciples, Acts xx, 30, doubtless had as itching palms: II Pet. ii, 15, "Following the way of Balaam, the son of Bosor, who loved the wages of unrighteousness." Jude 11, "They ran greedily after the error of Balaam for reward." Thus we see that not only the excess of hire in wealthiest times, but also the undue and vicious taking or giving it, though but small or mean, as in the primitive times, gave to hirelings occasion, though not intended, yet sufficient, to creep at first into the church. Which argues also the difficulty, or rather the impossibility, to remove them quite, unless every minister were, as St. Paul, contented to preach gratis;[9] but few such are to be found. As therefore we cannot justly take away all hire in the church, because we cannot otherwise quite remove all hirelings, so are we not, for the impossibility of removing them all, to use therefore no endeavor that fewest may come in; but rather, in regard the evil, do what we can, will always be incumbent and unavoidable, to use our utmost diligence how it may be least dangerous: which will be likeliest effected, if we consider, first, what recompense God hath ordained should be given to ministers of the church (for that a recompense ought to be given them, and may by them justly be received, our Savior himself from the very light of reason and of equity hath declared, Luke x, 7, "The laborer is worthy of his hire"); next, by whom; and lastly, in what manner.

What recompense ought to be given to church ministers, God hath answerably ordained according to that difference which he hath manifestly put between those his two great dispensations, the law and the gospel. Under the law he gave them tithes; under the gospel, having left all things in his church to charity and Christian freedom, he hath given them only what is justly given them. That, as well under the gospel as under the law, say our English divines, and they only of all protestants, is tithes; and they say true, if any man be so minded to give them of his own the tenth or twentieth: but that the law therefore of

tithes is in force under the gospel, all other protestant divines, though equally concerned, yet constantly deny. For although hire to the laborer be of moral and perpetual right, yet that special kind of hire, the tenth, can be of no right or necessity but to that special labor for which God ordained it.[10] That special labor was the Levitical and ceremonial service of the tabernacle, Num. xviii, 21, 31, which is now abolished: the right therefore of that special hire must needs be withal abolished, as being also ceremonial. That tithes were ceremonial, is plain, not being given to the Levites till they had been first offered a heave-offering to the Lord, verses 24, 28. He then who by that law brings tithes into the gospel, of necessity brings in withal a sacrifice and an altar; without which tithes by that law were unsanctified and polluted, verse 32, and therefore never thought on in the first Christian times, till ceremonies, altars, and oblations, by an ancienter corruption, were brought back long before.

And yet the Jews, ever since their temple was destroyed, though they have rabbis and teachers of their law, yet pay no tithes, as having no Levites to whom, no temple where to pay them, no altar whereon to hallow them; which argues that the Jews themselves never thought tithes moral, but ceremonial only. That Christians therefore should take them up when Jews have laid them down, must needs be very absurd and preposterous. Next, it is as clear in the same chapter that the priests and Levites had not tithes for their labor only in the tabernacle, but in regard they were to have no other part nor inheritance in the land, verses 20, 24, and by that means for a tenth, lost a twelfth. But our Levites, undergo-

---

[9] Milton had in mind the account of Paul's self-support as a tent-maker in Acts xviii, 1–4, and his own profession in I Cor. ix, 17, that his preaching was its own reward.

[10] In the opening chapter of William Prynne's *A Gospel Plea* (*Interwoven with a Rational and Legal) for the Lawfulnes & Continuance of the Ancient Settled Maintenance and Tithes Of the Ministers of the Gospel* (1653) a strong case is made on the basis of John vi, 30–38, for the payment of hire to the laborer. The argument runs from p. 5 to p. 15, pleading that, "They which preach the Gospel should live of the Gospel" (I Cor. ix, 14) and that "Learned Ministers are at great charges to furnish themselves with Bookes and Libraries," etc. The general tone of Prynne's work is hectoring and violent, for he insisted that all works questioning the right of the clergy to tithes were "*clamorous cavils* and false *absurd Allegations* of Sacrilegious, Covetous, Impious, Violent, Unreasonable, Brutish men" (p. 2).

ing no such law of deprivement, can have no right to any such compensation: nay, if by this law they will have tithes, can have no inheritance of land, but forfeit what they have. Besides this, tithes were of two sorts, those of every year and those of every third year: of the former, everyone that brought his tithes was to eat his share: Deut. xiv, 23, "Thou shalt eat before the Lord thy God, in the place which he shall choose to place his name there, the tithe of thy corn, of thy wine, and of thine oil," &c. Nay, though he could not bring his tithe in kind, by reason of his distant dwelling from the tabernacle or temple, but was thereby forced to turn it into money, he was to bestow that money on whatsoever pleased him, oxen, sheep, wine, or strong drink; and to eat and drink thereof there before the Lord, both he and his household, verses 24, 25, 26. As for the tithes of every third year, they were not given only to the Levite, but to the stranger, the fatherless, and the widow, verses 28, 29, and chapter xxvi, 12, 13. So that ours, if they will have tithes, must admit of these sharers with them. Nay, these tithes were not paid in at all to the Levite, but the Levite himself was to come with those his fellow guests, and eat his share of them only at his house who provided them; and this not in regard of his ministerial office, but because he had no part nor inheritance in the land. Lastly, the priests and Levites, a tribe, were of a far different constitution from this of our ministers under the gospel: in them were orders and degrees both by family, dignity, and office, mainly distinguished; the high priest, his brethren and his sons, to whom the Levites themselves paid tithes, and of the best, were eminently superior, Num. xviii, 28, 29.

No protestant, I suppose, will liken one of our ministers to a high priest, but rather to a common Levite. Unless then, to keep their tithes, they mean to bring back again bishops, archbishops, and the whole gang of prelatry, to whom will they themselves pay tithes, as by that law it was a sin to them if they did not? Verse 32. Certainly this must needs put them to a deep demur, while the desire of holding fast their tithes without sin may tempt them to bring back again bishops, as the likeness of that hierarchy that should receive tithes from them, and the desire to pay none may advise them

to keep out of the church all orders above them. But if we have to do at present, as I suppose we have, with true reformed protestants, not with papists or prelates, it will not be denied that in the gospel there are but two ministerial degrees, presbyters and deacons;[11] which if they contend to have any succession, reference, or conformity with those two degrees under the law, priests and Levites, it must needs be such whereby our presbyters or ministers may be answerable to priests, and our deacons to Levites; by which rule of proportion it will follow that we must pay our tithes to the deacons only, and they only to the ministers. But if it be truer yet, that the priesthood of Aaron typified a better reality, I Pet. ii, 5, signifying the Christian true and "holy priesthood, to offer up spiritual sacrifice," it follows hence that we are now justly exempt from paying tithes to any who claim from Aaron, since that priesthood is in us now real, which in him was but a shadow. Seeing then by all this which has been shown that the law of tithes is partly ceremonial, as the work was for which they were given, partly judicial, not of common, but of particular right to the tribe of Levi, nor to them alone, but to the owner also and his household at the time of their offering, and every three years to the stranger, the fatherless, and the widow, their appointed sharers, and that they were a tribe of priests and deacons improperly compared to the constitution of our ministry, and the tithes given by that people to those deacons only; it follows that our ministers at this day, being neither priests nor Levites, nor fitly answering to either of them, can have no just title or pretense to tithes by any consequence drawn from the law of Moses. But they think they have yet a better plea in the example of Melchisedec,[12] who took tithes of Abram ere the

11 Cf. the denial of any distinction between priests and bishops in *CG*, notes 8 and 34. The stoutest challenger of the claims of the English bishops had been William Prynne in his *A Catalogue of such Testimonies in all Ages as Plainly evidence Bishops and Presbyters to be both one, equall, and the same in Jurisdiction and Office* (1641).

12 The simple statement in Gen. xiv, 20, that in return for the Hospitality and blessing of the King of Salem, *Melchisedek*, Abraham "gave him tithes of all" the spoil taken in a recent battle, is interpreted by Prynne in *A Plea*, pp. 57–61, 80–84, and

law was given; whence they would infer tithes to be of moral right. But they ought to know or to remember that not examples, but express commands oblige our obedience to God or man: next, that whatsoever was done in religion before the law written, is not presently to be counted moral, whenas so many things were then done both ceremonial and judaically judicial that we need not doubt to conclude all times before Christ more or less under the ceremonial law. To what end served else those altars and sacrifices, that distinction of clean and unclean entering into the ark, circumcision, and the raising up of seed to the elder brother, Gen. xxxviii, 8? If these things be not moral, though before the law, how are tithes, though in the example of Abram and Melchisedec? But this instance is so far from being the just ground of a law, that after all circumstances duly weighed both from Gen. xiv and Heb. vii, it will not be allowed them so much as an example. Melchisedec, besides his priestly benediction, brought with him bread and wine sufficient to refresh Abram and his whole army; incited to do so, first, by the secret providence of God, intending him for a type of Christ and his priesthood; next, by his due thankfulness and honor to Abram, who had freed his borders of Salem from a potent enemy: Abram on the other side honors him with the tenth of all, that is to say (for he took not sure his whole estate with him to that war), of the spoils, Heb. vii, 4. Incited he also by the same secret providence, to signify as grandfather of Levi,[13] that the Levitical priesthood was excelled by the priesthood

147, as clearly providing a precedent for the payment of tithes to the English clergy. His elaborate and tortured reasoning gets a hardly less elaborate answer from Milton in the pages which now follow.

[13] Abraham was, of course, the great grandfather of Levi. Milton's loose use of the word "grandfather" does not affect his criticism of Prynne's argument. Prynne had made the most that he could of St. Paul's comparison of Melchisedek, who was a priest as well as a king, and resembled Christ, who "abideth a priest continually" (Heb. vii, 3). St. Paul then goes on, in a way which is really irrelevant to Prynne's reasoning, to observe that Christ, who is greater than Melchisedek, accepts tithes in heaven of a kind of which "the sons of Levi" had a mere type when they "had a commandment to take of the people . . . according to the law, that is, of their brethren, though they come out of the loins of Abraham."

of Christ. For the giving of a tenth declared, it seems, in those countries and times, him the greater who received it. That which next incited him was partly his gratitude to requite the present, partly his reverence to the person and his benediction: to his person, as a king and priest, greater therefore than Abram, who was a priest also, but not a king. And who unhired will be so hardy as to say that Abram at any other time ever paid him tithes, either before or after; or had then, but for this accidental meeting and obligement; or that else Melchisedec had demanded or exacted them, or took them otherwise than as the voluntary gift of Abram? But our ministers, though neither priests nor kings more than any other Christian, greater in their own esteem than Abraham and all his seed, for the verbal labor of a seventh day's preachment, not bringing, like Melchisedec, bread or wine at their own cost, would not take only at the willing hand of liberality or gratitude, but require and exact as due, the tenth, not of spoils, but of our whole estates and labors; nor once, but yearly. We then it seems, by the example of Abram, must pay tithes to these *Melchisedecs:* but what if the person of Abram can either no way represent us, or will oblige the ministers to pay tithes no less than other men? Abram had not only a priest in his loins, but was himself a priest, and gave tithes to Melchisedec either as grandfather of Levi, or as father of the faithful. If as grandfather (though he understood it not) of Levi, he obliged not us, but Levi only, the inferior priest, by that homage (as the apostle to the Hebrews clearly enough explains) to acknowledge the greater. And they who by Melchisedec claim from Abram as Levi's grandfather, have none to seek their tithes of but the Levites, where they can find them. If Abram, as father of the faithful, paid tithes to Melchisedec, then certainly the ministers also, if they be of that number, paid in him equally with the rest. Which may induce us to believe that as both Abram and Melchisedec, so tithes also in that action typical and ceremonial, signified nothing else but that subjection which all the faithful, both ministers and people, owe to Christ, our high priest and king.

In any literal sense from this example

they never will be able to extort that the people in those days paid tithes to priests; but this only, that one priest once in his life, of spoils only and in requital partly of a liberal present, partly of a benediction, gave voluntary tithes, not to a greater priest than himself, as far as Abram could then understand, but rather to a priest and king joined in one person. They will reply perhaps that if one priest paid tithes to another, it must needs be understood that the people did no less to the priest. But I shall easily remove that necessity by remembering them that in those days was no priest, but the father, or the first-born of each family; and by consequence no people to pay him tithes but his own children and servants, who had not wherewithal to pay him but of his own. Yet grant that the people then paid tithes, there will not yet be the like reason to enjoin us—they being then under ceremonies, a mere laity, we now under Christ, a royal priesthood, I Pet. ii, 9, as we are coheirs, kings and priests with him, a priest for ever after the order, or manner, of Melchisedec. As therefore Abram paid tithes to Melchisedec because Levi was in him, so we ought to pay none because the true Melchisedec is in us and we in him who can pay to none greater and hath freed us by our union with himself from all compulsive tributes and taxes in his church. Neither doth the collateral place, Heb. vii, make other use of this story than to prove Christ, personated by Melchisedec, a greater priest than Aaron: verse 4, "Now consider how great this man was," &c.; and proves not in the least manner that tithes be of any right to ministers, but the contrary: first, the Levites had "a commandment to take tithes of the people according to the law, that is, of their brethren, though they come out of the loins of Abraham, verse 5. The commandment then was, it seems, to take the tithes of the Jews only and according to the law. That law changing of necessity with the priesthood, no other sort of ministers, as they must needs be another sort under another priesthood, can receive that tribute of tithes which fell with that law, unless renewed by another express command and according to another law: no such law is extant. Next, Melchisedec not as a minister, but as Christ himself in person, blessed "Abraham," who "had the promises," verse 6, and

in him blessed all, both ministers and people, both of the law and gospel: that blessing declared him greater and the better than whom he blessed, verse 7, receiving tithes from them all, not as a maintenance, which Melchisedec needed not, but as a sign of homage and subjection to their king and priest: whereas ministers bear not the person of Christ in his priesthood or kingship, bless not as he blesses, are not by their blessing greater than Abraham, and all the faithful with themselves included in him; cannot both give and take tithes in the same respect; cannot claim to themselves that sign of our allegiance due only to our eternal king and priest; cannot therefore derive tithes from Melchisedec.

Lastly, the eighth verse hath thus; "Here men that die receive tithes: there he received them, of whom it is witnessed that he liveth."[14] Which words intimate that as he offered himself once for us, so he received once of us in Abraham, and in that place the typical acknowledgement of our redemption: which had it been a perpetual annuity to Christ, by him claimed as his due, Levi must have paid it yearly as well as then, verse 9; and our ministers ought still, to some Melchisedec or other, as well now as they did in Abraham. But that Christ never claimed any such tenth as his annual due, much less resigned it to the ministers, his so officious receivers, without express commission or assignment, will be yet clearer as we proceed. Thus much may at length assure us that this example of Abram and Melchisedec, though I see of late they build most upon it, can so little be the ground of any law to us, that it will not so much avail them as to the authority of an example.

Of like impertinence is that example of Jacob,[15] Gen. xxviii, 22, who of his free choice, not enjoined by any law, vowed the tenth of all that God should give him; which, for aught appears to the contrary, he vowed as a thing no less indifferent before his vow than the foregoing part thereof; that the

[14] The reference is still to the seventh chapter of Hebrews.

[15] A very dogmatic contemporary application to tithes was made by Prynne of the story of *Jacob's* wrestling with the angel in honor of whose blessing at Beth-el he set up a stone there and made the vow to him: "And of all that thou shalt give me I will surely give the tenth unto thee."

stone, which he had set there for a pillar, should be God's house. And to whom vowed he this tenth but to God? Not to any priest, for we read of none to him greater than himself. And to God, no doubt but he paid what he vowed, both in the building of that Bethel, with other altars elsewhere, and the expense of his continual sacrifices, which none but he had right to offer. However, therefore, he paid his tenth, it could in no likelihood, unless by such an occasion as befell his grandfather, be to any priest.

But, say they, "All the tithe of the land, whether of the seed of the land, or of the fruit of the tree, is the Lord's, holy unto the Lord," Lev. xxvii, 30. And this before it was given to the Levites; therefore since they ceased. No question; for "the whole earth is the Lord's, and the fulness thereof," Psal. xxiv, 1; and the light of nature shows us no less: but that the tenth is his more than the rest, how know I, but as he so declares it? He declares it so here of the land of Canaan only, as by all circumstance appears; and passes, by deed of gift, this tenth to the Levite; yet so as offered to him first a heave-offering, and consecrated on his altar, Num. xviii, all which I had as little known, but by that evidence. The Levites are ceased, the gift returns to the giver. How then can we know that he hath given it to any other? Or how can these men presume to take it unoffered first to God, unconsecrated, without another clear and express donation, whereof they show no evidence or writing? Besides, he hath now alienated that holy land: who can warrantably affirm that he hath since hallowed the tenth of this land, which none but God hath power to do or can warrant?

Their[16] last proof they cite out of the gospel, which makes as little for them, Matt. xxiii, 23, where our Savior, denouncing woe to the scribes and Pharisees, who paid tithes so exactly and omitted weightier matters, tells them that these they ought to have done, that is, to have paid tithes. For our Savior spake then to those who observed

the law of Moses, which was yet not fully abrogated till the destruction of the temple. And by the way here we may observe out of their own proof that the scribes and Pharisees, though then chief teachers of the people, such at least as were not Levites, did not take tithes, but paid them: so much less covetous were the scribes and Pharisees in those worse times than ours at this day. This is so apparent to the reformed divines of other countries, that when any one of ours hath attempted in Latin to maintain this argument of tithes, though a man would think they might suffer him without opposition in a point equally tending to the advantage of all ministers, yet they forbear not to oppose him, as in a doctrine not fit to pass unopposed under the gospel. Which shows the modesty, the contentedness of those foreign pastors with the maintenance given them, their sincerity also in the truth, though less gainful, and the avarice of ours: who through the love of their old papistical tithes, consider not the weak arguments or rather conjectures and surmises, which they bring to defend them.

On the other side, although it be sufficient to have proved in general the abolishing of tithes, as part of the Judaical or ceremonial law, which is abolished all, as well that before as that after Moses, yet I shall further prove them abrogated by an express ordinance of the gospel, founded not on any type, or that municipal law of Moses, but on moral and general equity given us instead: I Cor. ix, 13, 14, "Know ye not, that they who minister about holy things, live of the things of the temple; and they which wait at the altar, are partakers with the altar? So also the Lord hath ordained, that they who preach the gospel, should live of the gospel."[17] He saith not, should live on things which were of the temple or of the altar, of which were tithes, for that had given them a clear title: but abrogating that former law of Moses, which determined what and how much, by a later ordinance of Christ, which leaves the what and how much indefinite and free, so it be sufficient to live on, he saith, "The Lord hath so ordained, that they who preach the gospel, should live of the gospel"; which hath neither temple, altar, nor sacrifice: Heb. vii, 13, "For he of whom these things are

16 Milton takes up another of Prynne's arguments, but he is thinking also of Sir Henry Spelman's *Concilia* (see n. 21 below), to which he now refers as having been opposed by many Protestant clergy on the Continent. They had always seemed to him to contrast favorably with the English clergy in this respect. Cf. *TKM*, n. 29.

17 Cf. n. 10, above.

spoken, pertaineth to another tribe, of which no man gave attendance at the altar:" his ministers therefore cannot thence have tithes. And where the Lord hath so ordained, we may find easily in more than one evangelist: Luke x, 7, 8, "In the same house remain, eating and drinking such things as they give: for the laborer is worthy of his hire," &c. "And into whatsoever city you enter, and they receive you, eat such things as are set before you." To which ordinance of Christ it may seem likeliest that the apostle refers us both here and I Tim. v, 18, where he cites this as the saying of our Savior, that "the laborer is worthy of his hire." And both by this place of Luke and that of Matt. x, 9–11, it evidently appears that our Savior ordained no certain maintenance for his apostles or ministers publicly or privately in house or city received, but that, whatever it were, which might suffice to live on: and this not commanded or proportioned by Abram or by Moses, whom he might easily have here cited, as his manner was, but declared only by a rule of common equity which proportions the hire as well to the ability of him who gives as to the labor of him who receives, and recommends him only as worthy, not invests him with a legal right. And mark whereon he grounds this his ordinance; not on a perpetual right of tithes from Melchisedec, as hirelings pretend, which he never claimed either for himself or for his ministers, but on the plain and common equity of rewarding the laborer; worthy sometimes of single, sometimes of double honor, not proportionable by tithes. And the apostle in this forecited chapter to the Corinthians, verse 11, affirms it to be no great recompense, if carnal things be reaped for spiritual sown; but to mention tithes, neglects here the fittest occasion that could be offered him, and leaves the rest free and undetermined. Certainly if Christ or his apostles had approved of tithes, they would have, either by writing or tradition, recommended them to the church: and that soon would have appeared in the practise of those primitive and the next ages. But for the first three hundred years and more, in all the ecclesiastical story I find no such doctrine or example: though error by that time had brought back again priests, altars, and obla-

tions; and in many other points of religion had miserably Judaized the church.

So that the defenders of tithes,[18] after a long pomp and tedious preparation out of heathen authors telling us that tithes were paid to Hercules and Apollo, which perhaps was imitated from the Jews, and as it were bespeaking our expectation that they will abound much more with authorities out of Christian story, have nothing of general approbation to begin with from the first three or four ages but that which abundantly serves to the confutation of their tithes; while they confess that churchmen in those ages lived merely upon freewill offerings. Neither can they say that tithes were not then paid for want of a civil magistrate to ordain them, for Christians had then also lands and might give out of them what they pleased; and yet of tithes then given we find no mention. And the first Christian emperors, who did all things as bishops advised them, supplied what was wanting to the clergy not out of tithes, which were never motioned, but out of their own imperial revenues; as is manifest in Eusebius, Theodoret, and Sozomen,[19] from Constantine to Arcadius.

[18] After quoting Grotius, On War and Peace (De Jure Belli et Pacis III, vi, 4), and Selden "at large in his History of Tithes" on the relevance of the ancient pagan practice of dedicating the tenth part of spoils in war to the gods, Prynne's Plea goes on (p. 73), in a passage deserving Milton's description of "pompous," to say in large capitals that by this "CUSTOM THE GRECIANS ALSO, WITH THE CARTHAGINIANS AND ROMANS, DECIMAM DE PRAEDA SACRIFICAVERUNT, CONSECRATED A TENTH PART OF THEIR PREY TO THEIR GODS, AS TO APOLLO, HERCULES, JOVE."

[19] Eusebius (c260–340), to whose authority as "the ancientest writer extant on church history" Milton appealed repeatedly in Of Prelatical Episcopacy and elsewhere, and Theodoret (c386–458), for whom he had less respect, both wrote Ecclesiastical Histories, as did Hermias Salamenes Sozomenus (c400–443), bringing the record down to the reign of the emperor Arcadius (died 408). It is interesting to find Sozomenus cited here in close proximity to The History of the Bohemian Persecution, From the beginning of their Conversion to Christianity in the year 894 to the year 1632 (London, 1650), as is the case in Eikon, Chap. 17. The Bohemian History was a rough translation by a group of exiles from Bohemia of a much earlier work which had been published in Prague in 1541 under the title, Kronyka (Vaclav) & Libočan. Much is made in this work of the common ground between the followers of John Hus in Bohemia and the Waldenses in Italy.

Hence those ancientest reformed churches of the Waldenses, if they rather continued not pure since the apostles, denied that tithes were to be given, or that they were ever given in the primitive church, as appears by an ancient tractate in the *Bohemian History*. Thus far hath the church been always, whether in her prime or in her ancientest reformation, from the approving of tithes: nor without reason; for they might easily perceive that tithes were fitted to the Jews only, a national church of many incomplete synagogues, uniting the accomplishment of divine worship in one temple; and the Levites there had their tithes paid where they did their bodily work; to which a particular tribe was set apart by divine appointment, not by the people's election: but the Christian church is universal; not tied to nation, diocese, or parish, but consisting of many particular churches complete in themselves, gathered not by compulsion or the accident of dwelling nigh together, but by free consent, choosing both their particular church and their church officers. Whereas if tithes be set up, all these Christian privileges will be disturbed and soon lost, and with them Christian liberty.

The first authority which our adversaries bring, after those fabulous apostolic canons which they dare not insist upon, is a provincial council held at Cullen, where they voted tithes to be "God's rent," in the year 356;[20] at the same time perhaps when the three kings reigned there, and of like authority. For to what purpose do they bring these trivial testimonies, by which they might as well prove altars, candles at noon, and the greatest part of those superstitions fetched from paganism or Jewism, which the papist, inveigled by this fond argument of antiquity, retains to this day? To what purpose those decrees of I know not what bishops, to a Parliament and people who have thrown out both bishops and altars, and promised all reformation by the word of God? And that altars brought tithes hither, as one corruption begot another, is evident by one of those

questions which the monk Austin propounded to the pope, "concerning those things, which by offerings of the faithful came to the altar," as Beda[21] writes, Book 1, Chapter 27. If then by these testimonies we must have tithes continued, we must again have altars. Of fathers, by custom so called, they quote Ambrose, Augustin, and some other ceremonial doctors of the same leaven: whose assertion without pertinent scripture, no reformed church can admit; and what they vouch is founded on the law of Moses, with which, everywhere pitifully mistaken, they again incorporate the gospel; as did the rest also of those titular fathers, perhaps an age or two before them, by many rites and ceremonies, both Jewish and heathenish, introduced; whereby thinking to gain all, they lost all: and instead of winning Jews and pagans to be Christians, by too much condescending they turned Christians into Jews and pagans. To heap such unconvincing citations as these in religion, whereof the scripture only is our rule, argues not much learning nor judgment but the lost labor of much unprofitable reading. And yet a late hot querist[22] for tithes, whom ye may know by his wits lying ever beside him in the margin, to be ever beside his wits in the text, a fierce reformer once, now rankled with a contrary heat, would send us back, very reformedly indeed, to learn reformation from Tyndarus and Rebuffus, two canonical promoters. They produce next the ancient constitutions of this land, Saxon

---

[20] Milton doubts clerical claims that a council authorized tithes at Cologne in 346 and that the Cathedral there possessed relics of the three kings or "wise men from the east" who visited the infant Jesus (Matt. ii, 1).

[21] In the translation of the Venerable *Bede's The History of the Church of England* by Thomas Stapleton (Antwerp, 1565), p. 56, Milton found the passage to which he refers. He was probably interested in the answer which the question of the founder of English Christianity drew from Gregory; who ordered that "all maner oblation that are geven be divided into iiii portions. And the one thereof geven unto the bishop towards his hospitalitie, thother to the clergy, the third to the poore, the fourth to the reparation of the churches."

[22] Again the *querist* is Prynne, who on p. 145 of *A Plea* quotes Spelman's *Concilia*, p. 396, as his authority for his point about Athelstan's edict in 928. In *Ten Considerable Queries about Tithes* (1659), p. 3, among other works defending tithes, he quoted Tyndarus and Rebuffus "in their Treatises *de Decimis*." Alfanus Tindarus was the author of a hardly relevant *Tractatus de materia compensationum*, which was published at Siena in 1493. The still less relevant *Brevis caeterum utilis tractatus de decimis tam feudalibus quam aliis* of Pierre Rebuffus was published at Venice in 1585.

laws, edicts of kings and their councils, from Athelstan,[23] in the year 928, that tithes by statute were paid: and might produce from Ina,[24] above 200 years before, that Romescot or Peter's penny was by as good statute law paid to the pope from 725, and almost as long continued. And who knows not that this law of tithes was enacted by those kings and barons upon the opinion they had of their divine right? As the very words import of Edward the Confessor, in the close of that law: "For so blessed Austin preached and taught," meaning the monk who first brought the Romish religion into England from Gregory the pope. And by the way I add that by these laws, imitating the law of Moses, the third part of tithes only was the priest's due; the other two were appointed for the poor, and to adorn or repair churches; as the canons of Ecbert and Elfric witness. *Concil. Brit.* If then these laws were founded upon the opinion of divine authority, and that authority be found mistaken and erroneous, as hath been fully manifested, it follows that these laws fall of themselves with their false foundation.

But with what face or conscience can they allege Moses or these laws for tithes, as they now enjoy or exact them? Whereof Moses ordains the owner, as we heard before, the stranger, the fatherless, and the widow,[25] partakers with the Levite; and these fathers which they cite, and these though Romish rather than English laws, allotted both to priest and bishop the third part only. But these our protestant, these our new reformed English presbyterian divines, against their own cited authors and to the shame of their pretended reformation, would engross to themselves all tithes by statute; and, supported more by their wilful obstinacy and desire of filthy lucre than by these both insufficient and impertinent authorities, would persuade a Christian magistracy and parliament, whom we trust God hath restored for a happier

reformation, to impose upon us a Judaical ceremonial law, and yet from that law to be more irregular and unwarrantable, more complying with a covetous clergy, than any of those popish kings and parliaments alleged. Another shift they have to plead, that tithes may be moral as well as the sabbath, a tenth of fruits as well as a seventh of days. I answer that the prelates who urge this argument have least reason to use it, denying morality in the sabbath and therein better agreeing with reformed churches abroad than the rest of our divines. As therefore the seventh day is not moral, but a convenient recourse of worship in fit season, whether seventh or other number, so neither is the tenth of our goods, but only a convenient subsistence morally due to ministers.

The last and lowest sort of their arguments, that men purchased not their tithe with their land, and such like pettifoggery, I omit, as refuted sufficiently by others. I omit also their violent and irreligious exactions, related no less credibly: their seizing of pots and pans from the poor, who have as good right to tithes as they; from some, the very beds; their suing and imprisoning, worse than when the canon law was in force; worse than when those wicked sons of Eli were priests, whose manner was thus to seize their pretended priestly due by force; I Sam. ii, 12, &c., "Whereby men abhorred the offering of the Lord." And it may be feared that many will as much abhor the gospel, if such violence as this be suffered in her ministers, and in that which they also pretend to be the offering of the Lord. For those sons of Belial within some limits made seizure of what they knew was their own by an undoubted law; but these, from whom there is no sanctuary, seize out of men's grounds, out of men's houses, their other goods of double, sometimes of treble value, for that which, did not covetousness and rapine blind them, they know to be not their own by the gospel which they preach. Of some more tolerable than these, thus severely God hath spoken, Isa. lvi, 11, &c., "They are greedy dogs; they all look to their own way, every one for his gain, from his quarter." With what anger then will he judge them who stand not looking, but, under color of a divine right, fetch by

[23] See Milton's account of *Ina's* laws, "the first of Saxon extant today," *Britain* (C.E. X, 178).

[24] Milton found this bit of ammunition in Spelman's *Concilia*, p. 259. Cf. n. 21 above.

[25] In Deut. x, 8 and 18, the motive for God's separation of the Tribe of Levi for priestly duties is stated as the will for "judgment of the fatherless and the widow," and love of "the stranger, in giving him food and raiment."

force that which is not their own, taking his name not in vain, but in violence? Nor content, as Gehazi[26] was, to make a cunning, but a constrained advantage of what their master bids them give freely, how can they but return smitten, worse than that sharking minister, with a spiritual leprosy? And yet they cry out sacrilege, that men will not be gulled and baffled the tenth of their estates by giving credit to frivolous pretenses of divine right. Where did God ever clearly declare to all nations, or in all lands (and none but fools part with their estates without clearest evidence, on bare supposals and presumptions of them who are the gainers thereby) that he required the tenth as due to him or his son perpetually and in all places? Where did he demand it, that we might certainly know, as in all claims of temporal right is just and reasonable? Or if demanded, where did he assign it, or by what evident conveyance to ministers? Unless they can demonstrate this by more than conjectures, their title can be no better to tithes than the title of Gehazi was to those things which by abusing his master's name he rooked from Naaman. Much less where did he command that tithes should be fetched by force, where left not under the gospel, whatever his right was, to the freewill offerings of men? Which is the greater sacrilege, to belie divine authority, to make the name of Christ accessory to violence, and, robbing him of the very honor which he aimed at in bestowing freely the gospel, to commit simony and rapine, both secular and ecclesiastical; or, on the other side, not to give up the tenth of civil right and propriety to the tricks and impostures of clergymen, contrived with all the art and argument that their bellies can invent or suggest; yet so ridiculous and presuming on the people's dullness and superstition as to think they prove the divine right of their maintenance by

Abraham paying tithes to Melchisedec, whenas Melchisedec in that passage rather gave maintenance to Abram; in whom all, both priests and ministers as well as laymen, paid tithes, not received them.

And because I affirmed above, beginning this first part of my discourse, that God hath given to ministers of the gospel that maintenance only which is justly given them, let us see a little what hath been thought of that other maintenance besides tithes, which of all protestants our English divines either only or most apparently both require and take. Those are fees for christenings, marriages, and burials: which, though whoso will may give freely, yet being not of right but of free gift, if they be exacted or established, they become unjust to them who are otherwise maintained; and of such evil note that even the *Council of Trent,* II, p. 240, makes them liable to the laws against simony who take or demand fees for the administering of any sacrament: *Che la sinodo volendo levare gli abusi introdotti,* &c.[27] And in the next page, with like severity condemns the giving or taking for a benefice, and the celebrating of marriages, christenings, and burials, for fees exacted or demanded: nor counts it less simony to sell the ground or place of burial. And in a state assembly at Orleans, 1561, it was decreed, *Che non si potesse essiger cosa alcuna,* &c., p. 429: "That nothing should be exacted for the administering of sacraments, burials, or any other spiritual function." Thus much that council of all others the most popish, and this assembly of papists, though by their own principles in bondage to the clergy, were induced, either by their own reason and shame, or by the light of reformation then shining in upon them, or rather by the known canons of many councils and synods long before, to condemn of simony spiritual fees demanded. For if the minister be maintained for his whole ministry, why should he be twice paid for any part thereof? Why should he, like a servant, seek vails[28] over and above his wages? As for christenings, either they themselves call

---

[26] After Elisha had healed Naaman the Syrian of leprosy and refused any reward, "Gehazi, the servant of Elisha, . . . followed after Naaman . . . and said, . . . My master hath sent me saying, Behold, even now there be come to me from the mount Ephraim two young men of the sons of the prophets: give them, I pray thee, a talent of silver, and two changes of garments. And Naaman said, Be content, take two talents" (II Kings v, 20–23).

[27] For the *History of the Council of Trent* and its author, Fra Paolo Sarpi, see *Areop,* n. 59. Milton quotes from the original edition of 1619: ". . . the Council wishing to alleviate the abuses which have been brought in."

[28] *vails:* gratuities, tips.

men to baptism, or men of themselves come: if ministers invite, how ill had it become John the Baptist to demand fees for his baptizing, or Christ for his christenings? Far less becomes it these now, with a greediness lower than that of tradesmen calling passengers to their shop, and yet paid beforehand, to ask again for doing that which those their founders did freely. If men of themselves come to be baptized, they are either brought by such as already pay the minister, or come to be one of his disciples and maintainers: of whom to ask a fee, as it were for entrance, is a piece of paltry craft or caution befitting none but beggarly artists.[29] Burials and marriages are so little to be any part of their gain, that they who consider well may find them to be no part of their function. At burials their attendance they allege on the corpse; all the guests do as much unhired. But their prayers at the grave; superstitiously required: yet if required, their last performance to the deceased of their own flock. But the funeral sermon: at their choice; or if not, an occasion offered them to preach out of season, which is one part of their office.

But something must be spoken in praise: if due, their duty; if undue, their corruption: a peculiar simony of our divines in England only. But the ground is broken, and especially their unrighteous possession, the chancel. To sell that will not only raise up in judgment the council of Trent against them, but will lose them the best champion of tithes, their zealous antiquary, Sir Henry Spelman;[30] who in a book written to that purpose, by many cited canons, and some even of times corruptest in the church, proves that fees exacted or demanded for sacraments, marriages, burials, and especially for interring, are wicked, accursed, simoniacal, and abominable. Yet thus is the church, for all this noise of reformation, left still unreformed, by the censure of their own synods, their own favorers; a den of thieves and robbers. As for marriages, that ministers should meddle with them as not

sanctified or legitimate without their celebration, I find no ground in scripture either of precept or example. Likeliest it is (which our Selden[31] hath well observed, II, c. 58, *Ux. Eb.*) that in imitation of heathen priests who were wont at nuptials to use many rites and ceremonies, and especially, judging it would be profitable and the increase of their authority not to be spectators only in business of such concernment to the life of man, they insinuated that marriage was not holy without their benediction, and for the better color, made it a sacrament; being of itself a civil ordinance, a household contract,[32] a thing indifferent and free to the whole race of mankind, not as religious, but as men: best, indeed, undertaken to religious ends, and, as the apostle saith, I Cor. vii, "in the Lord." Yet not therefore invalid or unholy without a minister and his pretended necessary hallowing, more than any other act, enterprise, or contract of civil life, which ought all to be done also in the Lord and to his glory. All which, no less than marriage, were by the cunning of priests heretofore, as material to their profit, transacted at the altar. Our divines deny it to be a sacrament; yet retained the celebration, till prudently a late parliament recovered the civil liberty of marriage from their encroachment, and transferred the ratifying and registering thereof from the canonical shop to the proper cognizance of civil magistrates.[33] Seeing then that God hath given to ministers under the gospel that only which is justly given them, that is to say, a due and moderate livelihood, the hire of their labor, and that the heave-offering of tithes is abolished with the altar; yea, though not abolished, yet lawless, as they enjoy them; their Melchisedecian right also trivial and groundless, and both tithes and fees, if exacted or established, unjust and scandalous: we may hope, with them removed, to remove hirelings in some good measure, whom these tempting baits, by law especially to be recovered, allure into the church.

The next thing to be considered in the

---

[29] *artists* is used in a sense approximating the modern "quick-change artist."

[30] Milton has in mind a passage quoted by *Spelman* from the Laws of Egbert; "12. Item, Ut nullus Presbyter" etc. "That no priest shall presume to perform any religious service, or baptise, or bestow any spiritual gift for any kind of price" (Concilia, I, 259).

[31] Milton refers to a passage from *John Selden's Uxor Ebraica* (*Hebrew Wife*) which he had copied long before in CB (C.E. XVIII, 151). Cf. *DDD* Book I, Chap. xiii, and II, Chap. xx.

[32] Masson notes that Milton's second marriage was civil (Life of Milton, V, 281 and 612).

[33] Milton refers to the Marriage Act of 1653.

maintenance of ministers is by whom it should be given. Wherein though the light of reason might sufficiently inform us, it will be best to consult the scripture. Gal. vi, 6, "Let him that is taught in the word, communicate, to him that teacheth, in all good things": that is to say, in all manner of gratitude, to his ability. I Cor. ix, 11, "If we have sown unto you spiritual things, is it a great matter if we reap your carnal things?" To whom therefore hath not been sown, from him wherefore should be reaped? I Tim. v, 17, "Let the elders that rule well, be counted worthy of double honor; especially they who labor in word and doctrine." By these places we see that recompense was given either by everyone in particular who had been instructed, or by them all in common, brought into the church treasury, and distributed to the ministers according to their several labors: and that was judged either by some extraordinary person, as Timothy, who by the apostle was then left evangelist at Ephesus, II Tim. iv, 5, or by some to whom the church deputed that care. This is so agreeable to reason, and so clear, that anyone may perceive what iniquity and violence hath prevailed since in the church, whereby it hath been so ordered that they also shall be compelled to recompense the parochial minister, who neither chose him for their teacher, nor have received instruction from him, as being either insufficient, or not resident, or inferior to whom they follow; wherein to bar them their choice is to violate Christian liberty. Our law books testify that before the council of Lateran, in the year 1179, and the fifth of our Henry II, or rather before a decretal Epistle of Pope Innocent the Third, about 1200, and the first of King John, "any man might have given his tithes to what spiritual person he would:" and as the Lord Coke[34] notes on that place, *Institutes* part ii, that "this decretal bound not the subjects of this realm, but as it seemed just and reasonable." The pope took his reason rightly from the above cited place, I Cor. ix, 11, but falsely supposed everyone to be instructed by his parish priest. Whether this

were then first so decreed, or rather long before, as may seem by the laws of Edgar and Canute, that tithes were to be paid, not to whom he would that paid them, but to the cathedral church or the parish priest, it imports not; since the reason which they themselves bring, built on false supposition, becomes alike infirm and absurd, that he should reap from me, who sows not to me; be the cause either his defect, or my free choice.

But here it will be readily objected, What if they who are to be instructed be not able to maintain a minister, as in many villages? I answer that the scripture shows in many places what ought to be done herein. First, I offer it to the reason of any man, whether he think the knowledge of Christian religion harder than any other art or science to attain. I suppose he will grant that it is far easier; both of itself and in regard of God's assisting spirit, not particularly promised us to the attainment of any other knowledge, but of this only: since it was preached as well to the shepherds of Bethlehem by angels, as to the Eastern wise men by that star: and our Savior declares himself anointed to preach the gospel to the poor, Luke iv, 18; then surely to their capacity. They who after him first taught it, were otherwise unlearned men: they who before Hus[35] and Luther first reformed it, were for the meanness of their condition called, "the poor men of Lyons,"[36] and in Flanders at this day, *les gueus*,[37] which is to say, beggars. Therefore are the scriptures translated into every vulgar tongue, as being held in main matters of belief and salvation, plain and easy to the poorest: and such no less than their teachers have the spirit to guide them in all truth, John xiv, 26, and xvi, 13.

Hence we may conclude, if men be not all their lifetime under a teacher to learn logic, natural philosophy, ethics, or mathematics, which are more difficult, that certainly it

---

[34] Milton's primary authority here is doubtless Sir Edward Coke's *Second Part of The Institutes of the Laws of England*, which was published first in 1642.

[35] Cf. the reference to *Hus* in *CG*, n. 119.

[36] *poor men of Lyons*: the Waldensians. Pierre Gilles calls them so in the first sentence of his *History*. See n. 41 below.

[37] *Les gueus* in Holland in the time of the Dutch wars for independence from Spain in the late sixteenth century were men whose religion often took a form much like that of resistance movements in countries recently occupied by German troops.

is not necessary to the attainment of Christian knowledge that men should sit all their life long at the feet of a pulpited divine; while he, a lollard[38] indeed over his elbow cushion, in almost the seventh part of forty or fifty years teaches them scarce half the principles of religion; and his sheep ofttimes sit the while to as little purpose of benefiting, as the sheep in their pews at Smithfield;[39] and for the most part by some simony or other bought and sold like them: or if this comparison be too low, like those women, I Tim. iii, 7, "Ever learning and never attaining;" yet not so much through their own fault as through the unskilful and immethodical teaching of their pastor, teaching here and there at random out of this or that text, as his ease or fancy, and ofttimes as his stealth, guides him.

Seeing then that Christian religion may be so easily attained, and by meanest capacities, it cannot be much difficult to find ways, both how the poor, yea, all men, may be soon taught what is to be known of Christianity, and they who teach them, recompensed. First, if ministers of their own accord, who pretend that they are called and sent to preach the gospel, those especially who have no particular flock, would imitate our Savior and his disciples, who went preaching through the villages, not only through the cities, Matt. ix, 35, Mark vi, 6, Luke xiii, 22, Acts viii, 25, and there preached to the poor as well as to the rich, looking for no recompense but in heaven: John iv, 35, 36, "Look on the fields; for they are white already to harvest: and he that reapeth, receiveth wages, and gathereth fruit unto life eternal." This was their wages. But they will soon reply, "We ourselves have not wherewithal; who shall bear the charges of our journey?" To whom it may as soon be answered that in likelihood they are not poorer than they who did thus; and if they have not the same faith which those disciples had to trust in God and the promise of Christ for their maintenance as they did, and yet intrude into the ministry without any livelihood of their own, they cast themselves into a miserable hazard or

temptation, and ofttimes into a more miserable necessity, either to starve, or to please their paymasters rather than God: and give men just cause to suspect that they came neither called nor sent from above to preach the word, but from below, by the instinct of their own hunger, to feed upon the church.

Yet grant it needful to allow them both the charges of their journey and the hire of their labor, it will belong next to the charity of richer congregations, where most commonly they abound with teachers, to send some of their number to the villages round, as the apostles from Jerusalem sent Peter and John to the city and villages of Samaria, Acts viii, 14, 25; or as the church at Jerusalem sent Barnabas to Antioch, Chap. xi, 22, and other churches joining sent Luke to travel with Paul, II Cor. viii, 19: though whether they had their charges borne by the church or no, it be not recorded. If it be objected that this itinerary preaching will not serve to plant the gospel in those places, unless they who are sent abide there some competent time, I answer that if they stay there a year or two, which was the longest time usually stayed by the apostles in one place, it may suffice to teach them who will attend and learn, all the points of religion necessary to salvation; then sorting them into several congregations of a moderate number, out of the ablest and zealousest among them to create elders, who, exercising and requiring from themselves what they have learned, (for no learning is retained without constant exercise and methodical repetition) may teach and govern the rest: and so exhorted to continue faithful and steadfast, they may securely be committed to the providence of God and the guidance of his Holy Spirit, till God may offer some opportunity to visit them again and to confirm them: which when they have done, they have done as much as the apostles were wont to do in propagating the gospel, Acts xiv, 23, "And when they had ordained them elders in every church, and had prayed with fasting, they commended them to the Lord, on whom they believed." And in the same chapter, verses 21, 22, "When they had preached the gospel to that city, and had taught many, they returned again to Lystra, and to Iconium and Antioch, confirming the souls of the dis-

[38] Milton puns on the name commonly given to followers of Wycliffe in the fourteenth century and still loosely given to Puritans in his day. The etymology and origin of the word are doubtful.

[39] *pews:* pens. *Smithfield* was London's meat market.

ciples, and exhorting them to continue in the faith." And Chap. xv, 36, "Let us go again, and visit our brethren." And verse 41, "He went through Syria and Cilicia, confirming the churches."

To these I might add other helps, which we enjoy now, to make more easy the attainment of Christian religion by the meanest: the entire scripture translated into English with plenty of notes; and somewhere or other, I trust, may be found some wholesome body of divinity, as they call it, without school terms and metaphysical notions, which have obscured rather than explained our religion, and made it seem difficult without cause. Thus taught once for all, and thus now and then visited and confirmed, in the most destitute and poorest places of the land, under the government of their own elders performing all ministerial offices among them, they may be trusted to meet and edify one another, whether in church or chapel, or, to save them the trudging of many miles thither, nearer home, though in a house or barn. For notwithstanding the gaudy superstition of some devoted still ignorantly to temples, we may be well assured that he who disdained not to be laid in a manger, disdains not to be preached in a barn; and that by such meetings as these, being indeed most apostolical and primitive, they will in a short time advance more in Christian knowledge and reformation of life than by the many years' preaching of such an incumbent, I may say, such an incubus ofttimes, as will be meanly hired to abide long in those places.

They have this left perhaps to object further; that to send thus and to maintain, though but for a year or two, ministers and teachers in several places, would prove chargeable to the churches, though in towns and cities round about. To whom again I answer that it was not thought so by them who first thus propagated the gospel, though but few in number to us and much less able to sustain the expense. Yet this expense would be much less than to hire incumbents, or rather incumbrances, for lifetime; and a great means (which is the subject of this discourse) to diminish hirelings. But be the expense less or more, if it be found burdensome to the churches, they have in this land an easy remedy in their recourse to the civil magistrate; who hath in his hands the disposal of no small revenues, left perhaps anciently to superstitious, but meant undoubtedly to good and best uses; and therefore, once made public, appliable by the present magistrate to such uses as the church, or solid reason from whomsoever, shall convince him to think best. And those uses may be, no doubt, much rather than as glebes and augmentations are now bestowed, to grant such requests as these of the churches; or to erect in greater number, all over the land, schools and competent libraries to those schools, where languages and arts may be taught free together, without the needless, unprofitable, and inconvient removing to another place. So all the land would be soon better civilized, and they who are taught freely at the public cost might have their education given them on this condition, that therewith content, they should not gad for preferment out of their own country, but continue there thankful for what they received freely, bestowing it as freely on their country, without soaring above the meanness wherein they were born.

But how they shall live when they are thus bred and dismissed, will be still the sluggish objection. To which is answered that those public foundations may be so instituted as the youth therein may be at once brought up to a competence of learning and to an honest trade; and the hours of teaching so ordered as their study may be no hindrance to their labor or other calling. This was the breeding of St. Paul, though born of no mean parents, a free citizen of the Roman empire: so little did his trade debase him that it rather enabled him to use that magnanimity of preaching the gospel through Asia and Europe at his own charges.[40] Thus those preachers among the poor Waldenses, the ancient stock of our reformation, without these helps which I speak of, bred up themselves in trades, and especially in physic and surgery, as well as in the study of scripture (which is the only true theology) that they might be no burden to the church; and by the example of Christ might cure both soul and body, through industry joining that to their ministry which he joined to his by

---

40 Cf. n. 9 above. Prynne's reply to the argument from Paul's self-support is indicated in n. 10.

gift of the spirit. Thus relates Peter Gilles[41] in his *History of the Waldenses in Piemont*. But our ministers think scorn to use a trade, and count it the reproach of this age that tradesmen preach the gospel. It were to be wished they were all tradesmen; they would not then so many of them, for want of another trade, make a trade of their preaching: and yet they clamor that tradesmen preach; and yet they preach, while they themselves are the worst tradesmen of all.

As for church endowments and possessions, I meet with none considerable before Constantine, but the houses and gardens where they met and their places of burial; and I persuade me that from them the ancient Waldenses, whom deservedly I cite so often, held, "That to endow churches is an evil thing"; and that the church then fell off and turned whore, sitting on that beast in the Revelation, when under pope Sylvester she received those temporal donations.[42] So the forecited tractate of their doctrine testifies. This also their own traditions of that heavenly voice witnessed, and some of the ancient fathers then living foresaw and deplored. And, indeed, how could these endowments thrive better with the church, being unjustly taken by those emperors, without suffrage of the people, out of the tributes and public lands of each city, whereby the people became liable to be oppressed with other taxes. Being therefore given for the most part by kings and other public persons, and so likeliest out of the public, and if without the people's consent, unjustly, however to public ends of much concernment to the good or evil of a commonwealth, and in that regard made public though given by private persons, or, which is worse, given, as the clergy then persuaded men, for their souls' health, a pious gift; but as the truth was, ofttimes a bribe to God or to Christ for absolution, as they were then taught, from murders, adulteries, and other heinous crimes; what shall be found heretofore given by kings or princes out of the public, may justly by the magistrate be recalled and reappropriated to the civil revenue: what by private or public persons out of their own, the price of blood or lust, or to some such purgatorious and superstitious uses, not only may, but ought to be taken off from Christ, as a foul dishonor laid upon him, or not impiously given, nor in particular to any one, but in general to the church's good, may be converted to that use which shall be judged tending more directly to that general end.

Thus did the princes and cities of Germany in the first reformation; and defended their so doing by many reasons, as are set down at large in Sleidan,[43] Book vi, anno 1526, and Book xi, anno 1537, and Book xiii, anno 1540. But that the magistrate either out of that church revenue which remains yet in his hand, or establishing any other maintenance instead of tithe, should take into his own power the stipendiary maintenance of church ministers, or compel it by law, can stand neither with the people's right, nor with Christian liberty, but would suspend the church wholly upon the state and turn her ministers into state pensioners. And for the magistrate in person of a nursing father to make the church his mere ward, as always in minority, the church to whom he ought as a magistrate, Isa. xlix, 23, "to bow down with his face toward the earth, and lick up the dust of her feet"; her to subject to his political drifts or conceived opinions by mastering her revenue; and so by his examinant committees to circumscribe her free election of ministers, is neither just nor pious; no honor done to the church, but a plain dishonor: and upon her whose only head is in heaven, yea, upon him who is her only head, sets another in effect, and, which is most monstrous, a human on a heavenly, a carnal on a spiritual, a political head on an ecclesiastical body; which at length by such heterogeneal, such incestuous conjunction, transforms her ofttimes into a beast of many

---

[41] Milton was familiar with the *Histoire Ecclesiastique des eglises reformées recuilles en quelques Valées de Piedmont, & Circonvoisines, autrefois appelées Eglises Vaudoises* (Geneva, 1644) by *Pierre Gilles*, and his rather idyllic conception of the Waldensians was in part colored by Gilles' statement (pp. 15–16) that a part of the training of every Waldensian clergyman was in a trade or profession such as medicine to enable him to be useful to his congregation and not to be a financial burden to them.

[42] Cf. the note on the *donation* of Constantine (n. 7) above.

[43] For *Sleidan* and his account of the reply of the princes of the League of Schmalkald to the ambassador of the emperor Charles V see *TKM*, n. 120.

heads and many horns.[44] For if the church be of all societies the holiest on earth, and so to be reverenced by the magistrate, not to trust her with her own belief and integrity, and therefore not with the keeping, at least with the disposing, of what revenue should be found justly and lawfully her own, is to count the church not a holy congregation, but a pack of giddy or dishonest persons, to be ruled by civil power in sacred affairs.

But to proceed further in the truth yet more freely, seeing the Christian church is not national, but consisting of many particular congregations, subject to many changes, as well through civil accidents as through schism and various opinions not to be decided by any outward judge, being matters of conscience, whereby these pretended church revenues, as they have been ever, so are like to continue endless matter of dissension both between the church and magistrate, and the churches among themselves, there will be found no better remedy to these evils, otherwise incurable, than by the incorruptest council of those Waldenses, or first reformers, to remove them as a pest, an apple of discord in the church (for what else can be the effect of riches and the snare of money in religion?) and to convert them to those more profitable uses above expressed, or other such as shall be judged most necessary; considering that the church of Christ was founded in poverty rather than in revenues, stood purest and prospered best without them, received them unlawfully from them who both erroneously and unjustly, sometimes impiously, gave them, and so justly was ensnared and corrupted by them. And lest it be thought that, these revenues withdrawn and better employed, the magistrate ought instead to settle by statute some maintenance of ministers, let this be considered first, that it concerns every man's conscience to what religion he contributes; and that the civil magistrate is entrusted with civil rights only, not with conscience, which can have no deputy or representer of itself but one of the same mind: next, that what each man gives to the minister, he gives either as to God, or as to his teacher: if as to God, no civil power can justly consecrate to religious uses any part either of civil revenue,

which is the people's and must save them from other taxes, or of any man's propriety, but God by special command, as he did by Moses,[45] or the owner himself by voluntary intention and the persuasion of his giving it to God.

Forced consecrations out of another man's estate are no better than forced vows, hateful to God who "loves a cheerful giver;" but much more hateful, wrung out of men's purses to maintain a disapproved ministry against their conscience; however unholy, infamous, and dishonorable to his ministers and the free gospel, maintained in such unworthy manner as by violence and extortion. If he give it as to his teacher, what justice or equity compels him to pay for learning that religion which leaves freely to his choice whether he will learn it or no, whether of this teacher or another, and especially to pay for what he never learned, or approves not; whereby, besides the wound of his conscience, he becomes the less able to recompense his true teacher? Thus far hath been inquired by whom church ministers ought to be maintained, and hath been proved most natural, most equal and agreeable with scripture, to be by them who receive their teaching; and by whom, if they be unable. Which ways well observed can discourage none but hirelings, and will much lessen their number in the church.

It remains lastly to consider in what manner God hath ordained that recompense be given to ministers of the gospel: and by all scripture it will appear that he hath given it them not by civil law and freehold, as they claim, but by the benevolence and free gratitude of such as receive them: Luke x, 7, 8, "Eating and drinking such things as they give you. If they receive you, eat such things as are set before you." Matt. x, 7, 8, "As ye go, preach, saying, The kingdom of God is at hand," &c. "Freely ye have received, freely give." If God have ordained ministers to preach freely, whether they receive recompense or not, then certainly he hath forbid both them to compel it and others to compel it for them. But freely given, he accounts it as given to himself: Phil. iv, 16–18, "Ye sent once and again to my necessity. Not because I desire a gift;

---

[44] Again an allusion to the *beast* of Rev. xiii.

[45] The law of *Moses* authorized the Levites to take tithes of the Hebrews. Cf. n. 13 above.

but I desire fruit that may abound to your account. Having received of Epaphroditus the things which were sent from you, an odor of sweet smell, a sacrifice acceptable, well pleasing to God"; which cannot be from force or unwillingness. The same is said of alms: Heb. xiii, 16, "To do good and to communicate, forget not; for with such sacrifices God is well pleased." Whence the primitive church thought it no shame to receive all their maintenance as the alms of their auditors. Which they who defend tithes, as if it made for their cause, whenas it utterly confutes them, omit not to set down at large; proving to our hands out of Origen, Tertullian, Cyprian,[46] and others, that the clergy lived at first upon the mere benevolence of their hearers; who gave what they gave, not to the clergy, but to the church; out of which the clergy had their portions given them in baskets, and were thence called *sportularii, basket-clerks:* that their portion was a very mean allowance, only for a bare livelihood; according to those precepts of our Savior, Matt. x, 7, &c., the rest was distributed to the poor. They cite also out of Prosper, the disciple of St. Austin, that such of the clergy as had means of their own might not without sin partake of church maintenance; not receiving thereby food which they abound with, but feeding on the sins of other men: that the Holy Ghost saith of such clergymen, they eat the sins of my people; and that a council at Antioch, in the year 340, suffered not either priest or bishop to live on church maintenance without necessity. Thus far tithers themselves have contributed to their own confutation by confessing that the church lived primitively on alms. And I add that about the year 359, Constantius the emperor having summoned a general council of bishops to Ariminum in Italy, and provided for their subsistence there, the British and French bishops judging it not decent to live on the public, chose rather to be at their own charges. Three only out of Britain, constrained through want, yet refusing offered

assistance from the rest, accepted the emperor's provision; judging it more convenient to subsist by public than by private sustenance. Whence we may conclude that bishops then in this island had their livelihood only from benevolence; in which regard this relater, Sulpitius Severus, a good author of the same time, highly praises them. And the Waldenses, our first reformers, both from the scripture and these primitive examples, maintained those among them who bore the office of ministers, by alms only. Take their very words from the history written of them in French, part III, Book ii, Chap. 2: *La nourriture et ce de quoy nous sommes couverts,* &c. "Our food and clothing is sufficiently administered and given to us by way of gratuity and alms, by the good people whom we teach."

If then by alms and benevolence, not by legal force, not by tenure of freehold or copyhold: for alms, though just, cannot be compelled; and benevolence forced is malevolence rather, violent and inconsistent with the gospel; and declares him no true minister thereof, but a rapacious hireling rather, who by force receiving it, eats the bread of violence and exaction, no holy or just livelihood, no, not civilly counted honest; much less beseeming such a spiritual ministry. But, say they, our maintenance is our due, tithes the right of Christ, unseparable from the priest, nowhere repealed; if then, not otherwise to be had, by law to be recovered: for though Paul were pleased to forego his due and not to use his power, I Cor. ix, 12, yet he had a power, verse 4, and bound not others. I answer first, because I see them still so loth to unlearn their decimal arithmetic, and still grasp their tithes as inseparable from a priest, that ministers of the gospel are not priests; and therefore separated from tithes by their own exclusion, being neither called priests in the New Testament, nor of any order known in scripture: not of Melchisedec, proper to Christ only; not of Aaron, as they themselves will confess; and the third priesthood only remaining, is common to all the faithful. But they are ministers of our high priest. True, but not of his priesthood, as the Levites were to Aaron; for he performs that whole office himself incommunicably. Yet tithes remain, say they, still unreleased, the due of Christ; and to whom payable,

---

[46] In this account of the independence of the British and French bishops at the Council of Arminum in 359 A.D. Milton closely follows Sulpicius Severus in the second book of his *Historia Sacra,* which was published at Geneva in 1644. In Sulpicius' *Opera* (Leipsic, 1709) the passage occurs on pp. 267-68.

but to his ministers? I say again that no man can so understand them, unless Christ in some place or other so claim them. That example of Abram argues nothing but his voluntary act; honor once only done, but on what consideration, whether to a priest or to a king, whether due the honor, arbitrary that kind of honor or not, will after all contending be left still in mere conjecture: which must not be permitted in the claim of such a needy and subtle spiritual corporation pretending by divine right to the tenth of all other men's estates; nor can it be allowed by wise men or the verdict of common law.

And the tenth part, though once declared holy, is declared now to be no holier than the other nine, by that command to Peter, Acts x, 15, 28, whereby all distinction of holy and unholy is removed from all things. Tithes therefore, though claimed, and holy under the law, yet are now released and quit both by that command to Peter, and by this to all ministers, above cited, Luke x: "Eating and drinking such things as they give you": made holy now by their free gift only. And therefore St. Paul, I Cor. ix, 4, asserts his power indeed; but of what? not of tithes, but "to eat and drink such things as are given" in reference to this command: which he calls not holy things or things of the gospel, as if the gospel had any consecrated things in answer to things of the temple, verse 13; but he calls them "your carnal things," verse 11, without changing their property. And what power had he? Not the power of force, but of conscience only, whereby he might lawfully and without scruple live on the gospel; receiving what was given him, as the recompense of his labor. For if Christ the Master hath professed his kingdom to be not of this world,[47] it suits not with that profession, either in him or his ministers, to claim temporal right from spiritual respects. He who refused to be the divider of an inheritance between two brethren,[48] cannot approve his ministers, by pretended right from him, to be dividers of tenths and freeholds out of other men's pos-

sessions, making thereby the gospel but a cloak of carnal interest, and, to the contradiction of their master, turning his heavenly kingdom into a kingdom of this world, a kingdom of force and rapine. To whom it will be one day thundered more terribly than to Gehazi, for thus dishonoring a far greater master and his gospel, "is this a time to receive money, and to receive garments, and oliveyards, and vineyards, and sheep, and oxen?" The leprosy of Naaman linked with that apostolic curse of *perishing* imprecated on Simon Magus,[49] may be feared, will "cleave to 'such' and to their seed for ever." So that when all is done, and belly hath used in vain all her cunning shifts, I doubt not but all true ministers, considering the demonstration of what hath been here proved, will be wise, and think it much more tolerable to hear that no maintenance of ministers, whether tithes or any other, can be settled by statute, but must be given by them who receive instruction; and freely given, as God hath ordained.

And indeed what can be a more honorable maintenance to them than such, whether alms or willing oblations, as these, which being accounted both alike as given to God, the only acceptable sacrifices now remaining, must needs represent him who receives them much in the care of God and nearly related to him, when not by worldly force and constraint, but with religious awe and reverence, what is given to God, is given to him; and what to him, accounted as given to God. This would be well enough, say they; but how many will so give? I answer, "As many, doubtless, as shall be well taught; as many as God shall so move." Why are ye so distrustful, both of your own doctrine and of God's promises fulfilled in the experience of those disciples first sent? Luke xxii, 35, "When I sent you without purse, and scrip, and shoes, lacked ye anything? And they said, Nothing." How then came ours, or who sent them thus destitute, thus poor and empty both of purse and faith? who style themselves ambassadors of Jesus Christ and seem to be his tithe-gatherers, though an office of their own setting up to his dishonor, his exactors, his publicans rather, not trusting that he will maintain them in their embassy,

[47] John xviii, 36.

[48] And one of the company said unto him, Master, speak to my brother, that he divide the inheritance with me. And he said unto him, Man, who made me a judge or a divider over you? Luke xii, 13–14.

[49] II Kings v, 26, and Acts viii, 20–23.

unless they bind him to his promise by a statute-law that we shall maintain them. Lay down for shame that magnific title, while ye seek maintenance from the people: it is not the manner of ambassadors to ask maintenance of them to whom they are sent. But he who is Lord of all things, hath so ordained. Trust him then; he doubtless will command the people to make good his promises of maintenance more honorably unasked, unraked for. This they know, this they preach, yet believe not: but think it as impossible, without a statute law, to live of the gospel, as if by those words they were bid go eat their Bibles, as Ezekiel and John[50] did their books; and such doctrines as these are as bitter to their bellies; but will serve so much the better to discover hirelings, who can have nothing, though but in appearance, just and solid to answer for themselves against what hath been here spoken, unless perhaps this one remaining pretense, which we shall quickly see to be either false or uningenuous.

They pretend that their education either at school or university, hath been very chargeable and therefore ought to be repaired in future by a plentiful maintenance: whenas it is well known that the better half of them (and ofttimes poor and pitiful boys of no merit or promising hopes that might entitle them to the public provision, but their poverty and the unjust favor of friends) have had the most of their breeding both at school and university by scholarships, exhibitions, and fellowships at the public cost, which might engage them the rather to give freely as they have freely received. Or if they have missed of these helps at the latter place, they have after two or three years left the course of their studies there, if they ever well began them, and undertaken, though furnished with little else but ignorance, boldness, and ambition, if with no worse vices, a chaplainship in some gentleman's house, to the frequent embasing of his sons with illiterate and narrow principles. Or if they have lived there upon their own, who knows not that seven years' charge of living there, to them who fly not from the government of their parents to the license of a university, but come seriously to study, is no more than may be well

defrayed and reimbursed by one year's revenue of an ordinary good benefice? If they had then means of breeding from their parents, 'tis likely they have more now; and if they have, it needs must be mechanic and uningenuous in them to bring a bill of charges for the learning of those liberal arts and sciences which they have learned (if they have indeed learned them, as they seldom have) to their own benefit and accomplishment. But they will say, we had betaken us to some other trade or profession, had we not expected to find a better livelihood by the ministry. This is that which I looked for, to discover them openly neither true lovers of learning, and so very seldom guilty of it, nor true ministers of the gospel. So long ago out of date is that old "true saying," I Tim. iii, 1: "If a man desire a bishopric, he desires a good work." For now commonly he who desires to be a minister looks not at the work but at the wages; and by that lure or lowbell may be tolled from parish to parish all the town over. But what can be plainer simony than thus to be at charges beforehand, to no other end than to make their ministry doubly or trebly beneficial? To whom it might be said, as justly as to that Simon,[51] "Thy money perish with thee, because thou hast thought that the gift of God may be purchased with money: thou hast neither part nor lot in this matter."

Next, it is a fond error, though too much believed among us, to think that the university makes a minister of the gospel; what it may conduce to other arts and sciences, I dispute not now: but that which makes fit a minister, the scripture can best inform us to be only from above, whence also we are bid to seek them: Matt. ix, 38, "Pray ye therefore to the Lord of the harvest, that he will send forth laborers into his harvest." Acts xx, 28, "The flock, over which the holy ghost hath made you overseers." Rom. x, 15, "How shall they preach, unless they be sent?" By whom sent? by the university, or the magistrate, or their belly? No, surely; but sent from God only, and that God who is not their belly. And whether he be sent from God or from Simon Magus, the inward sense of his calling and spiritual ability will sufficiently tell him; and that strong obligation felt within

---

[50] Ezek. iii, 1, and Rev. x, 10.

[51] Cf. n. 49 above.

him, which was felt by the apostle, will often express from him the same words: I Cor. ix, 16, "Necessity is laid upon me, yea, woe is me if I preach not the gospel." Not a beggarly necessity, and the woe feared otherwise of perpetual want, but such a necessity as made him willing to preach the gospel gratis, and to embrace poverty, rather than as a woe to fear it. I Cor. xii, 28, "God hath set some in the church, first apostles," &c. Ephes. iv, 11, &c. "He gave some apostles," &c. "For the perfecting of the saints, for the work of the ministry, for the edifying of the body of Christ, till we all come to the unity of the faith." Whereby we may know that as he made them at the first, so he makes them still, and to the world's end. II Cor. iii, 6, "Who hath also made us fit or able ministers of the New Testament." I Tim. iv, 14, "The gift that is in thee, which was given thee by prophecy and the laying on of the hands of the presbytery." These are all the means, which we read of, required in scripture to the making of a minister.

All this is granted you will say: but yet that it is also requisite he should be trained in other learning; which can be nowhere better had than at universities. I answer that what learning, either human or divine, can be necessary to a minister, may as easily and less chargeably be had in any private house. How deficient else, and to how little purpose, are all those piles of sermons, notes, and comments on all parts of the Bible, bodies and marrows of divinity,[52] besides all other sciences, in our English tongue; many of the same books which in Latin they read at the university? And the small necessity of going thither to learn divinity, I prove first from the most part of themselves, who seldom continue there till they have well got through logic, their first rudiments; though, to say truth, logic also may much better be wanting in disputes of divinity, than in the subtle debates of lawyers and statesmen, who yet seldom or never

deal with syllogisms. And those theological disputations there held by professors and graduates are such as tend least of all to the edification or capacity of the people, but rather perplex and leaven pure doctrine with scholastical trash than enable any minister to the better preaching of the gospel. Whence we may also compute, since they come to reckonings, the charges of his needful library;[53] which, though some shame not to value at £600, may be competently furnished for £60. If any man for his own curiosity or delight be in books further expensive, that is not to be reckoned as necessary to his ministerial, either breeding or function. But papists and other adversaries cannot be confuted without fathers and councils, immense volumes, and of vast charges. I will show them therefore a shorter and a better way of confutation: Tit. i, 9, "Holding fast the faithful word, as he hath been taught, that he may be able by sound doctrine, both to exhort and to convince gainsayers:" who are confuted as soon as heard, bringing that which is either not in scripture, or against it. To pursue them further through the obscure and entangled wood of antiquity, fathers and councils fighting one against another, is needless, endless, not requisite in a minister, and refused by the first reformers of our religion. And yet we may be confident, if these things be thought needful, let the state but erect in public good store of libraries, and there will not want men in the church, who of their own inclinations will become able in this kind against papist or any other adversary.

I have thus at large examined the usual pretenses of hirelings, colored over most commonly with the cause of learning and universities, as if with divines learning stood and fell, wherein for the most part their pittance is so small: and, to speak freely, it were much better there were not one divine in the universities, no school divinity known, the idle sophistry of monks, the canker of religion; and that they who intended to be ministers were trained up in the church only, by the scripture and in the original languages thereof at school; without fetching the compass of other arts and sciences more than what they can well

[52] *marrows of divinity:* short manuals of theology such as William Ames, *Marrow of Divinity* (*Medulla Theologica*) fourth edition, 1630. Earlier editions in Rotterdam. Together with Johannes Wollebius' *Compendium · Theologiae Christianae* (1626) it is recognized by Arthur Sewell in *A Study of Milton's Christian Doctrine* (London, 1939), pp. 35–44, and by Maurice Kelley (*Argument*, p. 27) as having contributed to the plan of Milton's *CD*.

[53] The plea for clerical *libraries* had been strongly urged by Prynne. Cf. n. 10 above.

learn at secondary leisure and at home. Neither speak I this in contempt of learning or the ministry, but hating the common cheats of both; hating that they who have preached out bishops, prelates, and canonists, should, in what serves their own ends, retain their false opinions, their pharisaical leaven, their avarice, and closely their ambition, their pluralities,[54] their nonresidences, their odious fees, and use their legal and popish arguments for tithes: that Independents should take that name, as they may justly from the true freedom of Christian doctrine and church discipline, subject to no superior judge but God only, and seek to be dependents on the magistrate for their maintenance; which two things, independence and state hire in religion, can never consist long or certainly together. For magistrates at one time or other, not like these at present our patrons of Christian liberty, will pay none but such whom by their committees of examination they find conformable to their interests and opinions: and hirelings will soon frame themselves to that interest and those opinions which they see best pleasing to their paymasters; and to seem right themselves, will force others as to the truth. But most of all they are to be reviled and shamed who cry out with the distinct voice of notorious hirelings that if ye settle not our maintenance by law, farewell the gospel; than which nothing can be uttered more false, more ignominious, and, I may say, more blasphemous against our Savior; who hath promised without this condition, both his Holy Spirit, and his own presence with his church to the world's end: nothing more false (unless with their own mouths they condemn themselves for the unworthiest and most mercenary of all other ministers) by the experience of three hundred years after Christ, and the churches at this day in France, Austria, Polonia, and other places, witnessing the contrary under an adverse magistrate, not a favorable: nothing more ignominious, levelling, or rather undervaluing Christ beneath Mahomet.

For if it must be thus, how can any Christian object it to a Turk, that his religion stands by force only; and not justly fear from him this reply, Yours both by force and money, in the judgment of your own preachers. This is that which makes atheists in the land, whom they so much complain of: not the want of maintenance or preachers, as they allege, but the many hirelings and cheaters that have the gospel in their hands; hands that still crave, and are never satisfied. Likely ministers indeed, to proclaim the faith or to exhort our trust in God, when they themselves will not trust him to provide for them in the message whereon, they say, he sent them; but threaten, for want of temporal means, to desert it; calling that want of means which is nothing else but the want of their own faith; and would force us to pay the hire of building our faith to their covetous incredulity! Doubtless, if God only be he who gives ministers to his church till the world's end; and through the whole gospel never sent us for ministers to the schools of philosophy, but rather bids us beware of such "vain deceit," Col. ii, 8 (which the primitive church, after two or three ages not remembering, brought herself quickly to confusion) if all the faithful be now "a holy and a royal priesthood," I Pet. ii, 5, 9, not excluded from the dispensation of things holiest, after free election of the church and imposition of hands, there will not want ministers elected out of all sorts and orders of men, for the gospel makes no difference from the magistrate himself to the meanest artificer, if God evidently favor him with spiritual gifts, as he can easily and oft hath done, while those bachelor divines and doctors of the tippet[55] have been passed by. Heretofore in the first evangelic times (and it were happy for Christendom if it were so again) ministers of the gospel were by nothing else distinguished from other Christians but by their spiritual knowledge and sanctity of life, for which the church elected them to be her teachers and overseers,

---

[54] The Independents, of whom Milton was one, all stood in various ways and degrees to the left of the Presbyterians in their challenge to the authority of the clergy and to their claim to a professional income and status. Milton regretted the concessions which the moderate Independents, especially the group known in 1659 by their headquarters at the Savoy, were willing to make to the principle of an established church. In the later years of the Protectorate he had come to feel that Cromwell was losing the victory of peace because he supported the principle of a religious establishment with a salaried clergy supported by some form of taxation.

[55] tippet: scarf worn by bishops.

though not thereby to separate them from whatever calling she then found them following besides, as the example of St. Paul declares, and the first times of Christianity. When once they affected to be called a clergy, and became, as it were, a peculiar tribe of Levites, a party, a distinct order in the commonwealth, bred up for divines in babbling schools and fed at the public cost, good for nothing else but what was good for nothing, they soon grew idle: that idleness, with fulness of bread, begat pride and perpetual contention with their feeders, the despised laity, through all ages ever since; to the perverting of religion and the disturbance of all Christendom.

And we may confidently conclude it never will be otherwise while they are thus upheld undepending on the church, on which alone they anciently depended, and are by the magistrate publicly maintained, a numerous faction of indigent persons, crept for the most part out of extreme want and bad nurture, claiming by divine right and freehold the tenth of our estates, to monopolize the ministry as their peculiar,[56] which is free and open to all able Christians, elected by any church. Under this pretense exempt from all other employment and enriching themselves on the public, they last of all prove common incendiaries and exalt their horns against the magistrate himself that maintains them, as the priest of Rome did soon after against his benefactor the emperor,[57] and the presbyters of late in Scotland.[58] Of which hireling crew, together

with all the mischiefs, dissensions, troubles, wars merely of their kindling, Christendom might soon rid herself and be happy, if Christians would but know their own dignity, their liberty, their adoption, and let it not be wondered if I say, their spiritual priesthood, whereby they have all equally access to any ministerial function, whenever called by their own abilities and the church, though they never came near commencement or university. But while protestants, to avoid the due labor of understanding their own religion, are content to lodge it in the breast, or rather in the books, of a clergyman, and to take it thence by scraps and mammocks as he dispenses it in his Sunday's dole, they will be always learning and never knowing, always infants; always either his vassals, as lay papists are to their priests; or at odds with him, as reformed principles give them some light to be not wholly conformable; whence infinite disturbances in the state, as they do, must needs follow. Thus much I had to say; and, I suppose, what may be enough to them who are not avariciously bent otherwise, touching the likeliest means to remove hirelings out of the church; than which nothing can more conduce to truth, to peace and all happiness, both in church and state. If I be not heard nor believed, the event will bear me witness to have spoken truth: and I in the meanwhile have borne my witness, not out of season, to the church and to my country.

[56] *peculiar:* property available only to a particular owner.

[57] Cf. Milton's comment on the donation of Constantine above, and n. 7.

[58] So, in *The Articles of Peace* (C.E. VI, 257),

Milton inveighed against the insolence of the Scottish presbyters in Scotland and in Ulster for meddling in "State disputes wherein they are now grown such busie Bodies, to preach of Titles, Interest, and alterations in government."

THE READY AND EASY WAY

TO ESTABLISH

A FREE COMMONWEALTH,

AND THE EXCELLENCE THEREOF

COMPARED WITH THE INCONVENIENCES AND DANGERS OF

READMITTING KINGSHIP IN THIS NATION.

——————— "Et nos

Consilium dedimus Syllæ, demus populo nunc."[1]

BIBLIOGRAPHICAL NOTE—The *Way* was written in haste after General George Monk entered London on Feb. 6, 1660, and betrayed his wavering attachment to republican principles in a speech to the "Rump" Parliament. "March 3" is the date on the Thomason copy of the first edition in the British Museum. The second edition, "revis'd and augmented," was written after writs for the new Parliament had been issued and when the danger of Charles II's restoration was imminent; it seems to have been published very close to Charles' restoration in May. The present text is based upon the unique copy of the second edition in the Houghton Library at Harvard. Excellent modern editions exist by Evert M. Clark (New Haven, 1915) and by Laura E. Lockwood in her edition of *Of Education, Areopagitica, The Commonwealth* (Boston, 1911).

Although since the writing of this treatise the face of things hath had some change, writs for new elections have been recalled, and the members at first chosen readmitted[2] from exclusion, yet not a little rejoicing to hear declared the resolution[3] of those who are in power tending to the establishment of a free commonwealth, and to remove, if it be possible, this noxious humor of returning to bondage—instilled of late by some deceivers,[4] and nourished from bad principles and false apprehensions among too many of the people—I thought best not to suppress what I had written, hoping that it may now be of much more use and concernment to be freely published in the midst of our elections to a free parliament, or their sitting to consider freely of the government, whom it behoves to have all things represented to them that may direct their judgment therein. And I never read of any state, scarce of any tyrant, grown so incurable as to refuse counsel from any in a time of public deliberation, much less to be offended. If their absolute determination be to enthral us, before so long a Lent of servitude they may permit us a little shroving time first, wherein to speak freely and take our leaves of liberty. And because in the former edi-

[1] The motto, an adaptation of Juvenal's first *Satire*, 15–17:
Because we have advised Sulla himself,
We may now advise the people.
After urging General Monk to support a republican government in the form of a perpetual grand council (in an open letter of *Brief Declaration of a Free Commonwealth*, C.E. VI, 107–109), Milton now addresses all his compatriots. He compares himself to a Roman bold enough to remonstrate with the dictator Sulla after he had massacred thousands of members of the popular party in Rome in 82 B.C.

[2] On 21 February, 1660, under pressure from General Monk, the Rump Parliament admitted the members who had been "purged" by Colonel Pride in 1648. They were, of course, Presbyterian and prevailingly Royalist in sympathy.

[3] Before dissolving, the Rump provided that, although the elections for the new Parliament to meet on 26 April were to be free, Royalists should at least nominally be incapable of being elected.

[4] Milton points at Matthew Wren (who soon was to become Bishop of Ely), the recent author of *Monarchy Asserted, Or the State of Monarchicall and Popular Government* (1660), and at the author of the sermon which he attacked in *Brief Notes upon a late Sermon titl'd The Fear of God and the King; Preach'd and since Publish'd, by Matthew Griffith, D.D.* (C.E. VI, 151–64). Cf. n. 38 below.

tion, through haste, many faults escaped, and many books were suddenly dispersed ere the note to mend them could be sent, I took the opportunity from this occasion to revise and somewhat to enlarge the whole discourse, especially that part which argues for a perpetual senate. The treatise thus revised and enlarged, is as follows:

The Parliament of England, assisted by a great number of the people who appeared and stuck to them faithfulest in defense of religion and their civil liberties, judging kingship by long experience a government unnecessary, burdensome, and dangerous, justly and magnanimously abolished it,[5] turning regal bondage into a free commonwealth, to the admiration and terror of our emulous[6] neighbors. They took themselves not bound by the light of nature[7] or religion to any former covenant,[8] from which the king himself, by many forfeitures of a latter date or discovery, and our own longer consideration thereon, had more and more unbound us, both to himself and his posterity, as hath been ever the justice and the prudence of all wise nations that have ejected tyranny. They covenanted "to preserve the king's person and authority in the preservation of the true religion and our liberties," not in his endeavoring to bring in upon our consciences a popish religion,[9] upon our liberties, thraldom; upon our lives, destruction by his occasioning (if not complotting, as was after discovered) the Irish massacre;[10] his fomenting and arming the rebellion, his covert leaguing with the rebels against us, his refusing, more than seven times, propositions[11] most just and necessary to the true religion and our liberties, tendered him by the parliament both of England and Scotland. They made not their covenant concerning him with no difference between a king and a god, or promised him, as Job did to the Almighty, "to trust in him though he slay us":[12] they understood that the solemn engagement wherein we all forswore kingship, was no more a breach of the covenant than the covenant was of the protestation before,[13] but a faithful and prudent going on both in the words, well weighed, and in the true sense of the covenant, "without respect of persons,"[14] when we could not serve two contrary masters, God and the king, or the king and that more supreme law sworn in the first place to maintain our safety and our liberty.

They knew the people of England to be a free people, themselves the representers of that freedom; and although many were excluded, and as many fled (so they pretended) from tumults to Oxford,[15] yet they were left a sufficient number to act in parliament: therefore not bound by any statute of preceding parliaments but by the law of nature only, which is the only law of laws truly and properly to all man-

[5] By resolution on 7 February, 1649,—just nine days after the execution of Charles I—the Rump had declared the office and power of a king unnecessary, burdensome, and dangerous to liberty, safety, and public interest.

[6] England's diplomatic position was hardly improved by the execution of Charles, but by 1658 naval successes against the Dutch and later military successes jointly with the French against the Spaniards in Flanders had made England perhaps the most powerful country in Europe.

[7] Cf. *TKM*, n. 34, and *PL* VI, 42; IX, 352; and XII, 79–85.

[8] For the Solemn League and Covenant see *Eikon*, Preface, n. 33, and *TKM*, n. 7.

[9] Puritan fears of Charles I's sympathy with the Papacy are documented in *TKM*, n. 30, *CG*, notes 6 and 111, and *Eikon*, chaps. vii and xvii.

[10] In the attacks of the Irish on the English in Ulster, which began with the massacre of 23 October, 1641, Charles had no interest; but in 1643 he authorized Lord Ormond to offer the Irish a free parliament in order to secure their military

support. Various Irish negotiations were continued until 1648. Cf. *TKM*, notes 35 and 36.

[11] The Nineteen Propositions submitted to Charles by parliamentary commissioners on 2 June, 1642, the Treaty of Oxford, February, 1643, the Treaty of Uxbridge, February, 1645, the Proposals of the Scots, February and March, 1646, the Propositions of 21 April, 1647, and the Treaty of Newport, October, 1648, *may* be the seven propositions which Milton had in mind.

[12] Job xiii, 15.

[13] The formal protest of Parliament on 3 May, 1641, against "a Popish Army levied in Ireland, and Two Armies brought into the Bowels of this Kingdom, to the hazard of His Majesty's Royal Person." It bound its signers to support "the Doctrine of the Church of England" and to "defend His Majesty's Royal Person and Estate."

[14] The Solemn League and Covenant, which had been restored on 5 March, 1660, used the words "without respect of persons" of the engagement to extirpate popery.

[15] About 175 members of both houses, most of them from the House of Lords, withdrew from Westminster to set up a Royalist Parliament at the king's military headquarters in *Oxford*, and on 22 January, 1644, Charles opened its first and only sitting, which lasted about three months. Nearly 300 remained at Westminster.

kind fundamental,[16] the beginning and the end of all government, to which no parliament or people that will thoroughly reform but may and must have recourse—as they had, and must yet have, in church reformation (if they thoroughly intend it) to evangelic rules, not to ecclesiastical canons[17] though never so ancient, so ratified and established in the land by statutes which for the most part are mere positive laws,[18] neither natural nor moral—and so by any parliament, for just and serious considerations, without scruple to be at any time repealed.

If others of their number in these things were under force, they were not, but under free conscience; if others were excluded by a power which they could not resist, they were not therefore to leave the helm of government in no hands, to discontinue their care of the public peace and safety, to desert the people in anarchy and confusion, no more than when so many of their members left them as made up in outward formality a more legal parliament of three estates[19] against them. The best affected[20] also and best principled of the people stood not numbering or computing on which side were most voices in parliament, but on which side appeared to them most reason, most safety, when the house divided upon main matters. What was well motioned and advised, they examined not whether fear or persuasion carried it in the vote, neither did they measure votes and counsels by the intentions of them that voted, knowing that intentions either are but guessed at, or not soon enough known, and, although good, can neither make the deed such, nor prevent the consequence from being bad. Suppose bad intentions in things otherwise well done; what was well done was by them who so thought not the less obeyed or followed in the state, since in the church who had not rather follow Iscariot[21] or Simon[22] the magician, though to covetous ends, preaching, than Saul, though in the uprightness of his heart persecuting the gospel?

Safer they therefore judged what they thought the better counsels, though carried on by some perhaps to bad ends, than the worse by others, though endeavored with best intentions. And yet they were not to learn that a greater number might be corrupt within the walls of a parliament as well as of a city; whereof in matters of nearest concernment all men will be judges, nor easily permit that the odds of voices in their greatest council shall more endanger them by corrupt or credulous votes than the odds of enemies by open assaults; judging that most voices ought not always to prevail where main matters are in question. If others hence will pretend to disturb all counsels, what is that to them who pretend not, but are in real danger—not they only so judging, but a great, though not the greatest, number of their chosen patriots, who might be more in weight than the others in number: there being in number little virtue, but by weight and measure wisdom working all things, and the dangers on either side they seriously thus weighed:

From the treaty,[23] short fruits of long

---

[16] The appeal to the classical principle of the Law of Nature as basic to all human law, to which Milton constantly appealed, was first made in defense of Parliament's stand against Charles I by Henry Parker in his declaration in 1641, in his *Discourse concerning Puritans*, p. 47, that "the Law of Nature . . . determines that all Princes (are) public Ministers for the common good." Cf. *PL* XII, 29, and *TKM, passim*. A detailed study of Milton's conception of natural law by Ernest Sirluck is in preparation for Vol. II of the *Complete Prose Works of John Milton*, edited by Don Wolfe and to be published by the Yale University Press.

[17] Cf. Milton's respectful reference to Canon Law in *CG* I, vi, and his many disrespectful references to it in *DDD*.

[18] From the Declaration of the Army on 15 June, 1647, which asked that Parliament be purged and agree to several other severe demands, until Pride's purge on 6 December, 1648, Parliament was under constant pressure from the Army. Here Milton answers the charge which Sir Roger L'Estrange had just brought in *Reply to Plain English* that Cromwell had extorted Parliament's decision on 3 January, 1648, to attempt no more negotiation with Charles by personally threatening it in a speech delivered with his hand on his sword.

[19] *three estates*: the bishops or lords spiritual, the nobles or lords temporal, and the commons.

[20] *best affected*: favorably inclined (i.e., to the virtual republic or Commonwealth which was established after the execution of Charles).

[21] Milton recalls the "thirty pieces of silver" (Matt. xxvi, 15) for which Judas *Iscariot* betrayed Jesus.

[22] Cf. *TKM,* n. 228.

[23] The Commons rejected Charles's proposals in the Treaty of Newport, 27 October, 1648, because he would not grant more than ten of the twenty years' control of the army for which they

labors, and seven years' war; security for twenty years, if we can hold it; reformation in the church for three years, then put to shift again with our vanquished master. His justice, his honor, his conscience declared quite contrary to ours, which would have furnished him with many such evasions as in a book entitled *An Inquisition for Blood*[24] soon after were not concealed: bishops not totally removed but left, as it were in ambush, a reserve, with ordination in their sole power; their lands already sold, not to be alienated, but rented, and the sale of them called "sacrilege";[25] delinquents, few of many brought to condign punishment; accessories punished,[26] the chief author above pardon, though after utmost resistance vanquished; not to give, but to receive, laws; yet besought, treated with, and to be thanked for his gracious concessions, to be honored, worshipped, glorified.

If this we swore to do, with what righteousness in the sight of God, with what assurance that we bring not by such an oath the whole sea of bloodguiltiness upon our own heads?[27] If on the other side we prefer a free government, though for the present not obtained, yet all those suggested fears and difficulties, as the event will prove, easily overcome, we remain finally secure from the exasperated regal power and out of snares shall retain the best part of our liberty, which is our religion; and the civil part will be from these who defer us, much more easily recovered, being neither so subtle nor so awful as a king reënthroned. Nor were their actions less both at home and abroad than might become the hopes of a glorious, rising commonwealth: nor were the expressions both of army and people, whether in their public declarations or several writings, other than such as testified a spirit in this nation no less noble and well-fitted to the liberty of a commonwealth than in the ancient Greeks or Romans.[28] Nor was the heroic cause unsuccessfully defended to all Christendom against the tongue of a famous and thought invincible adversary,[29] nor the constancy and fortitude that so nobly vindicated our liberty, our victory at once against two the most prevailing usurpers over mankind, superstition and tyranny, unpraised or uncelebrated in a written monument likely to outlive detraction, as it hath hitherto convinced or silenced not a few of our detractors, especially in parts abroad.

After our liberty and religion thus prosperously fought for, gained, and many years possessed (except in those unhappy interruptions which God hath removed), now that nothing remains but in all reason the certain hopes of a speedy and immediate settlement for ever in a firm and free commonwealth, for this extolled and magnified nation—regardless both of honor won or deliverances vouchsafed from heaven—to fall back, or rather to creep back so poorly as it seems the multitude would to their once abjured and detested thraldom of kingship, to be ourselves the slanderers of our own just and religious deeds (though done by some to covetous and ambitious ends, yet not therefore to be stained with their infamy, or they to asperse the integrity of others; and yet these now by revolting from the conscience of deeds well

asked, and because he refused (1) to abolish episcopacy, (2) to permit final alienation of the bishops' lands, (3) to bind himself to mor than three years' guarantee of a Presbyterian establishment, or (4) drop his demand for an act of oblivion in favor of his supporters, many of whom Parliament had treated as delinquents and punished by sequestrating and selling their estates.

[24] James Howell's *An Inquisition for Blood, to the Parliament and the Army*, was published in July, 1649. It asserted, p. 4, that "those Lawes *that so strictly inhibit English subjects to* raise Armes against their king are still in force." In "the transactions of the late Treaty," it pleaded that Charles had acted "in his *politic* capacity," and so had not been in any way personally prejudiced by his pledges, or bound by them.

[25] In the discussion of the Treaty of Newport Charles took the attitude expressed in *Eikon Basilike;* that his conscience would not let him "swallow down such camels as others do of sacrilege and injustice both to God and man." In reply in *Eikon*, Chap. xi, Milton said that what the king called sacrilege was "taking from the clergy that superfluous wealth, which antiquity as old as Constantine . . . counted 'poison in the church' " (C.E. V, 187). Cf. *Hirelings*, n. 7.

[26] *accessories:* principally, the Earl of Strafford and Archbishop Laud.

[27] If Charles was a "murderer," as Milton calls him below for his "bloodguiltiness" in the civil wars, leniency to him would make his judges participators in his guilt.

[28] For the background of the inspiration of Milton's republican faith the reader should go to Z. S. Fink's *The Classical Republicans* (Evanston, 1945).

[29] Cf. *CG*, n. 99, and *Def 2*, the Bibliographical Note.

done, both in church and state, to throw away and forsake, or rather to betray a just and noble cause for the mixture of bad men who have ill-managed and abused it—which had our fathers done heretofore, and on the same pretense deserted true religion, what had long ere this become of our gospel and all protestant reformation so much intermixed with the avarice and ambition of some reformers?) and by thus relapsing to verify all the bitter predictions of our triumphing enemies, who will now think they wisely discerned and justly censured both us and all our actions as rash, rebellious, hypocritical, and impious; not only argues a strange, degenerate contagion suddenly spread among us, fitted and prepared for new slavery, but will render us a scorn and derision to all our neighbors.

And what will they at best say of us and of the whole English name but scoffingly, as of that foolish builder, mentioned by our Savior, who began to build a tower and was not able to finish it?[30] Where is this goodly tower of a commonwealth which the English boasted they would build to overshadow kings and be another Rome[31] in the west? The foundation indeed they laid gallantly, but fell into a worse confusion, not of tongues but of factions, than those at the tower of Babel; and have left no memorial of their work behind them remaining but in the common laughter of Europe! Which must needs redound the more to our shame if we but look on our neighbors the United Provinces,[32] to us inferior in all outward advantages; who notwithstanding, in the midst of greater difficulties, courageously, wisely, constantly went through with the same work and are settled in all the happy enjoyments of a potent and flourishing republic to this day.

Besides this, if we return to kingship and soon repent (as undoubtedly we shall when we begin to find the old encroachments coming on by little and little upon our consciences, which must necessarily proceed from king and bishop united inseparably in one interest), we may be forced perhaps to fight over again all that we have fought, and spend over again all that we have spent, but are never like to attain thus far as we are now advanced to the recovery of our freedom, never to have it in possession as we now have it, never to be vouchsafed hereafter the like mercies and signal assistances from Heaven[33] in our cause, if by our ungrateful backsliding we make these fruitless; flying now to regal concessions from his divine condescensions and gracious answers to our once importuning prayers against the tyranny which we then groaned under; making vain and viler than dirt the blood of so many thousand faithful and valiant Englishmen who left us in this liberty, bought with their lives; losing by a strange aftergame of folly all the battles we have won, together with all Scotland as to our conquest,[34] hereby lost, which never any of our kings could conquer, all the treasure we have spent, not that corruptible treasure only, but that far more precious of all our late miraculous deliverances; treading back again with lost labor all our happy steps in the progress of reformation, and most pitifully depriving ourselves the instant fruition of that free government which we have so dearly purchased, a free commonwealth, not only held by wisest men in all ages the noblest, the manliest, the equallest, the justest government, the most agreeable to all due liberty and proportioned equality, both human, civil, and Christian, most cherishing to virtue and true religion, but also (I may say it with greatest probability) plainly commended, or rather enjoined by our Savior himself to all Christians, not without remarkable disallowance and the brand of "gentilism" upon kingship.[35]

---

[30] The parable in Luke xiv, 28–30, is a rebuke to the half-hearted.

[31] Milton hoped that England would have a future as a republic no less glorious than *Rome's* destiny after expelling the Tarquin kings. Cf. *Eikon,* Chap. xxviii, n. 22, and *TKM,* n. 71.

[32] *United Provinces:* the Netherlands.

[33] The faith of the Puritans in their victories as proof of divine approval of their cause was provoking rejoinders like the question in *The Censure of the Rota* (1660), p. 9: "Are you not ashamed to rob *O. Cromwell* himselfe, and make use of his Canting with signall Assistances from Heaven?"

[34] If Charles II, whom the Presbyterian majority in Scotland favored, were to be restored to the thrones of both Scotland and England, then from Milton's point of view, Cromwell's victories over the Scots at Dunbar and Worcester would be thrown away.

[35] Milton thought of Christ's rebuke of the ambition of James and John to sit on his left and right hand in his glory: "Ye know that they which are accounted to rule over the Gentiles exercise lord-

God in much displeasure gave a king to the Israelites, and imputed it a sin to them that they sought one;[36] but Christ apparently forbids his disciples to admit of any such heathenish government. "The kings of the Gentiles," saith he, "exercise lordship over them," and they that "exercise authority upon them are called benefactors: but ye shall not be so; but he that is greatest among you, let him be as the younger, and he that is chief, as he that serveth." The occasion of these his words was the ambitious desire of Zebedee's two sons to be exalted above their brethren in his kingdom, which they thought was to be ere long upon earth. That he speaks of civil government is manifest by the former part of the comparison, which infers the other part to be always in the same kind. And what government comes nearer to this precept of Christ than a free commonwealth, wherein they who are greatest, are perpetual servants and drudges to the public at their own cost and charges,[37] neglect their own affairs, yet are not elevated above their brethren, live soberly in their families, walk the streets as other men, may be spoken to freely, familiarly, friendly, without adoration? Whereas a king must be adored like a demigod, with a dissolute and haughty court about him, of vast expense and luxury, masks and revels, to the debauching of our prime gentry, both male and female; not in their pastimes only, but in earnest, by the loose employments of court service, which will be then thought honorable. There will be a queen also of no less charge, in most likelihood outlandish and a papist, besides a queen mother such already, together with both their courts and numerous train: then a

royal issue, and ere long severally their sumptuous courts; to the multiplying of a servile crew, not of servants only, but of nobility[38] and gentry, bred up then to the hopes not of public, but of court offices, to be stewards, chamberlains, ushers, grooms even of the close-stool;[39] and the lower their minds debased with court opinions, contrary to all virtue and reformation, the haughtier will be their pride and profuseness. We may well remember this not long since at home, or need but look at present into the French court,[40] where enticements and preferments daily draw away and pervert the Protestant nobility.

As to the burden of expense, to our cost we shall soon know it; for any good to us deserving to be termed no better than the vast and lavish price of our subjection and their debauchery, which we are now so greedily cheapening,[41] and would so fain be paying most inconsiderately to a single person: who, for anything wherein the public really needs him, will have little else to do but to bestow the eating and drinking of excessive dainties, to set a pompous face upon the superficial actings of state, to pageant himself up and down in progress among the perpetual bowings and cringings of an abject people, on either side deifying and adoring him for nothing done that can deserve it. For what can he more than another man, who, even in the expression of a late court poet, sits only like a great cipher set to no purpose before a long row of other significant figures?[42]

ship over them. . . . But so shall it not be among you" (Mark x, 42). Cf. *PL* XI, 793; XII, 516.
[36] So the Puritans interpreted the warning in I Sam. viii, 11–18, cf the exactions which they would suffer if they insisted upon having a king. Cf. *Eikon*, Chap. xxvii, n. 19.
[37] Although Milton's salary as Secretary was moderate, those of many members of Cromwell's government have been described as too princely to support Milton's statement here. It is interesting to find Pepys confiding to his diary on 10 August, 1667, that most people agreed with him, "that we shall fall into a commonwealth in a few years, whether we will or no; for the charges of a monarchy is such that the kingdom cannot be brought to bear willingly, nor are things managed so well now-a-days under it, as heretofore."

[38] Milton was disgusted with the servile tone of pleas for the restoration of the monarchy like Wren's *Monarchy Asserted, or the State of Monarchicall and Popular Government* which included a defense of the value and the privileges of a strong *nobility*. Cf. n. 4 above.
[39] For appointments of a "groom of the king's stool" in the fifteenth and sixteenth centuries see *Ordinances and Regulations of the . . . Royal Household*, London, 1790, pp. 18 and 156.
[40] Where Louis XIV had been king since 1643.
[41] *cheapening*: bargaining over. The terms of Charles's restoration involved possibilities of loss and gain for thousands of people.
[42] In *Notes & Queries*, n.s. I (1954), 473, Elsie Duncan-Jones identifies the *court poet* with Sir William Davenant. Mark Eccles draws attention to Henry's indignant denial that he should "sit within the throne but for a cipher" (*The True and Honourable Historie of Sir John Oldcastle* IV, i, 20) and to Monsieur's say-

Nay, it is well and happy for the people if their king be but a cipher, being ofttimes a mischief, a pest, a scourge of the nation, and, which is worse, not to be removed, not to be controlled (much less accused or brought to punishment) without the danger of a common ruin, without the shaking and almost subversion of the whole land: whereas in a free commonwealth, any governor or chief counsellor offending may be removed and punished without the least commotion.

Certainly then that people must needs be mad or strangely infatuated that build the chief hope of their common happiness or safety on a single person;[43] who, if he happen to be good, can do no more than another man; if to be bad, hath in his hands to do more evil without check than millions of other men. The happiness of a nation must needs be firmest and certainest in a full and free council[44] of their own electing, where no single person, but reason only, sways. And what madness is it for them who might manage nobly their own affairs themselves, sluggishly and weakly to devolve all on a single person; and, more like boys under age than men, to commit all to his patronage and disposal who neither can perform what he undertakes, and yet for undertaking it, though royally paid, will not be their servant, but their lord! How unmanly must it needs be to count such a one the breath of our nostrils, to hang all our felicity on him, all our safety, our well-being; for which, if we were aught else but sluggards or babies, we need depend on none but God and our own counsels, our own active virtue and industry! "Go to the ant, thou sluggard," saith solomon; "consider her ways, and be wise;

which having no prince, ruler, or lord, provides her meat in the summer and gathers her food in the harvest:"[45] which evidently shows us that they who think the nation undone without a king, though they look grave or haughty, have not so much true spirit and understanding in them as a pismire: neither are these diligent creatures hence concluded to live in lawless anarchy, or that commended, but art set the examples to imprudent and ungoverned men of a frugal and self-governing democracy or commonwealth, safer and more thriving in the joint providence and counsel of many industrious equals than under the single domination of one imperious lord.

It may be well wondered that any nation styling themselves free, can suffer any man to pretend hereditary right over them as their lord, whenas, by acknowledging that right, they conclude[46] themselves his servants and his vassals, and so renounce their own freedom. Which how a people and their leaders especially can do, who have fought so gloriously for liberty, how they can change their noble words and actions, heretofore so becoming the majesty of a free people, into the base necessity of court flatteries and prostrations, is not only strange and admirable,[47] but lamentable to think on. That a nation should be so valorous and courageous to win their liberty in the field, and when they have won it, should be so heartless[48] and unwise in their counsels as not to know how to use it, value it, what to do with it, or with themselves; but after ten or twelve years' prosperous war and contestation with tyranny, basely and besottedly to run their necks again into the yoke which they have broken, and prostrate all the fruits of their victory for

---

ing in Chapman's *Bussy d'Ambois* (I, i, 34–36) that

> "There is no second place in numerous state
> That holds more than a cipher; in a king
> All places are contained."

[43] "One person" was a term much in vogue to refer to a monarch. Wren used it skilfully in *Monarchy Asserted* to indicate a kind of mathematical inevitability in his case for kingship as the strongest form of government because it secured the greatest concentration of power.

[44] *a full and free council*: the first mention of Milton's main proposal for a permanent governing body. The plan was in part a recognition of the Rump's desire to hold its power, but, as the more aristocratic form given to it in the second edition shows, it was fundamental to Milton's thought.

[45] The allusion is to Prov. vi, 6. Milton is replying to the favorite Royalist argument from the royal institutions of bees, which had figured largely in Edward Simmons' *A Loyal Subjects Belief* (1643) and the *Jura Majestatis* of Griffith Williams. Any candid observer, said Godfrey Goodman in *The Fall of Man* (London, 1616), p. 100, "will easily confesse that the greatest temporal happiness of man, which consists in a good government . . . , is much more eminently discerned amongst beasts, than amongst men. I . . . insist on the Bee, who seemes to teach us a platforme and precedent of perfect Monarchie; it is long since agreed and concluded in philosophie."

[46] *conclude*: demonstrate, prove.

[47] *admirable*: wonderful, astounding.

[48] *heartless*: lacking in heart or courage.

nought at the feet of the vanquished, besides our loss of glory and such an example as kings or tyrants never yet had the like to boast of, will be an ignominy if it befall us, that never yet befell any nation possessed of their liberty; worthy indeed themselves, whatsoever they be, to be for ever slaves, but that part of the nation which consents not with them, as I persuade me of a great number, far worthier than by their means to be brought into the same bondage.

Considering these things, so plain, so rational, I cannot but yet further admire on the other side how any man who hath the true principles of justice and religion in him, can presume or take upon him to be a king and lord over his brethren, whom he cannot but know, whether as men or Christians, to be for the most part every way equal or superior to himself: how he can display with such vanity and ostentation his regal splendor, so supereminently above other mortal men; or, being a Christian, can assume such extraordinary honor and worship to himself, while the kingdom of Christ, our common king and lord, is hid to this world, and such "gentilish"[49] imitation forbid in express words by himself to all his disciples. All protestants hold that Christ in his church hath left no vicegerent of his power; but himself,[50] without deputy, is the only head thereof, governing it from heaven: how then can any Christian man derive his kingship from Christ, but with worse usurpation than the pope his headship over the church, since Christ not only hath not left the least shadow of a command for any such vicegerence from him in the state, as the pope pretends for his in the church, but hath expressly declared that such regal dominion is from the gentiles, not from him, and

hath strictly charged us not to imitate them therein?

I doubt not but all ingenuous and knowing men will easily agree with me that a free commonwealth without single person or house of lords[51] is by far the best government, if it can be had. "But we have all this while," say they, "been expecting it,[52] and cannot yet attain it." 'Tis true, indeed, when monarchy was dissolved, the form of a commonwealth should have forthwith been framed, and the practice thereof immediately begun, that the people might have soon been satisfied and delighted with the decent order, ease, and benefit thereof. We had been then by this time firmly rooted past fear of commotions or mutations, and now flourishing. This care of timely settling a new government instead of the old, too much neglected, hath been our mischief. Yet the cause thereof may be ascribed with most reason to the frequent disturbances, interruptions, and dissolutions which the parliament hath had, partly from the impatient or disaffected people, partly from some ambitious leaders in the army[53]; much contrary, I believe, to the mind and approbation of the army itself, and their other commanders, once undeceived, or in their own power.

Now is the opportunity, now the very season wherein we may obtain a free commonwealth and establish it for ever in the land, without difficulty or much delay. Writs are sent out for elections, and, which is worth observing, in the name, not of any king, but of the keepers of our liberty, to summon a free parliament;[54] which then

---

[49] gentilish: cf. gentilism above, and note 45.

[50] So in CD I, xv, pp. 297-99, "the Kingly function of Christ" is defined as the government of his church "by an inward law and spiritual power." "Hence," Milton, like other Independents, argued that "external force ought never to be employed in the administration of the kingdom of Christ, which is the church." Here he applies the doctrine that no church should have the aid of civil magistrates in enforcing its discipline and beliefs to discredit the Royalist contention that the spiritual kingship of Christ obliged good Christians to accept monarchy as the only human form of government with divine sanction.

[51] Milton is recalling the act of Parliament in May, 1649, declaring England to be a free commonwealth. The resolutions and acts abolishing kingship and the House of Lords were passed in the previous February. These decisions were reaffirmed by the Rump on 7 May, 1659.

[52] expecting—waiting for (it).

[53] Can Milton have included Cromwell's personal dissolution of Parliament on 20 April, 1653? Doubtless he did include Richard Cromwell's dissolution of Parliament on 20 April, 1659, under pressure from the ambitious leaders of the army, Lambert, Desborough, and Fleetwood, whose notorious Wallingford House group the Parliament had tried to outlaw. In October, 1659, Lambert again dissolved the reconstituted Rump.

[54] On 16 March, 1660, the Long Parliament, after issuing writs "in the name of the Keepers of the Liberties of England" for a free election, finally dissolved itself.

only will indeed be free and deserve the true honor of that supreme title, if they preserve us a free people—which never parliament was more free to do, being now called not as heretofore, by the summons of a king, but by the voice of liberty.

And if the people, laying aside prejudice and impatience, will seriously and calmly now consider their own good, both religious and civil, their own liberty and the only means thereof, as shall be here laid before them, and will elect their knights and burgesses[55] able men, and according to the just and necessary qualifications (which, for aught I hear, remain yet in force unrepealed, as they were formerly decreed in parliament),[56] men not addicted to a single person or house of lords, the work is done; at least the foundation firmly laid of a free commonwealth, and good part also erected of the main structure. For the ground and basis of every just and free government (since men have smarted so oft for committing all to one person) is a general council of ablest men, chosen by the people to consult of public affairs from time to time for the common good. In this grand council must the sovereignty (not transferred but delegated only, and as it were deposited) reside, with this caution: they must have the forces by sea and land committed to them for preservation of the common peace and liberty; must raise and manage the public revenue, at least with some inspectors deputed for satisfaction of the people, how it is employed; must make or propose, as more expressly shall be said anon, civil laws, treat of commerce, peace or war with foreign nations; and, for the carrying on some particular affairs with more secrecy and expedition, must elect, as they have already out of their own number and others, a council of state.[57]

And, although it may seem strange at first hearing by reason that men's minds are prepossessed with the notion of successive parliaments, I affirm that the grand or general council, being well chosen, should be perpetual: for so their business is or may be, and ofttimes urgent, the opportunity of affairs gained or lost in a moment. The day of council cannot be set as the day of a festival, but must be ready always to prevent,[58] or answer[59] all occasions.[60] By this continuance they will become every way skilfullest, best provided of intelligence from abroad, best acquainted with the people at home, and the people with them. The ship of the commonwealth[61] is always under sail. They sit at the stern, and if they steer well, what need is there to change them, it being rather dangerous? Add to this that the grand council is both foundation and main pillar of the whole state; and to move pillars and foundations not faulty, cannot be safe for the building.

I see not, therefore, how we can be advantaged by successive and transitory parliaments; but that they are much likelier continually to unsettle rather than to settle a free government, to breed commotions, changes, novelties, and uncertainties, to bring neglect upon present affairs and opportunities, while all minds are suspense[62] with expectation of a new assembly, and the assembly, for a good space, taken up with the new settling of itself. After which, if they find no great work to do, they will make it by altering or repealing former acts, or making and multiplying

Venice, Holland, and Switzerland were being discussed. The essentially English nature of Milton's idea emerges in his "brief delineation of a free commonwealth" in his *Letter to General Monk* (C.E. VI, 108–9), where he flanks his design for a general council for the nation with a proposal of similar councils for all principal cities, "with a competent territory adjoined," so as to set up a balance of local and national governments faintly suggesting that between the federal and state governments in the U. S. A.

[58] *prevent:* anticipate, forestall.

[59] *answer:* handle, control.

[60] *occasions:* situations, emergencies.

[61] The idea of the *ship* of state may be older than Plato's elaborate parable of the mutinous crew in the *Republic* VI. An equally impressive instance is Bodin's account in the Preface to his *Commonweale* of the ship of state as so storm-tossed that the passengers have to lend a hand to the professional mariners.

[62] *suspense:* in suspense, gripped by uncertainty.

[55] Representatives of the counties in the House of Commons were traditionally called *knights,* and those from the boroughs, towns, and universities were called *burgesses.*

[56] In January and February, 1660, the Rump had passed a series of acts disabling all who could in any way be described as Royalist sympathizers from election to the new Parliament.

[57] Milton may have been thinking less of something like Cromwell's *Council of State,* in which he had served as Latin Secretary, than of a council patterned on continental models. In the "Rump" Parliament, as he wrote, several proposals for an executive council more or less like those in

new; that they may seem to see what their predecessors saw not and not to have assembled for nothing; till all law be lost in the multitude of clashing statutes. But if the ambition of such as think themselves injured that they also partake not of the government, and are impatient till they be chosen, cannot brook the perpetuity of others chosen before them, or if it be feared that long continuance of power may corrupt sincerest men, the known expedient is, and by some lately propounded, that annually (or if the space be longer, so much perhaps the better) the third part of senators may go out according to the precedence of their election,[63] and the like number be chosen in their places, to prevent the settling of too absolute a power, if it should be perpetual: and this they call "partial rotation."

But I could wish that this wheel or partial wheel[64] in state, if it be possible, might be avoided, as having too much affinity with the wheel of Fortune. For it appears not how this can be done without danger and mischance of putting out a great number of the best and ablest, in whose stead new elections may bring in as many raw, inexperienced, and otherwise affected, to the weakening and much altering for the worse of public transactions. Neither do I think a perpetual senate, especially chosen and entrusted by the people, much in this land to be feared, where the well-affected,[65] either in a standing army or in a settled militia, have their arms in their own hands. Safest therefore to me it seems, and of least hazard or interruption to affairs, that none of the grand council be moved, unless by death or just conviction of some crime: for what can be expected firm or steadfast from a floating foundation? However, I forejudge not any probable expedient, any temperament that can be found in things of this nature so disputable on either side.

Yet lest this which I affirm be thought my single opinion, I shall add sufficient testimony. Kingship itself is therefore

counted the more safe and durable because the king, and for the most part his council, is not changed during life. But a commonwealth is held immortal, and therein firmest, safest, and most above fortune. For the death of a king causeth ofttimes many dangerous alterations, but the death now and then of a senator is not felt, the main body of them still continuing permanent in greatest and noblest commonwealths and as it were eternal. Therefore, among the Jews the supreme council of seventy, called the Sanhedrim,[66] founded by Moses, in Athens that of Areopagus,[67] in Sparta[68] that of the ancients, in Rome the senate,[69] consisted of members chosen for term of life; and by that means remained as it were still the same to generations. In Venice[70] they change indeed ofter than every year some particular councils of state, as that of six, or such other: but the true senate, which upholds and sustains the government, is the whole aristocracy immovable. So in the United Provinces, the States-General, which are indeed but a council of state deputed by the whole union, are not usually the same persons for above three or six years; but the states of every city, in whom the sovereignty hath been placed time out of mind, are a standing senate, without succession, and accounted chiefly in that regard the main prop of their liberty. And why they should be so in every well-ordered commonwealth, they who write of policy give these reasons: That to make the senate successive not only impairs the dignity and luster of the senate, but weakens the whole commonwealth and

66 For Milton's view of the origin of the *Sanhedrim* see *PL* XII, 225–6, n.

67 Cf. *Aerop*, Bibliographical Note, and *Eikon,* Chap. xxviii, n. 20.

68 Under Lycurgus' constitution, as Plutarch describes it in the *Life of Lycurgus,* the council of thirty ancients, all over sixty years of age and elected for life, was the supreme authority in the government. Cf. *Educ,* n. 63.

69 Roman senators held office for life and assumed it by virtue of completion of service as Consuls or Praetors.

70 In *Venice* the Doge and his cabinet were in office for terms too short for them easily to take control of the state from the Senate and the Great Council, the latter of which was—by modern standards—a small body of nobles. It was recruited as Milton proposed that his grand council should be, only as vacancies occurred through the death of members or their individual removal for some extraordinary reason.

63 Harrington was pressing the principle of partial rotation, which had been a main defense of popular government in his blue-print constitution in *Oceana,* four years earlier.

64 A play on the idea of the *wheel* of rotation (Latin *rota,* a wheel) and of the wheel as the traditional symbol of the Goddess of Fortune.

65 *well-affected:* well-disposed, loyal.

brings it into manifest danger; while by this means the secrets of state are frequently divulged and matters of greatest consequence committed to inexpert and novice counsellors, utterly to seek in the full and intimate knowledge of affairs past.

I know not therefore what should be peculiar in England to make successive parliaments thought safest, or convenient here more than in other nations, unless it be the fickleness which is attributed to us as we are islanders.[71] But good education and acquisite[72] wisdom ought to correct the fluxible[73] fault, if any such be, of our watery situation. It will be objected that in those places where they had perpetual senates, they had also popular remedies against their growing too imperious: as in Athens, besides Areopagus, another senate of four or five hundred; in Sparta, the Ephori;[74] in Rome, the tribunes of the people.[75] But the event tells us that these remedies either little availed the people, or brought them to such a licentious and unbridled democracy as in fine ruined themselves with their own excessive power. So that the main reason urged why popular assemblies are to be trusted with the people's liberty, rather than a senate of principal men, because great men will be still endeavoring to enlarge their power, but the common sort will be contented to maintain their own liberty, is by experience found false, none being more immoderate and

ambitious to amplify their power than such popularities; which was seen in the people of Rome, who, at first contented to have their tribunes, at length contended with the senate that one consul, then both— soon after, that the censors and prætors also—should be created plebeian, and the whole empire put into their hands; adoring lastly those who most were adverse to the senate; till Marius,[76] by fulfilling their inordinate desires, quite lost them all the power for which they had so long been striving, and left them under the tyranny of Sulla.[77]

The balance therefore must be exactly so set as to preserve and keep up due authority on either side, as well in the senate as in the people. And this annual rotation of a senate to consist of three hundred, as is lately propounded, requires also another popular assembly upward of a thousand,[78] with an answerable rotation. Which, besides that it will be liable to all those inconveniences found in the foresaid reme-dies, cannot but be troublesome and chargeable, both in their motion[79] and their session, to the whole land, unwieldy with their own bulk, unable in so great a number to mature their consultations as they ought, if any be allotted them, and that they meet not from so many parts remote to sit a whole year lieger in one place, only now and then to hold up a forest of fingers, or to convey each man his bean or ballot into the box, without reason shown or common deliberation; incontinent[80] of secrets, if any be imparted to them, emulous and always jarring with the other senate. The much better way doubtless will be, in this wavering condition of our affairs, to defer

---

[71] In a passage which is based on Plato's warning in the *Laws* IV, 704, and which is a development of his own favorite doctrine of the influence of climate on national character, Bodin says: "As for the inhabitants vpon the Sea coast, and of great townes of traffique, all writers have observed, That they are more subtill, politike, and cunning, than those that lie farre from the sea and traffique. . . . For which cause *Plato* forbids them to build his Commonweale neere vnto the sea, saying, That such men are deceitfull and treacherous" (The *Commonweale* V, i, p. 564).

[72] *acquisite:* acquired.

[73] *fluxible:* fluid, volatile, inconstant.

[74] The five Spartan *Ephors* were originally created as a curb on the Ancients, but their power in time became a kind of inverted aristocracy. Milton was familiar with Aristotle's criticism of them (*Politics* II, ix) as poor because of their popular origin, therefore easily tempted by bribes, and tyrannous in action.

[75] The Roman *Tribunes* of the Plebeians were originally two officers, established first in 495 B.C., with power of veto over acts of the Senate. In 457 they were increased to ten, and their power became greater in fact than that of the Consuls.

[76] *Caius Marius* (157–86 B.C.), the great plebeian general who conquered Jugurtha, annihilated the invading Gauls in northern Italy, and was seven times Consul, secured his popular power in his later years by conspiring with the most unscrupulous Roman demagogues, and in the year before his death was responsible for the massacre of many aristocrats by his soldiers.

[77] *L. Cornelius Sulla* (138–78 B.C.), who served against Jugurtha under Marius and had a great military career, seized power and became dictator in 82 B.C. Cf. n. 1 above.

[78] Such a plan is mentioned by Miss Lockwood as figuring in the Commons' *Journal* of Sept. 8, 1659.

[79] *motion:* commuting between their homes and Westminster.

[80] *incontinent:* unwithholding, i.e., indiscreet.

the changing or circumscribing of our senate, more than may be done with ease, till the commonwealth be thoroughly settled in peace and safety, and they themselves give us the occasion.

Military men hold it dangerous to change the form of battle in view of an enemy: neither did the people of Rome bandy with their senate while any of the Tarquins[81] lived, the enemies of their liberty; nor sought, by creating tribunes, to defend themselves against the fear of their patricians, till (sixteen years after the expulsion of their kings, and in full security of their state) they had or thought they had just cause given them by the senate. Another way will be to well qualify and refine elections,[82] not committing all to the noise and shouting of a rude multitude, but permitting only those of them who are rightly qualified to nominate as many as they will; and out of that number others of a better breeding to choose a less number more judiciously, till after a third or fourth sifting and refining of exactest choice, they only be left chosen who are the due number and seem by most voices the worthiest.

To make the people fittest to choose, and the chosen fittest to govern, will be to mend our corrupt and faulty education, to teach the people faith, not without virtue, temperance, modesty, sobriety, parsimony, justice; not to admire wealth or honor; to hate turbulence and ambition; to place every one his private welfare and happiness in the public peace, liberty, and safety. They shall not then need to be much mistrustful of their chosen patriots in the grand council, who will be then rightly called the true keepers of our liberty, though the most of their business will be in foreign affairs. But to prevent all mistrust, the people then will have their several ordinary assemblies (which will henceforth quite annihilate the odious power and name of committees[83]) in the chief

towns of every county—without the trouble, charge, or time lost of summoning and assembling from far in so great a number, and so long residing from their own houses, or removing of their families—to do as much at home in their several shires, entire or subdivided, toward the securing of their liberty, as a numerous assembly of them all formed and convened on purpose with the wariest rotation. Whereof I shall speak more ere the end of this discourse, for it may be referred to time, so we be still going on by degrees to perfection. The people well weighing and performing these things, I suppose would have no cause to fear, though the parliament, abolishing that name as originally signifying but the "parley" of our lords and commons with their Norman king[84] when he pleased to call them, should, with certain limitations of their power, sit perpetual, if their ends be faithful and for a free commonwealth, under the name of a grand or general council.

Till this be done, I am in doubt whether our state will be ever certainly and thoroughly settled; never likely till then to see an end of our troubles and continual changes, or at least never the true settlement and assurance of our liberty. The grand council being thus firmly constituted to perpetuity, and still, upon the death or default of any member, supplied and kept in full number, there can be no cause alleged why peace, justice, plentiful trade, and all prosperity should not thereupon ensue throughout the whole land; with as much assurance as can be of human things that they shall so continue (if God favor us, and our wilful sins provoke him not) even to the coming of our true and rightful and only to be expected King, only worthy as he is our only Savior, the Messiah, the Christ, the only heir of his eternal Father, the only by him anointed and ordained

---

81 Cf. n. 31 above.

82 In *Milton in the Puritan Revolution* (New York, 1941), p. 301, Don Wolfe reduces Milton's election scheme to a graph.

83 As early as 1647 local *committees* were established to forward the Parliamentary cause. Though they "had no definite authority to govern the Church" (S. R. Gardiner, *History of the Great Civil War*, III, 202) and interfered only moderately in religious affairs, they were active against Royalist

conspiracies and under the Protectorate, when their presidents were the notorious eleven major generals who enforced the rule of Cromwell's Council of State throughout England, they were unpopular.

84 In the Army debates at Putney and Whitehall in 1647–1649 the popular leaders often betrayed a naive faith in the liberties of Englishmen before the Norman conquest. "In Alfred's time," said Commissary Nicholas Cowling, "the Commons had all the power" (quoted by Woodhouse in *Puritanism and Liberty*, p. 120). Cf. *TKM*, n. 5, and *Eikon*, Chap. xxviii, n. 29.

since the work of our redemption finished, universal Lord of all mankind.

The way propounded is plain, easy, and open before us, without intricacies, without the introducement of new or obsolete forms or terms, or exotic models—ideas that would effect nothing but with a number of new injunctions to manacle the native liberty of mankind, turning all virtue into prescription, servitude, and necessity, to the great impairing and frustrating of Christian liberty.[85] I say again, this way lies free and smooth before us, is not tangled with inconveniences, invents no new encumbrances, requires no perilous, no injurious alteration or circumscription of men's lands and properties; secure, that in this commonwealth, temporal and spiritual lords removed, no man or number of men can attain to such wealth or vast possession as will need the hedge of an agrarian law[86] (never successful, but the cause rather of sedition, save only where it began seasonably with first possession) to confine them from endangering our public liberty. To conclude, it can have no considerable objection made against it that it is not practicable; lest it be said hereafter that we gave up our liberty for want of a ready way or distinct form proposed of a free commonwealth. And this facility we shall have above our next neighboring commonwealth (if we can keep us from the fond conceit of something like a duke of Venice,[87] put lately into many men's heads by someone or other subtly driving on under that notion his own ambitious ends to lurch a crown) that our liberty shall not be hampered or hovered over by any engagement to such a potent family as the house of Nassau,[88] of whom to stand in perpetual doubt and suspicion, but we shall

live the clearest and absolutest free nation in the world.

On the contrary, if there be a king, which the inconsiderate multitude are now so mad upon, mark how far short we are like to come of all those happinesses which in a free state we shall immediately be possessed of. First, the grand council, which, as I showed before, should sit perpetually (unless their leisure give them now and then some intermissions or vacations, easily manageable by the council of state left sitting), shall be called, by the king's good will and utmost endeavor, as seldom as may be. For it is only the king's right, he will say, to call a parliament; and this he will do most commonly about his own affairs rather than the kingdom's, as will appear plainly so soon as they are called. For what will their business then be, and the chief expense of their time, but an endless tugging between petition of right and royal prerogative,[89] especially about the negative voice,[90] militia, or subsidies, demanded and ofttimes extorted without reasonable cause appearing to the commons, who are the only true representatives of the people and their liberty, but will be then mingled with a court faction. Besides which, within their own walls, the sincere part of them who stand faithful to the people will again have to deal with two troublesome counterworking adversaries from without, mere creatures of the king, spiritual, and the greater part, as is likeliest, of temporal lords, nothing concerned with the people's liberty.

If these prevail not in what they please, though never so much against the people's interest, the parliament shall be soon dissolved, or sit and do nothing; not suffered to remedy the least grievance, or enact aught advantageous to the people. Next, the council of state shall not be chosen by the parliament, but by the king, still his own creatures, courtiers and favorites, who will be sure in all their counsels to set their master's grandeur and absolute power, in

---

[85] Cf. CG, n. 48.

[86] The classic example of failure of *agrarian* legislation was that of the Tribunes Tiberius and Gaius Gracchus in Rome in 133–123 B.C. Cf. n. 75 above. Milton may be replying to Harrington's serious proposal of an agrarian law in *Oceana*, and he may have recalled Plato's disapproval of such laws (in *Laws*, 684c).

[87] Probably a suggestion for returning Richard Cromwell to nominal power with a status like that of the Doge of *Venice*. Cf. n. 70 above.

[88] The heirs of William, Prince of Orange, of the *house of Nassau*, inherited the power which he secured for himself as Stadtholder in the republic which was established by the provinces of the Netherlands in 1579.

[89] Milton looks back to the beginning of Parliament's resistance to Charles I's assertion of the *royal prerogative* when, in 1628, he was forced to consent to the Petition of Right. Cf. *TKM*, n. 86, and *Eikon*, Preface, n. 31, and Chap. xxvii, n. 8.

[90] Cf. Milton's discussion of the royal veto power in *Eikon*, Chap. vi, and again in Chap. xxvii, notes 11 and 14.

what they are able, far above the people's liberty. I deny not but that there may be such a king who may regard the common good before his own, may have no vicious favorite, may hearken only to the wisest and incorruptest of his parliament: but this rarely happens in a monarchy not elective, and it behoves not a wise nation to commit the sum of their well-being, the whole state of their safety to fortune. What need they? and how absurd would it be, whenas they themselves, to whom his chief virtue will be but to hearken, may with much better management and dispatch, with much more commendation of their own worth and magnanimity, govern without a master? Can the folly be paralleled, to adore and be the slaves of a single person for doing that which it is ten thousand to one whether he can or will do, and we without him might do more easily, more effectually, more laudably ourselves? Shall we never grow old enough to be wise to make seasonable use of gravest authorities, experiences, examples? Is it such an unspeakable joy to serve, such felicity to wear a yoke, to clink our shackles locked on by pretended law of subjection, more intolerable and hopeless to be ever shaken off than those which are knocked on by illegal injury and violence?

Aristotle,[91] our chief instructor in the universities (lest this doctrine be thought sectarian, as the royalist would have it thought), tells us in the third of his *Politics* that certain men at first, for the matchless excellence of their virtue above others, or some great public benefit, were created kings by the people, in small cities and territories, and in the scarcity of others to be found like them: but when they abused their power and governments grew larger and the number of prudent men increased, that then the people, soon deposing their tyrants, betook them, in all civilest places, to the form of a free commonwealth. And why should we thus disparage and prejudicate our own nation as to fear a scarcity of able and worthy men united in counsel to govern us, if we will but use diligence and impartiality to find them out and choose them, rather yoking ourselves to a single person, the natural adversary and oppressor of liberty; though good, yet far easier

corruptible by the excess of his singular power and exaltation, or at best, not comparably sufficient to bear the weight of government, nor equally disposed to make us happy in the enjoyment of our liberty under him?

But admit that monarchy of itself may be convenient to some nations,[92] yet to us who have thrown it out, received back again, it cannot but prove pernicious. For kings to come, never forgetting their former ejection, will be sure to fortify and arm themselves sufficiently for the future against all such attempts hereafter from the people; who shall be then so narrowly watched and kept so low[93] that though they would never so fain, and at the same rate of their blood and treasure, they never shall be able to regain what they now have purchased and may enjoy, or to free themselves from any yoke imposed upon them. Nor will they dare to go about it—utterly disheartened for the future, if these their highest attempts prove unsuccessful—which will be the triumph of all tyrants hereafter over any people that shall resist oppression. And their song will then be, to others, "How sped the rebellious English?"—to our posterity, "How sped the rebels, your fathers?"

This is not my conjecture, but drawn from God's known denouncement against the gentilizing Israelites, who, though they were governed in a commonwealth of God's own ordaining, he only their king, they his peculiar people, yet affecting rather to resemble heathen, but pretending the misgovernment of Samuel's sons[94] (no more a reason to dislike their commonwealth than the violence of Eli's sons[95] was imputable to that priesthood or religion) clamored for a king. They had their longing, but with this testimony of God's wrath: "Ye shall cry out in that day because of your king whom ye shall have chosen, and the Lord will not hear you in that

[91] Cf. *TKM*, notes 42 and 47.

[92] In the *Commonplace Book* Milton had recorded his interest in the theory that various forms of government suit various nations (C.E. XVIII, 163).
[93] Again in the *Commonplace Book* (C. E. XVIII, 176) Milton quotes Guicciardini's *History of Italy* on the tendency of tyrants to suppress popular military activity.
[94] Cf. *TKM*, n. 72, and *Eikon*, Chap. xxvii, n. 19.
[95] The story of the *sons of Eli*, who "were sons of Belial, and knew not the Lord," is found in I Sam. ii, 12–17.

day."[96] Us if he shall hear now, how much less will he hear when we cry hereafter, who once delivered by him from a king, and not without wondrous acts of his providence, insensible and unworthy of those high mercies, are returning precipitantly, if he withhold us not, back to the captivity from whence he freed us!

Yet neither shall we obtain or buy at any easy rate this new gilded yoke which thus transports us. A new royal revenue must be found, a new episcopal, for those are individual:[97] both which being wholly dissipated, or bought by private persons, or assigned for service done (and especially to the army), cannot be recovered without a general detriment and confusion to men's estates, or a heavy imposition on all men's purses—benefit to none but to the worst and ignoblest sort of men whose hope is to be either the ministers of court riot and excess, or the gainers by it. But not to speak more of losses and extraordinary levies on our estates, what will then be the revenges and offenses remembered and returned, not only by the chief person, but by all his adherents; accounts and reparations that will be required, suits, indictments, inquiries, discoveries, complaints, informations, who knows against whom or how many, though perhaps neuters,[98] if not to utmost infliction, yet to imprisonment, fines, banishment, or molestation?—if not these, yet disfavor, discountenance, disregard, and contempt on all but the known royalist, or whom he favors, will be plenteous.

Nor let the new royalized presbyterians[99] persuade themselves that their old doings, though now recanted, will be forgotten, whatever conditions be contrived or trusted on. Will they not believe this, nor remember the pacification;[100] how it was kept to the Scots; how other solemn promises many a time to us? Let them but now read the diabolical forerunning libels,[101] the faces, the gestures that now appear foremost and briskest in all public places, as the harbingers of those that are in expectation to reign over us. Let them but hear the insolencies, the menaces, the insultings of our newly animated common enemies crept lately out of their holes, their hell I might say by the language of their infernal pamphlets, the spew of every drunkard, every ribald; nameless, yet not for want of license, but for very shame of their own vile persons, not daring to name themselves, while they traduce others by name; and give us to foresee that they intend to second their wicked words, if ever they have power, with more wicked deeds.

Let our zealous backsliders forethink now with themselves how their necks yoked with these tigers of Bacchus[102]—these new fanatics of not the preaching-, but the sweating-tub,[103] inspired with nothing holier than the venereal pox—can draw one way under monarchy to the establishing of church discipline with these new-disgorged atheisms. Yet shall they not have the honor to yoke with these, but shall be yoked under them. These shall plough on their backs. And do they among them who are so forward to bring in the single person, think to be by him trusted or long regarded? So trusted they shall be and so regarded, as by kings are wont reconciled enemies; neglected and soon after discarded, if not prosecuted for old traitors; the first inciters, beginners, and more than to the third part actors, of all that followed.

It will be found also that there must be then as necessarily as now (for the contrary part will be still feared) a standing army, which for certain shall not be this, but of the fiercest Cavaliers, of no less expense, and perhaps again under Rupert.[104]

---

[96] I Sam. viii, 18.

[97] *individual:* privately owned. No compensation was, in fact, ever paid to the purchasers of the alienated lands of the bishops and nobles who had supported Charles I when they were restored by act of Parliament to their former owners after the restoration of Charles II.

[98] *neuters:* persons siding with neither side in the Civil War.

[99] For the strong support of Charles during his confinement and the trial by the *Presbyterians,* whom Milton calls "our Zealous backsliders," below, see *TKM* in many passages.

[100] For the *Pacification* which Charles signed with the Scots in December, 1647, see *TKM,* n. 151.

[101] In Appendix A to his edition of the *Way* Mr. Clark reprints some choice examples of the "libels."

[102] With the god of wine, says Conti (V, xiii), lynxes, tigers, and panthers are wont to go. Here, of course, *tigers* is used in a double sense.

[103] The fanatic Fifth Monarchy men had been preaching for more than a decade from tubs in the streets. The *sweating tubs* that Milton recommends for the preachers of a return to monarchy were used in treating venereal disease.

[104] *Prince Rupert* (1619–82), the son of Eliza-

But let this army[105] be sure they shall be soon disbanded (and likeliest without arrear or pay) and being disbanded, not be sure but they may as soon be questioned for being in arms against their king. The same let them fear who have contributed money, which will amount to no small number that must then take their turn to be made delinquents[106] and compounders. They who past reason and recovery are devoted to kingship perhaps will answer that a greater part by far of the nation will have it so: the rest therefore must yield.

Not so much to convince these, which I little hope, as to confirm them who yield not, I reply that this greatest part have both in reason and the trial of just battle lost the right of their election what the government shall be. Of them who have not lost that right, whether they for kingship be the greater number, who can certainly determine? Suppose they be, yet of freedom they partake all alike, one main end of government; which if the greater part value not, but will degenerately forego, is it just or reasonable that most voices against the main end of government should enslave the less number that would be free?[107] More just it is, doubtless, if it come to force, that a less number compel a greater to retain (which can be no wrong to them) their liberty, than that a greater number, for the pleasure of their baseness, compel a less most injuriously to be their fellow slaves. They who seek nothing but their own just liberty, have always right to win it and to keep it, whenever they have power, be the voices never so numerous

that oppose it. And how much we above others are concerned to defend it from kingship, and from them who in pursuance thereof so perniciously would betray us and themselves to most certain misery and thraldom, will be needless to repeat.

Having thus far shown with what ease we may now obtain a free commonwealth, and by it, with as much ease, all the freedom, peace, justice, plenty, that we can desire; on the other side, the difficulties, troubles, uncertainties, nay, rather impossibilities, to enjoy these things constantly under a monarch; I will now proceed to show more particularly wherein our freedom and flourishing condition will be more ample and secure to us under a free commonwealth than under kingship.

The whole freedom of man consists either in spiritual or civil liberty. As for spiritual, who can be at rest, who can enjoy anything in this world with contentment who hath not liberty to serve God and to save his own soul according to the best light which God hath planted in him to that purpose, by the reading of his revealed will and the guidance of his Holy Spirit?[108] That this is best pleasing to God, and that the whole protestant church allows no supreme judge or rule in matters of religion but the scriptures—and these to be interpreted by the scriptures themselves, which necessarily infers liberty of conscience—I have heretofore proved at large in another treatise;[109] and might yet further, by the public declarations, confessions, and admonitions of whole churches and states,[110] obvious in all history since the reformation.

This liberty of conscience, which above all other things ought to be to all men dearest and most precious, no government more inclinable not to favor only, but to protect, than a free commonwealth, as being most magnanimous, most fearless,

---

beth, Queen of Bohemia, and Charles I's nephew, joined his uncle early in the Civil War, led brilliant cavalry charges at Edgehill and the first Battle of Newbury, forced the defeat of Marston Moor on his superiors by insisting on fighting against heavy odds, was commander-in-chief of the royal army when it was defeated at Naseby, and later commanded Charles's fleet.

105 *this army*: the veterans who had fought with Cromwell and were at the moment still strongly republican in outlook.

106 Royalist landowners in large numbers had been declared *delinquents* by the Long Parliament and their estates seized and sold.

107 As he wrote this paragraph Milton may have thought of Plato's "greatest principle of all" (in the *Laws* III, 690): "that the wise should lead and command, and the ignorant follow and obey." His conception of the leadership of Parliament in the Puritan Revolution had always involved that principle.

108 This sounds very like the Preface to *CD*, which Milton must at least have been meditating by this time, and to which he might refer as naturally as he does to *Civil Power* below.

109 The *Treatise of Civil Power in Ecclesiastical Causes.*

110 Cf. the Westminster Confession of 1647: "The infallible rule of interpretation of Scripture is the Scripture itself; and therefore, when there is a question about the true and full sense of any Scripture (which is not manifold, but one), it must be searched and known by other places that speak more clearly."

and confident of its own fair proceedings. Whereas kingship, though looking big, yet indeed most pusillanimous, full of fears, full of jealousies, startled at every umbrage,[111] as it hath been observed of old to have ever suspected most and mistrusted them who were in most esteem for virtue and generosity of mind, so it is now known to have most in doubt and suspicion them who are most reputed to be religious. Queen Elizabeth, though herself accounted so good a protestant, so moderate, so confident of her subjects' love, would never give way so much as to presbyterian reformation in this land, though once and again besought, as Camden relates;[112] but imprisoned and persecuted the very proposers thereof, alleging it as her mind and maxim unalterable, that such reformation would diminish regal authority.

What liberty of conscience can we then expect of others, far worse principled from the cradle, trained up and governed by popish and Spanish counsels,[113] and on such depending hitherto for subsistence? Especially what can this last parliament expect, who having revived lately and published the covenant, have re-engaged themselves never to readmit episcopacy? Which no son of Charles returning but will most certainly bring back with him, if he regard the last and strictest charge of his father, "to persevere in, not the doctrine only, but government of the church of England, not to neglect the speedy and effectual suppressing of errors and schisms";[114] among which he accounted presbytery one of the chief.

Or if, notwithstanding that charge of

his father, he submit to the covenant, how will he keep faith to us with disobedience to him, or regard that faith given, which must be founded on the breach of that last and solemnest paternal charge, and the reluctance, I may say the antipathy, which is in all kings against presbyterian and independent discipline? For they hear the gospel speaking much of liberty—a word which monarchy and her bishops both fear and hate, but a free commonwealth both favors and promotes, and not the word only, but the thing itself. But let our governors beware in time lest their hard measure to liberty of conscience be found the rock whereon they shipwreck themselves (as others have now done before them in the course wherein God was directing their steerage to a free commonwealth), and the abandoning of all those whom they call "sectaries" (for the detected falsehood and ambition of some) be a wilful rejection of their own chief strength and interest in the freedom of all protestant religion, under what abusive name soever calumniated.

The other part of our freedom consists in the civil rights and advancements of every person according to his merit: the enjoyment of those never more certain, and the access to these never more open, than in a free commonwealth. Both which, in my opinion, may be best and soonest obtained, if every county in the land were made a kind of subordinate commonalty or commonwealth, and one chief town or more, according as the shire is in circuit, made cities, if they be not so called already; where the nobility and chief gentry from a proportionable compass of territory annexed to each city may build houses or palaces befitting their quality, may bear part in the government, make their own judicial laws, or use these that are, and execute them by their own elected judicatures and judges without appeal, in all things of civil government between man and man. So they shall have justice in their own hands, law executed fully and finally in their own counties and precincts, long wished and spoken of, but never yet obtained. They shall have none then to blame but themselves if it be not well administered, and fewer laws to expect or fear from the supreme authority. Or to

---

[111] *umbrage:* shadow.

[112] Cf. the appeal to *Camden* in *CG* I, vii (n. 140). Here Milton refers to the *History of Elizabeth*: "The Reform'd Religion being now Establish'd by Parliament, the Queen's chief Care and Concern was how to guard and protect it from the several Attacks and Practices of . . . its profess'd Enemies. . . . And as she would admit of no innovations herein, so she studied to square her own Life and Actions by so even a balance, as to preserve the character of one not given to change."

[113] Milton thought of Charles II's upbringing by a French, Catholic mother, and of his recent attachment to the Spaniards, on whose part he had fought in Flanders when Cromwell's expeditionary force helped Turenne defeat the Spaniards on 4 June, 1658, at the Battle of the Dunes.

[114] The words are quoted in *Eikon*, Chap. xxvii (see p. 801 above) from the *Eikon Basilike*.

those that shall be made, of any great concernment to public liberty, they may without much trouble in these commonalties, or in more general assemblies called to their cities from the whole territory on such occasion, declare and publish their assent or dissent by deputies within a time limited sent to the grand council. Yet so as this their judgment declared shall submit to the greater number of other counties or commonalties, and not avail them to any exemption of themselves, or refusal of agreement with the rest, as it may in any of the United Provinces, being sovereign within itself, ofttimes to the great disadvantage of that union.[115]

In these employments they may, much better than they do now, exercise and fit themselves till their lot fall to be chosen into the grand council, according as their worth and merit shall be taken notice of by the people. As for controversies that shall happen between men of several counties, they may repair, as they do now, to the capital city, or any other more commodious, indifferent place, and equal judges. And this I find to have been practised in the old Athenian commonwealth, reputed the first and ancientest place of civility in all Greece; that they had in their several cities a peculiar, in Athens a common, government; and their right, as it befell them, to the administration of both.[116]

They should have here also schools and academies at their own choice, wherein their children may be bred up in their own sight to all learning and noble education—not in grammar only, but in all liberal arts and exercises. This would soon spread much more knowledge and civility, yea, religion, through all parts of the land, by communicating the natural heat of government and culture more distributively to all extreme parts which now lie numb and neglected; would soon make the whole nation more industrious, more ingenuous at home, more potent, more honorable abroad. To this a free commonwealth will easily assent, nay, the parliament hath had already some such thing in design; for of all governments a commonwealth aims most to make the people flourishing, virtuous, noble, and high-spirited. Monarchs will never permit, whose aim is to make the people wealthy indeed perhaps, and well fleeced for their own shearing[117] and the supply of regal prodigality, but otherwise softest, basest, viciousest, servilest, easiest to be kept under. And not only in fleece, but in mind also sheepishest, and will have all the benches of judicature annexed to the throne, as a gift of royal grace that we have justice done us; whenas nothing can be more essential to the freedom of a people than to have the administration of justice and all public ornaments in their own election and within their own bounds, without long travelling or depending on remote places to obtain their right, or any civil accomplishment, so it be not supreme, but subordinate to the general power and union of the whole republic.

In which happy firmness, as in the particular above-mentioned, we shall also far exceed the United Provinces by having, not as they (to the retarding and distracting ofttimes of their counsels or urgentest occasions), many sovereignties united in one commonwealth, but many commonwealths under one united and entrusted sovereignty. And when we have our forces by sea and land, either of a faithful army or a settled militia, in our own hands to the firm establishing of a free commonwealth, public accounts under our own inspection, general laws and taxes, with their causes, in our own domestic suffrages, judicial laws, offices, and ornaments at home in our own ordering and administration, all distinction of lords and commoners that may any way divide or sever the public interest, removed—what can a perpetual senate have then wherein to grow corrupt, wherein to encroach upon us, or usurp? Or if they do, wherein to be formidable? Yet if all this

---

[115] A practical result of the lack of centralized power in Holland had recently been the failure of some of the *United Provinces* to give their admirals, Martin Tromp and de Ruyter, the support necessary to secure victory over the English in the naval war in 1652–3.

[116] In 510 B.C. Cleisthenes ended civil strife in Attica by decentralizing government and stopping the control over the agricultural districts and smaller towns which the rich oligarchs of Athens had exercised. Ten new tribes were established, and the demes or towns were given the right to elect their demarchs or mayors locally.

[117] The figure goes back to Plato's description (*Rep.* I, 343) of true kings as never thinking of their subjects as sheep, but rather working for their advantage day and night.

avail not to remove the fear or envy of a perpetual sitting, it may be easily provided to change a third part of them yearly, or every two or three years, as was above mentioned: or that it be at those times in the people's choice, whether they will change them, or renew their power, as they shall find cause.

I have no more to say at present. Few words will save us, well considered; few and easy things, now seasonably done. But if the people be so affected as to prostitute religion and liberty to the vain and groundless apprehension that nothing but kingship can restore trade—not remembering the frequent plagues and pestilences that then wasted this city, such as through God's mercy we never have felt since,[118] and that trade flourishes nowhere more than in the free commonwealths of Italy, Germany, and the Low Countries, before their eyes at this day (yet if trade be grown so craving and importunate through the profuse living of tradesmen that nothing can support it but the luxurious expenses of a nation upon trifles or superfluities; so as if the people generally should betake themselves to frugality, it might prove a dangerous matter, lest tradesmen should mutiny for want of trading, and that therefore we must forego and set to sale religion, liberty, honor, safety, all concernments divine or human, to keep up trading)—if, lastly, after all this light among us, the same reason shall pass for current to put our necks again under kingship as was made use of by the Jews to return back to Egypt[119] and to the worship of their idol queen, because they falsely imagined that they then lived in more plenty and prosperity, our condition is not sound, but rotten, both in religion and all civil prudence; and will bring us soon, the way we are marching, to those calamities which attend always and unavoidably on luxury, all national judgments under foreign or domestic slavery. So far we shall be from mending our condition by monarchizing our government, whatever new conceit now possesses us.

However, with all hazard I have ventured what I thought my duty to speak in season, and to forewarn my country in time, wherein I doubt not but there be many wise men in all places and degrees, but am sorry the effects of wisdom are so little seen among us. Many circumstances and particulars I could have added in those things whereof I have spoken; but a few main matters now put speedily in execution, will suffice to recover us and set all right. And there will want at no time who are good at circumstances; but men who set their minds on main matters and sufficiently urge them, in these most difficult times I find not many.

What I have spoken is the language of that which is not called amiss "The good old Cause."[120] If it seem strange to any, it will not seem more strange, I hope, than convincing to backsliders. Thus much I should perhaps have said, though I were sure I should have spoken only to trees and stones, and had none to cry to, but with the prophet, "O earth, earth, earth!" to tell the very soil itself what her perverse inhabitants are deaf to.[121] Nay, though what I have spoke should happen (which thou suffer not, who didst create mankind free! nor thou next, who didst redeem us from being servants of men!)[122] to be the last words of our expiring liberty. But I trust I shall have spoken persuasion to abundance of sensible and ingenuous men; to some, perhaps, whom God may raise of these stones to become children of reviving liberty,[128] and may reclaim, though they seem now choosing them a captain back for

---

[118] Since 1625 there had been no great outbreak of the plague which had been dreaded with good cause in the reigns of Elizabeth and James I, and was often regarded as a divine judgment. In 1665 Milton lived through its last and perhaps its worst epidemic outbreak in London.

[119] Cf. the story of the desire of the Hebrews in the desert to return to "the cucumbers, and the melons, and the leeks, and the onions, and the garlick" of *Egypt* (Num. xi, 5).

[120] Milton glances at the insult that was being put upon the traditional name of his cause among its supporters by pamphlets like *A Coffin for the Good Old Cause, Or, A Sober Word by way of Caution to the Parliament and Army*, etc. . . . By an Affectionate Friend to it and them, which was anonymously published in 1660.

[121] Jeremiah xxii, 29.

[122] Christ has redeemed us from "being servants of men" either on the religious level or the political, because "in Christ we are all alike priests" (*CD* I, xxviii; C.E. XVI, 212), and because the whole political meaning of the gospel is that God "human left from human free" (*PL* XII, 71).

[128] Cf. Ezekiel's vision of the dry bones which gradually revive as he preaches to them (Ezek. xxxvii).

Egypt, to bethink themselves a little and consider whither they are rushing; to exhort this torrent also of the people not to be so impetuous, but to keep their due channel; and at length recovering and uniting their better resolutions, now that they see already how open and unbounded the insolence and rage is of our common enemies, to stay these ruinous proceedings, justly and timely fearing to what a precipice of destruction the deluge of this epidemic madness would hurry us, through the general defection of a misguided and abused multitude.

THE CHRISTIAN DOCTRINE

JOHN MILTON,

TO ALL THE CHURCHES OF CHRIST,

AND TO ALL

WHO PROFESS THE CHRISTIAN

FAITH THROUGHOUT THE WORLD,

PEACE, AND THE RECOGNITION OF THE TRUTH,

AND ETERNAL SALVATION

IN GOD THE FATHER, AND IN OUR LORD JESUS CHRIST.

BIBLIOGRAPHICAL NOTE—The chapters of *CD* which are reproduced here (Book I, Chaps. i–x and xxvii; Book II, Chap. ix) are taken from Bishop Charles R. Sumner's translation in its first edition (Cambridge University Press, 1825). For the story of the thwarted effort of Daniel Skinner to have Milton's original Latin text published in Amsterdam in 1675 and of the discovery of Milton's original manuscript in the Record Office in London in 1823, the reader may go to the Columbia *Milton,* Vol. XVII, 425–28. For the most authoritative account of the composition, state, and revisions of the original manuscript he should turn to Maurice Kelley's *This Great Argument,* A Study of Milton's *De Doctrina Christiana* as a Gloss upon *Paradise Lost* (Princeton University Press, 1941). Arthur Sewell's interesting *A Study in Milton's Christian Doctrine* (London, 1939) is superseded by Kelley's treatment of the problems of the dating of the revisions of the manuscript and of the relevancy of the work to interpretation of *PL.* Sumner's many notes paralleling individual passages in *PL* and *CD* are not reproduced here, but the present editor is indebted to them and to Kelley's tabulations of all such parallels in Chaps. iv–vii and in the Index to Passages from *PL* on pp. 264–69 in his *Argument* for many of the notes to *PL.*

Since the commencement of the last century, when religion began to be restored from the corruptions of more than thirteen hundred years to something of its original purity, many treatises of theology have been published, conducted according to sounder principles, wherein the chief heads of Christian doctrine are set forth sometimes briefly, sometimes in a more enlarged and methodical order. I think myself obliged, therefore, to declare in the first instance why, if any works have already appeared as perfect as the nature of the subject will admit, I have not remained contented with them—or, if all my predecessors have treated it unsuccessfully, why their failure has not deterred me from attempting an undertaking of a similar kind.

If I were to say that I had devoted myself to the study of the Christian religion because nothing else can so effectually rescue the lives and minds of men from those two detestable curses, slavery and superstition, I should seem to have acted rather from a regard to my highest earthly comforts, than from a religious motive.

But since it is only to the individual faith of each that the Deity has opened the way of eternal salvation, and as he requires that he who would be saved should have a personal belief of his own, I resolved not to repose on the faith or judgment of others in matters relating to God; but on the one hand, having taken the grounds of my faith from divine revelation alone, and on the other, having neglected nothing which depended on my own industry, I thought fit to scrutinize and ascertain for myself the several points of my religious belief, by the most careful perusal and meditation of the Holy Scriptures themselves.

If therefore I mention what has proved beneficial in my own practice, it is in the hope that others, who have a similar wish of improving themselves, may be thereby invited to pursue the same method. I entered upon an assiduous course of study in my youth, beginning with the books of the Old and New Testament in their original languages and going diligently through a few of the shorter systems of divines, in imitation of whom I was in the habit of classing under certain heads whatever passages of Scripture occurred for extraction, to be made use of hereafter as occasion might require. At length I resorted with increased confidence to some of the more copious theological treatises, and to the examination of the arguments advanced by the conflicting parties respecting certain disputed points of faith. But, to speak the truth with freedom as well as candour, I was concerned to discover in many instances adverse reasonings either evaded by wretched shifts, or attempted to be refuted, rather speciously than with solidity, by an affected display of formal sophisms, or by a constant recourse to the quibbles of the grammarians; while what was most pertinaciously espoused as the true doctrine, seemed often defended, with more vehemence than strength of argument, by misconstructions of Scripture, or by the hasty deduction of erroneous inferences. Owing to these causes, the truth was sometimes as strenuously opposed as if it had been an error or a heresy—while errors and heresies were substituted for the truth, and valued rather from deference to custom and the spirit of party than from the authority of Scripture.

According to my judgment, therefore, neither my creed nor my hope of salvation could be safely trusted to such guides; and yet it appeared highly requisite to possess some methodical tractate of Christian doctrine, or at least to attempt such a disquisition as might be useful in establishing my faith or assisting my memory. I deemed it therefore safest and most advisable to compile for myself, by my own labour and study, some original treatise which should be always at hand, derived solely from the word of God itself, and executed with all possible fidelity, seeing that I could have no wish to practise any imposition on myself in such a matter.

After a diligent perseverance in this plan for several years, I perceived that the strong holds of the reformed religion were sufficiently fortified, as far as it was in danger from the Papists,—but neglected in many other quarters; neither competently strengthened with works of defence, nor adequately provided with champions. It was also evident to me, that, in religion as in other things, the offers of God were all directed, not to an indolent credulity, but to constant diligence, and to an unwearied search after truth; and that more than I was aware of still remained, which required to be more rigidly examined by the rule of Scripture, and reformed after a more accurate model. I so far satisfied myself in the prosecution of this plan as at length to trust that I had discovered, with regard to religion, what was matter of belief, and what only matter of opinion. It was also a great solace to me to have compiled, by God's assistance, a precious aid for my faith, —or rather to have laid up for myself a treasure which would be a provision for my future life, and would remove from my mind all grounds for hesitation, as often as it behoved me to render an account of the principles of my belief.

If I communicate the result of my inquiries to the world at large; if, as God is my witness, it be with a friendly and benignant feeling towards mankind, that I readily give as wide a circulation as possible to what I esteem my best and richest possession, I hope to meet with a candid reception from all parties, and that none at least will take unjust offence, even though many things should be brought to light which will at once be seen to differ from certain received opinions. I earnestly beseech all lovers of truth, not to cry out that the Church is thrown into confusion by that freedom of discussion and inquiry which is granted to the schools, and ought certainly to be refused to no believer, since we are ordered *to prove all things,* and since the daily progress of the light of truth is productive far less of disturbance to the Church, than of illumination and edification. Nor do I see how the Church can be more disturbed by the investigation of truth, than were the Gentiles by the first promulgation of the gospel; since so far from recommending or imposing anything on my own authority, it is my particular advice that every one should suspend his opinion on whatever points he may not feel himself fully satisfied, till the evidence of Scripture prevail, and persuade his reason into assent and faith. Concealment is not my object; it is to the learned that I address myself, or if it be thought that the learned are not the best umpires and judges of such things, I should at least wish to submit my opinions to men of a mature and manly understanding, possessing a thorough knowledge of the doctrines of the gospel; on whose judgements I should rely with far more confidence, than on those of novices in these matters. And whereas the greater part of those who have written most largely on these subjects have been wont to fill whole pages with explanations of their own opinions, thrusting into the margin the texts in support of their doctrine with a summary reference to the chapter and verse, I have chosen, on the contrary, to fill my pages even to redundance with quotations from Scripture, that so as little space as possible might be left for my own words, even when they arise from the context of revelation itself.

It has also been my object to make it appear from the opinions I shall be found to have advanced, whether new or old, of how much consequence to the Christian religion is the liberty not only of winnowing and sifting every doctrine, but also of thinking and even writing respecting it, according to our individual faith and persuasion; an inference which will be stronger in proportion to the weight and importance of those opinions, or rather in proportion to the authority of Scripture, on the abundant testimony of which they rest. Without this liberty there is neither religion nor gospel —force alone prevails,—by which it is disgraceful for the Christian religion to be supported. Without this liberty we are still enslaved, not indeed, as formerly, under the divine law, but, what is worst of all, under the law of man, or to speak more truly, under a barbarous tyranny. But I do not expect from candid and judicious readers a conduct so unworthy of them,— that like certain unjust and foolish men, they should stamp with the invidious name of heretic or heresy whatever appears to them to differ from the received opinions, without trying the doctrine by a comparison with Scripture testimonies. According to their notions, to have branded any one at random with this opprobrious mark, is to have refuted him without any trouble, by a single word. By the simple imputation of the name of heretic, they think that they have despatched their man at one blow. To men of this kind I answer, that in the time of the apostles, ere the New Testament was written, whenever the charge of heresy was applied as a term of reproach, that alone was considered as heresy which was at variance with their doctrine orally delivered, —and that those only were looked upon as heretics, who according to Rom. xvi. 17, 18. *caused divisions and offences contrary to the doctrine of the apostles . . . serving not our Lord Jesus Christ, but their own belly.* By parity of reasoning therefore, since the compilation of the New Testament, I maintain that nothing but what is in contradiction to it can properly be called heresy.

For my own part, I adhere to the Holy Scriptures alone—I follow no other heresy or sect. I had not even read any of the works of heretics, so called, when the mistakes of those who are reckoned for orthodox, and their incautious handling of Scripture, first taught me to agree with their opponents whenever those opponents agreed with Scripture. If this be heresy, I confess with St. Paul, Acts xxiv. 14. *that after the way which they call heresy, so worship I the God of my fathers, believing all things which are written in the law and the prophets*—to which I add, whatever is written in the New Testament. Any other judges or chief interpreters of the Christian belief, together with all implicit faith, as it is called, I, in common with the whole Protestant Church, refuse to recognize.

For the rest, brethren, cultivate truth with brotherly love. Judge of my present undertaking according to the admonishing of the Spirit of God—and neither adopt my sentiments, nor reject them, unless every doubt has been removed from your belief by the clear testimony of revelation. Finally, live in the faith of our Lord and Saviour Jesus Christ. Farewell.

A POSTHUMOUS TREATISE

ON

THE CHRISTIAN DOCTRINE,

COMPILED FROM THE HOLY SCRIPTURES ALONE:

IN TWO BOOKS:

BY

JOHN MILTON.

BOOK I.

CHAPTER I.

OF THE CHRISTIAN DOCTRINE, AND THE
NUMBER OF ITS DIVISIONS.

The Christian Doctrine is that DIVINE REV-ELATION disclosed to all ages by CHRIST (though he was not known under that name in the beginning) concerning the nature and worship of the Deity, for the promotion of the glory of God, and the salvation of mankind.

It is not unreasonable to assume that Christians believe in the Scriptures whence this doctrine is derived—but the authority of those Scriptures will be examined in the proper place.

CHRIST. Matt. xi. 27. *neither knoweth any man the Father, save the Son, and he to whomsoever the Son will reveal him.* John i. 4. *in him was life, and the life was the light of men.* v. 9. *that was the true light which lighteth every man that cometh into the world.* 1 Pet. iii. 19. *by which also he went and preached unto the spirits in prison.*

Under the definition of CHRIST are also comprehended Moses and the Prophets, who were his forerunners, and the Apostles whom he sent. Gal. iii. 24. *the law was our schoolmaster to bring us unto Christ, that we might be justified by faith.* Heb. xiii. 8. *Jesus Christ, the same yesterday, to-day, and for ever.* Col. ii. 17. *which are a shadow of things to come: but the body is of Christ.* 1 Pet. i. 10, 11. *who prophesied of the grace that should come unto you: searching what, or what manner of time the Spirit of Christ which was in them did signify.* Rom. i. 1. *Paul, a servant of Jesus*

Christ: in which manner he begins nearly all the rest of his epistles. 1 Cor. iv. 1. *let a man so account of us, as of the ministers of Christ.*

DIVINE REVELATION. Isai. li. 4. *a law shall proceed from me.* Matt. xvi. 17. *flesh and blood hath not revealed it unto thee, but my Father which is in heaven.* John vi. 46. *they shall be all taught of God.* ix. 29. *we know that God spake unto Moses.* Gal. i. 11, 12. *the gospel which was preached of me is not after man; for I neither received it of man.* 1 Thess. iv. 9. *ye yourselves are taught of God.*

This doctrine, therefore, is to be obtained, not from the schools of the philosophers, nor from the laws of man, but from the Holy Scriptures alone, under the guidance of the Holy Spirit. 2 Tim. i. 14. *that good thing which was committed unto thee keep by the Holy Ghost which dwelleth in us.* Col. ii. 8. *lest any man spoil you through philosophy.* Dan. iii. 16. *we are not careful to answer thee in this matter.* Acts iv. 19. *whether it be right in the sight of God to hearken unto you more than unto God, judge ye.*

In this treatise then no novelties of doctrine are taught; but, for the sake of assisting the memory, what is dispersed throughout the different parts of the Holy Scriptures is conveniently reduced into one compact body as it were, and digested under certain heads. This method might be easily defended on the ground of Christian prudence, but it seems better to rest its authority on the divine command; Matt. xiii. 52. *every scribe which is instructed unto the kingdom of heaven is like unto a man which is an householder, which bringeth forth out of his treasure things new and old.* So also the Apostle says, 2 Tim. i. 13. *hold fast the form*—which the author of the Epistle to the Hebrews seems to have determined to adopt as the rule of his own conduct for teaching the heads of Christian doctrine in methodical arrangement: vi. 1–3. *of repentance from dead works, and of faith toward God, of the doctrine of baptisms, and of laying on of hands, and of resurrection of the dead, and of eternal judgement; and this will we do, if God permit.* This usage of the Christians was admirably suited for Catechumens when first professing their faith in the Church. Allusion is made to the same system in Rom. vi. 17. *ye have obeyed from the heart that form of doctrine which was delivered you.* In this passage the Greek word τυπὸς, as well as ὑποτύπωσις 2 Tim. i. 13. seems to signify either that part of the evangelical Scriptures which were then written (as in Rom. ii. 20. μόρφωσις, *the form of knowledge and of the truth in the law,* signified the law itself) or some systematic course of instruction derived from them or from the whole doctrine of the gospel. Acts xx. 27. *I have not shunned to declare unto you all the counsel of God*—which must mean some entire body of doctrine, formed according to a certain plan, though probably not of great extent, since the whole was gone through, and perhaps even repeated several times during St. Paul's stay at Ephesus, which was about the space of three years.

Christian doctrine is comprehended under two divisions,—FAITH, or THE KNOWLEDGE OF GOD,—and LOVE, or THE WORSHIP OF GOD. Gen. xvii. 1. *walk before me, and be thou perfect.* Psal. xxxvii. 3. *trust in Jehovah, and do good.* Luke xi. 28. *blessed are they that hear the word of God, and keep it.* Acts xxiv. 14. *believing all things* —and v. 16. *herein do I exercise myself.* 2 Tim. i. 13. *hold fast the form of sound words which thou hast heard of me, in faith and in love which is in Christ Jesus.* 1 Tim. i. 19. *holding faith and a good conscience.* Tit. iii. 8. *that they which have believed might be careful—.* 1 John. iii. 23. *that we should believe and love.*

These two divisions, though they are distinct in their own nature, and put asunder for the convenience of teaching, cannot be separated in practice. Rom. ii. 13. *not the hearers of the law, but the doers of the law shall be justified.* James i. 22. *be ye doers of the word, and not hearers only.* Besides, obedience and love are always the best guides to knowledge, and often lead the way from small beginnings, to a greater and more flourishing degree of proficiency. Psal. xxv. 14. *the secret of Jehovah is with them that fear him.* John vii. 17. *if any man will do his will, he shall know of the doctrine.* viii. 31, 32. *if ye continue in my word . . . ye shall know the truth, and the truth shall make you free.* 1 John ii. 3. *hereby we do know that we know him, if we keep his commandments.*

It must be observed, that Faith in this division does not mean the habit of believing, but the things to be habitually believed. So Acts vi. 7. *were obedient to the faith.* Gal. i. 23. *he preacheth the faith.*

CHAP. II.
OF GOD.

Though there be not a few who deny the existence of GOD, for *the fool hath said in his heart, There is no God,* Psal. xiv. 1. yet the Deity has imprinted upon the human mind so many unquestionable tokens of himself, and so many traces of him are apparent throughout the whole of nature, that no one in his senses can remain ignorant of the truth. Job xii. 9. *who knoweth not in all these that the hand of Jehovah hath wrought this?* Psal. xix. 1. *the heavens declare the glory of God.* Acts xiv. 17. *he left not himself without witness.* xvii. 27, 28. *he is not far from every one of us.* Rom. i. 19, 20. *that which may be known of God is manifest in them.* and ii. 14, 15. *the Gentiles . . . shew the work of the law written in their hearts, their conscience also bearing witness.* 1 Cor. i. 21. *after that in the wisdom of God, the world by wisdom knew not God, it pleased God by the foolishness of preaching to save them that believe.* There can be no doubt but that every thing in the world, by the beauty of its order, and the evidence of a determinate and beneficial purpose which pervades it, testifies that some supreme efficient Power must have pre-existed, by which the whole was ordained for a specific end.

There are some who pretend that nature or fate is this supreme Power: but the very name of nature implies that it must owe its birth to some prior agent, or, to speak properly, signifies in itself nothing; but means either the essence of a thing, or that general law which is the origin of every thing, and under which every thing acts,—and fate can be nothing but a divine decree emanating from some almighty power.

Further, those who attribute the creation of every thing to nature, must necessarily associate chance with nature as a joint divinity; so that they gain nothing by this theory, except that in the place of that one God, whom they cannot tolerate, they are obliged, however reluctantly, to substitute two sovereign rulers of affairs, who must almost always be in opposition to each other. In short, many ocular demonstrations, many true predictions verified, many wonderful works have compelled all nations to believe, either that God, or that some evil power whose name was unknown, presided over the affairs of the world. Now that evil should prevail over good, and be the true supreme power, is as unmeet as it is incredible. Hence it follows as a necessary consequence, that God exists.

Again: the existence of God is further proved by that feeling, whether we term it conscience, or right reason, which even in the worst of characters is not altogether extinguished. If there were no God, there would be no distinction between right and wrong; the estimate of virtue and vice would entirely depend on the blind opinion of men; no one would follow virtue, no one would be restrained from vice by any sense of shame, or fear of the laws, unless conscience or right reason did from time to time convince every one, however unwilling, of the existence of God, the Lord and ruler of all things, to whom, sooner or later, each must give an account of his own actions, whether good or bad.

The whole tenor of Scripture proves the same thing; and the disciples of the doctrine of Christ may fairly be required to give assent to this truth in the first instance, according to the expression in Heb. xi. 6. *he that cometh to God, must believe that he is.* It is proved also by the dispersion of the ancient nation of the Jews throughout the whole world, according to what God often forewarned them would happen on account of their sins. Nor is it only to pay the penalty of their own guilt that they have been reserved in their scattered state, among the rest of the nations, through the revolution of successive ages, and even to the present day; but rather to be a perpetual and living testimony to all people under heaven, of the existence of God, and of the truth of the Holy Scriptures.

No one, however, can have right thoughts of God, with nature or reason alone as his guide, independent of the word, or message of God. Rom. x. 14. *how shall they believe in him of whom they have not heard?*

God is known, so far as he is pleased to make us acquainted with himself, either from his own nature, or from his efficient power.

When we speak of knowing God, it must be understood with reference to the imperfect comprehension of man; for to know God as he really is, far transcends the powers of man's thoughts, much more of his perception. 1 Tim. vi. 16. *dwelling in the light which no man can approach unto.* God therefore has made as full a revelation of himself as our minds can conceive, or the weakness of our nature can bear. Exod. xxxiii. 20, 23. *there shall no man see me, and live . . . but thou shalt see my back parts.* Isai. vi. 1. *I saw the Lord sitting upon a throne, high and lifted up, and his train filled the temple.* John i. 18. *no man hath seen God at any time.* vi. 46. *not that any man hath seen the Father, save he which is of God, he hath seen the Father.* v. 37. *ye have neither heard his voice at any time.* 1 Cor. xiii. 12. *we see through a glass, darkly . . . in part.*

Our safest way is to form in our minds such a conception of God, as shall correspond with his own delineation and representation of himself in the sacred writings. For granting that both in the literal and figurative descriptions of God, he is exhibited not as he really is, but in such a manner as may be within the scope of our comprehensions, yet we ought to entertain such a conception of him, as he, in condescending to accommodate himself to our capacities, has shewn that he desires we should conceive. For it is on this very account that he has lowered himself to our level, lest in our flights above the reach of human understanding, and beyond the written word of Scripture, we should be tempted to indulge in vague cogitations and subtleties.

There is no need then that theologians should have recourse here to what they call anthropopathy—a figure invented by the grammarians to excuse the absurdities of the poets on the subject of the heathen divinities. We may be sure that sufficient care has been taken that the Holy Scriptures should contain nothing unsuitable to the character or dignity of God, and that God should say nothing of himself which could derogate from his own majesty. It is better therefore to contemplate the Deity, and to conceive of him, not with reference to human passions, that is, after the manner of men, who are never weary of forming subtle imaginations respecting him, but after the manner of Scripture, that is, in the way in which God has offered himself to our contemplation; nor should we think that he would say or direct anything to be written of himself, which is inconsistent with the opinion he wishes us to entertain of his character. Let us require no better authority than God himself for determining what is worthy or unworthy of him. If *it repented Jehovah that he had made man,* Gen. vi. 6. and *because of their groanings,* Judges ii. 18, let us believe that it did repent him, only taking care to remember that what is called repentance when applied to God, does not arise from inadvertency, as in men; for so he has himself cautioned us, Num. xxiii. 19. *God is not a man that he should lie, neither the son of man that he should repent.* See also 1 Sam. xv. 29. Again, if *it grieved the Lord at his heart,* Gen. vi. 6. and if *his soul were grieved for the misery of Israel,* Judges x. 16, let us believe that it did grieve him. For the affections which in a good man are good, and rank with virtues, in God are holy. If after the work of six days it be said of God that *he rested and was refreshed,* Exod. xxxi. 17. if it be said that *he feared the wrath of the enemy,* Deut. xxxii. 27, let us believe that it is not beneath the dignity of God to grieve in that for which he is grieved, or to be refreshed in that which refresheth him, or to fear in that which he feareth. For however we may attempt to soften down such expressions by a latitude of interpretation, when applied to the Deity, it comes in the end to precisely the same. If God be said *to have made man in his own image, after his likeness,* Gen. i. 26.

and that too not only as to his soul, but also as to his outward form (unless the same words have different significations here and in chap. v. 3. *Adam begat a son in his own likeness, after his image*) and if God habitually assign to himself the members and form of man, why should we be afraid of attributing to him what he attributes to himself, so long as what is imperfection and weakness when viewed in reference to ourselves be considered as most complete and excellent whenever it is imputed to God. Questionless the glory and majesty of the Deity must have been so dear to him, that he would never say anything of himself which could be humiliating or degrading, and would ascribe to himself no personal attribute which he would not willingly have ascribed to him by his creatures. Let us be convinced that those have acquired the truest apprehension of the nature of God who submit their understandings to his word; inasmuch as he has accommodated his word to their understandings, and has shown what he wishes their notion of the Deity should be.

To speak summarily, God either is, or is not, such as he represents himself to be. If he be really such, why should we think otherwise of him? If he be not such, on what authority do we say what God has not said? If at least it be his will that we should thus think of him, why does our imagination wander into some other conception? Why should we hesitate to conceive of God according to what he has not hesitated to declare explicitly respecting himself? For such knowledge of the Deity as was necessary for the salvation of man, he has himself of his goodness been pleased to reveal abundantly. Deut. xxix. 29. *the secret things belong unto Jehovah, but those things which are revealed belong unto us . . . that we may do them.*

In arguing thus, we do not say that God is in fashion like unto man in all his parts and members, but that as far as we are concerned to know, he is of that form which he attributes to himself in the sacred writings. If therefore we persist in entertaining a different conception of the Deity than that which it is to be presumed he desires should be cherished, inasmuch as he has himself disclosed it to us, we frustrate the purposes of God instead of rendering him submissive obedience. As if, forsooth, we wished to show that it was not we who had thought too meanly of God, but God who had thought too meanly of us.

It is impossible to comprehend accurately under any form of definition the *divine nature,* for so it is called, 2 Pet. i. 4. *that ye might be partakers of the divine nature*—though nature does not here signify essence, but the divine image, as in Gal. iv. 8. *which by nature are no Gods,* and θεοτὴς Col. ii. 9. θεοτὴς Rom. i. 20. τὸ θεῖον Acts xvii. 29. which words are all translated *Godhead.* But though the nature of God cannot be defined, since he who has no efficient cause is essentially greatest of all, Isai. xxviii. 29. some description of it at least may be collected from his names and attributes.

The NAMES and ATTRIBUTES of God either show his nature, or his divine power and excellence. There are three names which seem principally to intimate the nature of God,— יְהֹוָה *Jehovah*— יָהּ *Jah*— אֶהְיֶה *Ehie.*

Even the name of Jehovah was not forbidden to be pronounced, provided it was with due reverence. Exod. iii. 15. *Jehovah, God of your fathers . . . this is my name for ever, and this is my memorial.* xx. 7. *thou shalt not take the name of Jehovah thy God in vain.* Again, it occurs pronounced, 1 Kings xvii. 12. *as Jehovah thy God liveth,* and so in many other places. This name both in the New Testament and in the Greek version of the Old is always translated Κύριος—THE LORD,—probably for no other reason than because the word Jehovah could not be expressed in Greek letters. Its signification is, *he who is,* or, *which is, and which was, and which is to come,* Rev. i. 4. Jah, which is a sort of contraction of the former name, has the same signification. Exod. xvii. 16. *Jah hath sworn*—and in other places. Exod. iii. 14. אֶהְיֶה *Ehie,*

I am that I am or *will be;* and if the first person be changed into the third of the kindred verb, *Jave, who is,* or *will be,*—meaning the same as Jehovah, as some think, and more properly expressed thus than by the other words; but the name Jave appears to signify not only the existence of his nature, but also of his promises, or rather the completion of his promises; whence it is said, Exod. vi. 3. *by my name* JEHOVAH *was I not known to them.* And with what vowel points this name Jehovah ought to be pronounced, is shown by those proper names into the composition of which two of them enter, as Jehosaphat, Jehoram, Jehoiada, and the like. The third, or final vowel point may be supplied by analogy from the two other divine names, אֲדֹנָי and יָהּ.

I. The first of the attributes which show the inherent nature of God, is TRUTH. Jer. x. 10. *Jehovah is the true God.* John xvii. 3. *that they might know thee the only true God.* 1 Thess. i. 9. *the living and true God.* 1 John v. 20. *that we may know him that is true.*

II. Secondly, God considered in his most simple nature is a SPIRIT. Exod. iii. 14, 15. *I am that I am.* Rom. xi. 36. *of him and through him are all things.* John iv. 24. *God is a spirit.* What a spirit is, or rather what it is not, is shown, Isai. xxxi. 3. *flesh, and not spirit.* Luke xxiv. 39. *a spirit hath not flesh and bones.* Whence it is evident that the essence of God, being in itself most simple, can admit no compound quality; so that the term *hypostasis* Heb. i. 3. which is differently translated *substance,* or *subsistence,* or *person,* can be nothing else but that most perfect essence by which God subsists by himself, in himself, and through himself. For neither *substance* nor *subsistence* make any addition to what is already a most perfect essence; and the word *person* in its later acceptation signifies any individual thing gifted with intelligence, while *hypostasis* denotes not the *ens* itself, but the essence of the *ens* in the abstract. Hypostasis, therefore, is clearly the same as essence, and thus many of the Latin commentators render it in the passage already quoted. Therefore, as God is a most simple essence, so is he also a most simple subsistence.

III. IMMENSITY and INFINITY. 1 Kings viii. 27. *the heaven and heaven of heavens cannot contain thee.* Job xi. 8. *it is as high as heaven . . . deeper than hell.* xxxvi. 26. *God is great, and we know him not.*

IV. ETERNITY. It is universally acknowledged that nothing is eternal, strictly speaking, but what has neither beginning nor end, both which properties are attributed to God, not indeed in each of the following passages separately, but as a plain deduction from the several texts when compared together. Job xxxvi. 26. *neither can the number of his years be searched out.* Gen. xxi. 33. *the everlasting God,* literally, *the God of old time* or *ages.* Psal. xc. 2. *from everlasting to everlasting, thou art God,* or *from age to age.* cii. 12. *but thou, O Jehovah, shalt endure for ever.* v. 24. *thy years are through all generations.* v. 27. *but thou art the same, and thy years shall have no end.* Psal. cxlv. 13. *thy kingdom is an everlasting kingdom.* Isai. xliii. 10. *before me there was no God formed, neither shall there be after me.* xliv. 6. *I am the first, and I am the last.* Habak. i. 12. *art thou not from everlasting,* literally, *from old time.*

The evidence of the New Testament is still clearer, because the Greek word signifies *to exist for ever.* Rom. xvi. 26. *according to the commandment of the everlasting God.* 1 Tim. i. 17. *unto the King eternal.* Rev. i. 4. *from him which is, and which was, and which is to come.*

But all the words used in Scripture to denote eternity, often signify only of old time, or antiquity. Gen. vi. 4. *mighty men which were of old.* Job xx. 4. *knowest thou not this of old,* or *from eternity, since man was placed upon earth?* Isai. xlii. 14. *I have long time holden my peace.* David also seems to have understood that the term *for ever* only intimated *a great while to come.* 2 Sam. vii. 13. *I will stablish the throne of his kingdom for ever,* compared with v. 19. *thou hast spoken also of thy servant's house for a great while to come.* See also 1 Chron. xvii. 12, 14, 17. John ix. 32. *since the world began was it not heard that any man opened the eyes of one that was born blind.* Acts iii. 21. *which God hath spoken by the mouth of all his holy prophets since the world began.* 2 Tim. i. 9. and Tit. i. 2. *before the world began:* and in Heb. xi. 3. the word is also used to signify this world, where the Syriac version translates it,—*before the worlds were framed.* From these and many similar texts it appears that the idea of eternity, properly so called, is conveyed in the Hebrew language rather by comparison and deduction than in express words.

V. The IMMUTABILITY of God has an immediate connection with the last attribute. Psal. cii. 27. *but thou art the same.* Mal.

iii. 6. *I am Jehovah, I change not.* James i. 17. *with whom is no variableness, neither shadow of turning.*

VI. His INCORRUPTIBILITY is also derived from the fourth attribute. Psal. cii. 26. *thou shalt endure.* Rom. i. 23. *the uncorruptible God.* 1 Tim. i. 17. *unto the King immortal.*

VII. The next attribute of God, his OMNIPRESENCE, arises from his infinity. Psal. cxxxix. 8, 9. *if I ascend up into heaven, thou art there,* &c. &c. Prov. xv. 3. *the eyes of Jehovah are in every place.* Jer. xxiii. 24. *do not I fill heaven and earth?* Eph. iv. 6. *who is above all, and through all, and in you all.* Our thoughts of the omnipresence of God, whatever may be the nature of the attribute, should be such as appear most suitable to the reverence due to the Deity.

VIII. OMNIPOTENCE. 2 Chron. xx. 6. *in thine hand is there not power and might?* Job xlii. 2. *I know that thou canst do every thing.* Psal. xxxiii. 9. *he spake, and it was done.* cxv. 3. *he hath done whatsoever he hath pleased.* See also cxxxv. 6. Matt. xix. 26. *with God all things are possible.* Luke i. 37. *with God nothing shall be impossible.* Hence the name of El Shaddai, applied to the Deity, Gen. xvii. 1. *I am the Almighty God,* literally, *sufficient.* Ruth i. 21. *the Almighty hath afflicted me.* Jer. xxxii. 18. *the Great, the Mighty God, the Lord of Hosts.* Gen. xiv. 22. *Jehovah, the most high God, the possessor of heaven and earth.* Thus also the name אֲדֹנָי frequently occurs. In the New Testament, *the Lord Almighty,* 2 Cor. vi. 18, and Rev. i. 8. *the only Potentate, the King of kings and Lord of lords,* 1 Tim. vi. 15. There seems, therefore, an impropriety in the term of *actus purus,* or the active principle, which Aristotle applies to God, for thus the Deity would have no choice of act, but what he did he would do of necessity, and could do in no other way, which would be inconsistent with his omnipotence and free agency. But it must be observed, that the power of God is not exerted in things which imply a contradiction. 2 Tim. ii. 13. *he cannot deny himself.* Tit. i. 2. *God, that cannot lie.* Heb. vi. 18. *in which it was impossible for God to lie.*

IX. All the preceding attributes may be regarded as necessary causes of the ninth attribute, the UNITY of God; of which, however, other proofs are not wanting. Deut. iv. 35. *Jehovah he is God, there is none also beside him.* v. 39. *Jehovah he is God in heaven above, and upon the earth beneath: there is none else.* vi. 4. *hear, O Israel, Jehovah our God is one Jehovah.* xxxii. 39. *I, even I, am he, and there is no God with me.* 1 Kings viii. 60. *that all the people of the earth may know that Jehovah is God, and that there is none else.* 2 Kings xix. 15. *thou art the God, even thou alone, of all the kingdoms of the earth.* Isai. xliv. 6. *beside me there is no God.* v. 8. *is there a God beside me? yea, there is no God; I know not any.* xlv. 5. *I am Jehovah, and there is none else; there is no God beside me.* v. 21. *there is no God else beside me . . . there is none beside me.* v. 22. *I am God, and there is none else*—that is, no spirit, no person, no being beside him is God; for *none* is an universal negative. xlvi. 9. *I am God, and there is none else; I am God, and there is none like me.* What can be plainer, what more distinct, what more suitable to general comprehension and the ordinary forms of speech in order that the people of God might understand that there was numerically one God and one Spirit, in the common acceptation of numerical unity?

For it was fitting and highly agreeable to reason, that what was the first and consequently the greatest commandment, scrupulous obedience to which was required by God even from the lowest of all the people, should be delivered in so plain a manner, that nothing ambiguous or obscure in its terms could lead his worshippers into error, or keep them in suspense or doubt. And thus the Israelites under the law and the prophets always understood it to mean, that God was numerically one God, that beside him there was none other, much less any equal. For those disputants of the schools had not yet appeared, who depending on their own sagacity, or rather on arguments of a purely contradictory tendency, cast a doubt upon that very unity of God which they pretended to assert. But as with regard to the omnipotence of the Deity, it is universally allowed, as has been stated before, that he can do nothing which involves a contradiction; so must it also be remembered in this place, that nothing can

be said of the one God, which is inconsistent with his unity, and which implies at the same time the unity and plurality of the Godhead.

Proceeding to the evidence of the New Testament, we find it equally clear, in so far as it goes over the former ground, and in one respect even clearer, inasmuch as it testifies that the Father of our Lord Jesus Christ is that One God. Mark xii. 28, Christ having been asked, which was the first commandment of all, answers, v. 29. from Deut. vi. 4.—a passage quoted before, and evidently understood by our Lord in the same sense which had been always applied to it—*hear, O Israel, the Lord our God is one Lord.* To which answer the scribe assented, v. 32. *well, Master, thou hast said the truth; for there is one God, and there is none other but he.* John xvii. 3. *This is life eternal, that they might know thee, the only true God.* Rom. iii. 30. *seeing it is one God.* 1 Cor. viii. 4. *we know . . . that there is none other God but one.* v. 6. *to us there is but one God, the Father, of whom are all things.* Gal. iii. 20. *a mediator is not a mediator of one; but God is one.* Eph. iv. 6. *one God and Father of all.* 1 Tim. ii. 5. *there is one God.* So too, though אֱלֹהִים be plural in the Hebrew, it is used notwithstanding for the One God, Gen. i. 1. אֱלֹהִים בָּרָא· Psal. vii. 10. and lxxxvi. 10. אֱלֹהִים־בַּדִּיף; and elsewhere. But אֱלֹהַ is also used in the singular, Psal. xviii. 31. *who is God save Jehovah, or who is a rock save our God?* which verse is sufficient to show that the singular and plural of this word both mean the same thing. More will be found on this subject in the fifth Chapter.

Hitherto those attributes only have been mentioned which describe the nature of God, partly in an affirmative sense, partly negatively, as where they deny the existence of those imperfections in the Deity, which belong to created things,—as, for instance, when we speak of his immensity, his infinity, his incorruptibility. The succeeding attributes are such as show his divine power and excellence under the ideas of VITALITY, INTELLIGENCE and WILL.

I. VITALITY. Deut. xxxii. 40. *I live for ever*, whence he is called *the living God.* Psal. xlii. 2. and in many other passages. John v. 26. *the Father hath life in himself.*

II. The attribute of OMNISCIENCE refers to the INTELLIGENCE of God. Gen. vi. 5. *God saw . . . every imagination of the thoughts of his heart.* Gen. xviii. 14. *is anything too hard for Jehovah?* 1 Chron. xxviii. 9. *Jehovah searcheth all hearts.* 2 Chron. vi. 30. *thou only knowest the hearts of the children of men.* Psal. xxxiii. 15. *he fashioneth their hearts alike; he considereth all their works.* cxxxix. 2. *thou understandest my thought afar off.* v. 4. *for there is not a word in my tongue, but, lo, O Jehovah, thou knowest it altogether.* cxlvii. 5. *his understanding is infinite.* Job xi. 7–9. *canst thou by searching find out God?* &c. xxvi. 6. *hell is naked before him.* Prov. xv. 11. *hell and destruction are before Jehovah; how much more then the hearts of the children of men.* xvi. 2. *Jehovah weigheth the spirits.* xvii. 3. *Jehovah trieth the hearts.* Isai. xl. 28. *there is no searching of his understanding.* Jer. xvii. 10. *I Jehovah search the heart, I try the reins,* whence, Acts i. 24. he is called *the Lord which knoweth the hearts of all men.* Jer. xxiii. 23, 24. *am I a God at hand, saith Jehovah, and not a God afar off? can any hide himself in secret places that I shall not see him?* Heb. iv. 13. *all things are naked and opened unto the eyes of him,* whence he is called the *only wise*, Dan. ii. 10. Rom. xvi. 27. 1 Tim. i. 17. So extensive is the prescience of God, that he knows beforehand the thoughts and actions of free agents as yet unborn, and many ages before those thoughts or actions have their origin. Deut. xxxi. 16. *behold, thou shalt sleep with thy fathers; and this people will rise up, and go a whoring after the gods of the strangers of the land,* &c. v. 20, 21. *then will they turn unto other gods,* &c. *for I know the imagination which they go about even now, before I have brought them into the land which I sware.* 2 Kings viii. 12. *I know the evil that thou wilt do unto the children of Israel.*

III. With reference to the WILL, God is, 1ˢᵗ. INFINITELY PURE AND HOLY. Exod. xv. 11. *glorious in holiness.* Josh. xxiv. 19. *he is an holy God.* 1 Sam. ii. 2. *there is none holy as Jehovah.* vi. 20. *before this holy God Jehovah.* Job xv. 15. *the heavens are not clean in his sight.* Isai. vi. 2, 3. *he covered his face . . . and said, Holy, holy, holy, is the Lord of Hosts.* xl. 25. *saith the Holy One.* xli. 20. *the Holy One of Israel.* Habak. i. 13. *thou art of purer eyes than to behold evil.*

2. He is MOST GRACIOUS. Exod. xxxiv. 6. *merciful and gracious, long-suffering, and abundant in goodness and truth.* See also Psal. lxxxvi. 15. and ciii. 8. v. 4. *neither shall evil dwell with thee.* xxv. 6. *thy loving-kindnesses . . . have been ever of old.* ciii. 11. *great is his mercy toward them that fear him.* v. 17. *the mercy of Jehovah is from everlasting to everlasting.* cxix. 68. *thou art good, and doest good.* Lam. iii. 22. *it is of the mercies of Jehovah that we are not consumed.* Matt. xix. 17. *there is none good but one, that is, God.* Luke vi. 36. *be ye merciful, as your Father also is merciful.* 2 Cor. i. 3. *the Father of mercies.* Eph. ii. 4. *rich in mercy.* 1 John iv. 8. *God is love.* And thus again God may be proved to be immutable, from the consideration of his infinite wisdom and goodness; since a being of infinite wisdom and goodness would neither wish to change an infinitely good state for another, nor would he be able to change it without contradicting his own attributes.

3. As God is true by nature, so is he also TRUE and FAITHFUL in respect of his will. Psal. xix. 7. *the testimony of Jehovah is sure.* John vii. 28. *he that sent me is true.* Rom. iii. 4. *let God be true, but every man a liar.* 2 Tim. ii. 13. *if we believe not, yet he abideth faithful.* 1 Cor. i. 9. and x. 13. *God is faithful.* Rev. vi. 10. *O Lord, holy and true.*

4. He is also JUST. Deut. xxxii. 4. *all his ways are judgment, a God of truth and without iniquity, just and right is he.* Psal. xxxvi. 6. *thy righteousness is like the great mountains.* cxix. 137. *righteous art thou, O Jehovah, and upright are thy judgements.* Isai. v. 16. *God . . . shall be sanctified in righteousness.* It is not requisite to discuss at large in this place what is consistent or inconsistent with the justice of God, since if it be necessary to say anything on so clear a subject, occasions will arise for introducing such observations as may be required in other parts of this work.

Severity also is attributed to God. Rom. xi. 22. *on them which fell, severity.*

From all these attributes springs that infinite excellence of God which constitutes his true perfection, and causes him to abound in glory, and to be most deservedly and justly the supreme Lord of all things, according to the qualities so frequently ascribed to him. Psal. xvi. 11. *in thy presence is fulness of joy.* civ. 1. *thou art clothed with honour and majesty.* Dan. vii. 10. *thousand thousands ministered unto him.* Matt. v. 48. *as your Father which is in heaven is perfect.* 1 Tim. i. 11. *the blessed God.* vi. 15. *who is the blessed . . . potentate.*

Some description of this divine glory has been revealed, so far as it falls within the scope of human comprehension. Exod. xix. 18, &c. *mount Sinai was altogether on a smoke—.* xxiv. 10, &c. *they saw the God of Israel, and there was under his feet as it were a paved work of a sapphire stone, and as it were the body of heaven in his clearness.* xxxiii. 9, 10. *the cloudy pillar descended, &c. &c.—* and v. 18, &c. 1 Kings xix. 11. *behold, Jehovah passed by.* viii. 10, 11. *the cloud filled the house of Jehovah.* xxii. 19. *I saw Jehovah sitting on his throne.* Psal. xviii. 8, &c. and civ. Micah i. 3, &c. Nahum i. 3, &c. Isai. vi. Ezek. i. and viii. 1–3. and x. 1, &c. and xliii. 2, 3. Habak. iii. 3, &c. Dan. vii. 9. Rev. iv.

It follows, finally, that God must be styled by us WONDERFUL, and INCOMPREHENSIBLE. Judges xiii. 18. *why askest thou thus after my name, seeing it is secret?* Psal. cxlv. 3. *his greatness is unsearchable.* Isai. xl. 28. *there is no searching of his understanding.*

CHAP. III.

OF THE DIVINE DECREES.

Hitherto I have considered that knowledge of God which is to be obtained from his nature. That which is derived from his efficiency is the next subject of inquiry.

The EFFICIENCY OF GOD is either INTERNAL or EXTERNAL.

The INTERNAL EFFICIENCY of God is that which is independent of all extraneous agency. Such are his decrees. Eph. i. 9. *which he hath purposed in himself.*

The DECREES OF GOD are GENERAL or SPECIAL. GOD'S GENERAL DECREE is that WHEREBY HE HAS DECREED FROM ALL ETERNITY OF HIS OWN MOST FREE AND WISE AND HOLY PURPOSE, WHATEVER HE WILLED, OR WHATEVER HE WAS HIMSELF ABOUT TO DO.

WHATEVER, &c. Eph. i. 11. *who worketh all things after the counsel of his own will;* which comprehends whatever he himself works or wills singly, not what is done by others, or by himself in co-operation with those to whom he has conceded the natural power of free agency. The creation of the world, and the removal of the curse from the ground, Gen. viii. 21. are among his sole decrees.

FROM ALL ETERNITY. Acts xv. 18. *known unto God are all his works from the beginning of the world.* 1 Cor. ii. 7. *even the hidden wisdom which God ordained before the world.*

OF HIS OWN MOST FREE—; that is, without controul, impelled by no necessity, but according to his own will. Eph. i. 11. as before.

MOST WISE—; that is, according to his perfect foreknowledge of all things that were to be created. Acts ii. 23. *by the determinate counsel and foreknowledge of God.* iv. 28. *for to do whatsoever thy hand and thy counsel determined before to be done.* xv. 18. *known unto God are all his works from the beginning of the world.* 1 Cor. ii. 7. *the hidden wisdom which God ordained before the world.* Eph. iii. 10, 11. *the manifold wisdom of God, according to the eternal purpose which he purposed.*

There is an absurdity, therefore, in separating the decrees or will of the Deity from his eternal counsel and foreknowledge, or in giving them priority of order. For the foreknowledge of God is nothing but the wisdom of God, under another name, or that idea of every thing, which he had in his mind, to use the language of men, before he decreed any thing.

Thus it is to be understood that God decreed nothing absolutely, which he left in the power of free agents,—a doctrine which is shewn by the whole canon of Scripture. Gen. xix. 17, 21. *escape to the mountain, lest thou be consumed . . . see, I have accepted thee concerning this thing also, that I will not overthrow this city for the which thou hast spoken.* Exod. iii. 8,

17. *I am come down to deliver them . . .
and to bring them up unto a good land*—
though these very individuals actually perished in the wilderness. God also had determined to deliver his people by the hand
of Moses, yet he would have killed that
same Moses, Exod. iv. 24. if he had not
immediately circumcised his son. 1 Sam.
ii. 30. *I said indeed . . . but now Jehovah
saith, Be it far from me;*—and the reason
for this change is added,—*for, them that
honour me I will honour.* xiii. 13, 14. *now
would Jehovah have established thy kingdom . . . but now thy kingdom shall not
continue.* Again, God had said, 2 Kings
xx. 1. that Hezekiah should die immediately, which however did not happen, and
therefore could not have been decreed without reservation. The death of Josiah was
not decreed peremptorily, but he would not
hearken to the voice of Necho when he
warned him according to the word of the
Lord, not to come out against him; 2 Chron.
xxxv. 22. Again, Jer. xviii. 9, 10. *at what
instant I shall speak concerning a nation,
and concerning a kingdom, to build and to
plant it; if it do evil in my sight, that it
obey not my voice, then I will repent of the
good wherewith I said I would benefit
them,*—that is, I will rescind the decree,
because that people hath not kept the condition on which the decree rested. Here
then is a rule laid down by God himself,
according to which he would always have
his decrees understood,—namely, that regard should be paid to the conditionate
terms attached to them. Jer. xxvi. 3. *if so
be they will hearken, and turn every man
from his evil way, that I may repent me of
the evil, which I purpose to do unto them
because of the evil of their doings.* So also
God had not even decreed absolutely the
burning of Jerusalem. Jer. xxxviii. 17, &c.
*thus saith Jehovah . . . if thou wilt assur-
edly go forth unto the king of Babylon's
princes, then thy soul shall live, and this
city shall not be burned with fire.* Jonah
iii. 4. *yet forty days, and Nineveh shall be
overthrown*—but it appears from the tenth
verse, that when God saw that they turned
from their evil way, he repented of his purpose, though Jonah was angry and thought
the change unworthy of God. Acts xxvii.
24, 31. *God hath given thee all them that
sail with thee*—and again—*except these*

abide in the ship, ye cannot be saved, where
Paul revokes the declaration he had previously made on the authority of God; or
rather, God revokes the gift he had made
to Paul, except on condition that they should
consult for their own safety by their own
personal exertions.

It appears, therefore, from these passages
of Scripture, and from many others which
occur of the same kind, to the paramount
authority of which we must bow, that the
most high God has not decreed all things
absolutely.

If, however, it be allowable to examine
the divine decrees by the laws of human
reason, since so many arguments have been
maintained on this subject by controvertists
on both sides with more of subtlety than
of solid argument, this theory of contingent decrees may be defended even on the
principles of men, as most wise, and in no
respect unworthy of the Deity. For if
those decrees of God which have been referred to above, and such others of the
same class as occur perpetually, were to be
understood in an absolute sense, without
any implied conditions, God would contradict himself, and appear inconsistent.

It is argued, however, that in such instances not only was the ultimate purpose
predestinated, but even the means themselves were predestinated with a view to
it. So indeed it is asserted, but Scripture
nowhere confirms the rule, which alone
would be a sufficient reason for rejecting
it. But it is also attended by this additional inconvenience, that it would entirely
take away from human affairs all liberty
of action, all endeavour and desire to do
right. For the course of argument would
be of this kind—If God have at all events
decreed my salvation, whatever I may do
against it, I shall not perish. But God
has also decreed as the means of salvation
that you should do rightly. I cannot, therefore, but do rightly at some time or other,
since God has decreed that also,—in the
mean time I will act as I please; if I never
do rightly, it will be seen that I was never
predestinated to salvation, and that whatever good I might have done would have
been to no purpose. See more on this
subject in the following Chapter.

Nor is it sufficient to affirm in reply,
that the kind of necessity intended is not

compulsory, but a necessity arising from the immutability of God, whereby all things are decreed, or a necessity arising from his infallibility or prescience, whereby all things are foreknown. I shall satisfactorily dispose in another place of these two alleged species of necessity recognized by the schools: in the mean time no other law of necessity can be admitted than what logic, or in other words, what sound reason teaches; that is to say, when the efficient either causes some determinate and uniform effect by its own inherent propensity, as for example, when fire burns, which kind is denominated physical necessity; or when the efficient is compelled by some extraneous force to operate the effect, which is called compulsory necessity, and in the latter case, whatever effect the efficient produces, it produces *per accidens*. Now any necessity arising from external causes influences the agent either determinately or compulsorily; and it is apparent that in either alternative his liberty would be wholly annihilated. But though a certain immutable and internal necessity of acting right, independent of all extraneous influence whatever, may exist in God conjointly with the most perfect liberty, both which principles in the same divine nature tend to the same point, it does not therefore follow that the same thing can be conceded with regard to two different natures, as the nature of God and the nature of man, in which case the external immutability of one party may be in opposition to the internal liberty of the other, and may prevent unity of will. Nor is it admitted that the actions of God are in themselves necessary, but only that he has a necessary existence; for Scripture itself testifies that his decrees, and therefore his actions, of what kind soever they be, are perfectly free.

But it is objected that no constraint is put upon the liberty of free agents by divine necessity or first causes. I answer,—if it do not constrain, it either determines, or co-operates, or is wholly inefficient. If it determine or co-operate, it is either the sole or the joint and principal cause of all the actions, whether good or bad, of free agents. If it be wholly inefficient, it cannot be called a cause in any sense, much less can it be termed necessity.

Nor do we imagine anything unworthy of God, when we assert that those conditional events depend on the human will, which God himself has chosen to place at the free disposal of man; since the Deity purposely framed his own decrees with reference to particular circumstances, in order that he might permit free causes to act conformably to that liberty with which he had endued them. On the contrary, it would be much more unworthy of God, that man should nominally enjoy a liberty of which he was virtually deprived, which would be the case were that liberty to be oppressed or even obscured under the pretext of some sophistical necessity of immutability or infallibility, though not of compulsion,—a notion which has led, and still continues to lead many individuals into error.

However, properly speaking, the divine counsels can be said to depend on nothing, but on the wisdom of God himself, whereby he perfectly foreknew in his own mind from the beginning what would be the nature and event of every future occurrence when its appointed season should arrive.

But it is asked how events, which are uncertain, inasmuch as they depend on the human will, can harmonize with the decrees of God, which are immutably fixed? for it is written, Psal. xxxiii. 11. *the counsel of Jehovah standeth for ever.* See also Prov. xix. 21. and Isai. xlvi. 10. Heb. vi. 17. *the immutability of his counsel.* To this objection it may be answered, first, that to God the issue of events is not uncertain, but foreknown with the utmost certainty, though they be not decreed necessarily, as will appear afterwards.—Secondly, in all the passages referred to, the divine counsel is said to stand against all human power and counsel, but not against the liberty of will with regard to such things as God himself had placed at man's disposal, and had determined so to place from all eternity. For otherwise one of God's decrees would be in direct opposition to another, and that very consequence would ensue which the objector imputes to the doctrine of his opponents, namely, that by considering those things as necessary which the Deity had left to the uncontrouled decision of man, God would be rendered mutable. But God is not mutable, so long as he decrees nothing absolutely which could happen otherwise through the liberty assigned to man; whereas he would then be mutable, then his counsel would not stand, if he were to obstruct by another decree that liberty which he had already decreed, or were to darken it with the least shadow of necessity.

It follows, therefore, that the liberty of man must be considered entirely independent of necessity, and no admission can be made in favour of that modification of the principle which is founded on the doctrine of God's immutability and prescience. If there be any necessity at all, as has been stated before, it either determines free agents to a particular line of conduct, or it constrains them against their will, or it co-operates with them in conjunction with their will, or it is altogether inoperative. If it determine free agents to a particular line of conduct, man will be rendered the natural cause of all his actions, and consequently of his sins, and formed as it were with an inclination for sinning. If it constrain them against their will, man who is subject to this compulsory decree will be rendered the cause of sins only *per accidens,* God being the cause of sins *per se.* If it co-operate with them in conjunction with their will, then God becomes either the principal or the joint cause of sins with man. If finally it be altogether inoperative, there is no such thing as necessity, it virtually destroys itself by being without operation. For it is wholly impossible, that God should have decreed necessarily what we know at the same time to be in the power of man; or that that should be immutable which it remains for subsequent contingent circumstances either to fulfil or frustrate.

Whatever, therefore, was left to the free will of our first parents, could not have been decreed immutably or absolutely from all eternity; and questionless, either nothing was ever placed in man's power, or if it were, God cannot be said to have determined finally respecting it without reference to possible contingencies.

If it be objected, that this doctrine leads to absurd consequences, we reply, either the consequences are not absurd, or they are not the consequences of the doctrine. For it is neither impious nor absurd to say, that the idea of certain things or events might be suggested to God from some extraneous source; for since God had determined from all eternity, that man should so far be a free agent, that it remained with himself to decide whether he would stand or fall, the idea of that evil event, or of the fall of man, was suggested to God from an extraneous source,—a truth which all confess.

Nor does it follow from hence, that what is merely temporal becomes the cause of, or a restriction upon what is eternal, for it was not any thing temporal, but the wisdom of the eternal mind that gave occasion for framing the divine counsel.

Whatever therefore was the subject of the divine counsel, whether man or angel who was to be gifted with free will, so that his fall might depend upon his own volition, such without doubt was the nature of the decree itself, so that all the evil consequences which ensued were contingent upon man's will; wherefore the covenant stood thus—if thou remain faithful, thou shalt abide in Paradise; if thou fall, thou shalt be cast out: if thou dost not eat the forbidden fruit, thou shalt live; if thou eat, thou shalt die.

Hence, those who contend that the liberty of actions is subject to an absolute decree, erroneously conclude that the decree of God is the cause of his foreknowledge, and antecedent in order of time. If we must apply to God a phraseology borrowed from our own habits and understanding, that his decrees should have been the consequence of his foreknowledge seems more agreeable to reason, as well as to Scripture, and to the nature of God himself, who, as has just been proved, decreed every thing according to his infinite wisdom by virtue of his foreknowledge.

It is not intended to deny that the will of God is the first cause of all things, but we do not separate his prescience and wisdom from his will, much less do we think them subsequent to the latter in point of time. Finally, the will of God is not less the universal first cause, because he has himself decreed that some things should be left to our own free will, than if each particular event had been decreed necessarily.

To comprehend the whole matter in a few words, the sum of the argument may be thus stated in strict conformity with reason. God of his wisdom determined to create men and angels reasonable beings, and therefore free agents; at the same time he foresaw which way the bias of their will would incline, in the exercise of their own uncontrouled liberty. What then? shall we say that this foresight or foreknowledge on the part of God imposed on them the necessity of acting in any definite way? No more than if the future event had been foreseen by any human being. For what any human being has foreseen as certain to happen, will not less certainly happen than what God himself has predicted. Thus Elisha foresaw how much evil Hazael would bring upon the children of Israel in the course of a few years, 2 Kings viii. 12. Yet no one would affirm that the evil took place necessarily on account of the foreknowledge of Elisha; for had he never foreknown it, the event would have occurred with equal certainty, through the free will of the agent. So neither does any thing happen because God has foreseen it; but he foresees the event of every action, because he is acquainted with their natural causes, which, in pursuance of his own decree, are left at liberty to exert their legitimate influence. Consequently the issue does not depend on God who foresees it, but on him alone who is the object of his foresight. Since therefore, as has before been shown, there can be no absolute decree of God regarding free agents, undoubtedly the prescience of the Deity (which can no more bias free agents than the prescience of man, that is, not at all, since the action in both cases is intransitive, and has no external influence,) can neither impose any necessity of itself, nor can it be considered at all the cause of free actions. If it be so considered, the very name of liberty must be altogether abolished as an unmeaning sound; and that not only in matters of religion, but even in questions of morality and indifferent things. There can be nothing but what will happen necessarily, since there is nothing but what is foreknown by God.

That this long discussion may be at length concluded by a brief summary of the whole matter, we must hold that God foreknows all future events, but that he has not decreed them all absolutely: lest all sin should be imputed to the Deity, and evil spirits and wicked men should be exempted from blame. Does my opponent avail himself of this, and think the concession enough to prove either that God does not foreknow every thing, or that all future events must therefore happen necessarily, because God has foreknown them? I allow that future events which God has foreseen, will happen certainly, but not of necessity. They will happen certainly, because the divine prescience cannot be deceived, but they will not happen necessarily, because prescience can have no influence on the object foreknown, inasmuch as it is only an intransitive action. What therefore is to happen according to contingency and the free will of man, is not the effect of God's prescience, but is produced by the free agency of its own natural causes, the future spontaneous inclination of which is perfectly known to God. Thus God foreknew that Adam would fall of his own free will; his fall therefore was certain, but not necessary, since it proceeded from his own free will, which is incompatible with necessity. Thus too God foreknew that the Israelites would revolt from the true worship to strange gods, Deut. xxxi. 16. If they were to be led to revolt necessarily on account of this prescience on the part of God, it was unjust to threaten them with the many evils which he was about to send upon them, ver. 17. it would have been to no purpose that a song was ordered to be written, which should be a witness for him against the children of Israel, because their sin would have been of necessity. But the prescience of God, like that of Moses, v. 27. had no extraneous influence, and God testifies, v. 16. that he foreknew they would sin from their own voluntary impulse, and of their own accord,—*this people will rise up,* &c. and v. 18. *I will surely hide my face in that day . . . in that they are turned unto other gods.* Now the revolt of the Israelites which subsequently took place, was not the consequence of God's foreknowledge of that event, but God foreknew that, although they were free agents, they would certainly revolt, owing to causes with which he was well acquainted. v. 20, 21. *when they shall have eaten and filled themselves, and waxen fat, then will they turn unto other gods . . . I know their imagination which they go about, even now before I have brought them into the land which I sware.*

From what has been said it is sufficiently evident, that free causes are not impeded by any law of necessity arising from the decrees or prescience of God. There are some who in their zeal to oppose this doctrine, do not hesitate even to assert that God is himself the cause and origin of sin. Such men, if they are not to be looked upon as misguided rather than mischievous, should be ranked among the most abandoned of all blasphemers. An attempt to refute them, would be nothing more than an argument to prove that God was not the evil spirit.

Thus far of the GENERAL DECREE of God. Of his SPECIAL DECREES the first and most important is that which regards his SON, and from which he primarily derives his name of FATHER. Psal. ii. 7. *I will declare the decree: Jehovah hath said unto me, Thou art my Son, this day have I begotten thee.* Heb. i. 5. *unto which of the angels said he at any time, Thou art my son, this day have I begotten thee? And again, I will be to him a Father, and he shall be to me a Son.* 1 Pet. i. 19, 20. *Christ . . . who verily was fore-ordained before the foundation of the world.* Isai. xlii. 1. *mine elect, in whom my soul delighteth.* 1 Pet. ii. 4. *chosen of God, and precious.* From all these passages it appears that the Son of God was begotten by the decree of the Father.

There is no express mention made of any SPECIAL DECREE respecting THE ANGELS, but its existence seems to be implied, 1 Tim. v. 21. *the elect angels.* Eph. i. 9, 10. *the mystery of his will . . . that he might gather together in one all things in Christ, both which are in heaven, and which are on earth.*

CHAP. IV.

OF PREDESTINATION.

The principal SPECIAL DECREE of God RELATING TO MAN is termed PREDESTINATION, whereby God IN PITY TO MANKIND, THROUGH FORESEEING THAT THEY WOULD FALL OF THEIR OWN ACCORD, PREDESTINATED TO ETERNAL SALVATION BEFORE THE FOUNDATION OF THE WORLD THOSE WHO SHOULD BELIEVE AND CONTINUE IN THE FAITH; FOR A MANIFESTATION OF THE GLORY OF HIS MERCY, GRACE, AND WISDOM, ACCORDING TO HIS PURPOSE IN CHRIST.

It has been the practice of the schools to use the word predestination, not only in the sense of election, but also of reprobation. This is not consistent with the caution necessary on so momentous a subject, since wherever it is mentioned in Scripture, election alone is uniformly intended. Rom. viii. 29, 30. *whom he did predestinate to be conformed to the image of his Son . . . moreover whom he did predestinate, them he also called: and whom he called, them he also justified: and whom he justified, them he also glorified.* 1 Cor. ii. 7. *the hidden wisdom, which God ordained before the world unto our glory.* Eph. i. 5. *having predestinated us unto the adoption.* v. 11. *in whom also we have obtained an inheritance, being predestinated according to his purpose.* Acts ii. 23. compared with iv. 28. *him being delivered by the determinate counsel and foreknowledge of God they have taken . . . for to do whatsoever thy hand and thy counsel determined before to be done,* namely, as a means of procuring the salvation of man.

In other modes of expression, where predestination is alluded to, it is always in the same sense of election alone. Rom. viii. 28. *to them who are the called according to his purpose.* ix. 23, 24. *the vessels of mercy which he had afore prepared unto glory, even us, whom he hath called.* Eph. iii. 11. *according to the eternal purpose which he purposed in Christ Jesus.* 2 Tim. i. 9. *according to his own purpose and grace.* For when it is said negatively, 1 Thess. v. 9. *God hath not appointed us to wrath, but to obtain salvation by our Lord Jesus Christ,* it does not follow by implication that there are others who are appointed to wrath. Nor does the expression in 1 Pet. ii. 8. *whereunto also they were appointed,* signify that they were appointed from all eternity, but from some time subsequent to their defection, as the Apostles are said to be *chosen* in time, *and ordained* by Christ to their office, John xv. 16.

Again, if an argument of any weight in the discussion of so controverted a subject can be derived from allegory and metaphorical expressions, mention is frequently made of those who are written among the living, and of the book of life, but never of the book of death. Isai. iv. 3. *written among the living.* Dan. xii. 1. *at that time thy people shall be delivered, every one that shall be found written in the book.* Luke

x. 20. *rather rejoice, because your names are written in heaven.* Philipp. iv. 3. *whose names are in the book of life.* At the same time this figure of enrolment in the book of life does not appear to signify eternal predestination, which is general, but some temporary and particular decision of God applied to certain men, on account of their works. Psal. lxix. 28. *let them be blotted out of the book of the living, and not be written with the righteous;* whence it appears that they had not been written from everlasting. Isai. lxv. 6. *behold it is written before me; I will not keep silence, but will recompense.* Rev. xx. 12. *the dead were judged out of those things which were written in the books, according to their works.* It is clear, therefore, that it was not the book of eternal predestination, but of their works. In the same way neither were those ordained from everlasting who are said, Jude 4. to have been *before of old ordained to this condemnation.* For why should we give so extensive a signification to the term *of old,* instead of defining it to mean, from the time when they had become inveterate and hardened sinners? Why must we understand it to imply so remote a period, either in this text, or in the passage whence it seems to be taken? 2 Pet. ii. 3. *whose judgment now of a long time lingereth not, and their damnation slumbereth not,*—that is, from the time of their apostasy, however long they had dissembled it.

The text, Prov. xvi. 4. is also objected,— *Jehovah hath made all things for himself; yea, even the wicked for the day of evil.* But God did not make him wicked, much less did he make him so *for himself.* All that he did was to sentence the wicked to deserved punishment, as was most fitting, but he did not predestinate him, if innocent, to the same fate. It is more clearly expressed, Eccles. vii. 29. *God hath made man upright; but they have sought out many inventions,* whence the day of evil ensues as certainly, as if the wicked had been made for it.

PREDESTINATION, therefore, must always be referred to election, and seems often to be put for it. What St. Paul says, Rom. viii. 29. *whom he did foreknow, he also did predestinate,* is thus expressed 1 Pet. i. 2. *elect according to the foreknowledge.* Rom. ix. 11. *the purpose of God according to elec-* tion. xi. 5. *according to the election of grace.* Eph. i. 4. *he hath chosen us in him.* Col. iii. 12. *as the elect of God, holy and beloved.* 2 Thess. ii. 13. *because God hath from the beginning chosen you to salvation.* Reprobation, therefore, could not be included under the title of predestination. 1 Tim. ii. 4. *who will have all men to be saved, and to come unto the knowledge of the truth.* 2 Pet. iii. 9. *the Lord . . . is long-suffering to us-ward, not willing that any should perish, but that all should come to repentance,*—to us-ward, that is, towards all men, not towards the elect only, as some interpret it, but particularly towards the wicked, as it is said, Rom. ix. 22. *God endured . . . the vessels of wrath.* For if, as some object, Peter would scarcely have included himself among the unbelievers, much less would he have numbered himself among such of the elect as had not yet come to repentance. Nor does God delay on account of the elect, but rather hastens the time. Matt. xxiv. 22. *for the elect's sake those days shall be shortened.*

I understand by the term election, not that general or national election, by which God chose the whole nation of Israel for his own people, Deut. iv. 37. *because he loved thy fathers, therefore he chose their seed after them,* and vii. 6–8. *Jehovah thy God hath chosen thee to be a special people unto himself,* Isai. xlv. 4. *for Israel mine elect.* Nor do I mean that election by which God, after rejecting the Jews, chose the Gentiles as those to whom the Gospel should be announced in preference, of which the apostle speaks particularly Rom. ix. and xi. Nor am I referring to that election by which an individual is selected for the performance of some office, as 1 Sam. x. 24. *see ye him whom the Lord hath chosen?* John vi. 70. *have not I chosen you twelve, and one of you is a devil?* whence those are sometimes called elect who are eminent for any particular excellence, as 2 John 1. *the elect lady,* that is, most precious, and v. 13. *thy elect sister.* 1 Pet. ii. 6. *a chief corner stone, elect and precious.* 1 Tim. v. 21. *the elect angels.* But that special election is here intended, which is nearly synonymous with eternal predestination. Election, therefore, is not a part of predestination; much less then is reprobation. For, speaking accurately, the ultimate purpose of predestination is the salvation of believers,—a thing in itself desirable,—but on the contrary the object which reprobation has in view is the destruction of unbelievers, a thing in itself ungrateful and odious; whence it is clear that God could never have predestinated reprobation, or proposed it to himself as an end. Ezek. xviii. 32. *I have no pleasure in the death of him that dieth.* xxxiii. 11. *as I live, saith the Lord God, I have no pleasure in the death of the wicked, but that the wicked should turn from his way and live.* If therefore the Deity have no pleasure either in sin, or in the death of the sinner, that is, either in the cause or the effect of reprobation, certainly he cannot delight in reprobation itself. It follows, that reprobation forms no part of what is meant by God's predestination.

WHEREBY GOD, &c. that is, God the Father. Luke xii. 32. *it is your Father's good pleasure.* So it is stated wherever mention is made of the divine decrees or counsel: John xvii. 2. *as many as thou hast given him.* v. 6, 11, 24. *the men which thou gavest me out of the world.* Eph. i. 4. *he hath chosen us in him.* v. 5. *having predestinated us.* v. 11. *being predestinated according to his purpose.*

BEFORE THE FOUNDATION OF THE WORLD, Eph. i. 4. 2 Tim. i. 9. *before the world began.* See also Tit. i. 2.

IN PITY TO MANKIND, THROUGH FORESEE-ING THAT THEY WOULD FALL OF THEIR OWN ACCORD. It was not simply man as a being who was to be created, but man as a being who was to fall of his own accord, that was the matter or object of predestination; for that manifestation of divine grace and mercy which God designed as the ultimate purpose of predestination, presupposes the existence of sin and misery in man, originating from himself alone. It is universally admitted that the fall of man was not necessary; but if on the other hand the nature of the divine decree was such, that his fall became really inevitable,—which contradictory opinions are sometimes held in conjunction by the same persons,—then the restoration of man, who had fallen of necessity, became no longer a matter of grace, but of simple justice on the part of God. For if it be granted that he lapsed, though not against his own will, yet of necessity, it will be impossible not to think that the admitted

necessity must have overruled or influenced his will by some secret force or guidance. But if God foresaw that man would fall of his own free will, there was no occasion for any decree relative to the fall itself, but only relative to the provision to be made for man, whose future fall was foreseen. Since then the apostacy of the first man was not decreed, but only foreknown by the infinite wisdom of God, it follows that predestination was not an absolute decree before the fall of man; and even after his fall, it ought always to be considered and defined as arising, not so much from a decree itself, as from the immutable conditions of a decree.

PREDESTINATED; that is, designated, elected: proposed to himself the salvation of man as the scope and end of his counsel. Hence may be refuted the notion of an abandonment and desertion from all eternity, in direct opposition to which God explicitly and frequently declares, as has been quoted above, that he desires not the death of any one, but the salvation of all; that he hates nothing that he has made; and that he has omitted nothing which might suffice for universal salvation.

FOR A MANIFESTATION OF THE GLORY OF HIS MERCY, GRACE, AND WISDOM. This is the chief end of predestination. Rom. ix. 23. *that he might make known the riches of his glory on the vessels of mercy.* 1 Cor. ii. 7. *we speak the wisdom of God in a mystery, even the hidden wisdom which God ordained before the world unto our glory.* Eph. i. 6. *to the praise of the glory of his grace.*

ACCORDING TO HIS PURPOSE IN CHRIST. Eph. iii. 10, 11. *the manifold wisdom of God, according to the eternal purpose which he purposed in Christ Jesus our Lord.* i. 4, 5. *he hath chosen us in him; having predestinated us unto the adoption of children by Jesus Christ.* v. 11. *in him, in whom also we have obtained an inheritance, being predestinated according to his purpose.* This is the source of that love of God, declared to us in Christ. John iii. 16. *God so loved the world, that he gave his only begotten Son.* Eph. ii. 4, 5. *for his great love wherewith he loved us . . . by grace ye are saved.* 1 John iv. 9, 10. *in this was manifested the love of God toward us, because that God sent his only begotten Son into the world,* &c. Wherefore there was no grace decreed for man who was to fall, no mode of reconciliation with God, independently of the foreknown sacrifice of Christ; and since God has so plainly declared that predestination is the effect of his mercy, and love, and grace, and wisdom in Christ, it is to these qualities that we ought to attribute it, and not, as is generally done, to his absolute and secret will, even in those passages where mention is made of his will only. Exod. xxxiii. 19. *I will be gracious to whom I will be gracious,* that is, not to enter more largely into the causes of this graciousness at present, Rom. ix. 18. *he hath mercy on whom he will have mercy,* by that method, namely, which he had appointed in Christ. Or it will appear on an examination of the particular texts, that in passages of this kind God is generally speaking of some extraordinary manifestation of his grace and mercy. Thus Luke xii. 32. *it is your Father's good pleasure.* Eph. i. 5, 11. *by Jesus Christ to himself, according to the good pleasure of his will: in whom also we have obtained an inheritance . . . after the counsel of his own will.* James i. 18. *of his own will,*—that is, in Christ, who is the word and truth of God,—*begat he us with the word of truth.*

THOSE WHO SHOULD BELIEVE, AND CONTINUE IN THE FAITH. This condition is immutably attached to the decree; it attributes no mutability, either to God or to his decrees; 2 Tim. ii. 19. *the foundation of God standeth sure, having this seal, The Lord knoweth them that are his:* or according to the explanation in the same verse, all who *name the name of Christ, and depart from iniquity;* that is, whoever believes: the mutability is entirely on the side of them who renounce their faith, as it is said, 2 Tim. ii. 13. *if we believe not, yet he abideth faithful; he cannot deny himself.* It seems then that there is no particular predestination or election, but only general,—or in other words, that the privilege belongs to all who heartily believe and continue in their belief,—that none are predestinated or elected irrespectively, e.g. that Peter is not elected as Peter, or John as John, but inasmuch as they are believers, and continue in their belief,—and that thus the general decree of election becomes personally applicable to each particu-

lar believer, and is ratified to all who remain stedfast in the faith.

This is most explicitly declared by the whole of Scripture, which offers salvation and eternal life equally to all, under the condition of obedience in the Old Testament, and of faith in the New. There can be no doubt that the tenor of the decree in its promulgation was in conformity with the decree itself,—otherwise the integrity of God would be impugned, as expressing one intention, and concealing another within his breast. Such a charge is in effect made by the scholastic distinction which ascribes a two-fold will to God; his revealed will, whereby he prescribes the way in which he desires us to act, and his hidden will, whereby he decrees that we shall never so act: which is much the same as to attribute to the Deity two distinct wills, whereof one is in direct contradiction to the other. It is, however, asserted that the Scriptures contain two opposite statements respecting the same thing;—it was the will of God that Pharaoh should let the people go, for such was the divine command,—but it was also not his will, for he hardened Pharaoh's heart. The truth however is, that it was God alone who willed their departure, and Pharaoh alone who was unwilling; and that he might be the more unwilling, God hardened his heart, and himself deferred the execution of his own pleasure, which was in opposition to that of Pharaoh, that he might afflict him with heavier punishment on account of the reluctance of his will. Neither in his mode of dealing with our common father Adam, nor with those whom he calls and invites to accept of grace, can God be charged with commanding righteousness, while he decrees our disobedience to the command. What can be imagined more absurd than a necessity which does not necessitate, and a will without volition?

The tenor of the decree in its promulgation (which was the other point to be proved) is uniformly conditional. Gen. ii. 17. *thou shalt not eat of it; for in the day that thou eatest thereof thou shalt surely die,*—which is the same as if God had said, I will that thou shalt not eat of it; I have not therefore decreed that thou shalt eat of it; for if thou eat, thou shalt die; if thou eat not, thou shalt live. Thus the decree itself was conditional before the fall; which from numberless other passages appears to have been also the case after the fall.   Gen. iv. 7. *if thou doest well, shalt thou not be accepted? and if thou doest not well, sin lieth at the door*, or, *the punishment of sin watcheth for thee*.   Exod. xxxii. 32, 33. *blot me, I pray thee, out of thy book which thou hast written . . . whosoever hath sinned against me, him will I blot out of my book*. Such was the love of Moses for his nation, that he either did not remember that believers, so long as they continued such, could not be blotted out, or the expression must be understood in a modified sense, as in Rom. ix. 1, &c. *I could wish, if it were possible—*: but the answer of God, although metaphorical, explains with sufficient clearness that the principle of predestination is founded upon a condition,—*whosoever hath sinned, him will I blot out*. This is announced more fully in the enforcement of the legal covenant, Deut. vii. 6–8. where God particularly declares his choice and love of his people to have been gratuitous; and in v. 9. where he desires to be known as *a faithful God which keepeth his covenant and mercy*, he yet adds as a condition, *with them that love him and keep his commandments*.   Again, it is said still more clearly, v. 12. *it shall come to pass, if ye hearken to these judgements, and keep and do them, that Jehovah thy God shall keep unto thee the covenant and the mercy which he sware unto thy fathers*.   Though these and similar passages seem chiefly to refer either to the universal election of a nation to the service of God, or of a particular individual or family to some office (for in the Old Testament it is perhaps difficult to trace even a single expression which refers to election properly so called, that is, election to eternal life), yet the principle of the divine decree is in all cases the same.   Thus it is said of Solomon, as of another Christ, 1 Chron. xxviii. 6, 7, 9. *I have chosen him to be my son, and I will be his father*.   But what are the terms of the covenant?—*if he be constant to do my commandments and my judgments, as at this day . . . if thou seek him, he will be found of thee; but if thou forsake him, he will cast thee off for ever*.   The election of his posterity also depended on the same stipulation. 2 Chron. vi. 16. *so that thy children take heed to their way, to walk in my law*.   See also xxxiii. 8. and xv. 2. *the Lord is with you, while ye be with him . . . but if ye forsake him, he will forsake you;* whence Isaiah does not scruple to say, xiv. 1, *the Lord will yet choose Israel*.   See also Zech. i. 16. Isaiah also shows who are the elect; lxv. 9, 10. *mine elect shall inherit it . . . and Sharon shall be . . . for my people that have sought me*.   Jer. xxii. 24. *though Coniah were the signet upon my right hand, yet would I pluck thee thence*.

The same thing must be observed in the covenant of grace, wherever the condition is not added.   This however seldom happens.   Mark xvi. 16. *he that believeth and is baptized shall be saved; but he that believeth not shall be damned*.   If we could conceive God originally predestinating mankind on such conditional terms as these, endless controversies might be decided by this single sentence, or by John iii. 16. *God so loved the world, that he gave his only begotten Son, that whosoever believeth in him should not perish, but have everlasting life*.   xv. 6. *if a man abide not in me, he is cast forth as a branch*.   v. 10. *if ye keep my commandments, ye shall abide in my love, even as I have kept my Father's commandment*.   xvii. 20. *neither pray I for these alone, but for them also which shall believe on me through their word*.   Such therefore were those who were predestinated by the Father.   So also, Luke vii. 30. *the Pharisees and lawyers rejected the counsel of God against themselves, being not baptized of him;* whence it appears that even they might previously have been predestinated, if they would have believed.   Who was more certainly chosen than Peter? and yet a condition is expressly interposed, John xiii. 8. *if I wash thee not, thou hast no part with me*.   What then ensued?   Peter readily complied, and consequently had part with his Lord: had he not complied, he would have had no part with him.   For though Judas is not only said to have been chosen, which may refer to his apostleship, but even to have been given to Christ by the Father, he yet attained not salvation. John xvii. 12. *those that thou gavest me I have kept, and none of them is lost, but the son of perdition; that the Scripture might be fulfilled*. i. 11, 12. *he came unto his own, and his own received him not*.   But as many as received him, to them gave he power, &c., that is, to those who believed in his name; to whom he did not give power before they had received and believed in him, not even to those who were specially called his own. So St. Paul, Eph. i. 13. *in whom also after that ye believed, ye were sealed with that holy spirit of promise.* Undoubtedly those whom in the beginning of his epistle he calls holy, who were not sealed till after that they had believed, were not individually predestinated before that period. 2 Cor. vi. 1. *we beseech you also that ye receive not the grace of God in vain.* Rev. iii. 5. *he that overcometh, the same shall be clothed in white raiment, and I will not blot out his name out of the book of life.* On the other hand it is said, xxii. 19. *if any man shall take away from the words of the book of this prophecy, God shall take away his part out of the book of life.*

Again, if God have predestinated us *in Christ*, as has been proved already, it certainly must be on the condition of faith in Christ. 2 Thess. ii. 13. *God hath from the beginning chosen you to salvation through sanctification of the Spirit, and belief of the truth.* Therefore it is only future *believers* who are chosen. Tit. i. 1. *according to the faith of God's elect, and the acknowledging of the truth which is after godliness.* Heb. xi. 6. *without faith it is impossible to please God,*—and thus become one of the elect; whence I conclude that believers are the same as the elect, and that the terms are used indiscriminately. So Matt. xx. 16. *many be called, but few chosen,* only signifies that they which believe are few. Rom. viii. 33. *who shall lay anything to the charge of God's elect?* that is, of believers: otherwise by separating election from faith, and therefore from Christ, we should be entangled in hard, not to say detestable and absurd doctrines. So also, Rom. xi. 7. *the election have obtained it;* that is, believers, as is clear from the twentieth verse, *thou,* that is, thou that art elect, *standest by faith;* and v. 22. *if thou continue in his goodness; otherwise thou also shalt be cut off.* Such is St. Paul's interpretation of the doctrine in his own case; 1 Cor. ix. 27. *lest that by any means when I have preached to others, I myself should be a castaway.* Philipp. iii. 12. *not as though I had already attained,*

either were already perfect; but I follow after, if that I may apprehend that for which also I am apprehended of Christ Jesus. 2 Tim. ii. 10, 12. *I endure all things for the elect's sakes, that they may also obtain the salvation which is in Christ Jesus,* &c. yet it is said in the next verse, *if we believe not, yet he abideth,* &c.

Two difficult texts remain to be explained from analogy by the aid of so many plainer passages; for what is obscure must be illustrated by what is clear, not what is clear by what is obscure. The first passage occurs Acts xiii. 48. the other Rom. viii. 28–30. which, as being in my judgement the least difficult of the two, I shall discuss first. The words are as follow: *we know that all things work together for good to them that love God, to them who are the called according to his purpose: for whom he did foreknow, he also did predestinate to be conformed to the image of his Son,* &c. *moreover whom he did predestinate, them he also called; and whom he called, them he also justified; and whom he justified, them he also glorified.*

In the first place it must be remarked, that it appears from v. 28, that those *who love God* are the same as those *who are the called according to his purpose,* and consequently as those *whom he did foreknow,* and *whom he did predestinate,* for *them he also called,* as is said in v. 30. Hence it is apparent that the apostle is here propounding the scheme and order of predestination in general, not of the predestination of certain individuals in preference to others. As if he had said, We know that all things work together for good to those who love God, that is, to those who believe, for those who love God believe in him. The order of this scheme is also explained. First, God foreknew those who should believe, that is, he decreed or announced it as his pleasure that it should be those alone who should find grace in his sight through Christ, that is, all men, if they would believe. These he predestinated to salvation, and to this end he, in various ways, called all mankind to believe, or in other words, to acknowledge God in truth; those who actually thus believed he justified; and those who continued in the faith unto the end he finally glorified. But that it may be more clear who those are whom God has foreknown, it must be observed that there are three ways in which any person or thing is said to be known to God. First, by his universal knowledge, as Acts xv. 18. *known unto God are all his works from the beginning of the world.* Secondly, by his approving or gracious knowledge, which is an Hebraism, and therefore requires more explanation. Exod. xxxiii. 12. *I know thee by name, and thou hast also found grace in my sight.* Psal. i. 6. *Jehovah knoweth the way of the righteous.* Matt. vii. 23. *I never knew you.* Thirdly, by a knowledge attended with displeasure. Deut. xxxi. 21. *I know their imagination which they go about,* &c. 2 Kings xix. 27. *I know . . . thy coming in, and thy rage against me.* Rev. iii. 1. *I know thy works, that thou hast a name that thou livest, and art dead.* In the passage under discussion it is evident that the approving knowledge of God can be alone intended; but he foreknew or approved no one, except in Christ, and no one in Christ except a believer. Those therefore who were about to love, that is, to believe in God, God foreknew or approved; —or in general all men, if they should believe; those whom he thus foreknew, he predestinated, and called them that they might believe; those who believed, he justified. But if God justified believers, and believers only, inasmuch as it is faith alone that justifieth, he foreknew those only who would believe, for those whom he foreknew he justified; those therefore whom he justified he also foreknew, namely, those alone who were about to believe. So Rom. xi. 2. *God hath not cast away his people which he foreknew,* that is, believers, as appears from v. 20. 2 Tim. ii. 19. *the Lord knoweth them that are his,* that is, *all who name the name of Christ, and depart from iniquity;* or in other words, all believers. 1 Pet. i. 2. *elect according to the foreknowledge of God the Father, through sanctification of the Spirit, unto obedience and sprinkling of the blood of Jesus Christ.* This can be applicable to none but believers, whom the Father has chosen, according to his foreknowledge and approbation of them, through the sanctification of the Spirit and faith, without which the sprinkling of the blood of Christ would avail them nothing. Hence it seems that the generality of commentators are wrong in interpreting the

foreknowledge of God in these passages in the sense of prescience; since the prescience of God seems to have no connection with the principle or essence of predestination; for God has predestinated and elected whoever believes and continues in the faith. Of what consequence is it to us to know whether the prescience of God foresees who will, or will not, subsequently believe? for no one believes because God has foreseen his belief, but God foresees his belief because he was about to believe. Nor is it easy to understand how the prescience or foreknowledge of God with regard to particular persons can be brought to bear at all upon the doctrine of predestination, except for the purpose of raising a number of useless and utterly inapplicable questions. For why should God foreknow particular individuals, or what could he foreknow in them which should induce him to predestinate them in particular, rather than all in general, seeing that the common condition of faith had been established? Without searching deeper into this subject, let us be contented with only knowing, that God, out of his infinite mercy and grace in Christ, has predestinated to salvation all who should believe.

The other passage is Acts xiii. 48. *when the Gentiles heard this, they were glad, and glorified the word of the Lord; and as many as were ordained to eternal life, believed.* The difficulty is caused by the abrupt introduction of an opinion of the historian, in which he at first sight appears to contradict himself as well as the rest of Scripture, for he had before attributed to Peter this saying, chap. x. 34, 35. *of a truth I perceive that God is no respecter of persons; but in every nation he that feareth him, and worketh righteousness, is accepted with him.* *Accepted* certainly means chosen; and lest it should be urged that Cornelius had already been a proselyte before, St. Paul says the same thing even of those who had never known the law, Rom. ii. 10, 14. *there is no respect of persons with God,* &c. *when the Gentiles which have not the law,* &c. 1 Pet. i. 17. *the Father, who without respect of persons judgeth according to every man's work.* Now those who hold the doctrine that a man believes because he is ordained to eternal life, not that he is ordained to eternal life because he will believe, cannot avoid attributing to God the character of a respecter of persons, which he so constantly disclaims. Besides, if the Gentiles believed because they were ordained to eternal life, the same must have been the primary cause of the unbelief of the Jews, v. 46. which will plead greatly in their excuse, since it would seem that eternal life had only been placed in their view, not offered to their acceptance. Nor would such a dispensation be calculated to encourage the other nations, who would immediately conclude from it that there was no occasion for any will or works of their own in order to obtain eternal life, but that the whole depended on some fatal ordinance; whereas on the contrary Scripture uniformly shows in the clearest manner, that as many as have been ordained to eternal life believe, not simply because they have been so ordained, but because they have been ordained on condition of believing.

For these reasons other interpreters of more sagacity, according to my judgment, have thought that there is some ambiguity in the Greek word τεταγμένος, which is translated *ordained,* and that it has the same force as εὖ ἤτοι μετρίως διατεθειμένοι, *well or moderately disposed or affected,* of a composed, attentive, upright, and not disorderly mind; of a different spirit from those Jews, as touching eternal life, who had *put from them the word of God,* and had shown themselves *unworthy of everlasting life.* The Greeks use the word in a similar sense, as in Plutarch, and 2 Thess. iii. 6, 11. *there are some which walk disorderly,* certainly with reference to eternal life. This sense of the word, and even the particular application which is here intended, frequently occurs in Scripture in other terms. Luke ix. 62. εὔθετος, *well disposed or fit for the kingdom of God.* Mark xii. 34. *not far from the kingdom of God.* 2 Tim. ii. 21. *a vessel . . . meet for the master's use, and prepared for every good work.* For, as will be shown hereafter, there are some remnants of the divine image left in man, the union of which in one individual renders him more fit and disposed for the kingdom of God than another. Since therefore we are not merely senseless stocks, some cause at least must be discovered in the nature of man himself,

why divine grace is rejected by some and embraced by others. One thing appears certain, that though all men be dead in sin and children of wrath, yet some are worse than others; and this difference may not only be perceived daily in the nature, disposition and habits of those who are most alienated from the grace of God, but may also be inferred from the expressions used in the parable, Matt. xiii. where the nature of the soil is variously described in three or four ways, part as stony ground, part overrun with thorns, part good ground, at least in comparison of the others, before it had as yet received any seed. See also Matt. x. 11, &c. *inquire who in it is worthy, &c. . . . and if the house be worthy, let your peace come upon it.* How could any one be worthy before the Gospel had been preached, unless on account of his being *ordained,* that is, well inclined or disposed, to eternal life? which Christ teaches that the rest will perceive in their own punishments after death. Matt. xi. 22. *it shall be more tolerable for Tyre and Sidon at the day of judgement, than for you.* Luke xii. 47, 48. *that servant which knew his Lord's will . . . shall be beaten with many stripes: but he that knew not . . . shall be beaten with few stripes.* And, lastly, the gift of reason has been implanted in all, by which they may of themselves resist bad desires, so that no one can complain of, or allege in excuse, the depravity of his own nature compared with that of others.

But, it is objected, God has no regard to the less depraved among the wicked in his choice, but often prefers the worse to the better. Deut. ix. 5. *not for thy righteousness, or for the uprightness of thine heart, dost thou go to possess their land.* Luke x. 13. *if the mighty works had been done in Tyre and Sidon, which have been done in you, they had a great while ago repented, sitting in sackcloth and ashes.* I answer, that it cannot be determined from these passages, what God regards in those whom he chooses; for in the first place, I have not argued that he has regarded righteousness even in the least degree. Secondly, in the former passage the question is not respecting election to life eternal, but concerning the gift of the land of Canaan to the Israelites, a gift assigned them for other reasons than those for which eternal life would have been given,—partly on account of the wickedness of the original inhabitants, and partly that the promise might be fulfilled which had been ratified by an oath to their forefathers; wherein there is nothing that contradicts my doctrine. In the latter passage, it is not the elect who are compared with the reprobate, but the reprobate who are compared with each other, the Tyrians with the unbelieving Jews, neither of which nations had repented. Nor would the Tyrians ever have truly repented, even if these miracles had been wrought among them, for if God had foreseen that they would have repented, he would never have forsaken them; but the expression is to be understood in the same sense as Matt. xxi. 31. *the publicans and the harlots go into the kingdom of God before you.*

Lastly, it will be objected that *it is not of him that willeth, nor of him that runneth, but of God that showeth mercy,* Rom. ix. 16. I answer, that my argument does not presuppose one that willeth or that runneth, but one that is less reluctant, less backward, less resisting than another—that it is, nevertheless, God who showeth mercy, and who is at the same time infinitely wise and just. Meanwhile, when it is said that *it is not of him that willeth nor of him that runneth,* it is not denied that there is one who wills, and one who runs, only care is taken not to assign to him any portion of merit or praise. But when God determined to restore mankind, he also without doubt decreed that the liberty of will which had been lost should be at least partially regained by them, which was but reasonable. Whomsoever therefore in the exercise of that degree of freedom which their will had acquired either previously to their call, or by reason of the call itself, God had seen in any respect willing or running, (who it is probable are here meant by the ordained) to them he gave a greater power of willing and running, that is, of believing. Thus it is said, 1 Sam. xvi. 7. *Jehovah looketh on the heart,* namely, on the disposition of men either as it is by nature, or after grace has been received from him that calleth them. To the same purport is that well known saying,—*to him that hath shall be given.* This may be illustrated by the example of the centurion,

Matt. viii. 10. *I have not found so great faith, no, not in Israel,*—of the woman of Canaan, Matt. xv. 28. *O woman, great is thy faith,*—of the father of the demoniac, Mark ix. 24. *Lord, I believe; help thou mine unbelief,*—and of Zaccheus, Luke xix. 3. *he sought to see Jesus who he was,* whence, v. 9. *Jesus said unto him, This day is salvation come to this house.* Zaccheus therefore had not been ordained from all eternity, but from the time when he had shewn himself eagerly desirous of knowing Christ.

Nor is it less on this account *of God that showeth mercy,* since the principal is often put for the sole cause without impropriety, not only in common discourse, but even in the language of logicians; and certainly unless God had first shown mercy, it would have been in the power of no one either to will or to run. Philipp. ii. 13. *for it is God that worketh in you both to will and to do of his good pleasure.* 2 Cor. iii. 5. *not that we are sufficient of ourselves to think any thing as of ourselves; but our sufficiency is of God,* without whose mercy he that willeth or he that runneth would gain nothing.

I think therefore it must be sufficiently clear from the analogy of all the rest of Scripture, who those are that are said in the passage quoted from the Acts to have been ordained to eternal life. On a review of the whole, I should conjecture, that Luke had not intended to advance in so abrupt a manner any new doctrine, but simply to confirm by a fresh example the saying of Peter respecting Cornelius, Acts x. 34, 35. Cornelius and the Gentiles with him believed, as many at least as feared God and worked righteousness, for such were accepted of God in every nation. So in the other passage, those of the Gentiles whose thoughts were already devoted to serious subjects, worthy the attention of men, believed, and gave themselves up to instruction with docility and gladness of heart, glorifying the word of the Lord. Such Peter declared were accepted of God in every nation, and such Luke in conformity with Peter's opinion asserts to be ordained to, that is, qualified for eternal life, even though they were Gentiles.

But an objection of another kind may perhaps be made. If God be said to have predestinated men only on condition that they believe and continue in the faith, predestination will not be altogether of grace, but will depend on the will and belief of mankind; which will be derogatory to the exclusive efficacy of divine grace. But this is so far from being true, that the doctrine of grace is thus placed in a much clearer light than by the theory of those who make the objection. For the grace of God is acknowledged to be infinite, in the first place, inasmuch as he showed any pity at all for man whose fall was to happen through his own fault. Secondly, because he *so loved the world, that he gave his only begotten Son* for its salvation. Thirdly, because he has again granted us the power of volition, that is, of acting freely, in consequence of recovering the liberty of the will by the renewing of the Spirit. It was thus that he opened the heart of Lydia, Acts xvi. 14. But if the condition whereon the decree depends, that is to say, the will enfranchised by God himself, and faith which is required of mankind be left in the power of beings who are free agents, there is nothing in the doctrine either derogatory to grace, or inconsistent with justice; since the power of willing and believing is either the gift of God, or, so far as it is inherent in man, partakes not of the nature of merit or of good works, but only of a natural faculty. Nor does this reasoning represent God as depending upon the human will, but as fulfilling his own pleasure, whereby he has chosen that man should always use his own will with a regard to the love and worship of the Deity, and consequently with a regard to his own salvation. If this use of the will be not admitted, whatever worship or love we render to God is entirely vain and of no value; the acceptableness of duties done under a law of necessity is diminished, or rather is annihilated altogether, and freedom can no longer be attributed to that will over which some fixed decree is inevitably suspended.

The objections, therefore, which are so vehemently urged by some against this doctrine, are of no force whatever;—namely, that on this theory, the repentance and faith of the predestinated having been foreseen, predestination becomes posterior in point of time to works,—that it is rendered dependent on the will of man,—that God

is defrauded of part of the glory of our salvation,—that man is puffed up with pride,—that the foundations of all Christian consolation in life and in death are shaken,—that gratuitous justification is denied. On the contrary, the scheme, and consequently the glory, not only of the divine grace, but also of the divine wisdom and justice, is thus displayed in a clearer manner than on the opposite hypothesis; which was the principal end that God proposed to himself in predestination.

Since then it is so clear that God has predestinated from eternity all those who should believe and continue in the faith, it follows that there can be no reprobation, except of those who do not believe or continue in the faith, and even this rather as a consequence than a decree; there can therefore be no reprobation of individuals from all eternity. For God has predestinated to salvation, on the proviso of a general condition, all who enjoy freedom of will; while none are predestinated to destruction, except through their own fault, and as it were *per accidens,* in the same manner as there are some to whom the gospel itself is said to be a stumbling-block and a savour of death. Of this assertion proof shall be given from the testimony of Scripture no less explicit than of the doctrine asserted in the former part of the chapter. Isai. l. 1. *where is the bill of your mother's divorcement, whom I have put away? . . . behold for your iniquities have ye sold yourselves.* Hos. iv. 6. *because thou hast rejected knowledge, I will also reject thee . . . seeing thou hast forgotten the law of thy God, I will also forget thy children.* Rev. xiii. 8. *all that dwell upon the earth shall worship him, whose names are not written in the book of life of the Lamb slain from the foundation of the world.* And who are they but such as have not believed? whom God has therefore deserted because they *wandered after the beast,* v. 3. Nor should I call the decree mentioned in Zephaniah ii. 1–3. a decree of eternal reprobation, but rather of temporal punishment, and at any rate not an absolute decree, as the passage itself is sufficient to show: *gather yourselves together, &c. before the decree bring forth . . . &c. &c. it may be ye shall be hid in the day of the anger of Jehovah.*

For if God had decreed any to absolute reprobation, which we do not read, he must, even according to their system who affirm that reprobation is an absolute decree, have likewise decreed the means without which his own decree could not be fulfilled. Now these means are neither more nor less than sin. Nor will the common subterfuge avail, namely, that God did not decree sin, but only its permission: this is a contradiction in terms; for at this rate he does more than simply permit it: he who permits a thing does not decree it, but leaves it free.

But even if there be any decree of reprobation, Scripture everywhere declares, that as election is established and confirmed by faith, so reprobation is rescinded by repentance. Jer. vi. 30. *reprobate silver shall men call them, because Jehovah hath rejected them;* and yet in the third verse of the following chapter God addresses himself to the same people—*amend your ways and your doings, and I will cause you to dwell in this place.* So too in chap. xviii. 6, &c. where God compares his own right with that of the potter, (whence St. Paul seems to have taken his metaphor, Rom. ix.) *if that nation, against whom I have pronounced, turn from their evil, I will repent of the evil that I thought to do unto them.* So too, where God defends in the clearest manner the justice of his ways, Ezek. xviii. 25-27. *when the wicked man turneth away from the wickedness that he hath committed, and doeth that which is lawful and right, he shall save his soul alive.* xxxiii. 14, 15. *when I say unto the wicked, Thou shalt surely die, if he turn from his sin, and do that which is lawful and right, &c. &c. he shall surely live, he shall not die.* The same is inculcated in other parts of the chapters just quoted: xviii. 31, 32. *why will ye die, O house of Israel? for I have no pleasure in the death of him that dieth, saith the Lord Jehovah; wherefore turn yourselves, and live ye.* xxxiii. 11. *say unto them, As I live, saith the Lord Jehovah, I have no pleasure in the death of the wicked; but that the wicked turn from his way and live; turn ye, turn ye from your evil ways, for why will ye die, O house of Israel?* Luke xiii. 5. *except ye repent, ye shall all likewise perish:* therefore, if ye repent, ye shall not perish. If then there be no repentance, of what advantage is election; or if there be repentance, of what injury is reprobation? Accordingly St. Paul, in speaking of those whom he describes as blinded, and whom he opposes to the elect, Rom. xi. 7. *the election hath obtained it, and the rest were blinded,* subjoins immediately, v. 11. *have they stumbled that they should fall? God forbid;* and v. 23, &c. *and they also, if they abide not in unbelief, shall be graffed in; for God is able to graff them in again, &c.* lastly, he adds, v. 32. *God hath concluded them all in unbelief, that he might have mercy upon all.*

If then God reject none but the disobedient and unbelieving, he undoubtedly gives grace to all, though not in equal measure, yet sufficient for attaining knowledge of the truth and final salvation;—I have said, not in equal measure, because not even to the reprobate, as they are called, has he imparted uniformly the same degree of grace. Matt. xi. 21, 23. *woe unto thee, Chorazin, &c. for if the mighty works which have been done in you, had been done in Tyre and Sidon,—&c.* See also Luke x. 13. For God, as any other proprietor might do with regard to his private possessions, claims to himself the right of determining concerning his own creatures according to his pleasure, nor can he be called to account for his decision, though, if he chose, he could give the best reasons for it. Rom. ix. 20, 21. *nay but, O man, who art thou that repliest against God? shall the thing formed say to him that formed it, Why hast thou made me thus? hath not the potter power over the clay?* It is owing, therefore, to his supreme will that God does not vouchsafe equal grace to all; but it is owing to his justice that there are none to whom he does not vouchsafe grace sufficient for their salvation. Isai. v. 4. *what could have been done more in my vineyard, that I have not done in it?* which words are spoken of the whole nation of the Jews, not of the elect only. xxvi. 10. *let favour be showed to the wicked, yet will he not learn righteousness.* Ezek. xii. 2. *which have eyes to see, and see not, they have ears to hear, and hear not; for they are a rebellious house.* 2 Kings xvii. 13. *Jehovah testified against Israel, and against Judah, by all the prophets, and by all the seers, saying, Turn ye from your evil ways,* &c. . . . *notwith-standing they would not hear, but hard-ened their necks.* See also 2 Chron. xxxvi. 15, 16. John i. 9. *that was the true light, which lighteth every man that cometh into the world.* ix. 41. *if ye were blind, ye should have no sin; but now ye say, We see, therefore your sin remaineth,* namely, because your sin is the fruit of pride, not of ignorance. xv. 22. *if I had not come and spoken unto them, they had not had sin: but now they have no cloak for their sin.* xii. 34-41. *yet a little while is the light with you: walk while ye have the light, lest darkness come upon you,* &c. *while ye have light, believe in the light, that ye may be the children of light.* Acts xiii. 46. *it was necessary that the word of God should first have been spoken to you, but seeing ye put it from you, and judge yourselves un-worthy of everlasting life, lo, we turn to the Gentiles.* xiv. 16, 17. *who in times past suffered all nations to walk in their own ways: nevertheless he left not himself without witness.* Rom. x. 20, 21. *I was found of them that sought me not; I was made manifest unto them that asked not after me: but to Israel he saith, All day long I have stretched forth my hands unto a disobedient and gainsaying people.* 2 Cor. vi. 1, 2. *behold, now is the accepted time; behold, now is the day of salvation.* Heb. iii. 7, 8. compared with Psal. xcv. 7, 9. *to-day if ye will hear his voice, harden not your hearts.* Undoubtedly if he desire that the wicked should turn from their way and live, Ezek. xxxiii. 11.—if he would have all men to be saved, 1 Tim. ii. 4.—if he be unwilling that any should perish, 2 Pet. iii. 9. he must also will that an adequate pro-portion of saving grace shall be withholden from no man; for if otherwise, it does not appear how his truth towards mankind can be justified. Nor is it enough that only so much grace shall be bestowed, as will suffice to take away all excuse; for our condemna-tion would have been reasonable, even had no grace at all been bestowed. But the offer of grace having been once proclaimed, those who perish will always have some excuse, and will perish unjustly, unless it be evident that it is actually sufficient for salvation. So that what Moses said in his address to the Israelites, Deut. xxix. 4. *Je-hovah hath not given you an heart to per-ceive, and eyes to see, and ears to hear, unto this day,* must be understood as having been dictated by the kindness and tenderness of his feelings, lest he should have been ac-cused of harshness and asperity towards so large an assembly of the people, who were then on the point of entering into covenant with God, if he had chosen that particular time for openly reproving the hardness of their hearts. When, there-fore, there were two causes to which their impenitence was capable of being ascribed, —either that a heart had not yet been given by God, who was at liberty to give it when he pleased, or, that they had not yielded obedience to God,—he made men-tion only of the freedom of God's will, and left their hardness of heart to be suggested silently by their own consciences; for no one could be at a loss to perceive, that if God to that day had not given them an understanding heart, their own stubborn-ness must have been the principal cause; or else that God, who had wrought so many miracles for their sakes, had abundantly given them a heart to perceive, and eyes to see, and ears to hear, but that they had refused to make use of these gifts.

Thus much, therefore, may be consid-ered as certain and irrefragable truth—that God excludes no one from the pale of re-pentance and eternal salvation, till he has despised and rejected the propositions of sufficient grace, offered even to a late hour, for the sake of manifesting the glory of his long-suffering and justice. Nor has God anywhere declared in direct and precise terms that his will is the cause of reproba-tion, but the reasons which influence his will in the case at issue are frequently pro-pounded,—namely, the grievous sins of the reprobate previously committed, or fore-seen before actual commission,—want of repentance,—contempt of grace,—deafness to the repeated calls of God. For reproba-tion must not be attributed, like the elec-tion of grace, to the divine will alone. Deut. ix. 5. *not for thy righteousness, or for the uprightness of thine heart, dost thou go to possess their land: but for the wickedness of these nations Jehovah thy God doth drive them out before thee.* For the exercise of mercy requires no vindi-cation; it is unnecessary to assign any cause for it, except God's own merciful will; but, that reprobation, the consequence of which is punishment, may be reconciled with justice, it must be owing to man's sin alone, and not to the arbitrary will of God—to sin either committed or foreseen, after the constant rejection of grace, or after it has been sought at length too late, and only through fear of punishment, when the appointed day of grace is past. For God does not reprobate for one cause, and condemn or assign to death for another, according to the distinction commonly made; but those whom he has condemned on account of sin, he has also reprobated on account of sin, as in time, so from all eternity. And this reprobation lies not so much in the divine will, as in the obstinacy of their own minds; it is not God who decrees it, but the reprobate themselves who determine on refusing to repent while it is in their power. Acts xiii. 46. *ye put it from you, and judge yourselves unworthy of everlasting life.* Matt. xxi. 43. *the stone which the builders rejected, &c. therefore the kingdom of God shall be taken from you.* See also 1 Pet. ii. 7, 8. Matt. xxiii. 37. *how often would I have gathered thy children together, &c. and ye would not.* Nor would it be less unjust to decree reprobation, than to condemn for any other cause than sin. As, therefore, there is no condemnation except on account of unbelief or of sin, (John iii. 18, 19. *he that believeth not is condemned already, because he hath not believed, &c. this is the condemnation, that light is come into the world, and men loved darkness rather than light:* xii. 48. *he that rejecteth me, and receiveth not my words, hath one that judgeth him; the word that I have spoken. &c.* 2 Thess. ii. 12. *that they all might be damned who believed not the truth,*) so we will prove from all the passages that are alleged in confirmation of the decree of reprobation, that no one is excluded by any decree of God from the pale of repentance and eternal salvation, unless it be after the contempt and rejection of grace, and that at a very late hour.

We may begin our proofs of this assertion from the instance of Jacob and Esau, Rom. ix. since in the opinion of many the question seems to turn on that case. It will be seen that the subject of discussion in this passage is not so much predestination, as the unmerited calling of the Gentiles after the Jews had been deservedly rejected.

St. Paul shows in the sixth verse that the word which God spake to Abraham, had not therefore taken none effect because all his posterity had not received Christ, and more had believed among the Gentiles than among the Jews; inasmuch as the promise was not made in all the children of Abraham, but in Isaac, v. 7; that is to say, *they which are the children of the flesh, these are not the children of God, but the children of the promise are counted for the seed,* v. 8. The promise therefore was not made to the children of Abraham according to the flesh, but to the children of God, who are therefore called the children of the promise. But since Paul does not say in this passage who are the children of God, an explanation must be sought from John i. 11, 12. where this very promise is briefly referred to; *he came unto his own, and his own received him not: but as many as received him, to them gave he power to become the sons of God, even to them that believe on his name.* The promise therefore is not to the children of Abraham in the flesh, but to as many of the children of his faith as received Christ, namely, to the children of God and of the promise, that is, to believers; for where there is a promise, it behoves that there be also a faith in that promise.

St. Paul then shows by another example, that God did not grant mercy in the same degree to all the posterity even of Isaac, but much more abundantly to the children of the promise, that is, to believers; and that this difference originates in his own will: lest any one should arrogate any thing to himself on the score of his own merits. v. 11, 12. *for the children being not yet born, neither having done any good or evil, that the purpose of God according to election might stand, not of works, but of him that calleth, it was said unto her, The elder shall serve the younger.* The purpose of God, according to what election? Doubtless according to the election to some benefit, to some privilege, and in this instance specially to the right of primogeniture transferred from the elder to the younger of the sons or of the nations; whence it arises that God now prefers the Gentiles to the Jews. Here then his purpose of election is expressly mentioned, but to reprobation there is no allusion. St. Paul is satisfied with employing this example to establish the general principle of election to any mercy or benefit whatever. Why should we endeavour to extort from the words a harsh and severe meaning, which does not belong to them? If the elder shall serve the younger, whether the individual or the people be intended, (and in this case it certainly applies best to the people) it does not therefore follow that the elder shall be reprobated by a perpetual decree; nor, if the younger be favoured with a larger measure of grace, does it follow that the elder shall be favoured with none. For this can neither be said of Esau, who was taught the true worship of God in the house of his father, nor of his posterity, whom we know to have been called to the faith with the rest of the Gentiles. Hence this clause is added in Esau's blessing, Gen. xxvii. 40. *it shall come to pass when thou shalt have the dominion, that thou shalt break his yoke from off thy neck.* Now if the servitude of Esau implied his reprobation, these words must certainly imply that it was not to last for ever. But an expression which occurs in the same chapter is alleged as decisive: *Jacob have I loved, but Esau have I hated,* v. 13. But how did God evince his love or hatred? He gives his own answer, Mal. i. 2, 3. *I hated Esau, and laid his mountains and his heritage waste.* He evinced his love therefore to Jacob, by bringing him back again into his country from the land of Babylon; according to the purpose of that same election by which he now calls the Gentiles, and abandons the Jews. At the same time even this text does not prove the existence of any decree of reprobation, though St. Paul subjoins it incidentally as it were, to illustrate the former phrase,—*the elder shall serve the younger;* for the text in Mal. i. 2, 3. differs from the present passage, inasmuch as it does not speak of the children yet unborn, but of the children when they had been long dead, after the one had eagerly accepted, and the other had despised the grace of God. Nor does this derogate in the least from the freedom of grace, because Jacob himself openly confesses that he was undeserving of the favour which he had obtained; Gen. xxxiii. 10. St. Paul

therefore asserts the right of God to impart whatever grace he chooses even to the undeserving, v. 14, 15. and concludes—*so then it is not of him that willeth, or of him that runneth,* (not even of Jacob, who had openly confessed himself undeserving, nor of the Jews who followed after the law of righteousness) *but of God that showeth mercy,* v. 16. Thus St. Paul establishes the right of God with respect to any election whatever, even of the undeserving, such as the Gentiles then seemed to be.

The apostle then proceeds to prove the same thing with regard to the rejection of the Jews, by considering God's right to exercise justice upon sinners in general; which justice, however, he does not display by means of reprobation, and hatred towards children yet unborn, but by the judicial hardening of the heart, and punishment of flagrant offenders. v. 17, 18. *for the Scripture saith unto Pharaoh, Even for this same purpose have I raised thee up,* &c. He does not say, *I have decreed,* but, *I have raised up;* that is, in raising up Pharaoh he only called into action, by means of a most reasonable command, that hardness of heart, with which he was already acquainted. So Exod. iii. 19. *I am sure that the king of Egypt will not let you go.* So too I Pet. ii. (in which chapter much has been borrowed from the ninth of Romans,) v. 7, 8. *unto them which be disobedient, the stone which the builders disallowed . . . &c. even to them that stumble at the word, being disobedient; whereunto also they were appointed.* They therefore first disallowed Christ, before they were disallowed by him; they were then finally appointed for punishment, from the time that they had persisted in disobedience.

To return however to the chapter in Romans. It follows in the next verses, 19–21. *thou wilt say then unto me, Why doth he yet find fault?* &c. *why hast thou made me thus*—that is, hard-hearted, and a vessel unto dishonour, whilst thou showest mercy to others? In answer to which the apostle proves the reasonableness, not indeed of a decree of reprobation, but of that penal hardness of heart, which, after much long-suffering on the part of God, is generally the final punishment reserved for the more atrocious sins. v. 21. *hath not the potter power over the clay?* that is, the material fitted for his own purposes, to put honour upon whom he chooses, provided it be not on the disobedient; as it is said 2 Tim. ii. 21. *if a man purge himself from these, he shall be a vessel unto honour,* &c. whilst he hardens still more the hearts of the contumacious, that is, he punishes them, according to the next verse of this chapter— *he endured with much long-suffering the vessels of wrath fitted to destruction.* Whence then were they fitted, except from their own hardness of heart, whereby the measure of their iniquity was completed! See Gen. xv. 16. and Eph. v. 6. *because of these things cometh the wrath of God upon the children of disobedience.* Nor does the use of the passive voice always imply the sufferance of some external force; for we speak of one being given up to vice, or inclined to this or that propensity, meaning only that such is the bias of his own disposition. Finally, the three last verses of the chapter, which contain the conclusion of the whole question, are a convincing proof that St. Paul only intended to show the free and gratuitous mercy of God in calling the Gentiles to salvation, who should be obedient to the faith, and at the same time the justice of his judgments in hardening the hearts of the Jews and others, who obstinately adhered to the law of works. v. 30–32. *what shall we say then? that the Gentiles . . . have attained to righteousness which is of faith*—not therefore through election independent of faith: *but Israel . . . hath not attained: wherefore? because they sought it not by faith*—not therefore through a decree of reprobation independent of unbelief.

After having passed this difficulty, those which remain will scarcely interrupt our course. Psal. xcv. 10, 11. *forty years long was I grieved with this generation,* &c. *unto whom I sware in my wrath that they should not enter into my rest.* It must be observed here how long it was before God passed his decree, and that (if we may reason by analogy respecting spiritual things, from types of this kind, as was done before in the case of Esau) he excluded from his eternal rest only those who tempted him, and whose hearts were hardened. 2 Chron. xxxvi. 15, 16. *and Jehovah God of their fathers sent to them by his messengers,* &c. *because he had compassion on his people and on his dwelling-place: but they mocked the messengers of God,* &c. *until the wrath of Jehovah arose against his people, till there was no remedy.* Isai. xxviii. 12, 13. *to whom he said, This is the rest wherewith ye may cause the weary to rest,* &c. *yet they would not hear: but the word of Jehovah was unto them precept upon precept,* &c. *that they might go, and fall backward,* &c. *wherefore hear the word of Jehovah, ye scornful men,* &c. xxix. 10. *for Jehovah hath poured out upon you the spirit of deep sleep, and hath closed your eyes.* The reason is given, v. 13, 14. whence it appears that it was not on account of God's decree, but of their own grievous wickedness: *forasmuch as this people draw near me with their mouth,* &c. *but have removed their heart far from me . . . therefore the wisdom of their wise men shall perish,* &c. Matt. xi. 25, 26. *I thank thee, O Father, because thou hast hid these things from the wise and prudent, and hast revealed them unto babes: even so, Father, for so it seemed good in thy sight.* Lest we should attribute this solely to the arbitrary will of God, the verses preceding will explain why it so seemed good, and why Christ ascribes glory to the Father on this account, v. 21–23; in which it is disclosed what those wise men had first been themselves, namely, despisers of the divine grace. See also xiii. 11. *because it is given unto you to know the mysteries of the kingdom of heaven, but to them it is not given.* And why? the next verse subjoins the reason: *whosoever hath, to him shall be given, and he shall have more abundance; but whosoever hath not, from him shall be taken away even that he hath.* It is impossible to apply this sentence otherwise, than to those who have first voluntarily rejected divine grace, in the sense in which nearly the same words are addressed, chap. xxv. 29. to the slothful servant. A passage to the same purpose occurs, chap. xiii. 13. *therefore speak I to them in parables, because they seeing see not,* &c. Hence an easy solution is afforded for other texts. John viii. 43. *ye cannot hear my word;*—because when ye were able, ye would not, ye are now unable on account of your unbelief in which you are hardened, not on account of any decree of God; or in consequence of your pride, through which you cannot endure to hear the word; or lastly, as it is expressed in the following verse, 44, because *ye are of your father the devil, and the lusts of your father ye will do.* Again, v. 46. *if I say the truth, why do ye not believe me?* Christ himself answers the question, v. 47. *ye therefore hear not, because ye are not of God.* What is the meaning of *ye are not of God?* not surely, ye are not elect: it implies the same as *to be of the devil,* v. 44. that is, to follow the devil rather than God. So too, x. 26. *ye believe not, because ye are not of my sheep.* Why not of my sheep? Because it was so decreed? By no means,—but because ye do not hear the word; because ye do not follow me; *my sheep hear my voice, and they follow me,* v. 27. Ye, as I repeatedly tell you, do not believe. v. 25, 26. *I told you, and ye believed not; the works that I do in my Father's name, they bear witness of me: but ye believe not, because ye are not of my sheep, as I said unto you.* The argument runs thus—ye do not believe, because ye are not of my sheep; ye are not of my sheep, because ye neither hear my word, nor follow me. Christ certainly intended to give some such reason for their unbelief as would throw the fault of it upon themselves, not such a one as would exempt them from blame; but if not to be of his sheep, be interpreted to mean not to be of the elect, a privilege which had never been within their option, his words would contain an excuse for their conduct, rather than a reproof, which would be contrary to his obvious purpose. Again, xii. 39, 40, compared with Isai. vi. 10. *therefore they could not believe, because that Esaias saith again, He hath blinded their eyes,* &c. Not because the words of Isaiah, or the decree of God delivered by his mouth, had previously taken away from them the power or grace of belief irrespectively; but according to the reason declared by the prophet why they could not believe, namely, because God had blinded their eyes. And why he had thus blinded their eyes the preceding chapter explains, v. 4, &c. because nothing more remained to be done to his unfruitful vineyard, but to cut it down. This appears still more clearly Luke xiii. 24, 25. *many will seek to enter in, and shall not be able: when once the master of the house is risen up, and hath shut to the door.* xiv. 24. *I say unto you, that none of those men that were bidden shall taste of my supper.* xix. 42. *if thou hadst known, at least in this thy day, the things which belong unto thy peace! but now they are hid from thine eyes.* Rom. i. 21, 24, 26. *because that when they knew God, they glorified him not as God,* &c. *wherefore God also gave them up,* &c. *for this cause God gave them up,* &c. 2 Thess. ii. 10–12. *with all deceivableness of unrighteousness in them that perish; because they received not the love of the truth, that they might be saved: and for this cause God shall send them strong delusion, that they should believe a lie: that they all might be damned who believed not the truth, but had pleasure in unrighteousness.* iii. 2. *for all men have not faith;* that is, obstinate and unreasonable sinners have it not; which the context shows is the sense intended. 1 Pet. ii. 7, 8. *the stone which the builders disallowed,* &c. *and a stone of stumbling and rock of offence, even to them which stumble at the word, being disobedient; whereunto also they were appointed,*—that is, to be disobedient. And why? Because they had disallowed that stone, and had stumbled upon it, disallowing Christ themselves before they were disallowed by him. Whoever has paid attention to what has been urged, will easily perceive that the difficulties respecting this doctrine have arisen from the want of making the proper distinction between the punishment of hardening the heart and the decree of reprobation; according to Prov. xix. 3. *the foolishness of man perverteth his way, and his heart fretteth against Jehovah.* For such do in effect impugn the justice of God, however vehemently they may disclaim the intention; and might justly be reproved in the words of the heathen Homer:

Αὐτῶν γὰρ σφετέρῃσιν ἀτασθαλίῃσιν ὄλοντο.
Odyss. I. 7.

.... they perish'd self-destroy'd
By their own fault.   Book I. l. 9.

And again, in the person of Jupiter:

Ὢ πόποι, οἷον δή νυ θεοὺς βροτοὶ αἰτιόωνται!
ἐξ ἡμέων γάρ φασι κάκ' ἔμμεναι· οἱ δὲ καὶ
αὐτοὶ
σφῇσιν ἀτασθαλίῃσιν, ὑπὲρ μόρον, ἄλγε'
ἔχουσιν.   *Odyss.* I. 32.

Perverse mankind! whose wills, created free,
Charge all their woes on absolute decree:

All to the dooming gods their guilt translate,
And follies are miscall'd the crimes of fate.
                Book I. l. 40. Pope's Translation.

CHAP. V.

PREFATORY REMARKS.

I cannot enter upon subjects of so much difficulty as the SON OF GOD and the HOLY SPIRIT, without again premising a few introductory words. If indeed I were a member of the Church of Rome, which requires implicit obedience to its creed on all points of faith, I should have acquiesced from education or habit in its simple decree and authority, even though it denies that the doctrine of the Trinity, as now received, is capable of being proved from any passage of Scripture. But since I enrol myself among the number of those who acknowledge the word of God alone as the rule of faith, and freely advance what appears to me much more clearly deducible from the Holy Scriptures than the commonly received opinion, I see no reason why any one who belongs to the same Protestant or Reformed Church, and professes to acknowledge the same rule of faith as myself, should take offence at my freedom, particularly as I impose my authority on no one, but merely propose what I think more worthy of belief than the creed in general acceptation. I only entreat that my readers will ponder and examine my statements in a spirit which desires to discover nothing but the truth, and with a mind free from prejudice. For without intending to oppose the authority of Scripture, which I consider inviolably sacred, I only take upon myself to refute human interpretations as often as the occasion requires, conformably to my right, or rather to my duty as a man. If indeed those with whom I have to contend were able to produce direct attestation from heaven to the truth of the doctrine which they espouse, it would be nothing less than impiety to venture to raise, I do not say a clamour, but so much as a murmur against it. But inasmuch as they can lay claim to nothing more than human powers, assisted by that spiritual illumination which is common to all, it is not unreasonable that they should on their part allow the privileges of diligent research and free discussion to another inquirer, who is seeking truth through the same means and in the same way as themselves, and whose desire of benefiting mankind is equal to their own.

In reliance, therefore, upon the divine assistance, let us now enter upon the subject itself.

OF THE SON OF GOD.

Hitherto I have considered the INTERNAL EFFICIENCY of God, as shown in his decrees.

His EXTERNAL EFFICIENCY, or the execution of his decrees, whereby he carries into effect by external agency whatever decrees he has purposed within himself, may be comprised under the heads of GENERATION, CREATION, and the GOVERNMENT OF THE UNIVERSE.

First, GENERATION, whereby God, in pursuance of his decree, has begotten his only Son; whence he chiefly derives his appellation of Father.

Generation must be an external efficiency, since the Father and Son are different persons; and the divines themselves acknowledge this, who argue that there is a certain emanation of the Son from the Father (which will be explained when the doctrine concerning the Holy Spirit is under examination); for though they teach that the Spirit is co-essential with the Father, they do not deny that it emanates, and goes out, and proceeds, and is breathed from the Father,—which are all expressions denoting external efficiency. In conjunction with this doctrine they hold that the Son is also co-essential with the Father, and generated from all eternity. Hence this question, which is naturally very obscure, becomes involved in still greater difficulties if the received opinion respecting it be followed; for though the Father be said in Scripture to have begotten the Son in a double sense, the one literal, with reference to the production of the Son, the other metaphorical, with reference to his exaltation, many commentators have applied the passages which allude to the exaltation and mediatorial functions of Christ as proofs of his generation from all eternity. They have indeed this excuse for their proceeding, if any excuse can be offered in such a case, that it was impossible to find a single text in all Scripture to prove the eternal generation of the Son. This point appears certain, notwithstanding the arguments of some of the moderns to the contrary, that the Son existed in the beginning, under the name of the logos or word, and was the first of the whole creation, by whom afterwards all other things were made both in heaven and earth. John i. 1–3. *in the beginning was the Word, and the Word was with God, and the Word was God,* &c. xvii. 5. *and now, O Father, glorify me with thine own self with the glory which I had with thee before the world was.* Col. i. 15, 18. *the first-born of every creature.* Rev. iii. 14. *the beginning of the creation of God.* 1 Cor. viii. 6. *Jesus Christ, by whom are all things.* Eph. iii. 9. *who created all things by Jesus Christ.* Col. i. 16. *all things were created by him and for him.* Heb. i. 2. *by whom also he made the worlds,* whence it is said, v. 10, *thou, Lord, in the beginning hast laid the foundation of the earth;* on which point more will be said in the seventh Chapter, on the Creation.

All these passages prove the existence of the Son before the world was made, but they conclude nothing respecting his generation from all eternity. The other texts which are produced relate only to his metaphorical generation, that is, to his resuscitation from the dead, or to his unction to the mediatorial office, according to St. Paul's own interpretation of the second Psalm: *I will declare the decree; Jehovah hath said unto me, Thou art my Son; this day have I begotten thee*—which the apostle thus explains, Acts xiii. 32, 33. *God hath fulfilled the promise unto us their children, in that he hath raised up Jesus again; as it is also written in the second Psalm, Thou art my Son; this day have I begotten thee.* Rom. i. 4. *declared to be the Son of God with power, according to the Spirit of holiness, by the resurrection from the dead.* Hence, Col. i. 18. Rev. i. 4. *the first begotten of the dead.* Heb. i. 5, speaking of the exaltation of the Son above the angels; *for unto which of the angels said he at any time, Thou art my Son, this day have I begotten thee? and again, I will be to him a Father, and he shall be to me a Son.* Again, v. 5, 6, with reference to the priesthood of Christ; *so also Christ glorified not himself to be made an High Priest, but he*

that said unto him, Thou art my Son, this day have I begotten thee: as he saith also in another place, Thou art a priest for ever, &c. Further, it will be apparent from the second Psalm, that God has begotten the Son, that is, has made him a king: v. 6. *yet have I set my King upon my holy hill of Sion;* and then in the next verse, after having anointed his King, whence the name of Christ is derived, he says, *this day have I begotten thee.* Heb. i. 4, 5. *being made so much better than the angels, as he hath by inheritance obtained a more excellent name than they.* No other name can be intended but that of Son, as the following verse proves: *for unto which of the angels said he at any time, Thou art my Son; this day have I begotten thee?* The Son also declares the same of himself. John x. 35, 36. *say ye of Him whom the Father hath sanctified, and sent into the world, Thou blasphemest, because I said, I am the Son of God?* By a similar figure of speech, though in a much lower sense, the saints are also said to be begotten of God.

It is evident however upon a careful comparison and examination of all these passages, and particularly from the whole of the second Psalm, that however the generation of the Son may have taken place, it arose from no natural necessity, as is generally contended, but was no less owing to the decree and will of the Father than his priesthood or kingly power, or his resuscitation from the dead. Nor does this form any objection to his bearing the title of begotten, in whatever sense that expression is to be understood, or of God's *own Son,* Rom. viii. 32. For he is called the own Son of God merely because he had no other Father besides God, whence he himself said, that *God was his Father,* John v. 18. For to Adam God stood less in the relation of Father, than of Creator, having only formed him from the dust of the earth; whereas he was properly the Father of the Son made of his own substance. Yet it does not follow from hence that the Son is co-essential with the Father, for then the title of Son would be least of all applicable to him, since he who is properly the Son is not coeval with the Father, much less of the same numerical essence, otherwise the Father and the Son would be one person;

nor did the Father beget him from any natural necessity, but of his own free will,— a mode more perfect and more agreeable to the paternal dignity; particularly since the Father is God, all whose works, as has been already proved from Scripture, are executed freely according to his own good pleasure, and consequently the work of generation.

For questionless, it was in God's power consistently with the perfection of his own essence not to have begotten the Son, inasmuch as generation does not pertain to the nature of the Deity, who stands in no need of propagation; but whatever does not pertain to his own essence or nature, he does not effect like a natural agent from any physical necessity. If the generation of the Son proceeded from a physical necessity, the Father impaired himself by physically begetting a co-equal; which God could no more do than he could deny himself; therefore the generation of the Son cannot have proceeded otherwise than from a decree, and of the Father's own free will.

Thus the Son was begotten of the Father in consequence of his decree, and therefore within the limits of time, for the decree itself must have been anterior to the execution of the decree, as is sufficiently clear from the insertion of the word *to-day*. Nor can I discover on what passage of Scripture the assertors of the eternal generation of the Son ground their opinion, for the text in Micah v. 2. does not speak of his generation, but of his works, which are only said to have been wrought *from of old*. But this will be discussed more at large hereafter.

The Son is also called *only begotten*. John i. 14. *and we beheld his glory, the glory as of the only begotten of the Father.* v. 18. *the only begotten Son which is in the bosom of the Father.* iii. 16, 18. *he gave his only begotten Son.* 1 John iv. 9. *God sent his only begotten Son.* Yet he is not called essentially one with the Father, inasmuch as he was visible to sight, and given by the Father, by whom also he was sent, and from whom he proceeded; but he enjoys the title of only begotten by way of superiority, as distinguished from many others who are also said to have been born of God. John i. 13. *which were born of God.* 1 John iii. 9. *whosoever is born of*

God, doth not commit sin. James i. 18. *of his own will begat he us with the word of truth.* 1 John v. 1. *whosoever believeth, &c. is born of God.* 1 Pet. i. 3. *which according to his abundant mercy hath begotten us again unto a lively hope.* But since throughout the Scriptures the Son is never said to be begotten, except, as above, in a metaphorical sense, it seems probable that he is called *only begotten* principally because he is the one mediator between God and man.

So also the Son is called the *first born.* Rom. viii. 29. *that he might be the first born among many brethren.* Col. i. 15. *the first born of every creature.* v. 18. *the first born from the dead.* Heb. i. 6. *when he bringeth in the first begotten into the world.* Rev. iii. 14. *the beginning of the creation of God,*—all which passages preclude the idea of his co-essentiality with the Father, and of his generation from all eternity. Thus it is said of Israel, Exod. iv. 22. *thus saith Jehovah, Israel is my son, even my first born;* and of Ephraim, Jer. xxxi. 9. *Ephraim is my first born;* and of all the saints, Heb. xii. 23. *to the general assembly of the first born.*

Hitherto only the metaphorical generation of Christ has been considered; but since to generate another who had no previous existence, is to give him being, and that if God generate by a physical necessity, he can generate nothing but a co-equal Deity, which would be inconsistent with self-existence, an essential attribute of Divinity; (so that according to the one hypothesis there would be two infinite Gods, or according to the other the *first* or *efficient cause* would become the *effect,* which no man in his senses will admit) it becomes necessary to inquire how or in what sense God the Father can have begotten the Son. This point also will be easily explained by reference to Scripture. For when the Son is said to be *the first born of every creature,* and *the beginning of the creation of God,* nothing can be more evident than that God of his own will created, or generated, or produced the Son before all things, endued with the divine nature, as in the fulness of time he miraculously begat him in his human nature of the Virgin Mary. The generation of the divine nature is described by no one with more sublimity and copiousness than by the apostle to the Hebrews, i. 2, 3. *whom he hath appointed heir of all things, by whom also he made the worlds; who being the brightness of his glory, and the express image of his person,* &c. It must be understood from this, that God imparted to the Son as much as he pleased of the divine nature, nay of the divine substance itself, care being taken not to confound the substance with the whole essence, which would imply, that the Father had given to the Son what he retained numerically the same himself; which would be a contradiction of terms instead of a mode of generation. This is the whole that is revealed concerning the generation of the Son of God. Whoever wishes to be wiser than this, becomes foiled in his pursuit after wisdom, entangled in the deceitfulness of vain philosophy, or rather of sophistry, and involved in darkness.

Since, however, Christ not only bears the name of the only begotten Son of God, but is also several times called in Scripture God, notwithstanding the universal doctrine that there is but one God, it appeared to many, who had no mean opinion of their own acuteness, that there was an inconsistency in this; which gave rise to an hypothesis no less strange than repugnant to reason, namely, that the Son, although personally and numerically another, was yet essentially one with the Father, and that thus the unity of God was preserved.

But unless the terms unity and duality be signs of the same ideas to God which they represent to men, it would have been to no purpose that God had so repeatedly inculcated that first commandment, that he was the one and only God, if another could be said to exist besides, who also himself ought to be believed in as the one God. Unity and duality cannot consist of one and the same essence. God is one ens, not two; one essence and one subsistence, which is nothing but a substantial essence, appertain to one ens; if two subsistences or two persons be assigned to one essence, it involves a contradiction of terms, by representing the essence as at once simple and compound. If one divine essence be common to two persons, that essence or divinity will either be in the relation of a whole to its several parts, or of a genus to its several species, or lastly of a common subject to

its accidents. If none of these alternatives be conceded, there is no mode of escaping from the absurd consequences that follow, such as that one essence may be the third part of two or more.

There would have been no occasion for the supporters of these opinions to have offered such violence to reason, nay even to so much plain scriptural evidence, if they had duly considered God's own words addressed to kings and princes, Psal. lxxxii. 6. *I have said, Ye are gods, and all of you are children of the Most High;* or those of Christ himself, John x. 35. *if he called them Gods, unto whom the word of God came, and the Scripture cannot be broken—;* or those of St. Paul, I Cor. viii. 5, 6. *for though there be that are called gods, whether in heaven or earth, (for there be gods many and lords many,) but to us there is but one God, the Father, of whom are all things,* &c. or lastly of St. Peter, ii. 1, 4. *that by these ye might be partakers of the divine nature,* which implies much more than the title of gods in the sense in which that title is applied to kings; though no one would conclude from this expression that the saints were co-essential with God.

Let us then discard reason in sacred matters, and follow the doctrine of Holy Scripture exclusively. Accordingly, no one need expect that I should here premise a long metaphysical discussion, and introduce all that commonly received drama of the personalities in the Godhead: since it is most evident, in the first place, from numberless passages of Scripture, that there is in reality but one true independent and supreme God; and as he is called one, (inasmuch as human reason and the common language of mankind, and the Jews, the people of God, have always considered him as one person only, that is, one in a numerical sense) let us have recourse to the sacred writings in order to know who this one true and supreme God is. This knowledge ought to be derived in the first instance from the gospel, since the clearest doctrine respecting the one God must necessarily be that copious and explanatory revelation concerning him which was delivered by Christ himself to his apostles, and by the apostles to their followers. Nor is it to be supposed that the gospel would be ambiguous or obscure on this subject; for it was not given for the purpose of promulgating new and incredible doctrines respecting the nature of God, hitherto utterly unheard of by his own people, but to announce salvation to the Gentiles through Messiah the Son of God, according to the promise of the God of Abraham. *No man hath seen God at any time; the only begotten Son, which is in the bosom of the Father, he hath declared him,* John i. 18. Let us therefore consult the Son in the first place respecting God.

According to the testimony of the Son, delivered in the clearest terms, the Father is that one true God, by whom are all things. Being asked by one of the scribes, Mark xii. 28, 29, 32. which was the first commandment of all, he answered from Deut. vi. 4. *the first of all the commandments is, Hear, O Israel, the Lord our God is one Lord;* or as it is in the Hebrew, *Jehovah our God is one Jehovah.* The scribe assented; *there is one God, and there is none other one but he;* and in the following verse Christ expresses his approbation of this answer. Nothing can be more clear than that it was the opinion of the scribe, as well as of the other Jews, that by the unity of God is intended his oneness of person. That this God was no other than God the Father, is proved from John viii. 41, 54. *we have one Father, even God. It is my Father that honoureth me; of whom ye say that he is your God.* iv. 21. *neither in this mountain, nor yet at Jerusalem, shall ye worship the Father.* Christ therefore agrees with the whole people of God, that the Father is that one and only God. For who can believe that the very first of the commandments would have been so obscure, and so ill understood by the Church through such a succession of ages, that two other persons, equally entitled to worship, should have remained wholly unknown to the people of God, and debarred of divine honours even to that very day? especially as God, where he is teaching his own people respecting the nature of their worship under the gospel, forewarns them that they would have for their God the one Jehovah whom they had always served, and David, that is, Christ, for their King and Lord. Jer. xxx. 9. *they shall serve Jehovah their God, and David their King, whom I will raise up unto them.* In this passage Christ, such

as God willed that he should be known or served by his people under the gospel, is expressly distinguished from the one God Jehovah, both by nature and title. Christ himself therefore, the Son of God, teaches us nothing in the gospel respecting the one God but what the law had before taught, and everywhere clearly asserts him to be his Father. John xvii. 3. *this is life eternal, that they might know thee, the only true God, and Jesus Christ whom thou hast sent.* xx. 17. *I ascend unto my Father and your Father; and to my God and your God:* if therefore the Father be the God of Christ, and the same be our God, and if there be none other God but one, there can be no God beside the Father.

Paul, the apostle and interpreter of Christ, teaches the same in so clear and perspicuous a manner, that one might almost imagine the inculcation of this truth to have been his sole object. No teacher of catechumens in the Church could have spoken more plainly and expressly of the one God, according to the sense in which the universal consent of mankind has agreed to understand unity of number. 1 Cor. viii. 4–6. *we know that an idol is nothing in the world, and that there is none other God but one: for though there be that are called gods, whether in heaven or in earth, (as there be gods many and lords many), but to us there is but one God, the Father, of whom are all things, and we in him; and one Lord Jesus Christ, by whom are all things, and we by him.* Here the expression *there is none other God but one* excludes not only all other essences, but all other persons whatever; for it is expressly said in the sixth verse, that *the Father is that one God;* wherefore there is no other person but one: at least in that sense which is intended by divines, when they argue from John xiv. 16. that there is another God, for the sake of asserting the personality of the Holy Spirit. Again, to those *who are called gods, whether in heaven or in earth, God the Father of whom are all things* is opposed singly; he who is numerically *one God,* to *many gods.* Though the Son be another God, yet in this passage he is called merely *Lord;* he *of whom are all things* is clearly distinguished from him *by whom are all things,* and if a difference of causation prove a difference of essence, he is distinguished also in essence. Besides, since a numerical difference originates in difference of essence, those who are two numerically, must be also two essentially. There is *one Lord,* namely he whom *God the Father hath made,* Acts ii. 36. much more therefore is the Father Lord, who made him, though he be not here called Lord. For he who calls the Father *one God,* also calls him one Lord above all, as Psal. cx. 1. *the Lord said unto my Lord,* —a passage which will be more fully discussed hereafter. He who calls Jesus Christ *one Lord,* does not call him one God, for this reason among others, that *God the Father hath made him both Lord and Christ,* Acts ii. 36. Elsewhere therefore he calls the Father both God and Lord of him whom he here calls *one Lord Jesus Christ.* Eph. i. 17. *the God of our Lord Jesus Christ.* 1 Cor. xi. 3. *the head of Christ is God.* xv. 28. *the Son also himself shall be subject unto him.* If in truth the Father be called *the Father of Christ,* if he be called *the God of Christ,* if he be called *the head of Christ,* if he be called the God to whom Christ described as the Lord, nay, even as *the Son himself, is subject, and shall be subjected,* why should not the Father be also the Lord of the same Lord Christ, and the God of the same God Christ; since Christ must also be God in the same relative manner that he is Lord and Son? Lastly, the Father is he *of whom,* and *from whom,* and *by whom,* and *for whom are all things;* Rom. xi. 36. Heb. ii. 10. The Son is not he *of whom,* but only *by whom;* and that not without an exception, *all things,* namely, *which were made,* John i. 3. *all things, except him which did put all things under him,* 1 Cor. xv. 27. It is evident therefore that when it is said *all things were by him,* it must be understood of a secondary and delegated power; and that when the particle *by* is used in reference to the Father, it denotes the primary cause, as John vi. 57. *I live by the Father;* when in reference to the Son, the secondary and instrumental cause: which will be explained more clearly on a future occasion.

Again, Eph. iv. 4–6. *there is one body and one Spirit, even as ye are called in one hope of your calling; one Lord, one faith, one baptism; one God and Father of all,* *who is above all, and through all, and in you all.* Here there is one Spirit, and one Lord; but the Father is one, and therefore God is one in the same sense as the remaining objects of which unity is predicated, that is, numerically one, and therefore one also in person. 1 Tim. ii. 5. *there is one God, and one mediator between God and men, the man Christ Jesus.* Here the mediator, though not purely human, is purposely named man, by the title derived from his inferior nature, lest he should be thought equal to the Father, or the same God, whereas the argument distinctly and expressly refers to one God. Besides, it cannot be explained how any one can be a mediator to himself on his own behalf; according to Gal. iii. 20. *a mediator is not a mediator of one, but God is one.* How then can God be a mediator of God? Not to mention that he himself uniformly testifies of himself, John viii. 28. *I do nothing of myself,* and v. 42. *neither came I of myself.* Undoubtedly therefore he does not act as a mediator to himself; nor return as a mediator to himself. Rom. v. 10. *we were reconciled to God by the death of his Son.* To whatever God we were reconciled, if he be one God, he cannot be the God by whom we are reconciled, inasmuch as that God is another person; for if he be one and the same, he must be a mediator between himself and us, and reconcile us to himself by himself; which is an insurmountable difficulty.

Though all this be so self-evident as to require no explanation,—namely, that the Father alone is a self-existent God, and that a being which is not self-existent cannot be God,—it is wonderful with what futile subtleties, or rather with what juggling artifices, certain individuals have endeavoured to elude or obscure the plain meaning of these passages; leaving no stone unturned, recurring to every shift, attempting every means, as if their object were not to preach the pure and unadulterated truth of the gospel to the poor and simple, but rather by dint of vehemence and obstinacy to sustain some absurd paradox from falling, by the treacherous aid of sophisms and verbal distinctions, borrowed from the barbarous ignorance of the schools.

They defend their conduct, however, on the ground, that though these opinions may seem inconsistent with reason, they are to be held for the sake of other passages of Scripture, and that otherwise Scripture will not be consistent with itself. Setting aside reason therefore, let us have recourse again to the language of Scripture.

The passages in question are two only. The first is John x. 30. *I and my Father are one,*—that is, one in essence, as it is commonly interpreted. But God forbid that we should decide rashly on any point relative to the Deity. Two things may be called one in more than one way. Scripture saith, and the Son saith, *I and my Father are one,*—I bow to their authority. Certain commentators conjecture that they are one in essence,—I reject what is merely man's invention. For the Son has not left us to conjecture in what manner he is one with the Father, (whatever member of the Church may have first arrogated to himself the merit of the discovery,) but explains the doctrine himself most fully, so far as we are concerned to know it. The Father and the Son are one, not indeed in essence, for he had himself said the contrary in the preceding verse, *my Father, which gave them me, is greater than all,* (see also xiv. 28. *my Father is greater than I,*) and in the following verses he distinctly denies that he made himself God in saying, *I and my Father are one;* he insists that he had only said as follows, which implies far less, v. 36. *say ye of him whom the Father hath sanctified, and sent into the world, Thou blasphemest; because I said, I am the Son of God?* This must be spoken of two persons not only not co-essential, but not co-equal. Now if the Son be laying down a doctrine respecting the unity of the divine essence in two persons of the Trinity, how is it that he does not rather attribute the same unity of essence to the three persons? Why does he divide the indivisible Trinity? For there cannot be unity without totality. Therefore, on the authority of the opinions holden by my opponents themselves, the Son and the Father without the Spirit are not one in essence. How then are they one? It is the province of Christ alone to acquaint us with this, and accordingly he does acquaint us with it. In the first place, they are one, inasmuch as they speak and act with unanimity; and so he explains himself in the same chapter, after the Jews had misunderstood his saying: x. 38. *believe the works; that ye may know and believe that the Father is in me, and I in him.* xiv. 10. *believest thou not that I am in the Father, and the Father in me? the words that I speak unto you, I speak not of myself, but the Father that dwelleth in me, he doeth the works.* Here he evidently distinguishes the Father from himself in his whole capacity, but asserts at the same time that the Father remains in him; which does not denote unity of essence, but only intimacy of communion. Secondly, he declares himself to be one with the Father in the same manner as we are one with him,—that is, not in essence, but in love, in communion, in agreement, in charity, in spirit, in glory. John xiv. 20, 21. *at that day ye shall know that I am in the Father, and ye in me, and I in you: he that hath my commandments, and keepeth them, he it is that loveth me; and he that loveth me, shall be loved of my Father.* xvii. 21. *that they all may be one, as thou, Father, art in me, and I in thee; that they also may be one in us.* v. 23. *I in them, and thou in me, that they may be made perfect in one, and that the world may know that thou hast sent me, and hast loved them as thou hast loved me.* v. 22. *the glory which thou gavest me I have given them, that they may be one, even as we are one.* When the Son has shown in so many modes how he and the Father are one, why should I set them all aside? why should I, on the strength of my own reasoning, though in opposition to reason itself, devise another mode, which makes them one in essence; or why, if already devised by some other person, adopt it, in preference to Christ's own mode? If it be proposed on the single authority of the Church, the true doctrine of the orthodox Church herself teaches me otherwise; inasmuch as it instructs me to listen to the words of Christ before all other.

The other passage, which according to the general opinion affords the clearest foundation for the received doctrine of the essential unity of the three persons, is I John v. 7. *there are three that bear record in heaven, the Father, the Word, and the Holy Ghost, and these three are one.* But not to mention that this verse is wanting in the Syriac and the other two Oriental versions, the Arabic and the Ethiopic, as well as in the greater part of the ancient Greek manuscripts, and that in those manuscripts which actually contain it many various readings occur, it no more necessarily proves those to be essentially one, who are said to be one in heaven, than it proves those to be essentially one, who are said to be one on earth in the following verse. And not only Erasmus, but even Beza, however unwillingly, acknowledged (as may be seen in their own writings) that if John be really the author of the verse, he is only speaking here, as in the last quoted passage, of an unity of agreement and testimony. Besides, who are the three who are said to bear witness? That they are three Gods, will not be admitted; therefore neither is it the one God, but one record or one testimony of three witnesses, which is implied. But he who is not co-essential with God the Father, cannot be co-equal with the Father. This text however will be discussed more at large in the following chapter.

But, it is objected, although Scripture does not say in express words that the Father and the Son are one in essence, yet reason proves the truth of the doctrine from these, as well as from other passages of Scripture.

In the first place, granting, (which I am far from doing,) that this is the case, yet on a subject so sublime, and so far above our reason, where the very elements and first postulates, as it were, of our faith are concerned, belief must be founded, not on mere reason, but on the word of God exclusively, where the language of the revelation is most clear and particular. Reason itself, however, protests strongly against the doctrine in question; for how can reason establish (as it must in the present case) a position contrary to reason? Undoubtedly the product of reason must be something consistent with reason, not a notion as absurd as it is removed from all human comprehension. Hence we conclude, that this opinion is agreeable neither to Scripture nor reason. The other alternative therefore must be adopted, namely, that if God be one God, and that one God be the Father, and if notwithstanding the Son be also called God, the Son must have received the name and nature of Deity from God

the Father, in conformity with his decree and will, after the manner stated before. This doctrine is not disproved by reason, and Scripture teaches it in innumerable passages.

But those who insist that the Son is one God with the Father, consider their point as susceptible of ample proof, even without the two texts already examined, (on which indeed some admit that no reliance is to be placed) if it can be demonstrated from a sufficient number of Scripture testimonies that the name and attributes and works of God, as well as divine honours, are habitually ascribed to the Son. To proceed therefore in the same line of argument, I do not ask them to believe that the Father alone and none else is God, unless I shall have proved, first, that in every passage each of the particulars above mentioned is attributed in express terms only to one God the Father, as well by the Son himself as by his apostles. Secondly, that wherever they are attributed to the Son, it is in such a manner that they are easily understood to be attributable in their original and proper sense to the Father alone; and that the Son acknowledges himself to possess whatever share of Deity is assigned to him, by virtue of the peculiar gift and kindness of the Father; to which the apostles also bear their testimony. And lastly, that the Son himself and his apostles acknowledge throughout the whole of their discourses and writings, that the Father is greater than the Son in all things.

I am aware of the answer which will be here made by those who, while they believe in the unity of God, yet maintain that the Father alone is not God. I shall therefore meet their objection in the outset, lest they should raise a difficulty and outcry at each individual passage. They twice beg the question, or rather request us to make two gratuitous concessions. In the first place, they insist, that wherever the name of God is attributed to the Father alone, it should be understood οὐσιωδῶς, not ὑποστατικῶς, that is to say, that the name of the Father, who is unity, should be understood to signify the three persons, or the whole essence of the Trinity, not the single person of the Father. This is on many accounts a ridiculous distinction, and invented solely for the purpose of supporting their peculiar opinion; although in reality, instead of supporting it, it will be found to be dependent on it, and therefore if the opinion itself be invalidated, for which purpose a simple denial is sufficient, the futile distinction falls to the ground at the same time. For the fact is, not merely that the distinction is a futile one, but that it is no distinction at all; it is a mere verbal quibble, founded on the use of synonymous words, and cunningly dressed up in terms borrowed from the Greek to dazzle the eyes of novices. For since *essence* and *hypostasis* mean the same thing, as has been shown in the second Chapter, it follows that there can be no real difference of meaning between the adverbs *essentially* and *substantially,* which are derived from them. If then the name of God be attributed to the Father alone *essentially,* it must also be attributed to the Father alone *substantially;* since one substantial essence means nothing else than one hypostasis, and vice versa. I would therefore ask my adversaries, whether they hold the Father to be an abstract ens or not? Questionless they will reply, the primary ens of all. I answer, therefore, that as he has one hypostasis, so must he have one essence proper to himself, incommunicable in the highest degree, and participated by no one, that is, by no person besides, for he cannot have his own proper hypostasis, without having his own proper essence. For it is impossible for any ens to retain its own essence in common with any other thing whatever, since by this essence it is what it is, and is numerically distinguished from all others. If therefore the Son, who has his own proper hypostasis, have not also his own proper essence, but the essence of the Father, he becomes on their hypothesis either no ens at all, or the same ens with the Father; which strikes at the very foundation of the Christian religion. The answer which is commonly made, is ridiculous—namely, that although one finite essence can pertain to one person only, one infinite essence may pertain to a plurality of persons; whereas in reality the infinitude of the essence affords an additional reason why it can pertain to only one person. All acknowledge that both the essence and the person of the Father are infinite; therefore the essence of the Father cannot be communicated to another person, for otherwise there might be two, or any imaginable number of infinite persons.

The second postulate is, that wherever the Son attributes Deity to the Father alone, and as to one greater than himself, he must be understood to speak in his human character, or as mediator. Wherever the context and the fact itself require this interpretation, I shall readily concede it, without losing anything by the concession; for however strongly it may be contended, that when the Son attributes every thing to the Father alone, he speaks in his human or mediatorial capacity, it can never be inferred from hence that he is one God with the Father. On the other hand I shall not scruple to deny the proposition, whenever it is to be conceded not to the sense of the passage, but merely to serve their own theory; and shall prove that what the Son attributes to the Father, he attributes in his filial or even in his divine character to the Father as God of God, and not to himself under any title or pretence whatever.

With regard to the name of God, wherever simultaneous mention is made of the Father and the Son, that name is uniformly ascribed to the Father alone, except in such passages as shall be hereafter separately considered. I shall quote in the first place the texts of the former class, which are by far the more considerable in point of number, and form a large and compact body of proofs. John iii. 16. *so God loved the world, that he gave his own Son,* &c. vi. 27. *him hath God the Father sealed.* v. 29. *this is the work of God, that ye believe on him whom he hath sent.* xiv. 1. *ye believe in God, believe also in me.* What is meant by believing in any one, will be explained hereafter; in the mean time it is clear that two distinct things are here intended—*in God* and *in me.* Thus all the apostles in conjunction, Acts iv. 24. *lifted up their voice to God with one accord, and said, Lord, thou art God which hast made heaven and earth . . . who by the mouth of thy servant David hast said, Why did the heathen rage . . . against the Lord, and against his Christ?* Rom. viii. 3. *God sending his own Son.* 1 Thess. iii. 11. *now God himself, and our Father, and our Lord Jesus Christ, direct our way unto you.* Col. ii. 2. *to the acknowledgement of the mystery of God, and of the Father, and of Christ.* iii. 3. *your life is hid with Christ in God.* 2 Tim. iv. 1. *I charge thee therefore before God and the Lord Jesus Christ.* 1 John iv. 9. *the love of God toward us, because that God sent his only begotten Son.* So also where Christ is named first in order. Gal. i. 1. *by Jesus Christ, and God the Father, who raised him from the dead.* 2 Thess. ii. 16. *now our Lord Jesus Christ himself, and God, even our Father.* The same thing may be observed in the very outset of all the Epistles of St. Paul and of the other apostles, where, as is natural, it is their custom to declare in express and distinct terms who he is by whose divine authority they have been sent. Rom. i. 7, 8. 1 Cor. i. 1–3. 2 Cor. i. 1–3. and so throughout to the book of Revelations. See also Mark i. 1.

The Son likewise teaches that the attributes of divinity belong to the Father alone, to the exclusion even of himself. With regard to omniscience. Matt. xxiv. 36. *of that day and hour knoweth no man, no not the angels of heaven, but my Father only;* and still more explicitly, Mark xiii. 32. *not the angels which are in heaven, neither the Son, but the Father.*

With regard to supreme dominion both in heaven and earth, the unlimited authority and full power of decreeing according to his own independent will. Matt. vi. 13. *thine is the kingdom and the power and the glory for ever.* xviii. 35. *so likewise shall my heavenly Father do also unto you, if ye from your hearts forgive not,* &c.— xxvi. 29. *in my Father's kingdom.* xx. 23. *to sit on my right hand and on my left, is not mine to give, but it shall be given to them for whom it is prepared of my Father. It is not mine—,* in my mediatorial capacity, as it is commonly interpreted. But questionless when the ambition of the mother and her two sons incited them to prefer this important petition, they addressed their petition to the entire nature of Christ, how exalted soever it might be, praying him to grant their request to the utmost extent of his power whether as God or man; v. 20. *worshipping him, and desiring a certain thing of him,* and v. 21. *grant that they may sit.* Christ also answers with reference to his whole nature—*it is not mine to give;* and lest for some reason

they might still fancy the gift belonged to him, he declares that it was altogether out of his province, and the exclusive privilege of the Father. If his reply was meant solely to refer to his mediatorial capacity, it would have bordered on sophistry, which God forbid that we should attribute to him; as if he were capable of evading the request of Salome and her sons by the quibble which the logicians call *expositio prava* or *æquivoca,* when the respondent answers in a sense or with a mental intention different from the meaning of the questioner. The same must be said of other passages of the same kind, where Christ speaks of himself; for after the hypostatical union of two natures in one person, it follows that whatever Christ says of himself, he says not as the possessor of either nature separately, but with reference to the whole of his character, and in his entire person, except where he himself makes a distinction. Those who divide this hypostatical union at their own discretion, strip the discourses and answers of Christ of all their sincerity; they represent every thing as ambiguous and uncertain, as true and false at the same time; it is not Christ that speaks, but some unknown substitute, sometimes one, and sometimes another; so that the words of Horace may be justly applied to such disputants:

Quo teneam vultus mutantem Protea nodo?

Luke xxiii. 34. *Father, forgive them,* &c. John xiv. 2. *in my Father's house.* So also Christ himself says, Matt. xxvi. 39. *O my Father, if it be possible, let this cup pass from me; nevertheless not as I will, but as thou wilt.* Now it is manifest that those who have not the same will, cannot have the same essence. It appears however from many passages, that the Father and Son have not, in a numerical sense, the same intelligence or will. Matt. xxiv. 36. *no man knoweth . . . but my Father only.* Mark xiii. 32. *neither the Son, but the Father.* John vi. 38. *I came down from heaven, not to do mine own will, but the will of him that sent me.* Those therefore whose understanding and will are not numerically the same, cannot have the same essence. Nor is there any mode of evading this conclusion, inasmuch as the Son himself has thus expressed himself even with regard to his own divine nature. See also Matt.

xxvi. 42. *and* v. 53. *thinkest thou that I cannot now pray to my Father, and he shall presently give me more than twelve legions of angels?* Mark xiv. 36. *Abba, Father, all things are possible unto thee; take away this cup from me, &c.* Luke xxii. 29. *I appoint unto you a kingdom, as my Father hath appointed unto me.* xxiii. 46. *Father, into thy hands I commend my spirit.* John xii. 27. *Father, save me from this hour.* If these prayers be uttered only in his human capacity, which is the common solution, why does he petition these things from the Father alone instead of from himself, if he were God? Or rather, supposing him to be at once man and the supreme God, why does he ask at all for what was in his own power? What need was there for the union of the divine and human nature in one person, if he himself, being equal to the Father, gave back again into his hands every thing that he had received from him?

With regard to his supreme goodness. Matt. xix. 17. *why callest thou me good? there is none good but one, that is, God.* We need not be surprised that Christ should refuse to accept the adulatory titles which were wont to be given to the Pharisees, and on this account should receive the young man with less kindness than usual; but when he says, *there is none good but one, that is, God,* it is evident that he did not choose to be considered essentially the same with that one God; for otherwise this would only have been disclaiming the credit of goodness in one character, for the purpose of assuming it in another. John vi. 32. *my Father giveth you the true bread from heaven.* v. 65. *no man can come unto me*—that is, to me, both God and man—*except it were given unto him of my Father.*

With regard to his supreme glory. Matt. xviii. 10. *their angels do always behold the face of my Father which is in heaven.* John xvii. 4. *I have glorified thee on the earth.* Nay, it is to those who obey the Father that the promise of true wisdom is made even with regard to the knowing Christ himself, which is the very point now in question. John vii. 17, 18. *if any man will do his will, he shall know of the doctrine whether it be of God, or whether I speak of myself: he that speaketh of him-*self *seeketh his own glory; but he that seeketh his glory that sent him, the same is true, and no unrighteousness is in him.* xv. 8. *herein is my Father glorified, that ye bear much fruit; so shall ye be my disciples.* Matt. vii. 21. *not every one that saith unto me, Lord, Lord, shall enter into the kingdom of heaven, but he that doeth the will of my Father that is in heaven.* xii. 50. *whosoever shall do the will of my Father which is in heaven, the same is my brother, and sister, and mother.*

Thus Christ assigns every attribute of the Deity to the Father alone. The apostles uniformly speak in a similar manner. Rom. xv. 5, 6. *the God of patience and consolation grant you to be like minded one toward another, according to Christ Jesus.* xvi. 25–27. *to him that is of power to stablish you . . . according to the commandment of the everlasting God . . . to God only wise, be glory through Jesus Christ—our Lord,* as the Vetus Interpres and some of the Greek manuscripts read it. 1 Tim. vi. 13–16. *I give thee charge in the sight of God, who quickeneth all things, and before Christ Jesus, who witnessed a good confession . . . until the appearing of our Lord Jesus Christ, which in his times he shall show, who is the blessed and only Potentate, the King of kings and Lord of lords; who alone hath immortality, dwelling in the light which no man can approach unto, whom no man hath seen, nor can see; to whom be honour and power everlasting. Amen.*

With regard to his works. See Rom. xvi. 25–27. 1 Tim. vi. 13–16. as quoted above. 2 Cor. i. 21, 22. *now he which stablisheth us with you in Christ, and hath anointed us, is God; who hath also sealed us.* Now the God which stablisheth us, is one God. 1 Pet. i. 2. *elect according to the foreknowledge of God the Father, through sanctification of the Spirit unto obedience and sprinkling of the blood of Jesus Christ.* Even those works which regard the Son himself, or which were done in him. Acts v. 30–33. *the God of our fathers raised up Jesus . . . him hath God exalted with his right hand to be a Prince and a Saviour, for to give repentance to Israel, and forgiveness of sins.* Gal. i. 1. *by Jesus Christ, and God the Father, who raised him from the dead.* Rom. x. 9. *if thou shalt believe in thine heart that God hath raised him from the dead, thou shalt be saved.* 1 Cor. vi. 14. *God hath both raised up the Lord, and will also raise us up by his own power.* 1 Thess. i. 10. *to wait for his Son from heaven, whom he raised from the dead.* Heb. x. 5. *sacrifice and offering thou wouldest not, but a body hast thou prepared me.* 1 Pet. i. 21. *who by him do believe in God that raised him up from the dead.* So many are the texts wherein the Son is said to be raised up by the Father alone, which ought to have greater weight than the single passage in St. John, ii. 19. *destroy this temple, and in three days I will raise it up*—where he spake briefly and enigmatically, without explaining his meaning to enemies who were unworthy of a fuller answer, on which account he thought it unnecessary to mention the power of the Father.

With regard to divine honours. For as the Son uniformly pays worship and reverence to the Father alone, so he teaches us to follow the same practice. Matt. vi. 6. *pray to thy Father.* v. 9. *after this manner therefore pray ye; Our Father, which art in heaven,* &c. xviii. 19. *as touching any thing that they shall ask, it shall be done for them of my Father which is in heaven.* Luke xi. 1, 2. *teach us to pray,* &c. *and he said unto them, When ye pray, say, Our Father, which art in heaven.* John ii. 16. *make not my Father's house an house of merchandise.* iv. 21–23. *the hour cometh, and now is, when the true worshippers shall worship the Father in spirit and in truth; for the Father seeketh such to worship him.* xv. 16. *that whatsoever ye shall ask of the Father in my name, he may give it you.* xvi. 23. *in that day ye shall ask me nothing; . . . whatsoever ye shall ask the Father in my name, he will give it you.* Rom. i. 8, 9. *first, I thank my God through Jesus Christ for you all . . . for God is my witness, whom I serve with my spirit in the gospel of his Son,* &c. v. 11. *we also joy in God through our Lord Jesus Christ.* vii. 25. *I thank God, through Jesus Christ our Lord.* xv. 6. *that ye may with one mind and one mouth glorify God, even the Father of our Lord Jesus Christ.* 1 Cor. i. 4. *I thank my God always on your behalf, for the grace of God which is given you by Jesus Christ.* 2 Cor.

i. 3. *blessed be God, even the Father of our Lord Jesus Christ, the Father of mercies, and the God of all comfort.* Gal. i. 4, 5. *who gave himself . . . according to the will of God and our Father; to whom be glory for ever and ever.* Eph. i. 3. *blessed be the God and Father of our Lord Jesus Christ,* &c. ii. 18. *for through him we both have access by one Spirit unto the Father.* iii. 14. *for this cause I bow my knees unto the Father of our Lord Jesus Christ.* v. 20, 21. *now unto him that is able to do exceeding abundantly, above all that we ask or think, according to the power that worketh in us, unto him be glory in the Church by Christ Jesus, throughout all ages, world without end.* Philipp. i. 2, 3. *grace be unto you and peace from God our Father, and from the Lord Jesus Christ. I thank my God upon every remembrance of you.* See also Col. i. 3. and iii. 17. *whatsoever ye do . . . do all in the name of the Lord Jesus, giving thanks to God and the Father by him.* 1 Thess. i. 2, 3. *we give thanks to God for you all, making mention of you in our prayers; remembering without ceasing your work of faith, and labour of love, and patience of hope in our Lord Jesus Christ, in the sight of God and our Father.* v. 9, 10. *to serve the living and true God; and to wait for his Son from heaven, whom he raised from the dead.* See also 2 Thess. i. 2, 3. and 2 Tim. i. 3. *I thank God, whom I serve from my forefathers.* Now the forefathers of Paul served God the Father alone. See also Philem. 4, 5. and 1 Pet. i. 3. and iv. 10. *as every man hath received the gift . . . let him speak as the oracles of God . . . as of the ability which God giveth, that God in all things may be glorified through Jesus Christ.* James i. 27. *pure religion and undefiled before God and the Father, is this.* 1 John ii. 1. *we have an advocate with the Father, Jesus Christ the righteous.* 2 John 4–6. *walking in truth, as we have received a commandment from the Father . . . this is love, that we walk after his commandments.* Rev. i. 6. *who made us kings and priests unto God and His Father; to him be glory and dominion for ever and ever.* Matt. xxi. 12. *Jesus went into the temple of God.* Here however my opponents quote the passage from Malachi, iii. 1. *the Lord whom ye seek shall suddenly come to his temple, even the messen-*

ger of the covenant. I answer, that in prophetical language these words signify the coming of the Lord into the flesh, or into the temple of the body, as it is expressed John ii. 21. For the Jews sought no one in the temple as an object of worship, except the Father; and Christ himself in the same chapter has called the temple his Father's house, and not his own. Nor were they seeking God, but *that Lord and messenger of the covenant;* that is, him who was sent from God as the mediator of the covenant;—he it was who should come to his Church, which the prophets generally express figuratively under the image of the temple. So also where the terms God and man are put in opposition to each other, the Father stands exclusively for the one God. James iii. 9. *therewith bless we God, even the Father; and therewith curse we men, which are made after the similitude of God.* 1 John ii. 15, 16. *if any man love the world, the love of the Father is not in him: for all that is in the world . . . is not of the Father, but of the world.*

But it is strenuously urged on the other hand, that the Son is sometimes called God, and even Jehovah; and that all the attributes of the Deity are assigned to him likewise in many passages both of the Old and New Testament. We arrive therefore at the other point which I originally undertook to prove; and since it has been already shown from the analogy of Scripture, that where the Father and the Son are mentioned together, the name, and attributes, and works of the Deity, as well as divine honours, are always assigned to the one and only God the Father, I will now demonstrate, that whenever the same properties are assigned to the Son, it is in such a manner as to make it easily intelligible that they ought all primarily and properly to be attributed to the Father alone.

It must be observed in the first place, that the name of God is not unfrequently ascribed, by the will and concession of God the Father, even to angels and men,—how much more then to the only begotten Son, the image of the Father. To angels. Psal. xcvii. 7, 9. *worship him all ye gods . . . thou art high above all the earth; thou art exalted far above all gods,* compared with Heb. i. 6. See also Psal. viii. 5. To judges. Exod. xxii. 28. *thou shalt not re-vile the gods, nor curse the ruler of thy people.* See also, in the Hebrew, Exod. xxi. 6. xxii. 8, 9. Psal. lxxxii. 1, 6. *he judgeth among the gods. I have said, Ye are gods, and all of you are children of the Most High.* To the whole house of David, or to all the saints. Zech. xii. 8. *the house of David shall be as God, as the angel of the Lord before them.* The word אֱלֹהִים, though it be of the plural number, is also employed to signify a single angel, in case it should be thought that the use of the plural implies a plurality of persons in the Godhead: Judges xiii. 21. *then Manoah knew that he was an angel of Jehovah: and Manoah said unto his wife, We shall surely die, because we have seen God.* The same word is also applied to a single false god. Exod. xx. 3. *thou shalt have no other gods before me.* To Dagon. Judges xvi. 23. To single idols. 1 Kings xi. 33. To Moses. Exod. iv. 16. and vii. 1. To God the Father alone. Psal. ii. 7. xlv. 7. and in many other places. Similar to this is the use of the word אֲדֹנִים, *the Lord,* in the plural number with a singular meaning; and with a plural affix according to the Hebrew mode. The word אֲדֹנָי also with the vowel *Patha* is frequently employed to signify one man, and with the vowel *Kamets* to signify one God, or one angel bearing the character of God. This peculiarity in the above words has been carefully noticed by the grammarians and lexicographers themselves, as well as in בַּעַל used appellatively. The same thing may perhaps be remarked of the proper names בְּעָלִים and עַשְׁתָּרוֹת. For even among the Greeks the word δεσπότης, that is, Lord, is also used in the plural number in the sense of the singular, when extraordinary respect and honour are intended to be paid. Thus in the *Iphigenia in Aulis* of Euripides, λίαν δεσπόταισι πιστὸς εἶ, (l. 394, Beck's edition) for δεσπότῃ, and again εὐκλεές τοι δεσποτῶν θνήσκειν ὑπὲρ (l. 312) for δεσπότου. It is also used in the *Rhesus* and the *Bacchæ* in the same manner.

Attention must be paid to these circumstances, lest any one through ignorance of the language should erroneously suppose, that whenever the word Elohim is joined with a singular, it is intended to intimate a plurality of persons in unity of essence. But if there be any significance at all in this peculiarity, the word must imply as many Gods, as it does persons. Besides, a plural adjective or a plural verb is sometimes joined to the word Elohim, which, if a construction of this kind could mean anything, would signify not a plurality of persons only, but also of natures. See in the Hebrew Deut. v. 26. Josh. xxiv. 19. Jer. x. 10. Gen. xx. 13. Further, the singular אֱלֹהַּ also sometimes occurs, Deut. xxxii. 18.

and elsewhere. It is also attributed to Christ with the singular affix. Psal. cx. 1. לַאדֹנִי *Jehovah said unto my Lord,* in which passage the Psalmist speaks of Christ (to whom the name of *Lord* is assigned as a title of the highest honour) both as distinct from Jehovah, and, if any reliance can be placed on the affix, as inferior to Jehovah. But when he addresses the Father, the affix is changed, and he says, v. 5. אֲדֹנָי, *the Lord at thy right hand shall strike through kings in the day of his wrath.*

The name of God seems to be attributed to angels, because as heavenly messengers they bear the appearance of the divine glory and person, and even speak in the very words of the Deity. Gen. xxi. 17, 18. xxii. 11, 12, 15, 16. *by myself have I sworn, saith Jehovah.* For the expression which was so frequently in the mouth of the prophets, and which is elsewhere often omitted, is here inserted, that it may be understood that angels and messengers do not declare their own words, but the commands of God who sends them, even though the speaker seem to bear the name and character of the Deity himself. So believed the patriarch Jacob; Gen. xxxi. 11-13. *the angel of God spake unto me, saying . . . I have seen all that Laban doeth unto thee. I am the God of Bethel,* &c. xxxii. 30. *I have seen God face to face;* compared with Hos. xii. 4, 5. *he had power with God, yea, he had power over the angel.* Exod. xxiv. 10, 11. *they saw the God of Israel . . . also they saw God.* Deut. ix. 33. *did ever peo-*

ple hear the voice of God speaking out of the midst of the fire, as thou hast heard, and live? Yet it is said, Exod. xxxiii. 20. *there shall no man see me, and live.* John i. 18. *no man hath seen God at any time.* v. 37. *ye have neither heard his voice at any time, nor seen his shape.* 1 Tim. vi. 16. *dwelling in the light which no man can approach unto, whom no man hath seen, nor can see.* It follows therefore that whoever was heard or seen, it was not God; not even where mention is made of God, nay even of Jehovah himself, and of the angels in the same sentence. Gen. xxviii. 12, 13. *behold the angels of God . . . and behold, Jehovah stood above them.* 1 Kings xxii. 19. *I saw Jehovah sitting on his throne, and all the host of heaven standing by him.* Isai. vi. 1, 2. *I saw the Lord sitting upon a throne . . . above it stood the seraphim.* I repeat, it was not God himself that he saw, but perhaps one of the angels clothed in some modification of the divine glory, or the Son of God himself, the image of the glory of his Father, as John understands the vision, xii. 41. *these things said Esaias, when he saw his glory.* For if he had been of the same essence, he could no more have been seen or heard than the Father himself, as will be more fully shewn hereafter. Hence even the holiest of men were troubled in mind when they had seen an angel, as if they had seen God himself. Gen. xxxii. 30. *I have seen God.* Judges vi. 22. *when Gideon perceived that he was an angel of Jehovah, Gideon said, Alas, O Lord Jehovah, for because I have seen an angel of Jehovah face to face.* See also xiii. 21, 22. as before.

The name of God is ascribed to judges, because they occupy the place of God to a certain degree in the administration of judgement. The Son, who was entitled to the name of God both in the capacity of a messenger and of a judge, and indeed in virtue of a much better right, did not think it foreign to his character, when the Jews accused him of blasphemy because he made himself God, to allege in his own defence the very reason which has been advanced. John x. 34-36. *Jesus answered them, Is it not written in your law, I said, Ye are gods? If he called them gods unto whom the word of God came, and the Scripture cannot be broken; say ye of him whom the*

Father hath sanctified and sent into the world, Thou blasphemest; because I said, I am the Son of God?—especially when God himself had called the judges, sons of the Most High, as has been stated before. Hence 1 Cor. viii. 4, 5. *for though there be that are called gods, whether in heaven or in earth, (as there be gods many, and lords many,) but to us there is but one God, the Father, of whom are all things, and we in him; and one Lord Jesus Christ, by whom are all things, and we by him.*

Even the principal texts themselves which are brought forward to prove the divinity of the Son, if carefully weighed and considered, are sufficient to show that the Son is God in the manner which has been explained. John i. 1. *in the beginning was the Word, and the Word was with God, and the Word was God.* It is not said, from everlasting, but *in the beginning.* The Word,—therefore the Word was audible. But God, as he cannot be seen, so neither can he be heard; John v. 37. The Word therefore is not of the same essence with God. *The Word was with God, and was God,*—namely, because he was with God, that is, in the bosom of the Father, as it is expressed v. 18. Does it follow therefore that he is essentially one with him with whom he was? It no more follows, than that the disciple *who was lying on Jesus' breast,* John xiii. 23. was essentially one with Christ. Reason rejects the doctrine; Scripture nowhere asserts it; let us therefore abandon human devices, and follow the evangelist himself; who is his own interpreter. Rev. xix. 13. *his name is called The Word of God*—that is, of the one God: he himself is a distinct person. If therefore he be a distinct person, he is distinct from God, who is unity. How then is he himself also God? By the same right as he enjoys the title of the Word, or of the only begotten Son, namely, by the will of the one God. This seems to be the reason why it is repeated in the second verse—*the same was in the beginning with God;* which enforces what the apostle wished we should principally observe, not that he was in the beginning God, but in the beginning with God; that he might show him to be God only by proximity and love, not in essence; which doctrine is consistent with the subsequent explanations of the evange-

list in numberless passages of his gospel.

Another passage is the speech of Thomas, John xx. 28. *my Lord and my God.* He must have an immoderate share of credulity who attempts to elicit a new confession of faith, unknown to the rest of the disciples, from this abrupt exclamation of the apostle, who invokes in his surprize not only Christ his own Lord, but the God of his ancestors, namely, God the Father;—as if he had said, Lord! what do I see—what do I hear—what do I handle with my hands? He whom Thomas is supposed to call God in this passage, had acknowledged respecting himself not long before, v. 17. *I ascend unto my God and your God.* Now the God of God cannot be essentially one with him whose God he is. On whose word therefore can we ground our faith with most security; on that of Christ, whose doctrine is clear, or of Thomas, a new disciple, first incredulous, then suddenly breaking out into an abrupt exclamation in an ecstasy of wonder, if indeed he really called Christ his God? For having reached out his fingers, he called the man whom he touched, as if unconscious of what he was saying, by the name of God. Neither is it credible that he should have so quickly understood the hypostatic union of that person whose resurrection he had just before disbelieved. Accordingly the faith of Peter is commended—*blessed art thou, Simon*—for having only said—*thou art the Son of the living God,* Matt. xvi. 16, 17. The faith of Thomas, although as it is commonly explained, it asserts the divinity of Christ in a much more remarkable manner, is so far from being praised, that it is undervalued, and almost reproved in the next verse—*Thomas, because thou hast seen me, thou hast believed; blessed are they that have not seen, and yet have believed.* And yet, though the slowness of his belief may have deserved blame, the testimony borne by him to Christ as God, which, if the common interpretation be received as true, is clearer than occurs in any other passage, would undoubtedly have met with some commendation; whereas it obtains none whatever. Hence there is nothing to invalidate that interpretation of the passage which has been already suggested, referring the words—*my Lord*—to Christ,—*my God*—to God the Father, who had just testified that Christ was his Son, by raising him up from the dead in so wonderful a manner.

So too Heb. i. 8. *unto the Son*—or *of the Son*—*he saith, Thy throne, O God, is for ever and ever.* But in the next verse it follows, *thou hast loved righteousness, &c. therefore God, even thy God, hath anointed thee with the oil of gladness above thy fellows,* where almost every word indicates the sense in which Christ is here termed God; and the words of Jehovah put into the mouth of the bridal virgins, Psal. xlv. might have been more properly quoted by this writer for any other purpose than to prove that the Son is co-equal with the Father, since they are originally applied to Solomon, to whom, as properly as to Christ, the title of God might have been given on account of his kingly power, conformably to the language of Scripture.

These three passages are the most distinct of all that are brought forward; for the text in Matt. i. 23. *they shall call* (for so the great majority of the Greek manuscripts read it) *his name Immanuel, which being interpreted is, God with us,* does not prove that he whom they were so to call should necessarily be God, but only a messenger from God, according to the song of Zacharias, Luke i. 68, 69. *blessed be the Lord God of Israel; for he hath visited and redeemed his people, and hath raised up an horn of salvation for us,* &c. Nor can anything certain be inferred from Acts xvi. 31, 34. *believe on the Lord Jesus Christ,*—and *he rejoiced, believing in God with all his house.* For it does not follow from hence that Christ is God, since the apostles have never distinctly pointed out Christ as the ultimate object of faith; but these are merely the words of the historian, expressing that briefly which there can be no doubt that the apostles inculcated in a more detailed manner,—faith in God the Father through Christ. Nor is the passage in Acts xx. 28. more decisive,—*the Church of God, which he hath purchased with his own blood;* that is, with his own Son, as it is elsewhere expressed, for God properly speaking has no blood; and no usage is more common than the substitution of the figurative term blood for offspring. But the Syriac version reads, not *the Church of God,* but *the Church of Christ;* and in our own recent translation it is, *the Church of the Lord.* Nor can any

certain dependence be placed on the authority of the Greek manuscripts, five of which read τοῦ Κυρίου καὶ Θεοῦ, according to Beza, who suspects that the words τοῦ Κυρίου have crept in from the margin, though it is more natural to suppose the words καὶ Θεοῦ to have crept in, on account of their being an addition to the former. The same must be said respecting Rom. ix. 5. *who is over all, God blessed for ever. Amen.* For in the first place, Hilary and Cyprian do not read the word *God* in this passage, nor do some of the other Fathers, if we may believe the authority of Erasmus; who has also shown that the difference of punctuation may raise a doubt with regard to the true meaning of the passage, namely, whether the clause in question should not rather be understood of the Father than of the Son. But waiving these objections, and supposing that the words are spoken of the Son; they have nothing to do with his essence, but only intimate that divine honour is communicated to the Son by the Father, and particularly that he is called God; which has been already fully shown by other arguments. But, they rejoin, the same words which were spoken of the Father, Rom. i. 25. *more than the Creator, who is blessed for ever. Amen,* are here repeated of the Son; therefore the Son is equal to the Father. If there be any force in this reasoning, it will rather prove that the Son is greater than the Father; for according to the ninth chapter, he is *over all,* which however, they remind us, ought to be understood in the same sense as John iii. 31, 32. *he that cometh from above, is above all; he that cometh from heaven is above all.* In these words even the divine nature is clearly implied, and yet, *what he hath seen and heard, that he testifieth,* which language affirms that he came not of himself, but was sent from the Father, and was obedient to him. It will be answered, that it is only his mediatorial character which is intended. But he never could have become a mediator, nor could he have been sent from God, or have been obedient to him, unless he had been inferior to God and the Father as to his nature. Therefore also after he shall have laid aside his functions as mediator, whatever may be his greatness, or whatever it may previously have been, he must be subject to God and the Father. Hence he is to be accounted above all, with his reservation, that he is always to be excepted *who did put all things under him,* 1 Cor. xv. 27. and who consequently is above him under whom he has put all things. If lastly he be termed *blessed,* it must be observed that he received blessing as well as divine honour, not only as God, but even as man. Rev. v. 12. *worthy is the Lamb that was slain to receive power and riches and wisdom and strength and honour and glory and blessing;* and hence, v. 13. *blessing, and honour, and glory, and power, be unto him that sitteth upon the throne, and unto the Lamb for ever and ever.*

There is a still greater doubt respecting the reading in 1 Tim. iii. 16. *God was manifest in the flesh.* Here again Erasmus asserts that neither Ambrose nor the Vetus Interpres read the word God in this verse, and that it does not appear in a considerable number of the early copies. However this may be, it will be clear, when the context is duly examined, that the whole passage must be understood of God the Father in conjunction with the Son. For it is not Christ who is *the great mystery of godliness,* but God the Father in Christ, as appears from Col. ii. 2. *the mystery of God and of the Father, and of Christ.* 2 Cor. v. 18, 19. *all things are of God, who hath reconciled us to himself by Jesus Christ . . . to wit, that God was in Christ, reconciling the world unto himself, not imputing their trespasses unto them.* Why therefore should God the Father not be in Christ through the medium of all those offices of reconciliation which the apostle enumerates in this passage of Timothy? *God was manifest in the flesh*—namely in the Son, his own image; in any other way he is invisible: nor did Christ come to manifest himself, but his Father, John xiv. 8, 9. *Justified in the Spirit*—and who should be thereby justified, if not the Father? *Seen of angels*—inasmuch as they desired to look into this mystery, 1 Pet. i. 12. *Preached unto the Gentiles*—that is, the Father in Christ. *Believed on in the world*—and to whom is faith so applicable, as to the Father through Christ? *Received up into glory*—namely, he who was in the Son from the beginning, after reconciliation had been made, returned with the Son into glory, or was received

into that supreme glory which he had obtained in the Son. But there is no need of discussing this text at greater length: those who are determined to defend at all events the received opinion, according to which these several propositions are predicated not of the Father but of the Son alone, when they are in fact applicable both to the one and the other, though on different grounds, may easily establish that the Son is God, a truth which I am far from denying—but they will in vain attempt to prove from this passage that he is the supreme God, and one with the Father.

The next passage is Tit. ii. 13. *the glorious appearing of the great God and our Saviour Jesus Christ.* Here also the glory of God the Father may be intended, with which Christ is to be invested on his second advent, Matt. xvi. 27. as Ambrose understands the passage from the analogy of Scripture. For the whole force of the proof depends upon the definitive article, which may be inserted or omitted before the two nouns in the Greek without affecting the sense; or the article prefixed to one may be common to both. Besides, in other languages, where the article is not used, the words may be understood to apply indifferently either to one or two persons; and nearly the same words are employed without the article in reference to two persons, Philipp. i. 2. and Philem. 3. except that in the latter passages the word *Father* is substituted for *great.* So also 2 Pet. i. 1. *through the righteousness of [our] God and our Saviour Jesus Christ.* Here the repetition of the pronoun ἡμῶν without the article, as it is read by some of the Greek manuscripts, shows that two distinct persons are spoken of. And surely what is proposed to us as an object of belief, especially in a matter involving a primary article of faith, ought not to be an inference forced and extorted from passages relating to an entirely different subject, in which the readings are sometimes various, and the sense doubtful,—nor hunted out by careful research from among articles and particles, —nor elicited by dint of ingenuity, like the answers of an oracle, from sentences of dark or equivocal meaning—but should be susceptible of abundant proof from the clearest sources. For it is in this that the superiority of the gospel to the law consists; this, and this alone, is consistent with its open simplicity; this is that true light and clearness which we had been taught to expect would be its characteristic. Lastly, he who calls God, *great,* does not necessarily call him supreme, or essentially one with the Father; nor on the other hand does he thereby deny that Christ is *the great God,* in the sense in which he has been above proved to be such.

Another passage which is also produced is 1 John iii. 16. *hereby perceive we the love of God, because he laid down his life for us.* Here however the Syriac version reads *illius* instead of *Dei,* and it remains to be seen whether other manuscripts do the same. The pronoun *he,* ἐκεῖνος, seems not to be referred to God, but to the Son of God, as may be concluded from a comparison of the former chapters of this epistle, and the first, second, fifth and eighth verses of the chapter before us, as well as from Rom. v. 8. *God commendeth his love toward us, in that, while we were yet sinners, Christ died for us. The love of God,* therefore, is the love of the Father, whereby he so loved the world, that *he purchased it with his own blood,* Acts xx. 28. and for it *laid down his life,* that is, the life of his only begotten Son, as it may be explained from John iii. 16. and by analogy from many other passages. Nor is it extraordinary that by the phrase, *his life,* should be understood the life of his beloved Son, since we are ourselves in the habit of calling any much-loved friend by the title of life, or part of our life, as a term of endearment in familiar discourse.

But the passage which is considered most important of all, is 1 John v. part of the twentieth verse—for if the whole be taken, it will not prove what it is adduced to support. *We know that the Son of God is come, and hath given us an understanding, that we may know him that is true, and we are in him that is true, (even) in his Son Jesus Christ: this is the true God, and eternal life.* For *we are in him that is true in his Son,*—that is, so far as we are in the Son of him that is true:—*this is the true God;* namely, he who was just before called *him that was true,* the word *God* being omitted in the one clause, and subjoined in the other. For he it is that is *he that is true* (whom that we might know, *we know*

that the Son of God is come, and hath given us an understanding) not he who is called *the Son of him that is true,* though that be the nearest antecedent,—for common sense itself requires that the article *this* should be referred to *him that is true,* (to whom the subject of the context principally relates,) not to *the Son of him that is true.* Examples of a similar construction are not wanting. See Acts iv. 10, 11. and x. 16. 2 Thess. ii. 8, 9. 2 John 7. Compare also John xvii. 3. with which passage the verse in question seems to correspond exactly in sense, the position of the words alone being changed. But it will be objected, that according to some of the texts quoted before, Christ is God; now if the Father be the only true God, Christ is not the true God; but if he be not the true God, he must be a false God. I answer, that the conclusion is too hastily drawn; for it may be that he is not *he that is true,* either because he is only the image of him that is true, or because he uniformly declares himself to be inferior to him that is true. We are not obliged to say of Christ what the Scriptures do not say. The Scriptures call him *God,* but not *him that is the true God;* why are we not at liberty to acquiesce in the same distinction? At all events *he* is not to be called a false God, to whom, as to his beloved Son, he that is the true God has communicated his divine power and glory.

They also adduce Philipp. ii. 6. *who being in the form of God*— But this no more proves him to be God than the phrase which follows—*took upon him the form of a servant*—proves that he was really a servant, as the sacred writers nowhere use the word *form* for actual being. But if it be contended that *the form of God* is here taken in a philosophical sense for the essential form, the consequence cannot be avoided, that when Christ laid aside the form, he laid aside also the substance and the efficiency of God; a doctrine against which they protest, and with justice. *To be in the form of God,* therefore, seems to be synonymous with being in the image of God; which is often predicated of Christ, even as man is also said, though in a much lower sense, to be the image of God, and to be in the image of God, that is, by creation. More will be added respecting this passage hereafter.

The last passage that is quoted is from the epistle of Jude, v. 4. *denying the only Lord God, and our Lord Jesus Christ.* Who will not agree that this is too verbose a mode of description, if all these words are intended to apply to one person? or who would not rather conclude, on a comparison of many other passages which tend to confirm the same opinion, that they were spoken of two persons, namely, the Father the only God, and our Lord Jesus Christ? Those, however, who are accustomed to discover some extraordinary force in the use of the article, contend that both names must refer to the same person, because the article is prefixed in the Greek to the first of them only, which is done to avoid weakening the structure of the sentence. If the force of the articles is so great, I do not see how other languages can dispense with them.

The passages quoted in the New Testament from the Old will have still less weight, if they be produced to prove anything more than what the writer who quoted them intended. Of this class are, Psal. lxviii. 17-19. *the chariots of God are twenty thousand, &c. . . . the Lord is among them, &c. thou hast ascended on high . . . thou hast received gifts for men.* Here (to say nothing of several ellipses, which the interpreters are bold enough to fill up in various ways, as they think proper) mention is made of two persons, *God* and *the Lord,* which is in contradiction to the opinions of those who attempt to elicit a testimony to the supreme divinity of Christ, by comparing this passage with Eph. iv. 5-8. Such a doctrine was never intended by the apostle, who argues very differently in the ninth verse—*now that he ascended, what is it but that he also descended first into the lower parts of the earth?*—from which he only meant to show that the Lord Christ, who had lately died, and was now received into heaven, *gave gifts unto men* which he had received from the Father.

It is singular, however, that those who maintain the Father and the Son to be one in essence, should revert from the gospel to the times of the law, as if they would make a fruitless attempt to illustrate light by darkness. They say that the Son is not only called God, but also Jehovah, as ap-

pears from a comparison of several passages in both testaments. Now Jehovah is the one supreme God; therefore the Son and the Father are one in essence. It will be easy to expose the weakness of such an argument as this, which is derived from the ascription of the name of Jehovah to the Son. For the name of Jehovah is conceded even to the angels, in the same sense as it has been already shown that the name of God is applied to them, namely, when they represent the divine presence and person, and utter the very words of Jehovah. Gen. xvi. 7. *the angel of Jehovah found her,* compared with v. 10. *the angel of Jehovah said unto her, I will multiply thy seed exceedingly,* and v. 13. *she called the name of Jehovah who spake unto her—.* xviii. 13. *and Jehovah said, &c.* whereas it appears that the three men whom Abraham entertained were angels. Gen. xix. 1. *there came two angels.* v. 13. *and Jehovah hath sent us*—compared with v. 18, 21, 24. *Oh, not so, אֲדֹנָי: and he said unto him, See, I have accepted thee . . . then Jehovah rained . . . from Jehovah out of heaven.* Gen. xxi. 17. *the angel of God called to Hagar out of heaven, &c. . . . God hath heard*—compared with v. 18. *I will make him a great nation.* So Exod. iii. 2, 4. *the angel of Jehovah . . . when Jehovah saw that he turned aside to see, God called unto him*—compared with Acts vii. 30. *there appeared to him an angel of the Lord in a flame of fire in a bush.* If that angel had been Christ or the supreme God, it is natural to suppose that Stephen would have declared it openly, especially on such an occasion, where it might have tended to strengthen the faith of the other believers, and strike his judges with alarm. In Exod. xx. when the law was delivered, no mention is made of any one who gave it to Moses, except Jehovah, and yet Acts vii. 38. the same Stephen says, *this is he that was in the church in the wilderness with the angel which spake to him in the mount Sina;* and verse 53. he declares that *the law was received by the disposition of angels.* Gal. iii. 19. *it was ordained by angels.* Heb. ii. 2. *if the word spoken by angels was steadfast, &c.* Therefore what is said in Exodus to have been spoken by Jehovah, was not spoken by himself personally, but by angels in the name of Jehovah. Nor is this extraordinary, for it does not seem to have been suitable that Christ who was the minister of the gospel should also be the minister of the law: *by how much more also he is the mediator of a better covenant,* Heb. viii. 6. But it would indeed have been wonderful if Christ had actually appeared as the mediator of the law, and none of the apostles had ever intimated it. Nay, the contrary seems to be asserted Heb. i. 1. *God who at sundry times and in divers manners spake in times past unto the fathers by the prophets, hath in these last days spoken unto us by his Son.* Again it is said, Num. xxii. 22. *God's anger was kindled . . . and the angel of Jehovah stood in the way for an adversary unto him.* v. 31. *then Jehovah opened the eyes of Balaam, and he saw the angel of Jehovah.* Afterwards the same angel speaks as if he were Jehovah himself, v. 32. *behold I went out to withstand thee, because thy way is perverse before me:* and Balaam says, v. 34. *if it displease thee—;* to which the angel answers—*only the word that I shall speak unto thee, that thou shalt speak.* v. 35. compared with v. 20. and with chap. xxiii. 8, 20. Josh. v. 14. *as captain of the host of Jehovah am I come,* compared with vi. 2. *Jehovah said unto Joshua.* Judg. vi. 11, 12. *an angel of Jehovah . . . the angel of Jehovah*—compared with v. 14. *Jehovah looked upon him, and said—.* Again, v. 20, 21. *the angel of God . . . the angel of Jehovah:* and v. 22. *Gideon perceived that he was an angel of Jehovah*—compared with v. 23. *Jehovah said unto him*—although the angel here, as in other instances, personated the character of Jehovah:—v. 14. *have not I sent thee?* v. 16. *surely I will be with thee, and thou shalt smite the Midianites:* and Gideon himself addresses him as Jehovah, v. 17. *show me a sign that thou talkest with me.* 1 Chron. xxi. 15. *God sent an angel—.* v. 16, 17. *and David saw the angel of Jehovah . . . and fell upon his face, and said unto God—.* v. 18, 19. *then the angel of Jehovah commanded Gad to say unto David . . . and David went up at the saying of Gad, which he spake in the name of Jehovah.*

But it may be urged, that the name of Jehovah is sometimes assigned to two persons in the same sentence. Gen. xix. 24. *Jehovah rained . . . from Jehovah out of heaven.* 1 Sam. iii. 21. *Jehovah revealed himself to Samuel in Shiloh by the word of Jehovah.* Jer. xxxiv. 12. *the word of Jehovah came to Jeremiah from Jehovah, saying—.* Hos. i. 7. *I will save them by Jehovah their God.* Zech. iii. 1-3. *standing before the angel . . . and Jehovah said unto Satan, Jehovah rebuke thee*—and again, *before the angel.* I answer, that in these passages either one of the two persons is an angel, according to that usage of the word which has been already explained; or it is to be considered as a peculiar form of speaking, in which, for the sake of emphasis, the name of Jehovah is repeated, though with reference to the same person; *for Jehovah the God of Israel is one Jehovah.* If in such texts as these both persons are to be understood properly and in their own nature as Jehovah, there is no longer one Jehovah, but two; whence it follows that the repetition of the name can only have been employed for the purpose of giving additional force to the sentence. A similar form of speech occurs Gen. ix. 16. *I will look upon it, that I may remember the everlasting covenant between God and every living creature:* and 1 Cor. i. 7, 8. *waiting for the coming of our Lord Jesus Christ.* 1 Thess. iii. 12, 13. *the Lord make you to increase, &c. to the end he may stablish your hearts . . . before God, even our Father, at the coming of our Lord Jesus Christ.* Here whether it be *God, even our Father,* or *our Lord Jesus,* who is in the former verse called *Lord,* in either case there is the same redundance. If the Jews had understood the passages quoted above, and others of the same kind, as implying that there were two persons, both of whom were Jehovah, and both of whom had an equal right to the appellation, there can be no doubt that, seeing the doctrine so frequently enforced by the prophets, they would have adopted the same belief which now prevails among us, or would at least have laboured under considerable scruples on the subject: whereas I suppose no one in his senses will venture to affirm that the Jewish Church ever so understood the passages in question, or believed that there were two persons, each of whom was Jehovah, and had an equal right to assume the title. It would seem, therefore, that they interpreted them in the manner above mentioned. Thus in allusion to a human being, I Kings viii. I. *then Solomon assembled the elders of Israel . . . unto king Solomon in Jerusalem.* No one is so absurd as to suppose that the name of Solomon is here applied to two persons in the same sentence. It is evident, therefore, both from the declaration of the sacred writer himself, and from the belief of those very persons to whom the angels appeared, that the name of Jehovah was attributed to an angel; and not to an angel only, but also to the whole Church, Jer. xxxiii. 16.

But as Placæus of Saumur thinks it incredible than an angel should bear the name of Jehovah, and that the dignity of the supreme Deity should be degraded by being personated, as it were, on a stage, I will produce a passage in which God himself declares that his name is in an angel. Exod. xxiii. 20, 21. *behold, I send an angel before thee, to keep thee in the way,* &c. *beware of him, and obey his voice; provoke him not, for he will not pardon your transgressions; for my name is in him.* The angel who from that time forward addressed the Israelites, and whose voice they were commanded to hear, was always called Jehovah, though the appellation did not properly belong to him. To this they reply, that he was really Jehovah, for that angel was Christ; I Cor. x. 9. *neither let us tempt Christ,* &c. I answer, that it is of no importance to the present question, whether it were Christ or not; the subject of inquiry now is, whether the children of Israel understood that angel to be really Jehovah? If they did so understand, it follows that they must have conceived either that there were two Jehovahs, or that Jehovah and the angel were one in essence; which no rational person will affirm to have been their belief. But even if such an assertion were advanced, it would be refuted by chap. xxxiii. 2, 3, 5. *I will send an angel before thee . . . for I will not go up in the midst of thee . . . lest I consume thee in the way. And when the people heard these evil tidings, they mourned.* If the people had believed that Jehovah and that angel were one in essence, equal in divinity and glory, why did they mourn, and desire that Jehovah should go up before them, notwithstanding his anger, rather than the

angel? who, if he had indeed been Christ, would have acted as a mediator and peacemaker. If, on the contrary, they did not consider the angel as Jehovah, they must necessarily have understood that he bore the name of Jehovah in the sense in which I suppose him to have borne it, wherein there is nothing either absurd or theatrical. Being at length prevailed upon to go up with them in person, he grants thus much only, v. 14.—*my presence shall go with thee*—which can imply nothing else than a representation of his name and glory in the person of some angel. But whoever this was, whether Christ, or some angel different from the preceding, the very words of Jehovah himself show that he was neither one with Jehovah, nor co-equal, for the Israelites are commanded to hear his voice, not on the authority of his own name, but because the name of Jehovah was in him. If on the other hand it is contended that the angel was Christ, this proves no more than that Christ was an angel, according to their interpretation of Gen. xlviii. 16. *the angel which redeemed me from all evil;* and Isai. lxiii. 9. *the angel of his presence saved them*—that is, he who represented his presence or glory, and bore his character; an angel, as they say, by office, but Jehovah by nature. But to whose satisfaction will they be able to prove this? He is called indeed, Mal. iii. 1. *the messenger of the covenant:* see also Exod. xxiii. 20, 21. compared with I Cor. x. 9. as before. But it does not therefore follow, that whenever an angel is sent from heaven, that angel is to be considered as Christ; nor where Christ is sent, that he is to be considered as one God with the Father. Besides that the obscurity of the law and the prophets ought not to be brought forward to refute the light of the gospel, but on the contrary the light of the gospel ought to be employed to illustrate the obscurity necessarily arising from the figurative language of the prophets. However this may be, Moses says, prophesying of Christ, Deut. xviii. 15. *Jehovah thy God will raise up unto thee a prophet from the midst of thee, of thy brethren, like unto me; unto him ye shall hearken.* It will be answered, that he here predicts the human nature of Christ. I reply that in the following verse he plainly takes away from Christ that divine nature which it is wished to make co-essential with the Father—*according to all that thou desiredst of Jehovah thy God in Horeb . . . saying, Let me not hear again the voice of Jehovah my God,* &c. In hearing Christ therefore, as Moses himself predicts and testifies, they were not to hear the God Jehovah, nor were they to consider Christ as Jehovah.

The style of the prophetical book of Revelations, as respects this subject, must be regarded in the same light. Chap. i. 1, 8, 11. *he sent and signified it by his angel.* Afterwards this angel (who is described nearly in the same words as the angel, Dan. x. 5, &c.) says, *I am Alpha and Omega, the beginning and the ending, saith the Lord, which is, and which was, and which is to come.* v. 13. *like unto the Son of man.* v. 17. *I am the first and the last.* ii. 7, &c. *what the Spirit saith unto the churches.* xxii. 6. *the Lord God sent his angel.* v. 8. *before the feet of the angel which showed me these things.* v. 9. *see thou do it not; for I am thy fellow-servant,* &c. Again, the same angel says, v. 12. *behold I come quickly, and my reward is with me,* &c. and again, v. 13. *I am Alpha and Omega,* &c. and v. 14. *blessed are they that do his commandments;* and v. 16. *I Jesus have sent my angel,* &c. These passages so perplexed Beza, that he was compelled to reconcile the imaginary difficulty by supposing that the order of a few verses in the last chapter had been confused and transposed by some Arian, (which he attributed to the circumstance of the book having been acknowledged as canonical by the Church at a comparatively late period, and therefore less carefully preserved,) whence he thought it necessary to restore them to what he considered their proper order. This supposition would have been unnecessary, had he remarked, what may be uniformly observed throughout the Old Testament, that angels are accustomed to assume the name and person, and the very words of God and Jehovah, as their own; and that occasionally an angel represents the person and the very words of God, without taking the name either of Jehovah or God, but only in the character of an angel, or even of a man, as Junius himself acknowledges, Judges ii. 1, &c. But according to divines the name of Jehovah signifies two things, either the na-

ture of God, or the completion of his word and promises. If it signify the nature, and therefore the person of God, why should not he who is invested with his person and presence, be also invested with the name which represents them? If it signify the completion of his word and promises, why should not he, to whom words suitable to God alone are so frequently attributed, be permitted also to assume the name of Jehovah, whereby the completion of these words and promises is represented? Or if that name be so acceptable to God, that he has always chosen to consider it as sacred and peculiar to himself alone, why has he uniformly disused it in the New Testament, which contains the most important fulfilment of his prophecies; retaining only the name of the Lord, which had always been common to him with angels and men? If, lastly, any name whatever can be so pleasing to God, why has he exhibited himself to us in the gospel without any proper name at all?

They urge, however, that Christ himself is sometimes called Jehovah in his own name and person; as in Isai. viii. 13, 14. *sanctify Jehovah of hosts himself, and let him be your fear, and let him be your dread: and he shall be for a sanctuary; but for a stone of stumbling and for a rock of offence to both the houses of Israel,* &c. compared with 1 Pet. ii. 7. *the same is made the head of the corner, and a stone of stumbling,* &c. I answer, that it appears on a comparison of the thirteenth with the eleventh verse,—*for Jehovah spake thus to me,* &c.—that these are not the words of Christ exhorting the Israelites to sanctify and fear himself, whom they had not yet known, but of the Father threatening, as in other places, that he would be *for a stone of stumbling,* &c. *to both the houses of Israel,* that is, to the Israelites, and especially to those of that age. But supposing the words to refer to Christ, it is not unusual among the prophets for God the Father to declare that he would work himself, what afterwards under the gospel he wrought by means of his Son. Hence Peter says—*the same is made the head of the corner, and a stone of stumbling.* By whom made, except by the Father? And in the third chapter, a quotation of part of the same passage of Isaiah clearly proves that the Father was speaking of himself; v. 15. *but sanctify the Lord God*—under which name no one will assert that Christ is intended. Again, they quote Zech. xi. 13. *Jehovah said unto me, Cast it unto the potter; a goodly price that I was prized at of them.* That this relates to Christ I do not deny; only it must be remembered, that this is not his own name, but that the name of Jehovah is in him, Exod. xxiii. 21. as will presently appear more plainly. At the same time there is no reason why the words should not be understood of the Father speaking in his own name, who would consider the offences which the Jews should commit against his Son, as offences against himself; in the same sense as the Son declares that whatever is done to those who believed in him, is done to himself. Matt. xxv. 35, 40. *I was an hungred, and ye gave me meat, &c. inasmuch as ye have done it unto one of the least of these my brethren, ye have done it unto me.* An instance of the same kind occurs Acts ix. 4, 5. *Saul, Saul, why persecutest thou me?* The same answer must be given respecting Zech. xii. 10. especially on a comparison with Rev. i. 7. *every eye shall see him, and they also that pierced him:* for none have seen Jehovah at any time, much less have they seen him as a man; least of all have they pierced him. Secondly, they pierced him who *poured upon them the spirit of grace,* v. 10. Now it was the Father who poured the spirit of grace through the Son; Acts ii. 33. *having received of the Father the promise of the Holy Ghost, he hath shed forth this.* Therefore it was the Father whom they pierced in the Son. Accordingly, John does not say, *they shall look upon me,* but, *they shall look upon him whom they pierced,* chap. xix. 37. So also in the verse of Zechariah alluded to a change of persons takes place— *they shall look upon me whom they have pierced, and they shall mourn for him as one mourneth for his only son;* as if Jehovah were not properly alluding to himself, but spoke of another, that is, of the Son. The passage in Malachi iii. 1. admits of a similar interpretation: *behold I will send my messenger, and he shall prepare the way before me, and Jehovah, whom ye seek, shall suddenly come to his temple, even the messenger of the covenant, whom ye delight in: behold he shall come, saith Jehovah of hosts.* From which passage Placæus argues thus: He before whose face the Baptist is to be sent as a messenger, is the God of Israel; but the Baptist was not sent before the face of the Father; therefore Christ is that God of Israel. But if the name of Elias could be ascribed to John the Baptist, Matt. xi. 14. inasmuch as he *went before him in the spirit and power of Elias,* Luke i. 17. why may not the Father be said to send him before his own face, inasmuch as he sends him before the face of him who was to come in the name of the Father? for that it was the Father who sent the messenger, is proved by the subsequent words of the same verse, since the phrases *I who sent,* and *the messenger of the covenant who shall come,* and *Jehovah of hosts who saith these things,* can scarcely be understood to apply all to the same person. Nay, even according to Christ's own interpretation, the verse implies that it was the Father who sent the messenger; Matt. xi. 10. *behold, I send my messenger before thy face.* Who was it that sent?—the Son, according to Placæus. Before the face of whom?—of the Son:—therefore the Son addresses himself in this passage, and sends himself before his own face, which is a new and unheard of figure of speech; not to mention that the Baptist himself testifies that he was sent by the Father, John i. 33. *I knew him not, but he that sent me . . the same said unto me,* &c. God the Father therefore sent the messenger before the face of his Son, inasmuch as that messenger preceded the advent of the Son; he sent him before his own face, inasmuch as he was himself in Christ, or, which is the same thing, in the Son, *reconciling the world unto himself,* 2 Cor. v. 19. That the name and presence of God is used to imply his vicarious power and might resident in the Son, is proved by another prophecy concerning John the Baptist, Isai. xl. 3. *the voice of him that crieth in the wilderness, Prepare ye the way of Jehovah; make straight in the desert a highway for our God.* For the Baptist was never heard to cry that Christ was *Jehovah,* or *our God.*

Recurring, however, to the Gospel itself, on which, as on a foundation, our dependence should chiefly be placed, and adducing my proofs more especially from the evangelist John, the leading purpose of whose work was to declare explicitly the nature of the Son's divinity, I proceed to demonstrate the other proposition announced in my original division of the subject—namely, that the Son himself professes to have received from the Father, not only the name of God and of Jehovah, but all that pertains to his own being,—that is to say, his individuality, his existence itself, his attributes, his works, his divine honours; to which doctrine the apostles also, subsequent to Christ, bear their testimony. John iii. 35. *the Father loveth the Son, and hath given all things unto him.* xiii. 3. *Jesus knowing that the Father had given all things unto him, and that he was come from God.* Matt. xi. 27. *all things are delivered unto me of my Father.*

But here perhaps the advocates of the contrary opinion will interpose with the same argument which was advanced before; for they are constantly shifting the form of their reasoning, Vertumnus-like, and using the twofold nature of Christ dedeveloped in his office of mediator, as a ready subterfuge by which to evade any arguments that may be brought against them. What Scripture says of the Son generally, they apply, as suits their purpose, in a partial and restricted sense; at one time to the Son of God, at another to the Son of Man,—now to the Mediator in his divine, now in his human capacity, and now again in his union of both natures. But the Son himself says expressly, *the Father loveth the Son, and hath given all things into his hand,* John iii. 35.—namely, because *he loveth him,* not because he hath begotten him—and he hath given all things to him as *the Son,* not as Mediator only. If the words had been meant to convey the sense attributed to them by my opponents, it would have been more satisfactory and intelligible to have said, *the Father loveth Christ,* or *the Mediator,* or *the Son of Man.* None of these modes of expression are adopted, but it is simply said, *the Father loveth the Son;* that is, whatever is comprehended under the name of the Son. The same question may also be repeated which was asked before, whether from the time that he became the Mediator, his Deity, in their opinion, remained what it had previously been, or not? If it remained the same, why does he ask and receive every

thing from the Father, and not from himself? If all things come from the Father, why is it necessary (as they maintain it to be) for the mediatorial office, that he should be the true and supreme God; since he has received from the Father whatever belongs to him, not only in his mediatorial, but in his filial character? If his Deity be not the same as before, he was never the Supreme God. From hence may be understood John xvi. 15. *all things that the Father hath are mine*—that is, by the Father's gift. And xvii. 9, 10. *them which thou hast given me, for they are thine; and all mine are thine, and thine are mine.*

In the first place, then, it is most evident that he receives his name from the Father. Isai. ix. 6. *his name shall be called Wonderful,* &c. *the everlasting Father;* if indeed this elliptical passage be rightly understood; for, strictly speaking, the Son is not the Father, and cannot properly bear the name, nor is it elsewhere ascribed to him, even if we should allow that in some sense or other it is applied to him in the passage before us. The last clause, however, is generally translated not *the everlasting Father,* but *the Father of the age to come,* —that is, its teacher, the name of father being often attributed to a teacher. Philipp. ii. 9. *wherefore God also hath highly exalted him, and hath given him* (καὶ ἐχαρίσατο) *a name which is above every name.* Heb. i. 4. *being made so much better than the angels, as he hath by inheritance obtained a more excellent name than they.* Eph. i. 20, 21. *when he set him at his own right hand . . . far above all principality,* &c. *and every name that is named, not only in this world, but also in that which is to come.* There is no reason why that name should not be Jehovah, or any other name pertaining to the Deity, if there be any still higher: but the imposition of a name is allowed to be uniformly the privilege of the greater personage, whether father or lord.

We need be under no concern, however, respecting the name, seeing that the Son receives his very being in like manner from the Father. John vii. 29. *I am from him.* The same thing is implied John i. 1. *in the beginning.* For the notion of his eternity is here excluded not only by the decree, as has been stated before, but by the name of Son, and by the phrases—*this day have I begotten thee,* and, *I will be to him a father.* Besides, the word *beginning* can only here mean *before the foundation of the world,* according to John xvii. 5. as is evident from Col. i. 15–17. *the first born of every creature: for by him were all things created that are in heaven, and that are in earth,* &c. *and he is before all things, and by him all things consist.* Here the Son, not in his human or mediatorial character, but in his capacity of creator, is himself called the first born of every creature. So too Heb. ii. 11. *for both he that sanctifieth, and they that are sanctified, are all of one;* and iii. 2. *faithful to him that appointed him.* Him who was begotten from all eternity the Father cannot have begotten, for what was made from all eternity was never in the act of being made; him whom the Father begat from all eternity he still begets; he whom he still begets is not yet begotten, and therefore is not yet a son; for an action which has no beginning can have no completion. Besides, it seems to be altogether impossible that the Son should be either begotten or born from all eternity. If he is the Son, either he must have been originally in the Father, and have proceeded from him, or he must always have been as he is now, separate from the Father, self-existent and independent. If he was originally in the Father, but now exists separately, he has undergone a certain change at some time or other, and is therefore mutable. If he always existed separately from, and independently of, the Father, how is he from the Father, how begotten, how the Son, how separate in subsistence, unless he be also separate in essence? since (laying aside metaphysical trifling) a substantial essence and a subsistence are the same thing. However this may be, it will be universally acknowledged that the Son now at least differs numerically from the Father; but that those who differ numerically must differ also in their proper essences, as the logicians express it, is too clear to be denied by any one possessed of common reason. Hence it follows that the Father and the Son differ in essence.

That this is the true doctrine, reason shows on every view of the subject; that it is contrary to Scripture, which my opponents persist in maintaining, remains to be proved by those who make the assertion.

Nor does the type of Melchisedec, on which so much reliance is placed, involve any difficulty. Heb. vii. 3. *without father, without mother, without descent; having neither beginning of days, nor end of life; but made like unto the Son of God.* For inasmuch as the Son was without any earthly father, he is in one sense said to have had no beginning of days; but it no more appears that he had no beginning of days from all eternity, than that he had no Father, or was not a Son. If however he derived his essence from the Father, let it be shown how that essence can have been supremely divine, that is, identically the same with the essence of the Father; since the divine essence, whose property it is to be always one, cannot possibly generate the same essence by which it is generated, nor can a subsistence or person become an agent or patient under either of the circumstances supposed, unless the entire essence be simultaneously agent or patient in the same manner also. Now as the effect of generation is to produce something which shall exist independently of the generator, it follows that God cannot beget a co-equal Deity, because unity and infinity are two of his essential attributes. Since therefore the Son derives his essence from the Father, he is posterior to the Father not merely in rank (a distinction unauthorized by Scripture, and by which many are deceived) but also in essence; and the filial character itself, on the strength of which they are chiefly wont to build his claim to supreme divinity, affords the best refutation of their opinion. For the supreme God is self-existent; but he who is not self-existent, who did not beget, but was begotten, is not the first cause, but the effect, and therefore is not the supreme God. He who was begotten from all eternity, must have been from all eternity; but if he can have been begotten who was from all eternity, there is no reason why the Father himself should not have been begotten, and have derived his origin also from some paternal essence. Besides, since father and son are relative terms, distinguished from each other both in theory and in fact, and since according to the laws of contraries the father cannot be the son, nor the son the father, if (which is impossible from the nature of relation) they were of one essence, it would follow that the father stood in a filial relation to the son, and the son in a paternal relation to the father,—a position, of the extravagance of which any rational being may judge. For the doctrine which holds that a plurality of hypostasis is consistent with a unity of essence, has already been sufficiently confuted. Lastly, if the Son be of the same essence with the Father, and the same Son after his hypostatical union coalesce in one person with man, I do not see how to evade the inference, that man also is the same person with the Father, an hypothesis which would give birth to not a few paradoxes. But more may perhaps be said on this point, when the incarnation of Christ comes under consideration.

With regard to his existence. John v. 26. *as the Father hath life in himself, so hath he given to the Son to have life in himself.* vi. 57. *as the living Father hath sent me, and I live by the Father, so he that eateth me,* &c. This gift of life is for ever. Heb. ii. 8. *unto the Son he saith, Thy throne, O God, is for ever and ever,*—hence xi. 12. *they shall perish, but thou remainest . . . but thou art the same, and thy years shall not fail.*

With regard to the divine attributes. And first, that of Omnipresence; for if the Father has given all things to the Son, even his very being and life, he has also given him to be wherever he is. In this sense is to be understood John i. 48. *before that Philip called thee . . . I saw thee.* For Nathanael inferred nothing more from this than what he professes in the next verse,—*thou art the Son of God,* and iii. 13. *the Son of man which is in heaven.* These words can never prove that the Son, whether of man or of God, is of the same essence with the Father; but only that the Son of man came down from heaven at the time when he was conceived in the womb of the Virgin, that though he was ministering on earth in the body, his whole spirit and mind, as befitted a great prophet, were in the Father,—or that he, who when made man was endowed with the highest degree of virtue, is, by reason of that virtue, or of a superior nature given to him in the beginning, even now in heaven; or rather *which was in heaven,* the Greek ὤν having both significations. Again, Matt. xviii. 20.

there am I in the midst of them. xxviii. 20. *I am with you alway, even unto the end of the world.* Even these texts, however, do not amount to an assertion of absolute omnipresence, as will be demonstrated in the following chapter.

Omniscience. Matt. xi. 27. *all things are delivered unto me of my Father, and no man knoweth the Son, but the Father, neither knoweth any man the Father, save the Son, and he to whomsoever the Son will reveal him.* John v. 20. *the Father loveth the Son, and showeth him all things.* viii. 26. *I speak those things that I have heard of him.* v. 28. *then shall ye know that . . . as my Father hath taught me, I speak these things.* v. 38. *I speak that which I have seen with my Father.* xv. 15. *all things that I have heard of my Father, I have made known unto you.* ii. 24, 25. *he knew all men . . . for he knew what was in man.* xxi. 17. *thou knowest all things.* xvi. 30. *now are we sure that thou knowest all things . . . by this we believe that thou camest forth from God.* iii. 31–34. *he that cometh from heaven . . . what he hath seen and heard . . . he whom God hath sent speaketh the words of God; for God giveth not the Spirit by measure unto him.* Rev. i. 1. *the revelation of Jesus Christ, which God gave unto him,*—whence it is written of him, ii. 23. *I am he which searcheth the reins and hearts,*—even as it is said of the faithful, that they know all things; 1 John ii. 20. *ye have an unction from the Holy One, and ye know all things.* Even the Son, however, knows not all things absolutely; there being some secret purposes, the knowledge of which the Father has reserved to himself alone. Mark xiii. 32. *of that day and that hour knoweth no man, no not the angels which are in heaven, neither the Son, but the Father;* or as it is in Matt. xxiv. 36. *my Father only.* Acts i. 7. *the times and the seasons, which the Father hath put in his own power.*

Authority. Matt. xxviii. 18. *all power is given unto me in heaven and in earth.* Luke xxii. 29. *I appoint unto you a kingdom, as my Father hath appointed unto me.* John v. 22. *the Father hath committed all judgment unto the Son.* v. 43. *I am come in my Father's name.* vii. 16. *my doctrine is not mine, but his that sent me.* viii. 42.

I proceeded forth and came from God; neither came I of myself, but he sent me. xii. 49, 50. *I have not spoken of myself, but the Father which sent me, he gave me a commandment what I should say, and what I should speak.* xiv. 24. *the word which ye hear is not mine, but the Father's which sent me.* xvii. 2. *as thou hast given him power over all flesh.* Rev. ii. 26, 27. *to him will I give power . . . even as I received of my Father.*

Omnipotence. John v. 19. *the Son can do nothing of himself, but what he seeth the Father do; for what things soever he doeth, these also doeth the Son likewise.* v. 30. *I can of my own self do nothing.* x. 18. *I have power to lay it down, and I have power to take it again: this commandment have I received of my Father.* Hence Philipp. iii. 21. *he is able even to subdue all things unto himself.* Rev. i. 8. *I am . . . the Almighty:* though it may be questioned whether this is not said of God the Father by the Son or the angel representing his authority, as has been explained before: so also Psal. ii. 7.

Works. John v. 20, 21. *for the Father . . . will show him greater works than these . . . for as the Father raiseth up the dead, and quickeneth them; even so the Son quickeneth whom he will.* v. 36. *the works that my Father hath given me to finish, the same works that I do, bear witness of me that the Father hath sent me:*— it is not therefore his divinity of which they bear witness, but his mission from God; and so in other places. viii. 28. *then shall ye know that I am he, and that I do nothing of myself.* x. 32. *many good works have I showed you from my Father.* xi. 22. *I know that even now, whatsoever thou wilt ask of God, God will give it thee.* v. 41. *Father, I thank thee that thou hast heard me.* So likewise in working miracles, even where he does not expressly implore the divine assistance, he nevertheless acknowledges it. Matt. xii. 28. compared with Luke xi. 20. *I cast out devils by the spirit,* or *finger, of God.* John xiv. 10. *the Father that dwelleth in me, he doeth the works.* Yet the nature of these works, although divine, was such, that angels were not precluded from performing similar miracles at the same time and in the same place where Christ himself abode daily:

John v. 4. *an angel went down at a certain season into the pool.* The disciples also performed the same works. John xiv. 12. *he that believeth on me, the works that I do shall he do also; and greater works than these shall he do.*

The following gifts also, great as they are, were received by him from the Father. First, the power of conversion. John vi. 44. *no man can come to me, except the Father which hath sent me draw him.* xvii. 2. *that he should give eternal life to as many as thou hast given him:* and so uniformly; whence arises the expression, Matt. xxiv. 31.—*his elect.* Wherever therefore Christ is said to have chosen any one, as John xiii. 18. and xv. 16, 19. he must be understood to speak only of the election to the apostolical office.

Secondly, creation—but with this peculiarity, that it is always said to have taken place *per eum,* through him, not by him, but by the Father. Isai. li. 16. *I have put my words in thy mouth, and I have covered thee in the shadow of mine hand, that I may plant the heavens, and lay the foundations of the earth, and say unto Zion, Thou art my people.* Whether this be understood of the old or the new creation, the inference is the same. Rom. xi. 36. *for of him,—that is, of the Father,—and through him, and to him are all things; to whom be glory for ever.* 1 Cor. viii. 6. *to us there is but one God, the Father, of whom are all things, and we in him; and one Lord Jesus Christ, by whom are all things.* The remaining passages on the same subject will be cited in the seventh chapter, on the Creation. But the preposition *per* must signify the secondary efficient cause, whenever the *efficiens a quo,* that is, the principal efficient cause, is either expressed or understood. Now it appears from all the texts which have been already quoted, as well as from those which will be produced hereafter, that the Father is the first or chief cause of all things. This is evident even from the single passage, Heb. iii. 1–6. *consider the Apostle . . . who was faithful to him that appointed him . . . who hath builded the house,* that is, the Church. But he *that appointed him,* v. 2. and *builded all things, is God,* that is, the Father, v. 4.

Thirdly, the remission of sins, even in his human nature. John v. 22. *the Father hath committed all judgment unto the Son.* Matt. ix. 6. *but that ye may know that the Son of man hath power on earth to forgive sins, then saith he,* &c. Acts v. 31. *him hath God exalted with his right hand to be a Prince and a Saviour, for to give repentance to Israel, and forgiveness of sins.* Hence Stephen says, vii. 60. *Lord, lay not this sin to their charge.* It clearly appears from these passages that the following expression in Isaiah refers primarily to God the Father, xxxv. 4–6. *behold, your God will come with vengeance, even God with a recompense, he will come and save you: then the eyes of the blind shall be opened,* &c. For it was the Father who appointed Christ *to be a Saviour,* Acts v. 31. and the Father is said *to come unto him,* John xiv. 23. and *do the works,* as has been proved before.

Fourthly, preservation. John xvii. 11, 12. *holy Father, keep through thine own name those whom thou hast given me . . . I kept them in thy name.* v. 15. *I pray . . . that thou shouldest keep them from the evil.* Col. i. 17. *by him all things consist.* Heb. i. 3. *upholding all things by the word of his power,* where it is read in the Greek, not *of his own power,* but *of his,* namely, of the Father's power. But this subject will come under consideration again in the eighth chapter, on Providence, where the chief government of all things will be shown to belong primarily to the Father alone; whence the Father, Jehovah, is often called by the prophets not only the Preserver, but also the Saviour. Those who refer these passages to the Son, on account of the appellation of Saviour, seem to fancy that they hereby gain an important argument for his divinity; as if the same title were not frequently applied to the Father in the New Testament, as will be shown in the thirteenth chapter.

Fifthly, renovation. Acts v. 31. *him hath God exalted with his right hand, to be a Prince and a Saviour, for to give repentance to Israel.* 1 Cor. i. 30. *of him are ye in Christ Jesus, who of God is made unto us wisdom, and righteousness, and sanctification, and redemption.* 2 Cor. iv. 6. *for God, who commanded the light to shine out of darkness, hath shined in our hearts to give the light of the knowledge of the glory of God in the face of Jesus Christ.*

v. 17–21. *behold, all things are become new, and all things are of God, who hath reconciled himself to us by Jesus Christ . . . we pray you in Christ's stead, be ye reconciled unto God: for he hath made him to be sin for us, who knew no sin, that we might be made the righteousness of God in him.* Hence Jer. xxiii. 6. may be explained without difficulty; *this is his name whereby he shall be called, Jehovah our righteousness,* and xxxiii. 16. *this is the name wherewith she shall be called* (that is, the Church, which does not thereby become essentially one with God) *Jehovah our righteousness.*

Sixthly, the power of conferring gifts—namely, that vicarious power which he has received from the Father. John xvii. 18. *as thou hast sent me into the world, even so have I also sent them into the world.* See also xx. 21. Hence Matt. x. 1. *he gave them power against unclean spirits.* Acts iii. 6. *in the name of Jesus Christ of Nazareth, rise up and walk.* ix. 34. *Jesus Christ maketh thee whole.* What was said before of his works, may be repeated here. John xiv. 16. *I will pray the Father, and he shall give you another Comforter.* xvi. 13, &c. *the Spirit shall receive of mine . . . all things that the Father hath are mine, therefore said I that he shall take of mine.* xx. 21, 22. *as my Father hath sent me, even so send I you . . . receive the Holy Ghost.* Hence Eph. iv. 8. *he gave gifts to men;* compared with Psal. lxviii. 18. whence it is taken—*thou hast received gifts for men.*

Seventhly, his mediatorial work itself, or rather his passion. Matt. xxvi. 39. *O my Father, if it be possible, let this cup pass from me.* Luke xxii. 43. *there appeared an angel unto him from heaven, strengthening him.* Heb. v. 7, 8. *who in the days of his flesh, when he had offered up prayers and supplications with strong crying and tears unto him that was able to save him from death, and was heard in that he feared: though he were a Son, yet learned he obedience by the things which he suffered.* For if the Son was able to accomplish by his own independent power the work of his passion, why did he forsake himself; why did he implore the assistance of his Father; why was an angel sent to strengthen him? How then can the Son be considered co-essential and co-equal with the Father? So too he exclaimed upon the cross—*My God, my God, why hast thou forsaken me?* He whom the Son, himself God, addresses as God, must be the Father, —why then did the Son call upon the Father? Because he felt even his divine nature insufficient to support him under the pains of death. Thus also he said, when at the point of death, Luke xxiii. 46. *Father, into thy hands I commend my spirit.* To whom rather than to himself as God would he have commended himself in his human nature, if by his own divine nature alone he had possessed sufficient power to deliver himself from death? It was therefore the Father only who raised him again to life; which is the next particular to be noticed.

Eighthly, his resuscitation from death. 2 Cor. iv. 14. *knowing that he which raised up the Lord Jesus, shall raise up us also by Jesus, and shall present us with you.* 1 Thess. iv. 14. *them also which sleep in Jesus shall God bring with him.* But this point has been sufficiently illustrated by ample quotations in a former part of the chapter.

Ninthly, his future judicial advent. Rom. ii. 16. *in the day when God shall judge the secrets of men by Jesus Christ according to my gospel.* 1 Tim. vi. 14. *until the appearing of our Lord Jesus Christ.*

Tenthly, divine honours. John v. 22, 23. *the Father hath committed all judgement unto the Son; that all men should honor the Son, even as they honour the Father . . . which hath sent him.* Philipp. ii. 9–11. *God hath highly exalted him, and hath given him a name . . . that at the name of Jesus every knee should bow . . . and that every tongue should confess that Jesus Christ is Lord, to the glory of God the Father.* Heb. i. 6. *when he bringeth in the first-begotten into the world, he saith, And let all the angels of God worship him.* Rev. v. 12. *worthy is the Lamb that was slain to receive power,* &c. Hence Acts vii. 59. *calling upon God, and saying, Lord Jesus, receive my spirit.* ix. 14. *all that call upon thy name.* 1 Cor. i. 2. *with all that in every place call upon the name of Jesus Christ our Lord.* 2 Tim. ii. 22. *with them that call upon the Lord out of a pure heart,* that is, as it is explained Col. iii. 17. *whatsoever ye do . . . do it in the name of the Lord Jesus, giving thanks to God and the Father by him.* 2 Tim. ii. 19. *every one*

that nameth the name of Christ. It appears therefore that when we call upon the Son of God, it is only in his capacity of advocate with the Father. So Rev. xxii. 20. *even so, come, Lord Jesus*—namely, to execute judgement, *which the Father hath committed unto him, that all men might honour the Son,* &c. John v. 22, 23.

Eleventhly, baptism in his name. Matt. xxviii. 18, 19. *all power is given unto me in heaven and in earth; go ye therefore and teach all nations, baptizing them in the name of the Father, and of the Son, and of the Holy Ghost.* More will be said on this subject in the next chapter.

Twelfthly, belief in him; if indeed this should be considered as an honour peculiar to divinity; for the Israelites are said, Exod. xiv. 31. *to believe Jehovah and his servant Moses.* Again, *to believe the prophets* occurs 2 Chron. xx. 20. and *faith toward all saints* Philem. 5. and *Moses in whom ye trust,* John v. 45. Whence it would seem, that *to believe in any one* is nothing more than an Hebraism, which the Greeks or Latins express by the phrase *to believe any one;* so that whatever trifling distinction may be made between the two, originates in the schools, and not in Scripture. For in some cases *to believe in any one* implies no faith at all. John ii. 23, 24. *many believed in his name . . . but Jesus did not commit himself unto them.* xii. 42. *many believed on him, but because of the Pharisees they did not confess him.* On the other hand, *to believe any one* often signifies the highest degree of faith. John v. 24. *he that believeth on him* (qui credit ei) *that sent me, hath everlasting life.* Rom. iv. 3. *Abraham believed God, and it was counted unto him for righteousness.* 1 John v. 10. *he that believeth not God.* See also Tit. iii. 8. This honour, however, like the others, is derived from the Father. John iii. 35, 36. *the Father hath given all things into his hand: he that believeth on the Son hath everlasting life.* vi. 40. *this is the will of him that sent me, that every one which seeth the Son, and believeth on him, may have everlasting life.* xii. 44. *Jesus cried and said, He that believeth on me, believeth not on me, but on him that sent me.* Hence xiv. 1. *ye believe in God, believe also in me.* 1 John iii. 23. *this is his commandment, that we should believe on the name of his Son Jesus Christ.* It may therefore be laid down as certain, that *believing in Christ* implies nothing more than that we believe Christ to be the Son of God, sent from the Father for our salvation. John xi. 25–27. *Jesus said unto her, I am the resurrection and the life; he that believeth in me, though he were dead, yet shall he live: and whosoever liveth and believeth in me shall never die. Believest thou this? She saith unto him, Yea, Lord; I believe that thou art the Christ, the Son of God, which should come into the world.*

Thirteenthly, divine glory. John i. 1. *the Word was with God, and the Word was God.* v. 14. *we beheld his glory, the glory as of the only-begotten of the Father,* παρὰ Πατρός. v. 18. *no man hath seen God at any time; the only-begotten Son, which is in the bosom of the Father, he hath declared him.* vi. 46. *not that any man hath seen the Father, save he which is of God,* ὁ ὢν παρὰ τοῦ Θεοῦ. xvii. 5. *glorify thou me with thine own self with the glory which I had with thee before the world was.* No one doubts that the Father restored the Son, on his ascent into heaven, to that original place of glory of which he here speaks. That place will be universally acknowledged to be the right hand of God; the same therefore was his place of glory in the beginning, and from which he had descended. But the right hand of God primarily signifies a glory, not in the highest sense divine, but only next in dignity to God. So v. 24. *that they may behold my glory which thou hast given me; for thou lovedst me before the foundation of the world.* In these, as in other passages, we are taught that the nature of the Son is indeed divine, but distinct from and clearly inferior to the nature of the Father, —for to be with God, πρὸς Θεὸν, and to be from God, παρὰ Θεῷ,—to be God, and to be in the bosom of God the Father,—to be God, and to be from God,—to be the one invisible God, and to be the only-begotten and visible, are things so different that they cannot be predicated of one and the same essence. Besides, the fact that the glory which he had even in his divine nature before the foundation of the world, was not self-derived, but given by the love of the Father, plainly demonstrates him to be inferior to the Father. So Matt. xvi. 27. *in*

the glory of his Father. Acts iii. 13. *the God of Abraham, and of Isaac, and of Jacob, the God of our fathers, hath glorified his Son Jesus.* Col. i. 19. *it pleased the Father that in him should all fulness dwell.* ii. 9. *in him dwelleth all the fulness of the Godhead bodily.* Eph. iii. 19. *that ye might be filled with all the fulness of God.* These passages most clearly evince that Christ has received his fulness from God, in the sense in which we shall receive our fulness from Christ. For the term *bodily,* which is subjoined, either means *substantially,* in opposition to the *vain deceit* mentioned in the preceding verse, or is of no weight in proving that Christ is of the same essence with God. 1 Pet. i. 21. *who gave him glory, that your faith and hope might be in God.* ii. 4. *chosen of God and precious.* 2 Pet. i. 16, 17. *we were eye-witnesses of his majesty; for he received from God the Father honour and glory, when there came such a voice to him—.* 1 Pet. iv. 11. compared with 2 Pet. iii. 18. *that God in all things may be glorified, through Jesus Christ, to whom be praise and dominion for ever and ever: but grow in grace, and in the knowledge of our Lord and Saviour Jesus Christ; to whom be glory both now and for ever.* On a collation of the two passages, it would seem that the phrase *our Lord,* in the latter, must be understood of the Father, as is frequently the case. If however it be applied to the Son, the inference is the same, for it does not alter the doctrine of the former passage. John xii. 41. citing Isai. lxiii. 5. *these things said Esaias, when he saw his glory, and spake of him,*—that is, the glory of the only-begotten, given to the Son by the Father. Nor is any difficulty created by Isai. xlii. 8. *I am Jehovah, that is my name; and my glory will I not give to another, neither my praise to graven images.* For though the Son be *another* than the Father, God's meaning is merely that he will not give his glory to graven images and strange gods,—not that he will not give it to the Son, who is the brightness of his glory, and the express image of his person, and upon whom he had promised that he would put his Spirit, v. 1. For the Father does not alienate his glory from himself in imparting it to the Son, inasmuch as the Son uniformly glorifies the Father. John xiii. 31. *now is the Son of man glorified, and God is glorified in him.* viii. 50. *I seek not mine own glory; there is one that seeketh and judgeth.*

Hence it becomes evident on what principle the attributes of the Father are said to pertain to the Son. John xvi. 15. *all things that the Father hath are mine.* xvii. 6, 7. *thine they were, and thou gavest them me; . . . now they have known that all things whatsoever thou hast given me are of thee.* It is therefore said, v. 10. *all mine are thine, and thine are mine*—namely, in the same sense in which he had called the kingdom his, Luke xxii. 30. for he had said in the preceding verse, *I appoint unto you a kingdom, as my Father hath appointed unto me.*

Lastly, his coming to judgment. 1 Tim. vi. 14. *until the appearing of our Lord Jesus Christ, which in his time he shall show, who is the blessed and only Potentate, the King of kings and Lord of lords; who only hath immortality, dwelling in the light which no man can approach unto; whom no man hath seen, nor can see.*

Christ therefore, having received all these things from the Father, and *being in the form of God, thought it not robbery to be equal with God,* Philipp. ii. 5. namely, because he had obtained them by gift, not by robbery. For if this passage imply his co-equality with the Father, it rather refutes than proves his unity of essence; since equality cannot exist but between two or more essences. Further, the phrases *he did not think it,—he made himself of no reputation,* (literally, *he emptied himself,*) appear inapplicable to the supreme God. For *to think* is nothing else than to entertain an opinion, which cannot be properly said of God. Nor can the infinite God be said to empty himself, any more than to contradict himself; for infinity and emptiness are opposite terms. But since he emptied himself of that form of God in which he had previously existed, if the form of God is to be taken for the essence of the Deity itself, it would prove him to have emptied himself of that essence, which is impossible.

Again, the Son himself acknowledges and declares openly, that the Father is greater than the Son; which was the last proposition I undertook to prove. John x. 29. *my Father is greater than all.* xiv. 28. *my Father is greater than I.* It will be answered, that Christ is speaking of his human nature. But did his disciples understand him as speaking merely of his human nature? Was this the belief in himself which Christ required? Such an opinion will scarcely be maintained. If therefore he said this, not of his human nature only, (for that the Father was greater than he in his human nature could not admit of a doubt) but in the sense in which he himself wished his followers to conceive of him both as God and man, it ought undoubtedly to be understood as if he had said, My Father is greater than I, whatsoever I am, both in my human and divine nature; otherwise the speaker would not have been he in whom they believed, and instead of teaching them, he would only have been imposing upon them with an equivocation. He must therefore have intended to compare the nature with the person, not the nature of God the Father with the nature of the Son in his human form. So v. 31. *as the Father gave me commandment, even so I do.* John v. 18, 19. Being accused by the Jews of having made himself equal with God, he expressly denies it: *the Son can do nothing of himself,* v. 30. *as I hear I judge, and my judgement is just; because I seek not mine own will, but the will of my Father which sent me.* vi. 38. *I came down from heaven, not to do mine own will, but the will of him that sent me.* Now he that was sent was the only begotten Son; therefore the will of the Father is other and greater than the will of the only begotten Son. vii. 28. *Jesus cried in the temple, saying . . . I am not come of myself.* viii. 29. *he that sent me is with me: the Father hath not left me alone; for I do always those things that please him.* If he says this as God, how could he be left by the Father, with whom he was essentially one? if as man, what is meant by his being *left alone,* who was sustained by a God head of equal power? And why *did not the Father leave him alone?*—not because he was essentially one with him, but because he *did always those things that pleased him,* that is, as the less conforms himself to the will of the greater. v. 42. *neither came I of myself,*—not therefore of his own Godhead,—*but he sent me:* he that sent him was therefore another and greater than himself. v. 49. *I honour my Father.* v. 50. *I seek not mine own glory.*

v. 54. *if I honour myself, my glory is nothing;* it is therefore less than the Father's glory. x. 24, 25. *if thou be the Christ, tell us plainly . . . the works that I do in my Father's name, they bear witness of me.* xv. 10. *as I have kept my Father's commandments, and abide in his love.* xvi. 25. *the time cometh when I shall no more speak to you in proverbs, but I shall shew you plainly of the Father.* xx. 17. *I ascend unto my Father and your Father; and to my God, and your God.* Compare also Rev. i. 11. *I am Alpha and Omega,* and v. 17. *I am the first and the last.* See also ii. 8. iii. 12. *him that overcometh will I make a pillar in the temple of my God,* which is repeated three times successively. Here he, who had just before styled himself *the first and the last,* acknowledges that the Father was his God. Matt. xi. 25, 26. *I thank thee, O Father, Lord of heaven and earth; because thou hast hid these things, &c. even so, Father, for so it seemed good in thy sight.*

Thus far we have considered the testimony of the Son respecting the Father; let us now enquire what is the testimony of the Father respecting the Son: for it is written, Matt. xi. 27. *no man knoweth the Son, but the Father; neither knoweth any man the Father, save the Son, and he to whomsoever the Son will reveal him.* 1 John v. 9. *this is the witness of God which he hath testified of his Son.* Here the Father, when about to testify of the Son, is called God absolutely; and his witness is most explicit. Matt. iii. 17. *this is my beloved Son, in whom I am well pleased.* Isai. xlii. 1. compared with Matt. xii. 18. *behold my servant, whom I uphold; mine elect in whom my soul delighteth; I have put my spirit upon him:*—see also Matt. xvii. 5. 2 Pet. i. 17. *for he received from God the Father honour and glory, when there came such a voice to him from the excellent glory, This is my beloved Son, in whom I am well pleased.* Mal. iii. 1. *even the messenger of the covenant, behold he shall come, saith Jehovah of hosts:* and still more clearly Psal. ii. where God the Father is introduced in his own person as explicitly declaring the nature and offices of his Son. Psal. vii. 8, 11, 12. *I will declare the decree; Jehovah hath said unto me, Thou art my Son . . . ask of me and I shall give . . .*

serve Jehovah . . . kiss the Son. Heb. i. 8, 9. *unto the Son he saith, Thy throne, O God, is for ever and ever . . . thou hast loved righteousness, and hated iniquity; therefore God, even thy God, hath anointed thee with the oil of gladness above thy fellows.* To the above may also be added the testimony of the angel Gabriel, Luke i. 32. *he shall be great, and shall be called the Son of the Highest, and the Lord God shall give unto him the throne of his father David.* If then he be the Son of the Most High, he is not himself the Most High.

The apostles every where teach the same doctrine; as the Baptist had done before them. John i. 29. *behold the Lamb of God.* v. 33, 34. *I knew him not, but he that sent me to baptize with water, the same said unto me, &c. and I saw, and bare record that this is the Son of God.* iii. 32. *what he hath seen and heard, that he testifieth,* &c.—not he alone that was *earthly,* nor did he speak only of *earthly things,* but he that is *above all,* and that *cometh from heaven,* v. 31. lest it should be still contended that this and similar texts refer to the human nature of Christ. 2 Cor. iv. 4, 6. *lest the light of the glorious Gospel of Christ, who is the image of God, should shine unto them.* Col. i. 15. *who is the image of the invisible God, the first-born of every creature.* Philipp. ii. 6. *in the form of God.* Heb. i. 2. *whom he hath appointed heir.* v. 3. *the brightness of his glory, and the express image of his person.* The terms here used, being all relative, and applied numerically to two persons, prove, first, that there is no unity of essence, and secondly, that the one is inferior to the other. So v. 4. *being made so much better than the angels, as he hath by inheritance obtained a more excellent name than they.* 1 Cor. iii. 23. *ye are Christ's, and Christ is God's.* Here, if any where, it might have been expected that Christ would have been designated by the title of God; yet it is only said that he is *God's.* The same appears even more clearly in what follows; xi. 3. *I would have you know that . . . the head of Christ is God.* Eph. i. 17. *the God of our Lord Jesus Christ.* 1 Cor. xv. 27. *when he saith, all things are put under him, it is manifest that he is excepted, which did put all things under him: and when all things shall be subdued unto him, then shall the Son also himself be subject unto him that put all things under him, that God may be all in all.* Here the usual subterfuge of the opponents of this doctrine, that of alleging the mediatorial office of Christ can be of no avail; since it is expressly declared, that when the Son shall have completed his functions as mediator, and nothing shall remain to prevent him from resuming his original glory as only begotten Son, he shall nevertheless be subject unto the Father.

Such was the faith of the saints respecting the Son of God; such is the tenor of the celebrated confession of that faith; such is the doctrine which alone is taught in Scripture, which is acceptable to God, and has the promise of eternal salvation. Matt. xvi. 15-19. *whom say ye that I am? and Simon Peter answered and said, Thou art the Christ, the Son of the living God: and Jesus answered and said unto him; Blessed art thou, Simon Bar-jona: for flesh and blood hath not revealed it unto thee, but my Father which is in heaven . . . upon this rock I will build my Church.* Luke ix. 20. *the Christ of God.* John i. 49, 50. *Nathanael answered and saith unto him, Rabbi, thou art the Son of God; thou art the King of Israel.* vi. 69. *we believe and are sure that thou art that Christ, the Son of the living God.* ix. 35-38. *dost thou believe on the Son of God? he answered and said, Who is he, Lord, that I might believe on him? and Jesus saith unto him, Thou hast both seen him, and it is he that talketh with thee: and he said, Lord, I believe; and he worshipped him.* xi. 22, 26, 27. *I know that even now, whatsoever thou wilt ask of God, God will give it thee: whosoever liveth and believeth in me, shall never die: believest thou this? she said unto him, Yea, Lord, I believe that thou art the Christ, the Son of God, which should come into the world.* xvi. 27, 30, 31. *the Father himself loveth you, because ye have loved me, and have believed that I came out from God: now are we sure that thou knowest all things; by this we believe that thou camest forth from God.* xvii. 3, 7, 8, 21. *this is life eternal, that they might know thee the only true God, and Jesus Christ whom thou hast sent: now they have known that all things, whatsoever thou hast given me, are of thee; for I have given unto them the words which thou gavest me; and they have re-*

ceived them, and have known surely that I came out from thee: that the world may believe that thou hast sent me. xx. 31. *these are written, that ye might believe that Jesus is the Christ, the Son of God, and that believing, ye might have life through his name.* Acts viii. 37. *if thou believest, thou mayest. . . . I believe that Jesus Christ is the Son of God.* Rom. x. 9. *if thou shalt believe in thine heart that God hath raised him from the dead, thou shalt be saved.* Col. ii. 2. *that their hearts might be comforted, being knit together in love, and unto all riches of the full assurance of understanding, to the acknowledgement of the mystery of God, and of the Father, and of Christ.* Philipp. iv. 6, 7. *let your requests be made known unto God: and the peace of God, which passeth all understanding, shall keep your hearts and minds through Christ Jesus.* 1 Pet. i. 21. *who by him do believe in God, that raised him up from the dead, and gave him glory; that your faith and hope might be in God.* 1 John iv. 15. *whosoever shall confess that Jesus is the Son of God, God dwelleth in him, and he in God.* v. 1. *whosoever believeth that Jesus is the Christ, is born of God.* v. 5. *who is he that overcometh the world, but he that believeth that Jesus is the Son of God?* Finally, this is the faith proposed to us in the Apostles' Creed, the most ancient and universally received compendium of belief in the possession of the Church.

CHAP. VI.

OF THE
HOLY SPIRIT.

Having concluded what relates to the Father and the Son, the next subject to be discussed is that of the Holy Spirit, inasmuch as this latter is called the Spirit of the Father and the Son. With regard to the nature of the Spirit, in what manner it exists, or whence it arose, Scripture is silent; which is a caution to us not to be too hasty in our conclusions on the subject. For though it be a Spirit, in the same sense in which the Father and Son are properly called Spirits; though we read that Christ by breathing on his disciples gave to them the Holy Ghost, or rather perhaps some symbol or pledge of the Holy Ghost, John xx. 22.—yet in treating of the nature of the Holy Spirit, we are not authorized to infer from such expressions, that the Spirit was breathed from the Father and the Son. The terms *emanation* and *procession,* employed by theologians on the authority of John xv. 26. do not relate to the nature of the Holy Spirit; *the Spirit of truth, ὁ παρὰ τοῦ Πατρὸς ἐκπορεύεται, who proceedeth* or *goeth forth from the Father;* which single expression is too slender a foundation for the full establishment of so great a mystery, especially as these words relate rather to the mission than to the nature of the Spirit; in which sense the Son also is often said ἐξελθεῖν, which in my opinion may be translated either *to go forth* or to *proceed* from the Father, without making any difference in the meaning. Nay, we are even said *to live by every word* (ἐκπορευομένῳ) *that proceedeth,* or *goeth forth from the mouth of God,* Matt. iv. 4. Since therefore the Spirit is neither said to be generated nor created, nor is any other mode of existence specifically attributed to it in Scripture, we must be content to leave undetermined a point on which the sacred writers have preserved so uniform a silence.

The name of Spirit is also frequently applied to God and angels, and to the human mind. When the phrase, the Spirit of God, or the Holy Spirit, occurs in the Old Testament, it is to be variously interpreted; sometimes it signifies God the Father himself, —as Gen. vi. 3. *my Spirit shall not alway strive with man;* sometimes the power and virtue of the Father, and particularly that divine breath or influence by which every thing is created and nourished. In this sense many both of the ancient and modern interpreters understand the passage in Gen. i. 2. *the Spirit of God moved upon the face of the waters.* Here, however, it appears to be used with reference to the Son, through whom the Father is so often said to have created all things. Job xxvi. 13. *by his Spirit he hath garnished the heavens.* xxvii. 3. *the Spirit of God is in my nostrils.* xxxiii. 4. *the Spirit of God hath made me, and the breath of the Almighty hath given me life.* Psal. civ. 30. *thou sendest forth thy Spirit, they are created.* cxxxix. 7. *whither shall I go then from thy Spirit?* Ezek. xxxvii. 14. *I shall put my Spirit in*

you, and ye shall live. See also many other similar passages.

Sometimes it means an angel. Isai. xlviii. 16. *the Lord Jehovah and his Spirit hath sent me.* Ezek. iii. 12. *then the Spirit took me up.* See also v. 14, 24, &c.

Sometimes it means Christ, who according to the common opinion was sent by the Father to lead the Israelites into the land of Canaan. Isai. lxiii. 10, 11. *they rebelled, and vexed his Holy Spirit . . . where is he that put his Holy Spirit within them?*— that is, the angel to whom he transferred his own name, namely, Christ *whom they tempted,* Numb. xxi. 5, &c. compared with 1 Cor. x. 9.

Sometimes it means that impulse or voice of God by which the prophets were inspired. Nehem. ix. 30. *thou testifiedst against them by thy Spirit in thy prophets.*

Sometimes it means that light of truth, whether ordinary or extraordinary, wherewith God enlightens and leads his people. Numb. xiv. 24. *my servant Caleb, because he had another Spirit within him—.* Nehem. ix. 20. *thou gavest also thy good Spirit to instruct them.* Psal. li. 11, 12. *take not thy Holy Spirit from me . . . renew a right Spirit within me.* cxliii. 10. *thy Spirit is good; lead me into the land of uprightness.* Undoubtedly neither David, nor any other Hebrew, under the old covenant, believed in the personality of that *good* and *Holy Spirit,* unless perhaps as an angel.

More particularly, it implies that light which was shed on Christ himself. Isai. xi. 2. *the Spirit of Jehovah shall rest upon him, the Spirit of wisdom and understanding, the Spirit of counsel and might, the Spirit of knowledge and of the fear of Jehovah.* xlii. 1. *I have put my Spirit upon him,* compared with Acts x. 38. *how God anointed Jesus of Nazareth with the Holy Ghost and with power.*

It is also used to signify the spiritual gifts conferred by God on individuals, and the act of gift itself. Gen. xli. 38. *a man in whom the Spirit of God is.* Numb. xi. 17, 25, 26, 29. *I will take of the Spirit which is upon thee, and will put it upon them.* 2 Kings ii. 9. *I pray thee, let a double portion of thy Spirit be upon me.* v. 15. *the Spirit of Elijah doth rest upon Elisha.*

Nothing can be more certain, than that

all these passages, and many others of a similar kind in the Old Testament, were understood of the virtue and power of God the Father, inasmuch as the Holy Spirit was not yet given, nor believed in, even by those who prophesied that it should be poured forth in the latter times.

So likewise under the Gospel, what is called the Holy Spirit, or the Spirit of God, sometimes means the Father himself. Matt. i. 18, 20. *that which is conceived in her is of the Holy Ghost.* Luke i. 35. *the Holy Ghost shall come upon thee, and the power of the Highest shall overshadow thee; therefore also that holy thing which shall be born of thee, shall be called the Son of God.*

Again, it sometimes means the virtue and power of the Father. Matt. xii. 28. compared with Luke xi. 20. *I cast out devils by the Spirit* or *finger of God.* Rom. i. 4. *declared to be the Son of God with power, according to the Spirit of holiness, by the resurrection from the dead.* For thus the Scripture teaches throughout, that Christ was raised by the power of the Father, and thereby declared to be the Son of God. See particularly Acts xiii. 32, 33. quoted in the beginning of the last chapter. But the phrase, *according to the Spirit* (secundum Spiritum) seems to have the same signification as Eph. iv. 24. *which after God* (secundum Deum) *is created in righteousness and true holiness;* and 1 Pet. iv. 6. *that they might live according to God* (secundum Deum) *in the Spirit.* Isai. xlii. 1. compared with Heb. ix. 14. *I have put my Spirit upon him . . . who through the eternal Spirit offered himself without spot to God.* Luke iv. 1. *Jesus, being full of the Holy Ghost,* and v. 18. compared with Isai. lxi. 1. *the Spirit of the Lord Jehovah is upon me, because he hath anointed me to preach the gospel to the poor; he hath sent me,* &c. Acts x. 38. *God anointed Jesus of Nazareth with the Holy Ghost and with power.* i. 2. *after that he through the Holy Ghost had given commandments unto the apostles whom he had chosen.* It is more probable that these phrases are to be understood of the power of the Father, than of the Holy Spirit itself; for how could it be necessary that Christ should be filled with the Holy Spirit, of whom he had himself said, John xvi. 15. *he shall take of mine?* For the

same reason I am inclined to believe that the Spirit descended upon Christ at his baptism, not so much in his own name, as in virtue of a mission from the Father, and as a symbol and minister of the divine power. For what could the Spirit confer on Christ, from whom he was himself to be sent, and to receive all things? Was his purpose to bear witness to Christ? But as yet he was himself not so much as known. Was it meant that the Spirit should be then manifested for the first time to the church? But at the time of his appearance nothing was said of him or of this office; nor did that voice from heaven bear any testimony to the Spirit, but only to the Son. The descent therefore and appearance of the Holy Spirit in the likeness of a dove, seems to have been nothing more than a representation of the ineffable affection of the Father for the Son, communicated by the Holy Spirit under the appropriate image of a dove, and accompanied by a voice from heaven declaratory of that affection.

Thirdly, the Spirit signifies a divine impulse, or light, or voice, or word, transmitted from above either through Christ, who is the Word of God, or by some other channel. Mark xii. 36. *David himself said by the Holy Ghost.* Acts i. 16. *the Holy Ghost by the mouth of David spake before concerning Judas.* xxviii. 25. *well spake the Holy Ghost by Esaias the prophet.* Heb. iii. 7. *wherefore, as the Holy Ghost saith, To-day if ye will hear his voice,* &c. ix. 8. *the Holy Ghost this signifying, that the way into the holiest of all was not yet made manifest.* x. 15. *whereof the Holy Ghost also is a witness to us.* 2 Pet. i. 21. *holy men of God spake as they were moved by the Holy Ghost.* Luke ii. 25, 26. *the Holy Ghost was upon him: and it was revealed unto him by the Holy Ghost—.* It appears to me, that these and similar passages cannot be considered as referring to the express person of the Spirit, both because the Spirit was not yet given, and because Christ alone, as has been said before, is, properly speaking, and in a primary sense, the Word of God, and the Prophet of the Church; though *God at sundry times and in divers manners spake in time past unto the fathers by the prophets,* Heb. i. 1. whence it appears that he did not speak by the Holy Spirit alone, unless the term be understood in the signification which I have proposed, and in a much wider sense than was subsequently attributed to it. Hence, I Pet. i. 11. *searching what or what manner of time the Spirit of Christ which was in them*—that is, in the prophets—*did signify,* must either be understood of Christ himself,—as iii. 18, 19. *quickened by the Spirit, by which also he went and preached unto the spirits in prison,*—or it must be understood of the Spirit which supplied the place of Christ the Word and the Chief Prophet.

Further, the Spirit signifies the person itself of the Holy Spirit, or its symbol. Matt. iii. 16. Mark i. 10. *he saw the Spirit of God descending like a dove, and lighting upon him.* Luke iii. 22. *in a bodily shape like a dove.* John i. 32, 33. *like a dove.* Nor let it be objected, that a dove is not a person; for an intelligent substance, under any form whatever, is a person; as for instance, the four living creatures seen in Ezekiel's vision, ch. i. John xiv. 16, 17. *another Comforter.* See also v. 26. xv. 26. xvi. 7, 13. xx. 22. *he breathed on them, and saith unto them, Receive ye the Holy Ghost,*—which was a kind of symbol, and sure pledge of that promise, the fulfilment of which is recorded Acts ii. 2-4, 33. *having received of the Father the promise of the Holy Ghost, he hath shed forth this.* Matt. xxviii. 19. *in the name of the Father, and of the Son, and of the Holy Ghost.* Acts xv. 28. *it seemed good to the Holy Ghost.* Rom. viii. 16. *the Spirit itself beareth witness with our spirit.* v. 26. *it helpeth our infirmities . . . it maketh intercession for us.* Eph. i. 13, 14. τῷ πνεύματι τῷ ἁγίῳ, ὅς ἐστιν ἀρραβών· *ye were sealed with that Holy Spirit of promise which* (*who,* Whitby, Macknight) *is the earnest of our inheritance.* iv. 30. *grieve not the Holy Spirit of God.*

Lastly, it signifies the donation of the Spirit itself, and of its attendant gifts. John vii. 39. *but this spake he of the Spirit, which they that believe on him should receive; for the Holy Ghost was not yet given.* Matt. iii. 11. *he shall baptize you with the Holy Ghost and with fire.* See also Acts i. 5. and xi. 16. 1 Thess. v. 19. *quench not the Spirit.*

Who this Holy Spirit is, and whence he comes, and what are his offices, no one has taught us more explicitly than the Son of God himself, Matt. x. 20. *it is not ye that speak, but the Spirit of your Father that speaketh in you.* Luke xi. 13. *how much more shall your heavenly Father give the Holy Spirit to them that ask him.* xxiv. 49. *behold, I send the promise of my Father upon you; but tarry ye in the city of Jerusalem, until ye be endued with power from on high.* John xiv. 16, 17. *I will pray the Father, and he shall give you another Comforter, that he may abide with you for ever, even the Spirit of truth.* v. 26. *the Comforter, which is the Holy Ghost, whom the Father will send in my name.* xv. 26. *the Comforter, whom I will send unto you from the Father, . . . which proceedeth from the Father, he shall testify of me.* xvi. 7. *I will send him unto you.* v. 8. *when he is come, he will reprove the world—.* v. 13. *he shall not speak of himself; but whatsoever he shall hear, that shall he speak.* v. 14. *he shall glorify me, for he shall receive of mine.* v. 15. *all things that the Father hath are mine; therefore said I that he shall take of mine.* xx. 22. *when he had said this, he breathed on them, and saith unto them, Receive ye the Holy Ghost.* Acts ii. 2-4, 33. *having received of the Father the promise of the Holy Ghost, he hath shed forth this—.* v. 32. *we are his witnesses of these things, and so is also the Holy Ghost whom God hath given to them that obey him.* Rom. xv. 13. *now the God of hope fill you with all joy and peace in believing, that ye may abound in hope through the power of the Holy Ghost.* 1 Cor. xii. 3. *no man can say that Jesus is the Lord, but by the Holy Ghost.* Heb. ii. 4. *God also bearing them witness both with signs and wonders, and with divers miracles, and gifts of the Holy Ghost, according to his own will.* Hence he is called the Spirit of the Father, the Spirit of God, and even the Spirit of Christ. Matt. x. 20. *it is the Spirit of your Father that speaketh in you.* Rom. viii. 9. *but ye are not in the flesh, but in the Spirit, if so be that the Spirit of God dwell in you: now if any man have not the Spirit of Christ, he is none of his.* v. 15, 16. *ye have received the spirit of adoption, whereby we cry, Abba, Father; the Spirit itself beareth witness with our spirit, that we are the sons of God.* 1 Cor. vi. 11. *by the Spirit of our God.* 2 Cor. i. 21, 22. *he which stablisheth us with you in Christ, and hath anointed us, is God; who hath also sealed us, and given the earnest of the Spirit in our hearts.* Gal. iv. 6. *God hath sent forth the Spirit of his Son into your hearts, crying, Abba, Father.* Eph. i. 13, 14. *that holy Spirit of promise, which is the earnest of our inheritance.* iv. 30. *grieve not the holy Spirit of God, whereby ye are sealed.* ii. 18. *through him we both have access by one Spirit unto the Father.* 1 Pet. i. 12. *the Holy Ghost sent down from heaven.* From all which results the command in Matthew xxviii. 19. *baptizing them in the name of the Father, and of the Son, and of the Holy Ghost.* 1 John v. 7. *there are three that bear witness in heaven, the Father, the Word, and the Holy Ghost; and these three are one.* The latter passage has been considered in the preceding chapter; but both will undergo a further examination in a subsequent part of the present.

If it be the divine will that a doctrine which is to be understood and believed as one of the primary articles of our faith, should be delivered without obscurity or confusion, and explained, as is fitting, in clear and precise terms,—if it be certain that particular care ought to be taken in every thing connected with religion, lest the objection urged by Christ against the Samaritans should be applicable to us—*ye worship ye know not what,* John iv. 22.—if our Lord's saying should be held sacred wherever points of faith are in question—*we know what we worship*—the particulars which have been stated seem to contain all that we are capable of knowing, or are required to know respecting the Holy Spirit, inasmuch as revelation has declared nothing else expressly on the subject. The nature of these particulars is such, that although the Holy Spirit be nowhere said to have taken upon himself any mediatorial functions, as is said of Christ, nor to be engaged by the obligations of a filial relation to pay obedience to the Father, yet he must evidently be considered as inferior to both Father and Son, inasmuch as he is represented and declared to be subservient and obedient in all things; to have been promised, and sent, and given; to speak nothing of himself; and even to have been given as an earnest. There is no room here for any sophistical distinction founded on a twofold nature; all these expressions refer to the Holy Spirit, who is maintained to be

the supreme God; whence it follows, that wherever similar phrases are applied to the Son of God, in which he is distinctly declared to be inferior to the Father, they ought to be understood in reference to his divine as well as to his human character. For what those, who believe in the Holy Spirit's co-equality with the Father, deem to be not unworthy of him, cannot be considered unworthy of the Son, however exalted may be the dignity of his Godhead. Wherefore it remains now to be seen on what grounds, and by what arguments, we are constrained to believe that the Holy Spirit is God, if Scripture nowhere expressly teach the doctrine of his divinity, not even in the passages where his office is explained at large, nor in those where the unity of God is explicitly asserted, as in John xvii. 3. 1 Cor. viii. 4, &c. nor where God is either described, or introduced as sitting upon his throne,—if, further, the Spirit be frequently named the Spirit of God, and the Holy Spirit of God, Eph. iv. 30. so that the Spirit of God being actually and numerically distinct from God himself, cannot possibly be essentially one God with him whose Spirit he is, (except on certain strange and absurd hypotheses, which have no foundation in Holy Scripture, but were devised by human ingenuity for the sole purpose of supporting this particular doctrine)—if, wherever the Father and the Holy Spirit are mentioned together, the Father alone be called God, and the Father alone, omitting all notice of the Spirit, be acknowledged by Christ himself to be the one true God, as has been proved in the former chapter by abundant testimony;—if he be God who *stablisheth us in Christ,* who *hath anointed us,* who *hath sealed us,* and *given us the earnest of the Spirit,* 2 Cor. i. 22. if that God be one God, and that one God the Father;—if, finally, *God hath sent forth the Spirit of his Son into our hearts, crying, Abba, Father,* Gal. iv. 6. whence it follows that he who sent both the Spirit of his Son and the Son himself, he on whom we are taught to call, and on whom the Spirit himself calls, is the one God and the only Father. It seems exceedingly unreasonable, not to say dangerous, that in a matter of so much difficulty, believers should be required to receive a doctrine, represented by its advocates as of primary importance and of undoubted certainty, on anything less than the clearest testimony of Scripture; and that a point which is confessedly contrary to human reason, should nevertheless be considered as susceptible of proof from human reason only, or rather from doubtful and obscure disputations.

First, then, it is usual to defend the divinity of the Holy Spirit on the ground, that the name of God seems to be attributed to the Spirit: Acts v. 3, 4. *why hath Satan filled thine heart to lie to the Holy Ghost? . . . thou hast not lied unto men, but unto God.* But if attention be paid to what has been stated before respecting the Holy Ghost on the authority of the Son, this passage will appear too weak for the support of so great a doctrinal mystery. For since the Spirit is expressly said to be sent by the Father, and in the name of the Son, he who lies to the Spirit must lie to God, in the same sense as he who receives an apostle, receives God who sent him, Matt. x. 40. John xiii. 20. St. Paul himself removes all ground of controversy from this passage, and explains it most appositely by implication, 1 Thess. iv. 8. where his intention is evidently to express the same truth more at large: *he therefore that despiseth, despiseth not man, but God, who hath also given unto us his Holy Spirit.* Besides, it may be doubted whether the Holy Spirit in this passage does not signify God the Father; for Peter afterwards says, v. 9. *how is it that ye have agreed together to tempt the Spirit of the Lord?* that is, God the Father himself, and his divine intelligence, which no one can elude or deceive. And in v. 32. the Holy Spirit is not called God, but a witness of Christ with the apostles, *whom God hath given to them that obey him.* So also Acts ii. 38. *ye shall receive the gift of the Holy Ghost,* given, that is, by God. But how can the gift of God be himself God, much more the supreme God?

The second passage is Acts xxviii. 25. compared with Isai. vi. 8, 9. *I heard the voice of the Lord, saying—&c. . . . well spake the Holy Ghost by Esaias the prophet,* &c. See also Jer. xxxi. 31. compared with Heb. x. 15. But it has been shewn above, that the names Lord and Jehovah are throughout the Old Testament attributed to whatever angel God may entrust with

the execution of his commands; and in the New Testament the Son himself openly testifies of the Holy Spirit, John xvi. 13. that *he shall not speak of himself, but whatsoever he shall hear, that shall he speak. It* cannot therefore be inferred from this passage, any more than from the preceding, that the Holy Ghost is God.

The third place is 1 Cor. iii. 16. compared with vi. 19. and 2 Cor. vi. 16. *the temple of God . . . the temple of the Holy Ghost.* But neither is it here said, nor does it in any way follow from hence, that the Holy Spirit is God; for it is not because the Spirit alone, but because the Father also and the Son *make their abode with us,* that we are called *the temple of God.* Therefore in 1 Cor. vi. 19. where we are called *the temple of the Holy Ghost,* Paul has added, *which ye have of God,* as if with the purpose of guarding against any error which might arise respecting the Holy Spirit in consequence of his expression. How then can it be deduced from this passage, that he whom we have of God, is God himself? In what sense we are called *the temple of the Holy Ghost,* the same apostle has explained more fully Eph. ii. 22. *in whom ye also are builded together for an habitation of God through the Spirit.*

The next evidence which is produced for this purpose, is the ascription of the divine attributes to the Spirit. And first, Omniscience; as if the Spirit were altogether of the same essence with God. 1 Cor. ii. 10, 11. *the Spirit searcheth all things, yea the deep things of God: for what man knoweth the things of a man, save the spirit of a man which is in him? even so the things of God knoweth no man, but the Spirit of God.* With regard to the tenth verse, I reply, that in the opinion of divines, the question here is not respecting the divine omniscience, but only respecting those deep things *which God hath revealed unto us by his Spirit*—the words immediately preceding. Besides, the phrase *all things* must be restricted to mean whatever it is expedient for us to know: not to mention that it would be absurd to speak of God searching God, with whom he was one in essence. Next, with regard to the eleventh verse, the essence of the Spirit is not the subject in question; for the consequences would be full of absurdity, if it were to be understood that the Spirit of God was with regard to God, as the spirit of a man is with regard to man. Allusion therefore is made only to the intimate relationship and communion of the Spirit with God, from whom he originally proceeded. That no doubt may remain as to the truth of this interpretation, the following verse is of the same import: *we have received . . . the Spirit which is of God.* That which is *of* God, cannot be actually God, who is unity. The Son himself disallows the omniscience of the Spirit still more plainly. Matt. xi. 27. *no man knoweth the Son, but the Father, neither knoweth any man the Father, save the Son, and he to whomsoever the Son will reveal him.* What then becomes of the Holy Spirit? for according to this passage, no third person whatever knoweth either the Father or the Son, except through their medium. Mark xiii. 32. *of that day and that hour knoweth no man, no, not the angels which are in heaven, neither the Son, but the Father.* If not even the Son himself, who is also in heaven, then certainly not the Spirit of the Son, who receiveth all things from the Son himself; John xvi. 14.

Secondly, Omnipresence, on the ground that *the Spirit of God dwelleth in us.* But even if it filled with its presence the whole circle of the earth, with all the heavens, that is, the entire fabrick of this world, it would not follow that the Spirit is omnipresent. For why should not the Spirit easily fill with the influence of its power, what the Sun fills with its light; though it does not necessarily follow that we are to believe it infinite? If that lying spirit, 1 Kings xxii. 22. were able to fill four hundred prophets at once, how many thousands ought we not to think the Holy Spirit capable of pervading, even without the attributes of infinity or immensity?

Thirdly, divine works. Acts ii. 4. *the Spirit gave them utterance.* xiii. 2. *the Holy Ghost said, Separate me Barnabas and Saul for the work.* Acts xx. 28. *the Holy Ghost hath made you overseers to feed the Church of God.* 2 Pet. i. 21. *holy men of God spake as they were moved by the Holy Ghost.* A single remark will suffice for the solution of all these passages, if it be only remembered what was the language of Christ respecting the Holy Spirit, the Comforter; namely, that he was sent by the Son

from the Father, that he spake not of himself, nor in his own name, and consequently that he did not act in his own name; therefore that he did not even move others to speak of his own power, but that what he gave he had himself received. Again, 1 Cor. xii. 11. the Spirit is said *to divide to every man severally as he will.* In answer to this it may be observed, that the Spirit himself is also said to be divided to each according to the will of God the Father, Heb. ii. 4. and that even *the wind bloweth where it listeth,* John iii. 8. With regard to the annunciation made to Joseph and Mary, that the Holy Spirit was the author of the miraculous conception, Matt. i. 18, 20. Luke i. 35. it is not to be understood with reference to his own person alone. For it is certain that, in the Old Testament, under the name of the Spirit of God, or of the Holy Spirit, either God the Father himself, or his divine power was signified; nor had Joseph and Mary at that time heard anything of any other Holy Spirit, inasmuch as the personality and divinity of the Holy Spirit are not acknowledged by the Jews even to the present day. Accordingly, in both the passages quoted, πνεῦμα ἅγιον is without the customary article; or if this be not considered as sufficiently decisive, the angel speaks in a more circumstantial manner in St. Luke: *the Holy Ghost shall come upon thee, and the power of the Highest shall overshadow thee; therefore that holy thing which shall be born of thee shall be called the Son of God,*—that is, of the Father: unless we suppose that there are two Fathers,—one Father of the Son of God, another Father of the Son of man.

Fourthly, divine honours. Matt. xxviii. 19. *baptizing them in the name of the Father, and of the Son, and of the Holy Ghost.* Here mention is undoubtedly made of three persons; but there is not a word that determines the divinity, or unity, or equality of these three. For we read, Matt. x. 41. John xiii. 20. of receiving a prophet in the name of a prophet, and a righteous man in the name of a righteous man, and of giving a cup of cold water in the name of a disciple; which evidently means nothing more, than because he is a prophet, or a righteous man, or a disciple. Thus too the Israelites *were baptized unto Moses,* 1 Cor. x. 2. that is, unto the law or doctrine of Moses; and *unto the baptism of John* occurs in the same sense, Acts xix. 3. and *in the name of Jesus Christ for the remission of sins*, Acts ii. 38. and *into Jesus Christ* and *into his death*, Rom. vi. 3. and *into one body*, 1 Cor. xii. 13. To be baptized therefore *in their name*, is to be admitted to those benefits and gifts which we have received through the Son and the Holy Spirit. Hence Paul rejoiced that no one could say he had been baptized in his name, 1 Cor. i. 13–15. It was not the imputation of making himself God that he feared, but that of affecting greater authority than was suitable to his character. From all which it is clear that when we are baptized in the name of the Father, Son, and Holy Ghost, this is not done to impress upon our minds the inherent or relative natures of these three persons, but the benefits conferred by them in baptism on those who believe,—namely, that our eternal salvation is owing to the Father, our redemption to the Son, and our sanctification to the Spirit. The power of the Father is inherent in himself, that of the Son and the Spirit is received from the Father; for it has been already proved on the authority of the Son, that the Son does every thing in the name of the Father, and the Spirit every thing in the name of the Father and the Son; and a confirmation of the same truth may be derived from the words immediately preceding the verse under discussion; v. 18. *all power is given unto me . . . go ye therefore . . . baptizing in the name*, &c. and still more plainly by 1 Cor. vi. 11. *but ye are washed, but ye are sanctified, but ye are justified in the name of the Lord Jesus, and by the Spirit of our God.* Here the same three are mentioned as in baptism, *the Son, the Spirit,* and *our God;* it follows therefore that the Father alone is our God, of whom are both the Son and the Spirit.

But invocation is made to the Spirit. 2 Cor. xiii. 14. *the grace of the Lord Jesus Christ, and the love of God, and the communion of the Holy Ghost, be with you all.* This, however, is not so much an invocation as a benediction, in which the Spirit is not addressed as a person, but sought as a gift from him who alone is there called God, namely, the Father, from whom Christ himself directs us to seek the communication of the Spirit, Luke xi. 13. If the

Spirit were ever to be invoked personally, it would be then especially, when we pray for him; yet we are commanded not to ask him of himself, but only of the Father. Why do we not call upon the Spirit himself, if he be God, to give himself to us? He who is sought from the Father, and given by him, not by himself, can neither be God, nor an object of invocation. The same form of benediction occurs Gen. xlviii. 15, 16. *the God before whom my fathers did walk . . . the angel which redeemed me from all evil, bless the lads:* and Rev. i. 4. *grace be unto you and peace from him which is . . . and from the seven spirits.* It is clear that in this passage the seven spirits, of whom more will be said hereafter, are not meant to be invoked. Besides that in this benediction the order or dignity of the things signified should be considered, rather than that of the persons; for it is by the Son that we come to the Father, from whom finally the Holy Spirit is sent. So 1 Cor. xii. 4–6. *there are diversities of gifts, but the same Spirit: and there are differences of administrations, but the same Lord: and there are diversities of operations, but it is the same God which worketh all in all.* Here the three are again mentioned in an inverse order; but it is one God which worketh all in all, even in the Son and the Spirit, as we are taught throughout the whole of Scripture.

Hence it appears that what is said Matt. xii. 31, 32. has no reference to the personality of the Holy Spirit. For if to sin against the Holy Spirit were worse than to sin against the Father and Son, and if that alone were an unpardonable sin, the Spirit truly would be greater than the Father and the Son. The words must therefore apply to that illumination, which, as it is highest in degree, so it is last in order of time, whereby the Father enlightens us through the Spirit, and which if any one resist, no method of salvation remains open to him. I am inclined to believe, however, that it is the Father himself who is here called the Holy Spirit, by whose *Spirit,* v. 28. or *finger,* Luke xi. 20. Christ professed to cast out devils; when therefore the Pharisees accused him falsely of acting in concert with Beelzebub, they are declared to sin unpardonably, because they said of him who had the Spirit of his Father, *he hath an unclean spirit,* Mark iii. 30. Besides, it was to the Pharisees that he spoke thus, who acknowledged no other Spirit than the Father himself. If this be the true interpretation of the passage, which will not be doubted by any one who examines the whole context from v. 24 to v. 32. that dreaded sin against the Holy Spirit will be in reality a sin against the Father, who is the Spirit of holiness; of which he would be guilty, who should affirm that the Spirit of the Father which was working in Christ was the prince of the devils, or an unclean spirit;—as Mark clearly shows in the passage quoted above.

But the Spirit bestows grace and blessing upon the churches in conjunction with the Father and the Son; Rev. i. 4, 5. *grace be unto you and peace from him which is . . . and from the seven spirits which are before his throne, and from Jesus Christ.* It is clear, however, that the Holy Spirit is not here meant to be implied; the number of the spirits is inconsistent with such a supposition, as well as the place which they are said to occupy, standing like angels before the throne. See also iv. 5. and v. 6. where the same spirits are called *seven lamps of fire burning before the throne,* and the *seven horns* and *seven eyes* of the Lamb. Those who reduce these spirits to one Holy Spirit, and consider them as synonymous with his sevenfold grace, (an opinion which is deservedly refuted by Beza) ought to beware, lest, by attributing to mere virtues the properties of persons, they furnish arguments to those commentators who interpret the Holy Spirit as nothing more than the virtue and power of the Father. This may suffice to convince us, that in this kind of threefold enumerations the sacred writers have no view whatever to the doctrine of three divine persons, or to the equality or order of those persons;—not even in that verse which has been mentioned above, and on which commentators in general lay so much stress, 1 John v. 7. *there are three that bear record in heaven, the Father, the Word, and the Holy Ghost, and these three are one,* where there is in reality nothing which implies either divinity or unity of essence. As to divinity, God is not the only one who is said to bear record in heaven; 1 Tim. v. 21. *1 charge thee before God, and the Lord Jesus Christ, and the elect angels,*—where

it might have been expected that the Holy Spirit would have been named in the third place, if such ternary forms of expression really contained the meaning which is commonly ascribed to them. What kind of unity is intended, is sufficiently plain from the next verse, in which *the spirit, the water, and the blood* are mentioned, which *are to bear record to one,* or *to that one thing.* Beza himself, who is generally a staunch defender of the Trinity, understands the phrase *unum sunt* to mean, *agree in one.* What it is that they testify, appears in the fifth and sixth verses— namely, that *he that overcometh the world is he that believeth that Jesus is the Son of God, even Jesus Christ,* that is, *the anointed;* therefore he is not one with, nor equal to, him that anointed him. Thus the very record that they bear is inconsistent with the essential unity of the witnesses, which is attempted to be deduced from the passage. For the Word is both the Son and Christ, that is, as has been said, *the anointed;* and as he is the image, as it were, by which we see God, so is he the word by which we hear him. But if such be his nature, he cannot be essentially one with God, whom no one can see or hear. The same has been already proved, by other arguments, with regard to the Spirit; it follows, therefore, that these three are not one in essence. I say nothing of the suspicion of spuriousness attached to the passage, which is a matter of criticism rather than of doctrine. Further, I would ask whether there is one Spirit that bears record in heaven, and another which bears record in earth, or whether both are the same Spirit. If the same, it is extraordinary that we nowhere else read of his bearing witness in heaven, although his witness has been always most conspicuously manifested in earth, that is, in our hearts. Christ certainly brings forward himself and his Father as the only witnesses of himself, John viii. 16, 19. Why then, in addition to two other perfectly competent witnesses, should the Spirit twice bear witness to the same thing? On the other hand, if it be another Spirit, we have here a new and unheard-of doctrine. There are besides other circumstances, which in the opinion of many render the passage suspicious; and yet it is on the authority of this text, almost exclusively, that the whole doctrine of the Trinity has been hastily adopted.

Lest however we should be altogether ignorant who or what the Holy Spirit is, although Scripture nowhere teaches us in express terms, it may be collected from the passages quoted above, that the Holy Spirit, inasmuch as he is a minister of God, and therefore a creature, was created or produced of the substance of God, not by a natural necessity, but by the free will of the agent, probably before the foundations of the world were laid, but later than the Son, and far inferior to him. It will be objected, that thus the Holy Spirit is not sufficiently distinguished from the Son. I reply, that the Scriptural expressions themselves, *to come forth, to go out from the Father, to proceed from the Father,* which mean the same in the Greek, do not distinguish the Son from the Holy Spirit, inasmuch as these terms are used indiscriminately with reference to both persons, and signify their mission, not their nature. There is however sufficient reason for placing the name as well as the nature of the Son above that of the Holy Spirit in the discussion of topics relative to the Deity; inasmuch as the brightness of the glory of God, and the express image of his person, are said to have been impressed on the one, and not on the other.

CHAP. VII.

OF THE
CREATION.

The second species of external efficiency is commonly called CREATION. As to the actions of God before the foundation of the world, it would be the height of folly to inquire into them, and almost equally so to attempt a solution of the question. With regard to the account which is generally given from 1 Cor. ii. 7. *he ordained his wisdom in a mystery, even the hidden mystery which God ordained before the world,* —or, as it is explained, that he was occupied with election and reprobation, and with decreeing other things relative to these subjects,—it is not imaginable that God should have been wholly occupied from eternity in decreeing that which was to be created in a period of six days, and which, after having been governed in diverse manners for a few thousand years, was finally to be received into an immutable state with himself, or to be rejected from his presence for all eternity.

That the world was created, is an article of faith: Heb. xi. 3. *through faith we understand that the worlds were framed by the word of God.*

CREATION is that act whereby GOD THE FATHER PRODUCED EVERY THING THAT EXISTS BY HIS WORD AND SPIRIT, that is, BY HIS WILL, FOR THE MANIFESTATION OF THE GLORY OF HIS POWER AND GOODNESS.

WHEREBY GOD THE FATHER. Job ix. 8. *which alone spreadeth out the heavens.* Isai. xliv. 24. *I am Jehovah that maketh all things; that stretcheth forth the heavens alone; that spreadeth abroad the earth by myself.* xlv. 6, 7. *that they may know from the rising of the sun, and from the west, that there is none beside me: I am Jehovah, and there is none else: I form the light, and create darkness.* If there be any thing like a common meaning, or universally received usage of words, this language not only precludes the possibility of there being any other God, but also of there being any co-equal person, of any kind whatever. Neh. ix. 6. *thou art Jehovah alone; thou hast made heaven, the heaven of heavens.* Mal. ii. 10. *have we not all one Father? hath not one God created us?* Hence Christ himself says, Matt. xi. 25. *I thank thee, O Father, Lord of heaven and earth.* So too all the apostles, Acts iv. 24. compared with v. 27. *Lord, thou art God, which hast made heaven and earth, and the sea, and all that in them is . . . the kings of the earth stood up . . . against thy holy child Jesus.* Rom. xi. 36. *for of him, and through him, and to him are all things.* 1 Cor. viii. 6. *to us there is but one God, the Father, of whom are all things.* 2 Cor. iv. 6. *for God who commanded the light to shine out of darkness, hath shined in our hearts, to give the light of the knowledge of the glory of God in the face of Jesus Christ.* Heb. ii. 10. *him, for whom are all things, and by whom are all things.* iii. 4. *he that built all things is God.*

BY HIS WORD. Gen. i. throughout the whole chapter—*God said.* Psal. xxxiii. 6. *by the word of Jehovah were the heavens* made. v. 9. *for he spake, and it was done.* cxlviii. 5. *he commanded, and they were created.* 2 Pet. iii. 5. *by the word of God the heavens were of old,*—that is, as is evident from other passages, by the Son, who appears hence to derive his title of Word. John i. 3, 10. *all things were made by him: by him the world was made.* 1 Cor. viii. 6. *to us there is but one God, the Father, of whom are all things, and we in him; and one Lord Jesus Christ, by whom are all things.* Eph. iii. 9. *who created all things by Jesus Christ.* Col. i. 16. *by him were all things created.* Heb. i. 2. *by whom also he made the worlds;* whence it is said, v. 10. *thou hast laid the foundation of the earth.* The preposition *per* sometimes signifies the primary cause, as Matt. xii. 28. *I cast out devils* (per Spiritum) *by the Spirit of God.* 1 Cor. i. 9. *God is faithful,* (per quem) *by whom ye are called,*—sometimes the instrumental, or less principal cause, as in the passages quoted above, where it cannot be taken as the primary cause, for if so, the Father himself, of whom are all things, would not be the primary cause; nor is it the joint cause, for in such case it would have been said that the Father created all things, not by, but with the Word and Spirit; or collectively, the Father, the Word, and the Spirit created; which phrases are nowhere to be found in Scripture. Besides, the expressions *to be of the Father,* and *to be by the Son,* do not denote the same kind of efficient cause. If it be not the same cause, neither is it a joint cause; and if not a joint cause, certainly the Father, of whom are all things, must be the principal cause, rather than the Son by whom are all things; for the Father is not only he *of* whom, but also from whom, and for whom, and through whom, and on account of whom are all things, as has been proved above, inasmuch as he comprehends within himself all lesser causes; whereas the Son is only he by whom are all things; wherefore he is the less principal cause. Hence it is often said that the Father created the world by the Son,—but never, in the same sense, that the Son created the world by the Father. It is however sometimes attempted to be proved from Rev. iii. 14. that the Son was the joint, or even the principal cause of the creation with the Father; *the beginning of the crea-*

tion of God; where the word *beginning* is interpreted in an active sense, on the authority of Aristotle. But in the first place, the Hebrew language, whence the expression is taken, nowhere admits of this sense, but rather requires a contrary usage, as Gen. xlix. 3. *Reuben, thou art . . . the beginning of my strength.* Secondly, there are two passages in St. Paul referring to Christ himself, which clearly prove that the word *beginning* is here used in a passive signification. Col. i. 15, 18. *the first born of every creature, . . . the beginning, the first born from the dead,*—where the position of the Greek accent, and the passive verbal πρωτό-τοκος, show that the Son of God was the first born of every creature precisely in the same sense as the Son of man was the first born of Mary, πρωτότοκος, Matt. i. 25. The other passage is Rom. viii. 29. *first born among many brethren;* that is, in a passive signification. Lastly, it should be remarked, that he is not called simply *the beginning of the creation,* but *of the creation of God;* which can mean nothing else than the first of those things which God created; how therefore can he be himself God? Nor can we admit the reason devised by some of the Fathers for his being called, Col. i. 15. *the first born of every creature,*—namely, because it is said v. 16. *by him all things were created.* For had St. Paul intended to convey the meaning supposed, he would have said, *who was before every creature,* (which is what these Fathers contend the words signify, though not without violence to the language) not, *who was the first born of every creature,* an expression which clearly has a superlative, and at the same time to a certain extent partitive sense, in so far as production may be considered as a kind of generation and creation; but by no means in so far as the title of first born among men may be here applied to Christ, seeing that he is termed first born, not only in respect of dignity, but also of time. v. 16. *for by him were all things created that are in heaven.*

Nor is the passage in Prov. viii. 22, 23. of more weight, even if it be admitted that the chapter in general is to be understood with reference to Christ: *Jehovah possessed me in the beginning of his way before his works of old: I was set up from everlasting.* For that which was *possessed* and *set up,* could not be the primary cause. Even a creature, however, is called the beginning of the ways of God, Job xl. 19. *he (behemoth) is the chief* (principium) *of the ways of God.* As to the eighth chapter of Proverbs, it appears to me that it is not the Son of God who is there introduced as the speaker, but a poetical personification of wisdom, as in Job xxviii. 20-27. *whence then cometh wisdom?—then did he see it.*

Another argument is brought from Isai. xlv. 12, 23. *I have made the earth . . . unto me every knee shall bow.* It is contended that this is spoken of Christ, on the authority of St. Paul, Rom. xiv. 10, 11. *we shall all stand before the judgement seat of Christ: for it is written, As I live, saith the Lord, every knee shall bow to me.* But it is evident from the parallel passage Philipp. ii. 9-11. that this is said of God the Father, by whose gift the Son has received that judgement seat, and all judgement, *that at the name of Jesus every knee should bow . . . to the glory of God the Father;* or, which means the same thing, *every tongue shall confess to God.*

AND SPIRIT. Gen. i. 2. *the Spirit of God moved upon the face of the waters;* that is, his divine power, rather than any person, as has been already shown in the sixth chapter, on the Holy Spirit. For if it were a person, why is the Spirit named, to the exclusion of the Son, by whom we so often read that the world was created? unless indeed that Spirit were Christ, to whom, as has been before proved, the name of Spirit is sometimes given in the Old Testament. However this may be, and even if it should be admitted to have been a person, it seems at all events to have been only a subordinate minister: God is first described as creating the heaven and the earth; the Spirit is only represented as moving upon the face of the waters already created. So Job xxvi. 13. *by his Spirit he hath garnished the heavens.* Psal. xxxiii. 6. *by the word of Jehovah were the heavens made, and all the host of them by the breath* (spiritu) *of his mouth.* Now the person of the Spirit does not seem to have proceeded more from the mouth of God than from that of Christ, who *shall consume that wicked one with the spirit of his mouth,* 2 Thess. ii. 8. compared with Isai. xi. 4. *the rod of his mouth.*

BY HIS WILL. Psal. cxxxv. 6. *whatsoever*

Jehovah pleased, that did he in heaven and earth. Rev. iv. 11. *for thy pleasure they are and were created.*

FOR THE MANIFESTATION OF THE GLORY OF HIS POWER AND GOODNESS. Gen. i. 31. *God saw every thing that he had made, and behold, it was very good.* See also 1 Tim. iv. 4. Psal. xix. 1. *the heavens declare the glory of God.* Prov. xvi. 4. *Jehovah hath made all things for himself.* Acts xiv. 15. *that ye should turn from these vanities unto the living God which made heaven and earth and the sea, and all things that are therein.* xvii. 24. *God that made the world and all things therein.* Rom. i. 20. *for his eternal power and Godhead are clearly seen.*

Thus far it has appeared that God the Father is the primary and efficient cause of all things. With regard to the original matter of the universe, however, there has been much difference of opinion. Most of the moderns contend that it was formed from nothing, a basis as unsubstantial as that of their own theory. In the first place, it is certain that neither the Hebrew verb בָּרָא, nor the Greek κτίζειν, nor the Latin *creare,* can signify to create out of nothing. On the contrary, these words uniformly signify to create out of matter. Gen. i. 21, 27. *God created . . . every living creature which the waters brought forth abundantly . . . male and female created he them.* Isai. liv. 16. *behold, I have created the smith . . . I have created the waster to destroy.* To allege, therefore, that creation signifies production out of nothing, is, as logicians say, to lay down premises without a proof; for the passages of Scripture commonly quoted for this purpose, are so far from confirming the received opinion, that they rather imply the contrary, namely, that all things were not made out of nothing. 2 Cor. iv. 6. *God, who commanded the light to shine out of darkness.* That this darkness was far from being a mere negation, is clear from Isai. xlv. 7. *I am Jehovah; I form the light, and create darkness.* If the darkness be nothing, God in creating darkness created nothing, or in other words, he created and did not create, which is a contradiction. Again, what we are required *to understand through faith* respecting *the worlds,* is merely this, that *the things which were seen were not made of things which do appear,* Heb. xi. 3. Now *the things which do not appear* are not to be considered as synonymous with nothing, (for nothing does not admit of a plural, nor can a thing be made and compacted together out of nothing, as out of a number of things) but the meaning is, that they do not appear as they now are. The apocryphal writers, whose authority may be considered as next to that of the Scriptures, speak to the same effect. Wisd. xi. 17. *thy almighty hand that made the world of matter without form.* 2 Macc. vii. 28. *God made the earth and all that is therein of things that were not.* The expression in Matt. ii. 18. may be quoted, *the children of Rachel are not.* This, however, does not mean properly that they are nothing, but that (according to a common Hebraism) they are no longer amongst the living.

It is clear then that the world was framed out of matter of some kind or other. For since action and passion are relative terms, and since, consequently, no agent can act externally, unless there be some patient, such as matter, it appears impossible that God could have created this world out of nothing; not from any defect of power on his part, but because it was necessary that something should have previously existed capable of receiving passively the exertion of the divine efficacy. Since, therefore, both Scripture and reason concur in pronouncing that all these things were made, not out of nothing, but out of matter, it necessarily follows, that matter must either have always existed independently of God, or have originated from God at some particular point of time. That matter should have been always independent of God, (seeing that it is only a passive principle, dependent on the Deity, and subservient to him; and seeing, moreover, that, as in number, considered abstractedly, so also in time or eternity there is no inherent force or efficacy) that matter, I say, should have existed of itself from all eternity, is inconceivable. If on the contrary it did not exist from all eternity, it is difficult to understand from whence it derives its origin. There remains, therefore, but one solution of the difficulty, for which moreover we have the authority of Scripture, namely, that all things are of God. Rom. xi. 36. *for of him, and through him, and to him are all things.*

1 Cor. viii. 6. *there is but one God, the Father, of whom are all things:* where the same Greek preposition is used in both cases. Heb. ii. 11. *for both he that sanctifieth, and they who are sanctified, are all of one.*

In the first place, there are, as is well known to all, four kinds of causes,—*efficient, material, formal,* and *final.* Inasmuch then as God is the primary, and absolute, and sole cause of all things, there can be no doubt but that he comprehends and embraces within himself all the causes above-mentioned. Therefore the material cause must be either God, or nothing. Now nothing is no cause at all; and yet it is contended that forms, and above all, that human forms, were created out of nothing. But matter and form, considered as internal causes, constitute the thing itself; so that either all things must have had two causes only, and those external, or God will not have been the perfect and absolute cause of every thing. Secondly, it is an argument of supreme power and goodness, that such diversified, multiform, and inexhaustible virtue should exist and be *substantially* inherent in God (for that virtue cannot be *accidental* which admits of degrees, and of augmentation or remission, according to his pleasure) and that this diversified and substantial virtue should not remain dormant within the Deity, but should be diffused and propagated and extended as far and in such manner as he himself may will. For the original matter of which we speak, is not to be looked upon as an evil or trivial thing, but as intrinsically good, and the chief productive stock of every subsequent good. It was a substance, and derivable from no other source than from the fountain of every substance, though at first confused and formless, being afterwards adorned and digested into order by the hand of God.

Those who are dissatisfied because, according to this view, substance was imperfect, must also be dissatisfied with God for having originally produced it out of nothing in an imperfect state, and without form. For what difference does it make, whether God produced it in this imperfect state out of nothing, or out of himself? By this reasoning, they only transfer that imperfection to the divine efficiency, which they are unwilling to admit can properly be attributed to substance considered as an efflux of the Deity. For why did not God create all things out of nothing in an absolutely perfect state at first? It is not true, however, that matter was in its own nature originally imperfect; it merely received embellishment from the accession of forms, which are themselves material. And if it be asked how what is corruptible can proceed from incorruption, it may be asked in return how the virtue and efficacy of God can proceed out of nothing. Matter, like the form and nature of the angels itself, proceeded incorruptible from God; and even since the fall it remains incorruptible as far as concerns its essence.

But the same, or even a greater difficulty still remains—how that which is in its nature peccable can have proceeded (if I may so speak) from God? I ask in reply, how anything peccable can have originated from the virtue and efficacy which proceeded from God? Strictly speaking indeed it is neither matter nor form that sins; and yet having proceeded from God, and become in the power of another party, what is there to prevent them, inasmuch as they have now become mutable, from contracting taint and contamination through the enticements of the devil, or those which originate in man himself? It is objected, however, that body cannot emanate from spirit. I reply, much less then can body emanate from nothing. For spirit being the more excellent substance, virtually and essentially contains within itself the inferior one; as the spiritual and rational faculty contains the corporeal, that is, the sentient and vegetative faculty. For not even divine virtue and efficiency could produce bodies out of nothing, according to the commonly received opinion, unless there had been some bodily power in the substance of God; since no one can give to another what he does not himself possess. Nor did St. Paul hesitate to attribute to God something corporeal; Col. ii. 9. *in him dwelleth all the fulness of the God head bodily.* Neither is it more incredible that a bodily power should issue from a spiritual substance, than that what is spiritual should arise from body; which nevertheless we believe will be the case with our own bodies at the resurrection. Nor, lastly, can it be understood in what sense God can properly be called infinite, if he be capable of receiving any accession whatever; which would be the case if anything could exist in the nature of things, which had not first been of God and in God.

Since therefore it has (as I conceive) been satisfactorily proved, under the guidance of Scripture, that God did not produce everything out of nothing, but of himself, I proceed to consider the necessary consequence of this doctrine, namely, that if all things are not only from God, but of God, no created thing can be finally annihilated. And, not to mention that not a word is said of this annihilation in the sacred writings, there are other reasons, besides that which has been just alleged, and which is the strongest of all, why this doctrine should be altogether exploded. First, because God is neither willing, nor, properly speaking, able to annihilate anything altogether. He is not willing, because he does everything with a view to some end,—but nothing can be the end neither of God, nor of anything whatever. Not of God, because he is himself the end of himself; not of anything whatever, because good of some kind is the end of everything. Now nothing is neither good, nor in fact anything. Entity is good, non-entity consequently is not good; wherefore it is neither consistent with the goodness or wisdom of God to make out of entity, which is good, that which is not good, or nothing. Again, God is not able to annihilate anything altogether, because by creating nothing he would create and not create at the same time, which involves a contradiction. If it be said that the creative power of God continues to operate, inasmuch as he makes that not to exist which did exist; I answer, that there are two things necessary to constitute a perfect action, motion and the effect of motion: in the present instance the motion is the act of annihilation; the effect of motion is none, that is, nothing, no effect. Where then there is no effect there is no efficient.

Creation is either of things invisible or visible.

The things invisible, or which are at least such to us, are, the highest heaven, which is the throne and habitation of God, and the heavenly powers, or angels.

Such is the division of the apostle, Col. i.

16. The first place is due to things invisible, if not in respect of origin, at least of dignity. For the highest heaven is as it were the supreme citadel and habitation of God. See Deut. xxvi. 15. 1 Kings viii. 27, 30, *heaven of heavens.* Neh. ix. 6. Isai. lxiii. 15. *far above all heavens,* Eph. iv. 10. where God *dwelleth in the light which no man can approach unto,* 1 Tim. vi. 16. Out of this light it appears that pleasures and glories, and a kind of perpetual heaven, have emanated and subsist. Psal. xvi. 11. *at thy right hand there are pleasure for evermore.* Isai. lvii. 15. *the high and lofty one that inhabiteth eternity, whose name is Holy; I dwell in the high and holy place.*

It is improbable that God should have formed to himself such an abode for his majesty only at so recent a period as at the beginning of the world. For if there be any one habitation of God, where he diffuses in an eminent manner the glory and brightness of his majesty, why should it be thought that its foundations are only coeval with the fabrick of this world, and not of much more ancient origin? At the same time it does not follow that heaven should be eternal, nor, if eternal, that it should be God; for it was always in the power of God to produce any effect he pleased at whatever time and in whatever manner seemed good to him. We cannot form any conception of light independent of a luminary; but we do not therefore infer that a luminary is the same as light, or equal in dignity. In the same manner we do not think that what are called *the back parts* of God, Exod. xxxiii. are, properly speaking, God; though we nevertheless consider them to be eternal. It seems more reasonable to conceive in the same manner of the heaven of heavens, the throne and habitation of God, than to imagine that God should have been without a heaven till the first of the six days of creation. At the same time I give this opinion, not as venturing to determine anything certain on such a subject, but rather with a view of showing that others have been too bold in affirming that the invisible and highest heaven was made on the first day, contemporaneously with that heaven which is within our sight. For since it was of the latter heaven alone, and of the visible world, that Moses undertook to write, it would have been foreign to his purpose to have said anything of what was above the world.

In this highest heaven seems to be situated the heaven of the blessed; which is sometimes called Paradise, Luke xxiii. 43. 2 Cor. xii. 2, 4. and Abraham's bosom, Luke xvi. 22. compared with Matt. viii. 11. where also God permits himself to be seen by the angels and saints (as far as they are capable of enduring his glory), and will unfold himself still more fully to their view at the end of the world, 1 Cor. xiii. 12. John xiv. 2, 3. *in my Father's house are many mansions.* Heb. xi. 10, 16. *he looked for a city which hath foundations . . . they desire a better country, that is, an heavenly . . . for he hath prepared for them a city.*

It is generally supposed that the angels were created at the same time with the visible universe, and that they are to be considered as comprehended under the general name of *heavens.* That the angels were created at some particular period, we have the testimony of Numb. xvi. 22. and xxvii. 16. *God of the spirits,* Heb. i. 7. Col. i. 16. *by him were all things created . . . visible and invisible, whether they be thrones,* &c. But that they were created on the first, or on any one of the six days, seems to be asserted (like most received opinions) with more confidence than reason, chiefly on the authority of the repetition in Gen. ii. 1. *thus the heavens and the earth were finished, and all the host of them,*— unless we are to suppose that more was meant to be implied in the concluding summary than in the previous narration itself, and that the angels are to be considered as the host who inhabit the visible heavens. For what is said Job xxxviii. 7. that they shouted for joy before God at the creation, proves rather that they were then already in existence, than that they were then first created. Many at least of the Greek, and some of the Latin Fathers, are of opinion that angels, as being spirits, must have existed long before the material world; and it seems even probable, that the apostasy which caused the expulsion of so many thousands from heaven, took place before the foundations of this world were laid. Certainly there is no sufficient foundation for the common opinion, that motion and time (which is the measure of motion) could not, according to the ratio of priority and subsequence, have existed before this world was made; since Aristotle, who teaches that no ideas of motion and time can be formed except in reference to this world, nevertheless pronounces the world itself to be eternal.

Angels are spirits, Matt. viii. 16. and xii. 45. inasmuch as a legion of devils is represented as having taken possession of one man, Luke viii. 30. Heb. i. 14. *ministering spirits*. They are of ethereal nature, 1 Kings xxii. 21. Psal. civ. 4. compared with Matt. viii. 31. Heb. i. 7. *as lightning*, Luke x. 18. whence also they are called Seraphim. Immortal, Luke xx. 36. *neither can they die any more*. Excellent in wisdom; 2 Sam. xiv. 20. Most powerful in strength; Psal. ciii. 20. 2 Pet. ii. 11. 2 Kings xix. 35. 2 Thess. i. 7. Endued with the greatest swiftness, which is figuratively denoted by the attribute of wings; Ezek. i. 6. In number almost infinite; Deut. xxxiii. 2. Job xxv. 3. Dan. vii. 10. Matt. xxvi. 53. Heb. xii. 22. Rev. v. 11, 12. Created in perfect holiness and righteousness; Luke ix. 26. John viii. 44. 2 Cor. xi. 14, 15. *angels of light . . . ministers of righteousness*. Matt. vi. 10. *thy will be done in earth as it is in heaven*. xxv. 31. *holy angels*. Hence they are also called sons of God, Job. i. 6. and xxxviii. 7. Dan. iii. 25. compared with v. 28. and even Gods, Psal. viii. 5. xcvii. 7. But they are not to be compared with God; Job iv. 18. *his angels he charged with folly*. xv. 15. *the heavens are not clean in his sight*. xxv. 5. *yea, the stars are not pure in his sight*. Isai. vi. 2. *with two wings he covered his face*. They are distinguished one from another by offices and degrees; Matt. xxv. 41. Rom. viii. 38. Col. i. 16. Eph. i. 21. and iii. 10. 1 Pet. iii. 22. Rev. xii. 7. Cherubim, Gen. iii. 24. Seraphim, Isai. vi. 2. and by proper names; Dan. viii. 16. ix. 21. x. 13. Luke i. 19. Michael, Jude 9. Rev. xii. 7. 1 Thess. iv. 16. *with the voice of the Archangel*. Josh. v. 14. See more on this subject in the ninth chapter. To push our speculations further on this subject, is to incur the apostle's reprehension, Col. ii. 18. *intruding into those things which he hath not seen, vainly puffed up by his fleshly mind*.

THE VISIBLE CREATION comprises the material universe, and all that is contained therein; and more especially the human race.

The creation of the world in general, and of its individual parts, is related Gen. i. It is also described Job xxvi. 7, &c. and xxxviii. and in various passages of the Psalms and Prophets. Psal. xxxiii. 6–9. civ. cxlviii. 5. Prov. viii. 26, &c. Amos iv. 13. 2 Pet. iii. 5. Previously, however, to the creation of man, as if to intimate the superior importance of the work, the Deity speaks like to a man deliberating: Gen. i. 26. *God said, Let us make man in our own image, after our own likeness*. So that it was not the body alone that was then made, but the soul of man also (in which our likeness to God principally consists); which precludes us from attributing pre-existence to the soul which was then formed,—a groundless notion sometimes entertained, but refuted by Gen. ii. 7. *God formed man of the dust of the ground, and breathed into his nostrils the breath of life; thus man became a living soul*. Job xxxii. 8. *there is a spirit in man, and the inspiration of the Almighty giveth them understanding*. Nor did God merely breathe that spirit into man, but moulded it in each individual, and infused it throughout, enduing and embellishing it with its proper faculties. Zech. xii. 1. *he formeth the spirit of man within him*.

We may understand from other passages of Scripture, that when God infused the breath of life into man, what man thereby received was not a portion of God's essence, or a participation of the divine nature, but that measure of the divine virtue or influence, which was commensurate to the capabilities of the recipient. For it appears from Psal. civ. 29. 30. that he infused the breath of life into other living beings also; —*thou takest away their breath, they die . . . thou sendest forth thy spirit, they are created;* whence we learn that every living thing receives animation from one and the same source of life and breath; inasmuch as when God takes back to himself that spirit or breath of life, they cease to exist. Eccles. iii. 19. *they have all one breath*. Nor has the word *spirit* any other meaning in the sacred writings, but that breath of life which we inspire, or the vital, or sensitive, or rational faculty, or some action or affection belonging to those faculties.

Man having been created after this manner, it is said, as a consequence, that *man became a living soul;* whence it may be inferred (unless we had rather take the heathen writers for our teachers respecting the nature of the soul) that man is a living being, intrinsically and properly one and individual, not compound or separable, not, according to the common opinion, made up and framed of two distinct and different natures, as of soul and body,—but that the whole man is soul, and the soul man, that is to say, a body, or substance individual, animated, sensitive, and rational; and that the breath of life was neither a part of the divine essence, nor the soul itself, but as it were an inspiration of some divine virtue fitted for the exercise of life and reason, and infused into the organic body; for man himself, the whole man, when finally created, is called in express terms *a living soul.* Hence the word used in Genesis to signify *soul,* is interpreted by the apostle, 1 Cor. xv. 45. *animal.* Again, all the attributes of the body are assigned in common to the soul: the touch, Lev. v. 2, &c. *if a soul touch any unclean thing,*—the act of eating, vii. 18. *the soul that eateth of it shall bear his iniquity;* v. 20. *the soul that eateth of the flesh,* and in other places:—hunger, Prov. xiii. 25. xxvii. 7.—thirst, xxv. 25. *as cold waters to a thirsty soul.* Isai. xxix. 8.—capture, 1 Sam. xxiv. 11. *thou huntest my soul to take it.* Psal. vii. 5. *let the enemy persecute my soul, and take it.*

Where however we speak of the body as of a mere senseless stock, there the soul must be understood as signifying either the spirit, or its secondary faculties, the vital or sensitive faculty for instance. Thus it is as often distinguished from the spirit, as from the body itself. Luke i. 46, 47. 1 Thess. v. 23. *your whole spirit and soul and body.* Heb. iv. 12. *to the dividing asunder of soul and spirit.* But that the spirit of man should be separate from the body, so as to have a perfect and intelligent existence independently of it, is nowhere said in Scripture, and the doctrine is evidently at variance both with nature and reason, as will be shown more fully hereafter. For the word *soul* is also applied to every kind of living being; Gen. i. 30. *to every beast of the earth,* &c. *wherein there is life* (anima vivens, Tremell.) vii. 22. *all in whose nostrils was the breath of life, of all that was in the dry land, died;* yet it is never inferred from these expressions that the soul exists separate from the body in any of the brute creation.

On the seventh day God ceased from his work, and ended the whole business of creation; Gen. ii. 2, 3.

It would seem therefore, that the human soul is not created daily by the immediate act of God, but propagated from father to son in a natural order; which was considered as the more probable opinion by Tertullian and Apollinarius, as well as by Augustine, and the whole western church in the time of Jerome, as he himself testifies, Tom. II. Epist. 82. and Gregory of Nyssa in his treatise on the soul. God would in fact have left his creation imperfect, and a vast, not to say a servile task would yet remain to be performed, without even allowing time for rest on each successive sabbath, if he still continued to create as many souls daily as there are bodies multiplied throughout the whole world, at the bidding of what is not seldom the flagitious wantonness of man. Nor is there any reason to suppose that the influence of the divine blessing is less efficacious in imparting to man the power of producing after his kind, than to the other parts of animated nature; Gen. i. 22, 28. Thus it was from one of the ribs of the man that God made the mother of all mankind, without the necessity of infusing the breath of life a second time, Gen. ii. 22. and Adam himself begat a son in his own likeness after his image, v. 3. Thus 1 Cor. xv. 49. *as we have borne the image of the earthy;* and this not only in the body, but in the soul, as it was chiefly with respect to the soul that Adam was made in the divine image. So Gen. xlvi. 26. *all the souls which came with Jacob out of Egypt, which came out of his loins.* Heb. vii. 10. *Levi was in the loins of Abraham:* whence in Scripture an offspring is called *seed,* and Christ is denominated *the seed of the woman.* Gen. xvii. 7. *I will be a God unto thee, and to thy seed after thee.* 1 Cor. xv. 44. *it is sown a natural body.* v. 46. *that was not first which is spiritual, but that which is natural.*

But besides the testimony of revelation,

some arguments from reason may be alleged in confirmation of this doctrine. Whoever is born, or shapen and conceived, in sin, (as we all are, not David only, Psal. li. 5.) if he receive his soul immediately from God, cannot but receive it from him shapen in sin; for to be generated and conceived, means nothing else than to receive a soul in conjunction with the body. If we receive the soul immediately from God, it must be pure, for who in such case will venture to call it impure? But if it be pure, how are we conceived in sin in consequence of receiving a pure soul, which would rather have the effect of cleansing the impurities of the body; or with what justice is the pure soul charged with the sin of the body? But, it is contended, God does not create souls impure, but only impaired in their nature, and destitute of original righteousness. I answer, that to create pure souls destitute of original righteousness,—to send them into contaminated and corrupt bodies,—to deliver them up in their innocence and helplessness to the prison house of the body, as to an enemy, with understanding blinded and with will enslaved,—in other words, wholly deprived of sufficient strength for resisting the vicious propensities of the body—to create souls thus circumstanced, would argue as much injustice, as to have created them impure would have argued impurity; it would have argued as much injustice, as to have created the first man Adam himself impaired in his nature, and destitute of original righteousness.

Again, if sin be communicated by generation, and transmitted from father to son, it follows that what is the πρῶτον δεκτικὸν, or original subject of sin, namely, the rational soul, must be propagated in the same manner; for that it is from the soul that all sin in the first instance proceeds, will not be denied. Lastly, on what principle of justice can sin be imputed through Adam to that soul, which was never either in Adam, or derived from Adam? In confirmation of which Aristotle's argument may be added, the truth of which in my opinion is indisputable. If the soul be equally diffused throughout any given whole, and throughout every part of that whole, how can the human seed, the noblest and most intimate part of all the body, be imagined destitute and devoid of the soul of the parents, or at least of the father, when communicated to the son by the laws of generation? It is acknowledged by the common consent of almost all philosophers, that every form, to which class the human soul must be considered as belonging, is produced by the power of matter.

It was probably by some such considerations as these that Augustine was led to confess that he could neither discover by study, nor prayer, nor any process of reasoning, how the doctrine of original sin could be defended on the supposition of the creation of souls. The texts which are usually advanced, Eccles. xii. 7. Isai. lvii. 16. Zech. xii. 1. certainly indicate that nobler origin of the soul implied in its being breathed from the mouth of God; but they no more prove that each soul is severally and immediately created by the Deity, than certain other texts, which might be quoted, prove that each individual body is formed in the womb by the immediate hand of God. Job x. 8–10. *thine hands have made me . . . hast not thou poured me out as milk?* Psal. xxxiii. 15. *he fashioneth their hearts alike.* Job xxxi. 15. *did not he that made me in the womb make him?* Isai. xliv. 24. *thus saith Jehovah . . . he that formed thee from the womb.* Acts xvii. 26. *he hath made of one blood all nations of men.* We are not to infer from these passages, that natural causes do not contribute their ordinary efficacy for the propagation of the body; nor on the other hand that the soul is not received by traduction from the father, because at the time of death it again betakes itself to different elements than the body, in conformity with its own origin.

With regard to the passage, Heb. xii. 9. where *the fathers of the flesh* are opposed to *the Father of spirits,* I answer, that it is to be understood in a theological, not in a physical sense, as if the father of the body were opposed to the father of the soul; for *flesh* is taken neither in this passage, nor probably any where else, for the body without the soul; nor *the father of spirits* for the father of the soul, in respect of the work of generation; but *the father of the flesh* here means nothing else than the earthly or natural father, whose offspring are begotten in sin; *the father of spirits* is either the heavenly father, who in the beginning created all spirits, angels as well as the human race, or the spiritual father, who bestows a second birth on the faithful; according to John iii. 6. *that which is born of the flesh is flesh, and that which is born of the Spirit is spirit.* The argument, too, will proceed better, if the whole be understood as referring to edification and correction, not to generation; for the point in question is not, from what source each individual originated, or what part of him thence originated, but who had proved most successful in the employment of chastisement and instruction. By parity of reasoning, the apostle might exhort the converts to bear with his rebuke, on the ground that he was their spiritual father. God indeed is as truly the father of the flesh as of *the spirits of flesh,* Numb. xvi. 22. but this is not the sense intended here, and all arguments are weak which are deduced from passages of Scripture originally relating to a different subject.

With regard to the soul of Christ, it will be sufficient to answer that its generation was supernatural, and therefore cannot be cited as an argument in the discussion of this controversy. Nevertheless, even he is called *the seed of the woman, the seed of David according to the flesh;* that is, undoubtedly, according to his human nature.

There seems therefore no reason, why the soul of man should be made an exception to the general law of creation. For, as has been shown before, God breathed the breath of life into the other living beings, and blended it so intimately with matter, that the propagation and production of the human form were analogous to those of other forms, and the proper effect of that power which had been communicated to matter by the Deity.

Man being formed after the image of God, it followed as a necessary consequence that he should be endued with natural wisdom, holiness, and righteousness. Gen. i. 27, 31. ii. 25. Eccles. vii. 29. Eph. iv. 24. Col. iii. 10. 2 Cor. iii. 18. Certainly without extraordinary wisdom he could not have given names to the whole animal creation with such sudden intelligence, Gen. ii. 20.

CHAP. VIII.

OF THE
PROVIDENCE OF GOD,
OR OF HIS
GENERAL GOVERNMENT OF THE UNIVERSE.

The remaining species of God's external efficiency, is his GOVERNMENT OF THE WHOLE CREATION.

This government is either GENERAL or SPECIAL.

His GENERAL GOVERNMENT is that whereby GOD THE FATHER REGARDS, PRESERVES, AND GOVERNS THE WHOLE OF CREATION WITH INFINITE WISDOM AND HOLINESS ACCORDING TO THE CONDITIONS OF HIS DECREE.

GOD THE FATHER. Neh. ix. 6. *thou, even thou, art Jehovah alone . . . thou hast made, and thou preservest them all.* To this truth Christ himself bears witness everywhere. Matt. v. 45. *that ye may be the children of your Father which is in heaven; for he maketh his sun to rise . . . and sendeth rain,* &c. vi. 4. *thy Father which seeth in secret.* v. 8. *your Father knoweth.* v. 13. *thine is the kingdom and the power and the glory.* v. 26. *your heavenly Father feedeth them.* v. 32. *your heavenly Father knoweth that ye have need of all these things.* vii. 11. *your Father which is in heaven shall give good things unto them that ask him.* x. 29. *one of them shall not fall on the ground without your Father.* Acts i. 7. *the times and the seasons which the Father hath put in his own power.* Eph. i. 11. *according to the purpose of him who worketh all things after the counsel of his own will.* James i. 17. *every good gift and every perfect gift is from above, and cometh down from the Father of lights.* Even as regards the Son himself. Acts iv. 27. *against thy holy child Jesus, whom thou hast anointed . . . for to do whatsoever thy hand and thy counsel determined before to be done.* The preservation of the universe is attributed to the Son also, but in what sense, and on what grounds, may be seen in the fifth chapter, on the Son of God. Col. i. 17. *by him all things consist,*—but both the preceding and following verses explain on what account; namely, because the Father, v. 13. *hath translated us into the kingdom of his dear Son,* and because, v. 19. *it pleased the Father that in him should all fulness dwell.* Heb. i. 3. *upholding all things by the word of his power,* namely, because, v. 2. *the Father hath appointed him heir of all things.* Further, it will appear on an examination of the passage, that the original ought to be translated, not of *his own* power, but of *his,* namely, the Father's, of whose person he was the express image: and the right reading in the Greek is αὑτοῦ, not αὐτοῦ, since δι ἑαυτοῦ immediately follows, as if put expressly for the sake of distinction. Lastly, Christ testifies of himself, Matt. xxviii. 18. *all power is given unto me in heaven and in earth;* and to the same effect in many other places.

REGARDS. Job xxxi. 4. *doth not he count all my steps?* 2 Chron. xvi. 9. *the eyes of Jehovah run to and fro throughout the whole earth.* Psal. xxxiii. 15. *he fashioneth their hearts alike; he considereth all their works.* Jer. xxxii. 19. *Thine eyes are open upon all the ways of the sons of men.* Hos. ii. 21. *I will hear the heavens.*

PRESERVES. Deut. viii. 3. *man doth not live by bread only, but by every word that proceedeth out of the mouth of Jehovah.* Job vii. 20. *O thou preserver of men.* Psal. xxx. 7. *thou didst hide thy face, and I was troubled.* lxxx. 1. *O Shepherd of Israel, thou that leadest Joseph like a flock . . . shine forth.* v. 3. *cause thy face to shine and we shall be saved.* civ. 29. *thou takest away their breath, they die.* Nehem. ix. 6. *thou hast made . . . and thou preservest them all.* Acts xiv. 17. *he left not himself without witness.* xvii. 25. *he giveth to all life.* v. 28. *in him we live.*

ACCORDING TO THE CONDITIONS OF HIS DECREE. It is necessary to add this qualification, inasmuch as God preserves neither angels, nor men, nor any other part of creation absolutely, but always with reference to the conditions of his decree. For he preserves mankind, since their spontaneous fall, and all other things with them, only so far as regards their existence, and not as regards their primitive perfection.

GOVERNS. Job xiv. 5. *thou hast appointed his bounds.* Psal. xxix. 10. *Jehovah sitteth king for ever.* xciii. 1. *Jehovah reigneth . . . the world also is established.* ciii. 19. *his kingdom ruleth over all.* Prov. xx. 24. *man's goings are of Jehovah.* xxi. 1. *the king's heart is in the hand of Jehovah . . . he turneth it whithersoever he will.*

WITH INFINITE WISDOM AND HOLINESS. Job ix. 10. *which doeth great things past finding out, yea, and wonders without number.* Prov. x. 24. *the fear of the wicked it shall come upon him; but the desire of the righteous shall be granted.* xii. 3. *a man shall not be established by wickedness.* xiii. 9. *the light of the righteous rejoiceth.* Isai. lv. 9. *my ways are higher than your ways.* Deut. xxxii. 4. *all his ways are judgment.* Psal. xix. 9. *the judgments of Jehovah are true and righteous altogether.* lxxvii. 13. *thy way, O God, is in the sanctuary.* Generally speaking, however, no distinction is made between the righteous and the wicked, with regard to the final issue of events, at least in this life. Job xii. 6. *the tabernacles of robbers prosper.* xxi. 7. *wherefore do the wicked live, become old?* Eccles. vii. 15. *there is a just man that perisheth in his righteousness, and there is a wicked man that prolongeth his life in his wickedness.* viii. 14. *there be just men unto whom it happeneth according to the work of the wicked; again, there be wicked men, to whom it happeneth according to the work of the righteous.* ix. 2. *there is one event to the righteous and to the wicked.* The reason for this may be seen Job v. 7. *man is born unto trouble as the sparks fly upward.* xxiv. 23. *though it be given him to be in safety, whereon he resteth; yet his eyes are upon their ways,* &c. Psal. lxxiii. 12, &c. *behold, these are the ungodly who prosper in the world,* &c. . . . *until I went into the sanctuary of God; then understood I their end.* xcii. 7. *when the wicked spring as the grass,* &c. . . . *it is that they shall be destroyed for ever.* Eccles. vii. 18. *it is good that thou shouldest take hold of this; yea also from this withdraw not thine hand; for he that feareth God shall come forth of them all.* viii. 12. *though a sinner do evil an hundred times, and his days be prolonged; yet surely I know that it shall be well with them that fear God.* Jer. xii. 1. *wherefore doth the way of the wicked prosper?* Dan. xii. 10. *many shall be purified, and made white, and tried.*

THE WHOLE OF CREATION. Gen. viii. 1. *God remembered Noah, and every living thing, and all the cattle.* ix. 9, 10, 12, 15.

I, behold I establish my covenant with you . . . and every living creature that is with you. Prov. xv. 3. *the eyes of Jehovah are in every place, beholding the evil and the good.*

Even the smallest objects. Job. xxxiv. 21. *for his eyes are upon the ways of man, and he seeth all his goings.* Psal. civ. 21. *the young lions roar after their prey, and seek their meat from God.* cxlvii. 9. *he giveth to the beast his food.* Matt. vi. 26. x. 29, 30. *a sparrow shall not fall on the ground without your Father: but the very hairs of your head are all numbered.*

At the same time, God does not extend an equal share of his providential care to all things indiscriminately. 1 Cor. ix. 9. *doth God take care for oxen?* that is, as much care as he takes for man? Zech. ii. 8. *he that toucheth you, toucheth the apple of his eye.* 1 Tim. iv. 10. *the Saviour of all men, specially of those that believe.*

Natural things. Exod. iii. 21. *I will give this people favour in the sight of the Egyptians;* that is, by operating a change in their natural affections. Jer. li. 16. *he uttereth his voice, there is a multitude of waters in the heavens; and he causeth the vapours to ascend from the ends of the earth.* Amos v. 8. *that calleth for the waters of the sea, and poureth them out upon the face of the earth; Jehovah is his name.*

Even such as are supernatural. Lev. xxv. 20, 21. *and if ye shall say, What shall we eat the seventh year? . . . it shall bring forth fruit for three years.* Deut. viii. 3, 4. *he fed thee with manna . . . thy raiment waxed not old upon thee, neither did thy foot swell these forty years.* See also xxix. 5. 1 Kings xvii. 4. *I have commanded the ravens to feed thee there.* v. 14. *the barrel of meal shall not waste,* &c.

Events contingent or fortuitous. Exod. xxi. 13. *if God deliver him into his hand.* Prov. xvi. 33. *the whole disposing of the lot is of Jehovah.* Nor is anything derogatory to divine providence intended by Scripture, even where (as sometimes happens) it scruples not to employ the names of fortune or chance; all that is meant is to exclude the idea of human causation. Eccles. ix. 11. *time and chance happeneth to them all.* Luke x. 31. *by chance there came down a certain priest that way.*

Voluntary actions. 2 Chron. x. 15. *so the king hearkened not unto the people: for the cause was of God.* Prov. xvi. 9. *a man's heart deviseth his way; but Jehovah directeth his steps.* xx. 24. *man's goings are of Jehovah.* xxi. 1. *the king's heart is in the hand of Jehovah as the rivers of water; he turneth it whithersoever he will.* Jer. x. 23. *O Jehovah, I know that the way of man is not in himself.* In this, however, there is no infringement on the liberty of the human will; otherwise man would be deprived of the power of free agency, not only with regard to what is right, but with regard to what is indifferent, or even positively wrong.

Lastly, temporal evils no less than blessings. Exod. xxi. 13. *if God deliver him into his hand.* Isai. xlv. 7. *I make peace and create evil,*—that is, what afterwards became evil, and now remains so; for whatever God created was originally good, as he himself testifies, Gen. i. Matt. xvii. 7. *woe unto the world because of offences; for it must needs be that offences come: but woe to that man by whom the offence cometh.* 1 Cor. xi. 19. *for there must be also heresies amongst you, that they which are approved may be made manifest amongst you.*

God, however, is concerned in the production of evil only in one of these two ways; either he permits its existence by throwing no impediment in the way of natural causes and free agents, (as, Acts ii. 23. *him being delivered by the determinate counsel of God . . . ye have slain.* xiv. 16. *who in times past suffered all nations to walk in their own ways.* 1 Pet. iii. 17. *it is better, if the will of God be so, that ye suffer for well-doing.* iv. 19. *them that suffer according to the will of God,*) or, secondly, he causes evil by the infliction of judgments, which is called the evil of punishment. 2 Sam. xii. 11. *behold I will raise up evil against thee out of thine own house,*—that is, punishment. Prov. xvi. 4. *Jehovah hath made all things for himself; yea, even the wicked for the day of evil;* that is, him who, having been created good, became subsequently wicked by his own fault, in conformity with the explanation already given of Isai. xlv. 7. liv. 16. *I created the waster to destroy.* Lam. iii. 38, 39. *out of the mouth of the Most High proceedeth not evil and good? wherefore doth a living man complain, a man for the punishment of his sins?* Amos iii. 6. *shall there be evil in a city, and Jehovah hath not done it?* For God, who is infinitely good, cannot be the doer of wickedness, or of the evil of sin; on the contrary, out of the wickedness of men he produces good. Gen. xlv. 5. *God did send me before you to preserve life.* l. 20. *as for you, ye thought evil against me; but God meant it unto good.*

If (inasmuch as I do not address myself to such as are wholly ignorant, but to those who are already competently acquainted with the outlines of Christian doctrine) I may be permitted, in discoursing on the general providence of God, so far to anticipate the natural order of arrangement, as to make an allusion to a subject which belongs properly to another part of my treatise, that of sin, I might remark, that even in the matter of sin God's providence finds its exercise, not only in permitting its existence, or in withdrawing his grace, but also in impelling sinners to the commission of sin, in hardening their hearts, and in blinding their understandings.

In impelling sinners to the commission of sin. Exod. ix. 16. *for this cause have I raised thee up.* Judges ix. 23. *God sent an evil spirit between Abimelech and the men of Shechem.* 2 Sam. xii. 11, 12. *I will raise up evil against thee out of thine own house, and I will take thy wives before thine eyes, and give them unto thy neighbour . . . I will do this thing.* xvi. 10. *Jehovah hath said unto him, Curse David.* xxiv. 1. *Jehovah moved David against them to say, Go, number Israel and Judah.* Compare 1 Chron. xxi. 1. 1 Kings xxii. 20. *who shall persuade Ahab?* Psal. cv. 25. *he turned their heart to hate his people.* Ezek. xiv. 9. *I Jehovah have deceived that prophet.*

In hardening their hearts. Exod. iv. 21. vii. 3. *I will harden Pharaoh's heart.* Deut. ii. 30. *Jehovah thy God hardened his spirit.* Josh. xi. 20. *it was of Jehovah to harden their hearts.* John xii. 39, 40. *therefore they could not believe, because that Esaias said again . . . he hath hardened their heart.* Rom. ix. 18. *whom he will he hardeneth.*

In blinding their understandings. Deut. xxviii. 28. *Jehovah shall smite thee with madness, and blindness, and astonishment of heart.* 1 Sam. xvi. 14. *an evil spirit from Jehovah troubled him.* 1 Kings xxii. 22. *I will be a lying spirit in the mouth of all his prophets: and Jehovah said, Thou shalt persuade him.* Isai. viii. 14. *he shall be for a stone of stumbling and for a rock of offence to both the houses of Israel; for a gin and for a snare—.* xix. 14. *Jehovah hath mingled a perverse spirit in the midst thereof, and they have caused Egypt to err.* xxix. 10. *Jehovah hath poured out upon you the spirit of deep sleep, and hath closed your eyes.* Matt. xiii. 13. *therefore speak I to them in parables, because they seeing see not.* John xii. 40. compared with Isai. vi. 9. *he hath blinded their eyes.* Rom. i. 28. *God gave them over to a reprobate mind.* 2 Thess. ii. 11. *God shall send them a strong delusion, that they should believe a lie.*

But though in these, as well as in many other passages of the Old and New Testament, God distinctly declares that it is himself who impels the sinner to sin, who hardens his heart, who blinds his understanding, and leads him into error; yet on account of the infinite holiness of the Deity, it is not allowable to consider him as in the smallest instance the author of sin. Hos. xiv. 9. *the ways of Jehovah are right, and the just shall walk in them; but the transgressors shall fall therein.* Psal. v. 4. *thou art not a God that hath pleasure in wickedness, neither shall evil dwell with thee.* Rom. vii. 8. *sin, taking occasion by the commandment, wrought in me all manner of concupiscence.* James i. 13, 14. *let no man say when he is tempted, I am tempted of God; for God cannot be tempted with evil, neither tempteth he any man: but every man is tempted when he is drawn away of his own lust and enticed.* iv. 1. *from whence come wars and fightings amongst you? come they not hence, even of your lusts which war in your members?* 1 John ii. 16. *for all that is in the world, the lust of the flesh, and the lust of the eyes, and the pride of life, is not of the Father, but is of the world.* For it is not the human heart in a state of innocence and purity, and repugnance to evil, that is induced by him to act wickedly and deceitfully; but after it has conceived sin, and when it is about to bring forth, he, in his character of sovereign disposer of all things, inclines and biasses it in this or that direction, or towards this or that object. Psal. xciv. 23. *he shall bring upon them their own iniquity, and shall cut them off in their own wickedness, yea, Jehovah our God shall cut them off;*—that is to say, by the infliction of punishment. Nor does God make that will evil which was before good, but the will being already in a state of perversion, he influences it in such a manner, that out of its own wickedness it either operates good for others, or punishment for itself, though unknowingly, and with the intent of producing a very different result. Prov. xvi. 9. *a man's heart deviseth his way, but Jehovah directeth his steps.* Thus Ezek. xxi. 21, 22. when the king of Babylon stood at the parting of the way in doubt whether he should go to war against the Ammonites or against the Jews, God so ordered the divination, as to determine him on going against Jerusalem. Or, to use the common simile, as a rider who urges on a stumbling horse in a particular direction is the cause of its increasing its speed, but not of its stumbling,—so God, who is the supreme governor of the universe, may instigate an evil agent, without being in the least degree the cause of the evil. I shall recur again to this simile hereafter. For example,—God saw that the mind of David was so elated and puffed up by the increase of his power, that even without any external impulse he was on the point of giving some remarkable token of his pride; he therefore excited in him the desire of numbering the people: he did not inspire him with the passion of vain glory, but impelled him to display in this manner, rather than in any other, that latent arrogance of his heart which was ready to break forth. God therefore was the author of the act itself, but David alone was responsible for its pride and wickedness. Further, the end which a sinner has in view is generally something evil and unjust, from which God uniformly educes a good and just result, thus as it were creating light out of darkness. By this means he proves the inmost intentions of men, that is, he makes man to have a thorough insight into the latent wickedness of his own heart, that he may either be induced thereby to forsake his sins, or if not, that he may become notorious and inexcusable in the sight of all; or lastly, to the end that

both the author and the sufferer of the evil may be punished for some former transgression. At the same time, the common maxim, that God makes sin subservient to the punishment of sin, must be received with caution; for the Deity does not effect his purpose by compelling any one to commit crime, or by abetting him in it, but by withdrawing the ordinary grace of his enlightening spirit, and ceasing to strengthen him against sin. There is indeed a proverb which says, that he who is able to forbid an action, and forbids it not, virtually commands it. This maxim is indeed binding on man, as a moral precept; but it is otherwise with regard to God. When, in conformity with the language of mankind, he is spoken of as instigating, where he only does not prohibit evil, it does not follow that he therefore bids it, inasmuch as there is no obligation by which he is bound to forbid it. Psal. lxxxi. 11, 12. *my people would not hearken to my voice, and Israel would none of me: so I gave them up unto their own hearts' lust, and they walked in their own counsels.* Hence it is said, Rom. i. 24. *wherefore God also gave them up to uncleanness,*—that is, he left them to be actuated by their own lusts, to walk in them; for properly speaking God does not instigate, or give up, him whom he leaves entirely to himself, that is, to his own desires and counsels, and to the suggestions of his ever active spiritual enemy. In the same sense the Church is said to give up to Satan the contumacious member, whom it interdicts from its communion. With regard to the case of David's numbering the people, a single word will be sufficient. For it is not God, but Satan who is said to have instigated him, 2 Sam. xxiv. 1. 1 Chron. xxi. 1. A similar explanation applies to the passage in 2 Sam. xii. 11, 12. *behold, I will raise up evil against thee out of thine own house,*—that is, the evil of punishment,—*and I will take thy wives before thine eyes, and give them unto thy neighbour,*—that is, I will permit thy son to go in unto them, according to the counsel of Ahithophel; for this is the meaning of the word *give,* as has been just shown. As to the popular simile of the stumbling horse, the argument drawn from it is itself a lame one; for the sinner, if he be really instigated, is not instigated simply to act, as in the case of the horse, but to act amiss,—or in other words, he is instigated to stumble, because he stumbles. In both the instances above adduced, God had determined to punish openly the secret adultery of David: he saw Absalom's propensity to every kind of wickedness; he saw the mischievous counsels of Ahithophel, and did nothing more than influence their minds, which were already in a state of preparation for any atrocity, to perpetrate one crime in preference to another, when opportunity should offer; according to the passage of Proverbs quoted above, xvi. 9. *a man's heart deviseth his way; but Jehovah directeth his steps.* For to offer an occasion of sinning, is only to manifest the wickedness of the sinner, not to create it. The other position, that God eventually converts every evil deed into an instrument of good, contrary to the expectation of sinners, and overcomes evil with good, is sufficiently illustrated in the example of Joseph's sale by his brethren, Gen. xlv. 8. Thus also in the crucifixion of Christ, the sole aim of Pilate was to preserve the favour of Cæsar; that of the Jews to satisfy their own hatred and vengeance; but God, whose *hand and counsel had determined before every thing that was to be done,* Acts iv. 28. made use of their cruelty and violence as instruments for effecting the general redemption of mankind. Rom. xi. 11. *through their fall salvation is come unto the Gentiles.* 1 Cor. xi. 19. *there must be also heresies among you, that they which are approved may be made manifest among you.* Philipp. i. 12, 14. *the things which happened unto me have fallen out rather unto the furtherance of the gospel.*

Again, as God's instigating the sinner does not render him the author of sin, so neither does his hardening the heart or blinding the understanding involve that consequence; inasmuch as he does not produce these effects by infusing an evil disposition, but on the contrary by employing such just and kind methods, as ought rather to soften the hearts of sinners than harden them. First, by his long-suffering. Rom. ii. 4, 5. *despisest thou the riches of his long-suffering . . . but after thy hardness and impenitent heart treasurest up unto thyself wrath?* Secondly, by urging his own good and reasonable commands in opposition to

the obstinacy of the wicked; as an anvil, or adamant, is said to be hardened under the hammer. Thus Pharaoh became more furious and obdurate in proportion as he resisted the commands of God. Exod. v. 2. *who is Jehovah?* vii. 2, 3. *thou shalt speak all that I command thee . . . and I will harden Pharaoh's heart.* Isai. vi. 10. *make the heart of this people fat,*—that is to say, by the repeated inculcation of the divine commands, as in xxviii. 13. *the word of Jehovah was unto them precept upon precept . . . that they might go and fall backward.* Thirdly, by correction or punishment. Ezek. iii. 20. *when a righteous man doth turn from his righteousness and commit iniquity, and I lay a stumbling-block before him, he shall die.* Jer. v. 3. *thou hast stricken them, but they have not grieved . . . they have made their faces harder than a rock.* The hardening of the heart, therefore, is usually the last punishment inflicted on inveterate wickedness and unbelief in this life. 1 Sam. ii. 25. *they hearkened not unto the voice of their father, because the Lord would slay them.* God often hardens in a remarkable manner the powerful and rebellious princes of this world, in order that through their insolence and haughtiness his glory may be magnified among the nations. Exod. ix. 16. *for this cause have I raised thee up, for to show in thee my power.* See also x. 2. compared with Rom. ix. 17. *even for this same purpose have I raised thee up, that I might show my power in thee.* Exod. xiv. 4, 17. *I will be honoured upon Pharaoh.* Yet the act of hardening is not so exclusively the work of God, but that the wicked themselves fully co-operate in it, though with any view but that of fulfilling the divine will. Hence Pharaoh is said to harden his own heart, Exod. ix. 34. *when he saw that the rain and the hail and the thunders were ceased, he sinned yet more, and hardened his heart, he and his servants.* 2 Chron. xxxvi. 13. *he stiffened his neck, and hardened his heart from turning unto Jehovah.* Psal. xcv. 8. *harden not your heart.* Zech. vii. 12. *they made their hearts as an adamant stone, lest they should hear the law and the words which Jehovah of hosts hath sent.*

Thus also with regard to the blinding of the understanding. Deut. xxviii. 15.

compared with v. 28. *it shall come to pass, if thou wilt not hearken unto the voice of Jehovah thy God . . . Jehovah shall smite thee with madness, and blindness, and astonishment of heart,* that is, by withdrawing the light of his grace, by confounding or stupefying the faculties of the mind, or by simply permitting Satan to work these effects in the sinner. Rom. i. 28. *even as they did not like to retain God in their knowledge, God gave them over to a reprobate mind.* 2 Cor. iv. 4. *in whom the god of this world hath blinded the minds of them which believe not.* Eph. ii. 2. *the spirit that now worketh in the children of disobedience.* 2 Thess. ii. 11. *for this cause God shall send them strong delusion.* Lastly, God is said to deceive men, not in the sense of seducing them to sin, but of beguiling them to their own punishment, or even to the production of some good end. Ezek. xiv. 9–11. *if the prophet be deceived when he hath spoken a thing, I Jehovah have deceived that prophet, and I will stretch out my hand upon him,* &c. *. . . and they shall bear the punishment of their iniquity . . . that the house of Israel may go no more astray from me.* God first deceived the already corrupt and covetous prophet, by disposing his mind to prophesy things acceptable to the people, and then deservedly cut off both the people who inquired of him, and the prophet of whom they inquired, to deter others from sinning in a similar manner; because on the one hand a bad intention had been displayed on the part of the inquirers, and on the other a false answer had been returned, which God had not commanded.

To this view of providence must be referred what is called temptation, whereby God either tempts men, or permits them to be tempted by the devil or his agents.

Temptation is either for evil or for good.

An evil temptation is when God, as above described, either withdraws his grace, or presents occasions of sin, or hardens the heart, or blinds the understanding. This is generally an evil temptation in respect of him who is tempted, but most equitable on the part of the Deity, for the reasons abovementioned. It also serves the purpose of unmasking hypocrisy; for God tempts no one in the sense of enticing or persuading to sin, (see James i. 13. as above,) though

there be some towards whom he deservedly permits the devil to employ such temptations. We are taught in the Lord's prayer to deprecate temptations of this kind; Matt. vi. 13. *lead us not into temptation, but deliver us from evil.*

A good temptation is that whereby God tempts even the righteous for the purpose of proving them, not as though he were ignorant of the disposition of their hearts, but for the purpose of exercising or manifesting their faith or patience, as in the case of Abraham and Job; or of lessening their self-confidence, and reproving their weakness, that both they themselves may become wiser by experience, and others may profit by their example: as in the case of Hezekiah, 2 Chron. xxxii. 31. whom *God left*—partially, or for a time—*to try him, that he might know all that was in his heart.* He tempted the Israelites in the wilderness with the same view. Deut. viii. 2. *to humble thee, and to prove thee, to know what was in thine heart, whether thou wouldest keep his commandments or no.* Psal. lxvi. 10. *thou, O God, hast proved us, thou hast tried us as silver is tried.* 1 Pet. i. 7. *that the trial of your faith . . . might be found unto praise.* iv. 12. *beloved, think it not strange concerning the fiery trial which is to try you, as though some strange thing happened unto you.* Rev. ii. 10. *behold, the devil shall cast some of you into prison, that ye may be tried.*

This kind of temptation is therefore rather to be desired. Psal. xxvi. 2. *examine me, O Jehovah, and prove me; try my reins and my heart.* James i. 2, 3. *my brethren, count it all joy when ye fall into divers temptations; knowing this, that the trying of your faith worketh patience.*

God also promises a happy issue. 1 Cor. x. 13. *there hath no temptation taken you but such as is common to man: but God is faithful, who will not suffer you to be tempted above that ye are able, but will with the temptation also make a way to escape, that ye may be able to bear it.* James i. 12. *blessed is the man that endureth temptation; for when he is tried, he shall receive the crown of life.*

Yet even believers are not always sufficiently observant of these various operations of divine providence, until they are led to investigate the subject more deeply, and become more intimately conversant with the word of God. Psal. lxxiii. 2, 17. *my feet were almost gone . . . until I went into the sanctuary of God: then understood I their end.* Dan. xii. 10. *many shall be purified, and made white, and tried; but the wicked shall do wickedly: and none of the wicked shall understand, but the wise shall understand.*

Having said in the prefatory definition, that the providence of God extends to all things, and that it has enacted certain immutable laws, by which every part of the creation is administered, it may not be an useless digression to inquire in this place, whether, among other fixed regulations, a limit has been set to the duration of human life, which is not to be passed. That such is the case, Scripture clearly intimates. Job xiv. 5. *seeing his days are determined, the number of his months are with thee, thou hast appointed his bounds that he cannot pass.* Psal. xc. 10. *the days of our years are three score years and ten, and if by reason of strength they be fourscore years, yet is their strength labour and sorrow; for it is soon cut off, and we fly away.* From these and similar passages, and especially from the early history of the world, it is evident that God, at least after the fall of man, limited human life to a certain term, which in the progress of ages, from Adam to David, gradually became more and more contracted; so that whether this term be one and the same to all, or appointed differently to each individual, it is in the power of no one to prolong or exceed its limits. This is the province of God alone, as is proved beyond all doubt by the promise of long life made by him to his people, and by his addition of fifteen years to the life of Hezekiah when at the point of death. The power of shortening or anticipating the term in question, on the contrary, is not the exclusive privilege of God, though this also is exercised by him, both for purposes of reward and punishment; the same effect may be, and in fact frequently is, produced by the crimes or vices of mortals themselves. Prov. x. 27. *the fear of Jehovah prolongeth days, but the years of the wicked shall be shortened.* Exod. xx. 12. *honour thy father and thy mother, that thy days may be long upon the land,* &c. See also numerous passages to the

same purpose, during the time of the law. Psal. lv. 23. *bloody and deceitful men shall not live out half their days,* that is, they shall not live to the end of that term, to which by the constitution of their bodies they might otherwise have arrived; in which class are to be placed all those who lay violent hands on themselves, or who accelerate death by intemperate living.

The providence of God is either ordinary or extraordinary.

His ordinary providence is that whereby he upholds and preserves the immutable order of causes appointed by him in the beginning. This is commonly, and indeed too frequently, described by the name of nature; for nature cannot possibly mean anything but the mysterious power and efficacy of that divine voice which went forth in the beginning, and to which, as to a perpetual command, all things have since paid obedience. Job xxxviii. 12. *hast thou commanded the morning since thy days?* v. 33. *knowest thou the ordinances of heaven?* Psal. cxlviii. 8. *fire and hail, snow and vapours, stormy wind fulfilling his word.* Isai. xlv. 12. *I have stretched out the heavens, and all their host have I commanded.* Jer. xxxi. 36. *if those ordinances depart from before me.* xxxiii. 20. *my covenant of the day and my covenant of the night.*

The extraordinary providence of God is that whereby God produces some effect out of the usual order of nature, or gives the power of producing the same effect to whomsoever he may appoint. This is what we call a miracle. Hence God alone is the primary author of miracles, as he only is able to invert that order of things which he has himself appointed. Psal. lxxii. 18. *who only doeth wondrous things.* John x. 21. *can a devil open the eyes of the blind?* 2 Thess. ii. 9. *whose coming is after the power of Satan, with all power and signs and lying wonders.*

The use of miracles is to manifest the divine power, and confirm our faith. Exod. vi. 6, 7. *I will redeem you . . . with great judgments . . . and ye shall know that I am Jehovah your God.* viii. 22. *I will sever in that day the land of Goshen . . . to the end thou mayest know that I am Jehovah.* 1 Kings xvii. 24. *now by this I know that thou art a man of God.* Mark xvi. 20. *the*

Lord working with them, and confirming the word with signs following. Heb. ii. 4. *God also bearing them witness, both with signs and wonders and with divers miracles, and gifts of the Holy Ghost, according to his own will.*

Miracles are also designed to increase the condemnation of unbelievers, by taking away all excuse for unbelief. Matt. xi. 21. *woe unto thee, Chorazin . . . for if the mighty works which were done in you had been done in Tyre and Sidon, they would have repented long ago—.* John xv. 24. *if I had not done among them the works which none other man did, they had not had sin: but now they have no cloke for their sin.*

CHAP. IX.

OF THE
SPECIAL GOVERNMENT
OF
ANGELS.

THE GENERAL GOVERNMENT OF PROVIDENCE has been hitherto the subject of consideration. The SPECIAL GOVERNMENT is that which embraces with peculiar regard angels and men, as beings far superior to the rest of the creation.

Angels are either good or evil, Luke ix. 26. viii. 2. for it appears that many of them revolted from God of their own accord before the fall of man. John viii. 44. *he abode not in the truth, because there is no truth in him: when he speaketh a lie, he speaketh of his own, for he is a liar and the father of it.* 2 Pet. ii. 4. *God spared not the angels that sinned.* Jude 6. *the angels which kept not their first estate.* 1 John iii. 8. *the devil sinneth from the beginning.* Psal. cvi. 37. *they sacrificed unto devils.*

Some are of opinion that the good angels are now upheld, not so much by their own strength, as by the grace of God. 1 Tim. v. 21. *the elect angels,* that is, who have not revolted. Eph. i. 10. *that he might gather together in one all things in Christ, both which are in heaven and which are on earth.* Job iv. 18. *his angels he charged with folly.* See also xv. 15. Hence arises, in their opinion, the delighted interest which the angels take in the mystery of

man's salvation; 1 Pet. i. 12. *which things the angels desire to look into.* Eph. iii. 10. *that now unto the principalities and powers in heavenly places might be known by the church the manifold wisdom of God.* Luke ii. 13, 14. *a multitude of the heavenly host praising God,* namely, on account of the birth of Christ. xv. 10. *there is joy in the presence of the angels of God over one sinner that repenteth.* They assign the same reason for their worshipping Christ. Heb. i. 6. *let all the angels of God worship him.* Matt. iv. 11. *angels came and ministered unto him.* Philipp. ii. 10. *at the name of Jesus every knee should bow, of things in heaven—.* 2 Thess. i. 7. *the Lord Jesus shall be revealed from heaven with his mighty angels.* 1 Pet. iii. 22. *angels being made subject unto him.* Rev. v. 11, 12. *worthy is the Lamb that was slain.* It seems, however, more agreeable to reason, to suppose that the good angels are upheld by their own strength no less than man himself was before his fall;—that they are called *elect,* in the sense of beloved, or excellent;—that it is not from any interest of their own, but from their love to mankind, that they desire to look into the mystery of our salvation;—that they are not comprehended in the covenant of reconciliation; —that, finally, they are included under Christ as their head, not as their Redeemer.

For the rest, they are represented as standing dispersed around the throne of God in the capacity of ministering agents. Deut. xxxiii. 2. *he came with ten thousands of saints.* 1 Kings xxii. 19. *I saw Jehovah sitting on his throne, and all the host of heaven standing by him on his right hand and on his left.* Job. i. 6. *there was a day when the sons of God came to present themselves before Jehovah.* See also ii. 1. Dan. vii. 10. *ten thousand times ten thousand stood before him.* Matt. xviii. 10. *their angels do always behold the face of my Father which is in heaven.* Luke i. 19. *I am Gabriel who stand in the presence of God.*

Praising God. Job xxxviii. 7. *all the sons of God shouted for joy.* Psal. cxlviii. 2. *praise ye him, all his angels.* Neh. ix. 6. *the host of heaven worshippeth thee.* Isai. vi. 3. *one cried unto another and said, Holy, holy, holy.* See also Rev. iv. 8. vii. 11. *the angels fall before the throne on their faces.*

They are obedient to God in all respects.

Gen. xxviii. 12. *behold the angels of God ascending and descending on it.* Psal. ciii. 20. *his angels . . . that do his commandments.* Zech. i. 10. *these are they whom Jehovah hath sent to walk to and fro through the earth.*

Their ministry relates especially to believers. Heb. i. 14. *are they not all ministering spirits, sent forth to minister for them who shall be heirs of salvation?.* Psal. xxxiv. 7. *the angel of Jehovah encampeth round about them that fear him.* xci. 11. *he shall give his angels charge over thee.* Isai. lxiii. 9. *the angel of his presence saved them.* Matt. xviii. 10. *their angels do always behold the face of my Father.* xiii. 41. *the Son of man shall send forth his angels, and they shall gather out of his kingdom all things that offend.* xxiv. 31. *they shall gather together his elect from the four winds.* Acts xii. 15. *it is his angel.* 1 Cor. xi. 10. *for this cause ought the woman to have power on her head because of the angels,* namely, as some thing, (and numerous examples in confirmation of their opinion are not wanting) those angels whose office it was to be present at the religious assemblies of believers.

Seven of these, in particular, are described as traversing the earth in the execution of their ministry. Zech. iv. 10. *those seven are the eyes of Jehovah which run to and fro through the whole earth.* Rev. v. 6. *which are the seven Spirits of God sent forth into all the earth.* See also i. 4. and iv. 5.

It appears also probable that there are certain angels appointed to preside over nations, kingdoms, and particular districts. Dan. iv. 13, 17. *this matter is by the decree of the watchers.* xii. 1. *Michael . . . the great prince which standeth for the children of thy people.* x. 13. *I remained there with the kings of Persia.* 2 Pet. ii. 11. *whereas angels, which are greater in power and might, bring not railing accusation against them before the Lord.* Gen. iii. 24. *to keep the way of the tree of life.*

They are sometimes sent from heaven as messengers of the divine vengeance, to punish the sins of men. They destroy cities and nations. Gen. xix. 13. 2 Sam. xxiv. 16. 1 Chron. xxi. 16. *David saw the angel of Jehovah . . . having a drawn sword in his hand stretched out over Jerusalem.* They lay waste whole armies with unexpected destruction. 2 Kings xix. 35. Compare also other passages to the same effect. Hence they are frequently represented as making their appearance in the shape of an armed host. Gen. xxxii. 1, 2. *this is God's host.* Josh. v. 15. *the captain of the host of Jehovah.* 2 Kings vi. 17. *the mountain was full of horses and chariots of fire.* Psal. lxviii. 17. *the chariots of God are twenty thousand.* Luke ii. 13. *a multitude of the heavenly host.*

Angels are also described Isai. vi. Hos. i. 7. Matt. xxviii. 2, 3. Rev. x. 1.

There appears to be one who presides over the rest of the good angels, to whom the name of Michael is often given. Josh. vi. 14. *as captain of the host of Jehovah am I come.* Dan. xi. 13. *Michael, one of the chief princes, came to help me.* xii. 1. *Michael shall stand up, the great prince.* Rev. xii. 7, 8. *Michael and his angels fought against the dragon.* It is generally thought that Michael is Christ. But Christ vanquished the devil, and trampled him under foot singly; Michael, the leader of the angels, is introduced in the capacity of a hostile commander waging war with the prince of the devils, the armies on both sides being drawn out in battle array, and separating after a doubtful conflict. Rev. xii. 7, 8. Jude also says of the same angel, *when contending with the devil he disputed about the body of Moses, he durst not bring against him a railing accusation,*—which would be an improper expression to use with reference to Christ, especially if he be God. 1 Thess. iv. 16. *the Lord himself shall descend from heaven with the voice of the archangel.* Besides, it seems strange that an apostle of Christ, in revealing things till then so new and unheard-of concerning his master, should express himself thus obscurely, and should even shadow the person of Christ under a difference of name.

The good angels do not look into all the secret things of God, as the Papists pretend; some things indeed they know by revelation, and others by means of the excellent intelligence with which they are gifted; there is much, however, of which they are ignorant. An angel is introduced inquiring Dan. viii. 13. *how long shall be the vision?* xii. 6. *how long shall it be to the end of these wonders?* Matt. xxiv. 36. *of that day knoweth no man, no not even the angels in heaven.* Eph. iii. 10. *to the intent that now unto the principalities and powers in heavenly places might be known by the church the manifold wisdom of God.* Rev. v. 3. *no man in heaven was able to open the book.*

The evil angels are reserved for punishment. Matt. viii. 29. *art thou come hither to torment us before the time?* 2 Pet. ii. 4. *God cast them down to hell, and delivered them into chains of darkness, to be reserved unto judgement.* Jude 6. *he hath reserved them in everlasting chains under darkness unto the judgement of the great day.* 1 Cor. vi. 3. *know ye not that we shall judge angels?* Matt. xxv. 41. *everlasting fire, prepared for the devil and his angels.* Rev. xx. 10. *they shall be tormented for ever and ever.*

They are sometimes, however, permitted to wander throughout the whole earth, the air, and heaven itself, to execute the judgements of God. Job i. 7. *from going to and fro in the earth.* 1 Sam. xvi. 15. *the Spirit of Jehovah departed from Saul, and an evil spirit from Jehovah troubled him.* 1 Pet. v. 8. *the devil, as a roaring lion, walketh about.* John xii. 31. *the prince of this world.* 2 Cor. iv. 4. *the god of this world.* Matt. xii. 43. *he walketh through dry places.* Eph. ii. 2. *according to the prince of the power of the air.* vi. 12. *against spiritual wickedness in high places.* They are even admitted into the presence of God. Job i. 6. ii. 1. 1 Kings xxii. 21. *there came forth a spirit, and stood before Jehovah.* Zech. iii. 1. *he showed me Joshua the high priest standing before the angel of Jehovah, and Satan standing at his right hand to resist him.* Luke x. 18. *I beheld Satan as lightning fall from heaven.* Rev. xii. 12. *woe to the inhabiters of the earth, for the devil is come down unto you.* Their proper place, however, is the bottomless pit, from which they cannot escape without permission. Luke viii. 31. *they besought him that he would not command them to go out into the deep.* Matt. xii. 43. *he walketh through dry places, seeking rest, and findeth none.* Mark v. 10. *he besought him much that he would not send them away out of the country.* Rev. xx. 3. *and cast him into the bottomless pit, and shut him up.* Nor can they do anything without the command of God. Job i. 12. *Jehovah said unto Satan, Behold, all that he hath is in thy power.*

Matt. viii. 31. *suffer us to go away into the herd of swine.* Rev. xx. 2. *he laid hold on the dragon . . . and bound him a thousand years.*

Their knowledge is great, but such as tends rather to aggravate than diminish their misery; so that they utterly despair of their salvation. Matt. viii. 29. *what have we to do with thee, Jesus, thou Son of God? art thou come hither to torment us before the time?* See also Luke iv. 34. James ii. 19. *the devils believe and tremble,* knowing that they are reserved for punishment, as has been shown.

The devils also have their prince. Matt. xii. 24. *Beelzebub, the prince of the devils.* See also Luke xi. 15. Matt. xxv. 41. *the devil and his angels.* Rev. xii. 9. *the great dragon was cast out . . . and his angels.* They retain likewise their respective ranks. Col. ii. 15. *having spoiled principalities and powers.* Eph. vi. 12. *against principalities, against powers.* Their leader is the author of all wickedness, and the opponent of all good. Job i. and ii. Zech. iii. 1. *Satan.* John viii. 44. *the father of lies.* 1 Thess. ii. 18. *Satan hindered us.* Acts v. 3. *Satan hath filled thine heart.* Rev. xx. 3, 8. *that he should deceive the nations no more.* Eph. ii. 2. *the spirit that now worketh in the children of disobedience.* Hence he has obtained many names corresponding to his actions. He is frequently called *Satan,* that is, an enemy or adversary, Job i. 6. 1 Chron. xxi. 1. *the great dragon, that old serpent, the devil,* that is, the false accuser, Rev. xii. 9. *the accuser of the brethren,* v. 10. *the unclean spirit,* Matt. xii. 43. *the tempter,* iv. 3. *Abaddon, Apollyon,* that is, the destroyer, Rev. ix. 11. *a great red dragon,* xii. 3.

CHAP. X.

OF THE

SPECIAL GOVERNMENT OF MAN

BEFORE THE FALL,

INCLUDING

THE INSTITUTIONS OF THE SABBATH

AND OF MARRIAGE.

The Providence of God as regards mankind, relates to man either in his state of rectitude, or since his fall.

With regard to that which relates to man in his state of rectitude, God, having placed him in the garden of Eden, and furnished him with whatever was calculated to make life happy, commanded him, as a test of his obedience, to refrain from eating of the single tree of knowledge of good and evil, under penalty of death if he should disregard the injunction. Gen. i. 28. *subdue the earth, and have dominion—*. ii. 15–17. *he put him into the garden of Eden . . . of every tree in the garden thou mayest freely eat; but in the day that thou eatest of the tree of the knowledge of good and evil, thou shalt surely die.*

This is sometimes called *the covenant of works,* though it does not appear from any passage of Scripture to have been either a covenant, or of works. No works whatever are required of Adam; a particular act only is forbidden. It was necessary that something should be forbidden or commanded as a test of fidelity, and that an act in its own nature indifferent, in order that man's obedience might be thereby manifested. For since it was the disposition of man to do what was right, as a being naturally good and holy, it was not necessary that he should be bound by the obligation of a covenant to perform that to which he was of himself inclined; nor would he have given any proof of obedience by the performance of works to which he was led by a natural impulse, independently of the divine command. Not to mention, that no command, whether proceeding from God or from a magistrate, can properly be called a covenant, even where rewards and punishments are attached to it; but rather an exercise of jurisdiction.

The tree of knowledge of good and evil was not a sacrament, as it is generally called; for a sacrament is a thing to be used, not abstained from: but a pledge, as it were, and memorial of obedience.

It was called the tree of knowledge of good and evil from the event; for since Adam tasted it, we not only know evil, but we know good only by means of evil. For it is by evil that virtue is chiefly exercised, and shines with greater brightness.

The tree of life, in my opinion, ought not to be considered so much a sacrament, as a symbol of eternal life, or rather perhaps the nutriment by which that life is sustained. Gen. iii. 22. *lest he take also of the tree of life, and eat, and live for ever.* Rev. ii. 7. *to him that overcometh, will I give to eat of the tree of life.*

Seeing, however, that man was made in the image of God, and had the whole law of nature so implanted and innate in him, that he needed no precept to enforce its observance, it follows, that if he received any additional commands, whether respecting the tree of knowledge, or the institution of marriage, these commands formed no part of the law of nature, which is sufficient of itself to teach whatever is agreeable to right reason, that is to say, whatever is intrinsically good. Such commands must therefore have been founded on what is called positive right, whereby God, or any one invested with lawful power, commands or forbids what is in itself neither good nor bad, and what therefore would not have been obligatory on any one, had there been no law to enjoin or prohibit it. With regard to the Sabbath, it is clear that God hallowed it to himself, and dedicated it to rest, in remembrance of the consummation of his work; Gen. ii. 2, 3. Exod. xxxi. 17. Whether its institution was ever made known to Adam, or whether any commandment relative to its observance was given previous to the delivery of the law on Mount Sinai, much less whether any such was given before the fall of man, cannot be ascertained, Scripture being silent on the subject. The most probable supposition is, that Moses, who seems to have written the book of Genesis much later than the promulgation of the law, inserted this sentence from the fourth commandment, into what appeared a suitable place for it; where an opportunity was afforded for reminding the Israelites, by a natural and easy transition, of the reason assigned by God, many ages after the event itself, for his command with regard to the observance of the Sabbath by the covenanted people. An instance of a similar insertion occurs Exod. xvi. 33, 34. *Moses said unto Aaron, Take a pot, and put an omer full of manna therein . . . so Aaron laid it up;* which however did not take place till long afterwards. The injunction respecting the celebration of the Sabbath in the wilderness, Exod. xvi. a short time previous to the delivery of the law, namely, that no one should go out to gather manna on the seventh morning, because God had said that he would not rain it from heaven on that day, seems rather to have been intended as a preparatory notice, the groundwork, as it were, of a law for the Israelites, to be delivered shortly afterwards in a clearer manner; they having been previously ignorant of the mode of observing the Sabbath. Compare v. 5. with v. 22–30. For the rulers of the congregation, who ought to have been better acquainted than the rest with the commandment of the Sabbath, if any such institution then existed, wondered why the people gathered twice as much on the sixth day, and appealed to Moses; who then, as if announcing something new, proclaimed to them that the morrow would be the Sabbath. After which, as if he had already related in what manner the Sabbath was for the first time observed, he proceeds, v. 30. *so the people rested on the seventh day.*

That the Israelites had not so much as heard of the Sabbath before this time, seems to be confirmed by several passages of the prophets. Ezek. xx. 10–12. *I caused them to go forth out of the land of Egypt, and brought them into the wilderness; and I gave them my statutes, and showed them my judgements, . . . moreover also I gave them my sabbaths, to be a sign between me and them, that they might know that I am Jehovah that sanctify them.* Neh. ix. 13, 14. *thou camest down also upon mount Sinai . . . and gavest them right judgements . . . and madest known unto them thy holy sabbath, and commandedst them precepts, statutes and laws, by the hand of Moses thy servant.* This subject, however, will come again under discussion, Book II. Chap. vii.

With regard to marriage, it is clear that it was instituted, if not commanded, at the creation, and that it consisted in the mutual love, society, help, and comfort of the husband and wife, though with a reservation of superior rights to the husband. Gen. ii. 18. *it is not good that the man should be alone; I will make him an help meet for him.* 1 Cor. xi. 7–9. *for a man . . . is the image of the glory of God, but the woman is the glory of the man: for the man is not of the woman, but the woman of the man; neither was the man created for the woman, but the woman for the man.* The power of the husband was even increased after the fall. Gen. iii. 16. *thy desire shall be to thy husband, and he shall rule over thee.*

Therefore the word בַּעַל in the Hebrew signifies both husband and lord. Thus Sarah is represented as calling her husband Abraham *lord,* 1 Pet. iii. 6. 1 Tim. ii. 12–14. *I suffer not a woman to teach, nor to usurp authority over the man, but to be in silence: for Adam was first formed, then Eve; and Adam was not deceived, but the woman being deceived, was in the transgression.*

Marriage, therefore, is a most intimate connection of man with woman, ordained by God, for the purpose either of the procreation of children, or of the relief and solace of life. Hence it is said, Gen. ii. 24. *therefore shall a man leave his father and his mother, and shall cleave unto his wife, and they shall be one flesh.* This is neither a law nor a commandment, but an effect or natural consequence of that most intimate union which would have existed between them in the perfect state of man; nor is the passage intended to serve any other purpose, than to account for the origin of families.

In the definition which I have given, I have not said, in compliance with the common opinion, *of one man with one woman,* lest I should by implication charge the holy patriarchs and pillars of our faith, Abraham, and the others who had more than one wife at the same time, with habitual fornication and adultery; and lest I should be forced to exclude from the sanctuary of God as spurious, the holy offspring which sprang from them, yea, the whole of the sons of Israel, for whom the sanctuary itself was made. For it is said, Deut. xxiii. 2. *a bastard shall not enter into the congregation of Jehovah, even to his tenth generation.* Either therefore polygamy is a true marriage, or all children born in that state are spurious; which would include the whole race of Jacob, the twelve holy tribes chosen by God. But as such an assertion would be absurd in the extreme, not to say impious, and as it is the height of injustice, as well as an example of most dangerous tendency in religion, to account as sin what is not such in reality; it appears to me, that, so far from the question respecting the lawfulness of polygamy being a trivial, it is of the highest importance that it should be decided.

Those who deny its lawfulness, attempt to prove their position from Gen. ii. 24. *a man shall cleave unto his wife, and they shall be one flesh,* compared with Matt. xix. 5. *they twain shall be one flesh.* A man shall cleave, they say, to his wife, not to his wives, and they twain, and no more, shall be one flesh. This is certainly ingenious; and I therefore subjoin the passage in Exod. xx. 17. *thou shalt not covet thy neighbour's house, nor his man-servant, nor his maid-servant, nor his ox, nor his ass:* whence it would follow that no one had more than a single house, a single man-servant, a single maid-servant, a single ox or ass. It would be ridiculous to argue, that it is not said houses, but house, not man-servants, but man-servant, not even neighbours, but neighbour; as if it were not the general custom, in laying down commandments of this kind, to use the singular number, not in a numerical sense, but as designating the species of the thing intended. With regard to the phrase, *they twain,* and not more, *shall be one flesh,* it is to be observed, first, that the context refers to the husband and that wife only whom he was seeking to divorce, without intending any allusion to the number of his wives, whether one or more. Secondly, marriage is in the nature of a relation; and to one relation there can be no more than two parties. In the same sense therefore as if a man has many sons, his paternal relation towards them all is manifold, but towards each individually is single and complete in itself; by parity of reasoning, if a man has many wives, the relation which he bears to each will not be less perfect in itself, nor will the husband be less *one flesh* with each of them, than if he had only one wife. Thus it might be properly said of Abraham, with regard to Sarah and Hagar respectively, *these twain were one flesh.* And with good reason; for whoever consorts with harlots, however many in number, is still said to be *one flesh* with each; 1 Cor. vi. 16. *what, know ye not, that he which is joined to an harlot is one body? for two, saith he, shall be one flesh.* The expression may therefore be applied as properly to the husband who has many wives, as to him who has only

one. Hence it follows that the commandment in question (though in fact it is no commandment at all, as has been shown) contains nothing against polygamy, either in the way of direct prohibition or implied censure; unless we are to suppose that the law of God, as delivered by Moses, was at variance with his prior declarations; or that, though the passage in question had been frequently inspected by a multitude of priests, and Levites, and prophets, men of all ranks, of holiest lives and most acceptable to God, the fury of their passions was such as to hurry them by a blind impulse into habitual fornication; for to this supposition are we reduced, if there be anything in the present precept which renders polygamy incompatible with lawful marriage.

Another text from which the unlawfulness of polygamy is maintained, is Lev. xviii. 18. *neither shalt thou take a wife to her sister, to vex her, to uncover her nakedness, beside the other in her life time.* Here Junius translates the passage *mulierem unam ad alteram,* instead of *mulierem ad sororem suam,* in order that from this forced and inadmissible interpretation he may elicit an argument against polygamy. In drawing up a law, as in composing a definition, it is necessary that the most exact and appropriate words should be used, and that they should be interpreted not in their metaphorical, but in their proper signification. He says, indeed, that the same words are found in the same sense in other passages. This is true; but it is only where the context precludes the possibility of any ambiguity, as in Gen. xxvi. 31. *juraverunt vir fratri suo,* that is, *alteri, they sware one to another.* No one would infer from this passage that Isaac was the brother of Abimelech; nor would any one, on the other hand, entertain a doubt that the passage in Leviticus was intended as a prohibition against taking a wife to her sister; particularly as the preceding verses of this chapter treat of the degrees of affinity to which intermarriage is forbidden. Moreover, this would be *to uncover her nakedness,* the evil against which the law in question was intended to guard; whereas the caution would be unnecessary in the case of taking another wife not related or allied to the former; for no nakedness would be thereby uncovered.

Lastly, why is the clause *in her life time* added? For there could be no doubt of its being lawful after her death to marry another who was neither related nor allied to her, though it might be questionable whether it were lawful to marry a wife's sister. It is objected, that marriage with a wife's sister is forbidden by analogy in the sixteenth verse, and that therefore a second prohibition was unnecessary. I answer, first, that there is in reality no analogy between the two passages; for that by marrying a brother's wife, the brother's nakedness is uncovered; whereas by marrying a wife's sister, it is not a sister's nakedness, but only that of a kinswoman by marriage, which is uncovered. Besides, if nothing were to be prohibited which had been before prohibited by analogy, why is marriage with a mother forbidden, when marriage with a father had been already declared unlawful? or why marriage with a mother's sister, when marriage with a father's sister had been prohibited? If this reasoning be allowed, it follows that more than half the laws relating to incest are unnecessary. Lastly, whereas the prevention of enmity is alleged as the principal motive for the law before us, it is obvious, that if the intention had been to condemn polygamy, reasons of a much stronger kind might have been urged from the nature of the original institution, as was done in the ordinance of the Sabbath.

A third passage which is advanced, Deut. xvii. 17. is so far from condemning polygamy, either in a king, or in any one else, that it expressly allows it; and only imposes the same restraints upon this condition which are laid upon the multiplication of horses, or the accumulation of treasure; as will appear from the seventeenth and eighteenth verses.

Except the three passages which are thus irrelevantly adduced, not a trace appears of the interdiction of polygamy throughout the whole law; nor even in any of the prophets, who were at once the rigid interpreters of the law, and the habitual reprovers of the vices of the people. The only shadow of an exception occurs in a passage of Malachi, the last of the prophets, which some consider as decisive against polygamy. It would be indeed a late and postliminous enactment, if that were for the first time prohibited after the Babylonish captivity which ought to have been prohibited many ages before. For if it had been really a sin, how could it have escaped the reprehension of so many prophets who preceded him? We may safely conclude that if polygamy be not forbidden in the law, neither is it forbidden here; for Malachi was not the author of a new law. Let us however see the words themselves as translated by Junius, ii. 15. *Nonne unum effecit? quamvis reliqui spiritus ipsi essent: quid autem unum?* It would be rash and unreasonable indeed, if, on the authority of so obscure a passage, and one which has been tortured and twisted by different interpreters into such a variety of meanings, we were to form a conclusion on so important a subject, and to impose it upon others as an article of faith. But whatever be the signification of the words *nonne unum effecit,* what do they prove? are we, for the sake of drawing an inference against polygamy, to understand the phrase thus—*did not he make one woman?* But the gender, and even the case, are at variance with this interpretation; for nearly all the other commentators render the words as follows: *annon unus fecit? et residuum spiritus ipsi? et quid ille unus?* We ought not therefore to draw any conclusion from a passage like the present in behalf of a doctrine which is either not mentioned elsewhere, or only in doubtful terms; but rather conclude that the prophet's design was to reprove a practice which the whole of Scripture concurs in reproving, and which forms the principal subject of the very chapter in question, v. 11–16. namely, marriage with *the daughter of a strange god;* a corruption very prevalent among the Jews of that time, as we learn from Ezra and Nehemiah.

With regard to the words of Christ, Matt. v. 32. and xix. 5. the passage from Gen. ii. 24. is repeated not for the purpose of condemning polygamy, but of reproving the unrestrained liberty of divorce, which is a very different thing; nor can the words be made to apply to any other subject without evident violence to their meaning. For the argument which is deduced from Matt. v. 32. that if a man who marries another after putting away his first wife, committeth adultery, much more must he commit adultery who retains the first and marries another, ought itself to be repudiated as an illegitimate conclusion. For in the first place, it is the divine precepts themselves that are obligatory, not the consequences deduced from them by human reasoning; for what appears a reasonable inference to one individual, may not be equally obvious to another of similar discernment. Secondly, he who puts away his wife and marries another, is not said to commit adultery because he marries another, but because in consequence of his marriage with another he does not retain his former wife, to whom also he owed the performance of conjugal duties; whence it is expressly said, ark x. 11. *he committeth adultery against her.* That he is in a condition to perform his conjugal duties to the one, after having taken another to her, is shown by God himself, Exod. xxi. 10. *if he take him another wife, her food, her raiment, and her duty of marriage shall he not diminish.* It cannot be supposed that the divine forethought intended to provide for adultery.

Nor is it allowable to argue, from 1 Cor. vii. 2. *let every man have his own wife,* that therefore none should have more than one; for the meaning of the precept is, that every man should have his own wife to himself, not that he should have but one wife. That bishops and elders should have no more than one wife is explicitly enjoined 1 Tim. iii. 2. and Tit. i. 6. *he must be the husband of one wife,* in order probably that they may discharge with greater diligence the ecclesiastical duties which they have undertaken. The command itself, however, is a sufficient proof that polygamy was not forbidden to the rest, and that it was common in the church at that time.

Lastly, in answer to what is urged from 1 Cor. vii. 4. *likewise also the husband hath not power of his own body, but the wife,* it is easy to reply, as was done above, that the word *wife* in this passage is used with reference to the species, and not to the number. Nor can the power of the wife over the body of her husband be different now from what it was under the law, where it is called עוֹבה , Exod. xxi. 10. and signifies *her stated* times, which St. Paul

expresses in the present chapter by the phrase, *her due benevolence.* With regard to what is *due,* the Hebrew word is sufficiently explicit.

On the other hand, the following passages clearly admit the lawfulness of polygamy. Exod. xxi. 10. *if he take him another wife, her food, her raiment, and her duty of marriage shall he not diminish.* Deut. xvii. 17. *neither shall he multiply wives to himself, that his heart turn not away.* Would the law have been so loosely worded, if it had not been allowable to take more wives than one at the same time? Who would venture to subjoin as an inference from this language, therefore let him have one only? In such case, since it is said in the preceding verse, *he shall not multiply horses to himself,* it would be necessary to subjoin there also, therefore he shall have one horse only. Nor do we want any proof to assure us, that the first institution of marriage was intended to bind the prince equally with the people; if therefore it permits only one wife, it permits no more even to the prince. But the reason given for the law is this, *that his heart turn not away;* a danger which would arise if he were to marry many, and especially strange women, as Solomon afterwards did. Now if the present law had been intended merely as a confirmation and vindication of the primary institution of marriage, nothing could have been more appropriate than to have recited the institution itself in this place, and not to have advanced that reason alone which has been mentioned.

Let us hear the words of God himself, the author of the law, and the best interpreter of his own will. 2 Sam. xii. 8. *I gave thee thy master's wives into thy bosom . . . and if that had been too little, I would moreover have given unto thee such and such things.* Here there can be no subterfuge; God gave him wives, he gave them to the man whom he loved, as one among a number of great benefits; he would have given him more, if these had not been enough. Besides, the very argument which God uses towards David, is of more force when applied to the gift of wives, than to any other,—thou oughtest at least to have abstained from the wife of another person, not so much because I had given thee thy master's house, or thy master's kingdom, as because I had given thee the wives of the king. Beza indeed objects, that David herein committed incest, namely, with the wives of his father-in-law. But he had forgotten what is indicated by Esther ii. 12, 13. that the kings of Israel had two houses for the women, one appointed for the virgins, the other for the concubines, and that it was the former and not the latter which were given to David. This appears also from 1 Kings i. 4. *the king knew her not.* Cantic. vi. 8. *there are fourscore concubines, and virgins without number.* At the same time, it might be said with perfect propriety that God had given him his master's wives, even supposing that he had only given him as many in number and of the same description, though not the very same; even as he gave him, not indeed the identical house and retinue of his master, but one equally magnificent and royal.

It is not wonderful, therefore, that what the authority of the law, and the voice of God himself has sanctioned, should be alluded to by the holy prophets in their inspired hymns as a thing lawful and honourable. Psal. xlv. 9. (which is entitled *A song of loves*) *kings' daughters were among thy honourable women.* v. 14. *the virgins her companions that follow her shall be brought unto thee.* Nay, the words of this very song are quoted by the apostle to the Hebrews, i. 8. *unto the Son he saith, Thy throne, O God,* &c. as the words wherein God the Father himself addresses the Son, and in which his divinity is asserted more clearly than in any other passage. Would it have been proper for God the Father to speak by the mouth of harlots, and to manifest his holy Son to mankind as God in the amatory songs of adulteresses? Thus also in Cantic. vi. 8–10. the queens and concubines are evidently mentioned with honour, and are all without distinction considered worthy of celebrating the praises of the bride: *there are threescore queens, and fourscore concubines, and virgins without number . . . the daughters saw her and blessed her; yea, the queens and the concubines, and they praised her.* Nor must we omit 2 Chron. xxiv. 2, 3. *Joash did that which was right in the sight of the Lord all the days of Jehoiada the priest: and Jehoiada took for him two wives.* For the two clauses are not placed in contrast, or disjoined from each other, but it is said in one and the same connection that under the guidance of Jehoiada he did that which was right, and that by the authority of the same individual he married two wives. This is contrary to the usual practice in the eulogies of the kings, where, if to the general character anything blameable be subjoined, it is expressly excepted; 1 Kings xv. 5. *save only in the matter of Uriah the Hittite.* v. 11, 14. *and Asa did that which was right . . . but the high places were not removed: nevertheless Asa's heart was perfect.* Since therefore the right conduct of Joash is mentioned in unqualified terms, in conjunction with his double marriage, it is evident that the latter was not considered matter of censure; for the sacred historian would not have neglected so suitable an opportunity of making the customary exception, if there had really been anything which deserved disapprobation.

Moreover, God himself, in an allegorical fiction, Ezek. xxiii. 4. represents himself as having espoused two wives, Aholah and Aholibah; a mode of speaking which he would by no means have employed, especially at such length, even in a parable, nor indeed have taken on himself such a character at all, if the practice which it implied had been intrinsically dishonourable or shameful.

On what grounds, however, can a practice be considered dishonourable or shameful, which is prohibited to no one even under the gospel? for that dispensation annuls none of the merely civil regulations which existed previous to its introduction. It is only enjoined that elders and deacons should be chosen from such as were husbands of one wife, 1 Tim. iii. 2. and Tit. i. 6. This implies, not that to be the husband of more than one wife would be a sin, for in that case the restriction would have been equally imposed on all; but that, in proportion as they were less entangled in domestic affairs, they would be more at leisure for the business of the church. Since therefore polygamy is interdicted in this passage to the ministers of the church alone, and that not on account of any sinfulness in the practice, and since none of the other members are precluded from it either here or elsewhere, it follows that it was permitted, as abovesaid, to all the remaining members of the church, and that it was adopted by many without offence.

Lastly, I argue as follows from Heb. xiii. 4. Polygamy is either marriage, or fornication, or adultery; the apostle recognizes no fourth state. Reverence for so many patriarchs who were polygamists will, I trust, deter any one from considering it as fornication or adultery; for *whoremongers and adulterers God will judge;* whereas the patriarchs were the objects of his especial favour, as he himself witnesses. If then polygamy be marriage properly so called, it is also lawful and honourable, according to the same apostle: *marriage is honourable in all, and the bed undefiled.*

It appears to me sufficiently established by the above arguments that polygamy is allowed by the law of God; lest however any doubt should remain, I will subjoin abundant examples of men whose holiness renders them fit patterns for imitation, and who are among the lights of our faith. Foremost I place Abraham, the father of all the faithful, and of the holy seed, Gen. xvi. 1, &c. Jacob, chap. xxx. and, if I mistake not, Moses, Numb. xii. 1. *for he had married [a Cushite,* Marginal Translation, or] *an Ethiopian woman.* It is not likely that the wife of Moses, who had been so often spoken of before by her proper name of Zipporah, should now be called by the new title of a Cushite; or that the anger of Aaron and Miriam should at this time be suddenly kindled, because Moses forty years before had married Zipporah; nor would they have acted thus scornfully towards one whom the whole house of Israel had gone out to meet on her arrival with her father Jethro. If then he married the Cushite during the lifetime of Zipporah, his conduct in this particular received the express approbation of God himself, who moreover punished with severity the unnatural opposition of Aaron and his sister. Next I place Gideon, that signal example of faith and piety, Judg. viii. 30, 31. and Elkanah, a rigid Levite, the father of Samuel; who was so far from believing himself less acceptable to God on account of his double marriage, that he took with him his two wives every year to the sacrifices and annual worship, into the immediate presence of God; nor was he therefore reproved, but went home blessed with Samuel, a child of excellent promise, 1 Sam. ii. 10. Passing over several other examples, though illustrious, such as Caleb, 1 Chron. ii. 46, 48. vii. 1, 4. the sons of Issachar, in number *six and thirty thousand men, for they had many wives and sons,* contrary to the modern European practice, where in many places the land is suffered to remain uncultivated for want of population; and also Manasseh, the son of Joseph, 1 Chron. vii. 14. I come to the prophet David, whom God loved beyond all men, and who took two wives, besides Michal; and this not in a time of pride and prosperity, but when he was almost bowed down by adversity, and when, as we learn from many of the psalms, he was entirely occupied in the study of the word of God, and in the right regulation of his conduct. 1 Sam. xxv. 42, 43. and afterwards, 2 Sam. v. 12, 13. *David perceived that Jehovah had established him king over Israel, and that he had exalted his kingdom for his people Israel's sake: and David took him more concubines and wives out of Jerusalem.* Such were the motives, such the honourable and holy thoughts whereby he was influenced, namely, by the consideration of God's kindness towards him for his people's sake. His heavenly and prophetic understanding saw not in that primitive institution what we in our blindness fancy we discern so clearly; nor did he hesitate to proclaim in the supreme council of the nation the pure and honourable motives to which, as he trusted, his children born in polygamy owed their existence. 1 Chron. xxviii. 5. *of all my sons, for Jehovah hath given me many sons, he hath chosen,* &c. I say nothing of Solomon, notwithstanding his wisdom, because he seems to have exceeded due bounds; although it is not objected to him that he had taken many wives, but that he had married strange women; 1 Kings xi. 1. Nehem. xiii. 26. His son Rehoboam *desired many wives,* not in the time of his iniquity, but during the three years in which he is said to have walked in the way of David, 2 Chron. xi. 17, 21, 23. Of Joash mention has already been made; who was induced to take two wives, not by licentious passion, or the wanton desires incident to uncontrolled power, but by the sanction and advice of a most wise and holy man, Jehoiada the priest. Who can believe, either that so many men of the highest character should have sinned through ignorance for so many ages; or that their hearts should have been so hardened; or that God should have tolerated such conduct in his people? Let therefore the rule received among theologians have the same weight here as in other cases: "The practice of the saints is the best interpretation of the commandments."

It is the peculiar province of God to make marriage prosperous and happy. Prov. xix. 14. *a prudent wife is from Jehovah.* xviii. 22. *whoso findeth a wife, findeth a good thing, and obtaineth favour of Jehovah.*

The consent of parents, if living, should not be wanting. Exod. xxii. 17. *if his father utterly refuse to give her unto him—.* Deut. vii. 3. *thy daughter thou shalt not give unto his son.* Jer. xxix. 6. *take wives for your sons.* But the mutual consent of the parties themselves is naturally the first and most important requisite; for there can be no love or good will, and consequently no marriage, without mutual consent.

In order that marriage may be valid, the consent must be free from every kind of fraud, especially in respect of chastity. Deut. xxii. 20, 21, 23. It will be obvious to every sensible person that maturity of age is requisite.

The degrees of affinity which constitute incest are to be determined by the law of God, Lev. xviii. Deut. xxvii. and not by ecclesiastical canons or legal decrees. We are moreover to interpret the text in its plain and obvious meaning, without attempting to elicit more from it than it really contains. To be wise beyond this point, savours of superstitious folly, and a spurious preciseness.

It is also necessary that the parties should be of one mind in matters of religion. Under the law this precept was understood as applying to marriages already contracted, as well as those in contemplation. Exod. xxxiv. 15, 16. Deut. vii. 3, 4. compared with Ezra x. 11, &c. and Nehem. xiii. 23, 30. A similar provision was made under the gospel for preventing the contraction of any marriage where a difference of religious opinion might exist: 1 Cor. vii. 39. *she is at liberty to be married to whom she will, only in the Lord.* 2 Cor. vi. 14. *be ye not unequally yoked together with unbelievers.* But if the marriage be already contracted, it is not to be dissolved, while any hope remains of doing good to the unbeliever. 1 Cor. vii. 12. For the rest, what kind of issue generally follows such marriages may be seen in the case of the antediluvian world, Gen. vi. of Solomon, 1 Kings xi. 1, &c. of Ahab, xxi. 25. of Jehoshaphat, who gave his son Jehoram a wife of the daughters of Ahab, 2 Kings viii.

The *form* of marriage consists in the mutual exercise of benevolence, love, help, and solace between the espoused parties, as the institution itself, or its definition, indicates.

The end of marriage is nearly the same with the form. Its proper fruit is the procreation of children; but since Adam's fall, the provision of a remedy against incontinency has become in some degree a secondary end. 1 Cor. vii. 2. Hence marriage is not a command binding on all, but only on those who are unable to live with chastity out of this state. Matt. xix. 11. *all men cannot receive this saying.*

Marriage is honourable in itself, and prohibited to no order of men; wherefore the Papists act contrary to religion in excluding the ministers of the church from this rite. Heb. xiii. 4. *marriage is honourable in all.* Gen. ii. 24. 1 Cor. ix. 5. *have we not power to lead about a sister, a wife, as well as other apostles?* 1 Tim. iii. 2. *a bishop must be blameless, the husband of one wife.* v. 4. *one that ruleth well his own house, having his children in subjection.*

Marriage, by its definition, is an union of the most intimate nature; but not indissoluble or indivisible, as some contend, on the ground of its being subjoined, Matt. xix. 5. *they two shall be one flesh.* These words, properly considered, do not imply that marriage is absolutely indissoluble, but only that it ought not to be lightly dissolved. For it is upon the institution itself, and the due observance of all its parts, that what follows respecting the indissolubility of marriage depends, whether the words be considered in the light of a command, or of a natural consequence. Hence it is said, *for this cause shall a man leave father and mother . . . and they two shall be one flesh;* that is to say, if, according to the nature of the institution as laid down in the preceding verses, Gen. ii. 18, 20. the wife be an help meet for the husband; or in other words, if good will, love, help, comfort, fidelity, remain unshaken on both sides, which, according to universal acknowledgement, is the *essential form* of marriage. But if the essential form be dissolved, it follows that the marriage itself is virtually dissolved.

Great stress, however, is laid upon an expression in the next verse; *what God hath joined together, let not man put asunder.* What it is that God has joined together, the institution of marriage itself declares. God has joined only what admits of union, what is suitable, what is good, what is honourable; he has not made provision for unnatural and monstrous associations, pregnant only with dishonour, with misery, with hatred, and with calamity. It is not God who forms such unions, but violence, or rashness, or error, or the influence of some evil genius. Why then should it be unlawful to deliver ourselves from so pressing an intestine evil? Further, our doctrine does not separate those whom God has joined together in the spirit of his sacred institution, but only those whom God has himself separated by the authority of his equally sacred law; an authority which ought to have the same force with us now, as with his people of old. As to Christian perfection, the promotion of which is urged by some as an argument for the indissolubility of marriage, that perfection is not to be forced upon us by compulsion and penal laws, but must be produced, if at all, by exhortation and Christian admonition. Then only can man be properly said to dissolve a marriage lawfully contracted, when, adding to the divine ordinance what the ordinance itself does not contain, he separates, under pretence of religion, whomsoever it suits his purpose. For it ought to be remembered that God in his just, and pure, and holy law, has not only permitted divorce on a variety of grounds, but has even ratified it in some cases, and enjoined it in others, under the severest penalties, Exod. xxi. 4, 10, 11. Deut. xxi. 14. xxiv. 1. Ezra x. 3. Nehem. xiii. 23, 30.

But this, it is objected, was *because of the hardness of their hearts,* Matt. xix. 8.

I reply, that these words of Christ, though a very appropriate answer to the Pharisees who tempted him, were never meant as a general explanation of the question of divorce. His intention was, as usual, to repress the arrogance of the Pharisees, and elude their snares; for his answer was only addressed to those who taught from Deut. xxiv. 1. that it was lawful to put away a wife for any cause whatever, provided a bill of divorcement was given. This is evident from the former part of the same chapter, v. 3. *is it lawful for a man to put away his wife for every cause?* not for the sole reason allowed by Moses, namely, if *some uncleanness were found in her,* which might convert love into hatred; but because it had become a common practice to give bills of divorce, under the pretence of uncleanness, without just cause; an abuse which, since the law was unable to restrain it, he thought it advisable to tolerate, notwithstanding the hardness of heart which it implied, rather than to prevent the dissolution of unfortunate marriages, considering that the balance of earthly happiness or misery rested principally on this institution.

For, if we examine the several causes of divorce enumerated in the law, we shall find that wherever divorce was permitted, it was not in compliance with the hardness of the human heart, but on grounds of the highest equity and justice. The first passage is Exod. xxi. 1-4. *these are the judgments which thou shalt set before them: if thou buy an Hebrew servant . . . in the seventh year he shall go out free for nothing . . . if he were married, then his wife shall go out with him: if his master have given him a wife, and she have borne him sons or daughters, the wife and her children shall be her master's, and he shall go out by himself.* Nothing could be more just than this law, which, so far from conceding anything to the hardness of their hearts, rather restrained it; inasmuch as, while it provided against the possibility of any Hebrew, at whatever price he might have been purchased, remaining more than seven years in bondage, it at the same time established the claim of the master as prior to that of the husband. Again, v. 10, 11. *if he take him another wife, her food, her raiment, and her duty of marriage shall he not diminish: and if he do not these three unto her, then shall she go out free without money.* This law is remarkable for its consummate humanity and equity; for while it does not permit the husband to put away his wife through the mere hardness of his heart, it allows the wife to leave her husband on the most reasonable of all grounds, that of inhumanity and unkindness. Again, Deut. xxi. 13, 14. it was permitted by the right of war, both to take a female captive to wife, and to divorce her afterwards; but it was not conceded to the hardness of their hearts, that she should be subsequently sold, or that the master should derive any profit from the possession of her person as a slave.

The third passage is Deut. xxiv. 1. *when a man hath taken a wife, and married her, and it come to pass that she find no favour in his eyes, because he hath found some uncleanness in her, then let him write her a bill of divorcement, and give it in her hand, and send her out of his house.* There is no room here for the charge of hardness of heart, supposing the cause alleged to be a true, and not a fictitious one. For since, as is evident from the institution itself, God gave a wife to man at the beginning to the intent that she should be his help and solace and delight, if, as often happens, she should eventually prove to be rather a source of sorrow, of disgrace, of ruin, of torment, of calamity, why should we think that we are displeasing God by divorcing such a one? I should attribute hardness of heart rather to him who retained her, than to him who sent her away under such circumstances; and not I alone, but Solomon himself, or rather the Spirit of God itself speaking by the mouth of Solomon; Prov. xxx. 21, 23. *for three things the earth is disquieted, and for four which it cannot bear; for an odious woman when she is married—*. On the contrary, Eccles. ix. 9. *live joyfully with the wife whom thou lovest all the days of the life of thy vanity, which he hath given thee;* the wife therefore *which he hath given thee* is she *whom thou lovest,* not she whom thou hatest: and thus Mal. ii. 16. *whoever hateth,* or, *because he hateth, let him dismiss her,* as all before Junius explain the passage. God therefore appears to have enacted this law by the mouth of Moses, and reiterated it by that of the prophet, with the view, not of giving scope to the hard-heartedness of the husband, but of rescuing the unhappy wife from its influence, wherever the case required it. For there is no hard-heartedness in dismissing honourably and freely her whose own fault it is that she is not loved. That one who is not beloved, who is, on the contrary, deservedly neglected, and an object of dislike and hatred; that a wife thus situated should be retained, in pursuance of a most vexatious law, under a yoke of the heaviest slavery (for such is marriage without love) to one who entertains for her neither attachment nor friendship, would indeed be a hardship more cruel than any divorce whatever. God therefore gave laws of divorce, in their proper use most equitable and humane; he even extended the benefit of them to those whom he knew would abuse them through the hardness of their hearts, thinking it better to bear with the obduracy of the wicked, than to refrain from alleviating the misery of the righteous, or suffer the institution itself to be subverted, which, from a divine blessing, was in danger of becoming the bitterest of all calamities.

The two next passages, Ezra x. 3. and Nehem. xiii. 23, 30. do not permit divorce on account of the people's hardness of heart, but positively command it for the most sacred religious reasons. On what authority did these prophets found their precept? They were not the promulgators of a new law; the law of Moses alone could be their warrant. But the law of Moses nowhere commands the dissolution of marriages of this kind; it only forbids the contracting of such: Exod. xxiv. 15, 16. Deut. vii. 3, 4. whence they argued, that the marriage which ought never to have been contracted, ought, if contracted, to be dissolved. So groundless is the vulgar maxim, that what ought not to have been done, is valid when done.

Marriage therefore gives place to religion; it gives place, as has been seen, to the right of a master; and the right of a husband, as appears from the passages of Scripture above quoted, as well as from the whole tenor of the civil law, and the universal custom of nations, is nearly the same as that of the master. It gives way, finally, to irresistible antipathies, and to that natural aversion with which we turn from whatever is unclean; but it is nowhere represented as giving way to hardness of heart, if this latter be really alleged as the sole or principal reason for enacting the law. This appears still more evidently from Deut. xxii. 19. *because he hath brought up an evil name upon a virgin of Israel, she shall be his wife; he may not put her away all his days:* and v. 29. *she shall be his wife, because he hath humbled her; he may not put her away all his days.* Now if the law of Moses did not give way to his hardness of heart who was desirous of putting away the virgin whom he had humbled, or to his who was willing to put away the wife against whom he had brought up an evil report, why should we imagine that it would give way to his alone who was averse from uncleanness, supposing that such aversion could properly be included under the definition of hardness of heart? Christ therefore reproves the hardness of heart of those who abused this law, that is, of the Pharisees and others, when he says, *on account of the hardness of your hearts he permitted you to put away your wives;* but he does not abrogate the law itself, or the legitimate use of it; for he says that Moses permitted it on account of the hardness of their hearts, not that he permitted it wrongfully or improperly. In this sense almost the whole of the civil law might be said to have been given on account of the hardness of their hearts; whence Paul reproves the brethren, 1 Cor. vi. 6. because they had recourse to it, though no one argues from hence that the civil law is, or ought to be abrogated. How much less then can any one who understands the spirit of the Gospel believe, that this latter denies what the law did not scruple to concede, either as a matter of right or of indulgence, to the infirmity of human nature?

The clause in the eighth verse, *from the beginning it was not so,* means nothing more than what was more clearly intimated above in the fourth verse, *he which made them at the beginning, made them male and female;* namely, that marriage in its original institution was not capable of being dissolved even by death, for sin and death were not then in existence. If however the purpose of the institution should be violated by the offence of either, it was obvious that death, the consequence of that

offence, must in the course of things dissolve the bond; and reason taught them that separation must frequently take place even before that period. No age or record, since the fall of man, gives a tradition of any other *beginning* in which *it was not so.* In the earliest ages of our faith, Abraham himself, the father of the faithful, put away his contentious and turbulent wife Hagar by the command of God, Gen. xxi. 10, 12, 14.

Christ himself, v. 9. permitted divorce for the cause of fornication; which could not have been, if those whom God had once joined in the bands of matrimony were never afterwards to be disunited. According to the idiom of the eastern languages, however, the word fornication signifies, not adultery only, but either what is called *any unclean thing,* or a defect in some particular which might justly be required in a wife, Deut. xxiv. 1. (as Selden was the first to prove by numerous Rabbinical testimonies in his *Uxor Hebræa*) or it signifies whatever is found to be irreconcilably at variance with love, or fidelity, or help, or society, that is, with the objects of the original institution; as Seldon proves, and as I have myself shown in another treatise from several texts of Scripture. For it would have been absurd, when the Pharisees asked, whether it was allowable to put away a wife for every cause, to answer, that it was not lawful except in case of adultery, when it was well known already to be not only lawful but necessary to put away an adulteress, and that not by divorce, but by death. Fornication, therefore, must be here understood in a much wider sense than that of simple adultery, as is clear from many passages of Scripture, and particularly from Judg. xix. 2. *his concubine played the whore against him;* not by committing adultery, for in that case she would not have dared to flee to her father's house, but by refractory behaviour towards her husband. Nor could Paul have allowed divorce in consequence of the departure of an unbeliever, unless this also were a species of fornication. It does not affect the question, that the case alluded to is that of a heathen; since whoever deserts her family *is worse than an infidel,* 1 Tim. v. 8. Nor could anything be more natural, or more agreeable to the original institution, than that the bond which had been formed by love, and the hope of mutual assistance through life, and honourable motives, should be dissolved by hatred and implacable enmity, and disgraceful conduct on either side. For man, therefore, in his state of innocence in Paradise, previously to the entrance of sin into the world, God ordained that marriage should be indissoluble; after the fall, in compliance with the alteration of circumstances, and to prevent the innocent from being exposed to perpetual injury from the wicked, he permitted its dissolution; and this permission forms part of the law of nature and of Moses, and is not disallowed by Christ. Thus every covenant, when originally concluded, is intended to be perpetual and indissoluble, however soon it may be broken by the bad faith of one of the parties; nor has any good reason yet been given why marriage should differ in this respect from all other compacts; especially since the apostle has pronounced that *a brother or a sister is not under bondage,* not merely in a case of desertion, but *in such cases,* that is, in all cases that produce an unworthy bondage. 1 Cor. vii. 15. *a brother or a sister is not under bondage in such cases, but God hath called us in peace,* or *to peace:* he has not therefore called us to the end that we should be harassed with constant discord and vexations; for the object of our call is peace and liberty, not marriage, much less perpetual discord and the slavish bondage of an unhappy union, which the apostle declares to be above all things unworthy of a free man and a Christian. It is not to be supposed that Christ would expunge from the Mosaic law any enactment which could afford scope for the exercise of mercy towards the wretched and afflicted, or that his declaration on the present occasion was intended to have the force of a judicial decree, ordaining new and severer regulations on the subject; but that, having exposed the abuses of the law, he proceeded after his usual manner to lay down a more perfect rule of conduct, disclaiming on this, as on all other occasions, the office of a judge, and inculcating truth by simple admonition, not by compulsory decrees. It is therefore a most flagrant error to convert a gospel precept into a civil statute, and enforce it by legal penalties.

It may perhaps be asked, if the disciples understood Christ as promulgating nothing new or more severe than the existing law on the subject of divorce, how it happened that they were so little satisfied with his explanation, as to say, v. 10. *if the case of the man be so with his wife, it is not good to marry?* I answer, that it is no wonder if the disciples, who had imbibed the doctrines of their time, thought and felt like the Pharisees with regard to divorce; so that the declaration of our Lord, that it was not lawful to put away a wife for every cause, only having given her a writing of divorcement, must have appeared to them a new and hard saying.

The whole argument may be summed up in brief as follows. It is universally admitted that marriage may lawfully be dissolved, if the prime end and form of the institution be violated; which is generally alleged as the reason why Christ allowed divorce in cases of adultery only. But the prime end and form of marriage, as almost all acknowledge, is not the nuptial bed, but conjugal love, and mutual assistance through life; for that must be regarded as the prime end and form of a rite, which is alone specified in the original institution. Mention is there made of the pleasures of society, which are incompatible with the isolation consequent upon aversion, and of conjugal assistance, which is afforded by love alone; not of the nuptial bed, or of the production of offspring, which may take place even without love: from whence it is evident that conjugal affection is of more importance and higher excellence than the nuptial bed itself, and more worthy to be considered as the prime end and form of the institution. No one can surely be so base and sensual as to deny this. The very cause which renders the pollution of the marriage bed so heavy a calamity, is, that in its consequences it interrupts peace and affection; much more therefore must the perpetual interruption of peace and affection by mutual differences and unkindness be a sufficient reason for granting the liberty of divorce. And that it is such, Christ himself declares in the above passage; for it is certain, and has been proved already, that fornication signifies, not so much adultery, as the constant enmity, faithlessness, and disobedience of the wife, arising from the manifest and palpable alienation of the mind, rather than of the body. Not to mention, that the common, though false interpretation, by which adultery is made the sole ground of divorce, so far from vindicating the law, does in effect abrogate it; for it was ordained by the law of Moses, not that an adulteress should be put away, but that she should be brought to judgement, and punished with death.

.   .   .   .   .

CHAP. XXVII.

OF

THE GOSPEL

AND

CHRISTIAN LIBERTY.

THE GOSPEL IS THE NEW DISPENSATION OF THE COVENANT OF GRACE, FAR MORE EXCELLENT AND PERFECT THAN THE LAW, ANNOUNCED FIRST OBSCURELY BY MOSES AND THE PROPHETS, AFTERWARDS IN THE CLEAREST TERMS BY CHRIST HIMSELF, AND HIS APOSTLES AND EVANGELISTS, WRITTEN SINCE BY THE HOLY SPIRIT IN THE HEARTS OF BELIEVERS, AND ORDAINED TO CONTINUE EVEN TO THE END OF THE WORLD, CONTAINING A PROMISE OF ETERNAL LIFE TO ALL IN ALL NATIONS WHO SHALL BELIEVE IN CHRIST WHEN REVEALED TO THEM, AND A THREAT OF ETERNAL DEATH TO SUCH AS SHALL NOT BELIEVE.

THE NEW DISPENSATION. Jer. xxxi. 31-33, compared with Heb. viii. 8, 9. *I will make a new covenant with the house of Israel, and with the house of Judah, not according to the covenant that I made with their fathers.* It is called *the new testament,* Matt. xxvi. 28. Mark xiv. 24. Luke xxii. 20. 1 Cor. xi. 25. 2 Cor. iii. 6. But the word διαθήκη, in the Hebrew בְּרִית, is generally

used by the inspired writers for συνθήκη, *covenant,* and is rendered in Latin by the word *pactum,* 2 Cor. iii. 14. Gal. iv. 24. *veteris pacti.* The Gospel is only once called *testament* in a proper sense, for a particular reason which is there subjoined. Heb. ix. 15, 16, &c. *for this cause he is the mediator of the new testament, that by means of death for the redemption of the*

transgressions that were under the first testament, they which are called might receive the promise of eternal inheritance; for where a testament is, there must also of necessity be the death of the testator.

MORE EXCELLENT AND PERFECT THAN THE LAW. Matt. xiii. 17. *many prophets and righteous men have desired to see those things which ye see, and have not seen them, and to hear those things which ye hear, and have not heard them.* 2 Cor. iii. 11, &c. *if that which was done away was glorious, much more that which remaineth is glorious. Seeing then that we have such hope, we use great plainness of speech; and not as Moses—.* Heb. vii. 18-20, 22. *the law made nothing perfect, but the bringing in of better hope did, by the which we draw nigh unto God: and inasmuch as not without an oath he was made priest; for those priests were made without an oath, but this with an oath . . . by so much was Jesus made a surety of a better covenant.* viii. 6, &c. *by how much more also he is the mediator of a better covenant, which was established upon better promises, &c. . . . I will put my laws into their mind.* James i. 25. *whoso looketh into the perfect law of liberty, and continueth therein, he being not a forgetful hearer, but a doer of the work, this man shall be blessed in his deed.* 1 Pet. i. 10, &c. *of which salvation the prophets have inquired and searched diligently, who prophesied of the grace that should come unto you . . . with the Holy Ghost sent down from heaven; which things the angels desire to look into.* The Gospel is also called *the ministry* and *word of reconciliation,* 2 Cor. v. 18, 19. whereas on the contrary *the law worketh wrath,* Rom. iv. 15.

BY MOSES AND THE PROPHETS. John v. 39. *they are they which testify of me.* v. 46. *had ye believed Moses, ye would have believed me, for he wrote of me;* namely Gen. iii. 15. xxii. 18. xlix. 10. Deut. xviii. 15. Luke xxiv. 27. *beginning at Moses and all the prophets, he expounded unto them in all the scriptures the things concerning himself.* Acts xvii. 11. *searching the scriptures daily, whether those things were so.* xxvi. 22, 23. *saying none other things than those which the prophets and Moses did say should come.* Rom. iii. 21. *being witnessed by the law and the prophets.* 1 Pet.

i. 10. *who prophesied of the grace which should come unto you.*

WRITTEN IN THE HEARTS OF BELIEVERS. Isai. lix. 21. *as for me, this is my covenant with them, saith Jehovah; My Spirit which is upon thee, and my words which I have put in thy mouth, shall not depart out of thy mouth, nor out of the mouth of thy seed, nor out of the mouth of thy seed's seed, saith Jehovah, from henceforth and for ever.* Jer. xxxi. 31–33. *behold the days come . . . but this shall be the covenant that I will make with the house of Israel; After those days, saith Jehovah,* (a declaration particularly worthy of attention, as it specifies in what respect the new covenant is more excellent than the old) *I will put my law in their inward parts, and write it in their hearts—,* compared with Heb. viii. 10, &c. *this is the covenant . . . I will put my laws into their mind . . . and I will be to them a God, and they shall be to me a people.* Joel ii. 28. *it shall come to pass afterward, that I will pour out my Spirit upon all flesh . . . and also upon the servants and upon the handmaids in those days will I pour out my Spirit.* To these may be added, from the chapter of Jeremiah quoted above, v. 34. *they shall all know me, from the least of them unto the greatest of them.* Joel ii. 28. *your sons and your daughters shall prophesy, your old men shall dream dreams, your young men shall see visions.* Compare Acts ii. 16–18. For although all real believers have not the gift of prophecy, the Holy Spirit is to them an equivalent and substitute for prophecy, dreams, and visions. 2 Cor. iii. 3. *ye are manifestly declared to be the epistle of Christ ministered by us, written not with ink, but with the Spirit of the living God, not in tables of stone, but in fleshy tables of the heart.* v. 6. *ministers of the new testament, not of the letter, but of the spirit; for the letter killeth, but the spirit giveth life.* James i. 21. *receive with meekness the engrafted word, which is able to save your souls.*

BY THE HOLY SPIRIT, the gift of God, and peculiar to the gospel. John vii. 39. *the Holy Ghost was not yet given, because that Jesus was not yet glorified.* xiv. 26. *the Comforter, which is the Holy Ghost, whom the Father will send in my name, he shall teach you all things.* See also Luke xii. 12. Acts i. 8. *ye shall receive power after that the Holy Ghost is come upon you.* See also ii. 1, &c. v. 38. *repent, &c. . . . and ye shall receive the gift of the Holy Ghost.* Rom. v. 5. *by the Holy Ghost which is given unto us.* 1 Cor. ii. 13. *in words which the Holy Ghost teacheth.* 2 Cor. xiii. 14. *the communion of the Holy Ghost.* 1 Thess. iv. 8. *who hath also given unto us his Holy Spirit.* See also Rom. viii. 9. 1 Cor. xii. 3. 1 Pet. i. 12. 1 John iv. 13.

ORDAINED TO CONTINUE EVEN TO THE END OF THE WORLD. 2 Cor. iii. 11. *much more that which remaineth is glorious.* Eph. iv. 13. *till we all come . . . unto a perfect man, unto the measure of the stature of the fulness of Christ.*

A PROMISE OF ETERNAL LIFE. Mark xvi. 15, 16. *go ye into all the world, and preach the gospel . . . he that believeth and is baptized shall be saved.* Rom. i. 16. *the power of God unto salvation.*

TO ALL WHO SHALL BELIEVE. John iii. 15, 16. *whosoever believeth in him,* &c. Rom. i. 16, 17. *to every one that believeth.* 1 John ii. 25. *this is the promise that he hath promised us, even eternal life.* See other passages to the same effect above, in the chapter on faith and its objects. Under the name of believers the penitent are comprehended, inasmuch as in the original annunciation of the gospel repentance and faith are jointly proposed as conditions of salvation. Matt. iii. 1, &c. iv. 17. Mark i. 15. Luke xxiv. 47. Acts ii. 39–41. x. 35. *he that feareth him and worketh righteousness, is accepted of him.* xix. 3, 4. xx. 21. and elsewhere.

A THREAT OF ETERNAL DEATH TO SUCH AS SHALL NOT BELIEVE. Matt. x. 14, 15. *whosoever shall not receive you nor hear your words, when ye depart out of that city, shake off the dust of your feet: verily I say unto you, It shall be more tolerable for the land of Sodom—.* xxi. 37, &c. *he sent unto them his son . . . but when the husbandmen saw the son, they said . . . let us kill him . . . they say unto him, He will miserably destroy those wicked men.* Mark xvi. 16. *he that believeth not shall be damned.* John iii. 19. *this is the condemnation, that light is come into the world, and men loved darkness rather than light.* Acts iii. 23. *every soul which will not hear that prophet, shall be destroyed from among*

the people. 2 Thess. i. 8, 9. *taking venge-*
ance on them that know not God, and that
obey not the gospel. Heb. x. 26, &c. *if we*
sin wilfully after that we have received the
knowledge of the truth, there remaineth no
more sacrifice for sins, but a certain fearful
looking for of judgement. By unbelievers,
however, those only can be meant to whom
Christ has been announced in the gospel;
for *how shall they believe in him of whom*
they have not heard? Rom. x. 14.

IN ALL NATIONS. Matt. xxiv. 14. *this gos-*
pel of the kingdom shall be preached in all
the world, for a witness unto all nations,
and then shall the end come. Mark xvi.
15. *to every creature.* John x. 16. *other*
sheep I have, which are not of this fold.
Acts x. 34, 35. *of a truth I perceive that*
God is no respecter of persons; but in every
nation he that feareth him, and worketh
righteousness, is accepted of him. Rom. x.
18. *their sound went into all the earth, and*
their words unto the ends of the world.
This was predicted, Isai. ii. 2, &c. *it shall*
come to pass in the last days, &c. See also
Mic. iv. 1. Isai. xix. 18, &c. *in that day*
shall five cities in the land of Egypt speak
the language of Canaan, &c. xxv. 6, &c.
unto all people. xlii. 4, &c. *the isles shall*
wait for his law. xlv. 22, 23. *look unto*
me, and be ye saved, all the ends of the
earth. lv. 4, 5. *a witness to the people,* &c.
lvi. 3, &c. *neither let the son of the stranger*
. . . speak, saying, Jehovah hath utterly
separated me from his people. lxvi. 21.
I will also take of them for priests and
Levites, saith Jehovah. Jer. iii. 17. *all the*
nations shall be gathered unto it. xxv. 8,
&c. *because ye have not heard my words,*
behold, I will send and take all the families
of the north—. Hagg. ii. 7. *the desire of*
all nations shall come. Zech. viii. 20. *there*
shall come people, and the inhabitants of
many cities.

On the introduction of the gospel, or
new covenant through faith in Christ, the
whole of the preceding covenant, in other
words the entire Mosaic law, was abolished.
Jer. xxxi. 31–33. as above. Luke xvi. 16.
the law and the prophets were until John.
Acts xv. 10. *now therefore why tempt ye*
God, to put a yoke upon the neck of the
disciples, which neither our fathers nor we
were able to bear? Rom. iii. 21. *now the*
righteousness of God without the law is

manifested. vi. 14. *ye are not under the*
law, but under grace. vii. 4. *ye also are*
become dead to the law by the body of
Christ, that ye should be married to an-
other, even to him that is raised from the
dead, that we should bring forth fruit unto
God. v. 6. *now we are delivered from the*
law, that being dead wherein we were held,
that we should serve in newness of spirit,
and not in the oldness of the letter. In the
beginning of the same chapter the apostle
illustrates our emancipation from the law
by the instance of a wife who is loosed from
her husband that is dead. v. 7. *I had not*
known sin but by the law (that is, the whole
law, for the expression is unlimited) *for I*
had not known lust, except the law had said,
Thou shalt not covet. It is in the decalogue
that the injunction here specified is contained; we are therefore absolved from subjection to the decalogue as fully as to the
rest of the law. viii. 15. *ye have not re-*
ceived the spirit of bondage again to fear.
xiv. 20. *all things indeed are pure,* compared with Tit. i. 15. *unto the pure all*
things are pure; but unto them that are de-
filed and unbelieving is nothing pure, but
even their mind and conscience is defiled.
1 Cor. vi. 12. *all things are lawful to me,*
but all things are not expedient; all things
are lawful for me, but I will not be brought
under the power of any. x. 23. *all things*
are lawful for me, but all things are not ex-
pedient; all things are lawful for me, but
all things edify not. 2 Cor. iii. 3. *not in*
tables of stone, but in fleshy tables of the
heart. v. 6–8. *ministers of the new testa-*
ment, not of the letter, but of the spirit; for
the letter killeth, but the spirit giveth life:
but if the ministration of death, written and
engraven in stones, was glorious . . . how
shall not the ministration of the spirit be
rather glorious? v. 11. *if that which was*
done away was glorious, much more that
which remaineth is glorious. v. 15. *the*
children of Israel could not stedfastly look
to the end of that which is abolished. v.
17. *if any man be in Christ, he is a new*
creature; old things are passed away; be-
hold, all things are become new. Gal. iii.
19. *wherefore then serveth the law? it was*
added because of transgressions, till the seed
should come, to whom the promise was
made. v. 25. *after that faith is come, we*
are no longer under a schoolmaster. iv. 1,

&c. *the heir, as long as he is a child, differeth nothing from a servant . . . until the time appointed of the father: even so we, when we were children, were in bondage under the elements of the world; but when the fulness of the time was come, God sent forth his Son, made of a woman, made under the law, to redeem them that were under the law, that we might receive the adoption of sons.* Compare also v. 21, addressed to those who desired to be under the law; and v. 24, of Hagar and Sarah, *these are the two covenants; the one from the mount Sinai, which gendereth to bondage, which is Agar . . . but Jerusalem which is above,* v. 26. *is free:* hence v. 30. *cast out the bondwoman and her son; for the son of the bondwoman shall not be heir with the son of the freewoman.* v. 18. *if ye be led of the Spirit, ye are not under the law.* Eph ii. 14, 15. *who hath broken down the middle wall of partition between us, having abolished in his flesh the enmity, even the law of commandments contained in ordinances.* Now not only the ceremonial code, but the whole positive law of Moses, was a law of commandments, and contained in ordinances; nor was it the ceremonial law which formed the sole ground of distinction between the Jews and Gentiles, as Zanchius on this passage contends, but the whole law; seeing that the Gentiles, v. 12. *were aliens from the commonwealth of Israel, and strangers from the covenant of promise,* which promise was made to the works of the whole law, not to those of the ceremonial alone; nor was it to these latter only that the enmity between God and us was owing, v. 16. So Coloss. ii. 14–17. *blotting out the hand-writing of ordinances that was against us . . . he took it out of the way,* &c. Heb. vii. 12, 15, 16. *the priesthood being changed, there is made of necessity a change also in the law . . . there ariseth another priest, who is made not after the law of a carnal commandment.* v. 18. *there is verily a disannulling of the commandment going before,* (that is, of the commandment of works) *for the weakness and unprofitableness thereof.* viii. 13. *in that he saith, a new covenant, he hath made the first old; now that which decayeth and waxeth old, is ready to vanish away.* xii. 18, &c. *ye are not come unto the mount that might be touched, and that burned with fire, nor unto blackness, and darkness, and tempest, and the sound of a trumpet, and the voice of words; which voice they that heard entreated that the word should not be spoken to them any more . . . but ye are come unto mount Sion . . . and to Jesus the mediator of the new covenant.*

It is generally replied, that all these passages are to be understood only of the abolition of the ceremonial law. This is refuted, first, by the definition of the law itself, as given in the preceding chapter, in which are specified all the various reasons for its enactment: if therefore, of the causes which led to the enactment of the law considered as a whole, every one is revoked or obsolete, it follows that the whole law itself must be annulled also. The principal reasons then which are given for the enactment of the law are as follows; that it might call forth and develope our natural depravity; that by this means it might work wrath; that it might impress us with a slavish fear through consciousness of divine enmity, and of the hand-writing of accusation that was against us; that it might be a schoolmaster to bring us to the righteousness of Christ; and others of a similar description. Now the texts quoted above prove clearly, both that all these causes are now abrogated, and that they have not the least connection with the ceremonial law.

First then, the law is abolished principally on the ground of its being a law of works; that it might give place to the law of grace. Rom. iii. 27. *by what law? of works? nay, but by the law of faith.* xi. 6. *if by grace, then is it no more of works; otherwise grace is no more grace.* Now the law of works was not solely the ceremonial law, but the whole law.

Secondly, iv. 15. *the law worketh wrath; for where no law is, there is no transgression.* It is not however a part, but the whole of the law that worketh wrath; inasmuch as the transgression is of the whole, and not of a part only. Seeing then that the law worketh wrath, but the gospel grace, and that wrath is incompatible with grace, it is obvious that the law cannot co-exist with the gospel.

Thirdly, the law of which it was written, *the man that doeth them shall live in them,* Gal. iii. 12. Lev. xviii. 5. and, *cursed is every one that continueth not in all things which are written in the book of the law to do them,* Deut. xxvii. 26. Gal. iii. 10. was the whole law. From *the curse of this law Christ hath redeemed us,* v. 13. inasmuch as we were unable to fulfil it ourselves. Now to fulfil the ceremonial law could not have been a matter of difficulty; it must therefore have been the entire Mosaic law from which Christ delivered us. Again, as it was against those who did not fulfil the whole law that the curse was denounced, it follows that Christ could not have redeemed us from that curse, unless he had abrogated the whole law; if therefore he abrogated the whole, no part of it can be now binding upon us.

Fourthly, we are taught, 2 Cor. iii. 7. that the law *written and engraven in stones* was *the ministration of death,* and therefore *was done away.* Now the law engraven in stones was not the ceremonial law, but the decalogue.

Fifthly, that which was, as just stated, a law of sin and death, (of sin, because it is a provocative to sin; of death, because it produces death, and is in opposition to the law of the spirit of life,) is certainly not the ceremonial law alone, but the whole law. But the law to which the above description applies, is abolished; Rom. viii. 2. *the law of the spirit of life in Christ Jesus hath made me free from the law of sin and death.*

Sixthly, it was undoubtedly not by the ceremonial law alone that *the motions of sin which were by the law, wrought in our members to bring forth fruit unto death,* Rom. vii. 5. But of the law which thus operated it is said that we *are become dead thereto,* v. 4. and *that being dead wherein we were held,* v. 6. *we are delivered from it,* as a wife is free *from the law of her husband who is dead,* v. 3. We are therefore delivered, v. 6. not from the ceremonial law alone, but from the whole law of Moses.

Seventhly, all believers, inasmuch as they are justified by God through faith, are undoubtedly to be accounted righteous; but Paul expressly asserts that *the law is not made for a righteous man,* 1 Tim. i. 9. Gal. v. 22, 23. If however any law were to be made for the righteous, it must needs be a law which should justify. Now the ceremonial law alone was so far from justifying, that even the entire Mosaic law had not

power to effect this, as has been already shown in treating of justification: Gal. iii. 11, &c. therefore it must be the whole law, and not the ceremonial part alone, which is abrogated by reason of its inability in this respect.

To these considerations we may add, that that law which not only cannot justify, but is the source of trouble and subversion to believers; which even tempts God if we endeavour to perform its requisitions; which has no promise attached to it, or, to speak more properly, which takes away and frustrates all promises, whether of inheritance, or adoption, or grace, or of the Spirit itself; nay, which even subjects us to a curse; must necessarily have been abolished. If then it can be shown that the above effects result, not from the ceremonial law alone, but from the whole law, that is to say, the law of works in a comprehensive sense, it will follow that the whole law is abolished; and that they do so result, I shall proceed to show from the clearest passages of Scripture. With regard to the first point, Acts xv. 24. *we have heard that certain which went out from us have troubled you with words, subverting your souls, saying, Ye must be circumcised, and keep the law.* v. 10. *why tempt ye God, to put a yoke upon the neck of the disciples?* Certain of the Pharisees which believed, said that *it was needful for them to keep the whole law,* v. 5. when therefore Peter in opposition to this doctrine contends, that the yoke of the law ought to be removed from the necks of the disciples, it is clear that he must mean the whole law. Secondly, that the law which had not the promise was not the ceremonial law only, but the whole law, is clear from the consideration, that it would be sufficient if one part had the promise, although the other were without it; whereas the law which is so often the subject of discussion with Paul has no promise attached to either of its branches. Rom. iv. 13, 16. *the promise that he should be the heir of the world, was not to Abraham, or to his seed through the law, but through the righteousness of faith.* Gal. iii. 18. *if the inheritance be of the law, it is no more of promise; but God gave it to Abraham by promise;* and therefore not by the law, or any part of it; whence Paul shows that either the whole law, or the promise itself, must of necessity be abolished, Rom. iv. 14. *if they which are of the law be heirs, faith is made void, and the promise is made of none effect.* Compare also Gal. iii. 18. as above. By the abolition of the promise, the inheritance and adoption are abolished; fear and bondage, which are incompatible with adoption, are brought back, Rom. viii. 15. Gal. iv. 1, &c. v. 21, 24, 26, 30. as above; union and fellowship with Christ are dissolved, Gal. v. 4. *Christ is become of no effect unto you, whosoever of you are justified by the law,* whence follows the loss of glorification; nay, grace itself is abolished, unless the abolition of the law be an entire abolition: Gal. v. 4. *whosoever of you are justified by the law, ye are fallen from grace,* where by the word *law* is intended the entire code, as appears not only from the preceding verse, *he is a debtor to do the whole law,* but from other considerations; finally, the Spirit itself is excluded; Gal. v. 18. *if ye be led of the Spirit, ye are not under the law;* therefore, vice versa, if ye be under the law, ye are not led of the Spirit. We are consequently left under the curse: Gal. iii. 10. *as many as are of the works of the law, are under the curse; for it is written, Cursed is every one that continueth not in all things which are written in the book of the law, to do them;* therefore *all things which are written in the law,* and not the things of the ceremonial law alone, render us obnoxious to the curse. Christ therefore, when he *redeemed us from the curse,* v. 13. redeemed us also from the causes of the curse, namely, the works of the law, or, which is the same, from the whole law of works; which, as has been shown above, is not the ceremonial part alone. Even supposing, however, that no such consequences followed, there could be but little inducement to observe the conditions of a law which has not the promise; it would be even ridiculous to attempt to observe that which is of no avail unless it be fulfilled in every part, and which nevertheless it is impossible for man so to fulfil; especially as it has been superseded by the more excellent law of faith, which God in Christ has given us both will and power to fulfil.

It appears therefore as well from the evidence of Scripture, as from the arguments above adduced, that the whole of the Mosaic law is abolished by the gospel. It is to be observed, however, that the sum and essence of the law is not hereby abrogated; its purpose being attained in that love of God and our neighbour, which is born of the Spirit through faith. It was with justice therefore that Christ asserted the permanence of the law, Matt. v. 17. *think not that I am come to destroy the law, or the prophets; I am not come to destroy, but to fulfil.* Rom. iii. 31. *do we then make void the law through faith? God forbid: yea, we establish the law.* viii. 4. *that the righteousness of the law might be fulfilled in us, who walk not after the flesh, but after the Spirit.*

The common objection to this doctrine is anticipated by Paul himself, who expressly teaches that by this abrogation of the law, sin, if not taken away, is at least weakened rather than increased in power: Rom. vi. 14, 15. *sin shall not have dominion over you; for ye are not under the law, but under grace: what then? shall we sin, because we are not under the law, but under grace? God forbid.* Therefore, as was said above, the end for which the law was instituted, namely, the love of God and our neighbour, is by no means to be considered as abolished; it is the tablet of the law, so to speak, that is alone changed, its injunctions being now written by the Spirit in the hearts of believers; with this difference, that in certain precepts the Spirit appears to be at variance with the letter, namely, wherever by departing from the letter we can more effectually consult the love of God and our neighbour. Thus Christ departed from the letter of the law, Mark ii. 27. *the sabbath was made for man, and not man for the sabbath,* if we compare his words with the fourth commandment. Paul did the same in declaring that a marriage with an unbeliever was not to be dissolved, contrary to the express injunction of the law; 1 Cor. vii. 12. *to the rest speak I, not the Lord.* In the interpretation of these two commandments, of the sabbath and marriage, a regard to the law of love is declared to be better than a compliance with the whole written law; a rule which applies equally to every other instance. Matt. xxii. 37-40. *on these two commandments* (namely, the love of God and our neighbour) *hang all the law and the prophets.* Now neither of these is propounded in express terms among the ten commandments, the former occurring for the first time Deut. vi. 5. the latter, Lev. xix. 18. and yet these two precepts are represented as comprehending emphatically, not only the ten commandments, but the whole law and the prophets. Matt. vii. 12. *all things whatsoever ye would that men should do unto you, do we even so to them; for this is the law and the prophets.* Rom. xiii. 8, 10. *he that loveth another hath fulfilled the law; love is the fulfilling of the law.* Gal. v. 14. *all the law is fulfilled in one word, even in this, Thou shalt love thy neighbour as thyself.* 1 Tim. i. 5. *the end of the commandment is charity out of a pure heart, and of a good conscience, and of faith unfeigned.* If this is the end of the Mosaic commandment, much more is it the end of the evangelic. James ii. 8. *if ye fulfil the royal law according to the scripture, Thou shalt love thy neighbour as thyself, thou shalt do well.* Hence all rational interpreters have explained the precepts of Christ, in his sermon on the mount, not according to the letter, but in the spirit of the law of love. So also that of Paul, 1 Cor. xi. 4. *every man praying or prophesying, having his head covered, dishonoureth his head;* a text which will come under consideration in Book II. chap. iv. on the outward deportment befitting prayer. Hence it is said, Rom. iv. 15. *where no law is, there is no transgression;* that is, no transgression in disregarding the letter of the law, provided that under the direction of the Spirit the end of the institution be attained in the love of God and our neighbour.

On the united authority of so many passages of Scripture, I conceived that I had satisfactorily established the truth in question against the whole body of theologians, who, so far as my knowledge then extended, concurred in denying the abrogation of the entire Mosaic law. I have since however discovered, that Zanchius, in his commentary on the second chapter of Ephesians, declares himself of the same opinion, remarking, very justly, that 'no inconsiderable part of divinity depends on the right explanation of this question; and that it is impossible to comprehend the Scriptures properly, especially those parts which relate to justification and good works,' (he might have added, the whole of the New Testament) 'unless the subject of the abrogation of the law be thoroughly understood.' He proves his point with sufficient accuracy, but neglects to follow up his conclusions; losing himself in a multitude of minute exceptions, and apparently fluctuating between the two opinions, so as to leave the reader, if not extremely attentive, in a state of uncertainty. I have also observed that Cameron somewhere expresses the same opinion respecting the abolition of the whole law.

It is asserted, however, by divines in general, who still maintain the tenet of the converted Pharisees, that it is needful for those who are under the gospel to observe the law (a doctrine which in the infancy of the church was productive of much mischief) that the law may be highly useful, in various ways, even to us who are Christians; inasmuch as we are thereby led to a truer conviction of sin, and consequently to a more thankful acceptance of grace; as well as to a more perfect knowledge of the will of God. With regard to the first point, I reply, that I am not speaking of sinners, who stand in need of a preliminary impulse to come to Christ, but of such as are already believers, and consequently in the most intimate union with Christ; as to the second, the will of God is best learnt from the gospel itself under the promised guidance of the Spirit of truth, and from the divine law written in the hearts of believers. Besides, if the law be the means of leading us to a conviction of sin and an acceptance of the grace of Christ, this is effected by a knowledge of the law itself, not by the performance of its works; inasmuch as through the works of the law, instead of drawing nearer to Christ, we depart farther from him; as Scripture is perpetually inculcating.

In the next place, a distinction is made; and Polanus in particular observes, that 'when it is said that we are not under the law, it is not meant that we are not under an obligation to obey it, but that we are exempt from the curse and restraint of the law, as well as from the provocation to sin which results from it.' If this be the case, what advantage do believers reap from the gospel? since even under the law they at least were exempted from the curse and provocation to sin; and since to be free from the restraint of the law can mean nothing but that for which I contend, an entire exemption from the obligation of the law. For as long as the law exists, it constrains, because it is a law of bondage; constraint and bondage being as inseparable from the dispensation of the law, as liberty from the dispensation of the gospel; of which shortly.

Polanus contends, on Gal. iv. 4, 5. *to redeem them that were under the law,* that 'when Christians are said to be redeemed from subjection to the law, and to be no longer under the law, this is not to be taken in an absolute sense, as if they owed no more obedience to it. What then do the words imply? They signify, that Christians are no longer under the necessity of perfectly fulfilling the law of God in this life, inasmuch as Christ has fulfilled it for them.' That this is contrary to the truth, is too obvious not to be acknowledged. So far from a less degree of perfection being exacted from Christians, it is expected of them that they should be more perfect than those who were under the law; as the whole tenour of Christ's precepts evinces. The only difference is, that Moses imposed the letter, or external law, even on those who were not willing to receive it; whereas Christ writes the inward law of God by his Spirit on the hearts of believers, and leads them as willing followers. Under the law, those who trusted in God were justified by faith indeed, but not without the works of the law; Rom. iv. 12. *the father of circumcision to them who are not of the circumcision only, but who also walk in the steps of that faith of our father Abraham, which he had being yet uncircumcised.* The gospel, on the contrary, justifies by faith without the works of the law. Wherefore, we being freed from the works of the law, no longer follow the letter, but the spirit; doing the works of faith, not of the law. Neither is it said to us, *whatever is not of the law is sin,* but, *whatever is not of faith is sin;* faith consequently, and not the law, is our rule. It follows, therefore, that as faith cannot be made matter of compulsion, so neither can the works of faith. See more on this subject in the fifteenth chapter, on Christ's kingly office, and on the inward spiritual law by which he governs the church. Compare also Book II. chap. i. where the form of good works is considered.

From the abrogation, through the gospel, of the law of servitude, results Christian liberty; though liberty, strictly speaking, is the peculiar fruit of adoption, and consequently was not unknown during the time of the law, as observed in the twenty-third chapter. Inasmuch, however, as it was not possible for our liberty either to be perfected or made fully manifest till the coming of Christ our deliverer, liberty must be considered as belonging in an especial manner to the gospel, and as consorting therewith: first, because truth is principally known by the gospel, John i. 17. *grace and truth came by Jesus Christ,* and truth has an essential connection with liberty; viii. 31, 32. *if ye continue in my word, then are ye my disciples indeed; and ye shall know the truth, and the truth shall make you free.* v. 36. *if the Son therefore shall make you free, ye shall be free indeed.* Secondly, because the peculiar gift of the gospel is the Spirit; but *where the Spirit of the Lord is, there is liberty,* 2 Cor. iii. 17.

CHRISTIAN LIBERTY is that whereby WE ARE LOOSED AS IT WERE BY ENFRANCHISEMENT, THROUGH CHRIST OUR DELIVERER, FROM THE BONDAGE OF SIN, AND CONSEQUENTLY FROM THE RULE OF THE LAW AND OF MAN; TO THE INTENT THAT BEING MADE SONS INSTEAD OF SERVANTS, AND PERFECT MEN INSTEAD OF CHILDREN, WE MAY SERVE GOD IN LOVE THROUGH THE GUIDANCE OF THE SPIRIT OF TRUTH. Gal. v. 1. *stand fast therefore in the liberty wherewith Christ hath made us free; and be not entangled again with the yoke of bondage.* Rom. viii. 2. *the law of the Spirit of life in Christ Jesus hath made me free from the law of sin and death.* v. 15. *ye have not received the spirit of bondage again to fear; but ye have received the Spirit of adoption, whereby we cry, Abba, Father.* Gal. iv. 7. *wherefore thou art no more a servant, but a son.* Heb. ii. 15. *that he might deliver them who through fear of death were all their lifetime subject to bondage.* 1 Cor. vii. 23. *ye are bought with a price; be not ye the servants of men.* James i. 25. *whoso looketh into the perfect law of liberty, and continueth therein.* ii. 12. *so speak ye, and so do, as they that shall be judged by the law of liberty.*

THAT WE MAY SERVE GOD. Matt. xi. 29, 30. *take my yoke upon you . . . for my yoke is easy, and my burden is light,* compared with 1 John v. 3–5. *this is the love of God, that we keep his commandments, and his commandments are not grievous.* Rom. vi. 18. *being then made free from sin, ye became the servants of righteousness.* v. 22. *now being made free from sin, and become servants to God, ye have your fruit unto holiness.* vii. 6. *now we are delivered from the law, that being dead wherein we were held, that we should serve in newness of spirit, and not in the oldness of the letter.* xii. 1, 2. *present your bodies . . . a reasonable service; and be not conformed to this world; but be ye transformed by the renewing of your mind, that ye may prove what is that good and acceptable and perfect will of God.* James i. 25. *whoso looketh into the perfect law of liberty, and continueth therein, he being not a forgetful hearer, but a doer of the work, this man shall be blessed in his deed.* 1 Pet. ii. 16. *as free, and not using your liberty for a cloke of maliciousness, but as the servants of God.* Hence we are freed from the yoke of human judgements, much more of civil decrees and penalties in religious matters. Rom. xiv. 4. *who art thou that judgest another man's servant? to his own master he standeth or falleth.* v. 8. *whether we live or die, we are the Lord's.* Matt. vii. 1. *judge not, that ye be not judged.* Rom. xiv. 10. *why dost thou judge thy brother? or why dost thou set at nought thy brother? for we shall all stand before the judgement-seat of Christ.* If we are forbidden to judge (or condemn) our brethren respecting matters of religion or conscience in common discourse, how much more in a court of law, which has confessedly no jurisdiction here; since Paul refers all such matters to the judgement-seat of Christ, not of man? James ii. 12. *so speak ye, and so do, as they that shall be judged by the law of liberty;* namely, by God, not by fallible men in things appertaining to religion; wherein if he will judge us according to the law of liberty, why should man prejudge us according to the law of bondage?

BY THE GUIDANCE OF THE SPIRIT OF TRUTH IN LOVE. Rom. xiv. throughout the whole of the chapter; and chap. xv. 1–15. In these chapters Paul lays down two especial cautions to be observed; first, that whatever we do in pursuance of this our liberty, we should do it in full assurance of faith, nothing doubting that it is permitted us. v. 5. *let every man be fully persuaded in his own mind.* v. 23. *whatever is not of faith, is sin.* Secondly, that we should give no just cause of offence to a weak brother, v. 20, 21. *for meat destroy not the work of God: all things indeed are pure, but it is evil for that man who eateth with offence.* 1 Cor. viii. 13. *if meat make my brother to offend, I will eat no flesh while the world standeth, lest I make my brother to offend;* which resolution, however, must be considered as an effect of the extraordinary love which the apostle bore his brethren, rather than a religious obligation binding on every believer to abstain from flesh for ever, in case a weak brother should think vegetable food alone lawful. ix. 19–22. *though I be free from all men, yet have I made myself servant unto all, that I might gain the more; unto the Jews I became as a Jew . . . to them that are under the law, as under the law . . . to them that are without law, as without law; being not without law to God, but under the law to Christ . . . to the weak became I as weak . . . I am made all things to all men.* x. 23. *all things are lawful for me, but all things are not expedient.* Gal. v. 13. *for, brethren, ye have been called unto liberty; only use not liberty for an occasion to the flesh; but by love serve one another.* 2 Pet. ii. 19. *while they promise themselves liberty, they themselves are the servants of corruption.* 1 Cor. viii. 9. *take heed lest by any means this liberty of yours become a stumbling-block to them that are weak.*

This appears to have been the sole motive for the command given to the churches, Acts xv. 28, 29. *to abstain from blood, and from things strangled;* namely, lest the Jews who were not yet sufficiently established in the faith should take offence. For that the abstinence from blood was purely ceremonial, is evident from the reason assigned Lev. xvii. 11. *the life of the flesh is in the blood, and I have given it to you upon the altar to make an atonement for your souls.* Thus the eating of fat was forbidden by the law, vii. 23, &c. yet no one infers from hence that the use of fat is unlawful, this prohibition applying only to the sacrificial times: Acts x. 13, &c.

No regard, however, is to be paid to the

scruples of the malicious or obstinate. Gal. ii. 4, 5. *and that because of false brethren unawares brought in, who came in privily to spy out our liberty which we have in Christ Jesus, that they might bring us into bondage; to whom we gave place by subjection, no, not for an hour; that the truth of the gospel might continue with you.* 1 Cor. xiv. 38. *if any man be ignorant, let him be ignorant.* Christ was not deterred by the fear of giving offence to the Pharisees, from defending the practice of his disciples in eating bread with unwashen hands, Matt. xv. 2, 3. and plucking the ears of corn, which it was considered unlawful to do on the sabbath-day, Luke vi. 1, &c. Nor would he have suffered a woman of condition to anoint his feet with precious ointment, and to wipe them with her hair, still less would he have vindicated and praised the action, John xii. 3, &c. neither would he have availed himself of the good offices and kindness of the women who ministered unto him whithersoever he went, if it were necessary on all occasions to satisfy the unreasonable scruples of malicious or envious persons. Nay, we must withstand the opinions of the brethren themselves, if they are influenced by motives unworthy of the gospel. Gal. ii. 11, &c. *when Peter was come to Antioch, I withstood him to the face, because he was to be blamed.* Nor ought the weak believer to judge rashly of the liberty of a Christian brother whose faith is stronger than his own, but rather to give himself up to be instructed with the more willingness. Rom. xiv. 13. *let us not therefore judge one another any more.*

Neither this reason, therefore, nor a pretended consideration for the weaker brethren, afford a sufficient warrant for those edicts of the magistrate which constrain believers, or deprive them in any respect of their religious liberty. For so the apostle argues 1 Cor. ix. 19. *though I be free from all men, yet have I made myself servant unto all;* I was not made so by others, but became so of my own accord; *free from all men,* and consequently from the magistrate, in these matters at least. When the magistrate takes away this liberty, he takes away the gospel itself; he deprives the good and the bad indiscriminately of their privilege of free judgement, contrary to the spirit of the well known precept, Matt. xiii. 29, 30.

lest while ye gather up the tares ye root up also the wheat with them: let both grow together until the harvest.

.   .   .   .   .   .

BOOK II

CHAP. IX.

OF

THE FIRST CLASS OF SPECIAL VIRTUES
CONNECTED WITH
THE DUTY OF MAN TOWARDS
HIMSELF.

The special virtues which regulate our desire of external advantages, have reference either to bodily gratifications, or to the possessions which enrich and adorn life.

The virtue which prescribes bounds to the desire of bodily gratification, is called TEMPERANCE. Tit. ii. 11, 12. *the grace of God that bringeth salvation hath appeared unto all men, teaching us that denying ungodliness and worldly lusts, we should live soberly, righteously, and godly in this present world.* 1 Pet. ii. 11. *as strangers and pilgrims, abstain from fleshly lusts which war against the soul.* 2 Pet. ii. 9. *the Lord knoweth how . . . to reserve the unjust unto the day of judgement to be punished; but chiefly them that walk after the flesh in the lust of uncleanness.*

Under temperance are comprehended sobriety and chastity, modesty and decency.

SOBRIETY consists in abstinence from immoderate eating and drinking. 1 Thess. v. 8. *let us, who are of the day, be sober.* 1 Pet. i. 13. *wherefore gird up the loins of your mind, be sober.* iv. 7. *the end of all things is at hand; be ye therefore sober, and watch unto prayer.* v. 8. *be sober, be vigilant; because your adversary the devil, as a roaring lion, walketh about seeking whom he may devour.* Esther i. 8. *the drinking was according to law; none did compel: for so the king had appointed to all the officers of his house, that they should do according to every man's pleasure.*

The opposites of this virtue are drunkenness and gluttony; instances of which may be seen in Noah, Gen. ix. Lot, Gen. xix. and Benhadad, 1 Kings xx. 16. Prov. xx. 1. *wine is a mocker.* xxi. 17. *he that loveth wine . . . shall not be rich.* xxiii. 3, &c. *be not desirous of his dainties, for they are deceitful meat.* v. 20, 21. *be not among winebibbers, among riotous eaters of flesh—.* v. 29–32. *who hath woe? who hath sorrow? who hath contentions? who hath babbling? who hath wounds without cause? who hath redness of eyes? they that tarry long at the wine.* Isai. v. 11, 12. *woe unto them that rise up early in the morning, that they may follow strong drink . . . but they regard not the work of Jehovah.* v. 22. *woe unto them that are mighty to drink wine.* xxviii. 1, 3, 7, 8. *woe to the crown of pride, to the drunkards of Ephraim—.* Ezek. xvi. 49. *behold, this was the iniquity of thy sister Sodom, pride, fulness of bread.* Luke xxi. 34. *take heed to yourselves, lest at any time your hearts be overcharged with surfeiting, and drunkenness, and cares of this life, and so that day come upon you unawares.* Rom. xiii. 13. *let us walk honestly, as in the day; not in rioting and drunkenness.* 1 Cor. vi. 10. *nor drunkards . . . shall inherit the kingdom of God.* Gal. v. 21. *drunkenness, revellings, and such like . . . shall not inherit the kingdom of God.* Hos. iv. 10. *they shall eat, and not have enough.* vii. 5. *in the day of our king the princes have made him sick with bottles of wine.* Habak. ii. 15. *woe unto him that giveth his neighbour drink.* Eph. v. 18. *be not drunk with wine, wherein is excess; but—.* 1 Pet. iv. 3, 4. *the time past of our lives may suffice us . . . when we walked in lasciviousness, lusts, excess of wine, revellings, banquetings . . . wherein they think it strange that ye run not with them to the same excess of riot.*

Allied to sobriety is watchfulness. Matt. xxiv. 42. *watch therefore; for ye know not what hour your lord doth come.* See also xxv. 13. xxvi. 41. Mark xiii. 35. v. 37. *what I say unto you, I say unto all, Watch.* Luke xii. 37. *blessed are those servants, whom the lord when he cometh shall find watching.* xxi. 36. *watch ye therefore and pray always, that ye may be accounted worthy to escape all these things that shall come to pass.* Col. iv. 2. *continue in prayer, and watch—.* 1 Thess. v. 6. *therefore let us not sleep, as do others; but let us watch and be sober.* 1 Pet. v. 8. *be sober, be vigilant.* Rev. iii. 3. *if therefore thou shalt not watch, I will come upon thee as a thief*

in the night. xvi. 15. *blessed is he that watcheth, and keepeth his garments, lest he walk naked.* In most of these passages it appears that the watchfulness spoken of refers less to the sleep of the body, than to the lethargy of the mind.

The opposite to this is an excessive love of sleep. Prov. xx. 13. *love not sleep, lest thou come to poverty.*

CHASTITY consists in temperance as regards the unlawful lusts of the flesh; which is also called sanctification. 1 Thess. iv. 3. *this is the will of God, even your sanctification, that ye should abstain from fornication.* Rev. xiv. 4. *these are they which were not defiled with women, for they are virgins: these are they which follow the Lamb.*

To chastity are opposed all kinds of impurity; effeminacy, sodomy, bestiality, &c. which are offences against ourselves in the first instance, and tending to our own especial injury. 1 Cor. vi. 15, 16. *know ye not that your bodies are the members of Christ? shall I then take, &c.—? what, know ye not that he which is joined to an harlot is one body?—.* v. 18. *flee fornication: every sin that man doeth is without the body; but he that committeth fornication, sinneth against his own body.* See also Prov. vi. 24, &c. Gen. xxxviii. 9, 10. *the thing which he did displeased the Lord.* Exod. xxii. 19. *whosoever lieth with a beast shall surely be put to death.* Lev. xviii. 22, 23. *thou shalt not lie with mankind.* Deut. xxiii. 17. *there shall be no whore of the daughters of Israel, nor, &c.* xxvii. 21. *cursed is he that lieth with any manner of beast.* Prov. ii. 16. *to deliver thee from the strange woman.* v. 3, &c. *the lips of a strange woman drop as an honeycomb.* vi. 24. *to keep thee from the evil woman.* See also v. 32. vii. 25. *let not thine heart decline to her ways.* ix. 18. *he knoweth not that the dead are there—.* xxii. 14. *the mouth of strange women is a deep pit.* See also xxiii. 26, 27. xxx. 20. *such is the way of an adulterous woman; she eateth, and wipeth her mouth, and saith, I have done no wickedness.* 1 Kings xiv. 24. *there were also sodomites in the land.* Rom. xiii. 13. *not in chambering and wantonness.* 1 Cor. vi. 9, 10. *be not deceived; neither fornicators . . . nor adulterers, nor effeminate, nor abusers of themselves with mankind*

. . . shall inherit the kingdom of God. v. 13, &c. the body is not for fornication, but for the Lord, and the Lord for the body. Eph. v. 3–5. *fornication and all uncleanness . . . let it not be once named among you, as becometh saints . . . nor filthiness . . . which are not convenient . . . for this ye know, that no whoremonger, nor unclean person . . . hath any inheritance in the kingdom of Christ and of God.*

MODESTY consists in refraining from all obscenity of language or action, in short, from whatever is inconsistent with the strictest decency of behaviour in reference to sex or person. Deut. xxv. 11, 12. *when men strive together, &c.* Job xxxi. 1. *I made a covenant with mine eyes, &c.* 1 Cor. xi. 10. *for this cause ought the woman to have power on her head, because of the angels.* Heb. xii. 28. *we may serve God acceptably, with reverence and godly fear.* 2 Kings iv. 15. *when he had called her, she stood in the door.* The same ideas of womanly decorum existed even among the Gentiles. Thus Homer introduces Penelope:

στῆ ῥα παρὰ σταθμὸν τέγεος πύκα ποιητοῖο. *Odyss. á.* 333.

She . . . beneath
The portal of her stately mansion stood.
I. 414. *Cowper's Translation.*

Opposed to this are obscene conversation, and filthy and licentious gestures. Isai. iii. 16, &c. *therefore Jehovah will smite with a scab the crown of the head of the daughters of Zion, and Jehovah will discover their secret parts.* Matt. v. 28. *whosoever looketh on a woman, &c.* Eph. v. 4. *neither filthiness, nor foolish talking, nor jesting, which are not convenient.* 2 Pet. ii. 14. *having eyes full of adultery.*

DECENCY consists in refraining from indecorum or lasciviousness in dress or personal appearance. Exod. xx. 26. *neither shalt thou go up by steps unto mine altar, that thy nakedness be not discovered thereon.* Deut. xxii. 5. *the woman shall not wear that which pertaineth unto a man, neither shall a man put on a woman's garment; for all that do so are abomination unto Jehovah thy God.* Zeph. i. 8. *it shall come to pass . . . that I will punish all such as are clothed in strange apparel.* Matt. xi. 8. *they that wear soft clothing are in kings' houses.* 1 Tim. ii. 9. *in like manner also that women adorn themselves in*

modest apparel, with shamefacedness and sobriety, not with broidered hair, or gold, or pearls, or costly array. 1 Pet. iii. 3. *whose adorning let it not be that outward adorning of plaiting the hair, and of wearing of gold, or of putting on of apparel.* 2 Kings ix. 30. *she painted her face, &c.*

Moderation in the enjoyment of temporal possessions manifests itself in the virtues of contentment, frugality, industry, and a liberal spirit.

CONTENTMENT is that virtue whereby a man is inwardly satisfied with the lot assigned him by divine providence. Prov. x. 22. *the blessing of Jehovah, it maketh rich.* xxx. 8. *give me neither poverty nor riches; feed me with food convenient for me.* Eccles. iii. 12, 13. *I know that there is no good in them, but for a man to rejoice and to do good in his life; and also that every man should eat and drink, and enjoy the good of all his labour, it is the gift of God.* v. 18, &c. *behold that which I have seen; it is good and comely for one to eat and to drink, and to enjoy the good of all the labour that he taketh under the sun all the days of his life which God giveth him, for it is his portion; every man also to whom God hath given riches and wealth, and hath given him power to eat thereof, and to take his portion and rejoice in his labour; this is the gift of God: for he shall not much remember the days of his life; because God answereth him in the joy of his heart.* vi. 1, 2. *there is an evil which I have seen under the sun, and it is common among men; a man to whom God hath given riches, wealth, and honour, so that he wanteth nothing for his soul of all that he desireth, yet God giveth him not power to eat thereof, but a stranger eateth it.* ix. 9, 10. *live joyfully with the wife whom thou lovest—.* Zech. ix. 16, 17. *how great is his goodness, and how great is his beauty!—.* Philipp. iv. 11, 12. *not that I speak in respect of want; for I have learned in whatsoever state I am, therewith to be content: I know both how to be abased, and I know how to abound; every where, and in all things, I am instructed both to be full and to be hungry, both to abound and to suffer need.* 1 Tim. vi. 6, 7. *godliness with contentment is great gain; for we brought nothing into this world, and it is certain we can carry nothing out: and having food* and raiment let us therewith be content. Heb. xiii. 5. *be content with such things as ye have.* Even in poverty. Psal. xxiii. 1, 2. *Jehovah is my shepherd; I shall not want.* xxxiv. 9, &c. *there is no want to them that fear him; the young lions do lack and suffer hunger—.* xxxvii. 16, 18, 19. *a little that a righteous man hath is better,* &c. . . . *they shall not be ashamed in the evil time, and in the days of famine they shall be satisfied.* xl. 17. *I am poor and needy, yet Jehovah thinketh upon me—.* lxviii. 10. *thou hast prepared of thy goodness for the poor.* Prov. x. 3. *Jehovah will not suffer the soul of the righteous to famish.* Hence poverty is not to be accounted a disgrace. Prov. xvii. 5. *whoso mocketh the poor, reproacheth his maker.* xix. 1. *better is the poor that walketh in his integrity, than he that is perverse in his lips.* xxviii. 6. *better is the poor that walketh in his uprightness, than he that is perverse in his ways, though he be rich.* v. 11. *the rich man is wise in his own conceit, but the poor that hath understanding searcheth him out.* We are forbidden to glory in riches, or to put our confidence in them. Prov. xi. 28. *he that trusteth in his riches shall fall.* Eccles. vi. 11. *seeing there be many things that multiply vanity—.* Mark x. 23–25. *how hardly shall they that have riches enter into the kingdom of God! . . . it is easier for a camel to go through the eye of a needle—.* 1 Tim. vi. 17, 18. *charge them that are rich in this world that they be not high-minded, nor trust in uncertain riches, but in the living God.* 2 Kings xx. 13, 14. *Hezekiah hearkened unto them, and showed them all the house of his precious things.*

Opposed to this are, first, anxiety respecting the necessaries of life. Matt. vi. 25, &c. *take no thought for your life, what ye shall eat, or what ye shall drink, nor yet for your body, what ye shall put on.* v. 33. *seek ye first the kingdom of God and his righteousness, and all these things shall be added unto you.*

Secondly, covetousness. Job xx. 15. *he hath swallowed down riches, and he shall vomit them up again.* Josh. vii. 21. *when I saw among the spoils,* &c. . . . *then I coveted them and took them.* Psal. cxix. 36. *incline my heart unto thy testimonies, and not to covetousness.* Prov. i. 19. *so are the ways of every one that is greedy of gain, which taketh away the life of the owners thereof.* xv. 27. *he that is greedy of gain troubleth his own house.* xx. 21. *an inheritance may be gotten hastily at the beginning, but the end thereof shall not be blessed.* Eccles. ii. 26. *to the sinner he giveth travail, to gather and to heap up, that he may give to him that is good before God.* iv. 8. *there is one alone, and there is not a second; yea, he hath neither child nor brother, yet is there no end of all his labour, neither is his eye satisfied with riches.* v. 10. *he that loveth silver, shall not be satisfied with silver.* Isai. lvii. 17. *for the iniquity of his covetousness was I wroth, and smote him.* Matt. vi. 19. *lay not up for yourselves treasures upon earth, where moth and rust doth corrupt.* xxvii. 5. *he cast down the pieces of silver,* &c. Luke xii. 15. *take heed and beware of covetousness: for a man's life consisteth not in the abundance of the things that he possesseth.* 1 Tim. vi. 9, &c. *they that will be rich fall into temptation and a snare, and into many foolish and hurtful lusts.* Heb. xiii. 5. *let your conversation be without covetousness.* For covetousness is idolatry. Matt. vi. 24. *ye cannot serve God and mammon.* Eph. v. 5. *nor covetous man, who is an idolater.* Col. iii. 5. *covetousness, which is idolatry.* It is likewise styled the root of all evil. 1 Tim. vi. 10. *the love of money is the root of all evil; which while some coveted after, they have erred from the faith.*

Thirdly, a murmuring against the wisdom of God in making provision for the wants of this life. Jude 16. *these are murmurers, complainers, walking after their own lusts, and their mouth speaketh great swelling words, having men's persons in admiration because of advantage.*

FRUGALITY consists in avoiding expense, so far as is seemly, and in wasting nothing which is capable of being applied to an useful purpose. John vi. 12. *gather up the fragments that remain.*

The opposite of this is penuriousness. 1 Sam. xxv. 3. *the man was churlish.* v. 11. *shall I then take my bread, and my water . . . and give it unto men?* Eccles. vi. 2. *a man to whom God hath given riches, wealth, and honour, so that he wanteth nothing for his soul of all that he desireth, yet God giveth him not power to eat thereof, but a stranger eateth it.*

INDUSTRY is that by which we honestly provide for ourselves the means of comfortable living. Gen. ii. 15. *to dress it and to keep it.* iii. 19. *in the sweat of thy face thou shalt eat bread.* Prov. x. 4. *he becometh poor that dealeth with a slack hand.* v. 5. *he that gathereth in summer is a wise son.* xii. 11. *he that tilleth his land shall be satisfied with bread.* xiv. 23. *in all labour there is profit.* xxi. 5. *the thoughts of the diligent tend only to plenteousness, but of every one that is hasty only to want.* xxii. 29. *seest thou a man diligent in his business? he shall stand before kings.* 1 Thess. iv. 11, 12. *work with your own hands, as we commanded you; that ye may walk honestly toward them that are without, and that ye may have lack of nothing.* 2 Thess. iii. 12. *we exhort by our Lord Jesus Christ, that with quietness they work, and eat their own bread.*

The opposite of this is remissness in making provision for the necessaries of life. Prov. vi. 6. *go to the ant, thou sluggard.* x. 5. *he that sleepeth in harvest is a son that causeth shame.* xiii. 4. *the soul of the sluggard desireth, and hath nothing.* xix. 24. *a slothful man hideth his hand in his bosom.* xx. 4. *the sluggard will not plow by reason of the cold; therefore shall he beg in harvest and have nothing.* xxi. 25. *the desire of the slothful killeth him, for his hands refuse to labour.* xxii. 13. *the slothful man says, There is a lion in the streets.* xxiv. 30. *I went by the field of the slothful.* xxvi. 14. *as the door turneth upon his hinges, &c.* xxviii. 19. *he that followeth after vain persons shall have poverty enough.* Eccles. iv. 5, 6. *the fool foldeth his hands together, and eateth his own flesh: better is an handful with quietness, than both the hands full with travail and vexation of spirit.* 2 Thess. iii. 10. *if any would not work, neither should he eat.*

LIBERALITY is a temperate use of our honest acquisitions in the provision of food and raiment, and of the elegancies of life.

In the provision of food. Gen. xxi. 8. *Abraham made a great feast.* Job. i. 5. *it was so, when the days of their feasting were gone about, that Job sent and sanctified them.* Psal. xxiii. 5. *thou preparest a table before me in the presence of mine enemies; thou anointest mine head with oil; my cup runneth over.* civ. 15. *wine that maketh glad the heart of man, and oil to make his face to shine—.* Prov. xxxi. 6. *give strong drink unto him that is ready to perish.* Dan. x. 3. *I ate no pleasant bread.* Luke v. 29. *Levi made him a great feast.* John xii. 2, 3. *there they made him a supper . . . then took Mary a pound of ointment of spikenard, very costly.* Acts xiv. 17. *filling our hearts with food and gladness.*

Of the elegancies of life. Gen. xxiv. 22. *the man took a golden ear-ring of half a shekel weight—.* 2 Sam. i. 24. *who clothed you in scarlet, with other delights, who put on ornaments of gold upon your apparel.* Prov. xiv. 24. *the crown of the wise is their riches.* xxxi. 22, 25. *she maketh herself coverings of tapestry—.* Eccles. ix. 8. *let thy garments be always white, and let thy head lack no ointment.*

The opposite of this is luxury. Prov. xxi. 17. *he that loveth pleasure shall be a poor man; he that loveth wine and oil shall not be rich.* Luke xvi. 19. *there was a certain rich man which was clothed in purple and fine linen, and fared sumptuously every day.*

The virtues more peculiarly appropriate to a high station are lowliness of mind and magnanimity.

Lowliness of mind consists in thinking humbly of ourselves, and in abstaining from self-commendation, except where occasion requires it. Exod. iii. 11. *who am I, that I should go unto Pharaoh?* Psal. cxxxi. 1. *my heart is not haughty, nor mine eyes lofty, neither do I exercise myself in great matters, or in things too high for me.* Prov. xi. 2. *with the lowly is wisdom.* xii. 9. *a man that is despised and hath a servant, is better than he that honoureth himself.* xv. 33. *before honour is humility.* See also xviii. 12. xvi. 19. *better is it to be of an humble spirit with the lowly, than to divide the spoil with the proud.* xxix. 23. *honour shall uphold the humble in spirit.* Jer. i. 6, 7. *ah Lord . . . I am a child.* Dan. ii. 31. *this secret is not revealed to me for any wisdom that I have more than any living.* Matt. xxiii. 12. *he that humbleth himself shall be exalted.* Rom. xii. 10. *in honour preferring one another.* 2 Cor. x. 13. *we will not boast of things without our measure, but according to the measure of the rule, &c.* v. 15. *not boasting of things without our measure—.* Eph. iii. 8. *unto* me who am less than the least of all saints—. v. 21. submitting yourselves one to another in the fear of God. Philipp. ii. 3. in lowliness of mind let each esteem other better than themselves.

In abstaining from self-commendation, except where occasion requires it. Job xii. 3. I have understanding as well as you, I am not inferior to you. xiii. 2. what ye know, the same do I know also. xxix. 8, &c. the young men saw me, and hid themselves, and the aged arose and stood up. Judges v. 7. until I Deborah arose, that I arose a mother in Israel. Eccles. i. 16. lo, I am come to great estate, and have gotten more wisdom than all they that have been before me.

Opposed to this are, first, arrogance. Prov. xx. 6. most men will proclaim every one his own goodness. xxvi. 16. the sluggard is wiser in his own conceit, than seven men that can render a reason. James iii. 1. be not many masters, knowing that we shall receive the greater condemnation.

Secondly, a desire of vain glory. Matt. xxii. 12. whosoever shall exalt himself shall be abased. John v. 41. I receive not honour from men. v. 44. how can ye believe, which receive honour one of another? xii. 42, 43. they loved the praise of men more than the praise of God. Gal. v. 26. let us not be desirous of vain glory. 1 Thess. ii. 6. nor of men sought we glory, neither of you, nor yet of others.

Thirdly, boasting. Prov. xxv. 14. whoso boasteth himself of a false gift, is like clouds and wind without rain.

Fourthly, a crafty or hypocritical extenuation of our own merits, for the purpose of extorting greater praises.

Fifthly, a glorying in iniquity and misdeeds. Psal. lii. 1. why boastest thou thyself in mischief, O thou mighty man? Isai. iii. 9. they declare their sin as Sodom, they hide it not; woe unto their soul, for they have rewarded evil unto themselves.

Allied to lowliness is the love of an unspotted reputation, and of the praises of good men, with a proportionate contempt for those of the wicked. Psal. cxix. 22. remove from me reproach and contempt; for I have kept thy testimonies. v. 39. turn away my reproach, which I fear. Prov. xxii. 1. a good name is rather to be chosen than great riches, and loving favour rather

than silver and gold. Eccles. vii. 1. a good name is better than precious ointment. 1 Kings xviii. 13. was it not told my lord what I did, when Jezebel slew the prophets of Jehovah? Neh. v. 14, 15. so did not I, because of the fear of God. Matt. v. 11. blessed are ye when men . . . shall say all manner of evil against you falsely for my sake. 2 Cor. vi. 8. by honour and dishonour, by evil report and good report, as deceivers and yet true. Heb. xi. 24–26. esteeming the reproach of Christ greater riches than the treasures in Egypt. xiii. 13. let us go forth therefore unto him without the camp, bearing his reproach.

Opposed to this is a shameless disregard of reputation. Luke xviii. 2. which feared not God, neither regarded man.

Secondly, an excessive and indiscriminate passion for esteem and praise, from whatever quarter. Prov. xxvii. 2. let another man praise thee, and not thine own mouth. Matt. xxiii. 5. all their works they do for to be seen of men. Luke vi. 26. woe unto you, when all men shall speak well of you.

MAGNANIMITY is shown, when in the seeking or avoiding, the acceptance or refusal of riches, advantages, or honours, we are actuated by a regard to our own dignity, rightly understood. Thus Abraham did not refuse the gifts of the king of Egypt, Gen. xii. 13. xx. 14. though he rejected those of the king of Sodom, xiv. 22, 23. and though he declined to accept the field offered him by Ephron the Hittite, except on payment of its full value, xxiii. 13. Thus also Job, although restored to his former health and prosperity, did not disdain the congratulatory offerings of his friends, xlii. 11. In this spirit Gideon refused the kingdom, Judges viii. 23. The same disposition accompanied Joseph in his exaltation from a prison to the first honours of the empire, Gen. xli. So also Daniel ii. 48, 49. then the king made Daniel a great man, and gave him many great gifts. On the other hand, chap. v. 17. he answered and said before the king, Let thy gifts be to thyself, and give thy rewards to another; but v. 29. Belshazzar commanded, and they clothed Daniel with scarlet. He was actuated by the same temper in refusing and in accepting dignities. vi. 2. over these were three presidents, of whom Daniel was first. Such was also the spirit of Nehemiah in asking honours, ii. 5. *I said unto the king, If it please the king, and if thy servant hath found favour in thy sight, that thou wouldest send me into Judah;* of Samuel in laying down his authority, 1 Sam. x. 1. *then Samuel took a vial of oil, and poured it upon his head, and kissed him, and said, Is it not because Jehovah hath anointed thee—?* of Elisha in refusing a reward for the cure he had wrought, 2 Kings v. 15, 16. *as Jehovah liveth, before whom I stand, I will receive none;* of Christ in rejecting the empire of the world, Matt. iv. 9. *all these things will I give thee, if,* &c.   Luke iv. 6. John vi. 15. *when Jesus therefore perceived that they would come and take him by force to make him a king, he departed—;* in despising riches, 2 Cor. viii. 9. *though he was rich, yet for your sakes he became poor;* in accepting honours, Matt. xxi. 7, &c. *they brought the ass, and the colt . . . and they set him thereon.* Such, finally, is the spirit by which every true Christian is guided in his estimate of himself. James i. 9, 10. *let the brother of low degree rejoice in that he is exalted; but the rich in that he is made low.*

Allied to this is indignation at the unfounded praises or undeserved prosperity of the wicked.   Prov. xxx. 21, &c. *for three things the earth is disquieted, and for four which it cannot bear; for a servant when he reigneth, and a fool when he is filled with meat; for an odious woman when she is married, and an handmaid that is heir to her mistress.* When however this feeling exceeds due bounds, it ceases to be praiseworthy. Psal. xxxvii. 1. *fret not thyself because of evil doers.* v. 7, 8. *fret not thyself because of him who prospereth in his way, because of the man who bringeth wicked devices to pass.* Prov. iii. 31. *envy thou not the oppressor, and choose none of his*

ways.   The language of indignation is used, Job xxx. 1, &c. Psal. xv. 4. *in whose eyes a vile person is contemned, but he honoureth them that fear Jehovah.* The vehemence of its expression sometimes borders on indecency.   See Ezek. xvi. 25, 36.

Opposed to magnanimity are, first, an ambitious spirit.   Numb. xii. 2. *hath Jehovah indeed spoken only by Moses? hath he not spoken also by us?* xvi. 3. *seeing all the congregation are holy, every one of them, and Jehovah is among them: wherefore then lift ye up yourselves above the congregation of Jehovah?* Judges ix. 1, 2. *Abimelech went to Shechem . . . and communed with them . . . saying, Speak, I pray you, in the ears of all the men of Shechem,* &c. 2 Sam. xv. 2. *Absalom rose up early, and stood beside the way of the gate—.* v. 4. *O that I were made judge in this land—.* Prov. xxv. 27. *for men to search their own glory is not glory.*

Secondly, pride, when a man values himself without merit, or more highly than his merits deserve, or is elated by some insignificant circumstance.   2 Sam. xxii. 28. *thine eyes are upon the haughty, that thou mayest bring them down.* Prov. vi. 16, 17. *these six things doth Jehovah hate . . . a proud look—.* xv. 25. *Jehovah will destroy the house of the proud.* xvi. 5. *every one that is proud in heart is an abomination to Jehovah.* v. 18. *pride goeth before destruction.* xviii. 12. *before destruction the heart of man is haughty.* xxi. 4. *an high look, and a proud heart—.* xxix. 23. *a man's pride shall bring him low.*

Thirdly, pusillanimity; of which Saul when chosen king is an example, 1 Sam. x. 21, 22. *when they sought him, he could not be found . . . behold, he hath hid himself among the stuff.*

Appendix

SOME EARLY LIVES OF MILTON

COLLECTIONS FOR THE LIFE OF MILTON

By John Aubrey, F.R.S.

Mr. John Milton

Was of an Oxfordshire family: his grandfather . . . [a Rom. Cath.] of Holten, in Oxfordshire, near Shotover. His father was brought up in the University of Oxon, at Christ Church, [his mother was a Bradshaw, Chpr. Milton (his brother, the Inner Temple) barrister], and his gr. father disinherited him because he kept not to the Catholic religion [He found a Bible, in English, in his chamber]; so thereupon he came to London, and became a scrivener (brought up by a friend of his, was not an apprentice), and got a plentiful estate by it, and left it off many years before he died. He was an ingenious man, delighted in music, composed many songs now in print, especially that of Oriana.

His son John was born in Bread Street, in London, at the Spread Eagle, which was his house (he had also in that street another house, the Rose, and other houses in other places). He was borne *Anno Domini* . . . the . . . day of . . . about . . . a clock in the . . . He went to school to old Mr. Gill, at Paul's school; went, at his own charge only, to Christ College in Cambr. [at fifteen], where he stayed eight years at least; then he travelled into France and Italy. At Geneva he contracted a great friendship with the learned Dr. Deodati, of Geneva (*vide* his poems). [Had Sir H. Wotton's commendatory letters.] He was acquainted with Sir Henry Wotton, who delighted in his company, Ambassador at Venice. He was several years [*qu.* How many? *Resp.* Two years] beyond sea, and returned to England just upon the breaking out of the civil wars. He was Latin Secretary to the Parliament.

Anno Domini 1619 he was ten years old, as by his picture, and was then a poet. His school-master then was a Puritan, in Essex, who cut his hair short.

He married his first wife . . . Powell, of Fost-hill, in Oxonshire. She went without her husband's consent to her mother in the King's quarters. [She went from him to her mother's at . . . the King's quarters, near Oxford . . . and wrote the triple cord, about Divorce.] She died *Anno Domini* . . .

Anno Domini . . . [*sic*] by whom he had 4 children. Hath two daughters living; Deborah was his amanuensis; he taught her Latin, and to read Greek (and Hebrew, qu. *erased*,) to him when he lost his eyesight, which was *Anno Domini* . . .

He was scarce so tall as I am [*Qu. quot* feet I am high? *Resp.* Of middle stature]. He had light brown [auburn] hair. His complexion exceeding fair [he was so fair that they called him the Lady of Christ College]. Oval face, his eye a dark gray. His widow has his picture drawn (very well and like) when a Cambridge scholar. She has his picture when a Cambridge scholar, which ought to be engraven; for the pictures before his books are not *at all* like him.

He married his 2d wife, Mistress Eliz. Minshull, *Anno* . . . (the year before the sickness), a gentle person, a peaceful and agreeable humor.

After he was blind, he wrote these following books, *viz.*

Paradise Lost,
Paradise Regained,
Grammar,
Dictionary, imperfect.

He was a spare man.

[Different rell.] Two opinions do not well on the same bolster. She was a . . . royalist, and went to her mother near Oxford [the K's quarters]. I have so much charity for her that she might not wrong his bed, but what man (especially contemplative) would like to have a young wife environed [and stormed] by the sons of Mars, and those of the enemy party.

He lived in several places, e.g. Holborn near K's gate. He died in Bunhill opposite the Artillery-garden wall.

His harmonical and ingenious soul did lodge in a beautiful and well-proportioned body.

In toto nusquam corpore menda fuit.

Ovid.

He had a very good memory; but I believe that his excellent method of thinking and disposing did much help his memory.

I heard that after he was blind, that he was writing, a [Latin] dictionary in the hands of Moses P.H. *Vidua affirmat.* She gave all his papers (among which this dictionary imperfect) to his nephew, that he brought up, a sister's son, . . . Philips, who lives near the Maypole in the Strand. She has a great many letters by her from learned men, his acquaintance, both of England, and beyond sea.

His eye-sight was decaying about 20 years before his death. (*Qu.* when quite [stark] blind?) His father read without spectacles at 84. His mother had very weak eyes, and used spectacles presently after she was thirty years old.

Of a very cheerful humor.

Seldom took any physic, only sometimes he took manna.

He was very healthy, and free from all diseases; only toward his later end, he was visited with the gout, spring and fall. He would be cheerful even in his gout-fits, and sing.

He died of the gout struck in, the 9th or 10th of November, 1674, as appears by his apothecary's book.

He lies buried in St. Giles, Cripplegate, [upper end of] chancel at the right hand. *Mdm.* his stone is now removed; for about 2 years since (now 1681) the two steps to the communion-table were raised. I guess Jo. Speed and he lie together.

Qu. His nephew, Mr. Edw. Philips, for a perfect catalogue of his writings. *Mdm.* he wrote a little tract of *Education.*

Mdm. Mr. Theodore Haak, R.S.S. hath translated half his Paradise Lost into High Dutch, in such blank verse, which is very well liked of by Germanus Fabricius, professor at Heidelberg, who sent to Mr. Haak a letter upon this translation. *Incredible est quantum nos omnes affecerit gravitas styli, et copia lectissimorum verborum, et . . .* vide the letter.

He was an early riser, *sc.* at 4 o'clock *manè,* yea, after he lost his sight. He had a man read to him. The first thing he read was the Hebrew Bible, and that was at 4*h. manè*-4/2 *h.* +. Then he contemplated. At 7 his man came to him again, and then read to him and wrote till dinner; the writing was as much as the reading. His 2d daughter, Deborah, [married in Dublin to one Mr. Clarke (a mercer, sells silk); very like her father.] could read to him Latin, Ital. and French, and Greek. The other sister is Mary, more like her mother. After dinner he used to walk 3 to 4 hours at a time (he always had a garden where he lived): went to bed about 9. Temperate, rarely drank between meals. Extreme pleasant in his conversation, and at dinner, supper, &c. but satirical.

He pronounced the letter R very hard [*Litera canina*. A certain sign of a satirical wit. From Jo. Dryden].

He had a delicate, tuneable voice, and had good skill. His father instructed him. He had an organ in his house; he played on that most. His exercise was chiefly walking.

He was visited much by learned, more than he did desire.

He was mightily importuned to go into Fr. and Italy. Foreigners came much to see him, and much admired him, and offered to him great preferments to come over to them, and the only inducement of several foreigners that came over into England, was chiefly to see O. Protector, and Mr. J. Milton; and would see the *house and chamber* where *he* was born. He was much more admired abroad than at home.

His familiar learned acquaintance were Mr. Andrew Marvell, Mr. Skinner, Dr. Paget, M.D.

Mr. . . . . Skinner, who was his disciple.

Jo. Dryden, Esq., Poet Laureate, who very much admires him, and went to him to have leave to put his Paradise Lost into a drama in rhyme. Mr. Milton received him civilly, and told him he would give him leave to tag his verses.

His widow assures me that Mr. Hobbs was not one of his acquaintance, that her husband did not like him at all, but he would acknowledge him to be a man of great parts, and a learned man. Their interests and tenets were diametrically opposite—vide Mr. Hobbes *Behemoth*.

From his bro. Chr. Milton:—

When he went to school, when he was very young, he studied very hard, and sat up very late; commonly till 12 or one o'clock at night, and his father ordered the maid to sit up for him, and in those years (10) composed many copies of verses, which might well become a riper age. And was a very hard student in the university, and performed all his exercises there with very good applause. His 1st tutor there was Mr. Chapell, from whom receiving some unkindness [whipped him], he was afterwards (though it seemed opposite to the rules of the college), transferred to the tuition of one Mr. Tovell, who died parson of Lutterworth.

I have been told that the father composed a song of fourscore parts of the Landgrave of Hesse for which highness sent a medal of gold or a noble present. He died, about 1647, buried in Cripplegate ch. from his house in the Barbican.

Mr. Chr. Milton to see the date of his bro. birth.

1. Of Reformation.   } *Qu.* whether two
     Against Prelatical Episcopacy. }   books.
2. The reason of Church Government.
3. A Defence of Smectymnuus.
4. The Doctrine and Discipline of
        Divorce.   } All these in prosecu-
5. Colasterion.   } tion of the same
6. The Judgment of Martin Bucer. } subject.
7. Tetrachordon (of Divorce). }

Areopagitica, viz., for the Liberty of the Press.
Of Education.
Iconoclastes.
Tenure of Kings and Magistrates.
Defensio Populi Anglicani.

Defensio Secunda contra Morum.   His Logic.
Defensio Tertia.
Of the Power of the Civil Magistrate in Ecclesiastical
    Affairs.
Against Hirelings (against Tithes).
Of a Commonwealth.
Against Dr. Griffith.
Of Toleration, Heresy, and Schism.

He went to travel about the year 1638, and was abroad about a year's space, chiefly in Italy: immediately after his return he took a lodging at Mr. Russell's, a tailor, in St. Bride's Churchyard, and took into his tuition his sister's two sons, Edw. and John Philips, the first 10, the other 9 years of age; and in a year's time made them capable of interpreting a Latin author at sight, &c. and within 3 years they went through the best of Latin and Greek poets: Lucretius and Manilius (and with him the use of the globes, and some rudiments of arithm. and geom.) of the Latins; Hesiod, Aratus, Dionysius Afer, Oppian, Apollonii *Argonautica,* and Quintus Calaber.   Cato, Varro, and Columella *de Re Rustica* were the very first authors they learned.

As he was severe on one hand, so he was most familiar and free in his conversation to those to whom most sour in his way of education.   N. B.   He made his nephews songsters, and sing from the time they were with him.

John Milton was born the 9th of December, 1608, *die Veneris,* half an hour after 6 in the morning.

From Mr. E. Philips:—All the time of writing his Paradise Lost, his vein began at the autumnal equinoctial, and ceased at the vernal, or thereabouts (I believe about May), and this was 4 or 5 years of his doing it.   He began about 2 years before the K. came in, and finished about 3 years after the K.'s restoration.

Qu.   Mr. J. Playford *pro* Wilby's Set of Orianas.

In the [4th] book of Paradise Lost there are about 6 verses of Satan's exclamation to the sun, which Mr. E. Philips remembers about 15 or 16 years before ever his Poem was thought of; which verses were intended for the beginning of a tragedy, which he had designed, but was diverted from it by other business.

Whatever he wrote against monarchy was out of no animosity to the King's person, or out of any faction or interest, but out of a pure zeal to the liberty of mankind, which he thought would be greater under a free state than under a monarchial government.   His being so conversant in Livy and the Roman authors, and the greatness he saw done by the Roman commonwealth, and the virtue of their great commanders induced him to.

His first wife (Mrs. Powell, a royalist) was brought up and lived where there was a great deal of company and merriment, dancing, &c.   And when she came to live with her husband at Mr. Russell's, in St. Bride's ch. yard, she found it very solitary; no company came to her, oftentimes heard his nephews beaten and cry.   This life was irksome to her, and so she went to her parents at Foste-hill.   He sent for her (after some time), and I think his servant was evilly entreated, but as for wronging his bed, I never heard the least suspicions, nor had he of that any jealousy.

From Mr. Abr. Hill:—*Memorand.*   His sharp writing against Alexander More, of Holland, upon a mistake notwithstanding he had given him by the ambassador [*Qu.* the ambassador's name of Mr. Hill?   *Resp.*   Newport, the Dutch ambassador] all satisfaction to the contrary: *viz.* that the book called *"Clamor"* was writ by Peter du Moulin. Well, that was all one; he having writ it, it should go into the world; one of them was as bad as the other.

His sight began to fail him at first upon his writing against Salmasius, and before 'twas fully completed, one eye absolutely failed. Upon the writing of other books after that, his other eye decayed.

Write his name in red letters on his pictures with his widow to preserve.

THE LIFE OF MILTON

By Edward Phillips *

Of all the several parts of history, that which sets forth the lives, and commemorates the most remarkable actions, sayings, or writings of famous and illustrious persons, whether in war or peace, whether many together, or any one in particular, as it is not the least useful in itself, so it is in highest vogue and esteem among the studious and reading part of mankind.

The most eminent in this way of history were, among the ancients, Plutarch and Diogenes Laertius, of the Greeks; the first wrote the lives, for the most part, of the most renowned heroes and warriors of the Greeks and Romans; the other, the lives of the ancient Greek philosophers. And Cornelius Nepos (or as some will have it Æmilius Probus) of the Latins, who wrote the lives of the most illustrious Greek and Roman generals.

Among the moderns, Machiavelli, a noble Florentine, who elegantly wrote the life of Castruccio Castracani, Lord of Lucca. And of our nation, Sir Fulke Greville, who wrote the life of his most intimate friend, Sir Philip Sidney; Mr. Thomas Stanley of Cumberlo-Green, who made a most elaborate improvement to the foresaid Laertius, by adding to what he found in him, what by diligent search and enquiry he collected from other authors of best authority; [and] Isaac Walton, who wrote the lives of Sir Henry Wotton, Dr. Donne, and for his divine poems, the admired Mr. George Herbert. Lastly, not to mention several other biographers of considerable note, the great Gassendus of France, the worthy celebrator of two no less worthy subjects of his impartial pen; *viz.* the noble philosopher Epicurus, and the most politely learned virtuoso of his age, his countryman, Monsieur Peiresk.

And pity it is the person whose memory we have here undertaken to perpetuate by recounting the most memorable transactions of his life (though his works sufficiently recommend him to the world), finds not a well-informed pen able to set him forth, equal with the best of those here mentioned; for doubtless, had his fame been as much spread through Europe in Thuanus's time, as now it is and hath been for several years, he had justly merited from that great historian, an eulogy not inferior to the highest by him given to all the learned and ingenious that lived within the compass of his history. For we may safely and justly affirm, that take him in all respects, for acumen of wit, quickness of apprehension, sagacity of judgment, depth of argument, and elegancy of style, as well in Latin as English, as well in verse as prose, he is scarce to be paralleled by any the best of writers our nation hath in any age brought forth.

He was born in London, in a house in Breadstreet, the lease whereof, as I take it, but for certain it was a house in Breadstreet, became in time part of his estate, in the year of our Lord 1606.[1] His father John Milton, an honest, worthy, and substantial citizen of London, by profession a scrivener; to which he voluntarily betook himself by the advice

---

* Edward Phillips left the fullest and least unreliable of the early biographies of his uncle. He was the son of Anne Milton Phillips (the poet's sister) and Edward Phillips, senior, and was born in the autumn of 1630. He and his brother John were both pupils of Milton and must have lived with him for several years, but in the end both of them seem to have become sympathizers with the position of the Royalists. Edward, however, remained personally loyal to Milton and translated his *Letters of State* into English after his death.

[1] The correct date of Milton's birth was Dec. 9. 1608.

and assistance of an intimate friend of his eminent in that calling, upon his being cast out by his father, a bigoted Roman Catholic, for embracing, when young, the protestant faith, and abjuring the popish tenets. For he is said to have been descended of an ancient family of the Miltons, of Milton near Abingdon in Oxfordshire; where they had been a long time seated, as appears by the monuments still to be seen in Milton church; till one of the family having taken the wrong side, in the contest between the Houses of York and Lancaster, was sequestered of all his estate, but what he held by his wife. However, certain it is that this vocation he followed for many years, at his said house in Breadstreet, with success suitable to his industry and prudent conduct of his affairs. Yet he did not so far quit his own generous and ingenious inclinations as to make himself wholly a slave to the world; for he sometimes found vacant hours to the study (which he made his recreation) of the noble science of music, in which he advanced to that perfection that as I have been told, and as I take it by our author himself, he composed an *In Nomine* of forty parts; for which he was rewarded with a gold medal and chain by a Polish prince, to whom he presented it. However, this is a truth not to be denied, that for several songs of his composition after the way of these times (three or four of which are still to be seen in Old Wilby's set of Airs, besides some compositions of his in Ravenscroft's Psalms) he gained the reputation of a considerable master in this most charming of all the liberal sciences. Yet all this while he managed his grand affair of this world with such prudence and diligence that by the assistance of divine Providence favoring his honest endeavors, he gained a competent estate, whereby he was enabled to make a handsome provision both for the education and maintenance of his children; for three he had, and no more, all by one wife, Sarah, of the family of the Castons, derived originally from Wales, a woman of incomparable virtue and goodness: John the eldest, the subject of our present work, Christopher, and an only daughter Ann.

Christopher, being principally designed for the study of the common law of England, was entered young a student of the Inner Temple, of which house he lived to be an ancient bencher, and keeping close to that study and profession all his life time, except in the time of the civil wars of England; when being a great favorer and asserter of the King's cause, and obnoxious to the Parliament's side, by acting to his utmost power against them, so long as he kept his station at Reading; and after that town was taken by the Parliament forces, being forced to quit his house there, he steered his course according to the motion of the King's army. But when the war was ended with victory and success to the Parliament party by the valor of General Fairfax and the craft and conduct of Cromwell, and his composition made by the help of his brother's interest with the then prevailing power, he betook himself again to his former study and profession, following chamber-practice every term; yet came to no advancement in the world in a long time, except some small employ in the town of Ipswich, where (and near it) he lived all the latter time of his life; for he was a person of a modest, quiet temper, preferring justice and virtue before all worldly pleasure or grandeur. But in the beginning of the reign of King James the II, for his known integrity and ability in the law, he was by some persons of quality recommended to the King, and at a call of sergeants received the coif, and the same day was sworn one of the barons of the Exchequer, and soon after made one of the judges of the Common Pleas. But his years and indisposition not well brooking the fatigue of public employment, he continued not long in either of these stations; but having his *quietus est,* retired to a country life, his study and devotion.

Ann, the only daughter of the said John Milton, the elder, had a considerable dowry given her by her father in marriage with Edward Philips, the son of Edward Philips of Shrewsbury, who, coming up young to town, was bred up in the crown-office in Chancery, and at length came to be secondary of the office under old Mr. Bembo. By him she had, besides other children that died infants, two sons yet surviving, of whom more hereafter; and by a second husband, Mr. Thomas Agar (who, upon the death of his intimate friend Mr. Philips, worthily succeeded in the place, which, except some time of exclusion before and during the Interregnum, he held for many years, and left it to Mr. Thomas Milton, the son of the aforementioned Sir Christopher, who at this day executes it with great reputation and ability), two daughters, Mary who died very young, and Ann yet surviving.

But to hasten back to our matter in hand. John, our author, who was destined to be the ornament and glory of his country, was sent, together with his brother, to Paul's school, whereof Dr. Gill the elder was then chief master; where he was entered into the first rudiments of learning, and advanced therein with that admirable success, not more by the discipline of the school and good instructions of his masters (for that he had another master, possibly at his father's house, appears by the *Fourth Elegy* of his Latin poems written in his 18th year, to Thomas Young, pastor of the English Company of Merchants at Hamburg, wherein he owns and styles him his master), than by his own happy genius, prompt wit and apprehension, and insuperable industry: for he generally sat up half the night, as well in voluntary improvements of his own choice, as the exact perfecting of his school exercises. So that at the age of 15 he was full ripe for academic learning, and accordingly was sent to the University of Cambridge; where in Christ's College under the tuition of a very eminent learned man, whose name I cannot call to mind, he studied seven years and took his degree of Master of Arts; and for the extraordinary wit and reading he had shown in his performances to attain his degree (some whereof, spoken at a *Vacation Exercise* in his 19th year of age, are to be yet seen in his *Miscellaneous Poems*), he was loved and admired by the whole university, particularly by the fellows and most ingenious persons of his house. Among the rest there was a young gentleman, one Mr. King, with whom, for his great learning and parts, he had contracted a particular friendship and intimacy; whose death (for he was drowned on the Irish seas in his passage from Chester to Ireland) he bewails in that most excellent monody in his forementioned poems, entitled *Lycidas*. Never was the loss of friend so elegantly lamented; and among the rest of his *Juvenile Poems*, some he wrote at the age of 15, which contain a poetical genius scarce to be paralleled by any English writer.

Soon after he had taken his Master's degree, he thought fit to leave the university: not upon any disgust or discontent for want of preferment, as some ill-willers have reported; nor upon any cause whatsoever forced to fly, as his detractors maliciously feign; but from which aspersion he sufficiently clears himself in his *Second Answer to Alexander Morus,* the author of a book called, *Clamor Regii Sanguinis ad Coelum,* the chief of his calumniators; in which he plainly makes it out that after his leaving the university, to the no small trouble of his fellow-collegiates, who in general regretted his absence, he for the space of five years lived for the most part with his father and mother at their house at Horton near Colebrook in Berkshire; whither his father, having got an estate to his content and left off all business, was retired from the cares and fatigues of the world.

After the said term of five years, his mother then dying, he was willing to add to his acquired learning the observation of foreign customs, manners, and institutions; and thereupon took a resolution to travel, more especially designing for Italy; and accordingly, with his father's consent and assistance, he put himself into an equipage suitable to such a design; and so, intending to go by the way of France, he set out for Paris, accompanied only with one man, who attended him through all his travels; for his prudence was his guide, and his learning his introduction and presentation to persons of most eminent quality. However, he had also a most civil and obliging letter of direction and advice from Sir Henry Wotton, then Provost of Eton, and formerly resident Ambassador from King James the First to the state of Venice; which letter is to be seen in the first edition of his *Miscellaneous Poems.*

At Paris, being recommended by the said Sir Henry and other persons of quality, he went first to wait upon my Lord Scudamore, then Ambassador in France from King Charles the First. My Lord received him with wonderful civility; and understanding he had a desire to make a visit to the great Hugo Grotius, he sent several of his attendants to wait upon him and to present him in his name to that renowned doctor and statesman, who was at that time Ambassador from Christina, Queen of Sweden, to the French king. Grotius took the visit kindly, and gave him entertainment suitable to his worth and the high commendations he had heard of him. After a few days, not intending to make the usual tour of France, he took his leave of my Lord, who at his departure from Paris, gave him letters to the English merchants residing in any part through which he was to travel, in which they were requested to show him all the kindness and do him all the good offices that lay in their power.

From Paris he hastened on his journey to Nice, where he took shipping, and in a short space arrived at Genoa; from whence he went to Leghorn, thence to Pisa, and so to Florence. In this city he met with many charming objects, which invited him to stay a longer time than he intended; the pleasant situation of the place, the nobleness of the structures, the exact humanity and civility of the inhabitants, the more polite and refined sort of language there than elsewhere. During the time of his stay here, which was about two months, he visited all the private academies of the city, which are places established for the improvement of wit and learning, and maintained a correspondence and perpetual friendship among gentlemen fitly qualified for such an institution; and such sort of academies there are in all or most of the most noted cities in Italy. Visiting these places he was soon taken notice of by the most learned and ingenious of the nobility and the grand wits of Florence, who caressed him with all the honors and civilities imaginable; particularly Jacobo Gaddi, Carlo Dati, Antonio Francini, Frescobaldo, Cultellino, Bonmatthei and Clementillo: whereof Gaddi hath a large, elegant Italian canzonet in his praise, [and] Dati, a Latin epistle, both printed before his Latin poems, together with a Latin distich of the Marquis of Villa, and another of Selvaggi, and a Latin tetrastich of Giovanni Salsilli, a Roman.

From Florence he took his journey to Siena, from thence to Rome, where he was detained much about the same time he had been at Florence; as well by his desire of seeing all the rarities and antiquities of that most glorious and renowned city, as by the conversation of Lucas Holstenius and other learned and ingenious men, who highly valued his acquaintance and treated him with all possible respect.

From Rome he travelled to Naples, where he was introduced by a certain hermit who accompanied him in his journey from Rome thither, into the knowledge of Giovanni Baptista Manso, Marquis of Villa, a Neapolitan by birth, a person of high nobility, virtue, and honor, to whom the famous Italian poet, Torquato Tasso, wrote his treatise *De Amicitia;* and moreover mentions him with great honor in that illustrious poem of his, entitled *Gierusalemme Liberata.* This noble marquis received him with extraordinary respect and civility, and went with him himself to give him a sight of all that was of note and remark in the city, particularly the viceroy's palace, and was often in person to visit him at his lodging. Moreover, this noble marquis honored him so far, as to make a Latin distich in his praise, as hath been already mentioned; which being no less pithy than short, though already in print, it will not be unworth the while here to repeat.

> *Ut mens, forma, decor, facies, [mos,] si pietas sic*
> *Non Anglus, verum hercle Angelus ipse foret.*

In return of this honor, and in gratitude for the many favors and civilities received of him, he presented him at his departure with a large Latin eclogue, entitled *Mansus,* afterwards published among his *Latin Poems*. The marquis at his taking leave of him, gave him this compliment: that he would have done him many more offices of kindness and civility, but was therefore rendered incapable, in regard he had been over-liberal in his speech against the religion of the country.

He had entertained some thoughts of passing over into Sicily and Greece, but was diverted by the news he received from England that affairs there were tending toward a civil war; thinking it a thing unworthy in him to be taking his pleasure in foreign parts while his countrymen at home were fighting for their liberty: but first resolved to see Rome once more; and though the merchants gave him a caution that the Jesuits were hatching designs against him in case he should return thither, by reason of the freedom he took in all his discourses of religion; nevertheless he ventured to prosecute his resolution, and to Rome the second time he went; determining with himself not industriously to begin to fall into any discourse about religion, but, being asked, not to deny or endeavor to conceal his own sentiments. Two months he stayed at Rome, and in all that time never flinched, but was ready to defend the orthodox faith against all opposers; and so well he succeeded therein, that, good Providence guarding him, he went safe from Rome back to Florence, where his return to his friends of that city was welcomed with as much joy and affection as had it been to his friends and relations in his own country, he could not have come a more joyful and welcome guest.

Here, having stayed as long as at his first coming, excepting an excursion of a few days to Lucca, crossing the Apennine and passing through Bononia and Ferrara, he arrived at Venice; where when he had spent a month's time in viewing of that stately city and shipped up a parcel of curious and rare books which he had picked up in his travels (particularly a chest or two of choice music-books of the best masters flourishing about that time in Italy, namely, Luca Marenzo, Monte Verde, Horatio Vecchi, Cifa, the Prince of Venosa, and several others), he took his course through Verona, Milan, and the Poenine Alps, and so by the lake Leman to Geneva, where he stayed for some time, and had daily converse with the most learned Giovanni Deodati, theology professor in that city; and so returning through France, by the same way he had passed it going to Italy, he, after a peregrination of one complete year and about three months, arrived safe in England about the time of the King's making his second expedition against the Scots.

Soon after his return and visits paid to his father and other friends, he took him a lodging in St. Bride's Churchyard, at the house of one Russel, a tailor, where he first undertook the education and instruction of his sister's two sons, the younger whereof had been wholly committed to his charge and care.

And here by the way, I judge it not impertinent to mention the many authors both of the Latin and Greek, which through his excellent judgment and way of teaching, far above the pedantry of common public schools (where such authors are scarce ever heard of), were run over within no greater compass of time, than from ten to fifteen or sixteen years of age. Of the Latin, the four grand authors *De Re Rustica,* Cato, Varro, Columella and Palladius; Cornelius Celsus, an ancient physician of the Romans; a great part of Pliny's *Natural History;* Vitruvius his *Architecture;* Frontinus his *Stratagems;* with the two egregious poets, Lucretius and Manilius. Of the Greek, Hesiod, a poet equal with Homer; Aratus his *Phaenomena,* and *Diosemeia;* Dionysius Afer *De Situ Orbis;* Oppian's *Cynegetics* and *Halieutics;* Quintus Calaber his *Poem of the Trojan War* continued from Homer; Apollonius Rhodius his *Argonautics:* and in prose, Plutarch's *Placita Philosophorum,* and Περι Παιδων 'Αγογιας [*sic*]; Geminus's *Astronomy;* Xenophon's *Cyri Institutio,* and *Anabasis;* Ælian's *Tactics;* and Polyænus his *Warlike Stratagems.* Thus by teaching he in some measure increased his own knowledge, having the reading of all these authors as it were by proxy; and all this might possibly have conduced to the preserving of his eyesight, had he not moreover been perpetually busied in his own laborious undertakings of the book and pen.

Nor did the time thus studiously employed in conquering the Greek and Latin tongues, hinder the attaining to the chief oriental languages, *viz.*, the Hebrew, Chaldee, and Syriac, so far as to go through the *Pentateuch*, or Five Books of Moses in Hebrew, to make a good entrance into the *Targum*, or Chaldee Paraphrase, and to understand several chapters of St. Matthew in the Syriac Testament: besides an introduction into several arts and sciences, by reading Urstisius his *Arithmetic*, Riff's *Geometry*, Petiscus his *Trigonometry*, Johannes de Sacro Bosco *De Sphæra;* and into the Italian and French tongues, by reading in Italian Giovan Villani's *History of the Transactions between several petty States of Italy;* and in French a great part of Pierre Davity, the famous geographer of France in his time.

The Sunday's work was, for the most part, the reading each day a chapter of the Greek Testament, and hearing his learned exposition upon the same (and how this savored of atheism in him, I leave to the courteous backbiter to judge). The next work after this was the writing from his own dictation, some part, from time to time, of a tractate which he thought fit to collect from the ablest of divines who had written of that subject: Amesius, Wollebius, &c., *viz. A perfect System of Divinity*, of which more hereafter.

Now persons so far manuducted into the highest paths of literature both divine and human, had they received his documents with the same acuteness of wit and apprehension, the same industry, alacrity, and thirst after knowledge, as the instructor was indued with, what prodigies of wit and learning might they have proved! The scholars might in some degree have come near to the equalling of the master, or at least have in some sort made good what he seems to predict in the close of an elegy he made in the seventeenth year of his age, upon the death of one of his sister's children (a daughter), who died in her infancy:

> Then thou, the mother of so sweet a child,
> Her false, imagin'd loss cease to lament,
> And wisely learn to curb thy sorrows wild:
> This if thou do, he will an offspring give,
> That till the world's last end shall make thy name to live.

But to return to the thread of our discourse. He made no long stay in his lodgings in St. Bride's Church-yard; necessity of having a place to dispose his books in, and other goods fit for the furnishing of a good, handsome house, hastening him to take one; and, accordingly, a pretty garden-house he took in Aldersgate-street, at the end of an entry and therefore the fitter for his turn by the reason of the privacy; besides that there are few streets in London more free from noise than that. Here first it was that his academic erudition was put in practice, and vigorously proceeded, he himself giving an example to those under him (for it was not long after his taking this house, ere his elder nephew was put to board with him also) of hard study and spare diet; only this advantage he had, that once in three weeks or a month, he would drop into the society of some young sparks of his acquaintance, the chief whereof were Mr. Alphry and Mr. Miller, two gentlemen of Gray's Inn, the beaux of those times, but nothing near so bad as those now-a-days; with these gentlemen he would so far make bold with his body as now and then to keep a gawdy-day.

In this house he continued several years, in the one or two first whereof he set out several treatises, *viz.*, that *Of Reformation;* that *Against Prelatical Episcopacy; The Reason of Church-Government; The Defence of Smectymnuus*, at least the greatest part of them, but as I take it, all; and some time after, one sheet *Of Education* which he dedicated to Mr. Samuel Hartlib, he that wrote so much of husbandry (this sheet is printed at the end of the second edition of his *Poems*), and lastly *Areopagitica*.

During the time also of his continuance in this house, there fell out several occasions of the increasing of his family.   His father, who till the taking of Reading by the Earl of Essex his forces, had lived with his other son at his house there, was upon that son's dissettlement necessitated to betake himself to this his eldest son, with whom he lived for some years, even to his dying day.   In the next place he had an addition of some scholars; to which may be added, his entering into matrimony; but he had his wife's company so small a time, that he may well be said to have become a single man again soon after.

About Whitsuntide it was, or a little after, that he took a journey into the country; no body about him certainly knowing the reason, or that it was any more than a journey of recreation; after a month's stay, home he returns a married man, that went out a bachelor; his wife being Mary, the eldest daughter of Mr. Richard Powell, then a justice of peace, of Forresthill, near Shotover in Oxfordshire; some few of her nearest relations accompanying the bride to her new habitation; which by reason the father nor any body else were yet come, was able to receive them; where the feasting held for some days in celebration of the nuptials and for entertainment of the bride's friends.   At length they took their leave and returning to Forresthill left the sister behind, probably not much to her satisfaction as appeared by the sequel.   By that time she had for a month or thereabout led a philosophical life (after having been used to a great house, and much company and joviality), her friends, possibly incited by her own desire, made earnest suit by letter, to have her company the remaining part of the summer, which was granted, on condition of her return at the time appointed, Michaelmas, or thereabout.   In the meantime came his father, and some of the forementioned disciples.

And now the studies went on with so much the more vigor, as there were more hands and heads employed; the old gentleman living wholly retired to his rest and devotion, without the least trouble imaginable.   Our author, now as it were a single man again, made it his chief diversion now and then in an evening, to visit the lady Margaret Lee, daughter to the —— Lee, Earl of Marlborough, Lord High Treasurer of England, and President of the Privy Council to King James the First.   This lady being a woman of great wit and ingenuity, had a particular honor for him and took much delight in his company, as likewise her husband Captain Hobson, a very accomplished gentleman; and what esteem he at the same time had for her, appears by a sonnet he made in praise of her, to be seen among his other *Sonnets* in his extant *Poems*.

Michaelmas being come, and no news of his wife's return, he sent for her by letter; and receiving no answer, sent several other letters, which were also unanswered; so that at last he dispatched down a foot messenger with a letter, desiring her return.   But the messenger came back not only without an answer, at least a satisfactory one, but to the best of my remembrance, reported that he was dismissed with some sort of contempt.   This proceeding in all probability was grounded upon no other cause but this, namely, that the family being generally addicted to the cavalier party, as they called it, and some of them possibly engaged in the King's service, who by this time had his headquarters at Oxford, and was in some prospect of success, they began to repent them of having matched the eldest daughter of the family to a person so contrary to them in opinion; and thought it would be a blot in their escutcheon, whenever that court should come to flourish again.

However, it so incensed our author that he thought it would be dishonorable ever to receive her again, after such a repulse; so that he forthwith prepared to fortify himself with arguments for such a resolution, and accordingly wrote two treatises, by which he undertook to maintain, that it was against reason, and the enjoinment of it not provable by Scripture, for any married couple disagreeable in humor and temper, or having an aversion to each other, to be forced to live yoked together all their days.   The first was his *Doctrine and Discipline of Divorce,* of which there was printed a second edition with some additions. The other in prosecution of the first, was styled *Tetrachordon.*   Then the better to confirm his own opinion by the attestation of others, he set out a piece called *The Judgment of Martin Bucer,* a protestant minister, being a translation out of that reverend divine, of some part of his works exactly agreeing with him in sentiment. Lastly, he wrote in answer to a pragmatical clerk, who would needs give himself the honor of writing against so great a man, his *Colasterion,* or *Rod of Correction for a Saucy Impertinent.*

Not very long after the setting forth of these treatises, having application made to him by several gentlemen of his acquaintance for the education of their sons, as understanding haply the progress he had infixed by his first undertakings of that nature, he laid out for a larger house, and soon found it out.

But in the interim before he removed, there fell out a passage, which though it altered not the whole course he was going to steer, yet it put a stop or rather an end to a grand affair, which was more than probably thought to be then in agitation; it was indeed a design of marrying one of Dr. Davis's daughters, a very handsome and witty gentlewoman, but averse, as it is said, to this motion. However, the intelligence hereof, and the then declining state of the King's cause, and consequently of the circumstances of Justice Powell's family, caused them to set all engines on work to restore the late married woman to the station wherein they a little before had planted her. At last this device was pitched upon. There dwelt in the lane of St. Martin's le Grand, which was hard by, a relation of our author's, one Blackborough, whom it was known he often visited, and upon this occasion the visits were the more narrowly observed, and possibly there might be a combination between both parties; the friends on both sides concentring in the same action, though on different behalfs. One time above the rest, he making his usual visit, the wife was ready in another room, and on a sudden he was surprised to see one whom he thought to have never seen more, making submission and begging pardon on her knees before him. He might probably at first make some show of aversion and rejection; but partly his own generous nature, more inclinable to reconciliation than to perseverance in anger and revenge, and partly the strong intercession of friends on both sides, soon brought him to an act of oblivion and a firm league of peace for the future; and it was at length concluded that she should remain at a friend's house till such time as he was settled in his new house at Barbican, and all things for her reception in order; the place agreed on for her present abode was the widow Webber's house in St. Clement's Church-yard, whose second daughter had been married to the other brother many years before. The first fruits of her return to her husband was a brave girl, born within a year after; though, whether by ill constitution or want of care, she grew more and more decrepit.

But it was not only by children that she increased the number of the family; for in no very long time after her coming, she had a great resort of her kindred with her in the house, *viz.* her father and mother, and several of her brothers and sisters, which were in all pretty numerous; who upon his father's sickening and dying soon after, went away.

And now the house looked again like a house of the Muses only, though the accession of scholars was not great. Possibly his proceeding thus far in the education of youth may have been the occasion of some of his adversaries calling him pedagogue and schoolmaster; whereas it is well known he never set up for a public school to teach all the young fry of the parish, but only was willing to impart his learning and knowledge to relations, and the sons of some gentlemen that were his intimate friends; besides, that neither his converse, nor his writings, nor his manner of teaching ever savored in the least anything of pedantry; and probably he might have some prospect of putting in practice his academical institution, according to the model laid down in his sheet *Of Education.* The progress of which design was afterwards diverted by a series of alteration in the affairs of state; for I am much mistaken if there were not about this time a design in agitation of making him adjutant-general in Sir William Waller's army. But the new modeling of the army soon following proved an obstruction to that design; and Sir William, his commission being laid down, began, as the common saying is, to turn *cat in pan*.

It was not long after the march of Fairfax and Cromwell through the city of London with the whole army, to quell the insurrections Brown and Massey, now malcontents also, were endeavoring to raise in the city against the army's proceedings, ere he left his great house in Barbican, and betook himself to a smaller in High Holburn, among those that open backward into Lincoln's Inn Fields. Here he lived a private and quiet life, still prosecuting his studies and curious search into knowledge, the grand affair perpetually of his life; till such time as, the war being now at an end, with complete victory to the Parliament's side, as the Parliament then stood purged of all its dissenting members, and the King after some treaties with the army *re infecta,* brought to his trial; the form of government being now changed into a free state, he was hereupon obliged to write a treatise, called *The Tenure of Kings and Magistrates.*

After which his thoughts were bent upon retiring again to his own private studies, and falling upon such subjects as his proper genius prompted him to write of, among which was the history of our own nation from the beginning till the Norman Conquest, wherein he had made some progress. When (for this his last treatise, reviving the fame of other things he had formerly published) being more and more taken notice of for his excellency of style, and depth of judgment, he was courted into the service of this new commonwealth and at last prevailed with (for he never hunted after preferment, nor affected the tintamar and hurry of public business) to take upon him the office of Latin secretary to the Council of State, for all their letters to foreign princes and states; for they stuck to this noble and generous resolution, not to write to any, or to receive answers from them, but in a language most proper to maintain a correspondence among the learned of all nations in this part of the world; scorning to carry on their affairs in the wheedling, lisping jargon of the cringing French, especially having a minister of state able to cope with the ablest any prince or state could employ, for the Latin tongue. And so well he acquitted himself in this station that he gained from abroad both reputation to himself and credit to the state that employed him.

And it was well the business of his office came not very fast upon him, for he was scarce well warm in his secretaryship before other work flowed in upon him, which took him up for some considerable time. In the first place there came out a book said to have been written by the king, and finished a little before his death, entitled εἰκὼν βασιλική, that is, *The Royal Image;* a book highly cried up for its smooth style, and pathetical composure; wherefore to obviate the impression it was like to make among the many, he was obliged to write an answer, which he entitled εἰκονοκλάστης or *Image-Breaker.*

And upon the heels of that, out comes in public the great kill-cow of Christendom, with his *Defensio Regis contra Populum Anglicanum;* a man so famous and cried up for his Plinian Exercitations and other pieces of reputed learning, that there could no where have been found a champion that durst lift up the pen against so formidable an adversary, had not our little English David had the courage to undertake this great French Goliath, to whom he gave such a hit in the forehead, that he presently staggered, and soon after fell. For immediately upon the coming out of the answer, entitled, *Defensio Populi Anglicani contra Claudium Anonymum,* &c. he that till then had been chief minister and superintendent in the court of the learned Christina, Queen of Sweden, dwindled in esteem to that degree that he at last vouchsafed to speak to the meanest servant. In short, he was dismissed with so cold and slighting an adieu, that after a faint dying reply, he was glad to have recourse to death, the remedy of evils and ender of controversies.

And now I presume our author had some breathing space, but it was not long. For though Salmasius was departed, he left some stings behind; new enemies started up barkers, though no great biters. Who the first asserter of Salmasius his cause was, is not certainly known but variously conjectured at, some supposing it to be one Janus, a lawyer of Gray's Inn, some Dr. Bramhal, made by King Charles the Second, after his restoration, Archbishop of Armagh in Ireland; but whoever the author was, the book was thought fit to be taken into correction; and our author not thinking it worth his own undertaking, to the disturbing the progress of whatever more chosen work he had then in hands, committed this task to the youngest of his nephews; but with such exact emendations before it went to the press that it might have very well passed for his, but that he was willing the person that took the pains to prepare it for his examination and polishment should have the name and credit of being the author; so that it came forth under this title, *Joannis Philippi Angli Defensio pro Populo Anglicano contra,* &c.

During the writing and publishing of this book, he lodged at one Thomson's next door to the Bull-head tavern at Charing-Cross, opening into the Spring-Garden; which seems to have been only a lodging taken till his designed apartment in Scotland-Yard was prepared for him. For hither he soon removed from the aforesaid place; and here his third child, a son, was born, which through the ill usage, or bad constitution, of an ill chosen nurse, died an infant.

From this apartment, whether he thought it not healthy, or otherwise convenient for his use, or whatever else was the reason, he soon after took a pretty garden-house in Petty-France in Westminster, next door to the Lord Scudamore's, and opening into St. James's Park. Here he remained no less than eight years, namely, from the year 1652, till within a few weeks of King Charles the Second's restoration.

In this house his first wife dying in childbed, he married a second, who after a year's time died in childbed also. This his second marriage was about two or three years after his being wholly deprived of sight, which was just going about the time of his answering Salmasius; whereupon his adversaries gladly take occasion of imputing his blindness as a judgment upon him for his answering the King's book, &c. whereas it is most certainly known that his sight, what with his continual study, his being subject to the headache, and his perpetual tampering with physic to preserve it, had been decaying for above a dozen years before, and the sight of one for a long time clearly lost. Here he wrote, by his amanuensis, his two *Answers to Alexander More,* who upon the last answer quitted the field.

So that being now quiet from state adversaries and public contests, he had leisure again for his own studies and private designs; which were his aforesaid *History of England,* and a new *Thesaurus Linguæ Latinæ,* according to the manner of Stephanus, a work he had been long since collecting from his own reading, and still went on with it at times, even very near to his dying day; but the papers after his death were so discomposed and deficient that it could not be made fit for the press; however, what there was of it was made use of for another dictionary.

But the height of his noble fancy and invention began now to be seriously and mainly employed in a subject worthy of such a Muse, *viz.* a heroic poem, entitled *Paradise Lost;* the noblest in the general esteem of learned and judicious persons of any yet written by any either ancient or modern. This subject was first designed a tragedy, and in the fourth book of the poem there are six verses, which several years before the poem was begun, were shown to me and some others, as designed for the very beginning of the said tragedy. The verses are these:—

O thou that with surpassing glory crown'd!
Look'st from thy sole dominion, like the god
Of this new world; at whose sight all the stars
Hide their diminish'd heads; to thee I call,

> But with no friendly voice; and add thy name,
> O Sun! to tell thee how I hate thy beams
> That bring to my remembrance, from what state
> I fell, how glorious once above thy sphere;
> Till pride and worse ambition threw me down,
> Warring in Heaven, against Heaven's glorious King.

There is another very remarkable passage in the composure of this poem, which I have a particular occasion to remember; for whereas I had the perusal of it from the very beginning, for some years, as I went from time to time to visit him, in a parcel of ten, twenty, or thirty verses at a time, which being written by whatever hand came next, might possibly want correction as to the orthography and pointing; having as the summer came on, not having been showed any for a considerable while, and, desiring the reason thereof, was answered: That his vein never happily flowed but from the autumnal equinoctial to the vernal,[2] and that whatever he attempted [otherwise] was never to his satisfaction, though he courted his fancy never so much, so that in all the years he was about this poem, he may be said to have spent but half his time therein.

It was but a little before the King's restoration that he wrote and published his book *In Defence of a Commonwealth*, so undaunted he was in declaring his true sentiments to the world; and not long before, his *Power of the Civil Magistrate in Ecclesiastical Affairs*, and his *Treatise against Hirelings*, just upon the King's coming over; having a little before been sequestered from his office of Latin secretary and the salary thereunto belonging.

He was forced to leave his house also in Petty-France, where all the time of his abode there, which was eight years as above-mentioned, he was frequently visited by persons of quality, particularly my Lady Ranalagh, whose son for some time he instructed; all learned foreigners of note, who could not part out of this city, without giving a visit to a person so eminent; and lastly, by particular friends that had a high esteem for him, *viz.* Mr. Andrew Marvel, young Lawrence (the son of him that was president of Oliver's council), to whom there is a sonnet among the rest, in his printed *Poems;* Mr. Marchamont Needham, the writer of *Politicus;* but above all, Mr. Cyriac Skinner whom he honored with two sonnets, one long since public among his *Poems,* the other but newly printed.

His next removal was, by the advice of those that wished him well and had a concern for his preservation, into a place of retirement and abscondance, till such time as the current of affairs for the future should instruct him what farther course to take. It was a friend's house in Bartholomew Close, where he lived till the act of oblivion came forth; which it pleased God, proved as favorable to him as could be hoped or expected, through the intercession of some that stood his friends both in Council and Parliament; particularly in the House of Commons, Mr. Andrew Marvel, a member for Hull, acted vigorously in his behalf and made a considerable party for him; so that, together with John Goodwin of Coleman Street, he was only so far excepted as not to bear any office in the Commonwealth.

Soon after appearing again in public, he took a house in Holborn near Red Lyon Fields; where he stayed not long, before his pardon having passed the seal, he removed to Jewin Street. There he lived when he married his 3d wife, recommended to him by his old friend Dr. Paget in Coleman Street. But he stayed not long after his new marriage, ere he removed to a house in the Artillery-walk leading to Bunhill Fields. And this

---

[2] The evidence about this much-controverted point has been reviewed by T. B. Stroup in "Climatic Influence on Milton," in *MLQ*, IV (1943), 185–89, incidentally showing that another of Milton's early biographers, John Toland, understood that he "composed best in warm weather."

was his last stage in this world, but it was of many years continuance, more perhaps than he had had in any other place besides.

Here he finished his noble poem, and published it in the year 1666. The first edition was printed in quarto by one Simons, a printer in Aldersgate Street; the other in a large octavo, by Starky near Temple-Bar, amended, enlarged, and differently disposed as to the number of books by his own hand, that is by his own appointment; the last set forth, many years since his death, in a large folio, with cuts added, by Jacob Tonson.

Here it was also that he finished and published his history of our nation till the Conquest, all complete so far as he went, some passages only excepted; which, being thought too sharp against the clergy, could not pass the hand of the licenser, were in the hands of the late Earl of Anglesey while he lived; where at present is uncertain.

It cannot certainly be concluded when he wrote his excellent tragedy entitled *Samson Agonistes,* but sure enough it is that it came forth after his publication of *Paradise Lost,* together with his other poem called *Paradise Regained,* which doubtless was begun and finished and printed after the other was published, and that in a wonderful short space considering the sublimeness of it; however, it is generally censured to be much inferior to the other, though he could not hear with patience any such thing when related to him. Possibly the subject may not afford such variety of invention, but it is thought by the most judicious to be little or nothing inferior to the other for style and decorum.

The said Earl of Anglesey, whom he presented with a copy of the unlicensed papers of his history, came often here to visit him, as very much coveting his society and converse; as likewise others of the nobility and many persons of eminent quality; nor were the visits of foreigners ever more frequent than in this place, almost to his dying day.

His treatise *Of True Religion, Heresy, Schism and Toleration,* &c. was doubtless the last thing of his writing that was published before his death. He had, as I remember, prepared for the press an answer to some little scribing quack in London, who had written a scurrilous libel against him; but whether by the dissuasion of friends, as thinking him a fellow not worth his notice, or for what other cause I know not, this answer was never published.

He died in the year 1673 towards the latter end of the summer and had a very decent interment according to his quality, in the church of St. Giles, Cripplegate, being attended from his house to the church by several gentlemen then in town, his principal well-wishers and admirers.

He had three daughters who survived him many years (and a son) all by his first wife (of whom sufficient mention hath been made): Anne his eldest as above said, and Mary his second, who were both born at his house in Barbican; and Deborah the youngest, who is yet living, born at his house in Petty-France, between whom and his second daughter, the son, named John, was born as above-mentioned, at his apartment in Scotland Yard. By his second wife, Catharine, the daughter of captain Woodcock of Hackney, he had only one daughter, of which the mother, the first year after her marriage, died in childbed, and the child also within a month after. By his third wife Elizabeth, the daughter of one Mr. Minshal of Cheshire, (and kinswoman to Dr. Paget), who survived him, and is said to be yet living, he never had any child.

And those he had by the first he made serviceable to him in that very particular in which he most wanted their service, and supplied his want of eyesight by their eyes and tongue. For though he had daily about him one or other to read to him; some persons of man's estate, who of their own accord greedily catched at the opportunity of being his readers, that they might as well reap the benefit of what they read to him as oblige him by the benefit of their reading; others of younger years sent by their parents to the same end; yet, excusing only the eldest daughter by reason of her bodily infirmity and difficult utterance of speech (which to say truth I doubt was the principal cause of excusing her), the other two were condemned to the performance of reading and exactly pronouncing of all the languages of whatever book he should at one time or other think fit to peruse; *viz.* the Hebrew (and I think the Syriac), the Greek, the Latin, the Italian, Spanish, and French. All which sorts of books to be confined to read, without understanding one word, must needs be a trial of patience almost beyond endurance; yet it was endured by both for a long time. Yet the irksomeness of this employment could not always be concealed, but broke out more and more into expressions of uneasiness; so that at length they were all (even the eldest also) sent out to learn some curious and ingenious sorts of manufacture that are proper for women to learn, particularly embroideries in gold or silver. It had been happy indeed if the daughters of such a person had been made in some measure inheritrixes of their father's learning; but since fate otherwise decreed, the greatest honor that can be ascribed to this now living (and so would have been to the others had they lived) is to be daughter to a man of his extraordinary character.

He is said to have died worth 1500 £ in money (a considerable estate, all things considered) besides household goods; for he sustained such losses as might well have broke any person less frugal and temperate than himself; no less than 2000 £ which he had put for security and improvement into the excise office, but neglecting to recall it in time could never after get it out, with all the power and interest he had in the great ones of those times; besides another great sum by mismanagement and for want of good advice.

Thus I have reduced into form and order whatever I have been able to rally up, either from the recollection of my own memory of things transacted while I was with him, or the information of others equally conversant afterwards, or from his own mouth by frequent visits to the last.

I shall conclude with two material passages which though they relate not immediately to our author, or his own particular concerns, yet in regard they happened during his public employ and consequently fell especially most under his cognizance, it will not be amiss here to subjoin them. The first was this:

Before the war broke forth between the States of England and the Dutch, the Hollanders sent over three ambassadors in order to an accommodation; but they returning *re infecta,* the Dutch sent away a plenipotentiary, to offer peace upon much milder terms, or at least to gain more time. But this plenipotentiary could not make such haste but that the Parliament had procured a copy of their instructions in Holland, which were delivered by our author to his kinsman that was then with him, to translate for the Council to view before the said plenipotentiary had taken shipping for England; an answer to all he had in charge lay ready for him, before he made his public entry into London.

In the next place there came a person with a very sumptuous train, pretending himself an agent from the prince of Condé, then in arms against Cardinal Mazarin: the Parliament mistrusting him, set their instrument so busily at work, that in four or five days they had procured intelligence from Paris that he was a spy from King Charles; whereupon the very next morning our author's kinsman was sent to him with an order of Council commanding him to depart the kingdom within three days, or expect the punishment of a spy.

By these two remarkable passages, we may clearly discover the industry and good intelligence of those times.

AN ANONYMOUS *LIFE OF MILTON**

To write the lives of single persons is then a commendable undertaking, when by it some moral benefit is designed to mankind. He who has that in aim, will not employ his time or pen to record the history of bad men, how successful or great soever they may have been; unless by relating their tragical ends (which, through the just judgment of the Almighty, most commonly overtakes them) or by discriminating, with a due note of infamy, whatever is criminal in their actions, he warn the reader to flee their example.

But to celebrate, whether the gifts or graces, the natural endowments, or acquitted laudable habits of persons eminent in their generations, while it gives glory to God, the bestower of all good things, and (by furnishing a model) tends to the edification of our brethren, is little less than the duty of every Christian; which seems acknowledged by the late supervisors of our Common Prayer when they added to the Collect for the church militant, a clause commemorating the *Saints and Servants of God departed this life in his Fear.*

That he who is the subject of this discourse made it his endeavor to be thought worthy of that high character, will, I make no doubt, appear to the impartial reader from the particulars which I shall with all sincerity relate of his life and works.

The learned Mr. John Milton, born about the year sixteen hundred and eight, is said to be descended from an ancient knightly family in Buckinghamshire, that gave name to the chief place of their abode. However that be, his father was entitled to a true nobility in the Apostle Paul's Heraldry; having been disinherited about the beginning of Queen Elizabeth's reign by his father, a Romanist, who had an estate of five hundred pound a year at Stainton St. John in Oxfordshire, for reading the Bible. Upon this occasion he came young to London, and being taken care of by a relation of his, a scrivener, he became free of that profession; and was so prosperous in it, and the consortship of a prudent, virtuous wife, as to be able to breed up in a liberal manner, and provide a competency for two sons and a daughter. After which, out of a moderation not usual with such as have tasted the sweets of gain, and perhaps naturally inclined rather to a retired life by his addiction to music (for his skill in which he stands registered among the composers of his time), he gave over his trade and went to live in the country.

This his eldest son had his institution to learning both under public and private masters; under whom, through the pregnancy of his parts and his indefatigable industry (sitting up constantly at his study till midnight), he profited exceedingly; and early in that time wrote several grave and religious poems, and paraphrased some of David's Psalms.

At about eighteen years of age he went to Christ's College in Cambridge; where for his diligent study, his performance of public exercises, and for choice verses, written on the occasions usually solemnized by the universities, as well for his virtuous and sober life, he was in high esteem with the best of his time.

After taking his degree of Master of Arts he left the university, and, having no design to take upon him any of the particular learned professions, applied himself for five years, at his father's house in the country, to the diligent reading of the best classic authors,

---

*In "Concerning 'The Earliest Life of Milton,'" in *ELH,* IX (1942), 106–15, Edward S. Parsons accepts Malone's date of 1686 or 1687 for this work. In the same issue of *ELH,* pp. 116–17, Allan R. Benham presents evidence that it was written in reply to Anthony Wood's treatment of Milton in *Athenae Oxonienses* in 1691. On the evidence of the handwriting of Milton's younger nephew, John Phillips, Miss Darbishire has attributed this Life to him, but her judgment of the handwriting is challenged by W. R. Parker, who attributes it to Cyriack Skinner in *TLS,* 13 Sept., 1957, and justifies his attribution in *Milton. A Biography* (Oxford University Press, 1968), pp. xiv–xv.

both divine and human; sometimes repairing to London, from which he was not far distant, for learning music and the mathematics.

Being now become master of what useful knowledge was to be had in books, and competently skilled amongst others, in the Italian language, he made choice of that country to travel into, in order to polish his conversation, and learn to know men. And having received instructions how to demean himself with that wise, observing nation, as well as how to shape his journey, from Sir Henry Wotton, whose esteem of him appears in an elegant letter to him upon that subject, he took his way through France. In this kingdom, the manners and genius of which he had in no admiration, he made small stay, nor contracted any acquaintance; save that, with the recommendation of Lord Scudamore, our King's Ambassador at Paris, he waited on Hugo Grotius, who was there under that character from the Crown of Sweden.

Hasting to Italy by the way of Nice, and passing through Genoa, Leghorn, and Pisa he arrived at Florence. Here he lived two months in familiar and elegant conversation with the choice wits of that city, and was admitted by them to their private academies; an economy much practised among the virtuosi of those parts, for the communication of polite literature, as well as for the cementing of friendships. The reputation he had with them they expressed in several commendatory verses, which are extant in his book of poems. From Florence he went to Rome, where, as in all places, he spent his time in the choicest company; and amongst others there, in that of Lucas Holstein.

At Naples, which was his next remove, he became acquainted with Marquis Manso, a learned person, and so aged as to have been contemporary and intimate with Torquato Tasso, the famous Italian heroic. This nobleman obliged him by very particular civilities, accompanying him to see the rarities of the place, and paying him visits at his lodging; also sent him the testimony of a great esteem in this distich:

> Ut Mens, Forma, Decor Facies, Mos, si Pietas sic,
> Non Anglus, verum herclè Angelus ipse fores.

Yet excused himself at parting for not having been able to do him more honor by reason of his resolute owning his religion. This he did whensoever by any one's enquiry occasion was offered; not otherwise forward to enter upon discourses of that nature. Nor did he decline its defense in the like circumstances even in Rome itself on his return thither; though he had been advised by letters from some friends to Naples, that the English Jesuits designed to do him mischief on that account. Before his leaving Naples he returned the Marquis an acknowledgement of his great favors in an elegant copy of verses entitled *Mansus,* which is extant amongst his other Latin poems.

From Rome he revisited Florence for the sake of his charming friends there; and then proceeded to Venice, where he shipped what books he had bought, and through the delicious country of Lombardy, and over the Alps to Geneva, where he lived in familiar conversation with the famous Diodati. Thence through France he returned home, having, with no ill management of his time, spent about fifteen months abroad.

He had by this time laid in a large stock of knowledge, which as he designed not for the purchase of wealth, so neither intended he it, as a miser's hoard, to lie useless. Having therefore taken a house, to be at full ease and quiet, and gotten his books about him, he set himself upon compositions, tending either to the public benefit of mankind, and especially his countrymen, or to the advancement of the Commonwealth of Learning. And his first labors were very happily dedicated to what had the chiefest place in his affections, and had been no small part of his study, the service of religion.

It was now the year 1640, and the nation was much divided upon the controversies about church government, between the Prelatical party, and the Dissenters, or, as they were commonly then called, Puritans. He had studied religion in the Bible and the best authors, had strictly lived up to its rules, and had no temporal concern depending upon any hierarchy to render him suspected, either to himself or others, as one that writ for interest; and, therefore, with great boldness and zeal offered his judgment, first in two *Books of Reformation* by way of address to a friend, and then, in answer to a bishop, he writ of *Prelatical Episcopacy* and *The Reason of Church Government*. After that, *Animadversions upon the Remonstrants defence* (the work of Bishop Hall) *against Smectymnuus* and *Apology for those Animadversions*.

In this while, his manner of settlement fitting him for the reception of a wife, he in a month's time (according to his practice of not wasting that precious talent) courted, married, and brought home from Forresthall, near Oxford, a daughter of Mr. Powell. But she, that was very young, and had been bred in a family of plenty and freedom, being not well pleased with his reserved manner of life, within a few days left him, and went back into the country with her mother. Nor though he sent several pressing invitations could he prevail with her to return, till about four years after, when Oxford was surrendered (the nighness of her father's house to that garrison having for the most part of the meantime hindered any communication between them), she of her own accord came, and submitted to him, pleading that her mother had been the inciter of her to that frowardness. He, in the interval, who had entered into that state for the end designed by God and nature, and was then in the full vigor of his manhood, could ill bear the disappointment he met with by her obstinate absenting; and, therefore, thought upon a divorce, that he might be free to marry another; concerning which he also was in treaty. The lawfulness and expedience of this, duly regulate in order to all those purposes for which marriage was at first instituted, had upon full consideration and reading good authors been formerly his opinion; and the necessity of justifying himself now concurring with the opportunity, acceptable to him, of instructing others in a point of so great concern to the peace and preservation of families, and so likely to prevent temptations as well as mischiefs, he first writ *The Doctrine and Discipline of Divorce,* then *Colasterion,* and after *Tetrachordon.* In these he taught the right use and design of marriage; then the original and practice of divorces amongst the Jews, and showed that our Savior, in those four places of the Evangelists, meant not the abrogating but rectifying the abuses of it; rendering to that purpose another sense of the word fornication (and which is also the opinion amongst others of Mr. Selden in his *Uxor Hebraea*) than what is commonly received. Martin Bucer's *Judgment* in this matter he likewise translated into English. The Assembly of Divines then sitting at Westminster, though formerly obliged by his learned pen in the defense of Smectymnuus, and other their controversies with the bishops, now impatient of having the clergies' jurisdiction, as they reckoned it, invaded, instead of answering, or disproving what those books had asserted, caused him to be summoned for them before the Lords. But that house, whether approving the doctrine, or not favoring his accusers, soon dismissed him.

This was the mending of a decay in the superstructure, and had for object only the well-being of private persons, or at most of families. His small treatise *of Education,* addressed to Mr. Hartlib, was the laying a foundation also of public weal. In it he prescribed an easy and delightful method for training up gentry in such a manner to all sorts of literature, as that they might at the same time by like degrees advance in virtue and abilities to serve their country, subjoining directions for their attaining other necessary or ornamental accomplishments; and it seemed he designed in some measure to put this in practise. He had, from his first settling, taken care of instructing his two nephews by his sister Phillips, and, as it happened, the son of some friend. Now he took a large house, where the Earle of Barrimore, sent by his aunt the Lady Ranalagh, Sir Thomas Gardiner of Essex, and others were under his tuition. But whether it were that the tempers of our gentry would not bear the strictness of his discipline, or for what other reason, he continued that course but a while.

His next public work, and which seemed to be his particular province, who was so jealous in promoting knowledge, was *Areopagitica,* written in manner of an oration, to vindicate the freedom of the press from the tyranny of licensers; who either enslaved to the dictates of those that put them into office, or prejudiced by their own ignorance, are wont to hinder the coming out of any thing which is not consonant to the common received opinions, and by that means deprive the public of the benefit of many useful labors.

Hitherto all his writings had for subject the propagation of religion or learning, or the bettering some more private concerns of mankind. In political matters he had published nothing. And it was now the time of the King's coming upon his trial, when some of the Presbyterian ministers, out of malignity to the Independent party, who had supplanted them, more than from any principles of loyalty, asserted clamorously in their sermons and writings the privilege of kings from all accountableness. Or (to speak in the language of this time) non-resistance and passive obedience to be the doctrine of all the Reformed Churches. This general thesis, which encouraged all manner of tyranny, he opposed by good arguments, and the authorities of several eminently learned protestants in a book titled *The Tenure of Kings,* but without any particular application to the dispute then on foot in this nation.

Upon the change of government which succeeded the King's death he was, without any seeking of his, by the means of a private acquaintance, who was a member of the new Council of State, chosen Latin Secretary. In this public station his abilities and the acuteness of his parts, which had lain hid in his privacy, were soon taken notice of, and he was pitched upon to elude the artifice of Εἰκὼν Βασιλική. This he had no sooner performed answerably to the expectation from his wit and pen, in Εἰκονοκλάστης, but another adventure expected him.

Salmasius, a professor in Holland, who had in a large treatise, not long before, maintained the parity of church governors against Episcopacy, put out *Defensio Caroli Regis,* and in it, amongst other absurdities, justified (as indeed it was unavoidable in the defense of that cause, which was styled *Bellum Episcopale*) to the contradiction of his former book, the pretensions of the bishops. Him Mr. Milton, by the order of his masters, answered in *Defensio pro populo Anglicano,* both in more correct Latin, to the shame of the other's grammarship, and by much better reasoning. For Salmasius being a foreigner, and grossly ignorant of our laws and constitution (which in all nations are the respective distinguishing principles of government), either brought no arguments from thence, or such only (and by him not seldom mistaken or misapplied) as were partially suggested to him by those whose cause he had undertaken; and which, having during the many years of our divisions been often ventilated, received an easy solution. Nor had he given proof of deeper learning in that which is properly called politics, while he made use of trite instances, as that of the government of bees, and such like to prove the preëminency of monarchy; and all along so confounded it with tyranny (as also he did the Episcopal with the Papal government), that he might better have passed for a defender of the grand Signor, and the Council of Trent, than of a lawful king and a reformed church. For this and reneging his former principles he was by Mr. Milton facetiously exposed; nor did he ever reply, though he lived three years after.

But what he wisely declined, the further provoking such an adversary, or persisting to defend a cause he so ill understood, was attempted in *Clamor Regii Sanguinis,* etc., in which Salmasius was hugely extolled, and Mr. Milton as falsely defamed. The anonymous author, Mr. Milton, who had by his last book gained great esteem and many friends among the learned abroad, by whom, and by public ministers coming hither he was often visited, soon discovered to be Morus, formerly a professor and minister at Geneva, then living in Holland. Him, in *Secunda Defensio pro populo Anglicano,* he rendered ridiculous for his trivial and weak treatise under so tragical a title, containing little of argument, which had not before suffered with Salmasius. And because it consisted most of railing and false reproaches, he, in no unpleasant manner, from very good testimonies retorted upon him the true history of his notorious impurities, both at Geneva and Leyden. Himself he also, by giving a particular ingenuous account of his whole life, vindicated from those scurrilous aspersions, with which that book had endeavored to blemish him; adding perhaps thereby also reputation to the cause he defended, at least with impartial readers, when they should reflect upon the different qualifications of the respective champions. And when Morus afterwards strove to clear himself of being the author, and to represent Mr. Milton as an injurious defamer in that particular, he in *Defensio pro se* by very good testimonies, and other circumstantial proofs justified his having fixed it there, and made good sport of the other's shallow evasions.

While he was thus employed his eyesight totally failed him; not through any immediate or sudden judgment, as his adversaries insultingly affirmed, but from a weakness which his hard, nightly study in his youth had first occasioned, and which by degrees had for some time before deprived him of the use of one eye. And the issues and seatons, made use of to save or retrieve that, were thought by drawing away the spirits, which should have supplied the optic vessels, to have hastened the loss of the other. He was, indeed, advised by his physicians of the danger, in his condition, attending so great intentness as that work required. But he, who was resolute in going through with what upon good consideration he at any time designed, and to whom the love of truth and his country was dearer than all things, would not for any danger decline their defense.

Nor did his darkness discourage or disable him from prosecuting, with the help of amanuenses, the former design of his calmer studies. And he had now more leisure, being dispensed with by having a substitute allowed him, and sometimes instructions sent home to him, from attending in his office of secretary.

It was now that he began that laborious work of amassing out of all the classic authors, both in prose and verse, a *Latin Thesaurus* to the emendation of that done by Stephanus; also the composing *Paradise Lost,* and the framing a body of divinity out of the Bible. All which, notwithstanding the several calamities befalling him in his fortunes, he finished after the Restoration: as also the *British History* down to the Conquest, *Paradise Regained, Samson Agonistes,* a tragedy, *Logica and Accedence, commenced Grammar* and had begun a *Greek Thesaurus;* having scarce left any part of learning unimproved by him, as in *Paradise Lost* and *Regained* he more especially taught all virtue.

In these works, and the instruction of some youth or other at the entreaty of his friends, he in great serenity spent his time and expired no less calmly in the year 1674.

He had naturally a sharp wit, and steady judgment; which helps toward attaining learning he improved by an indefatigable attention to his study; and was supported in that by a temperance, always observed by him, but in his youth even with great nicety. Yet did he not reckon this talent but as entrusted with him; and therefore dedicated all his labors to the glory of God and some public good; neither binding himself to any of the gainful professions, nor having any worldly interest for aim in what he taught. He made no address or court for the employment of Latin secretary, though his eminent fitness for it appears by his printed letters of that time. And he was so far from being concerned in the corrupt designs of his masters, that whilst in his first and second *Defensio pro populo Anglicano* he was an advocate for liberty against tyranny and oppression (which to him seemed the case, as well by the public declarations on the one side [and he was a stranger to their private counsels], as by the arguments on the other side, which run mainly upon the justifying of exorbitant and lawless power), he took care all along strictly to define and persuade to true liberty, and especially in very solemn perorations at the close of those books; where he also, little less than prophetically, denounced the punishments due to the abusers of that specious name. And as he was not linked to one party by self interest, so neither was he divided from the other by animosity; but was forward to do any of them good offices, when their particular cases afforded him ground to appear on their behalf. And especially, if on the score of wit or learning, they could lay claim to his peculiar patronage. Of which were instances, among others, the grandchild of the famous Spenser, a papist suffering in his concerns in Ireland, and Sir William Davenant when taken prisoner, for both whom he procured relief.

This his sincerity, and disentanglement of any private ends with his sentiments relating to the public, proceeded no doubt from a higher principle, but was in great part supported, and temptations to the contrary avoided by his constant frugality; which enabled him at first to live within compass of the moderate patrimony his father left him, and afterwards to bear with patience, and no discomposure of his way of living, the great losses which befell him in his fortunes. Yet he was not sparing to buy good books, of which he left a fair collection; and was generous in relieving the wants of his friends. Of his gentleness and humanity he likewise gave signal proof in receiving home, and living in good accord till her death with his first wife, after she had so obstinately absented from him. During which time, as neither in any other scene of his life, was he blemished with the least unchastity.

From so Christian a life, so great learning, and so unbiassed a search after truth it is not probable any errors in doctrine should spring. And, therefore, his judgment in his body of divinity concerning some speculative points, differing perhaps from that commonly received, (and which is thought to be the reason that never was printed) neither ought rashly to be condemned, and however himself not to be uncharitably censured; who, by being a constant champion for the liberty of opining, expressed much candor towards others. But that this age is insensible of the great obligations it has to him, is too apparent in that he has no better a pen to celebrate his memory.

He was of a moderate stature, and well proportioned, of a ruddy complexion, light brown hair, and handsome features; save that his eyes were none of the quickest. But his blindness, which proceeded from a gutta serena, added no further blemish to them. His deportment was sweet and affable; and his gait erect and manly, bespeaking courage and undauntedness (or a *nil conscire*), on which account he wore a sword while he had his sight, and was skilled in using it. He had an excellent ear, and could bear a part both in vocal and instrumental music. His moderate estate left him by his father was, through his good economy, sufficient to maintain him. Out of his secretary's salary he had saved two thousand pounds, which, being lodged in the excise, and that bank failing upon the Restoration, he utterly lost. Besides which, and the ceasing of his employment, he had no damage by that change of affairs. For he early sued out his pardon; and by means of that, when the Sergeant of the house of Commons had officiously seized him, was quickly set at liberty. He had, too, at the first return of the Court in good manners left his house in Petty France, which had a door into the park; and in all other things demeaning himself peaceable, was so far from being reckoned disaffected, that he was visited at his house on Bunhill by a chief officer of state, and desired to employ his pen on their behalf. And when the subject of divorce was under consideration with the Lords, upon the account of the Lord Ross, he was consulted by an eminent member of that house. By the great fire in 1666 he had a house in Bread Street burnt, which was all the real estate he had.

He rendered his studies and various works more easy and pleasant by allotting them their several portions of the day. Of these the time friendly to the Muses fell to his poetry;

and he, waking early (as is the use of temperate men), had commonly a good stock of verses ready against his amanuensis came; which if it happened to be later then ordinary, he would complain, saying *he wanted to be milked*.   The evenings he likewise spent in reading some choice poets, by way of refreshment after the day's toil, and to store his fancy against morning.   Besides his ordinary lectures out of the Bible and the best commentators on the week day, that was his sole subject on Sundays.   And David's Psalms were in esteem with him above all poetry.   The youths that he instructed from time to time served him often as amanuenses, and some elderly persons were glad for the benefit of his learned conversation, to perform that office.   His first wife died a while after his blindness seized him, leaving him three daughters, that lived to be women.   He married two more, whereof one survived him.   He died in a fit of the gout, but with so little pain or emotion that the time of his expiring was not perceived by those in the room.   And though he had been long troubled with that disease, insomuch that his knuckles were all callous, yet was he not ever observed to be very impatient.   He had this elegy in common with the patriarchs and kings of Israel, that he was gathered to his people; for he happened to be buried in Cripplegate, where about thirty years before he had by chance also interred his father.

Index of Names

The names included in this index are those of historical persons to whom Milton refers or who are mentioned in the footnotes. No biblical characters are included, nor is there any attempt to index Milton's countless and often hidden biblical references, but references to persons and books of the Apocrypha are listed. Milton's own name is not indexed, but the names of his Milton and Phillips relatives will be found. Writers and their works are not distinguished unless more than one work is involved. Although many of the authors and works in this index were expressly mentioned by Milton, or were consciously recalled by him as he wrote, the student should not be misled into thinking that all the works here listed (especially those by Robert Burton and Shakespeare) should be regarded as having shaped Milton's thought or language.

Abbas, Shah, 442
Abelard, 472
Achaemenes, 9
Aelian, 225, 1029
Aelius Spartianus, 782
Aemilius Probus, 1025
Aeschines, 614
Aeschylus
  Agamemnon, 8, 39
  Choephorae, 554
  Eumenides, 8, 419
  Libation Bearers, 8
  Prometheus Bound, 174, 214, 236, 278, 300, 383, 549, 556, 567
  Seven against Thebes, 74, 226
Agar, Thomas, 1027
Agesilaus, 616
Agricola, 742
Agrippa I, Herod, 803
Agrippa, Henry Cornelius, 182, 213, 225, 274, 336, 420
Alaric, 611
Ahasuerus, 644
Albert, Duke of Prussia, 706
Albertus Magnus, 295
Alcaeus, 126
Alciati, Andreas, 59, 711
Alcibiades, 26
Alcuin, 701, 763
Aldo Manuzio, 721
Aldovrandus, Ulisse, 418
Alexander the Great, 26, 32, 140, 283, 286, 390, 474, 498, 506, 507, 511, 521, 621, 626, 627
Alexander of Jerusalem, 679
Alexander V, Pope, 659

Alexander, Sir William, 254
Alfray, Thomas, 1030
Alfred the Great, 796, 798, 810, 891
Almansor, 442
Alphrey, *see* Alfray, Thomas
Amaury de Bene, 217
Ambrose, Saint, 139, 284, 809, 845, 865
Ames, William, 194, 701, 843, 877
Ammianus Marcellinus, 512
Anacreon, 51
Andreini, Giambattista, 174, 183, 250, 388, 391, 400, 538, 539
Andrewes, Lancelot, 21, 640, 647, 650-653 *passim*
Andronicus Comnenus, 792
Anglesea, Arthur Annesley, Earl of, 1036
Anselm, Saint, 654
Anthony, Saint, 478
Antigonus, 513
Antiochus Epiphanes, 508, 770
Antipater the Idumaean, 462, 503
Antony, Marc, 784
Apelles 40, 600
Apian, Peter, 187, 423
Apicius Caelius, 618
Apocrypha
  Bel, 780
  Ecclesiasticus, 348, 569
  I Esdras, 359, 806
  I Maccabees, 508, 770
  II Maccabees, 462
  Tobit, 281, 307, 497
  Wisdom of Solomon, 345
Apollinarius, Claudius, 726, 980
Apollodorus, 11, 607, 614
Apollonius of Perga, 778